Medieval Germany

An Encyclopedia

Medieval Germany

An Encyclopedia

Edited by
John M. Jeep
Miami University

Garland Publishing, Inc.
New York & London
2001

Published in 2001 by
Garland Publishing, Inc.
29 West 35th Street
New York, NY 10001

Garland is an imprint of the Taylor & Francis Group.

Editorial Staff

Laura Kathleen Smid
Project Editor

Edward Cone
Melissa Dobson
Margery Heffron
Copyeditors

Alexis Skinner
Production Editor

Laura-Ann Robb
Production Director

Richard Steins
Development Manager

Sylvia K. Miller
Publishing Director, Reference

10   9   8   7   6   5   4   3   2   1

Library of Congress Cataloging-in-Publication Data
Medieval Germany / edited by John M. Jeep.
      p. cm.
   Includes bibliographical references and index.
   ISBN 0-8240-7644-3 (alk. paper)
   1. Germany—History—1273–1517—Encyclopedias 2,   Civilization,
Medieval—Encyclopedias. 3. Netherlands—History—To 1384—Encyclopedias. 4.
Netherlands—History—House of Burgundy, 1384–1477—Encyclopedias. 5.
Netherlands—History—House of Burgundy, 1477–1556—Encyclopedias. I. Jeep, John M.

DD157 .M43 2001
943'.02'03—dc21   00-061780

Printed on acid-free, 250-year-life paper
Manufactured in the United States of America

0012968370

Contents

v

Alphabetical List of Entries

Alphabetical List of Entries

Alphabetical List of Entries

List of Entries by Category

Art and Architecture

Bernward of Hildesheim
Bertram, Meister
Charles IV, Art
Cistercian Art and Architecture
Cologne, Art
Constance, Art
E. S., Master
Egbert
Erhart, Gregor
Erhart, Michel
Erwin von Steinbach
Franciscan Art and Architecture
Francke, Master
Frederick I Barbarossa, Art
Frederick III, Art
Gothic Art and Architecture
Gothic Art and Architecture, Late
Gottfried von Straßburg, *Tristan,* Illustrations
Grasser, Erasmus
Heinrich von Veldeke, *Eneide,* Illustrations
Henry II, Art
Henry the Lion, Art
Heraldry
Herlin, Friedrich
Herrad von Hohenburg
Heselloher, Hans
Holbein, Hans, the Elder
Holy Lance
Housebook, Master of the
Iconographies, Innovative
International Style
Jewish Art and Architecture
Kaiserchronik, Latin, Illuminated
Koerbecke, Johann
Kraft, Adam
Lauber, Diebolt
Leinberger, Hans
Liederhandschriften, Illustrations
Life of Mary, Master of
Liturgical Vestments, Manuscripts, and Objects
Liturgy, Furniture
Lochner, Stefan
Manuals, Artists', and Modelbooks
Manuscripts, Painting and Production
Multscher, Hans
Nicholaus of Verdun
Nicolaus Gerhaert von Leyden
Otto I, Art
Otto II, Art

Otto III, Art
Ottonian Art and Architecture
Pacher, Michael
Paleography
Pilgram, Anton
Pilgrim's Badges
Playing Cards, Master of
Pleydenwurff, Hans
Potter, Dirc
Printmaking
Riemenschneider, Tillmann
Romanesque Art and Architecture
Rosary
Runkelstein
Sankt Bartholomew Altarpiece, Master of
Sankt Veronica, Master of
Schongauer, Martin
Siegburg, Art
Stoss, Veit
Syrlin, Jörg (Elder and Younger)
Theoderic, Master
Theophanu, Art
Trier, Art
Van Meckenem, Israhel
Warbeck, Veit
Weckmann, Nicolaus, the Elder
Witz, Konrad
Wolfram von Eschenbach, *Parzival,* Illustrations
Wolfram von Eschenbach, *Willehalm,* Illustrations
Wolgemut, Michael
Women and Art
World Maps
Zeitblom, Bartholomäus

Daily Life

Alphabet
Charms
Childhood
Clothing, Costume, and Fashion
Cookbooks
Diet and Nutrition
Family
Fishing
Gardens and Gardening
Hunting and Hunting Literature
Magic
Magic and Charms, Dutch
Marriage and Divorce

Medicine
Nobility and Farmers
Pilgrim's Badges
Pregnancy and Childbirth
Runes
Tournaments
Town Planning and Urbanism

Education

Alphabet
Block Book
Bookmaking and Production
Dhuoda
Education
Encyclopedic Literature, Dutch
Encyclopedic Literature, German
Gutenberg, Johann
Herrad von Hohenburg
Hrabanus Maurus
Hunting and Hunting Literature
Johannes Scottus
Libraries
Manuals, Artists', and Modelbooks
Manuscripts, Painting and Production
Ministerials
Numbers and Calculation
Paleography
Prayer Books
Preaching and Sermons, Dutch
Preaching and Sermons, German
Printing Press
Printmaking
Roland and Charlemagne, Illustrations
Sachliteratur
Universities
Walahfrid Strabo
World Maps

Language

Abrogans
Alphabet
Boethius
Boethius, Dutch
Dutch Language, Dialects
German Language, Dialects
Glosses, Old High German
Gothic Language
Isidore
Latin Language
Onomastics
Paleography
Strasbourg Oaths

Law

Eike von Repgow, Legal
Empire
Law and Lawbooks
Seals and Sigillography

Literature

Albrecht von Johansdorf
Albrecht von Kemenaten
Albrecht von Scharfenberg
Alexander Literature, Dutch
Alexanderlied
Alpharts Tod
Anegenge
Animal Epics, Dutch
Annolied
Archpoet
Aristoteles und Phyllis
Armenbibel
Armer Hartmann
Arnolt, Priester
Ars Moriendi
Arthurian Literature, Dutch
Arthurian Literature, German
Beheim, Michael
Berthold von Holle
Beyeren, Herald
Bible Epic, Saxon
Block Book
Boner, Ulrich
Bookmaking and Production
Boppe, Meister
Brendan
Bruno of Magdeburg
Buch von Bern and *Rabenschlacht*
Carmina Burana
Charlemagne Epics, Dutch
Charlemagne Epics, German
Charms
Chronicles, City, Dutch
Chronicles, City, German
Chronicles, Regional/National, Dutch
Chronicles, Regional/Territorial, German
Chronicles, World, Dutch
Chronicles, World, German
Crusades, Literature, Dutch
De Heinrico
Dietrich and *Wenezlan*
Dietrichepik
Drama
Drama, Christmas Plays
Drama, Dutch
Drama, Easter Plays

List of Entries by Category

Philosophy

Places and Place Study

Religion and Theology

Women, Gender, and Families

List of Entries by Category

Introduction

Medieval Germany: An Encyclopedia is an introduction to the society and culture of German- and Dutch-speaking Europe from approximately C.E. 500 to 1500. By presenting articles on major persons, places, historical occurrences, artistic and technological accomplishments, intellectual developments, and daily life of the period roughly outlined, this reference work intends to answer readers' questions and supply further information on major topics from the broad field of medieval German studies. Its 647 entries were suggested and written by an international team of scholars from North America and Europe.

The editors conceived the entries as covering the fields of German and Dutch art history, language and literature, history, music, philosophy, religion, and general (social structure, daily life). Tangential articles such as "Boethius" or "Latin Language" reflect significant influences on the medieval German- and Dutch-speaking world.

How to Use This Book

Entries are arranged alphabetically. Article headings appear in English or German, depending on the authors' perception of the most common usage in English. Works of literature are discussed under the author's name, when known or supposed. Names are listed according to English-language customs, Wolfram von Eschenbach under "W," Ulrich Fuetrer under "F." Cross references ("See also . . .") follow articles when called for. An analytical index also serves to point users to the appropriate article. Blind entries ("John Ruusbroec. *See* Jan van Ruusbroec"; "Teutonic Knights. *See Deutschorden*") in both the text and the index lead nonspecialists to the information they seek.

Authors were asked to keep the general reader in mind; bibliographies, listing primary sources, translations, and secondary sources, were severely limited. They provide orientation into the vast field of medieval German studies; the works cited in turn contain a wealth of references for further reading and research. Thus, articles can be perused gainfully by nonspecialists and experts alike. English language sources were preferred but not always available.

Acknowledgments

Medieval Germany: An Encyclopedia, was conceived in 1986, when Edward R. Haymes was approached by Gary Kuris, then of Garland Publishing, at the Medieval Studies Conference at Western Michigan University in Kalamazoo, Michigan, about a German volume within Garland Publishing's Medieval Encyclopedia series. After serving as general editor during the initial phase, during which a first master list of articles was drawn up and many collaborators were won, Haymes passed on the general editorship to a former associate editor, Stephanie Cain Van D'Elden, who in turn relinquished the position in 1996 to the undersigned. I had been associated with the project from early on as a contributor and as a consulting editor (Old High German). I assumed the general editor position with the vast majority of entries chosen, very many of them assigned, a good number of them already submitted. In addition to Haymes and Van D'Elden, Joan A. Holladay (art) and Geert Claassens (Dutch) have been with the project since its inception, and have demonstrated near-saintly patience and stick-to-it-iveness. In addition, Holladay assumed the sizable burden of selecting, acquiring, and authoring labels for the many illustrations. She has been ably assisted by, among others, her husband, Daniel Hofmann, and Anne Rudloff Stanton. Michael Frassetto agreed to take over the vacated associate editor position for history late in 1996. Consulting editors Frank Gentry (Middle High German literature), Donna Mayer-Martin (music), Frank Tobin (religion and philosophy), and Jan Ziolkowski (Latin), have been invaluable over the years. Wesley Stevens (history) provided useful input.

It is indeed a pleasant duty to thank a veritable host of scholars who shall, for fear I might omit someone, remain unnamed, who responded to requests for suggestions for potential entries and authors. Without their selfless support, this would be a far inferior reference work. You know who you are, and many of you appear in a significant way in the bibliographies. A further group of individuals responded to my many requests for address information, or otherwise helped me locate persons whose whereabouts were or had become unknown to me. This encyclopedia is, then, truly the result of a team effort.

Introduction

Each article is signed. This gives credit where credit is due. The contributors have, in some cases, waited years for their work to see the light of day. Those collaborators whose work has been listed as "done" for a long period of time are to be thanked for their timely responses and submissions. Without them, the time-consuming efforts to gather less punctual submissions would not have been possible. Various factors contributed to the delays over the years. The editors are most grateful to the authors for their expertise, their collegiality, and their patience. It has been a pleasure to be in contact with so many selfless, considerate, and talented individuals. Most readers will not have the delight of reading as many articles as the editors have, and we have profited from our exposure to such a wide range of scholarship.

I have benefited from the support of the department of German, Russian, and East Asian Languages (Robert Di Donato, chair) and the College of Arts and Science (John Skillings, acting dean) of Miami University, who provided student staff support, technical support, and an atmosphere conducive to research. My colleagues David Siebenhar, Charlotte Wharton, and Dan Meyers cheer-fully provided helpful answers to my many computer-related questions. Erin Brown assisted the general editor for one semester. Marianne Lown was my initial editorial contact at Garland Publishing; from 1997–1999, Joanne Daniels guided me. Richard Steins and Tim Roberts provided welcome support and expertise during an editorial transition phase. For the final stages, Laura Kathleen Smid has been a most conscientious and supportive editor. Finally, Cliff Kallemeyn has been a careful production editor. As always, Lynda Hoffman-Jeep and L. Cariña Jeep have supported me and my work.

The atmosphere generated at the medieval studies conferences at the Medieval Institute of Western Michigan University has always been encouraging and stimulating. The association with these conferences has been very productive in this undertaking.

I dedicate this book to the memory of my father, Charles W. Jeep, Jr., whose natural inquisitiveness and broad interests represent the kind of reader the collaborators on this volume hope to engage.

John M. Jeep
Miami University

Abbreviations

b.	born
B.C.E	Before Common Era
c.	century
ca.	circa
C.E.	Common Era
chap.	chapter
col., cols.	column, columns
d.	died
ed., eds.	editor, editors
e.g.	for example
esp.	especially
fl.	flourished
fol.	folio (manuscript page)
i.e.	that is
ills.	illustrations
introd.	introduction
l., ll.	line, lines
m.	married
MHG	Middle High German
no.	number
n.p.	no place, no publisher
OHG	Old High German
p., pp.	page, pages
pbk.	paperback
pl., pls.	plate, plates
r.	ruled, reigned
rev.	revised
rpt.	reprint, reprinted
St.	Saint (German *Sankt*)
supp.	supplement
trans.	translator(s)
UMI	University Microfilms Inc.
v., vv.	verse, verses
vol., vols.	volume, volumes

Contributors

Melitta Weiss Adamson
University of Western Ontario
Cookbooks; Diet and Nutrition

Andrew E. Anderson
Southern Methodist University
Adam von Fulda

Marian Andringa
Rijksuniversiteit te Leiden
Alexander Literature, Dutch

Wim van Anrooij
Rijksuniversiteit te Leiden
Beyeren, Herald; Stoke, Melis

David Appleby
U.S. Naval Academy
Synod of Frankfurt

Amanda Athey
University of Georgia
Hadewijch

Wolfgang Augustyn
Zentralinstitut für Kunstgeschichte
Schaffhausen

Piet Avonds
Antwerp, Belgium
Brabant, Duchy of

Peter Barnet
Metropolitan Museum of Art
Gothic Art and Architecture—Textiles; Riemenschneider,
Tillmann; Romanesque Art and Architecture—Metalwork,
—Textiles; Weckmann, Nicolaus, the Elder

Bas J. P. van Bavel
Universiteit van Amsterdam
Monasticism, Dutch

Bruce A. Beatie
Cleveland State University
Carmina Burana

Patricia Zimmerman Beckman
University of Chicago
Beguines; Visionary Literature

Brigitte Bedos-Rezak
University of Maryland at College Park
Heraldry; Seals and Sigillography

Thomas Bein
Universität Bonn
Frauenlob

Donald P. Beistle
University of Georgia
Mithras

Dean Phillip Bell
Spertus Institute of Jewish Studies
Jews

Ingrid Bennewitz
Universität Bamberg
Neidhart

Florin Berindeanu
University of Georgia
Mariendichtungen

John W. Bernhardt
San Jose State University
Fodrum, Gistum, Servitium Regis; Itinerant Kingship;
Kunigunde; Renovatio Regni Francorum

Amand Berteloot
Westfälische Wilhelms—Universität Münster
Saints' Lives, Dutch

David R. Blanks
American University in Cairo
Family; Rural Settlement; Slavery

Uta-Renate Blumenthal
Catholic University of America
Canossa; Concordat of Worms; Gregory VII; Henry IV;
Investiture Controversy

Hans J. Böker
McGill University, Montreal, Que.
Corvey; Frederick III, Art; Goslar; Kleve; Lübeck; Lüneburg;
Maria Saal; Minden; Neubrandenburg; Paderborn; Prenzlau;
Stendal; Stralsund; Vienna; Wismar; Zwettl

Frank P. C. Brandsma
Riijksuniversiteit te Utrecht
Arthurian Literature, Dutch

Daniel F. Callahan
University of Delaware
Leo IX; Sylvester II

William F. Carroll
Harvard University
Education

Stephen M. Carey
Washington University in St. Louis
Exemplum; Heinrich der Teichner; Konrad von Mure; Konrad von Würzburg; *Minneallegorie, Minnerede;* Otte

Amelia Carr
Allegheny College, Meadville, Pa.
Heiligenkreuz; Klosterneuburg; Linz; Regensburg; Seckau; Tegernsee

Kristin M. Christensen
University of Notre Dame
Mysticism

Geert H. M. Claassens
Katholieke Universiteit Leuven
Animal Epics, Dutch; Bible Translations, Dutch; Bible Translator of 1360, Dutch; Crusades, Literature, Dutch; *Grimbergse Oorlag, De;* Herrad von Hohenburg; Jacob van Maerlant; Jan van Boendale; Literature, Dutch; *Reynard* the Fox, Dutch; *Seghelijn van Jherusalem;* Segher Diengotgaf

Albrecht Classen
University of Arizona
Alexanderlied; Boner, Ulrich; Chronicles, World, German; Eilhart von Oberge; Hadlaub, Johannes; Hugo von Langenstein; Hugo von Montfort; Johann von Würzburg; Kaufringer, Heinrich; Oswald von Wolkenstein; Püterich von Reichertshausen, Jacob; Thomasîn von Zerklaere; *Ulenspegel;* Ulrich von Etzenbach; Ulrich von Türheim; Warbeck, Veit

Adam S. Cohen
Washington, DC
Einsiedeln; Freising; Gandersheim; Gernrode; Henry II, Art; Otto I, Art; Otto II, Art; Otto III, Art; Ottonian Art and Architecture—Manuscript Illumination

Kristen M. Collins
University of Texas at Austin
Echternach; Hildesheim; Ottonian Art and Architecture—Wall Painting; Reichenau

Leo A. Connolly
University of Memphis
Bible; *De Heinrico;* German Language, Dialects; *Ludwigslied;* Otfrid

John J. Contreni
Purdue University
Charlemagne; Charles III, the Fat; Johannes Scottus; Lothar I; Louis the Pious; Louis II; Theodulf of Orléans

Brigitte Corley
London, Eng.
Bertram, Meister; Conrad von Soest; Francke, Master

Melanie Gesink Cornelisse
University of Texas at Austin
Iconographies, Innovative—Dance of Death, —Man of Sorrows; *Pietà;* Van Meckenem, Israhel

Rebecca W. Corrie
Bates College, Lewiston, Maine
Gothic Art and Architecture—Panel Painting, —Stained Glass; Gurk; Iconographies, Innovative—*Schutzmantelmadonna;* Lambach; Romanesque Art and Architecture—Mural Painting; Salzburg; Seligenstadt

William C. Crossgrove
Brown University
Encyclopedic Literature, German; *Sachliteratur*

Pia F. Cuneo
University of Arizona
Augsburg; Holbein, Hans, the Elder

Guido O. E. J. De Baere
University of Antwerpen
Jan van Ruusbroec

Kelly DeVries
Loyola College in Maryland
Archer/Bowman; Armor; Crossbow; Fortification; Warfare; Weapons

Ernst S. Dick
University of Kansas
Heinrich von dem Türlin

Madelyn Bergen Dick
Atkinson College, York University, Toronto, Ont.
Adelheid of Burgundy; Conrad I; Eike von Repgkow, Legal; Henry I; Henry the Lion; Holy Lance; Welfs

William J. Diebold
Reed College, Portland, Ore.
Carolingian Art and Architecture—Introduction, —Architecture, —Mural Painting

Martina Dlugaiczyk
Universität Gesamthochschule Kassel
Clothing, Costume, and Fashion; Gothic Art and Architecture—Sculpture, Tombs

Contributors

Maria Dobozy
University of Utah
Eike von Repgow; Law and Lawbooks; *Spielmannsepen*

Michael R. Dodds
Southern Methodist University
Berno von Reichenau

Edelgard E. DuBruck
Marygrove College, Detroit, Mich.
Fastnachtspiele

Lawrence G. Duggan
University of Delaware
Conversion; Diocese; Empire; *Fürstbischof; Landfrieden;*
Monasteries

Graeme Dunphy
Universität Regensburg
Drama, Paradise Plays; *Gesta Romanorum; Physiologus;*
Tannhäuser, Der; *Wartburgkrieg*

Matthias Exner
Bayerisches Landesamt für Denkmalpflege
Müstair; Steinbach; Werden

An Faems
Katholieke Universiteit Leuven
Beatrijs van Nazareth; *Brendan;* Dirc van Delf; Willem of
Hildegaersberch

Robert C. Figueira
Lander University, Greenwood, S.C.
Frederick II

Ruth H. Firestone
Fort Hays State University, Hays, Kans.
Albrecht von Kemenaten; *Alpharts Tod;* Boethius; *Buch von
Bern* and *Rabenschlacht; Dietrich und Wenezlan; Eckenlied;
Sigenot; Virginal*

Jacqueline A. Frank
Long Island University, C. W. Post Campus
Jewish Art and Architecture

Michael Frassetto
Encyclopedia Britannica
Admonitio Generalis; Carolingians; Clovis; Conradin of
Hohenstaufen; Crusades; Donation of Constantine; Frederick
I Barbarossa; Gerhoh of Reichersberg; Hanseatic League;
Henry the Raspe; Lechfeld, Battle of; Louis the Child;
Manfred of Sicily; *Ordinatio Imperii;* Otto IV; Otto of
Freising; Rahewin; Staufen; Succession

Peter Frenzel
Wesleyan University
Mönch von Salzburg, Der; Reinmar von Zwetter; *Sangspruch;*
Walther von der Vogelweide

Paul J. J. van Geest
Titus Brandsma Instituut
Thomas à Kempis

Edda Gentry
Pennsylvania State University
Muskatblüt

Francis G. Gentry
Pennsylvania State University
Annolied; Armer Hartmann; Ezzo; Heinrich von Melk;
Kaiserchronik; Notker von Zwiefalten

Richard Gerberding
University of Alabama, Huntsville
Pippin

Patricia A. Giangrosso
New Orleans, La.
Benedict, Rule of Saint; Charms

Jason Glenn
University of Southern California
Charles III, the Simple; Robertians

Hans-Peter Glimme
Philipps-Universität Marburg
Romanesque Art and Architecture—Introduction,
—Architecture

Jutta Goheen
Carleton University, Ottawa, Ont.
Hugo von Trimberg

Eric J. Goldberg
Claremont McKenna College, Claremont, Calif.
Strasbourg Oaths

Elsa Gontrum
Brookline, Mass.
Bern; Sion; Winterthur; Zug

Eileen P. McKiernan González
University of Texas at Austin
Iconographies, Innovative—*Anna Selbdritt,* —Holy Kinship

Mariken Goris and Wilma Wissink
Katholieke Universiteit Nijmegen
Boethius, Dutch

Karen Gould
University of Texas at Austin
Gutenberg, Johann; Iconographies, Innovative—Throne of Solomon; Manuals, Artists', and Modelbooks; Manuscripts, Painting and Production; Printing Press; Strasbourg

Anna A. Grotans
Ohio State University
Notker Labeo

A. L. H. Hage
Chronicles, City, Dutch; Chronicles, Regional/National, Dutch; Chronicles, World, Dutch; Historiography, Dutch

Rosemary Drage Hale
Concordia University, Montreal, Que.
Caesarius of Heisterbach; Ebner, Margaretha; Langmann, Adelheid; Legends; Preaching and Sermons, German

Leslie Anne Hamel
University of Maryland University College at Schwäbisch Gmünd
Esslingen am Neckar; Lorch; Maulbronn; Schwäbisch Gmünd; Stuttgart; Wimpfen

Tracy Chapman Hamilton
University of Texas at Austin
Charles IV, Art; Parler Family; Prague; Theoderic, Master

Melissa Thorson Hause
Marburg, Ger.
Marburg; Town Planning and Urbanism

Edward R. Haymes
Cleveland State University
Dietrichepik; Heldenbücher; Nibelungia Minora; Walther und Hildegund; Wolfdietrich and *Ortnit*

M. F. Hearn
University of Pittsburgh
Ottonian Art and Architecture—Sculpture

Hubert P. Heinen
University of Texas at Austin
Friedrich von Hausen; Heinrich der Glîchezâere; Marner, Der; *Minnesang;* Reinmar der Alte; Ulrich von Lichtenstein; Versification

Matthew Z. Heintzelman
University of Chicago
Drama, Christmas Plays; Drama, Easter Plays; Drama, Passion Plays

Wolfgang Hempel
University of Toronto
Muspilli

Ingeborg Henderson
University of California, Davis
Drama, Last Judgment Plays; Konrad von Heimesfurt; Stricker, Der; *Wigamur;* Wirnt von Grafenberg

David Hiley
Universität Regensburg
Liturgy, Music

Ernst Ralf Hintz
Fort Hays State University, Hays, Kans.
Arnolt, Priester; Chronicles, City, German; Chronicles, Regional/Territorial, German; Entechrist, Linzer; Frau Ava

Maartin J. F. M. Hoenen
Katholieke Universiteit Nijmegen
Agricola, Rodolphus; Marsilius van Inghen; Siger of Brabant

Melanie Holcomb
University of Michigan
Lorsch; Metz; Ottonian Art and Architecture—Textiles; Romanesque Art and Architecture—Ivories

Joan A. Holladay
University of Texas at Austin
Basel; Bonn; Cologne, Art; Constance, Art; Elizabeth of Hungary; Erfurt; Frankfurt am Main; Frueauf, Rueland the Elder; Gerthener, Madern; Gothic Art and Architecture—Manuscript Painting, —Sculpture, Introduction; Guelph Treasure; Hirsau; Ingelheim; Iconographies, Innovative—Introduction, —Acts of Charity, —Holy Graves, —*Johannesschüssel, —Palmesel,* —Saint John on the Bosom of Christ, —Wise and Foolish Virgins; International Style; Limburg an der Lahn; Magdeburg; Merseburg; Metalworking; Moser, Lucas; Mühlhausen; Quedlinburg; Romanesque Art and Architecture—Stained Glass; Rottweil; Sankt Paul in Lavanttal; Wartburg; Xanten; Zurich

Franz-Josef Holznagel
Cologne, Ger.
Liederhandschriften

Bram van den Hoven van Genderen
Rijksuniversiteit te Utrecht
Utrecht

Gert Hübner
Universität Bamberg
Berthold von Holle; Boppe, Meister; Hornburg, Lupold

Caroline Huey
University of Texas at Austin
Folz, Hans

Contributors

Joseph P. Huffman
Messiah College, Grantham, Penn.
Cologne, Archdiocese; Cologne, History; Matilda, Empress; Siegburg, Abbey; Westphalia

Larry Hunt
University of Georgia
Prayer Books

W. N. M. Hüsken
Nijmegen, Netherlands
Drama, Dutch; Drama, Latin, Netherlands

Jane Campbell Hutchison
University of Wisconsin, Madison
E. S., Master; Playing Cards, Master of

William H. Jackson
University of St. Andrews, St. Andrews, Scot.
Herbort von Fritzlar; Tournaments

Anteuen Jansen
Rijksuniversiteit te Leiden
Holland

Virginia Jansen
University of California, Santa Cruz
Gothic Art and Architecture, Late—Architecture

John M. Jeep
Miami University
Abrogans; *Georgslied; Isidore*

Sibylle Jefferis
University of Pennsylvania
Aristoteles und Phyllis; Heiligenleben; Hermann von Fritzlar; *Legenda Aurea,* Alsatian; *Maget Kron, Der; Märtyrerbuch; Passienbüchlein; Passional;* Rudolf von Ems; Schondoch; *Väterbuch*

Phyllis G. Jestice
California State University, Hayward
Coronation; Gottschalk of Orbais; Otto I; Otto II; Otto III; *Privilegium Ottonianum;* Theophanu

Sidney M. Johnson
Indiana University
Hochzeit, Die; Nabuchodonosor; Song of Songs; *Vom Rechte;* Wolfram von Eschenbach

Christine M. Kallinger-Allen
Berlitz Translation Services
Fuetrer, Ulrich

Virginia Roehrig Kaufmann
Princeton Research Forum
Franciscan Art and Architecture; Gothic Art and Architecture—Manuscript Painting; Helmarshausen; Henry the Lion, Art; Iconographies, Innovative—Equestrian Figures; Roger of Helmarshausen; Theophilius Presbyter

Rhonda L. Kelley
University of Georgia
Devotio Moderna

Peter Klein
Universität Hamburg
Dendrochronology

Genevra Kornbluth
University of Maryland, College Park
Carolingian Art and Architecture—Sculpture and Metalwork

Mikel M. Kors
Katholieke Universiteit Nijmegen
Peters, Gerlach

Jerry Krauel
Concordia University
Hildebrandslied

Kelly Kucaba
University of Kentucky
Gottfried von Straßburg

Marcia Kupfer
Washington, DC
World Maps

Richard H. Lawson
University of North Carolina, Chapel Hill
Tatian

M. Rebecca Leuchak
Roger Williams University, Bristol, R.I.
Gothic Art and Architecture—Metalwork; Ottonian Art and Architecture—Metalwork

Daniel M. Levine
Savannah College of Art and Design
Lochner, Stefan; Sankt Bartholomew Altarpiece, Master of; Sankt Veronica, Master of

Gertrud Jaron Lewis
Laurentian University, Sudbury, Ont.
Elisabeth von Schönau; Gertrud von Helfta; Hildegard von Bingen; Sister-Books

Orlanda S. H. Lie
Rijksuniversiteit te Utrecht
Encyclopedic Literature, Dutch; Magic and Charms, Dutch

Karen E. Loaiza
State University of New York at Plattsburgh
Bernward of Hildesheim; Ottonian Art and Architecture—
Introduction, —Ivories; *Registrum Gregorii,* Master of; Sankt
Gall; Theophanu, Art

Douglas W. Lumsden
University of California, Santa Barbara
Alcuin

Winder McConnell
University of California, Davis
Kudrun

John M. McCulloh
Kansas State University
Martyrology

William C. McDonald
University of Virginia
Beheim, Michael; Heselloher, Hans; Laufenberg, Heinrich;
Patronage, Literary; Stainreuter, Leopold

James W. Marchand
The University of Illinois at Urbana-Champagne
Alphabet; Fishing; Gothic Language; Hunting and Hunting
Literature; Mythology; Onomastics; Runes

John Margetts
University of Liverpool
Herrand von Wildonie

Susan Marti
University of Dortmund
Chur; Engelberg; Königsfelden; Sankt Katharinenthal

Lesa Mason
Savannah College of Art and Design
Liturgical Vestments, Manuscripts, and Objects; Relics and
Reliquaries

Hartwig Mayer
University of Toronto
Glosses, Old High German

Claudia A. Meier
Johannes Gutenberg-Universität Mainz
Kaiserchronik, Latin, Illuminated

Robert Melzak
Carolingian Art and Architecture—Ivories

Kerstin Merkel
Universität Gesamthochschule Kassel
Mainz

Thom Mertens
Antwerp, Belgium
Mande, Henrik; Radewijns, Florens

Kathleen J. Meyer
Bemidji State University
Jans Enikel; Lutwin; Ulrich von Zatzikhoven

Clyde Lee Miller
State University of New York at Stony Brook
Albertus Magnus; Nicholas of Cusa

Scott Bradford Montgomery
University of North Texas
Gothic Art and Architecture, Late—Metalwork; Iconographies,
Innovative—*Pestkreuz;* Melk; Münster; Sankt Wolfgang; Zillis

Ruth M. W. Moskop
East Carolina University
Aschaffenburg; Coburg; Dinkelsbühl; Hamburg; Landshut;
Maria Wörth; Mariazell; Munich; Passau; Sankt Veit an der
Glan; Viktring; Wiener Neustadt; Würzburg

William North
Carleton College, Northfield, Minn.
Adam of Bremen; Billunger; Bruno of Magdeburg; *Comes/Graf;*
Conrad II; *Dux/Herzog;* Henry III; Saxon War

Jim Ogier
Roanoke College, Salem, Va.
Wittenweiler, Heinrich

Judith H. Oliver
Colgate University
Iconographies, Innovative—*Gnadenstuhl;* Osnabrück; Soest

Lea T. Olsan
Northeast Louisiana University
Magic

Linda B. Parshall
Portland State University
Albrecht von Scharfenberg

Brian A. Pavlac
King's College, Pa.
Berthold von Henneberg; Bouvines, Battle of; Burchard of
Worms; Frederick III; Golden Bull; Hammer of Witches;
Henry VI; Lothar III; Marchfeld, Battle of; Maximilian;
Morgarten, Battle of; Nancy, Battle of; *Reichskirche;* Sempach,
Battle of; Trier; Worrington, Battle of

Contributors

Paul B. Pixton
Brigham Young University
    Adolf of Nassau; Burg; Coblenz; Conrad of Marburg; Conrad of Urach; Constance; Councils/Synods; Crusades, Recruitment; Engelbert of Berg; Judith the Welf; Lahn River; Lorraine; Luxemburger; Matfridings; Meuse River; Ministerials; Moselle River; Nobility and Farmers; Oliver of Paderborn; *Reich;* Rhenish Palatinate; Salians; *Statutum in Favorem Principum;* Toul; Verdun

Sara S. Poor
Stanford University
    Marriage and Divorce; Women

Irmengard Rauch
University of California, Berkeley
    Bible Epic, Saxon

Susanne Reece
Ohio State University
    Koerbecke, Johann; Pilgram, Anton; Pleydenwurff, Hans; Schongauer, Martin

Marta O. Renger
Rheinische Friedrich-Wilhelms Universität Bonn
    Block Book; Freiberg; Gothic Art and Architecture, Late—Painting; Housebook, Master of the; Life of Mary, Master of; Nicolaus Gerhaert von Leyden; Pilgrim's Badges; Wienhausen; Witz, Konrad

Bert Roest
Rijksuniversiteit te Groningen
    Preaching and Sermons, Dutch

Jonathan Rotondo-McCord
Xavier University of Louisiana
    Anno; Birth, Marriage, Burial; Ezzonids; Feudalism; Historiography, German; Land Ownership; Rainald of Dassel

Elisabeth Rüber-Schütte
Landesamt für Denkmalpflege Sachsen-Anhalt
    Halberstadt; Halle

James A. Rushing Jr.
Rutgers University, Camden
    Gottfried von Straßburg, *Tristan,* Illustrations; Heinrich von Veldeke, *Eneide,* Illustrations; *Liederhandschriften,* Illustrations; Rodenegg; Roland and Charlemagne, Illustrations; Runkelstein; Schmalkalden; Wolfram von Eschenbach, *Parzival,* Illustrations; Wolfram von Eschenbach, *Willehalm,* Illustrations

Warren Sanderson
Concordia University, Montreal, Que.
    Ottonian Art and Architecture—Architecture

Lieselotte E. Saurma-Jeltsch
Universität Heidelberg
    Lauber, Diebolt

J. Anda Schippers
Nijmegen, Netherlands
    Fables, Dutch

Corine Schleif
Arizona State University
    Gothic Art and Architecture, Late—Introduction; Iconographies, Innovative—*Schreinmadonna;* Kraft, Adam; Women and Art

Margaret Schleissner
Rider University, Lawrenceville, N.J.
    Hartlieb, Johannes; Medicine; Pregnancy and Childbirth

Brigitte Schliewen
Vaterstetten, Ger.
    Erhart, Gregor; Erhart, Michel; Grasser, Erasmus; Herlin, Friedrich; Leinberger, Hans; Pacher, Michael; Zeitblom, Bartholomäus

Klaus M. Schmidt
Bowling Green State University
    Arthurian Literature, German; Charlemage Epics, German

Carol M. Schuler
The Cloisters, Metropolitan Museum of Art
    Gothic Art and Architecture—Sculpture, Devotional Images; Iconographies, Innovative—*Arma Christi,* —Sorrows of the Virgin; Ludolf of Saxony

James A. Schultz
University of California, Los Angeles
    Childhood

Jenny H. Shaffer
New York
    Aachen; Essen; Fulda

Dorothy M. Shepard
Pratt Institute
    Admont; Millstatt; Romanesque Art and Architecture—Manuscript Illumination; Schwäbisch-Hall

Audrey Shinner
University of Georgia
    Saints' Cult

Elizabeth Siberry
London, Eng.
    Crusades, Opposition

Jeffrey Chipps Smith
University of Texas at Austin
Gothic Art and Architecture, Late—Sculpture; Multscher, Hans; Nuremberg; Rothenburg ob der Tauber; Stoss, Veit; Syrlin, Jörg (Elder and Younger); Ulm; Wolgemut, Michael

Susan L. Smith
University of California, San Diego
Armenbibel

William Bradford Smith
Oglethorpe University, Atlanta, Ga.
Charles IV; Hohenzollern; Wenceslas

Kristine K. Sneeringer
Washington University in St. Louis
Heinrich von Veldeke; Meistersinger

Irene Spijker
Houten, Netherlands
Charlemagne Epics, Dutch

Charlotte Stanford
Pennsylvania State University
Erwin von Steinbach

Mark Stansbury-O'Donnell
University of St. Thomas
Egbert; Speyer; Trier, Art

Kathryn Starkey
University of North Carolina, Chapel Hill
Paleography

Alexandra Sterling-Hellenbrand
Goshen College, Goshen, Ind.
Albrecht von Johansdorf; Heinrich von Morungen

Alison G. Stewart
University of Nebraska, Lincoln
Printmaking

Steven A. Stofferahn
Purdue University
Dhuoda; Judith, Empress

Debra L. Stoudt
University of Toledo
Berthold von Regensburg; David von Augsburg; Friends of God; Mechthild von Hackeborn; Seuse, Heinrich

Robert G. Sullivan
University of Massachusetts
Anegenge; *Genesis* and *Exodus*

Pegatha Taylor
University of California, Berkeley
Capitularies; *Eigenkirche*

Rita Tekippe
University of Central Arkansas
Frederick I Barbarossa, Art; Gothic Art and Architecture—Ivories; Siegburg, Art

Lynn D. Thelen
Ursinus College, Collegeville, Pa.
Nibelungenlied; Werner der Gärtner

J. W. Thomas
University of Kentucky
Pleier, Der

David F. Tinsley
University of Puget Sound
Hermann von Sachsenheim

Frank Tobin
University of Nevada, Reno
Mechthild von Magdeburg; Meister Eckhart

Jens Ulff-Møller
Lyngby, Denmark
Coinage and Mints; Numbers and Calculation

William Urban
Monmouth College, Monmouth, Ill.
Deutschorden

Alphons M. J. van Buuren
Amersfort, Netherlands
Potter, Dirc

Stephanie Cain Van D'Elden
University of Minnesota
Graf Rudolf; Helbling, Seifried; Kürenberc, Der von; *Moriz von Craûn;* Suchenwirt, Peter

Evert van den Berg
Zwolle, Netherlands
Dutch Language, Dialects

Dieuwke van der Poel
Rijksuniversiteit te Utrecht
Heinric; *Roman de la Rose,* Dutch

Kim Vivian
Augustana College, Rock Island, Ill.
Hartmann von Aue

Contributors

Susan von Daum Tholl
Simmons College, Boston
    Carolingian Art and Architecture—Painting

Oebele Vries
Rijksuniversiteit Groningen
    Friesland

Stephen L. Wailes
Indiana University
    Drama

Richard Ernest Walker
University of Maryland at College Park
    Literature and Historiography; Peter von Staufenberg

James K. Walter
Ohio Northern University
    Servatius; *Sylvester, Trierer; Tnugdalus*

Susan L. Ward
Rhode Island School of Design
    Ars Moriendi; Bamberg; Braunschweig; Cistercian Art and
    Architecture; Gothic Art and Architecture—Introduction,
    —Sculpture, Early Altarpieces, —Sculpture, Interior
    Programs, —Sculpture, Portal Programs; Iconographies,
    Innovative—Mass of Saint Gregory; Liturgy, Furniture; Maria
    Laach; Naumburg; Nicholas of Verdun; Notke, Brent;
    Romanesque Art and Architecture—Sculpture; Roriczer,
    Matthew; Rostock; *Schleswig*

David A. Warner
Rhode Island School of Design
    Liudolfinger; Magdeburg; *Renovatio Imperii Romanorum;*
    Thietmar of Merseburg; Widukind of Corvey

Sarah Westphal
McGill University, Montreal, Que.
    Sammelhandschrift

William Whobrey
Yale University
    Bookmaking and Production; Libraries; Universities

Katharina M. Wilson
University of Georgia
    Hrosvit of Gandersheim

Anne Winston-Allen
Southern Illinois University at Carbondale
    Johannes von Tepl; Gardens and Gardening; Rosary

Gregory H. Wolf
St. Louis University
    Koblenz; Lucerne; Meißen; Schwerin; Worms

Manfred Zimmermann
University of Cincinnati
    Heinrich von Neustadt

Jan M. Ziolkowski
Harvard University
    Archpoet; *Ecbasis Captivi;* Hrabanus Maurus; Latin Language;
    Poeta Saxo; *Ruodlieb;* Walahfrid Strabo; *Waltharius*

Detlef Zinke
Augustinermuseum, Freiburg im Breisgau
    Freiburg

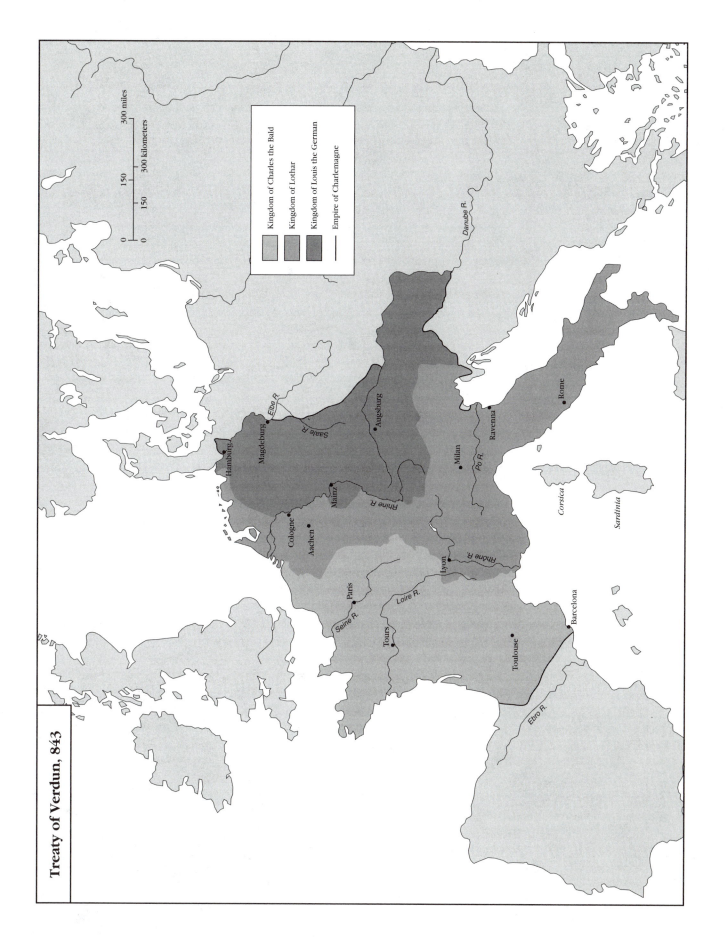

Treaty of Verdun, 843

Kingdom of Charles the Bald
Kingdom of Lothar
Kingdom of Louis the German
Empire of Charlemagne

300 miles
300 kilometers
150
150
0
0

Danube R.
Elbe R.
Saale R.
Augsburg
Magdeburg
Hamburg
Mainz
Cologne
Aachen
Rhine R.
Milan
Po R.
Ravenna
Rome
Corsica
Sardinia
Rhône R.
Lyon
Paris
Loire R.
Seine R.
Tours
Toulouse
Barcelona
Ebro R.

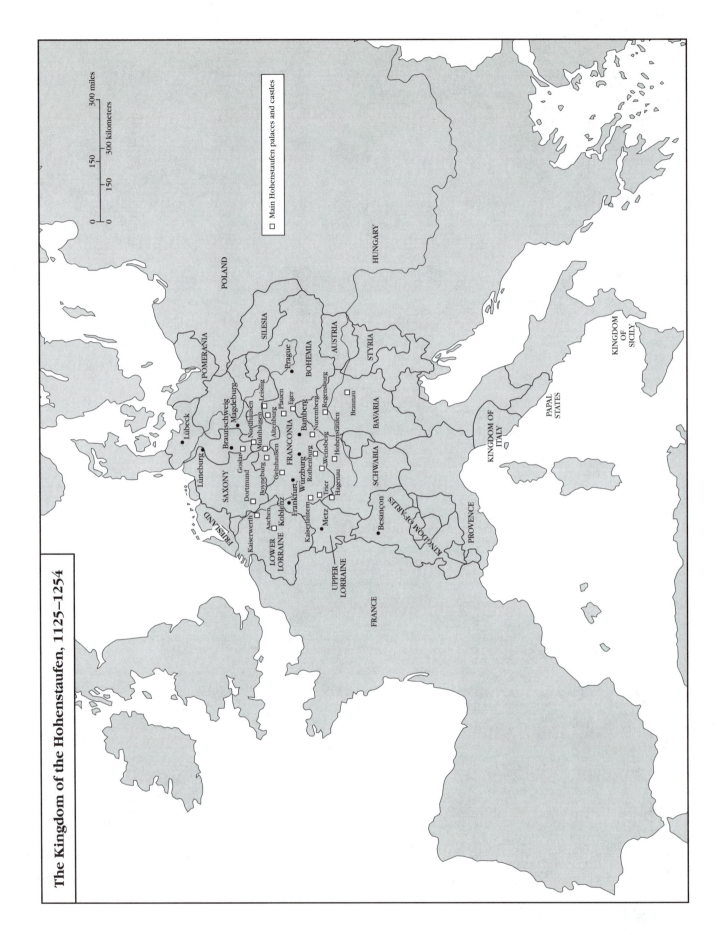

The Kingdom of the Hohenstaufen, 1125–1254

□ Main Hohenstaufen palaces and castles

300 miles
300 kilometers

POLAND

POMERANIA

SILESIA

BOHEMIA

AUSTRIA

STYRIA

HUNGARY

KINGDOM OF SICILY

Prague

Lübeck

Braunschweig
Magdeburg
Nordhausen
Mühlhausen Leisnig
Plauen
Altenburg
Eger
Bamberg
Nuremberg
Regensburg

Braunau

BAVARIA

Lüneburg

SAXONY

Goslar
Dortmund
Boyneburg
Gelnhausen
FRANCONIA
Würzburg
Rothenburg
Weinsberg
Hohenstaufen

SCHWABIA

Kaiserwerth

Aachen
Koblenz
FRANKFURT
Kaiserslautern
Metz
Trier
Hagenau

FRIESLAND

LOWER
LORRAINE

UPPER
LORRAINE

Besançon

KINGDOM OF ARLES

PROVENCE

KINGDOM OF ITALY

PAPAL STATES

FRANCE

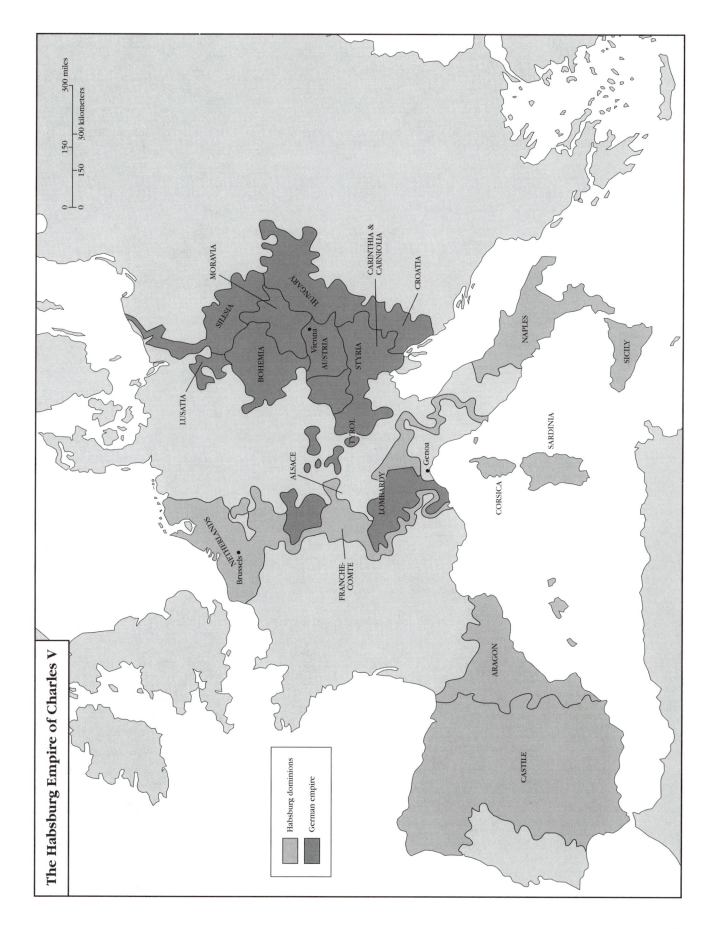

The Habsburg Empire of Charles V

300 miles

300 kilometers

Habsburg dominions

German empire

MORAVIA

SILESIA

BOHEMIA

LUSATIA

HUNGARY

Vienna

AUSTRIA

STYRIA

CARINTHIA & CARNIOLIA

CROATIA

TYROL

ALSACE

Genoa

LOMBARDY

FRANCHE-COMTE

NETHERLANDS

Brussels

NAPLES

SICILY

SARDINIA

CORSICA

ARAGON

CASTILE

A

Aachen

A cultural and strategic center during the Carolingian dynasty and Holy Roman Empire, Aachen, known for its hot springs, was the location of first-century Roman baths. By the late fourth or early fifth century, Roman structures had been transformed into a Christian cult site. Perhaps lured by the waters, Pippin (Pépin) III, founder of the Carolingian dyansty, wintered in Aachen with his itinerant court in 766 and erected a residence. While little is known of Pippin's activities, evidence of his continuation of the cult site exists in scanty archaeological remains beneath the church built by his son, Charlemagne. Aachen's unparalleled renown and complex, changing significance may be tied to Charlemagne, who erected a palace—his favored residence—from ca. 792–805. This ambitious "capital," located within the Frankish stronghold of Austrasia, created a political, ecclesiastical, and artistic center for Charlemagne's empire and became the kernel of the medieval city.

While excavations shed light on aspects of the extensive complex, Charlemagne's palace, located in what is still Aachen's center, is no longer extant, save for portions of his chapel to the Virgin and the *Granusturm,* a square, multistoried, staired structure punctured by round-arched windows. The chapel, a two-story polygonal structure with a multistoried westwork (western entry structure), preceded by a forecourt and flanked to the north and south by (now lost) basilical structures, exists today in much altered form, partially masked by nineteenth-century restorations. The chapel forecourt communicated with the audience hall to the north through a walkway with a central gatehouse. The extant *Granusturm* stood at the east end of the audience hall (atop which a Gothic town hall was built), giving access to the build-ing's upper reaches as well as to a neighboring two-story building.

Aspects of the palace structures may be likened formally to Roman and Byzantine works—the chapel to San Vitale in Ravenna and the audience hall to Constantine's audience hall in Trier. From what is known of the buildings and the chapel's lavish outfitting, however, it is evident that Charlemagne mined, and thus assumed and directed, a number of pasts to create a multivalent, malleable image. The chapel's bronze doors, the *spolia* (recycled) columns of the interior columnar screen juxtaposed with the second-story bronze grills and now-lost dome mosaic, as well as the rich production of the "court school," all bear witness to diverse, evocative artistic preoccupations.

With Charlemagne's death at Aachen in 814, Louis the Pious (Louis I) ruled from the center established by his father. Throughout the Middle Ages, possession of Aachen, and thus of Charlemagne, was seen as a conferral of authority and legitimacy, a notion evidenced early, in the unsuccessful attempt by Charles II (Charles the Bald) to take the city in 876. Aachen's multilayered and changing importance as a power center became increasingly complex as successive rulers took up residence, augmenting the palace as well as the burgeoning city.

The 936 coronation of Otto I (Otto the Great) initiated a tradition in which the chapel at Aachen was the locus for the coronation of "German" rulers until 1531. The Ottonian focus on their appropriated imperial center is evidenced by the rulers' extant commissions for the chapel, including the Lothar Cross (ca. 1000), the Gospel Book of Otto III (ca. 990), the altar frontal known as the Pala d'Oro (ca. 1020), and the ambo (lectern) of Henry II (r. 1002–1024). Otto III as well augmented the cityscape

Aachen, palace chapel, view from north. *Photograph: Joan A. Holladay*

through a ring of foundations: the Church of the Savior, a Benedictine foundation for women, to the north (on the site of the late-ninth-century funerary church of Louis the Pious); the basilical collegiate church dedicated to the emperor's friend, the martyr Saint Adalbert, to the east; and the Benedictine abbey of Burtscheid to the south. These foundations, completed under Henry II, have subsequently undergone numerous rebuildings. Otto III's particular interest in Aachen, and in Charlemagne, reached an apogee with his "discovery" of Charlemagne's tomb within the chapel on Pentecost in the year 1000.

The twelfth century saw another spate of imperial interest in Aachen, as Frederick I Barbarossa, who walled the growing city in the late twelfth century (expanded in the thirteenth and fourteenth centuries), purportedly opened Charlemagne's tomb in 1165 and removed the remains. While the ruler again lavished great attention on Aachen, the elaborate chandelier (the *Barbarossaleuchter*), probably created in connection with Charlemagne's canonization after the exhumation, stands today as his significant commission. The creation of the shrine (ca. 1182–1215) for

Charlemagne's relics and the *Marienschrein* (shrine of the Virgin), begun in 1238 to hold relics of Christ, the Virgin, and John the Baptist donated by Charlemagne, anchored the status of Aachen as a multivalent holy site.

The growing cult gave rise, beginning in the fourteenth century, to the city's prominence as a pilgrimage site, the goal of the *Aachenfahrt* (pilgrimage to Aachen). The numerous chapels attached to the perimeter of Charlemagne's building—the *Matthiaskapelle* (first quarter of the fourteenth century); the *Annakapelle* (thirteenth and fourteenth centuries); the *Karlskapelle* (1455–1474); the *Nikolaskapelle* (second half of the fifteenth century); and the vast choir (1355–1414)—together with additions to the chapel's treasury, bear testimony to the changing yet persistently central importance of Aachen in the Middle Ages.

BIBLIOGRAPHY

Faymonville, Karl. *Die Kunstdenkmäler der Stadt Aachen.* 2 vols. 1916; rpt. Düsseldorf: Schwann, 1981.

Grimme, Ernst Günther. *Der Dom zu Aachen: Architektur und Ausstattung.* Aachen: Einhard-Verlag, 1994.

Heitz, Carol. *L'architecture religieuse carolingienne: Les formes et leurs fonctions.* Paris: Picard, 1980.

Kubach, Hans Erich, and Albert Verbeek. *Romanische Baukunst an Rhein und Maas: Katalog der vorromanischen und romanischen Denkmäler,* vol. 1. Berlin: Deutscher Verlag für Kunstwissenschaft, 1976, pp. 1–19.

Jenny H. Shaffer

SEE ALSO

Carolingian Art and Architecture; Charlemagne; Frederick I Barbarossa; Gothic Art and Architecture; Henry II, Art; Louis the Pious; Otto I; Otto III; Romanesque Art and Architecture

Abrogans

Preserved in three mansucripts, this Latin–Old High German glossary is "the oldest German book," the first German-Latin bilingual dictionary and the first German dictionary of any kind. The eighth-century manuscript from St. Gall includes the OHG Lord's Prayer and Creed (written by a different scribe), and also contains a significant source for the Latin *Abrogans,* the *Abavus maior* glossary. Some 3,670 Old High German glosses (circa 14,700 attestations) of an alphabetical Latin thesaurus of obscure biblical terms were compiled from various older Latin, largely patristic glossaries (see heading: *Incipiunt closas ex novo et veteris testamenti,* "Here begin glosses from the New and Old Testament"). Manuscript K (St. Gall) is a late-eighth-century copy from the southwestern German-speaking area, perhaps Murbach; Pa was copied circa 810 in Murbach; Ra represents an early ninth-century copy from Reichenau. K and Ra are copies made from the same version. The original *Abrogans deutsch* is perhaps from the mid–eighth century. The manuscripts show Irish/Anglo-Saxon scribal influence, corresponding to the introduction of glossaries to Germany by English missionaries.

Abrogans is an alphabetical listing by Latin headword [L], followed by Latin synonym(s) [S], each with Old High German translation [T]. Beginning with the title headword (K, p. 4): *Abrogans* [L1] = *dheomodi* [T1], *humilis* [S1] = *samftmoati* [T2]; *abba* [L2] = *faterlih* [T3], *pater* [S2] = *vater* [T4]; and so on. The glosses, an invaluable source of early OHG vocabulary and grammar, are evidence of intense lexicographical labor, aimed primarily at careful Bible study. *Samanunga-uuorto,* an abridged reworking of the Latin-German glossary, appeared later.

BIBLIOGRAPHY

Bischoff, Bernhard, Johannes Duft, and Stefan Sonderegger (transcription), eds. Die *"Abrogans"-Handschrift der Stiftsbibliothek St. Gallen: das älteste deutsche Buch.* 2 vols. St. Gallen: Zollikofer, 1977.

Sievers, Eduard, and Elias Steinmeyer, eds. *Die althochdeutschen Glossen,* vol. 1. 1879; rpt. Dublin and Zurich: Weidmann, 1969, pp. 1–270.

Splett, Jochen. "Abrogans (deutsch)." In *Die deutsche Literatur des Mittelalters: Verfasserlexikon,* vol. 1. 2d ed. Berlin: de Gruyer, 1978, cols. 12–15.

———. *Abrogans-Studien.* Stuttgart: Steiner, 1976.

John M. Jeep

SEE ALSO
Glosses, Old High German; Latin Language

Adam of Bremen (fl. 2nd half of the 11th c.)

Author of the *Gesta Hammaburgensis ecclesiae Pontificum* (History of the Archbishops of Hamburg-Bremen), Adam of Bremen is widely regarded as one of the finest historians of the Early Middle Ages, yet little is known about the man himself beyond the hints and allusions embedded in his history and its extensive marginalia. These suggest that Adam was born in Franconia and was probably trained in the cathedral school of either Bamberg or Würzburg. In 1066/1067 he joined the church of Bremen, having been recruited by the mercurial and ambitious Archbishop Adalbert (1043–1072), who probably saw in him a means to improve the literary reputation of his see. By 1069, Adam was in charge of the cathedral school at Bremen, appearing in a document as *magister scolarum* (master of learning). Soon thereafter, Adam began working on his *Gesta.* In his search for information on the history of his church and its privileges, he drew upon—often quite critically—a wide range of sources including Carolingian hagiography, diplomata, papal letters, and the accounts of eyewitnesses such as King Sven II Estridsen of Denmark, one of Adam's principal informants on the peoples of and Christian missions to Scandinavia. Completed just after Adalbert's death (1072), the first "edition" of the history (1075/1076) was dedicated to Adalbert's successor Liemar (1072–1101). Adam continued to revise and augment his history in marginalia until his death in the early 1080s.

In the first two of the four books comprising his work, Adam traced the history of the church of Hamburg-Bremen from its foundation in the eighth century until

1043, attentively documenting the vicissitudes of its wealth and power in the region and the role played by its bishops in the politics of the German Reich. In book 3, Adam turned to the pontificate of Bishop Adalbert and rendered a portrait of his late patron that is remarkable for its subtle portrayal of this tragic, complex man; indeed, it is recognized as a milestone in medieval biography. Having repeatedly highlighted his church's leading role in the conversion of the northern peoples to Christianity, Adam devoted the whole of book 4 to detailed descriptions of the geography, people, and customs of the Scandinavian lands as well as the progress of missionary efforts in those areas. Although perhaps intended to aid and inspire later missionaries, Adam's relatively balanced account of these non-Christian peoples makes his work a monument of medieval geographical writing and one of the most important sources of information concerning pre-Christian Scandinavia.

BIBLIOGRAPHY

Adam of Bremen. *History of the Archbishops of Hamburg-Bremen,* trans. F. J. Tschan. New York: Columbia University Press, 1959.

———. *Magistri Adam Bremensis Gesta Hammaburgensis Ecclesiae Pontificum,* ed. B. Schmeidler. Monumenta Germaniae istorica. Scriptores Rerum Germanicarum 2. Hannover: Hahn, 1917.

Misch, Georg. *Geschichte der Autobiographie,* vol. 3, pt. 1. Frankfurt am Main: G. Schulte-Bulmke, 1959, pp. 168–214.

Theuerkauf, G. "Die Hamburgische Kirchengeschichte Adams von Bremen. Gesellschaftsformen und Weltbilder im elften Jahrhundert." In *Historiographia Mediaevalis . . . Festschrift für Franz-Josef Schmale,* ed. Dieter Berg and Hans-Werner Goetz. Darmstadt: Wissenschaftliche Buchgesellschaft, 1988, pp. 118–137.

William North

SEE ALSO

Carolingians; *Fürstbischof; Reich*

Adam von Fulda (ca. 1445–1505)

Generally remembered as a musician, Adam von Fulda was a remarkably versatile scholar who was respected for his poetry and historiography as well as for his musical accomplishments. He was probably born in Fulda around 1445 and was a member of the Benedictine order at Vormbach until his marriage in 1490. In that year he went to work for Frederick the Wise, Elector of Saxony, entering court service at Torgau as a singer. In 1492 Frederick appointed him court historiographer, suggesting that he compile a history of the Saxons. By 1498 he was in charge of musical activities at Frederick's court. In 1502 he was appointed professor of music at Wittenberg University, a post he held until his death from the plague in 1505.

His music theory treatise *De musica,* the work for which he is best remembered, dates from his years at Vormbach; it was completed the year he left the order. The four parts of this work deal with music in general, the modes and their application in composition, musical meter and notation, and musical intervals. While Adam's rules for composition may be regarded today as vague and general, they are nevertheless a competent codification of contemporary practice. Noteworthy is his attack on those responsible for the damage done to music by instrumentation of vocal compositions and inaccurate musical notation.

Most of Adam's surviving music is liturgical, including seven hymns, one mass, a magnificat, two antiphons, and a respond. The compositional style of these works owes less to the composer's contemporaries such as Josquin des Prez and more to the Burgundian composers of the preceding generation, principally Guillaume Dufay, whom Adam regarded as a composer worthy of imitation. Yet Adam was most highly regarded in his time for his secular songs, three of which have survived: "Ach Jupiter" (Oh, Jupiter), "Apollo aller Kunst" (Apollo of all art), and "Ach hülff mich leyd" (Oh, help me sorrow), the last of which the Swiss music theorist Heinrich Loris (Henricus Glareanus, 1488–1563) recommended as a skillfully composed and justly famous work. Indeed, in addition to appearing in the *Dodecachordon* (Basel, 1547) with a sacred text added by Loris himself, versions of the song are found in many other musical collections of the time, such as in a songbook from Aachen and in transcription for keyboard in two collections from Poland.

Adam's publications outside of music include a collection of religious poetry compiled by Wolf Cyklops of Zwickau. This volume, published by Symphorian Reinhart in 1512 and known for its eight woodcuts by Lucas Cranach, was dedicated to Duke John of Saxony, brother of Frederick the Wise. Johannes Heidenberg (Johannes Trithemius, 1462–1516), abbot of Würzburg, used Adam's unfinished history of the Saxons in his own historical writings, but he attributes Adam's contributions to a fictitious eleventh-century monk, Megenfrid of Fulda.

BIBLIOGRAPHY

Adam de Fulda. "De Musica." 1490. *Scriptores ecclesiastici de musica sacra potissimum,* ed. Martin Gerbert. Vol. 3. St. Blaise: Typis San-Blasianis, 1784; rpt. Hildesheim: Olms, 1963, pp. 329–381.

Borchardt, Frank L. *German Antiquity in Renaissance Myth.* Baltimore: Johns Hopkins Press, 1971.

Bridgman, Nanie. "The Age of Ockeghem and Josquin." In *The New Oxford History of Music,* vol. 3, *Ars Nova and the Renaissance, 1300–1400,* ed. Dom Anselm Hughes and Gerald Abraham. London: Oxford University Press, 1960. Glareanus Henricus. *Dodecachordon,* trans. Clement A. Miller. N.p.: American Institute of Musicology, 1965.

Niemöller, Klaus Wolfgang. "Adam von Fulda." In *The New Grove Dictionary of Music and Musicians,* ed. Stanley Sadie. Vol. 1. London: Macmillan, 1980, p. 120.

Riemann, Hugo. *History of Music Theory,* trans. Raymond Haagh. Lincoln: University of Nebraska Press, 1962.

Seton-Watson, R. W. "The Abbot Trithemius." In *Tudor Studies.* Freeport, N.Y.: Books for Libraries Press, 1969.

Andrew E. Anderson

Adelheid of Burgundy
(ca. 931–December 16/17, 999)

Holy Roman Empress and saint, Adelheid (Adelaide) of Burgundy (Adelheid von Burgund) was the daughter of Rudolf II of Burgundy (r. 912–937) and Bertha of Swabia (d. 960). In 937 Adelheid was betrothed to Lothar of Italy, marrying him in 947. After Lothar's death in 950, Berengar II of Ivrea seized the throne and in April 951 Adelheid was incarcerated; she escaped in August. Her plight came to the attention of the German king Otto I, who traveled to Italy in September 951; they were married in October. Between 952 and 955 Adelheid had four children: Henry and Brun, both of whom died in childhood, and Mathilda and Otto. Adelheid was politically active during Otto's reign, but after his death in 973, she retired to Italy when her relationship with her son Otto II and his Byzantine wife Theophanu deteriorated.

After Otto II's death in 983, Theophanu's assumption of the regency for Otto III restricted Adelheid's influence. But Theophanu died in 991 and Adelheid continued the regency to 995. Adelheid spent her remaining years at the monastery of Selz, her foundation in Alsace. She died at Selz on the night of December 16/17, 999.

Adelheid was called "Companion of Kings" *(consors regni);* Pope Sylvester II called her "Mother of Kingdoms." Abbot Odilo of Cluny wrote her epitaph and Pope Urban II canonized her in 1097. No descriptions or personal letters exist, but the memorial book of the Ottonians contains the dates April 20, 950 and August 20, 950 with the details of Adelheid's imprisonment. These incidents defined Adelheid's personality, and it was through these deeds that she wished to be remembered.

BIBLIOGRAPHY

Baumer, Gertrud. *Otto I und Adelheid.* Tübingen: Wunderlich, 1951.

Eickhoff, Ekkehard. *Theophanu und der König: Otto III und seine Welt.* Stuttgart: Klett-Cotta, 1996.

Glocker, Winfrid. *Die Verwandten der Ottonen und ihre Bedeutung in der Politik.* Cologne: Böhlau, 1989.

Odilo of Cluny. "Epitaphium domine Adelheide auguste." In *Mitteilungen des Instituts fur Österreichische Geschichte: Ergänzungsband 20/2.* ed. Herbert Paulhart Graz: Böhlaus Nachfolger, 1962. [Odilo's life of Adelheid.]

Madelyn Bergen Dick

SEE ALSO

Otto I; Otto II; Otto III; Sylvester II; Theophanu

Admonitio Generalis

The *Admonitio Generalis* (General Admonition) is the capitulary, or collection of ordinaces, issued by Charlemagne in 789 that most clearly states the educational and religious goals and ideals of the great Frankish king and that also laid the foundation for the Carolingian renaissance. Consisting of eighty-two chapters (fifty-nine of which borrowed extensively from the eighth-century canon law collection *Dionysio-Hadriana*), the *Admonitio* reveals the level of cultural sophistication achieved at Charlemagne's court and the greater goals the court sought to reach. In this capitulary, Charlemagne asserted his understanding that he was a new Josiah with the responsibility to rule over God's new chosen people and the duty to reform their moral and spiritual lives so that they could achieve salvation. To accomplish this goal, and to create "peace, concord, and unanimity" among the Christian people, the *Admonitio* contains legislation concerning the moral reform and discipline of the priesthood. The capitulary emphasizes the responsibility of the priesthood to preach "rightly and honestly" and to avoid innovation and teachings contrary to the canons. Priests are expected to live moral lives, to teach their flocks to follow their example, and to be guided in the performance of their duties by the bishops. Chapter 72 of the *Admonitio* asserts the responsibility of the bishops and monks to establish schools to teach boys to read and write and to correct books important to the faith. The *Admonitio Generalis* established the religious reform program of Charlemagne's reign and, with the *Epistola de litteris colendis,* the revival of learning associated with his broader reform program.

BIBLIOGRAPHY

Admonitio Generalis. Monumenta Germaniae historica 22, pt. 1. Hannover: Hahn, n.d., pp. 53–62.

McKitterick, Rosamond. *The Frankish Church and the Carolingian Reforms, 789–895.* London: Longman, 1977.

Michael Frassetto

SEE ALSO

Capitularies; Carolingians; Charlemagne

Admont

In 1074 Archbishop Gebehard of Salzburg founded a Benedictine monastery in Styria with monks form the monastery of St. Peter at Salzburg. Gebehard, who presented the foundation books, vestments, chalices, and other liturgical necessities, was buried there. Among the manuscripts he gave Admont are an eleventh-century Italian giant Bible (Admont manuscripts C/D) and a gospel book (manuscript no. 511). The latter was made in Salzburg in the late eleventh century and is decorated with architectually framed portraits of the gospel writers on gold grounds.

Admont's scholarly life and scriptorium were very active in the Romanesque period. It produced manuscripts of intellectual vigor, some of them illuminated. The fact that some of these were signed by women is a reminder that Admont also housed a group of nuns. Their conventual buildings and the abbey church were both dedicated in 1121.

The Admont Bible, a giant Bible made in Salzburg circa 1140–1150 (now Vienna, Österreichische National-biblothek, no. Cod. Series nova 2701–2702), was owned by the monastery from the fourteenth century until 1937. This important Bible, known for its numerous framed miniatures, also contains many historiated and decorated initials. Much of its iconography and the modeling of its faces derive from Byzantine models, which is characteristic of Salzburg painting of the twelfth century.

The contents of the library, including around 1,100 manuscripts, are all that are left of the medieval monastery after the fire of 1865.

BIBILOGRAPHY

Beach, Alison I. "The Female Scribes of Twelfth-Century Bavaria." Ph.d. diss., Columbia University, 1996.

Buberl, Paul. *Die illuminierten Handschriften in Steiermark 1: Die Stiftsbibliothek zu Admont und Vorau.* Beschreibendes Verzeichnis der illuminierten Handschriften in Österreich 4. Leipzig: Hiersemann, 1911, pp. 1–160.

Mannewitz, Martin. *Stift Admont: Untersuchungen zu Entwicklungsgeschichte, Ausstattung und Ikonographie der Klosteranlage.* Munich: Scaneg, 1989.

Mazal, Otto. *Katalog der abendländischen Handschriften der Österreichischen Nationalbibliothek, Series nova,* 4 vols. Vienna: George Prachner, 1963, vol. 2/1, pp. 359–368.

Swarzenski, Georg. *Die Salzburger Malerei von den ersten Anfängen bis zur Blütezeit des romanischen Stils: Studien zur Geschichte der deutschen Malerei und Handschriftenkunde des Mittelalters,* 2 vols. Lepizig: Hiersemann, 1980–1913, pp. 72–77; figs. 92–113.

Swarzenski, Hanns. "Two Unnoticed Leaves from the Admont Bible." *Scriptorium* 10 (1956): 94–96.

Swoboda, Karl M. "Die Bilder der Admonter Bibel des 12. Jahrhunderts." *Neue Aufgaben der Kunstgeschichte* (1935): 47–63.

"Vitae Gebehardi et successorum eius." *Monumenta Germaniae Historica, Scriptores* 11, ed. G.H. Pertz. Hannover: Hahn, 1854, pp. 17–51.

Wehli, Tünde. "Die Admonter Bibel." *Acta Historiae Artium* 23/3–4 (1977): 173–285.

Dorothy M. Shepard

SEE ALSO

Romanesque Art and Architecture; Salzburg

Adolf of Nassau (1250–July 2, 1298)

The son of Count Walram II of Nassau, Adolf was the German King from 1292 to 1298. Born in 1250, he married Imagina of Limburg and acquired a reputation as a warrior early on. His brief rise to prominence came about following the failure of King Rudolf I of Habsburg to win over King Wenceslas II of Bohemia to the election of Rudolf's son, Duke Albert of Austria, as successor to the throne at a diet held at Frankfurt in 1291, just weeks before his death. Duke Albert of Saxony and probably also Margrave Otto of Brandenburg gave their votes to Bohemia at Zittau for a sum of money. This coalition was broken up by Archbishop Siegfried of Cologne, who supported Count Adolf of Nassau, to whom he had been obligated since the battle of Worringen in 1288. Archbishop Siegfried in turn persuaded Archbishop Gerhard II of Mainz to join him. Adolf was elected in the Dominican church at Frankfurt on May 5, 1292 with the votes of Mainz (voting also for Bohemia), Cologne, Saxony, and perhaps also Brandenburg. Pfalzgrave (Count Palatine) Ludwig II was alone in supporting the candidacy of Albert of Austria.

Adolf's election was in part a reaction against the pro-French policy of the Habsburgs, but it was also due to the fact that Adolf was territorially weak and thus posed no threat to the great princes of the empire. Rudolf, too, had begun his reign as a weak king, but the acquisition of Austria had made him one of the most powerful princes in the empire, and a king with an extensive power base was not to their liking. Prior to his coronation on June 24, 1292, Adolf had capitulated to exorbitant demands by the electors which pushed his modest resources to the limit: Cologne was promised 25,000 marks, with several Nassau fortresses taken as security; he was also obligated to hand over various lands, including some fortresses which did not even belong to him; Wenceslas II of Bohemia apparently received the promise that Adolf's son Rupert would marry Agnes of Bohemia, and that until the marriage, imperial lands in Pleißen (around Altenburg) and Eger would be held as security; Archbishop Gerhard of Mainz insisted that Adolf assume his debts incurred with the curia at his (Gerhard's) election, and that Landgrave (territorial ruler) Henry of Hesse be elevated to the status of an imperial prince; Archbishop Bohemund of Trier made rather modest demands.

Adolf's policy thereafter was dictated by the need to relieve his staggering financial burdens, while at the same time securing a better territorial basis for his monarchy. In 1293 he bought the *Landgrafschaft* (provincial ducal property) of Thuringia (in some sources also Meißen) from the always-needy Albert the Entarteter, Landgrave of Thuringia for 11,000–12,000 marks of silver. While this increased Adolf's debt substantially, it gave him a significant territorial base, something he had previously lacked. Adolf's presence in Thuringia was perceived as a threat to the archbishop of Mainz, however, whose church had extensive holdings there also. The king's position vis-à-vis the princes took an even bolder upturn in June 1294 when Edward I of England offered an alliance against France which included a £25,000 subsidy. Backed with such resources, Adolf made a move to actually take possession of his Thuringian and other middle-Germany lands from the landgrave's disinherited sons, Frederick the Dauntless and Dietzmann (Dietrich).

Adolf's growing power so close to Bohemia eventually drove King Wenceslas into the camp of his former archrival, Duke Albert of Austria. Criticism of Adolf was voiced in 1297 while Archbishop Gerhard was in Prague to conduct the belated consecration of Wenceslas as king. By February 1298 Brandenburg and Saxony had joined the conspiracy as well: they had persuaded Duke Albert to bring his army to the Rhine and attack Adolf, following which they would declare the latter deposed and Albert his successor. The plot unfolded almost as scripted: while Albert busied Adolf with his army on the Upper Rhine, Archbishop Gerhard of Mainz, who had been excommunicated by the pope, set about to orchestrate the deposition; this action took place on June 23, 1298 with five of the seven electoral votes.

Adolf tried to reclaim in battle what he had lost through the electors' treachery: he fell at Göllheim, near Worms, on July 2, 1298, and was buried at the monastery Rosenthal. He was remembered in two long, contemporary poems.

BIBLIOGRAPHY

Patze, H. "Erzbischof Gerhard II von Mainz und König Adolf von Nassau." *Hessisches Jahrbuch für Landesgeschichte* 13 (1963): 83–140.

Samanek, Vincenz. *Studien zur Geschichte König Adolfs von Nassau.* Sitzungsberichte der österreichischen Akademie der Wissenschaft, philosophisch-historische Klasse 207, no. 2. Vienna: Holder-Pichler-Tempsky, 1930.

Schliephake, F. W. Theodor. *Geschichte von Nassau*, vols. 2–3. Wiesbaden: Kreidel, 1867, 1869.

Trautz, Fritz. "Studien zur Geschichte und Würdigung König Adolfs von Nassau." *Geschichtliche Landeskunde* 2 (1965): 1–65.

Paul B. Pixton

SEE ALSO
Wenceslas

Agricola, Rodolphus (Roelof Huysman; 1443/1444–October 27, 1485)

One of the earliest and most important humanists of the Low Countries, Agricola was multitalented and had a great influence on the development of northern humanism.

He was born in 1443/1444 in Baflo near Groningen, studied medieval liberal arts in Erfurt (B.A. 1458) and Louvain (M.A. 1465), and law during his stay at Pavia (1468/1469–1475, with several interruptions). In Pavia he also became influenced by Italian humanists. In 1484 he lectured on Pliny the Younger at Heidelberg, where he died October 27, 1485.

Agricola was not a prolific writer; his oeuvre is rather limited and heterogeneous. It includes a treatise on the art of dialectical invention entitled *De inventione dialectica,* and a number of Latin poems, letters, and orations, most of which are available only in manuscripts and early printed editions.

In *De inventione dialectica,* completed in 1479 and considered to be his main work, Agricola puts forward a theory for finding arguments and for developing and structuring reasoning. In opposition to the medieval tradition, it combines dialectics and rhetoric. The work has a practical, not a theoretical, orientation and examines and uncovers the laws of speech and argumentation. It teaches how to use language correctly and persuasively, in literature, politics, preaching, science, and so on. The book became very popular in the sixteenth century and was issued in a large number of editions.

BIBLIOGRAPHY

Agricola, Rodolphus. *De inventione dialectica lucubrationes.* Cologne, 1539; rpt. Nieuwkoop: De Graaf, 1967.

———. *De inventione dialectica libri omnes.* Cologne, 1539; repr. Frankfurt am Main: Minerva, 1967.

———. *De inventione libri tres. Drei Bücher über die Inventio dialectica,* ed. Lothar Mundt. Tübingen: Niemeyer, 1992.

———. *Over dialectica en humanisme,* ed. Marc van der Poel. Baarn: Ambo, 1991.

———. "Rudolph Agricola's De Inventione Libri Tres: A Translation of Selected Chapters," ed. J. R. McNally. *Speech Monographs* 34 (1967): 393–422.

Akkerman, Fokke, and Arjo Vanderjagt, eds. *Rodolpus Agricola Phrisius 1444–1485.* Leiden: Brill, 1988 [bibliography pp. 314–344].

Maarten J. F. M. Hoenen

Agriculture

See Feudalism; Gardens and Gardening; Nobility and Farmers

Albertus Magnus (ca. 1200–1280)

Also known as "Albert the Great" and "Universal Doctor," Albertus Magnus was a Dominican theologian, philosopher, scientist, and saint. One of the most famous medieval precursors of modern science and best known today as the teacher of Thomas Aquinas, Albert was renowned in his own day for his encyclopedic knowledge, his voluminous writings, and his interpretive rendering of Arabic Aristotelian sources into Latin. In part due to spurious works given his name, he gained further repute after his death and into the Renaissance as a magician and alchemist. Albert introduced his own sort of Aristotelian scholasticism to the Dominican houses of study he founded in Germany, and Albertist Aristotelianism became one strain of the scholastic *via antiqua* (old path) that endured in German universities.

Born in Lauingen, Bavaria, Albert first studied at Padua, joined the Dominicans in 1223, and went to Cologne to study theology. He moved to Paris (1241) to complete his master in theology (1245), and was the first German to hold a chair of theology there. He lectured at Paris until returning to Cologne (1248) to found the Dominican precursor to the university, *studium generale.* Thomas Aquinas, Ulrich of Strassburg, and Giles of Lessines were among his students during these years. Made provincial of German Dominicans (1254), Albert acted as arbiter in many difficult ecclesial and political disputes, one of which led to his being made bishop of Regensburg briefly in the 1260s. Sent to all Germany by Pope Urban IV to preach the Crusade in 1263–1264, he thereafter resided mostly in Cologne, although he traveled on foot continuously throughout Germany, as well as to France and to Italy. Albert preached, taught theology, and wrote continuously from the 1230s until just before his death in 1280.

In Paris in the 1240s he wrote his *Summa de creaturis* (Book of the Creatures) and commented on Peter Lombard's *Sentences.* Already making extensive use of Arabic and Greek Aristotelianism, Albert greeted the newly available Aristotle materials with enthusiasm. He decided to present the whole of human knowledge as found in Aristotle and his Arabic commentators to the Latin West and to correct or add to Aristotelian thinking by means of knowledge that had not been available to Aristotle. This monumental project of paraphrase and explanation took two decades and included mathematics, logic, natural philosophy and science—including botany, mineralogy, biology, and zoology—as well as ethics, politics, and metaphysics. Because of the suspicion cast on Aristotle by theological traditionalists, Albert's project amounted to a defense of philosophy and reason in its own right.

These commentaries, because of the nature of his sources, manifest the modified view of Aristotle in Neoplatonic commentators that was also adopted by Arabic Aristotelians such as Avicenna (Ibn Sīnā) and Averroës (Ibn Rushd). Albert generally adopted Aristotle's views of the physical world and repudiated what he believed were mistaken interpretations of Aristotle on such matters, while indicating where he himself thought the Stagirite incorrect. But Albert's view of what transcends the physical universe reflects the Christian Neoplatonic (and Augustinian) Aristotelianism that was the dominant view among later scholastics. In contrast, Aquinas's ideas, while arguably closer to Aristotle himself, were a minority view in the late Middle Ages.

A careful observer of natural phenomena, Albert often incorporated his own experience to correct and supplement his sources in his writings about the natural world. His discussion of place and time follows that of Avicenna, but with his own emphases: only two dimensions, length and width, are essential to place, while time's matter is the uninterrupted flow of indivisible nows, and its form is number. In logic Albert gave classic expression to the medieval doctrine of three types or modes of being of universals (*ante rem:* in divine thought; *in re:* in natural things; *post rem:* in human thought); this doctrine subordinated logic to metaphysics.

Albert elaborated on his own metaphysical ideas in *De causis et processu universitatis* (The Causes and Development of the Universe) during the 1260s when he was completing his commentary on Aristotle's *Metaphysics.* In this original synthesis he adopts Aristotle's cosmology and accepts the system of Intelligences governing the spheres (while denying that they are angels). But Albert modifies Avicenna's emanation doctrine so that it becomes primarily a causality of higher *attracting* lower rather than overflowing or emanating into lower. Within this concept, the first principle's goodness calls and brings together all the forms found inchoate in matter, calling them to resemble the first. This Neoplatonism thus completes a metaphysics of being with a natural theology of the cause of being—the one or good found in *The Book of Causes* (by the Greek philosopher Proclus, ca. 410–485) and Pseudo-Dionysius, an early theologian. Linking the phys-

ical universe with the spiritual is the function of intellect. Albert's psychology criticized the view that there was only one intellect for all human beings. Yet he also attempted to harmonize Averroës's ideas about the intellect with his own commitment to the nobility and immortality of the human soul, leaving the unity of soul and body at best ambiguous. For Albert the process of abstraction is not merely from experienced particulars, but the result of a complex illumination (and use) of the human soul by the Intelligences en route to making everything one in God.

That divine first cause thereby provides the object of his ethical ideal of the contemplative or speculative life as surpassing all others. This ideal entails what Albert calls the acquisition of intellect (*intellectus adeptus*), where the separate agent intellect becomes the form of the soul, producing a state of happiness or contemplative wisdom that consists in contemplation of the separated beings. It rewards philosophical effort that progressively detaches the soul from the world of perceptual experience and aims at acquisition of intellect, thus dovetailing nicely with Albert's religious beliefs and mystical leanings. For him theology based on religious faith is not merely speculative but also affective, however intellectual. All of his theological writings and commentaries concentrate on the reality of God, not just on ideas about him. For Albert there is no knowledge of the ultimate mystery that is not at once transformative of the knower's mind and heart and life.

BIBLIOGRAPHY

Albertus Magnus. *Alberti Magni Opera omnia,* ed. Auguste Borgnet and E. Borgnet. 38 vols. Paris: Vives, 1890–1899.

———. *Alberti Magni Opera omnia edenda curavit Institutum Alberti Magni Coloniense Bernhardo Geyer praeside.* Muenster: Aschendorff, 1951–.

———. *Book of Minerals,* trans. Dorothy Wyckoff. Oxford: Clarendon, 1967.

Albertus Magnus and Thomas Aquinas. *Albert and Thomas: Selected Writings,* trans. Simon Tugwell, New York: Paulist, 1988.

Hoenen, Maarten J. F. M., and Alain de Libera, eds. *Albertus Magnus und der Albertismus: Deutsche philosophische Kultur des Mittelalters.* Leiden: Brill, 1995.

Kovach, Francis J., and Robert W. Shahan, eds. *Albert the Great: Commemorative Essays.* Norman: University of Oklahoma Press, 1980.

Libera, Alain de. *Albert le Grand et la Philosophie.* Paris: Vrin, 1990.

Wallace, William A., ed. *American Catholic Philosophical Quarterly* 70, no. 1 (1996). [Special Albertus Magnus issue.]

Weisheipl, J. A. ed. *Albertus Magnus and the Sciences: Commemorative Essays 1980,* Toronto: Pontifical Institute of Medieval Studies, 1980.

Clyde Lee Miller

SEE ALSO
Cologne, History

Albrecht von Johansdorf (fl. ca. 1200)

A contemporary of the Middle High German poets Heinrich von Morungen and Reinmar der Alte, Albrecht von Johansdorf wrote *Minnesang* (courtly love poetry) and Crusade lyric around 1200 in southern Germany. Documents show record of a certain Albertus de Janestorf, who served as a *ministerial* (cleric) of the bishop of Passau from approximately 1180 or 1185 to 1209.

Albrecht is known primarily as an author of *Minnelieder* (courtly love songs). Thirteen of his poems appear in the collection *Minnesangs Frühling* (Springtime of Minnesang, henceforth MF). His preference for long lines in his verse indicate that he had a thorough knowledge of the older form of *Minnesang* that had originated in the Danube region of Bavaria earlier in the twelfth century. However, Albrecht's own style of verse is entirely modern and surpasses even Frederick von Hausen in its use of the canzone stanza. In his poems, Albrecht favors the dialogue structure known as the *Wechsel* (exchange), in which the man and the woman speak in alternating strophes. This form recalls the typical dialogue of a Provençal *tenzone* but at the same time changes the traditional structure to reflect a courtly conversation between a knight and his lady; we no longer see a quarrel or debate. In these discussions, the emphasis is on the moral improvement of the knight through service to the lady. The lady is, however, spiritually involved in this process and she is an integral part of it.

Albrecht seems to have suffered a bit in his reputation as a poet of *Minnelieder,* mainly because of a dichotomy that some scholars have perceived in his work between love poetry and Crusade poetry, between the desire for the love of a lady and the love of God. The poem MF 87 illustrates this conflict in lines 13–18. As the lady gazes upon the Crusader's cross of her lover, she cannot help but wonder how he will manage both *"varn über mer und iedoch wesen hie"* (to travel across the sea and yet be here). Hugo Bekker postulates that this conflict may show that the lady's qualities are not necessarily reflections of divine attributes but that their influence may be confined to the temporal earthly plane alone. Thus we are perhaps dealing "not with *hohe Minne* [high or courtly love] but with the early budding of what we may conventionally call romantic love" (Bekker 1978, 97). In an effort to offer new criteria for reevaluating Albrecht's reputation as a poet of *Minnesang*, Bekker suggests that perhaps the concept of *hohe Minne* may not be the best standard by which to gauge the value of Albrecht's work. In Albrecht's ability to understand the conflict between *minne* and God in a more evenhanded fashion, using MF 91, lines 22–28 as an example, de Boor sees a precursor of the more equitable relationship that Walther von der Vogelweide describes as *ebene Minne* (even or equal love).

By general scholarly consensus, however, Albrecht's five Crusade poems mark an artistic high point for this genre in German medieval poetry. As Albrecht seeks to unite the call of God and the love of the lady under the common goal of service in the Crusade lyric, these poems may remain his most enduring legacy. Albrecht attempts to strike an equitable balance between the religious commitment of the Crusade and courtly service to ladies by offering the idea that courtly love has a component of higher moral (or even of religious) value. In resolving the opposition of Crusade and love (or *minne*), in allowing God and the lady to coexist in the same loving human heart, Albrecht von Johansdorf manages to transform the conflicts depicted in the works of his contemporaries Frederick von Hausen and Hartmann von Aue.

BIBLIOGRAPHY
Bekker, Hugo. *The Poetry of Albrecht von Johansdorf.* Davis Medieval Texts and Studies. Leiden: Brill, 1978.

Bertau, Karl. *Deutsche Literatur im europäischen Mittelalter,* vol. 1, *800–1197.* Munich: Beck, 1972, pp. 676–677.

Boor, Helmut de. *Geschichte der deutschen Literatur von den Anfängen bis zur Gegenwart,* vol. 2, *Die höfische Literatur: Vorbereitung, Blüte, Ausklang, 1170-1250.* 11th ed. Munich: Beck, 1991.

Bumke, Joachim. *Geschichte der deutschen Literatur im hohen Mittelalter,* vol. 2. Munich: Deutscher Taschenbuchverlag, l990.

Moser, Hugo, and Helmut Tervooren, eds. *Des Minnesangs Frühling.* 37th rev. ed. Stuttgart: Hirzel, 1981.

Alexandra Sterling-Hellenbrand

SEE ALSO

Crusades; Friedrich von Hausen; Hartmann von Aue; Heinrich von Morungen; *Minnesang;* Reinmar der Alte; Versification; Walther von der Vogelweide

Albrecht von Kemenaten (fl. ca. 1230–1240)

Possibly a member of a Swabian ministerial family located near modern-day Gross-Kemnat, Albrecht names himself in the fragmentary Dietrich epic *Goldemar* (Strophe 2, line 2), preserved in a fourteenth-century Swabian manuscript. References to him in other sources suggest that he wrote ca. 1230–1240.

Only a bit more than the first nine strophes of *Goldemar* remain, but the formal elegance of its thirteen-line stanza (*Bernerton-* or *Eckenstrophe*) and its adaptation of heroic material in reaction to courtly literature are seen in other epics in which the medieval popular hero Dietrich von Bern, named after Theodoric the Great, the fifth century king of the Ostrogoths, plays a central role. Critics at first attributed *Eckenlied, Sigenot,* and *Virginal,* other Dietrich epics in *Bernerton,* to Albrecht. More recent studies of differences in dialect, transmission, and attitudes toward courtly customs have disproved this hypothesis.

All of the Dietrich epics in *Bernerton* depict Dietrich in conflict with dwarfs, giants, and dragons, unwilling to fight without serious reason, and, although naturally virtuous, unaware of the meaning of love and chivalry. To distinguish them from another, more serious group, usually called the "historical" Dietrich epics (see *Alpharts Tod*), these and other Dietrich epics in which he is motivated in a chivalric cause are called *aventiurehaft* (like a knightly quest).

Goldemar is an exception with regard to love: Dietrich falls in love with a maiden he sees in the company of Goldemar, the dwarf king. A reference in the prose supplement to the first printed version of the *Heldenbuch* (a collection of heroic tales printed after 1480) informs readers that Goldemar had abducted the maiden, Hertlin, daughter of the king of Portugal. Dietrich defeated Goldemar, rescued Hertlin, and took her as his first wife before Herrat (Heinzle 1981, 4r). Another reference in *Reinfried von Braunschweig* (an anonymous Middle High German verse romance, ca. 1300) says that Dietrich's relatives the Wülfinge helped him, and giants fought on Goldemar's side.

BIBLIOGRAPHY

Albrecht von Kemenaten. *Goldemar,* ed. Julius Zupitza. Deutsches Heldenbuch 5. 2d ed. 1870; rpt. Dublin and Zurich: Weidmann, 1968, pp. 203–204.

Heinzle, Joachim. *Heldenbuch: Nach dem ältesten Druck in Abbildung.* 2 vols. Göppingen: Kümerle, 1981–87. [Facsimile of first printed version.]

———. *Mittelhochdeutsche Dietrichepik.* Zurich and Munich: Artemis, 1978.

Ruth H. Firestone

SEE ALSO

Alpharts Tod; Dietrichepik; Eckenlied; Heldenbücher; Sigenot; Virginal

Albrecht von Scharfenberg (fl. late 13th c.)

This Middle High German poet was named by the fifteenth-century writer Ulrich Füetrer as one of the greatest German poets, and revealed by him as the author of two otherwise unknown courtly romances, "Seifrid de Ardemont" and "Merlin." Albrecht was long considered identical with Wolfram von Eschenbach, since throughout most of his lengthy work, *Der jüngere Titurel* (the Later Titurel), he masqueraded as Wolfram, author of the *Titurel* fragments, finally naming himself, Albrecht, in stanza 5883. Seven stanzas inserted at two earlier points in the text (the so-called *Hinweisstrophen,* or reference stanzas), also claim that Wolfram is not the author, although without naming Albrecht. The *Jüngerer Titurel* has been dated ca. 1270–1275 through textual evidence and a fragmentary dedication poem (the *Verfasserfragment,* or author fragment). Albrecht, perhaps born in Bavaria and active to the north (in Thuringia?), has not been further identified.

From the later Middle Ages until well into the nineteenth century, *Der jüngere Titurel* was highly esteemed, considered by many to be Wolfram's greatest work. Its reputation faltered after 1829 when the scholar Karl Lachmann declared it tedious and not by Wolfram, but its standing recovered in the late twentieth century. There are eleven complete manuscripts and nearly fifty fragments extant; an incunabulum version was printed in Strasbourg in 1477.

The complex plot of the *Jüngerer Titurel* revolves around a love story based on the fragmentary account of

Sigune and Tschionatulander found in Wolfram's *Parzival* and *Titurel.* Their tragic tale becomes part of a moralizing saga with a worldwide sweep encompassing an enormous cast of characters, the Christian West and the heathen East, Arthur's court and the Grail kingdom—the entire story subordinated to a didactic message of Christian virtue. The verse form is a refined version of Wolfram's *Titurel* stanza.

BIBLIOGRAPHY

Albrecht von Scharfenberg. *Albrechts von Scharfenberg Jüngerer Titurel,* ed. Wolf Werner and Kurt Nyholm. 3 vols. Berlin: Akademie-Verlag, 1955–1992.

Borchling, Conrad. *Der jüngere Titurel und sein Verhältnis Wolfram von Eschenbach.* Göttingen: [n.p.], 1897.

Guggenberger, Herbert. *Albrechts Jüngerer Titurel. Studien zur Minnethematik und zur Werkkonzeption.* Göppingen: Kümmerle, 1992.

Parshall, Linda B. *The Art of Narration in Wolfram's "Parzival" and Albrecht's "Jüngerer Titurel."* Cambridge: Cambridge University Press, 1981.

Schröder, Werner, ed. *Wolfram Studien VIII.* Berlin: Schmidt, 1984.

Linda B. Parshall

SEE ALSO

Füetrer, Ulrich; Wolfram von Eschenbach

Alcuin (ca. 735–May 19, 804)

Leading scholar and adviser in the court of Charlemagne and architect of the Carolingian renaissance, Alcuin and his fellow intellectuals eagerly promoted and perhaps engineered Charlemagne's imperial coronation. Alcuin envisioned Charlemagne leading a Christian empire in the manner of Plato's philosopher-king. Although reality fell short of this dream, Alcuin's vision lived on as an ideal toward which all later medieval rulers continued to strive.

Arriving in Aachen from York in the 780s at Charlemagne's invitation, Alcuin brought the vital tradition of Northumbrian scholarship to Charlemagne's court. He established himself as the head of a court school; among his students was Charlemagne himself. A lifelong educator, Alcuin used education as a means of reforming and regulating the clergy. He founded many new schools. He wrote texts on grammar and composed the first treatises on rhetoric and dialectics since Boethius. Setting up a scriptorium, Alcuin assigned an unprecedented number of scribes to the task of preserving classic and patristic manuscripts.

As a theologian, Alcuin emphasized the authority of the fathers of the church over original thought. Alcuin authored numerous commentaries on Scripture, always following in the tradition of the church fathers and carefully avoiding innovation. Nevertheless, in the very act of establishing the boundaries for discussions of doctrine, Alcuin contributed to a lasting theological framework for Christian discourse.

In 796, Alcuin became the abbot of St. Martin, near Tours. From the comfort of this prestigious and wealthy monastery, he continued to council Charlemagne and his advisers by means of a stream of steady correspondence, which the scholar maintained until his death.

BIBLIOGRAPHY

Alcuin. *Alcuin of York c. AD 732 to 804: His Life and Letters,* trans. Stephen Allott. York: Sessions, 1974.

Bullough, Donald A. "Alcuin and the Kingdom of Heaven: Liturgy, Theology, and the Carolingian Age." In *Carolingian Essays,* ed. Uta-Renate Blumenthal. Washington, D.C.: Catholic University of America, 1983, pp. 1–69.

Cavadini, John C. *The Last Christology of the West: Adoptionism in Spain and Gaul.* Philadelphia: University of Pennsylvania Press, 1993.

Marenbon, John. *From the Circle of Alcuin to the School of Auxerre.* Cambridge: Cambridge University Press, 1981, pp. 30–66.

Douglas W. Lumsden

SEE ALSO

Aachen; Boethius; Charlemagne; Coronation; Education; Manuscripts, Painting and Production

Alexander Literature, Dutch

In the Low Countries various literary and historical texts about Alexander the Great were written in the vernacular in the Middle Ages. The most significant and eldest literary work is *Alexanders Geesten,* an epic poem of about 14,200 verses in rhyming couplets, composed by the important Flemish author Jacob van Maerlant around 1260. It was commissioned by a lady, most probably Aleide van Avesnes, sister of King William (Willem) II of Holland. The main source of inspiration for Maerlant was the *Alexandreis* by Walter (Gautier) of Châtillon, a Latin epic in Virgilian style, written somewhere between 1170 and

1180 for the archbishop of Reims. Like the author of his source Maerlant divided his text into ten books. He simplified the style of the flowery language of Walter and Christianized his text by eliminating mythological figures and by using Christian imagery and terminology. By portraying Alexander more as a medieval sovereign than as a classical hero, the poet made *Alexanders Geesten* seem like a work of guidance for a young prince, a so-called "mirror of princes." To his adaptation Maerlant also added an exhaustive description of the world, treatises on Babylonian Persian and Roman history, biblical history, and narratives about nature. For this addition the author consulted a further seventeen sources. The text of *Alexanders Geesten* has survived in only one complete manuscript and in four fragments. The main manuscript (Munich, Bayerische Staatsbibliothek, manuscript no. cgm. 41) is written in a language containing many dialect features used around 1400 in the Lower Rhine area between Kleve (Cleves) and Gulik.

Jacob van Maerlant again gives a detailed treatment of Alexander in his last work, *Spiegel historiael* (Mirror of History), an adaptation in Middle Dutch rhyming couplets of Vincent of Beauvais's *Speculum historiale.*

Far into the Middle Ages, Alexander continued to be popular in the Low Countries, witnessed by the fifteenth-century *Die historie van den groten Koninc Alexander* (History of the Great King Alexander). This literary work in Middle Dutch prose, a so-called *volksboek* (folk book) and first printed in 1477, is based on the section on Alexander in a fourteenth-century history Bible. Considering that the composer of this Bible used Maerlant's *Spiegel historiael* as well as his *Alexanders Geesten* for this section, the Flemish poet seems to have contributed considerably to the disclosure of Alexander's history meant for an illiterate audience.

BIBLIOGRAPHY

Hoogstra, S. S., ed. *Proza-bewerkingen van het leven van Alexander den Groote in het Middelnederlandsch.* The Hague: Martinus Nijhoff, 1898.

Jacob van Maerlant. *Alexanders Geesten van Jacob van Maerlant,* ed. Johannes Franck. Groningen: Wolters, 1882.

———. *Jacob van Maerlant's Spiegel historiael,* ed. Matthijs de Vries and Eelco Verwijs. 4 vols. Leiden: Brill, 1863–1879.

Voorbij, J. B. "The History of Alexander the Great in Jacob van Maerlants *Spiegel historiael.*" In *Vincent of Beauvais and Alexander the Great: Studies on the Speculum Maius and its translations into Medieval Vernaculars,* ed. W. J. Aerts, E. R. Smits, and J. B. Voorbij. Groningen: Egbert Forsten, 1986, pp. 57–84.

Marian Andringa

SEE ALSO
Alexanderlied; Bible Translations, Dutch; Jacob van Maerlant

Alexanderlied

Throughout the Middle Ages the story of Alexander the Great, based on at least five accounts by ancient authors—among which the *Historiae Alexandri Magni* written by Quintus Curtius Rufus (first century C.E.) and the prose romance by Pseudo-Callisthenes (second century B.C.E.) were most prominent— enjoyed tremendous popularity and was retold in almost all European languages. Sometime between 1150 and 1170 the *Pfaffe* (priest) Lambrecht recreated the story in Middle High German poem *Alexanderlied* on the basis of the Old French *Roman d'Alexandre* composed by Alberic of Bisinzo, which has come down to us in only 105 verses. Lambrecht's poem *(The Song of Alexander)* has survived only in the famous *Vorau Sammelhandschrift* (manuscript no. 276) from the second half of the twelfth century, where it was copied down between material from the Old Testament *(Jüngere Judith)* and the New Testament (Frau Ava's *Leben Jesu)* and obviously served as a historical-fictional document to support the biblical statements.

Little is known about Lambrecht except that he was well versed in Latin and French and composed a fragmentary sermon-like legend, *Tobias,* derived from the eponymous biblical book. On the basis of his language we may assume that he came from the Moselle region, probably from Trier, but he seems to have composed his works in Cologne. From allusions in the text we know that Lambrecht was familiar with Germanic heroic poetry and Homer's *Iliad.* Lambrecht's *Alexander* was further developed sometime in the 1170s by an anonymous poet and copied in a Strasbourg manuscript which was lost to fire in 1870.

The *Vorau Alexander* comprises 1,533 verses and describes the life of Alexander the Great from his childhood to his first major military successes, concluding, against historical fact, with the death of the Persian king Darius at the hands of Alexander in their first battle. In his prologue Lambrecht emphasizes the transitory nature of this world and presents Alexander as an example of the vainglory of secular fame and wealth. However, despite explicit criticism of Alexander's greed for ever new conquests, the text is dominated by a profound admiration for the Greek ruler and his military accomplishments. In contrast to the later *Alexander* versions, the *Vorau Alexander* does not dwell on the miraculous events and observations pertaining to the world of the East, which Alexander conquered. Instead Lambrecht emphasizes the impact of Alexander's six teachers, among them Aristotle, and invests much energy in the descriptions of the ferocious siege of Tyre. The poet characterizes Alexander as *wunderlîche* (v. 45), that is, as impressive and amazing, but refrains from highlighting his intellectual curiosity and desire to explore the unknown world, so typical of the later versions.

Scholarship is divided over the question of whether the fragmentary ending was intended or not. Lambrecht refrained from extrapolating his French source and perceived his role to be more that of a historian who weighs the validity and truthfulness of the various sources available to him. Alexander's heathenness explains why he destroyed Jerusalem and Bethlehem, among other holy sites in Palestine, and the poet contrasts him negatively with King Solomon (v. 25ff.), pointing out the Greek ruler's vengefulness and cruelty.

The protagonist's main quest, to fight against Darius, rests in the latter's request for tribute payments to him as a sign of the Greeks' submission under the Persian rule (v. 82f.). Alexander battles for his personal honor and glory and does not allow any religious arguments to influence his thinking. Ultimately, the poem's main purpose emerges to be a warning against *vanitas* (vanity) and of God's punishment of human sinfulness. But Alexander also serves as God's instrument in fulfilling the biblical prophecy in his destruction of the Persian empire.

BIBLIOGRAPHY

Bertau, Karl. *Deutsche Literatur im europäischen Mittelalter,* vol. 1. Munich: Beck, 1972, pp. 329–337.

Degering, Hermann, ed. "Tobias." *Beiträge zur Geschichte der deutschen Sprache und Literatur* 41 (1916): 528–536.

Fischer, Wolfgang. *Die Alexanderliedkonzeption des Pfaffen Lambreht.* Munich: Eidos, 1964.

Maurer, Friedrich, ed. "Die Werke des Pfaffen Lamprecht." In his *Die religiösen Dichtungen des 11. und 12. Jahrhunderts,* vol. 2. Tübingen: Niemeyer, 1965, pp. 517–566.

Schröder, Werner. "Pfaffe Lambrecht." In *Deutsche Dichter,* ed. Gunter E. Grimm und Frank Rainer Max. Stuttgart: Reclam, 1989, pp. 73–80.

Albrecht Classen

SEE ALSO
Alexander Literature, Dutch; Frau Ava

Alphabet

All writing systems that use linear symbols for vowels are derived ultimately from the Greek alphabet, in which Phoenician letter names such as aleph, which were consonants in the Phoenician alphabet, were taken by the acrophonic principle (whereby the letter has the same meaning as the first sound of its name) to be vowels.

German was most frequently written in the Latin alphabet in the Middle Ages, and Otfrid has left us a treatise on the problems this created in his prefatory poem *Ad Liutpertum.* Only a few modifications were made, for example in the use of *k, w,* and *z.* It is to be noted that *u* and *v* and *i* and *j,* though used in the Middle Ages, did not indicate the distinction found today.

In the elementary education of the Middle Ages and throughout, the theory of the connection between the letter and the sound was that of Greek grammarians. A letter had three elements: shape (*figura*), name (*nomen*), and meaning (*potestas,* the sound or sounds it represented), with the meaning being read from the first sound of the letter name. It is thus important to investigate the letter names along with their shapes. The investigation of the shapes of the letters is the realm of paleography.

The alphabet was not as well known in the Middle Ages as it is now, and it was often thought to be great art to write so-called abecedaria or *abc* poems, with each division beginning with a different letter of the alphabet. Wolfram von Eschenbach could speak of "the art of abc" (*die kunst von abece; Parzival,* v. 453.15) as if it were great learning. In this same passage, Wolfram mentions necromancy. The alphabet was used in the Middle Ages for magic purposes in many different ways. We also already encounter in Isidore of Seville the notion of the meaning of each letter of the alphabet, and this notion is continued and extended in later works, so that, for example, *Q* was considered the "shameful letter" (*suntleich oder schentleich leben*). Alphabetization was thought to be a great art, and where used is quite often not strict, so that *ab* may appear after *at,* for example.

The alphabet was also used for "secret" writing by use of various codes. In literature, we find names imbedded within the lines, as in *Tristan,* as well as acrostic (whereby the first letters of a line or verse spell a name) and *teleosticha* (in which the final letters of a line or verse spell a name). The opening verses of Otfrid's *Evangelienbuch* offer the best known example, employing both. The letters of a word are often taken to form an acronym for the etymology; e.g., *Devs* (God) is said to have the etymology dans eternam vitam suis, "He Who grants eternal life to His people." Play with the alphabet was not uncommon, especially in the case of names, so that we find anagrams, reversals, and so on. Most of the secret writings are simple substitution codes, but some have resisted all attempts at decipherment even until today, as is the case of the famous Bacon Cipher (Voynich Manuscript), a text in Latin script attributed to Roger Bacon. Monograms are also found, some quite elaborate.

Other alphabets were used for the writing of German, most notably runes and the Hebrew alphabet. There is a sizable literature in German in Hebrew script, beginning with the Old High German lullaby *(Schlummerlied).* Of course, works in Early Yiddish, such as the early sixteenth-century *Bovobukh* (Buovo d'Ancona Book) of Elija Levita, are written in Hebrew script. Much work is left to be done in editing and deciphering such works, and their attribution is much disputed.

BIBLIOGRAPHY

Bischoff, Bernhard. *Übersicht über die nichtdiplomatischen Geheimschriften des Mittelalters.* Graz and Cologne Böhlaus Nachfolger, 1954.

Diringer, David. *The alphabet: A Key to the History of Mankind.* 3d ed. rev. with Reinhold Regensburger. 2 vols. New York: Funk and Wagnalls, 1968.

Dornseiff, Franz., *Das Alphabet in Mystik und Magie.* 2d ed. 1925; rpt. Leipzig: Zentralantiquariat, 1975.

Hakkarainen, Heikki J. *Studien zum Cambridger Codex T-S. 10. K. 22.* 3 vols. Vol 1. Turku: Turun Yliopisto, 1967. Vols. 2 and 3, Annales Academiae Scientiarum Fennicae. Helsinki: Suomalainen Tiedeakatemia, 1971, 1973. [Vol. 2, "Graphemik und Phonemik," is a fine study of the problems involved in using Hebrew script for Middle High German.]

Howard, John Anderson. "Hebrew-German and Early Yiddish Literature: A Survey of Problems." Ph.D. Diss. University of Illinois, 1972 [corpus, treatment, bibliography of each item].

Jellinek, Max Hermann. *Über Aussprache des Lateinischen und deutsche Buchstabennamen.* Akademie der Wissenschaften in Wien, Philosophisch-Historische Klasse, Sitzungsberichte, 212. Band 2. Abhandlung. Vienna and Leipzig: Holder-Pichler-Tempsky, 1930.

Wilhelm, Frederick *Denkmäler deutscher Prosa des 11. und 12. Jahrhunderts.* 1914; rpt. Munich: Max Hueber Verlag, 1960, no. XLI [German medieval texts on the meanings of letters].

James W. Marchand

SEE ALSO
Gottfried von Straßburg; Otfrid; Runes; Wolfram von Eschenbach

Alpharts Tod

This fragmentary narrative is composed as a sequel and response to *Buch von Bern* (also called *Dietrichs Flucht*) and *Rabenschlacht;* all three narratives are usually classified as "historical" Dietrich epics, or heroic narratives featuring Theodoric (Dietrich von Bern), fifth-century king of the Ostrogoths. The names of some of the characters reflect those of historical figures from the period of the Germanic migrations, but narrative events, assimilated to traditional story patterns or schemata, are literary, not historical. On the other hand, the three narratives reflect political realities of the thirteenth century more directly than do the episodic, or *aventiurehafte* Dietrich epics (see *Albrecht von Kemenaten*). *Alpharts Tod* is preserved on thirty-three leaves of a fifteenth-century Hanau manuscript that once also contained Johann von Würzburg's *Wilhelm von Österreich* and the epic *Nibelungenlied.* Manuscript evidence shows that *Alphart* once covered forty-six leaves, of which leaves 1, 18, and 23–34 are now missing. Of its 469 four-line strophes 236 are Nibelungen strophes, 231 are in the verse form known as *Hildebrandston.* Its dialect is West Central German, but linguistic and literary evidence indicates that it was based on a mid- to late-thirteenth-century Alemannic version.

The plot of *Alpharte Tod* is easily summarized. Kaiser Ementrich, Dietrich's uncle, has declared war against him to force Dietrich to receive land from him in fief. He sends Hen, Dietrich's former vassal, to bring Dietrich this information.

Young Alphart, Dietrich's man, insists upon standing watch alone. Alphart's uncle Hylbrand, who has brought him up as his own son, fights a duel with him to prevent him from doing so. Alphart wins.

On watch, Alphart defeats, one by one, an eighty-man detachment sent by Ementrich. Ementrich, desperate, forces Wytdich, also a former vassal of Dietrich's, to duel with Alphart. Alphart is close to victory when Hen comes to Wytdich's aid. Fighting unethically, two against one, and also breaking their oath as former vassals not to fight against Dietrich, they kill Alphart. (Lacuna, or gap, between leaf 23–34.)

Hylbrand obtains help from nobles living at Breisach. To avenge Alphart's death and to defend Bern, Dietrich and his men engage in battle. They win, but Ementrich, Wytdich, and Hen escape to Ravenna. Dietrich laments for his men and rewards the survivors. There is a great feast at Bern, whereupon the Breisach nobles return home.

Paralleling similar developments in the French historical tales known as *chansons de geste, Alphart* was composed to solidify the tendency toward the formation of a Dietrich cycle (represented by *Buch von Bern* and *Rabenschlacht*), by depicting the beginning of the feud between Dietrich and Ementrich. All three narratives were inspired by the *Nibelungenlied,* in which Dietrich is depicted as an exile who loses his men. *Alphart's* plot somewhat resembles that of the *Chanson de Roland* (Song of Roland), either because of literary influence or because both epics are composed according to schemata common to heroic narrative. As a late addition to the Dietrich story, *Alphart* documents the fact that a productive, heroic, narrative tradition survived in Germany until late in the Middle Ages.

BIBLIOGRAPHY

Behr, Hans-Joachim. "Der Held und seine Krieger oder über die Schwierigkeiten, ein Gefolgsherr zu sein: Überlegungen zu 'Alpharts Tod.'" In *2. Pöchlarner Heldenliedgespräch: Die historische Dietrichepik,* ed. Klaus Zatloukal. Vienna: Fassbaender, 1992, pp. 13–23.

Firestone, Ruth H. "Aside from That, What's Wrong with Alphart?" In *Canon and Canon Transgression in Medieval German Literature,* ed. Albrecht Classen. Göppingen: Kümerle, 1993, pp. 123–134.

Zimmer, Uwe. *Studien zu 'Alpharts Tod' nebst einem verbesserten Abdruck der Handschrift.* Göppingen: Kümerle, 1972.

Zimmermann, Günter. "Wo beginnt der Übermut? Zu 'Alpharts Tod.'" In *2. Pöchlarner Heldenliedgespräch:*

Die historische Dietrichepik, ed. Klaus Zatloukal. Vienna: Fassbaender, 1992, pp. 165–182.

Ruth H. Firestone

SEE ALSO

Albrecht von Kemenaten; *Buch von Bern* and *Rabenschlacht Dietrichepik; Hildebrandslied;* Johann von Würzburg; *Nibelungenlied;* Versification

Anegenge

Das Anegenge (The Beginning) is an anonymous poem of 3,242 lines in the southern Bavarian dialect of Middle High German, from the last quarter of the twelfth century. Its author expounds some of the theological questions that arise from the story of the Creation up through the Flood (Genesis 1–9). Although there are long passages of narrative based on the Bible, *Das Anegenge* is not a biblical epic, strictly speaking. In its often discursive and analytical approach to questions of dogma, the poem is unique in the German vernacular religious literature of the twelfth century. Like most of these works, it contains pastoral elements, including direct admonishment of the audience, but the author, a priest or monk, is not content with conveying basic doctrine or ethics in poetic form. He is intellectually far more ambitious, however much one might fault his execution.

Following a conventional opening prayer asking for God's guidance, the author warns his lay audience not to try to penetrate God's mysteries too deeply lest they drown themselves in their effort. The author then announces the themes for which he will provide guidance: (1) God's mode of existence before the Creation, (2) the Trinity, (3) God's prescience of Lucifer's fall and (4) that of Adam and Eve, (5) the Incarnation, and (6) the fate of unbaptized children. There is much repetition and overlap. The author typically states his position, then dismisses contrary views by citing authorities, or by providing arguments based on reason, or by constructing skillful allegories. To call this method "scholastic" would be to reach too high. As a document of laypeople's theological sophistication, however, the work provides fascinating witness.

BIBLIOGRAPHY

Neuschäfer, Dietrich, ed. *Das Anegenge: Textkristische Studien.* Munich: Fink, 1966.

Rupp, Heinz. *Deutsche religiöse Dichtungen des 11. und 12. Jahrhunderts. Untersuchungen und Interpretationen.* 2d. ed. Bern: Francke, 1971, pp. 217–260.

Tveitane, Mattias. "The Four Daughters of God: A Supplement." *Neuphilologische Mitteilunge* 81 (1980): 409–415.

Robert G. Sullivan

SEE ALSO
Bible

Animal Epics, Dutch

Middle Ages texts about animals can be divided into three genres. The first, natural history, aims at passing on to the audience "real knowledge" about animals, often in the form of the so-called book of beasts (Latin *bestiarium*). In the second, the fable, animals are often the main characters in a short moralistic tale that focuses on an aspect of human behavior. The third, the animal epic, has the same moralizing function as the fable, but it is usually a story in which animal characters act in a longer and more complex narrative. In all three of these genres the animal is described with respect to its meaning for man.

The genre of the natural history, belonging to the *artes*-literature (liberal arts), ultimately goes back to the Greek book of animals *Physiologus* and the works of Pliny the Elder (d. 79). A fine representative in Middle Dutch is *Der naturen bloeme* (The Flowers of Nature, ca. 1266), an adaptation of Thomas of Cantimpré's *Liber de natura rerum* (The Book of Nature's Things) by the Flemish poet Jacob van Maerlant. This highly organized "encyclopedia" combines empirical knowledge (though fantasy has its part in it) of Aristotelian background with frequent moralizing apostrophes in which the world of the animals is used as a source of social knowledge. Another example is the translation of Richard de Fournival's *Bestiaire d'amour* (Fables of Love, 1245–1260), in which the behavior of animals from the older stories is compared with the experiences and lamentations of the rejected lover. This translation, in the dialect of the Lower Rhine area, is preserved in a richly illuminated manuscript and was made by an anonymous translator, probably commissioned by count Reinoud I van Gelre (d. 1326).

The fable is also an inheritance of antiquity. Seminal for the genre is the collection of the semilegendary Aesop(us) (Greece, 6th c. B.C.E.), but before him exemplary tales with animals as protagonists must have been circulating in India, Egypt, and Mesopotamia. The most famous collection of fables in Middle Dutch is the *Esopet* (sixty-seven of Aesop's fables), translated from Latin in the thirteenth century (perhaps in Flanders).

A tributary to the fable, but of a different form and nature, is the animal epic. With respect to the form—a large-scale narrative with complex intrigue—it is related to chivalric literature. Animals are the leading characters, as in the fable, and the didactic element is very important. But the didactics are combined with satire, the world of the animal very often being a derisive imitation of human society. Instrumental in this imitation is the fact that the animals use language, a feature which classifies the animal epic as fiction (*fabula*) in the eyes of the medieval audience. In the *Speculum stultorum* (The Fools' Mirror, 1179/1180) by Nigellus de Longo Campo, the ass Burnellus is the main character, a role usually reserved in European animal epic for the wolf and the fox.

The first animal epic of the Low Countries is in Latin, the *Ysengrimus*. This poem of 6,574 lines was written in Gent (1148–1149) by an author that has a different name in every preserved manuscript: Nivardus, Balduinus Cecus, or Bernardus. It is likely that he belonged to the clergy, but otherwise nothing is known about him. The *Ysengrimus* in itself is not entirely original, drawing from the Aesopian fable and the Latin *Ecbasis captivi* (11th c.), and was in its turn a major source for the Old French *Roman de Renart*.

From the *Roman de Renart* the first branch, *Li Plaid* (after 1173), was the most important source of the Middle Dutch *Van den vos Reynaerde*, a beautiful poem in coupled rhyme (3,468 lines), by the otherwise unknown Flemish poet Willem. He used other parts of the *Roman de Renart* as additional sources, but managed to mould this material into a flawless animal epic that defies the notion of "adaptation." The dating is uncertain, but there is a consensus about 1230–1260 as being the most plausible period. Of *Van den vos Reynaerde* three complete manuscripts and fragments of four more have been preserved, one of them combining this epic with a copy of Maerlant's *Der naturen bloeme*. Another of the complete manuscripts and one of the fragments have a special place in the manuscript tradition, because they actually contain a younger, enlarged version of *Van den vos Reynaerde*, in which this text is completely incorporated.

This enlarged version, called *Reinaerts historie*, was written around 1375 by an anonymous poet and is almost twice the size of *Van den vos Reynaerde*, some 7,800 lines. The poet incorporated this text, but not altogether unaltered: he follows the intrigue of *Van den vos Reynaerde* very closely, but changed many details as a preparation for his continuation. The continuation itself is mainly based on the sixth branch of the *Roman de Renart*, entitled *Le combat judiciaire* (The Legal Battle), which the poet follows in an independent way. Of his additional sources the Middle Dutch *Esopet,* the Old French *Cléomades* of Adenet li Roi, and works of the Latin poet Seneca should be mentioned. For a long time *Reinaerts historie* was neglected in favor of Willem's story, yet recent research has shown that it is a well-composed text in its own right, which vigorously denounces the perversion of human ethics. It is in this form that the story of Reynard the Fox became popular in Dutch and European literature. William Caxton used it as a source for his *The historye of reynart the foxe* (1481) and it was also the source for the oldest printed version in Middle Low German, the *Reynke de vos* (Lübeck 1498). Ultimately a large part of the postmedieval printed versions in many European languages—e.g., Johann Wolfgang von Goethe's *Reineke Fuchs*—can be traced back to the Middle Dutch *Reinaerts historie.*

Another descendant of *Van den vos Reynaerde* came into being shortly after the original. Not later than 1279 a certain Balduinus Iuvenis from Bruges translated and adapted the text into Latin. This *Reynardus vulpes* (1,850 lines) is the first known adaptation of a Middle Dutch text into that language.

BIBLIOGRAPHY

Bosch, J. *Reynaert-perspectief.* Kampen, Kok, 1972.

Bouwman, Andre Th. *Reinaert en Renart: Het dierenepos Van den vos Reynaerde vergeleken met de Oudfranse Roman de Renart.* 2 vols. Amsterdam, Prometheus, 1991.

Colledge, Edmund, and Adriaan J. Barnouw, trans. *Reynard the Fox and other Mediaeval Netherlands Secular Literature.* Leiden, Sijthoff, 1967.

Daele, Rik van. *Ruimte en naamgeving in "Van den vos Reynaerde."* Gent: Koninklijke Academie voor nederlandse Taal- en Letterkunde, 1994.

Daele, Rik van, et al., eds. *Van den vos Reynaerde: Het Comburgse handschrift.* Leuven, Davidsfonds, 1991. [Facsimile of the Comburg mansucript, with transcription.]

Engels, Louk J. "Reynardus vulpes als bewerking van de Reinaert," in *Verraders en bruggenbouwers: Verkenningen naar de relatie tussen Latinitas en Middelnederlandse letterkunde.* ed. Paul Wackers et al. Amsterdam: Prometheus, 1996, pp. 63–84 and 282–291.

Flinn, John. *Le Roman de Renart dans la littérature française et dans les littératures étrangères au Moyen Age.* Toronto: University of Toronto Press, 1963, pp. 598–671.

Goossens, Jan. *Die Reynaert-Ikonographie.* Darmstadt: Wissenschaftliche Buchgesellschaft, 1983.

Gysseling, Maurits, ed. *Corpus van Middelnederlandse teksten (tot en met het jaar 1300).* Reeks II: Literaire handschriften, dl. 6. Leiden: Nijhoff, 1987, pp. 403–422. [*Bestiare d'amour* translation.]

Heeroma, Klaas. *De andere Reinaert.* The Hague: Bakker, 1970.

Huygens, Robert B. C., ed. *Reynardus vulpes. De Latijnse Reinaert-vertaling van Balduinus Iuvenis.* Zwolle, Tjeenk Willink, 1968.

Lulofs, Frank, ed. *Van den vos Reynaerde.* Groningen, Wolters-Noordhoff, 1983.

Mann, Jill, ed. *Ysengrimus: Text with translation, Commentary, and Introduction.* Leiden: Brill, 1987.

Martin, Ernst, ed. *Reinaert. Willems Gedicht Van Den Vos Reynaerde und die Fortsetzung Reinaerts Historie.* Paderborn: Schöningh, 1874, pp. 107–341.

Stuiveling, Garmt, ed. *Esopet. Facsimile-uitgave naar het enig bewaarde handschrift.* 2 vols. Amsterdam: Menno Hertzberger, 1965.

Van Oostrom, Frits Pieter. "Benaderingswijzen van de Reinaert." In *Historische letterkunde. Facetten van vakbeoefening,* ed. Marijke Spies. Groningen: Wolters-Noordhoff, 1984, pp. 13–33.

Verwijs, Eelco, ed. *Jacob van Maerlant's Naturen Bloeme.* 2 vols. Groningen: Wolters, 1872–1878. Verzandvoort, Erwin, and Paul Wackers. *Reynaert den vos; oft, Der dieren oordeel.* Antwerp/Apeldoorn: Berghmans, 1988 [chapbook version].

Wackers, Paul. *De waarheid als leugen: Een interpretatie van Reynaerts historie.* Utrecht: HES, 1986.

Geert H. M. Claassens

SEE ALSO

Ecbasis captivi; Fables, Dutch; Jacob van Maerlant; *Reynard the Fox,* Dutch

Anno (r. 1056–1075)

Born to a minor noble family in Swabia, Anno II, archbishop of Cologne, became one of medieval Germany's most powerful ecclesiastics. Driven by the ambition to advance the see of Cologne during his tenure as archbishop from 1056 to 1075, Anno left a controversial legacy as saint on the one hand and manipulative power player on the other.

Anno built or renovated several of Cologne's churches, including St. Mary's ad gradus ("on the steps"), St. George, St. Mary-in-the-Capitol, St. Gereon, and Great St. Martin. He also took on political rivals, especially the aristocratic Ezzonid family. In the late 1050s, Anno persuaded Ezzo's daughter Richeza to assign a number of important family properties to Cologne. In 1060, a bitter conflict between Anno and Richeza's cousin, Count Palatine Henry, resulted in Henry's loss of the Siegberg (Southeast of Cologne), where Anno founded a monastic community. With Ezzonid power broken, Anno focused his political acumen on the affairs of the realm. The death of Emperor Henry III in 1056 quickly led to instability in the Reich. The young Henry IV was barely six years old, and the regency exercised by the empress Agnes was unpopular with the German aristocracy. In 1062, Anno took matters into his own hands by kidnapping the boy-king at Kaiserswerth on the Rhine. Temporarily, Anno, as new regent, was the most powerful person in Germany. In 1064, however, Anno was called to Italy in the wake of a papal schism. Upon his return, Anno found that his rival Adalbert, archbishop of Hamburg-Bremen, had ingratiated himself with the young king. In 1065, Henry IV celebrated his coming of age, and promptly shook off whatever was left of the authority Anno had once exercised over him.

Despite his role as archchancellor of Italy and the Roman church, Anno distanced himself in the 1070s from papal reform developments south of the Alps. More important for Anno was monastic reform as a means of furthering the influence of Cologne. Monks from Anno's Siegberg foundation reformed a number of important communities in Germany. Other storms were brewing in the twilight years of Anno's pontificate. Cologne was a wealthy city with a substantial middle class, and early yearnings for urban liberty clashed with the archbishop's grip as lord of the city. In 1074, after Anno's servants impounded a merchant boat, the city rebelled. Anno locked himself in the cathedral to escape rioting burghers, and in disguise that evening fled through a hole in the city wall. The rebellion was brutally suppressed by Anno a few days later, but left a bitter memory for both city and bishop. When Anno died in 1075, he was buried in his beloved monastery on the Siegberg, where he was soon honored for his personal sanctity. His career, on the eve of the Investiture Controversy, cannot be stereotyped as either proimperial or propapal. Anno fought for the rights not of the Roman church as much as for those of his own see.

BIBLIOGRAPHY

Arnold, Benjamin. "From Warfare on Earth to Eternal Paradise: Archbishop Anno II of Cologne, the History of the Western Empire in the Annolied, and the Salvation of Mankind." *Viator* 23 (1992): 95–113.

Jenal, Georg. *Erzbischof Anno II. von Köln (1056–75) und sein politisches Wirken: Ein Beitrag zur Geschichte der Reichs—und Territorialpolitik im 11. Jahrhundert.* Stuttgart: Hiersemann, 1974/1975.

Oediger, Frederick Wilhelm. *Die Regesten der Erzbischöfe von Köln im Mittelalter,* vol. 1. Düsseldorf: Droste, 1978, pp. 313–1099.

Rotondo-McCord, Jonathan. "Body Snatching and Episcopal Power: Archbishop Anno II of Cologne, Burials in St. Mary's ad gradus, and the Minority of Henry IV." *Journal of Medieval History* 22 (1996): 297–312.

Jonathan Rotondo-McCord

SEE ALSO

Annolied; Cologne, Archdiocese; Ezzonids; Henry III; Henry IV; Investiture Controversy; Siegburg, Abbey;

Annolied

Written down circa 1077, *Das Annolied* (the Song of Anno) is one of the most fascinating works of the Early Middle High German period and second only to the *Kaiserchronik* for insights into important aspects of the medieval worldview, especially the medieval concept of historical progression *(translatio imperii)* and its allegorical interpretation. The complete work is preserved through most fortunate chance; it exists only in a very late edition by Martin Opitz (1639), and vv. 19–78 in an edition of *De literis & lingua getarum, siue, Gothorum* by Bonaventura Vulcanius (d. 1614) from 1597. Each edition appears to be based on a different manuscript—not, however, on a different redaction of the poem. The complete work consists of 878 lines contained in forty-nine strophes of unequal length.

The most pressing reason for the composition of the *Annolied* was the glorification of Anno the prince, Anno the bishop, and Anno the "good shepherd" of his Cologne flock (ca. 1010–1075, archbishop 1056–1075), no mean task, since Anno was and is an extremely controversial political figure. It is clear that Anno is being proposed as a candidate for sainthood, an event that did ultimately take place roughly one hundred years later in 1183. The skillfulness of the poet in situating Anno and in weaving the events of the bishop's life into the broad tapestry of the history of salvation and the history of the world is quite unique in early Middle High German poetry.

It is conjectured that the immediate source for the "Anno" portion of the *Annolied* (strophes 34–48) was a now-lost *Vita Annonis* (Life of Anno) by Reginhard, the abbot of Siegburg (1076–1105). A most important source for the *Vita Annonis* is the annals of Lampert, monk of Hersfeld (ca. 1078). Unfortunately the identity of the *Annolied* poet is not known, and the place and time of composition can likewise not be determined with certainty. Since Anno died in December 1075 and the text reports his death, we do at least have a terminus a quo. And although scholarly opinion is somewhat divided on these topics, in more recent scholarship consensus is nonetheless forming around the conjecture that the work was composed sometime between March 1077 and December 1081 by a monk of the reform monastery of Siegburg. The poet skillfully weaves the account of Creation, the history of the city, the progression of empires from East to West, the relationship of the Romans with the Franks, and the case for Anno's canonization into a seamless whole. In addition, we encounter, for the first time in the vernacular, an episode about the legendary feats of Alexander the Great. The anecdote involves the familiar narrative of Alexander exploring the depths of the sea in a type of ancient bathysphere. But in the *Annolied* something new is added: Alexander is betrayed by his faithless men and abandoned to die on the ocean floor. (Although occurring in later versions of the Alexander story, the motif of the faithless men is not attested in any sources up to the time of the composition of the *Annolied*.) After seeing fear-inspiring merpeople and other marvels of the deep, Alexander devised a plan for his rescue. He caused some of his blood to spill into the water. The blood irritated the ocean to the extent that it spat Alexander out upon dry land.

The *Annolied* can justly be labeled a phenomenon of eleventh-century vernacular literature. Not only do we find the first mentionings in the vernacular of a hitherto unknown aspect of the Alexander legend, as well as the fleshed out account of the *translatio imperii*, the notion that the ancient Roman Empire would pass on to the German rulers, which would enjoy great popularity in later centuries but which was by no means a pressing concern in the eleventh century. We also are confronted with an extraordinary work of art whose complexity and clear spirit of dedication inspire admiration and great respect for the unknown monk-poet and his labor of love as well as thanks to Martin Opitz for having rescued this tale.

BIBLIOGRAPHY

Bulst, Walter, ed. *Das Annolied,* ed. Martin Opitz, 1639; rpt. Heidelberg: Winter, [1946].

Curschmann, Michael, and Ingeborg Glier, eds. *Deutsche Dichtung des Mittelalters.* vol. 1. *Von den Anfängen bis zum hohen Mittelalter.* Frankfurt am Main: Fischer, 1987, pp. 92–147 [trans. into modern German].

Gentry, Francis G. *Bibliographie zur frühmittelhochdeutschen geistlichen Dichtung.* Berlin: Schmidt, 1992, pp. 43–53.

Hellgardt, Ernst. "Die Rezeption des Annoliedes bei Martin Opitz." In *Mittelalter-Rezeption: Ein Symposion,* ed. Peter Wapnewski. Stuttgart: Metzler, 1986, pp. 60–79.

Knab, Doris. *Das Annolied: Probleme seiner literarischen Einordnung.* Tübingen: Niemeyer, 1962. Knoch, Peter. "Untersuchungen zum Ideengehalt und zur Datierung des Annoliedes." *Zeitschrift für deutsche Philologie* 83 (1964): 275–301.

Liebertz-Grün, Ursula. "Zum Annolied: Atypische Struktur und singuläre politische Konzeption." *Euphorion* 74 (1980).

Maurer, Frederick, ed. *Die religiösen Dichtungen des 11. und 12. Jahrhunderts. Nach ihren Formen besprochen,* vol. 2. Tübingen: Niemeyer, 1965.

Nellmann, Eberhard. "Annolied." In *Die deutsche Literatur des Mittelalters: Verfasserlexikon,* ed. Kurt Ruh, et al., vol. 1. Berlin and New York: Gruyter, 1978, cols. 366–371.

———. *Die Reichsidee in der deutschen Dichtung der Salier- und frühen Stauferzeit: Annolied, Kaiserchronik, Rolandslied, Eraclius.* Berlin: Schmidt, 1963, pp. 35–81.

———, ed. *Das Annolied. Mittelhochdeutsch und Neuhochdeutsch.* Stuttgart: Reclam, 1975 [trans. into modern German].

Thomas, Heinz. "Bemerkungen zu Datierung, Gestalt und Gehalt des Annoliede." *Zeitschrift für deutsche Philologie* 96 (1977): 24–61.

Vollmann-Profe, Giseala. *Geschichte der deutschen Literatur von den Anfängen bis zum Beginn der Neuzeit.* Vol. 1, pt. 2, *Von den Anfängen zum Hohen Mittelalter.* Tübingen: Niemeyer, 1994.

Wehrli, Max. *Geschichte der deutschen Literatur vom frühen Mittelalter bis zum Ende des 16. Jahrhunderts.* Stuttgart: Reclam, 1980.

Francis G. Gentry

SEE ALSO
Anno; *Kaiserchronik*

Archer/Bowman

Archers and archery were a traditional part of the German army during the Middle Ages. Because of the large number of arrowheads found in premedieval Germanic graves, it is thought that Germanic tribes operated the bow as a weapon even before they entered the borders of the Roman Empire, and that they continued to use the bow once they had settled beyond the Rhine and Danube Rivers. These early archers generally were equipped with a bow of simple wood construction, but in later centuries bows were improved by the addition of horn, sinew, and glue in a composite construction complete with angled ears to give more pull to the bowstring. By the end of the eleventh century the crossbow had also joined the more traditional bow in the German army, with units of crossbow men as well as other archers participating in military endeavors both in the Holy Roman Empire and in the Holy Land. The traditional bow continued to be used in Germany, both in war and in hunting, although by the end of the Middle Ages the crossbow was the most prominent archery weapon among soldiers. Some German armies also hired crossbow-armed foreign mercenaries, principally from Italy and Switzerland.

BIBLIOGRAPHY
Bradbury, Jim. *The Medieval Archer.* New York: St. Martin, 1985.
Contamine, Philippe. *War in the Middle Ages,* trans. M. Jones. London: Blackwell, 1984.
DeVries, Kelly. *Medieval Military Technology.* Peterborough: Broadview, 1992.
Hardy, Robert. *Longbow: A Social and Military History.* 3d ed. London: Bois d'Arc, 1994.
Nicolle, David C. *Arms and Armour of the Crusading Period, 1050–1350.* 2 vols. White Plains: Kraus, 1988.

Kelly DeVries

Architecture

See individual locations and styles.

Archpoet

The so-called Archpoet (the Latin form *Archipoeta* is followed in German), whose real name is unknown, was probably born around 1130 in Germany or eastern France. Nothing is known of him except what he reveals in ten surviving poems. Despite a knightly background, he disliked martial arts and preferred poetry. His nickname, which is found as a subscription in the main manuscript of his poems, may have been given to him because of the esteem in which his audience held him, or it may play upon the "arch-" elements in the titles of his chief patron, Reinald of Dassel (d. 1167), who was the archbishop of Cologne and the archchancellor of Frederick I Barbarossa (ca. 1122–1190). Because Frederick was king of Germany and Holy Roman Emperor, Reinald's court moved frequently in Germany, Burgundy, and northern Italy.

The Archpoet's poems date from the early and mid-1160s, and all of them can be classed as occasional poems, relating to the chief concerns and events of Reinald's court. In them the Archpoet gives signs of knowing the trivium of grammar, rhetoric, and dialectic as well as the basics of theology, whereas his short-lived study of medicine leaves almost no marks. He alludes with apparent ease to the Vulgate Bible and Roman poets, and he incorporates parody of confessions, sermons, and liturgy. Although his poems often constitute petitions for food, drink (especially wine), money, and clothing, and although they seem always to have been meant for public recitation at the court, the Archpoet differentiates himself sharply from professional entertainers of a humbler sort.

Two of the poems are in leonine hexameters, but the rest are based on accentual rhythms. The most famous of the poems is the Archpoet's confession to the archchancellor (incipit, or first line, "Aestuans intrinsecus"). Whereas the other nine poems survive mostly in only a single manuscript, this one is extant in more than thirty, most famously in the *Carmina burana;* Carl Orff set its first five strophes to music in his oratorio (1937). The confession is one of four in the *Vagantenstrophe,* with dissyllabic rhyme.

One remarkable aspect of the Archpoet—or of his persona as a poet, if his name does not in itself indicate such distancing—is his candor about his shortcomings. He discusses his proclivity for love affairs, drinking, gambling, and keeping bad company. Nor is his physical condition much better than his moral, to judge by his complaints about his cough and his proximity to death. The former failings may be little more than a stance struck by the poet to entertain his audience; the persona could be as far from the reality as that of Chaucer the character was from Chaucer the poet or man. Unfortunately the latter defects may well have taken the life of the Archpoet at a young age, since he disappears from our view in 1167 at the latest.

BIBLIOGRAPHY

Adcock, Fleur, ed. and trans. *Hugh Primas and the Archpoet.* Cambridge: Cambridge University Press, 1994.

Krefeld, Heinrich, ed. and trans. *Der Archipoeta.* Berlin: Akademie, 1992.

Dronke, Peter. "The Archpoet and the Classics." In *Latin Poetry and the Classical Tradition. Essays in Medieval and Renaissance Literature,* ed. Peter Godman and Oswyn Murray. Oxford: Clarendon Press, 1990, pp. 57–72.

Pucci, Joseph. "Job and Ovid in the Archpoet's *Confession.*" *Classica et mediaevalia* 40 (1989): 235–250.

Shurtleff, Steven. "The Archpoet as Poet, Persona, and Self: The Problem of Individuality in the Confession." *Philological Quarterly* 73 (1994): 373–384.

Jan Ziolkowski

SEE ALSO

Frederick I Barbarossa; Latin Language

Aristoteles und Phyllis

Together with *Dulciflorie* and *Moriz von Craûn, Aristoteles und Phyllis* is one of the three earliest German novellas *(maeren),* all anonymous short tales in verse based on French sources. *Le Lai d' Aristote* by Henri d' Andeli, the Old French courtly version of the narrative, was composed around 1230, and *Aristoteles und Phyllis* followed shortly thereafter.

The oldest and single manuscript of this version, B, was written in the second quarter of the thirteenth century in an Alemannic dialect (originally in Rhine-Franconian). This manuscript, in fragments, comprises only 204 verses and contains in addition *Der arme Heinrich* (E) of Hartmann von Aue. Version B of *Aristoteles und Phyllis* was slightly influenced in style and motifs by Hartmann's *Erec,* but especially by Gottfried von Straßburg's *Tristan.* In the later version, S, of about 1290 (554 verses), complete interpolations of *Tristan* are added in several places to make a parody out of the behavior of Aristoteles, since Tristan's love is paralleled with Phyllis's humorous seduction of Aristoteles. But the real love between Alexander (Aristotle's pupil) and Phyllis, who is angry at Aristotle's attempts to keep the two apart, is also based on *Tristan.*

In both versions, Alexander's parents appear, and Alexander and Phyllis are still adolescents. Aristoteles gets reprimanded for letting Phyllis ride him like a horse. Only in the older version B, which is more elegant and courtly, do Alexander and Phyllis stay together. And Phyllis wanted to be carried on Aristoteles's back, because her feet were tired. There were three manuscripts of version S in collections in Strasbourg (ca. 1330/1350, in Alemannic), Regensburg (fourteenth century, in Bavarian) and in Karlsruhe (ca. 1430/1435, in Swabian/Bavarian/East-Franconian).

From circa 1430/1440, a Moselle-Franconian manuscript contains a play titled *Aristoteles und die Königin* (Phyllis is not named here), which does not include the *Tristan* interpolations but is just as farcical as version S. The parents of Alexander do not appear. Alexander and Phyllis are adults, and Aristoteles praises love at the end and does not flee. The play includes motifs of both versions, B and S.

The story of *Aristoteles und Phyllis* is also adapted as a scene (114 verses) in the *Alexandreis* of Ulrich von Etzenbach. Alexander is grown up, and the foreign queen, who stays with him, is Candacis. The role of Aristoteles is played by the teacher Aristander, whereas Aristoteles stayed home in Athens in the Alexander epic. This episode is based on the old version B of *Aristoteles und Phyllis* and secondarily on the Latin exemplum of *Aristoteles* by Jacques de Vitry of ca. 1230.

While the German *maere* of *Aristoteles und Phyllis* has a two-part schema, first the love affair between Alexander and Phyllis, which gets disturbed by Aristoteles, and second Phyllis's revenge by tricking Aristoteles into a compromising situation and ridicule, the Latin exemplum, on the other hand, is a misogynous clerical version, where it is Alexander's wife, the queen, who, after a brief introduction, gets reprimanded for trying to take revenge, and Aristoteles gets away with an excuse not to trust women. This literary tradition is conveyed in three later *Fastnachtspiele* and a play by Hans Sachs.

BIBLIOGRAPHY

Fischer, Hanns. *Studien zur deutschen Märendichtung.* 2d ed. Tübingen: Niemeyer, 1983, pp. 309–311; 443.

Jefferis, Sibylle. "Das Spiel *Aristoteles und die Königin* (University of Pennsylvania Cod. Ger. 4): Ein Vergleich mit seiner Hauptvorlage, dem Märe *Aristoteles und Phyllis." Fifteenth Century Studies* 15 (1989): 165–181.

———. "Aristoteles (and Phyllis): *Fabliau, maere, spiel.*" In *The Medieval Text, Methods and Hermeneutics: A Volume of Essays in Honor of Edelgard E. DuBruck,* ed. William C. McDonald and Guy R. Mermier. *Fifteenth Century Studies* 17 (1990): 169–183.

———. "The *fabliau* or *maere Aristoteles und Phyllis:* A Comparison of the Two Versions." *Medieval Perspectives* 4/5 (1991): 80–90.

———. "Die Szene des "gerittenen Aristoteles" in der Alexandreis Ulrichs von Etzenbach." In *Canon and Canon Transgression in Medieval German Literature,* ed. Albrecht Classen. Göppingen: Kümerle, 1993, pp. 135–152.

Sibylle Jefferis

SEE ALSO

Fastnachtspiele; Gottfried von Straßburg; Hartmann von Aue; Ulrich von Etzenbach

Armenbibel

The term *Armenbibel,* or *Biblia Pauperum* (Paupers' Bible), is the designation applied to a category of manuscripts and early printed books that narrate the lives of Christ and the Virgin within the framework of biblical typology. In a sequence of pictures and short texts, these works explicate the typological relationship between persons, objects, and events in the New Testament, called the antitypes, and the persons, objects, and events in the Old Testament that prefigure or foreshadow them, called the types, by virtue of some significant parallel between the two. For example, Christ on the cross is prefigured by the brazen serpent raised up on a tree by Moses.

A total of seventy-nine complete or fragmentary examples survive. The earliest date from the beginning of the fourteenth century, but these were probably preceded by one or more lost models perhaps dating as far back as the twelfth century. Manuscript versions were produced until the late fifteenth century, the preponderance in Germany and Austria. A few block book (printed from blocks of engraved wood) versions appeared in the Netherlands and in Germany in the mid–fifteenth century, and the first of several fifteenth- and sixteenth-century editions printed with moveable type were published by Albrecht Pfister in Bamberg in 1462–1463. The earliest texts are Latin; German and dual German/Latin texts began to appear in the late fourteenth century.

Armenbibel (Vienna, Österreichische Nationalbibliothek, Cod. 1198), fol. 7r: Old Testament types for the Crucifixion. *Photograph: Bildarchiv, ÖNB Wien*

The *Biblia Pauperum* differs from other typological treatises such as the *Speculum Humanae Salvationis* (Mirror of Human Salvation) and the *Concordantia Caritatis* (Concordance of Charity) in its narrative structure and in the importance of pictures relative to text. It is further characterized by a schematic organization in which each antitype is typically accompanied by two types, with identifying labels, or *tituli,* by four Old Testament prophets and their relevant prophetic verses, and by short texts, or *lectiones,* that explain the typological relationships. A core sequence of thirty-four antitypes that begins with the Annunciation and concludes with the death of the Virgin is present from the beginning; starting in the late fourteenth century, that sequence was frequently augmented by additional scenes from the Passion, reflecting the intensified preoccupation with Christ's suffering and death that marks late medieval devotional practice. Extant examples have been grouped into three families associated with Austria, Weimar, and Bavaria respectively, based chiefly on the selection and sequence of antitypes and on the compositional arrangement of pictorial and textual elements on the page. Within these families, individual manuscripts vary considerably in the nature and quality of execution. Most are illustrated with pen-and-ink drawings; only a few are fully illuminated.

The authorship, intended audience, and purpose of the *Biblia Pauperum* remain obscure. The title *Biblia Pauperum,* which appears in just two fairly late manuscripts, inspired the once current view that it was produced for the use of poor, semiliterate clergy who had to rely on pictures as a source of religious knowledge. More recently, authorities have suggested that it was more likely directed to laypeople who likewise needed pictures for instruction and were wealthy enough to afford books. Both views must be approached cautiously, as scholars of later medieval religious life have come to appreciate that religious images did not function merely as substitutes for texts but were accorded independent importance as objects of devotion and meditation and as mnemonic devices for a broad spectrum of beholders that included highly literate individuals, among them monks and nuns.

BIBLIOGRAPHY

Cornell, Henrik. *Biblia Pauperum.* Stockholm: Thuletryck, 1925.

Henry, Avril. *Biblia Pauperum: A Facsimile and Edition.* Aldershot: Scolar, 1987.

Nellhaus, Tobin. "Mementos of Things to Come: Orality, Literacy, and Typology in the *Biblia Pauperum.*" In *Printing the Written Word: The Social History of Books circa 1450–1520,* ed. Sandra Hindman, Ithaca N.Y.: Cornell University Press, 1991, pp. 292–321.

Schmidt, Gerhard. *Die Armenbibeln des XIV. Jahrhunderts.* Graz: H. Böhlaus Nachfolger, 1959.

Schmidt, Gerhard, and W. Weckwerth, "Biblia Pauperum (Armenbibel)." *Lexikon zur christlichen Ikonographie.* Vol. 1. Rome: Herder, 1968, pp. 293–298.

Soltész, Elizabeth. *Biblia Pauperum: Facsimile Edition of the Forty-Leaf Blockbook in the Library of the Esztergom Cathedral.* Budapest: Corvina, 1967.

Zimmermann, Hildegard. "Armenbibel.' *Reallexikon zur deutschen Kunstgeschichte,* vol. 1. Stuttgart: Metzler, 1937, pp. 1072–1084.

Susan L. Smith

SEE ALSO

Bible; Block Book; Gothic Art and Architecture; Ludolf of Saxony

Armer Hartmann (fl. ca. 1140–1160)

The presumed author of the thirty-eight-hundred-line *Rede vom heiligen Glouben* (Treatise on Holy Faith) identifies himself in line 3737 of the work with the phrase "ich arme Hartman," utilizing the fairly common epithet *arm,* a translation of Latin *miser* (poor). A more exact identification of Hartmann was not possible in 2000. Although probably written ca. 1140–1160, the work itself was contained in the Strasbourg-Molsheimer manuscript (ca. 1187) that was burned during the French siege of Strasbourg in 1870. Fortunately, the work was faithfully copied and printed prior to the conflagration—there is a postulated four-hundred-line lacuna (gap) between lines 3224 and 3625.

The work is an exposition of the Christian *credo* (the Apostles' Creed) as it appears in the Sunday liturgy and is best described as a rhymed theological tract. Although Hartmann displays more than a passing familiarity with Platonist discourse, the *Rede vom heiligen Glouben* is not a learned theological document on the intricacies of the *credo* and the subtleties of interpretation, but rather can be viewed as a primer to aid the laity in comprehending the central mysteries of Christianity contained in the creed. The text evidences a cohesive internal structure proceeding from Creation to Redemption and its significance to the proper conduct of life on earth and to the certainty of the final judgment and reward for the just.

Hartmann concentrates much energy on descriptions of the emerging noble lifestyle in the twelfth century, which he views as a possible threat to the soul. Thus he admonishes his listeners to renounce their possessions and enter a monastery as *conversi* (converts). If they cannot do that, they should help the poor; remember the one who is the author of all their wealth and joy; and control their sexual appetites. Moderation in all things and a life of active Christianity will ensure the salvation of the soul regardless of one's station in life.

BIBLIOGRAPHY

Gentry, Francis G. *Bibliographie zur frühmittelhochdeutschen geistlichen Dichtung.* Berlin: Schmidt, 1992, pp. 75–79.

Frederick Leyen, von der. *Des Armen Hartman Rede vom Glouven. Eine deutsche Reimpredigt des 12. Jahrhun-*

derts. Breslau (Wroclaw), 1897; rpt. Hildesheim and New York: Olms, 1977.

Massmann, Hans Ferdinand. *Deutsche Gedichte des zwölften Jahrhunderts und der nächstverwand ten Zeit. I. Theil: Die Strassburg-Molsheimische Handschrift.* Quedlinburg/Leipzig: Druck und Verlag von Gottfried Basse, 1837, pp. 1–42.

Maurer, Frederick, ed. *Die religiösen Dichtungen des 11. und 12. Jahrhunderts,* vol. 2. Tübingen: Niemeyer, 1965, pp. 573–628.

Rupp, Heinz. *Deutsche religiöse Dichtungen des 11. und 12. Jahrhunderts. Untersuchungen und Interpretationen.* 2d ed. Bern and Munich: Francke, 1971, pp. 134–216.

Vollmann-Profe, Gisela. *Geschichte der deutschen Literatur von den Anfängen bis zum Beginn der Neuzeit.* Vol. 1, pt. 2, *Wiederbeginn volkssprachiger Schriftlichkeit im hohen Mittelalter.* 2d ed. Tübingen: Niemeyer, 1994.

Francis G. Gentry

Armor

There were three types of defensive armaments worn during the Middle Ages: that to cover the body, or armor, that to cover the head, or helmets, and that carried by the nonweapon-wielding hand, or shields. Each of these, unlike their offensive counterparts, descended directly from that worn by late imperial Roman soldiers and changed little in the style, choice of metal for construction, and method of manufacture throughout all of Europe until the end of the Middle Ages.

By the fall of Rome an imperial soldier would be outfitted either in a *lorica squamata* cuirass, which was made of a large number of metallic scales attached to each other by wire or leather laces and affixed to a linen textile undergarment by linen cord, or, becoming increasingly more popular, a *lorica hamata,* which was constructed of metal rings. Alternate rows of these rings were punched out of sheet metal, with the connecting row in between made from metal wire, the ring ends butted or riveted together; each ring was interlocked with four others, two in the row above and two in the row below. Thirty-five thousand to forty thousand of these rings were needed to make a cuirass. Both styles covered the torso from the shoulder to at least the middle of the thigh and some seem to have stretched as far down as the knee. Both could be worn by either an infantry or a cavalry soldier. There were also two different types of helmets. The infantry helmet was bowl-shaped, made of two iron halves joined together by a metal strip. It was lined by a leather cap, not attached to the outer helmet, on which was affixed an iron neck guard and iron cheek pieces. The cavalry helmet was also bowl-shaped, but instead of having an inner leather cap on which the neck and cheek guards were affixed, it was constructed of four to six pieces, including a ridge, nose guard, and extremely wide cheekpieces, all of which were attached by rivets or hinges to the helmet itself. The shield carried by these soldiers was quite long, rectangular in shape and curved to fit the body. It was made of plywood and was covered in leather, on which was fastened gilded and silvered bronze decoration and a metallic boss. Around its edges was a rim of wrought iron or bronze.

During most of the Middle Ages, the *lorica squamata* and the *lorica hamata* continued to be made and worn for defensive protection. The *lorica squamata* is the lesser known of the two styles; nevertheless, as cloth-covered armor it continued to be popular, if not the preferred armor of infantry soldiers, as excavations of grave mounds at the site of the Battle of Visby have shown. The *lorica hamata,* or chain mail suit of armor, is much better known, and was undoubtedly a much more protective body armor; it was also extraordinarily expensive. Chain mail armor remained the primary body armor of knights and cavalry soldiers—in other words, of those who could afford it—into the late Middle Ages. Sometimes it was short, covering only the torso and thighs of the wearer, while at other times it enclosed even the feet, hands, and head. It was also usually worn over, but not attached to, a heavy quilted undergarment (known as a *haubergeon*), which added to the defensive capability of the armor. Chain mail continued to be used and favored by soldiers in the fourteenth century, but as high-powered crossbows and longbows were able to break the rings and penetrate the armor, new, more capable defense was needed. This led to the next significant change in defensive armaments: plate armor. After a series of experimental and evolutionary developments, full suits of plate armor, covering from the head to the feet, became constructed and worn, initially only in tournaments, but eventually in warfare as well. This change was initiated in the late thirteenth and early fourteenth centuries and lasted well into the sixteenth century.

During the Middle Ages, soldiers of all European lands wore metal helmets made of several pieces which were formed to protect the head and face. For the cavalry, especially the knights, helmets eventually enclosed the entire head, first in the can-shaped manner of the high medieval great helm, then in the *bascinet*, a conical helmet truncated at the top and sometimes ending in a slight point, with a moveable visor, and finally in the famous "frog-mouthed" helmet, which developed in the late Middle Ages and became extremely popular for use in tournaments as well as in warfare. The infantry preferred the open "kettle hat" which, although acquiring a much larger brim, did not differ much from the late Roman infantry helmet.

The late Roman shield changed frequently in shape and size throughout the Middle Ages, but not in materials or method of manufacture. Carolingian shields were large and round, but by the eleventh century they had given way to the narrower, "kite-shaped" shield. Both, however, remained made of wood, and at least some were covered, perhaps on both sides, by leather. The kite-shaped shield would dominate shield design for nearly two centuries until it evolved into a more triangular shape, shorter, wider, probably lighter and almost always flat. At the same time, the shape of the new shield allowed for more maneuverability on horseback; infantry troops continued to use the kite-shaped shield for a while until they too switched to the newer triangular design. The flat or slightly curved triangular shield of moderate size popular in the thirteenth century continued to be popular in the fourteenth and fifteenth centuries as well, but, it seems, only among cavalry soldiers.

After the turn of the fifteenth century, the triangular cavalry shield was supplanted by shields of a variety of shapes and sizes. The most common of these was an oblong, either rounded or pointed on the lower edge, and often bent forward at the top and bottom. Leaf-shaped and round shields were also known. Cavalry shields also began to be made of metal, and sometimes, if used exclusively in tournaments, they were reinforced by extra metallic plates. Infantry soldiers also rejected their thirteenth-century triangular shields, returning sometime in the early fourteenth century to the round shield not seen in regular use in western Europe since Charlemagne's day. Three styles of late medieval infantry shields developed: the medium-sized target or targe, the small buckler, and the very large pavis. Most infantry shields continued to be made of wood covered by leather.

BIBLIOGRAPHY

Contamine, Philippe. *War in the Middle Ages,* trans. M. Jones. London: Blackwell, 1984.

DeVries, Kelly. *Medieval Military Technology.* Peterborough: Broadview, 1992.

Nicolle, David C. *Arms and Armour of the Crusading Period, 1050–1350.* 2 vols. White Plains: Kraus, 1988.

———. *Medieval Warfare Source Book.* 2 vols. London: Arms and Armour, 1995–1996.

Kelly DeVries

SEE ALSO

Carolingians; Charlemagne; Crossbow; Warfare; Weapons

Arnolt, Priester (fl. 12th c.)

Author of the Middle High German poem known chiefly as the *Loblied auf den Heiligen Geist* (Song of Praise to the Holy Spirit), preserved in a Vorau manuscript (no. 276, fol. 129vb–133vb). Scholars may also refer to the poem as *Gedicht von der Siebenzahl* (Poem on Number Seven; not to be confused with *De septem sigillis,* On the Seven Signs, from a MHG Innsbruck manuscript). The Bavarian dialect in which the work is written and the given name of the poet have led some scholars to believe that the author may have been that of the Juliana (also Juliane) legend, the prior of the Premonstratenser monastery of Schäftlarn near Munich from 1158 until the year of his death in 1163. Known as "ein priester der hiez Arnolth" (a priest called Arnolth, v. 919), the author examines the significance and symbolism of the sacred number seven. The short poem of 955 rhymed verses addresses a lay audience, *vil tumpen leigen* (very uneducated laypersons, v. 937) to impart religious knowledge on topics such as the seven supplications in the Lord's Prayer, the seven gifts of the Holy Spirit, and the seven seals of the Apocalypse, as well as natural knowledge of the physical universe as a macrocosmos, with its seven planets, phases of the moon, and days of the week, complemented by human existence as a microcosmos with its seven *artes* (liberal arts), seven ages of man, and so on. The rhyme and verse technique indicate the work as dating from the middle of the twelfth century. A further indication is that scholars have noted similarities between Arnolt's "Song of Praise to the Holy Spirit" (v. 640–695) and the *Kaiserchronik* (v. 605–642), whose final entry dates from Christmas 1146. Arnolt's use of number symbolism highlights the divine order of creation and its meaning for life in this world. The author concludes his poem as he began with a hymn of praise to the Holy Spirit.

The other work attributed to Arnolt is the Juliane legend: "ein ewart do,/Arnolt was er geheizen" (a priest there, Arnolt he was called; Juliana, v. 4f.). A holy woman, Juliane renounces pagan gods and refuses to marry her promised suitor, Count Aulesius, unless he becomes Christian. Divine intercession enables her to endure the tribulations that await in prison and joyfully gain the crown of martyrdom. Though the work is preserved only in a fourteenth-century manuscript from the womens' monastery of the Augustiner-Chorherrenstift Seckau (University Library in Graz, cod. 1501, 12th c. fol. 95r–134r), Arnolt is still likely to have been the author. Scholars note that the "burlesque" scene, where Juliane not only resists temptation by the devil, but subdues the ancient foe and forces him to confess his transgressions, belongs to the Latin tradition of the legend and need not indicate late medieval authorship.

BIBLIOGRAPHY

Bartsch, Karl. "Zu Priester Arnolts Juliana." *Germania* 28 (1883): 257–267. Berschin, W. "Zur lateinischen und deutschen Juliane-Legende." *Studi Medievali* 14 (1973): 1003–1012.

Brunöhler, Ernst. "Über einige lateinische, englische, französische und deutsche Fassungen der Julianenlegende mit einem Abdruck des lateinischen Textes dreier Münchener Handschriften." Ph.D. diss., Bonn, 1912, p. 119.

Ganz, Peter. "Priester Arnolt." In *Die deutsche Literatur des Mittelalters Verfasserlexikon,* ed. Kurt Ruh, Gundlof Keil, Werner Schröder, Burghart Wachinger, and Franz Josef Worstbrock, vol. 1. 2d ed. Berlin and New York: Gruyter, 1978, cols. 489–493.

Geith, Karl-Ernst. "Die Edition der Juliane-Legende des Priester Arnolt." In *Kolloquium über Probleme altgermanistischer Editionen.* Wiesbaden, 1968, pp. 72–80.

———. "Ein deutsches Gedicht aus dem Kloster Schäftlarn." *Analecta Praemonstratensia* 45 (1969): 56–64.

———. "Priester Arnolts Legende von der heiligen Juliana. Untersuchungen zur lateinischen Juliana-Legende und zum Text des deutschen Gedichtes." Ph.D. diss., Freiburg, 1965, pp. 205–258.

Gentry, Francis G. "Ex oriente lux: 'Translatio' Theory in Early Middle High German Literature." In *Spectrum Medii Aevi: Essays in Early German Literature in Honor of George Fenwick Jones.* Göppingen: Kümerle, 1983, pp. 119–137.

———. "The Development of the Concept of 'Simplicity' from Classical Antiquity to the Vernacular Literature of the German Middle Ages." In *From the Greeks to the Greens: Images of the Simple Life,* ed. Reinhold Grimm and Jost Hermand. Madison: University of Wisconsin Press, 1989.

Hofmann, Sieglinde. "Reimtechnik und Formkunst des Priester Arnold. Studien zum 'Loblied auf den Heiligen Geist' und zur 'Legende von der heiligen Julianna.'" Ph.D., diss Freiburg, 1973.

Leitzmann, Albert. "Zu Arnolds 'Juliane.'" *Beiträge zur Geschichte der deutschen Sprache und Literatur* 73 (1954): 319.

Maurer, Frederick I, ed. "Loblied auf den Heiligen Geist" [Von der Siebenzahl]. In his *Die religiösen Dichtungen des 11. und 12. Jahrhunderts,* vol. 3. Tübingen: Niemeyer, 1970, pp. 57–85.

Mohr, Wolfgang. "Vorstudien zum Aufbau von Priester Arnolds 'Loblied auf den Heiligen Geist' ('Siebenzahl')." In *Die Wissenschaft von deutscher Sprache und Dichtung: Methoden, Probleme, Aufgaben. Festschrift für Frederick I Maurer.* Stuttgart: Klett, 1963, pp. 320–351.

Polzer-van Kol, Herman. "Priester Arnolds Gedicht von der Siebenzahl." Ph.D. diss. Berlin, 1913.

Ranke, Kurt. "Volkskundliches zu Priester Arnolds Gedicht von der Siebenzahl." *Zeitschrift für deutsche Philologie* 71 (1951/1952): 343–365.

Schönbach, Anton. "Priester Arnolds Legende von St. Juliane." *Sitzungsberichte der philosophisch-historischen Klasse der österreichischen* [formerly *Kaiserlichen*] *Adademie der Wissenschaften in Wien* 101, no. 1 (1882): 445–536, esp. 491–517.

Ernst Ralf Hintz

SEE ALSO
Kaiserchronik

Ars Moriendi

Written by an anonymous author, probably in the early fifteenth century, the text of the *Ars Moriendi* (The Art of Dying Well) developed out of a series of writings about the way to die in the Christian faith. It first appears after the Council of Constance (1414–1418) and may have actually been composed at the council. Its original audience seems to have been the laity, who were increasingly emulating a variety of clerical practices in the later Middle Ages, including participating in elaborate death rituals. The *Ars Moriendi,* now preserved in over three hundred Latin and vernacular versions, recounts the final hours of the protagonist, the dying Moriens, as he is tempted to turn away from his faith but successfully resists and finally achieves a good death.

Germany was particularly important in the development of the illustrated *Ars Moriendi,* and the largest group of texts can be associated with southern Germany, specifically Bavaria and Swabia. Although the text appears in a long version that is rarely illustrated, its great popularity was as a block book, where both text and images are printed from carved wood blocks. Almost all of these block books were printed at Augsburg in southern Germany. In such books the text was radically shortened to suit the format and accompanied by a standardized series of eleven woodcuts. Each image centers on Moriens in his bed. In five prints, demons tempt Moriens by trying to get him to renounce his faith, to turn to despair, to impatience, to vainglory, and to avarice. Each image of temptation is followed by an illustration showing angels supporting Moriens in corresponding virtuous behavior. The final print shows Moriens achieving a good death surrounded by his family and endorsed by the Church.

The block book illustrations may have been created for that format. Most of the illuminated manuscript versions have miniatures that seem dependent on the printed versions rather than vice versa. There is a series of copper plate engravings of the *Ars Moriendi* images attributed to Master E. S., which are very similar to the illustrations of the block books, and scholars have speculated that they may have been made as a model for the books.

Block books were a popular media that provided information to medieval users through a variety of means. In addition to their visual presence, the characters in the *Ars Moriendi* woodcuts hold scrolls with short written messages that paraphrase elements contained in the already reduced text. Sometimes the *Ars Moriendi* was printed on a single sheet, which could be hung on the wall. In this case the text was reduced to the scrolls held by various participants.

The *Ars Moriendi* was part of a late medieval interest in the societal mediation of death. This preoccupation encompassed a greater prevalence of wills and an interest in the sacrament of extreme unction. It also included the appearance of other visual programs related to the idea of dying well, including the Three Living and the Three Dead, which shows three healthy young men confronting three skeletonalized dead, and the Dance of Death, where death in the form of a skeleton comes to a variety of people in different stations of life.

BIBLIOGRAPHY

Binski, Paul. *Medieval Death: Ritual and Representation.* Ithaca, N.Y.: Cornell University Press, 1996.

O'Connor, Mary. *The Art of Dying Well: The Developement of the Ars Moriendi.* New York: Columbia University Press, 1942.

Susan L. Ward

SEE ALSO
Augsburg; Block Book; E. S., Master; Iconographies, Innovative

Arthurian Literature, German

Stories revolving around King Arthur, or the *matière de Bretagne* (Breton material), found their way into German-speaking areas primarily through France. The first Arthurian romance in German, *Erec* (ca. 1180), by Hartmann von Aue (ca. 1160–1210), appeared in the southwestern corner of the German empire, where the house of Zähringen, probable candidate for Hartmann's sponsors, maintained extended personal, political, and cultural relationships with their French neighbors. Centers of patronage in Thuringia, Bavaria, and Austria later became focal points for this modern genre, which rapidly gained popularity among the educated nobility. It is not clear what role the oral tradition of wandering storytellers played in the spread of the genre throughout Europe, and in German-speaking areas in particular. Many German adaptations of French narrations, containing elements that cannot be traced directly to their putative sources, appear only in later versions of the stories. However, in general, the written versions of the romances of Chrétien de Troyes (ca. 1140–1190) became the standard for a certain type of Arthurian narrative in the German vernacular during the early stages of the genre. Three of Chrétien's four Arthurian romances (*Erec et Enide, Yvain,* and *Le conte du Graal*) were adapted into German coinciding with the first high period of German literature, between 1180 and 1220. Along with the usual motifs, Chrétien's narrative form of the double turning point in the hero's development is carried over into German versions. It shows the initial rise of an individual to glory at King Arthur's court, an incident that turns the hero's fate to shame, a period of despair followed by a reassessment of values, a quest for gradual redemption, and the hero's final rise to the status of an exemplary knight.

Hartmann's *Erec* serves as a typical example of this narrative technique: Erec gains his beautiful wife, Enite, by winning the grand prize at a tournament in King Arthur's court. Hailed as the premier knight, he ascends to rulership of the parental empire. But blinded by Enite's beauty, he spends most of his time in bed with his wife instead of looking to the business of government, leading to public shame. Enraged, he tears himself and his wife away from the comforts of the court. Through a series of dangerous adventures, he gradually realizes his true duty as a responsible ruler and husband. Supported by the unwavering love of his wife, he is victorious in a final duel with the ruler of an enchanted court, which ultimately leads the royal couple, now back at court, to even higher fame and glory and an ideal state of governance.

Hartmann's adaptation has been preserved through only one fairly complete sixteenth-century manuscript included in Hans Ried's *Ambraser Heldenbuch* (Book of Heroes from Ambras Castle) and fragments of three manuscripts from the thirteenth and fourteenth centuries. *Erec* is not a mere translation but an expansion of Chrétien's model through a process that has been identified by French scholars as *adaptation courtoise,* or courtly adaptation. Authorial comments are lengthened or inserted and elaborate descriptions of courtly ambiance are interpolated at the expense of dialogue. Greater emphasis is placed on the key role and depth of the evolving love between the royal couple in serving as a basis for a sound system of government. The same technique, yet more limited, can be observed in Hartmann's *Iwein* (ca. 1202), which is similar to *Erec* in its thematic development.

The flagship of Arthurian narrative based on Chrétien is Wolfram von Eschenbach's *Parzival* (ca. 1200–1210). No other courtly romance has been preserved in so many manuscripts. More than eighty have survived, sixteen complete versions and sixty-six fragments. Wolfram seems to have been by far the most popular writer of courtly romances throughout the German Middle Ages. It may be assumed that Chrétien's *Le conte du Graal* (the Count of the Grail), a fragment, was Wolfram's primary source. But Wolfram turned it into a true masterpiece of his own, vastly expanding the family history of the dynasty of the Grail kings, placing love and marriage at the center of the Grail quest, which in Chrétien's version focused primarily on the theme of sin and atonement, and sharpening the dichotomy between the worldly and fallible Arthurian court and the ideal, selfless rulership of the Grail dynasty.

Wolfram expands even further upon the theme of the Grail dynasty through a second romance in stanzas, *Titurel,* which remained a fragment. It is the story of the tragic youthful love affair between Sigune, Parzival's aunt, and Schionatulander, who dies early in combat because of Sigune's capricious wish to possess an elaborate hound's leash inscribed with a love story.

This romance was continued and expanded by Albrecht von Scharfenberg, probably a well-educated cleric, origin unknown, whose language places him into the Bavarian/East Middle German region. His work, *Der Jüngere Titurel* (the Younger Titurel; ca. 1260–1275), is a vast compendium of the history of the Grail kings, in great detail, dating back to ancient Troy and the Roman emperors. This history, which is the complete story of Sigune and Tschinotulander, was only alluded to by Wolfram, in both *Parzival* and *Titurel*. The narration continues far beyond Parzival's ascension to the Grail kingdom, relating the story of the legendary priest-king Johann, whose empire extended into India. Fifty-eight manuscripts and a print from 1477 testify to a great popularity of the work. Until the nineteenth century the narrative had been considered Wolfram's masterpiece, and throughout the late Middle Ages Wolfram was probably better known through Albrecht's romance than through his own works. Another expansion of Wolfram's *Parzival* was compiled by two goldsmiths from Strasbourg, Philipp Colin and Claus Wisse, in their *Rappoltsteiner Parzifal* (1331–1336). A relatively faithful copy of Wolfram's *Parzival* was expanded by translations from Chrétien's *Le conte du Graal* and its various French continuations.

A second and later type of Arthurian literature juxtaposes the almost classical narrative structure based on Chrétien with a complex web of plots and subplots. These romances are oriented around one or two exemplary heroes outside the traditional circle of the round table, who use the passive and sometimes foolish Arthurian court mainly to mirror their own superior qualities. This type of narrative vastly expanded on fantastic, otherworldly elements, including dwarfs, giants, humanoid monsters, and numerous miraculous events. The first representative of this genre is *Wigalois* (1210–1215) by Wirnt von Grafenberg (ca. 1170–1235). The romance begins as a narrative with Gawein (Arthur's nephew) as its central character, but later Wigalois, Gawein's son, follows his father's footsteps and surpasses him. Other representatives of the genre are *Daniel von dem blühenden Tal* (Daniel of the Blossoming Valley; 1210–1225) by a poet identified as Der Stricker (ca. 1190–1250), which features Arthur as active hero next to the central character. Stricker's Daniel triggered a later version by Der Pleier, *Garel von dem blühenden Tal* (Garel of the Blossoming Valley), followed by another romance by the same author, *Meleranz* (both works composed

ca. 1240–1270). Of the same type is Konrad von Stoffeln's *Gauriel von Muntabel* (after 1250). Heinrich von
dem Türlîn's complex work, *Diu Crône* (the Crown, ca.
1230), featuring Gawain as its central character, constitutes the most representative model for this type of
Arthurian literature.

The stories involving Lancelot, Guinevere, and King
Arthur as central characters make up a third and less popular type of Arthurian literature in Germany. The earliest
version, *Lanzelet* (ca. 1200) by Ulrich von Zatzikhoven,
has a narrative structure quite distinct from Chrétien's,
and its motifs differ from most other sources of Lancelot
stories. Lanzelet represents a type of hero whose development never takes a negative turn. He is complete and perfect from beginning to end. He gets involved with King
Arthur's court only in order to rescue Guinevere from her
abductor, Vâlerîn, a feat of which Arthur and his champi-
ons seem to be totally incapable. Ulrich's actual source
cannot be identified. The Middle High German *Prosa-
Lancelot* (Prose Lancelot; before 1250), on the other
hand, is a faithful translation of the French *Lancelot en
prose* (1215–1230), perhaps mediated by a Middle Dutch
version. It is preserved through nine fragmentary manuscripts from the thirteenth to sixteenth centuries.

A key element within the general European context of
the Arthurian tradition, the Merlin figure, found limited
and late entrance into German literature. Only a fragment of that story cycle is preserved in the so-called
Rheinischer Merlin (Rhenish Merlin; 1250–1300), while
the *Prosa-Lancelot* includes a narrative section on Merlin
of merely seventy lines. *Der theure Mörlin* (the Dear Mörlin) by Albrecht von Scharfenberg is preserved only in a
late medieval compilation of stories, Ulrich Füetrer's
Buch der Abenteuer (Book of Adventures, 1473–1483). It
is the sole complete German representative of the cycle
that has such a prominent place in Geoffrey of Monmouth, the French Arthurian cycle of narratives by
Robert de Boron, and the Vulgate cycle.

The fourth type of the German Arthurian tradition
is the stories involving the tragic couple Tristan and
Isolt, which probably was not originally related to the
Arthurian tradition but became linked with it at a later
stage of its development. Both early German versions of
the story show a loose, almost casual connection to the
Arthurian cycle of stories. Eilhart von Oberge's *Tristrant*
(ca. 1170–1190) was preserved in fragments from three
early manuscripts dating back to the late twelfth to
early thirteenth centuries. It is generally accepted to be
based on the so-called *Estoire*, the earliest French Tristan

romance, which has been lost but is considered as the
basis of all later adaptations of the subject matter. In
the narrative, Tristrant woos Isalde of Ireland for his
master, King Mark of Cornwall. On their journey from
Ireland to Cornwall they accidentally drink some of the
love potion meant for King Mark before his wedding
night. An inextricable passionate love thereafter con-
sumes the couple throughout a series of persecutions
and attempts to separate them until they find their
tragic end. In Eilhart's version, the love affair unfolds in
a fairy-tale-like atmosphere, in which the responsibility
for the couple's transgression against the prevalent
moral codes is tied firmly to the mechanism of the
magic potion.

Gottfried von Straßburg's (died before 1230) *Tristan
und Isolde* (ca. 1210), based on the narration by Thomas
d'Angleterre, is generally considered the masterpiece of
the genre. However, the work breaks off shortly after the
final separation of the couple, omitting Tristan's marriage
to Isolt of the White Hands and the final reunification of
the lovers in death. Early continuations of the story claim
that the work was unfinished due to the premature death
of the poet, but theories prevail that Gottfried simply
gave up on it. The romance has been preserved through
eleven complete manuscripts and sixteen fragments, most
of them dating back to the early thirteenth century. Gottfried's work is much more than a translation of Thomas's
version into German. His extensive commentaries on
love as a special force that rules the lives of individuals
and brings them into opposition with society make it one
of the most complex works of the period. The conflicts of
erotic relationships vis-à-vis the rigid codes of a feudal society are presented without simple solutions. The ambiguous function of the love potion has been the subject
of controversies among interpreting scholars since the
nineteenth century.

The *Tristan* of Ulrich von Türheim (Swabian, fl.
1236–1244 in Augsburg), composed before 1243 under
the patronage of territorial princes close to the imperial
dynasty of the Staufen family, claims to be a continuation
of Gottfried's work. But although Ulrich seems stylistically indebted to Gottfried, most of his motif developments point to Eilhart's *Tristrant* as a direct source. The
story begins where Gottfried breaks off, with Tristan marrying Isolt of the White Hands, and continues to the
tragic demise of the couple, with King Mark planting the
rose and vine on their grave. The ensuing intertwining of
these symbolizes the final unification of the lovers in
death. Ulrich seems preoccupied with the end of the story

and deals very little with the social and ethical issues raised by Gottfried.

A second continuation of Gottfried's *Tristan* was written by the burgher Heinrich von Freiberg, under the patronage of Bohemian nobility. His *Tristan* is based partly on Ulrich von Türheim's version and partly on Eilhart's. It also includes and expands motifs that occur before Gottfried breaks off. Like Ulrich, Heinrich fully integrates Tristan with King Arthur's court and his model knights. In a sense, Heinrich turns Gottfried's ideas around by playing down the importance of erotic love, seen here as a mere machination of the devil, who is ultimately responsible for the moral transgressions of the lovers and their ensuing sufferings. The symbols of the rose and the vine are interpreted in a traditional Christian sense, whereby the lovers find only peace and salvation after death, when the human vine finally embraces Christ, represented by the rosebush.

An episodic spin-off from the larger cycle is *Tristan als Mönch* (Tristan as Monk; 1210–1260, perhaps Alsatian, South Franconian/Allemanic, Switzerland). The story concerns the episode of Tristan's return to Cornwall after his marriage to Isolt of the White Hands. Believed dead and disguised as a monk, Tristan travels from home and is rejoined with his beloved Isolt the Fair. The episode is triggered by Guinevere and Arthur, who invite the entire high nobility to festivities at Carduel. Each knight is supposed to be accompanied by his dearest love. Tristan is torn between betraying his wife and acknowledging his one and only love, Isolt, the Blonde. He takes his wife to Cornwall but then disappears. Compared to Gottfried's work, the short romance seems to upgrade the importance of the institution of marriage, while the effect of the love potion is never mentioned.

The fragment of a Middle Low German Tristan romance (ca. 1350) contains the adaptation of the episode of Tristan and the dwarf. In this narrative, Tristan is approached by a dwarf, also named Tristan, for assistance in finding his lost lover. When the former declines, the dwarf, believing Tristan is dead, claims Tristan would have helped him for sure. Contrary to Gottfried and Thomas, his sources, the writer places the exemplary knight above the exemplary lover as the essence of his narration. Toward the end of the medieval period the prose novel *Tristrant und Isalde* (first printing 1484), a streamlined version of the entire narrative material, was aimed primarily at an audience of burghers. Knightly values are downplayed in this work in favor of a more sentimental approach to the theme of the unfortunate lovers,

whose negative example was intended to instruct people in the importance of placing obedience to Christian values above the entrapments of erotic love.

Having reached their heyday during the thirteenth and early fourteenth centuries, with a brief revival from the viewpoint of story collecting during the fifteenth and early sixteenth centuries, literary treatments of Arthurian matter gradually faded away during the sixteenth and seventeenth centuries, only to be rediscovered and revived during the late eighteenth and early nineteenth centuries. One common feature of the German Arthurian literature is the relative weak role King Arthur plays in most of the narratives. This phenomenon may be explained by the ambivalent attitude toward centralized rulership taken by most of the territorial lords who sponsored this type of literature.

BIBLIOGRAPHY

Albrecht von Scharfenberg

Albrecht von Scharfenberg. *Albrechts von Scharfenberg Jüngerer Titurel*, vol. 4, ed. Kurt Nyholm. Deutsche Texte des Mittelalters 79. Berlin: Akademie-Verlag, 1995.

Eilhart von Oberge

Eilhart von Oberge. *Tristrant und Isalde*, ed. and trans. Danielle Buschinger and Wolfgang Spiewok. WODAN 27. Greifswald: Reineke-Verlag, 1993.

———. *Eilhart von Oberge's Tristrant*, trans. J. W. Thomas. Lincoln: University of Nebraska Press, 1978.

Gottfried von Straßburg

Chinca, Mark. *Gottfried von Strassburg, Tristan*. Cambridge: Cambridge University Press, 1997.

Gottfried von Straßburg. *Tristan*, ed. Reinhold Bechstein and Peter Ganz. Deutsche Klassiker des Mittelalters 4. Wiesbaden: Brockhaus, 1978.

———. *Tristan*, ed. Frederick I Ranke. Berlin: de Gruyter, 1930.

———. *Tristan*, trans. Rüdiger Krohn. 3 vols. Stuttgart: Reclam, 1980 [German trans.].

———. *Tristan*, trans. A. T. Hatto. Harmondsworth: Penguin Books, 1960 [with fragments by Thomas].

Mikasch-Köthner, Dagmar. *Zur Konzeption der Tristan-minne bei Eilhart von Oberg und Gottfried von Strassburg*. Helfant Studien S 7. Stuttgart: Helfant, 1991.

Steinhoff, Hans-Hugo. *Bibliographie zu Gottfried von Strassburg: II. Berichtszeitraum 1970–1983*. Berlin: Schmidt, 1986.

Stevens, Adrian, and Roy Wisbey, eds. *Gottfried Von Strassburg and the Medieval Tristan Legend: Papers from an Anglo-North American Symposium.* Rochester, NY: Boydell and Brewer; London: Institute of Germanic Studies, 1990.

Tasker Grimbert, Joan, ed. *Tristan and Isolde: A Casebook.* New York: Garland, 1995.

Hartmann von Aue

Hartmann von Aue. *Erec,* ed. Christoph Cormeau and Kurt Gärtner. 6th ed. Tübingen: Niemeyer, 1985.

———. *Erec,* ed. and trans. Thomas Cramer. Bücher des Wissens. Frankfurt am Main: Fischer-Taschenbuch Verlag, 1972 [German trans.].

———. *Erec,* trans. Thomas L. Keller. Garland Library of Medieval Literature 12. Series B. New York: Garland, 1987.

———. *Erec,* trans. and introd. J. W. Thomas. Lincoln: University of Nebraska Press, 1982.

———. *Iwein,* ed. G. F. Benecke, Karl Lachmann, and L. Wolff, trans. Thomas Cramer. Rev. ed. Berlin: de Gruyter, 1974.

———. *Iwein,* trans. Wolfgang Mohr. Göppingen: Kümerle, 1985 [German trans.].

———. *Iwein,* ed. and trans. Patrick M. McConeghy. Garland Library Of Medieval Literature 19. Series A. New York: Garland, 1984.

Hasty, Will. *Adventures in Interpretation: The Works of Hartmann Von Aue and Their Critical Reception.* Columbia, S.C.: Camden House, 1996.

Jackson, W. H. *Chivalry in Twelfth-Century Germany: The Works of Hartmann Von Aue.* Cambridge and Rochester, N.Y.: Brewer, 1994.

Heinrich von dem Türlin

Dick, Ernst S. "The German Gawein: Diu Crone and Wigalois." *Interpretations* 15 (1984): 11–17.

Heinrich von dem Türlin. *Diu Crône von Heinrich von dem Türlîn,* ed. Gottlob Heinrich Frederick I Scholl. Bibliothek des Litterarischen vereins in Stuttgart 27. Stuttgart: Litterarischer Verein, 1852.

———. *The Crown: A Tale of Sir Gawein and King Arthur's Court,* trans. J. W. Thomas. Lincoln: University of Nebraska Press, 1989.

Maksymiuk, Stephan. "Knowledge, Politics and Magic: The Magician Gansguoter in Heinrich von dem Türhein's Crone." *German Quarterly* 67 (1994): 470–483.

Read, Ralph R. "Heinrich von dem Türhein's Diu Krone and Wolfram's Parzival." *Modern Language Quarterly* 35 (1974): 129–139.

Thomas, Neil. "Heinrich von dem Turlin's Diu Crone: An Arthurian Fantasy?" *Amsterdamer Beitrage zur Älteren Germanistik* 36 (1992): 169–179.

Heinrich von Freiberg

Heinrich von Freiberg. *Tristan,* ed. Alois Bernt. Halle an der Saale: Niemeyer, 1906; repr. Hildesheim and New York: G. Olms, 1978.

Konrad von Stoffeln

Konrad von Stoffeln. *Gauriel von Muntabel. Der Ritter mit dem Bock,* ed. Wolfgang Achnitz. Tübingen: Niemeyer, 1997.

Schiewer, Hans-Jochen. "Ein bisher unbekanntes 'Gauriel'-Fragment in München." *Zeitschrift fur Deutsches Altertum und Deutsche Literatur* 118 (1989): 57–76.

Pleier, Der

Kern, Peter. *Die Artusromane des Pleiers: Untersuchungen uber den Zusammenhang von Dichtung und literarischer Situation.* Berlin: Schmidt, 1981.

Pleier, Der. *Garel von dem blünden Tal von dem Pleier,* ed. Wolfgang Herles. Vienna: Halosar, 1981.

———. *Meleranz,* ed. Karl Bartsch. Bibliothek des Litterarischen Vereins in Stuttgart 60. Stuttgart: Litterarischer Verein, 1861.

———. *The Pleier's Arthurian Romances: Garel of the Blooming Valley, Tandareis and Flordibel, Meleranz;* trans. J. W. Thomas. Garland Library of Medieval Literature 91. New York: Garland, 1992.

Rossbacher, Roland Franz. *Artusroman und Herrschaftsnachfolge: Darstellungsform und Aussagekategorien in Ulrichs von Zatzikhoven "Lanzelet," Strickers "Daniel von dem blühenden Tal" und Pleiers "Meleranz".* Göppingen: Kümerle, 1998.

Thomas, Neil. "The Arthurian Trilogy of Der Pleier: A Reassessment." *Reading Medieval Studies* 20 (1994): 89–105.

Prosa-Lancelot

Huber, Christoph. "Von der Gral-Queste zum Tod des Königs Artus: Zum Einheitsproblem des Prosa Lancelot.' In *Positionen des Romans im späten Mittelalter,* ed. Walter Haug and Burghart Wachinger. Tübingen: Niemeyer, 1991, pp. 21–38.

Reil, Cornelia. *Liebe und Herrschaft: Studien zum altfranzösischen und mittelhochdeutschen Prosa-Lancelot.* Tübingen: Niemeyer, 1996.

Remakel, Michèle. *Rittertum zwischen Minne und Gral: Untersuchungen zum mittelhochdeutschen Prosa-Lancelot.* Frankfurt am Main: P. Lang, 1995.

Schröder, Werner, ed. *Schweinfurter "Lancelot"-Kolloquium 1984*. Berlin: Schmidt, 1986.

Steinhoff, Hans-Hugo, ed. and trans. *Prosalancelot*. Frankfurt am Main: Deutscher Klassiker Verlag, 1995.

Wolfzettel, Frederick, ed. *Artusrittertum im späten Mittelalter: Ethos und Ideologie*. Giessen: Schmitz, 1984, pp. 138–145.

Rappoltsteiner Parzival

Wisse, Claus, and Philipp Colin. "Parzifal: eine Ergänzung der Dichtung Wolframs von Eschenbach." In *Elsässische Litteraturdenkmäler aus dem XIV–XVII. Jahrhundert,* ed. Ernst Martin and Erich Schmidt. Strasbourg: K. J. Trübner, 1878–1888.

Wittmann-Klemm, Dorothee. *Studien zum "Rappoltsteiner Parzifal"*. Göppinger Arbeiten zur Germanistik 224. Göppingen: Kümerle, 1977.

Rheinischer Merlin

Beckers, Hartmut, ed. *Der rheinische Merlin: Text, Übersetzung, Untersuchungen der Merlin-und Lüthild-Fragmente nach der Handschrift Ms. germ. qu. 1409 der Staatsbibliothek Preussischer Kulturbesitz Berlin,* trans. and study Gerd Bauer et al. Schöninghs mediävistische Editionen 1. Paderborn: Schöningh, 1991.

Stricker, Der

Böhm, Sabine. *Der Stricker: ein Dichterprofil anhand seines Gesamtwerkes*. Frankfurt am Main and New York: P. Lang, 1995.

Stricker, Der. *Daniel von dem blühenden Tal,* ed. Michael Resler. Tübingen: Niemeyer, 1983; rev. ed. 1995.

———. Daniel of the Blossoming Valley, trans. Michael Resler. New York: Garland, 1990.

Wailes, Stephen L. "Wolfram's Parzival and Der Stricker's Daniel von dem Blühenden Tal." *Colloquia Germanica* 26 (1993): 299–315.

Wambach, Annemarie. "Strickers Daniel von dem bluhenden Tal: Ein 'klassischer' Artusroman?" *Arthuriana* 6 (1996): 53–76.

Tristrant und Isalde

Brandstetter, Alois, ed. *Tristrant und Isalde*. Tübingen: Niemeyer, 1966 [two printed versions from 1484 and 1498].

Buschinger, Danielle, and Wolfgang Spiewok, eds. *Prosaroman.*Greifswald: Reineke Verlag, 1993 [facsimile of 1484 edition].

Ulrich von Türheim

Ulrich von Türheim. *Tristan und Isolde des Gottfried von Strassburg. Tristan: eine Fortsetzung,* trans. Dieter Kühn; ed. Lambertus Okken. Frankfurt am Main: Insel, 1991.

———.*Das Tristan-Epos Gottfrieds von Straßburg: mit der Fortsetzung des Ulrich von Türheim; nach der Heidelberger Handschrift Cod. Pal. germ. 360,* ed. Wolfgang Spiewok. Berlin: Akademie-Verlag, 1989.

Ulrich von Zatzikhoven

Ulrich von Zatzikhoven. *Lanzelet: Mittelhochdeutsch/ Neuhochdeutsch,* trans. Wolfgang Spiewok. Greifswald: Reineke-Verlag, 1997 [German trans.].

———. *Lanzelet; A Romance of Lancelot,.* trans. Kenneth G. T. Webster. Rev. ed., introd. Roger Sherman Loomis. New York: Columbia University Press, 1951.

Zellmann, Ulrike. *Lanzelet: der biographische Artusroman als Auslegungsschema dynastischer Wissensbildung*. Düsseldorf: Droste, 1996.

Wigamur

Blamires, David. "The Sources and Literary Structure of Wigamur." In *Studies in Medieval Literature and Languages in Memory of Frederick Whitehead,* ed. W. Rothwell et al. Manchester: Manchester University Press, 1973, pp. 27–46.

Buschinger, Danielle, ed. and introd. *Wigamur.* Göppingen: Kümerle Verlag, 1987.

Martin, Ann G. "The Concept of *Reht* in *Wigamur.*" *Colloquia Germanica* 20 (1987): 1–14.

Thomas, Neil. "The Sources of 'Wigamur' and the German Reception of the Fair Unknown Tradition." *Reading Medieval Studies* 19 (1993): 97–111.

Wirnt von Grafenberg

Wirnt von Grafenberg. *Wigalois, der Ritter mit dem Rade,* ed. J. M. N. Kapteyn. Bonn: F. Klopp, 1926.

———. *Wigalois: The Knight of Fortune's Wheel,* trans. J. W. Thomas. Lincoln: University of Nebraska Press, 1977.

Wolfram von Eschenbach

Kühn, Dieter. *Der Parzival des Wolfram von Eschenbach.* Frankfurt am Main: Insel, 1986.

Wolfram von Eschenback. *Wolfram von Eschenback,* ed. Karl Lachmann. 6th ed. introd. Eduard Hartl. Berlin and New York: de Gruyter, 1926; rpt. 1997 [1st ed. Berlin: G. Reimer, 1833].

———. *Parzival. Mittelhochdeutscher Text,* ed. Karl Lachmann; trans. Peter Knecht; introd. Bernd Schirok. Berlin and New York: de Gruyter, 1998.

———. *Parzival,* ed. Karl Lachmann; trans. and introd. Wolfgang Spiewok. Stuttgart: Reclam, 1981.

———. *Parzival,* trans. and introd. Helen M. Mustard and Charles E. Passage. New York: Vintage, 1961; rpt. 1990.

———. *Parzival,* trans. A. T. Hatto. Penguin Classics. Harmondsworth: Penguin, 1980.

———. *Willehalm. Titurel,* ed. Walter Johannes Schröder and Gisela Hollandt. Darmstadt, Wissenschaftliche Buchgesellschaft, 1971.

———. *Titurel,* trans. Charles E. Passage. New York: Ungar, 1984.

Klaus M. Schmidt

SEE ALSO

Albrecht von Scharfenberg; Arthurian Romance, Dutch; Eilhart von Oberge; Füetrer, Ulrich; Gottfried von Straßburg; Hartmann von Aue; Heinrich von dem Türheim; Pleier, Der; Stricker, Der; Ulrich von Türheim; Ulrich von Zatzikhoven; Wirnt von Grafenberg; Wolfram von Eschenbach

Arthurian Literature, Dutch

Although the manuscripts date mainly from the fourteenth and fifteenth centuries, the heyday of Middle Dutch Arthurian literature occurred in the second half of the thirteenth century, when most of the romances were created; at the beginning of the fourteenth century many of them were collected in the so-called *Lancelot Compilation.* Flanders, where French manuscripts were produced (and illustrated), where the counts were important patrons of French authors (Philippe d'Alsace, for example, sponsored Chrétien de Troyes's *Conte du Graal,* ca. 1190), and where Middle Dutch variants of Arthurian names appear in the charters very early, was by far the most productive region, as the dialect features of the manuscripts indicate. Rhymed couplets of three or four beats were the literary form for Arthurian romance throughout the period, as well as for Middle Dutch Charlemagne epics and chronicles. Only rarely is the patron for a given romance mentioned. The texts often are anonymous and the date of their creation can usually be indicated only approximately; even the dates of the (often fragmented) manuscripts are far from certain.

In the decades just before 1250, one of the first texts to be translated into Middle Dutch was the *Conte du Graal* (Count of the Grail, with its first continuation). Of Conte du Graal, the *Perchevael,* only fragments remain, but the episodes concerning Walewein (Gauvain) have been edited to fit into the *Lancelot Compilation,* as is the case for most of the romances. Other early translations and/or adaptations are the *Wrake van Ragisel* (an adaptation of the *Vengeance Raguidel*) and *Tristan* (a fragment of a translation of the version by Thomas of Britain). Around 1260 a poet, probably Jacob van Maerlant, translated *Torec,* using a now lost French text about a knight and a golden circlet. The first half of the *Ferguut* is a translation of Guillaume le Clerc's *Fergus,* but the second part of the text has no direct relation to the French original. Not only in new versions or endings did the Middle Dutch authors express their creativity, however. There are also original romances, such as *Walewein; Ridder metter mouwen* (the story of "the knight with the sleeve"), a love story and search for the father *(Vatersuche),* and *Moriaen,* a tale of a Moorish knight's chivalric education and quest for his father. Written by two authors, Penninc and Pieter Vostaert, *Walewein* (11,200 lines) follows the fairy tale motif of the Golden Bird and describes how Walewein, aided by a prince in the guise of a fox, finds a beautiful damsel and a magic sword in order to meet the challenge of bringing a floating chess set to Arthur's court. The frontispiece of the Leiden manuscript (ca. 1350) shows Walewein setting out on his quest. The text was influential: the authors of the *Ridder metter mouwen* and *Moriaen* both adapted episodes from *Walewein.*

Apart from these "episodic" texts, there also are translations of the more "biographical" and "historical" Old French prose texts. Probably the first of these are Jacob van Maerlant's renderings of the prose *Joseph d'Arimathie* and *Merlin:* the *Historie vanden Grale* and the *Boek van Merline,* composed around 1261 for Albrecht van Voorne (a nobleman from the inner circle of the count of Holland). The principal French text in this genre, the *Lancelot en prose,* was translated into Middle Dutch at least three times. The fragments of *Lantsloot vander Haghedochte* (Lancelot of the Cave) reveal that this first adaptation in verse reduced most of the innovative features, especially the geographical and chronological "realism" of the original, to a more traditional format. Probably created probably around 1280, the second rhymed Flemish version—the *Lanceloet-Queeste vanden Grale-Arturs Doet* (preserved in the *Lancelot Compilation*)—

maintained the innovations and provided a more faithful translation. The two fragments of the third translation show that its author went one step further and rendered the story in Middle Dutch prose. Other Dutch versions of the *Lancelot en prose* may be the basis of German translations. Finally, the Brabantine poet Lodewijk van Velthem translated in 1326 the *Suite-Vulgate du Merlin*, attaching his *Merlijn Continuatie* to Maerlant's Grail and Merlin texts. Apart from Middle Dutch fragments, this trilogy is preserved in a Middle Low German retelling *(Umschreibung)* from ca. 1425, included in a manuscript at Burgsteinfurt (North Rhine-Westphalia).

The combination of already existing works with new and/or adapted texts also resulted in a manuscript now in The Hague, the aforementioned *Lancelot Compilation* (early fourteenth century). The last leaf of this manuscript states that *her* (lord) Lodewijc van Velthem was the owner. One of its most intriguing aspects is the markings of the contemporaneous medieval editor, who corrected scribal errors but also added marginal signs and words to facilitate the oral delivery of the text. The creator of the *Lancelot Compilation* used the Flemish *Lanceloet-Queeste-Arturs Doet* as the framework and added seven romances to this history of Arthur's reign. Some of these romances have come down to us only in this codex and may have been adapted or created especially for their insertion by the compiler: *Walewein ende Keye,* a story of the rivalry between Gauvain and Kay, with no known parallel in Old French, *Lanceloet en het hert met de witte voet* (Lancelot and the White-footed Deer), a tale reminiscent of the "Dragon's tongue" episode in *Tristan* and of the *Lai de Tyolet,* and *Torec.* Fragments of the other texts exist, but their full story is preserved (in a rewritten form, as comparison with the fragments shows) only here. Between the *Lanceloet* and the *Queeste,* the *Perchevael* (the Gauvain episodes), and the *Moriaen* were inserted, whereas the *Wrake van Ragisel, Ridder metter mouwen, Walewein ende Keye, Lanceloet en het hert met de witte voet,* and *Torec* were placed between the *Queeste* and *Arturs Doet.* In the first decades of the fourteenth century, most of the Middle Dutch Arthurian romances were thus brought together in two collections of texts, both in some relation to Lodewijk van Velthem. By concept and contents, these collections may have been conceived as one great Arthurian summa, or definitive collection.

The probable dates of the manuscripts indicate that the Middle Dutch Arthurian romances were copied, and enjoyed by their audiences, in the fourteenth and fifteenth centuries, even though none of the texts has come to us in a great number of copies. Later on, printers favored Charlemagne epics over Arthurian romances. Two quires of the *Historie van Merlijn,* printed ca. 1535–1540 by Simon Cock in Antwerp, are the only witness to interest in the Arthurian realm in the days of early printing in the Low Countries.

BIBLIOGRAPHY

Besamusca, Bart, Frank Brandsma, and Ada Postma, eds. *Lanceloet.* Vol. 1. Hilversum: Verloren, 1997. Vols. 2–3. Assen: Van Gorcum, 1991, 1992. Vol. 4. Hilversum: Verloren, 1998.

Claassens, Geert H. M., and David F. Johnson, eds. *King Arthur in the Medieval Low Countries.* Louvain: Louvain University Press, 1998.

Draak, Maartje, ed. *Lanceloet en het hert met de witte voet.* 4th ed. Culemborg: Tjeenk Willink-Noorduijn, 1971.

Es, G. A. van, ed. *Penninc en Pieter Vostaert, Roman van Walewein.* Zwolle: Tjeenk-Willink, 1957; rpt. 1976.

Gerritsen, Willem P. *Die Wrake van Ragisel.* 2 vols. Assen: Van Gorcum, 1963.

———, ed. *Lantsloot vander Haghedochte.* Amsterdam: Noord-Hollandsche Uitg. Mij., 1987.

Gysseling, Maurits, ed. *Corpus van Middelnederlandse teksten (tot en met het jaar 1300).* Vol 1, *Perchevael and Tristan.* The Hague: Nijhoff, 1980, pp. 501–519 and pp. 337–342.

Haan, Max J. M. de, ed. *Ferguut.* Leiden: New Rhine Publ., 1974 [facsimile].

———. *Roman van den Riddere metter Mouwen.* Utrecht: HES, 1983.

Hogenhout, Jan, and Maaike Hogenhout. [n.p.] *Torec.* Abcoude, 1978.

Janssens, Jozef D. "Le roman arthurien 'non historique' en moyen néerlandais: traduction ou création originale?" In *Arturus Rex.,* ed. Willy van Hoecke. Vol. 2. Louvain: Louvain University Press, 1991, pp. 330–351.

Johnson, David F., trans. and ed. *Penninc and Pieter Vostaert, Roman van Walewein.* New York: Garland, 1992.

Jonckbloet, Willem J. A., ed. *Roman van Lancelot (XIIIe eeuw).* The Hague: Van Stockum, 1846–1849 [compilation].

Kruyter, C. W. de, ed. *Die riddere metter mouwen.* Leiden: New Rhine Publ., 1975 [facsimile].

Kuiper, Willem. *Die riddere metten witten scilde.* Amsterdam: Schiphouwer en Brinkman, 1989.

Lie, Orlanda S. H. *The Middle Dutch Prose Lancelot.* Amsterdam: Noord-Hollandsche Uitg. Mij., 1987.

Lodewijk van Velthem, *Merlijn Continuatie.* In J. van Vloten, *Jacob van Maerlants Merlijn,* ed. J. van Vloten. Leiden: Brill, 1880.

Oostrom, Frits P. van *Lantsloot vander Haghedochte.* Amsterdam: Noord-Hollandsche, 1981.

Paardekooper-van Buuren, Hanneke, and Maurits Gysseling. *Moriaen.* Zutphen: Thieme, 1971.

Prins-s'Jacob, Johanna C. "The Middle Dutch version of La Queste del Saint Graal." *De nieuwe taalgids* 73 (1980): 120–132.

Rombauts, Edward, et al. *Ferguut.* Culemborg: Tjeenk Willink–Noorduijn, 1976; rpt. 1994.

Sodmann, Timothy. *Jacob van Maerlant: Historie van den Grale und Boek van Merline.* Cologne and Vienna: Böhlau, 1980.

Weston, Jessie L., trans. *Moriaen.* New York: New Amsterdam Book Co., 1901.

Zemel, Roel. *Op zoek naar Galiene.* Amsterdam: Schiphouwer en Brinkman, 1991.

Frank P. C. Brandsma

SEE ALSO

Arthurian Literature, German; Charlemagne Epics, Dutch; Gottfried von Straßburg; Jacob van Maerlant

Aschaffenburg

A city in present-day Bavaria, on the right bank of the Main River, Aschaffenburg was an important ecclesiastial center in the late Middle Ages. Although the early history of Aschaffenburg is clouded with uncertainty, the city is thought to be located at the site of the Roman, then Alemannic, settlement referred to as Ascapha in a late-seventh-century geography text. Evidence suggests that the present-day *Kilianskapelle* (Chapel of St. Kilian) is located where the settlement's first church was built between 711 and 716. Aschaffenburg is remembered as the place where King Ludwig III (ca. 835–882) married the Saxon princess Liutgard in 869. Duke Luitolf of Swabia and his wife Ida established the collegiate foundation St. Peter and Alexander in 957. After this church and surrounding lands were given to the archbishop of Mainz in 982–983, a close relationship between Aschaffenburg and the archdiocese of Mainz developed.

A bridge over the Main, completed in 986, fostered growth of the settlement, but markets, tolls, and other requirements for an actual town were not present until the twelfth century. Early in that century, the archbishop, having become involved in a dispute with the emperor, renewed the settlement's fortifications and presumably laid out the rudiments of the medieval castle as well. A new church dedicated to Saints Peter and Alexander but referred to as the *Stiftskirche* was built during the twelfth and thirteenth centuries; it combines Romanesque and Gothic elements.

From the middle of the thirteenth century, Aschaffenburg's importance increased as a result of its being the second residence of the archbishops of Mainz who, after the pope, held the highest ecclesiastical rank in the Holy Roman Empire. As the location of assemblies, synods, and numerous official visits, the city prospered into the sixteenth century. Beginning in 1509, Matthias Gothardt (Matthias Grünewald) directed building projects at the castle. He served as fountain and waterworks director, master mechanic, and court painter. On August 10, 1552, troops of Margrave Albert Alcibiades of Brandenburg plundered and destroyed the Gothic structure. The medieval castle keep, however, still stands in the courtyard of the seventeenth-century Johannisburg Palace.

BIBLIOGRAPHY

Rhoda, Burkard von. *Aschaffenburg Castle and Pompeiianum.* 4th ed. Munich: Bayerische Verwaltung der Staatlichen Schlösser, 1989.

Schneider, Ernst. *Aschaffenburg.* Amorbach: Hermann Emig, 1982.

Ruth M. W. Moskop

SEE ALSO

Gothic Art and Architecture; Mainz; Romanesque Art and Architecture

Augsburg

Augsburg, located in present-day Bavaria on the Lech River, was an important political, economic, and cultural center throughout the Middle Ages and into the early modern period. It had become a Roman city around 30 C.E. Christians were present from the early fourth century C.E.; in 304, the young Christian woman Afra was martyred in Augsburg for refusing to make offerings to the emperor. Saint Afra became one of the two patron saints of the city, and her grave was one of the most important sites of pilgrimage, local worship, and architectural activity. Exactly when Augsburg became an episcopal seat is debated. However, the first document clearly referring to an Augsburg bishop (Wikterp) is dated 738.

Wikterp's successor, Bishop Simpert (778–807) began construction of the cathedral, which was consecrated in 805–807. The cathedral was rebuilt and expanded several times: under Bishop Ulrich (924–973), who joined Saint Afra as the city's second patron saint; under Bishop Embrico between 1056 and 1065, when the bronze double doors with their thirty-five scenes from the Old Testament and ancient mythology were added; and then between 1331 and 1431, when the structure's nave and side aisles were expanded and rebuilt in the Gothic style, and a large choir with ambulatory and radiating chapels was added to the east end. The bronze doors are one of the most important surviving examples of Romanesque bronze relief sculpture, and the Romanesque stained glass windows depicting five Old Testament prophets (ca. 1140) on the south wall of the cathedral's nave are the oldest extant stained glass windows.

In addition to the cathedral, other churches were built and decorated for the growing number of parishes. When the Franciscans and Dominicans came to Augsburg in the 1220s, many monastic institutions were established, requiring the construction and decoration of residences and places of worship. The church erected to honor Saint Afra had been expanded to include the worship of Saint Ulrich. From 1474 to 1500 this church, with its double patrocinium, was substantially expanded.

Augsburg was also rich in secular architecture. First mention of a city hall was made in 1260. This wooden structure was replaced in 1385 by a masonry one. The last decades of the fourteenth century also saw the construction of guild halls, including those for the weavers, butchers, and bakers.

In the fifteenth century Hans Burgkmair, Ulrich Apt, Hans Holbein the Elder, and other Augsburg painters achieved local prominence. Augsburg also became one of the earliest major centers for printing, which had begun there by 1468. Printers included Erhard Ratdolt and Anton Sorg.

BIBLIOGRAPHY

Blendinger, F., and W. Zorn, ed. *Augsburg: Geschichte in Bilddokumenten.* Munich: Beck, 1976.

Gottlieb, Günther, et al. *Geschichte der Stadt Augsburg.* 2d ed. Stuttgart: Theiss, 1985.

Zorn, Wolfgang. *Augsburg: Geschichte einer deutschen Stadt.* 2d ed. Augsburg: Hieronymus Mühlberger, 1972.

Pia F. Cuneo

SEE ALSO
Hans Holbein the Elder; Libraries

B

Badges
See Pilgrim's Badges

Bamberg

A bishopric and city in Bavaria, Bamberg was especially important during the Ottonian through Gothic periods. A small settlement seems to have existed on the site since the seventh century, but Bamberg was essentially founded in the early eleventh century when the Holy Roman Emperor Henry II and his wife, the Empress Kunigunde, established a bishopric there in 1007. Henry hoped to create a "new Rome" in the eastern part of his domain, and to this end a cathedral, palace, market, and settlement were built, forming a center of imperial power. Henry showed his devotion to his foundation by lavishing gifts on Bamberg Cathedral, including vestments, especially an embroidered cope known as the Sternenmantel for its unique star design (Bamberg, Diözesanmuseum), ivory book covers, and manuscripts. The status of Bamberg was enhanced by the burial of the imperial couple in the cathedral that they had founded. An additional consequential figure associated with Ottonian Bamberg was Pope Clement II (1046–1047), who was bishop of Bamberg before his elevation and was also buried in Bamberg Cathedral.

Bamberg cathedral's connections with both a holy emperor and a pope gave the church a unique character that continued to be reflected in the building's decorative programs through the Middle Ages. The importance of the emperor and his wife was heightened by Henry's canonization in 1146 and Kunigunde's in 1200. Although the present building dates from the thirteenth century, Henry II was the patron of the original cathedral, which was consecrated in 1012. The Ottonian cathedral had a high choir in the west and a second choir in the east with a crypt under it. While nothing of this church remains above ground, its plan and masonry fragments are known through excavation; perhaps because of the great status of the original patron, the Ottonian cathedral's plan influenced the layout of the later larger church.

The present cathedral, dedicated to St. Peter and St. George, was built after a fire in 1183 under Bishop Ekbert von Andechs (1203–1237) and consecrated on May 6, 1237. This church follows the general plan of the earlier Ottonian church with two choirs. There is a transept on the western end of the building and four exterior towers. Because of the double choir, the main entrance to the cathedral, the Prince's Portal, (Fürstenpforte) is located in the middle of the nave's north side. The cathedral's interior exhibits the heavy mural surface and regular spatial organization typical of the German interpretation of Gothic architecture. The nave is divided into square bays with four-part ribbed groin vaulting, and the building has a two-story elevation, consisting of a pointed nave arcade and a single window per bay.

The sculpture at Bamberg Cathedral represents one of the finest ensembles in any German cathedral. The work consists of three sculpted portals: the Mercy Portal (Gnadenpforte), next to the east choir on the north side; the Adam Portal (Adamspforte), also next to the east choir but on the south side; and the already mentioned Prince's Portal on the north side of the nave. Additional sculpture is found in the interior of the building, including a choir screen, figures placed against interior columns, and tombs. Of the three portals, the work on the Mercy Portal is the earliest. It has a semicircular tympanum (arch above doorway) showing the Virgin and Child surrounded by the cathedral's patron saints, Peter and George, and its

Bamberg, cathedral, Princes' Portal: Last Judgment. *Photograph: Joan A. Holladay*

founders, Henry II and Kunigunde, with two smaller scale ecclesiastics in the outer corners. The only other sculpted decoration in this portal is a capital frieze of martyrs. The Mercy Portal's style is similar to contemporary sculpture in Cologne and ultimately probably related to a figure and drapery style found in Mosan metalwork. In addition to the Mercy Portal, this workshop carved the eastern face of the choir screen with pairs of apostles. The sculptors of the Mercy Portal created some of the jamb figures for the Prince's Portal. Most of that portal is sculpted by a different workshop, however, with a very close association to Reims Cathedral. This Bamberg/ Reims group sculpted the semi-circular Last Judgment tympanum and the remaining jamb figures (side posts) on the Prince's Portal in a program that represents a compressed version of Reims's north transept facade. The Reims-related workshop also carved jamb figures of Henry II, Kunigunde, St. Peter, St. Stephen, Adam, and Eve for the Adam Portal and additional sculpture presently inside the cathedral, including the famous Bamberg Rider. This workshop represents one of the most direct connections between French and German sculpture during the Gothic period, and many German sites in the thirteenth century including Magdeburg, Mainz, and Naumburg exhibit styles derived from the Bamberg workshop's interpretation of French cathedral sculpture. Stylistically this Bamberg/Reims workshop is characterized by an interest in classical sources (seen especially in the Visitation groups at both cathedrals) and in natural observation apparent in both faces and vegetal forms. At Bamberg there is also a heightened emotional expressiveness, seen in the grinning and grimacing faces of the Last Judgment tympanum on the Prince's Portal, which is absent at Reims.

The interior sculpture at the cathedral includes a Visitation group, the renowned Bamberg Rider, and several other figures associated with the Bamberg/Reims workshop. There are considerable problems with the original placement of much of this interior sculpture. The Rider is presently positioned on the north pier in the entrance to the east choir. He sits firmly on his horse looking away from the wall with the reins in one hand and the strings of his mantel in the other, and seems to embody the knightly virtues so important in the medieval domestication of those who fight. Along with the figure of Uta from Naumburg, the Bamberg Rider has become one of the popular icons of German medieval art. The figure, horse, and plinth (base) are made of seven pieces of sandstone and represent a considerable technical achievement, although the Rider's specific identity is uncertain. Stylistically the figure resembles the figure of Philip Augustus at Reims, and proposed identifications include Henry II or another German ruler, Constantine, the first Christian emperor, and St. Stephen of Hungary, who was the brother-in-law of Henry II. Most of these identifications would support the concepts of saintly ruler, church foundation, and association of secular and religious power, so important in the imagery at Bamberg Cathedral. There are significant parallels between the Bamberg Rider and the slightly later Magdeburg Rider. But unlike the Magdeburg Rider, the Bamberg Rider is not freestanding and may have always had an interior placement.

A tomb for Pope Clement was also sculpted during this campaign. The original form of the monument is open to question, but it consisted of two components—an effigy, presently mounted on a pier in the east choir, and a tomb chest of gray marble. The effigy, also by the Bamberg/Reims workshop, is very similar to jamb figures of clerics on French cathedrals. The marble tomb chest has a rare iconography, with St. John the Baptist and the Death of the Pope on the short sides of the chest and the Cardinal Virtues on the long sides.

Bamberg Cathedral continued to receive sculptural embellishment during the later Middle Ages. Wooden sculpted choir stalls dating from around 1380 were originally present in both the east and the west choirs of the cathedral. Reliefs of Henry II and Kunigunde appear in the decorative program of the choir stalls along with saints, prophets, and a collection of hybrid creatures. Tillmann Riemenschneider sculpted the tomb of Henry II and Kunigunde between 1499 and 1513. Originally located in the east end of the nave, it consists of effigies of the emperor and empress on a tomb chest decorated with narrative panels of their lives, drawn mostly from the Golden Legend of Jacobus de Vorragine. A Virgin altarpiece of 1523 by Veit Stoss, originally made for a Carmelite convent in Nuremberg, was subsequently transferred to Bamberg by Stoss's son during the Reformation.

While the cathedral is the most notable medieval structure in Bamberg, several other churches date from the Middle Ages, although most received extensive baroque remodeling during a period of prosperity in the seventeenth century. The Benedictine abbey of St. Michel's, founded in 1015 by Bamberg's first bishop, Eberhard, had a plan that originally related to that of Hirsau, but the church received extensive later remodeling. Bishop St. Otto (d. 1139), who converted the Pomeranians, is buried in a sculpted tomb (first half of the fifteenth century) located in St. Michael's Abbey. Bamberg also has a fine late Gothic example of a parish church dedicated to the Virgin (1375–1387), which has been related to the architectural style of the Parler family. The Cistercian cloister of Ebrach is near Bamberg. Secular buildings from the Middle Ages include the palace, founded by Henry II but rebuilt between 1475 and 1511, and some of the canon's half-timbered houses in the area around the cathedral.

BIBLIOGRAPHY

Neundorfer, Bruno. *Der Dom zu Bamberg: Mutterkirche des Erzbistums.* Bamberg: St. Otto-Verlag, 1987.

Schuller, Manfred, et al. *Das Fürstenportal des Bamberger Domes.* Bamberg: Bayerische Verlagsanstalt, 1993.

Traeger, Jörg. "Der verschollene Name: Zur Deutungsgeschichte des Bamberger Reiters." *Zeitschrift des Deutschen Vereins für Kunstwissenschaft* 49/50 (1995–1996): 44–76.

Valentiner, Wilhelm. *The Bamberg Rider: Studies of Mediaeval German Sculpture.* Los Angeles: Zeitlin and Ver Brugge, 1956.

Weinfurter, Stefan. *Heinrich II (1002–1024): Herrscher am Ende der Zeiten.* Regensburg: Verlag Friedrich Pustet, 1999, pp. 263–268.

Winterfeld, Dethard von. *Der Dom in Bamberg.* Ph.D. diss., University of Bonn, 1969, 2 vols. Berlin: Mann, 1979.

———. "Zur Baugeschichte des Bamberger Fürstenportales." *Zeitschrift für Kunstgeschichte* 39 (1976): 147–166.

Susan L. Ward

SEE ALSO

Cistercian Art and Architecture; Gothic Art and Architecture; Henry II, Art; Hirsau; Iconographies, Innovative; Magdeburg; Mainz; Naumburg; Nuremberg; Ottonian Art and Architecture; Parler Family; Riemenschneider, Tillmann; Romanesque Art and Architecture; Stoss, Veit

Barbarossa
See Frederick I Barbarossa.

Basel

Located on the Rhine, Basel was an ecclesiastical and intellectual center throughout the Middle Ages, and the site of the Council of Basel, a general council of the Roman Catholic Church, in the fifteenth century. While a Celtic settlement had existed from the middle of the first century B.C.E. on the hill over the Rhine now occupied by a cathedral, the Roman colony that shares its early history with Basel (also Basle) was founded upstream at Augusta Raurica, seven miles to the east. Settled in 44 B.C.E., the Roman town thrived until the third century, when it was moved, for the purposes of better defense, to the hill where the cathedral now stands. The name *Basilia* (English also Basle) is documented as early as 374. In 455 the Romans abandoned the site to the local Alemannic tribes. Isolated bishops are documented from the fifth century; a continuous succession is known only from the middle of the eighth. The city was Frankish from the beginning of the sixth century; from about 900 it belonged to the kingdom of Burgundy; under Emperor Henry II, at the beginning of the eleventh century, it was incorporated into the empire.

Under the Celts a cult building may have stood on the site of the present cathedral, and the Romans seem to have continued religious activities in this area after their move there. While one might hypothesize a Merovingian building on the same site, archaeological excavations have documented only two earlier church buildings in the area of the present cathedral. A ninth- or tenth-century building traced the dimensions of the present building's nave and aisles. An Ottonian structure was dedicated in 1019 in the presence of the emperor Henry II. It is not possible to say whether the earlier of the two buildings was the much-praised church finished by Bishop Hatto (891–913) in the early ninth century or a replacement for this building after the Magyar invasion of 917; it is also possible that the rebuilding after 917 took a full century. Henry's presence at the dedication and his gift of the golden altar antependium (now in Paris, Musée de Cluny) gave him a reputation as the cathedral's founder.

Basel, *Münster*, west façade, detail: portal. *Photograph: Joan A. Holladay*

The present building was erected in the last third of the twelfth century in late Romanesque style. At least the choir, which includes the first use of an ambulatory in a German bishop's church, was finished by 1205. The majestic interior is marked by a three-story elevation, wide proportions, and heavy walls. The exterior of the Romanesque building has been almost entirely obscured: first by the addition of chapels along the aisles in the late thirteenth and first half of the fourteenth centuries, then by the reerection of the upper levels of the towers and choir after an earthquake in 1356. Johannes Parler, then at work on the cathedral of Freiburg im Breisgau, undertook the rebuilding; his influence is most visible in the triforium and clerestory of the choir. After a rededication of the high altar in 1363, work on the crossing and west facade proceeded more slowly; the towers were completed by 1500.

Contemporary with the late Romanesque building campaign is the north transept door, the so-called Gallus portal, named after the altar to the missionary Saint Gall inside the transept. The late twelfth-century portal is noteworthy as one of the earliest figural portals in German-speaking areas and as one of the earliest representations of the Acts of Charity according to Matt. 25:34–36. Six two-figure reliefs representing care for the hungry, the thirsty, the homeless, the naked, the sick, and the incarcerated frame the doorway. As in the biblical text, these good deeds are portrayed in the typanum as preparation for the Last Judgment. The lintel shows the Wise and Foolish Virgins, a related theme, also from Matthew 25. The jamb figures represent the Evangelists.

After about 1258, the west facade was reconfigured with a narthex between the two towers. The sculptured portal opened from the narthex into the nave. After the 1356 earthquake, the portal was moved forward to the exterior facade of the narthex and four remaining large-scale figures mounted in the spandrels at tympanum level. The program centered on a narrative tympanum representing the Passion and culminating in an image of the Last Judgment; only the archivolts survived the Reformation. They represent prophets and angels in a style close to that of the Erminold Master, a noted sculptor whose preserved works at Prüfening and Regensburg date from the 1260s. The four large-scale figures, usually dated about 1290, are related in style and iconography to the nearly contemporary portals at Strasbourg and Freiburg. The figure of a Foolish Virgin, along with the heads of two others preserved in the Cathedral Museum, must have come from a full group of the Wise and Foolish Virgins; this figure is now paired with the so-called Prince of the World. The Prince, who represents temptation, was added to the portal program at Strasbourg for the sake of the portal's symmetry; as the Bridegroom-Christ figure of the biblical parable lets the Wise Virgins into the garden of Paradise, the Prince tempts their foolish counterparts with worldly pleasures. The Basel program must have comprised the full group of twelve figures. Their original placement is difficult to ascertain. The textual source and the understanding of the Wise and Foolish Virgins as an allegory of preparedness for entry into heaven account for the association of the group elsewhere with the Last Judgment and for its typical location on the doorway. However, the preserved archivolts are not deep enough to have had corresponding jambs with space for the full twelve-figure group, and the quarter-century chronological gap between the execution of the archivolts and these figures would also argue against a placement in the immediate portal context. Equally difficult to explain in the context of the portal are the two remaining figures in large scale, which represent the emperor Henry II and his wife Kunigunde. It seems likely that they stood around the interior walls of the deep narthex, analogous to the arrangement at the Münster at Freiberg im Breisgau.

The Franciscan church (*Barfüsserkirche,* now the Historical Museum), to the south of the cathedral, was erected about 1300. On their arrival in Basel in 1231, the Franciscans had settled outside the city wall to the west, near the preserved thirteenth- or fourteenth-century gate known as the *Spalentor.* In 1250 they moved to the city center, to the site of the current church. A fire in the cloister in 1298 may have necessitated the replacement of the mid-thirteenth-century building; the new church was built at the turn of the century immediately to the north of its predecessor and in a similar form. The lay church is separated from the monks' choir not only by a deep choir screen but by a striking difference in the form of the two spaces. The monks preached to the lay community in the spacious aisled nave with its flat wood ceiling. Beyond the choir screen the single vessel of the vaulted choir, its walls dissolved in a continuous band of stained glass windows, marked a hierarchically more important space.

The church of the Dominican monks (*Predigerkirche*) was erected between 1233 and 1269 and rebuilt in part after 1356, and that of the Dominican nuns, at Klingental in Kleinbasel across the river, was built in the 1280s and 1290s. Both used a form similar to that of the Franciscan church. The Klingental cloister and the wall around the cemetery near the Dominican church were both decorated with painted cycles of the Dance of Death. The series in the cloister at Klingental seems to have predated slightly that on the wall of the cemetery near the men's house, ca. 1445–1450. Portions of the latter, preserved when the wall was dismantled in the nineteenth century, are preserved in the Historical Museum.

The Council of Basel, held in the city from 1431 to 1448, debated the growing reform movements within the Church. It marks the beginning of the city's important role in the intellectual life of late medieval Europe. The first university in Switzerland was founded in Basel in 1459–1460. By the end of the century, Basel had become a major center of the newly founded printing industry. Scholars from all over Europe came to live and work in Basel, where they had access to the means to publish their works. Their presence there attracted not only students but artists, who hoped to find work decorating and illustrating their books. After 1500, these included such well-known figures as the Dutch humanist Erasmus (d. 1536 in Basel) and the German painter and printmaker Hans Holbein the Younger (d. 1545) and his brother Ambrosius (d. ca. 1519).

BIBLIOGRAPHY

Die Kunstdenkmäler des Kantons Basel Stadt. Basel: Birkhauser, 1932–1966.

Furger-Gunti, Andres. *Die Ausgrabungen im Basler Münster, 1: Die spätkeltische und augusteische Zeit (1. Jahrhundert v. Chr.), vol. 1, Untersuchungen zur spätkeltisch-frührömischen Übergangszeit in Basel 1. Basler Beiträge zur Ur- und Frühgeschichte 6.* Derendingen-Solothurn: Habegger, 1979.

Reinhardt, Hans. *Das Basler Münster.* Basel: Werner, 1939.

Sauerländer, Willibald. "Das Stiftergrabmal des Grafen Eberhard in der Klosterkirche zu Murbach." In *Amici Amico: Festschrift für Werner Gross zu seinem 65. Geburtstag am 25.11.1966,* ed. Krut Badt and Martin Gosebruch. Munich: Fink, 1968, pp. 59–77.

Joan A. Holladay

SEE ALSO

Freiburg; Iconographies, Innovative; Libraries; Parler Family; Regensburg; Universities

Battle

See Warfare; names of individual battles.

Beatrijs van Nazareth (1200–1268)

The Brabantine mystic Beatrijs van Nazareth was born in 1200, the youngest child of a burgher family in Tienen (in the present-day Belgian province of Flemish-Brabant); for that reason she is also known as Beatrijs van Tienen. She evidently was trained in the medieval liberal arts *(artes liberales),* showing a good knowledge of Latin. In 1215 she took the solemn vows as a Cistercian nun. In 1236 she moved to the convent in Nazareth (near the town of Lier), where she was prioress until her death in 1268.

Quite a lot is known about the life of this mystic thanks to the Latin text *Vita Beatricis,* written in the last quarter of the thirteenth century by an anonymous Cistercian monk. Allegedly this *vita* was based on a diary that Beatrijs kept in Middle Dutch, but which is now lost. The only surviving work by her is entitled *Van seven manieren van heileger minne* (The Seven Steps of Holy Love), a short treatise in prose, dealing with seven aspects of the love for God. This work dates back to 1250 and is therefore one of the oldest Middle Dutch texts in prose (together with some works by the other Brabantine mystic, Hadewijch). *Van seuen manieren van heileger minne* has come down to us in three manuscripts from the fourteenth and fifteenth centuries, always in combination with other texts.

Beatrijs van Nazareth is, alongside Hadewijch, one of the most prominent representatives of female mysticism in the medieval Low Countries. Her treatise was probably meant for people within her own circle, possibly as an introduction into the spiritual life for the novices of her own convent. Beatrijs considers the love of man for God to be a gift of God and describes in seven steps the experience of joy and longing as well as tension and agony caused by this spiritual *minne.* The ultimate goal of mystical ascent, according to Beatrijs, is the fulfillment of love and the union of the soul with its heavenly bridegroom.

Beatrijs's treatise reveals influences of the *amor* (love of God) concept as was current in twelfth-century Northern French spirituality, prominently expressed in texts of Cistercian origin. In the *minne,* then, God reveals Himself and man is free to comply with that love; in love, man can meet God.

The works of Beatrijs and Hadewijch are of the utmost importance for the development of Middle Dutch as a written language. Both mystics tried to express the role of the divine and the experiencing of God in their lives, while realizing that their vernacular falls short vis-à-vis such an endeavor. Thus they frequently made use of neologisms, using the language in a creative way. They laid the foundations of a Middle Dutch mystical language, which made itself felt in the oeuvre of Jan van Ruusbroec and, through him, in the writings of the Modern Devotion, a later religious movement.

BIBLIOGRAPHY

Carton, M. J., trans. "Beatrice of Nazareth. The Seven Steps of Love." *Cistercian Studies* 19 (1984): 31–42.

Vekeman, Herman W. J. "Beatrijs van Nazareth. Die Mystik einer Zisterzienserin." In Peter Dinzelbacher and Dieter R. Bauer, ed. *Frauenmystik im Mittelalter.* Ostfildern: Schwabenverlag, 1985, pp. 78–98.

———. *Hoezeer heeft God mij bemind. Beatrijs van Nazareth (1200–1268).* Vertaling van de Latijnse *Vita* met inleiding en commentaar. Kampen/Averbode: Kok/Altiora, 1993.

Vekeman, Herman W. J., and Jacques J. Th. M. Tersteeg, ed. *Beatrijs van Nazareth. Van seuen manieren van heileger minnen.* Zutphen: Thieme, 1971.

An Faems

SEE ALSO

Beguines; *Devotio Moderna;* Hadewijch; Jan van Ruusbroec

Beguines

Flourishing in thirteenth-century Germany and the Low Countries, Beguines were urban laywomen devoted to imitating Christ through poverty, chastity, and the apostolic life, without formalized rule or official order. They lived a hybrid of religious and secular lives as part of a broader renewal called *mulieres religiosae* (religious women). They attributed their movement to no single founder, but had roots in Gregorian reform. Enjoining moderation rather than extreme asceticism, they supported themselves through hospital work, weaving, and acts of charity. Beguines (and Beghards, their fewer male counterparts) lived either individually, in group homes, or in protected clusters of residences and churches called *beguinages.*

The most prominent Beguine communities in Germanic areas thrived in Cologne (eventually including over one hundred houses), Mainz, Strasbourg, Basel, and Wesel. Most German Beguines lived in the small sororities that could be found interspersed throughout nearly all German cities. They represented a significant portion of the population, and records show their notable economic and material contributions.

Beguines evoked both praise and censure from ecclesiastical authorities. Their fate rode the oscillating tide of the Church's attempts to respond to and regulate the swell of religious lay movements. Thus, although Jacques de Vitry, bishop of Acrer, courted and secured approval for the holy women from Pope Honorius III (1216–1227), the Fourth Lateran Council (1215) banned new forms of religious life. Pope Gregory IX's bull (1233) offered protection for northern spiritual women, while a Mainz synod of the same year confiscated Beguine property. Most of the specific synodic legislation against Beguines voiced suspicion over unauthorized teaching and unregulated practice. For example, Eichstätt (1284) opposed unauthorized lay leaders delivering sermons. Mainz (1261) objected to women donning a habit and maintaining chastity without the supervision of enclosure. Magdeburg (1261) reminded Beguines to obey parish priests. Church authorities gradually associated Beguines with antinomianism because some women taught complex theological doctrines. As a result, the Council of Vienne (1311) censured them more forcefully with two decisive decrees (1317). *Ad nostrum* turned the Inquisition on Beguines and outlined specific errors. *Cum de quibusdam mulieribus* called for the dissolution of Beguines, but left a degree of latitude in enforcement. As pressure increased, many Beguines joined stable tertiary and mendicant orders, with whom they had already sustained productive, collaborative relationships.

Beguines authored some of the earliest, most artful theologies in European vernaculars. These mystical teachings constitute their most lasting legacy. The most influential German Beguine is inarguably Mechthild von Magdeburg (d. ca. 1282). In *Das Fließende Licht der Gottheit* she develops a language of images, paradox, and courtly convention to teach about the soul, God, and mystical union. The lesser-known German Beguines Agnes Blannbekin (d. 1312) and Christina of Stammeln (d. 1315) contribute to our growing awareness of Beguine devotion. Because of the fluidity of medieval linguistic borders, we may also include two Flemish Beguines, Beatrijs van Nazareth (d. 1268) and Hadewijch of Antwerp (fl. thirteenth century), as contributors to medieval religious culture in the Rhine region. The Beguine writers influenced later German mystical authors including Meister Eckhart (also Eckehart, Eckart; d. 1327) and Margaretha Ebner (d. 1351).

BIBLIOGRAPHY

Freed, John B. "Urban Development and the 'Cura Monialium' in Thirteenth-Century Germany." *Viator* 3 (1972): 311–327.

Grundmann, Herbert. *Religious Movements in the Middle Ages,* trans. Steven Rowan. Notre Dame, Ind.: University of Notre Dame Press, 1995.

Lerner, Robert E. "Beguines and Beghards." In *Dictionary of the Middle Ages,* ed. Joseph R. Strayer. Vol. 2. New York: Scribner, 1982–1989, coll. 157–162.

McDonnell, Ernst. *The Beguines and Beghards in Medieval Culture, with Special Emphasis on the Belgian Scene.* New Brunswick, N.J.: Rutgers University Press, 1954.

Murk-Jansen, Saskia. *Brides in the Desert: The Spirituality of the Beguines.* Maryknoll, N.Y.: Orbis, 1998.

Patricia Zimmerman Beckman

SEE ALSO

Basel; Beatrijs van Nazareth; Cologne; Ebner, Margaretha; Hadewijch; Mechthild von Magdeburg; Mainz; Meister Eckhart; Strasbourg

Beheim, Michael (1416/1421–1472/1479)

A prolific author and composer of almost five hundred song-poems, Michael (or Michel) Beheim (also Behaim; Beham) was until the late twentieth century dismissed as a *Vielschreiber* (scribbler) and mere cultural-historical curiosity. He is now recognized as one of the most important singers, composers, and publishers (*Liedpublizisten*) of the fifteenth century. Beheim's reevaluation, facilitated by the appearance of a critical edition of his poems (*Gedichte,* published 1968–1972), coincided with the reassessment of fifteenth-century aesthetics in general. Beheim is an important figure because of his poetic range and the range of his ambition. A manuscript scribe, poet, and composer, he produced a virtual summa of medieval themes and poetic forms, creating religious songs, moral and ethical poetry, political and historical writings, autobiographical verse, love songs, fables, and songs on the nature and status of the singer's art. (He even writes on Dracula, Vlad the Impaler.) As a poetic musician *(musicus poeticus)* and lay theologian, Beheim championed *rechte kunst* (proper art) and artistic individuality, the latter grounded in the composition of original songs, or *Töne* (occasion pieces with titles such as *Zugweise, Kurze Weise, Verkehrte Weise, Osterweise, Trummetenweise, Gekrönte Weise, Slecht guldin Weise, Hohe guldin Weise, Hofweise,*

Slegweise, Lange Weise, Angstweise). Beheim also fashioned lengthy chronicles in verse: *Pfälzische Reimchronik,* (Palatine Rhyme Chronicle), *Buch von der statt Triest* (The Book of the City Treist), and *Buch von den Wienern* (The Book of the Viennese). Since the poet set these chronicles to music, thus making them sung epics (*Sangvers-Epen*), they hold the distinction of being the final specimens of Middle High German epic material that was sung. All of Beheim's oeuvre can in fact be performed to music, and he perhaps surprisingly leaves to his audience a choice of modes of reception. In the foreword to the *Buch von der statt Triest* he states, for example, that "you can read it like a rhymed book or sing it like a song" *(man es lesen mag als ein gereimptes puch oder singen als ain lied).* By presenting an alternative to traditional, communal, oral song performance, Beheim makes one of the first appeals in German literature to silent readers.

Literary criticism on Michael Beheim is devoted to taxonomy; for example, whether he was a medieval or modern poet, whether he was a Meistersinger, and if the term "professional poet" (*Berufsdichter*), frequently applied to him in research, helps us to understand him any better. That his work is difficult to pigeonhole arises from Beheim's status as a transition poet par excellence; as such, he embodies clashing and contradictory, but not mutually exclusive, tendencies. For instance, although he was a conservative author who cataloged and recapitulated the entire repertoire of fourteenth- and fifteenth-century German political writers, or *Spruchdichter,* Beheim sanctioned, and made a specific appeal to, a modern reading audience, recognizing the power and place of the book. Similarly, his great concern for the accurate textual transmission of his "collected works" on the manuscript page marks him as both a conservator and a protohumanistic student of the word. Although Beheim esteemed tradition, imitating and paraphrasing revered masters (Johann von Neumarkt, Heinrich von Mügeln, Heinrich Seuse, Heinrich von Langenstein, Thomas Peuntner, the Nicholas von Dinkelsbühl redactor, Muskatblüt), he reanimated not only poetry but theology, promulgating an Augustinian renewal in the vernacular that deserves the name of pre-Lutheran biblical humanism. Using song-poetry as a medium for proselytism among the laity, Beheim stylized himself as a poet-theologian and transmitter of patristic theology, who translated, versified, and set to music Scripture, sacred tractates, and sermons.

It is uncertain whether Michael Beheim was born in 1416 or 1421, or if he died before 1472 or after 1479, but it is possible to reconstruct his life in otherwise remarkable detail from rich autobiographical verses, for example, Song 24, "On Michael Peham's [sic] birth and his travels to this country" (*Von Michel Pehams gepurt und seinem her chomen in dis lannd*). In strophes bearing the traces of emendation as authorial intervention, Beheim alludes to his humble origins as a weaver's son, and sketches a career path that leads to no less than the imperial court of Frederick III of Habsburg. Among his prominent patrons were King Christian I of Denmark, Konrad von Weinsberg (the imperial archchamberlain), Count Ulrich II von Cilli, and Margrave Albrecht III, ("Achilles") von Brandenburg-Ansbach. For another noble sponsor, Frederick I of Wittelsbach, elector and Count Palatine, the poet reformulates the centuries-old adage concerning medieval German literary patronage, "Whose bread I eat, their song I sing" *(Wes' Brot ich eß, des Lied ich sing)*. These words have had an extraordinarily negative resonance in Beheim scholarship because they are deemed an expression of personal ethics rather than a rhetorical formula. A master of the rhetorical art, he was a loquacious, self-conscious artist with a sharp eye for accuracy of textual transmission and a strong belief that poetry should serve a moral purpose. His melodies and strophic structures, his wide-ranging and varied themes, his ecumenical impulses and his promotion of sacred subject matter as appropriate to secular audiences, all make him the architect of a rich compendium of songs and song types.

BIBLIOGRAPHY

Gille, Hans, and Ingeborg Spriewald, ed. *Die Gedichte des Michel Beheim*. 3 vols. Berlin: Akademie-Verlag, 1968–1972.

McDonald, William C. *"Whose Bread I Eat": The Song-Poetry of Michel Beheim*. Göppingen: Kümmerle, 1981.

Müller, Ulrich. "Autobiographische Tendenzen im deutschsprachigen Mittelalter: Probleme und Perspektiven der Edition. Vorgeführt am exemplarischen Fall der Sangvers-Lyrik und Sangvers-Epik des Michel Beheim." *Editio* 9 (1995): 63–79.

Schanze, Frieder. *Meisterliche Liedkunst zwischen Heinrich von Mügeln und Hans Sachs*. 2 vols. Munich: Artemis, 1983–1984.

Scholz, Manfred Günter. *Zum Verhältnis von Mäzen, Autor und Publikum im 14. und 15. Jahrhundert: "Wilhelm von Österreich" "Rappoltsteiner Parzifal," Michel Beheim*. Darmstadt: Wissenschaftliche Buchgesellschaft, 1987.

William C. McDonald

SEE ALSO
Seuse, Heinrich; Muskatblüt; Versification

Benedict, Rule of Saint

One of the most important documents of western Christendom is the rule for monks written in the early sixth century by Saint Benedict of Nursia (b. ca. 480), founder of the monastery at Monte Cassino as well as others in the area around Rome. Although probably meant as no more than a guide for those monasteries Benedict himself had established, the Rule of Saint Benedict gradually became the guiding principle for the governance and functioning of monasteries and nunneries throughout western Europe, which were then termed "Benedictine."

In 787, after a visit to Monte Cassino, Charlemagne had an exact copy of the Latin text made, possibly from Saint Benedict's autograph manuscript, and sent to Aachen. This authentic copy became the standard text guiding Carolingian monastic reform after the Synod of Aachen in 802 urged the adoption of the Rule of Saint Benedict in Frankish monasteries.

The rule itself requires that the text be read to the whole community of monks each year (chapter 60) and that the entire text be read three times to novices during their first year (chapter 58), a time when they are unlikely to have much knowledge of Latin. Thus, not only did every monastery library have its own copy of the rule, but the Latin text soon became an object of glossing and translating efforts.

Six Old High German glosses of the Latin text of the Rule of Saint Benedict are extant. Although only a single ninth-century OHG translation of the rule still exists (St. Gall, Stiftsbibliothek, Codex 916), it is known that two others once belonged to the same St. Gall Abbey library.

In the later Middle Ages, translating efforts increased. A single monastery might have several translations of the rule made in succeeding generations. Of the seventy extant MHG translations dating from the twelfth to the early sixteenth centuries, only seventeen have been edited and published in entirety.

The Old High German translation of the rule is an interlinear version with the German words written above the Latin words they translate, without regard for German word order. Studies show that the German text is not a translation of the Latin text above which it appears, but of a slightly different Latin text of the rule. For roughly the first third of the Latin text, virtually every word is translated; thereafter, the translation becomes a gloss with only certain words translated.

The earliest extant MHG version of the Benedictine rule is the Rule of Zwiefalten, from a monastery in Württemberg, written in Swabian dialect. (Published MHG rules are named after the monastery of origin or, occasionally, the present location, e.g., the London Rule.) Like the OHG rule, Zwiefalten is an interlinear version of an older text, copied in the mid- to late twelfth century.

The Rule of Oxford, early fourteenth century, once belonged to the monastery at Eberbach in the Rhineland. However, the fact that its language was adapted for use by nuns indicates that it was not likely used there, but perhaps at one of the Rhenish foundations affiliated with Eberbach.

No definitive studies of the MHG rules establish relationships and affinities between the various translations. Preliminary comparisons indicate a remarkable amount of freedom exercised by medieval translators in rendering this important religious document into German.

BIBLIOGRAPHY

Daab, Ursula. *Die Althochdeutsche Benediktinerregel des Cod. Sang. 916.* Tübingen: Niemeyer, 1959.

———. *Studien zur Althochdeutschen Benediktinerregel.* Halle an der Saale: Niemeyer, 1929.

Petri, Edda. "Die mittelhochdeutschen Übersetzungen der Regula Benedicti." *Regulae Benedicti Studia* 8/9 (1979/1980): 67–71.

Petri, Edda, and John E. Crean, Jr. "Handschriftenverzeichnis mittelhochdeutscher Benediktinerregeln bis 1600." *Regulae Benedicti Studia* 6/7 (1981): 151–154.

Schmidt, Konrad. "Vier deutsche Benediktinerregeln aus dem späten Mittelalter." Ph.D. diss., Berlin, 1969.

Selmer, Carl. *Middle High German Translations of the Regula Sancti Benedicti: The Eight Oldest Versions.* Cambrige, Mass.: Medieval Academy of America, 1933; rpt. New York: Kraus, 1970.

Simmler, Franz. *Aus Benediktinerregeln des 9. bis 20. Jahrhunderts: Quellen zur Geschichte einer Textsorte.* Heidelberg: Winter, 1985.

Patricia A. Giangrosso

Bern

The city of Bern (Switzerland) owes its founding to Duke Berthold V of Zähringen, who chose the site on the Aare peninsula in 1191 as a point of defense against the French-speaking regions. Bern was granted free imperial status in 1218, but by the end of the fourteenth century the citizenry governed the city. Bern's strong local nobility and appetite for property alienated the neighboring regions as its importance and power grew. Its entrance into the Swiss Confederation in 1353 is attributed in part to Bern's attempt to quell various uprisings of its own subjects, who sympathized with the Confederates (Uri, Schwyz, Unterwalden).

Bern's planning and architecture reflect its prosperity in the late Middle Ages. The city, with its three parallel main streets, was divided into modules which were then leased, subdivided into housing, and subleased. Its infrastructure was impressively progressive: canals for transport, sewers and canals for drinking water, as well as fortifications; four gates survive from the twelfth and fourteenth centuries. A fire in 1405 destroyed all private houses, but Bern's two smaller churches, the Französische Kirche (French Church) and the Nydeggkirche, survived. After building a city hall (1406–1417), Bern's citizens saw the need for an equally impressive ecclesiastical structure. A cathedral dedicated to Saint Vincent was built on the site of the original twelfth-century parish church. Matthäus Ensinger, who was also working on the cathedrals in Ulm and Strasbourg, planned and oversaw the building of the Bern cathedral for twenty-five years beginning in 1421. The result is a basilica with few alterations made to the original plan. Of note is the choir, with stained glass windows of iconographic interest. The decorative vaults with sculpted capstones were erected by Daniel Heinz between 1571 and 1575. The sculpture decorating the three portals of the facade was executed by Erhart Küng from Westphalia between 1458 and 1505. Represented in the tympanum of the central portal is the scene of the Last Judgment, which, in its images of the classes in late medieval society, demonstrates the influence of the mystery plays of the period.

BIBLIOGRAPHY

Divorne, Françoise. *Bern et les villes fondées par les ducs de Zähringen au XIIe siècle: Culture médiévale et modernité.* Brussels: Archives d'architecture moderne, 1991.

Furrer, Bernhard. "Das Weltgericht am Berner Münster und seine Restaurierung." *Unsere Kunstdenkmäler 3* (1993): 323–332.

Hofer, Paul, and Luc Mojon. *Die Kunstdenkmäler des Kantons Bern: Die Stadt Bern.* 5 vols. Basel: Birkhäuser, 1947–1969.

Kurmann-Schwarz, Brigitte. "Das 10,000-Ritter Fenster im Berner Münster und seine Auftraggeber." *Zeit-*

schrift für schweizerische Archäologie und Kunstgeschichte 49 (1992): 39–54.

Schläppi, Christoph. *Das Berner Münster.* Bern: Gesellschaft für schweizerische Kunstgeschichte, 1993.

Sladeczek, Franz-Josef. *Erhart Küng: Bildhauer und Baumeister am Münster zu Bern (um 1420–1507).* Ph.D diss., Universität Giessen, 1986; Bern: Paul Haupt, 1990.

Elsa Gontrum

SEE ALSO
Gothic Art and Architecture, Late; Strasbourg; Ulm

Berno von Reichenau (d. June 7, 1048)

The abbot of one of southern Germany's leading monasteries, Berno von Reichenau (also Bern, Bernardus, Berno Augiensis) contributed richly to medieval German culture. His writings encompass treatises on music theory, liturgy, and theology, as well as saints' lives, sermons, letters, and musical compositions. His most famous pupil was the music theorist, composer, and historian Hermann von Reichenau (also Hermannus Contractus), whose historical writings provide essential information concerning Berno's biography.

The circumstances of Berno's birth are unknown, although he was probably born to a German family of some prominence. He is first associated with the monastery of Prüm. In 1008 Emperor Henry II appointed him abbot of the island monastery of Reichenau. In 1014 Berno traveled to Rome for Henry's coronation, a measure of his high political standing. In 1022 he again accompanied Henry to Rome, this time also visiting Monte Cassino. These journeys, as well as a third trip in 1027 to attend the coronation of Emperor Conrad II, doubtless gave him access to sources important for his musical and liturgical research. Upon the accession of the unsympathetic Conrad, Berno was embroiled in disputes over encroachments upon previously granted ecclesiastical privileges. Emperor Henry III, son of Conrad II, proved to be a more supportive sovereign than his predecessor, and visited Berno at Reichenau on February 4, 1040. Berno died there on June 7, 1048, having in his forty years as abbot guided the monastery to new levels of artistic and scholarly achievement. He was buried in the newly consecrated choir of the abbey church. Berno's tomb was rediscovered in 1929; measurements of his remains show that he stood an imposing six feet three inches tall.

As a music theorist, Berno struck a balance between practical application and abstract theory. His most significant contributions are three tonaries (lists of chants ordered by mode). Most important of these is the *Prologus in tonarium,* a tonary with explanatory prologue that was widely distributed during the eleventh and twelfth centuries, sometimes with later interpolations. By Berno's own admission it is mainly a compendium from earlier sources. Another, abridged, tonary, *De consona tonorum diversitate,* was apparently intended for teaching novices at Reichenau. In addition to the tonaries, a treatise entitled *De mensurando monochordo* (On measuring monochords) has been tentatively attributed to Berno. Berno's views on mode appear to have been relatively conservative, and do not reflect the growing influence of the Italian music theorist Guido of Arezzo. Berno's treatment of transposition and modal affinity forms an important background to Hermann's highly original work. In the area of rhythm, Berno warns against the failure to distinguish between long and short notes.

Berno's musical compositions include three hymns, an Epiphany trope, three sequences, and an office for Saint Ulrich; an office for Saint Meinrad is also tentatively ascribed to him.

As hagiographer, liturgist, and theologian, Berno's contributions are also rich. His *Vita sancti Udalrici* (Life of Saint Ulrich) is noteworthy for its fine literary style. Also ascribed to Berno are treatises on religious topics including Advent, prayer (in hexameter), fasting, and heresy, as well as on the Mass *(De quibusdam rebus ad missae officium pertinentibus,* On Certain Things Pertaining to the Office of the Mass) and on differences between the Gallic and Roman Psalters (*De varia psalmorum*); Berno's authorship of these latter two treatises has been questioned by modern scholars, however. More than a dozen sermons and sermon fragments are preserved, many of them on Marian topics, as well as about twenty letters to emperors, bishops, abbots, and other leaders. That numerous other works of music theory, history, and poetry came to be attributed to Berno, often on weak grounds, testifies to the esteem in which he was held by later generations of medieval scribes.

BIBLIOGRAPHY
Gerbert, Martin. *Scriptores ecclesiastici de musica sacra potissimum.* Sankt-Blasien, 1784; Graecii, Styria, 1905; rpt. Hildesheim: Olms, 1963, 1990.

Hiley, David. *Western Plainchant: A Handbook.* Oxford: Oxford University Press, 1993.

Migne, Jacques-Paul. *Patrologiae cursus completus.* Series Latina. Paris, 1844–1864; on CD-ROM: Arlington, Va: Chadwyck-Healey, 1995.

Oesch, Hans. *Berno und Hermann von Reichenau als Musiktheoretiker.* Publikationen der Schweizerischen Musikforschenden Gesellschaft, ser. II, vol. 9. Bern: Haupt, 1961.

Rausch, Andreas. "Die Musiktraktate des Abtes Bern von Reichenau." Ph.D diss., Universität Wien, 1996.

Waesberghe, J. Smits van. *Bernonis Augiensis Abbatis: De arte musica disputationes traditae. Pars A. Bernonis Augiensis de Mensurando Monochordo. Pars B. Quae ratio est inter tria opera de arte musica Bernonis Augiensis.* Divitiae Musicae Artis ser. A, lib. VI. 2 vols. Buren: Knuf, 1979 [includes facsimiles].

Michael R. Dodds

SEE ALSO
Conrad II; Henry III; Liturgy, Music; Reichenau

Bernward of Hildesheim (960–1022)

Bishop of Hildesheim and abbot of St. Michael's, Hildesheim (1007–1022), Bernward was a pivotal member of the Ottonian court, and his patronage stimulated the arts at Hildesheim. He was born in 960 into a noble Saxon family that enjoyed the friendship of the Ottonian emperors. By 977 he had joined the imperial chancellery as a notary. He subsequently became court chaplain and tutor to Otto III. As bishop of Hildesheim, Bernward continued to advise and represent Otto III and Henry II. His imperial service entailed considerable travel. Under Otto II, during the regency, and under Otto III, he was frequently in Italy, especially Rome. As Henry II's diplomatic representative to Robert II of France in 1007, he visited Paris, Saint-Denis, and Tours. The various cultural sources to which Bernward was exposed on these occasions were fundamental with respect to his patronage of the arts at Hildesheim.

As bishop of Hildesheim, Bernward was responsible for several major commissions. In addition to the Benedictine monastery church of St. Michael's, his patronage is represented by a series of illuminated manuscripts and several important works in metal, especially the hollow-cast bronze column and doors now in the cathedral at Hildesheim. The complex program of the doors, which relates to the fall of man and his redemption through Christ, depends on a typological reading of paired Old and New Testament scenes and indicates the erudition of the patron. Formally and iconographically, the doors and the column derive from Carolingian sources from Tours, Reims, and Metz, but the general concept as well as the hollow-cast technique reflect Bernward's acquaintance with classical and early Christian Roman monuments.

BIBLIOGRAPHY
Brandt, Michael, and Arne Eggebrecht, ed. *Bernward von Hildesheim und das Zeitalter der Ottonen.* Hildesheim: Dom- und Diözesanmuseum, 1993.

Karen E. Loaiza

SEE ALSO
Henry II, Art; Hildesheim; Metz; Otto II; Otto III

Berthold von Henneberg (1441/1442–1504)

A prelate who wielded considerable political influence under Maximilian I, Berthold, after twenty years as a cathedral canon and dean of Mainz, succeeded as archbishop in 1484. The diocese was in somewhat desolate condition after many wars with regional dynastic families over territorial lordship. Like many other contemporaries, Berthold believed that a reform of the Holy Roman Empire, which should establish an effective central government dominated by the princes, might end the recurrent warfare. At the *Reichstag* of Worms (Diet of Worms) in 1495, Berthold's leadership gained the passage of the "eternal territorial peace" (*ewige Landfriede*) and the founding of an imperial chamber court (*Reichskammergericht*). Both were helpful in promoting lasting stability in the empire.

But Berthold and the reformers were not satisfied with these accomplishments, thinking that Emperor Maximilian I was too distracted by his "foreign" wars and territorial ambitions. So at Augsburg in 1500 Berthold restricted Maximilian with an imperial regime *(Reichsregiment)* run by the princes. Long archchancellor in name and by tradition, Berthold briefly became so in fact as he gained control of the imperial chancery and seal. By the time of Berthold's death in 1504, however, Emperor Maximilian had exploited the disagreements among the princes and estates and successfully regained his authority.

BIBLIOGRAPHY
Bader, Karl S. *Ein Staatsmann vom Mittelrhein: Gestalt und Werk des Mainzer Kurfürsten und Erzbischofs Berthold von Henneberg.* Forschungen und Studien aus

dem Raume Pfalz, Rhein, Mosel und Saar. Mainz: Druckhaus Schmidt, 1955.

Hartung, Fritz. "Berthold von Henneberg, Kurfürst von Mainz." *Historische Zeitschrift* 103 (1909): 527–551.

Helm, Claudia, and Jost Hausmann. *1495. Kaiser, Reich, Reformen: Der Reichstag zu Worms: Austellung des Landeshauptarchives Koblenz in Verbindung mit der Stadt Worms zum 500jährigen Jubiläum des Wormser Reichstags von 1495.* Veröffentlichungen der landessarchivverwaltung Rheinland Pfalz, Katalogreihe. Coblenz: Landesarchivverwaltung Rheinland-Pfalz, 1995.

Brian A. Pavlac

SEE ALSO

Fürstbischof; Landfrieden; Maximilian

Berthold von Holle

The author of three courtly love romances, *Demantin, Crane,* and *Darifant,* named for their heroes, was probably the scion of a Hildesheim ministerial family who is attested from 1251 to 1270. Berthold, who mentions Duke Johann of Brunswick in the *Crane* prologue, apparently had connections to the Guelph court.

Demantin (11,761 verses) and *Crane* (4,919 verses) are each preserved in one manuscript and three fragments. A fragment of 265 verses survives of *Darifant,* leaving its content largely unclear. The reception of the texts remained confined to northern Germany, and in the fifteenth century, the first half of *Crane* was adapted for prose in Cologne. Berthold's exceptional position in German thirteenth-century courtly romance rests on his northern sphere of activity and his hybrid language, a mixture of Middle High and Low German.

In *Demantin,* the prince Demantin woos the Greek king's daughter Sirgamot in vain. Her father marries her to the old king of Antioch, who does not consummate the union. Demantin elopes with her and defends their love in a war against both her father and her husband, who finally renounces her. The rather strictly composed plot structure is determined by the succession of fight, adventure, and festivity. Love is the highest value for the noble-minded protagonists and, according to the old ideals of knightly service, the unrivaled motivation of masculine action. Conflicts with honor and marriage are settled in love's favor without enduringly endangering the social order. Berthold's depiction of chivalric standards, courtly lifestyle, and ceremonial splendor is decidedly nostalgic. The mainly realistic setting is mingled with reminiscences of the fairy-tale world of Arthurian romance, as a dwarf king who advises Demantin's friend Firganant of princely ideals is familiar with France and Germany, and a fairy queen is the sovereign of German fairies.

Crane, the hero of the title, is the nickname of the Hungarian king's son Gayol, who wanders to the imperial court with his friends Stare (starling) and Valke (falcon), sons of the dukes of Bavaria and Austria. He falls in love with the emperor's daughter Acheloyde and, after some complications are resolved, marries her. In the second half of the romance, he demonstrates his princely skills in a series of adventures. In the decisive tournament for Acheloyde, Crane fights in disguise, initiating what seems to be a conflict of social rank. Unaware of his real position, Acheloyde proves the honest loyalty *(triuwe)* of her love by consenting to an alliance that would deprive her of her social status. Just as she exemplifies loyalty in love, Crane's marshal Assundin incarnates political loyalty, the three companions loyalty in friendship, and Crane himself knightly and princely loyalty. Therefore, the romance is entirely concentrated on the praise of *triuwe* as the central virtue of nobility.

Berthold takes his motifs from the courtly epic tradition, but no concrete sources have been discovered. Wolfram von Eschenbach, whom he names as his model, only marginally influenced his style and poetic technique. Compared to other love romances of the thirteenth century, such as Rudolf von Ems's *Willehalm von Orlens* and Konrad von Würzburg's *Partonopier* and *Engelhard,* the simplicity and stereotypy of his language and the lack of rhetorical pretension are striking.

BIBLIOGRAPHY

Bartsch, Karl, ed. *Berthold von Holle.* Nuremberg: Bauer and Raspe, 1858.

———. *Demantin von Berthold von Holle.* Tübingen: Laupp, 1875.

Beckers, Hartmut. "Die Kölner Prosabearbeitung des Crane-Romans Bertholds von Holle. Untersuchung und Textausgabe." *Niederdeutsches Wort* 23 (1983): 83–135.

Malsen-Tilborch, Gabriele von. *Repräsentation und Reduktion. Strukturen späthöfischen Erzählens bei Berthold von Holle.* Munich: Beck, 1973.

Wermke, Matthias. *Elemente mündlicher Komposition in der ritterlichen Epik des späten 13. Jahrhunderts. Die Versromane Bertholds von Holle.* Frankfurt am Main: Lang, 1988.

Zimmermann, Manfred. "Nachklassische Artusepik ohne Artus. Die Dichtungen Bertholds von Holle." In *Artusroman und Intertextualität,* ed. Friedrich Wolfzettel. Giessen: Schmitz, 1990, pp. 235–244.

Gert Hübner

SEE ALSO
Konrad von Würzburg; Rudolf von Ems; Welfs; Wolfram von Eschenbach

Berthold von Regensburg (ca. 1210–1272)

The most well-known and effectual preacher in the vernacular in the German Middle Ages was the Franciscan priest Berthold von Regensburg. Neither Berthold's birthdate nor birthplace has been established, but he is identified with the Minorite order in Regensburg, of which he became a member, possibly after years of study in Magdeburg. While Berthold acted as confessor to the women of nearby Obermünster and Niedermünster, his fellow Franciscan David von Augsburg probably served as his assistant. Beginning in 1240 and continuing until his death, Berthold preached to religious and lay audiences first in southern Germany, then Bohemia, Switzerland, Styria, and France. In 1263 Pope Urban IV requested that Berthold assist Albertus Magnus in preaching the Crusades. Berthold's preaching to the masses took place outside the church and in the vernacular; embellished descriptions of his sermonizing assert that the lay crowds sometimes numbered forty thousand to two hundred thousand. Such exaggerated estimates substantiate Berthold's popularity and the respect in which he was held. Because of his notoriety he also was called upon to settle disputes in the political and religious spheres.

The only extant works by and attributed to Berthold are Latin and German sermons. Five collections of sermons comprise the Latin corpus. Of these only the first three collections—*Rusticanus de Dominicis* (Rural Sunday Sermons), *Rusticanus de Sanctis* (Holy Day), and *Commune Sanctorum Rusticani* (Rural Saints' Day Sermons)—numbering 254 works, are indisputably by Berthold; they were prepared between 1250 and 1255 for his fellow preachers. The authenticity of the remaining 135 Latin sermons is uncertain. In the preface to the sermons Berthold states that he undertook the editing of the works to counter the error-ridden versions being produced by enthusiastic but unskilled clerics.

The authorship of the German sermons cannot be ascertained with any degree of certainty. More than two hundred pieces have at one time or another been attributed to Berthold, but today fewer than one hundred are identified as works based on the sermons of the Franciscan. It is presumed that the vernacular sermons were copied and edited by Franciscan monks in or around Augsburg beginning in the 1260s, before Berthold's death, until approximately 1275; nonetheless, it is unlikely that Berthold read or approved of many of the works. The editor's hand is clearly discernible; thus these sermons should not be viewed as mere transcriptions of the sermons as preached by Berthold. The German sermons reveal a dependence on the earlier Latin homiletic works, but none is a translation from the Latin.

More than three hundred manuscripts containing Berthold's Latin sermons have been identified; in contrast only eight principal manuscripts that include the vernacular sermons are extant. The Latin homiletic works follow the tradition of the thematic or university-style sermon of the Scholastics, whereas the vernacular sermons emphasize *exempla* (examples) as opposed to a rigid structure or an interpretation of Scripture. In general Berthold would have preached the Latin sermons to a learned, religious audience and the vernacular sermons to the laity; the notable exceptions are the German *Sermones ad Religiosas* (*Klosterpredigten,* Sermons for the Religious), which were preached to women in Berthold's spiritual care.

The frequency of Berthold's name in medieval chronicles, the wealth of extant sermons by and attributed to him, and the esteem in which his contemporaries held him and successors attest to his influence and importance.

BIBLIOGRAPHY
Banta, Frank G. "Berthold von Regensburg: Investigations Past and Present." *Traditio* 25 (1969): 472–479.
De Alcantara Hoetzl, Petrus, ed. *Sermones ad religiosos XX ex Erlangensi codice Unacum sermone in honorem S. Francisci e duobus codicibus monacensibus in centenarium septimum familiae franciscanae.* Munich: Huttler, 1882 [Latin works].
Pfeiffer, Franz, and Joseph Strobl, eds. *Berthold von Regensburg. Vollständige Ausgabe seiner deutschen Predigten.* Vienna: Braumüller, 1862 and 1880; rpt. ed. Kurt Ruh [with supplementary material]. Deutsche Neudrucke, Texte des Mittelalters. Berlin: de Gruyter, 1965 [German works].
Richter, Dieter. *Die deutsche Überlieferung der Predigten Bertholds von Regensburg.* Munich: Beck, 1969.
Schönbach, Anton. "Studien zur Geschichte der altdeutschen Predigt, I–VIII." *Sitzungsberichte der*

Kaiserlichen Akademie der Wissenschaften in Wien, Philosophisch-historische Klasse 142 (1900), 147 (1904), and 151–155 (1905–1907); rpt. Hildesheim: Olms, 1968.

Debra L. Stoudt

SEE ALSO

Albertus Magnus; David von Augsburg; Preaching and Sermons, Dutch; Preaching and Sermons, German

Bertram, Meister (ca. 1340–1415)

A painter who was born in Minden in Westphalia, Bertram is documented in Hamburg from 1367, and is known to have led a prospering and influential workshop there. A testament of 1390 speaks of an intended pilgrimage to Rome; one dated 1410 disposes of a considerable fortune.

Master Bertram, God Creating the Animals from the Grabow Altarpiece (Hamburg, Hamburger Kunsthalle, Inv. 500f). *Photograph: © Elke Walford, Hamburg*

Twenty-four painted scenes survive from the first opening of a double-winged carved altarpiece from the church of Saint Peter (moved to Grabow in 1731; now Kunsthalle, Hamburg). They were painted by Bertram in 1379 and narrate the Latin poem *Speculum humanae salvationis* (1324, Mirror of Human Salvation) from Creation to the flight into Egypt. The initial scenes are dominated by the single image of the Creator, silhouetted against a gold ground. This monumental, eloquent figure is created in color and light without visible drawing lines, reminiscent of the painting style of Master Theoderic in Prague. Powerful limbs can be discerned below heavy garments. The narrative is convincingly carried by a sense of movement in the figure and by the forceful gestures of the large hands. Here, as in the later multifigured scenes, nature and architecture merely create a sparse stage setting for the vigorous protagonists.

An altarpiece, painted around 1410 for a convent at Buxtehude, is decorated with eighteen apocryphal and biblical scenes from the life of the Virgin. There, in tune with stylistic trends, Bertram's figures are reduced in scale and dressed in lighter materials, and they inhabit a more furnished stage. However, the distinct figure style of the workshop persists. It was echoed in many German workshops, and reflections have even been noted in wall paintings in the Chapterhouse of Westminster Abbey, London.

BIBLIOGRAPHY

Jensen, Jens Christian. "Meister Bertram, Quellen und Untersuchungen." *Zeitschrift des Vereins für Hamburgische Geschichte* 44 (1958): 141–203.

Lichtwark, Alfred. *Meister Bertram tätig in Hamburg 1367–1415*. Bilderhefte der Hamburger Kunsthalle 1. Hamburg: Lütcke und Wulff, 1905.

Platte, Hans. *Meister Bertram in der Hamburger Kunsthalle*. 4th ed. Hanover: T. Schäfer, 1982.

Portmann, Paul. *Meister Bertram*. Zurich: Rabe, 1963.

Brigitte Corley

SEE ALSO

Hamburg; Ludolf of Saxony; Prague; Theoderic, Master

Beyeren, Herald (ca. 1345–1414)

The son of Claes Heynen, Beyeren was a court poet and historian. Born in the county of Holland, from 1371 he was employed as a messenger by Jan van Blois, one of the count of Holland's nobles, and nine years later he worked at the court of Duke Willem I of Gelre (d. February 16,

1402) as Gelre Herald. He wrote *Ehrenreden,* a German genre of short elegiac poems in honor of specific knights, usually written after they had died, in which the knight's arms were described according to the rules of blazon. In these and other works, he defended the old chivalric ideal. Around 1395 he was invested with the title of King of Arms of the Ruyers, which made him the most important herald in the area between the Meuse and the Rhine. For his own use, he compiled the *Gelre Wapenboek* (Gelve Book of Arms), in which he not only brought together arms of the European nobility, but also recorded his poems and included a portrait of himself. He took this manuscript with him to the court of Holland, with which he took service as Beyeren Herald in 1402. In his new surroundings, the genre of the *Ehrenreden* slowly receded into the background and he began to concentrate on writing long historiographical works, such as the *Wereldkroniek* (World Chronicle) and the *Hollandse kroniek* (Dutch Chronicle). These writings reveal his knowledge of the earlier literary tradition; he used works by Martin of Troppan (Martinus Polonus), Jacob van Maerlant, Melis Stokes, Jan van Boendale, and Johannes de Beka, among others. The form in which his work has come down to us may be called remarkable: six illuminated autographs have survived.

BIBLIOGRAPHY
Anrooij, Wim van. "Heralds, Knights and Travelling." In *Medieval Dutch Literature in Its European Context,* ed. Erik S. Kooper, Willem P. Gerritsen, and Frits P. van Oostrom. Cambridge: Cambridge University Press, 1994, pp. 46–61.
Bouton, V. *Wapenboeck ou armorial de 1334 à 1372* [. . .]. *Précédé de poésies héraldiques par Gelre, héraut d'armes.* 10 vols. Paris, 1881–1905.
Oostrom, Frits P. van. *Court and Culture: Dutch Literature, 1350–1450.* Berkeley: University of California Press, 1992, pp. 126–71.

Wim van Anrooij

SEE ALSO
Jacob van Maerlant; Jan van Boendale; Stokes, Melis

Bible

From the time of the Christianization of Germany, the Bible influenced almost every area of life. Biblical influence was utterly pervasive throughout the Carolingian and Ottonian periods and continued even after the rise of chivalry. Especially before the thirteenth century, this influence was often indirect; for most Germans of that time, the Bible was a Latin document, available mainly to the educated.

Several different forms of the Latin Bible were in use. Although the Vulgate text produced by Saint Jerome soon dominated, older manuscripts often contain the earlier and less accurate Old Latin (*Itala*) version. Since the Bible is very large, most manuscripts are incomplete, containing, for example, only the Gospels or the Psalms. Instead of the Gospels, some offer the diatessaron attributed to the second-century Syrian theologian Tatian; a diatessaron combines portions of the four Gospels, omitting redundant passages.

A famous ninth-century manuscript from Fulda contains, in parallel columns, a Latin diatessaron and a slightly divergent Old High German translation. The German *Tatian* (the modern title given to the OHG text) was not unique; we possess fragments of a slightly earlier translation of Matthew (in a collection of fragments known as *Isidor*). We also have several early translations of the Lord's Prayer (Matt. 6:9–13) and of various Psalms, meant for prayer and sometimes instruction. Williram's (Abbot of Eversberg, Bavaria) eleventh-century annotated translation of the Song of Songs was a particular favorite (at least eighteen manuscripts). Later, we find more ambitious translation projects: hints of a (possibly heretical) translation about 1260, and a complete New Testament in Augsburg in 1350. Although the famous Gutenberg Bibles are in Latin, the Strasbourg printer Johann Mentelin printed the first German Bible in 1466, using a clumsy translation perhaps 150 years old. Even before Mentelin, German texts are not rare; more than eight hundred earlier manuscripts contain all or part of the Bible in German. These translations were not used in the Mass; throughout the Middle Ages, even in parish churches, the Epistle and Gospel passages assigned for the day were chanted or read in Latin. Yet even before translations became common, the contents and teachings of the Bible were well known. As the Scriptures were proclaimed in Latin, German churchgoers could meditate on the biblical scenes and motifs often painted on church walls and ceilings. Outside, carved images might be found on the doors or over the portals. Later, stained or painted glass, and sometimes statues, presented biblical themes. Studying any book on medieval pictorial arts, one is struck by how many paintings, illuminations, and even simple decorations represent biblical scenes.

The Bible also figured heavily in German literature. Until the appearance of courtly literature shortly before 1200, the most significant German poetic works dealt with biblical topics. Many of these are finely crafted and strikingly original. The ninth-century Old Saxon *Heliand* portrays Christ as a Germanic king-hero; like the Old Saxon *Genesis* poem, it used the traditional alliterative verse form to which the newly converted Saxons were accustomed. Slightly later, Otfrid of Weißenburg created a new, rhyming verse form for his monumental Gospel poem. His new meter was quickly imitated, becoming the basis for almost all subsequent Old High German poetry, and eventually developed into the courtly couplet favored in Middle High German epics. While it is not entirely clear for whom these poems were intended—Otfrid says his is meant to keep the "laymen's disgusting singing" *(laicorum cantus obscoenus)* from disturbing pious ears—we still find poems such as "Christ and the Samaritan Woman" (tenth century) and the longer "Vienna-Millstätt *Genesis* and *Exodus*" (eleventh and twelfth century, respectively). Later, however, religious poetry strays farther from the Bible. Hartmann von Aue's *Armer Heinrich* slightly resembles Job but is completely independent. Other poets use extracanonical material; Konrad of Fussesbrunnen reworked the apocryphal Gospel of the Infancy of Jesus.

As elsewhere in Europe, early medieval German interpretation of the Bible followed the principle of the three senses of Scripture, first formalized by Origen in the third century: besides the obvious "literal sense," Scripture had a "moral sense" and, most important, a "spiritual sense." Many narrative passages of Otfrid's poem are followed by reflective and interpretive sections labeled *mystice* ("in a mystical sense"), which may be longer than the narrative. Some scholars, including Origen himself, even claimed that the literal sense of a passage might sometimes be false, at least in details, if this helped to express the spiritual sense. The Frankish theologian Hrabanus Maurus (ca. 784–856) apparently thought it below Christ's dignity to ride into Jerusalem on an ass, as the four Gospels say. According to this scholar, the ass was included because spiritually it represented the synagogue; as indicated in the *Heliand,* Jesus must have walked.

The spiritual sense was particularly important for interpreting the Old Testament, where scholars looked for "types" foreshadowing persons and events of the New Testament. The Israelites' passage through the Red Sea was a type of baptism; Eve and the serpent a type of the Annunciation. Typology reaches a peak in the so-called

Biblia pauperum (Paupers' Bible), printed from woodblocks in the Netherlands ca. 1460 but known in manuscript a few centuries earlier. Each page depicts an incident from the New Testament flanked by two counterparts (types) from the Old Testament: the Crucifixion is matched with Abraham's near-sacrifice of Isaac (Gen. 22:1–18) and with Moses raising up the bronze serpent (Num. 21:8–9). But not all spiritual-typological interpretations were so reasonable. The eleventh-century German didactic treatise *Elder Physiologus,* having explained that the lion signifies Christ because of its strength, makes it a type of the Resurrection: the lion is born dead, but is brought to life by the father on the third day. We are further told, with muddled metaphors and unnatural history, that the elephant and its mate represent Adam and Eve.

The development of Scholasticism in the twelfth century greatly affected the role of Scripture in theology, which now concentrated its interest on theological and philosophical speculation rather than biblical interpretation. Increasingly, dissident or reform-minded groups, such as the Waldenses and Hussites, invoked the Bible as the supreme authority in religious matters, trumping policies of an often corrupt papacy and ineffectual general councils. This led in turn to suspicion by the Church of vernacular Bible reading by "unqualified" laymen.

BIBLIOGRAPHY

Ferrante, Joan M. "The Bible as Thesaurus for Secular Literature." In *The Bible in the Middle Ages: Its Influence on Literature and Art,* ed. Bernard S. Levy. Binghamton, N.Y.: Center for Medieval and Early Renaissance Studies, 1992, pp. 23–49.

Henry, Avril, ed. *Biblia pauperum: A Facsimile and Edition.* Ithaca, N.Y.: Cornell University Press, 1987.

Kartschoke, Dieter. *Altdeutsche Bibeldichtung.* Stuttgart: Metzler, 1975.

Lamper, J. W. H., ed. *Cambridge History of the Bible,* vol. 2. Cambridge: Cambridge University Press, 1969.

New Catholic Encyclopedia, vol. 2, s.v. "Bible," esp. pp. 436–449 [text of Vulgate], 476–479 [German versions], 498–503 [exegesis], 525-529 [Bible cycles in art]. New York: McGraw-Hill, 1967.

Smalley, Beryl. *The Study of the Bible in the Middle Ages.* 2d ed. Oxford: Blackwell, 1952; rpt. Notre Dame, Ind: University of Notre Dame Press, 1964.

Sonderegger, Stefan. "Geschichte deutscher Bibelübersetzung in Grundzügen." In *Sprachgeschichte: Ein*

Handbuch zur Geschichte der deutschen Sprache und ihrer Erforschung, ed. Werner Besch, et al. 2d ed. vol. 1. Berlin: de Gruyter, 1998, pp. 229–284.

Leo A. Connolly

SEE ALSO

Bible Epic, Saxon; Hartmann von Aue; Hrabanus Maurus; Latin Language; Otfrid; Song of Songs; Versification

Bible Epic, Saxon

The *Heliand,* the nearly six-thousand-line Old Saxon (OS) epic narrative that was titled by its first editor, Andreas Schmeller, in 1830, is the earliest heroic epic of continental Germanic (Gmc.). Most likely composed during the reign of Louis the Pious (814–840), as evidenced in the prose preface A attributed to the *Heliand,* this New Testament epic (together with the Old Saxon Old Testament poem *Genesis*) fulfills the proselytizing intent of Louis the Pious while foiling his reputed destruction of heroic Germanic literature. For it is the unique achievement of the *Heliand* author(s) to have portrayed the life of Christ in the guise of a Germanic lord (OS *drohtin*) with a retinue of twelve thanes (OS *thegnos*) in the wooded environs (OS *waldos*) of northern Germany and the North Sea coast.

The language of the *Heliand* is not German. It is Saxon and, accordingly, genetically aligned with English and Frisian of a thousand years ago (Old English [OE] and Old Frisian [OF]). That the descendant languages of Old Saxon develop into what are termed Middle Low German and Modern Low German is indicative of the ever increasing linguistic interference from German in the course of the second millennium. Still, the indigenous, heterogeneous nature of Old Saxon cannot be denied.

Old Saxon's filiation with Frisian and English is considered by far older, originally allied in the Ingvaeonic (or North Sea Germanic) *Sprachbund* (group of languages) accountable for such isoglosses (linguistic markers) as the loss of nasal before *f, s,* and *þ,* with compensatory lengthening of the preceding vowel (e.g., OS/OE/OF *fîf* but OHG *fimf).* Another telltale North Sea Germanic isogloss reflected in the Old Saxon language is the syncretism (identicalness) of persons in the plural verb suffixes in both of the synthetic (not using helping verbs) tenses and moods; thus the present indicative *-ad,* the present subjunctive *-en,* the preterite indicative *-un,* and the preterite subjunctive *-in* for all three persons of the

plural verb. The rholess (lacking *r*) pronominal morphology (e.g., OS *he,* "he" and *mi,* "me," in contrast with OHG *er* and *mir,* respectively), as well as the syncretism of the OS dative *mi* with the accusative *mi* and the dative/accusative *us,* "us," *unk,* "us two," *thi,* "you" singular, *eu,* "you" plural, and *ink,* "you two," are Ingvaeonisms. A hallmark of North Sea Germanic is the masculine plural nominative/accusative noun morphology in *-s* (e.g., OS *waldos,* "forests").

On the other hand, Old High German interference in Old Saxon is repeatedly understood as such, rather than as being autochthonous (occurring independently). Thus, the Old Saxon *Heliand* manuscripts evince ambivalence, albeit inconsistently, with regard to the Ingvaeonic loss of nasal discussed above (e.g., *ôdran,* "other" [manuscript M] and *andran* [manuscript C]). Similarly, consider the accusative/dative case syncretism (e.g., *mik,* "me" [manuscript M] and *mi* [manuscript C]). Nowhere in the Old Saxon phonology is graphemic interference from Old High German so widely invoked as in the case of the Old Saxon digraphs (two letter spellings) <ie> and <uo>, frequently interpreted as mere graphemic representation of Gmc. (Germanic) *ê2 and *ô (*denotes unattested forms), which diphthongize (evolve into two vowels) in Old High German to *ie* and *uo,* respectively. The *Heliand* data are typically ambiguous. For the reflexes of Gmc. *ô, for example, manuscript M overwhelmingly yields <ô>, while manuscript C strongly prefers <uo>. However, collateral phonological strategies in manuscript C allow the extrapolation of a paralinguistic conditioner, *drawl,* which speaks to glided vowels, if not full diphthongs, for the digraphs of manuscript C.

Lexically the *Heliand* yields isoglosses shared with Old High German, such as OS *slutil ,* "key," OHG *sluzzil,* but OE *cæg,* OF *sletel* and *kei,* while OS *ant-, bilukan,* "unlock, lock," are cognate with OE *-lucan* and OF *-luka* rather than with OHG *-sliozan.* Old Saxon's bipartate nature is displayed in the semantics of, for example, the *Heliand* word *drom,* which incorporates both the OE gloss "joy" and the OHG gloss "dream," of OE *dream* and OHG *troum,* respectively.

The *Heliand* manuscripts C and M transmit most of the Bible epic; in addition three *Heliand* fragments are extant, namely manuscripts P, V, and S. The tenth-century manuscript C (Cotton Caligula, no. A. VII), housed in the British Library, London, consists of lines 1 through 5,968 with a few small lacunas; it is the most complete *Heliand* manuscript, numbering 165 leaves. The remaining four manuscripts are dated in the ninth century.

Manuscript M (no. Cgm. 25) is housed in the Bayerische Staatsbibliothek in Munich. More than one-sixth of the lines contained in manuscript C are missing from manuscript M, which contains 74 leaves and a half leaf that supplies the final lines 5,959–5,983 of the *Heliand*. Fragment P, formerly housed in Prague, now in the Museum für deutsche Geschichte in Berlin, consists of a single leaf. Numbered R56/2537, the manuscript P fragment contains lines 958–1006 of the *Heliand*. Lines 1279–1356 of the *Heliand* are recorded in one of four Vatican fragments, designated manuscript V (Palatinus Latinus 1447) and housed in the Vatican Library, Rome. (The remaining three manuscript V fragments comprise the Old Saxon *Genesis*, discussed below). The most recently discovered *Heliand* fragment, Manuscript S, was found in the Staatliche Bibliothek am Johannes-Turmeier-Gymnasium in Straubing. Manuscript S contains discontinuous portions from the *Heliand* fits V through IX. Now housed in the Bayerische Staatsbibliothek, Munich, the manuscript S fragment consists of eight leaf sides, with only the top and the bottom third of the first two and the last two sides preserved.

The provenance of the *Heliand* manuscripts and their possible (i.e., hypothesized) archetype are difficult to ascertain; the varying viewpoints are not only complex but also frequently contradictory. Possible sites targeted for the writing of the *Heliand* and/or its prototype are Werden on the Ruhr in the southwestern part of the Old Saxon territory, or Corvey on the Weser River farther to the east. Strong arguments are invoked for a Fulda origin, the influential and prestigious scriptorium on Old High German territory founded by Boniface, née Wynfrith of Wessex. Indeed, the *Heliand* poet may have moved between one or more of these scriptoria in the writing of manuscript M. Manuscript C is widely held to have been written in southern England, while the newly found manuscript S fragments, which share features with manuscript M, have been claimed for Werden. The richness of linguistic variation, which is amply evident in all parts of the grammar, is such that the *Heliand* manuscript evidence defies conclusive dialect identification.

The confusing nature of the *Heliand* data has led to speculation that the language of the *Heliand* represents a quasi-pidgin language, used for the purpose of proselytizing. On the one hand this is consonant with the conversion mission of the superstratum (invading group) Franks; on the other hand, it makes little sense if the ordinary Old Saxon native speaker had difficulties understanding a specialized level of usage. Alternately, the *Heliand* is viewed as a literary work representative of a more formal register that may have been the province of the more educated proselytizers. Transversing dialects and registers is time; a feature such as the conspicuous sequence *-cht*, which correlates with *-ft*, as in OS *craft:cracht*, "power," has long been viewed as a later (tenth century) western change in progress from *f* to *h*, in addition to possibly being representative of a formal register. The newly found manuscript S (dating from the ninth century) evinces exclusively *ht*. However, this may also be accountable to the limited remains of manuscript S.

The V manuscript, which delivers but one fragment of the *Heliand*, yields three fragments of an Old Saxon *Genesis*: verses 1–26a depicting the fall of Adam and Eve; verses 27–150 telling the story of Cain and Abel, and the Antichrist; verses 151–337 dealing with Abraham, Sodom, and Lot's salvation. The Old Saxon *Genesis* fragments, discovered by Karl Zangmeister in 1894 in the Vatican Library, confirmed the brilliant 1875 conjecture of Eduard Sievers that the so-called Old English *Later Genesis*, or *Genesis B*, is a translation of a lost Old Saxon *Genesis*. Sievers hypothesized an Old Saxon original *Genesis* purely on the basis of internal linguistic evidence comparing, for example, the OE *Genesis B gieng* (l. 626; 3rd person, singular, preterite), "went," with OS *Heliand geng*, rather than with expected OE *eode*.

The alliance of the Old Saxon *Genesis* with the *Heliand* is postulated via external evidence, specifically through their alleged attribution by a Latin prose preface, *Praefatio in librum antiquum lingua Saxonica conscriptum* (Preface to an old book written in the Saxon language), consisting of two parts, A and B, and of a Latin verse preface, *Versus de poeta et interprete huius codicis* (Verses about the poet and interpreter of this book), both of which provide a rationale for the composition of the *Heliand* and *Genesis* narrative epics. The prefaces also give clues to such questions as the time of composition (in or shortly after the reign of *Ludouicus piissimus Augustus* (August Louis the Most Pious) and to the personage of the author(s) of the *Heliand* and *Genesis*. Preface A reveals that the purpose of Louis in commissioning the Saxon poet (*de gente Saxonum*) was to make the Scriptures accessible to all his subjects, noneducated and educated alike (*non solum literis verum etiam illiteratis*).

A labyrinth of linguistic and textual problems is associated with the Latin prefaces, and not only with regard to their putative linkage to the *Heliand* and *Genesis*. The time, place, and author of the prefaces come into question; indeed, the problem of the legitimacy of the prefaces relative to the *Heliand* and *Genesis* occupies a large portion of the *Heliand's* textual history. Of the innumerable bits of evidence produced by the prefaces, preface A provides the word *vitteas* (fits) by which the *Heliand* sections or chapters are designated. In fact manuscript C confirms the existence of such running chapter heads. The word *vitteas* itself helps identify preface A as of early medieval origin rather than as belonging to the Renaissance. *Vitteas* is a contamination of the Gmc. root **fit* (posited Indo-European form **ped,* "foot") and the Latin (Lat.) feminine accusative plural desinence *as.* Genetically related to Old Norse (ON) *fitja,* "to tie the ends of yarn on a warp," and to OHG *fizza,* "a tied set of wound yarns," the metaphor of sectioning in weaving appears to fall within the semantic features of *vitteas.* This semantic trope extends to varying morphology such as ON *tattr,* which incorporates the features "thread, strand," and "section," and relates genetically with Latin *texere,* "weave." Notice also that English *rhapsody,* which can refer to a section of an epic poem, again derives from the weaving concept, Greek *rhaptein,* "to sew." The poet, *vates* of preface A, reoccurs in preface B (*Vatem*) and in the verse preface (*Vates*). Both the prose preface B and the verse preface, in particular the latter, exploit the Caedmonian metaphor of a naive but divinely inspired poet.

The *Heliand* and *Genesis* poet(s) are hardly surpassed in choice of relatively simple yet sublime words and phrases and their elegantly crafted interdigitation. The quality of the epics is profusely praised in preface B as surpassing all German poetry in its elegance (*cuncta Theudisca poëmata suo vincat decore*). All three Latin prefaces bear witness to the texts' sweet decor (Preface A: *sui decoris dulcedinem*); wealth of vocabulary, excellence of meaning (Preface B: *copia verborum . . . excellentia sensuum*); and skillful diction (Versus: *docta . . . carmina*). True to Germanic style (compare the kennings of Old Norse and Old English), a wealth of compounds infuses the Old Saxon Bible epics. Thus, for example, the Old Saxon copulative compound *gisunfader,* "son(s) and father," referring to the disciples John, James, and their father, as matched by the OHG *sunufaterungo* of the *Lay of Hildebrand,* attests to the astounding sophistication of the *Heliand* poet(s) in partaking of the rich bequeathment of heroic Germanic lexicon.

Similarly, the verse form of the *Heliand* and *Genesis* is Germanic in employing alliterative technique, for which the opening line of the *Heliand* can serve as a prototype: "*Mánega uuáron, the sia iro mód gespón*" (There were many whose mood impelled them.) The line is divided into two half lines by caesura. Each half line has two primary stressed syllables, of which two alliterate in *m,* the latter being the principal stave. Old Saxon allows a great number of nonprimary stressed syllables leading to extended lines, as well as alliteration of word classes other than the nominal and verbal classes more standard to Germanic alliterative verse. The verse form of the *Heliand* thus evinces modifications of paradigm Germanic alliterative poetry engendered by linguistic change, foremost the weakening of the intensity of Germanic stress, disabling alliteration and proliferating tertiary stressed syllables as found, for example, in vowel epenthesis (loss) and end-syllable weakening. Not at all to be regarded as diminishing their beauty, the interplay of the evolution of the Old Saxon language with the form of the Bible epics yields stunning pragmatic effects. Notice the loquaciousness of the Old Saxon Adam in the *Genesis* long line *Uuela, that thu nu Eua . . .* (Woe, that you now Eve) compared with the Old English *Genesis B Hwæt, ᚦ *u Eue . . .* (What, you Eve). Further, the numerical-architectonic structuring of the *Heliand* emulates an architectural feat reminiscent of a medieval stained glass window.

Beyond the phonology, morphology, and lexicon, the syntax infuses the Old Saxon Bible epics with powerful narrative strategies. In the linear syntax finite verb-first order, in particular with introductory word, is the unmarked order, thus (X)VSO (optional element X, verb V, subject S, object O). Frequently the X position is filled by a particle; the negative particle OS *ne* is constrained proclitically to the finite verb. The striking verb-first order in Germanic finds explanation in the concatenative (linking) function of the particles and, indeed, of the bare finite verb itself in advancing the epic narrative. The linguist Otto Behaghel's law, whereby semantically associated concepts are syntactically adjacent, together with his law of old information before new, in this case anaphoric suturing by the particle or verb with the previous discourse, intersect with Wilhelm Wackernagel's law of metrically light elements, of which the verb is one, placed to the left. Enhancing the epic narrative strategies of the linear syntax are those of the nonlinear syntax, that is, the morphology. The unmarked finite verb in the (X)VS order is a statal auxiliary (OS *werðan,* "become," *wesan,* "be," *hebbian,* "have") in syntagm with past participle. As past perfect forms, they function to portray action previous to an action more proximate in time, and within their own proposition they are imperfective and accordingly serve to background rather than to foreground the narrative action. The affective meaning is low-keyed, "laid-back," in contrast to proximate, on-the-spot action, yielding a continuative, conjunctive pragmatic effect produced by the interaction of the adjectival participle plus auxiliary and compounded by the latter's position in verb-first order.

Thus it is that the internal linguistic machinery of Old Saxon helps encode a Gospel harmony, in keeping with a popular Christian trope of the waning first millennium, which is also a heroic Bible epic deeply in synchrony with the essential native Germanic culture of the Old Saxons.

BIBLIOGRAPHY

Behaghel, Otto, and Burkhard Taeger, ed. *Heliand und Genesis*. 9th ed. Tübingen: Max Niemeyer, 1984.

Belkin, Johanna and Jürgen Meier. *Bibliographie zu Otfrid von Weißenburg und zur altsächsischen Bibeldichtung (Heliand und Genesis)*. Bibliographie zur deutschen Literatur des Mittelalters 7. Berlin: Schmidt, 1975.

Eichhoff, Jürgen, and Irmengard Rauch, ed. *Der Heliand*. Wege der Forschung 321. Darmstadt: Wissenschaftliche Buchgesellschaft, 1973.

Murphy, G. Ronald. *The Saxon Savior: The Germanic Transformation of the Gospel in the Ninth-Century Heliand*. Oxford: Oxford University Press, 1989.

———, trans. *The Heliand: The Saxon Gospel*. Oxford: Oxford University Press, 1992.

Rauch, Irmengard. *The Old Saxon Language: Grammar, Epic Narrative, Linguistic Interference*. Berkeley Models of Grammar 1. New York: Lang, 1992.

Irmengard Rauch

SEE ALSO
Bible; *Hildebrandslied;* Louis the Pious; Versification

Bible Translations, Dutch

During the Middle Ages, no complete translation of the Bible into the vernacular of the Low Countries was produced, although partial translations were made perhaps as early as the ninth century. From this period stem the so-called *Wachtendonckse Psalmen*, an interlinear translation of twenty-five Psalms into Old Dutch. They have only been preserved in a copy from the sixteenth century and are named after their last known possessor, the canon Arnoldus van Wachtendonck of Liège. Early Middle Dutch translations of the Psalter probably circulated, but have not come down to us.

Though not a Bible translation in the strict sense, the *Rijmbijbel* (or *Scolastica*) by the Flemish poet Jacob van Maerlant marks the beginning of the popularization of the Bible in the Dutch language. Jacob finished this abridged adaptation of Petrus Comestor's *Historia Scolastica* in 1271, adding an adaptation of Flavius Josephus's *De Bello Iudaïco* (The Jewish War) to it. This poem of almost thirty-five thousand lines in rhymed couplets was in all probability commissioned by a nobleman and intended to serve an audience of noble laymen. From the period 1270 to 1360 several witnesses of a Middle Dutch tradition of Bible translations have been preserved, yet the exact and relative chronology of these translations as well as their interdependencies are still a matter of debate. The so-called Southern Dutch translation of the New Testament is only preserved in six relatively young manuscripts (not all of them contain all the books of the New Testament), which has led to the opinion that this translation was produced around 1390. Yet twentieth-century research came up with arguments for a much earlier dating, perhaps even before Jacob's *Rijmbijbel*. This translation of the Gospels, letters of Saint Paul, canonical letters, Acts of the Apostles, and the Revelations sticks very close to the Latin text and contains many untranslated Latin words.

Perhaps at the end of the thirteenth century, a brilliant harmony (retelling) of the Gospels was made, which is usually referred to as the Liège diatesseron. This diatesseron, preserved completely in only one manuscript, was made by an anonymous monk from Flanders or Brabant. The main source was probably the Latin *Vita Christi* (in the version of a manuscript now at Fulda, Germany); its structure can be compared to Tatian's history of the life of Jesus. Additional sources were the *Glossa ordinaria* and Jacob's *Rijmbijbel*. The fact that it contained readings which were not corroborated by the Latin version of the Bible, or Vulgate, gives the work a particular place in the tradition of Middle Dutch Bible translations. The translator underpins his text with glosses from Gospel commentaries by Augustin, Jerome, Gregory the Great, and Bede. In the same period some other harmonies of the Gospels were made, which were more in accordance with the Vulgate. Some twenty manuscripts are known (though some just contain excerpts or have come down fragmentarily), in which sometimes features of the Liège diatesseron appear. A good representative of these Vulgate-oriented harmonies is the so-called *Diatesseron Harense*. Probably related to these harmonies is the *Amsterdam Lectionary,* a translation of the Gospel pericopes (liturgical readings). This lectionary belongs to a group of lectionaries and epistolaries that had their origin in (West) Flanders. A younger representative is the *Lectionary of Gruuthuse.* Of this group some seven manuscripts have been preserved. Often they contain other texts (e.g. a Middle Dutch translation of the *Credo* or a calendar) useful in liturgical practice, or a translation of a separate Bible book (e.g., the Apocalypse).

Around 1400 an anonymous translator (from Flanders or Brabant) produced the first Middle Dutch translation of the Psalms that actually has been preserved. Yet linguistic features of this translation, of which six manuscripts remain, testify to the fact that previously other translations of the Psalms must have circulated in the Low Countries. In the same period and region, the Apocalypse was translated. In one of the three manuscripts preserved, it is combined with the Psalms translation mentioned above. Another manuscript (Paris, Bibliothéque National, manuscript no. Néerl. 3) occupies a special place in the tradition because it contains twenty-three magnificent, full-page miniatures.

In the middle of the fourteenth century the so-called Bible Translator of 1360 started his activities as a translator. This anonymous monk, most probably from the Carthusian abbey of Herne (some thirty miles southwest of Brussels), is responsible for a great number of Middle Dutch translations of important Latin texts. He derives his name from his second translation, a "history bible" (retelling), which he made at the request of Jan Tay, a citizen of Brussels. With the Vulgate as his main source he translated the Pentateuch, Joshua, Judges, Ruth, 1 and 2 Samuel, 1 and 2 Kings, Tobias, Daniel, Judith, Esther, Job, and 1 and 2 Maccabees. From Petrus Comestor's *Historia Scolastica* he drew Ezekiel, Habakkuk, Ezra, and Nehemiah. For the New Testament he used an older Middle Dutch harmony of the Gospels and translated the *Actus apostolorum* from the Vulgate. The first part of this history bible was completed on June 12, 1360, the second part on June 23, 1361. In some manuscripts of this history bible we also find the texts *Cyrus, Jan Hyrcanus* (III Maccabees), and *Destruxie van Jerusalem* (Destruction of Jerusalem); as well as *Alexanders Historie,* which has led some scholars to believe that the Bible Translator translated or adapted these texts too for inclusion in his history bible. In his translation, the Bible Translator used additional sources such as the *Glossa ordinaria,* Jacob's *Rijmbijbel,* and the *Bible historiale* of Guiard des Moulins. Later he translated some parts again, and adding new translations of other parts—Isaiah (before 1384), Jere-

miah, Lamentations, Ezekiel, Proverbs, Ecclesiastes, Song of Songs, The Wisdom of Solomon, Ecclesiasticus (Jezus Sirach), and the Psalms—all with the Vulgate as his source, he almost came to produce a complete Bible in the vernacular. This history bible was widespread, as more than thirty preserved manuscripts witness. Remarkable features of his work as a translator are his reflections on the difficulties he met in translating the Vulgate (e.g., in the prologue to the Pentateuch) and his habit of outlining glosses or quotations from his additional sources with a rubric, thus explicitly separating them from his main text.

Around 1400 a second (North Dutch) history bible, the so-called *Noordnederlandse historiebijbel,* was made in the county of Holland. The main source was the Vulgate, yet in composition the *Historia scolastica* by Petrus Comestor was followed. It contains Pentateuch, Joshua, Judges, Ruth, 1 and 2 Samuel, 1 and 2 Kings, Tobias, Godolias (an extract from Jeremiah), Daniel, Judith, Ezra, and Maccabees, with interpolations of secular materials (e.g., a history of Alexander). Of this history bible only seven manuscripts remain, six of which were written by the same scribe.

At the end of his life, the founder of the Devotio moderna, Geert Grote (1340–1384), made a book of hours, for which he translated fifty-four Psalms completely and six Psalms partially. Probably at the beginning of the fifteenth century a follower of Grote continued his translation and completed what is now known as the *Psalms and Cantica in the Standard Redaction of the Modern Devotion.* Generally it is assumed that this continuator was Johan Scutken (d. 1423), a cleric from the convent of Windesheim. Of this standard redaction, the third complete Psalms translation in Middle Dutch, fifty-six manuscripts are known (although some are now lost or damaged).

The same Johan Scutken was responsible for the so-called Northern Dutch translation of the New Testament, and this attribution is of a much greater certainty. He must have made this translation—which contains the four Gospels, letters of Saint Paul, canonical letters, Acts of the Apostles, and the Apocalypse, but also the pericopes (readings) from the Old Testament—between 1387 and 1391. The great number of manuscripts (more than 120) which contain it completely or partially testifies to the popularity of this translation. Scutken's translation formed the basis for several lectionaries (readers) and harmonies of the Gospels.

A separate branch of the tradition of Middle Dutch Bible translations is formed by the so-called Utrecht

Bibles. In some thirty manuscripts, large parts of the history bible by the Bible Translator of 1360 were combined with parts of Scutken's translation (especially the letters of the Apostles and the Apocalypse) and the *Psalms and Cantica in the Standard Redaction of the Modern Devotion.* Several of the manuscripts are lavishly illuminated.

The first printed book in Middle Dutch was a Bible, printed in Delft in 1477, by Jacob Jacobsoen van der Meer and Mauricius Yemantsoen van Middelborch. It was an edition in two volumes of the Old Testament (but without the Psalms). They used the translation of the Bible Translator of 1360, even printed his prologue, but ommitted his glosses and his interpolations from Comestor's *Historia Scolastica.* The books Chronicles, Ezekiel, and the lesser prophets were translated especially for this printed Bible. A complete printed Bible was not to be printed until the Reformation.

BIBLIOGRAPHY

Berg, Marinus K. A. van den. *De Noordnederlandse Historiebijbel.* Hilversum: Verloren, 1998.

Biemans, Jos A. A. M. *Middelnederlandse bijbelhandschriften.* Leiden: Brill, 1984.

Bruin, Cebus C. de. "Bespiegelingen over de 'Bijbelvertaler van 1360'. Zijn milieu, werk en persoon." *Nederlands Archief voor Kerkgeschiedenis* 48 (1967–1968): 39–59; 49 (1968–1969): 135–154; 50 (1969–1970): 11–41; 51 (1970–1971): 16–41.

———. *Middelnederlandse vertalingen van het Nieuwe Testament.* Groningen: Wolters, 1935.

Bruin, Cebus C. de, Christoph Gerhardt, and Jo G. Heymans, eds. *Corpus Sacrae Scripturae Neerlandicae Medii Aevi.* 20 vols. Leiden: Brill, 1970–1984 [editions of most of the translations named in this article].

Bruin, Cebus C. de, and F. G. M. Broeyer. *De Statenbijbel en zijn voorgangers.* Haarlem: Nederlands Bijbelgenootschap; Brussels: Belgisch Bijbelgenootschap, 1993.

Coun, Theo. "De Zuidnederlandse vertalingen van de vier evangeliën." In *Boeken voor de eeuwigheid: Middelnederlands geestelijk proza,* ed. Thom Mertens et al. Amsterdam: Prometheus, 1993, pp. 87–107 and 395–400.

Gysseling, Maurits, ed. *Corpus van Middelnederlandse teksten.* Reeks II: Literaire handschriften, vol. 3, *Rijmbijbel/tekst.* Leiden: Nijhoff, 1983 [Jacob van Maerlant].

Ebbinge Wubben, and Claudius Henricus. *Over Middelnederlandsche vertalingen van het Oude Testament.* *Bouwstoffen voor de geschiedenis der Nederlandsche Bijbelvertaling.* The Hague: Nijhoff, 1903.

Geert H. M. Claassens

SEE ALSO
Bible; Bible Epic, Saxon; Bible Translator of 1360, Dutch; *Devotio Moderna;* Jacob van Maerlant; Literature, Dutch

Bible Translator of 1360, Dutch (fl. mid-14th c.)

This anonymous monk, most probably from the Carthusian abbey of Herne (some thirty miles southwest of Brussels), is one of the most enigmatic figures of Middle Dutch literature. His biography can to some extent be deduced from his works: his first known translation dates from 1358, the last from 1388. He is called the "Bible Translator of 1360" because in that year he finished the first part of his *Historijenibel* (history Bible), a narrative retelling of the Bible. In the thirty years of his activity he did not write any original work as far as we know, but translated a great number of important Latin texts into Middle Dutch, thus playing an important role in intellectual, spiritual, and devotional developments in the Low Countries during the fourteenth century.

The attribution of texts to the Bible Translator is based on diverse criteria. In the prologues added to his translations, he sometimes mentions texts he already translated or wants to translate in the future. In these prologues (or in colophons) he occasionally gives statements of a more personal nature, concerning his health, or mentions the work's date of completion. His vocabulary shows some idiosyncrasies and his translation technique has its peculiarities (although it is not unique in itself), and reveals a thorough command of Latin. On these criteria scholars have come to a consensus concerning his oeuvre.

In 1357 and the beginning of 1358 he translated the *Legenda aurea* (Golden Legend) of Jacobus de Voragine. In a colophon he gives January 10, 1357 as the day of completion, but because the Bible Translator in all probability used the Easter style, the dates of all the works he completed between January 1 and Easter must be revised. The *Gulden legende* is the first Middle Dutch translation of this hagiographic collection, but a second was soon to follow in the northern parts of the Low Countries (which dates from circa 1400). Of both this translation and the second, more than one hundred manuscripts are known (some only fragmentary); some contain sections from both translations.

His second work was the production of his history Bible, which he made at the request of Jan Tay, a citizen of Brussels. With the Vulgate (Latin version) as his main source, he translated the following books: Pentateuch, Joshua, Judges, Ruth, Samuel 1 and 2, Kings 1 and 2, Tobias, Daniel, Judith, Esther, Job, and 1 and 2 Maccabees. From the twelfth-century writer Petrus Comestor's *Historia Scolastica* (Scholastic History) he took Ezekiel, Habakkuk, Ezra, and Nehemiah. For the New Testament he used an older Middle Dutch harmony (or compilation) of the Gospels and translated the Acts (*Actas apostolorum*) from the Vulgate. The first part of this history Bible was completed on June 12, 1360, the second part on June 23, 1361. In some manuscripts we also find the texts *Cyrus, Jan Hyrcanus* (Maccabees III), *Destruxie van Jerusalem* (Destruction of Jerusalem) and *Alexanders Historie* (Story of Alexander), which led some scholars to believe that the Bible Translator also translated or adapted these texts for inclusion in his history Bible. In his translation, the Bible Translator used additional sources such as a Latin glossary (*Glossa ordinaria*), the Dutch *Rijmbijbel* (Rhymed Bible, or *Scolastica*) of Jacob van Maerlant, and the French *Bible historiale* (History Bible) of Guiard des Moulins. Later he retranslated some parts and, adding new translations of other sections, all with the Vulgate as his source, he ended up producing a nearly complete Bible in the vernacular. This text was widespread, as more than thirty preserved manuscripts attest. Around 1400, a second history Bible was produced in the county of Holland which was made virtually independent of the Bible Translation of 1360. Of it, only seven manuscripts remain.

On request of Lodewijc Thonijs, a noble citizen of Brussels, the Bible Translator produced the first Middle Dutch version of the Benedictine Rule (*Regula Sancti Benedicti*). This translation, *Benedictus regule,* was completed on or around January 13, 1373. The colophon states that Lodewijc Thonijs intended it as a gift to his sister Maria Thonijs, a Benedictine nun in the convent of Vorst, as a means to better acquaint the nuns with the rule. In this translation some flaws occur, which makes it quite certain that the Bible Translator did not belong to the Benedictine order. Fourteen manuscripts of this translation survive.

Sente Gregorius omeliën op de evangeliën (St. Gregory's Sermons on the Gospels) was completed in Lent of 1381, a translation of the Latin *Homiliae XL in Evangelia*

(Forty Sermons on the Gospels) of Gregory the Great (ca. 540–604). Of this translation some seventeen manuscripts are known, as well as two manuscripts containing only excerpts. The Bible Translator altered the order of the sermons from the Latin manuscripts.

A translation of the *Collationes patrum* (learned commentaries on religious topics) of Johannes Cassianus (ca. 360–435) was finished on January 5th, 1383, also on request of Lodewijc Thonijs (he donated a copy of it to the Benedictine convent to which his sister belonged). The Bible Translator did not give a translation of the full text; he omitted *collationes* 13 (on free will and grace) and 17 (on essentials and accidentia in spiritual life). The semi-pelagianistic (refuting the notion of original sin) tendencies in these *collationes* were apparently well understood by the Bible Translator, and he thus deemed these parts to be spiritually dangerous for the "simple" folk, the *illiterati,* for whom he was translating. Two manuscripts have come down to us, yet both are lacking *collationes* 1–12. Cassianus's *Collationes patrum* were to be translated a second time in Middle Dutch, at the beginning of the fifteenth century, by an anonymous translator within the circles of the "New Piety" (*Devotio moderna*), to which Cassianus's text was very dear. Remarkably enough, one of the manuscripts combines *collationes* 16 and 18–24 in the translation of the Bible Translator with *collationes* 1–14 and 17 in the second translation.

Then he returned to the Bible, translating Isaiah, Jeremiah, Lamentations, and Ezekiel from the Vulgate. The date of completion of these books of the Bible is unknown, but Isaiah must have been completed before 1384.

Bonaventura's *Lignum vitae,* a mystical-ascetic treatise, was translated as *Vanden houte slevens,* completed on August 2, 1386. Of this translation three manuscripts and an excerpt remain. In the colophon of the most important manuscript (Brussels, Koninklijke Bibliotheek, 15087–15090, fol. 154ra), the Latin text is wrongly attributed to the Carthusian theologian Henry of Balma.

On March 1, 1387 he completed *Der minnen gaert,* a translation of the *Stimulus amoris* by Pseudo-Bonaventura. In the colophon of the most important of the two preserved manuscripts (Brussels, Koninklijke Bibliotheek, 15087–15090, fol. 129ra), the Latin text is also wrongly attributed to the same Henry of Balma.

His *Sente Gregorius Dyalogus* was completed on November 4, 1388, a translation of the saints' lives (*Libri IV dialogorum de vita et miraculis patrum Italicorum et de aeternitate animarum)* by Gregory the Great. Four copies of this translation remain. It is thought to be his last, because in the prologue the Bible Translator complains about his health and old age. A second translation, from within circles of the Modern Devotion, was made around 1400 and had far greater dissemination.

These are the translations that can be dated, but some others cannot. It is still plausible that the undated works were produced between 1361 and 1372 and 1373 and 1380. These are:

1. A translation of Proverbs, Ecclesiastes, Song of Songs, The Wisdom of Solomon, and Ecclesiasticus *(Jezus Sirach)* from the Vulgate.

2. A separate translation of the Psalms after the Vulgate.

3. *Der vader boec,* a translation of the *Historia monachorum in Aegypto* (ca. 412) by Thimotheus of Alexandria (book 2 of the *Vitae Patrum*), with additional saints' lives from book 1 of the *Vitae Patrum* and other hagiographical texts. As the Bible Translator in the prologue refers to his translations of the Old and New Testament, this must have been done after 1361, but before his translation of the *Verba Seniorum.* Seven manuscripts with the complete translation have been preserved, but additionally some ten manuscripts are known to contain parts of it.

4. A translation of the so-called *Verba Seniorum,* which is books 5 and 6 of the famous *Vitae Patrum.* This translation, entitled *Der heiligher vadere collacien,* is also undated but surely came after *Der vader boec.* A first comparison with the *Verba seniorum* as edited in Migne's *Patrologia Latina* shows the Bible Translator either reshuffled the *dicta* in his source or used a hitherto unknown version of the Latin text. Five manuscripts with this translation have come down to us. A second Middle Dutch translation was soon made, probably by Wermbold van Buscop, a kindred soul of Geert Groote, founder of the *Devotio moderna.*

5. *Vier omeliën van Sinte Bernardus op dat evangelie Missus est Gabriël angelus* (Four Sermons by Saint Bernard on the Gospel words "An angel, Gabriel, is sent"), a translation of Saint Bernard's Latin work of the same title, *Homliae IV de laudibus Virginis Matris super verba Evangelii Missus est angelus Gabriel.* Four manuscripts are known of this translation, which has scarcely been investigated.

6. *Homiliae in Ezechielem prophetam* (Sermons on the Prophet Ezekiel) by Gregory the Great. In the pro-

logue to his translation of Jeremiah, the Bible Translator explicitly states his intention to translate this work, but no manuscript of the translation has as yet been found. Of some other translations the attribution to the Bible Translator is still a matter of dispute.

The preserved manuscripts show that most of the Bible Translator's texts were widespread throughout the Low Countries. The fact that some texts were copied alongside translations made by members of the *Devotio moderna* testifies to the profound influence that the Bible Translator had on their spiritual development. Why, especially in this environment, so many of the texts mentioned above were retranslated remains a subject for further research.

Remarkable is the fact that the Bible Translator made some of his translations at the behest of certain citizens of Brussels. Such an involvement of laymen in the dissemination of sacred literature is far from common in a time when the clergy jealously guarded its monopoly as mediators between God and His revelation and the great mass of nonclerics. In many prologues this issue is addressed, with the Bible Translator complaining about the opposition he meets from the clergy. Yet we must not see the Bible Translator as a precursor of the Reformation: in a time when the Church was in upheaval and clerical discipline both within and outside of the monasteries waned, he merely wanted to meet the needs of the laymen—as well as that of the illiterate members of the clergy—for spiritual guidance, by providing vernacular versions of important religious and devotional texts.

The Bible Translator has had an extraordinary influence on the development of Middle Dutch as a literary language. Translating *uten herden swaren ghewapenden Latine te Dietschen* ("from the very difficult Latin into Dutch," cited in the colophon to Cassianus's *Collationes*) was not a simple task, as the Bible Translator was confronted with syntactic and lexical differences between Latin and Middle Dutch. This often resulted in an extension of the semantic realm of Middle Dutch words or in slightly adjusted use of Latin terms (with or without an explicative gloss). Very important are his explicit reflections on the technique of translating, as in the prologue to the Pentateuch translation, which reveal him to be a careful scholar, well aware of the difficulties of his task.

BIBLIOGRAPHY

Biemans, Jos A. A. M. *Middelnederlandse bijbelhandschriften.* Leiden: Brill, 1984.

Bruin, Cebus C. de. "Bespiegelingen over de 'Bijbelvertaler van 1360'. Zijn milieu, werk en persoon." *Nederlands Archief voor Kerkgeschiedenis* 48 (1967–1968): 39–59; 49 (1968–1969): 135–154; 50 (1969–1970): 11–41; 51 (1970–1971): 16–41.

———, ed. *Corpus Sacrae Scripturae Neerlandicae Medii Aevi.* Series Maior, Tomus I, 1–3. Leiden: Brill, 1977–1978.

Claassens, Geert H. M. "The *Dialogues* of Gregory the Great in Middle Dutch Literature." In ed. Rolf Bremer and David F. Johnson, *Gregory the Great and the Germanic World* [forthcoming].

Coun, Theo. "De Zuidnederlandse vertalingen van de vier evangeliën." In *Boeken voor de eeuwigheid. Middelnederlands geestelijk proza,* ed. Thom Mertens et al. Amsterdam: Prometheus, 1993, pp. 87–107 and 395–400.

———. "De lokalisering van de Bijbelvertaler van 1360." In *Lingua Theodisca. Beiträge zur Sprach- und Literaturwissenschaft. Jan Goossens zum 65. Geburtstag,* ed. Vranke Callaert, et al. Vol. 1. Münster: LIT-verlag, 1995, pp. 153–161.

———, ed. *De oudste Middelnederlandse vertaling van de Regula S. Benedicti.* Hildesheim: Gerstenberg, 1980 [Benedictine Rule in Middle Dutch, introd. in English].

Ruh, Kurt. *Bonaventura deutsch. Ein Beitrag zur deutschen Franziskaner-Mystik und -Scholastik.* Bern: Francke, 1956 [on the *Lignum vitae* trans., pp. 159–163].

Scheurkogel, Leonard. "De overlevering van de Noord- en Zuidnederlandse *Legenda aurea.*" *Verslagen en Mededelingen van de Koninklijke Academie voor Nederlandse Taal- en Letterkunde* (1997): 60–118.

Geert H. M. Claassens

SEE ALSO
Bible; Bible Translations, Dutch; *Devotio Moderna;* Saints' Lives, Dutch

Billunger

Historians recognize two noble lines associated with the family name Billung (German plural Billunger). The "Older Billungs" were active in the time of Charlemagne (ca. 742–814) in the regions of Ostfalen (Eastphaelia) and Hessia, while the "Younger Billungs" first came to prominence in the reign of Saxon king Otto I (936–973) with the brothers Wichmann I and Hermann I. The precise genealogical relationship between these two lines is not known.

The older of the two brothers and a nobleman of excellent reputation in the eyes of the historian Widukind of Corvey, Wichmann I (d. 944) expanded Billung territorial holdings on the middle Weser, Lippe, and lower Rhine Rivers through his marriage to Frideruna, sister of Queen Matilda, wife of King Henry I (r. 919–936). When King Otto I (r. 936–973) passed him over for a position of command on Saxony's eastern frontier and chose his younger brother Hermann, the elder Billung rebelled briefly against the king, but was eventually and permanently reconciled with him. Wichmann I's son, Wichmann II, died young (d. 967), a rebel against the king, an outlaw, and a figure who fascinated his contemporaries.

Hermann I (d. 973) was declared *princeps militiae* (prince of the military) by Otto I in 936 and was charged with leading military expeditions and given oversight *(procuratio)* of Saxony in the king's absence. Through the opportunities provided by his command of the Slavic frontier on the lower Elbe, Hermann greatly expanded the patrimony of his branch of the Billungs in the Bardengau in lower Saxony and on the middle Weser. During the life of his son Bernhard I (d. 1011), the ducal title of the Billungs came to mark the family's own position of leadership among the Saxon nobility rather than a royal office (such as *princeps militiae*) with determinate powers and privileges. The change in the title means that the role of the Billungs, now the most highly regarded Saxon dynasty, had switched from king's representative to the tribe to the tribe's representative to the king.

In the time of Duke Bernhard II (d. 1059) the Billungs lost their favored position at the Saxon royal court, a decline in status accelerated by the increasing strife among the dukes, the bishops of Paderborn, and the archbishops of Hamburg-Bremen. The Billungs' relation to the German emperors worsened rapidly during the rule of Archbishop Adalbert (1043–1072), who attempted to use his unique influence at the royal court to minimize, if not eliminate, the ducal family's power in the region. This hostility continued under Bernhard II's son Duke Ordulf (1059–1072), further undermining, at least in part, the political preeminence of the Billung dukes within the Saxon nobility. Thus, while the Billung dukes participated in the first phases of the Saxon War (1073–1088) against Henry IV, they were not its leaders, and eventually Ordulf's son, Duke Magnus (1059–1106) went over to the side of Henry IV. Dying without male heirs, Magnus was the last Billung duke. King Henry V (r. 1106–1125) divided the Billung patrimony between the Welf and Ascanian houses into which the Billungs had married. He conferred the Billungs' ducal title, however, upon Lothar III of Supplinburg.

BIBLIOGRAPHY

Althoff, Gerd. "Die Billunger in der Salierzeit." In *Die Salier und das Reich*, Vol. 1, *Salier, Adel und Reichsverfassung,* ed. S. Weinfurter. Sigmaringen: Thorbecke, 1991, pp. 309–330 [extensive bibliography].

Freytag, H.-J. *Die Herrschaft der Billunger in Sachsen.* Studien und Vorarbeiten zum historischen Atlas Niedersachsens 20. Göttingen: Vandenhoeck and Ruprecht, 1951.

Jordan, Karl. "Herzogtum und Stamm in Sachsen während des Hohen Mittelalters." *Niedersächsisches Jahrbuch für Landesgeschichte* 30 (1958): 1–27; rpt. in Karl Jordan, *Ausgewählte Aufsätze zur Geschichte des Mittelalters.* Kieler Historische Studien 29. Stuttgart: Klett-Cotta, 1980.

William North

SEE ALSO

Carolingians; Charlemagne; Henry I; Henry IV; Otto I; Saxon War; Welfs; Widukind of Corvey

Birth, Marriage, Burial

Although statistical evidence to support the claim is almost completely lacking, childbirth in medieval Germany among all levels of society probably did not differ substantially from the experience of birth elsewhere in Europe. Labor was dangerous for both mother and child, and high rates of maternal and infant mortality can be assumed. Normally, midwives attended a woman in labor; physicians were present in rare circumstances, and only when mother and child were in grave danger. While fictional, the scene of Herzeloyde's labor described in Wolfram von Eschenbach's *Parzival* was probably not uncommon in real life. Herzeloyde lapsed into a coma-like state for some time while pregnant, but those around her would not or could not help her. Only a "wise old man" knew the "proper" remedy of forcing her teeth apart and splashing water into her mouth to revive her. Having endured this questionable procedure, she barely survived big-boned Parzival's birth. In fact, cesarean section to save the life of both mother and child

does not seem to have been practiced until the later Middle Ages.

Complex economic, legal, and political issues affected marriage. A woman was transferred from the *munt,* or protection, of her father to that of her husband, who was obligated to compensate the father. The morning after the wedding, the groom also traditionally gave his bride a gift, or *Morgengabe.* A dowry given by the woman's family was not as substantial or important as the man's payments during most of the German Middle Ages. Church law insisted that all baptized Christians had the right to contract marriage regardless of social status, but also forbade marriages within prohibited degrees of kinship. The former right was often in practice restricted by lords who did not want unfree dependents—which included peasant serfs as well as powerful ministerials—to marry outside of a lordship. The latter prohibition was subject to sometimes spectacular violations, such as the marriage of Otto of Hammerstein and Irmingard in the early eleventh-century Rhineland. The attempt to dissolve their marriage against their will led to a dispute involving king, archbishops, pope, and other aristocrats.

Among aristocrats at least, burial was an important means of forging and preserving family identity. The preservation of liturgical and spiritual *memoria* (memorial records) was not left to chance, and numerous donations to religious communities were tied to a donor's right to be buried in a church so benefited. By the twelfth century (and anticipated by the Salian dynastic necropolis at Speyer), many elite families (such as the Welfs) had begun to designate burial sites within family monasteries on ancestral family land. This has often been taken as evidence of an emerging consciousness of the family as patrilineal dynasty rather than broad kin-group characterized by both paternal and maternal inheritance. Although this thesis remains controversial, members of the medieval German elite were increasingly specific about their wishes concerning place of burial. One striking example is that of Arnold II of Wied, archbishop of Cologne from 1151 to 1156, who endowed the splendid double-chapel Schwarzrheindorf as his burial site.

BIBLIOGRAPHY

Bergdolt, K. "Schwangerschaft und Geburt." In *Lexikon des Mittelalters,* vol. 7. Munich: LexMA Verlag, 1995, cols. 1612–1616.

Ehlers, Joachim. "Magdeburg, Rom, Aachen, Bamberg: Grablege des Königs und Herrschaftsverständnis in ottonischer Zeit." In *Otto III–Heinrich II. Eine Wende,* ed. Bernd Schneidmüller and Stefan Weinfurter. Mittelalter-Forschungen, vol. 1. Sigmaringen: Jan Thorbecke, 1997.

Freed, John. *The Counts of Falkenstein: Noble Self-Consciousness in Twelfth-Century Germany.* Transactions of the American Philosophical Society, vol. 74, pt. 6, 1984. Philadelphia: American Philosophical Society, 1984.

———. *Noble Bondsmen: Ministerial Marriages in the Archdiocese of Salzburg, 1100–1343.* Ithaca, N.Y.: Cornell University Press, 1995.

Leyser, Karl J. *Rule and Conflict in an Early Medieval Society: Ottonian Saxony.* Bloomington: Indiana University Press, 1979.

Streich, Gerhard. *Burg und Kirche während des deutschen Mittelalters: Untersuchungen zur Sakraltopographie von Pfalzen, Burgen und Herrensitze.* Vorträge und Forschungen, Sonderband 29. 2 vols. Sigmaringen: Jan Thorbecke Verlag, 1984.

Jonahtan Rotondo-McCord

SEE ALSO
Cologne, Archdiocese; Family; Ministerials; Salians; Speyer; Welfs; Wolfram von Eschenbach

Block Book

A fifteenth- and early-sixteenth-century book whose pages, both text and picture, are printed from wood blocks on paper (xylography). Made mainly in the Netherlands and in Germany, block books contain texts of religious, moral, and theological subjects, printed on only one side of the page. The blank backs were often pasted together to provide a continuous sequence. The pictures serve to make visible the story told by the less important short texts accompanying them, in contrast to illuminated manuscripts, in which the text dominates. Three different combinations of text and picture are found: (1) picture and text together on one page, (2) text and picture facing one another on two pages, and (3) text alone or with small pictures integrated into the text. Although it was earlier assumed that the block books preceded the invention of printing, a study of the watermarks of the paper on which they were printed showed that the most popular first editions were printed after 1460 and thus were produced simultaneously with incunabula. Most of the texts, such as the typological *Biblia Pauperum* (Paupers' Bible) and *Speculum humanae salva-*

tionis (Mirror of Human Salvation), *Revelation,* or *Antichrist,* were well-known in manuscript form. Didactic texts, such as the *Ars moriendi* (On the Art of Dying), *Canticum canticorum* (Song of Songs), *Defensorium virginitatis Mariae* (Defense of the Virgin Mary), and *Ars memorandi* (The Art of Memory), were also numerous. In contrast, there are relatively few secular texts. Although they were less expensive than handmade manuscripts, block books were also luxury items available only to the nobility and well-situated citizens, or to teachers or clergy who used them in their work. Since most were written in the vernacular, they were apparently intended for people who did not read Latin.

BIBLIOGRAPHY
Mertens, Sabinet, Elke Purpas, and Cornelia Schneider. *Blockbücher des Mittelalters: Bilderfolgen als Lektüre.* Mainz: P. von Zabern, 1991.

Stevenson, Allen. "The Quincentennial of Netherlandish Blockbooks." *British Museum Quarterly* 31 (1966–1967): 83–87.

Marta O. Renger

SEE ALSO
Armenbibel; Ars Moriendi; Bookmaking and Production; Latin Language; Ludolf of Saxony; Manuscripts, Painting and Production; Printmaking

Boethius (ca. 480–ca. 525 C.E.)

Anicius Manlius Severinus Boethius was a Roman philosopher whose Latin translations and commentaries on Aristotle, Plato, and the Greek Neoplatonists introduced the work of these thinkers to western Europe. He was a member of a prominent Roman Christian family and possibly educated in Alexandria and/or Athens. In 510 he was appointed Roman consul and in 522 Master of the Offices in the court of Theoderic the Great, but he soon fell from favor: found guilty of treason and sorcery, he was sentenced to death. Imprisoned and awaiting execution, he wrote *De consolatione philosophiae* (*The Consolation of Philosophy*), a Platonic dialogue in the form of a Menippian satire (after the Greek writer Menippus, third century B.C.E.), as an attempt to give transcendent meaning to his fall.

His works, rediscovered in the ninth century by Alcuin in the Carolingian empire, under Alfred the Great in Britain, helped determine the development of western European civilization. Boethian concepts of education, explained in his two surviving treatises on the *quadrivium* (a term he invented, designating four of the seven liberal arts), defined the structure and content of the monastic school system. His translations and commentaries on Aristotle, two of which were translated into Old German at St. Gall by Notker Labeo, introduced Aristotelian logic to the West. These and his theological tractates appealed primarily to scholars. There is some evidence that the *De institutione musica,* the primary authority on music theory throughout the Middle Ages, also influenced medieval literature, most notably Gottfried von Straßburg's *Tristan.*

The *Consolation of Philosophy* was undoubtedly the best-known and most influential work of Boethius. Accompanied by glosses and commentaries and used as a textbook in monastery schools, it directly and indirectly influenced the language, style, thought, and imagery of later generations. Notker Labeo and others translated it into German. Meister Eckhart quoted it in his homilies. Its image of the goddess Fortuna with her wheel recurred frequently in secular literature and art. Its influence on medieval English literature is well known, but investigation of the nature and extent of its influence on medieval German literature is just beginning.

BIBLIOGRAPHY

Bieler, Ludwig. *Anicii Manlii Severini Boethii Philosophiae Consolatio.* Turnhout: Brepols, 1957.

Pickering, F. P. *Augustinus oder Boethius?* 2 vols. Berlin: Erich Schmidt, 1967, 1976.

Ruth H. Firestone

SEE ALSO

Alcuin; Gottfried von Straßburg; Meister Eckhart; Notker Labeo; Sankt Gall

Boethius, Dutch

The Middle Dutch tradition of Boethius's (d. 524) *De consolatione philosophiae* (*The Consolation of Philosophy*) is clearly a phenomenon of the later Middle Ages, and probably not without reason. In the thirteenth century, Jacob van Maerlant translated minor parts of this work in his *Spieghel historiael* (Mirror of History). But it was not until the second half of the fifteenth century that the complete text of the *Consolatio* was translated into Middle Dutch. And it is striking that in that period, almost simultaneously, two full Middle Dutch translations were carried out.

Probably the oldest integral translation is from Jacob Vilt, a goldsmith in Bruges. He completed his Middle Dutch translation of the *Consolatio* in 1466. The autograph is not preserved, but we have one manuscript copied in 1470 by Drubbel (Utrecht, University Library, manuscript no. 1335), hitherto unedited. Vilt's translation is only partly based on the original Latin. In the prologue he mentions that an Old French translation of Jean de Meun was used—in fact a copy of a pseudo de Meun. As in the Boethian and pseudo de Meun traditions, Vilt translates into both prose and verse. In marginal glosses he locates his commentary (especially on passages in prose): he elucidates ideas, historical persons, and images. In general, his translation is detailed and comprehensive. As for the poems, much attention is paid to their form. Vilt uses various rhyme schemes, following in the so-called *Rederijkers* (Dutch poets' society) tradition.

The second integral translation, the so-called *Ghent Boethius,* is preserved in an impressive yet hitherto unedited incunable (book printed before 1500). It was printed by Arend de Keysere in 1485 in Ghent. Over fifty copies of this incunable have survived. It is printed onto 360 large folios, and is set in two Gothic type fonts. Some copies have miniatures. It contains the complete Latin text of the *Consolatio,* a Middle Dutch translation in verse and prose, and an extensive Middle Dutch commentary, probably the most extensive commentary comprised on the *Consolatio* during the Middle Ages. Translation and commentary were written sometime between 1444 and 1477. In the incunable, the text of the *Consolatio* is divided into short fragments, each fragment followed by its Middle Dutch translation and the commentary relating to the fragment. The author is unknown, but it is assumed that he was from Ghent because of the dialect coloring of the translation and the commentary. In the prologue the author explains his method of translation, especially regarding the meters. Because of the rules he imposed on himself—no more lines than the Latin verses, no more than ten syllables per line—he was not always able to translate the complete contents of the Latin poems. However, he usually translates the missing parts in the commentary, where he offers the complete text by means of paraphrase. He seems to have tried to translate in a faithful way, although that did not prevent him from adding some obvious Christian accents to his translation. The commentary is a peculiar compilation of all kinds of explanations ranging from textual analysis to elucidations on topics only remotely concerning the actual text of the *Consolatio.* These explanations are accompanied by citations from the Bible and from a wide range of classical and medieval authorities. It is notable that hardly any contemporary authorities are cited. The main source of the commentary is the Latin commentary of Renier of St. Trudon, probably the rector of the Latin school in Mechelen (ca. 1370). This Latin commentary is preserved in four manuscripts.

BIBLIOGRAPHY

Angenent, M. P. "Het Gentse Boethiuscommentaar en Renier van Sint-Truiden." *Tijdschrift voor Nederlandse Taal- en Letterkunde* 107 (1991): 274–310.

Arnould, Alain, and Jean Michel Massing. *Splendours of Flanders.* Cambridge: Cambridge Univesity Press, 1993, pp. 168–169 and 182–183.

Gerritsen, Willem P. "Desen fabule es elken toegescreven. De Gentse Boethiusvertaler en de mythe van Orpheus." *De Nieuwe Taalgids* 73 (1980): 471–491.

Goris, Mariken, ed. *The Second Book of the Ghent Boethius.* Forthcoming.

Goris, Mariken, and Wilma Wissink. "The Medieval Dutch Tradition of Boethius' *Consolatio Philosophiae.*" In *Boethius in the Middle Ages. Latin and Vernacular Traditions of the Consolatio Philosophiae,* ed. Maarten J. F. M. Hoenen and Lodi Nauta. Leiden: Brill, 1997, pp. 121–165.

Hoek, Jacob M. *De Middelnederlandse vertalingen van Boethius' De Consolatione Philosophiae.* Harderwijk: Flevo, 1943.

Wissink, Wilma. "Dit jeghewordighe lied of rijm es twijfelic ende hoghe omme wel verstaen." *Millennium 3* (1989): 128–150.

———, ed. *The First Book of the Ghent Boethius.* Forthcoming.

Mariken Goris
Wilma Wissink

SEE ALSO
Boethius; Jacob van Maerlant

Boner, Ulrich (fl. mid-13th c.)

One of the most successful composers of fables or didactic narrative was the Dominican monk Ulrich Boner, whose name appears in documents between 1324 and 1350 produced in Bern, Switzerland. Late medieval audiences tremendously enjoyed reading fables for entertainment and moral instruction. Boner was the first to put together a major collection of these works in the tradition of Aesop, which he called *Edelstein* (precious stone), completed around 1350. The name implies that the fables function analogously to precious stones, which reveal their true salutory and divinatory character only after a thorough investigation. With his fables Boner wanted to teach his audience general moral and ethical lessons. He combined many medieval fables from the Latin tradition, especially from the text corpus of the Anonymus Neveleti (fables 1–62) and of Avian (fables 63–91). Boner's *Edelstein* remained the most influential and popular fable collection in Germany for the following century. When a Bamberg printer published it in 1461, it was one of the first secular texts written in German and printed for the book market. Each fable has a title and a subtitle; the latter serves as an indicator of the specific theme to be dealt with in the fable. At the end is the epimython, the moral, didactic explanation. Although Boner pursued religious intentions with his *Edelstein,* often the fables convey worldly messages, such as the advantages of specific types of behavior and the value of political freedom.

The rediscovery of the Middle Ages by enlightened intellectuals such as Johann Jakob Bodmer (1698–1783) and Gotthold Ephraim Lessing (1729–1781) began with their editorial work of Boner's fables.

BIBLIOGRAPHY

Blaser, Robert Henri. *Ulrich Boner, un fabuliste suisse du XIVe siècle.* Diss., Université de Paris. Mulhouse: [n.p.], 1949.

Boner, Ulrich. *Der Edelstein,* ed. Friedrich Pfeiffer. Leipzig 1844.

———. *Der Edelstein. Faksimile der ersten Druckausgabe Bamberg 1461,* ed. Doris Fouquet. Stuttgart: Müller and Schindler, 1972.

Grubmüller, Klaus. *Meister Esopus: Untersuchungen zur Geschichte und Funktion der Fabel im Mittelalter.* Munich: Artemis, 1977.

Waas, Christian. "Quellen des Bonerius." *Zeitschrift für deutsches Altertum und deutsche Literatur* 46 (1902): 341–59.

Albrecht Classen

Bonn

The medieval city of Bonn, on the river Rhine, achieved political prominence in the fourteenth century as the site of the coronation of two German kings. The city lay to the south of the site of a Roman camp founded in the time of Augustus. Here the church known as the *Münster*

Schwarzrheindorf, chapel, view from east. *Photograph: Joan A. Holladay*

choir exterior and the integrated towers are definitive elements of the Rhenish Romanesque.

Arnold von Wied, prior of Cologne Cathedral and chancellor, erected on the opposite side of the Rhine the chapel at Schwarzrheindorf (d. 1151). It was subsequently enlarged by his sisters about 1170. The two-story chapel is decorated with mid-twelfth-century wall paintings juxtaposing the visions of Ezekiel and scenes from the New Testament.

The city gained in political importance after 1288, when the archbishop, driven from Cologne by the citizens, took up residence in his palace in Bonn (on the site now occupied by the University of Bonn). After disputed elections, the archbishop crowned two German kings, Frederick III the Fair in 1314 and Charles IV in 1346, in the Bonn Münster rather than the traditional palace chapel at Aachen.

BIBLIOGRAPHY

Clemen, Paul. *Die Kunstdenkmäler der Stadt und des Kreises Bonn.* Kunstdenkmäler der Rheinprovinz 3. 1905. Düsseldorf: Pädagogischer Verlag Schwann, 1981.

Joan A. Holladay

SEE ALSO
Cologne, Archdiocese

Bookmaking and Production

In late antiquity, the parchment codex had replaced the papyrus role. This represented a leap in bookmaking technology that brought with it obvious advantages of endurance and ease of use. It was in this form that the book as we still know it was produced throughout the Middle Ages in Europe. Leaves of parchment were folded and gathered into convenient groupings, usually four, and then bound with two facing pages, making any page as easily accessible as the first. In Germany, as throughout Europe, early medieval book production was exclusively the work of the monasteries. Encouraged by their rules to pray and meditate on God's Word, it became imperative to produce the books that would permit such study, given the total absence of larger public or private book collections. Book production was then, from the transition of late antiquity to the early Middle Ages, in the hands of those who made books for their own use. The manufacture of books was both labor intensive and expensive, even for the most ordinary of codices. Great care was

(now the parish church St. Martin) rose over the site of a memorial chapel erected in the Roman cemetery in the second half of the third or first half of the fourth century. Legend credits Saint Helena, the mother of the Roman emperor Constantine, with the church's foundation; as at Xanten and the church of St. Gereon at Cologne, her patronage is associated with the veneration of martyrs from the Theban legion, in this case Saints Cassius and Florentius. The current building is the fifth on this site: the early Christian *memoria* (memorial site) was succeeded by a small hall church erected about 400, a larger Carolingian building about 780, and a stately Salian church with a double choir built in the mid-eleventh century. The choir of the present church was consecrated in 1153, with work on the nave continuing until about 1220. The sharply demarcated stories of rhythmic arcades that articulate the

taken in producing any book, and certain examples meant for display or use in special circumstances were created as works of art, as costly and beautiful as any painting or sculpture.

The labor to produce the materials needed for making books was time intensive and represented a wide range of skills. The most basic material was parchment, most often the skins of cows or sheep, and each skin had to undergo a lengthy finishing process in order to provide a suitable writing surface. Scores of animals, sometimes hundreds, would be needed for a single book. Once the parchment was delivered to the scriptorium, it underwent further preparation: arrangement by hair and flesh sides, so that like sides faced each other, and ruling by pricking or lead point. On very rare occasions the parchment might be colored to add further drama to the writing surface. Other basic materials that had to be fabricated were ink and writing utensils. Ink was manufactured from natural materials, either carbon (soot) or iron gall, mixed with wine, water, or vinegar. Colored inks, mostly red, were produced from vermilion or cinnabar. Finally, very costly books could be written with gold or silver. The actual writing utensil was most often a quill feather, cut and sharpened to specification. A typical scribe's tool set thus consisted of a sharp knife, several quills, ink horns, chalk, razor and sponge for corrections, a lead point, a ruler, and an awl (and, from the fourteenth century on, glasses).

The actual hand copying of texts was preceded by the need to decide upon a text to be copied, not an inconsequential task when confronted with the reality that not all texts could be produced in sufficient quantities. If the desired text was not available, arrangements had to be made to borrow it from some other monastery. If parchment was unavailable or in short supply, the master scribe, or *armarius,* might decide to erase the text of an older, possibly no longer comprehensible or useful, codex. The production of books from erased texts, or palimpsests, was most common in the early Middle Ages. The role of the monastic school and its teachers was crucial in determining not only the texts and the type of script to be used, but also the layout and assignment of tasks. Many manuscripts were produced in a kind of assembly line. Several scribes would work on the same manuscript simultaneously, each having been assigned a gathering of leaves and a particular portion of text. It seems that most copying was done silently, since it was necessary for several scribes to work side by side on different texts. Once a portion of the text was completed, it might be given to a corrector for proofreading and emendation. Next it was handed to a rubricator for the highlighting of initials and parts of text in red. For more elaborate efforts, an illuminator would furnish the text with images in the form of initials or full-page paintings in spaces left by the copyist. Finally, a book had to be bound in order to protect the text and allow for ease of use over a long period of time. The leaves first had to be ordered, often with the help of numbers or catchwords indicating the next gathering. Bindings could be parchment or leather covers, simply wrapping the pages; more commonly the leaves were sewn together and placed between wooden boards covered with leather. This process often involved the destruction of older books for the use of parchment scraps to strengthen the bindings themselves. The boards could be decorated with pressed stamps or engravings. Bindings were then often marked in some way by the librarian to indicate title and location. In some cases, the binding was itself a work of art and representation, encrusted with precious stones and gold or worked in ivory.

With the growth of universities in Germany in the late fourteenth century, book use and its production moved away from the exclusive realm of the monasteries. University texts were usually dictated by faculty to students, and the university often paid secular scribes to produce approved texts. Even monasteries began to produce books on request for well-paying citizens who wanted to exhibit their literary taste. Various monastic orders, especially women's, specialized in text copying for a fee. The most important development in medieval bookmaking was the introduction of paper. This material could be produced relatively inexpensively in great quantities, was durable and long lasting, and was well-suited for handwriting. Since its introduction in the thirteenth century and its manufacture in Germany as of 1390, paper was to revolutionize the production of books, quadrupling the production rate of the previous century. Over half of all manuscripts still extant from medieval Germany are from the fifteenth century and written on paper. This revolution was to be consummated with the invention of movable type around 1450. Expensive books made for the exclusive use of certain closed communities were replaced by printed books that combined inexpensive materials and textual replication on a commercial scale.

BIBLIOGRAPHY

Avrin, Leila. *Scribes, Script and Books: The Book Arts from Antiquity to the Renaissance.* Chicago: American Library Association, 1991.

Banks, Doris. *Medieval Manuscript Bookmaking: A Bibliography.* Metuchen, N.J.: Scarecrow, 1989.

Bischoff, Bernhard. *Latin Paleography: Antiquity and the Middle Ages,* trans. Daibhi O Croinin and David Ganz. Cambridge: Cambridge University Press, 1990.

Brownrigg, Linda, ed. *Making the Medieval Book: Techniques of Production.* Los Altos Hills, Calif.: Anderson-Lovelace, 1995.

Diringer, David. *The Hand-Produced Book.* New York: Hutchinson's, 1953; rpt. New York: Dover, 1982.

Ganz, Peter, ed. *The Role of the Book in Medieval Culture.* Brepols: Turnhout, 1986.

Harmon, James A. *Codocology of the Court School of Charlemagne: Gospel Book Production, Illuminatiion, and Emphasized Script.* Frankfurt: Lang, 1984.

Levarie, Norma. *The Art and History of Books.* New Castle, Del.: Oak Knoll, 1995.

Maniace, Marilena, and Paola Munafò, ed. *Ancient and Medieval Book Materials and Techniques.* 2 vols. Città del Vaticano: Biblioteca Apostolica Vaticana, 1993.

Putnam, George. *Books and Their Makers During the Middle Ages.* 2 vols. New York: Putnam's, 1896.

Rück, Peter, and Martin Boghardt, ed. *Rationalisierung der Buchherstellung im Mittelalter und in der frühen Neuzeit.* Marburg: Institut für Historische Hilfswissenschaften, 1994.

Wattenbach, Wilhelm. *Das Schriftwesen im Mittelalter.* 3d ed. Leipzig: Hirzel, 1896; rpt. 1958.

William Whobrey

SEE ALSO
Block Book; Education; Libraries; Liturgical Vestments, Manuscripts, and Objects; Manuscripts, Painting and Production; Paleography; Universities

Boppe, Meister (fl. end of the 13th c.)

Boppe was a poet and composer best known for didactic lyrics. References to fellow poet Konrad von Würzburg (d. 1287) in an obituary prayer to King Rudolf of Habsburg (1273–1291) and to the margraves of Baden indicate that Boppe had composed his verses and music in southern Germany by the end of the thirteenth century. As for most of the didactic lyrical poets (*Sangspruchdichter*), however, there is no external documentary evidence of this. The famous Heidelberg University *Codex Manesse* attributes forty stanzas in eight different metrical and melodical forms (*Töne*) to him, but other manuscripts ascribe six of these *Töne* and seven of the strophes to other poets. The Jena manuscript, which gives Boppe the title *Meister* (master) preserves only the first *Ton,* later named *Hofton* (court verse form), with eighteen stanzas. A nine-strophical *Ave Maria* in the *Hofton* survives in a fourteenth-century Heidelberg manuscript. As Boppe ranks with a group of twelve famous old *Sangspruch* masters, more than two hundred further stanzas in the *Hofton* are recorded in *Meistersang* manuscripts of the fifteenth and sixteenth centuries. Boppe is commonly regarded as the composer of the *Hofton* and the author of the *Hofton* stanzas in the older manuscripts, with the exception of the religious *Ave Maria.* The stanzas of the other *Töne* not attributed to other poets may be his. The number of the *Meistersang* texts that are his work—and to what extent they are his work—remains uncertain.

Boppe's poems treat the common themes of the thirteenth-century didactic lyric (*Sangspruchdichtung*) in conventional ways. In the role of teacher and counselor, the poet gives instruction and advice to his courtly audience, praising secular chivalric ideals and female virtues as well as God and the Virgin Mary. While divine grace is the highest value in one stanza, earthly love's rewards outrank everything else in another, and in a satirical strophe money is the ultimate ideal. The poet laments his own poverty and extols decency, charity, and princely generosity, a merit particularly important for the wandering artists; he decries miserliness, self-praise, and unjustified eulogy. He has knowledge of the mysteries of Redemption, the dignity of the priesthood and of mankind, the preexistence of the Virgin and her identity as God's mercy, the contrasts between outer appearance and inner worth, good advice and false counsel. In the role of the minnesinger, he gives a satirical catalog of the lady's preposterous demands. Boppe's technical devices indicate considerable rhetorical skill. He repeatedly uses the traditional bestiary imagery to exemplify good and false behavior and has a special preference for cumulative enumerations, displayed by catalogs of countries and peoples, values and virtues, biblical *exempla* (examples), and series of parallel statements and rhetorical questions, often combined with anaphora.

BIBLIOGRAPHY

Alex, Heidrun. *Der Spruchdichter Boppe: Edition, Übersetzung, -Kommentar.* Tübingen: Niemeyer, 1998.

Brunner, Horst, and Burghart Wachinger, eds. *Repertorium der Sangsprüche und Meisterlieder des 12. bis 18. Jahrhunderts.* Vol. 3. Tübingen: Niemeyer, 1986, pp. 209–245.

Tolle, Georg. *Der Spruchdichter Boppe. Versuch einer kritischen Ausgabe seiner Dichtungen.* Sondershausen: Programm der fürstlichen Realschule, 1894.

Gert Hübner

SEE ALSO
Konrad von Würzburg; Meistersinger; *Sangspruch;*
Versification

Bouvines, Battle of (July 27, 1214)

In France's war with Flanders in 1213–1214, King Philip II Augustus of France fought against King John of England, who was allied with both the Flemish and Emperor Otto IV of Brunswick. The Flemish plan called for a broad coordinated attack toward Paris, with English forces moving from the south while the Germans and Flemings advanced from the northeast, thus dividing Philip's resources. Unfortunately, the English advance failed and Otto's army faced Philip's concentrated forces when they met at Bouvines, south of Tournai. Philip's larger and better organized knights overwhelmed Otto's in cavalry charges and melees. The French killed over 150 nobles and knights and captured over another 150, while sustaining hardly any losses of their own.

As a consequence, Otto, who was fighting for control of the empire with Frederick II, Staufer, lost any chance of reclaiming his former imperial authority. And the defeat both sealed John's loss of Normandy and Anjou and fueled the discontent in England that led to the Magna Carta. Meanwhile Philip II, confiscating John's lands and encroaching into the Lowlands, achieved a lasting dominance for the monarchy in France.

BIBLIOGRAPHY
Duby, Georges. *The Legend of Bouvines: War, Religion and Culture in the Middle Ages,* trans. Catherine Tihanyi. Berkeley: University of California Press, 1990.
Delbrück, Hans. *Medieval Warfare,* trans. Walter J. Renfroe, Jr. History of the Art of War 3. Lincoln: University of Nebraska Press, 1982.
Oman, Charles. *A History of the Art of War in the Middle Ages.* 2 vols. 2d ed. London: Methuen, 1924.

Brian A. Pavlac

SEE ALSO
Frederick II; Otto IV; Staufen

Bowman

See Archer/Bowman.

Brabant, Duchy of

The duchy of Brabant (now the Belgian provinces Antwerp and Brabant and the Dutch province North Brabant) constituted one of the largest principalities in the western part of the German empire. As early as 870, the Treaty of Meersen mentions the *gau* (district) of Brabant. The history of the duchy of Brabant is generally thought to begin by the end of the twelfth century. This duchy was situated on territory of the older and larger duchy Lower Lorraine, founded around 959. Its nucleus consisted of the territorial possessions of the Reiniers, an important ducal house of Lorraine. In 977 the West Frankish Carolingian Charles of Lower Lorraine obtained the title of duke of Lower Lorraine. His daughter Gerberga (d. 1008) married Lambert I (d. 1015), count of Louvain and of Brabant (of which Brussels was the center). Lambert was the founding father of the dukes of Brabant, who, referring to Lambert's marriage, rightfully claimed to descend from Charlemagne. This background explains why the Brabantine dukes continuously tried, using the Brabantine territory as a stepping-stone, to regain the territory of the old Lower Lorraine.

The title of duke of Lower Lorraine had meanwhile passed to the house of the Ardennes. In 1066 Godfrey (Godfried) I the Bearded (1095–1139), count of Louvain, received the ducal title of Lower Lorraine from King Henry V of Germany. In that same year Godfrey I was enfeoffed with the margravate Antwerp. In general his reign is considered to mark the beginning of the history of the duchy of Brabant. The ducal title of Lower Lorraine would remain in the possession of the Brabantine dynasty: Godfrey II (1139–1142), Godfrey III (1142–1190), Henry I (1190–1235), Henry II (1235–1248), Henry III (1248–1261), Henry IV (1261–1267). The last was the oldest son of Henry III, but he was underage and weak minded. A regency was established and exercised by the widowed duchess Aleidis of Burgundy until Henry IV resigned his right to the duchy in 1267 in Kortenberg in favor of his younger brother John I (1267–1294); thereafter followed John II (1294–1312), John III (1312–1355, the last duke from the Brabantine dynasty), and Johanna (1355–1406). Johanna, the oldest daughter of John III, was married to Duke Wenceslas of Luxembourg (d. 1383). The marriage remained childless and, after Wenceslas's demise, the Burgundy dynasty under the reign of Johanna became anchored in Brabant. This meant the definitive end of the autonomous history of the duchy. The dukes of Brabant from the house of Burgundy were Antoine of Burgundy (1406–1415); John IV

(1415–1427); Philip of Saint-Pol (1427–1430); Philip the Good, duke of Burgundy (1430–1467); Charles the Bold, duke of Burgundy (1467–1477); and Maria of Burgundy (1477–1482), daughter of Charles the Bold. She was succeeded by Philip the Fair (1482–1506), the son from her marriage with the Habsburg Maximilian of Austria. And thus Brabant passed to the Habsburgs.

By 1106 the title duke of Lorraine was nothing more than an empty box, an honor no longer connected to any real power. Still, the dukes of Brabant always proudly carried the designation. In addition, they tried to establish sovereign authority over this part of the old Carolingian "Middle Kingdom," especially after the reign of Henry I. In scholarly literature this policy is known as the Brabantine dukes' *Drang nach Osten* (push toward the East). Its Lorraine character has traditionally been denied by scholars. Until the late twentieth century, the motives behind the strategy were misinterpreted, due largely to the Belgian historian Henri Pirenne (1862–1935) and his *Histoire de Belgique* (1900–1932). The *éminence grise* (gray eminence) of Belgian historiography, Pirenne believed that the Brabantine expansion policy stemmed from the pursuit by the Brabantines of a strong state that would be independent of the German empire. Brabantine expansionism, however, meant more than mere imperialism. It was inspired by a legitimate quest for the restoration of the Brabantines' authority as dukes of Lower Lorraine. From this viewpoint, the battle of Woeringen in 1288 and the subsequent annexation of the duchy of Limburg by Brabant in 1289 can be interpreted as a partial realization of the Brabantine dukes' Lorraine dream, for the duchy of Limburg was part of the old Lower Lorraine. In contrast to what Pirenne and his followers claimed, this battle had nothing to do with a political project aimed at dominating the trade route between Bruges and Cologne. The trade route did not even run through the duchy of Limburg (though some negligible kilometers ran through 's-Hertogenrade, the possession of which was traditionally linked with the title of the duke of Limburg). When Duke Philip the Good of Burgundy became duke of Brabant in 1430, he also inherited the dream of the Brabantine dynasty of restoring Brabantine sovereinty over Lower Lorraine. However, his plan to establish a Lorraine kingdom failed. His son and successor Charles the Bold in turn wanted to unify Lower and Upper Lorraine under his rule, to form a kingdom with Nancy as capital. When he was killed in a battle with Duke René of Upper Lorraine in 1477 before the gates of Nancy, this undertaking, too, failed.

From an ecclesiastical point of view, the territory of the duchy of Brabant was largely situated within the boundaries of the diocese of Liège (archbishopric of Cologne). The remaining part resided in the diocese of Cambrai (archbishopric of Reims). In 1332 and 1336 Duke John III of Brabant requested of the pope (first John XXII and then Benedict XII) the establishment of a separate diocese of Brabant. This request, however, was denied. Brabant's position between the dioceses of Liège and Cambrai would remain unchanged until the establishment of new dioceses in the Low Countries under Philip II (1559). The duchy was predominantly Dutch speaking. Only a small part of the territory, the *Roman Pays de Brabant* (Romance Territory of Brabant), was French speaking.

The relationship between the dukes of Brabant and their Brabantine subjects was dominated by the opposition between the external aims of the dukes (the realization of their Lorraine ambitions) and the internally focused popular priorities of the prominent Brabantine cities , especially the seven that were known as the "good cities" (Louvain, Brussels, Antwerp, 's-Hertogenbosch, Tienen, Nijvel, and Zoutleeuw). Inspired by the ideology of popular sovereignty, the cities judged that the dukes' main priority was to serve the general interest of Brabant. From the cities' perspective, the realization of the dynasty's ambitions required too great a risk. Wars cost money and the region's textile industry, the import of raw materials and the export of final products, would suffer heavily from the disruption caused by a military conflict. The leading role that the Brabantine cities played in the production of luxury cloth in Europe would then be threatened.

On a national level, the political community of Brabant was organized into three estates. The First Estate consisted of the prelates of the old Brabantine abbeys. The convents of the mendicant orders and the secular clergy were represented in the Second Estate, together with the Brabantine knights. The Third Estate contained the "good cities" and was the most powerful in the duchy due to its economic strength. Consequently, the cities were the dynasty's most important opponents, especially in the thirteenth and fourteenth centuries. Within the Third Estate, Louvain and Brussels were most prominent. These two cities de facto determined the policy of their estate and heavily influenced national politics. The Brabantine knights were active as an estate only in the wake of the great cities. For instance, at a time when the death of John III was expected to cause a succession crisis, they concluded a treaty on May 17, 1355 in which the treaty of the Brabantine cities of March 8, 1355 was literally included, thereby avoiding a succession struggle. The prelates (First Estate) were at first only politically active when their contribution was demanded in a general poll. Their resistance to a poll in 1314 and in 1335, for example, led to the oldest known confederations of the Brabantine abbeys.

Characteristic of the political culture in Brabant was the early development of constitutionalism. As many aspects as possible of the relationship between the duke and his subjects were laid down in written privileges (constitutions) granted by the duke. These documents increasingly and systematically restricted the duke's power. The list of constitutions is impressive: the wills of Henry II (1248) and Henry III (1261); the Charter of Kortenberg (1312) and the Privilege of the Brabantine abbeys, both granted by John II on his deathbed; the Flemish and Walloon Charter of 1314 (John III); and, most important, the famous Ceremonial Entry (*Blijde Inkomst*) of Johanna and Wenceslas (granted on January 3, 1356, but legally valid only a few months from the end of February 1356 onward). Henceforth and until the end of the Ancient Regime, all dukes of Brabant would have to grant their subjects a Ceremonial Entry, a sign of acknowledgment, at the commencement of their reign. In this context the *Nieuw Regiment* (New Regiment) of John IV is also important (1422).

The ideology of popular sovereignty played an important role in the duchy and was applied in specific political situations. This can be illustrated by various examples, such as the case of John III, who was only twelve years old when his father, John II, died in 1312. Because of the indebtedness of the ducal treasury, partly due to the Limburg succession-war (1283–1289) and the battle of Woeringen (June 5, 1288), Brabantine merchants abroad were arrested and their merchandise confiscated. The ransom and the sales profit of the confiscated goods served to settle the duke's debts. This situation proved catastrophic for the foreign trade of the duchy. To handle the crisis, a regency consisting of Floris Berthout, Lord of Mechelen, and the count of Gulik was established. However, the regents did not succeed in resolving the trade problem. Hence the cities assumed control in 1314. They extended the legal age of John III for six more years, until 1320. From 1314 until 1320 the duchy was governed by a municipal regency. This council proved successful and consequently ended the crisis in the foreign trade.

The Third Estate was instrumental in the preservation of the territorial integrity of the duchy. For instance in 1354–1355, a succession crisis loomed after the death of John III. The three legal sons of the duke were deceased. His three legal daughters were married: Johanna to Duke Wenceslas of Luxembourg, Margaretha to Count Louis of Mâle of Flanders, and Mary to Duke Reinald of Gelre. With the cities' consent, the duke had named his oldest daughter, Johanna, as his successor. The other daughters inherited a sum of money. This was not sufficient in the opinion of Louis of Mâle, who claimed Mechelen and sovereignty over the Scheldt region on behalf of his wife. War and a possible disintegration of the Brabantine territory were possible, as it was feared that the Duke of Gelre might also assert his territorial rights. Thus, after the death of John III, representatives of the cities and Johanna immediately commenced to negotiate in John's castle in Tervuren on December 5, 1355. When Johanna granted Brabant the Ceremonial Entry on January 3, 1356, measures for the preservation of the territorial integrity of the duchy were central to the document. They constituted the *sine qua non* for the cities—and thereby the country's—recognition of Johanna as duchess.

Brabant also had a tradition of written political treaties, as evidenced by the town pacts (*stedenbonden*) of 1261–1262, 1313, 1355, 1372, and 1428, the *Ridderbond* (pact of the members of the Second Estate) of 1355, and the confederations of Brabantine abbeys of 1314 and 1335. The Brabantine-Flemish treaty of December 3, 1339, agreed upon by the major Brabantine and Flemish towns, also belongs to this tradition. All stipulations from these texts form a sort of "democratic" constitution, admired by the other regions of the Low Countries, which were not as politically evolved (in the North it would take until the schism in 1581–1585 and in the South until the end of the sixteenth century). The duchy of Brabant (and not the county of Flanders, as Pirenne had claimed) became the most prominent region of the Low Countries, of fundamental importance to the development of a sense of solidarity in this region in the period before the House of Burgundy came to power in Brabant.

In addition to the ambition of the Brabantine dukes to regain sovereignty over Lower Lorraine, the actions of the Brabant dynasts within the German empire caused strife between the dukes and their subjects. The dukes were German princes and members of the *Reichfürstenstand* (upper noble class). They paid homage to the German king/emperor. As guardian of the coronation city of

Aachen, which boasted the throne of Charlemagne and his descendants, they shared in the Carolingian prestige. In the famous Heidelberg *Minnesang* manuscript (Codex Manesse), the lyrical poetry of John I appears among those of other Middle High German poets. In addition, various dukes were considered to be successors to the German throne.

John III, grandson of John I, the hero of Woeringen he so admired, was the patron of the Middle High German epic *Lohengrin*, written between September 16, 1332, and November 1333. The protagonist of the epic, Lohengrin, refers to the historical John III of Brabant. This identification throws a special light on the role the duke wished to play in the German empire. The anonymous author was granted the commission during the first phase of a great coalition against Brabant (1332–1334). This coalition aligned all of the landlords of the principalities surrounding Brabant. Their main goal was to take revenge on John III for the victory of John I in the battle of Woeringen in 1288 and to break the power and esteem of Brabant. In this tense atmosphere, when the future of Brabant was at stake, the duke commissioned the writing the *Lohengrin* (7,670 verses). This patronage clarifies the position of the Brabantine dukes as German *Reichsfürsten* (imperial dukes).

During the composition of the *Lohengrin,* Brabant, as part of the Middle Kingdom and of the duchy of Lower Lorraine, was threatened with extinction. John III successfully resisted the coalition against him. But other parts of the former Carolingian Middle Kingdom, Upper Lorraine and the Arelaat, were at risk of being irretrievably lost to the German empire due to increasing French influence in these territories and the lax, even passive, response of Louis of Bavaria. In the epic, Lohengrin (John III) is presented as the indispensable savior, the defender of the empire's interests, sent by the community of the Grail. He unconditionally pays homage to the German king for Brabant/Lower Lorraine. Acts of homage for Upper Lorraine and the Arelaat follow. These three acts of homage are the only ones mentioned in the *Lohengrin.* The homage for Upper Lorraine is instigated after an arbitrational decision by Lohengrin, who declares that the duchy would forever remain within the German empire. After this declaration the king of the Arelaat pays homage as well.

The message of the epic is clear: as Lorraine is defended by Duke Lohengrin, so must the other parts of the Middle Kingdom be safeguarded in order to preserve

them for the empire. In contrast to the lax action of Louis of Bavaria when confronted with the impending loss of Upper Lorraine and of the Arelaat, all means must be employed to fully reintegrate these territories into the empire. This is the clear political message of the patron of the epic, John III. The reproach addressed to Louis of Bavaria is beyond misinterpretation.

But what was the motive behind this literary, propagandistic initiative of John III? Why choose that moment to commission such a work? The epic was written at a time when the abdication of Louis of Bavaria was possible. If this were to occur, a new king would have to be chosen. In *Lohengrin,* John III let himself be pictured as the savior of the German empire, as someone who, with God's help, could defend its interests. In other words, he ensured that he would be seen as the ideal candidate for the throne in the event that Louis of Bavaria stepped down. The intended audience of this epic was first and foremost the electors and their courts and other powerful leading figures who were thought to influence the choice for a new king.

Presumably, the involvement of John III in matters concerning the empire is representative of the involvement of his predecessors. Only *Lohengrin* allows us to imagine its extent. With respect to Belgian historiography, John III's commitment to imperial state matters has traditionally been discounted. Until recently it was believed that at that time, although Brabant juridically still belonged to the empire, the dukes operated largely independently of the empire, especially after John I. Here again the misconception can be attributed to Henri Pirenne, whose *Histoire de Belgique* attempted to trace the fundaments of Belgian independence in order to legitimize the new state following the revolution of 1830. As a consequence his conception of Belgian history was deterministic in character. He took into account only those past events and tendencies that more or less prefigured the 1830 revolution. He systematically disregarded indications of unrealized possibilities, such as the annexation of Brabant by the German empire, a consequence of the Lorraine ambitions of the Brabantine dynasty. The medieval history of the duchy of Brabant, then, at least until the beginning of Burgundian rule, should henceforth be linked with German history. The medieval history of Germany continues to be written starting from the boundaries of the contemporary Federal Republic of Germany. Hence, Brabant is only briefly or coincidentally mentioned, when it is mentioned at all.

BIBLIOGRAPHY

Avonds, Piet. *Brabant tijdens de regering van hertog Jan III (1312–1356). De grote politieke krisissen.* Brussels: Koninklijke Academie voor Wetenschappen, Letteren en Schone Kunsten van België, 1984.

———. *Brabant tijdens de regering van hertog Jan III (1312–1356). Land en Instellingen.* Brussels: Koninklijke Academie voor Wetenschappen, Letteren en Schone Kunsten van België, 1991.

———. "Ghemeyn oirbaer. Volkssoevereniteit en politieke ethiek in Brabant in de veertiende eeuw." In *Wat is wijsheid? Lekenethiek in de Middelnederlandse letterkunde,* ed. Joris Reynaert et al. Amsterdam: Prometheus, 1994, pp. 223–239 and 422–427.

———. "Waar blijven dan toch Bohort, Galaad, Perceval en de anderen? De verspreiding van de Arturepiek in Brabant (twaalfde—begin veertiende eeuw)." In *Op avontuur. Middeleeuwse epiek in de Lage Landen,* ed. Jozef D. Janssens et al. Amsterdam: Prometheus, 1998, pp. 37–49 and 285–293.

Avonds, Piet, and Jozef D. Janssens. *Politiek en Literatuur. Brabant en de Slag bij Woeringen (1288).* Brussels: UFSAL-Centrum voor Brabantse Geschiedenis, 1989.

Avonds, Piet, H. Thomas, and J. A. van Houtte. "Brabant." In *Lexikon des Mittelalters,* ed. Robert Auty et al. Vol. 2. Munich and Zurich: Artemis, 1977ff., coll. 526–534.

Bautier, Robert-Henri. "La place de la draperie brabançonne et plus particulièrement bruxelloise dans l'industrie textile du moyen âge." *Annales de la Société Royale d'Archéologie de Bruxelles* 51 (1956-1966): 31–63.

Blok, Dirk Peter et al., eds. *Algemene Geschiedenis der Nederlanden.* Vols. 1–4. Haarlem: Fibula-van Dishoeck, 1977–1983.

Bonenfant, Paul, and Anne-Marie Bonenfant-Feytmans. "Du duché de Basse-Lotharingie au duché de Brabant." *Revue Belge de Philologie et d'Histoire* 46 (1968): 1129–1165.

Camps, Henricus P. H. *Oorkondenboek van Noord-Brabant tot 1312.* Vol. 1, *De meierij van 's-Hertogenbosch.* The Hague: Nijhoff, 1979 [charters].

Cauchie, A., and Alphonse Bayot. "Rapport sur les chroniques de Brabant." *Bulletin de la Commission Royale d'Histoire de Belgique,* ser. 5, no. 10 (1900): xxxvii–xciii.

Knetsch, Carl. *Das Haus Brabant. Genealogie der Herzoge von Brabant und der Landgrafen von Hessen.* Darmstadt: Historische Verein für das Grossherzogtum Hessen, 1917.

Laurent, Henri, and Fritz Quicke. *Les origines de l'état Bourguignon. L'accession de la Maison de Bourgogne aux duchées de Brabant et de Limbourg (1383–1407).* Brussels: Palais des Académies, 1939.

Prevenier, Walter, and Willem Pieter Blockmans. *De Bourgondische Nederlanden.* Antwerp: Mercatorfonds, 1983.

Quicke, Fritz. *Les Pays-Bas à la veille de la période bourguignonne, 1356–1384.* Brussels: Ed. Universitaires, 1947.

Smets, Georges. *Henri Ier, duc de Brabant.* Brussels: Lamertin, 1908.

Stein, Robert. *Politiek en historiografie. Het ontstaansmilieu van Brabantse kronieken in de eerste helft van de vijftiende eeuw.* Louvain: Peeters, 1994.

Steurs, Willy. *Naissance d'une région. Aux origines de la Mairie de Bois-le-Duc. Recherches sur le Brabant septentrional aux 12e et 13e siècles.* Brussels: Academie Royale de Belgique, 1993.

Uyttebrouck, Andre. *Le gouvernement du duché de Brabant au bas moyen âge (1355–1430).* 2 vols. Brussels: ULB, 1975.

Van Uytven, Raymond. "La draperie brabançonne et malinoise du XIIe au XVIIe siècle: Grandeur éphémère et décadence." In *Produzione, commercio e consumo dei panni di lana,* ed. Marco Spallanzami. Florence: Olschki, 1976, pp. 85–97.

Verkooren, Alphonse. *Inventaire des chartes et cartulaires des duchés de Brabant et de Limbourg et des Pays d'Outremeuse.* Part I, *Chartes originales et vidimées* (8 vols.) and Part II, *Cartulaires* (15 vols.). Brussels: Hayez, 1910-1988 [archival material].

Wauters, Alphonse. *Le duc Jean Ier et le Brabant sous le règne de ce prince (1267–1294).* Brussels: Decq, 1862.

Piet Avonds

SEE ALSO

Jan van Boendale; Charlemagne; Chronicles, Regional, Dutch; Historiography, German; Maximilian I Habsburg

Braunschweig

Chronicles relate that Braunschweig, a city in Lower Saxony, was founded in 861 by two brothers, Bruno and Dankward. The first castle, the Dankwarderode, was built in the early eleventh century by Count Liudolf and his wife, Gertrude, who also founded a collegiate church next to their castle where Liudolf was buried in 1038. Later Braunschweig passed first to the imperial family (1090) then through marriage to Henry the Proud, duke of Saxony and leader of the Guelph party. His son, the Guelph duke Henry the Lion (1129–1195), made Braunschweig his capital. While retaining and improving the core of castle and church, Henry also constructed much new town fabric. Interested in expansion of the empire north and east, and the role of merchants, Henry was involved with the founding of the Hanse city of Lübeck and created new merchant quarters in Braunschweig.

Henry the Lion completed a series of impressive architectural and artistic projects in the old center of Braunschweig, which reflected his desires to create a worthy ducal capital. He rebuilt the Dankwarderode around a courtyard with the rebuilt church of St. Blasius forming the south side. One of the most impressive monuments of Henry's reign is the over-life-size lion erected in the castle courtyard in 1166. This sculpture, made of gilt bronze, stands poised with open mouth. It has an elaborately detailed mane and originally had glass eyes. As the first fully freestanding sculpture since antiquity, the sources for the lion are a matter of considerable interest. Sculpture in Italy such as the Etruscan she-wolf may have been a source, especially since the she-wolf was in the prestigious collection of the pope and displayed outside the Lateran palace during the Middle Ages, providing a model for both the form and the placement of such an animal figure. More precise stylistic antecedents for the Braunschweig lion may be found in small bronze aquamanile (vessel) common in Germany in the twelfth century that often took the form of lions. The lion's association with Henry's name (Guelph = Leo in Latin = lion) provides additional reasons for the public display of this sculpture.

Henry rebuilt the ducal church adjoining the Dankwarderode and dedicated it to St. Blasius and St. John the Baptist (1173–1194). The church later became the cathedral of Braunschweig. A major function of the rebuilt church was to hold the relics Henry brought back from a pilgrimage to the Holy Land in 1172–1173. The twelfth-century building had a basilican plan with a single side aisle, transept, and massive two-towered westwork. The entrance from the palace courtyard was in the transept arm. The church is groin-vaulted in square bays with a simple two-story elevation, and the east end has an elevated choir with a semicircular apse above a crypt. This eastern part of the church contains an extensive cycle of wall painting from the second quarter of the thirteenth century showing the lives of the patron saints, Blasius and John the Baptist; it is stylistically related to the manuscript group of the Goslar Evangeliary.

The interior of the church contained several important large sculptures and pieces of church furniture, including the Imervard Cross of the mid-twelfth century, a wooden sculpture of the clothed Christ on the Cross, and from 1188 a bronze candelabra decorated with enamels and an altar dedicated to the Virgin with a marble slab and five bronze columns. Tombs of Henry the Lion and Matilda Plantagenet, his wife, commissioned circa 1235–1240 by their sons, including Emperor Otto IV, were placed at the entrance to the choir. They represent the first example of a double tomb in Germany, although the type already existed in France. The royal couple is depicted as of an ideal age. The effigy of the duke holds a sword and model of a church. Matilda's hands are clasped in prayer. While consoles are placed under the effigies' feet, the drapery falls as if the figures were lying down. The style of the figures is full-bodied with deep, three-dimensional drapery in rather excited folds, which have been related to the *Zackenstil* (jagged or zigzag style). The style is similar to German thirteenth-century cathedral sculpture such as that of the Goldene Pforte at Freiberg Cathedral. It is possible that the Braunschweig tombs conceptually related to tombs of Matilda's parents, the Plantagenet tombs at Fontevrault in France.

The church of St. Blasius was the medieval repository of the collection of metalwork known as the Guelph Treasure. This collection of metalwork, presently dispersed in many collections, dates from the Ottonian, Romanesque, and Gothic periods, and was first inventoried in 1482. The chronicler Arnold von Lübeck refers to Henry's zeal in enriching the House of God, and this is thought to include his components of the Guelph Treasure. It is known that Henry brought relics and reliquaries back from Constantinople, where the Emperor Manuel Comnenus was trying to win Henry's favor, and these objects were subsequently donated to St. Blasius. But a large number of the works in the Guelph Treasure are German, reflecting German expertise in metalwork. These objects include portable altars, reliquaries, and several arm reliquaries (Berlin, Staatlichen Museen, Preussischer Kultureebesitz, Kunstgewerbemeuseum, nos. Inv. W. 12, W. 19, W. 20, W. 23).

Henry the Lion was also a donor of manuscripts; one of his most impressive donations was the Gospels of Henry the Lion (Wolfenbüttel, Herzog August-Bibliothek Cod. Guelf., no. 105 Noviss. 2), made at the scriptorium of the abbey of Helmarshausen and originally placed on the high altar at St. Blasius. The famous coronation miniature (fol. 171v) shows Henry and Matilda crowned by Christ and surrounded by their famous ancestors.

While the late twelfth century was the apogee of Braunschweig's medieval history, another period of artistic achievement began during the reign of Duke Otto the Mild (1318–1346). At this time Braunschweig became a center in the Hanseatic League, ushering in a new period of prosperity. The city market square with its Rathaus (town hall, 1393–1396) was laid out, and modifications were made to the adjoining church of St. Martin. This church, which had a westwork, was erected around 1250 and was remodeled in the early fifteenth century. Architectural modifications were also undertaken at the ducal church of St. Blasius around this time (1469–1474). The north aisle was modified into a double hall with elaborate ribbed groin vaulting on decorated columns. The mendicants were active in late medieval Braunschweig, and the Franciscan cloister and church, the Brüdernkirche, were built between 1343 and 1361. Other impressive medieval churches in Braunschweig include St. Michaelis, begun in 1158 and the second-oldest in the city; St. Peter's, a Gothic hall church from the end of the thirteenth century; and the Benedictine abbey of St. Aegidien and its cloister, rebuilt as a Gothic hall church after a fire of 1278.

BIBLIOGRAPHY

Helmarshausen und das Evangeliar Heinrichs des Löwen: Bericht über ein wissenschaftliches Symposium in Braunschweig und Helmarshausen vom 9. Oktober bis 11. Oktober 1985, ed. Martin Gosebruch and Frank N. Steigerwald. Schriftenreihe der Kommission für Niedersächsischen Bau- und Kunstgeschichte bei der Braunschweigischen Wissenschaftlichen Gesellschaft 4. Göttingen: Goltze, 1992.

Heinrich der Löwe und seine Zeit: Herrschaft und Repräsentation der Welfen 1125–1235, ed. Jochen Luckhardt and Franz Niehoff, 3 vols. Munich: Hirmer Verlag, 1995.

Kimpflinger, Wolfgang. *Stadt Braunschweig,* 2 vols. Baudenkmale in Niedersachsen 1. Hameln: C.W. Niemeyer, 1993–1996.

Möhle, Martin. *Der Braunschweiger Dom Heinrichs des Löwen: Die Architecktur der Stiftskirche St. Blasius von 1173–1250.* Braunschweig: Selbstverlag des Braunschweigischen Geschichtsverlag, 1995.

Steigerwald, Frank. *Das Grabmal Heinrichs des Löwen und Mathildes im Dom zu Braunschweig: Eine Studie zur figürlichen Kunst des frühen 13. Jahrhunderts, insbesondere der bildhauerischen.* Ph.D diss., Braunschweig Technical University, Braunschweiger Werkstücke 47. Braunschweig: Waisenhaus Buchdruckerei und Verlag, 1972.

Winter, Patrick De. *The Sacral Treasure of the Guelphs.* Cleveland and Bloomington: Cleveland Museum of Art and Indiana University Press, 1985.

Susan L. Ward

SEE ALSO

Franciscan Art and Architecture; Freiberg; Gothic Art and Architecture; Hanseatic League; Helmarshausen; Henry the Lion; Lübeck; Metalworking; Ottonian Art and Architecture; Relics and Reliquaries; Romanesque Art and Architecture; Town Planning and Urbanism

Brendan

A Middle Dutch poem (2,284 verses) probably composed in the second half of the twelfth century, *De reis van Sint Brandaan* (The Voyage of Saint Brendan), tells the story of the Irish abbot Brandaan, who, during a sea voyage of nine years, lands on miraculous coasts where he encounters many wonderful and strange creatures. The reason for the voyage is Brandaan's lack of faith: enraged by so many lies, he has thrown a book describing the wonders of God's creation into the fire. An angel appears and gives him the divine order to make a sea voyage to discover for himself what is truth and what is falsehood. The voyage and the written report of it are to replace the book that Brandaan has burned.

In the narrative's various episodes, Brandaan stays at heavenly and infernal places, is confronted with sea monsters, and meets hermits, devils, and the strange people of the *Walseranden*. In addition to information on natural and supernatural phenomena, some theological problems are raised.

The Middle Dutch *Reis van Sint Brandaan* has come down to us in two manuscripts from around 1400. The text in the Van Hulthem manuscript is not complete: 332 verses (presumably) are lacking due to a missing first page. The Comburg manuscript offers us a complete text. The two versions diverge in word choice and formulation. Together with two German texts in verse and a High

German prose version, they go back to a now-lost original that was composed around 1150 in the Middle Franconian area. The text was meant for a twelfth-century lay audience.

Investigating the sources of *De reis van Sint Brandaan* is a complex business. The author used older and contemporary works, Latin and vernacular texts, and books of a discursive as well as a narrative character. The text has some episodes in common with the Latin prose *Navigatio Sancti Brendani Abbatis,* which possibly dates back to the ninth century. The Latin text in turn is related to the old Irish genre of the *immrama* (sea voyage stories that recount landings on miraculous coasts), and especially to one of those stories, the *Immram curaig Máele Dúin* (The Sea Voyage of Mael Duin's Ship). The genre was very popular. The Latin text is preserved in more than one hundred manuscripts and was translated into several medieval vernacular languages. In addition to this Latin text, the author of the Middle Dutch version made use of other sources, such as texts about the marvels of the East. Some episodes resemble parts of the twelfth-century German text *Herzog Ernst* (Duke Henry). The author also used discursive sources belonging to the medieval Latin *physiologus* and bestiary tradition. The text also contains innovations, such as the instigating event of the burned book that must be replaced by Brandaan.

The Irish abbot Brendan is a historical figure. *Brénaind moccu Altai* was born in 500 near Tralee in the north of the county of Kerry (southwest Ireland). He was an important religious leader who founded several monasteries in the west of Ireland. He died around 580. In the eighth century he was known as a famous sailor. Later on he was invoked as a saint against fire. Several versions of the life of Saint Brendan (*Vita Brendani*) have survived, in which biographical data are mixed with episodes of a miraculous voyage. This *Vita* probably had some influence on the *Navigatio Sancti Brendani Abbatis.*

BIBLIOGRAPHY

Gerritsen, W. P., ed., and Willem Wilmink, trans., *De reis van Sint Brandaan. Een reisverhaal uit de twaalfde eeuw.* Amsterdam: Prometheus/Bert Bakker, 1994.

Gerritsen, W. P., Doris Edel, and Mieke de Kreek. *De wereld van Sint Brandaan.* Utrecht: HES, 1986.

Strijbosch, Clara. *De bronnen van De reis van Sint Brandaan.* Hilversum: Verloren, 1995 [with a summary in English].

An Faems

SEE ALSO

Hartlieb, Johannes

Bruno of Magdeburg (fl. late 11th c.)

The chronicler Bruno of Magdeburg (also Bruno of Merseburg) served in the episcopal *familiae* of Archbishop Werner of Magdeburg (1063–1078), then Bishop Werner of Merseburg (1059–1093), two of the principal ecclesiastical leaders of the rebellion known as the Saxon War (1073–1088). It is to Werner of Merseburg that Bruno dedicated the historical narrative for which he is known, the *Liber de bello saxonico* (Book on the Saxon War) probably early in 1082. In his history, Bruno defended the Saxons' rebellion against charges of *lèse-majesté* (crime against the crown) through a vivid portrayal of the "unkingly" deeds of Henry IV's youth and a highly partisan account of the first eight years (1073–1081) of the Saxons' rebellion against that king. Far from opponents of God-ordained kingship, Bruno strove to portray the Saxon rebels as spokesmen and restorers of the right Christian political order. He was therefore at pains to highlight and document the absolute obedience of the rebel leaders to the voice of the divine order, the reform papacy under Pope Gregory VII (1073–1085), and did so by including verbatim transcriptions of key letters from Pope Gregory VII, Henry IV, and the Saxon princes; indeed, he is our only source for the latter. Yet, although a vigorous apologist for the Saxon cause and adherent of the reform papacy, Bruno was also willing to criticize the Saxon princes for ignorance, overconfidence, and self-interest, and the papacy and its legates for vacillation and double-dealing. A tightly constructed, incisive, at times eloquent and dryly humorous work, the *Book on the Saxon War* reveals the author to have been not only a well-trained Latin stylist who was particularly influenced by the classical historian Sallust's works, but a perceptive observer of his society and its politics.

BIBLIOGRAPHY

Bruno of Magdeburg. *Brunos Buch vom sächsischenkriege,* ed. H.-E. Lohmann. Monumenta Germaniae historica. Deutsches Mittelalter. Kritische Studientexte 2. Leipzig: Hiersmann, 1937; rpt. 1980.

Eggert, W. "Wie 'pragmatisch' ist Brunos Buch vom Sachsenkrieg?" *Deutsches Archiv* 51 (1995): 543–553.

Kost, Otto-Hubert. *Das östliche Niedersachsen im Investiturstreit: Studien zum Brunos Buch vom Sachsenkrieg.*

Studien zur Kirchengeschichte Niedersachsens 13. Göttingen: Vandenhoeck and Ruprecht, 1962.

Sprigade, K. "Über die Datierung von Brunos Buch vom Sachsenkrieg." *Deutsches Archiv* 23 (1967): 544–548.

William North

SEE ALSO
Henry IV; Gregory VII

Buch von Bern and *Rabenschlacht*

Also known as the "historical" Dietrich epics, *Buch von Bern* (also called *Dietrichs Flucht*) and *Rabenschlacht* were composed in Bavarian-Austrian dialect and transmitted together in four complete manuscripts, showing that they were perceived as a double epic by their audience, the Austrian nobility. Two fragments survived to modern times. One, now lost, contained 318 lines of *Buch von Bern,* the other, 58 strophes from *Rabenschlacht.* The two narratives are interrelated in plot, but different in other respects. *Buch von Bern* is written in the rhymed couplets of chronicles and courtly romances; in an excursus decrying unjust treatment of the lower nobility by princes, one Heinrich der Vogler (a pseudonym) names himself as the author (line 8,000). Heinrich might have written only this and similar excursuses, or he might be the author in the sense that he reworked a traditional tale to depict a thirteenth-century political situation. *Rabenschlacht* is anonymous and written in a unique six-line strophe. Its many inconsistencies and high proportion of native terms for warfare are characteristic of oral-traditional style, but other elements of style and content mark it as a work of the mid- to late thirteenth century.

The two oldest manuscripts of *Buch von Bern* (the late-thirteenth-century Riedegg and early-fourteenth-century Windhagen manuscripts) lack the extended prologue (over two thousand lines), recounting the succession of kings of Italy (including Ortnit and Wolfdietrich) that characterizes later versions (a Heidelberg manuscript from 1447 and the Ambras manuscript prepared by Hans Ried for Kaiser Maximilian). There are no variations in the main plot. Prior to Dietrich's birth Italy has been divided among his father, Dietmar, and his two uncles, Diether and Ermrich. Ermrich, ruler of Rome, attacks young Dietrich in order to take over northern Italy. Advisers help Dietrich win a battle at Milan. The hero's plans to reward his men are foiled when Ermrich's men take a number of Dietrich's men hostage. Dietrich goes into exile so that the hostages can be released. He obtains the support of Etzel (Attila) in order to go back to Bern (Verona) and face Ermrich again. He wins a partial victory. Returning to Etzel, he must marry Herrat, Queen Helche's niece, in order to obtain further support. A third battle occurs when the treacherous Witege gives Raben (Ravenna) back to Ermrich. Although Dietrich again wins a partial victory, he suffers heavy losses. He laments for the dead on both sides (especially for his man, young Alphart, who has been killed), then returns to Etzel.

Rabenschlacht begins between the second and third battle. Dietrich, in exile, laments the loss of his men, especially that of Alphart (strophe 10, line 5). To assuage his grief, Helche arranges for his marriage to Herrat. The army prepares to leave for Raben. The sons of Helche and Etzel are only children, but they insist on going with the army. Helche and Etzel reluctantly agree to let them go in Dietrich's care. The boys and Dietrich's younger brother are forbidden to leave Bern. They insist upon taking a ride outside the gates. The weather is foggy, which causes them to take a wrong path into the vicinity of the battle. The next morning all three children are killed by Witege, one of Ermrich's men, in unfair combat (see *Alpharts Tod,* in which the murder of the youthful hero takes place two against one at the hands of Wytdich and Hen). After the first part of the battle, Dietrich discovers that the boys are dead, laments, and pursues Witege, who, aided by a mermaid, escapes into the sea. The battle continues. Dietrich wins, but Ermrich escapes. Rüedeger pleads Dietrich's case with Helche and Etzel, who reluctantly forgive him.

The chronological relationship of *Buch von Bern* and *Rabenschlacht* is not entirely clear, but because *Buch von Bern* can be interpreted as a response to *Rabenschlacht* in many respects, it seems probable that *Rabenschlacht* is the earlier of the two.

BIBLIOGRAPHY

Curschmann, Michael. "Zu Struktur und Thematik des Buchs von Bern." *Beiträge zur Geschichte der deutschen Sprache und Literatur* 98 (1976): 367–374.

Firestone, Ruth H. "An Investigation of the Ethical Meaning of Dietrich von Bern in the Nibelungenlied, *Rabenschlacht,* and *Buch von Bern.*" In *In hôhem prîse: A Festschrift in Honor of Ernst S. Dick,* ed. Winder McConnell. Göppingen: Kümmerle, 1989, pp. 61–75.

Haug, Walter. "Hyperbolik und Zeremonialität: Zu Struktur und Welt von *Dietrichs Flucht und Rabenschlacht.*" In *Deutsche Heldenepik in Tirol,* ed. Egon Kühebacher. Bozen: Athesia, 1979, pp. 367–374.

Martin, Ernst. *Alpharts Tod, Dietrichs Flucht, Rabenschlacht.* Deutsches Heldenbuch 2. 1866; rpt. Dublin and Zurich: Weidmann, 1967, pp. 57–215; 219–326.

Ruth H. Firestone

SEE ALSO
Alpharts Tod; Dietrichepik; Maximilian

Burchard of Worms (965–1025)

Burchard (also Buggo) was bishop of Worms and a codifier of the laws of both court and Church. Probably from a comital, or ducal family in Hesse, he served in the diocese of Mainz for Archbishop Willigis, who brought him to the attention of the Emperor Otto III. Otto named him bishop of Worms in 1000. Burchard was respected enough to be entrusted with raising the future emperor Conrad II. Burchard tried to restore order to his see, which had been devastated by the Hungarian invasions. He rebuilt old and established new churches and monasteries. Even more important, two documents attest to his far-sighted planning and organization. First, he compiled a collection of laws known as the *Decretum Collectarium* or the *Brocardus,* after himself. Burchard's *Decretum* had widespread use; later canonists such as Ivo of Chartres and Gratian drew heavily from it. Second, he wrote the Laws and Statutes for the Familia of St. Peter of Worms, the first example of a law book for court vassals and ministerials.

BIBLIOGRAPHY

Hoffmann, Hartmut, and Rudolf Pokorny. *Das Dekret des Bischofs Burchard von Worms: Textstufen—Frühe Verbreitung—Vorlagen.* Munich: Monumenta Germaniae Historica, 1991.

Will, Johanna B. *Die Rechtsverhältnisse zwischen Bischof und Klerus im Dekret des Bischofs Burchard von Worms: eine kanonistische Untersuchung.* Würzburg: Echter, 1992.

Brian A. Pavlac

SEE ALSO
Conrad II; *Fürstbischof;* Law and Lawbooks; Otto III

Burg

Members of the landed aristocracy during the Carolingian period tended to be itinerant, moving about from one unfortified manor house to another. Where fortification (*burg* = castle) did exist, it tended to be large scale, providing protection for both the owner and the neighboring rural populace in the uncertainties of the ninth and tenth centuries. Most often, burgs were built of timber, not unlike forts on the Russian and American frontiers in the eighteenth and nineteenth centuries. Already in the early tenth century, however, certain families were beginning to build smaller-scale residences of stone, intended for the use of their *familia*—that is, of their household alone.

Unlike England, where numerous, very large royal castles were erected during the reign of William the Conqueror, German kings as late as the reign of Henry III (d. 1056) owned few castles, apart from the citadels in towns like Goslar, Nuremberg, and Regensburg, which were provincial headquarters, and nobles and kings alike lived in rambling unfortified manor houses. With the outbreak of the civil war, the situation changed and castles sprang up throughout Germany, built by temporal and spiritual lords as well as by the emperors themselves. An important acquisition was the fortress Trifels, perched high above Annweiler in the Wasgau forest of the Rhineland, which dates from 1040–1060 and was surrendered by the archbishop of Mainz to Emperor Henry V in 1113. Custom dictated that upon the death of an emperor, the imperial insignia be taken to Trifels. At the end of the twelfth century, the English king Richard I was brought to Trifels while his fate was being decided.

Whereas the private castles built in England during the reign of King Stephen (1135–1154) were frequently torn down by his successor, Henry II, the process of building castles on the hereditary estates of the German nobility during the eleventh century could not be halted once the civil war was over. The earliest reference to the Zollerburg, ancestral home of the imperial house of Hohenzollern, is 1061; Frederick of Büren built the castle of Staufen about 1077 and was thenceforward known as Frederick of Staufen; the family of Berthold began to call itself von Zähringen about 1100. One of the most famous of the Rhine castles, that of Stahleck above the town of Bacharach, is first mentioned in 1135. Few German castles are more famous than the Wartburg, home of the landgraves of Thuringia; it was the setting for a dazzling courtly culture at the end of the twelfth and the early thirteenth centuries, but also the stage on which Saint Elizabeth of Hungary (d. 1231) played out her short adult life.

The proliferation of castles continued into the thirteenth and fourteenth centuries. The archbishops of

Mainz, for example, built the castle Lahneck above Oberlahnstein in 1240, while the Martinsburg in Oberlahnstein itself dates from the late fourteenth century. Throughout Germany, control of the countryside rested in the hands of hundreds of counts, lesser nobles, and *ministeriales* (administrators), who generally styled themselves after their castle or burg. It was from the castle that their authority was exerted, and it was in a large degree the castle upon which their authority was constructed. As ecclesiastical princes such as the archbishops of Cologne extended their temporal lordship during the twelfth and thirteenth centuries, they acquired fortresses (such as the Homburg and the Godesburg, near Bonn) which they garrisoned with their own *ministeriales,* and they compelled the noble occupants of other burgs to become their vassals.

BIBLIOGRAPHY
Duncker, Alexander. *Rheinlands Schlösser und Burgen.* 1857–1883. Rev. ed. with commentary by Wilfried Hansmann and Gisbert Knopp. Düsseldorf: Schwann, 1981.
Friedrichs, J. *Burg und territoriale Grafschaften.* Bonn: Georgi, 1907.
Patze, Hans, ed. *Die Burgen im deutschen Sprachraum: Ihre rechts- und verfassungsgeschichtliche Bedeutung.* Vol. 1. Sigmaringen: Thorbecke, 1976.

Paul B. Pixton

SEE ALSO
Family; Fortifications; Henry III; Hohenzollern; Ministerials; Staufen

Burial
See Birth, Marriage, Burial.

C

Caesarius of Heisterbach (1180–ca. 1240)

A Cistercian monk educated in Cologne, Caesarius became the prior and master of novices at the monastery of Heisterbach. His extant writings include a number of sermons and a few saints' lives, but Caesarius is most noted for his *Dialogus miraculorum* (Dialogue on Miracles), compiled and written in Latin between 1219 and 1223. As novice master, he gathered the material together in a collection of stories intended to illustrate Christian doctrine for the monks in his charge and aid in the development and preparation of sermons on particular topics. Hence, the stories are divided into a variety of thematic units, with subject headings such as conversion, contrition, confession, temptation, demons, the Eucharist, and the Miracles of the Virgin Mary. The collection is framed by a dialogue between a novice monk *(novicius interrogans)* and the master *(monachus respondens)*. The content, owing as much to an oral tradition as to religious sources, straddles the border between official canonical doctrine and that of folk legend. Many of the stories depict scenes drawn from the everyday life of the region and time period, including that of emperors, peasants, townspeople, beggars, and clergy. Because the stories are meant to serve as examples to live by, they are called *exempla,* and while they are shaped as miracle tales, weaving religious doctrine with popular material, each has a particular moral point. While the primary audience for the *Dialogus miraculorum* was that of male Cistercian monasteries, there is evidence that the works of Caesarius are important in the history of medieval women's spirituality in Germany. There are over two hundred references to women's cloisters in Caesarius's works and evidence that he personally knew six Cistercian women's monasteries in the Lower Rhineland.

BIBLIOGRAPHY

Caesarius of Heisterbach. *Caesari Heisterbacensis Monachi Ordinis Cisterciensis Dialogus miraculorum,* ed. Joseph Strange. 2 vols. Bonn: Colonia, 1871.

———. *The Dialogue on Miracles,* trans. H. von E. Scott and C. C. Swinton Bland. London: Routledge, 1929.

Moolenbroek, J. J. van. "Caesarius von Heisterbach über Zisterzienserinnes." *Citeaux* 41 (1990): 45–65.

Rosemary Drage Hale

SEE ALSO
Cologne, Archdiocese; Exemplum; Legends

Calculation

See Numbers and Calculation.

Canossa

One of the four regional fortresses of the Countess Matilda of Tuscany in Reggion Emilia, Canossa was constructed with triple walls on a steep rock that jutted out from the Appenines over the plain. Ruins, in particular of its church St. Apollonio, have remained as a reminder of the famous encounter there in January 1077 between Pope Gregory VII (1073–1085) and King Henry IV (1056–1106). The pope had deposed and excommunicated Henry at the Roman synod of February 1076 in response to letters brought by messengers from the assembly (diet) meeting at Worms in January 1076, renouncing on the part of the archbishops and bishops their obedience to "Brother Hildebrand" and on the part of the king calling on Gregory to resign. When the deposition became known in Germany, Henry found himself deserted.

The opposition gathered at Tribur in October 1076 together with papal legates. They declared that they would no longer recognize Henry as king if he would not succeed in obtaining absolution from the pope within a year. They also invited Gregory to come to Augsburg in February 1077 to act as mediator between themselves and the king. In desperation Henry decided to meet Gregory in Italy, crossing with his wife Bertha and their two-year-old son Conrad in a particularly severe winter the six-thousand-feet-high Mont Cenis, the only pass that was open to the king. It was an almost suicidal undertaking. When Gregory, on his way to Augsburg, heard in Mantua of Henry's arrival, he retreated to Matilda's castle of Canossa. Henry appeared as a penitent, barefoot and in sackcloth, in the castle yard asking for admittance. Gregory could not easily refuse reconciliation, especially since Henry's cause was supported by others present, the Countess Matilda, Abbot Hugh of Cluny who was Henry's godfather, and Countess Adelheid of Turin, Henry's mother-in-law. Gregory secured a written promise and an oath from Henry that he would accept the pope's judgment and allow him free passage. The pope then lifted up Henry from the ground and gave him and his companions communion. The events were judged differently even by contemporaries. Penance per se was not an act that would detract from the royal dignity, but Henry certainly had recognized Gregory as judge and thus as an intermediary between himself and God. He was visibly subordinate to the sovereignty of the Church and his status as king by the grace of God was bound to suffer.

BIBLIOGRAPHY

Fuhrmann, Horst. *Germany in the High Middle Ages, c. 1050–1200,* trans. Timothy Reuter. Cambridge: Cambridge University Press, 1986.

Kämpf, Hellmut, ed. *Canossa als Wende: Ausgewählte Aufsätze zur neueren Forschung.* Darmstadt: Wissenschaftliche Buchgesellschaft, 1963; rpt. 1976.

Uta-Renate Blumenthal

SEE ALSO

Gregory VII, Henry IV; Investiture Controversy

Capitularies

Capitularies were instruments of government used by the Carolingians, consisting of collections of written articles *(capitula).* The articles summarized oral proclamations made by the king in consultation with an assembly of lay and ecclesiastical leaders. The Carolingians used capitularies to regulate the royal administration and to bolster the national laws governing the different peoples of the Carolingian empire. The collections also contained measures related to Church dogma, ecclesiastical organization, and the liturgy. The kings' authority to issue capitularies derived from the royal ban *(bannum):* his right to command subjects to perform services for the realm and punish them for disobedience. Charlemagne and Louis the Pious issued the most important capitularies between 779 and 805, frequently following on revolts or other crises. These articles promoted an image of the Carolingian empire as a unified Christian polity. Several collections were also produced for the provinces east of the Rhine (Bavaria, Alemania, Frisia, and Saxony). Most notably, Charlemagne dictated harsh measures to eradicate Saxon paganism. With the division of the empire in 843, the production of capitularies decreased. The legal authority of the advisory assembly also tended to grow in relation to royal authority, especially east of the Rhine. The practice of issuing capitularies died out in the late ninth century.

BIBLIOGRAPHY

Ganshof, F. L. *The Carolingians and the Frankish Monarchy,* trans. Janet Sondheimer. London: Longman, 1971.

Loyn, H. R., and John Percival. *The Reign of Charlemagne: Documents on Carolingian Government and Administration.* London: Arnold, 1975.

Mordek, Hubert. "Zur Bedeutung des Frankfurter Kapitulars." In *794—Karl der Große in Frankfurt am Main. Ein König bei der Arbeit.* Exhibition of the City of Frankfurt am Main. Sigmaringen: Thorbecke, 1994, pp. 46–50.

Societas Aperiendis Fontibus Rerum Germanicum Medii Aevi, ed. *Capitularia Regum Francorum.* In *Monumenta Germaniae Historica, Leges,* section 2. Hannover: Hahn, 1883–1897.

Pegatha Taylor

SEE ALSO

Admonitio Generalis; Carolingians; Charlemagne

Cards

See Playing Cards, Master of.

Carmina Burana

The *Carmina Burana* is not only the richest surviving collection of Medieval Latin lyric poetry, but because of the German composer Carl Orff's 1938 setting of twenty-four of the songs as a "secular cantata," doubtless also the most well-known to the general public. It is also unique both in being the only collection organized by thematic categories, and in containing forty-seven "German strophes" attached to Latin songs whose strophic form they usually share, as well as a number of Latin-German and Latin-French macaronic (bilingual) poems and Latin liturgical dramas. Moreover, if current theories about its origin are correct, the collection was not only put together in medieval Germany, but its creators were probably a group of bilingual (or even multilingual) German-speaking clerics in the Tyrol who themselves wrote a number both of the Latin lyrics and the German strophes unique to the manuscript.

A loose translation of "Songs of Benediktbeuron," *Carmina Burana* is the popular name given to the manuscript, no. Clm 4660 in the Bavarian State Library in Munich, by its first editor, Johannes Schmeller. The history of the manuscript *(Codex Buranus)* before 1803 is unknown. Though a later editor, Otto Schumann, had argued for a late-thirteenth-century date for the original manuscript, its final editor, Bernhard Bischoff, has suggested on paleographic grounds a date closer to 1230, and scholarship has generally supported that date. In 1803 the manuscript was in the monastic library of Benediktbeuron, south of Munich. At some previous time it had been rebound in an order different from the original order, and some of the leaves had become separated; these were discovered by Wilhelm Meyer and published as the *Fragmenta Burana* (Fragments from Benediktbeuron) in 1901. When the monasteries were secularized in 1803, the rebound manuscript and the separate leaves went to the Bavarian State Library, where the manuscript was discovered and published in a semidiplomatic edition by Johannes Schmeller in 1847. A critical edition of the manuscript was begun in 1930 by Alfons Hilka and Otto Schumann, and was completed by Bernhard Bischoff in 1970.

The critical edition, following the organization of the manuscript before it was rebound, is divided into four sections: (1) moral-satiric poems (nos. 1–55), (2) love songs (56–186), (3) drinking and gaming songs (187–226), and (4) liturgical plays (227–228). The *Fragmenta Burana* form a final section (1*–26*). That would indicate a total of 254 poems in the manuscript. The numbering system initiated by Hilka and Schumann, however, assigns letters (e.g., CB 48, CB 48a) to stanzas or sections considered not part of the basic song (e.g., the so-called German strophes) but apparently considered part of it by the original scribes, and Roman numerals to quantitative poems that parallel tradition shows to have independent status (e.g., CB 32 I and II); finally, the notes to the critical texts often contain additional stanzas or verses (some from the *Codex Buranus* itself, some from parallel manuscripts) that the editors consider to be inauthentic. As a result, the actual number of different poems or poem fragments in the critical edition is far higher than the numbering would indicate. Counting all of the separately identified stanzas and songs, section 1 contains 89 poems; section 2, 222; section 3, 73; section 4, 2, and the *Fragmenta,* 32, for a total of 418 individual works or fragments.

If Schmeller's 1847 edition was for the most part a diplomatic printing of the extant manuscript in its rebound form and without the *Fragmenta,* the Hilka-Schumann-Bischoff edition presents a text that reflects the original manuscript only in its ordering. Hilka and Schumann established as their editorial principle the consultation of the entire parallel transmission for each separate work. Although a number of the poems are unique to the *Codex Buranus,* the greater number are also transmitted elsewhere, often with a different text, and often with many parallel manuscripts (there are 502 manuscripts in the final accounting of the parallel tradition, 106 of them containing two or more songs also in the *Codex Buranus*). The result is that each poem in their edition amounts to a separate critical edition: e.g., the metrical poem "Pergama flere volo" (CB 101) is based on 61 parallel manuscripts.

Though the parallel manuscript tradition is extensive (53 manuscripts in Paris, 48 in Munich, 34 in London, 24 in Cambridge), only a few overlap significantly with the *Codex Buranus.* The most important is Florence Laurenziana Plut. 29,1, a manuscript, originally French, from the end of the thirteenth century, which not only contains nineteen songs from the *Carmina Burana* (CB 12, 14, 15, 19, 21, 22, 26, 27, 31, 33, 34, 36, 47, 63, 67, 131, 131a, 188, 189), but also the music for these songs in mensural notation.

The *Codex Buranus* itself is a "musical" manuscript: 43 of the poems are "notated" with lineless neumes (a notation system that shows the general melodic contours without indication of intervals or rhythm), and neumatic notation had been intended by the scribes for another sixteen poems. Of those 59 poems, only eighteen have parallel manuscripts with mensural notation. Those songs with music in parallel manuscripts have been edited in performing versions by Ulrich Müller (1979), and there have been two recordings of the "complete" music of the *Carmina Burana* (by the Clemencic Consort in 1978 and the Mew London Consort in 1994). The two collections do not completely duplicate one another, and both directors include speculative melodies based either upon interpretation of the neumes or upon "contrafacture"—the use of a surviving melody by another poem with the same strophic form.

The notion of contrafacture is central, finally, to most theories about the German strophes of the *Carmina Burana*. Most of these 47 strophes in Middle High German attached to Latin songs show the same strophic form as the parallel Latin poem (or a very similar form, considering the different languages), and nine of them occur in other manuscripts: CB 48a is a stanza from Otto von Botenlauben, CB 113a from Dietmar von Aist, CB 143a, 147a, and 166a from Reinmar von Hagenau, CB 150a from Heinrich von Mohrungen, CB 151a from Lutolt von Seven, CB 168a from Neidhart von Reuental, and CB 169a and 211a from Walther von der Vogelweide (211a is a stanza from Walther's famous "Palastine Song," *Palästinalied*); CB 203a is a stanza from the Middle High German poem *Eckenlied*. Earlier theories argued, therefore, that the melodies of the German strophes had served as models for the Latin poems, and that is certainly true in some instances. Given, however, the multilingual nature of the manuscript, the fact that many of the German strophes unique to the *Codex Buranus* have little literary merit, and that a number are significantly different in form from "their" Latin poems, it now seems likely that many of the unique German strophes are jeux d'esprit attributed to the Tyrolean compilers of the manuscript, who may indeed be the authors also of a number of the Latin poems.

BIBLIOGRAPHY

Beatie, Bruce A. "Carmina Burana 48-48a: A Case of 'Irregular Contrafacture'." *Modern Language Notes* 80 (1965): 470–478.

Bernt, Günter, trans. *Carmina Burana: Die Lieder der Benediktbeurer Handschrift.* Munich: Deutscher Taschenbuch Verlag, 1974, rpt. 1979 [modern German].

Carmina Burana. Clemencic Consort, René Clemencic, director. Three compact disks. Harmonia Mundi musique d'abord HMA 190336–190338. Recorded 1975–1978.

Carmina Burana. New London Consort, Philip Pickett, director. Four compact disks. L'Oiseau Lyre 443 143. Recorded 1986–1987, issued 1994.

Dronke, Peter. "Poetic Meaning in the *Carmina Burana.*" *Mittellateinisches Jahrbuch* 10 (1975): 116–137.

Eder, Christine, trans. *Carmina Burana.* Facsimile Reproduction of the Manuscript Clm 4660 and Clm 4660a (Bayerische Staatsbibliothek München). Introd. Bernhard Bischoff. Brooklyn, NY: Institute of Mediaeval Music, 1967; rpt. in two volumes, Munich: Prestel, 1967; rpt. 1970.

Hilka, Alfons, and Otto Schumann, eds. *Carmina Burana. Mit Benutzung der Vorarbeiten Wilhelm Meyers.* Heidelberg: Carl Winter, 1930–1970.

Lehtonen, Tuomas M. S. *Fortuna, Money, and the Sublunar World: Twelfth-Century Ethical Poetics and the Satirical Poetry of the Carmina Burana.* Bibliotheca historica 9. Helsinki: Finnish Historical Society, 1995.

Meyer, Wilhelm, ed. *Fragmenta Burana.* Berlin: Weidmann, 1901

Müller, Ulrich, Michael North, and René Clemencic, eds. *Carmina Burana: lateinisch-deutsch. Gesamtausgabe der mittelalterlichen Melodien mit den dazugehörigen Texten.* Munich: Heimeran, 1979.

Sayce, Olive. *Plurilingualism in the Carmina Burana: A Study of the Linguistic and Literary Influences on the Codex.* Göppingen: Kümmerle, 1992.

Schmeller, Johann Andreas. *Carmina Burana. Lateinische und deutsche Lieder und Gedichte einer Handschrift des XIII. Jahrhunderts aus Benedictbeuern auf der K. Bibliothek zu München.* 1847; 4th ed., Breslau: Marcus, 1904.

Steer, Georg. "*Carmina Burana* in Südtirol: Zur Herkunft des clm 4660." *Zeitschrift für deutsches Altertum und deutsche Literatur* 112 (1983): 1–37.

Vollmann, Benedikt Konrad, ed. *Carmina Burana: Texte und Übersetzungen.* Mit den Miniaturen aus der Handschrift und einem Aufsatz von Peter und Dorothee Diemer. 1. Aufl. Frankfurt am Main: Deutscher Klassiker Verlag, 1987 [modern German].

Walsh, P. G., ed. and trans. *Love Lyrics from the Carmina Burana.* Chapel Hill: University of North Carolina Press, 1993.

Bruce A. Beatie

SEE ALSO
Eckenlied; Heinrich von Mohrungen; Neidhart; Walther von der Vogelweide

Carolingian Art and Architecture

[This entry includes six subentries:
Introduction
Architecture
Ivories
Mural Painting
Painting
Sculpture and Metalwork]

Introduction

The term Carolingian derives from "Carolus Magnus," Charlemagne's name in Latin, and refers, literally, to art produced in areas ruled by a monarch of the Carolingian family. Georgaphically, this included the western half of Germany, the Low Countries, most of France, and parts of Italy. Chronologically, Carolingian rule in what is now Germany extended from 751 until 910. In this instance the historicopolitical definition of an artistic period is not arbitrary, for the leading centers of Carolingian art production were the royal courts and the monasteries with close ties to them. And members of the Carolingian family were among the chief patrons of early medieval art.

The most important Carolingian court was Charlemagne's at Aachen, but the Carolingian pattern of royal succession, with all of a ruler's sons dividing his lands, meant that the boundaries of kingdoms and the locations of courts shifted. This makes it difficult to generalize about the centers of Carolingian art. Monasteries, which were not transient, were somewhat less susceptible to shifting political currents; important German monasteries active in Carolingian art production include those at St. Gall, Fulda, Reichenau, and Lorsch.

Carolingian art is generally characterized by great material richness, technical excellence, and iconography that is often extremely sophisticated. Formally it manifests various syntheses between the abstract art of the Carolingians' barbarian ancestors and the illusionistic representational styles of Rome and Byzantium, centers that Carolingian kings and monks saw as political and intellectual models. Carolingian art was tremendously influential throughout much of the Middle Ages because of the success of this formal synthesis and the immense prestige of the Carolingians, typically looked on as the first kings of France and Germany. In Germany, the Ottonians and Salians drew on Carolingian models with especial frequency.

BIBLIOGRAPHY
Barral i Altet, Xavier. *The Early Middle Ages from Late Antiquity to A.D. 1000.* Taschens World Architecture. Cologne: Taschen, 1997.
Conant, Kenneth John. *Carolingian and Romanesque Architecture, 800 to 1200.* Pelican History of Art. Baltimore: Penguin, 1966.
Dodwell, C. R. *The Pictorial Arts of the West 800–1200.* Yale University Press Pelican History of Art. New haven Conn.: Yale University Press, 1993.
Hubert, Jean, Jean Porcher, and W. Volbach. *The Carolingian Renaissance.* The Arts of Mankind. New York: George Braziller, 1970.
Lasko, Peter. *Ars Sacra, 800–1200,* 2d ed. Yale University Press Pelican History of Art. New Haven, Conn.: Yale University Press, 1994.

William J. Diebold

SEE ALSO
Aachen; Fulda; Lorsch; Ottonian Art and Architecture; Reichenau; Sankt Gall

Architecture

As with much of Carolingian culture, Carolingian architecture was not innovative, but involved the standardization of previously established types. Nonetheless, Carolingian buildings were of great importance in the Middle Ages thanks to the exceptional prestige of the ruling dynasty and the sheer extent of Carolingian construction: over four hundred monasteries were built or rebuilt in the century before 855.

Carolingian architecture is difficult to characterize because the evidence is scant. Only a handful of buildings remain and they are not representative of the full range of construction, for they include no structures in wood, the material used in the early Middle Ages for almost every building that was not a church. Even among the stone churches, few are well preserved; many fell into ruin, were destroyed (typically by fire to their wooden roofs), or became outmoded and were replaced.

Based on the extant buildings and what can be gleaned from history and archeology, however, Carolingian churches can be divided into two main groups: basilicas and centrally-planned structures. Throughout the early Middle Ages the basic church building was the hall-shaped basilica; the Carolingians codified rather than challenged this tradition. Extant Carolingian basilicas include the churches constructed for Charlemagne's courtier Einhard at Seligenstadt and Michelstadt-Steinbach. There were prestigious, but now-last Carolingian basilicas at Fulda and St. -Denis. Basilicas have an entrance facade, almost without exception in the west, and in the east an apse, a semicircular sanctuary sheltering the altar. The rectangular area between entrance and apse, the nave, varied in length and width and was sometimes flanked by two or four aisles. The nave connected the door to the most important part of the building and gave the basilica its characteristic axis. In the Carolingian period, when stone vaulting was rarely used, such churches were covered with a simple peaked timber roof. The large blank spaces of the nave and apse walls provided ample room for mural decoration in fresco or mosaic.

The basilica's popularity as a building type for the Carolingians is easy to understand; it was simple to construct and highly adaptable in size and scale. More important, it was well suited to the Christian liturgy, since its layout directed the viewer's attention to the altar as soon as he or she stepped through the door. In a church that served a large populace, the nave sheltered the worshippers, with the clergy or monks around the altar. In churches without large congregations, such as that of St. Riquier at Centula, the nave was the site of additional altars, used in the monastery's complex processional liturgy. A final, significant reason for the widespread popularity of the basilica among the Carolingians was the prestige they ascribed to its form. The fourth-century Roman basilicas, especially that of St. Peter, were the most important churches in medieval Christendom; Carolingian basilicas, such as those at Fulda and St. -Denis, followed these early Christian models closely in an attempt to link the Carolingians to Mediterranean Christianity.

The adoption of the traditional basilican form and the more consistent use of stone as a building material illustrate a systematization characteristic of Carolingian administration and culture. The best architectural expression of this Carolingian tendency to regularize is the so-called plan of St. Gall, a unique architectural ground plan for a never-built monastery, made in the first decades of the ninth century. In its completeness—every one of the monastery's many functions finds architectural expression—and consistent use of a modular system of proportions, the St. Gall plan, which featured a basilican church at its heart, is a fine architectural example of the Carolingian desire to standardize.

Not all Carolingian churches were basilicas; some were centrally planned, dominated not by an axis but by a single central point or area. Like the basilica, this is a building type with a long history, going back to classical antiquity and subsequently adopted by Christians for structures with a central focal point. The most famous centrally-planned structure of the Middle Ages, the palace chapel at Aachen, is Carolingian, part of a large complex established by Charlemagne around 790. The chapel has two stories, with a ring-like corridor surrounding the open central space on each level; Charlemagne's throne was in the second-floor gallery. The form of the Aachen chapel is likely derived form the octagonal church of San Vitale in the Adriatic city of Ravenna, built in the sixth century by the Byzantine emperor Justinian as a foothold in his attempt to reconquer Italy. Ravenna was not simply an abstract model for Charlemagne's builders; Einhard's biography of the emperor reports that the columns inside the chapel were taken from Ravenna and Rome, the imperial capital of the pagan Caesars and, more important for Charlemagne, of Constantine and his Christian successors. The evocation and spoliation of these cities at Aachen invokes the two great imperial models, Rome and Byzantium, and this invocation was fulfilled in 800 when Charlemagne himself was crowned Roman emperor. Both the complex intellectual program of the palace chapel and its dependence on earlier models are characteristic of Carolingian building.

Another characteristic Carolingian structure is found at Lorsch, a monastery with close ties to the royal court. Often called a gatehouse, its function is debated. It is a small freestanding building, with three arches at ground level and a room on the first floor. In its combination of classical elements (such as the Corinthian capitals of the engaged columns and the triple opening on the ground floor, which evokes the Arch of Constantine in Rome) and more typically medieval elements (such as the brightly colored stonework and the stone reminders of timber construction in the second story) this building encapsulates several aspects of Carolingian architecture, otherwise a difficult subject to define.

BIBLIOGRAPHY

Barral i Altet, Xavier. *The Early Middle Ages from Late Antiquity to A.D. 1000.* Cologne and New York: Taschen, 1997.

Conant, Kenneth John. *Carolingian and Romanesque Architecture, 800 to 1200.* Baltimore and Harmondsworth: Penguin, 1966.

Heitz, Carol. *L'architecture religieuse carolingienne: Les formes et leurs fonctions.* Paris: Picard, 1980.

Horn, Walter, and Ernest Born. *The Plan of St. Gall: A Study of the Architecture and Economy of and Life in a Paradigmatic Carolingian Monastery.* 3 vols. Berkeley: University of California Press, 1979. More easily available in the abridged form by Lorna Price: *The Plan of St. Gall in Brief: An Overview Based on the 3-volume Work by Walter Horn and Ernest Born.* Berkeley: University of California Press, 1982.

Hubert, Jean, Jean Porcher, and Wolfgang Volbach. *The Carolingian Renaissance.* New York: Georges Braziller, 1970.

Jacobsen, Werner. *Der Klosterplan von St. Gallen und die karolingische Architektur: Entwicklung und Wandel von Form und Bedeutung im fränkischen Kirchenbau zwischen 751 und 840.* Ph.D. diss. Philipps-Universität Marburg an der Lahn, 1981. Berlin: Deutscher Verlag für Kunstwissenschaft, 1992.

Krautheimer, Richard. "The Carolingian Revival of Early Christian Architecture." *Art Bulletin* 34 (1942): 1–38; rpt. Richard Krautheimer, *Studies in Early Christian, Medieval, and Renaissance Art.* New York: New York University Press, 1969.

Stalley, R. A. *Early Medieval Architecture.* Oxford and New York: Oxford University Press, 1999.

William J. Diebold

SEE ALSO

Aachen; Charlemagne; Fulda; Lorsch; Seligenstadt; Steinbach; Sankt Gall

Ivories

Elephant ivory was a luxury material in Carolingian Germany, available via trade, gifts, or reuse of older pieces. Plaques frequently served as bookcover decoration, reflecting the Carolingian revival of manuscript production. Several caskets and combs also survive.

Among early products are the Dagulf Psalter bookcovers (Paris, Louvre), made for Charlemagne at Aachen to give to Pope Hadrian I (d. 795). They depict King David, to whom Charlemagne was often compared, and Saint Jerome as, respectively, composer and reviser of the Psalms. The rounded figures with busily fluttering draperies are translations of late Antique forms. Similar figures occur on the cover of a Gospel Book in Oxford (Bodleian Library): Christ is shown treading the Beasts surrounded by Infancy and Miracle scenes. The surrounding of a triumphal motif with narrative generally has antique sources, and several scenes copy extant fifth-century ivories. The Lorsch Gospel covers, largest of the group, came late in Charlemagne's reign. The front (Vatican), relatively more linear, is centered on Christ treading the beasts and the back, with more varied drapery, on Mary holding the infant Christ. The overall five-part format and the flying angels holding medallions recall early Byzantine diptychs.

Charlemagne's son Drogo became bishop of Metz (823–855), where he patronized ivory carving. The Drogo Sacramentary covers (Paris, Bibliothèque Nationale) show a series of episcopal rites. Their rustic style, with large heads, also appears in the surrounding Infancy scenes on a bookcover in Frankfurt (Liebieghaus), whose format resembles the earlier Oxford cover. The center panel here is a Temptation of Christ in a more classical style, with more natural proportions and clinging drapery.

Under Drogo's successor at Metz, Bishop Adventius (858–875), two groups of ivories were produced. The earlier, with relatively flat and linear figures, includes the Ascension on the Coburg Gospels (early 860s) and a matching Crucifixion plaque in the Victoria and Albert Museum (London). The Crucifixion scene is expanded with personifications: the Church receives Christ's blood in a chalice as Synagogue turns away, while below are seated the Sea and Earth, an imperial motif of universal triumph. The Ascension cover has border panels of birds in vine scrolls with jagged leaves typical of Metz ornament. A Metz ivory in Florence (Bargello Museum) shows a layman, probably the centurion Cornelius, welcoming and being baptized by Saint Peter. In 863, Adventius recovered the wealthy nearby monastery of St. Peter at Gorze from lay control, an event probably underlying this ivory.

Later in Adventius's episcopate, further carvings, in a more solid and rounder style, can be grouped around the ivory-inlaid throne (St. Peter's, Vatican) made circa 870–875 for Charles the Bald. The pair of panels on the Metz Gospelbooks (Paris Bibliothèque Nationale, lat. 9383 and 9390) includes a Crucifixion showing new personifications imported from Charles's more westerly workshop. Its companion shows scenes of Christ's Resurrection in an order following the liturgical calendar. A similar liturgical ordering occurs in the Miracle scenes on a Metz ivory in Berlin (Staatliche Museen).

The monastery of St. Gall produced ivories under Abbot Salomon, who was also bishop of Constance (890–920). The covers of Gospel-Lectionary Ms. 53 at St. Gall, ascribed to the monk Tuotilo, combine scenes of

Christ in Majesty and the Assumption of the Virgin with Saint Gall's encounter with a bear. The figural scenes, in a linear style, are juxtaposed with fields of leaf-scroll ornament related to north Italian art. The emphasis on ornament brings the end of Carolingian art back to pre-Carolingian tendencies.

BIBLIOGRAPHY

Euw, Anton von. "Studien zu den Elfenbeinarbeiten der Hofschule Karls der Grossen." *Aachener Kunstblätter* 34 (1967): 37–60.

Fillitz, Hermann. "Die religiöse Reform und die bildende Kunst der Karolingerzeit: Die Elfenbeine." *Riforma religiosa e arti nell'epoca carolingia.* Atti del 24 Congresso internazionale di storia dell'arte. Bologna: CLUEB, 1983, 1: 59–69.

Gaborit-Chopin, Danielle. *Ivoires du moyen âge.* Fribourg: Office du Livre, 1978, 44–78, 185–192.

Goldschmidt, Adolf with P.G. Hübner and O. Homburger. *Die Elfenbeinskulpturen aus der Zeit der karolingischen und sächsischen Kaiser 1.* Denkmäler der deutschen Kunst. Berlin: Bruno Cassirer, 1914.

Melzak, Robert. "Antiquarianism in the Time of Louis the Pious and Its Influence on the Art of Metz." in *Charlemagne's Heir: New Perspectives on the Reign of Louis the Pious,* ed. Peter Godman and Roger Collins. Oxford: Clarendon Press, 1990, pp. 629–640.

———. "Petrine Iconography and Politics in the Carolingian Metz Ivories." *Arte medievale,* 2d series, 9/2 (1995): 1–9.

Menz-Vonder Mühll, Marguerite. "Die St. Galler Elfenbeine um 900." *Frühmittelalterliche Studien* 15 (1981): 387–434.

Ribbert, Margret. *Untersuchungen zu den Elfenbeinarbeiten der älteren Metz Gruppe.* Ph.D. diss., University of Bonn, 1992. Beiträge zur Kunstgeschichte 7. Witterschlick/Bonn: M. Wehle, 1992.

Schnitzler, Hermann, and Dietrich Kötzsche. "Die Elfenbeinarbeiten der Hofschule." in *Karl der Grosse: Werk und Wirkung.* Aachen: Schwann, 1965, pp. 309–359.

Robert Melzak

SEE ALSO

Aachen; Charlemagne; Charles II; Constance; Metz; Sankt Gall

Mural Painting

Very little Carolingian mural, or wall, painting has survived, but the scant remains, the archaeological evidence, and written records all indicate that it was a common pictorial form although, because its raw materials were not of great value, not an especially prestigious one. Wall painting was found in many Carolingian buildings, both secular and religious, but it is difficult to distinguish the Carolingian uses of this medium from those of their predecessors or successors. Most Carolingian churches were basilicas with relatively small windows, leaving large areas of wall space in both the nave and the apse available for painted decoration. Following the example of the prestigious early Christian Roman basilicas such as Old St. Peter's or St. Paul outside the Walls, these areas were often decorated with scenes from the Life of Christ or important saints. Surviving examples from the ninth century include the Alpine churches of Müstair (Switzerland), Malles, and Naturno (both Italy); the church of St. Maximin in Trier (now Trier, Landesmuseum); and the gateway to the monastery at Lorsch. Carolingian secular buildings were also decorated with frescoes. The most famous were the paintings in the church and royal hall of the Carolingian royal palace at Ingelheim, frescoes now lost but described in an important poem by Ermoldus Nigellus written in the 820s. These depicted events from the Old and New Testaments in the church and, in the royal hall, scenes from pagan and Christian history, including images of the Carolingian monarchs themselves.

BIBLIOGRAPHY

Dodwell, C.R. *The Pictorial Arts of the West, 800–1200.* Yale University Press Pelican History of Art. New Haven, Conn.: Yale University Press, 1993.

Exner, Matthias. "Carolingian Art, IV,1 (ii) Wall Painting." *Dictionary of Art,* ed. Jane Turner. Vol. 5. London: Macmillan, 1996, pp. 797–800.

Grabar, André. *Early Medieval Painting from the Fourth to the Eleventh Century.* Great Centuries of Painting. Lausanne, Switzerland: Skira, 1957.

Hubert, Jean, Jean Porcher, and Wolfgang Volbach. *The Carolingian Renaissance.* The Arts of Mankind. New York: George Braziller, 1970.

William J. Diebold

SEE ALSO

Ingelheim; Lorsch; Müstair; Trier

Painting

Although Carolingian painting survives in fragmentary wall paintings from Brescia, Müstair, Málles Venosta, Lorsch, Corvey, and Trier, it is preserved primarily in illu-

Lorsch Evangeliary (Vatican City, Bibliotheca Apostolica Vaticana, Pal. Lat. 50, and Alba Julia, Biblioteca Documentara Batthyaneum), fol. 18v: Christ in Majesty. *Photograph: Faksimile Verlag Luzern.*

minated manuscripts. The art historical term *Carolingian* has traditionally referred to those manuscripts associated with the court of Charlemagne, sole ruler of the Franks from 771 until his death in 814; with monastic and humanistic production under his son, Louis the Pious (814–840); and with the court of Charlemagne's grandson, Charles the Bald (840–877). This literature has assumed Charlemagne's deliberate revival of late Antique forms and has defined Carolingian primarily in relation to court production. Despite a presumed, inherent unity, however, historians of the period have repeatedly uncovered a pluralism, an internationalism characteristic of the scholars assembled by Charlemagne. The complex political, cultural, and social strands of the age are mirrored in developments in the art of illumination.

Charlemagne's success seems to lie not in effecting a conscious renaissance but in his ability to identify the

need for reform. The reforms initiated during his rule called for new books. The large number of manuscripts that survive from the later eighth to mid–ninth century witness an organized effort to integrate visual components, such as evangelist portraits from the best available models, into books that would serve the practical needs created by the reform of script from numerous local hands into a clear, standardized minuscule; the reform of the gradually corrupted text of the Vulgate Bible; and a standardization of the liturgy.

The traditional corpus of Carolingian manuscripts begins with those service books and Gospels made for Charlemagne and known collectively as the works of the Court School. These include the Godescalc Evangeliary, 781–783 (Paris, Bibliothèque Nationale, n.a. lat. 1203); the Dagulf Psalter, 783–794 (Vienna, National Library, Cod. 1861); the late-eighth-century Vienna Coronation Gospels in the Vienna Treasury; the early-ninth-century Soissons Gospels (Paris, Bibliothèque Nationale, n.a. lat. 1203); and the Bibles made under Alcuin (d. 804), abbot of St. Martin at Tours. The earliest manuscripts from the period before 800, including the Dagulf Psalter and a Gospel book in Paris (Bibliothèque de l'Arsenal, ms. 4), contain no figural representations and rely on insular, geometric decorative forms with which their northern artists were familiar and comfortable. Aniconic tendencies are later implied in a Gospel book made, probably at Fleury around 820 for Theodulf, bishop of Orléans, the author of the *Libri Carolini* and a major force in the iconoclastic debate in the west (Bern, Burgerbibliothek, Cod. 348; Mütherich and Gaehde 1976: pl. 11). The influence of the Byzantine east is apparent in the evangelist portraits of the Vienna Coronation Gospels, in which oversized halos and an illusionism reminiscent of late Antiquity differentiate these miniatures form their contemporaries found in books made for Charlemagne. The nascent works of the Carolingian production reflect the diversity of the period. Other writing centers active during the early Carolingian period have traditionally been excluded form the discussion, but both political and textual ties indicate that books made at Salzburg in the later eight century also deserve to be considered Carolingian. Salzburg, ruled until 784 by Tassilo, Duke of Bavaria and a cousin of Charlemagne, was later governed by an appointee of the emperor himself. Eighth-century text connections further support Salzburg's ties to the early Court School. For instance, the Canticles in a psalter made for Tassilo before 788 (Montpellier, Bibliothèque de l'Université, ms. 409) are textually related to the Dagulf

Psalter, one of the earliest books made for Charlemagne and intended as a gift for Pope Adrian I (d. 795) (*Der Goldene Psalter,* commentary, 42–43). After Charlemagne's death in 814, book production centered in monasteries in those areas overseen by strong archbishops like Ebbo at Reims (816–835) and Drogo at Metz (823–855).

The second generation of Carolingian painting circa 814–840 (Koehler and Mütherich IV–VI) exemplifies a true appreciation for late Antique texts both secular and religious. These books are arguably the most significant of all Carolingian production in that they preserve otherwise unknown luxury books form the fourth and fifth centuries. During the rule of Louis the Pious, copies were made of late Antique treatises such as the fourth-century copy of the *Phenomenon* by the Greek poet Aratos of the third century B.C.E. (Leiden, Bibliotheek der Rijksuniversiteit, Voss. lat. Q 79; Aratea 1989). Scientific concerns are also apparent in astronomic and computistic manuscripts made during the first half of the ninth century (Madrid, Biblioteca Nacional, Cod. 3307, made at Metz, ca. 840; and Vienna, National Library, Cod. 387, made at Salzburg, 809–818). A Carolingian copy of the *Psychomachia,* a poem depicting the battle of virtues and vices by the fourth-century Christian poet Prudentius (Bern, Burgerbibliothek, Cod. 264), spawned numerous copies between the ninth and the twelfth centuries. Similarly, ninth-century copies of comedies by the Roman poet Terence were recopied throughout the Middle Ages for teaching Latin grammar (Rome, Biblioteca Vaticana, Vat. lat. 3868, ca. 820; and Paris, Bibliothèque Nationale lat. 7899, after 850). The antique figural poem, or *carmina figurata,* a device created in the early fourth century by Constantine the Great's court poet, in which the text is arranged on the page to form an image, was used by artists in the Madrid *Aratea* manuscript. A similarly intimate text-image connection was created by the Fulda scribes and artists who designed the acrostic poems in a copy of Hrabanus Maurus's *De laudibus sanctae crucis,* made for the Emperor Louis the Pious (Rome, Biblioteca Vaticana, Reg. lat. 124, ca. 840–842; Mütherich and Gaehde 1976: pl. 12, Irblich 1994: no. 48).

The final phase of Carolingian painting spans the rule of Charlemagne's grandson Charles the Bald (840–877), whose court school produced densely ornamented Gospel books and illuminated Bibles (Koehler and Mütherich V). The practical functions of these manuscripts are overshadowed by the presence of the book as an object indicative of wealth and power. In one of the most elaborate images in the Codex Aureus of St. Emmeram dated 870 (Munich, Bavarian State Library, Clm. 14000), the emperor is portrayed in a liturgical context among the heavenly hosts and twenty-four Elders of the Apocalypse as they adore the Lamb in an eschatological composition that fills two pages (Mütherich and Gaehde 1976: pls. 37–38). In the frontispiece to the Book of Psalms in a Bible presented to Charles the Bald by Count Vivian, lay abbot of Tours (845–846, Paris, Bibliothèque Nationale lat. 1), the emperor is associated with the biblical King David. The image revolves around a crowned figure of Charles wrapped only in a mantle and boots as he plays a harp and dances as did David before the Ark (I Chron. 13:8). Four musicians and his honor guard surround the emperor. This page also combines theological and humanistic concerns by combining female allegories of the Christian cardinal virtues with inscribed portraits of the king's chief musicians. With the Court School of Charles the Bald, Carolingian painting reached a baroque phase; at Charles's death in 877, the empire was divided and lost centralized power. It soon became too weak to withstand invasions from the north.

Style in the Carolingian period is a function of several components: individual artists interpreting the style of models mainly imported from central Italy, indigenous artistic traditions creating cohesive regional systems of decoration and figure types, and external influences from the British Isles and Byzantium. Insular influences are a consistent component of Carolingian painting. The earliest manuscripts compose the page around geometric decorative forms and panel-style frames borrowed from the insular artistic tradition. Northern artists working for Charlemagne, for instance, in the Evangelist portraits of the Soissons Gospels, deconstruct the spatial compositions of their southern models and reconstruct spatial relationships in the manner of insular artists. As late as 870, the opacity of the dense patterns characteristic of insular carpet pages is reappropriated in the decoration of the Codex Aureus of Charles the Bald (Mütherich and Gaehde 1976: pl. 36).

The evangelist portraits of the Coronation Gospels in Vienna (Mütherich and Gaehde 1976: pls. 8, 10) exhibit a distinctive flaking of white and blue pigments like their Byzantine counterparts, suggesting that the pigments were prepared in the west according to an eastern recipe. However, these portraits also display a reduced three-dimensionality, spatially ambiguous furnishings, and an atmospheric illusionism less subtly rendered than in eastern examples. The Vienna evangelist portraits also contain contradictions between frame and field that are anticlassicizing and betray a northern artist's hand. (For instance, John's footstool overlaps the portrait's frame, and the remnants of Mark's footrest reveal its oblique angle and unnatural slant.) The three-dimensional conception of the figures and a concern for comprehensible space in manuscripts made Charlemagne argue for the presence of high quality, late Antique models from central Italy. The rendering of the illusionism and the re-ordering of settings supports an interpretation by northern artists.

Carolingian painting style is characterized by diverse regional interpretations of available models. Hasty renderings from late Antique books are echoed in the sketchy, diminutive figures from the scriptorium of the monastery at Hautvilliers near Reims (Koehler and Mütherich VI) in manuscripts like the Utrecht Psalter, made for Archbishop Ebbo (Utrecht, Bibliotheek der Rijksuniversiteit, Cat. Cod. MS Bibl. Rhenotraiectinae, I, Nr. 32, 816–835). The active, often calligraphic Reimois style that also marks the illustrations of the Paris Terence tenaciously survives in later medieval copies. A ninth-century Reimois copy of the *Psychomachia* now in Bern (Burgerbibliothek Cod. 264) retains heavily contoured figures that rest comfortably in credible space and attest to fine late Antique origins. Bible production at Tours continued past the mid–ninth century and produced large-format illustrated Bibles whose figure style is a northern artist's reinterpretation of late Antique images. The regional style of each of these manuscripts reflects a sense of the place of their production, which often overwhelms individual artists' approach to the model.

The manuscripts made at Metz during the rule of Charles the Bald display their own distinct style, which follows the design of contemporary ivory carving form the same area. The acanthus openwork of the decorated initials in the Drogo Sacramentary (Paris, Bibliothèque Nationale lat. 9428; *Drogo Sakramentar* 1974) creates elegant compositions silhouetted against reserved parchment. The tendrils that entwine the shafts of each decorated letter also serve as settings for small scenes depicting biblical events that refer literally or allegorically to the liturgical readings of the Sacramentary. The leafy acanthus and faux metallic, marble, and cabochon surfaces organized within paneled frames in a Sacramentary fragment made in Metz around 870 relate to the heavily decorated pages produced at the court School of Charles the Bald (Paris, Bibliothèque Nationale lat. 1141; Mütherich and Gaehde 1976: pls. 32–34).

The elegant geometric compositions found in the so-called Second Bible of Charles the Bald (871–873; Paris, Bibliothèque Nationale lat. 2) contrast with Charles's earlier manuscript decoration. Here reserved parchment serves as a background for beaked beast heads, panel-style frames filled with interlace, and fields of dotting, which are borrowed form the ornamental pages of seventh-century Hiberno-Saxon decoration to create a new Franco-Saxon style.

Charlemagne, like most great leaders, was able to surround himself with key people, led by Alcuin of York, who identified certain needs for reform of script, Bible text, and liturgy. He set in motion the establishment of book production, supplying his northern artists with a network of the best available models from central Italy. This Carolingian system of churchmen and artists continued to produce for three generations. To recognize the divergent styles in these manuscripts is to increase the appreciation of this artistic period. Areas that have traditionally been labeled peripheral to the Carolingian corpus should be brought into the fold of this diverse production. To consider writing centers like that at Salzburg under Tassilo as Carolingian is not only historically correct but also advantageous to our understanding of the period. Stylistic diversity and the variety of manuscript types and texts selected to be copied create the richness of the phenomenon of Carolingian painting.

BIBLIOGRAPHY

Bierbrauer, Katharina. *Die vorkarolingischen und karolingischen Handschriften,* 2 vols. Katalog der illuminierten Handschriften der Bayerischen Staatsbibliothek in München 1. Wiesbaden: L. Reichert, 1990.

Bischoff, Bernhard. "Die Hofbibliothek Karls des Grossen." *Mittelalterliche Studien: Ausgewählte Aufsätze zur Schriftkunde und Literaturgeschichte,* 3 vols. Stuttgart: Anton Hiersemann, 1966–1981, 3: 149–169.

———. *Manuscripts and Libraries in the Age of Charlemagne,* trans. and ed. Michael Gorman. Cambridge: Cambridge University Press, 1994.

Bischoff, Bernhard, et al., eds. *Aratea: Kommentar zum Aratus des Germanicus MS. Voss. Lat. Q. 79, Bibliothek der Rijksuniversiteit Leiden,* 2 vols. Lucerne: Faksimile-Verlag, 1987–1989.

Bullough, Donald. "*Albuinus deliciousus Karoli regis:* Alcuin of York and the Shaping of the Early Carolingian Court." In *Institutionen, Kultur und Gesellschaft im Mittelalter: Festschrift für Josef Fleckenstein zu seinem 65. Geburtstag,* ed. Lutz Fenski, Werner Rösener, and

Thomas Zotz. Sigmaringen: Jan Thorbecke, 1984, 73–92.

Der Goldene Psalter—Dagulf-Psalter: Vollständige Faksimile-Ausgabe im Originalformat von Codex 1861 der Österreichischen Nationalbibliothek, ed. Kurt Holter, 2 vols. Codices Selecti 59. Graz: Akademische Druck- und Verlagsanstalt, 1980.

Drogo Sakramentar, Ms. Lat. 9428, Bibliothèque Nationale, Paris, intro. by Florentine Mütherich. 2 vols. Codices selecti 49. Graz: Akademische Druck- und Verlagsanstalt, 1974.

Irblich, Eva. *Karl der Grosse und die Wissenschaft: Ausstellung Karolingischer Handschriften der Österreichischen Nationalbibliothek zum Europa-Jahr 1993,* 2d ed. Vienna: Die Nationalbibliothek, 1994.

Jones, Leslie W., and Charles Rufus Morey. *The Miniatures of the Manuscripts of Terence prior to the Thirteenth Century.* 2 vols. Princeton, N.J.: Princeton University Press, 1930.

Karl der Grosse: Werk und Wirkung. Düsseldorf: Schwann, 1965.

Kessler, Herbert L. *The Illustrated Bibles from Tours.* Princeton, N.J.: Princeton University Press, 1977.

Koehler, Wilhelm, and Florentine Mütherich. *Die karolingischen Miniaturen.* 6 vols. Berlin: Cassirer, 1930–1994.

McKitterick, Rosamond. *The Carolingians and the Written Word.* Cambridge: Cambridge University Press, 1989.

Mütherich, Florentine. "Carolingian Art, IV, 3, Manuscript Painting." In *Dictionary of Art,* ed. Jane Turner. London: Macmillan, 1996. 5: 800–805.

Mütherich, Florentine, and Joachim Gaehde. *Carolingian Painting.* New York: Braziller, 1976.

Physiologus Bernensis. Voll-Faksimile-Ausgabe des Codex Borgensarius 318 der Burgerbibliothek Bern. Commentary C. Steiger and O. Homburger. Basel: Alkuin-Verlag, 1964.

Salzman, Michele. *On Roman Time: The Codex Calendar of 354 and the Rhythm of Urban Life in Late Antiquity.* The Transformation of Classical Heritage 17. Berkeley: University of California Press, 1990.

Stettiner, Richard. *Die illustrierten Prudentius Handschriften.* 2 vols. Berlin: J.S. Preuss, 1985; Berlin: Grote, 1905.

Stevens, Wesley M. *Cycles of Time and Scientific Learning in Medieval Europe.* Collected Studies Series CS 482. London: Variorum, 1995.

Sullivan, Richard E. "The Carolingian Age: Reflections on Its place in the History of the Middle Ages." *Speculum: A Journal of Medieval Studies* 64 (1989): 267–306.

Susan von Daum Tholl

SEE ALSO

Charlemagne; Charles II; Corvey; Lorsch; Louis the Pious; Metz; Müstair; Salzburg; Trier

Sculpture and Metalwork

Metalwork, coins, engrave gems, seal dies, and life-size stone and stucco figures were made from Lotharingia to Bavaria. Large sculpture survives in fragments such as the Lorsch head form circa 800; it may derive from the cult of relics, from the Marian cult, or from ruler images. Texts document many lost works but describe only their materials, which were of monetary and symbolic value, not their imagery. Most metalwork objects had wooden cores sheathed in precious metals.

The classification of surviving works is uncertain. Brooches were enameled with saints throughout the eastern empire. Scandinavian finds may be Carolingian or local imitations. Style may reflect outside influences, patrons' wishes, or regional habits. Sculpture is nonetheless provenanced by stylistic comparison to manuscripts and ivories, attributed to Aachen and Metz. Gem mounts

Aachen, palace chapel, bronze door, detail. *Photograph: Joan A. Holladay*

changing from bands to filigree arcades also indicate relative chronology. Monumental cast bronze doors and railings remain in their original setting at the palace chapel in Aachen, near an archaeologically attested workshop. Use of ornament links them to Charlemagne's Court School of the early 790s, which also produced brooches.

Clerics and later rulers are also identified as patrons by inscriptions on coins and seals; on the lost reliquary of Einhard, which took the form of a small triumphal arch with Christian imagery; and on a rock crystal disk engraved with scenes from the Old Testament story of Susanna for Lothar II (855–869). Another inscription links Duke Tassilo of Bavaria with the liturgical cup (768/769–788) that defines the "Tassilo chalice style," also called "Anglo-Carolingian" in reference to its strong Insular (Great Britain) flavor. Eighty-five known metalwork objects use this style (ca. 750–850). A book cover on the Lindau Gospels shows the group's inconographic complexity, with the animals of Creation, Adoration of the Cross, and universal renewal in the Crucifixion.

Liturgical functions are common for Carolingian sculpture. Many processional crosses probably resembled the so-called Ardennes Cross (ca. 825–875)—one face a Tree of Life, the other a gemmed triumphal cross with a transparent center stone covering a relic. Several crystal Crucifixions shared this function; others were set on altars. Relics were also kept in purse or house reliquaries. Among the most elaborate is a late-eighth-century example from Enger; one side is decorated with overlapping crosses and enameled animals, the others with reliefs of Christ, angels, Mary, and saints, all guarded by lions above: a typical mix of Frankish and Mediterranean motifs recalling Creation and Christian salvation. Equally elaborate altars and book covers abounded, but the portable Adelhausen altar (ca. 800–850) and the tenth-century metalwork on the book cover (now Paris, Bibliothèque Nationale, lat. 9383) are among the few surviving German examples. The Aachen bronzes were both liturgical and political. Likewise political were figures that substituted for rulers (as had Roman busts), probably including the miniature bronze equestrian known as the Metz Rider (ca. 800 or ca. 870).

Portrait coins and seals imitating Roman models claim authority for Carolingian rulers and demonstrate interest in Roman and early Christian art. Other objects physically incorporate earlier works, as does the ewer reliquary at St.-Maurice d'Agaune in Switzerland. More frequent are innovative compositions inspired by Roman forms. Most Carolingian sculpture expresses contemporary ideas, as On a Crystal Baptism (855–869) that uses liturgical elements to examine the roles of bishops and catechumens.

BIBLIOGRAPHY

Elbern, Victor H. *Die Goldschmiedekunst im frühen Mittelalter.* Darmstadt: Wissenschaftliche Buchgesellschaft, 1988.

Fraenkel-Schoorl, Neeke. "Carolingian Jewellery with Plant Ornament." *Berichten van de Rijksdienst voor het Oudheidkundig Bodemonderzoek* 28 (1978): 345–397.

Hamann-MacLean, Richard. "Das problem der karolingischen Grossplastik." In *Kolloquium über Spätantike und frühmittelalterliche Skulptur 3: Vortragstexte (1972).* Mainz: Philipp von Zabern, 1974, 21–37.

Haseloff, Günther. *E-mail in frühen Mittelalter: Frühchristliche Kunst von der Spätantike bis zu den Karolingern.* Marburger Studien zur Vor- und Frühgeschichte, Sonderband 1. Marburg: Wolfgang Hitzeroth Verlag, 1990.

Kornbluth, Genevra. *Engraved Gems of the Carolingian Empire.* University Park: Pennsylvania State University Press, 1995.

———. *"Bibliothèque Nationale MS Lat. 9383: Archaeology and Function of a late Carolingian Treasure Binding."* Forthcoming in *Aachener Kunstblätter* 62. (2001).

Lasko, Peter. *Ars Sacra 800–1200,* 2d. ed. New Haven, Conn.: Yale University Press, 1994.

Pawelec, Katharina. *Aachener Bronzegitter: Studien zur karolingischen Ornamentik um 800.* Bonner Beiträge zur Kunstwissenschaft 12. Cologne: Rheinland-Verlag, 1990.

Wamers, Egon. "Insular Art in Carolingian Europe: The Reception of Old Ideas in a New Empire." In *the Age of Migrating Ideas: Early Medieval Art in Northern Britain and Ireland,* ed. R. Michael Spearman and John Higgitt. Edinburgh: National Museums of Scotland and Stroud, Gloucestershire: Alan Sutton, 1993, 35–44.

Genevra Kornbluth

SEE ALSO

Aachen; Charlemagne; Clothing, Costume, and Fashion; Lorsch; Metz; Relics and Reliquaries; Seals and Sigillography

Carolingians

Ruling much of Europe from the eighth to the tenth centuries, the Carolingians, so-called for their greatest member, Charlemagne (742–814), and for their tendency to name children in each generation Charles (Carolus), laid the foundation for later medieval civilization. The Carolingian tradition of coronation and their governmental ideas would serve as the model for the medieval German empire, and the breakup of the Carolingian empire would lead to the emergence of medieval France and Germany. Their reign witnessed, too, a great cultural flowering traditionally called the Carolingian renaissance.

The dynasty's origins can be traced to a marriage alliance between the Austrasian nobles Arnulf, bishop of Metz (d. ca. 645), and Pippin I (also Pepin the Elder) of Landen (d. 640). The fortunes of the family rested upon its control of the office of mayor of the palace *(major domus)*, a reward to Pippin for his help to the Merovingian king Chlotar II (584–629). Pippin became one of the most powerful figures in the kingdom and passed this legacy on to his son Grimoald (d. 656). The family suffered a setback as a result of Grimoald's political ambitions and his effort to replace the reigning Merovingian with his own son. This premature usurpation led to the murder of Grimoald.

The fortunes of the family were revived by Pippin II of Heristal (687–714) and Charles Martel (714–741). Pippin recovered the office of mayor and united the Frankish kingdom at the battle of Tertry in 687. Civil strife broke out after Pippin's death between his widow, Plectrude, and his illegitimate son, Charles. After initial setbacks, it was Charles who prevailed and assumed the office of mayor.

Charles Martel's term as mayor witnessed the increasing prestige and power of the family. A fierce warrior, Charles successfully imposed his authority on the kingdom during the 720s and won victories against foreign foes. His most important battle was in 732 near Poitiers, where he defeated a Muslim army from Spain. Although subsequent battles were necessary to expel the raiders, the battle of Poitiers established Martel's reputation as a great warrior. Charles further strengthened the alliance between his family and the Frankish church. Although he would alienate much church land to compensate the nobility and ensure their loyalty—an effort that would seriously weaken the church—Charles established strong ties with the royal abbey of St. Denis, promoted the activities of Anglo-Saxon missionaries, and received a proposal from the pope for an alliance against the Lombards in

Italy. So great was Charles's power in the kingdom by the end of his life that he ruled without a Merovingian king and, in Frankish royal tradition, divided the succession between his two sons, Pippin (also Pépin) III the Short (d. 768) and Carloman (d. 754).

The brothers ruled effectively—appointing a new Merovingian king and promoting needed religious and political reform—until Carloman withdrew to a monastery in 747. This action left Pippin as sole mayor and led him to petition the pope, Zacharias (741–752), to order by apostolic authority that Pippin be made king. Zacharias responded as Pippin had hoped and in November 751, Pippin was elected king by the Frankish nobles and crowned and anointed by the bishops of the realm. Coronation and unction were repeated in 754 by Pope Stephen II and led to the establishment of a firm alliance between Rome and the kingdom of the Franks.

Pippin's reign as king (751–768) was a critical time in the history of the dynasty because it was Pippin who established the foundation of Carolingian royal policy. He continued the program of reform of the church and strengthened ties with Rome by two invasions to protect the pope from his Lombard enemies. He undertook the vigorous expansion of the realm and promoted the idea of sacral kingship. Despite his many achievements, Pippin's reign is often overshadowed by that of his illustrious son, Charlemagne.

When Pippin died in 768 he left the kingdom to his sons Carloman and Charlemagne. Tensions existed between the two brothers and civil war nearly broke out but Carloman's death in 771 opened the way for the sole rule of his brother as king until 800 and then as emperor until 814. Charlemagne's success was, in part, the result of his abilities as a warrior; his reign witnessed the dramatic expansion of the territory of the kingdom. Charles undertook a campaign lasting from 772 to 804 to conquer and convert the Saxons. This process saw nearly annual campaigns into Saxony, the mass execution of Saxons, destruction of pagan shrines, and the deportation of large numbers of Saxons. Renewing his father's efforts with even greater enthusiasm, Charles invaded Italy, defeated the Lombards, and became king of the Lombards. He overcame the duke of Bavaria, Tassilo, in 787 and smashed the Avars in the early 790s. His first venture into Muslim Spain had disastrous results but, undaunted, he returned to create the Spanish March, his foray into Spanish territory.

A successful empire builder, Charlemagne was also an innovator in government. The basic unit of government was the county, which was ruled in the king's name by local nobles whose responsibilities included maintaining peace and order, implementing royal law, and dispensing justice. New local judicial officers *(scabini)* were established to adjudicate local disputes. The local authorities were overseen by special representatives of the king, the *missi dominici,* who were usually dispensed in pairs, one noble and one ecclesiastic, to ensure the proper administration of justice, publish new laws, and hear oaths of loyalty. Charles also issued a new type of law, the capitulary, and generally increased the use of writing in government. The capitularies addressed a wide range of issues including religious reform, education, and administration of royal palaces. The most famous of these, the *Admonitio Generalis* of 789, laid the foundation for the great cultural revival known as the Carolingian renaissance. Charles himself invited scholars from throughout Europe, including Alcuin, Theodulf of Orleans, and Paul the Deacon, to participate in his court.

Charlemagne was also responsible for reviving the empire in the west. This occurred when Charles went to Rome to investigate an attack on Pope Leo III (795–816). On December 25, 800, Charles attended Christmas mass and while rising from prayer Leo crowned him emperor and those in the church hailed him as emperor and augustus. Although doubts about Charlemagne's interest in the imperial title were raised by his biographer, Einhard, who declared that Charles would not have entered the church that day had he known what was to happen, many of the court scholars had already asserted Charlemagne's imperial stature in the 790s. And Charles would employ the title in his last years and would rededicate himself to his program of renewal with a new "imperial" capitulary in 802.

Although Charles first saw the title as a special honor for himself alone, he passed on the imperial dignity intact to his sole surviving son, Louis the Pious (778–840). Louis's reign was characterized by continued cultural and religious reform but also by civil war. Louis emphasized his imperial authority in ways that his father did not and sought to ensure the empire's indissolubility by a sophisticated plan of succession in 817. The *Ordinatio Imperii* made provision for all of Louis's sons but reserved imperial and sovereign authority for his eldest son, Lothar (795–855), who would be associated with his father as emperor and then made his successor. Dissatisfaction with the plan emerged almost immediately and was the cause of the revolt in 817 of Louis's nephew, Bernard, who died in the forceful suppression of the uprising. De-

spite this, Louis's reign during the 810s and 820s saw important achievements, including monastic reform, which was a precursor of the Cluniac reform (renewal of monasteries using the Benedictive Rule) and governmental reform that provided legal and constitutional grounds for Carolingian power in Italy.

Despite these positive developments, Louis's reign became troubled in the late 820s and 830s. The birth of a fourth son, Charles the Bald (823–877), and the reorganization of his succession plan provided the other sons, and many nobles and bishops, reason to revolt against Louis's authority. The 830s witnessed much turmoil in the empire and even the deposition of Louis by Lothar. But Louis would regain his throne and rule until his death in 840 when he was succeeded by Lothar, Charles, and Louis the German (804–876).

Civil war intensified in the years after Louis's death as his surviving sons struggled for preeminence in the empire. After several bloody battles, the brothers agreed to the Treaty of Verdun, 843, which divided the realm between them, with Charles getting western Francia, Louis eastern Francia, and Lothar central Francia and Italy as well as the imperial title. Lothar's territory was the least defensible, a problem in the face of civil tensions but also in the face of Viking, Muslim, and Magyar invasions. His acceptance of the tradition of division of inheritance further undermined the territorial integrity of the central kingdom. Indeed, the treaty of Meerssen, 870, saw the division of the northern parts of Lothar's territory between Charles and Louis. Charles survived the wars of the 830s and 840s to establish a strong kingship and to resurrect the dynamic court culture of his grandfather. He also assumed the imperial crown and captured Aachen before his death in 877. It was the kings of West Francia that would preserve the dynasty the longest, lasting until 987, when death and betrayal brought an end to the line.

In East Francia, the dynasty would be replaced much sooner but it would leave an important legacy on its successors and on the medieval empire. After the wars of the 840s, Louis the German continued the Carolingian line in East Francia but was faced with many challenges. He ruled over a diverse kingdom comprising Bavaria, Franconia, Saxony, Swabia, and Thuringia. He was plagued by attacks from Slavs and Vikings and faced the rising power of the nobility, especially the Liudolfings, and suffered revolts from within his family, including two by his son Carloman (d. 880). His dependence on the church, especially the monasteries of his realm, was, in part, the result of the special problems of his kingdom. He divided the realm between his three sons, who succeeded him on his death on August 28, 876, but it would be Louis's son, Charles the Fat (r. 876–887, d. 888) who would receive the imperial title and, for a short time, reunite the empire.

Despite a strong start to his reign and early success against invaders, Charles' ill health and the growing success of Viking raiders led to his deposition in 887. He was succeeded in East Francia by the illegitimate son of his brother, Arnulf of Carinthia (887–899), who ruled with much early success and was crowned emperor in Rome. But Arnulf too was plagued by ill health in his later years and was succeeded after his death by his six-year-old son, Louis the Child (899–911). Louis was the last of the Carolingians to rule in East Francia. His reign was marked by destructive Magyar invasions and the deaths of powerful nobles who were critical to the defense of the realm. On the death of Louis, the nobles of East Francia elected Conrad I king, thereby laying the foundation for the rise of the medieval German kingdom. Conrad and his successors inherited a realm divided into numerous duchies and threatened by foreign invaders, but they also became heir to Carolingian traditions of government and strong ties with the Church.

BIBLIOGRAPHY

Fichtenau, Heinrich. *The Carolingian Empire,* trans. Peter Munz. Toronto: University of Toronto Press, 1979.

Ganshof, François L. *The Carolingians and the Frankish Monarchy: Studies in Carolingian History,* trans. Janet L. Sondheimer. London: Longman, 1971.

———. *Frankish Institution Under Charlemagne,* trans. Bryce and Mary Lyon. Providence, R.I: Brown University Press, 1968.

Halphen, Louis. *Charlemagne and the Carolingian Empire,* trans. Giselle de Nie. Amsterdam: North-Holland, 1977.

McKitterick, Rosamond. *The Frankish Kingdoms Under the Carolingians, 751–987.* London: Longman, 1983.

———. *The Carolingians and the Written Word.* Cambridge: Cambridge University Press, 1989.

Reuter, Timothy. *Germany in the Early Middle Ages, c. 800–1056.* London: Longman, 1991.

Riché, Pierre. *The Carolingians: A Family Who Forged Europe,* trans. Michael I. Allen. Philadelphia: University of Pennsylvania Press, 1993.

Scholz, Bernhard Walter, trans. *Carolingian Chronicles.* Ann Arbor: The University of Michigan Press, 1970.

Sullivan, Richard E. "The Carolingian Age: Reflections on Its Place in the History of the Middle Ages." *Speculum* 64 (1989): 257–306.

Thorpe, Lewis, trans. *Two Lives of Charlemagne.* Harmondsworth, England: Penguin Press, 1969.

Michael Frassetto

SEE ALSO

Admonitio Generalis; Aachen; Capitularies; Charlemagne; Charles III, the Fat; Coronation; Dhuoda; Donation of Constantine; Empire; Liudolfinger; Louis the Pious; *Ordinatio Imperii;* Pippin; Succession; Theodulf of Orléans; Verdun

Castles and Manor Houses

See individual locations.

Cathedrals and Churches

See individual locations.

Charlemagne (747–814)

Charles the Great (*magnus,* whence the French "Charlemagne"), King of the Franks (768–814) and emperor of the West (800–814) was born in 747 to Pippin (Pépin) III and his wife, Bertha, daughter of the powerful Count Caribert of Laon. Pippin, mayor of the palace of the Franks, named his son after his own father, the redoubtable Charles Martel (d. 742). In 751 when Charles was still a boy, Pippin became king after deposing Childeric III (743–751), the last member of the Merovingian dynasty established by Clovis (481–511). The legitimacy of the new dynasty was bolstered when Pope Stephen II (also III, 752–757) came to Francia to bless Bertrada (Bertha) and in the name of Saint Peter anoint Pippin and his sons Charles and Carloman as "patricians of the Romans." The pope forbade the Franks from choosing anyone as king other than a Carolingian (from the Latin Carolus, Charles). This dynastic change and the relationship binding the political and military power of the Carolingian family to the spiritual power of the papacy were revolutionary events. Pippin III proved to be a resourceful and energetic king whose conquest of Aquitaine, two successful expeditions against the Lombards, and promotion of religious reform demonstrated the potential and direction of the new dynasty.

During his long reign Charles more fully realized and amplified Pippin's initiatives. So spectacular was his achievement that his posthumous reputation assumed legendary proportions. Einhard (ca. 770–840), who grew up at Charles's court, in his valuable *Life of Charles* borrowed language from Suetonius's *Lives of the Caesars* (second-century C.E.) to add rhetorical luster appropriate to his subject. In later centuries crusading and romance legends inspired by Charles's memory enriched medieval vernacular literature. In the twentieth century his memory served to advance the prospects of a united Europe. Since 1949, the citizens of Aachen, Germany, have annually awarded the International Charlemagne Prize *(Karlpries)* to individuals whose activities further "the creation of a United States of Europe." In his own time, Charles grappled with the implications of a new style of kingship, faced the challenges of conquest, revolt, and the future of the dynasty, and attempted to unify and reform a society embracing a welter of different peoples within a community that eventually stretched over one million square kilometers.

The kingdom Charles inherited from his father in 768 was much smaller, essentially modern France, Belgium, the Netherlands, Luxembourg, and western Germany. At first Charles shared the kingdom with his younger brother Carloman. Corulership set the stage for rivalry within the family, especially when Carloman refused to aid in suppressing rebellions in Aquitaine, but Carloman's death in December 771 averted serious dynastic tension. As sole king, Charles turned his attention to solidifying control of political and military resources and to crises outside his realm. A successful king in the early Middle Ages was a successful warlord. Charles, as had Pippin III and Charles Martel before him, succeeded as a leader because he succeeded as a warrior. Charles drew the warrior class, some 250 to 300 counts and their followers, to his cause by sharing with them the spoils of war and political authority. Aristocratic loyalty and support provided the mainstay of Charles's war machine. Charles's detailed orders to his warriors stipulating when and where to mobilize and what equipment and manpower to bring offer an unparalleled insight to his command and control structure. His ability to make war almost continually and most often successfully for more than thirty years on many fronts attests to Charles's success as a military commander.

After Carloman's death Charles's armies began to campaign outside Francia. In 772, rejecting his mother's efforts to ally with the Lombard kingdom (Charles had even married a soon to be repudiated Lombard princess),

Charles responded to calls of Pope Hadrian I (772–795) for help against the "pestiferous" Lombards. After a siege of nine months the Lombard capital of Pavia fell in 774 and Desiderius, the last Lombard king of the two-century-old kingdom, was captured and confined to the monastery of Corbie in northern Francia. Charles became the king of the Lombards. During the siege of Pavia, he made the first ever visit by a Frankish king to Rome. Charles's political relationship to the pope was ambiguous and Hadrian soon chafed under the growing presence and influence of Frankish counts and ecclesiastics in Italy. Although linked to Desiderius by family ties, Duke Tassilo III of Bavaria did not intervene in the Lombard war. Tassilo earlier had agreed to become a vassal of Pippin. When Charles required Tassilo to renew his pledges in 781, the semi-independent duke balked. After military threats and a decade of diplomatic intrigue, Tassilo was confined to a monastery and in 794 "abdicated." The annexation of Lombardy and Bavaria is all the more impressive when viewed together with the continuous conflict in Saxony. One of the last centers of vibrant Germanic paganism, the Saxon homeland east of the Rhine was a hotbed of political resistance to Carolingian aggression fueled by devotion to Saxon culture and skillful exploitation of Frankish preoccupation in other regions. Earlier in the eighth century Charles Martel fought against the Saxons, a struggle his grandson continued in 772. Saxony was finally subdued in 804, but not until after several uprisings led by the spirited Widukind (also Wittekind), the massacre of forty-five hundred Saxon prisoners, and the forced deportation of Saxons to Francia. The conquest and eventual Christianization of Saxony extended Carolingian power into a region never controlled by the Roman Empire.

In 777 the emir of Barcelona, no doubt encouraged by the success of Frankish arms, persuaded Charles to invade Spain, which had been under Muslim control since 711. This bold venture ended in 778 in a disaster immortalized in the *Song of Roland,* the attack on Charles's rear guard by Basques in the Pyrenees. Operations in the 790s in the Danube basin where the Avars had been settled from the sixth century, met greater success. As the partisans of the Lombards and of Tassilo, these "new Huns" defined themselves as enemies of the Carolingians. In 791 Charles initiated an eastern campaign that Einhard described as second only to the Saxon wars in its intensity and significance. By 796 Charles had crushed Avar power. Significantly, Einhard seemed most impressed by the fifteen wagons, each drawn by four oxen, that were required to haul Avar treasure back to Francia. Three years later in 799 the Bretons in Brittany, who had long been foes of the Franks, surrendered to Charles's armies.

Charles's ceaseless campaigns enriched and transformed his kingdom. As the lands under his control expanded to cover most of western Europe, the Carolingians established contact with peoples on their periphery including Scandinavians, Slavs, Byzantines, Muslims, and Anglo-Saxons. The patriarch of Jerusalem as well as Hārūn ar-Rashīd, the caliph of Baghdad, and the imperial court at Constantinople exchanged embassies and correspondence with Charles's court. But Charles's primary focus lay in controlling the heterogeneous lands and peoples of his vast domain measuring some six hundred miles along each axis from Scandinavia to the Mediterranean and from the Atlantic to the Danube. Charles's administrative and political structure was multilayered. Although master of all, Charles delegated power and authority to trusted followers. His sons Louis and Pippin were appointed sub-kings of Aquitaine and Italy, respectively, while his brother-in-law Gerold was put in charge of Bavaria. Charles established marches in dangerous border regions whose governors controlled the local counts. Elsewhere counts exercised military, judicial, and fiscal authority. Charles tried to hold this centrifugal system of shared authority together by several means. Royal capitularies, documents organized by topics *(capitula)*, established and broadcast policy. The subjects of these—including farm management, minting, heresy, religious reform, justice, famine, warfare, education, feuds, homicide, rape, widows, and orphans—suggests the range of his concept of governance. Several capitularies addressed specifically to the *missi,* the king's personal representatives dispatched throughout the kingdom to carry out his wishes and to investigate local problems, point to another level of administrative and political control. *Missi* (from the Latin *missus,* "one who is sent out") had been used by Merovingian kings, but Charles extended and regularized their use as agents of government, who linked a highly fragmented political system to the king's household.

When he was not campaigning Charles settled in favorite palaces at Frankfurt, Herstal, Ingelheim, Mainz, Worms, and Thionville, in the heartlands of the Frankish kingdom. After 794 he resided semipermanently at the new palace complex at Aachen. The king's household, with its feasts, rituals, comings and goings, hunting expeditions, and, in Aachen's warm springs, group bathing, formed a dynamic community. Carolingian poets memorialized the conviviality of the royal entourage. Charles's

household consisted of the seneschal who maintained provisions, butlers, cupbearers, chamberlains, who took care of the living quarters, the constable, who attended the stable, a host of domestics, and family members. By the end of his long life, Charles presided over a large, three-generation family. Einhard mentions five wives as well as four concubines who were a part of Charles's household and bore at least sixteen children who survived infancy. His wives, especially Hildegard, Fastrada, and Liutgard played important political and public roles, as did his sons and daughters, some of whom became bishops, abbots, and abbesses. Ironically, the religious reform that Charles encouraged would shortly after his death lead to condemnation of his Germanic warlord lifestyle. In a widely reported dream, the monk Wetti related in 824 that he had observed in the afterlife a wild beast gnawing at Charles's genitals as punishment for his sexual sins.

The system of governance and administration that Charles gradually built up depended on loyalty and commitment to his policies. In practice the system was often compromised by the personal and family interests of officials who used their positions to enrich themselves. Charges of corruption and abuse of power by rapacious counts, judges, and even *missi* who succumbed to bribery occur commonly in the sources, especially during the last decade of Charles's reign. Important family connections made it difficult to bring corrupt officials to justice. In addition to periodic rebellions of conquered peoples, Charles also faced serious challenges to his regime. In 785–786, a rebellion led by Count Hadrad of Thuringia had to be brutally suppressed. A few years later in 792 one of Charles's sons was discovered at the center of a plot against the king's life involving Frankish aristocrats. After dealing swiftly with the rebels, Charles attempted to enforce loyalty by legal and religious means. In 786, 789, 792, and again in 802 after he became emperor, he required an ever widening group, which eventually embraced all freemen, lay and clerical, over the age of twelve, to swear personal loyalty to him. The 802 oath was especially significant, since it bound oath takers not only to obey the emperor and protect his life, but also to live Christian lives.

The nexus between politics and religion had long been a feature of Frankish life and culture. Charles Martel and Pippin III enjoyed close relations with clergy and identified with religious reform. The prologue to the mid-eighth-century revision of the Salic Law unabashedly depicted the Franks as God's new Chosen People. Within this tradition Charles enacted religious reforms and promoted Christianity as vigorously as he waged war and managed his kingdom. He drew talented churchmen to his court as advisers, many of whom he was able to place strategically in bishoprics and monasteries throughout his realm. These churchmen often performed important political duties as well. Court scholars honored Charles's patronage of their work by calling him David after the biblical king. In religious matters, however, Charles modeled himself on Josiah, the Hebrew king who undertook a root and branch reform of Israel based on biblical precepts. His great reform capitulary, the *Admonitio Generalis* of 789, outlines the king's blueprint for a biblically based society. With the biblical kings of old, Charles confidently determined religious policy and used his court to define religious orthodoxy in the West, especially opposing Spanish views on the nature of Christ and Byzantine views of images in worship.

The centrality of the Bible in Carolingian political culture sparked reform in education and stimulated literary culture. During Charles's reign political authority in a massive, sustained, and visible way promoted intellectual culture as essential to the well-being of society. Charles's patronage attracted the leading scholars of Europe to his court, often non-Franks such as the Anglo-Saxon Alcuin, the Visigoth Theodulf, the Italian Peter of Pisa, and the Irishman Dungal. Alcuin, who enjoyed a close personal relationship with Charles, played an especially significant role in establishing a new pedagogy and in training Frankish students to serve as "soldiers of Christ" in the parishes, cathedrals, and monasteries of Carolingian Europe. Charles interacted comfortably with his court scholars, admired Augustine's *City of God,* spoke Latin fluently, and was particularly interested in astronomy and time reckoning. In their pursuit of biblical wisdom as a guide for the reform of their society, Carolingian scholars produced a more legible form of Latin script, Carolingian minuscule. In their efforts to improve learning in Latin and the liberal arts as a stepping-stone to more profound comprehension of sacred wisdom, they copied Roman texts that might otherwise have perished. Carolingian masters and students composed the first audience to systematically read and interpret the works of the Christian church fathers. In their numerous commentaries, technical schoolbooks, theological, philosophical, and political treatises, histories, poetry, and letters, they attempted to integrate secular learning and sacred wisdom in the services of Carolingian society. The emergence of controversy and debate on fundamental theological, philosophical,

political, and legal issues testifies to the sophistication and originality of the new culture. Charles's patronage and the wealth flowing into the hands of aristocrats and ecclesiastics also stimulated artistic production in the form of metalwork, elaborate book covers, jewelry, crystal, ivory carving, painting, and manuscript illumination. Some six hundred new buildings went up in the Carolingian realms, including cathedrals, monasteries, and palace complexes at Aachen and Paderborn.

On December 25, 800, Pope Leo III (795–816) crowned Charles emperor in Rome. Charles's continent-wide conquests and strong leadership certainly justified the title, but contemporary sources are unclear about the meaning of the coronation and modern scholars continue to debate its significance. Not even the participants seemed fully aware of the implication of the revival of the imperial title in the West. Certainly the coronation was not a surprise, as Einhard reported, since Charles's circle in the late 790s had already begun to describe him in imperial terms. Charles had come to Rome to rescue the city from his political enemies. The pope no doubt saw conferral of the imperial title as a means to draw Charles even closer to the see of St. Peter and to forge new links with a Western emperor to replace the fractured links with the emperor in Constantinople. "David" was to become Constantine. Again, Rome was disappointed in the new arrangement since Charles dominated the Roman church as he had the church to the north of the Alps. The great programmatic Capitulary of 802 defining an imperial Christian political culture for Europe was crafted in Aachen, not Rome. What the imperial office meant to the relationship between pope and emperor, religion and politics, would be debated for centuries to come. For Charles the emperorship was a personal honor. When in 806 he outlined the future division of the empire among his legitimate sons, Charles, Pippin, and Louis, the question of the imperial title was ignored. In 813, with two of his three heirs dead, Charles bestowed the title on Louis without benefit of papal consultation or approval.

The division of 806 and Louis's coronation in 813 were the actions of a man contemplating his last years. Charles died on January 28, 814 at Aachen and was buried there. His long reign strengthened the power of his family in Europe, entrenched warrior-aristocrats as partners with kings in governing, promoted a distinctly European Christian religion and culture, defined a new sacral kingship, and revived the ambiguous ideology of empire. More than anything, Charles consolidated the fundamental elements of an emerging

European identity that late generations would refine and burnish.

BIBLIOGRAPHY

Bullough, Donald. *The Age of Charlemagne.* 2d ed. London: Paul Elek, 1973.

Collins, Roger. *Charlemagne.* Toronto: University of Toronto Press, 1998.

Contreni, John J. "The Carolingian Renaissance: Education and Literary Culture." In *The New Cambridge Medieval History,* ed. Rosamond McKitterick. *Vol. 2, c. 700–c. 900.* Cambridge: Cambridge University Press, 1997, pp. 709–757.

———. "Carolingian Biblical Culture." In *Iohannes Scottus Eriugena: The Bible and Hermeneutics,* ed. Gerd Van Riel, Carlos Steel, and James McEvoy. Ancient and Medieval Philosophy, De-Wulf-Mansion Centre, Series 1, XX. Louvain: Louvain University Press, 1996, pp. 1–23.

Dutton, Paul Edward. *The Politics of Dreaming in the Carolingian Empire.* Lincoln: University of Nebraska Press, 1994.

———, ed. *Carolingian Civilization: A Reader.* Peterborough, Ont.: Broadview Press, 1993.

Fichtenau, Heinrich. *The Carolingian Empire: The Age of Charlemagne,* trans. Peter Munz. Oxford: Basil Blackwell, 1957.

Ganshof, François Louis. *Frankish Institutions Under Charlemagne,* trans. Bryce and Mary Lyon. Providence, R.I.: Brown University Press, 1968.

Godman, Peter. *Poets and Emperors: Frankish Politics and Carolingian Poetry.* Oxford: Clarendon Press, 1987.

———, trans. *Poetry of the Carolingian Empire.* Norman: University of Oklahoma Press, 1985.

King, P. D., trans. *Charlemagne: Translated Sources.* Lambrigg, England: P. D. King, 1987.

Loyn, H. R., and John Percival, trans. *The Reign of Charlemagne: Documents on Carolingian Government and Administration.* London: Edward Arnold, 1975.

McKitterick, Rosamond. *The Frankish Kingdoms Under the Carolingians, 751–987.* London and New York: Longman, 1983.

Nees, Lawrence. *A Tainted Mantle: Hercules and the Classical Tradition at the Carolingian Court.* Philadelphia: University of Pennsylvania Press, 1991.

Nelson, Janet. "Women at the Court of Charlemagne: A Case of Monstrous Regiment?" In Janet Nelson, *The Frankish World, 750–900.* London: Hambledon Press, 1996, pp. 223–242.

Riché, Pierre. *The Carolingians: A Family Who Forged Europe,* trans. Michael Idomir Allen. Philadelphia: University of Pennsylvania Press, 1993.

Sullivan, Richard E. *Aix-la-Chapelle in the Age of Charlemagne.* Norman: University of Oklahoma Press, 1963.

John J. Contreni

SEE ALSO

Admonitio Generalis; Capitularies; Carolingians; Coronation; Louis the Pious; Pippin: *Servatius;* Succession

Charlemagne Epics, Dutch

Throughout the Middle Ages, Charlemagne epics were popular in the Low Countries. Some of them are among the oldest known literature written in Middle Dutch: *Van den bere Wisselau,* the *Roelantslied,* and *Renout van Montalbaen* probably date to the late twelfth century. An example of a more recent text is *Hughe van Bordeus,* which originated presumably in the fourteenth century. Charlemagne epics were copied through the end of the Middle Ages. Unfortunately, all of these epics save one *(Karel ende Elegast)* have been preserved only fragmentarily. Nevertheless, each of the three cycles that the medieval French poet Bertrand de Bar-sur-Aube distinguished with regard to the French *chansons de geste* (song of deeds) is represented. The cycle of the king is represented by, for example, *Aspremont, Beerte metten breden voeten, Karel ende Elegast,* and the *Roelantslied; Van den bere Wisselau,* a text that seems to stem from a Germanic tradition, can also be assigned to this cycle. *Gheraert van Viane* and *Willem van Oringen,* among others, belong to the cycle of Guillaume d'Orange *(geste de Garin de Monglane).* The cycle of the rebellious vassals is represented by *Madelgijs, Ogier van Denemarken,* and *Renout van Montalbaen.* In addition, there are fragments of texts not belonging to any of these three major cycles: *Hughe van Bordeus* and the *Roman der Lorreinen,* for example. Finally, fragments exist which have not yet been identified.

All of the Dutch Charlemagne epics are written in rhyming couplets. It has been argued that texts such as the Limburg *Aiol, Renout van Montalbaen,* and the *Roelantslied,* which show the oldest stage in the development of versification techniques, were originally written in long internally rhyming verses. Most Charlemagne epics are thought to have been composed in Flanders. The majority of the manuscripts in which they have come down to us were probably also executed in this region. In other regions too, however, Charlemagne epics were composed or copied. The *Roman der Lorreinen* and *Van den bere Wisselau* are thought to be Brabantine; besides a Flemish *Aiol* there is a Limburg one; and we know that a poet from Holland composed a *Willem van Oringen,* which might be identified with the *Willem van Oringen* of which some hundreds of verses have been preserved.

The source of most Middle Dutch Charlemagne epics has been a French *chanson de geste,* but this in no way means that the Dutch texts are slavish imitations of their French parallels. Some of them can be labeled as (free) translations. The *Roelantslied,* for example, is a translation of the *Chanson de Roland.* The Limburg *Aiol,* too, is a translation. The Flemish *Aiol* and a number of other texts, on the other hand, must instead be characterized as free adaptations or retellings. Sometimes, the differences between the Middle Dutch text and its Old French counterpart are such as to evoke the idea that, while composing his text, the Dutch poet had no manuscript containing the French text within reach, but based it on his recollection of one or more performances of a chanson de geste he had attended. The Middle Dutch *Ogier* and *Renout van Montalbaen* may have been composed in this way. Worthy of mention is the special place among the Charlemagne epics occupied by *Karel ende Elegast,* in which we are told how Charles, obeying an order of God, sets out stealing and so discovers that a conspiracy has been planned against him. No *chanson de geste* telling of this story has been preserved, but we may assume that one existed: *Renaut de Montauban* and *Le restor du paon* both contain a brief summary of the story. Whereas the majority of the Middle Dutch Charlemagne epics are considered to be dependent on French texts, there is an intriguing hypothesis stating that in the case of *Karel ende Elegast* the dependency is in the opposite direction: according to this hypothesis, the creator of the lost *chanson de geste* (the *Chanson de Basin*) used a Middle Dutch *Karel ende Elegast.*

Karel ende Elegast appeared in print from the late fifteenth century on. In all printed editions that have been preserved, it kept its original metrical form: it is a text in rhymed verses. In employing this meter, *Karel ende Elegast* constitutes an exception to the printed Dutch Charlemagne literature: all of the other printed texts are prose romances. The sixteenth-century *Historie vander coninghinnen Sibilla,* a text that has come down to us only in a prose version in print, appears to derive from a Spanish prose text. Other romances are prose adaptations of Middle Dutch rhymed epics. Some of these romances,

like the *Historie vanden vier Heemskinderen* (a prose adaptation of *Renout van Montalbaen*) were popular for centuries.

BIBLIOGRAPHY

Bennett, Philip E. et al., eds. *Charlemagne in the North: Proceedings of the Twelfth International Conference of the Société Rencesvals, Edinburgh 4th to 11th August 1991.* Edinburgh: Société Rencesvals. British Branch, 1993, pp. 31–63, 81–88, 95–102.

Farrier, Susan E. *The Medieval Charlemagne Legend: An Annotated Bibliography.* New York and London: Garland, 1993 [Dutch materials by Geert H. M. Claassens].

Gerritsen, Willem P., and Anton G. van Melle, eds. *Van Aiol tot de Zwaanridder; personages uit de middeleeuwse verhaalkunst en hun voortleven in literatuur, theater en beeldende kunst.* Nijmegen: Sun, 1993.

Irene Spijker

SEE ALSO
Charlemagne; Charlemagne Epics, German; Legends

Charlemagne Epics, German

After Charlemagne's death in 814, his son, Louis the Pious (814–840) shifted the focus on education away from the royal court and into the monasteries. In general, this had a numbing effect on the development of secular literature. Einhard wrote the first secular biography, *Vita Caroli Magni* (Life of Charlemagne), in Latin prose under the reign of Louis. Nevertheless, for the next 350 years, secular literary works, especially those written in the German vernacular, remained scarce in contrast to the massive body of spiritual literature in Latin. Interest in Charlemagne and his times did not rise again at the secular courts until the middle of the twelfth century, when influenced by the second Crusade (1147–1149), Charlemagne was rediscovered as the great defender of Christianity against the heathen onslaught and as the force that had reunified the Roman empire into the Holy Roman Empire.

According to German scholarly tradition, the term *Heldenepik* (heroic epics) has been reserved for the "genuine" Germanic poetic narrations oriented around the historical Dietrich figure, King Theoderic (471–526) of the Ostrogoths. Centerpiece of that Germanic tradition is the *Nibelungenlied,* which became the German national epic. The French national heroic epic, *Chanson de Roland*

(Song of Roland, early twelfth century), on the other hand, along with the entire literary genre *chanson de geste* (song of deeds), centered around Charlemagne, never received the attention as *Heldenepik* by the early German scholars, although its first representative, *Rolandslied* (Song of Roland, 1170) appeared at least thirty years before the so-called German national epic. No other epic of the twelfth century found such a rapid and wide acceptance. It has been preserved through two complete and four fragmentary manuscripts dating back to the twelfth century or around 1200. The *Rolandslied* was written in Regensburg by a priest who called himself Chuonrat (Konrad), probably under the patronage of Duke Henry the Lion, the most powerful territorial lord in Germany, and his English wife Mathilda. The historical background to the epic is the annihilation of Charlemagne's rear guard in the Pyrenees by Basque warriors upon his return from Spain. The French source highlights the leader of the rear guard, Roland, a legendary hero, who in defense of his *dulce France* (sweet France) and his king refuses to call for help after being ambushed by the traitors, until with his last gasp he blows his horn Olifant, thus bringing back Charlemagne to witness his heroic death and punish the traitors. Konrad follows the plot of his source carefully but shifts the emphasis away from the theme of French nationalism in order to emphasize the crusading spirit of the fight against the heathens, thus almost doubling the original length of the epic. The figure of Charlemagne is highlighted as the exemplary Christian ruler and legitimate bearer of the crown of the Holy Roman Empire, reflecting the canonization of Charlemagne that took place around that time. It is possible that Konrad's patron, Henry the Lion, seeing himself as Charlemagne's descendant, wanted to underline his own claims to the imperial throne against the dynasty of the Staufer family.

Three types of the French heroic epic tradition, the *chanson de geste,* were adapted into German, the first being epics that deal with Charlemagne's legendary biography in a more or less panegyric fashion. The *chanson de Roland* is the most prominent representative of this type. Another German adaptation of this work was composed by a professional writer from East Franconia, who called himself Der Stricker and worked most of the time in Austria for various patrons. His work, known under the title *Karl* (1215–1233), is probably based on Konrad's earlier version but uses several other French sources as well. Der Stricker's main motive may have been to give Konrad's version the smooth formal surface of the courtly romance, which was then in fashion. No less than twenty-

four complete and twenty-three fragmentarily preserved manuscripts testify to its success. The only other German adaptation of the *chanson de Roland* is a Low German version, based on Konrad's *Rolandslied* and other French sources, which are responsible for an interpolated episode on Roland's and Olivier's meeting with a heathen prince, Ospinel, and a final episode after Roland's death that deviates completely from Konrad's version. Although it may have been originally composed during the early thirteenth century, the Low German *Rolandslied* is completely preserved only as part five of a loose compilation of originally independent works that deal with Charlemagne's life. Their independence is evidenced by manuscript fragments clearly different from the versions preserved in the compilation. This magnum opus of thirty-six thousand verse lines, known under the title *Karlmeinet,* is written in the Ripuarian dialect of the region around Cologne and Aachen and was probably compiled after the first decade of the fourteenth century. The compiler has made a conscious effort to give the work a semblance of wholeness through introductory and linking segments, the longest of which, part three, tells about Charlemagne's conquests, his fight against the Saracens, and his coronation as Holy Roman Emperor. The final segment of *Karlmeinet* dealing with Charlemagne's last years and death originated from the compiler's pen as well. The first part of the compilation is the independent work *Karl und Galie.* It tells the story of the young orphaned heir to the throne, who flees from treacherous usurpers to Spain, where he finds refuge under the pseudonym (Karl) Meinet at the court of King Galafer of Toledo, with whose help he regains his realm. Secretly engaged to Galafer's daughter, Galie, Charlemagne returns to Spain to abduct her, is pursued by the Saracens, but finally brings her home, where she converts to Christianity and becomes his queen. The second part of *Karlmeinet, Morant und Galie,* has also been identified as an originally independent work. It is the story of treacherous courtiers who accuse one of Charlemagne's confidants, Morant, of having an affair with Galie. Eventually, Morant remains victorious in the decisive duel and marries Galie's friend Florette.

A second type of *chanson de geste* has been identified as *gestes des vassaux rebelles* (tales of rebellious vassals), narratives that feature vassals who are either falsely accused of treason or rebel against unjust treatment by Charlemagne. These epics, created toward the end of the twelfth century, originally reflected the struggle of the territorial lords against the idea of a centralized kingdom pushed by the house of Capet, whose members claimed to be directly descended from Charlemagne. The conflict, which in France was finally settled in favor of centralism around 1200 by Philippe II Auguste, continued to fester in Germany without ever being resolved. This may explain the continued interest in these epics in German-speaking areas. One of them is represented in *Karlmeinet* as *Karl und Elegast*. Like this work, most of the other epics of this type, named for individual heroes like Gerart van Rossiliun, Ogier von Dänemark, and Reinolt von Montelban, found their way into Germany via Dutch adaptations and are fully preserved only in fifteenth- and sixteenth-century manuscripts. Others, like Herpin, Sibille, Loher und Maller, appear in fifteenth-century novels by Elisabeth von Nassau-Saarbrücken, which have been adapted directly from French sources.

A third type of *chanson de geste* is only loosely associated with Charlemagne's biography. These epics are focused on the figure of Guillaume d'Orange, who was historically related to Charlemagne and fought under him and Louis the Pious against the Saracens. The literary Guillaume (Willehalm, in German) fights against his own father-in-law, Terramer, leader of the Muslim armies, who wants to recapture his daughter Arabele for the "right" faith. Willehalm and Arabele had fallen in love and fled to France. Arabele is baptized under the name of Gyburc before they get married. All this is cause for two horrible battles at Aliscanz that wipe out thousands of warriors. The earliest and most outstanding representative of this genre is Wolfram von Eschenbach's *Willehalm* (ca. 1210–1220). Wolfram's direct source may have been a version of the French epic *Bataille d'Aliscanz*, but he may also have used sources from oral tradition. Although unfinished, Wolfram's epic is a masterpiece of Crusade literature. He strips the rough edges off the warrior world of the *chanson de geste* and creates an elaborate and refined courtly setting for the enormous holy war. By building such extreme contrasts he directs attention to the sheer cruelty—or madness—of pitting the noblest representatives of both cultures, which he presents as virtually equal in quality, in deadly battles against each other over the issue of baptism. Wolfram's *Willehalm* seems to have enjoyed almost the same popularity as his *Parzival*. Twelve complete manuscripts—some of them with precious illuminations—and fifty-eight fragments have survived. Ulrich von Türheim continued the unfinished work with his *Rennewart* (before 1250) and Ulrich von dem Türlin wrote its pre-history, *Arabel* (after 1253, before 1278), thus creating a trilogy of more than sixty thousand verse

lines. Aside from *Die Schlacht von Alischanz* (The Battle of Alischanz), an early fourteenth-century independent Low German translation of the French epic, the material was frequently viewed as a historical record and thus found entry in many fifteenth- and sixteenth-century chronicles. In general, Charlemagne epics are to be considered among histories, folkloric legends, and courtly romances throughout the Middle Ages in Germany.

BIBLIOGRAPHY

Rolandslied

Buschinger, Danielle, and Wolfgang Spiewok. *Das "Rolandslied" des Konrad: gesammelte Aufsätze.* Greifswald: Reineke-Verlag, 1996.

Konrad, der Pfaffe. *Das Rolandslied des Pfaffen Konrad: Mittelhochdeutch/Neuhochdeutsch,* ed. and trans. Dieter Kartschoke. Stuttgart: Reclam, 1993 [German trans.].

———. *Priest Konrad's Song of Roland,* trans. J. W. Thomas. Columbia, S.C.: Camden House, 1994.

Karl Meinet

Burg, Udo von der. "Konrads Rolandslied und das Rolandslied des Karlmeinet." *Rheinische Vierteljahrsblätter* 39 (1975): 321–341.

Frings, Theodor, and Elisabeth Linke, eds. *Morant und Galie.* Deutsche Texte des Mittelalters 69. Berlin: Akademie-Verlag, 1976.

Helm, Dagmar, ed. *Karl und Galie: Karlmeinet, Teil I: Abdruck der Handschrift A (2290) der Hessischen Landes- und Hochschulbibliothek Darmstadt und der 8 Fragmente.* Deutsche Texte des Mittelalters 74. Berlin: Akademie-Verlag, 1986.

Keller, Adelbert von, ed. *Karl Meinet.* Bibliothek des Litterarischen Vereins in Stuttgart 45; rpt. Amsterdam: Rodolpi, 1971.

Zagolla, Rüdiger. *Der Karlmeinet und seine Fassung vom Rolandslied des Pfaffen Konrad.* Göppinger Arbeiten zur Germanistik 497. Göppingen: Kümmerle, 1988.

Stricker, Der

Burg, Udo von der. *Strickers Karl der Grosse als Bearbeitung des Rolandsliedes: Studien zu Form und Inhalt.* Göppinger Arbeiten zur Germanistik 131. Göppingen: Kümmerle, 1974.

Schnell, Rüdiger. "Strickers Karl der Grosse: Literarische Tradition und politische Wirklichkeit." *Zeitschrift für Deutsche Philologie* 93 (Sonderheft, 1974): 50–80.

Stricker, Der. *Karl der Grosse,* ed. Karl Bartsch (1857); rpt. with afterward by Dieter Kartschoke. Deutsche

Neudrucke: Reihe: Texte des Mittelalters. Berlin and New York: de Gruyter, 1965.

Wolfram von Eschenbach

Gibbs, Marion E. *Narrative Art in Wolfram's Willehalm.* Göppinger Arbeiten zur Germanistik 159. Göppingen: Kümmerle, 1976.

Greenfield, John, and Lydia Miklautsch. *Der "Willehalm" Wolframs von Eschenbach: eine Einführung.* Berlin and New York: de Gruyter, 1998.

Lachmann, Karl, ed., *Wolfram von Eschenbach.* 6th ed., introd. Eduard Hartl (1926); rpt. Berlin and New York: de Gruyter, 1997.

Lefèvere, André, ed., *Wolfram von Eschenbach.* German Library 2. New York: Continuum, 1991.

Ulrich von dem Türlin. *Arabel.* Eine alemannische Bearbeitung der "Arabel" Ulrichs von dem Türlin. Die Exzerpte aus Wolframs "Willehalm" in der "Weltchronik" Heinrichs von München, ed. Werner Schröder. Texte und Untersuchungen zur "Willehalm"-Rezeption. Vols. 1–2. Berlin and New York: de Gruyter, 1981.

———. *Willehalm: mit der Vorgeschichte des Ulrich von dem Türlin und der Fortsetzung des Ulrich von Türheim: vollständige Faksimile-Ausgabe im Originalformat des Codex Vindobonensis 2670 der Österreichischen Nationalbibliothek.* Codices selecti phototypice impressi; v. 46, 46*. Graz: Akademische Druck- und Verlagsanstalt, 1974 [facsimile].

Wolfram von Eschenbach. *Willehalm: nach der Handschrift 857 der Stiftsbibliothek St. Gallen,* trans. and ed. Joachim Heinzle. Frankfurt am Main: Deutscher Klassiker Verlag, 1991 [with illustrations and an essay].

———. *Willehalm,* ed. Werner Schröder; trans. and introd. Dieter Kartschoke. Berlin and New York: de Gruyter, 1989.

———. *Willehalm,* trans. Marion E. Gibbs and Sidney M. Johnson. Penguin Classics. Harmondsworth, England and New York: Penguin, 1984.

Other Studies

Burchert, Bernhard. *Die Anfänge des Prosaromans in Deutschland: die Prosaerzählungen Elisabeths von Nassau-Saarbrücken.* Frankfurt am Main and New York: P. Lang, 1987.

Morrison, Susan Signe. "Women Writers and Women Rulers: Rhetorical and Political Empowerment in the Fifteenth Century." *Women in German Yearbook* (1993): 25–48.

Müller, Jan-Dirk. "Späte Chanson de geste-Rezeption und Landesgeschichte: Zu den Übersetzungen der Elisabeth von Nassau-Saarbrücken." In *Wolfram-Studien XI: Chansons de geste in Deutschland,* ed. Joachim Heinzle, L. Peter Johnson, and Gisela Vollmann-Profe. Berlin: Schmidt, 1989, pp. 206–226.

Klaus M. Schmidt

SEE ALSO

Charlemagne; Charlemagne Epics, Dutch; *Nibelungenlied;* Stricker, Der; Wolfram von Eschenbach

Charles III, the Fat (839–January 13, 888)

The third son of Louis the German (r. 840–876), Charles the Fat became king of Alemmannia upon his father's death and king of Italy in 879; he was the last Carolingian emperor. In 881, Pope John VIII, hoping to involve Charles in the defense of Italy, crowned the king and his wife, Richardis, emperor and empress. When his younger brother Louis the Younger (r. 876–882) died, Charles gained control of Franconia, Saxony, and Bavaria. Finally, after the death of King Carloman (r. 879–884) of West Francia, magnates in the west invited Charles to be their king and pledged him their loyalty in June 885. Although nominally reunited, the union of the Carolingian empire under Charles was ephemeral. Saracens, Northmen, Slavs, resistance from important magnates such as Arnulf of Carinthia, his failure to produce a legitimate heir, and a debilitating illness (he suffered a spectacular seizure at the royal synod of Frankfurt on January 26, 873) led to Charles's forced retirement in November 887.

Charles had a lasting impact on medieval literature. He commissioned Notker, a monk of St. Gall, to compose the *Deeds of Charlemagne,* an engaging portrait of exemplary kingship that includes edifying lessons from the reigns of Louis the Pious and Louis the German. Charles is also the center of the vivid *Vision of Karl III,* an account, probably composed at Reims in the entourage of Bishop Fulk, that conveys considerable anxiety about Carolingian dynastic succession.

BIBLIOGRAPHY

Dutton, Paul Edward. *The Politics of Dreaming in the Carolingian Empire.* Lincoln: University of Nebraska Press, 1994.

Reuter, Timothy. *Germany in the Early Middle Ages, 800–1056.* London and New York: Longman, 1991.

Riché, Pierre. *The Carolingians: A Family Who Forged Europe,* trans. Michael Idomir Allen. Philadelphia: University of Pennsylvania Press, 1993.

John J. Contreni

SEE ALSO

Carolingians; Charlemagne; Louis the Pious

Charles III, the Simple (879–929)

King of the West Frankish kingdom, Charles III is also known to modern scholars as Charles the Simple or Charles the Straightforward, a more accurate translation of posthumous references to him as *simplex* (simple).

Charles was born on September 17, 879, just five months after his father, King Louis the Stammerer, had died and less than two years after the death of his illustrious paternal grandfather, Emperor Charles the Bald. Before he was six years old, both of his half brothers (Louis III and Carloman), heirs to their father's kingdom, had suffered accidental deaths. Before he was nine, his uncle, Emperor Charles the Fat, whom the West Frankish magnates had invited to be their king, had abdicated and died. When Charles was thirteen, a group of magnates, disgruntled with King Odo, the emperor's successor, crowned the boy as their king, but they were unable to wrest the kingdom from Odo's control. Charles would not actually rule until Odo's death in 898.

Historical evidence for Charles' reign is sparse, most details of the period are elusive, and interpretations must be speculative. Nonetheless, a few important moments can be ascertained. In 911, for example, in a meeting at Saint-Clair-sur-Epte with the Northmen (Norse) of the Seine basin, Charles seems to have named their leader, Rollo, count of the region around Rouen in exchange for Rollo's defense against other Norse bands and for his conversion to Christianity.

In that same year, the nobles of Lotharingia, a neighboring kingdom, recognized Charles as their king, and, over the next decade, he sought to solidify his dynastic claim to the Lotharingian throne. But his authority in the region was challenged, and eventually undermined, by a series of conflicts with the Lotharingian aristocracy. Most notable was his clash with a Count Gislebert who rebelled in 915 when Charles did not invest him with the dukedom previously held by his father. Gislebert and his supporters were able to enlist the support of Henry of Saxony who hoped to extend his influence into Lotharingia. But Charles and Henry made a truce in 921 and recognized one another, respectively, as "King of the Western Franks" *(rex Francorum occidentalium)*—Charles was the first king to take this title—and "King of the Eastern Franks" *(rex Francorum orientalium)*. The Lotharingians continued to recognize Charles as their king, but not for long. By 925 Lotharingia was firmly in the hands of Henry and his newly named duke, Gislebert.

By that time, Charles had also lost authority over the West Frankish lands. Led by the powerful Robert of Neustria, brother of the deceased King Odo and a loyal supporter of Charles at the beginning of his reign, the magnates rebelled against the king, ostensibly because Charles seemed to be too greatly influenced by a Lotharingian adviser named Hagano. Whether or not this was indeed the cause of simmering tensions between Charles and his magnates, or merely a symptom of a more profound dissatisfaction with Charles' rule, support for the king remained low among the West Frankish aristocracy from about 917 onward. In 922 tensions reached a head. The rebels declared Robert their king and then, when he died in a battle against Charles at Soissons in 923—a battle the rebels won—they elected Rudolf of Burgundy as Robert's successor. Before Charles had an opportunity to face the challenge presented by his new rival, he was captured by the treacherous Count Herbert of Vermandois and held captive until he died on October 7, 929.

Although we cannot reconstruct in great detail Charles' reign, we can identify some changes in West Frankish politics and kingship within his lifetime. As Janet Nelson points out, unlike his namesake Charles the Bald, Charles the Simple appears to have been unable to distribute honors *(honores)* stategically among his magnates, to transfer dukes or counts from one office to another, or to intervene effectively in ecclesiastical appointments within his kingdom. Nor is there any evidence that he sent out *missi* (decrees) or issued capitularies, as had previous Carolingian kings. By the end of his life, the political landscape of his grandfather's empire had undergone a major change. The West Frankish lands, the heartland of that empire, now consisted of a handful of territorial principalities ruled more directly by heads of aristocratic dynasties than by the king.

BIBLIOGRAPHY

Eckel, A. *Charles le Simple.* Paris: Bouillon, 1899.

McKitterick, Rosamond. *The Frankish Kingdoms under the Carolingians.* London: Longman, 1983, pp. 306–313.

Nelson, Janet. *Charles the Bald.* London: Longman 1992, pp. 256–264.

Sassier, Y. *Hugues Capet.* Paris: Fayard, 1987.

Jason Glenn

SEE ALSO
Capitularies; Carolingians; Henry I

Charles IV (1316–1378)

Emperor Charles IV (r. 1346–1378) was born in Prague, May 14, 1316, the eldest son of John of Luxembourg and Elizabeth of Bohemia. He was baptized under the name of Wenceslas, following the tradition of the Premyslid (Bohemian) dynasty. At the age of seven he was sent to Paris to be educated at the court of Charles IV of France. At his confirmation Wenceslas was given the name of Charles. In Paris he met the Benedictine abbot Pierre Roger de Fécamp, later Pope Clement VI, whose sermons made a major impact on young Charles' spiritual development. He also studied briefly at the University of Paris.

Nuremberg, *Frauenkirche,* west façade. *Photograph: Joan A. Holladay*

Following campaigns in Italy to secure Luxembourg interests (1331–1333), Charles administered the kingdom of Bohemia during his father's absence. During his stay in Bohemia (1334–1336) Charles retrieved mortgaged crown lands and negotiated two very important treaties with Poland (Trencin and Visegrád). These teaties established one of the basic aspects of Charles's foreign policy: the abandonment of military expansion in favor of a policy based on treaties and alliances. Charles consistently aimed to maintain the balance of power between Poland, Hungary, the Teutonic Knights, the Habsburg dominions, and his own Bohemian crown lands.

In 1340, when his father became blind, Charles assumed control over the Luxembourg domains, opening the way for his eventual acquisition of the imperial throne. Emperor Louis the Bavarian's policies, particularly his attempts to obtain Tyrol and his renewed conflicts with the papacy, had aroused the enmity of other German the princes. In 1344 an assembly of princes demanded that Louis do sufficient penance to lift the ban of excommunication within two years or face deposition. When Louis failed to do so, the electors met, declared Louis deposed, and elected Charles as emperor on July 1, 1346. Charles' uncle, Archbishop Baldwin of Trier, played a leading role in the negotiations with the princes and the papacy that led to the election.

Initially, Charles' position was rather weak. Because of his support from Clement VI, he was identified by some as yet another "clergy king" *(Pfaffenkönig).* Many bishops and nearly all the imperial cities remained loyal to Louis. Worse for Charles, shortly after his election, he lost a good number of supporters, including his father blind King John, who died fighting for the French at Crècy (August 26, 1346). Civil war was prevented when Louis the Bavarian died bear hunting in October 1347. Although supporters of the Wittelsbach dynasty elected Günther of Schwarzburg king of Germany in January 1349, he was dead by the end of summer.

Prague served as the political, cultural, and spiritual center of Charles' domain. The city had already risen to prominence under the Premyslid rulers, but had suffered serious neglect under King John. Charles began reconstruction of the Hradschin castle during his first long stay in Bohemia in the 1330s. In 1344 he arranged for the bishop of Prague to be elevated to the rank of archbishop. After his coronation as King of Bohemia in 1347, Charles initiated a number of projects that substantially reshaped the city. A new cathedral dedicated to St. Veit was begun on the Hradschin. Within the cathedral,

Charles had built a special chapel to hold the relics of St. Wenceslas. He also founded a university in 1348, the first in the empire. With the foundation of the New Town (Nové Mesto) in Prague, Charles nearly tripled the size of the city.

Charles' political views and his religious ideas were closely connected. From his early years in Paris and Italy, he had developed a sense of his own divine mission. This ideal was represented in the new coronation ordo, or rites, devised for Bohemia in 1347. The coronation ordo, like his mania for collecting religious relics, reflected the conservative side of Charles' religiosity. But, although his personal religious views connected him most strongly with the Devotio Antiqua, he was not without sympathy for the Devotio Moderna. He was acquainted with Johannes Tauler and Christina Ebner among the German mystics. In 1363 Charles brought the fiery preacher Conrad Waldhauser to Prague and later supported and defended Waldhauser's student Jan Milic, albeit after Milic stopped identifying the emperor as the Antichrist.

Charles's Italian policies reflected a realization that it would be nearly impossible to restore imperial authority in that region. He made two trips to Rome after his election as emperor. In the winter of 1354–1355 Charles traveled to Rome for his imperial coronation (January 6, 1355) and to settle affairs in the Holy City following the revolt and death of the tribunal official Cola de Rienzo the previous fall. During his trip, Charles met the poet Petrarch in Mantua on December 15, 1354. Two years later Petrarch traveled to Prague as part of a diplomatic mission from the Visconti, a Lombard noble family. During that visit, Charles failed to convince the poet to remain at his court. He likewise refused Petrarch's invitation to intervene more forcibly in Italian affairs.

In Bohemia, Charles sought to establish a more centralized administration. Much of his effort was aimed at increasing the size and scope of the area that compromised the Bohemian crown lands. He transferred the Silesian duchies from their status as fiefs of the empire to the Bohemian crown. Charles also undertook to create "New Bohemia," a string of possessions in the Upper Palatinate and Franconia that would link Bohemia with the Rhineland. The Bohemian nobles were not wholly supportive of these ventures, however, and sharply resisted Charles's attempts to codify Bohemian law in the Majestas Carolina of 1355.

Charles was much more successful in dealing with the states of the empire. Three general trends typify his German policy. First, he devoted his dynastic policy (Haus-machtpolitik), to maintaining and increasing the power of the Luxembourg dynasty within and without the empire. Secondly, Charles sought to fill vacant bishoprics with his supporters, revivifying the imperial church as a political tool for the emperors. Finally, he made alliances with leading states and cities in the empire and sponsored leagues, in particular, city leagues, to help maintain the public peace. The cities of Nuremberg and Lübeck, as well as the Hohenzollern burggraves (districts) of Nurembert and the margraves of Miessen, benefited from Charles' patronage. In general, Charles's German policy focused on maintaining a balance of power within the empire.

One of the main achievements of Charles' reign was the promulgation of the Golden Bull on January 10, 1356. The Golden Bull regulated the conduct of imperial elections, fixing the number of electors at seven: the archbishops of Mainz, Trier, and Cologne, the king of Bohemia, the margraves of Miessen and Brandenburg, and the counts Palatine of the Rhine. Succession in the secular electoral principalities was to follow primogeniture. The Golden Bull gave the electoral princes extensive rights, including the jus de non appellando et de non evocando, or priviledge of nomination and selection, and elevated the position of the king of Bohemia over that of the other electors. Charles sought to create unity among the electoral princes, and ultimately, to ensure hereditary succession through the regulated process of election.

Charles leaned heavily on the imperial cities, particularly those in Swabia, as executors of the public peace (Landfriede). Although the Golden Bull forbade leagues in principle, city leagues and princely leagues created by the emperor in order to secure the peace became a fixed part of Charles' Landfrieden policy. The Swabian Landfriede of 1370, comprised almost entirely of imperial cities, was clearly directed against a growing alliance of the Habsburgs and the counts of Württemberg.

In 1377 Charles returned to France, accompanied by his son Wenceslas, to gain French support for his plans to put his younger son, Sigismund, on the Polish throne. During the negotiations, Charles agreed to recognize the French dauphin as imperial vicar in the kingdom of Arles, effectively ceding the Arelat to France in perpetuity.

In the last years of his reign, Charles occupied himself largely with the succession and with returning the papacy to Rome. The emperor needed to acquire the mark (territory) of Brandenburg in order to secure the election to emperor of his eldest son Wenceslas (June 10, 1376). To raise money, Charles opted to mortgage a number of imperial cities. On July 4, 1376, in opposition to this decision, a group of Swabian cities formed a league. War broke out the following spring, by which time twenty-eight cities had joined the Swabian city league, with the aim of achieving the status of free imperial cities.

Conflect also ensured from Charles' determination to reutrn the papacy to Rome. He was able to convince Pope Gregory XI and the curia to return to Rome in September 1377, but after Gregory's death (March 26, 1378), a series of disputes between the newly elected Pope Urban VI and Charles ultimately resulted in the Great Schism.

Charles IV died in Prague on November 29, 1378. He was married four times: to Blanche of Valois (1316–1348), Anna of Wittelsbach (1329–1353), Anna von Schweidnitz (1339–1362), and Elizabeth of Pomerania (1347–1393). At his death the Luxembourg lands were divided between his sons, Wenceslas IV (Bohemia and Silesia), Sigismund (Brandenburg), and Johann (Görlitz), and his brothers Johann Heinrich (Moravia) and Wenceslas (Luxembourg and Brabant).

BIBLIOGRAPHY

Seibt, Ferdinand. *Karl IV. und Sein Kreis.* Munich: Oldenbourg, 1978.

———, ed. *Karl IV. Staatsmann und Mäzen.* Munich: Prezel, 1978.

Spevacek, Jirí. *Karel IV. Zivot a dílo.* Prague: Svoboda (Rudé právo), 1979.

———. *Karl IV. Sein Leben und seine staatsmänische Leistung.* Prague: Academie nakladatelstri Ceskoslovenské akademi ved, 1978.

Werunsky, E. *Geschishte Kaiser Karls IV. und seiner Zeit.* Innsbruck: Wagner, 1880–1892.

Zeumer, Karl. *Die Goldene Bulle Kaiser Karls IV.* Weimar: Hermann Böhlaus Nachfolger, 1908.

William Bradford Smith

SEE ALSO

Charles IV, Art; Golden Bull; Hohenzollern; *Landfrieden;* Luxemberger; Succession; Wenceslas

Charles IV, Art

The son born to John, Count of Luxembourg, and Elizabeth Přemyslid, Queen of Bohemia, on May 14, 1316, in Prague was baptized Wenceslas, a dynastically rich name that honored Elizabeth's Přemyslid past. In April 1323, he accompanied his father to the court of Charles IV of France, where he remained during the following decade.

Soon after his arrival in Paris, he was confirmed, and the king gave the boy his own name; the reference to Charlemagne would prove useful in Charles' later imperial politics. While in Paris, Charles attended the university, where he acquired a lifelong dedication to learning that resulted in his later introducing education to the people of his empire.

After reaching his majority in 1333, Charles returned to Prague where he ruled jointly with his father. (His mother had died in 1330.) Upon the death of John in 1346, Charles was crowned king of Bohemia. With the backing of a majority of the German electors, the pope, and the French crown, he was elected king of the Romans. On Easter in 1355, in Rome, Charles was crowned Holy Roman Emperor by the pope.

During the course of his rule, Charles was responsible for nearly tripling the size of Bohemia and, by consolidating the power of the kings of Bohemia through political alliances, turning the German kingship into an office of primogeniture rather than election. These two goals were primarily achieved through his four marriages: to Blanche of Valois (m. 1323–d. 1348), Anne of the Palatinate and Wittelsbach (m. 1349–d. 1353), Anne of Swidnica (m. 1353–d. 1362), and Elizabeth of Pomerania (m. 1363–d. 1393). Each of his wives, contributed extensive lands to Charles' kingdom, either in the form of dowries or through inheritance. These marriages were just as critical, though, for forging relations with members of his wives' families, some of whom were electors who had been less than supportive of his causes in the past. By securing votes through marriage alliances, Charles was able to see his fifteen-year-old son, Wenceslas, crowned king of the Romans in 1376.

As a student in Paris Charles acquired a love for, and understanding of, the political potential of architecture, sculpture, painting, and literature. His imprint is most noticeable in the city he chose for his imperial seat, Prague, but his patronage also touched many smaller towns. In the capital he renovated the Přemyslid Palace in Hradčany, continued work on St. Vitus Cathedral as part of the recent promotion of Prague to an archbishopric, founded the University—the first in central Europe—and the New Town, and, through these measures, increased trade and pilgrimage. His palace at Karlstein outside Prague remains one of the most stunning examples of eastern Gothic architecture, and his patronage of Peter Parler as the designer of St. Vitus and the Charles Bridge testifies to Charles's ability as a connoisseur and adventurous patron. He gathered around him many foreign artists and local masters, two of whom were Tommaso da Modena and Theodericus of Prague. The exchange between these varied artistic traditions resulted in the vital "Bohemian school" of visual arts.

In the realms of history and literature, not only did Charles actively assemble a vast local and international library, as well as commission chronicles of Bohemia, he himself composed an autobiography and a *vita* of his ancestor, Saint Wenceslas. By having many of these works translated into the vernacular, Charles promoted learning of the less-esteemed German and Czech languages in addition to Latin, Italian, and French. The importance he placed on language as a unifying tool is also apparent in the political document that codified the German electoral process, the Golden Bull.

BIBLIOGRAPHY

Jarrett, Bede. *The Emperor Charles IV.* London: Eyre and Spottiswoode, 1935.

Seibt, Ferdinand, ed. *Kaiser Karl IV.: Staatsmann und Mäzen.* Munich: Prestel, 1978.

Stejskal, Karel. *European Art in the 14th Century,* trans. Till Gottheinerová. London: Octopus Books, 1978.

Thompson, Samuel H. "Learning at the Court of Charles IV." *Speculum* 25 (1950): 1–20.

Via Caroli Quarti: Die Autobiographie Karls IV. Einfuhrung, Ubersetzung und Kommentar, ed. Eugen Hillenbrand. Stuttgart: Fleischhauer & Spohn, 1979.

Tracy Chapman Hamilton

SEE ALSO

Charles IV; Parler Family; Prague; Theodoric, Master; Wenceslas

Charms

Also known as *Zaubersprüche* or *Heilsegen,* charms are usually short, often formulaic, texts, either spoken or written, used to elicit a desired outcome. They might be as simple as a single word or string of characters, or elaborate compilations of several charms incorporating various motifs.

Charms were used and recorded throughout the medieval period in all parts of Germany. Texts are found in psalters, prayer books and liturgical manuscripts (often as marginalia) in herbals, and in medical and veterinary compendia, scattered among the herbal recipes and other remedies. In the late Middle Ages, charms were recorded in *Hausrezeptbucher,* books containing practical information for running a household. If named at all, *Segen* or *Benedictio* ("blessing") was the designation applied to these texts in the manuscripts. (The term *Zauberspruch,* charm, cannot be dated earlier than the seventeenth century.)

Some individual medieval German charms have been studied intensively, e.g., the Merseburg charms (see below), but there has been no truly definitive study of the corpus of Old High German (OHG) and Middle High German (MHG) charms. It is doubtful that any OHG charms are still undiscovered; however, there may be German charms from the later medieval period still to be found in manuscripts. Thus, one cannot speak conclusively about medieval German charms, but only point out tendencies in these texts.

Charms may be a mixture of German and Latin. Early mixed-language texts often had a Latin heading and instructions accompanying a German charm, while the situation in later macaronic texts tended to the reverse. Many early critics often omitted the Latin segments in their editions of the OHG charms, obscuring the Christian context in which the charms were found.

Charms may manifest literary characteristics similar to longer contemporary works and be in verse, prose, or a mixed form. While the earliest charms seldom follow the metrical rules of Germanic poetry, these older texts do exhibit some features of *Stabreim,* e.g., the Bavarian worm charm (*Pro nessia,* Munich, Bayersiche Staatsbibliothek, manuscript no. Clm. 18524, 2, fol. 203b, 9th c.), the Merseburg charms (10th c.) and the Viennese dog charm (Vienna, Nationalbibliothek, manuscript no. Cod. 552, fol. 107r, 10th c.). A twelfth-century charm for a lame horse (*Ad equum errehet,* Paris, Bibliothèque Nationale, no. nouv. acq. lat. 229, p. 251) is considered to be in Otfridian, an Old High German end-rhyming verse. (It is, however, important to note that critics have not all been in agreement about the forms of individual OHG charms.) An elaborate wound charm in a British Library (BL) manuscript (BL Arundelm, no. 295, fol. 113r, 13th c.) is written in rhymed pairs suggestive of the meter of *Parzival.*

In their "classical" form, charms consist of a heading, often naming the purpose, instructions for use or accompanying ritual (frequently including the recitation of the Lord's Prayer and/or Hail Mary, typically three of each), a historiola (in narrative charms) and the incantation proper. By no means do all charms exhibit all parts, nor is a charm without one of these parts incomplete. Nor do the parts, if present, always follow "classical" order. In particular, the heading and instructions might follow the charm itself.

Examples of headings include: *Contra vermes* (Old Saxon worm charm, Vienna, Nationalbibliothek, no. Cod. 751, fol. 188v, 10th c.); *Ad pestem equi quod dicitur morth* (horse charm, Vatican, Pal. lat. 1158, fol. 68v, 12th c.); *Vor dy worme* (BL Arundel 33, fol. 95a, manuscript dated 1432); and *Item dis ist ain bewärtte segen fur das blütten wa das ist* (blood charm, St. Gall, Stiftsbibliothek, no. Cod. 755, p. 71, 15th c.). Where a series of charms with the same purpose follow one another in a manuscript, the only heading of the succeeding texts might be *Item*.

Instructions may be as simple as *dic* at the beginning and *Pater noster. ter.* at the end of the Vatican horse charm, or complex, e.g., *Item des ersten leg din hand uff die wunden oder uff die nasen und sprich dise wortt* (Like the first one, place your hand on the wound or on the nose and say these words,) at the beginning and *wenn du dise wortt gesprichest so sprich drü pater noster und aue maria* (when you say those words, also say three Our Fathers and Hail Marys) at the end of the St. Gall blood charm.

Narrative charms begin with an historiola *(epische Einleitung* an "epic introduction") which relates an anecdote, often involving a cure analogous to the one sought or promised by the charm. With the exception of the Merseburg charms (see below), the narrative motifs are manifestly Christian, paraphrasing Biblical or apocryphal events. Frequent motifs include: "Three Angels" confronting a disease demon; "Three Brothers," who meet Christ while searching for a cure; "Longinus," who pierces Christ's side with a spear; and "Job" sitting on a dung heap. Particular motifs were associated with certain ailments. For example, Job charms were for worms; Longinus appeared in blood and wound charms, as well as in charms for removing arrow and spear heads.

The majority of extant charms are healing blessings *(Heilsegen).* Their purpose was to contribute to the health and well-being of humans or valuable domestic beasts, especially horses. As such, *Heilsegen* may be either prophylactic or curative. They were used to treat epilepsy, lameness, bleeding, fevers, worms (in German society, not worms *per se,* but worms as the cause of disease and pain, e.g., toothache worms) and as birthing aids, to name only a few uses. Even those earlier charms not specifically medical in purpose, e.g., the Lorsch Bee charm (Vatican Library, no. Pal. lat. 220, fol. 58r, 10th c.), nevertheless address the concerns of a largely agrarian society. Later in the period, charms served a much broader range of purposes, including aiding lovers, fighting fires, winning horse races, controlling pests and curing sleeplessness in children. Charms of particular use to a chivalrous and crusading society included weapon blessings, and journey and wound charms.

In the late Middle Ages, charms tended to exhibit more "magical" characteristics, i.e., mysterious words, characters, or figures. They also became more elaborate, conflating charms and motifs that earlier had appeared singly and broadening the application of traditional motifs.

Also in the later period, charms were sometimes recorded in the court proceedings of witchcraft trials. With these charms, the "black" magical element crept in, with reported charms often being directed towards harm rather than good. How the context in which these charms were recorded might have affected their content and form has not yet been studied.

The Merseburg Charms

Of all the German charms so far published, none have aroused more interest or engendered more discussion and debate among Germanists than the two Merseburg charms. The texts of the charms, generally based on Steinmeyer's edition (see below), and a literal translation, follow:

First Merseburg charm:

1	*Eiris sazun idisi, sazun hera duoder.*	Once sat women, they sat here then there.
	suma hapt heptidun,	some fastened bonds,
	suma heri lezidun,	some impeded an army,
5	*suma clubodun umbi cuoniouuidi insprinc haptbandun, inuar uigandun! .H.*	some unraveled fetters: escape the bonds, flee the enemy! .H.

Second Merseburg charm:

1	*Phol ende Uuodan uuorun zi holza. du uuart demo Balderes uolon sin uuoz birenkit.*	Phol and Wodan rode to the woods. Then, Balder's foal wrenched his foot.
5	*thu biguolen Sinthgunt, Sunna era suister, thu biguolen Friia,*	Then did Sinthgunt enchant it, Sunna her sister, then did Freya enchant it,

	Uolla era suister,	Fulla her sister,
	thu biguolen Uuodan,	then did Wodan enchant it,
10	*so he uuola conda:*	as he well could:
	sose benrenki,	if a bone-wrenching,
	sose bluotrenki	if a blood-wrenching,
	sose lidirenki:	if a limb-wrenching:
	ben zi bena,	bone to bone,
15	*bluot zi bluoda,*	blood to blood,
	lid zi geliden	limb to limb,
	sose gelimida sin!	as if bonded!

The texts, discovered in 1841 by Georg Waitz in a theological manuscript (Merseburg Cathedral Library, Codex 136, f. 84r [85r old numbering]), were first published and analyzed by Jacob Grimm in 1842.

As is true of perhaps most medieval German charms, both are narrative charms, with historiola (first charm, ll. 1–6; second charm, ll. 1–13) and incantation (first charm, ll. 7–8; second charm, ll. 14–17). The second charm clearly belongs to the tradition of healing charms. (For whatever the cause, there were a number of charms for curing lameness in horses and humans.) In nearly every other respect, the Merseburg charms differ from most other extant OHG and MHG charm texts.

No other charms show so clearly a structure based on the number three. This is especially striking in the second charm. Moreover, the second Merseburg charm is the only medieval German charm to specify gods from the pagan, Germanic past. This doubtless led Grimm to characterize both charms as pagan, an attribute most critics have since accepted. Critics also almost universally agree that the purpose of the first charm is to free captives, a purpose not only unique among medieval German charms, but also among other medieval western European charms.

Virtually every other point concerning these texts has been disputed by scholars and not yet conclusively settled. From the exact meaning of *idisi* and *umbi cuoniouuidi* to the significance of the apparent *H* at the end of the first Merseburg charm, and from the question of who or what was *Phol,* and whether *Balderes* is a reference to the god "Baldr" or an appellative referring to Phol or Uuodan, to how many goddesses speak in the second charm, critics disagree on interpretations of both texts. Since the charms are recorded in a theological manuscript, most likely by a monk, and are followed by a liturgical prayer, even the question of whether or not they are pagan has been disputed by some modern critics. Indeed, it would be more accurate to say that the charms are not clearly Christian, than to state categorically that they are pagan. Both representative of their genre and unique in their details, the Merseburg charms serve as a reminder that, as much as is known about life in medieval Germany, there is still much to be learned. Charms can provide an extraordinary insight into that life.

BIBLIOGRAPHY

Abernethy, George William. "The Germanic Metrical Charms." Ph.D. diss., University of Wisconsin/ Madison, 1983. UMI 83-06654.

Grimm, Jacob. "Über zwei entdeckte Gedichte aus der Zeit des deutschen Heidentums." In *Abhandlungen der kgl. preussischen Akademie, phil.-hist. Klasse.* Berlin, 1842, pp. 1–24; rpt. in Jacob Grimm.

———. *Kleinere Schriften,* II. Berlin: Dummler, 1865, rpt. Hildesheim: Olms, 1965, pp. 1–28 [with facsimile].

Halsig, Friedrich. *Der Zauberspruch bei den Germanen bis um die Mitte des XVI. Jahrhunderts.* Leipzig: Dr. Seele & Co., 1910.

Hampp, Irmgard. *Beschwörung - Segen - Gebet: Untersuchungen zum Zauberspruch aus dem Bereich der Volksheilkunde.* Stuttgart: Silberburg, 1961.

Miller, Carol L. "The Old High German and Old Saxon Charms. Text, Commentary and Critical Bibliography." Ph.D. diss., Washington University, 1963. UMI 64-2323.

Müllenhoff, K[arl] and W[ilhelm] Scherer. *Denkmaler deutscher Poesie and Prosa aus dem VIII-XII Jahrhundert.* 4th ed., Berlin/Zurich: Weidmannische Verlagsbuchhandlung, 1892; rpt. 1964.

Müller, Martin. *Über die stilform der altdeutschen zaubersprüche bis 1300.* Gotha: Perthes, 1901.

Murdoch, Brian. "But Did They Work? Interpreting the Old High German Merseburg Charms in Their Medieval Context." *Neuphilologische Mitteilungen* 89 (1988): 358–369.

Pinto, Lucille B. "The Worm Charm in the German Middle Ages." Ph.D. diss., University of Chicago, 1969.

Piper, Paul. "Segen aus Sanct Gallen." *Germania* 25 (1880): 67–71. [St. Gall blood charm]

Priebsch, Robert. "Segen aus Londoner Hss." *Zeitschrift für deutsches Altertum und deutsche Literatur* 38 (1894): 14–21. [Worm charm: BL Arundel 33, f. 95a]

Sievers, Eduard. "Drei deutsche Segensspruche." *Zeitschrift für deutsches Altertum und deutsche Literatur* 15 (1872): 452–456. [Wound charm: BL Arundel 295, f. 113r.]

von Steinmeyer. Elias. *Die kleineren althochdeutschen Sprachdenkmäler.* Berlin: Weidmannische Verlagsbuchhandlung, 1916.

Patricia Giangrosso

SEE ALSO
Otfrid; Wolfram von Eschenbach

Childbirth
See Pregnancy and Childbirth.

Childhood

Children in medieval Germany, for the most part, were regarded as deficient adults. Because children lacked speech, they cried to make their wishes known; because they lacked sense and experience, they were foolish and indiscreet; and because they lacked gravity, they played games and sought pleasure. From this point of view, the best that could be said was that, not having had much opportunity to sin, children were purer than adults. Middle High German *tump* means "young," "inexperienced," and "foolish," suggesting that deficiencies of age, experience, and wisdom inevitably go hand in hand.

That medieval Germans viewed children as deficient adults does not mark them as particularly benighted in their attitude towards their young. Most Europeans, from antiquity into the eighteenth century, believed the same thing. Nor does it support the theory that people in the Middle Ages had no "idea of childhood" because they failed to perceive the difference between children and adults, a claim that has gained wide currency since it was made almost forty years ago by Philippe Ariès. A period of life defined by its lack of adult qualities and skills is a period of life defined precisely by its difference from adulthood. Nor did the medieval belief that children were deficient adults mean that medieval children were not loved by their parents—another widely held view that can be traced to Ariès. Nearly all contemporary texts assumed that parents' love for their children was powerful and inevitable.

Evidence about childhood in medieval Germany is hard to come by since the usual historical sources spend hardly a word on children, even those, like Frederick Barbarossa or St. Elizabeth, who were born into the highest nobility and grew up to capture the imagination of their contemporaries. In order to learn about the medieval German idea of childhood, therefore, one must draw on less orthodox sources: narrative, didactic, homiletic, and other sorts of texts. About the childhood of social groups that did not figure in texts—the vast majority of the population—we still know virtually nothing.

Childhood in medieval Germany was more disruptive than we would find tolerable. Mortality rates were high, especially for children and mothers, so that even if a child reached adulthood—between 30 and 50 percent did not—one or both parents might well have already died. Social practices, too, took children away from their parents. Among these customs were oblation (which placed children in religious houses) and fosterage (which sent them to other households to be educated). In 1211, when she was only four, Saint Elizabeth was sent by her parents, the king and queen of Hungary, to the Thuringian court, where she grew up alongside her future husband. Childhood dislocation was common in literary texts as well: Tristan was orphaned at birth, raised by foster parents, and then abducted and abandoned on an unknown coast.

Since we now believe that childhood experiences have a profound effect on later development, we would expect the disruptions Elizabeth or Tristan suffered as children would have left permanent psychological scars. Medieval Germans did not. They believed that a child's nature was determined at birth, largely as a consequence of his or her lineage. One's nature could be very specific: a person could inherit a predisposition to noble love, skill at jousting, or a sense of decorum. Because individual nature was fixed at birth, children were assumed to come of age with that nature intact, regardless of the disruptions they had endured. Childhood was not understood as a stage of life in which the individual, moving through a series of developmental stages, was shaped by education, experience, and environment but as one in which the deficiencies of childhood gradually disappeared and the immutable nature of the individual was gradually revealed. Childhood was seen as a period not of development, but of revelation.

As a consequence, education played a smaller role than we would expect. To be sure, children, especially future clerics, were educated in monasteries and cathedral schools, at courts and at universities, in fact and in fiction. But the child's nature determined how much could be accomplished and the techniques that would be required. Educating ordinary children was viewed as a thankless task: such children had to be disciplined frequently and taught to fear their masters if there was to be any hope of inculcating good habits in them. Children with exceptional natures, on the other hand, hardly required education at all. Although Parzival was kept ignorant of knighthood until he was nearly grown up, he needed only a few words of instruction before defeating the first five knights against whom he jousted. He succeeded because of "the nature that he had inherited from Gahmuret," his father (Wolfram von Eschenbach, *Parzival*, 174,24). In medieval Germany education was considered merely the catalyst that released the nature that was always there, unaffected by childhood deprivations or dislocations.

Although medieval Germans, in general, found little to recommend childhood, childhood seems to have enjoyed enhanced status at court. Narrative texts written for secular courts between 1150 and 1300 paid particular attention to children. These texts represent detailed programs of courtly education and elaborate rites of passage, such as knighting and marriage. Between 1200 and 1250 writers expanded the depiction of childhood in their sources *(Parzival)* and added stories of childhood to narratives that had none *(Nibelungenlied)*. Vernacular didactic texts, which appeared for the first time during this period, were optimistic in tone, unlike those written later in the century. Literary texts exhibited an increased sentimentality: children cried and played with toys; parents displayed greater tenderness to their children; children fell in love. During precisely those years when courtly culture flourished, childhood, like eating, fighting, sexual desire, and other aspects of life, was refined, stylized, and given a courtly form. Courtly childhood, like festivals, chivalry, and courtly love, became an attribute of courtly life, a mark of distinction whereby the secular elite staked its claim to cultural status. The courtly revaluation of childhood marked an important step in the transformation of childhood from a period of life defined by its failure to measure up to adulthood into one believed to be different from adulthood, but special and of interest for its own sake.

BIBLIOGRAPHY

Ariès, Philippe. *Centuries of Childhood: A Social History of Family Life,* trans. Robert Baldick. New York: Vintage, 1962.

Arnold, Klaus. *Kind und Gesellschaft in Mittelalter und Renaissance: Beiträge und Texte zur Geschichte der Kindheit.* Paderborn: Schöningh and Munich: Lurz, 1980.

Gray, Ursula. *Das Bild des Kindes im Spiegel der altdeutschen Dichtung und Literatur: Mit textkritischer Ausgabe von Metlingers "Regiment der jungen Kinder."* Bern: Lang, 1974.

Loffl-Haag, Elisabeth. *Hört ihr die Kinder lachen? Zur Kindheit im Spätmittelalter.* Pfaffenweiler: Centaurus, 1991.

McLaughlin, Mary Martin. "Survivors and Surrogates: Children and Parents from the Ninth to the Thirteenth Centuries." In *The History of Childhood,* Lloyd de Mause, ed. New York: Psychohistory Press, 1974; rpt. New York: Harper & Row, 1975, pp. 101–181.

Schultz, James A. *The Knowledge of Childhood in the German Middle Ages, 1100–1350.* Philadelphia: University of Pennsylvania Press, 1995.

Shahar, Shulamith. *Childhood in the Middle Ages.* London: Routledge, 1990.

Ta-Shma, Israel. "Children in Medieval German Jewry: A Perspective on Ariès from Jewish Sources." *Studies in Medieval and Renaissance History* n.s. 12 (1991): 261–280.

Wenzel, Horst. "'kindes zuht und wibes reht': Zu einigen Aspekten von Kindheit im Mittelalter." In *Ordnung und Lust: Bilder von Liebe, Ehe und Sexualität in Spätmittelalter und früher Neuzeit,* ed. Hans-Jürgen Bachorski. Trier: Wissenschaftlicher Verlag, 1991, pp. 141–163.

James A. Schultz

SEE ALSO
Frederick I Barbarossa; Gottfried von Straßburg; *Nibelungenlied;* Wolfram von Eschenbach

Christmas Plays
See Drama, Christmas Plays.

Chronicles, City, Dutch

Although towns (or cities) appeared in the northern parts of the Low Countries from the twelfth century onwards, chronicles treating the history of a town or reporting urban events did not come into being—probably because urban self-consciousness was still absent—before the second half of the fifteenth century. The first chronicles were in the form of small treatises (*Chronicle of Haarlem to 1328,* ca. 1490; the *Descriptio oppidi Amstelodamensis,* ca. 1490, a description of the towns of the county of Holland with special emphasis on Amsterdam; and the *Libellus de Traiecto instaurato,* ca. 1485, a survey of the buildings of Maastricht) or short poems about local events.

The first real town chronicle was written by Jacob Bijndorp, town secretary of Kampen (from 1466 until 1482), a prospering town because of its membership of the North-German Hanseatic League. His chronicle, with several continuations by other town secretaries until 1547, demonstrates the origin of a new genre: it starts as a history of the world and does not concentrate on local events until sometime in the 15th century.

In the southern parts of the Low Countries urban development came earlier. Yet, town chronicles did not flourish there. It is true that the *Annales Gandenses,* written by a friar of Ghent, contains an account of the struggle between the Flemish towns and the King of France during the years 1297–1310, and Jean d'Outremeuse of Liège (1338–1400) wrote an enormous rhymed chronicle of his native town, the *Geste de Liège,* from its legendary Trojan origin until his own times. But, although those chronicles, just like the unreliable *Liber de antiquitate urbis Tornacensis* (Tournai) or the *Chronica Tornacensis,* pay much attention to the history of those towns, they are not, strictly speaking, town chronicles, since their primary focus is world history.

BIBLIOGRAPHY

Balau, S. *Etude critique des sources de l'histoire du pays de Liège.* Brussels: Kiessling. 1902–1903.

Bormans, Stanislas, ed. *Ly Myreur des histors,* Vol. 6. Brussels: M. Hayez, 1880 [*Geste de Liège*].

Carasso-Kok, Marijke. *Repertorium van verhalende historische bronnen uit de middeleeuwen.* The Hague: Nijhoff, 1981.

de Ram, P. F. X. ed. *Bulletin de la Commission Royale d'Histoire* 12 (1846–47): 6–44 [*Libellus de Traiecto*].

de Smet, J.-J., ed. *Corpus chronicorum Flandriae,* Vol. 3. Brussels: M. Hayez, 1841, pp. 479–563 [*Liber de antiquitate urbis Tornacensis* and *Chronica Tornacensis*].

De Vereeniging tot beoefening van Overijsselsch Regt en Geschiedenis Vol. 5 (1862): 1–40, 40–46, 46–62 and Vol. 6 (1864): 1–135, 135–146 [*Kamper Kronieken*].

Gier, A. Jean d'Outremeuse, "*La Geste de Liège*. L'histoire régionale au xive siècle." *Fifteenth-Century Studies* 14 (1988): 87–94.

Johnstone, Hilda, trans. *Annales Gandenses.* New York: Nelson, 1951.

A. L. H. Hage

SEE ALSO
Chronicles, Regional/National, Dutch; Chronicles, World, Dutch; Historiography, Dutch; Jan von Boendale

Chronicles, City, German

Written in Middle High German and early New High German, the German city chronicles are a collection of chiefly secular texts with religious underpinnings that deal with the economic, political, and social events comprising the history of medieval German municipalities and the lives of their citizens.

City chronicles, written in the vernacular between the thirteenth and the end of the sixteenth century, are descendants of the earliest German language chronicles: *das Annolied* (Song of [Bishop] Anno [of Cologne]) from the late eleventh century, and *die Kaiserchronik* or *Chronica* (Chronicle of the Kings) in 17,283 rhymed verses, from the middle of the twelfth century. These works promoted and conceptualized the attributes and legimacy of the ideal ruler. The former, a propagandistic work attributed to the monastery of Siegburg, advocated the canonization of archbishop Anno of Cologne (ca. 1010–1075). In this chronicle, the city of Cologne is merely the setting for the idealized depiction of Anno as the personification of justice and Christian charity. The latter, the "Imperial Chronicle," was written by a monk or cleric from Regensburg in 1147 at the behest of a high-ranking nobleman—possibly the Bavarian duke, Henry the Proud. It tells of imperial rulers and the qualities they require—the foremost being justice—and of the proper role of emperors and popes within the empire.

The vernacular rhymed chronicles aimed to legitimize and preserve the traditional privileges of the feudal nobility. Unlike Latin chronicles addressed chiefly to a monastic audience, these vernacular rhymed chronicles instructed an increasingly lay public on the just exercise of monarchical power within the divine plan for salvation. Traditional allusions to saints, miracles, and fabulous occurrences were still prevalent in historical works of the period, however, as a means of edification and delight.

While these rhymed chronicles legitimized feudal nobility and its privileges by using traditional themes, the city chronicles, predominantly in vernacular prose, highlighted the burghers' interest in topical events by rendering them with greater factualness. For instance, one of the oldest vernacular prose chronicles, the *Straßburger Chronik,* completed in 1362 by Fritsche Klosener, a minor official *(summissarius)* of the Strasbourg cathedral, reveals both an emphasis on facts and a logical organization of materials, though not always in strict chronological order. Klosener includes both papal and imperial history, but he devotes more than half of his chronicle to the history of Strasbourg as a bishopric and city. The chronicler documents specific Strasbourg events, such as the earthquake of 1357, the persecution of the Jews in 1298, 1337, and 1349, the unrest in the guilds during the years 1308, 1332–1348, and 1349, and the ensuing changes to the charter of the city council. This emphasis on facts and topicality reflected the social values of urban communities founded chiefly on practical economic and political concerns.

During the thirteenth and fourteenth centuries, the German kings and emperors of the Holy Roman Empire granted increasing privileges to imperial cities *(Reichsstädte),* such as Nuremberg and Frankfurt, that were directly subject to the emperor rather than to surrounding territorial principalities. These cities, together with the so-called *Freie Städte* (free cities) of Cologne, Augsburg, Basel, Regensburg, Speyer, and Worms, all of which were freed by their citizenry from the rule of lordly bishops, came to consider such privileges as *reht,* their lawful right. The inhabitants of both types of cities—the legal and constitutional distinction between them all but disappeared by the sixteenth century—began to identify the *Reich* no longer with a transient king, as was customary during the earlier medieval period, but with their own cities as bulwarks of the empire, and eventually as the empire per se. The *Nürnberger Chronik* of Sigmund Meisterlin (1488), for example, demonstrates the assertive, political self-image of the most influential imperial city of the period—the city of the *Reichstage,* where the imperial diet of the Holy Roman Empire convened—through the use of the interchangeable terms *fürsten und städt* and *städt und fürsten.* The use of one formulation for the other attests to Meisterlin's belief in the equality of his city with the nobility, deferring only to the higher authority of the pope and the emperor. The chronicler depicts the municipality of Nuremberg as the embodiment of the empire and, indeed, of the apprehensible world itself.

The compilation of often diverse and seemingly unrelated materials in city chronicles underscores the conviction that city and empire were one and the same. As a consequence of this perceived unity, local and imperial history became inseparable. Nevertheless, the relationships of these municipalities—and even territorial cities *(landesherrliche Städte)* subject to the immediate jurisdiction of regional rulers—with the powerful nobility of the German-speaking lands and beyond, could range from alliances of convenience and necessity to open aggression in the struggle for power, land, and economic advantage. In particular, the increasing consolidation of disparate regions into geographically contiguous states *(Flächen-*

staaten) by ambitious territorial rulers heightened the anxiety of municipal citizens and found resonance in numerous city chronicles.

It was, however, during the late medieval period of the fourteenth and fifteenth centuries that the often conflicting interests of cities with those of territorial rulers achieved their greatest prominence in city chronicles. These histories are primarily based on official sources compiled by city clerks *(Stadtschreiber).* One such chronicler was Konrad Justinger (d. 1425), who was commissioned by the *Stadtrat,* the governing body of Bern, in 1421. Justinger's *Chronik der Stadt Bern* (City Chronicle of Bern) encompasses the history of the city from the election of Frederick Barbarossa in 1152 to the laying of the cornerstone for the cathedral in 1421. The chronicler not only evaluated and compiled official documents for this work, but also collected songs of his day.

In 1474, almost sixty years after Justinger's death, the *Stadtrat* of Bern commissioned another chronicler, Diebold Schilling the Elder, to provide an official history of the city, and Justinger's chronicle provided him with the first part of his three-part continuation.

Unofficial municipal and personal histories by individual citizens were also complied. From 1450 to 1468, out of personal interest in his city's welfare, Burkhart Zink, a naturalized citizen of Augsburg, recorded local events of the years 1368 to 1468. In the second chapter of his *Augsburger Chronik,* Zink included his autobiography. The account of his youth, up to his becoming a citizen of Augsburg—an expensive and prestigious privilege that granted social and economic advantage—was not without intrinsic, exemplary value for the city. The story of Zink as an *Augsburger* merged and coincided with the continuing history of Augsburg itself. The city became the vibrant, active subject, rather than the mere object of the chronicle.

Unofficial and official chroniclers alike viewed their prosperity as inextricably bound to their municipality, but they also identified themselves as members of the civic community, the empire, and Christendom. During the later medieval period the status of *Reichsstadt* heightened this identification. Imperial cities came to regard themselves as the very embodiment of the empire and imperial *reht* as a legal, judicial, and political entity. City chroniclers thus strove to expatiate upon the theme of city government by singing its praises and affirming its legitimacy.

In a later Augsburger chronicle of the city's Weavers' Guild, the so-called *Weberchronik* from the year 1544,

Clemens Jäger, a guild master and civil servant, likened the municipal government of the imperial city of Augsburg to that of the Roman republic. By designating the mayor as consul, the village administrator as praetor, and other officials as their republican counterparts, Clemens employed historical precedents to extol his city's form of government as one founded on ancient and venerable tradition. The chronicle also served a political purpose. A guild-dominated city council had originated during the fourteenth-century uprisings of numerous influential artisans against the confining rule of hereditary oligarchy. Hence, the chronicler's appeal to the authority of well-known historical precedents encouraged citizens to retain the established tradition of their city's government.

The city chronicles also recounted the role played by their respective civic communities in the progression of Christian history toward salvation. In doing so, they documented municipal history as a meaningful series of divine acts and interventions in the affairs of cities and of citizens who considered themselves to be agents of God's design. The chroniclers strove to demonstrate that even deleterious events and disruptions of civic life, whether from natural disasters, usurpation of power, or moral laxity, were not merely accidental occurrences but divine admonitions for repentance and reform. The dreadful appearance of comets, for example, commonly presaged ominous events. The comet of 1435 (noted in the *Konstanzer Chronik),* was interpreted as a warning of the election of an unworthy pope, and the comet of 1472 (recorded in the *Lübecker Ratschronik),* by turning its tail toward the Southwest, was seen to have foretold a plague in the Rhine area and war in France and Burgundy. Thus, city chronicles provided instruction on how to gain salvation and prosperity by learning from lessons past, present, and, perhaps, the future.

Late medieval city chronicles commonly rendered past, present, and anticipated future events as contemporaneous with the life of the chronicler and his city. As such, the perception of temporal history was a static one that focused on lasting values and enduring beliefs preserved within the "eternal" present. This view affirmed municipal rights and privileges not only for the fleeting moment, but in perpetuity.

As a record of at least nominally Christian communities, city chronicles also sought to promote some certainty of redemption through timeless, immediate examples of God's ongoing benevolence toward their city and citizenry, as well as of His occasional displeasure, in order to spur moral reform. What distinguishes these chronicles from their earlier counterparts, however, is the value city chroniclers of the later medieval period placed on the rendering of history as verifiable facts and events. As scholars have noted, the city acquired its own *persona* during this period. City chronicles portrayed the city itself as playing a central role in the formation of its own history and in the definition of its urban identity and that of its citizens.

BIBLIOGRAPHY

Cramer, Thomas. *Geschichte der deutschen Literatur im späten Mittelalter.* Munich: Deutscher Taschenbuch Verlag, 1990.

Green, D. H. *Medieval Listening and Reading.* Cambridge: Cambridge University Press, 1994.

Heinzle, Joachim. *Vom hohen zum späten Mittelalter. Wandlungen und Neuansätze im 13. Jahrhundert (1220/30–1280/90).* Geschichte der deutschen Literatur von den Anfängen bis zum Beginn der Neuzeit. Vol. 2, pt. 2; 2nd ed. Tübingen: Niemeyer, 1994.

Leuschner, Joachim. *Deutschland im späten Mittelalter.* Göttingen: Vandenhoeck & Ruprecht, 1975.

Rupprich, Hans. *Vom späten Mittelalter bis zum Barock: Das ausgehende Mittelalter, Humanismus und Renaissance 1370–1520.* Munich: Beck, 1970.

Schmale, Franz-Josef. *Funktion und Formen mittelalterlicher Geschichtsschreibung.* Darmstadt: Wissenschaftliche Buchgesellschaft, 1985.

Schmidt, Heinrich. *Die Deutschen Städtechroniken als Spiegel des bürgerlichen Selbstverständnisses im Spätmittelalter.* Göttingen: Vandenhoeck & Ruprecht, 1958.

Schmidt, Wieland. "Vom Lesen und Schreiben im späten Mittelalter." In *Festschrift für Ingeborg Schröbler zum 65 Geburtstag,* ed. Dietrich Schmidtke and Helga Schüppert. Tübingen: Niemeyer, 1973, pp. 309–327.

Vollmann-Profe, Gisela. *Von den Anfängen zum hohen Mittelalter: Wiederbeginn volkssprachiger Schriftlichkeit im hohen Mittelalter (1050–1160/70).* Geschichte der deutschen Literatur von den Anfängen bis zum Beginn der Neuzeit. Vol. 1, pt. 2; 2nd ed. Tübingen: Niemeyer, 1994.

Wenzel, Horst. "Aristokratisches Selbstverständnis im städtischen Patriziat von Köln, dargestellt an der Kölner Chronik Gottfried Hagens." In *Literatur–Publikum–historischer Kontext,* ed. Gert Kaiser. Bern: Lang, 1977, pp. 9–28.

———. "Zur Repräsentation von Herrschaft im mittelalterlichen Texten. Plädoyer für eine Literaturgeschichte der Herrschaftsbereiche und ihrer Institutionen." *Adelsherrschaft und Literatur,* ed. Horst Wenzel. Bern: Lang, 1980, pp. 339–375.

Ernst Ralf Hintz

SEE ALSO
Anno; *Annolied;* Augsburg; Chronicles, City, Dutch; Chronicles, World, German; Cologne, History; Empire; Latin Language; Nuremberg; *Reich;* Town Planning and Urbanism

Chronicles, Regional/National, Dutch

The origin of Dutch regional chronicles, a widespread and prevailing genre of historiography in the Low Countries, is related to the rise of territorial principalities and dynasties. Chronicles with regional interest also originated in monasteries and other spiritual centers, and, incidentally, in towns. The formation of the Burgundian state, in which most areas of the Netherlands of the fourteenth and fifteenth centuries were successively incorporated, gave the genre a new impulse. On the one hand, chronicle-writing was stimulated by the political aspirations of the Burgundian dukes; on the other, it reflected growing territorial self-consciousness.

Holland, where the counts took advantage of the monastery of Egmond as an intellectual center, was the undisputed historiographic center of the North. Several sources became important in chronicling the history of the rise of the county of Holland: the twelfth-century *Annales Egmundanenses,* with a fourteenth-century continuation by Willem, Procurator of Egmond, who also considers international affairs; the thirteenth-century *Chronicon Egmundanum,* an adaptation of the *Annales;* the Middle Dutch rhymed chronicle of Melis Stoke (ca. 1300), who was closely connected with the court, as was Claes Heynenzoon (*Hollantsche cronike* until 1409); the prose chronicle of the unoriginal *Clerc uten Lagen Landen,* a member of the chancery of the counts of Holland; and the influential *Chronographia* of Johannes Beka (ca. 1350), whose well-written chronicle was later translated into Middle Dutch. Beka also described the history of the diocese of Utrecht, Holland's constant enemy, and advocated a reconciliation between Holland and Utrecht because of their common origin. Jan Gerbrandszoon of Leyden (Johannis à Leydis), prior of a Haarlem monastery (ca. 1470), in his comprehensive *Chronicum comitum Hollandie et episcoporum Ultraiectensium* (Chronicle of the

Duchy of Holland and the Bishopric of Utrecht) and the *Chronicon* by the Gorkum cleric Theodericus Pauli dealt with the same territories.

The historiographic output in the diocese of Utrecht, whose worldly authority was far-reaching but ineffective, lagged very much behind that of Holland. Around 1020 the monk Alpertus of Metz, who was related to the spiritual and secular aristocracy in the diocese, wrote his *De diversitate temporum* (On various times), an important source for our knowledge of the influential noble dynasties of the time. Two centuries later, an anonymous but competent writer, close to the bishop, wrote the *Quaedam narracio de Groninghe,* which dealt particularly with the bishops' military campaigns and other events in the northern part of their diocese.

In Frisia, which was able to withdraw from the authority of neighboring principalities, historiography flourished mainly in monasteries. The Premonstratensian monastery Bloemhof near Wittewierum and the monastery Thabor, of canons regular, were especially influential centers. They were the cradle of the *Chronica* of the abbots Emo and Menko (thirteenth century).

An important historical source for the county of Gelre, a duchy since 1339, is *De nobili principatu Gelrie et eius origine* by the cleric Willem de Berchen (who lived near Nijmegen), characterized by its reaction against the Burgundian penetration into the region.

In the South, the duchy of Brabant, the counties of Flanders, Hainault, and Namur, and the diocese of Liège were the main principalities. The chronicle genre flourished especially in the first two. In Brabant, territorial historiography began with a compilation of several genealogies of the ducal dynasty in order to legitimate its Carolingian descent: the *Chronica de origine ducum Brabantiae* (ca. 1300). Around 1290 the *Yeeste van de slag bij Woeringen,* by Jan van Heelu, was written. In light of Brabant's successful annexation of Limburg, Heelu defended the claims of the dynasty and demonstrated the loyalty to his sovereign lord. The *Brabantsche Yeesten* (ca. 1316) by the Antwerp alderman-clerk Jan van Boendale also attempted to reconcile the diverging interests of the Brabantine towns and the dynasty. In Hennen van Merchtenen's *Cronike van Brabant* (to 1414) Brabantian nationalism was harmoniously connected with the Burgundian transfer of power. For the duchy's new rulers, Edmond de Dynter, secretary to John and Philip of Burgundy, wrote a documented chronicle of Brabant until 1442: *Chronica nobilissimorum ducum Lotharingiae et*

Branbantiae. Die alder excellentste cronyke van Brabant—published in 1497 by the printer Roland van den Dorpe of Antwerp—which traced the Burgundian dynasty to the Trojans via the Brabantine dukes and the Carolingians. This chronicle marked the end as well as the height of Brabantine historiography.

Flanders had many of the same characteristics as Brabant. The number of texts is considerable; their mutual relationship, however, is complex. The starting point is the *Flandria generosa* (ca. 1164), begun in the abbey at Saint-Omer and continued until 1347. This genealogy of the Flemish counts influenced the principal Flemish vernacular chronicles: the *Chronique de Flandre,* of which the oldest version—also called *Ancienne chronique de Flandre*—covers the period to 1342 and the latest version, to 1383; the *Rijmkroniek van Vlaanderen* (to 1405), which describes social disturbances in the fourteenth century; and the *Kronijk van Vlaanderen* (to 1467). Via the pro-Burgundian *Cronike ende genealogie van den princen ende graven van [. . .] Vlaenderlant* (to 1440), attributed to Johannes of Dixmude, the chronicle genre comes to a close in *Die excellente Cronike van Vlaenderen,* printed in Antwerp in 1531 by Willem Vorsterman.

The history of Hainault is partially treated by the well-informed Gislebert of Mons (d. 1225), chancellor and ambassador of Count Baudouin V, in his *Chronicon Hanoniense.* For the territories of Liège, two works are important: the *Historia et res gestae pontificum Leodiensium* by the Liegian canon and lawyer Jan van Hocsem (d. 1348), whose attention to economic issues is remarkable; and the legendary *Geste de Liège* by Jean d'Outremeuse (1338–1400), a chronicle interlacing the genres of the town chronicle and the Charlemagne romances.

In addition to regional chronicles, the history of the Low Country territories is, though often incidentally, treated by several well-known Burgundian historiographers, including Froissart and others.

BIBLIOGRAPHY

Balau, Sylvain. *Etude critique des sources de l'histoire du pays de Liège au moyen âge.* Brussels: M. Hayez, 1902–03.

Bethmann, Ludwig C., ed. *Monumenta Germaniae Historica.* SS no. 9. Hannover: Hahn, 1851, pp. 317–334 [*Flandria generosa*].

Borgnet, Adolphe, and Stanislas Bormans, ed. *Ly myreur des histors,* Vol. 6. Brussels: M. Hayez, 1880 [*Geste de Liège*].

Bruch, H. *Chronographia Johannis de Beke.* Rijks Geschiedkundige Publicatien, Grote serie, Vol. 143. The Hague: M. Nijhoff, 1973.

———, ed. *Croniken van den Stichte van Utrecht ende van Hollant.* Rijks Geschiedkundige Publicatien, Grote serie, Vol. 180. The Hague: M. Nijhoff, 1982.

Carasso-Kok, Marijke. *Repertorium van verhalende historische bronnen uit de middeleeuwen.* The Hague: M. Nijhoff, 1981.

Cauchie, Alfred, and Alphonse Bayot. "Chroniques du Brabant." *Bulletin de la Commission Royale d'Histoire* 69 (1900): 37–93.

de Geer van Jutphaas, B. J. L., ed. *Bronnen van de geschiedenis der Nederlanden in de middeleeuwen. Kronijk van Holland van een ongenoemden geestelijke.* Werken van het Historisch Genootschap, no. 6. Groningen: Wolters, 1867 [*Clerc uten Lagen Landen*].

De Mooy, Albertus J., ed. *De Gelderse kroniek van Willem van Berchen.* Arnhem: Brouwer, 1950.

de Ram, Petrus F. X., ed. *Chronica nobilissimorum ducum Lotharingiae et Brabantiae.* 3 vols. Brussels: M. Hayez, 1854–1860.

de Smet, Joseph-Jean, ed. *Corpus chronicorum Flandriae,* vol. 3. Brussels: M. Hayez, 1856, pp. 35–109 [Johannes of Dixmude].

———, Joseph-Jean, ed. *Corpus chronicorum Flandriae,* vol. 4. Brussels: M. Hayez, 1865, pp. 587–898 [*Rijmkroniek van Vlaanderen*].

Feith, H. O., and G. Acker Stratingh, ed. *Kronijken van Emo en Menko.* Werken van het Historisch Genootschap, no. 4. Groningen: Wolters, 1866.

Gezelle, Guido, ed. *Hennen van Merchtenen's Cornicke van Brabant (1414).* Gent: Siffer, 1896.

Heller, J., ed. *Monumenta Germaniae Historica.* SS, no. 25. Hannover: Hahn, 1851, pp. 405–413 [*Chronica de origine ducum Brabantiae*].

Hulshof, A., ed. *Alperti Mettensis De diversitate temporum.* Werken van het Historisch Genootschap, 3rd ser., no. 37. Groningen: Wolters, 1916.

Kervyn de Lettenhove, [Josef], ed. *Istore et croniques de Flandres,* 2 vols. Brussels: M. Hayez, 1879–1880 [*Ancienne chronique de Flandre*].

Kurth, Godefroid, ed. *La chronique de Jean de Hocsem.* Brussels: Kiessling, 1927.

Oppermann, Otto, ed. *Fontes Egmundenses.* Werken van het Historisch Genootschap, 3rd ser., no. 61. Groningen: Wolters, 1933.

Pertz, G. H., ed. *Annales Egmundanenses.* In *Monumenta Germaniae Historica* SS XVI. Hannover: Hahn, 1859, pp. 445–479.

Pijnacker Hordijk, C., ed. *Willelmi capellani Chronicon.* Werken van het Historisch Genootschap, 3rd ser., no. 20. Groningen: Wolters, 1904.

———. *Quedam narracio de Groninghe.* Werken van het Historisch Genootschap, n.s., no. 49. Utrecht: Kemink, 1888.

Prevenier, Walter, and Wims Blockmans. *The Burgundian Netherlands.* Cambridge: Cambridge University Press, 1986, pp. 214–240.

Repertorium fontium historiae medii aevi primum ab Augusto Pottharst digestum, nunc cura collegii historicorum e pluribus nationibus emendatum et auctum, 6 vols. Rome: Instituto storico italiano per il medio evo, 1978ff. [in progress].

Serrure, Constant P., and J. Ph. Blommaert, ed. *Maetschappij der Vlaemsche Bibliophielen.* The Hague: M. Nijhoff, 1839–1840 [*Kronijk van Vlaanderen*].

Sloet van de Beele, L. A. J. W., ed. *Wilhelmus de Berchen, De nobili principatu Gelrie.* The Hague: M. Nijhoff, 1870.

Vanderkindere, Leon, ed. *La chronique de Gislebert de Mons.* Brussels: Kiessling, 1904.

van Oostrom, Frits P. *Court and Culture. Dutch Literature, 1350–1450.* Berkeley: University of California Press, 1992.

Weiland, Ludwig, ed. *Monumenta Germaniae Historica,* SS no. 23. Hannover: Hahn, 1874, pp. 465–523 [Emo en Menko].

———. *Monumenta Germaniae Historica,* SS no. 23. Hannover: Hahn, 1874, pp. 402–426 [Groningen chronicle].

Willems, Jan Frans, ed. *Rymkronyk van Jan van Heelu betreffende den slag van Woeringen, van het jaer 1288.* Brussels: M. Hayez, 1836.

———. *De Brabantsche Yeesten of Rymkronyk van Braband,* 3 vols. Brussels: M. Hayez, 1839–69.

A. L. H. Hage

SEE ALSO
Brabant, Duchy of; Chronicles, City, Dutch; Holland; Stokes, Melis; Utrecht

Chronicles, Regional/Territorial, German

Middle High German and early New High German compendia recounted the social, political, economic, and military history of a region or territory, chiefly to legitimize the territorial claims of the ruling nobility. The primary expression of these claims were chronicles which supported the *Landesfürsten* (regional princes) in their efforts to consolidate and expand their newly emerging territorial states. Numerous examples of such chronicles appear from the end of the thirteenth century and throughout the late medieval period.

Prominent among them is a prodigious early fourteenth-century work of nearly 100,000 verses, the Austrian Rhyme Chronicle (*Österreichische Reimchronik*) of Ottokar von Steiermark. The chronicler (ca. 1260/1265 to 1319/1321), possibly Ottokar aus der Geul, was a member of an administerial family in the service of the regional prince Otto II of Lichtenstein (son of Ulrich von Lichtenstein, the author of *Frauendienst*). Ottokar documents the reign of the Habsburg kings Rudolf and Albrecht as an amalgam of Austrian-Steiermark (Styrian) regional and imperial history. The work begins with the death of Emperor Frederick II in 1250 and ends with the uprising in Lower Austria against Duke Frederick I in 1309. The author's familiarity with vernacular literary works provided models for the chronicle's depiction of courtly life and its rendering of courtly speech. He refers to courtly epics such as *Iwein, Parzival,* and *Willehalm,* and, among others, to works such as *Meier Helmbrecht* and the heroic epics, the *Nibelungenlied* and the *Dietrichepik.*

Ottokar chronicles the struggle between Ottokar II of Bohemia and the Habsburger Rudolf I, and favorably depicts the landed nobility's energetic support of the Habsburgs in putting an end to the Bohemian king's "unjust" territorial expansion. Although deemed worthy of praise by the chronicler as an exemplary king and brave knight, Ottokar II incurs God's wrath by chasing after worldly renown (*nach der Werlde lone,* l. 16738). In addition to opinionated commentary, Ottokar, the chronicler, combines contrived materials such as fictitious accounts and dialogues with actual written and oral sources to promulgate what scholars have characterized as pro-Habsburg sentiment, albeit one in the interest of the Styrian-Austrian landed nobility.

Preceding Ottokar von Steiermark's work was the Book of Princes, or *Fürstenbuch,* by Jans Enikel. The author refers to himself in the prologue as a *rehter Wienner* (v. 19–23), a Viennese burgher in good standing, and he may well have been a property owner who enjoyed patrician status. Although his name is not documented in Viennese archives, that of his grandfather (noted in the prologue) appears frequently. Writing in the last quarter of the thirteenth century, Jans recounts the ancient founding of Vienna and the inception and dominant role of the Babenberger dynasty after Albrecht, names the first margrave to become a Christian, and describes in detail the final Babenberg rulers, Count Ludwig II and, in particular, Duke Frederick II (1230–1246). And though the laudable qualities of Duke Frederick II, *der vogt was in Ôster-rîch* (ll. 2119–2136), receive ample mention, the chronicler does not refrain from depicting the duke's attributes in a revealing account of his excesses. These include not only the fleecing of certain citizens of Vienna by devious financial means, but the rape of a young Viennese woman named Brünhild at an official court function—a despotic incident that led the outraged townspeople to drive the transgressor from their city.

It is during the account of these final Babenberg rulers that the chronicler first mentions the Viennese citizenry. In this context, he promotes the interests of the Viennese upper strata as patrician knights, "Ritterbürger" (*miles et civis*), and decidedly exaggerates their political and economic importance. In addition to the Book of Princes, a regional chronicle, Jans Enikel is also believed to be the author of a world chronicle (*Die Weltchronik*) which expresses emerging Austrian national pride.

Another prominent work of the period is the Braunschweiger (Brunswick) Rhymed Chronicle (*Braunschweigische Reimchronik*). This history of the Welf dynasty and that of the city of Braunschweig promoted the territorialization process under the Welf duke Albrecht I, the possible patron of the chronicle. Writing toward the end of the thirteenth century, the chronicler, possibly of the St. Blasius cloister in Braunschweig, advocated the interests of the Welf ruling house by hyperbolizing Albrecht I as a paragon of knightly virtues and the flower of his dynasty. Although the chronicle may have been completed during Albrecht's lifetime, it is likely that the patron at the time the work was completed was his oldest son and duke, Heinrich der Wunderliche, whose death was in 1322.

Many other regional chronicles from the fourteenth to the sixteenth century from the German-speaking lands have been preserved. Examples of these later works can be found in the *Kronike von Pruzinlant*, compiled by Nikolaus von Jeroschin (ca. 1290–1345) as a history of the Teutonic Order; *Deutscher Orden*, completed circa 1331–1341, and based on a Prussian chronicle (*Chronicon terrae Prussiae*) by the Teutonic knight Peter Dusburg from

1326; the Rhymed Mecklenburg Chronicle (*Mecklenburgische Reimchronik*) by Ernst von Kirchberg, commissioned by Duke Albrecht II of Mecklenburg during the second half of the fourteenth century; and the *Chronica de principibus terrae Bavarorum,* the first Bavarian regional chronicle (*Landeschronik*), compiled by Andreas von Regensburg, a religious chronicler from the local cloister St. Mang (*Augustinerchorherrenstift*), at the behest of Ludwig VII of Bavaria in 1425 and continued from 1428 until 1436.

Andreas von Regensburg also translated his work into German in *Die Chronik von den Fürsten von Bayern.* Another German-language chronicle was the *Schwäbische Chronik,* from the second half of the fifteenth century, compiled in prose by Thomas Lirer and printed in Ulm in several editions by Konrad Dinckmuth in 1485 and 1486. The latter edition is renowned as one of the finest illustrated histories of the period. The *Chronica Baioariorum* (Bavarian Chronicle) by Veit Arnpeck (ca. 1435–96), was translated into German, *Chronik der Bayern,* by 1493. Other chronicles included the *Chronik von den Fürsten aus Bayern,* compiled by Hans Ebran von Wildenberg (1426–ca. 1502) chiefly as a genealogy of the Wittelsbach dynasty; the *Hand- und Hausbuch* (Handbook and Housebook), written by Konrad Stolle (ca. 1430–1505) as a regional history of Thuringia; and the *Landeschronik von Thüringen und Hessen,* by Wigand Gestenberg (1457–1522), who probably completed it after 1515.

Scholars have noted that the regional chronicles of the Swiss Confederation, e.g., the *Berner Chronik* (1420) by Konrad Justinger (d. 1438) and his later collaborators such as Diebold Schilling, the Elder (ca. 1430–1486) and Diebold Schilling, the Younger (1460–ca. 1520), comprise a pronounced variant of the genre in their glorification of the confederation's separation from the empire and its struggle for sovereignty. The sixteenth-century historical source that Friedrich Schiller used for his *Wilhelm Tell,* the *Chronicon helveticum,* by Aegidius Tschudi (1505–1572), may well be deemed the zenith of Swiss regional chronicles.

BIBLIOGRAPHY

Brunner, Otto. *Adeliges Landleben und Europäischer Geist.* Salzburg: Müller, 1949.

Bumke, Joachim. *Mäzene im Mittelalter.* Munich: Beck, 1979.

Cramer, Thomas. *Geschichte der deutschen Literatur im späten Mittelalter*. Munich: Deutscher Taschenbuch Verlag, 1990.

de Boor, Helmut. *Die deutsche Literatur im späten Mittelalter: Zerfall und Neubeginn*. Pt. 1. Munich: Beck, 1962.

Heinzle, Joachim. *Vom hohen zum späten Mittelalter. Wandlungen und Neuansätze im 13. Jahrhundert (1220/30–1280/90)*. Königstein im Taunus: Athenäum, 1984; 2nd ed. Tübingen: Niemeyer, 1994.

Leuschner, Joachim. *Deutschland im späten Mittelalter*. Göttingen: Vandenhoeck & Ruprecht, 1975.

Liebertz-Grün, Ursula. *Das andere Mittelalter. Erzählte Geschichte und Geschichtserkenntnis um 1300. Studien zu Ottokar von Steiermark, Jans Enikel, Seifried Helbling*. Munich: Fink, 1984.

Loehr, Maja. "Der Steirische Reimchronist: her Otacher ouz der Geul." *Mitteilungen des Instituts für Österreichische Geschichtsforschung*. 51 (1937): 89–130.

Rupprich, Hans. *Vom späten Mittelalter bis zum Barock*. Pt. 1. *Das ausgehende Mittelalter, Humanismus und Renaissance 1370–1520*. Munich: Beck, 1970.

Schmale, Franz-Josef. *Funktion und Formen mittelalterlicher Geschichtsschreibung*. Darmstadt: Wissenschaftliche Buchgesellschaft, 1985.

Schmidt, Wieland. "Vom Lesen und Schreiben im späten Mittelalter." In *Festschrift für Ingeborg Schröbler zum 65. Geburtstag*, ed. Dietrich Schmidtke and Helga Schüppert. Tübingen: Niemeyer, 1973, pp. 309–327.

Scholz, Manfred Günter. *Zum Verhältnis von Mäzen, Autor und Publikum im 14. und 15. Jahrhundert*. Darmstadt: Wissenschaftliche Buchgesellschaft, 1987.

Vollmann-Profe, Gisela. *Von den Anfängen zum hohen Mittelalter (1050–1160/70)*. Königstein im Taunus: Athenäum, 1986; 2nd ed. Tübingen: Niemeyer, 1994.

Weinacht, Helmut. "Ottokar von Steiermark (O. aus der Geul)." In *Die deutsche Literatur des Mittelalters: Verfasserlexikon*, ed. Kurt Ruh. Vol. 7. Berlin and New York: de Gruyter, 1989.

Wenzel, Horst. "Zur Repräsentation von Herrschaft im mittelalterlichen Texten. Plädoyer für eine Literaturgeschichte der Herrschaftsbereiche und ihrer Institutionen." In *Adelsherrschaft und Literatur*, ed. Horst Wenzel. Bern: Lang, 1980, pp. 339–375.

———. "Aristokratisches Selbstverständnis im städtischen Patriziat von Köln, dargestellt an der Kölner Chronik Gottfried Hagens." In *Literatur–Publikum–historischer Kontext*, ed. Gert Kaiser. Bern: Lang, 1977, pp. 9–28.

Ernst Ralf Hintz

SEE ALSO

Dietrichepik; Hartmann von Aue; Jans Enikel; *Nibelungenlied;* Ulrich von Lichtenstein; Wolfram von Eschenbach

Chronicles, World, Dutch

Historical writings that deal with biblical, ecclesiastical, and profane history, starting from the Creation or the birth of Christ, world chronicles operate within a universal and salvation-oriented system. The chronicles are organized around biblically founded periods (*aetates*), according to the theory of four world empires or periods of rule.

The genre originated in the Low Countries in the eleventh century in spiritual and, especially, monastic circles. The monumental *Chronographica sive Chronica* by the learned Benedictine Sigebert of Gembloux (1029–1112), who continued the world chronicle of Eusebius/Hieronymus from 381 until his own time, is an early and very influential specimen of the genre. Several authors extended the chronicle, including some from the monasteries of Affligem and Ourscamps.

The genre remained popular in monastic circles until the end of the Middle Ages. At the end of the thirteenth century, Balduinus, a Norbertine monk of the monastery Ninove, in East Flanders, and Johannes de Thielrode, monk of St. Baaf's Abbey in Gent, each completed a world chronicle. The latter, covering the period up to 1130, is principally based on the *Flandria generosa*. In the fifteenth century, Cornelius Zantfliet (d. 1461), a monk in Liege, wrote a relatively accurate world chronicle and, in a Cistercian abbey, Ter Duinen Jan Brandon (d. 1428), Egidius de Roye (d. 1478), and Adriaan de Budt (d. 1488) produced their *Chronodromon*, a chronicle with a particularly Burgundian viewpoint, based on several Flemish sources.

From the second half of the thirteenth century, the *Chronicon summorum pontificum imperatorumque ac de septem aetatibus mundi* by Martinus van Troppau (d. 1278) and the *Speculum historiale* by Vincentius of Beauvais (d. 1264) surpassed Sigebert's chronicle in influence. Both works were frequently used by authors of world chronicles in the vernacular. These had begun to appear during the same period and were written by clerics commissioned by secular principals. Among them was a world chronicle by Jacob van Maerlant and the priest Lodewijk van Velthem (near Louvain), who continued Maerlant's translation to 1250 for Maria van Berlaer. For

Gerard van Voorne, viscount of Zeeland, Velthem wrote a continuation of the chronicle to 1316, with special attention to the end of time and contemporary events.

In courtly circles, around 1400, Claes Heynenzoon produced a world chronicle, also based on Vincentius and Martinus. Claes was a herald, first in the service of the duke of Gelre and afterwards of Willem VI, count of Holland, to whom he dedicated his work. A few decades later a world chronicle appeared with no direct connection to monasteries or principalities: the *Chronicon Tielense*, written by a layman from the area near Tiel, (begun ca. 1425; a definitive version ca. 1450) and based on, among others, chronicles by Martinus of Troppau and Johannes Beka. Especially in its final sections, this chronicle recounts the history of adjacent territorial principalities.

Around the year 1480, the historian Theodericus Pauli, a priest in Gorkum, began his tripartite *Chronicon universale*, which extends until 1488, a skillful compilation based on an impressive number of sources. At about the same time, the first printed world chronicle appeared: the *Fasciculus temporum* by Werner Rolevinck in Cologne in 1474; a translated and extensive edition was produced a few years later by the printer Jan Veldenaer (Utrecht, 1480).

BIBLIOGRAPHY

Balau, Sylvian. *Etude critique des sources de l'histoire du pays de Liège au moyen âge.* Brussels: M. Hayez, 1902–1903.

Bethmann, Ludwig C., ed. *Monumenta Germaniae historica,* SS no. 6. Hannover: Hahn, 1844, pp. 300–374 [Sigebert of Gembloux].

Carasso-Kok, Marijke. *Repertorium van verhalende historische bronnen uit de middeleeuwen.* The Hague: M. Nijhoff, 1981.

de Smet, Joseph-Jean, ed. *Corpus chronicorum Flandriae,* vol. 2. Brussels: M. Hayez, 1841, pp. 587–731.

———. *Corpus chronicorum Flandriae,* vol. 1. Brussels: M. Hayez, 1837, pp. 261–367 [*Chronodromon*].

Gorissen, Pieter, ed. *Sigeberti Gemblacensis chronographiae auctarium Affligemense.* Brussels: Koninklijke Vlaamse Academie voor wetenschappen, letteren en schone kunsten van België, 1952.

Heller, J., ed. *Monumenta Germaniae historica,* SS no. 25. Hannover: Hahn, 1880, pp. 559–584 [Johannes de Thielrode].

Holder-Egger, Oswald, ed. *Monumenta Germaniae historica,* SS no. 25. Hannover: Hahn, 1880, pp. 521–546 [Balduinus].

Kervyn de Lettenhove, Josef, ed. *Chroniques relatives à l'histoire de la Belgique sous la domination des ducs de Bourgogne,* vol. 3. Brussels: M. Hayez, 1876, pp. 235-328 [Pauli; Latin texts].

———. *Chroniques relatives à l'histoire de la Belgique sous la domination des ducs de Bourgogne,* vol. 1. Brussels: M. Hayez, 1870, pp. 1–166.

Krüger, Karl Heinrich. *Die Universalchroniken.* Typologie des sources du Moyen Age occidental, fascicle 16. Turhout: Brepols, 1976.

Lettinck, Nico. "The Character of Later Medieval Universal Histories in the Netherlands." In *L'Historiographie médiévale en Europe,* Jean-Philippe Genet, ed. Paris: CNRS, 1991, pp. 321–331.

van der Linden, Herman, Paul de Keyser, and Adolf van Loey. *Lodewijk van Velthem's Voortzetting van den Spiegel historiael.* 3 vols. Brussels: M. Hayez, 1906–1938.

van Oostrom, P. *Court and Literature: Dutch Literature 1350–1450.* Berkeley: University of California Press, 1992.

A. L. H. Hage

SEE ALSO

Beyeren, Herald; Chronicles, City, Dutch; Chronicles, City, German; Chronicles, Regional/National, Dutch; Chronicles, World, German; Historiography, Dutch; Jacob van Maerlant; Jan van Boendale

Chronicles, World, German

Although medieval Latin historiography was fully developed and highly advanced by the mid-twelfth century (examples include Ekkehard of Aura's world chronicle completed by 1125, Otto of Freising's world chronicle composed between 1143 and 1146, and the chronicle by Frutolf of Michelsberg in the early twelfth century), world chronicles in German were not composed until the thirteenth century. The anonymous poet of the *Annolied* (ca. 1080/1085 or shortly after 1105) and the composer of the *Kaiserchronik* (Chronicle of the Emperors, ca. 1135–1147) had already incorporated extensive historighical information into their texts, but their dominant framework continued to be the literary and hagiographical narrative.

Shortly before 1218, the priest Eberhard wrote the *Gandersheimer Reimchronik,* in which the history of his convent, seen from a global perspective, received primary attention. This world chronicle was written in Low German and based on local oral traditions, but the author also mentioned political events in Rome and in the German empire. Eberhard intended his work primarily as a way to authenticate the convent's claims of independence from the bishop's jurisdiction, and he strongly criticized courtly culture and the vices of the nobility as a class.

Another Low German writer (Eike von Repgow?) created the enormously popular *Sächsische Weltchronik* (Saxon World Chronicle) sometime in the middle of the thirteenth century. In this chronicle, the usual verse is almost completely replaced by prose. The text takes the reader form biblical times (Genesis) to the thirteenth century C.E. but focuses on the history of the Roman Empire. Various versions of this chronicle exist; one was translated into Middle High German, and another, into Latin.

Rudolf von Ems was the first to write a true world chronicle in Middle High German. Commissioned by German king Conrad IV sometime in the 1240s, the chronicle was designed to serve as political propaganda. Since Conrad had to struggle to maintain the power base of the Hohenstaufens, Rudolf portrayed the imperial family as sacrosanct and included within the text an extensive hymn on the Hohenstaufen. This was all to no avail, however, as Conrad died in 1251 while in Italy, and the German empire subsequently collapsed. Rudolf himself had accompanied Conrad on his military campaign and died in the same year, leaving his chronicle as a fragment of 33,500 verses.

The chronicle, divided into six major historical periods, begins in biblical times and first breaks off after an account of King Solomon. An anonymous writer continued the chronicle for 2,900 verses, ending his work with the prophet Eli. Didactic elements were mostly missing in Rudolf's work; instead, the author emphasized a theological worldview by contrasting the divine world (*Gotis stat*) with the secular world (*der weltlichen stat*). In addition, Rudolf included accounts of ancient Greece, Troy, and Italy, developed a cosmography, and discussed the current geopolitical situation in Germany in the context of the history of royal rulers from the time of the Old Testament to the Hohenstaufen family (Conrad IV). Both stylistically and conceptually, Rudolf closely followed the model of the courtly romance in his world chronicle—one reason for the great popularity of his work.

An anonymous author created the *Christherre-Chronik* at the request of the margrave Henry III of Meißen (1247–1288) sometime in the second half of the thirteenth century. He relied heavily on the Bible, especially the Book of Judges, and closely followed the model of

clerical literature aimed at religious teaching. Around 1270/1280 the prose chronicle *Buch der Könige* (Book of Kings) was written by a member of the Augsburg Franciscans, who also included a *Prosa-Kaiserchronik,* a prose version modeled after the twelfth-century rhymed *Kaiserchronik.*

One of the most popular world chronicles proved to be Jans Enikel's *Weltchronik* (World Chronicle) from the second half of the thirteenth century. Enikel, Viennese and of noble origin, found a very enthusiastic audience, as is evident by the surviving thirty-nine manuscripts (this was a lot for the time). He emphasized the Old Testament period and history since the foundation of Rome, but dealt very little with the present. Enikel used the *Imago mundi* (Image of the World) of the theologian Honorius Augustodunensis as his model, but he also incorporated many narrative texts for the entertainment of his readers.

The Magdeburger *Weichbildchronik* (Town Chronicle), composed in prose at about the same time, served as introductory text to a law book and combined world history with local history up to the time of King William of Holland (d. 1256). Other German world chronicles from the late thirteenth century were the *Braunschweigische Reimchronik* (Braunschweig/Brunswick Rhymed Chronicle), the *Livländische Reimchronik* (Livland Rhymed Chronicle), and the *Österreichische Reimchronik* (Austrian Rhymed Chronicle).

In the first half of the fourteenth century Heinrich von München composed a massive world chronicle, which consisted of 56,000 to 100,000 verses, the length varying among the eighteen surviving manuscripts. Apart from a chronological survey, Heinrich also included legends, hagiographic narratives, and even pieces from secular literature. In 1337 an unknown author wrote the *Oberrheinische Chronik* (Upper Rhenish Chronicle) with particular focus on the history of the papacy and the German emperors. Jacob Twinger von Königshofen's *Deutsche Chronik* (German Chronicle) from 1386 combines global history with local history. Dietrich Engelhus (ca. 1362–1434) composed a world chronicle in Latin, which he translated into German in 1424. On the basis of his *Cronica Novella* (New Chronicle), Hermann Korner (ca. 1365–1438), a Lübeck Dominican, created a Low German translation in which he traced world history until the time of his own death. The Ulm city doctor and translator Heinrich Steinhöwel printed a world chronicle in 1473 entitled *Tütsche Cronica* (German Chronicle), which purported to cover the entire time period from

Genesis to Emperor Frederick II. Jacob Köbel extended the chronicle to the year 1531. The two Nuremberg council scribes Johannes Plattenberger and Theodorich Truchsess produced a German world chronicle in 1459 entitled *Excerpta chronicarum* (Excerpts form the Chronicles), a massive compilation from previous works. This, in turn, was an influential source for Hartmann Schedel (1440–1514), a Nuremberg medical doctor and the author of the monumental *Liber Chronicarum* (Book of Chronicles), first printed in 1493.

Many of these world chronicles were constantly rewritten, expanded, copied, and modified to meet new expectations, widen historical horizons, and offer different evaluations of past events. Often deriving their basic material from Latin chronicles, they were extremely well received by learned audiences, as we can tell from the many manuscript copies (e.g., there are more than one hundred manuscripts and fragments of the *Christherre-Chronik*). In many cases, however, they were more religious than historical, and often included literary elements for general entertainment. Many of the world chronicles were richly illustrated.

BIBLIOGRAPHY

Bumke, Joachim. *Geschichte der deutschen Literatur im hohen Mittelalter.* Munich: dtv, 1990.

Cramer, Thomas *Geschichte der deutschen Literatur im späten Mittelalter.* Munich: dtv, 1990.

Gernentz, Hans-Joachim. "Historiographisches und juristisches Schrifttum." In *Geschichte der deutschen Literatur. Mitte des 12. bis Mitte des 13. Jahrhunderts,* ed. Rolf Bräuer. Berlin: Volk und Wissen, 1990, 719–746.

Grundmann, Hermann. *Geschichtsschreibung im Mittelalter,* 2nd ed. Göttingen; Vandenhoeck und Ruprecht, 1965.

Haeusler, Martin. *Das Ende der Geschichte in der mittelalterlichen Weltchronistik.* Ph.D. diss. Cologne, 1979 [revised]. Cologne and Vienna: Böhlau, 1980.

Maschek, Hermann. *Deutsche Chroniken.* Leipzig: Reclam, 1936.

Wolf, Jürgen. *Die Sächsische Weltchronik im Spiegel ihrer Handschriften.* Munich: Fink, 1997.

Albrecht Classen

SEE ALSO

Anno; Chronicles, Regional/Territorial, German; Holland; Jans Enikel; *Kaiserchronik;* Rudolf von Ems; Vienna

Chur

The only urban settlement in the Roman province of *Raetia prima,* the capital of the present canton of Graubünden in Switzerland, Chur lies at the confluence of the Plessur and Rhine rivers in the foothills of the Alps. At the heart of the medieval city is the so-called *Hof* (court) on an elevated rock plateau inside the late Roman fort. Here the bishops, documented from 451, erected their cathedral.

Several early medieval churches have been documented archeologically. The most important is the two-story St. Stephen's from the fifth and sixth centuries, the tomb site for the bishops of Chur; remains of its once rich decoration with mosaics and paintings are preserved. Typical for the Carolingian period are the single-aisled longitudinal churches with three half-round apses, as seen in the parish church of St. Martin, rebuilt in the late Gothic period. The church of St. Luzi, also of this type, was rebuilt as a Premonstratensian church in the twelfth century. The only remnant of the earlier church is the Carolingian ring crypt for the relics of the "apostle" Saint Luzius, who was thought to be responsible for the conversion of the bishopric to Christianity.

The predecessors to the Romanesque cathedral of St. Mary's on the Hof have only been partially excavated. The choir of the vaulted three-bay basilica is elevated over a hall crypt; a rectangular choir bay precedes the square apse. The final dedication is dated 1272. The building contains important architectural sculpture on the interior: the capitals increase in quality from west to east with the most significant in the choir. Indirect stylistic influences from northern Italy seem probable. At the entrance to the crypt, four statue columns from about 1200 represent apostles standing on lions; these nearly life-sized figures may have come from a lectern. The late Gothic winged altarpiece on the high altar was made between 1486 and 1492 by Jacob Russ of Ravensburg. The cathedral treasury preserves numerous late antique and medieval relics, reliquaries, crosses, sculptures, and panel paintings, which document the uninterrupted continuity of the bishopric back into the early Christian period.

BIBLIOGRAPHY

Beckerath, Astrid von. *Der Hochaltar in der Kathedrale von Chur: Meister und Auftraggeber am Vorabend der Reformation.* Ammersbek bei Hamburg: Verlag an der Lottbek, 1994.

Meier, Hans-Rudolf. *Romanische Schweiz.* Zodiaque. Würzburg: Echter, 1996, pp. 49–76.

Poeschel, Erwin. *Die Kunstdenkmäler des Kantons Graubünden 7: Chur und der Kreis der fünf Dörfer.* Basel: Birkhäuser, 1948.

Sennhauser, Hans Rudolf. "Spätantike und frühmittelalterliche Kirchen Churrätiens." In *Von der Antike zum frühen Mittelalter,* ed. J. Werner and E. Ewig. Sigmaringen: Thorbecke, 1979, pp. 193–218.

Sulser, Walter, and Hilde Claussen. *Sankt Stephan in Chur: Frühchristliche Grabkammer und Friedhofskirche.* Zurich: Manesse, 1978.

Susan Marti

Churches

See Carolingian Art and Architecture; Cistercian Art and Architecture; Franciscan Art and Architecture; Gothic Art and Architecture; Ottonian Art and Architecture; Romanesque Art and Architecture.

Cistercian Art and Architecture

The Cistercian order began as a reform of Benedictine monasticism at the monasteries of Cîteaux and Clairvaux in the eastern French region of Burgundy. This reform included a different, more austere, attitude towards the visual arts and architecture than was common in contemporary Benedictine practice. These restrictions, believed necessary to preserve monastic life from distraction and to save money for the poor, were promulgated in a series of general canons restricting most kinds of liturgical art.

With its rigorous reforms and with a spokesman of extremely high caliber in Saint Bernard of Clairvaux (d. 1153), the Cistercian order became extremely popular during the twelfth century and spread rapidly. The original house of Cîteaux (1098) had four daughter houses founded by 1115, including Morimond (1115). Most of the early German Cistercian houses for men were dependencies of Morimond, with several important houses founded before 1150 including Ebrach (1127), Altenberg (1133), Heiligenkreuz (1135), and Georgenthal (1142), each of which founded numerous dependencies of its own. German Cistercian houses for women included Wechterswinkel (before 1144), which had ties to the male house at Ebrach or Bildhausen, and later had a large group of women's houses as dependencies.

Architecturally, monasteries were supposed to be plain and functional. The earliest Cistercian churches consisted of a nave with a simple square east end without towers or crypt. The pointed arches and meticulous stone work of French Cistercian architecture are closely related to the emerging Gothic style of the Île-de-France, and the Cistercians are frequently credited with bringing elements of that style to Germany.

Although the strong central control of Cîteaux created overall uniformity in Cistercian architecture, German Cistercian buildings also reflect local Romanesque architectural traditions. Square apses, like that at Ebrach, were typical, but other types of apses were preferred in certain regions; these include the polygon, as at Bronnbach, and the apse *en échelon* (in stepped formation), which can be seen, for example, at Altenberg. Cistercian churches do not usually have crypts, but German churches built for cloistered women include crypts under the raised nun's gallery, as at Frauental.

Because of demands that monasteries of this order be in isolated locations and be self-sufficient, and that all monks participate in manual labor, Cistercians were involved in considerable technical innovation, especially mining and metallurgy, which were practiced at the German Cistercian houses of Walkenreid, Sittichenbach, and Altzelle.

Many Cistercian abbeys illuminated manuscripts; the abbey of Ebrach, for example, had a celebrated scriptorium active from the thirteenth to the fifteenth century. Sifridus Vitulus was a particularly notable scribe and illuminator working at Ebrach in the early fourteenth century. Cistercian women were also active as illuminators, as is suggested by a gradual from a Cistercian convent at Frauenroth (Stuttgart, Württembergische Landesbibliothek, manuscript no. HB I 246, 14th c.).

BIBLIOGRAPHY

Brückner, Wolfgang, and Jürgen Lenssen, ed. *Zisterzienser in Franken: Das alte Bistum Würzburg und sein einstigen Zisterzen.* Würzburg: Echter, 1991.

Dahmen, Jost. *Deutsche Zisterzienserkunst.* Cologne and Vienna: Böhlau, 1974.

Die Zisterzienser: Ordensleben zwischen Ideal und Wirklichkeit. Schriften des Rheinischen Museumsamtes 10. Cologne: Rheinland-Verlag, 1980, pp. 311–400, 530–578.

Susan L. Ward

SEE ALSO
Gothic Art and Architecture; Hirsau; Wienhausen

City Chronicles
See Chronicles, City.

Class

See Feudalism; Nobility and Farmers.

Clothing, Costume, and Fashion

In addition to its protective function, dress in medieval Germany also served purposes of social differentiation. Already under the Franks, clothing followed strict rules: both sexes wore similar tunic-like garments dependent on Roman models. Women's robes reached to the ground; men complemented their shorter garment with a mantle clasped on the right shoulder and leggings held up by fabric bands twisted around the legs. Functionality and poverty dictated the farmers' typical smocks and pants; people of lower social position were forbidden to wear the robes, fabrics, and colors reserved for feudal lords.

In the tenth and eleventh centuries, the lengthening of the man's robe led to a single look for members of the upper classes, lay and religious, men and women; common people continued to wear the shorter robe. Byzantine influence became apparent in women's clothing in the eleventh century in the use of expensive fabrics and decoration and the lengthening of the undergarment to form a train.

Extravagant cuts mark the clothing of the twelfth and thirteenth centuries: tightly cut upper garments that emphasized the body, overgarments (*Suckenie*) with removable decorative sleeves, and mantles with tassels. Wimples, chaplets, and various forms of veils were the most common forms of headwear. In the course of the thirteenth century, how the clothes were worn became important: the gathering up of overlong robes revealed the underdress in a contrasting color as well as the masses of fabric that marked the wearer's wealth. The arrangement of folds and the use of coded gestures, such as the linking of the finger through the tassel cord, conveyed information about the wearer's social status. Men's clothing was similar to women's but used less fabric and fewer folds; robes of different colors worn over one another and garments divided vertically into two colors (*mi-parti*) also made clothing more colorful.

Unusually slim proportions are characteristic of fourteenth-century clothing: garments were cut more tightly, and trains, sleeves, and toes of pointed shoes were lengthened according to the status of the wearer. The most striking innovations were the decolleté and the *Kruseler,* a veil with a crimped or pleated edge. In the middle of the fourteenth century, men's clothing changed fundamentally when the long outer garment, one of the most important privileges of the nobility, was replaced by the *Schecke,* a short garment that accentuated the body. The new fitted style made buttons and buttonholes necessary; like belts (*Dupsing*), they were also fashionable accessories. Little bells attached to the belt were a typically German fashion statement, epitomizing elegant dress for both sexes.

In the fifteenth century, the *Schecke* was increasingly shortened, becoming a doublet, and the leggings became the pants with codpiece preferred by younger men. Characteristic of the second half of the century is the *Schaube,* a long cloak with collar open in the front, and the beret. The tight bodice with a shirt underneath similar to a man's developed from the women's upper garment to cover the bosom.

Thirteenth-century fashion: Empress Adelheid and Emperor Otto I, Meissen, Cathedral, choir, north wall. *Photograph: Joan A. Holladay*

BIBLIOGRAPHY

Boehn, Max von. *Die Mode.* 8 vols. Munich, 1963.

Eisenbart, Liselotte Constanze. "Kleiderordnungen der deutschen Städte zwischen 1350 und 1700." Ph.D. Diss. Göttingen, 1962.

Kühnel, Harry. *Bildwörterbuch der Kleidung und Rüstung: Vom Alten Orient bis zum ausgehenden Mittelalter.* Stuttgart: Kröner, 1992.

Rady, Ottille. *Das weltliche Kostüm von 1250–1410 nach Ausweis der figürlichen Grabsteine im mittelrheinischen Gebiet.* Dachau, 1976.

Thiel, Erika. *Geschichte des Kostüms: Die europäische Mode von den Anfängen bis zur Gegenwart.* 6th, rev. ed. Berlin: Henschel, 1997.

Martina Dlugaiczyk

Clovis (481–511)

The most important king of the Merovingian dynasty, Clovis was a *magnus et egregius pugnator,* according to Gregory of Tours. A "brutal and treacherous warrior," he unified the Frankish kingdoms and laid the foundation for later Frankish power and influence. He cultivated good relations with the bishops in his realm and was the first Frankish king to convert to Christianity.

Clovis waged a series of wars to expand the boundaries of his realm. Although there exists much debate over the exact chronology of these events and even over the extent of Clovis' war-making, it is likely that he pursued an aggressive foreign policy that led to an enlarged Frankish kingdom. His many battles included victories over Syagrius in 486, the Alamans at the battle of Tolbiac in 496, the Burgundians in 500, the Visigoths in 507, and various lesser Frankish kings in his last years.

The wars against the Alamans and Visigoths were given religious significance by Gregory, an interpretation of these events that reveals how important the conversion of Clovis was to this Gallo-Roman bishop. The king's conversion, under the influence of his wife Chlothild and in the face of defeat at the battle of Tolbiac, may be little more than pious legend, but Clovis did convert to Catholic Christianity at some point between 496 and 508. It is no longer generally held that Clovis converted directly to Catholic Christianity from paganism, but it is believed that he converted first to Arian Christianity or, at least, was sympathetic to the Arian confession. His conversion did not greatly influence Frankish belief, but it did solidify relations with the Catholic hierarchy in his realm.

In his last years, Clovis' power came to be recognized by the emperor in Constantinople—who may have granted him an honorary consulship—and in Ostrogothic (East Gothic) Italy. Also in his last years, Clovis focused more on domestic policy by holding a church council at Orléans and by issuing the Salic (Salian) Law, an act which suggests the influence of Roman legal and administrative traditions on the king. At his death, the kingdom was divided among his sons, establishing a tradition that would continue throughout Merovingian history.

BIBLIOGRAPHY

Gregory of Tours. *History of the Franks,* trans. Lewis Thorpe. Harmondsworth, England: Penguin, 1974.

Daly, William M. "Clovis: How Barbaric, How Pagan?" *Speculum* 69 (1994): 619–664.

Wallace-Hadrill, J. M. *The Long-Haired Kings.* Toronto: Medieval Academy Reprints, 1982.

Wood, Ian. *The Merovingian Kingdoms, 450–751.* London: Longman, 1994.

Michael Frassetto

SEE ALSO
Law and Lawbooks

Coblenz

Coblenz lies at the confluence of the Moselle and Rhine rivers and at the meeting point of four Rhine schist massifs. Founded by the Romans in 9 B.C.E. as *Castrum ad Confluentes* (whence the corrupted form *Coblenz*) on the left bank of the Rhine, it was an important point along the frontier or *limes*. In the fifth century, it was destroyed by the Franks, who then built a *Königshof* (regal court) on the ruins. The settlement that grew around this fortification had little importance early on: according to Gregory of Tours, the Frankish Coblenz of 585 was too small to accommodate a royal delegation from King Guntrans to his cousin Sigebert within its walls.

In 807 Charlemagne held a *Gerichtstag,* or session of the imperial court, here. From this point onward, the medieval town began to grow in importance. At the assemblies and *Fürstentage* (princely diets) which were held here, important decisions were made concerning affairs of the Carolingian empire. Louis the Pious spent time at Coblenz in 819 and 823, and the presence of Louis and his wife at the consecration of the original St. Castor church at Coblenz in 836 by Archbishop Hetti of Trier, added special significance as well.

Six years later (842), and again in 848 and 860, Coblenz was the site where the three kings—Lothar, Louis the German, and Charles the Bald—negotiated the partition of their father's and grandfather's empire. In 886, Coblenz, together with Andernach and Sinzig, was the price for which the Viking Gottfried would cease his ravaging and make peace with Charles the Fat.

What had originally been an imperial town became an episcopal one in 1018 when Emperor Henry II granted the *Königshof* to the archbishop of Trier; at the same time, Trier acquired the strategically located fortress Ehrenbreitstein, which had been built on the opposite bank of the Rhine in the tenth century. The new lords attempted to improve the appearance and well-being of the town, which, by the twelfth century, had become an important trading center, controlling trade on both rivers.

At times, the town was the residence of the archbishops. Reflecting the growing significance of Coblenz was the church of St. Florin, which dates from ca. 1100, and the Liebfraukirche, the choir of which was begun in the twelfth century. A "customs roll" from the early twelfth century provides a unique look into where people traded goods—both raw materials and finished products—at the time. The town was chartered in 1214.

In 1208 Archbishop John I of Trier expanded the collegiate church of St. Castor. Eight years later, the Teutonic Knights established a *Komturei* (fortified residence) next to this church on the triangle of land where the Mosel joins the Rhine. From this point onward, the name *Deutsches Eck* (German Corner) has remained as the designation for this geographical nexus. The Dominicans were introduced into Coblenz in 1233, providing a bulwark against heretical activities that had been noticed at Coblenz, Mainz, and Cologne during the latter part of the previous century.

Archbishop Arnold of Trier secured the rights of advocacy over Coblenz in 1253 from the counts of Nassau. In the previous year, he had begun to build a wall around that portion of the residential area that had outgrown the old Frankish town. Additional portions of the new town wall were built by the burghers, who complained to Archbishop Henry of Vinstingen about the lack of protection on the land side. Fearing a diminution of his authority in the town, Henry in 1280 erected an archiepiscopal fortress nearby.

Coblenz was the favorite residence of Baldwin of Luxemburg, Archbishop of Trier in the fourteenth century, who was the most powerful and influential of the medieval metropolitans. In 1343 he began constructing a fourteen-arch bridge across the Rhine, something that had not existed at Coblenz for more than 800 years. Named for him, the structure still stands today. At nearby Rens, Baldwin helped secure the election of his brother Henry as German emperor in 1308. During his regime, the German princes, under the presidency of Louis the Bavarian, came to Coblenz in 1338 for a dazzling assembly. King Edward III of England appeared as well, seeking help against France from the Germans.

BIBLIOGRAPHY

Bellinghausen, Hans. *2000 Jahre Koblenz: Geschichte der Stadt an Rhein und Mosel.* Boppard (am Rhein): Boldt, 1973.

Diederich, Anton. *Das Stift St. Florin zu Koblenz.* Göttingen: Vandenhoeck & Ruprecht, 1967.

Geschichte der Stadt Koblenz: Von den Anfängen bis zum Ende der kurfürstlichen Zeit, ed. Ingrid Bátori, Dieter Kerber, and Hans Josef Schmidt. Stuttgart: Theiss, 1992.

Paul B. Pixton

SEE ALSO

Charlemagne; Charles III, the Fat; Lothar; Moselle River

Coburg

Very little information about Coburg's early history has survived. The name is first mentioned in 1056 when Queen Richeza of Poland transferred her holdings in Coburg to the archbishop of Cologne. Other documents from the late eleventh century attest to the presence of a church that was surrounded by a walled settlement strategically located on a hill overlooking the Itz valley. The fortified castle, *Veste Coburg,* was probably begun by the dukes of Andechs-Meran. By the thirteenth century, a town existed in the valley below the earlier settlement. Before 1217, construction of a parish church and priory began. The church was named after the town patron, Saint Mauritius, a Moor whose head is represented in the city seal. The present church of St. Moritz is a late Gothic, fourteenth century, three-aisle *Hallenkirche* (hall church), the interior of which was later ornamented in Baroque style.

The establishment of a mint in 1268 presupposes the presence of thriving trade and commerce in Coburg. Louis of Bavaria granted the rights of self-government to the city in 1331. The dukes of Wettin (Saxony) made Coburg their center of government in 1353, and in establishing residence there during the sixteenth century, increased the political and cultural importance of the city. The painter Lucas Cranach the Elder visited Coburg several times between 1500 and 1506 while working on commissions for the dukes. Cranach is responsible for the oldest extant representations of the fortress, one of which is found on the left wing of the altarpiece in Dresden known as the *Katarinenaltar* (Catherine Altar, 1506).

BIBLIOGRAPHY

Schneier, Walter. *Coburg im Spiegel der Geschichte.* Coburg: Neue Presse, 1985, pp. 25–86.

Ruth M. W. Moskop

SEE ALSO

Cologne, History; Gothic Art and Architecture; Gothic Art and Architecture, Late; Louis of Bavaria

Coinage and Mints

The first German coins created in the time of the great migrations by the Franks and Merovingians (fifth century) were modeled on Roman-Byzantine coinage. The gold coin *solidus* was the main unit, but its third, the *triens* was the more common (ca. 1.4 grams). The fines of the Salian Law (508–511) mention a silver coinage in which 40 *denarii* equalled one *solidus.*

With the reforms of Pepin III (751–768), the silver *denarius* replaced the gold coin, and minting became solely a royal perogative. The name of the king began to appear on the coins, and private coins disappeared. The number of mints was reduced.

In the 790s, Charlemagne (768–814) reformed the coinage by increasing the weight of the minting pound to 408.24 gr., which equalled 240 *denar/pfennig* coins (1.7 gr.). This system became almost universal in Europe in the eighth to twelfth centuries. The accounting system defined twelve *pfennig* as a *solidus/schilling,* and twenty *schilling* as a *libra/pfund,* but only the penny, halfpenny, and farthing (a quarter of a penny) were minted. Most mints were located in the Rhineland towns of Aachen, Bonn, Cologne, Mainz, and Trier.

The Ottonian and Salian period (ca. 950–1125) was the age of the *Fernhandelsdenar* (foreign trade denar), when coins were used in foreign trade. Most coins left Germany and later appeared in Scandinavian, Polish, Baltic, and Russian hoards, apparently as a result of a well established Baltic trade. One hundred thousand *pfennig* have been found in Scandinavia, and 94,000, in Poland

and Pomerania; the fact that only 30,000 have been found in Germany may indicate a weak internal economy. The coins continued to be of almost the same weight, even though several ecclesiastical institutions obtained minting privileges in the tenth century. The great variety of types was a threat to the unity of the German coinage.

Another base, the *mark,* was first mentioned in 1015. It was of Scandinavian origin and weighed eight Roman ounces (*øre,* 218.3 gr.). Around 1100 the *mark* began to supplant the *pfund.* Most prominent was the *mark* of Cologne, which had various values: The currency *mark* (210.24 gr.) consisted of 12 *schilling,* or 144 *pfennig;* the *mark* of weight (215.5 gr.) equalled 16 *Lot* (of 4 *Kvintin* of 16 *ort* each). The commercial *mark* weight was 200 g. The *mark* of Cologne (233.85 gr.) became the basis of currency in Germany 1559–1857.

During the Hohenstaufen period (1138–1254), the national minting system disintegrated. Only the coinage of Cologne and Westphalia kept their value, while the weight of the *pfennig* declined by half. When ecclesiastical and feudal lords obtained the privilege of minting, the coinage became regional and valid only in the area where it was produced. The individual areas were clearly distinguished by different weight standards. In the east, the coins were repeatedly called in and renewed *(abjectio et renovatio).* Typical coinage of the period 1150–1350 was the artistic *hohlpfennig* or *bracteates,* which had a relief on one side only.

With the explosive growth in the number of towns, trade also expanded, resulting in the need for rationalization of money circulation in the thirteenth and fourteenth centuries. Since the Emperor *(Kaiser)* no longer controlled coinage, minting had become strictly local.

To overcome the confusing variety of local coinage, districts allied with one another to mint coins of similar value and type. These alliances, called *Münzverein* (also *Münzbund,* minting alliances), blossomed in the fourteenth century; they appear in Lübeck-Hamburg from 1255 onward and in the Wendische *Münzbund* 1373/1379 to 1570. The Upper Rhenian *Münzbund* consisted of 74 mints (*Rappenmünzbund*) and lasted from 1386 to 1537.

In the late Middle Ages, the *Groschen* and the *Gulden* became the standard coinage in Europe. The *Groschen* was modeled on the silver coin, *Gros tournois* (4.22 gr.), introduced by Louis IX of France in 1266. The *Groschen* was especially popular in northern and western Germany between Oldenburg and the Rhineland, in Saxony,

Thuringia, Hesse, and in the Netherlands. The coin flourished in the period 1360–1380 but became obsolete in 1400, except in Frankfurt, where it lasted to the sixteenth century. The *Gulden* (3.54 gr., 1252), a Florentine gold coin, was widely imitated and became standard coinage in the Rhenish *Münzbund*.

BIBLIOGRAPHY

Dannenberg, Hermann. *Die deutschen Münzen der sächischen und fränkischen Kaiserzeit.* 11 vols. Berlin: Weidmann, 1876–1894.

Grierson, Philip, and Mark Blackburn. *Medieval European Coinage, Vol. 1: The Early Middle Ages (5th–10th Centuries).* Cambridge: Cambridge University Press, 1986 [bibliography, illustrations: 65 plates].

Kluge, Bernd. *Deutsche Münzgeschichte von der späten Karolingerzeit bis zum Ende der Salier (Ca. 900 bis 1125).* Sigmaringen: Thorbecke, 1991.

Morrison, Karl F., and Henry Grunthal. *Carolingian Coinage.* New York: The American Numismatic Society, 1967.

North, Michael. *Das Geld und seine Geschichte vom Mittelalter bis zur Gegenwart.* Munich: Beck, 1994.

———, *Von Aktie bis Zoll: Ein historisches Lexikon des Geldes.* Munich: Beck, 1995.

Jens Ulff-Møller

SEE ALSO
Charlemagne; Laws and Lawbooks; Numbers and Calculation; Pippin; Salians

Cologne, Archdiocese

Bishop Irenaeus of Lyons records the existence of a Christian community in Cologne *(Köln)* by the late second century. Maternus, later bishop of Trier and the first documented bishop of Cologne, was present at the synod of Rome (313) and Arles (314). The troubles attending the arrival of the Franks in Cologne produced a gap in the list of bishops from the death of Bishop Severin (397) to ca. 565–567, but, through the patronage of the bishops of Trier and of the Frankish ruling house, the Cologne church was revived by the time of Bishop Kunibert's pontificate (ca. 626–648).

The late sixth century began a long period of close relations between the Cologne bishopric and the German monarchy that would last until the thirteenth century. The bishops served Merovingian kings as royal councilors, as ambassadors, and as regents for the Austrasian court in Cologne. The Carolingians established a special *amicitia* (friendly relationship) with the Cologne bishops, which found its fullest expression when Charlemagne raised Bishop Hildebald to metropolitan status over a vast province in 794/795. The archbishopric of Cologne would eventually encompass most of northwest Germany from Friesland and Saxony to lower Lotharingia, and include the bishoprics of Utrecht, Osnabrück, Minden, Münster, and Liège. The Norman destruction of the city interrupted Cologne's rise to predominance in the lower Rhineland and western Saxony, but the see was quickly revived under the Saxon monarchy. Emperor Otto I (936–973) appointed his youngest brother, Bruno, as both archbishop of Cologne and *archidux* of Lotharingia. Bruno I (r. 953–965) also served as imperial regent from 961–965 and laid the foundations for archiepiscopal lordship over the city of Cologne and its environs which would last until 1288. During this period, archbishops of Cologne exercised royal rights of high justice, tolls, weights and measures, mints, markets, and defense.

By the mid-eleventh century the archbishops of Cologne had emerged as the preeminent ecclesiastics of the German episcopate. Since the pontificate of Archbishop Heribert (999–1021) they had enjoyed the right to crown and anoint the king-elect at Aachen, thereby playing a central role in all royal elections. As imperial princes, the archbishops became deeply involved in the emperors' Italian affairs; to expand their authority in this realm, they were given the office of chancellor of Italy from 1031 onward. Anno II (1256–1275) and Engelbert I (1215–1225) would also periodically continue to fulfill the role of imperial regent. Pope Leo IX confirmed these prerogatives in 1052, and added to them the authority to preside over the provincial synod.

Of course, this mixture of secular and spiritual lordship drew the archbishops of Cologne directly into the Investiture Controversy. In general the archbishops stood on the side of the Salian monarchs; yet, after the Concordat of Worms (1122), imperial influence over episcopal elections dwindled. Rainald of Dassel (1159–1167) and Philip of Heinsberg (1167–1191) were the last two archbishops who were raised to the see by imperial command without allowing for canonical elections. Thereafter, the local noble houses of Berg and Hochstaden competed within the cathedral chapter for the archiepiscopal honor, placing a combined eleven of the seventeen archbishops during the years 1132–1297.

In 1180 the archbishops added the duchy of Westphalia to their ducal domains in lower Lotharingia. Philip of Heinsberg received the newly created duchy by virtue of Emperor Frederick Barbarossa's dismantling of Welf ducal lands in Saxony. This period marks the high point of archiepiscopal involvement in imperial politics, a role requiring the archbishops to be away from Cologne for extended periods for embassies throughout Europe and for military campaigns in Italy during the papal schism.

By the early thirteenth century, however, the archbishops of Cologne moved away from a pro-Staufen policy and began to establish their own independent territorial principality. Archbishop Adolf I of Altena (1193–1203; 1212–16), during the Welf-Staufen struggle for the throne *(Thronstreit),* alternately supported Welf or Staufen candidates depending on the advantage that might pertain to his territorial independence. His coronation prerogative ensured that the Cologne archbishop would be at the center of political intrigue surrounding royal elections, but in Adolf I's case, this proved a mixed blessing. Although he was able, with English financial support, to obtain the election of Otto IV, his subsequent abandonment of the Welf for Philip of Swabia led to excommunication and deposition by Pope Innocent III as well as to deep discord with the burghers of Cologne.

Although Archbishop Engelbert I of Berg returned to the Staufen camp as regent of the young Henry (VII) and imperial regent for Emperor Frederick II, by the 1240s, Archbishop Conrad of Hochstaden (1238–1261) had joined the pope and archbishop of Mainz in an effective anti-Staufen policy that curtailed imperial power in Germany. The result was the establishment of the archbishop's territorial principality based on two duchies and provincial ecclesiastical authority.

Thereafter, the archbishops of Cologne were the real holders of royal authority in northwest Germany. In 1258 the archbishop Conrad of Hochstaden confirmed this status by obtaining from his personal candidate for royal election, Richard of Cornwall, not only confirmation of full imperial authority throughout the territorial principality, but, also, the right to install new bishops in the name of the king. By this time many nobles held fiefs of the archbishop of Cologne: the duke of Limburg, the counts of Saffenberg, Jülich, Berg, Are, Geldern, Kleve, Kessel, Zutphen, Armsberg, Altena, Mark, and Tecklenburg, and the lords of Hochstaden, Isenburg, Tomburg, Heinsberg, and Lippe.

At the peak of princely power in the mid-thirteenth century, the archbishops sought to tighten control over the autonomous burghers of Cologne and the local nobility of lower Lotharingia and Westphalia. This led to a half-century of civil wars, which culminated in the collapse of the archbishop's ducal power when Archbishop Siegfried of Westerburg was defeated at the Battle of Worringen (1288) at the hands of a coalition of Cologners and nobles from Brabant, Jülich, Berg, and Kleve. From this time on, the archbishops no longer resided in Cologne, but rather at their palaces in Bonn and Brühl.

By the late thirteenth century, the papacy had secured the right to appoint the archbishops of Cologne, and subsequent archbishops maintained good relations with Rome throughout the fourteenth and fifteenth centuries. As loyalists to the Avignon papacy, Archbishops Henry II of Virneburg (1304–1332) and Walram of Jülich (1332–1349) refused to recognize Ludwig of Bavaria's kingship. Archbishop William von Gennep (1349–1362) was influential in the kingship of Charles IV (1346–1378) and in the editing of the Golden Bull (1356). But, by the mid-fifteenth century, the archbishopric had declined to a second-class power and no longer played a leading role in imperial politics.

Evidence for the beginning of a parish system on the left bank of the Rhine can be found in the sixth century, and for Westphalia by the end of the eighth century. Many of these episcopal parishes and tithes were eventually given to religious foundations and cloisters during the ninth and tenth centuries. By the eleventh century, the archdiaconate and the college of priors were fully functioning in the archdiocese. The cathedral chapter of canons is first documented in 866, but evidence suggests its origin in the seventh century. By the end of the twelfth century, there were thirty-six benefices for canons, sixteen supplementary benefices, and twenty benefices for cathedral scholars *(magistri).* Since around 1216, eight of the benefices had been reserved for canon priests.

As a sign of its importance in the archdiocese, the cathedral chapter had its own seal by 1106/1109. It often struggled with the college of priors in episcopal elections however, and by the mid-thirteenth century, had successfully asserted its independence and power. The chapter separated from the archbishopric *(Erzstift)* through the establishment of its own assembly and independent benefices, and by removing itself from liability for the archbishop's debts. Final success was achieved in 1250, when the college of priors was removed from episcopal elections and sons of ministerials and burghers were no longer accepted as candidates for the cathedral chapter. Thereafter, the canons lived the life of independent, powerful, and princely churchmen, certain to become archbishops.

BIBLIOGRAPHY

Droege, G. "Das kölnische Herzogtum Westfalen." In *Heinrich der Löwe,* ed. Wolf-Dieter Mohrmann. Göttingen: Vandenhoeck & Ruprecht, 1980, pp. 275–304.

Ennen, Edith. "Erzbishof und Stadtgemeinde in Köln bis zur Schlacht von Worringen (1288)." In *Gesammelte Abhandlungen.* Bonn: Rohrscheid, 1977, vol. 1, pp. 388–404.

Erkens, Franz-Reiner. *Der Erzbischof von Köln un die deutsche Königswahl.* Siegburg: F. Schmitt, 1987.

Janssen, Wilhelm. "Die Erzbischöfe von Köln un ihr "Land" Westfalen im Spätmittelalter." *Westfalen* 58 (1980): 82–95.

———. "Die Kanzlei der Erzbischöfe von Köln im Spätmittelalter." *Münchener Beiträge zur Mediävistik und Renaissane-Forschung* 35 (1984): 147–169.

Kallen, Gerhard. "Das Kölner Erzstift und der *'ducatus Westfalie et Angarie'* (1180)." *Jahrbuch des Kölnischen Geschichtsveriens* 31/32 (1956–57): 78–107.

Knipping, Richard, et al., ed. *Die Regensten der Erzbischöfe von Köln im Mittelalter,* 4 vols. Bonn: P. Hanstein, 1901–61.

Oediger, Frederick Wilhelm. *Das Bistum Köln von den Anfängen bis zum Ende des 12. Jahrhunderts,* 2nd ed. Cologne: J. P. Bachem, 1972.

Pötter, Wilhelm. *Die Ministerialität der Erzbischöfe von Köln vom Ende des 11. bis zum Ausgang des 13. Jahrhunderts.* Düsseldorf: Schwann, 1967.

Vollrath, Hanna and Stefan Weinfurter, ed. *Köln: Stadt und Bistum in Kirche und Reich des Mittelalters: Festschrift fur Odilo Engels zum 65. Geburtstag.* Cologne: Böhlau, 1993.

Joseph P. Huffman

SEE ALSO

Anno; Charlemagne; Cologne, Art; Cologne, History; Concordat of Worms; Frederick Barbarossa; Golden Bull; Investiture Controversy; Leo IX; Otto I; Otto IV; Rainald of Dassel; Welfs; Westphalia; Worringen, Battle of

Cologne, Art

Medieval Cologne grew up over a Roman settlement founded in 38 B.C.E. and elevated to the status of colony in 50 C.E. Christians were present in the city from the second century; bishops were named from the fourth. In the fourth century Saint Ursula and her 11,000 virgin

Cologne, cathedral, west façade, Peter's Portal. *Photograph: Joan A. Holladay*

companions and Saint Gereon and soldiers from the Theban legion are supposed to have been martyred here and buried in the Roman cemeteries outside the city walls. At the beginning of the fifth century, a Frankish king replaced the Roman governor. The Franks occupied the Roman buildings, in many cases using them for their intended functions. Thus, both the street plan and the location of major public buildings in modern Cologne date back 2000 years to Roman times.

Cologne's important role in Charlemagne's campaign to Christianize Eastern Europe was acknowledged with its elevation to an archbishopric at the end of the eighth century. The archbishop was simultaneously the city's political and ecclesiastical overlord until Archbishop Siegfried's expulsion after his defeat at the Battle of Worringen in 1288. Thereafter, the city was ruled by a council comprised of patricians, tradesmen and representatives of the guilds. At this time the city, with a population of about 40,000, was the largest in Germany, and, with Paris and London, one of the largest in Europe. Its strategic position on the Rhine and its alliance with the Hansa made it an important trading center. It was also an important center of learning. From the mid-thirteenth century, the Franciscans, Dominicans, and Augustinians each established a *studium generale* or "college" here, and Albertus Magnus, Master Eckhart, and Duns Scotus were among those called to teach. The university was founded in 1389.

The late antique bishops of Cologne had their cathedral on the same site as the present church. Two richly endowed graves from the mid-sixth century attest to continued use of the site for religious purposes under the Franks. As early as the end of the sixth century, a new cathedral was erected on the easternmost part of the present site. It was replaced in the ninth century by a stately double-choir basilica, whose large scale corresponded to the political importance of the new archbishopric. This political claim was made more visible in renovations carried out in the middle of the tenth century under Archbishop Bruno, brother of the Holy Roman Emperor Otto I. Two additional aisles added along the sides of the nave heightened the resemblance to Old St. Peter's in Rome. This likeness, already established by the western choir dedicated to Saint Peter, reflected Cologne's reputation among German churches as *quasi mater et matrona* ("like a mother and a matron").

The acquisition of the relics of the Three Magi for the cathedral in 1164 and the resulting increase in pilgrim traffic, as well as the introduction of the new Gothic style in France, made the Carolingian cathedral appear small and out of date. Archbishop Konrad von Hochstaden laid the cornerstone of the present building in 1248. The choir, closely related to that of the cathedral at Amiens, was consecrated in 1322. After completion of the south portal of the west façade by sculptors of the Parler school about 1380, work slowed and finally came to a complete halt in 1560. The building was finished, largely according to medieval plan, between 1842 and 1880 as a symbol of the newly united Germany.

The decoration of the church interior centers on two main themes: the role of the Virgin, with Saint Peter, the cathedral's patron, in the history of salvation; and the place of the cathedral in the political life of the German realm. The Virgin stands with Christ at the head of the apostles on the piers of the choir (1280s), and the relief scenes at the center of each side of the high altar (1310s) describe episodes from her life. Paintings of scenes from her life also decorate the south choir screen (1330s).

The shrine of the Three Kings (ca. 1181–1230), attributed to Nicholas of Verdun, serves as the nexus for a program of overtly political content. As the first kings recognized by Christ, the Magi were seen as worthy forebears of the German kings who claimed divine sanction for their rule. This idea is expressed concretely on the front of the shrine where Otto IV, who donated the gold for this panel, is represented as the fourth magus. The status of the Archbishop of Cologne, who traditionally crowned newly elected kings at Aachen, was also enhanced by association with the magi.

The interdependence of the cathedral and the German kings is further highlighted in the program of the clerestory windows (1311), where forty-eight kings attend the Adoration of the Magi in the axis window; in the choir stalls (1308–1311), whose easternmost seats were reserved for the emperor and the pope; and on the choir screen (1330s), where painted sequences oppose images of the archbishops of Cologne with representations of the Roman and Holy Roman emperors.

The great churches of the tenth and eleventh centuries owe their origins to three of the city's archbishops: Bruno (953–965), Heribert (999–1021), and Anno (1056–1075). Simultaneously with his renovations to the cathedral, Archbishop Bruno founded the Benedictine abbey of St. Pantaleon on the site of a Carolingian oratory just outside the city wall to the west. Bruno's patronage was continued by the Empress Theophanu, wife of Otto II; his successor, Warin, dedicated the building in 980. The powerful entry tract, known as a *Westwerk,* refers to the building's imperial connections.

Across the river at Deutz, Archbishop Heribert founded a Benedictine abbey in 1002 over the ruins of a Roman fort. Dedicated in 1020, the church made deliberate reference to the palace chapel at Aachen, not only in the centralized ground plan, but in the double dedication to the Virgin and the Savior. The church was completely rebuilt in the seventeenth century.

Of the two churches founded by Archbishop Anno, only the church of St. George, founded in 1059 and dedicated in 1067, still stands. The patrocinium of the church of Sta. Maria ad gradus, dedicated in 1057, and its location at the east end of the cathedral were intended to further heighten Cologne's resemblance to Rome.

As the result of a dream, Anno added the long choir to the fourth-century church of St. Gereon, whose original structure is associated with Saint Helena, the mother of the Emperor Constantine. The centralized plan of the earlier structure marks its function as a martyrium, commemorating the saint and his martyred companions of the Theban legion.

Anno also dedicated the church of Sta. Maria im Kapitol, built over the site of the city's major Roman temple by the Abbess Ida, granddaughter of Emperor Otto II and Theophanu. Here, too, the choice of models was intended to heighten the importance of the foundation: as at the Early Christian Church of the Nativity in Bethlehem, the transept ends and choir are given almost identical rounded forms, resulting in a triconch. Of the well-preserved furnishings from the Middle Ages, only the wood doors date from the period before the church's dedication in 1065. The left door describes the Infancy of Christ in eleven relief scenes, while the right door depicts episodes from the Entry into Jerusalem to Pentecost.

A second period of intense building activity occurred from the early twelfth to the early thirteenth century. Many of the churches built in previous centuries were enlarged or remodeled, and a number of buildings preserved from still earlier periods were replaced. Aisles were added along the nave of St. Pantaleon. In the middle of the twelfth century, the nave and choir of St. George were given stone vaults, and, a few years later, the west choir was completely rebuilt on an extended plan. The enlarged choir at St. Gereon, now flanked by square towers, was dedicated in 1156. The membering of the exterior of the east end took up the arcaded pattern articulated at the church of St. Cassius and Florentius at Bonn three years earlier and became a standard for the Cologne churches of this period. It can be seen at both Great St. Martin (1150–1240) and the Church of the Apostles (1192–ca. 1220), which also reuse the triconch form first articulated in Cologne at Sta. Maria im Kapitol.

The Carolingian church at the burial site of the Holy Virgins, now St. Ursula, was replaced soon after excavators working on the city wall in 1106 discovered a Roman cemetery, which was presumed to contain the relics of the entire virgin band. The church of St. Severin, also built over a fourth-century cult site in a Roman cemetery, was finished with the consecration of the choir in 1237. St. Kunibert, the last of Cologne's corona of Romanesque churches, was dedicated in 1247, the year before work began on the new Gothic cathedral. The stylistic similarity of these numerous Romanesque churches gives Cologne's religious architecture a unified look even today.

In this period, too, should be placed the great golden shrines that once marked the treasuries of nearly all Cologne's churches. These copper- and silver-gilt shrines typically take a simplified church-form and measure over one and a half meters long. Seated apostles or other saints in *repoussé* (repose) fill the arcades along the long sides, and relief or enamel scenes of the saint's life and martyrdom decorate the sloped roof. The shrine of Saint Heribert, ca. 1160–1170, is among the best preserved of these works, but the contemporary shrine for Saint Ursula, now heavily restored, and that of her fiancé Aetherius (ca. 1170) are still housed at the church of St. Ursula. Those for Saint Maurinus (ca. 1170) and Saint Albinus (1186) are at St. Pantaleon. The Three Kings' shrine in the cathedral (ca. 1181–1230) is the latest and grandest of the series.

Even before the decision to build a new cathedral, the Franciscans had begun construction of a church in the Gothic style near the city center in 1246. The churches of the Dominicans and the Poor Clares, erected in the next decades, are no longer preserved. The new Gothic choir erected at St. Ursula's echoes the forms of the Sainte-Chapelle, the royal chapel built in the palace at Paris between 1241 and 1248. The choir of St. Ursula's, together with that added to the palace chapel at Aachen in the middle of the fourteenth century, another follower of the Sainte-Chapelle, in turn influenced the new choir added to the church of St. Andreas between 1414 and 1420. In 1466 and 1493, two of Cologne's leading patrician families constructed small chapels in Late Gothic style in the corners between the lobes of the triconch at Sta. Maria im Kapitol.

Until 1106, when areas to the north, west, and south were incorporated into the city, Cologne was contained within the Roman wall. A new wall, erected between about 1180 and the middle of the thirteenth century, was razed in the nineteenth century to provide space for the ring road surrounding the inner city. A number of the gates that gave access through the wall are preserved: the *Ulrepforte* and *Severinstor* at the south and the *Eigelsteintor* at the north.

Of the stately houses built by the local patricians, only the house of the Overstolz family still stands. Its arcaded front and fragments of interior painting attest to its decoratively representative intentions.

The *Rathaus* (city hall), erected over the site of the Roman *praetorium*, was also intended to proclaim the city's status. The oldest preserved part, the Hansa Hall, dates to the 1330s. Here, larger than life-sized sculptured figures of the Nine Heroes present Old Testament, Early Christian, and medieval role models for the decision makers in the room below. Prophet figures on the opposite wall and the building's tower, one of the defining monuments of the cityscape, date to the beginning of the fifteenth century.

As early as the Ottonian period, Cologne was a center for both sculpture and painting. In addition to the doors at Sta. Maria im Kapitol, the Gero cross (969–976) and some twenty illuminated manuscripts provide evidence of the high quality of artistic production in the city around the time of the millennium.

The paintings in the vaults of the parish church of St. Maria Lyskirchen (1220/30–1270) precede the numerous works created in a fully developed Gothic style in the years around 1300. In addition to the painted and sculpted decoration created for the cathedral choir in the years of its construction, polychromed (multi-colored) wood sculptures were produced in the city in great numbers, especially figures of the Virgin and wooden busts for the relics of Saint Ursula and her companions. Illuminators were also active, producing manuscripts for religious foundations and private patrons both inside and outside the city.

The International Style is represented in Cologne by the paintings of the so-called Master of Saint Veronica and a number of so-called Soft Style Madonnas, including figures at the cathedral, Sta. Maria Lyskirhen, and St. Gereon. The work of Stefan Lochner (d. 1451) exemplifies the increasing realism of the succeeding period. The city's two best known sculptors in the fifteenth century were Konrad Kuyn, who also served as master of the works at the cathedral, and Tilman van der Burch.

BIBLIOGRAPHY

Binding, Gunther. *Städtebau und Heilsordnung: Künstlerische Gestaltung der Stadt Köln in ottonischer Zeit.* Düsseldorf: Droste, 1986.

Bloch, Peter and Hermann Schnitzler. *Die ottonische Kölner Malerschule.* 2 vols. Düsseldorf: Schwann, 1967–1970.

Die Kunstdenkmäler der Stadt Köln. 8 vols. Düsseldorf: Schwann, 1906–1938.

Die Parler und der Schöne Stil 1350–1400: Kunst unter den Luxemburgern. Cologne: Museen der Stadt Köln, 1978.

Holladay, Joan A. "Relics, Reliquaries, and Religious Women: Visualizing the Holy Virgins of Cologne." *Studies in Iconography* 18 (1997): 67–118.

———. "Some Arguments for a Wider View of Cologne Painting in the Early Fourteenth Century." *Georges-Bloch-Jahrbuch des Kunstgeschichtlichen Seminars der Universität Zürich* 4 (1997): 1–16.

Monumenta Annonis: Köln und Siegburg. Weltbild und Kunst im hohen Mittelalter. Cologne: Schnütgen Museum, 1975.

Ornamenta ecclesiae: Kunst und Künstler der Romanik. Cologne: Stadt Köln, 1985.

Rode, Herbert. *Die mittelalterlichen Glasmalereien des Kölner Doms.* Berlin: Deutscher Verlag für Kunstwissenschaft, 1974.

Schnütgen Museum: Die Holzbildwerke des Mittelalters 1000–1400. Cologne: Schnütgen Museum, 1989.

Stefan Lochner, Meister zu Köln: Herkunft, Werke, Wirkung. Cologne: Wallraf-Richartz Museum, 1994.

Vor Stefan Lochner: Die Kölner Maler von 1300 bis 1430. Cologne: Wallraf-Richartz Museum, 1974.

Zehnder, Frank Gunter. *Katalog der Altkölner Malerei.* Cologne: Stadt Köln, 1990.

Joan A. Holladay

SEE ALSO

Bonn; Cologne, Archdiocese; Cologne, History; International Style; Lochner, Stefan; Metalworking; Nicolaus of Verdun; Parler Family; Relics and Reliquaries; Sankt Veronika, Master of; Theophanu

Cologne, History

Cologne (German *Köln,* from Latin *colonia* "colony") was the largest medieval German city, with a population of ca. 40,000 by the early fourteenth century. Geographically favored as a commercial and administrative center, the city was located at the southern end of the lower Rhineland where its natural harbor converged with the east-west land routes. Cologne was famous throughout Europe for its exports of wine (especially to England), metals, and manufactured goods such as textiles, armor and weapons, dressed furs, leather and felt goods, glass ceramics, and goldwork. It was also a major trade emporium, hosting three yearly fairs from the eleventh century onward and enjoying the right of staple (commercial supplier) from 1259.

The Romans initially resettled a Germanic tribe known as the Ubii on this site in 38 B.C.E. This *oppidium Ubiorum* was then superseded in 50 C.E. by a Roman colony named after the empress Agrippina (who had been born there), complete with a stone wall and nine gates. Hence, the modern name Cologne is derived from the Latin appellation: *Colonia Claudia Ara Agrippinensium.* The emperor Constantine further fortified this city of 98.6 hectares with a fort *(Kastell Divitia)* on the right bank of the Rhine (Deutz) and joined the two with a bridge across the river during the years 310–315 C.E. By 90 C.E, Cologne had become the Roman capital of Lower Germany. Upon the arrival of the Franks in the mid-fourth century the colony declined rapidly, although it became a residence for the Ripuarian Frankish kings and retained a bishop's see and three churches of martyrs (St. Severin, St. Gereon, St. Ursula). Charlemagne eventually raised the bishopric to metropolitan status, thus assuring the archbishops of Cologne a vast archdiocese in northern Germany.

After Cologne's destruction by the Vikings in 881–882, a distinctly medieval city began to emerge. The Saxon emperor Otto I appointed his youngest brother, Bruno, archbishop of Cologne, and under Bruno I (ca. 925–985), the *portus* was once again a fortified wall and mercantile activity quickly expanded. The emperor also gave Bruno the duchy of Lotharingia (Lorraine) with all its attendant rights of jurisdiction (high justice, tolls, weights and measures, mints, markets, defense). The archbishops of Cologne became imperial princes, with Cologne as the capital of their domains. This meant that their ducal authority also extended to the city itself, although the archbishops' jurisdiction directly affected most of the population only in the areas of the courts and economic policy. An independent-minded citizenry proceeded to settle Cologne, and friction soon developed. In 1074 the burghers rebelled against the heavy hand of Archbishop Anno II's rule. In subsequent years, municipal leaders often turned to the monarch for relief against their *Stadtherr;* they even defended the Salian Henry IV against his rebellious son Henry V in 1106 and were rewarded with imperial authorization to extend and maintain the city's fortifications—until then the prerogative of the archbishops.

Few conflicts developed during the twelfth century because the archbishops were most often away from the city on imperial business. As archchancellors of Italy, they were deeply involved in the emperor's Italian campaigns during the Staufen era. Their absence allowed the burghers to further increase their autonomy and experience in self-governance. The positions of *Burggraf* (nobleman) and *Stadtvogt* (ministerial, or court administrator)

were increasingly replaced by the burghers (called *scabini* or *Schöffen*) in the administration of archiepiscopal and parish courts. A council of wealthy burgher families called the *Richerzeche* (or *Meliorat*) was formed, which elected two mayors and assumed increasing control over craft regulations and municipal economic policy (mint, tolls, taxes).

In 1180 the city's leaders obtained imperial authority to extend the city walls yet again; this initiative went against the express wishes of the archbishop and gave Cologne the highest and strongest walls in Germany. At this time the city had reached the size of just over 400 hectares.

By the early thirteenth century, effective control of the city had passed from the archbishop to some fifteen powerful patrician families *(Geschlechter),* who administered local government through twelve districts *(Sondergemeinden),* based mostly on parish boundaries. At these parish courts the *scabini* and *Amtsleute* (officials) administered low justice and managed the affairs of the districts. From 1130 onward, municipal records *(Schreinsurkunden)* were kept. Inheritances, purchases, mortgages, and bequests of houses and property were recorded and citizens were enrolled for taxation purposes. In 1216 a City Council *(Rat)* was formed in order to widen political participation beyond the patrician *Geschlechter* in the *Richerzeche (Meliorat)* and college of *scabini.* At first the *Rat* was suppressed by both the archbishop and the *Geschlechter,* but it had replaced the *Richerzeche (Meliorat)* as the leading municipal institution by the mid-thirteenth century. The *Geschlechter* were able to maintain control of the *Rat,* however, throughout the remainder of the century.

During the thirteenth century, latent tensions between the archbishops and the autonomous patrician families reemerged. The *Thronstreit* between the Staufen and Welf dynasties during the first two decades of the century produced an open split between the two parties. The Cologners supported Otto IV out of economic motives while the archbishops and their ministerials, out of territorial motives, wavered between Staufen and the alternate anti-Welf candidates. In reaction to this hostile situation, the archbishops sought creative ways to regain authority over the city.

By 1258 hostilities had reached such a level that Albertus Magnus was invited to head the Great Arbitration commission, which was to settle disputed claims of jurisdiction once and for all. The commission's settlement proved unhelpful in resolving tensions, however, since it determined that ultimate jurisdictional authority derived from the archbishop's lordship but had traditionally been delegated to and exercised by the burghers. The archbishops, thereafter, sought to use longstanding disputes among the patrician families to dismantle the settlement.

In 1259 Archbishop Conrad Hochstaden failed in his effort to pit the craftsmen against the *Geschlechter*. His successor, Engelbert II of Falkenburg, was imprisoned after breaching the terms of the Great Arbitration by attempting to fortify the municipal tower with his soldiers. Engelbert was held in the count of Jülich's castle for over a year while bloody battles raged between the patrician factions of the city of Cologne. The archbishop supported the losing faction in this conflict, and after release from prison, he abandoned Cologne for palaces in Bonn and Brühl.

Archbishop Siegfried of Westerburg was the last to make a concerted effort at recovering power. In 1279 he purchased the favor of the high court of the *Burggraf* in order to retain legal jurisdiction in the city and surrounding countryside, and then struck directly by leading an army against the city in 1288. When a coalition of Cologne citizens and local nobles defeated the archbishop's army at the Battle of Worringen, they secured permanent municipal autonomy.

Cooperation among the patrician *Geschlechter* would last until the fourteenth century, when growing factional discord provided the craftsmen and lesser merchants the chance to overthrow them. The weavers led a revolt in 1370–1371 that resulted in a mixed government of patricians and craft guilds. This experiment failed, but, in 1396, a substantial alliance of merchant corporations (*Gaffeln*) and craft guilds finally overthrew the patrician *Geschlechter* regime and produced a *Verbundbrief* that would serve as the municipal constitution of Cologne until the end of the eighteenth century. The *Richerzeche (Meliorat)* was abolished in favor of a reconstituted City Council (*Rat)*, thus assuring broader representation. By the mid-fifteenth century the last vestige of patrician privilege, the office of *scabini (Schöffen)*, was open to anyone with proper professional qualifications. Cologne was granted the status of a free imperial city in 1475 by Emperor Frederick III.

Medieval Cologne was famous for its abundance and variety of religious institutions. The cathedral was dedicated to St. Peter and the Virgin Mary in 870, and an ambitious rebuilding project in the Gothic style was initiated in 1248 after the original edifice had burned down. The massive cathedral was not completed, however, until 1880. After Archbishop Rainald of Dassel translated the relics of the Three Kings (Magi) from Milan to the cathedral's high altar in 1164, these patron saints joined Saint Ursula and her minions to make Cologne a Europe-wide pilgrimage site. *Sancta Colonia*, as the city was called, possessed dozens of religious foundations from every order, from Benedictines to the Brethren of the Common Life, and over 150 Beguine houses in addition to its eighteen parish churches and numerous chapels. Great intellectuals like Duns Scotus, Albertus Magnus, Gerard Pucelle, and Meister Eckhart lived in Cologne, and the city joined with Dominicans to found a university in 1388.

Cologne's Jewish community can be traced back to late antiquity and, though restricted to a ghetto in St. Laurence parish and viciously persecuted during the Crusades and the Black Death, it maintained a synagogue and vital socio-economic ties to other Jewish communities from Basle to York. The community was driven out of Cologne in 1349 during the panic of the plague, but allowed back in 1372. The Jews were expelled again in 1424, and their synagogue was transformed into the City Council's chapel dedicated to St. Maria in Jerusalem.

BIBLIOGRAPHY

Ennen, Leonard and Gottfried Eckertz, ed. *Quellen zur Geschichte der Stadt Köln.* 6 vols. Cologne, 1860–1879; rpt. Aalen: Scientia, 1970.

Groten, Manfred. *Köln im 13. Jahrhundert. Gesellschaftlicher Wandle und Verfassungsgeschichte.* Cologne: Böhlau, 1995.

Heborn, Wolfgang. *Die politische Führungsschicht der Stadt Köln im Spämittelalter.* Bonn: Rohrscheid, 1977.

Hoeniger, Robert, ed. *Kölner Schreinsurkunden des zwölften Jahrhunderts: Quellen zur Rechts- und Wirtschaftsgeschichte der Stadt Köln.* 2 vols. Bonn: E. Weber, 1884–1894.

Irsigler, Franz. *Die wirtschaftliche Stellung der Stadt Köln im 14. Und 15. Jahrhundert.* Wiesbaden: Steiner, 1979.

Kellenbenz, Hermann, ed. *Zwei Jahrtausende Kölner Wirtschaft.* 2 vols. Cologne: Greven, 1975.

Keussen, Hermann. *Topographie der Stadt Köln im Mittelalter.* 2 vols. Bonn: Hanstein, 1918, rpt. Düsseldorf: Droste, 1986.

Koebner, Richard. *Die Anfänge des Gemeinwesens der Stadt Köln.* Bonn: Hanstein, 1922.

Kuske, Bruno, ed. *Quellen zur Geschichte des Kölner Handels und Verkehres im Mittelalter.* 4 vols. Bonn: Hanstein, 1917–1934.

Loesch, Heinrich von. *Die Kölner Kaufmannsgilde im zwölften Jahrhundert.* Trier: Lintz, 1904.

Planitz, Hans and Thea Buyken, ed. *Die Kölner Schreinsbücher des 13. und 14. Jahrhunderts.* Weimar: Hermann Bohlaus, 1937.

Stehkämper, Hugo. "Die Stadt Köln in der Salierzeit." In *Die Salier und das Reich,* ed. Stefan Weinfurter. Sigmaringen: Thorbecke, 1991–1992.

———, ed. *Köln, das Reich und Europa.* Cologne: Neubner, 1971.

Strait, Paul. *Cologne in the Twelfth Century.* Gainesville: University Presses of Florida, 1974.

Joseph P. Huffman

SEE ALSO

Anno; Beguines; Cologne, Archdiocese; Cologne, Art; Lorraine; Meister Eckhart; Mysticism; Rainald of Dassel; Visionary Literature

Comes/Graf

The Latin word *comes,* or "count," meant "companion" and retained this basic meaning throughout the Middle Ages. In the late Roman Empire, however, *comes* also came to designate a "companion of the prince" and, by extension, a range of high governmental functionaries. During the Merovingian period, counts and similar officials, known as *graviones* or *graffiones* (whence the German word *Graf* "count" is derived), were responsible for a variety of military and civilian functions, playing a particularly important role in local and royal justice. By the end of the eighth century, the offices of *Graf* and *comes* had become almost synonymous, and *Graf* remains the usual German translation of *comes.*

In theory, counts were administrative officers directly dependent on the king; in practice, many comital (ducal) lands and rights became the private possessions of local noble families in a process known as "allodialization." Thus, while the early Carolingians had effectively used counts as flexible instruments for the direct administration of royal lands and the control of the local nobility, by the late ninth century, counts in many regions were recognized as princes in their own right, owing fealty to the king but having a high degree of autonomy within their territories.

Although German kings attempted to limit the development of comital autonomy by a variety of means, from the eleventh century onwards many older comital families were able to strengthen their domination of a defined

region centered around a key castle or monastery (which often gave the family its name). It should be noted, however, that, throughout the later Middle Ages, many new counts continued to be directly subordinate to the king and were used effectively to administer royal lands and justice. Counts also held, at different times and places, extensive economic and juridical rights over medieval cities and occupied important positions in regional ecclesiastical affairs as the advocates and patrons of religious houses and churches.

BIBLIOGRAPHY

Arnold, Benjamin. *Count and Bishop in Medieval Germany. A Study of Regional Power, 1100–1350.* Philadelphia: University of Pennsylvania Press, 1991.

Borgolte, Michael. "Graf", "Grafschaft". In *Lexikon des Mittelalters,* vol. 3. Munich and Zurich: Artemis, 1984.

Leyser, Karl. "The German Aristocracy from the Ninth to the Early Twelfth Century." *Past and Present* 41 (1968): 25–53; rpt. in *Medieval Germany and Its Neighbors, 900–1250.* London: Hambledon, 1982.

Tellenbach, Gerd. "From the Carolingian Nobility to the German Estate of Imperial Princes." In *The Medieval Nobility. Studies on the Ruling Classes of France and Germany from the Sixth to the Twelfth Century,* ed. and trans. Timothy Reuter. Amsterdam/New York: North-Holland, 1978, pp. 203–242.

Werner, Karl-Ferdinand. "*Missus-Marchio-Comes.* Entre l'administration centrale et l'administration locale de l'Empire carolingien." In *Histoire comparée de l'administration I'VE-XVIIIe.* Actes du XIVe colloque historique franco-allemand, Tours, March 27–April 1, 1977. Munich and Zurich: Artemis, 1980; rpt. in *Vom Frankenreich zur Entfaltung Deutschlands und Frankreichs. Ursprünge, Strukturen, Beziehungen: Ausgewählte Beitrage: Festgabe zu seinem sechzigsten Geburtstag.* Sigmaringen: Thorbecke, 1984.

William North

SEE ALSO

Carolingians

Concordat of Worms

Since the eighteenth century, the documents which three legates of Pope Calixtus II (1119–1124) exchanged with Emperor Henry V on September 23, 1122, near Worms, have been known as the Concordat of Worms. The concordat put an end to the struggle between the papacy and the empire over investitures and ended the schism in the church. Henry V solemnly promised to renounce the practice of investiture of bishops and abbots with ring and staff and to permit free canonical elections and consecration of the elected ecclesiastics. At the same time, the emperor pledged to return all church properties and the *regalia* (relic possessions) of Saint Peter, which had fallen into his hands or those of his supporters during the Investiture Controversy.

The privilege document of Calixtus II has come down to us only in secondary copies, but the copy signed by Henry V is still preserved in the *Archivio Segreto* (Secret Archives) of the Vatican. In the case of Germany, the pope agreed that bishops and abbots would be elected in the presence of the king. Moreover, the king would be allowed to invest the elected ecclesiastics with the temporalities *(regalia)* of the future see using a staff as a symbol. The investiture would take place before the consecration of the elected bishop or abbot, thus giving the king a chance to veto a candidate.

In other parts of the empire (Burgundy and Italy) prelates would be invested with their temporalities by the emperor within six months of their elections. All of the ecclesiastics would be obliged to fulfill all of the duties to the emperor which they incurred through their investiture.

The documents exchanged at Worms constituted a compromise and were only a partial victory for the papal party. Even so, Calixtus II, at first could only succeed in obtaining the grudging approval of the First Lateran Council (1123) by emphasizing the dispensatory character of the privilege. Nevertheless, the concordat determined the future relationship between church and monarchy. Since it had been concluded at the insistence and with the assistance of the secular and ecclesiastical princes of Germany, it also established the basic structure of the German constitution in the Middle Ages.

BIBLIOGRAPHY

Benson, Robert. *The Bishop Elect.* Princeton: Princeton University Press, 1968.

Bernheim, Ernst. *Das Wormser Konkordat und sein Vorurkunden hinsichtlich Entstehung, Formulierung, Rechtsgültigkeit.* Breslau: Marcus, 1906; rpt. Aalen: Scientia, 1970.

Classen, Peter. "Das Wormser Konkordat in der deutschen Verfassungsgeschichte." In *Investiturstreit und Reichsverfassung,* ed. Josef Fleckenstein. Sigmaringen: Thorbecke, 1973, pp. 411–460.

Tellenbach, Gerd. *The Church in Western Europe from the Tenth to the Early Twelfth Century,* trans. Timothy Reuter. Cambridge: Cambridge University Press, 1993.

Uta-Renate Blumenthal

SEE ALSO
Investiture Controversy

Conrad I (ca. 880–December 23, 918)

Conrad I (Konrad I) was born about 880, the son of Glismoda and her husband Conrad the Elder of the house of the Konradiner. This family, originally from the Trier/Lahn/Alsace area, made a belated entry into the high politics of East Francia when Arnulf of Carinthia married Oda, a Konradiner family member. As the secular guardians of Arnulf's son, Louis the Child (Ludwig das Kind), the Konradiner family increased their wealth and power in the Main-Franconia region during Louis' short reign (900–911). They achieved this success at the expense of the Babenbergers, whose almost total collapse they engineered in 906, aided by the subtle diplomacy of Hatto, archbishop of Mainz.

When Louis the Child died, Conrad was chosen as his successor at a meeting of mostly Franconian nobles in November 911 at Forchheim. Conrad was the first non-Carolingian ruler of East Francia, but his succession seems to have been carefully planned, and the new king gave every indication that he wished to exercise the prerogatives of his Carolingian predecessors. His charters indicate a strong desire to follow tradition, and his chancery was filled with clerks from the previous reign. Between 911 and 913, Conrad developed an energetic program of governmental renewal, but putting it into action proved very difficult. Only those members of the higher clergy who needed royal protection for their churches were in favor of Conrad's plans. The secular nobility was less amenable.

Conrad could not prevent the nobles of Lotharingia from immediately allying themselves with the West Frankish Carolingian ruler. In the northern part of his realm, Conrad was recognized as king by Duke Otto of Saxony, a revered elder statesman. But Otto died in 912, and his son and successor Henry (Heinrich) discouraged any royal interference in his duchy after 915.

Nor was Conrad any more effective in the southern part of his realm. In Bavaria the weakness of royal authority since 899 had enabled Duke Liutpold, and, after 907, his son Arnulf, to create a strong local power base in spite of continuous struggle with the Magyars. In 913 Conrad married Kunigunde, the widow of Liutpold, and Arnulf of Bavaria became his stepson; this did not improve their relationship. Neither repeated invasions nor the temporary exile of the young duke with the Magyars allowed Conrad to have any say in Bavaria. The defeat of the Magyars in 913 at the battle of the Inn, undertaken by the Bavarians and Swabians without royal aid, did nothing to enhance Conrad's reputation as a strong defender of the realm.

Royal government had also ceased to function in Swabia. In the late ninth century, Arnulf of Carinthia had guarded this western frontier against both West Francia and the kingdom of Burgundy. Around 910 the Hunfridinger Burchard had attempted to become duke, but he was killed in 911 and his son exiled. The brothers Erchanger and Berthold sought to take his place. They seem to have expected Conrad's tacit approval for their actions since his wife Kunigunde was their sister. Conrad tried to prevent strong ducal government in Swabia, but in 915 Erchanger and his adherents defeated the king's forces and Erchanger became duke.

This did not mean peace in Swabia, however. Erchanger and his brother Berthold feuded continuously with Bishop Solomon of Constance, abbot of St. Gall and Conrad's chancellor, whom they imprisoned and attempted to blind. Thereupon, a group of bishops called a synod at Hohenaltheim (near Nordlingen) in 916, under the leadership of the papal legate Peter of Orta, and condemned the offenders to incarceration in a monastery. But Conrad, who was not present and who was not pleased over this clerical interference in his royal prerogatives, reversed the episcopal verdict, captured Erchanger, Berthold, and their nephew and had them beheaded on January 21, 917. The real beneficiary of Conrad's move was the young Burchard II, who had returned in 915 and may have been involved in the elimination of his rivals. Burchard became duke late in 918.

After 917 Conrad retreated to Franconia, and his sphere of power became more restricted. In 918 he did make one final attempt to defeat Arnulf of Bavaria, but he was badly wounded in this attack and did not recover. Not yet 40, he died on December 23, 918. He was buried in the monastery of Fulda.

It was in death that Conrad achieved most renown. According to contemporary accounts, he recognized in his final days that he had failed as king because he had neither luck nor charisma. Conrad commanded his brother Eberhard to take the royal insignia: the sword, the crown, the scepter, the mantle, and the arm rings to Henry of Saxony, the one person who might succeed where Conrad had failed. Whatever the truth of these stories—and most of them come from the pens of the court historians of the Ottonians—Eberhard did approach Henry and, after several months of negotiations, Henry was chosen king by the nobles of the *regnum Franconium* and *Saxonum* in May 919. The era of the Ottonian kings had begun.

The annals and chronicles composed in the opening decades of the tenth century had little information about Conrad I beyond noting his election in 911 and death in 918. Additional details depended upon the writer's location; the execution of the Swabian rebels is the most frequently cited story. In modern scholarship Conrad has usually been perceived as a footnote in works dealing with the origins of the German monarchy. More recently, however, investigations have shown that Conrad's policies were not so far removed from those of his successor, Henry, but that his early death prevented him from achieving any of his goals. Conrad the King (*Conradus rex*) was perhaps a better ruler than he realized.

BIBLIOGRAPHY

Arnold, Benjamin. *Medieval Germany 500–1300: A Political Interpretation.* Toronto: University of Toronto Press, 1997.

Dümmler, Ernst. *Geschichte des ostfränkischen Reiches.* 2nd. ed. Leipzig: Dunker und Humblot, 1887–1888.

Fuhrmann, Horst. "Die Synode von Hohenaltheim (916)—quellenkundlich betrachtet." *Deutsches Archiv* 43 (1987): 440–468.

Goetz, Hans-Werner, "Der letzte 'Karolinger'? Die Regierung Konrad I. im Spiegel seiner Urkunden." *Archiv für Diplomatik* 26 (1980): 56–125.

Reuter, Timothy. *Germany in the Early Middle Ages 800–1056.* London: Longman, 1991.

Madelyn Bergen Dick

SEE ALSO

Henry I; Lahn River; Louis the Child; Succession; Trier

Conrad II (ca. 990–June 4, 1039)

The first monarch of the new royal dynasty of the Salians, Conrad (Konrad) II was born circa 990 to Heinrich, son of Duke Otto of Carinthia and grandson of Duke Conrad of Lotharingia (d. 955). After his father's death, he was raised by his grandfather and uncle Conrad until he was taken into the episcopal household of Bishop Burchard of Worms (1000–d. 1025), supposedly because of ill-treatment at the hands of his relatives. In 1016, he married Gisela (d. 1043), daughter of Hermann II of Bavaria, thereby allying himself with one of the noblest families in the *Reich* (empire). The future king Henry III was born to the couple one year later in 1017.

When King Henry II died childless early in 1024, the nobility of the *Reich* was presented with the opportunity to elect a new monarch and ruling house. The royal election, recounted in unusual detail by the royal biographer and chaplain Wipo, was held at Kamba on the Rhine on September 4, 1024. Chosen over his rival and cousin Conrad the Younger (d. 1039), Conrad II was consecrated and crowned king by Archbishop Aribo of Mainz on September 8.

Once crowned king, Conrad had to make his kingship, his royal *presentia,* felt throughout his realm by establishing the personal bonds with local ecclesiastics, monasteries, and nobles that were the true guarantees of his kingship's power and stability. Furthermore, he had to gain the support of the Saxons and the members of the Lotharingian nobility who had not consented to his election. Therefore, following the tradition of his Ottonian predecessors, he devoted the next fifteen months to a royal *iter* (journey) that enabled him to meet and negotiate with nobles from Lotharingia to Saxony as well as those in Alemannia, Bavaria, Franconia, and Swabia.

With his rule thus consolidated by late 1025, Conrad embarked upon an expedition to Italy that lasted from the spring of 1026 until early summer of 1027. There he reestablished his authority over such rebellious cities of northern Italy as Pavia and Ravenna and broke down the opposition to royal rule within the Italian nobility through a combination of diplomacy and military might. Crowned Roman emperor by Pope John XIX (1024–1032) on Easter (March 26) of 1027 with King Cnut of England and Denmark and King Rudolf III of Burgundy in attendance, Conrad then headed south into Apulia, where he reestablished nominal German sovereignty over the Lombard princes and attempted to secure the frontier with Byzantine southern Italy.

Back in Germany, Conrad pondered the future of the dynasty. At Regensburg in June of 1027, he elevated his son Henry as duke of Bavaria and, on Easter of 1028, had

him crowned king at Aachen with the consent of the princes of the *Reich.* The death in 1033 of King Rudolf III enabled the Salian monarch to expand his hegemony by incorporating the kingdom of Burgundy into the *Reich.* Around 1034, after his earlier bid for a marriage alliance with Byzantium had failed, Conrad turned to Denmark for a bride for his son; Henry III married King Cnut's (1017–1035) daughter Kunigunde in 1036. With the deaths of the reigning dukes of Swabia and Carinthia in 1038 and 1039 respectively, Conrad invested Henry III with those duchies, thereby giving him a unique position of power in the three southernmost duchies of the German *Reich.*

Despite the extent of his power, Conrad II faced several internal rebellions and significant foreign challenges during his reign. Just two years after Conrad's election, a group of conspirators led by his rival Conrad the Younger rebelled during the king's first expedition to Italy. After an initial show of loyalty, the king's stepson Duke Ernst II of Swabia later joined this rebellion; he persisted in his opposition to Conrad, despite brief returns to grace and appointments to office, until he was killed in August of 1030.

In 1036 Conrad journeyed again to Lombardy to settle widespread disputes between subvassals and their lay and ecclesiastical overlords over the security of the subvassals' legal status and rights. After overcoming the resistance of the Italian episcopate and their attempt to introduce Count Odo of Champagne (995–1037) as king, Conrad finally settled the dispute in favor of the subvassals with his decree *Constitutio de feudis* of 1037, which represented a major departure from the earlier, proepiscopal policies of his Ottonian predecessors.

On his eastern frontiers, Conrad responded to the repeated political challenges posed by Poland, Bohemia, and Hungary through a combination of military might, alliances with neighboring princes, territorial exchanges, and diplomacy, designed essentially to maintain the status quo rather than expand German hegemony.

Perhaps the most debated aspect today of Conrad's kingship is his ecclesiastical policy. Earlier scholarship stressed the secularity of Conrad II's reign and the king's calculated development and exploitation of the *Reichskirche* (imperial church) to achieve secular political aims. More recent studies, however, while not ignoring Conrad's political and economic reliance on ecclesiastical and monastic structures, have offered a more balanced assessment that highlights Conrad's personal association with leading monastic reformers of his time, including Odilo of Cluny, William of Dijon, and Poppo of Stablo; his efforts to further their reforms; his swift change in policy after a unique case of simony reported by Wipo; and his support of reformers such as Bruno of Egisheim, the future Pope Leo IX. Finally, they argue that, although Conrad undoubtedly saw himself as the head of the imperial Church, this position of leadership remained, in his mind, a religious as well as a secular office, an attitude certainly manifested by his son Henry III.

Dying on June 4, 1039, Conrad II was laid to rest by Empress Gisela and King Henry III in the cathedral of Speyer.

BIBLIOGRAPHY

Boshof, Egon. *Die Salier,* 3rd ed. Stuttgart and Berlin: Kohlhammer, 1995, pp. 33–91.

Die Urkunden Conrads II., ed. Harry Bresslau and P. Kehr. Munich: Monumenta Germaniae Historica, 1909; rpt. 1980.

Hoffmann, Hartmut. *Monchskönig und "rex idiota". Studien zur Kirchenpolitik Heinrichs II. und Conrads II.* Hannover: Hahn, 1995.

Morrison, K. F. "The Deeds of Conrad II." In *Imperial Lives and Letters of the Eleventh Century,* ed. Theodor E. Mommsen and Karl F. Morrison. New York: Columbia University Press, 1962.

Trillmich, Werner. *Kaiser Conrad II. und seine Zeit,* ed. Otto Bardong. Bonn: Europa Union Verlag, 1991.

Wipo. *Gesta Chuonradi,* ed. Harry Bresslau. Hannover: Hahn, 1878; rpt. 1993.

W. L. North

SEE ALSO

Burchard of Worms; Coronation; *Reich;* Henry III; Leo IX; *Reichskirche;* Succession

Conrad of Marburg (ca. 1180–1233)

One of medieval Germany's most fascinating personalities was born about 1180, probably near Marburg, in Hesse. Eventually he became a Premonstratensian priest. In 1214 he was commissioned by Pope Innocent III to press the crusade against the Albigensians, a mandate which resulted in a series of bloody massacres. Two years later he appeared as a different type of crusade preacher, this time as a recruiter of men to participate in the Fifth Crusade which had been called into being in 1213 by

Pope Innocent. According to the chronicler Burchard of Ursberg, most recruiting activity slowed down following the death of Innocent in July 1216, but Conrad of Marburg and Conrad of Krosigk were two who apparently continued their efforts without ceasing.

By 1226 Conrad of Marburg had acquired an influential position at the court of Ludwig IV, landgrave of Thuringia; a year earlier he became the confessor of Ludwig's wife, Elizabeth, whom he disciplined with physical brutality. The prolonged fasts which he prescribed for her eventually wore down her health and ultimately may have caused her early death, but in the process she developed a reputation for piety which served to promote her beatification almost immediately. Here too, Conrad of Marburg was influential, just as he had been in determining her place of burial at Marburg where St. Elizabeth's church soon arose as a fitting shrine for her relics.

Conrad had meanwhile obtained another papal assignment: Pope Gregory IX made him the chief inquisitor in Germany, with the mandate to exterminate heresy, denounce clerical marriages, and reform the monasteries. His methods were so severe that a plea went out from the German bishops to have the pope remove him. Their plea was ignored, however.

In 1233 he took his maniacal inquisition to the final extreme by accusing one of the highest members of German society—Count Henry of Sayn—of various forms of heretical activity, including such bizarre behavior as riding on turtles. Henry in turn appealed to a court of his peers, an assembly of princes. Such a diet, held at Mainz under the presidency of King Henry VII declared him innocent. Speaking for the others, Archbishop Dietrich II of Trier declared that Count Henry was departing from the session "a free man and a Christian." Conrad of Marburg is said to have muttered that, had he been found guilty, things would have been very different.

The hatred toward Conrad was by now difficult to control. As he and his companions rode away from Mainz toward Marburg, he was brutally murdered on July 30, 1233. When news of this event reached Rome, the pope merely accepted it; no effort was made to punish the perpetrators. The contemporary chronicles report that, with the death of Conrad, peace and quiet returned to Germany once again.

BIBLIOGRAPHY

Förg, Ludwig. *Die Ketzerverfolgung in Deutschland unter Gregor IX.* Historische Studien 218. Berlin: Ebering, 1932.

Kaltner, Balthasar. *Konrad von Marburg und die Inquisition in Deutschland.* Prague: F. Tempsky, A. Haase, 1882.

Maurer, Wilhelm. "Zum Verständnis der heiligen Elisabeth von Thüringen." *Zeitschrift der Geschichte und Kunst* 65 (1953/1954).

Shannon, Albert Clement. *The Popes and Heresy in the Thirteenth Century.* Villanova, Pa: Augustinian, 1949.

Paul B. Pixton

SEE ALSO
Crusades

Conrad of Urach (fl. late 12th c.)

Conrad of Urach was the son of Count Egino the Bearded of Urach; his mother came from the family of the dukes of Zähringen. His birth fell before 1170. Apparently determined for a clerical career early on, he received his training at the cathedral school of Liège (St. Lambert's), where his maternal great-uncle, Rudolf of Zähringen, sat as bishop 1167–1191. At some point (probably while his uncle was still bishop), Conrad acquired a canonate in the cathedral; in 1196 he appears as cathedral dean, charged with maintaining order among the community. That the canons were in need of reform can be seen from the statutes issued in 1202 by Cardinal legate Guy Poré. By that time, however, Conrad had left the chapter.

Conrad's uncle, Duke Berthold V of Zähringen, was a candidate for the throne of Germany in the disputed election which followed the untimely death of Henry VI in 1197. As guarantees that he would produce the money needed to secure his election, Berthold offered his nephews—Conrad and Berthold of Urach—to the archbishops of Cologne and Trier; meanwhile, most other German princes had elected Philip of Swabia, brother of the deceased king. Hearing this, the duke renounced his claims, but the two archbishops retained their hostages for some time longer. This use of them as pawns in the political game of chess apparently had a profound effect upon both hostages: should they be released, they vowed to become monks, and, in fact, both became Cistercians. In 1199, Conrad entered the Cistercian house at Villers-on-the-Dyle in Brabant.

Meanwhile, on February 1, 1200, Albert of Cuyck, the successor to Rudolf of Zähringen as bishop of Liège, died, and the see was left vacant. Part of the cathedral chapter elected Conrad of Urach, who had not yet made his final profession at Villers, as bishop; another faction elected an archdeacon who was studying at Paris at the time. Conrad renounced any claim to the office, however, apparently preferring the *vita contemplativa* (contemplative life) to the *vita activa* (active life) required of a German prince bishop. He made his final vows at Villers. His family ties, as well as his obvious abilities, led to his becoming prior at Villers by ca. 1204, and in 1208/1209 he was elected abbot. His reputation as an ardent reformer and as a rigorous administrator led to his elevation as abbot of Clairvaux in 1214, and, as such, he attended the Fourth Lateran Council.

Despite his having become a monk, Conrad could not escape the responsibilities placed on him as one of the most influential individuals in the Latin Christendom of his day. In December 1216, he was sent with Abbot Arnald of Citeaux to Philip II and Louis of France to negotiate peace with England. In 1217 Conrad became abbot of Citeaux and general of the Cistercian Order; he probably assumed office at the general meeting of the chapter of the order held at the end of the year.

In January 1219, Pope Honorius III consecrated Conrad as cardinal bishop of Porto and San Rufina. At the time, there were twenty members of the College of Cardinals: four cardinal bishops, eight cardinal priests, and eight cardinal deacons. Of these, sixteen were from Italian provinces, two from Iberia, one from England, and one from Languedoc. Conrad thus joined the college as its only German member and remained so thus until 1225. During Lent 1220, he was appointed as the successor of Cardinal Bertrand as legate to the Albigensian lands, and given a mandate to support Amalrich de Montfort against Count Raymond of Toulouse. His fame spread, to the extent that soon thereafter, he was nominated to the archbishopric of Besançon. Honorius III would not allow this, however, claiming that Conrad's talents were needed throughout the Church.

In 1224 Conrad was given the legation as crusade preacher in Germany, but he also participated in various other activities, such as the condemnation of the accused renegade prior Henry Minneke at Hildesheim in October 1224, the national synod held at Mainz in November and December 1225, and the burial of Archbishop Engelbert of Cologne in December 1225. By May 1226 he was back in Rome, and he was present on March 18, 1227, when Honorius III died. According to tradition, Conrad was the first to be offered the tiara, but, again, he rejected an episcopal office. Only then was Gregory IX chosen. Even had Conrad accepted, however, his pontificate might well have been a brief one: he died on September

29, 1227, and was buried at Clairvaux, at the side of the smaller altar.

BIBLIOGRAPHY

Neiningen, Fulk. *Konrad von Urach († 1227): Zähringer, Zisterzienser, Kardinallegat.* Paderborn: Schöningh, 1994.

Pixton, Paul B. "Cardinal Bishop Conrad of Porto and S. Rufina and the Implementation of Innocent III's Conciliar Decrees in Germany, 1224–1226." In *Proceedings of the Tenth International Congress of Medieval Canon Law* [. . .] 1996 [to appear].

Schreckenstein, Karl Heinrich Freiherr Roth von. "Konrad von Urach, Bischof von Porto und S. Rufina, als Cardinallegat in Deutschland 1224–1226." *Forschungen zur deutschen Geschichte*, 7 (1867):319–393.

Winter, F. "Ergänzungen der Regesten zur Geschichte des Cardinallegaten Conrad von Urach, Bischof von Porto und St. Rufina." *Forschungen zur deutschen Geschichte* 11 (1871):631–632.

Paul B. Pixton

SEE ALSO
Crusades; Henry VI

Conrad von Soest (ca. 1360–ca. 1422)

One of the most significant German painters of the late Middle Ages, Conrad von Soest played a pivotal role in the diffusion of the International Courtly Style in northern Europe. His name is known through signatures on two altarpieces. A marriage contract, dated February 11, 1394, can plausibly be connected with the painter. It was signed by six of the most prominent patricians of Dortmund and attests to the painter's considerable wealth and high social standing. He was a member of the confraternities of the Marienkirche (1396—?) and of the Nikolaikirche (1412–1422).

Iconographic and stylistic evidence suggests that, following his apprenticeship in Dortmund, Conrad joined the workshop of the Parement Master in Paris in the 1380s. There he seems to have had access also to designs by Jacquemart de Hesdin. The creative and vigorous style of Conrad's underdrawing, consistent in the two signed altarpieces, refutes any notion of an imitative artist dependent on Burgundian patterns. Instead, Conrad achieved a synthesis of the style and technique learned in the royal workshops in Paris with this Westphalian inheritance, without forsaking originality.

His earliest surviving work, the signed Niederwildungen Altarpiece from 1403 (Stadtkirche, Bad Wildungen), was painted under the patronage of the Order of St. John. The Closed altarpiece depicts four saints venerated in the church. When open, twelve painted scenes, arranged in two rows around a central full-height Crucifixion, describe the life of Christ from the Annunciation to the Last Judgment. In the multifigured Crucifixion, the courtly elegance of some attendants contrasts with the realism of bucolic figures. The noted art historian Erwin Panofsky (1953, p. 71) spoke of precocious naturalism when he extolled the sharp characterization and powerful modeling of the thieves, and he compared the linear description of the noble figures to work by the universally esteemed Limbourg brothers. Conrad was a gifted and observant storyteller. The tender humanity of his elegant protagonists combined with selective naturalistic description, together with the outstanding craftsmanship, decorative surface pattern created by sinuous line, and a sophisticated iconography, place the altarpiece in the forefront of artistic development around 1400.

By around 1420, when Conrad painted his other signed work, the altarpiece for the church of the Virgin *(Marienkirche)* in Dortmund, he concentrated on the dramatic potential of his now monumental figures and the emotional power of color. The altarpiece was commissioned by his own confraternity. The panels were cut in 1720 to fit into a (lost) baroque framework. They originally showed a central Death of the Virgin, surmounted by a lunette, flanked by the Nativity and Adoration on the obverse, and the Annunciation and Coronation on the reverse sides of the wings. Conrad's subtle and varied palette was now supported by a sensitive awareness of the effect of light and shade in the modeling of forms. His courtly figures, careful characterization, costly pigments, and exquisite punchwork would have gratified the taste and chivalric ideals of his cosmopolitan patrons.

The patrician members of the confraternity belonged to an exclusive, well-educated, and prosperous group who played a leading part in the influential international trading association, the Hanseatic League. Their lifestyle eased the diffusion of Conrad's last perpetuated style abroad. Conrad's influence was most profoundly felt in Cologne; his style was introduced there by the immigrant Veronica Master and still reflected in the work of Stefan Lochner.

BIBLIOGRAPHY

Corley, Brigitte. *Conrad von Soest: Painter among Merchant Princes.* London: Harvey Miller, 1996.

Conrad von Soest, *Death of the Virgin* from the Dortmund Altarpiece. *Photograph: Westfälisches Amt für Denkmalpflege, Münster.*

———. "A Plausible Provenance for Stefan Lochner?" *Zeitschrift für Kunstgeschicte* 59 (1996): 78–96.

———. "A Nineteenth Century Photograph and the Reconstruction of the Dortmund Altarpiece." *Visual Resources: An International Journal of Documentation* 13 (1997): 169–188.

———. "Historical Links and Artistic Reflections: England and Northern Germany in the Late Middle Ages," in *Harlaxton Medieval Studies,* ed. John Mitchell [forthcoming].

———. "Meister Konrad von Soest, ein geborener Dortmunder Bürger, und andere Dortmunder Maler." *Beiträge zur Geschichte Dortumnds und der Grafschaft Mark* 32 (1925): 141–145.

Fritz, Rolf. "Conrad von Soest als Zeichner." Westfalen 28 (1953): 10–19.

Panofsky, Erwin. *Early Netherlandish Painting: Its Origins and Character.* Cambridge, Mass.: Harvard University press, 1953, pp. 71, 93–94, 129.

Steinbart, Kurt. *Konrad von Soest.* Vienna: Schroll, 1946.

Winterfeld, Luise von. *Geschichte der freien Reichs- und Hansestadt Dortumnd,* 7th ed. Dortmund: F. W. Ruhfus, 1981.

Brigitte Corley

SEE ALSO

Cologne, Art; International Style; Lochner, Stefan; Sankt Veronica, Master of; Soest

Conradin of Hohenstaufen (1252–1268)

Grandson of Frederick II (1194–1250) and son of Conrad IV (1228–1254), Conradin or "little Conrad," the titular king of Jerusalem and king of Sicily, faced many difficulties in his short life. His father's untimely death in 1254, when Conradin was only two years old, hampered his efforts to secure his rights to the succession. He was displaced from his Hohenstaufen legacy in 1258 by Manfred of Sicily (1232–1266), his uncle and illegitimate son of Frederick II. He also faced opposition from the papacy which continued its anti-Hohenstaufen crusade.

But the most serious opposition came from Charles of Anjou who had been invited by Pope Urban IV to launch a crusade to conquer Sicily. Charles had defeated Manfred at the Battle of Benevento in 1266 where the Hohenstaufen leader died. Opponents of the Angevin and of the papacy turned to the young Conradin after Manfred's death to lead them against their enemies. Conradin met

with much support from the Italians as he traveled south to Sicily to claim his birthright. But despite Italian support and a substantial army, Conradin's youth and inexperience proved no match for Charles. Although Conradin's approach forced Charles to abandon the siege of Lucera, a Hohenstaufen stronghold, he would not be able to overcome his rival. At the battle of Tagliacozzo, Conradin was defeated and taken captive by Charles, who had the young king beheaded on October 29, 1268. Conradin's death brought to a close the illustrious line of the Hohenstaufen.

BIBLIOGRAPHY

Abulafia, David. *Frederick II: A Medieval Emperor.* Oxford: Oxford University Press, 1988, pp. 408–422.

Runciman, Steve. *The Sicilian Vespers: A History of the Mediterranean World in the Late Thirteenth Century.* Cambridge: Cambridge University Press, 1958.

Michael Frassetto

SEE ALSO

Frederick II

Constance

Located on the Rhine River at its exit from Lake Constance (German, *Bodensee*), the Roman fortress of *Constantia* was known as early as the third century (C.E.) when it was captured by the Alemanni. In 560 or 570 the bishopric of Windisch *(Vindonissa)* was transferred to Constance, and remained one of the most powerful in Germany throughout the Middle Ages. Tradition has it that Fridolin erected a monastery here in 511 and that another monastery had been established outside the city by Irish monks in the seventh century. In the suburb of Petershausen lies the monastery which Bishop Gebhard established in 953; the equally famous abbey of Kreuzlingen lay before the south gate.

The location of the city attracted merchants and, even in the early Middle Ages, Constance was a major trade center. About 900 it acquired market rights, and by the eleventh and twelfth centuries, it was one of the most important markets in Germany, specializing in linen processing. Over time, the burghers became more and more independent, a condition which led to friction with the bishops who had acquired the rights of lordship over the city. In 1192 Constance became a free imperial city when Henry VI declared it free from all duties to the bishop.

The favorable location of Constance between Germany and Northern Italy meant that emperors frequently spent time there. Charlemagne, Louis the Pious, and Otto II all sojourned in the city and granted the bishops various rights and privileges. It was here that Henry III delivered his speech against simony and established a general peace. In 1076, 3600 clerics assembled in a synod at Constance and repudiated the papal order on celibacy. In 1358 the Emperor Charles IV held a dazzling *Fürstentag* at Constance.

Three other events at Constance stand out for their high drama: the peace concluded between Frederick Barbarossa and Pope Eugenius III in June 1183; the sudden appearance of Frederick of Sicily before the city gates in 1212; and the Council of Constance, 1414–1418.

The Treaty of Constance (1183) brought to an end the struggle between the emperor and the towns of the Lombard League. Frederick renounced his claims to royal rights in northern Italy; the cities in turn recognized the overlordship of the empire. A house on the upper marketplace of the city, the Barbarossa Inn, carries the inscription *Curia Pacis,* indicating the spot where this accord took place.

Young Frederick of Staufen successfully evaded his rival Otto IV's loyal forces in northern Italy in the summer of 1212 by crossing the Alps through the Engadine to the lands of a friendly prelate, the bishop of Chur. He finally reached Germany where he had allies of his own. Moving swiftly from one Swiss abbey to another, the news of his arrival rallied loyal forces, and by mid-September Frederick had about three hundred cavalry, largely supplied by churchmen. The last significant hurdle before he could seriously challenge the Welf was the city of Constance, towards which Otto was progressing with some speed. The challenge for Frederick was to get there first, persuade the bishop to receive him, and deny access to his rival. Otto's cooks had already entered the city, a great reception was being prepared, and Otto himself was across the lake and expected in Constance within a matter of hours. Suddenly, seemingly out of nowhere, Frederick appeared before the gates of the city and demanded admission. The hour of decision had come for the bishop; after some hesitation, he opened the gates. Frederick entered, quickly won the allegiance of the burghers, and, successfully and literally, slammed the door in Otto's face. From Constance he progressed down the Rhine where he received the submission of the great episcopal cities and their prelates. Without the triumph at Constance, Frederick II of Staufen would most likely have failed in his attempt to assert his claim to the German throne in 1212, and the history of the empire thereafter would have been much different.

Two centuries later, nearly 100,000 people jammed Constance when an ecumenical council of the Church was held 1414–1417 to heal the Great Schism and deal with various matters of Church discipline, including heresy. Once again an emperor was present. This was Sigismund, under whose protection Jan Hus and Jerome of Prague had come to the council to defend themselves against charges of heresy. Hus was imprisoned from December 6, 1414, until March 24, 1415, at the Dominican monastery on an island in Lake Constance while the council fathers met in the cathedral to discuss his errors and decide his fate. He was declared a heretic and burned at the stake on July 6, 1415, in the plaza which lies in the western part of the city in an area called "Paradise." The following year, the burgrave of Nürnberg was enfiefed with (granted control of) the Mark Brandenburg by Emperor Sigismund in the marketplace of Constance. Two more years were required before the Schism was healed, however. In 1417 a conclave held in the *Kaufhaus* (merchants' hall) proclaimed the election of Martin V as pope and settling the schism.

BIBLIOGRAPHY

Bäumer, Remigius, ed. *Das Constanceer Konzil.* Darmstadt: Wissenschaftliche Buchgesellschaft, 1977.

Loomis, Louise Ropes. *The Council of Constance.* New York: Columbia University Press, 1961.

Maurer, Helmut. *Constance im Mittelalter, Geschichte der Stadt Constance,* vol. I. Constance: Stadler 1989.

Paul. B. Pixton

SEE ALSO

Charles IV; Chur; Constance, Art; Frederick I Barbarossa; Frederick II; Henry III, Henry VI; Louis the Pious; Otto II; Otto IV; Welfs

Constance, Art

As a result of its strategic location and the political significance of its bishop, Constance (German, *Konstanz*) also became a major center of art production. Especially in the late thirteenth and early fourteenth century, paintings, sculptures, and metalwork objects from Constance were exported throughout southern Germany and present-day

Constance, cathedral, chapel of St. Maurice, Holy Grave. *Photograph: Joan A. Holladay*

zur Kunkel and the church of the Dominican cloister (now the Insel Hotel) exhibit two-dimensional versions of this same style.

BIBLIOGRAPHY

Das Graduale von St. Katharinenthal um 1312. 2 vols., ed. Johannes Duft, et al. Lucerne: Faksimile-Verlag, 1980–1983.

Futterer, Ilse. *Gotische Bildwerke der deutschen Schweiz.* Diss. Universität Zürich, 1928. Augsburg: Dr. Benno Filser Verlag, 1930.

Konstanz: Ein Mittelpunkt der Kunst um 1300. Constance: Seekreis Verlag, 1973.

Michler, Jürgen. *Gotische Wandmalerei am Bodensee.* Friedrichshafen: Verlag Robert Gessler, 1992, pp. 14–33.

Joan A. Holladay

SEE ALSO

Constance; Gothic Art and Architecture; Iconographies, Innovative; Sankt Katharinenthal

Constantine

See Donation of Constantine.

Conversion

Conversion, meant primarily as conversion of non-Christians to Christianity, has played a more central role in German history than one might initially think. The Germanic peoples were the first outside the Roman Empire to be systematically converted to Christianity. It was for the Goths that Bishop Ulphilas (ca. 311–383), the "Apostle of the Goths," translated the Bible into Gothic—the first known transcription of any Germanic language into writing. Other bishops, including those of Rome, also pressed on with the work of conversion, sometimes advocating the use of pressure and force.

Charlemagne took this aggressiveness one step further by linking conversion with conquest in his long wars with the Saxons. (He does not seem to have pursued this kind of policy with respect to the Avars and Slavs, however.) The Saxons, in their turn, combined conversion with conquest, beginning in the 920s and sporadically thereafter until full resumption of the policy in the twelfth century. Missionary activity was promoted by the founding of new sees, especially the archbishopric of Magde-

Switzerland, where they influenced works of other, less active, centers. The squat, expressive figures of the Holy Grave in the circular chapel at the eastern end of the cathedral predict the characteristic Constance style of circa 1300, which finds its fully developed form in the wood sculptures associated with Master Heinrich of Constance. His images of Saint John resting on the bosom of Christ (now in Museum Mayer van den Bergh, Antwerp) and the standing Virgin and Child, made for the convent of Dominican nuns at St. Katharinenthal—and still located there—share heart-shaped faces with slightly pinched features and sweet expressions, elegant, expressive gestures, and lyrically flowing draperies. The lavishly decorated gradual painted for St. Katharinenthal in 1312 (now in Zurich, Schweizerisches Landesmuseum, Inv. No. LM 29329) and wall paintings preserved in the Haus

burg around 968. The bishopric of Bamberg was explicitly established by Henry II in 1007 "so that the paganism of the Slavs would be destroyed, and the memory of the name of Christ would always be remembered there." In the thirteenth and fourteenth centuries, the Teutonic Knights continued this work against the Slavs and extended it to the Baltic peoples. As a result, the boundaries of the Christian Empire were progressively pushed far to the east of where the Romans had dared to go. In this respect, as in so many others, medieval Germany was the heir of Charlemagne.

Germany was also an important base for the conversion of the Scandinavian peoples to Christianity. Even as these dreaded "Northmen" devastated the Continent and the British Isles in the ninth and tenth centuries, St. Anskar (801–865), the "Apostle of the North" and first archbishop of Hamburg-Bremen (ca. 848), used his sees to try to convert the Danes. Anskar was a Picard by background, but monks from Anglo-Saxon England and elsewhere similarly labored among the Norsemen. The extent of the Christian imperial ambition of the Germans however, was revealed two centuries later when Adalbert, archbishop of Hamburg-Bremen from 1045 to 1072 and regent from 1056 to 1066, so vigorously promoted missionary activity in the Orkneys, Iceland, and Greenland, as well as Scandinavia, that Pope Leo IX named him papal legate and vicar of the North. Adalbert had hoped to be appointed primate of the North, but his hopes were frustrated by the opposition of his enemies, the destruction of Hamburg by the Wends in 1071–1072, and the papal creation of separate churches in Denmark, Norway, and Sweden in 1004, 1153, and 1164, respectively. Despite later imperial claims and the ever sensitive issue of Schleswig and Holstein, the northern borders of the empire were now effectively rounded off, more or less concluding the conversion efforts.

There is a second meaning of "conversion," which became particularly important after the Roman emperors adopted Christianity as the sole official religion of the empire in the fourth century. Christianity was no longer a matter of choice, and infant baptism became the norm. "Conversion," which had previously preceded baptism, was now to be experienced later in life as a call to conversion of heart, to a life of sacrifice in imitation of Christ, especially in forgoing wealth, sex, and one's own will in submission to the will of God. For the next thousand years, in Germany as in the rest of Christendom, this ordinarily meant withdrawing from the world, becoming a hermit, a monk, or a nun, and embracing the vows of poverty, chastity, and obedience. Without a doubt, the most famous German who ever underwent "conversion" was the one who ended up challenging this understanding of the word—Martin Luther.

BIBLIOGRAPHY

Bartlett, Robert. "The Conversion of a Pagan Society in the Middle Ages." *History* 70 (1985): 185–201.

Beumann, Helmut, ed. *Heidenmission und Krezzugsgedanke in der deutschen Ostpolitik des Mittelalters.* 2nd ed. Darmstadt: Wissenschaftliche Buchgesellschaft, 1973.

Christiansen, Eric. *The Northern Crusades: the Baltic and the Catholic Frontier, 1100–1525.* 2nd ed. Harmondsworth: Penguin Books, 1997.

Fletcher, R. A. *The Barbarian Conversion: from Paganism to Christianity.* New York: Henry Holt, 1998.

Hillgarth, J. N., ed. *Christianity and Paganism, 350-750: The Conversion of Western Europe.* Philadelphia: University of Pennsylvania Press, 1986.

Muldoon, James, ed. *Varieties of Religious Conversion in the Middle Ages.* Gainesville: University Press of Florida, 1997.

Lawrence G. Duggan

SEE ALSO

Bamberg; Charlemagne; *Deutschorden;* Gothic Language; Leo IX; Magdeburg

Cookbooks

The *Répertoire des manuscrits médiévaux contenant des recettes culinaires* lists forty-five late-medieval codices containing culinary recipes in High and Low German. The collections range from miscellaneous recipes to extensive cookbooks of 200 to 300 recipes. Most of the culinary manuscripts were written in the 15th century, and often appear in composite codices together with such standard treatises as *Regimen sanitatis,* or *Regimen duodecim mensium,* (a book of horse remedies and a book on grafting respectively).

The oldest German cookbook is contained in the Universitätsbibliothek in Munich (no. 2° Cod. ms. 731) and is known as *Daz buoch von guoter spîse* (The Book of Good Food). It was entered into the codex between 1345 and 1354 at the request of Michael de Leone, notary to the Bishop of Würzburg, and compiled from two different sources. Part I consists of a rhymed prologue, fifty-five culinary recipes, and two recipe-parodies; Part II, of forty-four recipes. Two cookbooks in the tradition of the *Buoch von guoter spise* are in Vienna (Nationalbibliothek, Cod. Vind. 2897, *Wiener Kochbuch*, "The Viennese Cookbook", and Cod. Vind. 4995, *Mondseer Kochbuch)*.

Unlike modern cookbooks, which give precise cooking instructions and usually divide the recipes into appetizers, soups, side dishes, salads, fish, meat, fowl, desserts, and breads, their medieval counterparts provide hardly any quantities and often list the recipes in little or no apparent order. The *Buoch von guoter spise* starts with a sweet dish, followed by deer liver, two chicken dishes, and a sweet rice dish. Small groupings of recipes, which share a certain ingredient, shape, or consistency, are sometimes discernable. In Part II of the *Buoch* a distinction is made between dishes for fast and feast days. Most of the medieval cookbooks reflect an aristocratic or monastic cuisine, which later became accessible to a larger bourgeois audience through early printed editions such as the *Kuchenmeysterey* published in Passau ca. 1486. The ingredients most frequently mentioned in German cookbooks are pepper, saffron, apples, almonds and almond milk, honey, sugar, rice, fish, pork, bacon, chicken, butter, lard, vinegar, milk, water, wine, bread, eggs, cheese, flour, and salt. Popular dishes included purees, puddings, pies, *blanc manger,* casseroles, fritters, roasts, flat cakes, sauces, and special presentations *(Schaugerichte).*

Only two German cookbooks provide the names of aristocratic cooks: the *Kochbuch Meister Eberhards,* and the *Kochbuch Meister Hannsens.* Eberhard's German-language treatise consists of twenty-four culinary recipes and a dietetic list of foodstuffs based on Konrad von Eichstätt's *Sanitatis Conservator;* Hannsen's collection includes 289 recipes, of which twelve are for colors, dyes, and miscellaneous remedies. Culinary recipes can also be found in the vast dietetic literature of the Middle Ages.

BIBLIOGRAPHY

Feyl, Anita. *Das Kochbuch Meister Eberhards. Ein Beitrag zur altdeutschen Fachliteratur.* Ph.D. diss. Freiburg im Breisgau, 1963.

Hajek, Hans. *Daz buoch von guoter spise. Aus der Würzburg-Münchener Handschrift neu herausgegeben.* Berlin: Schmidt, 1958.

Lambert, Carole, ed. *Du manuscrit à la table. Essais sur la cuisine au Moyen Age et Répertoire des manuscrits médiévaux contenant des recettes culinaires.* Paris: Champion-Slatkine and Montreal: Les Presses de l'Université de Montréal, 1992.

Wiswe, Hans. *Kulturgeschichte der Kochkunst. Kochbücher und Rezepte aus zwei Jahrtausenden mit einem lexikalischen Anhang zur Fachsprache von Eva Hepp.* Munich: Moos, 1970.

Melitta Weiss Adamson

SEE ALSO
Diet and Nutrition

Coronation

The early German kings were installed by a single constitutive act: their election and acclamation by the nobles of the realm. To this was added the ecclesiastical rite of unction, anointing the candidate with consecrated oil. This act symbolized the new birth in Christ of the ruler-elect and was drawn from the rite of baptismal unction. (The link to Old Testament royal unction is only indirect.) The rite of unction was first recorded in Frankish lands when Pippin the Short assumed the throne and was anointed by a papal emissary in 751. Anointing was not considered necessary until around 850, after which it became standard in the West Frankish kingdom. The first authenticated case of unction of an East Frankish ruler was that of Conrad I in 911, and the ceremony only became standard from the time of Otto I. Otto also fixed the place for German royal coronations at Aachen for the remainder of the Middle Ages and decreed that the ceremony would be performed by the archbishop of Mainz.

The liturgy of coronation developed in the second half of the ninth century, defining more clearly the sacred duty and character of the ruler. Unction especially emphasized the ruler's duty to defend the Church and his answerability to the clergy. From 962 on, most German kings were also crowned as emperor, and the imperial *ordo* (or rites) reinforced the close relationship between emperor and Church. Imperial coronation was in the gift of the pope and was conferred along with a special duty to defend the Church, especially the Roman Church, against its foes.

The coronation *ordo* adopted by the Ottonians probably dates from the first third of the tenth century. It became standard through its inclusion in the widely-circulated Romano-German pontifical of circa 960. According to this rite, the ruler shares the ministry of a bishop and is mediator between clergy and people. The coronation rite has four main parts: first, the emperor promises protection and defense of the Roman Church; second, after three consecrating prayers, the emperor-elect prostrates himself and then is anointed with the oil of exorcism on his right arm and between his shoulders; third, the pope places the crown on the emperor's head before the main altar; and finally, mass is celebrated.

The first certain unction of a queen was that of Judith, daughter of Charles the Bald, upon her marriage to Aethelwulf of Wessex in 856. The cermony was probably conducted to safeguard her position in a foreign land. It became standard with West Frankish queens, but was only introduced to Germany in the tenth century, perhaps with the coronation of Edith, Otto I's first wife, in 936, but certainly upon his marriage to Adelheid in 951.

For both kings and queens, the ceremony of coronation served to set the ruler apart as God's special child by adoption. It conferred divine protection and made attack upon the ruler sacrilege. In female coronations, the prayers also stressed fecundity. Election and unction together signified the assent of all nobles, both secular and ecclesiastical, to the ruler's authority.

BIBLIOGRAPHY

Elze, Reinhard, ed. *Die Ordines für die Weihe und Krönung des Kaisers under der Kaiserin.* Monumenta Germaniae Historica. Fontes iuris germanici antiqui in usum scholarum 9. Hannover: Hahnsche Buchhandlung, 1960.

Le sacre des rois. Actes du Colloque international d'histoire sur les sacres et coronnements royaux (Reims 1975), ed. Jean Sainsaulien Paris: Les Belles Lettres, 1985.

Nelson, Janet L. *Politics and Ritual in Early Medieval Europe.* London: Hambledon, 1986.

Wallace-Hadrill, J. M. "The Via Regia of the Carolingian Age." In *Trends in Medieval Political Thought*, ed. Beryl Smalley. Oxford: Blackwell, 1965, pp. 22–41.

Phyllis G. Jestice

SEE ALSO

Adelheid of Burgundy; Carolingians; Charlemagne; Conrad I; Otto I; Succession

Corvey

The Benedictine abbey of Corvey (Northrhine-Westphalia) was founded in 822 by Emperor Louis the Pious on the west bank of the river Weser. The first Carolingian abbey church—consecrated in 844 and replaced in 1665 by the present post-Gothic structure—is known from excavations to have been a basilica with a rectangular choir and axial chapel. Later, this first church was enlarged with transepts and a choir with apse, surrounded by an annular outer crypt that terminated in a cruciform axial chapel.

To this church was added in 873–885 the westwork (entrance structure on west side), which, though altered, has survived intact. Through the monumental massing of its three towers and its use as a setting for court ceremonies, this westwork represents a monument to imperial presence in the abbey church and the region. Its square core continues from the crypt-like entrance hall up into tower, where the choir of St. John is surrounded on three sides by galleries and screened off from the church by similar arcades. Traces of Carolingian wall decoration have been found, depicting, besides architectural elements, scenes from the myth of the Argonauts. More recently, the outlines of large-scale figures on the high walls have been detected. In addition, fragments of the painted ceiling of the destroyed cruciform chapel have been uncovered by excavation.

Under Abbot Wibald of Stavelot and Corvey (1147–1158), the westwork was transformed into the present two-towered façade. The dramatic change was achieved by reducing the central tower to the roof level of the church and by incorporating the central space as a western gallery (now reserved primarily for liturgical use) into the church structure.

BIBLIOGRAPHY

Kreusch, Felix. *Beobachtungen an der Westanlage der Klosterkirche zu Corvey: Ein Beitrag zur Frage ihrer Form und Zweckbestimmung.* Cologne: Böhlau, 1963.

Lobbedey, Uwe. "Neue Ausgrabungsergebnisse zur Baugeschichte der Corveyer Abteikirche." *Westfalen* 55 (1977): 285–297.

Möbius, Friedrich. *Westwerkstudien.* Jena: Friedrich Schiller-Universität, 1968.

Hans J. Böker

SEE ALSO

Carolingian Art and Architecture; Louis the Pious

Costume

See Clothing, Costume, and Fashion.

Councils/Synods

Councils and synods in medieval Germany derived from a tradition in the primitive Church when disciples of

Christ gathered to establish policies and clarify doctrines. In the post-Apostolic era, bishops of the various Roman provinces developed the practice of gathering to discuss and reach decisions on matters of both theological and disciplinary nature. Various ecumenical councils held between 325 and 787 dealt with a host of issues, the most controversial of which tended to involve definitions of the Godhead.

In the Latin West several councils were held from the ninth century on: the great royal-imperial assemblies of the Carolingian age; the general councils convened under papal auspices in the eleventh century and thereafter (including the four Lateran, or papal councils of 1123, 1139, 1179, and 1215); provincial gatherings directed by a papal legate or the metropolitan; and diocesan synods at which the clergy of a diocese assembled under the presidency of the local bishop. During the twelfth century, synods on a national scale, which had been quite customary during the Salian period, became less common. While some dioceses, such as Halberstadt and Hildesheim, maintained strong synodal traditions throughout the century, the practice of holding annual synods with the clergy of their diocese seems to have died out in many bishoprics.

Whereas the early Christian councils were preoccupied with doctrinal matters, those of the Latin West from ca. 1050 to 1122 gave much greater attention to various aspects of "reform" as constantly redefined in each new generation; such issues as simony, clerical continence, and lay investiture were paramount. While eighteen German bishops were present at the Third Lateran Council in 1179, twenty-one attended the Fourth Lateran in 1215, together with a significant number of abbots and other ecclesiastical representatives.

Canon 6 of the Lateran IV constitutions ordained that a provincial synod be held each year, during which the metropolitan would read the decrees of the general council and treat other matters of concern with his suffragans (subordinates); they in turn were obligated to meet once annually with their diocesan clergy in order to improve the discipline of the clergy and their ability to perform their pastoral duties (cura animarum). Recent studies have concluded that this mandate was only partially carried out, and that, throughout the thirteenth century, synods at both the diocesan and provincial levels were held only sporadically. Relatively few examples exist of statutes issued by German prelates during this time.

One of the most spectacular synods in thirteenth-century Germany was held during November and De-

cember 1225 at Mainz under the direction of Cardinal-legate Conrad of Urach who had spent the previous year traversing the realm on various matters of papal business, and whose knowledge of the German church was perhaps unrivaled at the time. The statutes issued on this occasion served as the nucleus for several later collections of the thirteenth and early fourteenth centuries.

The increased in the number of sets of diocesan and provincial synodal statutes in Germany after 1300 indicates, perhaps, that the synodal tradition was still alive, but, by and large, it failed to achieve the regeneration of the medieval Church for which Innocent III had expressed hope in 1215.

BIBLIOGRAPHY

Binterim, Anton Joseph. *Pragmatische Geschichte der deutschen National-, Provincial-, und vorzüglichsten Diöcesanconcilien, vom vierten Jahrhunderts bis auf das Konzilium zu Trent,* vols. 4–5. Mainz: Kircheim, Scott und Thielmann, 1840–1843.

Hinschius, Paul. *Das Kirchenrecht der Katholiken und Protestanten in Deutschland,* vol. 3. Berlin: Guttentag, 1869ff.; rpt. Berlin: Akademische Druck-und Verlagsanfalt, 1959.

Schannat, Johann Friedrich. *Concilia Germaniae,* vols. 3–4. Cologne: Krakamp et Haerdum C. Simonis, 1759ff.

Pixton, Paul B. *The German Episcopacy and the Implementation of the Decrees of the Fourth Lateran Council, 1216–1245: Watchmen on the Tower.* Leyden: Brill, 1995.

Paul B. Pixton

SEE ALSO

Carolingians; Conrad of Urach; Salians; Synod of Frankfurt

Crossbow

The crossbow was a mechanical bow that became the standard archery weapon in Germany during the Middle Ages. The basic construction of the weapon was a small bow attached to a stock that provided a groove for the bolt and handle, with a bowstring that was held in place ready for release by a trigger mechanism.

Descended from the ancient Greek *gastraphetes* (or "belly bow"), the crossbow became popular in western Europe during the late eleventh century. Because of its brutality in war, both Pope Urban II (r. 1088–1099) and the Second Lateran Council (1139) condemned its use among Christians. However, this condemnation was rarely heeded as the crossbow became increasingly popular in Europe. This was especially the case in Germany, where most emperors and nobles used crossbowmen in their armies between the twelfth and fifteenth centuries, frequently employing foreign mercenary crossbowmen if they failed to recruit sufficient numbers of these troops from among their own subjects. Crossbowmen were used tactically at the beginning of a battle and on the flanks as harassers of opposing forces. By the late Middle Ages, the crossbow had increased in use and efficiency. The composite crossbow, made of horn, sinew, and glue, was considerably more powerful than earlier bows. Stirrups, windlasses, and *cranequins* were added to the stock to enable the bow to be strung with greater tension, increasing immensely the power of the pull. Improvements to the release mechanism and to the bolt also added to the efficiency of the weapon. By the early thirteenth century, castles were being designed with openings for crossbows and ships were being outfitted with the weapon. By the early fifteenth century, crossbows were being replaced in the defense of castles by small-caliber cannons, and, ultimately, by the middle of the sixteenth century, the weapon had been replaced on the battlefield by handguns.

BIBLIOGRAPHY

Bradbury, Jim. *The Medieval Archer.* New York: St. Martin, 1985.

Contamine, Philippe. *War in the Middle Ages,* trans. M. Jones. London: Blackwell, 1984.

DeVries, Kelly. *Medieval Military Technology.* Peterborough: Broadview, 1992.

Foley, V., G. Palmer, and W. Soedel. "The Crossbow." *Scientific American* 252 (1985): 104–110.

Nicolle, David C. *Arms and Armour of the Crusading Period, 1050–1350.* 2 vols. White Plains: Kraus, 1988.

Kelly DeVries

SEE ALSO

Archer/Bowman; Fortification; Warfare; Weapons

Crusades

Although generally recognized as a French phenomenon, the crusading movement, and the ideals associated with it, was not without influence in Germany. Absent from the successful First Crusade, German knights and their kings and emperors participated in the Second and Third Crusades. The emperor Frederick II Hohenstaufen himself led a Crusade to rescue Jerusalem in the thirteenth century and faced a Crusade against him led by a hostile papacy. Moreover, the crusading ideal influenced relations with Germany's pagan neighbors on its eastern frontier and inspired the creation of a military order which, ultimately, would help push Christianity eastward.

The origins of the idea of the Crusade are rooted in the social, cultural, and religious transformation occurring at the turn of the millennium. As the invasions of the tenth century waned, and western knights turned their aggression against their neighbors, an effort emerged to redefine the function of the knight and focus his energy against a common, non-Christian foe. The effort to Christianize knighthood and sanctify war can be traced to the *vita* (life) of Gerald of Aurillac and the Peace of God movement of the early eleventh century. The sanctification of knighthood was also part of the broader reform movement of the eleventh century, especially the Gregorian reform movement. Indeed, Pope Gregory VII planned to lead a Crusade himself in 1074. Finally, the growing interest in the Holy Land and the increasing number of pilgrims journeying there—including the mass pilgrimage from Germany in 1064–1065—contributed to the idea of the Crusade. In part, the Crusades were designed to protect pilgrims traveling to Jerusalem and to protect Jerusalem itself from Muslims, who were deemed the enemies of the faith.

The First Crusade began with Pope Urban II's call to arms at the Council of Clermont in 1095. Inspired by Byzantine defeats at the hands of the Turks and reports of the persecution of Christians and their requests for aid, Urban appealed to the knights of Christendom to end their conflicts against each other and to make war on their enemies, the Turks, thereby rescuing the Holy Land. Urban's call to arms was received enthusiastically by the people of Europe and inspired peasants and warriors to make the journey to defend the Holy Land. In the empire, however, the call to arms was not well received. This was due, not to any lack of religious zeal on the part of the military aristocracy of the Empire, but, as Otto of Freising noted, to "the hostility which existed at the time between the king and pope." Indeed, one of the consequences of the ongoing Investiture Controversy was the near complete absence of German knights from the First Crusade.

The First Crusade was not, however, without consequences for Germany. It was in the empire that some of the worst excesses and greatest atrocities of the Crusade were committed. Inspired by the call to defeat the enemies of Jesus Christ, a number of crusaders attacked the Jews living in several cities in the empire. The pogroms were led by the Rhineland noble Emich of Leiningen, who gained much support despite the official prohibition against violence towards the Jews issued by Henry IV. The first city to suffer was Speyer, but here, thanks to a generous bribe, the Jews were protected by the bishop, and only a small number suffered from crusader violence. Far worse massacres would follow in the late spring and summer of 1096. From May 25 to May 29, the Jewish community at Mainz suffered the persecutions of Emich and his crusaders. This was followed by an assault on the community of Jews in Cologne and by attacks on the Jews in Trier and Metz by a branch of the main army. A separate army led by Peter the Hermit forced the community of Regensburg to accept baptism, and a third, attacked towns in Bohemia. The crusaders offered the Jews the choice between conversion and death in these cities and desecrated their holy books, synagogues, and cemeteries. Religious fervor, greed, and the desire to avenge the death of Christ led to the violent pogroms that occurred in a number of cities in the empire as the crusaders traveled to the Holy Lands.

Although they did not participate in the First Crusade, Germans would involve themselves in several subsequent Crusades. The fall of Edessa to the Turkish leader 'Imad ad-Din Zengi inspired the call for the Second Crusade (1147–1149) and for active participation in that Crusade by German knights and their king, Conrad III. Although at first reluctant to participate because of internal difficulties in Germany and Italy, Conrad was persuaded to take the cross after hearing a sermon delivered by Bernard of Clairvaux at the Christmas mass at the king's court in Speyer in 1146. Indeed, so great was the enthusiasm for a Crusade that a large number of Saxons petitioned for the right to launch a separate Crusade against the pagan Wends. Conrad's attention, however, was directed toward the Holy Land, toward which he headed with a substantial army of knights and nobles, including his nephew and heir, Frederick Barbarossa. Warmly received and provisioned by the Byzantine emperor Manuel I, Conrad would not have similar good fortune when he entered Islamic territory. On October 25, 1147, he and his army were ambushed near Dorylaeum, site of a great crusader victory in 1097, and decisively defeated. Many of the survivors returned home, leaving Conrad with a much reduced force, with which he would join the main crusader army. The ambush near

Dorylaeum was but one of many disasters to plague the ill-fated Second Crusade, whose final disaster would come with the attempt to take Damascus in July 1148. Although Conrad and the Crusade leaders had early success at Damascus, they maneuvered themselves into an untenable position and were forced to withdraw. Conrad himself would leave the Holy Land in the fall of 1148 and, after a brief stay in Constantinople, return to Germany in early 1149, having had little success as a crusader.

The Third Crusade (1189–1192) similarly precipitated by a disaster in the Holy Lands, also witnessed the enthusiastic, but ultimately doomed, participation of German warriors. The defeat at the Battle of Hattin and the fall of Jerusalem to the great general Saladin moved secular and ecclesiastical leaders in Western Christendom to call for a crusade. The Third Crusade boasted leadership by the greatest of Europe's rulers: Richard I of England, Philip II Augustus of France, and Emperor Frederick Barbarossa. The emperor had participated in the unfortunate Second Crusade and had long been enamored with the idea of crusading. He and many nobles took the cross in the presence of a papal legate during mass on the fourth Sunday of Lent in 1188. Barbarossa organized and led the largest, most organized, and best disciplined army the Crusades had ever seen. The army, numbered by contemporaries at 100,000, journeyed eastward until it reached Constantinople, where the emperor Isaac Angelus proved difficult. Barbarossa was able, however, to persuade Isaac to support and provision the crusading force. The army then proceeded into Asia Minor. After early difficulties, the crusaders managed to take Konya and then move into the friendly territory of Cilicia. Shortly thereafter, Barbarossa, still vigorous at age 70, apparently attempted to swim the river Gösku, but drowned at midstream. Leaderless, the German army fragmented; some crusaders returned home, and others proceeded to Syria, suffering losses along the way. The loss of the emperor greatly demoralized the remaining crusaders and weakened the overall effort of the Crusade.

Despite the lack of success of the Second and Third Crusades and the calamity of the Fourth Crusade, the crusading ideal remained attractive in the empire, and German crusaders continued to participate in the great campaigns of the thirteenth century. Children from the Rhineland, led by a boy named Nicholas, participated in the Children's Crusade in 1212, and Leopold of Austria and many other German knights participated in the Fifth Crusade (1217–1221).

Among the supporters of the Fifth Crusade was the emperor Frederick II Hohenstaufen, who delayed embarking for the Holy Land until 1228 so that he could resolve political difficulties in the empire. In many ways a conventional Christian ruler who recognized his obligation to God and the Church, Frederick's sense of imperial authority and responsibility informed his crusading sensibility. He launched a Crusade that was as complex and unconventional as he himself is often claimed to have been. Among the unusual characteristics of this Crusade was the size of his army, which was much smaller than conventional crusading armies, and its much greater focus.

Frederick had a better grasp of the politics of the Islamic world than most Western leaders and sought to use that knowledge to his advantage; paradoxically, he had a poor understanding of Latin politics in the eastern Mediterranean. His affairs in the Holy Land were complicated by his status as king of Jerusalem through his marriage to Yolande (Isabella), the heiress to the throne. Although he crowned himself king of Jerusalem and later celebrated a crown-wearing ceremony while in Jerusalem—consciously suggesting the legend of himself as the Last Emperor—the death of his wife made his claims to the throne somewhat tenuous. Nonetheless, he ruled as king and waged his Crusade as king of Jerusalem rather than as a traditional Western crusader.

Two characteristics made his crusade truly unique. Frederick himself waged no real war; instead, in a treaty signed on February 18, 1229, negotiated with the sultan, he received Bethlehem, Nazareth, much of Jerusalem, and a strip of land from the coast to the Holy City. Meanwhile, he faced a Crusade against him led by Pope Gregory IX, who had excommunicated the emperor before the latter's departure for the Holy Land. Frederick may have acquired Jerusalem, but his Crusade brought little benefit and worsened the already difficult situation for him in Italy and the empire.

German crusading activities were not limited to the Holy Land or participation in the armies of the various individual crusades. Beginning at the time of the Second Crusade and lasting into the sixteenth century, German knights received approval to wage Crusades against pagans living along the eastern frontier of the empire. Crusades were launched against Estonia and Livonia in the early thirteenth century and against Prussia in 1230. A series of particularly ruthless Crusades against Prussia in the 1260s and 1270s hastened the Christianization of Prussia and its colonization by Germans. Of critical importance

in these Crusades was the Order of the Hospital of St. Mary of the Germans of Jerusalem which was founded in 1189/1190 and is more commonly known as the Teutonic Knights (Deutschorden). Founded in the Holy Land, the Teutonic Knights were involved in building castles, creating settlements, and fighting wars of conquest along the empire's frontier. These activities, lasting into the sixteenth century, were part of the longstanding policy of the empire's push to the east. They also reveal the flexibility of the idea of the crusade and its popularity and importance in Germany.

BIBLIOGRAPHY

Christiansen, Eric. *The Northern Crusades. The Baltic and the Catholic Frontier, 1100–1525.* Minneapolis: University of Minnesota Press, 1980.

Erdmann, Carl. *The Origin of the Idea of the Crusade,* trans. Marshall Baldwin and Walter Goffart. Princeton: Princeton University Press, 1977.

Mayer, Hans E. *The Crusades,* trans. John Gillingham. 2nd ed. Oxford: Oxford University Press, 1988.

Riley-Smith, Jonathan. *The Crusades: A Short History.* New Haven: Yale University Press. 1987.

Runciman, Steven. *A History of the Crusades.* 3 vols. Cambridge: Cambridge University Press, 1951.

Setton, Kenneth M., ed. *A History of the Crusades.* 2nd ed. 6 vols. Madison: University of Wisconsin Press, 1974.

Urban, William. *The Baltic Crusade.* 2d ed., rev. and enl. Chicago: Lithuanian Research and Studies Center, 1994.

Michael Frassetto

SEE ALSO

Crusades, Opposition; *Deutschorden;* Frederick I Barbarossa; Frederick II; Henry IV; Mainz; Otto of Freising; *Seghelijn von Jherusalem;* Speyer; Trier

Crusades, Literature, Dutch

Most of the Middle Dutch Crusade literature survives only in fragments and consists mainly of translations (in rhymed couplets) from Old French sources. From the *Roman van Antiochië* (Old French: *Chanson d'Antioche*) some 175 lines remain; from the *Godevaerts Kinsthede* (Old French: *Enfances Godefroi),* only sixty. Both fragments stem from the same manuscript and seem to indicate that the complete Old French Crusade cycle was translated into Middle Dutch, probably commissioned by the dukes of Brabant (between 1250 and ca. 1300). The *Boudewijn van Seborch* (Old French: *Baudouin de Sebourc),* of which some 430 verses remain in fragments of two manuscripts, was perhaps written for the court of Hainault, Holland in the second half of fourteenth century.

The *Roman van Saladin* has a Flemish background. Of this text, only 160 verses remain. It is a translation of the lost Old French proto-*Saladin.* The *Roman van Cassant* is also a translation from an Old French source (proved by references in other texts), but this source has left no other traces. The fragments stem from the late fourteenth century and contain some sixty-five, mostly damaged or illegible verses. It has, perhaps, a Flemish background.

The only complete Middle Dutch crusade texts are in printed form. *Dystorie van Saladine* was printed between 1479–1483 at Oudenaarde (Belgium) by Arend de Keysere. It is a reworking of the *Roman van Saladin* in 2111/2112 eight-line stanzas. This incunabulum, perhaps printed on the occasion of the siege of Rhodos in 1480, is the best representative of the lost Old French proto-*Saladin.*

The *Ridder metter Swane,* containing the Swan Knight legend traditionally connected with the Crusade story (the Swan Knight was the grandfather of Godfrey of Bouillon), also survives only in printed form. This popular tale in prose (with rhymed monologues and dialogues) was printed more than twenty-five times in the Low Countries between the early sixteenth century and 1930. The *Historie van Godevaert van Boloen* is a translation from the *Historia de itinere contra Turcos,* a printed Crusade chronicle (Cologne, ca. 1472) containing a combination of the chronicles of Robert of Reims and Fulkert of Chartres. The Middle Dutch translation, as yet unedited, is a beautiful incunabulum printed in 1486 at Gouda. It seems to mark the beginning of the "scientific" study of Crusade historiography in Dutch vernacular.

BIBLIOGRAPHY

Boekenoogen, G. J. *Een schone ende miraculeuse historie vanden Ridder metter Swane etc.* Leyden: Brill, 1931.

Claassens, Geert H. M., ed. *De Middelnederlandse kruisvaartromans.* Amsterdam: Schiphouwer en Brinkman, 1993.

———. "The Middle Dutch Crusade Epics: A Survey." *Olifant* 14 (1989): 165–178.

———. "Some notes on the proto-*Saladin.*" In *Aspects de l'épopée romane. Mentalités-Idéologies-Intertextuelités,* ed. W. Noomen and H. van Dijk. Groningen: Forsten, 1995, pp. 131–140.

Serrure, C. P. *Dystorie van Saladine.* Ghent: Annoot-Braeckman, 1848.

Geert H. M. Claassens

SEE ALSO
Crusades; Historiography; *Segelijn van Jherusalem*

Crusades, Opposition

Opposition to crusading, which can be traced from the time of the First Crusade, came from different quarters and took a variety of forms. As major military enterprises, leaving for an extended and uncertain period, the crusading armies attracted large numbers of camp followers and noncombatants. The presence of these people prompted criticism from those who, with good reason, argued that they impeded the military effectiveness of the army. The presence of women, especially, became the standard explanation for defeat as a divine punishment for human sinfulness. Failures were also attributed to the consequences of the crusaders' pride and avarice. One finds the Latin phrase *peccatis exigentibus hominum* ("great human sinfulness") in numerous chronicle accounts of military reverses, such as the disastrous outcome of the Second Crusade. This belief in divine retribution prompted calls for reform in the crusading armies. On the Third Crusade, for example, the Emperor Frederick Barbarossa ruled that those guilty of fornication would be punished severely.

There was also criticism of lay rulers for their delay in taking up the cross. The prompt departure of Frederick Barbarossa in response to Saladin's defeat of the forces of the Latin kingdom at Hattin was contrasted with the vacillation of Richard I of England and Philip Augustus of France. Three decades later, however, the Emperor Frederick II was subject to similar criticism for his tardiness in departing on the Fifth Crusade and was even blamed by some for the defeat of the crusaders at Damietta. Predictably, one can also find opposition to the introduction of taxation in order to finance the Crusades. The German minnesinger Walther von der Vogelweide denounced the papal levies as a cunning scheme to enrich the papacy and its allies, and there was further criticism of the redemption of indulgences in the thirteenth century.

All this, however, was directed at the crusaders or aspects of the crusading movement rather than at the concept itself. Opposition to the crusades as such came in two forms—criticism of specific expeditions and fundamental criticism. Although the idea of crusading against heretics and opponents of the papacy in Europe can be traced back to the twelfth century, it was the thirteenth century when major expeditions were launched against the Albigensian heretics in Southern France and against Frederick II and his heirs, Conrad, Manfred, and Conradin. The use of the Crusade against the Hohenstaufen aroused fierce criticism from a number of sources. Chroniclers and vernacular poets from the Languedoc, Northern Italy, and the imperial heartland of Germany were forthright in their attacks upon the papacy and its supporters. Critics lamented that aid was wrongly being diverted from the Holy Land to the detriment of the campaign against the Muslims. Of the opponents of later crusades in Italy, some were known enemies of the papal curia; others came from Ghibelline territory.

It has been argued in the past that, largely because of the diversion of the crusades from the East, criticism of crusading grew stronger during the thirteenth century, and that the seeds of decline were well established by the time of the Second Council of Lyons in 1274. The real picture is more complex. Except for the occasional pacifist or group such as the Joachites, there was very little fundamental criticism of crusading in the twelfth and thirteenth centuries. The crusading movement was very much alive and well in the late Middle Ages. After the fall of Acre in 1291, attempts continued to be made to regain Jerusalem, but crusading had become much more diverse: there were now numerous theaters of operation from Spain to northeastern Europe and against a range of Christian opponents of the Church.

Disillusionment with the very idea of crusading, expressed in some of the most virulent attacks upon the movement, originated in the mid-twelfth century in the bitter aftermath of the Second Crusade. Two key critics were German—Gerhoh of Reichersberg and the annalist of Würzburg. Initially a supporter of the expedition, Gerhoh's position had changed dramatically by 1160 when he began work on his "On the Study of the Antichrist" (De investigatione antichristi). As the title suggests, he drew a connection between the failure of the Crusade and the presence of the Antichrist. The Würzburg annalist, like other contemporaries, criticized the behavior of the crusaders. He then went on to suggest that the crusade itself was inspired by the devil against God's righteous punishment of the world. The devil, he wrote, had deceived men into taking the cross at the peril of their bodies and souls. There is nothing like this in the reaction to either the battle of Hattin and the subsequent fall of Jerusalem to Saladin, or the later fall of Acre to the Mamluks. En-

thusiasm for the Crusades remained, even when political difficulties in Western Europe undermined attempts to launch new expeditions to the Holy Land.

BIBLIOGRAPHY

Gerhoh of Reichersberg. *De investigatione antichristi.* Monumenta Germaniae historica Libelli de lite. 3. Hanover: Hahn, 1897.

Housely, N. J. *The Italian Crusades: The Papal Angevin Alliance and the Crusades against Christian Laypowers, 1254–1343.* Oxford: Clarendon Press, 1982.

Siberry, J. E. *Criticism of Crusading, 1095–1274.* Oxford: Clarendon Press, 1985.

———. "Troubadours, trouveres, minnesingers and the crusades." *Studi medievali* 29 (1988): 19–43.

Throop, P. A. *Criticism of the Crusade: A Study of Public Opinion and Crusade Propaganda.* Amsterdam: Swetst Zeitlinger, 1940.

Würzburg Annalist. *Annales herbipolenses.* Monumenta Germaniae historica SS 16. Hanover: Hahn.

Elizabeth Siberry

SEE ALSO

Conradin of Hohenstaufen; Crusades; Crusades, Recruitment; Frederick I Barbarossa; Frederick II; Gerhoh of Reichersberg; Manfred of Sicily; Minnesinger; Walther von der Vogelweide

Crusades, Recruitment

Following the announcement of a Crusade in 1095 at Clermont, various charismatic preachers set out to recruit an army that could liberate the Holy Land from Muslim hands. There appears to have been little such preaching done in Germany, however, for the evidence suggests that an awareness of an impending crusade developed only as crusaders from France were passing through the region.

In 1146, Pope Eugenius III initially tried to keep the preaching of the Second Crusade limited to France and Italy, hoping that the German king, Conrad III, could be persuaded to help him regain control of Rome from the Normans of Sicily. The task of preaching the Crusade was entrusted to Abbot Bernard of Clairvaux, who adhered to the papal plan. He was forced to change course, however, when an unauthorized Cistercian monk named Rudolf began to preach to the inhabitants of northern France and the Rhineland in the style of one of the millenarian preachers of the First Crusade. Above all, it was Rudolf's urging of renewed pogroms against the Jews that necessitated Bernard's traveling to Germany. Arriving in the Rhineland, Bernard dealt quickly with Rudolf, and then remained to preach; at Christmas, Conrad III, together with numerous other Germans, took up the cross.

The Third Crusade came on the heels of the fall of Jerusalem to the Muslims in 1187, and recruitment north of the Alps was entrusted to Archbishop Joscius of Tyre and Cardinal Legate Henry of Albano. The first men to take the cross did so at an imperial diet at Strasbourg in December 1187; the emperor, Frederick Barbarossa, delayed until March 1188 at Mainz. His decision to enlist in the Crusade caught the attention of his generation, but his tragic drowning en route to the Holy Land resulted in minimal German involvement in subsequent military engagements.

Two formal Crusades occurred during the pontificate of Innocent III (1198–1216)—the Fourth and the Fifth. German participation in the Fourth Crusade was limited, although some German prelates such as Bishop Conrad of Halberstadt were present. The events of 1204, including discussions leading to the redirection of crusade efforts toward Constantinople, only served to convince the pontiff that greater control was necessary, however, and in 1213 he announced a new Crusade in the encyclical *Quia maior nunc*. In each realm, men of proven talent and loyalty were chosen as preacher-recruiters and were given limited powers to use in that effort. In Germany we find *magister* (master) Oliver of Paderborn and *magister* Hermann of Bonn in the province of Cologne; *magister* Conrad of Speyer and others in the province of Mainz; the Cistercian abbot of Villers-en-Brabant, Conrad of Urach, and the abbot of Rommersdorf in the province of Trier; the former bishop of Halberstadt, Conrad of Krosigk, in the province of Magdeburg; and Albert, cathedral provost of Salzburg, in the province of Salzburg.

The recruiting effort was reinforced at the Fourth *Lateranum* (council at Rome) where Innocent III issued the decree *Ad liberandum* aimed at raising the necessary money for the enterprise. The crusade preachers were given the task of collecting the half-tithe and of procuring the necessary supplies and ships. The crusade preachers traveled throughout Germany, agitating the populace whenever they could and capitalizing on occasions, such as knightly tournaments and local feast days, which brought together large numbers of people. The resulting army of German warriors was substantial.

Later Crusades also sought to find support in Germany; in 1225 Pope Honorius III recalled several experienced recruiters, including Oliver of Paderborn, Conrad of Speyer, and Conrad of Krosigk, to preach. Later in the thirteenth century, in 1263 and 1264, Albert the Great served as a Crusade legate in Germany as well.

BIBLIOGRAPHY

Cramer, Valmar. "Albert der Große als Kreuzzugslegat für Deutschland 1263/1264," *Palästina-Hefte des deutschen Vereins vom Heiligen Lande* (1933): 3–87.

Pixton, Paul B. "Erwerbung des Heeres Christi: Prediger des Fünften Kreuzzuges in Deutschland," *Deutsches Archiv* 34 (1978): 166–191.

Powell, James M. *Anatomy of a Crusade, 1213–1221.* Phildelphia: University of Pennsylvania Press, 1986.

Paul B. Pixton

SEE ALSO

Crusades; Crusades, Opposition; Frederick I Barbarossa; Warfare

Cult

See Saints' Cult.

D

David von Augsburg (1200/1210–1272)

The Franciscan teacher and preacher David von Augsburg profoundly influenced his contemporaries and successors through his vernacular and Latin tracts on the ascetic and mystical nature of religious life. Around 1240 David became the novice master at the Franciscan monastery in Regensburg, which along with Augsburg was the spiritual center of the Franciscans in the thirteenth century. In 1246 he was appointed papal visitator of two abbeys in the vicinity, a position he shared with Berthold von Regensburg and several other Minorites. As Berthold's assistant, David accompanied the renowned preacher on homiletic and mission tours.

David's extant works consist solely of his Latin and German tracts and letters; in many instances the authenticity is still disputed. His *De exterioris et interioris hominis compositione secundum triplicem statum incipientium, proficientium et perfectorum* is one of the most significant works on the spiritual life in the Middle Ages and survives in some four hundred manuscripts, including many German and Dutch translations. The work consists of three treatises, each devoted to one aspect of the threefold way. The first part focuses on the life of the spiritual neophyte and how the novice must free himself of the world and its enticements and be educated. In part two the inner person is called to reform in light of the image of the trinity. The third part enumerates seven steps to be followed by a religious person seeking perfection, i.e., divine knowledge. Speculative mystical theology predominates as well in the *Sieben Staffeln des Gebetes* (The Seven Steps of Prayer), which survives in three German versions as well as a Latin source; only the German version "B" is unquestionably by David. David's tracts proved particularly influential in the Netherlands among the Windesheimer and the adherents of the *Devotio moderna* (New Piety).

BIBLIOGRAPHY

De exterioris et interioris hominis compositione secundum triplicem statum: incipientium, proficientium et perfectorum, ed. PP. Collegii S. Bonaventurae. Ad Claras Aquas (Quaracchi): Ex Typographia Eiusdem Collegii, 1899 [Latin works].

Pfeiffer, Franz, ed. *Deutsche Mystiker des 14. Jahrhunderts.* Vol. 1. 1845; rpt. Aalen: Scientia, 1962, pp. 309–397 [German works].

Schwab, Francis Mary. *David of Augsburg's "Paternoster" and the Authenticity of his German Works.* Munich: Beck, 1971.

Spiritual Life and Progress, trans. Dominic Devas. London: Burns, Oates, and Washbourne, 1937.

Debra L. Stoudt

SEE ALSO
Devotio Moderna; Preaching and Sermons, German

De Heinrico

A macaronic (bilingual) Latin-German poem commemorating the reconciliation of Henry, duke of Bavaria, with Holy Roman Emperor Otto, *De Heinrico* (About Henry) is written in the new meter seen in Otfrid's gospel poem, with assonance but—being bilingual—little rhyme. Each long line contains both languages: typically, a Latin half line followed by a syntactically connected German half line. Thus the anonymous poet writes:

> de quodam duce / themo hêron Heinrîche,
> qui cum dignitate / thero Beiaro rîche bewarode.

of a certain duke, / the Lord Henry,
who with honor / took care of the Bavarians'
realm. (vv. 3–4)

Whether the Old High German poem refers to Emperor Otto I (936–973) and his brother Henry, whom he made Duke of Bavaria in 941, or to Otto III (983–1002) and Henry the Quarrelsome (son of the preceding Henry) is unknown; both interpretations entail chronological difficulties. Though both pairs quarreled, the poem does not speak directly of reconciliation: Otto receives Henry with honor, attends mass with him, again receives him and leads him to the Council, where he accepts Henry's advice:

Then all the discussion stood / under Henry's control:
whatever Otto did, / Henry had counseled it all:
and whatever he omitted / Henry had also counseled that (vv. 22–24)

Though found in the eleventh-century manuscript of the "Cambridge Songs," the poem is unambiguously of German origin. The author stresses the honor shown to the duke of Bavaria; nevertheless, though some have posited an original Bavarian version, the dialect is North Rhenish Franconian, except that Otto, because of his Saxon origins, is made to speak Old Saxon.

BIBLIOGRAPHY

Jungandreas, Wolfgang. "De Heinrico." *Leuvense Bijdragen: Tijdschrift voor germaansche filologie* 57 (1968): 75–91.
Murdoch, Brian O. *Old High German Literature.* Boston: Twayne, 1983, pp. 100–102.

Leo A. Connolly

SEE ALSO
Otfrid; Otto I; Otto III; Versification

Dendrochronology

Tree-ring dating, or dendrochronology, is a method for dating wood or objects in which wood has been used, based on measurements of the variation in the width of annual growth rings of the wood.

Dendrochronology was developed using the well-defined rings of temperate and subpolar gymnosperm and angiosperm species (e.g., oak, beech, fir, pine, spruce).

The method has not been successfully applied in the tropics.

The width of annual growth-rings of trees varies from year to year, depending on climatic and other environmental conditions in each year during the life of a tree. Over a number of years, the pattern of variation from year to year becomes increasingly distinctive and unique for the specific time and place in which a given tree grew.

The measured sequence of an undated sample can be compared with a continuous dated sequence of measured tree-ring widths for a specific region. If the bark or the terminal growth-ring is preserved in an undated sample, the exact felling year of a tree from which it came is also determined. If the bark and outer rings have been trimmed, it is possible to estimate the felling year for a given sample by adding to the date of the last reserved ring a specified number of years. The value is an average number of sapwood rings for a particular region.

As an example for a dendrochronological dating, the analysis of the Wartburg will be described. The construction of its palace is dated with construction starting shortly before 1157. The tie-beams of the ground floor and of the first upper story were cut around 1162 (+5/−3). The construction (without the second story) may have taken five to ten years. The so-called Elizabeth Gallery was built not before 1477 and the Margaret Gallery not before 1478; the construction of the Luther Gallery (Vogtei) was started in 1480. Further building activities from the seventeenth and nineteenth centuries can also be identified dendrochronologically.

BIBLIOGRAPHY

Baillie, M. G. L. *Tree-Ring Dating and Archaeology.* Ph.D. diss., Queen's University, 1973. Chicago: University of Chicago Press, 1982.
Eckstein, Dieter. *Dendrochronological Dating.* Handbooks for Archaeologists 2. Strasbourg: European Science Foundation, 1984.
Eckstein, Dieter, Thomas Eissing, and Peter Klein. *Dendrochronologische Datierung der Wartburg.* Cologne: Abteilung Architekturgeschichte des Kunsthistorischen Instituts der Universität zu Köln, 1992.
Hollstein, Ernst. *Mitteleuropäische Eichenchronologie: Trierer Dendrochronologische Forschungen zur Archäologie und Kunstgeschichte.* Trierer Grabungen und Forschungen 11. Mainz: Philipp von Zabern, 1980.
Schweingruber, Fritz Hans. *Tree Rings: Basics and Applications of Dendrochronology.* Dordrecht: Reidel, 1988.

Peter Klein

Deutschorden

Der Deutsche Orden (*Ordo Theutonicorum,* literally "The German Order," but more commonly known as the Teutonic Knights) was founded 1189/1190 at the siege of Acre to provide spiritual and hospital services for German crusaders. Its duties were enlarged in 1198 to include military service; within a few years its military role was more prominent than its hospital duties. The *Deutschorden,* like other military orders, could not maintain itself in the Holy Land solely from the lands it held there. Money, recruits, and reinforcements came from Germany and Italy, where it possessed lands, churches, and hospitals—gifts of friends, admirers, and relatives of members. By the early thirteenth century it was clear that the Crusade to the Holy Land was not going well. Christian territories had shrunk to the point that the military orders could not deploy the knights whom they had recruited and trained. Seeking to employ his knights usefully, Grandmaster Hermann von Salza (1210–1239) sent knights to Transylvania (1211–1225), Prussia (1226), and Livonia (1237). After the loss of Acre in 1291, the order concentrated on the struggle against Lithuanian pagans and Orthodox Russians. In 1309 the grandmaster moved his residence to Marienburg in Prussia.

There were three classes of membership: knights, often of ministerial and burgher ancestry, but as time passed, ever more of noble ancestry; priests; and serving brothers ("graymantles") who were men-at-arms and administrators rather than actual servants. They lived in convents like other orders of friars, but the knights spent their time training for war. Hunting was a popular pastime that kept men and horses in peak condition. In the fourteenth century, when grandmasters such as Winrich von Kniprode (1352–1382) were attracting prominent Western nobles to join summer and winter expeditions into Lithuania, the order became famous for chivalric display. Chaucer's knight came to Prussia in this era. In the fifteenth century, after the English, French, and German crusaders ceased to come to Prussia, the banquets degenerated into all-male drinking parties; nobles began to look on the order as a sinecure for their younger sons.

The order was especially well known for its Realpolitik. Rational planning can be seen in the organization of the Prussian state and its commerce, military strategy, and diplomacy to a degree unusual in this era. The officers did not hesitate to defy the pope when necessary, as was often the case when their interests were threatened by ambitious and capable ecclesiastical opponents and Christian monarchs.

Still, it would be a mistake to underestimate the members' piety. Religious duties were carried out faithfully under the supervision of officers often known for their personal zeal and of the priest brothers. Fast days and vigils were taken seriously. At one time the order petitioned the pope for permission to hear Matins before dawn because the days were so short during the Prussian winter that they needed every moment of light for warfare against the pagan foe.

There were three important regional groupings, each led by a master elected for life: Prussia, Livonia, and Germany. Each held annual chapter meetings, to which convents sent representatives and grand chapter meetings when necessary to discuss important business or elect a new grandmaster. There were disputes between these bodies, often acrimonious ones, even schisms; on a few occasions these resulted in civil war, coups, and threats of war. On the whole, however, the principles of poverty, obedience, and chastity prevailed over personal honor, individual or group ambition, and differing views concerning political and military strategy.

In 1308 the Prussian branch of the order became the dominant power of the region by annexing Pomerellia. Though the purchase of Brandenburg rights was technically correct, the action angered the Poles. For the rest of the century the Polish king was often an ally in the wars against the pagans, but occasionally hostile and always a potential enemy. At the Battle of Tannenberg (1410) King Jagiello of Poland and Duke Vytautas of Lithuania crushed the order's army. The balance of power shifted rapidly, with the order sinking ever deeper into impotence and irrelevance.

After 1525, when the last grandmaster in Prussia, Albrecht von Hohenzollern, converted that branch of the order to Protestantism, rendered homage to the king of Poland, and became duke of Prussia, the German master adopted his titles and authority. This reorganized order contained mixed convents, some part Roman Catholic, part Lutheran, part Evangelical. By 1590 the Roman Catholic convents of the order had evolved into a branch of the Habsburg military machine, providing officers and troops for the wars against the Turks in the Balkans. In 1809 this order was abolished and its possessions confiscated, but it was revived in 1834 as the *Deutschritterorden* (Order of German Knights) to provide hospital services and in 1866 as an honorary organization of the upper nobility. In 1918 the Habsburg connection dissolved. In 1929 the organization returned to its original function, a hospital order. Today it also provides ministerial services, providing priests to German-speaking congregations in countries where Germans are minorities.

BIBLIOGRAPHY

Burleigh, Michael. *Prussian Society and the German Order: An Aristocratic Corporation in Crisis c. 1410–1460.* Cambridge, England: Cambridge University Press, 1984.

Christiansen, Eric. *The Northern Crusades: The Baltic and the Catholic Frontier, 1100–1525.* Minneapolis: University of Minnesota Press, 1980.

Gli inizi del cristianesimo in Livonia-Lettonia and La cristianizzazione della Lituania. Vatican: Libreria editrice Vaticana, 1986–1987 [essays on the role of the crusaders in the conversion of the Baltic peoples].

Nicholson, Helen. *Templars, Hospitallers and Teutonic Knights: Images of the Military Orders, 1128–1291.* Leicester: Leicester University Press, 1993.

Riley-Smith, Jonathan. *The Crusades: A Short History.* New Haven, Conn.: Yale University Press, 1987.

Urban, William *The Samogitian Crusade.* Chicago: Lithuanian Research and Studies Center, 1989.

———. *The Baltic Crusade.* 1975. 2d rev. ed. Chicago: Lithuanian Research and Studies Center, 1994.

———. "The Teutonic Knights and the Baltic Crusades." *Historian* 56 (1994): 519–530.

William Urban

SEE ALSO

Crusades; Crusades, Recruitment; Ministeriales; Monasteries; Warfare

Devotio Moderna

The *Devotio moderna* (renewed, literally "modern devotion") was a Dutch religious movement begun in the 1370s consisting of houses of brothers and sisters living in common. Master Geert Grote founded the *Devotio moderna* in 1375 when he opened up his own home to the first sisters. The movement was characterized by a commitment to evangelical work, the surrender of private property to the community, and prayerful meditations. The brothers and sisters of the *Devotio moderna* produced some original texts (collations, exercises, and customaries), collections of excerpted spiritual writings, and copy work. The last of these documents were written around 1500.

The term "Devotio moderna" is usually rendered into English as the "Modern Devotion" and its adherents referred to as the "New Devout," but a more accurate translation of *moderna* is "renewed," as it was the renewal of apostolic devotion and not a new form of devotion that Master Geert and his students sought. This distinction between renewed and new was an important one to the New Devout because the movement never declared a new or different doctrinal position from that of the Roman Catholic Church. Although the houses often had their own rectors and confessors and heard in-house sermons (collations), their members, nevertheless, attended mass daily. Still, the New Devout distinguished themselves from other parishioners by attending mass separately and by prostrating themselves during mass.

The *Devotio moderna* was dedicated to evangelical work, that is, the conversion or "saving" of their neighbors. Such evangelizing took the form of "preaching" publicly in the town square and "teaching" individuals who came to the common house for instruction. The evangelical message, like their private meditations, focused on vice and virtue, judgment and salvation, and the life and Passion of Christ. The movement required chastity, charity, humility, and obedience of all its adherents. It stressed a characterization of God as a loving and compassionate father and as a nurturing mother, with frequent references to the milk of God feeding the Christian child.

Though Master Geert and a few of the movement's brothers and sisters were from the upper classes and were university educated, the vast majority of its members were of the middle and lower classes and were educated by the brothers and sisters in the group of teachers known as the Common Life. The adherents of the *Devotio moderna* regarded education and wealth with suspicion, declaring that any activity not also useful to spiritual progression was not a worthy pursuit. Members of the houses were required to surrender all their personal property to the common fund and demonstrate proper Christian humility at all times. For these reasons (voluntary poverty and a humble disposition), the community was suspicious of and in turn suspected by those of wealth or social pretension, including local patricians and the wealthy, often corrupt religious orders.

In addition to giving over their property and incomes to the common life, each brother and sister performed manual labor that served both practical and spiritual purposes. Practically, it provided the brothers and sisters with the financial support necessary to maintain the community chest. Spiritually, manual labor, seen as a necessary distraction from the world, was incorporated into their meditations. From the spiritual point of view the most highly regarded form of manual labor was the copying of religious texts, an activity that both brothers and sisters performed. In addition to copying, the sisters also participated in more traditional female work, such as sewing, tatting, and brewing.

In many respects the *Devotio moderna* resembled other spiritual separatist movements that were eventually declared heretical by the church, and, because of its criticism of corrupt clergy and its tendency to elevate the laity to positions of authority, the movement has been called proto-Protestant and is even credited with contributing to the Reformation. However, the *Devotio moderna* did not consider itself to be anti-Catholic or anti-church, having never taken up a doctrinal position in contradiction to the Catholic Church. In fact, the movement's main criticism of the church—excesses and corruption within the Roman Catholic hierarchy—was a concern that the Catholic or Counter-Reformation addressed. Furthermore, wherever the Protestant Reformation took hold, the houses of the common life disappeared, surviving the longest in the Catholic regions of Germany.

BIBLIOGRAPHY

Van Engen, John H., trans. *Devotio Moderna: Basic Writings.* New York: Paulist, 1988.

Rhonda L. Kelley

SEE ALSO

Mysticism; Preaching and Sermons, Dutch; Visionary Literature; Women

Dhuoda (ca. 800–ca. 845)

Few biographical details remain on Dhuoda, the only known female author of the Carolingian Renaissance. This well-educated noblewoman from a powerful Austrasian family married Bernard, duke of Septimania, at the royal palace at Aachen on June 29, 824. Bernard, a powerful imperial magnate, played an important but unpredictable role in the turbulent 830s and 840s. During the duke's extended absences between the births of their two sons, William (826) and Bernard (841), Dhuoda played a key role administering the province. To counter Bernard's emerging disloyalty, King Charles the Bald summoned William to court as a royal hostage in 841. In response, Dhuoda crafted her *Liber manualis* (Handbook) to guide her teenage son through his perilous stay at the palace. Tragically, she may have witnessed her husband's execu-

tion for treason in 844, and perhaps also that of William in 849 after his failed attempts to avenge his father's death. The younger Bernard (d. 886) lived long enough to carry on the family line, for it was his son, William the Pious of Aquitaine, who founded the monastery Cluny in 910. Dhuoda's own death date is unknown, but the *Liber*'s references to her recurring sickness, as well as its detailed instructions for her funeral, indicate that she may have died shortly after finishing her book in 843.

Although much of what is known of Dhuoda centers around the men in her life, her own work has commanded far greater scholarly interest. Written in the genre of the "mirror for princes," the *Liber manualis* endeavored to help William fulfill his complementary and sometimes contradictory roles of son, vassal, and Christian. Despite the author's protestations of ignorance, her advice exhibits an intimate and wide-ranging familiarity with scripture and patristics well situated within the broader literary and theological currents of the Carolingian era. Recent studies of Dhuoda's book have uncovered veiled critiques of Bernard's political inconstancy, as well as several inherent assertions of matriarchal authority. Once dismissed as artless and incoherent, the *Liber manualis* is a monument of medieval women's literature.

BIBLIOGRAPHY

Dhuoda. *Manuel pour mon fils,* ed. Pierre Riché, trans. Bernard de Vregille and Claude Mondésert. Sources chrétiennes 225. Paris: Les Éditions du Cerf, 1975.

———. *Handbook for William: A Carolingian Woman's Counsel for Her Son,* ed. and trans. Carol Neel. Lincoln: University of Nebraska Press, 1991.

Dronke, Peter. *Women Writers of the Middle Ages: A Critical Study of Texts from Perpetua (d. 203) to Marguerite Porete († 1310).* Cambridge: Cambridge University Press, 1984.

Claussen, Martin A. "Fathers of Power and Mothers of Authority: Dhuoda and the *Liber manualis.*" *French Historical Studies.* 19 (1996): 785–809.

Nelson, Janet. *Charles the Bald.* London: Longman, 1992.

Riché, Pierre. *The Carolingians: A Family Who Forged Europe,* trans. Michael Idomir Allen. Philadelphia: University of Pennsylvania Press, 1993.

Steven A. Stofferahn

Dialects

See Dutch Language, Dialects; German Language, Dialects; Gothic Language; Latin Language.

Diet and Nutrition

In medieval German literature the diet of the nobility is described as consisting of game, fish, and white bread; that of the peasants as dark bread, porridge, turnips, and sidemeat, i.e. the cheap cuts of pork. In these texts aristocrats drink wine, while peasants drink water, milk, cider, or beer. This rather simplistic view of the medieval diet does not yet take into account the bourgeoisie, which was becoming a significant cultural force in the later Middle Ages. Although the quantity of meat eaten in castles was higher than that in towns or in the countryside, only a small percentage of it was game. Domestic animals such as pigs, cattle, sheep, goats, and chickens were a much bigger source of meat. In addition, all classes depended heavily on grain and fruit. In Germany, oats and barley were preferred over millet. Studies of fecal waste have shown that cherries, plums, sloes, damsons, apples, pears, medlars, hazel- and walnuts, other types of berries, rose hips, and elderberries were the most popular fruit. Foodstuffs such as fruit and vegetables were normally eaten when in season; foods that had been preserved through marinating (kraut), salting (fish), smoking (meat), and drying (fruit, electuary), or fresh fruit (apples), were stored for the winter in cellars and larders. Whenever possible, animals such as fish and chickens were kept alive until they were needed in the kitchen. Small animals no longer a part of German cuisine included squirrels, hedgehogs, beavers, starlings, sparrows, and jays. Cooks, especially those of more modest households, used all the parts of an animal (meat, blood, head, inner organs) and turned them into purees, pies, and sausages. Finely chopped or mashed, foodstuffs were colored and/or filled in molds in the shape of mushrooms, fish, crayfish, eggs, and birds. Leftovers, too, were used to prepare new dishes. Herbs such as mint, sage, rue, leeks, onions, parsley, fennel, dill, caraway, lovage, mustard, watercress, juniper berries, celery, and horseradish were used fresh in the summer and dried in the winter. Most spices had to be imported and were therefore very expensive. The most affordable were pepper and ginger, followed by cinnamon, cloves, nutmeg, and saffron, which was approximately seven times more expensive than pepper. Other luxury goods were almonds, rice, and sugar, which were also in high esteem as foods for the sick and convalescent.

Fasting laws prohibited the consumption of meat, fowl, lard, eggs, and dairy products on every Friday and Saturday, all church holidays, during Lent, and before saints' holidays, which amounted to more than a third of the days of the Christian calendar. Those who could not afford fish had to live on hemp, lentils, beans, and bread. Poppy-, lin-, and rapeseed oil were substitutes for butter and lard in Germany.

The main meals of the day were eaten at sunrise, noon, and sundown and usually consisted of several courses. Most of the tableware was made of wood, metal, and pottery. Glass was still rare, and the cutlery included a knife and spoon, but no fork. According to medieval medicine, the right quantity, composition, and sequence of dishes was essential for maintaining or restoring the balance of the four humors (hot, cold, wet, dry) in the human body. German physicians such as Konrad von Eichstätt and Arnold von Bamberg wrote dietetic treatises (*Regimen sanitatis literature*) in which they described the humoral qualities of individual foodstuffs, and occasioanlly provided culinary recipes. This dietetic information later found its way into medieval German cookbooks.

New in the diet of fifteenth-century Germany are salads prepared from raw vegetables, pasta, and a variety of imported foods such as capers, figs, dates, lemons, limes, oranges, pomegranates, pine nuts, and carob beans. Wine, initially drunk by the nobility and on special occasions, had now become a drink consumed by everybody who could afford it, regardless of status.

BIBLIOGRAPHY

Adamson, Melitta Weiss. *Medieval Dietetics: Food and Drink in "Regimen Sanitatis" Literature from 800 to 1400.* Frankfurt am Main: Peter Lang, 1995.

Elsas, M. J. *Umriß einer Geschichte der Preise und Löhne in Deutschland. Vom ausgehenden Mittelalter bis zum Beginn des neunzehnten Jahrhunderts.* Leyden: Sijthoff's, 1936.

Janssen, Walter. "Essen und Trinken im frühen und hohen Mittelalter. Aus archäologischer Sicht." In *feestbundel voor prof. dr. J. G. N. Renaud.* Zutphen: De Walburg Pers, 1981, pp. 324–331.

Jones, George Fenwick. "The Function of Food in Mediaeval German Literature." *Speculum* 35 (1960): 78–86.

Kühnel, Harry, ed. "Nahrung." In *Alltag im Spätmittelalter.* Graz: Edition Kaleidoskop, 1984, pp. 196–236.

Wiegelmann, Günter. "Ethnologische Nahrungsforschung in Deutschland." *Ethnologia Europaea* 5 (1971): 99–108.

Melitta Weiss Adamson

SEE ALSO
Cookbooks

Dietrich und Wenezlan

This fragmentary Dietrich epic (499 lines), composed in rhymed couplets of Bavarian dialect, is preserved on two leaves of a parchment manuscript from the middle of the thirteenth century. It is the second-oldest surviving Dietrich epic; only the *Eckenlied* strophe from the *Carmina Burana* is older. The fragment might be the only surviving part of an epic called by der Marner *Der Riuzen Sturm*.

The fragment begins as Wolfhart, Dietrich's man, brings Dietrich a challenge from Wenezlan, a Polish prince. Wenezlan has taken both Wolfhart and Hildebrand hostage. Having heard of Dietrich's great strength, Wenezlan challenges him to a duel with the understanding that, if Dietrich does not accept the challenge, Wenezlan will kill the hostages. Dietrich hesitates. Wolfhart mentions that he and Hildebrand accompanied Dietrich into exile; such loyalty deserves support. Also, if Dietrich does not accept the challenge, Wenezlan will attack Etzel, with whom Dietrich is now allied.

Saying he was only joking, Dietrich accepts the challenge and informs Etzel of it. They order the army to fold its tents and march with them across the Salzach River into Wenezlan's territory. They arrive at nightfall and make camp (Lacuna).

Ladies watch from a magnificent tent as the duel begins. Wolfhart, seeing Dietrich in distress, urges him on to greater feats. The duel continues until evening. As the fragment ends, Dietrich wonders how long he will have to go on fighting.

The narrative combines elements of the historical and *aventiurehaften* (knightly quest) Dietrich epics in such a way that it is ambiguous with regard to its predominant tradition (see entries for *Alpharts Tod* and Albrecht von Kemenaten). As in many of the *aventiurehaften* texts, Dietrich refuses to accept a courtly challenge, and this results in unnecessary combat (see entry for Albrecht von Kemenaten). But the situation is also political, as in the "historical" Dietrich epics (see entry for *Alpharts Tod*). As in the *Nibelungenlied, Rabenschlacht,* and *Buch von Bern,* Dietrich is in exile with Etzel. When he understands that the situation threatens Etzel's interests and the lives of his men, he accepts the challenge. The duel in the presence of ladies is thus both necessary conflict and courtly game. In content, style, and composition, *Dietrich und Wenezlan* is most similar to *Biterolf und Dietleib,* another narrative in rhymed couplets that is ambiguous with regard to its predominant tradition and also involves an encounter with a prince of Poland.

BIBLIOGRAPHY

Firestone, Ruth H. "The Literary Classification of *Dietrich und Wenezlan:* A Reevaluation." *German Studies Review* 5 (1982): 9–20.

———. "On the Similarity of *Biterolf und Dietleib* and *Dietrich und Wenezlan.*" In *Comparative Research on Oral Traditions: A Memorial for Milman Parry,* ed. John Miles Foley. Columbus, Ohio: Slavica, 1987, pp. 161–183.

Heinzle, Joachim. *Mittelhochdeutsche Dietrichepik.* Zurich: Artemis, 1978, pp. 187–191, 290.

Zupitza, Julius. "Dietrich und Wenezlan." *Deutsches Heldenbuch 5.* Dublin: Weidmann, 1870; rpt. 1968, pp. 265–274.

Ruth H. Firestone

SEE ALSO

Buch von Bern and *Rabenschlacht; Carmina Burana; Dietrichepik; Eckenlied; Marner, Der; Nibelungenlied*

Dietrichepik

The figure of Dietrich von Bern, based loosely on the historical Ostrogothic king in Italy Theoderic the Great (r. 493–526), became the central figure of a wide variety of verse narratives composed during the High Middle Ages in Germany. The variety of these narratives along with the profusion of variant versions and their adaptations in the Norwegian *Thidrekssaga af Bern* suggests a wide distribution of oral tales in verse throughout the German-speaking world. The stories are composed in four-line strophes similar to that of the *Nibelungenlied (Alpharts Tod, der Wunderer, Rabenschlacht),* in rhymed couplets (*Biterolf und Dietleip, Laurin, Walberan, Dietrich und Wenzeland, Das Buch von Bern),* and in a clumsy thirteen-line stanza known as the *Bernerton,* or "Melody of Verona" *(Virginal, Eckenlied, Sigenot, Goldemar).* As far as content is concerned, it is traditional to divide the narratives into the historical *(Buch von Bern, Rabenschlacht, Alpharts Tod)* and the remainder, generally referred to as *märchenhaft* (fairy-tale-like) narratives. Dietrich also appears in the *Nibelungenlied* and in the *Rosengarten zu Worms* as a major character, and in some versions of the *Wolfdietrich* he is inserted as Wolfdietrich's grandson. The legendary *history* "story" of Dietrich appears all together only in the Norwegian saga. Dietrich is presented as a king of the Amelungs in Bern (Verona), who is the nephew of the Roman emperor Ermenrich. After being falsely accused by his uncle's evil adviser, he is driven from his lands and spends thirty years in exile at the court of Etzel (Attila the Hun). During this time he takes part in an attempt to retake his lands that is militarily successful but leads to the death of the sons of Etzel and his return to Etzel in mourning. He is also involved in the cataclysmic battle with the Nibelungs/Burgundians that concludes the *Nibelungenlied,* and most of his men are killed. He finally returns to his land and rules until his death.

The legendary history of Dietrich arose soon after his lifetime in heroic stories. It essentially turns his historical career on its head, since he ruled competently over his kingdom for thrity-three years and was never driven from it. The story was well established by the time of composition of the ninth-century *Hildebrandslied,* which features Dietrich's weapons-master and also refers to Dietrich's enemy as Otachre, a name clearly derived from that of the historical enemy of Theoderic, Odoacer. The villainous Ermanaric was later substituted for Odoacer, in spite of his having died more than a century before Dietrich's reign.

BIBLIOGRAPHY

Firestone, Ruth H. *Elements of Traditional Structure in the Couplet Epics of the Late Middle High German Dietrich Cycle.* Göppingen: Kümmerle, 1975.

Haymes, Edward R., and Susann T. Samples. *Heroic Legends of the North: An Introduction to the Nibelung and Dietrich Cycles.* Garland Reference Library of the Humanities 1403. New York: Garland, 1996.

Heinzle, Joachim. *Mittelhochdeutsche Dietrichsepik.* Zurich: Artemis, 1978.

Hoffmann, Werner. *Mittelhochdeutsche Heldendichtung.* Berlin: Schmidt, 1974.

Wisniewski, Roswitha. *Mittelalterliche Dietrichdichtung.* Stuttgart: Metzler, 1986.

Edward R. Haymes

SEE ALSO

Alpharts Tod; Buch von Bern and *Rabenschlacht;* Chronicles, Regional/Territorial, German; *Dietrich und Wenezlan; Hildebrandslied; Nibelungenlied*

Dinkelsbühl

Founded between 1170 and 1180 at the site of a preexisting settlement on the Wörnitz River, Dinkelsbühl is one of the most noteworthy medieval settlements in Franconia. The town developed around the crossing of an important north-south road used as part of a pilgrimage route to Rome and an east-west road that led to a ford across the Wörnitz. Travel logs attest to visits from kings and emperors, and under Rudolf von Habsburg, who came to Dinkelsbühl in 1285, the town became a *Reichsstadt* (imperial city). The economy of Dinkelsbühl depended primarily on market trade, and its craftsmen were respected particularly for the production of woven goods, scythes, and sickles.

The wall around Dinkelsbühl, completed in 1430, and an early Gothic gate tower, the Wörnitz Tor, are well preserved to this day. Between 1448 and 1492, the late Gothic, three-aisle church dedicated to St. George, the Georgskirche, was constructed on the foundation of the first parish church, the Romanesque Bartholomäuskirche. Although the exterior of the Georgskirche was never completed, it is one of the most remarkable *Hallenkirchen* (hall churches) in southern Germany. The Gothic church tower incorporates the Romanesque base and portal of the earlier west facade.

From the late fifteenth century, the economy of Dinkelsbühl began to decline so that its craftsmen produced wares primarily to serve the needs of the immediately surrounding areas. Spared serious damage during the Thirty Years' War, the town retains much of its fifteenth-century character even today.

BIBLIOGRAPHY

Bunting, James. *Bavaria.* New York: Hastings House, 1972, pp. 49–51.

Gluth, Paul. *Dinkelsbühl.* Dinkelsbühl: Wenng, 1985.

Ruth M. W. Moskop

SEE ALSO

Gothic Art and Architecture; Romanesque Art and Architecture

Diocese

The diocese is a telling marker of the decline of the Roman Empire, the concomitant rise of Christianity, and the growth of medieval Germany. Originally an occasional unit of Roman civil administration, the diocese was employed by Diocletian (284–305) in his reorganization of the empire when, on top of the existing provincial structure, he added four prefectures and twelve dioceses. As the emperors of the following century adopted Christianity as the sole official religion of the empire, what had been largely an urban religion now necessarily had to expand into the countryside *(pagus)* to embrace the *pagani* (pagans) living there. And in the rapidly disintegrating West in particular, bishops came to govern these areas increasingly called "dioceses," although these were much smaller than those of Diocletian.

The original eight dioceses of what later became medieval Germany were largely defined by the outer limits of Roman occupation, in a line along the Rhine running from Constance to Cologne and including Trier on the Moselle. According to tradition, bishops are attested in all these cities in the fourth century. While it is unclear whether Augsburg had bishops this early, in these cities it is problematical whether bishops continued to rule during the disasters of the fifth and sixth centuries. Continuity does exist from the seventh century onward here as well as in Augsburg, Brixen, and Regensburg. Thereafter the progress was steady and marched pari passu (side by side) with the work of conversion and, increasingly, of conquest conducted by both the Franks and the Bavarians. Thus around 700 Salzburg came into being, and in the eighth century the Bavarian dioceses of Freising, Passau, Würzburg, Eichstätt, and Bremen were founded. In the ninth no fewer than eight new dioceses were created, and at least another ten in the tenth. To provide order for this extraordinary growth, metropolitan or archiepiscopal sees were established de novo (as new) or by elevation of existing bishoprics: Mainz, Salzburg, Trier, and Cologne between circa 780 and 800; Hamburg-Bremen in 848; and Magdeburg by 968. New dioceses continued to be founded into the thirteenth century as expansion into Scandinavian and especially Slavic lands continued. Thus for the Teutonic Knights (Die Deutschorden) Prussia was divided in 1243 into four exempt dioceses whose bishops were completely subject to the order. But elsewhere the outer limits of the German church and empire had already been demarcated by the popes' creation between circa 1000 and 1164 of archdioceses and primatial (church officials') sees for Poland, Hungary, Denmark, Norway, and Sweden. Significantly, however, the diocese of Prague, created in 973, remained in the province of Mainz until its separation and elevation to an archbishopric in 1344—a clear sign of the special place of the kingdom of Bohemia in the empire.

By 1500 there were about sixty dioceses in Germany. It is difficult to be precise about the number, for much depends on whether one counts exempt dioceses and especially those in the penumbra of the empire (e.g., Metz, Toul, Verdun, Besançon, Breslau). Although German dioceses varied greatly in size, they were on average much larger than those in Italy (where there were nearly 250) or

even England (17). Even more distinctive was the fact that from the High Middle Ages about four dozen of them developed into prince-bishoprics whose incumbents ruled both dioceses as bishops and territories (usually called *Hochstifte, Erzstifte* in the case of archbishoprics) as princes. Dioceses and *Hochstifte* were never coterminous, and in the case of Constance the bishop ruled the largest diocese and one of the smallest *Hochstifte* in the empire. This disparity became increasingly significant in the fourteenth and especially the fifteenth centuries with the progressive extension of princely power over the church. In those regions where one form or another of "Reformation" was introduced in the sixteenth century, the "diocese" subject to Catholic bishops came to be effectively restricted to the confines of the *Hochstifte* until the end of the Old Reich (empire).

BIBLIOGRAPHY

Gatz, Erwin, and Clemens Brotkorb, ed. *Die Bischöfe des Heiligen Römischen Reiches 1448 bis 1648. Ein biographisches Lexikon.* Berlin: Duncker and Humblot, 1996.

Hauck, Albert. *Kirchengeschichte Deutschlands.* 5 vols. in 6, 1911–1929; rpt. Berlin: Akademie-Verlag, 1954.

Jedin, Hubert, et al., eds. *Atlas zur Kirchengeschichte.* Freiburg: Herder, 1970.

Lawrence G. Duggan

SEE ALSO

Augsburg; Constance; Cologne, Archdiocese; *Deutschorden;* Eichstätt; Empire; Freising; Metz; Moselle; Regensburg; *Reich;* Trier; Würzburg

Dirc van Delf (ca. 1365–ca. 1404)

Dirc van Delf, author of Dutch religious texts, was one of the most learned men of his time. He was probably born in Delft (county of Holland) around 1365. At an early age he entered the Dominican convent at Utrecht. After many years of study he became doctor of theology. From December 1399 onward we find him at the court of Duke Albrecht of Bavaria, count of Holland, in The Hague. There he had the function of court chaplain, but he also lectured at German universities, such as Cologne and Erfurt. We lose all trace of Dirc van Delf after the death of his patron Albrecht in the year 1404.

In 1401, a book presumably written by Dirc for countess Margaret of Cleves, wife of Albrecht, is mentioned in the accounts of the court in The Hague, but unfortunately it has not survived. For Duke Albrecht he started writing around 1403 the *Tafel van den Kersten Ghelove (Handbook of the Christian Faith),* a scholastic summa, or compendium, in the vernacular. Stylistically, it is one of the best Middle Dutch prose works, and is indeed one of the most learned encyclopedias of all European vernacular languages. The text consists of two large parts: the Winterstuc (Winter Piece) and the Somerstuc (Summer Piece). The main source of the *Tafel van den Kersten Ghelove* is the *Compendium of Religious Truths (Compendium theologicae veritatis)* by Hugh Ripelin of Strasbourg (also known as Hugo Argentinensis, ca. 1210–ca. 1270), but Dirc made use of many other Latin sources as well. Dirc's personal achievement consists in his regrouping and reformulating of this large amount of knowledge. He always takes into account the intellectual level of his audience, and his use of images often corresponds with the experiences of the members of the court. His work deals with the whole creation: there are, among others, chapters about God, the creation of the world, the creation of humankind, the angels, more scientific subjects like the planets, the four elements, physiognomy, and also virtues and vices, God's mercy, the life of Christ, the acts of the apostles, the ecclesiastical hierarchy, works of mercy, liturgy, the sacraments, social order, the Antichrist, and the Last Judgment. Using the Aristotelian system of dialectical reasoning, Dirc expounds God's perfect plan for the laity: nothing is without sense or reason. Finally, he significantly enriched the Middle Dutch vocabulary with neologisms from scholasticism.

His dedication manuscript that has come down to us is illuminated with superb miniatures with an aesthetic as well as a didactic function. They form a concrete support of the text. Besides richly illuminated manuscripts for the aristocracy, less luxuriously executed manuscripts have survived as well. The latter were used by the clergy and especially in nunneries and Beguine communities. In an environment where knowledge of Latin could be problematic, the vernacular *Tafel van den Kersten Ghelove* filled a need for religious reading material. In addition, many miscellanies with religious texts contain excerpts from the *Tafel van den Kersten Ghelove.* A Middle Low German adaptation exists as well.

BIBLIOGRAPHY

Daniëls, F. A. M. *Meester Dirc van Delf. Zijn persoon en zijn werk.* Utrecht: N. V. Dekker en Van de Vegt en J. W. van Leeuwen, 1932.

———, ed. *Meester Dirc van Delf, Tafel van den Kersten Ghelove.* 4 vols. Utrecht: N. V. Dekker and Van de Vegt en J. W. van Leeuwen, 1937–1939.

van Oostrom, Frits P. *Court and Culture: Dutch Literature, 1350–1450.* Berkeley: University of California Press, 1992.

An Faems

Divorce
See Marriage and Divorce.

Donation of Constantine

Although one of the most important and well-known forgeries of the Middles Ages, the date of composition and purpose of the Donation (German, *Schenkung*) of Constantine, or *Constitutum Constantini,* remain unclear. It has been seen as a document designed to support papal efforts to strengthen ties with the Frankish kingdom or to undermine Byzantine rights in Italy. Others have argued that the forgery was designed to legitimize papal claims to the Exarchate (Eastern Church). The Donation is thought to have been intended to assert the papacy's emancipation from the constitutional structure of the Eastern Empire, and may have also asserted the papacy's own independence and political legitimacy in Italy. The Donation, whatever its origin, would have a long career in defense or in opposition to papal authority until proved a forgery by Lorenzo Valla in 1439.

There is consensus that the Donation was written in the 750s by a Lateran cleric, possibly with the knowledge of Pope Stephen II, and was associated with the coronation and Donation of Pippin, by which Ravenna was given to the papacy. The forgery was based on the legends of Pope Sylvester I, which had existed since the fifth century. The first part of the Donation describes the events of Constantine's conversion, including being cured of leprosy and instructed in matters of the faith by Sylvester. In this section, Constantine asserts the importance of Rome as the city of Peter and Paul and as the ultimate authority in matters of orthodoxy. In the second part, Constantine makes his donation to the papacy prior to his own departure for the new capital in the east. He grants the pope supremacy over the sees of Antioch, Alexandria, Constantinople, Jerusalem, and all the churches of the world, and he grants temporal authority over "Judea, Greece, Asia, Thrace, Africa, Italy, and various islands." Most important, Constantine bestows on the pope "our palace [the Lateran], the city of Rome and all the provinces, districts, and cities of Italy or of the western regions."

Although its origins remain unclear, the later history of the Donation is more definite. The forgery was involved in the struggles between church and state and manipulated by advocates on both sides. In the late ninth century, Frankish bishops inserted the Donation into canon law collections to secure ecclesiastical property rights. In the eleventh century emperors and popes passed judgment on the document. Otto III questioned the authenticity of the Donation and rejected the "mendacious privileges" and "fictitious writings" found in the document. The Gregorian Reformers found support for their territorial claims in Italy and rights to primacy in the Donation. It also provided a framework for the ceremonial and political programs of the Gregorians, especially their claim to control of the imperial dignity. In the twelfth century, Innocent II saw in the Donation justification for the continued "imperialization" of the papacy, and in the thirteenth century Innocent III inferred from the Donation rights to intervene in imperial elections. Indeed, the Donation influenced political and religious affairs long after its origins in the Carolingian period.

BIBLIOGRAPHY

The Donation of Constantine, in *Carolingian Civilization: A Reader,* ed. Paul Edward Dutton. Peterborough, Ontario: Broadview, 1993.

Furhman, Horst, ed. *Constitutum Constantini.* Monumenta Germaniae Historica, Fontes 10. Hanover: Hahn, 1968.

Noble, Thomas. *The Republic of St. Peter: The Birth of the Papal State, 680–825.* Philadelphia: University of Pennsylvania Press, 1984.

Ullmann, Walter. *The Growth of Papal Government in the Middle Ages,* 3d ed. London: Methuen, 1970.

Michael Frassetto

SEE ALSO
Carolingians; Charlemagne; Otto III; Pippin

Drama

Those who think of "drama" as a branch of literature practiced by writers of talent or genius from classical Antiquity to the present must abandon this notion when investigating drama in medieval Germany. Nearly all German plays are anonymous, and most are the work of civic committees or of clerks hired for the occasion, not of "writers" esteemed for their craft. Men could make their living in medieval Germany writing and performing love songs or religious and gnomic poetry, or writing sacred or secular stories in verse, but we do not know that anyone in medieval Germany made a living writing, performing, directing, or producing plays. These activities fell to amateurs who were fully engaged by other professions most of the year. At a given season they might fill roles in a dramatic performance for a particular audience, whether this was the congregation of a church or the townspeople and visitors assembled on a city square. The scripts for these plays were not regarded as "literature" and so were often not preserved—at least the paucity of play texts in comparison with documented performances supports this inference. In these respects, medieval drama has much in common with the amateur theatricals and civic pageants of today.

Modern assumptions about the nature of drama are also a poor guide to the medieval phenomenon because they are largely derived from tenets in Aristotle's *Poetics,* as these have been embodied in and modified by centuries of European and American dramaturgy. One often meets the criticism that medieval plays are incoherent and disorganized. It is a commonplace of Hrosvit criticism, for example, that her *Gallicanus* consists of two independent actions loosely connected by the presence of the titular hero, but what criteria are appropriate to Hrosvit's tenth-century work? She had no knowledge of, hence no concern with, Aristotelian unities. The aesthetics of medieval drama do not arise in classical antiquity, and one must not approach it with modern assumptions about the literary construction of "drama" or the characteristics of a "good play."

Although there were no theaters in medieval Germany, there were stages (at the simplest, platforms indoors or outdoors that permitted spectators better lines of sight). Costumes and properties were used, and special effects could be created. One may accordingly speak of the drama as "staged impersonation for dramatic effect," i.e., role playing intended to move spectators emotionally and (sometimes) cognitively.

The great majority of plays depict events from Christian sacred history with the purpose of confirming the spectators' understanding of their religious significance. These plays do not so much teach new lessons as confirm old ones; they justify Christian tradition and many offices and activities of both church and state, serving in this way a deeply conservative social purpose. Medieval German drama as a communal activity sponsored and financed by institutions of governance (often city councils) was no place for the questioning of commonly held beliefs. Secular drama had greater freedom in this regard than did sacred, partly because of its close connection to Carnival, and seems thus to have enjoyed the seasonal license of transgression. Even so, it restricted its sharpest barbs to common human failings in such areas as sexuality and business life.

The beginnings of German drama can be traced back at least to the tenth century (Easter plays). Key moments in the gospel narrative of Jesus' death and resurrection were expanded verbally and accompanied by gestures and movements. Just how elaborate these expansions could become at an early date is shown by the tenth-century *Regularis concordia,* in which costumes, props, and body language are specified, but this *English* document can only be suggestive for German practices. Nonetheless, twelfth-century German manuscripts from the monastery of St. Lambrecht (Rhineland Palatinate) transmit an Easter liturgical drama in Latin that calls for dramatic action ("let the cantor appoint two, one old and the other young, who, after the shouting of the crowd has been finished, should come to the sepulcher, the youth first and let him wait; let the old man, following, gaze attentively into the tomb . . . ," Bevington 1975: 38) in which the congregation was to participate by singing hymns in German ("the shouting of the crowd"). It is a very long way from this playlet to the Easter spectacles staged in the fifteenth and even sixteenth centuries, which could involve hundreds of people, last for days, and cost a lot of money, nor is the development linear—i.e., the relatively simple dramatizations of the early centuries do not give way uniformly and progressively to elaborate productions. In the chapbook *Til Eulenspiegel,* published in 1515, the thirteenth prank is about Til sabotaging a little Easter play traditionally staged in the village church, in which the priest plays Jesus, his maid the angel, and two peasants the three (sic) Marys. Such village enactments, as well as grand urban spectacles, must have been familiar to the readership of the book.

The roots of serious drama in Christian liturgy connect it firmly to the Latin language. By the end of the Middle Ages, however, the use of Latin had shrunk to a few moments of highly liturgical character (in Til Eulenspiegel's prank, both the maid and one of the peasants recites in Latin). In general, the reduction of Latin and the growing predominance of German in religious plays parallels their progression out of the church and into the marketplace for performance, as well as their textual expansion: it became ever more necessary to give access through vernacular speech to the content of the impersonations, which moved ever further from their familiar gospel origins. This general development does not, however, serve to explain the relations of Latin and German in each specific play. The complex dramas found in the thirteenth-century manuscript of the *Carmina Burana* are basically Latin, but the long Passion play includes German lyrics for songs sung by Mary Magdalene. Almost contemporary is the Easter play transmitted (in fragments) by a manuscript once in the monastic library at Muri, Switzerland, which is entirely in German. This was long regarded as "the first drama in German," but recent scholarship has argued persuasively that this particular manuscript, written for a prompter, included only the German portion of the play, which was original, and omitted all the traditional Latin material, which was so familiar that no performer would have stumbled over it. The relationship of Latin and the vernacular in medieval German dramas is a basic research problem.

As the language of educated discourse, Latin was also used for nonbiblical dramas in the earlier centuries. Hrosvit, a cannoness at the abbey Gandersheim (Saxony), wrote six short plays in Latin, supposedly in imitation of Terence, around the middle of the tenth century. Although these did not influence the development of mainstream German drama, they are little jewels from a person who had the intuitions and instincts of a fine playwright as well as a keen, subtle mind, a good measure of self-esteem, and pride in her gender. Three plays featuring Roman emperors (*Gallicanus; Agape, Chionia and Irene; Sapientia*) study the relationship of political power and Christian truth, and thus constitute oblique advice to the Ottonian imperial court. Hrosvit was closely connected with this court through her abbess, teacher, and friend Gerberg, a niece of Emperor Otto the Great. Her pair of prostitute dramas, *Maria* and *Thais,* are similar in showing young women lost in the carnal world and apparently redeemed through the efforts of elderly, celibate monks, but these formidable heroines pursue holiness passionately once their ignorance (their despair of forgiveness) is removed, and in the case of Maria this ignorance must be charged to her well-intentioned but bumbling male mentor, the hermit Abraham. Hrosvit was a writer many centuries ahead of her time.

Another Latin play of remarkable originality and depth is the *Play of Antichrist* from the late twelfth century, preserved in a manuscript from the Tegernsee monastery (Bavaria). It presents a complex political action involving the German king (who is also the Holy Roman emperor) and the kings of France, Greece, Jerusalem, and Babylon. After a first section, in which the German emperor subdues the Western world for the Faith, Antichrist appears and confounds the entire empire—last of all the emperor himself, and then only through false miracles—before God strikes him down. This play glorifies in eschatological perspective the Hohenstaufen dynasty of Frederick I Barbarossa. It has been argued that a performance must have required an outdoor arena the size of a polo field, on which elaborate equestrian and martial exercises could be presented, as well as the dialog and singing contained in the manuscript.

One gains good insights into fully fledged German religious drama of the Middle Ages from the *Frankfurt Director's Script,* written in the first half of the fourteenth century. The manuscript, a roll made of seven parchment pages glued together, contains stage directions in red ink and the first words of speeches and songs in black. These outline a Passion play that lasted two days and was a huge undertaking, requiring more than eighty actors on the first day alone and giving cues for some four hundred speeches and songs. It begins with a series of messianic prophecies from seven Old Testament authorities brought forward by St. Augustine in an effort to persuade Jews of the truth of Christianity. They are scorned by the Jews, however, so Augustine calls for a dramatization of sacred history to be performed as another way to convince the unbelievers. The following Passion play is thus a play within the play. It begins with the story of John the Baptist and scenes from Jesus' public life, from his baptism through various healings; there follow the Sermon on the Mount, the raising of Lazarus, the entry into Jerusalem, the meal with Simon the Pharisee and the anointing by Mary Magdalene, then the heart of the Passion story, the Last Supper through the Crucifixion. The play does not end here, however, but includes the Resurrection and standard scenes from Easter play tradition, culminating in Jesus' Ascension. The final two scenes are a return to the frame, the conflict between Christians and Jews regarding the true faith, and Church disputes successfully with Synagogue, from whom a group of "eight or ten" Jews fall away and request baptism. This baptism is staged, as the insignia of authority (robe and crown) fall from the figure of Synagogue. Both the main action and the frame demonstrate to the play's audience the correctness of Christian belief and the eventual triumph of the Faith over even the obdurate Jews.

Medieval religious drama is centered on the events of Holy Week, to which by far the greatest number of texts pertains. The Christmas season was also dramatically productive, though to a lesser degree, and there is at least one play each transmitted for Corpus Christi, Whitsuntide, the Ascension, the Assumption, and other feasts. There are also saints' plays, and a group about the Last Judgment. In contrast with this fecundity of staged impersonations dealing with Christianity, plays treating purely secular themes are very few before the middle of the fifteenth century, when the urban Shrovetide (Carnival, or *Fastnachtspiel*) play tradition is preserved in manuscripts. One is sure that there were secular plays before the written evidence begins, but little can be said of them that is not conjecture.

Secular drama emerges toward the end of the fourteenth century. Manuscripts hold hints of a tradition of mummery or simple playmaking about *The Conflict of Spring [May] and Fall.* The merits of the seasons are advanced by comical advocates—"Lily Bush" praises spring as the time of natural beauty and refined love, "Bold Toper" extols fall as the season of the vintage. The form of the "plays" is that of a simple revue, serial speech making. This conflict between high and low culture was no doubt made comical by the exaggerations of the rivals not only in words but also in costumes, characterizations, and mime. Audience sympathy was certainly on the side of "Bold Toper," who stands for the indulgences of the vintage, hence by implication for instincts and appetites released from all the fetters of life in medieval communities.

There are plays from roughly the same period that feature Neidhart, a chivalric hero derived from a thirteenth-century troubadour of this name, in his entanglements with hostile peasants. The plot of the earliest "Neidhart play" (just sixty-six lines, in a manuscript dated 1360–1370) gives a feeling for the type: Who will find the first flower of spring? The duchess of Austria will bestow her special favor on that person. Neidhart spots a flower and places his hat over it for safekeeping, then hurries off to fetch the duchess and her court. She comes on stage, lifts the hat—and is disgusted, outraged at Neidhart! (The audience probably saw mimed what we can only deduce from parallel versions of this plot: that peasants observed Neidhart making his discovery, then one of them picked the flower when Neidhart had gone and promptly defecated on the very spot before replacing the hat). This scatological prank is at the center of the five Neidhart plays transmitted, the longest of which (around 2,600 lines) exceeds well-known Easter plays in textual length.

Secular drama achieves full growth in the fifteenth century with the proliferation of Carnival plays. About

150 have been preserved; most are from the major urban cultures of Lübeck and Nuremberg, but a cluster comes from Tyrol. In the prolific Nuremberg tradition, they are brief theatrical entertainments for the pre-Lenten period performed in taverns or private homes by apprentices and journeymen in the trades, and feature simple humor derived from bodily functions—reproductive or excretory—or social friction (dishonest workmen, shrewish wives). In form they vary from the simple revue, a sequence of autonomous speeches directed to a core problem or conflict, such as a wife's complaint that her husband is no good sexually, to one-act dramas with several roles and discernible development. The tradition in Lübeck, which can be dated back at least to 1430 and may thus be the earliest, was somewhat different. Performers were young men from well-to-do families, organized in fraternities, and performances took place on open-air stages. Unfortunately not one Lübeck play survives in manuscript, although we do possess a register of titles of seventy-three plays, from which it appears that many of these treated serious subjects in a serious manner.

From Nuremberg, over 100 late medieval Carnival plays are known (to which the eighty-three plays of this kind by the early modern author Hans Sachs could be added). The earliest play that can be dated with confidence was written in 1456 by the artisan Hans Rosenplüt—untypically, it is a serious piece on the menace of the Turk to Christian Europe—so the Nuremberg tradition (which was exported to Tyrol) is a phenomenon of the end of the Middle Ages. The plays are usually short and vulgar, suitable for the amusement of a crowd drinking strong beer and requiring little or no rehearsal. "The Doctor's Play" is 102 lines long, with four roles: three servants bring the urine of their master or mistress to a doctor for analysis; he concludes that a peasant has eaten bad meat and needs to empty his bowels, the young wife whose old husband can't satisfy her at night needs a young lover, and a housemaid is not sick but pregnant, for which the "cure" is a cradle. If the long and rich tradition of religious plays in medieval Germany expresses the spiritual hunger of the people and serves to legitimate the ecclesiastical and political status quo, then the Carnival plays that erupt in the fifteenth century express in a compensatory manner the carnality of urban populations and their skepticism of established, late medieval institutions.

BIBLIOGRAPHY

Bergmann, Rolf. "Spiele, Mittelalterliche geistliche." In *Reallexikon der deutschen Literaturgeschichte,* 2d ed., 5 vols. Berlin: de Gruyter, 1958–1988, vol. 4, pp. 64–100.

———. "Überlieferung, Interpretation und literaturgeschichtliche Stellung des Osterspiels von Muri." *Internationales Archiv für Sozialgeschichte der deutschen Literatur* 9 (1984): 1–21.

———. *Katalog der deutschsprachigen geistlichen Spiele und Marienklagen des Mittelalters.* Munich: Beck, 1986.

Bevington, David, comp. *Medieval Drama.* Boston: Houghton Mifflin, 1975

Brett-Evans, David. *Von Hrosvit bis Folz und Gengenbach. Eine Geschichte des mittelalterlichen deutschen Dramas.* 2 vols. Grundlagen der Germanistik 15, 18. Berlin: Erich Schmidt, 1975.

Die deutsche Literatur des Mittelalters. Verfasserlexikon, ed. Kurt Ruh et al., 2d ed. Berlin: de Gruyter, 1978ff. [authoritative reference work, in progress, articles on many individual works and authors important for medieval German drama] wherein: *Frankfurter Dirigierrolle* [Frankfurt Director's Script], vol. 2, cols. 808–812. *Hrosvit von Gandersheim,* vol. 4, cols. 196–210. *Osterfeiern* [Easter offices], vol. 7, cols. 92–108. *Osterspiel von Muri* [Easter Play from Muri], vol. 7, cols. 119–124. *Rosenplütsche Fastnachtspiele* [Carnival plays in the style of Hans Rosenplüt], vol. 8, cols. 211–232. *Tegernsee Ludus de Antichristo* [Play of Antichrist], vol. 9, cols. 673–679.

Dronke, Peter. "Hrosvitha." In *Women Writers of the Middle Ages: A Study of Texts from Perpetua († 203) to Marguerite Porete († 1310).* Cambridge: Cambridge University Press, 1984, pp. 55–83, 293–297.

Froning, Richard, ed. *Das Drama des Mittelalters.* Stuttgart, 1891f.; rpt. Darmstadt: Wissenschaftliche Buchgesellschaft, 1964.

Hardison, O. B., Jr. *Christian Rite and Christian Drama in the Middle Ages.* Baltimore: Johns Hopkins University Press, 1965.

von Keller, Adalbert. *Fastnachtspiele aus dem 15. Jahrhundert.* 4 vols. Stuttgart, 1853, 1858; rpt. Darmstadt: Wissenschaftliche Buchgesellschaft, no. 7, 1965.

Linke, Hansjürgen. "Vom Sakrament bis zum Exkrement. Ein Überblick über Drama und Theater des deutschen Mittelalters." In *Theaterwesen und dramatische Literatur,* ed. Günter Holtus. Tübingen: Francke, 1987, pp. 127–164.

———. "Germany and German-speaking Central Europe." In *The Theatre of Medieval Europe: New Research in Early Drama,* ed. Eckehard Simon. Cambridge:

Cambridge University Press, 1991, pp. 207–224 [trans. by the editor].

Michael, Wolfgang F. *Das deutsche Drama des Mittelalters.* Berlin: de Gruyter, 1971.

Neumann, Bernd. *Geistliches Schauspiel im Zeugnis der Zeit. Zur Aufführung mittelalterlicher Dramen im deutschen Sprachgebiet.* 2 vols. Munich: Artemis, 1987.

Simon, Eckehard. "Drama." In *Dictionary of the Middle Ages.* New York: Scribners, 1982–1989, vol. 4, pp. 266–272.

Wuttke, Dieter, ed. *Fastnachtspiele des 15. und 16. Jahrhunderts,* 4th ed. Stuttgart: Reclam, 1989.

Young, Karl. *The Drama of the Medieval Church.* 2 vols. London: Oxford University Press, 1933; rpt. 1951, 1962, 1967.

Stephen L. Wailes

SEE ALSO

Carmina Burana; Drama, Christmas Plays; Drama, Dutch; Drama, Easter Plays; Drama, Last Judgment Plays; Hrosvit of Gandersheim; Lübeck; Neidhart; Nuremberg

Drama, Christmas Plays

While not as widely performed and attested as Passion plays and Easter plays—there are only eight play manuscripts—Christmas plays still formed an essential part of the annual cycle of religious drama in the German-speaking part of Central Europe. As with Easter plays, Christmas plays were performed only during the appropriate liturgical season; however, Passion plays and Corpus Christi plays may also include representations of the Nativity. In contrast to the more expansive Passion and Easter plays, even the larger of the Christmas plays remains somewhat shorter—the Christmas play from Hesse (ca. 1450) has 870 lines and 27 parts.

In a wider sense, these plays present the story of Jesus' Nativity and closely related incidents: the Annunciation, the Visitation, his birth, the visits by the shepherds and Magi, the murder of the innocents, the flight to Egypt, and the purification of Mary. They may also include prophets plays in which the coming of Jesus is foretold. More narrowly, Christmas plays are those that depict the core moments of the Nativity. In the German tradition, however, a special scene is added in which the baby is rocked in a cradle (the *Kindelwiegen*), and he is entertained with special songs and dances. Some of these car-

ols—such as "Joseph, lieber neve mein" and "In dulci jubilo"—are still popular today.

The plays show Latin roots, having grown out of prophets plays and Christmas liturgies. As with all medieval religious drama, however, the role of apocryphal religious literature is also immense. Of the earlier plays, the most developed is the Latin Benediktbeuern Christmas Play (early thirteenth century). A major component of this play—based on the pseudo-Augustinian *Sermo contra Judeos, Paganos, et Arianos*—is its lengthy prophets play, in which the coming of Jesus is foretold by the prophets from the Old Testament. These prophecies are then opposed by Archisynagogus. The oldest theatrical Christmas scenes in German come not from an independent play but, rather, from the Himmelgarten Passion fragment (mid–thirteenth century). The first separate Christmas play comes from St. Gall (ca. 1330), but most texts date from the late fifteenth and early sixteenth centuries. From the Erlau collection, we have a crib play and a Magi play (fifteenth century). The Christmas play from Hesse (ca. 1450), with its numerous coarsely comical elements, is among the most developed of this genre: Joseph struggles with the maidservants and others; the shepherds bring to the baby their all-too-earthly requests, including protection of their sheep from wolves. There is also a play from Sterzing (1511) and a fragmentary Swabian Christmas play from the early fifteenth century, first published in the 1970s.

Current research has benefited most from the renewed interest in performance records and from a catalog of religious drama. These have shown that the performance of plays related to the Christmas season was more widespread than manuscript evidence indicates. There is also a newly edited Annunciation play from the "Debs Manuscript." No German-language Christmas play has been translated into English thus far, and only the Latin Benediktbeuern Christmas play is currently available in translation.

BIBLIOGRAPHY

Bergmann, Rolf. "Spiele, Mittelalterliche geistliche." In *Reallexikon der deutschen Literaturgeschichte,* ed. Werner Kohlschmidt and Wofgang Mohr. Berlin: de Gruyter, 1958ff.

Bevington, David, ed., comp. *Medieval Drama.* Boston: Houghton Mifflin, 1975.

Froning, Richard. *Das Drama des Mittelalters.* Stuttgart: 1891f.; rpt. Darmstadt: Wissenschaftliche Buchgesellschaft, 1964.

Katalog der deutschsprachigen geistlichen Spiele und Marienklagen des Mittelalters, ed. Rolf Bergmann et al. Munich: Beck, 1986.

Linke, Hansjürgen. "Germany and German-speaking Central Europe." In *The Theatre of Medieval Europe: New Research in Early Drama,* ed. Eckehard Simon. Cambridge: Cambridge University Press, 1991, pp. 207–224.

Neumann, Bernd. *Geistliches Schauspiel im Zeugnis der Zeit. Zur Aufführung mittelalterlicher religiöser Dramen im deutschen Sprachgebiet.* Munich: Artemis, 1987.

Simon, Eckehard. "Drama, German." In *Dictionary of the Middle Ages,* ed. Joseph R. Strayer. New York: Scribners, 1982–1989, vol. 4, pp. 266–272.

Matthew Z. Heintzelman

SEE ALSO

Drama, Easter Plays; Drama, Passion Plays

Drama, Dutch

Apart from some occasional fragments (*Abraham and Sarah* and *Antichrist;* see below) and a small number of plays (by Colijn—also Caillieu or Keyart—van Rijssele, and Anthonis de Roovere; see below) extant only in later copies, just one collection of Dutch plays has survived from before 1494—the beginning of the Habsburg dynasty in the Low Countries. The so-called Van Hulthem manuscript includes *Abele Spelen* and *Sotternieën.* Two fifteenth-century codices contain *Die Eerste Bliscap van Maria* and *Die Sevenste Bliscap onser Vrouwen,* representing the first and the last episodes of a Brussels cycle of Plays of our Lady. Finally, the oldest printed version of the famous play of *Elckerlyc* dates back to circa 1495.

Abele Spelen *and* Sotternieën

Among the oldest Western European manuscripts with secular plays in the vernacular, a Flemish one, the Van Hulthem codex, contains four *Abele Spelen,* one dramatized *Sotte Boerde,* and five *Sotternieën.* Whereas the last word refers to the genre of farce, the term *abel* is ambiguous. It has been explained as "refined," "artistic," "able," "fine," and the like. The plays are part of a larger manuscript, possibly used in a scriptorium for copying individual texts on demand. Originally, they may have been of the repertory of a group of professional actors (*camerspelers*) who, unlike the amateur rhetoricians, charged entrance fees for their private performances, presumably held for an aristocratic audience. The paper manuscript dates back to the early fifteenth century.

All four *abele spelen* deal with matters of the heart. In one, *Vanden Winter ende Vanden Somer,* we find an allegorical debate about which season is best suitable for love. Summer and Winter, both supported by two helpers, cannot find a solution to their dispute and decide to settle their argument by combat. Moiaert, follower of Summer and personification of the lover, urges Venus to solve the conflict. As soon as she appears on stage, Winter gives in. Yet Venus proclaims that neither can do without the other. A fragment of a play on the same theme is preserved in a single leaf manuscript at Ghent, dating back to circa 1436. *Esmoreit, Lanseloet van Denemerken,* and *Gloriant*—the three remaining *abele spelen*—display a chivalrous atmosphere and do not contain any explicit allegory. Each play is set in, alternately, a Christian and an Islamic environment. The play of *Esmoreit* is named after a Sicilian prince whose father is led to believe that his wife was unfaithful to him and that his son is illegitimate. Instead of killing the child, the deviser of these allegations, Robbrecht, sells it to a Saracen from Damascus. There Esmoreit is brought up by the king's daughter, Damiet, who is told that the boy is a foundling. Many years later she falls in love with her protégé. On discovering this and hearing about his uncertain background, Esmoreit wants to prove his noble birth and sets off on a quest. Back home his mother recognizes her son by the turban he wears, one in which she used to wrap him up as a baby. Thus Robbrecht's felony is revealed and he is sentenced to be hanged. After both have converted to Christianity, Damiet and Esmoreit are joined in matrimony.

Another prince, *Lanseloet,* has fallen in love with Sanderijn, a young woman of noble birth but lower in rank. His mother, to make an end to Lanseloet's lovesickness, sets a trap for the girl, making her believe that her son is ill and needs to be attended. After thus being lured into his room, she is raped by Lanseloet and then flees from the castle. Wandering about in the woods she meets a noble foreigner who invites her to become his spouse. The girl accepts and so they leave for Rawast, a town in a faraway country somewhere in Africa. Lanseloet soon mourns his loss. He commands his servant, Reinout, to find Sanderijn and bring her back to him. When she is found, Sanderijn refuses to obey Lanseloet's wishes. Fearing that he will start a war to conquer her, Reinout tells Lanseloet that Sanderijn died on hearing his master's name, whereupon the prince dies himself.

Gloriant, duke of Brunswick, is utterly reluctant to marry. Yet in Abelant lives a certain Florentijn who decides to test Gloriant's stubbornness. She has her portrait made and sends it to him. On seeing her image, Gloriant falls in love with the depicted woman. Despite warnings by his uncle, he travels to Abelant, where the two soon fall into each other's arms. Their amorous rendezvous, however, is watched over by Florentijn's cousin, Floerant, who betrays them to Roedelioen, the princess's father. The lovers are arrested and imprisoned, but the girl's servant releases Gloriant from the dungeon. When Florentijn is interrogated by her father about her misdeeds, Gloriant suddenly appears and chases away his opponent. He carries off Florentijn to Brunswick, where the couple is heartily welcomed. Once more, a conversion to Christianity is part of the play's climax.

Much research has been done to find sources for the three chivalrous *abele spelen.* Duinhoven regards *Esmoreit* as a profane version of the story of Moses. Tenacious claims by the same scholar see the tale dramatized in *Lanseloet van Denemerken* as related to the Old French romance of *Lancelot du Lac.* But since Esmoreit and Gloriant as well as other names in the latter play are found in the Old French *Baudouin de Sebourc* (a Middle Dutch translation of which is known to us), it seems likely that the chivalrous *abele spelen* rather stem from narrative sources related to the Crusades.

The play *Lanseloet* enjoyed great popularity at a very early period. In 1412, it was performed in Aachen, and as late as 1720, it still belonged to the repertory of a Dutch Zeeland Rhetoricians' Chamber. Moreover, during the fifteenth and sixteenth centuries, it was printed at least a dozen times, both in Dutch and in Low German. The chapbook version of the play is not directly copied from the text in the Van Hulthem manuscript. The latter reflects an older stage of development in which chivalric and bourgeois societies coexist, whereas the printed text expresses concepts more closely related to civic moral standards.

Each of the four *abele spelen* is followed by a farce, or *sotternie.* Hence *Vanden Winter ende vanden Somer* combines with *Rubben, Lanseloet van Denemerken* with *Die Hexe* (The Witch), *Esmoreit* with *Lippijn,* and *Gloriant* with *Die Buskenblaser* (The Boxblower). Finally, the incomplete *sotte boerde* (a genre, similar to the French *fabliau,* otherwise known in a narrative mode only) of *Drie Daghe Here* (Three Days Lord) is united with an incomplete *sotternie, Truwanten* (Truants). Most of the *sotternieën,* as well as *Drie Daghe Here,* deal with the stereotype problem of distorted marital relations in which wives dominate their spouses. In *Die Hexe* we find a conflict between two women and a farmer's wife who is under suspicion of being a witch. *Truwanten* is a most peculiar farce showing how a maidservant is carried off by the devil after her mistress has found out about her connections with a truant.

BIBLIOGRAPHY

Ayres, Harry Morgan, trans. *An Ingenious Play of Esmoreit.* The Hague: Nijhoff, n.d.

Beckers, Jozef J. M. *Een tekst voor alle tijden [. . .] Lanseloet van Denemerken.* Amsterdam: n.p., 1993.

Beidler, Peter, and Therese Decker. *"Lippijn:* A Middle Dutch Source for the Merchant's Tale?" *Chaucer Review* 23 (1989): 234–250.

[Brussels and Utrecht Study Group.] *Truwanten,* 3d ed. Utrecht: HES, 1987.

Colledge, Edmund, trans. "Lancelot of Denmark." In *Reynard the Fox and other Medieval Netherlands Secular Literature,* vol. 1. Leiden: Sijthoff, 1967, pp. 165–183.

Van Dijk, Hans, ed. *Lanseloet van Denemerken. Een abel spel.* Amsterdam: Amsterdam University Press, 1995.

Duinhoven, Anton M., ed. *Esmoreit.* Zutphen: Thieme, 1979.

———. "De bron van Lanseloet." *Tijdschrift voor Nederlandse Taal- en Letterkunde* 95 (1979): 262–287.

Geyl, Pieter, trans. *A Beautiful Play of Lancelot of Denmark.* The Hague: Nijhoff, 1924.

Hummelen, Wim M. H. "Performers and Performance in the Earliest Serious Secular Plays in the Netherlands." *Comparative Drama* 26 (1992): 19–33.

Hüsken, Wim, and Frans Schaars, eds. *Sandrijn en Lanslot.* Nijmegen: Alfa, 1985.

Judd, S. trans. "Two Short Pieces from Medieval Dutch: [. . .] Gloriant." *Dutch Crossing* 43 (1991): 52–93.

Leendertz, P., Jr., ed. *Middelnederlandsche Dramatische Poëzie.* Groningen: Wolters, 1900–1907.

Lerner, R. E. "Vagabonds and Little Women." *Modern Philology* 65 (1967–1968): 301–307.

Oakshott, Jane, and Elsa Strietman, trans. "Esmoreit." *Dutch Crossing* 30 (1986): 3–39; also as *An Excellent Play of Esmoreit, Prince of Sicily.* Preston, England: Alphaprint, 1989.

Stellinga, Govert, ed. *Het abel spel Vanden Winter ende Vanden Somer.* Zutphen: Thieme, 1966.

———, ed. *Het abel spel Gloriant van Bruuyswijc en de sotternie De buskenblazer na volghende.* Culemborg: Tjeenk Willink/Noorduijn, 1976.

Strietman, Elsa. "The Low Countries," in Eckehard Simon, ed. *The Theatre of Medieval Europe.* Cambridge: Cambridge University Press, 1991, pp. 225–252, 284–288.

Traver, H. "Religious Implications in the Abele Spelen." *Germanic Review* 26 (1951): 34–49.

W. N. M. Hüsken

SEE ALSO
Drama; *Sammelhandschrift*

Eerste Bliscap van Maria and Sevenste Bliscap Onser Vrouwen

Legend has it that, in 1348, the Holy Virgin instructed a woman to transport her miraculous statue from Antwerp to Brussels by boat. To commemorate this event the latter town inaugurated an annual procession. On the occasion of its centenary, the local authorities (possibly incorporating an older celebratory tradition) decided to establish a cycle of mystery plays on the Seven Joys of Mary. The texts of the first and the last plays, called *Die eerste bliscap van Maria* and *Die sevenste bliscap van onser vrouwen*, respectively, have been preserved for posterity. Manuscripts, in use until 1566, the year in which the *Ommegang* (procession) was last held, date back to the mid–fifteenth century. Fragments of *Die eerste bliscap* dating from the same era were recently discovered as well.

Die eerste bliscap van Maria (The First Joy of Our Lady) is a dramatization of the Annunciation, preceded by the history of Adam and Eve's Fall and by a Trial in Heaven. The play represents the only extant example in Dutch of a drama structure that resembles a Corpus Christi Cycle. Interspersed with scenes of Lucifer and Envy, the two instigators of Adam's misery, we successively find Adam and Eve's temptation, their expulsion from Eden, a Satan's Trial in which humankind is condemned to hell, Adam's death including the Legend of the Cross, and a prophet play. In a next sequence, Bitter Suffering persuades Passionate Prayer to try and convince Mercy to release the Patriarchs from hell. Demonstrating the effects of praying, Passionate Prayer drills a hole into the ceiling of the stage, thus getting access to heaven. At her request, Mercy successfully pleads to God against Justice on behalf of humankind, eventually resulting in the promise by God's Son to incarnate. Now the main topic of the play, the Annunciation, is arrived at. In the temple Joachim is denied his offerings to the priests because of his infertility. An angel nevertheless announces Anna's pregnancy. Mary's birth, her naming and presentation in the temple, the election of Joseph as her future spouse, and a scene showing Gabriel's Annunciation to the Virgin conclude the play.

Die sevenste bliscap van onser vrouwen (The Seventh Joy of Our Lady) dramatizes the Holy Virgin's death and assumption as described in Apocryphal writings. However, according to Mak the text is entirely based on Jacobus de Voragine's *Legenda aurea.* Once more, it is Gabriel who visits Mary. Now he announces God's decision that it is time to join her Son in heaven. The apostles are brought to Mary's dwelling to be present at her deathbed. All are transported by air on clouds. Shortly before she dies, devils try to tempt the Virgin but the Archangel Michael chases them away. After she has died, God commands the apostles to bury her body in the valley of Josaphat. While singing the antiphon *Exit de Egypto,* the procession is attacked by Jews. But as soon as they attempt to touch the bier their hands wither. How the Jews eventually retreat we do not know because here the manuscript lacks some 350 lines. The play continues with a tardy St. Thomas—after all, he was in India!—being the sole apostle to witness Mary's assumption in person. He explains the events to the others. Proving his claims, he shows them Mary's girdle, which he was given by one of the angels present. Her tomb is found empty. After having praised the Lord and the Virgin, the apostles separate again.

BIBLIOGRAPHY

Beuken, Willem H., ed. *Die Eerste Bliscap van Maria en Die Sevenste Bliscap van Vrouwen.* Zwolle: Tjeenk Willink, 1978.

Lievens, Robrecht. "De eerste bliscap van Maria," in Marcus De Schepper, ed. *Nederlandse letteren in de Leuvense Universiteitsbibliotheek.* Leuven: KUL afd. Ndl. Literatuur en Volkskunde, 1982, pp. 41–47.

Mak, Jacobus Johannes. "De bron van 'Die sevenste bliscap.'" *Verslagen en Mededelingen van de Koninklijke Vlaamse Academie* (1957): 293–307.

Meredith, Peter, and Lynette Muir. "The Trial in Heaven in the Eerste Bliscap and Other European Plays." *Dutch Crossing* 22 (1984): 84–92.

Strietman, Elsa. "Two Dutch Dramatic Explorations of *The Quality of Mercy*," in M. Chiabò, ed *Atti del IV Colloquio della Société internationale pour l'étude du théâtre médiéval: Viterbo 10-15 luglio.* Viterbo, Italy: Centro Studi sul Teatro Medioevale e Rinascimentale, 1984, pp. 179–201.

Elckerlyc

The Dutch version of the highly allegorized story in which humankind is summoned to give account of his earthly deeds is, as was finally confirmed by E.R. Tigg, older than its famous English counterpart, *Everyman.* Tigg proved his theory by indicating that rhyming stopgaps in the English text had been added to conceal the nonrhyming result of a literal translation from the Dutch. Moreover, *Everyman,* printed in 1525, is labeled anti-Reformation, whereas *Elckerlyc* is characterized as ante-Reformation. It seems very unlikely, however, that *Everyman* is a direct translation from any of the four extant Dutch versions. *Elckerlyc* survives in three late-fifteenth- to early-sixteenth-century chapbook versions and in a manuscript dating from the final decade of the sixteenth century. The latter play and *Everyman* frequently differ from the printed texts, thus suggesting that both go back to older versions.

The play may have been awarded a first prize during a drama competition in Antwerp. The source for the latter information, the title page of *Homulus* (1536), the play's first Latin translation by the Maastricht schoolmaster Ischyrius, also names Petrus Diesthemius as its alleged author. From a theological point of view, *Elckerlijc* proves to have been of utmost importance. Hence, Latin translations and adaptations made the text available to a scholarly world. As for the play's general story line, various sources have been cited. *Barlaam* and *Josaphat* in Jacobus de Voragine's *Legenda aurea* presents the closest analogy to the tale dramatized in *Elckerlyc.*

BIBLIOGRAPHY

Barnouw, Adriaan J., trans. *The Mirror of Salvation.* The Hague: Nijhoff, 1971.

Conley, John, et al., trans. *The Mirror of Everyman's Salvation.* Amsterdam: Rodopi, 1985.

Cooper, Geoffrey, and Christopher Wortham, eds. *The Summoning of Everyman,* 2d ed. Nedlands: University of Western Australia Press, 1984.

De Haan, Max J.M., and J. van Delden, eds. *De Spiegel der Zaligheid van Elkerlijk.* Leiden: Vakgroep Nederlandse Taal- en Letterkunde, 1979.

Tigg, E.R. "Is *Elckerlijc* Prior to Everyman?" *Journal of English and Germanic Philology* 38 (1939): 568–596.

Van Elslander, Antoon, ed. *Den spyeghel der salicheyt van Elckerlijc,* 8th ed. Antwerp: De Nederlandsche Boekhandel, 1985.

Vos, R. "Elckerlijc—Everyman—Homulus—Der Sünden Loin ist der Tod." *Tijdschrift voor Nederlandse Taal- en Letterkunde* 82 (1966): 129–143.

Vos, R., ed. *Den spieghel der salicheit van Elckerlijc.* Groningen: Wolters, 1967.

Other Plays

Town records, though not so far systematically studied, indicate that performing drama was common practice in most cities throughout the entire fifteenth century, both in the northern and southern provinces. J.A. Worp was one of the first Dutch scholars to give an extensive list of performances as found in city accounts. His list includes references to Christmas plays, Easter plays, Passion plays, Resurrection plays, and saints plays throughout the fifteenth century, related mainly to the southern provinces. Secular drama is scarcely represented. Most records, however, lack specific titles of plays. In more recent years, Worp's pioneering work is supplemented, particularly in relation to the archives of the northern provinces. In Arnhem, for example, performances independent of a Shrovetide tradition of *Neidhart* plays were discovered, dating back to 1395. A play, presumably a farce, on "Lizzy who wanted to have a husband who smells of a harness," was performed in Deventer in 1470. Four years later the town staged a *King Ahasverus,* and in 1484 the local Guild of Seafarers on Bergen (Norway) produced a play on *Susanna.* This is fairly exceptional, for some time during the fifteenth century, the Rhetoricians' Chambers assumed full responsibility for organizing drama performances. Some even claim to have been established in the early decades of the fifteenth century, such as the Chamber of "The Book" in Brussels (1401), the "The Holy Ghost" in Bruges (1428), and "The Jesse Flower" in Middelburg (1430).

Fragments of a fifteenth-century *Abraham-and-Sarah Play* were found in Zutphen, a small Hansa town in the eastern part of the Netherlands. The text is a dramatization of Gen. 18: 6–15. In the Liège State Archives, fragments were also discovered of a mid–fifteenth-century *Play of Antichrist.* The manuscript contains rubrics partly in Latin, but otherwise it reveals characteristics that point at the province of Limburg as its place of origin. Its contents mainly consist of a dialogue between Antichrist and the prophets Elijah and Enoch, ending in their deaths. In 1445, a Play on the Coming of Antichrist was performed in the town of Zwolle as well. Shortly after Margaret of Savoye's birth (January 10, 1480), Brussels's official town poet, Colijn Caillieu, composed an untitled *presentspel* (gift play) on this happy event. Caillieu may be identified as Colijn van Rijssele, author of *De spiegel der minnen,* and as the "amorous" Colijn Keyart, who wrote *Van Narcissus ende Echo* (see below). The play is inspired by seasonal tradition. It stages a dialogue among three Kings: the King of Clergy, the King of Nobility, and the King of Labor. Adorned with a profusion of references to biblical and classical literature, prefiguring Margaret's birth, the Kings inform one another about their descent and their ambitions. They intend to offer certain gifts to the newly born child: a rose, a golden apple, and the sweet leaves of Eden's Tree of Life. All three Kings had been instructed to do so by Experience. The latter allegorical person eventually ties the symbolic meaning of the three gifts together into one image: the leaves, the rose, and the apple can be found on a single branch of a tree. They can even be compared to gold, myrrh, and incense. Finally a stage compartment is opened revealing a mother and child to whom the Kings offer their gifts. The play gives an excellent example of how future sixteenth-century Rhetoricians would create their versions of similar occasional plays in countless numbers. The famous sixteenth-century humanist scholar and man of letters Dirck Volckertsz Coornhert (1522–1590) was the first person to edit, in 1561, Colijn van Rijssele's (d. ca. 1481) play of *De spiegel der minnen* (The Mirror of Love). The fairly lengthy text consists of six plays relating the story of two lovers who, because the girl's father refused to allow them to get married, recently died in a Zeeland town. The author proves to have been extremely well informed in matters of astrological and medical implication. A few years earlier, in 1552, a play by Colijn, nicknamed "amorous" alias Colijn Keyart, was copied out by a certain Reyer Gheurtz: *Van Narcissus ende Echo,* a dramatization of one of the tales in Ovid's *Metamorphosis.* Van Gijsen is convinced that this play, too, was composed by Van Rijssele; a 1621 edition of the text erroneously names Jan Baptist Houwaert (1533–1599) as its author.

Anthonis de Roovere (ca. 1430–1482), a bricklayer or master builder and official town poet of the city of Bruges, composed a play based on the Athanasian and Apostolic Creeds, *Quiconque vult salvus esse.* In 1527, it was copied out by his fellow townsman Cornelis Everaert (ca. 1480–1556). The play is built on disputations among a Christian, a Jew, and a Muslim, attacking each other's beliefs, changing sides throughout the entire discussion. Allegorical characters, named Law and Faith, present the Christian dogmas, which are commented on by the two non-Christians and a third critic, named Half

Wise Half Fool. The play ends in a *tableau vivant* (a scene in which actors remain in a fixed position), displaying a Crucifix.

BIBLIOGRAPHY

Arn, Mary-Jo, ed. "A Little-Known Fragment of a Dutch Abraham-and-Isaac Play." *Comparative Drama* 17 (1983): 318–26.

De Bock, Eugeen, ed. "Een presentspel van Colijn Cailleu." *Spiegel der Letteren* 6 (1963): 241–269.

Gessler, Ja, ed. "Fragmenten van een Limburgsch Antichrist-spel uit de XVᵉ eeuw," in Maurits Basse et al., eds. *Album opgedragen aan Prof. Dr. J. Vercoullie.* Brussels: Paginae, 1927, pp. 137–146.

Hollaar, Jeannette M., and E.W.F. van den Elzen. "Het vroegste toneelleven in enkele Noordnederlandse plaatsen." *De nieuwe taalgids* 73 (1980): 302–324.

———. "Toneelleven in Deventer in de vijftiende en zestiende eeuw." *De nieuwe taalgids* 73 (1980): 412–425.

Immink, Margaretha W., ed. *De Spiegel der Minnen door Colijn van Rijssele.* Utrecht: Oosthoek, 1913.

Scharpé, Lodewijk, ed. "De Rovere's spel van Quiconque vult salvus esse." *Leuvensche Bijdragen* 4 (1900–1902): 155–193.

Van Elslander, Antoon. "Lijst van Nederlandse rederijkerskamers uit de XVᵉ en XVIᵉ eeuw." *Jaarboek "De Fonteine"* 18 (1968): 29–60.

Van Gijsen, Annelies. *Liefde, Kosmos en Verbeelding: Mens- en Wereldbeeld in Colijn van Rijssele's Spiegel der Minnen.* Groningen: Wolters-Noordhoff, 1989.

Worp, Jacob Adolf. *Geschiedenis van het Drama en van het Tooneel in Nederland,* Vol. 1. Groningen: Wolters, 1904.

W. N. M. Hüsken

SEE ALSO
Drama; Neidhart

Drama, Easter Plays

Together with Passion plays, the Easter play represents the most widespread and most highly developed of the medieval theater traditions of the German Middle Ages. In a broader context, plays of the Easter season may include all manner of works that depict scenes from the story of Jesus' arrest, death, and Resurrection, thus including Passion plays, Easter plays, Marian lamentations *(Marienklage* or *planctus),* Emmaus (or pilgrim) plays,

Corpus Christi plays, as well as plays about Mary Magdalene, the Last Supper, and the Deposition from the Cross. In the narrower sense, the Easter play depicts the events of Jesus' Resurrection, from the setting of guards at the tomb, to the Harrowing of Hell, the mercator (merchant) scenes, the three Marys at the tomb, Jesus as gardener, the race between Peter and John, and other appearances by Jesus after the Resurrection. While Passion plays often contained the events of Easter Day as well, Easter plays themselves were shorter and generally confined to one day.

This article concentrates on the narrower sense of the term: plays about the events of Easter Day. There are still remains of thirty-two such vernacular plays (often under the heading *osterspil,* "Easter Play," or some form of the word *pascha/paschalis,* "Easter") with varying amounts of Latin text.

The roots of the Easter play go back to the *Quem queritis* Easter trope (tenth-century manuscripts from Limoges and St. Gall); that is, when the angel at the tomb asks the three Marys "Whom do you seek?" Out of this prototheatrical moment grew the Easter liturgical plays *(Osterfeiern),* which remained entirely in Latin, and thus were still suitable for use during the Latin mass. There are 528 such plays from the German-speaking parts of Central Europe. Easter liturgical plays were recorded and performed up to the end of the Middle Ages.

With the advent of Easter plays *(Osterspiele)* the tenor changed greatly. Certain satirical elements came to the fore, such as the mercator scene, with the often ribald antics of the unguent merchant, his wife, and his servant. Another major comical scene is the restocking of hell with new souls, the so-called *Ständesatire* (social satire). This grew out of one of the central episodes of the Easter play—based on the Gospel of Nicodemus—in which Jesus descends to hell and opens the gates to free the righteous souls (Adam, Isaiah, Seth, John the Baptist, and others) of those who had died before his coming. The newly emptied realm of hell was often then refilled with the souls of contemporary sinners and cheats, such as the baker who steals dough or the tailor who takes the extra fabric.

The first German-language example we have is the fragmentary Easter play from Muri (mid–thirteenth century), which is noteworthy in part because of its use of courtly language. From the fourteenth century we have fragments from Breslau (Wrocław), Munich, Berlin, and Linz. One of the more complete of the early plays is the Innsbruck Thuringian Easter Play of 1391, which includes both the mercator scenes and the *Ständesatire.* These plays reached their zenith in the mid– to late fifteenth century, with play texts and fragments from Low German areas (Redentin, Wolffenbüttel, Osnabrück), West Central German (Trier, Melk, Berlin), Alemannic areas (Feldkirch, Regensburg), and the Bavarian areas (Erlau, Bozen, Tyrol, Steinach, Vienna, Munich, Göttweig). The play traditions generally end in the course of the sixteenth century, often with the advent of the Protestant Reformation.

Since the 1960s, there has been an increased interest in all medieval German drama. For Easter plays, this has meant newly published texts from Tyrol (Debs Manuscript); inclusion in a catalog of all medieval German religious plays; and a collection of performance records for religious drama. Attempts have also been made to incorporate the plays' origins into the nomenclature for the Easter plays, using such hybrid forms as the Innsbruck Thuringian Easter Play.

Only the Redentin play (1464), with its expansive *Ständesatire* has thus far been translated into English.

BIBLIOGRAPHY

Bergmann, Rolf. "Spiele, Mittelalterliche geistliche," in *Reallexikon der deutschen Literaturgeschichte,* ed. Werner Kohlschmidt and Wolfgang Mohr. Berlin: de Gruyter, 1958ff.

Das Redentiner Osterspiel, ed., trans. Brigitta Schottmann. Stuttgart: Reclam, 1975.

Katalog der deutschsprachigen geistlichen Spiele und Marienklagen des Mittelalters, ed. Rolf Bergmann et al. Munich: Beck, 1986.

Linke, Hansjürgen. "Germany and German-speaking Central Europe" in *The Theatre of Medieval Europe: New Research in Early Drama,* ed. Eckehard Simon. Cambridge: Cambridge University Press, 1991, pp. 207–224.

Neumann, Bernd. *Geistliches Schauspiel im Zeugnis der Zeit. Zur Aufführung mittelalterlicher religiöser Dramen im deutschen Sprachgebiet.* Munich: Artemis, 1987.

The Redentin Easter Play, trans. A. E. Zucker. New York: Columbia University Press, 1941.

Steinbach, Rolf. *Die deutschen Osterspiele und Passionsspiele des Mittelalters.* Cologne: Böhlau, 1970.

Matthew Z. Heintzelman

SEE ALSO

Drama, Christmas Plays; Drama, Passion Plays; Melk; Trier

Drama, Last Judgment Plays

A corpus of religious plays predominantly associated with the Alemannic region whose core content is derived from Matthew 25: 31–46. They tell of Christ summoning humankind to the Last Judgment, rewarding those who have followed his commandments and punishing all sinners by casting them into hell. A characteristic feature of these plays is a basically tripartite composition, involving a prelude, the actual judgment scenes, and a conclusion. Typically, the plays' emphasis is on condemnation rather than salvation, since their historical purpose was to portray vividly the horrors of hell and to serve as a strong deterrent to those viewing the performance. Whereas Latin versions of the play were performed as far back as the end of the thirteenth century, we have no information regarding the genesis of the German variants. Hellmut Rosenfeld assumes a mid-fourteenth-century prototype. Written in rhymed couplets, the plays vary in length from 334 verses (Donaueschingen play) to 2,762 verses (Luzern play). They are transmitted in paper manuscripts from the fifteenth and sixteenth centuries. Since Reuschel's 1906 investigation, it has been commonplace among scholars to employ the somewhat dubious distinction between original and expanded versions. The former group encompasses the plays associated with the towns of Bern, Copenhagen, Donaueschingen, Güssingen, Rheinau (now called Schaffhausener Weltgerichtsspiel and located in Zurich), Walenstadt, and with the Jantz collection (consisting of the Berlin, Chur, Luzern, and Munich plays) Additional known variants of the play are lost.

Medieval German drama, conceivably the most important representative of urban literature, has received only scant attention when compared to other genres, and Last Judgment plays are no exception. It was not until the 1980s that they became a focal point of interest. Initial activities centered on editorial projects. Only the Munich and Luzern plays remain unedited, yet plans are under discussion for a definitive edition of all plays. Topics of scholarly inquiry have also included the sources and role of the illustrations in the Copenhagen and the Berlin variants as well as the actual purpose of specific manuscripts. Even a superficial comparison of the Munich and the Copenhagen play, for example, would seem to suggest on the basis of explicit stage directions in the former that some branches of the transmission were intended as scripts for a production, whereas others had undergone a transformation, most notably through the addition of a picture cycle, to a text intended for reading. This transformation, in turn, raised fundamental questions about appropriate generic labeling. Complicating the discussion of generic affiliation is the fact that plays containing a bare minimum of "stage directions," such as the Donaueschingen or Jantz variants, could conceivably serve as the basis for a performance. The 1984 production of the Bern play in the city's historical museum showed that the absence of detailed staging directions and a manuscript source clearly intended for reading purposes do not rule out a priori the possibility of performance.

BIBLIOGRAPHY

Blosen, Hans, and Ole Lauridsen. *Das Kopenhagener Weltgerichtsspiel.* Heidelberg: Winter, 1988.

Linke, Hansjürgen. *Das Güssinger Weltgerichtsspiel.* Heidelberg. Winter, 1995.

McConnell, Winder, and Ingeborg Henderson. "Das Weltgerichtsspiel der Sammlung Jantz mit der Donaueschinger Variante Handschrift Nr. 136." *Jahrbuch des Wiener Goethe-Vereins* 92/93 (1988/1989): 223–321.

Mone, Franz Joseph. *Der jüngste Tag* [= *Schaffhauser,* earlier *Rheinauer Weltgerichtsspiel*]. Schauspiele des Mittelalters l. Karlsruhe: Macklot, 1846, pp. 265–304.

Reuschel, Karl. *Die deutschen Weltgerichtsspiele des Mittelalters und der Reformationszeit.* Teutonia 4. Leipzig: Eduard Avenarius, 1906.

Schulze, Ursula. *Berliner Weltgerichtsspiel. Augsburger Buch vom Jüngsten Gericht,* Litterae 14. Göppingen: Kümmerle, 1991.

———. *Churer Weltgerichtsspiel.* Texte des späten Mittelalters und der frühen Neuzeit 35. Berlin: Erich Schmidt, 1993.

Senn von Buchs-Werdenberg, Nikolaus. *Daß Jüngste Gericht* [= *Walenstadt*]. Teufen: Niederer, 1869.

Stammler, Wolfgang. *Berner Weltgerichtsspiel.* Texte *des späten Mittelalters* 15. Berlin: Erich Schmidt, 1962.

Ingeborg Henderson

SEE ALSO
Drama

Drama, Latin, Netherlands

In the Low Countries, few manuscripts have been preserved containing liturgical drama. Hence there is no need to discriminate any further between different types of Easter plays and Christmas plays.

Easter Plays

Type I specimens of a *Visitatio Sepulchri,* consisting of a brief dialogue at the Tomb of Christ among the three Marys and the Angel, are present in codices from Postel, Tongres, and Utrecht. Type II versions, with an elaborate rendering of the original trope as well as including text having a bearing on the apostles Peter and John, were found in manuscripts from Haarlem and Utrecht.

In 1938, Jos. Smits van Waesberghe discovered a hitherto unknown *Ludus Paschalis* (Easter play, twelfth century) in a Maastricht *Evangelary* (book of gospel readings) preserved at the Royal Library at The Hague. An enlarged version of the same Easter play, including a mercator scene, was found in a hymnal (at Egmond, ca. 1491). A Delft manuscript (ca. 1496) merely states the words spoken by the Phisicus, i.e., Mercator, and has brief indications of the women's text on their way to Christ's sepulchre. In the same town, a record in the accounts of the church of St. Hippolytus informs us about the stage properties needed for a Resurrection play, as it used to be performed on Low Sunday at the end of the fifteenth century. Although records attest to a great number of performances in the vernacular of Easter and Passion plays in various towns and villages of the Low Countries, no play texts have survived.

The Maastricht *Ludus Paschalis,* the text that provides the best impression of a Dutch tradition of Easter plays, comprises eight characters: Christ, both as a gardener and as a pilgrim; two angels at the tomb; the three Marys carrying spices and ointments; and two disciples. Its story line, supplemented with various antiphons, basically concentrates on four elements: *Quem quaeritis* (Whom are you seeking) trope, *Hortulanus* (garden) scene, *Victimae Paschalis* (Easter victims), and *Peregrinus* sequence.

Christmas Plays

Bilsen—or, more precisely, Munsterbilsen—is the toponym related to a manuscript containing an *Officium Stellae* dating back to about 1130. Smits van Waesberghe, who tacitly combines the text in his recent edition of the play with the *Ordo Rachelis* of the Fleury play book, identifies Theodoric of St. Truiden (ca. 1040–1107) as its author. The Bilsen *Officium* is, in any case, the only liturgical Christmas play created in the Low Countries that has come down to us. It follows most of the tradition as it is found elsewhere. Exceptional, however, is the name of the first and most important king, Zoroastro. Two further remarkable characteristics of the play are the hexameters in the opening song of the choir and the use of rhyme in the stage directions.

References to *Magi* plays have been found in Delft, 's-Hertogenbosch, and Utrecht. In the southern Low Countries, similar plays were produced in Geraardsbergen, Gistel, and Loo. A Delft history dating back to the early eighteenth century gives a detailed description of the way a Christmas play was staged, in 1498, in St. Ursula's. *Magi* plays may also have been put on by puppeteers. In 1363, the French nobleman Jean de Blois, whose usual domicile was the province of Holland, supposedly attended such a performance in Bohemia.

BIBLIOGRAPHY

De Boor, Helmut. *Die Textgeschichte der lateinischen Osterfeiern.* Tübingen: Niemeyer, 1967.

———. "Das holländische Osterspiel." *Acta Germanica* 3 (1968): 47–62.

Hollaar, Jeannette M., and E. W. F. van den Elzen. "Het vroegste toneelleven in enkele Noordnederlandse plaatsen." *De nieuwe taalgids* 73 (1980): 302–324.

King, Norbert. *Mittelalterliche Dreikönigsspiele,* 2 vols. Freiburg: Universitätsverlag, 1979.

Lipphardt, Walter, ed. *Lateinische Osterfeiern und Osterspiele.* 9 vols. Berlin: de Gruyter, 1975–1990.

Oosterbaan, D. P., ed. "Het Delftse Paasspel van omstreeks 1496." *Tijdschrift voor Nederlandse Taal- en Letterkunde* 83 (1967): 1–26.

Smits van Waesberghe, Joseph. "A Dutch Easter Play." *Musica Disciplina* 7 (1953): 15–37.

———, ed. *Muziek en Drama in de Middeleeuwen.* Amsterdam: Bigot and Van Rossum, 1942, rpt. 1954.

———, ed. *Het Grote Herodesspel of Driekoningenspel van Munsterbilzen.* Hasselt: Provinciaal archief- en documentatiecentrum, 1987.

Van de Graft, Catharina C. "Over het Spel van Herodes in den Dom te Utrecht." *Jaarboekje van Oud-Utrecht* (1924): 71–102.

Van Mierlo, Jozef. "Een Utrechtsch Antiphonarium." *Leuvensche Bijdragen* 8 (1908–1909): 1–75.

Vellekoop, Cees. "Het Paasspel van Egmond," in Frederik W.M. Hugenholtz et al., eds. *Leven, wonen en werken in Holland aan het einde van de dertiende eeuw.* The Hague: Nijhoff, 1979, pp., 51–70.

Worp, Jacob Adolf. *Geschiedenis van het drama en van het tooneel in Nederland,* vol. 1. Groningen: Wolters, 1904.

Young, Karl. *The Drama of the Medieval Church.* Vol. 2. Oxford: Clarendon, 1933.

———. *The Drama of the Medieval Church.* 2 vols. Oxford: Clarendon, 1933.

W. N. M. Hüsken

SEE ALSO
Drama; Drama, Dutch

Drama, Paradise Plays

The story of the creation and fall of the protoplasts, Adam and Eve, is important in Christian thinking not just as a historical beginning but also as a theological rationalization of the need for salvation, and because it served, through typological connections, as a pointer to Christ, the new Adam. The paradise play, also called Genesis play, is a dramatization of this material. In Middle High German, the paradise play is not a distinct form. Liturgical considerations and the ecclesiastical calendar dictated that the principal forms of religious drama were the Christmas, Easter, Passion, and Corpus Christi plays. However, all these could use Old Testament events to prefigure the New Testament material central to their actual liturgical function. Plays that begin with the creation stories can be gathered under the general category of paradise plays, irrespective of their main emphasis. These can then be seen as precursors of the later plays that appear in German from early modern times with the creation story as their principal or sole subject.

The earliest evidence of a German paradise play is a reference in the Regensburg city annals to the performance in 1194 of a play dealing with the creation and fall, and with the prophets. The inclusion of the prophets indicates that, as with the plays with known texts, the Genesis material was used as an opening scene, subordinated to another purpose. The oldest surviving German paradise play is the *Wiener Passionsspiel (Viennese Passion Play),* early-fourteenth-century Austrian, but on linguistic evidence going back to a thirteenth-century central German (Rhenish-Franconian) original. Also fourteenth century is the *Maastrichter Osterspiel,* the oldest drama of any kind in Middle Dutch, and the Kassel Fragments, discovered in 1985 in the bindings of four later manuscripts. Examples from the fifteenth century are the *Egerer Passionsspiel (Eger Passion Play,* Cheb, ca. 1460), the *Künzelsauer Fronleichnamsspiel (Künzelsauer Corpus*

Christi Play, Swabian, 1479), and Arnold Immessen's *Sündenfall (Sin,* Low German, ca. 1480). The *Zerbster Fronleichnamsspiel (Zerbst Corpus Christi Play,* 1504) was apparently the last paradise play to appear before the Reformation radically altered the nature of religious drama.

The Protestant paradise play, which emerged in the sixteenth century and developed into a very broad popular tradition in both Protestant and Catholic areas, moves the story of the protoplasts firmly into the central position, with typological references to later salvation history becoming more marginal. We may mention three of the earliest. Valten Voith of Magdeburg was the author of a long and complex play entitled *Vom herrlichen Ursprung . . . des Menschen (On the Glorious Origin ... of Man,"* 1538). Hans Sachs's *Tragödia von Schöpfung, Fall und Austreibung (Creation Tragedy, Fall and Expulsion,* 1545) is relatively brief and close to the Bible yet proved extremely influential with whole sections being taken up into later folk plays. In Zwinglian Zürich, Jacob Ruff (or Ruf, Rüff, etc.) produced his *Adam und Heva (Adam and Eve,* 1550), a two-day pageant of impressive proportions with a cast of over a hundred.

Typical elements of a paradise play are the fall of rebel angels, the creation, temptation, and fall of the protoplasts, their expulsion from paradise, Cain's murder of Abel, and the death of Adam. An infernal council in which the demonic powers discuss their tactics may serve as an opening scene or be inserted after the creation of Eve. Apocryphal material such as Adam's attempt to return to paradise and Seth's quest for the Oil of Life may also appear. Paradise plays must be seen in the context of the vast tradition of medieval literary adaptations of Adam and Eve material. The Latin *Vita Adae et Evae* was by far the most influential; important Adam books in German include the *Wiener Genesis* (c. 1075), the *Millstätter Genesis* (ca. 1120), the *Anegenge* (1173/1180), and Lutwin's *Eva und Adam* (early fourteenth century).

Graeme Dunphy

SEE ALSO
Anegenge; Bible; Drama; *Genesis* and *Exodus*

Drama, Passion Plays

Major component of the overall cycle of plays related to the Easter season including the arrest, trial, death, and Resurrection of Jesus. In the later Middle Ages in Germany, these grew into one of the most important cultural expressions of urban society. As the name indicates, the Passion play focuses on Jesus' suffering *(passio)* and death. But unlike its closely related counterpart, the Easter play, the Passion play tradition grew to encompass the entire history of salvation and may include scenes such as the Nativity, ministry of Jesus, Resurrection, Ascension, the lament of the Virgin Mary at the cross *(Marienklage* or *planctus),* as well as those Old Testament scenes viewed as reflecting on the events of the New Testament. In this sense, the term "Passion play" is more inclusive than the term "Easter play," which is limited to the events of Easter Day itself. Unlike Corpus Christi processions, which have essentially the same contents range, the Passion play productions were not tied to a specific liturgical celebration or season, and were usually performed on a large, simultaneous stage. Such productions could last up to several days—four days in Frankfurt am Main in 1492, 1498, and 1506; seven days in Bozen in 1514—and for several hours each day.

Forty-nine Passion plays in German that are extant in complete or fragmentary manuscripts, and the majority of these use some form of the word *passio* (passion) to describe their contents. These are usually separated into four linguistic and regional groups: the Rhine-Hesse plays (Frankfurt, St. Gall, Alsfeld, Heidelberg, Fritzlar, Friedberg), the Tyrolian plays (Sterzing, Bozen, Brixen, Hall), the Swabian-Swiss plays (Lucerne, Donaueschingen), and other individual plays. Plays date already from the early thirteenth century, but the Passion play tradition reaches its zenith in the late fifteenth and early sixteenth centuries. While the form largely died out where the Protestant Reformation established itself, in some Catholic areas—notably in the Tyrol and Lucerne—play productions continued throughout the sixteenth century and even into the early seventeenth century, under the direction of production leaders such as Benedikt Debs and Vigil Raber.

The earliest Passion play containing much German is the *Benediktbeuern Play* (early thirteenth century). Fragments of other early plays have been found in Himmelgarten, Vienna, Maastricht, Kreuzenstein, and Osnabrück. As with all medieval religious drama, much of the nomenclature is based on the modern location of the manuscript, not on its probable origin or site of the production. Other major early examples of the Passion play include the St. Gall Rhenish-Franconian Passion play (St. Gall, Stiftsbibliothek, manuscript no. 919) and the Frankfurt Director's Scroll (between 1315 and 1345). This latter manuscript, interesting as well for its unusual format, forms the earliest record of one of the most important play traditions, since we can trace Frankfurt play productions from the early fourteenth century up through the 1493 manuscript—days two and three of a four-day play—and up to the end in 1515. In addition, we have numerous records concerning the last three performances in 1492, 1498, and 1506.

The *Lucerne Passion Play* (or *Lucerne Easter Play)* dates back as early as the mid–fifteenth century, and was performed up to the early seventeenth century. Coming somewhat later than many of the other plays, it is particularly well documented. The numerous Tyrolian plays date largely from the latter part of the fifteenth century and up to the mid–sixteenth century. As with the Lucerne play, numerous performance records, as well as manuscripts of both entire plays and parts of plays, are extant. This has led to much renewed editorial activity in recent years. An upswing in research in all medieval German drama since the mid-1960s has led to a vast new array of pertinent tools for scholars: new editions of plays, especially the Tyrolian plays, but also of previously published plays (e.g., Frankfurt, Alsfeld, and Donaueschingen); a comprehensive catalog of religious plays; standardization of the nomenclature for the plays; and an exhaustive collection of performance records for all religious drama. In thematic research, this has opened up new possibilities for studying the social aspects of religious drama— whether in its depiction of specific characters, the importance of the plays to the local society, or in the anti-Jewish content of many plays. Unfortunately, the lack of English translations—only the *Benediktbeuern Passion Play,* the *St. Gall Rhenish-Franconian Passion Play,* and the *Alsfeld Passion Play* have thus far been translated into English— continues to prevent many English speakers from working in this area.

BIBLIOGRAPHY

Bergmann, Rolf. "Spiele, Mittelalterliche geistliche," in *Reallexikon der deutschen Literaturgeschichte,* ed. Werner Kohlschmidt and Wolfgang Mohr et al. Berlin: de Gruyter, 1958ff.

———. *Studien zur Entstehung und Geschichte der deutschen Passionsspiele des 13. und 14. Jahrhunderts.* Munich: Fink, 1972.

Das Donaueschinger Passionsspiel, ed. Anthonius H. Touber. Stuttgart: Reclam, 1985.

Froning, Richard. *Das Drama des Mittelalters.* Stuttgart, 1891f.; rpt. Darmstadt: Wissenschaftliche Buchgesellschaft, 1964.

Katalog der deutschsprachigen geistlichen Spiele und Marienklagen des Mittelalters, ed. Rolf Bergmann et al. Munich: Beck, 1986.

Linke, Hansjürgen. "Germany and German-speaking Central Europe," in *The Theatre of Medieval Europe: New Research in Early Drama,* ed. Eckehard Simon. Cambridge: Cambridge University Press, 1991, pp. 207–224.

Neumann, Bernd. *Geistliches Schauspiel im Zeugnis der Zeit. Zur Aufführung mittelalterlicher religiöser Dramen im deutschen Sprachgebiet.* Munich: Artemis, 1987.

The Saint Gall Passion Play, trans. Larry E. West. Brookline, Mass.: Classical Folia Editions, 1976.

Steinbach, Rolf. *Die deutschen Osterspiele und Passionsspiele des Mittelalters.* Cologne: Böhlau, 1970.

Matthew Z. Heintzelman

SEE ALSO
Drama; Drama, Christmas Play; Drama, Easter Play

Dutch Language, Dialects

The first systematic trials to develop a transregional Dutch standard language take place in the sixteenth and seventeenth centuries, when under the influence of Renaissance ideals the desire arises to equalize Dutch to the classical languages—Latin and Greek. People start by writing grammars with which they try to lay down the norms. Afterwards one can see an accelerating growth toward a standard language in the Dutch area. That standard language increasingly supersedes the colloquial dialects. Certainly up to circa 1600, however, a more or less regionally colored language is written.

Hardly any documents containing coherent authentic Old Dutch texts have survived. The oldest official texts written in a Middle Dutch dialect originate from Ghent, the capital of the county of Flanders; they date from circa 1240. Soon afterward, Holland and Brabant also switch over to the national language, followed by the other regions in the fourteenth century. In those times, the frontier between Dutch and French was in about the same place as it is nowadays; but in northern France in later times it moved slightly to the north. In those days the frontier was a rather straight line south of Brussels, from Calais to the region between Maastricht and Liège. It is much more difficult to draw the frontier with Middle Low German, because it is not possible to indicate a group of isoglosses (linguistic characteristics) that divides a potential western language from an eastern one. For the sake of convenience, one currently takes the present-day national boundary with Germany in the north, but in the south one includes the dialects of the region boundaried by the Meuse and Rhine rivers, the area around Nijmegen, and the High German language boundary (the *maken/machen* isogloss), where necessary, which seems to be the most correct way in view of the cultural and political orientation of the region concerned: the origins of the county, later the duchy of Gelre, are situated there.

The earliest Middle Dutch literary codex, surviving very fragmentarily and containing the *Life of Saint Servaes* by Veldeke, originates from Limburg, the region of Maastricht. From the thirteenth century, (fragments of) similar manuscripts remain from Brabant, Flanders, and east of the Dutch language area. But the vast majority of Middle Dutch literary manuscripts date from the fourteenth century and originate in Flanders.

Middle Dutch literary works have been delivered mainly in three principal groups of dialects: Hollandish, Flemish, and Brabantish. The first two are strongly similar in a number of respects, because they have North Sea Germanic features that often remind one of English. They are as follows:

a. Unrounding of short *ü (/ü/)* to *i* in words like *stic* (compare English *stick* with German *Stück* and Brabantish *stuc*), *pit* (compare English *pit* with Brabantish *put*) and *brigghe* (compare English *bridge* with German *Brücke* and Brabantish *brugghe*). In Holland one sometimes find *e* instead of *i: pet, bregghe.*

b. Rounding of *a* to *o* in front of voiceless velar fricatives as in *brocht* (compare English *brought* with German *brachte* and Brabantish *brachte*).

c. Pronouns in the second person with *j: jou/ju* (compare English *you* and Brabantish *u*).

d. *M* as an ending of the first person singular of the verb *zijn (to be): ic bem* (compare English *I am* with German *ich bin* and Brabantish *ic ben*).

Moreover, in the West one finds a geminated consonant in the infinitive of (Flemish) *zullen* / (Hollandish) *sellen* (English *shall,* Brabantish *selen,* eastern *so(e)len*).

Furthermore, Flemish distinguishes itself from Hollandish because it makes no difference between the presence or absence of umlaut of former *eu;* in the first case Holland has *y:* (written *u* or *uu*): *lude, beduden,* otherwise *i:* (written *ie*): *bieden,* (cf. German *Leute, bedeuten, bieten*). West of Brabant one always finds *ie,* as in Flanders: *liede, bedieden, bieden.* A similar difference one finds in the case of former *ai:* Flemish *eghen* (with umlaut factor), *deel* (without such a factor), Hollandish (and Brabantish) *eighen, deel;* in Limburgish *ei* is found in the majority of both cases: *eigen, deil* (German *eigen, Teil*).

Brabantish (like Limburgish) differs further from the western dialects with respect to umlaut of long *û* (Brabantish *vueren,* German *führen,* western *voeren*) and long *â* (long *a*) (Brabantish *greve, bequeme,* western *grave, bequame* (German *Graf, bequem*). Here it agrees with western German dialects.

In the extreme eastern dialects one frequently finds *a* in places where farther to the west *o* is found in words like *apen* (elsewhere *open,* German *offen*), *baven* (elsewhere *boven,* English *above*), a spelling that indicates an open pronunciation of former short *o* in open syllables. Besides, these dialects differ from the other ones in lacking vocalization of *l* between *o* and dentals: here one finds *wolde, gold* instead of *woude, goud* (see German *wollte, Gold; ou* is pronounced approximately like *ow* in English *now*).

In these cases in northeastern dialects former *al* and *ol* have both become *ol,* being kept apart in the southeastern dialects as well as in German (Limburgish *ald,* German *alt,* northeastern *old,* western *oud*).

In this way it can be observed that the Middle Dutch dialects form a spectrum, the extremes of which are colored more "English" or more "German," respectively.

BIBLIOGRAPHY

Berteloot, Amand. *Bijdrage tot een klankatlas van het dertiende-eeuwse Middelnederlands.* 2 vols. Ghent: Koninklijke Academie voor Nederlandse Taal- en Letterkunde, 1984.

Mooijaart, Maartje A. *Atlas van Vroegmiddelnederlandse Taalvarianten,* Utrecht: LEd, 1992.

van Loey, A. *Middelnederlandse Spraakkunst.* 2 vols. Groningen: Wolters-Noordhoff, 1976.

van Loon, J. *Historische fonologie van het Nederlands.* Leuven: Acco, 1986.

Evert van den Berg

SEE ALSO
Literature, Dutch

Dux/Herzog

The Latin word *dux* originally signified the general function of "leader," especially the leader of a military contingent; later it became the title of an office. *Herzog,* the German translation of *dux,* has a similar history. Although its etymology remains contested, the most reasonable theory suggests that *Herzog* derived from the Old High German word *herizogo,* which meant the "bringer/leader of the army *(Heer)."* Throughout its medieval history, the position of *dux/Herzog* seems to have retained a primarily military character: the duke was responsible for assembling and leading a regional contingent in battle. But the ducal office also frequently included civil, juridical, and ambassadorial functions, depending on local conditions. In the later Middle Ages, the powers of the duke underwent a process of territorialization, with the duke holding the rights and powers of lordship within a clearly defined geographical area, the *Territorialherzogtum.*

Dukes were generally recognized as deriving their public authority from their position as representatives of the king. At the same time, kings were often led to choose members of local noble families who already held de facto private wealth, power, and prestige in an attempt to harness local elite nobles to royal ends. While this policy could enable kings to rule more effectively by entrusting authority to those already in a position to wield it effectively, it also permitted these local families over time to increase their own wealth, power, and regional autonomy, sometimes to the detriment of royal authority. This tense political symbiosis between kings and dukes, although varying considerably over time and by region, remains one of the leitmotifs of the political history of medieval German lands.

BIBLIOGRAPHY

Brunner, Karl. "Der frankische Fürstentitel im 9. und 10. Jahrhundert," in *Intitulatio* II, ed. Herwig Wolfram. Mitteilungen des Instituts fur Österreichische Geschichtsforschung. Ergänzungsband 24. Graz: Hermann Böhlaus, 1973, pp. 179–340.

Goez, H.-W. "Herzog, Herzogtum," in *Lexikon des Mittelalters,* vol. 3. Munich: Artemis, 1984, cols. 2189–2193.

Kienast, Walter. *Der Herzogstitel in Frankreich und Deutschland (9. bis 12. Jahrhundert). Mit Listen der ältesten deutschen Herzogsurkunden.* Munich: R. Oldenbourg, 1968.

Lewis, Andrew. "The Dukes in the Regnum Francorum, A.D. 550–710." *Speculum* 51 (1976): 381–410.

Werner, Karl-Ferdinand. "Les Duchés «nationaux» d'Allemagne au IXe et au Xe siècle," in *Vom Frankenreich zur Entfaltung Deutschlands und Frankreichs. Ursprünge, Strukturen, Beziehungen: Ausgewählte Beitrag : Festgabe zu seinem sechzigsten Geburtstag.* Sigmaringen: Thorbecke, 1984, pp. 311–328.

William North

SEE ALSO
Comes/Graf

E

E. S., Master (fl. ca. 1450–1467)

This Upper Rhenish engraver active circa 1450–1467 is named after the two Gothic letters inscribed on 18 of 318 engravings from the same group. Sixteen of the plates were also inscribed with dates, ranging from 1461 to 1467; they are the earliest "signed" and dated prints in Western art. The identity of the artist has never been successfully proven, although Erwin von Stege, mintmaster to Emperor Frederick III, was one of the possibilities considered. More recently it has been suggested that the initials may be those of a publishing house rather than of an individual.

The most influential of the first two generations of northern European printmakers, E.S. seems to have been trained initially as a goldsmith, for he made frequent use of goldsmiths' punches for decorative effect on the garments, arms, and armor of his engraved figures. Plates made in his workshop were the first to use the technique of cross-hatching, among a rich variety of other burin (engraving) effects. Although several have inscriptions in the Alemannic dialect of southwestern Germany, the exact location of E.S.'s workshop has never been determined. Signed plates were printed on papers traceable to both south German and Swiss mills—the Walking Bear watermark of the city of Bern among them. Three late engravings were indulgence sheets made for the Benedictine monastery of Einsiedeln (Switzerland)—one a pioneering "reproduction" of a known painting, the epitaph fresco of Otto III of Hachberg in the cathedral of Constance (1445), while others reflect the figure style of the sculptor Nicolaus Gerhaert von Leyden, active in Strasbourg around 1460.

BIBLIOGRAPHY

Bevers, Holm. *Meister E.S.: Ein oberrheinischer Kupferstecher der Spätgotik.* Munich: Staatliche Graphische Sammlung, 1987.

Geisberg, Max. *Die Kupferstiche des Meisters E.S.* Berlin: B. Cassirer, 1924.

Koreny, Fritz. Review of Holm Bevers, *Meister E.S. Print Quarterly* 4, 3 (1987): 304–308.

Landau, David, and Peter Parshall. *The Renaissance Print 1470–1550.* New Haven, Conn.: Yale University Press, 1994, pp. 46–50.

Lehrs, Max. *Geschichte und kritischer Katalog des deutschen, niederländischen und französischen Kupferstichs im 15. Jahrhundert* 2: Meister E.S. Vienna: Gesellschaft für vervielfältigende Kunst, 1910.

Shestack, Alan. *Master E.S.: Five Hundredth Anniversary Exhibition.* Philadelphia: Philadelphia Museum of Art, 1967.

Jane Campbell Hutchison

SEE ALSO
Bern; Einsiedeln; Frederick III; Metalwork; Nicolaus Gerhaert von Leyden; Printmaking; Strasbourg

Easter Plays
See Drama, Easter Plays.

Ebner, Margaretha (1291–1351)

Born in 1291 in Donauwörth, near Regensburg, to a patrician family, Margaretha Ebner entered the Dominican cloister of Maria-Mödingen at an early age and was buried there in 1351. In 1332, Heinrich von Nördlingen, her Dominican confessor, convinced her to write a record of her spiritual journey. Without the aid of an amanuensis, she wrote her *Offenbarungen* (Revelations) herself in Alemannic, a dialect of Middle High German. A lengthy manuscript for the Middle Ages (over 100 folio pages) Margaretha's *Revelations* follows a chronological description of her spiritual life from 1312 to 1348, the experiences arranged according to the liturgical calendar. The text belongs to a medieval religious genre referred to as autohagiography. In 1312 Margaretha became seriously ill and for three years endured a variety of afflictions described in the opening chapters of her book. Suffering a severe illness for an extended period of time is a feature commonly reported in medieval hagiography or autohagiography and figures prominently in the religious experiences of medieval women. Recovered, Margaretha undertook a rigorous program of asceticism, self-mortification, fasting, and flagellation. At one point she begged Mary to ask God that she be granted the miracle of stigmata. Quite in keeping with fourteenth-century piety, her devotions center on the humanity of Christ, primarily on his birth and death. Material images of both cradle and cross are, therefore, conspicuous in her devotional exercises. The religious experiences that Margaretha narrates in her writings typify those of ecstatic mystics described in a variety of texts in late medieval Europe, particularly prominent in late medieval Germany. It is also noteworthy that fifty-four letters from Heinrich von Nördlingen and other contemporaries are included in the nineteenth-century Strauch edition.

BIBLIOGRAPHY:

Hale, Drage Rosemary. "Rocking the Cradle: Margaretha Ebner (Be)Holds the Divine," in *Performance and Transformation: New Approaches to Late Medieval Spirituality,* ed. Mary A. Suydam and Joanna E. Ziegler. New York: St. Martin's Press, 1999, pp. 210–241.

Margaretha Ebner und Heinrich von Nördlingen, ed. Philipp Strauch. Frieburg im Breisgau: Mohr, 1882; rpt. Amsterdam: P. Shippers N. V., 1966.

Margaretha Ebner: Major Works, trans. Leonard P. Hindsley. New York: Paulist, 1993.

Rosemary Drage Hale

SEE ALSO

Langmann, Adelheid; Sister-Books

Ecbasis Captivi

An anonymous Latin poem of 1,229 hexameters, the *Ecbasis captivi* (full title: *Ecbasis cuiusdam captivi per t[r]opologiam,* "The Escape of a Certain Captive, Told Allegorically") survives in two twelfth-century manuscripts. It was discovered and first published by Jacob Grimm. Although dates throughout the tenth and eleventh centuries have been proposed, the poem was most likely composed 1043–1046. The poem is connected with Toul in its contents, Trier in its manuscript transmission. Replete with borrowings from earlier poetry, it is also intricate in narrative structure. A long inner story (ll. 392–1009, 1016–1097) is enclosed within an outer (69–391, 1010–1015, 1098–1223); both stories are encircled by a prologue (1–68) and an epilogue (1224–1229). In some ways this poem marks the start of the tradition that includes first Heinrich der Glîchezaere's *Reinhart Fuchs* and later *Reinke de Vos.*

The outer story tells of a calf who escapes one Holy Saturday only to fall into the clutches of a wolf, who takes him to his den to eat him. The calf receives a reprieve until the following day. Soon after daybreak on Easter Sunday, the calf's herd arrives outside the den. The wolf assures his two henchmen that he will win, provided that the fox has no part in the battle. At the request of his two allies, the wolf explains that his fear goes back to a dispute between his grandfather and the fox. This account makes up the inner story. Once the outer story resumes, the wolf suffers setbacks that culminate in his death through the fox's craftiness.

The inner story, which may be entitled "The Sick Lion, Fox, and Flayed Courtier," centers on a lion king and his court. When the lion falls ill, all animals except the fox assemble to suggest remedies. The wolf arranges to have the fox condemned to death for treason. Alerted, the fox piles worn-out shoes on her shoulders to convince everyone that she has traveled widely in search of a cure. The cure is to wrap the king in the wolf's hide.

Because of the poem's curious title, unusual style, and many mentions of Easter, the *Ecbasis captivi* has elicited numerous allegorical interpretations. For later beast literature it holds importance for its full depiction of the wolf-villain as a monk.

BIBLIOGRAPHY

Strecker, Karl, ed. *Ecbasis cuiusdam captivi per tropologiam.* Monumenta Germaniae Historica, Scriptores rerum Germanicarum in usum Scholarum 69. Hanover: Hahn, 1935.

Zeydel, Erwin H., ed. and trans. *Ecbasis cuiusdam captivi: Escape of a Certain Captive.* Chapel Hill: University of North Carolina Press, 1964.

Ziolkowski, Jan M. *Talking Animals: Medieval Latin Beast Poetry, 750–1150.* Philadelphia: University of Pennsylvania Press, 1993.

Jan M. Ziolkowski

SEE ALSO
Reynard the Fox, Dutch; Trier

Echternach

Situated in present-day Luxembourg, thirty kilometers to the west of Trier, the medieval monastery of Echternach witnessed two distinct periods of influence. During the eighth century Echternach functioned as an important center of Insular tradition, in terms of both ecclesiastical and artistic practice. The monastery's founder, Willibrord, was born in Northumbria. At the age of twenty he joined the community of English monks at Rath Melsigi in Ireland. He was sent to Frisia in 690 and in 695 was consecrated as archbishop of the Frisian church. He benefited from the protection and patronage of Pippin II, the Carolingian mayor of the palace, and his family. Pippin's mother-in-law, Abbess Irmina, made the initial alienation of land for the foundation of a *monasteriolum* (convent?) at Echternach. The community was established between 697 and 698, the date of the initial land grant, and 704, when Willibrord began construction of an entirely new monastery on the site.

The strongest evidence for a scriptorium at Echternach during this period rests in a group of four manuscripts: a Book of Prophets and the Hieronymian Martyrology, which have been bound together since the eighth century (Paris, Bibliothèque Nationale de France, no. MS lat. 9382), the Calendar of Saint Willibrord (Paris, Bibliothèque Nationale de France, no. MS lat. 10837), and the Augsburg Gospels (Augsburg, Universitätsbibliothek, no. Cod I.2.4°.2). These manuscripts are all written and illuminated in an Insular style and contain the names of scribes whose names and hands can also be identified in Echternach charters dating to the first quarter of the eighth century. The Echternach Gospels (Paris, Bibliothèque Nationale de France, no. MS lat. 9389) have been attributed to the same Lindisfarne scribe responsible for the Durham Gospels (Durham, Cathedral Library, no. MS A.II.17). It is not known if the Echternach Gospels came to the monastery from Lindisfarne with Willibrord in 690 or at a later time; however, the presence of this luxurious manuscript of the Northumbrian school at Echternach does attest to the artistic links between this community and the Hiberno-Saxon monasteries.

By the ninth century Echternach had become a community of canons governed by a lay abbot. With the Gorze reform (a reform of the Benedictine order and some of its practices) however, the monastery became a satellite foundation of St. Maximin's at Trier, one of the region's most powerful monasteries. St. Maximin's had become a center of the Gorze reform in 934, and in 973, at the wish of Otto I, Echternach returned to Benedictine rule. The canons were forcibly removed from the abbey and replaced by the reformed Abbot Ravanger and forty monks from St. Maximin's.

In 1028 Humbert, a monk from Saint Maximin's and a representative of the Cluniac movement, became abbot. This launched a second period of reform and a new wave of artistic activity at the monastery. In 1028 Humbert rebuilt the abbey church, which had been destroyed by fire in 1016; he is reported to have decorated it with images and painting. Under Abbot Humbert, the monastery's scriptorium took the role formerly held by Reichenau, as one of the great centers of Ottonian manuscript production and dissemination.

The Codex Aureus (Nuremberg, Germanisches Nationalmuseum, no. MS 156142/KG1138) is a luxurious gospel book dating to about 1031, and appears to have been made for the abbey itself. Its opening image of a Christ in Majesty bears stylistic and iconographic ties to that of the Sainte Chapelle Gospels made in Trier about 984 (Paris, Bibliothèque Nationale de France, no. MS lat. 8851). The sumptuous incipit pages of the Codex Aureus, with gold lettering on purple bands over green backgrounds, appear to borrow directly from the earlier manuscript. One of the most striking elements of the manuscript is its departure from the predominantly iconic approach to earlier Ottonian illumination. The arrangement of the figures in three tiers draws from Carolingian models, however; the sheer number of figures and frequent repetition of Christ on the same page represent a move toward a new narrative organization of the material.

Echternach is counted among the last great schools of Ottonian manuscript production; as such it maintained its connections with the imperial rulers into the following dynasty. A book of pericopes (Bremen, Universitätsbibliothek, no. MS b. 21) from 1039–1043, the Goslar Gospels (Uppsala, University Library, no. MS C.93) of

1047–1056, and the Speyer Gospels (Escorial, no. Cod. Virtr. 17) of 1045–1046 were all commissioned by the Salian emperor Henry III.

BIBLIOGRAPHY

Avril, François, and Claude Rabel. *Manuscrits enluminés d'origine germanique 1: X^e–XIVe siècle.* Paris: Bibliothèque Nationale de France, 1995, pp. 1–56.

Ferrari, Michele Camillo, Jena Schroeder, and Henri Trauffler, eds. *Die Abtei Echternach 698–1998.* Echternach: Cludem, 1999.

Hoffmann, Hartmut. *Buchkunst und Königtum im ottonischen und frühsalischen Reich.* 2 vols. Monumenta Germaniae Historica, Schriften 30. Stuttgart: Hiersemann, 1988.

Kahsnitz, Rainer, Ursula Mende, Elisabeth Rücker. *Das Goldene Evangelienbuch von Echternach: Eine Prunkhandschrift des 11. Jahrhunderts.* Frankfurt am Main: Fischer, 1982.

Mayr-Harting, Henry. *Ottonian Book Illumination: An Historical Study.* 2 vols. London: Harvey Miller, 1991.

Netzer, Nancy. *Cultural Interplay in the Eighth Century: The Trier Gospels and the Making of a Scriptorium at Echternach.* Cambridge, England: Cambridge University Press, 1994.

Schroeder, J. "Bibliothek und Schule der Abtei Echternach um die Jahrtausendwende." *Publications de la Section historique de l'Institut Grand-Ducal de Luxembourg* 111 (1977): 201–378.

Kristen M. Collins

SEE ALSO

Ottonian Art and Architecture; Trier

Eckenlied

A Dietrich epic in *Bernerton* strophes, *Eckenlied* is preserved in seven manuscript and eleven printed versions. Of these, manuscript *L,* a late-thirteenth-century Alemannic manuscript, the conclusion of which is missing; manuscript *d,* the version of the *Dresdener Heldenbuch* of 1472; and *s,* a Strasbourg printed version of 1559, best represent the three main variants of the plot. A strophe in the Bavarian *Carmina Burana* (ca. 1220) and the Ecca episode of the Norse *Thidrekssaga* (ca. 1250) show that the narrative was widely known in German-speaking areas by the early thirteenth century. Accurate descriptions of Tyrolian geography and loose connections to Tyrolian folklore suggest that it appeared there first.

The beginning of the story is similar in all versions: Ecke, a gigantic knight, wants to duel with Dietrich. Seburg, one of three queens at Jochgrimm, dispatches Ecke to bring Dietrich to her. Ecke forces a reluctant Dietrich to duel with and defeat him. Dietrich takes Ecke's sword, armor, and head. He then vanquishes Ecke's brother Vasolt and other giants. The texts then diverge. In complete versions, Dietrich eventually reaches Jochgrimm. In the *Dresdener Heldenbuch* (a criticism of courtly literature) he reproaches Seburg for frivolously sending Ecke to die, then throws Ecke's head at her feet. In the printed version (a traditional tale of rescue) the queens thank Dietrich with a feast, because he has rescued them from marriage to Ecke and his brothers.

Eckenlied originated as an etiological explanation for the name of Dietrich's sword Eckesachs (sharp blade). As is shown by its strophe, its close similarity to an episode in the French Arthurian prose romance *Chevalier au Papagau,* and Ecke's dispatch by a lady, it achieved its preserved form in reaction to courtly literature.

A few fragments of another Dietrich epic, involving a character named Vasolt as well as other giants, might be related to the *Eckenlied.* Since the fragments are not in *Bernerton* like all other versions of the *Eckenlied,* but in long lines suggestive of *Nibelungen-* or *Hildebrandsstrophen,* no definite connection can be established.

BIBLIOGRAPHY

Brévart, Francis B., ed. *Das Eckenlied: Mittelhochdeutsch/Neuhochdeutsch.* Stuttgart: Reclam, 1986 [manuscript L and continuations according to both the *Dresdener Heldenbuch* and a 1559 printed version].

———, ed. *Das Eckenlied: Sämtliche Fassungen.* 3 vols. Tübingen: Niemeyer, 1999.

Heinzle, Joachim. *Mittelhochdeutsche Dietrichepik.* Zurich: Artemis, 1978.

Zupitza, Julius, ed. *Eckenlied.* Deutsches Heldenbuch 5. 1870; rpt. Dublin: Weidmann, 1968, pp. 219–264.

Ruth H. Firestone

SEE ALSO

Albrecht von Kemenaten; *Dietrichepik; Nibelungenlied; Sigenot; Virginal*

Education

In medieval Germany, which had a very low literacy rate, three types of schools existed: those of monasteries, cathedrals, and towns. In the early Middle Ages, from the sixth through ninth centuries, monastery schools flourished alongside those of the bishoprics. Because the latter were affiliated with the church of the bishop, they are referred to today as cathedral schools. As populations increased, economies expanded, and more people began to congregate in towns, schools were founded for the laity. While some overlap occurred as these schools came into existence, a chronological development can be discerned that progressed from the monasteries to the towns, from the religious to the secular. Throughout the Middle Ages, private tutoring also existed in Germany as an important and prevalent method of education, particularly for the nobility.

At the beginning of the ninth century, three main monastic centers of learning in Germany were St. Gall (613/614–1798), Reichenau (724–1757), and Fulda (744–1802). Also of importance were Weißenburg (635–1789), Lorsch (764–1248), Murbach (727/764), Amorbach (734–1803), Niederalteich (741–1803), Tegernsee (756/761–1803), Hersfeld (769–1556), and St. Emmeram (739–1812). All these monasteries earned renown owing to the size of their libraries, the erudition of certain monks, and the significance of their literary production. In addition to these monasteries, many others flourished throughout Germany that undoubtedly possessed libraries and schools of their own.

In the tenth and eleventh centuries, when many monasteries in Germany were struggling for survival, cathedral schools were thriving in larger towns. Cologne, Mainz, Speyer, Trier, Worms, Straßburg, Constance, Augsburg, Freising, Passau, Regensburg, Salzburg, Eichstätt, Würzburg, Bamberg, Münster, Paderborn, Hildesheim, and Magdeburg were all important educational centers. Like the monasteries, these schools were renowned because of the bishops who presided over them, the quality of their teachers, and the importance of their literary production.

In what way did cathedral schools differ from monastic ones? The answer lies not in the curriculum, which in both cases encompassed to varying degrees the study (in Latin) of the seven liberal arts (*trivium* = grammar, rhetoric, dialectic; *quadrivium* = arithmetic, geometry, music, astronomy), but in the purpose for which the boys (ages seven to twenty-one) were educated. Many monasteries of the time, St. Gall, for example, had two schools—an interior one and an exterior one, also referred to, respectively, as claustral and canonical. In general, the interior schools trained oblates as monks, whereas the exterior schools concentrated on the education of secular clerics and laymen. Cathedral schools resembled the exterior schools of the monasteries.

As monastery and cathedral schools gradually lost their patronage, town schools supplanted them. Whereas monastery and cathedral schools operated under the aegis of the church and served its interests, town schools owed their existence to the common people and catered to their more worldly needs. By the end of the fourteenth century they existed in great number throughout Germany, even in towns of moderate size. At first, town schools imitated clerical institutions and offered a similar curriculum. Only in the fourteenth century, when the number of schools multiplied along with the population, did the needs of the laity become the focus of instruction and German the medium and object of it. *Schreibschulen* (writing schools) and *deutsche Schulen* (German schools) date from this time.

BIBLIOGRAPHY

Bumke, Joachim. *Höfische Kultur. Literatur und Gesellschaft im hohen Mittelalter.* 2 vols. Munich: dtv, 1986, pp. 92ff., 596ff.

Buzas, Ladislaus. *Deutsche Bibliotheksgeschichte des Mittelalters.* Wiesbaden: Reichert Verlag, 1975.

Fried, Johannes, ed. *Schulen und Studium im sozialen Wandel des hohen und späten Mittelalters.* Sigmaringen: Thorbecke, 1986.

Jaeger, C. Stephen. *The Envy of Angels: Cathedral Schools and Social Ideals in Medieval Europe, 950–1200.* Philadelphia: University of Pennsylvania Press, 1994.

Kämmel, Heinrich Julius. *Geschichte des deutschen Schulwesens im Übergange vom Mittelalter zur Neuzeit,* ed. Otto Kämmel. Leipzig: Duncker and Humblot, 1882.

Moeller, Bernd, et al., eds. *Studien zum städtischen Bildungswesen des späten Mittelalters und der frühen Neuzeit. Bericht über Kolloquien der Kommission zur Erforschung der Kultur des Spätmittelalters 1978– 1981.* Abhandlungen der Akademie der Wissenschaften in Göttingen, Philol.-hist. Klasse 3. Folge, Nr. 137. Göttingen: Vandenhoeck and Ruprecht, 1983.

Riché, Pierre. *Les Écoles et l'enseignement dans l'Occident chrétien de la fin du Ve siècle au milieu du XIe siècle.* Paris: Aubier Montaigne, 1979.

William F. Carroll

SEE ALSO

Egbert (r. 977–993)

Before becoming archbishop, Egbert, archbishop of Trier, served with Archbishop Bruno of Cologne and as chancellor of the court of the Holy Roman Empire. At Trier Egbert was active in promoting manuscript and metalwork production and began work on rebuilding the cathedral, of which only the four eastern piers survive. Under Egbert there was a concerted artistic and liturgical effort to express the position of the apostolic primacy of the see of Trier in Germany. Egbert retrieved the upper half of the staff of St. Peter from Cologne and brought it back to Trier, ordering an elaborate reliquary for the object (now in Limburg an der Lahn). The gold and enamel decoration and the inscription of the reliquary establish the succession of authority from Peter to the first three bishops of Trier—Eucharius, Valerius, and Maternus—and the succession of later popes and archbishops from Peter. Egbert also was active in promoting the cults of Eucharius, Valerius, and Maternus by undertaking the construction of a new church at the abbey of St. Eucharius around 980 and by commissioning Abbot Remigius of Mettlach to compose songs to the saints. New offices in honor of the first three bishops were also composed in this period. Egbert commissioned numerous reliquaries, manuscripts, and liturgical objects. Among the most noteworthy of these are the reliquaries containing a nail from the crucifixion and the sandal of the apostle Andrew and the manuscripts bearing his name, the Egbert Psalter and the Codex Egberti (manuscript of Egbert).

BIBLIOGRAPHY

Ronig, Franz J. *Codex Egberti: Das Perikopenbuch des Erzbischofs Egbert von Trier (977–993).* Trier: Spee-Verlag, 1977.

———. "Egbert, Erzbischof von Trier (977–993): Zum Jahrtausend seines Regierungsantritts." In *Festschrift 100 Jahre Rheinisches Landesmuseum Trier: Beiträge zur Archäologie und Kunst des Trierer Landes.* Trierer Grabungen und Forschungen 14. Mainz: P. von Zabern, 1979, pp. 347–365.

Sauerland, H. V., and Artur Haseloff. *Der Psalter Erzbischof Egberts von Trier, Codex Gertrudianus in Cividale: Historische-kritische Untersuchung.* Trier: Gesellschaft für nützliche Forschungen, 1901.

Westermann-Angerhausen, Hiltrud. *Die Goldschmiedarbeiten der Trierer Egbertwerkstatt.* Trier: Spee-Verlag, 1973.

Mark Stansbury-O'Donnell

SEE ALSO
Relics and Reliquaries; Trier

Eigenkirche

A German term coined in the 1890s by the historian Ulrich Stutz, *Eigenkirche* designates a form of privately owned *(eigen)* church *(Kirche)* common in Europe between the fifth and twelfth centuries. Typically, a layman who owned a large estate would found and endow a church using his own land. As the church's legal proprietor, he would retain control over its administration. He would appoint clerics and apportion the income—partly for his private use—derived from taxing the local population and exploiting the land. Stutz hypothesized that the private church derived from a pagan Germanic practice of maintaining house cults and priests. Subsequent research has demonstrated, however, that the practice was not peculiar to the Germanic tribes. It tended to develop in all societies in which large-scale land tenure existed, including notably the later Roman Empire. In the Frankish realm, the number of *Eigenkirchen* grew in the seventh and eighth centuries until the practice threatened to overwhelm a parallel legal tradition of diocesan church ownership. Bishops claimed the lands of all the churches within their diocese as a part of the general income attached to their office.

From the ninth to the eleventh centuries, the legal rights and economic customs associated with private churches diversified. The radical decentralization of secular power in the west Frankish (French) realm encouraged all levels of the aristocracy to sponsor private foundations—especially monasteries. Private ownership often went hand-in-hand with the promotion of new reformed monastic orders.

Without abolishing private churches, the German rulers also attempted to synthesize diocesan and private structures of ownership by forming an imperial church. They drew on the precedent set by the Carolingian emperors. The Ottonian and Salian emperors exercised similar rights over all bishoprics and some monasteries as private owners were allowed to exercise over their individual foundations. By associating the legal rights of proprietors with the imperial office, the emperors protected the majority of churches from being despoiled by individual nobles. In exchange they reserved the right to select bishops and abbots and to demand military and other services from these churches.

The church reform movement of the eleventh and twelfth centuries produced the single most concerted attack on the institution of private churches. Reformers wanted to assure the purity of the priesthood by isolating it from lay practices and interference, in order to protect the purity of the sacraments. The emperor was the lay ruler whose patronage of churches most directly challenged the pope's authority over the priesthood. The reformers therefore declared the emperors' control of ecclesiastical personnel to be illegal. The reformers' offensive resulted in the Investiture Controversy (1075–1122), during which the popes and the emperors disputed the right to appoint and invest bishops and abbots within the empire. By the mid–twelfth century canon law collections had declared all private possession of churches illegal. The Roman Church limited other forms of founders' rights to a largely symbolic "law of patronage." These successes helped to consolidate the church's exclusive rights as a property owner.

BIBLIOGRAPHY

Constable, G. "Monastic Possession of Churches and 'Spiritualis' in the Age of Reform." in *Il Monachesimo e la Riforma Ecclesiastica (1049–1122)*. Miscellanea del Centro di studi medioevali. Milan: Editrice Vita e Pensiero, 1971, pp. 304–331.

Dopsch, Alfons. *The Economic and Social Foundations of European Civilization,* trans. Erna Patzelt. New York: Harcourt, Brace and Company; London: Kegan Paul, Trench, Trübner, 1937.

Feine, H. E. "Ursprung, Wesen und Bedeutung des Eigenkirchentums." *Mitteilungen des Instituts für Österreichische Geschichte* (1956): 195–208.

Landau, P. *Jus Patronatus.* Cologne: Böhlau, 1975.

Linder, D. "Das kirchliche Benefizium in Gratians Dekret." *Studia Gratiana* 2 (1954): 375–386.

Stutz, Ulrich. *Die Eigenkirche als Element des mittelalterlich-germanichen Kirchenrechtes.* Berlin: H. W. Müller, 1895.

Tellenbach, Gerd. *Church, State and Christian Society at the Time of the Investiture Contest,* trans. R. F. Bennett. Toronto: University of Toronto Press, 1991.

Pegatha Taylor

SEE ALSO

Gregory VII; Investiture Controversy; Otto I; Salians

Eike von Repgow (fl. 1210–1235)

Beginning about 1150 we have records of a family living in Saxony between the rivers Saale and Mulde who called itself after the village of Reppichau near the city of Dessau. Eike von Repgow (also Eike von Reppichowe) probably belonged to this family of ministerials eligible to serve in the judiciary as *Schöffe,* that is, one of a group who determines judgments in a lawsuit. He is probably the person who appears as a witness in charters from 1209 to 1233. Although these charters place him in contact with Count Heinrich of Anhalt, Margrave Dietrich of Meißen, and Landgrave Ludwig of Thuringia and it is certain that he was liegeman to Count Hoyer of Falkenstein in Quedlinburg, we know little of the events in his life and cannot even be sure he was a *Schöffe.* What we do know is that he wrote arguably the most significant text of the German Middle Ages: the *Sachsenspiegel* (The Saxon Mirror, ca. 1225–1235). This is a compendium of the customary laws of thirteenth-century Saxony. Eike's text reveals an education in the seven liberal arts (possibly Halberstadt or Magdeburg), for he had learned Latin and was highly familiar with the Bible and canon law.

The reception of Eike's book was vast. Not only was it appropriated by the rest of Germany within forty years, including High German translations—*Deutschenspiegel* (Germans' Mirror), *Schwabenspiegel* (Swabians' Mirror), but as the four hundred extant manuscript versions demonstrate, it was frequently consulted and much of it remained in force for over three hundred years, thus confirming his contribution to German jurisprudence and culture. Authorship of the *Sächsische Weltchronik* (Saxon World Chronicle, 1260–1275), a lengthy summary of world history and catalog of Roman kings up to Eike's own age, is no longer attributed to Eike.

BIBLIOGRAPHY

Dobozy, Maria, trans. *The Saxon Mirror: A Sachsenspiegel of the Fourteenth Century.* Philadelphia: University of Pennsylvania Press, 1999.

Eckhardt, Karl August. *Sachsenspiegel Landrecht.* Monumenta Germaniae historica. Fontes juris Germanici antiqui, n.s. 1/1. Göttingen: Musterschmidt, 1955, rpt. 1973.

———. *Sachsenspiegel Lehnrecht.* Monumenta Germaniae historica. Fontes juris Germanici antiqui, n.s. 1/2. Göttingen: Musterschmidt, 1956, rpt. 1973.

Herkommer, Hubert. "Eike von Repgows *Sachsenspiegel und die Sächsische Weltchronik.*" *Niederdeutsches Jahrbuch* 100 (1977): 7–42.

Schmidt-Wiegand, Ruth, and Dagmar Hüpper, eds. *Der Sachsenspiegel als Buch.* New York: Lang, 1991.

Schmidt-Wiegand, Ruth, "Eike von Repgow," in *Die deutsche Literatur des Mittelalters: Verfasserlexikon,* ed. Kurt Ruh et al. Berlin: de Gruyter, 1980, vol. 2, cols. 400–409.

Schott, Clausdieter, ed. *Der Sachsenspiegel Eikes von Repgow,* trans. Ruth Schmidt-Wiegand [*Landrecht*] and Clausdieter Schott [*Lehnrecht*]. Zürich: Manesse, 1984.

Weiland, L. *Sächsische Weltchronik.* Monumenta Germaniae historica. Deutsche Chroniken 2. Hannover: Hahn, 1877, rpt. 1971, pp. 1–384.

Maria Dobozy

SEE ALSO

Eike von Repgow, Legal; Laws and Lawbooks

Eike von Repgow, Legal

The author of the *Sachsenspiegel* (Mirror of the Saxons), Eike von Repgow (also Repchow, Repgau) is perhaps the greatest German legal mind of the Middle Ages. He lived in eastern Saxony and may have had an estate at Reppichau near Madgeburg. He was born about 1180 and died sometime after 1235; there are six charters, between 1209 and 1233, that list him among the witnesses. He may have been present at these proceedings because of his legal expertise. Scholarly opinions are sharply divided on several areas of his life. One is his status either as *edelfrei,* a lesser noble, or as a *ministerial,* those serf-knights unique to German society, although he was probably a member of the free lower aristocracy. Another is his authorship of the *Sächsische Weltchronik,* a Saxon chronicle in German circa 1230. Nothing about Eike's life is very certain, and much is simply conjecture.

This elusive Saxon legal expert was responsible for a compilation of laws and customs called the *Sachsenspiegel.* This law code is not only unique in its scope and influence, it is also the first law book written in German, in the Middle Low German spoken in Eastphalia. As this language was predominantly oral, Eike, in writing down what was living law also invented the standard terminology to be used in the German law thereafter.

Sachsenspiegel is a law book in two volumes. Its first volume, the *Landrecht* (common/customary law), apply-

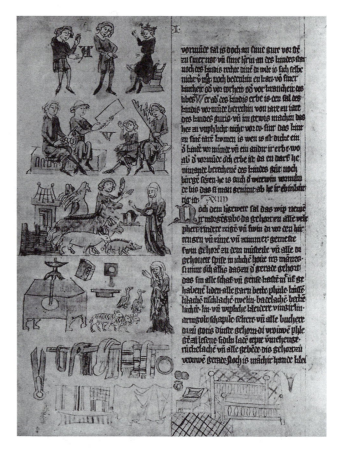

Sachsenspiegel (Dresden, Sächsische Landesbibliothek/Staats- und Universitätsbibliothek Dresden, Ms. 32), fol 11a: administration of the property of minors and widows. *Photograph: Sächsische Landesbibliothek/Staats- und Universitätsbibliothek Dresden, Deutsche Fotothek: Handrick*

ing to all members of the community, includes laws about inheritance, family customs, trial procedures, criminal law, and constitutional ideas about the nature of the German monarchy. It contains 675 sentences of law. The second volume, the *Lehnrecht* (feudal law), contains similar categories but is devoted to a single group: the *Ritter* (knights), an emerging mixture of freeborn lesser nobles and powerful *ministeriales,* the late medieval German gentry. The *Lehnrecht* contains 327 sentences of law.

Sachsenspiegel was enormously influential; it was illustrated in the thirteenth and fourteenth centuries, adapted to the customs and dialects of other parts of Germany, and annotated and supplemented by urban and regional legislation. As the Sachsenrecht (Saxon Law), it remained in use in German legal practice until the early twentieth century.

What were Eike's reasons for compiling the laws of the Saxons? Perhaps he wanted "to please both God and the world," thus aiding his contemporaries by a detailed description of trial procedures that he knew well, and serving God by discussing the traditional theories of the law as he understood them.

Eike strongly objected to bad laws, whether expressed in political turmoil, criminal actions, or human bondage—evils that ultimately had their origin in arbitrary action. He wished instead to uphold God's Eternal Order, the existence of good laws and the absolute necessity of freedom.

BIBLIOGRAPHY

Bergen (Dick), Madelyn. "The *Sachsenspiegel:* A Preliminary Study for a Translation." Ph.D. diss., Ohio State University, 1966.

Eike von Repchow. *Sachsenspiegel: Landrecht,* ed. Karl August Eckhardt, 2d rev. ed. Göttingen: Musterschmidt Verlag, 1955.

———. *Sachsenspiegel: Lehnrecht,* ed. Karl August Eckhardt, 2d rev. ed. Göttingen: Musterschmidt Verlag, 1956.

Ignor, Alexander. *Über das allgemeine Rechtsdenken Eikes von Repgow.* Paderborn: Schöningh, 1984.

Theuerkauf, Gerhard. *Lex, Speculum, Compendium Iuris. Rechtsaufzeichnung und Rechtsbewußtsein in Norddeutschland vom 8. bis zum 16. Jahrhundert.* Cologne: Böhlau, 1968.

Madelyn Bergen Dick

SEE ALSO

Eike von Repgow; Laws and Lawbooks; Ministerials

Eilhart von Oberg (fl. 1170–1190)

The history of Middle High German *Tristan* versions begins with Eilhart von Oberg's *Tristrant,* composed sometime between 1170 and 1190. In contrast to Gottfried von Straßburg's *Tristan* (ca. 1210), the older poem seems to have borrowed directly from a Celtic source, although a French intermediary story *(estoire)* is also possible. Hardly anything is known about the author except that he was a member of the noble family of Oberg who lived in the vicinity of Brunswick and were in the service of the bishops of Hildesheim and the Welf family. It seems highly likely that Eilhart created his *Tristrant* at the Brunswick court of his patroness, duchess Mechthild of England, who was married to Henry the Lion. Mechthild had been raised in London in a highly literate Anglo-Norman world where the Old French *Chanson de Roland* (Song of Roland) enjoyed considerable popularity. It can be assumed that she commissioned the translation of the latter into Middle High German *(Rolandslied),* and also promoted the creation of the goliardic epic *Herzog Ernst,* based on the *Chanson d'Aspremont,* and finally the composition of the *Tristrant* romance. Eilhart's text has been preserved in three fragmentary twelfth- and thirteenth-century manuscripts that contain altogether more than a thousand verses. The complete text is extant in three fifteenth-century paper manuscripts and was first printed by Anton Sorg in Augsburg as a prose version (chapbook) in 1484. This chapbook experienced a long-lasting popularity far into the eighteenth century. Eilhart's *Tristrant* was extensively used as an inspirational source for thirteenth-and fourteenth-century tapestry (e.g., Wienhausen).

In contrast to Gottfried's later version, Eilhart relies on simpler motivational elements to explain how Tristrant and the Irish princess Isalde meet and fall in love. The couple is eventually forced to leave the court and spends two miserable years in the woods until the effects of a love potion fade and each of them can return to his or her life. Tristrant marries Kehenis's sister, also named Isalde, but continues to love fair Isalde, his King's, Marke's, wife, whom he meets several times in secret. The lovers are caught flagrants delicto and are supposed to be executed. But a leper suggests that Isalde be turned over to his band to be raped by all of them, which then provides the opportunity for Tristrant to free himself and rescue his beloved mistress. Later Tristrant returns home from another adventure, mortally wounded, and calls his mistress for his rescue. When she arrives, however, he has already died, and so she also succumbs to death. Now King Marke learns about the love potion, forgives the lovers, and buries them together. Because Eilhart included more comical elements, gave a time limit to the power of the potion, and hence described love as a dangerous power undermining both King Marke's and Tristrant's marriage, this courtly romance had a more mundane and entertaining character than Gottfried's *Tristan.* Here the figure of King Arthur and his court also play a significant role.

BIBLIOGRAPHY

Bertau, Karl. *Deutsche Literatur im europäischen Mittelalter,* vol. 1, 800-1197. Munich: Beck, 1972.

Eilhart von Oberg. *Tristrant,* ed. Hadumond Bußmann. Tübingen: Niemeyer, 1969.

Eilhart von Oberg. *Tristrant und Isalde,* ed. Danielle Buschinger and Wolfgang Spiewok. Greifswald: Reineke, 1993.

———. *Tristrant,* trans. J.W. Thomas. Lincoln: University of Nebraska Press, 1978.

McDonald, William C. "King Mark, the Holy Penitent: On a Neglected Motif in the Eilhart Literary Tradition." *Zeitschrift für deutsches Altertum und deutsche Literatur* 120 (1991): 393–441.

Mertens, Volker. "Eilhart, der Herzog und der Truchseß. Der 'Tristrant' am Welfenhof." in *Tristan et Iseut, mythe européen et mondial,* ed. Danielle Buschinger. Göppingen: Kümmerle, 1987, pp. 262–281.

Strohschneider, Peter. "Herrschaft und Liebe: Strukturprobleme des Tristanromans bei Eilhart von Oberg." *Zeitschrift für deutsches Altertum und deutsche Literatur* 122 (1993): 36–61.

Albrecht Claasen

SEE ALSO
Gottfried von Straßburg

Einsiedeln

The martyrdom of the hermit monk Meinrad in 861 established the area east of Lake Zurich in central Switzerland as a focal point for local monasticism. A Benedictine foundation was inaugurated in 934 with support from the Swabian ducal family, and in 947 the monastery was placed under royal protection by Otto I. This status, with continued substantial grants throughout the Ottonian period, made Einsiedeln an important monastic center for Central Europe. As a pivotal link in the spread of the Gorze monastic reform, Einsiedeln supplied a steady stream of monks to serve as abbots and bishops throughout the realm, particularly in neighboring Bavaria. The abbacy of Gregory (964–996) saw the building of an enlarged church and an efflorescence of book production, including illuminated manuscripts that show links to Reichenau and especially St. Gall. The monastic library also preserves important liturgical and musical manuscripts, as well as the oldest extant copy of a German monastic *consuetudines,* or list of rules, from St. Emmeram in Regensburg (ca. 980–990).

In the thirteenth and fourteenth centuries, Einsiedeln suffered repeated attacks from various sides on its possessions, losing half its land in 1350. At the same time the monastery church became the object of increasing pilgrimage. The devotion to "Our Lady of the Hermits" was directed especially toward the famous mid-fifteenth-century "Black Madonna" statue (restoration in 1933 revealed that the Virgin and Child were originally flesh-toned). Three "Einsiedeln Madonna" engravings executed by Master E.S. in 1466, when the fire-damaged church was rededicated, attest to continued Marian devotion and the importance of the church as a pilgrimage destination on the eve of the Reformation. The now wholly baroque church and monastery continue to function as Switzerland's largest Benedictine foundation.

BIBLIOGRAPHY
Birchler, Linus. *Die Kunstdenkmäler des Kantons Schwyz* 1, *Einsiedeln, Höfe und March.* Basel: Birkhäuser, 1927, pp. 3–22, 178–202.

Euw, Anton von. *Liber Viventium Fabariensis: Das karolingische Memorialbuch von Pfäfers in seiner liturgie- und kunstgeschichtlichen Bedeutung.* Bern: Francke, 1989, pp. 189–192, 201–206.

Holzherr, George. *Einsiedeln: The Monastery and Church of Our Lady of the Hermits from the Carolingian Period to the Present.* Munich: Zurich: Schnell und Steiner, 1988.

Adam S. Cohen

SEE ALSO
E. S., Master; Otto I; Ottonian Art and Architecture; Regensburg; Reichenau; Sankt Gall

Elisabeth von Schönau (1129–1164)

A Benedictine nun, visionary, mystic, and women's *magistra* (teacher) in the double monastery of Schönau near St. Goarshausen, Elisabeth was strongly influenced by Hildegard von Bingen and yet her accomplishments were very different in scope and originality from the renowned contemporary visionary. Elisabeth's ecstasies, visions, and auditions started in 1152. In her visions, which were always accompanied by physical and mental suffering, Elisabeth sees herself guided by an angel.

Although she had begun to set down her own spiritual experiences in writing, in 1155 Elisabeth asked her brother, Ekbert (the author of *Sermones contra Catharos,* "Sermons against the Cathars," and later the abbot of Schönau), to join her at Schönau as her personal adviser and scribe. Much of her text, including some of her less orthodox visions (such as Christ as a woman), was reinterpreted by Ekbert. Similar to Hildegard, Elisabeth was deeply concerned with the corruption in the church of her time and pleaded for reform. Elisabeth faced strong clerical criticism throughout her life.

While never canonized, Elisabeth enjoyed a widespread saintly reputation among her contemporaries. Her work, less complicated than that of Hildegard von Bingen, was uniquely successful (becoming known as far away as twelfth-century Iceland); more than 150 medieval manuscripts are extant. The twelfth-century codex 3 of the Landesbibliothek at Wiesbaden, which contains her complete work, was compiled under Ekbert's supervision.

Besides over twenty letters (most of them written between 1154 and 1164), Elisabeth's work comprises the *Liber visionum,* a collection of her visions in three parts (1152–1160), which contains topical themes of interest today for the history of religion; the *Liber viarum dei* (Book of the Ways of God), 1156–1157, patterned after Hildegard von Bingen's *Scivias* (Know the Ways); and the *Liber revelationum de sacro exercitu virginum Coloniensium,* an imaginative embellishment of the then very popular Ursula legend, which had an enormous influence on medieval hagiography and iconography. While the Latin text of Elisabeth's work was edited (by F.W.E. Roth) in 1884, a critical edition is still outstanding.

BIBLIOGRAPHY

Clark, Anne L. *Elisabeth of Schönau: A Twelfth-Century Visionary.* Philadelphia: University of Pennsylvania Press, 1992.

Lewis, Gertrud Jaron. *Bibliographie zur deutschen Frauenmystik des Mittelalters.* Berlin: Erich Schmidt Verlag, 1989 [comprehensive list of primary texts and secondary sources up to 1988, pp. 146–158].

Ruh, Kurt. *Geschichte der abendländischen Mystik,* vol. 2, *Frauenmystik und Franziskanische Mystik der Frühzeit.* Munich: Beck, 1993, pp. 64–85.

Gertrud Jaron Lewis

SEE ALSO

Hildegeard von Bingen; Mysticism; Visionary Literature

Elizabeth of Hungary (1207–1231)

Saint Elizabeth (of Hungary, also of Thuringia) was born in 1207 to Andreas II, king of Hungary, and his wife, Gertrude of Andechs-Meranien. At the age of four she was betrothed to the eldest son of Hermann, landgrave of Thuringia, and was taken to be raised at his court. The marriage took place in 1221, four years after Hermann's death and his son's succession as Landgrave Ludwig IV.

Elizabeth bore two children, a son Hermann and a daughter Sophie, before her husband's departure on Crusade with Frederick II in 1227. A third child, Gertrude, was born three weeks after Ludwig's death on board ship off the coast of Italy. After her husband's death, Elizabeth left the court and moved to Marburg in the western part of Thuringia, where she established a hospital and spent the last four years of her life nursing the sick with her own hands. She was canonized in 1235, only four years after her death. The cornerstone for a new, Gothic church over her burial site was laid at that time. The testimony collected in support of Elizabeth's canonization soon augmented the bare facts of her life. She is said to have been unusually pious as a child, when she preferred praying to playing with other children and stole bread from the court kitchens to feed the poor. She was reputed to have tended the sick in her marriage bed and to have organized large-scale donations of grain from the landgraves' stores in time of famine. Popular legend too augmented the saint's image. An early story that she was chased from the Wartburg by her brothers-in-law after her husband's death is now thought to be apocryphal; it seems more likely that she left of her own volition to lead a life of piety and charity that was not possible at court. From the time of her death, she was venerated as a saint; the director of her ascetic spiritual practice during the last years of her life, Konrad of Marburg, quickly built a stone basilica over her burial site and began assembling testimony, particularly evidence of miracles, in support of her canonization. After Konrad's death in 1233, Elizabeth's powerful brothers-in-law actively supported the canonization; additional documentation accumulated at this time, including the *Libellus de dictis quatuor ancillarum,* (a brief treatise on her works) placed more emphasis on Elizabeth's earthly deeds. The pope's interest in Elizabeth's sainthood is clearly stated in the canonization documents: a new and popular saint was perceived to be a useful tool in the fight against heresy. Elizabeth's popularity in the eyes of the people seems to have relied not only on her generosity but, more specifically, on her adherence to the tenets of the new Franciscan order, which preached an ascetic lifestyle in which devotion to God was reflected in service to the less fortunate.

Two of the earliest works of art commemorating the new saint record scenes from her life. The roof panels from the great gilt shrine, probably underway by 1248, portray Ludwig's decision to take the cross, his departure from Elizabeth, the return of his bones to his wife, and Elizabeth clothing a beggar, taking the simple gray robes of a hospital worker as a sign of her poverty and devotion to others, distributing alms to the poor, feeding the hungry, and giving drink to the thirsty and washing the feet of a beggar. The nearly contemporary stained glass window, also in her church at Marburg, strengthens the emphasis on her charitable deeds by increasing their number to six, to correspond to the canonical Acts of Charity according to Matthew 25: 34–36, and organizing them together in the window's left lancet. Since a restoration in 1977–1979, they have been juxtaposed to single, unrepeated events from her life in the right lancet. All the scenes from the roof of the shrine also appear in the window in closely related compositions. In the roundel at the top of the window, Christ and the Virgin crown Francis and Elizabeth, respectively.

While later altarpieces both at St. Elizabeth's and elsewhere repeat scenes from her life (see *700 Jahre,* 1983: E, nos. 10 and 20, and II, nos. 2–4, 50–51), the preference in later works, both paintings and sculptures, is for single figures of the saint (see *700 Jahre:* II, nos. 3, 7–11, 14–15, 17–33, 40, 43–48). This type too derives from an early work, a window from the first stained glass campaign at St. Elizabeth's, circa 1240, which portrays the standing saint crowned and elegantly dressed. The single figures typically amplify this model with an attribute referring to Elizabeth's charity: a loaf of bread or a roll, a pitcher, or a garment. Frequently a beggar in smaller scale kneels at her feet awaiting her gift. Although the church dedicated to her at Marburg was not started until the day after her canonization, from the middle of the fourteenth century Elizabeth was also portrayed bearing a church model, the attribute typical of church founders and patrons (see *700 Jahre* 1983: II, nos. 57, 61–62, 64–66). Sometimes, especially in late medieval works produced in Hesse, the church is clearly identifiable as St. Elizabeth's, with its distinctive tri-conch (arched) apse and two tall facade towers.

BIBLIOGRAPHY

Bierschenk, Monika. *Glasmalereien der Elisabethkirche in Marburg: Die figürlichen Fenster um 1240.* Berlin: Deutscher Verlag für Kunstwissenschaft, 1991.

Demandt, Karl. "Verfremdung und Wiederkehr der heiligen Elisabeth." *Hessisches Jahrbuch für Landesgeschichte* 22 (1972): 112–161.

Der sog. Libellus de dictis quatuor ancillarum S. Elisabeth confectus, ed. Albert Huyskens. Kempten: Joseph Kosel, 1911.

Dinkler-von Schubert, Erika. *Der Schrein der hl. Elisabeth zu Marburg: Studien zur Schrein-Ikonographie.* Marburg: Verlag des Kunstgeschichtlichen Seminars der Universität, 1964.

Sankt Elisabeth: Fürstin, Dienerin, Heilige. Sigmaringen: Thorbecke, 1981.

Schmoll, Friedrich. *Die hl. Elisabeth in der bildenden Kunst des 13. bis 16. Jahrhunderts.* Marburg: Elwert, 1918.

700 Jahre Elisabethkirche in Marburg 1283–1983. 8 vols. Marburg: Elwert, 1983.

Werner, Matthias. "Die Heilige Elisabeth und die Anfänge des Deutschen Ordens in Marburg," in *Marburger Geschichte: Rückblick auf die Stadtgeschichte in Einzelbeiträgen,* ed. Erhart Dettmering and Rudolf Grenz. Marburg: Der Magistrat, 1980, pp. 121–164.

Joan A. Holladay

SEE ALSO
Iconographies, Innovative; Marburg

Empire

On Christmas day in the year 800, when Pope Leo III crowned the great Frankish king Charlemagne as Roman emperor, the Roman Empire in the West, vacant since 476, was legally revived. (This empire is altogether too often still referred to erroneously as the "Holy Roman Empire" or misleadingly as the "Carolingian empire." Legally, it was neither.) Charlemagne was fully cognizant of the dangerous implications of this act and in 813 sought to create a different precedent by presenting his sole surviving son Louis to the Frankish aristocracy as his successor and by crowning him Roman emperor. After his accession in 814, however, Louis had himself crowned again at Reims in 816 by Pope Stephen IV, and then his eldest son, Lothar, in Rome in 823 by Paschal I. The popes crowned every emperor thereafter until 1531.

Until 924 they steadily conferred the crown on members of the extended Carolingian family, with only an occasional interlude (e.g., 877–881); but after 924 the western empire was again vacant until the coronation on February 2, 962, of Otto I, duke of Saxony, king of the Germans since 936, and leader of great victories over the Magyars and Slavs in 955. With this act occurred the transfer or "translation" of the empire *(translatio imperii)* from the West Franks to the heirs of the East Franks— ironically, the Saxons, whom it had taken Charlemagne so long to subjugate. From then on, until the abolition of the empire in 1806, every candidate standing for election to the throne had to be able to trace his ancestry back to Otto I.

It was a crown well worth fighting for. Aside from the fact that the emperor enjoyed precedence over all other monarchs in Europe and that legally no other empire existed before Napoléon crowned himself emperor of the French in 1806, he presided over a rapidly growing realm thanks to the initiatives of the Franks. Whether or not Charlemagne was directly inspired by Roman claims to "the whole world" (as we are reminded in Luke 2:1), his biographer Einhard recounts with pride that he worked constantly to extend his empire and subdue foreign nations, and in fact he more than doubled the possessions he had inherited. In the Saxons and their successors, the Salians and the Hohenstaufens, he had worthy heirs. Lotharingia and Burgundy were acquired; Charlemagne's policy of conquest and conversion was now extended to the Slavs; efforts were undertaken to extend hegemony over Scandinavia, Poland, Hungary, and Bohemia; and more and more attention was devoted to Italy, the richest and most economically developed part of Europe and hence rightfully called "the garden of the Empire."

By the twelfth century, however, resistance was rising on many fronts, while the initiative in eastward expansion was passing to princes, bishops, and later the Teutonic Knights. Of the northern and eastern kingdoms, only Bohemia was incorporated into the empire, while Italy consumed more and more energy (the Hohenstaufen spent more than half their time there) in return for less and less. Although the popes have traditionally been blamed for frustrating these imperial ambitions, it was in fact the steady opposition of the Italian communes that did so, aided by the new arts of stone fortification.

The struggles with the popes from the later eleventh century onward did influence the empire in a different way, however. One of their many policies was the reversal of the sacralization of monarchy that had been developing during the previous centuries. Thus Bishop Liutprand of Cremona (d. ca. 972) had already written of the "holy emperor" and "most sacred emperor" in the tenth century. In response to these papal attempts to monopolize the sacred, Frederick Barbarossa (1152–1190) and his chancellor, Archbishop of Cologne Rainald von Dassel, began using the phrase *sacrum imperium* as a counterbalance to the *sancta ecclesia,* and after the mid-thirteenth century the full-blown term *sacrum Romanum imperium* (S.R.I.) stood in contrast to the *sancta Romana ecclesia* (S.R.E.)—the two claimants to the legacy of Rome.

There were two further significant developments in the formal nomenclature of empire in the fourteenth century. In response to French threats to retake the empire and reverse the *translatio* of the tenth century, the words "of the German Nation" came to be annexed to the phrase "Holy Roman Empire"; and then the long list of all the emperor's other titles ended with an allusion to late Roman practice, "at all times extender of the Empire" *(zu allen Zeiten Mehrer des Reiches).* Although all this terminological tinkering might be regarded as flights of fancy in the face of failure, it also represents a certain public willingness to abandon the old Roman empire, the full significance of which Petrarch finally realized in the fourteenth century. Renaissance historians have yet to grasp fully the significance of these facts, linking Germany and Italy, politics and culture, and to incorporate them into their construction of the Renaissance.

One final development of the twelfth and thirteenth centuries is worth noting: a decisive shift in the long-standing, delicate balance between the electoral rights of the princes and the claims to succession of a royal clan, in the direction of the former. In his early conflicts with Pope Alexander III (1159–1181), Frederick Barbarossa had inadvertently aided this development by arguing that the decisive moment in the making of an emperor was not coronation by the pope but election as king of the Romans by the German princes. What has deeply puzzled German historians for several generations is that as the electoral principle became ever more dominant, the circle of lay electors progressively shrank until there were only four entitled to participate (as recognized and enshrined as abiding law by Charles IV in the Golden Bull of 1356): the king of Bohemia, the count palatine of the Rhine, the duke of Saxony, and the margrave of Brandenburg. Why these four? Many explanations have been advanced, but none seems as convincing as that offered by Armin Wolf in 1983. He brilliantly argued that these were the sole surviving families that could trace their ancestry directly back to the sisters of Otto I, that in effect this was the criterion to determine the right to vote, and that by the late thirteenth century all the other families had died out. Like the right to stand for election itself, membership in the lay electoral circle depended on determinable descent from Otto I and his sisters. At the very top, the empire was very much a matter of extended family business.

But the empire was not merely German business, for the legitimacy of rulers and of rule elsewhere depended on it. In the High Middle Ages a very real question in law and political theory concerned the relationship between kings and the emperor, expressed in two questions in particular: What kind of authority did kings exercise? And did the emperor have any jurisdiction over them? The elegant solution to this conundrum was provided in the generally accepted principle, "The king is emperor in his own realm." Just to be sure, however, the rulers of Europe have long been eager to establish their connection with the imperial family of Otto I and, ultimately, of Charlemagne. Whether they are aware of it or not, this concern has lasted into the modern age. In the last hundred years it has been a commonplace that every ruler in Europe was related to Queen Victoria. Anglophiles will be crushed to learn, however, that her significance lay not in being queen of England, but instead a descendant of Otto I as a member of the house of Saxony-Coburg-Gotha (and, incidentally, empress).

BIBLIOGRAPHY

Folz, Robert. *The Concept of Empire in Western Europe from the Fifth to the Fourteenth Century.* London: Edward Arnold, 1969.

Heer, Friedrich. *The Holy Roman Empire.* New York: Praeger, 1968.

Matthew, D.J.A. "Reflections on the Medieval Roman Empire." *History* 77 (1992): 363–390.

Schramm, Percy Ernst. *Kaiser, Rom und Renovatio,* 2 vols., 1929; rpt. Darmstadt: Wissenschaftliche Buchgesellschaft, 1962.

Wolf, Armin. "Les deux Lorraine et l'origine des princes électeurs du Saint-Empire. L'impact de l'ascendance sur l'institution." *Francia* 11 (1983): 241–256.

———. "The Family of Dynasties in Medieval Europe: Dynasties, Kingdoms and *Tochterstämme.*" *Studies in Medieval and Renaissance History* 22 (1991): 183–260.

Lawrence G. Duggan

SEE ALSO

Carolingians; Charlemagne; Charles IV; Deutschorden; Frederick I Barbarossa; Golden Bull; Investiture Controversy; Louis the Pious; Lothar; Otto I; *Reich*

Encyclopedic Literature, Dutch

In general, Middle Dutch encyclopedic writings can be characterized as translations, adaptations, or compilations of authoritative Latin encyclopedias. The following selection lists only some of the most well-known encyclopedic works. In 1266 the Flemish poet Jacob van Maerlant rendered Thomas of Cantimpré's *Liber de natura rerum* (which was written for fellow Dominicans) into Middle Dutch verse for an aristocratic lay audience: *Der naturen bloeme.* During the years 1283–1288 Maerlant worked on his *Spiegel Historiael,* a (rhymed) world chronicle based on the *Speculum Historiale* of Vincent of Beauvais. The Middle Dutch prose translation of another thirteenth-century Latin encyclopedist, *De proprietatibus rerum* of Bartholomaeus Anglicus, has survived in a printed version of the fifteenth century. An anonymous thirteenth-century Flemish author wrote a popularized cosmological treatise in Middle Dutch verse derived from different Latin sources: *De Natuurkunde van het geheelal* (The Science of the Cosmos). The encyclopedic tradition of the fourteenth century is marked by its moralistic nature. In 1330 the Brabantine poet Jan van Boendale presented a moralistic picture of humankind's history in Middle Dutch verse: *Der leken spiegel* (The Laymen's Mirror), which consists of four books, beginning with a description of God and His Creation and ending with the Day of Judgment. Book 3, Chapter 15 contains the oldest Middle Dutch poetical treatise: *Hoe dichters dichten sullen* (How Writers Should Write). Another contemporary Antwerp writer produced a prose translation of the *Livre de Sidrac,* an original thirteenth-century French encyclopedic dialogue, also known as *Livre de la fontaine de toutes sciences.* Also a product of Antwerp is the Middle Dutch (verse) translation of Albertanus of Brescia's *De amore et dilectione Dei,* known in Dutch as the *Dietsche doctrinale* (Dutch Moralistic Teachings). In 1403 Dirc van Delf, commissioned by Albrecht of Bavaria, duke of Holland, wrote a theological encyclopedia in prose for laymen: *Tafel van den kersten ghelove* (Table of the Christian faith), based on several Latin sources.

BIBLIOGRAPHY

Daniëls, L.M.Fr., ed. *Meester Dirc van Delf, O.P., Tafel van den Kersten Ghelove.* 4 pts. in 3 vols. Antwerp: Neerlandia, 1937–1939.

de Vries, Matthijs, ed. *Jan van Boendale, gezegd Jan de Clerc: Der leken spieghel, leerdicht van den jare 1330,* 3 vols. Leyden: Du Mortier, 1844–1848.

de Vries, Matthijs, and Eelco Verwijs, eds. *Jacob van Maerlant's Spiegel Historiael, met de fragmenten der later toegevoegde gedeelten, bewerkt door Philip Utenbroeke en Lodewijc van Veltem,* 4 vols. Leyden: Brill, 1863–1879.

Gerritsen, Willem P. "Het spoor van de viervoetige Locusta." *De nieuwe taalgids* 61 (1968): 1–16.

Gerritsen, Willem P., et al. "A Fourteenth-century Vernacular Poetics: Jan van Boendale's 'How Writers Should Write'," in *Medieval Dutch Literature in its European Context,* ed. Erik Kooper. Cambridge: Cambridge University Press, 1994, pp. 245–260.

Gondrie, Irma M., ed. *Bartholomeus Engelsman. Van de werelt ende van de materialike lichamen des hemels. Het achtste boek van Bartholomaeus Anglicus' De proprietatibus rerum in een Middelnederlandse vertaling. Uitgegeven naar de druk van Jacob Bellaert. Haarlem, 24 dec. 1485.* 2 vols. Utrecht: Instituut De Vooys, 1981.

Jansen-Sieben, Ria, ed. *De natuurkunde van het geheelal. Een 13de-eeuws middelnederlands leerdicht.* 2 vols. Brussels: Paleis der Academien, 1968.

Jonckblet, Willem J. A., ed. *Die dietsche doctrinale. Leerdicht van den jare 1345, toegekend aan Jan Deckers.* The Hague: Schinkel, 1842.

Kinable, Dirk. *Facetten van Boendale. Literair-historische verkenningen van Jans teesteye en de Lekenspiegel.* Leyden: Dimensie/Internationaal Forum voor Afrikaanse en Nederlandse Taal en Letteren, 1998.

Nischik, Traude-Marie. *Das volkssprachliche Naturbuch im späten Mittelalter. Sachkunde und Dinginterpretation bei Jacob van Maerlant und Konrad von Megenberg.* Tübingen: Niemeyer, 1986.

Reynaert, Joris. "Ethiek en 'filosofie'voor leken: de *Dietsche Doctrinale,*" in *Wat is wijsheid. Lekenethiek in de Middelnederlandse letterkunde,* ed. Joris Reynaert et al. Amsterdam: Prometheus, 1994, pp. 199–214, 415–419.

van Oostrom, Frits P. *Court and Culture: Dutch Literature, 1350–1450.* Berkeley: University of California Press, 1992.

———. *Maerlants wereld.* Amsterdam: Prometheus 1996.

van Tol, J. F. J. *Het boek van Sidrac in de Nederlanden.* Amsterdam: H. J. Paris, 1936.

Verwijs, Eelco, ed. *Jacob van Maerlant's Naturen Bloeme,* Groningen: Wolters, 1878; rpt. Arnhem: Van Loon, 1980.

Orlanda S.H. Lie

SEE ALSO

Chronicles, World, Dutch; Dirc van Delf; Encyclopedic Literature, German; Jacob van Maerlant; Jan van Boendale; Latin Language

Encyclopedic Literature, German

Our modern encyclopedias with their alphabetical arrangement of articles are not lineal descendants of medieval encyclopedias. To the extent that they have medieval ancestors, these would be more readily found among Latin-German glossaries that were sometimes expanded with explanatory material. The only feature that medieval encyclopedias share with their modern namesakes is the attempt to provide information on a wide variety of subjects, but this information was presented systematically rather than alphabetically. Furthermore, all the medieval German encyclopedias were translations and reworkings of Latin originals. There was nothing in medieval German comparable to the *Livre du trésor* written in French in the thirteenth century by Brunetto Latini of Florence and soon translated into other Romance languages, including Latini's native Italian.

The first German encyclopedia, possibly written in the last decade of the twelfth century, provides information on natural phenomena as part of the Kingdom of God. This work identifies itself in its opening sentence as *Lucidarius* (Beacon), a name borrowed from the *Elucidarium* of Honorius Augustodunensis, a monk from Regensburg (d. 1137). The *Imago mundi* of the same author and the *Philosophia mundi* of William of Conches (d. 1154) were the chief sources used by the German author. The *Lucidarius* consists of three sections devoted to cosmology and geography, Christian history and practices, and life after death, including the Last Judgment. Even though its later transmissions often reveal special interest in the parts dealing with geography and natural history, its original structure suggests that it was produced by a cleric for courtly audiences.

The thirteenth century saw a number of Latin encyclopedias emerge from within the new religious orders, probably intended above all as compendia of knowledge for preachers. The best-known encyclopedists were the Dominicans Thomas of Cantimpré and Vincent of Beauvais, and the Franciscan friar Bartholomew of England. During the course of the following century, vernacular versions of these encyclopedias became extremely popular, but different regions favored different texts. In England, for example, Bartholomew's *De proprietatibus rerum* in the translation of John of Trevisa became the standard source of encyclopedic knowledge. In Germany, the *Liber de natura rerum* by Thomas of Cantimpré was the source for at least five German reworkings. Of these, the *Buch der Natur* (Treatise on the Natural World) by Conrad of Megenberg (1309–1363) was by far the most important. Conrad taught in Paris from 1334 to 1342, directed the cathedral school in Vienna from 1342 to 1348, and spent the remainder of his life as a canon in Regensburg. He wrote his encyclopedia specifically for the benefit of those who could not read Latin. Thomas had continued to revise his Latin encyclopedia during his lifetime and others had done so after his death. As Conrad came into possession of later versions, he also revised his German text, deleting and expanding and drawing on other sources as he saw fit. Conrad's encyclopedia is still extant in over one hundred manuscripts, and it was printed in 1475 and six more times before the end of the fifteenth century. It continued to be the most important encyclopedia in German well into the sixteenth century.

BIBLIOGRAPHY

Der deutsche "Lucidarius," vol. 1, *Kritischer Text nach den Handschriften,* ed. Dagmar Gottschalk and Georg Steer. Tübingen: Niemeyer, 1994.

Hayer, Gerold. *Konrad von Megenberg, "Das Buch der Natur": Untersuchungen zu seiner Text- und Überlieferungsgeschichte.* Tübingen: Niemeyer, 1998.

Hüne-mörder, Christian. "Antike und mittelalterliche Enzyklopädien und die Popularisierung naturkundlichen Wissens." *Sudhoffs Archiv* 65 (1961): 339–365.

Konrad von Megenberg. *Buch der Natur,* ed. Franz Pfeiffer. 1861; rpt. Hildesheim: Olms, 1994.

Meier, Christel. "Grundzüge der mittelalterlichen Enzyklopädik. Zu Inhalten, Formen und Funktionen einer problematischen Gattung," in *Literatur und Laienbildung im Spätmittelalter und in der Reformationszeit. Symposion Wolfenbüttel 1981,* ed. Ludger Grenzmann and Karl Stackmann. Stuttgart: Metzler, 1984, pp. 467–500.

William Crossgrove

SEE ALSO

Encyclopedic Literature, Dutch; Glosses, Old High German; *Sachliteratur*

Eneit
See Heinrich von Veldeke.

Engelberg

At the beginning of the twelfth century, the nobleman Konrad of Sellenbüren founded in a remote mountain valley in central Switzerland the Benedictine cloister Engelberg dedicated to Mary and saints Nicholas, Leonhard, and Theodore; it was settled by monks from the cloister Muri. The foundation flourished under Abbot Frowin (ca. 1143–1178), who came from the reformed Cluniac cloister of St. Blasien in the Black Forest. Engelberg was probably a double cloister from the beginning: the women's community was subordinated to the abbot of the men's cloister, and their buildings with the chapel dedicated to St. Andreas were located close by. The Benedictine cloister still exists, although none of the medieval buildings are preserved, as the church and convent buildings were rebuilt in 1730–1745. St. Andreas, the women's convent, was moved to Sarnen (Canton Obwalden) in 1615.

A flourishing scriptorium developed under Abbot Frowin. Some forty manuscripts with patristic and contemporary theological texts are preserved from this time, most of them still in the monastic library. The hands of three or four scribes can be identified. The manuscripts' decoration varies widely in quality and type from dedication images in colored pen drawing to figural and ornamental initials. How many artists worked on the decoration is unclear as the manuscripts have hardly been studied. Artistic influences from Burgundian Cistercian and Swabian illumination are assumed.

Until the early thirteenth century a group of able monks were active in the scriptorium. About 1200, the artist known as the Engelberg Master illustrated a manuscript of the texts of Augustine (manuscript no. Cod. 14) with several initials in colored washes. As in the illumination of the period of Abbot Frowin, these initials are marked by originality and free variation on traditional pictorial formulae; the bubbly vitality of the pen drawings, which cleverly combine figural and ornamental motifs, is new. Also from the time of Abbot Heinrich I (1197–1223) is a silver gilt reliquary cross with a particle of the True Cross. On the front the Evangelists surround the crucified Christ; over his head the relic is set behind a round disk. On the back, Abbot Heinrich is portrayed as the donor, with the patron saints of Engelberg; the Virgin is in the middle. No directly related works are known, but the iconographic program and the artistic forms of the cross indicate its manufacture in an experienced, first-rate workshop, perhaps in Alsace.

While the number of monks decreased in the course of the thirteenth century, the women's community, supported by the Habsburg queen Agnes of Hungary, grew to be the largest Benedictine convent in the territory of

Rule of St. Benedict (Engelberg, Stiftsbibliothek. Cod. 72), fol 1r: Abbot Walther with Guota, *Magistra* of the women's convent, and the monk Chuono, *Photograph: Susan Marti*

the Swiss confederation. A group of manuscripts in the vernacular reveal close connections to mystical circles on the Upper Rhine in the second half of the fourteenth century. A number of works of art associated with the convent of St. Andreas are preserved: illuminated psalters (still in the library at Engelberg), textiles (some in the Textile Museum in St. Gall), and several sculptures (some in the Swiss National Museum in Zurich), including a small baby Jesus, which is still used as a devotional image in Sarnen. Most of the textiles were probably embroidered by the nuns themselves.

BIBLIOGRAPHY

Durrer, Robert. *Die Kunstdenkmäler des Kantons Unterwalden.* Zurich: Verlag des Schweizerischen Landesmuseums, 1899, pp. 102–230, 647–697.

Eggenberger, Christoph, ed. *Die Bilderwelt des Klosters Engelberg: Das Skriptorium unter den Äbten Frowin (1143–1178), Berchtold (1178–1197), Heinrich (1197–1223).* Lucerne: Diopter, 1999.

Marti, Susan. "Illuminierte Psalterien aus Engelberg: Zur Handschriftenproduktion in der Frauengemeinschaft eines spätmittelalterlichen Doppelklosters." Ph.D. diss., University of Zurich, 1998.

Orden mit Benediktinerregel: Frühe Klöster—die Benediktiner und Benediktinerinnen in der Schweiz. Helvetia sacra 3, 1. Bern: Francke, 1986, pp. 595–657, 1733–1759.

Reinle, Adolf. "Die Kunst der Innerschweiz von 1200 bis 1450." *Innerschweiz und frühe Eidgenossenschaft: Jubiläumsschrift 700 Jahre Eidgenossenschaft.* 2 vols. Olten: Walter-Verlag, 1990, vol. 1, pp. 285–371.

Schilling, Rosy. "Die Engelberger Bildhandschriften aus Abt Frowins Zeit in ihrer Beziehung zu burgundischer und schwäbischer Buchmalerei." *Anzeiger für schweizerische Altertumskunde* (1933): 117–128.

Steinmann, Martin. "Abt Frowin von Engelberg (1143–1178) und seine Handschriften." *Der Geschichtsfreund* 146 (1993): 7–36.

Susan Marti

SEE ALSO
Metalwork

Engelbert of Berg (d. 1225)

A member of the noble family of the counts of Berg and Altena, Engelbert of Berg became a member of the cathedral chapter at Cologne during the episcopate of his cousin Adolf of Altena, who sat as archbishop 1193–1205. Over time he acquired the provostships of the collegiate churches of St. George, St. Severin, St. Mary in Aachen, Deventer, and Züften. In 1203, he was even elected bishop of Münster but declined, claiming he was too young for such an honor. In reality, he had his eye on the Cologne archiepiscopal chair. Adolf's political position in 1205 led to his being deposed, but the support of many of the prominent cathedral canons and other dignitaries of the archdiocese precipitated a schism that lasted until the Fourth Lateran Council in 1215. During the schism, Engelbert continued to support Adolf, and in 1216 the priors of Cologne elected Engelbert, who by now was cathedral provost as well as archdeacon, to be archbishop.

In 1220, just before returning to Sicily, Emperor Frederick II appointed Engelbert as regent for young Henry (VII), the not yet ten-year-old heir to the Staufen thrones. As regent, Engelbert displayed great administrative ability, though he did not always pursue policies in harmony with the emperor's intentions. He tried to create some stability in the political situation by instituting regional public peace agreements. But in his attempts to bring about closer relations with the English royal court, in line with Cologne tradition, and to bolster them by marriage projects between the Staufen king and the English royal family, he seems to have been more influenced by what was good for Cologne than by what was pleasing to Frederick II. Once war broke out anew between the English and French kings in 1224, Frederick sought to conclude a peace agreement with the Capetians. And instead of being wedded to one of the daughters of the English king, as urged by the archbishop, young Henry (VII), who was still a minor, was married to the daughter of the Babenberg Duke Leopold of Austria in November 1225.

There were also differences between the emperor in Sicily and the archiepiscopal regent concerning the treatment of King Valdemar of Denmark, who had been taken prisoner. Frederick endeavored to force Valdemar to give back former imperial areas between the Elbe and the Baltic that Otto IV and also he himself (in 1214) had granted to the Danish king.

Ultimately, Archbishop Engelbert fell victim to his own extensive family and territorial politics. He was ambushed and fatally wounded on the evening of November 7, 1225, while en route from Soest to Schwelm in Westfalia. The leader of the assailants was his cousin's son, Frederick of Isenberg, who himself had influential comrades-in-arms in his brothers, the bishops of Osnabrück and Münster. The immediate cause of the attack was the archbishop's efforts to remove a canoness foundation at Essen from the repressive actions of its lay advocates, the counts of Isenberg, but it was part of a larger policy aimed at placing as many ecclesiastical establishments as possible under the direct protection of Cologne's archbishop himself.

Engelbert's remains were buried in Cologne Cathedral on December 27, 1225, but they were ceremoniously transferred to a new grave in the cathedral during Lent 1226 in a ceremony presided over by Cardinal-bishop Conrad of Urach, then active in Germany as a papal legate. The legate also presided over a diet, during which a full investigation of the assassination was carried out. Both Walter von der Vogelweide and Caesarius of Heisterbach wrote pieces in honor of the slain prelate; the latter in fact began to collect anecdotal information that he eventually turned into a panegyric aimed at securing Engelbert's canonization as a martyr. Efforts to secure for Engelbert the martyr's crown similar to that of Thomas of Canterbury ultimately failed, however.

It is noteworthy that Frederick II did not appoint another prelate to the position of regent and guardian for his son; in place of the murdered archbishop he nominated Duke Ludwig of Bavaria. The move can be seen as an effort on Frederick's part to keep the German nobility from becoming totally alienated following Engelbert's ecclesiastical regime.

BIBLIOGRAPHY
Ficker, Julius. *Engelbert der Heilige, Erzbischof von Köln und Reichsverweser.* Cologne: Heberle, 1853.

Foerster, Hans. "Engelbert von Berg der Heilige." *Bergische Forschungen* 1 (1925): 108–123.

Greven, Joseph. "Die Entstehung der Vita Engelberti des Caesarius von Heisterbach." *Annalen des historischen Vereins für den Niederrhein* 102 (1918): 2ff.

Kleist, Wolfgang. "Der Tod des Erzbischofs Engelbert von Köln: eine kritische Studie." *Zeitschrift für vaterländische Geschichte und Altertumskunde Westfalens* 75 (1917): 182–249.

Lothmann, Josef. *Erzbischof Engelbert I. von Köln (1216-1225): Graf von Berg, Erzbischof und Herzog, Reichsverweser.* Cologne: Kölnischer Geschichtsverein, 1993.

Ribbeck, Walter. "Die Kölner Erzbischöfe und die Vogtei des Stiftes Essen 1221–1228." *Korrespondenzblatt des Gesamtvereins der deutschen Geschichte und Altertumsvereine.* 2 (1903): 35ff.

Paul B. Pixton

SEE ALSO

Caesarius of Heisterbach; Cologne, Archdiocese; Conrad of Urach; Frederick II; *Landfrieden;* Otto IV; Staufen

Entechrist, Linzer

The *Antichrist* from Linz is a Middle High German religious poem in strophes preserved in a thirteenth-century manuscript from the former monastery of Gleink in Trauntal. This tripartite work, written in 1170 by an anonymous author, depicts the reign of the Antichrist as a prelude to the Last Judgment. The poem comprises three sections with Latin headings: *De antichristo: Elia et Enoch; De signis XV dierum ante diem iudicii;* and *De adventu Christi ad iudicium.* The major segment of the poem that relates the origin, arrival, and demise of the Antichrist is nevertheless only a part of the whole. Arguably, a title more representative of the entire work may be *Von den letzten Dingen* (On the Last Things).

Because there are people who care to learn of the future, the poet tells of the Antichrist and the suffering that will befall the world. The Old Testament prophecy given by Jacob recounts the lineage of the antithetical figures of Christ and the Antichrist: the former from the tribe of Judah, which will bring forth the Virgin Mary, and the latter from the accursed tribe of Dan as depicted in the serpent metaphor. The poet offers instruction on interpreting eschatological portents of the Antichrist's coming, distinguishing divine miracles from demonic deceit and preparing wisely in perfecting vigilance. At the Mount of Olives, the Frankish king is to consummate the history of the empire and remove the final barrier to the progression of events that signal the Antichrist's reign. Although the Antichrist is to remain hidden from view until the age of thirty, he will secretly send false prophets to prepare his way. The vigilant will be able to discern them by their personal conduct and message, however, which disregard Christian charity and do violence to Christendom. The encounter with the Antichrist's cunning messengers is overshadowed by the confrontation of God's prophets, Elias and Enoch, with the Antichrist himself. The poem reveals the Antichrist's three means of false conversion: false miracles, bribes, and persecution. The conflict between good and evil escalates with each successive confrontation. When the Antichrist fails to persuade Elias that he is the Messiah, he slays both prophets with his sword and puts to death all who refuse to worship his image. The judgment and demise of Antichrist will take place on the Mount of Olives, where he is to be struck down by lightning.

After the Antichrist's reign, the poem tells of the interim before the Last Judgment and ends with Christ's testimony that the power of God the Father is unfathomable. The six strophes that form the second part of the poem, *De signis XV dierum ante diem iudicii,* render the fifteen days before the Last Judgment as a swift progression of eschatological time. The third part of the poem, *De adventu Christ ad iudicium,* introduces the themes of fire and transformation. This brief final segment tells of the awakening of the dead and the four groups who will stand at judgment before Christ as *rex iudicii.* The poet concludes the eschatological narrative by teaching that God's servants will take part in the renewal of creation: *ecce omnia novia facio* (all of this will be made new, v. 1176).

BIBLIOGRAPHY

de Boor, Helmut. *Die deutsche Literatur. Texte und Zeugnisse,* vol. 1. Munich: Beck, 1965, pp. 116–133.

Freytag, Hartmut. *Die Theorie der Allegorie in deutschen Texten besonders des 11. und 12. Jahrhunderts.* Bern: Francke, 1982.

Hintz, Ernst Ralf. *Learning and Persuasion in the German Middle Ages.* New York: Garland, 1997, pp. 139–179.

Hoffmann von Fallersleben, Heinrich, ed. *Fundgruben für Geschichte deutscher Sprache und Literatur.* Breslau: Grass, Barth, Aderholz, 1837, pp. 102–134.

Kettler, Wilfried. *Das jüngste Gericht. Philologische Studien zu den Eschatologie-Vorstellungen in den alt- und *frühmittelhochdeutschen Denkmälern.* Berlin: de Gruyter, 1977.

Kursawa, Hans-Peter. "Antichristsage, Weltende und jüngstes Gericht in mittelalterlicher deutscher Dichtung." Ph.D. diss., Cologne, 1976.

Maurer, Friedrich, ed. *Die religiösen Dichtungen des 11. und 12. Jahrhunderts,* vol. 3. Tübingen: Niemeyer, 1970, pp. 364–427.

Scheins, Martin. "Ist Hartmann der Alte der Verfasser des Linzer Entecrist?" *Zeitschrift für deutsches Altertum und deutsche Literatur* 16 (1873): 157–164.

Schiffmann, Konrad. "Die Handschrift des Linzer Entecrist." *Zeitschrift für deutsches Altertum und deutsche Literatur* 59 (1922): 163–164.

Schröder, Edward. "Zur Kritik des Linzer Entecrist." *Zeitschrift für deutsches Altertum und deutsche Literatur* 47 (1904): 289–291.

———. "Die Heimat des Linzer Entecrist." *Nachrichten von der Gesellschaft der Wissenschaften in Göttingen. Philologisch-historische Klasse* (1918): 340–346.

Wundrak, August. "Der Linzer Entecrist. Eine litterarhistorische Untersuchung." Ph.D. diss., Marburg, 1886.

Ernst Ralf Hintz

Erfurt

The early history of Erfurt is closely associated with St. Boniface, although tradition has a Benedictine cloister located on the Petersburg (Mount St. Peter) as early as 706, playing a role in missionary activity to the east. In 742 Boniface asked the pope to confirm establishment of a bishopric at Erfurt, and the church dedicated to the Virgin on the Domhügel (cathedral hill) was elevated to a cathedral. A new cathedral was begun a decade later, but in 754, Erfurt lost its bishopric to Mainz; it remained under the rule and influence of Mainz for the next millennium. Exactly how early a second church was erected on the hill next to the cathedral remains unclear, but in 836 the bones of St. Severus were transferred from Ravenna into the *altum monasterium* (high cloister). A Carolingian palace mentioned in 802 may have been located on the nearby Petersberg, and in 852 Louis the German held a *Reichstag* (imperial diet) here. The city's commercial center lay slightly to the east near the ford across the Gera.

The economy of the city in the Middle Ages was closely tied to the production and trade of woad, a plant that produces a blue dye. The city flourished from the twelfth to the fourteenth century; its favorable position for trade was enhanced when a bridge was built in 1156. The new Romanesque cathedral begun in 1154, after the collapse of the earlier building in the previous year, was consecrated in 1182. The church of St. Severus (Severikirche), rebuilt after a fire in 1079–1080, burned again in 1142 but was rebuilt quickly for a consecration in 1148. The church of Sts. Peter and Paul on the Petersberg was erected between 1103 and 1147 under the influence of the monastery church at Hirsau; only the exterior walls of the ground floor stand in anything like their original form. The so-called Schottenkirche, erected by Irish monks about 1200, preserves the only Romanesque interior in town.

By 1250, the city had achieved a measure of independence from Mainz, and in 1283, the city's tradesmen were granted a role in the city government, which they expanded in 1309–1310. The present cathedral and the church of St. Severus were rebuilt beginning about this time. The building sequence of the cathedral is particularly complex—the Romanesque building consecrated in 1182 continued to be a construction site as it was replaced, one part after another, over the course of the next three hundred years. The two towers flanking the choir were erected in the first third of the thirteenth century. A 1253 consecration is generally taken to relate to either an extension of the choir or the completion of the choir vaults, and another consecration, in 1290, marks an expansion of the choir to the east. The giant arches (*Kavaten*) that allow the extension of the choir beyond the natural profile of the hill were finished in 1329, but the transept and western section of the choir were rebuilt before work moved to the choir itself in 1349; the new choir which still possesses much of its original stained glass, was consecrated between 1370 and 1372. The Romanesque nave must have looked increasingly outdated against the light-flooded Gothic choir and the neighboring Severikirche, rebuilt between 1276 and circa 1332; it was rebuilt in the form of a late Gothic hall church in the decade between 1455 and 1465. Like the cathedral, the Severikirche is a hall church, built on the plan of the previous building.

The cathedral's long building history and the unusual location on the hill above town result in a number of unusual features. The narrow entrance to the choir and the nave that is narrower than the aisles relate to the earlier buildings on this site. The physical location to the west of town means that both the cathedral and the Severikirche are approached from the east—the choir end—rather than from the more typical west. The sculptural decora-

Erfurt, cathedral, north portal, right jamb, Foolish Virgins. *Photograph: Joan A. Holladay*

tion typical of a west facade is found on the cathedral in the two doorways of the so-called Triangel (triangle), the wedge-shaped structure that projects out toward St. Severus from the north transept. Here on the jambs of the door that faces toward the east—the first that one approaches on climbing the stair from the plaza below— stand the apostles; the Wise and Foolish Virgins decorate the western portal closer to St. Severus. The expressive, energized figures are contemporary with the structure of the Triangel circa 1330.

Two works from about 1160 remain from the medieval decoration of the Romanesque cathedral: a stucco retable surrounding a three-dimensional seated figure of the Virgin and Child, and the so-called Wolfram, a bronze in the shape of a man who supports candles in his outstretched arms. The cathedral choir stalls from about 1360–1370 are richly decorated, largely with single figures. Also preserved are numerous panel paintings, reliquaries, and textiles, including the so-called Elisa-

bethkasel, an elaborately embroidered chasuble of about 1300, and an embroidery with Tristan scenes from about 1380. The Severikirche preserves important stone sculptures from the fourteenth and fifteenth centuries. The sarcophagus of St. Severus, circa 1360–1370, features scenes from the life of the saint; the tomb slab with the effigy of the saint between figures of his wife Vincentia and daughter Innocentia is now installed as part of the altar dedicated to the saint in the south transept. The baptismal font with its elaborate blind tracery decoration and vault-high tracery superstructure dates from 1467; it still stands on its original site between the north inner and outer aisles near the west end. Its structure and quality suggest the work of a shop from southwestern Germany. The seated figures of angels are closely related in style to an especially fine alabaster relief of the Archangel Michael from the same year.

In addition to work on the cathedral and the Severikirche, the thirteenth century saw the establishment of the mendicant orders in Erfurt. The Franciscans settled outside the city walls in 1224, moving into the city a year later. Their church was already well advanced by 1231. Three windows from the original building were reinstalled in the new choir consecrated in 1316. Work on the nave of the new church continued through the fourteenth and fifteenth centuries. The Dominicans consecrated their cloister in 1230, a year after their arrival, and their first church in 1238. Gifts between 1240 and 1269 and indulgences dated 1263 and 1278 relate to the building of the new, five-bay choir finished in 1279. The nave proceeded more slowly, into the middle of the fourteenth century. The presence of the Dominican mystic Meister Eckhart here indicates the lively intellectual and spiritual climate; in 1303 he was elected the first provincial of the order's newly founded province of Saxony. The Augustinian Hermits made one of their earliest settlements in Germany in Erfurt in 1266. They were banned in 1273 but were reestablished by 1278, when their church is first mentioned. The present choir was begun in 1286, if not before; the date of the preserved stained glass around 1300 suggests that the choir may have been finished about this time. The nave was completed by 1335. By circa 1300, some twenty-one parish churches also dotted the city of ten thousand inhabitants.

The tradition of learning established by the schools of the mendicant orders in Erfurt was continued, in 1392, with the formation of the university. Even as the university became one of the leading scholarly centers in Germany in the fifteenth and sixteenth centuries, the city itself suffered an economic decline.

BIBLIOGRAPHY

Becker, Karl, Margarethe Brückner, Ernest Haetge, and Lisa Schürenberg. *Die Stadt Erfurt: Dom, Severikirche, Peterskloster, Zitadelle.* Die Kunstdenkmale der Provinz Sachsen 1. Burg: August Hopfer, 1929.

Berger, Rolf. *Die Peterskirche auf dem Petersberg zu Erfurt.* Ph.D. diss., University of Bonn, 1994. Beiträge zur Kunstgeschichte 10. Witterschlick/Bonn: M. Wehle, 1994.

Drachenberg, Erhard. *Die mittelalterliche Glasmalerei im Erfurter Dom.* Corpus vitrearum medii aevi, Deutsche Demokratische Republik 1.2. 2 vols. Berlin: Akademie-Verlag, and Vienna: Hermann Böhlaus Nachfolger, 1980–1983.

Drachenberg, Erhard, Karl-Joachim Maercker, and Christa Schmidt. *Die mittelalterliche Glasmalerei in den Ordenskirchen und im Angermuseum zu Erfurt.* Corpus vitrearum medii aevi, Deutsche Demokratische Republik 1.1. Berlin: Akademie-Verlag, and Vienna: Hermann Böhlaus Nachfolger, 1976.

Gutsche, Willibald. *Geschichte der Stadt Erfurt,* 2d ed. Weimar: H. Böhlaus Nachfolger, 1989. Lehmann, Edgar, and Ernst Schubert. *Dom und Severikirche Erfurt.* Leipzig: Koehler und Amelang, 1988.

Joan A. Holladay

SEE ALSO

Gothic Art and Architecture; Hirsau; Iconographies, Innovative; Liturgy, Furniture; Mainz; Meister Eckhart; Romanesque Art and Architecture

Erhart, Gregor (ca. 1470–1540)

Biographical dates for the stone and wood sculptor Gregor Erhart are known only after 1494, at which time he was already in Augsburg. His wife, Anna, whom he married about 1495–1496, was the sister of the Augsburg joiner Adolf Daucher; through this family, Erhart made close connections to the Holbein family of painters. Numerous commissions after 1498 attest to Erhart's growing reputation, which peaked about 1515 in Emperor Maximilian's commission for a Madonna of Mercy in Frauenstein in Upper Austria. The sources are silent about commissions after 1525; only the pen drawings of fencing lessons from 1533 testify to further artistic activity. Erhart died in Augsburg in 1540.

Gregor Erhart translated the aristocratic, self-confident art of his father, Michel Erhart of Ulm, into a more bourgeois version. The external contours of his works become softer; their expression tends toward the melancholy. Despite these changes, Gregor's artistic forms clearly adapt those of his father, and since the scholar Emil Spaeth identified their relationship in 1922, art historians have faced the task of separating the works of the two.

Not a single signed work exists from Gregor Erhart's hand. Attributions rely on the research of Wilhelm Vöge, who recognized the relationship between the over-life-size Madonna of Mercy from cloister Kaisheim in Bavaria (formerly in the Deutsches Museum in Berlin, destroyed in 1945), documented as a work of Erhart between 1502 and 1504, and the figure of the Virgin from the high altar of Blaubeuren. Current scholarship agrees that the shrine figures and the reliefs of the Blaubeuren altar, dated 1493 and 1494, respectively, were made jointly by the two Erharts under the direction of the father. With these religious works in wood belongs the Virgin figure, over two meters tall, from the cloister of Saints Ulrich and Afra, about 1495 (Augsburg, Städtische Kunstsammlungen). The heads of a girl and boy in the Victoria and Albert Museum in London and the female nude known as the *Belle Allemande* (Beautiful German Woman) in the Louvre in Paris, all about 1510, represent an increasing tendency toward secular works after 1500. The preserved works in stone include a tabernacle for the host in the Stadtkirche in Donauwörth, dated 1503, and several epitaphs and tomb stones in Augsburg, Eichstätt, and Jettingen. A second tabernacle and a stone crucifix for the church of St. Moritz in Augsburg (1502–1507) are known only through documents.

BIBLIOGRAPHY

Müller, Hannelore. "Michel und Gregor Erhart." *Lebensbilder aus dem bayerischen Schwaben,* ed. Götz Freiherr von Pölnitz. Veröffentlichungen der Schwäbischen Forschungsgemeinschaft bei der Kommission für Bayerische Landesgeschichte, 3d series, vol. 5. Munich: Hueber, 1956, pp. 16–44.

Otto, Gertrud. *Gregor Erhart.* Berlin: Deutscher Verein für Kunstwissenschaft, 1943.

Roth, Michael, and Hanns Westhoff. "Beobachtungen zu Malerei und Fassung des Blaubeurer Hochaltars," in *Flügelaltäre des späten Mittelalters,* ed. Hartmut Krohm and Eike Oellermann. Berlin: Dietrich Reimer, 1992, pp. 167–188.

Schädler, Alfred. "Gregor Erharts 'La Belle Allemande' im Louvre." *Aachener Kunstblätter* 60 (1994): 365–376.

Spaeth, Emil. "Quellenkundliche Beiträge zur Augsburger Plastik um 1500." *Monatshefte für Kunstwissenschaft* 15 (1922): 180–192.

Vöge, Wilhelm. "Der Meister des Blaubeurer Hochaltars und seine Madonnen." *Monatshefte für Kunstwissenschaft* 2 (1909): 11–21.

Brigitte Schliewen

SEE ALSO

Erhart, Michel; Holbein, Hans, the Elder; Ulm

Erhart, Michel (ca. 1440/1450–ca. 1520/1530)

Only a few concrete dates are known in the biography of Michel Erhart, who is always called *bildhower* (stone sculptor) in the documents. He is assumed to have been born between 1440 and 1450. Documented as a master in Ulm from 1469, he must have married the daughter of

Michel Erhart, *Schutzmantelmadonna* (Staatliche Museen zu Berlin—Preußischer Kulturbesitz, Skulpturensammlung). *Photograph: Staatliche Museen zu Berlin—Preußischer Kulturbesitz, Skulpturensammlung*

Vinzenz Ensinger, a masterbuilder in Constance, about this time; this familial relationship supports the thesis that Erhart probably served as a stone sculptor's apprentice in southern Germany. Repeated appearances as a sponsor for applicants for citizenship in the city of Ulm suggest that he possessed a position of considerable trust before the city council. He seems to have died at about eighty years of age. His son Gregor and at least one other son followed in their father's profession.

Of Erhart's nine works documented in archives between 1474 and 1516, which include the high altar for Ulm Cathedral finished in 1479, only two are preserved: a sandstone epitaph for the Abbot Konrad Mîrlin dated 1497 (now Augsburg, Städtische Kunstsammlungen) and five prophets created between 1517 and 1520 for a stone Mount of Olives group that originally comprised thirteen figures (Ulm, Ulmer Museum).

These works, together with an over-life-size Crucifix at St. Michael's in Schwäbisch-Hall, which is signed and dated 1494, serve as the point of departure for numerous attributions. With five further crucifixes, including one over five meters tall at St. Martin's in Landshut from 1495, a Madonna of Mercy dated about 1480 (Berlin, Bodemuseum) and an over-life-size standing Virgin from Kaufbeuren from about 1475–1480 (Munich, Bayerisches Nationalmuseum) number among the seventy major works attributed to the master by Anja Broschek. "The tightly composed figural forms" (Miller 1971:51), the radiant beauty of the virgins' faces, and the lively representation of details reveal the influence of Hans Multscher as well as Netherlandish sculptors on Erhart's aristocratic art.

The authorship of the busts on the end panels of the choir stalls in Ulm Cathedral between about 1469 and 1474 remains disputed. The high altar of Blaubeuren, however, is now considered as a joint work of Michel and his son Gregor, made while the son was active in the father's shop.

BIBLIOGRAPHY

Broschek, Anja. *Michel Erhart: Ein Beitrag zur schwäbischen Plastik der Spätgotik.* Berlin: de Gruyter, 1973.

Deutsch, Wolfgang. "Der ehemalige Hochaltar und das Chorgestühl: Zur Syrlin- und zur Bildhauerfrage," in *600 Jahre Ulmer Münster: Festschrift,* ed. Hans Eugen Specker and Reinhard Wortmann. Ulm: Kohlhammer, 1977, pp. 242–322.

Miller, Albrecht. "Der Kaufbeurer Altar des Michel Erhart." *Münchner Jahrbuch der Bildenden Kunst* 22 (1971): 46–62.

Müller, Hannelore. "Michel und Gregor Erhart," in *Lebensbilder aus dem bayerischen Schwaben,* ed. Götz Freiherr von Pölnitz. Veröffentlichungen der Schwäbischen Forschungsgemeinschaft bei der Kommission für Bayerische Landesgeschichte, 3d series, vol. 5. Munich: Max Hueber, 1956, pp. 16–44.

Roth, Michael, and Hanns Westhoff. "Beobachtungen zu Malerei und Fassung des Blaubeurer Hochaltars," in *Flügelaltäre des späten Mittelalters,* ed. Hartmut Krohm and Eike Oellermann. Berlin: Dietrich Reimer, 1992, pp. 167–188.

Schahl, Adolf. "Michel Erhart: Der Meister des Haller Kruzifixes." *Württembergisch-Franken* 47 (1963): 37–58.

Brigitte Schliewen

SEE ALSO
Constance; Erhart, Gregor; Iconographies, Innovative; Landshut; Multscher, Hans; Schwäbisch Hall; Ulm

Erwin von Steinbach (fl. ca. 1285–1318)

Master builder at Strasbourg Cathedral from about 1285 until his death in 1318, Master Erwin is the most famous of this building's architects, although the extent of his contribution has been much debated. He worked on the west facade of the cathedral, and has been credited with building it to the level of the rose window, or even designing the entire west facade.

The documentary sources for Erwin's life are few, consisting of sale contracts from 1284 and 1293; tomb inscriptions for his wife, Husa, and son John, master builder of the cathedral after his father; and two inscriptions, now missing today, on the cathedral itself. Yet the legend of Erwin has persisted. Although mentioned by earlier critics, the German writer Goethe amplified Erwin's fame. His 1772 essay, "*Von deutscher Baukunst, D. M. Ervini a Steinbach*" (On German Architecture, D[ivis] M[anibus] = to the divine spirit of Ervin of Steinbach) was addressed to Erwin and attributed Strasbourg Cathedral to him as a crowning German achievement. It should be noted that Goethe credited him with the spire, which was not built, however, until the fifteenth century.

Goethe's praise of Erwin established nationalistic tones in some later scholarship. Some scholars have seen him as responsible for the idea of the *Wandfassade* (literally, wall facade), incorporating the belfry. This would mean that much of Strasbourg Cathedral's west facade was an original design that was German in origin. But most scholars today view Erwin as responsible only for building to the level of the rose window. The question is not settled, but evidence is hard to find of Erwin's dates of tenure and authorship of the drawings of the west facade, now in the cathedral museum.

BIBLIOGRAPHY

Geyer, Marie-Jeanne. "Le Mythe d'Erwin de Steinbach," in *Les Bâtisseurs des cathédrales gothiques,* ed. Roland Recht. Strasbourg: Éditions les Musées de la Ville de Strasbourg, 1989, pp. 322–329.

Liess, Reinhard. "Das 'Kreßburger Fragment' im Hauptstaatsarchiv Stuttgart." *Jahrbuch der staatlichen Kunstsammlungen im Baden-Württemberg* 23 (1986): 6–31.

Wortmann, Reinhard. "Der Westbau des Straßburger Münsters und Meister Erwin." *Bonner Jahrbücher* 169 (1969): 290–318.

Charlotte Stanford

SEE ALSO

Gothic Art and Architecture; Strasbourg

Essen

The prominence of medieval Essen derived from its celebrated canonical foundation for aristocratic women, purportedly founded in circa 845–852 by Bishop Altfrid of Hildesheim (851–874). Altfrid probably also built the earlier, small chapel of St. Quintin, of which archaeological evidence was found on the north side of the foundation church; the first abbess of Essen, Altfrid's sister Gerswit, was buried there. While at the outset Essen was part of the patrimony of the Hildesheim bishops, under the Ottonians (sometime before 947), Essen gained protection, immunity—and distinction—as an independent royal foundation.

The 1943 bombings of the church during World War II necessitated repair from 1948 to 1957 but allowed for previously infeasible excavations and the ensuing clarification of the complex building history. The first church, a simple basilica dedicated to the Holy Trinity, the Virgin, and Saints Cosmos and Damien, was built circa 850–870. Partially destroyed in a fire of 946, the church was rebuilt, incorporating extensive remains of the previous structure. In the second half of the tenth century, a westwork (entrance structure) and outer crypt were added to the structure. The eleventh-century church, generally dated to the tenure of the abbess Theophanu (1039–1058), was constructed largely on the foundations of the expanded tenth-century structure. Fire necessitated the rebuilding of much of the church between 1276 and 1327, with the new structure built atop the partially razed nave, transept, and choir walls of its eleventh-century predecessor, again incorporating much of the previous building.

Golden Madonna, Essen, *Münster. Photograph: Rheinisches Bildarchiv der Stadt Köln*

The extant church, now the cathedral of Essen, bears witness to aspects of this extensive building activity. The nave and side aisles of the hall church (severely damaged during World War II), the transept, east end, and upper story of the outer crypt date to the late twelfth- and early thirteenth-century rebuilding. This Gothic campaign retained the still extant eleventh-century west atrium, west end structure, and lower outer crypt. The complex west end (the only part of the church relatively unscathed by the 1943 bombings) has received a great deal of attention, primarily owing to its formal comparison by scholars to the church of Charlemagne at Aachen. The eleventh-century western addition *(Westbau),* built in the area delineated by the tenth-century westwork, is preceded by a rectangular forecourt. On the exterior, the multistoried structure rises as an octagonal tower, while, on the interior, the elevation, which opens into the nave, presents three sides of an inscribed polygon that carries, above a first story of round arches, a two-story columnar screen.

The church of St. John the Baptist was built at the west end of the atrium preceding the foundation church. Established perhaps in the late tenth century as a baptismal church, by 1260 it was a parish church. St. John's was rebuilt a number of times throughout the Middle Ages, achieving its present form in 1471. Also tied to the city's main foundation, the church of St. Gertrude—the market church—was probably first built in the mid-eleventh century, and was replaced in the second half of the twelfth century by an aisled basilica. It too became a parish church in 1260.

The immense vitality of Essen under the Ottonians, reflected in its building history, may be gauged as well by the remarkable treasury, which includes works commissioned by the foundation's abbesses, drawn exclusively from the Ottonian house. Mathilde (d. 1011), the granddaughter of Otto the Great, and Theophanu, named for her grandmother, the wife of Otto II, stand out for their extraordinary patronage. Mathilde contributed the famous Golden Madonna and the seven-armed candelabra found today within the church, as well as three processional crosses found in the Treasury; she also was responsible for the now lost Marsusschrein, which held relics purportedly given to the foundation by Altfrid. Mathilde is suspected of having been the recipient of the Kinderkrone, the late-tenth-century child's crown thought to be a gift to the foundation from Otto III. In addition to her rebuilding of the church, Theophanu commissioned a cross containing a piece of the True Cross, a much-altered reliquary with a Nail from the Crucifixion, and a sumptuous book cover.

With the advent of the Salians, Essen lost a measure of the power and autonomy that was a hallmark of Ottonian female religious foundations. Yet the currency of Essen, particularly in the late Middle Ages, is reflected not only in the Gothic rebuilding but in the numerous works, primarily reliquaries, of the fourteenth and fifteenth centuries found today in the treasury. Another fortuitous survival is the well-known fourteenth-century *Liber ordinarius,* a liturgical text that allows insight into the uses of the church's complex spaces in the late Middle Ages.

BIBLIOGRAPHY

Der Liber Ordinarius der Essener Stiftskirche, ed. Franz Arens. Paderborn: Junfermann, 1908.

Heitz, Carol. *Recherches sur les rapports entre architecture et liturgie à l'époque carolingienne.* Paris, S.E.V.P.E.N., 1963.

Kubach, Hans Erich, and Albert Verbeek. *Romanische Baukunst an Rhein und Maas:Katalog der vorromanischen und romanischen Denkmäler.* 3 vols. Berlin: Deutscher Verlag für Kunstwissenschaft, 1976, vol. 1, pp. 268–280.

Pothman, Alfred. *Die Schatzkammer des Essener Münsters.* Munich: Schnell and Steiner, 1988.

———. *Der Essener Dom: Kathedralkirche des Ruhrbistums,* 4th ed. Regensburg: Schnell und Steiner, 1997.

Verbeek, Albert. "Die architektonische Nachfolge der Aachener Pfalzkapelle," in *Karl der Große: Lebenswerk und Nachleben,* ed. Wolfgang Braunfels and Percy Ernst Schramm. 4 vols. Düsseldorf: Schwann, 1967, vol. 4, pp. 113–156.

Zimmermann, Walther. *Das Münster zu Essen.* Kunstdenkmäler des Rheinlandes, Beiheft 3. Essen: Fredebeul und Koenen, 1956.

Jenny H. Shaffer

SEE ALSO
Aachen; Hildesheim; Otto I; Otto II; Otto III; Ottonian Art and Architecture; Relics and Reliquaries; Salians; Theophanu

Esslingen am Neckar

An important center of wine growing and making since Roman times, Esslingen am Neckar continued to owe much of its wealth and reputation to its fine wines throughout the Middle Ages. As early as the fourteenth century, southern German wine was measured in "Esslingen buckets." First documented in 777, the town was noted as an important gathering place for those traveling between the Rheinland and Italy.

Central in the old town, built on the foundations of an eighth-century church, the basilica of St. Dionysius dates to the thirteenth and fourteenth centuries. The squared-off eastern towers are essentially Romanesque in their overall design, although the south tower does show Gothic elements in its ornament. The seven bays of the nave are also clearly transitional, while the choir is High Gothic. Its fourteenth-century stained glass, of extremely high quality, was done primarily in Esslingen workshops. The subjects depicted are from the Old and New Testaments. Highly complex pier bases show the stonemason's interest in traditional wood carving techniques: spiral

Esslingen, Church of the Virgin, east portal on south nave wall: scenes from the life of the Virgin. *Photograph: Joan A. Holladay*

turnings, diamond patternings, and faceting. The fifteenth-century baptismal font is attributed to the Heidelberg master Lorenz Lechler.

The Dominican church of St. Paul, on the western end of the market square, was consecrated in 1268 by Albertus Magnus. It is the oldest existing church of the mendicant orders in Germany. The long basilica has ribbed cross vaults and a polygonal choir. Its severe forms and simplified decorations reflect mendicant ideals. Important objects in the interior include a late Gothic Crucifix over the altar and a fifteenth-century Madonna and Child originally made for the Church of Our Lady (Frauenkirche).

The High Gothic Frauenkirche stands outside the old city ring, to the north. The single western tower, with its fine tracery spire, was not completed until 1494. It was begun a hundred years earlier by Ulrich von Ensingen,

master builder of the cathedral of Ulm. Ulrich was succeeded by his sons Matthäus and Matthias. The upper octagon and spire were finally completed by Hans von Böblingen and his sons, Marx and Lux. Among the rich sculptural programs of the Frauenkirche are the southeastern portal representing scenes from the life of the Virgin (ca. 1350) and the southwestern portal depicting the Last Judgment (ca. 1400). The stained glass of the choir, dating to 1320–1330, was produced in Esslingen workshops.

Also at the heart of the old town is the late Gothic half-timbered Old Town Hall (Altes Rathaus), built in 1430. Carved console figures (ca. 1440) in its Bürgersaal (Citizens' Hall) depict saints, electors, and kings. Four of the oldest half-timbered houses in Germany, all dating to the fourteenth century, can be found on Esslingen's Harbor Market (Hafenmarkt, nos. 4, 6, 8, and 10). Another monument here, locally known as the "Yellow House," is a well-preserved tower residence from the second half of the thirteenth century.

Subsidiary to Esslingen's many monasteries were the so-called *Pfleghöfe*, which served as nursing and charity homes. Several of these survive from the Middle Ages. The oldest among them is the Salmannsweilder Pfleghof, east of the Frauenkirche. This massive stone structure is a survivor of the Hohenstaufen period. The Speyerer Pfleghof on the market square was built in the thirteenth century and the Konstanzer Pfleghof in 1327.

The Old Neckar Bridge, built in 1286, connects the old city center to the former river island of Pliensau. Most of this structure, one of Europe's oldest existing bridges, fell in the nineteenth century. It has since been restored.

Only fragments of the city fortress *(Burg)* in the north, above the old town, survive today. Built under the Hohenstaufen in the twelfth and thirteenth centuries, remnants of the once vast complex include the Fat Tower (Dicker Turm), the High Guard (Hohwacht), the cable gangway, and several sections of wall. A number of gates and towers of the old city wall also still stand. Most notable of these is the Wolfstor (Wolf's Gate), first documented in 1268. The late Romanesque gate bears the lion arms of the Hohenstaufen.

Esslingen's prosperity in the Middle Ages contributed to an increasing rivalry with the dukes of Württemberg. A period of war broke out as of 1246, ending in 1454 with the defeat of Esslingen. The Swabian Federation was founded here in 1488.

BIBLIOGRAPHY

Becksmann, Rüdiger. *Von der Ordnung der Welt: Mittelalterliche Glasmalereien aus Esslinger Kirchen.* Ostfildern: Hatje, 1997.

Bernhardt, Walter. *Die Pfleghöfe in Esslingen.* Esslingen: Stadtarchiv, 1982.

Borst, Otto. *Esslingen am Neckar: Geschichte und Kunst einer Stadt.* Esslingen: Bechtle, 1974.

Die Stadtkirche Sankt Dionyius in Esslingen am Neckar: Archäologie und Baugeschichte, ed. Landesdenkmalamt Baden-Württemberg. 3 vols. Forschungen und Berichte der Archäologie des Mittelalters in Baden-Württemberg 13. Stuttgart: Thieß, 1995.

Leslie Anne Hamel

SEE ALSO
Albertus Magnus; Carolingian Art and Architecture; Gothic Art and Architecture; Romanesque Art and Architecture; Ulm

Exemplum

An anecdote or short narrative, usually based on a maxim, precept, or proverb, that manifests a moral or dogmatic truth is called, following the Latin term for "example," exemplum (Middle High German *bîspel*, Middle English *bispell, besynan*). The exemplum shares several generic qualities with *Mären* and fables, and these similarities frustrate attempts to distinguish the forms from one another. Ulrich Boner, for example, based his *Edelstein* (1350) primarily on Aesop's fables, but he refers to the tales as *bîspel*. Some discern the exemplum from the fable by limiting exempla to narratives featuring human characters and a plausible turn of events. G.E. Lessing's *Abhandlungen über die Fabel* (1759), for example, advances this criterion. Ultimately, the function and context of the story, rather than the form, characterize an exemplum. Generally, an exemplum is a morally edifying tale within a longer didactic narrative. The exemplum illustrates, either through good or bad example, the proper moral behavior promoted in that narrative. A freestanding narrative of similar content might be identified as a *Märe* or a fable. However, in the absence of absolute generic distinctions, *Mären* and fables are often labeled exemplum as well. There are a number of antique collections of exempla, most notably Valerius Maximus's *Factorum et dictorum memorabilium* (ca. 20 C.E.), which was extremely popular in the Middle Ages. Exempla were employed by the church fathers, most notably in the *Dialogues* of Pope Gregory I (ca. 540–604). The exemplum experienced a drastic rise in popularity from the mid-twelfth century onward. Exempla can be found in a wide variety of ecclesiastical works of Alain de Lille (1128–1202) or in the *Speculum ecclesiae*, attributed to Edmund of Abington (1175–1240), as well as in moral-philosophical works from this period such as John of Salisbury's *Policratus* (1159) or the various *Fürstenspiegel* (guides for nobility). Vincent de Beauvais's *Speculum historiale* (ca. 1245; the first book of his monumental *Speculum majus*) and Caesarius von Heisterbach's *Dialogus miraculorum* (ca. 1220) are two of the most popular collections of exempla in the Middle Ages. This tradition continued well into the fourteenth century with historical works like the English *Gesta Romanorum*. Exempla also had a place in miraculous tales, legends, vitas, and, above all, sermons. Sermons provided the primary context for exempla. The production of exempla books like the *Alphabetum exemplorum* for preachers reflects the popularity of exempla in sermons. The exempla were intended to provide illustrations of the consequences of good and evil, to invoke the fear of God, or simply to enliven a boring sermon. The excessive use of exempla in sermons and the predilection of some preachers for particularly risqué or gruesome exempla led to their gradual waning in popularity and esteem. In Canto 29 of his *Paradiso* (ca. 1315), the Italian poet Dante bemoans that in church one is more likely to hear "jests and jibes" than the gospels. During the Reformation, the Catholic Church banned many of the more questionable exempla. In the vernacular literature, we find numerous references to exempla. There are several medieval German texts in which characters relate exempla but nothing as extensive as Boccaccio's Italian *Decameron* (1348–1353) or Chaucer's (ca. 1390) *Canterbury Tales*. Wolfram von Eschenbach strings together a number of exempla in the cryptic prologue of his Middle High German grail romance *Parzival* (ca. 1210). Indeed, reference to exempla has provided literary scholars with the key to understanding many obscure passages in epic literature and courtly lyric. Many works covered under the generic rubric of the *Märe* are also included under exemplum. Chief among these are the shorter works of the Stricker, but the works of Heinrich Kaufringer, Hans Rosenplüt, and even Konrad von Würzburg are sometimes included. Some critics even read Hartmann von Aue's *Der arme Heinrich* or Rudolf von Ems's *Der guote Gerhart* as exempla.

BIBLIOGRAPHY

Bremond, Claude. *L'"Exemplum."* Turnhout: Brepols, 1996.

Haug, Walter, and Burghart Wachinger, eds. *Exempel und Exempelsammlungen.* Tübingen: Niemeyer, 1991.

Menzel, Michael. *Predigt und Geschichte : historische Exempel in der geistlichen Rhetorik des Mittelalters.* Cologne: Böhlau, 1998.

Mosher, Joseph A. *The Exemplum in the Early Religious and Didactic Literature of England.* New York: Columbia University Press, 1911.

Scanlon, Larry. *Narrative, Authority, and Power: The Medieval Exemplum and the Chaucerian Tradition.* New York: Cambridge University Press, 1994.

Stephen M. Carey

SEE ALSO

Boner, Ulrich; Caesarius of Heisterbach; Hartman von Aue; Konrad von Würzburg; Legends; Rudolf von Ems; Wolfram von Eschenbach

Exodus

See Genesis and *Exodus.*

Ezzo (d. after 1065)

Presumed author of the *Cantilena de miraculis Christi* (Song on Christ's Miracles), more commonly known as the *Ezzolied* (Ezzo's Song), the first vernacular German work of mature literary quality since the Old High German *Christus und die Samariterin* (Christ and the Samaritin Woman, ca. 900). The earliest connection between the name Ezzo and a hymn composed around the middle of the eleventh century is found in the *Vita altmanni.* The *Vita* (ca. 1130) describes, among other events from the life of Altmann (d. 1091), a pilgrimage to the Holy Land in which the Passau bishop took part in 1064/1065. Also participating in this pilgrimage, according to the *Vita*, was a cleric named Ezzo who wrote a *Cantilena de miraculis Christi* in German. That the *cantilena* in the vernacular by someone named Ezzo and the *Ezzolied* are one and the same thing is a virtual certainty.

The work exists in two redactions, the *Strasbourg* (Bibliothèque Nationale et Universitaire, manuscript no. germ. 278, fol. 74v. "S"), and the *Vorau* (no. 276, Chorherrenstift, parchment, fol. 128r-129v "V"). The Strasbourg manuscript contains the older and without doubt more authentic, even if fragmentary version of the two (only seven strophes are preserved), whereas the Vorau redaction contains thirty-four strophes and is clearly a revision intended for a monastic audience. Both are probably revisions of a lost "Bamberg Ezzolied" original.

The hymn presents the immutable lessons of Christianity beginning with Creation ("S" 2–4; "V" 5–8), proceeding to the Fall ("S" 5–6; "V" 9–10), moving through the Old Testament period, culminating in the mission of John the Baptist ("S" 7; "V" 11–13), concentrating on the birth of Christ and his baptism ("V" 14–17), the miracles done during Christ's public ministry ("V" 18–19), the crucifixion and its significance, including the Harrowing of Hell ("V" 20–30), and concluding with a paean to the Cross ("V" 31–34).

The *Ezzolied* is a joyous celebration of the triumph of Christ over death and Satan. Emphasized is not the suffering Christ of later Gothic centuries but, rather, the victorious Christ the King of the Romanesque.

BIBLIOGRAPHY

Barack, K. A., ed. *Ezzos Gesang von den Wundern Christi und Nokers "Memento mori" in phototypischen Faksimile der Straßburger Handschrift.* Strasbourg: Trubner, 1879.

Barack, K. A. "Althochdeutsche Funde." *Zeitschrift für deutsches Altertum* 23 (1879): 210–212 ["S"].

Diemer, Joseph. "Beiträge zur älteren deutschen Sprache und Literatur, 22–23. Ezzo's Lied von dem Anegenge aus dem Jahr 1065." *Sitzungsberichte der philosophisch-historischen Klasse der österreichischen Akademie der Wissenschaften in Wien* 52 (1866): 183–202; 427–469 [notes; first complete edition of the Vorau version].

Freytag, Hartmut. "Ezzos Gesang. Text und Funktion." in *Geistliche Denkformen in der Literatur des Mittelalters.* Munich: Fink, 1984, pp. 154–170.

Gentry, Francis G. *Bibliographie zur frühmittel-hochdeutschen geistlichen Dichtung.* Berlin: Schmidt, 1992, pp. 184–191.

Maurer, Friedrich, ed. *Die religiösen Dichtungen des 11. und 12. Jahrhunderts. Nach ihren Formen besprochen und herausgegeben,* vol. 1. Tübingen: Niemeyer, 1964, pp. 284–303 ["V," "S"].

Polheim, Karl Konrad, ed. *Die deutschen Gedichte der Vorauer Handschrift (Kodex 276/2).* Graz: Akademischer Verlagsanstalt, 1958.

Rupp, Heinz. *Deutsche Religiöse Dichtungen des 11. und 12. Jahrhunderts. Untersuchungen und Interpretationen,* 2d ed. Bern: Francke, 1971, pp. 33–83.

Schmidt-Wiegand, Ruth. "Die Weltalter in Ezzos Gesang," in *Zeiten und Formen in Sprache und Dichtung: Festschrift für Fritz Tschirch zum 70. Geburtstag,* ed. Karl-Heinz Schirmer and Bernhard Sowinski. Cologne: Böhlau, 1972, pp. 42–51.

Schröder, Werner, ed. *Kleinere deutsche Gedichte des 11. und 12. Jahrhunderts.* Tübingen: Niemeyer, 1972, pp. 10–26 ["V," "S"].

Vollmann-Profe, Gisela. *Geschichte der deutschen Literatur von den Anfängen bis zum Beginn der Neuzeit, vol. 1, 2: Wiederbeginn volkssprachiger Schriftlichkeit im hohen Mittelalter,* 2d ed. Tübingen: Niemeyer, 1994, passim.

Francis G. Gentry

SEE ALSO
Ezzonids

Ezzonids

The Ezzonids were a family on the lower Rhine who rose to prominence by the year 1000, only to die out within a century. Their ascendancy was enabled by political developments after the incorporation of Lotharingia into the German kingdom in 925. Royal interests in the Rhineland prevented the formation of a powerful Rhenish duchy. Particularism to the advantage of local kin groups culminated in a regional power vacuum by the 990s. In response, Emperor Otto III and his mother, Theophanu, sought the support of regional elites. Around 990, a certain Hermann was appointed count palatine along the lower Rhine. In 991, the king's sister Mathilda was married to Hermann's son Ezzo, who became count palatine after his father's death in 996. Despite contemporaries' perception that Mathilda had married beneath her, the marriage seemed a happy one. Ten children were born to the couple. Of seven daughters, five became abbesses of important religious communities, while one (Richeza) became queen of Poland by marriage. One son (Otto) became duke of Swabia, while another (Hermann) was archbishop of Cologne from 1035 to 1056. By Ezzo's death in 1034 (Mathilda died in 1025), the Ezzonids exercised power and great influence throughout the realm.

However, the fact that so many of Ezzo and Mathilda's children pursued ecclesiastical careers had serious consequences for the longevity of the family. Otto, the son intended to assume his father's mantle, died childless in 1047. Otto's brother Ludolf had predeceased Ezzo in 1031, leaving behind two sons: Henry, who soon died, and Kuno (or Konrad). In the 1050s, Kuno perished in exile in Hungary after falling from favor with Emperor Henry III and losing the duchy of Bavaria. Richeza, after the death of her husband, King Mieszko II of Poland, in 1034, returned to Germany with Kazimir and took up residence at Brauweiler (west of Cologne), where Ezzo and Mathilda had founded a monastery. Kazimir dashed any expectations that he would uphold Ezzonid power in the Rhineland by returning to Poland in 1039 to reclaim his political inheritance there. Upon the deaths of Richeza and her sisters by the 1070s, there were no living descendants of Ezzo and Mathilda to assert family authority in western Germany. For a time, Ezzo's nephew Henry held the office of count palatine. But Henry soon became embroiled in a bitter conflict with Archbishop Anno II of Cologne (1056–1075). In 1060, Henry murdered his wife in a fit of madness and spent the rest of his life in monastic custody.

Chronic struggles between royal, ecclesiastical, and aristocratic powers advanced and then broke Ezzonid fortunes; such conflicts would soon deal an immense blow to the powers of the monarchy. More controversial is the presumed development of dynastic self-consciousness among the aristocracy of eleventh- and twelfth-century Germany. Though the Ezzonids seem to have favored fixed residences and had a family burial site (Brauweiler), they did not name themselves after these places, and in general did not view their family as a patrilineal dynasty.

BIBLIOGRAPHY

Beuckers, Klaus Gereon. *Die Ezzonen und ihre Stiftungen: Eine Untersuchung zur Stiftungstätigkeit im 11. Jahrhundert.* Münster: Lit, 1993.

Gerstner, Ruth. *Die Geschichte der lothringischen und rheinischen Pfalzgrafschaft von ihren Anfängen bis zur Ausbildung des Kurterritoriums Pfalz.* Bonn: Röhrscheid, 1941.

Lewald, Ursula. "Die Ezzonen: Das Schicksal eines rheinischen Fürstengeschlechtes." *Rheinische Vierteljahrsblätter* 43 (1979): 120–168.

Rotondo-McCord, Jonathan. *"Locum sepulturae meae . . . elegi:* Property, Graves, and Sacral Power in Eleventh-Century Germany." *Viator* 26 (1995): 77–106.

Steinbach, Franz. "Die Ezzonen: Ein Versuch territorialpolitischen Zusammenschlusses der fränkischen Rheinlande," in *Collectanea Franz Steinbach: Aufsätze und Abhandlungen zur Verfassungs-, Sozial- und Wirtschaftsgeschichte, geschichtlichen Landeskunde und Kulturraumforschung,* ed. Franz Petri and Georg Droege. Bonn: Röhrscheid, 1967, pp. 64–81.

Jonathan Rotondo-McCord

SEE ALSO

Anno; Henry III; Otto III; Theophanu

F

Fables, Dutch

In the medieval literature of the Low Countries, four fable collections are known, along with a number of stray fables found in other (literary) texts. The fable collections are called *Esopet, Parabelen van Cyrillus, Twispraec der creaturen,* and *Dye historien ende fabulen van Esopus.* All four are translations from Latin or French texts. Other fables are found, for example, in the work of Willem van Hildegaersberch; in *Van den vos Reynaerde* and *Reinaerts historie;* in the Hulthem manuscript; in the *Ridderboec* and in the *Pelgrimage van der menscheliker creaturen.*

The four fable collections can be characterized according to the ethics they represent. In the *Esopet* (containing sixty-seven Aesopic fables in verses) it is observed that evil things happen, and that the weak and the poor are usually the victims of the strong and the rich. It is also observed that nothing much can be done about it, except to try to avoid getting into trouble. People are encouraged to behave wisely and rightly, and it is made clear that bad behavior will—eventually—be punished. Although from a much later date, the collection *Dye historien ende fabulen van Esopus* (the *Esopet* was probably written in the thirteenth century, whereas *Dye historien* is a fifteenth-century text) is, in its contents and ethics, more closely related to the *Esopet* than to the other two collections (both fifteenth-century translations of fourteenth-century texts). *Dye historien* contains the history of Aesop's life, his fables, and numerous other fables by Avian and Rimicius, among others. Before and after each fable the moral is given. The ethics in this collection are much more influenced by Christian thought than those of the *Esopet,* and are more explicitly directed at maintaining the social status quo, often warning people against overstepping their place.

The *Parabelen van Cyrillus* consists of four books containing dialogues between animals or between other creatures, whereby the moral is explained with the help of quotations from classical authors (both Greek and Latin), the Bible, and other works. The four books treat the four cardinal vices: stupidity, pride, greed, and intemperance (as opposed to the virtues: wisdom, humility, justice, and temperance). The author's aim is to teach readers how to lead a virtuous life in order to lessen the sinfulness of the world; he stresses especially the importance of being led by wisdom in all one's deeds. The last collection, the *Twispraec der creaturen,* contains 122 fables or dialogues (featuring diverse creatures), each concluded by a *sententia* stating the moral, and then followed by a moralization in which the moral is repeated and enlarged on by exempla, historical anecdotes, stories from the Bible, parables, and sometimes an Aesopic fable. In many of the dialogues the main character is introduced together with some facts from medieval natural science, thereby linking this collection to the medieval tradition of the exegesis (learned explanation) of nature. In the *Twispraec der creaturen* the importance of justice is strongly represented; the author stresses that everyone will eventually be rewarded or, more likely, punished for their behavior on earth.

BIBLIOGRAPHY

Lelij, C. M., ed. *De Parabelen van Cyrillus.* Amsterdam: H. J. Paris, 1930.

Schippers, Anda. "Als wijt wel merken willen. Geestelijke interpretatie in de Twispraec der creaturen." *Millennium* 2 (1991): 147–164.

———. *Middelnederlandse fabels. Studie van het genre, beschrijving van collecties, catalogus van afzonderlijke fabels.* Nijmegen: n.p., 1995.

Stuiveling, Garmt, ed. *Esopet. Facsimile-uitgave naar het enig bewaard gebleven handschrift.* 2 vols. Amsterdam: Menno Hertzberger, 1965.

Wackers, Paul. "Middle Dutch Fables." *Reinardus, Yearbook of the International Reynard Society* 6 (1993): 203–216.

Anda Schippers

SEE ALSO

Animal Epics, Dutch; Exemplum; *Reynard the Fox,* Dutch; Willem of Hildegaersberch

Family

The nature and structure of medieval families changed considerably between the age of the German migrations and the church reform movement of the eleventh and twelfth centuries. Like so many other aspects of European culture, what came to be a consensus about the nuclear family as the basic cell of society was actually a synthesis of Roman, Christian, and German traditions. Although derived from the Latin word *familia,* the German term *Familie* did not appear until the sixteenth century, and by then conceptions about what constituted a family were very different from what they had been in the late ancient and early medieval worlds.

Roman law defined the *familia* in terms of both persons and property: it amounted to the people and things under the control of a *paterfamilias* (father of the family) and was therefore based on authority instead of on blood ties. A "family" in this sense need not even live in the same household. Medieval writers would eventually pick up the word and use it in much the same way in the context of manorialism to designate the serfs and other dependents of a seigneur, but the idea of the family as a domestic unit did not emerge before the Carolingian era.

The church's view of marriage and family life was equally slow to develop. Although early commentators such as Tertullian and Augustine recognized the importance of *amicitia* (friendship) and *caritas* (charity), they too employed "family" in a broad sense, not in terms of what later came to be thought of as a nuclear household consisting of a married couple and their unmarried children. What did concern the church, however, was the manner in which marriage was contracted and sexual relations practiced. By the ninth century theologians were arguing that marriage was an indissoluble union entered into by mutual consent, and by the twelfth century most agreed that marriage was also a sacrament and that the

ceremony should be performed if not by a priest then at least in one's presence.

Early on, however, these legal and religious constructions of the family were not easily reconcilable with German notions, which were based more on social and economic considerations than on legal or moral concerns. Most marriages were the result of negotiations between extended families and involved the exchange of gifts. Daughters could be married as early as age twelve without their consent, and while both maternal and paternal lineage was recognized, German fathers seemed to have had nearly as much power as the Roman *paterfamilias.* Among the Jutes, the right to beat children was recognized as long as no bones were broken, and a man could legally sell his children into slavery until the age of seven.

Marriages were fully recognized only through cohabitation, consummation, and the birth of children. Indeed, the first year was often seen as a trial period after which the relationship could be terminated if children were not produced. This and other customs allowing for the dissolution of marriages were universally condemned by the church, but Frankish, Visigothic, and Burgundian law codes permitted husbands to repudiate their wives for any number of reasons including adultery, inability to have children, infirmity, sorcery, or tampering with tombs. To make matters worse in the eyes of the church, concubinage was widespread among the noble elite, as was remarriage and, not infrequently, incest and polygamy. Many such instances are related by Gregory of Tours and other Merovingian and Frankish chroniclers. Charlemagne himself had five wives and at least as many concubines.

Another important component of early medieval family life was the role of the *Sippe* (clan, or kinship group). The *Sippe* guaranteed the safety of individuals through the blood feud, or vendetta. In addition to the gifts from her husband and family that a bride was supposed to hold as her own personal property, membership in her clan provided her with a measure of protection. She could turn to them in case her husband abused her, brought unsubstantiated charges of adultery, or tried to divorce her unjustly.

Eventually the view of marriage as a primarily socioeconomic arrangement and the tendency to focus more on the relationship of the couple to their extended families rather than to each other gave way to what we now think of as the "modern" family, that is, a nuclear household characterized by strong emotional bonds and relatively constrained ideas about sexual morality. Yet there has been considerable disagreement among scholars as to when this new family structure appeared in its definitive form. Several influential studies have suggested that it was not until the late sixteenth or early seventeenth century.

Yet there is strong evidence to the contrary. As scholars such as David Herlihy and James Brundage have demonstrated, although there may have been glaring exceptions in the upper echelons of society, the monogamous nuclear family as a moral domestic unit bound by conjugal love became the norm in western Europe no later than the ninth century. Carolingian administrators regularly assessed taxes on the basis of such family units, and theologians as esteemed as Thomas Aquinas recognized that domestic love was not only natural but of a greater intensity than love extended to friends and neighbors.

Although the church was never able to eliminate entirely all forms of adultery, repudiation, and remarriage, it was nonetheless successful in establishing impediments to marriage based on consanguinity and affinity and in assimilating German society to the notion of monogamy. Naturally other factors likewise had an impact on the shape of the medieval family, the most important of which was money—wealthy households tended to be larger—as well as location (city versus countryside), inheritance patterns, farming techniques, personal preferences, and individual circumstances; yet the institutionalization of the nuclear monogamous family, which became permanently embedded in European culture, was undoubtedly the church's greatest triumph in its long-standing efforts to overcome German traditions in the legislation of morality and family life.

BIBLIOGRAPHY

Brundage, James A. *Love, Sex and Christian Society in Medieval Europe.* Chicago: University of Chicago Press, 1987.

Goody, Jack. *The Development of the Family and Marriage in Europe.* New York: Cambridge University Press, 1983.

Herlihy, David. *Medieval Households.* Cambridge, Mass.: Harvard University Press, 1985.

———. "Family," *American Historical Review* 96 (1991): 1–16.

McNamara, Jo-Ann, and Suzanne F. Wemple. "Marriage and Divorce in the Frankish Kingdom," in *Women in Medieval Society,* ed. Susan Mosher Stuard. Philadelphia: University of Pennsylvania Press, 1976, pp. 95–124.

Mitterauer, Michael, and Reinhard Sieder. *The European Family: Patriarchy to Partnership from the Middle Ages to the Present,* trans. Karla Oosterveen and Manfred Hörzinger. Chicago: University of Chicago Press, 1982.

David R. Blanks

SEE ALSO
Carolingians; Charlemagne; Marriage and Divorce

Fastnachtspiele

Fifteenth-century comic plays (Carnival Plays) of varying length (rarely more than five hundred verses), which reflect many aspects of early modern German society. Secular, in Middle High German decasyllabic (of ten syllables) couplets, they exist in two varieties: serial, revuelike plays, where a number of male actors pronounce monologues competing with one another (*Reihenspiele,* for the favor of a woman or for anecdotes of courage, strength, wit, and obscenity); and well-structured pieces with an intrigue (*Handlungsspiele*); dialogues occur in judgment plays, visits to a doctor, or sales transactions. Many plays are linked to a specific festival of the church year, most often to Carnival in an urban setting. While the authors use persiflage to mock peasants for the benefit of the burghers, the rustics are also portrayed as witty and sometimes superior to the other estates (*Ständesatire*). The lower clergy appears here as love-starved, and the nobility as inept, degenerate, or questionable (e.g., in the so-called Neidhart plays). Married life and its occasions for irregularity are a favorable theme, where peasants may boast virility, and their wives top their partners in verbal insults, readiness for erotic escapades, or ingenuity in avoiding to be caught.

The first traces of Carnival plays stem from Hall/Tyrol; later centers are Nuremberg (some 120 plays), Sterzing/Tyrol, Lübeck (where only entries in a register are preserved), the Lower Rhine region, and Switzerland. It can be estimated that Carnival farces were staged in circa fifty-seven cities besides Nuremberg; unfortunately, few texts have come down to us. Subjects are the everyday life of burghers and peasants, courtly epics and chivalry (often in parody), classical mythology, biblical sources, or chapbook anecdotes (*fabliaux, Schwänke, Mären*) of unknown origins. The antics of street vendors and quacks can also be found, similar to the *mercator* episodes in passion plays, and scenes of marketing point to the many occasions for cheating. Authors were Pamphilius Gengenbach, Niklas Manuel, Hans Folz, Hans Rosenplüt (*Meistersinger*), Vigil Raber, Jacob Ayrer, the Lübeck

Zirkelbrüder, and Hans Sachs in the next century. Many plays remain anonymous.

Some representations took place on public stages, but most were performed in houses or inns. Money was collected during some shows, while considerable support came from the municipalities interested in providing an outlet for seasonal boisterousness. Props were minimal, though: a bench, a table, a chair; goods to be bought or sold. The actors were young men working in the different crafts or sons of patricians. A herald "ushered in" the play, asking for space and silence, while the same person (then called *Ausschreier)* ended the piece, inviting audience and actors to a drink and/or dance.

The Carnival plays, which need to be reedited and selectively translated, are a valuable mirror of fifteenth-century German society in all its aspects, and this despite the inevitable grotesque distortion of characters and situations. In an often inverted manner, the pieces point to the lasting significance of agriculture in spite of urban development; they opt for order, morality, and education, and persiflage ineptness, corruption, and deceit on all levels of society. In short, they teach how to avoid the Seven Deadly Sins—albeit in a very pleasant form.

BIBLIOGRAPHY

Bastian, Hagen. *Mummenschanz. Sinneslust und Gefühls-beherrschung im Fastnachtspiel des 15. Jahrhunderts.* Frankfurt am Main: Syndikat, 1983.

Catholy, Eckehard. *Das Fastnachtspiel des Spätmittelalters.* Tübingen: Niemeyer, 1961.

DuBruck, Edelgard E. *Aspects of Fifteenth-Century Society in the German Carnival Comedies.* Speculum Hominis. Lewiston, N.Y.: Mellen, 1993.

Keller, Adalbert von, ed. *Fastnachtspiele aus dem 15. Jahrhundert.* 3 vols. Stuttgart, 1853; rpt. Darmstadt: Wissenschaftliche Buchgesellschaft, 1965.

Lenk, Werner. *Das Nürnberger Fastnachtspiel des 15. Jahrhunderts.* Berlin: Akademieverlag, 1966.

Spiewok, Wolfgang. *Das deutsche Fastnachtspiel. Ursprung, Funktionen, Aufführungspraxis.* Greifswald: Reineke-Verlag, 1993, 2d ed. 1997.

Wuttke, Dieter, ed. *Fastnachtspiele des 15. und 16. Jahrhunderts.* Stuttgart: Reclam, 1978 [with extensive bibliography].

Edelgard E. DuBruck

SEE ALSO

Aristoteles und Phyllis; Drama; Drama, Passion Plays; Gottfried von Straßburg; Hartmann von Aue; *Mariendichtungen; Meistersinger;* Neidhart

Feudalism

The term *feudalism* was not known to the Middle Ages. Rather, it has been applied by later historians to various complexes or patterns of legal, social, and economic relations in medieval Europe and elsewhere. Many scholars now call into question the validity of feudalism as a concept for understanding medieval society, and reject the widespread existence of the classical feudal relationship, that of a vassal bound to a lord by ties of homage, loyalty, and military service, in return for the grant of a benefice or fief in the form of land. However, sources from medieval Germany do refer to benefices, fiefs, and (at least from the twelfth century on) feudal law, and feudalism (or its absence) has usually been regarded as an important factor in the course of medieval German history, especially at the level of the king and high aristocracy. Though debate continues about the actual nature of feudal ties, an overview of traditional views of feudalism and its consequences for German political developments is still of value.

Medieval Germany has often been labeled as feudally "archaic," especially when compared to post-Carolingian northern France. Germany shared with France the legacy of "Carolingian feudalism," in which vassalage (rooted in the Gallo-Roman practice of self-commendation and in the loyalty of the Germanic warrior band) was supposedly joined with the granting out of church land (at the command of the king) to the king's followers in benefice or precarial tenure *(precaria verbo regis).* The ability to grant such lands was important to Charles Martel in his wars with the Saracens, against whom the traditionally called-up army of freemen was not as effective as a host of professional mounted fighters who could be rewarded with grants of land in benefice. Other important moments in Carolingian feudalism have been judged to be Charlemagne's 799 Herstal capitulary, which allowed churches to grant benefices on their own (thus supposedly creating a group of *subvassals* loyal to the king through the church), as well as Charles the Bald's 877 capitulary of Quierzy, which allowed vassals participating in his Italian campaign to bequeath benefices to their heirs.

On the one hand, grants of land in benefice have been seen as tied to grants of office; legal and constitutional historians have debated whether the grant of land was a perquisite of the grant of office, or vice versa. On the other, however, the official character of Carolingian government appears to contrast sharply with the extreme localization of authority in post-Carolingian western Europe, where feudalism ostensibly put down its deepest roots, from which the Capetian kings of France would draw great strength only after the eleventh century. In Germany, the tenth-century Ottonians and eleventh-century Salians are held to have preserved official government more successfully than French rulers did during the same period. In theory, German kings did not necessarily grant offices as heritable fiefs, and could revoke a title or depose an officeholder for serious cause. Furthermore, the imperial church was a more dependable instrument of royal authority than a feudal nobility. As a consequence, many German regions saw little feudalization before the twelfth century. Local nobles continued to hold land as full property or allods (land held free of any feudal obligation).

German rulers were compelled to deal with feudal matters elsewhere, however. In 1037 in Milan, the emperor Conrad II (r. 1024–1039) ruled that no *miles* (soldiers to a lord) could be deprived arbitrarily of a benefice without judgment of peers. Inheritance of benefices was also protected by this legislation. Though the immediate goal of Conrad's decree was to gain the support of lower-ranking fighters for the king in Italian expeditions, its implications of royal protection for the rights of vassals would not have gone unnoticed in Germany. The 1037 ordinance also suggested the direction in which later Salians would go in their attempts to preserve royal authority. Although Henry III (r. 1039–1056) seemed to enjoy a relatively strong and stable kingship, German elite nobles chafed at Salian policies by the end of the reign. On the basis of extensive allodial holdings, lay nobles and churches alike had started to consolidate territorial power by the mid–eleventh century. The Salian ruler, in reaction, began to rely on the loyalty of powerful unfree retainers: the ministerials, tied to the king by bonds of legal servility, not (yet) vassalage in the usual sense. The reigns of Henry IV (1056–1106) and Henry V (1106–1125) saw royal attempts to retain power by relying on ministerials, castles, and friendly cities in the face of enormous aristocratic and ecclesiastical resistance. Feudalism was not an effective instrument for the Salians in their struggle to restore royal power battered and weakened by the Investiture Controversy. One result of the 1122 Concordat of Worms, however, was that high clerics could now be compelled to swear homage and fealty for their regalia of office, granted after election. Consequently, historians have usually seen a partial feudalization of Germany in the post-Salian period, though much evidence is Italian in origin. In 1131 in Liège, the Saxon ruler Lothar III of Supplingenburg (r. 1125–1137) performed the service of

strator for the pope, i.e., leading the pontiff's horse and holding the stirrup, a traditional gesture of vassalic subordination. One of the conditions of Lothar's imperial coronation in 1133 was that he receive the lands of Matilda of Tuscany as a papal fief, and a famed Lateran painting suggested that Lothar's imperial title was held feudally from the pope. In 1136, Lothar for his part decreed at Roncaglia in Italy that *milites* (soldiers) were not to alienate their benefices and so escape their obligation of military service to their lords—who in turn owed service to the empire. The Staufen ruler Frederick I Barbarossa (r. 1152–1190) renewed Lothar's ruling with his own legislation at Roncaglia in 1154 and again in 1158. Although all three ordinances were enacted in Italy, it is likely that they found resonance in Germany as well. They have been taken as evidence for a deliberate royal strategy of using feudal ties to strengthen imperial authority.

The reign of Barbarossa saw several significant feudal moments. On his way to his imperial coronation at the hands of Pope Adrian IV in 1155, the Hohenstaufen king at first declined to perform the service of strator and marshal at his meeting with the pope in Sutri. This symbolic gesture undoubtedly recalled, by way of contrast, Lothar of Supplingenburg's willingness to humble himself before a previous pope in 1131. At the imperial court of 1157 in Besançon, papal legates presented a letter from Pope Adrian IV (1154–1159) implying that the imperial dignity had been conferred upon Barbarossa by the pope as a *beneficium*. When translated into German as *lehen* or fief by Rainald of Dassel, imperial chancellor and archbishop of Cologne (1159–1167), the feudal connotations of this word provoked an uproar among the imperial party. The pope later explained that he intended by *beneficium* to express the grant of empire only as a "good deed" *(bonum factum)*, rather than a fief *(feodum,* which begins to appear frequently in twelfth-century sources). Though the Besançon incident has been interpreted variously, it betrays a sensitivity to changing feudal terminology, influenced in no small degree by the development and revival of professional and Roman law in Italy. Only a year before, in 1156, an Austrian duchy had been created and given as a hereditary benefice to Henry Jasomirgott in the edict *Privilegium minus* issued by Barbarossa. In 1180, one of the most celebrated cases of feudal law took place when Barbarossa convened an assembly of princes to depose the Welf Duke Henry the Lion (d. 1195), Barbarossa's cousin and erstwhile ally. Already charged by rivals with various misdeeds and condemned in 1179 at a court based on *Landrecht,* or customary "law of the land,"

Henry suffered the loss of his Saxon and Bavarian duchies by a feudal judgment of peers at Würzburg in January 1180; the fiefs were partitioned and granted out to Henry's rivals at Gelnhausen in April that year.

Significantly, one of the charges leveled against Henry was his failure to respond to a threefold summons issued "according to feudal law" *(sub feodali iure)*. Henry did not, however, lose his vast allodial holdings immediately. Barbarossa could not have deposed Henry solely by imperial authority—the cooperation of the German aristocracy was needed. Historians have traditionally seen Barbarossa's concessions to nobles on this occasion as an important step in the formation of a small, privileged body of imperial princes *(Reichsfürstenstand)*, though this process was by no means complete in 1180. It is also now agreed that the *Leihezwang*—the ruler's supposed obligation to grant out imperial fiefs within a year and a day—was not yet in force during Barbarossa's reign, though in this case Barbarossa did award the Welf's duchies to others fairly quickly. Despite Barbarossa's apparently successful use of feudal law to break dangerous rivals, the Staufen kings were not able to build a lasting royal authority on the basis of feudalism, just as they also failed to establish an exclusive principle of inheritance for royal succession.

The bitter struggle for the throne that broke out in 1198 between Philip of Swabia and Otto IV severely crippled the German monarchy and gave princes of the realm free rein to develop their own territorial positions based, perhaps ironically, on feudal lordship over lesser nobles. Frederick II (r. 1212-1250) was compelled to guarantee princely interests, first for ecclesiastical lords *(Confoederatio cum principibus ecclesiasticis,* 1220), then for both church and lay magnates *(Statutum in favorem principum,* 1232).

Feudal theory in Germany received its first extensive exposition in the *Sachsenspiegel* of Eike of Repgow *(Mirror of the Saxons,* ca. 1220). Divided into two main sections (treating, respectively, *Landrecht,* "law of the land," and *Lehnrecht,* or feudal law), Eike's "mirror" sets out an idealized hierarchy for the Heerschild *(clipeus militaris)* or system of military organization. In theory the Heerschild appears as a classic feudal pyramid of seven ranks, from the king at the top to ministerials at the bottom. Although the *Sachsenspiegel* does not provide a reliable portrait of medieval social hierarchies, it does reflect a thirteenth-century interest in establishing a theoretical base for feudal law, also picked up in the later *Schwabenspiegel*

(Mirror of the Swabians, ca. 1270). Emperors could draw little profit from such treatises, however. The double election of 1257 assured the formation of a princely college of royal electors *(Kurfürsten),* whose rights were guaranteed by Charles IV's Golden Bull of 1356. With the triumph of the electoral principle, princes used feudal law coupled with increasingly complex bureaucracies to forge the territorial states of late medieval Germany.

This commonly accepted model of the role of feudalism in German constitutional development has been seriously challenged by recent scholars, especially Susan Reynolds. In Reynolds's view, personal ties characteristic of what German scholars have called the *Personenverbandstaat* (state held together by bonds of loyalty between persons) were not nearly as important as a common set of political values shared by German kings and magnates. Even where these ties existed, they did not, in Reynolds's view, lead to vassalage territorialized in the form of fiefs. Although increasing numbers of properties might have been called fiefs in the twelfth and thirteenth centuries, Reynolds argues that this shift reflected the influence of rising professional law emanating especially from Italy; in other words, any change observed in the sources is more terminological than substantial. Free persons owed military service not because of fiefs, but because of their status in the kingdom as holders of full property, which remained the norm for types of property held in medieval Germany. Reynolds attributes the survival of allods in Germany not to a lack of feudalization but, rather, to strong government. Reynold's conclusions will no doubt remain controversial, but they have forced historians to reconsider commonly received interpretations of medieval German history and the place of feudalism in it.

BIBLIOGRAPHY

Althoff, Gerd. *Verwandte, Freunde und Getreue: Zum politischen Stellenwert der Gruppenbindungen im früheren Mittelalter.* Darmstadt: Wissenschaftliche Buchgesellschaft, 1990.

Bloch, Marc. *Feudal Society,* trans. L. A. Manyon, 2 vols. Chicago: University of Chicago Press, 1961.

Droege, Georg. *Landrecht und Lehnrecht im hohen Mittelalter.* Bonn: Ludwig Röhrscheid, 1969.

Ebel, Wilhelm. "Über den Leihegedanken in der deutschen Rechtsgeschichte, in *Studien zum mittelalterlichen Lehenswesen. Vorträge und Forschungen,* vol. 5, ed. Theodor Mayer. Lindau: Thorbecke, 1960, pp. 11–36.

Haverkamp, Alfred. *Medieval Germany 1056–1273,* trans. Helga Braun. Oxford: Oxford University Press, 1988.

Mitteis, Heinrich. *Lehnrecht und Staatsgewalt.* Weimar: Hermann Böhlau, 1933.

Prinz, Friedrich. *Grundlagen und Anfänge: Deutschland bis 1056.* Munich: Beck, 1985.

Reynolds, Susan. *Fiefs and Vassals: The Medieval Evidence Reinterpreted.* Oxford: Oxford University Press, 1994.

Jonathan Rotondo-McCord

SEE ALSO

Capitularies; Carolingians; Charlemagne; Charles IV; Conrad II; Eike von Repgow; Frederick I Barbarossa; Frederick II; Golden Bull; Henry III; Henry IV; Henry the Lion; Investiture Controversy; Law and Lawbooks; Ministerials; Otto IV; Rainald of Dassel; Salians; *Statutum in Favorem Principum*

Fishing

Often also called *halieutics,* fishing was important for the Middle Ages as a source of food and livelihood, as an amusement, but also because as one of the common aspects of medieval life, it offered a source for imagery and symbolism. The rivers, streams, and lakes of Germany offered a variety and abundance of fishes, as the fourth-century catalogue shows, of the fishes in the Moselle, from Bingen to Neumagen, written by Ausonius in his *Mosella.* Alongside these natural sources of fish, there were also fish farms and fisheries, and it was a poor manor that had no fishpond *(vivarium).*

We often hear of fishing as a sport or recreation, as in the case of the Fisher King of Arthurian legend, represented by Amfortas in Wolfram von Eschenbach's courtly romance *Parzival.* Note also the role played by the fish in Hartmann's legend tale *Gregorius.* In Wolfram's romance *Titurel,* the action begins with a fishing outing by Sigune and Schionatulander, and these are only a few of the many examples one could cite.

Since the world had entered into the sign *Pisces* at Christ's birth according to the horoscope of the world, the fish was seen as the image of Christianity. According to the well-known poem of the sibyl, *ICHTHYS,* Greek for "fish," stood as an acronym for Jesus Christ, Son of God, Savior. St. Peter was the great fisherman, and the church was known as the *Sagena Piscatoris* (the Seine of the Fisherman), according to the interpretation of

Matthew 13:47, or often as *Navicula Petri* (the little ship of Peter, or *"das Schifflein des Petrus"*). A person who spoke earnestly, but not always eloquently, could say that he spoke *piscatorie et non Aristotelice* (like a fisherman and not like Aristotle; cf. the historical poem *Kaiserchronik,* vv. 2561f.).

The famous scene of Thor fishing for the Midgard serpent is interpreted already by the "Old Icelandic Homily Book" (written down ca. 1200) as a reference to the image of Leviathan. The Leviathan of Job was taken throughout the Middle Ages as hell or Satan, as in the famous picture in Herrad of Landsberg's *Hortus deliciarum,* which shows God the Father fishing with Christ as bait on the hook of the cross, and there are many references to the bait and the hook in Middle High German literature and later in Luther and Schottel, for example. Of course, halieutic symbolism could also refer to love, with the *hamus* "hook" / *amor* "love" pair (*h* was not pronounced in Medieval Latin).

BIBLIOGRAPHY

Hagendahl, Harald. "Piscatorie et non Aristotelice. Zu einem Schlagwort bei den Kirchenvätern," in *Septentrionalia et Orientalia. Studia Bernhardo Karlgren Dedicata.* Kungliga vitterhets Historie och Antikvitets Akademiens Handlingar 91. Stockholm: Almqvist and Wiksell, 1959, pp. 184–193.

Marchand, James W. "Sagena Piscatoris: An Essay in Medieval Lexicography." in *Linguistic Method: Essays in Honor of Herbert Penzl,* ed. Irmengard Rauch and Gerold Carr. The Hague: Mouton, 1978, pp. 123–138.

von Koppenfels, Werner. *Esca et Hamus.* Bayrische Akademie der Wissenschaften. Philosophisch-Historische Klasse. Sitzungsberichte, Jahrgang 1973, no. 3 [On the bait and the hook theme].

James W. Marchand

SEE ALSO

Kaiserchronik; Wolfram von Eschenbach

Fodrum, Gistum, Servitium Regis

These terms (literally fodder, hospitality, service to the king) all refer in some way to an obligatory service or to various services claimed by medieval kings from the church in their realm, that is, the ecclesiastical institutions, and to a lesser degree from the nobility. At their core all relate to itinerant kingship and the king's right to accommodation and sustenance for himself and his retinue while traveling. This royal claim appears initially to have derived from the protection that the king provided to the church and his subjects. Like itinerant kingship, however, one finds a royal right to hospitality in many cultures.

Fodrum derived from the old Frankish word *fodar,* which meant "fodder for horses," and the *fodrum regis* referred to the duty of providing fodder to feed the horses and pack animals of the royal retinue. It retained this meaning throughout the Frankish period and in the German High Middle Ages north of the Alps. In Italy, however, in the High Middle Ages *fodrum regis* corresponded to the narrow concept of *servitium regis* north of the Alps. *Gistum regis* refers to the hospitality aspects of *servitium regis* as practiced in medieval France. *Servitium regis* in its narrow technical sense corresponds to the king's right to accommodation and upkeep. More generally, *servitium regis* encompassed a range of obligations or services owed to the king that included housing and feeding the royal court or sending provisions for the king's upkeep; for clergy to pray for the king and the realm; for officials of the bishop, abbot, and high nobles to give counsel at the royal court; and for the most wealthy and powerful to equip and supply a military contingent for the king.

In its broadest sense, *servitium regis* might include additional services exacted by the king, such as book production on royal commission, performance of diplomatic missions, maintenance of political prisons, manufacture of armor and weapons, and responsibility to maintain certain royal roads and bridges.

Beginning in the Frankish period, kings called on bishoprics and royal monasteries, along with royal properties, to provide them accommodation and upkeep. This tendency increased under the Carolingian Franks. As itinerant kingship advanced in the late ninth century, so did the intensity of the obligation to provide hospitality for the king; it reached its high point in the tenth and eleventh centuries under the Ottonian and Salian kings. The term *servitium regis* appears in charters, land registers, and narrative sources, but not frequently because it seems to have been a customary right and mainly received mention in the rare instances when the king granted an exemption from or reduction of the obligation. Initially, the *servitium regis* was paid in kind, and those obligated transferred much of the burden to their various dependents. Within episcopal and monastic communities, this

obligation, which fell on bishops, abbots, and abbesses, and whose exaction could lead to abuses, played a role in establishing property divisions between these officials and, respectively, the episcopal chapters of canons or the monastic communities. Increasingly, from the eleventh century in Italy and the twelfth in Germany, money payments appeared and by the thirteenth were generally established. Likewise, under the Hohenstaufen kings, towns became the mainstay of royal accommodation along with the royal residences and household properties listed in the registry know as the *Tafelgüterverzeichnis.* In Italy, the *fodrum regis,* which obligated payments from secular nobles and the communes as well, counted as the most important royal source of income. Limited attempts to create an annual tax from it nonetheless ultimately failed. By the late Middle Ages the material basis of kingship no longer depended on the *servitium regis,* which thus lost its importance.

BIBLIOGRAPHY

Bernhardt, John W. *Itinerant Kingship and Royal Monasteries in Early Medieval Germany, [circa] 936–1075.* Cambridge: Cambridge University Press, 1993, pp. 75-135.

Brühl, Carlrichard. *Fodrum, Gistum, Servitium Regis.* 2 vols. Cologne: Böhlau, 1968.

Haverkamp, Alfred. *Herrschaftsformen der Frühstaufer in Reichsitalien.* 2 vols. Stuttgart: Hiersemann, 1970–1971.

Heusinger, Bruno. *Servitium Regis in der deutschen Kaiserzeit: Untersuchungen über die wirtschaftlichen Verhältnisse des deutschen Königtums, 900–1250.* Berlin: de Gruyter, 1922.

Metz, Wolfgang. "Quellenstudien zum Servitium regis (900–1250)." *Archiv für Diplomatik* 22 (1976): 187–272; 24 (1978): 203–291; 31 (1985):273–327; 38 (1992):17–68.

———. *Das Servitium Regis.* Darmstadt: Wissenschaftliche Buchgesellschaft, 1978.

Peyer, Hans Conrad. *Von der Gastfreundschaft zum Gasthaus: Studien zur Gastlichkeit im Mittelalter.* Hanover: Hahn, 1987.

John W. Bernhardt

SEE ALSO

Carolingians; Itinerant Kingship; Otto I; Otto II; Otto III; Salians; Staufen

Folz, Hans (ca. 1450–1515)

Hans Folz is generally known in literary history as a master craftsman, Meistersinger, and carnival playwright, and as Hans Sachs's predecessor in the Nuremberg *Meistersang* and carnival play tradition.

Folz's first recorded residence was Worms. His profession as a barber/wound dresser, or *barbierer,* is apparent from the signature, or *impressum (hans von wurms barwirer),* that typically appears in his writings. In 1459 Folz applied for citizenship in the city of Nuremberg, and in a Nuremberg council document of 1486 he is referred to as a *Meister,* a master artisan or craftsman. In his works, Folz demonstrates an unusual amount of formal knowledge for an artisan. He shows a relatively developed understanding of Latin and also reveals knowledge of academic medicine, alchemy, and theology in his written work. Folz was one of the most multifaceted writers of his time. Scholars identify as his extant work approximately one hundred *Meisterlieder,* from twelve to thirty-five carnival plays, forty-eight fabliaux (poems), and two prose works.

Folz published almost all his work on his own printing press between 1479 and 1488. Most of the surviving prints are accompanied by woodcuts. He was probably the earliest Meistersinger to print his own songs, although only ten survive in print; the others exist in manuscript. It is possible that Folz intended his press as a means to a second income.

Folz's work varies widely in genre and theme, but was consistently popular at several levels of Nuremberg society. Records of personal libraries and Folz's own dedications reveal that he aspired to, and achieved, an elite readership in certain works. He addressed other works directly to lower levels of Nuremberg society.

Folz was one of the earliest authors in the Nuremberg carnival play tradition, writing plays and participating in their performance. Scholars have described his uniquely vehement use of carnival obscenity and scatological themes, and have described how Folz used the carnival play medium for an anti-Jewish agenda, revealing a strategic and political mindset that is apparent in much of his work.

Folz may have chosen the simple fabliau form (a rhyme-pair poem of varying length) to express himself most easily politically, humorously, or didactically. As his fabliaux are so varied thematically—they include religious, worldly, political, and traditional themes—one may deduce that Folz was giving free range to his every interest in this particular form.

The *Meisterlieder* (songs created within a guildlike group, for which Nuremberg was particularly well known) are primarily on spiritual-religious themes, especially the Virgin Mary, the Trinity, and the Incarnation. Also noteworthy is a series of songs in which Folz criticizes his fellow Meistersingers. Early scholarship identifies Folz as the author of a far-reaching *Meistersangsreform* "reform" through these songs, but later scholars deny this and convincingly characterize them simply as complaints against overregulation by the Nuremberg Meistersinger society. Other songs form thematic series as well.

Folz wrote six texts in his capacity as a wound dresser. The existence of subsequent editions shows that Folz succeeded in finding a popular audience for these instructional works.

No comprehensive edition of Folz's works exists at present. Separate German editions of his *Meisterlieder,* fabliaux, and carnival plays vary in reliability.

BIBLIOGRAPHY

Folz, Hans, in *Fastnachtspiele aus dem fünfzehnten Jahrhundert,* ed. Adelbert Keller. 3 vols. Stuttgart: Literarischer Verein, 1853.

———. *Die Meisterlieder des Hans Folz aus der Münchener Originalhandschrift und der Weimarer Handschrift Q. 566,* ed. August L. Mayer. Berlin: Weidmannsche Buchhandlung, 1908.

———. *Die Reimpaarsprüche,* ed. Hanns Fischer. Munich: Beck, 1961.

Janota, Johannes. "Hans Folz in Nürnberg: ein Autor etabliert sich in einer stadtbürgerlichen Gesellschaft," in *Philologie und Geschichtswissenschaft: Demonstrationen literarischer Texte des Mittelalters,* ed. Heinz Rupp. Heidelberg: Quelle and Meyer, 1977, pp. 74–91.

Price, David. "Hans Folz's Anti-Jewish Carnival Plays." *Fifteenth-Century Studies* 19 (1992): 209–228.

Caroline Huey

SEE ALSO
Drama; *Fastnachtspiele;* Meistersinger; Nuremberg

Fortification

The Roman Empire was a fortified empire. It consisted of large numbers of frontier fortifications—walls, camps, castles, and the like aimed to defend the borders of the empire from outside enemies—and of walled towns, which protected most of the population. With the onset of the Middle Ages, the Roman frontier forts had begun to deteriorate. Many were attacked and destroyed by invading barbarian forces, while others fell into disuse and ruin as borders changed and the need for protection against outside enemies diminished. The old Roman town walls, on the other hand, remained extremely important and continued to be maintained, repaired, and, when needed, rebuilt. These walls would remain the most extensive and important urban fortifications until the end of the Middle Ages.

As rural regions took on more economic and social importance in the early Middle Ages, it became apparent that there was a need for more and better rural fortifications. Initially, these were made of earthen ramparts and wooden palisades. Their chief means of defense was most often their inaccessibility to invading forces, and consequently most were constructed in the most inaccessible terrain available. Additionally, while more popular in France, the Low Countries, and England, motte-and-bailey castles also began to be constructed in Germany; their large, earthen mottes surmounted by a wooden castle and surrounded by a large bailey that itself was surrounded by an earthen rampart and wooden palisade made this style of castle the most defensible of all earth and wood fortifications.

Sometime during the early eleventh century, as near as can be dated from archaeological remains, the first masonry castles began to be constructed in Europe. Again initially more popular in the western European lands, with the return of the first Crusaders, Germany began to build many stone castles. Obviously influenced by what they saw in the more arid, less forested Middle East and Byzantium, these returning Crusaders took note of the very large and very powerful defensive structures built there, and once home in Europe they mimicked the style and method of construction of these fortifications.

There were two different styles of these stone masonry fortifications that appear in Germany from the twelfth through the fifteenth centuries. The earliest and simplest style of stone castle was the tower keep, which consisted primarily of a single tall, solid building meant to house the owner's entire family, servants, and garrison. Apartments, halls, chapels, kitchens, storage chambers, and even latrines were all incorporated into the castle structure. Most often the tower keep was built in a rectangular shape, although circular and multiangular-shaped castles were also constructed. Within a short time, tower keep castles began to be replaced by the more popular castle complex style of construction. Again influenced by Crusader predecessors, this style of castle relied not solely on

a large, solid keep to house all the inhabitants of the fortification but on a number of buildings, the largest and strongest of which served as the "keep," which were surrounded by high walls, flanking towers, crenellated wall-walks with machicolations (openings for releasing weapons), and extensive, secure gateways. Added protection came from their construction on the summits of precipitous hilltops and/or the digging of deep moats around the entire fortified structure.

While continuing to build both the tower keep and the castle complex types of fortifications until the end of the Middle Ages, by the fourteenth and fifteenth centuries the fortification needs of Europe had begun to change. The growth of urban areas, with their wealthy citizens needing defensive housing, necessitated urban fortifications. New town walls began to be built, while older Roman walls were enlarged and repaired. Also constructed were fortified residences. Built not unlike their rural tower keep cousins, these fortified residences were much more luxurious in their adornments, chambers, and furnishings; while still retaining as much defense capacity as possible, they did, however, surrender some traditional fortification strength for comfort. Soon these structures became popular in the countryside as well, and most late medieval fortifications are fortified residences. Eventually, too, gunpowder weapons began to change the nature of fortification construction as the large high medieval stone tower keeps and castle complexes with their long, straight walls fell quite quickly to the large cannons of besiegers. This required older castles to be adapted and new castles to be outfitted with antigunpowder weapon devices such as gunports, artillery towers, boulevards, and eventually bastions. But even these devices could not protect the traditional medieval fortification, and by the end of the Middle Ages a new style of fortification employing various lines of defense had begun to be built, the *trace italienne*.

BIBLIOGRAPHY

Contamine, Philippe. *War in the Middle Ages,* trans. M. Jones. London: Blackwell, 1984.

DeVries, Kelly. *Medieval Military Technology.* Peterborough: Broadview, 1992.

Kenyon, John R. *Medieval Fortifications.* New York: St. Martin's Press, 1990.

Thompson, M. W. *The Decline of the Castle.* Cambridge: Cambridge University Press, 1987.

———. *The Rise of the Castle.* Cambridge: Cambridge University Press, 1991.

Toy, Sidney. *A History of Fortification from 3000 BC to AD 1700.* London: Heineman, 1955.

Kelly DeVries

SEE ALSO
Burg; Warfare

Franciscan Art and Architecture

Much of the earliest art made for Franciscans and related to their teachings is found in Germany. Although German Franciscan architecture has long been a subject of study, painting has only recently been shown to have been an equally rich area of Franciscan patronage. Examples of mid-thirteenth-century German panel, glass, and manuscript painting have been related to Franciscan patronage and associated with work in Italy and especially at San Francesco in Assisi.

Basel, Franciscan church (*Barfüsserkirche,* now Historisches Museum), choir interior. *Photograph: Joan A. Holladay*

Franciscan churches were built in the major population centers beginning in the second quarter of the thirteenth century, and some are still preserved. Many were designed in a similar reductive Gothic style that has been related variously to Parisian forms and Italian variants of them. San Francesco in Bologna, itself after Parisian models, has been identified as a major source for the early German churches, including those in Cologne. The requirement of containing large groups of people desired by the order to fulfill its teaching function through preaching has been related to the significant development of hall churches in Cologne and then throughout Germany.

These churches, like San Francesco in Assisi, were decorated with stained glass and sometimes with painted crosses—the glass after German traditions and the crosses after the Italian type of *croce dipinti*. The Wimpassing Cross, first documented in the Franciscan (Minorite) church in Vienna, was destroyed in 1945 but is known from black-and-white photos (Berger-Fix 1980: 34–35). The type of *Christus patiens,* with a suffering or dead Christ figure, reflects a Byzantine type introduced in Italy by Giunta Pisano that might have appeared first in a cross made by him for the upper church at Assisi (illustration in Berger-Fix 1980: 47–48). Conversely, the German type of "Bible window" with typological pairs of Old and New Testament scenes, produced by German craftsmen for the apse of the upper church at Assisi, also appeared in the stained glass of some German Franciscan churches. Artists moving back and forth over the Alps seem to have brought techniques, styles, and themes back and forth, thus creating a certain homogeneity in many works identifiable as Franciscan. In some cases a specifically Franciscan vocabulary developed earlier in Germany and was brought later to Italy. The image of St. Francis receiving the stigmata in the stained glass of the Franciscan church (Barfüsserkirche) in Erfurt is, for example, one of the earliest and most significant.

Some of the most significant German manuscript illumination of the thirteenth century has also been related to the Franciscans, who quickly received considerable financial support. A magnificent mid-thirteenth-century lectionary fragment now in Hamburg (Staats- und Universitätsbibliothek, no. In scrinio 1) was indisputably made for Franciscans, as indicated by a prominent image of a monk wearing the characteristic Franciscan three-knotted cord belt. An elaborately illuminated Gospels, probably made for the archbishop of Mainz and now in Aschaffenburg (Hofbibliothek, no. Ms. 13), was made by the same artist(s) also associated with the workshop of the

Assisi windows. The Christological cycle of this manuscript has some of the earliest images of the Holy Family showing a range of emotional relations, with Christ from a tender embrace of his mother to extreme grief at the Lamentation; these became characteristic of Franciscan humanism in teaching and art.

BIBLIOGRAPHY

Berger-Fix, Andrea. "Das Wimpassinger Kreuz und seine Einordnung in die Kunst des 13. Jahrhunderts." *Wiener Jahrbuch für Kunstgeschichte* 33 (1980): 31–82.

Freed, John B. *The Friars and German Society in the Thirteenth Century.* Medieval Academy of America Publications 86. Cambridge, Mass.: Medieval Academy of America, 1977.

Kaufmann, Virginia Roehrig. "Iconographic Study of the Christological Cycle of the Miniatures of the Aschaffenburg Golden Gospels (Aschaffenburg, Hofbibliothek Ms. 13)." Ph.D. diss., Columbia University, 1986.

———. "Review of Frank Martin's *Apsisverglasung.*" *Speculum* 70 (1995): 581–586.

Manuskripte zur Kunstwissenschaft in der Wernerschen Verlagsgesellschaft 37. Worms: Wernersche Verlagsgesellschaft, 1993.

Martin, Frank. *Die Apsisverglasung der Oberkirche von S. Francesco in Assisi: Ihre Entstehung und Stellung innerhalb der Oberkirchenausstattung.* Ph.D. diss., University of Heidelberg, 1991–1992.

Schenkluhn, Wolfgang. *Ordines Studentes: Aspekte zur Kirchenarchitektur der Dominikaner und Franziskaner im 13. Jahrhundert.* Ph.D. diss., University of Marburg. Berlin: Gebr. Mann, 1985.

Virginia Roehrig Kaufmann

SEE ALSO
Cologne, Art; Erfurt; Gothic Art and Architecture; Mainz

Francke, Master (ca. 1380–ca. 1440)

A commission from the confraternity of "England-Travellers," dated 1424, names Master Francke. It has been suggested that, although working in a Hamburg monastery, he was a Dominican monk from Zutphen in Holland. This is the more plausible, as his intensely spiritual work differs profoundly from that of Bertram, the leading master in Hamburg. Francke's expressive linear style, figure canon, and iconography could derive from the Netherlands and certainly indicate an acquaintance,

around 1415, with French work from the Boucicaut and Rohan workshops.

Netherlandish influences dominate his double-winged St. Barbara Altarpiece (ca. 1420–1425; Kansallismuseo, Helsinki), especially in the realism and dramatic force of the male protagonists. The often friezelike arrangement of the figures in the painted martyrdom scenes is sculptural in character, and the designs in the carved shrine section have therefore also, controversially, been attributed to Francke.

The commission of 1424 is thought to relate to the St. Thomas Altarpiece, completed in 1436, of which only fragments survive (Kunsthalle, Hamburg). In the closed state, the altarpiece originally showed scenes from the childhood of Christ and the martyrdom of Saint Thomas; when opened, the drama of the passion of Christ was revealed. Francke employed steep hillside settings, silhouetted against a starred red ground for the outside scenes, and a gold ground on the festive side. In this altarpiece, certain motives, such as the women under the cross in the Crucifixion, suggest direct knowledge of the courtly art of Conrad von Soest. However, Francke favored poignant drama in contrast to Conrad's more lyrical mood.

Francke's work found numerous followers in Germany, but only in paintings by Rogier van der Weyden do we find a similar emotive use of line.

BIBLIOGRAPHY

Corley, Brigitte. *Conrad von Soest: Painter among Merchant Princes.* London: Harvey Miller, 1997, pp. 152–156.

Martens, Bella. *Meister Francke,* 2 vols. Hamburg: Friederichsen, de Gruyter, 1929.

Meister Francke und die Kunst um 1400. Hamburg: Kunsthalle, 1969.

Pylkkänen, Riitta. *Pyhän Barbaran legenda.* Helsinki: n. p., 1966.

Brigitte Corley

SEE ALSO
Bertram, Meister; Conrad von Soest; Hamburg

Frankfurt am Main

Fires in 1867 and 1944 destroyed much of the medieval city, but remains, excavations, and earlier documentation allow an understanding of its historical importance and visual appearance. Signs of Roman occupation of the topographically protected Domhügel (cathedral hill) date

Master Francke, Resurrection from the St. Thomas Altarpiece (Hamburg, Hamberger Kunsthalle, Inv. 498). *Photograph: © Elke Walford, Hamburg*

from the end of the first century C.E., but these military buildings do not seem to have comprised a proper fort. The Franks were present here from about 550; a *villa* served as the administrative center for royal lands in this area. Frankonofurd, or "ford of the Franks," is first mentioned by name in medieval documents and narrative sources in 794, when Charlemagne called a synod here to consider theological issues, including the adoptionist heresy and the use of images. The historian Orth finds it surprising that Charlemagne would have chosen this site for his synod as only a wooden *domus regis* (house of the king), rather than a proper palace, stood here. Although Charlemagne never visited Frankfurt again, it was a favorite stopping place of his successors. His son Louis the Pious undertook a new palace complex between 815 and 822–823, when he spent the winter and spring here. In its completed form, the three-part complex, as at Aachen, comprised the palace proper, which was connected by a covered walkway to a chapel; unlike Aachen, however, at Frankfurt all three buildings shared a single east-west axis. Notker Balbulus of St. Gall (late ninth century) credits Louis's son, Louis the German, with building the impressive new church, which was consecrated in 852. It shared its dedication to the Savior and the Virgin, its staffing with twelve clerics and an abbot, and the extensive gifts for its maintenance with Charlemagne's palace chapel at Aachen. On the basis of these similarities, the scholar Rexroth has suggested convincingly that the new church was intended as a substitute for the emperor's palace chapel, which was in the territory of Louis's older brother, Lothar, and that it served as part of Louis's campaign to extend the areas under his influence. As part of this campaign, Louis also arranged to have Lothar's son, Lothar II, elected in Frankfurt after the death of his father in 855.

The palace seems to have burned between 1018 and 1045; lacking an appropriate venue in which to hold court, the Salian kings largely avoided Frankfurt. Under the Staufer Konrad III (1138–1152), a new palace, the Saalhof, was erected at the south edge of the Domhügel. Part of the eastern wing and the chapel at the southeast corner today form part of the Historical Museum. On Konrad's departure on Crusade in 1147, he had his young son Henry VI elected king in Frankfurt. With the election of Frederick I Barbarossa in 1152, a tradition was established whereby the church of Louis the German became the site where the German kings were elected.

Indulgences in 1238 and 1239 indicate building underway at the ninth-century church: a Hallenkirche (hall church) only three bays long was erected between the

towers and transept of the Carolingian church. A dedication of some undetermined part of the new building in 1239 mentions St. Bartholomew, with the Savior, as the church's patron saint; relics of the apostle had been acquired at the latest by circa 1167. The new building seems to have been completed by about 1265; stylistic characteristics link it to the church of St. Elizabeth in Marburg. The remaining parts of the Carolingian building were replaced in the following centuries. In the first half of the fourteenth century, a wide transept and long choir were added at the building's east end; at the beginning of the fifteenth, the towers were razed and, under the local architect Madern Gerthener, replaced by a single tower, typically seen as a sign of independent cities' self-consciousness and pride. This must be related to two events. In 1356, in the codification of imperial law known as the Golden Bull, Charles IV had given Frankfurt the honor and the duty of holding the royal elections. Shortly thereafter, in 1372, the city council and citizens earned the right to name their own *Schultheiss* (mayor), and the city thus attained a status equivalent to that of an imperial free city (*freie Reichstadt*).

The fourteenth century was a period of financial well-being for the city, with a corresponding physical expansion and foundation of new institutions. In 1330 King Ludwig of Bavaria granted the city the right to hold a second annual fair, in addition to the fall fair documented since the late twelfth century, and the importance of Frankfurt as a trading center continued to grow throughout the fourteenth century. The boom was reflected in the building of a new city wall between 1333 and about 1350; the incorporation of the so-called Neustadt (New Town) tripled the size of the city. In 1348 the Grosse Kaufhaus (Large Market Building) was erected. In 1405–1406 the city purchased the houses known as the Römer (Roman) and the Goldener Schwan (Golden Swan) and began rebuilding them as the new town hall. Numerous religious foundations also date to this period of prosperity and growth. The church of St. Leonhard was established in 1317 where an earlier chapel to the Virgin and St. George had been built on land given to the citizens by Frederick II in 1219. A year later a wealthy patrician woman founded the Liebfrauenkapelle, a chapel dedicated to the Virgin, to the north of St. Bartholomew's, and at the end of the century, the church of St. Peter was established in the Neustadt. All these buildings, together with the church at the Carmelites, were renovated in the first third of the fifteenth century under the influence, perhaps even under the direction, of Madern Gerthener.

The official coronation site of the German kings remained at Aachen until 1562, when it was transferred to St. Bartholomew's in Frankfurt. In reality, however, most of the elections and coronations between 1356 and 1792 took place at St. Bartholomew's.

BIBLIOGRAPHY

Bund, Konrad. "Frankfurt am Main im Spätmittelalter 1311–1519," in *Frankfurt am Main: Die Geschichte der Stadt in neun Beiträgen.* Veröffentlichungen der Frankfurter Historischen Kommissio 17. Sigmaringen: Thorbecke, 1991, pp. 53–150.

Orth, Elsbeth. "Frankfurt am Main im Früh- und Hochmittelalter," in *Frankfurt am Main: Die Geschichte der Stadt in neun Beiträgen.* Veröffentlichungen der Frankfurter Historischen Kommission 17. Sigmaringen: Thorbecke, 1991, pp. 9–52.

750 Jahre Frankfurter Kaiserdom Sankt Bartholomäus 1239–1989, ed. Karl Heinrich Rexroth with Christoph Korneli. Frankfurt am Main: Historisches Museum, 1989.

Joan A. Holladay

SEE ALSO

Aachen; Charlemagne; Charles IV; Gerthener, Madern; Town Planning and Urbanism

Frau Ava (fl. first half the 12th c.)

Author ("Lady Ava") of a series of four religious Middle High German poems, written circa 1120 to 1125, transmitted in two versions known as the *Vorauer Handschrift* (manuscript "V") from the latter half of the twelfth century, and the missing fourteenth-century *Görlitzer Handschrift* (manuscript "G"). Frau Ava's work, viewed as a whole, provides a poetic rendering of the history of salvation. *Johannis,* the first poem of the series ("G" version only), begins with John the Baptist's future parents, Zacharias and his barren wife, Elizabeth, and Zacharias's failure to believe in the annunciation of the approaching birth of their son. Zacharias's lack of faith in the angelic message is punished by muteness. The poem next recounts the annunciation of Jesus to Mary, who in contrast to the doubting Zacharias, acknowledges her absolute faith in God. After the Baptist's birth and circumcision, and the restoration of speech to Zacharias through the intercession of the Holy Spirit, the exemplary character of Johannis highlights the need for repentance and vigilance. Johannis's ascetic discipline stands in opposition to Harod's lasciviousness. While the king enslaves himself to erotic passion, Johannis struggles to uphold the rule of reason and to bridle the desires of the flesh. The poem underscores the Baptist's role as a helper to all Christians. His spiritual orientation enables him to serve God and humankind, to bear witness as a martyr, and to merit the praise of Christendom. The major poem in the series, *Das Leben Jesu* (Life of Jesus), recapitulates the annunciation to Zacharias, the mission of John the Baptist, and the machinations of Herod. After the account of Jesus' baptism in the Jordan, Ava tells of his fast in the desert and encounter with Satan, his tempter. The defeat of the devil as tempter culminates in his actual subjection during Christ's triumphal Harrowing of Hell. Following the scenes of Jesus' temptations in the desert, the narrative recounts his miracles of healing. The capture, trial, and crucifixion of Jesus place charity—the central commandment to his disciples—in the context of giving one's own life for a friend. After depicting the Resurrection and the Ascension, the poem focuses on the arrival of the Holy Spirit in the upper room and the recipients' use of the divine gifts to teach others. The main body of *Das Leben Jesu* ends with Peter winning many converts as bishop in Antioch and Rome. The transitional verses that follow constitute *Die Sieben Gaben des Heiligen Geistes* (The Seven Gifts of the Holy Spirit) and offer a catalogue of virtues given by Jesus to his disciples. The third work in the series is *Der Antichrist.* This short poem of twelve strophes relates how the Antichrist will take possession of the world and overthrow the existing social order. Ava shows that his qualities are antithetical to the seven gifts of the Holy Spirit. Those who lack the correct orientation to God will succumb to the impostor's deception. Although the Antichrist's reign will last for four and one-half years and inflict great suffering on all Christians, the sin of pride will eventually lead to his fall and destruction. *Das jüngste Gericht,* the final poem in the series, previews the fifteen days that precede the Last Judgment and the purification of the world by fire. The second half of the poem describes the *Parousia,* the glorious second coming of Christ. Preceded by the four evangelists, he awakens the dead to reward the good and punish those who caused him suffering. As the requirements for salvation can no longer be fulfilled once Christ has returned, Ava advocates repentance and the immediate practice of redeeming virtues, particularly applicable to an aristocratic audience: protecting the poor, ransoming prisoners, holding court without bribe taking, showing mercy to those of lesser power, and generous giving of alms. After the account of the Last Judgment, the poem commemorates the beginning of the liturgical year at Easter as an appropriate time for spiritual reorientation.

Ava's poems are the earliest extent work of an identifiable woman author written in German. Little is known about the author apart from some autobiographical disclosures in her work and from records of her death. Only in the final poem of the series does Ava tell something about her life. Her sons are likely to have been clerics who advised her on interpreting Scripture and other religious sources. The record of Ava's death in the necrology of the Austrian monastery of Melk notes the year 1127 and her vocation as religious recluse.

BIBLIOGRAPHY

de Boor, Helmut. *Frühmittelhochdeutsche Studien. Zwei Untersuchungen.* Halle/Saale: Niemeyer, 1926.

Domitrovic, Martin. "Die Sprache in den Gedichten der Frau Ava, Vokalismus und Konsonantismus." Ph.D. diss., University of Graz, 1950.

Freytag, Wiebke. "Geistliches Leben und christliche Bildung. Hrotsvit und andere Autorinnen des frühen Mittelalters." *Deutsche Literatur von Frauen,* vol. 1. Munich: Beck, 1988, pp. 65–76.

Greinemann, S. Eoliba, OSB. "Die Gedichte der Frau Ava Untersuchungen zur Quellenfrage." Ph.D. diss., University of Freiburg im Breisgau, 1967.

Heer, Friedrich. *Aufgang Europas. Eine Studie zu den Zusammenhängen zwischen politischer Religiosität, Frömmigkeitsstil und dem Westen Europas im 12. Jahrhundert.* Vienna: Europa, 1949.

Helm, Karl. "Untersuchungen über Heinrich Heslers Evangelium Nicodemi." *Beiträge zur Geschichte der deutschen Sprache und Literatur* 24 (1899): 85–187.

Henschel, Erich. "Zu Ava 'Leben Jesu'." *Beiträge zur Geschichte der deutschen Sprache und Literatur* (Halle) 78 (1956): 479–484.

Hintz, Ernst Ralf. "Frau Ava," in *Semper idem et novus. Festschrift for Frank Banta,* ed. Francis G. Gentry. Göppingen: Kümmerle, 1988, pp. 209–230.

———. "Frau Ava (?–1127)." In *German Writers and Works of the Early Middle Ages: 800-1170,* ed. Will Hasty and James Hardin. Detroit: Gale, 1995, pp. 39–44.

———. *Learning and Persuasion in the German Middle Ages.* New York: Garland, 1997, pp. 103–137.

Hoffmann von Fallersleben, Heinrich. *Fundgruben für Geschichte deutscher Sprache und Literatur.* Breslau: Grass, Barth, 1830. [part 1, ("G") only, *Johannis* omitted].

Kienast, Richard. "Ava-Studien. 1–3" *Zeitschrift für deutsches Altertum und deutsche Literatur* 74 (1937): 1–36; 74 (1937): 277–308: 77 (1940): 45–104.

Maurer, Friedrich. *Die Dichtungen der Frau Ava.* Tübingen: Niemeyer, 1966.

Menhardt, Hermann. "Ein früher Teildruck der Görlitzer Ava-Handschrift." *Beiträge zur Geschichte der deutschen Sprache und Literatur* 81 (1959): 111–115.

Piper, Paul. "Die Gedichte der Ava." *Zeitschrift für deutsche Philologie* 19 (1887): 129–196, 275–321 [("V" and "G")].

Schacks, Kurt. *Die Dichtungen der Frau Ava.* Graz: Wiener Neudrucke, 1986.

Schröder, Edward. "Frau Ava und die Osterfeier." *Zeitschrift für deutsches Altertum und deutsche Literatur* 50 (1908): 312–313.

———. "Ava und Bettina." *Anzeiger für deutsches Altertum und deutsche Literatur* 42 (1923): 90–91.

———. "Aus der Gelehrsamkeit der Frau Ava." *Zeitschrift für deutsches Altertum und deutsche Literatur* 66 (1929): 171–172.

———. "Spiel und Spielmann." *Zeitschrift für deutsches Altertum und deutsche Literatur* 74 (1937): 45–46.

Stein, Peter K. "Stil, Struktur, historischer Ort und Funktion. Literarhistorische Beobachtungen und methodologische Überlegungen zu den Dichtungen Frau Avas," in *Festschrift für Adalbert Schmidt zum 70. Geburtstag.* Stuttgart: Heinz, 1976.

Wesenick, Gertrude. "Frühmittelhochdeutsche Dichtung des 12. Jahrhunderts aus der Wachau. Frau Avas Gedichte." Ph.D. diss., University of Tübingen, 1963.

Woelfert, Rosemarie. "Wandel der religiösen Epik zwischen 1100 und 1200 dargestellt an Frau Avas Leben Jesu und der Kindheit Jesu des Konrad von Fussesbrunnen." Ph.D. diss., University of Tübingen, 1963.

Ernst Ralf Hintz

Frauenlob (d. November 29, 1318)

Heinrich von Meißen, called *Frauenlob* (literally, Praise of Women), wrote Middle High German poetry in the late thirteenth and early fourteenth centuries. He died on November 29, 1318, and lies buried in Mainz. There being practically no nonliterary traces of his life, nearly all we know of him derives from his literary production. In later political poems *(Sangspruchdichtung),* Frauenlob names a series of historical personalities who provide dates for certain texts and may indicate a degree of mobility (e.g., Duke Heinrich von Breslau, King Eric of Denmark, among others); living and deceased poets of his time are named (e.g., Walther von der Vogelweide, Konrad von Würzburg, and many others) who offer hints of a relative chronology.

Frauenlob's literary production is broad, but many of the texts are extant in only one copy, thus making editing difficult. For example, numerous poems have been distorted by scribal misunderstandings and errors, and present a daunting philological challenge. Equally problematic is the question of authenticity. Owing to questionable reasoning on the part of the scholar Helmuth Thomas, the standard edition of Frauenlob's poems, edited by Stackmann and Bertau, contains an incomplete catalogue. To attain the broadest possible picture of Frauenlob's oeuvre, one must consult Ettmüllter's edition of 1843.

Frauenlob was comfortable composing in all genres: songs, political lyrics, disputes, and narrative poetry. Often his songs represent traditions common in the first half of the thirteenth century, employing topics such as courtly love *(minne),* nature, and religion. His series of songs, especially those on the Virgin Mary and the Trinity, are thematically and formally more ambitious. Frauenlob combines and refines traditional motives, often in a particular fashion: cryptic, encoded, aimed at a knowledgeable, elite audience. Within his *Spruchdichtung,* Frauenlob also expressed his own thoughts on poetry and his own role as a poet. Thus, on the one hand, he sees himself as a grateful successor to the great poets of the past (he especially honors Konrad von Würzburg), while, on the other hand, he presents himself as their superior: once he remarks, *ûz kezzels grunde gât mîn kunst* (from the depth of the caldron emerges my art), thereby setting himself apart from other poets.

A noteworthy composition is Frauenlob's "Dispute between Minne and the World," in which both allegorical partners—*minne* as courtly love personified—argue in learned fashion for their respective relative rank.

Frauenlob's *Leiche* are undoubtedly achievements of the highest order. He composed praises of the Crucifix, of *minne,* and of the Virgin Mary, and the melodies for each. It is because of the song to Mary, in praise of the heavenly woman, that Frauenlob received his nickname, Praise of Women, although his praise of worldly women may have also played a role. This song is Frauenlob's masterpiece: his theology, pious praise of Mary, and natural philosophy are combined in an immense concept and present a dimension of popular language praise of Mary hitherto unseen in this genre, a dimension that still today presents critical challenges. The love poem provides an unconventional concept of courtly love: *minne* is now founded in natural philosophy as a productive force of nature that unites opposites to create nature anew and to perpetuate the process of nature. The crucifix poem, finally, deals with the theological concepts of trinity, incarnation, salvation, and crucifix worship, at one unique linguistically and from the point of view of the motif.

Frauenlob marks a literary transition; he looks back on some one hundred years of tradition he knows well; intellectually he is well trained in many areas; he attempts to reapproach the great poetical topics aesthetically and substantively.

BIBLIOGRAPHY

Bein, Thomas. *Studien zu Frauenlobs Minneleich.* Frankfurt am Main: Lang, 1988.

Cambridger "Frauenlob"-Kolloquium 1986. Wolfram-Studien 10, ed. Werner Schröder. Berlin: Schmidt, 1988 [collection of papers from conference].

Ettmüller, Ludwig, ed. *Heinrich von Meißen, des Frauenlobs Leiche, Sprüche, Streitgedichte und Lieder.* Quedlinburg: Basse, 1843.

Huber, Christoph. *Die Aufnahme und Verbreitung des Alanus ab Insulis in mhd. Dichtungen.* Zurich: Artemis and Winkler, 1988.

März, Christoph. *Frauenlobs Marienliech Untersuchungen zur spätmittelalterlichen Monodie.* Erlangen: Palm and Enke, 1987.

Stackmann, Karle and Karl Bertau, eds. *Frauenlob (Heinrich von Meißen): Leichs, Sangsprüche, Lieder,* 2 vols. Göttingen: Vandenhoeck and Ruprecht, 1981.

Steinmetz, Ralf-Henning. *Liebe als universales Prinzip bei Frauenlob.* Tübingen: Niemeyer, 1994.

Thomas Bein

SEE ALSO
Sangspruch; Versification; Walther von der Vogelweide

Frederick I Barbarossa (d. 1190)

Perhaps the greatest figure of the twelfth century, Frederick I Barbarossa ruled the empire from 1152 until his untimely death while on crusade in 1190. Barbarossa was an effective and sometimes brutal ruler whose reign was marked by his efforts to establish his authority in Italy, often stormy relations with the papacy, and equally stormy relations with the princes in Germany. His efforts in one area often influenced the course of events in an-

Wimpfen am Berg, remains of the imperial palace, gallery. *Photograph: Joan A. Holladay*

other, and his reign strengthened the place of his family in the empire and laid the foundation for both subsequent successes and defeats.

According to his biographer Rahewin, Barbarossa had golden hair, a reddish beard, piercing eyes, and a cheerful face. He was also a devout son of the church who honored the clergy and was a great builder of palaces and other public buildings. A "lover of warfare, but only that peace may be secured thereby," Barbarossa, Rahewin tells us further, possessed the virtues of an emperor. Indeed, his military prowess and imperial bearing would be of value for Barbarossa when his uncle, Conrad III, chose him as his successor. Barbarossa was chosen because Conrad's son was still a minor and because of Barbarossa's relations to two of the greatest families in the empire, the Staufen and the Welfs (Guelfs).

Although he was chosen for his important family connections in the German lands of the empire, one of Bar-

barossa's primary concerns was the establishment of his authority in Italy. Relations with Italy, and especially with Rome, formed the core of his conception of the imperial authority because without formal coronation by the pope, Barbarossa could not claim the imperial title. As a consequence he spent much time in Italy, and shortly after the death of Conrad, Barbarossa made his first trip there. His relations began on a promising note as he and Pope Eugenius III (1145–1153) agreed to respect each other's interests in the Treaty of Constance (March 23, 1153). In 1155, Frederick was crowned emperor by the English pope, Hadrian IV (1154–1159), and restored Hadrian to the throne in Rome by suppressing a revolt led by Arnold of Brescia. But cordial relations would not last as both sides failed to adhere to the terms of the treaty, and advisers for both sides, including Rainald of Dassel and Roland Bandinelli, stressed principle over compromise. In 1157, the first great conflict erupted at the imperial court in Besançon over Hadrian's declaration that Barbarossa had received the empire as a *beneficium,* or fief, from the pope. Hadrian would apologize for the use of the term, explaining it meant "favor," but too late as relations had begun to sour.

An even greater breach would emerge during the reign of Alexander III (1159–1181), the former Roland Bandinelli. A disputed election in 1159 led to a schism and the emergence of two popes, Alexander III and Victor IV (1159–1164). The prolonged schism made Barbarossa's already complex dealings with Italy more difficult. The northern Italian cities that had opposed the expansion of the emperor's authority into Italy found a natural ally in Alexander, who, in turn, found much support from the king of France. Barbarossa's activities during the schism had mixed success. In the 1160s he managed to raze the northern Italian power of Milan and force Alexander out of Italy. He witnessed the succession of a series of imperial antipopes, including Paschal III (1164–1168), who crowned Barbarossa's wife, Beatrix, empress and who was enthroned in Rome by the emperor. Frederick's invasions of Italy witnessed victories over his rivals in northern Italy and Rome, and his efforts to establish a universal power to rival Rome that had begun in 1157 with the use of the term *sacrum imperium* (holy empire) were continued with his canonization of Charlemagne in 1165. But Frederick had been excommunicated by Alexander, and support for the pope was too strong throughout western Christendom and especially in Italy. The northern Italian cities formed a league at Verona that built a castle at Alessandria that would be a key stronghold and then rallied around the rebuilt city of Milan in the Lombard League. Moreover, although the emperor managed to take the city of Rome in 1166, he did so at great cost because many of his troops and key advisers, especially Rainald of Dassel, died from malaria. He never managed to take Alessandria and was defeated by the league in 1176 at the battle of Legnano. A peace conference followed the defeat and led to the peace of Venice in 1177. The settlement lifted the excommunication and recognized the imperial bishops appointed by Barbarossa. It also established a permanent peace between emperor and pope and a fifteen-year truce between emperor and the Lombard cities. Finally, it granted Barbarossa extensive rights in the much coveted Mathildine lands of Tuscany.

Much of the conflict with Rome involved the broader concerns of imperial rights in Italy, and relations with Rome were greatly complicated by Barbarossa's Italian policies. As emperor, Barbarossa saw control of Italy as essential to his authority, and, consequently, the emperor spent much time on the peninsula, undertaking a number of campaigns there. His efforts to establish his authority in Italy were shaped by his appreciation of Roman law and the teachings of the masters at Bologna. The clearest example of the influence of Roman law on Barbarossa and the desire to establish his rights in Italy can be found in the so-called Roncaglia decrees of 1158. The decrees were pronounced during the emperor's second Italian expedition and while tensions between Frederick and Pope Hadrian remained high. The decrees, the result of a council that included a number of jurists from Bologna, listed and defined royal rights *(regalia)* in Italy. The *regalia* included, as Rahewin notes, "dukedoms, marches, counties, consulates, mints, market tolls, forage tax, wagons tolls, transit tolls, mills, fisheries, bridges," and an annual tax on land and persons. The decrees also asserted Frederick's rights to nominate and confirm the various magistrates and judges of the cities of northern Italy. Finally, the decrees instituted the newly developing law of fiefs in Italy, limiting the rights of alienation of fiefs and defining more precisely the nature of a fief. The promulgation of the Roncaglian decrees was an effort by Frederick to establish himself as the governing authority in Italy, a legal pronouncement followed by ruthless enforcement. Although an important step for Barbarossa, the proclamation of the decrees was greatly resented by the northern Italian cities and led to much conflict between them and the emperor. In fact, the animosity generated by the decrees would complicate Barbarossa's efforts in Italy, a controversy that, in some ways, would not be resolved until the peace of Venice.

Frederick's other great concern was, of course, Germany and his relations with the German princes, especially with the Welf family and its greatest scion, Henry the Lion. To avoid the conflicts of his predecessor, Barbarossa needed to work at reconciliation with the major families of the realm from the very beginning of his reign. To satisfy the Staufen line he made his displaced cousin and son of Conrad III, the eight-year-old Frederick of Rothenburg, duke of Swabia. He granted the Babenberger Henry Jasomirgott the duchy of Austria after earlier depriving him of his Bavarian title. But the greatest grants were made to the Welf, Henry, who was granted the duchy of Bavaria and Saxony. And as duke of Saxony, Henry was allowed to expand his authority in the north by Frederick as a means of maintaining Henry's support for the emperor. Having placated the great families,

Barbarossa sought to strengthen his position and that of his family. A first step was taken when Barbarossa married Beatrix, the heiress to the county of Burgundy and parts of Provence. Barbarossa sought to expand familial and imperial lands throughout the realm, attaching Staufen territory to himself and also laying claim to possessions of other nobles when possible. Moreover, his willingness to allow Henry the Lion to fall for failure to attend imperial courts and for abuse of power as duke enabled Barbarossa to restructure the duchies of the realm, break up the larger duchies of the Lion, raise lesser noble families to higher authority, and establish feudal law in Germany. Finally, Barbarossa intervened in disputed episcopal elections and made greater use of *ministeriales* (clerics) during his reign to make his authority more effective.

Barbarossa's last great act was his participation in the Third Crusade. Long a supporter of these holy wars and a participant in the Second Crusade, Frederick took the cross at an assembly at Mainz in 1188. With great hope, Barbarossa led a large force toward the Holy Lands and enjoyed early success along the way. Unfortunately, while crossing the river Saleph on June 10, 1190, Barbarossa drowned. His army fragmented, with part returning home and part continuing on. The death of the emperor weakened the crusader army and, perhaps, undermined chances for success. Despite his unfortunate end, Barbarossa had made a lasting impact on the empire and left it at peace and in the relatively capable hands of his son, Henry VI (d. 1197).

BIBLIOGRAPHY

Benson, Robert L. "Political *Renovatio:* Two Models from Roman Antiquity," in *Renaissance and Renewal in the Twelfth Century,* ed. Robert L. Benson and Giles Constable with Carol D. Lanham. Toronto: University of Toronto Press, 1982, pp. 339–386.

Die Urkunden Friedrichs I, ed. Heinrich Appelt. Monumenta Germaniae historica. Die Urkunden der deutschen Konige und Kaiser 10, 1–3. Hannover: Hahn, 1975–1979.

Fuhrmann, Horst. *Germany in the High Middle Ages,* trans. Timothy Reuter. Cambridge: Cambridge University Press, 1986.

Gillingham, J. B. *The Kingdom of Germany in the High Middle Ages (900–1200).* London: Historical Association, 1971.

Leyser, Karl. "Frederick Barbarossa and the Hohenstaufen Polity," in *Communications and Power in Medieval Europe: The Gregorian Revolution and Beyond,* ed. Timothy Reuter. London: Hambledon Press, 1994, pp. 115-142.

———. "Frederick Barbarossa: Court and Country," in *Communications and Power in Medieval Europe: The Gregorian Revolution and Beyond,* ed. Timothy Reuter. London: Hambledon Press, 1994, pp. 143–155.

Morena, Otto. *Historia Frederici I,* ed. Ferdinand Güterbock. Monumenta Germaniae historica. Scriptores rerum germanicarum. Nova series 7. Berlin: Weidmann, 1930.

Munz, Peter. *Frederick Barbarossa: A Study in Medieval Politics.* Ithaca, N.Y.: Cornell University Press, 1969.

Otto of Freising and Rahewin. *Gesta Friderici Imperatoris,* ed. G. Waitz. Monumenta Germaniae historica. Scriptores rerum germanicarum 46. Hannover: Hahn, 1912.

———, and his Continuator, Rahewin. *The Deeds of Frederick Barbarossa,* trans. Charles Chrisopher Mierow. Toronto: University of Toronto Press, 1994.

Michael Frassetto

SEE ALSO

Crusades; Frederick I Barbarossa, Art; Gerhoh of Reichersberg; Henry VI; Henry the Lion; Ministerials; Otto of Freising; Rahewin; Rainald of Dassel; Staufen; Successsion; Welfs

Frederick I Barbarossa, Art

All the known artistic endeavors of Frederick I Barbarossa were politically motivated. Seeking rule over a wide geographic area and reinforcement of centers of power, he built castles in various locations, forgoing a centralized capital, while also taking advantage of Charlemagne's palace at Aachen, and of the ecclesiastical and ducal palaces of his allies. Vital to the history of medieval palace architecture, he restored Carolingian establishments at Nimwegen (1155) and Ingelheim (1160), and built new palaces at Eger (1180–1190), Wimpfen (1182), Kaiserslautern (1160), Gelnhausen (1170), Hagenau (1170–1184), and Kaiserswerth (1184). These defensive edifices all had compelling monumentality, simplified interior division, and carefully rusticated (tinted red) exteriors. Although physical remains are scant, excavations and archives disclose a penchant for strong walls, gate buildings and keeps, and palatine (royal) chapels. Local architectural and decorative idiom prevail, although German traits were exported for remote works, i.e., Rhenish/Saxon styles at Moravian Eger.

Palaces, chapels, and churches were splendidly furnished. Kaiserslautern, described in Rahewin's imperial chronicles, was richly appointed, and the tower chapel at Hagenau, intended to house the crown and spear of Christ, reflected the spirit of Jerusalem's Holy Sepulchre. Decoration for the apse and towers added to the hall church at Ingelheim circa 1160 included head consoles and friezes with lions and lambs. Stained glass in the Landesmuseum in Wiesbaden was perhaps a part of this renovation.

Attention to ecclesiastical foundations reflects Frederick's belief in imperial guardianship of the church. Patronage of Freising Cathedral resulted in portal sculptures of Frederick and Beatrix. They sponsored expansion of the church of St. Fides at Schlettstadt and donated choir windows there after his 1162 siege of Milan. Pictorial themes of royal lineage are pervasive, perhaps most notable in two reliquaries associated with the 1165 disentombment of Charlemagne. The arm of Charles, a specific and potent symbol of imperial power, was placed in a casket reliquary of gilded silver and enamel (now in the Louvre, Paris), while preparations proceeded for the larger gilded and jeweled Charlemagne shrine in Aachen. This latter was completed fifty years later and ceremonially nailed shut by Frederick II, as a pointed imperial gesture. Both shrine programs place Hohenstaufen rulers in a lineage with Charlemagne, while glorifying connections to the church and the Heavenly Jerusalem.

Also conceived as decorative enhancement, these shrines augmented a group of previous rulers' lavish gifts to Charles's palatine chapel. To illuminate the display space for the larger reliquary, Frederick and Beatrix also donated a gilded bronze chandelier, with a design echoing the octagonal chapel plan and including images from Revelations, the life and Passion of Christ, and the Eight Beatitudes.

Frederick is thought to have added a pair of gilt and enamel armbands (known from eighteenth-century sketches) to the imperial regalia: one with images of the Birth of Christ and the Annunciation to the Shepherds, the other with the Presentation in the Temple.

Two portraits, gifts from Frederick's godfather, Otto von Cappenberg, enhance the emperor's Christian reputation: the gilded bronze head, known as the Cappenberger reliquary, which pointedly revives an antique imperial type, and a gilded silver baptismal bowl, circa 1160. The bowl commemorates Frederick's christening in an image similar to that of Constantine's Baptism on the Stavelot Triptych of circa 1150, again suggesting a lineage of Christian rulers.

BIBLIOGRAPHY

Deér, Josef. "Die Siegel Kaiser Friedrichs I. Barbarossa und Heinrichs VI. in der Kunst und Politik ihrer Zeit," in *Festschrift Hans R. Hahnloser zum 60. Geburtstag,* ed. Ellen J. Beer et al. Basel: Birkhäuser, 1961, pp. 47–102.

Die Zeit der Staufer: Geschichte, Kunst, Kultur, ed. Rainer Haussherr. 5 vols. Stuttgart: Württembergisches Landesmuseum, 1979.

Faymonville, Karl. *Das Münster zu Aachen.* Die Kunstdenkmäler der Stadt Aachen 1. Düsseldorf: Schwann, 1916.

Folz, Robert. *Le Souvenir et la légende de Charlemagne dans l'empire germanique médiévale.* Paris: Société d'Édition Les Belles Lettres, 1950.

Grimme, Ernst Günther. *Aachener Goldschmiedekunst im Mittelalter von Karl dem Großen bis zu Karl V.* Cologne: Seeman, 1957.

———. "Das Bildprogramm des Aachener Karlsschreins." *Karl der Große und seine Schreine in Aachen—Eine Festschrift,* ed. Hans Müllejans. Mönchengladbach: Kühlen, 1988, pp. 124–135.

LeJeune, Rita, and Jacques Stiennon. *La légende de Roland dans l'art du moyen âge,* 2 vols. Brussels: Arcade, 1967.

Nilgen, Ursula. "Amtsgeneologie und Amtsheiligkeit: Königs- und Bischofsreihen in der Kunstpropaganda des Hochmittelalters," in *Studien zur Mittelalterlichen Kunst 800–1250: Festschrift für Florentine Mütherich zum 70. Geburtstag,* ed. Katherina Bierbauer et al. Munich: Prestel, 1985, pp. 217–234.

Schramm, Percy Ernst. *Die deutsche Kaiser und Könige in Bildern ihrer Zeit 751–1190.* Munich: Prestel, 1983.

Rita Tekippe

SEE ALSO
Aachen; Charlemagne; Metalwork; Relics and Reliquaries; Romanesque Art and Architecture; Wimpfen

Frederick II (December 26, 1194–December 13, 1250)

King of Sicily, Roman emperor, king of Jerusalem, Frederick was born on December 26, 1194, in Jesi (Ancona), the eldest child of Emperor Henry VI Hohenstaufen and Constance (daughter of Roger II and heiress to Sicily). Baptized Frederick Roger (after his grandfathers), his name signaled his two heritages, namely, rule over the empire and the Italian *regno* (reign) and their fateful fusion. The German princes elected him king of the Romans (1196), and he was crowned king of Sicily (1198) after his father's death. North of the Alps, the competing royal elections of Otto (IV) of Brunswick and Frederick's uncle, Philip of Swabia, plunged Germany into dynastic civil war. Before her own death, Constance named Pope Innocent III guardian over the four year old and regent of the kingdom.

As the young orphan grew into manhood, political disorder engulfed the *regno*. The child-king became a pawn of feuding native and German aristocratic factions while other outside parties pursued their own interest at the expense of the royal power. Childhood in cosmopolitan Palermo—scene of an intermingling of Arab, Norman, Italian, and Greek cultural impulses—favored Frederick's intellectual alertness, mental and emotional precocity, and polygon talents. His cheerfulness, amiability, and calculation were balanced by the capacity for mistrust, coldness, cruelty, misanthropy, a demonic temperament, and a general lack of scruples.

In June 1208, the murder of Frederick's uncle Philip paved the way for Otto's accession to royal power in Germany. Six months later Frederick attained his majority according to Sicilian law. A marriage was arranged by the pope to Constance of Aragon, sister of King Peter II; it brought Frederick the Aragonese military support that enabled him to bolster his political position in the kingdom before new danger arose. In return for various promises, including an undertaking not to interfere in Sicilian affairs, Otto IV secured imperial coronation at Pope Innocent's hands in 1209. But the new emperor's repudiation of his promise and his invasion of the kingdom triggered excommunication by the pope and papal support for a Hohenstaufen candidacy for the German and imperial crowns. In 1211 a group of German princes opposed to Otto met in Nuremberg and elected Frederick king of the Romans. In early 1212 Frederick decided to accept this election. Now he solidified the pope's support by confirming his mother's concessions regarding the Sicilian church; he also protected the dynasty's future by having his infant son, Henry, crowned co-king of Sicily.

During Autumn 1212 Frederick embarked on an unexpected and adventurous trip over the Alps to southwest Germany. Pro-Hohenstaufen princes, bishops, and towns now rallied to the support of the seemingly wondrous "boy of Apulia"; money and diplomatic support also came from Philip of France. Next Frederick moved north,

where he was elected king of the Romans (for the third time) in Frankfurt and crowned in Mainz. During 1213 Frederick solidified his political and military position against Otto and confirmed various concessions to the papacy and the German ecclesiastical princes. Otto now staked his future chances on an invasion of northern France, but Philip II won a decisive victory over him at Bouvines (1214). The chastened Welf withdrew to his Saxon strongholds, where he died in May 1218.

Now crowned king of the Romans a second time at Aachen (1215), an enthusiastic Frederick made a fateful vow to go on crusade to recover the Holy Places. A year later he renewed another commitment by formally promising Pope Innocent that he would turn the government of Sicily over to his young son Henry by right after he himself received the imperial crown. Innocent's death in 1216 was followed by the election of Honorius III, a decidedly less stern pope. In 1220 Frederick engineered Henry VIII's election as co-king of the Romans, thus assuring the union of Sicily and the empire that Innocent had feared. Frederick disingenuously informed Honorius that the election had occurred at the wish of the princes; in fact, the purchase price was not inconsiderable: to secure electoral support from the ecclesiastical princes Frederick promulgated the *Confoederatio* or *Privilegium cum principibus ecclesiasticis,* which contained the renunciation (at least in theory) of many royal rights in ecclesiastical territories. That same year Honorius crowned Frederick emperor in St. Peter's basilica.

For much of the next decade Frederick maintained his strong political position; despite his prior promises, the union of the imperial and Sicilian crowns meant a potential encirclement of the papacy. And now his attention could be turned to the *regno* for a five-year period of consolidation: the strengthening of fortifications and harbor facilities, establishment of a large war fleet and merchant navy, and restriction of the trading and extraterritorial privileges hitherto held by Pisan and Genoese merchants. In 1220 at Capua he promulgated assizes that included a requirement that all royal privileges granted since 1189 must be reviewed before given any further credence. In this manner, Frederick could recoup some royal rights and properties lost through usurpation or ill-advised concession. He also suppressed a Muslim revolt in Sicily and resettled many defeated Saracens in Lucera, where they established a Muslim enclave that in time became a center of royal support. To further the training of civil servants for a burgeoning royal bureaucracy, Frederick also founded the University of Naples.

His commitment to depart on crusade was postponed repeatedly as Frederick consolidated control over the *regno.* But it was never forgotten by Honorius and the papal curia. The pope even helped to arrange Frederick's marriage in 1225 to the heiress of the kingdom of Jerusalem, Isabella Yolande of Brienne. Frederick reiterated his crusade obligations: under pain of excommunication he would depart for the East before August 1227. In a related matter, Frederick promulgated, in 1226, for the Teutonic Knights the Golden Bull of Rimini, establishing the foundations of their autonomous state in Prussia. That same year the emperor attempted to convoke a diet to restore imperial rights in northern Italy, but his intentions were thwarted by the resistance of the reconstituted Lombard League under the leadership of Milan. The death of Honorius III in 1227 led to the election of Gregory IX, who as cardinal had been friendly to the emperor. But when plague struck the gathering crusaders in Brindisi during late summer 1227, the embarkation became a debacle; the emperor himself sailed but immediately became ill, returning three days later and postponing further departure to spring 1228. Yet Gregory, long impatient with the emperor's past excuses, held him strictly to the terms of his promises and excommunicated the emperor despite the latter's protestations.

Frederick nonetheless continued preparations for the voyage east despite the spiritual ban and Empress Yolande's death shortly after giving birth to Conrad (IV). In June 1228 the emperor reembarked with a small army and arrived in Acre, where he found little support from the local Syrian-Frankish baronage, the ecclesiastical hierarchy, or the military orders. Despite such handicaps, Frederick drew on his knowledge of Arabic and Muslim culture to negotiate a favorable treaty with the Egyptian sultan al-Kamil. The emperor next entered the Holy City and crowned himself king of Jerusalem, basing his title on his deceased wife's claim and on their son Conrad's minor status.

The pope's enmity did not slacken, however. War had already broken out in Italy. Since any further actions in Outremer were doomed to failure, the emperor set sail and returned to Brindisi. Frederick quickly assembled troops and swept the papal invaders back northward, taking care to halt his victorious advance at the border. Negotiations during the next year, 1230, culminated in the treaties of San Germano and Ceprano. Gregory absolved Frederick from excommunication, the territorial status quo was restored, and the emperor promised the Sicilian church freedom of prelatial elections and other privileges.

But otherwise nothing was decided regarding the threatened encirclement of papal territory, papal doubts regarding the emperor's stance toward ecclesiastical liberty, and the Lombard's autonomy.

A fragile peace now restored, Frederick embarked on his most memorable legal project—the codification of royal laws for the *regno* in *Liber Augustalis,* or Constitutions of Melfi (1231). This work of synthesis organized royal enactments with a view to centralize authority, bureaucratize royal government, and weaken all other nonroyal intermediate jurisdictions.

But trouble now loomed in Germany, where young King Henry's weakly executed and unsteady policy of alliance with imperial ministerials, towns, and lesser aristocrats provoked opposition and demands from the greater princes. Henry was compelled to issue the *Statutum in favorem principum* (1231), and his father had no choice but to confirm the same document a year later. In constitutional terms the autonomy of the princes was thereby somewhat strengthened, while restrictions on imperial cities were somewhat tightened. In 1232, Frederick imposed on his son an oath not to pursue in the future his former policies, but Henry nonetheless rebelled in 1234, and even allied himself with the Lombard League. When Frederick himself journeyed north in 1235, however, all resistance collapsed. Henry submitted unconditionally to his father, was stripped of his title and crown, and imprisoned for the rest of his life in various castles. He died by suicide in 1242.

Frederick now married again, this time to Isabella Plantagenet, sister of Henry III of England. The emperor proceeded to celebrate his triumphs at an imperial diet in Mainz, where he promulgated a peace edict that created the post of high court judge and proclaimed that all rights of governance originated in the monarchy. Frederick also staged a reconciliation with the Welfs by creating the feudal principality of Brunswick-Lüneburg for Otto, nephew of Otto IV.

Frederick returned to Italy, where he waged a military campaign during 1236 against the Lombards. Winter brought the emperor north again, this time to depose the outlawed rebel Frederick II of Austria and Styria. The emperor also arranged that his son Conrad was elected king of the Romans in Vienna (1237). He journeyed back to Italy, where his political fortunes now reached their zenith; Frederick led his army to victory over the League of Cortenuova, an alliance between Maitland and Lombard. The vanquished Lombards became eager to negotiate peace, but the emperor's intransigence encouraged instead a spirit of desperate resistance among a hard core of league members. Six cities chose to fight on. His relations with Pope Gregory also worsened. Frederick's illegitimate son Enzio married at his father's urging the heiress to a large portion of Sardinia and, in a calculated affront, immediately styled himself king of that island, thereby ignoring papal claims to overlordship. In 1239, the pope excommunicated Frederick a second time, charging that the emperor had oppressed the Sicilian church, impeded crusades, and assisted rebellious Romans. The real reasons for conflict, namely, the emperor's ongoing struggle with the Lombards and his perceived threat to papal autonomy, received no explicit mention.

The struggle quickly developed its apocalyptic as well as military aspects. Detractors called Frederick Antichrist; supporters hailed him as the expected messianic ruler of the Last Day. Crucial to Frederick's propaganda was his minister Petrus de Vinea, the architect of a new high rhetorical style that rivaled the fulminations of the papal chancery. On the military front the emperor and his subordinate commanders went from strength to strength. The disputed territories of Spoleto and the March were seized, and Frederick himself conducted an invasion of papal territories farther north. After a long siege Faenze surrendered. The emperor even managed to ruin the pope's impending Easter 1241 council in Rome, where Frederick expected further condemnations: his Pisan allies won a complete naval victory near the island of Montecristo over the Genoese fleet carrying many prelates to Rome. More than a hundred prospective council participants were captured and imprisoned under harsh conditions. But this triumph soon boomeranged to Frederick's discredit, for it confirmed the pope's characterization of him as an oppressor of the church.

The struggle consumed the emperor's political and military energies to such an extent that he played no role in confronting the Mongol storm that since 1273 had swept irresistibly through the Russian principalities, Poland, Hungary, and into Germany. At Liegnitz in Silesia in 1241, the Mongols annihilated a German-Polish army, but news of the death of their Great Khan Ogotai and the expectation of a succession struggle led to their withdrawal eastward. Nonetheless, Frederick was still castigated by many German subjects for his inactivity.

When Gregory IX died in August 1241, the emperor prudently awaited further developments. The election and short pontificate of Celestine IV led to a nineteen-month interregnum until a sufficient number of cardinals elected Innocent IV in 1243. Negotiations began immediately between Frederick and the new pope. The emperor offered several concessions, but Innocent continued to distrust his commitments and to fear his ultimate intentions. For their part, both papal and imperial partisans occasionally broke the truce. Eventually, the pope's unwillingness to abandon the Lombards convinced Frederick to break off negotiations and secure his own safety through flight across the Alps to Lyon in 1244.

To that city Innocent summoned a general council to meet the following summer in order to deal with the many accusations leveled against Frederick. When the synod met, the verdict was a foregone conclusion: the pope solemnly excommunicated the emperor again and deposed him from his imperial and royal offices. Under papal pressure in 1246 and 1247, several German princes elected in succession antikings Henry Raspe of Thuringia and William of Holland, but neither ultimately had much effect on Frederick's position in Germany.

More serious, however, were the conspiracies and revolts in Italy. A plot by some Apulian officials and aristocrats was discovered and crushed in 1246. Parma unexpectedly revolted in 1247 against Frederick and stymied his impending trip to Lyon and to Germany. To retake Parma the emperor now ordered construction of a new wooden siege town named Vittoria. But a sally by the besieged while Frederick was absent hunting scattered imperial forces, destroyed the siege town, and inflicted heavy casualties in 1248. The emperor had to discontinue the siege and withdraw. His misfortunes continued during 1249. First Frederick narrowly escaped an attempted poisoning by his personal physician. Next he had his close associate, Petrus de Vinea, arrested under mysterious circumstances as a traitor. Perhaps Petrus's actual crime was official corruption; in any event, he died shortly afterward, probably by suicide. Finally, the emperor's beloved son Enzio was captured by the Bolognese, never to be released until his death two decades later.

Despite these setbacks, Frederick's position in Germany, where Conrad IV defended his interests, was still strong. And while the emperor's political and military fortunes in northern and central Italy swung back and forth, he was still a force to be reckoned with. But a decisive reckoning would not occur. While in Apulia at the end of November 1250 Frederick became seriously ill, probably with dysentery. He managed to reach Castel Fiorentino; there he made his last testament, disposing of titles and territories, received absolution and extreme unction at the hands of a loyal bishop, and died on December 13. Frederick was buried in the cathedral of Palermo.

Frederick was an object of wonderment and fear during his life, but his death marked the beginning of the end for the Hohenstaufen dynasty; his sons and grandson were overwhelmed by premature and often violent deaths. The chronicler Matthew Paris called the emperor "wonder and marvelous transformer of the world" *(stupor mundi et immutator mirabilis)*. Frederick's three major constitutional documents for Germany—the *Confoederatio cum principibus ecclesiasticis,* the *Constitutio in favorem principum,* and the Mainz *Landfriede*—represented not the surrender of his political position there but, instead, the salvaging of royal prerogatives and a sober recognition of what the princes had already achieved. It was Frederick's death and the disappearance of his dynasty that created the interregnum that weakened forever the German monarchy's ability to imitate the piecemeal consolidations of English and French royal power. In Sicily, on the other hand, Frederick and his associates built on the strong royal traditions of the Norman kings and fashioned a government that rivaled other strong contemporary monarchies. Yet even there the time was not ripe for a thoroughly bureaucratic centralized state without autonomous communal, feudal, or ecclesiastical authorities. And whatever skepticism he may have possessed regarding the Catholic faith or religion in general, Frederick took great pains to stress his position as an orthodox Christian monarch.

When assessing Frederick's importance for the culture of his time, one must again note the mixed nature of his Sicilian milieu. Himself conversant in several languages, the emperor had a cosmopolitan outlook, eclectic tastes, and diverse interests in mathematics, the natural sciences, and philosophy. Frederick adopted startling Arab habits such as the harem and the traveling menagerie. He surrounded himself with intellectuals such as Petrus de Vinea, Michael Scot, and Leonardo Fibonacci. His Sicilian court witnessed the beginnings of literature in Italian *volgare* (popular tongue as opposed to Latin) as Frederick himself and his courtiers participated in a sudden flowering of lyric poetry. Architectural projects such as the stark Castel del Monte and the (now lost) Triumphal Gate in Capua expressed an originality that derived from both classical and nonclassical sources. His gold coinage—the *augustalis*—represented both a pioneering achievement of medieval European government as well as an enduring numismatic event. Finally, Frederick himself was a scientific author. His ornithological treatise on hunting with birds—the emperor's favorite sport—stressed the value of observation to correct received authority.

BIBLIOGRAPHY

Abulafia, David. *Frederick II: A Medieval Emperor.* London: Pimlico, 1988.

Fleckenstein, Josef, ed. *Probleme um Friedrich II.* Vorträge und Forschungen 16. Sigmaringen: Thorbecke, 1974.

Kantorowicz, Ernst. *Frederick the Second, 1194–1250,* trans. E. O. Lorimer. New York: Ungar, 1957.

Schaller, Hans Martin. *Kaiser Friedrich II. Verwandler der Welt.* Persönlichkeit un Geschichte 35. Göttingen: Musterschmidt, 1964.

Van Cleve, Thomas Curtis. *The Emperor Frederick II of Hohenstaufen.* "Immutator Mundi." Oxford: Clarendon Press, 1972.

Willemsen, C. A. *Bibliographie zur Geschichte Kaiser Friedrichs II. und der letzten Staufer.* Munich: Monumenta Germaniae Historica, 1986.

Wolf, Gunter G., ed. *Stupor mundi. Zur Geschichte Friedrichs II. von Hohenstaufen.* Darmstadt: Wissenschaftliche Buchgesellschaft, 1966.

Robert C. Figueira

SEE ALSO

Aachen; Bouvines, Battle of; Crusades; *Deutschorden;* Henry the Raspe; Landfrieden; Mainz; Ministerials; *Statutum in Favorem Principorum;* Staufen; Welfs

Frederick III (1415–1493)

Because of the early death of his parents, Duke Ernst of Austria and Cimburgis of Masovia, Frederic III Habsburg (1415–1493) became the ward of his uncle Duke Frederick IV "with the Empty Pockets" of the Tyrol. He was able to free himself from the guardianship only in 1435 at the late age of twenty, becoming in his own right duke of Styria, Carinthia, and Carniola. His first independent act was a pilgrimage to Jerusalem the next year, where he was knighted at the Holy Sepulchre.

The unexpected deaths of his uncle Frederick and cousin King Albrecht II in 1439 improved Frederick's situation, since he became the head of the House of Habsburg. As leader of the dynasty, he assumed the guardianship for younger relatives, reversing the situation of his own youth. First, he supervised the Tyrol for his nephew Sigismund for several years. But the Tyrolean and Alsatian possessions drew him into wasteful, inconclusive wars with the Swiss Confederation. Second, he controlled King Albrecht's son Ladislaus, born after his father's death, hence the sobriquet "Posthumous." Ladislaus was not only heir to lands in lower Austria but also the crowns of Hungary and Bohemia.

Frederick's preeminent position led the electoral princes unanimously to elevate the young duke to king of the Romans on February 2, 1440. Early in his reign, in August 1441, he issued a reform proposal for the empire, indicating the new king's intention to be an active monarch. A bad sign, however, was the long delay of more than two and a half years until his coronation in Aachen. Indeed, from 1444 to 1471 Frederick did not leave his hereditary lands. Hence royal influence, especially through the royal court of justice, wasted away while the power of the cities and princes grew correspondingly. Confined to Austria, Frederick's court nonetheless attracted some of the most important lawyers of the day, like Gregory Heimburg and Martin Mair. Frederick also tried to build a court promoting the newest arts and humanistic ideas, for a time attracting the support of the famous humanist Aeneus Silvius Piccolomini, the later Pope Pius II. Frederick's own interest in numerology, alchemy, and astrology may have prompted his frequent use of the mystical motto AEIOU, which centuries later was interpreted as "All the world is subject to Austria" (*Alles Erdreich Ist Oesterreich Untertan*).

Meanwhile, as leader of the Holy Roman Empire, Frederick did have some success with the church. At first neutral in the schism caused by the Council of Basel, he soon leaned toward supporting Rome. He gained lasting success by signing the Concordat of Vienna with Rome in 1448. Although not quite as advantageous to the monarchy as contemporary agreements in France or Hungary, it allowed Frederick control of seventeen episcopal sees. That agreement regulated papal-imperial relations for the rest of the empire's duration, leading to the continuing decline of papal influence on episcopal elections. Partially financed with money provided by the pope, Frederick went to Rome, where he was crowned emperor on March 19, 1452. He was the last emperor to undergo this traditional ceremony there. On a later trip to Rome in 1468, he gained the foundation of the diocese of Vienna.

Most important for Frederick was his position in his hereditary lands. He promoted its interests, for example, by accepting as genuine the forged *Privilegium Maius* (May Privilege), which claimed broad prerogatives for the Habsburgs and Austria. Yet dynastic quarrels with his relatives and rebellions by the estates continued to squander his resources. On his return from his imperial coronation in 1452, he found Austria in rebellion. Soon besieged in

Wiener Neustadt, he had to release Ladislaus from his guardianship. Again in 1462 the citizens of Vienna and then his brother Albrecht VI besieged Frederick. While Albrecht VI's unexpected death in 1463 quieted the situation, Frederick's territories remained exhausted.

And new, more energetic rivals appeared after the death of his nephew Ladislaus Posthumous in 1457. In Hungary Matthias Corvinus (r. 1458-1490) and in Bohemia George von Podiebrady (r. 1458–1471) became kings at the head of nationalistic movements. While George's influence was limited by his closeness to the Hussite heresy, Matthias of Hungary became a major force in Central Europe. Frederick at first tried to come to terms with Matthias, selling him back the famed Hungarian national Crown of St. Stephen in 1463. Matthias soon drove George from power in Bohemia. Then in 1477 Matthias went to war with Frederick, by 1485 conquering Vienna itself. In 1487 Matthias took Wiener Neustadt and lower Austria, forcing the emperor to retreat to Linz in Upper Austria.

Meanwhile in the west of the empire the dukes of Burgundy had been expanding what was once a French royal appanage into a vast territorial complex between France and Germany. Duke Charles the Rash, who hoped to transform his possessions into a kingdom, undertook negotiations with Frederick in Trier during 1473. Although the negotiations at first failed, Frederick's son Maximilian eventually gained the promise of marriage to Charles's daughter, Mary (although she had already been engaged six times). After Charles's death at the Battle of Nancy, Maximilian had to defend Mary's inheritance largely without any help from his father. Only when Maximilian was captured and held prisoner in Bruges in 1488 did Frederick arrive at the head of an imperial army and intimidate the city into freeing his son.

Slowly Frederick's position began to improve as Maximilian asserted his own authority. In 1490, Matthias Corvinus's death provided the opportunity for Maximilian to drive the Hungarian forces out of Austria. Maximilian seemed to be achieving success after success when his father, Frederick, died in Linz on August 19, 1493. He was finally interred in a magnificent tomb in St. Stephan's Cathedral in Vienna years later.

Although Frederick III had the longest reign of any German monarch, many historians have complained that he accomplished little. He has long been mocked as the *Heiliges Römisches Reiches Erzschlafmütze* (Holy Roman Empire's Arch-sleepingcap). Some say his greatest accomplishment was merely to outlive his enemies. Others maintain that while such an attitude may apply to the empire at large, in his own dynastic lands Frederick III was able to build for the future. By patiently insisting on his rights, helping to arrange his son's marriage, and insisting on his imperial prestige, Frederick helped to establish the future success of the Habsburgs.

BIBLIOGRAPHY

Hödl, Günther. "Habsburg und Österreich," in *Gestalten und Gestalt des österreichischen Spätmittelalters.* Vienna: Böhlau Verlag, 1988, pp. 173–193.

Nehring, Karl. *Matthias Corvinus, Kaiser Friedrich III., und das Reich: zum hunyadisch-habsburgischen Gegensatz im Donauraum.* Südosteuropäische Arbeiten 72. Munich: R. Oldenbourg, 1975.

Rill, Bernd. *Friedrich III.: Habsburgs europäischer Durchbruch.* Graz: Verlag Styria, 1987.

Thomas, Heinz. *Deutsche Geschichte des Spätmittelalters.* Stuttgart: Kohlhammer, 1983.

Brian A. Pavlac

SEE ALSO
Coronation; Maximilian

Frederick III, Art

Architectural and artistic patronage played an important role in the political career of Frederick III. In the first years of his independent rule after 1435, work on his two major residences at Wiener Neustadt and Graz formed the most important task. This included the rebuilding of both castles and, at Graz, the erection of a major court church, today's cathedral. His election as German king in 1440 was followed by construction work in Nuremberg. This work, undertaken by the city, saw both some changes to the imperial castle and, in 1439, the commencement of the ambulatory choir of St. Lawrence as a monumental court church; for this choir Frederick donated in 1477 the central, "imperial" window. The year 1440 saw the completion of the outer walls of the nave of St. Stephan at Vienna, which became the city's cathedral in 1468; its interior construction as a stepped hall church with star vaults was undertaken in 1446 by Hanns Puchspaum, while, at the same time, the westernmost gable of the south side, known as the Friedrichsgiebel, was constructed.

A second group of projects, starting around 1445 and reaching until 1455, comprised the chapels of his residences in Graz, Vienna, and Wiener Neustadt. The last is renowned for its heraldic facade (Wappenwand). Starting in 1444, the abbey church of the Habsburg family monastery at Neuberg was completed under Frederick's sponsorship, following to the detail the classical forms of the existing thirteenth-century choir; furthermore, the collegiate church of Maria Saal and several monasteries at Wiener Neustadt were built at this time, all of them serving the representational needs of the new emperor following Frederick's elevation to that position in 1452. This period is followed by more than a decade in which, owing to political difficulties, no major building was begun. Even a project like the northern tower of Vienna cathedral was postponed until 1466, when it was begun according to the new designs by Hans Spenyng from Dresden. Also in about 1467 a sudden concentration on military architecture is evidenced by the fortification of towns and the rebuilding of castles. Another ten years later, the castle of his new residence at Linz and other fortifications were begun in anticipation of Turkish and Hungarian attacks. Frederick's sojourn at Nuremberg in 1487 finally initiated some new building activity at the castle, where the imperial lodgings in the Romanesque palace were rebuilt. Among the churches of this city, the Frauenkirche of Charles IV received a new sacristy topped by an imperial lodge.

The works of art commissioned by Frederick include the Friedrichsaltar (1447) from Wiener Neustadt, now at Vienna, and his tomb monument, commissioned in 1468 and carved by Nikolaus Gerhaert van Leyden; the style of this artist influenced the sculptural cycles of several of Frederick's monuments. The architecture of his monuments is characterized by a strong tendency toward the classical style of the late thirteenth century, in allusion to the era of Emperor Rudolph of Habsburg.

BIBLIOGRAPHY

Feuchtmüller, Rupert. "Die kirchliche Baukunst am Hofe des Kaisers und ihre Auswirkungen." *Ausstellung Friedrich III. Kaiserresidenz Wiener Neustadt.* Katalog des Niederösterreichischen Landesmuseums N.F. 29. Vienna: Amt der Niederösterreichischen Landesregierung, Kulturreferat, 1966, pp. 197–213.

Wagner-Rieger, Renate. "Die Bautätigkeit Kaiser Friedrichs III." *Wiener Jahrbuch für Kunstgeschichte* 25 (1972): 128–153.

———. "Die steirische Baukunst unter Friedrich III." *Steirische Berichte* 2, 78 (1978): 11–13.

Hans J. Böker

Freiberg

Located on the upper Saxon "Silver Road," Freiberg was, during the Middle Ages, the largest and economically most important silver mining town of the region. A rich deposit of silver was discovered in a village named Christiansdorph in 1168, and it soon became a settlement named civitas Saxonum by the miners from the Harz region who settled there. The town was first documented as Friberch in 1218. Margrave Otto von Meißen built his fortress near it, later the Schloss (castle) Freudenstein, and by the beginning of the thirteenth century the town had a defensive wall with five towers. Craftsmen and merchants also settled and built in the prospering town and together with the miners formed what is now the Old Town. There were two periods of outstanding artistic production in Freiberg, which produced masterworks for the parish church originally belonging to the fortress.

Built from 1180 to 1212, the late Romanesque Marienkirche (Church of the Virgin), a basilica with cross-shaped columns, quickly became the most important church of the town. Often damaged by fires, it was completely rebuilt in 1484. Two sculptural groups survive from the first building: the figures of the late Romanesque Crucifixion group, from about 1225, are now installed above the entrance to the choir, and the Goldene Pforte (Golden Portal), the west front of the Romanesque building, is now on the south side of the church in the cloister. Finished about 1230, it is one of the earliest and most important German examples of a carved architectural portal inspired by French examples. Originally gilded and colored, its theme is the Last Judgment; the Resurrection of the Dead, who appear rising from their graves, occupies the outer archivolt (arch above the portal). In the center of the tympanum (curved triangle over a door) is the Virgin holding the Christ child with a globe in his hand. On the jambs (vertical sides of door) standing figures from the Old Testament and both John the Baptist and the Evangelist lead the eye of the visitor to this figure. On the innermost archivolt is the crowning of the Virgin by Christ, who also receives the Book of Life. In the next is Abraham with one child in his bosom who receives another from an angel, and following this, the Apostles with the dove representing the Holy Ghost in

the middle. A Pietà (Mary holding dead Christ in her lap) of about 1430 has also been preserved; the head of Christ wears a horsehair wig of about 1480.

Following the damage resulting from a town fire in 1484, the church was rebuilt and completed in 1512. What we see today is a three-aisle Hallenkirche (hall church), forty meters long, with ribbed vaulting and ten slender eight-sided pillars. Between the inside buttresses are galleries with balconylike projections. The Marienkirche had been dedicated as a cathedral in 1480 and a collegiate chapter established. New works of art were ordered for this building, initiating another artistic high point in Freiberg between 1500 and 1520. A cycle of wooden apostle figures on the buttresses, carved about 1500, and the Wise and Foolish Virgins on the inner columns, as well as the stone "tulip chancel," are the most important of these new works.

The entire chancel and its support were carved by Hans Witten from Chemnitz in 1510, as a fantastic plant culminating in the tulip-shaped chancel from which it received its name. The four church fathers are carved within the branches on the chancel, and the tree trunk stair is supported by a young miner; a seated figure with a rosary, identified as the prophet Daniel in the lion's den and understood as a symbol for the underground work of the miners, sits at its foot. The young man in the tree perhaps refers to the legend that the original silver discovery was made after he climbed a tree to search for treasure but was given advice to descend to the ground and dig. On the top of the pulpit canopy is the Virgin with Child holding grapes in his left hand and below them, the symbols of the four evangelists. Next to this stone pulpit is a wooden pulpit of 1638 supported by two miners. In 1537 Freiberg became Lutheran, and the choir of the church was converted to a memorial burial place. Outstanding here is the three-story cenotaph for Kurfürst Moritz of Saxony, built ten years after his death in 1563; it is the first freestanding Renaissance grave monument in middle Germany.

In addition to the church, many late medieval sites remain in Freiberg. The former Thürmerei (tower) built in 1488 near the church as the quarters for the new canons as well as extensive remains of the city walls with the 1490 Kornhaus (grain house) can still be seen. The Rathaus (city hall), built in 1470–1474, has been altered many times but still has medieval rooms inside. Outside the town the mine known as the Alte Elisabeth (Old Elizabeth) is now an historic monument; first documented in the sixteenth century, it was one of those that brought wealth to the town for eight hundred years.

248

BIBLIOGRAPHY

Magirius, Heinrich. *Der Dom zu Freiberg.* Berlin: Union, 1977.

Piltz, Georg. *Kunstführer durch die DDR,* 4th ed. Leipzig: Urania, 1973, pp. 467–473.

Schlemmer, Wilhelm. *Der Dom zu Freiberg.* Große Baudenkmäler 409, 4th ed. Munich: Deutscher Kunstverlag, 1994.

Marta O. Renger

SEE ALSO

Gothic Art and Architecture; Iconographies, Innovative; Romanesque Art and Architecture

Freiburg

Freiburg im Breisgau (Baden-Württemberg) is a foundation of the Swabian house of the dukes of Zähringen, who established a market beneath their main castle at the edge of the Black Forest about 1120. Berthold III and his brother Konrad included existing, slightly older settlements and an east-west trade route in the regular layout of the new town, whose characteristic crossed axes are still visible in Freiburg's street plan.

The founders allowed extensive privileges to merchants and tradesmen willing to settle in the new town. The growing community, which profited from nearby silver mining, soon took on the character of a city: a first city wall was established at the same time as the earliest forms of communal self-government, illustrated by the first city council charter in German-speaking lands, written before 1178. By 1200 the commune already numbered about eight thousand citizens. It was soon necessary to lay out walled suburbs; by the fourteenth century, the city's area had grown to about seventy-three hectares, or circa 175 acres.

Freiburg im Breisgau, *Münster, Vorhalle,* right wall: 5 Foolish Virgins, Grammar, Rhetoric, Arithmetic, Geometry. *Photograph: Joan A. Holladay*

The counts of Urach inherited the city in 1218 and from that time called themselves the Counts of Freiburg. Increasingly acute conflicts with the new lords led the city to buy its freedom in 1368 and to submit itself voluntarily to Habsburg rule. For four hundred years, Freiburg thus shared the fate of the Austrians. The university was founded here in the capital of their western "foreland" in 1457; it was the second institution of higher education in Habsburg territories after that at Vienna.

The parish church, which was almost certainly dedicated to the Virgin from the beginning, was founded to the northeast of the intersection of the two main streets. The decision to replace the modest original building, erected by Duke Konrad, about 1200 with a new, more representative structure modeled on the cathedral at Basle, was probably related to the plans of Duke Berthold V to move the dynastic necropolis here from the monastery of St. Peter in the Black Forest. From this structure the crossing and transept with its two flanking towers are still preserved. After a change of plan about 1230–1240, the nave of the basilica was executed in the High Gothic forms of the Île-de-France. It was finished at the beginning of the fourteenth century. The western tower was also begun about 1250; its characteristic tracery spire was completed about three decades later. This first openwork spire of the Gothic was widely imitated in Germany and elsewhere. The cathedral finally achieved its present form with the completion of the extended choir, consecrated in 1513; although begun in 1354, a long hiatus delayed its completion until about 1530.

The climax of the building's rich sculptural decoration is the program of the enclosed square porch under the tower. In this small space several themes of Christian dogma are united in a unique way. Incarnation and death of Christ, the Last Judgment, and especially the salvific meaning of the church, symbolized by the crowned Virgin on the trumeau (pillar), are at the center of this complicated program dated about 1300. Four enthroned figures of counts, on the outside of the tower, stand for earthly power and justice. Large parts of the medieval stained glass of the nave (about 1320–1330) are still preserved; the windows' proud donors—the guilds, who by this time were active in the city's political life, and the mining corporations—are represented in the lower panels. Single donors provided the means for glazing the chapels ringing the new choir: the Emperor Maximilian as the city's overlord, court functionaries situated in Freiburg, and members of the city patriciate (leaders) are depicted with their patron saints. Most of these images

rely on sketches of the young Hans Baldung Grien, a student of Dürer who was called from Strasbourg in 1512 to execute the panels of the monumental high altar.

In 1827 the parish church became the cathedral of the new archdiocese created out of the former diocese of Constance. Starting in about 1220 over a dozen orders and spiritual congregations, including the Franciscans (1229) and Dominicans (1233), erected cloisters in and around Freiburg. Encouraged by the city lords, the Franciscans and Dominicans also found strong support among the patriciate. The most important of these new institutions, partly because of its artistic decoration, was the Dominican cloister, in which Albertus Magnus was active for a short time about 1240. It was also the Dominicans who oversaw the majority of the women's cloisters, most of which were located just outside the city. Among these, Alt-Adelhausen, founded in 1234, was particularly well known as a site of female mysticism; one of the central texts of this movement, the chronicle of Anna von Munzingen, was composed here in 1318. Some of the rich furnishings of these women's foundations, mostly tapestries, embroideries, and liturgical manuscripts, have been preserved.

Minor parts of the medieval fortifications still stand, but only two gate towers have been preserved in large part. The Gate of St. Martin and the Swabian Gate, which gave entry into the two main streets, were erected after 1200; they have been disfigured by modern alterations. The city's rich municipal architecture is represented by the Gerichtslaube (Judgment Loggia), the oldest council hall, which was erected in 1303 and changed later, and the Kornhaus, built in 1498 for grain storage and trading but also used for dances. After the Second World War, only the facade of this latter was reerected. Two court functionaries of Emperor Maximilian, Jakob Villinger and Konrad Stürtzel, had palaces built for themselves about 1500; these too have been rebuilt.

BIBLIOGRAPHY

Die Zähringer: Anstoß und Wirkung, ed. Hans Schadek and Karl Schmid. Sigmaringen: Thorbecke, 1986.

Geschichte der Stadt Freiburg im Breisgau, vol. 1, *Von den Anfängen bis zum "Neuen Stadtrecht" von 1520,* ed. Heiko Haumann and Hans Schadek. Stuttgart: Theiss, 1996.

Hubel, Achim. "Das urspüngliche Programm der Skulpturen in der Vorhalle des Freiburger Münsters." *Jahrbuch der staatlichen Kunstsammlungen in Baden-Württemberg* 11 (1974): 21–46.

Kalchthaler, Peter. *Freiburg und seine Bauten,* 3d ed. Freiburg: Promo, 1994.

Kunstepochen der Stadt Freiburg. Freiburg: Augustinermuseum, 1970.

Detlef Zinke

Freising

Originally an early palace complex of the Agilolfings, the Freising Domberg became the center of the new diocese created during St. Boniface's organization of the Bavarian church in 739. The cathedral cloister under Bishop Arbeo (764/765–783) produced a vita (life) of St. Corbinianus, the Frankish missionary and copatron of the church, as well as manuscripts with decorated initials. Full-scale book illumination was apparently initiated under Bishop Anno (855–875). The unusually well-preserved libraries of Freising and other foundations in the bishopric, particularly Tegernsee, Weihenstephan, and Schäftlarn (all in the Munich State Library since 1803), provide a rich basis for studying the development of script and book illumination in medieval Bavaria.

The Freising bishops had particularly close ties to the Ottonian and Salian rulers, increasing the prestige and properties of the diocese. New foundations they supported near Freising included the rededicated Benedictine abbey of Weihenstephan (1020) and the Premonstratensian church of Sts. Peter and Paul, established by Bishop Otto I (1138–1158), author of *The Two Cities* chronicle and uncle of Frederick Barbarossa.

Despite the thoroughly baroque interior of Freising Cathedral, its architectural layout and scale are those of the Romanesque church built after a fire in 1159; that church itself had preserved something of the Carolingian plan. Gothic alterations of the thirteenth and fourteenth centuries were themselves effaced by later baroque campaigns. In the latter Middle Ages, the diocese of Freising, first under its Habsburg and then Wittelsbach bishops, continued to be an important ecclesiastic and artistic center. Jan Polack's *The Death of St. Corbinianus,* made for the high altar of Weihenstephan between 1484 and 1489 (Munich, Alte Pinakothek), contains the earliest topographical view of Freising.

BIBLIOGRAPHY

Benker, Sigmund. *Freising: Dom und Domberg.* Königstein im Taunus: Köster, 1975.

Branca, Emanuela von, Engelbert Gottsman, and Eberhard Wimmer. "Beiträge zur Baugeschichte des Freisinger Doms." *Architectura* 16 (1986): 149–180.

Mass, Josef. *Das Bistum Freising im Mittelalter.* Munich: E. Wewel, 1986.

Adam S. Cohen

SEE ALSO

Anno; Carolingian Art and Architecture; Frederick I Barbarossa; Gothic Art and Architecure; Ottonian Art and Architecture; Romanesque Art and Architecture; Tegernsee

Friedrich von Hausen (fl. late 12th c.)

By adopting and adapting the forms and motifs of Occitan lyrics, melding them with German ones, Friedrich von Hausen (present-day Rheinhausen, now a part of Mannheim) expanded and modernized German minnesong. Better documented as an historical figure, a *ministeriale* (court clerk) of Emperor Friedrich Barbarossa, than most minnesingers, he witnessed documents from 1171 to shortly before his death as a crusader in Anatolia in 1190 and was mentioned in many contemporary chronicles. His importance as a minnesinger can be seen in many apparent borrowings from his songs by others. The death of the minnesinger qua singer is lamented, a generation or so after the fact, in several songs and in Heinrich von dem Türlin's *Crône*. However, his contemporary fame, as attested, was as a political figure. From the twelfth to the fifteenth century, whenever singers are documented historical figures, their singing is never mentioned in official historical documents, and Hausen is no exception to this rule.

Hausen's love laments exalt the lady as desirable but unattainable; his general lack of concrete imagery and hypotactic style (employing subordinate clauses) adumbrate Reinmar. However, situational references such as those detailing a love reverie while riding, set him apart from the later singer. Though his songs of love from afar parallel similar songs by, for instance, the troubadour Jaufré Rudel, they also fit what we know about his history (he was often absent from home in the service of his liege lord). Though his praise of a lady and of ladies was part of a broader courtly fiction, there are definite parallels between the love at court he discusses and the life at court he led. He wrote several crusading songs in which, in contrast, for example, to Albrecht von Johansdorf, the service of God trumps service of his lady. In his scorn for the slackers who remained at home (*Des Minnesangs Frühling* [MF], song no. 53,21), he both echoes Romance lyric motifs and touches on a topic that doubtless resonated with the actual courtiers of his day. He is the first singer for whom a song (MF no. 42,1) is transmitted in three distinct versions, which examplifies minnesong's inherent mutability. His extended monologue in the woman's voice (MF no. 54,1, three strophes in C) presents a lady as skilled in lamenting the dilemma her intense love for her worthy suitor causes her as Reinmar's persona is in stating his (MF no. 165,10). This has led various scholars (probably incorrectly) to consider as spurious the song's ascription to Hausen.

BIBLIOGRAPHY

Bekker, Hugo. *Friedrich von Hausen: Inquiries into His Poetry.* Chapel Hill: University of North Carolina Press, 1977.

Moser, Hugo, and Helmut Tervooren, eds. *Des Minnesangs Frühling.* 2 vols., 36th ed. Stuttgart: Hirzel, 1977.

Mowatt, D.G. *Friderich von Hûsen: Introduction, Text, Commentary and Glossary.* Cambridge: Cambridge University Press, 1971.

Schweikle, Günther, ed. *Friedrich von Hausen: Lieder.* Stuttgart: Reclam, 1984.

Herbert Heinen

SEE ALSO

Albrecht von Johansdorf; Frederick I Barbarossa; Heinrich von dem Türlin; Ministerials; *Minnesang;* Reinmar der Alte; Versification

Friends of God

This loosely knit group of men and women *(Gottesfreunde)* from diverse socioeconomic backgrounds was inspired by and supportive of the mystical tradition in the fourteenth century. Devoted to prayer, meditation, and the apostolic life, these individuals congregated in and near Cologne and in Upper Germany around renowned religious figures such as the Dominicans Meister Eckhart and Johannes Tauler and the Franciscans Otto von Passau and Marquard von Lindau. Most of the sermons, visionary literature, tracts, and letters by the Friends of God appeared anonymously. Two notable figures among the group are Heinrich von Nördlingen and Rulman Merswin.

Heinrich von Nördlingen (died after 1356) was a secular priest who served as spiritual adviser and confessor for various female religious communities in and near his native Nördlingen and to the south. His extant correspondence, primarily with Margaretha Ebner of Medingen, constitutes the earliest personal letter exchange in German and the single source of information concerning his life. In 1338 Heinrich relocated to Basel, where he made the acquaintance of Johannes Tauler and other Friends of God. Here he shared in or directed the translation of Mechthild von Magdeburg's *Fließendes Licht der Gottheit (Flowing Light of the Godhead)* from Low German into Alemannic.

Rulman Merswin (1307–1382) was a successful merchant in Strasbourg who at age forty was encouraged by Heinrich von Nördlingen to embrace the religious life. Merswin leased and revitalized the impoverished Grünenwörth monastery, where he spent the remainder of his life. Some of the more than twenty devotional tracts produced at Grünenwörth, e.g., the *Neunfelsenbuch (The Book of the Nine Rocks),* survive as autographs by Merswin; Nikolaus von Löwen, Merswin's closest associate, apparently edited others. Several tracts have been attributed to a so-called *Gottesfreund vom Oberland,* who in all probability was the literary creation of either Merswin or Nikolaus, but whose identity remains uncertain.

BIBLIOGRAPHY

Jones, Rufus M. *The Flowering of Mysticism: The Friends of God in the Fourteenth Century.* New York: Macmillan, 1939; rpt. New York: Haffner, 1971.

Mystical Writings of Rulman Merswin, ed. and trans. Thomas S. Kepler. Philadelphia: Westminster Press, 1960.

Seeshotz, Anna Groh. *Friends of God: Practical Mystics of the Fourteenth Century.* New York: Columbia University Press, 1934; rpt. New York: AMS Press, 1970.

Debra L. Stoudt

SEE ALSO

Meister Eckhart; Mechthild von Magdeburg

Friesland

According to archaeological evidence the Frisians settled along the North Sea shore from about 500 B.C.E., eventually occupying the area between the mouths of the Old Rhine and Ems Rivers. At first they inhabited only the highest parts of the fertile salt marshes, which were transected by tidal inlets. To escape flooding they established their dwellings on artificially thrown-up elevations *(terpen* or *wierden).*

The Frisians are first mentioned by classical authors in the context of events of 12 B.C.E. They had close contacts with the Romans, but, except for a short period, remained outside the territory of the Roman Empire. During the Migration Age they swarmed out into the lower parts of the salt marsh area and spread farther along the coast in a southern as well as eastern direction (probably scattered settlements up to the Scheldt estuary and uninterrupted settlement up to the Weser estuary). After the eighth century the North Frisian islands, the west coast of Schleswig, the district of Wursten (east of the Weser estuary), and Saterland (to the east of the Ems) were colonized. During the Migration Age frequent contacts must have existed between Frisians and Anglo-Saxons. It is uncertain, however, whether Anglo-Saxons permanently settled in the Frisian territories.

The post-Roman period is characterized by an extreme scarcity of sources, Frisian ones even lacking totally. In the Old English *Beowulf* epic a Frisian king *(Fresena cyng)* is mentioned, called Finn. It is controversial whether the story of this ruler is based on historical events. From Anglo-Saxon sources the name of the Frisian king Aldgisl has come down to us. In 678 C.E. this ruler, who supposedly resided in Utrecht, extended hospitality to archbishop Wilfrid of York. Known from Anglo-Saxon as well as Frankish sources is the name of another Frisian king (or *dux,* as he is referred to in the latter ones): Radbod (Frisian *Redbad).* Shortly before 690 the Frankish mayor of the palace, Pippin II, expelled Radbod from a district, called citerior Fresia, on the possession of which Franks and Frisians repeatedly clashed. Its extent is not known, but it can be said with certainty that Utrecht and the famous trading center of Dorestad were part of it. After Pippin's death (714) Radbod reconquered citerior Fresia, but after his own passing five years later the northern frontier of the Frankish empire shifted to the Vlie estuary. Nothing is known of Radbod's succession. In the course of the eighth century the Franks conquered the remaining parts of Friesland: first (734) its supposed nucleus, situated between the Vlie and the rivulet Lauwers (this is the current Dutch province of Friesland, sometimes referred to as West Lauwers Friesland), and subsequently (785), simultaneously with Saxony, the section between the Lauwers and the Weser.

Targeted archaeological research of the period of kings has been taken up only recently. Attention is focused on the northwestern part of the *terpen* area of West Lauwers Friesland (Westergo), as many gold objects from this period have turned up here, the most remarkable being a (royal?) fibula (clasp) found in Tjitsma *terp* near Wijnaldum.

Little is known of paganism in Friesland. With regard to the Christianization of the Frisians, which took place in close connection with the Frankish conquest, more information is available. In 690 Pippin assigned citerior Fresia as sphere of activity to the Anglo-Saxon missionary Willibrord, who five years later was ordained archbishop of the Frisians by the Pope. The former Roman castellum in Utrecht was allotted to him as his residence. After Radbod's death Willibrord returned to his see, accompanied this time by another Anglo-Saxon, Boniface. In the course of time Boniface moved his activities to Hesse and Bavaria, but returned to Friesland in his old age. Soon after (754) he was killed by pagan Frisians in Dokkum (West Lauwers Friesland). After 785 a Frisian missionary, Liudger, who eventually was to be ordained the first bishop of Münster in Saxony (now Nordrhein-Westfalen), embarked on the Christianization of Friesland east of the Lauwers. The Frisian archbishopric was finally swallowed by the archbishopric of Cologne, the Frisian territories being divided among the bishoprics of Utrecht and Münster, both of them coming under Cologne, and the archbishopric of Bremen.

On the basis of archaeological research it is supposed that about 900 the *terpen* area was relatively densely populated. The main means of existence here was cattle breeding. The abundance of water resulted in an early development of navigation. From the end of the seventh until the middle of the ninth century Frisian trade flourished, reaching its zenith after the Frisians' integration into the Frankish empire. Frisian commercial activities developed in several directions, the main being England, Scandinavia (especially Sweden), and the Rhine area. Colonies of Frisian merchants are known to have existed in York, Duisburg, Cologne, Mainz, and Worms. At that time Friesland possessed Europe's most productive minting ateliers. Cloth constituted an important export commodity. It is a moot point whether the gift of *pallia fresonica* (frisian cloths) by Charlemagne to caliph Harun al-Rasid, which is mentioned by Notker Balbulus (end of the ninth century), refers to clothes produced in Friesland or to fabrics that were sold by Frisian merchants, but were manufactured elsewhere (in Flanders or England). A heavy blow was dealt to Frisian trade by the invasions of the Norsemen. Significantly enough, the first as well as the last to have been attested was directed against Friesland (810/1007). The Frankish conquest and the subsequent integration into the Frankish empire must have entailed fundamental changes in Frisian society. Most of the Frisian elite probably regained their properties in exchange for loyalty to the Frankish king. In the ninth century several large landowners bestowed goods on Frankish imperial abbeys (e.g. Fulda, Corvey, and Echternach), strengthening thus their ties with the king. In contrast to other tribes, like the Saxons, the Frisians failed to create a tribal duchy within the Frankish empire.

The earliest Frisian legal source that has been preserved is the *Lex Frisionum,* which goes back to about 800. This text perhaps represents part of a projected codification of Frisian law, made up by order of the Frankish king. Remarkably enough, the *Lex Frisionum* includes two pagan provisions—one regarding the allowed killing of newborn children, the other concerning the death penalty for temple desecrators. The legal provisions laid down in the *Lex Frisionum* concern West Lauwers Friesland, divergent provisions for the Frisian territories between the Vlie and the Sincfal (at the current Dutch-Belgian border on the Flemish coast) and between the Lauwers and the Weser being mentioned separately.

About 1000 a large-scale land reclamation movement gained momentum, in the course of which the vast peat zones situated behind the *terpen* area were reclaimed. Probably at a somewhat later time the first dikes were built. Gradually the dikes network expanded in such a way that building *terpen* was no longer necessary. Owing to reclamation and diking, agricultural production increased, laying the basis for a relatively large prosperity.

When the Frankish empire split up, Friesland became part of the *regnum* of Germany, eventually merging into the Holy Roman Empire. During the Frankish-German period Friesland was divided into several counties. In Holland, the name emerges in the sources at the beginning of the twelfth century, when the count's power came into the hands of an indigenous, i.e., Frisian, dynasty. By this time the idea of belonging to Friesland had been completely lost in this area. The name West Friesland, however, survived in the northeastern part of the current Dutch province of North Holland (this is why the name West Friesland, contrary to what is usual in English and German language publications, should not be applied to West Lauwers Friesland). West Friesland was subjugated by the count of Holland in 1289. After this the fortunes of Friesland west of the Vlie cease to be part of Frisian history.

It is not known how exactly Friesland between the Vlie and the Weser was divided into counties. The important thing here is that in this area the counts' authority rested not with Frisian but with foreign, mostly Saxon, lords.

Thus, in the eleventh century counts in West Lauwers Friesland were the Brunones, who resided in Brunswick. During the last quarter of this century the German king bestowed this part of Friesland on the bishop of Utrecht. In 1165, however, the emperor Frederick Barbarossa divided the count's authority of West Lauwers Friesland between the bishop of Utrecht and the count of Holland, the latter probably having inherited the Brunones' rights to Friesland. The resulting condominium undoubtedly hampered an effective exercise of power. Up to the middle of the thirteenth century the counts of Holland exercized some authority in West Lauwers Friesland (they, for example, appointed bailiffs), but their influence later decreased. In the territories between the Lauwers and the Weser the counts' authority was even weaker; here it vanished as early as about 1100. So to the west as well as to the east of the Lauwers, the rights attached to the count's authority, remarkably enough, failed to develop into sovereign rule. Parallel to this, feudalism did not take root in Friesland, owing to which the nobility did not develop beyond a prefeudal phase here. In the late Middle Ages already the absence of sovereign rule in the Frisian territories was known under the name "Frisian freedom."

The former counties in Friesland now disintegrated into a large number of self-governing districts (called *terrae*), the first being mentioned in 1220. The highest authority here rested with the "land community" *(universitas terrae;* known in German as *Landesgemeinde),* which seems to have been made up of the owners of farms to which a right of voting was attached. The bailiffs appointed by the counts were pushed aside now by communal judges, who changed places yearly. About 1200 and during the period 1323–1327, an alliance of, at least in principle, all Frisian territories, called *Upstallisbaem,* was in existence. Though judicial functionaries with special powers acted in its name, it failed to bring political unity. It is the more remarkable that all territories between the Vlie and the Weser made use of one and the same set of laws, known as the "Seventeen Privileges" and the "Twenty-Four Statutes." According to the latest research, these were drawn up in West Lauwers Friesland but were rewritten about 1225 to make them suitable for all Frisian territories free from sovereign rule.

Though frequently stricken by feuding, the Frisian *terrae* went through a period of prosperity that lasted until about 1350. Prosperity was shared by the monasteries, which from about 1160 were founded in large numbers, presumably on the initiative of local magnates. The imperial abbeys mentioned above gave up their Frisian possessions. In the absence of towns of any importance, the monasteries developed into the main centers of economic activity. They also played a prominent role in peacemaking. The prosperity of the Frisian *terrae* may also be demonstrated by the fact that among the participants of the crusades, there were remarkably many Frisians.

From about 1350 the Frisian territories suffered a severe economic crisis. Trade and navigation reached a low. The crisis was accompanied by social unrest, a decline of the monasteries, and erosion of communal institutions. During this period a social group, called (in Dutch) *hoofdelingen* or (in Latin) *capitales* or *capitanei* (literally headmen), rose to prominence. In it, prefeudal nobility appears to have amalgamated with those who distinguished themselves by extensive ownership of land and the possession of a fortified house. In the area between the Ems and the Weser, called East Friesland from the fifteenth century, the *hoofdelingen* not only absorbed the duties of the communal judicial functionaries but also took the village communities under their protection, which resulted in a disintegration of the "land communities." In the western half of East Friesland the tom Brok family managed to eclipse all its rivals, eventually acquiring a position reminiscent of that of a sovereign lord. In West Lauwers Friesland the "land communities" remained in existence, but here the internecine strife of the *hoofdelingen* resulted in an unbridled eruption of feuding. During this process two "parties" took shape, which more or less balanced each other: the Schieringers and the Vetkopers. Yet in this part of Friesland the influence of the towns, small as they were, gradually increased. In the area between the Lauwers and the Ems, which came to be called Ommelanden, both feuding and the rise of towns were checked by the neighboring city of Groningen, which managed to gain preponderance here.

A serious external threat to Frisian freedom was posed by the counts of Holland, who in 1291 assumed the title "lord of Friesland." In 1310 Count William III was recognized as lord by part of West Lauwers Friesland. His successor (William IV) failed to gain recognition, however. In 1345 he invaded this part of Friesland but was defeated (battle of Staveren). The boorish Frisians, who did not bother to ask ransoms, killed the count and many of his knights. In 1398 the then count of Holland, Albert, duke of Bavaria, subjugated West Lauwers Friesland, immediately making a start with feudalization of this area. After a year his rule collapsed, owing to a rebellion started by the *Schieringers*. The dukes of Burgundy, since 1433 counts of Holland, took up their predecessors' plans to conquer Friesland but never executed them. They were also unsuccessful in winning over the emperor to confer on them the title "king of Friesland."

According to the Seventeen Privileges, the Frisians owed their laws as well as their freedom to Charlemagne. On several occasions during the fourteenth and fifteenth centuries, they produced a false diploma ascribed to this ruler, in which the privileges they claimed were circumscribed. In 1417 the Schieringer "party" acquired a privilege from Sigismund, king of the Romans, by which the Frisians were recognized as being directly under imperial rule (German *reichsunmittelbar*). Thus for the first time they were officially freed from all claims to rule by sovereign lords. But this privilege had barely any practical consequences, as the empire was too weak to offer the Frisians protection and the Frisians failed to fulfil their financial commitments to the empire.

In East Friesland the power of the tom Brok family collapsed in 1427. After a short period of recovery of the "land communities" another *hoofdeling*, Ulrik Cirksena, won ascendancy. In 1464, at his request, he was made count in East Friesland by Emperor Frederick III. Thus eventually an indigenous dynasty managed to acquire the position of sovereign lord here. In 1480 the same emperor enfeoffed the burgomasters and council of Groningen with the Ommelanden, a decision that was never implemented, however.

In 1491 the burgomasters and council of Groningen won influence in the northeastern part of West Lauwers Friesland (Oostergo). When the Schieringers subsequently invoked the help of Emperor Frederick III, this ruler and his successor, Maximilian I, did promulgate new privileges but failed to offer active assistance. As a result some Schieringer leaders secretly appealed to Maximilian's stadtholder-general in the Netherlands, Albert duke of Saxony. By shrewd maneuvering this prince brought most of West Lauwers Friesland under control, after which he persuaded Maximilian and the electors of the Holy Roman Empire to commission him to be the ruler of the whole of Friesland. To save the fiction of the Frisians' imperial immediacy, the title conferred on him was not that of a count but of a gubernator and potestate (1498). Nevertheless, this event meant the end of Frisian freedom in West Lauwers Friesland. In 1515 Albert's successor sold his rights to Friesland to the count of Holland, the future emperor Charles V, an option that had been included in the 1498 commission. Thus West Lauwers Friesland became part of the Habsburg Netherlands, without any trace left of imperial immediacy. In 1536 the Ommelanden and Groningen subjugated themselves to the same prince and consequently were absorbed into the Netherlands as well. East Friesland stayed out of reach of the house of Habsburg, eventually not becoming part of the Dutch but of the German state.

The indigenous laws of the Frisians have been handed down in several law manuscripts, written in Old Frisian. From the thirteenth century canon and, to a lesser extent, Roman law penetrated Friesland. In West Lauwers Friesland indigenous law was abolished in 1504, after which, apart from some unimportant exceptions, only Roman law ruled here. In East Friesland and the Ommelanden the main indigenous law texts were translated into Low German. Here indigenous law was recodified in a modernized form, respectively about 1520 and in 1601. Some earlier law texts of the Frisians have won fame for their highly poetic form.

BIBLIOGRAPHY

Algra, N. E. *Zeventien Keuren en Vierentwintig Landrechten.* Graal Doorn, 1992.

Ehbrecht, Wilfried. *Landesherrschaft und Klosterwesen im ostfriesischen Fivelgo (970–1290).* Münster: Aschendorf, 1974.

Formsma, W. J., et al., eds. *Historie van Groningen Stad en Land.* Groningen: Tjeenk Willink, 1976.

Siems, Harald. *Studien zur Lex Frisionum.* Ebelsbach: Aktiv, 1980.

Halbertsma, H. *Frieslands oudheid.* 2 vols. n.p: n.p., 1982 [with English summary].

Janse, A. *Grenzen aan de macht. De Friese oorlog van de graven van Holland omstreeks 1400.* Hollandse historische reeks, 19. 's-Gravenhage: Stichting Hollandse historische reeks, 1993 [with English summary].

Kalma, J. J., et al., eds. *Geschiedenis van Friesland.* Fryske Akademy 325. Drachten: Laverman, 1968.

Knol, E. *De Noordnederlandse kustlanden in de vroege middeleeuwen.* Amsterdam: Vrije universiteit, 1993 [with English summary].

Lebecq, Stephane. *Marchands et navigateurs frisons du haut moyen âge,* 2 vols. Lille: Presses universitaires de Lille, 1983.

Mol, J. A. *De Friese huizen van de Duitse Orde.* Ljouwert: Fryske Akademy, 1991.

Mulder-Bakker, Anneke B. "*Oculus ecclesiae* or the Eyes of the People. Church and Society in Medieval Frisia." *Journal of Medieval History* 11 (1985): 295–314.

Russchen, A. *New Light on Dark-Age Frisia.* Fryske Akademy 311. Drachten: Laverman, 1967.

Schmidt, H. *Politische Geschichte Ostfrieslands.* Leer: Rautenberg, 1975.

Slicher van Bath, B. H. "The Economic and Social Conditions in the Frisian Districts from 900 to 1500." *AAG-Bijdragen* 13 (1965): 97–133.

van Lengen, Hajo. *Geschichte des Emsigerlandes: vom frühen 13. bis zum späten 15. Jahrhundert.* 2 vols. Aurich: Verlag Ostfriesische Landschaft, 1973–1976.

Vries, Oebele. *Het Heilige Roomse Rijk en de Friese vrijheid.* Leeuwarden: De Tille, 1986 [with English summary].

Oebele Vries

SEE ALSO

Charlemagne; Cologne, History; Frederick III; Fulda; Holland; Law and Lawbooks; Mainz; Maximilian; Worms

Frueauf, Rueland, the Elder (ca. 1440/1450–1507)

Both documents and signed paintings allow us to trace the career of Rueland Freauf, who divided his time between Passau and Salzburg. In the earliest records, in the 1470s, he is working for St. Peter's in Salzburg. The modern scholar Alfred Stange assumes that he received his training in Salzburg, perhaps with Conrad Laib, but also notes the influence of the anonoymous Bavarian painters known as the Master of 1467 and the Master of the Tegernsee Tabula Magna. In 1480, Freauf acquired citizenship in Passau, where in the next four years he completed the frescoes in the Rathaus (town hall), now lost, that a Master Ruprecht had begun a decade earlier.

In May 1484, Frueauf was called back to Salzburg to discuss the altar planned for the Franciscan church, but in August two donors, offering substantial sums for the altar's execution, managed to direct the commission to Michael Pacher. How these events are to be interpreted is a matter of debate. Stange sees the loss of the commission as a hard blow for Frueauf and the reason for his disappearance from the written records for three years, and proposes that he spent this time on a study trip, trying to update his style. Another scholar, Grete Ring, by contrast, thinks it unlikely that Frueauf was ever a candidate for the commission and that being asked to deliver an expertise on such an important project was an honor.

In any case, we next encounter Frueauf in Nuremberg, where, in 1487, he dated and signed a panel with his initials. Stange sees the influence of the Dutch painter known as the Master of Flémalle in Frueauf's work after this date, without proposing that his travels took him all the way to the Low Countries. By 1490, Frueauf was back in Salzburg, working on a major commission. In this year and the following he initialed and dated two of eight scenes intended to serve in the wings of an altarpiece. Scenes from the Passion—Christ in the Garden of Gethsemane, the Flagellation, the Road to Calvary, and the Crucifixion—were visible at the sides of the sculptured shrine when the altarpiece was open, while scenes from the life if the Virgin—Annunciation, Nativity, Adoration of the Magi, and Assumption—occupied the outsides of the wings (Vienna, Kunsthistorisches Museum, nos. 1397–1400).

In 1497 Frueauf is mentioned again as citizen of Passau, as is his son, the painter Rueland Frueauf the Younger. A year later the father's citizenship was revoked for failure to pay his debts, but it was soon reinstated on the recommendation of well-placed friends. From the last decade of Frueauf's life comes the initialed but undated portrait of Jobst Seyfried (Vienna, Kunsthistorisches Museum), the only preserved evidence of Frueauf's work in this genre.

This group of autograph works allows a clear definition of Frueauf's innovative style. Painted in bright colors with hard outlines, his figures are tall and slim. Individualized facial types convey a variety of expressions, which are heightened by dramatic gestures and lively drapery patterns. His figures tend to fill the foreground, prohibiting a view into the background, another device for concentrating the emotional impact of the works. On the basis of similarities to Frueauf's known paintings, a number of other works have been attributed to him; most common among these are twelve Passion scenes from an altarpiece, probably from circa 1480 (Regensburg, Historisches Verein), and a large, late panel representing Christ as Man of Sorrows (*Schmerzensmann*) (Munich, Alte Pinakothek, no. 10681).

BIBLIOGRAPHY

Baldass, Ludwig von. *Conrad Laib und die beiden Rueland Frueauf.* Vienna: Schroll, 1946.

Buchner, Ernst. "Ein Schmerzensmann von Rueland Frueauf d. é." *Pantheon* 16 (1943): 73–76.

Ring, Grete. "Frueauf, Rueland d. é." *Allgemeines Lexikon der bildenden Künstler von der Antike bis zur Gegenwart,* ed. Ulrich Thieme. Leipzig: Seemann, 1916, vol. 12, pp. 532–534.

Stange, Alfred. *Deutsche Malerei der Gotik.* vol. 10: *Salzburg, Bayern und Tirol in der Zeit von 1400 bis 1500.* Munich: Deutscher Kunstverlag, 1960, pp. 38–42.

Joan A. Holladay

SEE ALSO
Pacher, Michael; Passau; Salzburg

Fuetrer, Ulrich (ca. 1420–ca. 1496/1502)

The biographical facts surrounding Ulrich Fuetrer (also recorded as Füeterer, Füetrer), a fifteenth-century painter and writer, remain sketchy. Born about 1420 in Landshut, near Munich (Bavaria), Fuetrer most likely had some rudimentary education, for his knowledge of Latin is reflected in his writings. His name appears in Munich's accounting books, listing him as a decorative painter in 1453. Between 1476 and 1478, Fuetrer participated in a large commission of the annexation of Munich's city hall. He became a homeowner in 1482 (in today's Residenzstraße). Fuetrer might have died as late as 1502, but his death probably took place about 1496, shortly after some scandalous events took place in his house, for which his wife was banished from the city.

While the overall contour of his life remains uncertain, Fuetrer is best known for his writings, which fix him at the court in Munich during Albrecht IV's tenure. Evident in his literary works is his historiographic interest in the deeds and origins of chivalry. Fuetrer's major work, dedicated to Albrecht, *Das Buch der Abenteuer* (*The Book of Adventures,* 1473–1481/1487), is a reworking of some fifteen popular knightly romances of the thirteenth century written in a verse form also employed by Wolfram von Eschenbach (known as Titurel strophes), and contains *Der Trojanerkrieg* (*Trojan War*), *Merlin,* and other tales about the Holy Grail. This work also serves as a historical compendium about his patron Albrecht, who belonged to the house of Wittelsbach. Further works include *Die Bayerische Chronik* (*Bavarian Chronicle,* 1478–1481), a prose *Lanzelot* (ca. 1467), and a verse version of this latter work (ca. 1484–1487).

BIBLIOGRAPHY

Buschinger, Danielle, and Wolfgang Spiewok. "Ulrich Füeterer—ein Hofdichter?" *Jahrbuch der Oswald von Wolkenstein Gesellschaft* 4 (1986/87 [1988]): 95–102.

Cramer, Thomas. *Geschichte der deutschen Literatur im späten Mittelalter*. Munich: Deutscher Taschenbuch Verlag, 1990.

Füetrer, Ulrich. *Das Buch der Abenteuer. Nach der Handschrift A (Cgm. 1 der Bayerischen Staatsbibliothek)*, ed. Heinz Thoelen with Bernd Bastert, 2 vols. Göppingen: Kümmerle, 1997.

Nyholm, Kurt. "Fuetrer, Ulrich," in *Die deutsche Literatur des Mittelalters*. Verfasserlexikon, 2d ed., vol. 2, ed. Kurt Ruh. Berlin: de Gruyter, 1980, cols. 999–1007.

Christine M. Kallinger-Allen

SEE ALSO
Munich; Wolfram von Eschenbach

Fulda

While archaeological remains indicate Frankish-Merovingian habitation, Fulda achieved renown with Boniface's founding of the celebrated Benedictine monastery in 744. The interpretation of rich textual sources, coupled with analysis of extant structures and archaeological evidence, reveals a lively, evocative building history inaugurated with Fulda's auspicious beginnings. The first abbot, Boniface's disciple and friend Sturmi, erected the first church to the Savior. Boniface consecrated the main altar of the church, a basilica with a nave and side aisles, terminated to the east by a semicircular apse, in 751. In 754 Boniface died a martyr's death in Friesland and was interred at Fulda; speedy recognition of his sanctity drew many to the site.

In 791 Abbot Baugulf (779–802) undertook a larger church, and work began under the direction of the monk Ratgar. Conforming to the axis of Sturmi's church, the transeptless east end with a large semicircular apse was complete in 802 when Ratgar succeeded as Abbot. Under Ratgar, the rebuilding took on a grandiosity that enraged the monastic community, who complained to Charlemagne. Although relieved of his office in 817, Ratgar was able to articulate his architectural vision of Fulda's primacy as the resting place of the martyred Boniface through powerful reference to Old St. Peter's occidented (westernized) structure. Continuing from Baugulf's beginnings, the immense church had a nave and side aisles, and, to the west, a spacious projecting transept and large semicircular apse. With Ratgar's dismissal, Abbot Eigil (818–822) completed the structure, including crypts under the choirs. With the placement of St. Boniface's relics in the west apse, the church was consecrated in 819.

The structure remained relatively intact until 1704; the extant baroque cathedral incorporates aspects of Ratgar's plan and sizable portions of his western construction.

Eigil also built the small church to the Archangel Michael within the monastic cemetery. Of this centrally planned chapel, a round structure with eight columns and an eastern nichelike apse atop a crypt, only the crypt remains. This extraordinary structure centers on a squat column topped by an ionicizing (spiraled), reused, eighth-century capital, which visually supports a tunnel vault. An ambulatory-like structure, later subdivided, surrounds this central space. While often, and with reason, categorized an "imitation" of the Holy Sepulcher (a meaning perhaps obtained in later years and forms), Otfried Ellger has argued that this chapel, the eventual burial site of Eigil, reflects instead adherence to Antique sepulchral types, Fulda's commitment to the liturgical remembrance of its dead, and Eigil's desire to promote unity in the community after the unrest under Ratgar.

Destroyed in the tenth century, by the first half of the eleventh century the upper chapel was rebuilt in similar form, using remains of the old structure. Under Abbot Ruthard (1075–1096), the chapel received a second floor and was given a basilica-like cruciform shape through the construction of a two-story nave, without aisles, to the west, preceded by a tower, and transeptlike arms to the north and south. Consecrated in 1092, this structure still carries traces of possibly eleventh-century frescoes. In 1315, the west tower and nave roof were heightened. St. Michael's remains today, despite an overzealous "restoration" in the 1930s and damage during the Second World War, as testimony to aspects of Fulda's changing medieval building history.

BIBLIOGRAPHY

Ellger, Otfried. *Die Michaelskirche zu Fulda als Zeugnis der Totensorge: Zur Konzeption einer Friedhofs- und Grabkirche im karolingischen Kloster Fulda*. Ph.D. diss., University of Freiburg im Breisgau, 1985. Veröffentlichungen des Fuldaer Geschichtsvereins 55. Fulda: Parzeller, 1989.

Krautheimer, Richard. "The Carolingian Revival of Early Christian Architecture," in *Studies in Early Christian, Medieval, and Renaissance Art*. New York: New York University Press, 1969, pp. 203–256.

Landesamt für Denkmalpflege Hessen. *Stadt Fulda*. Braunschweig: Friedrich Vieweg, 1992.

Oswald, Friedrich, Leo Schäfer, and Hans Rudolf Sennhauser. *Vorromanische Kirchenbauten: Katalog der*

Denkmäler bis zum Ausgang der Ottonen. Munich: Prestel, 1966, vol. 1, pp. 84–89.

Sturm, Erwin. *Die Bau- und Kunstdenkmale der Stadt Fulda.* Fulda: Parzeller, 1984.

Jenny H. Shaffer

SEE ALSO
Carolingian Art and Architecture; Charlemagne

Funerals
See Birth, Marriage, Burial.

Furniture
See Liturgy, Furniture.

Fürstbischof

Prince-bishops, or ecclesiastical princes—church officials bestowed with secular powers—played a major role in medieval Germany. Although in some other parts of Europe bishops continued to administer extensive lands and some fairly autonomous temporal jurisdiction beyond the High Middle Ages (e.g., the bishops of Durham on the Scottish border), it was a distinctive feature of German history that so many prelates including some abbots and abbesses) continued to exercise so much temporal authority down to the end of the Old Reich. While some bishops from the very outset were firmly subject to their overlords (e.g., three sees dependent on the archbishops of Salzburg, and the four dioceses created in 1243 for the Prussian lands of the Teutonic Knights, or *Deutschorden*), by 1500 around four dozen governed their own principalities (called *Hochstifte*, or, in the case of archbishoprics, *Erzstifte),* and many of them were eligible to sit in the Prälatenbank of the College of Princes of the Reichstag, as it took on definitive form in the fourteenth and fifteenth centuries.

Bishops had become progressively more powerful and wealthy in the disintegrating western Roman Empire, especially in Gaul, and either eagerly or reluctantly took up the office of "defender of the city" *(defensor civitatis)* recorded in Emperor Justinian's (d. 565) law code. The Carolingian dynasty, as it ascended in the eighth century, coopted these powerful prelates, and then extended to other bishops rights, lands, and comital responsibilities in the governance of the expanding realm. The Saxon dynasty (Ottonians) continued this heavy reliance on

churchmen, so much so that the historian Leo Santifaller called it the Church System of the Reich *(Reichskirchensystem).* Although Timothy Reuter and others have questioned the usefulness of such a rigid term and its supposed uniqueness by comparison with royal reliance on the church elsewhere in Europe, it did come to pass that because of the nature of the empire, which had passed to the Saxons in 962, things turned out differently for the German church in the long run. The Investiture Controversy, or Gregorian reform, of the eleventh century (both misleading labels) culminated in the Concordat of Worms of 1122, according to which the emperor effectively surrendered control over the church in Italy and Burgundy in return for even greater control over the church in Germany than any of his royal counterparts legally enjoyed in their realms. Thus the emperor had the right to decide disputed elections of bishops and abbots in Germany (as opposed to the pope in the rest of Europe), and a bishop could not be consecrated until the emperor had invested him with his princely regalia. On the face of it, the emperors remained firmly in control.

Yet by 1300 prince-bishops were more clearly than ever pursuing their own policies and creating principalities with varying degrees of independence. Older interpretations have blamed the "loss" of imperial "control" on papal intransigence, the ambitions of the Hohenstaufen in Italy at the expense of Germany, the resistance of the Italian communes, the new stone fortifications in Europe that made conquest of castles and towns much more difficult, and the failure to develop specifically imperial institutions for the administration and enforcement of justice. Other historians have stressed the fundamental ungovernability from the top of such a large, expanding, and diverse empire. Recently, some historians such as Benjamin Arnold have argued that where we have tended to see conflict between emperors and princes and the failure of royal policies, we should instead discern patterns of cooperation and also royal successes, such as the surmounting of the problem of the dukes and the transformation of the title of duke in the twelfth century. All these arguments offer important insights and contain some truth. The indisputable fact nevertheless remains that in agreements made with the ecclesiastical and the secular princes in 1220 and 1232, respectively, Frederick II systematically extended to all of them rights and privileges that had been granted fitfully to individual princes over the course of several centuries. He thereby laid the legal foundation for the full emergence of principalities.

What prince-bishops would be able to do with those rights was another matter entirely. Ironically, it was in this period that their principalities largely ceased to grow. They had always depended first and foremost on royal largesse, which now became thinner and more complex (e.g., pawns). In addition, they faced revolts on the part of the burghers in their cathedral cities, leading to the withdrawal of the archbishops of Cologne to Bonn, those of Trier to Koblenz, those of Mainz to Aschaffenburg, and so on. Finally, they faced their greedy secular counterparts, who in the fourteenth and fifteenth centuries nibbled at their territories with an eye to gobbling them up, which in many cases they did in the course of the Reformation and which became one of the central factors precipitating the Thirty Years' War in 1618 (in the so-called ecclesiastical reservations clause of the Peace of Augsburg of 1555).

Three prince-archbishops stood out from all the rest. The Rhenish archbishops existing at the time of the *translatio imperii* (succession of the empire) in 962—Mainz, Cologne, and Trier—became the archchancellors of different parts of the empire and, ultimately, the three ecclesiastical electors of the empire enjoying precedence over the secular electors. Of the three archbishops, the archbishop of Mainz was the most important: head of the largest province in the Western church and arch-chancellor for Germany, he also had the additional right of convening and presiding over the College of Electors. Legally, he was the leading prince of the Holy Roman Empire.

Such powerful prince-bishops as these and their confreres in Münster, Osnabrück, and Salzburg (who survived for centuries between powerful Bavaria and Austria) were not necessarily pleasing to the prince-bishops of Rome, who raised few objections to talk of secularization in the eighteenth century. When secularization did come to pass in 1803, the last remaining rivals of the prince-bishops of Rome were eliminated, thereby paving the way for the unrestrained, restored papal monarchy of the nineteenth century—until it, too, was gobbled up by nascent Italy in 1871, for which the popes were unwilling to grant forgiveness until 1929.

BIBLIOGRAPHY

Arnold, Benjamin. "German Bishops and Their Military Retinues in the Medieval Empire." *German History* 7 (1989): 161–183.

———. *Medieval Germany, 500–1300: A Political Interpretation.* Toronto: University of Toronto Press, 1997.

Gatz, Erwin, and Brodkorb, Clemens, eds. *Die Bischöfe des Heiligen Römischen Reiches, 1448 bis 1648. Ein biographisches Lexikon.* Berlin: Duncker and Humblot, 1996.

Hauck, Albert. *Kirchengeschichte Deutschlands,* 5 vols. in 6 pts., 8th. ed. Berlin: Akademie-Verlag, 1954.

Reuter, Timothy. "The 'Imperial Church System' of the Ottonian and Salian Rulers: A Reconsideration." *Journal of Ecclesiastical History* 33 (1982): 347–374.

Schulte, Aloys. *Der Adel und die deutsche Kirche im Mittelalter,* 2d ed. Stuttgart: F. Enke, 1922.

Lawrence G. Duggan

SEE ALSO
Carolingians; Cologne, Archdiocese; Concordat of Worms; Frederick II; Investiture Controversy; Mainz; Staufen; Trier

G

Gandersheim

The oldest family foundation of the Liudolfing (eventually Ottonian) dynasty, Gandersheim was established in 852 by Count Liudolf and Countess Oda, in part as a result of Louis the German's missionary policy in Saxony. Located south of Hildesheim, the institution for female canonesses was amply endowed by the Ottonian and Salian houses, whose members held the position of abbess until 1125. Like Quedlinburg, the royal foundation of Gandersheim served as a center of political, liturgical, and historical consciousness for the Ottonian house. The canonry received imperial protection from Otto I during the abbacy of Gerberga of Bavaria, teacher and patroness of Hrotsvitha, whose works include a history of the foundation, the *Primordia coenobii Gandeshemensis.* Otto II and Theophanu placed their daughter Sophia in Gandersheim, and their magnificent purple-and-gold marriage charter, now in Wolfenbüttel, was at some point also deposited there. Sophia's election as abbess in 1001 was the catalyst for the *Gandersheimer Streit.* This dispute between Hildesheim and Mainz over privileges, control of the canonry, and seething political rivalries entangled the temporal and spiritual elite of the realm before its final resolution in 1030.

During the Investiture Controversy, the royal connection made Gandersheim a bastion of imperial support against the Saxon nobility. The following centuries were a continuous struggle against monastic reformers, the encroaching Hildesheim bishopric, and the increasingly powerful Welf family, who finally gained control of the abbacy in 1402. Despite economic decline and the change to Protestantism, Gandersheim remained a noble and independent foundation until its dissolution in 1810. Long a repository for precious art objects, the Romanesque church attained its present form, including the western "women's gallery," in the 1160s, though the building likely retains many features of its Ottonian predecessor.

BIBLIOGRAPHY

Althoff, Gerd. "Gandersheim und Quedlinburg: Ottonische Frauenklöster als Herrschafts- und Überlieferungszentren." *Frühmittelalterliche Studien* 25 (1991): 123–144.

Bernhardt, John W. *Itinerant Kingship and Royal Monasteries in Early Medieval Germany, c. 936–1075.* Cambridge: Cambridge University Press, 1993, pp. 149–161.

Goetting, Hans. *Das Bistum Hildesheim 1: Das reichsunmittelbare Kanonissenstift Gandersheim.* Germania Sacra N. F. 7. Berlin: de Gruyter, 1973.

Adam S. Cohen

SEE ALSO

Hildesheim; Hrosvit of Gandersheim; Investiture Controversy; Mainz; Otto I; Ottonian Art and Architecture; Quedlinburg; Romanesque Art and Architecture; Theophanu

Gardens and Gardening

The plan of St. Gall (816/820), a drawing of the layout for an ideal monastery, shows four separate gardens that correspond roughly to the main functions of gardens in the Middle Ages. The plan contains a vegetable garden, a physic garden, an orchard, and an enclosed cloister garden for meditation.

Whether adjacent to a peasant's hut or to the kitchen of a manor house, the ubiquitous kitchen garden with its wattle fence was essential for growing food and seasonings. Medicinal gardens likewise provided herbal treatments for the sick. In both types, plants were ideally grown in narrow, raised beds surrounded on all sides by paths for easier access. Larger estates and monasteries also had orchards where better fruit varieties were cultivated by grafting.

In patrician homes and larger estates the pleasure garden *(Lustgarten)* served as a place for dining, conversing, and social gatherings. Enclosed by a wall, fence, or rose hedge, the most elaborate of these gardens contained trellises, arbors, pergolas, a grassy mead with benches of turf or stone, raised beds for growing ornamentals, aromatic herbs, topiary plants, a fountain or well, perhaps a birdbath or dovecote, and some fruit or shade trees. Cloister gardens were usually divided into quarters by paths leading to a central fountain or shrub area. As a symbol of earthly and heavenly paradise, the garden provides the setting for significant episodes in courtly romances and a theme for numerous religious allegories.

BIBLIOGRAPHY

Harvey, John. *Mediaeval Gardens.* Beaverton, Ore.: Timber, 1981.

Hennebo, Dieter. *Gärten des Mittelalters.* Munich: Artemis, 1987.

Anne Winston-Allen

SEE ALSO
Sankt Gall

Genesis and *Exodus*

The early Middle High German *Genesis* and *Exodus,* two distinct and substantial verse epics based on the Bible, bear grand witness to the revival of German literature in the latter half of the eleventh century and at the beginning of the twelfth. Vernacular literature in the Old High German period, roughly 750–1050, had been full of promise in its variety of genres and approaches, but its production was isolated and sporadic, its history marked by severe discontinuity. Beginning around 1050, German literature again found its voice, no doubt significantly on the eve of the Investiture Controversy and the ensuing radical transformation of medieval German politics, society, and religiosity. The *Genesis* and *Exodus* poems are among the most important products of this new literary flourishing. Their poetic form and narrative techniques likely provided models or at least examples for subsequent authors, most important, those who began to turn to secular subjects after the middle of the twelfth century. If there is any continuity in German-language literature, its beginnings are to be sought here in these works. Beyond their obvious and uncontested literary-historical value, the *Genesis* and *Exodus* poems offer religious and social historians fascinating and sometimes unique insights into a turning point of German history. Historians would well profit from a better acquaintance with this too frequently neglected and often falsely characterized literature.

The *Genesis* and *Exodus* exist in different redactions, which are preserved in two codices, both illustrated with line drawings. The Vienna Codex is the older, perhaps from before 1150. It contains the full *Genesis* (6,062 lines) with seven illustrations, a prose translation of the *Physiologus,* the popular medieval bestiary, and an incomplete version of the *Exodus,* up to line 1,480 in the Millstatt equivalent. Now preserved at Klagenfurt, the Millstatt Codex is from the late twelfth century and is one of the most extensively illustrated vernacular manuscripts of the period. It begins with the *Genesis,* including eighty-seven illustrations inspired by the iconographic plan of the Vienna Codex. A rhymed *Physiologus* follows, including thirty-two drawings, and then a full version of the *Exodus* (3,316 lines). Five shorter religious works complete the codex, which is clearly arranged as a compilation of sacred history, beginning with the *Genesis* account of the creation of the orders of angels and closing with a fragmentary poem on the Heavenly Jerusalem. There are occasionally subtle and interesting differences between the Vienna and Millstatt versions of *Genesis* and *Exodus,* which appear to descend, independently of each other, from a lost archetype. For the most part, the discrepancies arise from the Millstatt redactor's attempts to modernize his material by changing linguistic forms and vocabulary and purifying rhymes. A third, partial version of the *Genesis,* the story of Joseph and his brothers, may be found as part of the *Vorau Books of Moses,* which are transmitted in the late-twelfth-century Vorau Codex.

The manuscript collections that preserve *Genesis* and *Exodus* offer clues to their reception and later interpretation. Art historians, for example, have argued that the illustrations point to the archiepiscopal court of Salzburg or perhaps to Regensburg and the Welf dynasty, specifically to Duke Henry the Lion (ca. 1129–1195), an important patron of vernacular literature. Linguistic evidence, however, proves that the poems themselves were composed much earlier than the codices. Both the *Genesis* and the *Exodus* are written in the Bavarian-Austrian dialect of early Middle High German. The Vienna version of *Genesis* is particularly archaic, suggesting an origin as early as 1050–1075. The *Exodus* is more recent, perhaps from around 1110–1130. The poetic form of the poems supports the proposed dating. Both are written in rhymed couplets with roughly four stressed syllables in a line. This scheme is followed more closely in the younger *Exodus;* the Vienna *Genesis* is far from regular in its metrical form and its rhymes are impure. Historical allusions in the poems are unfortunately too ambiguous to offer more precise conclusions about the date of composition.

The *Genesis* and *Exodus* are both anonymous, as are almost all vernacular poems from this period, and we are even uncertain whether the *Genesis* had a single author or was a collective effort. The religious matter of the poems, their authors' knowledge of Latin works, and indeed the very fact that they were written down at all show that the poets were churchmen, but whether lay priests or monks is unclear. Since the dominant trends in religiosity at this time were monastically inspired, this distinction, the subject of long debates, is perhaps irrelevant.

More tantalizing and pertinent is the question of the nature of the audience for whom these works were intended. The use of the vernacular would have been unlikely for a traditional monastic audience, which typically had recourse to the vernacular written word only in pedagogical settings. Regardless of how one judges the aesthetic merits of the *Genesis* and *Exodus* poems, they are clearly artistically ambitious works and far from being ancillary aids to translation. The eleventh-century institution of lay brethren associated with monasteries and their fast-growing numbers and importance in the second half of the eleventh century allow the speculation that the *Genesis* and *Exodus* may have been conceived for this interested, but incompletely "Latinized," audience. The *Genesis* was perhaps used as Lenten reading; the *Exodus* might have been connected with the Paschal liturgy. There is a marked interest in secular matters in both works, and the *Exodus,* especially, shows an intimate and enthusiastic knowledge of military affairs. The *Exodus* poet even addresses his audience as *mîne hêrren* (line 2907), or "my lords," possibly suggesting a lay audience at a secular court outside the monastery. Whoever the intended audience of these works, we may be certain of this much: The poets were clearly attempting to reach a wider spectrum of listeners than had been the case for the so-

phisticated Latin literature produced in the German-speaking lands prior to the Investiture Controversy. While there is nothing in the *Genesis* or *Exodus* to tie them to specifically Gregorian reform tenets, their transmission in the vernacular of monastic thinking and spirituality should be seen as an offshoot of the more general ecclesiastical attempt to reform the laity, which was initially favored by both the papal and the imperial parties.

The *Genesis* and *Exodus* authors' basic approach to their material is essentially identical. Their main source is the Vulgate Bible, and their goal is to give narratively coherent adaptations. Despite this similarity of conception, the *Genesis* and *Exodus* poems sometimes differ significantly in their narrative strategies, in part because of their authors' interpretative intentions, but also because of the nature of the biblical books they used as their sources. The *Genesis* is initially strongly episodic, discursive, and homiletic. In typical monastic fashion, the author frequently pauses to amplify his material, drawing on his knowledge of theological and hermeneutic commonplaces. Thus he happily describes in detail the functions of the parts of the human body, or he explains the origins of the various human races as a result of the herbs eaten by the sons of Cain and how slavery and human inequality arose from Noah's curse of his son Ham. The author consistently interprets his material as a foreshadowing or prefiguration of Christian truth. For instance, he explains the colors of the rainbow instituted by God after the Flood as signifying the blood and water that flowed from Christ's side at the crucifixion, which in turn signify the sacramental mixing of water and wine and the grace of Baptism. Isidore of Seville and the Venerable Bede (or his German adapter and transmitter Hrabanus Maurus) are ultimately the principal sources here; some have also detected the influence of the Virgilian biblical epic of Avitus (d. 518).

The episodic style changes as the *Genesis* author relates the history of Abraham, Isaac, Jacob, and most especially Joseph, whose story accounts for almost half of the text. Extraneous and nonessential elements—anything distracting from the narrative flow—are carefully excluded. The author develops an adroit epic style that is especially alive to the modern reader through its skillful characterizations and its anachronistic projection of the author's medieval surroundings into the world of the patriarchs. We hear, for example, of "retainers," "courtly feasts," "bold heroes," "ministerials," and "knights" (*guote chnechte* as well as the first literary use of the courtly term *rîter*).

The *Exodus* poet's ostensible purpose is typological, not homiletic. He states in his final lines that like Moses, we should flee from the Egypt of this world to journey to our true homeland, the heavenly Jerusalem. But the *Exodus* is not an extended allegory. Its author restricts himself to the first fifteen chapters of the biblical Exodus, avoiding theological commentary to focus on the conflict between Pharaoh and Moses. The poet clearly takes pleasure in constructing his bellicose narrative. Pharaoh's description of the Israelites, for example, could as well stem from a later secular poet: "They are good knights and well know how to battle" (*si sint guote chnehte, / geturren wole vehten,* ll. 95–96). These military elements have led Dennis Green to argue rightly that the *Exodus* breathes of the crusading spirit. Indeed, the presence of vernacular lay culture within the framework of a deep Latinate religiosity, much like the Crusaders' volatile mixture of piety and violence, is the essence of the fascination of *Genesis* and *Exodus.*

BIBLIOGRAPHY

Beyschlag, Siegfried. *Die Wiener Genesis. Idee, Stoff und Form.* Sitzungsberichte der Akademie der Wissenschaften in Wien. Philosophisch-historische Klasse 220. Vienna: Akademie der Wissenschaften, 1942.

Diemer, Joseph, ed. *Genesis und Exodus nach der Milstäter [sic] Handschrit.* 2 vols. Vienna: Gerold, 1862.

Dollmayer, Viktor, ed. *Die altdeutsche Genesis. Nach der Wiener Handschrift.* Halle: Niemeyer, 1932.

Essler, Josef. *Die Schöpfungsgeschichte in der "Altdeutschen Genesis" (Wiener Genesis V. 1–231). Kommentar und Interpretation.* Göppingen: Kümmerle, 1987.

Gentry, Francis G. *Bibliographie zur frühmittelhochdeutschen geistlichen Dichtung.* Berlin: Schmidt, 1992.

Green, Dennis Howard. *The Millstätter Exodus: A Crusading Epic.* London: Cambridge University Press, 1967.

Jacobson, Evelyn Margaret. "'Triuwe' and 'Minne' in the Millstätter Genesis." *Germanic Notes* 12 (1981): 51–54.

Kuhn, Hugo. "Gestalten und Lebenskräfte der frühmittelhochdeutschen Dichtung," in *Dichtung und Welt im Mittelalter.* Stuttgart: Metzler, 1969, pp. 112–132.

Menhardt, Hermann. "Die Bilder der Millstätter Genesis und ihre Verwandten," In *Beiträge zur älteren europäischen Kulturgeschichte. Festschrift für Rudolf Egger.* Klagenfurt: Verlag des Geschichtsvereines für Kärnten, 1954, pp. 248–371.

Papp, Edgar, ed. *Die altdeutsche Exodus.* Munich: Wilhelm Fink, 1968.

Smits, Kathryn, ed. *Die frühmittelhochdeutsche Wiener Genesis.* Berlin: Schmidt, 1972.

Voss, Hella. *Studien zur illustrierten Millstätter Genesis.* Munich: Beck, 1962.

Weller, Alfred. *Die frühmittelhochdeutsche Wiener Genesis nach Quellen, Übersetzungsart, Stil und Syntax.* Berlin: Schmidt, 1914.

Robert G. Sullivan

SEE ALSO
Bible; Bible Epic, Saxon

Georgslied

The sole surviving Old High German narrative hymn, "Georgslied" (Song of George) is preserved in one copy, a later addition also containing the Old High German scratched gloss "Kicila Verse" (Gisela's Verse) from the tenth (or early eleventh) century, composed of circa fifty-nine four-beat lines with interior rhyme, in ten strophes, perhaps incomplete at the end. Parchment and writing are damaged, the text in part illegible; scribal idiosyncrasies (especially transposition of letters) further encumber deciphering. A following entry *nequeo Vuisolf* (I, Wisolf, can't), is widely thought to be the complaint of a scribe frustrated by his task, i.e., writing down the "Georgslied." However, the hand of Wisolf does not match that of the "Georgslied."

The hymn, probably composed at or near the end of the ninth century (perhaps in or near Prüm or Reichenau) in connection with a celebration of St. George (for a church benediction, transfer of relics, or feast day on April 24), widely venerated in southwestern Germany, relates his trial, steadfastness (strophes 1–2), prison sentence, miraculous deeds (strophes 3–4), triple martyrdom and resurrection (strophes 5–7), raising a dead man, conversion of Queen Elessandria, and banishment of Abollin, the hell dog (strophes 8–10). Three variable refrains conclude each strophe (lacking in strophe 10), and were probably sung by a congregation in response to a cantor chanting the stanzas. Most episodes can be traced to various extant Latin prose legends surrounding St. George, but no one source contains all the elements of the Old High German rendition.

BIBLIOGRAPHY

Haubrichs, Wolfgang. *Die Kultur der Abtei Prüm zur Karolingerzeit: Studien zur Heimat des althochdeutschen Georgsliedes.* Bonn: Rohrscheid, 1979.

———. *Georgslied und Georgslegende im frühen Mittelalter: Text und Rekonstruktion.* Konigstein im Taunus: Scriptor, 1979.

Schützeichel, Rudolf. *Codex Pal. lat. 52: Studien zur Heidelberger Otfridhandschrift, zum Kicila-Vers und zum Georgslied.* Göttingen: Vandenhoeck and Ruprecht, 1982, pp. 53–97 [with photographs of manuscript].

von Steinmeyer, Elias. *Die kleineren althochdeutschen Sprachdenkmäler.* 1916; rpt. Zurich: Weidmann, 1963, pp. 94–97.

John M. Jeep

SEE ALSO

Glosses, Old High German; Otfrid; Versification

Gerhoh of Reichersberg (1093–1169)

Bavarian canon, controversialist, reformer, and correspondent with emperors and popes, Gerhoh, provost of Reichersberg, was a prolific writer and an important figure in twelfth-century literature and religion. Gerhoh was a strong advocate of continued reform of the church and was a vocal critic of the worldliness and wealth of the ecclesiastical hierarchy. Although critical of ecclesiastical abuses, Gerhoh was equally critical of secular abuses of power and was an important supporter of Innocent II in the papal schism of 1130 and a supporter, after initial neutrality, of Alexander III during the schism of that pope's reign. Gerhoh was also a representative of the new apostolic spirituality and the new urban milieu emerging in twelfth-century Europe. A canon and active preacher, Gerhoh's teaching offered an ideal of radical reform rooted in Gregorian ideals of the world. His definition of simony, the selling of indulgences, threatened the prebendary (grant-giving) system of the church and opened him to accusations of heresy in the autumn of 1130. He was saved from a heretic's fate only by the protection of powerful reform-minded members of the ecclesiastical hierarchy. But Gerhoh's criticism was not limited to the secular and religious elite; it extended to the representatives of the "new learning" including Peter Abelard, Gilbert de la Porée, and Peter Lombard. Finally, Gerhoh was a theologian of some note and author of a number of important treatises including *Liber de aedificio Dei* (On

God's House) and *Libellus de ordine donorum Spiritus sancti* (On the Order of the Gifts of the Holy Spirit). His most interesting theological work, however, can be found in his apocalyptic treatises, *De investigatione Antichristi* (The Investigation of Antichrist) and *De quarta vigilia noctis* (The Fourth Watch of the Night). In these works he develops a theology of history that posits the imminent end of time in his own day. He provides an outline of history based on the church's successful struggle against various antichrists culminating in the age of Pope Gregory VII. It was in the years following the reign of Gregory that the times of trouble and turmoil—evident for Gerhoh in the rampant simony and worldliness of many clerics and in the struggles between the pope and the emperor, Frederick Barbarossa—preceding the appearance of Antichrist occurred. Indeed, Gerhoh's work suggests that the biblical prophecies forewarning of Antichrist had been fulfilled and that his coming was imminent.

BIBLIOGRAPHY

Classen, Peter. "*Res Gestae,* Universal History, Apocalypse: Visions of Past and Future," in *Renaissance and Renewal in the Twelfth Century,* ed. Robert L. Benson and Giles Constable. Toronto: University of Toronto Press, 1991, pp. 387–417.

Meuthen, Erich. *Kirche und Heilsgeschichte bei Gerhoh von Reichersberg.* Leiden: Brill, 1959.

Morrison, Karl F. "The Exercise of Thoughtful Minds: The Apocalypse in Some German Historical Writings," in *The Apocalypse in the Middle Ages,* ed. Richard K. Emmerson and Bernard McGinn. Ithaca, N.Y: Cornell University Press, 1992, pp. 352–373.

Michael Frassetto

SEE ALSO

Frederick I Barbarossa; Gregory VII; Investiture Controversy; Otto of Freising

German Language, Dialects

A dialect is a distinctive speech form used only by a subset of the speakers of a language. Dialects are usually defined by region, sometimes also by class (British "received pronunciation") or ethnicity (African American English).

In the early Middle Ages, i.e., before around 1000, German was spoken not only in western Germany but also in Switzerland, Alsace, and parts of Austria. Early in this period, German was also spoken—at least by the

Frankish ruling class—in much of northern France and by the Lombards in northern Italy. This huge area was settled at different times by various Germanic tribes whose movements are sometimes difficult to trace. Their "West Germanic" dialects differed not only from the North Germanic of Scandinavia and the East Germanic of the Goths, but also from each other. They are not lineal descendants of a uniform "Proto-German" *(Urdeutsch)*, and, like the modern dialects, they are not "corrupt" forms of some earlier, "purer" language.

The oldest attestations of German proper are of German words incorporated in Latin texts. Soon we also find glosses *(Abrogans)* and connected texts (Old High German *Isidore*), all written by clerics who normally wrote in Latin. Manuscript spellings are often ambiguous: *uuir,* usually *wir* (we), also represents *vuir* (fire). Despite many inconsistencies, it is clear that several dialects were written. Traditionally, they are classified by the effects of the Second or High German Consonant Shift *(zweite Lautverschiebung)*, completed by about 700. Listing first those dialects most affected, we may distinguish:

Upper German, consisting of:

Alemannic (the southwest, including Switzerland and most of Alsace). Important texts include the translations known as the Murbach Hymns and translations with commentaries by Notker Labeo of St. Gall.

Bavarian (Bavaria and an increasing portion of Austria). Important texts include the poem *Muspilli* and a version of the Lord's Prayer from a monastery at Freising.

Middle German, including:

East Franconian (Würzburg, Bamberg), used for the Fulda translation of the Syrian monk Tatian's Life of Christ, or Gospel Harmony *(Evangelienharmonie)*. Of all older dialects, this most resembles modern standard German. From the twelfth century onward, it is usually classified as Upper German. Rhenish Franconian (Mainz, Frankfurt, Lorsch, Worms) is the language of the ninth-century (trilingual) Oaths from Strasbourg. The subdialect South Rhenish Franconian is exemplified by Otfrid's Gospel poem.

West Franconian in northern France, perhaps also Luxembourg and Lorraine. No surviving texts are unambiguously in this dialect, and by Carolingian times, the ruling class may have adopted Rhenish Franconian.

Middle Franconian, including Mosel Franconian (Trier) and (at least later) Ripuarian (Cologne).

Low German, containing:

Low Franconian (lower Rhine), known from some psalm translations.

Old Saxon (modern Lower Saxony), best known from the poem *Heliand.*

Upper and Middle German are collectively called High German. Low German was not affected by the consonant shift; Germanic /p t k/ remain as [p^h t^h k^h]. But Upper German dialects have [f s x] in some situations, [pf ts kx] in others; [x] is the sound written <ch> in modern *ma chen* (make). Examples, in characteristic Old High German spellings: *offan [offan]* "open," *uuazzar [wassar]* "water," *mahhôn [maxxo:n]* "to make" (<:> indicates a long vowel), *phad [pfad]* "path," *aphul [apful]* "apple," *zuei [tswei]* (not *[tswai]!*) "two," *chorn [kxorn]* "grain"— Middle German has [f s x] and [ts] as in Upper German, but has [k^h] rather than [kx], and many varieties have [p^h] rather than [pf]: Rhenish Franconian *korn, appul, pad.*

A further difference is that Germanic /b d g/ usually yield Upper German [p t k]: Bavarian and Alemannic *kepan* (give), *tak* (day). Rhenish Franconian writes rather *geban, dag,* while Mosel Franconian and Low German have *geven, dag.*

Almost until the present, German dialects have continued to diverge. Alemannic and Bavarian of the eighth or ninth century look nearly identical. Yet their modern descendants—Swiss, Swabian, Alsatian, and Bavarian dialects—are instantly identifiable and not necessarily mutually intelligible. Notker's careful Alemannic orthography (ca. 1000) already differs sharply from Bavarian and indicates development toward the tricky consonantism of modern Swiss German.

Migration produced further change. Already before 1000, German settlers moved east and south. For centuries, the ever-increasing size of the German-speaking world favored divergence. Low German was eventually spoken in Königsberg (Kaliningrad) and beyond, but it differed from varieties farther west. New "East Middle German" dialects developed when settlers from Upper and West Middle Germany colonized Thuringia, Upper Saxony, and Silesia, blending their dialects and creating new forms. Other colonial dialects (e.g., isolated Bavarian pockets in northern Italy) differed because they preserved archaic forms that had been replaced elsewhere.

Sometimes even shared developments split dialects apart. Beginning before 1200, *[i:]* in many dialects became a diphthong: *[mi:n]* "my" > *[mein], later [main]* or *[mɔ̃in]*. But German already had *[ei]* in words such as *ein* (one). Almost everywhere (though not in modern standard German), older *[ei]* made way for the new by changing first to *[ai]*, then variously to *[oa], [a:], [y:], or [e:]*. Although the High German consonant shift still provides a convenient way to classify dialects, it is the sheer number of later unshared changes (especially in the vowel system) that sometimes makes neighboring dialects difficult or even impossible to understand.

But not all changes led to greater diversity. By the twelfth century, many Alemannic (and perhaps already some Bavarian) dialects had abandoned Upper German *[kx p k]* < Germanic */k b g/,* using *[kʰ* b g] as in Franconian. This created a large new area of fairly uniform speech. When secular courtly literature arose shortly before 1200, it is perhaps no accident that the most significant courtly epics were written by Alemannic or East Franconian authors. Like the courts themselves, Gottfried von Strasbourg and the knight Hartmann von Aue (Alemannic) and Wolfram von Eschenbach (East Franconian) favored a more-than-regional language and style. Their model of courtly language was followed, if not always exactly, by many epic and lyric poets from other regions. But this model never became obligatory (the normalized spelling of modern editions is misleading); scribes even a few years later used more modern forms without compunction.

Another unifying force was the use of German for civil records after 1250. Though each city or court at first used something resembling the local dialect, the usage of certain chanceries gained increasing prestige and was widely imitated. Luther himself claimed to write the "common German language," created, he believed, by the chanceries of Duke Elector Frederick of Saxony and Emperor Maximilian, and his language became the basis for the modern standard written language. Yet the spoken dialects were long unaffected by chancery German (which was far from uniform) or even by Luther's language. It is telling that the Luther Bible had to be retranslated into Low German, the last edition appearing in 1621.

BIBLIOGRAPHY

Braune, Wilhelm. *Althochdeutsche Grammatik,* 14th ed. Hans Eggers. Tübingen: Niemeyer, 1987 [detailed descriptions of Old High German dialects].

Keller, Rudolf Ernst. *German Dialects: Phonology and Morphology, with Selected Texts.* Manchester: Manchester University Press, 1961 [treats several modern dialect types in depth, using extracts from dialect literature].

———. *The German Language.* London: Faber and Faber, 1978 [rev. ed. of Priebsch and Collinson, *The German Language*].

Lockwood, W. B. *An Informal History of the German Language.* London: André Deutsch, 1965; 2d ed. 1976 [especially helpful on dialects].

Priebsch, R., and W. E. Collinson. *The German Language,* 6th ed. London: Faber and Faber, 1956.

Leo A. Connolly

SEE ALSO

Abrogans; Bible; Bible Epic, Saxon; Gottfried von Straßburg; Hartmann von Aue; *Isidore;* Latin Language; Maximilian; Notker Labeo; Otfrid; *Tatian;* Wolfram von Eschenbach

Gernrode

Situated at the foot of the northeastern edge of the Harz mountain range just south of Quedlinburg (Sachsen-Anhalt), Gernrode was established as a foundation of canonesses in 959 by Gero, the foremost margrave in Ottonian Saxony. The canonry and its church served as a memorial for his two sons and as a family burial site; Hathui, Gero's widowed daughter-in-law, served as the first abbess, and Gero himself was interred there in 965. In 961 Gernrode received papal immunity from John XIII and royal protection and immunity from Otto I. The foundation's importance in the Ottonian period is indicated by its series of abbesses from the royal house, including Otto II and Theophanu's daughter Adelheid, who at one point ruled over Quedlinburg, Gernrode, and Gandersheim simultaneously.

The church, begun in 959, is the best surviving example of Ottonian architecture. The east end comprises a windowless apse, choir, and short transept with pronounced absidioles (projecting chapels). Underneath is a so-called hall crypt that, uncommonly, integrates features of ring- and cross-shaped crypts as well. A small adjacent *confessio* held the arm relic of St. Cyriacus, to whom the church was rededicated after Gero obtained the relic during a pilgrimage to Rome in 961. The unusual galleries above the aisles have been linked to Theophanu's presence in Quedlinburg, but in fact their origin and use remain

Gernrode, St. Cyruakus, view of westwork. *Photograph: Adam S. Cohen*

unclear. Another rare feature in the nave is the Holy Sepulcher in the south aisle, dated to circa 1080. Containing a sarcophagus and decorated with high and low relief sculpture, this small space was used for enactment of an Easter play. As a result of rebuilding in 1130, the original appearance of the church's west facade is uncertain; although the imposing towers are Ottonian, the west choir and crypt belong to the twelfth century.

BIBLIOGRAPHY

Erdmann, Wolfgang, Werner Jacobsen, Clemens Kosch, and Detlef von Winterfeld. "Neue Untersuchungen an der Stiftskirche zu Gernrode," in *Bernwardinische Kunst: Bericht über ein wissenschaftliches Symposium in Hildesheim vom 10.10. bis 13.10.1984,* ed. Martin Gosebruch and Frank N. Steigerwald. Schriftenreihe der Kommission für Niedersächsische Bau- und Kunstgeschichte bei der Braunschweigischen Wissenschaftlichen Gesellschaft 3. Göttingen: E. Goltze, 1988, pp. 245–285.

Schulze, Hans K. *Das Stift Gernrode.* Mitteldeutsche Forschungen 38. Cologne: Böhlau, 1965.

Striker, Cecil L. "The Byzantine Question in Ottonian Architecture Reconsidered." in *Architectural Studies in Memory of Richard Krautheimer,* ed. Cecil L. Striker. Mainz: Zabern, 1996, pp. 157–161.

Voigtlander, Klaus. *Die Stiftskirche zu Gernrode und ihre Restaurierung 1858–1872.* 2d ed. Berlin: Akademie-Verlag, 1982.

Adam S. Cohen

SEE ALSO

Drama, Easter Plays; Iconographies, Innovative; Otto I; Otto II; Ottonian Art and Architecture; Quedlinburg; Theophanu

Gerthener, Madern (1360/1370–1430)

Named with his father, Johann, among the stone masons of Frankfurt in 1387, Gerthener had taken over his father's shop by 1391. In 1395 he was taken onto the city payroll. In 1415 he calls himself *"der stadt frankenfurd werkmeister"* (master of the works of the city of Frankfurt), a position he had probably already held for some time. Most of his documented career was spent working on the church of St. Bartholomew: he was appointed head of the works in 1408. After finishing the transept here, he designed and, in 1415, began building the single tower that stood as a symbol of the city's independence. An octagonal story topped by a dome and an elaborate lantern surmounts the two lower stories on a square plan. The tracery decoration and especially the corner buttresses become increasingly ornate with each succeeding story. On the two portals we see the innovative uses of tracery forms, specifically hanging tracery and tracery vaults, that would become hallmarks of Gerthener's style.

In addition to his work on St. Bartholomew's, Gerthener was also involved in other projects in and around Frankfurt. In 1399 he guaranteed his work on the Alte Brücke (Old Bridge) across the Main, and in 1411 his work on the city wall is documented. Gerthener's mastery of the forms of late Gothic architecture, plus his visibility as head of the works on the coronation cathedral, drew his work to the attention of other patrons, and by the 1410s his reputation reached outside the city. Payments to Gerthener in 1407 from the funds of the so-called Gelnhausen tax, to which only King Ruprecht von der Pfalz (1400–1410) had access, may have been in compensation for the so-called Ruprechtsbau (Ruprecht building) at Heidelberg castle and/or the sacristy at Speyer Cathedral, begun in 1409. Gerthener's name appears in 1414–1415 in the financial records of the church of St. Katherine in Oppenheim, where he designed the west choir. The variety of the unusually fanciful tracery patterns in the tall windows and other details recall Gerthener's work in Frankfurt. In 1419 he was called to Strasbourg, where, with other masters, he advised on the continuation of the cathedral facade.

Other works sometimes associated with Gerthener fall into two groups: those on which his participation is assumed on the basis of his city positions and attributions on the basis of stylistic affinities with his secured works. Into the former category fall work on the town hall (the Römer), adapted from two patrician houses beginning in 1405, and the trade hall for linen, flax, and hemp products, the Leinwandhaus. Work on the city fortification system underway circa 1400 would also have been expected of the city's *Werkmeister*. This variety in the production of the medieval builder/architect—repair or rebuilding of existing structures, design and erection of both functional buildings, like bridges and fortification towers, and what we might today think of as "high" architecture, seen especially in churches—is typical of the era. The career of Peter Parler, for example, with whom Gerthener may have worked in Prague during his travels as a journeyman, also exhibits this diversity.

The high quality and use of architectural forms similar to those at Frankfurt produce general agreement that Gerthener was also at work on the so-called Memorienpforte (portal to the memorial chapel) at Mainz Cathedral about 1425. At Frankfurt, work on the church of the Virgin (Liebfrauenkirche), that of the Carmelites, and St. Leonhard's, all dated between 1415 and circa 1430, is sometimes associated with Gerthener on the basis of stylistic similarities to his documented works.

Three payment records indicate that Gerthener was also active as a sculptor. The sweet expressions and smoothed volumes of both the faces and the draperies of the two male saints on the cathedral side of the Memorienpforte are typically considered to exemplify his style. Other works sometimes assigned to Gerthener on stylistic grounds include the tympanum with the elaborate, multifigured scene of the Adoration of the Magi above the south portal of the Liebfrauenkirche in Frankfurt (ca. 1425), and the tomb of Anna von Dalberg (d. 1410) in the church of St. Katherine in Oppenheim. The art histo-

rian Kniffler argues that the epitaph of Siegfried zum Paradies, now in St. Nikolaus in Frankfurt (ca. 1420), and that of Johann II von Nassau (d. 1419), archbishop of Mainz, are more likely to be the master's own work.

Somewhat more problematic attributions are a print with the depiction of the Holy Grave (Berlin, Staatliche Museen Preussischer Kulturbesitz, Kupferstichkabinett), whose figures are close in style to those of the Memorienpforte, and a large-scale drawing with the design for Gerthener's tower at St. Bartholomew's (Frankfurt, Historisches Museum). Whether these are works by the master himself or by those who worked with him closely, Gerthener was an inventive artist of unusual energy and breadth.

BIBLIOGRAPHY

Beck, Herbert, Wolfgang Beeh, and Horst Bredekamp. *Kunst um 1400 am Mittelrhein: Ein Teil der Wirklichkeit.* Frankfurt am Main: Liebieghaus Museum alter Plastik, 1975, pp. 49–56.

Haberland, Ernst-Dietrich, and Hans-Otto Schrembs. *Madern Gerthener "der Stadt Franckenfurd Werkmeister": Baumeister und Bildhauer der Spätgotik.* Frankfurt am Main: Knecht, 1992.

Kniffler, Gisela. *Die Grabdenkmäler der Mainzer Erzbischöfe vom 13. bis zum frühen 16. Jahrhundert.* Ph.D. diss., University of Mainz, Dissertationen zur Kunstgeschichte 7. Cologne: Böhlau, 1978, pp. 51–109.

Ringshausen, Gerhard Johannes. "Madern Gerthener: Leben und Werk nach den Urkunden." Ph.D. diss., University of Göttingen, 1968.

Joan A. Holladay

SEE ALSO

Frankfurt am Main; Gothic Art and Architecture; Iconographies, Innovative; International Style; Mainz; Parler Family; Prague; Strasbourg

Gertrud von Helfta (1256–1301/1302)

A monastic, mystic author, Gertrud the Great *(die Größe)* entered the monastery of Helfta (near Eisleben) at the age of almost five. Her *Vita* (Life) presents her as a precocious child keenly interested in studying and eventually acquiring a comprehensive liberal arts education in Helfta. Under its abbess Gertrud von Hackeborn, the Helfta monastery had developed at that time into a center of culture and learning. Together with her older sisters in the community, Mechthild von Hackeborn (the abbess's sister) and the Beguine Mechthild von Magdeburg, Gertrud was instrumental in making Helfta into the focal point of thirteenth-century mysticism.

Gertrud's mystical conversion experience happened when she was twenty-five (on January 27, 1281). From a lukewarm monastic, avid in the pursuit of secular literature, she was turned into an ardent lover who dedicated herself wholeheartedly to a Christ-centered spirituality. Some eight years later, during Holy Week of 1289, Gertrud suddenly felt "violently compelled" by the Spirit to write the memorial of this pivotal experience (to be found in Book II of the *Legatus,* "Herald").

Gertrud never held an important office in her monastery. She spent her life studying theology (influences of Bernard of Clairvaux, William of St. Thierry, Hugh of St. Victor, and others are noticeable) and writing exegetical and spiritual texts in which scriptural and liturgical references abound, and where even nature plays a role. She also collaborated on Mechthild von Hackeborn's work, the *Liber specialis gratiae* (Book of Special Grace). Moreover, Gertrud functioned as a much sought-after pastoral counselor both of her sisters and of lay people. Gertrud died on November 17 at the age of forty-five or forty-six, but details of her death are not known. Gertrud von Helfta has been venerated as a saint first by the Benedictine Order (since 1674) and since 1734 officially by the entire Roman Catholic Church. She was also made the patron saint of the West Indies.

Presumably only a portion of Gertrud's writings has been preserved. Numerous prayer books that were published in many languages since the sixteenth century under the names of St. Gertrud and Mechthild (latest English edition, Philadelphia 1955) are not authentic. The *Legatus divinae pietatis* and her brief *Exercitia spiritualia,* consisting of prayerful meditations based on Scripture and the liturgy, are commonly listed as Gertrud von Helfta's works. The *Legatus* (The Herald of God's Loving-Kindness) consists of five parts: Books 3–5, roughly based on material provided by Gertrud, were composed by a sister in the Helfta community; Book 1 constitutes Gertrud's *vita* written after her death. Only Book 2 was written by Gertrud's own hand. Together with the equally authentic *Spiritual Exercises,* these two texts are unique jewels of medieval mysticism.

Gertrud's work was composed in Latin. An early fifteenth-century Middle High German translation, *ein botte der götlichen miltekeit* (its oldest mansucript is dated 1448) is a deliberately shortened version of Books 3–5 of the *Legatus.* The manuscript tradition of Gertrud von Helfta's work is meager. Of the *Legatus,* eight complete or partial fifteenth-century manuscripts are known. No manuscript is extant of the *Spiritual Exercises.* Its survival was made possible by the first publication of Gertrud von Helfta's Latin work in 1536 by the Carthusian Johannes Lanspergius of Cologne. Since then, most early editors and translators found it necessary to attach to Gertrud's work an initial *apologia* attesting to the orthodoxy of her writings.

To separate Gertrud von Helfta's specific way of thinking from the general mystical and intellectual atmosphere of Helfta, interpretation must focus on the *Exercitia* and her own Book 2 of the *Legatus.* Gertrud's "confessions" show her as profoundly humble. Yet simultaneously she sees all human beings invested with regal dignity through Christ's incarnation. Invisibly stigmatized and mystically united to Christ through an exchange of hearts, Gertrud encounters the divine as a self-confident woman. Her distinctive characteristic is her inner freedom *(libertas cordis),* which leaves her little patience with petty ecclesiastical regulations. The dominant tone of Gertrud von Helfta's work is that of intense joy, as best expressed in her mystical *jubilus (Exercitia).* Her God-language is notable for its imaginative inclusiveness. The theology of the Sacred Heart is to be credited more to the general Helfta community than to Gertrud.

BIBLIOGRAPHY

Barratt, Alexandra. *The Herald of God's Loving-Kindness by Gertrud the Great of Helfta, Books One and Two.* Kalamazoo, Mich.: Cistercian Publications, 1991.

Bynum, Caroline Walker. *Jesus as Mother: Studies in the Spirituality of the High Middle Ages.* Berkeley: University of California Press, 1982, pp. 170–262.

Finnegan, Mary Jeremy. *The Women of Helfta: Scholars and Mystics.* Athens: University of Georgia Press, 1991.

Hart, Mother Columba, trans. *The Exercises of St. Gertrude.* Westminster, Md.: Newman Press, 1956.

Hourlier, Jacques, et al. eds. *Gertrude d'Helfta. Oeuvres spirituelles.* Sources chrétiennes 127, 139, 143, 255, 331. Paris: du Cerf, 1967–1986 [bilingual, Latin-French].

Lewis, Gertrud Jaron. *Bibliographie zur deutschen Frauenmystik des Mittelalters.* Berlin: Erich Schmidt Verlag, 1989, pp.196–223 [comprehensive list of primary and secondary sources].

Lewis, Gertrud Jaron, and Jack Lewis, trans. *Gertrud the Great of Helfta: Spiritual Exercises*. Kalamazoo, Mich.: Cistercian Publications, 1989.

Shank, Lillian Thomas, and John A. Nichols. *Medieval Religious Women*, 2. Kalamazoo, Mich.: Cistercian Publications, 1987, pp. 239–273.

Winkworth, Margaret, trans. *Gertrude of Helfta: The Herald of Divine Love*. New York and Mahwah, N.J.: Paulist Press, 1993 [Books 1 and 2, and partially Book 3].

Gertrud Jaron Lewis

SEE ALSO
Mysticism; Visionary Literature

Gesta Romanorum

An anonymous collection of pious exempla (didactic tales), *The Deeds of the Romans* were in wide circulation from the early fourteenth century in Latin and various vernacular versions, mostly German, but also English and other languages. Scholars are divided about its country of origin, though this is likely to be England or Germany. The title (also *Romanorum historia, History of the Romans*) seeks to lend authority by emphasizing both the antiquity and the spiritual nature of the work.

Each "chapter" contains an exemplary story, generally set in classical Rome, with emperors as principal players in many. This is followed by a moral, invariably introduced by the invocation *carissimi* (dear ones; in the German version, *ir lieben*). Most commonly, the moral is typological, the characters being seen as representative of Christ, Mary, or the Church. Each chapter has a title that occasionally picks up on a motif from the story, more usually from the moral: "On the Sin of Conceit" (De peccato superbie); "On Forbidden Love" (De amore inordinato); "On Perfecting Life" (De perfectione vite); "On the Reign of the Heavens" (De regno celesti), and so on. The narrative style is sober and succinct; the anecdotes may be as short as one hundred words with morals of a similar length, though some of the tales are many times longer. The selection varies widely. In total there are almost three hundred exempla in the *Gesta Romanorum* tradition, though none of the manuscripts contain all of these and the German versions have considerably fewer. Two hundred fifty Latin and forty-four German manuscripts testify to the vast popularity of the work, and its influence on subsequent German literature was immense.

It is the direct source for numerous motifs in sacred and secular literature alike. The poet Lessing's story of the three rings in classic drama, *Nathan the Wise* (1779), became familiar in the German tradition through this medium, as did material of Jewish origin such as the legend of the animals that drank from Noah's vine and gave wine its properties. The *Gesta Romanorum* appeared in a series of printed editions from the late fifteenth century.

Graeme Dunphy

SEE ALSO
Exemplum

Gistum
See Fodrum, Gistum, Servitium.

Glosses, Old High German

The term "Old High German glosses" is understood to signify Old High German words or phrases (including parts of words) entered in Latin manuscripts to translate or explain Latin words or phrases, or make difficult grammatical and syntactical constructions transparent. Written with ink or scratched on the parchment with a stylus in order not to change the appearance of the manuscript (dry point glosses), they are placed between the lines (interlinear), in the margin (marginal), or within the text as a part of its form (context). In some manuscripts the glosses are in code. They vary in frequency from a few isolated glosses to word-for-word glossing, which represents the final step before actual translation. After a text had been glossed, the glosses together with their Latin *lemmata* (head words in a glossary) could be excerpted to form a glossary *(glossae collectae)*. Such glossaries could then be rearranged alphabetically or according to subject matter (class glossaries). Alphabetical or class glossaries may also be derived from Latin-Latin glossaries. There are almost 1,200 glossed manuscripts extant, which contain about 220,000 Old High German glosses, consisting of roughly 21,000 different words (including proper names). Latin and vernacular glossing went on in most monasteries. For vernacular glossing some important centers can be singled out: Echternach, Fulda, Mainz, Würzburg; Murbach, Reichenau, St. Gall; and Benediktbeuren, Freising, Regensburg. The most frequently glossed texts were the Bible; works of some pagan and early Christian poets (Vergil, Horace, Persius, Juvenal,

Prudentius, Arator, Alcimus Avitus, Juvencus); works of some ecclesiastical authors (Augustine, Orosius, Boethius); school texts (Priscian, Euthyches, Donatus); works of ecclesiastical instruction (Gregory the Great) and church law *(Canones)*. The glosses are the richest source material for the history of the German language from the beginning of written records in the eighth century to the early eleventh century. They are equally important for the cultural history of the Carolingian and Ottonian Middle Ages. In addition, they allow us a glimpse into the activities of the medieval classroom.

BIBLIOGRAPHY

Bergmann, Rolf. *Verzeichnis der althochdeutschen und altsächsischen Glossenhandschriften.* Berlin: de Gruyter, 1973.

Hildebrandt, Reiner. *Summarium Heinric.* 3 vols. Berlin: de Gruyter, 1974–1995.

Starck, Tayler, and John Wells. *Althochdeutsches Glossenwörterbuch.* Heidelberg: Winter, 1990 [list of gloss editions 25–35].

Steinmeyer, Elias, and Eduard Sievers. *Die althochdeutschen Glossen.* 5 vols. Berlin: Weidmann, 1879–1922.

Studien zum Althochdeutschen. Akademie der Wissenschaften in Göttingen, vols. 1ff. Göttingen: Vandenhoeck and Ruprecht, 1983ff. [especially students and collaborators of Rudolf Schützeichel, Münster].

Thoma, Herbert. "Glossen, althochdeutsche." *Reallexikon der deutschen Literaturgeschichte,* 2d ed., vol. 1. Berlin: de Gruyter, 1958, pp. 579–589 [with bibliography].

Hartwig Mayer

SEE ALSO

Abrogans; Boethius; Echternach; Freising; Fulda; Latin Language; Mainz; Regensburg; Reichenau; Sankt Gall; Würzburg

Golden Bull

The Golden Bull, or *Bulla Aurea,* named after its gold imperial seal, originated in Emperor Charles IV's desire for a broad imperial reform, hoping for an imperial peace and regulating coinage and tolls. At two different imperial courts, the first on January 10, 1356, in Nuremberg and the second in Metz on December 25, Charles instead promulgated a more narrowly focused reform. The "law book," as Charles called it, largely confined itself to regulating the election of the king and promoting the powers of the new electoral princes.

Concerning the election of the "king of the Romans," since the mid–thirteenth century fewer and fewer princes had been allowed to take part. The Golden Bull formally limited participation to seven electoral princes (*Kurfürsten),* specifically the three archbishops of Mainz, Cologne, and Trier, the king of Bohemia, the duke of Saxony, the margrave of Brandenburg, and the count Palatine by the Rhine. All other princes and prelates, as well as the pope, were excluded from direct collaboration. Proper procedures for an election were carefully spelled out. And a simple majority of four votes was sufficient for succession. The duly elected king of the Romans had the explicit right to become emperor of the Romans, to be crowned by the pope in Rome. Any papal rights to approve the candidate or to become regent or vicar of the empire during a vacancy were ignored.

Second, the Golden Bull codified many privileges of the seven electoral princes, who as "pillars" of the empire took on a new status as a "college" above the estates of the clergy, nobility, and townspeople. They were to meet yearly to advise the emperor (although that provision did not really succeed in practice). To prevent any possible trouble about dividing up electoral votes, their territories were made indivisible by inheritance. If an electoral dynasty died out, its vote and territory escheated, i.e., fell back to the king. Electoral princes gained full rights to capital justice as well as to the regalia or control of local mining, tolls, coinage, and the supervision of Jews. The law tried to constrain the growing power of city governments, which were forbidden to readily accept new citizens or to make alliances with one another against the princes. Seven copies of the document survive, preserved by several of the electoral princes, and by the cities of Frankfurt and Nuremberg. The Golden Bull can be considered as the foundational constitutional document of the Holy Roman Empire from the late Middle Ages to its end in 1806. While it technically ended the legal possibility of a hereditary kingdom, many emperors, like Charles IV himself, were later able to get their sons elected kings to succeed them through the control of electoral votes and influence on the electors. And while the Golden Bull strengthened the dominance of the electoral princes, other magnates soon sought similar rights.

BIBLIOGRAPHY

Fritz, Wolfgang D., ed. *Die Goldene Bulle Kaiser Karls IV. vom Jahre 1356.* Monumenta Germaniae Historica.

Fontes iuris in usum scholarum 11. Weimar: Hermann Böhlaus Nachfolger, 1972.

Mitteis, Heinrich. *Die Deutsche Königswahl*, 2d ed. 1944, rpt., Darmstadt: Wissenschaftliche Buchgesellschaft, 1981.

Moraw, Peter. *Von offener Verfassung zu gestalteter Verdichtung: Das Reich im späten Mittelalter 1250–1490*. Propyläen-Studienausgabe. Frankfurt am Main: Propyläen, 1989.

Müller, Konrad, trans. *Die Goldene Bulle Kaiser Karls IV. vom Jahre 1356.* Quellen zur neueren Geschichte 25. 2d ed. Bern: Lang, 1964.

Zeumer, Karl. *Die Goldene Bulle Kaiser Karls IV,* 2 vols. *Quellen und Studien zur Verfassungsgeschichte des deutschen Reiches in Mittelalter und Neuzeit,* vol. 2. Weimar: Hermann Böhlaus Nachfolger, 1908.

Brian A. Pavlac

SEE ALSO

Charles IV; Cologne, History; Mainz; Trier

Goslar

The economic importance of Goslar (Lower Saxony) was based on the silver deposits in the nearby Harz Mountains that were exploited from 968. As a consequence, Emperor Henry II erected in the years 1005–1015 the palatine complex, which was subsequently rebuilt under his successors of the Salian dynasty. Its center forms the palace hall, largely reconstructed in 1868–1879, flanked on either side by the double-storied chapels dedicated to St. Ulrich and Our Lady (now demolished), both of which displayed Byzantine elements in their architectural scheme. To the west of the palatine complex, the Romanesque collegiate church of St. Simeon and St. Jude, erected in 1047–1050 and demolished in 1819, served as the imperial court church. Only its northern porch, which now houses the imperial throne, has survived.

The imperial palatine complex was surrounded at a distance by monastic units. The church at Georgenberg, demolished for military reasons in 1527 but known through archaeological evidence, was a copy of Charlemagne's celebrated palatine chapel at Aachen. North of the town, the Augustinian monastery of Reichenberg was founded in 1117, and the church, today a ruin, was erected following the scheme of Hirsau. The parish church of Frankenberg became the western termination of the medieval town. After the foundation of an Augustinian nunnery, the original basilica with its western gallery for the territorial lord was vaulted. The church of St. Stephan in the eastern part of the town, mentioned for the first time in 1142, was also originally a Romanesque basilica; it was rebuilt after a fire in 1728. At the northern margins of the town, and connected to one of the town gates, the church of the Benedictine nunnery Neuwerk was founded circa 1175 by the imperial provost Volkmar of Wildenstein. Originally planned with groin vaults, the church, a cruciform basilica, was finally completed with heavy rib vaults.

At the center of the town is the market with the town hall and the main parish church of St. Cosmas and St. Damian, which was mentioned as *ecclesia forensis* (market church) in 1151. Like the monastic churches of the town, this church is a cruciform basilica that was vaulted in the thirteenth century.

In the late Middle Ages, Goslar acquired the status of an imperial city and developed its own territory. Around 1500, the renewed wealth is reflected in rebuilding projects at the churches and the fortification. Major reconstructions in late Gothic forms are still to be seen at the Frankenberg church and at St. Jacobi. The prestigious project of rebuilding the main parish church according to plans from Strasbourg, however, never materialized; its already constructed late Gothic south wall was finally demolished in the nineteenth century. The town hall, a double-storied building with its open market hall on the ground floor and an adjoining chapel, was erected as the western front of the market. Other monuments of this time are the houses of several guilds, for example, the Kaiserworth, erected in 1494 on south side of the market. The civic architecture of this time displays a richly decorated timber construction.

The town hall preserves the Goslar Evangeliary (or gospel lectionary), a manuscript in the Byzantine manner of the so-called *Zackenstil* (zigzag style) from the mid–thirteenth century.

BIBLIOGRAPHY

Das Goslarer Evangeliar, ed. Renate Kroos. Codices selecti 92. Graz: Akademische Druck- und Verlagsanstalt, 1991.

Frontzek, Wolfgang, Torsten Mennert, and Martin Möhle. *Goslarer Kaiserhaus: Eine baugeschichtliche Untersuchung.* Goslarer Fundus 2. Hildesheim: Olms, 1996.

Goslar: Bergstadt—Kaiserstadt in Geschichte und Kunst, ed. Frank Steigerwald. Schriftenreihe der Kommission für Niedersächsische Bau- und Kunstgeschichte bei der

Braunschweigischen Wissenschaftlichen Gesellschaft 6. Göttingen: Göltze, 1993.

von Behr, A., and U. Hölscher. *Die Kunstdenkmäler der Provinz Hannover 2–3: Stadt Goslar,* ed. Carl Wolff. Hanover: Selbstverlag der Provinzialverwaltung, 1901.

Hans J. Böker

SEE ALSO

Aachen; Gothic Art and Architecture; Henry II, Art; Hirsau; Ottonian Art and Architecture; Romanesque Art and Architecture; Strasbourg

Gothic Art and Architecture

[This entry includes fourteen subentries:

Introduction
Architecture
Ivories
Manuscript Painting
Metalwork
Panel Painting
Sculpture, Introduction
Sculpture, Devotional Images
Sculpture, Early Altarpieces
Sculpture, Interior Programs
Sculpture, Portal Programs
Sculpture, Tombs
Stained Glass
Textiles]

Introduction

Originally a derogatory term used to describe northern European architecture made before the fifteenth century, the word *Gothic* first appears in the works of the art historian Giorgio Vasari (1511–1574) and other humanist writers of the Italian Renaissance. In these writings architecture like that of Milan Cathedral is denigrated as the work of the Goths, the invaders who destroyed ancient Rome and the standards of classical art, which were being revived by Italian architects. These barbarian Gothic invaders were equated with the Germans by Vasari and other Italian Renaissance writers.

Perhaps because of this early association of the Gothic with Germany, German writers have long identified the Gothic as a particularly German style. As early as the sixteenth century, Strasbourg Cathedral was described as representing the high cultural level of the German people and was referred to as the eighth wonder of the world. By

the twentieth century even German popular culture perceived some works of German Gothic art, such as the figure of Uta from Naumburg (memorialized with her husband, Ekkehard II, in a statue as cathedral founder), as embodiments of the German national spirit.

Although the Gothic style was identified with Germanic invaders by Renaissance writers, the term has always described an art and architecture actually developed in France in the twelfth and thirteenth centuries. As the term *Gothic* was refined in art historical usage, French art and architecture became the standard for Gothic stylistic development. Thus its adaptation to other countries has always been somewhat problematic. German artworks do not always follow normative Gothic (i.e., French) development. This was especially the case during the twelfth and thirteenth centuries, when Germany developed independent artistic styles such as the *Zackenstil* (jagged style), and many German works of sculpture and architecture show combinations of Romanesque and Gothic elements, leaving art historians uncertain how to classify them.

BIBLIOGRAPHY

Brough, Sonia. *The Goths and the Concepts of Gothic in Germany from 1500–1700.* Frankfurt am Main: Peter Lang, 1985.

Ullrich, Wolfgang. *Uta von Naumburg: Eine deutsche Ikone.* Berlin: Verlag Klaus Wagenbach, 1998.

Susan L. Ward

SEE ALSO

Gothic Art and Architecture, Late; Naumburg; Romanesque Art and Architecture; Strasbourg

Architecture

As the Gothic style spread from northern France in the late twelfth century, it assumed different forms, creating myriad styles rather than one universalizing ideal. Early German Gothic, i.e., Gothic in German-speaking lands, encompasses various building types and forms, in which Romanesque values were often retained. Elements such as pointed arches, ribbed vaults, and linear articulation emphasizing verticality, thinness, and openness ran counter to the Romanesque of the cathedrals at Speyer, Mainz, and Worms and the hall at Goslar, where the power and continuity of imperial traditions were expressed in monumental volumes, blocky solidity, and solid wall planes. Gothic elements occurred first in the western areas of Germany (Limburg an der Lahn, Cologne, Bonn) and in the restrained architecture of the Cistercians (Maulbronn, Lilienfeld). By the second quarter of the thirteenth century, the luminous, diaphanous work of French Gothic began to be imported wholesale, first in what is termed "High Gothic" (Liebfrauenkirche, Trier; St. Elizabeth, Marburg), then in the rayonnant (Strasbourg and Cologne Cathedrals). German masons were sent to study the latest buildings in France, referred to as *opus francigenum* (ca. 1290, *Chronicle* of Burchard von Hall, cited in Frisch 1971: 56), or learned in cathedral building workshops. By the fourteenth century, however, German master masons had developed an inventive Gothic vocabulary far beyond French precedents. But German Gothic was never a unified style; the many regional variations have been grouped together historiographically mostly for nationalistic reasons, whereas in the Middle Ages connections were produced through relationships of geography, patronage, politics, and economics.

Beginnings of Gothic. Around 1200 on the Lower Rhine, Gothic elements appeared in the upper stories of buildings begun as Romanesque. In Cologne, responding to northeastern French Gothic forms, Gross St. Martin incorporated linear shafts and ribbed vaults, while St. Gereon (1219–1227) included pointed arches, thin double-wall construction, tracery, and flying buttresses. At the time of their expansion into Germany, the Cistercians built first in Romanesque style but often included pointed arches and ribbed vaults, disseminating them throughout Europe to earn the historians' appellation "missionaries of Gothic." By the thirteenth century, they adopted details from the Gothic of northeastern France, while retaining their order's ground plans and the sculptural roundedness and mural surfaces of early German Gothic.

The chapel of St. Michael's, Ebrach (ca. 1200), as well as at Maulbronn the south walk of the cloister (ca. 1220–1230), the entrance porch or *Paradies* (ca. 1210–1220), and the monks' refectory (ca. 1220) used trefoil arches, diagonally planted supports, and banded shafts *en délit* (detached colonnettes, or small columns) inspired by northeastern French practice from the regions of Noyon and Soissons. The refectory of Maulbronn is especially open with its slender columns and tall lancets. At Lilienfeld the ambulatory is impressively Gothic, perhaps responding to requirements of its patron, Margrave Leopold VI.

Early Cathedral and Great Church Gothic. While German cathedrals were rebuilt slowly in the thirteenth century, builders produced a "gothicized" Romanesque hybrid, retaining a ceremonially weighty cathedral architecture. Two of the most powerful cathedrals are Bamberg (1220s–1230s, perhaps begun circa 1212), erected under Bishop Ekbert of Andechs-Meranien (1203–1237), and Naumburg, with blocky piers, mural surfaces, and ribbed vaults spanning the double bays of Romanesque Italo-German design. After midcentury, openwork towers modeled on those of Laon were added to both cathedrals, their Gothic airiness appropriate for high appendages. With Gothic detailing, the south transept arm of Strasbourg (ca. 1230–1240) is similarly powerful.

Begun in 1209, the choir of Magdeburg Cathedral reveals an idiosyncratic adaptation. It becomes increasingly Gothic as the elevation rises, using thin angle shafts, crocket capitals, and five-part ribbed vaults with dogtooth ornament, all derived form northeastern France. As several of these elements occur at Maulbronn, the same designer has been suggested. Mixed with reused materials, some previously donated by Otto the Great, this architecture manifests rich, sculptural power. However ungainly by French standards, it emphasizes the meaning of its venerable past at the expense of a simple style-consciousness. German Gothic means more than French-derived forms adopted for their own sake.

During the first quarter of the thirteenth century several Rhenish churches were built, drawing on Gothic architecture from nearby regions. St. Georg at Limburg an der Lahn (1213–1235) incorporated flying buttresses and four stories, inspired principally by Laon Cathedral, but its seven-tower grouping also acknowledged regional building as at Neuss and Gross St. Martin in Cologne; it thus demonstrates the difficulty of separating related traditions. The nave of the Münster at Bonn (upper stories, ca. 1220–1230) drew from the cathedrals of Lausanne (ca. 1190–1230) and Geneva (late 12th c.) for its double-wall skeletalization and emphasis on width.

High Gothic. By circa 1230, German plasticity and mural surfaces yielded to the lightness of French style, embraced in the Liebfrauenkirche (Church of the Virgin) at Trier (ca. 1227–1233) and St. Elizabeth's at Marburg (1235–1283). Perhaps designed by one master using the same foot-measure, both show knowledge of Reims work and Gothic verticality. The plan of Trier, however, responds to the diagonally planted chapels of Braine, extended on all four sides to create a centralized structure that, here as elsewhere, signifies the dedication to Mary. Along with proportions based on the square (design *ad quadratum*), the plan represents an ideal form. The beautiful unity of the Liebfrauenkirche was echoed at

Marburg, Church of St. Elizabeth, interior, view to east. *Photograph: Virginia Jansen*

midcentury in the west choir of Naumburg, famous for its moving founders' statues placed like the apostles at the Sainte-Chapelle, Paris.

The church of St. Elizabeth at Marburg was erected over her grave in her hospital chapel. Built by the Order of Teutonic Knights, involving both papal and imperial interests, it influenced a series of dynastic churches in German as well as Polish, Bohemian, and Hungarian regions. The design combined regional elements of a trefoil (like a three-pointed leaf, or clover) ground plan and hall church type with details from Reims and Cambrai to produce a light-filled structure.

Rayonnant Gothic. By 1240, French rayonnant style transformed Gothic architecture, intensified by prestigious association with the French monarch Louis IX. Its refinement, linear delicacy, and greater integration eradicated German massing, laying the ground for the dra-

matic changes of late Gotic. The style quickly spread to Metz and Strasbourg (naves ca. 1235–1275). The width of Strasbourg nave, supported on the earlier Romanesque foundations, reflects a spatial majesty, but the design follows the latest fashion from Paris, Saint-Denis, Troyes, and Auxerre. The same design—without triforium—appears later in the naves of the Münster at Freiburg and the church of St. Lorenz in Nuremberg.

With the cathedral of Cologne (begun 1248; nave and towers unfinished until the nineteenth century), German masons demonstrated such full command of the rayonnant style that may scholars regard Cologne as a French cathedral built on German land and associated its French forms with the archbishop's connections to the French king and political opposition to the deposed Emperor Frederick II. The ground plan and elevation with full upper glazing follow Amiens and Beauvais, but the statues adossed to columns in the choir and other elements recall Parisian work, particularly the Sainte-Chapelle. Like it, the dematerialized structure serves equally as a dazzling housing for the reliquary of the Three Magi and as a temple of episcopal power. Narrow proportions and great height create staggering verticality, while pinnacles and tracery fragment surfaces throughout. Nearby Cistercian Altenberg also reveals a thorough knowledge of both Cologne and French buildings, such as Tours and Royaumont, where the burials of members of the French royal house served as a model for Alternberg's patrons, the counts of Berg. Likewise the choir of Regensburg Cathedral (1273–ca. 1310) reflects knowledge of French architecture.

Soon German designs outpaced their French models. The west facade of Strasbourg Cathedral (ca. 1277), partly designed by Erwin of Steinbach, is covered in openwork paneling composed of brittle tracery, far surpassing the rayonnant design originally planned (drawing ca. 1265), based on the transept facades of Notre-Dame, Paris. The layered effects of multiple screening emphasize a design freedom fully developed in late Gothic architecture. Related are the west facade of Cologne (begun mid–14th c.) and the south wall of the nave at St. Katherine's, Oppenheim (ca. 1317–1328).

Other Gothic Architectures. During this time new religious orders of the mendicant friars vowed poverty, preached to the growing urban population, and built plain structures with unarticulated walls and simple tracery windows. Naves followed either the Cistercian two-story elevation, as in the Dominican church at Regensburg (ca. 1270s, choir begun ca. 1245) and the Minorite

Altenberg, east end, view from southeast. *Photograph: Virginia Jansen*

spective ignores many instances in France, Spain, and Italy. Its identification with town parish churches is also incorrect, given that both Romanesque cathedrals, as for example at Paderborn, and Gothic cathedrals exist in the hall church form. In northwestern Germany, the earliest Gothic example is the cathedral of Minden (1267–1290). With three square bays typical of Westphalian Romanesque, the nave displays Gothic openness and architectural details. At Verden (1272–1313) the hall format was extended to the choir, a solution exploited in the late Gothic period. The hall choir of Cistercian Heiligenkreuz, Austria (ca. 1288–1295), employs the traditional square format of three bays updated with rayonnant tracery, whereas the continuously molded piers beckon toward Late Gothic.

The Marienkirche (Church of St. Mary) at Lübeck (ca. 1260–1330) emulated cathedral architecture in brick *(Backsteingotik)* with its tall, vaulted volumes, flying buttresses, ambulatory with chapels, and two-towered west facade (begun 1304), which had the tallest towers completed in the Middle Ages. With its stunning scale and site at the market square, whose public scribes gave their name to the Briefkapelle (ca. 1310) at the southwest corner of the church, the Marienkirche symbolized this leading city of the Hanseatic League. Although brick forms are generally simplified, its choir piers, moldings, and vaulting shafts copied the complicated profiles of rayonnant stonework enhanced by colored glazed bricks. The combination of diagonally placed chapels and ambulatory may be related to Quimper Cathedral (Brittany, ca. 1239) and the Vrouwkerk (Church of the Virgin) in the abbey of Sint Pieter in Ghent (ca. 1250), both cities like Lübeck with distant trading connections. The progeny of Lübeck's Marienkirche include the nearby Cistercian abbey of Doberan, Schwerin Cathedral, and the church of St. Nikolai in Stralsund (all before 1300), as well as the Marienkirche in Rostock, St. Nikolai in Wismar, and the Marienkirche in Stralsund. The immense scale and tall towers of these great brick churches attest to the wealth, power, and civic pride of their merchant communities, indicative of major social changes in the late thirteenth and fourteenth centuries. These forces continued to drive the most ambitious German building projects in the subsequent late Gothic period.

(Franciscan) church at Cologne (ca. 1248), or the Italian open two-story timber-roofed type. The Franciscan church at Freiburg im Breisgau (begun ca. 1280–1300) and the Dominican church at Colmar (nave, ca. 1325) exemplify this latter type. The unvaulted nave of the Dominican church at Gebweiler (ca. 1306) is even simpler—with plain walls, cylindrical piers, no bay division nor capitals. Without large towers or a transept, the most significant external features in friars' churches are the high gable roof and tall windows.

German builders also began to construct Gothic hall churches, in which the aisles are as tall as the central nave. The hall church is often seen to typify German Gothic as distinguished from the basilica form of French cathedrals; it became perhaps the most significant type in late Gothic German architecture. It is inaccurate to understand the type as native, however, even in the Romanesque examples of Westphalia and Bavaria; such a nationalistic per-

BIBLIOGRAPHY

Baum, Julius, and Helga Schmidt-Glassner, photographer. *German Cathedrals.* London: Thames and Hudson, 1956.

Binding, Günther. *High Gothic: The Age of the Great Cathedrals.* Taschen's World Architecture. Cologne: Taschen, 1999.

Bony, Jean. *French Gothic Architecture of the 12th and 13th Centuries.* Berkeley: University of California Press, 1983.

Branner, Robert. *St. Louis and the Court Style in Gothic Architecture.* London: Zwemmer, 1965.

Crossley, Paul. "The Architecture of Queenship," in *Queens and Queenship in Medieval Europe,* ed. Anne J. Duggan. Proceedings of a Conference held at King's College, London, April 1995. Woodbridge, Suffolk: Boydell Press, 1997, pp. 263–287.

Frankl, Paul. *Gothic Architecture,* trans. Dieter Pevsner. Pelican History of Art. Baltimore: Penguin, 1962.

Frisch, Teresa G. *Gothic Art 1140–c. 1450.* 1971. Medieval Academy Reprints for Teaching. Toronto: University of Toronto Press in association with the Medieval Academy of America, 1987.

Gall, Ernst. *Cathedrals and Abbey Churches of the Rhine,* trans. And adapted by Olive Cook. London: Thames and Hudson, 1963.

Götz, Wolfgang. *Zentralbau und Zentralbautendenz in der gotischen Architektur.* Berlin: Mann, 1968.

Nussbaum, Norbert. *German Gothic Church Architecture.* New Haven: Yale University Press, 2000.

Wilson, Christopher. *The Gothic Cathedral: The Architecture of the Great Church 1130–1530.* London: Thames and Hudson, 1990.

Virginia Jansen

SEE ALSO

Bamberg; Bonn; Cistercian Art and Architecture; Cologne, Art; Erwin von Steinbach; Esslingen am Neckar; Franciscan Art and Architecture; Freiburg; Goslar; Heiligenkreuz; Limburg an der Lahn; Lübeck; Magdeburg; Mainz; Marburg; Maulbronn; Metz; Minden; Möhlhausen; Naumburg; Nuremberg; Otto I; Paderborn; Regensburg; Romanesque Art and Architecture; Rostock; Rothenburg ob der Tauber; Schwerin; Speyer; Stralsund; Strasbourg; Trier; Wismar; Worms

Ivories

Fine ivory carvings were created in Germany this period, but they are difficult to localize and workshops remain undocumented, although certainly a production center existed at Cologne. Style and iconography were long believed to originate in Paris, where foreign artisans trained. But outsiders imitated French style, and Parisian carvers worked abroad. Rapid diffusion of portable ivory goods and ideas in the early thirteenth century increased international similarities.

The scholar Koechlin labeled almost all ivories Parisian, neither correlating types nor comparing to other media. Gaborit-Chopin saw affinities among various Parisian carvings and similar relationships in the Rhineland. Little, finally, studied similarities with metalwork and monumental sculpture, strengthening discernment of German products.

Some wood and ivory carvings were known products of metal workshops, and some goldsmiths carved ivory. Romanesque-era carving workshops in Cologne continued into the mid–thirteenth century, but Gothic-era shops and markets changed, as in Paris, with less independent shops and workers.

Secular and religious ivories are related to the circa 1300 wooden choir stalls at Cologne Cathedral and to local painting, stained glass, and enamels. Diptychs of Christ and the Virgin (New York, Metropolitan Museum of Art) and of St. Martin (Cleveland Museum of Art) are related to mid-fourteenth-century Cologne sculpture. A fourteenth-century Virgin and Child type bears physical characteristics of coeval Cologne citizens: broad forehead, wide-set eyes, small mouth, and double chin.

Certain masters are named for cities now housing their works rather than their work sites. The master of Kremsmünster carved crowded, high-contrast compositions linked to monumental sculpture in Mainz from circa 1400. The Berlin master (1350–1375) created works of mannered elegance, comparable to Cologne painting.

Elegant French and German Gothic Madonnas gradually become more aristocratic and maternal, like monumental Virgins at St. Denis and Sainte-Chapelle. While ivories were once generally believed to reflect earlier monumental sculpture, neither is surely first, nor is either more expressive, grand, refined, or original.

By 1300, shallower carving, schematization, and iconographic uniformity are general rather than local trends. By 1350, a distinctive Rhenish type—with ovoid head, high forehead, pointed chin, undulating drapery, and sinuous line—relates to regional sculpture, giving way by 1400 to a newly homogenized international style, reflecting links between European courts and cities.

German iconography and motifs spread throughout Europe. Revered relics of the Magi in Cologne inspired images of the Three Kings wearing gloves. Two passion motifs from Rhenish mystical writings—Mary helping Christ carry the cross and blood issuing from the crucified Christ's side becoming a sword that pierces Mary's heart—quickly circulated through European monasteries. Later medieval items for personal devotion—statues, plaques, diptychs, and booklets—were also used for commemorative rites at cult centers. Themes derived from Bible stories, often arranged in registers like portal sculpture.

Chivalric motifs, for example, scenes from the story of Parzival, adorned luxury goods like tablets and mirror backs, were common in the late Gothic era. They were also known earlier, however, as a Tristan casket from about 1200 in the British Museum attests. Other secular items include combs, writing tablets, and games, with themes of romance, the hunt, and lyric poetry.

BIBLIOGRAPHY

Bänsch, Birgit. "Serienproduktion in Beinschnitzerei," in *Ornamenta Ecclesiae: Kunst und Künstler der Romanik in Köln,* ed. Anton Legner. Cologne: Schnütgen-Museum, 1985, vol. 2, p. 414.

Barnet, Peter, ed. *Images in Ivory: Precious Objects of the Gothic Age.* Princeton, N.J.: Princeton University Press, 1997.

Euw, Anton von. "Elfenbeinarbeiten des 9. bis 12. Jahrhunderts," in *Rhein und Maas: Kunst und Kultur 800–1400.* 2 vols. Cologne: Schnütgen-Museum, 1972–1973, vol. 2, pp. 377–386.

Gaborit-Chopin, Danielle. *Ivoires du moyen âge.* Fribourg: Office du Livre, 1978.

Koechlin, Raymond. *Les Ivoires gothiques français.* 3 vols. Paris: A. Picard, 1924.

Little, Charles T. "Ivoires et art gothique." *Revue de l'art* 46 (1979): 58–67.

———. "Gothic Ivory Carving in Germany," in *Images in Ivory: Precious Objects of the Gothic Age,* ed. Peter Barnet. Princeton, N.J.: Princeton University Press, 1997, pp. 80–93.

Niehoff, Franz. "Zur Kölner Werkstatt der gestichelten Walrossschnitzerein" in *Ornamenta Ecclesiae: Kunst und Kultur 800–1400.* Cologne: Schnütgen-Museum, 1972, vol. 2, pp. 428–432.

Randall, Richard H., Jr. *The Golden Age of Ivory: Gothic Carvings in North American Collections.* New York: Hudson Hills Press, 1993.

St. Aubyn, Fiona, ed. *Ivory: An International History and Illustrated Survey.* New York: Harry N. Abrams, 1987.
                                                    Rita Tekippe

SEE ALSO

Cologne, Art; Gottfried von Straßburg, *Tristan,* Illustrations; Mainz; Romanesque Art and Architecture; Wolfram von Eschenbach, *Parzival,* Illustrations

Manuscript Painting

Some scholars identify German painting of the thirteenth century as Gothic only in works of the later part of the century that display identifiably French characteristics related to Parisian court style. But earlier works, of the mid-century, begin to display the influence of sculpture: bodies are more solid and massive with a new plasticity, or *Körperlichkeit,* a characteristic that may also distinguish a change from Romanesque to Gothic. Before this time German painting style was more influenced by Byzantine features, which underlay the sharply pointed and occasionally zigzag lines of the *Zackenstil,* a transitional style between Romanesque and Gothic.

Gradual from Cloister Wettingen (Aarau, Kantonsbibliothek, MsWettFm 1, fol. 17v). *Photograph: Joan A. Holladay*

This Gothic plasticity of human forms appeared in all painting media and can be seen earliest along the Rhine in Cologne, as in the wall painting of the octagon at St. Gereon and in the Aschaffenburg Gospels likely made in Mainz (Aschaffenburg, Hofbibliothek, Ms. no. 13); it later appears to the east, as, for example, in the stained glass at Naumburg. Direct relations of the Mainz manuscript and Naumburg glass to the sculptural workshop that produced the founder figures at Naumburg support the influence of Gothic sculptural forms. By the late thirteenth century the illuminations of Johannes von Valkenburg display the elegant courtly forms that had originated in Paris but that were also reflected in court art in England and elsewhere.

By circa 1300, a number of distinctive regional styles had developed, and works from Cologne, Regensburg, and Constance are easily distinguished from one another. While secular ateliers had largely replaced the monastic scriptoria where book production had been localized up through the thirteenth century, some cloisters, including women's houses, continued producing illuminated manuscripts for their own use, for gifts, and perhaps for sale. An inscription in a gradual from 1300 (Osnabrück, Domschatz) gives the "virgin" Gysela von Kerzenbroeck, probably a nun at the Cistercian cloister Rulle in Westphalia, credit for writing, illuminating, notating, and decorating the book "with golden letters and beautiful images." In the middle of the fourteenth century, Loppa de Speculo, a nun at the Franciscan convent of St. Klara in Cologne, wrote and decorated an antiphonary (Stockholm, Royal Library, no. A172) and wrote and notated another (Cologne, Wallraf-Richartz Museum, 23 fragments), which was decorated by several hands.

The production of both lay and monastic workshops concentrated on books for the mass—graduals, missals, antiphonaries, and lectionaries—and for private devotions—psalters and prayerbooks. Increasingly, however, new secular book types also appeared. Isolated examples in the thirteenth century—the Berlin *Eneide* (Staatsbibliothek Preussischer Kulturbesitz, Ms. 282) and the Munich *Tristan* (Bayerische Staatsbibliothek, Cgm. No. 51) and *Parzival* (Bayerische Staatsbibliothek, Cgm. No. 19)—are followed by a veritable explosion in the numbers of secular texts after about 1300, suggesting new interests of readers and patrons. Manuscript collections of love poems organized by author *(Liederhandschriften)* were assembled and illuminated in Constance and Zurich; one or more workshops in Zurich seem to have specialized in the production of *Weltchronik* (world

chronicle) manuscripts. Likewise, Regensburg in the early fourteenth century may have been a center for the production of copies of Thomasîn von Zerklaere's *Der Welsche Gast.*

As in more traditional, religious book types, the decorative program of these new books as a whole helped to orient readers to their place within the text. Illuminations might signal especially important text passages, while a spectrum of initials of different sizes and levels of decoration highlight major and minor text divisions. Although the decoration of religious manuscripts tended to follow set patterns, each of these new book types presented special problems to the manuscript's designer or illuminator, and a wide variety of solutions in the placement and types of images is visible. The colored drawings illustrating the *Sachsenspiegel* (Law of the Saxons), for example, occupy their own column alongside the text, while the full-page, painted author portraits of the *Liederhandschriften* precede each author's oeuvre. Framed images illustrating the *Weltchronik* or the *Willehalm* are inserted into the text column; the gold leaf that is so ubiquitous in images and initials in high-quality religious manuscripts appears only in these texts and others concerned with the history of salvation and the related fields of imperial history and law.

BIBLIOGRAPHY

Belting, Hans. "Zwischen Gotik und Byzanz: Gedanken zur Geschichte der sächsischen Buchmalerei im 13. Jahrhundert." *Zeitschrift für Kunstgeschichte* 41 (1978): 217–257.

Holladay, Joan A. "Some Arguments for a Wider View of Cologne Book Painting in the Early 14th Century." *Georges-Bloch-Jahrbuch des Kunstgeschichtliches Seminars der Universität Zürich* 4 (1997): 5–21.

Kaufmann, Virginia Roehrig. "Iconographic Study of the Christological Cycle of the Miniatures of the Aschaffenburg Golden Gospels (Aschaffenburg, Hofbibliothek Ms. 13)." Ph.D. diss., Columbia University, 1986.

Mark, Claudia Marchitiello. "Manuscript Illumination in Metz in the Fourteenth Century: Books of Hours, Workshops, and Personal Devotion." Ph.D. diss., Princeton University, 1991.

Nordenfalk, Carl. "Die deutschen Miniaturen des 13. Jahrhunderts." *Acta Archaeologica* (1937): 251–266.

Oliver, Judith. "The Mosan Origins of Johannes von Valkenburg." *Wallraf-Richartz-Jahrbuch* 40 (1978): 23–37.

————. "The French Gothic Style in Cologne: Manuscripts before Johannes von Valkenburg," in *Opstelleln voor Dr. Jan Deschamps ter Gelegenheid van zijn zeventigste Verjaardag,* ed. E. Cockx-Indestege and F. Hendrickx. Miscellanea Neerlandica 1. Louvain: Peeters, 1987, pp. 381–396.

————. "Worship of the Word: Some Gothic *Nonnenbücher* in their Devotional Context," in *Women and the Book: Assessing the Visual Evidence,* ed. Jane Taylor and Lesley Smith. London: British Library and Toronto: University of Toronto Press, 1996, pp. 106–122.

Ott, Norbert. "Typen der Weltchronik-Ikonographie: Bemerkungen zu Illustration, Anspruch und Gebrauchssituation volkssprachlicher Chronistik aus überlieferungsgeschichtlicher Sicht." *Jahrbuch der Oswald von Wolkenstein Gesellschaft* 1 (1980–1981): 29–55.

Regensburger Buchmalerei: Von frühkarolingischer Zeit bis zum Ausgang des Mittelalters, ed. Florentine Mütherich and Karl Dachs. Ausstellungskataloge der Bayerische Staatsbibliothek 39. Munich: Prestel, 1987.

Swarzenski, Hanns. *Die lateinischen illuminierten Handschriften des 13. Jahrhunderts in den Ländern an Rhein, Main und Donau.* Denkmäler deutscher Kunst. Berlin: Deutscher Verein für Kunstwissenschaft, 1936.

Virginia Roehrig Kaufmann and Joan A. Holladay

SEE ALSO

Metalwork

In the thirteenth century, production of metalwork shifted from the renowned monastic workshops of the twelfth century to goldsmithing shops in flourishing towns where there was an increasing demand for liturgical items. Centers of production were primarily in the Upper Rhine region—Westphalia, Lower Saxony, and north Germany, with Cologne continuing as a leading city in the craft. The ranks of patronage, previously composed of imperial rulers, nobility, and clergy, were swelled by new groups: provincial rulers, patrician families, civic fraternities, and even private individuals. In this secular context guilds controlled the education of the apprentice goldsmith, the conditions by which a craftsman could become a master, and the quality of manufacture; the earliest surviving guild records are from Strasbourg (1363). The triple-aisled house shrine, based firmly on twelfth-century traditions, as well as other liturgical objects common to the Romanesque period—anthropomorphic arm and head reliquaries, chalices, crosses, and book covers—continued to be made.

Increasingly intimate spiritual practices and the emphasis on the transubstantive (consecrated) host led to the development of inventive forms of reliquaries, particularly the Gothic pointed spire, and monstrances (procession items to display the host) embellished with such architectural motifs as pointed arches, pier buttresses,

Reliquary bust of St. Pantalus from treasury of Basel cathedral (Basel, Historisches Museum). *Photograph: Joan A. Holladay*

pinnacles, and finials. These forms reflected stylistic developments in the architecture of the Île-de-France. The fourteenth century saw elaborate innovations in enameling techniques, metal etching, and cast silver decoration, producing an increasingly elegant and precious illusion of depth painted in glittering light and shadow, replacing the Romanesque preference for repoussée copperwork and decorative gems. Figure styles reflected a newly expressive naturalism, with fully rounded forms and soft, fluid drapery. From the fourteenth century the demand for secular gold and silverwork increased, and goldsmiths were required to use an identifying town mark. In the mid–to late fifteenth century, goldsmiths began to add their own maker's mark. During the late Gothic period the production of secular goldsmiths' work increased, and goldsmiths received large commissions from town councils for municipal treasuries.

BIBLIOGRAPHY

Fritz, J. F. *Goldschmiedekunst der Gotik in Mitteleuropa.* Munich: Beck, 1982.

Möbius, Frederick, and Helga Sciurie. *Geschichte der deutschen Kunst 1200–1350.* Leipzig: E. A. Seemann, 1989, pp. 379–391.

Rhein und Maas: Kunst und Kultur 800–1400, ed. Anton Legner. 2 vols. Cologne: Schnütgen—Museum, 1972–1973.

M. Rebecca Leuchak

SEE ALSO

Cologne, Art; Metalworking; Nicolaus of Verdun; Romanesque Art and Architecture—Metalwork; Strasbourg

Panel Painting

Although religious images painted on wooden panels constitute one of the leading art forms of the Renaissance in northern Europe, few examples remain to mark the mid-thirteenth-century transition from the late Romanesque to the Gothic in this medium. Of these, some are liturgical objects. Others adhere closely to types found in Italy. The Wimpassing Crucifix (now destroyed), probably made by an artist from Salzburg, was based on Italian painted crucifixes, and its commission was associated with the activity of Franciscans north of the Alps. The style of this painted crucifix resembles that of manuscripts produced in the Würzburg region of Germany in the 1260s. Such correspondence between the styles of illuminated manuscripts, wall paintings, and painted altar-

Wimpassing Crucifix, destroyed. *Photograph: Kunsthistorisches Museum, Vienna*

pieces is found in the local schools throughout Central Europe. Another example is the altarpiece form the Wiesenkirche in Soest, circa 1240, which is remarkably close to the Byzantinizing style of Goslar manuscripts. Many more diptychs, triptychs, and larger altarpieces remain from the following centuries, but their styles continue the relationship to other media and the art of other regions found in thirteenth-century practice. In the fourteenth century, altarpieces of the Cologne school, such as the diptych with the Virgin and Child and the Crucifixion, now in Berlin, combine elements of English and French painting with those of Italian art and show a correspondence to manuscript illumination. Indeed, in the fourteenth century the development of the painted altarpieces of Central Europe was affected by the presence of Italian painters as well as their work. This same combination of elements led to the development of the distinctive, highly elegant sculptural styles of works such as the altarpieces at Klosterneuburg, Heiligenkreuz, and Hohenfurth, and eventually to the work of painters such as Konrad von Soest, Master Francke, and Stephan Lochner in the fifteenth century.

BIBLIOGRAPHY

Berger-Fix, Andrea. "Das Wimpassinger Kreuz und seine Einordnung in die Kunst des 13. Jahrhunderts." *Wiener Jahrbuch für Kunstgeschichte* 33 (1980): 31–82.

Budde, Rainer. *Köln und seine Maler 1300–1500.* Dumont Dokumente. Cologne: Dumont, 1986.

Die Zeit der Staufer: Geschichte, Kunst, Kultur, ed. Rainer Haussherr. 5 vols. Stuttgart: Württembergisches Landesmuseum, 1977, vol. 1, pp. 303–309.

Dupont, Jacques, and Cesare Gnudi. *Gothic Painting,* trans. Stuart Gilbert, 2d ed. New York: Rizzoli, 1979.

Klemann, Walter. *Stimmen und Farben: Ein Buch von Soester Kunst.* Recklinghausen: Bongers, 1974.

Oberhaidacher, Jörg. "Der Meister der St. Lambrechter Votivpanel und Simone Martini: Ein Nachtrag zur Kreuztragungsikonographie der internationalen Gotik in Österreich." *Wiener Jahrbuch für Kunstgeschichte* 45 (1992): 173–181.

Pesina, Jaroslav. *The Master of the Hohenfurth Altarpiece and Bohemian gothic Panel Painting.* Prague: Odeon, 1989.

Pieper, Paul. *Die deutschen, niederländischen und italienischen Tafelbilder bis zum 1530.* Münster: Aschendorff, 1986.

Stange, Alfred. *Deutsche Malerei der Gotik,* 10 vols. Berlin: Deutscher Kunstverlag, 1934–1961.

———. *German Painting: 14–16 Centuries.* London: Hyperion, 1950.

Rebecca W. Corrie

Sculpture, Introduction

Contemporary with the introduction of the Gothic style in German sculpture in the first half of the thirteenth century is the veritable explosion in the numbers of objects decorated with figural sculpture and the new sites where it occurs. Portals develop in complexity, and choir stalls, choir screens, altarpieces, and fonts now regularly bear elaborate programs in sculptured relief. Single figures, installed on altars where they served as the focus of personal devotions, and tombs bearing an image of the decreased begin to appear in significantly greater numbers. The numbers of objects preserved allow, in addition to the study of their forms and functions, a good view of the stylistic variety of German sculpture in the period after the French-influenced portal decoration at Bamberg and the work of the so-called Naumburg Master and before the homogenizing tendencies of the International, or Soft, Style. Although most of the artists remain anonymous—and we know precious little about those who have been identified by name—a number of distinct regional styles can be easily recognized. Thus the elegant, sophisticated look of Cologne sculpture of circa 1300 is easily distinguished from the sweeter, more approachable one of Upper Rhenish sculpture of the same date, as well as from those of Regensburg, Munich, and the Baltic. In this the situation parallels that in painting of the period; in fact, the stylistic features typical of a given region are often common to the two media.

BIBLIOGRAPHY

Bergmann, Ulrike. *Schnütgen Museum: Die Holzskulpturen des Mittelalters 1000–1400.* Cologne: Stadt Köln, 1989.

Hamann, Richard. *Die Elisabethkirche zu Marburg und ihre künstlerische Nachfolge 2: Die Plastik.* Denkmäler deutscher Kunst. Marburg: Verlag des Kunstgeschichtlichen Seminars der Universität Marburg an der Lahn, 1929.

Konstanz: Ein Mittelpunkt der Kunst um 1300. Constance: Seekreis Verlag, 1973.

Möbius, Friedrich, and Helga Sciurie. *Geschichte der deutschen Kunst 1200–1350.* Leipzig: E. A. Seemann, 1989, 281–378.

Suckale, Robert. *Die Hofkunst Kaiser Ludwigs des Bayern.* Munich: Hirmer, 1993.

Wentzel, Hans. *Lübecker Plastik bis zur Mitte des 14. Jahrhunderts.* Denkmäler deutscher Kunst. Berlin: Deutscher Verein für Kunstwissenschaft, 1938.

Joan A. Holladay

Sculpture, Devotional Images

Around the year 1300, a number of new iconographic innovations began to appear in German sculpture. Most

Röttgen Pietá (Bonn, Rheinisches Landesmuseum). *Photograph: Rheinisches Bildarchiv der Stadt Köln*

characteristic of these are the Pietà, the Man of Sorrows, and Christ and the Sleeping St. John, a subject derived from the Last Supper. Additional themes sometimes included in this group are the Madonna of Mercy (*Schutzmantelmadonna*), Christ as a Child, and Mary in Childbed.

The term *Andachtsbild,* commonly translated as "devotional image," was originally coined by German scholars studying specifically this group of sculptures. Erwin Panofsky, in a seminal article on the Man of Sorrows (1927), expanded the group by including two-dimensional works of the same subjects; he identified this group in essentially negative terms as neither hieratic (priestly) cult images nor scenic narratives. He further described them as works designed to stimulate, or allow for the possibility of, contemplative meditation.

Later scholars have generally employed Panofsky's broadened definition of a devotional image, although his distinction based on function oversimplified the issue. Subsequent research does give evidence also of liturgical use for some devotional images; moreover, the increasing realization that both icons and narrative scenes could also be designed to stimulate compassionate meditation means that this devotional function can no longer be claimed exclusively for devotional images.

Other scholars focused on the sources and meanings of these new themes. Earlier attempts to trace their subjects to poetry or passion plays have been discredited on chronological grounds; it seems more fruitful to regard the production of these works as an integral part of Gothic religious practice, with its increasing variety of observances spread among a range of social classes and organizations. Most recently, Hans Belting has examined the reception of devotional images within collective religious experiences, while Johanna Ziegler has argued for a return to the study of Pietàs and their impact as tangible, sculptural objects. These works thus remain at the core of continuing debates about the nature of Gothic religiosity.

BIBLIOGRAPHY

Belting, Hans. *The Image and Its Public in the Middle Ages: Form and Function of Early Painting of the Passion,* trans. Mark Bartusis and Raymond Meyer. New Rochelle, N.Y.: A. D. Caratzas, 1990.

Mâle, Émile. *Religious Art in France: The Late Middle Ages: A Study of Medieval Iconography and Its Sources,* trans. Marthiel Mathews. Princeton, N.J.: Princeton University Press, 1986.

Panofsky, Erwin. "'Imago Pietatis': Ein Beitrag zur Typengeschichte des 'Schmerzensmanns' und der 'Maria Mediatrix,'" in *Festschrift für Max J. Friedländer zum 60. Geburtstag.* Leipzig: E. A. Seemann, 1927, pp. 261–308.

Pinder, Wilhelm. "Die dichterische Wurzel der Pietà." *Repertorium für Kunstwissenschaft* 42 (1920): 145–163.

Ziegler, Johanna E. *Sculpture of Compassion: The Pietà and the Beguines in the Southern Low Countries c. 1300–c. 1600.* Brussels/Rome: Institut Historique Belge de Rome, 1992.

Carol M. Schuler

SEE ALSO

Iconographies, Innovative

Sculpture, Early Altarpieces

Sculpted altarpieces with movable wings, frequently also including painted components, are a German invention, which became extremely important for later medieval and Renaissance art throughout Europe. These altarpieces first appear in North German and Rhenish art in the years around 1325. The sources for such altarpieces are debated. Since many of the early altarpieces contain sections for relics as well as sculpted wings, it has been argued that winged altarpieces derive from elaborate relic cabinets kept in the sacristies of some thirteenth-century Gothic churches. These cabinets have sculpture or painting on the doors and relics contained within, a similar arrangement to the earliest altarpieces. The relic cabinet at Doberan dated to 1275 seems to be especially closely related to the winged altarpiece made for the altar of this church between 1310 and 1320. It has been argued that an enlargement of the relic collection during this period (1275–1310) encouraged a new and more public presentation in which the relics would be more closely linked to the celebration of the Eucharist. Many other early folding altarpieces are found in Cistercian churches, which did not have crypts and therefore needed to find a different place for the relics.

Liturgical practice may also account for the first appearance of the winged altarpiece. The possibility of opening and shutting the wings allowed for different programs to be shown at different liturgical seasons. Early examples include the altarpieces at Altenberg, Marienstatt, and Oberwesel, and the *Klarenaltar,* made for the Franciscan nuns and now in the cathedral at Cologne.

BIBLIOGRAPHY

Ehresmann, Donald L. "Some Observations of the Role of Liturgy in the Early Winged Altarpiece." *Art Bulletin* 64 (1982): 359–369.

Hochgotischer Dialog: Die Skulpturen der Hochaltäre von Marienstatt und Oberwesel im Vergleich. Worms: Wernersche Verlagsgesellschaft, 1993.

Susan L. Ward

SEE ALSO

Cistercian Art and Architecture; Cologne, Art

Sculpture, Interior Programs

Interior sculpture was frequently linked, stylistically and programmatically, with exterior portals. The Judgment Pillar at Strasbourg, a floor-to-ceiling column in the south transept, with trumpeting angels and a seated Christ (1230s), has a figure style similar to the *Muldenfaltenstil* (trough-fold, or soft style) of the south transept facade and judgment iconography tied to the Solomon figure of the exterior. In the Judgment Pillar, architecture and sculpture are integrated in a particularly skillful way, indicating the important role of interior elements in the total development of German Gothic sculpture.

An especially accomplished set of interior figures is the group of founders in the west choir of Naumburg Cathedral (1240s). While the Naumburg figures' placement may be derived from the apostle figures of the Sainte-Chapelle in Pairs, their lively expressive style and iconography, which reflect the integration of local nobility with the church, are uniquely German. The west choir at

Strasbourg, cathedral, interior, south transept, Judgment pillar. *Photograph: Joan A. Holladay*

Naumburg is separated from the nave by a choir screen, or *Lettner,* decorated with narrative reliefs and sculpted in a style similar to that of the founder figures. The direct emotional effect of the founders can be seen in the life-size crucifix on the choir screen, whose arms are stretched out so that a visitor passes under them on the way into the choir. A related choir screen and interior figure group are found at Meißen (mid–thirteenth century).

In the late thirteenth century, interior programs that reflect both rayonnant architecture and the interior figures of Louis IX's Sainte-Chapelle (1244–1248) in Paris begin to appear in Germany. Documents tell us that the church at Wimpfen-im-Tal was to be built *opere francigeno* (in the French style), and the rayonnant architecture is accompanied by a program of interior figures (ca. 1280). At Cologne, figures of Christ, the Virgin, and the apostles are adossed to the choir piers (1280–1300); this also represents a direct response to the Sainte-Chapelle in Paris. The figure style at Cologne is courtly with piquant faces, and bodies in an elegant Gothic sway clothed in voluminous robes with beaklike drapery folds. The architecture reflects the new rayonnant style, and the interior figures, a college of apostles like the Sainte-Chapelle, are part of an elaborate ensemble, which originally included a choir screen and a sculpted altar that contained relics similar to the elaborate interior setting of Louis IX's project.

BIBLIOGRAPHY

Möbius, Frederich, and Helga Sciurie. *Geschichte der deutschen Kunst 1200–1350.* Leipzig: E. A. Seemann Verlag, 1989, pp. 281–378.

Williamson, Paul. *Gothic Sculpture 1100–1300.* New Haven, Conn.: Yale University Press, 1995, pp. 67–101, 174–199.

Susan L. Ward

SEE ALSO

Cologne, Art; Liturgy, Furniture; Meißen; Naumburg; Strasbourg; Wimpfen

Sculpture, Portal Programs

The Gothic portal, a combination of sculptured figures and architectural elements in the new Gothic style, was created initially in France, where the two elements developed concurrently. In Germany, Gothic architectural elements and sculptural style were employed independently, resulting in portals quite different from French models and responding to specific German artistic needs. A considerable group of twelfth- and thirteenth-century Ger-

Trier, Church of Our Lady, west portal, prophets from jambs (Staatliche Museen zu Berlin—Preußischer Kulturbesitz, Skulpturensammlung). *Photograph: Joan A. Holladay*

man portals have Romanesque architectural settings but sculptural styles that show a variety of French early Gothic elements. The earliest group shows the influence of French early Gothic models in the figure style and includes the tympanum from the church of St. Cecilia in Cologne, circa 1160 (now in the Schnütgen Museum), reflecting the west facade at Chartres. French High Gothic figure style appears in German lands in a detailed Virgin portal on the south transept of Strasbourg Cathedral (1230s). The portal has two semicircular tympana, representing the Death of the Virgin and her Coronation, accompanied by impressive jamb figures of Synagogue and Ecclesia. Programmatically, devotion to the Virgin is characteristic of Gothic ideas, and stylistically the *Muldenfaltenstil,* or soft-fold style (also trough-fold), is derived from the workshops of Chartres's north transept. The fluid, elegant postures of the figures and the highly expressive faces at Strasbourg reflect German sensibilities.

The arrival of a workshop trained at Reims at Bamberg Cathedral to complete the Prince's Portal (*Fürstenpforte*, ca. 1235) provides another important stimulus to German Gothic sculpture. The program represents a compressed version of the north transept facade at Reims, and figures of the apostles and prophets at Bamberg are stylistically close to their counterparts at Reims but display a non-French emotional aspect. The north transept porch at Magdeburg Cathedral (ca. 1245) reflects French stylistic influences but less directly.

The combination of Gothic rayonnant architecture with Gothic sculptural style occurs in the triple west portals at Strasbourg (ca. 1280–1300). The program, a Passion in the center tympanum, Christ's Infancy on the left, and a Last Judgment on the right, is designed for the location and reflects the tensional relationships between bishop and chapter, town and mendicant orders. The style represents a continuation of the earlier Strasbourg lodge but also new influences from Paris. Later examples of the rayonnant portal appear at the cathedral of Freiburg-im-Breisgau (ca. 1290–1295) and at Worms Cathedral (ca. 1280).

German cathedral sculpture continues into the fifteenth century with portals such as that at Ulm Cathedral that includes Hans Multcher's Man of Sorrows (1429), which has an emotional impact like an *Andachtsbild* and reflects the *weicher Stil*, or soft style, so prevalent in German sculpture of circa 1400.

BIBLIOGRAPHY

Möbius, Frederich, and Helga Sciurie. *Geschichte der deutschen Kunst 1200–1350.* Leipzig: E. A. Seemann Verlag, 1989, pp. 281–378.

Schubert, Dietrich. *Von Halberstadt nach Meißen: Bildewerke des 13. Jahrhunderts in Thüringen, Sachsen und Anhalt.* Cologne: DuMont Schauberg, 1974.

Williamson, Paul. *Gothic Sculpture 1100–1300.* New Haven, Conn.: Yale University Press, 1995, pp. 67–101, 174–199.

Susan L. Ward

SEE ALSO
Bamberg; Cologne, Art; Freiburg; Iconographies, Innovative; International Style; Magdeburg; Multscher, Hans; Romanesque Art and Architecture; Strasbourg; Ulm; Worms

Sculpture, Tombs

Although burial inside churches was generally forbidden, from the earliest times exceptions were granted for persons of high status: nobles, religious, rulers, founders, and donors were interred in the crypt—the most important burial site for its proximity to the bones of the local saint, as well as in the choir and aisles. A tomb marking the burial site was placed into the floor flush with the paving, slightly raised on a low base, or on an elevated *tumba*. The deceased was usually portrayed on the tomb top, in low or high relief, sometimes in the round, in inverted relief, or engraved. The most typical material was stone or, less frequently, bronze; the tomb of Heinrich III of Sayn (d. 1247; now in the Germanisches Nationalmuseum in Nuremberg) is an unusual example in wood. From the end of the eleventh century, tomb sculpture represented one of the most important types of medieval sculpture.

In the early Christian period general prohibitions against imagery and the rigorous resistance to figural cult images worked against the use of figural sarcophagi like those known to the Etruscans and Romans. This trend

Tomb of Dean Johannes von Poczta (d. 1414), from Meissen cathedral, now All Saints' Chapel. *Photograph: Joan A. Holladay*

continued into the High Middle Ages. The bronze tomb in low relief for the antiking Rudolf of Swabia (d. 1080) in Merseburg Cathedral represents the earliest preserved example of figural tomb sculpture in Germany. Its composition and execution contrast with those of the abbesses of Quedlinburg from the first third of the twelfth century; their massiveness, symmetry, and ornamental decoration embody the Romanesque style. Increasing plasticity characterizes the subsequent development of the figural tomb relief. Whereas the bronze relief for the archbishop of Magdeburg Frederick of Wettin (d. 1152; Magdeburg Cathedral) still has a closed, compact form, the figures of Duke Henry the Lion and his wife, Mathilda, on the oldest preserved double tomb (1230–1240; Braunschweig Cathedral) display deep folds and movement in the positioning of the body if not, as in the works of the slightly later Naumburg Master, in the face.

Typical of medieval tomb sculptures is ambivalence in the stance of the figure. Most frequently the effigy, which derives from jamb sculptures, is portrayed as if a standing figure were tipped over on its back. Only the pillow under the head, folds over the body and on the background slab, and relaxed body parts suggest a recumbent position, but in many cases these are combined with elements that indicate standing: a console under the feet, tubelike folds running from waist to feet, and gestures such as blessing. The dead person always appears in ideal form and age; individual portrait character first appears in isolated tombs of the fourteenth century, then more frequently in the fifteenth. Until this time, only the inscription links the tomb to a specific person. An important element of the inscription is the date of death, on which yearly anniversary masses would be said. In addition to clothing that marks the social standing and official position of the deceased, insignias, architectural and heraldic details, and animals—lions, dogs, dragons, and snakes—are often included; their iconographic meaning is often ambivalent. Their placement at the foot of the dead person usually refers to the triumph over evil but may characterize the person represented in a more specific way.

The thirteenth century saw the formation of nearly all the tomb types used for the rest of the Middle Ages. The type of commemorative—as opposed to liturgical—tombs developed in the mid–thirteenth century at St.-Denis was taken over but modified. An example is the tomb of the German king Rudolf von Habsburg (d. 1291) in the cathedral at Speyer, whose face no longer represents an ideal, noble type but shows instead the be-

ginnings of an interest in individual physiognomy. The tomb of Bishop Wolfhard von Roth (d. 1302) in Augsburg Cathedral goes even further, portraying him with the sunken features and closed eyes of a dead man. Although north of the Alps the deceased was always portrayed lying down, this unusual effigy shows, for the first time, a corpse; it remained isolated and without following. Only in the fifteenth century in southern Germany do we find a series of tombs, such as those of apothecary and mayor of Straubing Ulrich Kastenmeyer (d. 1431; Straubing, St. Jakob) and Deacon Bernhard von Breidenbach (d. 1497; Mainz Cathedral), that represent the commemorated in the process of dying rather than as dead.

Around 1330, production of tombs picked up and local features became more marked. The transition from a simple stance, as in the tomb of Archbishop Peter von Aspelt (d. 1320; Mainz Cathedral), to the harmonious, dynamic S-curve, as in that of Archbishop Matthias von Bucheck (d. 1328; Mainz Cathedral), represents the essential development of this period. The rituals of the burial ceremony played an important role in the further evolution of figural tombs; the monuments commemorating the landgraves of Hesse (Heinrich I, d. 1308, and Heinrich the Younger, d. 1298; Otto I, d. 1328) in the south conch at St. Elizabeth's in Marburg are the first examples of *pleurant* (weeping) tombs in Germany. In addition to the mourners around the tomb base, accompanying figures, such as praying monks, censing (dispensing incense) angels, and angels holding the soul of the deceased in the form of a tiny naked figure, remind the living of their duties to commemorate the dead liturgically. From the middle of the fourteenth century, the increasing negation of the horizontal position—the effigy comes more and more to resemble a standing figure seen from the front—and the lack of space resulting from the growing number of commissions led to the vertical installation of tomb slabs. From this developed the framed standing image, well illustrated in the series of tombs of the archbishops of Mainz, as well as the epitaph, a representation of the deceased in a scenic relief mounted on the wall and thus independent of the actual burial site.

Several new features mark fifteenth-century tomb sculpture. Social change gave rise to a new group of tomb patrons among members of the middle class. The broader figures typical of the soft style (also trough or soft fold) begin to appear in tomb sculpture as well, as, for example, in the tomb of Archbishop Konrad von Daun (entombed 1434; Mainz Cathedral). And in tomb sculpture as elsewhere, the names of individual artists, such as Nicolaus Gerhaert von Leyden and Madern Gerthener, begin to be associated with their works.

BIBLIOGRAPHY

Bauch, Kurt. *Das mittelalterliche Grabbild: Figürliche Grabmäler des 11. bis 15. Jahrhunderts in Europa.* Berlin: de Gruyter, 1976.

Böhm, Gabriele. *Mittelalterliche figürliche Grabmäler in Westfalen von den Anfängen bis 1400.* Münster: Lit, 1993.

Egli, Viviane. "Gebärdensprache und Bedeutung mittelalterlicher Rittergrabbilder." Ph.D. diss., University of Zurich, 1987.

Hinz, Berthold. *Das Grabdenkmal Rudolfs von Schwaben: Monument der Propaganda und Paradigma der Gattung.* Frankfurt am Main: Kunststück, 1996.

Holladay, Joan A. "Portrait Elements in Tomb Sculpture: identification and Iconography," in *Europäische Kunst um 1300,* ed. Gerhard Schmidt. Akten des 25. Internationalen Kongresses für Kunstgeschichte 6. Vienna: Böhlau, 1996, pp. 217–221.

———. *Illuminating the Epic: the Kassel 'Willehalm' Codex and the landgraves of Hesse in the Early Fourteenth Century.* College Art Association Monographs, 57. Seattle: University of Washington Press, 1997, pp. 56–65.

Hurtig, Judith. "The Armored Gisant before 1400." Ph.D. diss., New York University, 1978, *Outstanding Dissertations in the Fine Arts.* New York: Garland, 1979.

Körner, Hans. *Grabmonumente des Mittelalters.* Darmstadt: Primus, 1996.

Panofsky, Erwin. *Tomb Sculpture: Four Lectures on Its Changing Aspects from Ancient to Bernini.* New York: Harry N. Abrams, 1964.

Reinle, Adolf. *Das stellvertretende Bildnis: Plastiken und Gemälde von der Antike bis ins 19. Jahrhundert.* Zurich: Artemis, 1984.

Schaum-Benedum, Christa. *Die figürliche Grabsteine des 14. und 15. Jahrhunderts in Hessen.* Bonn: Habelt, 1969.

Schmid, Karl, and Joachim Wollasch, ed. *Memoria: Der geschichtliche Zeugniswert des liturgischen Gedenkens im Mittelalter.* Münstersche Mittelalter-Schriften 48. Munich: Fink, 1984.

Martina Dlugaiczyk

SEE ALSO
Augsburg; Braunschweig; Gerthener, Madern; Henry the Lion; International Style; Magdeburg; Mainz; Marburg; Merseburg; Nicolaus Gerhaert von Leyden; Quedlinburg; Speyer

Stained Glass

Stained glass windows dating from the twelfth century and earlier can be found in Germany and Central Europe, but the great period of production in this region begins in the middle of the thirteenth century. In France extensive production of stained glass, like the introduction of Gothic architecture, begins in the twelfth century, but neither the style of architecture nor the figure style and treatment of space associated with the term *Gothic* appears in Germany until after 1250. Furthermore, although stained glass was commissioned for great monasteries and bishops' churches, much of the Gothic stained glass in Central Europe is found in structures built by the new religious orders such as the Franciscans and the Dominicans, as well as in parish churches.

Musical angels (Cologne, Schnütgen Museum). *Photograph: Joan A. Holladay*

Among the first major stained glass programs are those of the mid–thirteenth century found, for example, in the Middle Rhine and Lower Saxony, and including examples at Marburg, Freiburg im Breisgau, Naumberg, Basel, Goslar, and Lohne. Although many occur in Gothic churches based on French models and some even show French inspiration in their figure types, most belong to the late Romanesque in their reference to Byzantine models, as in the *Zackenstil* (zigzag style), and their lack of three-dimensional spatial niches. But Gothic concerns were introduced in the Middle Rhine, from Strasbourg in the second half of the thirteenth century. It is in the fourteenth century at Freiburg, Esslingen, Königsfelden, Cologne, and Regensburg that figures standing in ornamental niches begin to dominate, and in their poses, their three-dimensional bodies, and drapery forms show clear adherence to the concerns of French artists. Nevertheless, in the middle of the fourteenth century in Austria, the elements of Romanesque style still persisted in many centers. In a last development in stained glass toward the end of the fourteenth century at centers like Ulm and Augsburg, large scenes that encompass the entire glass surface began to appear.

Currently scholars working in this field address a series of problems including those of technology, condition, restoration, and the related problems of attributing and localizing windows long since moved from their original sites. Other issues include workshop organization, patronage, including that of religious orders, the relationship of stained glass to manuscript illumination, the relationship between the styles of Central Europe and Byzantine and French art, specifically Paris, and the presence of Central European glaziers in Italy. Also of interest are issues of iconography: the depiction of donors, the use of Old and New Testament cycles, the Tree of Jesse, life cycles of new saints such as Saint Elizabeth and Saint Francis of Assisi, and the use of moral themes including the Wise and Foolish Virgins.

BIBLIOGRAPHY

Bacher, Ernst. *Die mittelalterlichen Glasgemälde in der Steiermark*, vol. 1. *Corpus Vitrearum Medii Aevi*, Austria 3. Vienna: Böhlau, 1979.

Becksmann, Rüdiger. *Deutsche Glasmalerei des Mittelalters: Eine exemplarische Auswahl.* Stuttgart: Institut für Auslandsbeziehungen, 1988.

———. "Die Bettelorden an Rhein, Main und Neckar und der hofische Stil der Pariser Kunst um 1300." *Deutsche Glasmalerei des Mittelalters: Bildprogramme, Auftraggeber, Werkstatten*, ed. Rüdiger Becksmann. Berlin: Deutscher Verlag für Kunstwissenschaft, 1992, pp. 52–75.

Bierschenk, Monika. *Glasmalereien der Elisabethkirche in Marburg: Die figürlichen Fenster um 1240.* Berlin: Deutscher Verlag für Kunstwissenschaft, 1991.

Fritzsche, Gabriela. *Die mittelalterlichen Glasmalerei im Regensburger Dom.* 2 vols. Corpus Vitrearum Medii Aevi, Deutschland 13; Regensburg und Oberfalz 1. Berlin: Deutscher Verlag für Kunstwissenschaft, 1987.

Frodl-Kraft, Eva. *Die mittelalterlichen Glasgemälde in Wien.* Corpus Vitrearum Medii Aevi, Austria 1. Graz: H. Böhlaus Nachfolger, 1962.

———. "Problems of Gothic Workshop Practices in Light of a Group of Mid-Fourteenth-Century Austrian Stained-Glass Panels," in *Corpus Vitrearum: Selected Papers from the 11th International Colloquium of the Corpus Vitrearum, New York, 1–6 June 1982*, ed. Madeline Caviness and Timothy Husband. CVMA Occasional Papers 1. New York: Metropolitan Museum of Art, 1985, pp. 107–123.

Grodecki, Louis, and Catherine Brisac. *Gothic Stained Glass 1200–1300.* London: Thames and Hudson, 1985.

Kronbichler, Johann. *Das Margaretenfenster aus Stift Ardagger.* St. Pölten: Bishöfliches Ordinariat St. Pölten, 1991.

Martin, Frank. *Die Apsisverglasung der Oberkirche von S. Francesco in Assisi: Ihre Entstehung und Stellung innerhalb der Oberkirchenausstattung.* Regensburg: Schnell und Steiner, 1993.

Rode, Hermann. *Die mittelalterlichen Glasmalereien des Kölner Domes.* Corpus Vitrearum Medii Aevi Deutschland 4, 1. Berlin: Deutscher Verlag für Kunstwissenschaft, 1974.

Rebecca W. Corrie

SEE ALSO

Augsburg; Basel; Cologne, Art; Esslingen am Neckar; Franciscan Art and Architecture; Freiburg; Goslar; Iconographies, Innovative; Königsfelden; Marburg; Naumburg; Regensburg; Romanesque Art and Architecture; Strasbourg; Ulm

Textiles

The history of German textiles in the Gothic period is largely a continuation of Romanesque traditions, with significant contributions to the history of tapestry-woven wall hangings and linen and wool embroideries. Silks and

Late Gothic tapestry: Wild people with Fabulous Animals, Switzerland, ca. 1430–1440 (Zurich, Schweizerisches Landesmuseum, LM-1178). *Photograph: Schweizerisches Landesmuseum, Neg. 45462*

other luxury textiles were still primarily produced around the Mediterranean and in the Byzantine and Islamic east.

Linen and wool embroideries were produced during the Romanesque period, but during the Gothic period Lower Saxony, Hesse, and Westphalia developed highly accomplished embroideries for the altar and church furnishings that came to be known as *opus teutonicum* (German work). Particularly notable is a large group of "whitework" pieces done in linen, occasionally with a dyed ground, but more often made with undyed linen. This technique is sophisticated in its utilization of a variety of stitches to create a subtle pictorial relief. Many of these pieces are associated with convents in Hesse and Westphalia, and their manufacture is usually attributed to the nuns of these regions. Notable examples are the altar cloth and Lenten cover from the Premonstratensian convent at Altenberg an der Lahn, now in New York City (Metropolitan Museum of Art) and Cleveland (Cleveland Museum of Art). The Lenten cloth in Cleveland dates from the second quarter of the fourteenth century and measures 60¾ by 147½ inches. A large central quatrefoil depicts the Crucifixion while surrounding quatrefoils illustrate the Resurrection, the four evangelists, and several saints. The fourteenth-century altar cloth in New York, measuring 62½ by 150 inches depicts Christ in Majesty flanked by saints. A particularly large group of linen embroideries is preserved at Kloster Lüne near Lüneburg.

More colorful wool embroideries were produced in several regions, but the needleworkers of Lower Saxony appear to have been the most prolific. In addition to decorations for the altar that represent the Life of the Virgin, the Passion, and other sacred themes, the embroiderers of Lower Saxony were fond of secular themes, such as romances. A large but partially fragmentary wall hanging at Wienhausen produced in the early fourteenth century measures 91¾ by 159 inches. With colorful dyed wools on a linen ground, it depicts twenty-three scenes from the story of Tristan in three horizontal registers alternating with four registers of coats of arms.

During the late fourteenth century, Bohemian embroiderers produced many highly accomplished orphreys (gold embroidered trim) for vestments, altar frontals, and other ecclesiastical pieces in silk and metallic thread. The Bohemian embroideries, produced at a time when Prague was a European cultural capital, are stylistically more closely linked to Paris than to German centers. Unlike the monastic products in linen and wool, the Bohemian pieces were likely produced by professional embroiderers working in organized guilds.

The early history of European tapestry production in the Romanesque period is known in large part through the German examples at Halberstadt. German tapestries, produced primarily in Nuremberg and the Upper Rhine beginning in the middle of the fourteenth century, are equally significant to the history of tapestries in the late Gothic period.

In keeping with the role of Nuremberg as a major artistic center, it appears that by the late fourteenth century, more than one workshop was active, producing accomplished tapestries in wool, usually on a linen warp. One of the earliest to be preserved, from about 1380, illustrates the Twelve Wise Men, each surrounded by a banderole (banner) inscribed with words of wisdom. This was probably a civic commission, made for the Small Council Chamber of the Town Hall. Most tapestries produced in Nuremberg had religious themes, but secular themes continued to appear through the fifteenth century.

By the fifteenth century, significant tapestry workshops had developed in the Upper Rhine at Basel and Strasbourg. These workshops favored such secular themes as wild men and allegories of love and virtue. Following the lead of Nuremberg and the Upper Rhine, tapestries were produced at Cologne and other German centers, but by about 1500 the German workshops could no longer compete with the high-quality products of Flemish workshops, and the distinguished history of medieval German tapestries comes to a conclusion.

BIBLIOGRAPHY

Rapp Buri, Anna, and Monica Stucky-Schürer. *Zahm und Wild: Basler and Strassburger Bildteppiche des 15. Jahrhunderts.* Mainz: von Zabern, 1990.

Wilckens, Leonie von. *Die textilen Künste: Von der Spätantike bis um 1500.* Munich: Beck, 1991.

Peter Barnet

SEE ALSO

Basel; Cologne, Art; Gottfried von Straßburg, *Tristan,* Illustrations; Lüneburg; Nuremberg; Prague; Strasbourg; Wienhausen; Women and Art

Gothic Art and Architecture, Late

[This entry includes five subentries:

Introduction
Architecture
Metalwork
Painting
Sculpture]

Introduction

Like most names for period styles, the term *Late Gothic* (German, *Spätgotik*) originated in the nineteenth century as historical categories were established in keeping with the emerging paradigms of the new discipline of art history. Unlike most such designations, the notion of a Late Gothic era was controversial from the start. Even today consensus in usage is lacking. Generally, the term describes a style that dominated north of the Alps during the fourteenth, fifteenth, and early sixteenth centuries. English-language literature usually treats the Late Gothic as the final decorative phase of Gothic, with variants produced all over Europe at different times during the late Middle Ages. German-language scholarship considers the *Spätgotik* a style distinct from both the earlier French Gothic and the contemporary Italian Renaissance. The term *Northern Renaissance* as a period designation never gained currency among German-speaking art historians. Nationalist and even racist motivations color much of the early scholarship that extolled the Late Gothic as distinctly Germanic. In more recent writing, the term is used in recognition of stylistic plurality. Perception of a Late Gothic style that lasted into the sixteenth century and employed neither the classical forms of Italy nor the detailed verism of the Netherlands facilitates a consideration not only of elaborate and innovative architectural forms, especially in vaulting and tracery, but also of exuberant, emotionally expressive painting and sculpture that often served devotional purposes. According to some observers, in German areas the Late Gothic persisted into the mannerist and baroque eras, passing over the Renaissance. It has been suggested that lay patrons of the bourgeois class employed and expanded Gothic vocabulary in an attempt to maintain an earlier style that would link them to ecclesiastical power and feudal authority.

BIBLIOGRAPHY

Bialostocki, Jan. "Late Gothic: Disagreements about the Concept." *Journal of the British Archaeological Association* n.s. 3, vol. 29 (1966): 76–105.

Dehio, Georg. "Über die Grenzen der Renaissance gegen die Gotik." *Kunstchronik* n.s. 11 (1899–1900): cols. 273–277.

Frankl, Paul. *The Gothic: Literary Sources and Interpretations through Eight Centuries.* Princeton, N.J.: Princeton University Press, 1960.

Gerstenberg, Kurt. *Deutsche Sondergotik: Eine Untersuchung über das Wesen der deutschen Baukunst im Mittelalter.* Munich: Delphin-Verlag, 1913.

Pevsner, Nikolaus. *Outline of European Architecture.* Harmondsworth: Penguin, 1942.

Schmarsow, August. "Reformvorschläge zur Geschichte der deutschen Renaissance." *Berichte über die Verhandlungen der königlich-sächsischen Gesellschaft der Wissenschaften zu Leipzig, Philologisch-historische Klasse* 51 (1899): 41–76.

"Spätgotik," in *Lexikon der Kunst: Architektur, Bildende Kunst, Angewandte Kunst, Industrieformgestaltung, Kunsttheorie,* ed. Harald Olbrich et al. 7 vols. Leipzig: E. A: Seemann, 1987–1994, vol. 6, pp. 787–789.

Weise, Georg. "Das 'gotische' oder 'barocke' Stilprinzip der deutschen und der nordischen Kunst." *Deutsche Vierteljahresschrift für Literaturwissenschaft und Geistesgeschichte* 10 (1932); 206–243.

Worringer, Wilhelm. *Form in Gothic.* 1912, trans. Herbert Read. London: A. Tiranti, 1964.

Corine Schleif

SEE ALSO
Gothic Art and Architecture

Architecture

After the middle of the thirteenth century, when French Gothic rayonnant forms fundamentally affected European architecture, much German building reflected the greater unification and dissolution of the wall surface and increased complication of tracery patterns. Beginning in the early fourteenth century, German masters added to these more lightweight designs open spatial effects and intricate vaulting patterns and forms that emphasized a sense of diagonal movement throughout the structure. These features were particularly seen to full advantage in smaller churches rather than large cathedrals, although there too the new *Sondergotik*, or Late Gothic style, appeared in architectural details and restricted parts, such as chapels, apart from the main ritual spaces. The term *Sondergotik* is often simply used as a synonym for Late Gothic architecture in Germany, but *sonder,* meaning "special" or "unusual," highlights the striving for dramatic effects. One of the earliest buildings to show these changes was the church of the Holy Cross *(Heiligkreuzkirche)* at Schwäbisch Gmünd, which Henrich Parler, perhaps called from the cathedral workshop at Cologne, redesigned in the 1320s. It shows the typical elements of German Late Gothic: slim, unarticulated columns that allow spatial openness and unity, dynamic tracery patterns and vaults (those in place now date from the late fifteenth century), emphasis on horizontal expansion of space rather than verticality, a compact exterior profile, and a building type, the hall church, that allows emphasis on these traits. A classic rendering of the open hall type is seen in the parish church of St. Mary, known as the *Wiesenkirche,* in Soest, begun probably by 1313. It is a nearly perfect example in plan, openness, and unity, with its continuous moldings from arches to pier framing virtually unobstructed space, and exposing the tall windows and their thin vertical mullions capped by rich, geometric patterns.

Such a definition of Late Gothic, however, fits only certain buildings in the period, and may thus reflect a modern ideal of unity *(Gerstenberg),* in which Late Gothic is construed as an extreme antithesis to the clearly articulated model of High Gothic. The actual history was much more varied. For example, the church of St. George in Dinkelsbühl (built 1448–1499) maintains rigidly defined aisles rather than opening up diagonal vistas. Moreover, the interest in lateral spaciousness as opposed to soaring heights is probably related to the typically smaller size of buildings or, if large, to their simplification (e.g., St. Mary at Straslund) compared with the normally very large, highly articulated structure of cathedrals. The diminution in scale and lack of complication are surely due to the municipal sponsorship of the churches built at this time, a reflection of the burgeoning prosperity of cities, which nevertheless lacked the enormous feudal wealth of the long-established cathedrals, most of which had been recently rebuilt. Contemporaneous secular buildings also use the decorative elements of the style, as exemplified by the splendid, spacious Vladislav Hall (built 1493–1503) of Prague castle by Benedikt Ried or, now that merchant wealth could afford the display, by town halls and their council chambers at Basel, Braunschweig, Lübeck, Nördlingen, Straslund, and other municipal structures. Thus, at least some of the stylistic features associated with the Late Gothic should be attributed to economic, social, institutional, and liturgical factors.

Although Late Gothic architecture is found throughout Europe, Late Gothic developments in German-speaking areas were strongly imprinted by the work of the Parler family. The word *Parler* or *Parlier* was a professional designation before its use as a family name. Derived from the French *parler,* to speak, it specified the intermediary between the master of the works and the stone masons on the site, the foreman. In cities such as Basel and Strasbourg, the masons had organized into guilds with other members of the building trade—plasterers and carpenters, for example—as early as the thirteenth century. By 1402, the stone masons of Strasbourg were represented by their own guild; their statutes of 1464, together with those of the stonemasons of Trier (1397), Erfurt (1423), Regensburg (1440), and other cities, are known. Like the so-called Regensburg Ordinance of 1459—a transregional document legislating the activities of the often itinerant masters across a wide area between Strasbourg and Vienna—the provisions of these local documents protected their members, regulated their work, and stipulated practices of apprenticeship. Eventually the profession was governed by the four main building lodges of the Empire, at Strasbourg, Cologne, Vienna, and Bern.

The church of the Holy Cross at Schwäbisch Gmünd is the benchmark work of the Parler family patriarch Heinrich, but the real progenitor of Late Gothic style was his son Peter. Peter's work at Prague after 1356 produced the vocabulary that influenced two centuries of Gothic architecture in central Europe. Almost a complete manual of design is shown: dynamic patterns of all kinds—in tracery, in vaulting, and in three-dimensional features that create movement in the piers and elevation. Some historians have posited that many of his forms were derived from the English Decorated Style, even hypothesizing that Peter Parler may have traveled in England, but others derive his work largely, or even solely, from continental prototypes. In any case, his display of forms inaugurated a sense of artistic competition for future masons, especially when a succession of designers was employed on a project, as was often the case. Their designs of piers, moldings, tracery, and vault patterns became increasingly intricate and exuberant. The increasing self-consciousness of their art signaled a change in their professional and social status, marked by the passage in modern terminology from the term "master mason" to "architect." Moreover, the complex work encouraged the development of drawings, many of which still survive. In fact, the vault surface became flattened, which acted as a drawing board for Late Gothic experimentation with complicated vaulting design.

In the cathedral of St. Vitus at Prague, Peter Parler's tracery designs take on agile, curvilinear forms, moving far beyond the developed geometric complication of even Schwäbisch-Gmünd and Cologne, showing twisting curvilinear tracery patterns, and all manner of continuous curving intersections and double-cusped figures. The vaulting designs in the various chapels amount to a pattern book; the south porch includes an openwork vault with so-called flying ribs, where the ribs cross space but the cells are not filled in so that spatial interpenetration results. The profile of the high choir vault is high and shallow, effecting a sense of weightlessness, as its simple but ingenious design moves continuously across the borders of the bays rather than defining them. Integration and movement are also pronounced in the elevation, particularly in the diagonally planted tabernacles and splay of the upper elevation bordering the vaulting shafts of each bay, an idea derived from the swinging cornice—which shoots out around each group of vaulting shafts—of the choir at Schwäbisch Gmünd, and taken up later in St. Lawrence, Nuremberg. At Prague, however, it allows for an exterior passage around the pier at these upper stories, related to several French examples. Pier moldings slide into the plinth rather than articulated shaft bases. All these effects are employed in the interests of greater integration and surprising effect rather than clear definition.

Late Gothic of the fifteenth and sixteenth centuries developed features such as these, emphasizing spectacular visual effects that challenged expectations in building. Extravagant examples may be seen in the faceted net vault, intersecting and dying moldings, and dynamic projecting cornice in the choir at St. Lawrence, Nuremberg (built 1439–after 1464); the spiraling shafts around the pier core of the north choir aisles at Braunschweig cathedral (built 1469); the cellular vaults at St. Mary, Danzig (built 1484–1502); and the star vault with startling curving, intersecting, and broken ribs at St. Barbara at Kutná Hora (Kuttenberg) in Bohemia (choir vaults built 1499, nave vaults built 1540–1548). The church of the Virgin (*Frauenkirche)* at Ingolstadt boasts chapel vaults of the most elaborate florid sort from circa 1520. The rich, precious visionary quality of what François Bucher has termed "micro-architecture" arises from the use of similar features. Examples include the 1467 font at St. Severus, Erfurt; the oratory built by Benedict Ried for King Vladislav in one of the south chapels of Prague cathedral between 1490 and 1493, which is covered with stone carving treated as growing branches; the swelling, curvilinear gallery of 1492–1496, known as the Simpertus arch, by Burkhard Engelberg in the church of Saints Ulrich and Afra, Augsburg; the 1493 eucharistic tabernacle by Adam Kraft in St. Lawrence, Nuremberg; and the one of 1511–1525 at Nördlingen.

On the exterior the domination of the churches was manifested by the enormously high pitched roof and by towers, which rose higher and higher, many of which were topped with filigree-like openwork spires. Impressive towers can be seen, for example, at Freiburg im Breisgau (built 1275–ca. 1340); St. Stephen's cathedral, Vienna, whose tower, begun ca. 1359 but built mainly 1407–1433, rises to a height of ca. 418 feet (137 meters); Ulm, where the tower designed first by Ulrich von Ensingen in 1392 and later revised by Matthäus Böblinger was completed in the nineteenth century; Strasbourg cathedral, where von Ensingen and Johannes Hültz, working in succession between 1399 and 1439, raised the north tower to 142 meters; and the cathedral at Bern, where the tower erected between the 1480s and 1521 (finished in the 1890s) may reflect the earlier intentions of von Ensingen's son Matthäus Ensinger, who was master of the works here from 1420 until 1446.

At the same time, however, simplicity reigned in the piers and elevation, with a focus on the windows and most especially the vaults. The most elaborate tracery and curving vaulting ribs set usually on thin, octogonal or columnar piers are used at Schwäbisch Gmünd, as well as in the churches of Hans von Burghausen at Landshut—St. Martin, built 1392–1407 and later, and the *Spitalkirche* (Hospital Church), completed in 1407—and Salzburg, where he began the spectacularly open Franciscan church in 1408. Similar forms appear at the following six churches: St. Martin at Amberg, begun in 1421; St. George at Nördlingen, erected between 1427 and 1505; St. Michael at Schwäbisch Hall, built between 1427 and 1456 (in the nave and especially in the tall, open choir of 1495); St. John, Dingolfing, begun in 1467; the *Frauenkirche* (Church of the Virgin) in Munich (built 1468–1488); and the church of St. Anne, begun in 1499 at Annaberg, rich from the silver mines. Ribs are often faceted with razor-sharp edges; at times they are broken off just beyond intersection with other ribs or criss-cross them, and vault mold-

ings often disappear into the body of the pier, denying the clear articulation of earlier Gothic architecture. All these features aid in the construction of a hovering, ethereal, mystical space.

BIBLIOGRAPHY

Bucher, François. "Micro-Architecture as the 'Idea' of Gothic Theory and Style." *Gesta* 15 (1976): 71–89.

Die Parler und der schöne Stil 1350–1400: Europäische Kunst unter den Luxemburgern. 5 vols. ed. Anton Legner. Cologne: Museen der Stadt Köln, 1978.

Frankl, Paul. *The Gothic: Literary Sources and Interpretations Through Eight Centuries.* Princeton, N.J.: Princeton University Press, 1960.

———. *Gothic Architecture.* trans., Dieter Pevsner. *Pelican History of Art.* Baltimore: Penguin, 1962.

Gerstenberg, Kurt. *Deutsche Sondergotik: Eine Untersuchung über das Wesen der deutschen Baukunst im späten Mittelalter.* 2nd ed. Darmstadt: Wissenschaftliche Buchgesellschaft, 1969.

Nussbaum, Norbert. *German Gothic Church Architecture.* New Haven, Conn.: Yale University Press, 2000.

Simson, Otto von. *Das Mittelalter II: Das Hohe Mittelalter.* Propyläen Kunstgeschichte 6. Frankfurt: Ullstein Verlag, 1972.

Wagner-Rieger, Renate. "Gothic Art. Architecture. Germany and Central Europe." *Encyclopedia of World Art,* 15 vols. New York: McGraw-Hill, 1959–1968. 6: 511–525.

Wilson, Christopher. *The Gothic Cathedral: The Architecture of the Great Church 1130–1530.* London: Thames and Hudson, 1990.

Virginia Jansen

SEE ALSO

Augsburg; Basel; Bern; Braunschweig; Cologne, Art; Erfurt; Freiburg; Landshut; Lübeck; Nuremberg; Parler Family; Prague; Salzburg; Schwäbisch Gmünd; Schwäbisch-Hall; Soest; Stralsund; Strasbourg; Ulm; Vienna

Metalwork

The fourteenth through sixteenth centuries witnessed a tremendous expansion of metalworking in the German regions. In addition to a continuation and increase of traditional applications, new forms and techniques were developed, and new centers of production arose. Perhaps most significantly, changes in trade and economic conditions led to a growing demand for domestic and utilitarian objects for use by an increasingly affluent merchant

Reliquary Bust of Charlemagne (Aachen, cathedral treasury).
Photograph: Rheinisches Bildarchiv der Stadt Köln

and urban middle class. Despite this varied patronage and function, late Gothic metalwork is almost universally characterized by a great degree of lavish decoration and ornamental profusion, paralleling stylistic tendencies in sculpture and architectural decoration.

Changes in the cult of relics and the rise of the cult of the Eucharist necessitated the development of new forms of liturgical furnishings, such as monstrances, ostensoria (display vessels), relic monstrances, and a wide array of figural reliquaries. The increasing desire for more direct visual contact with relics and the Host, after the institution of the Feast of Corpus Christi in 1264, led to the development of the monstrance. This can be seen in the silver monstrance made circa 1500 in Nuremberg for the parish church at Memmelsdorf. The Late Gothic period also witnessed the greatest proliferation of figural reliquaries, particularly reliquary busts. Fine examples include the reliquary bust of Charlemagne (ca. 1349) in the

cathedral treasury at Aachen and Hans von Reutlingen's reliquary bust of St. Lambert (1508–1512) in the treasury of the cathedral of Liège. Paralleling this desire for a more tangible reliquary form, a number of lavish, multifigural narrative reliquaries were produced, such as the St. Simeon reliquary from the second third of the fourteenth century (Aachen, cathedral treasury).

Aside from the development of the monstrance, little changed in the function of liturgical tools. However, the numerous chalices and other liturgical appurtenances produced during the fourteenth and fifteenth centuries show an increase in elegant, decorative forms. Late-fourteenth- and fifteenth-century chalices reveal abundant figural and foliate decoration on the knob and the base. During the later fifteenth and sixteenth centuries the decorations on the knob became increasingly elaborate, as seen in the gold chalice of 1494 from the friars' church in Braunschweig.

During the fifteenth century, secular objects became more abundant and lavishly decorated. The silver casket, made in 1438 by Hans Schesslitzer and Peter Ratzko to hold the state jewels in the Heiliggeistkirche (Church of the Holy Spirit) in Nuremberg is entirely covered with the Nuremberg coat of arms, illustrating a rise in lavish, secular patronage, civic self-awareness, and interest in heraldry. Luxury items, such as jewelry, particularly rings and pendants, mirrors, and containers, grew in popularity as burghers increasingly imitated court usage. Vessels made for great state and corporation meetings grew in size and ornamentation, as can be seen in the two silver-gilt ewers with enameled wild men adorning their lids, produced around 1500 for the Order of Teutonic Knights (New York, Cloisters). Tankards and ewers were particularly popular among the burghers and civic guilds by the late fifteenth century. Characteristic of the type is the spectacular gilded and enameled silver ewer of 1477 from the Rathaus (town hall) of Goslar, with its decorative bands of foliage, musical angels, and dragon-shaped handle. Another form characteristic of the early sixteenth century is the double goblet *(Doppelpokal)*, replete with bulbous ornamental forms, as seen in examples at Nuremberg, Zwolle, and Karlsruhe. The elaborate table ornament and drinking vessel, known as the Schlüsselfelder Ship, produced in Nuremberg in 1503, possibly by the father of Albrecht Dürer, illustrates both the taste for sumptuous utilitarian objects and the ability of the late Gothic goldsmiths to satisfy the demand.

Increases in living standards and the rise of a successful middle class facilitated an expansion of production of metal household objects. Paralleling the tendencies in painting and sculpture, kitchen and table utensils show marked gains in elegance and refinement. Utilitarian objects, such as door knockers, eating utensils, weights, and measures were often cast in baser metals such as bronze, brass, iron, and zinc. The last was commonly used for tankards, pitchers, and pilgrims' badges, although the Schöner Brunnen (Beautiful Fountain) of 1408 in the marketplace in Braunschweig attests to more lavish and decorative uses of even the so-called baser metals. Ever more elaborate iron door hinges, gates, and grilles indicate the tendency toward more complex pattern and profuse decoration in virtually all Late Gothic metalwork. German metalsmiths particularly excelled in the production of elaborate locks, with Nuremberg achieving status as the principal center.

Only in large, physically and economically secure cities could metalwork in costly materials be extensively developed. The high degree of craftsmanship seen in reliquaries produced in Aachen during the fourteenth and fifteenth centuries attests to the prominence of local metalsmiths. During the late Gothic period, Nuremberg stands out as one of the principal centers of metalwork in Europe, as seen in the shrine of St. Sebaldus (1519) by Peter Vischer the Elder. Prior to the mid–fourteenth century, the major brass casting areas in the German lands had been in Lower Saxony and the Rhine-Maas region. By the end of the century, Nuremberg had become the principal center of brass and bronze production. Important bronze foundries also existed in northern Germany, as evinced by the immense tabernacle of the Marien-kirche (Church of the Virgin) in Lübeck.

BIBLIOGRAPHY

Falk, Otto von, and Erich Meyer. *Bronzegeräte des Mittelalters.* 5 vols. to date. Denkmäler deutscher Kunst. Berlin: Deutscher Verlag für Kunstwissenschaft, 1935–1992.

Fritz, Johann Michael. *Gestochene Bilder: Gravierungen auf deutschen Goldschmiedearbeiten der Spätgotik.* Ph.D. diss., University of Freiburg im Breisgau, 1961. Beihefte der Bonner Jahrbücher 20. Cologne: Böhlau Verlag, 1966.

———. *Goldschmiedekunst der Gotik in Mitteleuropa.* Munich: C. H. Beck, 1982.

Grimme, Ernst Günther. *Aachener Godlschmiedekunst in Westfalen von Karl dem Großen bis zu Karl V.* Cologne: E. A. Seemann, 1957.

Heppe, Karl Bernd. "Gotische Goldschmiedekunst in Westfalen vom zweiten Drittel des 13. Jahrhunderts bis zur Mitte des 16. Jahrhunderts." Ph.D. diss., University Münster, 1973.

Kohlhaussen, Heinrich. *Nüremberger Goldschmiedekunst des Mittelalters und der Dürerzeit 1240 bis 1540.* Berlin: Deutscher Verlag für Kunstwissenschaft, 1968.

———. *Europäisches Kunsthandwerk,* vol. 2, *Gotik und Spätgotik.* Frankfurt am Main: Umschau Verlag, 1970.

Wixom, William. "The Art of Nuremberg Brass Work," in *Gothic and Renaissance Art in Nuremberg 1300–1550.* New York: Metropolitan Museum of Art, and Munich: Prestel, 1986, pp. 75–80.

Scott Bradford Montgomery

SEE ALSO

Braunschweig; Heraldry; Liturgical Vestments, Manuscripts, and Objects; Metalworking; Nuremberg; Relics and Reliquaries

Painting

Although much of that written about the Late Gothic era concerns architecture, painting from 1430 to 1500 underwent a sweeping change in the German-speaking lands. In the first half of the period, the art of the southern Netherlands—Robert Campin and Jan van Eyck—was influential. Later, the style of Rogier van der Weyden was even more widespread.

The contrast of the Upper and Lower Rhine with Lucas Moser and Stefan Lochner appears at the beginning of this change. Although nothing is known of Moser's life, his famous Magdalen Altar (1432) from the church of the Magdalen in Tiefenbronn, has an inscription that has never been satisfactorily interpreted: "Weep, art, weep, yourself deplore. No one loves you anymore. 1432 Lucas Moser, painter from Weil, master of this work, pray to God for him." The main panels of the outside show scenes from the life of the Magdalen from the *Legenda aurea.* In the gable is shown the conversion of the Magdalen as she washes Christ's feet; the central panels represent the voyage of the Magdalen to Marseilles with companions, the appearance of the Magdalen to the prince and princess in the palace above her sleeping companions, and the last communion of the Magdalen. The predella, or lower panel, shows Christ flanked by the wise and foolish Virgins.

The origin of Stefan Lochner in the Lake Constance region is certain, but his style shows little connection to the art of the area. Instead it is closer—especially in the soft modeling of forms—to the art of the Veronica Master of Cologne and the Westphalian painting of Conrad van Soest. Lochner's Last Judgment (ca. 1435), probably his earliest work in Cologne, served as a model for many later artists. His most famous painting, done for the chapel of the city council of Cologne, is the so-called *Dombild,* or Adoration of the Magi (1440–1445), now in the cathedral. St. Ursula, who was martyred in Cologne in the third century, stands with her companions on the left wing, and St. Gereon, the patron saint of Cologne, and his companions occupy the right wing. A limited palette of colors—red, blue, yellow or gold, and green for the ground—is used. The Annunciation on the outside of the wings is cooler in color. His Madonna in the Rose Bower, circa 1450 (Cologne, Wallraf-Richartz-Museum), shows rounded forms and circles throughout, with its gentle, religious spirit. The Presentation in the Temple of 1447 (Darmstadt, Landesmuseum) was given by the Knights of the Teutonic Order for their church, St. Catherine in Cologne. Lochner has added many people—men, women, and choirboys—to the scene. At the right, a frontal figure dressed as a member of the Teutonic Order faces the viewer; he holds a sign with the date and at one time probably held in his right hand a reliquary in the shape of a cross.

To the south, the Master of the Darmstadt passion, active between 1435 and 1450, was almost the only German artist to orient himself on the works of Jan van Eyck. His altar from Bad Orb is now in Darmstadt. His rich color, chiaroscuro lighting, and surface texture are all Eyckian. His tendency toward linear style and deeper color range, however, set him apart from his contemporaries. In Ulm, Hans Multscher, who became a citizen in 1427 and died in 1467, made paintings that show an interest in religious sculpture. The wings of his Wurzach Altar from 1437 (Berlin, Gemäldegalerie) show heavy, expressive figures casting shadows and painted in strong color.

Farther south, Konrad Witz (ca. 1410–1446), from Swabia, established himself in Basel in 1434. His earliest work, the Heilspiegel Altarpiece (Altar of Human Salvation), circa 1435, is now in the Kunstmuseum, Basel. The figures are short in proportion but solid and rounded with angular drapery folds with reflected light on the edges. His last known work, the Miraculous Draught of Fishes, the central panel of the Altarpiece of St. Peter, 1444 (Geneva, Musée d'Art et d'Histoire), gives a wonderful view of the Swiss countryside. The eye is led into the scene by forms seen underneath the sur-

face of the water, providing a harmonious unity of man and nature.

About the same time, in 1446, Johann Koerbecke was recorded in Münster. He died in 1491. In the altarpiece he painted in 1457 for the monastery of Marienfeld, his figures have solidity and vigorous movement, and the draperies more weight and texture. The work of Koerbecke and his contemporaries exemplifies the transformation of the International Style into a more angular and severe style in the first half of the fifteenth century.

In Austria, Konrad Laib became a Salzburg citizen in 1448 and adopted Netherlandish compositions as in the Crucifixion, 1449 (Vienna, Österreichische Galerie, Belvedere). The Death of the Virgin, circa 1450, by the Master of Schloss Liechtenstein shows the influence of Tournai painters, but with more elongated figures.

In the later fifteenth century, the work of Rogier van der Weyden with its linear, rhythmic compositions within a spatial setting found a closer following than earlier styles. In Cologne, not far from the Netherlandish border, the Netherlandish style was strong, but some of the Cologne style remains. The anonymous Master of the Life of Mary, active circa 1460–1495, is named after a large altarpiece from 1463 with eighteen panels representing scenes from the life of the Virgin (Munich, Alte Pinakothek); he also painted a panel for the church of St. Ursula in Cologne (London, National Gallery). Although his figures show the immobility of Dierc Bouts, the sky is gold and there is little focused light to cast shadows. Another anonymous painter, the Master of the St. Bartholomew Altarpiece, created his earliest work, the Book of Hours of Sophia von Bylant, circa 1475, in Utrecht or Arnhem. Around 1480 he arrived in Cologne, where he created his mature works. Among them, the St. Thomas Altar of 1499 (Cologne, Wallraf-Richartz-Museum) and the St. Bartholomew Altar (Munich, Alte Pinakothek) of circa 1503, after which the artist is named, exemplify his style of intricate drapery folds and a wide range of mixed colors, especially in the costumes—a striking contrast to the works of the Master of the Life of Mary.

On the Upper Rhine, the outstanding painter of the time was Martin Schongauer, although his reputation today depends on his prints. His father, a goldsmith, moved to Colmar in 1440. Close to Rogier van der Weyden, he leaves only one dated painting, the Virgin and Child in a Rose Bower of 1473 (Colmar, church of St. Martin). Monumental in conception, the figures are broader than Rogier's. His influence spread far beyond the region where he worked. In Schongauer's generation, one of the most original engravers was the anonymous Housebook Master, so-called from a manuscript of 1475 in Waldburg-Wolfegg Castle, who invented a new method of engraving called drypoint. He was also a talented painter whose *Lovers* (1479) in Gotha is more linear and delicate in light and modeling. Friedrich Herlin was the main follower of Netherlandish ideas in Nördlingen. He arrived there in 1459 and in 1462–1465 painted the St. George Altarpiece for the city church (Nördlingen, Städtisches Museum). Sharper modeling and lesser atmospheric quality give to Herlin's imitation of Flemish style a flattened space and provincialism. The Family Altarpiece of 1488 (Nördlingen, Town Hall) is his most mature work. The Virgin holds the Child in a position close to that found in the paintings of Memling, and there is a greater unity of form and spatial arrangement than in his earlier paintings.

Hans Pleydenwurff moved to Nuremberg about 1450 and died at the height of his career in 1472. His Descent from the Cross from the Breslau Altar, 1462 (Nuremberg, Germanisches Nationalmuseum), lacks a transition between foreground figures and background landscape. The flattened composition is emphasized by the patterned gold brocade as sky. In his late Crucifixion (Munich, Alte Pinakothek) of circa 1470, the composition is based on Rogier's types under the cross and a wide landscape. After the death of Pleydenwurff, Michael Wolgemut, Albrecht Dürer's teacher, married Pleydenwurff's widow and inherited the shop. Dürer's Apocalypse (1498) was the first woodcut series on which all future printed interpretations of the Apocalypse were based.

Michael Pacher, born near Brixen in today's Italy and died 1498, invented a style that was not dependent on Rogier. His St. Wolfgang Altar, completed 1479–1481, is still in the church for which it was made, the church of St. Wolfgang on the Abersee in Austria. Covering a sculptured inner shrine are two sets of wings with paintings. The sculpted pinnacles and canopies rise thirteen feet into the church vaults. The outer shutters have four scenes from the life of St. Wolfgang. When these wings are open, eight panels of the life of Christ are seen. The inner shutters show scenes from the Life of the Virgin. Pacher's style shows diagonal lines that take deep plunges into space along the lines of the architecture. The figures become smaller from foreground to far distance. He paints sweeping draperies, and the foreground figures are giants seen from below.

Rueland Frueauf the Elder was the leading master in Salzburg and Passau after 1470. In the 1490s his Rogier-influenced style changed to a calmer mode often referred to as a classicizing trend in Late Gothic art. His Annunciation from an altar of the Life of the Virgin, 1490 (Vienna, Österreichische Galerie), shows monumental forms similar to those of Michael Pacher, with a Flemish base that created a clear style with even lighting.

Since the forms of Late Gothic architecture had reduced the wall area of churches available for paintings, works in this medium played a lesser role, and artists made elaborate altarpieces with folding wings, sometimes combining wood carving and paintings. The spread of mysticism across Germany gave to the gospel story, especially the Passion of Christ and devotional images, an expressive interest.

BIBLIOGRAPHY

Bial-Ostocki. "Late Gothic: Disagreements about the Concept." *Journal of the British Archaeological Association,* n.s. 3, 29 (1966): 76–105.

———. *Spätmittelalter und Beginnende Neuzeit.* Propyläen Kunstgeschichte 7. Frankfurt am Main: Propyläen Verlag, 1972, pp. 62–63, 98–101.

———. "Late Gothic," in *Dictionary of Art,* ed. Jane Turner. 34 vols. London: Macmillan, 1996, vol. 18, pp. 826–828.

Stange, Alfred. *Deutsche Malerei der Gotik.* 10 vols. Berlin: Deutscher Kunstverlag, 1934–1960.

———. *German Painting XIV–XVI Centuries.* New York: Hyperion, 1951.

Marta O. Renger

SEE ALSO

Basel; Cologne; Conrad von Soest; Herlin, Friedrich; Housebook, Master of the; International Style; Koerbecke, Johann; Life of Mary, Master of; Lochner, Stefan; Moser, Lucas; Münster; Multscher, Hans; Nuremberg; Pacher, Michael; Pleydenwurff, Hans; Salzburg; Sankt Bartholomew Altarpiece, Master of; Sankt Veronica, Master of; Schongauer, Martin; Ulm; Witz, Konrad; Wolgemut, Michael

Sculpture

From the later fourteenth through the early sixteenth century there was a tremendous demand for all types of sculpture throughout Germany. Unlike the previous period in which much of the sculpture was cut in stone and destined to adorn a fixed architectural setting, Late Gothic sculpture was characterized by its diversity of both materials and uses. Fueled by a waxing lay and civic pa-

Tilmann Riemenschneider, Altar of the Holy Blood, central shrine and wings, Rothenburg ob der Tauber, Church of St. James (Jakobskirche). *Photograph: Joan A. Holladay*

tronage, sculpture increasingly embodied personal, social, and religious aspirations. Ambitious clerics, nobles, and above all, burghers, embellished their churches, their residences, and their cities. Individual and communal faith was manifested pictorially in the form of an altarpiece, holy statue, or memorial, such as a tomb or epitaph. Only the advent of the Protestant Reformation, with its fundamental questioning of the role of religious art and its attendant iconoclasm beginning in about 1520, stanched this demand, which may have already peaked around 1500. Ulm Münster (1377–1531) possessed fifty-two endowed altars; the cathedral at Constance had sixty-three altars. Even small parish churches were enriched with a carved and, often, painted retable as well as a wealth of secondary art.

As needs changed so did the character of the sculptor's workshop. The fifteenth century witnessed the rise of numerous large ateliers headed by a single master who was usually, although not always, a sculptor. Exceptions include the Syrlins—joiners active in Ulm and Blaubeuren—and painter Michael Wolgemut of Nuremberg. The production of an altarpiece required the collaboration of sculptors, painters, and joiners. Tillmann Riemenschneider of Würzburg is credited with carving no fewer than 143 altarpieces and other sculptures in wood and stone for patrons throughout Franconia. Rothenburg ob der Tauber alone possessed seven of his altars. To handle this demand, Riemenschneider is documented training twelve apprentices between 1501 and 1517 who supplemented the other highly skilled artisans in his workshop. For some of the most successful masters, such as Hans Multscher or the Erharts of Ulm, it is often difficult differentiating between the master's own hand and those of followers mimicking his forms. Increasingly many of the most talented masters developed personal styles that distinguished their creations or, at least, the style of their workshops, from those of their peers. Riemenschneider's grave, dignified saints contrast instantly with Master H. L.'s (d. ca. 1533, known for the altar in the Breisach Münster) agitated figures with the marvelous calligraphic excesses of their swirling draperies as in his Coronation of the Virgin altarpiece in the Münster at Breisach.

The artistic production of any individual workshop was shaped by its geographic location and its access to adequate materials for carving. The wealthy towns of Bavaria, Franconia, Swabia, and the Rhine demanded more sculpture than most other regions of Germany. Sculptors in southern Germany had ready supplies of limewood and, in the Alps, pine, while masters like Heinrick Douwermann in Kalkar or Bernt Notke in Lübeck worked in oak. Although the same florid effects found in limewood sculpture form the later fifteenth century may be achieved in the denser oak, as in Klaus Berg's apostles in Güstrow Cathedral, its soft and elastic character permits easier, more virtuoso carving, especially cross-grain. It could be polychromed (colored) or just lightly stained. Unlike Italy, Germany lacked indigenous marble other than the bright red-flecked stone found in limited quantities around Salzburg. Sculptors resorted instead to using either sandstone or limestone, especially for funerary monuments and other projects that demanded durability. Westphalia's coarse, whitish baumberger sandstone is quite different from the finer brownish sandstone of Strasbourg. Quarries near Eichstätt yielded exceptionally fine-grain Solnhofen limestone that was well suited for small, highly detailed and polished reliefs, such as those by Hans Daucher of Augsburg. Only a few towns other than Nuremberg and Augsburg could sustain metal sculptors such as the Vischer family, who pioneered the use of brass for everything from small statuettes to monumental shrines, like the tomb of Saint Sebaldus in Nuremberg, for patrons across Europe.

German sculpture underwent dramatic transformations during this period. The "Soft Style" of the beautiful virgins, like the Krumauer Madonna (ca. 1400; Vienna, Kunsthistorisches Museum) with its gentle sway and delicate features, yielded to the growing naturalism of Hans Multscher and other masters influenced by Netherlandish art. Multscher's Madonna and Child (1437) in the parish church in Landsberg conveys a better suggestion of a weighty body moving beneath the heavy robes. Idealization is replaced by a strong individualization. Particularly effective is Christ's delicate gesture of balancing himself as he clutches Mary's robe with his right hand. Multscher's powerful Man of Sorrows (1429), with its emphasis on the convincing physical wounds and spiritual agony of Christ, commands the attention of all who enter through the main portal of the Münster in Ulm. Nicolaus Gerhaert von Leyden, the Netherlandish master who was active along the Upper Rhine and around Vienna, proved to be a catalyst to this nascent trend toward ever greater naturalism. His bust of a man (1463–1467; Strasbourg, Musée de l'Oeuvre Notre-Dame) shows a man (the artist?) captured in a moment of reflection. The fingers of his right hand press into the yielding flesh of his chin. In the epitaph of Konrad von Busang (1464; Strasbourg Cathedral), the pious canon's prayer is transformed into an intimate mystical encounter with Mary and the playful Christ child who reaches out to touch the old man's hands. Gerhaert's statues, many of which were subsequently destroyed, inspired Master E. S. and, to a lesser degree, Martin Schongauer of Colmar, whose engravings made Gerhaert's style accessible to a broad audience. As the quality of prints improved from the 1460s, sculptors increasingly borrowed their compositions. Even inventive masters like Riemenschneider or Veit Stoss of Nuremberg occasionally turned to a Schongauer engraving for inspiration. With the concurrent rise in demand for elaborate altarpieces, sculptors often needed such models for the carved reliefs or painted panels of the wings. Michael Pacher of Bruneck, Michel Erhart of Ulm and his son Gregor in Augsburg, Riemenschneider, Stoss, Nikolaus Hagenower of Strasbourg, Niklaus Weckmann of Ulm, the Dauchers of Augsburg, Master H. L. at Breisach, and Hans Leinberger of Landshut are among the masters who produced large and ever more intricate altarpieces for churches through southern Germany and the Tyrol. There were far fewer examples of this complexity in the north, although the original corpus of works has been reduced sharply by Protestant iconoclasm and wars. Bernt Notke of Lübeck's high altars for Århus Cathedral (1479) in Denmark and the Heilig-Geist-Spital (1483) in Tallinn (Revel) are far simpler in design and lack the complex superstructures and architectural frames of the southern altarpieces. His creativity is revealed better in his moving Crucifixion group (1477) in Lübeck Cathedral and his St. George slaying the dragon (1489) in Stockholm (Storkyrka).

Sculptors during this period diversified their art. While most of their work was destined for a church setting, they carved fountains such as the Schöner Brunnen (Beautiful Fountain) of circa 1385–1396 or Peter Flötner's Apollo Fountain of 1532, both in Nuremberg; statues for city halls and public buildings like Multscher's Charlemagne figure of circa 1427–1429 in Ulm or Adam

Kraft's Weighing House relief of 1497 in Nuremberg; or the various house madonnas by Kraft and Stoss in the some city. Portrait sculpture, including medals, statuettes either carved in fruitwood or cast in bronze or bress, and allegorical reliefs became popular, especially in Augsburg and Nuremberg during the opening decades of the sixteenth century. This trend toward collectible personal sculpture and secular public projects would continue especially as the Reformation threatened religious art and sculptors' livelihoods.

BIBLIOGRAPHY

Baxandall, Michael. *The Limewood Sculptors of Renaissance Germany.* New Haven, Conn.: Yale University Press, 1980.

Decker, Bernhard. "Das Ende des mittelalterlichen Kultbildes und die Plastik Hans Leinbergers." Ph.D. diss., University of Frankfurt am Main, 1976. Bamberger Studien zur Kunstgeschichte und Denkmal-pflege 3. Bamberg: Lehrstuhl für Kunstgeschichte und Aufbaustudium Denkmalpflege an der Universität Bamberg, 1985.

Guillot de Suduiraut, Sophie. *Sculptures allemandes de la fin du moyen âge dans les collections publiques françaises 1400–1530.* Paris: Réunion des Musées Nationaux, 1991.

Huth, Hans. *Künstler und Werkstatt der Spätgotik,* 1925, rpt. Darmstadt: Wissenschaftliche Buchgesellschaft, 1967.

Karrenbrock, Reinhard. *Westfälische Steinskulptur des späten Mittelalters 1380–1540.* Unna: Kreis Unna, Oberkreisdirektor, 1992.

Krohm, Hartmut, and Eike Oellermann, eds. *Flügelaltäre des späten Mittelalters.* Berlin: Reimer, 1992.

Liebmann, Michael J. *Die deutsche Plastik 1350–1550,* trans. Hans Störel. Leipzig: VEB Seemann Buch- und Kunstverlag, 1982.

Meisterwerke massenhaft: Die Bildhauerwerkstatt des Niklaus Weckmann und die Malerei in Ulm um 1500. Stuttgart: Württembergisches Landesmuseum, 1993.

Müller, Theodor. *Sculpture in the Netherlands, Germany, France, and Spain 1400 to 1500.* Pelican History of Art. Baltimore: Penguin, 1966.

Rommé, Barbara. *Gegen den Strom: Meisterwerke niederrheinischer Skulptur in Zeiten der Reformation 1500–1550.* Berlin: Reimer, 1997.

Schädler, Alfred. *Deutsche Plastik der Spätgotik.* Die blauen Bücher. Königstein im Taunus: K.R. Langewiesche Nachfolger, 1962.

Schindler, Herbert. *Der Schnitzaltar: Meisterwerke und Meister in Süddeutschland, Österreich und Südtirol.* Regensburg: Pustet, 1978.

Schmidt, Wolfgang. *Altäre der Hoch- und Spätgotik.* Publikationen der Gesellschaft für Rheinische Geschichtskunde n. F. 12, Abt. 1b. Cologne: Rheinland-Verlag, 1985.

Jeffrey Chipps Smith

SEE ALSO

Augsburg; Constance; Erhart, Gregor; Erhart, Michel; E. S., Master; Iconographies, Innovative; International Style; Kraft, Adam; Leinberger, Hans; Lübeck; Multscher, Hans; Nicolaus Gerhaert von Leyden; Notke, Bernt; Nuremberg; Pacher, Michael; Riemenschneider, Tillmann; Rothenburg ob der Tauber; Salzburg; Schongauer, Martin; Stoss, Veit; Strasbourg; Ulm; Vienna; Weckmann, Nicolas; Wolgemut, Michael; Würzburg

Gothic Language

Gothic is the earliest attested of the Germanic languages, with the exception of scattered inscriptions. Although most of the manuscripts are of the sixth century, the texts are for the most part of the fourth century, when Wulfila (311–ca. 381), bishop of the Goths, devised an alphabet and translated the Bible into his native tongue. Though some have complained that it is overly literal, it is a splendid translation and reveals his careful thought in almost every word. Besides the translation of the Bible, we have a number of other precious fragments, such as the *Skeireins,* a commentary on the Gospel of John, some deeds concerning property of the Gothic Church in Italy, some remarks on Gothic pronunciation and some sentences in Gothic (a Salzburg-Vienna manuscript), and the like. Recently, some lead plates inscribed in Gothic, inserted in graves for apotropaic (prevention) purposes, have been found in Hungary.

The manuscripts containing Gothic have offered numerous problems to scholars. The best known of them is the *Codex argenteus,* or Golden Manuscript, preserved in the library of Uppsala University in Sweden. One of the most precious manuscripts in the world, thanks to the rarity of the language and the adornment, it is written in gold and silver ink on purple parchment, presumably for Theodorich the Great. (A reconstituted page of this manuscript can be seen at www.lang.uiuc.edu/LLL/lll.html) Most of the other manuscripts of biblical Gothic are palimpsests, that is, manuscripts in which the Gothic has been scraped off and another text has been written over the Gothic. This, coupled with the fact that nineteenth-century scholars treated the manuscripts with reagents such as nutgall, makes them quite difficult to decipher.

Gothic has had enough influence on Old High German that authorities such as Wrede have spoken of that language as "gotisiertes Westgermanisch" (West Germanic Gothic). For example, words like *Kirche* (church), *Pfaffe* (minister), *Engel* (angel), and *Teufel* (devil) are said to show Gothic influence, and the use of *ther wîho atum* (the Holy Breath) instead of *ther heilago geist* (the Holy Ghost/Spirit) is thought to show Gothic missionary activity in Germany. The *Codex argenteus* itself is thought to have been brought to Germany from Italy under Charlemagne, and many works, such as that of Walahfrid Strabo, reveal knowledge of the Goths and Gothic, as is also shown in the famous Salzburg-Vienna Alcuin manuscript.

Gothic is important also for the textual criticism of the New Testament. It is the oldest extant representative of the so-called Byzantine version. This, along with Wulfila's well-known fidelity to the original text and his care in translating, makes Gothic the most important witness to that most important version.

As the oldest well-attested Germanic language, as well as almost the only extant witness to East Germanic, Gothic is of primary importance in the reconstruction of Proto-Germanic and in the understanding of many of the processes of the other Germanic languages. It remains the foundation stone of comparative Germanic linguistics.

BIBLIOGRAPHY

Marchand, James W. "Gotisch," in *Kurzer Grundriß der germanischen Philologie bis 1500.* Berlin: de Gruyter, 1969, pp. 94–122.

Mossé, Fernand. "Bibliographica gothica." *Mediaeval Studies* 12 (1950): 237–324; First Supplement, 15 (1953): 169–183; Second Supplement (James W. Marchand), 19 (1957): 174–196; Third Supplement (Ernst A. Ebbinghaus), 29 (1967): 328–343; Fourth Supplement (Ernst A. Ebbinghaus): 199–214.

Streitberg, Wilhelm. *Die gotische Bibel,* 2 vols. Germanische Bibliothek, 2, 3. Heildelberg: winter, 1908–1910. 2d ed. corrected, 1919–1938. 3d ed., 1950. 4th ed., 1960–1965 [standard edition, with dictionary].

Stutz, Elfriede. "Die germanistische These vom "Donauweg" gotisch-arianischer Missionare im 5. und 6. Jahrhundert," in *Die Völker an der mittleren und unteren Donau im 5. und 6. Jahrhundert,* ed. Herwig Wolfram and Falko Daim. Vienna: Österreichische Akademie der Wissenschaften, 1980, pp. 207–224.

James W. Marchand

SEE ALSO
Alcuin; Bible; Charlemagne; Conversion; Walahfrid Strabo

Gottesfreunde
See Friends of Gods.

Gottfried von Straßburg (fl. 1210)

The greatest poet of the German Middle Ages, Gottfried is known for his Middle High German *Tristan* romance, a fragment of just under twenty thousand lines composed in rhymed couplets. Gottfried may also be the author of two poems in the famous Manesse manuscript (University of Heidelberg library) under Ulrich von Liechtenstein's name. Falsely attributed to him are three other poems that are found in various manuscripts. The contours of his biography remain vague owing to lack of historical evidence. Ulrich von Türheim and Heinrich von Freiberg, two thirteenth-century writers of continuations of his fragment, name Gottfried explicitly as its author. That the majority of the earliest manuscripts were probably produced in Alsace or even directly in Strasbourg (he is known by the German form Straßburg) locates Gottfried in this medieval cultural center.

Our clearest picture of him is provided by the romance itself. Its date of composition—generally put at around 1210—is based mainly on mention in its so-called literary excursus of the poets Heinrich von Veldeke and Reinmar von Hagenau as being deceased, and of Hartmann von Aue, Bligger von Steinach, and Walther von der Vogelweide as still living. Gottfried's remarkable erudition—so evident throughout the romance—in French, German, and classical Latin literature; rhetoric and poetics; theology; law; and music as well as the elegance and artistry of his language and style are a sure indication of a humanist cathedral school education.

Though familiar with several versions of the Tristan story, Gottfried claims allegiance to only one: Thomas of Britain, of whose work only the latter part, which Gottfried did not get to, has survived. Until recently, only two small fragments overlapped with Gottfried's version, thus hampering a precise determination of Gottfried's reliance on Thomas. In 1995, however, a new fragment of Thomas's work surfaced that coincides with key scenes in Gottfried, namely, Tristan's and Isolde's reactions to the love potion, their arrival in Cornwall, and the wedding night. Initial assessments have led scholars to revise the prevalent (though not unanimous) assumption of Gottfried's fairly high degree of faithfulness to Thomas. For one thing, Gottfried innovated more than was previously thought; for another, it is now supposed that Gottfried drew on a greater number of sources. Among these, Eilhart von Oberge has gained particular significance because of common elements not found in the new Thomas fragment.

Though it shares numerous features with chivalric Arthurian romance, Gottfried's *Tristan* has more accurately been termed a courtier romance, since its hero acts more often in the capacity of courtier and artist than of knight, and since the narrative action tends to occur in the worldly, political arena of the court, rather than to depict knights on marvelous quests for adventure. Not only is Gottfried thoroughly acquainted with, he also details and explores various facets of the decorum, mores, and material culture of the court.

What follows is a highly condensed summary of the romance. It begins with a prologue in which Gottfried's narrator persona sets a discriminating tone by describing the audience of "noble hearts" to whom he specifically addresses his work. This elite group distinguishes itself by seeking not merely joy but by accepting both joy and sorrow, sweetness and bitterness into their lives. Gottfried offers them his love story as a palliative for the pain they suffer from love, and introduces his hero and heroine as the epitome of true lovers. The first strophes of the prologue create the acrostic *GDIETÊRICHTI*. *Dietêrich* is assumed to be Gottfried's patron (an otherwise unknown Dietrich), the *G* may be short for "Gottfried," and the *TI* stands for Tristan and Isolde.

The plot opens with an account of Tristan's parents, Riwalin and Blancheflur. Riwalin of Parmenie journeys to Cornwall, where he intends to refine his manners and his knightly skills at the court of the highly reputable King Marke. He and Marke's sister Blancheflur fall in love and conceive a child. Blancheflur steals away with Riwalin to Parmenie, where they marry. Riwalin's death in battle at the hand of his overlord Morgan causes Blancheflur to die of grief on giving birth to Tristan. To protect Tristan from Morgan, Riwalin's loyal marshal Rual has Tristan grow up as his child, though he sees to it that Tristan receives an education befitting a future ruler.

At age fourteen Tristan is kidnapped by Norwegian ship merchants but is later released on the shores of Cornwall. He meets King Marke, who takes Tristan into close favor on the basis of his dazzling accomplishments in hunting, musical performance, and foreign languages. Not until Rual arrives after a three-and-a-half-year search are Marke and Tristan enlightened as to their relationship as uncle and nephew.

Tristan is knighted in a ceremony whose portrayal is extraordinary for its literary value and its contravention of reader expectations. Initially dispensing with literal depiction, Gottfried cloaks events in allegory instead. From here he shifts to a metapoetic level, where his narrator persona expresses (ironically) an inability to prepare Tristan appropriately for the ceremony. A eulogistic critique of style follows of the five contemporary German poets and minnesingers mentioned above; one unnamed poet (in all likelihood Wolfram von Eschenbach) receives scathing criticism. Now thoroughly "tongue-tied," however, the poet requests inspiration to complete his task in a two-part invocation: first to Apollo and the Muses, then to the supernal Christian God. Only after distinguishing Tristan from his compatriots by delineating his special inborn virtues does Gottfried descend to the literal level and describe the presentation of sword, spurs, and shield. In disdaining to tell of the tournament that concludes the ceremony, Gottfried both distances himself from and gets in a sly dig at contemporaries who go on and on about such spectacles in great detail. The literary excursus is significant for its unique vernacular contribution to literary criticism.

The next episodes involve Tristan in trials of battle, in politics, and at court. His journey to Parmenie includes an attempt to legitimize his right to hold his father's fief. The encounter between Tristan and his would-be overlord, Morgan, goes awry, however, and Tristan ends up killing Morgan and acquiring his lands by force.

Upon Tristan's return to Cornwall, he learns that Marke is not an autonomous ruler but has been obliged since childhood to pay tribute to King Gurmun of Ireland. Taking up their cause, Tristan delivers Marke's kingdoms from further subjection by killing Gurmun's envoy, Morolt. During their judicial duel, one of Tristan's blows leaves a piece of his sword lodged in Morolt's skull. By his turn, Morolt has wounded Tristan with his poisoned sword, informing him that only his sister, Queen Isolde of Ireland, can cure him of its fatal effect. Tristan sets off for Ireland disguised as the minstrel/merchant "Tantris," and gains access to the queen by means of his sweetly compelling musical performance. She cures him in exchange for tutoring her daughter, the princess Isolde, whom he educates in letters, music, and courteous manners. After his return to Cornwall, intrigues brew against him by barons envious of his position as Marke's heir. To appease them, Marke reluctantly agrees to marry Princess Isolde, hoping this venture will fail because of the hostility between the two countries. But Tristan, who heads the bridal quest, succeeds. First he kills the dragon who has been terrorizing the Irish countryside, a prerequisite to winning Isolde's hand. The dragon's tongue, however, which Tristan has cut out as proof, is poisonous, and causes Tristan to sink, unconscious, into a bog. Meanwhile, the cowardly Irish steward, having found and appropriated the carcass of the dragon, has claimed Isolde as his reward, much to the dismay of the royal family. Through concerted efforts, the queen and her daughter find "Tantris," and the queen cures him anew.

A combination of events leads to Princess Isolde's discovery of Tristan's identity, and she almost slays him in revenge for Morolt. Spared, Tristan conveys Marke's offer of marriage and, after assisting the queen in thwarting the steward with his testimony, Tristan sails for Cornwall with Princess Isolde and Brangaene, her maid, in tow. Brangaene is in possession of a love potion given her by the queen, who wishes to ensure her daughter's happiness with her new husband, King Marke. But Tristan and Isolde inadvertently drink the potion together on their voyage, sealing their eternal love for each other. Though they consummate their love on the ship, loyalty forces Tristan to deliver Isolde to Marke, whom she weds. On the wedding night, Brangaene stands in for Isolde in order to conceal Isolde's loss of virginity. Fearing treason, Isolde attempts to have Brangaene murdered, but Brangaene demonstrates her discretion and trustworthiness, and continues to help the lovers carry on their clandestine affair.

When the Cornish steward Marjodo chances to discover their adulterous relationship, he relates "rumors" of it to Marke, who embarks on a series of attempts designed to catch the lovers out. Finally, the growing threat to the king's reputation and authority by the rumors induces Marke to force Isolde to undergo an ordeal of the hot iron. In this famous episode, the king desires the queen to destroy the rumors. She performs this feat with such calculating ingenuity and winning courtesy that the iron does not burn her when she carries it. Thus she restores both her own and the king's honor.

At court the lovers, unable to restrain their display of mutual affection, provoke Marke to banish them. They take refuge in a cave of lovers whose qualities bear mention. Each of the architectural elements of the cave is allegorically appropriate to a true lover's environment: the white, smooth wall means love's integrity, the cave's width is love's strength, its green floor love's constancy, and the crystal bed love's purity. Moreover, the door to the cave is constructed so as to admit only true lovers. Miraculously, the lovers need not eat, but subsist solely on love and love's gazes. One day, Marke happens upon the cave while hunting. Anticipating detection, Tristan places a sword between Isolde and himself before they fall asleep together. The sword's position convinces Marke of their innocence, and he has them fetched back to court.

There Isolde plans a rendezvous with Tristan in the garden in the face of increased surveillance by her husband. Marke discovers them while they are sleeping, but Tristan awakens in time to see him depart. Realizing that they must part company, Tristan and Isolde say a tender farewell, and Tristan flees Cornwall before Marke returns with his councillors.

Tristan seeks combat in an attempt to divert himself (albeit unsuccessfully) from the pain of separation from Isolde. He travels to Arundel, a coastal duchy, where he assists the inhabitants to a victory. On meeting its ruler's daughter, Isolde of the White Hands, Tristan spirals into confusion; her beauty and her name remind him of his Isolde. Isolde of the White Hands meanwhile falls in love with Tristan. Their proximity to each other at court causes Tristan to waver in his original love, and the romance breaks off as he laments the unfairness of his situation.

The dialectic and the nature of Gottfried's concept of love, his unorthodox relationship to Christianity, his attitude toward courtliness, and the interplay between narrator excursuses and narrative action are only some of the many aspects of the romance that have served both to stimulate and to vex scholarly attempts at interpretation. And yet, despite the obstacles caused by the abundant ambivalences and ironies and, quite simply, the alterity (uniqueness) of the work, Gottfried continues to delight and seduce his readership, leaving the impression of a brilliant poet, an aesthete of aloof yet discerning eye, and a superb master in absolute control of his art.

BIBLIOGRAPHY

Batts, Michael. *Gottfried von Strassburg.* New York: Twayne, 1971.

Chinca, Mark. *Gottfried von Strassburg: Tristan.* Cambridge: Cambridge University Press, 1997.

Dietz, Reiner. *Der "Tristan" Gottfrieds von Strassburg. Probleme der Forschung (1902–1970).* Göppingen: Kümmerle, 1974.

Draesner, Ulrike. "Zeichen—Körper—Gesang. Das Lied in der Isolde-Weiss-Hand Episode des "Tristans" Gotfrits von Strassburg," in *Wechselspiele: Kommunikationsformen und Gattungsinterferenzen mittelhochdeutscher Lyrik,* ed. Michael Schilling and Peter Strohschneider. Heidelberg: Winter, 1996, pp. 77–101.

Gottfried von Straßburg. *Tristan,* ed. Peter Ganz. Wiesbaden: Brockhaus, 1978 [text of Reinhold Bechstein's edition 1890–1891].

———. *Tristan,* ed. and trans. Rüdiger Krohn, 3 vols. Stuttgart: Reclam, 1984–1995 [text of Friedrich Ranke's edition 1930].

———. *Tristan,* ed. Karl Marold and Werner Schröder. Berlin: de Gruyter, 1906, rpt. 1969.

———. *"Tristan"* with the *"Tristan"* of Thomas, trans. A. T. Hatto. Harmondsworth: Penguin, 1967.

Haug, Walter. "Reinterpreting the Tristan Romances of Thomas and Gotfrid: Implications of a Recent Discovery." *Arthuriana* 7 (1997): 45–59.

Jackson, W. T. H. *The Anatomy of Love: The "Tristan" of Gottfried von Strassburg.* New York: Columbia University Press, 1971.

Jaeger, C. Stephen. *Medieval Humanism in Gottfried von Strassburg's "Tristan und Isolde."* Heidelberg: Carl Winter, 1977.

Kucaba, Kelley. "Höfisch inszenierte Wahrheiten. Zu Isolds Gottesurteil bei Gottfried von Strassburg," in *Fremdes wahrnehmen—fremdes Wahrnehmen,* ed. Wolfgang Harms and C. Stephen Jaeger in connection with Alexandra Stein. Stuttgart: Hirzel, 1997, pp. 73–93.

Picozzi, Rosemary. *A History of Tristan Scholarship.* Bern: Lang, 1971.

Steinhoff, Hans-Hugo. *Bibliographie zu Gottfried von Srassburg,* 2 vols. Berlin: Schmidt, 1971–1986.

Stevens, Adrian, and Roy Wisbey, eds. *Gottfried von Strassburg and the Medieval Tristan Legend.* Papers from an Anglo–North American Symposium. Cambridge: Brewer, 1990.

Wenzel, Horst. "Öffentlichkeit und Heimlichkeit in Gottfrieds *Tristan.*" *Zeitschrift für deutsche Philologie* 107 (1988): 335–361.

Kelley Kucaba

SEE ALSO

Eilhart von Oberge; Hartmann von Aue; Ulrich von Liechtenstein; Ulrich von Türheim; Walter von der Vogelweide; Wolfram von Eschenbach

Gottfried von Straßburg, *Tristan,* Illustrations

Represented in some thirty-five art works in the German-speaking region, the Tristan story is rivaled only by the Charlemagne/Roland material among secular literary motives in the visual arts. Beyond the sheer number of artifacts, two things distinguish the iconography of Tristan from that of other romance materials: the popularity of the subject in nonbook settings and noncyclical works, and the thematic uniformity of Tristan pictorializations.

The most popular motive in noncyclical works is the "orchard scene," in which Tristan and Isolde deceive Marke, who spies on them from a tree. The standard depiction of the scene was influenced by the iconography of the Fall of Man: a man and a woman under a tree, with Marke visually analogous to the serpent in the tree. In general, however, the meaning of the Fall of Man was not transferred to the orchard scene, which became an iconic representation of love and lovers, albeit perhaps with different significances in different contexts.

Despite considerable variation in choice and number of scenes, the Tristan narrative cycles in the German language area are strikingly uniform in their basic response to the story, regarding Tristan as an exemplary knight and the love of Tristan and Isolde as an exemplary love—risky, perhaps, but ultimately triumphant, and never obviously depicted as sinful or antisocial. Among the most noteworthy of the numerous nonbook Tristan cycles from the German region area are the three Wienhausen wall hangings, the Erfurt embroidery, and the Runkelstein murals. Compared with the number of nonbook artifacts, the number of illuminated Tristan manuscripts is surprisingly small. Most spectacular is the Munich codex (Bayerische Staatsbibliothek, no. Cgm 51) of circa 1240, with approximately 118 miniatures. Other illuminated Gottfried texts are considerably later: one in Cologne (Historisches Archiv der Stadt, no. W88*), with nine line drawings, dates from 1323; another in Brussels (Bibliothèque Royale, no. 14697), with 92 large drawings, is a product of the Diebolt Lauber workshop (first third of fifteenth century). Eilhart's text is illustrated in a Swabian manuscript of 1465–1470 (Heidelberg, Universitätsbibliothek, no. Cpg 346) and the prose version, *Tristran und Isalde,* is illustrated with closely related woodcuts in two incunabula (pre-1500 printed books).

BIBLIOGRAPHY

Curschmann, Michael. "Images of Tristan," in *Gottfried von Strassburg and the Medieval Tristan Legend: Papers from an Anglo-North American Symposium,* ed. Adrian

Stevens and Roy Wisbey. London: D. S. Brewer, 1990, pp. 1–17.

Ott, Norbert H. "Katalog der Tristan-Bildzeugnissen," in Hella Frühmorgen-Voss. *Text und Illustration im Mittelalter: Aufsätze zu den Wechselbeziehungen zwischen Literatur und bildende Kunst,* ed. Norbert H. Ott. Munich: Beck, 1975, pp. 119–139.

———. "*Tristan* auf Runkelstein und die übrigen zyklischen Darstellungen des Tristanstoffes: Textrezeption oder medieninterne Eigengesetzlichkeit der Bildprogramme?" in *Runkelstein: Die Wandmalereien des Sommerhauses,* ed. Walter Haug et. al. Wiesbaden: Reichert, 1982, pp. 194–239.

Walworth, Julia. "Tristan in Medieval Art." *Tristan and Isolde: A Casebook,* ed. Joan Tasker Grimbert. New York: Garland, 1995, pp. 255–299.

James A. Rushing Jr.

SEE ALSO
Charlemagne; Erfurt; Gothic Art and Architecture; Lauber, Diebolt; Roland and Charlemange, Illustrations; Runkelstein; Wienhausen

Gottschalk of Orbais (ca. 803–ca. 868)

A Saxon monk, theologian, and poet, Gottschalk was one of the most controversial religious figures in western Europe in the ninth century. He had been offered as a child to the monastery of Fulda by his parents. Upon adulthood he demanded his release, on the ground that he himself had not taken the vows of profession, and the word of another could not be binding on him. This embroiled him in a controversy with his abbot, Hrabanus Maurus, who kept the young Gottschalk in the monastery by force. Eventually the synod of Mainz (829) ruled that Gottschalk must remain in the monastic state, but at least allowed his transfer to the less hostile monastery of Orbais.

Gottschalk was a talented theologian. He developed a doctrine of double predestination that went several steps further than Augustine, teaching that from birth the elect were destined for salvation and wrongdoers to damnation. This called into question the power of divine grace in the world and roused the hostility of other leading Carolingian theologians. His old enemy Hrabanus Maurus, by then archbishop of Mainz, secured Gottschalk's condemnation at another synod of Mainz in 848. He refused to recant his beliefs, and was excommunicated and imprisoned by Archbishop Hincmar of Reims at the monastery of Hautvillers. His treatise "De praedestinatione" (On Predestination) was rediscovered in 1930. This work, along with Gottschalk's extant poetry, reveals its author as a man of deep learning and piety.

BIBLIOGRAPHY
Gottschalk. *Oevres théologiques et grammaticales de Godescalc d'Orbais,* ed. Cyrille Lambot. Louvain: Spicilegium Sacrum Lovaniense, 1945.

———. *Die Gedichte des Gottschalk von Orbais,* ed. Marie-Luise Weber. Frankfurt: Lang, 1992.

Nincham, D. E. "Gottschalk of Orbais: Reactionary or Precursor of the Reformation?" *Journal of Ecclesiastical History* 40 (1989): 1–18.

Vielhaber, Klaus. *Gottschalk der Sachse.* Bonn: Ludwig Röhrscheid Verlag, 1956.

Phyllis G. Jestice

SEE ALSO
Carolingians; Hrabanus Maurus

Graf Rudolf

An early courtly crusader romance from the end of the twelfth century, *Graf Rudolf* is dated 1170–1173, based on lines in the "Db" fragment where the king of Jerusalem tells about the Roman emperor who serves a rich king as cupbearer. Approximately 1,400 lines of the poem in fourteen fragments from a single manuscript are extant (Braunschweig, Stadtbibliothek, no. 5 and Göttingen, Universitätsbibliothek, no. Cod. Ms. philol. 184,7); the beginning and conclusion are missing. The dialect is Middle German, possibly from Hesse or Thuringia. The names Gilot, Beatrise, Bonifait, Appollinart, and Bonthard point to a French model. The second half (from a fragment "E") has much in common with the Old French Beuve de Hantone, which was composed later than the dates posed for *Graf Rudolf.*

The Christian Rudolf appears at the beginning as a military commander, fighting against the Saracens in the service of a Christian king of Jerusalem, performing brilliantly at Ascalon. For reasons not specified, he quarrels with this king and deserts to the Muslim Sultan Halap, who is clearly a worthier person. Initially Rudolf is imbued with typical Crusader enthusiasm. Later the only concession that he makes to his fellow Christians in combat is that he strikes them with the flat of his sword instead of the edge. Rudolf easily moves back and forth between the heathen and Christian worlds with no condemnation from the author. The author describes at length splendid ceremonies and magnificent objects evoking the exotic atmosphere of the East. The two sides seem to be divided by political and military antipathy rather than religious differences; what unites them are the courtly values accepted by the Crusaders as well as the Muslims.

The second half of the poem is a love story in which Rudolf woos the Sultan's daughter in typical courtly fashion. When he is imprisoned on a mission for her father, the princess travels to Constantinople, where she learns about Christianity and requests baptism. There is no indication that this baptism is the result of love for Rudolf or of any religious feelings concerning Christianity. Her conversion and adoption of the Christian name of Irmengard does not seem to make much difference to Rudolf, although undoubtedly it will simplify their future life together in Flanders. Rudolf escapes from prison, finds Irmengard in Constantinople, marries her, and they return to Flanders with their servants Beatrise and Bonifait. Bonifait is killed trying to defend the sleepers from twelve robbers. The story ends with Rudolf deeply mourning Bonifait.

BIBLIOGRAPHY

Beckers, Hartmut. "*Wandel vor sine missetat:* Schuldverstrickung und Schulderkenntnis im *Graf Rudolf-Roman,*" in *Von wyßheit würt der mensch geert. . .*, ed. Ingrid Kuhn and Gotthard Lerchner. Frankfurt am Main: Lang, 1993, pp. 17–37.

Bethmann, Johannes. *Untersuchungen über die mittelhochdeutsche Dichtung vom Grafen Rudolf.* Berlin: Mayer und Müller, 1904.

Brackert, Hellmut. "Besprechung über Graf Rudolf, hersg. von Peter Ganz." *Euphorion* 54 (1966): 139–154.

Ganz, Peter F. *Graf Rudolf.* Berlin: Erich Schmidt, 1964.

———. "Graf Rudolf." in *Die deutsche Literatur des Mittelalters: Verfasserlexikon,* ed. Kurt Ruh et al., vol. 3. Berlin: de Gruyter, 1981, cols. 212–216.

Grimm, Wilhelm. *Grave Rudolf.* Göttingen: Dietrich, 1828.

Kaplowitt, Stephen J. "The Non-literary Sources of *Graf Rudolf:* A Re-evaluation." *Studies in Philology* 66 (1969): 584–608.

Mohr, Wolfgang. "Zum frühöfischen Menschenbild in Graf Rudolf." *Zeitschrift für deutsches Altertum und deutsche Literatur* 96 (1967): 97–109.

Ruh, Kurt. *Höfische Epik des deutschen Mittelalters.* Berlin: E. Schmidt, 1977.

Sanders, Willy. "Zur Heimatbestimmung des Graf Rudolfs." *Zeitschrift für deutsches Altertum und deutsche Literatur* 95 (1966): 122–149.

Schröder, Edward. "Zur Quellenfrage des 'Grafen Rudolf.'" *Zeitschrift für deutsches Altertum und deutsche Literatur* 67 (1930): 79–80.

Schupp, Volker. "Zur Datierung des *Grafen Rudolf.*" *Zeitschrift für deutsches Altertum und deutsche Literatur* 97 (1968): 37–56.

Sybel, Heinrich von. "Über die geschichtliche Grundlage des *grafen Rudolf.*" *Zeitschrift für deutsches Altertum und deutsche Literatur* 2 (1842): 235–248.

Szklenar, Hans. *Studien zum Bild des Orients in den vorhöfischen deutschen Epen.* Göttingen: Vandenhoeck und Ruprecht, 1966.

Wentzlaff-Eggebert, Friedrich-Wilhelm. *Kreuzzugsdichtung des Mittelalters. Studien zu ihrer geschichtlichen und dichterischen Wirklichkeit.* Berlin: de Gruyter, 1960.

Stephanie Cain Van d'Elden

SEE ALSO
Crusades

Grasser, Erasmus (1445/1450–1518)

Born between 1445 and 1450 in Schmidmühlen near Regensburg, this master builder and sculptor in both stone and wood spent his career in Munich. Here he acquired the status of master in 1477, repeatedly held the office of head of the painter's guild, and occupied an especially privileged position at the court of the dukes of Bavaria. The strength of his sensual temperament is apparent in the peculiar style of his early wood sculpture, suggesting almost grotesque movements, which gives way to calmer forms only in his late works. The series of preserved architectural and sculptural works, of which only the epitaph of Ulrich Aresinger from 1482 (Munich, St. Peter's) is signed and dated, allows the conclusion that Grasser completed at least a six-year apprenticeship as a builder and stonecutter before the "quarrelsome, confused, and deceitful" journeyman appeared unexpectedly in Munich about 1474 (Frankl 1942: 257).

Only one of Grasser's architectural projects still stands—the ingenious extension added to the church of the Virgin in Schwaz in Tyrol between 1490 and 1502. Three other monuments are known through documents: the cloister Mariaberg near Rorschach from 1487, the tabernacle for the host at Freising Cathedral from 1489,

Erasmus Grasser, Morris Dancer (Munich, Münchner Stadt-museum. *Photograph: Münchner Stadtmuseum/Dorothee Jordens-Meintker*

and the well-room with accompanying chapel at the salt works at Reichenhall. Likewise four sculptures or groups are documented from the oeuvre of *maister Erasem schnitzer* (Master Erasmus wood-carver). Of the original sixteen Morris Dancers carved for the Altes Rathaus (old town hall) in Munich about 1480, ten are preserved today in the city museum. Seven mourners from a Lamentation group in limestone dated 1492 are preserved in Freising Cathedral. Wood figures of the Virgin and Saints Leonhard and Eligius, carved between 1502 and 1505, and the altar of St. Achatius (1503–1506) are to be found in the church at Reichersdorf in Upper Bavaria (Otto 1988:31–37).

The attributed works are more numerous. A multifig-ured altar of the Holy Cross from about 1482 at the church of the Assumption at Ramersdorf and a similar small-scale monstrance altar from about 1483, now in the Bavarian National Museum in Munich, reveal a knowl-edge of Netherlandish carved altarpieces. The often-cited influence of Nicolaus Gerhaert von Leyden on Grasser's

style is visible in three groups representing the Virgin and John the Evangelist under the cross: at the church of St. Leonhard at Traidendorf in the Oberpfalz (after 1470), from the church of St. Wolfgang in Munich (now Bavar-ian National Museum, 1485–1490), and at St. Arsatius in Ilmmünster (about 1500). The high-quality wood fig-ure of a Throne of Grace *(Gnadenstuhl)* in Schliersee, from about 1480, depends closely on an engraving of the same subject by the anonymous Master E. S.

BIBLIOGRAPHY

Frankl, Paul. "Early Works of Erasmus Grasser." *Art Quarterly* 5 (1942): 242–258.

Fuhrmann, Franz. "Die Stadtpfarrkirche zu Unserer Lieben Frau in Schwaz," in *Festschrift Heinz Mack-owitz,* ed. Sybille-Karin Moser and Christoph Bertsch. Lustenau: Neufeld-Verlag, 1985, pp. 87–94.

Halm, Philipp Maria. *Erasmus Grasser.* Augsburg: Benno Filser Verlag, 1928.

Müller-Meiningen, Johanna. *Die Moriskentänzer und an-dere Arbeiten des Erasmus Grasser für das Alte Rathaus in München.* Munich: Schnell und Steiner, 1984.

Otto, Kornelius. *Erasmus Grasser und der Meister des Blutenburger Apostelzyklus.* Miscellanea Bavarica Monacensia 150; Neue Schriftenreihe des Stadtarchivs München. Munich: UNI-Druck, 1988.

Ramisch, Hans. "Funde und Bemerkungen zu Erasmus Grasser und seinem Umkreis." *Bayerische Landesamt für Denkmalpflege, Berichte* 26 (1968): 83–95.

Rorimer, James J. "Three Kings from Lichtenthal." *The Metropolitan Museum of Art Bulletin* 12 (1953): 81–91.

Brigitte Schliewen

SEE ALSO

E. S., Master; Freising; Iconographies, Innovative; Munich; Nicolaus Gerhaert von Leyden

Gregory VII (c. 1025–1085)

Certainly one of the great popes of the medieval Church, Gregory lent his name to the eleventh-century reform of the Church, known as the Gregorian reform or the In-vestiture Controversy. He was born Hildebrand around 1025 in southern Tuscany (Soana?), or, less likely, Rome, to a well-to-do family, but came to Rome as a young child. In his letters as pope, Gregory mentions that he had grown up in the bosom of the Roman Church and refers to the special guardianship of the Apostle Peter, as well as to a Roman palace, the Lateran, where he attended school with upper-class children.

January 1047 is the first verifiable date for him; however, he accompanied Pope Gregory VI (1045–1046) into exile in Germany after the latter's deposition by Henry III at the synod of Sutri (Italy), December 20, 1046, and spent some time among the canons of Cologne cathedral. There is no evidence, whatsoever, that he became a monk at Cluny. In early 1049, Hildebrand returned to Rome with Pope Leo IX (1049–1054), was made subdeacon, and rector/administrator of the abbey of St. Paul's Outside the Walls. He worked on behalf of the papacy as legate to France, Germany, and Italy, was elevated to the position of archdeacon in late 1058 or early 1059, and perhaps was responsible for the coronation of Pope Nicholas II in the latter year.

During the funeral of Pope Alexander II, on April 22, 1073, Hildebrand was acclaimed as Pope Gregory VII in a tumultuous election by the Roman clergy and people, an election that was only subsequently formalized by the cardinals. Gregory interpreted his election as a special call by God to continue without hesitation the fight for what he defined as *iustitia* (justice), meaning the restoration of the Church to what Gregory and his collaborators saw as her proper place in the world order. He linked the battle against simony and for celibacy of the clergy—the chief characteristics of Gregorian reform—with a marked emphasis on papal primacy based on the primacy of the Roman Church. Although this primacy included the subordination of all temporal Christian governments to the papal authority, it applied first of all to the ecclesiastical hierarchy. In Gregory's view, all Christians, including kings and emperors, owed the papacy unquestioned obedience because the pope alone would never deviate from the Christian faith, given his mystic connection with Saint Peter, whose successor he was. Obedience to God became obedience to the papacy.

Gregory's attitude had profound consequences in the realm of politics. In France and, especially, Germany, direct papal intervention in the appointment of bishops and the prohibition of their investiture with ring and staff (1078) created severe tensions. Despite some initial problems, there was no hint of this tension with Germany at the outset of Gregory's pontificate. Gregory saw in Henry IV the future emperor and always thought highly of Henry IV. In a letter of December 1074 he suggested that Henry IV was to protect Rome and the Roman Church during a papal expedition to the Holy Land that Gregory envisioned in the company of the Empress Agnes,

Henry's mother, and Countess Matilda of Tuscany. But his attitude changed. In December 1075, by letter and messenger (who may have threatened excommunication orally), the pope blamed Henry harshly for the customary royal appointment of bishops to the Italian bishoprics of Milan, Ferno, and Spoleto as well as for the king's continued contact with those of his advisers who had been previously excommunicated.

In response, on January 24, 1076, at the diet of Worms, Henry IV and the vast majority of the German bishops replied in even harsher terms. They renounced their obedience to "Brother Hildebrand," and the king called on Gregory to abdicate. The Romans were asked to elect a new pope. North Italian bishops immediately joined their German colleagues. The letters reached Gregory during the Lenten synod (February 14–20, 1076), and he replied immediately, declaring Henry excommunicated and deposed as king. In his prayer to the Apostle Peter, he also absolved all of Henry's subjects from their oath of fealty.

The effect of Henry's excommunication was tremendous. Never before had a pope deposed a king, even though Gregory assumed that he had historical precedents on his side. Then, as now, the deposition of Henry was the most hotly debated action of Gregory's papacy. He had pursued to its logical conclusion his conviction that papal primacy pertained not only to the spiritual, but to the secular sphere. Church reform now became a struggle over dominance between the pope and his princely as well as his episcopal opponents in the civil war that raged intermittently throughout Henry's reign.

In order to save his crown, Henry finally submitted to Gregory at Canossa (January 28, 1077), thus implicitly recognizing papal claims to supremacy. Gregory excommunicated Henry for a second time at the Lenten synod of 1080, when he recognized Rudolf of Rheinfelden as king. However, after the absolution of Canossa, Henry had reasserted himself; the new excommunication had little effect, and the king was victorious in the civil war. A royal synod at Brixen formally deposed Gregory (June 25, 1080) and elected Wibert of Ravenna (anti-)pope. He was eventually enthroned as Clement III after the successful conclusion of Henry's Italian campaign in March 1084. Gregory had fled to the Castello S. Angelo. He was freed by his Norman vassal, Robert Guiscard, in May and accompanied him to Salerno where he died on May 25, 1085. Pope Paul V canonized Gregory in 1606, and his feast day, May 25, was expanded from Salerno to the entire Church in 1728.

The history of papal primacy cannot be imagined without Gregory, especially, but not only, with regard to his views on secular power. In his lifetime, he attempted to translate his own religious experience, with its mystical core, into historical reality. Concepts which he grasped intuitively were legally and theoretically elaborated in the twelfth and thirteenth centuries, resulting in what is known as the papal monarchy.

BIBLIOGRAPHY

Caspar, Erich, ed. *Das Register Gregors. VII Monumenta Germaniae historica,* Epistolae selectae, vol. 2. 2 vols. Berlin: Weidmann, 1920/1923.

Cowdrey, H. E. J. *The epistolae vagantes of Pope Gregory VII.* Oxford: Clarendon Press, 1972.

———. *Pope Gregory VII, 1073–1085.* Oxford: Oxford University Press, 1998.

Emerton, Ephraim, trans. *The Correspondence of Pope Gregory VII: Selected Letters from the Registrum.* New York: Columbia University Press, 1932.

Englberger, Johann. *Gregor VII. und die Investiturfrage: quellenkritische Studien zum angeblichen Investiturstreit von 1075.* Cologne: Böhlau, 1996.

Santifaller, Leo. *Quellen und Forschungen zum Urkunden- und Kanzleiwesen Papst Gregors VII.* Città del Vaticano: Biblioteca apostolica vaticana, 1957.

Schieffer, Rudolf. *Die Entstehung des päpstlichen Investiturverbots für den deutschen König.* Stuttgart: Heirsemann, 1981.

Watterich, Johann Matthias, ed. *Vitae Gregorii VII.* In *Pontificum romanorum* [. . .] *vitae,* vol. 2. Leipzig: Sumptibus Guilhelmi Engelmanni, 1862.

Uta-Renate Blumenthal

SEE ALSO
Cologne, Archdiocese; Henry III; Henry IV; Investiture Controversy; Leo IX; Saxon War; Worms

Grimbergse Oorlog, De

This Middle Dutch (Brabantine) poem is named after its main theme, the war *(oorlog)* between the clan of the Berthouts, petty lords of Grimbergen (near Brussels) and the dukes of Brabant. Two anonymous poets wrote the extensive poem (more than twelve thousand lines in rhymed couplets) around 1350, about two hundred years after the events described in it. The poem combines references to verifiable historical facts with fictitious stories from the epic tradition, and glorifies the virtues of knightly warfare and noble bravery at a time when nobility had been defeated by peasants (Battle of Courtrai, 1302) and gunpowder.

The original work, perhaps commissioned by the lord of Wezemaal, survives only in three eighteenth- and nineteenth-century transcriptions, based on medieval manuscripts that are known to have existed but are now lost. Around 1500 the poem was rewritten, and this second version survives in two seventeenth- and eighteenth-century transcriptions. The importance of the poem is indicated by the fact that, shortly after 1500, a prose version, based on the second rhymed version, was made. Twenty manuscripts (sixteenth to eighteenth century) of the prose version are known, of which thirteen actually survive.

After a long introduction, describing the ancestry of the dukes of Brabant, beginning with the Trojans, and depicting the origins of their conflict with the Berthouts, the poem narrates the war between the dukes of Brabant—Godfried I, Godfried II, and Godfried III—and the lords of Grimbergen—Wouter II and his sons Wouter III and Gerard II. This war—fought between 1141 and 1159—was ultimately lost by the lords of Grimbergen, who then became loyal vassals of the Brabantine ducal house.

BIBLIOGRAPHY

Blommaert, P[hilippe] and C[onstant] P[hilippe] Serrure, eds. *De Grimbergsche oorlog. Ridderdicht uit de XIVde eeuw.* 2 vols. Ghent: Annoot-Braeckman, 1852–1854.

Cohen, A. E. "Grimbergen en Woeronc." In *De Nederlanden in de late middeleeuwen,* ed. D. E. H. de Boer and J. W. Marsilje. Utrecht: Spectrum, 1987, pp. 24–30.

Deschamps, J. "De Prozabewerking van *de Grimbergse oorlog.*" In *Album Moors,* ed. S. Theissen and J. Vromans. Luik: Cipl, 1989, pp. 31–54.

Krah, V. "De Grimberge oorlog, een curieuze tekst." *Literatuur* 2 (1985): 213–220.

Geert H. M. Claassens

SEE ALSO
Brabant

Guelph Treasure

The history of the group of reliquaries known since the nineteenth century as the Guelph Treasure (German,

Welfenschatz) is intimately linked to that of the Guelph family and to their foundation in the palace at Braunschweig. About 1030, when the Countess Gertrude established the church dedicated to the Virgin, John the Baptist, and Saints Peter, Paul, and Balsius, she also took responsibility for the building and its contents. Four elaborate metalwork objects—a portable altar and two reliquary crosses, all in the Cleveland Museum of Art, and the arm reliquary of Saint Blasius (Braunschweig, Herzog Anton Ulrich-Museum), the earliest known example of this reliquary type—are inscribed with her name. When Henry the Lion, her great-great-great-grandson, rebuilt the church, by then dedicated primarily to St. Blasius, between 1173 and 1188, he also contributed a group of relics to its treasury. The early-thirteenth-century chronicler Arnold of Lübeck relates that Heinrich had acquired these relics, including a second relic of St. Blasius, from the Emperor Manuel in Constantinople on his return from Crusade in 1173 and that he had had them mounted in expensive reliquaries. Inscriptions on the arm reliquaries of Sts. Theodore and Innocent associate them with Heinrich; a golden cross and a reliquary in the form of a church with five towers are known today only through the documents. Heinrich's son, the Emperor Otto IV, specified in his will of 1218 that, with a single exception, all his and his father's relics were to be held in perpetuity by the church of St. Blasius.

The earliest inventory of the treasury, made in 1482, lists 138 reliquaries, of which 81 can be identified today. They include numerous portable altars, a dozen arm reliquaries, and reliquary crosses, as well as types of reliquaries that became popular at a later period: head reliquaries, monstrances and ostensoria (vessels for display), and three examples of plenary reliquaries, in which relics are set into the cover of a book containing all the mass readings for the church year. Some of these objects were given by later family members, others by canons of St. Blasius and other church officials.

In addition to the significance of its individual objects and their documented association with a specific family and the church that played an important role in its dynastic identity, the Guelph Treasure is important for its role in bringing the issue of the alienability of cultural patrimony to public attention in the 1930s. The treasury had remained more or less intact at St. Blasius until 1671, when Duke Rudolf August of Braunschweig-Wolfenbüttel gave it, without the permission of the chapter, to his Catholic cousin, Duke Johann Friedrich of Hanover, in exchange for his help in suppressing the city of Braun-

schweig. In 1866, when Prussia annexed the kingdom of Hanover, the treasury was designated the private property of King George V, who took it with him into exile in Austria. The German government and the city of Hanover both failed to purchase the objects when George's grandson offered the entire treasury for sale in 1928, and in 1930, it was purchased by a consortium of art dealers, who allowed the works to be sold individually. After the Cleveland Museum of Art purchased a number of key pieces, including three of Gertrude's original four donations, in 1931, the state of Prussia succeeded in acquiring the remaining forty-four objects for the Kunstgewerbemuseum (Museum of Decorative Arts) in Berlin.

BIBLIOGRAPHY

De Winter, Patrick. *The Sacral Treasure of the Guelphs.* Cleveland: Cleveland Museum of Art, 1985.

Der Welfenschatz und sein Umkreis, ed. Joachim Ehlers and Dietrich Kötzsche. Mainz: Philip von Zabern, 1998.

The Guelph Treasure: Catalogue of the Exhibition. Detroit: Institute of Arts, 1931.

Kötzsche, Dietrich. *Der Welfenschatz im Berliner Kunstgewerbemuseum.* Bilderheft der Staatlichen Museen Preussischer Kulturbesitz 20–21. Berlin: Gebrüder Mann, 1973.

———. "Der Welfenschatz." *Heinrich der Löwe und seine Zeit,* ed. Jochen Luckhardt and Franz Niehoff. 3 vols. Munich: Hirmer, 1995, vol. 2, pp. 511–528.

Joan A. Holladay

SEE ALSO
Braunschweig; Henry the Lion; Lübeck; Metalworking; Relics and Reliquaries

Gurk

The village of Gurk in the Austrian province of Carinthia was first mentioned in the ninth century. Tradition holds that the cathedral, formerly the seat of the bishops of Gurk, was founded by Countess Hemma of Freisach-Zeltschach, following the death of her husband and son in battle. The current structure was begun around 1140 by Bishop Romanus I. It consists of a nave and side-aisles with a crypt and a twin-towered facade with a gallery over the porch. It is in this west gallery that the most important of the thirteenth-century frescoes can be found, although additional frescoes, including a St. Christopher near the main altar, and stained glass are also part of the building's decoration.

The extensive and superb fresco cycle of the two-bay vaulted gallery has drawn much attention from scholars, for it is possibly the most important remaining monument of mid-thirteenth-century Austrian wall painting, especially among those painted in the so-called *Zackenstil* (or zigzag style, see below). As described by Otto Demus, the program is extensive and well organized. Within the space, divided into two groin-vaulted bays, are depictions of the Earthly Paradise in the east and the Heavenly Jerusalem in the west with the Four Rivers of Paradise and Jacob's Ladder between them. Scenes include the Annunciations to the Virgin and Saint Anne, the Entry into Jerusalem, and the Journey of the Magi. On the west wall is a depiction of the Transfiguration with light from three windows, a series of medallions with saints below, and, formerly in the apse, a Christ in Majesty with Saints. In addition, in the quadrants of the east vault are scenes of the Fall of Man. Perhaps most significant and striking of all of the images is the Virgin and Child Enthroned as the Throne of Solomon, in which the standing child caresses the Virgin's chin, as she does his. This image connects the fresco cycle to other mid-century paintings, and, along with the details of the style of all of the paintings, raises the thorny problem of the dating of the cycle.

The initial difficulties in dating lie with attempts to reconcile the frescoes with existing documentation. Two donors are depicted: Bishop Otto I, who probably consecrated the chapel in 1214, the only year in which he was bishop, and Dietrich II who was bishop from 1253–1278. In addition, records mention a *Heinricus pictor de Gurk* fourteen times between 1196 and 1226. Some scholars have argued for the earlier date around 1214, in part because of suggestions that the frescoes were repaired later in the thirteenth century, which would account for the second dedication. But, more recently, others have argued convincingly for a date around 1250 or slightly later, and this date can be upheld on the basis of style and iconography. The image of the Virgin and Child as the Throne of Solomon, which has been called a *Glykophilousa*, is a type which appears with variations in Central Europe in the second half of the thirteenth century and the early fourteenth century, for example, in the fresco cycle of the court chapel at Stein an der Donau. Here, the Virgin and Child caress each other's chins in a reference to the Song of Solomon, which underscores the meaning of the lion-based throne.

A similar image appears in a window at Strasbourg usually dated to the middle of the thirteenth century. The style of this window belongs to the version of the *Zacken-stil* found at Gurk, a style characterized not only by the angular zigzag style of the drapery, but also by distinctive facial and hair types. Of the examples of this style found in Austria, including those at Krems from around 1277 and Göss of the 1280s, Gurk appears to be the earliest. While the *Zackenstil* first appears to the north in Saxony, a particular version has been associated with manuscripts and stained glass of the Middle Rhine and Regensburg areas in the 1250s. It also appears in manuscripts associated with the monastery of St. Florian in Austria, some of which are strikingly similar to Gurk in the facial types as well as in the abundant, fractured, and angular drapery. Such correspondences argue for the later date of the fresco cycle at Gurk at the time of the cathedral's second consecration, a date which also clarifies the history of the *Zackenstil* in Central Europe.

BIBLIOGRAPHY

Becksmann, Rüdiger. *Deutsche Glasmalerei des Mittelalters: Eine exemplarische Auswahl.* Stuttgart: Institut für Auslandsbeziehungen, 1988.

Demus, Otto. *Romanesque Mural Painting*, trans. Mary Whittall. New York: Harry N. Abrams, 1970, pp. 634–636; figs. 298–305.

Die Zeit der Staufer: Geschichte, Kunst, Kultur, ed. Reiner Haussherr. 5 vols. Stuttgart: Württembergisches Landesmuseum, 1977, Vol. 1, pp. 301–302.

Ginhart, Karl, and Bruno Grimschitz. *Der Dom zu Gurk.* Vienna: Krystall-Verlag, 1930.

Lanc, Elga. *Die mittelalterlichen Wandmalereien in Wien und Niederösterreich.* Corpus der mittelalterlichen Wandmalereien Österreichs 1. Vienna: Verlag der Österreichischen Akademie der Wissenschaften, 1983.

Schmidt, Gerhard. *Die Malerschule von St. Florian: Beiträge zur süddeutschen Malerei zu Ende des 13. und im 14. Jahrhundert.* Graz: H. Böhlaus Nachfolger, 1962.

Rebecca W. Corrie

SEE ALSO

Gothic Art and Achitecture; Iconographies, Innovative; Romanesque Art and Architecture

Gutenberg, Johann (ca. 1400–February 3, 1468)

Credited with the invention of printing with movable metal type, Johann Gutenberg probably learned metalworking from his father's family who worked for the archbishop's mint. Gutenberg lived in Strasbourg from about 1428 to 1448, when he returned to Mainz where he had been born. There, he produced the Gutenberg Bible, the first major printed book. He died in Mainz on February 3, 1468.

Gutenberg's historical significance arises from his role in the development of printing. Records of lawsuits during his residence in Strasbourg point to his early experiments with the craft. The heirs of one of his partners, for example, sued to be included in the partnership. Testimony mentions "materials pertaining to printing," including a press, *Formen* (a word for type), and a purchase of metal. These items suggest that Gutenberg was working out the printing process, but no printed material has survived to support this theory.

After Gutenberg returned to Mainz, his efforts at printing continued. Another lawsuit, the so-called Helmasperger Instrument of 1455, connects Gutenberg with the Gutenberg Bible. Johann Fust, a Mainz businessman, sued Gutenberg to recover loans made in 1450 and 1452 for expenses incurred in making equipment, paying wages, and purchasing parchment paper and ink for "the work of the books." This document combined with analysis of the paper and its watermarks, the ink, and typography in the Gutenberg Bible lead to the conclusion that Gutenberg, aided by several assistants, including future printers Peter Schoeffer, Berthold Ruppel, and Heinrich Kefer, printed this Bible between 1450 and 1455.

Attribution of other printed books to Gutenberg is more problematic. He probably continued printing in Mainz. He has been connected with several works in the so-called "B36" group that used a larger and less refined Gothic font than the Gutenberg Bible. He has also been associated with a Mainz press that produced a Latin dictionary known as the *Catholicon* in 1460. However, the aesthetic and technical quality of the Gutenberg Bible makes this book the high point of his achievement.

BIBLIOGRAPHY

Fuhrmann, Otto W. *Gutenberg and the Strasbourg Documents of 1439.* New York: Press of the Wooly Whale, 1940.

Gutenberg, Aventur und Kunst: Vom Geheimunternehmen zur ersten Medienrevolution. Das offizielle Buch der Stadt Mainz zum Gutenbergjahr. Mainz: Schmidt, 2000.

Ing, Janet Thompson. *Johann Gutenberg and His Bible: A Historical Study.* New York: Typophiles, 1988.

Kapr, Albert. *Johann Gutenberg: The Man and his Invention.* trans. Douglas Martin. Aldershot, England: Scolar Press, 1996.

McMurtrie, Douglas C., ed. and trans. *The Gutenberg Documents: With translations of the texts into English, based with authority on the compilation by Dr. Karl Schorbach.* New York: Oxford University Press, 1941.

Ruppel, Aloys. *Johannes Gutenberg: Sein Leben und sein Werk.* 3d ed. Nieuwkoop: B. de Graaf, 1967.

Scholderer, Victor. *Johann Gutenberg: The Inventor of Printing.* 2d ed. London: British Museum, 1970.

Karen Gould

SEE ALSO

Bookmaking and Production; Mainz; Strasbourg

H

Hadewijch (fl. mid-13th c.)

In the final line of her twelfth vision, the thirteenth-century Brabant mystic Hadewijch writes: "By that abyss I saw myself swallowed. And there I received certainty about my being received, in this form, in my beloved, and my beloved also in me." The line not only provides a glimpse into the ecstatic experience of the author, but also suggests the aesthetic sense which imbues all of Hadewijch's writings. Indeed, her letters, visions, and poems have recently been praised as eminent in the literature of the *minnemystiek* (love mystic) tradition for their description of an unmediated experience of the divine, which is perfected in *minne,* or love, and not in ecclesiastical worship. During her lifetime as a Beguine, however, Hadewijch was forced into exile and her literary reputation into obscurity.

Although there is a paucity of biographical information about Hadewijch, her writings in the vernacular Middle Dutch convey the imaginative force with which she appropriated the courtly love tradition to reveal her desire for union with love. Addressed variously as a persona and as an abstraction, love represents for Hadewijch both the experience of the divine and the achievement of perfection offered by that experience. Her letters and poems encourage her readers to devote themselves to love as a principle of engagement in both spiritual and mundane matters, while the visions record the account of her progression into love as a sublime experience. The three manuscripts of her writings illustrate the skill with which Hadewijch crafted enthralling examples of the language of love.

BIBLIOGRAPHY

Vanderauwera, Ria. "The Brabant Mystic: Hadewijch." In *Medieval Women Writers*. Athens: University of Georgia Press, 1984 [English trans.].

Fraeters, Veerle, "Hadewijch." In *Women Writing in Dutch,* ed. Kristiaan Aercke. (New York, 1994), pp. 18–60.

Amanda Athey

SEE ALSO
Mysticism; Visionary Literature

Hadlaub, Johannes (fl. early 14th c.)

Hadlaub was one of the best known Middle High German courtly love poets. His contributions to late-medieval *Minnesang* are characterized by a full command of the classical tradition and an obviously playful experimentation with new aspects of the form. Hadlaub demonstrates a clear familiarity with the poetry of Gottfried von Neifen, Ulrich von Winterstetten, and Konrad von Würzburg, although he does not quite reach their artistic mastery. He imitated many famous examples of courtly love poetry, including Walther von der Vogelweide's women songs, Neidhart's peasant satires, Steinmar's love parodies, as well as the latter's fall and harvest songs. A major thematic innovation can be found in Hadlaub's song about household worries and the financial miseries which make it difficult for the father to feed his wife and children (no. 7). He also developed a new type of dawn song (no. 51) in which he describes an entire lovers tryst from early evening to early morning.

Hadlaub is mentioned once in a 1302 Zurich document. Three of his lays *(Leiche)* and fifty-one of his songs are included in the famous Manesse songbook, better known as the "Large Heidelberg Song Manuscript" *(Große Heidelberger Liederhandschrift),* which represents the most important collection of Middle High German courtly love poetry. In one poem (no. 8), Hadlaub sings a song of praise about the collector and patron Rüdiger Manesse (d. 1304) and his son Jakob, indicating that he might have worked as a scribe or in another capacity for them. In several of his semi-ironic love songs, Hadlaub mentions the names of those people in upper Zurich society who supported him as a composer of courtly poetry. In modern times, Hadlaub has been immortalized by the Zurich writer Gottfried Keller, who published a charming novella, *Hadlaub,* in 1878.

BIBLIOGRAPHY

Adam, Wolfgang. *Die "wandelunge."* Heidelberg: Winter, 1979, pp. 26–94.

Hadlaub, Johannes. *Text und Übersetzung von Max Schiendorfer.* Zurich: Artemis, 1986.

Lang, Hedwig. *Johannes Hadlaub.* Berlin: Schmidt, 1959.

Sayce, Olive. *The Medieval German Lyric 1150–1300.* Oxford: Clarendon, 1982, pp. 339–345.

Schröder, Eduard. "Hadlaub und Manesse." *Zeitschrift für deutsche Philologie* 70 (1933): 136–142.

Albrecht Classen

SEE ALSO

Konrad von Würzburg; *Minnesang;* Neidhart; Versification; Walther von der Vogelweide

Halberstadt

The first attempts to Christianize the northern foothills of the Harz mountains were undertaken from the religious center at Osterwieck (Seligenstadt) at the time of Charlemagne (d. 814). Under Charlemagne's son and successor, Louis the Pious, the center of missionary activity was transferred to Halberstadt, and the bishopric there was formally founded and subordinated to the see of Mainz. The rapid rise of the bishopric, especially in the tenth century, slowed sharply as a result of the conflict of the Emperors Henry IV (d. 1106) and Henry V (d. 1125) with the Saxons, and, in 1179, Henry the Lion destroyed the city in the clash between Emperor Frederick I Barbarossa and Bishop Ulrich.

Halberstadt lies at the junction of important trade routes and was formed from several smaller settlements. The central area around the cathedral was already walled in the Carolingian period; originally, it comprised only the church with the cloister at the south and the bishop's residence to the north. The present-day cathedral plaza *(Domplatz)* took shape around the year 1000 with the in-

clusion of the Church of the Virgin in the now oval-shaped fortified area around the cathedral. The houses of the canons were arranged along the long sides of the plaza; the bishop's residence had been moved to the northwest corner of the plaza slightly earlier, and the two churches opposed one another at the ends. Already in the tenth century, a market settlement with the city's parish church, St. Martin, was located to the southeast of the cathedral fortification; the city hall *(Rathaus),* which was also in this area, was destroyed in the Second World War, as were most of the once numerous half-timbered buildings in the old town. The other settlements were integrated within the city walls by the fourteenth century.

Today's cathedral building is the third on this site. The oldest, a Carolingian church, characterized by three aisles, a transept-like cross arm, and a shortened rectangular altar area, was enlarged in the second quarter of the ninth century with the addition of a chamber crypt and a three-part choir; these changes probably correspond to the shift from a mission church to a cathedral. The church was enlarged a second time before 859, when a transept and a long choir ending in a rounded apse were added over a ring crypt with side galleries and a cross-shaped, exterior axial chapel; the arrangement reflects that at the abbey church at Corvey. At the opposite end of the building a west-front (*Westwork*-like) structure was attached in place of an earlier burial or memorial church; the unidentified tombs were retained in the new structure.

After the collapse of the Carolingian church in 965, the eastern parts were reerected in their old form, the nave was lengthened, and a *Westwork,* or west front, with two towers added. The decision to replace this building was probably due to ambition and desire for modernity: a Gothic structure was begun in 1236–1239 with a western two-tower façade. The west portal sculpture is unusual in that the Last Judgment, so frequently represented in this position, is abbreviated and portrayed in small relief figures. The portal originally opened onto a three-aisled open narthex, or vestibule.

After the erection of the western bays of the nave, work stopped until the second quarter of the fourteenth century; the new campaign began in the east with the erection of the chapel to the Virgin. This elegantly proportioned chapel, with its unusually fully preserved stained glass cycle and its high-quality sculptured figures from the original building, illustrates particularly clearly the medieval sense of space. The next part to be completed, the ambulatory, is equipped with altar niches rather than the radiating chapels typical of cathedral choirs. Also uncommon are the galleries in the transept; their design probably arose from liturgical as well as musical needs. The building was dedicated in 1491 with the completion of the three-aisle, extremely tall, nave without a triforium, or upper gallery.

Above the rood screen, dated 1510, the important wood Crucifixion group from the previous building was installed; it probably dates before 1220. The relief sculpture represents the dead Christ framed by the mourning figures of Mary and John, with the unusual addition of two seraphim or cherubim. The supporting beam is decorated on both sides with busts of apostles and prophets in high relief. The completeness and nearly original installation of the five-figure group gives an authentic impression of the sculptural decoration of medieval churches.

Halberstadt cathedral possesses one of the largest treasuries to have survived from the high and late Middle Ages. Among its holdings are some of the oldest preserved European woven textiles, from the twelfth and thirteenth centuries. A so-called sacristy cupboard from the late Romanesque period, which served to store altar objects and reliquaries, is of exceptional art historical importance as its doors are decorated with some of the earliest paintings on wood panel.

The Church of the Virgin was established as part of a foundation of Augustinian canons in 1005. The three-aisle eastern crypt of the first building has been partially excavated in the area of the present building's crossing; the choir above probably ended in a truncated apse. The two lower levels of the western towers changed their orientation from that of the earliest building, revealing new planning. The larger church building in its present form was begun in the second quarter of the twelfth century and apparently finished in the late thirteenth. The three-aisle basilica with a transept lacks a crypt. The side choirs are as long as the main choir; all three end in rounded apses. This simple structure corresponds to a nearly complete renunciation of architectural sculpture. The eastern towers, added later in the corners between nave and transept, and the three-part sanctuary allow comparison with the nearby collegiate church at Hamersleben and point to influence from Hirsau. About 1170, the so-called baptismal chapel was erected adjacent to the south side of the *Westbau*, or west front (entrance structure), in the mature forms of the Lower Saxon High Romanesque. In the first half of the fifteenth century, the Chapel of St. Barbara, with its high-quality vault paintings and thematically related altar retable, or ledge, was built and decorated.

The tall choir screens separating the crossing from the transept arms are the most important decorative elements in the Church of the Virgin. Soon after 1200 these wall-like dividers, originally decorated only with simple moldings, were given stucco figural decoration that belongs among the most significant works of German sculpture of this period. These reliefs, which still preserve much of their original polychromy, or colors, show the apostles in two groups of six, seated under arcades with a palmette (palm leaf ornamentation) frieze above and below. One group centers around Christ, the other around the Virgin, an arrangement that follows models from the minor arts. The individualized figures show a close relationship to those of the choir screen at Hildesheim. The program of the choir screens and the lost rood screen almost certainly culminated in a crucifixion group. Only the crucifix itself, from about 1230, is preserved.

The present Church of St. Martin was erected between the second half of the thirteenth century and the middle of the fourteenth over an earlier building about which little is known. Whereas the earliest, eastern parts with a choir polygon and low, straight side choirs presume the erection of a basilical nave, the nave was actually completed as a three-aisle hall church. The use of a hall church type, as well as the massive *Westbau*, or western front, facing the cathedral, might be understood as signs of the city's self-consciousness. The most valuable object preserved from the church's original decoration is a bronze baptismal font from the beginning of the fourteenth century. On the west exterior wall stands a stone image of Roland from 1433, replaced in 1686; it originally stood in front of the city hall.

BIBLIOGRAPHY

Exner, Matthias, ed. *Stuck des frühen und hohen Mittelalters*. ICOMOS: Hefte des Deutschen Nationalkomitees 19. Munich: Lipp, 1996.

Findeisen, Peter. *Halberstadt: Dom, Liebfrauenkirche, Domplatz*. 2nd ed. Königstein im Taunus: Langewiesche, 1996.

Flemming, Johanna, Edgar Lehmann, and Ernst Schubert. *Dom und Domschatz zu Halberstadt*. Leipzig: Koehler und Amelang, 1990.

Killen, Renate. *Die St.-Martini-Kirche zu Halberstadt*. Berlin: Evangelische Verlagsanstalt, 1988.

Leopold, Gerhard. *Die Liebfrauenkirche in Halberstadt*. 2nd ed. Munich and Berlin: Deutscher Kunstverlag, 1993.

Leopold, Gerhard, and Ernst Schubert. *Der Dom zu Halberstadt: Bis zum gotischen Neubau.* Berlin: Akademie-Verlag, 1984.

Militzer, Klaus, and Peter Przybilla. *Stadtentstehung, Bürgertum und Rat: Halberstadt und Quedlinburg bis zur Mitte des 14. Jahrhunderts.* Veröffentlichungen des Max-Planck-Instituts für Geschichte 67. Göttingen: Vandenhoeck und Ruprecht, 1980.

Niehr, Klaus. *Die mitteldeutsche Skulptur der ersten Hälfte des 13. Jahrhunderts.* Artefact 3. Weinheim: VCH Verlagsgesellschaft, 1992.

Oswald, Friedrich, Leo Schäfer, and Hans Rudolf Sennhauser. *Vorromanische Kirchenbauten: Katalog der denkmäler bis zum Ausgang der Ottonen.* 1966–1971. Munich: Prestel-Verlag, 1990. *Nachtragsband.* Munich: Prestel-Verlag, 1991 [supp. vol.].

Elisabeth Rüber-Schütte

SEE ALSO

Charlemagne; Corvey; Hildesheim; Hirsau; Louis the Pious; Quedlinburg

Halle

The city owes its name (older German, *hal,* "salt-mine") and its existence to the unending wealth of the salt springs and salt production that is attested to here at least from the Iron Age. In 806, during a military expedition against the Sorbs, Charlemagne's son, King Charles, had a fort erected here on the east shore of the Saale river; its exact location is not known. The center of the flourishing settlement, which came into the possession of the archbishopic of Magdeburg in 968, was the Old Market *(Alter Markt)* where important trading roads met. Further settlements developed around the castle and the salt works.

As a result of continued economic growth, the city underwent substantial restructuring and considerable expansion after 1120; at the same time, the citizens gained increasing autonomy from the bishop. A new three-layered city wall secured the city, whose market place represented a political and administrative, economic, religious, and representational center. After a lengthy conflict, the city, which had been governed by a council, lost its political independence to the archbishop at the end of the fifteenth century, and he erected a fortified castle, the Moritzburg, as a symbol of his power. Paradoxically, only a short time later, Halle enjoyed an unusual cultural flowering under the guidance of the archbishop of Magdeburg, Cardinal Albrecht of Brandenburg, a humanist and friend and patron of the arts and an adversary of Martin Luther.

The so-called *Dom* (cathedral), although never a bishop's church, was founded as a Dominican church, which Cardinal Albrecht converted into a collegiate foundation at the beginning of the sixteenth century. Its present name derives from the fact that Albrecht made this one of the preeminent artistic and spiritual centers in central Germany. The Dominicans, who had settled in Halle in 1271, had finished their towerless and transeptless hall church with a polygonal choir about 1300. Some two hundred years later, with the change in function, Cardinal Albrecht transferred the *Hallesche Heiltum* here; at the time, this was the largest relic collection in Germany. Subsequent alterations to the building produced a completely new and magnificent appearance. Cardinal Albrecht took with him most of the lavish decorative elements, together with the relic collection, however, when he left Halle in 1541.

In the area of the present market Church of the Virgin originally stood two medieval churches, both with imposing paired western towers: St. Gertrude's in the west and St. Mary's in the east. The older church, St. Gertrude's, oriented toward the salt works, is documented in the eleventh century. Its pair of western towers dates from the late medieval period. The Church of the Virgin was erected on the new market place at the time of the city's expansion in the twelfth century and acquired its towers in a late Romanesque building campaign. Between 1529 and 1554, the two churches were torn down, with the exception of their towers, and a new building, a three-aisle hall church, erected between them. The towers of St. Mary's were increased in height. The church was begun before the Reformation, but was decorated afterwards; the complete renunciation of figural imagery reflects a Protestant aesthetic.

In 1184, the archbishop of Magdeburg established a foundation of Augustinian canons on the site of an older parish church, where an arterial road near the Old Market pierced the city wall. The collegiate church, a cross-shaped basilica, was replaced by the present high Gothic structure, begun in 1388 in the area of the choir. The three-aisle hall church dedicated to Saint Moritz, with a single, unfinished tower in the center of the west facade, was erected according to the unified plan of the architect Conrad of Einbeck in several building campaigns continuing into the sixteenth century. The east end, characterized by three apses *en echelon,* the center one closing with

Halle an der Saale, Church of the Virgin, nave vaults. *Photograph: Joan A. Holladay*

a 5/8 polygon, faces the city and, therefore, receives the richest decoration: ornate filigreed sculptural decoration culminates in the upper reaches of the wall. The high-quality figural decoration from the period of construction, the middle of the fifteenth century, has been lost. The plan of the east end and the specific forms of the *choir facade* derive from the circle of the Parlers, especially the cathedral at Prague circa 1370–1380. It is of unusual importance as the first of a group of similar *choir facades* in this area of central Germany.

Several signed, and sometimes dated, large-scale works document the sculptural activity of Conrad of Einbeck: the figures of Saint Maurice, the *Schmerzensmann* (Suffering Man), a Virgin in sorrow, Christ being scourged, and the supposed self-portrait of the artist. In striking contrast to contemporary works in the Soft Style, these combine willful, personalized forms, a solid realism characterized by individualized facial features and heightened expression, and rough, massive body shapes.

Giebichenstein castle lies on the bank of the Saale to the north of the old town near important historic trade routes and in the middle of an old settlement where extensive salt production is confirmed since the late Bronze Age. A castle probably existed here from the tenth century; with the foundation of the archbishopric of Magdeburg in 968, it came into the possession of the archbishops, who made this their main residence from 1382. Excavations in the upper castle, erected on a porphyry cliff, have suggested that the earliest stone structure on this site dates no earlier than the twelfth century. Only the gate tower still stands; it once guarded access to the palace building, an elaborate tower with living quarters, and a high Romanesque chapel. The fortress-like lower castle with walls and five towers was expanded in the middle of the fifteenth century. The importance of the castle declined with the move of the archbishop's household to the newly erected Moritzburg at the edge of the city in 1503.

The Moritzburg was erected inside the city walls between 1484 and 1517 as protection against the citizens and a symbol of the Church's dominion over the town. This fortified castle served as an administrative center and residence for the archbishops of Magdeburg. The building forms point to the influence of the Albrechtsburg in Meißen. The fortress-like structure comprises three wings, a defensive wall, and four massive corner towers; it is surrounded on three sides by banks and moats and, on the river side, by an enclosure. The different functions of the interior—defense, living, trade, and administration—were clearly divided among the three wings. The archbishop's palace, with its characteristic windows, was especially richly decorated, as was the chapel of Mary Magdalene, where niches held altars on which the reliquaries of the *Hallesche Heiltum* were exhibited until their removal to the cathedral in 1520–1521. Partially destroyed by fire in 1637, the castle is now used as a museum.

BIBLIOGRAPHY

Dräger, Ulf. *Moritzburg—Halle/Saale.* Regensburg: Verlag Schnell und Steiner, 1995.

Könnemann, E. ed. *Halle: Geschichte der Stadt in Wort und Bild.* Berlin, 1983.

Krause, Hans-Joachim. "Die Marktkirche zu Halle," in *Literatur, Musik und Kunst im übergang vom Mittelalter zur Neuzeit,* ed. Hartmut Boockmann et al. Göttingen: Vandenhoeck & Ruprecht, 1995.

Legner, Anton, ed. *Die Parler und der Schöne Stil 1350–1400: Europäische Kunst unter den Luxemburg-*

ern, Cologne: Museen der Stadt Köln, 1978, vol. 2, pp. 549–584.

Nickel, Heinrich L. *Der Dom zu Halle.* Munich and Zurich: Verlag Schnell und Steiner, 1991.

Rüger, Reinhard. *Die Marktkirche Unser Lieben Frauen zu Halle.* Munich and Berlin: Deutscher Kunstverlag, 1991.

Schmitt, Reinhard. *Burg Giebichenstein in Halle/Saale.* Munich and Berlin: Deutscher Kunstverlag, 1993.

Soffner, Monika. *Halle — Moritzkirche.* Passau: Kunstverlag-Peda, 1994.

Elisabeth Rüber-Schütte

SEE ALSO

Parler Family; Iconographies, Innovative

Hamburg

Later a leading Hanseatic city, Hammaburg became a Christian missionary center for northern Europe as well as a military fortress from which Frankish troops set out to conquer the area. Around 810, Charlemagne's troops established a fortified settlement and a church near the point where the Alster River flows into the Elbe. The oldest known documentation of this settlement, referred to as Hammaburg (*Hamma,* mud flat), dates from 834. Under Louis the Pious, the settlement was elevated to an archbishopric. The mission church became a cathedral, and its first archbishop, Ansgar, a Benedictine, was installed in 831. Later a monastery was added to the early cathedral. During this early period, the presence of the archbishop and some measure of prosperity among the military of the settlement attracted a small number of German merchants who traveled north in search of precious stones, particularly amber, and metals.

Hammaburg's first 250 years were punctuated by military defeats which left it in ruins on at least three separate occasions. In 845, the Danes laid waste to the settlement. As a result, the archbishop moved to Bremen where better security could be provided. Hammaburg was destroyed again in 983 by the Slavs. Archbishop Adalbert, teacher of Henry IV, sought to restore Hammaburg as the center of Christian missionary work. He met there with Danish and Slavic princes and declined a call to become pope in order to continue his work in northern Europe. Whatever progress Adalbert achieved in restoring the frontier settlement was undone, however, when Hammaburg was attacked by Slavic tribes from Mecklenburg in 1066 and reduced to ashes in 1072.

Present-day Hamburg developed from a cluster of small agricultural villages, some of which were fortified or settled over one hundred years before Hammaburg was established. One neighboring village on the Alster, home to farmers and fishermen, many of whom also worked as artisans, merged with Hammaburg and the two became the "Free City" of Hamburg under the aegis of the counts of Schauenburg. These Holstein lords, who took control of the area in 1111 and are credited with the founding of Hamburg, ushered in a new era of growth. They fostered colonization of the town and established a port on the Alster River that was used as a transfer point for shippers and merchants. On May 7, 1189, Count Adolf III received from Emperor Frederick I Barbarossa independence rights and privileges for the town and harbor of Hamburg, its citizens, and their ships. During the twelfth century, the cathedral, which maintained its original status in spite of the bishop's continued residence in Bremen, became the center of a market place that attracted traveling merchants and artisans. By the end of the century, merchants came not only from Westphalia and Bavaria, but also from the Netherlands and Italy.

In the early thirteenth century, the new town faced continual raids from Danish warriors, local feudal lords, and Slavic tribesmen. The citizens' response was to build larger fortifications and to organize themselves into militia groups. Although the city was autonomous, the merchants had to continually repurchase their right to remain self-governing. They paid large sums to the Danish king, the dukes of Saxony, the dukes of Holstein, the archbishop, and the Holy Roman emperor as well.

By 1300, Hamburg had built a fortress at the mouth of the Elbe River to protect its maritime interests. During the fourteenth century, Hamburg's population ranged between seven and eight thousand people. City merchants applied for and obtained membership in the Hanseatic League in 1321. Originally, Hamburg was the North Sea port for Lübeck. In spite of continuous harassment by pirates and feudal lords, the merchants carried on extensive trade in salt, grain, furs, amber, metals, and crafted items. Trading partners included England, Scandinavia, Russia, and Mediterranean countries, as well as the Rhineland, Bavaria, and Austria.

By about 1400, Hamburg's military forces had defeated and executed the pirates who lived along the coast between the Elbe and Weser Rivers, and her merchants had bought strategically located islands in the Elbe to prevent others from building fortifications there against the city.

BIBLIOGRAPHY

Plagemann, Volker. *Kunstgeschichte der Stadt Hamburg.* Hamburg: Junius-Verlag, 1995, pp. 15–115.

Rodnick, David. *A Portrait of Two German Cities: Lübeck and Hamburg.* Lubbock, Tex: Caprock Press, 1980, pp. 193–195.

Ruth M. W. Moskop

SEE ALSO

Charlemagne; Frederick I Barbarossa; Louis the Pious; Lübeck

Hammer of Witches

In 1484, Henry Krämer (1430–1505), called Institoris, a Dominican inquisitor for southern Germany, helped convince Pope Innocent VIII to issue the bull *Summis desiderantes.* This bull established the use of the Inquisition to hunt down supposed witches. Armed with such papal support, Krämer returned to Germany. He probably had some small success at first with witch trials in Constance, but in Innsbruck he ran into difficulty. After briefly cooperating, the local authorities ordered him and his Inquisition to leave the Tyrol. Disappointed with these efforts, Krämer, with the help of Jacob Sprenger, codified his vast knowledge of witch-hunting lore into a handbook, the *Malleus Maleficarum,* or *The Hammer of Witches,* published in 1486 or 1487.

The handbook was immediately popular and went through dozens of editions over the next centuries. The book was clearly organized and replete with citations by church fathers, observed phenomena, and anecdotal evidence. It laid out a program for dealing with what the authors saw as the threat of witchcraft. The first part of the book asserted the reality of witches and explained how they were dangerous to the Christian community. The middle sections described the various powers of witches. Witches, the handbook asserted, could prevent sexual intercourse, kill babies, change people into beasts or deprive a man of his "virile member." They could also cause cows to stop giving milk, destroy crops with hailstorms, and kill with lightning. The concluding sections of the handbook prescribed various remedies against witchcraft and examined how to put on trial, torture, convict, and pass sentence on a witch.

Although it acknowledges that witches could be either male or female, the *Hammer* is extremely hostile toward women. In Krämer's view, since women were more credulous, impressionable, surreptitious, and, especially, more carnal than men, they were more prone to evil superstition and sexual temptation by the Devil.

Although his fellow Dominicans censured Krämer in 1490, his misogynistic and superstitious ideas spread throughout continental Europe. The *Hammer* laid a foundation for the "Witch craze," or period of witch hunting, which would last well into the eighteenth century, costing thousands of lives and causing much suffering.

BIBLIOGRAPHY

Brauner, Sigrid. *Fearless Wives and Frightened Shrews: The Construction of the Witch in Early Modern Germany.* Amherst, Mass.: University of Massachusetts Press, 1995.

Institoris (alias Krämer), Heinrich, and Jakob Sprenger. *Malleus Maleficarum,* ed. André Schnyder. Litterae 113. Göppingen, Germany: Kümmerle Verlag, 1991.

Scholz Williams, Gerhild. *Defining Dominion: The Discourses of Magic and Witchcraft in Early Modern France and Germany.* Studies in Medieval and Early Modern Civilization. Ann Arbor: The University of Michigan Press, 1995.

Segl, Peter, ed. *Der Hexenhammer: Entstehung und Umfeld des Malleus Maleficarum von 1487.* Bayreuther historische Kolloquien 2. Cologne: Böhlau Verlag, 1988.

Summers, Montague, trans. and ed. *The Malleus Maleficarum of Heinrich Institoris (Kraemer) and James Sprenger.* 1928/1948; rpt. New York: Dover, 1971.

Brian A. Pavlac

SEE ALSO

Constance

Hanseatic League

The league, also known as the Hansa, was the major trade association of the Baltic and North Sea regions and northern Europe in general from the mid–twelfth to the mid–seventeenth century. The main focus of the voluntary organization was the promotion and protection of trade among league towns. The league used a variety of methods to guarantee its commercal success, including diplomacy and trade blockages. It also negotiated favorable treaties with trading partners outside the league to further the interests of the association. The Hanseatic League numbered as many as 180 member towns and had trade contacts throughout Germany, Scandinavia, England, France, Italy, and Spain. But in its period of greatest power and influence there were roughly between fifty-five and eighty towns in a much more tightly knit and more disciplined association. The legaue began a period of decline in the fifteenth century because of internal differences, a lack of a dependable military protector (particularly after the defeat of their military ally the Teutonic Order, or *Deutschorden,* at Tannenberg in 1410), and broader changes in Europe. It maintained a role in northern trade until 1669, however, when the last diet was held in Lübeck.

The league was founded in 1160 in the town of Lübeck as an association of merchants designed to protect international commerce and to secure privileges in foreign countries. It was a successful alliance and grew dramatically over the next two centuries, evolving from an association of merchants to an association of towns. In 1356 the first Hansa diet was held in Lübeck, and the organization was now a tightly knit association of towns. Other important member towns included Lüneburg, Riga, Rostock, Tallinn, Stralsund, and Wismar. There were member towns in Prussia, Saxony, Westphalia, and much of northern Germany. The geographic diversity was one of the group's strengths because the numerous towns brought a variety of goods to trade. But the wide geographic distribution of member towns was also a fundamental weakness that contributed to the organization's ultimate demise. There were differing goals among the towns, particularly between the Wendish and the Prussian, that undermined the uniformity of purpose necessary for the commerical league lacking a strong military. One of the great weapons of the league, the trade blockage, broke down on several occasions as Wendish or Prussian towns refused to participate in it. Despite this fatal flaw, the league was a success because it maintained order and cooperation among it members.

The unity and size of the league brought it much benefit, and it also gained much advantage by the wide array of goods traded by its member towns. Hansa towns provided valuable raw materials such as copper, timber, and wax to its trading partners. They also exported important foodstuffs including dried or salted fish—especially cod and herring—grain, and furs. They imported such things as wool from England and cloth from Flanders.

BIBLIOGRAPHY

Dollinger, Phillipe. *The German Hansa,* trans. D. S. Ault and S. H. Steinberg. London: Macmillan, 1970.

Michael Frassetto

SEE ALSO
Deutschorden; Lübeck

Hartlieb, Johannes (fl. 2d half of the 15th c.)

Hartlieb studied medicine in Padua, where he became a master in 1437 (probably) and doctor in 1439. Before 1440 in Austria, perhaps in Vienna or Graz, he translated Andreas Capellanus's *De amore* (On Love) for Duke Albrecht VI, the first work which can be attributed to him with certainty. From 1441, he served Dukes Albrecht III and his son, Siegmund, of Bavaria-Munich as court physician. For Albrecht and his wife, Anna of Braunschweig, he adapted the romance of Alexander and the legend of St. Brendan (1450–1457), the latter for Anna only.

Upon his return from a diplomatic mission to Margrave Johann of Brandenburg in 1456, he wrote, at the margrave's request, the *Buch aller verpoten Kunst* (The Book of all Forbidden Art), a catalogue and repudiation of all forms of black magic. Between 1460 and 1467 he translated Book 2 of Caesarius of Heisterbach's *Dialogus miraculorum (Dialogue on Miracles)* for the Munich patrician Hans Püterich, as well as the treatise, *Secreta mulierum (The Secrets of Women),* ascribed to Albertus Magnus, and the gynecological treatises attributed to Trotula of Salerno for Duke Siegmund. His scientific and medical works also include an herbal of unknown date and a list of drug prices for the city of Munich from 1453. Treatises previously attributed to him, now thought to be inauthentic, include books on mnemonics, lunar prognosis, onomatomancy, geomancy, chiromancy, and baths.

BIBLIOGRAPHY

Fürbath, Frank. *Johannes Hartlieb. Untersuchungen zu Leben und Werk.* Tübingen: Niemeyer, 1992.

Schnell, Bernhard. "Arzt und Literat. Zum Anteil der Ärzte am spätmitterlalterlichen Literaturbetrieb." *Sudhoffs Archiv* 75 (1991).

Margaret Schleissner

SEE ALSO
Brendan; Magic

Hartmann von Aue (ca. 1160–after 1210)

Of the four major writers of the High Middle Ages during the Hohenstaufen dynsaty—Hartmann von Aue, Walther von der Vogelweide, Wolfram von Eschenbach, and Gottfried von Straβburg—Hartmann von Aue stands out as the most prolific and diverse. His works include a verse treatise on love, *Diu Klage* (The Lament, ca. 1180), two Arthurian epics, *Erec* (ca. 1180) and *Iwen* (ca. 1200), two verse tales, *Gregorius* (ca. 1190) and *Armer Heinrich* (Poor Heinrich, ca. 1195), and eighteen poems—some spurious—spread out over much of his writing career.

Both Gottfried von Strasbourg, author of *Tristan,* and Wolfram von Eschenbach, author of *Parzival,* mention Hartmann in their works, and their comments reveal the esteem in which he was held by contemporary writers. As the poet who introduced the Arthurian romance into German-language literature, Hartmann influenced not only his literary generation but those who followed, well into the thirteenth century.

Like all of the major writers of the period, very little is known about Hartmann's life, and what is known must be gleaned from comments in his works, as nothing has come down to us in contemporary documents. Setting aside the question of whether Hartmann speaks in his works in an autobiographical or a literary voice, current thinking generally agrees on a rough sketch of Hartmann's life. In *Poor Heinrich* Hartmann calls himself a *dienstman,* consigning himself in an unembarrassed way to the class of *ministeriales,* an important, emerging, diverse class of court functionaries dependent for their living on the largesse of the nobility. Whether Hartmann came from a family that was in the ascendant or one that had fallen from free indentured status, is uncertain. By designating himself a *rîter* (knight) in the prologues to *Poor Heinrich* and *Iwein,* Hartmann reveals his knowledge of country life, the backdrop not only of his Arthurian romances, but also his verse tales and poetry.

Where Hartmann obtained the education he speaks of in *Poor Heinrich,* and whose traces are evident throughout his writings, is not known. Such an education could only have been obtained at a cathedral school or in a monastery; the setting of the monastery in *Gregorius* and discussions of the life and education there would favor the latter supposition. It appears that, in addition to Latin, Hartmann knew Old French, the language of Chrétien de Troyes and the influential French courtly culture. His allusions to classical works and to church philosophers confirm that Hartmann was one of the most learned poets of the age.

Hartmann must have had a wealthy, and thus powerful, patron, for writers of Hartmann's *ministerial*-knightly class were dependent on the court not only for the expensive outfitting of a knight, but also for costly writing resources, access to a courtly audience, and the availability of precious manuscripts of the French sources that Hartmann must have read. Numerous attempts made to pinpoint Hartmann's homeland have been inconslusive. His Alemannic language—a dialect covering a swath from northern Switzerland, southwestern Germany, and southeastern France, that is, modern Alsace—and a few scant descriptions in his works point to modern southern or southwestern Germany as his home. Two powerful families, the Zähringer and the Hohenstaufen, have been posited as Hartmann's patrons, and the Zähringer, with their seat near Freiburg at the crossroads of French and German culture, seem more likely. Finally, it should be no surprise that even the dates of Hartmann's life are disputed, but the period from around 1160 to shortly after 1210 would seem to have encompassed most of his years.

The chronology of Hartmann's writings is also disputed. However, some consensus has been reached: the *Lament* and some of the lyric poetry belong to an early phase, followed by the Arthurian romance *Erec.* Most critics agree that a dramatic metamorphosis then took place in Hartmann's life, something that shaped the themes of his next two works, *Gregorius* and *Poor Heinrich,* and some of his later poetry. Finally, toward the end of his life, Hartmann again turned to the Arthurian epic, this time to *Iwein.* (The beginning of *Iwein* may, however, have been written earlier and set aside, possibly during the presumed upheaval in the poet's life.)

The *Lament* may trace its heritage to the contemporary scholastic *disputatio,* a learned argument between two universty professors, or to legal cases or classical models of disputation. The stichomythic (rapid dialogue exchange) give-and-take between the heart and body in the third part of the work points ahead to the debate between the abbot and the young knight-to-be in *Gregorius,* and to alternating dialogue in *Erec* and *Iwein.* Whatever the origin of the work, this early writing bears the imprint of Hartmann's education, whether in a monastery or a church school.

After the body and the heart exchange reproaches and offer their defenses in the *Lament*, and after the stichomythic exchange between the two, the body, having seen the wisdom of the heart's arguments, redirects its attention in the final exchange to the courtly lady in question. A striking feature of the *Lament* is the heart's paradigmatic explanation of what makes up courtly love. Ethical attributes that form the underpinnings of *Minnesang* find echoes in some of Hartmann's poetry, and, coupled with a Christian ethic, resonate throughout Hartmann's works in the striving of the heroes toward betterment and self-fulfillment.

Of all of Hartmann's writings, his lyric poetry has raised the most contention among critics. The nineteenth-century Romantic/positivist viewpoint held that the lyrics mirrored Hartmann's life and could thus be grouped in chronological fashion, tracing first Hartmann's obeisance to the concepts of *minne* (courtly love), then, his disillusionment with and subsequent rejection of it in poetry praising common women, and, finally, to an ethical-spiritual substitution for *minne*, as represented in his *Kreuzlieder* (crusading songs).

What can be said is that Hartmann's poems—eighteen in the canon, but some of these are spurious—can be divided thematically: (1) traditional *Minnesang*; (2) complaints, whether by a man or a woman—the latter being called a *Frauenklage*; (3) songs of anti-*minne*, comprising a rejection of the high ideals of *minne* and a turn to more worldly love for fulfillment; and (4) crusading songs. Taken as a whole, much of Hartmann's lyrical poetry reads like the poetry of his age, and influences from earlier *Minnesänger* are apparent. At times he uses some stunning imagery, and his anti-*minne* songs and crusading songs strike the reader as honest and bold; they certainly must have influenced his contemporaries, including Walther von der Vogelweide. But Hartmann is a more conventional, conservative poet than others of his time, disdaining the erotic and the comical.

Hartmann most likely composed his *Erec* sometime in the 1180s, when he was in his twenties, shortly after the *Lament*, and contemporaneously with some of his lyric poetry. Although the legend of King Arthur had nationalistic overtones in England and France, mirroring the court of Henry II Plantagenet, king of England and of large parts of western France through his marriage to Eleanor of Aquitaine, this nationalism gave way to the trappings of courtly society and chivalry when Hartmann introduced the large-scale Arthurian romance in Germany.

Though he may have also used other sources, written and oral, Hartmann based *Erec* largely on Chrétien de Troye's *Erec et Enide* and acknowledged that fact in line 4629. It would be more appropriate to call *Erec* a reworking, or an adaptation, rather than a translation, however, for Hartmann took great liberties with his French model and expanded Chrétien's version by over 3,000 lines: 10,192 versus 6,958.

The differences between the two *Erecs* illuminate the disparate intentions of the two authors and highlight the similarities and dissimilarities of the two courtly societies. What strikes the reader of both works is Hartmann's focus on courtly society, and its concomitant etiquette of chivalry, and on the relationship between Erec and Enite. One can justifiably call Hartmann didactic, moralistic, and possibly even preachy, for, behind the Arthurian façade, he had a point to make. Both Erec and Enite are guilty of failing to understand their roles in a courtly society. It is their perilous journey that leads them to the awareness that courtly love is more than just physical attraction; it entails a mutually supportive relationship integrated into and supportive of a courtly society. While *Erec* is not a *Fürstenspiegel* (a sort of primer for the education of a prince), Hartmann would probably not have been disappointed had all knights turned out like his hero.

Hartmann also modeled *Gregorius* after a French prototype, the popular *La Vie du Pape Saint Grégoire*. *Gregorius* shows similiarities with varying versions, leading to the conjecture that an *Ur-Gregorius* existed at some point. Whatever the exemplar of *Gregorius*, Hartmann's use of it, as with *Erec* and *Iwein*, amounts more to a reworking or adaptation than a strict translation. Compared to the extant Old French versions, *Gregorius* is between one-third and one-half again as long, showing once more that, for Hartmann, the French original served mainly as a foundation on which he could use his poetic skill to erect a vastly different structure.

Gregorius followed *Erec* and the *Lament*, perhaps toward the end of the 1180s, and this positioning of the work has led to one aspect of its interpretation, i.e., that *Gregorius* is "anti-*Erec*," or anti-chivalric, a rejection by a more mature author of his earlier work, namely *Erec*. The thread of individual self-realization, a kind of *rite de passage*, ties Hartmann's major works together. Gregorius, moving from infancy through boyhood to manhood and finally to a precocious middle age of insight and wisdom, comes closest among Hartmann's characters to the *Bil-*

dungsfigur (character undergoing formative changes) of Wolfram von Eschenbach's *Parzival.*

Perhaps the interpretive focus should not, as some scholarship suggests, rest so heavily on the incest of Gregorius' parents, and on his own incest with his mother—for these acts, due to mitigating circumstances, seem pardonable to both medieval and modern thinking—or even on his own *superbia* (pride) at leaving the monastic world, but rather on the journey that Gregorius undertakes, both physically and spiritually, on the path that is mentioned both in the prologue and toward the end of the tale, when Gregorius seeks to do penance in the wilderness. This path may be seen as the path we all take in life.

(Like Erec early on,) the knightly Gregorius leads an exemplary life, an indication that *Gregorius* is not an antichivalric work. He falls, as Erec does, but differently, and, like Erec, he must come to an understanding of what has happened to him. He takes the initiative, directs his mother's actions, and sets out to do penance, for, after all, as the prologue and ending make clear, none is so stricken with sin that he cannot rise again, cleansed, and attain grace.

Heinrich von Aue, the protagonist in *Poor Heinrich,* like Erec and Gregorius, has reached what appears to be the pinnacle of success and happiness, only to fall. In his case, leprosy, which must be seen as a curse from God, strikes him down. Unlike Erec and Gregorius, Heinrich, at the beginning of the story, does not have to set out on a path to attain his goal; he has already reached it. Because of the narrator's praise of Heinrich, readers may wonder initially what brought about the knight's fall, but the narrator's comparison of Heinrich with Absalom and the many repetitions of the adjective "worldly" reveal that hubris and the pursuit of worldly things bring about Heinrich's predicament. From the onset of Heinrich's leprosy till the change "in his old way of thinking," he takes a number of positive steps, but he also missteps, and readers must determine if or why Heinrich deserves the salvation granted to him at the end of the story.

When Heinrich disposes of much of his wordly goods and moves in with the family of one of his tenants, Hartmann introduces his most controversial character, a girl of eight who, for three years, rarely departs from her afflicted master's side. Heinrich ends up calling her his "bride," and she ultimately agrees to sacrifice herself for him, for she has learned that only the blood of a willing virgin can save him. The controversy revolves around her motivations: is she selfless or selfish? Is her willingness to sacrifice herself only an arrogant pursuit of salvation? Or is she motivated out of love for her parents and for Heinrich? After all, since the pursuit of salvation recurs in Hartmann's works, and, since salvation was a teaching of the Church, can she be faulted for pursuing what appears to her, a girl without means, as the only road to salvation?

The fairy-tale ending of the story (his healing), in addition to the girl's virtual disappearance from the action, and the couple's ultimate salvation leave some readers dissatisfied. Has Heinrich actually earned his happiness? Do his actions at the end reveal a real change of heart? Not for this reason alone does *Poor Heinrich* remain the most controversial of Hartmann's major works. Where it fits in the chronology of Hartmann's work is also uncertain. It seems to mitigate, with its happy ending, the somberness of *Gregorius,* and point ahead to *Iwein,* Hartmann's return to the Arthurian theme.

The large number of manuscripts and fragments of *Iwein,* its being most often mentioned among Hartmann's work by contemporary writers, and the many depictions of scenes from it in frescoes and tapestries, all point to its popularity. As with *Erec,* Hartmann based *Iwein* on a work by Chrétien de Troyes, *Yvain: Le Chevalier au lion,* and, as in *Erec,* Hartmann greatly expanded upon the French original, by about twenty percent; 8,166 lines versus 6,818. Nevertheless, in *Iwein,* Hartmann followed Chrétien's plot line more closely adding mainly dialogue and authorial reflection.

The theme in *Iwein,* as in *Erec,* is the reconciliation of individual actions and individual love with chivalric ideals and a higher, ethical love. Like Erec, Iwein undergoes a series of adventures before and after his marriage to Laudine. Some critics have questioned Iwein's behavior when he kills Ascalon, Laudin's husband; others have criticized the later adventures as being too inconsequential to fit in the overall structure of the epic. But even more than with *Erec,* Hartmann juxtaposes courtly society with one man's actions, and what is a more requisite component of chivalric society than adventures and quests?

Hartmann treats the court of King Arthur in *Iwein* differently than he presented it in *Erec.* In the earlier work he toned down or eliminated much of Chrétien's criticism of the court, but in *Iwein* the court not only plays a more essential role, but the reader gets glimpses of a courtly society where all is not well. This change in tone could be due to an older Hartmann's lifelong experience at court, but whatever the reason, the court's flaws underline the ethical and moral perfectibility of the individual. From Erec via Gregorius and Heirnch and finally to Iwein, this is the thread that connects Hartmann's major works, for, as with many great writers, Hartmann had an ethical ideal and set out to show how it might be attained.

BIBLIOGRAPHY

Bühne, Sheema Zeeban, trans. *Gregorius.* New York: Ungar, 1966.

Clark, Susan L. *Hartmann von Aue: Landscapes of Mind.* Houston: Rice University Press, 1989.

Fisher, R. W., trans. *Narrative Works of Hartmann von Aue.* Göppingen: Kümmerle, 1983.

Gibbs, Marion E., and Sidney M. Johnson. *Medieval German Literature: A Companion.* New York and London: Garland, 1997, pp. 132–156.

Hasty, Will. *Adventures in Interpretation: The Works of Hartmann von Aue and Their Critical Reception.* Columbia, S.C.: Camden House, 1996.

———. *Adventure as Social Performance. A Study of the German Court Epic.* Tübingen: Niemeyer, 1990.

Jackson, William Henry. *Chivalry in Twelfth-Century Germany: The Works of Hartmann von Aue.* Cambridge: Brewer, 1994.

Keller, Thomas L., trans. *Hartmann von Aue. Erec.* New York & London: Garland, 1987.

———. *Hartmann von Aue. Klagebüchlein.* Göppingen: Kümmerle, 1986.

McConeghy, Patrick M., trans. *Iwein.* New York: Garland, 1984.

McFarland, Timothy, and Silvia Ranawake, ed. *Hartmann von Aue. Changing Perspectives: London Hartmann Symposium.* Göppingen: Kümmerle, 1988.

Resler, Michael, trans. *Erec by Hartmann von Aue.* Philadelphia: University of Pennsylvania Press, 1987.

Thomas, John Wesley, trans. *Erec.* Lincoln: University of Nebraska Press, 1982.

——— *Iwein.* Lincoln: University of Nebraska Press, 1979.

———. *Medieval German Lyric Verse in English Translation.* Chapel Hill: University of North Carolina Press, 1968.

———. *Poor Heinrich.* In: *The Best Novellas of Medieval Germany.* Columbia, S.C.: Camden House, 1984.

Tobin, Frank, trans. *Der arme Heinrich* [Medieval text with facing literal English translation]. In: *McGraw-Hill Anthology of German Literature,* vol. I: *Early Middle Ages to Storm and Stress.* ed. Kim Vivian, Frank Tobin, and Richard H. Lawson. New York: McGraw-Hill, 1993; rpt. *Anthology of German Literature: Vom frühen Mittelalter bis zum Sturm und Drang.* Chicago: Waveland, 1998, pp. 69–104.

———. *The Unfortunate Lord Henry.* In: *German Medieval Tales,* ed. Francis G. Gentry. New York: Continuum, 1983, pp. 1–21.

Tobin, Frank, Kim Vivian, and Richard H. Lawson. *Hartmann von Aue. The Complete Arthurian Romances, Tales, and Lyric Poetry.* University Park: Pennsylvania State University Press, 2000.

Tobin, Frank. "High Middle Ages." *In A Concise History of German Literature,* ed. Kim Vivian. Columbia, S.C.: Camden House, 1992, pp. 30–34, 45–48.

Zeydel, Edwin H., trans. (with Bayard Quincy Morgan). *Gregorius: A Medieval Oedipus Legend by Hartmann von Aue.* Chapel Hill: University of North Carolina Press, 1955.

Kim Vivian

SEE ALSO
Arthurian Literature, German; Gottfried von Straßburg; Ministerials; Staufen; Walther von der Vogelweide; Wolfram von Eschenbach

Health
See Charms; Medicine.

Heiligenkreuz

A Cistercian monastery located in the Vienna Woods of Lower Austria, Heiligenkreuz (Latin, *Sancta Crux*) was founded in 1135–1136 by Margrave Leopold III of Babenberg (canonized in 1485) at the request of his son Otto, then abbot of Cistercian Morimund and later bishop of Freising. Its first abbot, Gottshalk, came from Morimund, and throughout the medieval period, Heiligenkreuz retained its close connections with Burgundian France.

Laid out on a geometric plan reminiscent of Fontenay, the architecture of Heiligenkreuz monastery is severe but harmonious. In the extant building, the Romanesque nave, with its alternating wider and narrower piers, broad expanse of wall and banded rib vaults, remains from the first church, consecrated in 1187. The transept and modest portal were added around 1200. The church's east end was elongated by the addition of a chevet, described as a hall, consisting of three aisles of equal height, consecrated in 1295. A large body of late thirteenth-century stained glass is preserved at Heiligenkreuz, including examples of typical Cistercian grisaille (grayish) patterns, and more unusually, intensely colored images in multifoil frames. The stained glass in the wellhouse represents members of the Babenberg family, while the lancets in the choir depict prophets. The chapterhouse served as the burial place for members of the ducal house, including the last Babenberg duke, Frederick II the Wrangler (d. 1246).

Heiligenkreuz was a center of Cistercian activity in Austria, sending monks to Zwettl in 1138, Czikador in Hungary (1142), Baumgarten (1142), Marienberg in Hungary (1194), Lilienfeld (1206), Goldenkron in Bohemia (1263) and Neuberg in Styria (1327). Heiligenkreuz housed an important scriptorium, noted both for its scholarship and for its restrained Cistercian style of figured initials and illustrations in red and brown inks with wash. A few late-thirteenth century missals also exhibit the unique angular *Zackenstil*. Under the patronage of Bohemian margrave Premysl Ottokar (1251–1276), scholarship flourished, particularly in the person of Gutolf (active 1265–1293), noted historian, jurist, and philologist, and later abbot of Marienberg. The large medieval library remains on the site, which functions today as a monastery, seminary, and college. A panel in the monastery museum gives a name to the early fifteenth-century painter known as the Master of Heiligenkreuz, but this wandering artist associated with the imperial court had no particular connection to the convent.

BIBLIOGRAPHY

Dahm, Friedrich. *Das Grabmal Friedrichs des Streitbaren im Zisterzienserstift Heiligenkreuz: Rekonstruktion, Typus, Stil, liturgische Funktionen.* Vienna: Verlag der österreichischen Akademie der Wissenschaften, 1996.

Die Gotik in Niederösterreich: Kunst, Kultur und Geschichte eines Landes im Spätmittelalter. Vienna: Österreichische Staatsdruckerei, 1959. Exhibition catalog.

Die Zeit der frühen Habsburger: Dome und Klöster 1179–1379. Katalog des Niederösterreichischen Landemuseums N. F. 85. Vienna: Amt der Niederösterreichischer Landesregierung, Kulturabteilung, 1979. Exhibition catalog.

Frey, Dagobert. *Die Denkmale des Stiftes Heiligenkreuz.* Österreichische Kunsttopographie 19. Vienna: Krystall Verlag, 1926.

Frodl-Kraft Eva. *Die mittelalterlichen Glasgemälde in Niederöstereich.* Corpus vitrearum medii aevi, Österreich 2. Vienna, Cologne, and Graz: Böhlau, 1972, pp. 95–145.

Gaumannmüller, Franz. *Die mittelalterliche Klosteranlage der Abtei Heiligenkreuz.* Heiligenkreuz: Heiligenkreuzer Verlag, 1967.

Niemetz, Paulus. *Die Grablege der Babenberger in der Abtei Heiligenkreuz.* Heiligenkreuz: Heiligenkreuzer Verlag, 1974.

1000 Jahre Babenberger in Österreich. Vienna: Amt der Niederösterreichischer Landesregierung, Kulturabteilung, 1976. Exhibition catalog.

Wagner-Rieger, Renate. *Mittelalterliche Architektur in Österreich.* 2nd ed. St Pölten and Vienna: Verlag Niederösterreichisches Pressehaus, 1991.

Walliser, Franz. *Cistercienser Buchkunst: Heiligenkreuzer Skriptorium in seinem ersten Jahrhundert, 1133–1230.* Heiligenkreuz: Heiligenkreuzer Verlag, 1969.

Amelia Carr

SEE ALSO

Freising; Gothic Art and Architecture; Romanesque Art and Architecture; Zwettl

Heiligenleben

The prose collection *Heiligenleben* (Lives of the Saints, ca. 1405–1420) reflects the ideals and intentions of the so-called *Wiener Schule* (Viennese School, Nikolaus von Dinkelsbühl, Thomas Peuntner) and the Melk Reform (1418) of the southern German Benedictine cloisters during the reign of Emperor Sigismund (1410–1437) and Duke Albert V of Austria (1404–1439). Non-noble laymen "converts" needed German prose to participate in the assigned reading of the day, with emphasis on a loving God and praise and consideration for all the German-speaking areas in the empire, their bishoprics, founders of religious orders, and their patrons. Production of the *Heiligenleben* (containing 250 legends), and its spread through Austria, Bavaria, and Swabia, was also part of an effort to keep the peace, avoid and later survive the Hussite Wars, and end the religious controversy leading to the Great Schism, a goal achieved by 1436.

The sixteen parchment manuscripts of the *Heiligenleben* indicate they were distributed through Austria, Bohemia, Hungary, and Germany. About half of the monastic manuscripts are located in reformed Benedictine cloisters. Others have been found in Dominican women's cloisters, which adopted the reforms as well. As other orders joined, each received a copy of the *Heiligenleben.* The manuscripts of single legends, such as *Katharina* (1421, the oldest dated manuscript), *Klara von Assisi,*

Sebald, Oswald, Allerseelen, or *Gregorius auf dem Stein,* often show a closer dependency on the source texts than does the complete copy of the *Heiligenleben* of 1431 from Nürnberg, the primary German text. The original is probably an Austrian text, which contains the original version of *Katharina* with its youth story, a part that was later left out. Later, in Germany, the legend of *Birgitta of Sweden* was added.

Of the approximately two hundred manuscripts, half belonged to monasteries and the rest to wealthy nobility, merchants, and clergy. The manuscripts were often produced in workshops and contained illustrations. The *Heiligenleben* appeared also in contamination with the *Alsatian Legenda aurea* (in the southwest) and even with the *South Middle Netherlandic Legenda aurea* (in the northwest of Germany).

Literary sources for the *Heiligenleben,* include the *Passional,* the *Märtyrerbuch,* and, for *Katharina,* also the *Legenda aurea.* Other sources were verse epics and legends (Hartmann's *Gregorius,* the Münchner *Oswald, Georg* by Reinbot von Durne, Ebernand's von Erfurt *Heinrich und Kunigunde,* and *Alexius A*). By 1430, a so-called *Heiligenleben Redaction* in three volumes with 365 legends was created, which served as a productive source for reading and copying. Forty-one printings of the *Heiligenleben* were produced in southern and northern Germany between 1471–1521.

The *Heiligenleben* became a secondary source for *Der maget krone* (1473/1475) and for the *Passienbüchlein von den vier Hauptjungfrauen* in the Low German version printed by Simon Koch in Magdeburg in 1500. Meisterlieder were made of *Alexius* by Jörg Preining in Augsburg (1488), of *Dorothea* by Michael Schrade, and by Hans Sachs (1518) of the miracle of *Katharinas Bräutigam.* Painters, such as Dürer and Cranach used the stories for their paintings as well.

BIBLIOGRAPHY

Brand, M., K. Freienhagen-Baumgardt, R. Meyer, and Werner Williams-Krapp, ed. *Der Heiligen Leben.* Vol. 1: *Der Sommerteil.* Tübingen: Niemeyer, 1994. Vol. 2: *Der Winterteil.* 1998.

Jefferis, Sibylle. "Ein spätmittelalterliches Katharinenspiel aus dem Cod. Ger. 4 der University of Pennsylvania: Text und Studien zu seiner legendengeschichtlichen Einordnung." Ph.D. diss. University of Pennsylvania 1982. UMI 8217130, pp. 220–231.

Kunze, Konrad. "Der Heiligen Leben" ("Prosa-", "Wenzelpassional"). In *Die deutsche Literatur des Mittelalters.*

Verfasserlexikon, ed. Kurt Ruh, et al. Berlin/New York: de Gruyter, 1981, vol. 3, coll. 617–627.

Williams-Krapp, Werner. *Die deutschen und niederländischen Legendare des Mittelalters: Studien zu ihrer Überlieferungs-, Text- und Wirkungsgeschichte.* Tübingen: Niemeyer, 1986, pp. 188–377.

Sibylle Jefferis

SEE ALSO

Hartmann von Aue; *Legenda Aurea,* Alsatian; Legends; Meistersinger; *Passional; Passienbüchlein; Väterbuch*

Heinric (fl. ca. 1300)

This Middle Dutch poet, also known as Hein van Aken, is mentioned as an author in a number of Middle Dutch texts.

One, *Van den coninc Saladijn ende van Tabaryen* (Of King Saladijn and of Tabaryen), is an adaption of the French courtesy book *l'Ordene de chevalerie* (The Chivalric Order). The text has been shortened by over two hundred verses and its metrical form has been altered as well. The Old French source is continuous text in paired rhyme, but the Middle Dutch adaptation is stanzaic, with the rhyme scheme *ABABABAB.* The contents of the two are similar: Hughe van Tabaryen, who is a prisoner of war, makes Sultan Saladijn a knight and talks to him about the essence of knighthood. In the final line of the poem, the author's name is revealed: Hein van Aken. This text is the only one to mention Heinric's surname.

In the past, scholars have attributed other works to this author, but their evidence is weak. The translator of *Die Rose* ("The Rose"), for example, calls himself *van Brusele Henrecke* (Henrecke from Brussels, l. 9901). In *Der leken spieghel,* Jan van Boendale mentions a certain "Van Bruesele Heyne van Aken" (Book III, cap. 17, l. 91). This line has been used to argue that the translator of *Die Rose* is Hein van Aken, but the argument is not convincing.

Two other Middle Dutch texts have wrongly been attributed to Hein van Aken: the second part of an adaptation of *Li miserere* by the Renclus de Moiliens (in which the Christian name *Heinrec* is mentioned), and the *Vierde Martijn,* a stanzaic poem following the *Martijns* by Jacob van Maerlant, which a modern editor supposed contained a reference to Saladijn.

The *Roman van Heinric ende Margriete van Limborch* (Tale of Heinric and Margriete of Limborch) is a very colorful and long epic text (ca. 22,000 lines in twelve books). The entire text has come down to us in two codices, presently in Brussels and Leyden. The latter codex contains an epilogue in which the poet calls himself Heinric. The notion that Heinric is identical with the translator of *Die Rose,* is a proposition that has never been proven. *Margriete van Limborch* was probably written between 1291 and 1318 and was meant for the Brabantine court. The work is an original Middle Dutch composition into which a large number of well-known medieval literary motifs have been incorporated. Margriete, the daughter of Duke van Limburg, gets lost during a hunt and eventually finds herself at the court in Athens where the count's son, Echites, falls in love with her. After many adventures, the couple marries. A number of subplots are interwoven into this basic story, including one which deals with Margriete's brother Heinric, who travels around from place to place looking for his sister. A tale about Evax, who seeks Echites, and descriptions of entire sieges and wars are also included in the epic.

BIBLIOGRAPHY

Asselbergs, Willem J. A. "Het landschap van de Vierde Martijn," in Asselbergs, Willem J. A. *Nijmeegse colleges.* Zwolle: Tjeenk Willink, 1967, pp. 43–91.

de Keyser, P., ed. *Hein van Aken, Van den coninc Saladijn ende van Hughen van Tabaryen.* Leyden: Brill, 1950.

De Wachter, Lieve. "Een literair-historisch onderzoek naar de effecten van ontleningen op de compositie en de zingeving van de Roman van Heinric en Margriete van Limborch." Dissertation University of Brussels, 1998.

Hegman, Willy A., ed. *Hein van Aken, Vierde Martijn.* Zwolle: Tjeenk-Willink, 1958.

Janssens, Jozef D. 'Brabantse knipoogjes' in de Roman van Heinric ende Margriete van Limborch, *Eigen schoon en de Brabander* 60 (1977): 1–16.

Leendertz, Pieter, ed. *Het Middelnederlandsche leerdicht Rinclus.* Amsterdam: Jan Leendertz en Zoon, 1893.

Lievens, Robrecht. "De dichter Hein van Aken." *Spiegel der Letteren* 4 (1960): 57–74.

Meesters, Rob, ed. *Roman van Heinric ende Margriete van Limborch.* Amsterdam/Antwerpen: Wereldbibliotheek, 1951.

van Uytven, Raymond. "Historische knipoogjes naar 'Heinric ende Margriete van Limborch.'" *Bijdragen tot de geschiedenis* 66 (1983): 3–11.

Verwijs, Eelco, ed. *Heinric van Aken, Die Rose.* 1868; rpt. Utrecht: HES, 1976.

Dieuwke van der Poel

SEE ALSO

Jacob van Maerlant; Jan van Boendale; *Roman de la Rose,* Dutch

Heinrich der Glîchezâre (fl. late 12th c.)

Heinrich, the Alsatian author of *Reinhart Fuchs* (*Reynard the Fox,* last decade of the twelfth century), was the first to utilize myriad tales about the adventures of the clever fox and his opponents already treated satirically in the Latin poem *Ysengrimus* and the various branches of the French episodic narrative *Roman de Renart,* several of which were his principal sources, to form an extended animal epic. The appellation often attached to his name in scholarship, *Glîchezâre* (hypocrite), was surely intended by him to refer to Reinhart, as a fragment of the work from the beginning of the thirteenth century makes clear, but in the two very similar manuscripts, both written between 1320 and 1330, that preserve the whole work (with a small lacuna, or gap) it seems to be part of his own name. Several brief German didactic poems witness that Heinrich's version continued to be read to some extent in later centuries, but the French branches were independently shaped into a longer narrative in French and in Dutch, and the Dutch version(s) became the basis for the Low German *Reynke de Vos* and the Middle Englich *Reynard the Fox.*

The lacuna in *Reinhart Fuchs* is intentional; the narrative breaks off (in one manuscript with the words *et cetera*) just before Ysengrin the wolf is castrated, and picks up again with his laments. Heinrich, however, was not as prudish as a later medieval editor. His explicit account can be reconstructed from a didactic song attacking false oaths by Der Marner that clearly utilizes it. In a way, such explicitness is unusual; such details are generally hinted at rather than stated. Nevertheless, it was apparently his own invention—his known sources do not contain the episode, though *Reynke de Vos* has a distant parallel, as does its source.

All versions of the material utilize beasts in two ways: essentially, in that animals behave according to their nature (as understood in the Middle Ages), and allegorically, in that the animals portray human vices. Even where allusions to human institutions and actions are clear, the animals are never totally anthropomorphized. But, they all can speak, and they interact as if their differences were less consequential than their similarities. Almost all the versions, although perhaps not all branches of the *Roman de Renart,* criticize the misuse of office, be it secular or clerical. Heinrich demonstrates, through the implications of the episodes he adds to those he adapts from his sources, an intimate knowledge of local politics in the late twelfth century; the position discernible in his work is opposed to the Hohenstaufen, imperial one. He also is knowledgeable in the intricacies of Germanic law, adjusting his French sources where necessary to make the trial scene at the end of the work accord with his audience's understanding of legal procedure.

BIBLIOGRAPHY

Düwel, Klaus, ed. *Der Reinhart Fuchs des Elsässers Heinrich.* Tübingen: Niemeyer, 1984.

Göttert, Karl-Heinz, ed. and trans. *Heinrich der Glîchezâre: Reinhart Fuchs.* Stuttgart: Reclam: 1978.

Hubert Heinen

SEE ALSO

Animal Epics, Dutch; Marner, Der; *Reynard* the Fox, Dutch; Staufen

Heinrich der Teichner (ca. 1310–1377)

Heinrich's epithet reflects regional affiliation, presumably to the Teichentäler near Kallwang in Austria. Heinrich was a wandering poet and later settled near Vienna. His œvre consists almost entirely of short didactic poems. Contemporary poet Peter Suchenwirt referred to him as a *schlechter lay* (a simple layman). This estimation coincides with Heinrich's self-stylization. Although he draws from a variety of scholarly sources, he never stresses his own learning. Reminiscent of Wolfram von Eschenbach, Heinrich even claims to be illiterate, *nach den puechstaben bin ich aller chunst beschaben* ("I lack all the skills of the letters").

Heinrich's literary program emulates the tradition of the *sermo humilis,* the lowly, everyday language of divine truth. He consistently cites the Bible, the church fathers, such as Augustine, and Gregory, sermons by Bernard de Clairvaux, Berthold von Regensberg and others, and common proverbs. Presumably composed between 1350–1365, all of the 798 poems attributed to Heinrich promote Christian morals with practical and unadorned language and images.

Heinrich's poems comprise a genre in themselves: the *Teichnerreden*. The *Teichnerreden* end with the signature verse, *also sprach der Teychnaer* ("thus spoke the Teichner"). This signature verse became a literary convention, and some of the poems attributed to Heinrich are proba-

bly the work of imitators and predecessors.

Heinrich also composed longer poems, including a hymn in praise of the Virgin Mary, a *vita* of the martyr Dorothea, and the legend of Crescentia. He also wrote *Roßhaut,* the strange tale of a man who slaughters his only horse in order to make a gown for his wife, who wishes to rival the beautiful duchess. Some of Heinrich's works may have been commissioned by an Order of Lay Brothers.

Heinrich is believed to be buried at St. Coloman in Vienna. The expensive manuscripts and wide distribution of his work testify to his popularity during his lifetime.

BIBLIOGRAPHY

Lämmert, Eberhard. *Reimsprecherkunst im Spätmittelalter: Eine Untersuchung der Teichnerreden.* Stuttgart: Metzler, 1970.

Niewöhner, Heinrich, ed. *Die Gedichte des Heinrichs des Teichners.* 3 vols. Berlin: Akademie-Verlag, 1953—1956.

Stephen M. Carey

SEE ALSO

Berthold von Regensburg; Suchenwirt, Peter; Versification; Wolfram von Eschenbach

Heinrich von dem Türlin (fl. first half of the 13th c.)

The author of *Diu Crône* (The Crown), a 30,000-line Middle High German Arthurian romance in rhymed couplets, with triplets marking the end of each section, may also have written *Der Mantel* (The Cloak), a fragment of 994 lines, the authorship of which is rather uncertain.

Heinrich lived in the first half of the 13th century. The *Crône* must have been completed by ca. 1230. The date is linked to Rudolf von Ems's *Alexander,* where Heinrich's work receives favorable mention as *Allr Aventiure Krône* ("Crown of all Adventures"). Of Heinrich's biographical background, virtually nothing is known with certainty. The previously accepted connection with the family name *von dem Türlin* (meaning "of the doorway") in the Carinthian town of St. Veit seems untenable. From his work we can identify only his name, his language (Bavarian-Austrian), the degree of his education (extensive knowledge of French and Latin, and some Italian), and possibly his social status (hardly a knight). Internal evidence also suggests strong ties with the area of the Eastern Alps. Since his work has been shown to be uniquely syncretistic and thus dependent on numerous

French and German literary sources, only a major court with strong dynastic connections to France could have enabled him to embark on a project of such scope. As potential patrons, recent research has considered the Counts of Görz and Otto of Andechs-Meran.

Diu Crône belongs to a later group of Arthurian romances often referred to as "postclassical." Apart from recasting much of the *matière de Bretagne* (Breton, i.e., French, material), it takes a new and innovative approach to the aesthetics of romance: in its form, as an unprecedented venture into the medium of the fantastic; in its theme, because of its new emphasis on *Fortuna* (fortune); and in its structure, by departing from the standard two-part scheme of Chrétien's classic form of romance.

The work is also unique in making Gawein the central hero. In a plot that synthesizes the exploits of a great many Arthurian heroes, Gawein turns into an almost operatic superhero and savior figure who makes their adventures part of his own mission. In essentially three narrative sequences, he rescues Arthur's court from the threat of losing Ginover, undergoes a sequence of adventures structured around his own role in the Grail romance, and finally—like a second Parzival—reaches a somewhat anticlimactic zenith in delivering the living dead at the Grail castle.

As a protégé of Lady Fortune *(Sælde),* Gawein's *raison d'être* is the preservation of Arthur's court. Instead of pursuing a search for spiritual perfection, Heinrich's new type of hero operates in the secular context of a model court. Arthurian romance, as redefined by Heinrich, turns into a romance of society, stressing the stability of a central court as an indispensable basis of chivalrous existence. Heinrich's view of Arthur's court, no longer utopian, rather aims at a mythic model whose basis is fragile and ultimately doomed.

BIBLIOGRAPHY

Cormeau, Christoph. *'Wigalois' und 'Diu Crône': Zwei Kapitel zur Gattungsgeschichte des nachklassischen Aventiureromans.* Munich: Artemis, 1977.

Dick, Ernst S. "Tradition and Emancipation: The Generic Aspect of Heinrich's *Crône.*" In *Genres in Medieval German Literature,* ed. Hubert Heinen and Ingeborg Henderson. Göppingen: Kümmerle, 1986, pp. 74–92.

Jillings, Lewis. *Diu Crone of Heinrich von dem Türlein: The Attempted Emancipation of Secular Narrative.* Göppingen: Kümmerle, 1980.

Kratz, Bernd. "Zur Biographie Heinrichs von dem Türlin." *Amsterdamer Beiträge zur älteren Germanistik* 11 (1976): 123–167.

Scholl, G. H. F. *Diu Crône von Heinrîch von dem Türlîn,* 1852; rpt. Amsterdam: Rodopi, 1966.

Thomas, J. W. *The Crown: A Tale of Sir Gawein and King Arthur's Court by Heinrich von dem Türlin.* Lincoln, Neb.: University of Neberaska Press, 1989.

Ernst S. Dick

SEE ALSO
Arthurian Literature, German; Rudolf von Ems

Heinrich von Melk (d. after 1150)

Heinrich is believed to be the author of *Vom Priesterleben* (On the Life of Priests) and *Von des todes gehugde* (On the Remembrance of Death), both written after 1150. Although the virtual identity of lines 397–402 in *Vom Priesterleben* with lines 181–186 in *Von des todes Gehugde,* as well as the closely related subject matter, suggest that the two poems were written by the same individual, the matter of common authorship continues to be the subject of lively speculation.

At the end of *Von des Todes gehugde,* in the midst of a description of Paradise, the following verses appear: "Lord God, bring to that place [i.e. Paradise] for the glory of your mother and for the sake of all your saints Heinrich, your humble servant, and the abbot Erkenfried" (1029–1033). These few lines represent a biographical hint, and from them a most ingenious biography has been constructed for Heinrich. He has been identified as a *conversus,* a lay brother associated with a monastery. The monastery in question was assumed to be the Benedictine monastery of Melk in Austria, since an abbot Erkenfried governed that monastery 1122–1163. Because of the sharpness of the poet's attacks and the depth of his acquaintanceship with courtly life, Heinrich was thought to be a noble who, becoming progressively repelled by the world and rejected by ungrateful children, withdrew to a monastery as an older man. There, he seemed to have immersed himself in studies and found it as his duty to admonish all classes of society, particularly disreputable priests, regarding their duties as Christians.

Unfortunately, this biography is not accurate. Abbot Erkenfried of Melk could scarcely be Heinrich's patron since the two poems exhibit verse and rhyme techniques that reflect a period later than 1163 (e.g., a very high percentage of pure rhymes and a minimum of overlong lines of twelve to fourteen syllables). In addition, the contents of the poems underscore concerns such as the validity of sacraments administered by unworthy priests, and display conventions regarding court customs and the secular love lyric of a time more accurately located within the last quarter of the twelfth century. In the final analysis, there is only reasonable certainty that the author of both works was a layman, possibly a *conversus,* who demonstrated in his writings many manifestations of the popular piety movement of the twelfth century. These included his diatribes against dishonorable priests, criticisms of violations of sumptuary laws, invectives against the pride of the nobility, and general hostility toward worldly affairs when they interfered with performing one's Christian duty.

The Heinrich of *Von des todes Gehugde* and *Vom Priesterleben* is a layman who speaks about theological matters on an equal level with members of the clergy. He not only addresses a noble lay audience in the one work, he represents the interests of this group to a clerical audience in the other. His writing affirms the worth of the lay nobility and its view of the vital role it plays within the Christian order, a role that is becoming a dominant one in relation to the clergy. This confidence and positive self-image finds its quintessential expression in the secular tales of the courtly period, in which society is improved by the actions of members of the nobility and not by representatives of the institutionalized Church. The path to salvation begins to lead not solely through priests, but, primarily, through the good works of each individual.

BIBLIOGRAPHY

Freytag, Wiebke. "Das Priesterleben des sogenannten Heinrich von Melk. Redeformen, Rezeptionsmo dus und Gattung." *Deutsche Vierteljahresschrift* 52 (1978): 558–580.

Gentry, Francis G. *Bibliographie zur frühmittel-hochdeutschen geistlichen Dichtung.* Berlin: Schmidt, 1992, pp. 233–239.

———. "*Owe armiu phaffheite:* Heinrich von Melk's Views on Clerical Life." In *Medieval Purity and Piety: Essays on Medieval Clerical Celibacy and Religious Reform,* ed. Michael Frassetto. New York and London: Garland, 1998, pp. 337–352.

Kienast, Richard. *Der sogenannte Heinrich von Melk. Nach R. Heinzels Ausgabe von 1867.* Heidelberg: Winter, 1946.

Maurer, Friedrich, ed. *Die religiösen Dichtungen des 11. und 12. Jahrhunderts. Nach ihren Formen Besprochen,* Vol. 3. Tübingen: Niemeyer, 1970, pp. 258–359.

Neuser, Peter-Erich. "Der sogenannte Heinrich von Melk." In *Die deutsche Literatur des Mittelalters: Verfasserlexikon,* ed. Kurt Ruh, et al, vol. 3. Berlin and New York: de Gruyter, 1981, cols. 787–797.

———. *Zum sogenannten Heinrich von Melk. Überlieferung, Forschungsgeschichte und Verfasserfrage der Dichtungen Vom Priesterleben und Von des todes gehugede.* Vienna and Cologne: Böhlau, 1973.

Scholz Williams, Gerhild. "Against Court and School. Heinrich of Melk and Hlinant of Froidmont as Critics of Twelfth-Century Society." *Neophilologus* 62 (1978): 513–526.

———. *The Vision of Death: A Study of the "Memento mori" Expressions in some Latin, German and French Didactic Texts of the 11th and 12th Centuries.* Göppingen: Kümmerle, 1976.

Vollmann-Profe, Gisela. *Geschichte der deutschen Literatur von den Anfängen bis zum Beginn der Neuzeit,* vol. 1, pt. 2: *Wiederbeginn volkssprachiger Schriftlichkeit im hohen Mittelalter.* 2nd ed. Tübingen: Niemeyer, 1994, pp. 93-97; 130–137.

Francis G. Gentry

SEE ALSO
Versification

Heinrich von Morungen (d. 1220)

A contemporary of Albrecht von Johansdorf and Hartmann von Aue, Heinrich von Morungen represents the pinnacle of "classical" *Minnesang* around 1200. He is considered to be one of the most important lyric poets writing in German during the courtly period, and perhaps the most important Minnesänger after Reinmar and Walther von der Vogelweide.

Traces of dialect in Morungen's poems show him to be from central eastern Germany. Morungen's family probably came from a manor near Sangershausen in Thuringia. The poet named as *Her Heinrich von Morunge* in the famous Heidelberg *Minnesang* manuscript is commonly identified with a certain *Hendricus/Henricus de Morungen,* who is mentioned in two documents from between 1213 and 1218 that bear the seal of the margrave Dietrich of Meissen. In one of the documents, Morungen is described as a retired soldier *(miles emeritus),* who has received for his good service a yearly pension of ten marks. He apparently gave this pension to the cloister of St. Thomas in Leipzig. According to later sources, Morungen died in the monastery in 1222. Since Dietrich of Meissen was the son-in-law of Hermann of Thuringia, patron of Wolfram von Eschenbach and others, the records thus place Morungen at a court that was a center of literary activity in the German-speaking area in the early thirteenth century. Since Morungen hailed from an area controlled by the Hohenstaufen family, it is quite possible that Heinrich could have learned his craft at the court of Frederick I Barbarossa. As a poet, then, Morungen could possibly have appeared and/or performed at the court of Meissen contemporaneously with poets such as Walther von der Vogelweide.

While it is not known whether Morungen was a professional poet, he was one of the first Latin-educated secular poets *(Minnesänger)* in Germany; probably there was no other poet of the time who owed so much to the Latin poet Ovid. Morungen's adaptations of classical Ovidian themes influenced such younger contemporaries, as Herbort von Fritzlar. Morungen's poems are dated approximately twenty years before the documents that show his name. Characteristic is his formal style, artistically advanced, yet owing much to the style of the earlier French troubadors. Formal stylistic connections to the school of Friedrich von Hausen (such as rhymed strophes and dactyls) and Morungen's later influence on Walther von der Vogelweide suggest that Morungen wrote before 1200. Although a definitive chronology has not been established, 115 strophes, arranged in 35 poems, are attributed to Morungen.

Morungen is known primarily, not for his style, but for his use of images and symbols. The images grow out of the senses; foremost among these is sight: mirrors, windows, dreams, colors, dawn and twilight. As a visual person *(Augenmensch),* Morungen describes love that centers around vision and the contemplation of the beloved. It is a woman's beauty, not her virtue, that awakens in men the desire for love. Morungen does not, however, focus on physical sensuality; rather it is the act of seeing, or of beholding physical beauty, that enables the looker to perceive actual or true love, a perfect happiness, an absolute love. The looker, like Narcissus, loses and forgets himself as he beholds the beauty before him; moreover, this experience also enables him to create his own identity as a subject. This act of creating the subject is epitomized in the poem *Mir ist geschehen als einem kindelîne* ("It happened to me like a child," no. 145, 1), known as the "Narcissus Song" *(Narzissuslied)* for its allusions to this myth. Here the speaker/lover/subject overcomes his narcissism by distinguishing himself from the object of his affections, and by speaking about his desire in the language of the text. Through the poem and through language, the act of looking transcends a purely erotic level of reflection, approaching a more existential one. Thus, looking also functions as a metaphor for the poetic process, for the search for truth and its representation through language. In this way, Morungen raises *Minnesang* from a purely social purpose to an art form, thereby creating an aesthetic of service to women *(Frauendienst).*

Motifs that previously played a relatively minor role in *Minnesang,* particularly those that show love as enchantment or a magic force that pulls human beings into its sphere, take on a central role. Classical in origin (Ovid), such motifs closely connect Morungen's lyric to the concept of love portrayed in the early courtly epic of the late twelfth century. In Veldeke's *Eneit* and in Gottfried's *Tristan,* for example, courtly love *(minne)* is a magical and sometimes deadly power. As the lyric subject, Morungen experiences the same fate as the epic heroes — submission through the magic of love despite the threat of sickness, madness, or death. This magic arises from the beauty of the beloved; she is the moon, the stars, the sun, who sends down her light from afar. In the poem known as the *Venus-Lied,* the lady is a noble Venus (*"ein Venus hêre,"* no. 138, 33), whose beauty shines like the sun from a window. This beauty can inspire pure joy, and the word *wunne* (joy) appears often in Morungen's poems. (A notable example is *In sô hôher swebender wunne* ["In joy floating so high," no. 125, 19].) The beloved can also be a sweet murderess in the poem *Vil süeziu, senftiu tôterinne* ("Very sweet, soft murderess," no. 147, 4), who inspires a love that will last into the next world beyond death. The intimate connection between love, death, and sorrow brings this love very close to a mystical experience; there is an obvious link to Gottfried here as well. But in the conflict it reveals between reality and dream or fantasy, the experience of the lover also harkens back to the metaphor of Narcissus, whose fascination with his own projection has deadly results.

Although Morungen cannot be said to have a school of his own like that of Friedrch von Hausen, one can find thematic and stylistic evidence of his influence on Walther von der Vogelweide. Interestingly, Morungen himself is the hero of a ballad, "On the Honorable Morunger" *(Vom Edlen Möringer),* that dates from the middle of the fifteenth century.

BIBLIOGRAPHY

Bertau, Karl. *Deutsche Literatur im europäischen Mittelalter,* vol. 1: 800–1197. Munich: Beck, 1972, pp. 676–677.

Bumke, Joachim. *Geschichte der deutschen Literatur im hohen Mittelalter,* vol. 2. Munich: Deutscher Taschenbuchverlag, 1990.

de Boor, Helmut. *Geschichte der deutschen Literatur von den Anfängen bis zur Gegenwart,* vol. 2. 11th ed. *Die höfische Literatur. Vorbereitung, Blüte, Ausklang. 1170–1250.* Munich: Beck, 1991.

Glaser, Horst Albert, ed. *Mündlichkeit in die Schriftlichkeit.* Hamburg: Rowohlt, 1988, pp. 164–185.

Hayes, Nancy Karl. "Negativizing Narcissus: Heinrich von Morungen at Julia Kristeva's Court." *The Journal of the Midwest Modern Language Association* 22 (1989): 43–60.

"Heinrich von Morungen." In *Lexikon des Mittelalters,* vol. 4. Munich and Zurich: Artemis, 1977, cols. 2101–2102.

Kasten, Ingrid. "Klassischer Minnesang." In: *Deutsche Literatur. Eine Sozialgeschichte. Bd. 1*

Moser, Hugo and Helmut Tervooren, ed. *Des Minnesangs Frühling,* 37th rev. ed. Stuttgart: Hirzel, 1981 [poems cited above by no.].

Schnell, Rüdiger. "Andreas Capellanus, Heinrich von Morungen und Herbort von Fritzlar." *Zeitschrift für Deutsches Altertum und Deutsche Literatur* 104 (1975): 131–151.

Alexandra Sterling-Hellenbrand

SEE ALSO

Friedrich von Hausen; Gottfried von Straßburg; Heinrich von Veldeke; *Minnesang;* Versification; Walther von der Vogelweide

Heinrich von Neustadt (fl. first half of the 14th c.)

An author of three works of uncertain chronology, this Middle High German author of the 13th–14th centuries probably came from Wiener Neustadt (Lower Austria). He received a master's degree *(magister)* in medicine, probably at an Italian university, and spent most of his life in Vienna, where he is documented in 1312.

Apollonius von Tyrland, Heinrich's novel of 20,600 verses contained in four manuscripts, is based on a third-century Latin history of the kings of Tyre, *Historia Apollonii Regis Tyri,* and, ultimately, on a lost late Greek novel.

Prince Apollonius, shipwrecked far from home, wins the hand of a princess. Seemingly dead after giving birth to a daughter, she is given a ship's burial, but is revived by a physician after being thrown ashore. The little girl is abducted by pirates. It takes Apollonius sixteen years full of travels and many adventures to reunite his family. Thereafter, he establishes the Round Table two hundred years before Arthur, conquers Jerusalem, and finally becomes emperor.

Heinrich's work is an example of a late medieval sentimental novel in verse, with an emphasis on adventures, miracles, strange countries, and exotic scenery. It is influenced by earlier German epics such *Iwein, Parzival, Wolfdietrich,* and *Alexander.*

Von Gottes Zuokunft, a religious poem of about 8,000 verses, is preserved in six manuscripts. Part One is an allegorical explanation of the incarnation of Christ based on the Latin religious tract *Compendium Anticlaudiani* (ca. 1300). Part Two gives an account of Christ's life, death, and resurrection; Part Three deals with the Last Judgment.

Visio Philiberti, Heinrich's adaptation of a French visionary tale, describes an argument between a hell-bound soul and the body. It is contained in only one manuscript of *Von Gottes Zuokunft,* and possibly was intended to be a part of it.

BIBLIOGRAPHY

Bockhoff, A. and Samuel Singer. *Apollonius von Tyrland und seine Quellen.* Tübingen: Mohr, 1911.

Marti, Marta. *Gottes Zukunft von Heinrich von Neustadt.* Tübingen: Mohr, 1911.

Ochsenbein, Peter. "Heinrich von Neustadt." In *Die deutsche Literatur des Mittelalters: Verfasserlexikon,* ed. Kurt Ruh, et al. 2nd ed. Berlin: de Gruyter, vol. 3, 1981, cols. 838–845.

Manfred Zimmermann

SEE ALSO

Alexanderlied; Hartmann von Aue; Wolfram von Eschenbach; *Wolfdietrich* and *Ornit*

Heinrich von Veldeke (ca. 1150–1200)

Uncertainty surrounds the poet Heinrich von Veldeke, known primarily for his *Eneasroman* (The Story of Aeneas), but known also as the composer of *St. Servatius* and several love lyrics. Heinrich finished only about four-fifths of his *Eneide* between 1170 and 1175, because someone purportedly stole his manuscript from a wedding celebration at Cleve. Through the intervention of Hermann, count of Thuringia, he regained access to it

Eneide (Vienna, Österreichische Nationalbibliothek, Cod. 2861), fol. 21V; Eneas's departure from Dido, Death of Dido. *Photograph: Bildarchiv, ÖNB Wien*

and completed it about 1185. Heinrich's works remain elusive due to a dearth of adequate critical research; and the literature that attempts to outline the circumstances of his life and his creative activity is also inconclusive. Nevertheless, he is considered the father of German vernacular literature of the Middle Ages, a model for immediate contemporaries and later imitators alike.

Heinrich must have been born in the first half of the twelfth century, perhaps in a place called *Veldeke* or *Velker Mole* near Hasselt and Maastricht in what was, at the time, Limburgian Belgium. Early witnesses recorded his identity variously as *Heinrich, Heynrijck, Hainrich,* or *Heinric,* from *(van or von) Veltkilche(n), Veldeckh, Veldeg,* and *Veldig,* as well as *Veldeke.* Some poets referred to him as "Lord" and "Master," indicating that he was a noble and educated. There was, in fact, a Veldeke family of the lesser nobility in the Maastricht region. Heinrich may have been related to and served the counts of Loon. Rem-

iniscences of other authors and texts in his own work are evidence of his familiarity with ancient and contemporary literature, suggesting that he might have studied in a cathedral or monastery school. He was knowledgeable in the literatures and languages of Germany, of France, and of antiquity, employing the *Straßburg Alexander,* the Old French *Roman d'Eneas* and Virgil's *Aeneid* as models for his own version of the epic. He was also acquainted with Dictys and Dares, Ovid, and Servius. Both German and Dutch scholars claim him as their own.

Whether or not the original language of Veldeke's major work was Old Limburgian or a more universal German literary language has occupied a great deal of time and effort among Veldeke scholars. Ludwig Ettmüller published the first edition of the *Eneasroman* in 1882 based upon the larger number of Upper German manuscripts. Ettmüller believed the original to have been transcribed in a lowland dialect, but he did not think it was possible to reconstruct the original text. Some thirty years later, Otto Behaghel attempted a *Rückübersetzung* (a translation back to the older language), as did Gabriele Schieb and Theodor Frings in the 1960s. All existing versions of the epic, however, are Middle German, Upper German, or High German *(Ober-deutsch and Hochdeutsch).*

Whatever the original language, the work's influence reached exclusively to Upper German regions rather than to Veldeke's supposed home in Limburg. Gottfried von Straßburg acknowledges Heinrich as the first graft upon the stem of German literature, and his influence can be traced in a number of later German authors. In addition, one of his sources seems to have been the *Straßburg Alexander,* composed in an Alemannic dialect (and thus Upper German). The *Eneide* also bears a close, but problematic, relationship to the German *Tristrant* of Eilhart von Oberge. The question of language is known in Veldeke studies as "The Veldeke Problem." Though no one has unequivocally settled the question, the interpolation of a Limburg dialect seems to be the invention of Ettmüller rather than an actual fact. Veldeke apparently sought the widest possible German-speaking audience for his work.

Among scholars, the most widely-discussed critical topics concerning the *Eneasroman,* include the romances of Eneas with Dido and Lavinia, and the comparison of these to the Old French versions and to Virgil. For instance, for pursuing his fate and the will of the gods, Virgil does not blame Aeneas for abandoning Dido. The Old French and Middle High German authors portray her love as undisciplined, unsanctioned by society, and unrequited by Eneas, but do so more sympathetically than does Virgil. Veldeke demonstrates even more compassion for Dido than does the French poet. In both vernacular versions, the poets expand upon the relationship of Virgil's Aeneas and Lavinia, providing a commentary on ideal love, Lavinia's "legitimate" love, overcoming the "illicit" love of Dido and Eneas. According to the critical literature, the love theme then blends with the notion of governing *(Herrschaft und Liebe),* and finally modulates until notions of peace and of rulership prevail.

Commentators have related various portions of the text, especially those known as the *Stauferpartien,* to the rule of Frederick I Barbarossa. These include references to the great *Hoffest* at Mainz in 1184 and the finding of Pallas's grave by the emperor. At least one scholar, however, believes the work may have been written, at least initially, on behalf of Henry the Lion. Although critics debate many details of this work, they agree that Veldeke refined and expanded upon his model, and in general created an important work of art. Finally, Veldeke was the first to imitate French models in composing love songs in the German vernacular.

Of less interest and importance is Heinrich's *St. Servatius,* a work that exists in total in a manuscript of the fifteenth century in a New Limburgian dialect. A fragment remains of an Old Limburg version, though there is also an Upper German *Servatius.* As with the *Eneasroman,* text and critical problems have significantly hampered understanding of this work. Like the *Eneide,* the transcription of Heinrich's lyric poetry is entirely Upper German, though the impurity of his rhymes in these poems and songs points to less care and perhaps a greater affinity for his mother tongue than does his romance.

BIBLIOGRAPHY

Bathgate, R. H. "Hendrik van Veldeke's *The Legend of St. Servaes* Translated." *Dutch Crossing* 40 (1990): 3–22.

Behaghel, Otto, ed. *Heinrichs von Veldeke Eneide,* Heilbronn: Gebr. Henninger, 1882.

Dittrich, Marie-Luise. *Die 'Eneide' Heinrichs von Veldeke.* Part 1. Wiesbaden: Steiner, 1966.

Fromm, Hans. *Arbeiten zur deutschen Literatur des Mittelalters.* Tübingen: Niemeyer, 1989.

Kasten, Ingrid. "Herrschaft und Liebe. Zur Rolle und Darstellung des 'Helden' im Roman d'Eneas und in Veldeke's Eneasroman." *Deutsche Vierteljahrsschrift für deutsche Literaturwissenschaft und Geistesgeschichte* 62 (1988): 227–245.

Kistler, Renate. *Heinrich von Veldeke und Ovid.* Tübingen: Niemeyer, 1993.

Klein, Thomas. "Heinrich von Veldeke und die mitteldeutschen Literatursprachen. Untersuchungen zum Veldeke-Problem." *Zwei Studien zu Veldeke und zum Strassburger Alexander.* Amsterdam: Rodopi, 1985.

von Veldeke, Heinrich. *Eneasroman. Mittelhochdeutsch / Neuhochdeutsch,* trans. Dieter Kartschoke. Stuttgart: Reclam, 1986.

———. *Eneide,* ed. Theodor Frings and Gabriele Schieb. 3 vols. Berlin: Akademie, 1964–1970.

———. *Eneit,* trans. J. W. Thomas. New York: Garland, 1985.

———. *Sente Servas, Sanctus Servatius,* ed. Theodor Frings and Gabriele Schieb. Die epischen Werke des Henric van Veldeken, vol. 1. Halle (Saale): Niemeyer, 1956.

Kristine K. Sneeringer

SEE ALSO

Alexanderlied; Dutch Language, Dialects; Eilhart von Oberge; Friedrich I Barbarossa; Gottfried von Straβburg; Heinrich von Veldeke, *Eneide,* Illustrations; Versification

Heinrich von Veldecke, *Eneide,* Illustrations

The Berlin manuscript of Heinrich von Veldecke's *Eneide* (Berlin, Staatsbibliothek, no. Ms. germ. fol. 282) is not only one of the earliest illuminated German manuscripts, but also one of the most studied. Two later illuminated *Eneide* manuscripts have received little of the scholarly attention they deserve.

The Berlin codex, made in the Regensburg area in the 1220s to circa 1230, attempts an unusually ambitious synthesis of picture and text: seventy-one picture pages (most in two registers) alternate with text pages so that readers generally have pictures and text before them at the same time.

Much more than other early schemes for the illustration of vernacular texts, such as the scattering of a relatively few pictures through the text, as in the Heidelberg *Rolandslied,* or the clustering of pictures in isolated groups, as in the Munich *Parzival* and *Tristan* manuscripts, the layout of the Berlin *Eneide* suggests an intended simultaneous reading of pictures and text. However, the picture in view does not always correspond to the text on the opposite page, and the pictorial narrative sometimes diverges from the text. Despite the large body of scholarship on the codex, its text-picture relationship still needs considerable study.

A different approach to illustration is found in Heidelberg, Universitätsbibliothek, Cpg 403 (Alsace [Strasbourg?], 1419), where thirty-eight colored pen drawings and accompanying rubrics introduce the chapters into which the scribe has divided the text. Spaces for six additional images were never filled. Vienna, Österreichische Nationalbibliothek, Cod. 2861 (Swabia, 1474), represents yet another approach. Here an abridged version of Veldecke's *Eneide* is combined with a prose chronicle of the emperors and popes. The *Eneide* is illustrated with 152 colored pen drawings, grouped together in sets of four to six per page and accompanied by short, simple rubrics.

BIBLIOGRAPHY

Boeckler, Albert. *Heinrich von Veldecke: Eneide: Die Bilder der Berliner Handschrift.* Leipzig: Harrasowitz, 1939.

Diemer, Peter, and Dorothea Diemer. "Die Bilder der Berliner Veldecke-Handschrift." In *Heinrich von Veldecke. Eneasroman: Die Berliner Bilderhandschrift mit Übersetzung und Kommentar,* ed. Hans Fromm. Frankfurt: Deutscher Klassiker Verlag, 1992, pp. 911–970.

Fromm, Hans, ed. *Heinrich von Veldecke: Eneasroman: Die Berliner Bilderhandschrift mit Übersetzung und Kommentar,* Frankfurt: Deutscher Klassiker Verlag, 1992.

Kindlers Literatur Lexikon. 8 vols. Zurich: Kindler, 1965. Vol. 2, pl. 36 [after col. 1920].

von Veldecke, Heinrich. *Eneas-Roman: Universitätsbibliothek Heidelberg, Cod. Pal. Germ. 403.* Farbmikrofiche-Edition, introd. Hans Fromm. Munich: Lengenfelder, 1987.

James A. Rushing Jr.

SEE ALSO
Arthurian Literature, German; Gottfried von Straβburg, *Tristan,* Illustrations; Regensburg; Strasbourg; Wolfram von Eschenbach, *Parzival,* Illustrations

Helbling, Seifried (fl. late 13th c.)

Fifteen poems that appear in two manuscripts now in Vienna, one (Nationalbibliothek, manuscript no. 2887) from the seventeenth century, and the other, just a fragment of poem XV (manuscript no. 19799) from the early fourteenth century, are ascribed to a Seifried Helbling, based on a reference in poem XIII. These poems are often identified as the "Smaller Lucidarius" *(der kleine Lucidarius),* a title that was suggested by the inscription to poem I and by the fact that many of the poems adhere to a model somewhat like the Latin *Elucidarius* of Honorius Augustodunensis i.e., a didactic dialogue between the poet/master and his young servant.

While the author's true identity is in question, the poems (eight of which are political in nature) can be dated with some degree of accuracy by events mentioned in them. Thus the oldest poem was written between 1282 and 1283; it mentions that the two sons of the Roman emperor Rudolf I were sharing the reign of Austria and Styria. Albrecht and Rudolf II shared this position from December 27, 1282 to June 1, 1283, when Albrecht assumed the rule of Austria. The last poem was written about 1299. In poem no. IX, written after 1298, the poet claims to be sixty years old. The poet writes with obvious knowledge of the geography of Lower Austria and Vienna and in the dialect of this region. While his knowledge of persons and events is considerable, he always appears as the outsider, the observer watching and reporting on the affairs of state. He may have been a retired politician, a knight, or a retired clerk who had held a position with the Kuenring family or at the court of the duke of Austria.

In addition to didactic and political poems, the corpus includes poems in praise of the Virgin Mary and poems of repentance and supplication; other topics include the Last Judgement, hunting, a love allegory, historical accounts, satire directed against women, and social criticism. There is also a poem in the tradition of *Psychomachia* describing a battle between the forces of good and evil. Besides citing *Lucidarius,* the poet refers to Konrad von Haslau, Freidank, Wolfram von Eschenbach, Walther von der Vogelweide, der Stricker, Neidhart von Reuenthal, Helmbrecht, Wernher der Gartenære, and Steinmar.

BIBLIOGRAPHY

Ehrismann, Gustav. "Zum Seifried Helbling." *Germania* 33 (1888): 371.

Glier, Ingeborg. "Helbling, Seifried." In *Die deutsche Literatur des Mittelalters: Verfasserlexikon,* ed. Kurt Ruh, et al, vol. 3. Berlin: de Gruyter, 1981, cols. 943–947.

Heinemann, Wolfgang. "Zur Ständedidaxe in der deutschen Dichtung des Mittelalters." *Beiträge zur Geschichte der deutschen Sprache und Literatur* (Halle)

88 (1966): 1–90; 89 (1967): 290–403; 92 (1970): 388–437.

Karajan, Theodor Georg von. "Seifreid Helbling." *Zeitschrift für deutsches Altertum und deutsche Literautr* 4 (1844): 1–284.

Seemüller, Joseph. *Seifried Helbling.* Halle an der Saale: Niemeyer, 1866.

———. "Studien zum kleinen Lucidarius (Seifried Helbling)." *Sitzungsberichte der Wiener Akademie der Wissenschaften* 102 (1882): 567–674.

Van D'Elden, Stephanie Cain. "Rhetorical Devices in Seifried Helbling's Political Poetry." *Monatshefte* 74/4 (1982): 451–462.

———. "Seifried Helbling's *Ein mær ist guot ze schrîben an:* A Reevaluation." *Amsterdamer Beiträge zur älteren Germanistik* 13 (1978): 167–179.

Wallner, Anton. "Seifried Helbling." *Zeitschrift für deutsches Altertum und deutsche Literatur* 72 (1935): 267–278.

Stephanie Cain Van D'Elden

SEE ALSO
Neidhart; Stricker, Der; Walther von der Vogelweide; Werner der Gärtner; Wolfram von Eschenbach

Heldenbücher

Collections of narrative poetry in the vernacular became more and more specialized as the Middle Ages progressed. During the fifteenth and sixteenth centuries the terms *Heldenbuch* (Book of Heroes) and *Riesenbuch* (Book of Giants) became common designators for collections of heroic poetry. Modern usage generally associates the terms with collections restricted largely to heroic materials.

A manuscript collection from Strasbourg from sometime after the middle of the fourteenth century (lost in the bombardment of the city in 1870), containing a prose introduction, *Ortnit, Wolfdietrich, Der Rosengarten, Laurin, Sigenot,* and the Stricker's *Pfaffe Amis,* seems to have been the basis for the first printed *Heldenbuch,* printed by Johann Prüβ around 1483, also in Strasbourg. The printed version added a rhymed preface and omits the non-heroic *Pfaffe Amis.* This collection was reprinted by a variety of printers over the next century and became for many the *Heldenbuch.* There are versions from Augsburg (1491), Strasbourg (1509), Augsburg (1545), Frankfurt (1560), and again in Frankfurt (1590). The prose that appears variously at the beginning and end of these collections presents an interesting overview of the heroic "history" as it was understood by the collectors of this literature at the end of the Middle Ages.

Three additional collections are often included under this term. The first is Lienhart Scheubel's *Heldenbuch,* which probably originated in Nuremberg although it has long been in Vienna, where it was known as the *Piaristenhandschrift* because of its having been found in the library of the Piarist house in Vienna. The manuscript is dated to 1480–1490, and it contains *Virginal, König Anteloy, Ortnit, Wolfdietrich,* the *Nibelungenlied,* and *Lorengel.* This is the only such collection to include the *Nibelungenlied.*

The so-called *Dresdener Heldenbuch* (Dresden Book of Heroes) is probably also a product of Nuremberg and is dated 1472. One of the scribes identifies himself as Kaspar von der Rhön, which has led to the identification of this manuscript as Kaspar von der Rhön's *Heldenbuch.* This extensive collection includes *Ortnit, Wolfdietrich, Eckenlied, Rosengarten, Meerwunder, Sigenot, Wunderer, Herzog Ernst, Laurin, Virginal,* and the *Jüngeres Hildebrandslied.* Many texts, especially those written by the anonymous second scribe, are drastically condensed by the omission of what the scribe called "unnecessary words." Each text is prefaced by an illustration, all of which have been severely damaged by poor storage.

The grandest collection known under this rubric is the *Ambraser Heldenbuch* (Book of Heroes from [Castle] Ambras), a sumptuous parchment manuscript prepared to order for the emperor Maximilian I by the customs clerk Hans Ried in Bozen (Bolzano) in the years from 1503–1516. The term *Heldenbuch* is something of a misnomer for this collection, if we associate it strictly with heroic poetry, since most of the twenty-five texts in this stately volume are not what is now called *Heldendichtung* (heroic poetry). Fifteen of these texts, including *Kudrun* and *Moritz von Craûn,* are known only from this collection. Here is also the only nearly complete text of the *Erec* by Hartmann von Aue. Hans Ried modernized the language, but he seems to have copied good early texts so that the manuscript retains its importance as a source in spite of its late date and relatively modern language.

BIBLIOGRAPHY
Bäuml, Franz H., ed. *Kudrun. Die Handschrift.* Berlin: de Gruyter, 1969.

Koppitz, Hans-Joachim. *Studien zur Tradierung der weltlichen mittelhochdeutschen Epik im 15. und beginnenden 16. Jahrhundert.* Munich: Fink, 1980.

Unterkircher, Franz, ed. *Ambraser Heldenbuch. Vollständige Faksimile-Ausgabe im Originalformat. Kommentar.* Codices selecti 43. Graz: Akademische Druck- und Verlagsanstalt, 1973.

Edward R. Haymes

SEE ALSO
Hartmann von Aue; *Hildebrandslied; Kudrun; Moritz von Craûn; Nibelungenlied;* Stricker, Der; *Wolfdietrich* and *Ortnit*

Helmarshausen

The Benedictine monastery at Helmarshausen was founded on the Diemel River in 997 by a Count Eckhard and his wife, Mathilda. Although Otto III established it as an imperial abbey under Corvey, in 1017 Meinwerk, bishop of Parderborn, took it into control of his diocese, where it remained throughout the High Middle Ages. In 1107 it received relics of St. Modualdus as a gift from its feudal lord, the count of Northeim. A church of the Holy Sepulchre based on that in Jerusalem was erected over a baptismal church on the hill known as Kurkenburg and consecrated in 1126. At the foot of the hill were the monastic buildings, including the abbey church of Saints Mary and Peter, which in its early form had apses at each end and a crypt at its west end. The western apse was transformed into a towered Romanesque western entryway at the time of the third reconstruction. The high point of the monastery's history was in the late twelfth century, after which it suffered from political frictions with Paderborn; in 1223 it put itself under the protection of the archbishop of Cologne.

Helmarshausen is best known for its illustrious metalworker, Roger of Helmarshausen, named as the maker of the portable altar *(scrinium)* commissioned by Henry of Werl, bishop of Paderborn, and preserved at Paderborn Cathedral. Roger seems to have been part of an artistic capability that, while undocumented, is traditionally believed to have been active at the abbey. Numerous illuminated manuscripts are also attributed to the workshops of the abbey. Artistic activity is believed to have spanned the middle two decades of the twelfth century; still later the dedicatory preface of the Gospels made for Henry the Lion documents that the monk Herimann of Helmarshausen was permitted by his abbot to script the text of the luxurious manuscript. Several illuminated manuscripts of the late twelfth century are paintd in the style of earlier illuminations associated with Helmarshausen, but combined with more modern styles, as, for example, in Ms. 142 of the cathedral treasury at Trier (Kaufmann, 1992). Since the abbey was no longer thriving at that time, it is unlikely that they were made there, and Braunschweig, the residence of Henry the Lion, has been suggested as a possibility (Klössel 1995).

BIBLIOGRAPHY
Binding, Günther. "Die Baugeschichte des Benediktinerklosters Helmarshausen," in *Helmarshausen und das Evangeliar Heinrichs des Löwen: Bericht über ein wissenschaftliches Symposium in Braunschweig und Helmarshausen vom 9. Oktober bis 11. Oktober 1985,* ed. Martin Gosebruch und Frank N. Steigeerwald. Schriftenreihe der Kommission für Niedersächsischen Bau- und Kunstgeschichte bei der Braunschweigischen Wissenschaftlichen Gesellschaft 4. Göttingen: Goltze, 1992, 31–41.

Helmarshausen und das Evangeliar Heinrichs des Löwen: Bericht über ein wissenschaftliches Symposium in Braunschweig und Helmarshausen vom 9. Oktober bis 11. Oktober 1985, ed. Martin Gosebruch und Frank N. Steigerwald. Schriftenreihe der Kommission für Niedersächsischen Bau- und Kunstgeschichte bei der Braunschweigischen Wissenschaftlichen Gesellschaft 4. Göttingen: Goltze, 1992.

Hoffmann, Hartmut. *Bücher und Urkunden aus Helmarshausen und Corvey.* Monumenta Germaniae Historica Studien und Texte 4. Hanover: Hahn, 1992.

Jansen, Franz. *Die Helmarshausener Buchmalerei zur Zeit Heinrichs des Löwen,* 1933, rpt. Bad Karlshafen: Verlag des Antiquariats Bernhard Schäfer, 1985.

Kaufmann, Virginia Roehrig. "The Brunn Missal: A New Addition to the Later Helmarshausen Group," in *Helmarshausen und das Evangeliar Heinrichs des Löwen: Bericht über ein wissenschaftliches Symposium in Braunschweig und Helmarshausen vom 9. Oktober bis 11. Oktober 1985,* ed. Martin Gosebruch und Frank N. Steigerwald. Schriftenreihe der Kommission für Niedersächsischen Bau- und Kunstgeschichte bei der Braunschweigischen Wissenschaftlichen Gesellschaft 4. Göttingen: Goltze, 1992, 255–290.

Klössel, Barbara. "Buchmalerei in Braunschweig." *Heinrich der Löwe und seine Zeit: Herrschaft und Repräsentation der Welfen 1125–1235,* 3 vols, ed. Jochen Luckhardt und Franz Niehoff. Munich: Hirmer, 1995, vol. 2, 452–467.

Virginia Roehrig Kaufmann

SEE ALSO

Braunschweig; Cologne, Art; Corvey; Henry the Lion; Otto III; Paderborn; Roger of Helmarshausen; Romanesque Art and Architecture

Henry I (ca. 876–July 2, 936)

King of East Francia/Germany (*König von Ostfranken*), Henry I (Heinrich I.) was born in ca. 876, the third son of Otto, duke of Saxony (ca. 830/40–912), a Liudolfing, and Hadwig (d. ca. 903), daughter of Henry of *Ostfranken,* a Babenberger. Henry was named after his maternal grandfather. (The name Henry was rare in the ninth century; its oldest form is *Haimeric* [lord of the house].)

About 900 Henry married Hatheburg (ca. 876–ca. 909) in order to gain her inheritance of Merseburg and other lands in East Saxony. Hatheburg was a widow; the local clergy objected to the marriage as she was said to have planned to become a nun. Their opposition did not deter Henry, however. They had one son, Thankmar (906–937). The marriage was dissolved in 909. Not long after, Henry married Mathilde (born ca. 894/897) of the family of Widukind of Saxony, Charlemagne's adversary. Though hardly love at first sight, contemporary sources noted a powerful attraction between the couple. Mathilde would become an influential wife and a formidable dowager before she died in March 968. Their eldest son Otto was born on November 23, 912, seven days before the death of the grandfather whose name he bore. There were four more children; Gerberga (919–968), Henry (922–955), Hadwig (923–958), and Brun (925–965).

Upon the death of his father in 912, Henry became duke of Saxony; there was immediate trouble with Conrad I (*Konrad I.*), king of East Francia since 911. Conrad distrusted Henry's power in Saxony. In addition, a long-standing feud existed between them over the execution in 906 of the Babenberger Adalbert, Henry's maternal uncle. Conrad's success in consolidating control over Saxony was minimal, however. When he died in late December 918, he requested his brother Eberhard to offer the crown to his former rival. Following several months of negotiations, Henry was chosen king at Fritzlar on May 5, 919. He was forty-three years old.

Henry declined to be crowned by the Church, as was the Carolingian custom, for reasons that are not altogether clear and have been debated by historians ever since. His first actions were designed to extend his rule beyond the Carolingian kingdom of the Saxons and the

Franks into the southern areas of East Francia. In Bavaria Duke Arnulf had declared himself king but eventually abandoned his ambitions. Henry wisely left Arnulf in control of Bavaria, demanding only that Arnulf acknowledge Henry's status as king. In Swabia the situation was more complicated. Burchard II, who had only recently become duke, acknowledged Henry as king in 919 and promptly defeated his Burgundian rival Rudolph II in battle. In 922 the two made peace, and Rudolph married Burchard's daughter, persuading his father-in-law to help him gain the crown of Italy. This adventure ended in Burchard's death in 926. Henry was now in a position to impose a settlement in Swabia, and he appointed Hermann (a Conradiner) as duke. Henry also made a pact of friendship with Rudolph II. In return for the Holy Lance, a valuable relic which the German king coveted, Rudolph was allowed to keep the area of Basel which he already controlled.

Diplomacy, military pressure, and waiting patiently for the right moment to put his plans into action characterized Henry's dealings with the West Frankish king Charles the Simple (d. 929) and his opponents, Robert (d. 923) and Raoul (d. 936). Henry also secured the submission of the volatile area of Lotharingia and its duke Gilbert (Giselbert), who married Henry's daughter Gerberga in 928.

Now in his fifties, Henry issued a charter in 929 detailing the dower rights of his wife, the clerical education of his youngest son, Brun, and the marriage of his son Otto. The chosen bride was an Anglo-Saxon princess called Edith (ca. 912–946), a daughter of Edward the Elder, who arrived in Saxony with a younger sister, Adiva. The marriage between Otto and Edith took place sometime early in 930, when Henry undertook a lengthy circuit of his kingdom.

Henry's greatest accomplishment, however, was his decisive action against the Magyars who had been attacking East and West Francia since about 900. In 924 Henry's soldiers captured a Magyar chief, and, for his safe return, Henry demanded a nine-year truce, also securing a yearly tribute. During this truce, Henry created a mounted troop of soldiers to fight the Magyars and tested his new model army against the Slavs. He may also have built fortifications (*Burgen*) on the Elbe frontier. In March 933 Henry met with the invading Magyar forces at the battle of Riade, which ended in victory for Henry's new cavalry. There was to be peace on the Elbe frontier for a number of years.

By 935 Henry had achieved many of his goals: his relations with the dukes were based on contracts of friendship; he had defeated the Magyars, and his diplomacy had secured a modicum of peace on his Western frontier. After a long illness, Henry held a diet at Erfurt where he designated his eldest son by Mathilde as his successor. The future Otto I was then 24, married with two children, and a well-trained soldier. Henry I died on July 2, 936, at Memleben. He was buried in the Abbey Church of Quedlinburg where his tomb can still be found.

Modern historians have given Henry an important place in the history of early medieval Germany, crediting him with laying the foundations upon which his son Otto the Great created his empire. Tenth century writers noted his prowess as a warrior and his physical beauty and charm. In the twelfth century, Henry and Mathilde were perceived as the ancestors of the kings of Europe. Henry was also surrounded by legends and stories. Perhaps the most enduring of these is the tale about his receiving the crown while hunting birds. Thus, Henry I would enter the popular imagination under the name "the Fowler" (der Vogler).

BIBLIOGRAPHY

Althoff, Gerd and Hagen Keller. *Heinrich I. und Otto der Grosse. Neubeginn auf karolingischem Erbe.* Göttingen: Musterschmidt, 1985.

Büttner, Heinrich. *Heinrichs I. Südwest- und Westpolitik.* Constance: Thorbecke, 1964.

Diwalt, Helmut. *Heinrich der Erste.* Bergisch Gladbach: Lübbe, 1987.

Leyser, Karl. *Medieval Germany and its Neighbours, 900–1250.* London: Hambledon, 1982.

Reuter, Timothy. *Germany in the Early Middle Ages 800–1056.* London: Longman, 1991.

Madelyn Bergen Dick

SEE ALSO

Carolingians; Charlemagne; Charles III, the Simple; Conrad I; Fortification; Liudolfinger; Otto I; *Servatius*; Succession

Henry II, Art

As is the case with his political agenda and accomplishments, Henry's artistic patronage is often compared to Otto III's; elements of both continuity and innovation are manifest. Two sumptuous manuscripts, a Book of Gospels and a book of pericopes, or epistle and gospel readings (Munich, Staatsbibliothek, manuscripts no. clm.

4454 and 4452), reveal Henry's continued patronage of Reichenau. The magnificent Bamberg *Apocalypse* (Bamberg, Staatsbibliothek, Manuscript no. bibl. 140) was also thought to have been commissioned by Henry. That the manuscript was, in fact, created for Otto indicates the stylistic continuity of Reichenau manuscript illumination in the service of successive patrons

Henry's seals and bulls are also essentially based on Otto III's, but the inscription *Renovatio Regni Francorum* (For the Renown of the Rulers of the Franks) on Henry's royal bull suggests a conscious move away from Otto's "Roman" policy toward one aimed at the consolidation of the German realm. In this regard, it may be significant that Henry's direct artistic patronage was spread more widely throughout the realm than any of his predecessors.

The greatest number of objects commissioned by Henry come from his home duchy of Bavaria. His Sacramentary (mass and prayer book) from St. Emmeram in Regensburg (Munich, Staatsbibliothek, Clm. 4456) contains, unusually, two ruler images. The first, essentially based on Byzantine iconography, shows Henry crowned directly by Christ, and holding the Holy Lance, the symbol of rule and the realm's most precious relic. Like the other miniatures of the manuscript, the second ruler image is based on the Carolingian models from the *Codex aureus* (golden manuscript) of Charles the Bald, housed in St. Emmeram. While both are powerful pictures of Henry's royal might, these images retreat from the overt expressions of Christocentric kingship found in images of Otto III. A Gospel manuscript from St. Emmeram was sent by Henry to the abbey of Montecassino, likely after his visit in 1022 (Rome, Vatican, Ottob. 74). He also substantially supported the recently founded Bavarian cloister of Seeon, which produced a number of illuminated manuscripts on Henry's behalf, many for his new cathedral in Bamberg.

The founding in 1007 of the new diocese of Bamberg, which was as much the work of his wife Kunigunde, provided the fulcrum for much of Henry's patronage. In addition to the Sacramentary, other Regensburg manuscripts, and the Seeon books, Henry transferred the library of Otto III to Bamberg, including numerous Reichenau manuscripts. He and Kunigunde also enriched the cathedral with precious silk embroideries decorated with complex iconographic programs, likely made in Regensburg and still in the cathedral.

Other important commissions show that Henry did not ignore other parts of the realm. Objects like the *ambo* (pulpit) in Aachen, richly decorated with jewels and ivories, and the Basel *Antependium* (altar decoration), indicate flourishing centers of goldsmith work in the western part of Germany. In their number, luxury, and complexity, the objects associated with Henry II and Kunigunde were meant to express the couple's sanctity, which would lead them to be revered as Germany's only imperial saints.

BIBLIOGRAPHY

Fillitz, Hermann, Rainer Kahsnitz, and Ulrich Kuder. *Zierde für Ewige Zeit: Das Perikopenbuch Heinrichs II.* Frankfurt am Main: Fischer, 1994.

Hoffmann, Hartmut. *Buchkunst und Königtum im ottonischen und frühsalischen Reich.* Stuttgart: Hiersemann, 1988.

Klein, P. "Die Apokalypse Ottos III. und das Perikopenbuch Heinrichs II." *Aachener Kunstblätter* 56/57 (1988–1989): 5–52.

Schramm, Percy Ernst, and Florentine Mütherich. *Denkmale der deutschen Könige und Kaiser,* vol. 1: *Ein Beitrag zur Herrschergeschichte von Karl dem Grossn bis Friedrich II, 768–1250.* Veröffentlichungen des Zentralinstituts für Kunstgeschichte 2. 2nd ed. Munich: Prestel, 1981.

Adam S. Cohen

SEE ALSO

Bamberg; Basel; Otto III, Art; Ottonian Art and Architecture; Regensburg; Reichenau; Relics and Reliquaries; *Servatius*

Henry III (1028/1046–1056)

Henry III, son of the Emperor Conrad II (d. 1039) and Queen Gisela, daughter of Duke Hermann II of Swabia, was born on October 28, 1017 and died at age 39 on October 5, 1056. Made duke of Bavaria at age ten, Henry was elevated by his father and the German magnates to the kingship of Germany in the following year (1028). He shared the throne with his father until Conrad's death in 1039. In 1036, as part of a move to secure the northern frontiers of the empire and perhaps control the Saxon nobility, Henry married his first wife, Kunigunde, daughter of King Cnut of Denmark. Their daughter Beatrix (d. 1060) later became abbess of the Ottonian foundation of Quedlinburg. Kunigunde died in 1038.

The year before his father's death, Henry had also ob-

tained the kingship of Burgundy and duchy of Swabia, the latter of which he held until 1045.

In 1043, after assuming sole kingship of Germany in 1039, he married his second wife, Agnes of Poitou (d. 1077), daughter of Duke William V of Aquitaine, with whom he had three daughters and a son. One daughter, Adelheid (d. 1095), became another abbess of Quedlinburg; the other two, Mathilda (d. 1060) and Judith (Sophia, d. 1092/1096), were married, respectively, to Rudolf of Rheinfelden and King Salamo of Hungary and later King Wladyslaw of Poland. Crowned Holy Roman Emperor in 1046, Henry ruled as king and emperor until his death in 1056, when he was succeeded by his young son Henry IV (1050–1106).

Henry III's assumption of full royal powers in 1039 was a smooth one, since the transition had been prepared over a decade before by Henry's elevation to cokingship during his father's lifetime and by his direct control of the duchies of Bavaria and Swabia and the kingdom of Burgundy. The addition of the southeastern duchy of Carinthia to the regions under his direct rule in 1039 only enhanced his already strong political hold on the southern portion of the German realm. He had also arrived at the pinnacle of royal power after a careful process of practical political and military training which rendered him familiar with both the protocols of royal justice and court business and the demands of military campaigns and the battlefield: in short, with the business of medieval rule. These experiences also prepared him to begin building the vital networks of personal connections with other magnates that enabled so much of royal rule in medieval Germany.

Ecclesiastics, such as the historian Wipo and the polymath Berno of Reichenau, ensured that Henry not only received a basic literary education but also absorbed the ideals of theocratic kingship and participated, to a degree, in contemporary currents of religious revival and reform.

Honored with the epithets *spes imperii* (hope of the empire) and *amicus pacis* (friend of peace), Henry III showed his commitment to the ideals of peace and justice early in his reign with his proclamation of public peace and forgiveness of his opponents. At gatherings in Constance (1043), Trier (Christmas 1043), Menfö in Hungary (1044), and Rome (1046), Henry exhorted, begged, and ordered his audiences to keep the peace and to forsake revenge upon enemies by following their king's example. Despite Henry's emphasis on and general success in establishing peace within his kingdom — a success which has led historians to consider his reign the "high-point of early medieval imperial rule" — his reign was not without both internal and external political crises.

Internally, Henry's aggressive assertion of royal prerogatives and control met with particularly stiff local resistance in Lotharingia and Saxony. In Saxony, Henry exploited royal and imperial domains more intensively than had his predecessors, established a new palace at Goslar, and exercised tighter control over ecclesiastical affairs in the region, all of which set him at odds with the regional nobility and, especially, the noble family of the Billungs. In contrast to the opposition of the Saxon nobility, which simmered until the reign of Henry's son and only erupted in the Saxon War (1073–1089), the nobility of Lotharingia presented Henry with a formidable rival in the person of Godfried the Bearded, Duke of Upper Lotharingia. After Henry had ignored the duke's legitimate claim to the duchy of Lower Lotharingia, deprived Godfried of his rule, and engaged in a program of ecclesiastical appointments designed to contain or weaken Godfried's power, the duke and his allies revolted in 1044. Defeated in 1049, the duke took refuge in Italy, where, in 1054, he married, without the king's approval, the heir to the margraviate of Tuscany, Beatrix, the former wife of the most powerful ruler in Italy, margrave Boniface. Fearing Godfried's potential control of both Lotharingia and northern Italy, Henry entered Italy in 1055 and captured Beatrix and her daughter Mathilda, while Godfried escaped north to Lotharingia. He submitted to Henry in the following year.

Externally, Henry III was occupied by a series of wars against the kings of Bohemia and Hungary. Taking advantage of political disorder in Poland, King Vratislav I of Bohemia (1034–1058) invaded Poland, thus challenging Henry's overlordship of the German kingdom. After a disastrous initial campaign in August of 1040, Henry emerged victorious over the Bohemians in 1041 and compelled their king to pay tribute and recognize German hegemony. Henry then responded to Hungarian attacks upon the southern frontier with a series of expeditions in 1042, 1043, and 1044, which resulted in victory and the submission of Hungary to Germany at Menfö. According to one scholar (Egon Boshof), Henry's aim was simple: the reduction of Germany's eastern neighbors from independent states to kingdoms subordinate to German rule. Relations with Capetian France in the West, though generally amicable, suffered a setback in 1043–1046, when Henry's marriage to Agnes of Poitou increased anxieties about an alliance between the German

kingdom and Aquitaine and provoked an abortive French invasion of Lotharingia.

Known for his largely successful attempts to expand and enforce royal and imperial prerogatives within the German kingdom, Henry III is perhaps most famous for his zealous support of efforts to purify the clergy and for his decisive action in reforming the Roman papacy. Like his predecessors, Henry had used clerics extensively both as administrative functionaries in his *Hofkapelle* and as loyal agents who, once established in bishoprics throughout Germany and Italy, enabled him to strengthen the network of allies used to control the empire's territories. But, touched by the contemporary ideals of a clergy free from the heretical taint of simony (which came to be defined as the acquisition of ecclesiastical office through any form of recompense) and sexual impurity, Henry vigorously forbade simoniacal elections, granted free elections to abbeys and churches, and took measures to raise the moral caliber of the clergy, efforts which brought him praise from monastic reformers like Peter Damian.

His most famous acts, however, came in 1046 when he entered Italy, deposed the three competing popes, Gregory VI, Benedict IX, and Sylvester III, at synods in Sutri and Rome, and appointed a succession of German bishops as popes: Clement II and Damasus II, both of whom died soon after their elections. Although his bold action at Sutri was criticized by some as an inappropriate invasion of the ecclesiastical sphere by a secular ruler, Henry was nonetheless widely recognized for his efforts to rid the papacy of corruption. His selection in 1048 of Bishop Bruno of Toul, who would become Pope Leo IX (1049–1054), ushered in a new era of the papacy and of ecclesiastical reform.

BIBLIOGRAPHY

Boshof, Egon. *Die Salier,* 3rd ed. Stuttgart and Cologne: Kohlhammer, 1995, pp. 143–166.

Henry III. *Monumenta Germaniae Historica Diplomata Heinrichs III.,* ed. H. Breβlau and P. Kehr. Berlin 1926–1931; rpt. Munich: Monumenta Germaniae Historica, 1993.

Prinz, Friedrich. "Kaiser Heinrich III. Seine widersprüchliche Beurteilung und deren Gründe." *Historische Zeitschrift* 246 (1988): 529–548.

Schnith, K. "Recht und Friede. Zum Königsgedanken im Umkreis Heinrichs III." *Historisches Jahrbuch* 81 (1962): 22–57.

Weinfurter, Stefan, et al., ed. *Die Salier und das Reich.* 3

vols. Sigmaringen: Thorbecke, 1992, *passim.*

Wipo. *The Deeds of Conrad II,* trans. K. F. Morrison and T. Mommsen, in *Imperial Lives and Letters.* New York: Columbia University Press, 1962.

William North

SEE ALSO

Billunger; Conrad II; Constance; Henry IV; Leo IX; Saxon War; *Servatius;* Toul; Trier

Henry IV (r. 1056–1106)

Born on November 11, 1050, the future Emperor Henry IV was the much longed-for son and heir of Emperor Henry III and Agnes of Poitou. He was baptized by Archbishop Hermann of Cologne at Easter 1051. Abbot Hugh of Cluny, who had come specially from Burgundy at the invitation of the emperor, lifted the baby from the font, thus becoming his godfather and, apparently, also naming him. Elected king at Tribur in November 1053, Henry was crowned July 17, 1054, at Aachen and betrothed the next year to Bertha, a girl of his own age and daughter of the count of Turin. He was not even six years old when his father died on October 5, 1056, at the palace of Bodfeld in the Harz mountains.

On his deathbed, Henry III had entrusted his heir to Pope Victor II (1055–1057), the former bishop of Eichstätt and imperial chancellor. Victor managed to obtain recognition of little Henry's succession to the throne. Nominally, Henry IV began his reign in 1056. The guardianship lay in the hands of his pious mother, the Empress Agnes, until April 1063, however, when a faction of conspirators, led by Archbishop Anno II of Cologne, abducted the young king, who tried to save himself by jumping overboard into the Rhine. Anno now became the leading influence at court, replacing another bishop, Adalbert of Bremen. Anno had good relations with ecclesiastical reformers in Rome and reversed an earlier imperial policy which had supported the election of Bishop Cadalus of Parma as (anti)pope Honorius III. In collaboration with Peter Damian a papal legate, Anno and the German court recognized, instead, Pope Alexander II (1061–1073), who had been elected by Hildebrand (the future Gregory VII) and other reformers.

Henry IV began to govern in his own name at age six in March 1056. In July 1066 he married Bertha of Turin but tried to divorce her three years later. He desisted in face of the remonstrations of Peter Damian, who had been sent to Germany by the pope as a legate.

Henry's relationship with several German nobles was tense from the beginning of the reign. His troubles increased from about 1068, when he began to try to recover the crown lands, originally in the hands of the Ottonian rulers, in eastern Saxony and Thuringia. Essentially continuing his father's policies, Henry strengthened and expanded them, forcing the Saxons to build and maintain fortifications that were garrisoned with southern German *ministeriales.* This policy provoked Saxon resistance, playing into the hands of Otto of Northeim. Otto had forfeited the duchy of Bavaria in 1070 and formed an alliance with Magnus Billung, the duke of Saxony, and other magnates who had made their fortunes under Ottonian emperors during their eastward expansion. Together with the region's bishops, and with massive support from the Saxons in general, the magnates confronted Henry IV in the summer of 1073 at Goslar. They demanded that the castles he had recently built should be razed, that lands unjustly confiscated should be restored by the council of princes, and that the king should stay in Saxony and dismiss his low-born advisers and instead follow the princes' advice. Henry, who had also lost the support of the south German dukes, was besieged by the Saxon army and barely escaped from his fortress, the Harzburg, to find protection in the town of Worms. The Harzburg was stormed by the Saxons, but their army was defeated in September 1075. By the end of the year, however, Henry seemed to have mastered the situation. At Christmas the nobles elected his son Conrad their king.

At the request of the higher clergy of Milan, who had defeated the Pataria reform movement in the spring of 1075, Henry nominated the imperial chaplain Tedald as archbishop of Milan instead of Atto, who had the support of Pope Gregory VII and the Pararia. Gregory expressed his furious opposition in a letter (December 8, 1075) and in a verbal message, perhaps threatening the king with excommunication. From Worms, where nobles and ecclesiastics met jointly in a diet on January 24, 1076, came the reply. The German bishops, who resented papal claims of hierocracy and centralization, renounced their obedience to the pontiff, whom they called "Brother Hildebrand," and claimed his election had been illegal; Henry IV called upon Gregory to resign, and the Romans were asked to elect a new pope. The north Italian episcopate supported these measures immediately.

From the Lenten synod he was holding in Rome from February 14–20, 1076, Gregory deposed Henry, absolved his subjects from the oath of fealty, and excommunicated the king. Many of the bishops then deserted Henry, joining forces with the Bavarian and Saxon opposition. By October 1076, at the meeting of Tribur, the king had to accept their terms and to declare his submission to the pontiff. Unless Henry was absolved from his excommunication by February 1077, the assembly of Tribur threatened, they would proceed with the election of a new king. The German princes invited Gregory to come as an arbitrator to a diet that was to be held at Augsburg in February 1077. With no way out, Henry decided in mid-December 1076 to meet Gregory, who had already left Rome on his way to Augsburg in northern Italy. With his wife Bertha and his two-year-old son Conrad, Henry managed to cross Mount Cernis in severe winter weather. When he learned of the king's arrival, Gregory withdrew to the fortress of Canossa, owned by Countess Matilda of Tuscany. Thanks to the mediation of Henry's godfather, Abbot Hugh of Cluny, of Matilda, and of Adelheid of Turin (mother of the queen), Gregory reconciled Henry IV with the Church on January 28, 1077. Henry was forced to appear barefoot and dressed in a penitent's hair shirt for three days in a row in the inner courtyard of the castle requesting permission to enter before he was absolved by the pope.

In fact, though not in theory, when he reconciled Henry with the church, Gregory again recognized Henry as king. At the Lenten synod of 1080, however, the pontiff recognized Rudolf of Rheinfelden, whom the German opposition had elected in March 1077 despite the absolution of Canossa, as king. Henry was once again excommunicated, but, this time, ineffectively. At the synod of Brixen, June 1080, Henry and the princes nominated Archbishop Wibert of Ravenna to replace Gregory, whom the synod then deposed. The death of Rudolf, and military as well as political successes, enabled Henry to enter Rome in March 1084 when Wibert was consecrated Pope Clement III. On Easter Sunday, Henry IV was crowned emperor. Meanwhile, Gregory, freed by his vassals from his place of refuge, the Castello S. Angelo in Rome withdrew to Salerno, where he died in May 1085.

After his return to Germany, Henry at first was able to consolidate his position. With the death of Clement III in 1100 the end of the schism in the Church seemed possible. However, the negotiations between Henry IV and Pope Paschal II (1099–1118) always ended in failure, since Henry refused to give up his right to invest bishops with the ring and staff, the one demand on which Paschal insisted.

The collapse of these negotiations with the papacy lay behind the rebellion of Henry V against his father in late 1104. Through a ruse, the younger Henry captured Henry IV in late 1105. At Ingelheim on December 31, 1105, Henry IV was forced to abdicate. He managed to flee, however, and attempted to regain power. He died at Liège on August 7, 1106, eventually to be buried in the cathedral of Speyer.

A contemporary, albeit anonymous, biographer most movingly bemoaned the death of the emperor, the protector of the poor, opening with the words of Jeremiah 9.1: "Oh that my head were waters, and mine eyes a fountain of tears, that I might weep day and night for the slain daughter of my people."

BIBLIOGRAPHY

Benson, Robert L. ed. *Imperial Lives and Letters of the Eleventh Century,* trans. Theodor E. Mommsen and Karl F. Morrison. New York: Columbia University Press, 1962.

Freed, John B. "Henry IV of Germany." In *Dictionary of the Middle Ages,* vol. 6. New York: Scribner, 1985, p. 163.

Fuhrman, Horst. *Germany in the High Middle Ages,* trans. Timothy Reuter. Cambridge: Cambridge University Press, 1986.

Leyser, Karl. "The Crisis in Medieval Germany." In Karl Leyser, *Communications and Power in Medieval Europe,* trans. Timothy Reuter. London: Hambledon, 1994, pp. 21–49.

Lynch, J. H. "Hugh I of Cluny's Sponsorship of Henry IV: Its Context and Consequences." *Speculum* 60 (1985): 800–826.

Struve, Tilman. "Heinrich IV." In *Lexikon des Mittelalters,* vol. 4. Munich: Artemis, 1989, pp. 2041–2043.

von Gladiss, Dietrich, et al., ed. *Die Urkunden Heinrichs IV,* pts. 1–3. Monumenta Germaniae Historica. Diplomata 6/1–3. Hanover: Hahn, 1977, 1959, 1978.

Wies, Erbst W. *Kaiser Heinrich IV: Canossa und der Kampf um die Weltherrschaft.* Munich and Esslingen: Bechtle, 1996.

Uta-Renate Blumenthal

SEE ALSO

Aachen; Anno; Fortification; Gregory VII; Henry III; Investiture Controversy; Ministerials; Speyer; Succession; Worms

Henry the Lion (1129/1131–August 6, 1195)

Duke of Saxony and Bavaria *(Heinrich der Löwe, Herzog von Sachsen und Bayern),* Henry the Lion was born 1129/1131, the son of the Welf Henry the Proud *(Heinrich der Stolze)* and Gertrude, daughter of Lothar III. His father died in 1139, dispossessed of all his titles in his feud with Conrad III, but the Empress Richenza, Henry's grandmother, and Count Adolf of Holstein secured the boy's northern inheritance. Henry was enfeoffed with Saxony in 1142. (Bavaria had already been granted to Conrad III's half-brother Henry of Babenberg [Heinrich Jasomirgott]). Henry became a tough soldier and a ruthless politician, particularly in his Saxon lands and in his relationship to the Archbishopric of Bremen, and participated in the Wendish Crusade in 1147.

Frederick I Barbarossa of Swabia, Henry's cousin, became king in 1152. Henry accompanied Frederick to Italy in 1154–1155, and, during the coronation riots in Rome, saved his cousin's life. In 1156 Frederick returned Bavaria to Henry, but without the East Mark, which became Austria. Frederick granted that fiefdom to his uncle Henry Babenberg in the *Privilegium minus* (Lesser Privilege).

Over the next twenty years Henry supported Frederick but also expanded his own power. He founded Munich in 1157 and Lübeck in 1159, and married Mathilda of England (daughter of Henry II and Eleanor of Aquitaine) in 1165. Henry also built the cathedral and the castle in Brunswick (Braunschweig), was in Italy twice, and went on a pilgrimage to Jerusalem in 1172.

In 1176, at Chiavenna, Frederick demanded Henry's support for his war with the papacy and the Italian communes, but the Saxon duke refused to help without a substantial reward. Frederick's war ended in defeat, and he had to make peace with the pope in 1177. Upon his return to Germany, Frederick began legal proceedings against his cousin. For non-appearance at his trial, Henry was outlawed at the diet of Würzburg in 1180. He had few allies, and an imperial army defeated him in Saxony. In 1181 Henry was deposed from all his possessions and exiled; he and his family fled to his father-in-law, Henry II, in England, where he remained until 1185. Saxony was split between the Archbishop of Cologne and the Ascanian counts of Brandenburg. Bavaria went to a member of the Wittelsbach family.

When Frederick went on crusade in 1189, he exiled his cousin again; but Mathilda stayed in Brunswick, where she died that year. Henry returned to Germany upon the news of his cousin's death. He was finally pardoned by Henry VI and spent his remaining years in Sax-

ony. Henry the Lion died on August 6, 1195 and was buried in the cathedral at Brunswick beside his wife.

A man who fascinated his contemporaries, Henry the Lion was one of the most controversial German princes of the twelfth century. Italian historian Acerbus Morena, who met him in 1163, described him as of medium height, but strong and agile, with dark eyes and hair. Henry was arrogant and ruthless, but his dealings with Frederick in the 1180s show that he could seriously overplay his hand.

Some historians have celebrated him as the champion of nationalism and the expansion eastward, while others have chided him for deserting Frederick I at a crucial time in the empire's history. It is perhaps time to lay the old controversies to rest.

BIBLIOGRAPHY

Jordan, Karl. *Henry the Lion,* trans. P. S. Falla. Oxford: Clarendon, 1986.

Luckhardt, Jochen, and Franz Niehoff, ed. *Heinrich der Löwe und seine Zeit: Herrschaft und Repräsentation der Welfen* 1125–1235. 3 vols. Munich: Hirmer, 1995.

Mohrmann, Wolf-Dieter, ed. *Heinrich der Löwe.* Göttingen: Vandenhoek & Ruprecht, 1980.

Madelyn Bergen Dick

SEE ALSO

Crusades; Frederick I Barbarossa; Matilda, Empress

Henry the Lion, Art

Henry the Lion inherited his Saxon lands and ducal title through his mother, Gertrude, sole heir of the dynasty of the Brunonen and daughter of the emperor Lothar of Supplinburg. Through his father, the Guelph (Welf) Henry the Proud, he inherited the ducal title to Bavaria and the rich family legacy of the Guelphs in south Germany and Italy. His great uncle Welf V, for example, had married Mathilda of Tuscany, and two female ancestors were wives of the Carolingian rulers Louis the German, king of the East Franks, and the emperor Louis the Pious, whose son Charles the Bald was king of the West Franks. Henry's wife and the mother of his children was Mathilda, the daughter of Henry II of England. Frederick I Barbarossa, heir of the Swabian Hohenstaufen dynasty and emperor, was his first cousin on the Guelph side. But because of the complex nature of German politics and particularly Henry's ancestors' enduring history of changing alliances for political gain, his kinship with Barbarossa did not insure their being allies. Indeed, since they had been competitors for the imperial title, which Henry failed to get despite his superior claim and wealth in land holdings and power, they were destined to be enemies. When Henry failed to support Barbarossa in his Italian compaigns, the emperor used his power to strip Henry of his title and lands in Bavaria.

Throughout his lfie Henry's activities centered on his domains in the north, where he took up the fixed residence in Braunschweig of his Brunonen forebears. He expanded his political control into the Wagrian lands of the heathen Obodrites and Polabians, whom he more or less successfully Christianized; for his efforts, which amounted to a crusade, he received papal support and indulgences but criticism from the twelfth-century chronicler Helmut of Bosau. He secured revenue sources by developing institutions as he found them into well-functioning administration. He also supported the growth of trade and a mercantile class throughout his north German lands. Henry used a considerable part of his wealth to expand and adorn his palace, Dankwarderode, its chapel St. Cyriacus, the larger palace church eventually dedicated to St. Blasius, where he and Mathilda were buried, and religious institutions in Braunschweig and the region.

Henry the Lion was a remarkable patron of architecture and the arts. In this he continued in the tradition of the Brunonen who had had the metalwork objects made that formed the initial core of the "Guelph Treasure," to which Henry added prodigiously. He commissioned works in Cologne and Hildesheim, where he could get the highest-quality craftsmanship at that time, and it is believed that he also eventually established his own workshops in Braunschweig. Most of the works he had made were for liturgical use at St. Cyriacus, St. Blasius, and elsewhere. High points of Henry's patronage include the objects commissioned in Cologne, including the portable altar of 1150 signed by Eilbertus and the dome reliquary of 1185; the Wilton chalice, paten, and fistulae given by Henry to Count Berthold III of Andechs and thought to have been made in Hildeshem around 1172; and the Oswald reliquary and other objects from the same workshop that may have been in operation in the 1180s in Hildesheim or Braunschweig.

Henry and Mathilda also commissioned monumental works in bronze. Already in 1166 Henry had arranged for casting the over-life-size bronze lion that was installed on a high stone pier between Dankwarderode and St. Blasius; here it functioned as a symbol of his personal power

and his family's strength. For St. Blasius, Mathilda commissioned the cast-bronze altar dedicated to Mary in 1189, and the sixteen-foot-high, seven-armed candelabra of the same period, also made for St. Blasius. The candelabra recalled the Jewish temple in Jerusalem, as did elements of the arthcitecutre of Henry's expanded nave of St. Blasius, and were probably intended to recall the pilgrimage of the ducal couple to Jerusalem.

Henry the Lion had sumptuous books made for liturgical use in church and house chapel. Of these the famous Gospels of Henry the Lion, now preserved in the Herzog August Biliothek in Wolfenbüttel (Cod. Guelf. 105 Noviss. 2°), is the most lavishly decorated with colorful and decorative Gospel scenes as well as two images where Henry and Mathilda are presented. They are depicted on the dedication page (fol. 194) giving the Gospel manuscript to St. Blasius and the Virgin, and again on the coronation page (fol. 171v), receiving crowns from Christ in the company of illustrious members of their families. Many early Mass books are also preserved, including a once lavishly decorated Missal, which traveled the same route as the Gospels through Bohemia, and is now in Brno in the Czech Republic (Universitni Knihovna, no. Ms. R. 396).

Henry the Lion's use of art as a means of shaping the memory of himself and his family has recently been revealed as a fertile topic. In shaping their own *memoria* in the visual arts and architecture they commissioned, the Guelphs followed on what had already been established in the writing of their family history. The *Historia Welforum,* written circa 1170 by an anonymous Swabian cleric in the entourage of Henry's uncle Duke Welf VI, already suggests the family's sense of its own self-importance. This skill in molding the memory of the Guelphs through art was advanced also by Henry's son, the emperior Otto IV, and his grandson, Otto the Child, who continued to commission art that further enhanced the positive memory of their family.

BIBLIOGRAPHY

DeWinter, Patrick. *The Sacral Treasure of the Guelphs.* Cleveland: Cleveland Museum of Art, 1985.

Die Welfen und ihr Braunschweiger Hof im hohen Mittelalter, ed. Bernd Schneidmüller.

Heinrich der Löwe und seine Zeit: Herrschaft und Repräsentation der Welfen 1125–1235, ed. Jochen Luckhardt and Franz Niehoff. 3 vols. Munich: Hirmer, 1995.

Helmarshausen und das Evangeliar Heinrichs des Löwen: Bericht über ein wissenschaftliches Symposium in Braun-

schweig und Helmarshausen vom 9. Oktober bis 11. Oktober 1985, ed. Martin Gosebruch and Frank N. Steigerwald. Schriftenreihe der Kommission für Niedersächsischen Bau- und Kunstgeschichte bei der Braunschweigischen Wissenschaftlichen Gesellschaft 4. Göttingen: Goltze, 1992.

Jordan, Karl. Henry the Lion: A Biography, trans. P. S. Falla. Oxford: Clarendon Press, 1986.

Kaufmann, Virginia Roehrig. "The Brunn Missal: A New Addition to the Later Helmarshausen Group," in Helmarshausen und das Evangeliar Heinrichs des Löwen: Bericht über ein wissenschaftliches Symposium in Braunschweig und Helmarshausen vom 9. Oktober bis 11. Oktober 1985, ed. Martin Gosebruch and Frank N. Steigerwald. Schriftenreihe der Kommission für Niedersächsischen Bau- und Kunstgeschichte bei der Braunschweigischen Wissenschaftlichen Gesellschaft 4. Göttingen: Goltze, 1992, p. 255–290.

Niehr, Klaus. "'Sehen und Erkennen': Anspruch, Ästhetik and Historizität der Ausstattung der Stiftskirche St. Blasius zu Braunschweig," in Heinrich der Löwe und seine Zeit: Herrschaft und Repräsentation der Welfen 1125–1235, ed. Jochen Luckhardt and Franz Niehoff, 3 vols. Munich: Hirmer, 1995, vol. 2, pp. 272–282.

Oexle, Otto Gerhard. "Die Memoria Heinrichs des Loewen," in Memoria in der Gesellschaft des Mittelalters, ed. Dieter Geuenich and Otto Gerhard Oexle. Veröffentlichungen des Max-Planck-Instituts für Geschichte 111. Göttingen: Vandenhoeck und Ruprecht, 1994, pp. 128–177.

Wolfenbütteler Mittelalter-Studien 7. Wiesbaden: Harrassowitz, 1995.

Virginia Roehrig Kaufmann

SEE ALSO
Braunschweig; Cologne, Art; Frederick I Barbarossa; Guelph Treasure; Hildesheim; Metalworking; Relics and Reliquaries; Romanesque Art and Architecture; Welfs

Henry the Raspe (d. 1247)

In the course of his prolonged struggle with the papacy, the emperor Frederick II Hohenstaufen faced opposition within Germany, including the creation of an anti-king. Frederick's rival, Pope Innocent IV, at the Council of Lyons in 1245 declared Frederick deposed because of perjury, oppression of the Church, and alleged heresy, and called for the election of a new king. Henry Raspe, landgrave of Thuringia and imperial regent since 1242, was elected (anti-)king by the archbishops of Cologne and Mainz with the support of the archbishop of Trier in May 1246.

Henry received great support from Innocent IV during his short reign. Indeed, it was Innocent and his legate who had engineered his election, and it was Innocent who provided Henry with the grant of some 25,000 marks of silver. Although he had significant backing from Rome and won a battle near Frankfurt against Frederick's son Conrad, Henry's impact on Germany and on Frederick's reign was limited. He did, for a short time, unite the duchies of Austria and Styria to the imperial authority, but this association ended with his death. It was his death in February 1247, after a very brief reign, and his appearing to be a papal tool that limited his impact on Germany and Frederick.

BIBLIOGRAPHY
Haverkampf, Alfred. Medieval Germany, 1056—1273, trans. Helga Braun and Richard Mortimer. Oxford: Oxford University Press, 1992.

Van Cleve, Thomas Curtis. The Emperor Frederick II Hohenstaufen "Immutator Mundi." Oxford: Clarendon Press, 1972.

Michael Frassetto

SEE ALSO
Cologne; Frederick II; Mainz; Staufen; Trier

Henry VI (1165–1197)

At the tender age of three, Henry VI Staufen was already an elected and crowned king. His father, Emperor Frederick I Barbarossa, not only had him participate in the imperial government, but even tried to get him elected co-emperor. Scholars, such as Godfrey of Viterbo, provided the young king's education, according to several songs that appear in medieval collections of *Minnesang* (courtly love poetry). His father granted Henry the belt of knighthood at the famous tournament at Mainz during Pentecost 1184. By that autumn, Henry had become betrothed to Constance, eleven years his senior and the aunt of King William II of Sicily. During Barbarossa's disputes with Pope Urban III, Henry successfully conducted military campaigns against the papal states; but Urban's successor, Clement III, promised to crown him emperor. Henry took over the regency while Barbarossa went off upon the third Crusade in the spring of 1189.

When Barbarossa died in July 1190, Henry should have quietly succeeded to his father's inheritance. But several obstacles soon arose. For example, the Welf Henry the Lion, Duke of Saxony, had returned from exile in England and defied the royal armies by reclaiming his old power in the north. The sudden death of King William II of Sicily in November had, in Henry's view, left his wife Constance as the heir to that rich kingdom. When the Sicilians, with papal cooperation, elected William's illegitimate cousin, Count Tancred of Lecce, as king, Henry resolved to attack that kingdom after being crowned emperor in Rome. Finally, after coming to a truce with the Welfs and turning to Italy, Henry found that Pope Celestine III had replaced Clement.

Meanwhile, the city leaders of Rome had been pressuring the pope to destroy Tusculum, a city which had been loyal to and garrisoned by the Staufen, but which the Romans considered a rival. The aged pope-elect demanded that the king abandon Tusculum before any imperial coronation. With Tusculum torn down stone by stone, the Romans gladly cheered the papal consecration of Celestine on Easter Sunday, April 14, and the imperial coronation of Henry on Easter Monday. The new emperor then turned to the conquest of Southern Italy and Sicily. But, after a few successes, he failed at a siege of Naples, largely because of the summer heat and the effects of diseases like dysentery, cholera, and malaria on his troops. Although Henry survived a bout with sickness, many others died, and the army retreated northward. Meanwhile, the Empress Constance briefly became a prisoner of Tancred, king of Sicily.

Back in Germany, Henry faced new problems, especially as he tried to solve a quarrel over the see of Liège by naming his own candidate. Another candidate, Albert of Louvain, brother of the Duke of Brabant, had the backing of Pope Celestine, however, and was consecrated bishop. Five days later, German knights murdered him, and many blamed Henry for instigating the deed. Encouraged by the Welfs and the papacy, widespread opposition to Henry began to organize itself into open rebellion.

At this juncture, Henry was rescued by the capture of the English king, Richard the Lionhearted, who was returning from a Crusade in December 1192. Henry forced Richard's captor, Duke Leopold V of Austria, to turn the king over to imperial control; he then demanded a huge ransom for Richard's freedom. By the time Richard was released in February 1194, Henry had extorted 150,000 marks, which he divided with Leopold, as well as Richard's pledge of England as a fief of the empire with a yearly tribute of five thousand marks. Although the promised payments were never entirely realized, Henry used the large ransom to finance his invasion of Sicily.

His efforts were aided by the death of Tancred in February 1194, leaving only an infant son as heir, and Henry and his armies quickly conquered Sicily. On Christmas day 1194 he celebrated his kingship in the cathedral in Palermo. The next day, in Jesi on the mainland, Henry's wife gave birth to his own son and heir, the future Frederick II.

Through ruthless policies, Henry quickly secured his rule in Sicily. An alleged plot against him gave the emperor an excuse to banish the usurper's family to Germany, and, allegedly, in Byzantine fashion, to blind the infant former king as well as some officials. The Sicilian treasury was carried to Henry's castle, Trifels, in Swabia by more than 150 pack animals. By Easter 1195 the emperor had proclaimed his wife as regent for the Sicilian lands and set one of his powerful ministerials in place as viceroy; arranged the betrothal of his brother, Philip of Swabia, to Tancred's widow, Irene, a Byzantine princess; installed Philip as margrave of Tuscany (including the oft-disputed Mathildine lands); and begun to proclaim and organize a Crusade to the Holy Land.

Returning to Germany, Henry convinced many other princes to participate in the Crusade. He also nearly managed to get his young son recognized as king of the Romans by right of inheritance instead of by election. Henry suggested what is known as the *Erbreichsplan*, a proposal to ensure that the royal, and hence imperial, title would be inherited in the Staufen dynasty. In return, for secular princes, Henry promised to make fiefs held by the crown inheritable in the female line; for spiritual princes, he promised not to practice the *spolia*, a king's exploitation of the temporal powers and royal rights during a vacancy. At first, most of the princes accepted the plan, but, when Henry returned to Italy, they began to express their dissatisfaction. Even more, the Roman Curia opposed both the idea of uniting the crown of the Holy Roman Empire with that of Sicily and of giving up papal prerogatives in the imperial coronation process. By November 1196 Henry offered the pope what he claimed was more than any other emperor had ever done, the so-called *höchstes Angebot* (highest offer). But by the end of the year, Henry had given up on the inheritance plan, and the princes elected his son as king the old-fashioned way.

Back in Sicily during the spring of 1197, Henry barely escaped an attempted assassination, plotted probably with the tacit knowledge of the pope and Henry's own wife. Henry crushed the rebellion, executing some of the rebels in a brutal fashion. At the beginning of September, the main Crusader fleet set off for the Holy Land, where they gained promising victories. Later that month however, the emperor was taken seriously ill. He died at the age of only thirty-one on September 28, 1197, in Palermo. Revolts in Sicily and Italy and civil war in Germany over control of the crown soon gravely weakened the monarchy.

Both contemporary and historical opinion on Henry has been severely divided between those who viewed his death as a blessing or as a curse. His critics worry he might have established world dominion had he lived long enough; his advocates note the breakdown of German imperial authority after his death. Certainly, his death provided the opportunity for Innocent III to seize the leadership of Christendom. Overshadowed by the reputations of his father and son, Henry VI's short reign is nonetheless remarkable both for it successes and its flaws.

BIBLIOGRAPHY

Csendes, Peter. *Heinrich VI.* Darmstadt: Wissenschaftliche Buchgesellschaft, 1993.

Naumann, Claudia. *Der Kreuzzug Kaiser Heinrichs VI.* Frankfurt am Main: Lang, 1994.

Pavlac, Brian A. "Emperor Henry VI (1191–97) and the Papacy: Influences on Innocent III's Staufen Policies." In *Pope Innocent III and His World,* ed. John C. Moore. London: Ashgate, 1998.

Seltmann, Ingeborg. *Heinrich VI: Herrschaftspraxis und Umgebung.* Erlangen: Palm & Enke, 1983.

Toeche, Theodor. *Heinrich VI.* Jahrbücher der deutschen Geschichte 18. Leipzig, 1867; rpt. Darmstadt: Wissenschaftliche Buchgesellschaft, 1965.

Brian A. Pavlac

SEE ALSO

Constance; Crusades; Frederick I Barbarossa; Frederick II; Henry the Lion; Ministerials; *Minnesang;* Staufen; Welfs

Heraldry

Heraldry is a system of personal and hereditary family devices (English "coat of arms" or "shield"; German *Wappen* or *Schild*) which developed in western Europe in the twelfth century and was thereafter regulated by the heralds. There have been other such systems in other times and places, including ancient Egypt, Assyria, China, Japan, India, Mexico, Greece, the Roman Empire, and Islam, but similarities do not necessarily imply either influence or historical continuity.

The history of western preheraldic emblems in the first millennium remains poorly defined, despite substantial research conducted by German, Austrian, and Scandinavian scholars. These scholars consider that the premillennial figures and colors adorning Germanic fighters' shields, weapons, and banners, later to be instrumental in the development of medieval Germanic heraldry, constituted a Germano-Scandinavian emblematic scheme that either articulated a clanish/tribal structure or was used by the elite nobles for their individual symbols. To this controversy about the meaning of early emblematic signs, French and British scholars bring a third ingredient, the military, to which they ascribe the origin of medieval heraldic practice. As personal armor developed, toward the end of the eleventh century, to the point where warriors were encased in mail from head to foot, the problem of personal recognition became acute and prompted the decorative paintings on shields to evolve into known individual devices ultimately functioning as marks of recognition. These marks are said to be heraldic when, by the mid-twelfth century, they became hereditary to particular families.

The first armorial devices appeared in the aristocratic lineages of Luxemburg (1123), Meulan and Vermandois (ca. 1136), Saxony (the Guelf lion on the seal of Henry the Lion in 1144, and on that of his kinsman Welf of Tuscany in 1152), and Anjou and Flanders (ca. 1160). Originally confined to the nobility, heraldry extended to men of knightly and ministerial ranks who tended to derive their arms from the aristocratic families in whose ministeriality their families belonged. Heraldry, thus, came to symbolize the bonds forged between the various ranks of aristocratic society and to be emblematic of birth and station. When it became necessary to differentiate within a family, that is, to set apart the shields of cadet branches, marks of cadency *(Beizeichen)* were used for this purpose. These marks consisted of variations on the main coat of arms, which thus remained an emblem of common and continuous lineage.

At first depicted on shields and military equipment, such as the helmet with crest and mantling and the surcoat (or tunic), heraldic devices were soon displayed on seals. This custom led, during the thirteenth century, to the adoption of armorial bearings by women, churchmen, urban and religious corporations, and commoners, such as craftsmen, burghers, and peasants. Individuals

Zurich Roll of Arms, detail: Coats of arms of Austria, Bavaria, Saxony, Styria, and Teck (upper row) and Asperg, Heiligberg, Wildenberg, Kirchberg, Walsee, and Vaz (lower row) (Zurich, Schweizerisches Landesmuseum, AG-2760). *Photograph: Schweizerisches Landesmuseum, Neg. 16748*

could chose and adopt family arms without the permission of a superior authority, as long as they did not infringe on the rights and devices of others. Princely grants of arms, the earliest of which was made by the Emperor Ludwig of Bavaria in 1338, began to be common by the second half of the fourteenth century but never precluded an individual's right to adopt armorial bearings.

Heraldic emblems, as hereditary signs of identity, came to serve as marks of property as well, and their use extended to tombs, effigies, objects, monuments, and other works of art. The medieval memorial shield developed out of the custom, documented from the twelfth century on, of hanging a knight's armor, especially his shield, above his tomb in a church. In time, actual shields increasingly were replaced by wooden ones — either painted or carved, and inscribed with the date of death, the name of the dead knight, and a formula in the vernacular: *dem Got Genedig sey* (May God be merciful to him).

If heredity characterized medieval heraldry so did the precise rules and terminology ("blazon") which, systematized by heralds from the mid-thirteenth century onward, governed the presentation and description of heraldic devices. These included ordinaries and lines of partition (figures constituted by the geometric division of the shield), tinctures (colors, metals, and furs), and charges (objects, animals, and plants). Heralds were originally members of the domestic household, serving as *jongleurs* and messengers. They rose to prominence through the part they came to play in the staging and ceremony of tournaments which, from the thirteenth century, required the compilation of rolls recording the participants' arms. In imperial Germany, rolls appeared in the fourteenth century: the *Wappenrolle von Zürich* (Swiss, ca. 1340), Claes van Heynen or Heinenszoon's *Gelre Roll* (Netherlandish, ca. 1375), and the *Wappenbuch* by Konrad Grünenberg (German, 1483). On the occasion of the Council of Constance, 1414–1418, the German Ulrich von

Richenthal produced the occasional roll called *Konzil-schronik* in which he registered the coats of all who attended the council. In the *Gelre Roll,* the finest of all the armorial books of the Middle Ages, recording knightly coats from all over Europe, we encounter a master of heraldic erudition. Such mastery demanded a knowledge of genealogy and blazon, a command of the entire literary and historical culture of chivalry, an understanding of the laws of nobility and inheritance, and a knowledge of the mystical properties ascribed to plants, beasts, birds, colors, and metals. Such charges could be made to bear symbolic and allegorical meaning, and to tell a story. Canting arms, particularly common in early German heraldry, play with names. Thus in the Zurich Roll, Affenstein's *argent* shield is charged with a red ape *(affe) gules* breaking a stone *(stein).*

Capable of learned exposition, literate and visual, practical and ideological, heraldry evolved into a twofold science, recording genealogical information, and manipulating a body of signs into which its practitioners, both bearers and heralds, infused a broad variety of symbolic and historical meaning. The whole range of human experience and values and the historical mythology of chivalry itself was translated into a visual symbolic system that bridged the written word and its iconographical expression. Buttressed by the heralds' textual production, heraldic emblems conveyed messages of pride in chivalric virtues, martial achievements, and family connections. Ultimately, medieval coats of arms, because of their representational significance, became assigned to practically every important person, real or mythological, from Hector of Troy, through King David and Charlemagne, to King Arthur and the knights of the Round Table.

BIBLIOGRAPHY

Berchem, Egon Freiherr von, Donald Lindsay Galbreath, and Otto Hupp. *Beiträge zur Geschichte der Heraldik: Die Wappenbücher des deutschen Mittelalters.* 1939. Neustadt an der Aisch: Bauer und Raspe, 1972.

Brault, Gerard J. *Early Blazon: Heraldic Terminology in the Twelfth and Thirteenth Centuries.* Oxford: Clarendon, 1972.

Brooke-Little, John Philip. *Boutell's Heraldry.* 7th ed. London and New York: Warne, 1973.

Henning, Eckart, and Gabrielle Jochums. *Bibliographie zur Heraldik.* Cologne: Böhlau, 1984.

Hildebrandt, Adolf Matthias. *Wappenfibel: Handbuch der Heraldik.* 16th ed. Neustadt an der Aisch: Degener, 1970.

Kittel, Erich. "Wappentheorien." *Archivum heraldicum* (1971): 18–26, 53–59.

Pastoureau, Michel. *Traité d'héraldique.* 2nd ed. Paris: Picard, 1993.

Scheibelreiter, Georg. *Tiernamen und Wappenwesen.* 2nd ed. Vienna: Böhlau, 1992.

Seyler, Gustav Adelbert. *Geschichte der Heraldik.* 2 vols. 1885–1889. Neustadt an der Aisch: Bauer und Raspe, 1970.

Stalins, Gaston. *Vocabulaire-atlas héraldique en six langues.* Paris: Société du grand armorial de France, 1952.

Brigitte Bedos-Rezak

SEE ALSO

Clothing, Costume and Fashion; Constance; Gothic Art and Architecture; Henry the Lion; Seals and Sigillography; Zurich

Herbort von Fritzlar (fl. 1190–1217)

Herbort's rhymed courtly epic, *Liet von Troye,* the earliest surviving German version of the Trojan War story, is based on the *French Roman de Troie* by Benoît de Sainte-Maure. In the *Liet von Troye* the author Herbort names himself, refers to his education, and states that his work was commissioned by the landgrave Hermann of Thuringia (1190–1217) and that his French source was provided by Count Frederick of Leiningen. Nothing else is known of his life. The *Liet von Troye* is variously dated between 1190–1217. One complete manuscript and three fragments are known, with sufficient variations to indicate parallel versions of the text.

Recent research views Herbort as an author of considerable character who makes a vigorous and complex statement at the interface of clerical learning and secular, aristocratic culture. He abbreviates his French source and draws on Latin rhetoric and learning, with plays on numbers, references to the seven liberal arts, and echoes of school authors. Herbort departs from the *Roman de Troie,* for example, in raising the moral status of the Greek Achilles. He plays down the courtly festivities of the French version and deploys irony and humour in presenting love as a destructive malady rather than a source of virtue, and warfare as unredeemed, even grotesque, suffering instead of an idealized chivalric enterprise. His point of view is that of a clerical author somewhat distanced from the military and erotic values of courtly culture.

A German treatment of the life of Pontius Pilate has also at times been attributed to Herbort.

BIBLIOGRAPHY

Bumke, Joachim. "Untersuchungen zur Überlieferungsgeschichte der höfischen Epik im 13. Jahrhundert: Die Herbort-Fragmente aus Skokloster." *Zeit-schrift für deutsches Altertum und deutsche Literatur* 120 (1991): 257–304.

Fromm, Hans. "Herbort von Fritzlar. Ein Plädoyer." *Beiträge zur Geschichte der deutschen Sprache und Literatur* 115 (1993): 244–278.

Frommann, G. Karl, ed. *Herborts von Fritslâr liet von Troye.* Quedlinburg and Leipzig: Basse, 1837; rpt. Amsterdam: Rodopi, 1966.

Mertens, Volker. "Herborts von Fritzlar *Liet von Troye* — ein Anti-Heldenlied?" *Jahrbücher der Reineke-Gesellschaft* 2 (1992): 151–171.

William H. Jackson

Herlin, Friedrich (1430–1500)

The life of the wealthy painter and polychromer Friedrich Herlin, also known as *Hîrlein* and *Herlein,* is richly documented in written sources. Born in Rothenburg ob der Tauber, Bavaria, in 1430, he soon achieved a supra-regional importance; when he became a citizen of Nördlingen in 1467, the city conceded him freedom from taxes for several years. The *Familienaltar* (family altar), which he painted in 1488 (Nördlingen, Stadtmuseum), shows Herlin with nine children; two of his sons took up the profession of their father, and a daughter married the painter Bartholomäus Zeitblom of Ulm. Herlin died in 1500.

In three signed and dated altars in Nördlingen (1462, St. Georg), Rothenburg (1466, St. Jakob), and Bopfingen (1472, Stadtkirche St. Blasius), Herlin combines painted panels, characterized by warm, saturated colors and naive realism, testifying to the influence of Roger van der Weyden, with cycles of wooden shrine figures. A fourth altar commission, from 1471, is known only through documents, while the epitaph for the Müller family, which represents a Crucifixion, names Herlin in the inscription (1463, Nördlingen, Stadtmuseum).

Among the attributed works, four small panels dated 1459 from the Church of the Savior in Nördlingen (Munich, Bayerisches Nationalmuseum; Nördlingen, Stadtmuseum) and eight panel paintings dated 1459, probably from cloister Kaisheim (Bavaria; now Karlsruhe, Kunsthalle), represent Herlin's early altar paintings. Some painted epitaphs are attributed to the painter as autograph works: the Fergen epitaph, dated 1467, represents an enthroned Madonna (Rothenburg, St. Jakob), and the Genger epitaph, dated in the following year, portrays the *Ecce Homo* (Christ with the crown of thorns; Nördlingen, Stadtmuseum).

The painter's long-term association with the joiner Hans Waidenlich allows recent scholarship to recognize in Herlin an early example of a painter-entrepreneur active across regional borders. While Herlin and Waidenlich worked together on numerous, important, large-scale commissions, other artists—such as Nicolaus Gerhaert and Simon Lainberger—were hired to execute the wooden figural sculpture of the altar shrines.

BIBLIOGRAPHY

Buchner, Ernst. "Die Werke Friedrich Herlins." *Münchener Jahrbuch der Bildenden Kunst* 13 (1923): 1–51.

Krohm, Hartmut. "Bemerkungen zur kunstgeschichtlichen Problematik des Herlin-Retabels in Rothenburg o.T." *Jahrbuch der Berliner Museen* 33 (1991): 185–208.

Oellermann, Eike. "Die Schnitzaltäre Friedrich Herlins im Vergleich der Erkenntnisse neuerer kunsttechnologischer Untersuchungen." *Jahrbuch der Berliner Museen* 33 (1991): 213–238.

Ramisch, Hans. "Zum Meister des Nördlinger Hochaltars." *Jahrbuch der Staatlichen Kunstsammlungen in Baden-Württemberg* 8 (1971): 19–34.

Rieber, F., and R. E. Straub. "The Herlin Altarpiece at Bopfingen (1472): Technique and Condition of the Painted Wings." *Studies in Conservation* 22 (1977): 129–145.

Schmid, Elmar Dionys. "Der Nördlinger Hochaltar und sein Bildhauerwerk." Dissertation Universität München, 1971.

Brigitte Schliewen

SEE ALSO
Nicolaus Gerhaert von Leyden; Rothenburg ob der Tauber; Zeitblom, Bartolomäus

Hermann von Fritzlar (ca. 1275–ca. 1350)

Hermann von Fritzlar is known as a hagiologist (chronicler of saints), who wrote the first prose legendary in German, the *Heiligenleben* (Lives of the Saints), in 1443/1449. He is also the author of mystical sermons, tractates, and similar pieces, which he composed before the *Heiligenleben* and partially integrated into the legendary.

The *Heiligenleben* also includes the *Bartholomäus* sermon by Eckhart Rube from the anonymous Dominican collection of sermons *Paradisus anime intelligentis* (in two manuscripts from Erfurt) with the saint's life added at the end. From the *Postille* of the Dominican Heinrich von Erfurt (in six manuscripts) the legendary incorporated ten sermons from the Christmas cycle. Two other sermons were borrowed: from Gerhard von Sterngassen, a Dominican, *Antonius;* and from Hermann von Schildesche, an Augustinian, the *Heiligkreuzauffindung* (Finding the Holy Cross). Besides these thirteen sermons by master preachers, which all fit into the church calendar of the *Heiligenleben,* starting with Advent, the remaining seventy-five feast days are devoted to saints' legends, which Hermann von Fritzlar composed using collections such as the *Legenda aurea,* the *Passional,* the *Väterbuch,* and the *Märtyrerbuch* as sources.

In the prologue to the *Heiligenleben,* Hermann von Fritzlar writes an exemplum about a secret "friend of God" *(Gottesfreund),* achieving a *Unio mystica* (mystical union). At the center of his philosophy (and religion) is the belief that "God is born in the soul." He expands on this theme in the *Annunciation of Mary,* noting that he purposely started the legendary in the last week of March, when the *Annunciation of Mary,* was celebrated, as if to be in the right spirit to write this mystical work. In the sermon on the *Annunciation (Maria Verkündigung),* he mentions his other work, the tractate *Die Blume der Schauung* (The Blossom of the Vision), which he had published anonymously, and in which he had written more about this topic than on all other central Christian teachings. Three later manuscripts exist of *Die Blume der Schauung,* in Nürnberg, Köln and Gent.

Another treatise on the same topic of *Geburt des Wortes (Gottes) in der Seele* (The Birth of the Word [of God] in the Soul), as a *Programmschrift* (treatise) of Meister Eckhart and mysticism, exists in two Swabian manuscripts in Augsburg and is integrated into the *Heiligenleben,* in three parts after *Barbara, Lucia,* and *Thomas.*

Of the ten manuscripts of the *Heiligenleben,* only the Heidelberg codex is complete. The illustrated Salem codex is in fragments, the *Darmstädter Legendar* is a reworking, and the others are selections of one of three legendary, either very early (manuscripts in Trier and Halberstadt) or later (Berlin, Göttingen, and Dessau). In the *Darmstädter Legendar* of 1420, seventy-one legends are the same as in the *Heiligenleben,* but only thirteen are

exact copies. Of the learned sermons, only *Antonius* was retained. The saints' legends were sorted into four thematic groups: male, female (mostly martyrs), and the rest following the church calendar in two groups. The *Heiligenleben* of Hermann von Fritzlar also served as a partial source for new verse legends of the fifteenth century: *Katharina* (manuscript in Bielefeld), *Dorothea* (Brussels, originally from Braunschweig), and the so-called *Alexius K.*

BIBLIOGRAPHY

Jefferis, Sibylle. "Die Überlieferung und Rezeption des *Heiligenlebens* Hermanns von Fritzlar, einschließlich des niederdeutschen Alexius." In *Mittelalterliche Literatur im niederdeutschen Raum (Tagung Braunschweig 1996),* ed. Hans-Joachim Behr. *Jahrbuch der Oswald-von-Wolkenstein-Gesellschaft* 10 (1998): 191–209.

Morvay, Karin and Dagmar Grube. *Bibliographie der deutschen Predigt des Mittelalters: Veröffentlichte Predigten,* ed. Kurt Ruh. Munich: Beck, 1974, pp. 102–110, 119–123, 123–125.

Steer, Georg. "Geistliche Prosa." In *Die deutsche Literatur im späten Mittelalter 1250-1370,* ed. Ingeborg Glier. Munich: Beck, 1987, pt. 2, pp. 306–307.

Wagner, Bettina. "Die Darmstädter Handschrift 1886: Ein deutsches Prosalegendar des späten Mittelalters." *Bibliothek und Wissenschaft* 21. (1987): 1–37.

Werner, Wilfried and Kurt Ruh. "Hermann von Fritzlar." In *Die deutsche Literatur des Mittelalters: Verfasserlexikon,* ed. Kurt Ruh, et al., vol. 3, coll. 1055–1059. Berlin and New York: de Gruyter, 1981.

Sibylle Jefferis

SEE ALSO

Heiligenleben; Legenda Aurea, Alsatian; *Märtyrerbuch; Passional; Väterbuch*

Hermann von Sachsenheim (ca. 1366–1458)

A contemporary of Oswald von Wolkenstein and steward to the Counts of Württemberg, Sachsenheim found patronage at the Rottenberg court of Mechthild of the Palatinate, wife of Albrecht VI of Austria. Composed in the last decade of his life, his works survive in fifteen manuscripts and five editions of the fifteenth and sixteenth centuries. His oeuvre features mastery of vernacular literary traditions, drastic rhetorical swings between the sophisticated and the colloquial, and frequent allusions to contemporary events.

In *Die Mörin* and *Der Spiegel,* both anti-*Minnereden,* or anti-love-poems, the narrator is judged by a Court of Love, at which Lady Aventiure, Wolfram of Eschenbach's personification of storytelling, presides. In *Der Spiegel,* Lady Aventiure condemns him to death for infidelity. Only the pleas of the twelve attending personifications make possible his release into the custody of Lady Fidelity and his return to Swabia. In *Die Mörin* the narrator is kidnapped and transported to the wondrous realm of Venus Mynn (*Unminne,* or the figure of "Un-Love" personified), her craven consort, Tannhäuser, and her brutal henchwoman, the *Mörin,* to be tried for oath-breaking. The narrator reminds the audience that he is the author and "writes in" (nominates) Aventiure as judge for his appeal. After a tournament in honor of Lady Dishonor, the narrator swears a false oath to win his release. Sachsenheim's other works include *Das Schleiertüchlein,* a combination of *Minnerede,* or love poem, and pilgrim's narrative, which tells of a sorrowful knight, who, while still a squire, falls in love with a noble lady and, as a gesture of devotion, journeys to the holy places of the East. The lady's veil, sanctified with her blood, is a symbol of courtly and spiritual devotion.

In *Die Grasmetze* the contrast between the knight's elaborately courtly language and his failure as a lover reverses the clichés of the pastourelle. *Die Unminne* presents a diatribe in verse against the antithesis of Minne and its prominence in Sachsenheim's world. *Der goldene Tempel* combines an allegory of the heavenly Jerusalem with a gloss of the Church and its chancel as the embodiment of a universal community of believers. *Jesus der Arzt* is a brief, medical allegory of spirituality in verse.

BIBLIOGRAPHY

Huschenbett, Dietrich. "Hermann von Sachsenheim." In *Die deutsche Literatur des Mittelalters: Verfasserlexikon,* ed. Kurt Ruh, et al. 2nd ed., vol. 3. Berlin: de Gruyter, 1981, cols. 1091–1106.

Kerth, Thomas, ed. *Des Spiegels Abenteuer.* Göppingen: Kümmerle, 1986.

Rosenberg, Donald K., ed. *Das Schleiertüchlein. The Schleiertüchlein of Hermann von Sachsenheim.* Göppingen: Kümmerle, 1980.

Schlosser, Horst Deiter, ed. *Die Mörin.* Wiesbaden: Brockhaus, 1974.

David F. Tinsley

SEE ALSO
Minnesang; Oswald von Wolkenstein

Heroic Literature
See Heldenbücher.

Herrad von Hohenburg (fl. late 12th c.)

The abbess Herrad of the Augustinian convent Hohenburg (Landsberg), today, Sainte-Odile, near Strasbourg, whose name appears in documents between 1178 and 1196, is famous for her monumental compilation *Hortus deliciarum* (Garden of Delights). This encyclopedic work of 324 folio pages contains some sixty poems by various medieval Latin poets, such as Hildebert of Lavardin, Petrus Pictor, and Walther of Châtillon, a number of songs with their musical notations, various prose texts excerpted from the Bible, biblical commentaries, historical chronicles, church laws, the liturgy, and scholarly studies. Philosophical and legal statements by Peter Lombard and scientific observations by Isidor of Seville are also extensively copied in the *Hortus,* often accompanied by German glosses.

The manuscript was richly illuminated and is nearly unparalleled in medieval book production. The 153 miniatures, often taking up a whole page, illustrate the meanings of biblical texts, aspects of Christian belief, and the arts. In many respects the *Hortus* served as an encyclopedia, structured by the principles of the divine plan for the salvation of mankind.

Although the original manuscript burned in a fire in the Strasbourg library in 1870, older copies and descriptions provide a good idea of the splendor and learnedness of the *Hortus.* The abbess Herrad initiated and supervised the production of the manuscript, which was to instruct the women in the convent on how to reach paradise through a virtuous life on earth. Many leading twelfth-century scholars, such as Honorius Augustodunensis, Rupert of Deutz, and Peter Comestor, are well represented in the *Hortus.*

Apart from her considerable editorial work, Herrad also contributed to the significant expansion of her convent in political and economic terms.

BIBLIOGRAPHY

Bertau, Karl. *Deutsche Literatur im europäischen Mittelalter,* vol. 1. Munich: Beck, 1972, pp. 585–590.

Curschmann, Michael. "Texte — Bilder — Strukturen: Der *hortus deliciarum,* und die frühmittelhochdeutsche Geistlichendichtung." *Deutsche Vierteljahrsschrift für Literaturwissenschaft und Geistesgeschichte* 55 (1981): 379–418.

Green, Rosalie, et al. *Herrad of Hohenburg, Hortus deliciarum.* 2 vols. London and Leiden: 1979.

Saxl, F. "Illustrated Medieval Encyclopaedias." In Saxl, Fritz. *Lectures.* London: Warburg, 1957, vol. 1, pp. 228–254; vol. 2, figures 169–174.

Albrecht Classen

Herrand von Wildonie (ca. 1230–1278/1282)

A Middle High German author of songs and narratives, Herrand II of Wildonie was descended from an important Styrian family holding the hereditary office of high steward of Styria. The family seat was the now ruined castle of Alt Wildon, near Graz, Austria, on the River Mur. He was born circa 1230 and died about 1278/1282. Herrand was married to Perhta, daughter of Ulrich von Lichtenstein. He was active politically in the Interregnum years, first for Bela of Hungary, then Ottokar of Bohemia, and finally for Rudolf of Habsburg.

His literary oeuvre comprises three extant courtly love songs and four short narratives *(maere).* The songs are contained in the famous Heidelberg manuscript named for the family which commissioned the collection of love songs, or *minnesang* (University Library, no. cpg 848, the "Manesse Codex"). On fol. 201rv, is a miniature of the poet with an incorrect coat of arms. The narratives are also contained in another famous manuscript in Vienna (National Library, no. Ser. Nov. 2663), the *Ambraser Heldenbuch* (Book of heroes from Ambras [Castle]), fol. 217ra–220va.

Herrand's songs are considered largely conventional in nature, but his short narratives show him to be a leading writer in this genre's "post-Stricker" phase. The texts all seem to deal with constancy and loyalty, arranged in contrasting pairs. The first pair, *Die treue Gattin* (The Faithful Wife) and *Der betrogene Gatte* (The Betrayed Husband), present, respectively, a wife moved by such intense love and devotion that she disfigures her face to match her old and injured ugly husband and a young wife who tries to deceive her old husband with a younger lover.

The second pair of stories, *Der nackte Kaiser* (The Naked Emperor) and *Die Katze* (The Cat), deals with, first, the obligation of the ruler to carry out his duties conscientiously — the negligent Emperor Gornäus, cast down in a lowly position and replaced by an angel, must witness the latter's exemplary success until he acknowledges his former errors and be reinstated by his Doppelgänger—and, then, the vassal's obligation to remain faithful to his overlord—a dissatisfied tom cat does the rounds among a series of incongruous partners only to return in the end to his cat queen. In a time of great political upheaval, after the deaths of the last Babenberg Duke of Austria (1246) and the last Staufen Emperor (1250), these apparently generalized political admonitions must have been particularly pointed. These four distinct narratives document their author's literary modernity, whereas the content of these narratives points to a conservative stance by the author and a dialectic possibly aimed at the "classless" didacticism of Der Stricker. There is evidence that Herrand's work was known outside Styrian aristocratic circles.

BIBLIOGRAPHY

Curschmann, Michael. "Herrand von Wildonie (Wildon)." In *Die deutsche Literatur des Mittelalters. Verfasserlexikon,* ed. Kurt Ruh, et al., vol. 3. Berlin and New York: de Gruyter, 1981, cols. 1144–1147.

Deighton, Alan. "Die 'nichtpolitischen' Erzählungen Herrands von Wildonie." In *Kleinere Erzählformen im Mittelalter. Paderborner Colloquium 1987,* ed. Klaus Grubmüller, et al. Paderborn: Schöningh, 1988, pp. 111–120.

Fischer, Hanns. *Herrand von Wildonie. Vier Erzählungen.* Tübingen: Niemeyer, 1959. 2nd ed. 1969 [narratives].

Hofmeister, Wernfried. *Die steierischen Minnesänger. Edition, Übersetzung, Kommentar.* Göppingen: Kümmerle, 1987.

Margetts, John. "Herrand von Wildonie: The Political Intentions of *Der blöze keiser* and *Diu katze.*" In *Court and Poet. Selected Proceedings of the Third Congress of the International Courtly Literature Society (Liverpool 1980),* ed. Glyn S. Burgess. Trowbridge: Francis Cairns, 1981, pp. 249–266.

Ortmann, Christa and Hedda Ragotzky. "Zur Funktion exemplarischer *triuwe*-Beweise in Minne-Mären: "Die treue Gattin" Herrands von Wildone, "Das Herzemäre" Konrads von Würzburg und die "Frauentreue." In *Kleinere Erzählformen im Mittelalter. Paderborner Colloquium 1987,* ed. Klaus Grubmüller, et al. Paderborn: Schöningh, 1988, pp. 89–109.

Thomas, J. W., trans. *The Tales and Songs of Herrand von Wildonie.* Kentucky: University Press of Kentucky, 1972.

von Kraus, Carl. *Deutsche Liederdichter des 13. Jahrhunderts,* Vol. 1. *Text.* Tübingen: Niemeyer, 1952, pp. 588–589 [songs]. Vol. 2. *Kommentar* ed. Hugo Kuhn. 1958, pp. 635–638 [commentary].

John Margetts

SEE ALSO
Minnesang; Stricker, Der; Ulrich von Liechtenstein

Herzog
See Dux/Herzog.

Heselloher, Hans (fl. 1450–1483)

Hans Heselloher contributed materially to the fifteenth-century revival of Neidhart von Reuental (d. ca. 1236), whose depiction in lyric poems of the hostile encounter between the world of the court and the world of the peasant *(dörper)* had become legendary. So popular was Neidhart, especially in the later Middle Ages, that poets wrote *Neidharte,* literature fictitiously ascribed to Neidhart himself. One sign of a sort of Neidhart cult was the re-burial of the poet at St. Stephen's Cathedral in Vienna between 1350 and 1400. Imitation of Neidhart's style and themes in every imaginable genre was the mark of his continuing veneration. Two examples from Heselloher's century are the comic peasant epic *Der Ring* (The Ring), ca. 1400, by Heinrich Wittenwiler and the anonymous collection of Neidhart-inspired songs and merry tales *Neidhart Fuchs* (The Fox), which appeared as an early German printed book (1491/1497). One dancing tune included in the latter was composed by Hans Heselloher, who is so closely associated with Neidhart von Reuenthal that scholars dub him the "second Neidhart."

Heselloher was a Bavarian nobleman who presided as county court judge. A very small corpus of his poetry — less than ten songs — has come down to us, the most famous being the immensely popular song *üppiklichen dingen* ("[Regarding] trifling goings-on"), which concerns a peasant brawl at a dance. It is unclear why, and when, Heselloher began to compose works in the Neidhart tradition *(Neidhartiana),* but he became Neidhart's truest disciple. Heselloher imitated, for instance, the familiar Neidhartian role of the socially superior singer/narrator as fictive participant in boorish festivities, skipping to the beat of an eponymous tune, here "the Heselloher" *(den Heselloher).* Neidhart and his followers dwelt on the class conflict between the nobility and the peasantry, mocking

the latter as upstart yokels who, in their gaudy manner of dress, crude behavior and bearing of arms, foolishly aspire to a higher station in society. By so emulating Neidhart, Heselloher carried forth the peasants' satire *(Bauernsatire, Bauernspott),* blending two poetic postures: the ironic, humorous stance of the "lyric I" as ineffectual Lothario, and the poetic persona as aggressive vituperator who heaps crude invective (in dialect) on his villager rivals.

Heselloher faithfully reproduces the scenery of Neidhart's so-called "Winter Songs" *(Winterlieder),* for example, in the poem *Wes sol ich beginnen?* ("What am I to do?"). The lyric voice laments the passing of summer, and, with it, the loss of joy. He can find no girl to love him. Then, he spots pretty girls who, to the singer's woe, soon flirt with peasant boys, dressed up as elegantly as if they were noblemen. A high-spirited sort of wooing dance breaks out, at which Heselloher is left to lament his own inadequacies, to curse the vainglorious rustics who are his rivals for love, and to be ridiculed himself by a beautiful girl: *ey, essellocher, es stat nit schon, / das du dich selbs singst dar an!* ("Ho, Heselloher, it doesn't look good / for you to sing your own praises!").

However one judges the merits of the songs of Hans Heselloher, they bear eloquent witness to the vivacity and adaptiveness of the Neidhart tradition in German medieval literature.

BIBLIOGRAPHY

Curshmann, Michael, ed. *Texte und Melodien zur Wirkungsgeschichte eines spätmittelalterlichen Liedes (Hans Heselloher: 'Von üppiglichen dingen').* Bern: Francke, 1970.
Hartmann, August. "Hans Hesellohers Lieder." *Romanische Forschungen* 5 (1890): 449–518.
Simon, Eckehard. *Neidhart von Reuental.* Boston: Twayne Publishers, 1975.

William C. McDonald

SEE ALSO
Neidhart; Wittenweiler, Heinrich

Hildebrandslied

An Old High German fragmentary heroic lay of sixty-four lines, "The Lay of Hildebrand" was composed in Germanic alliterative verse and entered on the first and last leaves of the Kassel Codex Theol. fol. 54, probably in Fulda in the fourth decade of the ninth century. The lay begins in expected narrative fashion ("I have heard it told" *ik gihorta δat seggen*), but breaks off in mid-line, probably near the end of the poem. It is generally held that two scribes copied the text from an earlier manuscript: the bulk was copied by scribe A (the apprentice), whose writing was larger and more erratic; scribe B (the master), using a more even, compact stroke, tried to provide a corrective model in lines 30a–40a of the second page.

Part of the Dietrich cycle of legends, the lay tells of the battlefield encounter between Hildebrand and his son Hadubrand. Forced by Odoacer to flee the country with Dietrich and leave behind his wife and new-born son, Hildebrand returns after thirty years in exile, only to meet his own son, now grown to a man, and a warrior in his own right. Believing his father to be dead, Hadubrand rejects the peace gestures of Hildebrand, and refuses to accept that his adversary is his father. The Germanic warrior's sense of honor and the allegiance of Hildebrand and Hadubrand to opposing masters make combat inevitable for both; but only Hildebrand truly senses the tragedy which is about to unfold. The poem ends abruptly with the battle in full force; because of the missing lines, the outcome of the encounter is left to the reader's imagination, though later German and Norse sources point to either a reconciliation or to Hildebrand slaying his son.

Discussion continues to center on the transmission of the text, as well as its curious High-Low German dialect mixture. Though the historical setting is the late fifth century Ostrogothic Kingdom (Dietrich became Western Roman ruler in 493), the names ending in *-brand* have prompted scholars to posit Lombardic origins for the lay. As part of the Dietrich cycle, the lay would have been current in several oral (and probably written) German versions from the seventh to the ninth centuries. The presence of both High and Low German features led to early speculation that the extant text was written in a border dialect of German. Current theory now holds that the text reflects an only partially successful attempt to translate a High German original into Low German, a view reiterated in a recent exhaustive treatment of the work by Rosemarie Lühr (1982: I 48–56). New research, however, presents convincing evidence in support of an Old Low Franconian written version as the basis for the existing High Germanized text.

BIBLIOGRAPHY

Braune, Wilhelm and Ernst A. Ebbinghaus, ed. *Althochdeutsches Lesebuch.* 17th ed. Tübingen: Niemeyer, 1994, no. 28, pp. 84–85.

d'Alquen, Richard and Hans-Georg Trevers. "The Lay of Hildebrand: A Case for a Low German Written Original." *Amsterdamer Beiträge zur älteren Germanistik* 22 (1984): 11–72.

Knight Bostock, J. *A Handbook on Old High German Literature.* 2nd ed. London: Oxford University Press, 1976, pp. 43–82 [trans. pp. 44–47].

Lühr, Rosemarie. *Studien zur Sprache des Hildebrandliedes.* 2 vols. Frankfurt am Main: Lang, 1982.

Jerry Krauel

Hildegard von Bingen (1098–1179)

Benedictine, visionary, author, composer, and Germany's first female physician, Hildegard was the tenth child of Hildebert and Mechthild von Bermersheim. She was raised by the recluse Jutta von Spanheim at the Benedictine monastery of Disibodenberg (near Bingen) and made her monastic profession between 1112–1115. In 1136 she was elected *magistra* (mistress) of the Disibodenberg women's community which had by then become quite large.

While aware of a "shadow of the living light" *(umbra viventis lucis)* from childhood on, Hildegard had her first clear vision in 1141 at the age of 43. She understood her insights as divine revelations concerning the meaning of Scripture and obeyed the command to write. The Cistercian Pope Eugene III officially recognized her visionary gift at the Trier Synod in 1147/1148.

That same year, Hildegard founded her own Benedictine women's monastery, St. Rupertsberg (opposite Bingen), whose abbess she became, and in 1165, a second monastery in Eibingen (today, the Abbey St. Hildegard).

Between 1160–1170, Hildegard undertook four public preaching tours to German cities and monasteries, as far away as Bamberg and Swabia. Known as the *prophetissa teutonica* (German, female prophet), she was consulted by and corresponded with popes, kings, including Frederick I Barbarossa, abbots and abbesses, and many other renowned contemporaries, among them, Bernard of Clairvaux. In composing her complex visionary, exegetical, speculative, and scientific works, Hildegard was at first assisted by her former teacher, the monk Volmar of Disibodenberg, and from 1177 on, by Guibert of Gembloux, who is also the author of a partial *vita* of the Beneductine nun. Her complete *vita* was written by the monks Gottfried and Theoderich between 1177–1181. Listed in the *Martyrologium romanum* (list of martyrs) since the fifteenth century, Hildegard is venerated as a saint in Germany.

Hildegard von Bingen's most famous work *Scivias* (Know the Ways) (1141–1151) constitutes the first part of her trilogy of visions whose second and third parts are the *Liber vitae meritorum* (Book of Meritorious Life) (1158–1163) and the *Liber divinorum operum* (Book of Divine Works), the latter also entitled *Liber de operatione dei* (Book of the Works of God, [1163–1173]). In these works she speaks both of what she was given to see and of a divine voice interpreting these visions to her. Hildegard also conducted comprehensive studies of natural science and medicine, which she described in *Physica (Subtilitatum diversarum naturarum creaturarum libri novem)*. Nine books on the nature of various creatures and *Causae et curae* (Afflictions and cures, between 1150–1160). Several hundred letters of her correspondence have been preserved as well as many musical compositions including some seventy-seven liturgical songs, and a drama, the *Ordo virtutum* (The Order of Virtue). Hildegard also wrote two *vitae*, a treatise against the contemporary Cathars, and a linguistic essay on a *lingua ignota* (unknown language).

Hildegard's visionary and prophetic work deals with complex theological, anthropological, and ecclesiological issues. Her idea of the church and society was a strictly hierarchical one. Anchored in the Benedictine liturgical tradition and the Bible, Hildegard was familiar with the church fathers as well as with the writings of her contemporaries, Honorius Augustodunensis, Rupert von Deutz, and Bernard of Clairvaux.

Hildegard von Bingen was well known in her own century. Manuscripts of her works, especially some containing resplendent illuminations made under her own supervision, stem from the twelfth century. Thereafter, forgotten for centuries, her work was finally published in the extensive series of medieval Latin works, *Patrologia latina* (Vol. 197, 1855) and by Joannes Baptista Pitra (*Analecta*, Vol. 8, 1882). The twentieth century gave rise to a revival of Hildegard's work through studies and translations initiated by the Benedictine nuns of Eibingen, notably by the meticulous manuscript study of Marianne Schrader and Adelgundis Führkötter: *Die Echtheit des Schrifttums der heiligen Hildegard von Bingen. Quellenkritische Untersuchungen*, 1956 (On the Authenticity of the Writing of St. Hildegard von Bingen: Source Studies). Extended concentrated research in Hildegard von Bingen's voluminous work began in Germany around 1979 in the context of the 800-year celebration of her death. Since then, she has become probably the most studied and the best known of all medieval women writers, not only among literary and feminist scholars, but also among theologians, historians, and musicologists. Unfortunately, her literary and musical works have sometimes been popularized and misinterpreted beyond recognition.

BIBLIOGRAPHY

Hildegard of Bingen. *The Book of the Rewards of Life— Liber vitae meritorum*, trans. Bruce W. Hozeski. New York: Garland, 1994.

Hildegard of Bingen. *Scivias*, trans. Mother Columba Hart and Jane Bishop. New York: Paulist Press, 1990.

Klaes, Monica. *Vita Sanctae Hildegardis*. CCCM 126. Turnhout: Brepols, 1993 [Latin "Life"].

Lewis, Gertrud Jaron. *Bibliographie zur deutschen Frauenmystik des Mittelalters*. Berlin: Erich Schmidt Verlag, 1989 [primary texts, pp. 70–84; secondary sources, pp. 66–70 and 84–145].

Newman, Barbara. *From Virile Woman to Woman Christ: Studies in Medieval Religion and Literature*. Philadelphia: University of Pennsylvania Press, 1995.

van Acker, L. *Hildegardis Bingensis Epistolarium*. 2 vols. Turnhout: Brepols, 1991–1993 [Latin letters].

Gertrud Jaron Lewis

SEE ALSO
Frederick I Barbarossa; Monasteries; Preaching and Sermons, German; Women

Hildesheim

Ludwig the Pious founded the diocese of Hildesheim in 815, erecting a baptistry on the site now occupied by the cathedral. In 872 the cathedral was consecrated in honor of the Virgin, who is credited as having a specific role in its establishment. According to an eleventh-century chronicle, Ludwig first came upon the site in the course of a hunt. His chaplain performed the mass, but afterwards was unable to remove the relics of the Virgin from the rosebush on which he had placed them. This event was taken as a sign of the Virgin's favor and prompted the transfer of the bishop's seat from Elze to Hildesheim. The "thousand-year-old rosebush" continues to grow outside of the choir's apse.

The cathedral building went through a series of reconstructions throughout the course of its history. A 1013 fire caused only minor structural damage but brought about the loss of many of the cathedral's treasures. A fire in 1046 destroyed the cathedral, which was then rebuilt

Gospels of Bishop Bernward (Hildesheim, Dom-Museum, DS 18), fol. 16v: Bernward offering this manuscript at the altar. *Photograph: Dom-Museum Hildesheim (Engelhardt)*

under Bishop Hezilo between 1055 and 1061. The triple-aisle, cross-shaped plan was augmented by the addition of an apse, western façade, and square tower during the course of the eleventh century, while subsequent renovations continued on into the nineteenth century. On March 22, 1945, the cathedral was completely destroyed in an air raid. The current cathedral, a reconstruction of 1950–1960, has been built according to the plan of Bishop Hezilo.

Hildesheim's rich artistic heritage is largely the legacy of Bernward, who served as thirteenth bishop of Hildesheim from 993 until his death in 1022. He was responsible not only for smaller scale artistic output, commissioning books and metalwork, but for the construction of a new monastery. The monastery of St. Michael's was founded in 996 with monks Bernward brought with him from Cologne. In doing so, Bernward created a diversified community, with the secular canons of the cathedral maintaining connections to the court, while he

established a place in his see for a more pure form of Benedictine monasticism. Bernward laid the foundation stone for Saint Michael's church in 1001 and consecrated the structure shortly before his death. The abbey church was completed under Bishop Godehard in 1031. St. Michael's tower groupings and westwork refer to earlier Carolingian architecture, but the second transept and apse lend an increased sense of balance to the structure. The building was renovated after a fire at the end of the twelfth century, and it was at this time, following the canonization of Bernward, that the western crypt was deepened to accommodate a new tomb chamber for the saint. Like the cathedral, the abbey church was destroyed in 1945 and reconstructed the following decade.

Bernward's teacher and biographer Thangmar wrote that Bernward's early education included instruction in metal craft as well as book illumination. None of the remaining Hildesheim works can be attributed to his hand, but the quality and variety of works produced under his patronage speak to his early training and the importance he placed on the visual arts.

Hildesheim possesses one of the earliest extant free-standing sculptures of the seated Virgin and Child. The gilded lindenwood sculpture is of the Throne of Wisdom type, with the Christ child seated frontally on the Virgin's lap, and has been dated to 1000–1010. Although this date could place the sculpture among those works commissioned by Bernward, no record of the work's provenance remains.

A Saxon aristocrat by birth, Bernward maintained close ties to the court. In 987 he became a member of the imperial chapel and chancellery, and at the request of the Empress Theophanu, he became one of the two primary teachers of her eight-year old son, Otto III. In 1006–1007 he supported Henry II in his war against Baldwin IV of Flanders. Court patronage did not greatly affect Hildesheim's artistic activity, but court art does seem to have presented a model for Bernward, particularly in the area of manuscript illumination. The images of the 1015 Bernward Gospels derive much of their iconography from a Carolingian Gospel Book now known as the Prague Gospels (Prague, Cathedral Library, Cim. 2) (Mayr-Harting 1991: I,104). New in Bernward's manuscript, however, is the image of a crowned Virgin in the frontispiece. This *Maria Regina* constitutes the first such image of a crowned and enthroned Virgin in Ottonian art. It shares certain iconographic qualities with contemporary ruler portraits, such as the portraits of Otto III in the Aachen Gospels (Aachen, Cathedral Treasury) and the Gospels of Otto III (Munich, Bayerische Staatsbibliothek, Clm 4453), which were in turn modeled after images of Christ in Majesty.

Bernward sent the leader of his scriptorium, Guntbald, to Regensburg, then a major ecclesiastical center that had benefited from contact with the cathedral schools in Northern France. Henry Mayr-Harting finds evidence for the Regensburg influence on Hildesheim art in stylistic similarities between books such as the 1011 Guntbald Gospels and the 1014 Sacramentary of Guntbald and those of the Regensburg school. Further, Mayr-Harting suggests that Regensburg provided Hildesheim with a schematized model for visual and theological representations of Christ (1991: I,101).

An inscription in the Bernward Gospels consigns the work to St. Michael's, the designated site for many of the bishop's commissions, such as the silver candlesticks and the bronze doors of 1015 (now in the cathedral). The doors were striking on both technical and iconographic levels. Each cast in a single piece, they were the first monumental bronzes since antiquity. They provide examples of Bernward's affinity for representations of the human Christ and demonstrate the sophisticated manner in which he communicated his theological messages. Each of the bronze doors had eight fields, the left valve representing Old Testament scenes, such as the presentation of Eve, the Temptation, the Fall, and the murder of Abel and the judgment of Cain. These images were to be contrasted with those on the right door: New Testament scenes, including the Nativity, the Adoration of the Magi, and the Presentation in the Temple. In this typological pairing Eve was shown to be the woman who closed the doors to Paradise, bringing about the fall of man and giving birth to the child who would commit the first act of murder, while the other, Mary, opened the doors in giving birth to the child who would provide salvation to mankind.

BIBLIOGRAPHY

Brandt, Michael. *Bernward von Hildesheim und das Zeitalter der Ottonen.* Mainz: Philipp von Zabern, 1993.

———. *Das Kostbare Evangeliar des Heiligen Bernward.* Munich: Prestel 1993.

Gosebruch, Martin, und Frank N. Steigerwald, ed. *Berwardinische Kunst: Bericht über ein wissenchaftliches Symposium in Hildesheim vom 10.10. bis 13.10.1984,* Schriftenreihe der Kommission für Niedersächsische Bau- und Kunstgeschichte bei der Braunschweigischen Wissenschaftlichen Gesellschaft 3. Göttingen: Erich Goltze Gurbl, 1988.

Mayr-Harting, Henry. *Ottonian Book Illumination. A Historical Study.* 2 vols. London: Harvey Miller, 1991.

Stähli, Marlis. *Die Handschriften im Domschatz zu Hildesheim.* Mittelalterliche Handschriften in Niedersachsen 7. Wiesbaden: Otto Harrassowitz, 1984.

Tschan, Francis J. *Saint Bernward of Hildesheim.* Publications in Medieval Studies, The University of Notre Dame. Indiana: Notre Dame, 1961.

Kristen M. Collins

SEE ALSO
Bernward of Hildesheim; Cologne, Art; Henry II, Art; Otto III; Ottonian Art and Architecture; Regensburg; Theophanu

Hirsau

The importance of Hirsau (Baden-Württemberg) rests in its role in the Cluniac religious reform movement and the establishment of an architecture that reflected this reform. The earliest tradition holds that a monastery was founded by the local count at this site near Calw in the Black Forest in the ninth century. The monastery stood empty by about 1000, but, during a visit in 1049, Pope Leo IX made the decision to resettle it. In 1065 twelve monks and their abbot transferred here from Einsiedeln. In 1075, during a visit to Rome, Abbot William, who had arrived from St. Emmeram in Regensburg in 1069, learned about the Cluniac reform and decided to institute its new, more stringent practices in Hirsau. The success of the reform led not only to the foundation of a number of dependent monasteries, both in southern Germany and further east, but to the need for a larger church and cloister; these were built on the opposite side of the river between 1082 and William's death in 1091.

Although the church of Saints Peter and Paul was destroyed in the seventeenth century, its basic forms are known through earlier drawings, the ruins, archaeological excavations, and the numerous churches built under its influence. The church was modeled on the second church at Cluny, and a number of its forms had already been predicted at the Church of All Saints at Schaffhausen, which itself was influenced by Hirsau. Unusual at this date, when the High Romanesque was already taking form at Speyer and Mainz, for example, were the flat, unvaulted ceiling, the use of simple columnar supports, the unarticulated wall surface, and the lack of a crypt. In these features, the church not only reflected the spiritual severity associated with the reform, it articulated its antiimperial allegiance to the pope in the Investiture Controversy. The dedication of the church to Peter and Paul, its unusually large scale, and the simplicity reminiscent of the Holy City's Early Christian basilicas also highlighted the visual reference to and support of Rome.

BIBLIOGRAPHY

Berger, Rolf. *Hirsauer Baukunst: Ihre Grundlagen, Geschichte und Bedeutung,* pt. 1. Beiträge zur Kunstgeschichte 12. Witterschlick/Bonn: M. Wehle, 1995.

Gförer, A. F., ed. *Codex Hirsaugiensis,* Stuttgart: Sumptibus Societatis Litterariae Stuttgardiensis, 1843.

Irtenkauf, Wolfgang. *Hirsau: Geschichte und Kultur.* Thorbecke Kunstbücherei 7. Lindau and Constance: Thorbecke, 1959.

Joan A. Holladay

SEE ALSO

Investiture Controversy; Romanesque Art and Architecture; Schaffhausen

Historiography, Dutch

In the Middle Ages, history was ordinarily defined as *rerum gestarum narratio* (stories of deeds) or as only containing *res verae quae factae sunt* (things which truly happened) and, at least formally, distinguished from *fabulae — quae nec factae sunt nec fieri possunt* (fables — which are neither factual nor possible) (Isidore of Seville, d. 636, *Etymologica,* 1,44,5).

In practice, however, a clear-cut delimitation of historiography did not exist, partly because, at that time, the distinction between fact and fiction was based on criteria other than ours today. In addition, history was not then an independent discipline, but studied and pursued within the frame of literature, especially as part of the subjects *grammatica* (grammar) and *rhetorica* (rhetoric), and *ars poetica* (poetic art). Thus, saints' lives (vitae), for example, were considered part of historiography, and vernacular texts, such as epics about Charlemagne or the Crusades, were sometimes presented and regarded as veracious histories. Nevertheless, within this broad field, several important historiographic genres developed in the course of time, such as *annales, historiae, chronica* and *gesta.* The boundaries between these genres are not distinct, yet each has its own characteristics.

Annals, for example, are usually unpretentious strings of meteorological, military, and biographical facts. In histories, the narrative aspect prevails; in chronicles, the chronological setting of facts in a universal, regional or local scope predominates; and in *gesta,* the deeds and actions of prominent figures take a central place. These genres flourished in the Low Countries, especially in the format of regional and national chronicles, written in Latin, from the tenth century onward. Beginning with the thirteenth century, the genres appear in Middle Dutch as *historie, kronie,* and *yeeste.*

BIBLIOGRAPHY

Gessler, J. and J. F. Niermeyer. *Florilegium chronicorum neerlandicorum. Een keuze uit de Latijnse kronieken van Noord- en Zuid-Nederland van de tiende tot de vijftiende eeuw,* The Hague: Nijhoff, 1948.

Guenée, Bernhard. *Histoire et Culture historique dans l'Occident médiéval.* Aubier: Montaigne, 1980.

Isidore of Seville. *Etymologiae.* 2 vols. Oxford: Clarendon Press, 1911.

McCormick, Michael. *Les Annales du Haut Moyen-Age.* Turnhout: Brepols, 1975.

Schmale, Franz-Josef. *Funktion und Formen mittelalterlicher Geschichtsschreibung. Eine Einführung,* Darmstadt: Wissenschaftliche Buchgesellschaft, 1985.

A. L. H. Hage

SEE ALSO

Charlemagne; Charlemagne Epics, Dutch; Chronicles, City, Dutch; Chronicles, City, German; Chronicles, Regional/National, Dutch; Chronicles, Regional/National, German; Chronicles, World, Dutch; Chronicles, World, German; Crusades, Literature, Dutch

Historiography, German

In the twentieth century, modern historiography on medieval Germany underwent several crucial developments, at times conditioned by political developments and ideological agenda. Through the 1920s, Western historians remained influenced by positivist views of history which asserted that objective historical truth could be achieved "as it really was" (Leopold von Ranke). Also influential was the conviction that a natural law of state evolution had led to the rise of the nineteenth-century liberal-democratic state. Especially in Germany, a strong tradition of legal and constitutional history arose, which saw the medieval state as an imperfect predecessor of the modern one.

A reaction against evolutionary views of European state formation set in during the 1920s and 1930s in France and Germany. French historians began to see the totality of society as an object of study in its own right, and as an alternative to conventional political and institutional history. This social historical approach became the hallmark of the French "new history" *(Nouvelle Histoire)*, best known in medieval history circles as that practiced by Marc Bloch, Georges Duby, and other members of the school of historians associated with the journal *Annales E. S. C.* Similar developments took place in Germany. The most important German-language practitioner of the new social history was the Austrian Otto Brunner, whose study on *Land und Herrschaft* (Land and Lordship) remains a controversial classic. In it, Brunner argued that medieval society could not be analyzed in intellectual categories applied to the modern state. Instead, a new methodology of medieval history had to be forged from the language and content of medieval sources themselves. Unfortunately, Brunner and his ideas willingly served the academic and political agenda of emergent Nazi ideology, which sought to reject traditional constitutional history as part of the liberal legacy of the failed Weimar republic. It is ironic that Otto Brunner and Marc Bloch, contemporary pioneers of social history, respectively benefited from and fell victim to the Nazi regime.

Other German medievalists continued their work during the war years without actively collaborating with Hitler's state, though controversy remains regarding the extent to which their scholarship was guided by the prevailing political ideology. In the post-war years Walter Schlesinger, Karl Bosl, Friedrich Prinz, and others focused attention on issues of lordship and status. Another ongoing initiative of tremendous importance has been the critical source work of the *Monumenta Germaniae historica* (MGH, or Monuments of German History) in Munich, in recent decades under the leadership of Horst Fuhrmann, and later, Rudolf Schieffer.

One of the most influential post-war scholars was Gerd Tellenbach, who, in the 1950s, inspired a group of young historians working at Freiburg, the Freiburg working group, to devote energy to prosopography, or, the study of persons. Distinct from traditional biography, this new method of *Personenforschung* was applied to medieval necrologies and memorial books, which contain tens of thousands of names of individuals, entered by monks obligated to pray for them. Members of the Freiburg working group asked new questions of these sources in an attempt to uncover kin groups' perceptions of themselves.

Karl Schmid, a brilliant pupil of Tellenbach and one of the most productive German historians in the twentieth century, argued that the way in which aristocratic families defined themselves changed from the early to the High Middle Ages. Before the eleventh century, individuals viewed themselves as belonging to broad horizontally defined kin-groups, with no firmly defined boundaries, in which blood relation to other family members through women was just as important as ties through males. After ca. 1050, however, as noble families began to name themselves after their castles, individuals began seeing themselves as members of vertical patrilineal dynasties, with their family identity tied to a physical site. This shift in self-consciousness was accompanied by the rise of primogeniture. Though Schmid's thesis is problematic in many respects, it exerted a powerful and creative influence on the practice of medieval social history. Georges Duby acknowledged his intellectual debt to it and admired Schmid's work.

The lasting influence of the Freiburg group on medieval German historiography is undeniable. From the 1960s through the 1980s, Karl Schmid's colleagues and students continued to work on noble self-consciousness and related social historical themes. Schmid's friend and collaborator Joachim Wollasch turned to the study of necrologies, and was among the first medievalists to use computer-assisted analysis in the field of prosopography. Otto Oexle's work has focused on relations between the living and the dead, while Gerd Althoff, the best-known popularizer of medieval history in contemporary Germany, has written extensively on ritual as a means of communication and power.

Significantly, German medievalists have tended to resist tendencies in Germany to renationalize history in recent years. Even before 1990, some strains of West German historiography began to reject the pluralistic approach of the critical historians of the 1970s; such renationalization of modern German history received a tremendous impetus from German unification. Most medieval historians in Germany have not shared this narrow politicization. Michael Borgolte, for example, has argued for the expansion of a strongly pluralistic approach to the writing of German medieval history, recalling the social historical method of Otto Brunner.

In terms of volume, English-language scholarship on medieval Germany cannot compete with what has been written on medieval English and French topics by British and North American scholars. However, those who have devoted themselves to medieval German history have achieved important results. The British historian Geoffrey Barraclough brought an awareness of medieval Germany to a wider audience in the immediate post-war period. Karl Leyser brilliantly set medieval German developments within the context of critical and profound issues of importance for all medieval European history. More recently, Benjamin Arnold has produced several studies attentive to the details of regional political developments, while Timothy Reuter, who spent many years at the MGH, has been able to bring the best of both English and German historical approaches to the study of Germany. Finally, the American John Freed has published several important works on ministerials and is noted for applying to medieval German history the methods of social history practiced by other North American medievalists.

BIBLIOGRAPHY

Althoff, Gerd. *Die Deutschen und ihr Mittelalter* Darmstadt: Wissenschaftliche Buchgesellschaft, 1992.

Borgolte, Michael, ed. *Mittelalterforschung nach der Wende 1989.* Oldenbourg: Munich, 1995.

Brunner, Otto. *Land and Lordship: Structures of Governance in Medieval Austria,* trans. Howard Kaminsky and James Van Horn Melton. Philadelphia: University of Pennsylvania Press, 1992.

Freed, John B. "Reflections on the Medieval German Nobility." *American Historical Review* 91 (1986): 553–575.

Oexle, Otto Gerhard. "Gruppen in der Gesellschaft: Das wissenschaftliche OEuvre von Karl Schmid. "*Frühmittelalterliche Studien* 28 (1994): 10–423.

Reuter, Timothy. *Germany in the Early Middle Ages c. 800–1056.* New York: Longman, 1991.

Schmid, Karl. *Gebetsgedenken und adliges Selbstverständnis im Mittelalter: Ausgewählte Beiträge.* Sigmaringen: Jan Thorbecke Verlag, 1983.

Jonathan Rotondo-McCord

SEE ALSO
Historiography, Dutch; Ministeriales

Hochzeit, Die

A longer allegorical poem, somewhat reminiscent of the "Song of Songs," a biblical allegory which suggests the wedding of the church to Christ, *Die Hochzeit* (The Marriage) begins with the story of a powerful king who has sent his disobedient servants into an abyss, from whence they continue to make trouble. The king decides to marry a beautiful maiden in order to produce an heir and to assure the proper order of things (Latin *ordo*). After the maiden gives her agreement to the king's messenger, preparations for a gorgeous wedding are begun, and the maiden then comes to her bridegroom for the splendid festival. Throughout the narration of the story, the poet explains the allegorical interpretation of almost all the elements; in almost every aspect, *Die Hochzeit* is not a consistent, single allegory, but rather a seemingly random, disconnected discussion. Nevertheless, the significance of each event invariably has reference to true Christian living and to the proper order of things — in sum, a moral, perhaps anagogical exegesis, in the manner of typical biblical exegesis in sermons, but here of the poet's own fictional story.

Die Hochzeit is a lengthy work, almost 1100 lines in stanzas of varying length. Found after *Vom Rechte* in the Millstatt manuscript, the text is in poor condition. The poem is usually dated to 1160.

BIBLIOGRAPHY

Dunstan, A. C. "Sources and Text of the MHG Poem *Die Hochzeit.*" *Modern Language Review* 21 (1926): 178–186.

Ganz, Peter. "'Die Hochzeit': *fabula et significatio.*" In *Studien zur frühmittelhochdeutschen Literatur. Cambridger Colloquium 1971,* ed. L. P. Johnson, et al. Berlin: Erich Schmidt, 1974, pp. 58–73.

Haug, Walter, and Benedikt Vollmann. *Frühe deutsche Literatur und lateinische Literatur in Deutschland, 800-1150.* Frankfurt am Main: Deutscher Klassiker Verlag, 1991, pp. 784–749.

Maurer, Friedrich, ed. *Die religiösen Dichtungen des 11. und 12.Jahrhunderts. Nach ihren Formen besprochen und herausgegeben,* vol. 2, no. 30. Tübingen: Niemeyer, 1964–1970.

Sidney M. Johnson

Hohenzollern

The Hohenzollern dynasty is perhaps best known for the exploits of its Brandenburg-Prussian line in modern times. The medieval origins of the Hohenzollern dynasty, are, however, somewhat misty. The Zollern took their name from a castle on the northern slope of the Swabian Alb, south of Tübingen, between the Neckar and the Danube. The earliest reference to the counts of Zollern comes from about 1061 when two brothers, "Burchardus et Wezil de Zolorin," were killed in battle. It is generally agreed that Count Frederick I (ca. 1085–1115) was the son of Burchard and the ancestor of the later counts of Zollern.

By the middle of the twelfth century, the Zollern were associated with the Hohenstaufens. Count Frederick II (ca. 1125–1145) appeared at the Staufer *Landtag* at Königstuhl in 1140. About this time, the first major division within the dynasty occurred. Frederick II's brother Burkhard established a cadet line of Zollern-Hohenberg. At the second *Landtag* at Königstuhl (1186), the counts of both Zollern (Hechingen) and Hohenberg were represented.

The counts of Hohenberg held lands on either side of the older Zollern domains, and effectively blocked further expansion into the Neckar valley. Initially, the Hohenberg line showed promise, seizing Rottenburg in 1124. To the south, they extended their domains across the Neckar to Schramberg. By the later Middle Ages, however, the Hohenberg lands had been splintered among several branches, and by the end of the fourteenth century, most of their territories had fallen to the counts of Württemberg and Habsburg. The dynasty died out completely in 1486.

The counts of Zollern-Hechingen fared much better. Count Frederick III (d. ca. 1200) served under the Hohenstaufen emperors Frederick I Barbarossa and Henry VI. The later enfeoffed him with the burgravate of Nuremberg in 1191/1192. Burgrave Frederick I established the Hohenzollern dynasty firmly on Franconian soil. After his death, the Zollern lands were divided by treaty in 1204. Burgrave Conrad I (ca. 1186–1261) received the burgravate while the Swabian inheritance went to his younger brother, Frederick I. The Swabian line was for many years restricted to the older family holdings in the Alb. Only in the sixteenth century, with the acquisition of Sigmaringen (1534) were the counts able to extend their domains beyond the Danube and, not until the year 1623, were they raised to the princely estate.

The reign of Burgrave Conrad I marks the beginning of an aggressive policy of territorial formation by the Franconian Hohenzollern. Through his wife, Conrad acquired the lands of the counts of Anenberg in middle Franconia. These estates later constituted the core of the *Land unter dem Gehrig,* or *Unterland.* Conrad also obtained the imperial fief of Creussen, the first acquisition in what would become the *Land ober dem Gehrig,* the *Oberland.*

Expansion continued under Frederick III (1261–1297). Through his wife, Elizabeth, Frederick claimed a part of the massive territorial complex assembled by the Dukes of Andechs-Merian in Franconia. By terms of the treaty of Langenstädte (1260), the Merianer inheritance was divided between the Hohenzollerns (Bayreuth and Cadolzburg) and the counts of Truhendingen and Orlemünde. In 1272 Frederick played a key role in the negotiations leading to the election of Rudolf of Habsburg as emperor. In return for his support, Frederick II was enfeoffed with the imperial court *Landgericht* of Nuremberg by Rudolf I in 1273.

Imperial loyalty played a leading role in Hohenzollern politics during the fourteenth century. In the double election of 1314, Burgrave Frederick IV (1300–1332) sided with Louis the Bavarian. The burgrave was later praised by Louis as the "savior of the Empire" *(salvator imperii)* for helping defeat Frederick of Austria at Mühldorf in 1322. In one of his last acts, Frederick obtained advocacy rights over Ansbach in 1331. Frederick's eldest sons, Johann (1332–1257) and Conrad (d. 1334), ruled the Franconian lands as co-regents until the latter's death. In 1340 Johann was able to acquire the Orlemünde inheritance, including Kulmbach and much of the upper Main valley. After 1346, Johann assumed the position of regent *(Statthalter)* in Brandenburg. Two younger brothers became bishops: Frederick of Regensburg and Berthold of Eichstätt. The youngest brother, Albrecht the Handsome (d. 1361), ended up as a knight at the court of Edward III of England and fought on the English side during the Scots' war and the early phases of the war with France.

Johann II's son Frederick V (1357–1398) emerged as one of the strongest supporters of the Luxembourg emperor Charles IV. Charles' attempts to construct a Luxembourg stronghold in Franconia and the Upper Palatinate brought him into close contact with the Hohenzollerns, whose lands he hoped to acquire. Marriages were proposed between Frederick's eldest daughters and Charles' sons Wenceslas and Sigismund. These plans came to naught after the birth of Frederick's sons, but the burgrave was able to acquire a number of imperial fiefs along the Bohemian border, including Hof. Charles also raised the Hohenzollerns to the princely estate in 1363.

The Franconian lands were divided between Frederick's sons. Johann III (1398–1420) received the *Oberland* and served as an advisor to King Wenceslas. He later was with Sigismund of Hungary at the battle of Nikopolis (1396). Frederick IV (1398–1440), regent of the *Unterland,* also fought alongside Sigismund, and later helped him put down a rebellion in Hungary in 1409. In 1411, Sigismund named Frederick administrator *(Hauptmann und Verweser)* in the Mark of Brandenburg. After 1415, he exercised all princely rights and was named elector in 1417. Margrave Frederick I sought with limited success to reassert princely authority over the towns and nobility in Brandenburg. After 1426, he devoted most of his energies to Franconian affairs, appointing his son Johann, "the Alchemist," regent in the Mark. Frederick took part in four campaigns against the Hussites (1420, 1422, 1427, and 1431) and later helped negotiate the peace settlement of 1433. He was also involved in the negotiations at the Council of Constance and was able to acquire extensive privileges for the margraves over the bishoprics in the Mark.

Frederick I was succeeded in the Mark by his eldest son Frederick II (1440–1470). Frederick II was able to reconquer Uckermark and Neumark and acquired Kottbus in Lusatia. He used newly acquired ecclesiastical privileges (1447) to establish the basis for a territorial church. In 1440, Frederick founded the Order of the Swan, after the Burgundian order of the Golden Fleece. Membership in the *Schwannenorden Bruderschaft* was initially limited to thirty nobles selected from the Mark. After 1457, the order was extended to Franconia by Albrecht Achilles.

Frederick I's lands in Franconia were divided between his younger sons, Albrecht Achilles (1440–1486) and Johann the Alchemist. After the latter's death (1464) and the retirement of Margrave Frederick II (1470), Albrecht Achilles took charge of the *Oberland* and the Mark. Albrecht Achilles was unusually well educated, charming, skillful in tournaments, debates, and on the dance floor, and in general "the darling of the south German nobility" (Hintz, *Die Hohenzollern*). He extended the size and scope of the *Swannenorden* to include Franconian nobles and political allies. Indeed, his attachment to the ideals of knighthood led him to set up a "round table" at his court in Ansbach.

In Franconia, Albrecht sought to extend his authority over the prince-bishoprics of Würzburg, Bamberg, and Eichstätt, as well as over the imperial cities, in order to create a revivified Duchy of Franconia. Nuremburg successfully resisted Albrecht during the five-year *Städtekrieg* (Cities' War, 1453–1458), while Bamberg and Würzburg were able to deal the margrave a losing blow at Roth in 1460. The entrance of the dukes of Bavaria into the conflict signaled the failure of Albrecht's plans, and, in the Peace of Prague (1463), he abandoned claims over the cities and the ecclesiastical estates.

In the Mark, Albrecht issued a carefully considered court order (*Hofordnung*, or rules of the court) in 1470, but he was unable to prevent the towns from reasserting their autonomy. He sought, without success, to extend his authority over Pommerania and Silesia. In the latter case, he was named ruler *(Oberster Hauptmann)* after the death of King Sigismund in 1437. He supported Albrecht II of Habsburg and later the claims of his son, Ladislas Postumus, but with the accession of George Podiebrad in 1457, plans for establishing Hohenzollern lordship in Silesia were put off.

Albrecht's most lasting legacy was the *Dispositio Achillea* (1473) which regulated the succession in the Hohenzollern lands. The *Dispositio* established a principle of primogeniture in the Mark and secundogeniture in Franconia, which would be followed from then on. Younger sons were required to seek a vocation in the church.

Albrecht Achilles was succeeded in the Mark by Johann Cicero (1486), who founded the University of Frankfurt an der Oder in 1498. Following the terms of the *Dispositio Achillea*, Johann's eldest son Joachim I (1499–1515) reigned in Franconia until he went mad and was deposed. While their cousins in the Mark were counted among the most vigorous opponents of Martin Luther, Casimir of Brandenburg-Kulmbach (1515–1527) and his brothers, Georg the Pious (1527–1542) and Albrecht, grand master of the Teutonic Knights *(Deutschorden),* were early supporters of the Reformation. After embracing the Lutheran reform, Albrecht secularized the *Ordensland*, becoming the first duke of Prussia. The Franconian lands, Prussia and Jägerndorf in Silesia, were united under Georg Friedrich of Ansbach-Bayreuth (1543–1603), who was instrumental in acquiring Jülich-Cleve for the Hohenzollern. The Franconian line died with him, and from 1603 until the end of the old *Reich*, Ansbach and Bayreuth were ruled by a cadet branch of the electoral line. While Brandenburg emerged as a leading Protestant state, the Swabian line of Hohenzollerns remained Catholic until their extinction in 1886.

BIBLIOGRAPHY

Guttenberg, Erich Freiherr von. *Territorienbildung am Obermain.* Bamberg: Historischer Verein, 1927.

Meyer, Christian. *Geschichte der Burggrafschaft Nürnberg und der Späteren Markgrafschaften Ansbach und Bayreuth.* Tübingen: Verlag der H. Laupp'schen Buchhandlung, 1908.

Schumann, Günther. *Die Markgrafen von Brandenburg-Ansbach.* Ansbach: Selbstverlag des Historischen Vereins für Mittelfranken, 1980.

Ulhorn, Friedrich, and Walter Schlesinger. *Die deutschen Territorien.* Gebhardt Handbuch der deutschen Geschichte 13. Munich: Deutscher Taschenbuch Verlag, 1974.

William Bradford Smith

SEE ALSO
Deutschorden; Frederick I Barbarossa; Luxemburger; Staufen, Wenceslas

Hoheslied
See Song of Songs.

Holbein, Hans, the Elder (ca. 1465–1524)

Hans Holbein the Elder was one of the most important German artists of the late Gothic period. He combined characteristic elements of South German painting (especially that of Ulm and Augsburg) with influences from Netherlandish art. Particularly well-known are his altarpieces made for a wide variety of religious institutions and his approximately 200 drawings done either in silverpoint or ink. In addition to his paintings, Holbein also provided designs for woodcuts, sculpture, stained glass, and metal works. His contributions to the art of this period include an unusually sensitive use of color and careful study and use of physiognomy and gesture as vehicles for expression and narrative.

Documentary evidence for Holbein's life and work is scant. He was born in Augsburg about 1465, probably to the tanner Michel Holbein and his wife. No documents exist regarding his training and activities as a journeyman, but stylistic evidence points to a trip to Cologne and possibly to the Netherlands. The first signed and dated extant altarpiece by Holbein is the St. Afra Altar, made in 1490 for the Benedictine church of Sts. Ulrich and Afra in Augsburg. A document from 1493 labels Holbein a citizen of nearby Ulm, where he worked with the sculptor Michel Erhart in making an altarpiece for the Benedictine monastery in Weingarten. However, Holbein was back in Augsburg the following year, and he appears regularly in the city's tax records until 1514.

During these years in Augsburg, Holbein trained one apprentice and his two sons, Hans the Younger and Ambrosius; he also engaged his brother Sigmund and the Augsburg artist Leonhard Beck in his workshop. Holbein received many commissions during this period: between 1499 and 1512, from the Dominican convent of St.

Katherine's in Augsburg for various panels including an altarpiece and epitaphs; around 1500, for the high altar at the Dominican church in Frankfurt; in the early 1500s, for the high altar at the Cistercian church in Kaisheim; in 1509, for an altar in the convent of Hohenburg (near Strasbourg); and, between 1508 and 1510, for the silver altar commissioned from several artists for Augsburg cathedral.

Scholars disagree as to whether Holbein actually moved away from Augsburg after 1514, or if he simply was traveling extensively. In any case, he is known to have worked in Lucerne, Switzerland, and in the Alsace region, including at the Antonine monastery at Isenheim. He continued to receive commissions from Augsburg, as attested by his St. Sebastian Altar from 1516 for St. Katherine's and the panel representing "The Fountain of Life," commissioned by the Augsburg merchant Georg Königsberger and completed in 1519. Holbein's death in 1524 is noted in the painters' guild records.

BIBLIOGRAPHY
Bushart, Bruno. *Hans Holbein der ältere.* Augsburg: Hofmann, 1987.
Hans Holbein der ältere und die Kunst der Spätgotik. Augsburg: Himmer, 1965. Exhibition catalog.
Lieb, Norbert, and Alfred Stange. *Hans Holbein der ältere.* Berlin: Deutscher Kunstverlag, 1960.

Pia F. Cuneo

SEE ALSO
Augsburg; Cologne, Art; Erhart, Michel; Frankfurt am Main; Lucerne; Gothic Art and Architecture; Ulm

Holland
County in the coastal area between Meuse and Vlie.

Formation (9th c.–12th c.)

A certain Gerulf, mentioned in a charter from 889, is generally considered to have been the ancestor of the counts of Holland. He probably was a descendant of the legendary Frisian king Radbod. Gerulf exercised comital (ducal) authority in the northern part of what later became the county of Holland. His son (?) Dirk I, mentioned in charters from 921 until 928, possessed comital rights in the Carolingian counties Tesselgouw and Kennemerland in the north and probably also in the region on both sides of the Old Rhine and in *Masaland*. Presumably, the Frankish king had all coastal counties united under one count in order to strengthen his defenses against the Vikings.

From the beginning, the comital family was related to the high Carolingian aristocracy. Dirk II (d. 988) married Hildegard of Flanders, who was of Carolingian birth. His son Arnulf married Liutgard of Luxemburg. These matrimonial alliances with distinguished princely families can be regarded as an indication of the political importance of the county and the prestige of the comital family, probably as a consequence of descending from the royal house of Friesland (King Radbod).

During the reign of Dirk's successors, the centre of comital authority shifted to the south. Dirk III (993–1039) built a stronghold in Vlaardingen. When Dirk came into conflict with some merchants, whose trade with England he was hindering by levying tolls on the Merwede, the German emperor sent an army led by Godfried I of Lower Lotharingia to support the merchants. Dirk, however, succeeded in defeating the imperial troops. His sons, Dirk IV (1039–1049) and Floris I (1049–1061), continued their father's politics of south- and eastward expansion, which led to several clashes with the emperor. In one of these battles, Dirk IV was killed.

When Floris I died in 1061, the emperor seized the opportunity to rid himself of these rebellious counts and granted their territories to the bishop of Utrecht. Floris' wife Geertruid, who remarried to Robrecht of Flanders (called "the Frisian"), initially was able to maintain her position as countess, but in 1070 she and her son Dirk V were driven from power by the bishop. In 1076 Dirk V came back with the help of his stepfather, Robrecht the Frisian, and re-conquered his territories, with the exception of the northern part, which would later be called Western Frisia. His son Floris II (1091–1121) received the county of Holland as a fief from the Utrecht bishop. In 1101 he became the first count to be called *comes de Hollant*. The name *Holland* afterwards was gradually extended to the environs of Dordrecht in the south and to Kennemerland, Amstelland, and Waterland in the north.

The country consisted of a large sandy area along the coast and extensive peat bogs further inland. About the year 1000, only a small portion of the land was inhabited. The population was concentrated on the coastal sand dunes with outlying settlements along the river banks. From the eleventh to the thirteenth centuries, however, the peat bogs were systematically reclaimed. A network of ditches was constructed in order to lower the water level, thus providing arable farmland. The first reclamations

can be traced in Kennemerland. By the year 1300, virtually all of the peat bogs had been reclaimed and settled.

When Floris II died young in 1121, his son Dirk VI was still a child. Floris' wife, Countess Petronilla, emerged as a strong ruler who defended her son's interests very well. In 1127, after the murder of Charles the Good, she intervened in Flanders, trying to obtain the Flemish county for her son. In this, she did not succeed, but a year later she managed to obtain a part of Zeeland—Walcheren and the Bevelanden (called *Zeeland Bewesterschelde*)—as a fief from the count of Flanders. This was the beginning of a long dispute about rights to that territory, which was not settled until the fourteenth century. In 1133 Petronilla founded the abbey of Rijnsburg, probably as a burial place for her second son, Floris the Black, who had been killed in a fight near Utrecht. Thereafter, most counts and their families were buried there, although their ancestors had all been buried in the abbey of Egmond, north of Alkmaar.

Development (12th c.–13th c.)

In the course of the twelfth and thirteenth centuries, the county of Holland developed into a powerful and independent principality. The counts constantly tried to enlarge their power and influence. Gradually they surpassed the bishops of Utrecht—who lost power after the Concordat of Worms (1122)—and assumed rights formerly exercised by the emperor. This process was a lengthy and complicated one. In 1156, for example, the count did not succeed in having his candidate elected bishop of Utrecht. Frederick I Barbarossa instead appointed Godfried of Rhenen, who proved to be an ardent supporter of the emperor. Count Floris III (1157–1190) was forced to behave as a loyal imperial vassal when, in 1165, in his struggle with the bishop regarding dominion of Frisia, he had to submit to an imperial judgment. In this case, both the count and the bishop claimed authority in Westergo and Ostergo. Frederick agreed to a *condominum* (collaborahic dominium) by count and bishop together, which lasted until the middle of the thirteenth century. At the same time, Floris battled Philip of the Elzas in Flanders in an attempt to put an end to the Flemish suzerainty over Zeeland *Bewesterschelde*. Floris was captured and subsequently forced to accept the humiliating Treaty of Bruges (1167), which determined that authority in that part of Zeeland would be shared by Holland and Flanders. Floris III was present at Legnano in 1176 and also took part in the Crusade of 1190. He died in Antioch, a few weeks after the emperor.

Dirk VII (1190–1203), like other counts, tried to enlarge his territory and increase his influence. These efforts put him into conflict with his neighbors on several occasions. In 1197 he defeated the count of Gelre, with whom he had struggled over the election of a new bishop in Utrecht. In Brabant his campaign was less successful. Duke Henry I turned out to be a formidable adversary, and Dirk had to recognize him as suzerain for Dordrecht. Dirk also clashed with his brother William, who had joined the rebellious Western Frisians in 1195. After Dirk's death in 1203, the country endured a severe crisis as both William and Lodewijk of Loon, who had married Dirk's daughter Ada, claimed to be his rightful successor. Each of the two pretenders to the throne succeeded in rallying a number of influential adherents. After a few years, however, William managed to win the whole country over to his side.

In the first half of the thirteenth century, the influence of the dukes of Brabant in Holland remained strong, particularly in light of several matrimonial alliances. William I, for example, who had been married to Aleid of Gelre during the war of succession in 1220 married Mary, daughter of Henry I of Brabant. Four years later, his son Floris IV wed Machteld, another daughter of Henry's. Relations between the comital family and their Brabant relatives remained close. After the death of Floris IV at a tournament in Corbie in 1234, the regency was occupied by, respectively, Floris' brothers William and Otto, the bishop-elect of Utrecht, but from circa 1240, Machteld of Brabant came into prominence once more. She and her son William II maintained close connections with their Brabant relatives, especially Henry II, which turned out to be an important factor in William's election as Roman king in 1247. William II used his influence as king to consolidate power in his own territories. In 1253, for example, he tried to solve a conflict with Flanders by enfeoffing a part of that county to his brother-in-law John of Avesnes, who claimed rights to the lordship of Flanders. In 1256 William led an army to West Frisia in an attempt to subjugate the Frisians. When his horse fell through the ice, William was killed by the Frisians, who, unfortunately, did not recognize their king.

Especially in the second half of the thirteenth century, the urban population of Holland increased. The towns developed into regional market centers, but before 1300, only Dordrecht grew into a commercial center of interregional importance. The comital administration developed considerably during this period. Following the example of Flanders, bailiffs were appointed in new administrative areas: South Holland around Dordrecht; North Holland between Haarlem, Leiden, and Gouda; Delfland and Schieland between Delft and Rotterdam; and Kennemerland, north of Haarlem. Later, other bailiwicks were added. A comital council slowly emerged from a larger group of advising vassals and the influence of the nobility increased. The prince could only realize his political aims by cooperating with his nobles, who were themselves constantly competing for their own family interests.

Floris V (1264–1296) succeeded in solving two of Holland's major traditional issues: relations with the Sticht of Utrecht and the submission of the Frisians. Due to severe financial problems, the Utrecht bishop in 1274 was forced to mortgage some border castles, and Floris was able to penetrate into the Sticht and extend his power considerably by annexing the lands of Amstel and Woerden to his territories.

The conquest of Western Frisia took more time and energy. Only after three major military campaigns — 1272, 1282, and 1289 — did the Frisians accept the count as their legitimate lord. In 1289 Floris successfully negotiated a series of treaties with his former enemies. His political wisdom was evident in his decision to cede to the Frisians some autonomy. About the same time, Floris ordered one of his clerks to write a chronicle to demonstrate, among other things, the legitimacy of comital power in Frisia. This chronicle is known as the *Rijmkroniek* by Melis Stoke. Jacob of Maerlant, who had earlier written a *vorstenspiegel* (prince's primer) for the young Floris, used some passages of Stoke's text in his famous *Spiegel Historiael.* The self-confidence and status of the prince was also expressed in the construction of the *Grote Zaal* (big hall) in The Hague, a city which had been a comital residence since the time of Floris IV. The building was constructed around 1290 after the example of the English royal hall. It was an imposing building, which would impress foreign visitors for centuries.

Floris V was not successful in solving the ongoing conflict over Zeeland. In 1290 the issue once again came to a war, in which Floris V was captured and forced to acknowledge Flemish suzerainty. In 1295 he tried to cancel the treaty and to settle the problem once and for all. Although he had always been an ally of the English king, in the first months of 1296, he allied himself with the French. Edward I of England could not tolerate this new alliance and ordered some nobles in Holland to kidnap the count. They succeeded in capturing Floris during a hunting party near Utrecht. When the conspirators were on their way with the count to England, the company was stopped by some countrymen. Some confusion arose in which the count, who tried to escape, was killed.

A political crisis followed the death of Floris V, which was only averted when John of Avesnes, count of Hainault, Floris' nephew, assumed power in 1299. In 1303, however, he could not prevent an invasion of Flemish troops, who were encouraged by their victory at Kortrijk in 1302. It was only after the defeat of the Flemish army at Zierikee that peace was restored.

During the reign of William III (1304–1337), who mostly remained in Hainault, comital prestige and power grew enormously. William was generally accepted as an arbitrator in international conflicts and married his children to distinguished partners. His oldest daughter, Margaret, married the Roman king, Louis of Bavaria, in 1324. In 1323, the conflict with Flanders was settled definitively to William's advantage. In Holland he delegated much of the administration of the country; extended the authority of the noble council; and improved financial accounting..

His son William IV (1337–1345), a chivalric character and an enthusiastic Crusader, organized a full-scale and expensive attack on Frisia in 1345. It was a total disaster, and the count was killed along with a great part of his noble army. As William had no legitimate children, the emperor then enfeoffed his wife Margaret with comital power in Holland and Zeeland.

Bavaria and Burgundy (14th c.–15th c.)

Margaret's reign witnessed the rise of conflicting interests, polarizing in parties which later would become known as *Hoeken* and *Kabeljauwen*. The *Kabeljauwen* kidnapped Margaret's son William from Hainault and declared him the rightful count. Margaret and the *Hoeken* were then defeated in a brief civil war, and William managed to restore full authority. In 1358 William either went insane or was seized with a cerebral hemorrhage. Since he could no longer govern his counties, he retired to a castle in Hainault, and his brother Albert took power.

Albert of Bavaria's reign covered the second half of the fourteenth century. During that period, he grew into one of the most influential princes of the Low Countries. He married his daughter Catherine to William of Gulik, and Joan to Wenceslas, king of Bohemia. Even more notable was the famous double wedding celebrated in Cambrai (1385), called "one of the most brilliant spectacles of the age," when John of Nevers married Margaret of Bavaria, Albert's third daughter, and Margaret of Burgundy wed

William of Bavaria, Albert's eldest son and heir to the throne. William received the county of Ostrevant and was appointed governor in Hainault. From that moment on, Albert increasingly remained in The Hague, where a small but thriving court, consisting of musicians, poets, rhetoricians, heralds, and a range of other artists, became a center for cultural and artistic life.

At home, Albert aimed at a balance of power to check party conflicts. Initially, he seemed to have succeeded, but, as his son William became more independent after 1385, struggles flared up again. In the summer of 1393 William fell in disgrace and some leading nobles were banished from Holland. Although William reconciled with his father in 1394, and both parties were active in the full-scale military campaigns against the Frisians in 1396, 1398, and 1399 (partly to confirm the reconciliation), the party spirit remained latent. In 1401 William bequeathed Frisia to his father and started preparations for military actions against his major enemy, the lord of Arkel. This war lasted until 1412.

During Albert's reign, Holland was transformed economically from a largely agrarian and rural society to an urban, commercial, and industrial one. This transformation was caused largely by changes in the physical geography of the countryside. A rising sea level, combined with a slow settling down of the soil, hampered the cultivation of cereals and compelled many farmers to switch over to industrial crops or cattle breeding. This led to a sharp rise of urban immigration. Several towns were enlarged, and an increasing part of the population became involved in export industries, such as the manufacture of textiles (Leiden, Amsterdam) and the brewing of beer (Haarlem, Delft, Gouda), and in foreign trade and shipping. The sea became more and more threatening. Dikes repeatedly had to be strengthened because of the danger of inundation. From the beginning of the fifteenth century, windmills were used to provide drainage.

Due to the continuing wars in the last decade of Albert's reign, Holland's financial and fiscal situations underwent a change. The need for regular income as well as extraordinary revenues increased. The towns were indispensable as a source of extra money. Therefore, the five big cities in Holland (Haarlem, Leiden, Delft, Gouda, and Amsterdam) became an important factor in politics. By 1425 their alliance was formalized in the Estates of Holland.

Albert's son William VI (1404–1417) was closely attached to France and Burgundy. After his death, he was succeeded by his only child, Jacqueline. Her reign can be regarded as a transitional period to the reign of the Burgundians. From the beginning, she was unable to obtain full recognition, because her uncle, John of Bavaria, also claimed comital authority. John was supported by Sigismund, the Roman king, and a revived *Kabeljauw party.* Jacqueline could rely on the *Hoeken,* but her husband, John, Duke of Brabant, a first cousin of Philip of Burgundy, was of little support to her. Personally, as well as politically, their marriage was a fiasco.

In 1419 the treaty of Woudrichem was concluded, by which John of Bavaria obtained actual power over a large part of Holland. After his sudden death in 1425, Jacqueline once again tried unsuccessfully to claim power. By the second quarter of the fifteenth century, Philip the Good had succeeded in absorbing Holland into his own political domains. In 1433, three years before her death, Jacqueline formally renounced the throne.

During the Burgundian reign, Holland was administered by governors, originating in the Hainault nobility. By the middle of the fifteenth century a specialization within the comital council had been established. Financial *(Rekenkamer)* and legal *(Hof van Holland)* departments, both seated in The Hague, were split off. Partisanship within the nobility, connected with faction struggle in the urban patriciate, flared up occasionally, especially in 1440–1445 when the governor, William of Lalaing, favored the *Hoeken.* The governorship of John of Lannoy (1448–1462) enjoyed a period of relative peace. When Charles the Bold was killed in battle against the Swiss (1477), the Estates forced the young duchess, Mary, to grant a "great privilege" which left effective control of political authority in the hands of the Estates. A few years later, Mary's husband, Maximilian, had to suppress several uprisings in the towns.

During the fifteenth century, the towns further developed into important centers of trade and industry. After two wars with the Hanseatic League, Holland was victorious. By 1500, a significant proportion of all Baltic trade and shipping had fallen into Holland's hands.

BIBLIOGRAPHY

Algemene Geschiedenis der Nederlanden. 4 vols. Haarlem: Fibula-Van Dishoeck, 1980–1982.

Cordfunke, E. H. P. *Gravinnen van Holland. Huwelijk en huwelijkspolitiek van de graven uit het Hollandse Huis.* Zutphen: Walburg, 1987.

de Boer, D. E. H. *Graaf en grafiek. Sociale en economische ontwikkelingen in het middeleeuwse 'Noord-Holland' tussen ± 1345 en ± 1415.* Leiden: New Rhine, 1978.

de Boer, D. E. H., E. H. P. Cordfunke and F. W. N. Hugenholtz, ed. *Holland in wording. De ontstaansgeschiedenis van het graafschap Holland tot het begin van de vijftiende eeuw.* Hilversum: Verloren, 1991.

Koch, A., and J. G. Krucisheer, ed. *Oorkondenboek van Holland en Zeeland tot 1299,* 3 vols. The Hague: Nijhoff, 1970, Assen and Maastricht: Van Gorcum, 1986, 1992.

Jansen, H. P. H. "Holland's Advance." *Acta Historicae Neerlandicae* 10 (1978): 1–19.

———. "Modernization of the government: the advent of Philip the Good in Holland." *Bijdragen en Mededelingen betreffende de Geschiedenis der Nederlanden* 95 (1980): 254–264.

Jansma, T. S. *Raad en rekenkamer in Holland en Zeeland tijdens hertog Philips van Bourgondië.* Utrecht: Kemink, 1932.

Oostrom, F. P. van. *Court and culture: Dutch literature, 1350–1450.* Berkeley: University of California Press, 1992.

Spading, K. *Holland und die Hanse im 15. Jahrhundert.* Weimar: Böhlau, 1973.

Anteuen Jansen

SEE ALSO
Concordat of Worms; Friesland; Jacob van Maerlant; Stokes, Melis; Utrecht; Wenceslas

Holy Lance

The *Heilige Lanze* is part of the royal insignia of the medieval empire; today, it is housed in Vienna. Both its origin and its arrival in Germany are controversial; it is not, however, the "holy lance" discovered by crusaders in 1099.

According to Liudprand of Cremona (*Liber Antapodosis,* 4, 24.25) the lance, containing a nail from Christ's cross, was given by Count Samson to Rudolph II of Burgundy circa 922. Probably in 926, after the failure of his Italian campaign, Rudolph presented the lance to the German king Henry I in return for Burgundian control over Basel.

Otto I began the lance's association with Saint Maurice by building a new monastery in Magdeburg in honour of this Roman-Burgundian warrior saint. Otto also carried it into battle at Birten (939) and at the Lech (955). Thus, the lance reflected the king's status as chief warrior of the realm.

BIBLIOGRAPHY

Büttner, Heinrich. *Heinrichs I. Südost- und Westpolitik.* Constance: Thorbecke, 1964.

Eickhoff, Ekkehard. *Theophanu und der König. Otto III und seine Welt.* Stuttgart: Klett Cotta, 1996.

Madelyn Bergen Dick

SEE ALSO

Henry I; Lechfeld, Battle of; Otto I; *Reich*

Hornburg, Lupold (fl. mid-14th c.)

Next to nothing is known about the life of Lupold Hornburg, whose four rhymed orations *(Reimreden)* and one strophical song are preserved in the *Hausbuch* (house book) of Michael de Leone, canon and protonotary in Würzburg. Compiled circa 1350, the manuscript names Rothenburg ob der Tauber as Hornburg's hometown.

All four *Reimreden* deal with the political circumstances of 1347/1348. Preaching as a layman, Hornburg denounces the defective rule of clerical and secular princes in his *Landpredigt* (rural sermon), alluding both to the late emperor, Louis the Bavarian, and the new king, Charles IV. In an extensive complaint about the era's bad times, he interprets contemporary plagues as divine warnings against the generally wicked behavior of the mighty, makes apocalyptic insinuations, and ends with a wish for a strong emperor.

Des Reiches Klage (complaint about the empire) is largely based on a poem by East Franconian cleric Otto Baldemann, which, in turn, is an augmented translation of Würzburg archdeacon Lupold von Bebenburg's Latin *Ritmaticum* (rhymed work). In a dream, the poet meets a lady who reveals herself as the Roman Empire personified. She gives a short survey of the empire's glorious history from Julius Caesar to Henry II, presenting Charlemagne as the ideal ruler, and then deplores the current reign of kings, pope, and princes. The lady urges the poet to deliver her lament to the assembly of princes in Passau in July 1348, which Hornburg reports having done. The appearance of the "false Waldemar," a pretender to the throne of Brandenburg, in the summer of 1348, gave Hornburg the occasion to further complain about bad times and rulers in *Der Zunge Streit* (dispute of the tongue), in which he claimed that both princes and the emperor were obliged to serve the empire and not their own interests.

The fourth *Reimrede* is considered an early specimen of the *Ehrenrede,* a genre more common in the late four-teenth century. Probably composed in September 1347, it is a eulogy upon the death of Franconian nobleman Konrad von Schlüsselberg, whom Hornburg praises as a dutiful, unselfish knight. As the manuscript indicates, the three strophes of *Von allen Singern* ("On all the Singers") are cast in the *Langer Ton* (long verse) of Der Marner, a thirteenth century *Spruchdichter* (poet). In the first stanza, Hornburg lists twelve poets, mostly thirteenth century *Spruchdichter,* repeating the enumeration in the third stanza. The second strophe praises Reinmar (von Zweter) as the best of them. Hornburg's song is the first to name twelve poets no longer living, but they correspond only partially with the *Meistersinger's* twelve old masters.

BIBLIOGRAPHY

Bell, Clair Hayden, and Erwin G. Gudde, ed. *The Poems of Lupold Hornburg,* Berkeley and Los Angeles: University of California Press, 1945.

Henkel, Nikolaus. "Die zwölf alten Meister." *Beiträge zur Geschichte der deutschen Sprache und Literatur.* 109 (1987): 375–389.

Schanze, Frieder. "Hornburg, Lupold." In *Die deutsche Literatur des Mittelalters: Verfasserlexikon,* ed. Kurt Ruh, et al. 2nd ed., vol. 4. Berlin: de Gruyter, 1983, cols. 143–146.

Gert Hübner

SEE ALSO

Marner, Der; Meistersinger; Preaching and Sermons, Dutch; Reinmar von Zweeter; Versification

Housebook, Master of the (fl. ca. 1470–1500)

Also known as Master of the Amsterdam Cabinet, this anonymous printmaker, draftsman, and painter was active in the Middle Rhine area from circa 1470 to about 1500. His various names are derived from two groups of works attributed to him with certainty: parts of *The Medieval Housebook* (Schloss Wolfegg, Private Collection) and a group of eighty-nine drypoint engravings, eighty of which are today in the print cabinet at the Rijksmuseum in Amsterdam. Although his style was very influential in Germany, it has proved difficult to decide exactly which other works may be attributed to the Master and to identify him. Newer research has focused on a description of his working style.

The drypoint group includes religious subjects, as well as others reflecting courtly life of the late Middle Ages.

Master of the Housebook. The Young Man and Death (Amsterdam: Rijksmuseum). *Photograph: Rijksmuseum-Stichting Amsterdam*

Humorous subjects are characterized by their naturalism and spontaneous character. Dated from circa 1470 to 1490, the engravings display a development from small size and simple and hesitant drawing in the early sheets to an assured spatial representation and a more refined technique in the later ones.

The illustrations in the so-called *Housebook* are mainly technical drawings connected with sections on mining and military affairs. Preceding this section are drawings of the planets of the royal children, and of courtly scenes. The best of the planet drawings, Mars, Sol, and Luna, are most often attributed to the Master because of their similarities to his drypoints. The attribution of the remaining drawings is controversial since, although some show similarity to his earlier work, there are stylistic differences in the drawing.

A few drawings and miniatures as well as paintings, including the *Pair of Lovers* in Gotha and the altarpieces of the Passion in Speyer and the Life of the Virgin in Mainz, have been wholly or partially attributed to him. He may also have provided designs for stained glass which reflect his work in the prints and the *Housebook*.

BIBLIOGRAPHY

Graf zu Waldburg Wolfegg, Christoph, ed. *Das mittelalterliche Hausbuch: Faksimile und Kommentar.* 2 vols. Munich: Prestel, 1997.

Hess, Daniel. *Meister um das "mittelalterliche Hausbuch": Studien zur Hausbuchmeisterfrage.* Mainz: P. von Zabern, 1994.

Hutchison, Jane Campbell. *The Master of the Housebook.* New York: Collectors Editions, 1972.

Livelier than Life: The Master of the Amsterdam Cabinet or the Housebook Master, ca. 1470–1500. Amsterdam: Rijksprentenkabinet, Rijksmuseum, 1985. Exhibition catalog.

Marta O. Renger

SEE ALSO
Gothic Art and Architecture, Late; Mainz; Printmaking; Speyer

Hrabanus Maurus (ca. 780–February 4, 856)

The name Hrabanus derives from the Old High German word for "raven"; Maurus is a nickname he acquired later, perhaps from his teacher Alcuin, and it pays tribute to his dutiful piety as a disciple: Saint Maurus was Saint Benedict's favorite pupil. For his encyclopedic learning and the energy he manifested in administration and teaching, Hrabanus Maurus was dubbed in early modern times *praeceptor Germaniae* (the teacher of Germany).

Born at Mainz around 780 of noble Frankish parents, Hrabanus was given as a child to the monastery of Fulda. There, he was ordained deacon (801) before being sent for further education under Alcuin at Tours. He returned to Fulda, first as head of the cloister school and later as abbot (822–842). Upon resigning as abbot, he went into seclusion near Fulda at Petersberg. Later, he was named archbishop of Mainz (847), an office he held until his death on February 4, 856.

Hrabanus made a major contribution in educating young men, such as Otfrid von Weißenburg, Lupus of Ferrières, and Walahfrid Strabo, who became the foremost churchmen, scholars, and poets of the next generation.

Unfortunately, he is also remembered for one major failure in mentoring: he first forced Gottschalk of Orbais, a monk at Fulda, to take the tonsure against his will and later persecuted him, with severe beatings and imprisonment, for his beliefs on predestination.

Many of Hrabanus' numerous writings are derivative compilations. He sought to make available the scholarship of earlier eras by taking extracts from original works and knitting them together into a coherent whole, so that students and churchmen who did not have extensive libraries at their disposal could find in his works the essentials they needed for building their faith and extending their intellectual training.

De institutione clericorum (On the education of the clergy) is typical of Hrabanus' oeuvre in being replete with excerpted material. The first book sets forth the various ecclesiastical grades, liturgical vestments, and instruction to be given to catechumens; the second deals with liturgy; and the third focuses on liberal education, especially with the goal of training preachers.

Hrabanus wrote biblical commentaries on the historical books of the Old Testament (Pentateuch), some prophets (Jeremiah and Ezekiel), one of the Gospels (Matthew), and the epistles of Paul. In his exegeses, Hrabanus consistently excerpts patristic writers, such as Isidore and Bede, and supplies little of his own writing apart from allegorical and mystical interpretations.

Hrabanus's erudition and writing ability perhaps culminated in his encyclopedic *De rerum naturis* (later called *De universo*), in which he relies on Isidore's *Etymologies* as both source and inspiration. As in his exegeses, Hrabanus distinguishes himself from his predecessor by supplying allegorical explications.

Among his poems, the most successful was the *De laudibus sanctae crucis,* the first book of which contains a collection of twenty-eight *carmina figurata* (pattern or figure poems) that are arranged to form intricate designs. The second book offers a prose paraphrase.

Most of his other poems are conventional compositions in distichs and hexameters, but he also wrote rhythmic poetry and hymns.

Hrabanus, although not original, was an erudite and prolific scholar, whose efforts in extracting and synthesizing the writings of earlier interpreters served well the needs of his contemporaries and successors.

BIBLIOGRAPHY

Brunhölzl, Franz. *Histoire de la littérature latine du moyen âge,* vol. 1 "De Cassiodore à la fin de la renaissance carolingienne"; vol. 2 "L'époque carolingienne," trans. Henri Rochais, with bibliographic supplements by Jean-Paul Bouhot. Turnhout: Brepols, 1991, pp. 84–98, 282–286.

Dümmler, Ernst, ed. *Hrabani Mauri carmina.* In: *Monumenta Germaniae Historica Poetae Latini Aevi Carolini 2.* Berlin: Weidmann, 1884, pp. 154–258.

Knöpfler, Alois, ed. *Rabani Mauri de institutione clericorum libri tres.* Veröffentlichungen aus dem Kirchenhistorischen Seminar München. Munich: Verlag der J. J. Lentner'schen Buchhandlung, 1900.

Kottje, Raymund. "Hrabanus Maurus." In *Die deutsche Literatur des Mittelalters: Verfasserlexikon,* ed. Kurt Ruh, et al. 2nd ed. Berlin and New York: de Gruyter, 1988, vol. 4, cols. 166–196.

Migne, J.-P., ed. *Patrologiae cursus completus; series latina,* 221 vols. Paris: J.-P. Migne, 1844–1864, vols. 107–112.

Jan M. Ziolkowski

SEE ALSO

Charlegmagne; *Isidore;* Latin Language; Otfrid; Walahfrid Strabo

Hrosvit of Gandersheim (10th c.)

Born in the fourth decade of the tenth century, Hrosvit lived and wrote in the Gandersheim Abbey in Saxony, during the abbey's "Golden Age" under Gerberga II's rule. Her name, "Strong Voice (or Testimony)," expresses her poetic mission; the glorification of Christian heroes, both secular and religious. The subject of her poems are the Ottonians and the whole Liudolf dynasty as well as the saints and martyrs of the Christian church. Writing in Latin, mostly in leonine hexameters and rhymed, rhythmic prose, Hrosvit chose hagiographic plots for her legends and plays and contemporary and near-contemporary events for her secular epics.

Her works are arranged in three books, organized generically and chronologically, and delineated as such by prefatory and dedicatory materials. Book One contains eight legends *(Marian, Ascencio, Gongolf, Pelagius, Basilius, Theolphilus, Dionysius, and Agnes);* all but *Pelagius,* which she claims to have composed based on an eyewitness report, are based on biblical, apocryphal, and hagiographic texts.

Book Two, Hrosvit's best-known and most controversial work, contains six dramas, based, she claimed, on the comedies of Terence. For his alluring, but morally perilous, mimetic powers, she said she wished to substitute the glorious and morally beneficial ideals of militantly chaste Christianity. She chose the dramatic form, she argued, because the sweetness of Terence's style attracted many readers who, in turn, became corrupted by the wickedness of his subject matter. Of her six plays, two (*Dulcitius* and Sapientia) deal with the martyrdom of three allegorical virgins during the persecution of Christians under Diocletian and Hadrian; two concern the salvation of repentant harlots (*Abraham* and *Paphnutius*); and two (*Gallicanus* and *Calimachus*) are conversion plays.

Her two extant epics in Book 3, narrate the rise of the Ottonian dynasty (*Gesta Ottonis,* or Deeds of the Ottonians) and the foundation of the Gandersheim Abbey *(Primordia).* Throughout all her works, Hrosvit extols the ideals of monastic Christianity and exhorts her audience and readers to imitate and emulate her saintly models.

BIBLIOGRAPHY

Wilson, Katharina, trans. and ed. *Hrotsvit of Gandersheim: a florilegium of her works.* Woodbridge (Suffolk) and Rochester, N.Y.: Brewer, 1998.
———. trans. *The plays of Hrotsvit of Gandersheim.* New York: Garland, 1989.

Katharina M. Wilson

SEE ALSO
Drama; Latin Language;

Hugo von Langenstein (fl. late 13th c.)

In the late Middle Ages, religious literature, both hagiographic or legendary, gained tremendously in popularity. The famous *Martina* legend was first composed by Hugo von Langenstein, who was born into a family of lower nobility in the vicinity of Constance. Together with his father, Arnold, and three brothers, he joined the Teutonic Order and is mentioned in documents produced in Basel and Freiburg im Breisgau between 1271 and 1298. Inspired by the Dominicans — possibly his own sister Adelheid — Hugo wrote *Martina,* completed in 1293, in the form of a Latin *vita* (saint's life). It consists of 32,588 verses and has come down to us in one manuscript.

In it, Hugo outlined the basic Christian principles using the story of the Roman woman martyr Martina as his narrative framework. According to the *vita,* when Martina turned Christian and refused to pray to pagan gods, Emperor Alexander Severus ordered her to be tor-

tured. But, with the help of God's grace, she survived all punishments, thereby converting many people to Christianity. Eventually, she was beheaded and, later, became a highly regarded martyr.

The extensive didactic sections in Hugo's *Martina* are partly based on Pope Innocence III's *De miseria conditionis humanae* (On the Misery of the Human Condition) and Hugo Ripelin of Strasbourg's (d. before 1270) treatise on "the true theology," *Compendium theologicae veritatis,* among other writings. The text probably served as reading material during dinner in the convents of the Teutonic Order and is, therefore, divided into 292 sections. Although *Martina* was aimed at providing theological teaching, Hugo also discussed the proper ways to lead one's life and dealt with such topics as salvation, the coming of the antichrist, and Christian virtues.

Konrad von Würzburg exerted considerable influence on Hugo von Langenstein's writing. *Martina* seems to have been well known among the Teutonic Knights in succeeding centuries, and Johannes von Saaz (Tepl) reflects certain aspects of Hugo's text in his dialogic prose dispute between the devil and a farmer in "The Plowman from Bohemia" (*Ackermann aus Böhmen,* ca. 1401).

BIBLIOGRAPHY

Borst, Arno. *Mönche am Bodensee, 610–1525.* Sigmaringen: Thorbecke, 1978.
Steer, Georg. "Hugo von Langenstein." In *Die deutsche Literatur des Mittelalters. Verfasserlexikon.* 2nd, rev. ed. Kurt Ruh, et al., vol. 4. Berlin: de Gruyter, 1983, cols. 233–239.
von Langenstein, Hugo. *Martina,* ed. Adalbert von Keller. Stuttgart: Litterarischer Verein, 1856.

Albrecht Classen

SEE ALSO
Deutschorden; Konrad von Würzburg; Legends

Hugo von Montfort (1357–April 4, 1423)

The Styrian poet Hugo von Montfort lived in a transitional period between the Middle Ages and the Renaissance. Hugo wrote in the style of traditional courtly love poetry, *Minnesang,* but his songs also reflected his personal life, his relationship with his three wives, and the literary scene of his time. Moreover, Hugo specifically addressed the question of what literary genres were available to him and how to use them for his lyrical compositions.

Hugo was the second son of the powerful Count Willhelm III of Montfort-Bregenz and founded, through his marriage with Margarete von Pfannberg (1373, d. 1392), a new family branch of the Montforts. Because of his social status, he received an excellent education and was thoroughly familiar with classical and medieval literature. His texts refer not only to medieval German heroic and courtly poetry, but also indicate his familiarity with the French *Roman de la Rose* (completed in ca. 1370). Throughout his life, Hugo held many influential posts as administrator and judge in the Hapsburgian lands of Styria, Tyrol, and Bregenz. He also participated in a Crusade against the heathen Prussians in 1377 and took an active part in the management of his own large estates. In 1396 Hugo married Clementia von Toggenburg, who died in 1400, and in 1402, Anna von Neuhaus, who survived her husband by at least five years. Between 1413 and 1415, Hugo served as governor of Styria for Duke Leopold IV, who also sent him to the Council of Constance in 1414. The wealth of extant historical documents pertaining to Hugo provides a picture of his life in great detail.

In his *Rede* (didactic poem) no. 31, composed in 1401, Hugo takes stock of his oeuvre, listing seventeen other *Reden,* three poetic letters, mostly addressed to his wives, and ten love songs. In the following years he composed three *Reden,* three letters, and one song — a sum of thirty-eight pieces comprising 3,694 verses. Hugo commissioned a scribe to copy his texts in a manuscript, today housed in the Heidelberg University Library (manuscript no. cpg. 329). Since he was not musically inclined the musician Bürk Mangolt created the melodies for his songs (see no. 31, 177).

Insofar as Hugo's texts dealt mainly with personal concerns and refrained from ideological, religious, and military themes, they seem not to have reached a wide audience and were quickly forgotten after his death. Like Oswald von Wolkenstein, Hugo was independently wealthy and did not need to rely on his poetry for income. Both in his more traditional dawn songs and in his highly innovative songs idealizing the happiness of married life, the poet deliberately turned from political reality into the ideal of his private life and emphasized the transitoriness of human existence.

BIBLIOGRAPHY

Classen, Albrecht. *Die autobiographische Lyrik des europäischen Spätmittelalters.* Amsterdam and Atlanta: Editions Rodopi, 1991.

———. "Hugo von Montfort,—a Reader of the 'Roman de la Rose?'" *Monatshefte* 83 (1991): 414–432.

Goheen, Jutta. "Hugos von Montfort Version vom Paradies auf Erden, eine spätmittelalterliche Interpretation des Gralswunders." *Carleton Germanic Papers* 7 (1979): 26–36.

Meyer, Anke Sophie. *Hugo von Montfort: Autorenrolle und Repräsentationstätigkeit.* Göppingen: Kümmerle, 1995.

Moczygemba, Gustav. *Hugo von Montfort.* Fürstenfeld: G. Moczygemba, 1967.

von Montfort, Hugo. *Die Texte und Melodien der Heidelberger Hs. cpg 329,* ed. F. V. Spechtler. Göppingen: Kümmerle, 1978.

Albrecht Classen

SEE ALSO
Minnesang; Oswald von Wolkenstein

Hugo von Trimberg (1230/1240–ca. 1313)

Documented (1290) as teacher *(magister/rector scolarum)* of St. Gangolfstift in Teuerstadt near Bamberg, Hugo composed twelve works, seven of which survive. Among his four Latin texts, aids for teaching and preaching, the *Registrum Multorum Auctorum,* listing some eighty authors from classical antiquity to the Middle Ages, established a canon of Latin literary learning which was still observed as late as the seventeenth century.

The surviving work in Middle High German, *Der Renner,* about 24,600 verses, lives on in seventy manuscripts, and was printed at Frankfurt am Main in 1549. This gnomic text rivalled Wolfram von Eschenbach's *Parzival* in popularity for some time. Its thematic scope made the *Renner* a forerunner of the *Narrenliteratur* of Heinrich Wittenweiler and Sebastian Brant. The schema of the seven cardinal sins (medieval German, *hôchvart / Latin, superbia, gîtikeit/avaritia, frâz/gula, zorn/ira, nît/ invidia, unkiusche/luxuria, lazheit/accedia)* structured a vision of late medieval *societas Christiana* (Christian society) ruled by greed, as demonstrated in commerce and usury. The *Renner* documents an anxious view of early capitalism, a system seen to be deriving its impetus from Satan. Striving for money in this text separates the foolish rich from the wise and willing poor.

The *Renner's* stylistic diversity exemplifies the art of gnomic writing in the vernacular. Biblical examples, folk narrative, well worn fables, and quotations from classical and medieval authorities are used to support the author's attempt to lead fellow Christians from sin to virtue. For the literary and social historian, this extensive gnomic text provides a rich source for research into (late) medieval mentality. It portrays a deep ambivalence in Christian morality in relation to social roles of women, in the relationship of Christians to Jews, and in the view of *litterati* (the educated) regarding *illitterati* (the uneducated), and peasants *(rustici)* in particular. The *Renner* is an important representative of a popular literary genre which has left deep traces in the cultural memory.

BIBLIOGRAPHY

Ehrismann, Gustav, ed. *Der Renner von Hugo von Trimberg.* 4 vols. 1908–1911; rpt. ed. Günther Schweikle. Berlin: de Gruyter, 1970–1971.

Goheen, Jutta. *Mensch und Moral im Mittelalter.* Darmstadt: Wissenschaftliche Buchgesellschaft, 1990.

Rosenplenter, Lutz. *Zitat und Autoritätenberufung im "Renner" Hugos von Trimberg.* Frankfurt am Main: Lang, 1982.

Sprandel, Rolf. "Der Adel des 13. Jahrhunderts im Spiegel des Renner von Hugo von Trimberg." In *Otto von Botenglauben: Minnesänger, Kreuzfahrer, Klostergründer.* Würzburg: Schöningh, 1994, pp. 296–308.

Jutta Goheen

SEE ALSO
Wittenwiler, Heinrich; Wolfram von Eschenbach

Hunting and Hunting Literature

Hunting, often called *cynegetics,* was important in the Middle Ages as a form of recreation, as a means of procuring food, and as a source of symbolism. Although most people hunted, it became more and more the prerogative of the knight and the noble. Hunting was inextricably interwoven with forestry especially as the clearing of the land reduced the free forest, and the nobles set up forest preserves, a situation familiar to us from the stories of Robin Hood. If falconry be considered as a part of hunting, the part that hunting played in the life of the knight is extended greatly. Most of our literature, though written by court clerks *(ministeriales),* is about knights, and hunting, trapping, and fowling are reflected throughout the literature; in fact, they penetrate all aspects of the knight's life and seem as natural as the use of the telephone today. Thus it is that the Middle High German language itself reflects the importance of hunting. The word *bejagen* (to chase down) is used over sixty times in *Parzival,* often with the meaning of "to win love."

There are many hunting scenes in Middle High German literature, such as the death of Siegfried in the *Nibelungenlied* and the dismemberment of the deer in *Tristan.* Both the patron saint of the hunter, Saint Hubert, and Saint Eustace have stories connected with the hunt of the stag, and courtly love poetry *(minnesang)* is filled with the falcon theme. In iconography we find the theme of the Unicorn Chase, particularly in German art, with the unicorn (Mary) chased by a hunter with three dogs, named after the three cardinal virtues, Faith, Hope, and Charity.

It was quite natural, then, that extended metaphors and allegories using hunting should develop. The extensive European literature on hunting is reflected in German hunting poems: *Der entflogene Falke, Das Königsberger Jagdgedicht, Die verfolgte Hindin, Die Brackenjagd, Die Jagd der Minne, Drei Hunde als Beschützer.* The major allegory of the chase in Middle High German literature is Hademar von Laber's *Jagd* ("The Hunt"), a sustained allegorical stag chase of the fourteenth century. Other authors of hunting poems include Burkhard von Hôhenfels, Mechthild von Magdeburg, Peter Suchenwirt and Hugo von Montfort. In Old High German we find fragments of hunting poems, such as *Hirsch und Hinde* (Buck and Deer) and Notker Labeo's (d. 1029) famous exaggeration concerning the boar in his *Rhetoric.*

There were also German tractates dealing with the technical aspects of hunting, such as the *De arte bersandi,* the *Beizbüchlein, Die Lehre von den Zeichen des Hirsches,* the *Vogel Buech,* the *Puech zu der Waidmanschaft,* as well as translations of (mostly Latin) tracts, such as those of Petrus de Crescentiis and Albertus Magnus, all edited in *Quellen und Studien zur Geschichte der Jagd.* Although Frederick II's *De arte venandi cum avibus* (On the Art of Hunting with Birds), is a treatise on falconry, the emperor was interested in all types of hunting.

The animals of the chase,—the bison, the bear, the hare, the stag and the boar—were studied intensively, and their habits were well-known. This familiarity led to the extension of the animal fable inherited from antiquity in works such as *Reineke Fuchs* (Reynard the Fox), along with characteristics attributed to each animal, such as cunning to the fox, shyness to the hare, stupidity to the bear, etc. Also inherited from antiquity, but extended in medieval times, was the *Physiologus,* a work devoted to allegorizing the characteristics attributed to each animal. Animals of the chase, especially fictitious animals such as the dragon, were frequently used as symbols.

In religious literature, Satan was often represented as a fowler or a hunter, but also as an animal, such as a lion. The same treatment was accorded to Christ, who might also be represented as a hunter or as a lion (the Lion of Judah). Mary, the Mother of Christ, was often called "turtledove." Each of the implements of hunting—the snare, the bow, the arrow, the trap—as well as the dog and the horse, might also have been allegorized.

The hunt, as an integral and important part of medieval life, can be found everywhere, as witnessed by the number of words in modern German which derive from hunting terminology (German, *Weidmannssprache*).

BIBLIOGRAPHY

Dalby, David. *Lexicon of the medieval German hunt; a lexicon of Middle High German terms (1050–1500) associated with the chase, hunting with bows, falconry, trapping, and fowling.* Berlin: de Gruyter, 1965.

Lindner, Kurt, ed. *Quellen und Studien zur Geschichte der Jagd,* Berlin: de Gruyter, 1954ff.

Rösener, Werner, ed. *Jagd und höfische Kultur im Mittelalter.* Veröffentlichungeen des Max-Planck-Instituts für Geschichte 135. Göttingen: Vandenhoeck & Ruprecht, 1997.

Schwappach, Adam. *Handbuch der Forst- und Jagdgeschichte Deutschlands.* 2 vols. Berlin: J. Springer, 1885, 1888.

Thiébaux, Marcelle. *The Stag of Love: The Chase in Medieval Literature.* Ithaca: Cornell University Press, 1974.

Tilander, Gunnar, ed. *Cynegetica.* Series of editions and studies published in Sweden.

James W. Marchand

SEE ALSO

Frederick II; Gottfried von Straßburg; *Nibelungenlied;* Notker Labeo; *Physiologus; Reynard* the Fox, Dutch; Wolfram von Eschenbach

I

Iconographies, Innovative

[This entry includes twenty-one subentries:

Introduction

Twentieth-century scholars' understanding of the Gothic as a primarily French phenomenon has often led to the perception of German art and architecture, particularly of the thirteenth and fourteenth centuries, as a provincial, underdeveloped, or even misunderstood variant of the French standard. If German art of this period does frequently adopt French precedents, always varying the model so that their German character is never in ques-

tion, one of the areas in which it is truly innovative is in the development of new themes and subjects. While some of these make brief appearances in the twelfth century or even earlier, it is in the late thirteenth and early fourteenth that a wealth of new themes come into their own. The Wise and Foolish Virgins, for example, after its first, modest appearance circa 1140 at the royal abbey of St. Denis outside Paris, is given a more prominent role on the lintel of the Gallus Portal at Basel Cathedral some thirty to forty years later; a century later still it begins to appear in large scale as the major subject of easily visible door jambs. A number of these subjects arise or become popular in the charged mystical climate along the Upper Rhine; the lives of nuns recorded in the Dominican convents of this region and elsewhere indicate both the strongly visual character of their visions and some of the specific motifs that appear in works of art at the same time. Other subjects, such as the equestrian figure, can be associated with political motives, while still others have been related to the changing roles of women or new devotional practices.

Joan A. Holladay

SEE ALSO

Gothic Art and Architecture; Romanesque Art and Architecture; Sankt Katharinethal; Sister-Books; Visionary Literature; Women

Acts of Charity

Also known as the Acts of Mercy, this series of six kindnesses performed for Christ is described in Matt. 25: 34–36: "Then the king shall say to them that shall be on his right hand: Come ye blessed of my Father, possess you the kingdom prepared for you from the foundation of the

Basel, *Münster*, north side, Gallus Portal. *Photograph: Joan A. Holladay*

often associated with the image of heavenly reward, typically the Last Judgment. The sequence seems to have been especially preferred in the area of the Upper Rhine; in addition to the cycles at Basle and Strasbourg, the subject was represented in the reliefs of the lost mid-thirteenth-century rood screen at Strasbourg cathedral and in a north transept window from Freiburg cathedral circa 1250.

BIBLIOGRAPHY

Beyer, Victor, Christiane Wild-Block, and Fridtjof Zschokke. *Les vitraux de la cathédrale Nôtre-Dame de Strasbourg.* Corpus vitrearum medii aevi, France 9/1. Paris: Éditions du Centre nationale de la Recherche scientifique, 1986, pp. 482–493.

Die Zeit der Staufer: Geschichte—Kunst—Kultur, ed. Reiner Haussherr. 5 vols. Stuttgart: Württembergisches Landesmuseum, 1972, vol. 1, no. 411.

Haug, H. "Les oeuvres de miséricorde du jubé de la cathédrale de Strasbourg." *Archives alsatiennes de l'histoire de l'art* 2e série (1931): 99–122.

Schmitt, Otto. "Barmherzigkeit, Werke der Barmherzigkeit." *Reallexikon zur deutschen Kunstgeschichte.* 8 vols. to date. Stuttgart: J. B. Metzler, 1937ff., vol. 1, cols. 1457–1468.

Schweicher, C. "Barmherzigkeit." *Lexikon der christlichen Ikonographie.* 8 vols. Rome: Herder, 1968–1976, vol. 1, pp. 245–251.

Joan A. Holladay

SEE ALSO
Basel; Elizabeth of Hungary

world. For I was hungry, and you gave me to eat; I was thirsty, and you gave me to drink; I was a stranger, and you took me in; naked, and you covered me; sick, and you visited me; I was in prison, and you came to me."

To these six deeds, caring for the hungry, the thirsty, strangers and the homeless, the naked, the sick, and the incarcerated, a seventh was added after the middle of the twelfth century: burying the dead. The Acts were typically portrayed as two-figure scenes with one of three figures in the active role: an anonymous Samaritan, a particular saint noted for his or her charity, or Christ himself. In the earliest known example, the six reliefs flanking the Gallus portal on the north side of Basle cathedral (about 1170), the Acts are accomplished anonymously. At the church of St. Elizabeth in Marburg, the saint known for her charity to others performs the deeds in the left lancet of the mid-thirteenth century window dedicated to her life. Christ himself, identified by the cruciform halo, is the main actor in the window from the narthex (entrance structure) at Strasbourg cathedral (ca. 1320–1325). As in the biblical text, visual representations of the Acts are

Anna Selbdritt

The cult of Saint Anne (German, Anna) permeated Europe; however, it was in the Low Countries that the veneration of Saint Anne evolved into a true mother cult. At the end of the thirteenth century, Saint Anne's depiction with the Virgin Mary as a child expanded to include the Christ Child. This representation, particularly popular in Germany, forms the *Anna Selbdritt* (literally, Anne in a threesome). Saint Anne takes over Joseph's position in the Holy Family and becomes the matriarch of Christ's lineage, creating an earthly Trinity in contrast with the divine Trinity.

Jacobus de Voragine popularized the story of Saint Anne and her extended family through the *Golden Legend* (*Legenda aurea,* ca. 1255–1266). Jan van Denemarken (d. ca. 1545) and Peter Dorlant (1454–1507),

Annaselbdritt, from an early fourteenth-century Psalter. Engelberg, Stiftsbibliothek, Cod. 60, fol. 42r. *Photograph: Susan Marti*

working in Antwerp, shaped their versions of her life from the *Golden Legend,* and their works spread throughout the Low Countries after being translated into vernacular. Johannes Trithemius (1462–1516), one of the writers most dedicated to promulgating Saint Anne, presented her as a guide for the moral life of both men and women. He believed Saint Anne's power as the mother of Mary and grandmother of Jesus was almost unlimited.

Devotion to Saint Anne thrived at the local level. Pope Sixtus IV established her feast day in 1471, but many German dioceses had approved her feast day centuries before Rome. Churches, cloisters, chapels, hospitals, pilgrimage sites, and even bells were named after Sant Anne and give evidence to the popularity of her cult.

The growing debate surrounding the Immaculate Conception was a contributing factor to the popularity of Saint Anne and particularly of her image in the *Anna Selbdritt.* By focusing on Anne's exemplary life, the special privileges attending Mary's conception could be more persuasively presented. The elimination of Joachim, like

Joseph before him, implied the unsullied purity of Mary's conception. Saint Anne's legend became increasingly complicated in reference to Mary's perpetual virginity and Christ's lineage. St. Anne was accorded two more daughters, by other husbands, contributing to the development of the Trinubium (Anne's three marriages) and the Holy Kinship.

The multiplication of confraternities, brotherhoods, and guilds during the fifteenth and sixteenth centuries contributed to Saint Anne's cult. The earliest and most respected confraternity dedicated to Saint Anne was in Bremen in 1328. Its limited membership consisted of archbishops, priests, knights, and nobles. Many guilds called upon her, although she was primarily associated with the miner's and carpenter's guilds. Carpenters believed she created the first tabernacle through the birth of Mary. The poor, and particularly women, called on her for assistance during childbirth, at marriage and death, and in cases of barrenness and illness.

As devotion to Saint Anne diminished throughout Europe in the sixteenth century, the image of the *Anna Selbdritt* disappeared. The Council of Trent forbade the representation of the Trinubium in 1543–1563. The Holy Kinship, an expansion of the Trinubium, disappeared as well. Saint Anne's role was considered "misplaced devotion," though not strictly forbidden. Martin Luther, who had made his vows to Saint Anne on entering the priesthood, rejected her in 1525.

BIBLIOGRAPHY

Ashley, Kathleen, and Pamela Sheingorn, ed. *Interpreting Cultural Symbols: Saint Anne in the Late Medieval Society.* Athens: University of Georgia Press, 1990.

Gohr, Siegfried. "Anna Selbdritt." In *Die Gottesmutter: Marienbild in Rheinland und in Westfalen,* ed. Leonhard Küppers. 2 vols. Recklinghausen: Aurel Bongers, 1974, vol. 2, pp. 243–254.

Kleinschmidt, Beda. *Die Heilige Anna: Ihre Verehrung in Geschichte, Kunst und Volkstum.* Düsseldorf: L. Schwann, 1930.

Schaumkell, E. "Der Kultus der heiligen Anna am Ausgange des Mittlealters: Ein Beitrag zur Geschichte des religiösen Lebens am Vorabend der Reformation." Dissertation Universität Gießen, 1893.

Eileen P. McKiernan González

Arma Christi

The term *Arma Christi* (literally, weapons of Christ), refers to a representation of the instruments of the Passion.

Arma Christi from the Passional of Abbess Kunigunde. Prague, National and University Library, Ms. XIV A 17, fol. 10r. *Photograph: Národni Knihovna; Czech National Library*

As early as the fourth century, the Holy Cross was venerated as a symbol of Christ's triumph over Satan. During the Carolingian period, artists added other objects associated with the Passion, notably the lance, crown of thorns, scourge, and rod with sponge.

By the Gothic period, the *Arma Christi* had become a common artistic theme used in a wide range of contexts. The objects were still given offensive overtones when depicted as weapons used by Christ to combat Satan, as well as defensive nuances when displayed on a shield as a coat of arms. Most often, however, the *Arma Christi* were associated with the sufferings of the Passion and were employed to provoke empathetic veneration of Christ's torments. In this guise, the *Arma Christi* appear both as the primary subject and as amplifications of other themes; often appended to a Man of Sorrows or a Crucifixion, they were also depicted in conjunction with the Christ Child, the Madonna and Child, the *Pietà,* and the Last Judgment.

In keeping with the increasingly elaborated accounts of Christ's ordeal that characterize Gothic representations of the Passion, artists continued to expand the range of

arma to include the pillar of the Flagellation, tools for erecting the Cross, pincers, hammer, nails, ladder, dice, and the Five Wounds. As a compilation of objects associated with the various incidents of the story, these representations refer to multiple narratives in a single image. This artistic shorthand could thus encapsulate and convey the totality of Christ's sufferings.

BIBLIOGRAPHY

Berliner, Rudolf, "Arma Christi." *Münchner Jahrbuch der bildenden Kunst* 3/6 (1955): 35–152.

———. "Bemerkungen zu einigen Darstellungen des Erlösers als Schmerzensmann." *Das Münster* 9 (1956): 97–117.

Suckale, Robert. "Arma Christi: Überlegungen zur Zeichenhaftigkeit mittelalterlicher Andachtsbilder." *Städel-Jahrbuch* 6 (1977): 177–207.

Carol M. Schuler

Dance of Death

This theme (German, *Totentanz*) depicts the figure of Death, shown as a skeleton or a decaying corpse, leading a parade of living figures to their deaths. The living figures who fall prey to Death include both young and old, wealthy and poor, royalty and clergy, and thus serve to remind the viewer of the inevitability of death. In its earliest forms, this theme appears in late fourteenth-century French dramas and may have also been performed as part of Church liturgy. Popular interest in this theme may have resulted from the Black Death and the epidemic of 1373. By the fifteenth century, the theme had become extremely popular throughout Europe and was represented in a variety of media, including manuscripts, mural paintings, sculptures, and prints.

The theme of the Dance of Death is related to the thirteenth-century French legend, "The Three Living and The Three Dead." In this tale, three young noblemen meet three figures of Death who warn the youths against human vanity and speak about the transience of life. Similarly, many Dance of Death images include the warning words of the figure of Death as he leads the living away. Images like this are meant to encourage the viewer to repent and to lead a more pious life. Because the living figures in the Dance of Death represent all sectors of society, these images also served to critique the clergy and the wealthy and powerful. In any case, the figure of Death is a mocking and derisive figure, the great equalizer, who comes to dance away with the living, regardless of their status or position.

BIBLIOGRAPHY

Kozáky, István. *Geschichte der Totentänze.* 3 vols. Budapest: Magyar Töreneti Museum, 1936.

Rosenfeld, Hellmut. *Der mittelalterliche Totentanz: Entstehung, Entwicklung, Bedeutung.* Münster: Bohlau, 1954.

Stammler, Wolfgang. *Der Totentanz: Entstehung and Deutung.* Munich: Hanser, 1948.

Melanie Gesink Cornelisse

SEE ALSO
Basel

Equestrian Figures

Life-size, freestanding ancient Roman equestrian sculptures were known in Germany throughout the Middle Ages. The bronze example in Augsburg is likely to have been there since Roman times; the famous "Theodoric" brought from Ravenna to Charlemagne's court in Aachen was also likely an ancient Roman example renamed, as was the Marcus Aurelius figure in Rome, later known as Constantine. The image of an equestrian emperor was also produced by medieval craftsmen as early as the Metz Charlemagne figure of the ninth century, but in miniature, probably because the technique of casting monumental figures had gone out of practice and perhaps even been forgotten.

Instead of monumental figures, early medieval equestrians appeared mainly in miniature, on seals and coins, and not associated with the emperor but rather with high nobility. Local rulers were also depicted as equestrian figures in stone relief, first in Italy, on the Broletto facade in Milan, but later also in Zurich. The figures may be related to similar French stone relief equestrians that appeared on churches in southwest France, often identified as Constantine. The identification and placement of these figures has related them to a judicial function since courts of law were held in their close proximity. These features may link them with later examples.

The revival of monumental, freestanding life-size equestrian sculptures after ancient Roman fashion was achieved in the mid–thirteenth century, most likely related to the Italian-born Emperor Frederick II, who was closely associated with the German patrons responsible for their production in Bamberg Cathedral by Bishop Eg-

bert of Andechs Meran and by the archbishop of Magdeburg for the Old Market square.

BIBLIOGRAPHY

Grabar, André. "La Soie byzantine de l'évêque Gunther à la cathédrale de Bamberg." *Münchner Jahrbuch der bildenden Kunst* 7 (1956): 7–26.

Kaufmann, Virginia Roehrig. "The Magdeburg Rider: An Aspect of the Reception of Frederick II's Roman Revival North of the Alps," in *Intellectual Life at the Court of Frederick II Hohenstaufen.* Studies in the History of Art 44; Center for Advanced Studies in the Visual Arts Papers 24. Washington, D.C.: National Gallery of Art, 1994, pp. 63–88.

Mütherich, Florentine. "Die Reiterstatuette aus der Metzer Kathedrale," in *Studien zur Geschichte der europäischen Plastik: Festschrift Theodor Müller zum 19. April 1965.* Munich: Hirmer, 1965, pp. 9–16.

Thürlemann, Felix. "Die Bedeutung der Aachener Theodorich-Statue für Karl den Grossen (801) und bei Walafrid Strabo (829): Materialien zu einer Semiotik visueller Objekte im frühen Mittelalter." *Archiv für Kulturgeschichte* 59 (1977): 25–65.

Virginia Roehrig Kaufmann

SEE ALSO
Aachen; Augsburg; Bamberg; Carolingian Art and Architecture; Frederick II; Magdeburg; Metz; Zurich

Gnadenstuhl

The distinctive form of Trinity representation known as the *Gnadenstuhl* (Throne of Grace) consists of an enthroned God the Father holding, in his outstretched hands, the Crucifix. This image has its origins in the early twelfth century and expresses God's acceptance of His Son's sacrifice. It is thus fundamentally eucharistic and is first represented in an early twelfth-century Cambrai Missal (Cambrai, Bibliothèque municipale manuscript no. 224 [234]) illustrating the canon of the mass prayer *Te igitur,* where God is petitioned to accept the eucharistic sacrifice. Equally early is its depiction on a Hildesheim portable altar (London, Victoria and Albert Museum). It achieves monumental form in a large painted altarpiece of circa 1250–1270 from the St. Maria zur Wiesenkirche in Soest (Berlin, Stiftung Preussischer Kulturbesitz, Gemäldegalerie).

The dove of the Holy Spirit hovers above or between the two figures, adding a Trinitarian meaning to the

Gnadenstuhl, from an early fourteen-century Psalter. Engleberg, Stiftsbibliothek, Cod. 60, fol. 194. *Photograph: Susan Marti*

eucharistic image. In the thirteenth century, the *Gnadenstuhl* appears on an engraved paten from Walcourt of circa 1230 by Hugo d'Oignies (Namur, Soeurs de Notre Dame, Trésor d'Oignies) and at Psalm 109, the Sunday Vespers psalm, in a number of Mosan Psalters, where the dove flies sideways with one wingtip in the mouth of each figure, literally illustrating the Nicene Creed formulation that the spirit proceeded equally from the Father and the Son. It was here in the Mosan region (which was part of the Holy Roman Empire) that the office and feast of the Trinity were established first in the tenth and eleventh centuries. The Trinitarian meaning of the image is also stressed in its appearance at the litany in the two early thirteenth-century psalters of Hermann of Thuringia and Elizabeth of Hungary (Stuttgart, Württembergische Landesbibliothek, manuscript no. H.B.II and Cividale, Museo archeologico nazionale, manuscript no. CXXXVII) for it is in the litany that the creed is found.

BIBLIOGRAPHY

Braunfels, Wolfgang. *Die Heilige Dreifaltigkeit.* Düsseldorf: Schwann, 1954.

Kirschbaum, Engelbert. "Dreifaltigkeit, D3: Gnadenstuhl," in *Lexikon der christlichen Ikonographie.* 8 vols. Rome: Herder, 1968–1976, vol. 1, cols. 535–536.

Ligtenberg, Raphaeel. *Over den oorsprong en de eerste beteekenis van den genadestoel.* Collectanea Franciscana Neerlandica 3/1. s'Hertogenbosch: Teuling, 1932.

Schiller, Gertrude. *Iconography of Christian Art,* trans. Janet Seligman. 2 vols. Greenwich: New York Graphic Society Ltd., 1971–1972, vol. 2, pp. 122–124.

Judith Oliver

SEE ALSO

Elizabeth of Hungary; Soest

Holy Graves

The play *Quem quaeritis,* documented from the tenth century, reenacted the events of Easter morning. Three clerics dressed as the three Marys approached the "angel" who asked them, "Whom do you seek?" *(Quem quaeritis?)* before inviting them to verify for themselves that the crucified Christ had risen. The contemporary biography of Bishop Ulrich of Augsburg (d. 973) talks of burying a Host on Good Friday in an otherwise undefined "grave" *(Grab),* from which it was secretly removed on Easter morning. At other sites a crucifix was substituted for the Host. Like these early plays, the oldest preserved Holy Grave, a late-eleventh-century structure at Gernrode, gives visible form to these historical events.

The Gernrode group predicts in general terms the form and iconography of the more numerous Holy Graves of the thirteenth and fourteenth centuries: a room-sized architectural structure, with sculptural decoration depicting the conversation of the three Marys with the angel at Christ's empty tomb. Likewise the location in the south aisle is taken up by many of the later works.

Between 1260 and 1350, a number of Holy Graves appeared in the region of the Upper Rhine. That at Constance, which Peter Kurmann has redated to circa 1260, is the earliest preserved. Located in the tenth-century chapel of St. Mauritius, itself a copy of the rotunda of the Holy Sepulchre in Jerusalem, the Holy Grave retains the dodecagonal form of its exemplar. Small sculptural figures between the gables on the outside narrate scenes from the early life of Christ; those on the inside depict the three holy women buying salve from the apothecary and meeting the angel at the empty tomb. A wooden figure of the Magdalen from the Dominican women's convent at Adelshausen from the last quarter of the thirteenth century and an over-life-size Christ figure from Maria

Holy Grave from Strasbourg cathedral (Strasbourg, Musée de l'Oeuvre Notre-Dame). *Photograph: Joan A. Holladay*

Mödingen from the last third indicate that the more standard form of Holy Grave appeared about the same time. Influenced by contemporary tombs for well-placed clerics and laypeople, these groups included a life-size effigy of the dead Christ lying atop the sarcophagus under an architectural canopy. Against the back wall stand the three Marys, typically accompanied by the angel. The nearly simultaneous appearance of the Constance work and the more usual type suggests that the attempts by the scholars Schwarzweber and Forsyth to distingiush sharply between Holy Sepulchres—typically an architectural structure without sculptural decoration—and Holy Graves, with life-size figures, are overdone. What seems more important is that for about a century, these groups, like many of the other objects now commonly known as *Andachtsbilder,* answered the needs of pious Christians for visual images of the truths of their faith. That the Holy Graves served as the object of devotions and the stimulus for mystical partcipation in the events of Christ's life is documented in the so-called *Schwesternbuch* (nuns' book) documenting the religious practice of the nuns of St. Katharinenthal. The Holy Grave there probably belonged to yet another type: a wooden box, which contained a removable effigy, usually smaller than life-size, of the dead Christ. The interior lids of these boxes were often decorated with painted or relief figures of the Marys and angel or angels. The scholar Beyer identifies ten examples of the permanent, large-scale Holy Graves in Strasbourg in the fourteenth century; whether that of the 1330s in the St. Catherine chapel in the cathedral is before or after the similar monument in the cathedral at Freiburg im Breisgau (ca. 1130) is a matter of nationalist debate. Examples of the portable box type are preserved from the cloister at Lichtental (Karlsruhe, Badisches Landesmuseum), at the Maigrauge convent in Fribourg (Switzerland), and in the Schweizerisches Landesmuseum in Zurich. Both the stone and the wooden Christ figures frequently contained recesses in the chest or side for deposit of the Host between Good Friday and Easter.

BIBLIOGRAPHY

Beyer, Victor. *La Sculpture strasbourgeoise au 14ᵉ siècle.* Strasbourg: Compagnie des arts photoméchaniques, 1955, pp. 27–40.

Brooks, Neil C. *The Sepulchre of Christ in Art and Literature.* University of Illinois Studies in Language and Literature 7. Urbana: University of Illinois Press, 1921.

Dalmann, D. Gustaf. *Das Grab Christi in Deutschland.* Leipzig: Dieterich, 1922.

Das "St. Katharinentaler Schwesternbuch": Untersuchung, Edition, Kommentar, ed. Ruth Meyer. Tübingen: Max Niemeyer, 1995.

Forsyth, William. *The Entombment of Christ: French Sculptures of the Fifteenth and Sixteenth Centuries.* Cambridge, Mass.: Harvard University Press, 1970, pp. 5–21.

Kurmann, Peter. "Das Heilige Grab zu Konstanz: Gedanken zu seinem Sinngehalt." *Neue Zürcher Zeitung* 601 (Dec. 24, 1972): 41–42.

Noack, Werner. "Ein erstes Heiliges Grab in Frieburg." *Zeitchrift für Kunstgeschichte* 23 (1960): 246–252.

Schwarzweber, Annemarie. *Das heilige Grab in der deutschen Bildnerei des Mittelalters.* Freiburg im Breisgau: Eberhard Albert Universitätsbuchhandlung, 1940.

Joan A. Holladay

SEE ALSO

Constance; Gernrode; Gothic Art and Architecture; Sankt Katharinenthal; Wienhausen

Holy Kinship

A development of the iconography of *Anna Selbdritt* (Anna with Mary and the Christ child), the image of the Holy Kinship included St. Anne's extended family. This image grew as an alternative to the Tree of Jesse, giving Saint Anne the central role. This form, developed in the twelfth century, became extremely popular in Germany during the fourteenth and fifteenth centuries. The image grew out of the interest not only in the Immaculate Conception but in reference to Mary's perpetual virginity and the extension of Christ's lineage to include various of his apostles.

The Holy Kinship was elaborated in response to a reference in Matt. 12:46–50. Saint Jerome dismissed the reference to the "brothers of the lord" by explaining that brothers were equivalent to "the sons of my mother's sisters" at the time of the Gospels' composition. In one of his Bible commentaries, Haimo of Auxerre (fl. ca. 840–860) concluded that Anne must have had other daughters. This, in conjunction with the three Marys who witnessed Christ's resurrection, contributed to the development of the images of both the Trinubium and the Holy Kinship. The reasoning proceeds as follows: after Joachim's death, following the old law, Anne married his brother Cleophas and gave birth to Mary Cleophas, whose sons include James the Younger, Simon, Joseph the Righteous, and Judas. Upon Cleophas' death, Anne married Salome and had another daughter, Mary Salome. Mary Salome is the mother of Jacob the Elder and John the Evangelist. The three marriages of Saint Anne make up the Trinubium, her extended family, the Holy Kinship.

The Gospel of Matthew traces Christ's male genealogy down through his earthly father, Joseph, but the Tree of Jesse imagery, derived from the Gospel in the twelfth century, eliminates Joseph in favor of the Virgin. The Holy Kinship provides a wholly female alternative, maintaining the format of the Tree of Jesse with Saint Anne as its source. Esmerentina, Saint Anne's mother, became the source in a later development, supported by the Carmelites, which allowed the inclusion of Elizabeth, John the Baptist, and Saint Servatius. Sometime in the fourteenth century, the image of the Holy Kinship became entwined with the idea of a *Hortus Conclusus,* the closed garden that is a symbol for Mary's virginity. Saint Anne is surrounded by her daughters and their children within the garden. The respective husbands look over the wall or are not present.

In Germany the veneration of Saint Anne resembled a mother cult that permeated all levels of society. Saint Anne commanded universal appeal. Confraternities of the wealthy and middle classes believed her to be a member of their class, while the poor thought of her as their protector, calling on her during childbirth, marriage, death, barrenness, and illness. Saint Anne's popularity grew along with the expansion of guilds. She was primarily associated with the carpenter's guild and with miners. In many areas of Germany, popularity of her name was greater than that of Mary. Devotion to Saint Anne diminished throughout Europe in the sixteenth century. The Council of Trent forbade the image of the Trinubium in 1543–1563. The Holy Kinship, an expansion of the Trinubium, disappeared as well.

BIBLIOGRAPHY

Ashley, Kathleen and Pamela Sheingorn, ed. *Interpreting Cultural Symbols: Saint Anne in the Late Medieval Society.* Athens: University of Georgia Press, 1990.

Brandenburg, Ton. "St. Anne and Her Family: The Veneration of St. Anne in Connection with Concepts of Marriage and the Family in the Early Modern Period." In *Saints and She-Devils: Images of Women in the Fifteenth and Sixteenth Centuries,* ed. Léne Dresen-Coenders. London: Rubicon, 1987, pp. 101–127.

Gohr, Siegfried. "Anna Selbdritt." In *Die Gottesmutter: Marienbild in Rheinland und in Westfalen,* ed. Leonhard Küppers. 2 vols. Recklinghausen: Aurel Bongers, 1974, vol. 2, pp. 243–254.

Kleinschmidt, Beda. *Die Heilige Anna: Ihre Verehrung in Geschichte, Kunst und Volkstum.* Düsseldorf: Schwann, 1930.

Eileen P. McKiernan González

Johannesschüssel

The Gospels of Matthew (14:6–11) and Mark (6:21–28) relate the beheading of John the Baptist. King Herod was so pleased with the dance of his wife's daughter Salome on his birthday that he offered her whatever she wanted. Coached by her mother, who was angered that John had forbidden her marriage with her brother-in-law, she asked for the head of the Baptist on a salver. Herod had John beheaded and the head brought to the girl, who presented it to her mother.

As early as the tenth or eleventh century, the isolated image of the Baptist's head on the plate or platter (German, *Schüssel*) had appeared in Byzantine painting, where it served as an attribute of Saint John. The use of the image in western Europe begins in the thirteenth century. Among the large numbers of relics, including numerous relics of the Baptist, brought back to Europe by western Crusaders after the sack of Constantinople in 1204 was a large round silver plate, one of two found near the old imperial palace. Beginning in the thirteenth century, the image of the Baptist's head on a platter begins to appear both on seals and in life-sized sculptures in the round. The use on seals, especially those associated with members of the Order of the Knights of St. John, contributed to its spread. The sculptures are mostly found in southern Germany, Austria, and Tyrol. No single type predominates: the salver may be either flat or footed, the head may lie flat with the neck stump exposed or may be tilted up slightly for better visibility. The isolation of a particularly dramatic detail from a larger scene and their use in private devotional exercises place these works in the category of *Andachtsbilder* (devotional images), a characteristic subgroup of German Gothic sculptures.

BIBLIOGRAPHY

Arndt, Hella, and Renate Kroos. "Zur Ikonographie der Johannesschüssel." *Aachener Kunstblätter* 38 (1969): 243–328.

Joan A. Holladay

SEE ALSO
Gothic Art and Architecture

Johannesschüssel (Munich, Bayerisches Nationalmuseum). *Photograph: Joan A. Holladay*

Man of Sorrows

Representing a half-length portrait of Christ after his crucifixion, the Man of Sorrows (German, *Schmerzensmann;* Latin, *Imago Pietatis* [Image of Piety]) image contains elements which refer simultaneously to both his life and death. Although the wounds in his hands and side are evident, and he is shown with his eyes closed and his head dropped to the side, he stands erect and, in some variations, points to the wound in his side.

It is difficult to determine precisely the origins and development of this theme, but Panofsky and others have shown that it was originally a Byzantine motif, which was known and used in Italy by the twelfth century. The image type was popularized throughout western Europe in the fourteenth and fifteenth centuries, in part due to the efforts of the Carthusians who claimed that they owned the earliest image of this type in their titular church in Rome. According to the myth promoted by the Carthusians, the seventh-century pope St. Gregory had commissioned this image in order to record accurately a miraculous vision of the Man of Sorrows that had appeared to him during the performance of the Mass. For this reason, worshippers and pilgrims who said prayers before this image were offered generous indulgences. Although the Carthusian's image had probably originated in Constantinople and arrived in Rome around 1380, the popularity of this cult inspired the replication of this image in devotional prints and other pilgrim trinkets that served to spread the theme to the rest of Europe.

Even in some of its earliest examples, the Man of Sorrows was seen in several variations—with other characters from the Deposition scene or with other holy figures. In most of the earliest western forms of the image, the top and arms of the cross complete with its placard are shown behind Christ. In other depictions of the theme, Christ is shown with the *Arma Christi,* the implements of the Passion, such as the whipping scourge and the crown of thorns that make reference to his suffering as well as his eventual triumph. At times, the Man of Sorrows is held by angels on either side, or he is shown between the Virgin Mary and John the Baptist. In a later development of the theme, the Man of Sorrows appears as part of the Trinity; he is held by God the Father, and the Holy Spirit appears as a dove.

As several art historians have shown, many of these formal variations on the theme should be understood as artistic responses to the late medieval desire for a more direct and personal relationship with devotional images. Because of the half-length presentation of the Man of Sorrows, the medieval viewer was presented with a close-up portrait of Christ that was highly descriptive in its detail and could thereby bring the viewer closer to the actual experience of the Passion.

BIBLIOGRAPHY

Belting, Hans. *The Image and its Public in the Middle Ages.* New Rochelle: Aristide D. Caratzas, 1990, pp. 29–40.

Bertelli, Carlo. "The Image of Pity in Santa Croce in Gerusalemme." *Essays in the History of Art Presented to Rudolph Wittkower.* Ed. Douglas Fraser. London: Phaidon Press, 1967, pp. 40–55.

Panofsky, Erwin. "Imago Pietatis: Ein Beitrag zur Typengeschichte des 'Schmerzensmanns' und der 'Maria Mediatrix.'" In *Festschrift für Max J. Friedländer zum 60. Geburtstage.* Leipzig: E. A. Seemann, 1927, pp. 261–308.

Ringbom, Sixten. *Icon to Narrative: The Rise of the Close-up in Fifteenth-Century Devotional Painting.* Doornspijk: Davaco, 1984, pp. 107–147.

Stubblebine, J. H. "Segna di Buonaventura and the Image of the Man of Sorrows." *Gesta* 8/2 (1969): 3–13.

van Os, Henk W. "The Discovery of an Early Man of Sorrows on a Dominican Triptych." *The Journal of the Warburg and Courtauld Institutes* 41 (1978): 65–75.

Melanie Gesink Cornelisse

Mass of Saint Gregory

A legend that became popular in German art in the first quarter of the fifteenth century, the Mass of Saint Gregory reports that Pope Gregory I (ca. 540–604) had a parishioner who doubted the real presence of Christ in the elements of the Mass. After praying, the pope and the congregation had a vision of the suffering Christ within the chalice. The origins of the legend seem tied to the church of Santa Croce in Gerusalemme in Rome, where Pope Gregory was reputed to have said Mass and where there was a wonder-working image of Christ, supposedly donated by Gregory. This image of Christ and the story of the pope saying Mass were conflated in Germany into a depiction of Gregory's vision represented in a variety of media, including panel paintings and early printed books. The iconography of the legend was somewhat flexible and used many elements from other passion imagery, especially the *Arma Christi* (Weapons of Christ) and the Man of Sorrows.

A devotional image, the Mass of Saint Gregory celebrated the miracle of transubstantiation, and connected the Passion of Christ with the celebration of the Mass. The subject was particularly popular at sites with Corpus Christi or other eucharistic relics including Andechs on the Amersee, which possessed three hosts used by Saint Gregory, and Weingarten Abbey, which possessed a relic of the Holy Blood and which had an extremely early depiction of the legend on a manuscript leaf from the twelfth century. Images of the Mass of Saint Gregory sometimes carried indulgences, which were supposed to reduce the owner's time in purgatory and undoubtedly added to the image's popularity.

BIBLIOGRAPHY

Heinlen, Michael. "An Early Image of a Mass of St. Gregory and Devotion to the Holy Blood at Weingarten Abbey." *Gesta* 37 (1998): 55–62.

Westfehling, Uwe. *Die Messe Gregors des Grossen: Vision, Kunst, Realitat.* Cologne: Schnütgen Museum, 1982.

Susan L. Ward

Palmesel

The name *Palmesel* refers to the donkey on which Christ rode into Jerusalem on Palm Sunday. Representations of

Palmesel from the region of Constance (Gottlieben?) (Basel, Historisches Museum). *Photograph: Joan A. Holladay*

more typical in southern Germany, Austria, and Switzerland, and most of the fifty-odd preserved objects can be localized to these regions. In Zurich, for example, the ordo of Konrad von Mure, written about 1260, records the long-standing annual procession (*Liber ordinarius* 1995:237–241). A procession of clerics and townspeople went to the elevation known as the Lindenhof to meet a second group accompanied by the *Palmesel*. Palms were distributed in front of the sculpture as the whole group made its way back to the *Grossmünster* (church).

The tradition of the Palm Sunday procession and the making and use of *Palmesel* groups continued right up to the Reformation.

BIBLIOGRAPHY

Leuppi, Heidi, ed. *Die Liber ordinarius des Konrad von Mure: Die Gottesdienstordnung am Grossmünster in Zürich,* Spicilegium Friburgense 37. Fribourg: Universitätsverlag, 1995.

Lipsmeyer, Elizabeth. "Devotion and Decorum: Intention and Quality in Medieval German Sculpture." *Gesta* 34 (1995): 20–27.

———. "The Liber Ordinarius by Konrad von Mure and Palm Sunday Observance in Thirteenth-Century Zurich." *Manuscripta* 32 (1988): 139–145.

———. "Palmsonntag-Christus and Palmesel." *Volkskunst: Zeitschrift für volkstümliche Sachkultur* 12 (1989): 50–58.

Ostoia, Vera K. "A Palmesel at the Cloisters." *Metropolitan Museum of Art Bulletin* 14 (1956): 170–173.

Wiepen, Eduard. *Palmsonntagsprozession und Palmesel: Ein kultur- und kunstgeschichtlich-volkskundliche Abhandlung zum Kölner Palmesel der kunsthistorischen Ausstellung zu Düsseldorf 1902 (Sammlung Schnuutgen).* Bonn: P. Hanstein, 1903.

Joan A. Holladay

SEE ALSO
Constance; Essen; Zurich

this subject were usually three-dimensional wood sculptures, large if not life-sized, and outfitted with wheels so that they could be pulled in reenactments of the events of Palm Sunday. While Palm Sunday processions are known from the seventh century in Europe, the earliest mention of the use of an effigy or image in this paraliturgical context is in the *vita* (life) of Saint Ulrich, Bishop of Augsburg (d. 973). The oldest preserved sculptural example, from about 1200, is from the central Swiss village of Steinen. This example is typical in that Christ sits upright, his gaze directed forward; his right hand is raised in a gesture of blessing, and he holds a book or, more typically, the donkey's reins in his left.

While the Palm Sunday procession with a *Palmesel* is documented in fourteenth-century Essen, its use was

Pestkreuz

With the development of devotional images known as *Andachtsbilder* in the Late Middle Ages, there arose in the Rhineland a new image of the crucified Christ, so terribly tortured and scarred as to appear stricken with the plague. These violently dramatic and graphic devotional images were therefore referred to as plague crosses (*Pestkreuze*). The plague-stricken appearance of Christ does not, however, seem to have been inspired by the

Pestkreuz, Cologne, Sta. Maria im Kapitol. *Photograph: Rheinisches Bildarchly der Stadt Köln*

calamitous epidemics of the Black Death which ravaged Europe in the mid-fourteenth century. Rather, it can be seen as stemming from the rising preoccupation with the Passion, as seen in the increasingly elaborate descriptions of the torments of Christ. Already present in the thirteenth-century works of Pseudo-Bernard and Pseudo-Anselm, these traits of relentless and violent narrative description of the Passion became more common in the fourteenth century, as seen in the Passion Tract of Heinrich of St. Gall, the *Christi Leiden in einer Vision geschaut* (Christ's Passion as seen in a Vision), and Ludolph of Saxony's *Vita Christi* (Life of Christ). These texts, intended to inspire an increasingly emotional, subjective meditative experience, expound in great detail upon Christ's suffering.

A crucial text in this imagery was the book of Isaiah, which describes "the man of sorrows...thought as it were a leper" (53:4). The authors of the late medieval Passion tracts interpolated this passage into their accounts of Christ's suffering, so that Christ is beaten and tormented to the point of appearing leprous. The staggeringly sadistic details of the torments of Christ were particularly related to the Flagellation, as suggested in Isa. 1:6 and 63:1–2. The recitation of these passages during Holy Week rendered familiar this notion of Christ as *quasi leprosus.* This, coupled with the widespread circulation of violent narrative Passion texts based on this Old Testament imagery, may account for the frequency of such imagery in the North.

Possibly due to influence from the Cologne mystics, the *Pestkreuz* originated in the Rhineland. Examples include: Santa Maria im Kapitol (Cologne, dated 1304); Schnütgen-Museum (Cologne, ca. 1370, from Borken, Westphalia); San Giorgio dei Teutonici (Pisa, ca. 1315); St. Quirin (Neuss, ca. 1370, formerly in the Maria-Ablaß-Kapelle, Cologne); and the Hospice de Brioude (Haute-Loire, mid-fourteenth century). The influence of the dramatic crucifixion images, such as the *Pestkreuze,* can be seen in the mid-fourteenth-century writings of Bridget of Sweden (*Revelationes,* book 4). By the fifteenth century this type of image appears to have largely fallen from favor. However, the sporadic continuation of the *Pestkreuz* type can be seen in Matthias Grünewald's Isenheim Altarpiece of circa 1510.

BIBLIOGRAPHY

Francovich, Geza de. "L'Origine e la Diffusione del Crocifisso Gotico Doloroso." *Kunstgeschichtliches Jahrbuch der Biblioteca Hertziana* 2 (1938): 145–261.

Marrow, James H. *Passion Iconography in Northern European Art of the Late Middle Ages and Early Renaissance: A Study of the Transformation of Sacred Metaphor into Descriptive Narrative.* Kortrijk: Van Ghemmert, 1979.

Mühlberg, Fried. "Crucifixus Dolorosus: Über Bedeutung und Herkunft des gotischen Gabelkruzifixes." *Wallraf-Richartz-Jahrbuch* 22 (1960): 69–86.

———. "Zwei rheinische Kruzifixe der Gotik." *Jahrbuch der rheinischen Denkmalpflege* 23 (1969): 179–205.

Ruh, Kurt, ed. *Der Passionstraktat des Heinrich von St. Gallen,* Thayngen: K. Augustin, 1940.

Thoby, Paul. *Le crucifix, des origines au Concile de Trente.* Nantes: Bellanger, 1959.

von Alemann-Schwarz, Monika. *Cruzifixus dolorosus. Beiträge zur Polychromie und Ikonographie der rheinischen Gabelkruzifixe.* Dissertation Universität Bonn, 1973. Bonn: [n.p.], 1976.

Witte, Fritz. "Mystik und Kreuzesbild um 1300." *Zeitschrift für christliche Kunst* 33 (1920): 117–124.

Scott Bradford Montgomery

SEE ALSO

Gothic Art and Architecture; Ludolf of Saxony

Pietà

Also known as the *Vesperbild,* the *Pietà* presents an image of the Virgin Mary, seated with the crucified Christ in her lap. While there exist two-dimensional depictions of this theme, the term *Pietà* usually refers to representations that were sculpted in the round and intended for devotional contemplation. The first *Pietàs* were created for German convents around the beginning of the fourteenth century. In part, this theme appears to have been motivated by the writings of German mystics, such as Mechthild of Hackeborn (1247–1289), who encouraged her readers to meditate on Christ's wounds as he lay in his mother's lap. Around 1300, the Good Friday vespers began to include a meditation on this theme, resulting in the term *Vesperbild* to describe the sculpted images. By the later fourteenth century, the *Pietà* became popular in France, but it did not appear in Italy until after 1400. By the fifteenth century, the theme became widespread throughout Europe.

Often, sculptures of the *Pietà* were located on the secondary altars of churches, in close proximity to worshippers. Many of them were believed to work wonders. Viewers of such works were meant to meditate on the five wounds of Christ, which were understood to have healing and redemptive powers. In some cases, the host was kept inside the wound in Christ's side. In addition to meditating on the Passion and suffering of Christ, the *Pietà* image was also intended to focus attention on the suffering of Mary. Visually, the depiction of Mary holding her dead son recalls images of the Virgin and Child, and the miracle of the Incarnation. In this way, Mary's grief is made more poignant as her maternal role is emphasized. In addition, the theme draws a parallel between the Incarnation and the Passion of Christ, as two integral aspects of Redemption.

Several scholars have examined the theme of the *Pietà* in comparison to the narrative scene of the Lamentation. These studies help to clarify the particular character of the *Pietà* as a private devotional theme. Where the Lamentation shows many mourners and a dramatic outpouring of grief, the *Pietà* presents a still and solemn configuration, a private moment between a mother and her dead son.

The earliest style of *Pietàs* in Germany was rather harsh and grim, showing a rigidly posed, upright Christ placed on the lap of his agony-stricken mother. However,

with the International Style in the second half of the fourteenth century, the *Schöne Pietà* became more popular, employing a gentler and more tender mood as well as more delicate modeling. In later works, Christ was usually placed diagonally across Mary's lap or on the ground with his head resting in Mary's lap.

BIBLIOGRAPHY

Beissel, Stephan. *Geschichte der Verehrung Marias in Deutschland während des Mittelalters: Ein Beitrag zur Religionswissenschaft und Kunstgeschichte.* Freiburg im Breisgau: Herder, 1909.

Passarge, Walter. *Das Deutsche Vesperbild im Mittelalter.* Deutsche Beiträge zur Kunstwissenschaft 1. Cologne: Marcan, 1924.

Pinder, Wilhelm. *Die Pietà.* Bibliothek der Kunstgeschichte 29. Leipzig: Seemann, 1922.

Schneider, Frida Karla. *Die mittelalterlichen deutschen Typen und die Vorformen des Vesperbildes.* Dissertation Universität Kiel, 1931. Rendsburg: Schleswig Holsteinische Verlagsanstalt, 1931.

Weitzmann, Kurt. "The Origin of the Threnos." In *De Artibus Opuscula XL: Essays in Honor of Erwin Panofsky.* 2 vols. New York: New York University Press, 1961, Vol. 1, pp. 476–490.

Melanie Gesink Cornelisse

SEE ALSO

International Style; Mechtild von Hackeborn; Mysticism

Saint John on the Bosom of Christ

The Gospel account of the Last Supper (John 13:23–25) relates how the apostle, "whom Jesus loved," rested his head on Christ's breast. In this sculptural group, the central pair of Christ and Saint John the Evangelist has been isolated from the rest of the apostles, and all indications of setting have been excluded in order to force concentration on and identification with the emotions and interactions of the main characters. In these aspects, this subject fits well with the typical definition of the German *Andachtsbild,* or devotional image.

Like other *Andachtsbilder,* the group of Christ and Saint John first appeared about 1300, probably in the heightened spiritual context of certain Dominican and Cistercian nuns' convents in southern Germany, along the Rhine, and in the area of Lake Constance. The numerous preserved examples of this subject indicate its widespread popularity, which must have derived from its numerous overlapping meanings relevant to the lives of

St. John on the Bosom of Christ (Stuttgart, Württembergisches Landesmuseum). *Photograph: Joan A. Holladay*

monastics and, especially, nuns. Both the Evangelist and the Baptist were understood as models of virginity, and sculptures of the two figures were sometimes installed as pendants on symmetrically placed altars. Sermons and commentary also identified the Evangelist as the bridegroom of the marriage at Cana, whom Christ called to the contemplative life, and as the bride of the Song of Songs, the embodiment of the loving soul in mystical union with God. The joining of the two figures' right hands as in the marriage rite reinforces this idea of bridal union. John thus presents himself as a model for the nun's identification as she strives for the ideal union of the soul with God.

Scholars have identified two slightly different versions of this subject. A group in Cleveland, perhaps the earliest preserved version of this subject, dating from about 1280, and a slightly later group, now in the Württembergisches Landesmuseum in Stuttgart, are characterized by the strictly vertical figure of Christ. In the far more popular

version of the subject, deriving from the work carved by Master Heinrich of Constance for the Dominican nuns' convent at St. Katharinenthal (now in the Museum Mayer van den Bergh in Antwerp), the poses, gestures, and drapery configuration create a more tender interaction between the two figures. The subject also appears in stained glass and mural and manuscript painting.

BIBLIOGRAPHY

Greenhill, Eleanor. "The Group of Christ and St. John as Author Portrait: Literary Sources, Pictorial Parallels." In *Festschrift Bernhard Bischoff zu seinem 65. Geburtstag,* ed. J. Autenrieth and F. Brunhölzl. Stuttgart: Hiersemann, 1971, pp. 406–416.

Haussherr, Reiner. "Über die Christus-Johannes-Gruppen: Zum Problem *Andachtsbilder* und deutsche Mystik." In *Beiträge zur Kunst des Mittelalters: Festschrift für Hans Wentzel zum 60. Geburtstag,* ed. Rüdiger Becksmann, et al. Berlin: Mann, 1975, pp. 79–103.

Wentzel, Hans. *Die Christus-Johannes-Gruppen des vierzehnten Jahrhunderts.* Werkmonographie zur bildenden Kunst 51. Stuttgart: Reclam, 1960.

Joan A. Holladay

SEE ALSO

Constance; Gothic Art and Architecture; Sankt Katharinenthal; Song of Songs

Schreinmadonna

A hollow sculpted image of the Virgin and Child that opens to form a triptych (French, *Vierge Ouvrante*), *Schreinmadonnas* of wood and, less frequently, ivory ranged from a quarter-meter to a meter-and-a-half in height. They proliferated in central Europe from the twelfth to the early sixteenth century and experienced a brief revival as replicated collectors' pieces in the nineteenth century. Most published scholarship has concentrated on establishing types, chronologies, dating, and authentication.

Open, the figures frequently reveal a second carved image of the *Gnadenstuhl,* the vertical representation of the Trinity in which God the Father holds Christ in his outstretched arms. Less often, they display narrative scenes, and, rarely, a combination of the two. Several German examples from the late fourteenth and fifteenth centuries represent the Virgin as the *Madonna Misericordia,* extending her cloak to protect the faithful as they gather to adore the Trinity. The Schreinmadonna expressed notions associated with *Maria Mediatrix, Maria Ecclesia,* and *Maria Thesaurus.* The faithful gained visual access to the Godhead through the Virgin; the figures thus portrayed the Church's function as mediator between God and humankind and as administrator of grace. A vast range of metaphors for the Virgin as the container of the Trinity proliferated in late medieval hymns and verses. The materialization of these notions in the carved figures was criticized by Jean Gerson in 1402 and Johannes Molanus in 1570. Concerns centered around a possible literal reading of the figures that could lead to the misunderstanding that the entire Godhead sprang from the Virgin.

BIBLIOGRAPHY

Baumer, Christoph. "Die Schreinmadonna." *Marian Library Studies* 9 (1977): 239–272.

Fries, Walter. "Die Schreinmadonna." *Anzeiger des Germanischen Nationalmuseums* (1928/1929): 5–69.

Holbert, Kelly. "The Vindication of a Controversial, Early Thirteenth-Century *Vierge Ouvrante.*" *The Journal of the Walters Art Gallery* 55/56 (1997/1998): 101–121.

Kroos, Renate. "'Gotes tabernackel': Zu Funktion und Interpretation von Schreinmadonnen." *Zeitschrift für schweizerische Archaeologie und Kunstgeschichte* 43 (1986): 58–64.

Radler, Gudrun. *Die Schreinmadonna "Vierge Ouvrante" von den bernhardinischen Anfängen bis zur Frauenmystik im Deutschordensland: Mit beschreibendem Katalog.* Frankfurt: Kunstgeschichtliches Institut der Johann Wolfgang Goethe-Universität, 1990.

Schleif, Corine. "Die Schreinmadonna im Diözesanmuseum zu Limburg: Ein verfemtes Bildwerk des Mittelalters." *Nassauische Annalen* 95 (1984): 39–54.

Corine Schleif

Schutzmantelmadonna

In images of the *Schutzmantelmadonna,* also known as the *Mater Misericordiae* and the Madonna of Mercy, the Virgin Mary takes a variety of figures under the protection of her robe. While the type appears suddenly in Central Europe and Italy in the late thirteenth century, figures with a sheltering mantle occur in antiquity. In Europe and Byzantium, legends of the Virgin and her mantle as the protectors of Constantinople appear in the early Middle Ages. By the twelfth century, references to the Virgin's mantle appear in such Cistercian sources as the writings of Bernard of Clairvaux.

Images depicting the Virgin with her robe spread probably began at the church of the Blachernae in Constantinople, which held her mantle as its major relic. But these images lack the sheltered human figures. In the thirteenth century, two forms of the Virgin with supplicants appear. Some scholars argue that one type, a seated Virgin with Child, was invented in Europe, citing Duccio's Madonna of the Franciscans as the earliest example. But the closest comparisons to Duccio's tiny panel are in slightly earlier Armenian and Cypriote works, suggesting that this version was invented in the East, although the presence of the Cistercians and other Western orders in Constantinople between 1204 and 1261 may have inspired this motif. It is the standing Virgin without the child who shelters figures under her mantle that dominates Central Europe. A version of this formulation also appeared in an Armenian Gospel of 1270, although there are reports of slightly earlier images of this Virgin in Italy. By the 1330s the standing type appeared throughout Central Italy. Over the centuries, it became associated with plague monuments in Central Europe, as well as with the Rosary. The *Schutzmantelmadonna* has persisted to the modern era in a variety of media. Most notable are images produced around 1500 by South German sculptors, including Gregor and Michel Erhart.

BIBLIOGRAPHY

Baxandall, Michael. *The Limewood Sculptors of Renaissance Germany.* New Haven: Yale University Press, 1980, pp. 165–172.

Belting, Hans. *Likeness and Presence: A History of the Image before the Era of Art.* Chicago: The University of Chicago Press, 1994, pp. 354–358.

Belting-Ihm, Christa. *Sub matris tutela: Untersuchungen zur Vorgeschichte der Schutzmantelmadonna.* Abhandlungen der Heidelberger Akademie der Wissenschaften, Phil.-hist. Klasse 1976, no. 3. Heidelberg: Winter, 1976.

Carr, Annemarie Weyl. "Art in the Court of the Lusignan Kings." In *Cyprus and Crusades: Papers Given at the International Conference Cyprus and the Crusades, 6–9 September 1994,* ed. N. Coureas and J. Riley Smith. Nicosia: Society for the Study of the Crusades and the Latin East and the Cyprus Research Institute, 1995. 239–256.

Derbes, Anne. "Siena and the Levant in the Later Dugento." *Gesta* 28 (1989): 190–204.

Mohr, Angela. *Schutzmantelmadonnen in Oberösterreich.* Steyr: Ennsthaler, 1987.

Ousterhout, Robert. "The Virgin in the Chora: An Image and Its Contents." In *The Sacred Image East and West,* ed. Robert Outsterhout and Leslie Brubaker. Illinois Byzantine Studies. Urbana: University of Illinois Press, 1995, pp. 91–109.

Perdrizet, Paul. *La Vierge de Miséricorde: Étude d'un thème iconographique.* Bibliothèque des Écoles françaises d'Athènes et de Rome 101. Paris: Fontemoing, 1908.

Sussmann, Vera. "Maria mit dem Schutzmantel." Dissertation Universität Marburg, 1929. Marburg: [n.p.], 1929; also *Marburger Jahrbuch für Kunstwissenschaft* 5 (1929): 285–351.

Rebecca W. Corrie

SEE ALSO
Erhart, Gregor; Erhart, Michel

Sorrows of the Virgin

Although the New Testament barely mentions the Virgin Mary's presence at the Crucifixion, medieval commentators greatly expanded her role. The Virgin's sufferings at the sight of her Son's multiple torments became a standard fixture in the increasingly detailed and elaborated versions of the Passion, transmitted during the late Middle Ages through Passion plays, Passion tracts, devotional imagery, etc. The Virgin served as a mediatory figure whose sufferings enhanced the emotional impact of the story, and whose compassionate response served as a model for worshippers seeking an affective understanding of Christ's ordeal. Ultimately, the *Mater dolorosa,* or sorrowing mother, became herself an object of adoration, a mother whose own ordeal would enhance her sympathy for individual supplicants.

Gothic artists depicted the sorrows of the Virgin within the context of Passion scenes and as an independent subject. Motifs and themes particularly popular in Germany include Mary's *spasmo,* or swoon by the Cross; the *Mater dolorosa*—either alone or combined with a Man of Sorrows; the *Pietà,* in which the symbolic sword of compassion piercing Mary's chest is derived from the High Priest Simeon's prophecy to Mary in Luke 2:34–35; and the multiple sorrows of the Virgin. The last three were invented by German artists, who were possibly inspired by the Dominican mystic movement's encouragement of affective devotion. The widespread popularity of this veneration in Germany is demonstrated by the large number of surviving images of the Virgin's sorrows in a range of media from crude woodcuts and small ivories, to monumental wall paintings, stained glass, and altarpieces.

BIBLIOGRAPHIES
Meier, Theo. *Die Gestalt Marias im geistlichen Schauspiel des deutschen Mittelalters.* Berlin: E. Schmidt, 1959.

Schuler, Carol M. "The Sword of Compassion: Images of the Sorrowing Virgin in late Medieval and Renaissance Art." Ph.D. diss. Columbia University, 1987.

Wimmer, Erich. "Maria im Leid: Die mater dolorosa insbesondere in der deutschen Literatur und Frömmigkeit des Mittelalters." Dissertation Würzburg, 1968.

Carol M. Schuler

Throne of Solomon

This iconographic subject is based on the biblical accounts (2 Chron. 9:17–20; 1 Kings 10:18–20) that describe the ivory and gold throne with six steps leading up to it. Two lions were positioned on each step with two additional lions placed on either side of the throne. In the Middle Ages, the throne of Solomon became associated with the Virgin and Child as the seat of wisdom *(sedes sapientiae).* It was also connected with the idea of judgment, either the Last Judgement or justice dispensed by secular monarchs.

Many representations of the Throne of Solomon come from German-speaking areas, especially the upper Rhineland and Austria. They date primarily from the Gothic period. An early example is a wall painting in the bishop's chapel of the Cathedral of Gurk dated 1210–1220. One of the most famous and prominent depictions is on the central portal gable of the west facade of Strasbourg cathedral dated in the late thirteenth century. Most of these images elaborate the association with the Virgin and the Incarnation. They add Virtues, who are interpreted as steps leading to the Throne, prophets, whose prophecies refer to the virtues of the Virgin, and doves, as gifts of the Holy Spirit. The lions on the steps represent the Apostles, while the two lions beside or just beneath the throne are *terror demonum* and *terror inimicorum* of the Last Judgment. This characteristically German iconographic theme thus becomes a *summa* of the Christian idea of salvation.

BIBLIOGRAPHY
Piper, Ferdinand. "Maria als Thron Salomos und ihre Tugenden bei der Verkündigung." *Jahrbücher für Kunstwissenschaft* 5 (1873): 97–137.

Ragusa, Isa. "*Terror demonum* and *terror inimicorum:* The Two Lions of the Throne of Solomon and the Open Door of Paradise." *Zeitschrift fur Kunstgeschichte* 40 (1972): 93–114.

Wormald, Francis. "The Throne of Solomon and St. Edward's Chair." In *De Artibus Opuscula XL: Essays in Honor of Erwin Panofsky,* ed. Millard Meiss. New York: New York University Press, 1961. 2 vols. Vol. 1, pp. 532–539; Vol. 2: pls. 175–177.

Karen Gould

Wise and Foolish Virgins

The theme of the Wise and Foolish Virgins had appeared in Gothic sculpture from its very beginnings. On Abbot Suger's new façade for the church of the royal abbey at St. Denis (1137–1140), small figures of the virgins in low relief are arranged vertically on the doorposts of the central portal. Oriented to the image of the Last Judgment in the tympanum above, the Wise Virgins appear on Christ's right, on the left doorpost, with their hapless couterparts opposite, on his left (Latin, *sinister*) side. Arranged thus, the Virgins function as the ultimate metaphor for preparedness for entry into heaven, symbolized architecturally in the church building beyond the door. According to the parable in Matt. 25:1–13, five of the ten virgins waiting for the bridegroom had brought oil for their lamps; the other five came unequipped. When the bridegroom opened the door to allow them access to the wedding, only those whose lamps were burning were prepared to enter.

In the portrayals of this theme in art, the Wise Virgins carefully hold their lamps upright; as those of the Foolish Virgins are not burning, they are allowed to hang or fall. The separation of the women into two distinct groups is further dramatized by their physical appearance: the Foolish Virgins, disheveled with open hair, form a decided contrast to their calmer, better groomed sisters.

The theme makes its earliest appearance in German-speaking lands circa 1180 on the so-called *Galluspforte* (Portal of St. Gall) on the north side of the cathedral at Basel. Still small in scale, the virgins have now been moved into the lintel, where the proximity to the Last Judgment in the tympanum immediately above highlights the logical relationship between the two subjects. Six relief panels at the sides of the door represent the Acts of Charity, another metaphor for preparing oneself for the Last Judgment, also drawn from the Gospel of Matthew (25:34–36).

With the appearance of Gothic portal formats and programs in this region, the Wise and Foolish Virgins take on a new importance. Unlike French portals (Sens, Chartres, Notre-Dame in Paris) where the virgins only appear in small scale, on the west façade at Strasbourg cathedral (ca. 1280), large-scale figures occupy the jambs of the right portal. The figure of Christ as the Bridegroom, who had separated the two groups on the Basel lintel, appears here with his charges; his position on the innermost jamb not only makes visible the allusion to Christ as the door (John 10:9), but he seems to lead the Wise Virgins, on the right jamb behind him, into the church. For the sake of symmetry, a corresponding male figure, not present in the biblical text, was invented for the group opposite: the Prince of the World (*Fürst der Welt*) or the Tempter, wearing courtly dress and a crown of roses, stands on the outermost jamb. From this position, he offers the Foolish Virgins an apple with a seductive gesture, luring them away from the heavenly realm of the Church and back out into the world. In case his negative role in not clear enough, his elegant robe is open at the back, revealing the toads and snakes that consume his corrupted flesh. Similar twelve-figure groups were included in the interiors of the west porch at Freiburg im Breisgau (1280–1285) and Basel (1280s). Stylistic similarities also link these three groups.

Two eastern German versions of this theme from after the turn of the century depart from the courtly elegance of the Upper Rhine groups. Exaggerated poses and dramatic gestures of mourning characterize the Foolish Virgins at Magdeburg (ca. 1240–1250) and Erfurt (ca. 1350). Although these ten-figure groups are located on the north portals of their respective churches, it is not clear that this is the original installation at Magdeburg.

The scholar Helga Sciurie has related the appearance of this theme in large scale on the Strasbourg cathedral façade to problems with local women in these years. In particular, the Beguines—women who chose a life of piety and charity outside the official institutions of the Church—provided a threat to ecclesiastical authority. Together with the personifications of the Virtues in female form on the jambs of the left façade portal, the Wise and Foolish Virgins would have provided an especially potent form of address to a female audience and a moralizing message to all viewers about the importance of one's own actions for personal salvation. At Bern, too, (ca. 1475), the use of this theme on the jambs of the cathedral's west façade portal has been related to local concerns, but the social, political, and religious contexts that may help to

Strasbourg, cathedral, west façade, right portal, right jamb: Christ and the Wise Virgins. *Photograph: Joan A. Holladay*

account for the use of this theme at other sites have not yet been investigated. Less well known and well researched are the Romanesque and Gothic painted versions, which also typically appear in association with other eschatological themes.

BIBLIOGRAPHY

Körkel-Hinkfoth, Regine. "Sinnbild des Jüngsten Gerichts: Darstellungen der Parabel von den klugen und törichten Jungfrauen am Basler Münster." *Unsere Kunstdenkmäler* 44 (1993): 309–322.

Schubert, Dietrich. *Von Halberstadt nach Meissen: Bildwerke des 13. Jahrhunderts in Thüringen, Sachsen und Anhalt.* Dumont Dokumente. Cologne: M. Dumont Schauberg, 1974, pp. 301–305.

Sciurie, Helga. "Die Frauenfrage in Andachtsbild und Bauskulptur." *Frauen, Kunst, Geschichte: Zur Korrektur des herrschenden Blicks,* ed. Cordula Bischoff, et al. Kunstwissenschaftliche Untersuchungen des Ulmer Vereins, Verband für Kunst- und Kulturwissenschaft 13. Gießen: Anabas, 1985, pp. 53–62.

Sladeczek, Franz-Josef. *Erhart Küng: Bildhauer und Baumeister am Münster zu Bern (um 1420–1507).* Dissertation Universität Gießen, 1986. Bern: Paul Haupt, 1990, pp. 47–68.

Joan A. Holladay

SEE ALSO

Basel; Bern; Erfurt; Freiburg; Magdeburg; Schwäbisch Gmünd; Strasbourg

Ingelheim

The terrace on the left bank of the Rhein between Mainz and Bingen was the site of an important Carolingian palace. Jacobsen suggests that the church of St. Remigius documented in 742, which stood some five hundred meters away, may have been the chapel of an earlier palace (1994:30), but the structure for which Ingelheim is best known was erected under Charlemagne and his son Louis the Pious. Excavations conducted by Christian Rauch between 1909 and 1914, by Walter Sage in the 1960s, and ongoing since 1993 have revealed the plan of this ambibious structure. A heavy gate opened at the center of a curving wall onto a large semicircular forecourt at the east. Access to the second, square courtyard, around which the ceremonial and living quarters were arranged, was gained through the straight line of buildings opposite the entrance. At the southwest corner of the second court stood the *aula regia* (royal hall).

In addition to the scale of the complex, a number of specific features reveal the political ambitions of its patrons. A colonnade in imitation of ancient architecture ran along the curved inner wall of the semicircular forecourt. The large scale of the *aula regia,* its plan, and the arrangement of the windows in the apse suggest that it was modeled after the *aula palatina* (palace hall) erected by the early Christian Emperor Constantine at Trier. The cycle of paintings in the *aula,* documented by the ninth-century poet Ermoldus Nigellus, contributed to the palace's political message. Walther Lammers has reconstructed the two apparently separate but related parts of the cycle. One, depicting paired scenes from the lives of seven ancient rulers from Babylon, Africa, Greece, and Rome, he thinks, was painted in the nave. In the second, five Christian rulers were also given two images each: a single ceremonial image was accompanied by a narrative scene from that ruler's life. Depicted in this series was Constantine, Theodosius, Charles Martel, his son Pepin the Short, and his son Charlemagne. The second cycle was likely located in the single apse on the building's south end. After his description of the sequence of Christian rulers, Ermoldus notes that this is the site from which the emperor ruled (1884: 66). Like other aspects of the palace, the decorative cycle too may depend on ancient models; the combination of single figures and narrative occurred in the naves of the great early Christian churches in Rome—Old St. Peter's and St. Paul's outside the Walls.

The dating of the palace and its decoration is not entirely clear. Charlemagne's biographer Einhard refers to the king's building activities at Ingelheim and notes the splendor of the palace he erected here. Ermoldus's attribution of the painted cycle to Louis the Pious would seem to be clear, and most authors consider that Louis continued work on the palace begun by his father. Whether it was started early in Charlemagne's rule or at the end of his life is disputed, however. Jacobsen argues that the palace would have been brought to some degree of completion by the time Charlemagne spent Christmas there in 787 and held a royal assembly the following spring (1994: 29–31) and that Ingelheim thus provides important evidence of an early date for Charlemagne's campaign to revive antique art and architecture to legitimize his own reign. Likewise Jacobsen dates the painted cycle in the *aula regia* to the years between 787 and 800 on the grounds that Charlemagne's imperial coronation in the latter year would certainly have closed the narrative cycle if it had been executed after this date.

The association of the palace at Ingelheim with Charlemagne and its importance in the emperor's artistic politics made it an attractive monument for later rulers wishing to ally themselves with the image of their predecessor. A palace church is first documented in 997, when Otto III gave it to the newly founded nuns' cloister at Aachen; excavations have located the single-aisled building with a transept and rounded apse in the south arm of the second, square courtyard, and ceramic finds have suggested that it may have been newly erected, perhaps by the emperor himself, about this date.

Frederick I Barbarossa renovated the palace in the early years of his reign. Referring to Charlemagne and his palace at Ingelheim, Frederick's biographer Rahewin mentions the role of these and other buildings in "hold[ing] the gift and the memory of such a great emperor in honor" (1986: 712–713). The fact that Frederick vsited Ingelheim only four times also supports the thesis that his goal in these renovations was not the practical one of greater comfort but, rather, part of his larger campaign claiming political descent from Charlemagne.

In 1354, the emperor Charles IV, who also drew widely on the image of his predecessor, established a foundation of Augustinian canons in the palace at Ingelheim as a dependency of the one he had founded at the Karlshof in Prague. Frederick and Charles IV also decorated their palaces at Hagenau and Prague, respectively, with painted cycles of their forebears and predecessors in office, perhaps under the influence of the painted cycle in the Carolingian palace.

BIBLIOGRAPHY

Einhard. *Vita Karoli Magni imperatoris*, in *Two Lives of Charlemagne*, trans. Lewis Thorpe. Penguin Classics. Harmondsworth: Penguin, 1969.

Erler, Adalbert. *Das Augustiner-Chorherrenstift in der Königspfalz zu Ingelheim am Rhein: Ein Arbeitsbericht.* Sitzungberichte der Wissenschaftlichen Gesellschaft an der Johann Wolfgang Goethe-Universität Frankfurt am Main 23/1. Stuttgart: Franz Steiner Verlag Wiesbaden GmbH, 1986.

Ermoldus Nigellus. *In honorem Hludovici christianissimi Caesaris Augusti Ermoldi Nigelli exulis elegiacum carmen,* in Monumenta Germaniae Historica, Poetarum latinorum 2, ed. Ernst Dümmler. Berlin: Weidmann, 1884, 4–79.

Grewe, Holger. "Die Königspfalz zu Ingelheim am Rhein," in *779 Kunst und Kultur der Karolingerzeit: Karl der Grosse und Papst Leo in Paderborn.* Ed. Christoph Stiegemann and Matthias Wemhoff. Mainz: Philipp von Zabern, 1999. 3: 142–151.

Jacobsen, Werner. "Die Pfalzkonzeptionen Karls des Grossen," in *Karl der Grosse als vielberufener Vorfahr: Sein Bild in der Kunst der Fürsten, Kirchen and Städte,* ed. Lieselotte Saurma-Jeltsch. Schriften des Historschen Museums. Sigmaringen: Jan Thorbecke Verlag, 1994, 28–33.

Lammers, Walther. "Ein karolingisches Bildprogramm in der Aula Regia von Ingelheim," in *Festschrift für Hermann Heimpel zum 70. Geburtstag am 19. September 1971,* 3 vols. Veröffentlichungen des Max-Planck-Instituts für Geschichte 36. Göttingen: Vandenhoeck und Ruprecht, 1972, vol. 3, pp. 226–289.

Oswald, Friedrich, Leo Schaefer, and Hans Rudolf Sennhauser. *Vorromanische Kirchenbauten: Katalog der Denkmäler bis zum Ausgang der Ottonen,* 4 vols. Veröffentlichungen des Zentralinstituts für Kunstgeschichte in München 3. Munich: Presetl, 1966–1991, vol. 1, pp. 129–130; vol. 4, pp. 193.

Otto of Freising and Rahewin. *Die Taten Friedrichs oder richtiger Cronica,* trans. Adolf Schmidt, ed. Franz-Josef Schmale. Freiherr vom Stein Gedächtnisausgabe 17/1. Darmstadt: Wissenschaftliche Buchgesellschaft, 1986.

Rauch, Christian, and Hans-Jörg Jacobi. *Die Ausgrabungen in der Königspfalz Ingelheim 1909–1914.* Monographie des Römisch-Germanischen Zentralmuseums Mainz 2. Mainz: Verlag des Römisch-Germanischen Zentralmuseums, 1976.

Joan A. Holladay

SEE ALSO

Carolingian Art and Architecture; Charlemagne; Charles IV; Frederick I Barbarossa; Otto III; Ottonian Art and Architecture; Prague

International Style

In contrast with the distinctive regional styles of the first half of the century, a pan-European quality characterizes works of the years around 1400. From Poland to northern Italy, from the Netherlands to Prague and Vienna, figural works in both two- and three-dimensional media share a lyrical quality created by sweet expressions and swinging, rhythmic drapery folds described by sinuous lines. These stylistic features give rise to the other common name for this style, the Soft Style *(Weicher Stil)*; German scholars also use the term *der schöne Stil* (the far, or beautiful, style). Usually counted among the well-known practitioners of this style are Andrè Beauneveu and the Limbourg brothers, all of whom worked for John, Duke of Berry, the brother of the king of France, as well as Lorenzo Monaco, active in Florence. Artists working in the Soft Style in German-speaking lands tend to remain anonymous, although the name Hans von Judenburg has been associated with a number of wood sculptures from Styria in southeast Austria, and the role of the later members of the Parler family in the development of the style seems to have been crucial. German painters whose work is typically associated with the International Style include the Master of St. Veronica and Konrad von Soest.

Although we use the word "style," these works also reveal preferences for certain subjects and formats. Gold ground images of the half-length Madonna holding her child tenderly before her are a favorite subject in panel painting. Examples include the closely related panels known as the Madonna of Roudnice, dated after 1380 (Prague, National Gallery, Inv. Nr. 0 7102), and the Madonna of the Church of the Trinity Cˆeskè Bude ˆjovice, a Prague work from circa 1410 or earlier (now Hluboká nad Vltavou, Southern Bohemian Alesˆ-Gallery (Inv. Nr. 0/2). Preferred subjects in sculpture include the full-length standing Madonna with Child, known as the schöne Madonna, and the schöne Pietà, in which the Virgin supports the broken body of her dead son in her lap. In the latter, the youthful sweetness of the Virgin often seems at odds with the sorrow one would expect at this event.

gional provenance to many works of this style remains difficult, however, as it is complicated by both the mobility of artists and the portability of their works.

BIBLIOGRAPHY

Clasen, Karl Heinz. *Der Meister der Schönen Madonnen: Herkunft, Entfaltung und Umkreis.* Berlin: de Gruyter, 1974.

Europäische Kunst um 1400. Vienna: Kunsthistorisches Museum, 1962.

Grossmann, Dieter. *Stabat Mater: Maria unter dem Kreuz in der Kunst um 1400.* Salzburg: Salzburger Domkapitel, 1970.

The International Style: The Arts in Euroupe around 1400. Baltimore: The Walters Art Gallery, 1962.

Kreuzer-Eccle, Eva. *Hans von Judenburg und die Plastik des Weichen Stiles in Südtirol.* Dissertation, Universität Innsbrück, 1969. Calliano: R. Manfrini, 1978.

Kutal, Albert. *Gothic Art in Bohemia and Moravia.* New York: Hamlyn Publishing Group Limited, 1971.

Legner, Anton, ed. *Die Parler und der Schöne Stil 1350–1400: Europäische Kunst unter den Luxemburgern.* 5 vols. Cologne: Schnütgen Museum, 1978–1980.

Pinder, Wolfgang. "Zum Problem der 'Schönen Madonnen' um 1400." *Jahrbuch der preußischen Kunstsammlungen* 44 (1923): 147–171.

Salinger, Arthur, ed. *Der Meister von Großlobming,* Vienna: Österreichische Galerie, 1994.

Schmidt, Gerhard. "Kunst um 1400: Forschungsstand und Forschungsperspektiven." In *Internationale Gotik in Mitteleuropa,* ed. Götz Pochat and Brigitte Hagenlocher-Wagner. Kunsthistorisches Jahrbuch Graz 24. Graz: Akademische Druck- und Verlagsanstalt, 1990, pp. 34–49.

Schöne Madonnen 1350–1450. Salzburg: Salzburger Domkapitel, 1965.

Joan A. Holladay

SEE ALSO

Charles IV; Gothic Art and Architecture; Iconographies, Innovative; Magdeburg; Parler Family; Prague; Sankt Veronika, Master of

Schöne Madonna, Würzburg, Marlenkapelle. *Photograph: Joan A. Holladay*

Scholarship on the International Style has concerned itself largely with two questions—sources for the style and the relationships between works. Already in 1923, the art historian Pinder suggested sources for the *schöne Madonnen* in Bohemian sculpture and painting of the era of Charles IV, while noting that both the basics of the style and certain details were already present in works like the late thirteenth-century Madonna at Magdeburg cathedral. He also identified centers of sculptural production in Prague and Salzburg, as well as on the Rhine and along the Baltic coast, and tried to trace the stylistic filiations between various works. Assigning even a general re-

Investiture Controversy

The Investiture Controversy refers to a late phase of eleventh-century Church reform, lasting from ca.

1078–1122. Sometimes, however, the term is used incorrectly to cover the entire period of reform from the 1050s to 1122, the date of the Concordat of Worms. The term describes the struggle between the papacy *(sacerdotium)* and the European monarchies *(regnum)* over the participation of the ruler in the making of bishops and abbots through the handing over of the ring and crosier (bishop's staff) with the words "receive the church." The wording of this phrase shows that an investiture referred to the bishopric or abbey in general and did not distinguish between the office and the rights and property that came with it.

The term "investiture" did not occur before the second half of the eleventh century, but the custom reached back to the tenth. The investiture ceremony differed according to place and time, but the handing over of the symbols of ring and staff—they had been sent to the royal court after the death of the previous bishop—often occurred in conjunction with the commendation of the candidate to the king and a promise of fealty. Both ceremonies had been described as homage *(hominium* or *homagium)* since the late eleventh century. In many sources these terms are implicitly included when only investiture is mentioned.

Investiture should not be confused with election or consecration, although investiture was the single most important factor in the success of a candidate. For many years popes did not object to investiture, which was seen as the natural and customary expression of secular influence and power. The ceremony assured rulers of the loyalty of the wealthy and politically powerful bishops and abbots who were required to fulfill the *servitium regis,* or obligations to royalty, consisting of property fees, hospitality, military support, and court attendance. In the Empire, the Ottonian and early Salian rulers at times added to those obligations the rights and properties of counties.

Pope Gregory VII pronounced the first general legally binding prohibition of investiture by any lay person at the Roman Council of November 1078. No cleric was allowed to obtain the investiture of a bishopric, abbey, or church from the hands of the emperor or king, or any layman or lay woman. The prohibition was strengthened at the Lenten synod of 1080. Gregory's successors continued to uphold these decrees, which Pope Urban II expanded to include homage at the Council of Clermont in 1095. Under Pope Paschal II the reference to homage was omitted in the case of England, but, apart from a short period in 1111/1112, when his hands were tied by the privilege Henry V had extorted from him, Paschal, too,

insisted on strict prohibition of investiture. He succeeded in obtaining the acceptance of these principles in France (1107) as well as England (1105/1106). The settlement of the dispute for the Empire had to wait until 1122.

When Gregory VII deposed and excommunicated King Henry IV for the first time in February 1076, the investiture prohibition had not yet been fully formalized, but Henry's investiture of bishops in Milan, Fermo, and Spoleto doubtless was the provocation behind his excommunication. Beginning in the tenth century, German kings and emperors had relied to such an extent on the collaboration with ecclesiastics (Ottonian-Salian Church system) that the prohibition of investiture, which had assured them of the control of bishoprics and abbeys, threatened to undermine the monarchy entirely. At the assembly of Worms in January 1076, the German and Italian episcopate, with a few exceptions, had remained united behind the king. However, the investiture prohibitions, the election of the anti-king Rudolf of Swabia (March 15, 1077), and the final condemnation of Henry IV by Gregory VII (March 7, 1080) forged a powerful coalition between the noble opponents of the monarchy and papal adherents among bishops and abbots. Negotiations and battles between the two parties, which varied only temporarily in composition, followed upon one another for nearly thirty years. Not until 1109 *(Tractatus de investitura)* were there any signs of compromise. Henry's nomination of Archbishop Wibert of Ravenna at the synod of Brixen (June 25, 1080; consecration in St. Peter's Basilica as Clement III, March 24, 1084) transformed the Investiture Controversy into a struggle between *regnum* and *sacerdotium,* as evidenced by the numerous polemical writings edited in the *Libelli de Lite.*

The Investiture Controversy in France was much less dogmatic than in the Empire. The French kings Philip I (1059–1108) and Louis VI (1098–1137), as well as the nobility, also used the wealth, power, and property of bishoprics and abbeys in order to strengthen their own positions, but their situation was very different than either Germany or England. The kings and nobles of France divided among themselves the secular influence over the French church. Only about twenty-five French dioceses out of a total of about seventy-seven were open to royal influence. The tensions between Rome and Philip I were acute, but the issues in this case were the introduction of ecclesiastical reform and Philip's marital problems. Philip's excommunication and the interdict pronounced against him were purely pastoral punishments and had nothing to do with investiture. In France the investiture prohibitions of 1077/1078, first pronounced by the legate Hugh of Die, were only a minor additional irritant in the exercise of royal influence in those dioceses where the Capetians had always had to anticipate difficulties. Both popes and kings were always willing to compromise on investiture when absolutely necessary.

As exemplified in writings of the canonist Ivo of Chartres at the turn of the century, the argument for a differentiation between the temporalities and spiritualities connected to bishoprics and abbeys slowly gained ground. This differentiation would allow a king to invest an ecclesiastic with the temporalities (secular rights and property) of a see not by the ring and crosier, but by using some other symbol. Ring and staff had come to be understood as spiritual symbols that were not to be touched by the hands of laymen. It appears that, at the meeting between Pope Paschal II and the French kings at St. Denis (April 30–May 3, 1107), an agreement was reached on this basis. If a candidate were elected canonically, the king could invest him with the temporalities of his see. The king renounced the use of investiture, but in the case of a bishop, the bishop would promise fealty.

William I (1066–1087) brought to an end the English isolation from continental developments. However, papal willingness to compromise postponed a struggle over investiture till the time of Henry I (1100–1135) and Archbishop Anselm of Canterbury. As an exile, Anselm had been present at the Roman synod of 1099 where Urban II had repeated the prohibition of investiture and homage. Anselm considered himself bound to obey the papal decrees and, therefore, refused to accept investiture from Henry I. After negotiations beginning in Normandy in July 1105, Henry I declared that he would no longer insist on investiture but would continue to require the homage of prelates. Relying on the papal right to grant dispensation, Paschal II allowed Anselm of Canturbury in March 1106 to consecrate bishops who had done homage to the king but had not been invested by him. This compromise was criticized at an assembly in August 1107.

BIBLIOGRAPHY

Blumenthal, Uta-Renate. *The Investiture Controversy: Church and Monarchy from the Ninth to the Twelfth Century.* Philadelphia: University of Pennsylvania Press, 1988.

Uta-Renate Blumenthal

SEE ALSO

Concordat of Worms; Gregory VII; Henry IV

Isidore

Also known as the "Old High German Isidore and Mon(d)see/Vienna Fragments," this group of very early Old High German (OHG) texts and fragments are the sole surviving OHG theological prose tracts. Copied in a parallel translation opposite the Latin original on the same leaf (similar to the OHG *Tatian* with bilingual Latin/OHG on opposite manuscript leaves), the texts are: "Isidore": *De fide catholica ex veteri et novo testamento contra Iudaeos* by Isidore of Seville (d. 636), a treatise arguing against Jewish and for Christian beliefs, and the "Mon(d)see Fragments": snippets of four works: Isidore's *De fide,* the gospel of Matthew, an anonymous religious Latin tract, *"De vocatione gentium,"* two sermons: one anonymous, and one by Augustine (sermon no. 76). As the OHG texts are Bavarian copies from circa 800/810, the original translations are thought to be from the late eighth century/circa 800, perhaps in the area of the western South Rhenish Franconian dialect (in or near Metz or Murbach). Considered by modern scholars to be prose of high stylistic quality, the texts were translated in connection with imperial church politics, possibly under Archbishop Hildebald of Cologne (785–818), who directed the monastery at Mon(d)see from 803. These very early OHG linguistic specimens were excerpted for some of the "Murbach-Oxford glosses" from the 820s.

BIBLIOGRAPHY

Hench, George A., ed. *Der althochdeutsche Isidor: Facsimile-Ausgabe des Pariser Codex nebst critischem Text der Pariser und Monseer Bruchstücke. Mit Einleitung, grammatischer Darstellung und einem ausführlichem Glossar.* Straßburg: Trübner, 1893.

———. *The Monsee Fragments: Newly collated Text with Introduction, Notes, Grammatical Treatise and Exhaustive Glossary and a Photo-Lithographic Facsimile.* Straßburg: Trübner, 1890.

Matzel, Klaus. *Untersuchungen zur Verfasserschaft, Sprache und Herkunft der althochdeutschen Übersetzungen der Isidor-Sippe.* Bonn: Rohrscheid, 1970.

John M. Jeep

SEE ALSO

Bible; Glosses, Old High German; *Tatian*

Itinerant Kingship

The concept of itinerant kingship (German, *Reisekönigtum*) refers to a method of government whereby a king carries out all of the functions and symbolic representations of governing, by periodically or constantly traveling throughout his dominion. Although especially well-documented and studied for the Frankish-Carolingian and the German realms of medieval Europe, itinerant kingship existed throughout Europe during most of the Middle Ages. It even existed beyond the geographical and cultural boundaries of Europe, lasting in some places beyond the end of the European Middle Ages. Itinerant kingship thus designates a method of government found widely in premodern societies and determined by various economic, social, political, religious, and cultural factors. Societies having this kind of rulership display certain common characteristics: a largely natural economy; the dominance of peasant farmers by warriors or a particular clan; governmental authority deriving from personal relationships and often from feudal relations; magical or sacred conceptions of rulership; and, often, only a marginal reliance on written administrative government. In such societies, kings or chiefs moved constantly throughout their territories making their presence felt and reinforcing the personal bonds of their rulership.

The use of itinerant kingship in medieval Germany and the frequency of the royal progress or perambulation varied greatly according to governmental structure and administrative institutions. Merovingian and Carolingian kings traveled extensively, although not constantly. They resided for long periods of time in favored residences. Moreover, the Carolingian kingdom and empire at its height governed through using representatives or written instructions sent out from court. The East Frankish Carolingian kings, and especially their Ottonian and Salian successors, however, traveled almost constantly, rarely staying in one place longer than a few days or weeks or, at most, a month, and they used the written word in governing less than the Carolingian Empire. These kingdoms, based on a highly personal kingship, lacking centralized institutions, and depending only marginally on written records, used the royal itinerary as an essential method of governance. It became the crucial vehicle for manifestation of the royal will and the integration of a large and structurally diverse realm.

During the late Ottonian and early Salian periods, the king's initial perambulation of the realm *(Umritt),* on which he gathered assent from the regional assemblies of nobles to his election and received their homage, held great importance for taking real and symbolic possession of the kingdom upon accession. Thereafter, the Ottonian and Salian kings used the annual cycle of the royal itinerary, first, to convey the sacral nature of their kingship through solemn liturgical displays and wearing the crown, and, second, to execute the political and judicial aspects of their kingship by rewarding vassals and punishing enemies and by holding court and dispensing justice. The planning and organization of the itinerary depended largely upon the material resources along the chosen route. These included royal properties and the *fodrum, gistum,* and *servitium regis* (literally, fodder, hospitality, service for the king), primarily of royal churches, but sometimes of secular nobles. Itinerant kingship reached its high point under the Ottonian and Salian kings. The Hohenstaufen kings continued it to a lesser degree, but the onus of royal accommodation and support had shifted by then to the towns.

BIBLIOGRAPHY

Arnold, Benjamin. *Medieval Germany, 500-1300: A Political Interpretation.* Toronto: University of Toronto Press, 1997, pp. 130–131, 158–174.

Bernhardt, John W. *Itinerant kingship and royal monasteries in early medieval Germany, c[irca] 936–1075.* Cambridge: Cambridge University Press, 1993.

Leyser, Karl J. "Ottonian Government." *English Historical Review* 96 (1981): 721–753.

Müller-Mertens, Eckhard. *Die Reichsstruktur im Spiegel der Herrschafts Praxis Otto des Großen.* Berlin: Akademie-Verlag, 1980.

Peyer, Hans Conrad. "Das Reisekönigtum des Mittelalters." *Vierteljahrschrift für Sozial- und Wirtschaftsgeschichte* 51 (1964): 1–21.

John W. Bernhardt

SEE ALSO

Carolingians; Empire; *Fodrum, Gistum, Servitium;* Otto I; Otto II; Otto III; *Reich;* Salians; Staufen

J

Jacob van Maerlant (ca. 1230–ca. 1290)

A Flemish poet, Maerlant came from Bruxambacht, or, the "Freedom of Bruges" *(het Brugse Vrije)*. His oeuvre, which shows strong didactic tendencies, clearly indicates that he was well educated, even though his exact place in society is unclear. He probably received minor orders and held several positions as a clerk *(clerc)*. In the late 1350s, Maerlant moved northward to the island of Voorne (in the estuary of the River Maas in the southern part of the county of Holland), taking his name from the village Maerlant (near Brielle) on that island. He became sexton *(coster, custos)* of the local church of St. Peter (if *Coster* is not his family name), a profession that agreed perfectly with his activities as an author. During his stay in Maerlant he was possibly a tutor to young Floris V (d. 1296), count of Holland. Around 1270 he returned to Flanders, to Damme, near Bruges, earning his livelihood as a civil servant (in toll regulations) and continuing his writing. Tradition (unproved) has it that he was buried after his death ca. 1290 "under the bells" of the church of Our Lady in Damme.

Some of Maerlant's works are only known from references in his other works, such as the *Sompniarijs* (a book on dream interpretation), the *Lapidarijs* (a book on the mineral qualities of stones), and a *vita* (life) of St. Clare of Assisi. Maerlant's authorship of some works is still a matter of dispute, but his oeuvre amounted to at least 225,000 lines in coupled rhyme.

The oldest surviving work is *Alexanders Geesten* [Deeds of Alexander (ca. 1260, 14,277 verses)]. Maerlant wrote this history of Alexander the Great on a commission from Aleide van Avesnes, to whom he gives the pseudonym *Gheile* in an acrostichon (series of first letters in lines of a poem which spell words). The text is a translation and adaptation of the *Alexandreïs* of Walter of Châtillon, which Maerlant took from a manuscript with glosses. But the poet used a broad range of additional sources, including the *Historia Scholastica* (Scholastic History) of Petrus Comestor, Lucanus's *De Bello Civile* (Civil War), Ovid's *Metamorphoses,* Virgil's *Aeneid,* the *Disciplina Clericalis* (Clerical Discipline) of Pedro Alfonso, the *Secreta Secretorum* (Secret of Secrets), and Honorius of Autun's *Imago Mundi* (Image of the World).

For Albrecht of Voorne, Maerlant wrote *Merlijn* in 1261. The text encompasses two separate tales: the *Historie van den Grale* (History of the Grail, 1607 verses) and *Boek van Merline* (Book of Merlin, 8485 verses), which were adaptations of Robert de Boron's *Joseph d'Arimathie* (Joseph of Arimathia) and *Roman de Merlin* (Tale of Merlin). The *Torec* (ca. 1262) is Maerlant's second Arthurian romance. This text (about 3,800 verses) has only been handed down to us in an abridged form, included in the vast *Lancelot Compilation* of The Hague.

Maerlant's *Historie van Troyen* (ca. 1264, 40,880 verses) renders the history of the Trojan War, from its preparatory stages to its aftermath. Among the sources he used were the *Roman de Troie* of Benoît of St. Maure, the *Achilleid* of Statius, the *Aeneid* of Virgil, Ovid's *Metamorphoses* and his own *Alexanders Geesten*. In addition, he incorporated the complete *Trojeroman* of Segher Diengotgaf into his text. The patron behind this work is not yet known, but it is likely the *Historie van Troyen* was intended for a noble audience.

The "Mirror of Princes," the *Heimelijkheid der Heimelijkheden* (ca. 1266, 2,158 verses), was possibly written for the young count of Holland, Floris V, and is a translation of the *Secreta Secretorum* of Pseudo-Aristoteles.(Maerlant's authorship of this text is sometimes disputed.) *Der naturen bloeme* [Flower of Nature (ca. 1266, 16,670 verses)], the first bestiary in the vernacular, assimilated Aristotle's books on biology. Maerlant derived his text from his immediate source, the *Liber de Natura Rerum* (Book of Natural Things) by Thomas of Cantimpré. The bestiary was commissioned by the nobleman Nicolaas of Cats (d. 1283).

In 1271 Maerlant finished his *Scolastica,* an abridged adaptation of Petrus Comestor's *Historia Scolastica.* To this book, of some 27,000 verses, he added an adaptation of Flavius Josephus' *De Bello Iudaïco* (On the Jewish War). Maerlant considered the total text of almost 35,000 verses as a single work. Probably commissioned by a noble patron, it was intended to serve an audience of noble laymen *(illiterati).* Even though it was not a translation of the Bible, the *Scolastica* marked the beginning of the popularization of the Bible in the Dutch language.

In the early seventies Maerlant wrote *Sente Franciscus Leven* (10,545 verses). This fairly literal translation of the *Legenda Maior* of St. Bonaventure is perhaps the first *vita* of Saint Francis in the vernacular. Maerlant wrote it at the request of the *fratres minores* (Order of the Lesser Brothers) in Utrecht. During his career as a poet, Maerlant composed several shorter stanzaic poems. These lyrical texts with a didactic aim show a fervent devotion to the Virgin Mary and a strong critical attitude towards society.

Maerlant's *magnum opus* is undoubtedly his *Spiegel Historiael.* He worked from 1283 until 1288 on this world chronicle, dedicated to Count Floris V of Holland. The major source by this text is Vincent of Beauvais's *Speculum Historiale* but Maerlant consulted and absorbed many more sources, among them the Vulgate, the *Secreta Secretorum, De Hormesta Mundi* of Orosius, *De Origine et Rebus Gestis Getarum* of Jordanes, two works by Martin of Braga (the *Liber de Moribus* and the *Formulae vitae honestae*), Paulus Diaconus's *Historia Miscella,* the *Historia Regum Brittanniae* by Geoffrey of Monmouth, as well as the Crusade chronicles by Albert of Aken and (probably) William of Tyre. As it has come down to us, the *Spiegel Historiael* (ca. 91,000 verses), is not solely from the hand of Maerlant. He had planned a work in four parts (which he called *partieën*), and he wrote the first, the third, and three "books" of the fourth part. He had postponed work on the second part, containing the years 54–367 C.E., and never was able to complete it. Apart from the lacuna of the second part and the remaining "books" of part four, Maerlant wrote a history from the Creation to the year

1113. The *Spiegel Historiael* was completed by two of his younger contemporaries, Philip Utenbroeke and Lodewijc van Velthem. The latter added a fifth part, bringing the history to the year 1316.

The extent and diversity of his oeuvre, and his exceptionally erudite and critical style, marks Jacob van Maerlant as a leading author of his time whose stature extended beyond his Dutch homeland.

BIBLIOGRAPHY

Berendrecht, Petra. *Proeven van bekwaamheid. Jacob van Maerlant en de omgang met zijn Latijnse bronnen.* Amsterdam: Prometheus, 1996.

Claassens, Geert H. M. "Maerlant on Muhammad and Islam." In *Medieval Christian Perceptions of Islam. A Book of Essays,* ed. John V. Tolan. New York & London: Garland, 1996, pp. 211–242 and 361–393.

de Pauw, Napoleon, and Edward Gaillard, ed. *Die Istory van Troyen.* 4 vols. Ghent: Siffer, 1889–1892.

de Vries, Matthijs, and Eelco Verwijs, ed. *Jacob van Maerlant's Spiegel Historiael, met de fragmenten der later toegevoegde gedeelten, bewerkt door Philip Utenbroeke and Lodewijc van Velthem.* 3 vols. Leyden: Brill, 1863–1879.

Franck, Johannes, ed. *Alexanders Geesten, van Jacob van Maerlant,* Groningen: Wolters, 1882.

Franck, Johannes, and Jakob Verdam, ed. *Jacob van Maerlants Strophische Gedichten.* Leyden: Sijthoff, 1898.

Gysseling, Maurits, ed. *Corpus van Middelnederlandse teksten. Reeks II: Literaire handschriften,* Vol. 3, *Rijmbijbel/tekst,* Leyden: Nijhoff, 1983.

Maximilianus, O. F. M., ed. *Sinte Franciscus Leven van Jacob van Maerlant.* 2 vols. Zwolle: Tjeenk-Willink, 1954.

Sodmann, Timothy, ed. *Jacob van Maerlant, Historie van den Grale und Boek van Merline.* Cologne/Vienna: Böhlau, 1980.

te Winkel, Jan. *Maerlant's werken beschouwd als spiegel van de 13de eeuw.* Ghent 1892; rpt. Utrecht: HES, 1979.

van Oostrom, Frits P. *Maerlants werteld.* Amsterdam: Prometheus, 1996.

Verdenius, Andries A., ed. *Jacob van Maerlant's Heimelijkheid der Heimelijkheden.* Amsterdam: Kruyt, 1917.

Verwijs, Eelco, ed. *Jacob van Maerlant's Naturen Bloem.* 2 vols. Groningen: Wolters, 1872–1878.

Geert H. M. Claassens

SEE ALSO
Alexander Literature, Dutch; Arthurian Literature, Dutch; Beyeren, Herald; Bible Translations, Dutch; Boethius, Dutch; Encylopedic Literature, Dutch; Saints' Lives, Dutch; Segher Diengotgaf

Jan van Boendale (ca. 1280–1351)

A Brabantine poet and a native of Tervuren, a small town between Leuven and Brussels, Jan van Boendale spent most of his working life as secretary to the aldermen of the city of Antwerp. In this position he dealt with all levels of society, an experience that affected his writing. His oeuvre consists of some seven works, although some of those texts cannot definitively be attributed to him. Boendale wrote several versions of some of his works, mainly updates of his historiographic texts, which were then dedicated to other patrons.

His first work, the *Brabantsche yeesten* (Brabantine Deeds), is a chronicle in coupled rhyme, dealing with the history of the Brabantine ducal house in the period from ca. 600 to ca. 1350. This chronicle is divided in five parts ("books"), of which the first four describe the history of Brabant before Boendale's own lifetime, and the fifth is devoted to the three dukes contemporaneous with him: Jan I (d. 1294), Jan II (d. 1312), and Jan III (d. 1355). This voluminous work of some 16,000 lines was not written in one effort; the first version dates from ca. 1316, the fifth from 1347, and a sixth version may have been written around 1351, each one providing an updated version of the history of the duchy. This does not imply that Boendale was completely original in his chronicle. Large parts of his text were copied from the *Spiegel historiael* (Mirror of History) by Jacob van Maerlant—whom Boendale elsewhere called "the father of all Dutch poets"—and the anonymous *Chronica de origine ducum Brabantiae* (Chronicle of the Origins of the Duchy of Brabant); only when writing about his own lifetime is Boendale original.

After completing a second version of the *Brabantsche yeesten* in 1318 he used the text in 1322 as the source for a very short rhyme-chronicle, the so-called *Korte kroniek van Brabant* (374 lines). He later wrote a second version of this text too, in the years 1332–1333.

But between 1325–1330, he composed an extensive didactic poem of more than 20,000 lines, called *Der leken spiegel* (The Layman's Mirror). In using this title, Boendale explicitly addresses an audience of non-readers *(illiterati),* offering them an encyclopedic text, dealing with cosmology, the nature of human body and soul, the history of the Old and New Testaments, church history, devotional practice, etc. The poem is structured according to the *Heilsgeschichte* (divine plan) and divided into four books. Books one and two deal with God's Creation, the structure of the universe, and the course of history; book three is concerned with the present, and book four with the future. *Der leken spiegel* contains the oldest poetical treatise in Dutch: in book three, chapter fifteen, Boendale presents, under the title *Hoe dichters dichten sullen ende wat si hantieren sullen* (How writers should write and what they should pay attention to), his views on literature. This is not a treatise on technical aspects of poetry, but a declaration by a self-conscious author concerning the cultural responsibilities inherent in authorship. Here, Boendale presents his ideas on, among other topics, the prerequisites of true authorship, the value of literary tradition, and the relationship between genre and fictionality.

Between 1330–1334 Boendale wrote his *Jans teesteye* (Jan's testimony), a dialogue in some 4100 lines of coupled rhyme. In this polemic-didactic dialogue the participants are "Jan," Boendale's *alter ego,* and "Wouter," probably a fictitious person, playing the role of the pupil. The topic of discussion is *grosso modo,* the quality of life in their time. Jan takes a positive, but not uncritical position; Wouter's position is negative: he is the "praiser of times past" *(laudator temporis acti).*

Shortly after 1340 Boendale wrote *Van den derden Eduwaert,* describing in 2,018 lines the role of the English king Edward III (d. 1377) in continental European politics. The poem was not only a tribute to this king, whom Boendale probably had met in person; it was first and foremost a panegyric to Duke Jan III of Brabant, an ally of the English king at the outbreak of the Hundred Year's War in 1337.

Boendale's authorship of two poems is disputed. The first is the very short *Hoemen ene stat regeren sal* (18 lines, before ca. 1350), a poem advising officials on "how to rule a town." The poem is known in several versions, some written on the tie-beams of city halls, including those in Brussels and Emmerich. The oldest known version is incorporated in a manuscript of *Der leken spiegel* (Brussels, Koninklijke Bibliotheek, manuscript no. 15.658, fol. 122r).

The second disputed poem is called the *Boec van der wraken* [The book of punishment (5,870 lines, ca. 1346)]. Reacting to the conflict between Pope Clemens VI and the German emperor Louis of Bavaria, in which he chose the imperial side, Boendale has written a pamphlet-like poem around the theme of God's punishment for human sinfulness, with strong eschatological overtones. A second, updated version was written in 1351.

Typical of Boendale's historiographic works is his orientation on Brabantine history, apparent in the recurrent *origo*-motive (the tracing back of the origin of the ducal house to the Trojans) and the *reditus*-motive (the dukes of Brabant as the true inheritors of Charlemagne). Boendale's didactic perspective revolves around the theme of the *ghemeyn oirbaer* ("the common good"), which is the basis for his social criticism. Boendale criticizes clergy, aristocracy, and commoners alike, but evidently tends to identify himself with his urban environment. This somewhat intermediate position shows itself clearly in the dedications of his poems. Though often explicitly intended for a broad audience of laymen, many of the manuscripts contain dedications to members of the aristocracy, including Willem van Bornecolve, alderman of Antwerp, Rogier van Leefdale, viscount of Brussels, and Duke Jan III of Brabant.

Jan van Boendale is an example of what is called the Antwerp School, a designation for the explosive literary output of Antwerp in the first half of the fourteenth century. When cities began to emerge as centers of literary activity in the late thirteenth century, Antwerp was the third most culturally important town of Brabant (after Brussels and Leuven). In Antwerp this increased literary activity resulted in a rather homogeneous group of texts, which included, besides Boendale's works, the *Sidrac*, the *Melibeus,* and the *Dietsche doctrinale*. The *Sidrac* is an extensive encyclopedic and didactic dialogue in prose, translated from French in 1318. The *Melibeus* (1342) is a translation of the *Liber consolationis et consilii* (Book of Consolation and Counsel) by Albertanus of Brescia (d. after 1246). In 3,771 lines, a moralizing dialogue between allegorical characters is presented.

The *Dietsche doctrinale* (German Doctrine 1345) is another translation of a misogynistic didactic text by Albertanus of Brescia, *De amore et dilectione Dei et proximi et aliorum rerum et de forma vitae* (On God's love...). This work of some 6,650 lines, divided in three "books," deals with love and friendship, virtues and vices, and closes with an interesting section on the nature of God. It thus presents a compendium of laymen's ethics. The thematic similarities between the *Melibeus*, the *Dietsche doctrinale*, and Boendale's oeuvre—that history is a framework for laymen's ethics as well as the central concept of the "common good"—has sometimes led to the attribution of these two texts to Jan van Boendale.

BIBLIOGRAPHY

Avonds, Piet. "*Ghemeyn Oirbaer*. Volkssoevereiniteit en politieke ethiek in Brabant in de veertiende eeuw." In Reynaert, Joris et al. *Wat is wijsheid? Lekenethiek in de Middelnederlandse letterkunde.* Amsterdam: Prometheus, 1994, pp. 164–180 and 405–411.

Gerritsen, Willem P., et al. "A fourteenth-century vernacular poetics: Jan van Boendale's 'How Writers Should Write'." In Erik Kooper, ed. *Medieval Dutch Literature in its European Context.* Cambridge, Cambridge University Press, 1994, pp. 245–260.

De Vries, Matthijs, ed. *Der leken spieghel, leerdicht van den jare 1330, door Jan Boendale, gezegd Jan de Clerc, schepenklerk te Antwerpen.* 3 vols. Leyden, Du Mortier, 1844–1848.

Heymans, Jo, ed. *Van den derden Eduwaert.* Nijmegen, Alfa, 1983.

Heymans, Jo. "Geschiedenis in *Der Leken Spiegel*." In Geert R. W. Dibbets and Paul W. M. Wackers, ed. *Wat duikers van is dit! Opstellen voor W.M.H. Hummelen.* Wijhe: Quarto, 1989, pp. 25–40.

Jonckbloet, Willem J. A., ed. *Die Dietsche Doctrinale, leerdicht van den jare 1345, toegekend aan Jan Deckers.* The Hague, 1842.

Kinable, Dirk, *Facetten van Boendale. Literair-historische verkenningen van Jans teesteye en de Lekenspiegel.* Leyden: Dimensie, 1998.

Lucas, H.S. "Edward III and the poet chronicler John Boendale." *Speculum* 12 (1937): 367–369.

Reynaert, Joris. "Ethiek en 'filosofie' voor leken: de *Dietsche doctrinale*." In Joris Reynaert, et al. *Wat is wijsheid? Lekenethiek in de Middelnederlandse letterkunde.* Amsterdam: Prometheus, 1994, pp. 199–214 and 415–419.

Snellaert, Ferdinand A., ed. *Nederlandsche gedichten uit de veertiende eeuw van Jan Boendale, Hein van Aken en anderen naar het Oxfordsch handschrift.* Brussels, Hayez, 1869 *[Jans teesteye; Boec van der Wraken; Melibeus].*

Van Anrooij, Wim, ed. "Hoemen ene stat regeren sal. Een vroege stadstekst uit de Zuidelijke Nederlanden." *Spiegel der Letteren* 34 (1992): 139–157.

Van Anrooij, Wim. "Recht en rechtvaardigheid binnen de Antwerpse School." In Reynaert, Joris et al. *Wat is wijsheid? Lekenethiek in de Middelnederlandse letterkunde.* Amsterdam: Prometheus, 1994, pp. 149–163 and 399–405.

Van Eerden, Peter C. "Eschatology in the *Boec van der wraken*." In Werner Verbeke, Daniel Verhelst, and Andries Welkenhuysen, ed. *The Use and Abuse of Escha-*

tology in the Middle Ages. Leuven: Leuven University Press, 1988, pp. 425–440.

Van Tol, J. F. J., ed. *Het boek van Sidrac in de Nederlanden.* Amsterdam: H. J. Paris, 1936.

Willems, Jan Frans, ed. *De Brabantsche yeesten of rymkronyk van Braband.* 2 vols. Brussels: Hayez, 1839, 1843 and J. H. Bormans, *De Brabantsche yeesten, of rijmkronijk van Braband,* vol. 3. Brussel, Hayez, 1869 [with the *Korte kronike van Brabant*].

Geert H. M. Claassens

SEE ALSO

Brabant, Duchy of; Jacob van Maerlant; Chronicles, Regional/National, Dutch; Encyclopedic Literature, Dutch

Jan van Ruusbroec (1293–1381)

Jan van Ruusbroec, a Brabantine mystic, was born in 1293 in the village of Ruisbroek southeast of Brussels. When he was eleven, he went to live in the city with a relative, John (Jan) Hinckaert (d. 1350/1358), who was a canon of the collegiate church of St. Gudula. The boy attended the school attached to the church, and after the required studies, he was ordained a priest in 1317 and became a chaplain there. In Brussels he began to compose his first treatises on mystical life, among which were some of his most important writings: *Die geestelike brulocht* (The Spiritual Espousals) and *Vanden blinkenden steen* (The Sparkling Stone).

The *Spiritual Espousals* is the most famous and most translated of his works. It describes the entire path to a mystic life from a humble beginning to complete development and indicates the risks and possible deviations at each stage. According to Ruusbroec, the essence of mystical life is the direct and passive experience of God. To describe the different stages, he uses three terms in the *Espousals* which recur in all his treatises: *dat werkende leven* (the active life), *dat innighe leven* (the interior life), *and dat schouwende leven* (the contemplative life). Each is a way to live one's relation with God. In the active life, love manifests itself in the exercise of virtue; in the interior life, a new dimension of love is discovered: to adhere intimately to the Beloved; finally, in the contemplative life, the loving person is elevated above him- or herself and introduced into the most intimate life of God, the love of the Father, Son and Spirit in one divine being. Ruusbroec strongly emphasizes the point that, at each level, the higher life does not neglect, let alone reject, the lower life.

A person who has discovered the interior life should not despise the active life. And, one who has been introduced into the contemplative life should not disdain God nor active service to his neighbor. Just as the interior life does not replace the need for an active life, but inspires and purifies it, the contemplative life enhances and elevates both.

Whereas the *Espousals* is famous for its all-encompassing view, Ruusbroec's small treatise, *The Sparkling Stone,* is a masterpiece of conciseness. It briefly describes the three lives of the *Espousals* and then concentrates on the highest of the three, the contemplative life.

In 1343 Ruusbroec, together with John Hinckaert and Frank of Coudenberg (d. 1386), another Canon of St. Gudula, left Brussels to live a contemplative life in Groenendaal (Green Valley), a site in the Wood of Soignes about ten kilometers south of Brussels. To cope with the juridical problems, resulting from their living together as a religious community without belonging to an established order or following a recognized rule, the group, which had meanwhile increased, became a provostry of canons regular of St. Augustine. Ruusbroec was the first prior of the newly founded monastery.

In Groenendaal he continued his work as a writer. There, he finished his largest work, *Van den geesteliken tabernakel* (The Spiritual Tabernacle). As the number of the manuscripts still preserved indicates, this treatise must have been very popular in its time. For the modern reader, access is difficult because the *Tabernacle* is a continuous allegory on some passages from the biblical books, Exodus and Leviticus, which describe the construction of the tabernacle and give ritual prescriptions during Israel's stay in the desert. The link between material image and spiritual reality may seem somewhat far-fetched today, but the way in which Ruusbroec masters the complex whole of image and reality is astonishing.

In Groenendaal Ruusbroec not only wrote books, but also met people who came to him with their questions about a life of prayer. Among the most famous was Geert Grote (1340-1384), the founder of the religious movement, the Modern Devotion. Very rarely, Ruusbroec left Groenendaal to visit those who were not allowed to leave their monasteries. At an advanced age, he traveled on foot to a monastery of Carthusians to help them with some difficulties concerning his description of the highest stages of mystical life. This visit gave rise to one of his last works, *Boecsken der verclaringhe* (Little Book of Enlightenment). By means of another tripartition, *enecheit met middel* (unity with intermediary), *sonder middel* (without intermediary), and *sonder differencie* (without difference), he tries to explain to his friends that—though the distinction between Creator and creature is eternal—there is a moment in mystical life when nothing of the opposition between the beloved "you" and the loving "I" is left.

In 1381 Ruusbroec died in Groenendaal at the age of eighty-eight, but his works have survived him. During his lifetime, some were translated from the Brabantine Middle Dutch into High German for the *Gottesfreunde* (Friends of God) in Strasbourg and Basle, and into Latin. About the middle of the sixteenth century his *Opera Omnia* (entire works) were translated into Latin by a Carthusian in Cologne, Laurentius Surius (1523–1578). This was the basis for many later translations into modern languages, including German and Spanish. Ruusbroec's influence is evident in the first generations of the Modern Devotion: the canons regular of the Windesheim Chapter, Gerlach Peters (d. 1411), Hendrik Mande (d. 1431), and Thomas à Kempis (1379/1380–1471). Another member of the Modern Devotion, Hendrik Herp (d. 1477), was so deeply influenced by Ruusbroec that he earned the name of "Herold of Ruusbroec." Through him, Ruusbroec's influence reached France through Benedict of Canfield (1562–1610) and John of Saint Samson (1571–1636). Born in England, Benedict passed much of his life in France, where he became a Capuchin. There, he introduced Ruusbroec to mystical circles, for example, to one Madame Acarie (1566–1618). John, blind from his early youth, joined the Carmelites and became one of the most outstanding mystical writers of his order.

BIBLIOGRAPHY

Dupré, Louis. *The Common Life: The Origins of Trinitarian Mysticism and its Development by Jan van Ruusbroec.* New York: Crossroad, 1984.

Mommaers, Paul and Norbert de Paepe, ed. *Jan van Ruusbroec: the sources, content and sequels of his mysticism.* Mediaevalia Lovaniensia ser. 1. Studia 12. Leuven: Leuven University Press, 1984.

Underhill, Evelyn. *Ruysbroeck.* London: Bell, 1915.

van Ruusbroec, Jan. *Werken.* Naar het standaardhandschrift van Groenendaal uitgegeven door het Ruusbroec-genootschap te Antwerpen. 4 vols. Mechelen/Amsterdam: Kompas, 1932–1934; 2nd ed. Tielt: Lannoo, 1944–1948.

———. *Opera Omnia.* Studiën en tekstuitgaven van Ons Geestelijk Erf, XX. Leiden: Brill; Tielt: Lannoo; Turnhout: Brepols, 1981ff. [Middle Dutch text, English and Latin trans.; Dutch and Latin introd.; 10 vols.

planned, 4 published].

———. *The Spiritual Espousals and Other Works,* Trans. James A. Wiseman. New York/Mahwah/Toronto: Paulist, 1985.

Wiseman, James A. "*Minne* in *Die gheestelike brulocht* of Jan van Ruusbroec." S.T.D. Thesis. Catholic University of America, 1979.

Guido O. E. J. De Baere

SEE ALSO
Dutch Language, Dialects; Mande, Hendrik; Peters, Gerlach; Thomas à Kempis; Visionary Literature

Jans Enikel (fl. second half of the 13th c.)

Author of the Middle High German *Weltchronik* (World Chronicle) and the *Fürstenbuch* (Princes's Book), which were probably written in the final quarter of the thirteenth century, Jans Enikel identifies himself in the *Weltchronik* as Johans *der Jansen enikel* (the grandson of Jans). He mentions that he owns a house and, in the *Fürstenbuch,* he emphasizes his status as a Viennese citizen *(ein rehter Wienner).* He, therefore, probably belonged to the upper levels of Viennese society.

The *Weltchronik* is a rhymed chronicle of some 28,000 lines. It was apparently quite popular, since it is found in thirty-nine manuscripts, either in pure form or mixed in with other chronicles. Beginning with the biblical Creation of the world and the story of Adam, the author narrates in anecdotal style the stories of biblical, Greek, and Roman figures, continuing into contemporary times with a catalogue of the popes and the emperors, and ending with Frederick II. The narrative technique is similar to that of the *Kaiserchronik,* while the narrative material itself is from different sources. In particular, there is a large amount from the apocryphal material of the Jewish tradition.

The *Fürstenbuch* is less widely transmitted, with four complete manuscripts and three fragments. It contains, in over 4,000 lines, the story of the founding of Vienna, followed by the history of the Austrian rulers from Markgraf Albrecht to Herzog Frederick II. The narrative breaks off with the events of the battle of Leitha (1246). Like the *Weltchronik,* the narrative style of the *Fürstenbuch* is anecdotal in nature.

The little research that has been done on Jans Enikel indicates a certain amount of freedom and creativity in his use of sources and models. The *Weltchronik* was particularly influential for subsequent chronicles, specifically the *Christherre-Chronik* and the chronicle of Heinrich von München.

BIBLIOGRAPHY

Liebertz-Grün, Ursula. *Das andere Mittelalter: Erzählte Geschichte und Geschichtserkenntnis um 1300: Studien zu Ottokar von Steiermark, Jans Enikel, Seifried Helbling.* Munich: Fink, 1984, pp. 71–100.

Strauch, Philipp, ed. *Jansen Enikels Werke,* Hanover and Leipzig: Hahnsche Buchhandlung, 1900.

Strauch, Philipp. "Studien über Jansen Enikel." *Zeitschrift für deutsches Altertum* 28 (1884): 34–64.

Kathleen J. Meyer

SEE ALSO

Chronicles, World, German; Frederick II; *Kaiserchronik;* Vienna

Jewish Art and Architecture

Jewish art centered on ritual objects whose ephemeral nature, along with the vicissitude of *Ashkenazis* (a geocultural term describing the German Jewish community) has led to the disappearance of almost all examples. The existence and form of various objects can be expanded on from descriptions of pillages and images in contemporary manuscripts.

Art in the synagogue centered around the external decoration of the Torah scrolls. The wooden staves of the scrolls were decorated. Crowns of precious metals were placed over the scrolls, which were protected by a sheath or cloth. A metal pointer completed the dressing of the Torah. Attention was lavished on curtains for the wooden Torah ark. A pattern emerged with a valance embellished with various temple accessories. Perpetual lamps located in front of the ark were of metal and were star-shaped—a form that was to become popular for Sabbath lamps.

Ritual objects for the home included hanging Sabbath lamps. Wine, blessed prior to the Sabbath meal, was placed in beakers made of precious metals, and decorated with biblical scenes. Lamps and spice boxes required for the ceremony ending the Sabbath were also decorated: the earlier turret shape of the former later changed to towers or steeples. The latter were made of glass, but metals such as silver and gold were also used. Passover plates were decorated with ritual scenes relating to the festival. Lamps used during the Festival of Lights evolved from

Machsor Mecholl Haschana (Dresden, Sächsische Landesbibliothek/Staats- und Universitätsbibliothek Dresden, Ms. A 46a), fol. 202v: Moses receiving the tablets of the law. *Photograph: Sächsische Landesbibliothek/Staats- und Universitätsbibliothek Dresden, Deutsche Fotothek: R. Richter*

clay examples to ones of metal, which could be hung against the wall.

Manuscript production included liturgical books such as the Torah, Bibles, codices containing the obligatory prayers and additional poetry for Sabbath and the cycle of festivals *(Machzorim)* and text read at the Passover meal *(Haggadot),* rabbinical writings such as the *mishneh* Torah, marriage contracts, medical treatises, fables, and bestiaries. Jews were excluded from craft guilds, so not much is known about Jewish scribes and illuminators, except when the names of the former were included in colophons. While no specific style developed, script, iconography, and some motifs were specifically Jewish. Absence of capital letters in Hebrew writing led to evolution of bold initial word panels. Micrography was popular, with incorporation of the text into carpet pages. Portraying God in human form was strictly prohibited. The practices of using bird or animal heads on human forms, and of portraying heads from behind or with faces left blank, developed in the thirteenth and fourteenth centuries. By the fifteenth century, complete representations of humans were no longer avoided. A specific iconography based on biblical and midrashic concepts, ritual, and custom evolved for decorating the *Mahzor* (prayer book) and *Haggadah* (book with Exodus text), with a stress on folklore and humor in the latter.

Communal buildings included ritual baths, community halls, schools, and hospitals. The heart of a Jewish community was the synagogue, whose architecture was defined by the requirements of religious law and local authorities. Exteriors were unpretentious, though the interiors could be quite sumptuously decorated. Liturgical requirements necessitated a Torah ark placed on the axis and a reading platform. The sexes were separated during prayer, at first with a curtain, and later by addition of an annex. Two principal building types evolved: two naves separated by columns, or a single nave. Vaults frequently were five-partite. Decoration of sculptured reliefs, frescoes with animal and floral motifs, and stained glass windows became increasingly popular.

BIBLIOGRAPHY

Encyclopaedia Judaica. 16 vols. Jerusalem: Macmillan, 1971.

Gutmann, Joseph. *Hebrew Manuscript Painting.* New York: Braziller, 1978.

Metzger, Thérèse, and Mendel Metzger. *Jewish Life in the Middle Ages: Illuminated Hebrew Manuscripts of the Thirteenth to Sixteenth Centuries.* New York: Alpine Fine Arts Collection, 1982.

Roth, Cecil. *Jewish Art: An Illustrated History,* ed. Bezalel Narkiss. 2nd, revised edition Jerusalem: Massada, 1971.

Sed-Rajna, Gabrielle. *Ancient Jewish Art: East and West.* Neuchâtel: Attinger, 1985.

A Sign and a Witness: 2000 Years of Hebrew Books and Manuscript Illuminations, ed. Leonard Singer Gold. Studies in Jewish History. New York: New York Public Library, 1988.

Jacqueline A. Frank

SEE ALSO

Jews; Manuscripts, Painting and Production

Jews

[This entry includes three subentries:
Introduction
Internal Development
External Relations]

Introduction

Jews traveled throughout Germany as merchants in the late Roman Empire and early Middle Ages. Jews may even have settled in cities such as Cologne as early as the fourth century, though there are few substantive records of permanent Jewish settlement in Germany before the ninth and tenth centuries, when a number of Jewish families, the most prominent the Kalonymos family from Lucca, likely made their way to the Rhineland from Italy.

From the ninth to eleventh centuries, the most important Jewish community was in Mainz. In the 960s and 970s, there is mention of royal protection for Jews in Magdeburg and Merseburg. Jews settled in Regensburg in the tenth century, and Cologne, Worms, Trier, and Speyer in the eleventh century. In general, Jews found homes in old episcopal and trade centers. The famous invitation of the Bishop of Speyer to the Jews of Mainz in 1084 offered protection and numerous privileges for settling in the city at the same time that it made clear the economic benefit that the bishop intended to reap through their businesses. The charter was thus indicative of the later development of medieval German Jewry. Similar charters were offered to Jews in other cities, such as Worms in 1090. Due to the favorable economic conditions, autonomous self-government, and strong systems of education bolstered by the settlement of important scholars, the Rhineland communities flourished in the High Middle Ages.

Initially, Jews settled in cities and were first involved in international and later, during the eleventh century, in regional business. In the twelfth and thirteenth centuries, Jews were also involved in the collection of tolls and taxes, as well as money handling and credit, in large part due to restrictions prohibiting them from other occupations. Some Jews practiced as doctors, and many also were employed in the service of the Jewish community itself, as teachers, rabbis, and butchers, for example. Despite occupational restrictions, there are traces of Jews in a vast diversity of occupational positions in the later Middle Ages, such as "engineers," glassblowers, barbers, bookmakers, printers, gold and silversmiths, traders of many products (precious metals, leather, textiles, wine, fruit, vegetables, saffron, weapons), handworkers, weapon makers, innkeepers, servants, and furriers.

In the ninth century there were only a few dozen Jewish families in Germany, probably a few hundred in the tenth century. It has been estimated that there were as many as 4,000 to 5,000 Jews by the end of tenth century, and 20,000 to 25,000 on the eve of First Crusade (1096) at the end of the eleventh century. At the end of the Middle Ages, the largest Jewish communities included Regensburg (with more than 500 Jews), and Nürnberg (with more than 200 Jews). In the largest Jewish communities, however, Jews typically comprised no more than 1 to 3 percent of the total city population. The number of Jewish communities, each rather small in size, increased dramatically during the second half of the thirteenth and the first half of the fourteenth centuries, before the massacres and persecution of the Jews during the Black Death (1348–1350). Jews were dispersed throughout Germany in the fourteenth and fifteenth centuries, and there were numerous small Jewish communities and traces of Jews in areas outside larger cities and in rural areas. In the High Middle Ages, Jewish settlement was particularly widespread in the Rhineland, Upper Germany, and Franconia, though much thinner in Bavaria and the north. After the thirteenth century there was a thick settlement in the east, in places such as Silesia, Moravia, and Lower Austria. During the fifteenth century there was a substantial growth in the number of communities in the southwest, particularly in Baden Württemberg and parts of Bavaria.

Internal Development

The Jewish community often consisted of a small number of Jews who entered into an association based on consensus through binding oaths in order to protect the rights of its members from external authority and to regulate internal communal life according to a shared body of Jewish law, primarily as brought down in the Talmud and the various medieval codifications of Talmudic law, rabbinic *responsa* (commentaries), and local or regional ordinances and customs. Such associations could be oligarchic and ineffectual, relying as they did on indirect authority and the revocation of particular, typically ritual, services.

The Jewish community in medieval Germany was, in a certain sense, a state within a state. On the one hand, the Jewish community possessed the privilege of self-government; on the other hand, Jewish autonomy depended heavily on the toleration, and often assistance, of the civil government. The result was that Jews functioned within two systems of government that could be overlapping or contradictory. Try as they might, leaders of the Jewish community at times even had difficulty in keeping legal cases that had primarily to do with Jewish law from Christian or civil courts.

Although the individual local community, especially before the end of the fourteenth century, came to regard itself as an autonomous jurisdictional area, communities often joined together to enact specific regulations or to judge particular legal cases. Throughout the Middle Ages there were a number of important rabbinic synods that attempted to create centralized authority and legal observance. Of particular importance were the combined synods of the three Rhineland communities Speyer, Worms, and Mainz, known as *SHUM*. Between 1196 and 1250, ordinances were discussed and approved regarding a broad array of topics such as trial procedures, debts, taxation, the ban of excommunication, sumptuary laws, synagogues, and relations with non-Jews.

Although some Jewish communities had strict laws regarding the settlement of other Jews, membership in the community was typically automatic once an individual resided in that city for more than twelve months, had bought a house, begun extensive business, or settled his whole family.

The community was governed by a community council, comprised originally of wealthy and scholarly members of the community and convened for religious and "civil" functions in order to initiate and regulate communal policy, and protect the community and its economic, judicial, and diplomatic interests. The council heard cases between local and foreign Jews, cases regarding informants, information about the declaration and collection of taxes, and at times might oversee the distribution of charity. In larger communities a body of offices, at times modeled after local non-Jewish structures, dispensed important administrative functions. There were, for example, such positions as the supervisor of charity, tax assessors, as well as positions requiring the upkeep of the cemetery or the synagogue. The number of members serving on the council varied from city to city, as did the exact procedures for electing them. Most cities appointed between seven and fourteen members. In some places, councilmen were elected by a majority vote of all residents, in other communities through an indirect election committee. Generally, in theory at least, the length of tenure of office was one year; practically, however, officers were not typically removed from office as long as they continued to fulfill their duties. Elections often required the additional approval of the civil or ecclesiastical authority and often stipulated that the person elected pay an election fee and take an oath of fealty to the civil authority. Smaller communities had only a few leaders, or *parnasim,* who oversaw the numerous administrative functions within the Jewish community and between the Jewish and non-Jewish authorities.

The instability and dramatic results of the pogroms following in the wake of the Black Death had a profound effect on the Jewish communities in Germany. In response to disintegrating communal structures, the position of the rabbi became more formalized or "professionalized," since the rabbi was the chief person who could interpret and apply the body of Jewish law. At the end of the fourteenth century, Rabbi Meir ben Baruch Halevi of Vienna adopted a policy of ordaining students in order to permit them to establish an academy and perform vital rabbinic functions. Such ordination became popular in the fifteenth century and made the rabbi the primary agent in the reconstitution of the shattered Jewish communities.

The Jewish community entailed more than just Jewish people. A number of physical structures typically made up a Jewish quarter, if they did not yet constitute an official Jewish ghetto. In addition to living spaces, there were synagogues, ritual baths, and cemeteries. In the later Middle Ages we also find in the larger Jewish communities such as Mainz traces of a bakery and a slaughterhouse.

The Jewish household often included several generations of extended family and servants, even though the core Jewish family in medieval Germany may have averaged less than two children. Women played a central role within the Jewish family and community and they possessed a number of legal rights, particularly regarding marriage and divorce. Women could also play important roles in business matters, especially widows, who often continued their husbands' trades. In fact, Jewish women frequently headed their families: 22.6 percent of all family heads on the Mainz list of Jews martyred during the First Crusade, for example, were women.

Jewish learning took place at a number of levels. Both private and community instruction was available at the elementary and advanced levels—for children and for Talmudic students. Talmudic students studied in a *yeshivah,* a small association of students and a prominent scholar, that resembled in some external ways the early universities of the Middle Ages. Throughout the Middle Ages, *yeshivot* (plural) were organized, as well as housed and financed, by particularly prominent rabbis who attracted a following of students, who wandered from *yeshivah* to *yeshivah* in search of instruction, legal decisions, and local customs. Unlike the Jewish academies of Babylonia in the Talmudic period, German *yeshivot* were typically small, ranging in size from several to perhaps as many as 100 students. Students were instructed in a variety of textual methods and with a number of sources, particularly the Talmud, important medieval commentaries, and the decisions of other prominent rabbis, as well as local customs. Throughout the Middle Ages, German Jews engaged and created legal works, liturgy, chronicles, books of customs, and biblical and Talmudic commentaries. Some Yiddish and German works were also produced and undoubtedly circulated, though these seem to have been more significant only toward the end of the Middle Ages. Some Jews were also involved in mystical speculation and writing, such as the *Hasidei Ashkenaz,* or German Pietists, who flourished at the end of the twelfth century, particularly in some of the Rhineland communities and in Regensburg.

External Relations

Throughout the Middle Ages there were serious points of conflict between Jews and Christians and deadly attacks against Jews by Christians in Germany. Among the most notorious physical attacks were the massacres associated with the First Crusade, in which Christians murdered thousands of Jews, particularly in the Rhineland communities, and the accusations of well-poisoning and subsequent pogroms against and expulsion of the Jews during the Black Death in the middle of the fourteenth century. Less well-known are the attacks against Jews in the late thirteenth and first half of the fourteenth centuries, particularly in south Germany, as well as the eventual and almost systematic expulsion of the Jews from a variety of German cities in the fifteenth, and German territories in the sixteenth century. Both ecclesiastical and secular authorities persecuted the Jews at times. In 1012, for example, the Jews of Mainz were expelled by Henry II, and after the first third of the thirteenth century, when Jews were granted imperial privileges of protection as serfs of the chamber, they became easy and frequent targets of financial extortion, forced to pay weighty taxes and make substantial contributions to the crown. The anti-Jewish stance of the church could be even more destructive. The archbishop of Mainz, for example, sought to expel the Jews of Mainz as early as 937, and the Fourth Lateran (papal) Council (Rome, 1215) legislated severe restrictions against Jews that were taken up throughout Germany. Jews were, for example, restricted in their travels and their social interaction with Christians and were forcibly distinguished from Christians by required articles of dress, such as the Jewish hat or the yellow patch. They were also at times subject to heavy Christian missionizing and forced conversion. Anti-Jewish sentiment could be generated among the populace as well as the elite. Political and social segregation within the cities and professional marginalization were combined with popular negative perceptions, which cast Jews as culprits in theft, sorcery, host desecration, and ritual murder (as in Würzburg in 1147 and Fulda in 1235).

It would, however, be a mistake to suggest that Jews and Christians in medieval Germany never had normal relations. Often Jews and Christians shared cultural and social, if not religious, identity. Even where Jews lived in physically separated areas from Christians there were unavoidable points of contact in business and everyday life. Although it is difficult to document such interaction, the proliferation of both Jewish and Christian calls for the social and cultural separation of Jews and Christians indicates that there was significant interaction between the two groups on a daily basis and at a variety of levels.

In the end the Jews were unique in an otherwise homogeneous Christian culture, and yet the history of their development and interaction with their Christian neighbors reflected many of the more general historical developments in medieval Germany.

BIBLIOGRAPHY

GENERAL

Agus, Irving. *The Heroic Age of Franco-German Jewry.* New York: Yeshivah University Press, 1969.

Breuer, Mordechai and Michael Graetz. *German-Jewish History in Modern Times,* vol. 1: *Tradition and Enlightenment 1600–1780,* trans. William Templer. New York: Columbia University Press, 1996.

Stow, Kenneth R. *Alienated Minority: The Jews of Medieval Latin Europe.* Cambridge, Mass: Harvard University Press, 1992.

Toch, Michael. *Die Juden im Mittelalterlichen Reich.* Munich: Oldenbourg Press, 1998.

INTERNAL DEVELOPMENT

Agus, Irving. *Rabbi Meir of Rothenburg: His Life and His Works as Sources for the Religious, Legal, and Social History of the Jews of Germany in the Thirteenth Century.* Philadelphia: Dropsie College, 1947.

Eidelberg, Shlomo. *Jewish Life in Austria in the Fifteenth Century as Reflected in the Legal Writings of Rabbi Israel Isserlein and His Contemporaries.* Philadelphia: Dropsie College, 1962.

Finkelstein, Louis. *Jewish Self-Government in the Middle Ages.* New York: Feldheim, 1972.

Kanarfogel, Ephraim. *Jewish Education and Society in the High Middle Ages.* Detroit: Wayne State University Press, 1992.

Katz, Jacob. *Tradition and Crisis: Jewish Society at the End of the Middle Ages.* New York: Free Press, 1961.

Marcus, Ivan. *Piety and Society: The Jewish Pietists of Medieval Germany.* Leiden: Brill, 1981.

Shohet, David Menahem. *The Jewish Court in the Middle Ages: Studies in Jewish Jurisprudence According to the Talmud, Geonic, and Medieval German Responsa.* New York: Hermon Press, 1974.

Straus, Raphael. *Regensburg and Augsburg,* trans. Felix N. Gerson. Philadelphia: Jewish Publication Society of America, 1939.

Zimmer, Eric. *Harmony and Discord: An Analysis of the Decline of Jewish Self-Government in Fifteenth-Century Central Europe.* New York: Yeshivah University Press, 1970.

EXTERNAL RELATIONS

Chazan, Robert. *European Jewry and the First Crusade.* Berkeley: University of California Press, 1987.

Cohen, Jeremy. *The Friars and the Jews: The Evolution of Medieval Anti-Judaism.* Ithaca, N.Y.: Cornell University Press, 1982.

Hsia, R. Po-chia, and Hartmut Lehmann, eds. *In and Out of the Ghetto: Jewish-Gentile Relations in Late Medieval and Early Modern Germany.* Cambridge, England: Cambridge University Press, 1995.

Katz, Jacob. *Exclusiveness and Tolerance: Studies in Jewish-Gentile Relations in Medieval and Modern Times.* London: Oxford University Press, 1961.

Kisch, Guido. *The Jews in Medieval Germany: A Study of Their Legal and Social Status.* Chicago: The University of Chicago Press, 1949; 2nd edition, New York: Ktav Publishing House, Inc., 1970.

SOURCES

Germania Judaica, vol. 1: *Von den ältesten Zeiten bis 1238,* eds. M. Brann, I. Elbogen, A. Freimann; and H. Tykocinski. Breslau, 1917–1934; rpt. Tübingen: Mohr, 1963, vol. 2: *Von 1238 bis zur Mitte des 14. Jahrhunderts,* edited by Zvi Avneri, 2 points Tübingen: Mohr,

1968, vol. 3: 1350–1519, point. 1, eds. Arye Maimon and Yacov Guggenheim. Tübingen: Mohr, 1987; point 2, eds. Arye Maimon, Mordechai Breuer, and Yacov Guggenheim. Tübingen: Mohr, 1995; point 3, eds. Mordechai Breuer and Yacov Guggenheim. Tübingen: Mohr, [in press].

Dean Phillip Bell

SEE ALSO
Cologne, History; Crusades; Jewish Art and Architecture; Magdeburg; Mainz; Merseburg; Nuremberg; Speyer; Trier; Worms

Johann von Würzburg (fl. ca. 1300)
As in most cases of medieval German literature, hardly anything is known about the author, except for some self-references in his courtly romance, *Wilhelm von Österreich*. He mentions that he was born in Würzburg and worked as a scribe, perhaps for the counts of Hohenberg and Haigerloch, especially Count Albrecht von Haigerloch (d. 1298). He also expresses his thanks to a citizen of Esslingen, Dieprecht, for helping him with his work. *Wilhelm von Österreich* was completed in May of 1314 and was dedicated to the Dukes Leopold and Frederick of Austria. It appears to have been rather popular, since it has come down to us in a large number of manuscripts (in Gießen, Gotha, The Hague, Heidelberg, etc.). In total, there are ten complete manuscripts and ten fragments extant.

Wilhelm von Österreich is a biographical romance combining chivalrous with amorous adventures providing a mythical-historical background for the ruling House of Hapsburg. Duke Leopold of Austria and the heathen king Agrant of Zyzia make a pilgrimage to the holy site of John of Ephesus to pray for an heir. They meet by chance and make their sacrifices together. Leopold's wife delivers a son, Wilhelm, and Agrant's wife has a daughter, Aglye. The goddess Venus awakens love in both children through dreams and instigates Wilhelm to leave home on a search for Aglye. After exotic travels he meets Aglye, and the children fall in love. Her father, Agrant, separates them, however, because he wants to marry his daughter to a heathen prince. The lovers exchange an extensive correspondence that documents the high level of literacy that members of the higher aristocracy could acquire in the later Middle Ages. Aglye is twice promised as wife to heathen princes, but Wilhelm kills them both in battles and jousts. Only after he has liberated Queen Crispin of Belgalgan's kingdom of monsters are the lovers able to meet again. Soon afterwards a massive battle involves the heathen and Christian forces, which concludes with the Christians' victory and the heathens' baptism. Finally, King Agrant agrees with the marriage of Aglye and Wilhelm, to whom a son is born called Friedrich. Wilhelm dies thereafter when he is ambushed by an envious brother-in-law. Aglye's heart breaks when she hears the news and dies as well.

Wilhelm experiences a large number of allegorical adventures throughout his quest for his beloved. These, and other aspects, are often commented on by the narrator, who fully enjoyed the use of the so-called *geblümter Stil* (flowery style). Johann von Würzburg refers to Gottfried von Straßburg, Wolfram von Eschenbach, and Rudolf von Ems as his literary models. He also knows Albrecht's *Jüngeren Titurel* and other thirteenth century romances.

Wilhelm von Österreich displays a surprising openness toward the heathen culture, although the paradigm of Christianity as the only true religion is not abandoned in favor of global tolerance. Johann von Würzburg enjoyed considerable success with his work, which glorifies the House of Austria and combines the exotic world of the Orient with the world of Arthurian romance. The text was copied far into the fifteenth century and discussed by other writers such as Püterich of Reichertshausen and Ulrich Fuetrer. Anton Sorg printed a prose version in 1481 and 1491 in Augsburg, which was also reprinted, probably in Wittenberg in 1530–1540. Wilhelm and Aglye, the main characters in the romance, are portrayed in the fifteenth-century frescoes on Castle Runkelstein as ideal lovers, next to Tristan and Isolde, and Wilhelm of Orleans and Amelie.

BIBLIOGRAPHY
Brackert, Helmut: *"Da stuont daz minne wol gezam," Zeitschrift für deutsche Philologie, Sonderheft*, 93 (1974): 1–18.

Juergens, Albrecht: *'Wilhelm von Österreich'. Johanns von Würzburg 'Historia Poetica' von 1314 und Aufgabenstellung einer narrativen Fürstenlehre*. Frankfurt am Main: Lang, 1990.

Johanns von Würzburg *"Wilhelm von Österreich." Aus der Gothaer Hs.*, ed. Ernst Regel. Berlin: Weidmann, 1906; rpt. Zurich: Weidmann, 1970.

Mayser, Eugen. *Studien zur Dichtung Johanns von Würzburg*. Berlin: Ebering, 1931.

Ridder, Klaus. *Mittelhochdeutsche Minne- und Aventiureromane: Fiktion, Geschichte und literarische Tradition im späthöfischen Roman: Reinfried von Braunschweig, Wilhelm von Österreich, Friedrich von Schwaben.* Berlin: de Gruyter, 1998.

Straub, Veronika: *Entstehung und Entwicklung des früh-neuhochdeutschen Prosaromans. Studien zur Prosaauflösung 'Wilhelm von Österreich'.* Amsterdam: Rodopi, 1974.

Wentzlaff-Eggebert, Friedrich-Wilhelm: *Kreuzzugsdichtung des Mittelalters.* Berlin: Walter de Gruyter, 1960, pp. 290–293.

Albrecht Classen

SEE ALSO

Fuetrer, Ulrich; Gottfried von Straβburg; Gottfried von Straßburg, *Tristan*, Illustrations; Püterich of Reichertshausen, Jacob; Wolfram von Eschenbach

Johannes Scottus (fl. 845/846–877/879)

Biographical details concerning one of the most original and influential scholars of ninth-century Carolingian Europe are sparse. John Scottus (Eriugena) left Ireland for the Continent probably in the 830s and by the 840s was attached to the west Frankish court of Charles the Bald (r. 840–877). His career oscillated between the court and the ecclesiastical and intellectual centers of northeastern France, especially Soissons, Laon, and Reims.

John's major work, the *Periphyseon* (On Predestination), an engaging, complex, and original philosophical meditation embracing elements from the Augustinian, Neoplatonic, Greek and Latin patristic, and liberal arts traditions, is justly regarded as his masterpiece and as the most impressive speculative work between Augustine and Abelard. John Scottus's intellectual and pedagogical interests ranged widely. His earliest works, glosses on the grammar of Priscian (sixth century), on Martianus Capella's allegory of the liberal arts, *The Marriage of Philology and Mercury*, and on the Bible, introduced John's students to both human and sacred wisdom. His reputation as a keen scholar led the bishops of Laon and Reims to ask him to counter the views of Godescalc (Gottschalk), a Saxon monk, who argued that humans were predestined by God to both salvation and to damnation. In his *Periphyseon*, John demonstrated that humans were predestined for salvation, but not damnation, and seemed to suggest that evil was not real. This approach prompted widespread condemnation of John, who was lumped together with other Irish scholars for seeming to privilege dialectic over biblical truth. John's career as a teacher and author might

well have ended at mid-century had not Charles the Bald continued to patronize and protect him.

John's early works show an unusual and deepening familiarity with the Greek language and with the works of Byzantine theologians. In the aftermath of the predestination controversy he translated a series of seminal Greek works into Latin, none more important than those of Pseudo-Dionysius, a sixth-century Neoplatonist mistakenly revered in the Middle Ages as the first-century Athenian disciple of the apostle Paul. He also translated works by Maximus the Confessor, Gregory of Nyssa, and Epiphanius of Salamis, and thereby opened up conduits to the Greek tradition of mystical theology. His translations influenced the development of his own thought. He commented on the Pseudo-Dionysius's *Celestial Hierarchy* and wove Byzantine theology into the *Periphyseon*. The popularity of John's homily on the prologue to the gospel of St. John (more than fifty-five manuscripts survive) is owed to the medieval misattribution of the homily to Origen and John Chrysostom, an understandable confusion given the patently Greek flavor of the homily.

Charles the Bald's emulation of Byzantine court ceremony and dress offers a political parallel to John Scottus's scholarship, especially since the scholar also participated in the life of the court. Much of the poetry he composed and recited in Greek and Latin at the court of Charles and Irmintrudis, his queen, celebrated the important religious feast days and battlefield victories. John Scottus died apparently while at work on an unfinished commentary on the gospel of John. The surviving manuscript contains notes in Scottus's own hand.

BIBLIOGRAPHY

Contreni, John J., and Pádraig P. Ó Néill. *Glossae Divinae Historiae: The Biblical Glosses of John Scottus Eriugena.* Florence: SISMEL-Edizioni del Galluzzo, 1997.

Jeauneau, Édouard and Paul Edward Dutton. *The Autograph of Eriugena.* Corpus Christianorum, Autographa Medii Aevi 3. Turnholt: Brepols, 1996.

John Scottus. *Iohannes Scottus Eriugena, Carmina.* Ed. and trans. Michael W. Herren. Scriptores Latini Hiberniae 12. Dublin: Dublin Institute for Advanced Studies, 1993.

Van Riel, Gerd, Carlos Steel, and James McEvoy, eds. *Iohannes Scottus Eriugena: The Bible and Hermeneutics,* Ancient and Medieval Philosophy, De-Wulf-Mansion Centre, Series 1, XX. Leuven: Leuven University Press, 1996.

John J. Contreni

SEE ALSO
Carolingians; Gottschalk of Orbais

Johannes von Tepl (ca. 1350–early 15th c.)

Born in German and Czech-speaking Bohemia, Tepl (also known as Johannes von Saaz or Johannes Henslini de Sitbor) has been identified as the author of the *Ackermann aus Böhmen* (The Bohemian Plowman) by means of the acrostic IOHANNES, and by the signature de Tepla ("of Tepl") in a letter accompanying the work sent to friend Peter Rothirsch of Prague. Appointments as rector of the Latin school and notary of the cities of Saaz and later Prague-Neustadt show Tepl to have been literate in both Czech and Latin as well as German. Besides the *Ackermann aus Böhmen,* only a few German and Latin verses, plus parts of a Latin votive office (1404), have been identified as Tepl's work. It is unclear whether the *Czech Tkadlecek* (ca. 1407), a text similar to the *Ackermann* in which a weaver laments the loss of his unfaithful sweetheart, might also have been composed by him. *The Ackermann* is preserved whole or in part in sixteen manuscript editions, mostly of upper German provenance, as well as in seventeen early printed editions. The Pfister edition of 1460 is one of the two earliest printed books in German.

The work, an audacious debate with death, is framed as a legal proceeding in which a grief-stricken widower, a "plowman of the pen" (i.e., a scribe) brings a complaint against the justice and justification of death in God's world order. The plowman bewails the loss of his virtuous young wife, Margaretha, and rails at Death's cruelty and unfairness. In sixteen rounds of spirited debate, the plowman condemns Death while defending life, love, and man, God's finest creation. Death, in his turn, denies any dignity of man and any right to life, vaunting, instead, his own power and arbitrariness. Only in chapter 33 is the argument silenced when God is called on to deliver a verdict in the case. Because the plaintiff has fought well, God awards him honor, but gives the victory to Death by affirming the status quo. The work ends with an impassioned prayer for the soul of Margaretha.

The emotional verisimilitude of the argumentation and the correspondence of biographical data in the text to certain facts of Tepl's life have raised the question whether the work might not have been precipitated by an actual bereavement of the author, perhaps his first wife, the mother of his two oldest children. Records show Tepl to have been survived by a widow, Clara (possibly a second wife), and five children. The autobiographical thesis seems to be at odds, however, with the tone of the author's letter to Rothirsch, which emphasizes the stylistic devices and rhetorical strategies deployed in the work.

More significant than the unresolved autobiographical issue is the controversy over whether the arguments and style place the work further within the realm of late medieval or of early humanist thought. Although thematically and formally the *Ackermann* remains largely indebted to earlier medieval traditions, stylistically its language echos that of Johann von Neumarkt's chancellery German, which shows the strong influence of the Latin rhetorical forms of Italian humanists.

BIBLIOGRAPHY

Hahn, Gerhard. *Der Ackermann aus Böhmen des Johannes von Tepl.* Erträge der Forschung 215. Darmstadt: Wissenschaftliche Buchgesellschaft, 1984.

Hruby, Antonín. *Der Ackermann und seine Vorlage.* Munich: Beck, 1971.

Hübner, Arthur. "Deutsches Mittelalter und italienische Renaissance im *Ackermann aus Böhmen.*" *Zeitschrift für Deutschkunde* 51 (1937): 225–239.

Jaffe, Samuel. "Des Witwers Verlangen nach Rat: Ironie und Struktureinheit im *Ackermann aus Böhmen.*" *Daphnis* 7 (1978): 1–53.

Johannes von Saaz. *Der Ackermann aus Böhmen,* ed. Günther Jungbluth. 2 vols. Heidelberg: Winter, 1969–1983.

Johannes von Tepl. *Death and the Plowman; or, The Bohemian Plowman,* trans. Ernst N. Kirrmann from the Modern German version of Alois Bernt. Chapel Hill: University of North Carolina Press, 1958.

Schwarz, Ernst, ed. *Der Ackermann aus Böhmen des Johannes von Tepl und seine Zeit.* Wege der Forschung 143. Darmstadt: Wissenschaftliche Buchgesellschaft, 1968.

Anne Winston-Allen

Judith, Empress (ca. 800–843)

Adulated as a Rachel, vilified as a Jezebel, Empress Judith (r. 819—840) has likely suffered more than any other Carolingian from a polarized historiography. Primarily known as the second wife of Emperor Louis the Pious (r. 814–840) and mother of King Charles the Bald (r. 840–877), she assumed a commanding role in the volatile world of ninth-century Frankish politics, earning the respect of many, and the enmity of many more.

Presented at the February, 819, Aachen assembly by her parents (Welf, count of Alemannia, and the Saxon noblewoman Heilwig), a beautiful Judith caught the recently-widowed emperor's eye; they were married immediately. Judith gave birth in 821 to a daughter, Gisela, but did not pose a real threat to her three stepsons until producing a rival male heir, Charles, on June 13, 823. From that day forth she strove to procure a stable future for her son (and herself) by arranging advantageous marriage alliances, installing relatives in key imperial offices, and using her proximity to her husband on behalf of several influential courtiers. She achieved her greatest successes in Louis's territorial grants to Charles in 829 (Alemannia), 832 (Aquitaine), and 837 (Neustria), followed by the actual crowning of Charles as "king" in August, 838. Among such auspicious occasions, however, lay a series of rebellions in 830 and 833–834, each led by Louis's eldest son, Lothar, in an attempt to assert his own imperial authority. He and his followers focused much of their hostility on Judith, accusing her in 830 of adultery and sorcery (charges later cleared by her oath of innocence at Aachen on February 2, 831), and banishing her to Poitiers. They exiled her again in the later revolt to a convent in Tortona, Lombardy. Lothar's overconfidence and the ephemeral help of his brothers (Louis and Pepin) assured his failure in both instances, however, leaving Judith and Charles several years to consolidate their position (and according to some accounts, to wreak revenge) before Louis died on June 20, 840.

Civil war ensued, despite Louis's revised division of the empire in 839 between Lothar and Charles. In the end, it was the help of Louis the Bavarian (who had married Judith's sister, Emma, in 827) that made possible Charles's and Judith's victory over Lothar at Fontenoy on June 25, 841. Afterward, Charles further shored up his power base, benefiting particularly from his mother's activities in Aquitaine from her base in Bourges. On December 13, 842, Judith witnessed the strategic marriage of her son to Ermentrude (niece of Adalard, count of Tours). Charles soon enhanced this declaration of independence by dispossessing his mother of her lands and placing her in "retirement" at Tours, probably in February, 843. She died there two months later, on April 19, 843, comforted, perhaps, that her consistent efforts on behalf of her son had changed the course of Carolingian history.

Acclaimed by several contemporary writers for both her beauty and erudition, Judith also fostered Carolingian learning. She arranged for Walahfrid Strabo to tutor Charles from 829 to 838, and commissioned the second book of Freculf of Lisieux's important *Chronicle*. Hrabanus Maurus's dedication of a commentary on the biblical books of Judith and Esther, as well as a figure poem to Judith also testifies to her literary patronage, and has supported the contention that she may have personally supervised the creation and expansion of Louis the Pious's court library.

BIBLIOGRAPHY

Bischoff, Bernhard. "Benedictine Monasteries and the Survival of Classical Literature." In *Manuscripts and Libraries in the Age of Charlemagne*, trans. Michael Gorman. Cambridge, England: Cambridge University Press, 1994, pp. 134–160.

Boshof, Egon. *Ludwig der Fromme*. Darmstadt: Primus, 1996.

Cabaniss, Allen. "Judith Augusta and Her Time." *Studies in English* 10 (1969): 67–109.

Konecny, Silvia. *Die Frauen des karolingischen Königshauses*. Vienna: VWGÖ, 1976.

McKitterick, Rosamond. *The Frankish Kingdoms under the Carolingians, 751-987*. London: Longman, 1983.

Nelson, Janet L. *Charles the Bald*. London: Longman, 1992.

Ward, Elizabeth. "Caesar's Wife: The Career of the Empress Judith, 819–829." In *Charlemagne's Heir: New Perspectives on the Reign of Louis the Pious (814–840)*, eds. Peter Godman and Roger Collins. Oxford: Clarendon, 1990, pp. 205–227.

Steven A. Stofferahn

SEE ALSO

Carolingians; Hrabanus Maurus; Lothar I; Louis the Pious; Walahfrid Strabo

Judith the Welf (ca. 1100—1130/1131)

Judith was born about the year 1100, the daughter of the Welf (also Guelf) Duke Henry IX the Black of Bavaria and his wife, Wulfhilde, the elder daughter of Duke Magnus of Saxony (from the Billunger family). When Magnus died in 1106, Wulfhilde and her sister, Eilika, wife of the Ascanian count Otto of Ballenstedt, inherited his lands. Judith's siblings were Henry the Proud, Conrad the Cistercian, a hermit who lived in the Holy Land and died about 1126, Sophie, who married Duke Berthold III of Zähringen, Mathilda, who married Margrave Diepold IV of Vohburg, Wulfhilde, who married Count Rudolf of Bregenz, and Welf VI.

About 1120, Judith married Frederick II of Staufen who had followed his father as duke of Swabia in 1105. The marriage was part of a calculated policy aimed at expanding Welf family power into southwestern Germany through union with the Staufen and Zähringer. Their children were Bertha, who became the wife of Duke Matthew of Lorraine, and Frederick Barbarossa, born in 1122.

The marriage of a Staufen to a Welf princess augured well for a close alliance between the two powerful Swabian dynasties, but events proved otherwise. When the last Salian emperor, Henry V, died childless in 1125, there were several candidates for the German throne: as nephew of Henry V, Frederick II of Staufen had the best right of blood; Margrave Leopold III of Austria and Count Charles of Flanders also sought support. The ecclesiastical princes, headed by Archbishop Adalbert I of Mainz, rejected Frederick's claims and promoted the election of Lothar of Supplinburg, duke of Saxony, who was proclaimed king at Mainz.

At first, the Bavarians objected out of loyalty to Duke Frederick, their kinsman, but in time they were won over to the side of Lothar. The cause of their defection was the promise given by the archbishop of Mainz and his supporters that Henry the Black's son, Henry the Proud, should marry Lothar's only daughter, Gertrude, then ten years old. As Lothar had no sons, she was the sole heiress to the extensive possessions amassed by her father. Above all, the marriage gave young Henry the expectation of inheriting Lothar's Saxon dukedom and the crown itself as well, should Lothar become king.

Duke Henry the Black died in 1126 and was succeeded by Henry the Proud. The latter's marriage to Gertrud of Supplinburg in 1127 produced but one child, Henry the Lion, who was born in 1129/1130. That same marriage, and the betrayal that lay behind it, turned Duke Frederick II into a bitter adversary of both King Lothar and of his Welf kinsfolk.

In the struggle during the years following 1125, Judith of Welf was personally involved in the defense of Speyer in 1129. She died on February 22, 1130/1131, and was buried at the cloister at Lorch. After her death, Frederick II married Agnes of Saarbrücken. The marriage to Judith had not resulted in the harmonious coexistence of the Hohenstaufens and the Welfs, but it did produce a king and emperor. Moreover, Frederick II used a precious gold reliquary cross from Byzantium that he had acquired through his Welf wife, Judith, to buy two of his numerous castles. From his mother, Frederick Barbarossa acquired the provostship at Öhningen.

BIBLIOGRAPHY

Hechberger, Werner. *Staufer und Welfen 1125-1190: Zur verwendung von Theorien in der Geschichtswissenschaft,* Passauer Historische Forschungen 10. Cologne: Böhlau, 1996.

Jordan, Karl. *Henry the Lion,* trans. P. S. Falla. Oxford: Clarendon, 1986.

Weller, Karl, and Arnold Weller. *Württembergische Geschichte im südwestdeutschen Raum.* 9th edition Stuttgart: Theiss, 1985.

Die Zeit der Staufer. Geschichte-, Kunst-, Kultur-Katalog der Ausstellung des württembergischen Landesmuseums Stuttgart. Stuttgart: Württembergisches Landesmuseum, 1977.

Paul B. Pixton

SEE ALSO

Frederick I Barbarossa; Lothar III; Staufen; Welfs

K

Kaiserchronik

"The Chronicle of Emperors" was composed circa 1150. It represents the first appearance in German of the traditional Latin genre, the historical chronicle, and it provides the model for all other vernacular chronicles that followed. Sixteen complete manuscripts and twenty-five fragments attest to the phenomenal popularity of the work. Further evidence of its importance is provided by numerous revised versions and continuations. Arranged in rhyme pairs, 17,283 verses relate the history of the emperors of the Roman and Holy Roman Empire from Caesar to Konrad III (1138–1152). The narrative abruptly breaks off at Christmas, 1146, after describing the crusade preaching of Bernard of Clairvaux (1090–1153), and it is not clear whether the poet intended to carry on with his writing at some later point, or whether he considered the work complete for all practical purposes. Indeed, this is but one of many questions about dating and authorship that remain unanswered.

Most scholars are in agreement, however, that the Kaiserchronik as it now exists was completed by a Regensburg cleric around 1147. Nonetheless, given the current state of research, other questions regarding the beginning date of composition—suggestions range from 1126 to the early 1140s—and whether one or more poets were in involved in the writing must remain open.

In the prologue, the poet addresses his audience and says that he is going to impart something of value to attentive listeners. Just who comprised the audience is not certain, but, given the use of the vernacular language, it is highly likely that the target group was composed of members of the feudal nobility and ministerials, possibly even members of a cloister who were not versed in Latin. The poet announces that he will not only be portraying emperors, but also those popes who played a role in the empire will be profiled. Further, he will present both good and bad emperors and popes. Thus, it seems clear that the main purpose, and thus the usefulness, of the Kaiserchronik was to depict rulers, both pagan and Christian, who could be taken as worthy role models by the secular nobility of the poet's time.

The chronicle is a mirror of medieval Christian society and its firmly-held belief system. Replete with fanciful tales and distortions of history, spurious emperors, nonexistent relationships, the work is brimming with fascinating episodes—real or imagined—from the lives of the—real or imagined—Roman emperors. Whether real or fictitious, however, was of little import in the grand scheme of medieval things. For the medieval individual there was only one history—the history of salvation that began with the Creation. The actions and maneuvering of mere humans were of little consequence, except insofar as they were part of the divine scheme and furthered the divinely-ordained order on earth. Thus, more important for the poet and his audience was not whether the chronology presented in the work was correct, for example, but rather how the secular and ecclesiastical rulers carried out their responsibilities toward society.

BIBLIOGRAPHY

Gellinek, Christian. *Die deutsche Kaiserchronik. Erzähltechnik und Kritik.* Frankfurt am Main: Athenäum, 1971.

Nellmann, Eberhard. "Kaiserchronik." In *Die deutsche Literatur des Mittelalters: Verfasserlexikon,* eds. Kurt Ruh, et al., vol. 4. Berlin and New York: de Gruyter, 1983, cols. 949–964.

———. *Die Reichsidee in der deutschen Dichtung der Salier- und frühen Stauferzeit: Annolied, Kaiserchronik, Rolandslied, Eraclius.* Berlin: Schmidt, 1963.

Ohly, Ernst Friedrich. *Sage und Legende in der Kaiserchronik: Untersuchungen über Quellen und Aufbau der Dichtung.* 1940; rpt. Darmstadt: Wissenschaftliche Buchgesellschaft, 1968.

Schröder, Edward, ed. *Die Kaiserchronik eines Regensburger Geistlichen.* Hannover: Hahn, 1892; 3rd edition. Dublin and Zurich: Weidmann, 1969.

Vollmann-Profe, Gisela. Geschichte der deutschen Literatur von den Anfängen bis zum Beginn der Neuzeit, vol. 1, part 2: *Wiederbeginn volkssprachiger Schriftlichkeit im hohen Mittelalter.* 2nd edition. Tübingen: Niemeyer, 1994.

Francis G. Gentry

SEE ALSO
Crusades; Historiography, German

Kaiserchronik, **Latin, Illuminated**

The so-called *Anonymi chronica imperatorum* (Anonymous Chronicle of the Emperors), composed in 1112–1114 at Würzburg (?) on the command of Emperor Henry V, is preserved in a single illustrated manuscript (Cambridge, Corpus Christi College manuscript no. Lat. fol. 373). The text is based on the *Chronica universale* (Chronicle of the Universe) of Ekkehard von Aura and the chronicle of Sigebert of Gembloux. New research shows that the part following the year 1106 was probably written by Bishop Otto of Bamberg. The three books of the *Kaiserchronik* beginning with *De origine Francorum* (On the Origin of the Franks) contain sixteen drawings showing the dynastic line of succession (*Amtsgenealogie* or *Sukzessionsreihe*) from Pippin and Charlemagne up to Henry IV; they are done in brown and red ink and follow the representational stereotype of the seated frontal king known from coins and seals. All the drawings are accompanied by the beginning of the corresponding text.

The only colored illumination, on folio 83r, shows Pope Pascal handing the scepter and orb to Henry V, labeled *HENRICUS QUINTUS,* on the occasion of the coronation in 1111, or perhaps the transfer of the insignia in Mainz by Archbishop Ruthbart in 1106. At the end of Book 3 (fol. 95v), another drawing represents the marriage of Mathilda of England and Emperor Henry V in 1114. Genealogy, coronation, and marriage are the main subjects of interest for the illuminator as well as the author.

BIBLIOGRAPHY

Frutolfi et Ekkehardi Chronica necnon anonymi Chronica imperatorum / Frutolfs und Ekkehards Chroniken und die anonyme Kaiserchronik, trans. Franz-Josef Schmale and Irene Schmale-Ott. Ausgewählte Quellen zur deutschen Geschichte des Mittelalters 15. Darmstadt: Wissenschaftliche Buchgesellschaft, 1972, pp. 211–265.

James, Montague Rhodes. *A Descriptive Catalogue of the Manuscripts in the Library of Corpus Christi College, Cambridge.* 2 vols. Cambridge, England: The University Press, 1912, vol. 2, pp. 215–218.

Meier, Claudia A. "Vom Wort zum Bild—Chronicon pictum: Von den Anfängen der Chronikenillustration zu den narrativen Bilderzyklen in den Weltchroniken des hohen Mittelalters." Habilitation Universität Mainz, 1995 [unpublished professorial qualification degree].

Schmid, Karl. "Die Salier als Kaiserdynastie: Zugleich ein Beitrag zur Bildausstattung der Chroniken Frutolfs und Ekkehards." In *Iconologia sacra: Mythos, Bildkunst und Dichtung in der Religion- und Sozialgschichte Alteuropas. Festschrift für Karl Hauck zum 75. Geburtstag,* eds. Hagen Keller and Nikolaus Staubach. Arbeiten zur Frühmittelalterforschung 23. Berlin: Walter de Gruyter, pp. 486–490.

Schramm, Percy Ernst, and Florentine Mütherich. *Denkmale der deutschen Könige und Kaiser 1: Ein Beitrag zur Herrschergeschichte von Karl dem Grossen bis Friedrich II. 768–1250.* 2nd edition. Veröffentlichungen des Zentralinstituts für Kunstgeschichte 2. Munich: Prestel, 1981, no. 167.

———. *Die deutschen Könige und Kaiser in Bildern ihrer Zeit 751–1190.* 2nd edition. Munich: Prestel, 1983, nos. 174, 184, 190.

Claudia A. Meier

SEE ALSO
Charlemagne; Henry IV

Kaufringer, Heinrich (fl. early 15th c.)

The author composed twenty-seven short verse couplet narratives *(Maeren),* religious tales *(Bîspeln),* and sermon-like discussions in the late fourteenth and early fifteenth centuries. The most important manuscript, the closest to the author's original, was written in 1464. Kaufringer lived, as far as we can tell on the basis of the family name, the poet's language, his rhyme schemes, and references to specific towns in his novellas, in the area of Augsburg and Landsberg am Lech in the border region between Bavaria and Swabia. The prior of the Landsberg Pfarrkirche (ca. 1369–ca. 1404) Heinrich Kaufringer and his son (same name), who is documented once in 1404, are both good candidates as the novellas' potential author. There is, however, no absolute certainty for the identification of either of them.

It has been speculated that the author was a craftsman like Hans Rosenplüt and Hans Folz in Nuremberg, a merchant, or a cleric. We can only say with certainty that he defended viewpoints typical of an urban dweller with rather conservative attitudes and who favored political unity and harmony within the city. He often refers to his literary model, Heinrich der Teichner

Kaufringer's *Maeren* are preserved in a Munich manuscript (no. cgm 270) from 1464 (no. 1–17), and in the Berlin manuscript (no. mgf 564) (nos. 18–27) from 1472. One narrative is also contained in a second Munich manuscript (no. cgm 1119) from the second half of the fifteenth century. Most of the texts are signed by Kaufringer, which allows us to determine in all likelihood which of the narratives were, in fact, written by him. The production of the Munich manuscript (cgm 270) seems to have been organized by Kaufringer himself. In six sermon-like texts Kaufringer versified older German prose works. One of them he even based on a sermon by Berthold of Regensburg, and one on Heinrich Seuse's *Büchlein der ewigen Weisheit* (Book of Eternal Wisdom).

The narratives deal with topical issues of daily life and are of didactic, though humorous, nature. Kaufringer argued for a rational approach to theological questions, urged his listeners to fulfill their duties, but to resist unfair demands by the authorities.

The majority of Kaufringer's *Maeren,* however, are of erotic nature, in which women generally win over their husbands with the help of their intelligence *(gescheidkait)* and thus manage to protect their secret lovers. At times Kaufringer emphasizes moral behavior, which can also include violence to defend one's own reputation and honor (*Die unschuldige Mörderin,* The innocent Murderess).

BIBLIOGRAPHY

Fischer, Hanns: *Studien zur deutschen Märendichtung.* 2nd edition. Tübingen: Niemeyer, 1983.

Mihm, Arend: *Überlieferung und Verbreitung der Märendichtung im Spätmittelalter.* Heidelberg: winter 1967.

Sappler, Paul: *Heinrich Kaufringer: Werke, Text.* Tübingen: Niemeyer, 1972.

Simmons, Cynthia Lynn. "Tales by Heinrich Kaufringer." M.A. thesis, University of Texas at Austin, 1985.

Stede, Marga: *Schreiben in der Krise. Die Texte des Heinrich Kaufringer.* Trier: WVT, 1993.

Albrecht Classen

Kingship

See Itinerant Kingship.

Kleve

The nucleus of the urban development of Kleve is the Schwanenburg castle (Swan Mountain) of the counts of Cleves, situated prominently on a cliff. After the dynasty's extinction in 1368, Kleve became part of the large territorial complex of the counts of Mark, who, after 1417, were known as the dukes of Cleves. The latter, supported by the dukes of Burgundy, created an important political unit in the Lower Rhineland. The Romanesque palace of the courts, built around 1100, was demolished in 1771; its donjon, which collapsed in 1439, had, by 1453, been replaced by the late Gothic *Schwanenturm* (Swan Tower).

Below the castle, the town was founded in 1242; under Count Dietrich VIII, the two were connected by a larger ring of fortifications in 1341. In the same year, the Romanesque parish church, or *Stiftskirche,* was demolished and subsequently rebuilt as a princely court church to which an existing collegiate chapter was transferred, and, in 1347, the founder was interred in the choir. Construction of the nave was completed by 1394, the two-towered western façade by 1425–1426. Largely destroyed by bombing in 1944, the main body of the church was reconstructed by 1956, the western towers only being finished by 1970. The church, a pseudo-basilica with blind clerestory (tall windows), was influential in the genesis of late Gothic church architecture of the Lower Rhineland and served as the prototype of a number of related buildings in other residences of the Cleve dynasty (Kranenburg, Kalkar). To the north, the ducal memorial chapel, the adjoining sacristy, and the ducal lodge are attached to the choir. As a brick building, partly covered by tufa (a porous stone), with its architectural details (portals, tracery, and pillars) executed in sandstone, the monument represents a major step in the development of building economy and technology, a development characterized by the existence of a general entrepreneur who subcontracted the different tasks to independent artisans.

The Franciscan church, originally the parish church of the lower town and in 1285 converted by Count Dietrich VII into a monastic church, is of typological interest as an asymmetrical hall church in which the northern aisle is reduced to a mere sequence of niches *(Wandpfeilerkirche)*.

The rich court culture at Kleve manifested itself beautifully in the book of hours produced in the second quarter of the fifteenth century for Catherine of Cleves (now New York, Pierpont Morgan Library).

BIBLIOGRAPHY

Hilger, Hans Peter. *Der Kreis Kleve 4: Kleve.* Die Denkmäler des Rheinlandes. Düsseldorf: Rheinland-Verlag, 1967.

The Hours of Catherine of Cleves, ed. John Plummer. New York: Braziller, 1966 [facsimile].

Hans J. Böker

SEE ALSO

Gothic Art and Architecture; Romanesque Art and Architecture

Klosterneuburg

The monastery of Klosterneuburg on the Danube just north of Vienna was founded on the site of a Roman settlement circa 1114 by Margrave Leopold III of Babenberg and his wife, Agnes, daughter of German Emperor Henry IV. In 1133, Leopold gave the site to the Augustinian canons, led by Hartmann, who departed from Klosterneuburg in 1140 to be bishop of Brixen, and was later canonized. Under the diverse influences of the reform of Bishop Konrad of Salzburg and the Hirsau traditions of Agnes's Saxon heritage, Klosterneuburg developed a unique liturgy and a preeminence among Austrian monastic houses.

Typical of the Augustinian practice, Klosterneuburg was a double foundation, with the larger male convent dedicated to Mary and a separate, more cloistered space, for the canonesses dedicated to Mary Magdalene. It was probably the canonesses who developed the unique "Klosterneuburger style" of musical notation featuring Laon neumes on four lines with a distinctive four-line clef.

The three-aisle Romanesque basilica was consecrated in 1136. Its refurbishing after a fire in 1158 brought the cloister into its first golden age, led by Abbot Wernher (1168–1185; 1192–1194). The magnificent ambo of Nicholas of Verdun was dedicated in 1181; its three ar-

caded tiers of gold enamel work display salvation history in typological imagery. Also from the late twelfth century is a great bronze seven-armed candlestick, now displayed in the well house. The famous Klosterneuburger Easter play from circa 1200 (Ms. 574) may not ever have been performed at the convent, but it became part of its literary tradition. The important Klosterneuburg scriptorium produced a medieval library of more than 2,000 manuscripts, still housed on the site.

Despite another fire in 1330, the cloister blossomed again under Abbot Stephan von Sierndorf (1317–1335). At this time, the choir was vaulted in the Gothic style, and Nicholas's ambo transformed into an altarpiece by the addition of four panels in the elegant Italianizing style of the Vienna school. Propst Stephan also commissioned the stained glass program of the cloister windows, featuring scenes from the life of Christ and portraits of the notable figures from the convent's history.

The monastery was reformed in 1418 under Abbot Georg Müstinger, inspired by the spiritual movement of the Augustinian canons of Raudnitz. An increasing number of canons attended the University of Vienna, and the convent became a center for scientific learning, particularly cartography. The convent produced significant chronicles, including the *Kleine Klosterneuburger Chronik* (Short Klosterneuburg Chronicle). Its financial records document the activities of major illuminators of the Vienna court school of the mid-fifteenth century, including Masters Nicholas and Michael. The Babenberger ducal family was always closely tied to Klosterneuburg, where one of their residences was located. By the thirteenth century, there is evidence of pilgrimage to the graves of Leopold and Agnes in the chapterhouse, culminating in Leopold's canonization in 1485.

Notable gothic paintings in the cloister include the 1456 Mary Magdalene Altar by the Albrechtsmeister, the 1489–1493 Babenberger *Stammtafel,* a painted genealogy of the Babenberg founders, and panels by Rueland Frueauf the Younger illustrating the life of St. Leopold. The present church building boasts a baroque interior and an medievalizing exterior heavily restored by Friedrich von Schmidt in the nineteenth century.

BIBLIOGRAPHY

Buchhausen, Helmut. *Der Verduner Altar: Das Emailwerk des Nikolaus von Verdun in Stift Klosterneuburg.* Vienna: Edition Tusch, 1980.

Durand, Dana Bennett. *The Vienna-Klosterneuburg Map Corpus of the Fifteenth Century: A Study in the Transi-*

tion from Medieval to Modern Science. Leiden: Brill, 1952.

Fritzsche, Gabriela. *Die Entwicklung des "Neuen Realismus" in der Wiener Malerei: 1331 bis Mitte des 14. Jahrhunderts*. Dissertation Universität Wien, 1979. Dissertationen zur Kunstgeschichte 18. Vienna: Böhlau, 1983.

Frodl-Kraft, Eva. *Gotische Glasmalereien aus dem Kreuzgang in Klosterneuburg*. Klosterneuburger Kunstschätze 3. Klosterneuburg: Klosterneuburger Buch- und Kunstverlag, 1963.

Die Gotik in Niederösterreich: Kunst, Kultur und Geschichte eines Landes im Spätmittelalter. Vienna: Österreichische Staatsdruckerei, 1959.

Haidinger, Alois. *Katalog der Handscriften des Augustiner Chorherrenstiftes Klosterneuburg*. 2 vols. Vienna: Verlag der Österreichischen Akademie der Wissenschaften, 1983–1991.

Der heilige Leopold: Landesfürst und Staatssymbol. Katalog des Niederösterreichischen Landesmuseums N.F. 155. Vienna: Die Kulturabteilung, 1985.

Klaar, Adalbert. "Eine bautechnische Untersuchung des Altstiftes von Klosterneuburg." *Jahrbuch des Stiftes Klosterneuburg* N.F. 9 (1975): 7–20; 149–152.

Röhrig, Floridus. "Das kunstgeschichtliche Material aus den Klosterneuburger Rechnungsbüchern des 14. und 15. Jahrhunderts." *Jahrbuch des Stiftes Klosterneuburg* N.F. 6 (1966): 137–178.

———. *Das Stift Klosterneuburg und seine Kunstschätze*. St. Pölten and Vienna: Verlag Niederösterreichisches Pressehaus, 1984.

Schabes, Leo. *Alte liturgische Gebräuche und Zeremonien an der Stiftskirche zu Klosterneuburg*. Klosterneuburg: Volksliturgisches Apostolat, 1930.

Wagner-Rieger, Renate. "Zur Baugeschichte der Stiftskirche von Klosterneuburg." *Jahrbuch des Stiftes Klosterneuburg* N.F. 3 (1963): 137–179.

Amelia Carr

Knights

See Arthurian Literature, Dutch; Arthurian Literature, German; Tournaments; Warfare; Weapons.

Koblenz

Located at the confluence of the Moselle and Rhine rivers, Koblenz was the sight of a Roman fort erected by Emperors Augustus and Tiberius between 10 and 37 C.E. to protect the region from Germanic attacks. The city was destroyed by the Franks in 259–260 and rebuilt as a walled city, parts of which still stand, in the fourth century under Emperor Constantine (323–337). In the first half of the ninth century, the city developed as a religious and political center. As a secondary residence for Emperor Louis the Pious and his successors, the city served as the site for important political councils; the Treaty of Verdun in 842, and the Treaty of Meersen 860, which divided the empire, were signed here.

The church of St. Kastor was built in the Carolingian style outside the city walls; it was consecrated in 836 by Archbishop Hetti and Emperor Louis the Pious. It is debated whether the church was destroyed during the Norman invasion of 882. The Carolingian church of St. Mary, located within the city walls, was constructed in the latter half of the ninth century and was renamed the church of St. Florin in 940 when Emperor Henry I, the church's benefactor, presented to it the relics of St. Florin.

After Emperor Henry II presented the city of Koblenz and St. Kastor to Archbishop Poppo of Trier in 1018, a great building phase began. From the eleventh to early thirteenth centuries, St. Kastor was reconstructed in Romanesque style on its Carolingian foundations. The choir was rebuilt from 1147 to 1158; it was destroyed in 1198, rebuilt and consecrated in 1202. Reconstruction of St. Florin in the Romanesque style began around 1100; its choir was completed in Gothic style in the mid-fourteenth century. The double-tower facades of St. Kastor and St. Florin ushered in this tradition in the Rhineland. The *Liebfraukirche* (Church of the Virgin), first mentioned in 1182, is on the site of a fifth- or sixth-century pagan structure. Construction began in the late twelfth century in Romanesque style; a late Gothic choir, constructed between 1404 and 1430, was added to the original Romanesque choir. The west facade is characterized by two imposing towers dating from the thirteenth century.

The city experienced marked growth in the early thirteenth century. In 1216, Archbishop Theoderich von Wied invited the Teutonic Knights to Koblenz. Their first settlement in the Rhineland was located next to St. Kastor on the land at the confluence of the Mosel and Rhine; they named the area the *Deutsches Eck* (German Corner). Dominican and Franciscan settlements were first mentioned in 1233 and 1236, respectively. The Dominican basilica, destroyed during World War II, was the oldest Gothic church on the Middle Rhine. The Franciscan church, with its early Gothic choir, met the same fate.

Because of regional political conflicts and instability, Archbishop Arnold of Isenberg initiated a tax around 1250 to expand the city wall. The project was continued by Archbishop Henry von Vinstingen, who constructed a castle with additional taxes. The castle, strategically located buttressing the Moselle, was begun in 1277, and expansion continued through the eighteenth century. Situated close to an earlier Roman bridge, the *Balduinsbrücke* (Baldwin's Bridge) over the Moselle was begun in 1332 and completed in 1363.

Located west of the confluence of the Moselle and Rhine Rivers is Fort Ehrenbreitstein, whose construction began in the tenth century. The structure, almost all of which still exists, was received by Archbishop Poppo in 1020; it was greatly expanded in the mid twelfth century under Archbishop Hillin and served as the main protection for the city through the nineteenth century.

BIBLIOGRAPHY

Backes, Magnus. *Koblenz*. Berlin: Deutscher Kunstverlag, 1973.

Bator, Ingrid. *Geschichte der Stadt Koblenz*. 2 vols. Stuttgart: Theiss, 1992–1993.

Bellinghausen, Hans. *2000 Jahre Koblenz: Geschichte der Stadt an Rhein und Mosel*. 2nd edition. Boppard: Boldt, 1973.

Caspary, Hans, et al. *Rheinland-Pfalz. Saarland*. Dehio Handbuch der Deutschen Kunstdenkmäler. 2nd edition. Berlin: Deutscher Kunstverlag, 1984.

Dellwig, Herbert, and Udo Liessem. *Stadt Koblenz*. Düsseldorf: Schwann, 1986.

Michel, Fritz. *Die Geschichte der Stadt Koblenz im Mittelalter*. Trautheim/Darmstadt: Mushake, 1963.

———. *Die kirchlichen Denkmäler der Stadt Koblenz*. Kunstdenkmäler der Rheinprovinz 20, 1. 1937. Düsseldorf: Schwann, 1981.

———. *Die Kunstdenkmäler der Stadt Koblenz: Die profane Denkmäler und die Vororte*. Kunstdenkmäler von Rheinland-Pfalz 1. 1954. Munich: Deutscher Kunstverlag, 1986.

Petri, Franz, and Georg Droege, eds. *Rheinische Geschichte*. 3 vols. Düsseldorf: Schwann, 1983.

Gregory H. Wolf

SEE ALSO

Carolingian Art and Architecture; *Deutschorden*; Gothic Art and Architecture; Henry I; Henry II, Art; Louis the Pious; Romanesque Art and Architecture

Koerbecke, Johann (ca. 1420–1491)

A contemporary of Stefan Lochner and Konrad Witz, this painter contributed to the transition from the international Gothic style to a more realistic one, inspired by Netherlandish art. Koerbecke was probably born circa 1420 in Coesfeld (Northrhine Westphalia). He is first recorded in Münster in 1443, when he purchased a house. He led an important workshop there until his death on June 13, 1491.

Koerbecke's sole documented work is the Marienfeld Altarpiece, for which he received payment in 1456. Installed on the high altar of the Marienfeld monastery church in 1457, it originally consisted of a carved shrine and painted wings with scenes from the life of the Virgin and the Passion. In the seventeenth century, the wings were sawn into sixteen panels, now located in several collections (Avignon, Musée Calvet; Berlin, Gemäldegalerie; Chicago, Art Institute; Cracow, National Museum; Madrid, Thyssen Collection; Moscow, Pushkin Museum; Münster, Westfälisches Landesmuseum; Nuremberg, Germanisches Nationalmuseum; Washington, National Gallery). They reveal knowledge of works by important painters of the preceding generation in Westphalia and Cologne. Koerbecke's Crucifixion is inspired by Conrad von Soest's paintings of that subject, his Presentation is an interpretation of Stephan Lochner's 1447 version (Darmstadt, Hessisches Landesmuseum), and his Resurrection is based on Master Francke's 1424 *Englandfahrer Altarpiece* (Hamburg, Kunsthalle). Koerbecke's volumetric figures and detailed, naturalistic treatment of interiors and landscapes derive from Netherlandish art.

Other attributed works are the wings of the Langenhorst Altarpiece with eight scenes from the Passion (Münster, Westfälisches Landesmuseum), ca. 1445, and three panels from an altarpiece with scenes from the life of Saint John the Baptist: the baptism of Christ and Christ with Saint John (Münster, Westfälisches Landesmuseum), and the beheading of the Baptist (The Hague, Meermanno-Westreenianum Museum), ca. 1470. A wing with Saints John the Baptist and George, and a fragment with Saint Christopher, survive from the Freckenhorst Altarpiece of ca. 1470–1480 (Münster, Westfälisches Landesmuseum).

BIBLIOGRAPHY

Kirchhoff, Karl-Heinz. "Maler und Malerfamilien in Münster." *Westfalen* 4 (1977): 98–110.

Luckhardt, Jochen. *Der Hochaltar der Zisterzienserklosterkirche Marienfeld.* Münster: Westfälisches Landesmuseum für Kunst und Kulturgeschichte, 1987.

Pieper, Paul. *Die deutschen, niederländischen und italienischen Tafelbilder bis um 1530.* Bestandskataloge des Westfälischen Landesmuseum für Kunst und Kulturgeschichte. Münster: Aschendorff, 1986, pp. 140–200.

Sommer, Johannes. *Johann Koerbecke: Der Meister des Marienfelder Altars von 1457.* Dissertation, Universität Bonn, 1937. Münster: Westfälische Vereinsdruckerei, 1937.

Susanne Reece

SEE ALSO
Cologne, Art; Conrad von Soest; Francke, Master; International Style; Lochner, Stefan; Münster; Witz, Konrad

Königsfelden

The Franciscan cloister was erected between 1309 and 1330 near the village of Brugg (Canton Aargau, Switzerland) on the site where the German king Albrecht was murdered on May 1, 1308. His widow, Queen Elizabeth, and his daughter, Queen Agnes of Hungary, provided the major support for the construction of the memorial site and family necropolis. In order to provide perpetual services for the dead, a Franciscan women's convent was erected to the south of the church; a small number of Franciscan priests who ministered to the nuns' spiritual needs lived in the convent buildings to the north of the church. During the Reformation, the cloister was suppressed (1528) and the buildings adapted to secular uses and renovated several times. Still standing are the church, most recently restored in 1982–1986, and parts of the former women's cloister (much rebuilt). The stained glass windows of the choir are widely known.

In plan and elevation, the church represents a building type characteristic of the Dominican province of upper Germany in the early fourteenth century: a three-aisled, flat-roofed basilica is separated by a choir screen from the long vaulted choir in which three rectangular bays precede the 5/8 polygon of the apse. In the nave a simple marble cenotaph from the period of the original building campaign stands over the crypt in which a number of Habsburg family members were buried. The architectural membering of the choir is more complex than that of the

Königsfelden, choir, detail of axis window, Flagellation and Crucifixion. *Photograph: Joan A. Holladay*

simple nave and the eleven tall triple-lancet windows with high Gothic tracery still have the largest part of their original stained glass. All the windows were donated by members of King Albrecht's family, who are represented as donors in the bottom panel of their respective windows. The axis window represents scenes from Christ's Passion; it is flanked by windows portraying the Incarnation and appearances after the Crucifixion. Also in the polygon is a window with scenes from the lives of John the Baptist and Catherine and one with episodes from the life of Saint Paul. Windows along the straight walls of the choir portray the twelve apostles as single figures. Closest to the entrance to the choir are narrative windows devoted to the lives of Francis and Clara; next to them are windows with scenes from the *vitae* or "lives" of Saints Nicholas and Anna. Little is left of the colored glass of the nave. Franciscan and Habsburg preferences determined the choice of scenes and iconographic details.

The arrangement of the images was carefully planned: the high altar stands on the exact spot on which King Albrecht was murdered, and only in the windows directly over it are scenes portrayed in which blood flows or murder is committed. The window with scenes from the life of Saint Clara is on the south side, toward the women's cloister; the Francis window is installed on the side of the men's convent on the north. The windows, among the highest quality examples on the Upper Rhine, are in an elegant, courtly style; they are attributed to a workshop from Strasbourg and/or Constance. Maurer dates the planning and execution of all the windows in the years 1325–1330; Schmidt, relying on style and costume, supposes that the four western windows, with their differentiated compositions and the figures' modern coiffures and robes, were donated and planned with the other windows, but finished only in the decade between 1340 and 1350.

The rich original furnishings of the church can be reconstructed from different sources. Only a Venetian altar diptych dated about 1290 and two embroidered antependia, or hangings, are preserved; all three pieces are now in the Historical Museum in Bern.

BIBLIOGRAPHY

Boner, Georg. "Klarissenkloster Königsfelden." *Helvetia sacra* 5 (1978): 561–576.

Gerber, Markus. "Die Verwechslung des Männer- und Frauenklosters zu Königsfelden." *Brugger Neujahrsblätter* 36 (1986): 105–120.

Jäggi, Carola. "Eastern Choir or Western Gallery? The Problem of the Nuns' Choir in Königsfelden and other Early Mendicant Nunneries." [forthcoming].

Kurmann-Schwartz, Brigitte. "Die Sorge um die Memoria: Das Habsburger Grab in Königsfelden im Lichte seiner Bildausstattung." *Kunst und Architektur in der Schweiz* 50/4 (1999): [in print].

Marti, Susan. "Königin Agnes und ihre Geschenke," *Kunst+Architektur in der Schweiz* 47 (1996): 169–180.

Maurer, Emil. *Das Kloster Königsfelden.* Die Kunstdenkmäler des Kantons Aargau 3. Basel: Berkhauser, 1954.

———. "Habsburg und Königsfelden im Bildprogramm der Chorfenster." *Kunst+Architektur in der Schweiz* 47 (1996): 206–209.

Schmidt, Gerhard. "Zur Datierung der Chorfenster von Königsfelden." *Österreichische Zeitschrift für Kunst und Denkmalpflege* 40 (1986): 161–171.

Schramm, Percy Ernst, Hermann Fillitz, and Florentine Mütherich. "Der ehemalige Kirchenschatz des Klosters Kvnigsfelden (Aargau)." In *Denkmale der deutschen Könige und Kaiser 2: Ein Beitrag zur Herrschergeschichte von Rudolf I. bis Maximilian I. 1273-1519.* Veröffentlichungen des Zentralinstituts für Kunstgeschichte in München 7. Munich: Prestel, 1978, pp. 30–31.

Susan Marti

Konrad von Heimesfurt (fl. first half of the 13th c.)

The only author known to us—besides Konrad von Fußesbrunnen—to write religious narratives in the vernacular at this time. His two works, *Von unser vrouwen hinvart* (*Transitus Mariae,* Ascension of Mary) and *Diu urstende* (*Resurrectio,* Resurrection), written in verse around or before 1225 and around 1230, respectively, address audiences not knowledgeable in Latin. Konrad names himself in both works and identifies himself as a cleric. It is generally assumed that he was associated with the bishopric of Eichstätt. *Hinvart* consists of 1,209 verses and is transmitted in three manuscripts, six fragments, and as an interpolation in a manuscript containing Phillipp's *Marienleben.* There is only one extant manuscript of *Diu urstende,* which consists of 2,162 verses. With the exception of the fifteenth-century Berlin manuscript of *Hinvart,* the writing surface for all manuscripts is parchment.

The main source for *Hinvart* is the *Transitus Mariä* by Pseudo-Melito of Sardis. The plot centers on the death of the Virgin, as foretold by Gabriel, with Christ by her side and the apostles who had been miraculously summoned to Jerusalem for the occasion. It tells of her burial disrupted by Jews in the valley of Josaphat and of her resurrection and assumption witnessed by the apostles. The text ends with a plea for Mary's intercession on behalf of mankind. The overtly religious subject matter is introduced by a prologue reminiscent of courtly romance. The use of hunting imagery, the praise of constancy, the poet's mention of his modest station and talents, and his assurance that humility is more pleasing to God than *superbia* all suggest familiarity with courtly literature.

Konrad's longer narrative, *Diu urstende,* extends well beyond the confines of the title, as indicated in the prologue. It begins with the New Testament account of Christ's entry into Jerusalem and ends with extensive testimonials of the events surrounding Pentecost based on the *Gospel of Nicodemus.* The text consists of six major episodes. The first, third, and fifth are short sections based on biblical sources. They provide the historical framework for Christ's Crucifixion and entombment, his Ascension, and the Descent of the Holy Spirit. Sections two, four, and six are expanded versions of apocryphal sources in which the poet sets his own emphasis through frequent use of dialogue and textual changes. In the trial scene he juxtaposes various groups of supporters with the accusers while Jesus himself remains silent. Part four tells of the Resurrection and the liberation of Joseph of Arimathaea while part six is devoted to lengthy interrogations aimed at bearing witness to Joseph's liberation, Christ's Resurrection and Ascension, and, most importantly, Christ's harrowing of Hell, which allows the virtuous heroes of the Old Testament to share the benefits of the Gospel. But rather than ending on this triumphant note, the poet resumes his theme from the conclusions of parts two and four by polemicizing against the Jews, whose stubbornness in the face of all the witnesses will lead to their damnation.

Konrad von Heimesfurt was known to Rudolf von Ems and subsequent authors relied on his works in their own writings. *Hinvart* influenced Reinbot von Durne and Lutwin. Heinrich von München, Gundacker von Judenburg, Hawich der Kellner, a prose translation of the *Gospel of Nicodemus* transmitted in a manuscript group known as "E," and a verse narrative, *Befreiung der Altväter* ("Liberation of the Old Fathers"), all attest to the popularity of *Diu urstende* in the fourteenth and fifteenth century.

BIBLIOGRAPHY

Gärtner, Kurt, and Werner J. Hoffmann. *Konrad von Heimesfurt: 'Unser vrouven hinvart' und 'Diu urstende.'* Tübingen: Niemeyer, 1989.

Ingeborg Henderson

SEE ALSO

Lutwin; Rudolf von Ems

Konrad von Mure (ca. 1210–March 30, 1281)

Born in Muri, a town in Aargau, Switzerland, Konrad began his studies at the Benedictine monastery there and went on to Zurich and possibly even on to universities in Bologna and Paris. Ordained a priest in 1244, Konrad served as the director of the cathedral school in Zurich until 1271. As of 1246, he also served as the canon of the cathedral and, in 1259, he took on the newly created position of cantor. Konrad produced numerous works in Latin, many of which reflect his role as school director. His *Novus Graecismus* ("New Greek," ca. 1250), for example, is an adaptation and expansion of Eberhard von Béthune's (d. 1212) rhyming grammar book *Graecismus*. Konrad's *Libellus de naturis animalium* (Little Book on the Animals of Nature, ca. 1255), provides an allegorical exposition of the natural history found in books 11 and 12 of Isidore of Seville's *Etymologiae*. The book also treats various medieval technologies, for example, manuscript preparation. Celebrated in the nineteenth century as the "first heraldic poem," Konrad's *Clipearius Teutonicorum*, (ca. 1264), is now recognized as a catalog of heraldic devices designed to help scribes identify various insignia. Konrad's *Fabularius* (ca. 1273), an alphabetized compendium of medieval knowledge and his most influential work, covers history, literature, mythology, hagiography, poetics, and grammar. Konrad also composed the *Summa de arte prosandi* (ca. 1276), a treatise on the composition of letters and official documents. Some of Konrad's works reflect his position as cantor, i.e., his *Liber Ordinarius*. Konrad enjoyed a close relationship with King Rudolf of Hapsburg and composed the *Commendatitia Rudolfi regis Romanourm* (1273) in commemoration of the king's victory at the battle of Marchfeld. No historical evidence exists, however, to support Konrad's relationship to the Manesse family or to Johannes Hadlaub, as portrayed in Gottfried Keller's *Züricher Novellen*. Konrad died on March 30, 1281, in Zurich.

BIBLIOGRAPHY

Kronblicher, Walter. *Die Summa de arte prosandi des Konrad von Mure*. Zurich: Fretz and Wasmuth, 1968.

Leuppi, Heidi, ed. *Der Liber ordinarius des Konrad von Mure: die Gottesdeinstordnung am Großmünster in Zürich*. Freiburg: Universitätsverlag Freiburg, 1995.

Orbán, Arpaád P., ed. *Konrad von Mure: De naturis animalium*. Heidelberg: Carl Wintet, 1989.

Stammler, Wolfgang and Karl Langosch, eds. *Die deutsche Literatur des Mittelalters: Verfasserlexikon*, vol. 5. Berlin and Leipzig: de Gruyter, 1955, cols. 561–565

Stephen M. Carey

SEE ALSO

Hadlaub, Johannes; Marchfeld, Battle of; Zurich

Konrad von Würzburg (ca. 1230–1287)

Included among the "twelve old masters" revered by Meistersingers, Konrad produced one of the largest and most varied oeuvres in all of Middle High German literature. Initially neglected by modern scholars as an epigone and mannerist, critics are now examining Konrad's work in its own context. Konrad embodies a turn in German literature, he was neither noble (Song 32, line 189: *waere ich edel,* if I were noble) nor a part of the court. Konrad plied his trade in the cities and wrote for the wealthy bourgeoisie and the urban nobility. Archives, official documents, and Konrad's works themselves provide us with an extraordinary amount of information about his life and patronage. Born in Würzburg, Konrad began as a wandering poet, spent time in Strasbourg and eventually settled in Basle. Konrad wrote two lays. *Got gewaltec waz du schickest* (Powerful God, what you send) is a religious lay in praise of the Virgin and the Trinity. *Vênus diu feine diust entslâfen* (Elegant Venus has fallen asleep) is a secular lay treating courtly love. Unfortunately, the melodies to both of these have been lost. Konrad's shorter love lyric consists primarily of nine summer songs and eleven winter songs characterized by floral metaphors and the *jârlanc* introduction (nos. 5, 6, 10, 13, 17, 21, 23, 27). Konrad also produced three dawn songs (nos. 14, 15, 30), as well as exempla (nos. 18, 24, 25), maxims, and religious poetry. In Konrad's short lyric, one finds all the qualities of literary mannerism. For example, in song 26, every single word is part of a rhyming pair: *Gar bar lît wît walt, kalt snê wê tuot: gluot sî bî mir.* The excessive, albeit impressive rhyme schemes, especially in songs 26, 27, 28 and 30, ultimately obscure the meaning and emotion of the poetry and Konrad's use of traditional imagery often undermines the originality of his stylistic innovations. Konrad's allegory, *Die Klage der Kunst* (Art's Complaint), appeals for patronage and support of "true art" *(rehte kunst).* His hymn in praise of the Virgin Mary, *Die goldene Schmiede* (The Golden Smith), draws on and synthesizes an extraordinary range of medieval images and symbols. This work may have been commissioned by the Strasbourg Bishop Konrad von Lichtenberg. Other religious-oriented works include Konrad's verse legends. *Silvester* (1260) was commissioned by Liutold von Roeteln, the legend of *Alexius* (1265), by Johannes von Bermeswil and Heinrich Iselin, and Konrad composed the story of Pantaleon (1258) for Johannes von Arguel. The patronage of Konrad's earliest narrative work, *Das Turnier von Nantes* (The Tournament of Nantes, 1257–1258) is unknown, but critics suspect that it was written for someone affiliated with the Lower Rhine region. The tournament takes place at the Arthurian capital of Nantes and pits the German princes under the leadership of Richard of England against the French princes, under the leadership of the king of France. This poem was probably intended to win the support of the lower German princes for the recently crowned king of the Romans, Richard, earl of Cornwall (May 17, 1257). Konrad's fragment, *Schwannritter* (Swan Knight), also seems to have been written during this period. The tale is related to the French *Chevalier au Cygne* (1200) and the Lohengrin story found at the end of Wolfram von Eschenbach's *Parzival* (1210). Undoubtedly, Konrad's *Mären* (lyric novellas) are the most impressive and well-known works in his oeuvre. *Das Herzemaere* relates the popular tale of the jealous lord who feeds his wife the heart of her beloved knight. Konrad's introduction to this story recalls the work of Gottfried von Straßburg. This reference serves to underscore Gottfried's conspicuous influence on Konrad's style. In *Der Welt Lohn* (Worldly Reward), Konrad describes Wirnt von Grafenberg's (the poet of the courtly verse novel *Wigalois*) encounter with *Frau Welt* (Lady World). Although no certain source has been identified for this tale, it belongs to the *contemptus mundi* (contempt of the world) tradition. After gazing upon the infested backside of *Frau Welt,* Wirnt rejects the world, takes up the cross, and achieves martyrdom in the Holy Land. The dark comedy *Heinrich von Kempten* (also called *Otte mit dem Bart,* Otto with the Beard, 1261), illustrates the benefits of loyalty. Composed for the dean of Strasbourg Cathedral, Berthold von Tiersberg, the story plays on the traditions of the ill-tempered Emperor Otte (probably Emperor Otto II). Critics dispute the authorship of other *Mären* attributed to Konrad (*Die halbe Birne,* Half of the Pear, *Der Mvnch als Liebesbote,* The Monk as Go-between, etc.).

Konrad composed three romances. *Engelhard,* set in the time of Charlemagne, tells a tale of fidelity *(triuwe)* in friendship. Engelhard and Dietrich resemble one another almost exactly and develop a close friendship at court in Denmark. Dietrich leaves the court to assume his position as the duke of Brabant but returns to Denmark to help Engelhard win the hand of Engeltrud, the daughter of the king of Denmark. Later, Dietrich is stricken with leprosy. Reminiscent of Hartmann von Aue's tale, *Der Arme Heinrich,* the poem culminates after Dietrich reveals that the blood of Engelhard's children is the only remedy for his illness. In *Partonopier und Meliur* (1277), Konrad draws on the extremely popular French romance *Partonopeus de Blois* (1200). While out hunting,

Partonopier chances on a boat that takes him to the invisible island castle of the heiress of the Byzantine imperial throne, an enchantress named Meliur. At the castle, invisible hands tend to the youth. Partonopier lies with the invisible Meliur each night. Meliur plans to marry him when he comes of age under the condition that he does not look upon her before the appointed time. After a year has passed, Partonopier, plagued by doubts, chances to look upon Meliur and she rejects him. A year later, the pair is reconciled. Partonopier wins Meliur's hand through knightly prowess and becomes the Byzantine emperor. The romance comprises a mix of several different traditions, including: fairy tales, antique epics, *matèrie de Bretange* (tales of Bretange), and the *chansons de geste* (songs of heroic deeds). Similar motifs appear in *Die Königen von Brennenden See* (The Queen of the Burning Lake, 1220–1240), Egenolf von Staufenberg's courtly tale, *Ritter Peter* (1310), and in Thüring von Ringoltingen's verse tale *Melusine* (1456).

Konrad's last and greatest endeavor, *Trojanerkrieg* (The Trojan War, 1281) surpasses, with its 40,424 verses, Herbert von Fritzlar's Middle High German rendition of the fall of Troy, *Liet von Troye* (1190–1217) in both length and quality. Benoît de Sainte-Maure's *Estoire de Troie* is the main source for both German works. Konrad's narrative includes the birth of Paris and Achilles, relates the tale of Jason and Medea, the kidnapping of Helen and the preparation for war. Konrad's tale breaks off in the middle of the siege of Troy. The poem, concluded by a lesser, anonymous poet, was well received. The exact nature of the relationship of Konrad's *Trojanerkrieg* to the *Göttweiger Trojanerkrieg* (1270–1300) has not yet been determined. However, at the very least, Konrad's Schwannritter seems to have influenced the anonymous poet of *Göttweiger Trojanerkrieg*, erroneously attributed to Wolfram von Eschenbach. Konrad died in Basle either on August 31 or between October 8–22, 1287. He and his wife, Bertcha, had two daughters, Gerina and Agnese. He was buried in Basle. Konrad von Würzburg was highly esteemed by contemporaries and successors. He is depicted dictating his work in the Codex Manesse. Hugo von Timberg praises Konrad in *Der Renner* (ll. 1202–1220), and Frauenlob (Heinrich von Meißen) mourns him with the lament that art itself had died with the passing of Konrad: *ach kunst ist tôt!* (313, 15–21).

BIBLIOGRAPHY

Brandt, Rüdiger. *Konrad von Würzburg*. Darmstadt: Wissenschaftliche Buchgesellschaft, 1989.

Kokott, Hartmut. *Konrad von Würzburg: Ein Autor zwischen Auftrag und Autonomie*. Stuttgart: Hirzel, 1989.

Konrad von Würzburg. *Der Trojanische Krieg*, ed. Adelbert von Keller. Amsterdam: Rodopi, 1965.

———. *Die goldene Schmiede*, ed. Edward Schröder. Göttingen: Vandenhoeck & Ruprecht, 1969.

———. *Die Legenden: Silvester, Alexius, Pantaleon*, ed. Paul Gereke. Halle: Niemeyer, 1925–1927

———. *Engelhard*, ed. Paul Gereke. Tübingen: Niemeyer, 1982.

———. *Kleinere Dichtungen*, ed. Edward Schröder. 3 vols. Berlin: Weidmann, 1959–1963 [*Der Welt Lohn, Das Herzmaere, Heinrich von Kempten, Der Schwanritter. Das Turnier von Nantes, Die Klage der Kunst*, songs].

———. *Partonopier und Meliur*, eds. Karl Bartsch and Franz Pfeiffer. Berlin: de Gruyter, 1871; rpt. 1970.

———. *Trojanerkrieg: Staatsbibliothek Preussischer Kulturbesitz, Ms. germ. fol. 1*. Munich: Lengenfelder, 1989 [color microfiche].

Musica practica. *Minnesänger und Meistersinger Lieder um Konrad von Würzburg*. Freiburg: Christophorus, 1988 [audio recording].

Stephen M. Carey

SEE ALSO

Exemplum; Frauenlob; Gottfried von Straßburg; Hartmann von Aue; Herbort von Fritzlar; Hugo von Trimberg; *Mariendichtungen;* Meistersinger; *Sangspruch;* Wirnt von Grafenberg; Wolfram von Eschenbach

Kraft, Adam (d. 1508)

Many of Adam Kraft's (also Krafft) stone sculptures are still in situ in Nuremberg where he lived and worked from 1490 until his death in 1508. His major monument is the towering eucharistic tabernacle in the church of St. Lorenz. The complex tracery, composed of crocketed finials (projecting ornaments) and slender attenuated filaments that form interlacing circles and intertwining nodding ogee (or S-shape curved) arches, has attracted the admiration of viewers for its expressive fantasy, delicate intricacy, and technical perfection. Art historians have lauded the tabernacle as a work that develops the late Gothic stylistic vocabulary to its fullest. At the base, nearly life-size figures of Adam Kraft and two members of his workshop appear to support the structure on their shoulders as they kneel and look out to meet the gaze of beholders.

Kraft's six stations of the cross once punctuated the way leading from the church of St. Sebald to the parish cemetery outside the city walls. Today the reliefs are housed in the Germanisches Nationalmuseum (Nürnberg), and copies replace the originals. The reliefs exhibit extremes of human pathos at close range, showing Christ falling under the weight of his cross as he endures the various tortures of his grimacing tormentors while grief-stricken women watch.

Kraft also carved epitaphs on or in Nuremberg churches. The largest is the mural-like Schreyer-Landauer epitaph on the exterior of St. Sebald, representing the *Via Dolorosa* (The Way of the Cross), entombment, and Resurrection. The Pergensdorf epitaph and the Rebeck epitaph, both today in the Frauenkirche, as well as the Landauer epitaph in the church of St. Egidien, present variants of the coronation of the Virgin. The Kraft workshop likewise sculpted various reliefs, heraldic decorations, and house signs, including house Madonnas, for public buildings and private homes.

BIBLIOGRAPHY

Daun, Berthold. *Adam Krafft und die Künstler seiner Zeit.* Berlin: W. Hertz, 1897.

Schleif, Corine. "500 Jahre Sakramentshaus: Erklärung — Verklärung, Deutung — Umdeutung." *St. Lorenz 96: Mitteilungen des Vereins zur Erhaltung der Lorenzkirche* N.F. 41 (1996): 3–47.

———. "Nicodemus und Sculptors: Self-Reflexivity in Works by Adam Kraft and Tilman Riemenschneider." *Art Bulletin* 75 (1993): 599–626.

Schwemmer, Wilhelm. *Adam Kraft.* Nuremberg: Hans Carl, 1958.

Steingräber, Erich. *Adam Kraft: Die Nürnberger Stadtwaage.* Werkmonographien zur bildenden Kunst 113. Stuttgart: Reclam, 1966.

Stern, Dorothea. *Der Nürnberger Bildhauer Adam Kraft: Stilentwicklung und Chronologie seiner Werke.* Studien zur deutschen Kunstgeschichte 191. Strasbourg: Heitz, 1916.

Zittlau, Reiner. *Heiliggrabkapelle und Kreuzweg: Eine Bauaufgabe in Nürnberg um 1500.* Dissertation, Universität Bamberg, 1988. Nürnberger Werkstücke zur Stadt- und Landesgeschichte 49. Nuremberg: Stadtarchiv, 1992.

Corine Schleif

SEE ALSO

Gothic Art and Architecture; Nuremberg

Kudrun

Transmitted in a sole manuscript dating from the first quarter of the sixteenth century and contained in the *Ambras Heldenbuch* (Book of Heroes from [Castle] Ambras), *Kudrun* is an anonymous Middle High German heroic narrative poem in 1,705 four-verse strophes with "AABB" rhyme scheme. The strophes are arranged in thirty-two *âventiuren*, or cantos, and relate the story of various generations of the family of Ger, an Irish king. Most scholars agree that the work was originally written down relatively soon after the appearance of the *Nibelungenlied*, probably between 1230 and 1240. In all likelihood, its roots lie in the same oral-formulaic tradition as the *Nibelungenlied*.

From a thematic perspective, *Kudrun* may be divided into three sections. The Hagen-section (*âventiuren* 1–4) deals with the abduction of the young Prince Hagen of Ireland by a devilish griffin; his escape and youthful adventures in an otherworld populated by marvelous beasts and three abducted princesses; his eventual return to Ireland and succession to the throne, where he gains notoriety as a *Vâlant aller künige* (Satan of all Kings). The "Hilde" section (*âventiuren* 5–8) tells the story of Hagen's daughter, Hilde, and her voluntary "abduction" by Hetel and Wate from the virtual captivity in which she is held by her father; Hagen's pursuit; the ensuing battle against the "abductors," and the subsequent reconciliation of the warring parties. The "Kudrun" section (*âventiuren* 9–32), which constitutes the main body of the work, describes the abduction of Kudrun, daughter of Hetel of Hegelingenland and Hilde of Ireland, by Hartmut of Normandy and his father, Ludwig; the slaughter of the Hegelings on the Wülpensand in the first rescue effort; Kudrun's many years of deprivation in Norman captivity; her rescue by Herwig, her later husband, and his ally, the indomitable and irascible Wate; once again the section culminates in a final reconciliation between warring parties, following the destruction of the elder Norman dynasty, and punctuated by a total of four marriages. Some scholars have speculated that the section dealing with Hilde represents the oldest part of the epic, and that the Hagen and Kudrun sections are actually later additions. All three parts involve abductions that initially disturb the order of society, but are ultimately resolved, allowing general harmony to be restored. Successful marriages as a conclusion are certainly of major significance in the epic, and the positive role of women in establishing and maintaining a balance within society is more prevalent in *Kudrun* than perhaps any other work of the Middle High German period.

With its emphasis on reconciliation and continuity, *Kudrun* has been justifiably regarded as an "answer" to the *Nibelungenlied,* with which the poet was undoubtedly familiar. The "spirit" of the epic is devoid of the deep tragedy associated with the latter, on both the individual and collective level. Kudrun's forgiving demeanor has been contrasted with the vengeful actions of Kriemhild, her inner stature being regarded as exemplary, and her heroic suffering interpreted as a "poetic projection and surmounting of the everyday degradation of medieval woman" (Nolte, 1985). A particularly problematic area in *Kudrun* research is the issue of generic categorization. While the epic conforms in some ways to the "criteria" employed to designate German "heroic epic," it also has much in common with MHG *Spielmannsepik* (the predominance of the wooing expedition and the burlesque elements revolving around the giant-like Wate figure), and courtly romance (fairy-tale motifs and the basic cyclical structure: joy/order -> sorrow/disorder -> joy/order). It is perhaps most appropriate to view *Kudrun* as an eclectic work that has drawn on various oral and narrative traditions to present a positive alternative to its great predecessor by allowing the feminine element to predominate over the masculine (without, however, negating the latter).

BIBLIOGRAPHY

Bartsch, Karl, ed. *Kudrun.* 5th edition. Karl Stackmann. Wiesbaden: Brockhaus, 1965.

Bäuml, Franz H. *Kudrun. Die Handschrift.* Berlin: de Gruyter, 1969.

Hoffmann, Werner. *Kudrun. Ein Beitrag zur nachnibelungischen Heldendichtung.* Stuttgart: Metzler, 1967.

McConnell, Winder. *The Epic of Kudrun. A Critical Commentary.* Göppingen: Kümmerle, 1988.

McConnell, Winder, trans. *Kudrun.* Columbia, S.C.: Camden Press, 1992

Nolte, Theodor. *Das Kudrunepos — Ein Frauenroman?* Tübingen: Niemeyer, 1985.

Schmidt, Klaus M. *Begriffsglossar und Index zur Kudrun.* Tübingen: Niemeyer, 1994.

Stackmann, Karl. "Kudrun." In *Die deutsche Literatur des Mittelalters: Verfasserlexikon,* eds. Kurt Ruh, et al. 2nd edition. Berlin: de Gruyter, 1984, vol. 5, cols. 410–426.

Wisniewski, Roswitha. *Kudrun.* 2nd edition. Stuttgart: Metzler, 1969.

Winder McConnell

SEE ALSO
Heldenbücher; Nibelungenlied

Kunigunde (d. 1033)

The daughter of Count Siegfried of Luxembourg and Hadwig, Kunigunde (?–1033) married (998–1000) Duke Henry IV of Bavaria, who became King Henry II of Germany in 1002. On August 10, 1002, Archbishop Willigis of Mainz at Paderborn anointed and crowned Kunigunde queen. On February 14, 1014, Henry II and Kunigunde received imperial coronation in Rome from Benedict VIII. Pope Innocent III canonized her on March 29, 1200.

Kunigunde played a significant role in government. During Henry's struggle for the throne she intervened with two of his opponents, and she served as the king's representative twice during wars against the Poles and at the reinstatement of her brother, Henry V, as duke of Bavaria. About one-third of Henry II's charters record Kunigunde's intervention and others designate her as co-regent *(consors regis)*. In 1007, Kunigunde donated properties from her marriage gift for the foundation of the bishopric Bamberg. This ignited a rebellion of her brothers, especially Bishop Dietrich of Metz. As compensation, Henry II granted Kunigunde a dower, the royal residence at Kassel and royal properties surrounding it. On these she founded the nunnery, Kaufungen. On Henry II's death (July 13, 1024), Kunigunde directed the government until the election of Conrad II, to whom she transferred the rule *(regalia)*. She withdrew to Kaufungen, entered the monastic community, and lived there until her death, after which she was buried next to Henry II in Bamberg.

Due to their childless marriage, a legend arose that they had a virginal marriage, and another claimed that Kunigunde, unjustly accused of adultery, confirmed her innocence by walking on red-hot plowshares. An anonymous *vita* (saint's life) of Kunigunde appeared in 1199 for her canonization and her cult spread widely in the late Middle Ages.

BIBLIOGRAPHY

Glocker, Winfrid. *Die Verwandten der Ottonen und ihre Bedeutung in der Politik. Studien zur Familienpolitik und zur Genealogie des sächsischen Kaiserhauses.* Cologne: B'auohlau, 1989, pp. 225–243.

Hamer, Pierre. *Kunigunde von Luxemburg. Die Rettung des Reiches.* Luxembourg: Imprimerie Saint-Paul, Société anonyme, 1985.

Vita Sanctae Cunegundis. In Monumenta Germania Historica: Scriptores, vol. 4, Hannover: Hahn, [n.d.], pp. 821–828.

John W. Bernhardt

SEE ALSO

Conrad II; Henry II, Art

Kürenberc, Der von (fl. late 12th c.)

Der von Kürenberc is the earliest named German lyric poet. His poems are preserved only in the famous Heidelberg University library *Minnesang* manuscript "C," where he is grouped among the barons. He is possibly a member of the Kürenberg family who had a castle near Linz, Austria, during the mid-twelfth century. He is part of what is known as the Danube or indigenous school, showing very little French influence.

Fifteen stanzas have been preserved. The basic metrical unit is the four-beat half-line; the long lines formed of two such halves are combined in rhyming couplets. There are two stanza patterns: the predominant one of four long lines, which is the basis of the so-called Nibelung stanza, or *Nibelungenstrophe,* and that where a rhymeless line is inserted as the odd fifth half-line. Several are so-called "Women's stanzas," or *Frauenstrophen,* written from the woman's point of view. In one poem, a lady stands at night on battlements, listening to a knight singing from among the crowd, in *kürenberges wîse (Minnesangs Frühling [MF],* no. 8,1). In another poem, the lady is compared with a falcon: women and falcons are easily tamed, if one entices them rightly, they will seek the man (*MF* 10, 17).

Kürenberc makes dramatic and effective use of the *Wechsel,* or lyrical dialogue, alternating speeches of identical length. Frequently the speeches do not make contact; the man and woman talk past each other. In a *Wechsel,* he parodies the figure of the lover who so idealizes the lady that he stands beside her bed and does not dare wake her up, much less think of enjoying her favors (*MF* 8, 9-15). He has a dramatic sense of situations; his lyrics often tell little stories. His best known song has the falcon as its subject, *Ich zôch mir einen valken,* for which many widely differing interpretations have been proposed (*MF* 8,33). A person rears a falcon for more than a year, trains and adorns it with gold wire and silken jesses. The falcon flies away "into other lands." Later, the person sees the falcon, still with the gold and the silk, and says: *Got sende si zesamene, die geliep wellen gerne sîn* (God bring those together who wish to be lovers!). The poem might be the literal story of the loss of a falcon or the falcon might be a symbol for a messenger of love, or for the yearning of lovers, or for an unfaithful lover. If the woman is speaking, the poem may be identified as *Frauenstrophen,* if a man, as a *Botenlied.* If it is first the man and then the lady, it is a *Wechsel.*

Der von Kürenberc introduces several elements that appear in later *minnesang:* the message and messenger taken from medieval Latin epistle form; the need for secrecy and fear of spies, *merkære* (slanderers) and *lügenære* (liars); the submissive role of the man.

BIBLIOGRAPHY

Agler-Beck, Gayle. *Der von Kürenberg: Edition, Notes, and Commentary.* German Language and Literature Monographs 4. Amsterdam: John Benjamins, 1978.

Heffner, R.-M.S, and Kathe Peterson. *A Word-Index to Des Minnesangs Frühling.* Madison: University of Wisconsin Press, 1942.

Koschorreck, Walter, and Wilfried Werner, eds. *Codex Manesse. Die Große* Heidelberger Liederhandschrift. Faksimile-Ausgage des Cod. Pal. Germ. 848 der Universitdts-Bibliothek Heidelberg. Kassel: Ganymed, 1981 [facsimile].

Moser, Hugo, and Helmut Tervooren. *Des Minnesangs Frühling unter Benutzung der Ausgaben von Karl Lachmann und Moriz Haupt, Friedrich Vogt und Carl von Kraus.* Stuttgart: Hirzel, 1982.

Räkel, Hans-Herbert S. *Der deutsche Minnesang. Eine Einfrührung mit Texten und Materialien.* Munich: Beck, 1986.

Sayce, Olive. *Poets of the Minnesang. Introduction, Notes and Glossary.* Oxford: University Press, 1967.

Schweikle, Günther. *Die mittelhochdeutsche Minnelyrik,* vol. 1. *Die frühe Minnelyrik. Texte und Übertragungen, Einführung und Kommentar.* Darmstadt: Wissenschaftliche Buchgesellschaft, 1977.

———. *Minnesang.* Stuttgart: Metzler, 1989.

Tervooren, Helmut. *Bibliographie zum Minnesang und zu den Dichtern aus "Des Minnesangs Frühling."* Berlin: Schmidt, 1969, pp. 55–58.

Wapnewski, Peter. "Des Kürenberger's Falkenlied." *Euphorion* 53 (1959): 1–19.

Stephanie Cain Van D'Elden

SEE ALSO

Minnesang; Nibelungenlied; Versification

L

Lahn River

The Lahn valley lay at the center of the medieval *Lahn-gau* (district), which formed part of the constitutional structure of Germany in the tenth through the twelfth centuries. The river originates in the southern Rothaarge-birge (on the east slope of the Westerwald) atop the Lahnkopf, about 610 meters above sea level, and from thence flows in a generally southwesterly direction before emptying into the Rhine River at Niederlahnstein, some seven miles above Koblenz. It separates the Westerwald and the Taunus schist massifs. For the most part the course is narrow and winding; the direct distance from the source to the exit is only 82 kilometers; the actual length is 245 kilometers (about 152 miles) because of the many bends and turns. It is fed by several tributaries as well, including the Dill, the Elbbach, and the Gehlbach on the right, and the Ohm, the Solms, the Weil, the Ems, the Aar, the Dörsbach, and the Mühlbach on the left.

During the Middle Ages, various towns grew up along its banks. The foundations of a fortification at Marburg date to the tenth century, while the present fortress was begun about 1140; market privileges were extended to the inhabitants of the settlement that grew up around its base at about the same time. About 1450, the town had an estimated 3,200 inhabitants and three churches, including St. Elizabeth's Church, resting place for the relics of St. Elizabeth of Hungary. The choice of Marburg in part rested on the fact that since 1122, the town was in the possession of the Ludowings, who in 1131 were elevated to the status of landgraves of Thuringia.

Downstream from Marburg lay Gießen, which lay near the eastern extent of the archdiocese of Trier in the Middle Ages. A twelfth century collegiate church domi-nated the town of Wetzlar; and the magnificent St. George's Church at Limburg, built in the Gothic transi-tional style between 1210 and 1250, rose alongside the river as well. The small town of Nassau was the cradle of the counts of Laurenburg, who took the name of Nassau in the twelfth century and produced a king, Adolf, at the end of the thirteenth century.

The numerous castles and fortifications above the river point to the complicated territorial history of the region, but also to the significance of the Lahn valley in commer-cial geography: e.g., the Martinsburg near Oberlahnstein was a customs castle *(Zollburg)* belonging to the arch-bishop of Mainz dating from the fourteenth and fifteenth centuries. The *Burg* Lahneck, a fortress belonging to the archbishop of Mainz, is mentioned in 1224. Niederlahn-stein, on the other hand, is mentioned as early as 1047, and received town privileges in 1332. The neighboring Oberlahnstein appears in 997, but did not acquire town privileges until after 1500.

During the fourteenth century, the archbishopric of Trier asserted a greater presence in the Lahn region, as witnessed by the fortress Baldwinstein, which was built in 1320 to rival that of Schaumburg by Baldwin of Luxem-burg, archbishop of Trier.

BIBLIOGRAPHY

Keyser, E. "Die städtebauliche Entstehung der Stadt Mar-burg." *Zeitschrift des Vereins für hessische Geschichte* 72 (1961): 77–98.

Krings, Bruno. *Das Prämonstratenserstift Arnstein an der Lahn im Mittelalter 1139–1527.* Wiesbaden: Selb-stverlag der Historischen Kommission für Nassau, 1990.

Metternich, Wolfgang. *Der Dom zu Limburg an der Lahn.* Darmstadt: Wissenschaftliche Buchgesellschaft, 1994.

Paul B. Pixton

SEE ALSO
Coblenz; Fortification; Marburg; Trier

Lambach

Located between Salzburg and Linz in Upper Austria, Lambach is best known for its baroque monastery originally built at the end of the eleventh century and containing an extensive cycle of some of the most significant and well-preserved Romanesque frescoes in Germany and Austria. It is also known for its important monastic scriptorium and library. The excellent site may have been in use from an early time, and references to it first appear in late eighth-century texts with subsequent mention of a church dedicated to the Virgin. The monastery present today may have been constructed on the same site after the founding of a chapter of secular canons in Lambach by Count Arnold II around 1050, following the deaths of his wife and some of his children in a single disaster, the nature of which eludes historians. The count's third son, Adalbero, named bishop of Würzburg in 1045, transformed this community into a Benedictine monastery in 1056. Adalbero was deeply involved in the power struggle over investiture between Henry IV and Pope Gregory VII. As a result, he was expelled from his bishopric in 1085 and retired to Lambach where he died in 1090. Adalbero's political and reformist interests affected his activities at Lambach. There he installed monks and an abbot, Ekkebert, from Münsterschwarzach, who followed the monastic reform movement begun at the Gorze monastery, which not only adhered to a strict discipline, but also recognized the authority of the bishop in monastic affairs.

The fresco cycle lies in the west choir of what may originally have been a double-apse church. Although the ceiling of the fresco cycle was rediscovered in the nineteenth century, it was only in 1956 that the work began that led to the full uncovering of twenty-three scenes after more than a decade of restoration. The frescoes had been preserved when the west choir, the main choir of the church, was blocked off for the installation of an organ in the seventeenth century. Although it is likely that what remains is only a portion of the original, scholars studying the frescoes have attempted to work out its program. They have tied the official consecration of the high altar in the west choir to the Virgin, and another consecration to John the Evangelist in 1089 by Altmann of Passau and Adalbero, and to the events surrounding its foundation to the execution of the frescoes as well as their iconography. In addition to four individual Old Testament figures, the frescoes depict the childhood and early career of Christ, with an unusually extensive series of scenes of the story of Herod. Scholars have suggested that among other messages in the frescoes, such images constitute a commentary on the kingship issues at the heart of the Investiture Controversy. Scholars have noted a variety of textual sources for the iconography, including the writing of Josephus and the Lambach play of the three Magi. As Demus has argued, the painters probably came from Salzburg, for similarities have been noted between the style of the frescoes and a group of manuscripts illuminated there, but the artists also drew on an apparent knowledge of north Italian and even Byzantine art at Venice.

BIBLIOGRAPHY
Babcock, Robert G. *Reconstructing a Medieval Library: Fragments from Lambach.* New Haven, Conn.: Beinecke Rare Book and Manuscript Library, 1993.
Demus, Otto. *Romanesque Mural Painting,* trans. Mary Whittall. New York: Harry N. Abrams, 1970, pp. 624–627.
Genge, Hans-Joachim. *Die liturgiegeschichtlichen Voraussetzungen des Lambacher Freskenzyklus.* Münsterschwarzach: Vier-Türme-Verlag, 1972.
900 Jahre Klosterkirche Lambach: 20. Mai bis 8. Oktober 1989 im Benediktinerstift Lambach. Linz: Landesverlag, 1989.

Rebecca W. Corrie

SEE ALSO
Investiture Controversy, Romanesque Art and Architecture; Salzburg; Würzburg

Land Ownership

No abstract concept of absolute ownership of property (such as existed in Roman law) seems to have existed in the early Middle Ages. Rather, what defined a person's rights to an object was his or her ability to use it, draw some benefit from it, and to alienate it freely to another. In the past, this immediate possession of the land has been termed *gewere,* a later Saxon term equivalent to the English *seizin;* however, this use has been questioned in recent scholarship.

Words such as *eigen* (from a Germanic root implying "have") and *alodis* (combination of Frankish *al* or "full" and *od* or "thing possessed") initially designated the practical possession of either a movable object or a piece of land. From the Carolingian era on, such words as *allodium, possessio, praedium,* and *proprietas* were applied (often indiscriminately) to landed property, both inherited and acquired by gift or purchase. *Hereditas, patrimonium,* and related terms indicated inherited land. *Hantgemal,* which occurs only about forty times in medieval sources, seems to indicate a special ancestral property indicative of a kin group's free status.

Landed property was the steadiest source of income for medieval lords, since a piece of land consisted not simply of soil, but rather of resources on the land, including the serfs who worked it *(mancipia).* Initially, medieval Germany's substantial free peasantry made up the majority of landowners (though not possessing the majority of land owned). Women in Germany, when compared with women elsewhere in medieval Europe, enjoyed extensive property rights. Like men, they could receive property by inheritance, purchase, or gift (often as a marriage gift from their husbands), and could dispose of this property, although the presence of a man as legal advocate was expected at the time of transaction.

Land could also be given away. It was the gift of choice to churches and religious communities, transferred typically for the salvation of the souls of the donor and his or her kin. Specific conditions might be attached to the gift, such as the expectation of burial rights *(sepultura),* or the beneficiary's obligation to pray for the donor and celebrate a yearly memorial anniversary. The actual use of the property *(usus fructuarius)* might be reserved to the donor until his or her death. Consent of kin to an alienation was often sought in order to forestall later challenges.

Land could be "loaned" to others as well. Precarial agreements, in which a person would convey land to another and receive it back for the term of his or her life, were popular. A landowner might grant property to another as a benefice *(beneficium)* or (from the twelfth century on) a fief *(feodum),* without such a grant being necessarily connected to vassalage or acts of homage or fealty. Roman law commentators developed the distinction between the lord's *dominium directum* and the tenant's *dominium utile,* but such legal theory was probably not felt in Germany until the thirteenth century, when in many regions a fief could be alienated without the lord's consent.

BIBLIOGRAPHY

Ebel, Wilhelm. "Über den Leihegedanken in der deutschen Rechtsgeschichte." In *Studien zum mittelalterlichen Lehenswesen,* ed. Theodor Mayer. Lindau: Thorbecke, 1960, pp. 11–36.

Ebner, Herwig. *Das freie Eigen: Ein Beitrag zur Verfassungsgeschichte des Mittelalters.* Klagenfurt: Verlag des Geschichtesvereines für Kärnten, 1969.

Freed, John. *The Counts of Falkenstein: Noble Self-Consciousness in Twelfth-Century Germany.* Transactions of the American Philosophical Society, vol. 74, part. 6, 1984. Philadelphia: The American Philosophical Society, 1984.

Leyser, Karl. "The Crisis of Medieval Germany." *Proceedings of the British Academy* 69 (1983): 409–443.

Reuter, Timothy. "Property transactions and social relations between rulers, bishops and nobles in early eleventh-century Saxony: the evidence of the Vita Meinwerci." In *Property and Power in the Early Middle Ages,* eds. Wendy Davies and Paul Fouracre. Cambridge, England: Cambridge University Press, 1995, pp. 165–199.

Reynolds, Susan. *Fiefs and Vassals: The Medieval Evidence Reinterpreted.* Oxford: Oxford University Press, 1994.

Scherner, K. O. "Gewere." In *Lexikon des Mittelalters,* vol. 4. Munich: Artemis, 1989, cols. 1420–1421.

Jonathan Rotondo-McCord

SEE ALSO

Carolingians; Feudalism; Law and Lawbooks

Landfrieden

Royal enactments aimed to ensure peace, *Landfrieden* "peace of the land," or "peace associations" recur throughout the medieval German era. While making and keeping peace was arguably the central task of medieval kingship, its forms and successes changed considerably over time. The incursions of the Northmen (Norse), Saracens, and Magyars of the ninth and tenth centuries threatened to wreck the Carolingian achievement, and the mounted knights who had arisen to repel the invaders were rapidly becoming part of the problem because of their ability to terrorize and subjugate those whom they were supposed to protect. Beginning in the 980s, the bishops of the West Frankish realm undertook measures to restrain knights and establish peace. Originally two distinct initiatives called the Peace of God and the Truce of God, which gradually melded, they ruled out-of-bounds for combat certain sacred times as well as certain categories of people, threatened excommunication to violators, and organized the common people under the leadership of parish priests to enforce these provisions. The Peace of God was proclaimed by Pope Urban II at Clermont in 1095 and became part of the general legislation of the church in the twelfth century.

In Germany, great disorder prevailed during the reign of Henry IV because of his minority (until 1065), Saxon rebellions, and his struggles with the popes. Small wonder, then, that peace legislation was enacted in at least four German dioceses in the 1080s and in the duchies of Saxony and Bavaria in 1084 and 1094, respectively. To reassert royal authority in the face of all these implicit challenges (including the pope's), Henry IV himself issued the first imperial *Landfrieden* at Mainz in 1103, and thereafter it was considered to be the most effective type of royal legislation in Germany until the enactment of the "Eternal Peace of the Land" (*Ewiger Landfrieden*) by the Reichstag in 1495. From Frederick Barbarossa's first *Landfrieden* of 1152 onward, it was accepted that enforcement was left to regional and local authorities, significantly both a sign and an accelerator of the "territorialization" of Germany. Beyond these common features, however, the *Landfrieden* was no less complex in its patterns than in its origins. Some were valid for the entire empire (e.g., those of 1152, 1235, and 1495), others for particular regions. Some sought to prohibit feuding absolutely (e.g., 1152), others to restrict it (e.g., 1179, where Barbarossa had to retreat from his earlier position). Nor was the crown the only authority to enact such peaces. Princes, nobles, towns, and even peasants decreed all kinds of peace and formed peace associations all through the later Middle Ages. The most famous of them was probably that of three Alpine cantons in 1291, which grew into the Swiss Confederation.

The fact that such public measures were undertaken at so many levels for 400 years in Germany is a distinctive feature of its history and attests to the limited success of these initiatives. The right of feuding came to be restricted, not abolished, at least not until 1495—and even that could not be really effectively enforced until the eighteenth century. The right of escort (*Geleit*) was therefore an important issue in the late Middle Ages; the Golden Bull of 1356 devotes no fewer than twenty paragraphs to this issue for the imperial electors alone. As for the causes of this endemic violence, it is customary to fix most of the blame on the knights, the "robber barons" (*Raubritter*) of the late Middle Ages. Although the passion for liberty

and rights pervaded all of medieval European society, it ran amok in Germany. Churchmen, princes, burghers, and peasants all wanted their independence and readily resorted to declarations of feud to secure and defend their rights—thus the famous feud that the city of Vienna announced against its overlord, Emperor Frederick III, in 1462. And the "peace association" sworn by the inhabitants of Uri, Schwyz, and Unterwalden in 1291 looked to the Habsburgs like revolt against their lawful overlords, for which both sides were prepared to fight to the death again, and again, and again.

BIBLIOGRAPHY

Arnold, Benjamin. *Medieval Germany, 500–1300: A Political Interpretation.* Toronto: University of Toronto Press, 1997.

Brunner, Otto. *Land and Lordship. Structures of Governance in Medieval Austria.* Philadelphia: University of Pennsylvania Press, 1992.

Kaufmann, Ekkehard, and H. Holzhauer "Landfrieden." In *Handwörterbuch zur deutschen Rechtsgeschichte,* ed. Adalbert Eder, et al., vol. 2. Berlin: Schmidt, 1978, pp. 1451–1485.

Lawrence G. Duggan

SEE ALSO

Carolingians; Henry IV; Frederick I Barbarossa; Frederick III; Golden Bull; Saxon War

Landshut

The settlement at Landshut (Bavaria) developed around a bridge over the Isar River where two major trade routes crossed, one along the Isar and the other between the Inn River and Regensburg. The local historian, Veit Arnpeck, writes that Ludwig I, son of Otto von Wittelsbach, duke of Bavaria, reacted to robberies in the area by establishing a guard post midway along the road. This point was referred to as *Hut und Schutz des Landes* (shelter and protection of the land), eventually, as Landshut. Fertile meadows provided good grazing for dairy cattle and encouraged settlement of the surroundings. In 1204, Ludwig I began building the town of Landshut and a residential castle there. The castle, with its Romanesque chapel dedicated to St. George, the *Georgskapelle* (ca. 1230), was named Trausnitz in the fifteenth century and converted into a Renaissance building during the sixteenth. Minnesinger Neidhart von Reuental spent several years in Landshut around 1215, and beginning in 1247, Tann-

Landshut, St. Martin, interior view to east. *Photograph: Virginia Jansen*

häuser also lived there. In 1232, Ludmilla, widow of Ludwig I, founded the Cistercian cloister, Seligenthal, with its chapel dedicated to Saint Afra *(Afrakapelle)*. Dominican and Franciscan cloisters were also founded in Landshut in 1271 and 1280, respectively.

Landshut became the central city of the Wittelsbach dukes and thus a center of regional government between 1225 and 1503. A building in which town meetings were held was mentioned in 1331. As the meetings outgrew this first small building, they moved to the Dominican house, then to the Franciscan, and finally, in 1380, to a large building in the center of town that forms the middle section of the present city hall *(Rathaus)*. Important buildings built or rebuilt after the fire of 1342, and residences such as those on Altstadt Street have been preserved since medieval times and provide a model of medieval architecture and craftsmanship. The number of construction projects initiated before 1400 attests to

Landshut's rapid growth during the fourteenth century when construction began on the Gothic basilica St. Jodok and on the church of St. Nikola. In 1407, construction of *Heiliggeistkirche* (Church of the Holy Spirit) began. Structural problems in the Romanesque church of St. Martin were exacerbated by the fire of 1342, and the church was rebuilt starting in 1380. The new church, a late Gothic hall church with a brick spire more than 130 meters high, was completed in 1500. While the foundation of St. Martin's was being cleaned in 1979, walls, columns, and much of the Romanesque portal of the older church were discovered just beneath the floor of the present building.

As the ducal residence and capital of an expansive duchy that included two-thirds of medieval Bavaria, Landshut flourished under the patronage of the three "rich" dukes of Bavaria-Landshut: Heinrich, Ludwig, and Georg (1392–1503). While the original castle served as the center of government, a second castle, Burghausen, was constructed to provide a quieter, private home for the noble families. The early fifteenth century was marked by civil unrest with which the duke dealt severely. The mid-century was punctuated in 1444 by an outbreak of plague that killed thousands of people in the city. Although Jewish residents were protected under Heinrich, they were driven from Landshut after his death in 1450 in spite of the significant contribution they had made to the city's economic prosperity. In 1472, Duke Ludwig founded Bavaria's first university in Landshut where it remained until 1826 when it moved to Munich. The learned Dr. Martin Maier served not only as foreign minister and minister of culture for the duchy, but as the first chancellor of the university as well. A monument of red marble carved by Hans Beierlein of Augsburg for Dr. Maier's grave is located just inside the main entrance to St. Martin's. The marriage of Ludwig's son, Georg, to Hedwig of Poland in 1475 provided the setting for what is remembered as the most glamorous of all medieval feasts. Every four years, the wedding procession, known as the *Landshuter Hochzeit,* is reenacted.

Important fifteenth-century religious art from Landshut, stained glass round windows from 1477 depicting Duke Heinrich and the Virgin Mary originally belonging to the *Georgskapelle* and a Gothic altar from the same period, are housed in the church of Jenkofen. Under the leadership of Duke Georg (1479–1503), the city continued to develop as a cultural center. In 1489, the first paper mill in Bavaria was constructed in Landshut, and in 1493, the city boasted twenty-two goldsmiths. Numerous artisans, including Nikolaus Alexander Mair, were active in the city around 1500. Duke Georg died without male heirs, and the war that ensued for sovereignty ended in the dissolution of Bavaria-Landshut as an independent duchy and the unification of all of Bavaria under the sovereignty of Bavaria-Munich in 1505. Nevertheless, Landshut continued to be an important center of learning, art, and government.

BIBLIOGRAPHY

Spitzlberger, Georg. *Das Herzogtum Bayern-Landshut und seine Residenzstadt, 1392–1503.* Landshut: Stadt- und Kreismuseum, Stadtarchiv Landshut, 1993.

———. *Landshut in Geschichte und Kunst.* Landshut: Hornung, 1989.

Zorn, Eberhard. *Landshut: Entwicklungstufen mittelalterlicher Stadtbaukunst.* Landshut: Verkehrsverein, 1979.

Ruth M. W. Moskop

SEE ALSO
Gothic Art and Architecture; Jews; Neidhart; Romanesque Art and Architecture; Tannhäuser, Der

Langmann, Adelheid (ca. 1312–1375)

Born to a politically and socially powerful family in Nuremberg around 1312, at the age of thirteen, Adelheid Langmann was betrothed to Gottfried Teufel, who died shortly afterward. Following what she describes as a lengthy spiritual struggle, around 1330, Adelheid entered the Franconian Dominican cloister of Engelthal. Regarded as a particularly prosperous and renown cloister, Engelthal housed the daughters of many of the prominent burghers of the area. Among them was Christina Ebner, whose widespread praise included bishops and kings. Adelheid was cloistered at Engelthal in 1350 when King Charles IV (later Emperor Charles) visited the monastery for spiritual advice. She was educated in Latin and learned to read and write in her vernacular German dialect. Shortly after Christina wrote her spiritual autobiography, Adelheid recorded her visions and revelations along with a lengthy prayer dedicated to the Trinity. Her *Revelations,* extant in three manuscript variations, were written in a Bavarian dialect and chronicle her spiritual life from 1330 to 1344. While the content is essentially autohagiographical, representing the religious experiences of its author, there are stylistic similarities and thematic parallels with the mystical lives narrated in the convent chronicles of Helfta, Toss, Unterlinden, Diessenhoven,

and Adlehausen. Influenced by biblical sources, especially the Song of Songs, Adelheid's ecstatic mysticism reflects the bride mysticism of the Middle Ages. Her texts, as well as several other manuscripts written by Dominican cloistered women in Southern Germany, were rediscovered and edited by nineteenth-century scholars interested in the linguistic history of German.

BIBLIOGRAPHY

Die Offenbarungen der Adelheid Langmann: Klosterfrau zu Englethal, ed. Phillip Strauch. Strasbourg: Trübner, 1878.

Hale, Rosemary Drage. "*Imitatio Mariae:* Motherhood Motifs in Devotional Memoirs." *Mystics Quarterly* 16 (1990): 193–214.

Hindsley, Leonard P. *The Mystics of Engelthal: Writings from a Medieval Monastery.* New York: St. Martin's Press, 1998.

Rosemary Drage Hale

SEE ALSO
Charles IV; Ebner, Margaretha; Sister-Books; Women

Last Judgment Plays

See Drama, Last Judgment Plays.

Latin Language

Latin was not only the first major written language of western Europe but also an enduring influence on the vernacular languages and literatures that eventually supplanted its own. To exert this sway on the spoken languages and literatures of Germany required more substantial accommodations than were needed in some Romance-speaking parts of Europe, where Latin and its literature had been established for much longer. Not only was German more remote linguistically from school Latin than were Romance dialects, but its oral culture and verse forms were also more different. In contrast to most Romance-speaking areas, German-speaking ones, because their languages had not yet acquired scripts suitable for more than brief inscriptions, had not had poetry except in oral performance before the Middle Ages.

Both Latin and German were changed by the prolonged encounter. Latin was an international language, but, as is the case with English today, it acquired distinctive characteristics in its phonology, orthography, vocabulary, and even syntax in response to the effects of the native languages in the regions where it was used: A German monk or cleric spoke Latin differently from his French or Irish counterpart. In the other direction, many Latin words entered into German in direct lexical borrowing that began already in late antiquity, as well as indirect borrowings that were transmitted through the native languages (such as Anglo-Saxon and Irish) of missionaries who brought Christianity into Germany. Furthermore, there was calquing through the combination of German elements to coin words or constructions that were modeled on ones in Latin.

The time of the most intense interchange was probably the Carolingian period. The Christian culture with which the Frankish-Roman church pervaded the public life and worship of Germany brought new objects and types of buildings, institutions and hierarchies, and concepts. This Christian culture was based largely on Latin manuscripts, access to which was attained by acquiring knowledge of the Latin language, especially as transmitted in classics of Roman and Christian Latin literature. Charlemagne (768–814) established the blueprint for the attainment of this Christian Latin culture, as in his capitulary *De litteris colendis* (ca. 780–800) when he expressed concern over the poor power of expression among the clergy and the consequent possibility of misinterpretation of the scriptures, and called for the foundation of schools to spread a standard orthography and grammar.

Throughout western Europe, the world of learning and literacy was a Latin world. To learn to read was to learn Latin, to be literate was to be a Latin user. Latin was a father tongue, a language that was spoken by no one from the cradle but that was employed routinely in both writing and speech by an elite of clerics in many of the most important institutions. The coexistence of the German mother tongue with Latin can be called cultural diglossia, as opposed to the bilingualism that exists when two fully spoken languages cohabit.

From the twelfth century on, Latin seems to have made fewer contributions to the lexicon of German than did French, although often it is difficult to ascertain from which of the two languages a given loanword derived. Nevertheless, because the world of learning remained Latin for many centuries to come, many elements of the learned language continued to enter into German throughout the Middle Ages. By the same token, living Latin never ceased borrowing from German, in place-names, words for political and social structures (e.g., *marcgravius*), legal terms, and words for objects found only in local culture.

BIBLIOGRAPHY

Henkel, Nikolaus and Nigel F. Palmer, eds. *Latein und Volkssprache im deutschen Mittelalter 1100–1500. Regensburger Colloquium 1988.* Tübingen: Niemeyer, 1992.

Keller, R. E. *The German Language.* London: Faber and Faber, 1978, esp. pp. 225–228, 320–325.

McKitterick, Rosamond. *The Carolingians and the Written Word.* Cambridge, England: Cambridge University Press, 1989.

Wittstock, Otto. *Latein und Griechiesch im deutschen Wortschatz: Lehn- und Fremdwörter altsprachlicher Herkunft.* Berlin: Volkseigener Verlag, 1979; 4th edition, 1988.

Ziolkowski, Jan M. "Cultural Diglossia and the Nature of Medieval Latin Literature." In *The Ballad and Oral Literature,* ed. Joseph Harris. Cambridge, Mass.: Harvard University Press, 1991, pp. 193–213.

Jan M. Ziolkowski

SEE ALSO

Abrogans; Charlemagne; Dutch Language, Dialects; Glosses, Old High German; Gothic Language; Hrabanus Maurus; Onomastics; Paleography; Walahfrid Strabo; *Waltharius*

Lauber, Diebolt (fl. 1427–1467)

A writer, teacher, and employer, Lauber was active in Hagenau, Alsace. From 1440 to 1470, his handwriting is contained in several manuscripts of the Lauber workshop. He very likely had already organized the production of illustrated manuscripts in the early 1420s with the assistance of a large number of (at least sixteen) copyists and artists. Evidently, he had drawn on the experience of a preceding organization, the so-called *Werkstatt* (Workshop) of 1418. He remained active until 1470. In the late period he attempted to ensure the sale of the books by way of advertising. Prior to that he had secured his clientele through his contacts to the Hagenau *Landvogtei* (provincial government). Because of his editorial work, he was probably also involved in publishing. The genuine achievement of his business was the clear arrangement of texts, which were by and large written in the vernacular of the day, and included indexing, headings, and pictures. More than seventy codices are known today to have come from his workshop; the spectrum ranges from Bible picture books *(Historienbibeln),* which dominated until 1440, to epic poems, devotional books, scientific and legal literature. Production was subject to frequent changes in organizational form and turnover in staff. Standardized layout and text arrangement created a form of trademark, which was shaped above all by the illustrators of a group known as "A," employed in the production of twenty-nine manuscripts in the period from 1425 to 1450. At this time the illustrations acted as a form of catchword pre-interpreting the text. In contrast, during the late period, when Hans Schilling collaborated, detailed descriptions and exact presentation were emphasized.

BIBLIOGRAPHY

Fechter, Werner. "Der Kundenkreis des Diebolt Lauber." *Zentralblatt für Bibliothekswesen* 55 (1938): 121–146.

Kautzsch, Rudolf. "Diebolt Lauber und seine Werkstatt in Hagenau." *Centralblatt für Bibliothekswesen* 12 (1895): 1–32, 57–113.

Koppitz, Hans-Joachim. *Studien zur Tradierung der weltlichen mittelhochdeutschen Epik.* Munich: Fink, 1980, pp. 34–50.

Saurma-Jeltsch, Lieselotte E. *Die Kommerzialisierung einer spätmittelalterlichen Kunstproduktion: Zum Wandel von Konzeption und Herstellungsweise illustrierter Handschriften bei Diebolt Lauber und seinem Umkreis.* 2 vols. Wiesbaden: Reichert, 1999.

Lieselotte E. Saurma-Jeltsch

SEE ALSO
Manuscripts, Painting and Production

Laufenberg, Heinrich (ca. 1390–1460)

Laufenberg, a cleric active in Freiburg im Breisgau and Zofingen, composed the bulk of his verses between 1413 and 1445. In the latter year he entered a cloister in Strasbourg that had been founded by Rulman Merswin (d. 1382), the lay mystic and guiding spirit for the so-called Friends of God. Laufenberg is best known as the author of some 120 sacred songs written in the German vernacular, among them Christmas and New Year's verses. His Christmas song *Jn einem krippfly lag ein kind* (In a little crib lay a child) is representative in its straightforward narration, plain diction, and heartfelt religious devotion. Especially pronounced is Laufenberg's veneration of the Virgin Mary; few medieval poets command his breadth of Mariological symbols and tropes. The culmination of his Mariology is the *Buch der Figuren* (1441), a massive versified catalogue and interpretative commentary on more than 100 prefigurations of the Virgin in the Old Testament. Another lengthy work from his pen is the *Regimen sanitatis* (1429), a combination cosmology and medical reference tool of more than 6,000 German verses based on many source texts, Avicenna among them. The *Regimen,* besides treating health concerns, pregnancy, and child-care, examines the solar system, the elements, and natural phenomena—including pestilence. Very popular, Laufenberg's *Regimen* was an early printed book. Rounding out his longer works is a 1437 translation, in 15,000 verses, of a fourteenth-century discourse on salvation, *Speculum humanae salvationis.*

The prolific author, who had regular ecclesiastical duties as pastor, curate, and dean, evinces broad learning, theological sophistication, and mastery of a wide range of vernacular and Latin literary forms. At home in verse and prose, Laufenberg translated Latin church hymns and sequences and composed "mixed" poetry, that is, songs in alternating Latin and German verses. Musical composer and self-aware author in one person (Laufenberg liked to sign and date his compositions), he influenced hymn writing in the Reformation and beyond. As Martin Luther was to do, Heinrich Laufenberg penned many pointed *contrafactura,* appropriating secular texts and melodies for the Christian sphere. His most famous example—and his most famous song—is *Ich wölt, daz ich doheime wer* (I wished I were at home). The "home" of which the singer speaks is heaven; he longs for a home far from earth where he can gaze eternally upon God. In like vein, Laufenberg wrote Christian dawn songs and adapted secular love songs for worship of the Virgin Mary. She appears typically in his verse as the *mülnerin* (the miller's wife/female operator of a mill), a figure who threshes, grinds, and bakes the biblical "corn of wheat" (John 12:24) that is Jesus Christ. Evident everywhere in Laufenberg's work is the desire to increase piety in his broad audience, be these nuns, religious societies, or laymen. That his texts were read silently by individual readers for meditation and private devotion is very probable.

Scholarly research on Heinrich Laufenberg has labored under the loss of unique versions of most of his creations, the result of destruction of manuscripts in Strasbourg during the Franco-Prussian War in 1870. A critical edition of his works has not yet appeared and would necessarily contain presumed transcriptions.

BIBLIOGRAPHY

Schiendorfer, Max. "Der Wächter und die Müllerin 'verkert,' 'geistlich.' Fußnoten zur Liedkontrafaktur bei Heinrich Laufenberg." In *Contemplata aliis tradere,*

Studien zum Verhältnis von Literatur und Spiritualität. Festschrift für Alois Haas zum 60. Geburtstag, eds. Claudia Brinker, et al. Bern: Lang, 1995, pp. 273–316.

Wachinger, Burghart. "Notizen zu den Liedern Heinrich Laufenbergs." In *Medium aevum deutsch, Beiträge zur deutschen Literatur des hohen und späten Mittelalters. Festschrift für Kurt Ruh zum 65. Geburtstag,* eds. Dietrich Huschenbett, et al. Tübingen: Niemeyer, 1979, pp. 349–385.

William C. McDonald

SEE ALSO
Friends of God

Law and Lawbooks

Medieval Germany knew no law code or act of legislation in the modern sense. Instead, most of the legal rules governing the lives of people existed as social custom, habit, and morally proper conduct in which all members of society participated. Law in this sense accorded both duties and privileges to individuals according to social status. This customary law, then, relied on the public knowledge of individuals and their participation in the legal adjudication process. Their oral memory was supported by formal procedure enhanced with symbolic gestures and formulaic speech such as oaths. This means that law was orally and locally transmitted so that even after the Carolingian kings established a centralized state, and even after lawbooks were written, knowledge of law remained local for a long time as far as practice and consistency of judgments are concerned.

From the earliest records of German law to the reception of Roman law in Germany in the sixteenth century, we find the following types of legal rules or accords: Latin laws of the Germanic kingdoms (*leges,* fifth to ninth century); vernacular customary laws applied as the general law of a territory, thirteenth to sixteenth century; vernacular city codes created and agreed to by the city councils, beginning in the thirteenth century; feudal laws governing land and fealty relations of the nobility; Peace ordinances and other promulgations by rulers, twelfth to thirteenth century.

The Leges

After the tribal migrations, when the Germanic kingdoms were created on the foundation of Roman rule, law codes were compiled in Latin. Collectively, these *leges* de- veloped uniquely out of the Germanic tribes' encounter with the Romans. At that time the Germans were an archaic society lacking the concept of a central governing institution and found themselves confronted with a very well developed Roman legal system and culture and, in addition, with the Christian religion as an institution. Their gradual acculturation determined the specific content of the *leges.* They typically recorded Roman law as practices in their own particular region. Their long-term interaction produced the principle of personal law, which means that each person is accountable to the law of his own tribe or confederation. Thus a Roman was tried under Roman law and a Frank was tried under Frankish law. Separate rules were established for regulating disputes between litigants belonging to different ethnic groups. And finally, the Germans recognized the need to establish and maintain an organized government.

The writing of *leges* began with the Goths who confederated earliest with the Romans and continued when the Franks emancipated themselves and conquered several other tribes. Our earliest records are the fifth-century West Gothic *Edictus Theoderici, Lex Visigothorum,* and *Les Romana Visigothorum.* The first two laws were for the Goths and the last for handling the interaction between Goths and Romans. The other extant *leges* are the sixth century Burgundian *Lex Gundobada, Lex Romana Burgundionum,* and the Franconian *Lex Salica.* In the seventh century we have the *Lex Ribuaria* (revised Salic laws), and the Lombard *Edictus Rothari* followed in the eighth century by the *Lex Alamannorum* and *Lex Baiuvariorum.* These last two were written once they were conquered by the Franks and brought into the Frankish empire. Shortly thereafter and probably prompted by Charlemagne, the *Lex Frisionum, Lex Saxonum,* and *Lex Thuringorum* were compiled.

Composed of Germanic, Roman, and Christian elements, it is impossible to isolate a uniquely German foundation in these texts. Moreover, the values within Roman society were already Christian and had also been assimilated. We do know, however, that orality was basic to Germanic law and cannot be recovered because the *leges* are already informed by literacy. We also know that Germanic law lacked both a concept of rulership and a concept of state. In contrast, law in these texts is already understood as a means to establish and maintain organized government. Hence, the purpose of the *leges* was to create the essential elements of rulership and to institute lasting structures that support central authority. The king appears as the giver of law and has control of governing institutions such as the law courts. The *leges* also replaced the legal blood feud with composition of payment (material restitution) to the injured family. Thus the *leges* document what the Germanic tribes learned and assimilated.

Land Peace

Land peaces *(Landfrieden)* were promulgations made repeatedly by the emperors and also by territorial princes in Latin. They continued the papacy's *Pax dei* (Peace of God) movement, which had first declared short periods of nonviolence. Beginning in 1103, the emperors provided rules for establishing and maintaining such periods of peace by suggesting means to resolve conflict and listing punishments for grave crimes against public peace such as kidnapping, imprisonment, mutilation, or patricide. Their purpose was to end blood feuds, a practice that the *leges* evidently had halted, to establish a royal judge who strove to produce consistency in the legal process throughout the territories, and to stabilize the ruler's rights vis à vis the princes. Of the several such land peace agreements, Heinrich's Truce *(Treuga Heinrici)* of 1224 and the imperial "Land peace" of Mainz (*Mainzer Reichslandfriede,* 1235), distributed in German, are best known for two significant concepts: first, a public peace that may not be violated, and second, the concept that criminal acts were to be punished by specified physical penalties regardless of the perpetrator's social status. These innovations were further developed in the vernacular lawbooks.

The Vernacular Lawbooks

The beginning of the thirteenth century marks the transformation of oral custom to a written legal tradition after 300 years of silence. This very same period marks the rise of German for official use in all types of legal texts, including the imperial land peace agreements. First the imperial city code, the *Mühlhäuser Reichsrechtsbuch,* 1223–1231, appeared for the use of imperial ministerials. It was immediately followed by Eike von Repgow's much larger compilation, *Sachsenspiegel* (*Saxon Mirror,* 1225–1235), which contains a compilation of the legal practices in Saxony, an ethnically mixed territory where the traditions of Eastfalians (*Ostfalen,* east of Saxony), Westfalians, Thuringians, Swabians, Dutch, and the indigenous Slavs merged.

The *Saxon Mirror* contains two parts. The first, the territorial law, encompasses the legal customs and procedures that regulated the daily life and concerns of all inhabitants including serfs, free peasants, women, children,

and ethnic minorities. These customary laws include grazing rights, property rights in marriage, ownership and transfer of land, inheritance, criminal penalties, and legal procedures. The second part, the feudal law, records the rights and obligations that bind male and female vassals and liege lords.

From the time of the *leges* to the vernacular customary law, legal thinking changed strikingly. The *Saxon Mirror* records a critical shift in German law from a purely oral authority and transmission to written documentation that allowed greater consistency in the adjudication process. In addition, there are four specific, fundamental, and far-reaching developments in content as well. Perhaps the most obvious development is the explicit integration of Christianity by accommodating German legal custom to the canonists. The second innovation is territorial law. Unlike personal law, the *Saxon Mirror* presents a primarily territorial law for Saxony, meaning that the customs apply to all Germans living in that territory. Nevertheless, custom still acknowledged personal law for the ethnic Slavs. Procedure also allows for multilingualism, guaranteeing that a defendant can hear the charges against him in his own language. The third and most radical change, however, is the grounding of law and justice in God and the secular state (and with it, the expansion of the judiciary). No longer are the forebears the primary source of law. Rather, the concept of legal custom is firmly rooted in the state. From the outset, the *Saxon Mirror* points to God as the source of law and justice and ascribes the specific, secular application of law to imperial governance that began with Constantine and Charlemagne, who gave certain privileges to the Saxons. The king is presented as judge above all people and promulgator of laws. This emphasizes that the administration of justice was delegated from a central, royal point (section III, part 26), meaning that the king delegated his royal judicial authority to the judges and thereby gave them the right to preside over a superior court. The fourth change is the formation of a rudimentary criminal code with corporal punishments that elaborated on the land peace.

The impact of the myriad *Saxon Mirror* versions cannot be overestimated in or outside Germany. Within thirty-five years, several copies, adaptations, and translations of Eike's text were produced. The most important of these are the Upper German translations, *Deutschenspiegel* (*German Mirror,* 1275–1275), *Schwabenspiegel* (*Swabian Mirror,* 1276), and the later, illuminated manuscripts: an Oldenburg manuscript from 1336 in Low German, one in Heidelberg from 1294ff., another in

Dresden from 1295–1363, and a fourth in Wolfenbüttel from 1358–1362.

The title of *German Mirror* testifies that the translator extended the jurisdiction of Eike's book to all German-speaking areas. It also became a paradigm for codified law books in Prussia, Silesia, Ukraine, Hungary, Bohemia, and Poland. Used, therefore, throughout Germany, the book achieved the authority of a code for 300 years in more than 450 manuscript copies until reception of Roman law in the sixteenth century, and in some areas its influence lasted until the nineteenth century.

City Codes

The process of compiling city codes—also written in German—began at about the same time as the *Saxon Mirror* and was completed by the end of the fourteenth century. For the most part, these law books contained rules for merchants and markets. In addition, they included sections from the *Saxon Mirror* in order to regulate disputes between citizens of municipal and rural jurisdictions. The Magdeburg city codes begun in 1188 and then greatly expanded were probably the most influential because the new cities in the colonial areas looked to Magdeburg for legal guidance. The best known, the *Magdeburger Weichbild*, ca. 1250, describes the different courts along with their competencies and procedures. Other early cities with codes include Halle, Augsburg, Cologne, Hamburg, and Vienna.

BIBLIOGRAPHY

Der Oldenburger Sachsenspiegel. Vollständige faksimile-Ausgabe im Originalformat des Codex Picturatus Oldenburgensis CIM 1410 des Landesbibliothek Oldenburg, ed. Ruth Schmidt-Wiegand. 2 vols. Graz, Austria: Akademischer Druck-und Verlagsanstalt, 1995.

Deutschenspiegel und Augsburger Sachsenspiegel, eds. Karl August Eckhardt and Alfred Hubner, revision. edition. Hanover: Hahnsche Buchhandlung, 1933.

Die Dresdner Bilderhandschrift des Sachsenspiegels, ed. Karl von Amira. 2 vols. Leipzig: Hiersemann, 1902.

Die Heidelberger Bilderhandschrift des Sachsenspiegels. Kommentar und Anmerkungen, ed. Walter Koschorreck. 2 vols. Frankfurt am Main: Insel Verlag, 1970.

Dilcher, Gerhard. "Mittelalterliche Rechtsgewohnheit als methodisch-theoretisches Problem." In *Gewohnheitsrecht und Rechtsgewohnheiten im Mittelalter,* eds. Gerhard Dilcher, et al. Berlin: Duncker und Humblot, 1992, pp. 21–66.

Eike von Repgow. *Sachsenspiegel. Die Wolfenbütteler Bilderhandschrift Cod. Guelf. 3.1 Aug. 2°,* ed. and trans. Ruth Schmidt-Wiegand. 3 vols. Berlin: Akademie Verlag, 1993.

Johanek, Peter. "Rechtsschrifttum." In *Geschichte der deutschen Literatur,* vol. 3, part. 2, ed. Ingeborg Glier. Munich: Beck, 1987, pp. 396–431.

Laws of the Alamans and Bavarians, trans. Theodore J. Rivers. Philadelphia: University of Pennsylvania Press, 1977.

Magdeburger Rechtsquellen, ed. Paul Laband. 1869; rpt. Aalen: Scientia, 1967.

Oppitz, Ulrich-Dieter. *Deutsche Rechtsbücher des Mittelalters.* 3 vols. Cologne: Böhlau, 1990.

Planck, Julius Wilhelm von. *Das Deutsche Gerichtsverfahren im Mittelalter nach dem Sachsenspiegel und den verwandten Rechtsquellen* [1879]; rpt. New York and Hildesheim: Olms, 1973.

The Saxon Mirror: A Sachsenspiegel of the Fourteenth Century, trans. Maria Dobozy. Philadelphia: University of Pennsylvania Press, 1999.

Schott, Clausdieter. "Der Stand der Leges-Forschung." *Frühmittelalterliche Studien* 13 (1979): 29–55.

Schulze, Ursula. *Lateinisch-deutsche Parallelurkunden des 13. Jahrhunderts. Ein Beitrag zur Syntx der mittelhochdeutschen Urkundsprache.* Munich: Fink, 1975.

Text- und Sachbezug in der Rechtssprachgeographie, ed. Ruth Schmidt-Wiegand. Munich: Fink, 1985.

Maria Dobozy

SEE ALSO

Carolingians; Charlemagne; Chronicles, City, German; Eike von Repgow; Eike von Repgow, Legal; *Landfrieden;* Ministerials

Lechfeld, Battle of

One of the great battles of the tenth century and one that ended the threat of Magyar (Hungarian) invasion to central and western Europe and confirmed the reputation of Otto I. The battle, fought near the Lech River (Bavaria) on August 10, 955, witnessed the decisive victory of Otto and his armies against a much larger invading force. The invasion was the culmination of a long series of Magyar raids that stretched back into the ninth century. These raids had plagued not only Germany but also Aquitaine, Burgundy, East Francia, and Italy. The Magyars, lightly-armored and highly skilled horsemen and archers, raided throughout the first half of the tenth century primarily to spread terror and acquire booty. Exploiting the political instabilities of the late Carolingian world, the Magyars were quite successful in their raids of plunder and pillage and even threatened the existence of Bavaria and Swabia. The invasion of 955 was similar to the earlier assaults in that it was inspired by political difficulties in Otto's realm. Indeed, the events of 955 should be associated with the revolt against Otto of Liudolf and Conrad of Franconia in 954. A Magyar raiding party invaded during this revolt and Liudolf was accused of inviting in the enemy army, an accusation that turned the tide against the rebels. The Magyars, aware of lingering tensions in Otto's realm and confident from successes in 954, waged a more serious assault in the next year. In the summer of 955, a rather large army of uncertain size invaded Bavaria and laid siege to Augsburg on August 8. Otto, armed with the Holy Lance, led a force of Saxons south to oppose the invaders and was joined by contingents of Bohemians, Swabians, and Franks under the former rebel Conrad. Otto's army of 3,000 to 8,000 was significantly smaller than that of his enemy but was a heavily armed and armored force. Once the battle was engaged on August 10, Otto's better armed force triumphed but only after a near disastrous moment at the beginning of the engagement. The Magyar army attacked Otto's rear guard, nearly routing it, before Conrad turned and scattered the enemy. The battle turned quickly in Otto's favor as he forced the Magyars into close, hand-to-hand combat. As Widukind of Corvey notes, "The more daring of the enemy host resisted, then, when they saw their comrades behind them turn and run, were stupefied and surrounded by our army and killed." The victorious army pursued and destroyed much of the defeated foe. The Magyar leaders were captured and executed by Otto in a successful attempt to prevent further invasions by leaving the enemy leaderless. Although not without losses himself, including Conrad, Otto was hailed *imperator* (emperor) by his troops after the victory and regarded as the great defender of Christendom. His victory was seen as divinely inspired and the great prestige he earned strengthened his position in Germany and strengthened his claim to the imperial title he revived in 962.

BIBLIOGRAPHY

Leyser, Karl. "The Battle at the Lech, 955: A Study in Tenth-Century Warfare." *History* 50 (1965): 1–25.

Widukind of Corvey. *Die Sachsengeschichte,* eds. H.-E. Lohmann and Paul Hirsch. Monumenta Germanicae Historia. Scriptores rerum Germanicarum 60. 5th edition. Hannover: Hahn, 1935; rpt. 1977.

Michael Frassetto

SEE ALSO

Holy Lance; Otto I; Widukind of Corvey

Legenda Aurea, **Alsatian**

The Alsatian *Legenda Aurea,* (Golden Legendary, the oldest manuscript from 1362), is one of the first three prose legendaries (collections of legends) in German, together with Hermann von Fritzlar's *Heiligenleben* (1343–1349), and the South Middle Netherlandic *Legenda Aurea* (oldest manuscript 1358), which served as sermons and communal reading material for laymen and religious alike within the German mystics' movement of the fourteenth century, and for its later followers. The 190 legends were written in a pastoral style, and regularly include the liturgy of the day, according to the church calendar. The anonymous author might have lived in Strasbourg.

Manuscripts were produced in workshops and sold to the nobility and clergy alike. The professional productions were more accurate and usually had illustrations (mostly by Diebold Lauber). Three manuscripts were on parchment, seven had all the legends of the church year in one volume, nine had only the winter-part, eight the summer-part, four had selected only the legends of apostles (all in Switzerland), several had contamination with the *South German Heiligenleben* (ca. 1385–1400).

Manuscripts spread to all of Alsace, Switzerland, Swabia, the Palatinate, and even to Austria, as the dialects of the texts demonstrate. The legendary received an appendix of twelve legends (mostly of Strasbourg dignitaries), which was later used in the *Straßburger Chronik* of Jakob Twinger von Königshofen (1382). Other legends were added, after the reform of Dominican women cloisters of the southwest set in (1419), up to fifty-one. By 1460, the legendary influenced the work of Sister Regula, *Das Buch von den heiligen Mägden und Frauen,* comprising fifty-seven legends of female saints.

BIBLIOGRAPHY

Kunze, Konrad. "Jacobus a (de) Voragine (Varagine)." In *Die deutsche Literatur des Mittelalters. Verfasserlexikon,* eds. Kurt Ruh, et al. Berlin and New York: de Gruyter, 1981, vol. 4, cols. 448–466.

Kunze, Konrad, ed. *Die Elsässische Legenda aurea. Bd. 2. Das Sondergut.* Texte und Textgeschichte 10. Tübingen: Niemeyer, 1983.

Williams, Ulla, and Werner Williams-Krapp, ed. *Die Elsässische Legenda aurea,* vol. 1. *Das Normalcorpus.* Tübingen: Niemeyer, 1980.

Williams-Krapp, Werner. *Die deutschen und niederländischen Legendare des Mittelalters: Studien zu ihrer überlieferungs-, Text- und Wirkungsgeschichte.* Tübingen: Niemeyer, 1986, pp. 35–52.

Sibylle Jefferis

SEE ALSO

Heiligenleben; Hermann von Fritzlar; Lauber, Diebolt; Legends

Legends

In medieval Europe, edifying narratives of exemplary holy figures were gathered into collections called *legenda* or legendaries. Often very lengthy manuscripts, the collections were comprised of a variety of stories that might include the life of Christ, the life of Mary; a variety of saints' stories, both local and pan-European; tales of the church fathers; the desert fathers; passion stories or the narrations of famous martyrdoms; and a host of miracle stories. Because the fundamental material of a legend was typically the *vita* (or life) of a saint or paradigmatic holy figure, the literary form of a legend was similar to and often indistinct from that of hagiography. Much of the material was drawn from popular oral tradition and was normally organized according to the liturgical year. Selections were read aloud in monastic settings during the lessons of the second nocturn (early morning prayer period) of matins on each saint's feast day. For the laity, the hagiographic material was integrated into sermons and was often iconographically depicted in church imagery, in frescoes, chapel paintings, and sculpted figures. Throughout medieval Europe, legendaries—the stories of notable holy figures—were second only to the Bible in oral and written circulation.

Without doubt the most famous and widely used collection was the *Legenda aurea* or "Golden Legend" written by Jacobus de Voragine (ca. 1230–1298). Containing more than 200 stories, *The Golden Legend* quickly became the benchmark collection for all other compilers to follow. It had a remarkable impact on the composition of German vernacular legendaries. The *Vers-Passional,* completed between 1290–1300, was the first medieval German legendary to use the *Legenda aurea.* This 110,000-verse legendary is divided into three books, the first treating the birth of Mary, the Annunciation, the Nativity, and the life and Passion of Christ all organized according to the liturgical calendar. The second book includes stories of the apostles and Mary Magdalene, and the third book tells the stories of seventy-five saints from St. Nicholas (December 6) to St. Catherine (November 25). Although nothing is known of the poet, scholars speculate that he may also have authored the 41,540-verse *Das Väterbuch* (Lives of the Fathers) patterned on the Latin compilation, *Vita Fratrum,* and includes stories of the early Christian Church fathers and saintly monks and hermits. Together, the *Vers-Passional* and *Das Väterbuch* had enormous impact on the widespread transmission of vernacular legendaries in medieval German-speaking areas.

From approximately 1300 to 1350, German vernacular legendaries were composed metrically, as were *Das Väterbuch* and the *Vers-Passional.* After 1350, however, verse legendaries virtually disappeared, as prose legendaries became the fashion and the metrical collections were used primarily as source material. The first prose legendary, extant in only one manuscript, was compiled by a wealthy patrician layman, Hermann von Fritzlar, between 1343–1349. Intended for contemplation and devotion among the laity, Hermann combined the narrative elements of the *vita* with a homiletic style of sermons. The first complete German vernacular prose translation of the *Legenda aurea* was the *Elsässische Legenda aurea* completed in 1362 by an anonymous clergyman from Strasbourg. Shortly afterward, a Low German translation, the *Mittelniederdeutsche Legenda aurea,* appeared.

Regarded as the most popular of German prose legendaries, *Der Heiligenleben* (Lives of the Saints) was composed by a Dominican friar from Nürnberg between 1396 and 1410. Substantially larger than the *Legenda aurea, Der Heligen Leben* contains 251 legends from multiple sources including the *Vers-Passional,* the *Märtyrerbuch,* the *Legenda aurea* and the *Speculum Historiale* of Vincent Beauvais, as well as the Latin *Vitae Patrum.* Only thirty-one of the lives recorded are drawn from the *Legenda aurea* and more than any other prior collection, *Der Heligen Leben* includes selections more focused on European and especially German lives. The collection is arranged according to the liturgical year and each *vita* is accompanied by a short prayer intended for communal recitation. This especially influential collection is extant in nearly 200 manuscripts in both High and Low German vernaculars.

The literary classification of *legenda* is by its nature complex and also includes compilations such as *Der Seelentrost* (Consolation of the Soul). Written in the latter half of the fourteenth century, this vernacular collection of *exempla* or stories is largely devoted to the Ten Commandments. It is framed by a series of dialogues between a spiritual master and a young man and like other legendaries, it drew on popular folk material and religious doctrine to arouse interest and offer moral edification. While written in Latin for a distinctly monastic audience and composed some 200 years earlier, the *Dialogus miraculorum* of Caesarius of Heisterbach is similar in its intent to teach through engagingly presented stories. In the mid-fourteenth century, a number of Dominican convents in southern Germany composed chronicles referred to as *Nonnenbücher* (Sister-Books). Because these chronicles are largely comprised of collected *vitae* of nuns whose exemplary lives were collected as models for others, the *Nonnenbücher* have been likened to that of the legendary. However, while the religious intent may bear similarities with the compilation the saints' lives in the legendaries, the style is more accurately described as that of chronicling the history of the particular monastery.

Throughout the late fourteenth and fifteenth centuries, the production of legendaries escalated. And, as literacy increased among the laity and cloistered women, smaller volumes with more limited scope, narrating the life of a single saint, became fashionable, and countless editions were printed. Especially popular among these were the legends of John the Baptist, John the Evangelist, Augustine, Anne, Barbara, Dorothy, and Margaret.

During the Middle Ages the word "legend" did not carry the connotation of myth or fiction. The Latin verb *lego* meant "to gather" or "collect" and "to read out" or "recite." The word *legenda* itself came to mean a "saint's life" and the stories of the saints—the legends—were accepted by many medieval Christians as representative of historical reality. Although the material was often derived from folk and fairy tale, there were few challenges to the historical accuracy of the legends until the sixteenth century when Martin Luther condemned them as incredulous papist propaganda. Taking one of the legends from *Der Heiligen Leben,* that of St. John Chrysostom, he wrote and published a parody of the story, *Die Lügend von St. Johanne Chrosostommo,* as evidence of what he regarded as the fictional absurdity of the tales. As an aggregate of folktale, fairy tale, romance, and sacred history, medieval German legendaries provide historians with a great deal of evidence about the popular culture of the day.

BIBLIOGRAPHY

Kalinke, Marianne E. *The Book of Reykjahólar: The Last of the Great Medieval Legendaries.* Toronto: University of Toronto Press, 1996 [esp. pp. 3–24 with excellent historical synopsis of medieval German legendaries].

Willams-Krapp, Werner. "German and Dutch Legendaries of the Middle Ages: A Survey." In *Hagiography and Medieval Literature: A Symposium,* Odense: Odense University Press, 1981.

———. "German and Dutch translations of the *Legenda aurea* ." in Brenda Dunn-Lardeau, ed. *Legenda aurea: Sept sièclesde diffusion. Actes du colloque international sur la Legenda aurea: texte latin et branches veraculaires à l'Université du Québec à Montréal 11–12 mai 1983.* Montréal: Éditions Bellarmin, 1986, pp. 227–232.

Rosemary Drage Hale

SEE ALSO

Caesarius of Heisterbach; Exemplum; *Heiligenleben;* Hermann von Fritzlar; *Legenda Aurea,* Alsatian; *Märtyrerbuch; Passional; Servatius;* Sister-Books; *Väterbuch*

Leinberger, Hans (ca. 1480–ca. 1531)

Only a few dates between 1511 and 1527 are recorded from the life of this sculptor in wood and stone; he was probably born in Lower Bavaria about 1480, but he lived and worked in Landshut. Only in 1978 was Hubel able to associate definitively the monogram HL, discovered by Sighart in 1862, with Leinberger. The question of his early training is still undecided, with Upper Austria and Nuremberg both entertained as possibilities in the scholarly literature.

Leinberger's virtuoso forms can be seen in monumental Madonnas and figures of saints as well as in small multi-figured reliefs carved with stupendous vitality and subtle precision. In his low reliefs he masterfully conveys exceptional depth in both landscapes and interiors, and he embeds "his dense scenic representations" (Schädler 1977: 68) in these convincing spaces. In a new technique, Leinberger replaces the usual polychromy (use of different colors) with the marks of up to twenty-three different tooling punches, creating a variety of effects on the unpainted wood surface. Together with the new interpretation of landscape, these features indicate Leinberger's leanings toward the expressionism of the Danube school.

The signed works include the Rorer epitaph, a limestone relief dated 1524 (Landshut, St. Martin), and wood

Hans Leinberger, Neumarkt Madonna (Munich, Bayerisches Nationalmuseum). *Photograph: Bayerisches Nationalmuseum*

reliefs representing the baptism of Christ from 1515 and the Lamentation from the following year, both in the Bodemuseum in Berlin, and a Calvary, also from 1516 (Munich, Bayerisches Nationalmuseum). The high altar at the church of St. Castulus in Moosburg from 1514 is documented as a work of Leinberger's, as are four reliefs from the Castulus altar and two reliefs from the Saint John altar, all made in the same year. An enthroned Virgin and a *Schmerzensmann*, from the lost high altar at Polling near Weilheim, are also documented in 1526–1527.

The works attributed to Leinberger are numerous. Among the most important figures in the round are a Madonna in the Rosary from 1516–1518 (Landshut, St. Martin) and an enthroned Virgin from Neumarkt, probably from about 1510–1515, now in the Bavarian National Museum in Munich. Also in the same location are an *Anna Selbdritt* from before 1513, and a large figure of Saint James from about 1525. Two crucifixes, dated about 1515 and a decade later, are located with Leinberger's numerous other works at St. Castulus in Moosburg; a third, from about 1530, is in the church of St. Johannes in Erding. In addition to the signed Rorer memorial, Leinberger also completed limestone epitaphs for the Mornauer family about 1513–1515, also at St. Castulus, and after 1520 and 1521, respectively, for the Walkheiners (St. Peter near Straubing), and the Notthaffts (Landshut, St. Martin).

BIBLIOGRAPHY

Behle, Claudia. *Hans Leinberger: Leben und Eigenart des Künstlers—Stilistische Entwicklung—Rekonstruktion der Gruppen und Altäre.* Miscellanea Bavarica Monacensia 124; Neue Schriftenreihe des Stadtarchivs. Munich: UNI-Druck, 1984.

Hubel, Achim. "Ein eigenhändiger Brief des Bildhauers Hans Leinberger." *Verhandlungen des historischen Vereins für Oberpfalz und Regensburg* 118 (1978): 217–219.

Liedke, Volker. *Hans Leinberger: Marginalien zur künstlerischen und genealogischen Herkunft des großen Landshuter Bildschnitzers.* Munich: Kunstbuchverlag Weber, 1976.

Lill, Georg. *Hans Leinberger, der Bildschnitzer von Landshut: Welt und Umwelt des Künstlers.* Munich: Bruckmann, 1942.

Müller, Theodor. *Hans Leinberger.* Bayerisches National Museum Katalog 13, 2. Berlin: Gustav Weise, 1938.

Schädler, Alfred. "Zur künstlerischen Entwicklung Hans Leinbergers." *Münchner Jahrbuch der Bildenden Kunst* 28 (1977): 59–90.

———. "Hans Leinberger—Meister von Rabenden—Stephan Rottaler: Große altbayerische Bildwerke in der Münchner Frauenkirche." In *Die Münchner Frauenkirche: Restaurierung, und Rückkehr ihrer Bildwerke zum 500. Jahrestag der Weihe am 14. April 1994,* eds. Hans Ramisch and Peter Bernhard Steiner. Kataloge und Schriften des Diîzensanmuseums Freising 14. Munich: Pfeiffer, 1994, pp. 36–67.

Taubert, Johannes. "Zur Oberflächenbehandlung der Castulus-Reliefs von Hans Leinberger." In *Farbige*

Skulpturen: Bedeutung, Fassung, Restaurierung. Munich: Callwey, 1983. 89–96.

Thoma, Hans. *Hans Leinberger: Seine Stadt, Seine Zeit, Sein Werk.* Regensburg: Pustet, 1979.

Brigitte Schliewen

SEE ALSO

Iconographies, Innovative; Nuremberg; Vienna

Leo IX (1002–1054)

Pope Leo IX was born as Bruno of Egisheim in 1002 into a noble Alsatian family. His early studies were at the regional center in Lorraine of Toul, where, in 1017, he became a canon at the cathedral. Related to the German ruler Conrad II, he served prominently in the royal army in Lombardy in 1026. Conrad appointed him the bishop of Toul in 1027. Inspired by the monastic reform efforts of the tenth and eleventh centuries, Bruno sought to bring the fruits of these movements to such monasteries in his diocese as St. Aper, St. Dié, Moyenmoutier, and Remiremont. Reform of the diocesan clergy also was the order of a number of the synods he held. His efforts to reinvigorate his diocese as the bishop of Toul would prepare him for extending these activities to the whole Western Church when he became pope.

The emperor Henry III, his cousin, selected him to be pope in 1048, after the brief reigns of Henry's previous two appointees, and he was crowned at St. Peter's with the acclamation of the Roman people. From Lorraine he would summon such like-minded reformers as Humbert, abbot of Moyenmoutiers; Frederick of Liege, the future Pope Stephen IX, and Hugh of Remiremont. Joining the men of the north would be such Italian churchmen as Peter Damian and Hildebrand, the future Pope Gregory VII, to become the nucleus of what became the college of cardinals. Aided by the efforts of these and other reforming churchmen, the new pope sought through the holding of numerous regional synods in Italy, Germany, and the kingdom of the French to curb the problems of simony, nicolaitism (opposition to celibacy), and violence against churchmen and the poor and to deal with numerous other problems facing the church in this period. Pope Leo presided over these gatherings and exhibited the presence of the papacy to a substantial portion of Western Christendom, quite unlike that of his predecessors. He extended papal protection to monasteries in a series of charters and in 1050 issued a canonical collection that drew on earlier rulings to support his papal activities. His aggressive attempt to deal with the problems faced by the church is also apparent in his personally leading an army into southern Italy in 1053, with the approval of Henry III, to oppose the Normans, a major preoccupation in the latter part of his papacy, because they were such a threat to the ecclesiastical and papal political holdings in the region. The Normans defeated the army of the pope in June of that year and held Leo captive. Incensed by this invasion into a region where the Byzantines had claims, Patriarch Michael Cerularius of Constantinople closed the Latin churches in his city. Humbert was dispatched from Rome to lead a papal embassy to try to solve the problem. The result was not the desired rapprochement but a mutual excommunication by Humbert and the patriarch and the beginning, in July of 1054, of the great schism between Rome and Constantinople, between the Western Church and the Eastern Church that continues to the present. Pope Leo, however, was not alive to witness the separation. He died in April of that year in Rome shortly after his release from Norman captivity.

John of Fécamp called Pope Leo "the marvelous pope" *(papa mirabilis),* a title that in many ways he well deserved. His papacy marks an important moment in the history of the church. His achievements provided the foundation for the Gregorian reform and the future papal monarchy. He brought the presence of the bishop of Rome to many parts of Western Christendom, in a manner comparable to the papal global travels in the late twentieth century. At the Council of Rheims, he used the title of universal to emphasize the scope of the power of the vicar of Peter. His very name demonstrates his awareness of the singular importance of his position, so clearly delineated in the Petrine doctrine of Leo the Great. But he also utilized the Donation of Constantine to justify his actions in southern Italy where he aggressively displayed his leadership in a new papal militarism that looked forward to the summons of the First Crusade by Urban II in 1095. This aggressive leadership, however, also led to the great schism of 1054, a separation that has had a profound importance in the history of the church and of Europe as a whole. Few papacies, if any, have marked such a major change in the direction of the church.

BIBLIOGRAPHY

Analecta Bollandiana 25 (1906): 258–297 [Brussels, 1892ff.; continues *Acta Sanctorum*].

Brucker, P. P. *L'Alsace et l'Eglise au temps du pape saint Léon IX (Bruno d'Egisheim) 1002-1054,* 2 vols. Strasbourg: F. X. Le Roux, 1889.

Fliche, A. *La réforme grégorienne,* vol. 1 Louvain: Spicilegium sacrum louvaniense, 1924.

Leo IX, in *Acta Sanctorum.* London: Snowden, 1641ff. April 11, pp. 641–673 [lives of saints by calendar].

Migne, Jaques-Paul, ed. *Patrologia Latina,* vol. 143. Paris: Migne, 1882, cols. 457–800.

Nicol, D. M. "Byzantium and the Papacy in the Eleventh Century." *Journal of Ecclesiastical History* 13 (1962): 1–20.

Tellenbach, Gerd. *The Church in Western Europe from the Tenth to the Early Twelfth Century,* trans. T. Reuter. Cambridge, England: Cambridge University Press, 1993.

Daniel F. Callahan

SEE ALSO

Conrad II; Donation of Constantine; Gregory VII; Henry III; Toul

Libraries

The great Roman tradition of large, state-sponsored public libraries did not exist in the Middle Ages. Charlemagne and his successors were able to revive book production and classical learning in Germany, but this effort was centered in the Benedictine monasteries and court schools. Although Charlemagne himself most likely had a modest personal library, this was the exception among Carolingian nobles. The libraries of the ninth century were small, the greatest holding only several hundred manuscripts, and were dependent on the monastic scriptorium (writing center) for growth and vitality. Serving monastic needs, worship, and education, they concentrated their holdings in the areas of biblical exegesis and certain Latin classics for the learning of grammar and style. The libraries of this period were seldom located in a separate room but were distributed among the sacristy and common areas. Manuscripts were stored in a locked closet or trunk, the *armarium,* but most reading was done in the monks' cells. Only the most rudimentary catalogs, or book lists, were prepared to inventory the holdings. Among the most significant centers of learning, with commensurate libraries, were St. Gall, Reichenau, Lorsch, Fulda, Freising, Regensburg, Trier, Salzburg, and Konstanz. Most of these centers were also responsible for the beginnings of writing in the German language.

The bridge from the ninth to the twelfth century and the advent of the university library was provided by several monastic reform movements. After a period of stagnation and the destruction of many libraries by Norman, Saracen, or Hungarian raids in the late ninth and tenth centuries, the reformed monastery of Hirsau revitalized an interest in renewing outdated or insubstantial holdings. The Carthusians saw book production and proper librarianship as keys to their ascetic vision. The new mendicant orders of the early thirteenth century, the Franciscans and Dominicans, guided by the great universities of Paris, emphasized scholastic literature and established a new kind of study library with chained books, usually in a separate room. The greatest German libraries of the thirteenth and fourteenth centuries were at Erfurt, Heilsbronn, Mainz, Regensburg, and Bamberg. Only a few possessed texts in German.

There was a period of considerable decline in monastic production and collection after the great plague years in the mid-fourteenth century. It was during this time, however, that universities became established in Prague (1348), Vienna (1364), Heidelberg (1386), Cologne (1388), and Erfurt (1392). The faculties of these universities chartered substantial libraries fairly early on, and the growth of these libraries was rapid because of the support given them by individual princes or towns and the considerable donations of faculty and students. With the introduction of paper toward the end of the fourteenth century, certain monasteries were able to increase considerably the size and scope of their libraries, most notably Tegernsee, with more than 900 fifteenth-century manuscripts still extant. It was also at this time that the first useful catalogs appear, sometimes organized alphabetically by author or title, providing a means to locate texts rather than just an inventory of them. As libraries became status symbols, wealthy merchants and noblemen and women began to actively pursue private collections, with an interest in secular texts in German as well. The availability of commercial scribes and later the availability of printed books made this pursuit feasible. Although private and city libraries were to grow in importance at the end of the medieval period, the large state-sponsored library would not emerge in Germany until the seventeenth century.

BIBLIOGRAPHY

Buzas, Ladislaus. *Deutsche Bibliotheksgeschichte des Mittelalters.* Elemente des Buch- und Bibliothekswesens 1. Wiesbaden: Reichert, 1975.

Löffler, Klemens. *Deutsche Klosterbibliotheken.* Bücherei der Kultur und Geschichte 27. Bonn: Schröder, 1922.

McKitterick, Rosamond. *The Carolingians and the Written Word.* Cambridge, England: Cambridge University Press, 1989.

Mehl, Ernst, and Kurt Hannemann. "Deutsche Bibliotheksgeschichte." In *Deutsche Philologie im Aufriß.* 2nd edition. Berlin: Schmidt, 1957, pp. 454–562.

Thompson, James W. *The Medieval Library.* Chicago: The University of Chicago Press, 1939; rpt. 1957.

William Whobrey

SEE ALSO

Bookmaking and Production; Charlemagne; Cologne, History; Education; Freising; Fulda; Lorsch; Manuscripts, Painting and Production; Paleography; Prague; Regensburg; Reichenau; *Sachliteratur;* Salzburg; Sankt Gall; Trier; Universities; Vienna

Liederhandschriften

The German term *Liederhandschrift* (manuscript of songs) encompasses in its widest sense all manuscripts (and other media) that contain written records of the art of the Middle High German songwriters, an art form originally conceived as oral, i.e., not to be written down. In a narrower sense, manuscripts containing only such songs are designated *Liederhand-schriften.* The earliest example of an independent German language song manuscript, known as "A," is in the University Library at Heidelberg (no. cpg. 357), written in Alsace around 1270–1280. However, since "A" is obviously based on earlier, if lost, written versions, this kind of manuscript must be older. One of the main characteristics of medieval German language song manuscripts is the attempt to attribute the songs, lays, and *Sangsprüche* (political verse) to an author (authorial principle), and to collect all the texts of a given author into one corpus *(corpus principle).* In this way they vary recognizably from the medieval compilations of Latin, French, Provençal, and Italian poetry, all of which employ a spectrum of basic ordering practices ranging from the author and corpus principle through thematic and genre related viewpoints all the way to alphabetical listing. As a rule, German language song manuscripts gather a rather large number of authors' texts together, whereby the four main manuscripts ("A," "B," "C," and "J"—discussed below), when compared with each other, reveal characteristic differences with respect to their selection and ordering of the au-

thors' collections and the texts and genres contained therein. These differences result in part from the interests of the respective patrons, in part from the source materials then available.

Manuscript "A," one of the major collections, contains in its main corpus 791 songs and two lays, listed under thirty-four authors' names. The manuscript opens with a series of well-known authors with a large number of songs, (Reinmar, Walther von der Vogelweide, Heinrich von Morungen, Ulrich von Singenberg, Rubin), followed by a second section of collections of erstwhile anonymous groups that probably were assigned to an author (Niune, Gedrut, Spervogel, Der Junge Spervogel, Leuthold von Seven) at a later date, in addition to small collections of authors known by name. Alongside the dominant reflective courtly love songs (*Minnelieder*), "A" also contains dawn songs, Neidhart songs, shephard poems *(pastourelles),* lays, and *Sangsprüche.* "A" clearly focuses on the classical and postclassical songs. At the beginning of the fourteenth century, a number of anonymous additions were made to the anthology.

Manuscript "B" (Stuttgart, Württembergische Landesbibliothek, no. HB XIII 1), written in Constance at the beginning of the fourteenth century, contains in its main body 602 songs under twenty-five authors introduced with a full- or half-page portrait of the author and in the order that supposedly reflects the standing of the poets. The texts are reflective courting songs with related genres (messenger's song, crusade song); *Sangsprüche* are marginal throughout; no lays were included. The texts are all so-called Middle High German classic and early romanticizing *Minnesang* (courtly love poetry). This conservative core collection was later expanded and updated by Neidhart songs, *Sangsprüche,* the so-called Winsbecke complex, and two *Minnereden* (poetic excurses on love). These additions, other than the core texts, provide no pictures nor author attributions.

The major manuscript of Middle High German poetry is the Codex Manesse ("C," Heidelberg, Universitätsbibliothek, no. cgm. 848), commissioned around 1300 by the Zurich patrons Rüdiger and Johannes Manesse. After their deaths, the project was continued until about 1340. The manuscript contains the amazing total of more than 5,200 songs and thirty-six lays listed under 137 authors' names. In its main stock of 110 authors' corpora, "C" is related to two sources common to "A" and "B" (referred to as "*BC" and "*AC"—the asterisk signals the fact that these collections are postulated, but not extant). It is clear that not only texts were transmitted by "*BC," but also two definitive ordering practices: the hierarchical listing of the collections and the intention of introducing each collection with an author portrait. "*AC" shares the openness of the anthologizing concept with "C," including all known sub-genres of Middle High German poetry. "C" may also have borrowed from other collections, which can be posited using comparisons with other textual evidence. Especially close relationships exist with other illustrated poetic collections (Budapest fragment, Fragment of Nagler and Troß).

The Jena song manuscript ("J") from the Low German (northern Germany) language area around 1330–1350 contains 919 songs, the majority of which are *Sangspruch* songs, two lays and one lay fragment. Unlike the southern German manuscripts, "J" also provides—in ninety-one instances—the melodies. Three characteristics of "J" are shared by other Low German fragments (Walther von der Vogelweide, no. Z; "KLD Mb," Frauenlob, no. Z): the preference for *Sangspruch* and lays, the transmission of the melodies, and an extensive colometric (counting cola, or metric units) system of combining distinctive song portions. These manuscripts and fragments form one of two major centers of song transmission—the other being the southwest German—which vary in time and place. The illustrated southwest German manuscripts of the thirteenth and early fourteenth century present the classical genres of *Minnensang*, but without the melodies. At the other end, within the Low German area, a number of decades later, a center of *Sangspruch* and lay manuscripts emerges with melodies but without illustrations, and with only weak representation of the classical *Minnelied*.

Two special cases within the German language realm are 1) manuscript "D" (Heidelberg, Universitätsbibliothek, no. cpg. 350, South Rhenish dialect, before 1300), concentrating only on one author's works (Reinmar von Zweter, *Sangspruch*), and 2) Ulrich von Liechtenstein's novel "In Service of Women" (*Frauendienst*, Munich, Bayerische Staatsbibliothek, manuscript no. cgm. 44, before 1300, written in the Bavarian dialect), a stylized biography in which Ulrich's songs and lays are integrated into the fictional plot of the novel. Perhaps French novels with songs included served as an inspiration for Ulrich.

Independent song anthologies do not have to be written into books, but can also be arranged on a *Pergament Rotolus* (parchment roll), which are written parallel to the cross page and can be rolled together for transport (see Los Angeles, University of California Research Library, manuscript no. 170/575, and Basle, Universitätsbibliothek, no. N.I.6.50).

In addition to the dominating manuscript form of the independent song codex, there are also other forms of written Middle High German poetry. Among those are: 1. Sporadic later entries of individual songs on originally blank pages or parts of pages in the manuscript (first or last pages, pages left blank, margins), usually with no connection to the other texts in the manuscript; 2. Individual Middle High German strophes integrated into the context of Latin texts to the extent that they were no longer intended to be read as independent texts (e.g., in *Carmina Burana* manuscript); 3. Systematically arranged collections of poems in turn entered as legitimate sections of larger manuscripts containing various genres. This last kind of transmission is more commonly organized by author or corpus, much like the Neidhart corpus (Riedegger Manuscript, Berlin, Staatsbibliothek, no. mgf 1062) or the Walther and Reinmar collection of the Würzburg *Hausbuch* (Munich, Universitätsbibliothek, no. 2° Cod. Ms. 731). Occasionally, the collection principle reveals the attempt to organize by theme or by genre, for example in usually smaller *Minnesang* anthologies or in anonymous *Sangspruch* collections.

BIBLIOGRAPHY

Brunner, Horst, and Burghart Wachinger. *Repertorium der Sangsprüche und Meisterlieder des 12. bis 18. Jahrhunderts,* vol. 1. *Einleitung.* Tübingen: Niemeyer, 1994. Vol. 3–5. *Katalog der Texte. Älterer Teil.* Tübingen: Niemeyer, 1986–1991.

Bumke, Joachim. *Höfische Kultur. Literatur und Gesellschaft im hohen Mittelalter.* 2 vols. Munich: dtv, 1986, pp. 751–783.

Codex Manesse. Die Große Heidelberger Liederhandschrift. Faksimile-Ausgabe des Codex Pal. Germ. 848 der Universitätsbibliothek Heidelberg. Frankfurt am Main: Insel, 1975–1979 [facsimile].

Die Kleine Heidelberger Liederhandschrift. Cod. Pal. Germ. 357 der Universitätsbibliothek Heidelberg, ed. Walter Blank. 2 vols. Wiesbaden: Reichert, 1972 [facsimile].

Die Weingartner Liederhandschrift. 2 vols. Stuttgart: Müller und Schindler, 1969 [facsimile].

Holznagel, Franz-Josef. *Wege in die Schriftlichkeit. Untersuchungen und Materialien zur Überlieferung der mittelhochdeutschen Lyrik.* Tübingen, Basle: Francke, 1995.

Kornrumpf, Gisela. "Heidelberger Liederhandschrift A." In *Die deutsche Literatur des Mittelalters: Verfasserlexikon,* eds. Kurt Ruh, et al. Berlin: de Gruyter, vol. 3, cols. 577–584.

———. "Heidelberger Liederhandschrift C." In *Die deutsche Literatur des Mittelalters: Verfasserlexikon,* eds. Kurt Ruh, et al. Berlin: de Gruyter, vol. 3, cols. 584–597.

Koschorreck, Walter, and Wilfried Werner, eds. *Codex Manesse. Die große Heidelberger Liederhandschrift. Kommentar zum Faksimile.* Kassel: Graphische Anstalt für Kunst und Wissenschaft Ganymed, 1981.

Mittler, Elmar, and Wilfried Werner, eds. *Codex Manesse. Die Große Heidelberger Liederhandschrift. Texte - Bilder - Sachen. Katalog zur Ausstellung vom 12. Juni bis 4. September 1988. Universitätsbibliothek Heidelberg.* 2nd edition. Heidelberg: Braus, 1988.

Mittelhochdeutsche Spruchdichtung. Früher Meistersang. Der Codex Palatinus Germanicus 350 der Universitätsbibliothek Heidelberg, ed. Walter Blank. 3 vols. Wiesbaden: Reichert, 1974 [facsimile].

Tervooren, Helmut, and Ulrich Müller, eds. *Die Jenaer Liederhandschrift. In Abbildung. Mit einem Anhang: Die Basler und Wolfenbütteler Fragment.* Göppingen: Kümmerle, 1972 [facsimile].

Wachinger, Burghart. "Heidelberger Liederhandschrift cpg 350." In *Die deutsche Literatur des Mittelalters: Verfasserlexikon,* eds. Kurt Ruh, et al. Berlin: de Gruyter, vol. 3, cols. 597–606.

———. "Jenaer Liederhandschrift" In *Die deutsche Literatur des Mittelalters: Verfasserlexikon,* eds. Kurt Ruh, et al. Berlin: de Gruyter, vol. 4, cols. 512–516.

Franz-Josef Holznagel

SEE ALSO

Carmina Burana; Heinrich von Morungen; *Liederhandschriften,* Illustrations; *Minnesang;* Neidhart; *Sammelhandschriften; Sangspruch;* Walther von der Vogelweide

Liederhandschriften, Illustrations

The great lyric compilations of the late thirteenth and early fourteenth centuries represent the literarization of a previously oral form of verbal art, which had resisted writing longer than other vernacular genres. Their illustration must be considered in this context.

Two of the major German *Liederhandschriften* (literally "manuscripts of songs") are lavishly illustrated, and a number of fragments suggest that similar works, although not necessarily all of the same size and scope, were not uncommon. The structure in every case involves the arrangement of the poems into author oeuvres,

as already in the unillustrated "Small Heidelberg Manuscript" (*Kleine Heidelberger Liederhandschrift,* Universitätsbibliothek no. cpg 357), from the late thirteenth century, and the illustration of each oeuvre with a picture of the author.

The Codex Manesse or *Große Heidelberger Liederhandschrift* ("C," Heidelberg, Universitätsbibliothek, no. cpg 848) was made in Zurich in the first third of the fourteenth century, probably under the patronage of the Manesse family. The earliest sections were probably written before 1304. The nearly contemporary manuscript of songs from Weingarten (*Weingartner Liederhandschrift,* or "B," Stuttgart, Württembergische Landesbibliothek, no. HB XIII 1) produced in Constance circa 1310–1320, with its twenty-five miniatures, is based on the same concept and shares several of the same image types. Textually, the two are derived from a (no longer extant) common source *BC (the asterix signifies a text assumed to have been extant but now lost); the relationship between the miniatures in the two is not entirely clear, but probably the most widely accepted theory is that they share a common source.

Roughly contemporary with the Codex Manesse and the *Weingartner Handschrift,* and quite possibly earlier than these are the Budapest (Széchényi-Nationalbibliothek, no. Cod. Germ. 92) and Nagler (Krakau, Biblioteka Jagiello ska, no. mgo 125 [formerly Berlin]) fragments, both with poems grouped by author and accompanied by author pictures. The former was made in Bavaria or Austria circa 1300 or somewhat earlier, the latter is Allemanic, circa 1300. The much later Troß fragment (Krakau, Biblioteka Jagiello ska, mgq 519 [formerly Berlin]), made in Württemberg in the first half of the fifteenth century, is apparently a direct copy of C.

The illustration of named oeuvres with author pictures was not the only option for the illustration of lyric manuscripts. The earlier *Carmina Burana* (Munich, Bayerische Staatsbibliothek, no. clm 4660) from South Tyrol [Neustift?], circa 1230, contains miniatures generally related to the contents of poems, a type of illustration also found in the mid fifteenth-century *Hohenfurter Liederbuch* (České Budějovice Krajská; Knihovna, Ms. 1 VB 8b), a collection of religious songs with three drawings illustrating specific verses.

The organization and illumination of the Manesse-type manuscript represents a significant step in the literarization of secular song—the association of worldly lyrics with the names and personae of authors who are endowed by the iconography with something of the authority and stature of classical and Christian authors. No consensus exists on the immediate sources and inspiration of the Manesse-type illumination program. However, the general art historical antecedents of the visual topos "author portrait" lie in classical antiquity and in the illumination of the Psalms, Gospels, and other Christian texts; indeed, the depiction of Kaiser Heinrich at the beginning of the Manessische and Weingartner manuscripts employs the iconography of "David, king and prophet."

Most of the poets, however, do not appear in traditional author poses. Instead, the "portraits" reflect a number of iconographic traditions and represent a great variety of frequently punning or metaphorical responses to aspects of the poets' personae, names, and works. As such, they can generally not be taken as independent evidence of biographical facts. Overall, these authors appear not as churchly or classical authors in the strict sense, but as courtly singers, whose activity is nevertheless endowed with something of the social, representative function of literate authors.

BIBLIOGRAPHY

Frühmorgen-Voss, Hella. "Bildtypen in der Manessischen Liederhandschrift." In Hella Frühmorgen-Voss. *Text und Illustration im Mittelalter: Aufsätze zu den Wechselbeziehungen zwischen Literatur und bildende Kunst,* ed. Norbert H. Ott. München: Beck, 1975, pp. 57–88.

Koschorreck, Walter, and Werner Wilfried, eds. *Codex Manesse: Die große Heidelberger Liederhandschrift: Kommentar zum Faksimile des Codex Palatinus Germanicus 848 der Universitätsbibliothek Heidelberg.* Kassel: Ganymed, 1981 [especially Ewald Vetter, "Die Bilder," pp. 43–100; Wilfred Werner, "Die Handschrift und ihre Geschichte," pp. 13–39].

Spahr, Gebhard. *Weingartner Liederhandschrift: Ihre Geschichte und ihre Miniaturen.* Weißenhorn: Konrad, 1986.

Walther, Ingo F. *Codex Manesse: Die Miniaturen der Großen Heidelberger Liederhandschrift.* Frankfurt: Insel, 1988.

James A. Rushing Jr.

SEE ALSO
Constance; *Liederhandschriften;* Zurich

Life of Mary, Master of (fl. ca. 1460–1490)

An anonymous Cologne painter, active from circa 1460–1490, whose work combined Netherlandish influence, especially from the works of Rogier van der Weyden and Dirk Bouts, with the style of the followers of Stefan Lochner. He received his name from the altar of the Life of Mary, formerly in the church of St. Ursula in Cologne and now divided between the Alte Pinakothek in Munich and the National Gallery in London. One of the most influential artists in Cologne after 1450, his style was characterized by emphasis on elegant single figures with little connection to one another placed in clearly defined compositions. His work is closely related in style to paintings that today have been assigned to the Master of the Lyversberg Passion with whom he was earlier sometimes identified and the Master of the Legend of St. George. Like the former master, his work displays such strong Netherlandish influence that a period of travel in that region has traditionally been assumed. It is also possible that the employment of journeymen in the Cologne workshops who brought model drawings from the Netherlands played a role, since both artists combine Netherlandish motifs with those from local styles. An approximate dating for his works has been established on the basis of stylistic criticism and the biographies of donors where they are known. Additional altar paintings attributed to him include the Passion Triptych in the St. Nikolaus Hospital in Kues and the center panel of the Triptych of Canon Gerhard de Monte in the Wallraf-Richartz-Museum in Cologne.

BIBLIOGRAPHY

Goldberg, Gisela, and Gisela Scheffler. *Altdeutsche Gemälde,* vol 1: *Köln und Nordwestdeutschland.* 2 vols. Gemäldekatalog Bayerische Staatsgemäldesammlung, Alte Pinakothek, München 14. Munich: Bayerische Staatgemäldesammlungen, 1972, vol. 1, pp. 307–333.

Schmidt, Hans M. *Der Meister des Marienlebens und sein Kreis: Studien zur spätgotischen Malerei in Köln.* Beiträge zu den Bau- und Kunstdenkmälern im Rheinland 22. Dissertatin University of Bonn, 1969. Düsseldorf: Schwann, 1978.

Marta O. Renger

SEE ALSO
Cologne, Art; Gothic Art and Architecture, Late; Lochner, Stefan

Limburg an der Lahn

The history of the earlier structures on the rocky outcrop overlooking the Lahn is not clear. A castle mentioned in

Limburg on the Lahn, cathedral, west façade. *Photograph: Joan A. Holladay*

the ninth century had probably been here long before that. A notice in the necrology of St. Kastor at Koblenz credits Archbishop Hetti of Trier (814–817) with dedicating a church in an unspecified location to Saint George, who is the patron of the church at Limburg, but a series of excavations undertaken on the site of the current church since 1935 have found no evidence to support the theory that there was a building at Limburg at this time. In 910, Count Konrad Kurzbold founded a monastery for noblemen; the first building that can be documented dates to this period. Gifts of the emperors Otto I and Conrad II are documented in 940 and circa 1030, respectively; those of Heinrich IV and his wife, Agnes, in 1059 and 1062 are often associated with the documented consecration of an oratorium (oratory) in 1058. It is not possible to determine whether it was a new structure or a remodeling of an existing one.

The present church of St. George (a cathedral since 1827) is important both as one of the last late Ro-

manesque churches in Germany and for the preservation of its interior painting scheme. The consecration of the high altar in 1235 is generally taken to mark the end of the major building work. Although the church was built relatively quickly, this late date means that the church mixes features of the Rhenish Romanesque with those of the French Gothic from the second half of the twelfth century. Typical of the former are the pilaster strips and corbel tables that give the west facade its characteristic look. The multiple towers—those on the west pulled out flush with the facade wall, the use of flying buttresses around the choir, and the four-story interior elevation— the first in Germany—are marks of the influence of French early Gothic buildings such as the cathedrals at Noyon, Laon, and Tournai.

Several layers of eighteenth- and nineteenth-century paint covering the interior wall surfaces were removed in 1934–1935, revealing the medieval painted decoration intact underneath. Geometric patterns highlight the moldings on the arcades of the nave walls, and foliate motifs decorate the wall and vault surfaces. Images of apostles, prophets, kings, and virtues and vices appear above and between the arcades, and archangels and personifications of elements decorate the vaults. Between 1968 and 1972, the paint on the exterior was restored on the basis of remaining fragments; here, solid colors and geometric patterns pick out architectural elements.

The cathedral treasury still preserves some extraordinarily important works, indicating, with the royal and imperial gifts mentioned above, the status of this church in the Middle Ages and later. The Byzantine reliquary for fragments of the True Cross known as the Limburger Staurothek frames an imperial commission from the mid-tenth century in an outer case that is only slightly later. The silver gilt, enamel work, and inset gems mark the quality of this work, which came into the possession of the count of Flanders soon after the sack of Constantinople in 1204, but arrived in Limburg only in the nineteenth century. Equally important is the reliquary of gold foil, enamels, and gems, made to encase the staff of St. Peter, a commission of Archbishop Egbert of Trier dated 988.

BIBLIOGRAPHY

Der Dom zu Limburg, ed. Wolfram Nicol. Quellen und Abhandlungen zur Mittelrheinische Kirchengeschichte 54. Mainz: Selbstverlag der Gesellschaft für Mittelrheinische Kirchengeschichte, 1985.

Luthmer, Ferdinand. *Die Bau- und Kunstdenkmäler des Lahngebiets.* Die Bau- und Kunstdenkmäler des Regierungsbezirks Wiesbaden 3. 1907. Walluf bei Wiesbaden: Dr. Martin Sändig, 1973.

Metternich, Wolfgang. *Der Dom zu Limburg an der Lahn.* Darmstadt: Wissenschaftliche Buchgesellschaft, 1994.

Weyres, Willi. *Der Georgsdom zu Limburg: Festschrift zur Siebenhundertjahrfeier.* Limburg: Steffan, 1935.

Joan A. Holladay

SEE ALSO

Egbert; Gothic Art and Architecture; Romanesque Art and Architecture; Trier

Linz

Founded as the Roman *castellum* (fort) Lentia, Linz's favorable site along the Danube positioned it as a trading center for the wood, salt, and iron of Styria. The medieval fortified settlement was documented in 799 and recognized as a legitimate market town *(legittiums mercatus)* as early as 903–906. The city was held by the archbishops of Passau from 823 to 1190, with its advocates from the family of Haunsberg. Around 1200, direct control of the city and surrounding area was acquired by the dukes of Babenberg, who held it in fief from the archbishop of Passau.

The city bears traces of its medieval layout: a castle on a low hill surrounded by a moat and a triangular marketplace reflecting the Roman plan. Some early houses remain, including the town residences of the nearby monastery of St. Florian. The church of St. Martin is documented in 799, although its foundations are earlier. Its Carolingian portion is a spacious hall decorated with blind arcades and featuring three apsed niches. To the late fifteenth century date the building's Gothic choir, facade, and some frescoes. The royal *Residenz* was expanded under Leopold VI circa 1210 and extended again by Emperor Frederick III, who died there in 1493. Frederick's coat of arms from 1481 appears on the rectangular, two-storied building with towers. An illustration in the *Stadtbuch* (City Book) of Grein circa 1490 depicts the castle connected to the Friedrichstor (Frederick's Gate) by a bridge. In 1497 a bridge was built from Linz across the Danube.

Today the third-largest city in Austria, Linz had its heyday in the baroque period, when much of the city, including earlier churches of the Teutonic Order and the Minorites, was rebuilt. During the medieval period, Linz was

subject to the bishops of Lorch, in the archdiocese of Passau, not becoming itself the set of a diocese until 1785.

BIBLIOGRAPHY

Lechner, Karl. *Die Babenberger: Markgrafen und Herzoge von Österreich 976–1246.* Vienna: Hermann Böhlaus Nachfolger, 1976.

Mayrhofer, Fritz. *Geschicte der Stadt Linz 1: Von den Anfängen zum Barock.* Linz: Wimmer, 1990.

Rittinger, B. "Die karolingische Martinskirche von Linz." *Kunstjahrbuch der Stadt Linz* (1986): 26–37.

Ruhsam, Otto, ed. *Historische Bibliographie der Stadt Linz.* Linzer Forschungen 1. Linz: Archiv der Stadt Linz, 1989.

Schmidt, Justus. *Die Linzer Kirchen.* Österreichische Kunsttopographie 36. Vienna: Schroll, 1964.

Wacha, Georg. *Linz im Bild.* Katalog des Stadtmuseums Linz 49. Linz: Stadtmuseum Linz-Nordico, 1990.

Wagner-Rieger, Renate. "Die Bautätigkeit Kaiser Friedrichs III." *Wiener Jahrbuch für Kunstgeschichte* 25 (1972): 128–153.

Wied, Alexander. *Die profanen Bau- und Kunstdenkmäler der Stadt Linz.* 2 vols. Österreichische Kunsttopographie 42, 50. Vienna; Anton Schroll, 1977, 1986.

Amelia Carr

SEE ALSO

Carolingian Art and Architecture; *Deutschorden;* Franciscan Art and Architecture; Frederick III; Lorch; Passau

Literature and Historiography

Literature and historiography in medieval Germany do not reflect the Aristotelian opposition that history speaks of what has happened while literature addresses what can or ought to happen. They are rather two sides of the same coin: the desire to preserve actions or events in memory. Initially, truth and reliability played no role in the status of the one over the other; this distinction became a value judgment in the twelfth century.

Tacitus's reference in his Latin discussion of the Germanic peoples, *Germania* (chapter 2), to old songs in which the Germanic tribes preserved memories of heroic deeds, is an early indication that Germanic people combined creative expression and a sense of history. The Old English epic *Beowulf* (vv. 867–874) also provides an account of the process to which Tacitus refers; a singer praises the deeds of the victorious hero, creating on the spot an oral record of a current event. The desire to record actions and events, orally and later in writing, highlights personality, time, place, and the importance of chronology. The prevailing sense of order in medieval Germany was the Augustinian linear chronology of a world with a beginning and an end. Recording events and actions in chronological order fell into two main categories: annals and chronicles. Annals, usually anonymous, practical records with limited use and distribution, are nonliterary; chronicles, literary works whose authors were open about their historical objectives, achieved wider distribution and recognition among literate audiences.

The overlap of history as literature and literature as history reflected, at one stage, an interest in human actions within a limited space and in a given time. The functional approach exemplified by annals, or yearly books, marked this earliest stage of historical writing in Germany. The producers were clerics and educated laymen writing in Latin. A second approach, the chronicle, used the Christian perspective of time as a finite entity surrounding a central event, the birth of Jesus Christ, extending into the past as well as into the future. This approach, world history as universal history, reflected a broader historical interest in the world from its point of origin, the Creation, up to the writer's lifetime. Annals relied primarily on memory or observation; chronicles, as universal histories, took their structure and their authority from Holy Scripture, especially Genesis and the Book of Daniel.

The twelfth-century transition from Latin to German in historical writing includes Otto von Freising's (ca. 1111–1158) Latin account of the deeds of Frederic Barbarossa alongside the *Kaiserchronik* (1135), the first German work to treat world history as a history of the deeds of the Roman emperors and their German successors. Historical writing subsequently reflected a variety of subjects: interest in Germanic tribal ancestries; accounts of the deeds of illustrious persons; histories of cities or cloisters; and, for moral and didactic reasons, the lives of saints.

The scope of literature and historiography as related concepts also includes German works based on historical events or personalities but are not reliable as historical sources. These works include, among others, heroic Germanic materials, the foreword to the *Evangelienbuch* of Otfrid von Weissenburg (ca. 800–ca. 871), and the thirteenth-century universal history of Rudolf von Ems (d. ca. 1254).

BIBLIOGRAPHY

Glaser, Horst Albert, ed. *Deutsche Literatur. Eine Sozialgeschichte,* vol. 1: *Aus der Mündlichkeit in die Schriftlichkeit: Höfische und andere Literatur 750–1320,* ed. Ursula Liebertz-Grün. Reinbek bei Hamburg: Rowohlt, 1991.

Gossman, Lionel. *Between History and Literature.* Cambridge, Mass.: Harvard University Press, 1990.

Grundmann, Herbert. "Geschichtsschreibung im Mittelalter." In *Deutsche Philologie im Aufriß,* ed. Wolfgang Stammler. Berlin: Erich Schmidt Verlag, 1957, 2nd revision edition 1962, vol. 3, cols. 2221–2283.

Hay, Denys. *Annalists & Historians. Western Historiography from the Eighth to the Eighteenth Century.* London: Methuen, 1977.

White, Hayden. *Tropics of Discourse. Essays in Cultural Criticism.* Baltimore: Johns Hopkins University Press, 1978; rpt. 1985.

Richard Ernest Walker

SEE ALSO

Frederick I Barbarossa; *Kaiserchronik;* Otfrid; Rudolf von Ems

Literature, Dutch

Old Dutch (also called Middle Dutch) is a collection of dialects antedating circa 1170. The corpus of Old Dutch literature is very small, consisting of six texts, ranging in size from a brief writing sample to a more extensive religious text.

1. The *Wachtendonck Psalms* are an Old Dutch rendering of an Old High German translation of the Psalms, these texts are named after their last known owner, Arnold Wachtendonck of Liège. The translation was made ca. 950 by a monk from the Venlo-Krefeld area working for the nuns of the Münsterbilzen convent. The OHG original as well as the Old Dutch version are now lost. Based on the evidence from the remnants of a transcription (and the accompanying glosses) made by the humanist Justus Lipsius (1547–1606), the text must have contained all the Psalms as well as several hymns.

2. The *Orosius glosses of St. Omer,* both interlinear and marginal glosses in Old Dutch, were added to a manuscript of Orosius's *Historiae Adversum Paganos.* The glosses in this early eleventh-century manuscript, written in the Abbey of St. Bertin in St. Omer, are of a geograph-

ical nature, containing translations of the Latin names for the four cardinal points of the compass and some place-names. A copy of this manuscript was made in the second half of the eleventh century, including the same glosses (with two minor variations).

3. The *Holland-Utrecht names of the months and the four cardinal points of the compass* appear in a manuscript of Einhard's life of Charlemagne *Vita Karoli Magni* written ca. 1050 at Utrecht. The names were adapted from Old High German into Old Dutch. The morphology of these words indicates that the scribe may have come from the county of Holland.

4. *The Leyden,* or *Egmond Willeram.* This paraphrase of the Song of Songs by Williram, abbot of Ebersberg (Bavaria), was written around 1059–1065 in an Old Frankish dialect. In a copy of ca. 1100, made in the Abbey of Egmond (county of Holland), the language of the text was adapted to that of Holland. *Willeram* is a very important document for the study of Old Dutch, as it contains the oldest source for some words as well as for some inflected forms. A few words in *Willeram* would later disappear from the Dutch language. Furthermore, the text proves that the linguistic ties among Holland, West Flanders, and Frisia were still very strong around 1100.

5. *A short West Flemish love poem,* perhaps the best known specimen of Old Dutch, is a writing sample (ca. 1100) from a Dutch monk living and working at Rochester Abbey (Kent) who originated from the southwestern-most corner of the Dutch language area. On the last page of a manuscript of Aelfric's *Catholic Homilies* this monk and his colleagues tried out their quills and ink. The lines *hebban olla vogala nestas hagunnan hinase hic / enda thu wat unbidan we nu* (all the birds have started their nests, except me / and you: what are we waiting for) are accompanied by a Latin translation.

6. The *Münsterbilzen List of names and eulogy* was written in 1130 by a monk from the eastern Betuwe region (Arhem-Nijmegen-Elten) on a blank half-page in a ninth-century evangelarium (at the end of the Gospel of Matthew). It contains a list of participants at a meeting at the Münsterbilzen convent. The monk, probably Arnoldus Battaviensis, ends the list with a remark partly in Old Dutch, partly in Latin: *tesi samanunga vvas edele unde scona.& omnivm virtutum pleniter plena* (this gathering was noble and fair and full of all virtues.)

BIBLIOGRAPHY

Gysseling, Maurits, ed. *Corpus van Middelnederlandse teksten (tot en met het jaar 1300),* vol. 2. Literaire handschriften, part. 1, Fragmenten. The Hague: Nijhoff, 1980. Goossens, Jan. "Oudnederlandse en Vroegmiddelnederlandse letterkunde." *Tijdschrift voor Nederlandse Taal- en Letterkunde* 98 (1982): 241–272.

van Oostrom, Frits P. "Omstreeks 1100: Twee monniken voeren in het Oudnederlands de pen over de liefde." In *Nederlandse literatuur, een geschiedenis,* ed. Schenkeveld-Van der Dussen, Maria A. Groningen: Nijhoff, 1993, pp. 1–6.

Geert H. M. Claassens

SEE ALSO
Glosses, Old High German; Song of Songs

Liturgical Vestments, Manuscripts, and Objects

Medieval liturgical vestments were an important part of the Catholic tradition and were worn during traditional ceremonies. Specific colors dominated the wardrobe including green, red, white, gold, purple, and black. The color chosen to be worn for the day symbolized the church season or celebration. Green was used during ordinary time; red was used for the feast of martyrs and Pentecost as it symbolized blood and fire; white and gold were interchangeable and used for solemnities and joyous occasions including Christmas and Easter; purple represented reflection and was worn during Advent, Lent, and at penitential feasts; black symbolized somber times and was worn at mourning and funeral ceremonies and/or processions.

Vestments represented the positions of priest, deacon, subdeacon, and laity. Priests and deacons wore the amice, alb, cingulum, stole, and the dalmatic, but the priest's attire was more formal. A white linen shawl, the amice was worn under the alb. The alb was the white tunic that had three square inserts sewn on each sleeve at the wrist and one at the base of the dress to symbolize the location of nails in Christ's body at the crucifixion. A linen belt called the cincture was twisted around the waist to shorten the length of the alb. Priests wore a stole with the ends crossed over the breast and the back and tucked into the cincture, and the deacons wore a stole that was not crossed but worn over one shoulder (lower right to the upper left on the back and upper left to lower right on the front). A linen insert called the maniple was worn along the sleeve at the forearm. The rochet (surplice) was a choir shirt. Artists embroidered and painted scenes of the life of Christ and Mary on the priest's tortoise-shell shaped cloak called the chasuble, and a similarly embroidered dalmatic was worn by the deacon. A priest wore an outer hanging stole over the rochet or chasuble to indicate his position. Priests and deacons also wore a formal raincoat called the pluviale, which was usually embellished with New Testament scenes. For ceremonial purposes, a velum was used to cover the hands of the celebrant before lifting the sacred chalice.

Additional marks of rank included the tiara or beehive-shaped headpiece worn by the pope; the bishop's hat, called the mitre, was distinguished by its long pointed shape and the two ribbons hanging at the back on each side. A staff called the crozier was carried by bishops and abbots as a symbol of their rank and referred to Christ's role as the good shepherd. The pallium, a wool cloth strip worn as a yoke around the neck, was given by the pope to archbishops. An adaptation of the pallium was the square-shaped cloth breastplate worn by the bishops and called the rationale.

Following the early Christian tradition, medieval altars contained the tomb or a relic of a dead saint covered with a slab of unbroken stone. A cross was incised in the center to mark the sacred spot for placement of the chalice. Objects used during the mass were situated around this spot: candles, a cross, and one or more manuscripts. During periods of vigilance or formal celebrations the monstrance was the receptacle that displayed the Eucharist.

The priest and concelebrants needed specific liturgical objects for the mass. The chalice held the wine, and the paten was the plate used for distributing the Eucharist. Two gold or silver servers held the water and wine prior to the consecration. During the consecration the Eucharist was placed on the white linen cloth called the corporale. The chalice was covered by a thin square linen-lined board called the pall and a veil with the color of the day. Incensors used in the church had a utilitarian and ecclesiastical function: incense removed miscellaneous odors and the rising smoke symbolized prayers ascending to heaven. New Testament scenes were incised into the metal and decorated with the *niello, repoussé, cloisonné* and/or *champlevé* enamel techniques. Cabochons and Roman cameos contained symbolic meanings and were used to decorate the bases, stems, and rims of chalices. Situated strategically around the stems of a chalice, amethysts were believed to ward off evil spirits and to contain protective forces.

Five liturgical books were essential for the mass. The *Kyriale* contained the hymns of the mass including the *Gloria, Credo, Sanctus, Agnus Dei,* and the Gregorian chants. The *Lectionary* was organized according to the church calendar and included the specific daily readings from the Old and New Testaments and the Epistles. The *Missal* contained the complete rite of the mass for all occasions and daily worship, and the text was read or sung by the celebrant, deacons, and the congregation. An *Evangeliary* contained the selections from the Gospels to be read by the deacon who assisted the priest during Mass. The *Gradual* was the choir book containing antiphons and psalms.

BIBLIOGRAPHY

Braun, Joseph. *Die liturgische Gewandung im Occident und Orient nach Ursprung und Entwicklung, Verwendung und Symbolik.* Freiburg im Breisgau: Herder, 1907.

Lexikon für Theologie und Kirche, eds. Joseph Höfer and Karl Rahner. 10 vols. Freiburg im Breisgau: Herder, 1960.

Ornamenta Ecclesia: Kunst und Künstler der Romanik, ed. Anton Legner. 3 vols. Cologne: Stadt Köln, 1985.

Reliquien: Verehrung und Verklärung, ed. Anton Legner. Cologne: Schnütgen Museum, 1989.

Lesa Mason

SEE ALSO

Liturgy, Music; Manuscripts, Painting and Production; Metalworking; Paleography

Liturgy, Furniture

The altar, where the Eucharist was celebrated, was the most important piece of liturgical furniture in the church. Early German altars were usually composed of three stone slabs, but later examples incorporate columns, such as the altar at Braunschweig cathedral, donated by Henry the Lion, with a marble slab on five bronze columns (1188). Gothic altars sometimes had carved reliefs, which had stylistic and programmatic connections with other interior sculpture, as at Cologne cathedral (ca. 1300). Further elaboration of the altar areas included antependia, or altar frontals, sometimes deluxe works in gold like the Basle antependium, (ca. 1022–1024), presently in the Cluny Museum in Paris. During the Gothic period, altarpieces were frequently placed on or above altars, as in the case of Oberwesel. The consecrated bread, or Host, was stored in a suspended metal dove, symbolizing the Holy Spirit, in the early Middle Ages. In later medieval periods, the Host was kept in a tower-shaped ciborium on the altar, as at Great St. Martin, Cologne, or in an independent cabinet usually decorated with Gothic tracery, called a Sacrament house, such as the example by Adam Kraft in the church of St. Lorenz in Nuremburg (1496–1500).

During the Gothic period, the choir (the part of the church associated with the clergy), was separated from the rest of the church by a choir screen, or *lettner,* a divider frequently decorated with narrative reliefs. A large crucifix with St. John and the Virgin Mary was also frequently placed in the choir or on or above the choir screen. These crucifixes become popular in the Romanesque period and continued in popularity until the Reformation. Carved seats for the choir had misericords, or seat rests for the choir to lean against while singing, which were decorated with secular, sometimes ribald, imagery, as at Cologne cathedral (1308–1311).

The nave of the church, frequently associated with the laity, often contained a reading stand and pulpit so that the lessons and sermons might be delivered. Pulpits, such as that at Wechselburg, were usually attached to one of the nave or crossing columns. Baptismal fonts, in bronze, as the example from Hildesheim Cathedral (ca. 1220–1225), or carved stone, were usually located near the entrances of the church. Because of the symbolic importance of water in the church, sometimes entire wells, as at Regensburg, were enclosed in elaborate gothic structures within the church.

Since light was another element that had symbolic as well as practical importance, candlesticks were placed on the altar and elaborate chandeliers were hung in the nave and choir. In the early Middle Ages the chandeliers were usually wheel-shaped and frequently evoked the heavenly Jerusalem such as that in the cathedral at Hildesheim (mid-eleventh-century), which features twelve small towers and statues of the apostles. Later Gothic chandeliers were sometimes multileveled and decorated with tracery, gables, and figures of angels, as can be seen at Dortmund.

BIBLIOGRAPHY

Lübke, Wilhelm. *Ecclesiastical Art in Germany in the Middle Ages,* trans. L. A. Wheatley. Edinburg: Thomas C. Jack, 1873.

Ornamenta Ecclesiae: Kunst und Künstler der Romanik, ed. Anton Legner. 3 vols. Cologne: Stadt Köln, 1985.

Reinle, Adolf. *Die Ausstattung deutscher Kirchen im Mittelalter: Eine Einführung.* Darmstadt: Wissenschaftliche Buchgeslleschaft, 1988.

Susan L. Ward

SEE ALSO
Basel; Braunschweig; Cologne, Art; Gothic Art and Architecture; Henry the Lion; Hildesheim; Kraft, Adam; Regensburg

Liturgy, Music

The annual cycle of acts of Christian public worship and their constituent elements, in particular the items sung in plainchant (monophonic chant).

In medieval Germany, like other countries of western Europe, the Roman liturgy was celebrated. This involved observance of the yearly cycle of days of greater or lesser importance, and the daily round of services, each consisting of a certain number of prayers, readings and chants. On the one hand were the office hours: vespers and compline in the evening, the night office (also known as nocturns or matins), lauds before daybreak, prime, terce, sext, and none. Each followed a weekly cycle of sung and spoken elements, which would be interrupted by days of special solemnity, such as Christmas, Easter, or saint's days, these having had their own "proper" items. Mass was also celebrated daily, again following a yearly cycle of prayers, readings, and chants.

The sung items of mass and office together constitute the body of plainchant known loosely as "Gregorian chant," for a solo singer, or group of singers in unison. The chants are of particular interest because of their great stylistic range, displaying a variety far greater than that of liturgical prayers and readings. The chief matter of the office hours was the singing of Psalms to a simple recitation formula, all 150 Psalms being sung during the course of the week. Each Psalm or set of Psalms was framed by an antiphon, usually of modest musical scope (antiphons framing the *Magnificat* canticle of vespers and the *Benedictus* canticle of lauds are more demanding). More extended were the responsories sung after each lesson during the night office. Strophic hymns with simple melodies were also sung at each of the hours. The chants of mass are usually divided into two groups: (1) the "ordinary" chants, whose texts do not vary from one day to the next, Kyrie, Gloria, Credo (from the eleventh century), Sanctus, and Agnus Dei; and (2) the "proper" chants, with texts special to each day in turn, the Introit, Gradual,

Alleluia or Tract (in Lent), Sequence (following the Alleluia on principal feast days), Offertory, and Communion. Of these the Gradual, Alleluia, Tract, and Offertory are ornate in style, surpassing any item of the office in musical complexity. The establishment of the Roman liturgy and its extensive repertory of Gregorian chant in Germany proceeded during the eighth and ninth centuries. Anglo-Saxon missionaries of the seventh and eighth centuries—Willibrord in Frisia, Wynfrith/Boniface in central Germany and Bavaria, and several others—would have brought Roman liturgical observances from England (whose tradition went back to Augustine of Canterbury, in the time of Gregory the Great). But it is unlikely that uniform practice encompassing the whole Gregorian chant repertory could have been set in place at once. The more settled conditions in the Frankish kingdom of Pippin III (751–768), and especially Charlemagne (768–814), were a prerequisite for the cultivation of chant. It may be supposed that the great ecclesiastical centers such as Mainz and Salzburg, together with important Benedictine monasteries such as Fulda, played a leading role, but unfortunately we have no actual chant books from these places to document the process in detail. Books with musical notation (the signs commonly known as "neumes") are in any case very rare in the ninth century, but even books with chant texts alone are lacking for the German area. It is typical that the liturgical practice of Metz, whose song school enjoyed great prestige in Carolingian times, can only be reconstructed from the writings of Amalarius (ca. 830) and the lists of chants in the tonary (chants listed by mode rather than by liturgical order) in Metz (Bibliothèque Municipale, no. 351; ca. 850, without musical notation).

During most of the ninth century, oral transmission of the chant melodies seems to have been the rule. At least for Regensburg during the time of Bishop Baturich (817–848), a handful of notated chants have survived, and they may be indicative of similar accomplishments elsewhere in Germany. We learn most about the cultivation of liturgical chant in Germany in the late ninth and tenth centuries from the impressive number of notated chant books from the Benedictine monastery of St. Gall, witness to a highly sophisticated chant practice. St. Gall, Stiftsbibliothek, no. 359 is one of the earliest of all manuscripts notating a year's cycle of liturgical chants (in this case those proper chant chants of mass performed by the most expert solo singers). Equally significant are the St. Gall manuscripts no. 484 and 381 (second quarter of the tenth century), containing, among other things, the se-

quences and tropes that enhanced the solemnity of mass on the greater feast days. Sequences seem originally to have been sung as wordless vocalizations extending the Alleluia at mass, but in the St. Gall manuscripts (and all subsequent German sources), they are texted according to the principle of one syllable per note. Most of the melodies contain frequent repetitions, which when texted result in pairs of verses to the same music. The great majority of the sequence texts sung at St. Gall were composed by the monk Notker Balbulus ("the Stammerer," d. 912). A dedicatory letter (addressed to Liutward, bishop of Vercelli, chancellor of the emperor Charles the Fat) explains how he came to compose the texts and what principles guided his work, which was completed in 884.

In surviving tenth-century manuscripts from Einsiedeln and Reichenau, and from further afield as well, St. Alban's at Mainz, Eichstätt, and Regensburg, Notker's sequence texts form the basis of the repertory. If similarly early sources had survived from other places they might well tell the same tale; later manuscripts certainly do. It is difficult to know if this is the only area where St. Gall was so influential, or whether its cultivation of the basic repertory of Gregorian chant was also taken as a model in other centers.

Fellow monks of Notker also contributed new chants. Ratpert (d. ca. 900) composed a new set of office chants for the feast day of the patron Saint Gallus himself. Tuotilo (d. ca. 913) composed tropes, and both Hartmann and Waltram new versus (strophic hymn-like pieces with intercessionary texts). Tropes of two kinds were sung at St. Gall: supplementary verses intercalated into the singing of the Introit at mass (occasionally the offertory and communion as well), and melodic extensions of phrases of the Introit, many of these subsequently being texted on the principle of one syllable per note. The latter type of trope was specially favored at St. Gall but not much cultivated elsewhere. Other important authors at St. Gall were Notker II (d. 975), composer of the office for St. Otmar, and Notker III ("Labeo," d. 1022) author of a treatise on music theory written in Old High German.

In the preservation of chant books other centers were less fortunate. Only one early manuscript (Bamberg, Staatsbibliothek, lit. 5, compiled ca. 1000) has survived from Reichenau, for example, a collection of tropes and sequences with a tonary. But Berno, abbot of Reichenau (d. 1048), and the Reichenau monk Hermannus Contractus (d. 1052) were both authors of important writings on music theory, an area in which St. Gall seems to have been less active.

The heyday of another important center, the Benedictine monastery of St. Emmeram at Regensburg, came in the second quarter of the eleventh century. The musical life of the monastery was enriched by contacts with not only Reichenau but also the cathedral school of Chartres. Apart from the establishment of trope and sequence repertories, this period saw the creation of new offices for Saint Emmeram (by the monk Arnold, ca. 1030) and Saint Dionysius (ca. 1040—part of a notorious "discovery" of the relics of this saint and his establishment as a second patron, in which the prime mover was the monk Otloh). Hermannus Contractus then composed a new office for the canonization in 1052 of the former Bishop Wolfgang. Pope Leo IX, the former Bishop Bruno of Toul, himself a composer of offices for St. Gregory the Great and other saints, was in Regensburg for this purpose. Among those present would have been the monk Wilhelm, author of a treatise on music theory and later to become abbot of Hirsau in the Black Forest.

Music theory at this time was chiefly concerned on the one hand with parts of the late classical theory transmitted to the Middle Ages by the Latin writers Boethius, Martianus Capella, and Cassiodorus, and on the other hand with providing a conceptual framework for understanding Gregorian chant, not easily reconcilable with the former. Regino, for some years abbot of Prüm, who died in Trier in 915, is one of the most important of tenth-century music theorists. Apart from Berno and Hermannus Contractus of Reichenau, and Wilhelm of St. Emmeram (later Hirsau, d. 1091), already mentioned, the following made valuable contributions: Aribo of Freising, Theoger of Metz (ca. 1050–1120), and Engelbert of Admont (ca. 1250–1331).

The pattern of events observed at St. Gall and Regensburg was no doubt followed at many other centers. The first priority would have been the establishment of the basic Gregorian chant repertory, with a cantor and song school to ensure its preservation, perhaps aided by books with musical notation. If musical resources were sufficient, festal tropes and sequences could be taken into the repertory, perhaps even a new cycle of chants for the feast day of the patron might be composed or commissioned. Hermannus Contractus composed a special office for St. Afra of Augsburg, which, like his Wolfgang office, is remarkably advanced in musical style. (Others by Hermannus are lost.) In the next century, Udalscalc of Maisach (d. 1149 or 1151), abbot of the monastery of St. Ulrich and St. Afra in Augsburg, composed offices for St. Ulrich and for St. Conrad. At least some of the (musically most

unorthodox) compositions of Hildegard of Bingen (1098–1179) are intended for liturgical use. After Notker of St. Gall, the most important German composer of sequences was Gottschalk of Limburg (d. 1098). A great deal of the new plainchant composed from the eleventh century onward (often in a nonclassical or "neo-Gregorian" style) is, however, anonymous.

The number and order of office chants differs slightly between monastic and nonmonastic customs. Some monasteries followed a nonmonastic order of service, for example, the numerous houses of Augustinian canons in Austria, which followed a liturgy patterned on that of the canons of Salzburg Cathedral.

Many German plainchant sources display what is sometimes called the "German chant dialect," where the notes E and B are avoided in favor of F and C, respectively. This is, however, no more than a slight (and inconsistent) coloring of the melodies, a sort of regional accent; neither the number of notes nor the shape of the melodies is affected.

The earliest description of how the performance of chant could be enriched by adding an extra voice or voices (polyphony) was probably written in Germany: the treatise *Musica Enchiriadis,* and its companion, the *Scolica Enchiriadis,* late ninth century, possibly written at Werden. Here the polyphony is to be improvised according to simple rules of thumb. But there is no evidence for more sophisticated types of liturgical polyphony in Germany before the fourteenth century, when French compositions began to have some impact. In this respect, Germany appears to have been more conservative than its western and southern neighbors.

St. Gall manuscript 484 (second quarter of the tenth century) is one of the earliest sources for the special ceremony performed on Easter morning, the dialogue between the angel(s) and the Marys (Virgin Mary and Mary Magdalene) at the tomb of Christ beginning *Quem queritis in sepulchro.* Since the earliest French source is of the same date, it is unlikely that the dialogue was composed in St. Gall. (Its actual origin is still debated.) Some time in the eleventh century, a new version of the scene was made, possibly in Augsburg, beginning *Quis revolvet nobis ab hostio lapidum;* a scene including the disciples Peter and John was also added. Verses from the Easter sequence *Victime paschali laudes* are worked in, and many versions end with the hymn *Christ ist erstanden* (Christ is risen). This ceremony, found in countless sources, remained typical of medieval Germany. The material was rarely extended further. One of the earliest sources of the dramatization of the Magi story and the slaughter of the innocents at Herod's command is from Freising (11th c.) and it is possible that this matter was originally composed for nonecclesiastical edification before being adapted for liturgical use, both in Germany and elsewhere. One of the principal sources for the dramatic ceremonies of Christmas, Epiphany, and Easter, as well as many types of medieval lyric, both liturgical and secular, is the so-called *Carmina Burana* manuscript (Munich, Bayerische Staatsbibliothek, no. Clm 4660), originating probably in South Tyrol in the mid-thirteenth century.

Characteristically, the intermittent musical notation in the *Carmina Burana* manuscript is still staffless neumes. The use of the staff to notate precise musical pitches was somewhat slow to gain ground in Germany, except in monasteries connected by the Hirsau reform, and Cistercian houses, from the twelfth century onward. (The liturgy of Hirsau has to be reconstructed from books of its daughter houses, since none from Hirsau itself have survived.) Aachen and Trier are among the churches with a chant record in staff notation from the thirteenth century onward. On the other hand, it seems that in many places, staff notation was not introduced until the campaigns to codify the chant repertory in large choirbooks in the fifteenth and sixteenth centuries. In contrast to the priceless collection of early medieval manuscripts from St. Gall, almost no St. Gall sources with staff notation survive to provide a key to transcribing the earlier manuscripts and to help chart the development of chant in later centuries. One of the few exceptions is St. Gall 546, made by Joachim Cuontz for the 600th anniversary of Notker in 1512, an attempt to preserve for posterity the sequences and ordinary of mass chants and tropes of monastery's venerable tradition.

BIBLIOGRAPHY

Antiphonaire de l'office monastique transcrit par Hartker: MSS. Saint-Gall 390–391 (980–1011). Paläographie musicale II/1. Solesmes: Abbaye Saint-Pierre, 1900 [from St. Gall].

Antiphonale Pataviense (Wien 1519), ed. Karlheinz Schlager. Das Erbe deutscher Musik 88. Kassel: Bärenreiter, 1985 [from Passau].

Antiphonar von St. Peter [*Wien, Nationalbibliothek, series nova 2700*]. Codices selecti 21. Graz: Akademische Druck- und Verlagsanstalt, 1969–1973, 1974 [from Salzburg].

Cantatorium, IXe siècle: No. 359 de la Bibliothèque de Saint-Gall. Paläographie musicale II/2. Solesmes: Abbaye Saint-Pierre, 1924 [from St. Gall].

Le Codex 121 de la Biblioth que d'Einsiedeln (IX-XI siècle): Antiphonale missarum sancti Gregorii. Paläographie musicale I/4. Solesmes: Abbaye Saint-Pierre, 1894; repr. Bern: Lang, 1974 [from Einsiedeln].

Codex 121 Einsiedeln. Graduale und Sequenzen Notkers von St. Gallen. Weinheim, 1991 [from Einsiedeln].

Le Codex 339 de la Bibliothèque de Saint-Gall (Xe siècle): Antiphonale missarum sancti Gregorii. Paläographie musicale I/1. Solesmes: Abbaye Saint-Pierre, 1889 [from St. Gall].

Crocker, Richard L. *The Early Medieval Sequence.* Berkeley, Calif.: California University Press, 1977.

Drinkwelder, Otto. *Ein deutsches Sequentiar aus dem Ende des 12. Jahrhunderts.* Veröffentlichungen der Gregorianischen Akademie zu Freiburg in der Schweiz 8. Graz, Vienna, 1914 [Manuscript Berlin, Staatsbibliothek Preußischer Kulturbesitz, no. Mus. 40048].

Echternacher Sakramentar und Antiphonar. Codices Selecti 74. Graz: Adademische Druck- und Verlagsanstalt, 1982 [from Echternach]

Graduale Pataviense (Wien 1511): Faksimile, ed. Christian Väterlein. Das Erbe deutscher Musik 87. Kassel: Bärenreiter, 1982 [from Passau].

Die Handschrift Bamberg Staatsbibliothek Lit. 6. Monumenta Palaeographica Gregoriana 2 Münsterschwarzach, [1986] [from Regensburg]

Hankeln, Roman. *Historiae Sancti Dionysii Areopagitae. St. Emmeram, Regensburg, ca. 1050 / 16. Jh.* Musicological Studies 65/3. Ottawa: Institute of Mediaeval Music, 1998.

Haug, Andreas. *Troparia tardiva. Repertorium später Tropenquellen aus dem deutschsprachigen Raum.* Monumenta Monodica Medii Aevi, Subsidia 1. Kassel: Bärenreiter, 1995.

Hiley, David. *Historia Sancti Emmerammi Arnoldi Vohburgensis circa 1030.* Musicological Studies LXV/2. Ottawa: Institute of Mediaeval Music, 1996.

Kohlhase, Thomas, and Günther Michael Paucker. "Bibliographie Gregorianischer Choral." *Beiträge zur Gregorianik* 9–10 (1990) [entire volume].

———. "Bibliographie Addenda I", *Beiträge zur Gregorianik* 15–16 (1993) [entire volume].

Labhardt, Frank. *Das Sequentiar Cod. 546 der Stiftsbibliothek von St. Gallen und seine Quellen.* Publikationen der Schweizerischen Musikforschenden Gesellschaft, Serial. 2/8. 2 vols. Bern: Haupt, 1959–1963.

Lipphardt, Walter. *Der karolingische Tonar von Metz.* Liturgiewissenschaftliche Quellen und Forschungen 43. Münster: Aschendorff, 1965.

Le Manuscrit 807, Universitätsbibliothek Graz (XIIe siècle):
Graduel de Klosterneuburg. Paläographie musicale I/19.
Berne 1974 [from Klosterneuburg].

Marxer, Otto. *Zur spätmittelalterlichen Choralgeschichte*
St. Gallens: Der Codex 546 der St. Galler Stiftsbiblio-
thek. Veröffentlichungen der Gregorianischen Akademie zu Freiburg in der Schweiz 3. St. Gall, 1908.

Missale Basileense Saec. XI, eds. Anton Hänggi and Pascal
Ladner. 2 vols. Spicilegium Friburgense 35A–35B.
Freiburg: Herder, 1994.

Missale plenarium, Bibl. Capit. Gnesnensis, ms. 149, eds.
Krzysztof Bieganski and Jerzy Woronczak. Antiqui-
tates musicae in Polonia 11–12. 2 vols. Warsaw and
Graz: Akademische Druck- und Verlagsanstalt, 1970-
1972 [from Niederaltaich]

Moosburger Graduale. München, Universitätsbibliothek,
Cod. ms. 156. Faksimile, ed. David Hiley. Tutzing:
Hans Schneider, 1996 [from Moosburg].

Müller, Hartmut. *Das Quedlinburger Antiphonar.* Berlin,
Staatsbibliothek Preußischer Kulturbesitz Mus. ms.
40047). Mainzer Studien zur Musikwissenschaft
25/1–3. Tutzing: Hans Schneider, 1990 [from Qued-
linburg].

Die Musik in Geschichte und Gegenwart. ed. Ludwig Fin-
scher, vol. 8. Kassel: Bärenreiter and Stuttgart: Metzler, 1998 [therein. Müller, Hartmut. "Reichenau";
Hankeln, Roman. "Sankt Emmeram"; Haug, Andreas.
"Sankt Gallen"].

Norton, Michael Lee. "Of "Stages" and "Types" in Visi-
tatione Sepulchri." *Comparative Drama* 21 (1987):
34–61, 127–144.

Le Prosaire d'Aix-la-Chapelle. Monumenta Musicae Sacrae 3. ed. Rene Jean Hesbert. Rouen: Rouen, 1960
[from Aachen].

Rankin, Susan K. "The song school of St. Gall in the later
ninth century." In *Sangallensia in Washington: The Arts*
and Letters in Medieval and Baroque St. Gall Viewed
from the Twentieth Century, ed. James C. King. New
York: Lang, 1993, pp. 173–198.

Sigl, Maximilian. *Zur Geschichte des Ordinarium Missae in*
der deutschen Choralüberlieferung. Regensburg, 1911.

Stäblein, Bruno. "Deutschland. B. Mittelalter." In *Die*
Musik in Geschichte und Gegenwart. Allgemeine Enzyk-
lopädie der Musik, ed. Friedrich Blume. Kassel: Bärenreiter, 1949–1979, vol. 3.

Stiftsbibliothek Sankt Gallen. Codices 484 & 381. 3 vols. eds.
Wulf Arlt and Susan Rankin. Winterthur: Amadeus,
1996 [facsimile of two manuscripts from St. Gall].

David Hiley

SEE ALSO
Berno von Reichenau; *Carmina Burana;* Fulda;
Hildegard von Bingen; Leo IX; Mainz; Regensburg;
Reichenau; Sankt Gall; Song of Songs

Liudolfinger

Saxon noble house named, according to modern conventions, after its earliest known representative, Duke
Liudolf (d. 866). Later representatives of the family ascended the throne of the east Frankish/German realm
and are commonly referred to as the Ottonian dynasty.
Only the pre-royal line (i.e., up to 919) will be considered here.

The early history of the Liudolfinger remains highly
speculative. That their origins lay in Thuringia is suggested by their substantial land holdings in this area. A
foothold in Saxony, in the region of the river Leine, may
have been their reward for supporting the Franks during
Charlemagne's wars of conquest. By the middle of the
ninth century, they were firmly rooted in the aristocracy
of eastern Saxony *(Ostfalia)* and had established a close
and mutually beneficial relationship with the Carolingian
ruling house to the west. Although the precise significance of Liudolf's title (i.e., duke) is subject to debate,
one can probably assume that he exercised some combination of political and military leadership, at least in Ostfalia. Duke Liudolf's wife, Oda (d. 913), was of Frankish
origin and reportedly lived to the age of 107.

An important moment in the history of Liudolfinger
occurred with the foundation of the house of canonesses
at Gandersheim (ca. 850). This was very much a family
affair. Liudolf assembled an endowment for the community and, with his wife, traveled to Rome to obtain relics
for its church. In 852, Bishop Altfried of Hildesheim
(851–874), a distant relative, consecrated and installed
the couple's twelve-year-old daughter, Hathumoda, as
abbess. He also contributed to the community's endowment. In 877, King Louis the Younger, husband of yet
another of Liudolf's daughters (Liutgard), granted the
community the basic privileges of royal status: immunity,
protection, and (with qualifications) the right to elect
their own abbess. Gandersheim provided the Liudolfinger with a focal point for their piety, a place to bury
their dead and, given contemporary legal practice, there
was no reason to doubt that the community's landed
wealth would continue under Liudolfing control. Hathumoda's sisters, Gerberga (874–896/897) and Christina
(896/897–919), succeeded her in the office of abbess.

Oda, Liudolf's wife, entered Gandersheim as a canoness after her husband's death (866) and appears to have exercised considerable influence over the community. In fact, in the period 877–1043, the convent was ruled by only two abbesses who did not descend from Liudolf's lineage. It is not surprising, then, that the historical tradition at Gandersheim emphasized the close bonds between the community and Liudolf's lineage (i.e., Agius of Corvey, Hrotsvitha of Gandersheim).

Liudolf and Oda's offspring also included two sons, Brun and Otto. On Liudolf's death, Brun (d. 880) assumed his father's position as duke. When Brun himself died, during a military campaign against the Danes, this position passed to his younger brother, Otto (d. 912). Although Brun's descendants no longer possessed the title of duke, it has been argued that they continued to play a role in the politics of the realm and that one of them, Count Bruno of Braunschweig, may have made a bid for the throne in 1002. Under the leadership of Duke Otto, known as "the Illustrious," the Liudolfinger strengthened their position within the Saxon aristocracy, expanded their landholdings within their traditional stronghold of Thuringia, and extended their influence to the western regions of the duchy (i.e., Westphalia). Indeed, Otto's stature was such that he may have been considered a viable candidate for the throne in 911. Otto's wife, Hadwig (or Hathui, d. 903), belonged to the Babenberger, a powerful clan with substantial landholdings in the regions of Franconia and Thuringia. As the Liudolfinger were already a powerful presence in the latter region, an alliance with that clan can only have worked to their benefit. Of Otto's two eldest sons, Thankmar and Liudolf, we know almost nothing beyond their names, but for Henry, the third son and future king, a particularly beneficial marriage was arranged with Hatheburg, daughter of Erwin of Merseburg (d. before 909). Erwin may have been a count, though this is disputed, but certainly possessed substantial landholdings in and around Merseburg. Moreover, as he had no sons, Hatheburg stood to inherit a substantial portion of this wealth, a prospect scarcely diminished by the fact that she was a widow and had taken veil. The marriage produced a son, Thankmar (d. 938), who would later figure among the bitterest enemies of King Otto I (936–973).

In tandem with the Babenberger, the Liudolfinger took a leading role in the defense of the the eastern frontier, enhancing their own stature in the process and, by the 890s and 900s, were reducing Slavic tribes, such as the Daleminzi, to tributary status. Ties to the royal house were strengthened when, in 897, Duke Otto's daughter, Oda, married Zwentibold, son of Emperor Arnulf of Carinthia. In the early years of the tenth century, a threat to the security of the Liudolfinger emerged with the outbreak of feud between the Babenberg and Conradian clans. Although Duke Otto seems to have remained aloof from the fighting, his surrender of the lay abbacy of Hersfeld to Archbishop Hatto of Mainz (891–913), in 908, may have been the price he paid for associating with the losing side. Further conflict would ensue, somewhat later, when a member of the Conradian house was elected king (i.e., Conrad I, r. 911–919). In 909, Henry repudiated his first wife, Hatheburg, and married Mathilda (d. 968), a member of the Immeding clan and descendent of Widukind, the ninth-century Saxon duke who had led indigenous opposition to Charlemagne's conquest. That he managed to do this without surrendering Hatheburg's inheritance or initiating a feud with her clan is testimony to his political acumen and suggests that some sort of compensation was negotiated. As with Henry's earlier marriage, the alliance with Mathilda brought certain advantages. In particular, it represented an expansion of the family's sphere of influence in the area of Westphalia where his new bride possessed an ample inheritance near Herford and Enger.

Duke Otto the Illustrious died in 912. Since Henry's two older brothers had predeceased their father, he now assumed both the title of duke and a position of leadership within the Liudolfing house. Almost immediately, hostilities broke out between Duke Henry and King Conrad I, who had tried to hinder his succession. Henry seized the Saxon and Thuringian possessions of the archbishopric of Mainz whose prelate (i.e., Hatto I) strongly supported both the king and the Conradian clan. He also expanded his influence in the region of the river Weser, threatening Conradian strongholds. In 915, a deteriorating political situation forced King Conrad to recognize the new status quo in Saxony and accord Henry virtual independence within his duchy. With Henry's election as king in 919, the history of the Liudolfinger entered a new phase. Up to this point, they had been one among many powerful aristocratic houses, albeit a remarkably successful one. Henceforth, they would rank among the preeminent royal lineages of western Europe.

BIBLIOGRAPHY

Beumann, Helmut. *Die Ottonen.* 2nd edition. Kohlhammer: Stuttgart; 1991, pp. 22–31.

Wolf, A. "*Quasi herditatem inter filios.* Zur Kontroverse über das Königswahlrecht im Jahre 1002 und die Genealogie der Konradiner." *Zeitschrift der Savigny Stiftung für Rechtsgeschichte. Germanistische Abteilung* 112 (1995) 64–157.

David A. Warner

SEE ALSO
Carolingians; Charlemagne; Conrad I; Gandersheim; Henry I; Hrosvit of Gandersheim; Otto I

Lives
See Saints' Lives.

Lochner, Stefan (1400/1410–1451)

The most important painter of the early Cologne school of painting, Lochner is the only artist whose name can be associated with individual works. However, the entire attribution of his body of works is based on Albrecht Dürer's 1530 diary entry, in which he mentions the altarpiece in Cologne he saw painted by a "Master Stefan." The work in question is presumed to be the altarpiece representing the patron saints of the city in attendance at the Adoration of the Magi (now in Cologne cathedral), the most significant altarpiece produced in Cologne. All other works associated with Lochner are attributed through stylistic affinity to this piece. As a result of the meager documentation, some scholarship has cast doubt on the identity of the creator of these works. The historical Stefan Lochner, the only Stefan in the Cologne guilds, was active ca. 1435–1451, and is presumed to have been born between 1400 and 1410 in Meersburg, on Lake Constance. Little is known of his life, but he was first documented as a master in Cologne in June, 1442, and died, probably of the plague, in September, 1451. His life was probably short, as he died within a year of his parents. Two works are dated: the 1445 Presentation in the Temple (Lisbon, Gulbenkian Collection), and the 1447 work of the same subject (Darmstadt, Hessisches Landesmuseum).

Lochner's work often shows traces of Flemish realism, causing some to question the nature of his training. His paintings show little stylistic relationship to works from Lochner's homeland near Constance. Also, Lochner introduced numerous innovations to the essentially conservative Cologne school of painting. Lochner's figures inhabited landscapes and architectural settings full of specific details that clearly reflect a familiarity with Flemish works. His work shows figures that have somewhat

Stefan Lochner, Madonna in the Rose Arbor (Cologne, Wallraf-Richartz Museum). *Photograph: Rheinisches Bildarchiv der Stadt Köln*

more volume than previously seen, and these figures exist in space far more effectively than those of his Cologne predecessors.

Several of his works, such as the Nativity (Munich, Alte Pinakothek), the Gulbenkian Presentation in the Temple, and the St. Jerome in his Cell (Raleigh, North Carolina Museum of Art), all bear numerous similarities to the works of Robert Campin and his followers, particularly in the representation of interior spaces. Lochner's largest extant work, and the best known, is the previously noted City Patrons' Altarpiece or *Dombild*. This work seems to reflect both the knowledge of the Ghent Altarpiece, particularly on the exterior Annunciation, and Lochner's characteristic sweetness, grace, and delicacy. The figures in this altarpiece are the first life-size figures painted in Cologne.

Nevertheless, Lochner's paintings maintained links to the past and are noted for a tension between their fully modeled forms and linear patterns. He also often used gold backgrounds and, like earlier Cologne painters, outlined figures in red. Lochner's paintings are also characterized by a distinctly personal quality of calm and sweetness, creating a sense of quiet mysticism. These qualities are created through idealization of features, particularly those of women, and rich, glowing colors, often created with oil glazes. All these qualities are perhaps best seen in his Madonna of the Rosebower (Cologne, Wallraf-Richartz-Museum).

BIBLIOGRAPHY

Corley, Brigitte. "A Plausible Provenance for Stefan Lochner?" *Zeitschrift für Kunstgeschichte* 59 (1996): 78–96.

Förstesr, Otto H. *Stefan Lochner: Ein Maler zu Köln.* Frankfurt am Main: Prestel, 1938.

Goldberg, Gisela, and Gisela Scheffler. *Altdeutsche Gemälde, Köln und Nordwestdeutschland. Alte Pinakotek, München.* 2 vols. Bayerische Staatsgemäldesammlung Gemäldekataloge 14. Munich: Bayerische Staatsgemäldesammlung, 1972, vol. 1, pp. 190–210.

Stefan Lochner, Meister zu Köln: Herkunft, Werke, Wirkung, ed. Frank Günter Zehnder. Cologne: Wallraf-Richartz-Museum, 1993.

Zehnder, Frank Günter. *Katalog der Altkölner Malerei.* Kataloge des Wallraf-Richartz-Museums 11. Cologne: Stadt Köln, 1990, pp. 212–244.

Daniel M. Levine

SEE ALSO

Cologne, Art; Constance; Meersburg

Lorch

In the Rems valley, west of Schwäbisch Gmünd (Baden-Württemberg), the nucleus of the city of Lorch is located on the site of a Roman garrison. Established as a defensive position on the defensive frontier of the Roman Empire, the post was abandoned in the late third century. In the early eleventh century, Lorch came under the control of the Hohenstaufen, who built an early castle there.

Before 1102, Frederick of Swabia founded the Benedictine monastery of St. Peter. Northeast over the old city, on the *Liebfrauenberg* (Mountain of the Virgin), the abbey was originally intended for private worship by Frederick and his family. The original monastery complex was completed by 1108. As of 1140, the abbey church became the royal burial site of the Hohenstaufen.

Seriously damaged in the *Bauernkriege* (Peasants' War) of 1525, surviving medieval structures include a gate house, the prelature, a steward's house *(Vogtei)*, the tithe barn (for storing an agricultural reserve to be paid to the papacy), a dormitory, the cloister, and the abbey church.

The three-aisled Romanesque basilica, recognized as an example of the school of Hirsau, was given a Gothic choir in 1469. The nave, with its timbered ceiling, is separated from the transept by a triumphal arch. The founder's tomb at the center of the nave is sculpted with figural and heraldic ornaments. Although it is not known for certain precisely how many members of the house of Hohenstaufen are interred here, it is clear that no crowned male ruler's remains are among them. Queen Irene, daughter of the Byzantine emperor and widow of King Philip, was laid to rest at Lorch, as was her young daughter, Beatrice. In the north transept (the chapel of St. Mauritius) are the tombs of the lords of Woellwarth, dating to the fifteenth and sixteenth centuries. On the eight piers of the nave, paintings depicting Hohenstaufen kings and emperors have been uncovered. These are shown wearing dress of approximately 1500. Of interest in the cloister are the fifteenth-century net vaults in the north wing.

The monastery accumulated a large collection of religious relics in the Middle Ages, as a result of the patrons' participation in the crusades. After the death of Conradin in 1268, ending the Hohenstaufen line, Lorch passed into the possession of the duchy of Württemberg.

BIBLIOGRAPHY

Lorch: Beiträge zur Geschichte von Stadt und Kloster. 2 vols. Lorch: Stadt Lorch, 1990.

Leslie Anne Hamel

SEE ALSO

Clothing, Costume, and Fashion; Conradin of Hohenstaufen; Crusades; Gothic Art and Architecture; Hirsau; Romanesque Art and Architecture; Schwäbisch Gmünd; Staufen

Lorraine

In 843, by the terms of the Treaty of Verdun, the region between the Scheldt, Meuse, and Rhine rivers fell to Lothar I as part of the middle of the three Frankish kingdoms. Lothar divided his kingdom among his three sons shortly before his death: Italy went to Louis II, already crowned king of Italy in 844 and (co-)emperor in 850; Provence, the central section of the middle kingdom, went to the youngest son, Charles; and the rich fiscal lands in the northern third went to Lothar II, after whom Lorraine *(Lotharii regnum* "Lothar's Reign," German *Lothringen,* English Lotharingia) is named. The instability of the region made it a particularly appealing target of aggression by its neighbors to the east and west, and the final chapters of this struggle did not play themselves out until the early twentieth century.

Lorraine passed under German rule from about 888 until 911 when it went over to France for a few years. Henry I reconquered it in 925, but remained concerned about it since the duke, Giselbert, was attempting to create an independent principality. Henry I confirmed Giselbert, who was elected duke by the Lotharingians; he also gave Giselbert his daughter, Gerberga, as wife. In league with the duke of Franconia, Eberhard, Giselbert rebelled against his brother-in-law, Otto I, and was killed in 939 near Andernach in the current of the Rhine. When Giselbert's minor son Henry died in 944, Otto elevated the count of the Wormsgau (district of Worms), Conrad the Red, to be duke of Lorraine. But Conrad also rebelled, and following his deposition in 954, the lordship in Lorraine was conferred upon Otto's brother, Archbishop Bruno of Cologne.

After five years of such administration, the region of Lorraine was divided into two independent duchies: Upper and Lower Lorraine. Upper Lorraine originally comprised the bishoprics of Metz, Toul, Verdun, and Trier, that is, the land from the sources of the Meuse and Moselle as far as the borders of the Eifel and the Ardennes, and over to the Rhine to include the Vosges and the Hunsrück. From 959 until 1027, Frederick I of Bar, his son, Dietrich, and his grandson, Frederick II, held the ducal office. On the extinction of their line, King Conrad II granted Upper Lorraine to Gozelo I, duke of Lower Lorraine, temporarily reuniting the two Lorraines. Gozelo's son, Gottfried the Bearded (d. 1070), married Beatrice, daughter of Duke Frederick II of Upper Lorraine and widow of Margrave Boniface of Tuscany (d. 1052). She thus united the patrimony of her father with that of her first husband in Tuscany, creating a powerful dynastic base in Germany and Italy. Her daughter by the first marriage was the famous Mathilda of Tuscany, countess of Canossa, who in turn married the son of Beatrice's second husband by his first wife, Gottfried the Hunchback, duke of Lower Lorraine. Yet Gottfried neither enjoyed the peaceful possession of both duchies, nor did he produce heirs with Mathilda. The Ardennes house in Lorraine died out with him in 1076.

Alongside the older dukes of Lorraine there was from the beginning of the eleventh century another family that grew powerful in Upper Lorraine—that of the Etichoner, or the dukes of Lorraine from the house of Alsace. Adalbert, the son of Eberhard of Egisheim, count in Alsace, appears in 1037 as *dux et marchio Lothoringiae* (duke and

margrave of Lothringia, d. 1038). His son Gerhard appears only as margrave (d. 1050), but the latter's two sons were styled duke: Adalbert (d. 1048) was named duke of Lorraine in 1046 by Emperor Henry III; and Gerhard (d. 1070), originally the count of Bitsch, became his brother's successor in 1048. The Alsatian house engaged in a major struggle against the Ardennes house for control of Upper Lorraine.

Gerhard's son Thierry (d. 1116), who appears, like Adalbert, as *Lothringie dux et marchio* and in 1078 as *dux Metensis* (duke of Metz), was the direct ancestor of all the later dukes of Lorraine and of the imperial house of Austria. He was followed by his son, Simon I, who was married to King Lothar's sister, Adelheid, and who engaged in a protracted conflict with Archbishop Adelbero of Trier. Matthew, who succeeded as duke of Lorraine in 1138, was the husband of Bertha or Judith, daughter of Duke Frederick of Swabia. Simon II, duke until 1205, died as a monk in 1207. His brother, Frederick I, count of Bitsch in 1196, became duke in 1205, but died the following year. His son Frederick died in 1213, and his grandson Theobald died in 1220.

Lower Lorraine (or *Lotrick* in Flemish) comprised in earliest times the bishoprics of Cambrai, Cologne, Liège, Tournai, and Utrecht, so that in addition to the northern end of the Middle Rhine region, Ripuaria (around Cologne) also belonged to it. The short existence of the duchy and the bitter contest for it resulted in the name being applied only to the Belgian lands beyond the Maas. Already in 977 we see two competing dukes: Gottfried (Godfrey) I, count of Verdun and Eenham, reputedly a brother's son of the contemporary duke of Upper Lorraine, Frederick, from the house of Ardennes, who died after 984, and a French Carolingian, Charles (d. 991), son of Louis IV *d'outremer* (from across the sea), successor of his father since 987 and enthroned by Hugh Capet in 990.

Gottfried I's son, Gottfried II (d. ca. 1023), continued the struggle with success (he was reputedly enfeoffed with Lower Lorraine in 1012 by King Henry II). His opponent was Charles of France's son, Otto, who died in 1005 as the last Carolingian, and his brothers-in-law, Count Lambert of Louvain and Count Reginher of Hainault. Gottfried's brother and successor, Gozelo (d. April 19, 1044), acquired Upper Lorraine in 1033 as well through enfeoffment by King Conrad II. Henry III revived Ottonian policy of dividing Lotharingia, however: on the death of Duke Gozelo in 1044, the duchy was divided between his two sons. The geographical position of Lorraine between France and Germany made it difficult for any German king to secure lasting success with any policy: within a few months of the division, the eldest brother, Gottfried III, entered into league with the French king and rose in rebellion.

Even during his father's lifetime, Gottfried the Bearded had played a role in the governance of the two duchies and had received Upper Lorraine; he expected to receive both. Gozelo's death in 1044 provided Henry III with the opportunity to grant Lower Lorraine to the second son of Gozelo II, who had the reputation as a coward or an incompetent. For Gottfried this meant a reduction of his power, an arbitrary act of the king, a lack of appreciation for the unique position of Lorraine in the structure of the empire. Due to the early development of powerful comital (ducal) families in this region, a ducal authority could only exist if it had an extraordinary power base. Gottfried saw his rights and responsibilities unappreciated; he therefore went on the offensive. The king, on the other hand, saw the dukedom as an office that he could give to any member of a wide circle of relatives. The rebellion was suppressed in 1044–1045, and again in 1047–1049; Gottfried was excommunicated in 1049, and although he was reconciled with the king the same year, he lost the duchy.

The long-term effects of the reduction in the power of the dukes in Lorraine were negative: the nobles of the area had less control in their own drive for territorial lordship, and this led to a fragmentation of the western region of the empire. One of the major benefactors was Count Baldwin V of Flanders, who occupied lands on the eastern border of his county; he had them confirmed by Henry IV in early December, 1056, at Cologne; he also got the county of Hainault (Hennegau) through marriage. The king of France also had designs on Lorraine. The ducal title of Lower Lorraine evolved into the title of duke of Brabant after 1169; the descendants of the former dukes styled themselves dukes of Limburg.

Lorraine was a major source of the reforming impulse that transformed Latin Christendom from the second third of the eleventh century: Pope Leo IX was the former Bishop Bruno of Toul, and Humbert, cardinal bishop of Candida, was a Lorrainer who had come to Rome with him. Humbert looked to dukes Gottfried and Frederick of Lorraine to anchor the reform efforts when Emperor Henry III died unexpectedly in 1056: Frederick had been created abbot of Monte Cassino in 1056/1057 by Humbert, and he was also raised to the status of cardinal; he became pope as Stephen IX in 1057. The massive mili-

tary support provided by Duke Gottfried in 1059 ensured the accession of Nicholas II, who issued the papal election decree at the Lateran Council.

BIBLIOGRAPHY

Barth, Rüdiger E. *Der Herzog in Lotharingien im 10. Jahrhundert.* Sigmaringen: Thorbecke, 1990.

Boshof, Egon. "Lothringen, Frankreich und das Reich in der Regierungszeit Heinrichs III." *Rheinische Vierteljahrsblätter* 42 (1978): 63–127.

Hermann, Hans-Walter. "Die Stellung Oberlothingens in der Auseinandersetzung zwischen Kaisen und Papsttum." *Saarbrücker Hefte* 3 (1956): 49–69.

Hlawitschka, Eduard. *Vom Frankenreich zur Formierung der europäischen Staaten-und Völkergemeinschaft 840–1046.* Darmstadt: Wissenschaftliche Buchgesellschaft, 1986.

Paul B. Pixton

SEE ALSO
Brabant, Duchy of; Carolingians; Cologne, Archdiocese; Conrad II; Henry I; Henry II, Art; Henry III; Henry IV; Leo IX; Lothar I; Otto I

Lorsch

From its beginning, the foundation at Lorsch (Hesse) had strong ties with the Carolingian house; when Count Chancor founded the monastery in 764, he immediately placed it under the authority of his relative, Bishop Chrodegang of Metz, powerful ecclesiastical advisor to Pippin III. Its identity quickly shifted from a family monastery to a designated imperial institution, receiving royal immunities in 772. Throughout the ninth century, its abbots maintained close ties with Charlemagne, Louis the Pious, and successive East Frankish Carolingian rulers.

Building at the monastery began early and progressed with speed. At its center was a basilica dedicated to Saint Nazarius, begun in 767 and completed within a short seven years. The church comprised three naves, a transept, a rectangular choir, and a *Westwerk* (western entrance structure) that housed a chapel dedicated to St. Michael. The church served as the culminating monument at the eastern end of a 200-meter-long approach—an imposing sequence of courtyards, punctuated by triumphal arches and fortress-like walls. Visitors first entered into a large atrium, where they encountered the freestanding *Torhalle* (Gate Hall). Beyond that arched gateway, at the eastern end of the atrium, stood a two-storied block of masonry, the *castellum*. A smaller atrium followed. Referred to as "Paradise" on account of its opulent decoration, this small courtyard gave access to St. Nazarius's impressive facade. The walled monastic complex also included a cloister to the south of the church, the abbot's quarters, a cemetery, and a small chapel dedicated to Saint Udalrich. In 876, a crypt was added to the east end of the basilica that served as a mausoleum for Louis the German and other members of the Carolingian royal family of Germany.

A rare and spectacular example of Carolingian architecture, the still-standing *Torhalle* likely served as a reception room for visiting royalty. The date of construction is disputed, but it was probably built between 784 and 791. Its lower level, with its three arches, engaged columns, and composite capitals, looks to the Roman triumphal arch for inspiration. The second level is articulated with zigzag molding and pilasters. The exterior of the whole is decorated with an inlay of cream and terra-cotta stone in a variegated pattern of squares, lozenges, and hexagons, an imitation of and variation on the Roman technique of *opus reticulatum* (a netlike creation).

As a royal monastery, Lorsch remained the recipient of great wealth well throughout the ninth century. There exist no fewer than four catalogues of the Lorsch library from this period, attesting to the monastery's place as a center of learning, book collecting, and book production. One of the catalogues lists an *evangelium scriptum cum auro pictum habens tabulas eburneas* (an illuminated evangeliary written with gold having ivory covers), presumably a reference to the still extant Lorsch gospels from circa 810. The manuscript, now divided between Bucharest and the Vatican, is considered one of the central members of the so-called Ada group of manuscripts associated with Charlemagne's court. The ivory covers, divided between the Victoria and Albert Museum and the Vatican, are the largest and among the most splendid book covers from the period to have survived. The form of the front and back covers, each composed of five separate panels, emulates late antique imperial diptychs.

All that remains on the grounds of the once resplendent abbey today is the *Torhalle* and a modest Romanesque church, built after a fire in 1090, standing at the east end of what had been the large atrium.

BIBLIOGRAPHY

Behn, Friedrich. *Die Karolingische Klosterkirche von Lorsch, nach den Ausgrabungen 1927–28 und 1932–33.* Berlin and Leipzig: de Gruyter, 1934.

Heitz, Carol. *L'architecture religieuse carolingienne.* Paris: Picard, 1980.

Longhurst, Margaret, and Charles Rufus Morey. "The Covers of the Lorsch Gospels." *Speculum* 3 (1928): 64–73.

The Lorsch Gospels, intro. Wolfgang Braunfels. 2 vols. New York: Braziller, 1967.

Melanie Holcomb

SEE ALSO

Bookmaking and Production; Carolingian Art and Architecture; Charlemagne; Libraries; Louis the Pious; Romanesque Art and Architecture

Lothar I (795–855)

The eldest son of Louis the Pious (r. 814–840), Lothar was born in 795. In 817, when he had three sons, Louis issued the *Ordinatio imperii,* a document intended to maintain the unity of the Carolingian empire and peace among his sons after his death. According to this plan, Lothar became co-emperor with his father in 817, while his junior brothers, Pippin and Louis the German, were appointed kings of Aquitaine and Bavaria, respectively, and made subject to Lothar. The *Ordinatio* anticipated almost every possibility except one—the death in 818 of Louis's wife, Ermengard, his remarriage to Judith in 819, and the birth of a fourth son, Charles, in 823.

Lothar, twenty-eight years old when Charles was born, spent the rest of his life trying to preserve the future promised him in the *Ordinatio* against a new reality created by the birth of his half-brother. Louis attempted to forestall tension between them by assigning Lothar the spiritually and politically significant role of godfather to Charles and by sending Lothar to rule Italy. Lothar must have felt marginalized in Italy and threatened by the knowledge that the politically astute Judith was busily securing a place in the crowded dynasty for her son. In 830, when Pippin and Louis the German rebelled against their father and Judith, Lothar raced from Italy to join in. But Louis I played Pippin and Louis the German off against Lothar and the rebellion collapsed with Lothar in disgrace and once more confined to Italy. The next year, Louis I replaced the *Ordinatio* with a new dispensation, the *Divisio regni,* which allotted four kingdoms to the four brothers without mentioning the empire or emperor. The new settlement provoked a more serious rebellion against Louis I and Judith, this time masterminded by

Lothar, who had the support of Pippin and Louis the German, and even of Pope Gregory IV. In 833, Louis I, Judith, and the young Charles were captured. The rebellion fell apart when Pippin and Louis feared the ascendancy of Lothar, and others regretted the outrage the sons visited on their father and his wife.

When Louis I died in 840, his three surviving sons, Pippin having died in 838, negotiated warily and unsuccessfully among each other, Louis and Charles allying against Lothar. In June, 841, Frank fought Frank for the first time since 717 in a horrendous battle between Lothar's forces and those of Louis, Charles, and Judith that saw Lothar soundly defeated. Lothar next tried to separate these brother-opponents through diplomacy, but Louis and Charles only cemented their concord when they took the oaths at Strasbourg in February, 842, in each other's vernacular languages. In August, 843, at Verdun, after long and complex negotiations that included a survey of the Carolingian kingdoms, the brothers agreed to a three-way partition of the empire with Lothar retaining the imperial title. His portion, flanked on the west by that of Charles and on the east by that of Louis, extended from the North Sea to Mediterranean Italy. It included the political capital of Aachen and the spiritual capital of Rome.

In the years after Verdun, Lothar and Charles supported each other, Lothar even commissioning a magnificent illustrated gospel book (the Lothar Gospels, in Paris, Bibliothéque Nationale, manuscript no. lat. 266, contains a very impressive portrait of Lothar) from the monks of St. Martin in his brother's territory. When Lothar died on September 29, 855, his kingdom was divided among his three sons.

BIBLIOGRAPHY

Nelson, Janet L. *Charles the Bald.* London and New York: Longman, 1992.

Reuter, Timothy. *Germany in the Early Middle Ages, 800–1056.* London and New York: Longman, 1991.

Riché, Pierre. *The Carolingians: A Family Who Forged Europe,* trans. Michael Idomir Allen. Philadelphia: University of Pennsylvania Press, 1993.

John J. Contreni

SEE ALSO

Carolingians; Louis the Pious; *Ordinatio Imperii;* Verdun

Lothar III (1075–1137)

Lothar III of Supplinburg was born shortly after his father, Count Gebhard of Supplinburg, died in battle against King Henry IV. Historians know little about his youth, his rise to prominence, or exactly why King Henry V named Lothar as successor to the late Magnus Billung, duke of Saxony, on August 25, 1106. Soon after, having grown still more powerful through other inheritances and his own political and military ability, Lothar became the leader of the opposition to Henry V.

With the death of Emperor Henry V in 1125 without a son, German princes reasserted their traditional right to elect a new king. Representative magnates of the four ethnic divisions of Swabia, Bavaria, Saxony, and Franconia were delegated to the election at Mainz under the leadership of the archbishop. Although Duke Frederick II of Swabia, Henry V's nephew and heir, and Margrave Leopold III of Austria found a great deal of support, the archbishop promoted the case of the duke of Saxony, Lothar von Supplinburg. Lothar's party probably gained the support of the main holdout, the Welf duke of Bavaria, Henry the Black, with a promised marriage alliance between Henry's son, Henry the Proud, and Lothar's only child and heir, Gertrude. Elected on August 30 as king of the Romans, Lothar was crowned in Aachen about two weeks later.

The succession did not go smoothly, however. Between the Staufen Frederick II of Swabia and Lothar a new rivalry developed. The new king needed to assert his control over royal and imperial rights and properties. But royal prerogatives were mixed together with the personal inheritance of Henry V and the Salian dynasty inherited by the Staufen. Because Frederick was reluctant to turn over certain possessions, Lothar outlawed him at Christmas, 1125. Distracted by the defiance of Sobeslav of Bohemia, Lothar could not begin a military campaign against the Staufen until summer 1127, when he began to besiege Nuremburg. There the Staufen party elected Frederick's younger brother Conrad as anti-king in December, 1127. This conflict disturbed the peace of the empire until Conrad's capitulation in 1135. Nineteenth-century historians inflated these disagreements into a grand vendetta between two dynasties, the Welf (or in Italian, Guelph) versus the Staufen (or in Italian, Ghibelline after the castle Waiblingen). While such a view oversimplified the issues involved, the competing interests of these powerful families would recurrently affect imperial affairs for decades.

Meanwhile, Lothar was capably handling the affairs of his kingdom. His exploitation of extinct noble dynasties changed the political landscape. Lothar helped establish the Zähringens in Burgundy as rivals to the Staufen. Lothar's intervention of the succession of the duchy of

Lower Lotharingia led to its breakup into the duchies of Brabant and Limburg. In Saxony, his home territory, he enfeoffed the Askaniens with the Nordmark and the Wettins with the Marches of Meissen and Lausitz, dynasties that would, however, later become rivals of the Welfs. Lothar made his will felt beyond his kingdom's borders. He carried out several campaigns against the Slavs, collecting tribute from Poland and granting Pomerania as a fief. And a quick military demonstration against the Danish, where rivalry for the throne had caused disorder, encouraged the various candidates to acknowledge his overlordship almost without bloodshed.

Most importantly, Lothar became entangled in the papal schism between Innocent II and Anacletus II. Since both sides had respectable claims to the papacy, Lothar faced a real dilemma about whom to recognize as legitimate pope. Under the influence of the important Cistercian Abbot Bernard of Clairvaux and Norbert of Xanten (the founder of the Premonstratentian order, whom Lothar had made archbishop of Magdeburg), Lothar decided at a synod at Würzburg in 1130 to give allegiance to Innocent. Greeting the pope in Liège in March, 1131, Lothar acted as a groom and horse-marshal (Strator- und Marschaldienst), leading the pope's horse by the bridle and holding his stirrup during dismounting. The memorialization of this act with a fresco in the Vatican, implying that Lothar served as a vassal of the pope, later caused tension between imperial and papal ideologues.

In return for offering to conquer Rome for Innocent, Lothar tried to get back the old rights of investiture of bishops that had been lost for the monarchy in the Concordat of Worms. But Innocent only gave a promise of the imperial election. In late summer 1132, Lothar began an expedition to Italy with a small army. His attack on Rome brought one success: Innocent crowned Lothar and his wife, Richenza, emperor and empress on June 4, 1133, although in the Lateran Palace, since Anacletus's forces still held the Vatican. Again Lothar tried to reclaim investiture, but only received confirmation that his rights would be the same as his predecessor's. In negotiations about the Mathildine lands, he gained more success. Lothar recognized the claims of overlordship by the church, but he gained use of the lands in exchange for an annual payment of 100 pounds silver. Although the emperor immediately enfeoffed his son-in-law Henry the Proud with the lands, the papacy tried to portray him as a vassal of the church.

Within months Lothar returned to Germany, unable to defeat Anacletus's main ally, King Roger II of Sicily.

Soon, Innocent was forced to flee Rome. Once the Staufen had reconciled with Lothar, however, the worsening plight of Innocent prompted Lothar to lead a second, much larger, Italian expedition in 1136. In northern Italy Lothar was triumphant; by the beginning of 1137 he invaded the kingdom of Roger of Sicily. But the quarrels between pope and emperor over the disposition of conquests and leadership, as well as the heat of summer, led to the breakup of the campaign before lasting success could be won. On the return northward Lothar sickened, finally dying in Breitenwang near Reutte in Tyrol on December 4, 1137.

Both his contemporaries and later historians have tended to judge Lothar harshly, especially those who resented his rather friendly relations with leaders of the church. Other modern historians reject his image as *Pfaffenkönig* (parson's king): his quarrels with the pope and his wars with local territorial bishops belie that charge. The conflicts after his death that ruined his legacy were largely caused by the change in dynasty, which Lothar had tried to forestall by giving the imperial insignia to Henry the Proud. In many ways Lothar successfully expanded political authority in Saxony, Germany, and the empire.

BIBLIOGRAPHY

Bernhardi, Wilhelm. *Lothar von Supplinburg (1125–1127)*. Jahrbücher der deutschen Geschichte 15. 1879; repr., Berlin: Duncker und Humblot, 1975.

Crone, Marie-Luise. *Untersuchungen zur Reichskirchenpolitik Lothars III. (1125–1137) zwischen reichskirchlicher Tradition und Reformkurie*. Frankfurt am Main: Lang, 1982.

Wadle, Elmar. *Reichsgut und Königsherrschaft unter Lothar III. (1125–1137): Ein Beitrag zur Verfassungsgeschichte des 12. Jahrhunderts*. Berlin: Duncker & Humblot, 1969.

Brian A. Pavlac

SEE ALSO

Aachen; Billunger; Concordat of Worms; Henry IV; Salians; Staufen; Welfs

Louis the Child (899–911)

The last member of the Carolingian dynasty to reign in the east Frankish kingdom, Louis the Child was the sole legitimate son of Arnulf of Carinthia (r. 887–899), who succeeded his father at the age of six years old. He received important support from the church, including the monastery of St. Gall, and the regents, archbishops Hatto of Mainz and Adalbero of Augsburg. Throughout his reign, Louis was plagued by invasions of Magyar horsemen and over-mighty subjects. It was Liutpold, margrave of Bavaria, who provided the greatest defense against the Magyars and, thereby, demonstrated the weakness of Louis. Liutpold, however, died in battle against the Magyars in 907 and the invaders ravaged Bavaria and other parts of the kingdom with impunity for the next several years. Louis's ineffectiveness continued from his minority into his majority, 906–911, and his personal rule had little positive effect on the kingdom. At his death in 911, the nobles of the kingdom elected Conrad I (911–918) as king and ended the rule of the Carolingian dynasty in Germany.

BIBLIOGRAPHY

Riché, Pierre. *The Carolingians: A Family Who Forged Europe,* trans. Michael Idomir Allen. Philadelphia: University of Pennsylvania Press, 1993.

Michael Frassetto

SEE ALSO

Carolingians; Conrad I

Louis the Pious (April 16, 778–June 20, 840)

Louis *(Hludowicus)* and Lothar, a twin who soon died, were born on April 16, 778, in the palace of Chasseneuil near Poitiers to Hildegard, the wife of Charles the Great (Charlemagne). "Pious," not a contemporary epithet, was applied to Louis only at the end of the ninth century. In 781, Charles appointed Louis king of Aquitaine, an office he would grow into and hold for the next thirty-three years. In 794, sixteen-year-old Louis, already the father of two children by concubines, married Irmingard (d. 818), the daughter of Count Ingram. The royal couple produced five children within the decade.

Louis, as Charles's only surviving legitimate son, was crowned co-emperor at Aachen on September 11, 813. The implications of the imperial title Charles received in 800 remained ambiguous during his last years. The increasing involvement of churchmen in the administration of his realm suggests that Charles's concept of empire embraced religious as well as political leadership. A capitulary from this period wonders, "Are we indeed Christians?" One of Louis's great tasks after his father's death in January, 814, was to continue to define a Christian empire. Under Louis, Aachen became a beehive of activity. Charles had issued twenty diplomas during his last thirteen years; Louis nearly doubled that in his first year as emperor. Louis regarded his empire as a divine gift for whose welfare and improvement he was chiefly responsible. Much of his early legislation focused on monastic and ecclesiastical reform. With the help of Benedict of Aniane, a monk who had joined his inner circle back in Aquitaine and whom he installed at Inden nearby Aachen, Louis crafted a vision of empire in which religion, society, and politics coalesced. Concern for the unity of the Christian people animated the *Ordinatio imperii* of 817, his attempt to establish the imperial succession in a manner that would preserve the integrity of the empire. Lothar (b. 795) became co-emperor with Louis while his other sons, Pippin (b. 797) and Louis the Younger (b. 806), were assigned subordinate roles. In placing the unity of the empire before division among his heirs, Louis proposed a transpersonal vision of empire that emulated the unity of the church. Louis saw himself as emperor of the Christian people, not of various ethnic groups. His reforms and concept of empire owed nothing to papal guidance or initiative. The historic *Pactum Hludowicianum* agreement of 817 for the first time outlined specifically the nature of the papal-imperial relationship, a relationship that Louis dominated. Elsewhere he referred to the pope as his helper *(adiutor)* in caring for God's people.

Louis was equally forceful in the political realm. When his nephew, King Bernard of Italy, challenged his authority in 817 he acted swiftly to quash the rebellion, blinding Bernard and exiling the conspirators. (When Bernard died of his injuries, Louis demonstrated the depth of his commitment to Christian kingship by performing public penance.) To preempt further dynastic challenges, he had his half-brothers Drogo, Hugo, and Theodoric tonsured and placed in monasteries. After the death of Irmingard (October 3, 818), Louis married Judith, daughter of Count Welf and his wife, Eigilwi, who bore him two children, Gisela (821) and Charles (June 13, 823). The birth of Louis's fourth son later triggered searing conflicts within the family and Carolingian society at large. Other problems also challenged his reign during its second decade. Churchmen such as Bishop Agobard of Lyon began to complain about rampant corruption in Carolingian society, including exploitation of church lands and oppression of the poor by the warrior class. With the expansion of Carolingian hegemony at an end, powerful nobles who little understood the ideals of Louis's empire ransacked the Christian people and churches for material gain. The many groups ranged along the empire's extensive borders required continual attention. In the southeast, the Slovenians proved troublesome, while in the northeast Louis was able to effectively manage the Danish threat, which was defused when the Danish king Harald was baptized and adopted by Louis in 826. In the west, Louis campaigned personally in Brittany where he established nominal authority. In Gascony and the Pyrenees borderlands chronic instability reigned, partly because counts Hugo and Matfrid failed to support Louis's military efforts, a dereliction for which the emperor stripped them of their positions. Count Bernard of Barcelona was much more effective and for his efforts was appointed in 829 as the emperor's chamberlain, an office that brought him into intimate contact with the imperial family. Judith saw Bernard as a protector while Louis regarded him as the second man in the empire. Louis's forceful handling of counts Hugo and Matfrid and the empowerment of Bernard and Judith combined with the fear that any provision made for the young Charles would come at the expense of his half-brothers provoked a palace revolt in 830. Pippin and the younger Louis, aided by Hugo and Matfrid, sought to "free" the emperor from the tyrant Bernard and the Jezebel Judith, but Louis's supporters, sowing discord among his older sons, restored him to authority in October, 830. Although abortive, the coup claimed a victim when the vision of empire outlined in the 817 *Ordinatio imperii* was annulled. The new *Divisio regnum* of 831 restored traditional Frankish practice when it partitioned the empire into four approximately equal kingdoms on Louis's death. The new status quo, however, was only temporary. Adherents of a unified empire agitated against the *Divisio,* while conflict among the brothers continued and was exacerbated when enterprising nobles took sides. On June 30, 833, Louis met with Lothar near Colmar in Alsace to compose their differences, but instead the emperor found himself on the "Field of Lies" facing a coalition of his older sons, their supporters, Pope Gregory IV, and several leading clergy, who took him and Judith into custody. Judith was sent to a monastery in Italy while Louis was confined to the monastery of Saint-Medard in Soissons. Leading clerics, including Agobard of Lyon and Ebbo of Reims, argued that Louis failed as a king and must abdicate the throne. In a humiliating ceremony, he acknowledged his crimes, removed his imperial regalia, and was condemned to perpetual penance. This mistreatment of a father by his sons, another round of conflict among the older brothers and

their supporters, and increasing violence soon swung sympathy and support back to Louis who, from his confinement, was orchestrating his return. Freed from captivity, his weapons, his wife, and his youngest son were restored to him.

Emperor once again, Louis continued to rule energetically, bestowing key appointments on his supporters and punishing those such as Agobard and Ebbo who had betrayed him. He continued successfully to provide for Charles against the resistance of the younger Louis. When Pippin died in 838, Louis ignored the complaints of Pippin's son and granted the kingdom of Aquitaine to Charles. Lothar dedicated himself to his Italian lands and never challenged his father again. Louis rebuilt his own political network by holding frequent assemblies after 835 and by presiding at ceremonial and ritual activities, especially hunting, his favorite pastime. He continued to see to the collection of public revenue and directed successful military campaigns. In 839, an embassy from the Byzantine Empire arrived to congratulate him for his stout defense of Christendom.

On June 20, 840, Louis died on Petersaue, an island in the Rhine near his palace at Ingelehim. His last words reportedly were *Hutz, hutz* (German for "Away, away"), shouted as his mourners imagined to circling evil spirits. He was laid to rest in the monastery of Saint-Arnulf of Metz beside his mother and his sisters, Rotrud and Hildegard. Bishop Drogo, his half-brother, chose a late antique sarcophagus for him that depicted the flight of the Israelites across the Red Sea before the pursuing Egyptians. The motif symbolized baptism and triumph. Bitter civil war broke out among his sons, resulting in 843 in the formal division of the empire recorded in the Treaty of Verdun.

BIBLIOGRAPHY

Boshof, Egon. *Ludwig der Fromme.* Darmstadt: Primus, 1996.

De Jong, Mayke. "Power and Humility in Carolingian Society: The Public Penance of Louis the Pious." *Early Medieval Europe* 1 (1992): 29–52.

Godman, Peter, and Roger Collins, eds. *Charlemagne's Heir: New Perspectives on the Reign of Louis the Pious.* Oxford: Clarendon Press, 1992.

John J. Contreni

SEE ALSO

Aachen; Capitularies; Carolingians; Charlemagne; Coronation; Judith, Empress; Lothar I; *Ordinatio Imperii;* Succession

Louis II (November 1, 846–April 10, 879)

The eldest son of Charles II, the Bald (r. 840–877), Louis II, the Stutterer (der Stammerer) was born on November 1, 846. He reigned as king of West Francia for sixteen months (December 8, 877–April 10, 879) before dying of illness at Compiègne. The first thirty-one years of his life were spent at the center of his father's struggle to balance Carolingian dynastic concerns and the competing loyalty of the kingdom's ambitious nobles. Although afflicted with a speech disorder, Louis played an active role in the fractious politics of the 860s and 870s, often allying himself with his father's opponents. Charles installed Louis as king of Aquitaine in 867 and made him lay abbot of several monasteries, but strictly limited his power. After Charles's death, Louis moved energetically to preserve royal power. His descendants include King Charles III (the Simple; r. 893–929), and King Louis V (r. 986–987), the last Carolingian monarch.

BIBLIOGRAPHY

Nelson, Janet L. *Charles the Bald.* London and New York: Longman, 1992.

Riché, Pierre. *The Carolingians: A Family Who Forged Europe,* trans. Michael Idomir Allen. Philadelphia: University of Pennsylvania Press, 1993.

John J. Contreni

SEE ALSO

Carolingians; Charles III, the Simple

Lübeck

The city of Lübeck was founded as a harbor town at its present location in 1143 by Count Adolph II of Schaumburg and Holstein. Some earthworks and the foundations of a church testify to the destruction of a previously existing Slavic castle and adjoining market Liubice. In 1158 Duke Henry the Lion of Saxon forced Adolph to surrender the site, which was strategically important to Henry's military aims toward the east and as a trading place for the Baltic. After his political downfall in 1180, however, the city came under imperial control; it remained an independent political unit until 1937.

Lübeck is located on a peninsula created by the Trave and Wakenity Rivers and surrounded by swamps. The former castle, later replaced by dominican priory (Burgkloster), and the adjacent castle gate (Burgtor) protect its northern access via a land bridge, now pierced by a canal. Its southernmost point is marked by the cathedral of a

bishopric that, in 1160, was transferred from nearby Oldenburg. A first wooden structure was replaced between 1173 or 1174 and 1247 by the Romanesque nave and transepts that still form the core of the present monument. With its square groin vaults, it transposes the cathedral of Henry the Lion's residence at Braunschweig into the regionally dominant medium of brick. The building type was copied, although on a smaller scale, by the first parish church of St. Maria (Marienkirche, or St. Mary's), next to the market area halfway between castle and cathedral, and by the church of the Benedictine monastery of St. Johannes. Founded in 1177, the monastery was transferred to Cistercian nuns in 1246; it was demolished between 1806 and 1819.

By the mid–thirteenth century, Lübeck had changed from a feudal to a bourgeois city. The main expresson of this change is the (forged) document of Emperor Frederick II that, in 1226, changed its status to that of imperial city. The previous year the city had evicted the Danish occupation garrison from its castle and established a Dominican monastery in it; although the church was demolished in 1818, the medieval convent buildings have survived. To commemorate the city's victory over the Danes at Bornhöved (July 22, 1227), a Franciscan monastery was founded in 1229; its church, St. Katherinen, was erected as a major basilica with extended crypt under the choir and transepts that do not appear as such in the interior. At the same time St. Maria was replaced by a large Gothic hall church, completed by 1270, of which the lower part of a single western tower has survived in the two-towered western facade. The civic and mercantile center of St. Maria was surrounded by other semi-independent neighborhoods and parishes within the city's enclosure. Parallel to St. Maria, the church of St. Jacobus (St. James) of the neighboring trading settlement on the Koberg plaza was begun as a hall church but was soon changed, under the influence of the subsequent rebuilding of St. Marien, to a pseudobasilica with triple apse. St. Peter, in a settlement of artisans next to the main bridge crossing the Trave, and St. Aegidius in the south, both with single towers, adopted this model.

The first century of the city's independence witnessed a major effort in architectural development. Between 1266 and 1335, the cathedral received a new hall choir; its plan with radiating hexagonal chapels that unite with the bays of the ambulatory established a prototype for churches along the Baltic coast. Possibly not before 1286, when the city council acquired the patronage of St. Marien, a further rebuilding was undertaken of the church as a major basilica with ambulatory choir and two-towered western facade, but without transepts. This monument introduced the complete system of a Gothic cathedral with high nave and flying buttresses from the cathedrals at Cologne and Utrecht to the Baltic and generated the model for the churches at Schwerin, Rostock, Wismar, Stralsund, and elsewhere.

Lübeck's economic and political importance is reflected by its prominent place in the Hanseatic League, a confederation of towns under the leadership of Cologne to protect their trading interests and to insure social stability within the communes. The city's main secular building was the town hall overlooking the main market square. Originally a long hall with a Romanesque gable, it was later expanded by a Gothic cloth hall built parallel to it. The courtyard was later built over while the ensemble received a major screen facade with wind holes to its north and south.

In 1285, the construction of the Heilig-Geist-Spital (Hospital of the Holy Spirit) was completed, a social institution that housed the city's elderly and poor. The semimonastic ensemble—nearly unchanged today—consists of a chapel, the adjoining dormitory, and the cloisters. Its chapel, which appears to the outside as three houses separated by slender towers, represents a vaulted hall church of two bays penetrated by the hall of the dormitory with its wooden barrel vault.

Despite an attempt to improve the conditions of Lübeck's trade by the building of the Stegnitz canal in 1390–1398 to connect Lübeck to the places of salt production at Lüneburg, the fifteenth century was a period of constant decline, generated by political and military ventures. In 1426–1435, the city waged war against Denmark and in 1475 against England, after uprisings and a constitutional crisis in 1408–1416 had already undermined the city's inner stability. Nevertheless, a series of major secular building projects was undertaken to demonstrate the city's apparently undisturbed position. In 1440–1442, the city's builder Nikolaus Peck erected the Kriegsstubenbau, an assembly room of the council's war department, over an open market hall, connected by a gallery to the main building. Peck was also responsible for the remodeling of the Burgtor in 1444. The famous Holstentor was built in 1466–1478 by the council's builder Helmstede; although designed for artillery, it follows the example of the two-towered city gates of Cologne from the early thirteenth century.

The end of the medieval period in Lübeck is marked by the introduction of the Reformation by Johannes Bu-

genhagen in 1530–1531 and the unsuccessful attempt of Mayor Jürgen Wullenweber to restore the Hanseatic predominance, which failed in the *Grafenfehde* (Counts' Feud) in 1535. Just before, in 1509, an Augustinian nunnery had been founded; although its church was demolished in 1819, the convent buildings remain intact and house the city's important medieval art collection.

BIBLIOGRAPHY

Böker, Hans J. *Die mittelalterliche Backsteinarchitektur Norddeutschlands.* Darmstadt: Wissenschaftliche Buchgesellschaft, 1988.

Ellger, Dietrich, and Johanna Kolbe. *St. Marien zu Lübeck und seine Wandmalereien.* Neumünster in Holstein: K. Wachholtz, 1951.

Kruse, Karl Bernhard. *Die Baugeschichte des Heiligen-Geist-Hospitals zu Lübeck.* Ph.D. diss., University of Hannover, 1994. Lübecker Schriften zur Archäologie und Kunstgeschichte 25. Bonn: Habelt, 1997.

Lübeck 1226: Reichsfreiheit und frühe Stadt. Lübeck: Hansisches Verlagskontor Scheffler, 1976.

Hans J. Böker

SEE ALSO
Cistercian Art and Architecture; Cologne, History; Franciscan Art and Architecture; Gothic Art and Architecture; Hanseatic League; Henry the Lion; Lüneburg; Rostock; Schwerin; Stralsund; Wismar

Lucerne

Located on the Reuss River in Switzerland, Lucerne's history extends back to the late eighth century, when the monastery of St. Leodegar was established. The monastery became a dependency of Murbach abbey in Alsace in 840. In the second half of the twelfth century, the church of St. Leodegar was built in Romanesque style reflecting Alsatian influence; a Gothic choir, consecrated in 1345, replaced the original Romanesque east choir. The entire church, except the Gothic facade towers, fell victim to fire in 1633.

Beginning in the mid-twelfth century, Lucerne began to develop on both sides of the bridge over the Reuss, and in 1178 the Murbach abbot Konrad von Eschenbach founded the city. With the opening of the St. Gotthard Pass around 1230, Lucerne grew in size and importance as a market town. In 1291, Emperor Rudolf of Hapsburg bought the city, which ignited a quest for independence lasting more than a century. Lucerne joined the Swiss

Federation in 1332 and gained its independence within the Holy Roman Empire in 1417.

Lucerne is surrounded by the Musegg wall, built in the later half of the fourteenth century; at 870 meters, it is one of the longest fortifications in Switzerland. The *Kapellbruecke*, the main river bridge, was built around 1300 and rebuilt after a fire in 1993. Owing to the city's economic and religious ties with Italy, Italian influence is evident in monuments beginning in the late Middle Ages.

BIBLIOGRAPHY

Felder, Peter. *Die Hofkirche St. Leodegar und St. Mauritius in Luzern.* Basle: Birkhäuser, 1958.

Hegglin, Clemens, and Fritz Glauser, eds. *Kloster und Pfarre zu Franziskanern in Luzern.* Lucerne: Rex, 1989.

Reinle, Adolf. *Die Kunstdenkmäler des Kantons Luzern,* vol. 2–3. *Die Stadt Luzern.* Die Kunstdenkmäler der Schweiz. Basel: Birkhäuser, 1953–1954.

Gregory H. Wolf

SEE ALSO

Gothic Art and Architecture; Romanesque Art and Architecture

Ludolf of Saxony (1295/1300–1378)

Also referred to as Ludolf the Carthusian, Ludolf of Saxony is principally known as the author of a lengthy, devotional life of Christ. Little is known of his personal history. By tradition, he is thought to have started his religious life as a Dominican; in 1340, however, he entered the Carthusian Charterhouse of Strasbourg. In 1343, he was appointed prior of the Charterhouse at Koblenz, a position he gave up in 1348. He spent the last thirty years of his life as a monk, first in Mainz and later in Strasbourg.

At different times, scholars have attributed various texts to Ludolf; current consensus definitively assigns two texts to him, a *Commentary Upon the Psalms* and the better-known *Vita Christi.* The latter became particularly popular, as evidenced by numerous manuscript copies as well as approximately sixty printed editions; the earliest was published in Cologne in 1472, followed by a second edition printed in Strasbourg in 1474. Although especially popular in Germany, by the sixteenth century the text had also been translated into Dutch, Catalonian, Portuguese, Italian, and French.

Bearing traces of both Dominican and Carthusian influence, the *Vita Christi* is a characteristically late me-dieval treatment of Christ's life, both in its abundant detail, and in its concern with instructing the reader on the practice of imaginative, affective veneration of Christ's life. The text contains not only biography, but also orations and meditations, and exegeses on the practice of contemplative devotion. Ludolf drew on approximately sixty different sources for this text, which was meant as a guide to individual worship, as well as a source for readings and prayers.

BIBLIOGRAPHY

Baier, Walter. *Untersuchungen zu den Passionsbetrachtungen in der Vita Christi des Ludolf von Sachsen: Ein quellenkritischer Beitrag zu Leben und Werk Ludolfs und zur Geschichte der Passionstheologie.* 3 vols. Salzburg: Institut für Englische Sprache und Literatur, 1977.

Bodenstedt, Sister Mary I. *The Vita Christi of Ludolphus the Carthusian.* Washington, D.C.: Catholic University of America Press, 1944.

The Hours of the Passion taken from the Life of Christ by Ludolph the Saxon, trans. H. J. C. [Henry James Coleridge]. London: Burns and Oats, 1887.

Vita Jesu Christi e quatuor Evangeliis et scriptoribus orthodoxis concinnata, ed. A.-C. Bolard, L.-M. Rigollot, J. Carnandet. Paris and Rome: Palmé, 1865.

Carol M. Schuler

SEE ALSO

Cologne, History; Koblenz; Mainz; Strasbourg

Ludwigslied

An Old High German poem ("Song of Louis") celebrating the victory of Louis III (r. 862–882) over Viking invaders at Saucourt in 881, written before Louis's sudden death. Though probably composed at the monastery of St. Amand, its language seems to be Rhenish Franconian rather than the native but moribund West Franconian dialect. It uses the new rhyming meter first seen in Otfrid's gospel poem.

After the death of the West Frankish king Louis the Stammerer, his two eldest sons, Louis and Karlmann, were jointly crowned in 879. Louis received Francia and Neustria when the kingdom was divided in 880. Though his victory at Saucourt seemed decisive, he faced renewed Viking invasion and died at Tours while negotiating with the invaders in 882. According to the anonymous poet, Louis is at once God's servant and His representative to the West Franks. After the Stammerer's death, Louis and

Karlmann were in the care of the powerful abbot Hugo; the poet says rather that God was his guardian, having selected him to receive the throne. The Vikings are sent by God to test Louis's mettle, as well as to urge the Franks to repentance. Louis moves against them only when God commands "Help my people." Louis then proclaims:

"God has sent me here / and has Himself commanded,
If you think it advisable, / that I should fight here,
Not sparing myself / until I have saved you."

The king goes into battle singing a hymn. After a conventional description of bravery and gore ("Some he sliced through, others he stabbed through"), the poet announces: "Praised be the power of God! / Louis was victorious."

BIBLIOGRAPHY

Berg, Elisabeth. "Das Ludwigslied und die Schlacht bei Saucourt." *Rheinische Vierteljahrsblätter* 29 (1964): 175–199 [both OHG text and trans. into modern German].

Müller, Robert. "Der historische Hintergrund des althochdeutschen *Ludwigliedes*." *Deutsche Vierteljahrsschrift für Literaturwissenschaft und Geistesgeschichte* 62 (1998): 221–226.

Murdoch, Brian O. *Old High German Literature.* Twayne's World Authors Series 68. Boston: Twayne, 1983, pp. 93–100.

Leo A. Connolly

SEE ALSO
De Heinrico; Otfrid; Notker Labeo

Lüneburg

The city of Lüneburg (Lower Saxony), founded in 1247 by Duke Otto (the Child), developed in the later Middle Ages into a leading trading center and capital of the duchy of Braunschweig-Lüneburg (later Hanover). Its primary economic importance rested on the exploitation of the large salt deposits that were extracted from wells. Due to its post-medieval decline, the city has preserved much of its historic appearance with all of its major buildings erected in brick.

The town plan, forming a rough rectangle of 800 by 500 meters, reveals several historical units that grew into the present urban structure and which correspond to the different social groups that constituted the medieval town. In the southeast, the older market—the *Sand,* which is situated at the crossing of two major roads, reaches back into the pre-urban era. It is dominated by the main parish church, St. Johannis, a five-aisle hall church with a monumental western tower. The opposite urban pole lay to the northwest at the *Kalkberg,* a chalk hill just outside the town's fortifications on which stood the castle of the town's feudal lords, the Guelphs (Welfs). Both the castle and the abbey church of St. Michaelis, the dukes' burial church, were destroyed in 1371, as a consequence of the struggle for power between feudal lord and commune, and the abbey was subsequently moved within the town walls; by 1434, it had been rebuilt as a hall church in the decidedly conservative architectural forms of the late thirteenth century. The third unit to the north is the second market with the town hall to the west, a building complex whose different parts, dating from the thirteenth to the eighteenth century, serve simultaneously for civic and ducal representation. The former princely residence was situated to the north side of the market, and in its vicinity the church of St. Nikolai was constructed in the years 1407–1460. As a basilica with ambulatory choir and rich star vaults, this building follows the prototype established for the churches of late medieval princely residences in the Baltic (e.g., Schwerin, Wismar). In the neighborhood of the port in the northeastern corner of the town, the church was later adopted by the merchants and sailors. To the southwest, the parish church St. Lamberti, a hall church with rich star vaults in its nave, formed the center of the quarter of the *Salzsieder* (salt boilers); damage resulting from uneven subsidence of the ground, caused by the exploitation of the salt stock underneath, necessitated its demolition in 1860.

BIBLIOGRAPHY

Krüger, Franz, and Wilhelm Reinecke. *Die Kunstdenkmäler der Provinz Hannover* 5–6: *Stadt Lüneburg,* ed. Carl Wolff. Hanover: Selbstverlag der Provinzialverwaltung, 1906.

Hans J. Böker

SEE ALSO
Braunschweig; Gothic Art and Architecture; Gothic Art and Architecture, Late; Schwerin; Wismar

Lutwin (fl. ca. 1300)

Author of *Eva und Adam,* a retelling in 3,939 rhymed couplets of the biblical Creation story and the apocryphal

Vita Adae et Evae, little is known of Lutwin apart from his written work, dated around 1300. In retelling the biblical story, Lutwin underscores Eve's sensual nature as opposed to Adam's rational one. To tempt her, Satan lures her with insight and intelligence. Ultimately, however, it is her sensual appetite that betrays her, for she is overcome by the sight and feel of the apple. Following the narration of the biblical events, Lutwin then narrates the events subsequent to the expulsion from Eden, which are found in the Latin *Vita Adae et Evae.* Briefly, it involves their search for food, the penance they undertake, the birth of their sons, and the death of Adam. Lutwin's version follows fairly closely the Latin versions (there are more than ninety extant manuscripts of the *Vita,* and no one version has been found to be the specific source for Lutwin). One episode, however, is unique to Lutwin. Following the penance where the two stand up to their necks in water, Adam for forty days in the Jordan and Eve for thirty-four days in the Tigris, the two separate. In the *Vita* the motivation for the separation is that Eve was duped for a second time by the devil, so that she came out of the water before the penance was completed. In Lutwin's version, Eve leaves Adam because of a lover's quarrel. She wanted to make love as they had done in Eden but Adam, being the more spiritual and sensible, declines. Thus, again, the baser appetites of Eve are underscored. In spite of Lutwin's stereotypical view of Eve, he nevertheless depicts her with a great deal of sympathy.

BIBLIOGRAPHY

Hofmann, Konrad, and Wilhelm Meyer, eds. *Lutwins Adam und Eva.* Tübingen: Litterarischer Verein, 1881.

Halford, Mary-Bess. *Lutwin's Eva und Adam.* Göppingen: Kümmerle, 1984 [translation].

Murdoch, Brian. "Das deutsche Adamsbuch und die Adamslegenden des Mittelalters." In *Deutsche Literatur des späten Mittelalters. Hamburger Colloquium,* ed. Wolfgang Harms and Leslie. P. Johnson. Berlin: Schmidt, 1975, pp. 209–224.

Kathleen J. Meyer

SEE ALSO
Bible

Luxemburger

In 963, Count Siegfried, the son of the Ardennes Count Wigerich, exchanged the fortress *Lucilinburhuc,* which belonged to the abbey of St. Maximin in Trier, for his own villa at Feulen. Siegfried was the Gaugraf in the Moselgau and in the Ardennesgau in 993, and he was also the advocate of the monastery at Echternach and of St. Maximin. Indicative of the family's power and importance is the fact that Emperor Henry II married Kunigunde of Luxemburg, daughter of Siegfried and his wife, Hedwig, sister of Adelbert of Alsace, margrave of Lorraine. Kunigunde's eldest brother, Henry I, was count in the Ardennesgau and in the Bedagau in 993, and in 1004, he was elevated to the office of duke of Bavaria by his brother-in-law, the king. The second son of Siegfried, Frederick I (d. 1019), appears to have acquired significant lands in Hesse through his wife, who came from the dynasty of the counts of the Lahngau. Thierry of Luxembourg (German *Luxemburg),* another sibling, sat as bishop of Metz 1004–1046; his brother Adelbert was provost of St. Paulin near Trier, and in 1008, he was elected archbishop of Trier. Their nephew, Adelbert (son of Frederick I), followed as bishop of Metz 1046–1072.

The rising power of the Luxemburger dynasty can be seen in the appointment of Henry II as duke of Bavaria in 1042, of Frederick II as duke of Lower Lorraine and margrave of Antwerp by Emperor Henry III in 1046, and the election of Hermann of Luxemburg-Salm as anti-king to Emperor Henry IV in 1081. The Luxemburger were also the ancestors of the counts of Saarbrücken and Glitzberg. Conrad II, who died in 1136, was the last count of Luxembourg from the older or Ardennes line. He was succeeded by Henry, count of Namur, the son of the Luxemburger heiress Ermesindis. Her thirteenth-century namesake, also heiress to the Luxemburger lands and titles, married three times: first, with Henry, count of Champagne, then with Count Theobald of Bar, who died in 1213, and finally with Walram IV, duke of Limburg and margrave of Arlon, a union whereby the countship of Luxembourg passed to the house of Limburg.

The possessions of the counts of Luxembourg at the beginning of the thirteenth century were very significant, and they were next to the dukes of Lorraine the largest landlords on the left bank of the Rhine. The countship of Luxembourg with the enclosed county of Arlon comprised the entire modern grand duchy of Luxembourg, together with regions of western Germany around Saarburg, Trier, Bidburg, and Prüm, and the northern portion of the French department of Moselle until near Metz; it contained approximately 150 square miles. The larger western half spoke a Romance dialect (Walloon), while the smaller eastern region spoke German. In the midtwelfth century, there were approximately thirty fortresses in the county; toward the end of the thirteenth, the number had risen to about 100. The vassals who owed service to the counts of Luxembourg at the beginning of the thirteenth century numbered more than thirty-five, and there were also many ministerial families in their service. It was thus not an exaggeration when one reads that Count Henry of Namur and Luxembourg went against Archbishop Adelbero of Trier with some 1,500 men.

In 1308, Count Henry of Luxembourg was elected king of the Romans and asserted his claim to the imperial crown as well. He found support among such as Dante Alighieri, the Florentine poet whose piece "On the Monarchy," *De monarchia,* was dedicated to Henry. Although the electors rejected Henry's son as emperor, John did succeed to the throne of Bohemia; his grandson became the German king, Charles IV, in 1349. At the end of the fourteenth century, Sigismund and Wenceslas, sons of Charles IV, each sat as king for periods of time. Sigismund was emperor in 1415 at the time of the Council of Konstanz.

BIBLIOGRAPHY

Barraclough, Geoffrey. *The Origins of Modern Germany;* rpt. New York: Capricorn, 1963.

Hlawitschka, Eduard. *Die Anfänge des Hauses Habsburg-Lothringen. Genealogische Untersuchungen zur Geschichte Lothringens und des Reiches im 9., 10. und 11. Jahrhundert.* Saarbrücken: Kommissionsverlag, Minerva-Verlag Thinnes and Nolte, 1969.

Renn, Heinz. *Das erste Luxemburger Grafenhaus 963–1136.* Bonn: Röhrscheid, 1941.

Paul B. Pixton

SEE ALSO
Charles IV; Henry II, Art; Henry III; Wenceslas

M

Magdeburg

The Frankish border fort *Magadaburg,* first mentioned in 805, stood on the location of the present cathedral complex in a strategic military and commercial site above the river Elbe. Sometime during the following century, the fort was replaced by a *Hof* (court), including the requisite chapel. With the advent of a Saxon royal dynasty, the Ottonians, Magdeburg increased in importance. Otto I (936–973) granted the city to his first wife, Edith, as her *dos* (dowry) ca. 929. In 936, Otto founded a monastery there, dedicating it to St. Mauritius and his companions in the Theban legion. Throughout Otto's reign, Magdeburg was a frequent recipient of royal visits, in particular because it provided a convenient staging point for military expeditions into the Slavic lands beyond the Elbe. The ruler's presence and continued interest brought substantial benefits to the monastic community, which soon figured among the wealthiest in the realm. It is generally accepted that, by 955, Otto had formulated a plan to elevate the monastery at Magdeburg to the status of an archbishopric. He started building a new, unusually large church, which he endowed with more extensive rights of jurisdiction and new territories. In 965, he gave it rights to hold markets, mint coins, and collect customs duties. In spite of his efforts, clerical opposition prevented the monarch's plans from being realized until 968. In that year, an archbishop and chapter were installed in the former monastery of St. Mauritius, and most of the monks moved to a new foundation, St. John the Baptist at Berge.

The forms of the Ottonian church are known from excavations carried out in 1926. A transept and round choir flanked by two towers marked the east end; it was balanced at the west by a westwork. The long nave flanked by two aisles stretched in between. Separating the nave from the aisles were antique columns of marble, porphyry, and granite topped with late Roman capitals; Otto's transport of these *spolia* from Rome in 962 emulated Charlemagne's transfer of similar fragments to Aachen and suggests again the important role Otto intended this site to play in his imperial politics. He also intended it as a dynastic necropolis. In 946, his first wife Edith had been buried in the first church of St. Mauritius; Otto himself was buried in the crypt of the still unfinished cathedral in 973. After his death the eastern parts were enlarged: the five-aisled crypt was rebuilt for a consecration in 1008, and the new sanctuary above was erected under Archbishop Hunfried (1023–1051).

Excavations have also revealed the foundations of an impressively large palace, probably built between 962 and 973. The structure may have been modeled on Charlemagne's palace at Aachen, which also incorporated a religious foundation. A rounded western entry may suggest Byzantine influence. Magdeburg remained important for the subsequent Ottonian emperors. They celebrated the great Christian feasts there and actively intervened in archiepiscopal elections. Henry II is said to have personally translated (moved) relics of the community's patron saint, Mauritius, processing with them to the cathedral in the dead of winter. The Salians, however, preferred the palace at Goslar and other sites. As Otto's palace fell into disuse, the archbishops, who replaced the emperor as the ruler of the city, built their palace over the ruins of the emperor's.

In the second half of the twelfth century Archibishop Wichmann (1152–1192) was responsible for building a city wall that enclosed both the cathedral complex and the merchant settlement. He also reorganized the streets of the town, laying out the *Breiter Weg* (the Wide Way), which still serves as a major north-south axis. During his administration, or slightly later, the cathedral cloister was also erected in a late Romanesque style. Only the south wing still stands; on Good Friday in 1207 a fire that broke out on the *Breiter Weg* moved south, severely damaging the Ottonian cathedral and the other three wings of the cloister.

Against opposition from the cathedral chapter and the townspeople, who wanted to repair the old building, Archbishop Albrecht II von Käfernburg (1205–1232) began building a new cathedral in the Gothic style. His ambitious project makes a political statement about the importance of the archbishopric even as concessions he was increasingly forced to grant to the town's citizens diminished his own power.

The scholar Ernst Schubert *(Der Magdeburger Dom,* 984) has divided the construction of the cathedral into six phases, marked by changes in workmen and plans. It was finally finished in 1520, just four years before Martin Luther preached the Reformation at Magdeburg in the church of St. John. Already in the first phase, beginning with the laying of the cornerstone at the east end of the building in 1209, the influence of the French Gothic is apparent. Pointed arches are used throughout; the wall surface is membered with columns, including Otto's ancient imports taken over from the previous building; and the ground plan takes the typical French form in which shallow chapels open off the ambulatory ringing the polygonal choir. The transept and first bays of the nave, laid out in the second building phase between about 1220 and 1232, show the influence of the cathedrals then underway at Bamberg and Naumberg. The upper parts of the choir, including the deep gallery at the second level known as the *Bischofsgang* (Bishop's Passage), erected in the third building phase, between 1232 and 1235, reveal the influence of Cistercian Maulbronn via Ebrach and Walkenried. In the fourth campaign (1235–1254), the choir was raised, the transept finished, the nave extended, and aisles widened. The nave was finished in the fifth phase, between 1274 and 1363.

During this last phase, the west portal was also erected, most likely according to its third design. Three large stone figures of apostles, executed in the 1220s for either the west portal or that of the north transept, were mounted. Three additional figures of saints, perhaps made specifically for this site, remained against the piers of the second level of the choir interior without ever being installed in their originally planned position. The Bamberg-influenced figures of the Wise and Foolish Vir-

gins of ca. 1250, now installed on the portal of the so-called *Paradies* (a single bay entry hall on the north end of the north transept) may have been intended for a Last Judgment portal later planned for the west facade; Schubert and the scholar Fritz Bellmann, however, posit their original placement on the predecessor to the present, mid-fifteenth-century choir screen. In its final form of ca. 1310, the west portal shows the mark of the Rayonnant facade at Strasbourg with its thin screen of attenuated, brittle verticals. The single figure on the trumeau (doorpost) represents the Emperor Otto I. The upper parts of the west facade, with sculptures of Christ and the apostles, the Madonna, and Saints Mauritius and Catherine, were finished in the sixth building campaign between 1477 and 1520.

The cathedral's rich sculptural decoration also includes tombs of several of its archbishops, including the monuments for Friedrich von Wettin (d. 1152) and Wichmann von Seeburg (d. 1192), products of the influential twelfth-century bronze-casting workshop at Magdeburg. The elaborate wooden choir stalls with relief scenes from the life of Christ were presumably finished for the consecration of the Gothic building in 1363.

The city government seems to have commissioned Magdeburg's best-known sculptural achievement, the so-called Magdeburg Rider, an equestrian figure that stands between two maidens carrying banners under a baldachin in the main Market Square. Exactly whom the Rider represents is a matter of debate, with Constantine and Otto I as the preferred identifications. Erected probably in the first half of the 1230s, the figure may well symbolize the city's pride in its imperial beginnings and the city government's claim to have received its rights from the emperor. In the second half of the decade, Archbishop Wilbrand (1235–1254) was forced to grant the burghers important concessions toward self-rule in the form of the first city constitution. This did not completely settle long-standing disputes between the archbishop and the town over rights and freedoms, however, and in 1325, Wilbrand's successor was murdered by the townspeople.

BIBLIOGRAPHY

Behling, Lottlise. "Die klugen und törichten Jungfrauen zu Magdeburg: Nachträge und Ergänzungen zur Erforschungen der Magdeburger Skulpturen." *Zeitschrift für Kunstwissenschaft* 8 (1954): 19–42.

Bellmann, Fritz. "Die klugen und törichten Jungfrauen und der Lettner im Magdeburger Dom." *Festschrift für Harald Keller zum sechzigsten Geburtstag dargebracht von seinen Schülern.* Darmstadt: E. Roether, 1963. 87–110.

Beyer, Klaus G., and Hans-Joachim Mrusek. *Drei deutsche Dome: Quedlinburg, Magdeburg, Halberstadt.* 1983. Die bibliophilen Taschenbücher 639. Dortmund: Harenberg Kommunikation, 1992. 93–234.

Binding, Günther. *Deutsche Königspfalzen: von Karl dem Grossen bis Friedrich II. (765–1240).* Darmstadt: Wissenschaftliche Buchgesellschaft, 1996. 155–161.

Claude, Dietrich. *Geschichte des Erzbistums Magdeburg bis in das 12. Jahrhundert.* 2 vols. Mitteldeutsche Forschungen 67. 1–2. Cologne and Vienna: Böhlau, 1972, 1975.

Der Magdeburger Dom: Ottonische Gründung und staufischer Neubau. Ed. Ernst Ullmann. Schriftenreihe der Kommission für Niedersächsische Bau- und Kunstgeschichte bei der Braunschweigischen Wissenschaftlichen Gesellschaft 5. Leipzig: VEB E. A. Seemann Verlag, 1989.

Einem, Herbert von. "Zur Deutung des Magdeburger Reiters." *Zeitschrift für Kunstgeschichte* 16 (1953): 43–56.

Kaufmann, Virginia Roehrig. "The Magdeburg Rider: An Aspect of the Reception of Frederick II's Roman Revival North of the Alps." *Intellectual Life at the Court of Frederick II Hohenstaufen.* Studies in the History of Art 44; Center for Advanced Studies in the Visual Arts Papers 24. Washington D.C.: National Gallery of Art, 1994. 63–88.

Niehr, Klaus. *Die mitteldeutsche Skulptur der ersten Hälfte des 13. Jahrhunderts.* Diss. Universität Bonn, 1987. Artefact 3. Weinheim: VCH, Acta Humaniora, 1992. 108–124, 290–310.

Schubert, Dietrich. *Von Halberstadt nach Meissen: Bildwerke des 13. Jahrhunderts in Thüringen, Sachsen und Anhalt.* DuMont Dokumente. Cologne: DuMont, 1974. 258–264, 285–305.

Schubert, Ernst, with photos by Klaus Günter Beyer. *Der Magdeburger Dom.* 2nd ed. Frankfurt: Weidlich, 1984.

Schwineköper, Berent. "Zur Deutung der Magdeburger Reitersäule." *Festschrift Percy Ernst Schramm zu seinem 70. Geburtstag von Schülern und Freunden zugeeignet.* 2 vols. Wiesbaden: F. Steiner, 1964. 1: 117–142.

Traeger, Jorg. "Der verschollene Name: Zur Deutungsgeschichte des Bamberger Reiters." *Zeitschrift des deutschen Vereins für Kunstwissenschaft* 49/50 (1995/1996): 44–76.

Ullmann, Wolfgang. "Magdeburg, das Konstantinopel des Nordens: Aspekte von Kaiser- und Papstpolitik bei der Gründung des Magdeburger Erzbistums 968." *Jahrbuch für die Geschichte Mittel- und Ostdeutschlands* 21 (1972): 1–44.

Warner, David A. "Henry II at Magdeburg: Kingship, Ritual and the Cult of Saints." *Early Medieval Europe* 3 (1994): 135–166.

Joan A. Holladay and David A. Warner

SEE ALSO

Bamberg; Cistercian Art and Architecture; Gothic Art and Architecture; Iconographies, Innovative—Equestrian Figures; Iconographies, Innovative—Wise and Foolish Virgins; Liturgy, Furniture; Maulbronn; Naumburg; Otto I; Ottonian Art and Architecture; Town Planning and Urbanism

Maget Kron, Der

The title of this verse legend, "The Crown of the Virgin" (or "The Crown of the Virgins"), refers to the Virgin Mary receiving a martyr crown from God in the form of a *Marienpreis* (laudatory poem to Mary), a *Marienleben* (life of Mary), followed by twelve *Legends of the Virgin Martyrs*. The poems of the virgin martyrs are *Katharina, Barbara, Dorothea, Margareta, Ursula, Agathe, Agnes, Lucia, Caecilia, Cristina, Anastasia,* and *Juliana.* Intended as a monograph for the daily *Tischlesung* (reading at mealtime), these approximately 8,400 verses were composed by a Cistercian nun soon after the first printing of the *South German Heiligenleben* (1471 or 1472) in Augsburg. The legends borrow partially from Latin sources (such as the *Ave Maria* and the *Legenda aurea*) and from legends already in verse, for example, *Barbara*—which by 1425 had been preserved as a single legend in Konstanz—from a manuscript of the *Alsatian Legenda aurea* (ca. 1450), as well as from another version of the same *Alsatian Legenda aurea* (manuscript ca. 1450 from Lichtental). But the major sources for all the legends were the *Alsatian Legenda aurea* (originally ca. 1360), the *Heiligenleben* (ca. 1420), and the Latin *Legenda aurea.* Although *Katharina* is lost now, *Barbara* has some 650 verses, *Dorothea* circa 450, and *Margareta* about 280.

The author, who found verses more pleasant for extensive reading aloud, may well have been the successor to a *Lesemeisterin* and *Schreibmeisterin* (reading and writing mistress) Sister Margarethe, called Regula (d. 1478), in the Cistercian cloister Lichtental near Baden-Baden, to whose monograph in prose, the *Buch von den heiligen Mägden und Frauen* (comprising fifty-seven female saints, ca. 1460), *Der Maget kron* is closely related. While she obviously worked diligently at her poetry, there have been objections raised to her "false rhymes."

BIBLIOGRAPHY

Feistner, Edith. *Historische Typologie der deutschen Heiligenlegende des Mittelalters von der Mitte des 12. Jahrhunderts bis zur Reformation.* Wiesbaden: Reichert, 1995, pp. 249–257, 292–306.

Kunze, Konrad, ed. *Die Elsässische Legenda aurea,* vol. 2. *Das Sondergut.* Tübingen: Niemeyer, 1983, pp. 91–93; 94–102.

Rosenfeld, Hans-Friedrich. "Der maget krone." In *Die deutsche Literatur des Mittelalters. Verfasserlexikon,* ed. Kurt Ruh et al. Berlin: de Gruyter, 1985, vol. 5, coll. 1148–1152.

Sibylle Jefferis

SEE ALSO

Heiligenleben; Legenda Aurea, Alsatian; *Mariendichtungen*

Magic

Between 800 and 1500 C.E., many different kinds of practices may be called magic. Some were ancient customs that still survive here and there as folklore and superstitions. Others involved more complicated rituals and secret knowledge of hidden powers in nature and the invisible world of the intellect and spirits. Astrology (which overlapped with astronomy in the Middle Ages) offered possibilities for magic, as did alchemy. Although commonly used magic is found in manuscripts written in Old High and Middle High German, Low German, and Anglo-Saxon, more learned forms appear in manuscripts written in Latin.

Among the earliest known magical practices are charms *(Zaubersprüche)* and amulets used for protection against sicknesses, to stop bleeding, and to help with other troubles like a lame horse or theft. Distinctive to Germanic regions were threats to health and peace of mind from disease-causing worms and elves, which could be staved off by such domestic magic.

Beginning in the eleventh century and intensifying significantly in the twelfth and thirteenth, magic reputed to derive from secret books was strongly denounced by Christian church authorities. After the translation of new knowledge from Arabic sources, widely educated medieval writers like Albert the Great at Cologne

(1193–1280) sometimes succeeded in distinguishing which uses were safe and which were dangerous. But authorities had long agreed that the materials of nature— metals and precious stones, plants, animals—as well as words, contained hidden powers (virtues) of a surprising variety. A sapphire might be used to relieve an eye problem, stop a feverish sweat, free a prisoner, or induce a peaceful reconciliation. Rituals intended to focus the inherent powers in nature on specific problems might or might not involve demonic powers in the process. Lynn Thorndike and others have argued that science itself developed out of medieval *experimenta* with the powers in nature.

The planets too possessed hidden powers that influenced human events and natural phenomena. Accurate astrological calculations of the exact location of the stars and planets in relation to the signs of the zodiac and constellations made it possible to predict favorable and unfavorable times for marriages, battles, or meetings with powerful people. German Emperor Frederick II (d. 1246), like many of his noble peers, retained astrologers, including Michael Scot, in his court. Alchemy, the art of transmutations, also lent itself to magical purposes, since success at producing the elixir or philosopher's stone promised unlimited wealth and youth. Thus, alchemists often wrote down their secrets in highly encrypted forms.

In imaginative literature such as the Middle High German *Nibelungenlied,* magic attaches to objects like a sword, a cloak of invisibility, and dragon's blood. In Gottfried von Straßburg's retelling of the courtly romance of *Tristan und Isolde,* magical healing and a love potion determine the fate of the noble couple. The work of evil magicians is overcome by famous knights in Wolfram von Eschenbach's *Parzival* and the Middle High German verse novel *Wigalois.*

The figure of the magician as a person of exceptional abilities in manipulating secret powers for specific purposes emerges in the fifteenth century. A recently edited Munich manuscript (Bayerische Staatsbibliothek, no. clm 849) displays typical purposes for which a magician might conjure spirits or demons: to know the future or other hidden things (divination), create illusions as of a banquet or a fast horse, and manipulate people's emotions or behavior. The magician claims to be able to make a woman passionately desire him, cause a person to hate another, secure the favor of some powerful person, or make someone appear physically ridiculous or ill. A different kind of learned, ritual magic was intended to bring intellectual gifts, knowledge, and visions to the scholar-magician who underwent a rigorous discipline and elaborate ceremonies to acquire powers and specific knowledge in the liberal arts. Whereas conjuring demons for low purposes was labeled black magic or necromancy, conjuring with images to obtain intellectual powers constituted the *ars notoria,* or "angelic" magic, which some argued was entirely beneficent and positive. Nevertheless, at the end of the fourteenth century, people began to be condemned to torture and death for what were believed to be magical and demonic practices, activities that associated them in the minds of their accusers like the authors of the *Malleus Maleficarum* with demons (making contracts with the devil, flying, summoning devils, etc.).

How medieval Germans understood or practiced magic differs from one era and cultural environment to another. Old practices like reciting charms or divining a person's future in some object or natural phenomenon do not disappear in the later centuries of this period but continue to appear in books of medical recipes or survive alongside utilitarian information and prayers in manor books, such as the Wolfsthurn Castle manuscript described by Kieckhefer.

BIBLIOGRAPHY

Cockayne, Thomas Oswald. *Leechdoms, Wortcunning and Starcraft of Early England.* rev. ed. 3 vols. 1864–1866; rpt. London: Holland, 1961.

Fanger, Claire, ed. *Conjuring Spirits: Texts and Traditions of Medieval Ritual Magic.* University Park: University of Pennsylvania Press, 1998.

Hampp, Irmgard. *Beschwörung, Segen, Gebet: Untersuchungen zum Zauberspruch aus dem Berich der Volksheilkunde.* Stuttgart: Silberburg, 1961.

Harmening, Dieter. *Superstitio: Überlieferungs- und theoriegeschichtliche Untersuchungen zur kirchlich-theologischen Aberglaubensliteratur des Mittelalters.* Berlin: Schmidt, 1979.

Kieckhefer, Richard. *Magic in the Middle Ages.* Cambridge: Cambridge University Press, 1990.

———. *Forbidden Rite: A Necromancer's Manual of the Fifteenth Century.* Phoenix Mill, England: Sutton, 1997.

Peters, Edward. *The Magician, the Witch, and the Law.* Philadelphia: University of Pennsylvania Press, 1978.

Thorndike, Lynn. *The History of Magic and Experimental Science.* 8 vols. New York: Macmillan and Columbia University Press, 1923–1963.

Lea T. Olsan

SEE ALSO

Albertus Magnus; Charms; Gottfried von Straßburg; Magic and Charms, Dutch; *Nibelungenlied;* Wolfram von Eschenbach

Magic and Charms, Dutch

The study of Middle Dutch magical writings has benefited greatly from the publication of the *Repertorium van de Middelnederlandse Artes-literatuur* (Jansen-Sieben, 1989), an inventory of Middle Dutch *Fachliteratur* (technical writing) up to 1600. The corpus of extant manuscripts reveals a variety of magical writings, ranging from "white" (constructive) to "black" (destructive) magic. A substantial number of magical texts (charms, love potions, medical magic, herbal magic) has survived in a fifteenth-century manuscript preserved at Ghent (University Library, manuscript no. 697). In another fifteenth-century manuscript (London, Wellcome Institute, manuscript no. 517), a large collection of Latin alchemical, medical, and technical treatises is interspersed with some twenty-four Middle Dutch magical recipes (love magic, adjurations, incantations, herbal magic, magical experiments). A third collection of Middle Dutch magical recipes has survived in a fifteenth-century manuscript at Hattem (Streekmuseum Hattem Voermanhuis, manuscript no. C 5). The impact of magic on medieval society can best be measured by the numerous denunciations and condemnations of magical practice voiced by the authors of Middle Dutch penitentials and catechetical treatises. According to these writers, the believers and practitioners of the *artes magicae* (magic arts) will burn in hell because they sinned against the first commandment or because they have chosen the devil above God in exchange for magical knowledge. These admonitions indicate that magic occupied an important place in the Middle Ages. Recent research has propagated the study of Middle Dutch magical writings as an important contribution to the understanding of medieval literature and culture.

BIBLIOGRAPHY

Braekman, Willy L. "Middelnederlandse zegeningen, bezweringsformulieren en toverplanten." In *Verslagen en Mededelingen van de Koninklijke Vlaamse Academie voor Taal- en Letterkunde.* The Hague: Staatsdrukkerij Uitgeverijbedrijf, 1963, pp. 275–386.

———. "Magische experimenten en toverpraktijken uit een Middelnederlands handschrift." In *Verslagen en*

Mededelingen van de Koninklijke Vlaamse Academie voor Taal- en Letterkunde. The Hague: Staatsdrukkerij Uitgeverijbedrijf, 1966, pp. 53–118.

———. Een merkwaardige collectie "secreten" uit de vijftiende eeuw." In *Verslagen en Mededelingen van de Koninklijke Vlaamse Academie voor Taal- en Letterkunde.* The Hague: Staatsdrukkerij Uitgeverijbedrijf, 1987, pp. 270–287.

———. *Middeleeuwse witte en zwarte magie in het Nederalnds taalgebied.* Gent: Koninklijke Academie voor Nederlandse Taal- en Letterkunde, 1997.

———, ed. *Den Sack der Consten (1528).* Bruges: Van de Wiele, 1989.

———. ed. *Dat Batement van Recepten. Een Secreetboek uit de zestiende Eeuw.* Brussels: UFSAL, 1990.

Jansen-Sieben, Ria. *Repertorium van Middelnederlandse Artes-literatuur.* Utrecht: HES, 1989.

Lie, Orlanda S. H. "Die hexe in het perspectief van Middelnederlandse toverboeken." *Madoc* 4 (1990): 212–220.

———. "Literaire verwijzingen in Middelnederlandse magische teksten." *De nieuwe taalgids* 85 (1992): 234–246.

———. "De wereld van middeleeuwse magische recepten." *Literatuur* 10 (1993–1994): 209–216.

van Haver, Jozef. *Nederlandse incantatieliteratuur. Een gecommentarieerd compendium van Nederlandse bezweringsformules.* Gent: Koninklijke Vlaamse Academie voor Taal- en Letterkunde, 1964.

Orlanda S. H. Lie

SEE ALSO
Charms; Magic

Mainz

Medieval Mainz grew up within the walls of the Roman military base and provincial capital Mogontiacum, located at the point where the Main River flows into the Rhine. In the Carolingian period, the city became the ecclesiastical center of Germany under Archbishop Saint Boniface (746/747–754). Boniface's successor, Lul, succeeded in getting the office of archbishop, which had originally been granted to Boniface personally, permanently associated with Mainz. Under Charlemagne, the archbishop of Mainz supervised a large number of suffragan bishops, governed the largest ecclesiastical province in the Western world, and was primate of the church in Germania. As chancellor, the archbishop represented the emperor, and as the highest-ranking elector, he cast the first vote for king. The accumulation of appointments and honors associated with the position of archbishop of Mainz made this one of the most desirable episcopal sees, but it also presented problems for the city in its progress toward self-government.

With the erection of the cathedral, Archbishop Willigis (975–1011) created a new spiritual center in the city. In the Ottonian and Salian eras, the establishment of cloisters, parish churches, and other foundations also depended largely on the bishop.

By the early Gothic, which should be considered Mainz's golden age, the artistic initiative of the archbishop had given way to that of the citizens and the monastic orders. The union of Rhenish cities in 1254, the privileges extracted by the city government from the archbishop, and the increasing wealth of the city's patriciate created the necessary conditions for extensive building activity. Archbishop Siegfried III (d. 1249) granted the citizens the right to elect their government and handle its finances, which made the city virtually independent of the archbishop's rule. In the next century this would lead to constant discord between the city's secular and religious leaders. The conflict peaked in 1462 in a catastrophe that brought the city's economy as well as its artistic production to a standstill. Archbishop Adolf II of Nassau conquered the burning city after a bloody ten-hour battle in its streets. Eight hundred men, including Johannes Gutenberg, were banished, and all rights gained by the city since the thirteenth century were revoked.

Although destroyed five times by fire, the cathedral of St. Martin still reflects the same plan as the first building erected by Archbishop Willigis. Its basilical form is modeled on that of Old St. Peter's in Rome, with the main choir in the west preceded by a transept. Like the earlier church at Fulda (791–819), also a foundation of Boniface, and the later churches at Bamberg, Augsburg, and Regensburg, the cathedral at Mainz combines this "reverse orientation" with a secondary choir in the east. The erection of a church dedicated to the Virgin of the Steps (St. Maria ad gradus) on axis outside the east choir also depends on the Roman model; with the cathedral it provided an appropriate space for the royal coronation ceremony, which took place seven times in Mainz. In 975 Willigis had the pope confirm the right of the archbishop of Mainz to crown the German kings.

On the day before the consecration in 1009, the cathedral burned; it was quickly rebuilt by Willigis's successor, Bardo, and consecrated in 1036. The eastern parts and the nave were rebuilt after a second fire in 1081. About 1200 the dilapidated vaults of the nave were replaced and a new west choir built on a triconch (with three apses) plan. The addition of side chapels with tracery windows along the aisles between 1279 and 1320 introduced the Gothic architectural vocabulary. At this point the cathedral had attained the state in which it remains today.

The unusual cycle of medieval archbishops' tombs documents the continuity of episcopal power. The two oldest preserved tomb reliefs show Siegfried III von Eppstein (d. 1249) and Peter von Aspelt (d. 1320) crowning two and three smaller kings, respectively, in a unique tomb iconography. The later tombs follow an almost formulaic type that continues into the seventeenth century: a Gothic arch in low relief frames the fully vested archbishop holding a crosier and a book. The episcopal power displayed by the tombs reveals the self-consciousness of the powerful archbishops. Rather than serving a primarily memorial or liturgical function, the tombs represent the continuity of the political institution of the office of archbishop.

Looting and destruction have been responsible for the loss of much of the cathedral's medieval decoration including Willigis's massive gold cross weighing six hundred pounds, all the stained glass windows, and the western rood screen, of which only fragments remain. The preserved bronze doors from about 1100 attest to the splendor of the church's furnishings. The inscription on the doors emphasizes that these were the first metal doors since Charlemagne's time, made by Master Berenger for Archbishop Willigis.

One of the churches in the cathedral complex, St. Johannis, the supposed predecessor of the cathedral, stands outside the cathedral's west choir. The earliest source mentioning this church dates from about 600; it tells of the king's daughter Berthoara, who supported the bishop Sidonius in the building of the church. In 754 the body of the martyred St. Boniface was prepared here for burial in Fulda. The building as reerected after World War II dates in large part to the building campaign of Archbishop Hatto (891–913), who simultaneously erected the church at Reichenau Oberzell. In both churches the individual spaces are separated by strongly projecting piers. As at the cathedral, the primary choir and transept at St. Johannis are in the west.

The archbishop's palace chapel dedicated to St. Gotthard (1137) is attached to the cathedral. The four supports divide each of the two stories of the chapel into nine bays, with the middle bay left open to allow contact between the two stories. The structure thus belongs in the tradition of palace chapels with an identical ground plan attached to cathedrals, as at Speyer and formerly at Trier and Cologne.

Apart from three eighteenth-century examples, all the churches of Mainz were erected in the few decades around 1300, when sixteen large-scale projects were realized. Among the buildings still standing today, St. Stephan's was built as a collegiate church in the first half of the fourteenth century. The wealthy citizens, eager to embellish their city with larger, more modern houses of worship, rebuilt the parish churches of St. Emmeran, for which an indulgence dated 1296 exists, St. Quintin (1300–1330), and St. Christoph (1292–1352). The cloister churches of the Poor Clares (about 1334), the Rich Clares (begun 1272), and the Carmelites (second half of the fourteenth century) still stand; destroyed are those of the Dominicans (mid-thirteenth century), the Franciscans (begun 1253), the Augustinians (founded before 1260), the Teutonic Order (1302), the Carthusians (1330), Our Lady (begun 1285), the Magdalens, as well as Dalheim (third quarter of the thirteenth century) and St. Agnes, for which indulgences in favor of the building project were issued between 1274 and 1295. The side chapels along the aisles in the cathedral and the west choir of St. Johannis also date in this period of rich building activity.

Among these Gothic churches St. Quintin, which is already mentioned in 774 as a parish church, is the oldest foundation. The plan shows the optimal use of the small space available. As at St. Stephan's and the church of the Virgin, the new building, begun about 1300 and finished in 1330, uses the hall church form favored in Mainz. The type was transferred to Mainz from St. Elizabeth's in Marburg via other sites in Hesse. The relatively short nave flanked by the tall aisles creates the unusual effect of a light-flooded, airy cube; the destroyed church of the Virgin outside the cathedral must have produced a similar impression.

St. Stephan's is the largest church after the cathedral. Founded by Willigis on an exposed hill inside the city walls, the church had become structurally unsound by the middle of the thirteenth century. The new building was financed by numerous indulgences, whose dates between 1257 and 1338 establish the period of construction. This building too takes the form of a hall church, but in the more typical oblong shape than the shortened churches of St. Quentin and the Virgin. In addition, St. Stephan's has a transept as in the Hessian hall churches at

Marburg, Haina, and Friedberg. Like the cathedral and St. Johannis, it exhibits a second choir in the west, which is accentuated by a tower. A late Gothic cloister with fine net vaults was erected between 1462 and 1499.

The cloister of the Antonite monks is first mentioned in 1334; it was taken over in 1620 by the Poor Clares and today is referred to by their name. Because the Antonites dedicated themselves to care of the sick and raising pigs, they chose a site outside the city center, although still within the walls. The small aisleless church in the Gothic style is unusual for its completely intact vault painting, executed before 1350. Framed by painted tracery, saints, apostles, and the fathers of the church surround the figure of Christ, who presides over the assembly from the choir vault.

Early-fifteenth-century paintings grace the choir vaults of the Carmelite church. These represent in grisaille the suffering Christ surrounded by angels and prophets. The church, erected between 1326 and 1404, has the long choir typical of churches of the Mendicant orders, which needed more room for the choir stalls; the basilical nave is relatively short.

When St. Maria ad gradus, the church within the cathedral complex dedicated to the Virgin, burned in 1285, the decision was made to rebuild in a high Gothic style; the citizens supported the new building with unusually generous donations. Finished in 1311, the new church, erected over a nearly square plan, provided, with the neighboring cathedral, a defining element in the city's silhouette until its destruction by French bombardment in 1793. In contrast to the other, undecorated churches of Mainz, the church of the Virgin possessed richly decorated portals; the sculpture is close in style to that of the Naumburg Master.

The Roman walls within which the medieval city developed traced a square of about one kilometer's distance on each side. This area sufficed for the city's growth into the nineteenth century, with the exception of a single extension along the Rhine in the thirteenth century. By 1300 some 20,000–25,000 people lived in the city, whose western slopes provided space for orchards and even vineyards. Most of the city's gates pierced the east wall, in order to accommodate trade from the ship traffic along the Rhine. With the exception of the Iron Tower (about 1200), the Wood Tower (fourteenth century), and short passages of the east wall between them, the city wall was entirely demolished in the eighteenth century.

After 1300 a sort of citizens' center developed to the northeast of the cathedral quarter. Here the market hall, the hospital, the city hall, and the surrounding market and business district clearly expressed the aspirations of the citizenry. The market hall, dated about 1320, was also used for large public festivals. Unlike the more typical wooden market halls with open sides, that at Mainz was a defensible building in stone, reflecting both the value of the goods stored there and the importance of trade in the city's economy. Only the sculptural decoration—reliefs representing the seven electors and the king from the crenellations of the building's upper defenses—is preserved.

The hospital dedicated to the Holy Spirit from the second quarter of the thirteenth century is one of the few preserved medieval hospitals in Germany. Its two-story elevation is comparable to that of St. John's Hospital in Niederweisel in Hesse. The lower story, originally a seven-aisled hall, probably served as the infirmary.

Despite conditions that were sometimes conducive, no particular style of painting, sculpture, goldsmith work, or manuscript illumination developed in Mainz, and the idea of a Middle Rhenish school, cultivated in art historical scholarship for decades, must be discarded. The patrons of Mainz repeatedly looked to other centers for artists, for example, the renowned Naumburg Master, who sculpted the cathedral's now fragmentary west choir screen before 1250. Characteristic for the art of the city is the constant reprocessing of new influences from Burgundy, France, Bohemia, Germany, and the Netherlands; works from Mainz are always up-to-date without having a typical local character.

Kerstin Merkel

BIBLIOGRAPHY

Arens, Fritz. *Das goldene Mainz: Bauten und Bilder aus zweitausend Jahren.* Mainz: Matthias-Grünewald-Verlag, 1952.

———. *Die Kunstdenkmäler der Stadt Mainz,* 1: Kirchen St. Agnes bis Hl. Kreuz. Die Kunstdenkmäler von Rheinland-Pfalz 4,1, ed. Werner Bornheim gen. Schilling. Munich: Deutscher Kunstverlag, 1961.

Brück, Anton P. *Mainz von Verlust der Stadtfreiheit bis zum Ende des dreissigjährigen Krieges (1462–1648).* Geschichte der Stadt Mainz 5. Düsseldorf: W. Rau, 1972.

Brush, Kathryn Louise. "The West Choir Screen at Mainz Cathedral: Studies in Program, Patronage and Meaning." (Ph.d. diss., Brown University, 1987.

Denkmaltopographie Bundesrepublik Deutschland; Kulturdenkmäler in Rheinland-Pfalz 2.2. Düsseldorf: Schwann, 1988.

Falck, Ludwig. *Mainz im frühen und hohen Mittelalter (Mitte 5. Jh. bis 1244).* Geschichte der Stadt Mainz 2. Düsseldorf: W. Rau, 1972.

——. *Mainz in seiner Blütezeit als Freie Stadt (1244–1328).* Geschichte der Stadt Mainz 3. Düsseldorf: W. Rau, 1973.

Hause, Melissa Thorsen. "A Place in Sacred History: Coronation Ritual and Architecture in Ottonian Mainz." *Journal of Ritual Studies,* no. 1 (1992): 133–157.

Nagel, Ewald. *Stadt Mainz: Altstadt.* Herausgegeben im Auftrag des Kultusministeriums vom Landesamt für Denkmalpflege.

Neeb, Ernst, and Fritz Arens. *Die Kunstdenkmäler in Hessen, Stadtkreis Mainz.* vol. 2, part 2: *Bestehende und verschwundene Mainzer Kirchen.* Darmstadt: A. Bergsträsser Nachfolger, 1940.

Kerstin Merkel

SEE ALSO

Fulda; Gothic Art and Architecture; Marburg; Reichenau

Mande, Henrik (d. 1431)

Exponent of the Modern Devotion and author of Middle Dutch religious prose treatises, Mande was born in Dordrecht and worked as a copyist in the service of the counts of Holland. Before 1382 he went to Deventer and Zwolle when the Brethren of the Common Life began to spread in those cities. In 1395 he became a redditus (canon regular without ordination) in the newly founded monastery of Windesheim. There he worked as a copyist and illuminator of manuscripts. In 1431 he died while on a journey in Beverwijk (Holland).

Mande wrote fourteen relatively short treatises, of which twelve (or eleven?) survive. As an author, Mande relies heavily on writings of spiritual masters like Hugo of St. Victor, Hadewijch, and Jan van Ruusbroec. Therefore many of his treatises are read like reports. Important themes of his spirituality are the inward revelation and spiritual sincerity of living. Man has to turn into himself to find the inner truth, and he has to live without hypocrisy according to the truth that gradually is revealed to him.

Mande's numerous visions of the state of the dead made him a widely known but also disputed attraction. Most famous was his *Apocalypsis.* In this apocalyptic vision, Mande sees saints clothed by their virtues in heaven. Among them he sees a procession of the deceased leaders and former brethren and sisters of the Modern Devotion. In its imagery, vivacity, and colorfulness this vision reminds the modern reader of Van Eyck's famous painting *Lam Gods (Lamb of God)* in the cathedral of Ghent.

BIBLIOGRAPHY

De Baere, Guido. "Hendrik Mandes «Liber de sapida sapientia» teruggevonden?" *Ons Geestelijk Erf* 63 (1989): 288–295.

Een minnentlike claege, ed. Thom Mertens. Erfstadt: Lukassen, 1984.

Een spiegel der waerheit, ed. Thom Mertens. Erfstadt: Lukassen, 1984.

Mertens, Thom. "Hendrik Mande." *Ons Geestelijk Erf* 52 (1978): 363–396 [bibliography].

——. *Hendrik Mande (?–1431), teksthistorische en literairhistorische studies.* Nijmegen: [n.p.], 1986.

——. "Hendrik Mande als visionair." *Millennium* 3 (1989): 116–124.

Post, Regnerus R. *The Modern Devotion.* Leiden: Brill, 1968, pp. 331–337.

Spaapen, B. "Henri Mande." In *Dictionnaire de Spiritualité,* ed. Marcel Viller. Paris: Beauchesne, 1969, vol. 7, coll. 222–225.

Vanden licht der waerheit, ed. Thom Mertens. Erfstadt: Lukassen, 1984.

Visser, Gerard. *Hendrik Mande: Bijdrage tot de kennis der Noord-Nederlandsche mystiek.* The Hague: M. Nijhoff, 1899.

Thom Mertens

SEE ALSO

Devotio Moderna; Hadewijch; Jan van Ruusbroec

Manfred of Sicily (1232–1266)

The illegitimate son of Frederick II Hohenstaufen, Manfred attempted to reconstitute the family's fortunes in Italy and Sicily after his father's death. Inheriting many of his father's talents, including a passion for falconry, Manfred also inherited papal hostility to the Hohenstaufen, and his attempts to establish himself in Italy faced the formidable opposition of the papacy. It was this papal antagonism that would bring about the demise of Manfred and his family and introduce a new power, and new complications, to southern Italy and Sicily.

At his death in 1250, Frederick was succeeded by his son Conrad IV, and Manfred was established as the prince of Taranto and regent in Italy. It was Manfred's energy, and ambition, that secured Hohenstaufen control in the south during Conrad's absence in Germany. So great was Manfred's success that Conrad felt able to negotiate with Pope Innocent IV from a position of strength but also felt obligated to limit Manfred's grab for power in Sicily. Conrad's death in 1254 and the youth of his heir, the two-year-old Conradin, offered Manfred the opportunity to establish himself as the king of Sicily and the opportunity to create a Mediterranean empire.

At first supportive of Conradin, Manfred soon removed this support and was crowned king of Sicily in 1258. He was emboldened to take these steps because of the support he found among the Sicilian nobility, a result of his own efforts in that regard, and his victories in the field. Indeed, Innocent IV was at first willing to come to terms with Manfred and an agreement was reached between the two that saw Manfred's titles and lands restored and the assertion of papal rights over Sicily. But neither side was willing to honor the terms, and the old papal-Hohenstaufen feud was revived. Manfred rose against the pope, an offensive that led to the capture of the royal treasury and a great victory in Foggia in late 1254. Shortly after his victory, Manfred's cause received a further boost with the death of Innocent. Although the new pope, Alexander IV, was no more favorable to Manfred, momentum was on the latter's side. Throughout the later 1250s, Manfred improved his position in Sicily—securing his patrimony, founding new cities, and reviving the University of Naples—and expanded his power throughout Italy.

Manfred's success in Italy inspired him to look beyond the peninsula. He involved himself in the fractious politics of the eastern empire and supported one of the Latin pretenders to imperial power in Constantinople. The restoration of Greek control of Constantinople in the person of the emperor Michael Palaeologus provided military defeat for Manfred and his allies but also provided Manfred with a means to escape papal censure. Manfred vowed to launch a crusade to restore Baldwin II, the deposed Latin emperor, to the throne in Constantinople, a promise that did not ease tensions with the pope but did find Manfred a great ally in Baldwin. Manfred was further strengthened by successful marriage alliances with eastern powers and with King James of Aragon, so that by the early 1260s he was at the height of his power.

Manfred's successes in the broader Mediterranean and, especially, in central and northern Italy increased papal animosity toward the king. Negotiations with various princes in northern Europe had been going on for several years when Pope Urban IV came to terms with Charles of Anjou, brother of King Louis IX of France. Although the pope had found a champion in Charles and preached crusade against Manfred, it was the Hohenstaufen king who took the initiative against his rival. But Manfred called off his campaign with Urban's death in the hope that the new pope, Clement IV, would be more accommodating. Unfortunately for Manfred this was not the case. During the cessation of hostilities Charles secured his place in Italy and received support from the people of Rome and a number of Manfred's allies. In early 1266, Charles moved south and was met by Manfred at Benevento on February 26. In that battle, Manfred's army was routed but in the face of defeat Manfred fought valiantly and died in battle. Charles granted Manfred a burial with honor even though as an excommunicate he was denied church burial. Charles's victory at Benevento was a serious blow to Hohenstaufen fortunes and witnessed the death or capture of many Hohenstaufen supporters. And although Charles would eventually defeat Conradin, Charles too would fall victim to the tumultuous politics of Sicily in the so-called Sicilian Vespers.

BIBLIOGRAPHY

Abulafia, David. *Frederick II: A Medieval Emperor.* Oxford: Oxford University Press, 1988, pp. 406–428.

Housely, Norman. *The Italian Crusades: The Papal-Angevin Alliance and the Crusades against Christian Lay Powers, 1254–1343.* Oxford: Clarendon, 1982.

Leuschner, Joachim. *Germany in the Later Middle Ages,* trans. Sabine MacCormack. Amsterdam: North-Holland, 1980, pp. 65–90.

Runciman, Steve. *The Sicilian Vespers: A History of the Mediterranean World in the Later Thirteenth Century.* Cambridge: Cambridge University Press, 1958, pp. 26–95.

Michael Frassetto

SEE ALSO
Conradin of Hohenstaufen; Frederick II; Staufen

Manuals, Artists', and Modelbooks

During the Middle Ages, the traditions of craftsmanship and apprentice training dominated the production of art objects. Accordingly, few medieval sources on the practice of the arts survive. The extant materials fall into two categories: technical manuals and modelbooks.

The technical writings provide recipes for paints and explain the technological procedures for arts such as metalworking. The most famous example of such a manual is the treatise *On Divers Arts (De diversis artibus)*. It is thought to have been composed between 1110 and 1140 by the German Benedictine monk and metal craftsman Roger of Helmarshausen. It contains three sections on painting, stained glass, and metalworking.

The second category consists of modelbooks that record patterns for decorative designs and figural subjects. Medieval examples survive from the tenth century into the Renaissance throughout Europe. Sometimes they are groups of leaves bound into a manuscript with diverse textual contents; at other times they form discrete books. Usually, the subjects are rendered as outline drawings. Several interesting examples come from German regions such as three leaves in a twelfth-century manuscript from Einsiedeln (Stiftsbibliothek, manuscript no. 112) and six leaves in a thirteenth-century miscellany from Saxony (Wolfenbüttel, Herzog August Bibliothek, manuscript no. Aug. oct. 61/62). While both of these modelbooks primarily depict figural motifs, the fifteenth-century Göttingen Model Book and a similar manuscript in Berlin represent a combination of artists' manual and modelbook. They contain written instruction complemented by painted illustration of the sequential steps in depicting acanthus foliage and diapered backgrounds. These varied types of manuals and modelbooks of German provenance demonstrate some of the working methods of German artists in the Middle Ages.

BIBLIOGRAPHY

Avril, François. *La Technique de l'enluminure d'après les textes mé dié vaux: Essai de bibliographie.* Paris: Bibliothèque Nationale, 1967.

Gullick, Michael. "A Bibliography of Medieval Painting Treatises." *Making the Medieval Book: Techniques of Production,* ed. Linda Brownrigg. Los Altos Hills: Calif. Anderson-Lovelace, 1995, pp. 241–244.

Lehmann-Haupt, Hellmut. *The Göttingen Model Book: A Facsimile Edition and Translations of a Fifteenth-Century Illuminators' Manual.* Columbia: University of Missouri Press, 1972.

Ploss, E. E. *Ein Buch von alten Farben.* Heidelberg: H. Moos, 1962.

Scheller, R. W. *A Survey of Medieval Model Books.* Haarlem: Erven F. Bohn, 1963.

Theophilus. *On Divers Arts. The Treatise of Theophilus,* ed. John G. Hawthorne; trans. Cyril Stanley Smith. Chicago: University of Chicago Press, 1963.

Thompson, D. V. "Trial Index to Some Unpublished Sources for the History of Medieval Craftsmanship." *Speculum* 10 (1935): 410–431.

Karen Gould

SEE ALSO
Einsiedeln

Manuscripts, Painting and Production

During the Middle Ages, books were constructed, copied, and illuminated by hand. Throughout this period, the basic materials and techniques remained fairly constant. Until the late Middle Ages with the advent of paper, the support for the manuscript was parchment. This material is the skin of an animal, often sheep or calf, that was soaked in a lime solution, scraped, and stretched to form a smooth, sturdy writing surface. The parchment leaves were trimmed to the size desired for a particular book. An open leaf, or bifolio, was folded in half to form two folios. The front side of the folio is called the *recto*, while the back side is the *verso*. Each *recto* and *verso* are the equivalent of modern pages, but most medieval manuscripts are numbered by the folio.

Groups of bifolios were assembled to make gatherings. The parchment bifolios were placed so that hair side faced hair side and flesh side faced flesh side. Gatherings usually consisted of four bifolios (eight folios, or sixteen pages) or five bifolios (ten folios, or twenty pages), although other size gatherings were possible. Sometimes one or more folios were added or excised, creating an irregular gathering.

The next stage was the layout of the manuscript's contents. Placement of the text and provision of spaces for decorative initials and illustrations were blocked out on the folios. The text could be in one, two, or more columns. In the later Middle Ages, the text layout often included columns for textual commentary or glosses. Illuminations could fall within a column or could span more than one column. They could be full-page or could occupy a portion of the page height. Usually the size and placement of textual and decorative elements was based on geometrical proportions in relation to the folio or bifolio. Rulings established the layout. Small prickings in the margins provided points of alignment for the straightedge. The marking instrument varied. In the early medieval period the rulings were in hard point, leaving only a ridge or furrow on the parchment. Beginning

Stages of manuscript production in the roundels framing St. Michael with monks of the Michelsberg cloister. St. Ambrose, *De officiis ministrorum* (Bamberg, Staatsbibliothek, Ms. Patr. 5, fol. 1v). *Photograph: Staatsbibliothek Bamberg*

around the twelfth century, ruling was usually done in lead point. By the fourteenth century, ink ruling became common.

The scribes then copied the text using quill pens and brown iron gall ink. Decorative initials, illumination, and marginal ornamentation was painted after the text was copied. Often specialized artists, the illuminators, did this work although scribes often added decorative initials or line endings. In its most simple form, the embellishment consisted of larger initials, often in alternating colors of red or blue. More lavish illumination utilized gold leaf for backgrounds and a wide range of pigments. The paints were water-based and the pigments derived from natural substances such as earth-colored ochres and browns and plant dyes. A number of medieval artists' manuals preserve recipes for the paints.

The completed manuscript was ready for binding. The gatherings were stacked in order on a sewing frame with

thongs secured tightly along the manuscript's spine. The sewing went through the gatherings and around the thongs, which were then inserted into wooden covers. Leather usually covered the wood; it was often tooled with figural or decorative designs. Metal bosses, clasps, and ornaments could be attached. Some liturgical manuscripts had covers with metalwork, ivory, and jewels. The upper cover of the Gospel Book of Otto III (Munich, Bayerische Staatsbibliothek, no. Clm. 4453), for example, has an ivory panel surrounded by jewels to make a rich "treasure" binding. Many German Romanesque and Gothic manuscripts retain their tooled and stamped leather bindings that can often be attributed to individual craftsmen or workshops.

Two manuscripts of German origin contain the most complete medieval illustrations of the manuscript production process. In an early twelfth-century copy of Ambrose, *De officiis ministrorum* (Bamberg, Staatsbibliothek, manuscript no. Patr. 5) from the Benedictine monastery of Michelsburg near Bamberg, roundels depicting stages of book production surround a prefatory miniature. The bust-length figures of monks, drawn in brown and red ink, are shown stretching and trimming the parchment sheets, cutting a quill pen, scraping out a copying error, using a sewing frame to join the gatherings along the spine, preparing the boards, and attaching metal clasps to the wooden cover of the binding.

A thirteenth-century Bible (Copenhagen, Kongelige Bibliotek, manuscript no. 4, 2°) copied for a deacon of Hamburg Cathedral in the mid-thirteenth century contains historiated (containing figures) initials beginning some of the books of the Bible that show other aspects of manuscript production. The parchmenter provides parchment sheets to a monk, and the sheets are trimmed to the desired size. A quill is cut while the parchment is smoothed with pumice. A scribe rules the layout using a straight edge to guide the pen. Several initials depict scribes copying with their pens, scrapers, and inkwells. Finally, an illuminator paints the head of a man on a parchment folio.

While the materials and techniques of making medieval manuscripts changed little throughout the Middle Ages, the organization of manuscript production reflected the social and economic shifts that occurred between the early and later Middle Ages. During the early medieval period, monastic scriptoria were almost exclusively responsible for the production of manuscript books. During the Carolingian and Ottonian periods, German monasteries were very active in making manuscripts and preserving them in their libraries. Much of the study of German medieval manuscripts dating through the twelfth century has focused on attribution of manuscripts on paleographical and artistic grounds to particular monasteries and examining how these monastic scriptoria functioned.

The emperor Charlemagne's interest in learning, literacy, and the Christian religion gave strong support to monastic manuscript production throughout his empire and established a tradition of imperial patronage for these endeavors that continued for centuries in the German empire. The exact nature of a palace school or scriptorium at Aachen and its manuscript production and illumination during Charlemagne's reign remain controversial, but many luxurious manuscripts such as a series of Gospel books were made under Charlemagne's patronage at monastic foundations in the Carolingian empire. Among the outstanding contributions of the Carolingian Renaissance to the development of the medieval manuscript are the creation of a clear, legible script termed Caroline minuscule and a style of illumination that drew inspiration from classical art for its monumental figure style.

Even after Charlemagne's empire disintegrated, German monasteries continued to produce manuscript books. Under the patronage of Ottonian rulers, manuscript production and illumination flourished at centers such as Fulda, Trier, and Reichenau, among others. While Ottonian manuscripts continued to be copied in the Caroline minuscule script, the illumination tended to become somewhat more stylized, with firmly outlined figures, sharper and more linear drapery, and the use of intense colors against flat gold backgrounds.

German Romanesque manuscript production reflected the changing political situation. The strengthening of the local nobility created diverse sources of patronage and correspondingly more regional variations in styles of script and illumination. Monasteries such as Weingarten continued to maintain scriptoria. At the same time, cities such as Salzburg, Hildesheim, Regensburg, and Cologne became major artistic centers on whose scriptoria the German nobility drew in commissioning manuscripts.

By the thirteenth century, manuscript production altered in response to changing economic and social conditions in Europe. The strengthening of the money economy, the growth of a middle class, the increase in literacy, and the burgeoning of vernacular literature contributed to the development of commercial manuscript production by secular artisans and an active book trade. The processes involved in making manuscripts became more specialized. Parchmenters made the parchment, scribes copied the text, illuminators painted the miniatures and marginal decoration, and binders bound the manuscripts. These artisans worked individually, perhaps in a small workshop with one or more assistants or apprentices. A stationer, often working on behalf of a patron, usually coordinated the collaborative efforts needed to produce a single manuscript. Most German cities such as Cologne and Regensburg had a thriving book trade. Studies of German Gothic manuscripts from various perspectives provide more detailed nuances of how late medieval manuscript production in Germany functioned in particular locales and situations.

The range of people commissioning manuscripts broadened. The greater and lesser nobility continued to acquire manuscripts, both religious and secular, usually made with costly materials and illuminations. In addition, a wider group of middle-class patrons, including merchants, tradespeople, and students, purchased books. Religious institutions now obtained books through the commercial book trade, although monastic manuscript production continued in orders such as the Carthusians. The Charterhouse of St. Barbara in Cologne presents one example of a monastic foundation that actively engaged in manuscript production including copying, decorating, and possibly binding their books in the fifteenth century.

In the middle of the fifteenth century the invention of printing by Johann Gutenberg in Mainz brought major changes to the production of books. The rapid spread of printing technology in German cities and towns did not immediately displace artisans engaged in manuscript production. Rather, a transitional period ensued when an interchange occurred between manuscript and printed books. Early printed books often relied on scribes to add rubrics in red. Illuminators painted decorative initials, borders, and sometimes miniatures into the books. Binders continued to practice their trade for both manuscript and printed volumes. By the early sixteenth century, however, the printing process perfected the techniques of reproducing decorative features and illustrations, and the production of manuscripts effectively ceased.

BIBLIOGRAPHY

Bischoff, Bernhard. *Die südostdeutschen Schreibschulen und Bibliotheken in der Karolingerzeit.* 2 vols. Leipzig: Harrossowitz, 1940–1980.

Björnbo, Axel Anthon. "Ein Beitrag zum Werdegang der mittelalterlichen Pergamenthandschriften." *Zeitschrift für Bücherfreunde* 11 (1907–1908): 329–335.

Dressler, Fridolin. *Scriptorum Opus: Schreiber-Mönche am Werk.* Wiesbaden: Reichert, 1971.

de Hamel, Christopher. *Scribes and Illuminators.* London: British Museum Press, 1992.

Harmon, James A. *Codicology of the Court School of Charlemagne: Gospel Book Production, Illumination, and Emphasized Script.* Frankfurt: Peter Lang, 1984.

Hoffmann, Hartmut. *Buchkunst und Königtum im ottonischen und frühsalischen Reich,* 2 vols. Stuttgart: Hiersemann, 1986.

Holladay, Joan A. "The Willehalm Master and His Colleagues: Collaborative Manuscript Decoration in Early Fourteenth-Century Cologne." In *Making the Medieval Book: Techniques of Production,* ed. Linda L. Brownrigg. Los Altos Hills, Calif.: Anderson-Lovelace, 1995, pp. 67–92.

König, Eberhard. "The Influence of the Invention of Printing on the Development of German Illumination." *Manuscripts in the Fifty Years After the Invention of Printing.* London: Warburg Institute, 1983, pp. 85–94.

Kyriss, Ernst. *Verzierte gotische Einbände im alten deutschen Sprachgebiet.* 4 vols. Stuttgart: Hettler, 1951–1958.

Marks, Richard. *The Medieval Manuscript Library of the Charterhouse of St. Barbara in Cologne.* Salzburg: Institut für Englische Sprache und Literatur, 1974.

Mütherich, Florentine, and Karl Dachs. *Regensburger Buchmalerei: Von frühkarolingischer Zeit bis zum Ausgang des Mittelalters.* Munich: Prestel, 1987.

Oliver, Judith. "The Walters Homilary and Westphalian Manuscripts." *Journal of the Walters Gallery* 54 (1996): 69–85.

Shailor, Barbara. *The Medieval Book.* New Haven, Conn.: Yale University Library, 1988.

Stamm, Lieselotte. "Buchmalerei in Serie: Zur Frühgeschichte der Vervielfältigungskunst." *Zeitschrift für schweizerische Archäologie und Kunstgeschichte* 40 (1983): 128–135.

Szirmai, J. A. "Carolingian Bindings in the Abbey Library of St. Gall." In *Making the Medieval Book: Techniques of Production,* ed. Linda L. Brownrigg. Los Altos Hills, Calif.: Anderson-Lovelace, 1995, pp. 157–179.

Tholl, Susan E. von Daum. "The Cutbrecht Gospels and the Earliest Writing Center at Salzburg." In *Making the Medieval Book: Techniques of Production,* ed. Linda L. Brownrigg. Los Altos Hills, Calif.: Anderson-Lovelace, 1995, pp. 17–37.

Wattenbach, W. *Das Schriftwesen im Mittelalters.* 3d ed. 1896; rpt. Graz: Akademische Druck- und Verlagsanstalt, 1958.

Karen Gould

SEE ALSO

Aachen; Bookmaking and Production; Carolingian Art and Architecture–Painting; Charlemagne; Cologne, Art; Fulda; Gothic Art and Architecture–Manuscript Painting; Gutenberg, Johann; Hildesheim; Mainz; Manuals, Artists', and Modelbooks; Ottonian Manuscript Painting; Regensburg; Reichenau; Salzburg; Trier

Marburg

With respect to both urban structure and art and architectural monuments, Marburg on the Lahn River in Hesse is one of the best-preserved medieval towns in Germany. It originated before the mid-twelfth century as a market settlement at the foot of a castle belonging to the landgraves of Thuringia. A fortress on the present hilltop site is first mentioned in 1138–1139; a reference to Marburg as a city *(civitas)* and to its citizens *(burgenses)* in a chronicle of 1222 first documents its legal status as a municipality.

Medieval Marburg reached its high point in the thirteenth and fourteenth centuries, both architecturally and politically. In 1228, Marburg became the home of the widowed landgravine St. Elisabeth of Thuringia (1207–1231, canonized 1235), whose many charitable deeds included the founding of a hospital dedicated to St. Francis of Assisi outside and to the north of the city. In 1234, patronage of the hospital as well as the parish church of Marburg was ceded to the Order of Teutonic Knights, and in 1235 the Order began construction of a new church over the grave of St. Elisabeth, along with a new hospital to the south. In 1255 Marburg was established as the seat of the Teutonic Order for the entire Bailiwick of Hesse. From the late thirteenth century on, the city gained increasing political autonomy from the Hessian landgraves; its growth in population and importance throughout the thirteenth and fourteenth centuries is reflected in the construction of a Franciscan abbey in 1234 (destroyed 1731–1732) and a Dominican one in 1291 (now the university church, *Universitätskirche,*) as well as expansions of the city wall circa 1234 and 1300. The cornerstone of the present town hall *(Rathaus)* on the market square, however, was not laid until 1512; before that, the town council met in the charnel house *(Kerner)* east of the parish church.

Marburg, castle of the Landgraves of Hessen, interior, knights' hall. *Photograph: Joan A. Holladay*

From the mid-thirteenth to the end of the sixteenth century, a separate Hessian line of landgraves, beginning with Heinrich I (1247–1308), grandson of St. Elisabeth, adopted Marburg as one of their primary residences, a situation that gave rise to repeated architectural additions to and elaborations of the castle. In 1526, under Landgrave Philip the Magnanimous, Hesse became Protestant, and in 1527 the Philipps-Universität was established in Marburg as the first Protestant university. In 1529 the famous *Religionsgespräch* on the doctrine of the Eucharist took place among Luther, Zwingli, and other reformers in the Marburg castle.

The most notable medieval monument in Marburg is the church of St. Elizabeth (Elisabethkirche). Begun in 1235, it represents one of the first churches built in Germany in the French Gothic style. A three-aisle hall church with a triconch (three-apse) choir and a two-towered facade, it evinces architectural forms related to the church of Our Lady (Liebfrauenkirche) in Trier and

the cathedral of Reims. By 1250 the triconch and the three easternmost bays of the nave were standing; the nave and west portal were completed in time for the dedication of the entire church in 1283, while construction on the two west towers continued until the mid-fourteenth century.

The Elisabethkirche was erected with its north conch over the burial site of St. Elisabeth in the former chapel of the Hospital of St. Francis. From the beginning the Elisabethkirche was intended as the church for the Marburg house of the Order of Teutonic Knights and as a pilgrimage church for visitors to the grave of St. Elisabeth; after 1298, it was also used as a necropolis for the Hessian landgraves. The present distribution of functions in the triconch choir reflects the development of this threefold purpose: the north conch accommodates the mausoleum of St. Elisabeth; the east conch the high altar dedicated to Mary, patron saint of the Teutonic Order; while the south conch houses the grave monuments of the Thuringian and Hessian landgraves from Konrad of Thuringia (d. 1240) to Wilhelm II of Hesse (d. 1509).

The Elisabethkirche also contains numerous works of sculpture, painting, and sacred art *(ars sacra)*. One of the most important of these is the golden shrine of St. Elisabeth (ca. 1248), located since the late thirteenth or early fourteenth century in the sacristy on the north side of the east conch; it shows the figures of Mary, Elisabeth, Christ in Majesty, and the twelve Apostles as well as scenes from the life of St. Elisabeth. Portions of the original stained glass are preserved in the six central windows of the east conch, including a cycle of scenes from the life of St. Elisabeth and other panels dating to the first half of the thirteenth century. Other painted and sculptural decoration includes the retable of the high altar (ca. 1290), the baldachin and tomb of the mausoleum of St. Elisabeth (ca. 1280; ca. 1350), the stone choir screen (before 1343), and the *Pietà* (ca. 1390) in the predella (lowest horizontal panel) of the *Marienaltar* (altar of Mary) in the north conch. The latter, a carved and painted wooden altarpiece, and four others like it in the Elisabethkirche date to around 1510 and are the work of Marburg sculptor Ludwig Juppe (or his workshop) and the painter Johann von der Leyten.

While the Elisabethkirche, located outside and to the north of the medieval city, was associated above all with the Order of Teutonic Knights, the parish church of St. Mary within the city walls (now the Lutheran parish church) constituted an important urban focal point and served the ecclesiastical needs of the citizenry. The choir of the present Gothic structure, which succeeded a Romanesque predecessor on the same site, was dedicated in 1297, while work on the nave continued until 1390–1395; the west tower was not built until 1447–1473. Stylistically, the choir shows similarity to the palace chapel of the castle (dedicated 1288), while the three-aisled nave continues the hall church tradition of the Elisabethkirche.

In the Middle Ages as now, the townscape of Marburg was dominated by the hilltop castle of the Thuringian and Hessian landgraves. Archaeological excavations since 1989 have uncovered the remains of a fortification on the site dating to the ninth century, with further construction in the eleventh century; in its present form, the castle complex consists of structures dating from the twelfth to the fifteenth centuries. Of particular note is the great audience hall *(Fürsten-* or *Rittersaal)* in the north wing of the castle, a double-aisle space articulated with a central row of four piers and massive Gothic cross vaults. Built circa 1300, it is one of the largest of its kind in Germany.

BIBLIOGRAPHY

Arnold, Udo, and Heinz Liebing, ed. *Elisabeth, der Deutsche Orden und ihre Kirche.* Marburg: Elwert, 1983.

Dettmering, Erhart, and Rudolf Grenz, ed. *Marburger Geschichte.* 2d ed. Marburg: Magistrat, 1982.

Holladay, Joan A. *Illuminating the Epic: The Kassel Willehalm Codex and the Landgraves of Hesse in the Early Fourteenth Century.* Seattle: University of Washington Press, 1997.

Köstler, Andreas. *Die Ausstattung der Marburger Elisabethkirche.* Berlin: Reimer, 1995.

Meiborg, Christa, and Helmut Roth. "Die Ausgrabungen auf dem Marburger Landgrafenschloß (1989–1990)." In *Hessen und Thüringen.* Marburg: Historische Kommission für Hessen, 1992, pp. 47–48.

Müller, Matthias. *Die Marburger Pfarrkirche St. Marien.* Marburg: Magistrat, 1991.

Sankt Elisabeth: Fürstin, Dienerin, Heilige. Sigmaringen: Thorbecke, 1981.

700 Jahre Elisabethkirche in Marburg 1283–1983, vol. 1. *Die Elisabethkirche—Architektur in der Geschichte.* Marburg: Elwert, 1983.

Verscharen, Franz-Josef. *Gesellschaft und Verfassung der Stadt Marburg beim Übergang vom Mittelalter zur Neuzeit.* Marburg: Presseamt, 1985.

Melissa Thorson Hause

SEE ALSO

Deutschorden; Elizabeth of Hungary; Gothic Art and Architecture; Iconographies, Innovative; Trier

Marchfeld, Battle of (August 26, 1278)

King Otakar II of Bohemia, who had managed to accumulate a large bloc of territories in the heart of Central Europe, suffered a major reversal in 1276 when King Rudolf of Habsburg forced him to surrender Austria, Styria, Carinthia, and Carniola. Many of the Austrians, and especially the Viennese, resented their new Habsburg rule and joined in Otakar's attempt to reclaim those possessions two years later. Otakar's slow advance gave Rudolf time to gather his forces, supported by allies like Hungary and Salzburg. The two forces met on a field by the river March, near the village of Dürnkrut, north of Vienna. The Hungarian mounted archers conducted a devastating attack on Otakar's right flank, causing it to break and retreat. Otakar and his left flank charged for Rudolf himself, who was briefly unhorsed. An attack by Rudolf's reserve broke Otakar's lines, and a retreat became a rout. During the confusion personal enemies murdered Otakar.

The Battle of Marchfeld, August 26, 1278, or Dürnkrut, was one of the largest cavalry battles of the Middle Ages. It was also decisive for Central European history, since it marked the beginning of the rise of the Austrian Habsburgs, while Bohemia's influence was greatly reduced.

BIBLIOGRAPHY

Delbrück, Hans. *Medieval Warfare,* trans. Walter J. Renfroe Jr. History of the Art of War 3. Lincoln: University of Nebraska Press, 1982.

Oman, Charles. *A History of the Art of War in the Middle Ages.* 2 vols. 2d ed. London: Methuen, 1924.

Peball, Kurt. *Die Schlacht bei Dürnkrut am 26. August 1278.* Vienna: Österreichischer Bundesverlag, 1968.

Brian A. Pavlac

SEE ALSO
Heinrich der Teichner; Warfare

Maria Laach

The Benedictine abbey of Maria Laach, located on the Laacher See and subject to the archbishop of Trier, was founded in 1093 by the palatine count Heinrich and his wife, Adelheid. Maria Laach was one of the later Benedictine foundations in the Middle Rhine region and was founded to provide a necropolis for Count Heinrich and his family. Initially the abbey had associations with St. Nicholas, the patron of an earlier chapel on the site, but by the mid-twelfth century, documentation refers to the Virgin Mary as the chief patroness of the abbey.

The abbey church was built predominantly during the twelfth century and consecrated in 1156. The crypt, dating from the late eleventh century immediately following Count Heinrich's death in 1095, represents the first building phase, and the main vessel of the church was constructed subsequently between 1130 and 1156. Construction on the upper stories of the western facade and the western atrium is believed to postdate the consecration, and work on this section seems to have continued into the early thirteenth century. Maria Laach represents a late example of several features common in earlier German architecture. The plan includes both eastern and

Maria Laach, west choir with *Paradies. Photograph: Joan A. Holladay*

western apses, and there is a developed west facade with three towers, which may ultimately derive from the early medieval church at St. Riquier and certainly has parallels in the architecture of St. Michael's at Hildesheim (1001–1033). The transept also has three towers resulting in a rich and complex exterior silhouette for the church. The building interior has a two-story elevation, and the nave is divided into rectangular bays separated by half columns on piers and transverse arches above. The nave is vaulted in unribbed groin vaults. Because of the semicircular section of the vaults and the rectangular shape of the bays, there appears to be considerable stilting in the vaults. This fact and the lack of continuation between the wall membering and the vaults has led to speculation that the building was originally planned with a flat wooden roof and that the vaulting was added as part of a late-twelfth-century modification of the original scheme.

Stained glass windows donated by Abbot Dietrich von Lehmen (1256–1295) remain in the eastern apse, and documents mention a rich array of original furnishings including tapestries and metalwork now lost. Maria Laach also had an active scriptorium, and a number of extant manuscripts, dating from the mid-twelfth until the early sixteenth century, may be assigned to it.

BIBLIOGRAPHY

Kubach, Hans, and Albert Verbeek. *Romanische Kirchen an Rhein und Maas.* Neuß: Gesellschaft für Buchdruckerei, 1971.

Resmini, Bertram. *Die Benediktinerabtei Laach.* Germania Sacra Neufolge 31; Erzbistum Trier 7. Berlin: de Gruyter, 1993.

Susan L. Ward

SEE ALSO

Hildesheim; Romanesque Art and Architecture

Maria Saal

The Austrian collegiate church was founded in the eighth century by the archbishop of Salzburg and developed later into a center of a regional pilgrimage; it served traditionally as the coronation church for the dukes of Carinthia, and their ceremonial stone throne, the *Herzogenstuhl,* has stood since the early Middle Ages in the valley below the church, in an area known as the Zollfeld, from which the church took its name *(ain Zol, apud solium, in solio* [a throne, near the throne, on the throne]). In 1480 when, together with the adjoining residential buildings of the convent and the chapter the church was enclosed by fortifications, it became the largest of the fortified churches in Carinthia.

The present late Gothic church was erected in different stages: the choir and transepts were completed in 1435, and the nave followed between 1450 and 1459 under the patronage of Emperor Frederick III. Unusual for the late Gothic period in Austria, the church terminates in a two-towered facade with an extensive western gallery. To stress the legitimistic aspect of rulership, the nave's vault is decorated with a painted Tree of Jesse, dated 1490. The western crossing arch, lower than the nave, displays within an open oculus (literally, eye) a sculptural representation of the Last Judgment, recalling the emperor's judicial role.

As a reflection of the humanistic tendencies at the court of Frederick III, the church exhibits on its exterior a number of reliefs and inscriptions derived from Roman funeral monuments, mainly from Virunum, the provincial capital of Roman Noricum. These reliefs depict, among others, a pair of panthers in clear allusion to the heraldic symbols of the duchies of Carinthia and Styria,

while a second relief with a traveling coach drawn by horses might have referred to the medieval system of traveling kingship *(Reisekönigtum).* Other reliefs represent a scene from the Trojan War, and the famous she-wolf with the twins Romulus and Remus, both relating clearly to the founding myth of the Roman Empire, which played an important ideological role in the self-esteem of the house of Habsburg in the late Middle Ages as its members sought to reconstruct a genealogy that reached back to ancient Rome and its emperors.

Hans J. Böker

SEE ALSO

Frederick III; Gothic Art and Architecture, Late; Salzburg

Maria Wörth

The earliest church in the area of Maria Wörth was established in 894 at the highest point of a rocky peninsula on the southern shore of the Wörthersee. Bishop Waldo of Freising probably directed that the church be built to provide for parish and missionary needs in Carinthia. When the relics of Saints Primus and Felician were later brought from Rome, the church was named after them. East of the parish church stands a two-story Romanesque charnel house from about 1279. The most significant medieval art at Maria Wörth is to be found just west of the parish church in a much smaller church, the Winterkirche (Winter Church) or Rosenkranzkirche (Rosary Church), where an important cycle of Romanesque frescoes (ca. 1155) were discovered in 1895. The choir of the Winterkirche holds a precious stained glass panel that depicts Mary holding the Christ child (ca. 1425).

BIBLIOGRAPHY

Fräss-Ehrfeld, Claudia. *Geschichte Kärntens.* vol. 1., *Das Mittelalter.* Klagenfurt: Heyn, 1984, pp. 207–208.

Ginhart, Karl. *Kärnten.* Die Kunstdenkmäler Österreichs. Vienna: Schroll, 1976, pp. 383–385.

Pagitz, F. Die *Geschichte des Kollegiatstiftes Maria Wörth: Ein Beitrag zur Austria Sacra.* Archiv für vaterländische Geschichte und Topographie 56. Klagenfurt: Verlag des Geschichtsvereins für Kärnten, 1960.

Ruth M. W. Moskop

Mariazell

The earliest mention of the area of northern Styria in which Mariazell is located dates from 1025 and refers to the region's salt and iron deposits. Duke Heinrich III von Eppenstein bequeathed the land to the Benedictine cloister of St. Lambrecht, which in turn founded a *Zelle,* or small cloister, there in 1157. Mariazell has been a popular pilgrimage goal since 1330 and is still one of the most frequently visited pilgrimage sites in Austria. In 1342, Duke Albrecht II helped secure the town economically when he gave it market privileges. Although the thirteenth-century Romanesque church was replaced by a Gothic building in the late fourteenth century, an important Romanesque wooden sculpture of a seated Virgin and Child has survived from the twelfth century. This piece, referred to as the *Gnadenbild* (Picture of Grace) in acknowledgment of its miracle-working powers, is perhaps the oldest of its kind in Austria. The portal beneath the central tower of the Gothic church, flanked by baroque towers since the seventeenth century, boasts stone reliefs commissioned by Abbot Heinrich II Moyker of St. Lambrecht (1438–1439); they depict the spiritual, historical, and political significance of the church.

BIBLIOGRAPHY

Waid, Immaculata. *Mariazell und das Zellertal: Aus Geschichte und Chronik.* Mariazell: Eigenverlag F. Weiss und J. Greissl, 1982.

Wonisch, Othmar. *Mariazell.* Munich: Schnell und Steiner, 1957.

Ruth M. W. Moskop

SEE ALSO

Gothic Art and Architecture; Romanesque Art and Architecture

Mariendichtungen

The cult and celebration of Mary in medieval Germany, specifically in literary works *(Mariendichtungen),* are closely connected to the presence of the Teutonic Order *(Deutschorden).* Owing their existence to the missionary purpose of the Crusades, the Order of the Knights Hospitallers of St. John, and that of the Knight Templars that preceded the Teutonic Order, tried to respond in an organized manner to the increasing need of representing Christianity as a commanding faith.

The third expedition against the Muslim people that echoed among the many Germans living in Jerusalem led to the necessity of creating a German military organization approved by the pope to defend the ecumenical Christian values within the Germanic community. Finally, Pope Innocent III confirmed in 1215 the already existent Order of the German Knights, while during the reign of the next pontiff, Innocent IV, the Teutonic Order received the constitutional acts regarding its existence.

The Rule of the Teutonic Order dates in its ultimate form from 1244, and it was strongly based on the Cistercian movement in what concerns its military organization. During the undefined period of probation before taking the vows as a new member, the novice had to declare, "I promise and swear chastity in body and to be without greed and to be obedient to God and St. Mary" *(ich entheize und gelobe kusheit mines libes unde ane eigenschaft ze sine unde gehorsam Gote und sente Marien).* Regardless of this requirement of the chapter, the members of the Teutonic Order became to be popularly known as Marians *(Mariani)* and Knights of Mary *(Marienritter).* However, among the many annual festivals the Order observed, four were dedicated to the Virgin. Along with the distinctive black cross worn as an emblem, the Teutonic Order could also be identified by its focused dedication to the image of Mary. Moreover, the presence of the Virgin was to take material shape through the statue placed by the eastern gate into the city of Marienburg (now in Poland).

Since the Order embodied a blend of monastic and chivalric attitude, the literature it sponsored had to pertain to the basic Christian commandments. Thus, whatever could be extracted from the Old and New Testament and then transformed for obvious educational purposes into didactic literature constituted the primordial goal of the Order. Even if the presence of Mary was not central in certain texts, as the patroness of the Order she was always a central figure in their literature.

In "Das Gedicht von Siben Ingesigeln" (Poem of the Seven Seals) by Tilo von Kulm, the Marian allegory appears in the way she is portrayed as the chosen and no less pure vessel through which God sent his Son in this world. Mary is the "golden gate" *(portas aurea),* who, as in Heinrich von Hesler's *Die Apokalypse,* conceives the immaculate Son, "thus God emerged from the depth of Mary's flesh" *(Also schiet Got uz die clien des vleisches an Marien).*

An anonymous work, *Der Sunden Widerstreit* (The Contest of the Sins), is another allegorical poem with strong didactic elements. If the Christian knights should have any doubts about the outcome of their chivalric enterprises, they ought to be dispelled at once, since the Order is under the protection of the Virgin. It is just enough for the doubtful knight to recite an Ave Maria for the demonic spirits to be defeated.

In this sense, the well-known legend "Maria und der Ritter" (Mary and the Knight) stresses the magical side of the Virgin and perpetuates the rich medieval thematic of the Miracles of Our Lady. In the legend, the knight, overwhelmed by the miracles the Virgin had performed for him, decides to exchange arms for a life dedicated to Mary, "he wanted to be a Knight of Mary, that the Queen be praised" *(Marien ritter wolde sin des si gelobet die kuningin)*.

In "Die Witwe und ihr Sohn" (The Widow and her Son), the widow prays to the Virgin to free her only son from the prison where he is being kept. She has almost no hope, yet one night Mary enters the dungeon and sets the young man free. Bewildered, he returns to his mother, who, having learned of the miracle, commits herself in return to renounce the chains of motherhood that had kept her son tied to her and offers, in an act of supreme sacrifice, the son to the Absolute Mother.

Within the realm of the Eastern patristic thought, the presence of Mary can be noted in Sermon 17 (Homilia XVII) of Origen (185–254 C.E.), where we find the first mention of the Virgin's compassion for the Passion of the Son. Later, Ephraim the Syriac composed a lament of the Virgin followed, among other contributions, by the collection of six hundred sacred hymns to the Virgin entitled *Mariale,* left to us by the Greek Joseph the Hymnographer (ca. 816–886).

Known as Planctus Mariae, the liturgical tradition of depicting the deep suffering through sympathy of the Virgin for the crucified Son will continue throughout the medieval period of which the German nonliturgical aspect has been discussed earlier.

If the early patristic output has almost entirely been born within the Eastern Church, beginning with the eleventh century the center of essential Marian literature will move to the West. Anselm of Canterbury's "Dialogues of Mary" *(Dialogus Mariae)* and Bernard of Clairvaux's "Book of the Passion of Christ and the Sufferings and Tears of His Mother" *(Liber de Passione Christi et doloribus et planctibus Matris eius)* will introduce even more forcefully the theme of the Mother and Son seen as identical in their suffering. While the nature of their suffering is different (Christ transcends his human condition through universal suffering), the sorrow of his Mother renders their relationship deeply human.

Ubertino da Casale explains the profound roots of the Virgin's *compassio* (compassion) as lying in her Son's decision to grant her "the primate of compassion" *primatum compassionis*. In Ubertino's "Arbor vitae crucifixae Jesu" (Tree of Life of the Crucifixion of Jesus) one finds an un-usual emotional expression of the relationship between Mother and Son that reveals the poetical values of the Marian mysticism.

As we advance beyond the twelfth century, we gradually approach the peak of the lyrical mysticism in the Marian literature, a sign of modernity at the level of the poetic expression. From now on, the poets are those responsible for this switch to a less dogmatic representation of the theme of compassion; thus, from the subject of theological discourse, it becomes an exemplary story of utmost humanity. Gradually, the Marian compassion passes from the pages of theological disputes onto the stage of theatrical representation. The dramatic account that meets the criteria and the taste for a "popular" reception given by Jacopone da Todi—author of the burlesque *Lodi*—in his "Stabat Mater dolorosa" (The Suffering Mother Stood [next to the cross]) is far from singular in the medieval and late medieval West.

Because of the extreme dramatic tones and their accessibility to a large audience, the theme of Passion is added another climactic moment by intertwining it with Mary's compassion. Theatrical representations of the painful watch of the Virgin of her Son's agony on the Mount of Calvary abound in the West. In England, the Northern and Southern Passion, in Germany Der Frankfurter Passionsspiel, the Sacre Rappresentazioni in Italy, or the Planto o duelo que fizo la Virgen de la Pasion de su Fijo Jesu Christo in Spain are few examples among many others of the kind.

In France La Passion de jongleurs, the Passion d'Arras, in Italy the Pianto from Montecassino, the Lamentatio from the Abruzzi, or the Pianto delle Marie from the Marche are all expressions of the increasingly popular desire to associate the drama of passion *(passio)* and compassion *(compassio)* with individual human fate and make it more accessible to the popular sensibility. It was the story of Mary's compassion for her Son and the latter's humility in accepting his sacrifice that set the paradigm for a human understanding of the individual suffering.

BIBLIOGRAPHY

Delius, Walter. *Geschichte der Marienverehrung.* Munich: Reinhardt, 1963.

Donahue, Charles. *The Testament of Mary.* New York: Fordham University Press, 1942.

Goenner, Mary. *Mary-Verse of the Teutonic Knights.* New York: AMS, 1944.

Graef, Hilda. *Mary: A History of Doctrine and Devotion:.* London: Sheed & Ward, 1994.

Greisenegger, Wolfgang. *Die Realität im religiösen Theater des Mittelalters.* Vienna: Bohlaus, 1978.

Konigson, Elie. *L'Espace théâtral médiéval.* Paris: Editions du Centre National de la Recherche, 1957.

Levasti, Arrigo. *Mistici del Dueccento e del Trecento.* Milan: Ricciardi, 1960.

Ramon, Francisco Ruiz. *Historia del teatro español.* vol. 1. Madrid: Alianza, 1967.

Florin Berindeanu

SEE ALSO

Deutschorden; Drama; Drama, Passion Plays; Walther von der Vogelweide

Marner, Der (fl. ca. 1225–1250)

A Swabian didactic singer from the second quarter of the thirteenth century assumed, as was common among the didactic singers, a performer's pseudonym, the Marner (mariner, or possibly pawn, as a chess figure). His didactic program and piety seem Franciscan; at any rate, he clearly had clerical training. He is the only German singer of his age to whom both German and Latin songs are ascribed, but the authenticity of the Latin songs has been questioned. His songs, though they contain puzzling passages, lack for the most part the excessive ornateness and desire to impress with arcane knowledge we find in those of many (mostly later) didactic singers, which may be less a reflection of a less educated or a modest person and more the result of his desire to teach clear lessons. In addition to his didactic songs he created minnesongs and prayers. Most of his songs, however, preach moral behavior and, more commonly, chastise sinfulness. Marner also attacks fellow singers (and audiences with fickle tastes), and these songs have attracted the most scholarly attention. Despite his relatively open style and, possibly, modesty in choice of name, he clearly is proud of and defends his artistry and the importance of his undertaking as a poet and performer; his large corpus of songs bears witness to his fecundity. He was influential; his songs appear in considerable number in several manuscripts and inspired new songs by later singers for over a century.

BIBLIOGRAPHY

Haustein, Jens. *Marner-Studien.* Tübingen: Niemeyer, 1995.

Strauch, Philipp, ed. *Der Marner.* Strasbourg: Trübner, 1876.

Hubert Heinen

SEE ALSO

Minnesang; Versification

Marriage and Divorce

The Early Middle High German term *ê* (modern German *Ehe,* "marriage") meant "law" and referred to the Old Testament. Only after 1000 did the term acquire other meanings, and only since the thirteenth century have those meanings included the political, social, and sexual bond between man and woman. Nevertheless, scholarship on early Germanic law identifies three forms of marriage practiced during the rise and fall of the Frankish empire (ca. 485–ca. 900): *Muntehe, Kebsehe,* and *Friedelehe.* Because women were thought to be unable to live independently in the world and thus to require guardianship, a marital union required the transfer of guardianship rights (Latin *mundium,* hence *Muntehe*) between a suitor and the woman's father or other male guardian. This exchange took place in two public transactions: the betrothal, in which the suitor negotiated over the gift, or dower, he would make to the bride's family (by the twelfth century, the dower is settled on the bride); and the wedding banquet, during which the bride's kin ceremoniously handed her over to her new husband and then led her in a procession to her new home. After the marriage was consummated, the groom gave his new wife the *Morgengabe* (morning gift), an acknowledgment of her legitimacy. Options beyond the *Muntehe* included the *Kebsehe,* in which free men could take a concubine from among their servants or slaves, and the *Friedelehe,* a relationship established on mutual agreement but that involved no exchange of guardianship rights. Historians suggest that couples favored the *Friedelehe* when a woman's different social position presented obstacles to her joining the man's family, and they debate about whether this arrangement offered women a degree of (financial) independence. These three customs were not universal throughout the empire, however, which at its height covered what is now France, Germany, and northern Italy. Indeed, rather than reflecting uniformity, the legal sources reveal the conflicts arising from practices that varied considerably among different social strata and by region.

In the twelfth century, Christian theologians turned their attention to this diversity as part of their efforts after the Gregorian reforms to involve themselves in the lives of the laity. This attention produced the doctrine of *Konsensehe,* a marriage made valid only if and after both parties consent to it. Hoping this requirement would combat both marriages by abduction and those made purely for political purposes, the church rejected *Friedelehe* and *Kebsehe* as forms of concubinage, brought the *Muntehe* ceremony to the steps of the church, and made marriage into a Christian sacrament.

In defining this new sacrament, theologians debated the relative importance of consent versus sexual consummation. While biblical authorities like Paul claimed that the marriage union both protected individuals from carnal sin and mirrored the mystery of God's union with humanity, twelfth-century scholars cited Mary and Joseph's chaste marriage as a model, concluding that consent was the defining essence. With the rise of mendicant piety among men and women in the thirteenth century, this doctrine engendered alternative forms of spiritual marriage: husbands and wives living together in chastity, and women religious becoming the brides of Christ.

Avowing not only the exclusivity of the marriage bond, but also its longevity, the church sought also to discourage polygamy, multiple marriages, and divorce. However, while divorce was forbidden, a marriage could be declared invalid in cases of incest, if one person were already married, if either partner had not consented, if the marriage remained unconsummated because of impotence, or if a Christian had married a Jew or heathen (Jewish marriage laws also forbade such intermarriages). In cases of adultery or other scurrilous crimes, partners could request separations, though men were more successful in such cases than women. Generally, canon law prohibited remarriage as long as the former spouse lived. Given high death rates, however, multiple marriages, especially among the nobility, were common.

In the world of literature, an ideal marriage involved not only consent but also love, particularly in Hartmann von Aue's *Iwein* and *Erec,* and in Wolfram von Eschenbach's *Parzival.* In Gottfried's *Tristan,* however, the deep love felt by Tristan and Isolde occurs outside the arranged and very political marriage between Isolde and King Mark. Marriages "arranged" through deception lead to massive death and ruin in the *Nibelungenlied.* Divorce or separation is less common in Middle High German literature, although one thinks of Gahmuret, in *Parzival,* who leaves his first wife, the exotic Belecâne, because she is a heathen.

BIBLIOGRAPHY

Bouchard, Constance Brittain. *"Strong of Body, Brave and Noble:" Chivalry and Society in Medieval France.* Ithaca, N.Y.: Cornell University Press, 1998.

Brundage, James A. *Sex, Law and Marriage in the Middle Ages.* Aldershot, Great Britain: Variorum, 1993.

Bumke, Joachim. *Courtly Culture: Literature and Society in the High Middle Ages,* trans. Thomas Dunlap. Berkeley: University of California, Press, 1991.

Duby, Georges. *Love and Marriage in the Middle Ages,* trans. Jane Dunnett. Cambridge: Polity Press, 1994.

Elliott, Dyan. *Spiritual Marriage: Sexual Abstinence in Medieval Wedlock.* Princeton, N.J.: Princeton University Press, 1993.

McNamara, Jo-Ann, and Suzanne F. Wemple. "Marriage and Divorce in the Frankish Kingdom." In *Women in Medieval Society,* ed. Susan Mosher Stuard. Philadelphia: University of Pennsylvania Press, 1976, pp. 95–124.

Tallan, Cheryl. "Opportunities for Medieval Northern European Jewish Widows in the Public and Domestic Spheres." In *Upon My Husband's Death: Widows in the Literature and Histories of Medieval Europe,* ed. Louise Mirrer. Ann Arbor: University of Michigan Press, 1992, pp. 115–127.

Sara S. Poor

SEE ALSO

Family; Gottfried von Straßburg; Hartmann von Aue; Jews; Laws and Lawbooks; *Nibelungenlied*; Wolfram von Eschenbach; Women

Marsilius van Inghen (ca. 1340–August 20, 1396)

A scholastic philosopher and theologian, Marsilius made an important contribution to the development of late medieval logic and philosophy of nature and advocated the use of logicosemantic techniques in philosophy and theology.

Marsilius was born around 1340, in Nijmegen and died on August 20, 1396 in Heidelberg. He began his career as master of arts at the University of Paris in 1362, where he was also rector in 1367 and 1371 and student of theology from 1366 onward. He turned away from Paris because of the schism in 1378. From 1386 onward, he was master at the University of Heidelberg, which he helped to found. In Heidelberg he was rector no fewer than nine times, from 1386 to 1392 and in 1396. In 1395 or 1396 he concluded his study of theology and so became the first theologian to obtain a doctorate in Heidelberg.

His works include treatises on logic, commentaries on Aristotle, and a voluminous *Sentences* commentary. His writings on logic in particular had great influence. They were part of the syllabus of many late medieval universities, such as Prague, Heidelberg, Vienna, Erfurt, and Basle. According to Marsilius, there exists no universality outside the human mind. Universal concepts such as "man" or "animal" are formed by human thinking. The object of scientific knowledge is the proposition and the thing signified by the terms of the proposition. Science in all its different branches deals not so much with reality itself as with one's speech and thought about reality. Largely because of these convictions, Marsilius has been characterized as a nominalist *(nominalista)* and a terminist *(terminista)* since the early fifteenth century.

BIBLIOGRAPHY

Bos, Egbert P., ed. *Marsilius of Inghen. Treatises on the Properties of Terms.* Dordrecht: Reidel, 1983.

Hoenen, Maarten J. F. M. "Marsilius van Inghen, Bibliographie." *Bulletin de Philosophie Médiévale* 31 (1989): 150–167; 32 (1990): 191–195.

———. *Marsilius of Inghen. Divine Knowledge in Late Medieval Thought.* Leyden: Brill, 1993.

Marsilius of Inghen. *Questiones super quattuor libros Sententiarum,* Strasbourg 1501, rpt. Frankfurt am Main: Minerva, 1966 [a critical edition is currently under preparation].

Ritter, Gerhard. *Studien zur Spätscholastik.* vol. 1. *Marsilius van Inghen und die okkamistische Schule in Deutschland.* Sitzungsberichte der Heidelberger Akademie der Wissenschaften, Philosophisch-historische Klasse, 1921, no. 4. Heidelberg: Winter, 1921.

Maarten J. F. M. Hoenen

SEE ALSO
Universities

Märtyrerbuch

The *Märtyrerbuch,* or *Buch der Märtyrer* (Book of Martyrs), is a rhymed German legendary comprising 28,450 verses. Commissioned by a duchess, *Gräfin von Rosenberg,* and written by an anonymous poet and cleric, it celebrates in 103 legends, following the church calendar from January to December 31 (St. Sylvester, whence the German term for New Year's Eve, *Sylvester),* the feast days of Mary, of the cross, and of the saints, varying between 36 verses and 902 *(Katharina).*

The text is extant in twenty manuscripts as collections, single legends, and fragments, to which a Göttingen fragment of *Katharina* was recently added. The oldest manuscript (in Eisenstadt), possibly the original, was written in the East Franconian dialect circa 1275–1285. The poet did not yet know the Latin collection *Legenda aurea* or the German *Passional.* The two Latin collections used as sources for the *Märtyrerbuch* were the *Kurzlegendar* (an abbreviated anthology) and a collection known as the Great Austrian legendary *(Magnum Legendarium Austriacum).* Both Latin texts were derived from the *Windberg Legendar* (Windberg Legendary, ca. 1200), all three located in or near Regensburg.

The surviving *Märtyrerbuch* manuscripts suggest three levels of production: first, complete copies of the original in Swabian, Alemannic, and Bavarian dialects; second, manuscripts with contamination of the *Passional,* which reached even the East Middle German and Bohemian areas as well as Austria and Tyrol; third, single legends and later, altered copies of older collections.

Sixty-four of the legends became a source for the *South German Heiligenleben* in prose (Saints' Lives, 1385–1400). But the *Margareten-Marter* (ca. 1300) was influenced by the *Märtyrerbuch,* as well as the *Katharinen-Marter* (ca. 1300), the *Katharinenspiel* (1350–1370), two legends of *Katharina* in Donaueschingen, and also the *Heiligenleben* of Hermann von Fritzlar (1343–1349).

BIBLIOGRAPHY

Jefferis, Sibylle. "Das Göttinger Fragment der *Katharinenlegende* aus dem *Märtyrerbuch." Zeitschrift für deutsches Altertum* 114 (1985): 146–149.

———. "The Middle High German Versions of the *Alexius Legend,* derived from the *Magnum Legendarium Austriacum." Medieval Perspectives* 2 (1987): 45–72.

Kunze, Konrad. "Buch der Märtyrer" ("Märterbuch"). In *Die deutsche Literatur des Mittelalters. Verfasserlexikon,* ed. Kurt Ruh et al. Berlin: de Gruyter, 1978, vol. 1, cols. 1093–1095.

Sibylle Jefferis

SEE ALSO
Heiligenleben; Martyrology; *Passional*

Martyrology

Commonly used within monasteries, the lists of saints—including confessors and virgins as well as martyrs—were arranged by calendar order on the dates of their commemorations. The basis of the medieval tradition was the so-called Jerome's List of Martyrs (Martyrologium Hieronymianum).

Accepted in the Middle Ages as an authentic work of St. Jerome, this text dates from the mid–fifth century. It includes saints from much of the Roman world, but its entries normally consist only of the names of saints and the places of their death or burial. From the Carolingian period onward, "historical" or narrative martyrologies, which include capsule accounts of the saints' lives or passions, became the most common form of the genre. The earliest known historical martyrology was the work of the English historian Bede (d. ca. 735), which probably came to the Continent with the Anglo-Saxon missionaries to Germany. Ninth-century reform legislation that required the reading of a martyrology in the daily monastic chapter contributed to a surge of composition in the Frankish kingdom.

In western Francia, a series of authors established an influential martyrological tradition. An anonymous writer in Lyon added to Bede's martyrology, nearly doubling its length, and Florus of Lyon (d. ca. 860) similarly expanded the work of his anonymous predecessor. Then Ado of Vienne revised and greatly augmented Florus's text. Finally, in the third quarter of the ninth century, Usuard of Saint-Germain-des-Prés drew upon both Florus and Ado, often reducing their lengthy commemorations, to produce a martyrology that became the standard text of the High Middle Ages.

In the East Frankish region Hrabanus Maurus compiled an independent expansion of Bede's work, Wandalbert of Prüm composed a poetic martyrology based on Florus, and Wolfhard of Herrieden borrowed heavily from Ado's martyrology. Usuard employed Wandalbert as one of his sources, but otherwise the eastern compositions had little influence in the west. Western works did become popular in Germany, however. In the tenth and eleventh centuries, a number of authors—including Notker the Stammerer, Hermann the Lame, and the so-called Pseudo-Bede of Cologne—produced compilations that combined materials from Ado and Hrabanus. During the High Middle Ages, Usuard's martyrology gradually supplanted most other texts in Germany as well as elsewhere, and Herman Greven's fifteenth-century compendium was a much expanded version of that work.

Beginning with the Cistercians in the twelfth century, religious orders adopted official martyrologies along with other liturgical books. German examples of such texts include those used by the congregations of Bursfeld (Benedictine) and Windesheim (Augustinian). The German region also produced a number of vernacular martyrologies, all of them anonymous. Most of these are essentially translations of Usuard, but some, such as the *Jenaer Martyrologium* (in Jena), represent more complex compilations.

Throughout most of the Middle Ages, German martyrologies remained less influential than those of the French cultural region, and Usuard's work formed the basis of the modern Roman Martyrology. However, the sixteenth-century authors of that compilation accepted the "Pseudo-Bede of Cologne" as an authentic Bede text, assuring medieval German influence on the cult of saints in modern Catholicism.

BIBLIOGRAPHY

Dubois, Jacques. *Les martyrologes du Moyen Age latin.* Turnhout: Brepols, 1978; rpt. 1985.

Dubois, Jacques, and Jean Loup Lemaître. *Sources et méthodes de l'hagiographie médiévale.* Paris: Cerf, 1993.

McCulloh, John M. "The 'Pseudo-Bede of Cologne': A Martyrology of the 'Gorzean' Reform." In Karl Borchardt and Enno Bünz, ed. *Forschungen zur Reichs-, Papst- und Landesgeschichte. Festschrift Peter Herde,* vol. 1. Stuttgart: Hiersemann, 1998, pp. 81–99.

Overgaauw, E. A. *Martyrologes manuscrits des anciens diocèses d'Utrecht et de Liège. Étude sur le développement et la diffusion du Martyrologe d'Usuard.* 2 vols. Hilversum: Verloren, 1993.

Quentin, Henri. *Les martyrologes historiques du moyenâge.* Paris: Librairie Victor Lecoffre, 1908.

John M. McCulloh

SEE ALSO

Carolingians; Hrabanus Maurus; Latin Language; Legends; Saints' Cults

Master of *Registrum Gregorii*
See Registrum Gregorii, Master of.

Master of Sankt Bartholomew Altarpiece
See Sankt Bartholomew Altarpiece, Master of.

Master of Sankt Veronica
See Sankt Veronica, Master of.

Master of the Housebook
See Housebook, Master of.

Master of the Playing Cards
See Playing Cards, Master of.

Matfridings

One of the powerful comital (ducal) families that arose in the Carolingian period has been identified as the Matfridings, because of the prominence of the name Matfrid over several generations. The first documented ancestor is Count Matfrid of Orleans, who from the beginning of Louis the Pious's reign was one of the most influential counselors for over a decade. In February 828 he and Count Hugo of Tours (who was married to Matfrid's sister Ava) were deprived of their fiefs and offices at an imperial assembly at Aachen, because both the previous year as leaders of an army called out against the Saracens had not met an attack by them in the Spanish March soon enough. Both counts were from that time onward bitter enemies of Louis the Pious, and in the rebellions of his sons in 830, 832, and 833, they stood on the side of the rebels. In each instance they were forgiven and restored to their lands, titles, and offices. Matfrid and Hugo were among those who followed Lothar I to Italy shortly thereafter, where they received grants of new lands. Most of them, including Matfrid, died in Italy in 836–837 from a contagious disease, however.

The Lotharingian Count Matfrid who flourished 843–860 in the Bietgau (or Biet District), and 844–855 in the Eifelgau just to the north, and in the Verduner Gau, was the son of the previous Count Matfrid I. Matfrid II appears often in the charters of Lothar I and of Lothar II, and he was probably among the magnates who gathered June 5, 860, at Coblenz to give counsel to the agreement among Louis the German, Charles the Bald, and Lothar II on June 7. He was also the lay abbot of St.-Vaast.

Matfrid III, the son of Matfrid II, flourished 867–878 as a count in Lotharingia and also in the Eifelgau. He appears to have property in that part of Lothar II's realm that went to Charles the Bald in 870, probably in the Waberngau and in the Verduner Gau. In 877, with other magnates he was appointed at Quierzy as counselor to Charles's son, as often as he should be in the Meuse region. Matfrid III followed his father as lay abbot of St.-Vaast, and died about 883. Members of the Matfriding kinship grouping occupied the episcopal chair at Verdun 870-920/933, while the Matfriding Richard was abbot of Prüm in 897 and bishop of Liège 920–945 as well.

At the end of the ninth century, the Matfridings were rivals for power in Lotharingia with Zwentibold, the ille-gitimate son of King Arnulf. In 939 the Matfridings acquired the lands of another Lotharingian count, Reginar III, who was sent into exile. Although female members of the family married into the prominent dynasties of Lorraine, and as such became the ancestresses of King Henry III (1024–1039) and Pope Leo IX (1049–1054), it was the male line of the *pfalzgrave* (duke) Gottfrid (fl. before 950) from which the later dukes of Upper Lorraine descended. The name Gerhard, which appears with the Matfriding count of Metz (fl. 1021), became a dominant appellation for the Lotharingian dukes of the eleventh century, and the preference given the name by the later counts of Jülich and Hochstaden suggests some direct or agnate relationship. The name Matfrid, on the other hand, gradually disappears among the known descendants of Matfrid III, but its preferment by the eleventh-century counts in the Engersgau and their direct descendants, the counts of Wied, suggests a tie along some female line as well.

BIBLIOGRAPHY

Hlawitschka, Eduard. *Die Anfänge des Hauses Habsburg-Lothringen. Genealogische Untersuchungen zur Geschichte Lothringens und des Reiches im 9., 10. und 11. Jahrhundert.* Saarbrücken: Kommissionsverlag: Minerva-Verlag Thinnes and Nolte, 1969.

Wisplinghoff, Erich. *Untersuchungen zur frühen Geschichte der Abtei S. Maximin bei Trier von den Anfängen bis etwa 1150.* Mainz: Gesellschaft für Mittelrheinische Kirchengeschichte, 1970.

Paul B. Pixton

SEE ALSO
Carolingians; Henry III; Lothar I; Louis the Pious

Matilda, Empress (1102–1167)

The daughter of King Henry I of England and his wife, Matilda of Scotland, Matilda became the empress by virtue of her marriage to the Salian emperor, Henry V. Her father accepted the marriage proposal during Whitsuntide of 1109, at which time she was only eight years old. In the spring of 1110 she was sent to Germany under the care of Bishop Burchard of Cambrai, betrothed to Henry V at Utrecht, and crowned at Mainz by Archbishop Frederick of Cologne. Henry V then dismissed all her English attendants, and the child was taken under the guardianship of Archbishop Bruno of Trier to learn the

German language and customs. The marriage finally took place in January 1114 at Worms, the new consort now being twelve years old and her husband some thirty years her elder. Henry V had used the years between the betrothal and marriage to spend Matilda's enormous dowry of ten thousand silver marks on a major Roman expedition, during which he extracted the short-lived treaty of Ponte Mammolo from Pope Paschal II in hopes of decisively ending the Investiture Conflict.

Matilda soon played the crucial roles of patron and intercessor at court; she appeared on charters in subsequent years as the sponsor of many royal grants, and acted as petitioner several times on behalf of nobles or prelates who sought reconciliation with the emperor. Her imperial role expanded when she joined her husband on a military campaign in Rome in 1117. The imperial army occupied the city, and Matilda was crowned with her husband on Pentecost in St. Peter's Basilica by the archbishop of Braga. Matilda would choose to retain the imperial dignity even after leaving Germany, at least as a courtesy title. When her husband's presence was required north of the Alps after the coronation, Matilda remained in Italy as imperial regent. She assisted in the administration of imperial territories and presided over courts such as the session at Rocca Capineta near Reggio. She appears to have continued in this capacity during the year 1118, and then rejoined the emperor in Lotharingia in 1119. This royal apprenticeship at such a tender age prepared her well for the tumultuous years ahead. She was with Henry V in Utrecht at his untimely death in 1125, which left her a childless widow in possession of the imperial insignia at the age of twenty-three.

Her husband's hopes that she would produce an heir for the Salian line were quickly replaced by her father's need for an heir to the Norman dynasty, since Henry I's only son died in 1120. He therefore recalled her to England, and Matilda handed over the imperial insignia to Archbishop Adalbert of Mainz before returning to her Anglo-Norman homeland in 1125. After a sixteen-year absence she began yet another new life, with the only tokens of her imperial childhood in Germany being a treasure of jewels and personal regalia (most of which she would give to religious houses) and the precious relic of the hand of St. James (which she gave to the family abbey at Reading). She was recognized as the legitimate heir of Henry I in England and Normandy, and in 1128 Henry I married her to the unpopular Angevin suitor, Geoffrey Plantagenet. Matilda was the child in her first marriage, but in this second union Geoffrey was the child, being

ten years her junior and only fifteen years old. Her second marriage of political expediency was a rocky one, but it did produce the needed heir in 1133 (Henry II Plantagenet). After her father's death in 1135 Matilda spent some twenty years asserting her son's claim to the Anglo-Norman throne against her cousin, Stephen of Blois.

Once Henry II succeeded Stephen in 1154, Matilda lived the remainder of her life in Normandy, and was buried at the abbey of Bec upon her death in 1167. She proved to be a valuable and trusted adviser to her royal son. Although she recommended against the appointment of Thomas à Becket as the archbishop of Canterbury, Matilda was turned to repeatedly by all sides as a mediator (*mediatrix*) in the subsequent dispute between the king and cleric. This remarkable woman's Anglo-Norman-German life was summed up in the epitaph on her tomb: "Great by birth, greater by marriage, greatest by offspring. Here lies the daughter, wife, and mother of Henry." Yet surely the legacy of this indomitable woman reaches beyond the men whose political needs set the boundaries of her life.

BIBLIOGRAPHY

Chibnall, Marjorie. *The Empress Matilda: Queen, Consort, Queen Mother and Lady of the English*. Oxford: Basil Blackwell, 1991.

Geldner, Ferdinand. "Kaiserin Mathilde, die deutsche Königswahl von 1125 und das Gegenkönigtum Konrads III." *Zeitschrift für bayerische Landesgeschichte* 40 (1977): 3–22.

Leyser, Karl. "Frederick Barbarossa, Henry II and the hand of St. James." *English Historical Review* 90 (1975): 481–506; rpt. in *Medieval Germany and its Neighbors*. London: Hambledon, 1980, pp. 215–40.

Pain, Nesta. *Matilda: Uncrowned Queen of England*. London: Weidenfeld and Nicolson, 1978.

Rössler, Oskar. *Kaiserin Mathilde, Mutter Heinrichs von Anjou, und das Zeitalter der Anarchie in England*. Berlin: E. Ebering, 1897; rpt. Vaduz: Kraus Reprint, 1965.

Schnith, Karl. "*Domina Anglorum*, Zur Bedeuntungsstreite eines hochmittelalterlichen Herrscherinentitels." In *Grundwissenschaften und Geschichte: Festschrift für Peter Acht*, ed. Waldemar Schlogl and Peter Herde. Kallmunz: Lassleben, 1976, pp. 101–111.

Joseph P. Huffman

SEE ALSO

Investiture Controversy; Salians

Maulbronn

The Cistercian monastery of Maulbronn (Baden-Württemberg), founded in 1147, remains almost unchanged since the Middle Ages. Legend reports that a group of traveling monks stopped to water their horses at this site and stayed, establishing their own religious house. A fresco in the vault of the monastery's fourteenth-century Fountain Chapel depicts this story.

At the heart of the walled complex is the monastery church, consecrated in 1178. The three-aisle Romanesque pillar basilica received Gothic net vaulting in the fifteenth century. Its richness and painted details contradict the strict Cistercian ban on church ornament. Among the most notable works at Maulbronn is a relief group created in the Parler workshop circa 1370; it depicts the Raising of the Cross, the Crucifixion, and the Entombment. Further interior ornaments and furnishings, such as the finely carved oak choir stalls (1470) and a monumental stone Crucifix over the lay altar (1473), date primarily to the fifteenth century.

The early Gothic narthex (entrance hall) of the church, known as the *Paradies,* is among the earliest interpretations of the Gothic style east of the Rhine. The unknown Master of the Maulbronn *Paradies* is believed to have been trained in northern France, probably at Laon in Picardy.

Both monks and lay brothers lived within the monastery walls, although somewhat separated. Ordained priests, many of noble birth, ate in the Lord's Refectory, while lay brothers had their own lay refectory and dormitory. In addition to these buildings, the nearly self-sufficient community contained a mill, bakery, barns, forge, fishpond, vineyards, and gardens. The monastic ideal of *ora et labora* (prayer and work), stated in the Rule

Maulbronn, west façade with *Paradies. Photograph: Joan A. Holladay*

of St. Benedict, was adhered to in the involvement of monks in the monastery's farming efforts. Despite the Cistercian rule's forbidding heated rooms, there is a kalefaktorium at Maulbronn. This room was heated from a lower level, with holes in the floor providing warm air.

Additional monastery structures include the abbot's house, a chapter house, cloister, oratorium (prayer room), and the parlatorium where monks would break the rule of silence. It is from the Gothic cloister that one approaches the fourteenth-century Fountain Chapel (Brunnenkapelle). At the center of the small room is a tiered fountain, at which the monks would have participated in ceremonial washings before meals.

Few changes were made to Maulbronn's Romanesque and Gothic monuments during the Protestant Reformation, largely owing to the dukes of Württemberg, who took over the complex in 1504. Secularized in 1530, a ducal residence was added in 1588. The monastery survived into the twentieth century as a school. Maulbronn serves today as a mirror of medieval monastic life and practice.

BIBLIOGRAPHY

Frank, Georg. *Das Zisterzienserkloster Maulbronn: Die Baugeschichte der Klausur von den Anfängen bis zur Säkularisierung.* Studien zur Kunstgeschichte 70. Hildesheim: Olms, 1993.

Knapp, Ulrich. *Das Kloster Maulbronn: Geschichte und Baugeschichte.* Darmstadt: Wissenschaftliche Buchgesellschaft, 1997.

Leslie Anne Hamel

SEE ALSO

Benedict, Rule of Saint; Cistercian Art and Architecture; Gothic Art and Architecture; Parler Family; Romanesque Art and Architecture

Maximilian (1459–1519)

Emperor, patron of the arts, "the last knight," Maximilian I Habsburg enjoys a popular modern reputation. As the son of Emperor Frederick III, Maximilian experienced a youth tarnished by the wars and defeats his father suffered. His first important step into politics came in 1473, when his father negotiated with Duke Charles the Rash of Burgundy for the hand of his daughter, Mary. Although Charles's original demand of a royal crown was too high, the negotiations continued over the next few years. Then when Charles died unexpectedly at the Battle

of Nancy in 1477, the king of France moved to seize Mary, who was holding out in Ghent. Maximilian sealed their marriage first through procurators in April, and finally concluded it in person when he arrived at the head of a rescuing army in August. Their marriage became a true love match. The emperor enfeoffed his son with the lands of the late duke of Burgundy. Yet Maximilian only truly secured most of the lands in a series of wars with France. His victory at the battle of Guinegate in 1479 guaranteed his possession of the Lowlands and most of Burgundy, some of the richest lands in Europe.

These new lands were not so easy to hold onto, however, since the citizens of the prosperous towns disputed the power of the new dynasty. After Mary died from a riding accident in 1482, many in the Lowlands openly rebelled against Maximilian's authority. Allied with France, town forces managed to wring from Maximilian the supervision of his children, Philip and Margaret. Even worse, the city of Bruges took him prisoner for fourteen weeks in 1488. His father, in a rare but certainly necessary act of support, actually gathered an army that marched on the city, frightening the town into freeing Maximilian. Returning at the head of his own army, Maximilian conquered Bruges and many other towns, completing their defeat by 1493 in the Treaty of Senlis.

In the midst of these conflicts Frederick had managed to get Maximilian elected king of the Romans in Frankfurt on February 16, 1486, and crowned in Aachen on April 9. For the first time in a century a son had followed as king an imperial father during the father's lifetime. In 1490 Maximilian replaced his incompetent cousin, Sigismund "the Rich in Coins," as duke of Tyrol. He made that province, located between Burgundy and Austria on the way to Italy, and its capital, Innsbruck, the center of his imperial organization. From there to Mecheln in the Netherlands he established the first regular postal route in Europe. The silver of Tyrol helped to finance the reconquest of Austria from Matthias Corvinus, while the growing business with the Fugger banking family helped to underwrite many more imperial schemes. But with interest rates of over 35 percent on loans, Maximilian rarely had enough cash to fund all his plans.

After Mary's death, Maximilian fathered several illegitimate children, but he knew the importance of political marriages. To gain both cash and leverage against France, in 1490 Maximilian arranged his marriage by proxy with the twelve-year-old Anne of Brittany, who had just inherited that important province on her father's death. The next year Charles VIII invaded Brittany, dissolved his (unconsummated) marriage to Maximilian's daughter Margaret, and, without returning Margaret or her dowry of Burgundy, married Anne. Maximilian tried to gather an army to oppose these actions but was hopelessly outnumbered by French forces and hampered by his daughter's hostage status. The Brittany affair gained France a strategic province, earned Maximilian frustration and humiliation, and helped engender a centuries-long rivalry between the Habsburg and Valois dynasties. In 1497 Maximilian found another marriage partner in Bianca Maria Sforza, sister of Ludovico il Moro Sforza, who had usurped control of Milan. She brought a dowry of four hundred thousand gulden (guilders), or about three times what Maximilian could draw annually from the Habsburg Austrian lands. That money quickly disappeared also.

Soon after his father's death in 1493, Maximilian responded to a call for an imperial reform proposed for the Reichstag (imperial council) of Worms in 1495. There the archbishop of Mainz, Berthold von Henneberg, tried to gain a reform suitable to the princes. At the Reichstag, Maximilian agreed to the "eternal territorial peace" *(Ewige Landfriede),* once and for all, legally forbidding the many private wars and feuds among nobles that had disturbed the empire. To keep the peace, the Reichstag also created the Imperial Chamber Court (Reichskammergericht) and established a general tax, the "common penny" *(gemeine Pfennig).* Afterward many princes wanted further reform and withheld the general tax to put pressure on Maximilian. After his defeat in a brief war against the Swiss, the princes temporarily were able to further restrict Maximilian's authority, imposing an imperial regime *(Reichsregiment)* at Augsburg in 1500. By 1504, however, he had largely defeated the fractious princes. The possibility of a unified, effective imperial government vanished in these quarrels.

Maximilian's involvement in wars on the empire's fringes brought mixed results. He encouraged new developments in military tactics, like cannon. Or he increasingly abandoned the cavalry charge of armored knights in favor of infantry on foot with sword and pike, his *Landsknechte.* Maximilian regularly participated in the shifting diplomatic alliances, and he managed to maintain a reputation as an able commander. But he lost many wars, often through lack of funds. He fought frequently in Italy, which had become an open battleground since the invasion in 1494 by Charles VII of France. In 1508 Pope Julius II, needing Maximilian's military support in the League of Cambrai against Venice, offered to crown him emperor. Yet Maximilian was unable to fight his way to Rome. So he proclaimed himself "elected emperor of the Romans" on February 4, 1508, in Trient. Thus, with Julius's belated acceptance, he became emperor without a papal coronation.

Maximilian gained lasting importance for both his dynasty and European history because of two important double marriages he arranged. First in 1496 he married his son Philip "the Handsome," and daughter Margaret from his marriage with Mary, to the heirs of Spain, Juana "the Mad" and Juan, the children of Ferdinand of Aragon and Isabella of Castille. Philip and Juana had several children. The elder son, Charles V, eventually inherited both the Spanish and Austrian possessions and had an empire "on which the sun never set." The second double marriage was arranged in 1515, when Maximilian married his grandson Ferdinand and granddaughter Mary to the children of King Ladislaus of Bohemia and Hungary. This arrangement provided the legal claims to reunite Hungary and Bohemia with the Habsburg lands in 1526.

But Maximilian's attempts at building stronger institutions of rule in his own inherited lands led to increasing opposition, including open rebellion in some territories. Even the citizens of Innsbruck resented the burden of debts run up by the often cash-poor Maximilian. At the beginning of 1519 they finally refused to accept his credit, or to find stalls for his horses. In disdain he left the city for Vienna but sickened along the way and died on January 12. As a result, his magnificent tomb in Innsbruck lies empty; his body is buried in Wiener Neustadt, while his heart lies in Bruges, next to the body of his first wife, Mary.

Maximilian enjoys lasting fame as a well-rounded Renaissance prince. He was a patron of the arts and new sciences at the summit of the German Renaissance. His portrait by Albrecht Dürer is the most famous image of the monarch. Skilled and literate in several languages, he himself helped to produce two autobiographical epic poems *(Theuerdank* and *Weisskunig),* a hunting manual, and other works, including the *Ambraser Heldenbuch (Ambray Book of Heroes,* a compilation manuscript of courtly literature named after Castle Ambras). Sometimes called "the last knight," he was a great promoter of tournaments, drawing on the chivalric traditions of the court of Burgundy and continuing the Order of the Golden Fleece. Maximilian's idea of the Holy Roman Empire of the German nation ended the Middle Ages and looked forward to the attempt at universal empire by his successor, his grandson Charles V.

BIBLIOGRAPHY

Benecke, Gerhard. *Maximilian I (1459–1519): An Analytical Biography.* London: Routledge and Kegan Paul, 1982.

Wiesflecker, Hermann. *Kaiser Maximilian I.: Das Reich, Österreich und Europa an der Wende zur Neuzeit.* 5 vols. Vienna: Verlag für Geschichte und Politik, 1971–1986.

Brian A. Pavlac

SEE ALSO

Arthurian Literature, German; Bookmaking and Production; Coronation; Frederick III; Hartmann von Aue; *Landfrieden*; Nancy, Battle of

Mechthild von Hackeborn (1241–1298/1299)

A Cistercian sister of the Helfta community, Mechthild von Hackeborn's mystical visions were recorded in the *Liber specialis gratiae (Book of Special Grace)*. At age seven, Mechthild entered the Rodersdorf cloister, where her sister Gertrud already resided. After the community had relocated to Helfta, Mechthild served in the capacities of magistra and cantrix. In 1261 the five-year-old Gertrud von Helfta *(die Große)* was given into her charge. Bedridden the last eight years of her life, Mechthild revealed her visions at this time to Gertrud and at least one other sister at Helfta, who recorded them without her knowledge; however, Mechthild did approve portions of the account before her death.

The original German version of Mechthild's visions has not survived. There are more than 250 contemporaneous and subsequent Latin and vernacular manuscript versions of the *Liber specialis gratiae,* but only one manuscript contains all seven books. Rich in allegory, the seven parts chronicle Mechthild's life and death, her visions, the special graces she experienced, her teachings concerning the true devotion to God and the virtuous life, and fragments of a correspondence with a female friend. In contrast to the *Fließendes Licht der Gottheit (Flowing Light of the Godhead)* of Mechthild's somewhat older namesake at Helfta, Mechthild von Magdeburg, the descriptions and observations found in the *Liber specialis gratiae* are based on liturgy, scripture, and the writings of the church fathers; however, like the *Fließendes Licht,* the *Liber* exhibits originality in imagery, language, and style. Of special note is Mechthild's description of the devotion to the Sacred Heart of Christ *(Herz-Jesu-Verehrung),* which she and Gertrud die Große promoted at Helfta.

BIBLIOGRAPHY

Bynum, Caroline Walker. "Women Mystics in the Thirteenth Century: The Case of the Nuns of Helfta." In *Jesus as Mother: Studies in the Spirituality of the High Middle Ages.* Berkeley: University of California Press, 1982, pp. 170–262.

Finnegan, Jeremy. "Saint Mechtild of Hackeborn: *Nemo Communior.*" In *Medieval Religious Women,* vol. 2. *Peace Weavers,* ed. Lillian Thomas Shank and John A. Nichols. Kalamazoo, Mich.: Cistercian Publications, 1987, pp. 213–221.

Finnegan, Mary Jeremy. *The Women of Helfta.* Athens: University of Georgia Press, 1991 [first published 1962 as *Scholars and Mystics*].

Haas, Alois Maria. "Mechthild von Hackeborn. Eine Form zisterziensischer Frauenfrömmigkeit." In *Die Zisterzienser. Ordensleben zwischen Ideal und Wirklichkeit.* Ergänzungsband, ed. Kaspar Elm. Cologne: Rheinland-Verlag, 1982, pp. 221–239; rpt. "Themen und Aspekte der Mystik Mechthilds von Hackeborn." In *Geistliches Mittelalter,* ed. Alois Maria Haas. Dokimion 8. Freiburg, Switzerland: Universitätsverlag, 1984), pp. 373–391.

Halligan, Theresa, ed. *The Booke of Gostlye Grace of Mechthild of Hackeborn.* Toronto: Pontifical Institute of Mediaeval Studies. 1979.

Lewis, Gertrud Jaron. *Bibliographie zur deutschen Frauenmystik des Mittelalters.* Berlin: Schmidt, 1989, pp. 184–195.

Paquelin, Ludwig, ed. "Sanctae Mechthildis Virginis Ordinis Sancti Benedicti Liber specialis gratiae." In *Revelationes Gertrudianae ac Mechthildianae,* vol. 2. Poitiers: Oudin, 1877, pp. 1–422.

Schmidt, Margot. "Mechthild von Hackeborn." In *Die deutsche Literatur des Mittelalters: Verfasserlexikon,* 2d ed., ed. Kurt Ruh. Berlin: de Gruyter, 1987, vol. 6, cols. 251–260.

Debra L. Stoudt

SEE ALSO

Gertrud von Helfta; Sister-Books; Visionary Literature; Women

Mechthild von Magdeburg (ca. 1207– ca. 1282)

Beguine, visionary, and mystic, known to us through her sole book, *Das fließende Licht der Gottheit (The Flowing Light of the Godhead).* Biographical information gleaned or inferred from her book and its introductory material written in Latin by others indicates that she was born to a family of lower nobility near Magdeburg. She experienced her first vision at age twelve and left home about 1230 to take up the life of a Beguine in Magdeburg, returning home occasionally perhaps because of sickness or troubles caused by her book. Just as she criticized the deportment of some Beguines, male and female religious, clergy, the pope, and others, she, too, was subjected to criticism and even threats. Equally evident, however, is the support she received, especially from the Dominicans, whose order she praised. Baldwin, her brother, was received into this order, became subprior of the Dominican house in Halle, and was esteemed for virtue and learning. Another Dominican, Heinrich von Halle, was her spiritual adviser for many years and helped her edit (and, no doubt, circulate) incomplete versions of her book. About 1270 she entered the Cistercian convent at Helfta, renowned, under the leadership of Gertrud von Hackeborn, for its thriving spiritual life and devotion to learning, as witnessed by the writings of Mechthild von Hackeborn and Gertrud (the Great) von Helfta. Here Mechthild was sheltered from the trials of the unprotected life of a Beguine but, if we can believe her, was more revered from a distance than accepted into the community. With her health weakening and her sight failing, she completed the seventh and final section of her book. Her death is described in Gertrud of Helfta's *Legatus divinae pietatis.*

The original text of her book, written in Middle Low German with some Middle German characteristics, has been lost. A Middle High German version of the complete work translated about 1345 under the direction of Heinrich von Nördlingen in Basel survives in a manuscript at Einsiedeln ("E") and provides the principal textual basis for the study of Mechthild. Parts and short fragments have been discovered in other manuscripts. A Latin translation of the first six books of the Middle Low German original, probably the work of Dominicans in Halle, has come down to us preceded by a lengthy prologue justifying the book and its author.

Das fließende Licht can be described as confessional, visionary-revelatory, mystical, poetic, and devotional. It was written, we are told, by divine command to bear witness to the unusual divine favors bestowed on its author. Mechthild describes her visions, some global and some personal in scope, as well as her ecstatic mystical experiences of union. She prophesies, exhorts, criticizes, and teaches, using a rich variety of literary and nonliterary

forms of expression, from highly lyrical courtly modes with their concomitant conventions to didactic expositions of moral and ascetical truths. She avails herself of prose, verse, and, most distinctively, colon rhyme—a short, verselike unit ending in rhyme or, more frequently, assonance. Much of this colon rhyme has been lost in the Middle High German version.

Because she knew little or no Latin, Mechthild acquired her knowledge of theology and spiritual traditions secondhand through instruction and the liturgy. The theological content of her book gives striking evidence of the care given religious education by her spiritual teachers and advisers, but more especially to Mechthild's own intellectual gifts and intuitive spiritual receptivity. Among the influences perceptible in her book are the Song of Songs, Augustine, Bernard of Clairvaux, Hugh and Richard of St. Victor, and Joachim of Fiore. More important, however, Mechthild's book must be seen as unique in its conception, without discernible predecessors or successors.

BIBLIOGRAPHY

Bynum, Caroline Walker. "Women Mystics in the Thirteenth Century: The Case of the Nuns of Helfta." In Bynum. *Jesus as Mother—Studies in the Spirituality of the High Middle Ages.* Berkeley: University of California Press, 1982, pp. 170–262.

Franklin, James C. *Mystical Transformations: The Imagery of Liquids in the Work of Mechthild von Magdeburg.* Rutherford, N.J.: Fairleigh Dickinson University Press, 1978.

Galvani, Christiana Mesch, trans. *Flowing Light of the Divinity.* New York: Garland, 1991.

Haug, Walter. "Das Gespräch mit dem unvergleichlichen Partner: Der mystische Dialog bei Mechthild von Magdeburg als Paradigma für eine personale Gesprächsstrutkur." *Poetik und Hermeneutik* 11 (1984): 251–279.

Lewis, Gertrud Jaron. *Bibliographie zur deutschen Frauenmystik des Mittelalters.* Berlin: Schmidt, 1989, pp. 164–183 [bibliography].

Neumann, Hans. "Mechthild von Magdeburg." In *Die deutsche Literatur des Mittelalters: Verfasserlexikon.* 2d ed, vol. 6. Berlin: de Gruyter, 1987, cols. 260–270.

Neumann, Hans, ed. *Mechthild von Magdeburg. Das fließende Licht der Gottheit.* 2 vols. Munich: Artemis, 1990.

Schmidt, Margot. "*Minne du gewaltige Kellerin:* On the Nature of *minne* in Mechthild of Magdeburg's *fliessendes licht der gottheit.*" *Vox Benedictina* 4 (1987): 100–125.

Scholl, Edith. "To Be a Full Grown Bride: Mechthild of Magdeburg." In *Medieval Religious Women. vol. 2.: Peace Weavers,* ed. John A. Nichols and Lillian Thomas Shank. Kalamazoo, Mich.: Cistercian,1987, pp. 223–238.

Tax, Petrus. "Die große Himmelsschau Mechthilds von Magdeburg und ihre Höllenvision." *Zeitschrift für deutsches Altertum* 108 (1979): 112–137.

Tobin, Frank. *Mechthild von Magdeburg—A Medieval Mystic in Modern Eyes.* Columbia, S.C.: Camden House, 1995.

von Balthasar, Hans Urs. "Mechthilds kirchlicher Auftrag." In *Das fließende Licht der Gottheit,* trans. Margot Schmidt. 1955. 2d ed. Stuttgart-Bad Canstatt: F. Frommann, 1995, pp. 19–45.

Frank Tobin

SEE ALSO

Beguines; Gertrud von Helfta; Mysticism; Visionary Literature

Medicine

To the extent that Western European medicine drew on ancient Greek and Islamic medical ideas, medical literature was oriented toward the preservation, organization, and transmission of authoritative texts.

Early medieval medicine has been characterized as monastic medicine, because, beginning around 800, monasteries became centers for copying texts and for their practical application. The earliest medical texts written in German arose in this context. Apart from individual recipes in Latin recipe collections and vernacular glosses on Latin texts, the second half of the twelfth century marks the beginning of German vernacular medical literature with two pharmacological texts, the *Prüller Steinbuch* (Prüll Stone Book) and *Prüller Kräuterbuch* (Prüll Herb Book), the *Arzenîbuoch Ipocratis* (Hippocratic Healing Book), a prognostic text known as the Pseudo-Hippocratic *Capsula eburnea* (The Little Ivory Chest), the *Innsbrucker Arzneibuch* (a recipe collection), and a gynecological fragment in the same manuscript.

Major German medical works are the Thuringian *Bartholomäus* and an herbal known as *Macer* (both ca. 1200), as well as the *Arzneibuch* (handbook of general medicine) of Ortolf of Baierland (ca. 1300). As early as the mid–tenth century a center for medical learning and practice arose in Salerno in southern Italy. Increasingly in the twelfth century, the locus of learned medicine shifted away from the monastery to the university and court. By around 1300 Montpellier, Paris, Bologna, and Padua had medical faculties with set curricula that attracted students from all Europe. Also in the course of the twelfth and thirteenth centuries translations were made, particularly in southern Italy and Spain of medical works (those of Hippocrates and Galen and their Arabic followers) from Arabic and Greek into Latin. In addition, the reception of Aristotelian natural philosophy and logic as well as Arabic astrology transformed the study of medicine.

Throughout the Middle Ages the variety of medical practitioners described a spectrum with considerable overlap between the learned and popular (or practical) traditions. Ranging from lay healers and family members to university-trained physicians, it included men and women, Christians and Jews, herbalists or apothecaries, surgeons, barber-surgeons, empirics, and midwives. Many of these groups came to be regulated either by professional licensing or by guilds.

Gradually, in the fourteenth and fifteenth centuries, academic medicine began to reach other groups through translations into the vernacular and printing. The year 1348 saw the establishment by Emperor Charles IV of the University of Prague and thereafter of universities with medical faculties in German-speaking lands. Yet the majority of German medical students took their degrees at northern Italian universities. The arrival of plague in 1348 and its recurrences in subsequent centuries focused attention on public health and public health institutions.

By and large, during the Middle Ages, diseases were classified according to humoral theory, diagnosed through uroscopy, and treated with diet, medication, or surgery (including cautery and phlebotomy), although magic, astrology, and religious healing also played a role.

BIBLIOGRAPHY

Crossgrove, William. *Die deutsche Sachliteratur des Mittelalters.* Bern: Lang, 1994.

Keil, Gundolf, ed. *"ein teutsch puech machen": Untersuchungen zur landessprachlichen Vermittlung medizinischen Wissens.* Wiesbaden: Reichert, 1993.

Park, Katharine. "Medicine and Society in Medieval Europe, 500–1500." In *Medicine in Society: Historical Essays,* ed. Andrew Wear. Cambridge: Cambridge University Press, 1992, pp. 59–90.

Schnell, Bernhard. "Prolegomena to a History of Medieval German Medical Literature." In *Manuscript*

Sources of Medieval Medicine: A Book of Essays, ed. Margaret R. Schleissner. New York: Garland, 1995, pp. 3–15.

Siraisi, Nancy G. *Medieval and Early Renaissance Medicine: An Introduction to Knowledge and Practice.* Chicago: University of Chicago Press, 1990.

Margaret Schleissner

SEE ALSO

Charms; Education; Magic; *Sachliteratur*

Meißen

Located twenty-five kilometers northwest of Dresden at the confluence of the Triebisch and Elbe Rivers, Meißen (Saxony) is dominated by the Burgberg, a strategically located cliff plateau on which Henry I, duke of Saxony, founded the Castle Misni in 928, as part of his eastward expansion into Slavic territory. The development of Meißen reflects both religious and secular powers: Emperor Otto I established the bishopric of Meißen in 968, the same year the first margrave of Meißen is mentioned. The cathedral of Meißen, which sits atop the Burgberg, is dedicated to Saints John the Baptist and Donatus and replaces a tenth-century chapel and an Ottonian basilica built between 1006 and 1073. Construction of the Gothic cathedral began in 1260 under Bishop Albert II (1259–1266) and continued by Bishop Withego I (1266–1293); its High Gothic polygonal choir was consecrated in 1268. The first phase of construction continued with interruptions until 1410. The *Fürstenkapelle,* the margraves' burial chapel, built after 1423, forms the west choir.

Within the cathedral are seven standing figures from about 1255–1270 attributed to the Naumburg Master. The figures, among the best examples of thirteenth-century German sculpture, include representations of Emperor Otto I and Empress Adelheid. The original position of the figures is still debated; ranging in size from 185 to 211 centimeters, excluding bases, they may have been carved originally for a portal of the Virgin on the west facade, although current theories suggest that the figures were created before the completion of the choir and were consequently placed on the walls of the choir and the chapel of Mary Magdalene, located directly behind the choir.

The second main part of the city, Afraberg, a tax-free settlement, developed in the tenth century to protect the Misni castle. After first settling here in 1064, the Augus-

Meissen cathedral, interior, view to east. *Photograph: Joan A. Holladay*

tinians dedicated their monastery of St. Afra in 1205, the oldest preserved structure of the area. An annual market was established at the foot of the Burgberg in the tenth century and first documented in 1002. In 1205 Margrave Dietrich began the systematic planning of the city, which was first documented in 1295, between the Burgberg and the St. Afra settlement. The fires of 1447 and 1455 destroyed the Church of Our Lady (Frauenkirche), first mentioned in 1205, and rebuilt as a Late Gothic hall church in 1457, and the Franciscan church, which was part of the monastery founded in 1258. The margraves retained possession of Meißen until 1423, when it became a free city after Frederick I, the Elector of Saxony, received the Duchy of Saxony-Wittenberg.

The city was not destroyed during World War II, and its medieval character is evident in its architectural harmony.

BIBLIOGRAPHY

Hannig, Peter. *Bildwerke des Mittelalters und des Barocks aus der Albrechtsburg.* Dresden: Verlag der Kunst, 1985.

Lehmann, Edgar. *Der Dom zu Meißen.* Berlin: Union, 1971.

Mrusek, Hans-Joachim, ed. *Die Albrechtsburg zu Meißen.* Leipzig: E. A. Seeman, 1973.

———. *Drei sächsische Kathedralen: Merseburg, Naumburg, Meißen.* Dresden: Verlag der Kunst, 1976, pp. 266–375.

Schubert, Dietrich. *Von Halberstadt nach Meißen: Bildwerke des 13. Jahrhunderts in Thüringen, Sachsen und Anhalt.* Dumont Dokumente. Cologne: Dumont Schauberg, 1974, pp. 319–322.

Gregory H. Wolf

SEE ALSO

Adelheid of Burgundy; Gothic Art and Architecture; Gothic Art and Architecture, Late; Naumburg; Otto I; Romanesque Art and Architecture; Town Planning and Urbanism

Meister Eckhart (ca. 1260–1327/1328)

Dominican theologian, preacher, administrator, and mystic. The title *meister,* a corruption of the Latin *magister* (teacher) refers both to his having received the highest academic degree then attainable and to his professional duties at the University of Paris. He was born in Thuringia, possibly in a village called Hochheim, of which there are two, one near Erfurt and one near Gotha. One document refers to him as *de* (from, of) Hochheim, but some scholars consider this a familial rather than a geographical designation and use it to bolster the claim that Eckhart was of noble origin. He most likely entered the Order of Preachers (Dominicans) at the priory in Erfurt at about the age of fifteen. Possibly he received his early training in the arts at Paris and was witness to Bishop Stephen Tempier's condemnation of 219 articles of theology including several taught by Thomas Aquinas (d. 1274), the Dominican order's most distinguished theologian. At any rate, Eckhart is documented in Paris lecturing on Peter Lombard's *Sentences* in 1293–1294. Prior to this he had absolved the various stages of Dominican formation: one year novitiate, two years studying the order's constitutions and the divine office, about five years studying philosophy, with three additional years devoted to theology. Eckhart was no doubt also among those chosen for further study, very likely at the order's *studium generale* (early form of university) in Cologne, where he might have had direct contact with Albert the Great. After lecturing in Paris Eckhart advances rapidly within the order. He is prior in Erfurt 1294–1298, professor in Paris 1302–1303, provincial of the newly formed German Dominican province of Saxony 1303–1311, and again professor in Paris 1312–1313. There followed several years of preaching in the vernacular, to Beguines and nuns among others, in Strasbourg and then later in Cologne, where he might also have had professorial duties at the *studium generale.*

In 1325 the first clouds appear when some of Eckhart's teachings are investigated as to their orthodoxy. Eckhart is cleared, but the following year Henry of Virneburg, archbishop of Cologne, begins inquisitorial proceedings against him. Eckhart responds to lists of suspect theses taken from a broad selection of his Latin and German works and, on January 24, 1327, citing delays and the public scandal the proceedings are causing, appeals to the pope. On February 13 he protests his innocence from the pulpit of the Dominican church in Cologne and soon thereafter travels to Avignon, where a papal commission begins an investigation. On March 27, 1329, some time after Eckhart's death, a papal bull, *In agro dominico,* definitively ends the investigation. In it seventeen articles are condemned as heretical, two of which Eckhart claimed never to have taught. Eleven others are judged to be evil sounding but capable of an orthodox interpretation. The bull states that Eckhart, before his death, recanted the articles and anything else that might have caused error in the minds of his audience *quoad illum sensum.* In other words, he recanted a heretical interpretation of his words, not the words themselves.

Eckhart's writings can be divided into Latin works (professional theological treatises, learned commentaries on scripture, and some sermons or sermon outlines) and German works (spiritual tracts and, especially, sermons). Because of Eckhart's sad fate, his Latin works were generally forgotten and only rediscovered in the late nineteenth century. His German works became mixed with those of other spiritual authors or were often passed on with false or no attribution. As a result, the task of creating a reliable critical edition of the German works begun by Josef Quint in 1936 is just now nearing completion. Disagreement still remains concerning the authenticity of many German sermons not yet included in the critical edition, and discussion of their chronology has just begun. Eckhart is admired both for the brilliance of his mystical thought and for his virtuosity in expressing it. The first admirers of Eckhart after his rediscovery in the nineteenth century, because of their unfamiliarity with medieval philosophy and theology, made uninformed judgments about his originality in thought and language. Although scholars still view him as an original thinker, he is now recognized as being original within the context of the already well-developed system of scholastic thought. His mysticism has been termed speculative to indicate both its imbeddedness in scholastic philosophy and theology as well as the fact that he does not talk about mystical union in terms of personal experience. Rather, he describes the metaphysical constitution of both the human soul and God's nature that makes union possible. For Eckhart mystical union between God and the soul rests on their metaphysical oneness. Eckhart sees creatures as differing from God, but they differ only through the nothingness limiting the being that they possess; and being is God. Eckhart distinguishes between two kinds of being in creatures: formal or limited being, which constitutes them in existence separate from God, and virtual being—the being of creatures in the mind of God existing from eternity. The virtual being of creatures at one with God's being is their more real and vital being. Their formal being is a mere shadow by comparison. This distinction between formal and virtual being in creatures provides the context for understanding most of Eckhart's characteristic doctrines. Thus, for example, he urges us to become as poor in spirit as we were (in the mind of God) before we were (formally existing). In other words, we are to "reduce" our existence to existence in God. So, too, in becoming the just man, we do so by uniting completely with justice, which is identical with God's being. Through our oneness with God's being the birth of the Son takes place in us, as it does in Bethlehem, and united with this divine action we become both the begotten (Son) and the "begetter" (Father). The human intellect, that faculty most essential in establishing our likeness with God, is in its purely spiritual activity the spark of the soul in which we most throw off the confines of our creatureliness and imitate divine activity. And through detachment, a key term in Eckhart's mystical asceticism, the creature frees himself from his own specific self or formal being, which is in essence the limiting factor separating us from God, to become whole or one with him.

The startling vigor of Eckhart's thought is matched by the power and artfulness with which he expresses it. Though the Latin works show skillful manipulation of language, it is his German works, especially the sermons, that display a rich variety of linguistic artistry, some of it best termed rhetorical and some clearly poetic. Often he overcomes the limitations of the young vernacular's ability to express his rarefied mysticism by placing a key term in a variety of juxtaposed contexts in the manner of a leitmotif and thus gradually reveals to his audience the treasures it contains. He employs such figures as accumulation, antithesis, parallelism, hyperbole, chiasmus, and paradox to great advantage. Word games and original verbal strategies of other kinds abound.

Eckhart influenced most immediately John Tauler and Henry Suso, Dominican mystics of the next generation, and less clearly their Flemish contemporary John (Jan van) Ruusbroec. From the library of the Swiss cardinal Nicholas of Cusa (Cusanus), Latin works by Eckhart have come down to us with comments by the cardinal scribbled in the margins. Cusanus shows much affinity in thought with Eckhart and defended him against the attacks of the Heidelberg theologian Johannes Wenck. The baroque poet Johann Scheffler (Angelus Silesius) was certainly touched by Eckhartian ideas, but, as in the case of many other authors and works of the reformation period and beyond, whether the influence was direct or indirect is impossible to tell. In more modern times the philosophers Hegel, Schelling, and Baader all admired his thought, though until the mid–twentieth century much of this admiration was based on misunderstandings arising from ignorance about Eckhart's own intellectual context. The last forty years have seen great progress in understanding this exhilarating mystic, though much of his uncharted profundity remains to be explored.

BIBLIOGRAPHY

Colledge, Edmund, and Bernard McGinn, trans. *Meister Eckhart: The Essential Sermons, Commentaries, Treatises, and Defense,* New York: Paulist, 1981.

Koch, Josef. "Zur Analogielehre Meister Eckharts." 1959; rpt. in Josef Koch. *Kleine Schriften,* vol. 1. Rome: [n.p.], 1973, pp. 367–409.

Largier, Niklaus. *Bibliographie zu Meister Eckhart.* Freiburg: Universitätsverlag, 1989 [bibliography].

McGinn, Bernard. "Eckhart's Condemnation Reconsidered." *Thomist* 44 (1980): 390–414.

———. "The God Beyond God: Theology and Mysticism in the Thought of Meister Eckhart." *Journal of Religion* 61 (1981): 1–19.

———. "Meister Eckhart on God as Absolute Unity." In *Neoplatonism and Christian Thought,* ed. Dominic J. O'Meara. Albany: State University of New York Press, 1982, pp. 128–139.

———, ed., *Meister Eckhart and the Beguine Mystics.* New York: Continuum, 1994.

McGinn, Bernard, Frank Tobin, and Elvira Borgstadt. *Meister Eckhart: Teacher and Preacher.* New York: Paulist, 1986.

Meister Eckhart. *Die deutschen und lateinischen Werke,* ed. Josef Quint. Stuttgart: Kohlhammer, 1936ff.

Ruh, Kurt. *Meister Eckhart: Theologe, Prediger, Mystiker.* Munich: Beck, 1985.

Schürmann, Reiner. *Meister Eckhart: Mystic and Philosopher.* Bloomington: University of Indiana Press, 1978.

Smith, Cyprian. *Meister Eckhart: The Way of Paradox.* London: Darton, Longman and Todd, 1987.

Tobin, Frank. *Meister Eckhart: Thought and Language.* Philadelphia: University of Pennsylvania Press, 1986.

Walshe, M. O'C. *Meister Eckhart: Sermons and Treatises.* Rockport, Me.: Element, 1992.

Frank Tobin

SEE ALSO
Beguines; Seuse, Heinrich; Jan van Ruusbroec

Meistersinger

The term "master singers" (German *Meistersänger*) denotes German poets and writers of song lyrics, originally vagrant minstrels of the late fourteenth and early fifteenth centuries. Some scholars consider them to be the bourgeois equivalent and successors of the courtly *Minnesinger,* a group of poets singing of courtly love *(Minne),* which declined simultaneously with the Hohenstaufen dynasty. Others maintain that laymen gathered in "schools" of singing to create religious and festive songs, and that these schools arose out of the craft guilds. The claims are not mutually exclusive, each having some basis in fact. To legitimate their art without any appearance of being rebellious, the Meistersingers claimed to be the inheritors of twelve skilled medieval masters of the arts. They were not professional musicians but practiced songwriting as a formalized hobby or pastime, the opportunity occasioned by sufficient wealth to enjoy free time. Some of them were Latin educated; others possessed only very rudimentary learning. A famous Colmar manuscript, completed about 1470 and containing nine hundred songs, is the most comprehensive surviving evidence of their craft.

The creations of the Meistersingers were pedantic songs, governed by stiff rules of form called *Tablatur,* while elaborating moral and political themes. When composed for church, the lyrics adhered faithfully to the Bible, but during the fifteenth century the singers included secular topics in their repertoire. The poets supplied new lyrics for the invariable melodies of the Old Masters, though the general quality failed to match the forerunners. In the fifteenth and sixteenth centuries in Nuremberg, for example, there were six thousand poems set to only two hundred tunes. Normally, a stanza of a song called a *Gesatz* consisted of two melodically identical *Stollen* that formed the *Aufgesang* (ascending song, or "a") and the melodically distinct *Abgesang* (descending song, or "b"). As a rule, three stanzas, though there could be five or seven, comprised the bar, a musical unit (a song) following the pattern of "aab." The rhyme scheme *(Gebänd)* was frequently complicated and the rhythm sometimes irregular. The *Meistergesang* was performed by the singer without the benefit of either instrumental or vocal accompaniment. Because the static form hindered creativity, the genre seemed destined for oblivion. At the turn of the fifteenth to sixteenth century, when the Meistersingers were firmly ensconced in guilds, Hans Folz, barber and surgeon from Worms, convinced the school at Nuremberg to allow a greater variety in both lyrics and melody, a victory that infused the genre with renewed life. Some critics consider singers such as Walter von der Vogelweide, Konrad von Würzburg, Der Marner, and Regenbogen to have been Meistersingers, recalling a poem about the battle of poets at the Wartburg. It is more generally accepted, however, that Heinrich von Meißen (ca. 1260–1318) initiated the tradition. Heinrich is more popularly known as *Frauenlob* (literally praise of women), a cognomen that he earned in competition. He represents the middle-class poets who succeeded the knightly minnesingers, adapting *Minnesang* to theology and learning. His most famous work is his *Marienleich (Hymn to Mary),* in which he unites traditional religious iconography with philosophy. A well-educated minstrel who wandered between Prague and Mainz, Frauenlob founded schools of singers. There were no actual unions of poets in the earlier Middle Ages, though singers met at competitions such as the legendary "singers' war" at the Wartburg. The earlier minstrels depended entirely for their livelihood on their individual patrons, so a federation would have benefited them little. But in the late fourteenth and early fifteenth centuries, when a financially independent class arose in the cities, groups of poets also emerged. The early Meistersinger formed guilds, spreading throughout southern Germany, Silesia, and Bohemia. Although singers performed in northern Germany as well, there were apparently no singing schools. Members of the small trades met on Sunday afternoons to practice their homemade songs. A good song was analogous to a fine product such as shoes or clothing produced by a guild artisan. The schools of singing ordered members in ranks after the fashion of the craft associations. One began as a *Schüler* (pupil) and progressed through the ranks of *Schulfreund* (friend of the school), *Singer,* and *Dichter* (poet), only becoming a *Meister* (master) by the adjudication of the *Merker* (judge). Like their predecessors and like courtly knights, singers loved competition, in this case not a war of poets nor a tournament but a *Wettsingen,* or singing contest. Though notions of individual honor were banned in favor of the common good, the winner customarily received a medal with a picture of King David or a floral wreath. In general the works of the singers were not very popular, largely ignored, and unpublished, and few produced songs of excellence. The most famous Meistersinger, an apprentice shoemaker from 1509 to 1519, was Hans Sachs of Nuremberg (November 5, 1494–January 19, 1576). He founded a Latin school and surpassed all others in popularity, and productivity, and in artistic and theological influence. He became the master at Nuremberg in 1517, moving on to conduct the school in Munich until 1554. He wrote thousands of songs (sources vary between 4,000 and 6,000), some of which were biblical comedies and stories from both Old and New Testaments. He composed an additional 200 dramas, many for Fastnacht (Shrovetide). In his songs, Sachs espoused, in accordance with the conservative-minded nature of the Meistersingers, the cooperative efforts of all citizens and the common good as the highest goal of each individual. We remember the Meistersingers today because Richard Wagner memorialized them, especially Sachs, in his opera *Die Meistersänger* and because he renewed the form of the meistersong in his opera *Tannhäuser.* The significance of the Meistersingers lies in their devotion to their art and their attempt to inculcate moral principles through the text of their songs. According to one source, the decline of the genre began as early as 1504, with Johan von Soest. Attempts to renew the movement after 1600 failed, though the last school of singers was not actually disbanded until 1875 at Memmingen, a school that continued to exist only because of its adaptation of literary principles elucidated by the sixteenth-century German writer and literary critic Martin Opitz.

BIBLIOGRAPHY

Bell, Clair Hayden. *The Meistersingerschule at Memmingen and Its "Kurze Entwerfung."* Berkeley: University of California Press, 1952.

Die Schulordnung und das Gemerkbuch der Augsburger Meistersinger, ed. Horst Brunner, et al. Tübingen: Niemeyer, 1991.

Friedmann, Clarence William. *Prefigurations in Meistergesang: Types from the Bible and Nature.* New York: AMS, 1970.

Hermand, Jost. *Die deutschen Dichterbünde.* Cologne: Böhlau, 1998, pp. 12–22.

Linker, Robert White. *Music of the Minnesinger and Early Meistersinger.* Chapel Hill: University of North Carolina Press, 1962.

Nagel, Bert. *Die deutsche Meistersang.* Heidelberg: Kerle, 1952.

———. *Meistersang.* Stuttgart: Metzler, 1962.

Kristine K. Sneeringer

SEE ALSO

Folz, Hans; Fraunelob; Konrad von Würzburg; *Minnesang;* Walther von der Vogelweide

Melk

The steep rocky cliff, rising between the Danube and the Danube road at Melk (Lower Austria), appears to have been inhabited long before the Romans built a fort at Namare in the vicinity. During the migration of the German's tribes, the region was overrun by the Avars. With the Carolingian expansion eastward, the region was colonized by German nobles and monasteries. In 831 Louis the German gave the location Medelicha to the Bavarian monastery of Hereiden. Around 900 the Magyar incursion brought an end to this colonization. In the post-Lechfeld expansion a castle at Melk (Medelicha) was occupied by margraves of the Bavarian dukes. Following the revolt of the duke of Bavaria in 975, Emperor Otto II gave the castle and the surrounding region to the Babenberg Leopold I as a guardian post of the eastern frontier. The castle became the residence and burial site of the house of Babenberger. The Middle High German epic *Nibelungenlied* (ca. 1200) mentions a castle at Mederlikke, notable for its hospitality. A monastery, dedicated to Saints Peter and Paul, was established on the site by 985.

The translation of the relics of the recently martyred pilgrim Coloman from Stockerau to Melk on October 13, 1014, initiated a new era in the history of the abbey. Following numerous miracles, the cult of St. Coloman spread rapidly, with Melk as the center of veneration. In 1170 a new altar was dedicated to St. Coloman. Around this time the abbey's other most precious relics, which had been brought to Melk in the eleventh century, were "rediscovered": the Melk Cross, a piece of the True Cross, and the lance of St. Mauritius. With the possession of these important relics, and the dynastic associations of the Babenberg tombs, Melk attained important status as a pilgrimage site and one of the oldest holy sites in Austria. Coloman's status as patron saint of Austria in the thirteenth century increased the importance of Melk as a site of pilgrimage.

On March 21, 1089, Margrave Leopold II handed the site over to the Benedictines of Lambach. Leopold III (1095–1136) bestowed great gifts on the monastery, including a privilege of exemption in 1110, by which the monastery was placed directly under control of the Holy See. Leopold III also gave the Babenberg castle to the Benedictines and rebuilt the abbey church. During the twelfth and thirteenth centuries Kloster Melk was known as a great center of learning and artistic production, boasting a thriving monastery school and scriptorium. During the twelfth and thirteenth centuries a women's convent also existed on the site. A fire of 1297 destroyed the Romanesque church, library, and archive.

A new three-aisle Gothic basilica with a west tower was begun around 1324 and consecrated in 1429. The women's convent appears not to have been rebuilt. An artistic revival occurred under Duke Rudolf IV (1358–1365), who gave new Gothic settings for the Melk Cross and the Mauritius Lance, as well as a splendid monumental Gothic canopy-shrine for St. Coloman. These relics held significance for the Austrian dukes as legitimizing insignias of office.

With the reform plan of Duke Albrecht V following the Council of Constance, Melk became the center for the renewal of Benedictine monasteries in Austria and south Germany known as the Melk Reform. Monks from Subiaco arrived in 1418 to help implement the reform, which included a simplification of the liturgy, correction and production of liturgical books, and rigorous ordering of monastic life. The resulting revival of religious, scientific, humanist, and literary energy can be seen in the vast production of manuscripts from the fifteenth century at Melk. As a center of learning and reform, Melk saw many visiting monks and scholars who came to learn the new observance and study at its school. This heyday of Kloster Melk lasted for a century until a slow decline set in during the sixteenth century, when the Reformation left the monastery virtually depopulated until the seventeenth century.

The town of Melk grew up at the foot of the cliff, in the shadow of the castle and monastery above. Already in the eleventh century it was mentioned as a *civitas* in the account of the translation of St. Coloman. During the twelfth century the poet Heinrich von Melk and the poetess Frau Ava lived in the vicinity. By the thirteenth century the modest town had acquired market rights. However, the town was dominated by the fortified monastery on the escarpment above.

BIBLIOGRAPHY

Fillitz, Hermann. "Der mittelalterliche Schatz des Stiftes Melk." *Jacob Prandtauer und sein Kunstkreis: Ausstellung zum 300. Geburtstag des großen österreichischen Baumeisters.* Vienna: Österreichische Staatsdruckerei, 1960, pp. 123–125.

Keiblinger, Ignaz Franz. *Geschichte des Benedictiner-Stiftes Melk in Niederösterreich, seiner Besitzungen und Umgebungen,* vol. 1.: *Geschichte des Stiftes.* Vienna: Fr. Beck's Universitäts-Buchhandlung, 1851.

Kummer, Edmund. "Stift Melk und seine Geschichte," "Melk und die Babenberger," and "St. Coloman." *Jacob Prandtauer und sein Kunstkreis: Ausstellung zum 300. Geburtstag des großen österreichischen Baumeisters.* Vienna: Österreichische Staatsdruckerei, 1960, pp. 106–109, 129, 131.

Lechner, Karl. "Die Anfänge des Stiftes Melk und des St.-Coloman-Kultes." *Jahrbuch für Landeskunde von Niederösterreich* 29 (1944–1948): 47–54. *900 Jahre Benediktiner in Melk: Jubiläumsausstellung 1989 Stift Melk.* Melk: Stift Melk, 1989.

Schier, Wilhelm. *Das Benediktinerstift Melk an der Donau.* Vienna: Dr. Benno Filser Verlag, 1928.

Scott Bradford Montgomery

SEE ALSO

Constance; Gothic Art and Architecture; Heinrich von Melk; Lambach; *Niebelungenlied;* Otto II; Relics and Reliquaries; Romanesque Art and Architecture

Merseburg

King Henry I (919–936) built a palace at Merseburg, but a settlement on the strategic site above the Saale River is already mentioned in Carolingian times. Henry's son, the emperor Otto I (936–973), promised that he would establish a bishopric there if he won the battle against the Hungarians at Lechfeld in 955, and he finally fulfilled his vow in 968. The newly founded bishopric was abolished in 981 and then reestablished by Henry II in 1004. Bishop Thietmar von Merseburg (d. 1018) laid the cornerstone for the new cathedral in 1015, and the building was consecrated in the presence of Henry II in 1021. As elsewhere, the Ottonian church was built on a modular plan. The dimensions of the square crossing bay repeat in each transept arm and in the single bay of the choir. A semicircular apse closes the choir, which collapsed twice and was subsequently rebuilt with flanking eastern towers for a consecration in 1042. The three nave bays and their flanking aisles were rebuilt in a late Gothic style in the second half of the fifteenth century, using the Ottonian foundations for both the exterior walls and the columns. The addition of a crossing tower and upper stories to the west towers in the twelfth century preceded more extensive work in the thirteenth: the rebuilding of the choir and transepts retaining the lower walls of the Ottonian building, the insertion of sanctuaries between the east towers and transepts and the addition of upper stories to the east towers, the vaulting of the nave, and the erection of a *Vorhalle* (entrance hall) at the west end of the building.

Judging by Henry's donations to his foundation at Bamberg, to Charlemagne's palace chapel at Aachen, and to the cathedral at Basel, we may safely assume that he outfitted the new church at Merseburg in a similarly lavish fashion. Nothing remains of these early liturgical objects and furnishings. But Merseburg Cathedral houses the tomb of the first antiking Rudolf of Swabia. The cast-bronze tomb, originally gilt and inset with semiprecious stones, was installed in the crossing soon after Rudolf's death in 1080. It is important not only as an early example of large-scale casting in bronze but as an early example of a figural tomb. At a time when the Salian kings were still buried under simple stone slabs with inscriptions, Rudolf is portrayed in low relief, wearing a crown and carrying an orb and scepter as marks of office. Probably a commission of the Merseburg bishop Werner von Wolkenburg (1059–1093), Rudolf's tomb marks the bishop's papal position in the Investiture Controversy, the battle between the pope and the German king Henry IV over the right to name bishops. It also records the direct connection to the highest levels of secular authority that the bishopric had enjoyed earlier in the century.

BIBLIOGRAPHY

Haesler, Friedrich. *Der Merseburger Dom des Jahres 1015.* Studien zur thüringisch-sächsischen Kunstgeschichte 3. Halle: Gebauer-Schwetzschke, 1932.

Hinz, Berthold. *Das Grabdenkmal Rudolfs von Schwaben: Monument der Propaganda und Paradigma der Gattung.* kunststück. Frankfurt am Main: Fischer Taschenbuch Verlag, 1996.

Schubert, Ernst. *Der Dom zu Merseburg: Eine Führung.* Das christliche Denkmal 44–45. Berlin: Union Verlag, 1985.

Thietmar von Merseburg. *Chronik,* ed. and trans. Werner Trillmilch, 6th ed. Darmstadt: Wissenschaftliche Buchgesellschaft, 1985.

Joan A. Holladay

SEE ALSO

Aachen; Bamberg; Basel; Gothic Art and Architecture; Henry II, Art; Investiture Controversy; Liturgy, Furniture; Metalworking; Otto I; Ottonian Art and Architecture

Metalworking

Grave finds indicate that the Germanic and Alemannic peoples who occupied pre-Carolingian Germany already knew and used most of the metalwork techniques that would characterize the works produced in the great Ottonian and Romanesque centers. Crosses of thin gold foil were pressed over or into molds of clay or wood and sewn onto veils or laid over the corpse. Silver and bronze were cast in molds to create *fibulae* (brooches) and belt buckles, as well as stirrups and decorative bosses for harnesses. Linear designs, geometric patterns, and stylized foliate and animal motifs in low relief often decorated the surface, which might be fire-gilt. Likewise visible at this early date is niello, a technique in which a mixture of lead, sulfur, silver, and copper was melted into cast or engraved grooves to create a color contrast with the lighter silver or gilt background. Filigree vine patterns in twisted wire or granulation, made of tiny balls of molten gold or silver dropped adjacent to one another, decorated hairpins and brooches. Knowledge of Byzantine objects is supposed to account for the use of cloisonné, a technique in which narrow bands of metal soldered on edge to the ground provide chambers into which enamel or semiprecious stones, often garnet, were inserted for a multicolored effect. Peoples recently converted to Christianity produced reliquaries using the same techniques as these small, portable, personal objects.

Charlemagne's building of a permanent capital at Aachen and his standardization of Christian texts and liturgical practices necessitated both larger-scale objects and those for use in the mass. The cast bronze doors of the palace chapel at Aachen and the grilles of the second-story openings are the first large-scale cast bronzes in the West since Antiquity and suggest the employment or influence of technicians from the East. The technique would be revived again circa 1000 for objects like the bronze doors of Bishop Bernward of Hildesheim and Archbishop Willigis of Mainz. After this it was used regularly for both large-scale church objects like crucifixes, such as the meter-high example of the late eleventh century moved from Helmstedt to Werden in 1547, and candelabra, for example, that commissioned by Henry the Lion near the end of the twelfth century for St. Blasius, his foundation at Braunschweig. Book covers enshrined the word of God contained in the Gospel texts within as if it were a relic. The covers of the *Codex aureus* of St. Emmeran at Regensburg, made at the Court School of Charles the Bald in 870, includes embossed panels with Christ in Majesty, the Evangelists, and scenes from Christ's life, and gems and pearls mounted in settings reminiscent of architecture against a filigree ground. The reuse of antique gems and cameos often served a political purpose. On the Ottonian Lothar cross, given by Theophanu or her son Otto III to Charlemagne's foundation at Aachen (Cathedral Treasury), for example, a Roman cameo representing Caesar Augustus that appears at the intersection of the cross arms links the image of the emperor to that of Christ. This idea is strengthened by the engraved image on the back of the crucifix, where the head of the crucified Christ also occurs at the same place as the cameo on the front. The hand of God holds a laurel wreath, a symbol of triumph similar to that worn by Augustus, over the head of Christ. Other works of the Ottonian period incorporated ivories, both contemporaneous and earlier, and Byzantine enamels.

Important single works of both the Ottonian and Romanesque periods often use the full repertory of techniques. On the front of the older cross given by Abbess Mathilda to the women's foundation at Essen between 973 and 982 (Essen, Cathedral Treasury), the body of the Christ is embossed against a flat ground of gold foil. The halo, edges of the cross, and ends of all four arms are defined with filigreed vines and insert with gems and pearls, while a cloisonné panel carries the inscription above Christ's head and another represents Duke Otto of Bavaria and his sister, the abbess Mathilda, beneath Christ's feet. The images on the back are engraved into gilt copper foil.

The appearance of three-dimensional architectural sculpture in the twelfth century coincides with the inclusion of three-dimensional figures in small scale on shrines. On the Three Kings Shrine of circa 1200 in Cologne Cathedral, for example, the figures of the apostles and prophets are presented fully in the round; their gold foil exterior covers an interior of wax. The figures appear against engraved gold grounds; the arches over their heads and the spandrels between the arches are inset with gems, many of them antique, against grounds decorated with filigree; inscriptions are in *émail brun (Braunfirnis),* a technique from the beginning of the eleventh century in which heated linseed oil gave a rich brown tone to the surfaces it covered. Some of the decorative borders are cast, and the haloes, columns supporting the arches, and decorative borders are in the enamel technique of champlevé, which was circa 1100 a cheaper alternative to cloisonné. Related to cloisonné in its materials and effects, champlevé inserted colored glass paste into fields cut out of the solid ground of a usually copper plate.

Little is known about the organization of metalsmiths' shops, although the treatise of circa 1100 by Theophilus instructs us on the technical details of medieval metalworking and other arts.

While art historians traditionally devote their attention to large-scale cast bronze objects and to those in precious materials associated with church services and private devotion, metalworkers also produced door knockers, handles, and locks; tableware; and military objects—swords, armor, and helmets—in baser metals.

BIBLIOGRAPHY

Die Alamannen, ed. Karlheinz Fuchs et al. Stuttgart: Theiss, 1997.

Grimme, Ernst Bünther. *Der Aachener Domschatz. Aachener Kunstblätter 42* (1972) [entire issue].

Lasko, Peter. *Ars Sacra 800–1200,* 2d ed. Pelican History of Art. New Haven, Conn.: Yale University Press, 1994.

Ornamenta Ecclesiae: Kunst und Künstler der Romanik, ed. Anton Legner. 3 vols. Cologne; Schnütgen-Museum, 1985.

Theophilus. *De diversis artibus,* trans. and ed. C. R. Dodwell. London: T. Nelson, 1961.

Joan A. Holladay

SEE ALSO

Aachen; Bernward of Hildesheim; Braunschweig; Charlemagne; Cologne, Art; Essen; Gothic Art and Architecture; Helmarshausen; Henry the Lion; Liturgy, Furniture; Liturgical Vestments, Manuscripts, and Objects; Mainz; Nicolas of Verdun; Otto III; Ottonian

Art and Architecture; Relics and Reliquaries; Roger of Helmarshausen; Romanesque Art and Architecture; Theophanu; Werden

Metz

Metz exists as both an historical site (France) and as an art historical notion. Primarily through the efforts of Bishop Chrodegang (742–766), adviser to Pippin III, Metz became the leading episcopal see in the Frankish kingdom. The city was widely admired in the Carolingian period for its distinctive liturgical practices that included an adaptation of the Roman stational liturgy and the Roman chant. It seems fitting that the manuscript most readily associated with the city, the Drogo Sacramentary, should be a highly decorated Mass book. Commissioned by Bishop Drogo (826–855) for his personal use in circa 850–855, it is unique among Carolingian manuscripts for its delicate historiated (including figural scenes) initials, its elaborate classical acanthus decorations, and its extensive New Testament cycle.

Metz was renowned for its many churches—some forty in the Carolingian period. Paul the Deacon, in his *History of the Bishops of Metz* (783), made much of the architecturally rich cathedral complex. At its center was the episcopal church of Saint Stephen, a small octagonal church just to the west, Notre-Dame-la-Ronde, and St.-Pierre-le-Majeur, a three-nave basilica to the south, all three of which Archbishop Chrodegang (d. 766) mentions in his *Rules for Canons (Regula canonicorum)*. The still-standing St.-Pierre-aux-Nonnains, a fourth-century Roman basilica that became a monastery in the seventh century; the sixth-century church of St.-Pierre-le-Vieux; the church of Saint Paul built by Chrodegang, and the late-eighth-century church dedicated to Saint Gorgon were among the cluster of ecclesiastical buildings surrounding the canons' cloister.

In 1248, the citizens of Metz wrested power from the bishop to create an independent and prosperous city-state. It was during this time of municipal reorganization that work began to replace the old cathedral with a new Gothic structure that would also incorporate the church of Notre-Dame-la-Ronde. Begun in 1220, work continued in fits and starts for some three centuries. The result is a cathedral impressive for its soaring nave (42 meters) and its array of stained glass, much of which was made in the fourteenth and fifteenth centuries. Other noteworthy buildings from the Gothic period include the octagonal chapel of the Templars and the abbey church of St. Vincent.

Metz is also a category assigned to a group of Carolingian manuscripts associated with Drogo and to important groups of ninth- and tenth-century ivories. The Metz manuscripts are characterized by their rich, vegetal ornamentation, classical motifs, and sketchy, impressionistic figural style. Goldschmidt, who derived his classificatory system for ivories from manuscript studies, devised both a Metz and a Later Metz group. The Metz group proper is a relatively cohesive group that includes the ivory book covers on the Drogo Sacramentary. These ivories are characterized by sharp and linear carving, cutout backgrounds, and flat relief. The Later Metz group is a less coherent group that Goldschmidt saw as a continuation of the earlier group. Christological narratives and elaborate crucifixions are the favored themes. An often shared figural style, repetitions of certain motifs, and the frequent appearance of a dense acanthus leaf frame provide some links among the members of this large group. Still, the term "Metz school" must be considered primarily a scholar's organizational tool rather than a documented location for the production of ivories.

BIBLIOGRAPHY

Aubert, Marcel. La *Cathédrale de Metz*. Paris: Picard, 1931.

Goldschmidt, Adolph. *Die Elfenbeinskulpturen aus der Zeit der karolingischen und sächsischen Kaiser, 8–11. Jahrhundert, vol. 1.: Elfenbeinskulpturen*. 1914. Berlin: Deutscher Verlag für Kunstwissenschaft, 1969.

Heitz, Carol. *L'Architecture religieuse carolingienne*. Paris: Picard, 1980.

Köhler, Wilhelm. *Die Karolingischen Miniaturen, vol. 3.: Metzer Handschriften*. Berlin: Deutscher Verein für Kunstwissenschaft, 1960.

Melanie Holcomb

SEE ALSO

Carolingian Art and Architecture; Gothic Art and Architecture

Meuse River

The Meuse (Latin *Mosa*, Dutch *Meuse*) River was one of the more important waterways in medieval Europe. Rising at Pouilly on the Langres Plateau in Lorraine, it flows 590 miles (950 km) past Verdun, Sedan, and Carleville-Meieres. At Namur, it is joined by the Sambre River and then courses east to Liège, Huy, Maastricht, Venlo, and Bergen. Here it divides into two branches: the northern branch flows northwest to join the Waal River; the southern branch empties into the North Sea.

From Merovingian times there were numerous ports *(portus)* along the river, which served as an important trade artery connecting the Mediterranean and the lands bordering the North Sea. Under Dagobert (about 629–639), for example, a moneyer (authorized coiner) from Maastricht set himself up at the Frisian port of Durstede on the Meuse delta. Evidence shows that even in the eighth century there was considerable freight traffic on the Meuse, and at the end of the eighth century tolls were collected at Durstede and at Maastricht.

The region between the Meuse (with the *palatii,* or fortifications, of Jupille and Herstal), the Moselle, and the Rhine was the axis of Carolingian Austrasia. As a result of the Treaty of Verdun (843), the Meuse formed in its upper reaches the boundary between the west and middle kingdoms. From the ninth to the thirteenth centuries, it was the venue of numerous meetings between the West Frankish (French) and East Frankish (German) rulers. Durstede served as the hub of a large-scale trade with Scandinavia, but that characteristic also determined that it was pillaged every year from 834 to 837. In 841 Lothar I ceded some Frisian territory, including Durstede, to the "Normans," and a Norman duchy was established in the region of the Rhine delta. The main outlet of the empire was thus in the hands of the northerners.

Under the Ottonians, however, the entire length of the river was in German hands, and the most economically active part of the empire was the area between the Rhine and the Meuse (Meuse River Valley, Maasland), including Verdun, Mainz, and Cologne. Contacts between Frisia, the Low Countries, and England became fairly extensive, causing Durstede to expand. Tin from Cornwall was the essential material for the Maasland bronze and brass work, and merchants from the Maasland were selling their goods in London as early as 1130.

In addition to its own specialization in metalwares, the Meuse formed the northern end of the longer trade route that linked the Mediterranean and Flanders by way of the valleys of the Rhône and the Saône. Along it moved such varied goods as stone, salt, grain, fish, wood, and wine. River trade stimulated the growth of towns, as well as reviving the economic activity of the countryside. Among the towns and cities that thrived from the eleventh to the fifteenth century were Verdun, Mézières, Dinant, Namur, Huy, Liège, Maastricht, Roermond, Venlo, and Durstede.

While the Meuse united the areas through which it passed, it also served in part as a boundary, between the archbishoprics of Rheims and Cologne, for example, and (along with the Scheldt and Rhône Rivers) between France and the Empire during the High Middle Ages. The weakness of imperial authority in the region eventually led to French annexation, however, which was completed by Philip IV the Fair in 1298.

BIBLIOGRAPHY

Breuer, Heinz. *Die Maas als Schiffahrtsweg* Wiesbaden: Steiner, 1969.

Chapman, Gretel. *Mosan Art: An Annotated Bibliography.* Boston: Hall, 1988.

Rousseau, Félix. *La Meuse et le pays mosan en Belgique: leur importance historique avant le 13ᵉ siècle,* rpt. Brussels: Éditions Culture et Civilisation, 1977.

Voss, Ingrid. *Herrschertreten im frühen und hohen Mittelalter.* Cologne: Böhlau 1987.

Paul B. Pixton

SEE ALSO
Lothar I; Otto I; Otto II; Otto III

Millstatt

This Benedictine abbey was located beside a lake of the same name seventy-five miles south of Salzburg in the Carinthia region of Austria. Although the abbey, founded before 1088, was dissolved in 1469, its High Romanesque church still stands. The monastery is remembered today for its manuscript production; beginning immediately upon its foundation, the scriptorium was active well into the thirteenth century. At least one eleventh-century, around twenty twelfth-century, and about fifteen of its thirteenth-century manuscripts survive.

Its most famous manuscript is known as the Millstatt Genesis and is now kept in the Museum Rudolfinum in Klagenfurt (Kärntner Geschichtsverein, no. Cod. VI/19). This twelfth-century manuscript begins with a rhymed version of Genesis in early Middle High German. In addition, it contains seven other metrical texts, of which the Physiologus section is also illustrated with line drawings. The manuscript contains eighty-seven pen drawings of Genesis scenes done in brown, red, and blue inks, distributed throughout the poem. These drawings seem to derive from an early Christian illustrated manuscript of the book of Genesis for two reasons. One, the drawings illustrate only biblical events, not interpretive passages added by the German poet; two, the drawings are close iconographically to many in a group of artistic monuments, ranging from manuscripts to mosaics, known as the Cotton Genesis recension. The Millstatt Genesis is thus highly regarded as a northern reflection of an early Christian manuscript of the Cotton Genesis recension.

BIBLIOGRAPHY

Millstätter Genesis und Physiologus Handschrift. 2 vols. Graz: Akademische Druck- und Verlagsanstalt, 1967.

Menart, H. "Die Bilder der Millstätter Genesis und ihre Verwandten," in *Festschrift für Rudolf Egger.* 3 vols. Klagenfurt: Verlag des Geschichtsvereines für Kärnten, 1954, vol. 3. pp. 248–371.

Dorothy M. Shepard

SEE ALSO

Physiologus; Romanesque Art and Architecture; Salzburg

Minden

The bishopric of Minden (North Rhine-Westphalia) was founded around 800 by Charlemagne at the margins of his empire on the west bank of the river Weser. The first Carolingian church was destroyed by fire in 947; its successor was consecrated in 952. Of this building, the westwork (massive entrance structure), an imitation of nearby Corvey, has partially survived. In the mid-twelfth century, this westwork was transformed into the present two-towered façade by suppressing the central tower and opening the central space as a western gallery with triple arcades leading directly into the church. The nave of the adjoining Romanesque basilica, one of the first vaulted churches in northern Germany, was replaced in the later thirteenth century by the present Gothic hall church (destroyed in 1945 and since rebuilt); the latter combines architectural and sculptural features from Reims Cathedral with those from Cologne.

The parochial administration of Minden was centered in the four monastic units of St. Johannis, St. Marien, St. Martini, and St. Simeon, all of which reflect different stages of the architectural development of the cathedral. West of the cathedral precinct (the Domburg) developed the medieval market with its Gothic town hall, erected in the late thirteenth century.

Under Bishop Sigward (r. 1120–1140), a political adviser of Emperor Lothar III, the small chapel of Idensen west of Minden was built as the bishop's mausoleum. It represents the first completely vaulted structure in northern Germany, based on the church of Elten, which Sigward had consecrated in 1129. The iconography of its completely preserved fresco cycle, a typological program with strong political overtones relating to the investiture controversy, is based on the writings of Rupert of Deutz (d. 1129).

BIBLIOGRAPHY

Böker, Hans J. Idensen: *Architektur und Ausmalungsprogramm einer romanischen Hofkapelle.* Berlin: Mann, 1995.

Nordsiek, Hans, ed. *Zwischen Dom und Rathaus: Beiträge zur Kunst- und Kulturgeschichte der Stadt Minden.* Minden: Stadt Minden, 1977.

Hans J. Böker

SEE ALSO

Charlemagne; Cologne, History; Corvey; Gothic Art and Architecture; Investiture Controversy; Ottonian Art and Architecture; Romanesque Art and Architecture

Ministerials

Comprising a class unique to medieval Germany, the ministerials (Latin *ministeriales*, German *Dienstmänner,* or men in service) arose out of the uncertainties of the post-Carolingian period, as various German magnates sought to find a remedy for their labor needs in a number of areas, including administration, personal bodyguard, and military operations. Opting against the free nobility, whom they considered too independent and thus less reliable, great churches of the tenth century turned to the unfree peasantry for such individuals. Since the *ministeriales* were unfree, they remained obligated to serve their lord, but they could also be granted to other lords; yet they were more than mere serfs. They were trained as warriors and endowed with both allods (ceded land) and fiefs from which they supported themselves in a manner similar to feudal vassals. References to such individuals are found at the beginning of the eleventh century in narrative sources, while texts from the 1020s regulate their rights and duties.

Under the Salian kings and continuing into the Hohenstaufen epoch, secular rulers turned to extensive use of *ministeriales* as well. Conrad II (1024–1039), in his efforts to establish a strong royal authority independent of the lay nobility, relied heavily on the *ministeriales,* while the growing power and influence of the *ministeriales* at the courts of Henry III (1039–1056) and Henry IV (1056–1106) caused great antagonism toward the kings by the nobles, which lasted into the reign of Henry V (1106–1125). Yet, despite princely opposition to the use of *ministeriales* to exclude them from participation in the governance of the empire, the status of the ministerial class improved during the era of the Investiture Controversy and the accompanying civil war. In time, many lay princes and lesser nobles acquired *ministeriales* as well.

Although the vast majority of the ministerial families remained modestly successful, the career of the imperial ministerial Werner II of Bolanden demonstrates the heights to which some of them rose. This man not only served Emperor Frederick Barbarossa, but he also owed service to forty-five other lords from whom he held property; he possessed seventeen castles, and he was the lord of eleven hundred knights. A descendant of his became archbishop of Mainz in the mid-thirteenth century. Equally successful was Markward of Anweiler, whom Henry VI had earlier manumitted and created duke of Ravenna and the Romagna, and to whom Henry in 1197, just prior to his death, entrusted the regency of Sicily; in short, the future of Henry's young son Frederick was placed in the hands of this loyal retainer.

After the collapse of the Hohenstaufen empire, the imperial ministerials formed the unruly estate of the imperial knights *(Reichsritterschaft)*. In many thirteenth-century German dioceses, cathedral canons of ministerial origin openly challenged older families of the higher nobility for the highest ecclesiastical offices. Thus, in Trier we find the family of de Ponte (von der Brücke) competing with the counts of Wied; at Speyer, Conrad of Daun (de Tanne) became bishop in 1233; while at Worms, Conrad of Dürkheim succeeded to the bishop's chair in 1247. Other members of various ministerial families married into the high nobility; in numerous cases we find them merging into the urban patriciate (ruling class) as well.

BIBLIOGRAPHY

Bosl, Karl. *Die Reichsministerialität der Salier und Staufer,* 2 vols. Stuttgart: Hiersmann, 1950–1951.

Pötter, Wilhelm. *Die Ministerialität der Erzbischöfe von Köln vom Ende des 11. bis zum Ausgang des 13. Jahrhunderts,* Studien zur kölner Kirchengeschichte 9. Düsseldorf: Schwann 1967.

Schulz, Knut. *Ministerialität und Bürgertum in Trier.* Rheinisches Archiv 66. Bonn: Röhrscheid, 1968.

Paul B. Pixton

SEE ALSO

Conrad II; Frederick I Barbarossa; Henry III; Henry IV; Henry VI; Investiture Controversy; Staufen

Minneallegorie, Minnerede

Two genres of courtly love writing, the first allegory and the other commentary, combine ecclesiastical traditions of allegory and spiritual love (Otfried's *Evangelienbuch, Das Sankt Trudperter Hohelied*) with secular traditions of treatises on the nature of carnal love (Ovid's *Ars Amartoria* and *Remedia Amoris,* Andreas Capallanus's *Tractatus de Amore*). The love allegory *(Minneallegorie)* became extremely popular in the fourteenth and fifteenth centuries. The Minnegrotto in Gottfried von Straßburg's *Tristan* (ca. 1210) is one of the earliest, and undoubtedly the most famous, *Minne* allegories in German literature. The *joie de la curt,* "joy of the court," in Hartmann von Aue's *Erec* (ca. 1185) also functions as an allegory of love. The French *Roman de la Rose* (ca. 1230–1275) represents one of the most spectacular expressions of the form. In this French poem, we find many of the qualities that would come to define the form in Germany. The typical *Minneallegorie* embeds didactic intent within epic structure. Personifications of love and of the virtues and vices associated with it are stock figures in the love allegory. A knight in search of love encounters *Vrou Minne* or *Vrou Liebe* and her handmaidens—personifications of the virtues of love: fidelity *(triuwe),* self-control *(zucht),* charity *(milde),* and so on. This encounter takes place in a setting loaded with allegorical significance: a grotto, a garden, a forest, or a castle. *Vrou Minne* and her court instruct in the ways of love *(Minnehof).* *Der Minne Regel* *(Rule of Love,* 1404) by Eberhard von Cersne offers one model of the love allegory. A knight chances upon the various personified virtues guarding the ramparts of the castle of the queen of Love. Once inside, the Queen gives the knight twenty-three commandments of love and provides him with the questions and answers to thirty-eight mysteries of love. She then commands the knight to go out and capture a hawk. (The hawk is the most common symbol for knightly sexual desire.) After several adventures, the knight succeeds and brings the hawk back to the queen, who then gives further instruction, using material taken directly from Capallanus's *De Amore.* Other variations of the love allegory include hunting allegories *(Jagdallegorien)* and the allegory of the Castle of Love *(Minneburg).* In Hadamar von Laber's *Jagd* (ca. 1335–1340), a hunter captures the prey with the aid of his dogs named resolve *(wille),* desire *(wunne)*, consolation *(trôst)*, constancy *(stæte)*, and fidelity *(triuwe)*. In the *Königsberger Jagdallegorie* (ca. 1350), a hunter who fails to catch a doe with the various virtues in canine form succeeds when he employs the dogs of vice: inconstancy *(zwîfel)*, infidelity *(wenken)*, and deception *(falsche)*. The most popular love allegory of all is that of the Castle of Love. The storming of the castle has obvious sexual connotations and is a standard erotic allusion. In 1214, revelers actually enacted the siege of the Castle of Love at a courtly celebration in Treviso. (Friedrich Schiller alludes to a similar celebration in his play *Maria Stuart*.) In the poem *Minneburg* (ca. 1340, erroneously ascribed to Egen von Bamberg), the castle represents a woman and her many virtues. Versions and variations of the poem in Middle English, *Castel off Loue*, and in French, *Chastel d' amours*, attest to its popularity. Hermann von Sachsenheim's *Moerin* (1453), the works of Meister Altswert *(Das alte Schwert, Der Kittel*, and *Der Tugenden Schatz, etc.*, ca. 1385), and Heinzelin von Kontanz's *Ritter oder Pfaffe* (*Knight or Minister*, ca. 1290) are other important *Minneallegorien*.

The love commentary or *Minnerede* is a form closely related to the *Minneallegorie* in its didactic intent but differs in that none of the virtues, emotions, or vices in the poems are personified. We find commentaries on love in the works of Heinrich der Teichner, Peter Suchenwirt, Zilies von Sayn, Johann von Konstanz, and Eberhard von Cersne.

BIBLIOGRAPHY

Blank, Walter. *Die deutsche Minneallegorie. Gestaltung und Funktion einer spätmittelalterlichen Dichtungsform.* Stuttgart: Metzler, 1970.

Lewis, C. S. *The Allegory of Love: A Study in Medieval Tradition.* Oxford: Oxford University Press, 1958.

Schmidt, Ronald Michael. *Studien zur deutschen Minnerede: Untersuchungen zu Zilies von Sayn, Johann von Konstanz und Eberhard von Cersne.* Göppingen: Kümmerle, 1982.

Stephen M. Carey

SEE ALSO

Gottfried von Straßburg; Heinrich der Teichner; Otfrid; Song of Songs; Suchenwirt, Peter

Minnesang (12th—13th c.)

Medieval German love poetry, or *Minnesang*, represents one of the German-speaking world's lasting contributions to world literature. Some medieval Latin love songs date from the eleventh century; William IX of Acquitaine, the "First troubadour," created his Occitan love songs around the beginning of the twelfth. The first Middle High German songs by named singers about love *(minne, liebe)* and relationships between the lovers and their society that survive stem from roughly 1150, though they first appear, as do most later songs, in manuscripts dating from the late thirteenth and early fourteenth centuries. Minnesongs interested some members of the nobility, the secular clergy, and the ruling patrician class in the cities and continued to be created into the fifteenth century. In common parlance, *Minnesang* refers not only to love songs but also to religious, political, or topical songs, and wisdom poetry that is directed to the same audience, the courts, and performed (predominately) in secular settings. The term excludes hymns and other songs written for a religious community or occasion (such as the songs within the mystical writings of Mechthild von Magdeburg or the vernacular songs within religious dramas), though such songs both influence and are influenced by *Minnesang*. It also excludes the rule-driven songs composed by and for artisans from the fourteenth into the seventeenth century *(Meistergesang)*, although the mastersingers knew and explicitly drew on the minnesang tradition in shaping their forms and melodies. For the most part, *Minnesang* also excludes various popular songs with both religious and secular themes that were collected in song books, predominately in the fifteenth and sixteenth centuries, or cited in city chronicles, even though some of these recast minnesong motifs.

The "first minnesinger" is Der von Kürenberg, and other older singers include Meinloh von Sevelingen, the burgraves of Regensburg and Rietenburg, and Dietmar von Eist. Scholars date these singers on formal and, to a lesser extent, thematic grounds: long-line or rhymed couplet strophes, occasional impure or slant rhymes *(liep : niet)*, relatively simple syntax, no overt borrowings from the troubadours and trouvères (northern French singers who started imitating the troubadours shortly before the minnesingers did). The archaic German singers seem to have flourished along the Danube (with Regensburg as a western limit). Despite their eschewing a direct imitation of Romance models, they probably were aware of them. One generally archaic singer can be dated more precisely, since many documents inform us about Kaiser Heinrich (Emperor Henry VI, 1165–1197), who was knighted in 1184 and reigned as emperor only six years, though none refers to him as a singer. He is a transitional figure (as is

Dietmar), since part of his oeuvre directly reflects Romance influences.

Early songs tend to be one strophe, or less commonly two or three strophes, long; later ones are often longer. Laments about fickle or unresponsive lovers, promises to serve the lover (with feudal overtones), complaints about the intrusions of spies and slanderers *(merkaere, lügenaere)* in the lovers' (hoped-for) relationship recur in early (and later) minnesongs (and are common in Occitan and northern French songs as well). The lover relationship is implicitly illicit (almost never expressly adulterous); appeals to secrecy are common. Public disclosure of the relationship would bring shame or even death. Loving and singing of love, despite the pain and suffering it so often causes the lover(s), contribute to courtly joy *(hôher muot)*. Fairly rare, apparently archaic, are narrative accounts of the plight of lovers other than the person speaking; when they occur, they often introduce the quotation of a woman speaker. Strophes in the woman's voice constitute a major portion of early *Minnesang*. Direct dialogues are rare; more commonly, the lady and her lover utter monologues on a related topic, talking past each other. This exchange (German, *Wechsel*), a key feature of archaic song, is imitated and modified by later singers such as Reinmar der Alte, Heinrich von Morungen, and Walther von der Vogelweide. Songs (strophes) in which the lover is addressed directly are rarely answered. Occasionally, a messenger serves as a go-between *(Botenlied)* or the sole partner in a (direct) dialogue.

Dawn songs—laments by lovers forced to part by the coming of the dawn (German, *Tagelied;* in Occitan *alba;* in northern French, aubade)—combine elements of narrative (setting the scene, commenting on actions taken), monologue, and dialogue. Though the first dawn song, ascribed to Dietmar (in the anthology *Minnesangs Frühling,* no. 38,18), is early, and songs by Morungen and Reinmar allude to the dawn song, only at the height of sophisticated minnesongs around 1200, with the dawn songs of Wolfram von Eschenbach, does the genre become clearly established among the songs transmitted. Throughout the subsequent centuries to the mid–fifteenth century, such songs remain popular. Far more of them (over a hundred) exist in German than in the otherwise more extensive troubadour and trouvère traditions.

Deriving early German (Portuguese, Spanish, even some Medieval Latin) songs (in part) from noncourtly folk traditions is disputed, but plausible. Note the heavy use of the woman's voice; the simple syntax; the absence of overt references to Ovid, the Song of Songs, or hymns in praise of Mary (major influences on Medieval Latin, Occitan, French, and later German songs); and the relatively unsophisticated strophic forms and slant rhymes. The songs themselves, however, clearly, even self-consciously, situate the joys and sorrows of love at court. The lovers fear the opprobrium and desire the approbation of the courtiers. A central paradox of medieval love songs in general—that one strives to keep secret what one very publicly proclaims—permeates early minnesongs as much as it does later ones, though only later, in the self-reflexivity of Walther's "Unter der linden" (Beneath the Linden Tree) is the paradox thematized.

Some medieval German songs *(Spruch, Spruchlied,* and *Sangspruch)* deal not with love per se but rather with general questions of wisdom, often morality or propriety. The earliest examples are ascribed to Spervogel (and, by modern editors, to Herger), but they represent a type of song that was surely more common than the manuscripts indicate. Occitan poems known as *sirventes* and many of the *coblas* (stanzas) as well as Latin wisdom poetry parallel, but do not clearly influence, Spervogel, but did probably serve as models for subsequent singers. Walther became the master of the sophisticated *Sangspruch* and *Spruchlied,* which in his hands often contained a political overtone, and his songs are a major influence on the didactic and political songs that constitute a major genre throughout the thirteenth, fourteenth, and fifteenth centuries.

Internal references and reports about the performance of songs in the Middle Ages make it clear that medieval vernacular songs were composed to be performed, to be sung, as were many Medieval Latin songs. A tradition of Latin poems written for a reading audience extends back to Antiquity, but such poems, though they provided motifs copied by the troubadours, trouvères, and minnesingers, cannot serve as a model for our understanding of medieval vernacular songs. This having been said, one must admit that our knowledge of minnesongs of the twelfth and thirteenth centuries is based almost entirely on manuscripts that do not contain musical notation. None of the songs, in the classic edition of twelfth-century minnesongs, *Des Minnesangs Frühling,* are transmitted with (readable) music. By the mid– to late thirteenth century our songs may well have become, in effect, poems, i.e., have been read (silently or aloud) and understood as written texts. However, although internal references to an implicit audience are doubtless inherently fictional, recurrent direct addresses to a courtly audience ("you nobles" or simply "you") and exhortations like "listen" or "behold" (an implied performance gesture) permeate Occitan and Middle High German lyrics up to and including Walther von der Vogelweide. Though one may, perhaps must, assume that devotees of even the earliest extant songs collected them in written form (and read them), what they had were the texts of songs originally sung. Apparent performance cues are singularly lacking in Medieval Latin and rare in northern French and most Middle High German songs from the mid–thirteenth century on. Later authors such as Konrad von Würzburg (last half of the thirteenth century) may have written consciously, in part at least, for readers.

Our information on the intended audience for the songs derives from the songs themselves and from depictions of performance situations in epics and romances of the time, as well as in miniatures. For instance, a lady opens a song by Der von Kürenberg (*Minnesangs Frühling,* no. 8, 1):

Ich stuont mir nehtint spâte	*an einer zinne,*
do hôrt ich einen rîter	*vil wol singen*
in Kürenberges wîse	*al ûz der menigîn*

"I was standing late last night at a rampart when I heard a knight sing excellently in Kürenberg's melody from amidst the throng."

In this clearly fictional account of a listener, we have a singer at court overheard by a lady who is so struck by his singing that she continues: *er muoz mir diu lant rûmen, / alder ich geniete mich sîn* (He must leave my lands / or I'll claim him for myself). Two possible continuations of the song are transmitted; in one the knight echoes the lady's opening words and says he was standing by her bed but dared not wake her, to which she responds with a curse that she was not a wild boar (*Minnesangs Frühling,* no. 8, 9). If genuine, this would represent an almost unique instance of true dialogue and the only exchange within a strophe of archaic minnesong; many editors consider the strophe a spurious addition by a later author. Later, the generally accepted strophe responding, in the form of a *Wechsel,* to her has the knight calling for horse and armor so that he can leave her lands to evade her clutches (*Minnesangs Frühling,* no. 9,29). Both sets of strophes are burlesque in tone; neither strikes us as a very reliable guide to the way songs were presented and received; nevertheless, from what information we have some conclusions can be drawn.

As best we can determine, those interested in songs and singing in the courtly fashion made up a small number of the members of the most advanced and powerful courts. Singing of love entertained a select coterie of connoisseurs. It competed during courtly festivities with other amusements. Dancing, music making by instrumentalists, the recitation of both short and long tales, slanging matches (witty repartee), juggling and acrobatics, feats of martial skill, ostentatious promenading to display one's expensive clothes were direct competition. Eating and especially drinking were even more important. Just as there were no concerts for passive audiences in the Middle Ages (music accompanied other activities), there were no song recitals in the modern style. A singer had to divert a few people's attention from all the other available pastimes. But for this very reason, a singer could assume that those few who deigned to listen were intensely interested and involved in what was being sung. Increasingly, the songs presuppose an intimate awareness of poetic conventions. From the very earliest extant songs we can discern both the existence of code words for unspoken norms and the singers' willingness to arouse and thwart their audience's expectations in turn.

Almost all the twelfth-century songs are transmitted solely in three anthologies, codices written down between roughly 1275 and the early part of the fourteenth century: the *Small Heidelberg Song Codex* (A), the *Stuttgart Song Codex* (B), and the *Large Heidelberg* ("*Manesse*") *Song Codex* (C). There are several fragmentary manuscripts with texts also found in C, most significantly the Budapest fragment (Bu), which includes, among other texts, the first nine of the fifteen strophes ascribed to Der von Kürenberg, following the same exemplar (thus leading to a lost source text referred to as *BuC). We can assume that at least one of the exemplars of B, C, and Bu was itself an anthology with miniature portraits representing the authors, similar to these collections. Another codex, the Würzburg one (E), contains songs ascribed to Reinmar and Walther. The earliest anthology to contain minnesong strophes is the codex of the *Carmina Burana* from the second fourth of the thirteenth century. Most of its songs are in Latin, but a few are in both Latin and German, and a number of the Latin songs conclude with a strophe in German. This codex includes neumes, an early form of musical notation. The form of neumes used cannot be read with any degree of precision; those reading them must have already known the melody and merely needed a reminder. A major fourteenth-century collection of songs with clearer musical notation, the *Jena Song Codex* (J), anthologizes almost exclusively didactic singers of the last half of the thirteenth and first part of the fourteenth century; it does have songs (with music) by Spervogel.

Almost always, the sorts of mistakes we find in these manuscripts were copying errors, not memory lapses; in addition, the song collections were clearly compiled primarily from previously extant (shorter) song collections. Often, when two codices have the same song, they transmit other songs in the same order. This is true, for instance, for extensive stretches of B and C (deriving from a lost source text *BC), of A and C (*AC), and of E and C (*EC). Though there are cases of divergent ascription (the same song or, more commonly, a related version of a song, ascribed to more than one singer), for the most part the manuscripts agree. Even if they were not fixed in writing on composition, as many may have been, it is unlikely that a large number of the songs spent a considerable time in oral transmission before they were collected and eventually, entered in A, B, C, E, and so on (or in the exemplars *AC, *BC, *EC); otherwise they would have lost the ascription to their authors. Though on occasion scribes may have arbitrarily assigned a song transmitted anonymously, whether orally or in writing, to a known author, the evidence speaks against this being a common practice. Many instances of multiple ascription arguably resulted from one singer appropriating (or, as we would say now, covering) another's song.

Friedrich von Hausen, Heinrich von Veldeke, and Rudolf von Fenis, whose works can be dated with some precision to the 1180s and early 1190s, were singers from western German-speaking areas (or, in the case of Veldeke, a Dutch-speaking one) who closely modeled their songs on Occitan models. Motifs such as love from afar, a suitor's being spurned by a haughty lady, and hyperbolic praise of the lady's excellence abound. The singers concentrate on discussions of their own feelings and situations. Not infrequently, songs examine the nature of love, which is depicted as a mysterious and somehow novel force. As Hausen (MF 53, 15–17) asks (in Middle High German 'dactyls'): "Waz mac daz sîn, daz diu werlt heizet minne, / und ez mir tuot sô wê ze aller stunde / und ez mir nimet sô vil mîner sinne?" (What can that be that the world calls love and that hurts me so at all times and deprives me of so much of my reason?) Typically, though not universally, the suitor's love is unrequited. Lovesickness, described in language echoing classical Antiquity, especially Ovid's love lyrics (but also reflecting symptoms dealt with in medical treatises), is foregrounded. While most minnesingers situate themselves, their actions, and their aspirations at court,

Veldeke delights in introducing a song with images of nature. He employs a *Natureingang*, a device common in Medieval Latin songs that also occurs, more sparingly, in Occitan and northern French ones. A few of the earlier minnesongs (anonymous ones and some ascribed to Dietmar von Eist) show traces of the device, but Veldeke is the first minnesinger to employ it schematically. Scholars differ as to whether such nature introductions reflect folk songs or are literary borrowings from Roman Antiquity. Veldeke, in any case, clearly was emulating, in form and content, Medieval Latin songs (which may themselves mingle a sprinkling of folk-song motifs among their overt classical allusions). The predominant strophic form from Hausen on (for several centuries), often termed *Kanzone*, is tripartite, with a bifurcated *Aufgesang* followed by an *Abgesang*. Impure (slant) rhymes are rare.

Perhaps beginning slightly later than Hausen, Veldeke, and Fenis, though probably roughly contemporary with them, Ulrich von Gutenberg and Heinrich von Rugge share, for the most part, their motifs and forms. They are less obviously directly dependent on romance models. For each of the two, however, an example of a new form is transmitted: the *Leich*, which suggests courtly listeners appreciated a singer's mastery of complicated forms and training in the sophisticated musical techniques of ecclesiastic circles. Rugge, especially, delighted in intricate internal rhyme schemes and wordplay of a sort that became typical of such thirteenth-century minnesingers as Gottfried von Neifen and especially Konrad von Würzburg. In one strophe, for example, he characterizes love with such a profusion of *minne* that nothing else is left: the first two lines of the *Abgesang* (Minnesangs Frühling, no. 102, 2–3) recount that *Der minne erzeige ich mit der minne, / daz ich ûf minne minne minne.* (I demonstrate to love through love that I love love for the sake of love.) He was apparently much admired by his younger contemporaries. Hartmann von Aue borrowed heavily from Rugge's crusading *Leich* in creating his own crusading songs. Reinmar der Alte not only emulated his love songs but may have sung some of them himself. Many songs attributed by the editors to Rugge are ascribed in the manuscripts to both. The thirteenth-century minnesinger Rubin, in turn, draws on both Rugge and Reinmar.

Two other minnesingers of the last decades of the twelfth century, Heinrich von Morungen and Albrecht von Johansdorf, utilize many of the same motifs and similar forms, but treat them with greater freshness and originality (traits that were not necessarily prized in their own times but have made their songs especially attractive to modern readers). Morungen has been thought to echo and heighten Romance and Medieval Latin traditions; interestingly enough, however, none of his songs seems to have a discrete model. Johansdorf, on the other hand, clearly shows familiarity with specific Occitan and northern French songs and singers.

Both couple fervor with wit, letting their suitors pant or even die for love while the poet/performer ironizes their plight. Johansdorf even carries this ironic stance into his crusading songs, all of which thematize the tension between service to the lady and service to God (since going on a crusade means leaving the lady behind). He concludes one such song with the statement and plea (*Minnesangs Frühling*, no. 90, 13–15): *alle sünde liez ich wol wan die; / ich minne ein wîp vor al der welte in mînem muote. / got herre, daz vervach zu guote!* (I would eschew all sins but one: I love a woman in my heart more than all the world. Lord God, solve this dilemma to my benefit!) On the face of it, this is a bold rejection of total subservience to God. However, when we consider that earlier in the song we learn that the only real reason to undertake a crusade is to avenge the Muslim assertion that Mary was not a virgin, things get less clear. On the one hand, Johansdorf has consistently identified the lady as a somewhat fickle and demanding but, nevertheless, desirable woman of the court; on the other, he leaves himself the out that if his somewhat reluctant crusader were to be accused of impiety, he could easily maintain that his "sin" was merely loving the Holy Virgin too much.

Extolling the virtues of the lady with attributes normally associated with Mary, Morungen invites us to wonder at times whether he celebrates secular or divine love. He probably uses intimations of the sacred merely to intensify the profane. Within the lively, light-filled, and varied imagery of his songs, he combines the fire of passion with hyperbole that suggests playfulness. In his *In sô hôher swebender wunne* (Such highly floating joy, *Minnesangs Frühling*, no. 125, 19), for example, the speaker heaps up ever more synonyms for joy about his requited love, ending with the assertion that his *liebe* (joy or love) is so great that he cannot express it—after, of course, he has devoted four strophes to doing so. Whether the revelation, in the *Aufgesang* of the fourth strophe, that the favor he has received was merely a word should lead us to find his joyful reaction risibly disproportionate or sublimely tactful depends on what we imagine the word to be. If the lady said yes, as Morungen has his suitor wish she would in another (overtly playful) song (*Minnesangs Frühling*, no. 137, 17), rapture is reasonable.

Better known for his narrative works, Hartmann von Aue is often underappreciated as a minnesinger, though his skill and range are indisputable. His themes range from stereotypical love laments to idiosyncratic rejections of love service. As he does in his narratives, especially in *Erec,* he actively addresses and draws in his listeners. In addition to developing a sense of the singer as performer, he introduces seemingly autobiographical elements into his songs. It is generally agreed that the poetic "I" of medieval courtly song is a convention; the would-be lover speaks not as a flesh-and-blood suitor but rather as a literary type. Hartmann, though he uses (and refers to) the conventions, also flouts them. His songs in the woman's voice and his crusading songs are remarkable for their diversity.

The most prolific minnesinger of the twelfth century, to judge from what has been transmitted, Reinmar der Alte, did not lack in wit, though scholars have tended to ignore it. Reinmar eschews imagery for the most part; the relatively infrequent images generally occur in only one of several versions of a song or in songs ascribed to him by the manuscripts that scholars attribute to other singers. His persona, the hapless suitor whose every attempt to win his lady's favors is rejected haughtily, weaves convoluted arguments and engages in intricate meditations on his pitiful plight, often losing sight almost completely of the putative object of his affections, so intent is he on bemoaning his fate. What scholars, put off by this stance, have tended to ignore is that Reinmar has more than one voice. Of all the minnesingers from the decades before and after 1200, he utilizes the woman's voice most frequently. Though Reinmar's ladies assume various stances (sometimes even different ones in different versions of the same song), in none of the songs and strophes in the woman's voice can we discern a haughty lady spurning a suitor's love. On the contrary, Reinmar's ladies typically yearn for the lover kept from them (and from their bed) by society or even by their suitor's diffidence. Clearly Reinmar plays literary motifs off against each other. It does seem, to be sure, that he is more than anything concerned about his status as a poet. He and other singers seem to have transformed stock figures, the spies and chaperones who are typically cursed for keeping lovers apart into critics whose concern is not with the lovers but with artistic skill and rivals—not (only) for the lady's favors but (even more) for the broader audience's approbation.

The minnesinger who vied most directly for Reinmar's audience and learned most from him (and others) and created an oeuvre of minnesongs more varied than any before (or since), as well as many other sorts of songs, was Walther von der Vogelweide, who flourished as a singer in the decade before and the three decades after 1200. No other singer has attracted, or deserved, so much attention. Walther created minnesongs in the conventional style but also borrowed and transformed love-song motifs from Medieval Latin and often reshaped tired motifs by introducing aspects of the pugnacious persona he developed so skillfully in his didactic and political songs: *Sangsprüche* and *Spruchlieder*—the former being single strophes devoted to a theme; the latter, multistrophic songs. The prominence of such nonamatory songs in his oeuvre make him unique among medieval German singers, most of whom either specialized in minnesong with at most an occasional *Sangspruch* or devoted themselves to didactic poetry virtually exclusively. Walther's *Leich* and a number of his other songs are notable for their religious fervor and their relative theological sophistication. He sang not only for secular courts but also for ecclesiastic ones, and it has been suggested that he was by training and possibly by station more closely aligned to the religious community than seems to have been the case for most minnesingers. Whatever his rank in society (probably a lower one than early scholars assumed, but perhaps higher than many more recent scholars have posited), he was intensely aware of privilege and propriety. He vigorously defends himself as a singer against rivals and other detractors, but his touchiness may in part stem from a sense of social inferiority.

Wolfram von Eschenbach, whose tilts with Walther occur in his narratives, devoted most of his creative powers as a minnesinger, as best we can determine from what is transmitted, to the dawn song. Five of the nine songs ascribed to him treat the joys and sorrows of loving and parting at daybreak, though one of them (*Minnesangs Frühling*, no. M/T IV), "Der helden minne ir klage," (The Complaint of the Love of Heroes), with its pithy observation that the heartbreak of parting could be ameliorated if one were married to the woman embraced, is more nearly an anti–dawn song. Wolfram's imitators in this genre were legion. The four conventional minnesongs, though they lack the weight, complexity, and power of Wolfram's dawn songs and were not similarly influential, do add a lyric grace note to the oeuvre of this titanic epic poet. The observation (*Minnesangs Frühling*, no. M/T IX 3, 7) *[m]anlîch dienst, wîplîch lôn gelîch ie wac* (manly service and womanly reward have always had equal weight) echoes the emphasis on knightly deeds as service of the lady so prominent in courtly romance.

Ulrich von Singenberg, a prolific minnesinger of the early thirteenth century who extols Walther as his master, borrowed from him some of the variety of song types, sharing a dual interest in minnesongs and the *Sangspruch*. He carried an enthusiasm for wordplay several of his models possessed to an extreme. His most striking departure from the conventional, preserved only in codex A (from *AC—the C scribe arguably deleted it as undecorous), is a two-strophe altercation between Ulrich's son and Ulrich about which of them should serve the lady that is appended to a five-strophe, conventional praise of her. Ulrich, whose aspirations do not seem to have included originality, may have gotten the notion of inserting himself and his son into courtly song from Neidhart, whose innovations reshaped the landscape of minnesong.

Neidhart drew on the traditions of courtly love songs and of the *postourelle* (a dialogue between a shepherdess or other peasant girl with a knight or cleric) to develop a wide range of satiric songs. Most of his songs set in the summer have dialogues between peasant girls or between a peasant girl and her mother or monologues by an older woman about an anticipated dalliance (often at a dance) with a knight of Riuwental (hence the appelation von Reuental often given Neidhart). The older woman becomes a comic figure through her fervent desire for pleasure (sometimes expressed with the tropes of conventional minnesongs). Some summer songs present a wry, disillusioned view of the crusade as far less heroic and desirable than it is depicted to be in songs by Hartmann and Walther, for example. Many of Neidhart's winter songs culminate in a barn-dance battle between village louts who preen themselves as knights. Neidhart laments the loss of his dance partner or her loss of her mirror (a token of love? of poetry? of virginity?) to such as these. Or he praises her ring of hair into which he can thrust his "finger." Other winter songs begin more like typical courtly love laments, only to have the "courtly" world transform itself into one of parvenu peasants or to conclude with the introduction of the persona of the singer as an impoverished knight von Riuwental (vale of sorrows). The rare songs without such a clash between the ideal world of courtly song and a harsh rural reality make us wonder if a strophe or two might not have gotten lost. Yet other winter songs are laments that one has been too long involved in and with the world, such as we find among the songs of Hartmann, Walther, or Singenberg, with the often abrupt intrusion of country bumpkins. Does Neidhart parody an uncouth (provincial?) court or mock a rich peasantry with airs above its station? Perhaps both. Some early songs ascribed in manuscript C to Neidhart already present him as the protagonist in a ribald tale. Neidhart then becomes a literary figure in the role of an enemy of the peasants. A relative profusion of melodies is transmitted for Neidhart's songs.

A large number of more conventional minnesingers flourished in the thirteenth century, though Neidhart's influence and popularity peek through when one least expects them. Otto von Botenlouben creates noteworthy dawn songs. Burkhard von Hohenfels draws his elaborate nature imagery as much from scholasticism as from the world around him. Ulrich von Winterstetten introduces refrains as a standard feature of German songs. Walther von Metze tracks the history of minnesong with his borrowings. Gottfried von Neifen glories in formal artificiality but also creates a "peasant" song. Ulrich von Liechtenstein not only tries himself in many genres and invents some of his own but also creates a narrative framework for himself as minnesinger in his *Frauendienst* and offers commentaries on his own songs. Tannhäuser's dance *Leichs* blend Neidart's world with that of a court enamored with French fashions and vocabulary (traces of which can already be seen in some of Neidhart's songs). Steinmar complements his traditional minnesongs with a rollicking harvest song, in which wine is preferred to women, and a bucolic dawn song, in which the lovers are peasants and the bed for their tryst is a pile of hay. Konrad von Würzburg, whose minnesongs make up only a small part of his extensive oeuvre, excels in the ornamental use of rhyme.

Most of the minnesingers are from the south. Though some of the most prolific didactic singers, such as Reinmar von Zweter and Marner, lived and sang in the south, didactic singers such as Meister Rumelant, Suchensinn, Regenbogen, and Frauenlob tend to be from or have flourished in the north. The minnesong codices A, B, and C, from the southwest, do contain didactic songs, but love songs dominate; the major anthology of didactic songs, J, from the northeast, has few love songs, among them the Low German songs of Wizlav von Rügen. Probably the provenance of the codices has skewed the evidence, but it may well be that the courts to the south of Thuringia were more receptive to love songs and those to the north to didactic ones. Those in the middle appreciated both. Many of the didactic singers were probably not noble; their names often appear to be literary ones, as von der Vogelweide or von Reuental may have been. Frauenlob, Heinrich von Meissen, gained his (nick)name for his songs in praise of Mary, especially his magnificent "Marienleich." Often the didactic songs reflect scholastic lore and some, though not all, of these singers will have had a clerical background. Increasingly, their language became obscure. Frauenlob and others at the end of the thirteenth and beginning of the fourteenth century prided themselves on their flowers of rhetoric *(geblümter Stil)*. most of the minnesingers were nobles or ministeriales, or at least identified themselves with noble courts. Clearly, however, there was no hard-and-fast rule dividing the two types of singers, and many songs could be considered either a minnesong or a didactic one.

Though the mastersingers held up members of both groups as exemplary *(alte Meister),* they tended to model their own songs on the didactic ones. The Colmar Song Codex from around 1470, the most extensive fifteenth-century mastersong codex, has some songs (erroneously) ascribed to Walther, Wolfram, Neidhart, and Tannhäuser (the ascription may have simply signaled that the form and melody were borrowed), as well as a generous number of songs by didactic singers.

BIBLIOGRAPHY

Cramer, Thomas. *Was hilfet âne sinne kunst? Lyrik im 13. Jahrhundert. Studien zu ihrer Ästhetik.* Berlin: Schmidt, 1998.

———, and Ingrid Kasten, eds. *Mittelalterliche Lyrik: Probleme der Poetik.* Berlin: Schmidt, 1999.

Des Minnesangs Frühling, ed. Hugo Moser und Helmut Tervooren. 3 vols. 37th ed. Stuttgart; Hirzel, 1977–1988 [anthology].

Heinen, Hubert. "Thwarted Expectations: Medieval and Modern Views of Genre in Germany," in *Medieval Lyric: Genres in Historical Context,* ed. William D. Paden. Urbana; University of Illinois Press, 2000, pp. 434–446.

Kasten, Ingrid. *Frauendienst bei Trobadors und Minnesängern im 12. Jahrhundert. Zur Entwicklung und Adaption eines literarischen Konzepts.* Heidelberg: Winter, 1986.

Krohn, Rüdiger, ed. *"Dâ hœret ouch geloube zuo." Überlieferungs- und Echtheitsfragen zum Minnesang.* Stuttgart; Hirzel, 1995.

Newberry Consort. *Wanderers' Voices: Medieval Cantigas and Minnesang.* Los Angeles: Harmonia Mundi France, 1993 [sound recording].

Sayce, Olive. *The Medieval German Lyric 1150–1300.* Oxford: Clarendon, 1982.

Schiendorfer, Max. *Ulrich von Singenberg, Walther und Wolfram. Zur Parodie in der höfischen Literatur.* Bonn: Bouvier, 1983.

Scholz, Manfred Günter. *Walther von der Vogelweide.* Stuttgart: Metzler, 1999.

Schweikle, Günther. *Neidhart.* Stuttgart; Metzler, 1990.

———. *Minnesang,* 2d ed. Stuttgart; Metzler, 1995.

Tervooren, Helmut. *Sangspruchdichtung.* Stuttgart: Metzler, 1995.

———. *Reinmar-Studien. Ein Kommentar zu den "unechten" Liedern Reinmars des Alten.* Stuttgart: Hirzel, 1991.

———. *Gedichte und Interpretationen. Mittelalter.* Stuttgart: Reclam, 1993.

Willms, Eva. *Liebesleid und Sangeslust. Untersuchungen zur deutschen Liebeslyrik des späten 12. und frühen 13. Jahhunderts.* Munich: Artemis, 1990.

Hubert Heinen

SEE ALSO

Albrecht von Johansdorf; Frauenlob; Hartmann von Aue; Heinrich von Morungen; Heinrich von Veldeke; Henry VI; Konrad von Würzburg; Kürenberg, Der von; *Liederhandschriften; Liederhandschriften,* Illustrations; Mechthild von Magdeburg; Meistersinger; Reinmar der Alte; Rudolf von Ems; *Sammelhandschriften; Sangspruch;* Tannhäuser, Der; Versification; Walther von der Vogelweide; Wolfram von Eschenbach

Mithras

The Roman army first introduced the cult of Mithras to the Germanic tribes living along the banks of the Rhine and Danube Rivers in the second century, and it remained the religion of choice for the military and merchant classes in the outer Roman provinces until the collapse of the western empire in the fifth century. Throughout this period the Romanized Germans embraced the cult to an extent unseen elsewhere in the Roman colonies, and Mithraism's influence among the Germans spread well beyond the imperial frontiers, reaching all the way to Scandinavia and the Baltic region. The depth of Mithraism's influence on the Germanic consciousness is as familiar as the names of the days of the week in the modern Germanic languages. The Roman day-names reflect Mithraic cosmology and—in a neat reversal of the familiar *interpretatio romani* (world view based on Roman perspectives)—were adopted by the Romanized Germans in the second century and translated to fit their native pantheon. About this same time, Scandinavian artisans began to produce amulets modeled on Roman coins featuring motifs borrowed from the coins themselves as well as from Mithraic monuments.

Evidence suggests that Mithraism was an exclusively male cult and that most of its adherents were soldiers. It was a mystery religion without a sacred literature, and its mysteries were preserved and transmitted via a body of elaborately symbolic art, an apparently no-less-elaborate liturgy, and a seven-tiered process of initiation. The central figure in Mithraism is the god Mithras, who was celebrated as savior, world renewer, invincible god, and ally both of the great god of the sun, or shining sky, and of mortal rulers. He always is depicted as a powerfully built youth clad (sometimes only) in a Phrygian cap and blue cloak and armed with a dagger or short sword. The central mystery of the cult was the regeneration of the universe through Mithras's slaying of the cosmic bull, a feat that was reenacted in its liturgy and also provided the favorite subject for its sacred art. It was especially popular in the heavily garrisoned Rhineland and around the seaports of the Low Countries.

Mithraism's influence on Germanic literature cannot be demonstrated directly because neither the cult nor the Germans of late antiquity recorded their myths or religious practices in writing. Nevertheless, Mithraic art and architecture offer many striking parallels to the pre-Christian mythology and heroic legends of the Germans, in particular to the figures of Sîfrit (Siegfried), Sîgmund, and Sîgurd and the dragon-slaying tradition associated with them. The names of all three heroes share the protheme *sîge-* (victory), a name element associated with the worship of the Germanic god Wotan, the decider of battles and patron of the noble class whose cult arose in the Migration Age under the influence of Mithraism. Sîfrit and the Nibelung legends express especially powerful affinities with Mithraism: Sîfrit is associated in the *Nibelungenlied* with the city of Xanten "down by the Rhine," his mysterious magic cloak (*tarnkappe*) recalls the distinctive cap and mantle of Mithras, and his most famous feat, the slaying of the dragon, has much in common with Mithras's sacrifice of the cosmic bull.

The ideal *mithreum,* or Mithraic temple, was a natural cave proximate to a spring or other source of fresh, running water. All *mithraea* were subterranean and built to imitate caves where natural caves were lacking. The cave is of central importance in Mithraism because the cult held the universe to be a cavelike pocket of ordered matter amid immaterial chaos, and Mithras performed the sacrifice of the cosmic bull in a cave after capturing it in open country. Representations of the bull sacrifice emphasize Mithras's reluctance at the very moment he plunges his blade into the bull's nape. Similarly, Sîfrit ambushes the dragon outside the beast's lair beside a stream while the hero himself lay in a trench that further recalls the Mithraic cave. This formula in which a hero engages a monstrous adversary in or just outside a cave or barrow proximate to water also is echoed in the dragon fights in *Beowulf,* in the Icelandic lays of Sîgurd and Fafnir, and again in the Norse epic *Volsunga saga.* Moreover, the Germanic dragon slayer typically engages his prey without rancor and at the behest of some third party, and his defeat of the beast brings immense wealth to his folk, just as Mithras's reluctant sacrifice of the bull liberates its life force and reinvigorates the universe.

BIBLIOGRAPHY

Davidson, H. R. E. "Mithras and Wodan." In *Der historische Horizont der Götterbild-Amulette aus der Übergangsepoche von Spätantike zum Frühmittelalter,* ed. Karl Hauck. Göttingen: Vandenhoeck and Ruprecht, 1992, pp. 99–110.

Vermaseren, M. J. *Mithras, the Secret God,* trans. Therese Megan and Vincent Megaw. New York: Barnes and Noble, 1963.

Donald P. Beistle

SEE ALSO
Mythology; *Nibelungenlied*

Modelbooks

See Manuals, Artists', and Modelbooks.

Modern Devotion

See Devotio Moderna.

Monarchy

See individual rulers; Itinerant Kingship; Nobility and Farmers.

Monasteries

Although monasteries and religious houses came to dot the landscape of medieval Germany no less than in the rest of Europe, their initial position was different. Most of "Germany" lay beyond the Roman Empire, which had adopted Christianity as its sole official religion in the fourth century. In the province of Gaul there were already about two hundred monasteries by the year 500, and about four hundred by the year 700. Across the Rhine, by comparison, monasteries were an integral part of the expansion, creation, and conversion of medieval Germany.

Thus Fulda was founded in 744 by the Anglo-Saxon monk Boniface, the "Apostle of the Germans," as a base for missionary work. Chrodegang, bishop of Metz (d. 766), wrote a rule for secular canons who lived in community and sang the Divine Office, but who, unlike monks, were not obliged to forgo private property. Charlemagne promoted the adoption of this rule by cathedrals and collegiate churches and of the Rule of St. Benedict by monasteries, and he ordained that all these institutions establish schools and copying-rooms *(scriptoria)* for the preservation of texts. Abbeys like St. Gall and Reichenau were great centers of Carolingian cultural activity.

With the advance of the Franks, the Bavarians, and their successors, monasteries came to be planted in the lands of the Saxons and the Slavs. Although the reform "order" of Cluny scarcely penetrated into Germany, in the tenth and eleventh centuries Gorze, Stavelot-Malmedy, and Hirsau and other houses played a definitive role in the monastic reform movement. Interestingly, the great religious orders founded during the flowering of the twelfth and thirteenth centuries—the Cistercians, Carthusians, Premonstratensians, and the mendicant Franciscans, Dominicans, Augustinians, and Carmelites—all had their origins elsewhere (especially in France and Italy). Two of these orders, however, were founded by Germans: Bruno of Cologne, who established the Carthusians, and Norbert of Xanten, who founded the Premonstratensians. Both orders were a bit eccentric: the Carthusians were austerely eremitical, living mostly in their individual cells and coming together at best weekly, and in the late Middle Ages celebrated as the only religious order not requiring reformation, while the Premonstratensians were regular canons, living communally as monks, but also actively engaged in pastoral work rather than withdrawal from the world. Significantly, Bruno and Norbert created their orders in France, not on German soil. Just as no major heretical movement came out of medieval Germany, so too no major religious *order.*

Yet in the late Middle Ages the Rhineland did produce some significant religious *movements* that modified monastic ideals and practices for lay people living in the world and thus tended to break down the barriers between clergy and laity, thus paving the way for Luther's assault on monasticism and insistence on the priesthood of all believers. Chief among these movements were the

Beguines, the Beghards, and the Brethren of the Common Life.

As in much of the rest of Europe, monasteries and religious orders in Germany were in trouble in the late Middle Ages. By the mid-fourteenth century, all save the Carthusians were thought in desperate need of reform, including the mendicants, which had arisen just a century earlier. The popes launched reform initiatives beginning in the 1330s, and during the next two centuries members of the orders, often aided by princes and governments, achieved varying levels of success. Among the more conspicuous were the Benedictines, for which the monasteries of Melk, Kastel, and Bursfeld created reform "congregations." No fewer than eighty houses belonged to the Bursfeld Congregation by circa 1520. Similarly, Augustinian canons could look to the congregation of Windesheim, which numbered eighty-seven houses by 1500. Yet many monasteries, including the famous abbey of Weißenburg in Alsace, refused to reform and found an escape by formal conversion to collegiate churches. The strongly aristocratic character of the German church proved to be a major impediment to reform.

Monasteries for women in Germany deserve a special note. As in England and a few other places in Europe, there were here a number of double monasteries, with branches for women and men, but ruled by abbesses. As in the rest of Europe, monasteries in Germany provided refuges and protection for women and their property, but they seem also to have been peculiarly nourishing of women. It is probably no accident that out of German monasteries came Hroswitha of Gandersheim, the first dramatist of the Middle Ages; Hildegard of Bingen (1098–1179), one of the most formidable figures of the twelfth century; and a significant number of mystics like Mechtild of Magdeburg. One possible factor was that in the political world of Germany it was possible for a woman like the imperial princess-abbess of Essen to cut a large swath. (Women also held their place in the guild system and the world of work longer in Germany than they did elsewhere.) Whatever the reasons may be, women in monasteries tended to resist the introduction of the Reformation in the sixteenth century more stoutly and successfully than men did.

On the eve of the Reformation, there were in Germany no fewer than 160 Benedictine, 120 Premonstratensian, 80 Cistercian, 125 Franciscan, 70 Dominican, 60 Augustinian, and 50 Carmelite houses, as well as around 300 collegiate churches of all sorts.

BIBLIOGRAPHY

Elm, Kaspar, ed. *Reformbemühungen und Observanzbestrebungen im spätmittelalterlichen Ordenswesen.* Berlin: Duncker and Humblot, 1989.

Freed, John B. *The Friars and German Society in the Thirteenth Century.* Cambridge, Mass.: Medieval Academy of America, 1977.

Grundmann, Herbert. *Religious Movements in the Middle Ages.* Notre Dame: University of Notre Dame Press, 1995.

Hauck, Albert. *Kirchengeschichte Deutschlands.* 5 vols. in 6. 8th unrev. ed. Berlin: Akademie-Verlag, 1954.

Heimbucher, Max. *Die Orden und Kongregationen der katholischen Kirche.* 2 vols. Paderborn: Verlag Ferdinand Schöningh, 1933.

Lawrence, C. E. *Medieval Monasticism.* 2d ed. London: Longman, 1989.

Nyhus, Paul. *The Franciscans in South Germany, 1400–1530: Reform and Revolution.* Philadelphia: American Philosophical Society, 1975.

Rocca, G., and G. Pelliccia eds. *Dizionario degli istituti di perfezione.* 9 vols. to date. Rome: Edizioni Paoline, 1974ff.

Schulte, Aloys. *Der Adel und die deutsche Kirche im Mittelalter,* 2d ed. Stuttgart: F. Enke, 1922.

Lawrence G. Duggan

SEE ALSO
Charlemagne; Hildegard von Bingen; Hrosvit of Gandersheim; Mechthild von Magdeburg; Reichenau; Sankt Gall

Monasticism, Dutch

Since the slow process of Christianization in the Low Countries took place from the south to the north, the oldest monasteries are situated in the southern Netherlands. Particularly the Irish missionaries, mostly monks themselves, were active here in the founding of monasteries, using them as outposts in a mainly pagan area. By the beginning of the eighth century, thus about forty monasteries were founded in the south, among which important abbeys as Lobbes (at the Sambre River), Sint-Truiden, Echternach (in present-day Luxemburg), and Sint-Baafs (in Ghent). The regions north of the river Rhine, only partly christianized in the ninth century, had no monasteries in the early Middle Ages. Even though there existed a chapter of canons at the cathedral church in Utrecht, it was not until circa 1000 that the first monastery in the northern Netherlands was founded, the abbey of Hohorst near Utrecht.

In most parts of the Low Countries, especially in the north, the number of monasteries therefore was only small at that time. This changed drastically, however, in the period around 1100. From the reform movement in the church then arose two new monastic orders, the Cistercian and the Premonstratensian, which really flourished in the Low Countries. The reasons for their success were many. In the first place, some of these regions thus far virtually had no monasteries, so the new orders found fertile soil here. In the second place, the bishops here supported these new orders vigorously and the laymen were eager to donate properties to them. As a result, in less than a century several dozens of Cistercian and Premonstratensian abbeys were founded in the Netherlands. Apart from monastic services, these institutions also devoted themselves to public tasks. Though not to the extent suggested in earlier literature, in some cases they played an active part in land reclamation, diking of rivers, and cultivation of wasteland. In addition, they played an important role in spiritual care in countryside parishes and also created huge farms operated in a comparatively rational fashion. Famous in this last respect are the Cistercian abbeys of Ten Duinen en Ter Doest, which owned ten thousands of acres in the coastal areas of Flanders and Zealand.

As in other parts of Europe, these abbeys grew richer and richer as a result of their religious and economic success. The wealth they acquired, however, evoked serious criticism from new monastic movements that placed special emphasis on the vow of poverty, such as the Franciscans and the Dominicans. These mendicant orders, whose members lived in extreme sobriety, became very popular in the economically and demographically fast-growing cities of Holland and Flanders, where dozens of new convents were founded during the thirteenth and fourteenth centuries. Yet as in the course of years these orders, too, lost some of their religious splendor, a new movement developed in the northeastern regions of the Netherlands at the beginning of the fifteenth century, called the Modern Devotion. Inspired by their religious leader, Geert Grote, groups of men and women (the brothers and sisters of the Common Life) started living together in poverty and devotion, but without adopting a monastic rule. This movement exercised a strong influence on the religious orders, which also tried to reform themselves, and on the spiritual life in general, in the Netherlands as well as elsewhere.

As a result of this strong reform movement on the eve of the Reformation, monastic life in the Netherlands was fairly sound. Notwithstanding this, in the late sixteenth century an abrupt end came to the monasteries in the northern parts, because the Calvinist rebels against the Catholic Habsburg regime gained military and political control over these regions. They prohibited the practice of Catholicism and abolished all monasteries. In the south, on the other hand, the Catholic government stood its ground. Here the monasteries were damaged by the Iconoclasm of 1567 and the frequent military clashes but anyhow continued their existence into the modern era.

BIBLIOGRAPHY

Mol, Johannes A. *De Friese huizen van de Duitse orde.* Leeuwarden: Fryske Akademy, 1991 [with summary in German].

Monasticon Belge. 4 vols. Liège: Centre national de recherches d'histoire religieuse, 1890–1960. [comprehensive repertory of monasteries].

Monasticon Batavum, ed. Micharl Schoengen. 3 vols. Amsterdam: Noord-Hollandsche Uitgevers Maatschappij, 1941–1942 [somewhat outdated repertory of Dutch monasteries].

Sanders, J. G. M. *Waterland als woestijn. Geschiedenis van het Kartuizerklooster 'Het Hollandse Huis' bij Geertruidenberg 1336–1595.* Hilversum: Verloren, 1990 [with summary in French].

van Bavel, Bas J. P. *Goederenverwerving en goederenbeheer van de abdij Mariënweerd (1129–1592).* Hilversum: Verloren, 1993 [with summary in French].

van Engen, John. "The Virtues, the Brothers, and the Schools." *Revue Bé né dictine* 98 (1988): 178–217.

van Zijl, Theodore P. *Gerard Groote.* Washington, D.C.: Catholic University of America Press, 1963.

Bas J. P. van Bavel

SEE ALSO
Devotio Moderna; Monasteries; Utrecht

Monasticism, German

See Monasteries.

Mönch von Salzburg, Der (fl. 2d half of the 14th c.)

Known variously as Hermann, Johanns, or Hans in the over one hundred manuscripts in which his songs are transmitted, the Monk of Salzburg was the most prolific and popular German singer of the fourteenth century. His six polyphonic pieces are the earliest surviving part-songs in German. His forty-nine secular and fifty-seven religious songs represent nearly every genre current in fourteenth-century German singing, including the hymn, the sequence, the new year's song, the alba, the drinking song, and the *Leich* (lay). Virtually nothing is known about his life except that he moved in the courtly circles of the archbishop of Salzburg, Pilgrim II von Puchheim (r. 1365–1396).

His melodies fall between those of two dominant medieval German genres, *Spruchdichtung* and *Meistergesang*. Some reflect the traditional German e-based modalities (phrygian), though many tend toward the modern major, beginning on E or B-natural and ending on C. The songs are frequently adorned with richly textured preludes, interludes, and postludes. He sometimes favors *melissmas* at the beginning and end of lines and makes frequent use of refrains. "Josef, liber neve min" (Joseph, My Dear Nephew), a German Christmas song still sung today, is attributed to him in one of the manuscripts.

The monk's secular poetry combines themes of the courtly lyric and folk songs, earthy but sometimes simple and affecting, with strong reminiscences of the rhetoric of *Minnesang* and of the Neidhart tradition. His religious songs, some translations of Latin hymns, are closely akin to and probably influenced the songs of the Meistersinger in the fifteenth century. The most gifted German-language lyric singer of the next generation, Oswald von Wolkenstein, was indebted to the monk in both text and melody.

BIBLIOGRAPHY

Meyer, Friedrich Arnold, and Heinrich Rietsch. *Die Mondsee-Wiener Liederhandschrift und der Mönch von Salzburg*. Berlin: Mayer and Müller, 1896 [texts and melodies of the secular songs].

Spechtler, Franz Viktor, ed. *Die geistlichen Lieder des Mönchs von Salzburg*. Berlin: de Gruyter, New York, 1972 [texts and melodies of his religious songs].

Wachinger, Burghart. *Der Mönch von Salzburg: Zur Überlieferung geistlicher Lieder im späten Mittelalter*. Tübingen: Niemeyer, 1989.

Peter Frenzel

SEE ALSO

Meistersinger; *Minnesang*; Neidhart; Oswald von Wolkenstein; *Sangspruch*; Versification

Morgarten, Battle of (November 15, 1315)

In 1291 the three Alpine communities of Uri, Unterwalden, and Schwytz swore an "Eternal Alliance," therewith seeking their independence from local dynasts, most particularly the Habsburgs. In the disputed royal election of 1314, they showed their support for Ludwig von Wittelsbach against his rival, Frederick "the Handsome" von Habsburg, by sacking the Abbey of Einsiedeln. To punish these upstarts, Duke Leopold I von Habsburg of Austria (1293–1326) collected a large army of several thousand and marched along the narrow path of Morgarten to reach and attack Schwytz. When the vanguard was halted by a hastily built rampart, the knights jammed up along the narrow mountain road. Then the Swiss tumbled boulders and logs down on the army. In the resulting panic, the knights trampled their own infantry or fell down the mountainside. Finally, the Swiss moved in and butchered the Austrian forces, probably using their famous weapon, the halberd.

Throughout Christendom many nobles were shocked by the defeat of knights by mere peasants. The battle helped to secure the growing strength of the Swiss Confederation and the reputation of its fighting men.

BIBLIOGRAPHY

Delbrück, Hans. *Medieval Warfare,* trans. Walter J. Renfroe Jr. History of the Art of War 3. Lincoln: University of Nebraska Press, 1982.

Oman, Charles. *A History of the Art of War in the Middle Ages.* 2 vols. 2d ed. London: Methuen, 1924.

Brian A. Pavlac

SEE ALSO

Warfare

Moriz von Craûn

The story of Moriz von Craûn exists today in only one early sixteenth-century manuscript, the *Ambraser Heldenbuch* (Seria nova, No. 2663, Austrian National Library, Vienna). *Moriz von Craûn,* 1,784 lines, appears on folios 2va–5vc, in the manuscript of 238 oversized folios (460 mm × 360 mm). The name of the original poet, the precise date of composition (somewhere between 1173 and 1250), and the source (probably French) are unknown. From the rhymes and the choice of vocabulary, we can deduce that the poem was composed in the language region between Low or Rhenish Alemannic and Rhenish Franconian, i.e., between Strasbourg and Worms.

The story begins with a lengthy prologue of 288 lines in which the poet summarizes the course of chivalry *(translatio imperii)* since its inception in Greece—from Troy to Rome to France. Moriz von Craûn is a perfect knight who serves the countess of Beaumont, demonstrating his claim to chivalry in a number of somewhat distorted ways: he builds a ship that sails across the land on wheels pulled by hidden horses; he performs in a tournament, defeating countless knights. He is generous to a fault, giving away all his possessions. Moriz comes to the countess after the tournament, dirty and bloody and thus showing his complete devotion, to claim his reward. The countess makes him wait for her and thus he is asleep when she arrives for the rendezvous. She stalks away. Moriz awakes and decides to claim his reward without her consent. He finds the count and countess in bed. The count wakes up, sees Moriz approaching, and believes him to be the ghost of the knight he accidentally killed in the tournament; he jumps up in fright and strikes his shinbone, rendering himself unconscious on the floor beside the bed. Moriz slides into bed exclaiming: "This bed is half empty." The countess, not knowing the fate of her husband, now decides to give Moriz his reward. When they are finished, Moriz stands up, gives her back her ring, and reproaches her for not immediately giving him his reward. He rides away from the castle, and the countess repents her deeds.

For years scholars have questioned the genre of *Moriz von Craûn:* novella, *Schwank* or farce, exemplum (didactic tale), parody, fabliau, *mære*, short story, or *Erzählung*, whether it is courtly or anticourtly, a serious didactic work, an outrageous parody, or all the above. The text contains many elements characteristic of medieval culture and medieval literature: a strict—even classical—form and structure; descriptions of nature, armor, a castle, a tent, a tournament, a ship on wheels, a fantastic bed, a lady's chamber, and exotic birds and animals; courtly love according to Andreas Capellanus and his modern interpreters, pushed to its ridiculous logical conclusion (the concept of *dienst/lôn)*; lessons on chivalry; possible parody, and certainly satire as well as evidence of medieval knowledge of history *(translatio imperii)* and the classics.

BIBLIOGRAPHY

Anderson, Robert R. *Wortindex und Reimregister zum Moriz von Craûn.* Amsterdam: Rodopi, 1975.

Classen, Albrecht, ed. *Moriz von Craûn.* Reclam Universal-Bibliothek 8796. Stuttgart: Reclam, 1992.

Fritsch-Rößler, Waltraud. "'Moriz von Craûn': Minnesang beim Wort genommen oder es schläft immer der Falsche." *Uf der mâze pfat: Festschrfit für Werner Hoffmann zum 60. Geburtstag,* ed. Waltraud Fritsch-Rößler. GAG 555. Göppingen: Kümmerle, 1991, pp. 227–254.

Gentry, G. Francis. "A Tale from a City: *Moriz von Craûn." In Semper idem et novus. Festschrift for Frank Banta,* ed. Francis G. Gentry. Göppingen: Kümmerle, 1988, pp. 193–207.

Harvey, Ruth. *Moriz von Craûn and the Chivalric World.* Oxford: Clarendon Press, 1961.

Ortmann, Christa. "Die Bedeutung der Minne im 'Moriz von Craun'." *Beiträge zur Geschichte der deutschen Sprache und Literatur* 108 (1986): 385–407.

Pretzel, Ulrich. *Moriz von Craûn.* ATB 45. Tübingen: Max Niemeyer, 1966.

Ruh, Kurt. "Moriz von Craun: Eine hofische Thesenerzahlung aus Frankreich. *Formen mittelalterlicher Literatur. Siegfried Beyschlag zu seinem 65. Geburtstag,* ed. Otmar Wergner and Bernd Naumann. Göppingen: Kümmerle, 1970, pp. 77–90.

———. "Zur Datierung, zum Verfasser und zur Interpretation des Moriz von Craûn." *Zeitschrift für deutsche Philologie* 103 (1984): 321-365.

Thomas, Heinz. "Ordo Equestris-Ornamentum Imperii. Zur Geschichte der Ritterschaft im 'Moriz von Craûn'." *Zeitschrift für deutsche Philologie* 106 (1987): 341–353.

Thomas, J. Wesley. "Structure and Interpretation in Four Medieval German Novellas." In *Spretrum medii aevi George Fenwick Jones,* ed. William C. McDonald. Göppingen: Kümmerle, 1983, pp. 509–520.

Tomasek, Tomas. "Die mhd. Verserzahlung 'Moriz von Craun.' Eine Werkdeutung mit Blick auf die Vor-Geschichte." *Zeitschrift für deutsches Altertum* 115 (1986): 254–283.

Unterkircher, Franz. *Ambraser Heldenbuch vollständige Faksimile-Ausgabe im Originalformat. Kommentar.* Codices selecti 43. Graz: Akademische Druck-und Verlagsanstalt, 1973 [facsimile].

Van D'Elden, Stephanie Cain, ed. *Moriz von Craûn.* New York: Garland, 1990.

Van D'Elden, Stephanie Cain. "Lessons on Chivalry: *Moriz von Craûn."* In *in hôhem prîse: A Festschrift in Honor of Ernst S. Dick,* ed. Winder McConnell. Göppingen: Kümmerle, 1989, pp. 1–9.

Ziegeler, Hans-Joachim. "Moriz von Craûn." In *Die deutsche Literatur des Mittelalters: Verfasserlexikon,* vol. 6. Berlin: de Gruyter, 1986, cols. 692–700.

Stephanie Cain Van D'Elden

Heldenbücher; Maximilian

Moselle River

The source of the Moselle (German Mosel; French Moselle) River lies at Col de Bussang in the southern part of the Vosges mountain range of Lorraine; it flows in a generally northern direction past Metz and Trier, before beginning its twisting and turning course between the Eifel and the Hundsrück Massifs, and emptying into the Rhine River at Coblenz. The length of the river is some 335 miles (about 545 kilometers), and its course, together with that of the tributary rivers Saar, Sauer, Kyll, Ruwer, and Lieser, has provided the setting for settlements since pre-Roman times. Metz, lying at the confluence of the Moselle and the Seille Rivers, became the capital of Merovingian Austrasia in the sixth century; Trier, founded in 15 B.C.E. as Augusta Treverorum at a point where the river valley widens out, took its name from the nearby settlement and tribal sanctuary of the Treveri; it became an imperial residence toward the end of the third century, and it was here that Constantine the Great resided 306–312.

Tradition has it that Caesar Augustus introduced the grape, the walnut, and various fruits and flowers into the Moselle valley in 15 B.C.E. Certainly the mild climate of the region made it attractive, as did the numerous hot springs. During the tenth century, viticulture experienced remarkable development in the Moselle region, typical of what was happening along the Lot, the Seine, the Oise, and the Yonne. Long before the eleventh century the Moselle region became densely settled, with both the Hunsrück and the Eifel exhibiting high levels of demographic growth in the eleventh and twelfth centuries. Towns such as Wasserbillig became market centers as early as 1140. The region was also home to religious communities, such as the monastery Springiersbach, founded about 1150.

The Moselle formed an important and ancient trade route, in connection with the Rhône and the Saône. During the Middle Ages it was navigable as far as Remiremont and Épinal, but large boats could travel only as far up as Toul. Its significance as a major transport route therefore began at Toul, and in the mid–eleventh century boats from Toul were paying tolls at Koblenz. Venantius Fortunatus reports of a boat trip taken in 588 from Metz to Andernach; Bishop Gregory of Tours mentions the salt trade between Metz and Trier on the Moselle. In addition to salt, Moselle commerce was in wine, grain, wood, honey, wool, and also cloth.

The Moselle valley lay at the center of the Moselgau, that administrative district that arose in the aftermath of the collapse of the Carolingian Empire; the counts of the Moselgau appear in documents well into the twelfth century. The role of the Moselle in the context of territorial lordships (among others, the archbishopric of Trier; the bishoprics of Metz, Toul, and Verdun; the duke of Lotharingia; and the counts of Bar, Luxemburg, and Sponheim) can be seen in the numerous fortresses that overlook the river. Cochem, sometime known as the Reichsburg (imperial castle) and a frequent residence of the Lotharingian pfalzgraves, dates from 1027; the Burg Eltz dates from about 1160; the Gravenburg was also built in the twelfth century near Traben-Trarbach; while the Burg Thurandt (at Alken, fifteen miles from Koblenz) belonged to the future Pfalzgrave Henry of Welf, the son of Duke Henry the Lion, in 1192. From Metz downward there were also numerous toll stations on the river.

In the later Middle Ages, the Moselle lost out to the Maas/Meuse as a major trade artery, and economic decline set in.

BIBLIOGRAPHY

Lamprecht, Karl. *Deutsche Wirtschaftsleben im Mittelalter.* Leipzig: A. Durr, 1885/1886.

Schneider, J. *La Ville de Metz aux XIIIe et XIVe siècles.* Nancy: G. Thomas, 1950.

Yante, J.-M. "Die Wirtschaftsverhnisse in Moselluxemburg 1200–1560," *Rheinische Vierteljahrsblätter* 51 (1987): 129–166.

Paul B. Pixton

SEE ALSO

Carolingians; Coblenz; Fortification; Henry the Lion; Meuse River; Toul; Trier; Welfs

Moser, Lucas (fl. ca. 1431/1432)

The reputation of the painter Lucas Moser rests on a single work, the altarpiece with scenes from the life of Mary Magdalene in the former chapel of the Virgin (now the parish church) in Tiefenbroon, near Pforzheim in southwestern Germany. An inscription dates the work 1431 or 1432—the last digit is hard to read with clarity—and names "Lucas Moser, painter from Weil," a nearby town, as its author. Apart from this brief mention, nothing is known of the artist's life or career, and attempts to link him with documentary mentions of painters named Lucas in this area and with other works have not been widely accepted. Even the attribution of the Magdalene altar to Moser was disputed in a highly controversial book on the altarpiece published by Gerhard Piccard in 1969. Considering the inscription as a nineteenth-century forgery, Piccard assigned the work to a follower of the Sienese painter Simone Martini and argued that it had been made for the church of the Magdalene at Vézelay in Burgundy. Piccard's book, which received much publicity in advance of its publication, occasioned numerous rebuttals afterward, many of them based on new art historical or technical work. Current consensus holds that the inscription is not modern; that the altarpiece was made for its present position, where its unusual shape reflects that of the wall painting underneath, which it replaced; and that the coats-of-arms, which may have been added very slightly later, represent the patrons of the work, Bernhard von Stein and his wife, Agnes (Engelin) Maiser von Berg.

The central part of the altarpiece is occupied by episodes from the life of Mary Magdalene as told in the *Legenda aurea.* At the left, the saint and her companions, set adrift by pagans in a rudderless boat, approach the coast of Marseille, portrayed here in a recognizable view. In the center, the saint's companions are asleep below, while in the attic room above, the Magdalene appears to the ruler's wife in her sleep to ask her to intervene with her husband on behalf of the Christians. In the final scene, angels deliver the saint, clothed only in her hair after long years in the desert, to a church where the Bishop Maximinus administers her the last rites. In the unusual arched upper panel, the Magdalene washes the feet of Christ, while bust-length figures representing Christ as the Man of Sorrows in the midst of the Wise and Foolish Virgins fill the long, horizontal predella below. On feast days the unusually narrow wings would have been opened to reveal the siblings of the Magdalene, Saints Martha and Lazarus, painted on their insides, flanking a sculpted figure of the Magdalene (now replaced) at the center of the shrine.

Moser's style provides some clues to his early training. His individualized head types, exceptional interest in detail, and use of disguised symbolism indicate knowledge of Flemish painting. Charles Sterling sees Moser as "a close follower of Robert Campin" and notes particularly the use of a continuous background across the four scenes of the center of the altarpiece, a device the Fleming had used as early as about 1420 (1972: 19–22). Sterling also

suggests the influence of Flemish and Franco-Flemish manuscript illumination and the possibility of a trip to Provence. What is clear is that Moser's only known work is a masterpiece in both its style and its virtuoso handling of material and technique.

BIBLIOGRAPHY

Haussherr, Rainer. "Der Magdalenenaltar in Tiefenbronn: Bericht über die wissenschaftliche Tagung am 9. und 10. März 1971 im Zentralinstitut für Kunstgeschichte in München." *Kunstchronik* 24 (1971): 177–212.

Köhler, Wilhelm. Review of Gerhard Piccard, *Der Magdalenenaltar des 'Lucas Moser' in Tiefenbronn. Zeitschrift für Kunstgeschichte* 35 (1972): 228–249.

Piccard, Gerhard, *Der Magdalenenaltar des 'Lucas Moser' in Tiefenbronn: Ein Beitrag zur europäischen Kunstgeschichte.* Wiesbaden: Harrossowitz, 1969.

Richter, Ernst-Ludwig. "Zur Rekonstruktion des Tiefenbronner Magdalenen-Altars." *Pantheon* 30 (1972): 33–38.

Sterling, Charles. "Observations on Moser's Tiefenbronn Altarpiece." *Pantheon* 30 (1972): 19–32.

Joan A. Holladay

SEE ALSO
Gothic Art and Architecture; Iconographies, Innovative

Mühlhausen
Archaeological finds indicate a fifth-century fortification and church at the strategic site where north/south and east/west trading routes intersect with the Unstrut River. Gregory of Tours reports that the Franks defeated the local Thuringians in 531; Christianizing missions and the establishment of an administrative center for both economic and military purposes followed. The first mention of Mühlhausen by name dates to 967, when Otto II, still during his father's lifetime, issued a document here; this is the first of a number of recorded visits by the Ottonian emperors and indicates that the site had a certain importance. It also suggests that a palace must have stood here by this date. A notice in an eighteenth-century chronicle credits Otto I with building a church here in 970. While this late mention has sometimes been discounted and the earliest incarnation of the Marienkirche (Church of the Virgin) dated to the reign of Henry III (1039–1056), Ul-

rike Gentz has argued for the earlier date on the basis of similarities to the cathedral Otto founded at Magdeburg in 955. In 974 Otto II gave his wife Theophanu *civitas* and *curtis* (city and court) at Mühlhausen.

From about 1000, the city was organized around several centers; the two most important of these were the Altstadt, or Unterstadt (Old Town, or Lower Town), around the parish church of St. Blasius and the Neustadt, or Oberstadt (New Town, or Upper Town), organized around the Marienkirche along a ridge. The association of the latter with the imperial interest in Mühlhausen can be seen in the long triumphal axis that stretched from the church of St. Johannes (St. John's) to the facade of the Marienkirche; similar processional routes existed at the imperial cities of Speyer, Würzburg, and Augsburg. As a result of its strategic location Mühlhausen continued to be of interest to the Salian and Staufer emperors; Henry IV held an assembly of princes here in 1069, and about 1180 Frederick I Barbarossa extended the palace and allowed the city to build a defensive wall.

Mühlhausen experienced a second flowering in the late Middle Ages. The city's financial well-being, largely a result of the cloth trade, expressed itself in a building boom. The extent of a fire in 1244 remains unclear; much of the area around St. Blasius was destroyed, and the historian Gentz sees the fire as grounds for rebuilding the south tower of the Marienkirche. Steps toward governmental independence culminated in the citizens' destruction of the royal palace in 1256; the choir of the Marienkirche was extended using stones from the razed buildings. A polygonal apse was added to the choir of St. Blasius about 1270 and a Gothic nave finished circa 1300–1310. Its hall church form is based on that of St. Elizabeth's at Marburg, which, like both St. Blasius and the Marienkirche, was under the control of the Teutonic Order. A fire in 1315 seems to have necessitated rebuilding the latter as well, and in 1317 the archbishop of Mainz issued an indulgence to support the building effort. Work proceeded haltingly, however, slowed by the political disturbances in the city in midcentury. The long choir with two shorter, parallel side chapels reflected the modern choir type recently erected at St. Stephen's in Vienna. Concentrated work on the transept and nave dates to the second half of the century. Twelve of Mühlhausen's sixteen medieval churches still stand; with the Marienkirche and St. Blasius, many of them date to the building boom of the late thirteenth and fourteenth centuries: the church of the Franciscan friars, also known as the Kornmarktkirche (church at the grain market); St.

Petrus (St. Peter's); and the Jakobikirche (church of St. James), among others.

The mention of the Rathaus (town hall) in 1310 and 1320 reflects the city's steps toward self-government, and in 1348, when Charles IV exempted the city from its tax obligations, it achieved the status of *freie Reichsstadt* (imperial free city). In 1362 Charles made a further decision to the city's advantage, when he settled a long-standing dispute between the Teutonic Order and the city council in the latter's favor. The unusual sculptural group installed on the Marienkirche after 1362, perhaps about 1380, mirrors the emperor's interest in and protection of the city. On the south transept exterior, facing toward the city center, four over-life-size figures lean out from a balustrade to address the passers-by below. The pair at center—a crowned male figure and veiled woman—must represent Charles IV and his wife, the two outer figures well-placed courtiers. As at the Frauenkirche (church of the Virgin) at Nuremberg, where a second-story balcony allowed the ceremonial presentation of the king to the crowds below, Charles addresses his subjects, in this case the members of the city council, who were required to pay homage to the king on this site once a year. There is no evidence that Charles ever visited Mühlhausen, but in these sculptures, the city council gave visual expression to the city's long and prosperous history of imperial connections.

BIBLIOGRAPHY

Aulepp, Rolf. "die frühe Besiedlung der Neustadt von Mühlhausen." *Mülhäuser Beiträge zu Geschichte, Kulturgeschichte, Natur und Umwelt* 9 (1986): 12–24.

Badstöbner, Ernst. *Das alte Mühlhausen; Kunstgeschichte einer mittelalterlichen Stadt.* Leipzig: Koehler und Amelang, 1989.

Beyreuther, Gerald. "Zur Bedeutung Mühlhausens unter den ottonischen Königen/Kaisern, besonders unter Heinrich II. (1002–1024)." *Mühlhäser Beiträge zu Geschichte, Kulturgeschichte, Natur und Umwelt* 9 (1986): 5–12.

Gentz, Ulrike. *Die Marienkirche zu Mühlhausen in Thüringen: Eine Baumonographie.* Magister Arbeit, Universität München, 1995. Schriften aus dem Institute für Kunstgeschichte 65. Munich: tuduv, 1995.

Hilger, Hans Peter. "Die Skulpturen an der südlichen Querhausfassade von St. Marien in Mühlhausen in Thüringen." *Wallraf-Richartz-Jahrbuch* 22 (1960): 159–164.

Neumeyer, Alfred. "The Meaning of the Balcony-Scene at the Church of Muehlhausen in Thuringia: A Contribution to the History of Illusionism." *Gazette des Beaux Arts* 50 (1957): 305–310.

Richter, Christa. *Die mittelalterlichen Glasmalereien in Mühlhausen/Thüringen.* Corpus Vitrearum Medii Aevi, Deutschland 16. Berlin: Akademie Verlag, 1993.

Joan A. Holladay

SEE ALSO
Augsburg; Charles IV; Magdeburg; Marburg; Otto I; Otto II; Speyer; Town Planning and Urbanism; Würzburg; Vienna

Multscher, Hans (ca. 1400–before March 13, 1467)

Working in stone, wood, and metal, Multscher was Ulm's foremost sculptor during the mid–fifteenth century. Originally from the countryside near Leutkirch in the Allgäu, he moved to Ulm by 1427, when he was accepted as a freeman, married Adelheid Kitzin, daughter of a local sculptor, and became a citizen. Since he already owned a house in Ulm, Multscher may have arrived a few years earlier. Where and with whom he trained are unknown. Artistic influences in his work suggest he traveled to the Rhineland, Burgundy, and the Low Countries during his *Wanderjahr* (year as a journeyman).

Multscher's large workshop produced both single figures and complex retables with painted panels. His name is inscribed on the Karg Altar of 1433 in the cathedral of Ulm, whose statues were destroyed during the Protestant iconoclasm of 1531. Multscher signed the painted wings of the large Wurzbach Altar from 1437, portions of which are in Berlin (Gemäldegalerie). This altarpiece may have been executed for the Church of the Assumption of the Virgin (St. Maria Himmelfahrt) in Landsberg am Lech, where the large stone Madonna and Child remains. Between 1456 and 1459 Multscher and his workshop prepared the high altar of the parish church at Sterzing (Vipiteno) in South Tyrol; the remnants of this altar, which was dismantled in 1779, are divided among the church and the Museo Multscher in Sterzing, the Ferdinandeum in Innsbruck, the Bayerisches Nationalmuseum in Munich, and a private collection in Basel. These works form the basis for other attributions. Although Multscher is often cited as a painter, there is little evidence that his personal involvement extended beyond his roles as workshop head, master designer, and sculptor of some of the statues.

The artist introduced a greater sense of realism into southern German art. At a time when the lyrical Soft

Hans Multscher, Man of Sorrows, Ulm, cathedral, porch. *Photograph: Joan A. Holladay*

Style with its Beautiful Virgins, gracefully curved poses, and elongated proportions was popular, Multscher developed solid, more naturalistic figures that display the general influence of Netherlandish post-Sluterian sculpture. The Landsberg Madonna and Child from 1437 still includes hints of the Soft Style with its swaying stance, yet her inherent stability, the clear treatment of the deeply cut drapery folds, and the marvelously animated Christ Child who squirms in Mary's grasp reveal Multscher's new aesthetic sensibilities. Using this and related works, scholars have attributed to Multscher several slightly earlier projects. The most significant of these are the images of Charlemagne and other figures made circa 1427–1430 to adorn the eastern window of Ulm's city hall (the originals are now in the Ulmer Museum), the life-size Man of Sorrows from 1429 above the western entry to the cathedral of Ulm, and the alabaster Trinity group from circa 1430 in the Liebieghaus in Frankfurt. The half-nude

Christ evocatively displays his wounds to all who enter the cathedral. Its spirit recalls similar Christ figures by both Claus Sluter and the Master of Flémalle. Related to the Man of Sorrows is the slightly later model for the tomb of Duke Ludwig the Bearded of Bavaria (1435, now in the Bayerisches Nationalmuseum, Munich). Employing fine Solnhofen limestone rather than the coarser sandstone that he typically used, Multscher devised a highly detailed scene of Ludwig kneeling before the Holy Trinity. The tomb, intended for Ingolstadt, was never executed.

In the ensuing decades Multscher and his shop supplied numerous Madonnas, crucifixions, and other religious figures for churches near Ulm. His most notable creations include the tomb effigy of Countess Mechthild von Württemberg-Urach (1450–1455), now in the Stiftskirche in Tübingen; the bronze reliquary bust (ca. 1460) in the Frick Collection in New York; the life-size wooden *Palmesel* (palm donkey, 1456, Ulm Museum), which was made initially for the church of St. Ulrich and Afra in Augsburg, and the now divided Sterzing High Altar. The latter was made in Ulm and then transported to Sterzing, where Multscher and several assistants spent about seven months erecting the altarpiece in 1458 and early 1459.

BIBLIOGRAPHY

Baxandall, Michael. *The Limewood Sculptors of Renaissance Germany.* New Haven, Conn.: Yale University Press, 1980, pp. 12–13, 245–247.

Beck, Herbert, and Maraike Bückling. *Hans Multscher: Das Frankfurter Trinitätsrelief, Ein Zeugnis spekulativer Künstlerindividualität.* Frankfurt: Fischer Taschenbuch Verlag, 1988.

Grosshans, Rainald. "'Hans Multscher hat das werk gemacht': die Flugel des 'Wurzacher Altars' und ihre Restaurierung." *Museums Journal* (Berlin) 10 (1996): 78–80.

Reisner, Sabine, and Peter Steckhan. "Ein Beitrag zur Grabmalvisier Hans Multschers für Herzog Ludwig den Bärtigen." In *Das geschnitzte und gemalte bild auf den altaren stehen ist nutzlich und christenlich: Aufsätze zur süddeutschen Skulptur und Malerei des 15. und 16. Jahrhunderts,* ed. Rupert Schreiber. Messkirch: A. Gmeiner, 1988, pp. 9–74.

Schädler, Alfred. "Bronzebildwerke von Hans Multscher." In *Intuition und Kunstwissenschaft: Festschrift Hanns Swarzenski zum 70. Geburtstag am 30. August 1973,* ed. Peter Bloch. Berlin: Gebrüder Mann, 1973, pp. 391–408.

Theil, Edmund. *Der Multscher-Altar in Sterzing.* Bozen: Athesia, 1992.

Tripps, Manfred. "*Hans Multscher: Seine Ulmer Schaffenszeit 1427–1467.*" Dissertatin, Heidelberg University, 1966–1967. Weissenhorn: A. H. Konrad, 1969.

———. *Hans Multscher: Meister der Spätgotik, sein Werk, seine Schule, seine Zeit.* Leutkirch: Heimatpflege Leutkirch, 1993.

Jeffrey Chipps Smith

SEE ALSO

Augsburg; Gothic Art and Architecture; Iconographies, Innovative; International Style; Ulm

Munich

Although the first written mention of a village at the site of Munich (Bavaria) dates from the eighth century, archaeological evidence attests to the presence of a settlement during the sixth and seventh centuries. Legendary etymology linking the earlier name Munichen to the phrase *zu den Monchen* (at the monks' place) is questionable. Excavations in 1945 revealed that a parish church built during the mid–eleventh century existed at the present site of St. Peter's, the oldest parish church in Munich (1181). As a city, however, Munich's development began in 1158 with an act of aggression on the part of Duke Henry the Lion. Endeavoring to secure toll revenues for himself from an important salt transport route and to increase his political power as well, Henry destroyed a bridge over the Isar River in Oberföhring that was controlled by Bishop Otto of Freising and built a new bridge a few miles further upstream in his own territory. He fortified the new bridge, instituted a court of law, and established a mint and a market in the existing town. In 1180, following an altercation between Duke Henry and Emperor Frederick Barbarossa, nephew of Bishop Otto and cousin to Henry, the emperor gave control of the city to the bishops of Freising. Munich remained under church rule until, in 1240, the emperor awarded the duchy of Bavaria to Otto of Wittelsbach in return for the latter's loyal service. Munich became the residence of the Wittelsbachs when Ludwig the Stern (der Strenge), grandson of Otto, built a palace (Alter Hof) there in 1253–1255. The city continued to be the dukes' residence throughout the medieval period, increasing in importance when it became the capital of all Bavaria in 1505 consequent to the death of the last duke of Landshut, George the Rich (der

Reiche), and the unification of Upper and Lower Bavaria under the Munich branch of the Wittelsbach family.

In 1327, fire destroyed one-third of all the buildings in Munich. After the fire, Duke Ludwig of Bavaria enlarged the Alter Hof and, since the city had outgrown its first wall, promoted construction of a second wall. This second wall contained Munich until it was taken down at the end of the eighteenth century. Three gates from the fourteenth century wall have survived: the Sendlinger Tor, the Karlstor, and the Isartor. Although the Holy Ghost Hospital (Heiliggeistspital) is thought to have been founded as early as 1208, construction of the present Holy Ghost Church (Heiliggeistkirche) did not begin until 1327 and was not complete until 1392. When Ludwig of Bavaria was elected king (Ludwig IV) in 1328, Munich's importance as a political center increased along with his status. The city thrived under Ludwig's reign as a result of his concern for civic peace and his promotion of commerce and communication. His Bavarian code of law was an important contribution to law and order during this period. Learned Franciscans like Marsilius of Padua and William of Ockham were centered in Munich and lent theoretical support to Ludwig's claim that the empire had a right to elect kings and emperors without ecclesiastical participation. Ludwig's death in 1347 was followed by half a century of civil unrest culminating with civil war in the city in 1397–1398.

By 1412, the population of Munich had reached ten thousand, and in the years that followed, the city experienced both economic growth and an increase in artistic activity. Two central buildings constructed during the second half of the fifteenth century bear witness to the self-determination of Munich's citizens and to the autonomy they enjoyed with regard to both secular and ecclesiastical authority: the city hall and the church that still distinguishes the skyline, the Frauenkirche. Both these projects were carried out under the direction of Jörg Ganghofer, master builder of Munich. The medieval city hall (Altes Rathaus), destroyed several times by fire, was rebuilt for the last time in 1470. Important late Gothic (1480) wood carvings of dancing figures, the *Maurisken-tänzer (Morris Dancers)* by Erasmus Grasser, which once adorned the interior of the old city hall, are now in the Stadtmuseum. Munich's Frauenkirche, one of the largest Gothic churches in Europe, was completed in just twenty years (1468–1488). This massive brick church with twin towers 120 meters high was planned and financed by the townspeople. In medieval times, the exterior would have been plastered and painted. Ludwig IV was the first of the

Wittelsbachs to be buried in Munich; although his body is not in this church, Albrecht IV placed a splendid red marble memorial sculpture there around 1500. With almost fourteen thousand inhabitants in 1500, Munich housed the largest urban population in Bavaria, approximately equal to that of Basle, Trier, or Frankfurt.

BIBLIOGRAPHY

Götz, Ernst, Heinrich Habel, Karlheinz Hemmeter, and Friedrich Kobler. *München.* Handbuch der deutschen Kunstdenkmäler. Munich: Deutscher Kunstverlag, 1996.

Hohoff, Curt. *München.* Munich: Prestel, 1970.

Maier, Lorenz. "Stadt und Herrschaft: Ein Beitrag zur Gründungs- und frühen Entwicklungsgeschichte Münchens." Dissertation, University of Munich, 1988.

Miscellaneaa Bavarica Monacensia 147. Munich: Kommissionsverlag UNI-Druck, 1989.

Solleder, Fridolin. *München im Mittelalter.* Aalen: Scientia Verlag, 1962.

Ruth M. W. Moskop

SEE ALSO

Frederick I Barbarossa; Freising; Grasser, Erasmus; Henry the Lion; Gothic Art and Architecture, Late

Münster

The name Münster, derived from the Latin *monasterium* (monastery), reflects the monastic origins of the church, bishopric, and subsequent town. The monastery stood on the site later occupied by the cathedral precinct, on the east bank of the river Aa at the intersection of old roads connecting the Rhineland to the east and the north. The oldest names of the site, Mimigernaford and Mimigardeford, may reflect the importance of a crossing over the river. A Germanic sacred site apparently was superseded by a Frankish royal residence. Sent by Charlemagne to Christianize the western Saxons, St. Liudger founded a monastery on the site under the rule of St. Benedict around 793. Shortly thereafter, the bishopric of Münster was established, with Liudger consecrated as the first bishop on March 30, 805. In 819 the apostle Paul is mentioned as patron of the church, and one of his teeth was acquired by 1022. This relic, encased in a golden head reliquary, may have prompted the construction of a larger cathedral. This second cathedral was dedicated in 1090 by Bishop Erpho. It was rebuilt following a fire in 1121. A grand westwork (entrance structure) was added under

Münster, cathedral, *Vorhalle,* apostles. *Photograph: Joan A. Holladay*

Bishop Hermann II (1174–1203). Following a disastrous fire of 1197, all but the westwork was rebuilt. The cornerstone of this third (present) cathedral was laid on July 22, 1225, and Bishop Gerhard von der Mark dedicated the new building on September 30, 1264. The new church, with its three-aisle basilica nave, polygonal choir, double transepts, and massive twin-towered westwork, while essentially Romanesque in form and detail, anticipates the *Sondergotik* (unusual Gothic style) hall church in its open flow of space. The statues of the apostles (ca. 1235) from the west portal are among the earliest works of Gothic sculpture in Germany. The question of the influence of French models or sculptors on these figures is

important in the understanding of the spread of the Gothic style into Germany. The fourteenth through sixteenth centuries saw a series of mostly ornamental additions to the cathedral fabric in the late Gothic style, best seen in the *Salvator-*(Savior)-gable on the southeast transept. The Domburg (cathedral precinct) also contains a second church, dedicated to the Virgin.

During the ninth century the Domburg stood in the middle of a large agrarian surrounding. A new town *(civitas)* developed around the cathedral enclosure. By the beginning of the eleventh century a market was established to the east of the cathedral immunity. Around 1100 the Domburg was expanded and the enclosure fortified by a stone wall. The principal roadways were relocated to the Domburg, initiating an expansion of trade in the area of the Prinzipalmarkt (Principal Market).

On May 7, 1121, during the Investiture Controversy, the town and cathedral stronghold were stormed by the forces of Lothar of Saxony. The rebuilding of the city and cathedral from the ensuing fire initiated a new chapter in the city's history. The market area was reconstructed in an orderly manner. Though the bishop remained the principal authority up to the thirteenth century, the rise of a burgher upper class can be traced to the twelfth century. The town grew dramatically during the twelfth and thirteenth centuries, with the establishment of numerous parishes and the granting of a civic charter on January 18, 1278. The earliest parish was centered around the city and market church of St. Lambert, first constructed in the late eleventh century at the intersection of the trade routes and the principal markets in town. Around the time of the granting of the civic charter, the church was reconstructed in the Gothic style to symbolize the ascendancy of the urban merchant class and its growing autonomy from the episcopal center. The present three-aisled hall church dates from the fourteenth and fifteenth centuries, the period of greatest economic growth in medieval Münster. These centuries are marked by tensions between the religious/political center and the mercantile/economic periphery. This is best seen in the mid–fourteenth century Rathaus (City Hall), constructed on the Prinzipalmarkt just across from the main entrance to the cathedral immunity.

The growth of Münster was largely predicated by its location on important trade routes. Market and minting rights, possibly granted as early as the 960s, were well established by the mid-eleventh century. The impetus for community stemmed from the market area of St. Lambert and not from the central cathedral immunity. Merchant guilds were established by the eleventh century. The economy of Münster was based largely on textile trade, particularly local linens and imported furs and wool. As a mercantile center, Münster joined the Westphalian city league in 1246. During the fourteenth and fifteenth centuries, Münster played an important role in the Hanseatic League.

Despite the polarities of cathedral and market, the seven hundred years of the medieval period in Münster (ca. 800–ca. 1500) are marked by religious unity and economic expansion. This came to an end during the turmoil of the sixteenth century. Perhaps the watershed year, marking the end of the medieval period in Münster, is

1534, at which time the Anabaptist leader Jan van Leiden (Leyden) proclaimed himself king of the New Zion and established Münster as his capital. In 1535 the Anabaptist stronghold was stormed by the troops of Prince Bishop Count Franz of Waldeck. Jan van Leiden and his followers were massacred and the bodies of the leaders suspended from cages on the tower of the market church of St. Lambert. This symbolic act illustrates the tensions and forces that shaped the form of the city throughout the medieval period, as the bishop thus expressed his resumed sovereignty over the town. To assert the reinstated episcopal authority, a great bastion was constructed on the west side of town. The medieval period in Münster comes to a close with this restructuring of the face of the city. In contrast to the development of Münster from the cathedral core outward, this new era is introduced by an alteration in the urban fabric—a great bastion now dominating the city from the outside.

BIBLIOGRAPHY

Geisberg, Max. *Die Stadt Münster.* 7 vols. Bau- und Kunstdenkmäler von Westfalen 41. Münster: Aschendorff, 1932–1942.

Imagination des Unsichtbaren: 1200 Jahre bildende Kunste im Bistum Münster. 2 vols. Münster: Westfälisches Landesmuseum für Kunst und Kulturgeschichte, 1993.

Kroeschell, Karl. *Weichbild: Untersuchungen zur Struktur und Entstehung der mittelalterlichen Stadtgemeinde in Westfalen.* Cologne: Böhlau, 1960.

Kunst und Kultur im Weserraum 800–1600. 2 vols. Münster: Aschendorff, 1967.

Münster 800–1800: 1000 Jahre Geschichte der Stadt. Münster: Stadtmuseum, 1984.

Prinz, Joseph. *Das Rathaus zu Münster.* Münster: Aschendorff, 1958.

———. *Mimigernaford-Münster: Die Entstehungsgeschichte einer Stadt.* Geschichtliche Arbeiten zur Westfälischen Landesforschung 4. Münster: Aschendorff, 1960.

———, ed. *Münsterisches Urkundenbuch.* Das Stadtarchiv Münster; Quellen und Forschungen zur Geschichte der Stadt Münster N.F. 1. Münster: Aschendorff, 1960.

Schröer, Alois, ed. *Monasterium: Festschrift zum siebenhundertjährigen Weihegedächtnis des Paulus-Domes zu Münster.* Münster: Verlag Regensberg, 1966.

Sternberg, Thomas, ed. *Der Paulus-Dom zu Münster: Eine Dokumentation zum Stand der neuen Grabungen und Forschungen.* Münster: Katholische-Soziale Akademie, 1990.

Scott Bradford Montgomery

SEE ALSO

Charlemagne; Gothic Art and Architecture; Investiture Conflict; Werden

Music

See Liturgy, Music.

Muskatblüt (ca. 1390–1458)

In all probability, the name Muskatblüt is the family name of a Franconian didactic and lyric poet, rather than a nom de plume. Between 1424 and 1458 a Konrad Muskatblüt is frequently mentioned—although not as a poet—as the recipient of remunerations and gifts from several lords and the free imperial cities of Regensburg and Nuremberg, as well as an annuity granted by the archbishop of Mainz. Thus we may assume that in addition to his attendance at several imperial diets he was employed as a diplomatic courier, undertook extended journeys, e.g. to the Teutonic Order in Prussia, and served as an escort of various nobles. However, we cannot determine with certainty whether this individual who appears in the archives is identical with the poet whose songs, with few exceptions, are collected in one manuscript from 1434, and whose final strophes contain the auctorial identification "thus speaks Muskatblüt." The poet Muskatblüt, however, has obvious political interests reflected in some of his works where he refers to important contemporary events like the Council of Constance (1415) and the Imperial Diets in Nuremberg (1422 and 1431) and Frankfurt (1427). Assuming they are the same person, his biography would be as follows: He made a name for himself as a poet in his youth, and then after a period of itinerant minstrelsy coupled with political tasks, he settled in Mainz in the service of the court. His life span would then be from roughly 1390 to 1458. The majority of his songs, which, as a result of his identification in the final strophes, can be confidently ascribed to him, are found in the 1434 Cologne manuscript (a), which is itself a copy of a lost original collection. A few more are found in scattered transmission. Thematically as well as formally, his songs are close to those of the Meistersinger, dealing with salvation history, praise of the Virgin, and the Seven Liberal Arts, and using the well-known *Töne* (literally, melodies, i.e. songs).

But as far as can be determined, he never belonged to a school. In more than forty songs he presents his main concerns in the role of an admonishing teacher probably to a noble as well as a bourgeois audience. He denounces the injustices of his time: arrogance, greed, and especially the corrupt morals of the nobility, the standard bearers of the empire. Comparing his time to the courtly period, he affirms traditional values: honor, decency, dignity, and conjugal fidelity as opposed to the existing decadent state of affairs abounding with murder, arson, usury, robbery, and lewdness, although his admonitions often fell on deaf ears, as he himself asserts. In his spiritual songs (among them eighteen or twenty hymns to the Virgin), most of which were composed on the occasion of religious feasts (Christmas, the Ascension, and the Epiphany) he employs an allegorical technique, e.g., the empire is presented as a maiden with torn clothes, vices are depicted as animals, and so on. Also his thirteen love songs must have been well received by the public, and the popularity and wide dissemination of his works is attested to by numerous laudatory comments of his younger contemporary, Michel Beheim (1416–ca. 1475), among others. Indeed, his poetry was so well known that the adapted form of his name, a *Muskatblüt,* was not only used as the title of several of his poems in the subsequent manuscript tradition but was also employed by later poets for audience appeal. Whole parts of his poems were taken over by other writers and were even integrated into everyday didactic texts (*Gebrauchsliteratur*).

BIBLIOGRAPHY

Muskatblüt: Abbildungen zur Überlieferung: die Kölner Handschrift und die Melodie-Überlieferung, ed. Eva Kiepe-Willms and Horst Brunner. Göppingen: Kümmerle Verlag, 1987.

Petzsch, Christoph. "Muskatblüt." *Zeitschrift für deutsche Philologie* 96 (1977): 433–436.

Schanze, Frieder. *Meisterliche Liedkunst zwischen Heinrich von Mugeln und Hans Sachs.* 2 vols. Munich: Artemis, 1983–1984.

Willms, Eva. "Muskatblüt." In *Die deutsche Literatur des Mittelalters: Verfasserlexikon,* ed. Kurt Ruh et al. Berlin: de Gruyter, 1987, vol. 6, cols. 816–821.

———. *Spruchdichtungen Muskatblüts: Vorstudien zu einer kritischen Ausgabe.* Munich: Artemis, 1976.

Edda Gentry

SEE ALSO

Beheim, Michael; *Deutschorden*; Meistersinger

Muspilli

This Old High German poem describes the fate of the soul after death and the Final Judgment, while admonishing its audience to do pennance. The *Muspilli* has often been called "the most desperate piece of OHG literature", as its study is fraught with difficulties. None of the philological basics can be established with any certainty. The anonymous piece has been transmitted in the margins of four pages in only one manuscript (Munich, no. clm 14098), a codex dated between 821 to 827, by an unskilled scribe in the later part of the ninth century. The *Muspilli* is a fragment of 103 lines with the beginning and the end missing. The time of composition is quite uncertain (dates between 790 and 871 have been proposed), and so is the place (linguistic evidence suggests Bavarian origin). The title itself reflects much of the aura of mystery that surrounds the poem, it being derived by the first modern editor from an enigmatic word in verse 57 ("Then no kinsman can help a kinsman before the *muspille*") whose etymology and meaning has been a main topic of research. The suggestions have ranged from "the name of a fire demon" to "world destruction" to "Final Judgment," and to "verdict." The content itself poses no general problems. The first thirty lines describe the fight of the angels and devils for the soul right after death, the bliss of heaven, and the torments of hell. The rest of the text deals with the end of the world and the Last Judgment: the summons (ll. 31–36), the battle between Elijah and the Antichrist (ll. 37–49), the destruction of the earth (ll. 50–62), and the beginning of the Judgment (ll. 73–103). At various points the narrative becomes a penitential sermon, especially in lines 63–72, which warn against judicial abuse through bribery.

Although no one specific source has been established, the *Muspilli* belongs in the tradition of eschatological narratives particularly popular toward the end of the millennium. The details, however, are quite peculiar. The destruction of the world and God's court of justice are described in images and terms that seem to come from a Germanic origin. Inconsistency and disunity in form and structure have rendered the poem troublesome for interpreters. The meter is that of Germanic alliterative verse, but it is often flawed and is mixed with end rhyme features. The style fluctuates between poetic and prosaic. The narrative seems to juxtapose two incompatible themes (two judgments of the soul), it tends to digress into homiletic admonition, and its parts are joined rather abruptly. Until fairly recently such incongruence caused great dissatisfaction among scholars approaching the poem with modern concepts such as "harmony." The re-sulting common view was that the piece was a patchwork compilation of two different texts or that the original had been corrupted by interpolations. In the last two decades, however, a new attitude has emerged, relinquishing ideas of unity and of philological determinacy in favor of reading the poem on its own terms: as a reflection of the discontinuity of the times, for example, or as a member of a literary genre of pastiche and compilation.

The ongoing fascination of the *Muspilli* probably stems from three sources: first, the challenge of a text about which so much is unknown; second, the echoes in rhythm and imagery of other, lost Germanic poetry; and third, the allure of its powerful language and images seen, for example, in lines 51–54: *so intprinnant die perga, poum ni kistentit / enihc in erdu, aha artruknent / muor uarsuilhit sih, suilizot lougiu der himil / mano uallit, prinnit mittilagart* (Then the mountains burst into flames, no tree remains standing on earth, the waters dry up, the marsh swallows up itself, in fire smoulders the sky, the moon falls, the world burns).

BIBLIOGRAPHY

Bell, A. Robert. *Muspilli:* Apocalypse as Political Threat." *Studies in the Literary Imagination* 8 (1975): 102–104.

Braune, Wilhelm, ed. *Althochdeutsches Lesebuch,* rev. Ernst Ebbinghaus. Tübingen: Niemeyer, 1979, pp. 86–89.

Haug, Walter. "Das *Muspilli* oder das Glück literaturwissenschaftlicher Verzweiflung." In *Strukturen als Schlüssel zur Welt: Kleine Schriften zur Erzählliteratur des Mittelalters.* Tübingen: Niemeyer, 1989, pp. 162–198.

Steinhoff, Hans-Hugo. "Muspilli." In *Die deutsche Literatur des Mittelalters: Verfasserlexikon,* ed. Kurt Ruh et al. Berlin: de Gruyter, 1987, vol. 4, cols. 821–828.

Sullivan, Robert G. "Muspilli." In *Dictionary of Literary Biography,* ed. James Hardin and Will Hasty, vol. 148, *German Writers and Works of the Early Middle Ages: 800–1170.* Detroit: Gale, 1995, pp. 221–226.

Wolfgang Hempel

SEE ALSO
Mythology

Müstair

A Benedictine cloister in the diocese of Chur, Müstair is located in a mountain valley among the Engadine, the Vintschgau, and the Veltlin in the Swiss canton of Graubünden. The extensive preserved and excavated remains

Müstair, cloister church, detail of Carolingian wall painting from east wall (now Zurich, Schweizerisches Landesmuseum, LM-11990.1): Ascension of Christ. *Photograph: Schweizerisches Landesmuseum, Neg. 100176*

of the early medieval cloister make this site one of the most important examples of Carolingian architecture and wall painting. The foundation, which tradition credits to Charlemagne, dates before 806, probably at the end of the eighth century. Originally a men's abbey, it was given over to nuns in 1163.

The Carolingian establishment, erected over the remains of Bronze Age and late Roman settlements, is a rectangular complex with extensive conventual and farm buildings to the north and west of the cloister. At least the west and south wings of the cloister were two stories in height. At the northeast of the complex, the three-aisle church dedicated to St. John the Baptist is marked by a triapsidal sanctuary; the exterior features flattened blind arcades and a profiled roof cornice. The north annex, which runs the full length of the church, was originally matched by a similar structure along the south, which contained the original entrance to the church. At the southeast corner of the complex stands the chapel of the Holy Cross, which apparently also dates to the ninth century.

The cloister church houses the most extensive known cycle of Carolingian wall paintings, which were discovered under a layer of whitewash in 1896. Five registers on the nave walls described, from top to bottom, the story of David and the Infancy, Public Life, and Passion of Christ. The paintings of the lowest zone are almost completely lost; they apparently represented saints' (perhaps apostles') martyrdoms. The heavily restored paintings in the apse vaults portray, in the center choir, Christ in Majesty, with Christ giving the law to Peter and Paul *(traditio legis)* in the left apse and the jeweled cross *(crux gemmata)* in the right. On the walls of the apses are represented scenes from the lives of the saints to whom the altars are dedicated: Peter and Paul on the left, John the Baptist in the center, and Stephen at the right, some of these covered over with Romanesque paintings of the same subjects. A monumental Last Judgment occupies the upper registers of the west wall. Originally nearly one hundred scenes were separated from one another by a decorative system consisting of staffs wound with garlands; the images combine decorative richness—for example, in the background architecture painted with precious stones and pearl strands—with richly contrasting effects of light and shade.

Not all the wall paintings have been preserved in situ (on site). The installation of a late Gothic vault at the end of the fifteenth century obscured significant parts of the upper register of paintings. In 1894, David scenes from the upper nave walls and the remains of an Ascension of Christ from the triumphal arch were discovered above the vaults. These were subsequently removed and transported to the Swiss National Museum in Zurich.

The scholarly literature on the painting cites relationships to contemporary northern Italian and Roman monuments, although the insecure dates of the comparative objects make the chronological results uncertain. A date of about 800 supported by the archaeological evidence has been superseded by a more convincing one in the second quarter of the ninth century; an attempt to narrow down the date still further to the years between 829 and 840 on historical and iconographic grounds remains hypothetical. Marble relief panels remain from the Carolingian choir enclosure; they are housed in the cloister museum, as are fragments of Romanesque wall painting from 1157–1170. A stucco figure of Charlemagne now installed to the south of the central apse probably also dates from the Romanesque period.

The cloister and the roof and wood ceiling of the church were restored after a fire in 1079. The interior of the church was transformed into a hall church between 1487 and 1492 with the addition of a late Gothic ribbed vault and a nuns' choir on the west side.

BIBLIOGRAPHY

Birchler, Linus. "Zur karolingischen Architektur und Malerei in Münster-Müstair." In *Frühmittelalterliche Kunst in den Alpenländern: Akten des 3. Internationalen Kongresses für Frühmittelalterforschung.* Olten, Switzerland: Urs Graf, 1954, pp. 167–252.

Brenk, Beat. "Die romanische Wandmalerei in der Schweiz." *Basler Studien zur Kunstgeschichte.* N. F. 5 (1963): 28–61.

Cwi, Joan S. "A Study in Carolingian Political Theology: The David Cycle at St. John, Müstair." In *Atti del XXIV Congresso internazionale di storia dell'arte (Bologna, 1979),* vol. 1, *Reforma religiosa e arti nell'epoca carolingia.* Bologna: CLUEB, 1983, pp. 117–127.

Davis-Weyer, Caecilia. "Müstair, Milano e l'Italia carolingia." In *Il millennio ambrosiano: La città del vescovo dai Carolingi al Barbarossa,* ed. Carlo Bertelli. Milan: Electa, 1988, pp. 202–237.

Emmenegger, Oskar. "Klosterkirche St. Johann in Müstair: Maltechnik und Restaurierungsprobleme." In *Wandmalerei des frühen Mittelalters: Bestand, Maltechnik, Konservierung,* ed. Matthias Exner. ICOMOS—Hefte des Deutschen Nationalkomitees 23. Munich: Lipp-Verlag, 1998, pp. 56–66.

Müller, Iso. *Geschichte des Klosters Müstair: Von den Anfängen bis zur Gegenwart,* 3d ed. Disentis, Italy: Desertina, 1986.

Sennhauser, Hans Rudolf. "Funktionale Bestimmung von Trakten und Räumen der karolingischen Klosteranlage von Müstair: Skizze zum Stand der Überlegungen Februar 1996." In *Wohn- und Wirtschaftsbauten frühmittelalterlicher Klöster: Acta,* ed. H.R. Sennhauser. Zurich: VDF, 1997, pp. 283–302.

Spada Pintarelli, Silvia. *Pittura carolingia nell'Alto Adige: Note Bibliographiche.* Bozen, Italy: [n.p.], 1981, pp. 27–35.

Vorromanische Kirchenbauten: Katalog der Denkmäler bis zum Ausgang der Ottonen. Veröffentlichungen des Zentralinstituts für Kunstgeschichte 3. 1966–1971. Munich: Prestel, 1990, pp. 227–228. *Nachtragsband.* Munich: Prestel, 1991, pp. 295–296.

Wüthrich, Lucas. *Wandgemälde: Von Müstair bis Hodler. Katalog der Sammlung des Schweizerischen Landesmuseums Zürich.* Zurich: Berichthaus, 1980, pp. 17–46.

Wyss, Alfred. "Müstair, Kloster St. Johann: Zur Pflege der Wandbilder in der Klosterkirche." In *Wandmalerei des frühen Mittelalters: Bestand, Maltechnik, Konservierung,* ed. Matthias Exner. ICOMOS–Hefte des Deutschen Nationalkomitees 23. Munich: Lipp-Verlag, 1998, pp. 49–55.

Zemp, Josef, and Robert Durrer. *Das Kloster St. Johann zu Münster in Graubünden.* Kunstdenkmäler der Schweiz. Mitteilungen der schweizerischen Gesellschaft für Erhaltung historischer Kunstdenkmäler. N. F. 5–7. Geneva: A.-G. Atar, 1906–1910.

Matthias Exner

SEE ALSO

Carolingian Art and Architecture; Charlemagne; Chur; Romanesque Art and Architecture

Mysticism

Mystical texts treat the process of attaining knowledge of the Divine through personal spiritual experience ranging from contemplation and prayer to near absorption of the human soul into the Divine. The mystical literature of medieval Germany includes writings that describe mystical experience, as well as those that probe the meaning of the mystical way. These distinctions can occur along gender lines. Writings of some male mystics, for example, tend not to emphasize their own mystical experiences, but instead analyze the road to union with God. Writings of many women mystics, in contrast, are often distinctive in the detail they offer of visions, Christ-like suffering, and other physical phenomena. Nevertheless, and unfortunately, some studies particularly on the German tradition have limited male mystics and their writings to *speculative* and female mystics (or the label *Frauenmystik*) to *experiential* mysticism. Scholars now generally acknowledge, however, that such generalizations can obscure the variety of mystical events and texts that both men and women experienced or produced. Rather, the medieval German mystical tradition is best understood by viewing male and female mystics and their writings in historical context, often as interacting and, at times, as distinct phenomena.

Besides the Bible and patristic writings, three major influences shaped the German medieval mystical tradition: the writings of Dionysius the Pseudo-Areopagite, a late-fifth- or early-sixth-century likely Syrian theologian; interpretations of the Song of Songs; and Franciscan spirituality. The teachings of Dionysius the Pseudo-Areopagite attempted a harmony between neo-Platonism and Christian doctrine. His core teachings on the possibility of the soul's union with God as a result of its passage through the three stages of purgation, illumination, and union reverberate through much of medieval Christian mysticism, especially in Germany. Among various patristic and medieval interpretations of the Song of Songs, Bernard of Clairvaux's series of eighty-six sermons on the topic is the most profoundly influential for German mysticism. Bernard describes the soul as the bride and Christ as the Bridegroom, and mystical union thus as nuptials. Such nuptial influence is evident, for example, in one of the earliest examples of German mystical literature, the *St. Trudperter Hoheslied,* written in early Middle High German around 1150 or 1160. Finally, many medieval German mystical writings are also deeply indebted to Franciscan spirituality, especially the asceticism and very physical *imitatio Christi* symbolized by Francis's reception of the stigmata (wounds of Christ at Crucifixion).

Catalogs of German medieval mystics often begin with the Benedictine Hildegard of Bingen (1098–1179), who journeyed throughout Germany preaching against the abuses of the church and also corresponded with Bernard of Clairvaux and other ecclesiastical leaders, as well as Emperor Frederick Barbarossa. She wrote numerous visionary and theological treatises, songs for use by nuns, and even medical and scientific tracts. Such remarkable accomplishments notwithstanding, some scholars argue that Hildegard should be considered apart from the German mystical tradition. The scholar Kurt Ruh, in particular, points out that, though visionary, Hildegard was not ecstatic. Indeed, she claims to have experienced her visions while fully within her senses, not while taken up outside (or within) herself in a rapture. Furthermore, her visions were not scenes of her own interaction with the Divine but were rather showings of things to come, for which she served as prophetic reporter.

The Latin writings of the Benedictine Elisabeth of Schönau (ca. 1129–1164), are, like those of Hildegard, sometimes prophetic. Written in collaboration with her brother Ekbert, Elisabeth's descriptions of her visions and ascetic and ecstatic experiences, however, identify her as more clearly mystical than Hildegard, with whom she corresponded. Although not as diverse as those of Hildegard, Elisabeth's writings were more widely available in the Middle Ages and were also translated into several vernaculars.

The thirteenth century was a period of a new spirituality, typified by a desire to return to the *vita apostolica,* or simple life of poverty and prayer exemplified by Christ and his apostles. The development of the mendicant orders (Dominicans and Franciscans) corresponded with this new spirituality. David of Augsburg (ca. 1200–1271), a Franciscan, wrote numerous mystical, pastoral treatises encouraging prayer and asceticism for those who would reach union with God. This same period also marked the beginning of increased prominence

of women in the European mystical tradition, associated in part with the formation of independent communities of laywomen not associated with any established religious order, now generally referred to as Beguines. Beguine communities flourished especially in the Low Countries, with such mystically and literarily gifted representatives as Marie of Oignies, Beatrice of Nazareth, and Hadewijch of Antwerp among them. This period also saw an increased cooperation, or "mutual enrichment," as Bernard McGinn (1998: 18) describes it, between men and women, due partly to the growth of pastoral duties for monks from the mendicant orders toward the rapidly developing women's communities. From these male-female interactions, some of the most important mystical literature of the Middle Ages arose, as the men wrote or urged the women to write of their remarkable spiritual lives. Men's participation in the texts is not at all unproblematic, however, and poses an interesting challenge for readers and scholars, since the men were often not simply scribes but also editors.

Mechthild of Magdeburg (ca. 1208–1284 or 1297), Germany's most famous Beguine, composed a masterwork of German vernacular mysticism, *The Flowing Light of the Godhead (Das fließende Licht der Gottheit).* It comprises seven books, the first six of which were written between 1250 and 1270, while she lived as a Beguine in Magdeburg. The seventh book was written sometime after 1270, after she had left the Beguine life to join the prominent Cistercian/Benedictine convent at Helfta. Mechthild's use of language from courtly literature indicates that she was of noble birth and that she enjoyed a basic education. Her writings span an impressive breadth of genres. Mechthild's mysticism describes the soul's striving to find eternal refuge in God's love. Like her predecessor Hildegard, Mechthild is sometimes prophetic and critical of the church. Mechthild's mysticism was influenced most profoundly by the divine "greeting" she received at the age of twelve, a sign of God's presence in her life that both motivated and authorized her writing. She did not begin the record of her spiritual journey, however, until her confessor, likely Heinrich of Halle, encouraged her to do so in 1250.

Mechthild's Middle Low German original is lost. Her text survives in a Latin translation of the first six books and, in testimony to her significance for later German mystics, also in a Middle High German (Allemanic) version from around 1345, produced in Basel by the secular preacher Heinrich of Nördlingen, or by others in his circle. Nördlingen is also known to have sent portions of this translation to the Dominican nun Margaretha Ebner in Bavaria.

Two nuns of the Helfta convent, Mechthild of Hackeborn and Gertrud (known as the Great), highly esteemed Mechthild of Magdeburg, and their writings reflect the influence of her mysticism. The fact that their writings were in Latin, however, assured that they were read more widely and for much longer in the Middle Ages than was the idiosyncratic vernacular of the *Flowing Light.* The revelations of Mechthild of Hackeborn (d. 1298/1299) were recorded by two of her sister nuns, one of which was certainly Gertrud, in *The Book of Special Grace (Liber specialis gratiae).* Mechthild's book teaches worship of Christ, the Virgin Mary, and the Saints, and expands on the relationship of the soul to God. It was translated and disseminated widely in Europe and England throughout the Middle Ages.

Gertrud of Helfta (d. 1301/1302) wrote an account of her spiritual journey in *The Herald of Divine Love (Legatus divinae pietatis),* which consists of five books. Book Two, written in 1289, contains Gertrud's account of the visions and other mystical experiences that shaped her spiritual life. Sometime after 1289, Gertrud also wrote the *Spiritual Exercises (Exercitia spiritualia).* Gertrud's works emphasize the liturgy, especially the Eucharist. They also promote devotion to the Sacred Heart of Jesus and were influential in the spread of that cult in the later Middle Ages.

The fourteenth century is generally considered the most vibrant period for German mysticism, and the Dominican Eckhart (ca. 1260–ca. 1328), known as Meister Eckhart, is its most acclaimed figure. Eckhart left a diverse and sizable corpus of teachings, both theological/philosophical and spiritual or mystical, written in Latin and in his German vernacular. Among Eckhart's German oeuvre, *The Book of Divine Comfort (Daz buoch der goetlichen troestunge,* 1314 or 1318), is considered his most important work. His eighty-six German sermons, which his listeners wrote down, offer the greatest insight into Eckhart's particular brand of mysticism, which is generally classified as speculative mysticism in its purest form. Indeed, Eckhart's writings reveal nothing of his own interior life, and he even ridicules mystical experiences such as visions. His mystical thought is indebted to neo-Platonism, including especially a negative theology, which comprises both God's unknowability and the necessity for the soul to become nothing in order to unite with God. Eckhart also emphasizes the importance of turning away from the things of the world to facilitate the birth of God in the soul. Eckhart does not teach of a mystical way per se in the sense of steps or a path to mystical union. His followers Johannes Tauler (ca. 1300–1361) and Henry Suso (ca. 1295–1366) are more traditional in this aspect. Tauler and Suso are also in large part responsible for the dissemination of Eckhart's ideas, which was otherwise hampered by papal condemnation, in 1329, of twenty-eight of Eckhart's sentences. In fact, Eckhart remained in obscurity for several centuries after his death until his rediscovery in the nineteenth century.

The Dominican Tauler may have come under the direct influence of Meister Eckhart while a student in Cologne, where he was also likely a compatriot of Suso. Tauler's mysticism was in any case deeply informed by Eckhart's teachings. Like Eckhart, Tauler left no writings that describe his interior life. In fact, Tauler's teachings survive at all only because of the recording efforts of a group of Dominican nuns to whom he preached. Tauler teaches a practical mysticism, outlining the pseudo-Dionysian three-step path to mystical union. Tauler was associated with a group of spiritually minded laymen and clergy known as the Friends of God (Gottesfreunde). One of them, a layman named Rulman Merswin, appears to have fabricated the existence of the so-called Great Friend of God (Großer Gottesfreund), the alleged author of a series of mystical writings that he circulated in an apparent attempt to increase piety among his contemporaries. The writings were most likely the work of Merswin himself.

Henry Suso (Heinrich Seuse) is something of a transitional figure between his contemporaries Eckhart and Tauler. Like them, Suso preached widely, and his mystical teachings survive in large part because of his sermons. Unlike the writings of Eckhart and Tauler, however, Suso's writings include his *Vita,* a detailed, at times graphic account of his spiritual life, which was marked in its early stages by extreme asceticism. The *Vita,* which is also rife with courtly imagery, was recorded secretly by Elsbeth Stagel, a Dominican nun who served as Suso's confidante. Although Suso destroyed a portion of the text on learning of its existence, a divine message later assured him of God's approval of the record, which Suso then edited and expanded after Stagel's death. Suso's writings also include numerous letters, as well as an apology for and expansion of the teachings of Eckhart *(The Book of Eternal Truth—Büchlein der Wahrheit,* ca. 1326–1328), with whom Suso studied in Cologne. Suso's *Book of Eternal Wisdom (Büchlein der ewigen Weisheit,* ca. 1330) emphasizes the imitation of Christ's example as a means to mystical union. Suso himself translated and expanded the *Book of Eternal Wisdom* into Latin between 1331 and 1334 *(Horologium sapientiae)*. The vernacular version was among the most widely read devotional texts of the late Middle Ages. The *Horologium* also enjoyed a vast manuscript (over three hundred) and print history (nine early prints) and circulation in clerical circles.

Heinrich of Nördlingen, a secular preacher who was likely in contact with Johannes Tauler and other Friends of God, is best known through his nineteen-year correspondence with the Dominican nun Margaretha Ebner (ca. 1291–1351). In fact, the years of their letter exchange provide the only known information on Nördlingen's life. Scholars debate whether or not Nördlingen himself was a mystic, but, in any case, he supported Ebner and was an eager disciple of her mystical gifts. Their correspondence is generally considered the earliest surviving letter exchange in the German vernacular.

Besides her correspondence with Nördlingen (only one of her letters is extant, compared with fifty-six from Nördlingen), Ebner also wrote an account of her remarkable spiritual life in her *Revelations*. This work is one of several records of the flowering of spiritual and literary activity, from the thirteenth to the fifteenth centuries, but especially in the mid–fourteenth century, in southern German Dominican convents. Ebner's contemporaries penned the so-called *Sisterbooks,* or convent chronicles, which depict the ecstatically infused spiritual life of the convents. These chronicles, which recent studies have shown to be similar, in many ways, to saints' lives, were written to document for later generations of nuns the presence of God's grace in their convents. Typical of these vitae are details of the subjects' extreme physical suffering, as well as of their visions, auditions, visitations, and ecstasies, which often surrounded some aspect of the life, especially the childhood and passion, of Christ. Christine Ebner (1277–1356) and Elsbeth of Oye (ca. 1290–ca. 1340) are two of the more well-known mystics whose lives these chronicles record.

Mystics and spiritual thinkers from the Low Countries also influenced German mysticism. Of particular significance is the so-called *Devotio moderna,* a movement found in both lay (Brothers and Sisters of the Common Life) and religious (e.g., Windesheim Congregation) circles that began in the northern Low Countries but also spread to the Rhineland and beyond. The movement encouraged contemplation and the strengthening of the inner life of the individual. Originated by Geert Groote and influenced by Bernard of Clairvaux, Franciscan spiri-

tuality, and Jan van Ruusbroec among others, the best-known literature from the *Devotio moderna* movement is unquestionably the popular *Imitatio Christi* (first circulated 1418), attributed to Thomas à Kempis.

The later Middle Ages and early modern period brought important reception of earlier medieval mysticism. Nicholas of Cusa (1401–1464), for example, is perhaps better known as a philosopher or theologian than a mystic. Nevertheless, his vast writings, which examine God's absolute unity and endlessness, are indebted to Christian/neo-Platonic thought, such as that of Dionysius the Pseudo-Areopagite, as well as to Meister Eckhart. The so-called *Theologia Deutsch (Theologia Germanica)* is a fourteenth-century treatise transmitted in three manuscripts from the fifteenth century and later edited and published by Martin Luther (1516 and 1518). The *Theologia Deutsch* describes the deification of the human soul through the complete relinquishment of the will and a total following of the life of Christ. Luther's enthusiastic promotion of this mystical treatise (which other reformers did not second) contributed to its popularity for many decades.

From the late fifteenth century well into the seventeenth century, the Cologne Carthusian monastery of St. Barbara was a major center for the reception and publication of medieval mystical literature. The Cologne Carthusians, whose order had, since its eleventh-century beginnings, been active manuscript copyists, printed editions and translations—most for the first time—of the works of many important medieval mystics, including Jan van Ruusbroec, Johannes Tauler, Henry Suso, Catherine of Siena, Gertrud the Great of Helfta, Dionysius of Rijkel (or Dionysius the Carthusian, the most prolific European medieval mystic), and others. The Carthusians directed their publishing efforts to religious and lay circles alike in an attempt to rejuvenate the devotional spirit in the church and, later, to address the Lutheran challenge.

BIBLIOGRAPHY

Dinzelbacher, Peter, ed. *Wörterbuch der Mystik.* Stuttgart: Kröner, 1989.

Grundmann, Herbert. *Religiöse Bewegungen im Mittelalter: Untersuchungen über die geschichtlichen Zusammenhänge zwischen der Ketzerei, den Bettelorden und der religiösen Frauenbewegung im 12. und 13. Jahrhundert und über die geschichtlichen Grundlagen der deutschen Mystik.* Berlin: Ebering, 1935, rpt. Hildesheim: Georg Olms, 1961; Steven Rowan, trans. *Religious movements in the Middle Ages: the historical* links between heresy, the Mendicant Orders, and the women's religious movement in the twelfth and thirteenth century, with the historical foundations of German mysticism. Notre Dame, Ind.: University of Notre Dame Press, 1995.

Haas, Alois M. "Deutsche Mystik." In *Geschichte der deutschen Literatur von den Anfängen bis zur Gegenwart*, vol. 3, *Die deutsche Literatur im späten Mittelalter*, part 2. *Reimpaargedichte, Drama, Prosa*, ed. Ingeborg Glier. Munich: Beck, 1987, pp. 234–305.

———. *Sermo mysticus: Studien zu Theologie und Sprache der deutschen Mystik*. Freiburg, Switzerland: Universitätsverlag, 1979.

Haas, Alois M., and Heinrich Stirnimann, ed. *Das "Einig Ein": Studien zu Theorie und Sprache der deutschen Mystik*. Freiburg, Switzerland: Universitätsverlag, 1980.

Lewis, Gertrud Jaron. *By Women, for Women, about Women: The Sister-books of Fourteenth-century Germany*. Toronto: Institute of Mediaeval Studies, 1996 [with bibliography].

———. *Bibliographie zur deutschen Frauenmystik des Mittelalters*. Berlin: Schmidt, 1989.

McGinn, Bernard. *The Presence of God: A History of Western Christian Mysticism*. 3 vols. New York: Crossroad, 1992–1998.

Oehl, Wilhelm, ed. *Deutsche Mystikerbriefe des Mittelalters 1100–1550*. Munich: Georg Müller, 1931; rpt. Darmstadt: Wissenschaftliche Buchgesellschaft, 1972.

Preger, Wilhelm. *Geschichte der deutschen Mystik im Mittelalter nach den Quellen untersucht und dargestellt*, 3 vols. 1874–1893, rpt. Aalen: Zeller, 1962.

Ruh, Kurt. *Geschichte der abendländischen Mystik*. Munich: Beck, 1990.

———. ed. *Abendländische Mystik im Mittelalter: Symposion Kloster Engelberg, 1984*. Stuttgart: Metzler, 1986.

———. *Vorbemerkungen zu einer neuen Geschichte der abendländischen Mystik im Mittelalter*. Munich: Verlag der Bayerischen Akademie der Wissenschaften, 1982.

———. ed. *Altdeutsche und altniederländische Mystik*. Darmstadt: Wissenschaftliche Buchgesellschaft, 1964.

Schmidt, Margot, and Dieter Bauer, ed. *Grundfragen christlicher Mystik*. Stuttgart: 1987.

Weeks, Andrew. *German Mysticism from Hildegard of Bingen to Ludwig Wittgenstein: A Literary and Intellectual History*. Albany: State University of New York Press, 1993.

Wentzlaff-Eggebert, Friedrich-Wilhelm. *Deutsche Mystik zwischen Mittelalter und Neuzeit: Einheit und Wandlung ihrer Erscheinungsformen*. Berlin: de Gruyter, 1969.

Kristin M. Christensen

SEE ALSO
David von Augsburg; *Devotio Moderna*; Ebner, Margareta; Elisabeth von Schönau; Gertrud von Helfta; Hadewijch; Hildegard von Bingen; Jan van Ruusbroec; Meister Eckhart; Mechthild von Hackeborn; Mechthild von Magdeburg; Nicholas of Cusa; Song of Songs; Visionary Literature; Women

Mythology

Mythology is the study of myth, and there is a great deal of discussion as to how to define myth. Mythology overlaps in part with comparative religion and with the history of religion *(Religionsgeschichte)*, even magic, and superstition. Myths are stories about gods and supernatural happenings. Germanic mythology concerns the beliefs of the Germanic peoples. In the study of Germanic mythology there is a tendency to speak of North Germanic and South Germanic (what philologists call West and East Germanic) myth. This article is devoted to South Germanic myth. We must avoid equating Old Norse mythology with Germanic mythology, though there are numerous similarities and much comparative material.

For sources we have few direct witnesses as to Germanic mythology and religion. Most of what we know has been reported by people who were either not Germanic (e.g., the Greek and Roman reports) or not heathen, so that we often are looking at Germanic religion and mythology through foreign eyes. The sources for South Germanic mythology are extremely sparse. We have scattered information in reports by Caesar, Tacitus, and other Roman writers and later writers. Direct information is available in such monumental works as rune stones (the Nordendorf *fibula*, or clasp), rock carvings, and, for Germany in particular, such things as "Jupiter columns" *(Thor/Donar)* and *matrona* (matron) statues. Archaeology, linguistics, names, and literary history also contribute to our knowledge of South Germanic mythology, and the Old Norse sources offer comparative material. One must also not forget the reports of the churchmen, as well as such official documents as the *Indiculus superstitionum et paganiarum,* from the middle of the eighth century, and the various *Capitularia* of Charlemagne, which can be precious sources as to customs they wish to combat and names of heathen practices. The same can be said of such things as the Old Saxon Baptismal Oath *(Sächsisches Taufgelöbnis),* which lists things one wishes to renounce.

The next complex of problems is caused by such sources. There is the *interpretatio romana,* in which Roman authors such as Tacitus use Latin names for Germanic deities, e.g., *Mercurius* for *Wotan.* The obverse of this is the attempt by the reporter to equate Germanic gods with Roman gods: *Tiu = Mars,* and so forth, which can even go to such extents as to equate *Gefjon* with *Diana.* We can also speak of *interpretatio christiana,* in which medieval Christian myths, such as the Leviathan myth, are equated with heathen myths, such as that of the Midgard serpent.

Using *interpretatio germanica* may help us, however, to understand the Germanic pantheon through the use of the names of the days of the week. *Lunae dies = Monday* (day of the moon), *Martis dies = Tuesday* (Alemannic *Ziestag* "day of *Tiu,* god of war"), *Mercurii dies = Wednesday* (day of *Wôdan), Jovis dies = Thursday* (day of *Thor/ Donar,* god of thunder), *Veneris dies = Friday* (day of *Frija,* goddess of beauty). The importance of the various members of the pantheon varies in space and in time. As one can see from the etymology of his name, *Wôdan* (Latin *vâtes* "poet, seer"; Old Irish *fâith* "poet, seer") was originally the poet of the gods; in Old Icelandic literature, he is, as *Ôdhin,* the chief god, but in South Germanic myth, the chief god may be Donar or Ziu *(Saxnôt).*

We learn of other gods from various sources. The *Nordendorf Fibula* (clasp) mentions *Wôdan,* *Loga<thorn> ore,* and *Wigi<thorn>onar,* the latter two the source of much speculation. From the second *Merseburg Charm,* we learn of a number of names: *Phol, Wotan, Balder, Uuodan,* along with the goddesses *Sinthgunt, Sunna, Friia,* and *Volla,* all the source of much discussion. One might add to these the many names of goddesses such as *Hariasa* and *Hludana,* found on inscriptions, a rich list indeed.

An interesting source of myth is the *origo gentis* theme, the myths held by a people as to their origins (ethnogenesis). Tacitus *(Germania,* Ch. 2.9), for example, tells us of Tuisto, the tribal father of the Germanic tribes, whose son, Mannus, bore the progenitors of the tribal groups of the Ingvaeones, Hermiones, and Istvaeones. The common myth of the royal twins *(dioscuri;* compare Romulus and Remus), called *Alcis,* is related by Tacitus *(Germania,* Ch. 43.12 ff.) of the Naharvali, and Paulus Diaconus tells us of the twin progenitors of the Langobards, *Ibur* and *Aio,* for example.

Nature myths were obviously quite common, but we know very little about them. The Germanic tribes worshiped nature and particular phenomena of nature. We know of sun worship, worship of trees, sacred groves, even worship of poles, erected for the purpose. The famous *Irmensûl,* chopped down by Charlemagne in 772, is a prime example. Tacitus tells us about the earth goddess, *Nerthus,* whose image was carried around in a cart and returned to an island sanctuary. Tacitus tells us of predicting the future from various natural phenomena, such as the flight of birds, and the *Indiculus* tells us about the use of birds, horses, cow dung, and even sneezing for such purposes, though this borders more on magic than mythology.

The belief in ghosts, revenants, wights, and the like was common. The famous relation of Ibn Fadlan of a Viking ship burial (reconstructed by Michael Crichton in his 1976 novel *Eaters of the Dead)* points to a form of suttee (burial of the widow with the dead husband), known also from archeological evidence. This indicates a belief in life after death. An Old High German charm, *Ad signandum domum* (For a spirit in a house), indicates a belief in wights (spirits), as was to be expected, and the comparison with Old English and more modern German phenomena shows a belief in witches. There was also a widespread belief in the Wild Hunt, called in Middle High German *Wuotanes her,* a course of spirits and demons through the night air, especially during the Twelve Days of Christmas. The *Idisi* women mentioned in the first of the *Merseburg Charms* seem to have been a kind of Walkyrie, perhaps connected with the Old Scandinavian *disir.* There was also a belief in dwarves and giants.

The casting of spells, predicting the future, and apotropaic devices were also common. Tacitus already tells us of "wise women" (seers, sibyls) who could foretell the future, and he leaves us the names of two: Veleda and Albruna. That there were heathen beliefs in an end of the world seems quite likely, based on the word *muspilli,* used in the Old High German poem *Muspilli,* for final conflagration. The Germanic people also believed in a sort of paradise, a heavenly "meadow," as revealed in the Old English *neorxnawang* (paradise).

BIBLIOGRAPHY

Baetke, Walter. *Die Religion der Germanen in Quellenzeugnissen,* 3d ed. Frankfurt: Diesterweg, 1944 [trans. into German of the most important sources, topically organized].

Betz, Werner. "Die altgermanische Religion." In *Deutsche Philologie im Aufriss,* ed. Wolfgang Stammler, 2d ed., vol. 3. Berlin: Schmidt, 1962, cols. 1547–1646.

de Vries, Jan. *Altgermanische Religionsgeschichte,* 2 vols., 2d ed. 1956; rpt. Berlin: de Gruyter, 1970.

Dictionary of Northern Mythology. Rochester, N.Y.: Brewer, 1993 [excellent one-volume handbook with good bibliographies].

Dumézil, Georges. *Gods of the Ancient Northmen,* ed. Einar Haugen. Berkeley: University of California Press, 1973 [trans. of his *Les Dieux des germains* and four articles written 1952–1959].

Grimm, Jacob. *Teutonic Mythology,* trans. and ed. James Steven Stallybrass. 4 vols. New York: Dover, 1883–1888; rpt. 1966.

Sebeok, Thomas A., ed. *Myth: A Symposium.* Bibliographical and Special Series of the American Folklore Society, vol. 5. Bloomington: Indiana University Press, 1955 [series of articles on the nature of myth].

Simek, Rudolf. *Lexikon der germanischen Mythologie.* Kröners Taschenausgabe, vol. 368. Stuttgart: Kröner, 1984; trans. Angela Hall.

Smith, Ron. "Norse/Teutonic Mythologies." In *Mythologies of the World: A Guide to Sources.* Urbana, Ill.: National Council of Teachers of English, 1981, pp. 194–205.

James W. Marchand

SEE ALSO
Charms; Magic; *Muspilli*

N

Nabuchodonosor

Derived from biblical origin, *Nabuchodonosor* is the name frequently used for two Early Middle High German religious poems linked together in a famous Vorau (Austria) manuscript of Middle High German poetry, *Drei Jünglinge im Feuerofen* and *Die ältere Judith*. Their common element is the biblical figure of Nebuchadnezzar, active in the first poem, but passive in the second. *Drei Jünglinge im Feuerofen* (*Three Young Men in the Fiery Furnace*), the first poem, contains a rhymed version of the familiar story of the three Israelite youths—Shadrak, Mishak, and Abednego—from the Old Testament Book of Daniel (Chapter 3). King Nebuchadnezzar rejects the true God of the Israelites and has a golden idol built, ordering all his people to bow down before it. The three youths are depicted as faithful servants of God who refuse to bow down to Nebuchadnezzar's golden idol; they are thrown into the fiery furnace but are saved from harm by an angel. It is a short poem (eighty-four verses in seven strophes of varying length), concise, and dramatic — not unlike a ballad — ending in the recognition of God's power by the heathens and the disgrace of Nebuchadnezzar and his idols.

Immediately following the *Drei Jünglinge* in the Vorau manuscript, almost without interruption, comes *Die ältere Judith* (the "earlier Judith" as opposed to a "later" version). This is an abbreviated story from the Apocryphal Book of Judith, which describes Judith's slaying of Nebuchadnezzar's general, Holofernes, in his own tent. The ensuing relief of the siege of the Israelites in Bethulia is not narrated, leading to the assumption that this version is fragmentary. The determination of Judith to save her people, who had almost given up hope of salvation from God, and her courage to go into the enemy camp and decapitate Holofernes are evidence of God's working through a woman to save His chosen people. The poem ends before the actual decapitation and comprises only 136 rhymed verses in 13 stanzas of varying length. Like *Die drei Jünglinge,* it resembles a ballad, with the action carried largely by the dialogue. However, *Die jüngere Judith* ("younger [poem about] Judith") that follows in the Vorau manuscript is considerably longer (1,821 verses) and is almost a rhymed translation of the biblical Book of Judith, which starts with the events leading up to the siege of Bethulia and ends with the release of the Israelites after Judith's heroic deed. A hint of incipient courtly behavior may be seen in the scenes at Holofernes's camp. There is little overt exegesis (learned biblical commentary) in any of these three poems. They are direct examples of divine power working through people of steadfast faith, and the moral interpretation is therefore obvious. All three poems are by different authors, probably from the first half of the twelfth century.

BIBLIOGRAPHY

Haug, Walter, and Benedikt Vollmann, eds. *Frühe deutsche Literatur und Lateinische Literatur in Deutschland, 800–1150.* Frankfurt am Main: Deutscher Klassiker Verlag, 1991, pp. 718–727 [with German translation].

Maurer, Friedrich, ed. *Die religiösen Dichtungen des 11. und 12. Jahrhunderts. Nach ihren Formen besprochen,* 3 vols. Tübingen: Niemeyer, 1964–1970, vol. 1, no. 15; vol. 2, no. 30.

Purdie, Edna. "The Story of Judith in German and English Literature." *Bibliothèque de la revue de littérature comparée* 39 (1927): 31–34.

Schröder, Werner. "Ältere Judith" and "Nabuchodonosor." In *Die deutsche Literatur des Mittelalters: Ver-*

fasserlexikon, ed. Kurt Ruh et al., 2d ed. Berlin: de Gruyter, 1978ff., vol. 1, cols. 288–294 [*Ältere Judith;* vol. 4, cols. 923–926 [*Drei Jünglinge*].

Waag, Albert, and Werner Schröder, eds. *Kleinere deutsche Gedichte des XI. und XII. Jahrhunderts.* 2 vols. Tübingen: Niemeyer, 1972, vol. 1, no. 4; vol. 2, no. 31.

Sidney M. Johnson

SEE ALSO
Bible

Nancy, Battle of

The duke of Burgundy, Charles the Bold (or, more properly, the Rash), had been trying to dominate the border regions of France and the Holy Roman Empire. In 1476 he swiftly conquered the Duchy of Lorraine, but its ally, the Swiss cantons, came to its aide. The Swiss inflicted two major defeats on Charles in 1476, at the battles of Grandson and Morat, or Murten. With Burgundy's forces weakened, Lorraine rose in rebellion. When Charles was forced to besiege Lorraine's capital of Nancy, the duke of Lorraine with Swiss allies and mercenaries arrived to relieve the city. On January 5, 1477, through clever strategy and under cover of a snowstorm, the Swiss attacked on Charles's front and the flanks at the same time. Burgundy's armies, outnumbered and outfought, broke and retreated. The duke was found two days later, his head smashed in, his body half-frozen and partially devoured by wolves.

Without a male successor, the Burgundian inheritance fell largely to Maximilian I Habsburg, who quickly married Charles's only daughter, Mary. The successful establishment of the Habsburgs in the Lowlands and part of Burgundy altered the balance of European politics and created an enduring rivalry between the French Valois and Austrian Habsburg dynasties.

BIBLIOGRAPHY

Delbrück, Hans. *Medieval Warfare,* trans. Walter J. Renfroe Jr. History of the Art of War 3. Lincoln: University of Nebraska Press, 1982.

Oman, Charles. *A History of the Art of War in the Middle Ages,* 2 vols. 2d. ed. London: Methuen, 1924.

Vaughan, Richard. *Charles the Bold: The Last Valois Duke of Burgundy.* New York: Barnes and Noble, 1973.

Brian A. Pavlac

National Chronicles

See Chronicles, Regional/National, Dutch; Chronicles, Regional/Territorial, German.

Naumburg

A bishopric was founded in Naumburg in the early eleventh century. This site on the Saale River in Saxony was selected when the local bishopric, originally founded in nearby Zeitz, came under Bohemian attacks. The newly founded town also became the major seat of Count Ekkehard and his descendants. Strategically located between the firmly settled German provinces and the Slavic hinterlands, the new town exploited its location to become a major center of trade between the two groups, a process that continued and grew throughout the Middle Ages. A major annual event was the fair held on the Feast of Saints Peter and Paul (June 29), which provided substantial revenue for the town. An increase in trade in the later Middle Ages allowed Naumburg to be admitted into the Hanseatic League in 1432, solidifying its position as an economic center.

The thirteenth-century bishops, including Bishop Engelhard (1207–1242), held considerable power in medieval Naumburg and were able to marshal the resources necessary to begin construction of a new cathedral. During the thirteenth century, however, controversy broke out between the bishop, who was supported by the chapter, and the town council, supported by the local count. The chapter was in considerable debt because of the construction of the cathedral, and the actual power of the bishop waned as the economic and political power of the town council grew. By the end of the century the bishop withdrew to Zeitz, leaving the chapter, headed by a provost, in Naumburg. While the bishop retained nominal rights, after the thirteenth century the town council, with some input from the cathedral chapter, actually governed the city.

Probably the best-known building from medieval Naumburg is the cathedral, dedicated to Saints Peter and Paul, originally constructed about 1050 and rebuilt in the thirteenth century to incorporate the burial church of Count Ekkehard, which originally stood to the cathedral's west. The building represents a combination of late Romanesque and early Gothic features typical in thirteenth-century German architecture. It retains the traditional exterior massing of Saxon Romanesque basilicas but has a greatly elaborated four-towered facade and a more imposing scale than earlier buildings. The cathedral has single side aisles and a two-story elevation in the ribbed groin-vaulted nave, common in German early Gothic architecture. The building has two choirs—an east choir for traditional liturgical uses and a west choir that incorporated the former burial church of Count

Ekkehard within the cathedral's space. The east choir was rebuilt in the High Gothic style during the fourteenth century and represents one of the few substantial structures built under the bishop's patronage at this date. In addition to the cathedral itself there is also a cloister containing a Three Kings' chapel and a church dedicated to the Virgin.

The cathedral's sculptural ensemble is one of the most celebrated examples of German Gothic sculpture. It is found in two locations—the west choir, with large figures representing the family of the founding count, Ekkehard, and on the choir screen, which provides an entrance into the west choir. The primary sculptor, known as the Naumburg Master, has been the subject of scholarship that is so fundamental that it may be used to trace the development of German medieval art history. The Naumburg sculpture incorporates French style, largely stemming from Reims Cathedral. However, it does not represent direct influence but rather a creative departure from a wave of French influence that had appeared earlier in the thirteenth century at Bamberg and Magdeburg. Although charting the history of the Naumburg sculptor or workshop is a complex task, it is generally accepted that the choir screen at Mainz represents an earlier project of sculptors who continued their work at Naumburg and were subsequently active at Meissen.

Twelve members of the founding Ekkardinger family are represented adorsed (set back to back) on columns in the west choir, which is composed of one square with a polygonal apse. A date of circa 1250 is likely for the work, since a document of 1249 promises indulgences for contributing to the work in the west choir, and the founders' positions are similar to those of the standing apostles of the Sainte Chapelle in Paris, completed 1248. The ensemble shows two couples facing each other across the square bay, Count Hermann (d. 1032) standing next to his wife, Reglindis, and his younger brother Count Ekkehard II (d. 1046) standing next to his wife, Uta. Two other countesses and six additional counts appear as single figures, including Counts Dietmar, Syzzo, Wilhelm, and Thimo, who are attached to the colonettes between the windows in the polygon. The figures are notable for the lifelike depictions of features and behavior. Uta, for example, shields her face with her cloak collar, while grasping the mantle with the long expressive fingers of her other hand. The west choir also contains a stained glass program of saints and bishops that complements the sculpture.

The choir screen, usually dated slightly after the founder figures (ca. 1250–1255), has a central crucifixion with a highly expressive mourning Virgin and St. John and a band of Passion reliefs. The placement of the crucified Christ with outstretched arms in the center of the screen's doorway means that each person entering the west choir would have to pass under the arms involving him or her immediately with the sculpture. The Passion reliefs are distinguished by an everyday realism. Apostles tip back their cups and put bread into their mouths in the Last Supper relief, and the Jews depicted in the Paying of Judas and the Arrest of Christ scenes wear the small, pointed hats associated with members of that religion in medieval Germany. The realistic detail combined with heightened expressiveness seen at Naumburg is absent in contemporary French work, and these unusual qualities are an important reason for the continued interest in the character and career of the people who sculpted the figures of the west choir.

Additional medieval architecture in Naumburg includes the original parts of churches dedicated to St. Moritz and St. Wenzel and a hospital dedicated to Mary Magdalen, which was erected by 1144. As the communal movement was established in Naumburg, buildings suitable for civic uses were constructed. The fourteenth century saw the erection of walls around the city including five towers containing city gates (although the original construction was in wood rather than stone). The original City Hall (Rathaus) on the town square dated from the fourteenth century, although it was destroyed and rebuilt after fires in 1384, 1408, and 1457; the present building was constructed after a fire in 1517.

BIBLIOGRAPHY

Brush, Kathryn. "The Naumburg Master: A Chapter in the Development of Medieval Art History." *Gazette des Beaux Arts,* 6th series, 122 (1993): 109–122.

Schubert, Ernst. *Naumburg: Dom und Alt Stadt,* 2d ed. Leipzig: Koehler and Amelang, 1989.

———. *Der Naumburger Dom.* Halle an der Saale: Janos Stekovics, 1997.

Susan L. Ward

SEE ALSO
Bamberg; Gothic Art and Architecture; Magdeburg; Mainz; Meißen

Neidhart (fl. ca. 1215–1230)

A Middle High German poet of some renown, there is no documentary evidence of Neidhart's name or of his origins. Under the title "Lord" *(her) nithart,* the so-called large ("C") and the small ("A") *Minnesang*-manuscripts at Heidelberg University Library record the stanzas attributed to him. The singer is apostrophized as der *von Riuwental* (the one from the Riuew Valley) in the *Summer Songs (Sommerlieder)* and the defiantly stated "responseverses" *(Trutzstrophen)* of the *Winter Songs (Winterlieder).* This explains the name Neidhart von Reuental, a term especially used by earlier scholars. Both names can also be interpreted allegorically (*nithart* is a medieval name for the devil); *riuwental* taken literally reads as "valley of grief"). The only indication for dating Neidhart's poems is through an allusion in Wolfram von Eschenbach's courtly novel *Willehalm* (l. 312,12; written ca. 1215), as well as references to contemporary political events or personalities in his songs (Archbishop Eberhard II of Salzburg, Duke Friedrich II of Austria). These clues lead to the conclusion that Neidhart may possibly have lived from circa 1190 to 1240. The author's occupation and social rank are just as unknown, although, like Walter von der Vogelweide, he was probably a professional poet. It is almost certain that Neidhart spent part of his early literary career in the area of Bavaria/Salzburg, which he was forced to leave for some unknown reason—possibly due to losing his patron and/or audience, as can perhaps be discerned in changes in his literary style. There are no definite clues that Neidhart might have belonged to the Wittelsbach court of Ludwig I the Kelheimer. On the other hand, Winter Song No. 37 directly addresses Archbishop Eberhard II of Salzburg. Later on Neidhart sang in the vicinity of the Babenberg court of Friedrich II the Valiant (der Streitbare) in Vienna. This may also have been the setting for a literary argument with Walter von der Vogelweide and his concept of *Minnesang* (see Song L 64,31). The writers of subsequent generations (Rubin, Der Marner, Hermann Damen) regarded Neidhart as a good example and "master". The special form of his poetry developed into a separate lyrical genre in the late Middle Ages, while the content partly underwent strong changes. These later poems were passed on under the name *ain nithart* (a Neidhart) in the manuscripts (these songs, regarded largely as imitations following the nineteenth-century scholar Moritz Haupt, have come to be put under the term "pseudo-Neidhart" by researchers). During the last stage of this reception Neidhart became the hero of the *Schwankroman Neidhart Fuchs Schwankerzählungen und -Lieder* (*Neidhart Fox's Comical Tales and Songs,* published 1491/1497, 1537, und 1566), and many Neidhart plays, which belong to the oldest ex-

isting secular plays written in German. Altogether the numerous manuscripts (from the end of the thirteenth to the fifteenth century) record about 140 songs under the name of Neidhart, of which, however, only 66 are considered to be authentic. In the field of *Minnesang,* well-preserved songs form the major exception, even though they were recorded mostly only at a later period (about 68 tunes in all).

As far as form and content are concerned, Neidhart's songs, often described as "rustic/rural poetry" *(dörperlich),* can be divided into Summer Songs and Winter Songs (according to the varying introductory natural settings) and *Schwanklieder* (comic songs). The Summer Songs, divided into scenes, render simple verse forms that have been worked out in detail *(raien),* while their content forms a clear contrast to traditional *Minnesang.* The plot is shifted from the courtly to the rural realm, the "Knight," or Ritter von Riuwental, is exposed to the unconcealed sexual desires of the farmer's daughters and wives. Whereas the mother, who is the representative of socially accepted moral conventions, warns her daughter of the consequences of having an affair with the impoverished knight—in the so-called *Songs of the Aged (Altenlieder)* the positions of mother and daughter are reverse—the girl struggles to participate in the summer dance and thus also to gain the opportunity of a rendezvous. In the Sommer Songs, thought by some to be later, there are frequently statements on the unsatisfactory position of the singer and the loss of *vreude* (happiness) in courtly society (demonstrated via the theme of Engelmar's mirror theft). The Winter Songs, structured by stollen, require an intimate acquaintance with form and content of "classical" *Minnesang* to be understood, since the patterns of content and representation in *Minnesang* are constantly referred to in quotations and opposed to the so-called *dörper,* or farmer-stanzas. They portray the threat posed to the singer by rural upstarts, who arrogate aristocratic clothing and lifestyles to themselves, and, even though they adopt only the superficial forms of courtly culture, but not its actual contents, alienate the singer from his *vrouwe* "lady" (who turns out to be a "farmer's daughter" or, in the so-called *werlt-süeze,* or "wordly delight" songs, "Hure Welt"/Whore World). In the *Schwanklieder* the knight Neidhart is promoted to the role of ever-victorious enemy of the physically and intellectually inferior peasants. According to massive tradition as well as extraliterary evidence, the Neidhart-*Lieder* (songs) with their transformations of content enjoyed sustained popularity from the thirteenth to the sixteenth century. Only in recent times has research begun to refrain from continuing the debate about authenticity and to accept instead the genre of the "Neidharts" in the fullness of its tradition and history.

BIBLIOGRAPHY

Bennewitz, Ingrid. *Original und Rezeption. Funktions- und überlieferungsgeschichtliche Studien zur Neidhart-Sammlung R.* Göppingen: Kümmerle, 1987.

Beyschlag, Siegfried, ed. *Die Lieder Neidharts.* Darmstadt: Wissenschaftliche Buchgesellschaft, 1975.

Fritz, Gerd, ed. *Abbildungen zur Neidhart-Überlieferung I. Die Berliner Neidhart-Hs. R und die Pergament-Fragmente Cb, K, O und M.* Göppingen: Kümmerle, 1973.

Haupt, Moriz, ed. *Neidhart von Reuenthal.* Leipzig, 1864. 2d ed. Edmund Wießner. Leipzig 1923; rpt. ed. Ingrid Bennewitz, Ulrich Müller, and Franz V. Spechtler. Stuttgart: Hirzel, 1986.

Herr Neidhart diesen Reihen sang. Die Texte und Melodien der Neidhartlieder mit 'Übersetzungen und Kommentaren, ed. Siegfried Beyschlag and Horst Brunner. Göppingen: Kümmerle, 1968.

Holznagel, Franz-Josef. *Wege in die Schriftlichkeit. Untersuchungen und Materialien zur Überlieferung der mittelhochdeutschen Lyrik.* Tübingen: Francke, 1995.

Jöst, Erhard, ed. *Die Historien des Neithart Fuchs. Nach dem Frankfurter Druck von 1566.* Göppingen: Kümmerle, 1980.

Margetts, John, ed. *Neidhartspiele.* Graz: Akademische Druck- und Verlagsanstalt, 1982.

Schweikle, Günther. *Neidhart.* Stuttgart: Metzler, 1990.

Simon, Eckehard. *Neidhart v. Reuental. Geschichte der Forschung und Bibliographie.* The Hague: Mouton, 1968.

Wenzel, Edith, ed. *Abbildungen zur Neidhart-Überlieferung II. Die Berliner Neidhart-Hs. c (mgf 779).* Göppingen: Kümmerle, 1975.

Ingrid Bennewitz

SEE ALSO

Drama; *Liederhandschriften; Minnesang;* Wolfram von Eschenbach

Neubrandenburg

Founded in 1248 by Margrave Johann of Brandenburg as a border fortress against Pomerania, Neubrandenburg, as part of the Stargard dominion, was integrated into Mecklenburg in 1317. As a model example of a colonial town of the thirteenth century, Neubrandenburg possesses a circular ground plan with regular street pattern; its four gates are deliberately not aligned in order to avoid creating continuous thoroughfares.

In this pattern, the central block is replaced by the market square on which the town hall, and later the castle, were built; the main ecclesiastical building, the Marienkirche (church of the Virgin), is positioned farther to the south, replacing another block of houses. Consecrated in 1298, the church represents an unusual type: its rectangular ground plan lacks all indication of a choir, and articulated arcades over heavy compound pillars subdivide the central nave from the narrower aisles. The nine-bay length expresses a clear sense of longitudinality. The straight east end of the church enabled the erection of a monumental gable with finials and traceries transforming, by the use of molded bricks, a High Gothic cathedral facade—like that of Cologne Cathedral—into brick. The Franciscan monastery was founded circa 1260 at the northern termination of the town's main axis, where it was incorporated into the defensive works. In the first half of the fourteenth century, its first building was replaced by the present hall church, which, although an asymmetrical hall with only a northern aisle and the monks' choir, imitated St. Marien.

The nearly complete destruction of Neubrandenburg at the end of World War II, including its town hall, castle, and historic houses, left the shell of St. Marien standing as a ruin, while the Franciscan church remained intact. The town's defense works, however, are among the best preserved of their kind. Their main elements are the four gates (Friedländer, Stargarder, Treptower, and Neues Tor) dating from the fourteenth and fifteenth centuries. Of these, the Neues Tor (New Gate) shows in the fields of its traceried (ornamented with interlacing lines) gable on the town side eight female statues assembled out of pieces of terra-cotta. In the fifteenth century, as in many other towns, barbicans and outer, lower gates were added; only at Neubrandenburg have these survived to give the impression of a fully fortified medieval town.

BIBLIOGRAPHY

Die Bau- und Kunstdenkmale in der DDR, Bezirk Neubrandenburg, ed. Institut für Denkmalpflege der DDR. Munich: Beck, 1982

Hans J. Böker

SEE ALSO

Franciscan Art and Architecture; Gothic Art and Architecture; Town Planning and Urbanism

Nibelungenlied

Germany's preeminent heroic epic, the *Nibelungenlied (Song of the Nibelungs),* recounts Kriemhild's love and loss of her husband, the mighty hero Siegfried, and her revenge on his slayers, culminating in the destruction of the entire Burgundian empire. The story was written at the outset of the thirteenth century, during the first golden age of German literature. Its origins lie in the Danube region of what is now Austria. Almost nothing is known of the poet, whom most scholars regard as an educated clerk employed in some official capacity at court. The *Nibelungenlied* is preserved in three principal thirteenth-century manuscripts: "A", the shortest, in the Staatsbibliothek in Munich (Cod. germ. 34); "B", the most authoritative, dated as early as the first half of the thirteenth century, in the Stiftsbibliothek in St. Gall, Switzerland (Ms. 857); and "C", the most "courtly" version, in the Fürstlich Fürstenbergische Hofbibliothek in Donaueschingen (Ms. 63). The wealth of manuscripts (ten complete, 24 fragments) attests to its popularity during the Middle Ages. All extant manuscripts include *Die Klage,* an epic poem in rhymed couplets that recounts how the fallen heroes are mourned. This courtly and sentimental continuation to the abrupt and catastrophic conclusion of the *Nibelungenlied* is inferior to the epic itself. The name "Nibelung" occurs in the first part of the poem to denote Siegfried's treasure and the heroes who guard it; throughout the second half, the attribute is used as an alternate designation for the Burgundians.

Nibelungenlied is divided into 29 cantos (*âventiuren*) and comprises well over 2,300 four-line strophes. Its distinctive metrical form, known as the *Nibelungenstrophe,* was also used by the early Minnesinger known as Der von Kürenberg. Each of the long lines is divided into two by a caesura (audible break), and each half line contains three full beats, except for the second half of the fourth line, which contains four. The story itself falls into two parts.

Cantos 1–19 recount the love and marriage of Kriemhild and Siegfried and the slaying of Siegfried at the hand of Gunther and Hagen. In cantos 20–39, the poet tells of Kriemhild's marriage to Etzel and of her plan for revenge, culminating in the death of all the Burgundians. Part I introduces the virtuous and beautiful Kriemhild, the sister of the Burgundian kings Gunther, Gernot, and Giselher, whose duty is to protect her. In a dream Kriemhild sees two eagles tear to pieces a falcon she has raised. Her mother, Uote, interprets the falcon to be a husband who will bring her joy and sorrow. News of Kriemhild's great beauty reaches Xanten, and the young Siegfried, King Siegmund's son, sets out to woo her. When Siegfried arrives in Worms, the grim Hagen, Gunther's chief vassal, identifies the newcomer for Gunther and recounts his earlier, heroic deeds: Siegfried had singlehandedly won a vast treasure, the Nibelungen hoard, and, after having bathed in the blood of a dragon that he had slain, became invulnerable save for one spot between his shoulder blades. When the Danes and Saxons subsequently declare war, Siegfried helps Gunther by leading the Burgundians and distinguishing himself in battle. Upon his return he meets Kriemhild for the first time and they fall in love. Hearing of Brünhild, a queen of remarkable strength and beauty who may be won only by a man capable of besting her in three athletic contests, Gunther determines to woo her. He enlists the aid of Siegfried, to whom he promises the hand of Kriemhild if successful. In Isenstein, Siegfried pretends to be Gunther's vassal and, with the aid of his Tarnkappe (cloak of invisibility) is able to help him defeat Brünhild. Gunther thus wins her under false pretenses, and a double wedding takes place in Worms. But Brünhild, who has grown suspicious, resists Gunther's advances during their wedding night. Siegfried, who agrees to help Gunther, again dons the Tarnkappe and subdues Brunhild; she is once again deceived into believing in Gunther's mastery. Ten years later, Brünhild, brooding over her unhappy marriage, prevails upon Gunther to invite Siegfried and Kriemhild to Worms. During a knightly contest, the queens quarrel over the prowess of their respective husbands, with Brünhild insisting that Gunther is the superior man. The quarrel escalates, until Kriemhild reveals to Brünhild the ring and girdle that Siegfried had stolen from her the night he helped Gunther take her maidenhood. Devastated by the import of such visible evidence, Brünhild leaves the court in tears. She recounts the incident to Hagen, who plans and carries out Siegfried's murder. Hagen tricks Kriemhild into revealing the location of Siegfried's vulnerable spot and later uses this information to kill him by stabbing him in the back. Kriemhild is inconsolable and lives only for revenge. The grief-stricken widow remains in Worms distributing the Nibelungen treasure among her supporters and hoping that they will help her avenge Siegfried's death. When Hagen learns of this, he steals the treasure and sinks it in the Rhine.

At the start of Part II, thirteen years have elapsed since Siegfried's death. Etzel, king of the Huns, hears of Kriemhild's great beauty and determines to wed her. He sends his Christian vassal, Margrave Rüdiger of Bechlaren, to Worms as his proxy wooer. Kriemhild agrees to marry the wealthy and powerful Etzel only after she exacts an oath from Rüdiger that he will avenge all wrongs done her. Her departure from Worms marks a turning point in her personality: she no longer passively grieves for her dead husband; she now actively plans her revenge. After ten years of marriage, Kriemhild persuades Etzel to invite her brothers and Hagen to Gran for a festival. Despite Hagen's warnings, the Burgundians, or Niblungs as they are now called, accept the invitation and Hagen leads the expedition. Before they cross the Danube, Hagen learns from two water sprites that none of them will return alive except the chaplain. To test the truth of their prophesy, Hagen tosses the chaplain, a nonswimmer, overboard during the river crossing and uses an oar to try to keep his head submerged. Despite Hagen's best efforts, the chaplain reaches the opposite shore. On their arrival at Bechlaren, Rüdiger receives them with great hospitality, and Giselher is betrothed to Rüdiger's daughter. As host, Rüdiger accompanies his guests to Etzel's court, and shortly thereafter hostilities break out. The Huns attack the Burgundians in the sleeping quarters and thousands die. Soon afterward in the great banquet hall, Etzel's generous hospitality turns to hatred as he witnesses Hagen behead the former's young son, Ortlieb, in battle, an act that incites a new wave of fighting. The death toll rises to devastating heights on both sides. The Burgundians are finally besieged in the great hall, which Kriemhild has set on fire. The warriors quench their thirst with the blood of the slain. The loyal vassal Rüdiger, after a desperate struggle with his conscience, is compelled to enter the fray and battles against his friends, the Burgundians. After horrific carnage, Dietrich von Bern defeats the two remaining Burgundians, Gunther and Hagen, and brings them shackled before Kriemhild. Kriemhild has Gunther killed and then, with Siegfried's sword, she beheads the bound and defenseless Hagen. She herself is struck down by Hildebrand, Dietrich's vassal. At the conclusion of the work, only Etzel, Dietrich, and Hildebrand remain alive.

Part I of the *Nibelungenlied* differs from Part II in its attempt to incorporate courtly conventions into the narrative. The poet took great pains to portray Siegfried and Kriemhild's love in the refined terms of his day, a concession to the cultured tastes of his audience. Despite its courtly overlay, the *Nibelungenlied* differs markedly from the fashionable, idealistic courtly epics of the early thirteenth century. Not compassion, repentance, and forgiveness but rather jealousy, betrayal, and vengeance carry the narrative of the *Nibelungenlied*.

The tragedy that the poet recounts offers the medieval audience a depiction of what befalls when loyalties are betrayed, when noble status *(ordo mundi)* is ignored, when greed rather than goodness, when self-interest rather than human compassion become the order of the day. Moderation, the cornerstone of all courtly virtues, is absent; deception is the watchword of this tragic tale. God's will does not determine the action but rather the repercussions of deception revealed. Duplicity forms the thematic core of many of the highly dramatic and memorable scenes that punctuate the narrative.

Nibelungenlied, the subject of prolific scholarly inquiry, continues to intrigue its readers and elicit new and original research. Numerous investigations, past and present, have focused on the identity of the author; the date and origins of the poem; its narrative structure and oral-formulaic content; the characters, motivation, and message of the poem; and its reception. Much of the early research addressed the source or sources of the poem. Karl Lachmann, who published his source study in 1816, viewed the poem as a compilation of individual lays by autonomous poets. In 1920 Andreas Heusler refuted Lachmann's celebrated *Liedertheorie* (theory of songs) by postulating that the poet fashioned his tale from two distinct sources. He submitted that the first half derived from the "Younger Lay of Brünhild" *(Jüngeres Brünhildlied),* a short lay that recounted the love of Siegfried and Brünhild, the artifice used during Gunther's wooing, the quarrel between the two queens, and Brünhild's terrible revenge. Heusler posited a longer epic, the so-called *Ältere Not* (older tale), an account of the destruction of the Burgundians, as the basis for the second half of the *Nibelungenlied.* Many recent critics have given credence to Heusler's theory and have adopted and revised it.

More recent source studies have investigated *Nibelungenlied*'s literary connections with the verse and the prose *Völsungasaga* in Old Norse and the Scandinavian *Thidrekssaga,* while the second part of the *Nibelungenlied,* based on the destruction of the Burgundians by the Huns in 436, also forms the content of an older Eddic poem, the *Atlakvitha* (Lay of Atli). However, the Eddic version, told from a completely different point of view, depicts Guthrun (Kriemhild) taking vengeance on her husband, the cruel and treacherous Atli (Etzel), not on Högni (Hagen) and her brothers. Modern scholarly research has moved from source studies to a consideration of the artistic merit of the work itself. Scholars who view the anonymous poet as a masterful artist with the ability to create his great two-part heroic epic of Kriemhild's love, loss, and revenge from two originally unrelated poems have studied the poet's use of parallelism, foreshadowing, symbolic imagery, and dramatic confrontations to inform and structure his tragic tale and to depict his all-too-human characters. For example, Kriemhild's invitation to her brothers and Hagen in Part II shares a similar framework and motivation with Brünhild's invitation to Kriemhild and Siegfried in Part I. Such interconnected scenes lend richness, coherence, and new meaning to the narrative. Of the numerous studies investigating the major characters of the work, several have dealt with Hagen, Gunther's mighty vassal. One of the problems with the *Nibelungenlied* is that Siegfried, the hero, dies at the conclusion of Part I. Some critics have argued that Hagen, who leads the Burgundians to Gran, changes from villain to hero, from treacherous murderer to compassionate friend in the second half of the poem. While he is praised by many as the quintessential vassal entrusted with the safekeeping of his king and his people, others view Hagen as demonic, self-interested, and villainous to the end. Kriemhild's role in Siegfried's death and her demand for the treasure at the conclusion of the poem have also formed the subject of scholarly inquiry, as has Brünhild's conspicuous absence from the story line after Siegfried's death. Numerous investigations focus on the Christian knight Rüdiger, a highly moral and much respected hero caught up in the web of conflicting loyalties. The *Nibelungenlied,* which has intrigued both the medieval listener and the modern scholar with its complex origins, purposeful structure, psychologically credible yet sometimes contradictory characters, and dramatic denouement, continues to inspire diverse and original scholarly interpretation.

BIBLIOGRAPHY

Das Nibelungenlied, ed. Helmut de Boor, 22d ed. Wiesbaden: Brockhaus, 1988.

Das Nibelungenlied. ed. and trans. Helmut Brackert. 2 vols. Frankfurt am Main: Fischer, 1971.

Das Nibelungenlied. ed. and trans. Siegfried Grosse. Stuttgart: Reclam, 1997.

The Nibelungenlied. trans. A.T. Hatto. Harmondsworth, Middlesex: Penguin, 1969.

Andersson, Theodore M. *A Preface to the Nibelungenlied.* Stanford, Calif.: Stanford University Press, 1987.

Bauml, Franz H., and Eva-Maria Fallone, comps. *A Concordance to the Nibelungenlied.* Leeds: Maney and Son, 1976.

Bekker, Hugo. *The Nibelungenlied: A Literary Analysis.* Toronto: University of Toronto Press, 1979.

Ehrismann, Otfrid. *Nibelungenlied: Epoche—Werk—Wirkung.* Munich: Beck, 1987.

Gentry, Francis G. *"Triuwe" and "Vriunt" in the Nibelungenlied."* Amsterdam: Rodopi, 1975.

Haymes, Edward R. *The Nibelungenlied. History and Interpretation.* Urbana: University of Illinois Press, 1986.

Heinzle, Joachim. *Das Nibelungenlied. Eine Einführung.* Munich: Artemis, 1987; rpt. Frankfurt am Main: Fischer, 1994.

———, and Annaliese Waldschmidt, ed. *Die Nibelungen. Ein deutscher Wahn, ein deutscher Alptraum. Studien und Dokumente zur Rezeption des Nibelungenstoffs im 19. und 20. Jahrhundert.* Frankfurt am Main: Suhrkamp, 1991.

Heusler, Andreas. *Nibelungensage und Nibelungenlied. Die Stoffgeschichte des deutschen Heldenepos,* 6th ed. Dortmund: Ruhfus, 1965.

Hoffmann, Werner. *Das Nibelungenlied.* Stuttgart: Metzler, 1992.

McConnell, Winder. *The Nibelungenlied.* Boston: Twayne, 1984.

McConnell, Winder, ed. *A Companion to the Nibelungenlied.* Columbia, S.C.: Camden House, 1998.

Mowatt, D. G., and Hugh Sacker. *The Nibelungenlied: An Interpretative Commentary.* Toronto: University of Toronto Press, 1967.

Müller, Jan-Dirk. *Spielregeln für den Untergang: die Welt des Nibelungenliedes.* Tübingen: Niemeyer, 1998.

Nagel, Bert. *Das Nibelungenlied: Stoff—Form—Ethos.* Frankfurt am Main.: Hirschgraben, 1965; 2d ed. 1970.

Panzer, Friedrich. *Das Nibelungenlied. Entstehung und Gestalt.* Stuttgart: Kohlhammer, 1955.

Schulze, Ursula. *Das Nibelungenlied.* Stuttgart: Reclam, 1997.

Thomas, Neil. *Reading the "Nibelungenlied."* Durham: University of Durham, 1995.

Wunderlich, Werner, and Ulrich Müller, ed. *"waz sider da geschach": American-German Studies on the Nibelungenlied. Text and Reception. With Bibliography 1980–1990/1991.* Göppingen: Kümmerle, 1992.

Lynn Thelen

SEE ALSO

Childhood; *Heldenbücher; Nibelungia Minora; Waltharius*

Nibelungia Minora

The *Nibelungenlied (Song of the Nibelungs)* is the earliest and greatest of medieval German treatments of what we call the Nibelung legend *(Nibelungensage),* but it is not the only one. Several lesser works *(Nibelungia Minora)* treat the legend directly or indirectly.

The most popular of these is the *Rosengarten zu Worms (The Rosegarden at Worms),* a poem also included in the general area of Dietrich poems, since it involves Dietrich and his men and is told generally from their point of view. Kriemhild, desirous of demonstrating the superiority of her fiancé Sîfrid (Siegfried), challenges Etzel, Dietrich, and their men to serial single combat with the men of Worms, including Gunther, Giselher, Gernot, and Hagen, along with Siegfried. Etzel, Dietrich, and the others accept the challenge after adding several heroes to their usual number, most notable of whom is the warrior-monk Ilsan. Twelve battles are fought with a kiss from the princess as the reward in each case. The men of Worms are beaten in all the battles, which culminate in the battle between Dietrich and Siegfried. Dietrich is loath to join battle and does so only when goaded by Hildebrand, who accuses him of cowardice. The *Rosengarten* survives in almost twenty manuscripts and fragments in some four clearly recognizable versions.

The Nibelung legend proper reappears only in a late strophic narration called *Das Lied vom hürnen Seyfrid (The Song of Horned Siegfried),* which derives its name from the notion that Siegfried's skin was invulnerable after his bath in dragon's blood because it turned to horn. The young Siegfried is here portrayed as being obstreperous at home and is given to a smith to be raised. The smith finds him equally difficult and sends him out to fight a large number of dragons who are killed and melted down in a great fire. One dragon's horny skin adheres to the youth's and gives him his protective coating. Princess Krimhilt, the daughter of king Gybich, has been carried away by a flying dragon who has imprisoned her on a mountain. Seyfrid hears of this from a dwarf, Eugel, who shows him the way to the mountain. The dragon's lair is guarded by a giant named Kuperan, and much of the poem is devoted to the long battle between Seyfrid and the giant. After defeating the giant he rescues the maiden from the dragon. In a brief epilogue we are told that Seyfrid's in-laws will kill him and that his wife will avenge him.

The poem is poorly constructed and shows evidence of having been assembled from a number of differing versions. It survives only in printed versions from the early sixteenth century onward. The poem shares a number of details with Norse versions that are missing in the *Nibelungenlied,* suggesting that there was "recontamination" of German tradition from the north or that there were varying versions of the story of young Siegfried in oral tradition in Germany.

BIBLIOGRAPHY

Die Gedichte vom Rosengarten zu Worms, ed. Georg Holz. Halle: Niemeyer, 1893.

Haymes, Edward R., and Susann T. Samples. *Heroic Legends of the North: An Introduction to the Nibelung and Dietrich Cycles.* Garland Reference Library of the Humanities 1403. New York: Garland, 1996.

Heinzle, Joachim. *Mittelhochdeutsche Dietrichepik.* Zurich: Artemis, 1978.

Hoffmann, Werner. *Mittelhochdeutsche Heldendichtung.* Berlin: Schmidt, 1974.

Hürnen Seyfrid, Das Lied vom, ed. K. C. King. Manchester: University of Manchester Press, 1958.

Edward R. Haymes

SEE ALSO
Nibelungenlied

Nicholas of Cusa (1401–1464)

Most important German thinker of the fifteenth century (Latin, Nicolaus Cusanus), ecclesiastical reformer, administrator, and cardinal. His lifelong effort, as canon law expert at church councils, as legate to Constantinople and later to German dioceses and houses of religion, in his own diocese, and even in the papal curia was to reform and unite the universal and Roman Church. This active life finds written expression in several hundred Latin sermons and more theoretical background in his writings on ecclesiology, ecumenism, mathematics, philosophy, and theology. Curious and open-minded, learned and steeped in the Neoplatonic tradition, well aware of both humanist and scholastic learning, yet self-taught in philosophy and theology, Nicholas anticipated many later ideas in mathematics, cosmology, astronomy, and experimental science while constructing his own original version of systematic Neoplatonism. A whole range of earlier medieval writers influenced Nicholas, but his important intellectual roots are in Proclus and Pseudo-Dionysius. In spite of his significance few later thinkers, apart from Giordano Bruno, understood or were influenced by him until the late nineteenth century.

Born in Kues (between Koblenz and Trier), Nicholas studied liberal arts (and perhaps some theology) at Heidelberg (1416–1417) and canon law at Padua, where he earned his *doctor decretorum* (1423) and made initial contacts with Italian humanists and mathematicians. He studied and taught canon law at Cologne (1425), where Heimericus de Campo introduced him to the ideas of Albertus Magnus, Ramon Llull, and Pseudo-Dionysius. He soon ended his formal schooling and became secretary, then chancellor, to the archbishop of Trier. He refused chairs of canon law at Louvain in 1428 and 1435, preferring administrative work in the church. As an expert at the Council of Basel (1432–1438), he wrote on the Hussites, papal authority, and reform of the calendar. His important conciliarist treatise, *De concordia catholica* (*On Catholic Harmony*, 1433), stressed the principles of representation and of consent of the governed and embodied his lifelong commitment to bring harmony and unity out of conflict and diversity.

In 1437 Nicholas changed his support from the conciliarists to the pope to better work for unity. He traveled in the delegation to Constantinople seeking to reunite Greek and Roman churches. Ordained a priest by 1440, he traveled as legate to Germany for the next ten years on behalf of the papal cause, and was named (1448) and made (1450) cardinal. He was appointed bishop of Brixen in Tyrol the same year, but traveled to Germany and the Low Countries to preach the jubilee year and issue edicts of reform. His efforts to reform his own diocese led to enmity with the local archduke; twice Nicholas had to flee to Rome. After 1458 he remained in the papal curia of Pius II at Rome. Nicholas died in 1464 en route to Ancona from Rome.

His important masterpiece of 1440, *On Learned Ignorance (De docta ignorantia)*, was the foundation for his writings over the next quarter century. While fully engaged in practical ecclesiastical affairs, Nicholas also wrote some twenty philosophical/theological treatises and dialogues, plus ten works on mathematics, focusing on the problem of squaring the circle and on using mathematics in philosophical theology. The three books of *On Learned Ignorance* expound his central ideas about God, the universe, and Christ. Nicholas was to extend, expand, and modify these speculations in later writings.

"Learned ignorance" is so called because it involves acknowledging the limits of human knowledge when we seek to know what God is (or, indeed, what the exact essence of anything amounts to). Our rational knowledge is a kind of conceptual measuring designed for the finite realm of more and less, but unable to reach the absolute maximum and thus inadequate for measuring the infinite God. There is no humanly conceivable proportion between God and creatures. Yet for Nicholas, we are supposed to move in ignorance beyond reason's inadequacies in hopes of touching God (*incomprehensibiliter comprehendere*) through a kind of intellectual-mystical vision wherein all things are one. Since God's fullness comprises everything, Nicholas invokes the idea of the coincidence of opposites (*coincidentia oppositorum*) as the ontological correlative of learned ignorance. By limiting the principle of contradiction to the realm of finite creatures and their differences, we recognize that in divinity all opposites coincide in the transcendent infinite oneness. The lack of resemblance between God and creatures means that all our knowledge of God must be metaphorical.

Nicholas's later writings propose conjectural metaphors for exploring the limits of our knowledge and at the same time seeking the God beyond. Of particular import are *De coniecturis: On conjectures* (ca. 1442), where Nicholas proposes a hierarchical Neoplatonic ontology as a speculative conjecture (while pointing out that all our conceptual knowledge is provisional or conjectural) and *Idiota de mente: The Layman — About Mind* (1450), which parallels our minds' creation of a conceptual universe and the divine mind's creation of the actual world. In *De visione Dei: The Vision of God* (1453), Nicholas proposes an all-seeing icon to hold together for imagination and thought how our striving to see God is one with God's seeing us.

De possest: On Actualized Possibility (1460) and *De li non aliud: On the Not-other* (1461–1462) work out two descriptions, or "names," of God. The first stresses how in God all possibilities are real or actually exist; thus in God possibility and actuality coincide. The second is concerned to express how God is and is not present to created things—intimately connected ("not other than") yet never identical with (*not* "nothing else but") creatures in space and time. Each of these metaphors and, indeed, all of Nicholas's later writings are calculated to initiate dialectical thinking so that one may move from thinking of God and creatures as exclusive and exhaustive alternatives to seeing them as identified, yet not identical. God is to be seen as both all and nothing of created things; creatures are limited images of the divine infinite oneness that they cannot resemble yet for which they ceaselessly strive.

BIBLIOGRAPHY

The Catholic Concordance, trans. Paul E. Sigmund. Cambridge: Cambridge University Press, 1991.

De ludo globi = The Game of Spheres, trans. Pauline Moffitt Watts. New York: Abaris, 1986.

Duclow, D. F. "Nicholas of Cusa." In *Dictionary of Literary Biography: Medieval Philosophers,* vol. 115, ed. J. Hackett. Detroit: Bruccoli Clark, 1992.

Flasch, K. *Nikolaus von Kues: Geschichte einer Entwicklung.* Frankfurt am Main: Klostermann, 1998.

Haubst, R. *Streifzuege in die cusanische Theologie.* Münster: Aschendorff, 1991.

————, et al., eds. *Mitteilungen und Forschungsbeiträge der Cusanus-Gesellschaft.* Mainz: Mattias-Grünewald, 1961 ff. [Cusanus journal, bibliographies in vols. 1, 3, 6, 10, 15].

Hopkins, Jasper, trans. *Nicholas of Cusa on Learned Ignorance.* Minneapolis: Banning, 1985.

Hopkins, J. *A Concise Introduction to the Philosophy of Nicholas of Cusa,* 3d ed. Minneapolis: Banning, 1986.

Idiota de mente = The Layman, about Mind, trans. Clyde Lee Miller. New York: Abaris, 1979.

Jacobi, K. ed. *Nikolaus von Kues: Einführung in sein philosophisches Denken.* Freiburg: Alber, 1979.

The Layman on Wisdom and the Mind, trans. M.L. Fuhrer. Ottawa: Dovehouse, 1989.

Li non aliud. English & Latin. Nicholas of Cusa on God as not-other, trans. Jasper Hopkins. 2d ed. Minneapolis: Banning, 1983.

Nicolai de Cusa Opera Omnia, Heidelberg Academy Edition. Lepzig/Hamburg: Miner, 1932 ff.

Nicholas of Cusa's Metaphysic of Contraction, trans. Jasper Hopkins. Minneapolis: Banning, 1983.

Nicholas of Cusa: Selected Spiritual Writings, trans. H. Lawrence Bond. New York: Paulist, 1997.

Opera. 3 vols., ed. Jacques LeFevre d'Etaples. Paris: J. Blade, 1514; rpt. Frankfurt: Minerva, 1962.

Clyde Lee Miller

Nicholas of Verdun (ca. 1150–ca. 1210)

A goldsmith and enamelist active in the late twelfth and early thirteenth centuries, Nicholas is known for the stylistic originality of his work. Two dated works inscribed with his name exist: the ambo, or pulpit, dated 1181 (and remodeled into an altarpiece in 1330), from the Augustinian Abbey of Klosterneuburg near Vienna, and the shrine of the Virgin in Tournai Cathedral, dated to 1205. The shrine of the Three Kings in Cologne Cathedral, usually dated to the 1190s, is also partially attributed to Nicholas. This large reliquary was built to house the relics of the Three Magi, which Archbishop Rainald von Dassel had received from Emperor Frederick Barbarossa in 1164. After Nicholas's creation of the shrine, the Magi, as examples of both the first Christian pilgrims and the first Christian kings, became closely associated with theories of German kingship and also with the city of Cologne, their crowns appearing on its coat of arms by the end of the thirteenth century.

In technical details and certain stylistic features, Nicholas's work is related to the general tradition of metalwork in the Rhine and Meuse valleys, a region known in the twelfth century for its sophistication. His work is particularly closely related to the Heribert Shrine, considered the major achievement in metalwork from this area in the second half of the century. As with other Mosan artists, Nicholas was accomplished in creating both champlevé (decorative enamel filling) plaques, such as those found on the Klosterneuburg ambo, and three-dimensional figures, which are found on the Three Kings' Shrine and that of the Virgin. In addition to reflecting Mosan traditions, Nicholas's work, both two- and three-dimensional, shows a new interest in the natural proportioning of the human body, the fall of cloth garments over it, and a type of soft drapery fold called *Muldenfaltenstil* (trough fold style), which is smoothly curved and unlike the angular, inorganic drapery found in Romanesque art. This drapery style, perhaps first appearing in Nicholas's work, becomes extremely popular in the years around 1200 in a variety of other works, including cathedral sculpture, such as that at Bamberg Cathedral, stained glass, and manuscripts. The sources for these components of Nicholas's art are a matter of controversy with contemporary Byzantine art, Ottonian art, early Christian art, and even Roman minor arts cited as possible works Nicholas may have studied to acquire classicizing elements.

In spite of great stylistic innovation, there is evidence that Nicholas had the help of theologians in designing the complex iconographies of his shrines. A plaque of the Mouth of Hell from the Klosterneuburg ambo features a sketch of the Three Marys at the Tomb on the back. This is believed to represent a trial composition whose subject was later modified by the theological advisers to better accommodate the typological meaning of the whole ambo. The complex relationships between the Three Magi and contemporary kings implied by the images of the Three Kings' Shrine are also thought to reflect the ideas of theologians, in this case persons associated with Cologne Cathedral.

BIBLIOGRAPHY

Dahm, Frederick. *Studien zur Ikonographie des Kloster-neuburger Emailwerkes des Nicholaus von Verdun.* Vienna: VWGO, 1989.

Ornamenta Ecclesiae: Kunst und Künstler der Romanik in Köln, ed. Anton Legner. 3 vols. Cologne: Schnütgen Museum, 1985, vol. 2, pp. 216–224, 447–455.

Swarzenski, Hans. "The Style of Nicholas of Verdun: Saint Armand and Reims," in *Gatherings in Honor of Dorothy R. Miner,* ed. U. E. McCracken et al. Baltimore: Walters Art Gallery, 1974, pp. 111–114.

Susan L. Ward

SEE ALSO

Cologne, Art; Klosterneuburg; Metalworking; Relics and Reliquaries

Nicolaus Gerhaert von Leyden, so-called Bärbel von Ottenheim (Frankfurt am Main, Liebieghaus-Museum alter Plastk). *Photograph: Liebieghaus-Museum/Werner Neumeister*

Nicolaus Gerhaert von Leyden (d. 1473)

A sculptor whose few surviving documented works are dispersed from Trier and Strasbourg to Vienna, Nicolaus Gerhaert von Leyden remains relatively unknown today even though his style influenced late Gothic sculpture throughout Germany. Of the surviving stone carvings attributed to him or to his school, only five are authenticated by documents or signatures. The earliest to display his new inner dynamism and portrait realism is the signed tomb effigy of Archbishop Jacob von Sierck, dated 1462, now in the Diocesan Museum in Trier. Originally the upper half of a two-tiered tomb with his decaying corpse below, the deeply cut effigy was undoubtedly made by a mature artist. His stay in Strasbourg, where Nicolaus was mentioned frequently in documents from 1463 to 1467 and where he became a citizen in 1464, is the best-documented and most productive period of his life. Here he was commissioned in 1464 to create the portal of the Neue Kanzlei (New Chancellery), on which busts appeared as if looking down from a window; only two heads survive: the so-called Bärbel von Ottenheim in the Liebieghaus Museum in Frankfurt and Count Jacob von Hanau-Lichtenberg in the Musée de l'Oeuvre Notre-Dame in Strasbourg. The Epitaph of Conrad von Busnang in the Chapel of St. John in the cathedral at Strasbourg, signed and dated 1464, provides the only comparison for Madonna statues attributed to his circle. In 1465–1467 he worked on the carved wood high altar for the Constance Minster that was later destroyed. His best-known work, the signed Crucifix for the Old Cemetery in Baden-Baden, now in the Stiftskirche there, was dated 1467. In the same year, in response to the second invitation of Emperor Frederick III, Nicolaus went to Vienna and Wiener Neustadt, where he was responsible for the tomb lid of the Emperor in the Apostle's Choir of St. Stephen in Vienna. Nicolaus died in 1473 and was buried in Wiener Neustadt. There are fewer documents from these last years, and they provide less certitude in regard to the extent of his work.

In spite of the widespread destruction of Netherlandish sculpture of the fifteenth century and a lack of study of French work of the same time, the stylistic origins of Nicolaus are generally agreed to lie in the Flemish-Burgundian region. The individualism of his portrait heads derives from those of Claus Sluter at Dijon, and his knowledge of the late work of Jan van Eyck is also generally accepted. His busts from the Chancellery at Strasbourg are often compared to the earlier figures above the entrance to the house of Jacques Coeur in Bourges. The new dynamism he infused into his figures together with their physical expressiveness and the drapery expanding into the surrounding space characterize his contribution to the new style. These characteristics also appear in the works of the Masters E.S. and Martin Schongauer, both working in the Rhineland at approximately the same time as Nicolaus; the engravings of these artists are partly responsible for the rapid spread of his style in the late fifteenth century.

The most convincing unsigned and undocumented work attributed to Nicolaus is the bust of a Meditating

Man in the Strasbourg museum, assumed to be a self-portrait, also from the New Chancellery. The Crucifixion Altar in Nördlingen and the Virgin of Dangolsheim in Berlin are frequently considered his early work or that of a sculptor close to him.

BIBLIOGRAPHY

Müller, Theodor. *Sculpture in the Netherlands, Germany, France and Spain 1400 to 1500.* Pelican History of Art 25. Harmondsworth: Penguin, 1966, pp. 79–87.

Recht, Roland. *"Nicolas de Leyde et la sculpture à Strasbourg (1460–1525)."* Ph.D. diss., Université des Sciences Humaines de Strasbourg, 1978. Strasbourg: Presses Universitaires de Strasbourg, 1987, pp. 115–151, 341–345.

Marta O. Renger

SEE ALSO

Constance; E. S., Master; Frederick III; Gothic Art and Architecture; Schongauer, Martin; Strasbourg; Trier; Vienna; Wiener Neustadt

Nobility and Farmers

Although there were aristocratic families in the Merovingian period descended from the Gallo-Roman population, there were clearly others who traced their roots to the Frankish past. By the Carolingian age, certain kindreds had asserted themselves to the forefront, claiming special privileges among the rest of the population. One such kindred was that of the Udalrichings, of which Charlemagne's wife, Hildegard, was a member. Her brothers, Ulrich and Gerold, took a prominent place, especially in Alemannia. During the reign of Louis the Pious, however, they were replaced by the "Welfs" from the area near Lake Constance.

It was from kinship groups such as the Udalrichings, Alahofings, Etichons, Hunfridings, and Matfridings that the Carolingian rulers chose those men whom they installed as dukes and counts throughout their realms. Some scholars argue that the real end of the Carolingian empire came at the end of the ninth century, as these royal appointees began to establish territorial lordships—or to regionalize, a process that continued into the thirteenth century and beyond. By about 1000 C.E., noble families and kinships began to style themselves after their residence and to push down roots where they held power and influence. At the same time, the old kindreds fragmented into various branches; for example, the comital

families of Bregenz, Buchhorn, Winterthur, Pfullendorf, and Heiligenberg, who flourished in the High Middle Ages, all claimed descent from the Udalrichings. In the sense of the period after about 1000, noble families did not exist in the Carolingian and Ottonian ages.

The society of ninth- and tenth-century Germany was predominantly agrarian; at the same time it was decidedly unequal. Nobles shared space with nonnoble freemen and with the unfree. If one accepts the image of the nobility found in the fragmentary late-eleventh-century Latin poem *Ruodlieb,* the nobility spent great amounts of time feasting, hunting, honing their skills with weapons of war, and engaging in various family- and church-oriented activities such as the establishment of religious foundations. Documents of the eleventh and twelfth centuries reveal that many members of the nobility were becoming vassals to both spiritual and temporal princes, often creating conflicts of interest as the same noble found it challenging to serve two lords.

Like the nobility, free peasants could have rights in land called allodial, and in Ottonian times at least they probably owed some sort of military service. Servile peasants did not enjoy these same privileges or obligations, although Germany seems to have had areas throughout the Middle Ages where serfdom barely reached, particularly in the Alpine regions of the south. In time, manumitted serfs, called *censuales,* appear who rendered an annual sum to their landlord. Peasants might occasionally rise above their status through intermarriage or preferment within the church, though in Cologne and several other bishoprics, membership in the cathedral chapter was restricted to members of the nobility. If literature accurately reflects reality, this upward striving turned to tragedy. The poem *Meier Helmbrecht,* composed about the middle of the thirteenth century by Werner "der Gärtner" (the Gardener), presents a vivid and realistic picture of the age of decaying chivalry, relating the story of a young peasant who, dissatisfied with his lowly social position, becomes a highwayman and is finally hanged by angry peasants.

The economic recovery of the Rhineland in the tenth century and the expansion of the arable land beyond the limits of the Merovingian and Carolingian periods contributed to the vitality of Ottonian Germany. This internal expansion was matched on the eastern frontier by agricultural expansion in the marks of Meißen and Lausitz, on Germany's eastern frontier, which saw peasant pioneers flow in from all over the realm. The effects of this migration, and the subsequent demographic changes, left its impact from the coasts of the Baltic to Bohemia and Carinthia. German peasants thus became major players in the economic development of Central and Eastern Europe during the High and later Middle Ages.

BIBLIOGRAPHY

Bergengruen, Alexander. *Adel und Grundherrschaft im Merowingerreich.* Wiesbaden: Steiner, 1958.

Brunner, Otto. *Land and Lordship: Stuctures of Governance in Medieval Austria,* trans. Howard Kaminsky and James Van Horn Melton. Philadelphia: University of Pennsylvania Press, 1984.

Dopsch, Alfons. *Die Wirtschaftsentwicklung der Karolingerzeit: vornehmlich in Deutschland.* 2 vols., 2d ed. Weimar, 1921; 3rd rev. ed. Cologne: Böhlau, 1962.

Hauck, Karl. "Haus- und sippengebundene Literatur mittelalterlicher Adelsgeschlechter." *Mitteilungen des Instituts für österreichischer Geschichtsforschung* 62 (1954).

Irsigler, Franz. *Untersuchung zur Geschichte des frühfränkischen Adels.* Bonn: Rohrscheid, 1969.

Mitteis, Heinrich. "Formen der Adelsherrschaft im Mittelalter," in *Festschrift Fritz Schulz.* Weimar: Böhlau, 1951.

Schmid, Karl. "Über die Struktur des Adels im früheren Mittelalter." *Jahrbuch für fränkische Landesforschung* 19 (1959).

———. "Zur Problematik von Familie, Sippe und Geschlecht, Haus und Dynastie beim mittelalterlichen Adel." *Zeitschrift für die Geschichte des Oberrheins* 105, N.F. 66 (1957): 1–62.

Schulte, Aloys. *Der Adel und die deutsche Kirche im Mittelalter: Studien zur Sozial-, Rechts- und Kirchengeschichte.* 1910, 3rd ed. Darmstadt: Wissenschaftliche Buchgesellschaft, 1958.

Schulze, Hans K. *Adelsherrschaft und Landesherrschaft.* Cologne: Böhlau, 1963.

Störmer, Wilhelm. *Früher Adel: Studien zur politischen Führungsschicht im fränkisch-deutschen Reich vom 8. bis 11. Jahrhundert.* 2 vols. Stuttgart: Hieremann, 1973.

Tellenbach, Gerd. "Vom karolingischen Reichsadel zum deutschen Reichsfürstenstand," in *Adel und Bauern im deutschen Staat des Mittelalters.* Leipzig, 1943; rpt. Darmstadt: Wissenschaftliche Buchgesellschaft, 1976.

Paul B. Pixton

SEE ALSO
Carolingians; Charlemagne; Louis the Pious; *Ruodlieb;* Welfs

Notke, Bernt (ca. 1440–1509)

Although born in Lassen in Pomerania, Notke centered his artistic career in northern Germany, in the Hansa city of Lübeck. He is best known for large sculpted altarpieces, which were installed in Hansa cities throughout the Baltic region including Tallinn, Estonia; Stockholm, Sweden; as well as Lübeck. Although known primarily for his sculpture, Notke was also a painter, printmaker, and goldsmith.

Notke's most notable projects include his triumphal cross in the Marenkirche in Lübeck and his St. George and the Dragon from the Storkyrka in Stockholm. The triumphal cross (1477) was a life-size wooden ensemble with Christ on the Cross, here in the form of a Tree of Jesse, accompanied by St. John, the Virgin, Mary Magdalene, the patron Bishop Krummedyk, and Adam and Eve. The St. George and the Dragon (1489) was made as a votive offering from Sten Sture, who defeated the Danes after praying to St. George in the Storkyrka; the sculpture also contained a burial place for Sture in the base. Although St. George's face is not individualized, his elaborate armor and horse are modeled on those of Sture. The fantastic dragon is decorated with real elk horns, and the princess looks on from a separate console, adding to the dramatic verve of the piece.

Notke's paintings include a Mass of St. Gregory in the Marienkirche in Lübeck and the wings of several altarpieces, including that at Aarhus. Notke created woodcuts of the Dance of Death (1480), perhaps related to his painted versions of the subject, and was also a talented metalworker, who was head of the Swedish mint (1490) and made the silver figure of St. George, now in the Museum für Kunst und Gerwerbe in Hamburg.

BIBLIOGRAPHY

Eimer, Gerhard. *Bernt Notke: Das Wirken eines niederdeutschen Küunstlers im Ostseeraum.* Bonn: Kulturstiftung der deutschen Vertriebenen, 1985.

Hasse, Max. *Das Triumphkreuz des Bernt Notke im Lübecker Dom.* Hamburg: Heinrich Ellermann, 1952.

Müller, Theodor. *Sculpture in the Netherlands, Germany, France, and Spain 1400–1500.* Pelican History of Art. Harmondsworth: Penguin, 1966, pp. 128–132.

Paatz, Walter. *Bernt Notke und sein Kreis.* Berlin: Deutscher Verein für Kunstwissenschaft, 1939.

Stoll, Karlheinz, Ewald M. Vettner, and Eike Oellermann. *Triumphkreuz im Dom zu Lübeck: Ein Meisterwerk Bert Notkes.* Wiesbaden: Reichert, 1977.

Susan L. Ward

SEE ALSO
Gothic Art and Architecture; Hanseatic League; Lübeck; Printmaking

Notker Labeo (ca. 950–1022)

Also known as Notker III and Notker Teutonicus (Notker the German), Notker Labeo (the lip) was a St. Gall monk and teacher best known for his Old High German translation-commentaries of Latin classroom texts. In a letter to Bishop Hugo of Sitten (ca. 1019–1020), Notker refers to the vernacular translation project on which he has embarked as something uncommon and revolutionary and notes that it may even shock his reader. He argues, however, that students can understand texts in their mother tongue much more easily than in Latin. Notker's translation method adopts contemporary glossing practices (syntactical, morphological, and lexical) and develops and integrates them into a continuous Latin/German text. First Notker often rearranges the word order of the original Latin into a variant of the so-called natural order, the *ordo naturalis,* a current pedagogic word order that roughly corresponds to a subject-verb-object typology. He then expands on the text with additional classroom commentary—either his own or culled from other sources—by providing synonyms, supplying any implied subjects or objects, expounding rhetorical figures and etymologies, and interpreting mythological figures. Finally Notker appends his Old High German translation, which is sprinkled with further explanation in the vernacular and occasional Latin terms, a kind of mixed prose *(Mischsprosa).*

In his letter to the bishop, Notker also includes a list of works he had finished, thereby providing us with a fairly accurate account of his corpus: Boethius, *De consolatione Philosophiae (On the Consolation of Philosophy);* Martianus Capella, *De nuptiis Philologiae et Mercurii* (On the Marriage of Philology and Mercury); Boethius's Latin versions of Aristotle's, *De categoriis* (Categories) and *De interpretatione* (On Interpretation), and, his most popular work, the Psalter (together with the *Cantica* and three catechistic texts). He also refers to several of his own classroom compositions, which contain translations of technical terms and/or examples in Old High German; among these are thought to be *De arte rhetorica* (On the Art of Rhetoric), *Computus* (Calculating the Calendar), *De definitione* (On Definition), *De musica* (On Music), *Partibus logicae* (On the Parts of Logic), and *De syllogismis* (On Syllogisms). A few Latin treatises produced in the St. Gall school may also have been compiled by him: *De dialectica* (On Dialectics), *Distributio* (Logic), and *The St. Gall Tractate.* Other translations listed by Notker have not survived: *Principia arithmetica* (Arithmetic Principles, by Boethius?), *De trinitate* (On the Trinity, by Boethius or Remigius of Auxerre?), Gregory the Great's *Moralia in Iob* (Moral Deliberations on the Book of Job), and Cato's *Distichs,* Vergil's *Bucolica,* and Terence's *Andria.* Notker's work did not find great resonance, and only the Psalter and several of the minor treatises are preserved outside of St. Gall.

Notker's late-tenth-century Alemannic marks an important transition period in the history of the German language. The extant eleventh-century St. Gall copies of his texts are recorded with a fairly consistent spelling, which modern scholars have interpreted to reflect guidelines that Notker imposed on the St. Gall scribes. They include the *Anlautgesetz* (devoicing initial voiced stops /b d g/ following a voiceless consonant and/or a pause and in compounds) and the use of the acute and circumflex accents to mark word and/or sentence stress and vowel length. Notker's lexicon has also received considerable scholarly attention, owing to the many new words he coined to render into Old High German the highly complex Latin terminology he was translating.

BIBLIOGRAPHY

Coleman, Evelyn S. "Bibliographie zu Notker III. von St. Gallen," in *Germanic Studies in Honor of Edward H. Sehrt.* Coral Gables, Fl.: University of Miami Press, 1968, pp. 61–76.

———. "Bibliographie zu Notker III. von St. Gallen: Zweiter Teil," in *Spectrum medii aevi.* Göppingen: Kümmerle, 1983, pp. 91–110.

De nuptiis Philologiae et Mercurii: Konkordanzen, Wortlisten und Abdruck des Textes nach dem Codex Sangallensis 872, ed. Evelyn S. Firchow. Hildesheim: Olms, 1999.

Ehrismann, Gustav. *Geschichte der deutschen Literatur bis zum Ausgang des Mittelalters.* Munich: Beck, 1932, pp. 416–458.

Hellgardt, Ernst. "Notker des Deutschen Brief an Bischof Hugo von Sitten," in *Befund und Deutung.* Tübingen: Niemeyer, 1979, pp. 169–192.

———. "Notker Teutonicus: Überlegungen zum Stand der Forschung." *Beiträge zur Geschichte der deutschen Sprache und Literatur* 108 (1986): 190–205 and 109 (1987): 202–221.

King, James, and Petrus Tax, eds. *Die Werke Notkers des Deutschen, Altdeutsche Textbibliothek.* 10 vols. Tübingen: Niemeyer, 1972–1996.

Notker der Deutsche. *De interpretatione: Boethius' Bearbeitung von Aristoteles' Schrift Peri hermeneias : Konkordanzen, Wortlisten und Abdruck des Textes nach dem Codex Sangallensis 818,* ed. Evelyn S. Firchow. Berlin: de Gruyter, 1995.

Notker der Deutsche von St. Gallen. Categoriae : Boethius' Bearbeitung von Aristoteles' Schrift Kategoriai : Konkordanzen, Wortlisten und Abdruck der Texte nach den Codices Sangallensis 818 and 825, ed. Evelyn S. Firchow. Berlin: de Gruyter, 1996.

Notker-Wortschatz, eds. Edward H. Sehrt und Wolfram K. Legner. Halle (Saale): Niemeyer, 1955. Sehrt, Edward H. *Notker-Glossar.* Tübingen: Niemeyer, 1962.

The St. Gall Tractate: A Rhetorical Guide to Classroom Syntax, eds. and trans. Anna Grotans and David Porter. Columbia, S.C.: Camden House, 1995.

Schröbler, Ingeborg. *Notker III. von St. Gallen als Übersetzer und Kommentator von Boethius' De consolatione Philosophiae.* Tübingen: Niemeyer, 1953.

Sonderegger, Stefan. *Althochdeutsch in St. Gallen.* St. Gallen: Ostschweiz, 1970.

———. *Althochdeutsche Sprache und Literatur,* 2d ed. Berlin: de Gruyter, 1987.

———. "Notker III. von St. Gallen," in *Die deutsche Literatur des Mittelalters: Verfasserlexikon,* vol. 6., 2d ed. Berlin: de Gruyter, 1987, cols. 1212–1236.

Tax, Petrus W. "Notker Teutonicus," in *Dictionary of the Middle Ages,* vol. 9. New York: Scribner's, 1987, pp. 188–190.

Anna A. Grotans

SEE ALSO
Bible; Boethius; Latin Language

Notker von Zwiefalten (fl. 1089–1090)

Postulated author of the *Memento mori* (remember death), a penitential rhymed sermon (nineteen strophes, seventy-six long lines with a lacuna, or gap, of indeterminate length between lines 61 and 62) composed between 1080 and 1090 by a monk named Notker, quite probably Notker the abbot of the reform monastery of Zwiefalten who died on March 6, 1095. The work exists only on the final pages of an eleventh-century parchment manuscript from the Monastery of Ochsenhausen in the Allgäu (Bibliothèque Nationale et Universitaire Strasbourg, manuscript no. cod. germ. 278, fol. 154v–155r), which also contains the seven strophes that comprise the Strasbourg version of the *Ezzolied.* The misleading title, *Memento mori,* was given to the work by its first editor, K. A. Barack, misleading because the work deals with life and not death, although it is likely that it was delivered during the season of penitence, Lent. The sermon was intended for members of the lay nobility.

The work, whose basic theme is the journey of the soul through the world toward ultimate union with God, comprises three parts: I, strophes 1–6, which describe the need for the journey and the dangers that beset the soul; II, strophes 7–11, in which a special danger is highlighted, namely, that the rich and powerful do not grant the poor and powerless the rights to which they have every just expectation. It is this one sin that can condemn the soul to hell (this section contains the lacuna); III, strophes 12–17, in which Notker returns to the theme of the journey through life with a concrete example of the type of correct behavior demanded, namely, the proper disposition of wealth. The final two strophes (18 and 19) are probably not original to the poem. Essentially, Notker is presenting the basic tenet of Christianity—love of neighbor—to demonstrate that while times may have indeed changed toward the end of the 11th century, the enduring admonitions of Christ have not.

BIBLIOGRAPHY

Barack, K. A., ed. *Ezzos Gesang von den Wundern Christi und Nokers "Memento mori" in phototypischen Faksimile der Straßburger Handschrift.* Strasbourg: Teubner, 1879.

Barack, K. A. "Althochdeutsche Funde." *Zeitschrift für deutsches Altertum* 23 (1879): 212–216.

Dittrich, Marlies. "Der Dichter des Memento mori." *Zeitschrift für deutsches Altertum* 72 (1935): 57–80.

Gentry, Francis G. "Noker's 'Memento mori'." *Allegorica* 5, no. 2. (1994): 7–18 [with trans. into English].

———. *Bibliographie zur frühmittelhochdeutschen geistlichen Dichtung.* Berlin: Schmidt, 1992, pp. 191–196.

———. "Noker's Memento mori and the Desire for Peace." *Amsterdamer Beiträge zur älteren Germanistik* 16 (1981): 25–62.

———. "Vruot . . . Verdamnot? Memento mori vv. 61–62." *Zeitschrift für deutsches Altertum* 108 (1979): 299–306.

Kaiser, Gert. "Das Memento mori. Ein Beitrag zum sozialgeschichtlichen Verständnis der Gleichheitsforderung im frühen Mittelalter." *Euphorion* 68 (1974): 337–370.

Kuhn, Hugo. "Minne oder reht," in *Dichtung und Welt im Mittelalter,* 2d ed. Stuttgart: Metzler, 1969.

Maurer, Friedrich, *Die religiösen Dichtungen des 11. und 12. Jahrhunderts. Nach ihren Formen besprochen und herausgegeben,* vol. 1. Tübingen: Niemeyer, 1964, pp. 249–259.

Rupp, Heinz. *Deutsche Religiöse Dichtungen des 11. und 12. Jahrhunderts. Untersuchungen und Interpretationen,* 2d ed. Bern: Francke, 1972, pp. 11–32.

Scholz-Williams, Gerhild. *The Vision of Death: A Study of the 'Memento mori' Expressions in some Latin, German and French Didactic Texts of the 11th and 12th Centuries.* Göppingen: Kümmerle, 1976, pp. 105–111.

Schützeichel, Rudolf. *Das alemanische Memento mori. Das Gedicht und der geistig-historische Hintergrund.* Tübingen: Niemeyer, 1962 [critical edition and trans. into German].

Francis G. Gentry

SEE ALSO
Ezzo

Numbers and Calculation

Ancient number systems were used for counting objects, and therefore the number concept was concrete and finite, consisting of unit fractions, submultiples (a new unit that is a fraction of a larger unit, e.g., foot/inch), and integers; "zero" represented the absence of objects. For higher bases, the linguistic and metrological number systems combined different multipliers chosen for their numerical qualities, such as those having many divisors (6, 10, 12, 20), often in combination with the numbers of sequence of doubling progression of base 2 (2,4,6,16,32, etc.). In these systems, early societies were able to perform the four basic operations of arithmetic.

The linguistic number words reveal that Germanic peoples mastered a decimal system of calculation based on the Indo-European system with terms for one, ten, and one hundred; the word *thousand* was common only to the Germanic language group. In all Germanic languages the numerals show vestiges of a peculiar duodecimal element, resulting in a change in the linguistic expression between twelve and thirteen, sixty and seventy, and an extension of the decades to 120, meaning "one hundred" (*Großhundert*—12 × 10, or six score *Stiege*) rather than "100"; "thousand" meant a *Großtausend* (120 × 10) rather than "1,000". Even though the Germanic languages had a decimal concept, it did not represent the concept of exponentiation of base ten because the numerals had several meanings. "Hundred" was a "long hundred" of "120" when counting objects, whereas in counting money, years, and in ecclesiastical contexts it was "100"; for weights "hundred" was 112 pounds (the "hundredweight"). The Roman numerals "C," "D," and "M" further complicate the issue, as their numerical values depended on what was being counted. A 20 count ("score") formed an alternative method of counting, and each multiple of the score had a specific name.

The earliest examples of "long hundreds" are indirect sources in Gothic (Ulfila's Gothic Bible translation, fourth century), whereas Salfranconian *chunntualepti* (in the *Salian Law*) meant "120". "Long hundred" numerals are found in Old Norse, Old English, and Middle Scottish grammars, and in coinage (1 pound = 20 shillings = 240 *denarii*). Counting "six score to the hundred" continued far into the modern period as a method of accounting in the Royal Scottish administration, in Icelandic land taxation (until 1915), and was used for counting the leaves of the renowned Irish manuscript *The Book of Kells* in 1588. Long after the "long hundred" had disappeared from the language, it was used for counting by the piece in Baltic and North Sea trade and fishing, for counting commodities such as turf, planks, fish, cloth, fruit, vegetables, and eggs.

Calculation was performed by casting counters on a counting table *(Rechenbrett).* The result was recorded by incisions on tally sticks *(Kerbholz)* or by writing the number word, which sometimes was abbreviated into peculiar Roman numerals.

Medieval arithmetic was a theoretical discipline (Boethius, Isidore of Seville) that did not relate to practical calculation. Walther von Speier studied the abacus in St. Gall and wrote on practical arithmetic in *Ritmimachia* (Number Fight, 983). Gerbert (later Pope Sylvester II) brought Arabic science from Spain after 967. Arabic numerals began to occur around 1300 and became widely used around 1500 and thereafter. The ten numerals, the positional system, and decimal fractions revolutionized calculation after the Middle Ages.

BIBLIOGRAPHY

Barnard, Francis Pierrepoint. *The Casting-Counter and the Counting-Board.* Oxford: Clarendon, 1916.

Menninger, Karl. *Number Words and Number Symbols: A Cultural History of Numbers,* trans. Paul Broneer. New York: Dover, 1992.

Neumann, H-P. "Duodezimalsystem," in *Reallexikon der germanischen Altertumskunde,* 2d ed., ed. Herbert Jankuhn et al. Berlin: de Gruyter, 1968ff.

Ulff-Møller, Jens. "Arithmetic and Metrology in the British Isles and Iceland," in *Acta Metrologicae Historicae,* no. 5, ed. Harald Witthöft and Karl Jürgen Roth. St. Katharinen, Austria: Scripta Mercaturae, 1999, pp. 63–82.

Jens Ulff-Møller

SEE ALSO

Nuremberg

From the mid fourteenth to the sixteenth centuries, the city (German, *Nürnberg*) was among Europe's foremost artistic and mercantile centers. Located in sandy forests of middle Franconia within the diocese of Bamberg, Nuremberg was selected by Emperor Henry III (r. 1039–1056) as the site for a small castle and, in 1050, a chartered town. Nuremberg's fate was long linked with both the Holy Roman emperors and the Hohenzollern kings and burggraves. Rudolf I (r. 1273–1291) made it an imperial free city. Ludwig the Bavarian (r. 1314–1347) granted Nuremberg freedom from external legal jurisdiction and gave it custodial control of the imperial castle. In the Golden Bull of 1356, which formalized the imperial election process, Charles IV (r. 1355–1378), a frequent visitor, designated Nuremberg as the site of the inaugural diet of each new emperor. Under Charles's son, King Sigismund, the imperial relics and regalia were permanently transferred to Nuremberg in 1424, where they were stored in the Heilig-Geist-Kirche (Church of the Holy Spirit) and displayed annually until 1523 in the main market. The city ordered the Schöner Brunnen (Beautiful Fountain; planned 1370, erected 1385–1396), with its statues of the electors, for the market to commemorate its special position as one of the important imperial cities. As the community grew on both sides of the Pegnitz River, it was ringed by a common wall in about 1320. The walls had to be expanded again between 1377 and 1430 to accommodate the burgeoning population,

Nuremberg, St. Sebaldus, north door: Death, Funeral, and Coronation of the Virgin. *Photograph: Joan A. Holladay*

Nuremberg, castle, entrance. *Photograph: Joan A. Holladay*

which by 1500 had doubled to about 45,000–50,000 inhabitants. These fortifications, much of which are still extant, included 128 observation towers and walls averaging almost eight meters high.

Early views of Nuremberg, such as in Hartmann Schedel's *Liber chronicarum (Nuremberg Chronicle, 1493),* stress the city's majestic skyline dominated by the castle (Kaiserburg), its many church spires, its rich stock of stone houses, and its mighty defensive walls. Nuremberg boasted two great parish churches (St. Sebaldus and St. Lorenz), two dependent churches (Frauenkirche and St. Jakob), nine major monasteries, and a host of cemetery churches, hospitals, chapels, and other religious establishments. St. Sebaldus, which served the northern half of the city, is mentioned as early as 1070, when the faithful came to worship the saint's relics. The present, double-choir church was begun in 1230 with its western choir and nave. These sections contrast vividly with the much wider, airier hall-style choir erected between 1361 and 1372. St. Lorenz, situated south of the river and on the

site of an earlier chapel, is slightly newer in date. Shortly after the nave and crossing (1270–1350) were finished, Charles IV helped to fund the elaborately sculptured west facade (1355–1360). Between 1439 and 1477 Konrad Heinzelmann, Konrad Roritzer, and Jakob Grimm built the substantial hall choir. Both St. Sebaldus and St. Lorenz still retain much of their original decoration. Unlike churches in many other important Protestant towns, only some of their art was removed when Nuremberg embraced Lutheranism in 1525. The local patrician families vied with each other in endowing altars, erecting epitaphs, and commissioning sculptures and stained glass windows. Both churches offer rich surveys of Nuremberg's artistic talent between about 1350 and the Reformation. Like the two parish churches, the small Frauenkirche (Church of Our Lady, 1352–1358) and the Augustinian monastery (1479–1485), demolished in 1816, were hall-style churches. The former stands between the main and fruit markets on the site of a Jewish synagogue that was razed in 1349. Just north of the main market is the Rathaus (city hall). Extensive portions of the medieval building survive, including the vast great hall (1332–1340) where imperial diets, patrician dances, a legal court, and other events were held.

Situated on major trade routes, Nuremberg thrived from its commercial ties with Italy, Bohemia, and the rest of Europe. In the fifteenth and early sixteenth centuries it supported a remarkably large community of artists and artisans. These were divided into two groups—the sworn and the free. The sworn artists, notably the metalworkers, were those whose productions were deemed essential to Nuremberg's economic well-being. Annually they pledged allegiance and promised not to leave Nuremberg without the city council's permission. By contrast, the council sought to encourage the other arts by removing most barriers other than basic rules about training. Painters, printmakers, sculptors, and glaziers, among others, could settle in Nuremberg far more easily than in most other towns. It was the city council rather than guilds, which had been dissolved in 1349, that regulated all the trades.

Nuremberg's metalworkers were especially renowned. Importing ores and other metals from Bohemia, Saxony, Thuringia, and Swabia, artisans produced everything from humble sewing needles to sumptuous goldsmith cups to ornamented armor, much of which was exported. In the 1490s Hans Frey devised intricate table fountains, while another anonymous goldsmith fashioned the renowned Schlüsselfelder Ship in 1503 (Nuremberg, Germanisches Nationalmuseum). At a height of 79 cm, this is a wine pitcher in the form of a three-masted sailing ship perched on a twin-tailed mermaid. Gilt silver sailors man the guns and climb the riggings. Such works were destined for a highly sophisticated clientele. Ludwig Krug, Melchior Baier, and their peers also supplied costly reliquaries and liturgical objects. In 1514 Nuremberg registered 129 goldsmiths. The city's redsmiths, who worked in brass and bronze, were also quite prominent. Between 1462 and 1496 Nuremberg was home to 165 master redsmiths. Foremost among these was the Vischer family, who supplied tombs, epitaphs, memorials, and, later, small-scale sculptures to clients across Central Europe. Their skill is evident in the huge Tomb of St. Sebaldus that Peter Vischer the Elder and his sons completed in 1519 for the parish church. Other metalworkers made Nuremberg a leader in the production of portrait medals beginning in the late 1510s.

The city reached its greatest fame during the lifetime of Albrecht Dürer (1471–1528). Talented sculptors such as Veit Stoss and Adam Krafft enriched both parish churches. For the St. Lorenzkirche Stoss carved the polychromed (multicolored) limewood Angelic Salutation (1517–1518), an over life-size Annunciation within a rosary, that hangs before the high altar. Nearby stands Krafft's sacrament house (1493) with its realistic self-portrait statue seemingly supporting the 18.7 meter tall stone tabernacle. Pioneers like Dürer's godfather, the publisher Anton Koberger, and his teacher, Michael Wolgemut, recognized the emerging potentials of the print and the illustrated book to reach audiences across the continent when they collaborated on the Schatzbehalter (Treasury, 1491) and the *Liber chronicarum* (*Book of Time,* 1493). Two decades later there were dozens of printmakers and publishers creating books, religious prints, and, with the advent of the Reformation, often polemical broadsheets.

The Reformation, with its attendant religious and political upheavals plus broader shifts in European trade toward the Atlantic, affected Nuremberg's artists. Goldsmiths suffered far less than painters and sculptors from the waning of religious commissions. The city rediscovered and celebrated its medieval and Renaissance heritage in the early nineteenth century. Nuremberg still retained most of its older architectural heritage until the devastating bombings of 1945. Only a fraction of these structures were reconstructed after the war.

BIBLIOGRAPHY

Fehring, Günter P., and Anton Ress. *Die Stadt Nürnberg.* Bayerische Kunstdenkmale 10, 2d ed., ed. Wilhelm Schwemmer. Munich: Deutscher Kunstverlag, 1977.

Gothic and Renaissance Art in Nuremberg, 1300–1550. New York: Metropolitan Museum of Art, 1986.

Kohlhaussen, Heinrich. *Nürnberger Goldschmiedekunst des Mittelalters und der Dürerzeit 1240 bis 1540.* Berlin: Deutscher Verlag für Kunstwissenschaft, 1968.

Mende, Matthias. *Das alte Nürnberger Rathaus,* vol. 1. Nuremberg: Stadtgeschichtliche Museen Nürnberg, 1979.

Mitteilungen des Vereins für Geschichte der Stadt Nürnberg. 1878ff. [series of publications].

Pfeiffer, Gerhard, ed. *Nürnberg: Geschichte einer europäischen Stadt.* Munich: Beck, 1971.

Pfeiffer, Gerhard, and Wilhelm Schwemmer. *Geschichte Nürnbergs in Bilddokumenten,* 3d ed. Munich: Beck, 1977.

Schleif, Corine. *Donatio et Memoria: Stifter, Stiftungen und Motivationen an Beispielen aus der Lorenzkirche in Nürnberg.* Munich: Deutscher Kunstverlag, 1990.

Schwemmer, Wilhelm. *Das Bürgerhaus in Nürnberg.* Das deutsche Bürgerhaus 16. Tübingen: E. Wasmuth, 1972.

Smith, Jeffrey Chipps. *Nuremberg: A Renaissance City, 1501–1618.* Austin: University of Texas Press, 1983.

Strauss, Gerald. *Nuremberg in the Sixteenth Century: City Politics and Life between Middle Ages and Modern Times,* 2d ed. Bloomington: Indiana University Press, 1976.

Strieder, Peter. *Tafelmalerei in Nürnberg 1350 bis 1550.* Königstein im Taunus: K. Robert, 1993.

Jeffrey Chipps Smith

SEE ALSO

Charles IV; Gothic Art and Architecture; Gutenberg, Johann; Jewish Art and Architecture; Kraft, Adam; Printmaking; Wolgemut, Michael

Nutrition

See Diet and Nutrition.

Oliver of Paderborn (d. 1224)

Oliver of Paderborn (North Rhine-Westphalia) appears as the scholastic at Paderborn in the waning years of the twelfth century. His reputation was such, however, that by 1202 he had been appointed scholastic at Cologne Cathedral. In 1207 we find him in Paris, where he acted as the mediator between a canon from Reims and the monastery of St. Remy. Presumably, he had been attending the schools of Paris at the time. The following year, he appears in southern France, apparently as a preacher against the Albigensians. At this time, he established his lifelong friendship with Jacques de Vitry and Robert de Courçon, both of whom became well-known preachers of the Fifth Crusade in France.

In the papal encyclical *Quia maior nunc* of May 1213, Oliver was named as one of several crusade-preachers for Germany, with specific duties in the ecclesiastical province of Cologne. Assisting him was *magister* (master) Hermann, dean of St. Cassius's Church in Bonn. Over the next four years, he and his colleagues crisscrossed Germany, convening assemblies of people and exploiting every opportunity to present their message and enlist support for the crusade. They were armed with letters of indulgence with which to entice and reward participants. Following the Fourth Lateran Council in Rome (at which Oliver was also present), he and the other preachers were also charged with collecting the half-tithe that Innocent III had imposed on the clergy as a means of providing financial support for the crusade.

In the summer of 1217 the first company of warriors departed by ship from the Lower Rhine. Among them was Oliver himself, who played a vital role in the campaign against Damietta in the Nile delta. His *Historia* of this event and his other writings and letters make him the best known of the German preachers. Only after the fall of Damietta to the Muslims on September 8, 1221, did Oliver return to Cologne, where he appears again in the spring of 1222.

In 1223 Oliver was elected bishop of Paderborn. He never really occupied the office, however, having first resumed his role as crusade-preacher in 1224, and shortly thereafter being elevated to the cardinal-bishopric of St. Sabina. One sees the influence of his fellow German, Conrad of Urach, and perhaps also of Cardinal Robert de Courçon, in this appointment. Like Conrad, however, Oliver lived but a short time after donning the cardinal's hat; he died the same year.

BIBLIOGRAPHY

Hoogeweg, Hermann. "Der Kölner Domscholaster Oliver als Kreuzprediger." *Westdeutsche Zeitschrift für Geschichte und Kunst* 7 (1888): 237ff.

———. *Die Schriften des Kölner Domscholasters, späteren Bischofs von Paderborn und Kardinalbischof von S. Sabina Oliverus.* Stuttgart: Litterarischer Verein, 1894.

———. "Die Kreuzpredigt des Jahres 1224 in Deutschland mit besonderer Rücksicht auf die Erzdiözese Köln." *Deutsche Zeitschrift für Geschichtswissenschaft* 4 (1890): 54ff.

Pixton, Paul B. "Die Anwerbung des Heeres Christi: Prediger des Fünften Kreuzzuges in Deutschland." *Deutsches Archiv* 34 (1978): 166–191.

Paul B. Pixton

SEE ALSO

Conrad of Urach; Crusades

Onomastics

[This entry includes four subentries:

Introduction
Personal Names
Toponyms
Chrematonyms]

Introduction

Onomastics is the study of names and how names are given. A name is one or more words designating an individual person, place, or thing as an entity. Names are important in that they allow the bearer to be located in space and time. *Sine nomine persona non est* (No name, no person) goes a Roman legal proverb. Since names (proper nouns) are of persons, places, or things, we usually divide the subject up into personal names (anthroponyms), place names (toponyms), and names of things (chrematonyms, a less commonly used term); these may then be broken into any number of subcategories: tribal names (ethnonyms), names of bodies of water (hydronyms), and so on.

Personal Names

Although one could have just a single-stem name, such as *Karl, Hengist, Wulfila,* or *Hraban,* the Germanic tribes inherited from their Indo-European ancestors the habit of dithematic (bipartite) personal names: *Hilti-brant, Wolf-ram, Diet-rich,* and the like. Common second components of men's names are *-hari, -wolf, -balt,* and *-helm;* of women's names, *-gund, -hilt, -rûn,* and *-lint.* There was a tendency to give a "first name" plus an attribute, *Karl der Große* (Charles the Great), *Ludwig der Fromme* (Louis the Pious), *Ludwig der Dicke* (Louis the Fat). Again, as in Indo-European, these bipartite names might be shortened, usually into *n*-stems, and names from baby talk were not unusual: *Pappo, Mammo, Pippo, Poppo, Dhuoda.* Hypocoristics such as *Ebbo* (Eberhard), *Ezzo,* and *Anno* are also common. There were in general no family names, though the family or place of origin might be indicated. One cannot say that the Germanic tribes used patronymics, but there was a tendency to refer to the parent: *Hiltibrant, Heribrantes sunu,* and Modern German *Mommsen.* Finally, there was a tendency to give (three) alliterating names within a family: *Heribrant, Hiltibrant, Hadubrant; Gunther, Gîselher, Gêrnôt.* Because of the Latinate nature of Carolingian culture and its transmission, many of our names are known primarily in Latin form: *Hrabanus Maurus, Walahfrid Strabo, Notker Labeo.*

As we move toward Middle High German, the old dithematic names become less common or lose their meaning, and foreign names become more common, such as saints' names and biblical names: *Johannes, Peter, Andreas.* There was a remarkable increase in shortening of names, and *Dietrich* might yield many variants: *Dieto, Dietel, Dietze, Dirk, Thilo, Tymme.* Even biblical and saints' names might yield hypocoristics: *Beppo (Josef), Tönnies (Antonius).* Cognomina naturally increased as a means of differentiation, and we see the beginning of surnames, often from place names: *von Eschenbach, von der Vogelweide, von Aue, von Straßburg,* then from occupations, and so on. Ecclesiastical *(Bischof, Probst),* and literary names *(Artus, Biterolf)* were often used.

There was a tradition of name play in literary onomastics, as in St. Jerome's *Nominum interpretatio.* We find such things as Otfrid's acrostic and teleostic, Wolfram's "etymology" of *Parzival* (140,16f.), such place names as *Munsalvæsche,* even the *argumentum a nomine (nomen est omen).* In the religious sphere, name play was already found in the Bible, and it was extended during our period. The use of cognomina led to such things as "the 72 names of God" and to the hundreds of epithets applied to Mary, collected by Salzer, such as *mersterne (Stella maris), Aarons gerte (virga Aaron), beslozzener garte (hortus conclusus),* used so effectively by Walther.

Toponyms

As in the case of personal names, place names may also be simple, as *Köln* (Cologne), *Rîn* (Rhine), or compound. In the case of the compounds, it is useful to divide them into a first component, an adjective or a noun (determinant), and a second component (nucleus). The nucleus normally refers to some natural feature of the landscape: 1. names connected with streams, bodies of water: *-bach, -ach, -furt, -bronn, -weiher;* 2. islands: *-werder, -werd, -wörth;* 3. mountains and hills: *-höhe, -berg, -halde;* 4. woods: *-hart, -lohe, -forst;* 5. fields: *-au, -ried, -lar, -heide;* and so on.

As we move toward Middle High German, we note that the clearing of land gives us new names reflecting this activity: *-reut, -rode, riute, -schwand, -brand, -hagen, -hain,* and so forth. Expansion to the east led to the use of Slavic names, for example, *Leipzig, Dresden,* and *Berlin.* The expansion of cities and knighthood led to an increase in such nuclei as *-stadt* and *-burg.* The wider contact with the outside world occasioned by the Crusades led to many new or renewed geographical names: *Pülle* (also called *Apulia),* and *Bern* (as in *Dietrich von Bern; also* called *Verona).*

Chrematonyms

Names for things reflect the native taxonomy of medieval Germany, and they do not always overlap with modern nomenclature. Favorite dogs, horses, swords get names, often foreign ones: *Hiudan, Buzival* (Alexander's horse), *Durendart* (Roland's sword). Along with pet names, the beast epic and the fable brought in such names as *Reinhart* and *Ysengrin.* In Latin, it was common to use such terms as *Brunellus* (ass), and kennings such as *sonipes* "horse" and *corniger* "cow." The rise of the chancellery languages, with their circumlocutions and alliterating formulas *(Land und Leute, Hand und Habe),* created many new words, and the increase in words in *-heit* in the language of the mystics has been noted.

Onomastics reflects the culture and history of the nation and forms a valuable resource for their study.

BIBLIOGRAPHY

Bach, Adolf. *Deutsche Namenkunde,* 2d ed. 3 vols. in 5. Heidelberg: Winter, 1952–1956 [the standard work].

Beiträge zur Namenforschung. Heidelberg: Winter, 1949 ff. [journal and series valuable particularly for its supplements].

Besch, Werner, Oskar Reichmann, and Stefan Sonderegger, eds. *Sprachgeschichte. Ein Handbuch zur Geschichte der deutschen Sprache und ihrer Erforschung.* vol. 2, no. 16. "Deutsche Namengeschichte im Überblick." Berlin: de Gruyter, 1985, cols. 2039–2163 [bibliography].

Förstemann, Ernst. *Altdeutsches Namenbuch,* vol. 1, 2d ed. Bonn, 1900; rpt. Munich, 1966; vol. 2, 3, ed. Hermann Jellinghaus. Bonn, 1913–1916; rpt. Munich: Beck, 1967.

Gillespie, George T. *A Catalogue of Persons Named in German Heroic Literature (700–1600) Including Named Animals and Objects and Ethnic Names.* Oxford: Oxford University Press, 1973.

Onoma. Louvain: International Centre of Onomastics, 1950 ff. [annual bibliography].

Salzer, Anselm. *Die Sinnbilder und Beiworte Mariens in der deutschen Literatur und lateinischen Hymnenpoesie des Mittelalters.* 1886–1894, rpt. Darmstadt: Wissenschaftliche Buchgesellschaft, 1967.

Schwarz, Ernst. *Deutsche Namenforschung.* 2 vols. Göttingen, 1949–1950.

Steger, Hugo, ed. *Probleme der Namenforschung im deutschsprachigen Raum.* Darmstadt: Wissenschaftliche Buchgesellschaft, 1977 [essays].

James W. Marchand

SEE ALSO

Hildebrandslied; Wolfram von Eschenbach

Oorlag

See Grimbergse Oorlag, De.

Ordinatio Imperii

In 817, Louis the Pious, perhaps motivated by a recent accident, met with the leaders of the realm to determine the Frankish empire's fate. Louis decided to establish a succession plan, the *Ordinatio Imperii,* based on the idea of the empire's unity. Louis, after seeking divine inspiration, bestowed the succession on his eldest son, Lothar, and granted his other sons, Louis and Pippin, royal authority over subkingdoms in the eastern and western parts of the empire. Sovereign in their own territory, the younger sons would be subject to the authority of Lothar once Louis died. This attempt at establishing the empire's unity was not met with uniform support. The settlement was met by passive resistance from the Franks, whose tradition favored divided succession, and by active opposition in the failed revolt of Louis's nephew, Bernard, king in Italy. The *Ordinatio*'s later history was troubling for Louis, who revised the plan of succession to include a fourth son, Charles the Bald, and was accused of violating the document, and thus violating God's will, by Louis's enemies in the revolts of the 830s.

BIBLIOGRAPHY

Ganshof, F. L. "Some Observations on the *Ordinatio Imperii* of 817," in *The Carolingians and the Frankish Monarchy,* trans. Janet Sondheimer. London: Longman, 1971, pp. 273–288.

Ordinatio Imperii. Monumenta Germaniae Historica. Ch. 1. Hannover: Hahn, pp. 270–273.

"The *Ordinatio Imperii* of 817." in *Carolingian Civilization: A Reader,* trans. Paul Edward Dutton. Peterborough, Ontario: Broadview Press, 1993, pp. 176–179.

Michael Frassetto

SEE ALSO
Carolingians; Louis the Pious

Ortnit

See Wolfdietrich *and* Ortnit.

Osnabrück

The medieval city of Osnabrück was established as a bishopric ca. 780 by Charlemagne, who donated relics of Saints Crispin and Crispinian of Soissons to the cathedral of St. Peter. (They are now preserved in two gable shrines of the 1220s in the Diocesan Museum.) The first city wall was erected in the twelfth century around the Altstadt (old town). Excavations under the Church of St. Katharine in 1990 unearthed a twelfth-century centrally planned cruciform church, its western arm polygonal and reminiscent of the Ottonian church of the women's abbey in Essen. An inner circle of eight columns, possibly forming a Holy Sepulchre, is located in the center of this western arm.

In the Middle Ages, the thirteenth century was the period of the greatest prosperity for Osnabrück, which joined the Hanseatic League in 1246 and gained increasing civic autonomy from the bishop. The Neustadt (new town) surrounding the Altstadt was incorporated into the town around 1300. The Kaiserpokal, a silver-gilt cup of the late thirteenth century preserved in the town hall, is the most important medieval secular artwork in Osnabrück, although its origin and early history are unknown. The present Rathaus (town hall), erected and decorated with statuary circa 1500, replaced earlier thirteenth-century buildings.

The present Gothic cathedral with three aisles and domical ribbed vaults was begun in 1218 and dedicated in 1277. Its furnishings include a bronze baptismal font of 1217 and a monumental wooden crucifix of the 1230s. A number of churches were built in the city during the second half of the thirteenth and early fourteenth centuries: the Johanniskirche, Marienkirche, and Katharinenkirche, dedicated respectively to Saint John, the Virgin, and Saint Katherine—all three-aisle hall churches—and the single-nave church of the Dominicans. From the portal of the Marienkirche, the Coronation of the Virgin from the tympanum and figures of the Church (*Ecclesia*) and Synagogue (*Synagoga*) and the Wise and Foolish Virgins from the jambs are all now preserved in the Kulturgeschichtliches Museum. Two thirteenth-century polychrome wooden (multicolored) crucifixes are preserved in

the church. A richly illuminated gradual of circa 1300, known as the Codex Gisle, from the Cistercian convent in the neighboring village of Rulle (now in the Bischöfliches Generalvikariat), a chalice from Rulle in the Diöcesanmuseum, and a silver-gilt abbess's staff of circa 1380 from the Benedictine convent of St. Gertrud (now in the Kestner Museum in Hanover) reflect the wealth of the local nunneries. The goldsmith Johannes Dalhoff was active in the city in the mid-fifteenth century. His extant works include the shrine of St. Cordula and a *Gnadenstuhl* (Throne of Grace) reliquary, both in the Diöcesanmuseum today.

By the late fifteenth century Osnabrück had a population of ten thousand, and its continued prosperity is reflected in the new square ambulatory added to the cathedral, the east end of the Marienkirche, the tower, east end, and vaulting of the Katharinenkirche, as well as the erection of the present Rathaus.

BIBLIOGRAPHY
Borchers, Walter, et al. *Der Osnabrücker Domschatz.* Osnabrück: Wenner, 1974.
Dolfen, Christain. *Codex Gisle.* Berlin: Buchenau und Reichert, 1926.
Feldwisch-Dentrup, Heinrich. *Dom und Domschatz in Osnabrück.* Die Blauen Bücher. Königstein im Taunus: K. Langwiesche, 1980.
Kühne, Udo, Bernhard Tönnies, and Anette Haucap. *Mittelalterliche Handschriften in Niedersachsen, Kurzkatalog 2: Handschriften in Osnabrück: Bischöfliches Archiv, Gymnasium Carolinum, Bischöfliches Generalvikariat,* Kulturgeschichtliches Museum, Niedersächsisches Staatsarchiv, Diözesanmuseum, Pfarrarchiv St. Johann. Wiesbaden: Harrasowitz, 1993.
Osnabrücker Kulturschätze vom Mittelalter bis zum Renaissance. Bonn: Niedersächsische Landesvertretung, 1989.
Stadt im Wandel: Kunst und Kultur des Bürgertums in Norddeutschland 1150–1650. 4 vols. Stuttgart: Cantz, 1985.

Judith H. Oliver

SEE ALSO
Charlemagne; Essen; Gothic Art and Architecture; Iconographies, Innovative

Oswald von Wolkenstein (1376 or 1377–1445)

No other medieval German poet is better known to us today than the South Tyrolean Oswald von Wolkenstein.

Apart from amazingly concrete autobiographical references contained in his large oeuvre of 133 songs, the poet also left a vast number of historical traces in more than one thousand still extant documents. Even though the poetic statements about his own life have often to be taken as tongue-in-cheek and as topical in nature, recent research by Anton Schwob and others who have studied the archival material has confirmed most of Oswald's claims in his songs regarding his personal experiences. Born as the second son of an aristocratic South Tyrolean family, Oswald had to struggle for many years to establish his own existence both on the local and the international level. In 1401 he participated in a military campaign in Italy of the German King Ruprecht of the Palatinate; in 1410 he went on a pilgrimage to the Holy Land; between 1413 and 1415 he served Bishop Ulrich of Brixen and subsequently joined the diplomatic service of King Sigismund, with whom he traveled through western Europe. In 1417 Oswald married Margaretha von Schwangau and thus gained the rank of an imperial knight. In 1420–1421 he participated in one of the several wars against the always victorious Hussites, but in one of his songs ("Kl[ein]. [no.] 27") Oswald ridiculed the opponents. In the following years the poet was involved in many struggles and military conflicts with his neighbors, both peasants and aristocrats, and so also with the duke of Tyrol, Frederick IV of Habsburg. A major bone of contention was the castle Hauenstein in Seis am Schlern, to which Oswald had only a partial claim but which he took in his total possession after his marriage. At one point he even ended up in the ducal prison (1421–1422) and had to pay a huge ransom to be released. Although Oswald's power position improved over the next years to some degree, he was imprisoned again in 1427 and then had finally to submit under the centralized government of Duke Frederick. In 1429 Oswald joined the secret but highly influential court of justice, Feme, which was active all over Germany, and he also managed to consolidate his power base back home through manifold political connections and public services. In recognition of his accomplishments as diplomat and imperial servant, Oswald was inducted into the Order of the Dragon in 1431. In 1432 King Sigismund, while he stayed in northern Italy, called him into his service again and soon after sent him as one of his representatives to the Council of Basel. In 1433 Oswald probably witnessed the coronation of Sigismund as emperor at the hand of Pope Eugene IV in Rome. In 1434 Oswald participated in the imperial diet of Ulm, where Sigismund commissioned him to collect fines and

taxes in South Tyrol and also confirmed his rank as imperial knight. After the death of Duke Frederick, Oswald and his allies successfully organized opposition against the Habsburgians in South Tyrol, as they could influence and dominate the young successor, Duke Sigmund, at that time still under age, for several years. Ultimately, however, the landed gentry, and so the Wolkenstein family, increasingly lost ground and had to submit to the centralized government, the growing weight of the urban class, and even the economic power of the peasants.

Whereas Oswald's political career sheds significant light on the political and economic history of the early fifteenth century, his poetic production has earned him greatest respect among modern philologists and musicologists since the full rediscovery of this amazing literary personality as of the early 1960s. In contrast to most other medieval poets Oswald created his songs for personal reasons and commissioned his first personal collection of his works in 1425, manuscript A, to which he added songs until 1436, perhaps even 1441. In 1432 the second collection was completed, manuscript "B," in which Oswald also incorporated a stunning portrait of himself created by the Italian Renaissance painter Antonio Pisanello or one of his disciples while the poet was staying in Piacenza, Italy, in the entourage of King Sigismund. Both manuscripts were most likely produced in Neustift, near Brixen, and contain melodies for many of the songs. In 1450 Oswald's family had another copy of his songs made in a paper manuscript ("c"—by convention, paper manuscripts are listed by lowercase, parchment by uppercase letters), which is almost identical with manuscript "B" but lacks the notations.

Although twenty of Oswald's more traditional songs were also copied in a number of other song collections all over Germany throughout the fifteenth and sixteenth centuries (the last one in 1572), the poet was soon forgotten after his death, probably because his most important songs were too autobiographical and idiosyncratic, and also too innovative for his time. Some of the texts contain surprisingly erotic elements and seem to reflect Oswald's private experiences with his wife. His prison songs and his dawn songs are unique for his time, and so the various polyglot songs in which he combined a string of languages to present his own linguistic mastership. On the one hand Oswald demonstrated a thorough familiarity with conventional German courtly love song, or *Minnesang;* on the other he introduced melodies and poetic images from French, Flemish, and Italian contemporaries. Many of Oswald's songs are polyphonic and reflect an amazing variety of musical forms, such as the *caccia* (hunt, Kl. 52), or the *lauda* (praise, Kl. 109).

Hardly any other poet before him had such an excellent command of the broadest range of lyrical genres, as his oeuvre contains marriage songs, spring songs, prison songs, war songs, autobiographical songs, travel songs, dawn songs, Marian hymns, calendar songs, Shrovetide songs, songs about city life, songs in which he criticized both the rich merchants and the arrogant courtiers, various religious songs, and repentance songs.

Oswald was also a master of onomatopoetic expressions, such as in his Kl. 50, where the arrival of spring is vividly conveyed through the imitation of birdsongs. He seems to have learned much both from the Middle High German Neidhart tradition and from the Middle Latin tradition of boisterous and vivacious love songs as in the *Carmina Burana*. In addition, the Italian trecento (thirteenth-century) poets Cecco Angiolieri, Giannozzo, and Franco Sacchetti might have provided Oswald with important poetic models, but in his many old-age songs we also discover possible influences from the French poet Charles d'Orléans. Moreover, some scholars have suggested François Villon as a possible source for Oswald's autobiographical songs. Considering Oswald's extensive travels throughout western and southern Europe, Spanish and Flemish poetry also might have had a considerable impact on his work, as he adapted his models by way of *contrafacture* (use of secular melody in religious song). Recently we have also learned that contemporary folk poetry, proverbs, and perhaps specific legal formulas can be discerned in Oswald's language. Even narrative epics such as the Old Spanish *El Cid* and the Italian *Decamerone* by Boccaccio might have influenced him in his compositions. Finally, the poet also translated several Latin sequences that were usually performed during the liturgy.

Oswald's poetic genius transformed all these sources and models into highly individual poetic expressions. We will probably never reach a full understanding of which elements the poet borrowed from his predecessors and contemporaries, but we know for sure that Oswald had an extremely open mind for novel ideas and thoroughly enjoyed experimenting with a wide variety of poetic genres, styles, and images. He was one of the first medieval German poets to correlate closely text and melody and also created astoundingly polyphonic effects typical of *Ars nova* and the Italian trecento culture. Curiously, though, Oswald does not seem to have been in contact with humanists and Renaissance writers, even though he once refers to Petrarch (Kl. 10, 28), whose concept of man's

sinfulness seems to have influenced Oswald's religious thinking. In this regard the poet is quite representative of his own time, as he still lived in the medieval tradition and yet also opened his mind to many new approaches to music *(Ars nova)* and poetry.

Oswald's oeuvre can be located at the crossroads between the late Middle Ages and the Renaissance, as the poet belonged to neither cultural period yet shared elements with both. His songs already reflect a strong sense of the modern individual with the emphasis on personal experiences, ideas, needs, and desires, but they are, at the same time, deeply drenched in the medieval concept of human sinfulness and of life as nothing but a transitional period here on earth.

BIBLIOGRAPHY

Classen, Albrecht. "Oswald von Wolkenstein," in *German Writers of the Renaissance and Reformation 1280–1580,* ed. James Hardin and Max Reinhart. Detroit: Gale, 1997, pp. 198–205.

Die Lieder Oswalds von Wolkenstein, ed. Karl Kurt Klein et al., 3d. ed. Tübingen: Niemeyer, 1987.

Jahrbuch der Oswald von Wolkenstein Gesellschaft, 1ff. (1980/1981ff.) [vol. 11 in print].

Joschko, Dirk. *Oswald von Wolkenstein. Eine Monographie zu Person, Werk und Forschungsgeschichte.* Göppingen: Kümmerle, 1985.

Oswald von Wolkenstein. *Sämtliche Lieder und Gedichte,* trans. Wernfried Hofmeister. Göppingen: Kümmerle, 1989 [modern German trans.].

Schwob, Anton. *Oswald von Wolkenstein. Eine Biographie,* 3d ed. Bozen: Athesia, 1979.

———. *Die Lebenszeugnisse Oswalds von Wolkenstein. Edition und Kommentar. Bd. 1, 1382–1419, Nr. 1–92.* Vienna: Böhlau, 1999.

Spicker, Johannes. *Literarische Stilisierung und artistische Kompetenz bei Oswald von Wolkenstein.* Stuttgart: Hirzel, 1993.

Albrecht Classen

SEE ALSO
Carmina Burana; Minnesang; Neidhart; Versification

Otfrid (ca. 800–ca. 875)

A monk of the abbey of Weißenburg (now Wissembourg in Alsace), Otfrid is the author of a remarkable poem based on the four gospels, completed by about 870 and preserved in four manuscripts, three of them complete or nearly so. The famous Vienna manuscript was carefully corrected, and perhaps written in part, by Otfrid himself.

Otfrid composed the poem in a new, stress-based strophic verse form with two long lines per strophe. Each long line contains two half lines joined by rhyme or at least assonance at the caesura (audible break at the middle of a line). Thus the Lord's Prayer begins:

> *Fáter unser gúato, bist drúhtin thu gim‡ato*
> *in hímilon io hóher, uuíh si námo thiner.*
> *Biquéme uns thinaz ríchi, thaz hoha hímilrichi,*
> *thára uuir zua io gíngen ioh émmizigen thíngen.*

> Our Father good, thou art a kindly king
> so high in the heavens, holy be thy name.
> Thy kingdom come to us, the high kingdom of heaven,
> toward which may we always strive and firmly
> believe. (2,22,27–30)

All four manuscripts show the caesura and use initials, indentation, and rhythmic accents to explicate and show off the new verse form. Otfrid describes the meter and his spelling innovations in a letter to archbishop Liutbert of Mainz (included in two manuscripts), where his pride of invention is everywhere apparent. Suggestions that Otfrid merely modified an existing German verse form are therefore unlikely. Neither did Otfrid slavishly imitate Latin hymnody of the period: though some contemporary Latin hymns also show assonance, rhyme, and/or alternating stress, the overall effect of his poem is quite different. Otfrid's verse form was quickly used in several other Old High German and early Middle High German poems and seems the likely basis for the couplets of the Middle High German courtly epics.

Otfrid portrays the life of Christ as described in the four gospels, but his work is not merely a verse translation. After many narrative sections, he includes passages for reflection, labeling them *mystice,* or in a mystical sense. As in Germanic alliterative verse, Otfrid constantly repeats and restates ideas and phrases, often for the sake of the rhyme or the rhythm. His writing seems prolix; in the passage above, he uses thirty words where the alliterating Old Saxon Heliand has twenty-one and the prose Weißenburg Catechism only thirteen.

Otfrid's attention to meter and orthography suggests that the poem was meant to be read aloud or even chanted (one manuscript has some neums, an early form of musical notation), but it could have had no place in the Latin liturgy of the time.

The dialect of the poem is Southern Rhenish Franconian, though in part because of Otfrid's orthographic innovations, it differs slightly from that of other Weißenburg documents.

BIBLIOGRAPHY

Haubrichs, Wolfgang. "Otfrid von Weißenburg: Übersetzer, Erzähler, Interpret. . . ." in *Übersetzer im Mittelalter,* ed. Joachim Heinzle et al. Wolfram-Studien 14. Berlin: Schmidt, 1996, pp. 13–45.

Kleiber, Wolfgang. *Otfrid von Weißenburg: Untersuchungen zur handschriftlichen Überlieferung und Studien zum Aufbau des Evangelienbuches.* Bern: Francke, 1971.

Murdoch, Brian O. *Old High German Literature.* Boston: Twayne, 1983.

Patzlaff, Rainer. *Otfrid von Weißenburg und die mittelalterliche versus-Tradition.* Tübingen: Niemeyer, 1975.

Schweikle, Gunther. "Die Herkunft des althochdeutschen Reimes: Zu Otfried von Weißenburgs formgeschichtlicher Stellung." *Zeitschrift für deutsches Altertum und deutsche Literatur* 96 (1967): 166–212.

Leo A. Connolly

SEE ALSO
Bible

Otte (fl. 1190–ca. 1230)

Known as the author of *Eraclius,* the poet identifies himself in his prologue: *ein gelerter man hiez Otte* (a learned man was called Otte, v. 40). The poem, based on the *Eracle* (1180) of Gautier d' Arras, may have been composed at the court of Landgrave Hermann I of Thüringia or at the court of Duke Ludwig I in Landshut. However, both the date and the place of composition are disputed. *Eraclius* (5,392 lines) borrows from secular and ecclesiastical legends, historical chronicles, and courtly romance. The story is loosely based on the life of Byzantine Emperor Heraclius (ca. 575–641) and radically deviates from the known historical facts. There are three main sections of *Eraclius.* In the first part of the story, a pious couple bears a son blessed by God with the ability to identify the worth of any stone, horse, or woman. Eraclius wins the favor of the Emperor Focas with his fantastic abilities and chooses a wife for the emperor. The second part of the story, believed to be based on legends of the marriage of Theodoius II (408–450), incorporates themes of courtly literature and implies a familiarity with Heinrich von

Veldeke's *Eneit* and perhaps even Gottfried von Straßburg's *Tristan*. Against the advice of Eraclius, Focas has his wife, Anthânais, locked up in a tower while he is away at war. From the tower, Anthânais falls in love with Parides. Otte's depiction of the lover's passion reveals a playful side of the poet: *swaz diu frouwe und der jüngelinc ein ander dâ tâten, daz möhte ein nunne errâten.* (Whatever the woman and the young man did there, it may be guessed by a nun, vv. 4010–4012). The lovers are discovered, but Focas acts upon Eraclius's advice and spares them. The third part of the story relates the capture of Jerusalem and the confiscation of the relics of the True Cross by Cosdrôas (Chrosoes II). Eraclius defeats the Persian king in battle and returns the True Cross to Jerusalem. Gautier's poem ends here, but Otte continues the story with the cautionary tale of Eraclius's hubris. Otte also draws on information found in Otto von Freising's *Historia de duabus civitatibus (History of Two Cities)* and the *Kaiserchronik (Chronicle of the Emperors)* to include historical accounts of Saint Anastasius, the Monotheletism heresy, and the birth of Muhammad.

BIBLIOGRAPHY

Otte. *Eraclius,* ed. Winfried Frey. Göppingen: Kümmerle, 1983.

Frey, Winfried. *Textkritische Untersuchungen zu Ottes "Eraclius."* Frankfurt: Selbstverlag, 1970.

Pratt, Karen. *Meister Ottes "Eraclius" as an adaptation of "Eracle" by Gautier d'Arras.* Göppingen: Kümmerle, 1987.

Stephen M. Carey

SEE ALSO

Gottfried von Straßburg; Heinrich von Veldeke; *Kaiserchronik;* Otto of Freising

Otto I (912–973)

King of Germany 936–973 and emperor 962–973, Otto (the Great) was a member of the Liudolfing, or Saxon, dynasty, born in 912 to the future Henry I and his wife, Mathilda. Little is known of his early years. In 930 Otto married Edith, the half sister of King Aethelstan of Wessex, beginning a policy of marriage to foreign princesses that became the norm in Germany. He was almost certainly designated at that time as the next king. After his father's death, Otto was acclaimed by the nobles and crowned in Aachen on August 7, 936, reviving the coronation ritual that Henry I had foregone. This is the first sign of Otto's new view of kingship, marked by a policy of systematically increasing the gap between king and dukes and rejecting the rule by personal pacts that had characterized his father's reign. Perhaps this attitude helped provoke the civil wars of 937–941, as nobles took advantage of an unestablished king to settle old feuds and reduce royal rights. The two most important rebels were Otto's elder half brother Thankmar (who deeply resented that Henry I had declared his first marriage to Thankmar's mother invalid) and his younger brother Henry, who was supported by their mother, Mathilda. This has been hailed as resistance against a new Ottonian principle that the realm could not be divided as it had been by Merovingians and Carolingians; the truth was that Henry I had not had enough control of the kingdom to make a division possible, although he did divide his personal lands and treasure among his sons. The period of rebellion concluded with Thankmar's death and the submission of the other important rebels. Henry was forgiven and, in 947, given the duchy of Bavaria.

Otto continued his father's vigorous eastern and northern policy. Margraves Hermann Billung and Gero, acting with Otto's support, won a series of victories against the Slavs, gaining territory that Otto strove to pacify with an active policy that included both the establishment of fortified garrison outposts and active royal activity in missionary enterprises. The latter included the erection of several bishoprics—Brandenburg and Havelberg in 948; Oldenburg, Merseburg, Meissen, and Zeitz later in 968—at which time Otto's beloved monastic foundation of Magdeburg was also elevated to an archbishopric with authority over much of the eastern frontier. The success of the Ottonian eastern policy culminated in a series of victories in 955. On August 10 of that year, Otto decisively defeated a Magyar coalition at the battle of Lechfeld near Augsburg, an event that marked the end of Magyar raiding in Germany. This was followed by a victory over the Slavs at Recknitz on October 16th. Further campaigns led to the subjection of the Slavs between the middle Elbe and the middle Oder by 960, as well as making Bohemia and Poland tributary to the German king.

From an early period Otto had imperial ambitions. He took advantage of the disorders caused by Bangor's seizure of power in Lombardy to establish a foothold in Italy in 951. Otto accepted Bangor's submission and reinstated him as subking. To strengthen his personal control of Lombardy, though, the widower Otto married Adelheid, the widowed queen of the Lombards. At that time,

Otto requested that the pope crown him as emperor, but the pope refused, probably from fear of a strong German presence in Italy. Otto had to cut short his time in Italy, returning to Germany to deal with the revolt of his eldest son, Liudulf, who apparently felt threatened by Otto's new marriage alliance. In 961, though, Pope John XII appealed for Otto's help against his enemies. Otto responded swiftly with a second expedition to Italy. He prepared for a long campaign, taking the precaution of having the six-year-old Otto II, his eldest son by Adelheid, elected and crowned as king, and establishing a regency in Germany. The pope's enemies fled before Otto's army, and John XII crowned Otto I as emperor on February 2, 962, reviving the imperial title that had fallen in abeyance early in the century, and creating a link to the prestige of Charlemagne.

The imperial coronation led to a major shift in Otto's interests, leading him to spend ten of the last twelve years of his life in Italy. John XII soon realized that Otto was exerting much more direct domination over Italian affairs than he had bargained for. The pope therefore took part in a conspiracy aimed at ending Ottonian involvement in Italy, which led Otto to drive John from Rome and arrange his deposition. Otto then set up a new pope of his own choice, initiating almost a century of German control of the papacy. Imperial interests also led to campaigns in southern Italy from 966 on, especially with the goal of gaining Byzantine recognition of Otto's imperial title.

Otto I was an even more peripatetic ruler than most of his contemporaries, ruling largely through verbal orders during constant travels throughout his realm. He received little formal education, learning to read only in 946, while mourning for his first wife, Edith. Despite this, Otto established a particularly strong and secure kingdom, thanks especially to his military successes, the wealth acquired through exploitation of the newly found silver mines at Goslar, and his alliance with the church, particularly with German monasteries. Beginning in the 940s, Otto gradually replaced the dukes of Germany with members of the Ottonian family, who on the whole proved to be loyal supporters of the throne. His personal prestige and close kinship to the top families in western Europe allowed Otto to act as mediator in Burgundy and in France between the last Carolingians and the rising Capetian (French kings, tenth to fourteenth century) family. By the time of Otto's death at Memleben on May 7, 973, his German-based empire was the strongest state in Europe, a position it held for the next century. He is buried in the church he founded at Magdeburg, beside his wife, Edith.

BIBLIOGRAPHY

Althoff, Gerd, and Hagen Keller. *Heinrich I. und Otto der Große: Neubeginn und karolingisches Erbe.* Göttingen: Muster-Schmidt, 1985.

Leyser, Karl. *Communications and Power in Medieval Europe: The Carolingian and Ottonian Centuries,* ed. Timothy Reuter. London: Hambledon Press, 1994.

Reuter, Timothy. *Germany in the Early Middle Ages, 800–1056.* London: Longman, 1991.

Phyllis G. Jestice

SEE ALSO

Adelheid of Burgundy; Carolingians; Charlemagne; Coronation; Henry I; Lechfeld, Battle of; Liudolfinger; Otto II; *Servatius;* Succession

Otto I, Art

The single extant artistic representation of Otto is found on one of the sixteen remaining ivories that once formed a larger series narrating the life of Jesus. The plaque (New York, Metropolitan Museum of Art) shows the ruler in diminutive scale presenting a church to Christ in Majesty, a depiction presumably related to Otto's elevation of the church of Magdeburg to metropolitan status in 967. The original group of forty to fifty ivories already shows the interest in extensive New Testament cycles that would become a hallmark of later Ottonian book illumination.

Though probably made in Milan, the ivories were used in Otto's favored foundation of Magdeburg, perhaps to decorate an ambo (pulpit) or cathedra (throne) but most probably within an altar antependium. They constitute one of the few remaining indications of the glory of Otto's Magdeburg, developed as an eastern Saxon counterpart to Aachen, the western Lotharingian center inherited from Charlemagne's empire. As in Aachen, Magdeburg contained an integrated church and palace complex, though the cathedral was likely unfinished at the time of Otto's death in 973; the palace may have fallen into disrepair already by the twelfth century. A suggestion of the richness of Otto's original cathedral can be seen in the marble, porphyry, and granite columns originally used in the nave but incorporated into the rebuilt thirteenth-century choir. These columns were late antique *spolia* (war booty) brought to Magdeburg from Italy, probably from Ravenna in imitation of Charlemagne's activities in

Aachen. As was his first wife, Edith, the emperor was buried in the cathedral, where his marble sarcophagus, also perhaps from Ravenna, is still preserved.

Accompanied in the Magdeburg ivory by St. Mauritius, patron of the cathedral, the bearded Otto wears the high-arched crown that was made for his imperial coronation in 962 and became an integral part of the German regalia (Vienna Schatzkammer). Otto's imperial coronation also produced an innovative change in his seals, from the depiction of a traditional military figure in profile with lance and shield to a more imposing frontal figure holding a scepter and orb; the possible influence of Byzantine sources is difficult to gauge. Equally unclear is the relative impact of Byzantine, Italian, and western prototypes on the so-called *Ottonianum* diploma issued by Otto in 962 as a compact with the papacy. This unusually large presentation copy measures 100 × 40 cm and was executed on purple vellum with gold calligraphic script (Vatican, Archivio Segreto).

As part of his Carolingian emulation, Otto drew together at his court intellectuals, like Stephen of Novara and Liutprand of Cremona, though certainly not to the same degree as Charlemagne or Charles the Bald. Rather, because of the itinerant nature of Ottonian kingship and the political structure of the realm, cultural and artistic production was not centrally located or controlled, but was distributed among various important ecclesiastic and monastic sites. These included Cologne, where Otto's brother Archbishop Brun led a cathedral school of unparalleled learning; Corvey; and Gandersheim, where Widukind and Hrotsvitha, respectively, composed their historical works extolling Otto the Great.

BIBLIOGRAPHY

Lasko, Peter. *Ars Sacra 800–1200,* 2d ed. Pelican History of Art. New Haven: Yale University Press, 1994, pp. 81–90.

McKitterick, Rosamond. "Ottonian Intellectual Culture in the Tenth Century and the Role of Theophanu." *Early Medieval Europe* 2 (1993): 53–74; repr. in Rosamond McKitterick, *The Frankish Kings and Culture in the Early Middle Ages.* Aldershot: Variorum, 1995, essay no. 13.

Schramm, Percy Ernst, and Florentine Mütherich. *Denkmale der deutschen Könige und Kaiser,* vol. 1, *Ein Beitrag zur Herrschergeschichte von Karl dem Grossen bis Friedrich II. 768–1250,* 2d ed. Munich: Prestel, 1981.

Adam S. Cohen

SEE ALSO
Aachen; Charlemagne; Cologne, Art; Corvey; Gandersheim; Magdeburg; Ottonian Art and Architecture

Otto II (955–983)

King 961–983, emperor 967–983, sole ruler of the German Empire from 973, Otto II was born in 955 to Otto I and his second wife, Adelheid. His father arranged for the six-year-old Otto's election and coronation as king of the Germans in May 961, before setting out on his second Italian expedition. To secure the imperial title to his dynasty, the elder Otto further arranged to have his son crowned co-emperor on Christmas Day 967; Otto II was the last western emperor to receive imperial coronation in his father's lifetime. Despite these honors, the future Otto II was not given an independent position even after he came of age, and has left only twenty-seven extant documents from the twelve years of his official shared rule with Otto I. At his father's death in 973, the eighteen-year-old Otto was accepted as ruler without opposition.

The early years of Otto II's reign were occupied by a series of rebellions in Bavaria and Lotharingia. These rebellions were provoked by an attempt Otto made in 974 to reduce the power of his overly mighty cousin, Henry II "the Quarrelsome" (the nickname is not contemporary), duke of the semiautonomous duchy of Bavaria. Henry's defeat in 976 gave Otto the opportunity to reorganize the southern duchies, weakening Bavaria by turning its province of Carinthia into a separate duchy. Henry, unsatisfied with his position, led a second uprising in 976–977, and Bavaria was pacified only with Henry's imprisonment in 978.

Otto II's early military campaigns were successful, as Otto continued the strong eastern and northern policies of his father and grandfather. A victory over the Danes in 974 led to an expansion of German efforts to evangelize in the north. He also invaded Bohemia several times, returning it to its earlier tributary status after its ruler had seceded by joining with Henry the Quarrelsome in the rebellions of 974–977. On the western front, though, Otto was unable to play as strong a role as his father had. An effort of the French King Lothar to gain control of Lotharingia in 978 caught Otto by surprise, forcing him to flee Aachen before the French army. Otto quickly retaliated with a raid that penetrated France to the gates of Paris, but that accomplished little besides salving Otto's pride.

In 972, Otto II had married the Byzantine princess Theophanu, a marriage arranged by his father to enhance the prestige of the Ottonian dynasty. Contemporary sources suggest that Theophanu exerted a very strong influence on Otto, including the belief that the empress's "childish advice" led to Otto's disastrous campaign in southern Italy in 982. In reality, the southern campaign needs little explanation. Otto decided in 981 on the conquest of southern Italy, split at that time among Saracens, Greeks, and Lombards. He probably planned the campaign as an extension of imperial policies begun by Otto I, who had conducted several inconclusive campaigns in the region. Otto II's army was, however, decisively defeated by a Saracen force at the battle of Cotrone (Cap Colonne) on July 13, 982. Almost the entire German army was destroyed; Otto himself escaped only by swimming his horse out to a Greek ship in the bay, then disguising his identity until he reached safety. The Saracen army was too badly weakened to press its advantage, so the battle had little effect on the balance of power in Italy. This defeat, though, dealt a severe blow to Otto's prestige. The Slavs responded to news of the German defeat with an uprising in the summer of 983. A Slavic confederation devastated the German border, destroyed the bishoprics of Havelberg and Brandenburg, and burned Hamburg, reversing most of Otto I's successes in Slavic territory. Perhaps the seriousness of the political situation can be seen in the fact that Otto II summoned an imperial diet at Verona on May 27, 983, where he had his three-year-old son Otto III elected to the German kingship, then sent the child on to Aachen to be crowned. Otto II remained in Italy, trying to subject Venice to imperial control. He died of malaria in Rome on December 7, 983, at the age of twenty-eight, and is the only emperor to be buried in St. Peter's Basilica.

Otto II appears to have been dominated and overshadowed throughout his life by people of stronger character, first his father, then his wife Theophanu, and also by his counselors, especially the loyal and talented Archbishop Willigis of Mainz. Physically Otto was not as impressive as his father; the exhumation of his body in 1609 revealed that he was a small man, and eleventh-century sources describe him as a redhead. Certainly his reputation has suffered by comparison to his great father and exotic son. In general, his reign is best seen as one of consolidation and growing sophistication. Unlike his predecessors, Otto II was well educated. His love of luxury and ostentation was notorious, although this perhaps should be taken more as a sign of the enormous wealth the Ottonians were able to command than of character weakness. His reign saw advances in the imperial chancery and greater cooperation between the German and Italian parts of the empire. It also saw a closer identification with the ancient Roman Empire and the city of Rome, setting aside the Byzantine emperor's claim to be the only true successor of the caesars. Otto's chancery in 982 adopted for the first time the title Roman empire (*imperator Romanorum augustus*) as the designation of a German emperor, a title that became standard to Otto's successors. Despite his reverses in Italy and on the Slavic frontier, Otto left a firmly established realm, increasingly self-assured and international, to his son.

BIBLIOGRAPHY

Beumann, Helmut. *Die Ottonen.* Stuttgart: Kohlhammer, 1987.

Reuter, Timothy. *Germany in the Early Middle Ages, 800–1056.* London: Longman, 1991.

Phyllis G. Jestice

SEE ALSO

Adelheid of Burgundy; Coronation; Empire; Otto I; Otto II, Art; Otto III; *Servatius;* Succession; Theophanu

Otto II, Art

That the royal and imperial seals of Otto II are almost identical to those of his father suggests the relative political stability and continuity that resulted from Otto's cocrowning as king and emperor during Otto I's lifetime. Perhaps in memory of his father, Otto II presented Magdeburg Cathedral with a now-lost manuscript whose gold and gem–encrusted cover depicted Otto II and his wife, Theophanu. Otto II's personal interest in manuscripts is evident from the fact that he took a quadripartite Psalter dated 909 from the monastery of St. Gall during a visit in 972 (now Bamberg, Staatsbibliothek, manuscript no. Bibl. 44), perhaps for the purpose of learning Greek.

His union with Theophanu figures prominently in the artistic objects associated with Otto II. The luxurious presentation copy of the marriage diploma from 972 is one of the greatest monuments of Ottonian art (Wolfenbüttel, Staatsarchiv). Measuring 144.5 × 39.5 cm, the unusually large and sumptuous diploma is written in calligraphic script in gold ink on purple parchment and decorated with pairs of medallions patterned after Byzantine textile designs. The conception and ornamental details of the contract have been called a "Byzantine paraphrase," a description that applies as well to the ivory plaque depicting Otto II and Theophanu (Paris, Musée de Cluny). The rulers, wearing Byzantine attire, flank Christ, who crowns them; the inscriptions in mixed Greek and Latin call Otto *imperator Romanorum* and Theophanu *imperatrix Augustus,* indicating a date of 982–983. The plaque was likely made in Italy at the instigation of John Philagathos, Otto's chancellor in Italy, who kneels in submission under the emperor's feet. Though not a direct copy, the Ottonian ivory is essentially modeled on an almost contemporary Byzantine plaque representing the imperial couple Romanos II and Eudokia, datable to around the middle of the tenth century (opinions ascribing the Byzantine ivory to Romanos IV, 1068–1071, are less convincing).

While the coming of Theophanu to the west can no longer be regarded as a unique catalyst for the influx of Byzantine art into the Ottonian realm, it is nonetheless true that the blossoming of Ottonian art occurred during the reign of Otto II. As in the period of Otto I, cultural and artistic production continued to be scattered among diverse ecclesiastic and monastic centers. Especially noteworthy is the patronage of Archbishop Egbert of Trier, who promoted the so-called Master of the *Registrum Gregorii,* an artist whose oeuvre can be reconstructed with some confidence, and who was fundamentally responsible for the reintroduction of the classical style into Ottonian art. The Registrum Master has also been credited with a hand in the creation of Theophanu's marriage diploma (Hoffmann 1986: 108–116). The now fragmentary manuscript from which the artist takes his name contains the first in a series of Ottonian images in which the enthroned ruler receives homage from personified provinces. Egbert's poetic verses in the manuscript bemoan the passing of his patron Otto II, so that the ruler image should be seen as Otto II. The only Ottonian ruler buried in St. Peter's in Rome, Otto II should be credited with a greater role in the development of the Ottonian idea of the *renovatio imperii Romanorum* usually ascribed primarily to his son Otto III.

BIBLIOGRAPHY

Hoffmann, Hartmut. *Buchkunst und Königtum im ottonischen und frühsalischen Reich.* Schriften der Monumenta Germaniae Historica 30. 2 vols. Stuttgart: Anton Hiersemann, 1986.

Kaiserin Theophanu: Begegnung des Ostens und Westens um die Wende des ersten Jahrtausends, ed. A. von Euw and P. Schreiner. 2 vols. Cologne: Schnütgen Museum, 1991.

Nordenfalk, Carl. "Archbishop Egbert's 'Registrum Gregorii'," in *Studien zur mittelalterlichen Kunst 800–1250: Festschrift für Florentine Mütherich zum 70. Geburtstag,* ed. K. Bierbrauer et al. Munich: Prestel, 1985, pp. 87–100.

Schramm, Percy Ernst, and Florentine Mütherich. *Denkmale der deutschen Könige und Kaiser,* vol. 1, *Ein Beitrag zur Herrschergeschichte von Karl dem Grossen bis Friedrich II. 768–1250,* 2d ed. Veröffentlichungen des Zentralinstituts für Kunstgeschichte 2. Munich: Prestel, 1981.

Adam S. Cohen

SEE ALSO

Egbert; Gregory VII; Otto I; Otto III; *Registrum Gregorii,* Master of; Sankt Gall; Theophanu

Otto III (980–1002)

King of the Germans, 983–1002, emperor 996–1002, Otto III was the most flamboyant and controversial of the German emperors. He was born in 980, the only son of Emperor Otto II and the Byzantine princess Theophanu. Otto II continued his own father's policy of assuring Ottonian rule by having the young Otto elected king at Verona, May 27, 983. He then dispatched the three-year-old Otto to Aachen for coronation on Christmas 983. This was several weeks after Otto II's death in Italy but before the news had reached the north.

A series of informal regents governed the empire for most of Otto's short life. By German custom, the young king's proper guardian was his closest adult male relative, Duke Henry II the Quarrelsome of Bavaria. Henry, though, soon tried to supplant his charge, claiming the kingship in his own name. Archbishop Willigis of Mainz, though, threw his support behind Otto III, summoning the young king's mother, Theophanu, and grandmother Adelheid from Italy to help him preserve Otto's rights. After a period of intense political maneuvering, Henry surrendered Otto to the two empresses on June 29, 984. Theophanu assumed the regency for her son. After her death in 991, Adelheid directed affairs until Otto III formally came of age in September 994.

Otto's role during his childhood was strictly symbolic. In 986 he was sent on a campaign against the Slavs—not to fight but so Mieszko of Poland could join the host and do homage. For the most part, though, Otto was not very visible in German affairs until he came of age. He was very well educated. His main tutor was Bernward, the future bishop of Hildesheim, but he also received instruction in Greek from his mother's friend John Philagathos, a southern Italian. After coming of age, Otto continued his education with the most learned man of the age, Gerbert of Aurillac.

Rome during Otto's minority had fallen into the hands of the local noble Crescentius II. Pope John XV asked for Otto's help in 995, leading to Otto's first Italian expedition. John died before his arrival, so Otto forced the Roman Church to accept his own cousin Bruno of Carinthia as pope, who took the name Gregory V. Gregory then crowned Otto as emperor on May 21, 996. The imposition of a German pope shows Otto's early determination to control Rome. This marked a new departure, since Gregory was the first non-Roman pope since the Byzantine emperors had appointed Greeks to the office in the seventh century. Gregory was soon driven from the city, forcing Otto to return and reinstate him in 998. This time Otto secured Rome by having Crescentius executed, and had Crescentius's antipope (none other than Otto's former tutor, John Philagathos) blinded and imprisoned. Afterward, Otto stayed in Rome, having decided to make the city the capital of his empire. He had a palace built for himself on the Aventine. This has been taken as evidence of Otto III's grandiose plan to create a new Roman empire. Certainly Otto greatly developed the idea of a western empire, but it was not inextricably linked to Rome. At first he wanted to set up Aachen as a "new Rome," placing the focus of the empire in the north. It is probable that political instability in Italy made Otto decide to stay closer, where he could intervene effectively in affairs. Naturally enough, this made him very unpopular with the Romans, who revolted in early 1001, besieging Otto for a time in his own palace. Otto sent for more troops and was preparing an attack on Rome at the time of his death.

The earlier Ottonians had ruled almost entirely by means of continual travel throughout their realm. The decision to reside in a permanent capital thus marked another new departure. It forced Otto to develop a larger bureaucracy and enabled him to acquire a larger and more glittering court. For a time Otto's aunt, Abbess Mathilda of Quedlinburg, acted as regent in Germany, but after her death the emperor relied ever more on bishops to perform the work of government, laying the groundwork for the "imperial Church system" of the late Ottonians and Salians. In Rome itself, Otto created a hierarchy of court officials, elaborate by German standards, most of whom had Greek titles in emulation of the Byzantine court. Otto also insisted on a higher degree of ceremony than had been known to earlier German rulers, modeled on Byzantine practice.

Otto clearly saw his role as emperor in terms of leadership over the Christian world, assuming the titles "servant of Jesus Christ," and "servant of the apostles." This strong development of the imperial idea was already visible in 996 with Otto's appointment of the first German pope; after Gregory V's death in 999, the emperor continued his effort to control the papacy by appointing his former tutor Gerbert of Aurillac, who took the name Sylvester II. The two cooperated closely, even declaring the Donation of Constantine to be invalid. Otto appears to have been personally pious; he was close to both St. Nilus and St. Romuald of Ravenna; Bruno of Querfurt claims that the emperor even swore an oath to abdicate and retire to the wilds of Poland as a hermit. While this is unlikely, Otto did take very seriously his duty toward the church. In 1000 he made a pilgrimage to the tomb of the martyred Bishop Adalbert of Prague in Gniezno, arranging at that time for Gniezno to become the archbishopric of Poland. He went on from there to Aachen, where he had Charlemagne's grave opened, taking the pectoral cross from the body. Certainly this was in part the effort of an upstart Ottonian to associate himself with the prestige of the Carolingian dynasty. It is very likely that the tomb opening was also the first step in a project to canonize Charlemagne, perhaps the best example of Otto III's belief in the divine nature of the empire *(imperium)*. He also planned to continue the family alliance with the Byzantine emperors, arranging to marry the porphyrogenita (female successor) Theodora, but she arrived in Italy only at about the time of Otto's death.

Otto III's history, though, is one of largely unrealized potential. He died unexpectedly on January 24, 1002, at the age of twenty-one.

BIBLIOGRAPHY

Althoff, Gerd. *Otto III.* Darmstadt: Wissenschaftliche Buchgesellschaft, 1996.

Beumann, Helmut. *Die Ottonen.* Stuttgart: Kohlhammer, 1987.

Leyser, Karl J. *Medieval Germany and Its Neighbours 900–1250.* London: Hambledon, 1982.

Phyllis G. Jestice

SEE ALSO

Adelheid of Burgundy; Charlemagne; Coronation; Donation of Constantine; Otto II; Salians; Theophanu

Otto III, Art

In contrast to the relative paucity of images connected to both his father and his grandfather, there are numerous representations of Otto III from throughout his short life. He appears as a child in the arms of his mother, Theophanu, on an ivory from circa 983 (Milan, Castello Sforzesco), and is paired with her again on the remarkable book cover made in Trier under Archbishop Egbert between 985 and 991 (*Codex Aureus,* or Golden Manuscript from Echternach; Nuremberg, Germanisches National-museum, manuscript no. 156142). From the same period of Otto's minority is the small prayer book written for the king by the female scribe Duriswint under the direction of Archbishop Willigis of Mainz and probably Theophanu. With its combination of late Antique, Carolingian, and Byzantine stylistic and iconographic elements, the book is characteristic of Ottonian art in general.

While Otto's library does not seem to reflect an interest in contemporary works, it was an extensive and scholarly collection that included, for example, a fifth-century Livy and numerous books given to him by his tutor, Gerbert of Aurillac, including a luxury Boethius originally owned by Charles the Bald. A late Antique illustrated *Itala* manuscript, like many other luxury items, may well have been passed by Otto to the foundation of Quedlinburg, ruled by his sister, Adelheid.

The sumptuous manuscripts produced for Otto III at Reichenau clearly express the imperial ideals and notion of Christocentric kingship promulgated by the ruler and his advisers. In the Gospel Books now in Aachen and Munich (Staatsbibliothek, manuscript no. clm. 4453), the portrait of Otto replaces the expected composition of Christ in Majesty; in the Aachen Gospels, Otto is depicted in a mandorla (body halo), surrounded by symbols of the evangelists and elevated into heaven in a direct and unparalleled imitation of Christ. Similarly, in the Lothar Cross also in Aachen, the obverse has an antique cameo of Augustus Caesar substituted for Otto's portrait, a taut exposition of Otto as the Holy Roman emperor.

Otto's seals and bulls show a variety of innovations, but none is so meaningful as the imperial bull with the inscription *Renovatio Imperii Romanorum,* which copies a bull of Charlemagne and so epitomizes both the imperial aspirations and Carolingian emulation of Otto III. Otto's gift of copies of the Holy Lance, the most important relic in the Ottonian realm, to the recently converted Boleslav Chrobry of Poland and perhaps Stephen of Hungary, is a concrete manifestation of the eastern conversion policy adopted by the Saxon king in imitation of Charlemagne.

A second bull, with a personification of *Aurea Roma,* is strong evidence of Otto's continued preoccupation with Rome, as is his renovation of the Roman imperial palace. Nevertheless, the writings of Gerbert of Aurillac (later Pope Silvester II), Leo of Vercelli, and the extensive artistic patronage of Bishop Bernward of Hildesheim make clear that the desire for a Roman imperium (empire) did not reside with Otto alone. Indeed, Bernward's bronze column, copied after the Column of Trajan but now expressing the victory of Christ, is a cautious reminder that the fascination with Rome usually ascribed to Otto is really seen only through the refracted lens of his teachers and advisers.

BIBLIOGRAPHY

Das Evangeliar Ottos III: Clm. 4453 der Bayerischen Staatsbibliothek München. Faksimile-Ausgabe und Kommentar, eds. Fridolin Dressler, Florentine Mütherich, and Helmut Beumann. 2 vols. Frankfurt am Main: Fischer, 1978.

Gebetbuch Ottos III. Clm. 30111. Essays by Knut Görich and Elisabeth Klemm. Patrimonia 84. Munich: Bayerische Staatsbibliothek, 1995.

Mütherich, Florentine. "The Library of Otto III," in *The Role of the Book in Medieval Culture,* ed. Peter Ganz. Turnhout: Brepols, 1986, pp. 11–26.

Schramm, Percy Ernst. *Die deutschen Kaiser und Könige in Bildern ihrer Zeit 751–1190,* rev. ed. F. Mütherich et al. Munich: Prestel, 1983.

Adam S. Cohen

SEE ALSO

Bernward of Hildesheim; Charlemagne; Echternach; Egbert; Hildesheim; Mainz; Otto I; Otto III; Ottonian Art and Architecture; Quedlinburg; Reichenau; Theophanu; Trier

Otto IV (1175/1182–May 19, 1218)

Emperor and sometime ally of Pope Innocent III (1198–1216), Otto's reign was a time of chaos after the premature death of Henry VI. Leader of the Welf house and son of Henry the Lion, Otto was involved in a civil war for control of the empire with candidates of the rival Hohenstaufen house, Philip of Swabia and Frederick II. The struggle for control of the imperial crown had international implications and involved the princes of Germany, the kings of England and France, and the pope. Otto would ultimately lose the struggle to maintain control of the empire to Frederick.

The unexpected death of Henry in 1197 left the empire in a difficult situation because his heir, Frederick, was only three years old. It also offered the papacy the opportunity to break free from encirclement by the Hohenstaufen, an opportunity Innocent would exploit by playing one side against the other in the civil strife in Germany or by acting as referee between them. The situation was complicated by shifting alliances both inside and outside the empire. Frederick was first supported by the Staufen, including his uncle, Philip of Swabia. But Philip, motivated by the activities of forces opposed to his family, presented himself as king and was crowned at Mainz in September 1198. He also revived the alliance between his family and the Capetian dynasty, headed by Philip Augustus, to improve his position in Germany and Europe. The anti-Staufen forces inside Germany, supported by King Richard I of England, did not stand idly by but promoted a Welf candidate. The eldest son of Henry the Lion was still on crusade, and therefore the younger son, Otto, became the anti-Staufen candidate.

Otto, who had been raised at the court of his uncle, Richard I, and had been made count of Poitou and duke of Aquitaine in 1190 and 1196, respectively, made the most of his opportunity. He was crowned before Philip by the proper ecclesiastic, the archbishop of Cologne, and in the right place, Aachen. His election also carried great weight because he was elected by those traditionally empowered to choose the king. Indeed, the nature of his election was of great importance to Innocent, who would involve himself in the succession crisis because of the close ties of empire and papacy and because of papal claims to superior jurisdiction. Innocent, suspicious of the Hohenstaufen family and fearful of their territorial gains in northern and southern Italy, came to support Otto. This was critical to the king's success because his situation in Germany was weak despite having been elected by the right people and crowned in the right place, and because his greatest international ally, Richard, died in early 1199. To maintain papal support, Otto made important territorial concessions to the pope in Italy.

Otto's difficulties did not end, however, even though he had papal support, which was reinforced by Otto's concessions. Despite his excommunication, Philip managed to increase his power in Germany in the opening decade of the thirteenth century. He managed to increase support among the bishops of the empire, including the very important archbishop of Cologne, Adolf. Perhaps motivated by hostility to Rome, many princes also came to support Philip. By 1207 the papal curia had come to support Philip's claim to the imperial dignity and kingship in Germany, and in the following year the pope himself recognized Philip as king. Negotiations over territory in Italy and the imperial coronation were held between Philip and the pope, but they made little headway before Philip was murdered by Otto of Wittelsbach over Philip's broken engagement to Otto's daughter.

In 1208, fortunes once again turned for Otto, and he now received widespread support in Germany. He was elected king by the German princes a second time in November in Frankfurt and was victorious over French attempts to establish a rival king. To further strengthen his position in Germany, Otto was betrothed to Philip's daughter Beatrix. He was then crowned emperor by Innocent in Rome in October 1209, after renewing his promises to respect papal territory in Italy and also to refrain from intervening in Sicilian affairs.

Otto's success, however, seems to have gotten the better of him and, following the advice of his ministerials, he decided to extend his authority in Italy. He sought to expand his rights into papal lands, and thus alienated an important ally and created a dangerous opponent, Innocent. He further raised the ire of the pope by occupying Tuscany and invading the Hohenstaufen kingdom of Sicily. His invasion and conquest of Sicily in November 1210 led to the very encirclement by a German ruler that Innocent had struggled to prevent. Otto's actions also led Innocent to excommunicate the emperor in the autumn of 1210, and in the spring of 1211 Innocent released Otto's vassals from their oaths to the emperor.

Otto's difficulties were not limited to the opposition from the pope. To secure his position in Germany, Otto married Beatrix in 1212, but she died shortly after their marriage. He faced revolts in northern Italy, where opposition to German domination had existed for more than a generation, and in Germany, where the nobility had been released from their obligation of loyalty by the pope. He faced a rival king because Frederick followed him to Germany, where the princely opposition to Otto, with papal support, crowned Frederick king at Mainz. Frederick was able to gain a solid foothold in southern Germany, thus undermining Otto's authority and blocking his access to Italy. And both Frederick and Otto benefited from their alliances with the kings of France and England.

Otto's alliance with King John, however, would prove his undoing. Fearing that Philip Augustus would take English territory in France, John invaded with his nephew and ally Otto, who hoped to weaken French support for his Hohenstaufen rival. First John was defeated on the Loire and then, on July 27, 1214, Otto was disastrously defeated at the Battle of Bouvines. His supporters melted away after the defeat, and Frederick went on the offensive in the empire, imposing himself on Otto's remaining allies. Otto was formally deposed the following July and was confined to his personal lands in Brunswick until his death on May 19, 1218.

BIBLIOGRAPHY

Abulafia, David. *Frederick II: A Medieval Emperor.* Oxford: Oxford University Press, 1988.

Duby, Georges. *The Legend of Bouvines: War, Religion and Culture in the Middle Ages,* trans. Catherine Tihanyi. Berkeley: University of California Press, 1990.

Haverkamp, Alfred. *Medieval Germany, 1056–1273.* 2d ed., trans. Helga Braun and Richard Mortimer. Oxford: Oxford University Press, 1992.

Michael Frassetto

SEE ALSO

Aachen; Bouvines, Battle of; Cologne, Archdiocese; Frederick II; Henry VI; Henry the Lion; Welfs

Otto of Freising (ca. 1112–1158)

The most important historian of the twelfth century, Otto of Freising was well placed to write his works of history. He was born into the most prominent families in the empire and was related to the imperial Salian and Staufen lines. His father was Leopold III of Austria and his mother was Agnes, daughter of Henry IV and whose first husband was Frederick I, duke of Swabia. Otto was thus half brother of Conrad III and uncle of Frederick I Barbarossa. His ecclesiastical career began while he was still a child, when he became provost of the house of canons at Klosterneuburg (near Vienna). In 1127 or 1128, Otto journeyed to France to study with the great masters at Paris, including Hugo of St. Victor, Gilbert de la Porrée, and, probably, Peter Abelard. He left Paris in 1133 and on his way home joined the Cistercian abbey at Morimond. He was later elected bishop of Freising, before the canonical age and as the result of family influence. He participated in the Second Crusade (1147–1148) and, while en route to a Cistercian general chapter, died in Morimond in 1158.

Otto is best known for two historical works, *The Two Cities* and *The Deeds of Frederick Barbarossa.* The first of the two, is the more pessimistic but also the more philo-sophical work. Written between 1143 and 1146, *The Two Cities* is a world chronicle that tells the tale of salvation history that was heavily influenced by the work of St. Augustine. The first seven books outline the history of the world from creation to 1146. Otto's history describes the struggles of good and evil and praises the monks, the true representatives of the City of God on earth. *The Two Cities* also is a history of the *translatio imperii,* describing the transfer of universal power from the Greeks to the Romans to the Franks and ultimately to the Germans. It was in the Christian empire of the Germans that Otto saw the possibility of the existence of the City of God on earth, but the troubled times facing the empire from the time of Henry IV to Conrad III left him with little hope. The eighth, and final, book of *The Two Cities* is thoroughly eschatological and describes the coming of Antichrist, the Final Judgment, and establishment of the heavenly Jerusalem. Otto's somber perspective is not continued, however, in his other great work, *The Deeds of Frederick Barbarossa.* Completing the first two books before his death in 1158, Otto followed the plan outlined in a letter requested by Otto from his sponsor, Barbarossa himself. The first book details the events of the tumultuous reigns of Barbarossa's predecessors, and the second describes the first four years of the reign of Barbarossa, a time of peace and glory for the empire. Although *Deeds* overlooks matters unfavorable to the Staufen line, misrepresents the state of the realm at Barbarossa's ascension, and overstates his successes in Italy, it remains the most important source for events in the early years of Barabarossa's reign.

BIBLIOGRAPHY

Otto of Freising. *Chronica sive Historia de Duabus Civitatibus,* ed. A. Hofmeister. Monumenta Germaniae Historica Scriptores Rerum Germanicarum 40. Hannover: Hahn, 1912.

Otto of Freising and Rahewin. *Gesta Friderici Imperatoris,* ed. G. Waitz. Monumenta Germaniae Historica Scriptores Rerum Germanicarum 46. Hannover: Hahn, 1912.

Otto of Freising. *The Two Cities, by Otto, Bishop of Freising,* trans. Charles Christopher Mierow. New York: Columbia University Press, 1928.

Otto of Freising and his continuator, Rahewin. *The Deeds of Frederick Barbarossa,* trans. Charles Christopher Mierow with Richard Emery, 1953; rpt. Toronto: University of Toronto Press, 1994.

Michael Frassetto

SEE ALSO
Frederick I Barbarossa; Henry IV; Peter von Staufenberg; Salians; Staufen

Ottonian Art and Architecture

[This entry includes eight subentries:

Introduction
Architecture
Ivories
Manuscript Illumination
Metalwork
Sculpture
Textiles
Wall Painting]

Introduction

Ottonian art is best represented by the surviving illuminations, frescoes, ivories, and metalwork dating from the reigns of the Emperors Otto II (973–983), Otto III (983–1002), and Henry II (1002–1024). The major patrons were the emperor and his kin and close associates, many of whom were leading churchmen and -women. The hieratic quality that characterizes Ottonian art reflects this synthesis of secular and sacred authority and results from style, iconography, and the use of costly materials, including precious metals, ivory, enamels, and gemstones. Most surviving works were intended for ecclesiastical use, but many include both sacred and imperial imagery: on the ivory situla (vessel) from circa 1000 in Aachen, for example, the emperor, Saint Peter, and a number of bishops are represented together.

A variety of monastic workshops flourished under Ottonian patronage. Most of the important centers were located along the Rhine and Meuse Rivers, and many of them achieved prominence because of their links to the imperial family. Cologne, for instance, was associated with the court from the time of Archbishop Bruno (953–965), brother of Otto I, and was patronized by the royal abbesses of Essen. Trier became prominent under Archbishop Egbert (977–993), a member of Otto II's chancellery. The manuscript painter known as the Gregory Master—the leading artistic personality of the Ottonian age and Egbert's contemporary—was apparently active at Trier. Hildesheim flourished in the eleventh century under Abbot Bernward (993–1022), tutor of Otto III. The hollow-cast bronze doors and column he commissioned (now at Hildesheim Cathedral) are among the most sophisticated and ambitious works of early medieval art. Other leading centers, distinguished by their scriptorium activity, include Reichenau, Regensburg, and Echternach.

BIBLIOGRAPHY
Grodecki, Louis. *Le Siècle de l'an mil.* Paris: Gallimard, 1973.
Lasko, Peter. *Ars Sacra 800–1200,* 2d ed. New Haven, Conn.: Yale University Press, 1994, pp. 76–141.
Ornamenta Ecclesiae: Kunst und Künstler der Romanik, ed. Anton Legner. 3 vols. Cologne: Schnütgen-Museum, 1985.

Karen E. Loaiza

SEE ALSO
Aachen; Bernward of Hildesheim; Cologne, Art; Echternach; Egbert; Essen; Hildesheim; Otto I; Otto II; Otto III; Regensburg; *Registrum Gregorii,* Master of; Reichenau; Trier

Architecture

Under Saxon rule (919–1024), Ottonian architecture in the Holy Roman Empire moved beyond the shadows of Carolingian interpretations of Christian Antiquity to coalesce with pan-European Romanesque building trends during the eleventh century. Many Ottonian buildings survive, but seldom unrestored. Many more are known only from archaeological remains postdating the mid–tenth century. From beginnings under Henry I the Fowler (king 929–936), and remarkable accomplishments under Otto the Great (king 936–962, emperor 962–973), Otto II (972–982), Otto III (983–1002), and Henry II (1002–1024), Ottonian architecture continued until approximately 1065 in Germany, especially along the Rhine, Moselle, and Danube Rivers.

Henry I shifted construction largely northeastward into Saxony. He resumed late Carolingian policies of erecting fortifications to defend palaces, castles, churches, and monasteries against fierce pagan invaders, for instance, at Quedlinburg, Merseburg, and Werla. Otto I's selection of Charlemagne's grand, central-type, palace church at Aachen for his own coronation in 936 signaled the continuing Ottonian esteem for the Carolingian Holy Roman past. The same is reflected in central buildings newly constructed at Bruges (before 950), Mettlach (983–984), Liège (972–1008), and Cologne-Deutz (999–1021), among others, while Aachen's interior elevation was quoted unmistakably in three vertical sections of

Cologne, St. Pantaleon, westwork. *Photograph: Joan A. Holladay*

Saint Michael's at Hildesheim was still consecrated traditionally to the Saviour but also to the Virgin, the Holy Cross, and especially to the Archangel Michael.

Ottonian architects were more engaged with the Byzantines than their predecessors had been. In the very small church of St. Cyriacus at Gernrode (959/961–965; –970s), the influences of the Byzantines, looked upon then as the contemporary living Romans, are seen in the short nave, the full gallery over either side aisle, and the articulation of nave and gallery elevations in complicated rhythmic combinations of columns and piers. Recalled were late-fifth-century galleries at Saint Demetrius in Thessaloníki that had become common in Byzantium's western provinces by the tenth century. Recalled too in the gallery's external blind arcading was an articulation seen more than thirty years before at Constantinople's Myrelaion church (930). Delays in construction at Gernrode suggest these Byzantine elements belonged to its last construction phase, probably under Otto II's wife, the former Byzantine "princess" Theophanu (972–991). In 1017–1018 Bishop Meinwerk of Paderborn called in *operarios graecos,* (Greek or Byzantine workmen) to erect his chapel of St. Bartholomew. Its walls, articulated in shallow niches, enclosed a rectangular, hall-like, three-aisled space, in which elegantly slim columns defined a bay structure that was buoyantly and delicately vaulted.

At the very large, galleried, wooden-roofed monastic basilica of St. Maximin at Trier (934–952), nave and side aisles were separated by alternating piers and columns supporting spanning and lesser arcades, respectively, while at either end were three parallel semicircular apses. There seems to have been only a north transept arm. One apsidal group belonged to a massive westwork (949) entered from a tall, semicircular exedra that mirrored the nave's west apse. Far to the east, the second group (942), that of the main choir, led into a two-storyed, five-aisled outer crypt (952) behind the church. From 934 into the eleventh century, St. Maximin was the center of a Benedictine reform movement that swept through the Germanic lands, often bringing with it the large outer crypt and the diminished Ottonian westwork. Later, this reform was overtaken and finally assimilated by that of Cluny.

Inculcated with the reform at Trier, Archbishop Bruno of Cologne (954–966), the younger brother of Otto the Great and a leading sponsor of religious architecture, enlarged Cologne's cathedral after 954 and founded or reformed many monasteries. Benedictine St. Pantaleon at Cologne, with its plump tower on a cruciform westwork,

the massive mid-eleventh-century west tower of Essen's Münster.

Although frequently grouped with Carolingian building as early Medieval, Ottonian architecture was itself often innovative. Typically, Ottonian architects simplified the Carolingian full westwork at Reims (ca. 976), made it more monumental in the mighty "turris sanctae Mariae" at Werden on the Ruhr (ca. 920–943), and both simplified and monumentalized it in the reduced westwork at Cologne's St. Pantaleon (984–1002). While Werden retained the dominant central tower and substantial high transept of Carolingian full westworks, it relinquished the low, vaulted, entry-level hall "crypta," leaving two remaining levels opening east into the church proper. Such spatial changes were so consistently followed in tenth- and early-eleventh-century German westworks that they suggest a diminution of the liturgy of the Saviour in the reduced Ottonian westwork. By 1015 the west choir of

was begun in 964, continued for a short time after Bruno's death (d. 965), and completed under Empress Theophanu (d. 991). Its monumental, wooden-roofed nave without side aisles extended east beyond screened spacious transept arms with apsidioles (smaller apses) to a shallow semicircular apse. Externally, continuous gigantic blind arcades must have evoked thoughts of Charlemagne's audience hall at Aachen (799–800) and the *aula* (great hall) of Emperor Constantine I at Trier (310). Bruno's architects went beyond Charlemagne's buildings at Aachen, however, when at St. Pantaleon for the first time they transformed the pagan Roman audience hall type into a sacred Christian space. When more delicately proportioned blind arcading was carried into the nave, the major Romanesque architectural motif that took form was destined to appear half a century later in the nave of Speyer's great Romanesque basilican cathedral (1030–1060). Clearly, St. Pantaleon at Cologne was a seminal Ottonian and early Romanesque building.

Ordinarily, Ottonian architects constructed churches similar to Carolingian masonry basilicas with nave and side aisles ending in one or three semicircular apses, and with the nave's long, timber roof posed on a clerestory over arcades on piers, rather than columns. Frequently, their eastern appendages were low transept arms, though some coursed continuously north to south (Gernrode 970s, Hildesheim Cathedral 852–872 and ca. 1035, and Magdeburg Cathedral 978). Many but not all had a west tower, westwork, or west building, and an external eastern crypt.

Outside Hildesheim, Abbot Bishop Bernward's monastic church of St. Michael (ca. 1013–1015) echoed Carolingian St. Riquier at Centula (799) in its east and west transepts and tower groupings. Yet St. Michael's also diverged considerably from its likeliest Carolingian models. Its proportional dimensions reflected the writings of the Roman architect Vitruvius, but its abstract geometrical capitals rejected the classical orders. An unusual, two-storied ambulatory, which coursed around the substantial, projecting apsidal west choir with low, vaulted crypt beneath, may be traced to the late-tenth-century ambulatory built into fifth-century Santo Stefano at Verona. Unlike Hildesheim's cathedral, where a traditional building was preserved, St. Michael's was subtly original in plan and elevation, and openly so in its capitals. Without direct followers, Bernward's St. Michael's was a uniquely personal building.

Three mid-eleventh-century churches illustrate the rich diversity of later Ottonian or Germanic Romanesque architecture. Two were mainly unvaulted: the moderately sized Santa Maria im Kapitol at Cologne, with its continuous trefoil choir-with-ambulatory concluding the nave and side aisles; and the huge, magnificently monumental St. Gertrude at Nivelles, with its stately long nave and side aisles broken by diaphragm arches into elongated spatial bays, with its multileveled, towering west building, and an external eastern corridor crypt. One, the north basilica of the double cathedral at Trier, rebuilt in the tenth century, received at its west front a most impressive apse surmounted by twin low set-back blocklike towers. Probably first wooden-roofed, it was completely vaulted in the twelfth century.

The Ottonians' search for a functioning monumental architecture to express their new alignments with early Christian Rome and the contemporaneous Byzantine Romans was followed throughout the eleventh century by an increasing preoccupation with the structural technologies of vaulted bay systems. As the conflict between secular and churchly authority heightened circa 1070, a more limited post-Ottonian world continued to build as before, and endured as one of the principal regions of Europe's "Romanesque."

BIBLIOGRAPHY

Binding, Günther. "Ottonische Baukunst in Köln." *Kaiserin Theophanu: Begegnung des Ostens und Westens um die Wende der ersten Jahrtausends,* ed. Anton von Euw and Peter Schreiner. 2 vols. Cologne: Schnütgen-Museum, 1991, vol. 1, pp. 281–298.

Grodecki, Louis. *Au Seuil de l'art roman: L'architecture ottonienne.* Paris: Armand Colin, 1958.

Grodecki, Louis, Florentine Mütherich, Jean Taralon, and Francis Wormald. "Architecture," in *Le Siècle de l'an mil 950–1150.* Paris: Gallimard, 1973, pp. 1–84.

Herzog, E. *Die ottonische Stadt: Die Anfänge der mittelalterlichen Stadtbaukunst in Deutschland.* Frankfurter Forschungen zur Architekturgeschichte 2. Berlin: Gebrüder Mann, 1964.

Oswald, Friedrich, Leo Schaefer, and Hans Rudolf Sennhauser, eds. *Vorromanische Kirchenbauten: Katalog der Denkmäler bis zum Ausgang der Ottonen,* 4 vols. Munich: Prestel, 1966–1971; supp. by Werner Jacobsen. Munich: Prestel, 1991.

Sanderson, Warren. *Monastic Reform in Lorraine and the Architecture of the Outer Crypt, 950–1100.* Transactions of the American Philosophical Society N.S. 61,6. Philadelphia: American Philosophical Society, 1971.

Warren Sanderson

Ivories

In the tenth and eleventh centuries, elephant ivory was used primarily in prestigious ecclesiastical commissions. The largest group of surviving objects is plaques with relief carvings, most of which originally decorated the covers of liturgical books. Three-dimensional ivory carvings are less common, but the situlae, or buckets for liturgical use, from late-tenth-century Milan (Milan, Cathedral, Treasury, and London, Victoria and Albert Museum) and the early-eleventh-century Mainz Virgin and Child (Altertumsmuseum) represent this type.

The attribution of Ottonian ivories to identifiable individuals, such as the Master of the Registrum Gregorii, and specific ateliers has proven problematic. Some artists may have traveled with the peripatetic Ottonian court. Others moved among the monastic workshops of the empire, so formal and iconographical influences were constantly exchanged. Furthermore, the imperial patrons favored numerous centers with their commissions. Ottonian ivories also exhibit a variety of influences ranging from late Carolingian to late Antique Roman and contemporary Byzantine. Thus, no single workshop and no homogeneous style dominated in the Ottonian period. However, the formal development indicated by ivories carved between the middle of the tenth and the middle of the eleventh century is characterized generally by an increasing monumentality and clarity of individual forms and entire designs, despite frequently complex and spatially ambitious compositions.

The largest surviving group of ivories dating to the beginning of this development is the series of plaques, now dispersed, from the so-called Magdeburg Antependium. The majority of these reliefs, which may originally have decorated a pulpit or bishop's throne rather than an altar frontal, depict the events of Christ's life and emphasize his ministry. In comparison to plaques carved in the first half of the century under the influence of late Carolingian models from Metz, the Magdeburg figures, displayed against a decorative geometric ground or contained within geometricized architectural enclosures, have gained in monumentality and dignity. The narrative emphasis of these clearly legible compositions suggests contact with Middle Byzantine lectionary illustration.

Contemporary Byzantine as well as late Antique western sources exerted increased influence on ivory carvers during the reigns of Otto II (973–983), who married the Byzantine princess Theophanu, and of their son, Otto III (983–1002). The adaptation of Constantinopolitan models on the one hand and of Roman sources on the other both resulted in a stronger concept of the three-dimensional human figure and of perspectival architecture and space. An ivory situla made at Milan around 980 in preparation for a visit by Otto II is decorated with seated figures of the evangelists and the Virgin and Child in high relief under arcades (Milan, Cathedral, Treasury). The figures have gained in volume and the drapery in complexity in comparison with the Magdeburg reliefs, and compositional clarity is retained. The situla reliefs and an approximately contemporary plaque from Milan with a standing figure of the evangelist John (Paris, Louvre) are consistent with Byzantine ivory carving of the mid–tenth century, such as the Harbaville Triptych (Paris, Louvre), and indicate the authority of eastern models and their transmission to imperial art via northern Italy. The high figural relief and interest in perspectival space evident in several contemporary ivories of northern origin, such as the Halberstadt plaque of circa 985–990 with the evangelist John (Cathedral Treasury), are influenced by the Registrum Master's adaptation of late Antique western models.

BIBLIOGRAPHY

Lasko, Peter. *Ars Sacra 800–1200.* 2d ed. Pelican History of Art. New Haven, Conn.: Yale University Press, 1994, pp. 76–141.

Little, Charles. "From Milan to Magdeburg: The Place of the Magdeburg Ivories in Ottonian Art," in *Atti del 10° congresso internazionale di studi sull'Alto Medioevo.* Spoleto: Presso La Sede del Centro Studi, 1986, pp. 441–451.

Karen E. Loaiza

Manuscript Illumination

Unlike the Carolingians, whose attempt to centralize government resulted in the establishment of a fixed court with an attendant school from which deluxe illuminated manuscripts emanated, the Ottonian rulers were essentially itinerant, and a central court school never developed. Rather, the production of illuminated manuscripts was the domain of various episcopal sees and monasteries throughout the realm. Scholarship on Ottonian manuscript production has thus focused on outlining the individual schools of manuscript painting; major schools not otherwise mentioned below include Corvey, St. Gall, Einsiedeln, Fulda, Essen, Seeon, Salzburg, Freising, Minden, Stavelot, and Liège.

While the court itself did not produce manuscripts, the close interdependence among court, church, and cloister (customarily termed the *ottonisch-salische Reichskirche*) meant that those foundations favored by the imperial house were at the forefront of manuscript production. The monasteries at Reichenau were particularly active in the manufacture of books on behalf of the royal house. Notable examples include three manuscripts for Otto III—the Aachen Gospels (Aachen, Münsterschatz), the Gospels of Otto III (Munich, Bayerische Staatsbibliothek, no. Clm. 4453), and the Bamberg Apocalypse (Bamberg, Staatsbibliothek, no. Ms. 140)—and the Pericopes (liturgical readings) of Henry II (Munich, Bayerische Staatsbibliothek, no. Clm. 4454). The numerous ruler portraits in these and other liturgical manuscripts both develop and depart from Carolingian practice and emphatically underscore the sacral nature of the ruler himself. The greatest exposition of this idea is the image of Otto III in the Aachen Gospels, where the enthroned ruler, surrounded by evangelist symbols and a mandorla (body halo), is lifted up into the heavenly sphere. The picture essentially substitutes Otto III for Christ in a *Maiestas* (in His Majesty) composition; in fact, the page appears just after the book's canon tables, where the representation of Christ in Majesty would normally be expected. The image also includes two pairs of soldiers and ecclesiastics, signifying the unified support of the realm for and under Otto. It was the distribution of such deluxe manuscripts by the ruler that not only forged ties with individual foundations throughout the realm but also reminded the recipients of the sacral nature of the ruler.

A change in king usually brought a change in the fortunes of specific sees or houses. Just as Reichenau flourished under Otto III around 1000, Regensburg saw increased manuscript production as a result of Henry II's patronage throughout the first quarter of the eleventh century (e.g., a Sacramentary and Gospel Book [Munich, Bayerische Staatsbibliothek, no. Clm. 4456; Vatican, Bib-

lioteca Apostolica, no. Ms. Ottob. 74]), while the rise of the Salian rulers Conrad II and Henry III meant new commissions for Echternach in the middle of the century (e.g., the *Codex Aureus* [Nuremberg, Germanisches Nationalmuseum, no. Ms. 156142], and the Gospels of Henry III for Speyer Cathedral [Escorial, no. Cod. Vitr. 17]).

Because of the devolution of power to individual sees and monasteries, ecclesiastics became important as patrons of art to a greater degree than they had been in the Carolingian world. Such individuals as Bishops Egbert of Trier and Bernward of Hildesheim were dynamic patrons whose commissions in manuscripts and in other media enriched the wealth and status of their foundations. Noble women, often from the royal family, who served as abbesses were particularly vigorous book patrons, and such deluxe works as the *Hitda Codex* from Cologne (Darmstadt, Hessisches Landes- und Hochschulbibliothek, no. Ms. 1640) and the *Uta Codex* from Regensburg (Munich, Bayerische Staatsbibliothek, no. Clm. 13601) indicate not only the remarkable fortunes these women controlled but also the great intellectual level embedded in the pictures made for them.

The *Codex Egberti* (Trier, Stadtbibliothek, no. Ms. 24), executed for Egbert around 974, manifests several trends in Ottonian manuscript illumination besides the importance of episcopal patronage. It is a lectionary, a collection of Gospel excerpts read in the mass, perhaps the most popular kind of book illuminated in the period. Like the Gospels of Otto III, its pictures of the Life of Christ are chronologically ordered throughout the book. Other books introduced different programmatic schemes. The *Codex Aureus* of Echternach, for example, grouped the cyclical narratives together at the beginning of each gospel; cycles of the life of Christ were also incorporated into the sacramentaries that were a speciality of Fulda. The increased attention to the representation of Christ is the result of a renewed eleventh-century interest in Christ as a model for the ruler in particular and for individuals in general.

With its red frames, illusionistic backgrounds, and naturalistically modeled figures, the pictures of the *Codex Egberti* reveal the influence of late Antique manuscript painting (as found, for example, in the Vatican Vergil); the foremost proponent of this classical style in the tenth century was the so-called Master of the Registrum Gregorii, who worked primarily for Egbert. Other examples of his work include a Gospel Book now in Manchester (Rylands Library, no. Ms. 98), which had a dramatic influence on the development of painting in Cologne, and the Sainte-Chapelle Gospels (Paris, Bibliothèque Nationale, no. Ms. lat. 8851), which was imitated in the *Codex Aureus* of Echternach. The copies of this master's work disclose the general stylistic trends in Ottonian manuscript painting. Three-dimensional illusionism, as found in late Antique manuscripts and revived in Carolingian works, is the exception. Backgrounds are normally rendered as broad fields of gold, purple, or other saturated colors; rich colors are rarely blended but are juxtaposed to produce dramatic contrasts. This contributes to the overall reduction in spatial depth, so that figures often hover in two-dimensional space. A predilection for expressive hands and facial features is a hallmark of Ottonian book painting. The reduction in modeling and plasticity and a tendency toward linearization in both individual figures and compositional structures would be further developed in the Romanesque period.

Identifying the sources of Ottonian book painting has long been a scholarly concern. Despite differences of opinion about specific motifs, it is agreed that three basic sources were used by Ottonian illuminators: late Antique/early Christian, Carolingian, and Byzantine. This is neatly exemplified by a prayer book made in Mainz for Otto III by his mother, Theophanu, and Archbishop Willigis around 984 (Munich, Bayerische Staatsbibliothek, no. Clm. 30111). The dedication picture with the king is derived from late Antique imagery, as seen, for example, in the Calendar of 354; the image of the orant Otto beneath a Deesis (i.e., Christ depicted between the Virgin Mary and John the Baptist) relies on roughly contemporary Byzantine iconography, like that of a triptych in the Palazzo Venezia, Rome; while the representation of Otto prostrate before Christ is a development of Carolingian ideology, as expressed, for example, in the Prayer Book of Charles the Bald (Munich, Residenz, Schatzkammer [treasury]).

In general, Ottonian book illumination relied foremost on Carolingian models, which often provided the original artistic impetus as the Ottonian schools emerged in the middle of the tenth century. The clearest example is the *Gero Codex* (Darmstadt, Hessische Landes- und Hochschulbibliothek, no. Ms. 1948), made in Reichenau shortly before 969; its pictures were modeled directly on the Lorsch Gospels (Alba Julia, Batthayneum Library and Vatican, Biblioteca Apostolica, no. Ms. Pal. lat. 50), made in Charlemagne's court school at the beginning of the ninth century. Likewise, the images in the Sacramentary of Henry II of 1002–1014 depend to a great degree on the *Codex Aureus* of Charles the Bald from circa 870, which was housed in St. Emmeram, Regensburg's main monastery. For all their theopolitical contention with the Byzantine Empire, with a concomitant importation and emulation of eastern ideas and objects, as seen, for example, in the Byzantine ivory on the cover of the Gospels of Otto III, the Ottonians looked above all to the western, Carolingian Empire as their primary conceptual model. This was evident in their quest for papal coronations as emperor, in their conversion policies toward the Slavs, and in the manner they adopted and transformed Carolingian manuscript painting—through a distinctive style and new iconographic motifs—to express an ever increasing spiritual and political abstraction.

BIBLIOGRAPHY

Bloch, Peter, and Hermann Schnitzler. *Die ottonische Kölner Malerschule.* 2 vols. Düsseldorf: Schwann, 1967–1970.

Brandt, Michael, ed. *Das Kostbare Evangeliar des Heiligen Bernward.* Munich: Prestel, 1993.

Codex Egberti der Stadtbibliothek Trier, ed. Hubert Schiel. Basel: Alkuin-Verlag, 1960.

Cohen, Adam S. *The Uta Codex: Art, Philosophy, and Reform in Eleventh-Century Germany.* University Park: Pennsylvania State University Press, 2000.

Das Evangeliar Ottos III. Clm. 4453 der Bayerischen Staatsbibliothek: Faksimile-Ausgabe, ed. Fridolin Dressler, Florentine Mütherich, Helmut Beumann. Frankfurt am Main: Fischer, 1978.

Görich, Knut, and Elisabeth Klemm. *Gebetbuch Ottos III.: Clm. 30111.* Patrimonia 84. Munich: Kulturstiftung der Länder, 1995.

Grimme, Ernst Günther. *Das Evangeliar Kaiser Ottos III. im Domschatz zu Aachen.* Freiburg im Breisgau: Herder, 1984.

Hoffmann, Hartmut. *Buchkunst und Königtum im ottonischen und frühsalischen Reich.* Monumenta Germaniae Historica, Schriften 30. Stuttgart: Hiersemann, 1988.

Kahsnitz, Rainer, Ursula Mende, and Elisabeth Rücker. *Das Goldene Evangelienbuch von Echternach: Eine Prunkhandschrift des 11. Jahrhunderts.* Frankfurt am Main: Fischer, 1982.

Keller, Hagen. "Herrscherbild und Herrschaftslegitimation: Zur Deutung der ottonischen Denkmäler." *Frühmittelalterliche Studien* 19 (1985): 290–311.

Mayr-Harting, Henry. *Ottonian Book Illumination: An Historical Study.* 2 vols. London: Harvey Miller, 1991.

Nordenfalk, Carl. "Archbishop Egbert's 'Registrum Gregorii,'" in *Studien zur mittelalterlichen Kunst: Fest-*

schrift für Florentine Mütherich zum 70. Geburtstag, ed. Katharina Bierbrauer, Peter Klein, and Willibald Sauerländer. Munich: Prestel, 1985, pp. 87–100.

Palazzo, Eric. *Les Sacramentaires de Fulda: Étude sur l'iconographie et la liturgie à l'époque ottonienne.* Liturgiewissenschaftliche Quellen und Forschungen 77. Münster: Aschendorff, 1994.

Regensburger Buchmalerei: Von frühkarolingischer Zeit bis zum Ausgang des Mittelalters, ed. Florentine Mütherich and Karl Dachs. Munich: Prestel, 1987.

Vor dem Jahr 1000: Abendländische Buchkunst zur Zeit der Kaiserin Theophanu, ed. Anton von Euw. Cologne: Stadt Köln, 1991.

Adam S. Cohen

SEE ALSO

Aachen; Bamberg; Bernward of Hildesheim; Carolingian Art and Architecture; Cologne, Art; Echternach; Egbert; Henry II, Art; Mainz; Otto III; Regensburg; Reichenau; *Registrum Gregorii,* Master of; Romanesque Art and Architecture; Speyer; Theophanu

Metalwork

The centralized patronage and clear development of style in the Carolingian period were replaced during the tenth and eleventh centuries by a far more complex situation under the rule of the Saxon emperors Otto I, Otto II, Otto III, and Henry II, and the Salian Conrad II. Metalwork reflected the ideals and roles of imperial and episcopal rule as well as monastic culture in Ottonian society. Receptiveness to Byzantine cultural influence was signaled by the marriage of Otto II to Theophanu, niece of the Byzantine emperor John Tsimiskes, and later by Henry the Lion's pilgrimage to the Holy Lands in 1172–1173. Throughout the period, relics and luxury and liturgical objects were imported in large numbers from the east. The patronage of the emperors, artistic activity of bishops and of notably active abbesses, and production at the great artistic centers of the empire, such as Reichenau, Regensberg, Cologne, Fulda, and Corvey, resulted in a variety of styles executed in traditional metalworking techniques. Among the imperial commissions number the crown probably made for Otto I (961–962, Vienna, Schatzkammer) and most notably the commissions of Henry II: the pulpit and the altar frontal known as the Pala d'Oro made for the palace chapel at Aachen circa 1002–1014 and circa 1020, respectively, and the golden altar frontal of circa 1022–1024 from Basel Cathedral (Paris, Musée de Cluny). Bernward, Bishop of

Cover of the Codex Aureus from Echternach (Nuremburg, Germanisches Nationalmuseum). *Photograph: Germanisches Nationalmuseum*

Hildesheim, commissioned a pair of silver candlesticks (ca. 996–1000) a cast bronze column (1000–1010) and a pair of cast bronze doors (ca. 1015). Mathilde and Theophanu, abbesses at Essen, granddaughters of Otto I and Otto II, respectively, commissioned a total of four processional or altar crosses to the abbey; Theophanu also donated an elaborate book cover circa 1050. These and other splendid crosses, such as the Lothar Cross (ca. 985–991, Aachen, Cathedral Treasury), crowns like that of the Golden Virgin at Essen (Minster, ca. 983), and book covers such as that from 983–991, that decorate the *Codex Aureus* from Echternach (Nuremberg, Germanisches Nationalmuseum), together with reliquaries, like that made for a fragment of the sandal of St. Andrew (977–993 Trier, Cathedral Treasury), were executed in cloisonné and champlevé enameling, filigree, niello, and repoussé, and were embellished with gems. With the death of Henry II in 1024, Conrad II, first emperor of the Salian dynasty, continued to support the arts, commissioning the imperial altar cross, (ca. 1023–1130, Vienna, Schatzkammer), and the cast bronze "Krodo Altar" of the late eleventh century (Goslar, Museum).

BIBLIOGRAPHY

Bauer, Rotraud, et al. *The Secular and Ecclesiastical Treasuries: Illustrated Guide,* trans. Sophie Kidd and Peter Waugh. Guide to the Collections of the Kunsthistorische Museum 35. Vienna: Residenz Verlag, 1991, 148–158.

Fillitz, Hermann. "Ottonische Goldschmiedekunst," in *Bernward von Hildesheim und das Zeitalter der Ottonen.* 2 vols. Ed. Michael Brandt and Arne Eggebrecht. Hildesheim: Bernward Verlag, and Mainz: Philipp von Zabern, 1993, vol. 1, pp. 173–190.

Lasko, Peter. *Ars Sacra 800–1200,* 2d ed. Pelican History of Art. New Haven, Conn.: Yale University Press, 1994, pp. 76–141.

Rebecca Leuchak

SEE ALSO

Bernward of Hildesheim; Carolingian Art and Architecture; Cologne, Art; Corvey; Essen; Fulda; Guelph Treasure; Henry II, Art; Metalworking; Otto I; Otto II; Otto III; Ottonian Art and Architecture; Quedlinburg; Regensburg; Reichenau; Theophanu

Sculpture

Ottonian sculpture is an elusive entity. The chronological limits are hard to discern, because its beginning occurred somewhere in the continuum of the Carolingian tradition of sumptuary art, around the middle of the tenth century, and its end fell somewhere in the genesis of the Romanesque revival of monumental stone sculpture, about a century later. It is difficult to decide what artistic work ought to count as sculpture as distinct from sumptuary art, because Ottonian objects that were embellished with carved, modeled, or cast relief images—mostly figures—run the gamut in scale from miniature to monumental. It is also difficult to define an Ottonian formal character because two stylistic strains coexisted side by side: a pictorial mode, miniature in conception, that stemmed from Carolingian illuminations, and a new volumetric mode, relatively monumental in conception, in which forms occupy either real space or an abstractly defined space but not a pictorial one. Emerging in the late tenth century, the volumetric mode became dominant only at the point that Ottonian sculpture was about to become Romanesque. There is yet one more difficulty, namely, validating Ottonian sculpture as an artistic tradi-

Gero Crucifix, Cologne, cathedral. *Photograph: Rheinisches Bildarchiv der Stadt Köln*

tion, because there was no continuum; its production was sporadic and scattered and was virtually limited to patronage from the most privileged level of society. Until the middle of the eleventh century, when production of large stone figures began, the crafting of images with a third dimension, either in relief or in the round, was more a function of employing precious metals such as ivory, gold, or bronze than it was a conscious urge to make sculpture as a medium distinct from painting.

Virtually all Ottonian objects with sculptural embellishment are related to Christian worship, serving either as liturgical implements, church furniture, or reliquaries. Although undoubtedly commissioned and executed in a spirit of piety, the most lavish among them imply the additional motivation of celebrating the magnificence of an imperial regime or ecclesiastical reign. The most outstanding objects in the first period, the decades flanking 970, are a large wooden crucifix in Cologne Cathedral, made for Archbishop Gero; a large freestanding Virgin and Child in Essen Münster, carved of wood and covered with gold, made to hold a relic; and fragments of monumental stone figures from the facade of St. Pantaleon in Cologne. In the second period, the decades flanking 1010, there are three: at Hildesheim a great double-valved bronze door with scenes of the Life of Christ and a tall bronze column with a spiral narrative of the mission of Christ, both made for Bishop Bernward; and for Basel Cathedral a gold altar frontal, given by Emperor Henry II, with Christ, three archangels, and St. Benedict framed in an arcade (now Paris, Musée de Cluny). In the third period, the decades flanking 1060, there are more: a free-standing wooden Madonna and Child, originally covered with gold and holding a relic, made for Bishop Imad of Paderborn; a wooden door with scenes of the Life of Christ, at Maria-im-Kapitol (Mary in the Capitol), Cologne; a nearly life-size funerary slab figure of the Anglo-Saxon missionary Widukind, a long-dead military-political hero, at Enger; and three stone reliefs of Christ Enthroned and two saints, now set above a portal at St. Emmeram, Regensburg. Among these monuments there is no connective thread and no pattern of development, leaving Ottonian sculpture with the exceptional characteristic of manifesting no historical trajectory.

BIBLIOGRAPHY

Bernward von Hildesheim und der Zeitalter der Ottonien: Katalog der Ausstellung Hildesheim 1993. Hildesheim: Bernward Verlag; Mainz am Rheim: Verlag Philipp von Zabern, 1993.

Buddensieg, Tilmann. "Die Basler Altartafel Heinricks II." *Wallraf-Richartz Jahrbuch* 19 (1957): 133–192.

Jantzen, Hans. *Ottonische Kunst.* Munich: Münchner Verlag, 1947.

Panofsky, Erwin. *Die deutsche Plastik des elften bis dreizehnten Jahrhunderts.* Munich: Wolff, 1924.

Wesenberg, Rudolf. *Bernwardinische Plastik: Zur ottonischen Kunst unter Bischof Bernward von Hildesheim.* Denkmäler deutscher Kunst. Berlin: Deutscher Verlag für Kunstwissenschaft, 1955.

Wesenberg, Rudolf. *Frühe mittelalterliche Bildwerke: Die Schulen rheinischer Skulptur und ihre Ausstrahlung.* Düsseldorf: Schwann, 1972.

                                                    M. F. Hearn

SEE ALSO

Basel; Bernward of Hildesheim; Carolingian Art and Architecture; Cologne, Art; Essen; Hildesheim; Metalworking; Paderborn; Regensburg; Romanesque Art and Architecture

Textiles

Many of the luxury textiles favored in the West during the Ottonian period, a number of which still survive in Rhenish treasuries, were imports and gifts from the Byzantine Empire. Acknowledging the Ottonian taste for Byzantine silks is not, however, to dismiss local production of fine textiles, particularly in the form of tablet-woven silk bands of which several from the late tenth century still exist. In addition to examples found at Augsburg and Speyer, Trier claims an extremely well-preserved stole that depicts along its length frontal portraits of each of the twelve apostles. In Bamberg resides a fragment of a particularly luxurious band once attached to a cope of St. Kunigunde. Brocaded with green and blue silk and gold, it is decorated with a series of confronting lions on either side of stylized trees.

The earliest example of Ottonian embroidery can be found on a reliquary cover at St. Kunibert in Cologne. Made of blue linen, embroidered with silk and strips of gilded leather, this piece showing Christ in the heavens was created in the second half of the tenth century. The many fine embroideries associated with Kunigunde and her husband, Henry II, in the Bamberg treasury attest to imperial interest in this highly developed art. The "Star Mantle," so called because of the zodiacal signs and constellations that adorn it, was a gift to the cathedral from the imperial couple. Another cloak there said to have belonged to Kunigunde is decorated with a row of embroidered roundels showing New Testament scenes, while another depicts rows of enthroned rulers. All three are made of silk and embroidered with silk and metal threads.

BIBLIOGRAPHY

Levey, Santina M. "Embroidery" in *Textiles, 5000 Years: An International History and Illustrated Survey,* ed. Jennifer Harris. New York: Harry N. Abrams, 1993, pp. 200–203.

Müller-Christensen, Sigrid. "Examples of Mediaeval Tablet-Woven Bands," in *Studies in Textile History,* ed. Veronika Gervers. Toronto: Royal Ontario Museum, 1977, pp. 232–237.

Wilckens, Leonie von. "Die Stola aus Neumagen in Trier." *Zeitschrift für Kunstgeschichte* 51 (1988): 301–312.

                                                    Melanie Holcomb

SEE ALSO

Augsburg; Bamberg; Cologne, Art; Henry II, Art; Speyer; Trier

Wall Painting

In the period when monumental sculpture was just beginning to experience a resurgence, wall painting constituted the dominant medium for the decoration of Ottonian churches. Contemporary chronicles mention these paintings in praiseworthy, albeit somewhat general terms. Thangmar, the contemporary biographer of Bernward of Hildesheim (r. 993–1022), described the bishop as having decorated the "walls and ceilings [of his cathedral] . . . with marvellous bright paintings, so that one had the feeling of being in a completely new church" (Thangmar 1841: 761). The paintings in the chapel of St. Gertrude at Eichstätt were described as "wonderful and almost living pictures" (Dodwell 1993: 126).

Despite the chronicles' mention of paintings in centers such as St. Gall, Peterhausen, Deutz, Cologne, Aachen, and Echternach, few examples remain today. From the extant works it appears that Ottonian wall painting followed the Carolingian goal of illustrating scenes from or prefiguring the New Testament. The two primary sites where examples of Ottonian wall painting are preserved today are at Fulda in Hesse and in the area of Lake Constance. The Fulda murals are found in the crypts of two churches: Petersburg and St. Andrew at Neuenberg. The Petersburg paintings are fragments of a larger mural, and include scenes of Christ's Baptism in the Jordan, the Lamb of God, angels, and saints. The images at St. Andrew's date to circa 1023 and display a limited palette. C. R. Dodwell describes these works as "tinted drawings" and suggests an Anglo-Saxon model for the images, which include Abraham, Melchizedek, Abel, and a Christ in Majesty (Dodwell 1993: 128).

The Reichenau murals in the church of St. George at Oberzell convey a sense of the scale and sophistication of wall painting during this period. Paintings in the nave are set off by a frieze and illustrate Christ's miracles, including the storm at sea, the healing of the leper, and the raising of Lazarus. The figures are shown against a backdrop

Reichenau-Oberzell, St. George, interior with Ottonian wall paintings. *Photograph: Joan A. Holladay*

of architecture and horizontal bands of color. Deterioration, compounded by an extensive restoration in 1880, has resulted in the loss of much of the modeling. In the first publication to deal with these works, F. X. Kraus assigned a date of 985–987, locating them within the tenure of Abbot Witigowo. Later scholarship broadened the sphere of prospective dates to 950 or later but generally agree on an Ottonian origin for these works. These arguments rest primarily on stylistic and iconographic similarities to contemporary Reichenau book painting. In the most recent study on these works, Koichi Koshi has suggested that the paintings actually date to the Carolingian period and were contemporary with the construction of the church under the Abbot Hatto (888–913). Koshi's argument examines these works from a stylistic point of view, placing them in the context of Carolingian mural painting rather than manuscript illumination. The paintings at St. Sylvester at Goldbach are more modest in scale and execution than those at Oberzell, but are significant in that they have never been restored. In addition to a cycle of the miracles of Christ, the Goldbach paintings include the figures of the twelve apostles and that of Winidhere, the founder of Goldbach and monk of Reichenau.

The discourse surrounding Reichenau's status as a major center of book production has also questioned whether the monastery had its own wall painters. Wall paintings went for the most part unsigned, making it difficult to trace the artists. It is known that Reichenau possessed monastic wall painters in the ninth century, when they are recorded as having worked for a time at St. Gall. Dodwell suggests that a century later, the Oberzell paintings could have been executed by itinerant artists. Others have argued for Reichenau as a center of a school of wall painting, however, on the basis of the amount of work found in the region and its stylistic links to the Reichenau manuscripts. Deschamps even suggests that the miniaturists were also wall painters, asserting that these two arts penetrated each other. This question of context appears to be the crux of the problem for future research. Only when scholars have reconsidered the relationship of Ottonian wall painting to both contemporary manuscript illumination and earlier Carolingian mural cycles will a more complete history emerge.

BIBLIOGRAPHY

Beckwith, John. *Early Medieval Art.* New York: Thames and Hudson, 1985, pp. 88–92.

Deschamps, Paul. "Goldbach." *Congrès archéologique de France* 105–106: *Souabe* (1947): 60–75.

Dodwell, C. R. *Painting in Europe 800 to 1200.* Pelican History of Art. Harmondsworth, England: Penguin, 1971, pp. 45–51.

———. *The Pictorial Arts of the West, 800–1200.* Pelican History of Art. New Haven, Conn.: Yale University Press, 1993, pp. 123–130.

Koshi, Koichi. *Die frühmittelalterlichen Wandmalereien der St.-Georges-Kirche zu Oberzell auf der Bodenseeinsel Reichenau.* 2 vols. Denkmäler deutscher Kunst. Berlin: Deutscher Verlag für Kunstwissenschaft, 1999.

Kraus, F. X. *Die Wandegemälde in der St. Sylvesterkapelle zu Goldbach am Bodensee.* Munich: Bruckmann, 1902.

Martin, Kurt. *Die ottonischen Wandbilder der St. Georgskirche Reichenau-Oberzell,* 2d ed. Sigmaringen: Thorbecke, 1975.

Mayr-Harting, Henry. *Ottonian Book Illumination: An Historical Study.* 2 vols. London: Harvey Miller, 1991, pp. 203–209.

Thangmar, *Vita S. Bernwardi Episcoppi Hildesheimensis.* Monumenta Germaniae Historica, Scriptores 4. Hanover: Hahn, 1841, pp. 754–786.

Thibout, M. "Les Peintures murales de l'église d'Oberzell." *Congrès archéologique de France* 105–106: *Souabe* (1947): 43–58.

Kristen M. Collins

SEE ALSO

Aachen; Carolingian Art and Architecture; Cologne, Art; Echternach; Fulda; Ottonian Art and Architecture; Reichenau; Sankt Gall

P

Pacher, Michael (ca. 1430/1435–1498)

Born in the Puster valley in south Tyrol, the painter and wood carver Michael Pacher was one of those rare double talents of the late Middle Ages whose reputation reached well beyond his native region. Contemporary documents reveal, however, that he was primarily a painter, like Friedrich Pacher, who is presumed to be a relative. Thus, in spite of his astounding professional activity as a sculptor, most of his religious works comprise panel paintings and frescoes, including the vault paintings in the old sacristy at the cloister Neustift from about 1470. By 1467 at the latest he directed a workshop in Bruneck.

Pacher's importance lies in his adaptation of new artistic forms from Italy, the Netherlands, and southern Germany, which, in combination with his Alpine piety, he transforms into a new pictorial language. A clear understanding of Mantegna's frescoes in Padua and Mantua with their bold foreshortening and deep spaces constructed in virtuoso perspective is already apparent in four early panel paintings preserved from an otherwise lost altar dedicated to Thomas Becket (about 1460; Graz, Joanneum). In the altarpiece of the church fathers from Neustift near Brixen (1482–1483; Munich, Alte Pinakothek), he developed these pictorial techniques fully, setting the monumental figures under diagonally arranged trompe l'oeil baldachins (realistic figures) that seem to spring out of the paintings. Realistic, portraitlike facial features characterize the four small panels with the apostles and the helpers in need that were located at Wilten after 1820 (about 1465; now divided among the Österreichische Galerie in Vienna, the Museum Ferdinandeum in Innsbruck, and a private collection in the United States). No trace remains of a documented altarpiece, probably dedicated to the Archangel Michael, made for the parish church in Bozen between 1481 and 1484.

Of four Virgin altarpieces, all with richly sculptured shrines, three are fragmentarily preserved. An enthroned Madonna from 1462–1465 in the parish church of St. Lorenz near Bruneck, probably accompanied by the figures of St. Michael (Munich, Bayerisches Landesmuseum) and St. Lawrence (Innsbruck, Museum Ferdinandeum), has lasted through the centuries, although without the original shrine structure. Single panels from the wings, which were painted on both sides, are now housed in Munich (Alte Pinakothek) and Vienna (Österreichische Galerie). Pacher set a Coronation of the Virgin, composed as a scene rather than a stiff row of saints, into the center of the polyptych at Gries near Bozen (1471–1475); polychromed and gilded reliefs occupy the wings of the chapel-like shrine. Pacher's representation of the coronation before a gold brocade curtain supported by angels is based on Hans Multscher's altar in Sterzing. The contract mentions guard figures, which would have flanked the shrine; these, along with the painted wing panels, have disappeared. The masterpiece among Pacher's altars is the double triptych in the choir of the pilgrimage church at St. Wolfgang in the Salzkammergut; the contract is dated 1471, the execution between 1475 and 1481. With this work Pacher set the artistic standards against which other paintings and sculptures of the last phase of the late Gothic are measured. Here this "genius among altar sculptors of south Tyrol" (Paatz 1963: 44, my trans.) developed his own artistic language in the shimmering gold coronation set onto a stage under a filigreed tracery superstructure that reaches up to the vaults, in the imposing figures of the church's patron and St. Benedict, in the militant knight-saints at the sides of the shrine, and in the accompanying painted cycles with scenes from the lives of Christ, the Virgin, and St. Wolfgang. Probably the largest of Pacher's Virgin altars was that commissioned for the Franciscan church in Salzburg in 1484 and finished in 1498. This structure, greater than seventeen meters, was dismantled in the baroque period; its enthroned Madonna, later inserted into an altar by Fischer von Erlach, and several panels are preserved (Vienna, Österreichische Galerie). The extraordinary sum of 3,300 Rhenish gold florins was likely the highest paid for an altarpiece of this period. Pacher died in 1498, shortly before its completion.

BIBLIOGRAPHY

Egg, Erich. *Gotik in Tirol: Die Flügelaltäre.* Innsbruck: Haymon-Verlag, 1985, pp. 177–189.

Evans, Mark. "Appropriation and Application: The Significance of the Sources of Michael Pacher's Altarpieces," in *The Altarpiece in the Renaissance,* ed. Peter Humphrey and Martin Kemp. Cambridge: Cambridge University Press, 1990, pp. 106–128.

Goldberg, Gisela. "Late Gothic Painting from South Tyrol: Michael Pacher and Marx Reichlich." *Apollo 116* (1982): 240–245.

Hempel, Erhard. *Michael Pacher.* Vienna: A. Schroll, 1931.

Koller, Manfred, and Norbert Wibiral. *Der Pacher-Altar von St. Wolfgang: Untersuchung, Konservierung, Restaurierung 1969–1976.* Studien zu Denkmalschutz und Denkmalpflege 11. Vienna: Hermann Böhlaus Nachfolger, 1981.

Michael Pacher und sein Kreis: Ein Tiroler Künstler der europäischen Spätgotik (1498–1998). Bozen: Südtiroler Landesregierung, 1998.

Paatz, Walter. "Süddeutsche Schnitzaltäre der Spätgotik." *Heidelberger kunstgeschichtliche Abhandlungen. Neue Folge* 8 (1963): 44–54.

Rasmo, Nicolo. *Michael Pacher.* London: Phaidon, 1971.

Brigitte Schliewen

SEE ALSO

Gothic Art and Architecture; Multscher, Hans; Salzburg; Sankt Wolfgang

Paderborn

In 777 Charlemagne held an imperial synod at Paderborn, and in 799, the royal palace witnessed the historic meeting between Charlemagne and Pope Leo III, during which the terms for the imperial coronation were determined. In 805, Paderborn became a bishopric and missionary center for Saxony. Both the Carolingian cathedral and the palace complex to its north are known through excavations.

Under the patronage of Bishop Meinwerk (1009–1036), a relative and adviser of Henry II, Paderborn experienced, following the conflagration of 1000, a major urban reconstruction. The center of this scheme was the cathedral, a basilica with eastern transepts and a westwork (massive entry structure) in the Carolingian tradition, flanked to its north by the imperial and to its southwest by the episcopal palace. This central complex was to become the nucleus of a cruciform arrangement of monuments, intended to present a sacred topography, or *mappa mundi,* but was left uncompleted by the death of the patron. To the east, the centrally planned abbey church of Busdorf—the burial church of Meinwerk consecrated shortly before his death in 1036—represented the Holy Sepulchre at Jerusalem; to ensure a likeness with the prototype, Meinwerk had actually sent Wino, Abbot of Helmarshausen, to Jerusalem to procure the measurements of this church. The western arm of the cross was formed by the abbey of Abdinghof, founded by introducing thirteen monks from Cluny. After the collapse of the original church, a simplified version of the second abbey church at Cluny, the very day before its consecration in 1015, it was rebuilt instead "in the Roman manner" *(more Romano)* with a western set of transepts, which might have been originally intended for the planned monastery of St. Alexis south of the cathedral. The chapel of St. Bartholomew, attached to the imperial palace and known to have been built in 1017 by Byzantine craftsmen *(per Grecos operarios),* corresponds in all its measurements and major architectural features—even though transformed from a centrally planned church of the "cross-in-square" -type into a small hall church—with the church of the Myrelaion in Constantinople, planned as the burial church of Emperor Romanos I Lekapenos (922–944). An even closer copy of this model existed in the episcopal chapel attached to the southern transept of the cathedral, one of the earliest examples of a double-storied chapel with four columns and a central dome. The place of the planned monastery south of the cathedral was finally taken by the parish church, or *Gaukirche,* dedicated to St. Ulrich, a vaulted basilica of the twelfth century to which a Cistercian nunnery was attached in 1228.

The two most important works of art dating from this period are the so-called Imad Madonna from the mid–eleventh century and the small portable altar created by the artist Roger of Helmarshausen, or Theophilus Presbyter, as the author of the *Schedula de diversis artibus* calls himself.

In the second third of the thirteenth century, a re-building of the cathedral took place. It started with the western tower and the adjoining basilica bay and western transept, and continued as a hall church of the "Westphalian" type, integrating late Romanesque elements from the Rhineland and Gothic forms from the Île-de-France. A porch, the *Paradies,* was added to the south end of the western transept; its monumental sculptures show the distinct influence of works from Reims Cathedral. Following work on the cathedral, a Gothic hall nave was attached in the late thirteenth century to the church of Busdorf, and its octagonal part was subsequently demolished, leaving only its two round facade towers as flanking towers to the new choir. The Gothic parish church of the market district, St. Mary's, was demolished around 1800. An interesting reception of medieval style exists in the church of the Jesuits, built between 1682 and 1692 as a post-Gothic basilica with galleries.

BIBLIOGRAPHY

Böker, Hans J. "*Per Grecos Operarios:* St. Bartholomäus in Paderborn und die Rezeption eines byzantinischen Bautypus." *Niederdeutsche Beiträge zur Kunstgeschichte* 36 (1997): 8–27.

Lobbedey, Uwe. *Die Ausgrabungen im Dom zu Paderborn 1978/80 und 1983.* Denkmalpflege und Forschung in Westfalen 11. Bonn: Habelt, 1986.

Mietke, Gabriele. *Die Bautätigkeit Bishof Meinwerks von Paderborn und die frühchristliche und byzantinische Architektur.* Paderborner Theologische Studien 21. Paderborn: Schöningh, 1991.

Hans J. Böker

SEE ALSO

Carolingian Art and Architecture; Charlemagne; Gothic Art and Architecture; Helmarshausen; Henry II, Art; Metalworking; Ottonian Art and Architecture; Roger of Helmarshausen; Romanesque Art and Architecture; Theophilus Presbyter; World Maps

Painting

See individual styles and painters.

Paleography

Etymologically the word *paleography* means "old writing" (from Greek *palais,* "old," and *graphia,* "writing" or "script"). However, the term has come more generally to refer to the study and history of writing. The most common objects of study for paleographers concerned with the Middle Ages are manuscripts and manuscript fragments. Paleographers examine the appearance of letters, abbreviations, the slant of writing, the size of the letters, the movement of the pen, the direction and quality of the pen strokes, and the nature of the writing material. They attempt to classify scripts and plot the development, persistence, and dissemination of types of scripts. The study of paleography can help to establish the number and the skill of the hands that wrote a given manuscript, to determine the origin of a given manuscript, and, more specifically, to localize a manuscript to a region, a scriptorium, and sometimes even a particular scribe. Paleography is an important auxiliary science to history, philology, anthropology, and literature.

Most written texts from the early Middle Ages are in Latin, but Old High German glosses appear in religious texts from the middle of the eighth century. These glosses are generally interlinear or marginal German translations or explanations of Latin words and passages. The glosses comprise the largest corpus of the Old High German language. The earliest extant text of significance written in the vernacular is a bilingual German and Latin dictionary of synonyms from around the year 770, called the *Abrogans* after the first entry. The first narratives in Old High German appear around the turn of the ninth century. The genres of these narratives include sermons and religious legends. Several charms have also come down to us. Charlemagne first initiated the translation of important religious texts into German for missionary purposes. His efforts resulted in an increase in the use of the vernacular for writing. In this early period writing took place exclusively at monasteries. Through the dialectal variation in written Old High German, philologists can often trace a given text to a particular scriptorium.

The first manuscripts containing narratives of a secular nature appear toward the end of the twelfth century. In the twelfth and thirteenth centuries—the High Middle Ages—the number of manuscripts written in the vernacular increases significantly. The most common genres of texts written in Middle High German are literary texts, legal codifications and documents, and chronicles.

The script used in medieval German manuscripts changed in style in the course of the Middle Ages. From the end of the ninth to the late eleventh century, documents were written primarily in Caroline minuscule. This script evolved in the late eighth century, during the period of Charlemagne (r. 771–814). The Caroline minuscule is thought to have originated in northern France or western Germany, but its precise origin is subject to debate. By the mid–ninth century, this script was used for copying books throughout the Carolingian Empire, except in the far southeastern regions. In the second half of the tenth century, it was introduced into northern Germany, Poland, Bohemia, Hungary, and Scandinavia as these areas were Christianized. Caroline minuscule is an economic script and is highly legible. Each letter is written as an individual character, and there is only limited use of abbreviations and ligatures. This script remained widespread for four centuries.

Starting around the end of the eleventh century, the Caroline minuscule was replaced by Gothic script. Gothic minuscule is popularly regarded as the typical medieval script. Far more books and documentary texts are preserved in the Gothic script than in any other. The name *Gothic* actually refers to a family of scripts that became increasingly differentiated in the course of the Middle Ages. Certain features are common to most Gothic scripts: preference for angularity over curves, angular finishes at the top and bottom of short vertical strokes used to form the letters *m, n, i,* and *u* (called minims), lateral compression that emphasizes height in letters, and thick perpendicular strokes. The Gothic script became the model for Fraktur (literally "fractured," i.e., the "broken," or forked, form of the shafts), the script used for printing texts in the German language by printing presses in Germany into the beginning of the twentieth century (By contrast, Latin was generally printed in Roman script). Standard German handwriting is a continuation of cursive Gothic script.

Scribes, rubricators (colorers), and illustrators each took part in creating a manuscript. Initials were painted in red by rubricators after the manuscript had been completed. Initials were also frequently adorned, sometimes with a simple design and sometimes with elaborate, figurative images. Both religious and secular manuscripts often contain illustrations. The quality of the illustrations varies considerably. In general, liturgical manuscripts are more ornately and expensively decorated than manuscripts of a secular nature. The choice of subject matter for the images, and the relationship between word and image, varies considerably in the High Middle Ages.

In the Middle Ages, the most common writing material was parchment made out of the skin of calves (vellum), goats, or sheep; quill pens usually made from goose feathers; and ink that was often made from a mixture of oak gall and copper vitriol. The sheets of parchment were folded into gatherings that were then sewn and bound into books called *codices*. A codex can be made up of one or more folded sheets. Book formats are classified as folio, quarto (4to), octavo (8vo), duodecimo (12mo), sextodecimo (16mo), and so forth, depending on whether the sheet was folded to make two, four, eight, or sixteen leaves. The codex was usually bound between two wooden boards fastened together with clasps.

BIBLIOGRAPHY

Alexander, J. J. G. *Medieval Illuminators and Their Methods of Work.* New Haven, Conn.: Yale University Press, 1992.

Bischoff, Bernhard. *Palographie des römischen Altertums und des abendlandischen Mittelalters.* Berlin: Schmidt, 1979; Daibhi O Croinin and David Ganz, trans. *Latin Palaeography: Antiquity and the Middle Ages.* Cambridge: Cambridge University Press, 1990.

Brown, Michelle P. *A Guide to Western Historical Scripts from Antiquity to 1600.* London: British Library, 1990.

Schneider, Karin. *Gotische Schriften in deutscher Sprache.* Wiesbaden: Reichert, 1987.

Kathryn Starkey

SEE ALSO

Abrogans; Bookmaking and Production; Carolingians; Charlemagne; Charms; Glosses, Old High German; Law and Lawbooks; Latin Language; Libraries

Paradise Plays

See Drama, Paradise Plays.

Parler Family

Centered in Germany in the mid– to late fourteenth century, the three generations of Parlers were both architects and sculptors. They worked throughout Germany and its eastern neighbors, and whether called Parler, von Gmünd (from Gmünd) or von Freiburg (from Freiburg), they shared the mason's and master's mark of a twice broken staff, in the shape of a hook. Diverse in their style, the members of the Parler family were nevertheless enormously influential and involved in many of the grandest building projects of the fourteenth century.

Cologne, cathedral, west façade, Peter's Portal, left jamb. *Photograph: Joan A. Holladay*

The patriarch of the family, Heinrich Parler (fl. ca. 1330s–1371/1377), an architect, was master of the works at the Heiligkreuzkirche (Church of the Holy Cross) in Schwäbisch Gmünd by the 1330s. He is credited with redesigning the eastern section of the nave to coordinate with his plans for a hall choir instead of the original basilican plan. In addition to altering the layout of the church, Heinrich combined architecture and sculpture here in a way not before experienced in Europe. Mentioned in an inscription above a portrait of his son, Peter Parler, in the triforium (short middle story) of St. Vitus Cathedral in Prague, he continued to work on the Swabian cathedral until his death in 1377.

Scholars also credit Heinrich with leading building campaigns at the Frauenkirche (Church of the Virgin) in Nuremburg, the Münster at Ulm, and the choir of Augsburg Cathedral, work on which was taken up by his

youngest son, Michael, after Heinrich's death. At the Frauenkirche, Heinrich once again utilized a hall church plan, basing his design on the local palatine chapel. With its profusion of sculpture, cubic form, round columns, and innovative segmented arches, this structure is typically Parleresque. Heinrich's direct contribution at Ulm is questionable because of his advanced age at the time its foundation was laid in 1377. Nevertheless, he and his son Michael (fl. ca. 1359–1383) were commissioned by the town council to design an expansive hall church that was later changed to a basilica in 1392.

The elder son of Heinrich, referred to as Johann von Gmünd (also Hans Parler, fl. Basel ca. 1356–1359), followed his father's conception of open space and unarticulated bays in both his work at Basel Minster and the cathedral of Freiburg im Breisgau, where he was named director for life in 1359. He was most likely responsible for the design of the choir, and stylistic details point to his involvement in the sacristy and the superstructures of the two "Cock Towers" flanking the choir.

Before being called to Prague in 1356 by the Holy Roman Emperor Charles IV, Heinrich's second son, Peter Parler ("von Gmünd", 1333–July 13, 1399), assisted his father on both the Heiligkreuzkirche in Schwäbisch Gmünd, where he was born, and the imperially funded Frauenkirche in Nuremburg. Peter Parler's reputation grew enormously with his imperial commissions, and he became one of the most celebrated architects and sculptors of the Middle Ages. Peter's innovative style suited Charles IV's desire for a new aesthetic to accompany his dynastic program.

Along with the cathedral of St. Vitus, Peter Parler also designed the Charles Bridge and Tower in Prague, begun in 1373. The ceilings of both these monuments are covered in a profusion of rib vaulting; in particular, the freestanding vaulting of the south porch at St. Vitus helps dissolve the walls from which it springs. He also included more subtly striking elements, such as pinnacles that pierce through their offsets in the exterior lower story of the cathedral's chevet (apsidal termination of the eastern choir), and shafts that unify the clerestory (tall upper windows) and triforium (short middle story) by piercing the undulating cornice that runs between these two levels. When Peter retired as master of the works of the cathedral in 1397, he was succeeded by his son Wenceslas.

Peter Parler, as sculptor, was responsible for a set of carved choir stalls for St. Vitus (destroyed), and the tomb program of Charles IV's ancestors, begun in 1377, of which only the effigies of Ottokar I and Ottokar II can be linked to his hand. Peter Parler's high status at the imperial court is as much attested to by the numerous burgher commissions he undertook, seen in the churches of St. Bartholomew in Kolin, with its polygonal choir vaults, St. Apollinarius at Tyn, Saint Barbara in Kuttenberg, and of the Knights of Malta in Prague, as by his inclusion as one of the elite few whose busts, sculpted after his design, look down from the triforium of his cathedral in Prague.

The two sons of Johann von Gmünd— Michael (III, fl. 1380–ca. 1387/1388) and Heinrich (IV, ca. 1354–after 1387)—referred to themselves as "von Freiburg" as well as "von Gmünd." Michael worked with his father in Basel, probably raising the Münster towers by 1380. He then became master of the works at Strasbourg Cathedral in 1383, where he completed the middle story of the west facade after the great fire in 1384.

Heinrich is known for his skills as a sculptor, which he seems to have acquired under the direction of his grandfather Heinrich I in Schwäbisch Gmünd. His Christ Carrying the Cross and Man of Sorrows survive in the Heiligkreuzkirche. He traveled to Vienna and by the 1370s was working under the direction of his uncle, Peter Parler, in Prague. His figure of Saint Wenceslas remains in the saint's chapel in the cathedral, his tomb effigies of Břetislav I and Spytihněv II in the axial chapel, and his bust of Duke Wenceslas I of Luxembourg in the triforium.

Heinrich was probably in Cologne by 1378, where he took up work on the Petersportal, the only medieval portal at the cathedral. Aided by a second Parler master, perhaps Michael II of Savoy, he executed the baldachins over the apostles in the jambs (sides of doors), the tympanum (triangle above doors), and the seated archivolt (tympanum molding) figures. Additional evidence for Heinrich's presence in Cologne during the 1380s is seen in the female corbel bust (Eve?, now in the Schnütgen-Museum in Cologne) bearing the Parler mark. Because of the tender, soft, less realistic style of his sculptures, he and his workshop are credited with helping to develop the *Schöne Madonna* (Lovely Virgin Mary) type.

Other members of the Parler family—Hans Parler, Heinrich Parler III, and Johann von Freiburg—were called to advise on plans for the enormous cathedral in Milan, where Hans was named master engineer in May 1392.

BIBLIOGRAPHY

Gothic Art in Bohemia: Architecture, Sculpture, Painting, ed. Karl Swoboda, trans. Gerald Onn. Oxford: Phaidon, 1977.

Gotik—Prag um 1400: Der schöne Stil, böhmische Malerei und Plastik in der Gotik. Vienna: Wien Kultur, 1991.

Kutal, Albert. *Gothic Art in Bohemia and M'ravia.* New York: Hamlyn, 1971.

Neuwirth, Josef. *Peter Parler von Gmünd, Dombaumeister in Prag, und seine Familie: Ein Beitrag zur deutsch-Österreichischen Künstlergeschichte.* Prague: Calve, 1891.

Opitz, Josef. *Die Plastik in Böhmen zur Zeit der Luxemburger.* Prague: Stenc, 1936.

Die Parler und der schöne Stil 1350–1400: Europäische Kunst unter den Luxemburgern, ed. Anton Legner. 6 vols. Cologne: Museen der Stadt Köln, 1978–1980, vol. 1, pp. 159–168, 184–187, 293–297, 315–333.

Schmidt, Gerhard. "Peter Parler und Heinrich IV. Parler als Bildhauer." *Wiener Jahrbuch für Kunstgeschichte* 23 (1970): 108–153.

Schock-Werner, Barbara. "Peter Parler, maître d'oeuvre à Prague," in *Les Batisseurs des cathédrales gothiques,* ed. Roland Recht.

Strasbourg: Éditions Les Musées de la ville de Strasbourg, 1989, pp. 200–203.

Stejskal, Karel. *European Art in the 14th Century,* trans. Till Gottheinerová. London: Octopus, 1978.

Tracy Chapman Hamilton

SEE ALSO

Augsburg; Basel; Cologne, Art; Freiburg im Breisgau; International Style; Nuremberg; Prague; Schwäbisch Gmünd; Ulm

Parzival

See Wolfram von Eschenbach.

Passau

Located at the confluence of the Danube, Ilz, and Inn Rivers, Passau is one of the oldest important, continuously occupied settlements north of the Alps. In the fifth century, it was already a bishop's see with a basilical church and cloister located on the east bank of the Inn. The center aisle of the Ottonian Severinikirche, the church dedicated to Saint Severin, who presided there during the fifth century, is built over the foundations of these early Christian buildings.

In 739, Saint Stephan's cloister was founded as the bishop's cloister on the peninsula between the Danube and the Inn. During the ninth and tenth centuries, bishops of Passau exerted missionary influence over Austria,

Hungary, and Bulgaria, even into the realm of the Orthodox Church. Indeed, Bishop Ermanrich (866–874) vied with Saints Cyril and Methodius over territory. Under Bishop Pilgrim (971–991), the cathedral school directed by Liudfrith came to be well respected. The two cloisters St. Nicola (ca. 1070) and St. Stephan were centers of manuscript illumination. The oldest extant part of St. Stephan is the Romanesque crypt; the cathedral was rebuilt beginning in 1264, and the late Gothic choir with its unusual dome was completed during the fifteenth century.

The Niedernburg cloister was also founded during the eighth century and designated as distinctly royal property. The dedication to the Virgin, documented in 976, is characteristic of the royal churches of the Carolingian period. The bases of its towers, decorated with Romanesque frescoes, have survived as has the portal, which dates from 1200. The minnesinger Albrecht von Johannsdorf, who is believed to have accompanied Hartmann von Aue on a crusade in 1197, was the son of a prominent Passau family.

Beginning in Carolingian times, a merchant district developed between the imperial quarter around Kloster Niedernburg in the west and the bishop's quarter around St. Stephan's in the east. Citizens of this middle section struggled for some independence from the king and the bishop. The city hall with its high tower was begun in 1298, but citizens' demands were not fully met until 1443, when Passau was granted the status of imperial city *(Reichstadt)*. The church of Sankt Bartholomäus with its Romanesque tower and late Gothic aisle and choir was completed in 1328.

Between 1410 and 1420, the walls of Passau were extended to include Innstadt as well as Ilzstadt. Ilzstadt developed beginning in the tenth century and increased in importance to become the starting point of the Bohemian trade route known as the Goldene Steige (Golden Staircase). During the fifteenth century, Ilzstadt was home to a large Jewish community.

BIBLIOGRAPHY

Kastner, Jörg. *Kostbare Handschriften aus Passau.* Passau: Universitäts Verlag, 1980.

Die Kunstdenkmäler von Niederbayern 3: Stadt Passau. 1912–1936. Munich: R. Oldenbourg, 1980.

Ruth M. W. Moskop

SEE ALSO

Albrecht von Johannsdorf; Carolingian Art and Architecture; Gothic Art and Architecture; Hartmann von Aue; Jews; *Minnesang;* Ottonian Art and Architecture; Romanesque Art and Architecture

Passienbüchlein

The *Passienbüchlein von den vier Hauptjungfrauen (Little Book of the Passion of the Four Major Virgins)* is a rhymed collection of legends (or legendary) of circa 2,200 verses on the passions of Katharina, Barbara, and Margareta, plus Dorothea, all four the major virgin martyrs from late Antiquity who were involved in the conversion of numerous heathens.

Conversion and catechism were topics within the Teutonic Order (Deutschorden), where Prussians, Lithuanians, and others were the objects of missionary activity, and from where the *Passienbüchlein* might have originated (ca. 1330/1340), under the Master (Hochmeister) Luder von Braunschweig (Brunswick, 1331–1335) and his chaplain Nikolaus von Jeroschin. The sources for *Katharina* (595 verses) were another collection of saints' trials and tribulations, the *Passional* (1300/1320), and a Latin Bible translation (known today as *Vulgata 1*); for *Margareta* the *Passional* and the *Margareten-Marter* (*The Martyrer of Margaret*, 760 verses); for *Barbara* (440 verses) and *Dorothea* (400 verses) only the Latin versions from the appendix of the *Legenda aurea (Golden Book of Legends)*. *Dorothea* served as the source for a religious play, the *Kremsmünsterer Dorotheenspiel* (ca. 1350).

The eighteen *Passienbüchlein* manuscripts (four on parchment before 1400)—most in East Middle German, three in Low German, one in Bavarian, and one in Rhine-Franconian—were spread as a complete set first, then as parts in collections, and finally as single legends up to the end of the fifteenth century. Three printed editions followed in Marienburg (ca. 1492) and Leipzig (1508 and 1517).

In Cologne, some six printings were produced (ca. 1492–1520), which were partly reprinted in Lübeck (ca. 1515 and 1521), whereby for *Margareta* the *Margarten-Marter* became an additional source. In a Magdeburg printing (1500, without *Katharina*), the *South German Heiligenleben* (in Low German) and the *Legenda aurea* were used as sources, while for *Margareta* the *Low German Margareta-Legend* (ca. 1450) was also employed. The legends of these saints were, at least in part, perceived as being interchangeable and enjoyed relatively widespread distribution.

BIBLIOGRAPHY

Jefferis, Sibylle. "*Das Passienbüchlein:* Ein Legendenbeitrag im städtischen Leben um 1500," in *Literatur und Stadtkultur im späten Mittelalter und in der frühen Neuzeit (Tagung 1991 in Basel),* ed. Sieglinde Hartmann und Ulrich Müller. *Jahrbuch der Oswald-von-Wolkenstein Gesellschaft* 7 (1992–1993): 227–254.

Ursula Rautenberg. *Überlieferung und Druck: Heiligenlegenden aus frühen Kölner Offizinen.* Frühe Neuzeit 30. Tübingen: Niemeyer, 1996, esp. pp. 8–87.

Jefferis, Sibylle, and Konrad Kunze. "Passienbüchlein von den vier Hauptjungfrauen," in *Die deutsche Literatur des Mittelalters. Verfasserlexikon,* ed. Kurt Ruh et al. Berlin: de Gruyter, 1988, vol. 7, cols. 325–328.

Sibylle Jefferis

SEE ALSO

Deutschorden; Drama; *Legenda Aurea,* Alsatian

Passion Plays

See Drama, Passion Plays.

Passional

The *Passional* (or *Verspassional,* ca. 1290–1320) was the most widely spread rhymed German legendary, originating from an anonymous poet and priest within the Teutonic Order *(Deutschorden)* who had also produced the *Väterbuch (Book of the Fathers).* In three parts (I Mary and Jesus; II Apostles; III seventy-five Saints' Legends), the work was quickly distributed to all its centers in Germany, Austria, and Bohemia for the purpose of preaching and communal reading. Besides the elegant Latin *Legenda aurea (Golden Legendary)* of Jacobus of Voragine, as the major source, in his late classical style, one notices the influence of the German writers Rudolf von Ems, the Stricker, and Konrad von Würzburg.

In 1978, 95 manuscripts of the *Passional* were discerned, 9 of them paper, the others parchment, 10 with pure text of the *Passional,* 15 collections, 70 made up of 106 fragments. Book I had 19,000 verses, Book II 23,600, and Book III 66,400. The saints' legends in the order of the church year, from Nikolaus to Katharina, varied in length between 64 verses and 3,564 *(Katharina).* Before 1350, Heinrich von München included a quarter of the text of Books I and II in his *Weltchronik (World Chronicle,* in eight manuscripts). The *Marienleben/Marienmirakel (Life of Mary, Miracles of Mary)* and *Apostelbuch (Book of the Apostles)* were widely received in similar works (like the *Münchner Apostelbuch).*

In 1982, it was demonstrated that the *Passional* formed the major source not only for the *South German Heiligenleben (Lives of the Saints),* 1385–1400, but also for

the *Heiligenleben* of Hermann von Fritzlar, 1343–1349; the *Darmstädter Legendar* of 1420; the *Passienbüchlein von den vier Hauptjungfrauen,* ca. 1330–1340; the *Katharinenspiel* of 1350–1370; and several legends of the life of Catherine *Katharinenlegenden (Passio-Katerine,* Heinrichau, Wolfenbüttel, and Bielefeld).

BIBLIOGRAPHY

Jefferis, Sibylle. "Ein spätmittelalterliches Katharinenspiel aus dem Cod. Ger. 4 der University of Pennsylvania: Text und Studien zu seiner legendengeschichtlichen Einordnung." Ph.d. diss., University of Pennsylvania, 1982.

Richert, Hans-Georg. *Wege und Formen der Passionalüberlieferung.* Tübingen: Niemeyer, 1978.

———. "Passional," in *Die deutsche Literatur des Mittelalters: Verfasserlexikon,* ed. Kurt Ruh et al. Berlin: de Gruyter, 1988, vol. 7, cols. 332–340.

Sibylle Jefferis

SEE ALSO

Deutschorden; Heiligenleben; Konrad von Würzburg; Legends; *Passienbüchlein;* Rudolf von Ems; Stricker, Der; *Väterbuch*

Patronage, Literary

The promotion of oral and written works by sponsors using property or protection as a procuring medium is a medieval German phenomenon. German has several words for "patron": *Gönner, Auftraggeber,* and *Mäzen,* the latter a loan-translation from the Latin, commemorating Gaius C. Maecenas, friend and sponsor of the Latin poets Horace and Virgil (thus the German term for "patronage," *Mäzenatentum).* Patrons advanced literature in two main ways: the issuance of concrete contracts with poets, and the creation of an environing influence—an intellectual climate in which the arts could flourish. A third sphere of influence was the poem of supplication, which arose in expectation that a would-be sponsor would confer favor. In Germany, secular patronage of literature flowered in the High Middle Ages, when social and political conditions enabled the so-called *weltliche Fürstenhöfe* (worldly courts) of the aristocracy residing in city and castle to displace the church as the chief impetus for, and donor of, the arts. A notable exception is Wolfger of Erla, bishop of Passau from 1191, who may have been the patron of the *Nibelungenlied* poet. A highly aristocratic form of society permits the most complete development of literary patronage, it is agreed, because inequalities of wealth and position bring forth individual protection or largess. The model for the sponsorship of literature in medieval Germany was the feudal contract itself. Poets, often drawn from the ranks of the *ministeriales* (administrators), received sanctuary within the noble *familia* (extended family) in barter for the *servitium* (service) of literary production, which, as an act of fealty, furthered the interests of the donor and recipient. Author and sponsor thus participated in a reciprocal, communal act, a covenant of "give-and-take," according to which the patron gave protection and sustenance to the poet-vassal and took literature as a means of exchange. Literary patronage was thus not only an institution but a ritual with well-defined rules: for support of the poet, the patron expected reflected glory and personal memorialization as a promoter of art. Visible evidence of sponsorship are verses of homage to the patron, traditionally appearing in prologues or epilogues, sometimes as acrostics.

German medieval literary patronage was marked by the intersection and mingling of value systems—the ethical, the economic, the sociological, and the religious. In the amalgam, virtue itself puts on a new face. Writers self-servingly celebrate generosity as the chief aristocratic virtue, even as they equate prudence and uprightness with enlightened literary sponsorship. Diplomacy and pecuniary considerations were vital to patronage, the former in the acquisition of foreign manuscripts, and the latter in the subsidization of the often circuitous route from source material to public performance. The sponsors of lengthy narrative poems, as for example the Arthurian romances, needed financial resources for parchment, manuscripts, scribes, and probably translators. Of the motives for literary patronage, the dominant one was memorialization *(Gedächtnis)* and the status that it brought. The desire for recognition by one's peers accounted for much literary patronage; sponsorship communicated the benefactor's sense of self as aristocrat and sense of predestination to occupy a position of power. In one person the patron was therefore feudal lord, financier, connoisseur, collector, founder of libraries, arbiter of taste, and prime mover behind the patron's own commemoration as a gesture of aristocratic *Repräsentation.* In sociological terms, the patron embodied society itself; the act of patronage was hence an act of social accommodation. Although the relation between patronage and literary style is well defined, the degree to which literary sponsorship influenced political ethics is still contested. Witness the case of Walther von der Vogelweide, who in the interest of his

current protector composed songs in support of opposing dynasties (Welf and Staufen). Scholarship on Walther traditionally excuses his opportunism, slighting the influence of literary patronage on his tendentious verse in general and on his choice of song types in particular.

The systematic study of German medieval literary patronage began in the 1970s, when critical attention turned to conditions giving rise to the flowering of the arts. Sponsorship of literature, first believed to be a mere appendage to the sociology of literature and a subject of marginal interest only, has since emerged as a bona fide academic discipline, and it is the rare book that fails to mention the circumstances of composition. However, since primary evidence for sponsorship (direct commissions and the like) is sparse, researchers turn to speculation and deductive reasoning. In most cases it is very difficult to puzzle out which poems had a connection with a particular court or court circle, or which writers were part of a patron's entourage. Nevertheless, it is possible to draw general conclusions. First, there is a marked difference between the patronage associated with the royal courts and the courts of the lesser nobles, especially the landed aristocracy. Whereas the former encouraged encomiastic literature and history, often in the Latin tongue, the latter promoted courtly romances, lyric and epic poems—in the vernacular. Second, there is more proof for sponsorship of *Sachliteratur* (nonliterary writing) in all its forms, than for belles lettres. Finally, literary patronage is able to shed light on heraldic poetry, the origins of libraries, practices of enfeoffment, and literary reception. Of German patrons, Landgrave Herman of Thuringia (d. 1217) and Henry the Lion (d. 1195) are the best known. The latter, the Welf duke who ruled over Saxony and Bavaria, promoted the arts and sciences, including architecture, mural paintings, statuary, illuminated manuscripts, goldsmithery, and literature. The *Lucidarius* arose at his behest; the *Rolandslied,* and even Eilhart von Oberge's *Tristrant,* are associated with his court. The desire for political power certainly inspired Henry to further the arts, but the pursuit and legitimation of power cannot alone account for his munificence. His generous, large-scale patronage was an avenue for grand self-definition. Other princes and clans fostering literature were the Zähringer, Wettiner, Manesse, Wittelsbachs, and Habsburgs. Bohemia and Tyrol among geographical regions, called forth scholarship, while Heidelberg, Innsbruck, Munich, Augsburg, Vienna, and Zurich were the cities attracting the most interest. Urban patronage held special fascination because municipalities, as home to patrician and plebeian alike, were early testing places for the cooperation of social strata in literary and manuscript production.

BIBLIOGRAPHY

Backes. Martina. *Das literarische Leben am kurpfälzischen Hof zu Heidelberg im 15. Jahrhundert.* Tübingen; Niemeyer, 1992.

Bastert, Bernd. *Der Münchner Hof und Fuetrers 'Buch der Abenteuer.'* Frankfurt am Main: Lang, 1993.

Behr, Hans-Joachim. *Literatur als Machtlegitimation.* Munich: Fink, 1989.

Brunner, Horst. "Deutsche Literatur des 13. und 14. Jahrhunderts im Umkreis der Wittelsbacher," in *Wittelsbach und Bayern,* ed. Hubert Glaser. Munich: Hirmer, 1980, vol. 1, pp. 496–505.

Bumke, Joachim. *Mäzene im Mittelalter.* Munich: Beck, 1979.

Green, Richard F. *Poets and Princepleasers.* Toronto: University of Toronto Press, 1980.

Hahn, Reinhard. *Das literarische Leben am Innsbrucker Hof des späteren 15. Jahrhunderts und der Prosaroman 'Pontus und Sidonia (A).'* Frankfurt am Main: Lang, 1990.

Holzknecht, Karl J. *Literary Patronage in the Middle Ages.* 1923, rpt. New York: Octagon, 1966.

Jordan, Karl. *Heinrich der Löwe.* Munich: Beck, 1979.

McDonald, William C. *German Medieval Literary Patronage.* Amsterdam: Rodopi, 1973.

Müller, Jan-Dirk. *Gedechtnus. Literatur und Hofgesellschaft um Maximilian I.* Munich: Fink, 1982.

Peters, Ursula. *Literatur in der Stadt.* Tübingen: Niemeyer, 1983.

Renk, Herta-Elisabeth. *Der Manessekreis, seine Dichter und die Manessische Handschrift.* Stuttgart: Kohlhammer, 1974.

Streich, Brigitte. *Der Wettinische Hof im späten Mittelalter.* Cologne: Böhlau, 1989.

Theil, Bernhard. "Literatur und Literaten am Hofe der Erzherzogin Mechthild in Rottenburg." *Zeitschrift für württembergische Landesgeschichte* 42 (1983): 124–144.

Wenzel, Horst. *Adelsherrschaft und Literatur.* Frankfurt am Main: Lang, 1980.

William C. McDonald

SEE ALSO

Arthurian Literature, German; Ausgsburg; Munich; *Sachliteratur;* Vienna; Walther von der Vogelweide; Zurich

Peasants
See Feudalism; Nobility and Farmers.

Peter von Staufenberg

A verse novella (1,192 verses) written in the first decade of the fourteenth century (ca. 1310) by Egenolf von Staufenberg, member of an Alsatian noble family. Egenolf was a proponent of the social values associated with courtly literature of the twelfth and thirteenth centuries and part of a German literary tradition linked to Gottfried von Strasbourg and Konrad von Würzburg. The emphasis on physical love and its tragic consequences places *Peter von Staufenberg* in a thematic context well known in the High and late Middle Ages. This work from the courtly epigonic (imitatory) period contains a number of motifs, including the rash promise of a pleasure-seeking male and subsequent punishment by a vindictive female, linking it with much older Celtic folk materials and later French adaptations, a line of development generally cited with respect only to the major French and German courtly epics. As regards the incorporation of folk material into courtly literature, *Peter von Staufenberg* shares themes and motifs with Konrad von Würzburg's *Partonopier und Meliur,* the anonymous lay *Guingamor,* the lay *Guigemer* of Marie de France, and the thirteenth-century work *Li Roman de Dolopathos.*

While Egenolf's specific family background remains vague, his noble status underlines the practical, personal, and social objective of his literary effort: to provide a behavioral model for young noblemen. In the tradition of the mirrors for princes—didactic texts stressing the duties and responsibilities of rulers—*Peter von Staufenberg* reveals the author's interest in problems of social obligation and individual responsibility. The story illustrates this conflict in the context of the attitudes and actions of the lower nobility in relationship to societal and imperial demands and desires. Egenolf uses social elements alongside traditional courtly literary themes and motifs to define the conventional world of the knight and his lady while introducing into that world asocial, supernatural elements bearing a forceful didactic message.

Thematically, *Peter von Staufenberg* belongs to the tradition of tales of the Swan Knight type (Konrad's *Schwanritter*) or, in the view of some, Melusine, tales of love, lust, and death as the ultimate form of retribution. Egenolf's hero accepts the sexual and material favors of a beautiful woman who appears and disappears at will, he agrees to reject marriage proposals so long as the favors continue, and he faces the crucial conflict when his family and advisers insist that he marry the emperor's niece. Acquiescing to social pressure and forsaking his mysterious paramour, who the clergy conclude to be an emissary of Satan, Peter's tragic end comes by means of a vengeful lightning bolt from a female leg thrust through the ceiling of the church during the wedding ceremony.

The moral-didactic nature of *Peter von Staufenberg* attracted writers beyond the medieval period. A late medieval version (1588), attributed to Johann Fischart, is the work of Bernhard Schmidt, with Fischart contributing only the introduction. Friedrich de la Motte Fouqué's *Undine* (1811), the opera adaptation by Gustav Lortzing (1845), and Jean Giradoux's play *Ondine* (1939) are variations on the same theme.

BIBLIOGRAPHY

Grunewald, Eckehard, ed. *Peter von Staufenberg. Abbildungen zur Text- und Illustrationsgeschichte.* Göppingen: Kümmerle, 1978.

Schröder, Edward, ed. *Zwei Altdeutsche Rittermaeren: Moriz von Craon, Peter von Staufenberg.* Berlin: Weidmannsche, 1894, rpt. 1929.

Walker, Richard Ernest. *Peter von Staufenberg: Its Origin, Development, and Later Adaptation.* Göppingen: Kümmerle, 1980.

Richard Ernest Walker

SEE ALSO
Gottfried von Straßburg; Konrad von Würzburg; Otto of Freising

Peters, Gerlach (d. November 30, 1411)

The most important mystical writer of the *Devotio moderna* (Modern Devotion) movement, Peters received his spiritual education from the Brethren of the Common Life in Deventer, especially from Florens Radewijns. On Radewijns's instigation, Gerlach went, at an uncertain date, to the monastery of Windesheim and entered the order of canons regular in 1403.

As far as we know Gerlach did not become a writer before entering the monastery. Of his works, sixty-five manuscripts have been traced so far. He wrote two Middle Dutch *Letters* to his sister Lubbe, a Sister of the Common Life in Deventer, and two Latin works, *Breuiloquium* and *Soliloquium.* In the first of the two *Letters* he advises Lubbe how to combine her development in the spiritual life with the daily routine of being a *procuratrix.* In the other one he gives her a short treatise on the mystical life, strongly influenced by John Ruusbroec. In his *Breuiloquium* Gerlach tries to make clear how to live a truly spiritual life within a community. The influence of other devotionalists in this text is evident. Gerlach is most famous for his *Soliloquium,* a mystical text written as a *rapiarium,* or abduction story, put together by his friend Johannes Schutken after his death. His mysticism is Christocentric and influenced by the mystical teaching of Jan van Ruusbroec. However, we find personal elements such as his spirituality of the Cross and his very remarkable discernment of spirits. This text was printed as early as 1580 and afterward printed many times in Latin and translated into six languages, also in this century. Yet the text has been contaminated by an editor with a conservative, Counter-Reformation background.

BIBLIOGRAPHY

Deblaere, Albert. "Gerlach Peters (1378–1411) mysticus van de onderscheiding der geesten," in *Liber alumnorum Prof. Dr. E. Rombauts,* ed. Norbert De and Lode Roose. Leuven: Faculteit der Wijsbegeerte en Letteren, 1968, pp. 95–109.

Gericke, Wolfgang. "Das Soliloquium des Gerlach Peters. Kritische Erstausgabe des Wolfenbütteler Textes und Würdigung." 3 vols.

Habilitationsschrift. Halle-Wittenberg: Martin Luther University, 1942.

Kors, Mikel M. *De Middelnederlandse Brieven van Gerlach Peters (? – 1411).* Nijmegen: Centrum voor Middeleeuwse Studies, 1991.

Kors, Mikel M., ed. *Gerlaci Petri Opera Omnia.* Turnhout, Belgium: Brepols, 1996.

Mikel M. Kors

SEE ALSO
Devotio Moderna; Jan van Ruusbroec; Radewijns, Florens

Philosophy
See articles on individual philosophers.

Physiologus

The *Physiologus* is an anonymous early Christian textbook on the theological meaning of nature, written in Greek, apparently in Alexandria, Egypt, in the second to fourth centuries C.E. Throughout the Middle Ages and on at least into the fifteenth century it was seen as a major authority. It circulated widely, particularly in Latin but with translations also in most vernaculars, and survives in over four hundred manuscripts. The text itself refers to the author simply as the *physiologos* (natural philosopher), but medieval sources attribute it to various of the Greek fathers.

The forty-eight chapters draw together natural history and salvation history, following the principle of divine economy that holds that everything in creation reflects spiritual truth. Typically, each chapter begins with a Bible verse, followed by one or more *proprietates,* images from nature describing elements of contemporary knowledge of the lives of animals. These are then interpreted allegorically with respect to Christ, the Devil, the Christian, the sinner, and so on. Some of the motifs are extended and contain fantastic material. Elephants, for example, cannot bend their knees and have to sleep leaning against a tree. Hunters catch them by cutting down the tree. If an elephant is thus brought to a fall, he calls for help, but the other large elephants can do nothing; only the smallest elephant can help him back to his feet. Likewise, when the Devil caused Adam to fall, all the great prophets and patriarchs could not save him; only the frailty of Christ could achieve this.

The Latin *Physiologus* exists in a number of variant forms, mainly resulting from attempts to shorten it. One of the most influential is the version "b," a prose text known from manuscripts from the tenth century on. Two important versions apparently of the eleventh century are the *Physiologus Theobaldi,* containing twelve to thirteen chapters in various metrical forms, and the *Dicta Johannis Chrysotomi de naturis bestiarum* (the *Dicta* version), with twenty-seven chapters. In addition to the *Physiologus* proper, many bestiaries and medieval encyclopedias contain related texts.

The German versions of the *Physiologus* fall chronologically into two groups —those of the eleventh and twelfth centuries, which are translations of the *Dicta* version, and those of the fifteenth century, which mainly follow the *Theobaldi* text. The Old High German fragment—the "older," or *Älterer Physiologus,* survives in a late-eleventh-century manuscript held in Vienna and contains the first twelve chapters. Two closely related twelfth-century texts in early Middle High German are the *Vienna Physiologus* and the *Millstätt Physiologus.* These are found in the same large manuscripts as the Vienna and Millstätt *Genesis.* A twelfth-century Schäftlarn (Bavaria) fragment, scribbled in the gaps in an otherwise Latin manuscript, is appar-

ently completely separate. The late medieval versions include three translations of the *Physiologus Theobaldi,* one prose, one verse, and one interlinear gloss. There is also a set of inscriptions from Celje, Slovenia, and the important *Melk Physiologus,* both of which stand out because of their relative independence of the known Latin traditions.

BIBLIOGRAPHY

Henkel, Nikolaus. *Studien zum Physiologus im Mittelalter.* Ph.d. diss., Munich University, 1974. Tübingen: Niemeyer, 1976.

Graeme Dunphy

SEE ALSO
Encyclopedic Literature, German

Pilgram, Anton (ca. 1450/1460–1515)

This Moravian architect and sculptor is best known today as master of works of St. Stephan's Cathedral in Vienna between about 1511 and 1515. His architectural designs are representative of the Flamboyant Gothic style and his sculptures of the late Gothic naturalism then prevalent in southern Germany and Austria.

Pilgram was born in Brno circa 1450–1460. He trained in Brno and Vienna. His earliest documented activity is in Swabia, at the parish church of Wimpfen, where his mason's mark appears twice, with the dates 1493 and 1497. He is credited with the choir's looped-ring vaulting. A corbel (projected bracket) angel in the nearby parish church of Schwieberdingen also bears his mason's mark.

Next documented in Brno, his mason's mark appears in the north aisle of the church of St. James, begun 1502. Of his now destroyed Judentor (Jews' Gate), completed in 1508, seven console masks, an inscription, and his mason's mark survive (Brno, Moravian Museum). He completed the portal of the Rathaus (Town Hall) at Brno circa 1511.

In 1511 the Vienna City Council selected Pilgram's design for the cathedral's organ pedestal, then already under construction by Jörg Öchsel, which resulted in a legal feud. Pilgram became master of works for the cathedral in 1511. The pedestal, dated 1513, features a bust-length self-portrait. Although a similar self-portrait is located beneath the pulpit, circa 1513–1514, which also features Pilgram's mason's mark, recent scholarship has questioned this attribution. The busts of the church fathers on the pulpit are inspired by late-fifteenth-century Swabian and Upper Rhenish sculpture.

Also attributed to Pilgram is a tabernacle from circa 1482–1487 in the church of St. Kilian at Heilbronn. Its two caryatid (supporting column) figures of stonemasons are similar to those from Heutingsheim (parish church), Öhringen (Berlin, Deutsches Museum), and Rottweil (Lorenzkapelle). An Entombment group (Munich, Bayerisches Nationalmuseum), circa 1496, and a figure of a falconer (Vienna, Kunsthistorisches Museum), circa 1500, both in wood, and the Keckmann-Epitaph from circa 1511–1512 (Vienna, Stephansdom) are also ascribed to Pilgram.

BIBLIOGRAPHY

Feuchtmüller, Rupert. *Die spätgotische Architektur und Anton Pilgram: Gedanken zu neuen Forschungen.* Vienna: Österreichische Staatdruckerei, 1951.

Leisching, P. "Werkstreit zu St. Stephan in Wien in den Jahren 1511–1513," in *Arbeitsleben und Rechtsordnung: Festschrift Gerhard Schnorr zum 65. Geburtstag.* Vienna: Manz, 1988, pp. 805–820.

Oettinger, Karl. *Anton Pilgram und die Bildhauer von St. Stephan.* Vienna: Herold, 1951.

Saliger, Arthur. "Zur Frage der künstlerischen Autorschaft der Kanzel im Stephansdom im Wien." *Wiener Geschichtsblätter* 47 (1992): 181–197.

Susanne Reece

SEE ALSO
Gothic Art and Architecture, Late; Vienna; Wimpfen

Pilgrim's Badges

From the twelfth through the fifteenth centuries, flat, often perforated *Pilgerzeichen,* or badges with one-sided relief representations of a saint or of venerated holy relics, were a visible sign of the visit to a particular pilgrimage shrine. Made and sold at the site and commissioned by the spiritual leaders, they were often produced in thousands and sold inexpensively. Usually made from easily melted metals, often a tin-and-lead alloy, they had rings on the side so that they could be sewn on hats or garments or hung from the pilgrim's staff or rosary. Badges secured a certain protection for those who wore them because the powers of the relics or honored saints were considered alive and active in them. Because of this vicarious power, they have been found in graves and in reliquaries and altars in churches, and they also played a part in su-

perstitious or popular medical practices. Very few of the original number have come down to us because of their fragile nature and small value. Some examples have been found cast on church bells or in bodies of water that preserved them. As the showing of relics was removed from the churches into the open air, small mirrors were added to the badges that were thought to capture the radiating power of the relic, bringing its benefits into the daily life of the pilgrim. In the late fifteenth century badges were made in the form of coins or medals without rings but with holes through which they could be sewed on hats and garments or into Books of Hours. In this period, they were often painted in the borders of miniatures or shown as part of the pilgrim's costume in paintings.

BIBLIOGRAPHY

Koldewey, A. M. "Pilgrim Badges Painted in Manuscripts: A North Netherlandish Example," in *Masters and Miniatures: Proceedings of the Congress on Medieval Manuscript Illumination in the Northern Netherlands. Utrecht, 10–13 December 1989,* ed. K. van der Horst and J.-C. Klamt. Doornspijk: Davaco, 1991, pp. 211–218.

Köster, Kurt. "Mittelalterliche Pilgerzeichen," in *Wallfahrt kennt keine Grenzen,* ed. Lenz Kriss-Rettenbeck and Gerda Möhler. Munich: Bayerisches Nationalmuseum, 1984, pp. 203–223.

———. "Mittelalterliche Pilgerzeichen und Wallfahrtsdevotionalien," in *Rhein und Maas: Kunst und Kultur 800–1400,* ed. Anton Legner. 2 vols. Cologne: Schnütgen Museum, 1972, vol. 1, pp. 146–160.

Marta O. Renger

SEE ALSO
Relics and Reliquaries

Pippin (d. 768)

Pippin (the Short)'s father, Charles Martel, died on October 22, 741, leaving control of the family and of Francia to two of his sons. The elder, Carloman, assumed the position of mayor of the palace in Austrasia, thereby controlling it along with Alemannia and Thuringia, while the younger, Pippin, became mayor in Neustria, controlling it along with Burgundy and Provence. The Aquitanians, Alemans, Saxons, Gascons, and Bavarians immediately revolted. The brothers also faced trouble within the family from Gripho, Martel's son by another wife. He became a focus for discontent and a leader of revolts against his half brothers until his death in 753. In 743, to bolster their position against these threats, Carloman and Pippin placed a legitimate Merovingian, King Childeric III (743–751), on a throne that had been vacant for six years. Childeric was the last Merovingian to reign.

In 746, in the midst of dealing with all this, Carloman retired to the monastic life at Rome, leaving governance of the whole Frankish realm and its problems to Pippin. By 749, Pippin had managed to calm the political waters north of the Alps somewhat, but in Italy, the pope's troubles with the Lombards were increasing, and these would open the door for Pippin's usurpation of the Frankish throne.

In 750 Pippin sent envoys to Rome asking Pope Zacharias (741–752) the famous question whether it was right for a king to rule without having any royal power. Zacharias responded that he who had the royal power should be king. This reply was a clear papal signal that Pippin would have apostolic approval to take the throne for himself. In 751 he deposed Childeric III, tonsured him, and imprisoned him in the monastery of St. Bertin. Then, in the ancient Merovingian seat of Soissons, he had himself proclaimed king by the assembled Frankish great. In 753 and 754 the new king caused Pope Stephen II (III) (752–757), who had crossed the Alps to personally ask for Pippin's help against the Lombards, to anoint him king in obvious and holy imitation of the Old Testament.

In 755, now as King Pippin I (751–768), he invaded Italy, making good on his pledge to the pope to deliver Rome from the Lombards' military threat. In the wake of this campaign, Pippin established the Papal States, a kingdom comprising most of central Italy, protected by Frankish arms and with the pope as its secular head.

Both as mayor and then as king, Pippin was a strong ruler. He built on the work of his father, keeping the basic policies that his son, Charlemagne (768–814), would also continue. He conducted successful wars of conquest against the Germans to the East and took every opportunity to increase the control of his own central government, especially over Aquitaine and the other areas south of the Loire. In these endeavors, he relied heavily on the Austrasian nobility, placing them in the important positions of the realm. He established close cooperation with the papacy and fostered much ecclesiastical reform and expansion (St. Boniface) and also supported the revival of learning. When he died in 768, he indeed passed on many problems to his sons, Carloman and Charlemagne, but in general the position of the new Carolingian dynasty was secure.

BIBLIOGRAPHY

Annales Mettenses Priores, ed. Bernhard von Simson. Monumenta Germaniae Historica, Scriptores rerum germanicarum. Hannover: Hahn, 1905.

Hlawitschka, Eduard. "Die Vorfahren Karls des Grossen," in *Karl der Große,* vol. 1, ed. W. Braunfels. Düsseldorf: Schwann, 1965, pp. 51–82.

McKitterick, Rosamond. *The Frankish Kingdoms Under the Carolingians 751–987.* London: Longman, 1983.

Miller, David Harry. "Sacred Kingship, Biblical Kingship, and the Elevation of Pepin the Short," in *Religion, Culture, and Society in the Early Middle Ages,* ed. Thomas Noble and John J. Contreni. Studies in Medieval Culture 23. Kalamazoo, Mich.: Medieval Institute Publications, 1987, pp. 131–154.

Wallace-Hadrill, J. M. *The Barbarian West 400–1000,* 3d ed. London: Hutchinson, 1967, pp. 90–94.

Wood, Ian. *The Merovingian Kingdoms, 450–751.* London: Longman, 1994, pp. 287–292.

Richard Gerberding

SEE ALSO

Carolingians; Charlemagne

Playing Cards, Master of (fl. ca. 1435–1450)

This anonymous Swiss or south German engraver, active circa 1435–1450, is known chiefly from a set of designs for a pack of sixty playing cards first described by the Nazarene artist and collector Johann David Passavant. Geisberg (1905), the first to examine the engravings thoroughly, noted that the court cards were printed from single plates, with the suit added by overprinting, while many of the remaining cards had been created by means of small multiple images arranged to form page layouts. Lehmann-Haupt, who discovered nearly identical playing-card motifs in the marginalia of the Giant Bible of Mainz and the Hours of Catherine of Cleves, theorized that a model book by the Cleves illuminator had been taken to Mainz and used by Johann Gutenberg in 1453–1454, and that Gutenberg restruck the small plates to print playing cards after his bankruptcy in 1455. More recently and definitively, Van Buren and Edmunds (1974: 12–29) have disproved the Gutenberg theory, which fails to account for the use of obsolete fashions for the queens and knaves of the pack—clothing no longer worn in the 1450s. They found further use of the playing-card motifs in a group of twenty-four Tyrolean, Franco-Flemish, Savoyard, and English manuscripts, all dated earlier than

1455. As Van Buren and Edmunds pointed out, none of the surviving cards had been mounted for play.

Virtually nothing is known of the game or games originally played with the cards, which are divided into suits of men, birds, deer, and beasts of prey. The Bibliothèque Nationale in Paris owns the largest and most important collection (forty cards), while smaller groups are found in the print rooms of Dresden (fourteen), Vienna (six), Berlin, London, and Nuremberg (one each).

BIBLIOGRAPHY

Geisberg, Max. *Das älteste gestochene deutsche Kartenspiel vom Meister der Spielkarten (vor 1446)*. Strasbourg: J. H. E. Heitz, 1905.

Hébert, Michèle. *Inventaire des gravures des Écoles du Nord,* 2 vols. Paris: Bibliothèque Nationale, 1982–1983, vol. 1, pp. 29–36.

Lehmann-Haupt, Hellmut. *Gutenberg and the Master of the Playing Cards*. New Haven, Conn.: Yale University Press, 1966.

Lehrs, Max. *Geschichte und kritischer Katalog des deutschen, niederländischen und französischen Kupferstichs im 15. Jahrhundert*. Vienna: Gesellschaft für vervielfältigende Kunst, 1908, vol. 1, pp. 63–207.

Van Buren, Anne H., and Sheila Edmunds. "Playing Cards and Manuscripts: Some Widely Disseminated Fifteenth-Century Model Sheets." *Art Bulletin* 61 (1974): 2–29.

Jane Campbell Hutchison

SEE ALSO
Johann Gutenberg; Mainz; Printmaking

Pleier, Der (fl. 1240–1280)

An Austrian or Bavarian author, Der Pleier wrote three Arthurian verse-romances between 1240 and 1280, all of which survived only in later manuscripts. Well-acquainted with courtly works in German, Pleier carefully fitted his heroes and their adventures into the Arthurian framework left to him by earlier poets. His *Garel von dem blühenden Tal (Garel of the Flowering Valley)* employs the basic structure of Stricker's *Daniel vom blühenden Tal (Daniel of the Flowering Valley)* but keeps only two of its episodes and drastically changes its spirit. Through a series of adventures, Pleier's hero wins a queen, gathers a great army, and defeats a monarch who intended to attack King Arthur's realm.

For *Tandareis und Flordibel,* Pleier varies the plot of a story that he probably knew from Konrad Fleck's *Flore und Blanscheflur.* It tells of the forced separation of two teenaged lovers and the many dangers the hero must survive before they are reunited.

The bare framework of *Meleranz* came ultimately from the anonymous Breton lay (short verse narrative) *Graelent,* but in Pleier's version the fairy of the lay is a human girl-queen whom the boy Meleranz meets on his way to become a page at Arthur's court. He falls in love and, years later, rides out as a knight to search for her. After many adventures and the winning of a kingdom, he finds her and they are married. The most distinctive features of Pleier's romances are their detailed descriptions and their emphasis on manners.

BIBLIOGRAPHY

Bartsch, Karl. *Der Pleier: Meleranz.* 1861; rpt. Hildesheim: Olms, 1974.

Herles, Wolfgang. *Garel von dem bluenden Tal.* Vienna: Halosar, 1981.

Kern, Peter. *Die Artusromane des Pleier: Untersuchungen über den Zusammenhang von Dichtung und literarischer Situation.* Berlin: Schmidt, 1981.

Khull, Ferdinand. *Tandareis und Flordibel.* Graz: Buchhandlung Styria, 1885.

Thomas, J. W. *The Pleier's Arthurian Romances.* New York: Garland, 1992.

J.W. Thomas

SEE ALSO
Stricker, Der

Pleydenwurff, Hans (ca. 1425–1472)

This panel and glass painter was active in Franconia from circa 1450 until about 1472. He established the first significant painting workshop in Nuremberg, which produced works inspired by Netherlandish art. Michel Wolgemut was his pupil and assistant.

Pleydenwurff was born circa 1425 in Bamberg. Nothing is known of his initial training, but he probably went to the Netherlands in the early 1450s. He worked in Bamberg then in Nuremberg, where he became a citizen in 1457. At his death there in 1472, Pleydenwurff was listed as a glass painter. That year, Michel Wolgemut married his widow, Barbara, and inherited the workshop.

Pleydenwurff's only documented work is the Breslau Altarpiece, of which only fragments survive. Installed in the church of St. Elizabeth in Breslau on June 30, 1462, this large double-winged retable with a carved shrine fea-

Hans Pleydenwurff, Descent from the Cross from the Breslau Altar (Nuremberg, Germanisches Nationalmuseum). *Photograph: Germanisches Nationalmuseum*

tured scenes from Christ's Infancy and Passion, and Saints Jerome and Vincent of Teate. The upper part of the Presentation survives (Warsaw, Nationalmuseum). An undamaged wing with the Descent from the Cross (Nuremberg, Germanisches Nationalmuseum) is based on Roger van der Weyden's Deposition Altarpiece of circa 1444 (Madrid, Prado).

Other works have been attributed to Pleydenwurff on the basis of style. Earliest is the half-length Löwenstein Diptych of about 1456. Based on a type popularized by Roger van der Weyden in the Netherlands, it consists of a Man of Sorrows (Basel, Kunstmuseum) and a portrait of the Bamberg canon and subdeacon, Count Georg von Löwenstein (Nuremberg, Germanisches Nationalmuseum). Also ascribed to Pleydenwurff are a large Crucifixion (Munich, Alte Pinakothek), circa 1470, an altarpiece wing with St. Lawrence (Raleigh, North Carolina Museum of Art), after 1462, and wings with Infancy and Passion scenes from the Hof Altarpiece (Munich, Alte Pinakothek), dated 1465. This last was a workshop production, executed by assistants, including Michel Wolgemut.

BIBLIOGRAPHY

Kahsnitz, Rainer. "Stained Glass in Nuremberg." *Gothic and Renaissance Art in Nuremberg 1300–1550.* New York: Metropolitan Museum of Art, 1986, pp. 87–92.

Löcher, Kurt. "Panel Painting in Nuremberg: 1350–1550." In *Gothic and Renaissance Art in Nuremberg 1300–1550.* New York: Metropolitan Museum of Art, 1986, pp. 81–86.

Stange, Alfred. *Deutsche Malerei der Gotik.* 10 vols. Berlin: Deutscher Kunstverlag, 1934–1960, vol. 9, pp. 41–44.

Strieder, Peter. *Tafelmalerei in Nürnberg 1350–1550.* Königstein im Taunus: Karl Robert Langewiesche Nachfolger, 1993, pp. 52–59.

Suckale, Robert. "Hans Pleydenwurff in Bamberg." *Berichte des historischen Vereins Bamberg* 120 (1984): 423–438.

Susanne Reece

SEE ALSO
Bamberg; Nuremberg; Wolgemut, Michael

Poeta Saxo (fl. late 9th c.)

Sometime between 888 and 891 an otherwise unidentified Saxon poet (hence the Latin name by which he is customarily known), perhaps a monk at the monastery of Corvey (now North Rhine–Westphalia), composed a five-book verse epic. The first four books, aptly entitled *Annals Concerning the Deeds of Emperor Charlemagne*, amount to 1,999 hexameters (a few have been lost) and follow Charlemagne from the beginning of his reign as sole ruler in 771. The fifth book of 347 distichs (two-line strophic units) presents a general view, in panegyric terms, of Charlemagne's achievements and character. The poet offered Charlemagne as an example to encourage

King Arnulf of Carinthia, during whose reign the Poeta Saxo wrote, to restore the Saxon realm to its rightful glory.

For Charlemagne's career from 771 to 801 (up to Book 4, line 70) the Poeta Saxo relied on the so-called *Einhard Annals;* for the portrait in the fifth book he drew mostly on Einhard's *Life of Charlemagne;* and for 802–813 he presumably tapped lost annals. Because of his indebtedness to earlier texts, the Poeta Saxo has not been highly regarded as a source for historians. Among literary critics he has been viewed as a versifier rather than as a creative poet, because his displays of familiarity with classical poetry and formal rhetoric lead to a recasting of his sources only occasionally in style and very seldom in content. Despite his low standing, the Poeta Saxo deserves recognition for having been the first to put annals into verse and for having produced a history that makes the Saxons a central focus.

BIBLIOGRAPHY

Bischoff, Bernhard. "Das Thema des Poeta Saxo," in Bernhard Bischoff, *Mittelalterliche Studien,* vol. 3. Stuttgart: Hiersemann, 1981, pp. 253–259.

von Winterfeld, Paul, ed. *Poetae Saxonis annalium de gestis Caroli Magni imperatoris libri quinque,* in *Monumenta Germaniae Historica Poetae Latini Medii Aevi,* vol. 4, pt. 1. Berlin: Weidmann, 1899, pp. 7–71.

Jan M. Ziolkowski

SEE ALSO

Bible Epic, Saxon; Charlemagne; Latin Language; Versification

Poetry

See individual poets; Meistersinger; *Minnesang;* Versification.

Potter, Dirc (ca. 1368/1370–April 30, 1428)

Dutch poet and diplomat. After he finished high school (the "Latin School,") Potter entered the service of the count of Holland. Having started as a treasury clerk, he was, after 1400, promoted to clerk of the court of justice, bailiff of The Hague, and secretary of the count. As a diplomat he went on a number of journeys to Rome (1411–1412). In his spare time he wrote works of literature: two discourses in prose (after March 1415), *Blome der doechden (Flowers of Virtue),* which goes back to the

Italian *Fiore di virtù,* and *Mellibeus,* translated from a French translation of Albertanus of Brescia's *Liber consolationis;* but his principal work is *Der minnen loep (The Course of Love,* 1411–1412), a treatise in verse about love, larded with stories largely taken from the Bible and from Ovid, in particular from the *Heroides.* The work consists of four books (over eleven thousand lines). Potter distinguishes "foolish," "good," "illicit," and "licit" love; one book is devoted to each of them. Potter derived the classification in Books I, III, and IV from medieval commentaries on *Heroides,* which discern in the *Heroides amor stultus, illicitus,* and *licitus.* The "good" love of Book II does not originate from the *Heroides* commentaries, but (at least from Potter's point of view) it forms a whole with "licit" love, which is the highest degree of "good" love. It turns out that Potter knew the complete "medieval Ovid": Ovid's works, the commentaries on these works, and the *accessus,* i.e., the medieval introductions to them. Within the tradition of the "pagan" *artes amandi* (treatises on the art of love), Potter created a Christianized *ars amatoria.* As such he is highly original: *Der minnen loep* is unique in the European context.

BIBLIOGRAPHY

Leendertz, Pieter, ed. *Der minnen loep,* 2 vols. Leiden: du Mortier, 1845–1847.

Overmaat, Bernard G. L. "Mellibeus. Arnhem." Ph.d. diss., University of Nijmegen, 1950.

Schoutens, Stephanus. *Dat bouck der bloemen.* Hoogstraten: Van Hoof-Roelans, 1904 *[Blome der doechden]*.

van Buuren, A. M. J. *Der minnen loep van Dirc Potter: studie over een Middelnederlandse ars amandi.* Utrecht: HES, 1979.

———. "Dirc Potter, a Medieval Ovid," in Erik Kooper, ed. *Medieval Dutch Literature in Its European Context.* Cambridge: Cambridge University Press, 1994, pp. 151–167.

van Oostrom, Frits P. *Court and Culture:. Dutch Literature, 1350–1450.* Berkeley: University of California Press, 1992.

Alfons M. J. van Buuren

Prague

Late in the ninth century, members of the Přemyslid dynasty chose this site on a bend in the river Vltava as their capital. There they erected the first castle in Hradčany, where a much modified version still stands today. During the course of the next century, Prague grew into a busy city linking the lands to its east and west. It expanded its limits across the river, where a second castle, Vyšehrad, was built and where the Old Town sprang up as the central market district. By 973, Prague was already a vital enough city to warrant the establishment of a bishopric, at which point Saint Vitus's Rotunda, formerly the church of Prague Castle, became the city's cathedral.

Nothing remains of this tenth-century town. Prague's oldest traces come from the Romanesque city built around the Old Town Square and Little Square, such as the houses that still stand on Husova, Jilská, Celetná, and Karlova Streets. Prague Castle (Prazsky Hrad) also has several authentic Romanesque interiors, such as the hall from the palace of the Přemyslid princes Sobeslav I (1125–1140) and Vladislav II (1140–1172). The hall, some fifty yards long and supported by columns carved with their original interlace design, is now under the Gothic palace built by the rulers of the Jagiello and the Luxembourg dynasties.

During the Romanesque period the cathedral of Saints Vitus, Wenceslas, and Adalbert was erected on the site of Saint Vitus's Rotunda on the orders of Spytihněv II. The project for replacing the centrally planned rotunda with a basilican church began in 1060 and finished with the consecration by Bishop Cosmos in 1096. The final building, with single, vaulted aisles, eastern and western choirs, a transept, and towers in the west, preserved the location of the tomb of the dynasty's family saint, Wenceslas, in the southern aisle. As with the largest part of the Romanesque castle, nothing survives of this church.

Prague continued to expand and reorganize during the course of the twelfth and thirteenth centuries. Both castles were modified, and the two sides of the river were linked by a new stone bridge, the Judith Bridge (later to become the Charles Bridge). A number of churches were constructed; the Dominican, Franciscan, and Clarissan mendicant orders became established; and the Old-New Synagogue (Altneuschul) was erected in the Jewish Quarter, an area located just north of the Old Town. This building, the oldest synagogue in Europe, retains both its early-thirteenth-century single cell with transverse ribs and pointed barrel vaults, and the double-aisle, rib-vaulted hall added in 1280.

Another effect on the direction and growth of Prague was the independence granted by Václav I (1230–1253) to the Old Town in the 1230s and the founding of the Little Quarter (Mala Strana) by King Přemysl Ottakar II

in 1257. Separated by the river, these two governmentally distinct sections defined the boundaries of Prague, until Emperor Charles IV established the New Town in the middle of the next century.

In 1310 Emperor Henry VII expanded his territorial base by marrying his son, John of Luxembourg, to the orphaned Elizabeth Přemyslid, Queen of Bohemia. The son of this match, who, in addition to his Bohemian kingship, would eventually be elected Charles IV, king of the Romans and Holy Roman emperor, initiated a program of rebuilding in Prague that was to transform it from a town into the most politically and culturally important city in Central Europe. Even before Charles transferred the seat of the empire to Prague, he had begun his renovations and foundations throughout the city. One of his first acts on returning to Prague in 1333 as coruler of Bohemia was to authorize reconstruction of the Hradčany Palace. His campaign for the promotion of Prague to an archbishopric proved successful. He inundated Prague with scholars and founded Central Europe's first university in 1348. Of great use to the citizens of Prague was Charles's rebuilding of the Judith Bridge, destroyed by floods in 1342. Essential for convenient travel from the Old Town to the Little Quarter and Hradčany, it was finished soon after 1373 and renamed the Charles Bridge; sculpted portraits of Charles IV, his heir (Wenceslas IV), and Saints Adelbert, Sigismund, and Vitus look down from the portal.

From his early years in France and Italy, Charles IV was open to the influences of foreign artistic currents. But he also employed architects, sculptors, and painters from closer to home with the combination of these multinational styles resulting in the magnificent medieval city still evident today, one of the few cities remaining in Europe where one can still experience the layout and architecture much as they existed in the Middle Ages. The best-known and most elaborate example of this style is the cathedral of St. Vitus. Built on the site of its Romanesque predecessor, this project was part of the larger renovations to the Hradčany, linked physically to the royal palace by its location, and ideologically as the site of royal coronations and the resting place of the imperial family. The cathedral's foundation stone had been placed on the order of Charles IV on November 21, 1344, in celebration of Prague's new status as an archbishopric. The first architect, Matthew of Arras, began building the new choir and chapels in the rayonnant style popular in contemporary France.

Peter Parler, an architect from Swabia, was summoned by Charles IV in 1356, a few years after the death of Matthew of Arras. Well-founded in established German architectural traditions, he transformed these to create his own innovative style, which was well suited to Charles IV's dynastic design. He distinctly altered the layout of Matthew's cathedral, introducing a less integrated design that stressed horizontal architectural units with the rayonnant verticals. He utilized star vaults punctuated by bosses and innovative linear molding profiles (seen clearly in the clerestory level of the choir) to break down the building into a series of discrete units. To the most sacred part of the church, above the original tomb of Saint Wenceslas and facing south to the palace, was added a much larger, symbolically charged chapel to the imperial saint encrusted with precious stones and a canopy of vaulting. Directly adjacent to the chapel of St. Wenceslas is the south porch, also known as the Golden Portal from its exterior decoration of mosaic depicting the Last Judgment with the six patron saints of Bohemia, Charles IV, and Empress Elizabeth of Pomerania in attendance. This is one of many references to the imperial dynasty contained in the cathedral. The new tombs that Charles commissioned for six of his Přemyslid ancestors were placed in the choir chapels by 1377, and the emperor, with his four wives, was included in a cycle of busts depicting the imperial family, the archbishops of Prague, and some of the artists responsible for the cathedral's construction, including Parler, in the triforium level.

BIBLIOGRAPHY

Gotik—Prag um 1400: Der schöne Stil, böhmische Malerei und Plastik in der Gotik. Vienna: Wien Kultur, 1991.

Kutal, Albert. *Gothic Art in Bohemia and Moravia.* New York: Hamlyn, 1971.

Münzer, Z. "The Old-New Synagogue in Prague: Its Architectural History." In *The Jews of Czechoslovakia: Historical Studies and Surveys.* 2 vols. Philadelphia: Jewish Publication Society of America, 1968–1971, vol. 2, pp. 520–546.

Die Parler und der schöne Stil 1350–1400: Europäische Kunst unter den Luxemburgern, ed. Anton Legner. 6 vols. Cologne: Museen der Stadt Köln, 1978–1980.

Schmidt, Gerhard. "Malerei bis 1450." *Gotik in Böhmen: Geschichte, Gesellschaftsgeschichte, Architektur, Plastik und Malerei,* ed. Karl M. Swoboda. Munich: Prestel, 1969.

Stejskal, Karel. *European Art in the 14th Century,* trans. Till Gottheinerová. London: Octopus Books, 1978.

Vojtísek, Václav, and Dobroslav Líbal. *The Carolinum, Pride of the Caroline University.* Prague: Orbis, 1948.

Tracy Chapman Hamilton

SEE ALSO
Charles IV; Parler Family

Prayer Books

The tradition of German prayer books extends as far back as the ninth century and represents an evolution in sophistication of the early Christian Psalter (Book of Psalms). Prayer books are collections of prayers, Psalms, and meditations intended for a specific individual's private devotions. They are small enough to be comfortably portable and, because of the high cost of production, were usually commissioned by the aristocracy.

The earliest surviving examples of Psalters and prayer books that can claim Germanic origin are Carolingian. The Reims school of illumination is credited with the execution of a mid-ninth-century Psalter and the famous Utrecht Psalter (preserved in the University Library of Utrecht), which boasts some of the most beautiful displays of illumination in Western art. The oldest extant prayer book made for a medieval king is that of Charles the Bald, a product of Charles's court school, the last great school of the Carolingian renaissance.

Later examples of prayer books are not as frequent in Germany as they are in other countries such as France and England. Particularly underrepresented are Books of Hours. (The Book of Hours, an extremely popular form of prayer book, derived its name from its texts, which were suitable for recitation at each of the eight divisions of the medieval day. The Hours of the Virgin was its central text, but other texts such as excerpts from the gospels or calendars of feast days were also often incorporated.) A few noteworthy examples of post Carolingian prayer books include the prayer book of Otto III, and Hildegard von Bingen's personal prayer book, preserved at Munich's state library. A prayer book out of fourteenth-century Saxony, written in the vernacular, has also been recovered.

Prayer books fell under scrutiny with the coming of the Reformation. Martin Luther considered them ornamental extravagances of the wealthy and objected that they often included devotions not derived specifically from the Bible. In response, he wrote the Personal Prayer

Book in 1522, in which he attempted to simplify the prayer book's essential nature. Despite such efforts, however, traditionally sumptuous prayer books flourished in Germany at this time. The prayer book of Emperor Maximilian I, illustrated in part by Albrecht Dürer, is an excellent example. Others include Nicholas Glockendon's "Missal Cum Prayer Book" for Albert of Brandenburg in 1524, and Albert Glockendon's prayer book of William of Bavaria, completed in 1534.

BIBLIOGRAPHY

Diniger, David. *The Illuminated Book: Its History and Production.* London: Faber and Faber, 1967.

The Dictionary of Art, ed. Jane Turner. London: Macmillan, 1996, vol. 3, p. 506; vol. 4, pp. 358, 759; vol. 20, pp. 692, 736f.; vol. 28, p. 146.

The Dictionary of the Middle Ages, ed. Theodore Anderson. New York: Scribner, 1983, vol. 2, pp. 325–327.

Luther, Martin. *Luther's Works,* ed. Jaroslav Pelican. Saint Louis: Concordia, 1958.

New Catholic Encyclopedia, ed. William McDonald. New York: McGraw-Hill, 1967, vol. 11, pp. 678–683.

Tikkanen, J. J. *Die Psalter-Illustrationen im Mittelalter.* Helsinki: Finnischen Litteratur Gesellschaft, 1903.

————. *Abendländische Psalter-Illustrationen des Utrecht Psalter.* Helsinki: Finnischen Litteratur Gesellschaft, 1900.

Larry Hunt

SEE ALSO
Bible; Hildegard von Bingen; Maximilian; Notker Labeo

Preaching and Sermons, Dutch

Preaching was a fundamental activity of the church throughout the Middle Ages. Sermons were preached to convert and to instruct the populace with an explanation of the divine word contained in the Bible, in order to strengthen its faith and implement Christian morals. Sermons formed part of the divine service on Sundays and feast days (liturgical sermons *de tempore* and *de sanctis*), but they were also held separately on other public occasions, and could be directed to various specific social groups within the community *(sermones ad status).*

As early as the late fourth century missionaries became active in the southern parts of the Low Countries, whereas serious Christianization in the north started only in the seventh and eighth centuries under Carolingian protection. These missionaries—such as Amandus, Willibrord, Boniface, Liudger, and Lebuin—and their successors probably composed Latin sermons, but they had to engage in vernacular preaching as well to reach the lay population. Thus from the outset preaching in the Low Countries implied working in a bilingual situation. In the course of the ninth century the process of Christianization and the establishment of an ecclesiastical organization was completed (the dioceses Utrecht, Münster, Liège, and Osnabrück under the archdiocese Cologne; Terwaan, Tournai, and Kamerrijk under the archdiocese of Reims). By then the times of wandering missionaries were over. As in the numerous (Benedictine) monasteries founded in the Low Countries from the Carolingian period onward, sermons were foremost composed for internal use, not for the edification of the population in the outside world; pastoral care of the laity was predominantly the responsibility of the bishops and their subordinates (auxiliary bishops, deacons, parish priests). In the smaller country parishes, which in principle had their own church with a parish priest to administer the sacraments, celebrate mass, and preach, nothing but the most elementary religious instruction would have been offered.

In the late eleventh and twelfth centuries new monastic orders, the Premonstratensian (or Norbertine) order in particular, displayed a serious interest in the struggle against heresies and the religious instructions of the laity. Norbert of Xanten (1080–1134) and other Premonstratensian monks traveled through the southern parts of the Low Countries as wandering priests, and in the neighborhood of their monasteries they often took responsibility for the ministry of parish churches. Even greater changes occurred in the thirteenth century, with the rapid ascent of the mendicant orders in these regions (Dominicans, Franciscans, Augustinian Hermits, Carmelites). Preachers from these new orders took an active part in the pastoral care of the urban laity, sometimes in rivalry with the local secular clergy. They preached in parish churches, in their own convent churches—which were designed to house many people—on the streets, and on the marketplace.

The oldest extant sermon collections in the Low Countries, such as the twelfth-century Latin sermons of Elias of Ter Duinen and Stephen of Tournai, were meant for a monastic audience. These are carefully composed literary works, foremost of a mystical and spiritual exegetical character. The extant (Latin and vernacular) sermons of the mendicant preachers, who preached for very diverse clerical and lay audiences, cover a far wider range of topics. The emphasis of these sermons was primarily on penance, straightforward religious instruction, and the stimulation of lay devotion for the Eucharist and for local saints. Very important for the history of religious literature and experience in the Low Countries and for sermon literature in particular were the pastoral and literary activities of preachers associated with the Modern Devotion, such as Geert Grote (1340–1384) and Willem Jordaens (ca. 1321–1372); and of "observantist" preachers such as the Fransiscan Jan Brugman (1400–1473), Jan Storm of Brussels (d. 1488), and Hendrik Herp (d. 1477). These and many other popular preachers left us an impressive corpus of sermon collections and related works in Latin and in the vernacular. These collections, e.g., the anonymous *Limburgse sermoenen* (ca. 1340), the anonymous *Zwolse sermoenen* (before 1380), and the collations of Dirc of Herxen (1381–1457) not only contain translations and adaptations of Latin originals, such as translations of Bernard of Clairvaux's liturgical sermons and *sermones ad status* of Guilbert of Tournai—works that were very popular in the Low Countries in the later fourteenth and fifteenth centuries—but also reflect an impressive production of original sermons in the vernacular tongue. Many of these sermons were meant for private reading and meditation as well as for public hearing. Together with an array of other devotional texts and treatises (which, like many sermon collections, have yet to be critically edited), these sermons played an important role in later medieval religious life and the formation of lay and religious affective spirituality in the Low Countries.

BIBLIOGRAPHY

Épiney-Burgard, Georgette, ed. Henri Herp. *De Processu Humani Profectus. Sermones de diversis materiis vitae contemplativae.* Wiesbaden: Steiner, 1982.

Lingier, Carine. "Over de verspreiding van sint-Bernardus' liturgische sermoenen in het middelnederlands." *Ons geestelijk erf* 64 (1990): 18–40.

Longère, Jean. *La Prédication médiévale.* Paris: Études augustiennes, 1983.

Martin, H. "Devotia moderna et prédication." *Publications du centre européen d'études bourguignons* 29 (1989): 97–110.

Morvay, Karin, and Dagmar Grube, ed. *Bibliographie der deutschen Predigt des Mittelalters. Veröffentliche Predigten.* Munich: Beck, 1974 [German, Dutch, Latin sermons].

Pegel, R. H. "Sermon studies report. Dutch/Flemish." *Medieval Sermon Studies Newsletter* 28 (1991): 31–36; 29 (1992): 30–32; 30 (1992): 29.

Schieffer, Theodor. *Winfrid Bonifatius und die christliche Grundlegung Europas,* 2d ed. Freiburg: Herder, 1972.

Schneyer, Johannes B. *Geschichte der katholischen Predigt.* Freiburg im Breisgau: Seelsorge Verlag, 1969.

Schneyer, Johannes B. *Repertorium der lateinischen Sermones des Mittelalters.* 9 vols. Münster: Aschendorff, 1969–1980 [Latin sermons].

Seidel, Kurt Otto, ed. *Sô predigent etelîche. Beiträge zur deutschen und niederländischen Predigt im Mittelalter.* Göppingen: Kümmerle, 1982.

Simons, Walter. *Stad en apostolaat. De vestiging van de bedelorden in het graafschap Vlaanderen.* Brussel: Koninklijke academie voor wetenschappen, letteren en schone kunsten van België, 1987.

Talbot, C. H., ed. *The Anglo-Saxon Missionaries in Germany.* New York: Sheed and Ward, 1954, rpt. 1981.

Willeumier-Schalij, Johanna M. "Hendrik Herp als Predikant." *Ons geestelijk erf* 60 (1986): 23–37.

Zieleman, Gerrit C. *Middelnederlandse Epistel—en Evangeliepreken.* Leyden: Brill, 1978.

———. *De preek bij de moderne devoten. Een verkenning.* Deventer: Geert Groote Genootschap, 1984.

Bert Roest

SEE ALSO

Charlemagne; *Devotio Moderna;* Preaching and Sermons, German

Preaching and Sermons, German

As an integral part of the medieval liturgy on Sundays, Saints' Days, and Feast Days, the sermon followed the reading of the Gospel, providing biblical exegesis as well as theological and moral instruction. From the fifth century through the Middle Ages, Augustine's treatise on homiletics, Book 4 of *De doctrina Christiana (On Christian Doctrine),* was the exegetical model for preaching. With wide-ranging diversity in rhetorical styles, the primary goals of all sermons were to teach, to please, and to persuade. Typically, sermons began with a scriptural text and followed a particular theme that related the text to the lives of the listeners or readers. Throughout medieval Germany, whether preached in monastic settings, cathedrals, university chapels, or small parish churches, sermons both reflected and shaped society. While the intent was similar, sermons preached to the clergy *(ad cleros)* and those to the laity *(ad populum)* were considerably different. Popular sermons focused less on issues of doctrine and more on vices and virtues and included a greater number of exempla and legends.

Prior to the rise of Scholasticism in the twelfth century and the emergence of the Dominican and Franciscan orders in the thirteenth century, there was little variation in the form and style of sermons. As popular preaching increased, so also did the available sources for preachers. Manuals for preaching, *artes praedicandi,* and collections of model sermons *(Musterpredigten),* as well as a vast number of collections of legends and exempla were in wide circulation by the fourteenth century to assist the preacher in the construction of a sermon and the manner of delivery. Not all sermons were preached, however. It was not uncommon for sermons to be written, sometimes in the form of a letter, for private or communal study. Universities such as Prague, Vienna, and Heidelberg placed homiletics—training in the writing and delivery of sermons—in the curriculum. Jordan of Saxony (1190–1237) actively recruited in the universities for the Dominican Order, a mendicant order of friars known for preaching. Albertus Magnus (1207–1280), a renowned Dominican theologian, was one of his recruits.

Collections of sermons were copied and circulated throughout the Middle Ages. Extant collections of notable German preachers provide historians a great deal of evidence about medieval German religious customs and daily life. The Franciscan preacher Berthold of Regensburg (ca. 1211–1272) and Dominican preachers Meister Eckhart (ca. 1260–1327) and John Tauler (1300–1361) are among those whose sermon collections have been edited and received scholarly attention. With a growing number of Dominican convents and the blossoming of women's mysticism in fourteenth-century Germany, Dominican preachers such as Eckhart, Tauler, Henrich Seuse, and Heinrich Nördlingen were responsible for the spiritual guidance *(cura monialium)* of nuns. In addition to preaching in universities and monasteries, Dominican friars such as John Herolt (1390–1468) also preached to the laity—to peasants and burghers—on topics such as marriage and child rearing, exhorting them to lead virtuous lives. Even as the preliterate society of the early Middle Ages gave way to the biblically literate populace of the fifteenth and sixteenth centuries, preaching continued to occupy a significant role in German religious life.

BIBLIOGRAPHY

Battaillon, Louis, J. "Approaches to the Study of Medieval Sermons." *Leeds Studies in English,* n.s. 11 (1980): 19–35.

De ore Domini: Preacher and Word in the Middle Ages, ed. Thomas L. Amos, Eugene A. Green, and Beverly Mayne Kienzle. Kalamazoo, Mich.: Medieval Institute Publications, 1989.

Medieval Sermons and Society: Cloister, City, University, ed. Jacqueline Hamesse et al. Louvain-la-Neuve: Fédération Internationale des Instituts d'Études Médiévales, 1998.

Ruh, Kurt. "Deutsche Predigtbücher des Mittelalters," in *Beiträge zur Geschichte der Predigt,* ed. Haimo Reintizer. Hamburg, 1981, pp. 11–30; rpt. in *Kleine Schriften,* ed. Volker Mertens, vol. 2. Berlin: de Gruyter, 1984, pp. 296–317.

Rosemary Drage Hale

SEE ALSO
Albertus Magnus; Berthold von Regensburg; Conversion; Ludolph of Saxony; Meister Eckhart; Preaching and Sermons, Dutch; Seuse, Heinrich

Pregnancy and Childbirth

With few exceptions, medieval written sources on pregnancy and childbirth were composed by learned men. Comprising a variety of discourses (legal, theological, medical, physiological, and social or domestic) that at times intersect, these sources do not, therefore, reflect women's experience either as healers or as patients. Within medical discourse on gynecology and obstetrics, theoretical and practical, learned and folk traditions overlap. Women's reproductive health care lay in the hands of a range of practitioners, male and female, trained and untrained, Christian and Jewish, which included physicians, apothecaries, barber-surgeons, midwives, lay healers, friends, and family members. In the course of the Middle Ages in cities, women's health care increasingly came to be supervised by city physicians and officially approved "honorable women" through the examination and licensing of midwives and, from the fourteenth century on, through midwives' oaths. To counteract the negative effects of plague on the European population, increased emphasis was placed on female reproductive health in the late Middle Ages.

Medieval explanatory models regarding conception, time of gestation, embryology, and the like derived from ancient (Hippocratic, Galenic, Aristotelian, and Methodist) sources, transmitted to the Latin West largely through Arabic translations and compilations. Competing theories regarding the nature and role of menstruation and sperm in conception and heredity (the Galenic two-seed theory versus Aristotelian hylomorphism with the rennet-milk analogy) all were products of a male-centered biological tradition that served to warn men of the dangers of women. These included the right-left theory of sex determination, the phases of embryological and fetal development including astrological influences and ensoulment, the mortality of the eighth-month child, the seven-celled uterus (of Salernitan origin), pica (the pregnant woman's craving for "unnatural" foods), *imaginatio* (the influence of the mother's mental state on the offspring), and the milk-menstruum continuum. Patriarchal interests also motivated the intense concern with sterility. Information on contraception and abortion was transmitted, by contrast, in haphazard fashion. The major source of information on obstetrics was Soranus of Ephesos (second century, C.E.) whose *Gynaikea* was translated and adapted by Muscio in the sixth century. This literature, addressed to midwives and pregnant women by physicians, treats such topics as birthing stools, the choice of suitable birth attendants, treatment of difficult labor, fetal positions and manual version, retention of the afterbirth, extraction of a dead fetus, tears in the perineum, uterine prolapse, and pre- and postnatal care. Two printed obstetrical handbooks in German from around 1500—Pseudo-Ortolf of Baierland's *Frauenbüchlein* (*Little Book for Women*, ca. 1495) and Eucharius Roesslin's *Der Swangern Frauwen und hebammen Rosegarten* (*Pregnant Women's and Midwives' Rose Garden*, 1513—addressed to women, are based on this tradition.

BIBLIOGRAPHY

Diepgen, Paul. *Frau and Frauenheilkunde in der Kultur des Mittelalters.* Stuttgart: Thieme, 1963.

Green, Monica H. "Women's Medical Practice and Health Care in Medieval Europe." *Signs* 14 (1989): 434–473.

Keil, Gundolf. "Die Frau als Ärztin und Patientin in der medizinischen Fachprosa des deutschen Mittelalters," in *Frau and spätmittelalterlicher Alltag. Internationaler Kongreß Krems an der Donau 2. bis 5. Oktober 1984.* Vienna: Verlag der Österreichischen Akademie der Wissenschaften, 1986, pp. 157–211.

Ortolf von Bayerland. *Das Frauenbüchlein des Ortolff von Bayerland, gedruckt vor 1500,* ed. Gustav Klein. Munich: Kuhn, 1910.

Riha, Ortrun. "Ortolfus Pseudepigraphus," in *"ein teutsch puech machen." Untersuchungen zur landessprachlichen Vermittlung medizinischen Wissens,* ed. Gundolf Keil. Wiesbaden: Reichert, 1993, pp. 70–111.

Roesslin, Eucharius. *Der Swangern Frauwen vnd hebammen Rosegarten,* ed. Huldrych M. Koelbing. Dietikon-Zurich: Verlag Bibliophilie Drucke von Josef Stocker, 1976 [facsimile of edition of 1513].

————. *When Midwifery Became the Male Physician's Province: The Sixteenth Century Handbook 'The Rose Garden for Pregnant Women and Midwives,'* trans. and introd. Wendy Arons. Jefferson, N.C.: McFarland, 1994.

Margaret Schleissner

Prenzlau

Now part of Berlin, Prenzlau, consisting of earlier settlements around the parish churches of St. Nikolai and St. Jakobi, is mentioned for the first time in 1188 as a market. In 1235, Prenzlau was given the status of a town by Duke Barnim of Pomerania, which started its subsequent urban development. The inclusion of the two rural settlements led to a shift of axis in the otherwise regular ground plan characteristic of a colonial town. In 1374, Emperor Charles IV held a diet with north German princes at Prenzlau. In 1415, the town came under the rule of the margraves of Brandenburg.

The road leading into town through the suburb known as the Neustadt (New Town) continued as the middle cross axis of the town, marked by the Marienkirche (church of the Virgin) and Rathaus (town hall). The latter is destroyed, but the Marienkirche has survived as a ruin without its roofs and vaults. It represents a hall church of the triple-apse type from the mid–fourteenth century, which received—after its completion—an elaborate eastern gable with tracery in brick. The church of the Franciscan monastery, dating from the mid–thirteenth century and still erected in fieldstone, represents an unusual single-aisled and square-ended hall of five square bays, cross-rib vaulted, with triple groups of narrow windows. The Dominican monastery, begun in 1275 and consecrated in 1343, consists of a hall church with narrow aisles and short choir, and the monastic complex with cloister, chapter house, refectory, and other double-aisle halls. Prenzlau has also preserved portions of its defensive walls with several gates (Schwedter Tor, Blindower Tor, and Mitteltor).

Hans J. Böker

Priester Arnolt

See Arnolt, Priester.

Printing Press

The mechanism of the wooden screw press was developed in Germany in the fifteenth century. The basic construction of the printing press consists of two major components: the vertical uprights (the cheeks) and the horizontal platform (the carriage). The screw is fitted into the head, a transverse board between the cheeks. A hose covers the screw, and a heavy flat board, the platen, is hung from the hose. A long pole or spindle attached to the screw allows the printer to raise and lower the platen to apply the pressure.

The composed form of type is placed on a horizontal bed or coffin that moves along the carriage. The paper is attached to a frame called the tympan, which is hinged to the coffin. A frisket (light parchment frame) that covers the margins of the paper can be folded over the tympan. Printing is accomplished by securing the paper to the tympan, inking the type, folding the tympan and frisket over the inked type, rolling the carriage under the platen, and applying pressure by turning the screw with the spindle to lower the platen.

The technology of the printing press probably developed gradually. Documents about Johann Gutenberg's early printing efforts circa 1440 in Strasbourg that mention a press and his association with a wood turner, Konrad Saspach, suggest that he was working out the mechanism of a press. The clear impressions and clean margins in the Gutenberg Bible printed in Mainz circa 1450–1455 indicate that he had solved many technical challenges of the printing press. The earliest illustrations of printing presses from around 1500 show the basic components in place. The perfection of the printing press in mid-fifteenth-century Germany was essential to the success of printing books and illustrations.

BIBLIOGRAPHY

Moran, James. *Printing Presses: History and Development from the Fifteenth Century to Modern Times.* London: Faber, 1973.

Karen Gould

SEE ALSO

Gutenberg, Johann; Mainz; Strasbourg

Printmaking

During the late fourteenth century, when paper became available in plentiful supply, the first printed works on paper were made in Europe in southeastern Germany and Austria. These first prints —woodcuts—had great significance because they were the first works of art that could be reproduced easily in large numbers. Earlier, panel painting was the least expensive artistic medium. The low cost of woodcuts thus expanded the audience for visual art beyond the well-off merchant families commissioning panels to those of lesser means. Woodcuts were printed from wood blocks and follow in the late medieval tradition of printing textiles from inked blocks of wood.

Early woodcuts employ simple designs emphasizing outlines corresponding to the areas left in relief in the wood block, thus not carved away with knives. Lines were then inked and printed. During the second quarter of the fifteenth century, woodcuts became technically and pictorially more sophisticated, yet still rather simple but elegant, adding texture and dark-light to their designs. Woodcut incunables (pages printed using woodcuts, dating before 1450 and the invention of movable type) were stamped face down onto paper in the method of printed textiles, rubbed face up with a wooden implement like a spoon, perhaps even printed face up on a press.

The simple style of early woodcuts was often complemented by the addition of color by hand, enlivening their increasing naturalism and continuing the late medieval taste for color. Subjects were mostly Christian, including saints and scenes from the life of Christ and Mary, although after mid-century secular subjects such as playing cards increased in number. By the early sixteenth century, subject matter shifted toward the secular and included popular festivals and contemporary historic events.

Engravings were added in the second quarter of the fifteenth century to these less costly printed works of art. Originating in the Rhineland, engravings were an extension of what was then considered to be the more noble craft of the goldsmith tradition, which worked precious materials including gold. From the beginning, engravings differed from woodcuts in appearance and subject. The earliest engravings were printed from copper plates into which designs were carved in fine lines using a burin (steel tool). Engraving plates were run through a cylinder press, face up with wet paper on top, with the press exerting considerable pressure pushing the paper into the incised, inked lines. In such prints, called intaglios, carving fine lines into metal was faster and easier than removing wood from a block for woodcuts, especially in areas with complex designs involving cross-hatching. Early on engravings achieved not only line but light, shade, and color. These were indicated by flicks and parallel lines, with cross-hatching first used soon after mid century by Master E.S. Consequently, color was needed less, and added less frequently to engravings than to early woodcuts.

From the beginning, therefore, engravings were more

detailed pictorially than woodcuts and made use of a wider range of subjects, including secular ones like bathhouses and playing cards. Based on this greater sophistication and the higher prices paid for engravings, their audience has been estimated to include wealthier and more educated individuals than for the audience of woodcuts. Further research, especially specific case studies, is needed to bear this out.

Early prints are generally unsigned, but their makers have often been assigned names based on the type of work or marks on the prints, thus the Master of the Playing Cards and Master E.S. The work of the first known named engraver, Martin Schongauer, dates from 1470 to his death in 1491. Schongauer was first and foremost a painter. Fifteenth-century engravers like Schongauer, trained in the engraving tradition, fashioned their own designs and cut their own plates. The designers of woodcuts, by contrast, made detailed drawings but left cutting the blocks to woodcutters. The division between designer and woodcutter was standard for woodcuts from the outset. Designs for both woodcuts and engravings were transferred onto block or plate in reverse, compensating for the design reversal during printing. Designs were either drawn directly onto the block or flopped and pounced for transfer or greased, increasing the paper's transparency and lucidity of design.

The introduction of printing from movable type on a flatbed press in the years around 1450 resulted in the production of woodcuts on a more sophisticated level by the end of the century. Wood blocks were placed face up on the press, paper on top, and a flat wooden bed pressed down on paper and block, exerting pressure created by a large wooden screw turned tight. These presses were used for both books and their texts, and the numbers of illustrations in books increased substantially by the turn of the century. Woodcut illustrations became part of a larger web of connections within the book industry with its marketing throughout Europe. The connection between woodcut and book industry had two major repercussions for woodcuts. First, woodcuts appeared in books more frequently and increased in size, from several inches to as large as a foot (thus, half or full-page format of large books) by the time of Albrecht Dürer at the end of the century. Second, by that last decade of the century, woodcuts were marketed by international publishers like Anton Koberger, who sent books in barrels throughout Europe. With the publication of Koberger's *Nuremberg Chronicle* in 1493, woodcuts became successful from a modern perspective—they were large-scale productions,

sophisticated pictorially with cross-hatching, and were no longer anonymous (Michael Wolgemut and Dürer were designers). Dürer's woodcuts began with book illustrations and can be considered the finest produced in the history of Western art. By the end of Dürer's life (d. 1528), woodcuts and some engravings took on new meaning and importance in support of the Lutheran Reformation.

Whether early prints are viewed today as communicators of ideas (Ivins 1969), mechanical reproductions of one pictorial image (Benjamin 1955), or as part of a new culture of print after Gutenberg (Chartier 1987: 1–10), the appeal of late-fifteenth-century prints to the modern viewer is undeniable. The first print catalogue published by Adam von Bartsch between 1803 and 1821 (known today as "Bartsch") gives short shrift to the earliest anonymous prints in favor of prints by painter-print designers like Schongauer. Bartsch's catalogues, neatly titled *Le peintre-graveur (The Painter-Engraver),* helped shape our modern taste for the named artist and placed prints on the art historical map.

BIBLIOGRAPHY

Benjamin, Walter. "The Work of Art in the Age of Mechanical Reproduction," in *Illuminations.* New York: Harcourt, Brace and World, 1955, pp. 219–253.

Chartier, Roger, ed. *The Culture of Print: Power and Uses of Print in Early Modern Europe.* Princeton, N.J.: Princeton University Press, 1987.

Hults, Linda C. *The Print in the Western World: An Introductory History.* Madison: University of Wisconsin Press, 1996, pp. 72–74, 132–135.

Ivins, William. *Prints and Visual Communication.* Cambridge, Mass.: MIT Press, 1978.

Landau, David, and Peter Parshall. *The Renaissance Print 1470–1550.* New Haven, Conn.: Yale University Press, 1994.

Stewart, Alison G. "Early Woodcut Workshops." *Art Journal* 39, no. 3 (Spring 1980): 189–194.

Suffield, Laura, Katharina Mayer Haunton, Ilja M. Veldman, and Elizabeth Miller. "Printing," in *The Dictionary of Art,* ed. Jane Shoaf Turner. New York: Grove, 1996, vol. 25, pp. 588–625.

Alison G. Stewart

SEE ALSO

E.S., Master; Housebook, Master of the; Playing Cards, Master of; Printing Press; Schongauer, Martin;

Wolgemut, Michael

Privilegium Ottonianum

A solemn privilege (Privilege of the Ottonen) granted to the papacy by Emperor Otto I on February 13, 962, eleven days after his own imperial coronation. This document confirmed the Carolingian "donations," grants of land and rights, to the popes. The *Ottonianum* did not grant any significant new concessions to the pope's temporal authority; indeed a provision, perhaps added the next year, gave the emperor the right to ratify papal elections. This provided a juridical basis for future imperial domination of Roman politics.

The intent of the *Ottonianum* was clearly to signal a new relationship between the papacy and the German Empire. A copy of the privilege was drawn up on empurpled parchment in letters of gold, emphasizing the significance of the act. This should best be seen as a statement that Otto I, in whom the moribund empire had been revived, understood protectorship of the papacy and the Roman Church to be an essential part of his imperium. The *Ottonianum* also marked what proved to be a very temporary alliance between Otto I and Pope John XII. John, finding that the new emperor was intent on dominating Italian politics, formed a coalition intended to end the German presence on the peninsula. Otto, returning in 963, first forced the pope to flee Rome, then arranged his deposition by a church council, using the imperial power agreed on in the *Ottonianum* to arrange the election of a more amenable pope.

BIBLIOGRAPHY

Beumann, Helmut. *Die Ottonen.* Stuttgart: Kohlhammer, 1987.

Reuter, Timothy. *Germany in the Early Middle Ages.* London: Longman, 1991.

Phyllis G. Jestice

SEE ALSO
Carolingians; Otto I

Püterich von Reichertshausen, Jacob (ca. 1400–1467)

Püterich belonged to the urban patrician class of Munich and served at the court of the Bavarian dukes. In 1462 he composed a dedicatory poem, the so-called "Letter of Honor" *(Ehrenbrief),* for the countess of the Palatinate, Mechthild, Duchess of Austria, who held her own retirement court in Rottenburg on the Neckar. In his poem Püterich lists all the books kept in Mechthild's and in his own library and compares both their collections. Mechthild had sent him a list of ninety-four titles in her library; of these twenty-three are unknown to him, obviously because they were part of contemporary vernacular literature, especially representatives of the *Volksbücher* (chapbooks). Püterich's own library comprises 164 titles that he had collected over forty years on travels between Brabant and Hungary, some of which he acquired by means of force, as he openly admits, others he purchased, and others again he had copied with his own hand. Püterich did not like contemporary literature very much; instead, he praised the books from the old days, i.e., courtly romances from the thirteenth and fourteenth centuries, such as Albrecht (von Scharfenberg's) *Jüngere Titurel.* Püterich still attributes it to Wolfram von Eschenbach and falsely claims it as the masterpiece of German literature. He also included a praise of the duchess, discussed the miserable conditions of this world, cast a stylized image of himself, and listed all Bavarian families socially entitled to participate in tournaments.

The *Ehrenbrief* plays a major role in literary research as it informs us about the prevalent taste at that time on the part of the intellectual elite. It has survived in only one manuscript, today housed in the Getty Museum in Malibu, California. Although the portion of secular books in Püterich's library was quite extensive for his time, it made up only about a sixth of his entire library, which was filled with theological texts.

BIBLIOGRAPHY

Der Ehrenbrief des Püterich von Reichertshausen, ed. Fritz Behrend and Rudolf Wolkan. Weimar: Gesellschaft der Bibliophilen, 1920.

Grubmüller, Klaus. "Der Hof als städtisches Literaturzentrum," in *Befund und Deutung: Zum Verhältnis von Empirie und Interpretation in Sprach- und Literaturwissenschaft,* ed. Klaus Grubmüller et al. Tübingen: Niemyer, 1979, pp. 405–427.

Rischer, Christelrose. *Literarische Rezeption und kulturelles Selbstverständnis in der deutschen Literatur der "Ritterrenaissance" des 15. Jahrhunderts.* Stuttgart: Kohlhammer, 1973.

Strohschneider, Peter. *Ritterromantische Versepik im ausgehenden Mittelalter.* Frankfurt am Main: Lang, 1986.

Albrecht Classen

SEE ALSO
Albrecht von Scharfenberg; Wolfram von Eschenbach

Q

Quedlinburg

The first documentary evidence of a settlement at the Saxon city of Quedlinburg dates to 922, but it seems likely that a Carolingian fortress had already stood for a century in this location on the Bode River at the northern edge of the Harz Mountains. The erection of this first, undated fortification and the early-tenth-century history of this site are linked to the protection of the Holy Roman Empire against barbarian incursions from the east and to the related attempts to expand the empire's borders and Christianize the populace in these areas. Begun under Charlemagne at the end of the eighth century, these attempts were revived in the tenth century by the local duke and later king, Heinrich of Saxony. In 926 he enlarged the castle there; a palace chapel may have been erected at this time. In 929 he gave the settlement and its inhabitants to his wife, Mathilda, as part of her widow's pension in the event that he should predecease her. On his death in 936, he was buried before the altar of the palace chapel.

Soon thereafter—and clearly with the intent of establishing the church as a fitting family necropolis—Mathilda replaced the twelve canons with canonesses and granted the foundation privileges intended to confer it with a special status. The abbey was placed under royal protection and exempted from local secular laws and those of the neighboring bishop of Halberstadt, and the canonesses were allowed to elect their own abbess rather than accept one imposed on them by outside authorities. Queen Mathilda herself took up residence in the newly founded cloister and assumed its direction until her death in 968, when she was buried at her husband's side.

The queen was succeeded by her granddaughter, also named Mathilda, who initiated a series of abbesses from the royal family. During this period the abbey was also home to other royal women: after the death of Otto II in 983, his mother, Empress Adelheid, and his widow, Theophanu, retired to Quedlinburg, where, with the Abbess Mathilda, they ruled for the child Otto III until he assumed the rule for himself in 994. Under Mathilda's leadership the church was enlarged in and after 997: the small palace chapel became the choir of the new building, chapels were added at its sides, and it was extended to the west with a transept and long nave.

On Mathilda's death in 999 she was buried at her grandparents' heads, and Otto III appointed his sister Adelheid to succeed her. Adelheid undertook a complete rebuilding of the tenth-century church on a larger scale; the new building was consecrated in the presence of Heinrich II, the Empress Kunigunde, numerous bishops, and members of the nobility in 1021. This building burned in 1070 and it was quickly rebuilt in a Romanesque style; its consecration, delayed until 1129, took place in the presence of the Emperor Lothar. The documentation of sixty-nine royal visits to Quedlinburg between 922 and 1207 suggests the continued political importance of the site even after its high point under the Ottonian rulers.

Quedlinburg has enjoyed unusual attention at two points in recent history. Since Heinrich I was considered the founder of the first German Christian Empire, the First Reich, he elicted considerable interest among the founders of the Third Reich. When the one-thousandth anniversary of Heinrich I's death fell conveniently in 1936, Heinrich Himmler, leader of Hitler's SS (secret police), who may have considered himself a reincarnation of Heinrich, conducted excavations at Quedlinburg to search for the king's bones.

In 1990, the return to Quedlinburg of the luxury manuscript known as the Samuhel Gospels, which had been missing since the end of World War II, was negotiated after it appeared mysteriously on the art market. The recovery of this early-ninth-century illuminated codex with certain connections to Charlemagne's Court School led to the discovery of a dozen objects from Quedlinburg in Whitewright, Texas, where they had been shipped by an American GI at the end of World War II. Among these were an ivory casket, or reliquary box, and a liturgical comb, long thought to be gifts of Heinrich I to the abbey, and numerous small crystal vessels, some containing relics, that may have come with Theophanu from Byzantium and were then given by her or her children to the royal foundation. Other objects in the impressive treasury are traditionally identified as donations from the early Ottonian emperors to their family foundation: a second casket with ivories of early-tenth-century date is held to be a gift to the abbey from Otto I, and on his trips to Italy in 951–952 and 961–965, he is known to have purchased relics for his mother's foundation at Quedlinburg. These included a hair of the Virgin, a drop of her milk, and one of the alabaster vases in which Christ changed water into wine at the wedding feast at Cana as well as the bodies of the early Christian Saints Laurentia and Stephana. Thietmar of Merseburg relates how Otto III gave a golden staff, which is still preserved at Quedlinburg, in honor of his sister's installation as abbess. Many of the abbey's rich collection of manuscripts have also been identified. The covers of two of them were remodeled and an important tapestry acquired for the abbey about 1200, in a new period of well-being under two successive abbesses from the house of the margraves of Meißen.

BIBLIOGRAPHY

Bromberg, Anne. *The Quedlinburg Treasury.* Dallas: Dallas Museum of Art, 1991.

Honan, William H. *Treasure Hunt: A New York Times Reporter Tracks the Quedlinburg Hoard.* New York: Fromm International, 1997.

Jacobsen, Werner. "Zur Frühgeschichte der Quedlinburger Stiftskirche," in *Denkmalkunde und Denkmalpflege—Wissen und Wirken: Festschrift für Heinrich Magirius zum 60. Geburtstag am 1. Februar 1994.* Dresden: Karl M. Lipp Verlag, 1995, pp. 63–72.

Mrusek, Hans-Joachim, and Klaus G. Beyer. *Drei deutsche Dome: Quedlinburg, Magdeburg, Halberstadt.* Die bibliophilen Taschenbücher 639. Dortmund: Harenberg Kommunikation, 1992.

Wäscher, Hermann. *Der Burgberg in Quedlinburg: Geschichte seiner Bauten bis zum ausgehenden 12. Jahrhundert nach den Ergebnissen der Grabungen von 1938 bis 1942.* Schriften des Instituts für Theorie und Geschichte der Baukunst. Berlin: Henschelverlag, 1959.

Joan A. Holladay

SEE ALSO

Carolingian Art and Architecture; Charlemagne; Halberstadt; Henry II, Art; Otto I; Otto II; Otto III; Ottonian Art and Architecture; Romanesque Art and Architecture; Theophanu

R

Rabenschlacht

See *Buch von Bern* and *Rabenschlact.*

Radewijns, Florens (ca. 1350–1400)

Exponent of the Modern Devotion, founder of the Brethren of the Common Life, founder of the monastery of Windesheim. Radewijns was born circa 1350 at Leerdam or Gorinchem and died at Deventer in 1400. He studied at Prague (master of arts) and became a canon in Utrecht. After a sermon of Geert Grote, he converted and accepted the lower position of vicar at Deventer, where Grote lived. For this vicariat he had to be ordained priest. He became the first leader of a congregation of Brethren of the Common Life. These Brethren gave guidance to a convict of schoolboys.

Radewijns compiled two little treatises, which are important because they influenced the treatises of his housemate Gerard Zerbolt of Zutphen. These widely spread treatises gave the Modern Devotion its spiritual fundament. We also have some fragments of Radewijns's letters. He also wrote a (lost?) *propositum,* a set of personal intentions.

In Radewijns's spirituality, humility is a central theme. The idea of externals pulling along the inner man leads to a severe asceticism, as did the idea that a humble inner self has to reflect itself in humble and austere exteriors. By fasting and waking Radewijns had broken his weak nature and almost lost his sense of taste and his appetite. This severe asceticism is colored by the spirituality of the Desert Fathers, which also seems to have influenced his fear of the demon. In his young days Thomas à Kempis lived together with Radewijns. In his biography of Radewijns, Thomas portrays him as a man who incites both love and fear with his straightforwardness.

BIBLIOGRAPHY

Goossens, Leonardus A. M., ed. *De meditatie in de eerste tijd van de Moderne Devotie.* Haarlem: Gottmer, 1952, pp. 213–254 *[Tractatulus devotus].*

Épiney-Burgard, Georgette. "Florent Radewijns," in *Die deutsche Literatur des Mittelalters: Verfasserlexikon,* ed. Kurt Ruh et al. Berlin: de Gruyter, 2d ed. vol. 7, coll. 968–972.

———. "La Vie et les écrits de Florent Radewijns en langue vernaculaire." *Ons Geestelijk Erf* 63 (1989): 370–384.

Pohl, Michael J., ed. *Thomae Hemerken a Kempis Opera Omnia.* Freiburg: Herder, 1902–1922, vol. 7, pp. 116–210 [with bibliography].

Post, Regnerus R. *The Modern Devotion.* Leyden: Brill, 1968, pp. 317–325.

van Woerkum, M. "Florentius Radewijns. Schets van zijn leven, geschriften, persoonlijkheid en ideeën." *Ons Geestelijk Erf* 24 (1950): 337–346.

———. "Het Libellus «Omnes, inquit, artes»: een rapiarium van Florentius Radewijns." *Ons Geestelijk Erf* 25 (1951): 113–158, 225–268.

———. "Florent Radewijns," in *Dictionnaire de Spiritualité,* ed. Marcel Viller, vol. 5. Paris: Beauchesne, 1964, pp. 427–434.

Thom Mertens

SEE ALSO

Devotio Moderna; Thomas à Kempis; Visionary Literature

Rahewin (d. before 1177)

Notary, canon, devoted servant and chaplain of Otto of Freising, provost of St. Vitus of Freising, Rahewin (died before 1177) is best known as the continuator of Otto of Freising's *The Deeds of Frederick Barbarossa*. Although frequently judged the lesser of the two authors of the *Deeds*, Rahewin made a contribution not without merit, and his work as a historian stands well above that of his successors. At the very least we are indebted to Rahewin for information on the life of Otto, including a description of Otto's deathbed scene in which Otto requested that his views concerning Gilbert de la Porrée be corrected.

Rahewin's other contributions to the *Deeds* are not insignificant. Continuing the work after Otto's death in 1158, Rahewin wrote books three and four of the *Deeds*, which covered the years 1157–1160. These books detail Barbarossa's relations with the Poles and Danes as well as his involvement in Italy. Rahewin describes Barbarossa's physical appearance and struggles with and success against Milan. These books tell of Barbarossa's often difficult relations with the papacy and includes an account of the incident at Besançon where, in 1511, a confrontation between papal representatives and Barbarossa occurred. Rahewin's literary style is also noteworthy. His continuation contains the same laudatory, almost propagandist tone found in Otto's section, but this should not surprise because Barbarossa himself commissioned the work. Rahewin's work is very florid and often incorporates whole passages "borrowed" from Einhard, Jordanes, Sidonius Apollinarus, and Sallust. He also incorporated in his continuation the complete texts of letters and other official documents issued by the emperor or the pope in their disputes. Despite the often critical assessment of his work, Rahewin's continuation provides valuable information on an important period in the empire's history.

BIBLIOGRAPHY

Otto of Freising and his continuator, Rahewin. *The Deeds of Frederick Barbarossa*, trans. Charles Christopher Mierow, with Richard Emery. Toronto: University of Toronto Press, 1994.

Michael Frassetto

SEE ALSO

Frederick I Barbarossa; Otto of Freising

Rainald of Dassel (ca. 1120–1167)

From 1156 until his death in 1167, Rainald of Dassel was Frederick Barbarossa's most loyal and powerful adviser.

Born to a family of Lower Saxon lesser nobility circa 1120, Rainald was educated first at the Hildesheim cathedral school, then in France in the 1140s. He returned to Hildesheim by 1146. Rainald cultivated an interest in arts and letters and would become the chief patron of the "Archpoet" circa 1060.

In 1156, Barbarossa chose Rainald as imperial chancellor. Rainald straightway committed himself to the Hohenstaufen agenda of rejecting papal claims to primacy and establishing German imperial hegemony over northern Italy. Rainald's leadership led to innovations in the chancery almost immediately, including the use of the phrase *sacrum imperium* (Holy Empire) and its variants.

Rainald played a consistently dramatic role in international relations after his elevation to the chancellorship. In 1157, papal legatees met Barbarossa's court in Besançon to protest the imprisonment of Archbishop Eskil of Lund. The Latin text of Pope Adrian IV's letter suggested that the imperial crown numbered among many possible *beneficia* that could be given by the pope. Rainald's translation of the document deliberately rendered *beneficium* as "fief" *(lehen)* rather than "good work" or "favor," Adrian's intended meaning. The subsequent uproar led to a propaganda victory for Rainald and a clear formulation of the imperial position: empire derived from election by the princes and the grace of God, not papal coronation, which was simply a ceremonial act incumbent upon the pope.

Elected archbishop of Cologne at Barbarossa's instigation in 1159, Rainald did not actually take major orders until 1165. Rainald's uncompromising attitude toward the Roman curia led Barbarossa to reject conciliatory papal offers; the result was formal schism with the election of the antipope Victor IV in 1159. In 1162, Rainald oversaw the brutal destruction of Milan, upon whose unconditional surrender he had insisted. Within a few months, however, he had to preside over the failed synod of Saint Jean de Losne, convoked to resolve the papal crisis, but ending in a diplomatic victory for Pope Alexander III, who stubbornly refused to appear and be judged. In April 1164, in Lucca, Rainald orchestrated the election of another antipope, Paschal III. In July 1164, Rainald brought the relics of the Three Kings from Milan to Cologne, where they became the object of a major cult. Late in 1165, Rainald presided over the canonization of Charlemagne in Aachen, the most dramatic step taken in the programmatic sacralization of Barbarossa's imperial rule.

Rainald's uncompromising policy toward the papacy meant that only open conflict could decide the schism. In

July 1167, the imperial army won a major victory at Tusculum. Rome was taken, and Alexander III fled in disguise. Triumph was short-lived, however: an epidemic, probably malaria, decimated the German host, killing Rainald and several other princes. Barbarossa returned to Germany with what was left of his army. The political approach of the rest of his reign was markedly more flexible than it had been during the era of Rainald of Dassel.

BIBLIOGRAPHY

Engels, Odilo. *Die Staufer,* 4th ed. Stuttgart: Kohlhammer, 1989.

Ficker, Julius. *Reinald von Dassel: Reichskanzler und Erzbischof von Köln 1156–1167.* Cologne, 1850; rpt. Aalen: Scientia, 1966.

Grebe, Werner. "Studien zur geistigen Welt Rainalds von Dassel." *Annalen des Historischen Vereins für den Niederrhein* 171 (1969): 5–44.

Munz, Peter. *Frederick Barbarossa: A Study in Medieval Politics.* London: Eyre and Spottiswoode, 1969.

Jonathan Rotondo-McCord

SEE ALSO
Aachen; Charlemagne; Frederick I Barbarossa; Staufen

Regensburg

Founded on the Danube as the Roman camp Castra Regina in 179 C.E., Regensburg (Latin, Ratisbon) was widely acknowledged in the Middle Ages to be the main city of the *terra bavarica* (Bavaria) and often claimed to be the largest city in Germany. Seat of the Bavarian dukes from the time of Charlemagne onward, it was also a favorite city of German kings and emperors. Regensburg was the capital of the East Frankish Empire; Louis the German met embassies from Constantinopolitan Emperor Basil I in the city in 871 and 873, and in 875 built the Alte Kapelle (Old Chapel) as his palace chapel.

On the site of the Alte Kornmarkt (Old Grain Market), rulers took up residence, first the Roman *quaestor* (magistrate), then Bavarian dukes, and Carolingian kings. Around 1200, the Wittelsbach dukes established themselves there, living in what is now the Herzogshof (duke's court).

The Old Stone Bridge (Steinerne Brücke) was built over the Danube between 1135 and 1146 and, in 1182, was granted toll-free status. Around 1184, the position of *Hansgraf* (hannisgrave) was instituted, elected by the citizens of the city to oversee civic matters. After 1205, struggles between bishops and Bavarian dukes for control of the city resulted in the granting of numerous privileges, particularly in favor of the Jewish and foreign trading communities. Evidence of the newfound sovereignty of the city was its entrance in 1256 into an alliance with Rhenish cities. By 1285, Regensburg was recognized as a *freie Reichstadt* (imperial free city), expanding to absorb the nearby towns of Donaustauf (1385) and Stadtamhof (1408). The city's trading network was far-flung, and the Regensburger Pfennig (penny) was a recognized currency from Paris to Warsaw. However, the city suffered during the political trials of the late fifteenth century, and a bankruptcy of 1485–1486. In 1475, Regensburg put itself freely under the protection of the dukes of Bavaria-Landshut and in 1479 passed to Duke Albrecht IV of Upper Bavaria (Oberbayern). Finally in 1492, Regensburg was returned to Frederick III as a free imperial city, although civic unrest remained. By this time, it was clear that the ducal seat would be established in Munich, and Regensburg increasingly took a back seat to competitor trade towns of Augsburg and Nuremberg. However, the town continued a favorite place for imperial meetings, and the Reichstag (Imperial Diet) met in Regensburg no fewer than sixty-two times between 788 and 1653–1654.

The bishopric of Regensburg was founded in 739, and until 975 the office of bishop was held simultaneously by the Benedictine abbots of St. Emmeram. The cathedral is first mentioned in documents in 778, but the present building, begun circa 1250 in imitation of French Gothic style, was not completed until the sixteenth century. The Roriczer/Roritzer family served as cathedral *Baumeisters* (builders), notably Wentzel (1350–1419) and Konrad (1454–1466). Matthew Roriczer went on to work at St. Lorenz in Nuremberg and published his architectural handbook, *Das Puechlein der Fialen Gerechtigkeit* (The Little Book on Building Correctly), in Regensburg and Nuremberg in 1486. The Regensburg Ordinances of 1459 and 1514 have provided evidence about the organization of Gothic architectural guilds. The last Roritzer, Wolfgang, was beheaded as a heretic in 1514. The cathedral sculpture from circa 1375–1410 is immediately connected with the Parler family of Prague. The present structures of the cathedral cloister date from the eleventh and twelfth centuries. Most notable is the All Saints Chapel (Allerheiligenkapelle), whose dome rests on squinches modeled on those in the Capella Palatina in Palermo. The chapel was intended for the burial of Bishop Hartwig II (1155–1164) and decorated with frescoes illustrating the feast of All Saints, as described in Chapters 4 and 5 of the Book of Revelation.

637

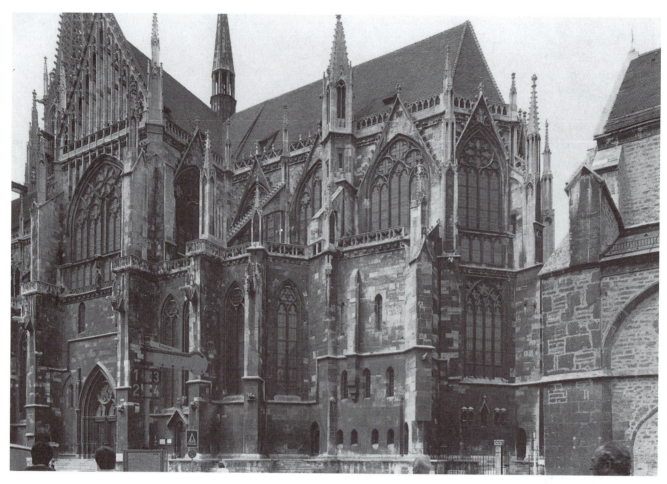

Regensburg cathedral, choir exterior. *Photograph: Virginia Jansen*

The powerful Benedictine abbey of St. Emmeram, an eighth-century foundation, was richly endowed by Carolingians, particularly Arnulf of Kärnten, who donated the precious *Codex Aureus (Golden Codex)* of circa 870 (Munich, Bayerische Staatsbibliothek, no. Clm 14000). The monastery was renewed by Wolfgang (972–994), who separated the offices of abbot and bishop. Abbot Ramwold (974–1001) spearheaded the Gorze reform of the monastery and was responsible for the exterior crypt dedicated in 980 and built on the model of St. Maximin of Trier. St. Emmeram boasted a significant scriptorium, an important school of music, and a school in the liberal arts tradition of Fulbert of Chartres. Manuscript production flourished particularly at the beginning of the eleventh century, when the convent produced the Sacramentary of Henry II (Munich, Bayerische Staatsbibliothek, Clm 4456). In the early eleventh century, the monastery became interested in the works of the pseudo-Dionysus, and even claimed to have the body of St.

Dionysius himself, supported by a vision and documents forged by the scribe Otloh. Under Abbot Reginward (1048–ca. 1060) the monastery reconstructed its western church to include a transept and a choir dedicated to St. Dionysius raised over the crypt of St. Wolfgang. While St. Emmeram's monks were never able to prove its ownership of Dionysius over the more convincing claims of St. Denis outside of Paris, their study of pseudo-Dionysian writings fueled the creation of typological poetry and artworks, including the magnificent ceiling of St. Emmeram, no longer extant.

Regensburg boasts numerous significant ecclesiastical foundations. Niedermünster was an imperial abbey of Benedictine nuns, founded circa 955 by Henry the Wrangler, whose wife, Judith, became abbess in 973 and was buried there. The Gospels illustrated for Abbess Uta between 1002 and 1025 (Munich, Bayerische Staatsbibliothek, no. Clm 13601) are another notable example of the Regensburg taste for deluxe manuscripts and typological iconography. The seventh-century itinerant bishop Erhard, who was buried in the church, was canonized in 1052. The Obermünster was a church of canonesses, a Carolingian foundation given in 833 to Hemma, wife of Louis the German, who served as abbess until her death in 876. A new church was consecrated in 1010 and reconsecrated in 1024 after a fire, but today stands in ruins. It was probably one of the women's convents that produced the magnificent mantles worn by the sainted imperial couple Henry II and Kunigunde, now preserved at Bamberg. The church of St. James (Jakobskirche), or the so-called Schottenkirche, was settled by Irish Benedictine monks circa 1067, and was probably the home of Honorius Augustodunensis in the mid–twelfth century. Honorius's works have been suggested as sources for the enigmatic north portal of the church, a three-leveled arched facade peopled with puzzling and archaizing figures that have been variously interpreted to represent the Easter mysteries, the Last Judgment of the Book of Revelations, or a cosmological vision.

Regensburg's output of medieval mural painting must have been enormous, though little survives. The most important extant material is found in Prüfening, ascribed to circa 1125 and 1150–1160, executed in a severe style related to the Hirsau reform movement that had inspired the church's foundation in 1109 by Bishop Otto of Bamberg. It is generally difficult to separate Regensburg from Prüfening artistic production in the third quarter of the twelfth century, and scholars attribute to the school both frescoes and the illustration of such manuscripts as the *Glossarium Salomonis* (Munich, Bayerische Staatsbibliothek, Clm 13002) or the *Laudes sanctae Crucis* (Munich, Bayerische Staatsbibliothek, Clm 14159).

The mendicant orders appeared early in Regensburg. The Franciscans were established by 1221 and nourished the noted vernacular preacher Berthold of Regensburg (ca. 1210–1272). The Dominican church of St. Blasius dates to 1230, and distinguished theologian Albertus Magnus served briefly as bishop of Regensburg (1260–1262) before returning to the Dominican order. By the midthirteenth century, mendicant influence had reoriented Regensburg scholarship and book production toward Paris. By the early fourteenth century, the city was also a center for illustrated manuscripts in the German vernacular, particularly Ottheinrich's Bible (Munich, Bayerische Staatsbibliothek, no. Cgm 8010/1 and 2) and the works of Martinus Opifex. Most of Regensburg's medieval manuscripts are now kept in the Bayerische Staatsbibliothek in Munich. Although the city was not a major center for printing, a few blockbooks and religious tracts, primarily Marian in subject matter, seem to have been printed there by Lienhart Wolff and Johannes Eysenhut.

Although many of Regensburg's structures were rebuilt in the seventeenth and eighteenth centuries, numerous medieval houses remain, and it has been remarked that the scale of the dense medieval town keyed to pack-animal traffic remains little changed today.

BIBLIOGRAPHY

Bischoff, Bernard. "Literarisches und künstlerisches Leben in St. Emmeram (Regensburg) während des frühen und hohen Mittelalters," in *Mittelalterliche Studien: Ausgewählte Aufsätze zur Schriftkunde und Literaturgeschichte*. 3 vols. Stuttgart: Anton Hiersemann, 1966–1981, vol. 2, pp. 77–115.

———. "Studien zur Geschichte des Klosters St. Emmeram im Spätmittelalter (1324–1525)," in *Mittelalterliche Studien: Ausgewählte Aufsätze zur Schriftkunde und Literaturgeschichte*. 3 vols. Stuttgart: Anton Hiersemann, 1966–1981, vol. 2, pp. 115–155.

Boeckler, Albert. *Die Regensburg-Prüfeninger Buchmalerei des 12. und 13. Jahrhunderts*. Munich: A. Reusch, 1924.

Bosl, Karl. "Die Sozialstruktur der mittelalterlichen Residenz- und Fernhandelsstadt Regensburg: Die Entwicklung ihres Bürgertums vom 9.–14. Jahrhundert." *Untersuchungen zur Gesellschaftlichen Struktur der Mittelalterlichen Städte in Europa: Vorträge und Forschungen herausgegeben vom konstanzer Arbeitskreis für mittelalterliche Geschichte* 11 (1966): 121–125.

Cohen, Adam S. *The Uta Codex: Art, Philosophy, and Reform in Eleventh-Century Germany*. University Park: Pennsylvania State University Press, 2000.

Demus, Otto. *Romanesque Mural Painting*. New York: Harry Abrams, 1970, pp. 36–38, 134–137, 610–613.

Dietheuer, Franz. *Die Bildersprache des Regensburger Schottenportals*. Regensburg: Verlag des Vereins für Regensburger Bistumsgeschichte, 1981.

Dietz, Karlheinz. *Die Römer in Regensburg*. Regensburg: Pustet Verlag, 1996.

Drexler, Jolanda, and Achim Hubel, eds. *Regensburg und die Oberpfalz*. Handbuch der deutschen Kunstdenkmäler, Bayern 5. Munich: Deutscher Kunstverlag, 1991.

DuBruck, Edelgard E., and Karl Heinz Göller, eds. *Crossroads of Medieval Civilization: The City of Regensburg and Its Intellectual Milieu*. Detroit: Michigan Consortium for Medieval and Early Modern Studies, 1984.

Flint, Valerie I. J. *Honorius Augustodunensis of Regensburg.* Aldershot: Variorum, 1995.

Frankl, Paul. *The Gothic: Literary Sources and Interpretations through Eight Centuries.* Princeton, N.J.: Princeton University Press, 1960.

Fritzsche, Gabriela. *Die mittelalterlichen Glasmalereien im Regensburger Dom.* Corpus vitrearum Medii Aevi, Deutschland 13, Regensburg und Oberpfalz. 2 vols. Berlin: Deutscher Verlag für Kunstwissenschaft, 1987.

Gimpel, Jean. *The Cathedral Builders.* New York: Grove Press, 1983.

Hubel, Achim, et al. *Der Dom zu Regensburg: Vom Bauen und Gestalten einer gotischen Kathedrale.* Regensburg: Friedrich Pustet, 1995.

Klemm, Elisabeth. *Die romanischen Handschriften der Bayerischen Staatsbibliothek 1: Die Bistümer Regensburg, Passau und Salzburg.* 2 vols. Katalog der illuminierten Handschriften der Bayerischen Staatsbibliothek in München 3. Wiesbaden: Ludwig Reichert, 1980, pp. 15–47.

Kraus, Andreas. *Civitas regia: Das Bild Regensburgs in der deutschen Geschichtsschreibung des Mittelalters.* Kallmünz: Lassleben, 1972.

Mader, Felix, Alois Mitterwieser, and Georg Lösti. *Stadt Regensburg.* Kunstdenkmäler von Bayern 2: Regierungsbezirk Oberpfalz 22, 3 vols. Munich: R. Oldenbourg, 1933.

Oswald, Friedrich, Leo Schaefer, and Hans Rudolf Sennhauser. *Vorromanische Kirchenbauten: Katalog der Denkmäler bis zum Ausgang der Ottonen.* 3 vols. Munich: Prestel, 1971, vol. 3, pp. 270–276.

Piendl, Max, ed. *Die Bibliotheken zu St. Emmeram in Regensburg.* Thurn-und-Taxis Studien 7. Kallmünz: Lassleben, 1971.

Regensburger Buchmalerei: Von frühkarolingischer Zeit bis zum Ausgang des Mittelalters. Munich: Prestel, 1987.

Sanderson, Warren. *Monastic Reform in Lorraine and Architecture of the Outer Crypt, 950–1100.* Transactions of the American Philosophical Society N.S. 61. Philadelphia: American Philosophical Society, 1971.

Schmid, Peter. *Regensburg: Stadt der Könige und Herzöge im Mittelalter.* Regensburger historische Forschungen 6. Källmunz: Lassleben, 1977

Shelby, Lon R., ed. and trans. *Gothic Design Techniques: The Fifteenth-century Design Booklets of Mathes Roriczer and Hanns Schmuttermayer.* Carbondale: Southern Illinois University Press, 1977.

Stein, Heidrun. *Die romanischen Wandmalereien in der Klosterkirche Prüfening.* Studien und Quellen zur Kunstgeschichte Regensburgs 1. Regensburg: Mittelbayerische Druckerei- und Verlags-Gesellschaft, 1987.

Strobel, Richard. "Das Nordportal des Schottenportals." *Zeitschrift des Deutschen Vereins für Kunstwissenschaft* 18 (1964): 1–24.

———. *Romanische Architektur in Regensburg: Kapitell, Säule, Raum.* Erlanger Beiträge zur Sprach- und Kunstwissenschaft 20. Nuremberg: Carl, 1965.

Swarzenski, Georg. *Die Regensburger Buchmalerei des 10. und 11. Jahrhunderts: Studien zur Geschichte der deutschen Malerei des frühen Mittelalters.* Universität Heidelberg. Leipzig: Hiersemann, 1901.

Wittelsbach und Bayern: Die Zeit der frühen Herzöge von Otto I. zu Ludwig dem Bayern. 2 vols. Munich: Hirmer Verlag, 1980.

Wunderle, Elisabeth. *Katalog der lateinischen Handschriften der Bayerischen Staatsbibliothek München: Die Handschriften aus St. Emmeram in Regensburg.* Wiesbaden: Harrassowitz, 1995.

1250 Jahre Kunst und Kultur im Bistum Regensburg: Berichte und Forschungen. Munich: Schnell und Steiner, 1989.

Amelia Carr

SEE ALSO

Augsburg; Bamberg; Berthold von Regensburg; Charlemagne; Frederick III; Henry II, Art; Henry the Lion; Hirsau; Munich; Nuremberg; Ottonian Art and Architecture; Parler Family; Romanesque Art and Architecture; Trier

Regional Chronicles

See Chronicles, Regional/National, Dutch; Chronicles, Regional/Territorial, German.

Registrum Gregorii, Master of (fl. late 10th c.)

Also known as the Registrum Master or Gregory Master, the Master of the *Registrum Gregorii* was the leading artistic personality in the Ottonian empire during the last quarter of the tenth century. Documentary evidence for him is lacking. He seems to have been active in Trier during the episcopate of Archbishop Egbert (977–993) and is known primarily from the miniatures he painted for Gospel and liturgical books. He may also have been an ivory carver. The Master's name derives from his miniatures depicting Pope Gregory the Great (Trier, Stadtbibliothek) and an Ottonian emperor, probably Otto II (Chantilly, Musée Condé, manuscript no. 14 bis), originally included in a compilation of Gregory's writings—a *Registrum Gregorii*—commissioned by Egbert. Both miniatures exhibit the Master's characteristic rounded, weighty figures and perspectival approach to space and architecture, representing his adaptation of classicizing Roman models of the fifth and sixth centuries to the medieval idiom.

The Registrum Master's style influenced illumination at many centers in the late tenth and eleventh centuries, but nowhere was his impact so evident as at Reichenau in the wake of the illumination of the *Codex Egberti* (Trier, Stadtbibliothek, manuscript no. 24). This Gospel lectionary was commissioned by Egbert and illustrated by the Registrum Master, to whom the first seven miniatures have been attributed, and two Reichenau monks. The circumstances surrounding the execution of the *Codex Egberti* continue to be debated, but the influence of the Master's style is fundamental for the evolution of Liuthar Group illustration at Reichenau, beginning in the mid-990s with such manuscripts as the Gospel lectionary in the Vatican (Biblioteca Apostolica, manuscript no. Barberini lat. 711) and the Gospel book in Aachen (Cathedral Treasury).

BIBLIOGRAPHY

Nordenfalk, Carl. "Archbishop Egbert's *Registrum Gregorii*," in *Studien zur mittelalterlichen Kunst 800–1250: Festschrift für Florentine Mütherich zum 70. Geburtstag,* ed. Katharina Bierbrauer et al. Munich: Prestel, 1985, pp. 87–100.

Karen E. Loaiza

SEE ALSO

Egbert; Otto II; Ottonian Art and Architecture; Reichenau; Trier

Reich

"Empire" *(Reich)* is a term used throughout the German Middle Ages to refer to various political constellations. To the inner circle at Charlemagne's court in 800, his adoption of the title "emperor" gave expression to the fact that he was more than just the king of the Franks, or king of the Lombards; with the exception of Anglo-Saxon England and Christian Spain, every Christian area of the Latin West was subject to him, and many non-Christian areas to the east recognized his suzerainty. There was to some large degree a correspondence between his realm and Latin Christendom.

Very quickly, however, the relationship between theory and practice changed. With the Treaty of Verdun (843), the idea of an ecumenical empire gave way to a more limited one. Lothar I received the title of emperor along with the Middle Kingdom, but when his lands were subdivided in 855, the imperial title went to his son Louis II as ruler of Italy. In short, the significance of the imperial title contracted almost to the point of meaninglessness.

In theory, however, the imperial title implied a claim to the disputed lands of the Middle Kingdom, and by the early tenth century it was a hotly contested prize. The winner in this go-around was the German king Otto I, who, in 962, assumed the imperial title, signifying the union of Germany, Italy, and Lorraine. His concept of empire, and the realities as well, looked back to Lothar I far more than to Charlemagne for its model. For the next three centuries, the term *Reich* had reference to this area, in which Germany exercised hegemony over the other two regions. Maintaining some substance for the theory required considerable effort, however, and from time to time German rulers ignored the imperial dimensions of their office, focusing on matters north of the Alps.

Otto I and Otto II both appeared as plain *imperator augustus* (noble emperor), but Otto III's chancery used the more pretentious *imperator Romanorum* (emperor of the Roman Empire). Though the Capetian kings of France were anxious to live on good terms with the empire, they were never prepared to admit to being imperial vassals. When Emperor Henry II and King Robert the Pious met on the banks of the Meuse in August 1023, they did so as equals; similarly, when Henry III and the French King Henry I met at Ivois in 1056, they did so on terms of equality. Henry III saw his imperial role not so much in territorial terms as in his obligation to purify and reinvigorate the papacy, the other universal head of the *respublica Christiana* (Christian republic). He did, however, object to the use of the title *Hispaniae imperator* (Hispanic emperor), which the Spanish king, Ferdinand the Great of Castile, had adopted after a great victory over the Moors.

German emperors often sought legitimization of their title and claims by marrying into the Byzantine imperial family. Otto II was the only one to do so, though appropriate spouses had been sought for both Otto III and Henry III. The securing of the hand of Isabella/Yolande of Brienne, heiress to the Latin kingdom of Jerusalem, by Frederick II of Staufen in 1223, gave a similar boost to the pretentions of the leader of the Christian world.

The accession of Frederick Barbarossa in 1152 brought a change in his attitude toward Italy, over what had prevailed for some time. In correspondence with the Byzantine emperor of Constantinople, he declared that the kings of Europe were constantly sending ambassadors to his court, to show their respect and obedience, and to offer oaths of loyalty and hostages. His chancery spoke disdainfully of the kinglets, or *reguli* (little kings), in at least one instance meaning thereby the kings of France, England, and Denmark who were *reges provinciales* (provincial kings). John of Salisbury waxed indignant over the implications of such claims for the king of France, but in the historian Rahewin's continuation of the *Gesta Friderici* (The *Deeds of Frederick*), we find a letter of Henry II of England that (although disputed) is made to say to Barbarossa: "We offer you our kingdom and all the lands under our dominion, we hand them over to your power, so that you may dispose of them as seems good to you, and so that your imperial will may be accomplished in all things." According to the English chronicler Hovedon, England's independence was compromised beyond that expressed in Henry's letter when Richard I, "by the advice of his mother Eleanor stripped himself of the kingdom of England and delivered it over to the emperor as lord of the world," a reference to the enforced homage of Richard to Barbarossa's son Henry VI in 1193.

Frederick Barbarossa found his plans for a reinvigorated empire challenged not only by the rising power of the Italian cities but by the theocratic pretensions of Pope Hadrian IV. To counter papal claims that the emperor held the empire as a "benefice conferred by the pope," Frederick declared that he held his kingdom and his empire from God alone. To buttress this argument, his chancery began to use the adjective *sacrum* (holy) or *sanctissimum* (most holy) in connection with the empire in 1157, contrasting it with *sacra ecclesia* (Holy Church). Several years later, Frederick secured the canonization of Charlemagne, who, in effect, became the patron saint of the empire; the beatification of Charles the Great symbolized the rebirth of the empire yet again under Frederick's rule.

Henry VI of Hohenstaufen's accession in 1190, and his abortive attempt to effect a union of the kingdom of Sicily with the empire, marked a decided departure from earlier imperial policy. Henry's son, Frederick II, in turn abandoned Germany in large measure, though there were still those who promoted the twelfth-century Staufen notion of the universal empire. At the Fourth Lateran (Papal) Council in 1215, Archbishop Siegfried II of Mainz, as arch-chancellor of the empire, objected to the announcement by Pope Innocent III that King John of England had surrendered his realm to the papacy and received it back as a fief during his efforts at reconciliation with Rome; the archbishop's protest that the empire exercised suzerainty over the *regnum Angliae* (rule of Anglia) was rejected.

Meanwhile, in 1202 Innocent III in the decretal *Per Venerabilem* had declared that the king of France was emperor within his own realm, "*cum rex superiorem in temporalibus minime recognoscat*"—he recognized no temporal superior. The epithet *Augustus* given to Philip II by his biographer and retained by history is a sharp reflection of his attitude to the imperial daydreams, and the collapse of the Hohenstaufen after 1250 placed the question of empire in the forefront of European politics. Pierre Dubois and John of Jandun maintained that the French king was the natural successor to the imperial dignity of the Hohenstaufen, and in fact the integrity of the western boundary of the empire began to erode toward the end of the century. Rudolf of Hapsburg was less interested in perpetuating the imperial ideas than in establishing an hereditary monarchy. It was during his reign that the lands of the bishopric of Toul west of the Meuse fell into French hands (1291), while in 1297 the French established control over the entire bishopric of Metz. But even in the fourteenth century there were still political theorists in France who recognized a certain validity to the emperor's claims of universal overlordship.

From 962 onward the rulers of Germany were, either actually or potentially, emperors. Only Otto II was consecrated emperor in his father's lifetime, and even then he had been king for some years before his imperial coronation. Otto III and Henry II did not become emperor until 996 and 1014, respectively, in each case more than a decade after they had succeeded to the throne. Conrad II was crowned in Rome in 1027 after a gap of only three years; his son Henry III waited seven years before crossing the Alps and receiving imperial coronation in 1046. Elected in 1212 and crowned at Aachen in 1215, Frederick II did not receive imperial consecration until November 1220. In short, the imperial crown could not simply be assumed; it had to be received from the pope at Rome.

This factor helps explain the frequent bitter struggles that went on between certain German monarchs and the papacy. Many German rulers made do with the title *rex Romanorum,* indicating that although they had been duly elected king, they had not yet received imperial coronation. Only in the fourteenth century did the German electors challenge this practice, and by then the imperial dignity was much less preoccupied with Italy than with Central Europe. Meeting at Rhens on the Rhine in July 1338, the German estates declared that the imperial dignity was held directly of God, and that a king elected by the majority was the legitimate ruler, entitled from the day of his election to exercise his functions without papal consent or confirmation. This was reaffirmed in the Golden Bull that Charles IV published in 1356.

The concept of the Holy Roman Empire—the full term appears first in 1254—lasted in one form or another until 1806, but a second empire was created in 1870–1871, to be followed by a third *Reich* in the early twentieth century. As a symbol of overlordship, the term emperor was also taken over by Napoléon in 1804, whose imperial coronation at the cathedral of Notre Dame in Paris was clearly influenced by that of Charlemagne on Christmas Day, 800, at Rome.

BIBLIOGRAPHY

Barraclough, Geoffrey. *The Medieval Empire: Idea and Reality.* London: G. Phillip, 1950, rpt. 1964.

Bryce, James. *The Holy Roman Empire.* New York: Macmillan, 1903, rpt. 1961.

Ficker, Julius. *Deutsches Königthum und Kaiserthum.* Innsbruck: Wagner, 1862.

Fichtenau, Heinrich. *The Carolingian Empire,* trans. Peter Munz. Toronto: University of Toronto Press, 1995.

Koch, Walter. *Die Reichskanzlei in den Jahren 1167 bis 1174.* Publicationen der historischen Kommission der österreichischen Akademie der Wissenschaft, Phil.-hist. Klasse, Denkschriften, 115. Vienna: Verlag der Österreichischen Akademien der Wissenschaften, 1973.

Leyser, Karl. *Medieval Germany and Its Neighbors, 900–1250.* London: Hambledon, 1982.

Michael, Wolfgang. *Die Formen des unmittelbaren Verkehrs zwischen den deutschen Kaisern und souveränen Fürsten vornehmlich in X., XI. und XII. Jahrhundert.* Hamburg: Voß, 1888.

Schramm, Percy Ernst. *Kaiser, Rom und Renovatio.* 2 vols.; rpt. Darmstadt: Wissenschaftliche Buchgesellschaft, 1962.

Struve, Tilman. "Kaisertum und Romgedanke in salischer Zeit." *Deutsches Archiv* 44 (1988): 424–454.

Paul B. Pixton

SEE ALSO

Carolingians; Charlemagne; Conrad II; Empire; Frederick I Barbarossa; Frederick II; Golden Bull; Henry II, Art; Henry III; Henry VI; Lothar I; Otto I; Otto II; Otto III; Staufen; Toul;

Reichenau

Located on Lake Constance (German, Bodensee) in what is today the state of Baden-Württemberg, the island monastery of Reichenau was founded by St. Pirmin in 724. Pirmin was a Visigothic monk who had come to the Frankish court from southern Gaul and was sent to Alemannia by Charles Martel. Although this region had succumbed to Frankish rule during the early sixth century, efforts to Christianize the Alemanni achieved widespread success only in the following century. The establishment of a monastery at Reichenau, like that of the nearby St. Gall (Switzerland) in 720, was meant to provide the region with a strong center of Christian and Frankish influence.

During the Ottonian period (919–1024), Reichenau continued to function as an outpost of royal influence. Eleventh-century documents attest to the monastery's policy of accepting only nobles into its community. As a royal abbey, it provided crucial support for the itinerant ruler, with its loyalty to the king providing a necessary check to the ambitions of the local nobility. Reichenau received land grants for its support of Otto I in the uprising of 953, and hosted the emperor in 965 and 972. Despite the ruler's infrequent appearance at the monastery, by the early eleventh century his presence was felt through the maintenance at Reichenau of a palace for his reception. One of the few East Frankish monasteries to have papal privileges confirming its authority, its abbot was subject to the authority of the king alone.

Reichenau, like St. Gall, was a major educational and artistic center during the Carolingian and Ottonian periods. In the ninth century the monastery's library contained four hundred codices. By the tenth and early eleventh centuries the collection had expanded to five hundred volumes. The Abbot Witigowo, who served from 985 to 997, is known for his patronage of the arts. He was eulogized by the monk Purchart in a lengthy poem describing his architectural projects, gifts of metalwork, and commission of wall paintings. While these paintings no longer remain, the church of St. Georg at Reichenau-Oberzell is one of the few sites to preserve examples of Ottonian wall painting.

Although recent scholarship has questioned whether Reichenau was indeed the site of a centralized scriptorium, the monastery continues to be widely recognized as

Reichenau-Oberzell, St. George, view from south. *Photograph: Joan A. Holladay*

a major center of Ottonian book production and transmission. The unfortunate disappearance of Reichenau's treasury explains why no significant illuminated manuscripts survive from the monastery itself. Instead, the manuscripts that remain are those that can be linked to the monastery through paleography and stylistic analysis.

The Gero Codex of circa 965–969 (Darmstadt, Landesbibliothek, mansucript no. 1948) is the earliest of the great Ottonian manuscripts attributed to Reichenau. The manuscript is a collection of pericopes, excerpts of Gospel texts to be read at the Mass, and derives its name from the dedication pages showing the patron Gero presenting the book to Saint Peter, and the scribe Anno extending the manuscript to Gero, the future archbishop of Cologne. It is the first extant book of the Ottonian period to utilize figurative art. Its evangelist portraits in particular have led scholars to name the Carolingian Lorsch Gospels (ca. 810) as a direct model. The materials and careful execution of its manufacture speak to the quality of the scriptorium that produced the manuscript, but it departs from its Carolingian model in several important ways. Whereas

Carolingian painting utilized modeling and architectural elements to convey the illusion of figures existing in space, the first move toward a specifically Ottonian aesthetic can be seen in the *Gero codex*. An emphasis on geometric patterning and the use of gold replaces the painterly style favored by the Carolingians. The figures in the *Gero codex* are sharply drawn and colored. Their large size and frontal poses further separate them from an illusionistic background.

Evidence for Reichenau's artistic ties to the imperial court can be found in the Gospel Book of Otto III of circa 998–1001 (Munich, Bayerische Staatsbibliothek, manuscript no. clm. 4453) and the Pericopes of Henry II of circa 1007–1012 (Munich, Bayerische Staatsbibliothek, no. clm. 4452). These two luxurious books fully realize the new aesthetic goals expressed in the earlier *Gero codex*. In the Pericopes of Henry II, large-scale figures float on gold grounds. Both manuscripts feature ruler portraits in the Christ Maiestas tradition, reinforcing through a visual synthesis of Christ and ruler the belief that the emperor was Christ's representative on Earth.

BIBLIOGRAPHY

Boeckler, Albert. "Die Reichenauer Buchmalerei," in *Die Kultur der Abtei Reichenau: Erinnerungsschrift zur zwölfhundertsten Wiederkehr des Gründungsjahres des Inselklosters 724–1924,* ed. Konrad Beyerle. Munich: Verlag der Münchner Drücke, 1925, vol. 2, pp. 956–998.

Dodwell, C. R., and D. H. Turner. *Reichenau Reconsidered: A Re-Assessment of the Place of Reichenau in Ottonian Art.* London: Warburg Institute, 1965.

Hoffmann, Hartmut. *Buchkunst und Königtum im ottonischen und frühsalischen Reich.* 2 vols. Monumenta Germaniae Historica, Schriften 30. Stuttgart: Anton Hiersemann, 1988.

Mayr-Harting, Henry. *Ottonian Book Illumination: An Historical Study.* 2 vols. London: Harvey Miller, 1991, pp. 203–209.

Purchard. "Gesta Witigowonis." *Die lateinischen Dichter des deutschen Mittelalters: Die Ottonenzeit,* ed. Karl Strecker and Gabriel Silagi. Monumenta Germaniae Historica, Poetae Latini Medii Aevi 5. Leipzig: Karl W. Hiersemann, 1937, pp. 260–279.

Reuter, Timothy. *Germany in the Early Middle Ages c. 800–1056.* London: Longman, 1991.

Schramm, Percy Ernst. *Die deutschen Kaiser und Könige in Bildern ihrer Zeit 751–1190,* rev. ed. Florentine Mütherich et al. Munich: Prestel, 1983.

Silagi. Monumenta Germaniae Historica, Poetae Latini Medii Aevi 5. Leipzig: Karl W. Hiersemann, 1937, pp. 260–279.

Kristen M. Collins

SEE ALSO

Carolingian Art and Architecture; Cologne, Art; Henry II; Lorsch; Otto I; Otto III; Ottonian Art and Architecture; Sankt Gall; Trier

Reichskirche

Most strictly, the term *Reichskirche* (imperial church) applies to the church properties, rights, and offices under the immunity protection of the king/emperor. This royal connection set nascent national churches, such as in England or France, somewhat apart from the developing Roman ecclesiastical hierarchy. In Germany, however, the kings of the Ottonian-Salian dynasty thoroughly expanded the secular authority of bishops and abbots as a counterweight to the competing dukes and locally entrenched magnates. Consequently, the kings often endowed churches with royal prerogatives, such as the right to hold markets, mint coins, carry out justice, and command warriors, in the process creating the powerful spiritual princes or prince-bishops. While historians once discussed the "Imperial Church System" *(Reichskirchensystem),* this term misleadingly implies a methodical organization. In practice, the king's influence on clerics, just as the pope's, varied widely depending on personalities and local circumstances.

BIBLIOGRAPHY

Fleckenstein, Josef. "Problematik und Gestalt der ottonisch-salischen Reichskirche," in *Reich und Kirche vor dem Investiturstreit: Vorträge beim wissenschaftlichen Kolloquium aus Anlaß des achtzigsten Geburtstags von Gerd Tellenbach,* ed. Karl Schmid. Sigmaringen: Thorbecke, 1985, pp. 83–98.

Reuter, Timothy. "The 'Imperial Church System' of the Ottonian and Salian Rulers: A Reconsideration." *Journal of Ecclesiastical History* 33 (1982): 347–374.

Brian A. Pavlac

Reinmar der Alte (fl. late 12th c.–early 13th c.)

Reinmar der Alte (the old) or, as he is often called by scholars, Reinmar von Hagenau, is the most prolific minnesinger of the twelfth century. He flourished (in the last fifteen or so years of the twelfth and the first years of the thirteenth) at the Babenberg court in Vienna, and probably also traveled widely, as did most courtiers and court retainers. He left no documentary record; we know him only as he presents himself and as other poets refer to him. He lacks the range of Walther von der Vogelweide; the only didactic lyrics he wrote were a few reflections on love, there is no *Leich* transmitted for him, and the only political songs ascribed to him are a widow's lament and two crusading songs. Yet the view of him as a singer of only one style of minnesong (courtly love song)—the lament of the hapless suitor—though influenced by his own stylization of his persona, is largely an artifact of scholarship during the past two centuries. Especially toward the end of the nineteenth and the first half of the twentieth century, scholars created an ever narrower image of Reinmar by claiming that songs and strophes ascribed to him were spurious, until the number of "pseudo-Reinmar" strophes exceeded those accepted as genuine. If we accept that he sang (and, in large part, created) most of the songs and strophes ascribed to him, it becomes clear that his oeuvre was rich and varied in addition to being extensive.

Even the narrow Reinmar canon is more nuanced than scholars were initially willing to perceive. For one thing, Reinmar utilizes the woman's voice more often and in more different ways than any minnesinger save Neidhart, whose peasant women and girls reflect the pastourelle (bucolic) rather than the *Wechsel* (exchange) that was Reinmar's inspiration. One thing becomes clear in the multifaceted roles the woman's voices depict: Reinmar's women cannot be equated with his persona's lady. The lady as the suitor describes her is recalcitrant, haughty, distant; the noble woman's voices show someone who, if she spurns her suitor, does so unwillingly, constrained by fear of social sanctions. Often, she demonstrates a desire for her lover far more impassioned (and physical) than that expressed by "Reinmar" in his stereotypical role. Indeed, she exposes his maunderings as misguided at best, ludicrous at worst. Of course, the woman's voice is Reinmar's projection just as much as the man's voice, but he surely intends the incongruity between the stances portrayed to be noted and relished. Just as Don Quixote is Cervantes's knight of the woeful countenance, Reinmar's suitor is doleful. Both are (tragi-) comic fictions. In many of the songs in the man's voice, the lady is marginalized, referred to sparingly and obliquely, and the primary subjects of the song are an examination of the suitor's feelings, the singer's singing, and the audience's reaction to songs or singer. The syntax is typically complex; abstractions and legalisms (casuistries) abound. Imagery is rare; it may be that where Reinmar tried to introduce imagery (in part, perhaps, by appropriating strophes from other singers), his audience rejected it. Several songs containing a strophe with some striking image omit this strophe in most versions and others are transmitted only once. For many minnesingers songs are transmitted in multiple versions; for no singer is this transmission tendency more common than for Reinmar. Not only was he prolific, he was apparently also intent on extending and varying his repertoire by changing the order and number of strophes and even, on occasion, the basic tenor of songs. Changes in wording, form, and most strikingly voice enable him to make new songs of old ones. Some of the variants we have are due to later singers (such as Niune) appropriating songs or scribes adding strophes from other versions or deleting ones they consider inappropriate or corrupt. And some of the textual variants are due to faulty copying, flawed memory, or scribal "improvements." Nevertheless, though most scholars dispute or disregard it, the texts make it abundantly clear that an authorial intention is behind most of the variance we find in Reinmar's (and other minnesingers') songs.

Many minnesingers thematize singing about singing; but Reinmar, with his unusually introspective and reflective persona, does so more than most. While focusing on the theme and engaging that segment of the listeners most concerned with singing, other singers, directly, he reacts to and may even borrow and adapt strophes from them. Such an interchange of allusions and even strophes gave rise to the notion that he feuded with Walther von der Vogelweide, with the latter objecting to Reinmar's ideology of love. Actually, their views on love are quite similar (and similarly diverse, depending on which genre they echo); nevertheless, both singers vie over which of the two is the superior artist. The *Wartburgkrieg,* a fictional account of a contest between singers at the Wartburg in Thuringia, probably reflects their competition (at considerable remove; Reinmar der Alte may have been conflated with Reinmar von Zweter). The coupling of the two singers in the Würzburg Song Codex may be another reflex of their strife. Gottfried von Straßburg pairs both "nightingales" as masters of minnesong. Walther, in his eulogies to Reinmar, praises his art but declares an antipathy toward his person; perhaps the latter is intended to lend veracity to the former, but it is also possible the two simply did not like each other very much. Reinmar arguably caused one of the most egregious instances of multiple ascription by copying a collection of Heinrich von Rugge's songs, or acquiring such a collection, to serve as models. A series of songs by Rugge, to which he may have added songs and strophes of his own, subsequently was copied into codex C twice, once under Rugge's name and once under Reinmar's. The affinities between the two singers are not restricted, however, to one block of songs, so the parallel transmission cannot be explained away as a mere scribal blunder, as scholars have tended to assume. Allusions to or strophes shared with Hartmann von Aue and Heinrich von Morungen probably also reflect Reinmar's willingness to appropriate; he in turn serves as a major model for such singers as Walther von Metze and Rubin.

BIBLIOGRAPHY

Heinen, Hubert, ed. *Mutabilität im Minnesang: mehrfach überlieferte Lieder des 12. und frühen 13. Jahrhunderts.* Göppingen: Kümmerle, 1989.

Jackson, William E. *Reinmar's Women: A Study of the Woman's Song ("Frauenlied" and "Frauenstrophe") of Reinmar der Alte.* Amsterdam: John Benjamin, 1981.

Obermaier, Sabine. *Von Nachtigallen und Handwerkern: 'Dichtung über Dichtung' in Minnesang und Sangspruchdichtung.* Tübingen: Niemeyer, 1995.

Schweikle, Günther. *Minnesang in neuer Sicht.* Stuttgart: Metzler, 1994.

Stange, Manfred. *Reinmars Lyrik: Forschungskritik und Überlegungen zu einem neuen Verständnis Reinmars des Alten.* Amsterdam: Rodopi, 1977.

Tervooren, Helmut. *Reinmar Studien: Ein Kommentar zu den "unechten" Liedern Reinmars des Alten.* Stuttgart: Hirzel, 1991.

Willms, Eva. *Liebesleid und Sangeslust: Untersuchungen zur deutschen Liebeslyrik des späten 12. und frühen 13. Jahrhunderts.* Munich: Artemis, 1992.

Ziegler, Vickie L. *The Leitword in* Minnesang: *Stylistic Analysis and Textual Criticism.* University Park: Penn State University Press, 1975.

Hubert Heinen

SEE ALSO

Hartmann von Aue; Heinrich von Morungen; *Minnesang;* Versification; Walther von der Vogelweide

Reinmar von Zwetter (ca. 1200–ca. 1250)

We know this prolific singer of *Sangspruchdichtung* (political and religious thought) only from his songs. They suggest he was born in the Rhineland, grew up in Austria, and was employed as a courtly singer by King Wenzel I of Bohemia in the 1230s. Other internal evidence indicates he sang at the court of the archbishop of Mainz in the 1240s. Reinmar's last datable piece stems from the years 1246 to 1248. He left some 230 single twelve-line, one-stanza songs, all sung to the same tune (called *Frauenehrenton* in manuscript "D") and a *Leich* (lay) without melody. There is also a handful of songs, probably spurious, in other stanzaic forms with which his name is associated. Only a few of his one-stanza songs can be thematically linked together. Most of Reinmar's work is contained in two sources, 219 stanzas in manuscript "C," the famous Manesse Song Manuscript (Heidelberg, no. Cod. Pal. Germ. 848), and 193 stanzas in manuscript "D" (Heidelberg, no. Cod. Pal. Germ. 350). Other stanzas are scattered over some twenty additional manuscripts. The illustration in "C" depicts him as a blind singer dictating his songs, though there is no evidence in the body of his work that he was sight-impaired.

The *Frauenehrenton,* Reinmar's only known melody, is a utilitarian d-based construction, a solid structure for the delivery of all his content-laden stanzas. It is possible that it is not an original composition, since one of Reinmar's confreres in courtly singing accuses him of being a tune thief *(doenediep).*

Reinmar's singing encompasses many of the popular subgenres of *Spruchdichtung,* e.g., political songs, religious songs, cautionary songs, songs of praise, songs about the nature of love, and songs extolling knightly virtue. In this he is a disciple of Walther von der Vogelweide, though his poetry lacks the nuance and lyricism of Walther. Many of his songs have a elegiac quality, lamenting the passing of the heyday of love, honor, and courtly values. In these Reinmar provides a canon for knightly behavior in the first half of the thirteenth century.

His rhetorical style is direct and convincing, underscoring his belief in the old-fashioned values of knighthood (especially *Minne*—courtly love—and honor) and reflecting a natural piety in which he pleads for righteousness, though never in a self-righteous way. His stanzas, especially the political ones, also afford glimpses of his life as a courtly singer. Like Walther before him, Reinmar had to generate political propaganda to suit the occasion. Illustrative are two songs composed in the 1230s, the first issuing a dire warning to those conspiring against Emperor Fredrick II (Roethe: No. 137), the second (composed after a change of patrons) urging willful resistance to the same monarch (Roethe: No. 149).

Pursuing the tradition of Walther's political and religious songs, Reinmar is the link to later singers of *Spruchdichtung* in the second half of the thirteenth century such as Bruder Werner, Meister Alexander, Meister Stolle, der Marner, and Frauenlob. That such a rich assortment of stanzas was collected in more than twenty manuscripts attests to his popularity. For three hundred years he was venerated by the Meistersinger, who counted him among the twelve old masters.

BIBLIOGRAPHY

Bonjour, Edgar. *Reimar von Zweter als politischer Dichter.* Bern: Haupt, 1922.

Gerhardt, Christoph. "Reinmars von Zweters Idealer Mann." *Beiträge zur Geschichte der deutschen Sprache und Literatur* (Tübingen) 109 (1987): 51–84, 222–251.

Roethe, Gustav. *Die Gedichte Reinmars von Zweter.* Leipzig: Hirzel, 1887.

Schubert, Martin J. "Die Form von Reinmars Leich." *Amsterdamer Beiträge zur älteren Germanistik* 41 (1995): 85–142.

Schupp, Volker. "Reinmar von Zweter, Dichter Kaisers Friedrichs II." *Wirkendes Wort* 19 (1969): 231–244.

Peter Frenzel

SEE ALSO

Frauenlob; Frederik II; Marner, Der; Meistersinger; *Sangspruch;* Versification; Walther von der Vogelweide; Wenceslas

Relics and Reliquaries

Medieval relics functioned as symbols of saintly life, served as instruments of intercession, and possessed a certain power as defined by the church and the believer. The relic constituted a part of a venerated person's physical remains or it was an object associated with his or her life. Relics conjured up the image of those who were faithful, filled with the Holy Spirit, connected to the mystical body of Christ, and as such were used as instruments of God to perform miracles. Medieval sensibility advocated veneration of the remains of the deceased who was considered holy and could intercede for the faithful before God. The reliquary was a container for the relic and emerged out of the need to enshrine the actual relic.

Relics are classified as primary, secondary, and tertiary types. Primary relics refer to the actual body parts of the deceased. An object that was used by or came into contact with the deceased is a secondary relic, and tertiary relics are those objects that came into contact with a primary relic and thereby possess a spiritual power. Popular examples of these types include the bones or tooth of a saint as a primary relic; a part of the true cross as a secondary relic; and a piece of cloth that has come into direct contact with the remains of a saint.

During the early Christian period a *memoria,* meaning the place of martyrdom, referred to a funerary place that was covered, housed the bones of the deceased, and was venerated. This tradition continued, and the bones of saints were considered sacred, called "relics," and housed in a crypt. The tradition that relics were hidden and could be touched rather than seen emerged in the Orthodox Church during Iconoclasm in Constantinople. By the mid–ninth century the western church replaced this hidden aspect and advocated actually seeing the relic. This visual emphasis led to the building of chapels for housing the sacred remains and to the creation of reliquaries for protecting and enshrining them.

Relics were transported throughout Christendom, especially during the Crusades. They were given as gifts to various cities. The possession of holy relics secured power and authority for the ruler and his kingdom by allying him with a holy object. Leaders vied to possess important relics as symbols of divinity and believed that their presence brought holiness to their city.

During the twelfth century, theological concerns conferred a new importance on sainthood, and the relic was elevated and moved from its original placement under the altar to a more prominent position above it. Believers visited relic sites and recognized the divine status of the saint who, as a result of her or his holy earthly life, had the power to cure and perform miracles with the help of God. Kings and queens, cardinals, and wealthy citizens commissioned metalsmiths to create reliquaries. Costly materials, such as cabochons and antique cameos, were used by artisans to embellish the containers. Inscriptions and images were sculpted into the surfaces to identify saints and the holy family.

The interest in the mystery and powers of the relics grew continuously, and the presentation of reliquaries added a theatrical aspect to worship. Reliquaries of all shapes and *picturae*—altarpieces with painted narrative images that often contained relics—formed a focal point for reflection at the high altar or at smaller subsidiary altars. Various relic forms conjure up some interesting images. Bust, foot, and arm reliquaries are known as "speaking reliquaries" because their shape reflects the relics they contain. Other popular types of reliquaries include the house, church, cross, purse, necklace, and triptych-shaped forms that survive today in cathedral treasuries and museums. The celebrated Shrine of the Three Magi (about 1190) contains bones believed to be those of the Three Kings, acquired by Emperor Frederick Barbarossa for Cologne. Nicolas of Verdun and his workshop sculpted gold repoussée (embellished with patterns) figures of the three Magi, Mary, and the Christ child, and the apostles and prophets. Rare gemstones, enamels, and filigree embellish the large shrine that was created for the archbishop as a symbol of holiness.

The legend of Saint Ursula told in the *Golden Legend* reads like a medieval romance and forms the basis for an incredible reliquary room in Cologne. At some unknown date in the early Christian era Ursula, who, with eleven thousands maiden companions, died in a massacre at Cologne upon returning from a pilgrimage from Rome. Excavations in Cologne (1106) revealed a large number of skeletons discovered not far from the Rhine, and these remains were believed to be Ursula's retinue. In the seventeenth century a special room, called the Goldene Kam-

Cologne, St. Ursula, Golden Chamber (Goldene Kammer), reliquary busts of the companions of St. Ursula. *Photograph: Joan A. Holladay*

mer (Golden Chamber), was built to enshrine the bones within the thirteenth-century church dedicated to this saint.

The cathedral at Aachen also exhibits exceptional examples of relics and reliquaries, including the head reliquary of Charlemagne containing part of the emperor's skull; the large house-shaped reliquary holding his bones located at the high altar; and the *Marienshrein* (shrine of the Virgin) containing a fragment from the dress of Mary, a piece of the loincloth of Christ worn on the cross, the cloth that wrapped the head of John the Baptist, and the swaddling clothes of the Christ child. To this day relics continue to mystify the beholder and their presence in Germany attests to the focus of medieval devotion.

BIBLIOGRAPHY

Angenendt, Arnold. *Heilige und Reliquien: Die Geschichte ihres Kultes vom frühen Christentum bis zur Gegenwart,* 2d ed. Munich: Beck, 1997.

Grimme, Ernst-Günther. "Der Aachner Domschatz." *Aachener Kunstblätter* 42 (1972): 1–409.

Jacobus de Voragine. *The Golden Legend: Readings on the Saints,* trans. William Granger Ryan. 2 vols. Princeton, N.J.: Princeton University Press, 1995.

Ornamenta Ecclesia. Kunst und Künstler der Romanik, ed. Anton Legner. 3 vols. Cologne: Stadt Köln, 1985.

Reliquien: Verehrung und Verklärung, ed. Anton Legner. Cologne: Stadt Köln, 1989.

Schmitz-Cliever-Lepie, Herta. *The Treasury of the Cathedral of Aachen.* Aachen: Chapter of the Cathedral, 1986.

Zehnder, Frank Günter. *Sankt Ursula: Legende, Verehrung, Bilderwelt.* Cologne: Wienand, 1987.

Lesa Mason

SEE ALSO

Aachen; Frederick I Barbarossa; Cologne, Art; Crusades; Metalworking; Nicholaus of Verdun

Renovatio Imperii Romanorum

A reference to efforts, real or rhetorical, to "revive the Roman Empire." Variations on the phrase appear already in Antiquity (e.g., *Renovatio Romanorum, Renovatio urbis Romae),* and especially under Charlemagne *(Renovatio Romanorum imperii).* In the form cited here, it appears on a lead seal attached to a *diploma* (no. D O III 285) issued at Rome, in 998, by Emperor Otto III (983–1002). In general, the phrase *Renovatio imperii Romanorum* has been taken as a reference to that emperor's ill-fated plan to create a renovated Roman Empire with its capital at Rome. The contours of this plan (or program) were established in a pioneering study published by Percy E. Schramm in 1929. Schramm argued that Otto had constructed the policies of his government around an ideal vision of Rome that was unique in being specifically secular, political, and universal. As evidence of this program, never explicitly witnessed by Otto himself, he cited a variety of literary, visual, and ritual sources. Although Schramm's interpretation of Otto III's *Rompolitik* (policy toward Rome) has long represented the basis for subsequent work on the topic, recent literature has cast doubt on his evidence and brought the whole character of Otto's program into question. In particular, a study by Görich concludes not only that the standard pool of evidence is insufficient to support the kind of theoretical structure proposed by Schramm, but perhaps is incapable of supporting any kind of *Rompolitik* at all. At this point, no clear alternative to Schramm's interpretation has emerged, but there seems to be general agreement that, whatever *Renovatio* may have meant to Otto III, it is unlikely to have represented a coherent program or a policy in any modern sense.

BIBLIOGRAPHY

Görich, Knut. *Otto III. Romanus Saxonicus et Italicus. Kaiserliche Rompolitik und sächsische Historiographie.* Historische Forschungen 18. Sigmaringen: Thorbecke, 1993.

Schramm, Percy Ernst. *Kaiser Rom und Renovatio. Studien zur Geschichte des römischen Erneuerungsgedankens vom Ende des karolingischen Reiches bis zum Investiturstreit.* 2 vols. Berlin: Teubner, 1929; vol. 1. rpt. Darmstadt: Wissenschaftliche Buchgesellschaft, 1984.

Warner, David A. "Ideals and Action in the reign of Otto III." *Journal of Medieval History* 25 (1998): 1–18.

David A. Warner

SEE ALSO

Charlemagne; *Reich;* Otto III

Renovatio Regni Francorum

The concept of the "Renewal of the Frankish Empire" occurs in the Carolingian and Ottonian periods of medieval Germany. It contains notions of internal renewal, both of a political and a religious nature, and a confirmation of the Franks and their East Frankish successors as leaders of a Western Christian empire on parity with the Byzantine Empire. The terminology first appeared on a metal seal of Louis the Pious—although some scholars argue that Charlemagne may have already used it in 813—and it has been linked with a program of reform activity that began late in Charlemagne's reign and intensified early in Louis's reign. Used sporadically in the ninth century, this inscription appears most dramatically again in 1003 on a lead seal of Henry II of Germany, who used it again to indicate a programmatic reform in his realm along Carolingian lines and to express the parity of the Western empire with Byzantium.

BIBLIOGRAPHY

Ohnsorge, Werner. *Abendland und Byzanz. Gesammelte Aufsätze zur Geschichte der byzantinisch-abendländischen Beziehungen und des Kaisertums.* Darmstadt: Wissenschaftliche Buchgesellschaft, 1958, pp. 111–130, 300–316.

Semmler, Josef. "Renovatio Regni Francorum: Die Herrschaft Ludwigs des Frommen in Frankenreich 814–829/830," in Peter Godman and Roger Collins, ed. *Charlemagne's Heir: New Perspectives on the Reign of Louis the Pious (814–840).* Oxford: Clarendon, 1990, pp. 125–126.

Weinfurter, Stefan. "Die Zentralisierung der Herrschaftsgewalt im Reich durch Kaiser Heinrich II." *Historisches Jahrbuch* 106 (1986): 241–297.

John W. Bernhardt

SEE ALSO

Carolingians; Charlemagne; Henry II, Art; Louis the Pious; *Renovatio Imperii Romanorum;* Seals and Sigillography

Reynard the Fox, Dutch

Van den vos Reynaerde, a Middle Dutch animal epic (3,469 lines in rhyming couplets), is one of the showpieces of Middle Dutch literature and probably the most widely studied Middle Dutch text. The author mentions his name, Willem, in the first line and adds that he previously had written a text named *Madock* (now lost); other than this, nothing is known about him. Nonetheless, dialect features and the use of many specific Flemish place-names make it quite certain that the author was of Flemish origin. The poem dates from the thirteenth century, probably from 1230–1260. The fact that Jacob van Maerlant refers to the poem in his *Rijmbijbel* (*Rhymed Bible,* 1270) and that the prime source Willem used, *Li plaid,* branch I of the Old French *Roman de Renart (The Story of Renart),* was written after 1173 set firm chronological limits. Because Willem also used other, younger branches of the *Roman de Renart* as additional sources, the year 1200 seems a plausible earliest possible date of composition *(terminus post quem).*

Three complete manuscripts and fragments of four more have been preserved. One of the complete manuscripts and one of the fragments have a special place in the manuscript tradition, actually they are manuscripts containing *Reinaerts historie,* a younger, enlarged version of Reynaert's story, in which *Van den vos Reynaerde* was completely incorporated.

Even though the nobility is severely criticized in *Van den vos Reynaerde,* it is plausible that the text was actually meant for an aristocratic audience. The good quality of the manuscripts is one of the arguments for this hypothesis.

In essence, *Van den vos Reynaerde* is the story of a trial. Many animals have complained to King Nobel about Reynaert's behavior. The king sends messengers to bring Reynaert to the court. The first two of them, Bruun the bear and Tybeert the cat, are lured into a trap by Reynaert, who uses their greed to bring them into a perilous situation. The third messenger is Grimbeert the badger, a relative of the fox. Reynaert agrees to accompany him to court, because otherwise his lair will be besieged by the king. At court Reynaert presents himself as a loyal servant to the crown and tries to challenge the plaintiffs. King Nobel furiously confronts him with his crimes against Bruun and Tybeert, but Reynaert replies that they were victims of their own vices. Once again a lot of animals bring in their complaints about Reynaert and he is sentenced to death by hanging. At this moment Grimbeert and Reynaert's other relatives leave the court. While the appointed executioners—Bruun, Tybeert, and Ysengrijn the wolf—are off to prepare the gallows, Reynaert makes a public confession of his sins. In this he comes up with a concoction about a treasure, hidden in a place called Kriekepit. This treasure was meant to overthrow King Nobel's throne in favor of Bruun. The other conspirators mentioned by Reynaert include Tybeert, Ysengrijn, Grimbeert (who had left the court), and his own deceased father. The implication of his father and Grimbeert lends credibility to Reynaert's story, and King Nobel and his wife cannot control their greed for gold. The king wants Reynaert to lead him to the treasure, but the fox refuses because he is under a papal ban and has to make a pilgrimage to Jerusalem. When the executioners return to the court they are immediately taken prisoner. Bruun is sentenced to give a pilgrim's bag to Reynaert, made of his own skin. Ysengrijn and his wife have to give him their "shoes," made in the same way. The next day

Reynaert wants to leave court and refuses Nobel's offer to escort him with his complete retinue. But he asks Cuwaert the hare and Belijn the ram to come along. At his "castle," Maupertuus, Reynaert entices Cuwaert to come inside and then kills the hare. He tells his wife, Hermeline, to prepare for flight, because the king will soon learn the truth. To the ram he gives the pilgrim's bag with the head of Cuwaert and tells him the bag contains a letter for King Nobel. At court Reynaert's deceit becomes apparent and the king is furious. Fyrapeel the leopard suggests that the ram be given to Bruun and Ysengrijn as a means of atonement. Thus peace is restored and Reynaert outlawed.

Many different interpretations have been suggested for *Van den vos Reynaerde.* Arendt (1965) interpreted it as a satire on the "wrong world," based on symbolic oppositions within the text (inside-outside, straight-crooked). Peeters (1973–1974) wanted to read it as an historical roman à clef, referring to the contemporary conflict between the Avesnes and the Dampierres over the county of Flanders. Most convincing are the interpretations of Lulofs (1975) and Wackers (1986, 1988). Both start from a contrast between the level of the narrative and the level of meaning. Lulofs stresses the importance of the trial as narrative framework, in which Reynaert appears to be a positive hero by outsmarting his opponents. On the level of meaning Reynaert is negative: he is a devilish seducer. Wackers opposed this interpretation by pointing out that in medieval literary theory the level of meaning always prevails over the level of the narrative. Especially the abuse of language makes it clear that Reynaert is evil incarnate on both levels. The brilliance of Willem is that he presents Reynaert as a very tempting protagonist: when the audience sympathizes with the fox in his viciously outwitting his opponents, it actually sympathizes with a way of life in which the end justifies every means.

Van den vos Reynaerde in its original form was never printed, but a prose version of *Reinaerts historie* was one of the first books to be printed in Dutch (Gouda 1479). It has been reprinted many times ever since, very often with beautiful illustrations and adapted to the needs of the period or to specific audiences (children). Very remarkable is the Latin translation, *Reynardus vulpes,* made by the Flemish poet Balduinus Iuvenis shortly after the Middle Dutch original.

BIBLIOGRAPHY

Arendt, Gerard-H. "Die satirische Struktur des mittelniederländischen Tierepos *Van den vos reynaerde.*" Ph.d. diss., University of Cologne, 1965.

Bosch, J. *Reynaert-perspectief.* Kampen: Kok, 1972.

Bouwman, Andre Th. *Reinaert en Renart. Het dierenepos Van den vos Reynaerde vergeleken met de Oudfranse Roman de Renart.* 2 vols. Amsterdam: Prometheus, 1991.

Colledge, E., and Adriaan J. Barnouw, trans. *Reynard the Fox and Other Mediaeval Netherlands Secular Literature.* Leiden: Sijthoff, 1967.

Goossens, Jan. *Die Reynaert-Ikonographie.* Darmstadt: Wissenschaftliche Buchgesellschaft, 1983.

Huygens, Robert B. C., ed. *Reynardus vulpes. De Latijnse Reinaert-vertaling van Balduinus Iuvenis.* Zwolle: Tjeenk Willink, 1968.

Lulofs, Frank. *Nu gaet reynaerde al huten spele.* Amsterdam: Thespa, 1975.

Lulofs, Frank, ed. *Van den vos Reynaerde.* Groningen: Wolters-Noordhoff, 1983.

Peeters, Leopold. "Historiciteit en chronologie in 'Van den vos reynaerde.'" *Spektator* 3 (1973–1974): 157–179, 347–369.

Van Daele, Rik, et al, eds. *Van den vos Reynaerde. Het Comburgse handschrift.* Leuven, Davidsfonds, 1991 [facsimile of the Comburg-mansucript, with transcription].

Van Daele, Rik. *Ruimte en naamgeving in Van den vos Reynaerde.* Gent: Koninklijke Academie voor nederlandse Taal- en Letterkunde, 1994.

Van Oostrom, Frits P. *Reinaert primair. Over het geïntendeerde publiek en de oorspronkelijke functie van "Van den vos reynaerde."* Utrecht: HES, 1983.

Verzandvoort, Erwin and Paul Wackers. "Bibliografie van de Reinaertvolksboeken." *Dokumentaal* 12 (1983): 7–21 [printed versions].

Wackers, Paul. *De waarheid als leugen. Een interpretatie van Reynaerts historie.* Utrecht: HES, 1986.

Wackers, Paul. "Mutorum Animalium Conloquium, or, Why Do Animals speak?" *Reinardus* 1 (1988): 163–174.

Geert H. M. Claassens

SEE ALSO
Animal Epics, Dutch; Fables, Dutch; Jacob van Maerlant

Rhenish Palatinate

About the year 1000 the greatest potential for power in the Rhenish (Rhine River) portion of the archdiocese of Cologne lay in the hands of the family of the Rhenish pfalzgrave (count Palatine). The office of *Pfalzgraf,* or *comes palatinus* (duke of the Palatinate, or palsgrave), was originally exercised by the highest *ministeriales* (ministerials, or officials) of the imperial Pfalz (*palatium,* whence Palatinate) at Aachen. Gradually, they appear as the representatives of the rights of the duke of Lower Lorraine in Ripuaria, that is, the area between the Meuse, the Rhine, and the diocese of Trier. In 916 a Widricus *comes palatii* appears; he is probably the same person as the contemporary count in the Ardennesgau, Bedagau, and Triergau (*gau* = district), the ancestor of the Ardennes dynasty. He was followed by a Herinbertus *comes palatinus* in 959, and by a Hermannus *comes palatinus* in 992 and 993 (this is probably the same Count Hermann who appears in 970 in the Bonngau, and in 975 and 980 in Eifelgau). Hermann in turn was the father of Ezzo (the short form for Ehrenfried), count in the Mühlgau in 996, in the Auelgau in 1015, and in the Bonngau in 1020; in 1023 Ezzo is called *comes palatinus* and in 1027 *advocatus Franciae*. The center of the ducal office in the Pfalz at Aachen gave its occupants on the Rhine axis an important power base.

Ezzo married Mathilda, daughter of Emperor Otto II and Theophanu, and thereby rose into the most prominent group of imperial princes. He was honored and granted lands by Henry II, and when he died in 1034, he was buried in the Abbey Brauweiler, west of Cologne. The Ezzonen (i.e., those of the house of Ezzo) held countships in the Bonngau, the Auelgau, the Ruhrgau, and the Keldachgau in the greater Cologne area; they also were counts in the Eifelgau and in the Zülpichgau, and they supervised the royal *fisci* (treasuries), extensive forests, and over certain trade routes. These latter were controlled by their fortified seats at Brauweiler, the Tomburg near Zülpich, and the Siegburg. They also held the rights of advocacy over important imperial monasteries and foundations (*Stifte*) in Essen, Vilich, Kornelimünster, and Maastricht. In short, the entire south region of the diocese of Cologne lay under the direct influence of the Ezzonen.

Ezzo's son Otto succeeded him as palsgrave, and from 1045 he was also duke of Swabia; he died without heirs in 1047 at the Tomburg. In 1036 another son, Hermann, became archbishop of Cologne, while daughters headed cloisters at Essen, Gerresheim, Nivelles, Gandersheim, Altmünster (near Mainz?), Neuß, Dietkirchen near Bonn, Vilich, and St. Maria in Capitol at Cologne. This generation clearly marked the apex of the family's power.

Tensions arose in the family as Henry I, the son of Ezzo's brother Hezelin (who appears as count in the

Zülpichgau in 1020) became palsgrave (1047–1061). Henry and Archbishop Hermann worked more and more in opposition, resulting in Hermann's transfer of the Hauskloster Brauweiler to St. Peter, the patron of the Cologne church, as well as other important pieces of family property. Of greatest significance was the grant of the Tomburg, which dominated the Aachen-to-Frankfurt military road *(Heerstrasse)* to Cologne. With this the archbishopric of Cologne began to encroach on the strategic points of support in the palsgrave's base of power. This was the situation when Anno became archbishop in 1056.

Anno was a stranger to the Cologne region, coming from the middling nobility of Swabia. As palsgrave, Henry used the minority of Henry IV to attempt to reestablish his power base; Anno opposed him. Henry was driven to his fortress at Cochem in 1060 (or 1061) where, in an insane rage, he murdered his own wife, Mathilda, countess of Ahr and heiress of Laach. He was eventually captured and taken to the monastery at Echternach where he died shortly thereafter.

Henry's successor was his minor son, Henry II, who came under the power of the archbishop and was forced to accept the changed realities: in the future, many of the former allodial (belonging to independent estates) possessions of the palsgravely family were held as fiefs of Cologne. The power of the palsgraves in the region of the Lower Rhine was forever gone; thereafter, it was centered in the Moselle area and on the Middle Rhine. Henry married Adelheid of Orlamünde; they were the cofounders of the abbey at Maria Laach about the year 1093. Henry II, who died April, 12 1095, as the last of the Ezzonen, lies buried there.

The office of *Pfalzgrave* now went to Adelheid's son by her first marriage, Siegfried, count of Ballenstädt, who appears in 1110 as principle advocate of the Treverene Church *(Treverensis ecclesiae principalis advocatus);* he died in 1113. His son and successor, William, was challenged by Count Gottfried of Calw in 1129, a supporter of Emperor Henry V. William prevailed over Gottfried, however, and appears as palsgrave of the Rhenish Franks and of the Palatinate on the Rhine *(comes palatinus Francorum Rheni, comes palatinus de Rheno)* from 1129 to 1140; he died without heirs. King Conrad III briefly designated Henry Jasomirgott, the margrave of Austria, as Rhenish *pfalzgrave,* but the latter could not establish himself on the Rhine. There was already a bitter struggle going on between Otto, count of Rheineck (from the house of Luxemburg-Salm), who was at once an heir to

the former *Pfalzgrave* Hermann and the husband of Gertrud of Nordheim, widow of *Pfalzgrave* Siegfried and mother of the previous *Pfalzgrave* William, who was a pretender to the pfalzgravely dignity, and Count Hermann of Stahleck, himself the husband of Gertrud, Margravine of Meissen.

Otto of Rheineck died in 1150, apparently out of grief over the death of his son Otto the Younger, who had been taken captive in 1148 by his rival Hermann. But Hermann of Stahleck did not occupy the Palsgrave's office for long. King Conrad III took from him in 1151 the fortresses Cochem, Clotten, and Rheineck, and his continued conflict with his ecclesiastical neighbors led to his being forced to submit to the humiliation of *Hundetragen* (carrying a dog over a prescribed distance) at an imperial diet at Worms in 1155. Deeply humbled, Hermann died 1158, leaving his ancestral lands near Bacharach to Conrad of Staufen, who in 1155 was enfeoffed by his half brother Frederick Barbarossa with the pfalzgravely dignity.

Conrad combined the ancient pfalzgravely possessions in Ripuaria and on the Mosel with the Stahleck allods (estates) on the Rhine; to these he added those lands inherited from his grandmother Agnes, daughter of Emperor Henry IV, in the Nahegau, Speyergau, and Wormsgau, and otherwise on the upper Rhine. These became the basis for the later Rhenish Palatinate. He fortified this all by building fortresses and towns, and although he initially continued the territorial-political quarrels with the archbishop of Trier, he eventually agreed to resign the rights of advocacy over Koblenz to the latter.

Palsgrave Conrad died in 1195 without male heirs, having first provided for the succession to his lands by his daughter Agnes, wife of Henry of Welf, the son of Henry the Lion and the brother of Otto of Brunswick. Pfalzgraf Henry in turn transferred the center of gravity of his possessions from the Middle Rhine (Tomburg, Laach, Cochem, Stahleck) to Heidelberg. He likewise surrendered an important set of rights in 1197, namely, the advocacy of Trier, which he renounced in favor of the archbishop. As had so many of his predecessors, Henry died without male heirs in 1227. His only son, Henry, had been enfeoffed in 1212 with the administration of the pfalzgraviate on Rhine, but he died two years later without heirs. As a consequence, the office of pfalzgrave went over to another line of the house of Welf, that of Bavaria.

During the thirteenth century, the count palatine of the Rhine emerged as one of the four temporal princes to whom, along with the three archbishops of Mainz, Cologne, and Trier, the exclusive right of electing the

German king belonged. In a fresco dating to 1355 in the Spanish Chapel in Santa Maria Novella at Florence, the Rhenish palsgrave is shown seated to the immediate left of the emperor, signifying some theoretical preeminence of this office in relation to other German nobles.

BIBLIOGRAPHY

Corsten, Severin. "Rheinische Adelsherrschaft im ersten Jahrtausend." *Rheinische Vierteljahrsblätter* 28 (1963): 84–130.

Droege, Georg. "Pfalzgrafschaft, Grafschaften und allodiale Herrschaften zwischen Maas und Rhein in salisch-staufischer Zeit." *Rheinische Vierteljahrsblätter* 26 (1961): 1–21.

Gerstner, Ruth. *Die Geschichte der lothringischen und rheinischen Pfalzgrafschaft.* Bonn: Röhrscheid, 1941.

Renn, Heinz. "Die Luxemburger in der lothringischen Pfalzgrafschaft." *Rheinische Vierteljahrsblätter* 11 (1941): 102–117.

Paul B. Pixton

SEE ALSO

Anno; Cologne, Archdiocese; Ezzo; Frederick I Barbarossa; Henry the Lion; Otto II; Theophanu

Riemenschneider, Tillmann (ca. 1460–1531)

Tillmann Riemenschneider is, perhaps, the best known of all German sculptors active during the years around 1500. His father, also Tillmann, was the mint master in Osterrode in Lower Saxony, but by 1483 the younger Riemenschneider was a journeyman carver in southern Germany. Documents place him in the guild of St. Luke in Würzburg, where he was a master by 1485. His workshop was large and successful, with twelve apprentices registered between 1501 and 1517.

Riemenschneider's two sons were also sculptors. From 1505 Riemenschneider served on the Würzburg Council, and he was burgomaster (mayor) in 1520–1521. In 1525 he was fined for refusing to support the bishop against a peasant revolt.

Riemenschneider's sculpture reveals familiarity with German and Netherlandish styles from a broad area. None of his travel is documented, however, and at least some of these regional styles could have been assimilated through the study of exported sculptures. In addition to his carefully worked surfaces, Riemenschneider is known for his excellence in wood, especially linden wood, as well as stone, primarily alabaster and sandstone. His training

Tillman Riemenschneider, Tomb of Rudolf von Scherenberg (d. 1485), Würzburg cathedral. *Photograph: Joan A. Holladay*

as a stone carver is usually attributed to his North German origins.

Riemenschneider was an innovative wood carver, experimenting with unpainted surfaces in such early works as the Münnerstadt altarpiece of 1490–1492, the artist's first dated work. This winged altarpiece, dedicated to Mary Magdalene, is currently divided between the Münnerstadt parish church and the museums in Munich (Bayersiches Nationalmuseum) and Berlin (Staatliche Museen Preussicher Kulturbesitz). Recent conservation has removed later gilding and polychromy (painting) to reveal Riemenschneider's extraordinarily careful attention to surface detail and nuance, akin to sculptures on a smaller scale, such as ivory carving. The success of Riemenschneider's unpolychromed sculpture is seen in such works as the great altarpiece of the Holy Blood (ca. 1499–1505) still in situ in the Jakobskirche in Rothenburg, and the lindenwood sculpture of Saints Christopher, Eustace, and Erasmus (1494), a fragment of a relief originally representing fourteen helper saints, now in the Metropolitan Museum of Art in New York City (The Cloisters). All these works reveal Riemenschneider's ability to carve refined drapery and flesh as well to reveal the underlying bone structure. Shortly after the completion of the Rothenburg altarpiece, Riemenschneider created the Creglingen altarpiece (Herrgottskirche, ca. 1505–1510) representing the Assumption of the Virgin in a more elaborate and complex style than the earlier works.

Riemenschneider's works in stone include the sandstone figures carved for the Marienkapelle in Würzburg, including the figures of Adam and Eve (1492–1493), and the nine apostle figures of 1500–1506 (all these now in the Mainfränkisches Museum, Würzburg). Among his most extraordinary achievements, however, are the few surviving works in alabaster such as the Angel and the Virgin Annunciate in Amsterdam of about 1480–1485 (Rijksmuseum), and the St. Jerome with the Lion in Cleveland (Museum of Art), which probably dates before circa 1495. Like some of the linden wood sculptures, these works are sparingly decorated with polychrome and gilt highlights, but they rely on the fineness of the carved surface for their impact.

In addition to altarpieces and architectural sculptures in wood and stone produced for churches in and around Franconia, Riemenschneider's career can be traced through several tomb monuments that attest to his prestige. As early as about 1488 Riemenschneider carved the monument of Eberhard von Grumbach (d. 1487) now in the parish church at Rimpar, depicting the knight in full Gothic armor in relief. The same format is repeated in the tomb monument of Konrad von Schaumberg (d. 1499) in the Marienkapelle in Würzburg. This work, however, of about 1502 is more mature in style, more portrait than effigy. Much grander in scale is the sandstone and marble monument of Archbishop Rudolf von Scherenberg (d. 1495) in the cathedral of Würzburg. Most impressive is the limestone and sandstone tomb of Emperor Heinrich II and Empress Kunigunde (1499–1513) in the cathedral of Bamberg. Below the relief of the imperial couple are a series of six relief panels illustrating scenes from their lives. Finally, around 1520 Riemenschneider carved the sandstone and marble monument of Archbishop Lorenz von Bibra in Würzburg Cathedral.

BIBLIOGRAPHY

Bier, Justus. *Tilmann Riemenschneider.* 4 vols. Würzburg: Verlagsdruckerei, 1925–1978.

———. *Tilman Riemenschneider: Frühe Werke.* Regensburg: Pustet, 1981.

———. *Tilmann Riemenschneider: His Life and Work.* Lexington: University Press of Kentucky, 1982.

Peter Barnet

SEE ALSO

Gothic Art and Architecture; Henry II, Art; Rothenburg ob der Tauber; Würzburg

Robertians

The Capetian kings ruled the west Frankish kingdom, lands that would come to be recognized as "France," from the accession of Hugh Capet in 987 to the death of Charles IV in 1328. The ancestors of this royal dynasty, however, are identified by modern scholars not as Capetians but rather as Robertians.

The Robertians can be traced with confidence back to the first half of the ninth century, when the family's namesake, known to us as Robert the Strong, moved west across the Rhine from the east Frankish lands into the kingdom of Charles the Bald. From the king he received some benefices and then, beginning in the early 850s, a number of offices and lands in Neustria. For the next decade, Robert was one of the most powerful and prominent men in the west Frankish kingdom and, despite his participation in a rebellion against the king, he was generally a loyal supporter of Charles. When he died in 866, he left behind two young sons who did not inherit his offices, but it was not long before most of Neustria was again under Robertian control. In fact, it was not long before there was a Robertian king of the Franks. In 888, after Charles and four other kings—Carolingian kings—had died in just over a decade, the west Frankish magnates deemed the only Carolingian heir too young to rule. Beset by threats of invasions from Northmen, they elected Robert's eldest son, Odo, as their ruler. Odo had, by that time, recovered most of his father's lands and offices, and as count of Paris, he had distinguished himself as a successful military leader in the defense of the city against Northmen in 886. During his reign, Odo bestowed numerous offices on his brother Robert, who built up and consolidated the Robertian lands in Neustria. When Odo died in 898, however, Robert did not become king. Rather, Odo was succeeded by the Carolingian Charles the Straightforward, whom the Franks had passed over a decade earlier and who had claimed the throne for himself in a rebellion against Odo in 893. Robert appears to have accepted the agreement for the succession reached by Odo and Charles, and he remained a loyal supporter of the king throughout much of Charles's reign. But the relationship between Charles and Robert and, for that matter, between the king and most of the west Frankish leaders, deteriorated in the late 910s. In 922, the Franks renounced Charles and elected Robert as their king. Robert was never able to establish his rule, however. He died in a battle with Charles in 923.

Although he never ruled as king, Robert's son Hugh—later nicknamed "the Great"—was no less prominent in Frankish politics than his father and uncle had been. In the mid 910s, while Robert and Charles were still on good terms, the king conferred on Hugh the inheritance of his father's lands. Hugh later orchestrated the accession of Charles's son, King Louis IV, in 936, and received from the new king the title dux Francorum (duke of the Franks), which enhanced his authority in Neustria and extended it north of the Loire. But like the rest of his lineage, Hugh found himself at times in conflict with the Carolingians. Indeed, during the late 930s and much of the 940s, Hugh and Louis had competing interests as they negotiated the hazards of shifting alliances among Frankish leaders. But the two men reconciled in the early 950s. And not long after their deaths in 954 (Louis) and 956 (Hugh), the king's son and heir, Lothar, granted Hugh's son, Hugh Capet, the ducal title. Although this Hugh jostled with other magnates and, at times, with the king to consolidate and extend his own power within the kingdom, like his father and grandfather, he appears to have had no evident royal ambitions—at least not until later in life. When Lothar died in 986, and his son Louis V died without a child in the following year, a gathering of Frankish leaders then elected Hugh as their king. Unlike any of his ancestors and in the face of some opposition, Hugh took steps to secure the throne for his dynasty: six months after his own accession he associated his son Robert to the throne, a move that, if only in retrospect, transformed the Robertians into the Capetians.

BIBLIOGRAPHY

Dunbabin, Jean. *France in the Making, 843–1180.* Oxford: Oxford University Press, 1985.

Favre, Edouard. *Eudes, comte de Paris et roi de France (882–888).* Paris: Bouillon, 1893.

Lauer, Phillipe. *Robert Iᵉʳ et Raoul de Bourgogne, rois de France, 923–936.* Paris: Champion, 1910.

Lot, Ferdinand. *Les derniers Carolingiens: Lothaire, Louis V, Charles de Lorraine, 954–991.* Paris: Bouillon, 1891.

———. *Études sur le règne d'Hugues Capet et la fin du Xᵉ siècle.* Paris: Bouillon, 1903.

McKitterick, Rosamond. *The Frankish Kingdoms under the Carolingians, 751–987.* London: Longman, 1983.

Sassier, Yves. *Hugues Capet: naissance d'une dynastie.* Paris: Fayard, 1987.

Jason Glenn

SEE ALSO

Carolingians; Charles III, the Simple.

Rodenegg

Murals in the castle at the village of Rodeneck/Rodengo, near Brixen (French/Bressanone) in South Tyrol, depict the story of Iwein. Eleven scenes start with the hero's departure to seek adventure, then continue with his encounter with the wild herdsman, his combat with Ascalon, the death of Ascalon, and the search for Iwein, and end with Iwein kneeling before Laudine as Lunete looks on. No evidence suggests that additional paintings have been lost. Stylistically related to religious works in Brixen, the paintings are the work of an anonymous painter and date from the 1220s to the 1230s. Early attempts to connect them with a "painter Hugo" and to place them in the first decade of the thirteenth century have proved untenable.

The "incompleteness" of the narrative as compared to Hartmann von Aue's *Iwein* has posed a challenge to literature-oriented interpreters, many of whom have assumed

Rodenegg Castle, final scene: Lunete presenting Ywain to Laudine. *Photograph: courtesty of Leonhard Graf von Wolkenstein-Rodenegg.*

that viewers were intended to read the final scene as standing for the entire episode of Iwein's marriage to Laudine. However, the rather bleak closing image gives no indication of future love, happiness, or marriage. Even pre-informed viewers who can mentally "complete" the story are left with a lingering image of grief and despair. Moreover, the artist has given a central position to the Lamentation-based rendering of Ascalon's death and visually juxtaposed scenes of adventure and combat with scenes of loss, despair, and grief. In general, the narrative appears to question sharply the values of knightly adventure and of the romance genre.

BIBLIOGRAPHY

Bonnet, Anne-Marie. *Rodenegg und Schmalkalden: Untersuchungen zur Illustration einer ritterlich-höfischen Erzählung und zur Entstehung profaner Epenillustration in den ersten Jahrzehnten des 13. Jahrhunderts.* Ph.d. diss. University of Heidelberg, 1981. Munich: tuduv, 1986, pp. 25–74 105–113.

Rasmo, Nicolò. "Überraschende Funde." *Merian—Monatshefte der Städte und Landschaften: Südtirol 26* no. 9 (1974): 48, 100.

Rushing, James A., Jr. *Images of Adventure: Ywain in the Visual Arts.* Philadelphia: University of Pennsylvania Press, 1995, pp. 30–90.

Schupp, Volker, and Hans Szklenar. *Ywain auf Schloß Rodenegg: Eine Bildergeschichte nach dem Iwein Hartmanns von Aue.* Sigmaringen: Thorbecke, 1996.

James A. Rushing Jr.

SEE ALSO

Hartmann von Aue; Romanesque Art and Architecture

Roger of Helmarshausen

An early-thirteenth-century copy of a document dated August 15, 1100, records the payments made by Henry of Werl, bishop of Paderborn, to the abbey of Helmarshausen for a cross and a container *(scrinium)* dedicated to Saints Kilian and Liborius made by the monk Roger (*Rogkerus monachus*). The container has been identified with the portable altar with images of the two saints and Henry preserved in the Diocesan Museum in Paderborn. The distinctive character of Roger's drawing style with characteristic nested V-folds, here conveyed in niello on silver, has led scholars to attribute a number of other high-quality works in metal to him. A second portable altar from the Abdinghof Monastery (now also preserved in the Diocesan Museum in Paderborn) has been identified with Roger's own hand by stylistic comparison of details of its movemented, narrative scenes with the more formal, hieratic images of the Kilian and Liborius altar; its images in silver-plated copper represent the martyrdoms of Sts. Blasius and Felix. The reliquary cross from the church of Saints Dionysius at Enger (Berlin, Kunstgewerbe Museum) has been associated with the cross mentioned in the Werl document cited above (Lasko 1992:79, 103). Many other works have also been associated with the hypothetical "workshop" of Roger based on stylistic and iconographic similarities; these include, for example, the cover of a Gospel book now in Trier (Cathedral Library, Ms. 139) and the backplate of a cross with the engraved image of St. Modoaldus, whose relics were transferred from Trier to Helmarshausen in 1107 (Cologne, Schnütgen Museum).

Eckhard Freise has found entries mentioning a monk Roger (with different spellings) in records of prayer confraternities at Benedictine houses in Stavelot and Cologne, as well as at Helmarshausen, and on this basis has constructed a hypothetical itinerary for Roger's monastic career. According to Freise, Roger would have been a monk at the Benedictine abbey at Stavelot until soon after 1100, when he moved to St. Pantaleon in Cologne; from 1107 until his death soon after 1125, he lived and worked at the abbey at Helmarshausen. Freise's chronology calls into question the date of 1100 for the document that has been used to date the Kilian and Liborius portable altar and to situate Roger in Helmarshausen at that time, since it places Roger in Cologne at the Benedictine monastery of St. Pantaleon until 1107. Westermann-Angerhausen has painstakingly reviewed many of the consequences of Freise's work on the accuracy of the date of the Werl document and traditional chronology of Roger's oeuvre, both of which assume him working already at Helmarshausen at the beginning of the twelfth century. By redating the portable altars in the 1120s, they are closer in date to the stylisti-

cally comparable illuminations from the scriptorium also associated with Helmarshausen, for example, the Gospels now in the J. Paul Getty Museum in Los Angeles (Ludwig Ms. II.3). So although Roger may lose his primacy as initiator of the nested-V fold style, his works now fit more comfortably with a larger group from the third decade of the twelfth century (Westermann-Angerhausen 1992: 70–71). It remains clear that Roger's nested V-fold style links him with Mosan metalwork, but questions as to where he was trained and the precise source of his metalworking traditions have not yet been satisfactorily resolved.

Interest in Roger's career is heightened by the widely accepted identification of him with the author of the *De diversis artibus (On Diverse Arts)*. The text is now generally dated early twelfth century, when Roger is known to have worked, and the existence of a rubric in the very early Vienna copy of the text (Österreichische Nationalbibliothek, Ms. 2527) states that its author, who calls himself Theophilus, was actually Roger. The treatise has been associated with a Benedictine monastery because of the prologues, which can be identified with Benedictine theology, and thus strengthens the identification of Roger with the author of the treatise. The text includes most extensive instructions for "how to do" metalwork, including many techniques used by Roger himself, but there is not complete congruence of Roger's techniques and those described in the treatise. Thus, if Roger was involved, he was adapting the knowledge of others and possibly material from earlier texts, since practices already out of date at the beginning of the twelfth century are included in the treatise.

BIBLIOGRAPHY

Fillitz, Hermann. "Rogerus von Helmarshausen," in *Helmarshausen und das Evangeliar Heinrich des Löwen*. ed. Martin Gosebruch und Frank N. Steigerwald. Schriftenreihe der Kommission für Niedersächsische Bau- und Kunstgeschichte bei der Braunschweigischen Wissenschaftlichen Gesellschaft 4. Göttingen: Goltze, 1992, 43–62.

Freise, Eckhard. "Roger von Helmarshausen in seiner monastischen Umwelt." *Frühmittelalterliche Studien* 15 (1981): 180–293.

Lasko, Peter. *Ars Sacra 800–1200*. Pelican History of Art. Harmondsworth: Penguin, 1972, 156–161.

———. "The Enger Cross." *Helmarshausen und das Evangeliar Heinrich des Löwen*, ed. Martin Gosebruch und Frank N. Steigerwald. Schriftenreihe der Kommission für Niedersächsische Bau- und Kunstgeschichte bei der Braunschweigischen Wissenschaftlichen Gesellschaft 4. Göttingen: Goltze, 1992, 79–108.

Westermann-Angerhausen, Hiltrud. "'Die Tragaltäre des Rogerus in Paderborn'—Der Wandel eines mittelalterlichen Künstlerbildes." *Helmarshausen und das Evangeliar Heinrich des Löwen,* ed. Martin Gosebruch und Frank N. Steigerwald. Schriftenreihe der Kommission für Niedersächsische Bau- und Kunstgeschichte bei der Braunschweigischen Wissenschaftlichen Gesellschaft 4. Göttingen: Goltze, 1992. 63–78.

Virginia Roehrig Kaufmann

SEE ALSO

Cologne, Art; Helmarshausen; Metalworking; Romanesque Art and Architecture; Theophanu, Art

Roland and Charlemagne, Illustrations

From the modern point of view it is easy to distinguish the historical realities of Charlemagne and Roland from the legendary and literary traditions that developed around these figures. From the medieval point of view it is probably impossible. Charles and Roland were historical figures, popular saints, and political icons of immense importance. The visual reception of these figures reflects this status. Throughout Europe, especially in the earlier period, Charlemagne and Roland tend to appear in monumental works of art in highly public places—church sculptures, stained glass windows, mural paintings. In the German language area, such public works include the golden shrine of Charlemagne in Aachen (ca. 1200–1215), decorated with scenes from the emperor's life, and two reliquaries also in Aachen, one for Charlemagne's arm (ca. 1165) and one (portraitlike) for his skull (ca. 1350). Charlemagne also appears in numerous representations of the Nine Worthies, for example, in the Hansasaal at Cologne and in the "triads" at Runkelstein. Highly visible today are close to forty statues of Roland, mostly in northern Germany, but scattered as far as Prague, Modena, Verona, and Dubrovnik.

The French *Song of Roland,* belonging to the oral sphere, remains unillustrated throughout its textual transmission, though in the thirteenth century and later the Charlemagne/Roland material is illustrated in a large number of *chansons de geste* and chronicle manuscripts from France. In Germany, the situation is different, reflecting the perceived "literariness" of the *Roland* adaptations and the political importance of the Charlemagne/Roland material. Pfaffe Konrad's *Rolandslied* was probably illustrated from the beginning of its manuscript tradition. The only complete manuscript (Heidelberg, Universitätsbibliothek, cpg. 112), dating from the end of the eleventh century (possibly as early as 1170), with its thirty-nine pen drawings, is one of the earliest illustrated German manuscripts of a secular text.

Der Stricker's *Karl der Große* is lavishly illuminated with full-color miniatures on gold ground in two luxury manuscripts: St. Gall, Stadtbibliothek und Bibliotheca Vadiana, manuscript no. 302 Vad., made in Zürich ca. 1300, has fifty-eight miniatures; and the twenty-three folios remaining from a southwestern German manuscript of the early fourteenth century (Berlin, Staatsbibliothek Preußischer Kulturbesitz, no. mgf 623) contain three full-page miniatures. Two mid fifteenth-century manuscripts (Bonn, Universitätsbibliothek, Ms. germ. fol. 136 and Hamburg, Staats- und Universitätsbibliothek, Cod. germ. 19) also contain Stricker's *Karl.* Beyond these, at least three German chronicle manuscripts contain visual responses to the legends of Charlemagne and Roland.

The sociopolitical, representative significance of Charlemagne and Roland persisted throughout the Middle Ages, as attested, for example, by the appearance of Charlemagne as representative ruler in a number of legal manuscripts. At the threshold of the modern era, Charles and Roland appear as saints in a work of propagandistic Habsburg genealogy, *Die Heiligen aus der Sipp-, Mag-* und Schwägerschaft Maximillians I, which exists both in illustrated manuscripts and as a woodcut series.

BIBLIOGRAPHY

Karl der Große: Lebenswerk und Nachleben 4: *Das Nachleben,* ed. Wolfgang Braunfels and Percy Ernst Schramm. Düsseldorf: Schwann, 1967.

Lejeune, Rita, and Jacques Stiennon. *La Légende de Roland dans l'art du Moyen Âge.* 2 vols. Brussels: Arcade, 1966.

Ott, Norbert H. "Pictura Docet: Zu Gebrauchsituation, Deutungsangebot und Appelcharakter ikonographischer Zeugnisse mittelalterlicher Literatur am Beispiel der Chansons de Geste" in *Grundlagen des Verstehens mittelalterlicher Literatur: Literarische Texte und ihr historischer Erkenntniswert,* ed. Gerhard Hahn and Hedda Ragotzky. Kröners Studienbibliothek 663. Stuttgart: Kröner, 1992, pp. 187–212.

Rempel, Hans. *Rolandstatuen: Herkunft und geschichtliche Wandlung.* Darmstadt: Wissenschaftliche Buchgesellschaft, 1989.

James A. Rushing Jr.

SEE ALSO
Aachen; Charlemagne; Cologne, Art; Prague;
Runkelstein; Stricker, Der

Roman de la Rose, Dutch

Two Middle Dutch translations of the French allegorical poem *Roman de la Rose* (Tale of the Rose) have come down to us: the anonymous Flemish *Rose* and Heinric's *Die Rose.* These two texts go back to two distinct groups of French manuscripts and must have come into being independently. We do not know which of the two Middle Dutch texts is older, nor whether the two poets knew each other's work.

The author of the Flemish *Rose* is not known, but the work reveals a poet of exceptional stature. The text is incomplete. Nine fragments have survived, originating from two codices and forming a total of nearly three thousand lines. The older manuscript is dated at about 1290, so the Flemish text must have come into being not long after the French model was completed (1269–1278). The story as we know it from the *Roman de la Rose* has been changed drastically. With the dream having been omitted, the Flemish *Rose* has a completely new framework. Here we have a first-person narrator who introduces himself as a clerk. He relates how he once met Jolijs and Florentine, a perfectly happy couple. Jolijs told him that he had received Florentine as a reward for his loyal services to Cupid. The clerk, who introduced himself as *Minre met Groter Quale* (lover with a Serious Illness), thereupon asked Jolijs to tell him the entire story as he hopes to learn what love is and how he himself should act to become a happy lover, too. In reply, Jolijs told him the story of the lover in the garden that in the Old French source is the account of the poet's dream. In the remainder of the Flemish text, Florentine reappears several times. Here, however, she has largely taken over the role of Bel Acueil in the original. For the most part, the discourses the allegorical figures deliver are faithful renderings of the Old French. This might mean that the poet considered these passages to be the essence of the text and therefore chose not to make major changes.

The other Middle Dutch translation, *Die Rose,* came into being at about the same time (the oldest manuscript dates back to ca. 1325), but originated in another region: Brabant rather than Flanders. The poet calls himself Heinric. He has been identified as Heinric van Aken, but there is no evidence for this. *Die Rose* is a fairly faithful translation with extensive abridgements, especially in the

part by Jean de Meun. The most conspicuous change is the omission of the episode on *Natura* (nature personified) and Genius.

BIBLIOGRAPHY
Heeroma, Klaas, ed. *De fragmenten van de tweede Rose.* Zwolle: Tjeenk Willink, 1958.
Verwijs, Eelco, ed. *Heinric van Aken, Die Rose.* 1868; rpt. Utrecht: HES, 1976.
van der Poel, Dieuwke E. *De Vlaamse Rose en Die Rose van Heinric. Onderzoekingen over twee Middelnederlandse bewerkingen van de Roman de la Rose.* Hilversum: Verloren, 1989 [with French summary].
———. "A romance of a Rose and Florentine. The Flemish adaptation of the Romance of the Rose." In *Rethinking the Romance of the Rose. Text, Image, Reception,* ed. Sylvia Huot and Kevin Brownlee. Philadelphia: University of Pennsylvania Press, 1992, pp. 304–315.

Dieuwke van der Poel

SEE ALSO
Heinric

Romanesque Art and Architecture

[This entry inclues nine subentries:

Introduction
Architecture
Ivories
Manuscript Illumination
Metalwork
Mural Painting
Sculpture
Stained Glass
Textiles]

Introduction

The term "Romanesque" derives from the resemblance of the monuments of this period to the works of ancient Rome, both the city and the larger empire; one thinks immediately of the Roman triumphal arch that served as a model for numerous church facades. But this label is an invention of the early nineteenth century, and thus the connection to Rome should not be drawn too insistently. Romanesque is primarily a style of churches and cloisters and the decorative arts associated with these sites, and as such is tied to imperial and papal tradition. Since Kubach, German scholarship has traditionally divided the period into the pre-Romanesque (eighth until early tenth century), the early (tenth to eleventh century), high (ca. 1100–1140), and late Romanesque (mid–twelfth to mid–thirteenth century). American scholars tend to label the two earlier subdivisions "Carolingian" and "Ottonian," corresponding to the political powers at the time and the family groups that provided the major patrons of these buildings.

BIBLIOGRAPHY

Kubach, Hans Erich. *Romanesque Architecture.* New York: Electa/Rizzoli, 1988 [trans. of 1964 German edition].

Hans-Peter Glimme

SEE ALSO
Carolingians

Architecture

While certain features characteristic of the Romanesque were already present in the tenth century, such as the ambulatory, which first appears in the cathedral of Clermont-Ferrand in France (consecrated in 946?), the full Romanesque style is marked by the use of modules, usually the square, in the plan and elevation and by the clarity of the spatial organization, especially visible from the building's exterior. Romanesque churches are further characterized by crypts, galleries, cross vaults, transepts, and nave bays that correspond to two bays of the aisle.

The facades of Romanesque churches derive from the Carolingian and Ottonian westwork, as seen in Corvey (873–885), where an almost independent structure precedes the nave, and St. Pantaleon in Cologne (late 10th c.). The three-tower group, found, for example, at the abbeys of Marmoutier in Alsace (mid-12th c.) or Maria Laach (ca. 1200), can be seen as a follower of the westwork, although it lacks the same independence. The two-tower facade, as seen in the abbey church at Königslutter, is also typical.

The double-choir arrangement, in which an apse at both the east and the west end of the church houses an altar and choir stalls, goes back to ancient Roman models. The type appears in the Carolingian period, at Fulda (ca. 800), for example, and in numerous Ottonian examples. Among them are the abbey church in Hersfeld (after 1037), and the church of St. Michael (1010–1033) in Hildesheim. The church of St. Godehard in Hildesheim (begun in 1133) and the cathedrals at Worms (after

Cologne, St. Kunibert, east end. *Photograph: Joan A. Holladay*

1171) and Mainz (1181–1239) provide examples of the double choir layout from the Romanesque period.

The double-choir church of St. Cyriakus at Gernrode in Saxony, built by Margrave Gero (d. 965) in the tenth century and supplied with a western choir in the twelfth, offers the earliest example of the use of galleries in Germany. They may be related to the building's function as a foundation for women, whose separation from other churchgoers was necessary.

The invention of the cubiform capital, which provides a perfect transition from the square abacus to the round column below, provides a clear geometric alternative to the more elaborate Corinthian capital. It appears first at the church of St. Michael at Hildesheim (1010–1033), from which it develops a variety of forms to become a standard feature of the Romanesque.

The windows of Romanesque buildings are typically round-headed, cut into the wall with tapered edges or decorated with columns at the sides. Sometimes they are grouped in twos or threes; in the late Romanesque, the

Cologne, St. Kunibert, interior. *Photograph: Joan A. Holladay*

cubiform capitals. The vaulting at Speyer plays an important role for the Romanesque. Here not only small spaces, such as crypt and aisle bays and chapels, were vaulted in stone, but, in a renovation to the originally wood-ceiling building, the nave too was, for the first time, given cruciform vaults about 1100. This represents a surpassing of the model, for in both ancient and medieval Rome, naves were typically left open to the wood roof.

The collegiate church at Königslutter in Lower Saxony, begun by Emperor Lothar of Süpplingenburg in 1135, marks the beginning of the late Romanesque, characterized by the more vertical multistoried structuring of the eastern apse. The figural ornament on the apse arcades indicates the participation of north Italian artisans. This building allies modest monastic architecture, now without a crypt, with late Romanesque decorative display. Cologne's numerous late Romanesque churches, for example, St. Gereon with its east choir dated between 1151 and 1156, predict the transition from Romanesque to Gothic in the thirteenth century, with their apses articulated in three or four stories (crypt, main story, upper story or gallery, and dwarves' gallery).

The monastic church of the Benedictines at Maria Laach (ca. 1220) is preceded to the west with an elaborately decorated Paradies or atrium, defined by three wings around an open courtyard. The round arcades are accented by moldings, and columns member the stepped portal at the west. Of the three towers over the west facade (12th and early 13th c.), the outer two are round with moldings while the center one is square in plan and structured with moldings, windows, and arcades.

The chapel of St. Gotthard at the cathedral of Mainz was completed about 1137 as the bishop's private chapel. It is typical of the court chapels of the period. It is built on a square plan with a small choir with rounded apse; its two stories are each supported by four columns. As at the palace chapel at Aachen, which served as a model for chapels of this type, the ruler, from his position at the western side of the upper story, would have had a direct view onto the mass performed at the altar below. Most of the Salian and Hohenstaufen palaces exist today in ruins; only parts of the fortification walls and palace buildings with their grouped window arcades still stand. Thus the remaining palace chapels are of particular importance. These take two basic forms: the extended form, as in Kaiserslautern (before 1160) and Gelnhausen (about 1180), and the two-story central structure with four interior supports, as in the chapel at Mainz. Examples of this

middle one is sometimes taller than those framing it. Elaborate portals, stepped back into the wall as at Speyer (mid-11th c.), or decorated with columns or figures, as at the so-called Golden Portal (Goldene Pforte) at the cathedral of Freiberg in Saxony about 1230, also begin to appear. The stone is always carefully worked in contrast to the fragments and found stones of earlier periods. The high quality is accentuated in the eleventh century by the use of ashlar (hewn and dressed stone) masonry; in the north, brick is also used, especially for cathedral and cloister churches.

As the necropolis for the Salian emperors, the cathedral at Speyer (begun ca. 1030) served as an important model for Romanesque churches. The still unfinished building was consecrated in 1061; it was completed in a second campaign between about 1080 and 1106. The building's crypt is divided into separate spaces under the choir, crossing, and transept. These spaces are all vaulted, with the vaults supported on columns with

latter type include the palace chapel of the landgraves of Thuringia at Landsberg near Halle (about 1170) and those at the imperial palaces at Hagenau in Alsace (about 1175, destroyed in the seventeenth century), Nuremberg (1170–1180), and Eger (1220–1230). The two-story chapel of St. Clement at Schwarzrheindorf, consecrated in 1151, deserves special mention for its painted interior and spatial clarity. In addition, the dwarves' gallery, which runs around the entire exterior of the building, is typical of late Romanesque.

Although the church of St. Elizabeth in Marburg, started in 1235, marks the beginning of the Gothic in Germany, buildings continued to be built in the Romanesque style for some time thereafter.

BIBLIOGRAPHY

Binding, Günther. *Deutsche Königspfalzen: Von Karl dem Grossen bis Friedrich II (765–1240).* Darmstadt: Wissenschaftliche Buchgesellschaft, 1996, pp. 199–396.

Conant, Kenneth John. *Carolingian and Romanesque Architecture 800–1200.* Baltimore: Penguin, 1959, pp. 255–267.

Kubach, Hans-Erich, and Albert Verbeek. *Romanische Baukunst an Rhein und Maas: Katalog der vorromanischen und romanischen Denkmäler.* 4 vols. Berlin: Deutscher Verlag für Kunstwissenschaft, 1976–1989.

Hans-Peter Glimme

SEE ALSO
Aachen; Bonn; Cologne, Art; Freiberg; Gernrode; Hildesheim; Mainz; Maria Laach; Marburg; Speyer; Worms

Ivories

A long-established workshop tradition made it possible for Germany to prosper in the area of ivory carving during the Romanesque period, in spite of a severe shortage of elephant tusks. While sculptors continued to work with small pieces of elephant ivory whenever possible, they more often turned to the more readily available materials of walrus ivory and bone. Eleven related plaques distributed in museums in Europe and the United States attest to the skills brought to the craft of walrus tusk carving during this period. The large square panels, perhaps created for the front of an ambo (pulpit), are each made up of several smaller pieces of walrus ivory. Characterized by small nicks that emphasize the folds of the drapery, these pieces of the so-called *gestichelte* (pricked) style are variously dated from 1110–1130 to 1170. They all depict scenes from the life of Christ, using iconographic schemes borrowed from Ottonian manuscript illumination. Their sinuous line, gently rounded volumes, and oval heads in three-quarter profile link them to monumental sculpture in Cologne.

With workshops specializing in book covers, game pieces, reliquaries, and portable altars, Cologne was a prominent ivory-producing center during the twelfth century with a thriving export business throughout Europe. Some thirty examples of octagonal or tower reliquaries all decorated with figures of the apostles still survive, a tribute to Cologne's "mass-production" of reliquaries made from bone. Rhenish carvers also collaborated with goldsmiths to create elaborate reliquaries that combined ivory or bone with gold, silver, and enamel. The Eltenberg Reliquary at the Victoria and Albert Museum in London demonstrates the proficiency with which these artists, using in this instance walrus ivory, could create large mixed-media objects dazzling for their rich effects.

BIBLIOGRAPHY

Euw, Anton von. "Elfenbeinarbeiten des 9. bis 12. Jahrhunderts," in *Rhein und Maas: Kunst und Kultur 800–1400.* Cologne: Schnütgen Museum, 1973, vol. 2, pp. 371–386.

Goldschmidt, Adolph. *Die Elfenbeinskulpturen aus der Zeit der karolingischen und sächsischen Kaiser 3–4: Die Elfenbeinskulpturen aus der romanischen Zeit.* 1914–1926. Berlin: Deutscher Verlag für Kunstwissenschaft, 1972.

Ornamenta Ecclesiae: Kunst und Künstler der Romanik in Köln, ed. Anton Legner. 3 vols. Cologne: Stadt Köln, 1985, vol. 2, pp. 414–439.

Melanie Holcomb

SEE ALSO
Cologne, Art; Relics and Reliquaries

Manuscript Illumination

Manuscripts painted in a Romanesque style were produced from the latter eleventh into the thirteenth centuries in the German provinces. This style, generally characterized as linear and stylized, concentrated on line and pattern in both figural treatments and backgrounds. The division of draperies into separate units and repetition of shapes within each unit contribute measurably to the stylized aspect of Romanesque painting. Figures and their settings were rendered by means of pen-and-ink drawing or full-body color in varying combinations. Major goals

Eneide (Staatsbibliothek zu Berlin—Preußischer Kulturbesitz, Ms. Germ. Fol. 282), fol. 17v: death of Dido. *Photograph: Staatsbibliothek zu Berlin—Preußischer Kulturbesitz*

rectly into text columns. German Romanesque manuscript production was chiefly the work of those committed to religious lives; knowledge of it can be only partial because the output of some of these monasteries is entirely lost. The names of some of the scribes and artists, among them women, have been preserved in dedicatory verses or illustrations.

Many new types of manuscripts were produced in the Romanesque period; among these were world chronicles, encyclopedias, saints' lives, modern and ancient authors, in addition to the liturgical texts, bibles, gospel books, psalters, and writings of the fathers of the church that had been the staples of manuscript production. Psalters were copied for private devotions as well as for community worship. Among liturgical texts, the development of the missal to combine the pericope (liturgical readings) book and the lectionary was a Romanesque phenomenon. An explosive growth in production of giant bibles took place during the Romanesque period, perhaps owing to increased demand as the number of monasteries grew or to the stimulus of the giant bibles created in Italy. These were generally multivolume illustrated bibles, approximately three feet by two feet in size.

A major characteristic of the Romanesque period was its compulsion to organize; thus every effort was made to arrange clearly both the contents and the decoration of manuscripts. Miniatures were devised to illustrate the moral allegories constructed in the encyclopedias and various teaching and devotional manuals. In the bestiary, some animals were associated with biblical figures, for example, the unicorn with the Virgin. The typological approach juxtaposed Old and New Testament events based on their prefiguring or fulfillment relationship.

The roots of German Romanesque painting lie in Ottonian art, and it was influenced by Mosan, northern French, Italian, and Byzantine art. Similar artistic objectives and styles prevailed throughout the five main manuscript-producing areas of Germany: the duchy of Swabia (which also included Alsace), the Rhineland, Saxony plus Westphalia and Thuringia, the Salzburg region, and Bavaria.

The German Romanesque style was inaugurated in Swabia, where the monasteries of Hirsau, Zwiefalten, and Weingarten were the most active manuscript producers. Hirsau's manuscript production was linked to its role as a pioneer in the reform movement of the early Romanesque period. Henry IV's gift to Hirsau of an Italian giant bible may have launched the period of greatest activity in its scriptorium. Hirsau provided its daughter

were to contour faces and to give figures substance and weight. Backgrounds were often composed of reiterated shapes, an inner area nesting into the outer, one usually blue, the other green. Gold backgrounds were chosen for the most elaborate productions.

Framed miniature paintings and ornamented initials were the primary decorations of Romanesque manuscripts, enriching the codices visually and conceptually as they indicated textual divisions. The size and complexity of these established a hierarchy of decoration that corresponded to the importance of the text being introduced. The initials were one of the most varied aspects of Romanesque book illumination; they were decorated with vinescroll ornament, single figures, or narrative scenes. Both miniatures and initials were often subdivided into compartments. Rather than use ornamental frames around introductory phrases as the Ottonian illuminators did, Romanesque scribes usually placed these phrases di-

houses their basic manuscripts; those became models for subsequent copies. Although much of the output of Hirsau is lost, many illuminated manuscripts produced at Zwiefalten, its daughter house, are extant and remain the single largest group of Swabian Romanesque manuscripts. In the eleventh century Judith of Flanders gave Weingarten—the Guelph (Welf) family monastery—a group of Anglo-Saxon and Flemish manuscripts that provided a wealth of models and ideas for those it made in the following century. The magnificently illuminated Berthold Sacramentary (New York, Pierpont Morgan Library, no. M. 710) was the culmination of this activity. The finest manuscript produced in Alsace was the *Hortus Deliciarum (Garden of Delights)*. Using texts and images drawn from a number of sources, Herrad, abbess of Hohenbourg, constructed in it a universal history of salvation centered on the life of Christ. Although the sole manuscript of this text was destroyed in 1870, much of its text and imagery had been recorded and has been reconstructed.

In the Rhineland, much manuscript production echoed Ottonian stylistic traits and drew on Ottonian models. Rhenish Romanesque depictions of single figures such as prophets mirrored its contemporary revival of stone sculpture. The close interplay between Mosan metalwork and manuscript painting here is revealed in the production of several scriptoria, among them Arnstein, St. Martin, and St. Pantaleon. Hildegard, abbess of Bingen, was a prolific writer best known for two books describing her visions, *Scivias* (Heidelberg, Universitätsbibliothek, Cod. Sal. X 16) and *Liber divinorum operum simplicis hominis* (Lucca, Bibliotheca Statale, no. Cod. lat. 1942). Important giant bibles copied in the Rhine region that have survived include the Arnstein (London, British Library, Harley Ms. 2799), Pommersfelden (Pommersfelden, Gräflich Schönborn'sche Schlossbibibliothek, Mss. 333–4), and Worms (London, British Library, Harley Ms. 2804) Bibles.

Saxony's Romanesque manuscripts also reveal clear stylistic and iconographic relationships with Mosan painting and metalwork. Corvey, Goslar, Hildesheim, Halberstadt, and Helmarshausen were the most important monasteries in this region. Theophilus, the author of an early-twelfth-century artist's handbook, *De diversis artibus,* was probably a monk of Helmarshausen. This scriptorium was active by mid-century, and in the late twelfth century it came under the direct patronage of Henry the Lion (Wolfenbüttel, Herzog-August Bibliothek, no. MS Guelph 105. Noviss. 20). Giant bibles produced in Saxony include the Hamersleben (Halberstadt, Dombibibliothek, Cod. 1–2), Merseburg (Domstiftsbibliothek, Cod. 1–3), and Mildenfurth (Jena, Universitätsbibliothek, Ms. Elect. theol., fols. 12 and 14) Bibles.

Salzburg was the center of Romanesque artistic developments in the area now known as Austria. Italian art was a great influence here; additionally, Byzantine stylistic and iconographic influences penetrated this region by way of Italy. The styles espoused in Salzburg were adopted throughout the whole region, with specific influences weakening as the distance from Salzburg increased. In Salzburg itself the monasteries of St. Peter and St. Erentrud produced many significant manuscripts, including the Antiphonary of St. Peter (Vienna, Österreichische Nationalbibliothek, Cod. Ser. Nova 2700) and the Admont Bible (Vienna, Österreichische Nationalbibliothek, Cod. Ser. Nova 2701–27102) at the former and a Pericope Book (Munich, Bayerische Staatsbibliothek, no. Clm 15903) and an Orational (Munich, Bayerische Staatsbibliothek, Clm 15902) at the latter. A giant Bible (Stiftsbibliothek, Cod. perg. 1) and a breviary (Munich, Bayerische Staatsbibliothek, Clm 8271) were produced for the nearby monastery of Michaelsbeuren. Other monasteries with active scriptoria at this time include Admont, St. Florian, and Mondsee, all significantly influenced by Salzburg's manuscript painting. Cistercian manuscripts produced by such houses as Zwettl and Heiligenkreuz were decorated more simply than those by the other Benedictine houses.

Bavarian manuscript illumination was impacted greatly by Salzburg, both stylistically and iconographically. Bavarian decoration was often pen-drawn rather than fully painted and characterized by conceptual lucidity and economy of detail. The major centers of Regensburg and Prüfening produced works so closely related in script and illumination that they are practically impossible to distinguish. Notable productions include copies of the works of Ambrose, Isidore, Rabanus Maurus, as well as saints' lives and miscellanies. The lavishly illustrated Erlangen Bible (Universitätsbibliothek, Cod. 1 perg.) was owned by a house of canons in Ansbach and may have been made in Regensburg.

Illuminated manuscripts are the best-preserved storehouse of German Romanesque painting styles. It is mainly through this body of evidence that we are able to trace stylistic developments from Ottonian through Romanesque into Gothic painting. By the 1230s the *Zackenstil* (zigzag style), a late Romanesque style transitional to Gothic, came into use in most of the German regions.

The *Zackenstil* was introduced in Thuringia in the early thirteenth century.

BIBLIOGRAPHY

Cahn, Walter. *Romanesque Bible Illumination.* Ithaca, N.Y.: Cornell University Press, 1982.

Dodwell, C. R. *The Pictorial Arts of the West 800–1200.* Pelican History of Art. New Haven, Conn.: Yale University Press, 1993, pp. 130–156, 269–315.

Grabar, André, and Carl Nordenfalk. *Romanesque Painting from the Eleventh to the Thirteenth Century.* New York: Skira, 1958.

Harrsen, Meta. *Central European Manuscripts in the Pierpont Morgan Library.* New York: Pierpont Morgan Library, 1958.

Klemm, Elisabeth. *Die romanischen Handschriften der Bayerischen Staatsbibliothek in München.* 3 vols. in 6. Katalog der illuminierten Handschriften der Bayerischen Staatsbibliothek in München 3. Wiesbaden: Reichert, 1980.

Legner, Anton. *Deutsche Kunst der Romanik.* Munich: Hirmer, 1982.

Mazal, Otto. *Buchkunst der Romanik.* Graz: Akademische Druck- und Verlagsanstalt, 1978.

Monumenta Annonis: Köln und Siegburg, Weltbild und Kunst im hohen Mittelalter, ed. Anton Legner. Cologne: Schnütgen Museum, 1975.

Mütherich, Florentine. "Malerei im 12. Jahrhundert," in *Das Mittelalter,* vol. 1, ed. Hermann Fillitz. Propyläen Kunstgeschichte 5. Berlin: Propyläen Verlag, 1969, pp. 264–269.

Ornamenta Ecclesiae: Kunst und Künstler der Romanik, ed. Anton Legner. 3 vols. Cologne: Stadt Köln, 1985.

Regensburger Buchmalerei von frühkarolingischer Zeit bis zum Ausgang des Mittelalters, ed. Florentine Mütherich and Karl Dachs. Munich: Prestel, 1987.

Rhein und Maas: Kunst und Kultur 800–1400. 2 vols. Cologne: Schnütgen Museum, 1972–1973.

Rothe, Edith. *Medieval Book Illumination in Europe: The Collections of the German Democratic Republic.* New York: Norton, 1968.

Suevia Sacra: Frühe Kunst in Schwaben. Augsburg: Mühlberger, 1973.

Swarzenski, Georg. *Die Salzburger Malerei von den ersten Anfängen bis zur Blütezeit des romanischen Stils: Studien zur Geschichte der Deutschen Malerei und Handschriftenkunde des Mittelalters.* 2 vols. Leipzig: K. W. Hiersemann, 1908–1913.

Turner, D. H. *Romanesque Illuminated Manuscripts in the British Museum.* London: British Museum, 1966.

Die Zeit der Staufer: Geschichte, Kunst, Kultur, ed. Reiner Haussherr. 5 vols. Stuttgart: Württembergisches Landesmuseum, 1977.

Dorothy M. Shepard

SEE ALSO

Admont; Corvey; Goslar; Halberstadt; Heiligenkreuz; Helmarshausen; Henry the Lion; Hildegard von Bingen; Hildesheim; Hirsau; Regensburg; Salzburg; Theophanu; Worms; Zwettl

Metalwork

We are fortunate to be informed about the craft of the Romanesque metalworker in Germany by one of its practitioners, identified as Theophilus Presbyter. Evidence suggests that Theophilus might be one and the same as the great Lower Saxon metalworker Roger of Helmarshausen. The treatise *De diversis artibus,* written in the early twelfth century, describes the tools of the workshop and a wide variety of techniques including casting and repoussé (relief on reverse side) decoration as well as niello (black incised designs) and enamel. The techniques and materials described by Theophilus correspond closely with extant examples of Romanesque metalwork.

The surviving monuments convey the range of the Romanesque craftsman in metal. In addition to precious liturgical objects for the altar, large-scale objects were among the major ornaments in Romanesque churches. Bronze doors decorated major buildings, and wooden doors were fitted with elaborate wrought iron hinges and cast bronze door pulls (or sanctuary rings) in the form of lions' heads. The font by Rainer of Huy in Liège demonstrates the mastery of bronze casting already available to metalworkers at the beginning of the twelfth century. Churches were decorated with monumental seven-branched candlesticks such as the example in the cathedral of Braunschweig, as well as great wheel-shaped chandeliers such as those at Aachen and Gross-Komburg. Large-scale bells also figure in the production of the Romanesque metalworker, although they are usually not elaborately decorated.

Smaller-scale objects include censers (incense-burning vessels), aquamaniles (ewers used in Mass), altar candlesticks, chalices and patens, crucifixes and cross bases, portable altars, retables (religious paintings on panels), and altar frontals. Reliquaries became increasingly large,

Shrine of St. Heribert (Cologne-Deutz, Church of St. Heribert). *Photograph: Rheinisches Bildarchiv der Stadt Köln*

particularly in the Meuse valley and Cologne, where the architectural form of the house-shrine became dominant.

German metalwork was concentrated in the Romanesque period primarily in two geographic regions—Lower Saxony, and the Meuse valley and Cologne—both of which had been metalworking centers in earlier times. The early Romanesque metalwork of Lower Saxony is best seen in the work of Roger of Helmarshausen from about 1100. Roger's surviving monuments include the portable altar in Paderborn (cathedral treasury), made for Bishop Henry of Werl (1084–1127), a portable altar from Abdinghof Abbey (Paderborn, Franciscan church), and the cover of a Gospel book from Helmarshausen in Trier (cathedral treasury). Roger's work is characterized generally by a strong graphic quality and a fondness for nested Gothic V-folds in particular. His work had a lasting influence throughout Germany during the twelfth century.

In the Meuse River valley just after 1100 the cast bronzes of Rainer of Huy had a seminal influence comparable to that of Roger of Helmarshausen in Lower Sax-

ony. Best seen in the great baptismal font now in the church of St. Bartholomew in Liège (1107–1118), Rainer's work is the most significant manifestation of classicism in early Romanesque metalwork. The classicizing tradition continued in the Meuse and Cologne areas throughout the twelfth century, as seen in such works as the great enameled objects made for Stavelot Abbey in the 1140s, the St. Bertin cross base of about 1150–1160, the great house shrines such as the St. Servatius shrine, and continuing to the work of Nicholas of Verdun in the late twelfth and early thirteenth centuries. Nicholas of Verdun's work, such as the Klosterneuberg Altarpiece (Klosterneuberg Abbey Church), the Shrine of the Three Kings (Cologne Cathedral), and the Shrine of the Virgin (Tournai Cathedral), is recognized as one of the strongest classicizing statements of the western Middle Ages.

BIBLIOGRAPHY

Bronzegeräte des Mittelalters. 6 vols. to date. Denkmäler deutscher Kunst. Berlin: Deutscher Verein für Kunstwissenschaft, 1935–.

Lasko, Peter. *Ars Sacra: 800–1200.* Pelican History of Art, 2d ed. New Haven, Conn.: Yale University Press, 1994, pp. 156–226, 240–253.

Swarzenski, Hanns. *Monuments of Romanesque Art: The Art of Church Treasures in North-Western Europe,* 2nd ed. London: Faber, 1974.

Theophilus. *De diversis artibus,* ed. and trans. C.R. Dodwell, 2d ed. Oxford Medieval Texts. Oxford: Clarendon, 1986.

Peter Barnet

SEE ALSO

Aachen; Braunschweig; Cologne, Art; Klosterneuburg; Liturgical Vestments, Manuscripts, and Objects; Metalworking, Nicholas of Verdun; Paderborn; Roger of Helmarshausen; Theophilus Presbyter; Trier

Mural Painting

Despite subsequent additions to the literature, Otto Demus's 1968 survey (published in English translation in 1970) provides other scholars with what remains the essential basis for the study of Romanesque wall painting. From Lower Saxony through Westphalia, Bavaria, and Austria and from the Ottonian antecedents of Romanesque painting to the last Gothic phases of the *Zackenstil* (zigzag or jagged style) in the thirteenth century, he outlines issues that scholars continue to address. Undoubtedly the most controversial has been his emphasis on the Byzantine sources of Central European painting, although especially with regard to thirteenth-century painting his observations have held up under the detailed scrutiny of other scholars. He also noted the importance of iconographic innovation in the formulation of the programs of wall paintings, for while the basis of many programs remained Old and New Testament cycles and saints' lives, changes were introduced, including program concepts based on Byzantine or Sicilian dome and apse decoration, as, for example, in the All Saints' Chapel at Regensburg dated around 1165. Other new programs were based on the writings of Rupert of Deutz and Honorius Augustodunensis and on political issues such as those addressed in the apse frescoes at Prüfening near Regensburg. Fresco painting was found throughout Europe before the Romanesque period, and thus Demus begins his discussion of Romanesque wall painting by looking at remaining Ottonian cycles, especially in churches at Reichenau dated around the year 1000. In their subject matter and their linear painting and facial types can be found the origins of twelfth-century paintings such as

those in the parish church of Idensen, which was founded as the private chapel of the Bishop of Minden, and was painted between about 1120 and 1140. As with other wall paintings, the best comparisons for these frescoes are in illuminated manuscripts, in this case from the major center at Helmarshausen. Mid-twelfth-century and slightly later frescoes found at the Nonnberg Convent at Salzburg, at Purgg, in the Rhineland at Schwarzrheindorf, and eventually at Prüll near Regensburg, among other sites, show familiarity with Byzantine or Byzantinizing church decoration or even manuscripts.

Among the most spectacular of the fresco programs are those remaining from the thirteenth century executed in the *Zackenstil.* The earlier examples, in the 1240s, appear to be in Lower Saxony at Braunschweig and Goslar, as well as at Soest and Cologne. Related images including the painted wooden ceiling at St. Michael's at Hildesheim, stained glass windows, and illuminated manuscripts help to establish approximate dating, as well as a relationship to Byzantine art, especially at Venice. Furthermore, the art of the *Zackenstil* has qualities of three-dimensionality and movement that resemble those of early Gothic painting in England and France. Nevertheless, the formality of the compositions and the linearity of the intense, angular, zig-zag drapery led Otto Demus to describe this style as Romanesque "mannerism" (Demus 1970a: 200–203; Demus 1970b: 615). In addition, he has argued that the zigzag style is, in fact, an emotionally charged exaggeration of the sort of drapery folds found in Byzantine art and Byzantinizing art, particularly that found in the mosaics of San Marco at Venice. Dates from the 1240s through the 1260s make comparisons with the volumetric figures of the early Palaeologan period of Byzantine wall painting convincing. Even more important is the motif book at Wolfenbüttel, which includes figures found on the Hildesheim ceiling and in the Goslar Gospel, dated around 1240. Buchthal (1979) among others has connected all these images with Byzantine manuscripts and the mosaics at San Marco. That the drawings are the work of a Venetian artist or a Saxon artist who had visited Venice or had seen a Byzantine Gospel provides insight into the manner in which Byzantine images became available to Central European painters. Moreover, frescoes at Matrei in Osttirol attributed to Paduan painters recruited to work at Salzburg demonstrate another manner in which Byzantine characteristics reached the north. By the third quarter of the thirteenth century the *Zackenstil* had reached Austria, and superb examples can be found in frescoes at

Gurk, Göss, Seckau, and Krems, where the elegance of Gothic paintings begins to be more evident.

BIBLIOGRAPHY

Belting, Hans. "Zwischen Gotik und Byzanz: Gedanken zur Geschichte der sächsischen Buchmalerei im 13. Jahrhundert." *Zeitschrift für Kunstgeschichte* 41 (1978): 217–257.

Buchthal, Hugo. *The "Musterbuch" of Wolfenbüttel and Its Position in the Art of the Thirteenth Century.* Byzantina Vindobonensia 12. Vienna: Verlag der Österreichischen Akademie der Wissenschaften, 1979.

Demus, Otto. *Byzantine Art and the West.* The Wrightsman Lectures 3. New York: New York University Press, 1970a.

———. *Romanesque Mural Painting,* trans. Mary Whittall. New York: Harry N. Abrams, 1970b.

Dodwell, C. R. *The Pictorial Arts of the West 800–1200.* New Haven, Conn.: Yale University Press, 1993.

Lanc, Elga. *Die mittelalterlichen Wandmalereien in Wien und Niederösterreich.* Corpus der mittelalterlichen Wandmalereien in Österreich 1. Vienna: Verlag der österreichischen Akademie der Wissenschaften, 1983.

Stein, Heidrun. *Die romanischen Wandmalereien in der Klosterkirche Prüfening.* Studien und Quellen zur Kunstgeschichte Regensburgs 1. Regensburg: Mittelbayerische Druckerei und Verlagsgesellschaft, 1987.

Die Zeit der Staufer: Geschichte, Kunst, Kultur, ed. Rainer Haussherr. 5 vols. Stuttgart: Württembergisches Landesmuseum, 1977, vol. 1, pp. 298–302.

Rebecca W. Corrie

SEE ALSO

Bonn; Braunschweig; Cologne, Art; Goslar; Gurk; Helmarshausen; Hildesheim; Minden; Ottonian Art and Architecture; Regensburg; Salzburg; Soest

Sculpture

Germany was one of the earliest regions in medieval Europe to develop large-scale sculpture. In the German empire there was continuity between Carolingian minor arts and larger works in a variety of sculptural media that began to appear during the late tenth century, such as monumental sculpted doorways and figures for devotional settings. Tomb sculptures were also an important early type of German Romanesque sculpture and include the cast bronze tomb of Rudolf of Swabia (ca. 1080) in the cathedral at Merseburg. Early projects of relief sculpture also characterize German Romanesque work and in-clude stone reliefs now above the doorway at St. Emmeran, Regensburg (ca. 1050), and reliefs associated with the tomb and crypt of St. Liudger in Werden (now in the Rheinisches Landesmuseum, Bonn, ca. 1050).

Although there is considerable continuity with Ottonian sculpture, after about 1100 German sculptors began to produce the historiated (containing figural scenes) capitals and monumental stone entrances commonly associated with the Romanesque style in other European regions. However, many of these works were less elaborate than contemporary church facades in other countries and seem dependent on foreign models, especially sculpture from France and Italy. Cologne was an important sculptural center throughout the period, but continuous traditions and interrelationships between workshops are uncommon in other regions. Historiated capitals, one of the most common types of Romanesque sculpture, are comparatively rare in Germany, and the examples that do exist tend to be derivative of northern Italian models, such as the capitals with figurative ornament found at Speyer Cathedral (before 1106), Mainz Cathedral (after 1106, with a second campaign around 1180), and the Chapel of the Holy Cross in Delecke/Soest (mid-12th c.). Portal decoration is more common than elaborate capital programs in Germany. However, exterior sculptural ensembles in Germany tend to have fewer subordinate parts than those in France, Spain, or Italy. While there are some elaborate multipart portals, such as Petershausen (1173–1180), Bamberg (1220–1235), Freiberg (ca. 1230), and the Galluspforte in Basel, Switzerland (end of the 12th c.), most portals consist of a tympanum (curved triangle above the door) alone. The most common iconography of these tympana is a central Christ surrounded by either the Virgin and St. John or by Peter and Paul. This group is sometimes accompanied by donor figures and/or local saints. Numerous examples of such portals exist in many parts of Germany and include the tympanum at the church in Gandersheim showing bust-length images of Christ, Peter, and Paul (ca. 1150), and a tympanum showing an enthroned Christ with the Virgin and St. Peter, a bishop, and a donor from Worms Cathedral (end of the twelfth century). German Romanesque tympana are located on various parts of the building. In addition to the traditional west entrance, other locations, especially the south side of the nave, were also common. Diverse materials also characterize German portal sculpture including limestone—the material almost universally used in France—and sandstone; even granite, a very hard stone, was employed in the Baltic re-

Fragment of so-called Gustorf choir screen, from St. Maria ad Gradus in Cologne (?): Adoration of the Magi and Annunciation to the Shepherds (Bonn, Rheinisches Landesmuseum). *Photograph: Joan A. Holladay*

gions. Moreover there is continuous production of sculpture in wood and stucco, which is closely related to the works produced in stone.

The style of German Romanesque sculpture varies considerably, from flat, minimally articulated shapes, seen in the west portal from Grossen-Linden (after 1230) and the granite tympanum from Norderbrarup (end of the 12th c.), to ornately draped, three-dimensional forms, some of which exhibit similarity to contemporary French sculpture. After 1150 the early Gothic style, consisting of simpler, more architectonic forms, was increasingly popular in northern France, and by 1200 a second wave of the Gothic style, characterized by greater three-dimensionality and smooth, sweeping folds, known as the *Muldenfaltenstil* (trough fold style), had become widespread in French sculpture. After 1160 these styles began to appear in Germany, especially in Cologne. For example, the tympanum from the church of St. Cecilia in Cologne (ca. 1160, now in the Schnütgen Museum) represents influence from the French early Gothic. Although occasionally a pure French style appears, as is the case in the Princesí Portal at Bamberg (ca. 1235), where a workshop trained at Reims Cathedral seems to have been active, it is more common for visual elements from French cathedral sculpture to appear in combination with local Romanesque art. Elements from the minor arts in the Mosan style, itself an important source for French sculptural style, sometimes appear to have been directly adapted by German sculptors. Other stylistic components in German sculpture, such as the *Zackenstil* (jagged style), seem to derive from contemporary book illumination. Such combinations produce dynamic visual hybrids common in Germany during the first half of the thirteenth century. By the second half of the thirteenth century most German sculpture is unmistakably Gothic in style.

Throughout the Romanesque period German sculptors continued to produce crucifixes, grave monuments, and sculptures of the Virgin and Child. In addition to examples in stone, many of these sculptures continue to be made in the traditionally employed materials of wood, metal, and stucco. Such works represent a continuous tradition from the eleventh century and suggest the important role of unbroken tradition in German Romanesque sculpture.

BIBLIOGRAPHY

Budde, Rainer. *Deutsche romanische Skulptur 1050–1250.* Munich: Hirmer, 1979.

Susan L. Ward

SEE ALSO

Bamberg; Basel; Cologne, Art; Essen; Freiberg; Gandersheim; Gothic Art and Architecture; Hildesheim; Mainz; Ottonian Art and Architecture; Paderborn; Speyer; Regensburg; Werden; Worms

Stained Glass

Although a few fragments of earlier glass are known, in the Romanesque period the medium comes into its own. Two basic types prevail: the narrow oblong windows typical of Romanesque architecture could each be filled with a single standing figure or with several multifigured scenes combined into a vertical narrative sequence. The latter would have been more appropriate for areas close to the spectator, while the large-scale, single figures would have been easily visible even in the clerestory windows far above the viewer. Biblical subjects predominate: the narrative programs typically juxtaposed typologically related scenes from the Old and New Testaments. The single figures lend themselves to programs that are linear rather than narrative or hierarchical: at the cathedral at Augsburg the prophets in the south nave clerestory probably faced figures of the apostles; the figures of German kings, apostles, female saints, and knights preserved at Strasbourg Cathedral were part of a larger All Saints program.

The windows at Augsburg, the earliest known programmatic cycle, are variously dated in the first half of the twelfth century; an association with the rebuilding begun in 1132 seems likely. Although the five preserved windows reveal an effort to differentiate the figures from one another in the color and details of costume and in the attributes and placement of the hands, they all share the strictly frontal pose, large staring eyes, and unfurled scrolls that drape down their bodies. The partitioning of body parts and drapery passages into abstract compartments with a logic of their own—a typical stylistic feature of the Romanesque—is furthered here by the nature of the stained glass medium, in which leads separate the colored glass fragments.

Although a similar program at Speyer is now known only through textual sources, the six kings preserved in Romanesque style at Strasbourg Cathedral represent the remains of an elaborate multilevel cycle from the late twelfth century. According to Zschokke's reconstruction (1942), the present position of the kings in the north aisle of the Gothic church corresponds to their placement in the earlier building. They would have faced apostles in the south aisle while figures of female saints occupied the south clerestory, and popes, deacons, and bishops of Strasbourg stood in the north clerestory. Execution of the cycle must have spread over a period of time, for twelve additional kings are in a Gothic style.

Five panels dated circa 1150–1160 remain from the Premonstratensian church of Arnstein on the Lahn (now Münster, Westfälisches Landesmuseum on loan from Schloá Cappenberg). Here five windows, each three panels high, developed an early narrative program in the choir. An abbreviated Tree of Jesse window at the center illustrated the genealogy of Christ; a narrative window on either side showed scenes from his life and after his death; the Old Testament scenes in the outermost windows represented types or prefigurations of the Christological scenes. Scenes preserved from the churches at Alpirsbach (ca. 1160–1170), St. Patrokli at Soest (ca. 1160–1166), and the cathedral at Strasbourg (last third of the twelfth century) indicate that these buildings also had narrative window programs with typological structures.

Romanesque stained glass, despite regional stylistic differences, presents a relatively unified picture, which will dissolve into technical, programmatic, and stylistic variety in the great glass programs of the Gothic.

BIBLIOGRAPHY

Becksmann, Rüdiger. *Deutsche Glasmalerei des Mittelalters: Eine exemplarische Auswahl.* Stuttgart-Bad Cannstatt: Dr. Cantz'sche Druckerei, 1988, pp. 92–99.

Beyer, Victor, Christiane Wild-Block, and Fridtjof Zschokke. *Les Vitraux de la cathédrale de Strasbourg.* Corpus vitrearum medii aevi, France 9/1. Paris: Éditions du Centre National de la Recherche Scientifique, 1986.

Frenzel, G., and G. Hinkes. "Die Prophetenfenster des Domes zu Augsburg." *Jahrbuch der Bayerischen Denkmalpflege* 28 (1970–1971): 83–100.

Haas, W. "Die alten Obergadenfenster des Augsburger Domes." *Jahrbuch der Bayerischen Denkmalpflege* 28 (1970–1971): 101–108.

Kalinowski, L. "*Virga versatur:* Remarques sur l'iconographie des vitraux romans d'Arnstein sur Lahn." *Revue de l'art* 62 (1983): 9–20.

Theophilus. *De diversis artibus,* ed. and trans. C. R. Dodwell, 2d ed. Oxford Medieval Texts. Oxford: Clarendon, 1986.

Zschokke, Fridtjof. *Die romanischen Glasmalereien des Strassburger Münsters.* Basel: Schwabe, 1942.

Joan A. Holladay

SEE ALSO

Augsburg; Soest; Speyer; Strasbourg

Textiles

German luxury garments, such as ecclesiastical and princely vestments, were most often made from silk woven in the eastern or southern Mediterranean, principally the Byzantine and Islamic east. Relatively few significant German textiles survive from the Romanesque period, but from them we learn that production consisted largely of wool and linen embroideries and woven tapestry wall hangings. Examples of both techniques were undoubtedly created for secular as well as ecclesiastical interiors, but few secular textiles are extant.

The earliest surviving European tapestries are at the cathedral of Halberstadt. The first of these, dating from the mid-twelfth century, is more than ten meters wide in its current, somewhat fragmentary state. It represents scenes of Abraham and Isaac, and it is generally consistent with Romanesque art of Lower Saxony. The second Halberstadt tapestry, of about 1170, is similar in style, depicting Christ in Majesty flanked by the Apostles. An early thirteenth-century tapestry at Halberstadt depicts the enthroned Charlemagne surrounded by four ancient philosophers. Roughly contemporary tapestry fragments depicting scenes from the Marriage of Philologia and Mercury, after a text of Martianus Capella, survive at Quedlinburg.

German embroidered altar decorations are best represented by late-twelfth-century linen fragment from the Rhineland, formerly preserved in Berlin but destroyed during World War II. It depicted scenes from the life of Christ in a fine linear style using linen chain stitch and silk thread for details. Still essentially Romanesque in style and also Rhenish is the silk antependium (decorative hanging) depicting Christ in Majesty flanked by saints and donors from Rupertsberg (Brussels, Musées Royaux d'Art et d'Histoire), embroidered in metallic threads about 1230.

BIBLIOGRAPHY

Dodwell, C. R. *The Pictorial Arts of the West: 800–1200.* Pelican History of Art. New Haven, Conn.: Yale University Press, 1993, pp. 16–30.

Wilckens, Leonie von. *Die textilen Künste: Von der Spätantike bis um 1500.* Munich: Beck, 1991.

Peter Barnet

SEE ALSO
Charlemagne; Halberstadt

Roriczer, Matthew (ca. 1430–ca. 1495)

A German master builder and printer, Roriczer was a member of a family of master builders associated with Regensburg Cathedral for three generations. Although Roriczer followed his father, Konrad, at Regensburg Cathedral, Roriczer is best known for his publications on architecture. After an early career in which he served as undermaster for his father at the church of St. Lorenz in Nuremberg and worked on the sacristy in Eichstätt, Matthew Roriczer succeeded his father as master builder of the cathedral of Regensburg circa 1476 and spent the remainder of his career in that position.

In 1486 Roriczer published "The Booklet on the Correct Design of Pinnacles" (Büchlein von der Fialen Gerechtigkeit) on his own press. This booklet, consisting of only ten folios, explains how to create the ground plan and, from that, to derive the elevation of a pinnacle using geometry. The language of the booklet is explanatory, spare, and clearly oriented to the practical process of creating the structure. There is great interest in this small piece of writing because it represents one of the first printed accounts by a medieval mason of his methods. In it Roriczer was revealing information, which was previously taught orally and that was the private province of the masons. The Regensburg Ordinance of 1459, a set of professional rules for the masons from many German centers, says that masons should not reveal technical information to nonmasons. An additional value of Roriczer's booklet is that it may describe a construction tradition used by much earlier Gothic builders, active in the thirteenth and fourteenth centuries, who left few written records.

BIBLIOGRAPHY

Frankl, Paul. *The Gothic: Literary Sources and Interpretations Through Eight Centuries.* Princeton, N.J.: Princeton University Press, 1960, pp. 148–150.

Gimpel, Jean. *The Cathedral Builders.* Trans. Carl Barnes. New York: Grove Press; London: Evergreen Books, 1961, pp. 122–126.

Shelby, Lon, ed., trans., and introduction. *Gothic Design Techniques: The Fifteenth-Century Design Booklets of Mathes Roriczer and Hanns Schmuttermayer.* Carbondale: Southern Illinois Press, 1977.

Susan L. Ward

SEE ALSO
Gothic Art and Architecture; Nuremberg; Regensburg

Rosary

From its remote beginnings in the seventh century, the Ave Maria (Hail Mary) prayer went on to become the most popular extraliturgical devotion of the Catholic Church. In its earliest form the prayer combined the Angel Gabriel's salutation in Luke 1: 28 with Elizabeth's words to Mary in Luke 1: 42. By the twelfth century the Ave salutation had become a popular way of greeting images of the Virgin. In the widely circulated thirteenth-century Marian miracle story, "Aves Seen as Roses" (*Marien Rosenkranz*, or "Mary's Rosary" in the Middle High German *Passional* "Passion Book"), 50 Ave-salutations are miraculously transformed into a rose chaplet. Three chaplets of 50 Aves—a substitute for the 150 Psalms—constituted a "psalter of Our Lady." In other forms, repetitions of the phrase "Ave Maria" were paired with 150 verse epithets for the Virgin. At least six Middle High German rosaries and Marian Psalters of this type can be found in manuscripts of the thirteenth and fourteenth centuries. Later, narrative meditations on the life of Christ came to be paired with repetitions of the Aves. A version with 50 such tags composed by Dominic of Prussia (1384–1460) is found in numerous fifteenth-century manuscripts and incunabula.

Around 1470 the Dominican Alanus de Rupe (1428–1475) tried to revive the older Marian Psalter form by founding a Brotherhood of Our Lady's Psalter at Douai. A more successful confraternity enrolling over 100,000 members within seven years was established in 1475 by Jacob Sprenger in Cologne and went on to become the largest such sodality. Although local chapters featured divergent methods of saying the devotion, the shorter form with fifteen meditations became the most popular and was made official by papal proclamation in 1569.

BIBLIOGRAPHY

Esser, Thomas. "Über die allmähliche Einführung der jetzt beim Rosenkranz üblichen Betrachtungspunkte." *Der Katholik* 30 (1904): 98–114, 192–217, 280–301, 351–373; 32 (1905): 201–216, 252–266, 323–350; 33 (1906): 49–66.

Winston, Anne. "Tracing the Origins of the Rosary: German Vernacular Texts." *Speculum* 68 (1993): 619–636.

Anne Winston-Allen

SEE ALSO
Mariendichtungen

Rostock

A city in northern Germany on the Warnow River and Baltic Sea, Rostock was founded as part of the German expansion into Baltic trade, which took place in the late twelfth and thirteenth centuries. Around 1200 a community of German merchants settled in Rostock, an area with a previous Slav town that had a market popular with Scandinavians. Rostock was recognized by the princes of Mecklenburg in 1218, and was granted a town council of ten and the law code of Lübeck. By 1262 two nearby small towns had been amalgamated with Rostock into a single city, and by circa 1300 a city wall enclosing all three settlements had been built. Rostock's prosperity and architectural character were determined by its role in the Hanseatic League, a trade consortium that flourished from the thirteenth through the fifteenth centuries, although in the late fourteenth century Rostock's wealth was augmented through the city's becoming a base for Baltic pirates.

As befits an important Hansa city, fine buildings in *Backsteingotik* (Gothic brick) characterize the medieval architecture of Rostock. This style, characteristic of northern Germany, uses locally manufactured brick instead of the stone more common in southern Germany and elsewhere. The Marienkirche (church of the Virgin), begun in 1230, is one of the most impressive medieval buildings in Rostock. It is a merchants' church, indicating the importance of this group as architectural patrons in Rostock, and is located next to the market square and Rathaus (town hall). The Marienkirche in Rostock is modeled on the Marienkirche in Lübeck, and both churches have multipart rib vaulting influenced by French Gothic architecture, perhaps through such intermediaries as the cathedral of Tournai, and east ends characterized by French-style radiating chapels. But unlike its counterpart in Lübeck, the Marienkirche in Rostock is a hall church, with a transept and aisles the same height as the nave. The Marienkirche in Rostock retains an original bronze font from 1290, which attests to continued north German expertise in that medium. The covered font is supported by figures representing the rivers of paradise and decorated with biblical scenes, which continue on the ornate cover with depictions of New Testament episodes. The church also contains an altar dating from around 1500 dedicated to St. Roch, protector from the plague; it is decorated by attenuated figures and detailed architectural elements.

Other churches in Rostock are less innovative than the Marienkirche. St. Nicholas, begun in the mid–thirteenth century, was built in brick in a Romanesque style. The church of St. Peter, constructed circa 1300, abandoned the French-influenced plan of the Marienkirche for a simple apse, rectangular aisled nave, and hall church form in *Backsteingotik*. Additional religious architecture in Rostock was created by the Cistercians and the mendicants, religious movements important in late medieval cities. The Cistercian women's convent of the Holy Cross founded in 1270 by the Danish Queen Margaret had a brick church, a large cloister, and additional monastic buildings, including a refectory decorated with painted floral motifs. The Franciscans and the Dominicans also had religious establishments in Rostock from the thirteenth century. Fragments remain from the Franciscan cloister St. Catherine's, founded in 1243, and the Dominican St. John's monastery, founded in 1256.

Medieval Rostock also had a considerable number of secular buildings, as was common in important Hansa towns. The city wall was erected around 1300. A section of the wall still remains, with two original medieval towers. Although the medieval Rathaus (town hall) was encased in an eighteenth-century facade, it preserves a mid–thirteenth-century core. Turrets and the tops of the tracery of lancet windows may be seen projecting above the later facade. Rostock also contained a large number of merchant's houses in the *Backsteingotik* style. A particularly fine example is the Kerkhofhaus from the first half of the sixteenth century, with its elaborate brick arcading, ornamented with terra-cotta plaques of male heads, female figures, mermen, and foliate motifs.

The university of Rostock, the oldest on the Baltic, was founded in 1419. Rostock was also important as an early center of printing in the Baltic region. In 1476 the Brethren of the Common Life set up a printing press in their monastery, which specialized in humanist works in German and Latin, as befitted a printing press in a university town.

BIBLIOGRAPHY
Ohle, Walter. *Rostock.* Leipzig: Seemann, 1970.
Piltz, George, and Constantin Beyer. *Backsteingotik: Zwischen Lübeck und Wolgast.* Würzburg: Stürtz, 1995.

Susan L. Ward

SEE ALSO
Cistercian Art and Architecture; Franciscan Art and Architecture; Gothic Art and Architecture; Hanseatic League; Lübeck

Rothenburg ob der Tauber

This small Franconian market town retains much of its medieval and Renaissance character because of its own historical misfortunes. During the Thirty Years' War (1618–1648), Protestant and Catholic armies repeatedly passed through its lands. Rothenburg was plundered by the count of Tilly's troops in 1631; three years later the town council paid the Swedish army not to attack. Since the town's economy never fully recovered, there were no funds for new construction. Rothenburg began in the ninth century as a fortification on a ridge about 305 feet (100 meters) above the Tauber River. With the death of the last count of Comburg-Rothenburg in 1116, control of Rothenburg gradually passed in 1142 to the Hohenstaufens, who immediately built a castle here. Emperor Rudolf of Habsburg elevated Rothenburg to an imperial free city in 1274. Emperor Charles IV sold the castle site to the city following the earthquake of 1356. Other than the Rödertor (Röder Gate) and the Weißertorturm (White Gate Tower), which date to the twelfth century, most of the city's extensive walls are from the fifteenth century. During Heinrich Toppler's tenure as mayor (1373–1408), Rothenburg reached its peak. In 1525 the city backed the peasants of the Tauber valley in their revolt against the bishop of Würzburg and other lords and was subsequently punished. The council embraced Lutheranism in 1544. It lost its free status in 1802–1803 when it was incorporated into the kingdom of Bavaria.

St. Jakob's, Rothenburg's parish church, stands on the site of a late-twelfth-century structure. The bishop of Würzburg transferred control of the church to the Knights of the Teutonic Order in 1258. They were the custodians of the Holy Blood Chapel, which houses a reliquary cross containing drops of Christ's blood. Within a decade this chapel was the focus of an active pilgrimage. In 1258 St. Jakob, formerly a dependent of nearby Detwang, became a parish church. The new structure reflects its three distinctive audiences. The Teutonic Knights erected the deep eastern choir and the two flanking towers around 1340 for their own services. The parishioners built the nave and aisles, which were largely finished in 1436 but not consecrated until 1471. Niclas Eseler and his son, Niclas the Younger, constructed the airy western choir (1452–1471) above an existing street for the Brotherhood of the Holy Blood when the old chapel proved too small for the number of pilgrims. The net vaults were completed in 1528. Between 1499 and 1506 the local joiner Erhard Harschner and the famed Würzburg sculptor Tillmann Riemenschneider created the monumental Holy Blood Altarpiece. Two angels holding the relic are incorporated into the elaborate superstructure of the altar. The artists structured the frame for the Last Supper in the corpus as a fictive room with bull's-eye windows. This innovation permits light to surround and accent Riemenschneider's expressive limewood statues. The wings of the church's high altar, located in the eastern choir, are signed and dated (1466) by Friedrich Herlin, a former Rothenburg citizen who had become the town painter of Nördlingen. His scenes depicting the lives of the Virgin on the interior and of St. Jakob (James Major) on the exterior reveal strongly the influence of Rogier van der Weyden. The sculptors are unknown, though Simon Lainberger of Nuremberg possibly carved the Crucifixion group while the style of the other standing saints suggests an Ulm master. The joiner was Hans Waidenbach of Nördlingen. The east choir retains its three stained glass windows including its central light with typological scenes (ca. 1340). The other pair date around 1400 and to the later fifteenth century. Much of St. Jakob's decoration was removed during the Reformation and especially after 1556, when this became a Lutheran church. Herlin's wings were painted over only to be rediscovered in 1922. New side galleries were built in 1614 but removed in the nineteenth century. Nevertheless, the church still contains its sacrament house (ca. 1400) and several notable sculptures.

Rothenburg's other religious establishments included a Franciscan monastery and a Dominican convent. The early Gothic-style Franciscan church, begun in 1285 and completed in the middle of the fourteenth century, still contains its screen separating the nave from the monks' choir, which was consecrated in 1309. The Dominican nunnery was founded in 1265 for local noble women and suppressed in 1524–1525. Today housing the Reichsstadtmuseum (Munincipal Museum), the church still retains its noted Passion Altarpiece from 1494, whose painted panels Hartmut Krohm attributes to Martin Schwarz, a local Franciscan monk. This is one of the few projects that one can link with a local artist. Rothenburg seems to have been too small to sustain a notable painter, sculptor, or architect, so that, repeatedly, the town had to import its art. Riemenschneider, working in the episcopal seat of Würzburg, supplied no fewer than seven altarpieces, including two for St. Jakob's, one for the Dominicans, and two for the Franciscans.

The city hall consists of two parallel buildings. The western wing dates to the years just after the fire of 1240. Leonhard Weidmann's imposing eastern wing from 1572 faces Rothenburg's main square and replaces an earlier structure that burned in 1501. Notable among Rothenburg's rich stock of houses, most of which are medieval or

Renaissance, is Heinrich Toppler's small castle from 1388, a stone and half-timber structure perched in the middle of the Tauber River.

BIBLIOGRAPHY

Bier, Justus. *Tilmann Riemenschneider,* 4 vols. Würzburg: Verlagsdruckerei, and Vienna: A. Schroll, 1925–1978.

Braunfels, Wolfgang. *Die Kunst im Heiligen Römischen Reich Deutscher Nation.* 6 vols. Munich: Beck, 1979–1989, vol. 3, pp. 193–200.

Krohm, Hartmut. *Die Rothenburger Passion im Reichsstadtmuseum Rothenburg-ob-der-Tauber.* Rothenburg: Verlag des Vereins Alt-Rothenburg, 1985.

Müller, Rainer A., and Brigitte Buberl, eds. *Reichsstädte in Franken.* 3 vols. Veröffentlichungen zur bayerischen Geschichte und Kultur 14–15. Munich: Haus der Bayerischen Geschichte, 1987.

Rau, Johannes, and Gerd Wachowski, eds. *500 Jahre St. Jakob Rothenburg o. d. T. 1485–1985.* Rothenburg: Evangelisch-Lutherische Kirchengemeinde St. Jakob, 1985.

Ress, Anton. *Die Kunstdenkmäler von Mittelfranken 8/1: Stadt Rothenburg o. d. T.—Kirchliche Bauten.* Munich: R. Oldenbourg, 1959.

Ulrich, Eva. *Die Jakobskirche in Rothenburg ob der Tauber.* Königstein im Taunus: Röster, 1975.

Jeffrey Chipps Smith

SEE ALSO

Deutschorden; Herlin, Friedrich; Riemenschneider, Tillmann; Würzburg

Rottweil

Located some 60 miles (100 kilometers) south-southwest of Stuttgart, Rottweil has an unusually complicated early history. Archaeological excavations carried out since 1967 have located the oldest settlement, from the second half of the sixth century B.C.E., on the left bank of the Neckar on a bluff surrounded on three sides by a bend in the river. After 72 C.E., the Romans erected a number of forts in this area; the largest, situated on a flatter plain on the opposite side of the river and several hundred meters to the south, developed into a significant town known as the Arae Flaviae. Coins from the late third and fourth centuries indicate a continued Roman presence, although the town's high point had certainly passed. The name Rotuvilla, which first appears in 771, and numerous tombs and building remains, including those of a stone structure, from the eighth century indicate Frankish re-settlement of the area. The scholars Gildhoff and Hecht suggest that still intact Roman roads may have made the advantageous position on the river even more attractive. The Carolingians administered their local territories from a palace erected on the left side of the Neckar along the Roman road, and both Carolingian and Salian rulers are documented visiting Rottweil, sometimes for longer periods.

The settlement flourished in the twelfth century. A large area around the palace known as the Mittelstadt (middle town) was walled, and a mint was established, perhaps as early as 1160 or 1170. This thriving town was abandoned about 1200, however; evidence points to a devastating fire as the cause. Instead of rebuilding on the same site or the Roman site across the river, where a small settlement, the so-called Altstadt (old town), was located, it was decided to move a kilometer to the north to a dramatic site on a high bluff almost entirely surrounded by the river and therefore easily defensible. The city center sat to the west of the entry into this horseshoe-shaped area, and in 1241 Frederick II remitted the city's taxes for use in building the defensive wall. At the center of town, streets were laid out in a grid pattern that is still visible, and buildings, including an unusual number of structures in stone, were built on oblong lots. From the thirteenth century, the city seems to have enjoyed increasingly independent forms of self-government; in the fourteenth century, the city was granted the status of an imperial free city (freie Reichsstadt). From 1299, it was the site of an important imperial court with jurisdiction over a large part of southwestern Germany.

At the end of the thirteenth and in the first half of the fourteenth century, galleries were built near the main intersection to serve as commercial centers. The two main religious foundations—the Heilig Kreuz Münster (the church of the Holy Cross) and the Kapellenkirche (chapel church), stand to the northwest and southeast of this intersection, respectively. The former, first erected with a Romanesque nave and a Gothic choir in the first half of the thirteenth century, was rebuilt in the fifteenth century, starting with the choir. The present, late Gothic nave with net vaults, dated 1497–1534, was erected according to the plans of Aberlin Jörg, who had built the similar Stiftskirche in Stuttgart. The Kapellenkirche stands on the site of—and probably gets its name from—an earlier pilgrimage church dedicated to the Virgin. A single tower, taken as a symbol of increased civic self-consciousness, was added beginning about 1325; Winfried Hecht has cautiously associated it with a Master Heinrich of Basel, probably a member of the Parler family, who is documented in Rottweil in 1342. By 1364, the nave and choir had been replaced. Aberlin Jörg added the two upper stories to the tower about 1473 and rebuilt the choir between 1478 and 1483. The three portals of the tower and the surrounding walls are decorated with an elaborate program of sculptures from the 1330s. The scenes from the life of Christ, apostles, and prophets can be attributed to several masters; the work of the most important, together with that of some of the same assistants who had aided him at Rottweil, also appears on the north portal of the cathedral at Augsburg.

The Dominicans were given an especially important site at the north edge of town, closing off the main axis out of town in this direction. Their new church was built beginning about 1266 and dedicated probably in 1282. As typical of Mendicant architecture of this region and elsewhere, the flat-roofed nave was separated from the narrow, vaulted choir by a choir screen. In the second half of the eighteenth century, the nave was completely rebuilt in the baroque style and the choir remodeled. The chapel dedicated to Saint Lawrence Lorenzkapelle, a late Gothic funerary chapel at the northwest edge of town, now houses the sculpture from the tower of the Kapellenkirche and other local works.

BIBLIOGRAPHY

Gildhoff, Christian, and Winfried Hecht. "Rottweil" in *Stadtluft, Hirsebrei und Bettelmönch: Die Stadt um 1300,* ed. Marianne and Niklaus Flüeler. Stuttgart: Theiss, 1992, pp. 108–125.

Hecht, Winfried. "Über Baumeister, Datierung und Brautrelief des Rottweiler Kapellenturms." *Alemannisches Jahrbuch* (1973/1975): 558–571.

Stähle, Willi. *Steinbildwerke der Kunstsammlung Lorenzkapelle Rottweil.* Veröffentlichungen des Stadtarchivs Rottweil 3. Rottweil: Stadtarchiv Rottweil, 1974.

Joan A. Holladay

SEE ALSO

Augsburg; Basel; Franciscan Art and Architecture; Liturgy, Furniture; Parler Family; Stuttgart; Town Planning and Urbanism

Rudolf von Ems (ca. 1190–ca. 1255)

The presumably Swiss author from Hohenems wrote five surviving quasi-historical epics in verse for important men close to the Staufer court (at first, during the reign of King Heinrich VII) and eventually for King Konrad IV himself, whom he might have accompanied on a campaign to Italy, where the king (and maybe the poet) died in 1254.

The works (based on French and Latin sources) in approximate chronological order are *Der gute Gerhard (Good Gerard)*, commissioned by Rudolf von Steinach (ministerial of the bishop of Constance) circa 1220; *Barlaam und Josaphat*, after a literary model of abbot Wido von Cappel (near Zürich); *Alexander*, without a known commissioner; *Willehalm von Orlens*, commissioned by Konrad von Winterstetten at the Staufer court in Swabia, before 1243; the French source was provided by Johannes von Ravensburg's *Weltchronik*, dedicated to King Konrad IV. Another theory is that Rudolf did not go to Italy and continued the *Weltchronik* beyond "Salomo," after which he added still two later excursus to *Alexander*. If Rudolf had also produced earlier courtly works, which he claimed in *Barlaam und Josaphat*, that is unproven. But an *Eustachius*-Legend, mentioned in *Alexander*, is lost.

Der gute Gerhard, after an unknown source, demonstrates courtly humanity toward a heathen (two manuscripts are extant). *Barlaam und Josaphat* describes the Indian Legend of Buddha after a Latin source of 1220–1223. (Extant in 47 manuscripts; the only illustrated manuscript, of 1469, was done by Diebold Lauber, with 138 drawings.) Alongside the *Laubacher Barlaam* of the Freisinger Bishop Otto II, Rudolf's is the second German version. In *Eustachius*, a high Roman general under Trajan converted to Christianity. *Willehalm von Orlens* is neither an *aventiure*, or courtly chivalric romance (Wolfram), nor a chanson de geste (heroic ballad, like Guillaume), but rather basically a courtly *Fürstenspiegel*, or guide for nobility. An ideal government, Staufer knighthood, exists also in France and England. (Of the twenty-nine extant manuscripts, seven are illustrated, mostly by Diebold Lauber.) A shorter narrative in rhymed couplets, *Wilhalm von Orlens*, was created in the fifteenth century, extant in four manuscripts and one print of Anton Sorg (Augsburg, 1491). Hans Sachs based his drama of 1559 on this print. In 1522, an anonymous Swabian writer reworked Rudolf's epic as strophic form in the Herzog-Ernst-Tone, a thirteen-line pattern. The story is also recounted in pictures, on a tapestry in Frankfurt of the first quarter of the fifteenth century, in fifteen scenes. The couple Wilhelm and Amelie is also found as a fresco at Runkelstein castle near Bozen. In *Alexander*, Rudolf wanted to portray history, not a heroic or courtly romance. Ten volumes were planned, which were stopped in the middle of the sixth book, however (death of Darius and victory over his followers). The two main sources were the *Historia de preliis* and Curtius Rufus. Fairy-tale portions were left out. (Of the three extant manuscripts, the Munich State Library manuscript was illustrated by Diebold Lauber.) The *Weltchronik* ends, after thirty-six thousand verses, in the middle of the Jewish history of the kings. (Over one hundred manuscripts are extant, as well as reworkings and rhymed bibles.)

BIBLIOGRAPHY

Green, Dennis. "On the Primary Reception of the Works of Rudolf von Ems." *Zeitschrift für deutsches Altertum* 115 (1986): 151–180.

Haug, Walter. "Wolframs 'Willehalm'—Prolog im Lichte seiner Bearbeitung durch Rudolf von Ems," in *Kritische Bewährung: Beiträge zur deutschen Philologie: Festschrift für Werner Schröder zum 60. Geburtstag*, ed. Ernst-Joachim Schmidt. Berlin: E. Schmidt, 1974, pp. 298–327.

Walliczek, Wolfgang. "Rudolf von Ems," in *Die deutsche Literatur des Mittelalters. Verfasserlexikon*, ed. Kurt Ruh et al. Berlin: de Gruyter, 1991, vol. 8, coll. 322–345.

Wenzel, Horst. "Höfische Geschichte." *Europäische Hochschulschriften* 1, 284 (1980): 71–87.

Wunderlich, Werner. *Der 'ritterliche' Kaufmann: literatursoziologische Studien zu Rudolf von Ems' "Der guote Gerhart."* Scriptor. Hochschulschriften. Literaturwissenschaft 7. Kronberg im Taunus: Scriptor, 1975.

Zaenker, Karl A. "The Manuscript Relationship of Rudolf von Ems' *Barlaam und Josaphat*." Ph.D. diss., University of British Columbia, 1974.

Sibylle Jefferies

SEE ALSO
Chronicles, World, German; Lauber, Diebold; Runkelstein; Staufen

Rule of Saint Benedict
See Benedict, Rule of Saint.

Runes
Runes form a writing system, an alphabet, used by some of the early Germanic peoples, mostly for epigraphic, but also occasionally for apotropaic (protective) purposes. They are derived from a Greco-Roman base, but specific

details are argued, as are also dates. It is usually assumed that the runes arose somewhere during the first century C.E., and most runologists today seem to lean toward derivation in the West, from North Italic alphabets. The runes were in use until early modern times in Scandinavia, so that they naturally developed geographical and temporal variants, ligatures, and the like. The word *rune* itself derives from a Germanic stem meaning something like "secret, secret meeting."

We usually divide runes into "older runes," three rows of eight each: *fuþarkgw—hnijėpRs—tbemłŋdo,* and "younger runes," a sixteen-rune alphabet: *fuþ ark— hnias—tbmly,* then divided into various national and subnational forms: Old English, Swedish, Danish, bind runes, dotted runes, staveless runes, and the like. Runes might be written in either direction, and even *boustrophedon* (one line one direction, next line opposite) inscriptions are known.

The runes found in German territory are all older runes (from the series of twenty-four), dating from circa 500 C.E. to circa 700 C.E. It is quite difficult to decide which runes are "German," and the term "South Germanic Runes" is used by many. There are fewer than fifty such runic inscriptions, mostly on movable objects, so that the place of the find cannot be used as a criterion in assigning them, and most of them consist of what seem to be names—of owners, rune masters, recipients, deities— one cannot say with certainty. A number of alphabet series are attested.

Though the use of runes thus ceased quite early in Germany, antiquarian interest in runes begins quite early also, even in Merovingian times (Venantius Fortunatus), but particularly under the Carolingians, with authorities such as Hrabanus Maurus, Alcuin, and Walahfrid Strabo. The so-called *Abecedarium Nordmannicum* offers in a mixed language (mostly Old Saxon) a short treatment of the younger runes and their names. The *Abrogans* (an eight-century Latin-German glossary) offers us the word *runstaba* as a gloss for Latin *litterae* (letters). The earlier use of runes is probably attested by such words as *rizan* (to write, scratch, Otfrid). Occasionally, runes were used within the Latin alphabet, for example, the *w*-rune in the *Hildebrandslied* manuscript, or the *g*-rune for *ga* in an Old High German prayer *(Wessobrunner Gebet),* and we have a letter from Swedish King Ansgar to Louis the Pious in 832 that mentions runes (doubtless Swedish).

Runes continued to be mentioned as an object of antiquarian interest and to be used in magical and medical texts throughout the Middle Ages. The so-called *Alcuin Treatise* of Manuscript 270 at St. Gall (Stiftsbibliothek) tells about the use of runes in a kind of rudimentary cryptography.

BIBLIOGRAPHY

Antonsen, Elmer. *A Concise Grammar of the Older Runic Inscriptions.* Tübingen: Niemeyer, 1975.

Arntz, Helmut. *Handbuch der Runenkunde,* 2d ed. Halle: Niemeyer, 1944 [Many prefer the first edition of 1935.].

Arntz, Helmut. "Die deutschen Runen," in *Deutsche Philologie im Aufriss,* ed. Wolfgang Stammler, 2d ed., vol. 3. Berlin: Erich Schmidt, 1957, pp. 1849–1870.

Krause, Wolfgang. *Die Runeninschriften im älteren Futhark.* 2 vols. Abhandlungen der Akademie der Wissenschaften in Göttingen. Philologisch-Historische Klasse, Dritte Folge 65. Göttingen: Vandenhoeck and Ruprecht, 1966.

James W. Marchand

SEE ALSO

Abrogans; Alcuin; *Hildebrandslied;* Hrabanus Maurus; Otfrid; Sankt Gall; Walahfrid Strabo

Runkelstein

Built in the 1230s, castle Runkelstein (Italian, Castel Roncolo) near Bozen (Italian, Bolzano) in South Tyrol was acquired in 1385 by the brothers Nicolaus and Franz Vintler, wealthy financiers who renovated and expanded the castle, added the Sommerhaus (summer house), and commissioned the extensive program of wall paintings for which the castle is known today. The restoration ordered by Maximilian I *von wegen der guten alten istori* (because of the good, old stories [i.e., the pictorial narratives]) was carried out in 1508 by Marx Reichlich. The north wall of the summer house collapsed in 1868, destroying signficiant portions of all three narrative cycles; Ignaz Seelos's 1857 drawings preserve several of the lost scenes.

The paintings appear to have been executed by local artists, those of the west palace between 1388 and 1395; those of the Sommerhaus and chapel between 1400 and 1407. Most of the chapel paintings can be attributed to the Bozen painter Hans Stocinger. The summer house paintings are stylistically similar, but precise evaluation is impossible, given Reichlich's extensive overpainting and the poor condition of the murals today.

Taken as a whole, the paintings add up to a representation of "courtliness" in terms of around 1400. The murals of the west palace are a direct representation of court culture, with courtly people standing in relaxed poses or engaged in conversation, sports, games, or dance. In one painting, the landscape background includes a realistic depiction of Runkelstein circa 1390; in another, two participants in a tournament are heraldically indentified as the Vintler brothers. The paintings of the Sommerhaus are devoted to historical, legendary, and literary motives. A series of portraits of the Holy Roman emperors stretches along the ground floor wall facing the courtyard; on the gallery wall above, the nine Triads begin with the traditional Nine Worthies and continue with figures from romance (three knights, three pairs of lovers) and heroic literature/popular legend (Germanic heroes, giants, giantesses, and dwarfs).

Inside on the ground floor, green grisaille murals depict scenes from the story of Wigalois, the hero of Wirnt von Gravenburg's early thirteenth-century romance. Twenty-one scenes in two registers, probably about half the original total, survived into modern times; about ten remain today, in poor condition. On the second floor, another set of green grisaille paintings depicts thirteen scenes (originally fifteen) from the story of Tristan and Isolde. In another room on the second floor, a series of colorful murals depicts scenes from the story of Garel from Der Pleier's late-thirteenth-century romance. Of the twenty-two scenes described in the nineteenth century, only about ten are extant today.

The paintings of the chapel include scenes from the legends of Sts. Christopher, Anthony, and Catherine, and a Crucifixion. The walls of the east palace were apparently painted as well, but only unidentifiable traces have survived into modern times.

BIBLIOGRAPHY

Haug, Walter, et al. *Runkelstein: Die Wandmalerei des Sommerhauses.* Wiesbaden: Reichert, 1982.

Loomis, Roger Sherman, and Laura Hibbard Loomis. *Arthurian Legends in Medieval Art.* MLA Monograph Series. New York: Modern Language Association, 1938.

Rasmo, Nicolò. "Runkelstein." *Tiroler Burgenbuch* 5, ed. Oswald Trapp. Bozen: Athesia, 1981, pp. 109–176.

James A. Rushing Jr.

SEE ALSO
Gothic Art and Architecture, Late; Gottfried von Straßburg, *Tristan,* Illustrations

Ruodlieb

The *Ruodlieb* is a Latin poem, probably mid-eleventh-century, in internally rhymed dactylic hexameters ("leonine hexameters"). It is extant only in fragments of two manuscripts, one apparently the poet's autograph, the other a clean copy produced under his direction. The surviving portion has been estimated to be only two-thirds of the original (2,320 verses of approximately 3,850), and even when intact the poem was probably unfinished.

Sometimes considered the earliest courtly romance, the *Ruodlieb* relates the adventures of a knightly hero who leaves his mother and ancestral home because his services as a courtier have brought him feuds rather than rewards. He becomes attached to the court of a foreign king ("the greater king"), is quickly promoted, and soon vanquishes an insurgent ("the lesser king"). Upon receiving a message that his mother needs him and that his opponents have died, Ruodlieb resolves to return home. Offered his choice of wealth or wisdom, Ruodlieb opts for the latter, which he receives in the form of a dozen precepts, but he also is given two loaves of bread that contain a treasure of riches and jewels. Ruodlieb's travels back to his native land begin with episodes (involving a redheaded rascal) that confirm the validity of the first three precepts, but the story then develops independently of the king's counsels. Ruodlieb encounters a nephew of his, they enter a castle, and the nephew falls in love with the daughter of the chatelaine. On arriving home, Ruodlieb announces the wedding. Pressed to take a wife himself, he has a farcical misbetrothal with a woman who turns out to be less than virginal. How the poem ended—if the poet ever completed it—is uncertain. The last two fragments give hints, in a dream that Ruodlieb's mother has and in a prophesy that a dwarf captured by Ruodlieb makes. Evidently Ruodlieb is destined to kill two kings, marry the surviving princess, and inherit the kingdom.

The narrative of the poem was a daring experiment. One indication that the *Ruodlieb* was a work in progress has already been mentioned: the poet starts to use the twelve counsels as a structuring device but then abandons them. Another is detectable in the poet's decision, apparently reached midstream in composition, to name his lead character: he seems to have added the name "Ruodlieb" (whence the title assigned the poem by modern editors) over an erasure in fragment no. 5 and to have employed it regularly only from fragment no. 12 on.

In its style too the poem is exceptional. Although its Latin has been faulted for its woodenness, it is living, much less bound by grammatical purism and emulation of influential classical authors than is usually the case in medieval Latin verse, especially hexameters. The poem also represents a new departure in its central themes, which anticipate those of later courtly romances in Old French and other medieval vernaculars a century or more later. It urges upon lords mercy, restraint, and generosity, and it promises good fortune to those who practice these virtues even in the face of adversity.

BIBLIOGRAPHY

Grocock, C.W., ed. and trans. *The Ruodlieb.* Chicago: Bolchazy-Carducci, 1985.

Haug, Walter, ed. *Ruodlieb. Faksimile-Ausgabe des Codex latinus Monacensis 19486 der Bayerischen Staatsbibliothek München und der Fragmente von St. Florian,* vol. 1 in 2 pts. [introd. and facsimile]. Wiesbaden: Reichert, 1974.

Kratz, Dennis, ed. and trans. *"Waltharius"* and *"Ruodlieb."* New York: Garland, 1984.

Vollmann, Benedikt Konrad, ed. *Ruodlieb. Faksimile-Ausgabe des Codex latinus Monacensis 19486 der Bayerischen Staatsbibliothek München und der Fragmente von St. Florian,* vol. 2, pt. 1 [Latin text]. Wiesbaden: Reichert, 1985.

———. *Ruodlieb.* Darmstadt: Wissenschaftliche Buchgesellschaft, 1993.

Jan M. Ziolkowski

SEE ALSO
Latin Language

Rural Settlement

Rural settlements in medieval Germany were diverse, ranging from hamlets and isolated farmsteads to a variety of planned nuclear villages such as Rundlinge, which had a central common, and Hufendörfer, which were arranged in straight lines. Although the theory has now been abandoned, legal scholars used to argue that these villages evolved from the so-called *Markgenossenschaften,* early medieval communities practicing a form of primitive communism. In Swabia, Bavaria, and Franconia—the heart of Old Germany—there was a long tradition of manorialism (the *Fronhof* system). Elsewhere such as in Saxony and Frisia there were large numbers of free peasants. Everywhere mountain communities tended to remain smaller and more independent.

It is difficult to identify common patterns of change amid this diversity, but generally speaking manorialism declined in the eleventh, twelfth, and thirteenth centuries as the population rose, the three-field system was introduced, and more land was cleared. East of the Elbe and Saale Rivers, a mixed population of indigenous Slavs and German and Dutch settlers was established in planned villages that formed increasingly self-conscious communities as they developed new legal, economic, political, and religious frameworks.

In the late Middle Ages, however, Germany experienced the same loss of population, due to plague and war, and decline in grain prices that affected the rest of Europe. In the heartland this led to the desertion of settlements, a rise in real wages, and greater freedoms as landowners tried to attract laborers and maintain levels of production; but in other regions, especially in the east and southwest, the agricultural crisis led to increased obligations and greater peasant dependence.

BIBLIOGRAPHY

Abel, Wilhelm. *Geschichte der deutschen Landwirtschaft vom frühen Mittelalter bis zum 19. Jahrhundert,* 3d ed. *Deutsche Agrargeschichte,* vol. 3. Stuttgart: Ulmer, 1978.

Bader, Karl S. *Studien zur Rechtsgeschichte des mittelalterlichen Dorfes.* 3 vols. Weimar: Böhlau, 1957, 1962, and 1973.

Genicot, Léopold. *Rural Communities in the Medieval West.* Baltimore: Johns Hopkins University Press, 1990.

Mayhew, Alan. *Rural Settlement and Farming in Germany.* London: Batsford, 1973.

Rösener, Werner. *Peasants in the Middle Ages,* trans. Alexander Stützer. Oxford: Polity Press, 1992 [German *Bauern im Mittelalter.* Munich: Beck, 1985].

David R. Blanks

S

Sachliteratur

The term *Sachliteratur* (literally, literature on a subject area), for which there is no good English equivalent, refers to texts dealing with the natural world and its inhabitants. By convention, fictional literature, history, law, and religion are excluded for various reasons, while science, medicine, and technology are included. German scholars working in the tradition established by Gerhard Eis, the pioneering scholar in studying German *Sachliteratur*, have preferred the terms *Fachprosa* (literally, prose writing in a discipline), *Artes-Literatur*, or *Fachliteratur*, because some medieval systematists categorized such literature according to the seven liberal arts, a corresponding seven mechanical arts, and even a third set of forbidden arts, or *Fächer*. In modern usage, the term *Fachliteratur* refers to specialized literature written for experts, and medieval German texts on scientific, medical, and technical subjects were neither exclusively nor even predominantly written for experts, hence the more inclusive term *Sachliteratur* is preferable.

Before the late twelfth century, German *Sachliteratur* was limited to Latin-German glossaries and a few short texts, often in the form of recipes written on the endpapers or in the margins of Latin manuscripts. Two early medical recipes from a manuscript at Basle, Switzerland, may be the oldest extant prose texts in the German language. The glossaries and other aids to understanding Latin texts continued to be produced throughout the Middle Ages, as did various other kinds of aids for learning Latin. The number and sophistication of Latin-German glossaries continued to grow, and the *Vocabularius Ex quo* (named after its first headword), produced around 1410, is extant in over two hundred manuscripts and forty printed editions from before 1500.

In the decades before and after 1200, anonymous authors first wrote lengthier prose texts in German on secular subjects, namely, the cosmological encyclopedia known as the *Lucidarius,* the medicinal herbal known as the *Older German "Macer,"* and the *Medical Handbook of Master Bartholomew.* The first two show signs of having been created for presentation to courtly audiences, while the last presupposes that there were readers interested in academic medicine in German. All three derive from Latin sources, and they all show signs of significant editorial intervention to adapt to a German-speaking audience. While the *Medical Handbook* by Ortolf of Baierland, written in the second half of the thirteenth century, soon replaced the *Bartholomew* as the most up-to-date medical treatise in German, excerpts from the latter are attested throughout the Middle Ages. The same can be said of the *Lucidarius,* which was superseded by the *Treatise on the Natural World* written by Conrad of Megenberg in the mid-fourteenth century. The variety of medicinal herbals attested after 1300 is so great that it is impossible to summarize their distribution here.

As already noted, medical literature occupied a particularly prominent role in the history of German *Sachliteratur,* with regimens of health, herbals, treatises on particular topics or individual medicinal plants, and surgery handbooks proliferating in the fourteenth and fifteenth centuries. One popular genre was the plague tract, following the appearance of the Black Death in Europe after 1347. While the most efficacious advice was usually the admonition to flee, these texts show how the medical establishment struggled to cope with a sudden, inexplicable, and deadly epidemic. The compilation of treatises into miscellanies—manuscripts containing texts on a variety of subjects—was especially characteristic of the late Middle Ages. These ranged from collections of medical treatises with additional recipes written into the margins, presumably by medical practitioners, to "house books"—collections of medical texts for private use along with treatises on subjects ranging from household management, cooking, agricultural practices, and wine making to veterinary medicine.

Magicians and conjurors were not necessarily distinguished from cheaters and swindlers by members of the late medieval elite, and texts describing their practices are often classified together as the "forbidden arts." In his *Book of All Forbidden Arts,* Johannes Hartlieb (d. 1468), a prominent Munich physician who wrote an overview of magic practices for a patron, Margrave Johann of Brandenburg, describes only methods for conjuring and prognostication. His creation of seven categories, following the seven liberal and seven mechanical arts mentioned above, is sometimes cited in support of dividing *Sachliteratur* into *Fächer.* Astrological prediction was officially one of the forbidden arts, but especially in the fifteenth century it played such a significant role in medical prognostication that astrological medicine assumed a prominent role in medical literature. The gradual expansion of literacy and the introduction of printing in the second half of the fifteenth century expanded the readership for German texts, especially after schools and pedagogical materials began to appear for teaching literacy in German to those with little or no previous knowledge of Latin. Texts describing technical skills date in some instances from the fourteenth century, but these were primarily in areas of direct interest to noblemen or clerics (e.g., veterinary medicine, hunting, hand-to-hand combat, cooking, cloth dyeing). Even these texts do not become common until the fifteenth century. Texts written by experts for fellow specialists are rare before 1400 but become more common before the end of the Middle Ages. One example is the *Book on Grafting and Wine-Making* by Gottfried of Franconia. Gottfried wrote his Latin tract before the middle of the fourteenth century, and it was already translated into German before the end of the century, but there are numerous manuscripts extant from the fifteenth century. Three tracts on using geometry to construct architectural features written and printed in the 1480s by Matthäus Roriczer, a Regensburg architect, fall into the same category.

Other texts, while usually containing technically accurate information, seem aimed at readers interested in learning about subjects of interest to them even though they are not themselves skilled in the area under discussion. There are tracts on gunnery, warfare, mining, distilling, and agriculture that seemingly fit into this category. It is indicative that the massive world chronicle produced in Nuremberg at the end of the fifteenth century by a group of prominent citizens under the leadership of Hartmann Schedel was immediately translated into German. This compendium of medieval knowledge, usually referred to as the *Nuremberg World Chronicle* and available in both Latin and German, marks the apotheosis of German as a language for serious scientific subjects. When German eventually replaced Latin as the language of academic discourse in the eighteenth and nineteenth centuries, the last vestiges of medieval *Sachliteratur* were traceable only in popular literature and beliefs as well as in specific subcultures such as astrology or so-called folk remedies. While these subcultures periodically experience bursts of renewed popularity even today, they also contribute to a skewed sense of the full range and value of medieval *Sachliteratur.*

BIBLIOGRAPHY

Assion, Peter. *Altdeutsche Fachliteratur.* Berlin: Erich Schmidt, 1973.

———. "Fachliteratur," in *Die deutsche Literatur im späten Mittelalter 1250–1370,* pt. 2. *Reimpaargedichte, Drama, Prosa,* ed. Ingeborg Glier. Munich: Beck, 1987, pp. 371–395 [bibliography, pp. 500–505].

Bein, Thomas. *'Wider allen den suhtin'. Deutsche medizinische Texte des Hoch- und Spätmittelalters.* Stuttgart: Helfant-Edition, 1989.

Crossgrove, William. *Die deutsche Sachliteratur des Mittelalters.* Langs germanistische Lehrbuch-Sammlung, vol. 63. Bern.: Lang, 1994.

Eis, Gerhard. *Mittelalterliche Fachliteratur,* 2d ed. Stuttgart: Metzler, 1967.

Haage, Bernhard Dietrich. "Deutsche Artesliteratur des Mittelalters. Überblick und Forschungsbericht." *LiLi. Zeitschrift für Literaturwissenschaft und Linguistik* 13 (1983): 185–205.

Jones, George Fenwick. "Fachschrifttum," in *Dictionary of the Middle Ages,* ed. Joseph R. Strayer, vol. 4. New York: Scribner, 1984, cols. 577a–580b.

Keil, Gundolf, and Peter Assion, ed. *Fachprosaforschung. Acht Vorträge zur mittelalterlichen Artesliteratur.* Berlin: Erich Schmitt, 1974.

Riha, Ortrun. "Kommunikationsprobleme in der medizinhistorischen Mittelalterforschung." *Gesnerus* 51 (1994): 20–33.

Schmitt, Wolfram. *Deutsch Fachprosa des Mittelalters. Ausgewählte Texte.* Berlin: de Gruyter, 1972.

William C. Crossgrove

SEE ALSO
Charms; Education; Encyclopedic Literature, German; Glosses, Old High German; Hartlieb, Johannes; Latin Language; Magic; Magic and Charms, Dutch; Medicine

Sachsenspiegel

See Eike von Repgow.

Saints' Cult

In the fourth century C.E., the cult of the saint developed from the Hellenic cult of the dead. The adoption of this Hellenic ritual by the Christian Church achieved far-reaching effects. Initially, it assisted in the conversion of pagans to Christianity. More important, it gave laypeople real faces to identify with in their quests for holiness and a method by which the church could promote social cohesion. In addition to the miraculous nature of saints and their relics, saints were perceived to be direct links to the divine.

In early Christian development, drama was perceived as an overt act of paganism because it was idolatrous and obscene. Saint Cyprian, bishop of Carthage, introduced this argument against the creation of Christian drama in the third century, and in the fourth century Chrysostom, patriarch of Constantinople, developed it. The identification of drama with paganism held until the tenth century, when the Saxon nun Hrotsvitha von Gandersheim began writing "comedies" and the English monk Ethelwold argued in favor of representative performance to elucidate church liturgy. The reintroduction of drama into Christian practice quickly gained popularity throughout Europe. Plays dramatizing the lives of saints, the Passion, the Harrowing of Hell, and the Last Judgment were widespread until the sixteenth century, when theater shifted its interest to more secular themes.

Medieval German drama is not so much a national literature as a liturgical one. The themes, subjects, and conventions used in it are common to medieval dramatic practices throughout Europe. Medieval German dramatic conventions stem directly from hagiographic conventions contemporary to these miracle plays.

Three salient features of medieval hagiography are the handling of the saintly ego, the experiences of the saints, and the conception of saintly time as paradoxical. The ego of the saint cannot be understood as that of one individual, but as closely linked, through the spirit of the divine, to the egos of other saints and ultimately to that of Christ himself. In addition, such saintly characteristics as grace and virtue cannot be seen, in the classical sense, as being qualities that can be nurtured by the individual. Grace and virtue, in the medieval mind, are perceived as gifts from God. The experiences of saints must be understood as being able to contradict logic. Time cannot be understood in the traditional Christian linear sense. The time of saints exists outside of traditional time. Although saints are categorized as humans, they represent manifestations of the grace of God on Earth as exemplars of ideal human behavior.

Another rhetorical convention common to the literature that surrounds saints is the use of *communio sanctorum* (community of saints): the connecting of the lives of the saints to one another and to the life of Christ through the co-option of experiences of other holy persons and the descriptions thereof.

Thus, the effect sought by liturgical drama and miracle plays was not achieved through the act of representation but through symbolic and stylized logic designed to evince the theological ethos that suffering on Earth led to redemption in the afterlife. In particular the German *Heiligenspiele* (plays of the saints) themselves were not an *imitatio Christi* (imitation of Christ) but a legitimization of the miracle of divine grace operating through the lives of the saints being portrayed.

The most famous German *Heiligenspiel* is the Oberammergau Passionspiel (Passion Play). It was first performed in the Bavarian town of the same name in 1633 to celebrate God's sparing the town from the plague. It has been performed approximately every ten years since that date and, true to its hagiographic origins, it has been rewritten a number of times.

Other German literary texts important to the understanding of the medieval cult of the saint include works by Hildegard von Bingen (1098–1179) and Mechtild von Magdeburg (1207–1282). Hildegard von Bingen's first major literary publication, *Scivias (Know the Ways)*, includes a musical play *Ordo Virtutum (Order of Virtue)* along with descriptions of her visions. Mechthild von Magdeburg, a visionary and bridal mystic, published *Das fließende Licht der Gottheit (The Flowing Light of God)*. The fourteenth-century translation of this text into Middle High German counts among the most forceful examples of women's writing from the Middle Ages.

The literature that surrounds the cult of the saints reflects a received tradition. In this sense, the artistry of the literature is secondary to the importance of the material that is conveyed. Thus, the literature of the saints must be seen as polymorphous, as rising out of the community of believers and changing as the needs of the community change, rather than as a static reflection of the genius of the author. Hence, the lives of saints retain the quality of presence; they never become historical artifacts.

BIBLIOGRAPHY

Brown, Peter. *The Cult of the Saints: Its Rise and Function in Latin Christianity.* Chicago: University of Chicago Press, 1980.

Cross, F.L., ed. *The Oxford Dictionary of the Christian Church.* London: Oxford, 1957.

Heffernan, Thomas J. *Sacred Biography: Saints and Their Biographers in the Middle Ages.* New York: Oxford, 1988.

Newald, Richard. *Geschichte der Deutschen Literatur,* vol. 3, pt. 2, ed. Ingeborg Glier. Munich: Beck, 1987, pp. 134–176, 242–254.

Wilson, Stephen, ed. *Saints and Their Cults: Studies in Religious Sociology, Folklore and History.* Cambridge: Cambridge University Press, 1983.

Audrey Shinner

SEE ALSO

Drama; Drama, Passion Plays; Hildegard von Bingen; Hrosvit of Gandersheim; Mechthild von Magdeburg

Saints' Lives, Dutch

In Middle Dutch literature, stories about the lives of saints play an important role. Not only the legends of local saints but also the lives of saints worshiped by the whole Christian world were adapted for the vernacular language. It is likely that there was already an oral tradition of stories of saints even before they were written down. This article first treats longer *vitae* (Lives), which circulated as independent issues, and second shorter versions, which were collected in often quite substantial anthologies.

The oldest Middle Dutch manuscript, which has been handed down only fragmentarily and which dates from the end of the twelfth century, is also the first example of Middle Dutch hagiography. It is the legend of St. Servatius written in verse by Heinric van Veldeke. About 1170 this poet from the region near the Meuse adapted the *Leven van Sint Servaes (Life of St. Servaes)* from a Latin original, presumably for the use of pilgrims and by order of the countess Agnes van Loon and Hessel, the custos (caretaker) of the church of St. Servaas in Maastricht in which the relics of this bishop were worshiped.

From the thirteenth century, a number of stories of saints written in verse have been passed down. Between 1276 and 1283 the West Flemish poet Jacob van Maerlant adapted the *Leven van Sint Franciscus (Life of St. Francis)* from a Latin biography written in 1261 by Bonaventure and accepted by the general chapter of the congregation of the Minorites in Pisa. Unfortunately, nothing has been preserved of the *Leven van Sinte Clara (Life of St. Clara),* which Maerlant claims to have written. Among mystics, some women from Limburger origin were highly worshiped. Willem van Affligem (1210–1279), abbot of the St. Truiden monastery, adapted the life of Saint Lutgart (1182–1246), abbess of the Cistercian convent of Aywières near Luik, from the Latin *Vita piae Lutgardis (Life of St. Lutgard),* written by Thomas van Cantimpré, a confidant of Lutgart. From this quite substantial *Leven van Sinte Lutgart,* only the second and the third book (together some twenty thousand verses) have been preserved. The same *vita* was again translated into the vernacular for nuns from the convent of Nonnemielen near St. Truiden by a Minorite named Brother Geraert, who came either from East Brabant or from West Limburg. This author also wrote the life of Christina (Kerstine, called "the Wonderful," about 1150–1224) from St. Truiden, who has never been officially canonized. Again a Latin *vita* written by Thomas van Cantimpré was used as a source. Also in the thirteenth century, the anonymous legends of Saint Trudo and Saint Alexius were written, which have been preserved only in fragments. Strictly speaking, the story of the miraculous sea voyage of the Irish abbot Saint Brendan (from Clonfert), which was translated from a Rhenish dialect into Middle Dutch, presumably at the beginning of the thirteenth century, does not belong to the genre of saints' lives.

During the following centuries, lives of saints were mostly written in prose. An important exception to the rule is the anonymous story of St. Kunera from Rheenen and the *Leven van Sint Amand (Life of St. Amand),* written by Gillis de Wevel in 1367, which is more than twelve thousand verses long. Among the rather long prose legends from a more recent date, the lives of Saint Katharina, Saint Hieronymus, and Saint Elisabeth deserve attention. All were written by unknown authors. The legend of the local Saint Godelieve from Gistel (about 1045–1070), which dates back to the fourteenth century, drew attention even outside West- and French-speaking Flanders. Above all, the period of religious reorientation known as *Devotio moderna* (new piety) highly stimulated the spread of lives of saints. That a work like the *vita* of Saint Lidwina from Schiedam (1380–1433), written by Jan Gerlachsz, was very popular is shown by the fact that this work was printed almost immediately after having been written and that it was still being reprinted in the fifteenth century in Gouda and Delft. Anonymous prose legends of Saint Francis, Saint Clara, and Saint Anna were also reprinted repeatedly.

Collecting the lives of saints for compilation started very early. Fragments of the so-called Enaamse Codex, in which, next to other texts, the lives of Saint Katharina, Saint Eustachius, Saint Agatha, Saint Werner, Saint Maria Egyptiaca, and Saint Zosimas, all written in verse, have been handed down, can be dated back as early as to the end of the thirteenth century. Some of these texts were written by a monk from the monastery Enaamse near Oudenaarde, but who composed the others is unknown. Also the *Spiegel Historiael* (*Mirror of History*, 1283–1288) includes numerous lives of saints. A part can be traced back to Jacob van Maerlant. The *Tweede partie* (second part) of this voluminous world chronicle, which almost exclusively contains stories of saints, is attributed to Philip Utenbroecke. It is unknown whether the anonymous author of *Der Ystorien Bloeme* ever succeeded in realizing his ambitious plan to relate the lives of the apostles, the martyrs, the confessors, and the virgins and widows. Fact is that only the first book containing the rhymed lives of the Twelve Apostles (4,280 verses) has been preserved. It is almost certain that the fourteenth-century author was inspired by the work of one of the most important Latin hagiographic collections of his time, i.e., by the *Legenda aurea* (*Golden Legend*) of Jacobus de Voragine (d. 1298).

This *Legenda aurea,* in the vernacular also called *Gulden Legende* (*Golden Legend*), or more often *Passionael,* was extremely popular. Apart from *Der Ystorien Bloeme,* this collection of saints' lives, which originally contained about 180 stories of saints, was presumably translated twice (or perhaps even three times) into Middle Dutch prose. The first adaptation dates back to about 1357 and was carried out by an anonymous monk, perhaps from the Carthusian monastery of Herne, some thirty miles (fifty kilometers) southwest of Brussels. As this monk also translated a number of books from the

Old Testament in 1360, he is often called the "Bible translator of 1360." Unfortunately only a part of the oldest copy of his translation of the *Legenda aurea* (1358) has been preserved. The quite numerous copies, mostly dating from the fifteenth century, vary substantially in composition. From the standard collection of Jacobus de Voragine, stories are regularly left out or are substituted by the lives of other saints, not infrequently local ones. Yet often stories are also divorced from their context and included either alone or in groups in other collections.

Probably about 1400, the so-called northern Dutch translation of the *Legenda aurea* came into being in Holland. It might be that it was a new translation. Another possibility is that someone from north Holland adapted one of the versions of the southern Dutch translation that circulated in Holland, using the Latin text as reference. It is also unclear whether the whole corpus of legends has been adapted or only a part of it. The fact is that no manuscript is preserved that contains a complete northern Dutch translation, whereas a mixture of legends from both the southern Dutch and northern Dutch version are found in a number of manuscripts. The distribution of the northern Dutch translation was restricted mainly to the north of the Netherlands and to the Dutch-German border region, whereas the southern Dutch translation spread all over the Dutch-speaking area, with the exception of Flanders in the southwest. It is not unlikely that this is closely connected with the movement of the *Devotio moderna* (Modern Devotion). The Dutch version was also read and copied in wide areas of Germany. A recent inventory registers about 110 manuscripts, fragments, and printed editions. For the sake of completeness let it be mentioned that in one of the manuscripts the legends of Saint Eustachius, Saint Basilius, and Saint Johannes de Aalmoezenier can be found in still another, perhaps even a third translation.

Parts of the *Vitae Patrum* (Books 1, 2, 5, and 6) with, among others, the life of Saint Anthonius written by Athanasius, the lives of the Desert Fathers written by Timotheus of Alexandria, and other legends have been adapted more than once in Dutch. The oldest translation is again one made by the Bible translator of 1360 and is known by the name of *The Book of Fathers (Der vader boec)*. In this case too a number of texts were translated for a second time in the north, presumably in Utrecht at the beginning of the fifteenth century. A third translation of the *Verba Seniorum (Words of the Elderly)* is supposed to have come to Limburg via a Ripuarian (Rhine Valley) link. The legends of *Der vader boec* were dealt with in exactly the same manner as those taken out of the *Passionael:* some copies contain the complete text of the *Vitae Patrum,* other copies chose only the lives of saints, and again others made another selection within this subgroup. Therefore it is sometimes difficult to distinguish exactly between the traditions of the *Passionael* and *Der vader boec,* respectively.

Gregory the Great's *Dialogi* were also translated twice in Middle Dutch. The first translation was made in 1388 by the Bible translator of 1360, the second probably in the early fifteenth century by an anonymous translator within the sphere of the *Devotio moderna.* The dissemination of excerpts from Gregory's *Dialogi* and other hagiographic sources in Latin sources through a wide variety of texts and collections defies any attempt at surveying, mainly because relevant research is still in progress.

It is strange that among this rich harvest of saints' lives, no story of the Blessed Virgin can be found. Therefore seven dramatized episodes out of the life of Mary, the so-called *Seven Bliscappen (Seven Joys),* out of which every year one episode has been performed in Brussels since 1448, are worth mentioning. Only the first and the last part of this cycle has been preserved. From the sixteenth century, dramatized stories of St. Trudo and St. George (St. Joris) have been handed down.

BIBLIOGRAPHY

Berteloot, Amand. "Herzog Librandus von Burgund. Ein frommer Fürst im Dickicht der niederländischen Legenda aurea-tradition." *Ons Geestelijk Erf* 70 (1996): 121–142.

Beuken, Willem H., ed. *Die eerste bliscap van Maria en Die sevenste bliscap van onser vrouwen.* Culemborg: Tjeenk Willink/Noorduijn, 1978 [*Eerste bliscap*].

Broeder Geraert. *Sinte Lutgart, Sinte Kerstine,* in Maurits Gysseling, ed. *Corpus van Middelnederlandse teksten (tot en met het jaar 1300).* Reeks II: Literaire handschriften. Deel 6. Leyden: Nijhoff, 1987, pp. 3–153.

Claassens, Geert H.M. "*Der ystorien bloeme.* Een mislukte *Legenda aurea*–bewerking in het Middelnederlands?" *Ons Geestelijk Erf* 70 (1996): 99–120.

———. "The *Dialogues* of Gregory the Great in Middle Dutch Literature," in Rolf Bremmer and David F. Johnson, eds. *Gregory the Great and the Germanic World* [forthcoming].

De Bruin, Cebus C., ed. *Middelnederlands geestelijk proza.* Zutphen: Thieme, 1940 [excerpts of some otherwise unpublished "Lives"].

De reis van Sint Brandaan. Een reisverhaal uit de twaalfde eeuw, ed. Willem P. Gerritsen. Amsterdam: Prometheus, 1994 [Saint Brandaan].

Deschamps, Jan, *Middelnederlandse handschriften uit Europese en Amerikaanse bibliotheken.* Leiden: Brill, 1972.

———, ed. "Fragmenten van twee Middelnederlandse levens van Sint-Trudo." *Handelingen der Koninklijke Zuidnederlandse Maatschappij voor Taal-, Letterkunde en Geschiedenis* 16 (1962): 219–284 [Saint Trudo].

Emonds, Edmond M. Th. "De legende van Sinte Kunera in de Middeleeuwen." Ph.d. diss., University of Leyden, 1922 [Saint Kunera of Rheenen].

Enaamse Codex: Gysseling, Maurits, ed. *Corpus van Middelnederlandse teksten (tot en met het jaar 1300).* Reeks II: Literaire handschriften. Deel 1, Fragmenten. The Hague: Nijhoff, 1980, pp. 393–500.

Gillis de Wevel. *Leven van Sint Amand, Patroon der Nederlanden, dichtstuk der XIV^{de} eeuw,* ed. Philip Marie Blommaert. 2 vols. Gent: Vanderhaeghen-Hulin, 1842–1843.

Goossens, Jan. "Die Servatiusbruchstücke. Mit einer Untersuchung und Edition der Fragmente Cgm 5249/18, 1b der Bayerischen Staatsbibliothek München." *Zeitschrift für deutsches Altertum und deutsche Literatur* 120 (1991): 1–65.

Gysseling, Maurits, ed. *Corpus van Middelnederlandse teksten (tot en met het jaar 1300).* Reeks II: Literaire handschriften. Deel 1, Fragmenten. The Hague: Nijhoff, 1980, pp. 526–528 [Saint Alexius].

Heinric van Veldeke. *Sinte Servaes,* ed. Theodor Frings and Gabriele Schieb. *Sente Servas Sanctus Servatius.* Halle an der Saale: Niemeyer, 1956.

———. Maurits Gysseling, ed. *Corpus van Middelnederlandse teksten (tot en met het jaar 1300).* Reeks II: Literaire handschriften, pt. 1, Fragmenten, The Hague: Nijhoff, 1980, pp. 287–298.

Jacob van Maerlant. Sinte Franciscus Leven, ed. Father Maximilianus, O.F.M. Cap. *Sinte Franciscus Leven van Jacob van Maerlant.* 2 vols. Zwolle: Tjeenk Willink, 1954.

Jacob van Maerlant's Spiegel Historiael, ed. Philip Utenbroeke et al. 3 vols. Leyden: Brill, 1863–1879.

Jan Gerlachsz. Sinte Lidwina van Schiedam, ed. Ludo Jongen et al. *Het leven van Liedewij, de maagd van Schiedam.* Schiedam: Fonds Historische Publikaties, 1989.

Jongen, Ludo, "Like a Pharmacy with Fragrant Herbs." The "Legenda Sanctae Clarae Virginis" in Middle Dutch, *Collectanea Franciscana* 65 (1995): 221–245.

———, et al., eds. and trans. *"Het leven van de zalige maagd Sint Clara." De Middelnederlandse bewerking van de "Legenda Sanctae Clarae Virginis" opnieuw naar het handschrift uitgegeven, vertaald en ingeleid.* Megen: San Damiano, 1998 [Saint Clara].

Kalff, Gerrit, ed. *Trou moet blycken. Toneelstukken der zestiende eeuw, voor het eerst naar de handschriften uitgegeven.* Groningen: Wolters, 1889, pp. 81–217 [Saint Trudo, play].

Leendertz, P., ed. *Middelnederlandsche dramatische poëzie.* 2 vols. Groningen: Wolters, 1900–1907, pp. 423–435 [Saint Joris, play].

Oudemans, Antonie C., ed. *Der ystorien bloeme. Dat is: de legende der heiligen, in Dietsche dichtmaat.* Naar het handschrift der Maatschappij van Nederlandsche Letterkunde te Leiden. Amsterdam: Van Langenhuysen, 1855.

Scharpé, Lodewijk, ed. "Sunte Elizabetten legende." *Leuvensche Bijdragen* 5 (1903–1904): 5–140 [Saint Elisabeth].

Scheurkogel, Leonard. "De overlevering van de Noord- en Zuidnederlandse Legenda aurea." *Verslagen en Mededelingen van de Koninklijke Academie voor Nederlandse Taal- en Letterkunde.* Amsterdam, 1997, pp. 60–118.

Van Mierlo, Jozef. *De Letterkunde van de Middeleeuwen,* in Frank Baur et al., *Geschiedenis van de Letterkunde der Nederlanden,* 2 vols. Hertogenbosch: Teulings Uitgevers Maatschappij/Brussels: Standaard Boekhandel [n.d.].

Willem van Affligem. *Sente Lutgart,* ed. Maurits Gysseling. *Corpus van Middelnederlandse teksten (tot en met het jaar 1300).* Reeks II: Literaire handschriften. Deel 5. Leyden: Nijhoff, 1985.

Williams-Krapp, Werner. *Die deutschen und niederländischen Legendare des Mittelalters.* Tübingen: Niemeyer, 1986.

Amand Berteloot

SEE ALSO

Bible Translator of 1360, Dutch; *Devotio Moderna;* Drama, Dutch; Heinric von Veldeke; Jacob van Maerlant

Salians

The Salian (German, *Salier*) dynasty, which produced four kings or emperors in the eleventh and early twelfth centuries, traced its roots back to at least the seventh century to a kinship group *(Adelssippe)* known as the Widonen that held high administrative positions and occasionally occupied the episcopal chair in Trier. At an early date they established a proprietary monastery *(Hauskloster)* at Mettlach on the Saar River, and by 742 or shortly before, they had founded a second such institution at Hornbach in the Bliesgau (Blies District, now in Rheinland-Pfalz). In about 760 a small monastery, that of St. Philip at Zell, west of Worms on the Pfrimm, belonged to the Widonen as well. The main center of Widonen power lay more or less in the area between Metz, Trier, Idar-Oberstein, and Pirmasens.

The Widonen appear as important helpers of the Carolingians. They and other noble families played a major role in building up the Frankish government as the Carolingians once again began to renew lordship rights east of the Rhine. At the end of the eighth century, the Widonen kinship split into various branches that established bases of power in Britanny, in the area of the lower Loire, and above all in the duchy of Spoleto. Duke Wido of Spoleto was ambitious and powerful enough that in 888 he laid claim to the throne of Burgundy. Though this lofty plan failed, he did manage to acquire the imperial crown in 891.

One branch of the family remained in the original homeland, and in the course of the ninth century their lordship spread outward from the Bliesgau (centered at Hornbach, since Mettlach was lost early on to the archbishop of Trier) into the Wormsgau and Speyergau. At the end of the ninth and the beginning of the tenth centuries, we encounter a Count Werner in the Wormsgau (891), Nahegau (891), and Speyergau (906), who was most probably a member of the Widonen kinship and from whom the line of Salian ancestors continues without interruption. Werner appears in the narrative sources as a violent man who gave his support to the Conradian monarchy; he even married one, probably a sister of Conrad I (911–919), which placed his family in the direct vicinity of the king.

Although the German crown passed to Henry I, duke of Saxony, in 919 and, upon his death, to his son Otto I, the Conradings struggled to create a Rhine-Frankish duchy for themselves; their defeat in the rebellion of 939 made way for the rise of the Salians as the dominant family on the Middle Rhine. Count Werner's son Conrad, surnamed "the Red," appears as count in the Nahegau, Wormsgau, and Speyergau, but also in the Niddagau, north of Frankfurt. As early as 941 he appears in the closest proximity of Otto I, and his ties to the Ottonian house were solidified by marriage in 947 to the daughter of Otto I, Liudgard. In 944 (or 945) he obtained the duchy of Lorraine from the king, i.e., the region from Alsace to the mouth of the Rhine, between the Meuse and the Rhine, with the tasks of defending the realm on the west and of subduing the Lotharingian nobility.

But Conrad the Red was perhaps too ambitious, and in 953 he joined a rebellion of Otto the Great's oldest son, Liudolf, against the king. Otto retaliated by stripping Conrad of his duchy in 953/4 and transferring important comital, or ducal, rights in the city of Mainz and in the area of Bingen to the archbishop. Conrad shortly thereafter made peace with the king, and in 955 he led the Frankish forces at the battle of Lechfeld; he died during the conflict and was buried at Worms Cathedral, in a fashion normally reserved for kings and bishops.

By now, Worms had become an important family center. It was the site of a Salian *Grafenburg*, an old Carolingian royal *pfalz*, or fortification, and it was also the center of family property and of important lands held by them. In 956, Conrad's son, Otto II, appears as count in the Nahegau, which he inherited from his father, and in the following years he united the Wormsgau, Speyergau, Niddagau, and other countships between the Neckar and the Rhine (Elsenzgau, Kraichgau, Enzgau, Pfinzgau, perhaps Uffgau)—an almost solid countships-complex in the Middle and Upper Rhine. This accumulation of power caused concern for Emperor Otto II, who, in an effort to remove him from his power base, appointed him duke of Carinthia and margrave of Verona in 978.

Deprived of his dukedom in 985, Otto II returned to his power base on the Rhine. Contemporary sources of the late tenth/early eleventh century refer to him as der Wormser (he of Worms) as a means of distinguishing him from a similarly named duke of Swabia and Bavaria who, like him, was a grandson of Otto the Great. Otto Wormatiensis also appears with the appellation Wormatiensis dux Francorum, a somewhat idiosyncratic term since he in fact had no duchy: he was simply put a "Frankish duke of Worms," and the royal court seems to have accepted this earliest instance of a "titular dukedom" in German history, a dukedom that rested on the ever increasing nobility and comital lordship with its center at Worms.

The prestige of Duke Otto of Worms helps account for the nomination of his son Bruno, now imperial chaplain (Hofkaplan), to be the successor of Pope John XV. He took the name Gregory V, and it was from him that Otto III, his kinsman, received the imperial crown on May 21, 996. His pontificate was painful, however; there

was great resistance from Rome and he was driven out. An antipope (John XVI) was installed briefly, and although Gregory V was restored in February 998, he died in February 999. Sylvester II (Gerbert of Aurillac) succeeded him.

The family position also came under attack closer to home. The concentration of power in the area of Worms inevitably brought about a struggle with the bishop for temporal control. Following the election of Henry II in 1002, the new king heaped favors on the church at Worms that had supported him. With the full backing of Bishop Burchard, King Henry II forced Otto to renounce claims over Worms in October 1002. The decreasing importance of the Salians can also be seen in the fact that, although Otto's son Conrad briefly held the duchy of Carinthia, when Conrad died in 1011, King Henry passed over Conrad Jr. in favor of Adalbero of Eppstein.

The fortunes of the Salians were dramatically altered by the death of Henry II in July 1024, which left the empire in shambles. Seeking a quick solution, the German princes selected Conrad the Elder, cousin to Conrad Jr., as king. He was consecrated at Mainz on September 24, 1024. He had previously married Gisela, daughter of Duke Hermann II of Swabia, to whom he was closely related. Their son, Henry III, succeeded virtually unopposed to the German throne in 1039, but his early death in 1056 left a small boy as heir. Born in 1050, Henry IV had received consecration as future king on July 17, 1054, and assumed personal rule on March 29, 1065, at Worms. His reign was characterized by the rising opposition of the German nobles to Salian policies and by the prolonged struggle with the papacy (particularly with Gregory VII) over the issue of lay investiture of high church offices. The conflict called forth the most bitter exchange of letters, bulls of excommunication, and depositions. For its shear dramatic value, nothing exceeded the picture of the emperor standing outside the walls of Countess Mathilda of Tuscany's fortress at Canossa in early 1077, seeking forgiveness from the pontiff, who was determined to travel to Germany, where he planned to preside over Henry's formal deposition. Canossa prevented that from occurring, and it clearly led to Henry's gaining the upper hand over Gregory. Henry died in August 1106, just weeks after he himself had escaped from confinement.

His son and the last Salian, Henry V, inherited a very different world than the one his grandfather had known. By 1100 the self-awareness of the nobles as representatives of the interests of the empire was on the rise. This required a new set of relationships between the king and the princes. For the ecclesiastical princes this was the Concordat of Worms of 1122; for the lay princes, it meant incorporating them into a new system during the twelfth century, the *Heerschildordnung* (order of the coat of arms). Henry V's death on May 23, 1125, without male heirs gave the German princes the opportunity for a free election: ignoring the blood-right claims of Duke Frederick I of Swabia, who had married Agnes, the daughter of Henry IV, they selected instead Conrad II of Franconia.

The Salian age was one of great building activity in Germany; hardly any Carolingian buildings survived past the mid–eleventh century. Recent scholarship has shown that Conrad II intended from the very beginning that Speyer and not the abbey of Limburg-on-the-Haardt become the family burial place. Speyer appears circa 1000 as a dilapidated bishopric and city, and he breathed new life into it. Construction began in 1025, and by the time Conrad II died in 1039, the crypt was sufficiently completed for his remains to be buried there; his wife, Gisela (d. 1043), and Henry III were buried alongside him. The cathedral was completed and consecrated Oct 4, 1061, by Bishop Gundekar II of Eichstätt. During the reign of his son Henry IV (1080s), however, it was expanded once again, under the direction of the *Bauleiter* Bishop Benno II of Osnabrück (1068–1088), who also built his own cathedral.

BIBLIOGRAPHY

Böhn, Georg Friedrich. "Salier, Emichonen und das Weistum des Pfalzgräflichen Hofes Alzey." *Veröffentlichungen des Instituts für Geschichtliche Landeskunde an der Universität Mainz* 10 (1974): 12–96.

Boshof, Egon. *Die Salier.* Stuttgart: Kohlhammer, 1987.

Büttner, Heinrich. "Das Bistum Worms und der Neckarraum während des früh- und Hochmittelalters." *Archiv für mittelrheinische Kirchengeschichte* 10 (1958): 9–38.

Das Reich der Salier 1024–1125: Katalog zur Ausstellung des Landes Rheinland-Pfalz. Sigmaringen: Thorbecke, 1992.

Weinfurter, Stefan. *Herrschaft und Reich der Salier: Grundlinien einer Umbruchzeit.* Sigmaringen: Thorbecke, 1992.

Paul B. Pixton

SEE ALSO

Burchard of Worms; Canossa; Carolingians; Concordat of Worms; Conrad II; Gregory VII; Henry I; Henry II, Art; Henry III; Henry IV; Investiture Controversy; Lechfield, Battle of; Otto I; Otto II

Salzburg

For much of its history, Salzburg was the residence of the archbishop of Salzburg, one of the most powerful figures in the Holy Roman Empire and ruler of the leading archbishopric in Germany. Often referred to as the "German Rome," the city was a political and cultural center, and especially in the eleventh, twelfth, and thirteenth centuries, its art had a major impact on the painting of Central Europe. The earliest settlement of the city appears to have been a Celtic one around 500 B.C.E. The Romans arrived around 40 C.E. Under the Romans, Christianity was introduced, and catacombs were built around 400 C.E. in the city, which was then known as Iuvavum. Among the

Orational from Salzburg (Munich, Bayerische Staatsbibliothek, Cim. 15902), fol. 72v: initial with Madonna and Child. *Photograph: Bayerische Staatsbibliothek.*

medieval churches, the most important are the monastery of St. Peter, founded around 696 by Saint Rupert, the Nonnberg Convent founded by Saint Erentrud at about the same time, the cathedral, the Franciscan church, and the church dedicated to Saint Michael. It is in connection with the first two that manuscripts and paintings are found today, in part because St. Peter's, the site of a major scriptorium, was the seat of the archbishop, who was also its abbot, for much of the early Middle Ages. Among other projects, the fortress on the Hohensalzburg was begun by Bishop Gebhard in the eleventh century.

Few frescoes remain. At St. Peter's, today a Romanesque church with a Gothic cloister, can be found a personification of the third hour of the monastic offices. This is the sole figure remaining from the twelfth-century redecoration of the church, which took place after a fire in 1127; it is painted in a Byzantinizing style similar to that found in manuscripts produced there at the same time. A mid-thirteenth-century image of St. Mary Magdalen with a donor has been connected with Salzburg manuscripts of that same period. The subject of much greater discussion has been a series of mid-twelfth-century frescoes at the Nonnberg Convent, said to be the oldest convent for women north of the Alps. Although portions of the structure's basis reach back to the Roman period, the present Romanesque building probably dates from the patronage of Henry II and Kunigunde around 1009. The remnants of its extensive fresco program, including the feet of an enthroned figure, can be seen on the west wall, below which is a series of niches with half-length figures of male saints, of which six survive intact. A number of scholars, including Paul Buberl and Otto Demus, have argued that the painters of these frescoes demonstrate a sensitive understanding of Byzantine art, probably transmitted through Italian examples at Venice.

Major activity in manuscript illumination at Salzburg dates from the eleventh century, after monastic life at St. Peter's was reformed from Regensburg in the tenth century following a period of violent upheaval. In several manuscripts dated to this era can be found evidence of both Carolingian and Byzantine models. In the twelfth century a period of spectacular production began, with a noticeable stylistic relationship to both Byzantine art and Italian art.

Manuscripts such as the Walther and Admont Bibles, from the second quarter of the twelfth century, share significant iconographic elements with both English and Byzantine works, and have been at the center of discussion of the history of Bible illustration. They also share a distinctive style that combines aspects taken from Byzantine models with a strong, linear treatment of figures with works such as the Pericope (Gospel Readings for the Mass) of St. Erentrud. Unquestionably the most impressive manuscript from this period is the St. Peter's Antiphonary, painted at mid-century. In this work the illuminators' familiarity with Byzantine facial and drapery types is even more striking. Some of the images are actually tinted drawings, a technique found in other Salzburg manuscripts from the second half of the twelfth century. By 1200 Salzburg illumination reached a superb level in the *Orationale* of Saint Erentrud, a luxurious manuscript that includes images of the Virgin demonstrating a profound familiarity with Byzantine models. The continued production of manuscripts at Salzburg into the middle of the thirteenth century is demonstrated in works such as the "Salzburg Lectionary" and the "Seitenstetten Missal," which has a calendar that directly copies the decoration of the calendar in the *Orationale*. These works mark the continued acquisition of Byzantine and Italian characteristics by Salzburg painters, in this case through the arrival of northern Italian illuminators in Salzburg, along with characteristics of the *Zackenstil* (zigzag style). The association of Salzburg artists with the Wimpassing Crucifixion panel and the stained glass in the upper church at Assisi argues for extensive production of art at Salzburg in the thirteenth century.

BIBLIOGRAPHY

Das Antiphonar von St. Peter: Vollständige Faksimile-Ausgabe im Originalformat des Codex Vindobonensis series nova 2700 der Österreichischen Nationalbibliothek, ed. Franz Unterkircher and Otto Demus. 2 vols. Codices selecti 21. Graz: Akademischer Druck- und Verlagsanstalt, 1974.

Das älteste Kloster im deutschen Sprachraum, St. Peter in Salzburg: 3. Landesausstellung 15. Mai–26. Oktober 1982, Schätze europäischer Kunst und Kultur. Salzburg: Salzburger Landesregierung, Kulturabteilung, 1982.

Berger-Fix, Andrea. "Das Wimpassinger Kreuz und seine Einordnung in die Kunst des 13. Jahrhunderts." *Wiener Jahrbuch für Kunstgeschichte* 33 (1980): 31–82.

Buberl, Paul. *Die romanischen Wandmalereien im Kloster Nonnberg in Salzburg und ihre Beziehungen zur salzburger Buchmalerei und zur byzantinischen Kunst.* Vienna: Anton Schroll, 1910.

Corrie, Rebecca W. "The Seitenstetten Missal and the Persistence of Italo-Byzantine Influence at Salzburg." *Dumbarton Oaks Papers* 41 (1987): 111–123.

Demus, Otto. *Byzantine Art and the West.* New York: New York University Press, 1970.

———. *Romanesque Mural Painting,* transl. Mary Whittall. New York: Harry N. Abrams, 1970.

Die Zeit der Staufer: Geschichte, Kunst, Kultur, ed. Reiner Haussherr. 5 vols. Stuttgart: Württembergisches Landesmuseum, 1977, vol. 1, pp. 569–573, nos. 743–745.

Dodwell, C.R. *The Pictorial Arts of the West 800–1200.* New Haven, Conn.: Yale University Press, 1993.

Martin, Frank. "Die Apsisverglasung der Oberkirche von S. Francesco in Assisi: Ihre Entstehung und Stellung innerhalb der Oberkirchenausstattung." Ph.d. diss., University of Heidelberg, 1991–1992. Worms: Wernersche Verlagsgesellschaft, 1993.

Swarzenski, Georg. *Die Salzburger Malerei von den ersten Anfängen bis zur Blütezeit des romanischen Stils: Studien zur Geschichte der deutschen Malerei und Handschriftenkunde des Mittelalters,* 2 vols. Leipzig: Hiersemann, 1908–1913.

von Eltz-Hoffmann, Lieselotte, and Oskar Anrather. *Die Kirchen Salzburgs: Irdische Metaphern einer überirdischen Welt.* Salzburg: A. Pustet, 1993.

Rebecca W. Corrie

SEE ALSO

Admont; Gothic Art and Architecture; Henry II, Art; Regensburg; Romanesque Art and Architecture

Sammelhandschrift

The term *Sammelhandschrift* refers, most simply, to a manuscript that has more than one text. The term itself can be translated into literal English as "collected manuscript." It contrasts with *Einzelhandschrift* (individual manuscript), referring to a manuscript with one text only. The number of texts in a *Sammelhandschrift* varies greatly; some preserve just two or three texts, while others have hundreds. The maximum number of texts in a manuscript is limited only by physical constraints such as the availability of writing material, the strength and width of the binding, or the size of the script; or by cultural constraints, such as the availability of texts in a given scribal milieu. Perhaps the main factor determining the number of texts in a *Sammelhandschrift* was the goal or intention of the scribe or compiler. Manuscripts whose text collection has some degree of coherence or focus have particular literary or cultural significance. Yet the contents of many *Sammelhandschriften* (plural) were collected randomly or haphazardly, for example, through the uncoordinated actions of several individuals over an extended period. Since many, perhaps most, manuscripts are *Sammelhandschriften,* the term designates a norm of medieval bookmaking. Collected manuscripts arose not only in German, but also in Latin and in the other European vernaculars. Examples of *Sammelhandschriften* are therefore numerous.

Although the word *Sammelhandschrift* is widely used in scholarly writing, its definition offers some surprising complications. For example, the variability of the medieval text, which includes adaptation, merger, fragmentation, and the like, makes the notion of the text itself unstable. For descriptive purposes, variability can make it difficult to count the number of texts present in a collected manuscript. From a more theoretical standpoint, the openness of the text to others in its folio environment may be a far more salient feature of the medieval book than the accumulation of textual units implied by the basic definition of the *Sammelhandschrift.* Glosses, marginalia, and occasional notations are not usually considered texts for the purpose of identifying a *Sammelhandschrift,* although this distinction is arbitrary. It is further doubtful whether a manuscript with a highly intentional composition should be classified as a *Sammelhandschrift,* simply because it has multiple texts. Examples of likely non-*Sammelhandschriften* include manuscripts whose contents are uniform and typically found together, such as the stories of the saints comprising the *Golden Legend;* or collections of Arthurian romances in which each romance has a chapterlike character; or manuscripts whose contents are arranged to follow the liturgical year. Still another complication arises with respect to language. Some scholars use the word *Mischhandschrift* (mixed manuscript) to designate a manuscript with both German and Latin texts, reserving *Sammelhandschrift* for manuscripts in either language exclusively. A distortion arises from this seemingly simple distinction, though, when a single Latin text or text cluster turns up in an otherwise German collection, or vice versa. Such occurrences are common. These complications indicate the poverty of our vocabulary for talking about the contents of medieval books and the rudimentary stage of our understanding of the manuscript's cultural dynamics—the factors that influenced their production and their use.

The concept of the *Sammelhandschrift* belongs fundamentally to the realm of bibliography. Decades of philological effort have solved most of the descriptive problems arising from collected manuscripts. A description of a manuscript indicates whether it is a *Sammelhandschrift* along with notes about the binding, materials, script, layout, marks of ownership, and so on. Each text is then enumerated, often with folio location, opening lines, manuscript and modern research titles, and a listing of other manuscripts in which each text is found. Particularly thorough descriptions also include references to important scholarship on individual texts. Such *Sammelhandschrift* descriptions are found in catalogues of manuscript collections, as well as in the apparatus of scholarly editions. Even when only one text from a *Sammelhandschrift* is edited, it has become standard practice to describe the entire manuscript in this manner. Bibliographic descriptions are essential because they provide a sense of the scope and diversity of the medieval book to readers who may rarely come into contact with the actual manuscript. They also make known the single text's most immediate historical context, the one offered by the collected manuscript.

This high bibliographic standard has developed hand in hand with an increasing awareness of the importance of *Sammelhandschriften* for rethinking aspects of medieval culture and history. Scholars in several text-based fields of medieval studies, working in a variety of medieval time periods, have become interested in the way texts are bundled in manuscripts as a key to how knowledge was organized. This research energy is especially productive for the field of vernacular cultural studies, with a focus on the later Middle Ages. In the fourteenth and fifteenth centuries, the use of German and other vernaculars as the written medium of all kinds of knowledge and information—religious, legal, medical, political, literary, etc.—simply exploded. This expanded use of German came in the wake of the disintegration of the cultural synthesis of the thirteenth century, in which an elite public produced, through patronage and direct authorship, and consumed, a stable set of literary genres. As more and more was written in German, and as the use of paper and the spread of literacy made manuscript production and ownership more common, manuscripts became ever more diverse in their contents. Text diversity is not necessarily randomness, though. Many *Sammelhandschriften* are a synchronic cross section of their historical moment of production and use. What has been called the typology of the *Sammelhandschrift,* or the stable "symbiosis" of text types in many manuscript collections, is the starting place for a cultural history of the text grounded in actual reading and bookmaking practices.

We are only beginning to know how to "read" *Sammelhandschriften* as cultural indices, aided by the publication of key *Sammelhandschriften* in their entirety. The rewards for this effort are significant. For example, *Sammelhandschriften* reveal aspects of performance when the sequence of texts reflects a performer's repertoire. The Middle Dutch Van Hulthem manuscript, dated about 1400, preserves the oldest known secular dramas from the German territories. These are paired so that a serious drama, usually on a courtly theme, is followed by a farce with a *märe*-like (comic) plot. These pairings represent the way the dramas were presented to medieval audiences. The entire group of drama pairs in van Hulthem was almost certainly copied from the repertoire of a theater company.

It is significant that whoever compiled the Van Hulthem manuscript kept these pairings so they became part of the reading experience for the manuscript's owners and users. The concept of reading experience is one of the most important ideas arising from the study of one important group of late medieval *Sammelhandschriften*—those with short texts in couplets. The notion of reading experience implies that texts in juxtaposition interpret each other, or resonate together, so that the process of sequential reading adds up to more than the mere sum of random parts. Some of the juxtapositions, such as the combination of eulogies with discourse on courtly love, are standard. They reveal not only the expectations of medieval readers but also tell modern readers far more about the reception of these genres (i.e., that a lover's absence was commensurate with a lover's loss through death) than could the study of either genre in isolation. Other juxtapositions one finds in *Sammelhandschriften* were clearly ad hoc but striking in their pointedness. By far the most common way of combining texts in *Sammelhandschriften* was through thematic pairing to form dyads. Dyads represent a textual equivalent of the couplet rhyme, and show how variance could occur among texts as well as among versions of the "same" text.

Along with readership experience, the concept readership practice has emerged from the study of *Sammelhandschriften.* Important insights have been achieved through the study of Middle English collected manuscripts, and these insights can be extended in the future to German manuscripts as well. Readership practice refers to all the ways readers could alter texts and text collections to suit their own tastes or needs. It begins with fairly simple incursions such as marginal notes or ownership marks, but extends to the addition of texts to a *Sammel-*

handschrift. Additions could accrue over time and represent the participation of several readers who thereby altered the overall character of the manuscript. The Middle English song collection known as the Findern manuscript is a good example; women especially can be documented among the manuscript's active readers. Readership practice also refers to the insight that scribes and compilers were themselves readers and editors; or that in the literate, vernacular culture of the later Middle Ages, the roles of scribe, collector, and manuscript user were no longer separated. Thus a literate person from any walk of life could adapt texts and tailor a *Sammelhandschrift* specifically to his or her own purposes, perhaps as a household book or a book of personal piety. A London green grocer named Richard Hill made a manuscript courtesy book (now British Museum, Balliol collection, manuscript no. 354) emphasizing ideal masculinity, including carefully selected extracts from Gower's *Confesio amantis.* This way of studying *Sammelhandschriften* brings in historical and sociological factors that greatly enrich the more formal approaches sketched above.

The study of *Sammelhandschriften* has had an impact on the way we think about literary history. It has been argued that the compilation of collected manuscripts is a powerful and autonomous witness to how medieval people organized and used their own textual heritage. Manuscript typology, or the prevailing ways of combining texts to produce *Sammelhandschriften,* is as important to historical reconstruction as more traditional categories such as genre or the author's oeuvre. In fact, a manuscript-centered approach to literary history can greatly improve our understanding of what an oeuvre or genre is by giving it a firm historical basis. Some late medieval manuscripts preserve the works of an author, but the authorization pertains less to the work itself than to the use to which it was to be put. Oswald von Wolkenstein's and Hugo von Montfort's oeuvres were preserved in manuscripts for family use and family inheritance (the Montfort and Wolkenstein family books, so to speak); Hans Rosenplüt's works, both authentic and spurious, were preserved in manuscripts with strong historical connections to Nuremberg by collections as concerned with the city's cultural identity as with the person of the author. Genre study has a similar, revisionary relationship to manuscript study. Thus manuscripts confirm the historical identity and autonomy of various genres, above all the song collections of the later Middle Ages. More often, though, they reveal the symbiosis of genres in patterns whose cultural significance we have only begun to suspect.

Finally, the new understanding of *Sammmelhandschriften* has provided powerful tools for the study of single medieval texts diachronically, during their period of active transmission. Variance is no longer regarded as a corruption of an author's original creation but, rather, as the trace of the text's historical reception. While certain kinds of variance can be interpreted without reference to manuscript context, variance tends to be much more meaningful in situ (on site), or with reference to the other texts around the one under scrutiny. Even texts that change little from manuscript copy to manuscript copy read very differently, depending on their immediate and overall manuscript context. Thus the same medieval tale can be read as a warning against the wiles of women in a *märe* (comic) context or as a high-minded reflection on the discipline demanded of the lover in a *minnerede* context, or as an allegory of salvation in a religious context.

BIBLIOGRAPHY

van Dijk, Hans. "The Structure of the 'Sotternieën' in the Hulthem Manuscript," in *The Theatre in the Middle Ages,* ed. Herman Braet, Johan Nowé, and Gilbert Tournoy. Leuven: Leuven University Press, 1985, pp. 238–250.

———. "De reeks Middeleeuwse Verzamelhaandschriften uit de Nederlanden." *Middeleeuwse Verzamelhandschriften uit de Nederlanden. Congres Nijmegen 14 Oktober 1994.* Hilversum: Verloren, 1996, pp. 93–98.

Glier, Ingeborg. *Artes Amandi: Untersuchung zu Geschichte, Überlieferung und Typologie der deutschen Minnereden.* Munich: Beck, 1971.

Kuhn, Hugo. "Versuch einer Literaturtypologie des deutschen 14. Jahrhunderts." *Liebe und Gesellschaft: Kleine Schhriften,* vol. 3, ed. Wolfgang Walliczek. Stuttgart: Metzler, 1980, pp. 121–134.

Rogers, Janine. "Gender and the Literate Culture of Late Medieval England." Ph.d. diss., McGill University, 1998.

Kirchner, Joachim. *Germanistische Handschriftenpraxis,* 2d ed. Munich: Beck, 1967.

Schneider, Karin. *Die deutschen Handschriften der Bayerischen Staatsbibliothek München,* vol. 5, pts. 2–6 of *Catalogus codicum manu scriptorum Bibliothecae Monacensis.* Wiesbaden: Harrassowitz, 1970–1991 [catalogues of important Bavarian State Library collection, Munich].

Westphal, Sarah. *Textual Poetics of German Manuscripts 1300–1500.* Columbia, S.C.: Camden House, 1993.

Sarah Westphal

SEE ALSO

Drama, Dutch; Hugo von Montfort; *Legenda Aurea,* Alsatian; *Mariendichtungen; Minnesang;* Oswald von Wolkenstein

Sangspruch

A lyric subgenre of courtly song, *Sangspruch* (also *Spruchdichtung*) encompassed a style of gnomic, mono-stanzaic song treating matters other than love. It coexisted with *Minnesang* (courtly love singing) at the German-speaking courts as a popular entertainment between the twelfth century and the fifteenth. The songs were often propaganda pieces commissioned by a patron, personal pleas to a lord for a reward (such as a house), or complaints about the indignities and discomforts inflicted on the singer (too little respect, too much travel, bad clothes, among others). Other themes included knightly virtues, courtly ethics, the condition of the world, laments about the chaotic present as opposed to the ordered past, the art of courtly singing (including polemics against rival singers), and Christian doctrine. A strong underlying theme was the preservation or restoration of traditional, conservative values.

The songs were composed and performed by professional singers not of the nobility, though their audiences were noble as were their pretensions. The livelihood of these paid courtly entertainers depended on the production and performance of songs to amuse, edify, and flatter their patrons. For most, the tenure at any one court was brief, so that they have been called *Fahrende* or *Wander-sänger* (traveling or wandering singers).

Unlike the polystanzaic songs of *Minnesang, Sang-spruch* was customarily confined to a single stanza. The stanzaic form echoed that of *Minnesang* (bar form), except that the lines and the stanzas of *Sangspruch* tended to be longer. The singers normally composed a number of one-stanza songs with the same metrical form, rhyme scheme, and melody, a melodic-poetic unit called the *Ton* (tune, plural *Töne*), and though the single stanza could stand by itself, thematic connections existed between some (though seldom all) of the stanzas within a *Ton.* A singer probably performed groups of stanzas together, though in a later performance he may have rearranged them or composed new ones in the same *Ton.* Early

redactors sometimes gave these *Töne* descriptive names, e.g., the "Long Tune," "Golden Tune," "Court Tune." *Sangspruch* is sometimes equated with the moral and didactic *sirventes* or the epigrammatic *cobla* of Old Provençal, though the *sirventes,* with its three to five stanzas, was typically longer.

Little is known about the singers and their circumstances, although the performance venue can frequently be identified. Only in rare cases (e.g., Walther von der Vogelweide and Konrad von Würzburg) did a singer compose both *Sangspruch* and *Minnesang.*

The term *Spruchdichtung (Spruch*-poetry) was coined in the nineteenth century by Karl Simrock as a designation for the vast body of lyric verse that did not treat love as its principal theme. Simrock and others erroneously concluded that this verse was recited and adopted the word *Spruch,* a "saying reflecting proverbial wisdom," a meaning often applicable to the content of *Sangspruch* but that ignores its musical aspect. The hundreds of melodies transmitted in the manuscripts make it clear, however, that the songs were sung in performance. More common today is the term *Sangspruch* (song-*Spruch*) or *Sangspruchdichtung* (song-*Spruch*-poetry).

There were a few early, sporadic singers of *Sangspruch* in the twelfth century (Spervogel, Herger, Friedrich von Hausen, among others), but Walther von der Vogelweide, the most notable lyric singer of the German Middle Ages, defined the art around the year 1200, shaping it into a powerful vehicle of serious public entertainment. His more than eighty stanzas of *Sangspruch* reflect the turbulence of imperial and papal politics, the travails of the singer's peripatetic professional life, and his reliance on and need for a dependable patron.

Walther's stanzas achieved a singular popularity in the decades after his death, influencing *Sangspruch* for two centuries. Some singers, such as Reinmar von Zweter (second quarter of the thirteenth century), were limited in their ability to produce a variety of *Töne.* Reinmar confined himself to a single *Ton,* though he lavished his inventiveness on a rich diversity of thematic material (God, the Trinity, instruction for patrons, and songs of praise and propaganda, both for and against the Hohenstaufen emperor Friedrich II). Other echoes of Walther's *Sang-spruch* can be heard in the stanzas of Marner and Bruder Werner (mid–thirteenth century), both of whom were skilled political propagandists. Konrad von Würzburg (d. 1287) is the first attested singer to have led a largely urban existence, perhaps pointing ahead to the middle-class art of the Meistersinger several centuries later. His large literary and musical output, produced primarily in Basle, reflect his bourgeois patronage. His *Sangspruch,* however, embraced many of the same themes and values of Walther and his followers.

Well before the end of the thirteenth century some singers had adopted (or had been given) fanciful names, perhaps following the example of Spervogel (Sparrow Bird), one of the few twelfth-century singers of *Sangspruch:* Singauf (Sing Out), Regenbogen (Rainbow), der Unversagte (the Undaunted One), der Wilde Alexander (Alexander the Wild), Rumeland (Leave-the-Land), der Kanzler (the chancellor), and Höllenfeuer (Hellfire).

The courtly popularity of *Sangspruch* continued through the thirteenth century. A devastating interregnum between 1256 and 1273 ended when Rudolf, the first royal Habsburg, was elected German king. Two singers, Friedrich von Sonnenberg and der Unverzagte (the Undaunted One) attached themselves to his court and performed before 1292. Der Unverzagte is remembered for an especially caustic complaint about the parsimonious proclivities of his patron, King Rudolf, toward his courtly singers and musicians.

All the singers of *Sangspruch* till about 1250 had learned their trade and sang in the central and south German areas. But later in the century north Germans such as Rumeland von Sachsen (Leave-the-Land from Saxony) and Hermann Damen began to appear. Most seem to have performed at central or south German courts, and their songs, copied into the manuscripts in a High German (i.e., south German) dialect, betray traces of their Low German (north German) origins.

The most important voice of *Sangspruch* around the year 1300 was that of Heinrich von Meißen, also called Frauenlob (Praise of Ladies). He, too, may have been in the service of King Rudolf as well as other south German patrons. The illustration in the Manesse Manuscript (ca. 1300) depicts him as an orchestra conductor leading an ensemble of nine singers and instrumentalists, possibly performing a *Leich.* According to legend he earned his nom de plume in a poetic debate with a singer named Regenbogen, defending the name *froue* (lady) against his opponent's predilection for *wîp* (woman).

Sangspruch after Frauenlob was practiced at the courts with dwindling enthusiasm. As the tradition aged, there was a growing dearth of inventiveness and a tendency to look back and imitate the old masters. Though a few singers such as Heinrich von Mügeln (second half of the fourteenth century), Muskatblüt, and Michel Beheim (both fifteenth century) produced *Sangspruch* in a courtly

context, the art was clearly in decline. But it was to serve as the basis of a new tradition of singing, *Meistergesang* (master singing), which took root in the cities of central and south Germany in the fifteenth century. It was now urban tradesmen and artisans who practiced the gnomic art. They organized themselves into guilds and based the composition of their songs on a set of strict rules. Though thoroughly middle class in social status, mentality, and audience, the Meistersinger took up the ethical and moral themes as well as the forms and melodies of the courtly singers. They paid homage to many of their predecessors by designating the "twelve old masters," among them Walther, Reinmar von Zweter, Frauenlob, and Marner, using the old *Töne* as templates for new texts.

BIBLIOGRAPHY

Brunner, Horst, and Burghart Wachinger, eds. *Repertorium der Spangsprüche und Meisterlieder des 12. bis 18. Jahrhunderts.* Tübingen: Niemeyer, 1986–1989

Cormeau, Christoph, ed. *Walther von der Vogelweide: Leich, Lieder, Sangsprüche.* Berlin: de Gruyter, 1996.

Huber, Christoph. *Wort sint der dinge zeichen: Untersuchungen zum Sprachdenken der mittelhochdeutschen Spruchdichtung bis Frauenlob.* Munich: Artemis, 1977.

Jones, George Fenwick. *Walther von der Vogelweide.* New York: Twayne, 1968.

Niles, Bernd. *Pragmatische Interpretationen zu den Spruchtönen Walthers von der Vogelweide: ein Beitrag zu einer kommunikationsorientierten Literaturwissenschaft.* Göppingen: Kümmerle, 1979.

Nix, Matthias. *Untersuchungen zur Funktion der politishen Spruchdichtung Walthers von der Vogelweide.* Göppingen: Kümmerle, 1993.

Roethe, Gustav, ed. *Gedichte Reinmars von Zweter.* Leipzig: Hirzel, 1887.

Schweikle, Günther. *Parodie und Polemik in mittelhochdeutscher Dichtung: 123 Texte von Kürenberg bis Frauenlob, samt dem Wartburgkrieg nach der Grossen Heidelberger Liederhandschrift.* Stuttgart: Helfant, 1986.

Tervooren, Helmut. *Sangspruchdichtung.* Stuttgart: Metzler, 1995.

Thomas, Helmuth, et al., eds. *Frauenlob (Heinrich von Meißen): Leichs, Sangsprüche, Lieder.* Göttingen: Vandenhoeck and Ruprecht, 1981.

von Kraus, Carl, ed. *Deutsche Liederdichter des 13. Jahrhunderts,* 2d ed. Gisela Kornrumpf, ed. Tübingen: Niemeyer, 1978.

Peter Frenzel

SEE ALSO
Beheim, Michael; Frauenlob; Friedrich von Hausen; Konrad von Würzburg; Marner, Der; Meistersinger; *Minnesang*; Muskatblüt; Reinmar von Zwetter; Versification; Walther von der Vogelweide

Sankt Bartholomew Altarpiece, Master of (ca. 1445–ca. 1515)

This master's name piece (Munich, Alte Pinakothek) was originally located in the church of St. Colomba in Cologne. He was known as both a painter and an illuminator of manuscripts. Most scholars believe that he was trained in the Netherlands, working in the area of Utrecht, and later settled in Cologne. He was probably born circa 1445 and died in Cologne around 1515, after moving there sometime about 1480. His only dated work is a manuscript, the 1475 Hours of Sophia van Bylant (Cologne, Wallraf-Richartz Museum), which was created in the area of either Utrecht or Arnheim. It has also been suggested that the Master was a Carthusian monk, and two of his works, the St. Thomas and Crucifixion altarpieces, were commissioned by Dr. Peter Rink for the Carthusian monastery in Cologne (now Wallraf-Richartz Museum).

His style was extremely distinctive, and he seems to have had no direct followers. He has been described as a "Late Gothic Mannerist," and his work is characterized by an intense mystical piety, with extremely volumetric treatment of form juxtaposed with rich, exaggerated, linear patterning. His figures also have distinctive characteristics, including long, bony, awkwardly articulated fingers and tiny mouths. Further, he has been called last of the Gothic painters in Cologne, owing in part to his adherence to standard iconographic patterns such as brocaded hangings in front of which stand rows of saints. However, behind these hangings one may often see deep, naturalistic landscapes, and his figures have a great deal of volume, although their poses are often rather contorted. His works are meticulously crafted, with a tremendous attention to detail. The overall effect is one of contrasts between naturalism and abstraction. The Master of the Saint Bartholomew Altarpiece also used extensive underdrawing, which is visible through some of the lighter pigments and has been verified throughout his works by technical means.

BIBLIOGRAPHY

Goldberg, Gisela, and Gisela Scheffler. *Katalog der Alten Pinakothek, München: Altdeutsche Gemälde, Köln und Nordwestdeutschland.* 2 vols. Bayerische Staatsgemäldesammlung Gemäldekataloge 14. Munich: Bayerische Staatsgemäldesammlung, 1972, vol. 1, pp. 223–243.

Hand, John Oliver. *German Paintings of the Fifteenth through Seventeeth Centuries.* The Collections of the National Gallery of Art Systematic Catalogue. Washington, D.C.: National Gallery of Art, 1993, pp. 133–140.

MacGregor, Neil. *A Victim of Anonymity: The Master of the Saint Bartholomew Altarpiece.* New York: Thames and Hudson, 1994.

Der Meister des Bartholomäus Altares, der Meister des Aachener Altares: Kölner Maler der Spätgotik. Cologne: Wallraf-Richartz-Museum, 1961.

Rath, Karl vom. Der Meister des Bartholomäusaltares. Bonn: L. Röhrscheid, 1941.

Zehnder, Frank Günter. *Katalog der Altkölner Malerei.* Kataloge des Wallraf-Richartz-Museums 11. Cologne: Stadt Köln, 1990, pp. 418–450.

Daniel M. Levine

SEE ALSO
Cologne, Art; Gothic Art and Architecture

Sankt Gall

The abbey of St. Gall, located in northern Switzerland near lake Constance (German, Bodensee), was an important cultural center in the early Middle Ages. Its history is related in the *Casus Sancti Galli,* an ongoing chronicle written between the ninth and fourteenth centuries. The monastery was founded in the first half of the eighth century and experienced its greatest prestige around the year 900, but declined in the tenth century in the aftermath of Hungarian and Saracen raids and a disastrous fire. Thereafter, St. Gall again achieved prominence in the fifteenth, seventeenth, and eighteenth centuries. The monastery was dissolved by the Council of the Canton of St. Gall in 1805. The extant buildings date to the seventeenth and eighteenth centuries, but the appearance of the abbey and town of medieval St. Gall can be ascertained from drawings and plans predating the Baroque rebuilding.

St. Gall's origins lie in the withdrawal to a hut along the Steinach tributary of the Rhine of the monk Gallus (d. ca. 650), a follower of the seventh-century Irish missionary St. Columba. Gallus built an oratory and monks' cells for a few companions, but the monastery proper was founded near Gallus's grave sometime before 744 by

Otmar, an Alemannic monk. Otmar built the first church dedicated to Saint Gall, and it was during his abbacy that the Benedictine rule and thus the Latin rite were adopted. The appearance of the medieval abbey was primarily determined by the building programs of the ninth century. Sometime before 830, Abbot Gozbert received from his counterpart at the neighboring abbey of Reichenau the famous plan of St. Gall, now in the St. Gall library. The plan, which measured about 43½ inches in length by 30 inches in width, was drawn and inscribed in red and black ink on parchment. It indicates the disposition of all the religious and secular spaces of a Benedictine monastery, from the great church at the center of the complex to utilitarian buildings, such as the houses for livestock and their keepers, at the perimeter. The contention that the plan reflects the priorities of the Carolingian court, including the emulation of early Christian, Roman models and reforms of the Benedictine order, has evoked considerable controversy, as has the suggestion that the plan builds on the system of square schematism. In any event, the plan was never carried out. Although Gozbert built a new abbey church in the 830s, archaeological investigation has revealed numerous deviations from the church of the plan, and subsequent building programs at St. Gall were likewise unrelated to it. The medieval buildings were replaced between about 1660 and 1800. The present monastery is dominated by the late Baroque church begun in 1755 by the architect Peter Thumb.

The monks of St. Gall made important contributions in many areas of medieval culture. Throughout the early Middle Ages, for example, they were active in the transmission of the liturgy, a scholarly interest indicated by such manuscripts as the *Rex Palimpsestorum* (St. Gall, Stiftsbibliothek, no. Ms. 908), which includes numerous liturgical texts dating from the sixth to the eighth century, and the Sacramentarium Triplex (St. Gall, Stiftsbibliothek, Ms. 43; ca. 1020–1030), with Gregorian, Gelasian, and Ambrosian sacramentary texts. In addition, three St. Gall monks contributed significantly to the development of church music. Four Latin hymns by Ratpert (d. ca. 890) have survived, Notker I the Stammerer (d. ca. 912) wrote sequences to be sung between the Epistle and Gospel readings, and the sculptor Tuotilo (d. 912) also wrote tropes, including those preserved in the *Evangelium Longum,* which bears the ivory covers he carved. The St. Gall library possesses some twenty books dating from the ninth to the twelfth century that include the neumes for liturgical singing, as well as theoretical texts.

The monastery of St. Gall is best known, however, for the illluminated manuscripts produced by its scriptorium. Surviving St. Gall manuscripts suggest that eight- and ninth-century efforts were restricted to initial illumination and depended on both Irish and continental models, as the initials in the Wolfcoz Psalter of circa 835 indicate (St. Gall, Stiftsbibliothek, Ms. 20). The earliest figural miniature known to have been painted at St. Gall appears in a mid-ninth-century Psalter now in Zurich (Zentralbibliothek, Ms. C 12, fol. 53r). In the second half of the ninth century, St. Gall illuminators exploited contemporary Carolingian models from Tours, Metz, and the Court School of Charles the Bald. Three manuscripts of this period—the Folchart Psalter of 872–873 (St. Gall, Stiftsbibliothek, Ms. 23), the *Evangelium Longum* (Stiftsbibliothek, Ms. 53), and the Golden Psalter (Stiftsbibliothek, Ms. 22), the latter two circa 900—together represent the apogee of initial and figural composition at St. Gall. Tuotilo's ivory covers on the Evangelium Longum, representing Christ in Majesty, the Assumption of the Virgin, and a miracle performed by Saint Gall, are characterized by a figural and spatial illusionism and coherent, disciplined composition that represent a continuation of the style of Carolingian Reims, in such works as the Utrecht Psalter, and of Metz. Tuotilo's understanding and appropriation of classical values is unequaled at St. Gall. He appears to have had no successors.

Cultural activity at St. Gall was curtailed in the tenth century by the invasions and fire. When the scriptorium resumed production around the year 1000, it was overshadowed by the imperial commissions of its neighbor and friendly rival, Reichenau. The early eleventh-century miniatures from St. Gall on the whole share neither the classicizing sophistication of the Carolingian painting nor the expressive stylisation of Ottonian Reichenau, although the illuminated antiphonary in St. Gall (Stiftsbibliothek, Manuscripts 390–391), written during the abbacy of Herker the Recluse (986–1017), has formal affinities with the Reichenau Ruodprecht group of the 980s.

BIBLIOGRAPHY

Horn, Walter, and Ernst Born. *The Plan of St. Gall.* 3 vols. Berkeley: University of California Press, 1979.

King, James C., and Werner Vogler, eds. *The Culture of the Abbey of St. Gall.* Stuttgart: Belser Verlag, 1991.

Nees, Lawrence. "The Plan of St. Gall and the Theory of the Program of Carolingian Art." *Gesta* 25 (1986): 1–8.

Karen E. Loaiza

Sankt Katharinenthal

The Dominican women's cloister, suppressed in 1869, lies on the left bank of the Rhine, downstream from the village of Diessenhofen in Canton Thurgau (Switzerland). It developed out of a house of Beguines founded near Winterthur at the beginning of the thirteenth century; in the middle of the century the convent was accepted into the Dominican order. The cloister was erected on territory of the counts of Kyburg. For topographical reasons, the conventual buildings stand on the north side of the church, which was dedicated to the Virgin, Katherine, Nicholas, John the Baptist, and John the Evangelist. The baroque rebuilding of the church, dating from 1732–1735, retains the spatial sequence of its medieval predecessor: a single-aisle nave, with two successive, flat-ended choirs at the east, an outer one (outside the cloistered area) and an inner one, the nuns' choir.

From the end of the thirteenth century, the cloister was a center of the south German mystical movement; visits are documented by Meister Eckhart, Albertus Magnus, and especially Heinrich Seuse (Suso), a member of the Dominican convent in Constance from 1327 to 1348. The nuns' lives recorded in the middle of the fourteenth century report the mystical experiences and visions of the sisters. Sculptures mentioned in the texts are now spread throughout the world. One of the best known is the life-size group of Christ and St. John the Evangelist in painted walnut from about 1305 (Antwerp, Museum Mayer van den Bergh). The work is considered a typical *Andachtsbild* (devotional image); it attempts to represent the theological concept of the *unio mystica* (mystical union) in pictorial terms. The sculpture was created by Master Heinrich of Constance, who, with other members of his workshop, made other sculptures for the convent: an over-life-size wood crucifix circa 1300 (St. Katharinenthal), a Madonna from the beginning of the fourteenth century, reworked in the baroque period (St. Katharinenthal), and a life-size, polychromed statue of John the Baptist about 1300 (now Paris, Musée des Arts Décoratifs, on long-term loan to the Badisches Landesmuseum, Karlsruhe). A small wooden Visitation group from about 1310–1320, now at the Metropolitan Museum of Art in New York, is attributed to the so-called Visitation Master. Two candlestick-bearing angels from about 1330 preserved in the Liebieghaus Museum in Frankfurt are supposed to come from a sculptured Entombment group that apparently stood in the nuns' choir. The so-called *croce dipinta* from circa 1250–1270 (Basel, Historisches Museum), a painted altar- and processional-cross, relies on a cross type especially favored in Italy.

Several liturgical codices, some lavishly illuminated, are preserved, including a group of seven manuscripts from the late thirteenth century in Rome (Biblioteca Apostolica Vaticana, Cod. vat. lat. 10769–10775) and the so-called Nuremberg Gradual, also from the late thirteenth century (Nuremberg, Germanisches Nationalmuseum, Hs. 21897), with twenty-six framed miniatures on gold ground. This latter served as a model for the manuscript known as the St. Katharinenthal Gradual (Zurich, Schweizerisches Landesmuseum). Dated to 1312, this manuscript, decorated with over seventy colored initials on gold ground, belongs to the most outstanding works

Gradual from St. Katharinenthal (Zurich, Schweizerisches Landesmuseum, LM-26117), fol. 183v: initial M with the beheading of John the Baptist, and John the Evangelist with text roll; sister Katharina de Radegge in the margin. *Photograph: Schweizerisches Landesmuseum, Neg. 49255*

of art from the Upper Rhine. The nuns must have copied the texts in the cloister's scriptorium themselves. The high-quality miniatures were painted in a workshop with far-reaching contacts, probably in Constance. The complex image program was designed by Dominican theologians, probably from the cloister in Constance, which was responsible for the care of the nuns' souls. It remains unclear whether the miniatures were executed in secular painting shops and/or in a monastic scriptorium.

BIBLIOGRAPHY

Das Graduale von Sankt Katharinenthal. Facsimile and Commentary. Lucerne: Faksimile-Verlag, 1980–1983.

Knöpfli, Alfred. *Das Kloster St. Katharinenthal.* Die Kunstdenkmäler des Kantons Thurgau 4. Basel: Wiese, 1989.

Meyer, Ruth. *Das St. Katharinenthaler Schwesternbuch: Untersuchung—Edition—Kommentar.* Tübingen: Niemeyer, 1995.

Michler, Jürgen. Review of Knöpfli 1989. *Zeitschrift für Kunstgeschichte* 53 (1990): 587–594.

Sciurie, Helga. "Die Todessymbolik der Christus-Johannes-Vorstellung." *Georges-Bloch-Jahrbuch des Kunstgeschichtlichen Seminars der Universität Zürich* 3 (1996): 132–156.

Susan Marti

SEE ALSO
Albertus Magnus; Constance; Gothic Art and Architecture; Meister Eckhart; Mysticism; Seuse, Heinrich; Sister-Books; Winterthur

Sankt Paul in Lavanttal

The importance of St. Paul in Lavanttal is twofold: in its own right as the oldest Cluniac cloister in Kärnten (Corinthia) in southeastern Austria, and as the successor to the royal monastery of St. Blasien in the Black Forest, whose monks were transferred to St. Paul after secularization in 1806–1807.

The castle at Lavant to the east of St. Veit and Klagenfurt had come into the possession of the counts of Spanheim with the marriage of Richardis of Aribon to Count Siegfried. Siegfried died on Crusade in 1065, and five years before his own death in 1096, their son Engelbert turned the castle into a cloister in his father's memory, calling twelve monks from Hirsau in Swabia. Remodeling of an existing church was finished for a consecration in 1093. The new church built during the tenures of Abbots Pilgram (1159–1192) and Ulrich I (1192–1222) shows the influence of the important church at Hirsau. The status of the abbey is marked by two papal favors: in 1099 Urban II took the abbey under his protection, and in 1177 Alexander III granted Abbot Pilgram the miter. Family burials continued here until 1256.

After a fire in 1367, the choir, transept, and part of the *chorus minor,* which extended three bays into the nave, were vaulted. The elaborate vaults added in the nave in 1468 were painted soon thereafter by the Pachers. The fifteenth century was a difficult period for the cloister, however; it suffered under ineffective leadership, the plague, unrest in the region, and the incursions of the Turks.

The monastic community was dissolved in 1787, but in 1809 monks from the tenth-century royal foundation with them not only liturgical objects and manuscripts from their earlier home but the bones of fourteen Habsburg family members from the thirteenth and fourteenth centuries that had been moved to St. Blasien from Basel and Königsfelden in 1770. The library now at St. Paul, consisting largely of manuscripts brought from St. Blasien, is one of the most important in Austria. The manuscripts located at the cloister before its dissolution have been transferred to Vienna and Klagenfurt.

BIBLIOGRAPHY

Festgabe zur 150-Jahr-Feier der Wiederbesiedlung des Benediktinerstiftes St. Paul im Lavanttal durch die Mönche von St. Blasien im Schwarzwald, ed. Gotbert Moro. Carinthia I 149 (1950). Klagenfurt: Verlag des Geschichtsvereines für Kärnten.

Ginhart, Karl. *Die Kunstdenkmäler des Benediktinerstiftes St. Paul im Lavanttal und seiner Filialkirchen.* Österreichische Kunsttopographie 37. Vienna: Anton Schroll, 1969.

Schroll, Beda. *Urkundenbuch des Benedictiner-Stiftes St. Paul in Kärnten.* Fontes rerum Austriacarum, 2. Abt. (Diplomataria et acta) 39. Vienna: Karl Gerold's Sohn, 1876.

Joan A. Holladay

SEE ALSO
Hirsau; Königsfelden; Pacher, Michael

Sankt Veit an der Glan

First mentioned as a village in 1131, St. Veit is located in Carinthia on the Glan River along the primary traffic artery between Vienna and Klagenfurt. By 1199, the village was known as a marketplace, and by 1224 it was considered a city. Originally, St. Veit belonged to the bishop of Bamberg, but during the second half of the twelfth century, it became a possession of the dukes of Carinthia. Under the sovereignty of Bernhard of Spanheim (1202–1256), the city, with a ducal residence within its walls and castles in the surrounding area, developed rapidly. Until 1518, St. Veit was the headquarters of the Carinthian dukes.

The parish church of St. Veit, or the Holy Trinity, dates from 1162; it is essentially a three-aisle, late Romanesque basilica that, in its restored state, has the appearance of a late Gothic structure. Just outside the west wall of St. Veit stands a Gothic church from 1323, which was originally a cloister church for the Poor Clares. Although the towered city gates were destroyed during the nineteenth century, the city wall still exists in its fifteenth-century form. St. Veit's city hall dates from 1468. The facades of buildings surrounding the central square were changed after a fire in 1829, but the old town retains its medieval character, and the structure of these buildings is otherwise undisturbed.

BIBLIOGRAPHY

Fräss-Ehrfeld, Claudia. *Geschichte Kärntens* 1: *Das Mittelalter.* Klagenfurt: J. Heyn, 1984, pp. 282–296.

Ginhart, Karl. *Kärnten.* Die Kunstdenkmäler Österreichs. Vienna: A. Schroll, 1976, pp. 619–635.

Ruth M. W. Moskop

SEE ALSO

Bamberg; Gothic Art and Architecture; Romanesque Art and Architecture; Vienna

Sankt Veronica, Master of (fl. ca. 1395– ca. 1415)

This anonymous master's name piece is the panel of Saint Veronica with the *Sudarium* (cloth), in Munich (Alte Pinakothek), a variation of which may be found in London (National Gallery). He was active in Cologne from circa 1395 until about 1415. There have been numerous attempts to associate the master with a name from Cologne's extensive guild lists, and Master Wilhelm from Cologne, Herman Wynrich von Wesel, and Hermann von Köln (Cologne) have been suggested. However, none of these names can be positively associated with the Master.

Scholars have seen the influence of French and Burgundian artists in his work. There has been some speculation as to the Master's association with the Carthusians and, in particular, the Chartreuse de Champmol in Dijon. In fact, authors have suggested the influence of Jean Malouel in the Master's work. His Crucifixion (Washington, D.C., National Gallery of Art) depicts a Carthusian monk kneeling at the foot of the cross recalling works executed by Malouel's teacher, Jean de Beaumetz, for the Chartreuse de Champmol. The Master's Small Calvary (Cologne, Wallraf-Richartz Museum) has been described as an enlarged version of a French illuminated manuscript.

The Master of St. Veronica's works are characterized by very fluid lines and expressive faces and gestures. The fluidity and gentle nature of his works is in keeping with the *weicher Stil* (soft style) of the International Gothic period. Through delicate modeling, the Master produced figures with a greater degree of plasticity than earlier Cologne painters, whose works tended to be flatter. His color sensibility, too, was very delicate and very original. He also created early examples of the typical painted *Andachtsbild* (devotional image). These small works depict half-length figures before a gold ground. Both versions of St. Veronica with the *Sudarium* fall into this category and were probably used for private devotion.

The Master of Saint Veronica was the most influential painter in Cologne before Stefan Lochner, and it has been suggested that other painters, such as the Master of St. Lawrence, were trained in his workshop.

BIBLIOGRAPHY

Goldberg, Gisela, and Gisela Scheffler. *Katalog der Alten Pinakothek, München: Altdeutsche Gemälde, Köln und Nordwestdeutschland.* 2 vols. Bayerische Staatsgemäldesammlung Gemäldekataloge 14. Munich: Bayerische Staatsgemäldesammlung, 1972, vol. 1, pp. 390–403.

Vor Stefan Lochner: Die Kölner Maler von 1300 bis 1430. Cologne: Wallraf-Richartz-Museum, 1974, pp. 36–39, 82–87.

Zehnder, Frank Günter. *Katalog der Altkölner Malerei.* Kataloge des Wallraf-Richartz-Museums 11. Cologne: Stadt Köln, 1990, pp. 316–329.

———. *"Der Meister der heiligen Veronika."* Ph.d. diss., University of Bonn, 1974. St. Augustin: [n.p.], 1981.

Daniel M. Levine

SEE ALSO

Cologne, Art; Gothic Art and Architecture; International Style; Lochner, Stefan

Sankt Wolfgang

About 994, Wolfgang, bishop of Regensberg, founded a hermitage for his retirement on a rocky spur above the Abersee (Lake Aber, also Lake St. Wolfgang, Upper Austria). The site attained cult status with Wolfgang's canonization in 1052, and by the twelfth century it had developed into a pilgrimage site. By 1380 a small market town had grown around the church, an estate of the Abbey of Mondsee (also in the region known as the Salzkammergut). After the destruction of the church by fire in 1429, a new, larger, three-aisle basilica was constructed, in response to the increased veneration of St. Wolfgang. Begun by Abbot Simon Reichlin of Mondsee Abbey, the new pilgrimage church was consecrated in 1477 by Abbot Benedikt Eck. The construction and decoration of the pilgrimage and parish church of St. Wolfgang am Abersee was also part of a general policy of the renewal of the estates of Kloster Mondsee during the second half of the fifteenth century.

The most significant monument associated with the church is the altarpiece created by Michael Pacher. Commissioned by Abbot Benedikt Eck in 1471, the altarpiece was completed and installed on the high altar in 1481. The contract of December 13, 1471, carefully stipulates the price—1,200 Hungarian guilders—and the iconographic program. The polychrome and gilded wooden corpus depicts the Coronation of the Virgin, flanked by Saints Wolfgang and Benedict. The predella (lowermost altar panel, *Sarg*) below portrays the Adoration of the Magi. In the florid pinnacles *(Aufzug)* are the Crucifixion, the Annunciation, and various saints. Two pairs of painted wings allow the altarpiece to variously display different scenes during distinct times of the liturgical calendar. For high feast days both wings would be opened, revealing the carved corpus flanked by four scenes of the life of the Virgin. For lesser feast days, only the outer wings would be opened, revealing a cycle of eight scenes of the Life of Christ. On the outer wings, seen in the closed position, are four episodes from the life of Saint Wolfgang.

The altarpiece, among the most significant works of Michael Pacher, reveals a variety of techniques and stylistic influences. The carved wooden corpus, predella, and pinnacles are in the tradition of late-fifteenth-century German carved altarpieces. The painted scenes on the wings, however, reveal a strong influence of north Italian painting of the fifteenth century, particularly the works of Andrea Mantegna. The combination of influences may be explained by Pacher's origins in the Tyrolian Alps.

Scholarly opinion varies over the attribution of different figures on the altarpiece. Despite the contractual stipulation that all work be by Michael Pacher himself, certain stylistic discrepancies are apparent. These slight variations may be attributable to the work of assistants, most likely Pacher's brother Friedrich and son Hans, and possibly to local artists working under Pacher's direction.

BIBLIOGRAPHY

Baxandall, Michael. *The Limewood Sculptors of Renaissance Germany.* New Haven, Conn.: Yale University Press, 1980.

Hempel, Eberhard. *Michael Pacher.* Vienna: Anton Schroll, 1931.

Rasmo, Nicolò. *Michael Pacher.* London: Phaidon, 1971.

Stechow, Wolfgang. *Northern Renaissance Art, 1400–1600.* Englewood Cliffs, N.J.: Prentice-Hall, 1966, pp. 77–78.

Stiassny, Robert. *Michael Pachers St. Wolfganger Altar.* 2 vols. Vienna: Schroll, 1919.

Zibermayr, Ignaz. "Michael Pacher's Vertrag über die Anfertigung des Altars in der Kirche zu St. Wolfgang." *Mitteilungen des Instituts für Österreichische Geschichtsforschung* 33 (1912): 468–482.

Scott Bradford Montgomery

SEE ALSO
Gothic Art and Architecture

Saxon War

The "Saxon War" (1073–1088) is the name given by both contemporaries and modern scholars to the period of intense political and military conflict between nobles of East Saxony and other regions and King Henry IV (1056–1106) that persisted from 1073 until 1088. According to contemporary sources, the Saxon princes and people, led by Otto of Northeim and Bishops Werner of Magdeburg, Werner of Merseburg, and Burchard of Halberstadt, conspired against the king in 1073 for several reasons: he had undertaken an aggressive campaign of castle building in Saxony intended to subjugate the Saxon people; he was attempting to usurp rights and privileges traditionally enjoyed by the Saxon princes; he had violated the norms of elite political behavior in his prosecution of injuries; and, finally, there were rumors of flamboyant immorality. Modern scholars have further suggested that the Saxon princes were also rebelling against a long-standing Salian policy of reacquiring, but not redistributing, royal lands in Saxony that had intensified during Henry's reign.

After initial success in 1073–1074, noble support for the Saxon cause in other regions waned as a result of political miscalculations and the sacrilegious destruction of the Hartzburg castle by Saxon peasants. At the battle of Unstrut in 1075, Henry IV wreaked a terrible defeat on Saxon forces and took their leaders into captivity, thus putting a temporary end to the rebellion. With Pope Gregory VII's excommunication of Henry IV during Lent of 1076, however, the rebellion regained momentum. The princes from Saxony and southern Germany allied themselves with the papal cause and called for an assembly in early 1077 at which the matter of the kingship would be decided by the German princes and the pope. When Gregory VII's journey to Germany was cut short by Henry IV's sudden appearance and penance at Canossa in Tuscany in January 1077, the princes assembled at Forchheim in February 1077 and elected Rudolf of Rheinfelden, duke of Swabia, as their king. The election at Forchheim is particularly noteworthy for the theory of purely elective monarchy articulated there. Although papal recognition of the legitimacy of Rudolf's kingship came only after Gregory VII's second excommunication of Henry IV in the Lenten synod of 1080, the election itself consolidated politically the alliance of Saxon and Swabian forces, and they enjoyed several military victories under Rudolf's leadership. He died in October 1080 as the result of battle wounds.

After electing Hermann of Salm as their king in December 1081, the rebellious princes continued to resist Henry IV for the next six years, although with diminishing success as key leaders like Otto of Northeim died (maybe in 1083) and others became reconciled to Henry IV, especially after Pope Gregory VII's death in 1085. With the deaths of Hermann of Salm and Bishop Burchard of Halberstadt in 1088 and the reconciliation of the remaining leaders to Henry IV, the Saxon War effectively ended, although the Salian monarchs continued to face occasional resistance in the region into the twelfth century.

In its effective challenge to the Salian style of kingship, in its vigorous assertion of noble rights, including the right to judge and elect the king, and in its recognition of and complex interaction with the legitimating power of the papacy, the Saxon War marked a crisis in the development of the medieval German polity and was a harbinger of the key diplomatic role the papacy would come to play in later medieval politics.

BIBLIOGRAPHY

Leyser, K. "The Crisis of Medieval Germany." *Proceedings of the British Academy* 69 (1983): 409–443.

Robinson, I. S. "Pope Gregory VII, the Princes and the Pactum of 1077." *English Historical Review* 373 (1979): 721–756.

William L. North

SEE ALSO

Gregory VII; Henry IV; Investiture Controversy; Salians

Schaffhausen

The city of Schaffhausen, Switzerland, owes its foundation to its strategic position on the right bank of the Rhine. The nearby rapids and the *Rheinfall,* or drop in the Rhine River bed, necessitated an interruption in shipping traffic between Basle and Constance, an important trading route since the tenth century. A settlement grew up around the storage depot set up for the transfer and warehousing of goods. Emperor Henry III granted the community the right to strike coins in 1045; in 1080 it received market rights from Count Eberhard III of Nellenburg. Until the thirteenth century, the abbot of the Benedictine cloister ruled the city. As of 1218, Schaffhausen was an imperial city with the exception of the period from 1330 to 1415, when it was under Austrian rule. In 1411 a government of the city's guilds was instituted. The first treaty of alliance with the Swiss confederation was drawn up in 1454; in 1501 Schaffhausen joined the confederation as the twelfth member canton. The city decided in favor of the Reformation in 1529 and dissolved the local cloisters, including the Benedictine monastery of All Saints and the Franciscan cloister.

About 1049–1050 Count Eberhard of Nellenburg, a wealthy noble related through his mother to the Salian dynasty of emperors, founded the monastery of All Saints. He held all the rights of the monastery himself as its lay owner; the monks are presumed to have numbered twelve and may have come from Einsiedeln. The founder's son, Burkhard of Nellenburg, augmented the gifts of his father to the house and renounced his rights as the cloister's head in favor of William of Hirsau, who became abbot. With the help of the monks of Hirsau, William succeeded in reforming the cloister according to stricter Cluniac principles. Pope Gregory VII confirmed the new order, and contemporary sources praised the discipline of the Schaffhausen cloister, a reputation it shared with Hirsau and St. Blasien. For this reason monks from

Schaffhausen, Church of All Saints, interior, view to east. *Photograph: Joan A. Holladay*

Schaffhausen were called to Benediktbeuren about 1106, to Lipporn in 1114, and to Rommersdorf, near Andernach, in 1117. Between the institution of the Hirsau reform and the middle of the twelfth century, a number of manuscripts were written in the cloister scriptorium. In the beginning these were illuminated on the model of manuscripts from the area of Lake Constance, which themselves reflected Reichenau illumination; under the influence of the Hirsau reform, illuminators renounced figural representation and limited themselves to foliate (full page) initials. Because the greatest part of the manuscripts have remained in Schaffhausen and an inventory from about 1100 allows us to know what is lost, the exact contents of the library of the reform cloister are known.

After the middle of the twelfth century, the influence of Hirsau in Schaffhausen waned, and as a result so did the importance of the cloister. The early history of the cloister church is not entirely clear. An altar dedication by Pope Leo IX is dated to 1049, but as work on a large church continued in the years after 1050, the dedication does not seem to mark the building's completion. In 1064 the bishop of Constance consecrated the church, which was never completed. Excavations have revealed that the structure had at least one and perhaps two aisles on each side of the nave, a transept, and a large semicircular apse flanked by two chapels. To the east of the church was a courtyard in which several chapels were arranged in a cross formation. With the introduction of the *Consuetudines,* or common law statutes, of Hirsau, the present church was erected, probably on the model of the mother church at Hirsau; it was finished in 1103–1104. The three-aisled, flat-roofed nave was preceded by a narthex and tower in the west; at the east, a salient transept separated the nave from the flat-ended choir. Nothing remains of the rich medieval furnishing of the church, which is known only from documents. Some fragments of architectural sculpture and the tombs of the founders, which date from about 1100, are preserved in the Allerheiligen Museum located in the former cloister.

BIBLIOGRAPHY

Butz, Annegret. *Katalog der illuminierten Handschriften des 11. und 12. Jh. aus dem Benediktinerkloster Aller-*

heiligen in Schaffhausen. Denkmäler der Buchkunst 11. Stuttgart: Hiersemann, 1994.

Frauenfelder, Reinhard. *Die Kunstdenkmäler des Kantons Schaffhausen,* vol. 1, Die Stadt Schaffhausen. Die Kunstdenkmäler der Schweiz 26/1. Basel: Birkhäuser, 1951.

Gamper-Schlund, Rudolf, Gaby Koch-Mund, Marlis Stähli. *Katalog der mittelalterlichen Handschriften der Ministerialbibliothek Schaffhausen.* Dietikon-Zurich: Graf, 1994.

Guyan, W. U. "Das Salvator-Kloster zu Schaffhausen: Ergebnisse der Allerheiligen-Grabung von 1963 bis 1965." *Zeitschrift für schweizerischen Archäologie und Kunstgeschichte* 36 (1979): 151–204.

Schudel, E. "Allerheiligen in Schaffhausen." *Frühe Klöster, Die Benediktiner und Benediktinerinnen in der Schweiz.* Helvetica sacra III/1/3. Bern: Francke, 1986, pp. 1490–1553.

Wolfgang Augustyn

SEE ALSO

Einsiedeln; Henry III; Hirsau; Reichenau

Schleswig

The location of Schleswig on the Jutland peninsula near the Danish border, where it sits on the north shore of the Baltic estuary of the river Schlei, gave it an important early role in Baltic trade, especially before the founding of Lübeck (1143) and the growth of the Hanseatic League. In the tenth century there was a Viking city, Haithabu, on the south shore of the Schlei, which was recognized by the German emperor Otto II and had a missionary bishop subject to the archbishop of Hamburg. After the destruction of Haithabu in 1066, the foundation on the north of the estuary, Schleswig, remained, and the bishop was transferred there. In the twelfth century, although its importance as a trade center decreased, Schleswig retained its episcopal stature and became the seat of the duchy of Schleswig. The first duke was Knud Laward (1115–1131). In 1139 the bishopric of Schleswig was transferred to the jurisdiction of the archbishop of Lund, Denmark. During the twelfth through fourteenth centuries the descendants of Knud Laward were frequently kings of Denmark as well as dukes of Schleswig, increasing the city's Danish ties. However, Schleswig retained its intermediary status between Germany and Denmark throughout the Middle Ages. Bishop Berthold (1287–1307), for example, was born in Copenhagen, while his successor, Johannes von Bokholt (1308–1331), was born in Lübeck.

The cathedral of St. Peter was first mentioned in a chronicle of 1134, which describes the burial of the Danish King Niels in the cathedral some years earlier (1120). Presumably the cathedral was begun circa 1100. The original building was in granite, and remains of the granite nave piers were discovered within the later brick piers. Sculpture from the twelfth-century campaigns includes a sculpted doorway (ca. 1180) on the south side of the cathedral with a granite tympanum (triangle above door) showing Christ in Majesty surrounded by St. Peter, St. Paul, and a donor. Its flat, minimally modulated Jutland style is also found in the tympana of the nearby churches of Munkbarup and Norderbarup. Granite reliefs with vibrant embracing lions biting each others' tails in a style reminiscent of earlier abstract animal interlace also date from this campaign. The church was largely destroyed in a fire circa 1200 and reconstructed in the brick common in the Hansa cities in the thirteenth century *(Backsteingotik)*. The nave was further reconstructed in brick in the fifteenth century, giving it a hall-church form and taller profile. The cathedral of St. Peter was originally decorated with an elaborate set of narrative wall paintings from the thirteenth and fourteenth centuries. The church retains a sculpted Three Kings altar from 1418 and a sculpted altar with passion scenes by Hans Brüggemann from 1521.

Schleswig was located on a peninsula whose shoreline changed considerably during the Middle Ages. In the eleventh and twelfth centuries the city was centered on a palace, the cathedral, and the harbor trading centers. The church of St. Nicholas also dates from this early period. By the thirteenth century the shoreline extended into the estuary, and a market square and cloisters for the new mendicant orders the Franciscans and the Dominicans were erected in the city. The earlier palace was covered over by the Franciscan cloister, suggesting a change in focus in the later medieval city.

BIBLIOGRAPHY

Ellger, Dietrich. *Die Kunstdenkmäler der Stadt Schleswig* 2: *Der Dom und der ehemalige Dombezirk.* Munich: Deutscher Kunstverlag, 1966.

Stange, Alfred. *Der Schleswiger Dom und seine Wandmalereien.* Berlin: Uhnenerbe Stiftung, 1940.

Vogel, Volker. *Schleswig im Mittelalter: Archäologie einer Stadt.* Neumünster: Karl Wachholtz Verlag, 1989.

Susan L. Ward

Schmalkalden

The early-thirteenth-century Hessenhof in this Thuringian city contains murals depicting scenes from the story of Iwein. Proposed dates for the paintings range from the 1220s to around 1250, with the 1240s perhaps most likely.

Twenty-three scenes in six rows on one wall and a vaulted ceiling narrate the Iwein story from Arthur's nap to Iwein's killing of the dragon, with significant omissions. Limited and inconclusive evidence suggests that a seventh register may originally have been present. A large painting of a courtly feast at one end of the room has often been read as part of the Iwein narrative, but the connection may be more thematic than narrative.

The pictorial narrative at Schmalkalden shows a high degree of independence from canonical versions of the Iwein story. The painter devotes fully half the scenes to images of courtly behavior—conversation, ceremony, and the bedroom—and an entire register to the wedding of Iwein and Laudine. On the other hand, the entire sequence of Iwein's missed deadline and his subsequent madness and recovery is omitted, and the murals thus offer no hint that Iwein's later adventures are undertaken for redemption, or that any of his adventures are problematic in any way. But adventure is also not endowed with any superior value, appearing, rather, as a kind of game played out in a context of courtly leisure reinforced by the room's apparent use for dining and drinking, as well as by the festive meal depicted on the end wall.

BIBLIOGRAPHY

Bonnet, Anne-Marie. *Rodenegg und Schmalkalden: Untersuchungen zur Illustration einer ritterlich-höfischen Erzählung und zur Entstehung profaner Epenillustration in den ersten Jahrzehnten des 13. Jahrhunderts.* Ph.d. diss., University of Heildelberg, 1981. Munich: tuduv, 1986, pp. 75–113.

Rushing, James A., Jr. *Images of Adventure: Ywain in the Visual Arts.* Philadelphia: University of Pennsylvania Press, 1995, pp. 91–132.

James A. Rushing Jr.

Schondoch (fl. 14th c.)

The Alemannic poet (also Schöndoch), who wrote the *Litauer (The Lithuanian),* a legendary short epic of 324 verses, and the *Königin von Frankreich und der ungetreue Marschall (The Queen of France and the Unfaithful Officer),* a courtly novella *(maere)* of about 720 verses (all twenty five manuscript copies considered), is known only by his pen name, since he was an itinerant poet *(Fahrender).* The *Litauer* focuses on the baptism of the historic Lithuanian king *(Großfürst)* Butawt in 1365, after he attended a mass at a church of the Teutonic Order *(Deutschorden),* in which he observed a miracle. A connection to the Teutonic Order is assumed because of the content of this quasi-historic epic and its transmission in just one manuscript, together with the legend *Martina* of Hugo von Langenstein, a very fervent work on behalf of the Teutonic Order.

The *Königin von Frankreich* had as its main hero Herzog Leopold III of Austria, who later died in the battle of Sempach in Switzerland in 1386 and became legendary. This novella, or *maere,* was the most copied in all southern and west Middle German dialects and can be seen as a work of propaganda for the Habsburgs. It is because Leopold creates justice for all classes and all good and bad persons in the plot of the novella, where the innocent exiled queen of France had to live in poverty for over four years, before she was brought back to the court of France. The story is based on the French chanson de geste *Reine Sébile,* but Schondoch changed the plot halfway through (without a fighting army and power, but simply by letting justice take its course). For its time, it must have been quite modern, enlightened, and even democratic, although as a metaphor for old, dependable justice, a fight between the murderer and the dog of the victim stood at the center, which was followed up by trustworthy councillors and knights of the king, as well as workers, merchants, the clergy, and justices in opposition to bad councillors. This story had universal appeal, as an exemplum with typecasts, and suited generations of German-speaking European courts. The story is also depicted in four picture cycles, known today as the *Königin von Frankreich.*

A prose version of this novella, *Cronica,* was composed by an anonymous author around 1460, extant in one Silesian manuscript of 1465. Only few changes occurred, for instance, that the queen was Leopold's sister. The novella was also used as the model for a *Meisterlied* in fifteen strophes, first printed by Hans Sporer 1498 in Erfurt and later six times between 1510 and 1570 in Nuremberg. The contents was mostly just shortened, but new emphasis and consideration was given to the king of France instead of Leopold. Finally, Hans Sachs wrote a drama of the *Meisterlied* in 1549.

Elisabeth von Nassau-Saarbrücken translated and transformed the French *Reine Sébile* into an Early German novel, after 1437; and the *Cronica* of the *Königin von Frankreich* might have been written with the knowledge of the *Sibille* (*Sébile*) novel, but not necessarily so. It was clearly derived from the novella.

BIBLIOGRAPHY

Arnold, Udo. "Schondoch." *Die deutsche Literatur des Mittelalters: Verfasserlexikon,* ed. Kurt Ruh et al. Berlin: de Gruyter, 1992, vol. 8, cols. 820–823.

Fischer, Hanns. *Studien zur deutschen Märendichtung,* 2d ed. Johannes Janota. Tübingen: Niemeyer, 1983, pp. 168–169; 397–399; 515–516.

Jefferis, Sibylle. "Die neuaufgefundene Heidelberger Handschrift von Schondochs *Königin von Frankreich und der ungetreue Marschall:* Ihre Einordnung in die übrige Handschriftenüberlieferung," in *New Texts, Methodologies, and Interpretations in Medieval German Literature (Kalamazoo Papers 1992–1995),* ed. Sibylle Jefferis. Göppingen: Kümmerle, 1999, pp. 209–228.

Liepe, Wolfgang. *Elisabeth von Nassau-Saarbrücken: Entstehung und Anfänge des Prosaromans in Deutschland.* Halle: Niemeyer, 1920, pp. 181–188; Jutta Strippel, ed. *Schondochs Königin von Frankreich: Untersuchungen zur handschriftlichen Überlieferung und kritischer Text.* Göppingen: Kümmerle, 1978, 273–277.

Sibylle Jefferis

SEE ALSO
Deutschorden; Hugo von Langenstein; Meistersinger; Sempach, Battle of

Schongauer, Martin (ca. 1450–1491)

Known today primarily as an engraver, this artist, active in Colmar and the Upper Rhine area from circa 1470 until about 1491, was nicknamed Hübsch Martin (Fair Martin) by his contemporaries in praise of his abilities as a painter. He is important as an assimilator of Netherlandish art. His work was influential in Germany, and he attracted many followers, including Albrecht Dürer.

Martin Schongauer was probably born circa 1450 in Colmar, a town south of Strasbourg. Although some have proposed a birth date of about 1430, this view has not found widespread acceptance. His father, Caspar, was a goldsmith, and Martin probably first trained in his shop. His father apparently wanted his son to become a cleric, for Schongauer's name appears in the 1465 matriculation records of the University of Leipzig. After only one semester, however, he returned to Colmar and began training as a painter. Caspar Isenmann, active in Colmar circa 1435–1472, is often cited as his teacher, but no evidence, documentary or stylistic, supports this assumption. As a journeyman, Schongauer likely traveled to Cologne, then to the Netherlands. His experience of works by the major Netherlandish masters—Roger van der Weyden, Robert Campin, Dieric Bouts, and Hugo van der Goes—is evident in his overall style and in his appropriation of Netherlandish compositions, motifs, and figure types. After his travels, Schongauer settled in Colmar, where he purchased a house in 1469 and again in 1477. He remained there until 1489, when he became a citizen of nearby Breisach. He died there in 1491.

None of Martin Schongauer's paintings are signed. The only dated work attributed to him is the Madonna of the Rose Arbor (Colmar, church of St. Martin), dated 1473 on the reverse. The figure types and detailed, naturalistic rendering of plants and birds are inspired by Netherlandish art. This work's date has been used to establish Schongauer's chronology.

Scholars agree that the earliest preserved works by Schongauer are two wings from the altarpiece commissioned by Jean d'Orlier, preceptor of the Antonite monastery of Isenheim, about 1470 (Colmar, Musée d'Unterlinden). They feature an Annunciation on the exterior, and on the interior, an Adoration and Jean d'Orlier presented by St. Anthony. Schongauer painted several small devotional paintings in the 1480s: two Holy Families (Munich, Alte Pinakothek; Vienna, Kunsthistorisches Museum), an Adoration of the Shepherds (Berlin, Gemäldegalerie), and two versions of the Virgin and Child at a Window (private collections). His last painting, a Last Judgment fresco in Breisach Minster, is based on Roger van der Weyden's Last Judgment Altarpiece of about 1445 (Beaune, Musée de l'Hôtel Dieu).

One-hundred sixteen monogrammed engravings survive, which include both religious and secular subjects. Schongauer's great contributions to the medium were his innovative use of stipling (dots), hatching (fine lines), and crosshatching to create tonal effects like those in paintings, and his adoption of complex compositions derived from paintings. The works are divided into two periods.

Martin Schongauer, Christ Carrying the Cross, engraving (Bartsch-21; Colmar, Musée d'Unterlinden). *Photograph: © Musée d'Unterlinden Colmar, photo O. Zimmermann*

The early engravings date to the early 1470s. Compositions, as in *Christ Carrying the Cross,* tend to be intricate and crowded with figures, and the system of modeling inconsistent. Mature works, from the late 1470s until his death, contain smaller groups, or single figures, and the modeling is more controlled and logical, as in the *Wise and Foolish Virgins.*

A number of drawings attributed to Schongauer also survive. The recent attribution of a watercolor *Study of Peonies* (private collection) provides insight into Schongauer's working methods (Koreny 1991: 591–596). It was probably executed as a preparatory study from nature for the 1473 *Madonna of the Rose Arbor.*

BIBLIOGRAPHY

Baum, Julius. *Martin Schongauer.* Vienna: A. Schroll, 1948.

Le beau Martin: Gravures et dessins de Martin Schongauer vers 1450–1491. Colmar: Museé d'Unterlinden, 1991.

Châtelet, Albert. "Martin Schongauer et les primitifs flamands." *Cahiers alsaciens d'archéologie, d'art et d'histoire* 22 (1979): 117–142.

Dvorak, Max. "Schongauer und die niederländische Malerei," in *Kunstgeschichte als Geistesgeschichte: Studien zur abendländischen Kunstentwicklung.* Munich: Piper, 1924, pp. 151–189.

Koreny, Fritz. "A Coloured Flower Study by Martin Schongauer and the Development of the Depiction of Nature from van der Weyden to Dürer," *Burlington Magazine* 133 (1991): 588–597.

Rosenberg, Jakob. *Martin Schongauer Handzeichnungen.* Munich: Piper, 1923.

Shestack, Alan. *The Complete Engravings of Martin Schongauer.* New York: Dover, 1969.

Susanne Reece

SEE ALSO

Cologne, Art; Gothic Art and Architecture; Printmaking; Strasbourg

Schwäbisch Gmünd

Situated on an upper stretch of the river Rems (Baden-Württemberg), the settlement of Schwäbisch Gmünd was first documented under the name of Gamundias in 782. Two Roman military roads crossed at this location (Rems and Fils), making the site attractive to craftsmen, horse traders, and small merchants serving the needs of travelers. King Konrad III of the house of Hohenstaufen (1138–1152) granted Schwäbisch Gmünd its city charter in 1155. Building campaigns commenced thereafter under the patronage of the house of Hohenstaufen and subsequently the dukes of Württemberg.

The nucleus of the settlement, roughly the area of today's market square, was fortified with walls and towers before gaining its city charter. A second ring of gates and towers encircled a broader area in the thirteenth century, only a small section of which remains today. The third

Schwäbisch Gmünd, Church of the Holy Cross, interior, nave and choir, view to east. *Photograph: Virginia Jansen*

city wall, with twenty four towers or half-towers, was enlarged again in the fourteenth and fifteenth centuries. Six towers from this period survive, among them the fourteenth-century Königsturm (King's Tower), which served as the medieval city's dungeon.

The late Romanesque church of St. Johannis, built between 1220 and 1250, stands on the site of an earlier Romanesque structure commissioned by Duchess Agnes of Swabia (d. 1105). The small basilica, with a simple rectangular form, uniform pillars, two-story elevation, and timber roof, relies heavily on early Christian models. Exterior ornament consists of corbel tables and rare sculptural works, depicting hunting-related imagery and fantastic beasts. An important enthroned Virgin and Child of sandstone, originally created for the church's southwestern exterior corner, is today displayed inside. Gothic alterations from the fifteenth century have since been removed.

Work on the church of the Holy Cross (Heilig-kreuzmünster) began about 1310, to replace a smaller twelfth-century parish church. Heinrich Parler, the second architect hired for the project, radically changed the plans of the first unknown builder, designing the first hall church in southern Germany. The nave was completed in 1350, and the foundation stone of the choir was laid in July 1351. Heinrich's son Peter Parler, born in Schwäbisch Gmünd in 1330, is believed to have been responsible for the design of the church's choir. Before its completion, however, the twenty-three-year-old Peter was called to Prague, where he was named master builder of the cathedral of St. Vitus. The work at Schwäbisch Gmünd was finalized by one "Master Johannes," who installed a flat wooden ceiling over the whole of the interior. Consecration took place on September 21, 1410. The Parler builders undoubtedly intended for the church to be fully vaulted, and by the late fifteenth century, this was realized with the decorative star vaulting of Burkhard Engelberg of Augsburg. The net vaulting of the choir dates to after 1500 and bears the mason's marks of Aberlin Jörg of Stuttgart and Hans von Urach.

The church's exterior and interior are richly ornamented with sculptural works, executed during the period of the Parlers' activity here. Among the finest of these is the southern portal, with its complex Last Judgment tympanum, dating to 1353. Fresco fragments from the fifteenth century, in a chapel behind the high altar, depict the Crucifixion and the Descent from the Cross.

As early as the fourteenth century, Schwäbisch Gmünd became known as a center of goldsmiths who enjoyed a widespread reputation for their superior work. Guilds were established here from the fourteenth century onward and exerted an increasing influence on the city administration and its building projects throughout the later part of the Middle Ages.

BIBLIOGRAPHY

Die Parler und der schöne Stil 1350–1400: Europäische Kunst unter den Luxemburgern, ed. Anton Legner. Cologne: Museen der Stadt Köln, 1978, vol. 1, pp. 315–324.

Schmitt, Otto. *Das Heiligkreuzmünster in Schwäbisch Gmünd.* Stuttgart: W. Kohlhammer, 1951.

Strobel, Richard. *Die Kunstdenkmäler der Stadt Schwäbisch Gmünd,* 2 vols. [to date]. Kunstdenkmäler in Baden-Württemberg 2–3. Munich: Deutscher Kunstverlag, 1995ff.

Leslie Anne Hamel

SEE ALSO

Augsburg; Gothic Art and Architecture; Parler Family; Prague; Romanesque Art and Architecture; Stuttgart

Schwäbisch-Hall

Originally a Celtic settlement on the hillside above the Kocher River, Schwäbisch-Hall prospered on its salt works. It received a charter from Frederick Barbarossa in 1156 and became an imperial free city in 1266. It was famous in medieval Europe for the imperial silver coins minted there: the Häller, or Heller, *pfennige* (pennies). Characteristically bearing an open hand and cross, these coins originated in the 1180s and were struck into the late fourteenth century.

Schwäbisch-Hall retains many reminders of its medieval past. Among these are a 1509 Gothic square fountain flanked by statues of Samson, St. Michael, and St. George. The town still has several medieval half-timbered houses. Its historical museum is in a ten-story Romanesque tower. On the opposite side of the river is the church of St. Katherine from the fourteenth and fifteenth centuries. An imposing flight of stairs leads up to St. Michael's; it still retains its Romanesque west tower, of which only the tower's top is a later replacement. Its Gothic hall-church interior dates to the fifteenth century; one of its chapels, added a century later, is in the flamboyant style. It contains altarpieces dating to the fifteenth and sixteenth centuries.

Two miles outside of Schwäbisch-Hall is Gross Comburg, a Benedictine abbey founded by Graf Burkhard II in 1078. In 1488 the abbey became a house of Augustinian canons. Known as Kloster Komburg in the Middle Ages, it was built as a fortified abbey on a hilltop. One of its entrances retains its twelfth-century Romanesque twin towers with a blind arcaded gallery and a hexagonal chapel dedicated to St. Erhard higher up on the left side.

Komburg's abbey church retains three Romanesque towers and two major monuments of Romanesque metalwork, a chandelier and an antependium or altar frontal. An inscription on the candelabrum names Abbot Hertwig, who ruled circa 1104–1139, as its donor. Made circa 1130 of copperplated and gilded iron, it is in the form of a crown nearly five feet in diameter. Its pierced scrollwork bands are decorated with towers and circular medallions, themselves decorated with three-dimensional standing figures and relief busts. The ensemble symbolizes the Heavenly Jerusalem, and the figures represent the just who inhabit the Holy City. The question of whether the candelabrum was actually made at Komburg has not been definitively settled.

The antependium of Komburg's high altar was also made circa 1120–1130. Of gilded copper and enamelwork, it depicts in relief with flattened folds Christ standing in a mandorla (body halo) flanked by evangelist symbols and apostles. Each stands in his own compartment with his name embossed, framed by bands of cloisonné (sectioned multicolor) enamel. Inscriptions appear on the rectangular frame and Christ's mandorla. Valentien argued convincingly that the Byzantine influence on its figural treatment, decorative patterns, and enamel technique came by way of Salzburg.

BIBLIOGRAPHY

Herrmann, Adolf. "Zum Komburger Kronleuchter und Antependium." *Zeitschrift des Deutschen Vereins für Kunstwissenschaft* 3 (1936): 174–195.

Valentien, Freerk. *Untersuchen zur Kunst des 12. Jahrhunderts im Kloster Komburg.* Ph.d. diss., University of Freiburg im Breisgau, 1963. Freiburg: Bissinger, 1963.

Die Zeit der Staufer: Geschichte, Kunst, Kultur, ed. Reiner Haussherr. 5 vols. Stuttgart: Württembergisches Landesmuseum, 1977, vol. 1, pp. 464–466.

Dorothy M. Shepard

SEE ALSO

Frederick I Barbarossa; Gothic Art and Architecture; Romanesque Art and Architecture; Salzburg

Schwerin

The chronicler Thietmar of Merseberg mentions Schwerin in 1018 as an outpost of a western Slavic tribe known as Obotrites (also Abotrites), who had built the castle Wallburg on the site of the current castle. After Henry the Lion, duke of Saxony, defeated the Slavs in 1160, he founded the margraviate of Schwerin and established the bishopric the same year. The early years of the bishopric were dominated by the Cistercians and Bishop Bernos, who built the Cistercian monasteries Doberan (1171) and Dargun (1172) in the immediate area. A Romanesque cathedral, of which only remnants of the west tower remain, was constructed in the latter half of the twelfth century; its choir was consecrated in 1248. Construction of the present brick Gothic basilica on the same site began in 1250; its choir was consecrated in 1327. Although construction lasted for almost two hundred years, the entire structure of the basilica is harmonious despite stylistic variances. The heyday of the bishopric was the thirteenth century after Margrave Henry I brought from Palestine a relic of the blood of Christ in 1222 and erected the Heilig-Bluts-Kapelle (Chapel of the Holy Blood) as a pilgrimage site. Emperor Charles IV made Schwerin a duchy in 1348; the ascension of Duke Albert II in 1358 brought an end to religious influence of the bishopric.

BIBLIOGRAPHY

Hahn, Gudrun, et al. *Schwerin*. Berlin: Verlag für Bauwesen, 1984.

Kaluza-Baumruker, Margit. *Das Schweriner Domkapitel*. Cologne: Böhlau, 1987.

Leupke, Gerd. *Dome, Kirchen und Kloster in Mecklenburg*. Frankfurt am Main: Wolfgang Weidlich, 1962.

Mueller, Hans, ed. *Denkmale in Mecklenburg: Ihre Erhaltung und Pflege in den Bezirken Rostock, Schwerin und Neubrandenburg*. Weimar: Hermann Böhlaus Nachfolger, 1976.

Strutz, Hans, ed. *Staatliches Museum Schwerin*. Leipzig: Seeman, 1984.

Gregory H. Wolf

SEE ALSO

Charles IV; Cistercian Art and Architecture; Gothic Art and Architecture; Henry the Lion; Romanesque Art and Architecture

Science

See Sachliteratur.

Sculpture

See individual styles.

Seals and Sigillography

Seals have a long history. Having originated alongside if not actually preceding the invention of writing, sealing was, in medieval Germany as in most other civilizations, a significant mechanism for marking and protecting ownership, signing commitment, designating identity, representing authority, and authenticating documentation. In parallel to their role in the sphere of practice, seals have also served as a metaphoric focus. Mesopotamian and biblical texts, Platonic and Aristotelian treatises, patristic and theological commentaries, literary texts—all incorporate sealing imagery as a conceptual tool. Such historical continuity need not imply congruence of the cultural and modal significance of the seals themselves. While partaking of the general Western cultural phenomenon, which between the twelfth and the fifteenth century privileged the seal as an authoritative mode for the representation of

Seal of Reinald von Dassel, Archbishop of Cologne, 1166 (Historisches Archiv der Stadt Köln Dom U3/11). *Photograph: Historisches Archiv*

individuals, officials, and corporations, German seals and sealing practices present distinctive features, in particular with respect to their sociology, their legal capacity, their aesthetics, and the circumstances of their diffusion.

The study of seals, or sigillography (German, *Siegelkunde* or *Sphragistik)*, achieved its disciplinary status and received its epistemological framework from Jean Mabillon's *De re diplomatica (On Diplomatics,* 1681), complemented for Germany by Johannes Michael Hennecius's *De veteribus Germanorum aliarumque nationum sigillis (On the Old Seals of the German and of Other Nations,* 1719). Sigillographic studies have, since their inception in the seventeenth century, been consistently pursued within the constraints of an auxiliary science required to serve the greater discipline of history. Seals have thus been defined as sources requiring specific heuristics, and a technique of conservation—the cast—has selectively privileged the most significant seals and the best extant impression of a given seal type. Such an epistemology, which fostered a scholarship based on cast collections, ultimately denatured seals, changing their locus (on documents) and their status (as signs), and erasing their fundamental signifying and operative principle: iteration, by which medieval seals (re)produced themselves as identity and as identical devices. Thus abstracted as object of knowledge and removed from the sphere of medieval discourse and practice, the medieval seal has literally been recast as a fixed type, all too often the prisoner of antiquarian agendas. In the last half of the twentieth century, however, electronic databases of medieval sealed charters, such as the LichtBildArchiv (photo archives) in Marburg, have permitted the consultation of seals in their original forms and loci. Computerized techniques of information retrieval, by enhancing the possibility of accumulating data along various thematic axes, have stimulated the formulation of newer approaches that have attempted to restore the historicity of seals as agents within the culture that produced and used them. A recent argument has been made, for instance, that seals, poised as they were at the nexus of the gestural, the visual, and the legible, fostered trust in writing and hence acculturation to literate modes. Seal iconography has lent itself to pioneering studies in ideology and iconology. A semiotic approach has redirected the analysis toward seals' modes and areas of signification (authority, identity), and contributed a methodology for retrieving the assumptions seals encode about the nature of their operation.

A medieval seal (Latin, *sigillum;* German, *Siegel)* is a mark pressed in relief on a plastic material (wax, lead, or

Seal of Elisabeth von Virenburg, Abbess at the Convent of the Holy Virgins (St. Ursula's), Cologne, 1310 (Historisches Archiv der Stadt Köln HUA 3/745A): *Schutzmantelursula. Photograph: Historisches Archiv*

gold) by the impact of a matrix, or die (Latin, *typarium;* German, *Siegelstempel, Petschaft, Typar),* intaglio-engraved with a text (the legend) and an iconographic device that, together, defined and personified the seal owner. In medieval as in modern terminology the term *seal* may designate both the matrix and the impressions issued from it. But for the sake of clarity, current usage tends to reserve the term *seal* for the impression (German, *Siegel* or *Siegelabdrücke).*

In western Europe following the disintegration of the Roman Empire, seal rings were widely used to communicate verbal orders and, imprinted in wax, to close personal letters. They belonged to private individuals, to bishops, and to rulers. Among the earliest royal extant rings are those of Childeric, king of the Franks (d. 481), Alaric II, king of the Visigoths (d. 507), and Theodoric the Great, king of the Ostrogoths (d. 507). By the seventh century, the royal sealing practice took on a specific, distinguishing feature as wax seal impressions bearing the king's image and title came to be attached to the diplomas given in his name. The western sealed diploma remained an exclusive royal and imperial prerogative until the tenth century. This documentary model was derived from the Byzantine imperial chancery, which, since the sixth century, had issued letters and documents sealed in lead and gold, inspiring further the use of metallic impressions (Latin, *bulla;* German, *Bulle*) by Western writing bureaus. Thus the pope, as both bishop of Rome and a Byzantine magistrate, sealed from the sixth century onward exclusively with lead *bullae,* introducing wax only in the thirteenth century and then exclusively for the papal secret seal known as the Fisherman's ring (Latin, *anulus piscatoris;* German, *Fischerring).* From the very year of his imperial coronation in 800, Charlemagne (d. 814) emulated the Byzantine *basileus* by resorting to gold and silver bulls for the sealing of his solemn diplomas, as did his successors. After his own assumption of the imperial crown in 962, Otto I (d. 973) resumed sealing with metallic bulls, a practice that Otto III (d. 1002), son of the Byzantine princess Theophanu, adopted systematically for a while. The leaden bull remained in use until the reign of Henry III (d. 1056). The much rarer golden *bullae,* exceptionally used by Louis the Pious, the Ottonians, and the Salians, became the exclusive prerogative of the Hohenstaufen chancery.

Whether wax or metal, medieval German seals were, at first, attached exclusively to royal or imperial deeds. The late Antique habit of closing letters with signet ring impressions became confined to the only part of society that still engaged in official epistolary exchanges, the bishops. The signet rings of Archbishop Ratbod of Trier (883–915) and of Liuthard, bishop of Paderborn (862–887) are still extant. The earliest western European instances of nonroyal documentary sealing occurred in tenth-century Germany, this usage deriving its momentum from the seal's role in both the definition and validation of kingship, and in ecclesiastical literate practice. The very use of sealed charters having already spread in parallel to the Carolingian multiplication of kingships, the Bavarian duke Arnulf (d. 937) undertook to seal documents issued in his own name, thus asserting his political independence from and opposition to the newly elected

non-Carolingian king of Germany, Conrad of Franconia (d. 918). This example was followed by the Salian Otto, as duke of Carinthia in 978, and in 1004 by the Saxon Duke Benno, thereafter extending to other potentates and to lesser lords. Episcopal documentary sealing also began in the tenth century, at Cologne (ca. 950), Trier (955), Mainz (976), Salzburg (ca. 958–991), Halberstadt (ca. 968–996), Liège (980), Tournai (994), Hildesheim (996), and Toul (971), paralleling the growing integration of the episcopacy into the royal/imperial administrative apparatus. By the eleventh century, cathedral chapters (Münster) and abbeys (St. Gall, Fulda, Corvey) had started to seal as well. Whereas the imperial chancery issued imperial documents exclusively, the schoolmen staffing episcopal and monastic writing bureaus undertook to write charters on behalf of laymen and women, thus further extending to these latter a practice of sealing informed by newly developed prescholastic theories of symbolic representation. Between the thirteenth and the fifteenth century, men and women from the lesser nobility, the church, the cities, and the crafts, as well as the peasantry, Jews, officials, towns, corporations, courts, and jurisdictions—all could, and many did, commit themselves by sealing the deeds recording their obligations. During the fifteenth century, such alternative modes for authorizing contracts as personal signatures and the notariate progressively replaced the seal for such purposes.

As seals spread socially, the originally empirical nature of their operations became an object of theory on the part of authorities, who introduced degrees within the seal's efficacy and fostered its function as a legal device for the authentication of written documents. Papal decretals, beginning with Pope Alexander III (r. 1159–1181), stipulated a distinction between seals that committed only their owners and users (private seals), and the *sigillum authenticum* (German, *authentisches Siegel),* which, emanating from those individuals, institutions, or corporate bodies invested with public authority, alone carried credibility and guaranteed systematically the contractants' transactions recorded in writing. The thirteenth-century Saxon law code, the *Sachsenspiegel,* written first in Latin and then in Low German between 1220 and 1235, displaying but little familiarity with canon law and no knowledge of Roman law, and based exclusively on the practical experience of the author, Eike von Repgow, in East Saxon law courts, distinguishes clearly between the personal seal validating only an act given in the seal owner's name, and the seal (that is, the *sigillum authenticum*) that validated documents given in the names of people other than the seal's owner. The Swabian legal code *Schwabenspiegel* (ca. 1275–1276), borrowing heavily from Roman and canon law, declared that only popes, emperors, kings, potentates, bishops, chapters, and convents had the right to validate documents by their seals; that minor landholding nobility might validate acts of their vassals; that the official or the town could validate those of their dependants.

Although such sociolegal regulations remained primarily prescriptive, as the large number of extant seals of knights, peasants, burghers, and Jews testify, seals belonging to public/official authorities nevertheless underwent a distinct fate. All seals had diversified, indeed multiplied into distinct categories, whereby a sealer would own several seals, each assigned a specific function. The great seal (Latin, *sigillum magnum;* German, *grosses Siegel, Hauptsiegel*) was the main seal used for solemn/formal documents. The small seal (Latin, *sigillum parvum* or *minus;* German, *kleines Siegel*) was affixed to writings dealing with internal administration, while the signet (Latin, *sigillum secretum;* German, *Sekretsiegel*) appeared on papers of personal matters. The counterseal (Latin, *contrasigillum;* German, *Rücksiegel*), which could also serve as small seal and signet, was a smaller impression made at the back of the wax to corroborate the principal seal and to discourage its forgery. Yet only public and official seals further diversified as seals of jurisdiction (German, *Gerichtssiegel, Geschäftssiegel; Latin, sigillum ad contractus, ad obligationes, ad recognitiones)*, which authorities used to supervise and certify contracts as part of their judicial and fiscal responsibilities. Seals of jurisdiction thus served as tools of the burgeoning administrative organization that reshaped both lay and ecclesiastical governance from the twelfth century onward.

Seal performance in the legal and administrative spheres has somewhat obscured other roles played by seals, roles deriving from and dependent on their iconic and symbolic language. For instance, in the cortege formed at the inauguration of the Imperial Diet *(Reichstag)*, the chancellor of the kingdom in which the diet was meeting preceded the emperor, carrying all imperial seals attached to a silver rod. At the end of the ceremony, the seals were returned to the imperial chancellor. During state rituals and travel throughout the empire, the emperor and his archchancellor wore the seal matrices around their necks.

Manufacture of imperial seal matrices, wherever documented, appears to have been entrusted to major artists and court advisers. Abbot Wibald of Stavelot (d. 1158), whose patronage of the greatest goldsmiths of his time

(such as Godfrey of Huy) led to his supervision of the execution of imperial seals, inspired the iconographic program on those of Frederic I Barbarossa (d. 1190) and his empress, Beatrix of Burgundy (d. 1184). However, little is known of seal engraving in general, and the more than hundred German seal makers (Latin, *taillatores, sculptores, incisores sigillorum;* German, *Stempelschneider*) who have been identified appear only in the fourteenth- and fifteenth-century accounts of those elite nobles or corporations and cities intent on possessing finely engraved items. Some places were then particularly famous for their seal-cutting workshops, such as Trier, Cologne, Nuremberg, and Augsburg, but fine engraving played little part in the manufacture of most medieval seals, which were simply cast. Relatively few medieval matrices are extant, for they were typically either destroyed or buried at the death of their owners, or used until they wore out.

Extant seal impressions, on the other hand, number over one million in western Germany and about three million in the whole of Europe; they are mostly round, pointed oval, or scutiform (shield shaped). Impressed on wax, which was the general method in the empire but for the use of (always round) metallic bulls by the imperial and a few episcopal chanceries (Cologne, Hamburg, Halberstadt), the seals' colors vary. At first, the wax was uncolored; by the thirteenth century it might be green (verdigris), red (vermilion), or brown. Occasionally the impression, in one color of wax, would be enclosed within wax of another color. From the early fifteenth century onward, red wax became a prerogative of the imperial chancery. Otherwise, the use and distribution of various colors in seals seem to have variously obeyed either taste, fashion, or local administrative practice. There were three standard ways of attaching the seal to the document, all used throughout the Middle Ages in imperial Germany. In one, the wax was laid on the surface of the parchment and stamped to produce an applied seal. A second method was to suspend the seal from a tag (parchment) or cord (silk, linen, woolen thread) that passed through slits made in the bottom edge of the document, usually folded back for added strength. The third technique involved attaching the seal to a strip of parchment (the tongue) partially cut away from the bottom edge of the document.

The system of figural representation on seals is the product of a dialectical tension between letters and images. The text (the legend) named the owner. It was normally displayed clockwise in an outer band, beginning at the top with a cross. This cross has been recently interpreted as a religious invocation by the German sigillographer Toni Diederich (1996), who notes that on certain seals, for example, the second city seal of Siegburg in Westphalia, the initial cross had been replaced by the verbal invocation *in nomine domini amen* (In the Name of God, Amen). In contradistinction to the individualizing legend, the image was emblematic of the seal's owner, pointing to status and to membership within specific categories: kingship, equestrian nobility, knighthood, office, occupation, religion, institution, kin (heraldry), holiness, or womanhood. Iconographic patterns, such as majesty, architecture, or sanctity, were meant to signify a concept rather than realistically to represent a person. Seals generated personal identity through a grammar that articulated the organizing principles of society. Personal identity was produced as an instance of social order, and thus served as the verifier of the system it substantiated. While seal images carry factual information about costume, architectural detail, and material culture in general, they also testify to concepts crucial to medieval thinking and praxis. Above all, they embody the medieval ability to invest the invisible with visibility.

BIBLIOGRAPHY

Bedos-Rezak, Brigitte. "Seals and Sigillography, Western," in *Dictionary of the Middle Ages,* ed. Joseph R. Strayer. New York: Scribners, 1982–1989, vol. 11, pp. 123–131.

Déer, Josef. "Die Siegel Kaiser Friedrichs I. Barbarossa und Heinrichs VI. in der Kunst und Politik ihrer Zeit." In *Festschrift Hans R. Hahnloser zum 60. Geburtstag,* ed. Ellen J. Beer. Basel: Birkhäuser, 1961, pp. 47–102.

Diederich, Toni. *Die alten Siegel der Stadt Köln.* Cologne: Greven, 1980.

———. "Prolegomena zu einer neuen Sigeltypologie." *Archiv für Diplomatik* 29 (1983): 242–284.

———. "Siegelforschung, Siegelerfassung und Siegelkonservierung." *Geschichte in Köln: Studentische Zeitschrift am historischen Seminar* 13 (1983): 5–39.

———. "Siegelkunst," in *Die Parler und der Schöne Stil 1350–1400: Europäische Kunst unter den Luxemburgern,* ed. Anton Legner. Cologne: Stadt Köln, 1978, vol. 3, pp. 151–163.

———. "Zum Quellenwert und Bedeutungsgehalt mittelalterlicher Städtesiegel." *Archiv für Diplomatik* 23 (1977): 269–285.

———. "Zur Bedeutung des Kreuzes am Anfang von Siegelumschriften," in *Graphische Symbole in mittelalterlichen Urkunden: Beiträge zur diplomatischen Semiotik,* ed. Peter Rück. Sigmaringen: Thorbecke, 1996, pp. 157–166.

Ewald, Wilhelm. *Siegelkunde.* Handbuch der mittelalterlichen und neueren Geschichte 4. 1914. Munich: Oldenbourg, 1969.

Ewe, Herbert. *Schiffe auf Siegeln.* Berlin: Bielefeld, 1972.

Friedenberg, Daniel M. *Medieval Jewish Seals from Europe.* Detroit: Wayne State University Press, 1987, pp. 145–309.

Gritzner, Erich. *Die Siegel der deutschen Universitäten in Deutschland, Österreich und der Schweiz.* 1906; rpt. Neustadt an der Aisch: Bauer und Raspe, 1976.

Henning, Eckart, and Gabriele Jochums. *Bibliographie zur Sphragistik: Schriftum Deutschlands, Österreichs und der Schweiz bis 1990.* Cologne: Böhlau, 1995.

Kahsnitz, Rainer. "*Imagines et signa:* Romanische Siegel aus Köln," in *Ornamenta ecclesiae: Kunst und Künstler der Romanik in Köln,* ed. Anton Legner. Cologne: Schnütgen Museum, 1985, vol. 2, pp. 21–60.

———. "Siegel und Goldbullen," in *Die Zeit der Staufer: Geschichte, Kunst, Kultur,* ed. Reiner Haussherr. Stuttgart: Württembergisches Landesmuseum, 1977, vol. 1, pp. 17–107, Catalogue. no. 27–162; vol. 2: ills. 11–92; vol. 3, ills. 1–30, 83–104.

Kittel, Erich. *Siegel.* Braunschweig: Klinkhardt u. Biermann, 1970.

———. "Die Siegelsammlungen in den westdeutschen Archiven." *Der Archivar* 2, no. 3 (1964): 225–238.

Pastoureau, Michel. *Les Sceaux.* Turnhout: Brepols, 1981.

Schramm, Percy Ernst. "Die Siegel, Bullen und Kronen der Karolinger," in *Kaiser, Könige und Päpste: Gesammelte Aufsätze zur Geschichte des Mittelalters,* 5 vols. Stuttgart: Hiersemann, 1968–1971, vol. 2, pp. 15–74, ills. 1–22.

Vocabulaire international de la sigillographie. Publicazioni degli Archivi di Stato. Rome: Ministerio per i Beni Culturali e Ambientali, 1990.

Wagner, Franz. "Goldschmiedekunst." In *Spätgotik in Salzburg: Skulptur und Kunstgewerbe 1400–1530.* Salzburg: Salzburger Museo Carolino Augusteum, 1976, pp. 75–92.

Brigitte Bedos-Rezak

SEE ALSO

Seghelijn van Jherusalem

This Middle Dutch (Flemish) romance is named after its main character, Seghelijn of Jerusalem. This extensive poem, almost twelve thousand lines in coupled rhyme, was written in the early fourteenth century by an anonymous poet (the attribution of it to Loy Latewaert is dubious). The poem is an original Middle Dutch work, though the poet used many different sources (e.g., the legends of St. Julian Hospitaller, St. Andrew and Judas, the *Bonne Florence de Rome, Fierabras,* and *Elie de St. Gilles*). He created an "anti-courtly romance" with a strong religious and hagiographic tone in which he also incorporated elements of (late) medieval crusade ideology and criticism. The text survives in one manuscript (ca. 1415), one incunabulum, five prints of the sixteenth century, and one excerpt in a fifteenth-century manuscript. The poem is an outstanding example of the late medieval narrative tradition in the Low Countries.

Seghelijn (meaning "the victorious and/or the blessed") is the son of Prides, the Muslim king of Jerusalem, and Queen Braffeleur. His mother, secretly converted to Christianity, fears for her son's life and abandons him. He grows up in a poor fisher family, but he returns to the court of his unsuspecting father to find out about his true identity and to become a knight. Refusing to swear an oath of fidelity to Muhammad, Seghelijn has to flee from court. He starts an adventurous life fighting the enemies of Christianity and collecting the relics of Christ's Passion. For fathering seven sons with seven unbaptized damsels—later to be known as the Seven Wise Men of Rome—he spends fifteen years in heathen prison, doing penance. After his release he continues his adventures as God's chosen knight, completing his collection of relics with the Holy Cross. Eventually he becomes emperor of Rome and ends his life as pope Benedict I.

BIBLIOGRAPHY

Claassens, Geert H. M. "Die Kerstenwet stercken. Kruisvaartideologie en -kritiek in de *Seghelijn van Jherusalem.*" *Tijdschrift voor Nederlandse Taal- en Letterkunde* 107 (1991): 235–273.

———. "Dat en is sonder reden. Over de zeven vragen van Seghelijn van Jherusalem." *Spiegel der Letteren* 40 (1998): 25–54.

Janssens, Jozef D. "Oorspronkelijkheid en traditionalisme in *Seghelijn van Jherusalem.*" *Leuvense Bijdragen* 67 (1978): 23–46.

van de Wijer, Ingrid. "*Segheliin van Iherusalem.* Tekstoverlevering van een Middelnederlands ridderdicht." *Quaerendo* 14 (1984): 273–304.

Verdam, Jakob, ed. *Seghelijn van Jherusalem.* Leyden: Brill, 1878.

Geert H. M. Claassens

SEE ALSO
Crusade Literature, Dutch; Crusades

Segher Diengotgaf (fl. 1200–ca. 1260)

Flemish-Brabantine poet, known for his *Trojeroman (Trojan Novel),* a courtly romance in circa 2,300 lines of coupled rhyme, not a comprehensive history of the Trojan War. Using a limited episode from this history as a narrative setting, Segher describes and debates some aspects of (courtly) love and virtues, with Trojan heroes as main characters. Segher's romance consists of three parts—*Tprieel van Trojen, Tpaerlement van Trojen,* and *Den groten strijt.* Formerly considered to be three separate romances, they are now viewed by modern scholarship as parts of one coherent text, in which the division in three parts is an important structural principle ("love debate"—"battle with words"—"battle in arms"). This structural principle also functions within the constituent parts (especially *Tprieel),* strongly drawing attention to love as the main theme (three dialogues and the general complaint on love). For the last two parts Segher used Benoît of St. Maure's *Roman de Troie. Tprieel,* however, is completely his own work (though he refers to Dares Phrygius as his source), in which he tries to emulate Benoît's concept of love. Benoît presented love and passion as destructive forces, Segher as a positive aspect of courtly culture, a force ennobling men and women. This concept forces Segher to leave the story of the Trojan War "unfinished," for it is passion that lays at the root of Troy's ultimate destruction.

Most likely Segher wrote his *Trojeroman* around 1240–1245 for the ducal court of Brabant (perhaps commissioned by Duke Henry II, d. 1261). The *Trojeroman* is preserved as an interpolation in Jacob van Maerlant's *Historie van Troyen* and as three separate texts in the famous Hulthem Manuscript (Brussels, Koninklijke Bibliotheek, manuscript no. 15,589–623); no independent manuscript survives of this very fine and early specimen of Middle Dutch courtly literature.

BIBLIOGRAPHY

de Pauw, Napoleon, and Edward Gaillard, eds. *Istory van Troyen.* 4 vols. Ghent: Siffer, 1889–1892, vol. 2, pp. 1–41, 59–88.

Janssens, Jozef D. "Segher Diengotgaf of Jacob van Maerlant aan het woord?" in 't Ondersoeck leert. Studies over middeleeuwse en 17de-eeuwse literatuur ter nagedachtenis van prof. dr. L. Rens, ed. G. van Eemeren and F. Willaerts. Leuven: Acco, 1986, pp. 43–53.

———. "De handschriftelijke overlevering van de Trojeroman van Segher Diengotgaf," in Miscellanea Neerlandica. Opstellen voor dr. J. Deschamps etc., ed. E. Cockx and F. Hendrickx. 3 vols. Leuven: Peeters, 1987, vol. 2, pp. 153–161.

van Anrooij, Wim. "Het wapenteken van Hector in Seghers Trojeroman," in Op avontuur. Middeleeuwse epiek in de Lage Landen, ed. Jozef. D. Janssens et al. Amsterdam: Prometheus, 1998, pp. 63–78, 296–307.

Geert H. M. Claassens

SEE ALSO

Brabant, Duchy of; Jacob van Maerlant

Seckau

Isolated in the Lower Tauern range of the high Alps, Seckau is the site of the oldest Augustinian foundation in Styria and was the seat of the diocese from 1218 until 1782. Established in 1140 in St. Marein on land given by Adalram von Wolfegg (Wolfeck) in penance for a murder, the community was organized under the first provost Wernher (1141–1196) and moved to its present location in 1142. A house for both male and female religious, Seckau was populated by Augustinian canons from Salzburg, making it part of the Augustinian reform circle of Salzburg Archbishop Konrad I (1106–1147). Konrad's earlier position as a canon in Hildesheim explains the Saxon stylistic features of the church at Seckau, a three-aisle, transeptless basilica, consecrated in 1164 by Bishop Hartmann of Brixen. Liturgically, Seckau was dependent on the Salzburg cathedral rite, but it also became a center for the development of the Augustinian sequence form. The vibrant community provided canons for the new foundation of Vorau in 1163.

In 1218, Eberhard II, archbishop of Salzburg, with the permission of Pope Honorius III, established Seckau as the seat of a small bishopric, and Frederick II consented, conferring on the bishop the dignity of prince of the Roman Empire. The first prince-bishop was Provost Karl von Friesach (1218–1230). Substantial rebuilding of the church precinct was necessitated after a fire of 1259. To the renewals of that period belong the no longer extant Liechtensteiner Chapel (consecrated in 1279), which extended the eastern end of the church. Probably executed circa 1290 is a Zackenstil fresco depicting in five tiers an extensive life of St. John the Baptist, now displayed in the south transept of the church. During the reigns of Provosts Andreas Ennstaler and Johannes Durnberger in the fifteenth century, the basilica was elaborately vaulted.

The convent of Seckau was rebuilt in the baroque period, vacated in 1782, and resettled in 1883 by Benedictines. The bishopric was moved to Graz by 1786, and the bulk of the medieval manuscript holdings of the monastery are today found in the Graz University Library.

BIBLIOGRAPHY

Amon, K., ed. Die Bischöfe von Graz-Seckau 1218–1968. Graz: Verlag Styria, 1969.

Augustiner-Chorherren zwischen Passau und Salzburg. Linz: Amt der Oberösterreichischer Landesregierung, Abteilung Kultur, 1984.

Demus, Otto. Romanesque Mural Painting. New York: Harry N. Abrams, 1970, p. 637.

Fest und Feier: Kirchenmusik in der Steiermark. Graz: Diözesanmuseum Graz, 1995.

Gotik in der Steiermark. Graz: Kulturreferat der Steiermarkische Landesregierung, 1978.

Roth, Benno. Quellen und Bibliographie zur Geschichte des ehemaligen Augustinerchorherren- und Domstiftes Seckau. Seckauer Geschichtliche Studien 13. Seckau: Selbstverlag des Verfassers, 1957.

———. Seckau: Geschichte und Kultur 1164–1964: Zur 800-Jahr-Feier der Weihe der Basilika. Vienna: Herold, 1964.

Weinfurter, Stefan. Salzburger Bistumsreform und Bischofspolitik im 12. Jahrhundert: Der Erzbischof Konrad von Salzburg (1106–1147) und die Regularkanoniker. Ph.d. diss., University of Cologne, 1973. Kölner Historische Abhandlungen 24. Cologne: Böhlau, 1975.

Wagner-Rieger, Renate. Mittelalterliche Architektur in Österreich. St. Pölten: Verlag Niederösterreichisches Pressehaus, 1991.

Amelia Carr

SEE ALSO

Frederick II; Gothic Art and Architecture; Hildesheim; Romanesque Art and Architecture; Salzburg

Seligenstadt

Although the most recent publication on the town is devoted to the restoration of the Romanesque House

(Ludwig, 1987), Seligenstadt, on the Main River east of Frankfurt, is best known for the Benedictine monastery founded by Einhard, Charlemagne's biographer and one of the most prominent members of the emperor's court. Einhard constructed the monastery to house the relics of Saints Marcellinus and Petrus, reputedly removed by his agent from the funerary basilica of that name on the edge of Rome. Although Einhard first constructed a church at Steinbach for these relics, and presumably for his own burial, by 830 he had begun building the larger monastery at Seligenstadt, then called Obermühlheim am Main, most likely the town or area in which he had been born to a noble family. The dedication of the monastery took place in 836 with Louis the Pious present.

On the basis of excavations and early descriptions, scholars have proposed reconstructions for Einhard's church building within the monastery complex. Seligenstadt is an important example of the Carolingian desire to build in the *more romano* (Roman style), also articulated at Lorsch and Fulda—an architectural extension of the interest in the ancient world that characterized the court of Charlemagne. Significant architectural motifs included a single raised apse with an annular crypt for the relics of the saints and a transept, elements that Krautheimer traced to St. Peter's at Rome, although he identified exact parallels for some of the characteristics of Seligenstadt in other Roman churches. At the west end of the nave with single side aisles was a narthex (entrance structure) that included the burials of Einhard and his wife Imma.

BIBLIOGRAPHY

Fleckenstein, Josef. "Einhard, seine Gründung und sein Vermächtnis in Seligenstadt," in *Das Einhardskreuz: Vorträge und Studien der Münsteraner Diskussion zum arcus Einhardi*. Abhandlungen der Akademie der Wissenschaften in Göttingen. Göttingen: Vandenhoeck und Ruprecht, 1974, pp. 96–121.

Krautheimer, Richard. "The Carolingian Revival of Early Christian Architecture." *Studies in Early Christian, Medieval, and Renaissance Art*. New York: New York University Press, 1969, pp. 203–256.

Ludwig, Thomas. *Das romanische Haus in Seligenstadt*. Ph.d. diss., Technische Hochschule Darmstadt, 1987. Stuttgart: K. Theiss, 1987.

Müller, Otto, and Carsten Waltjen with Wolfgang Einsingbach. *Seligenstadt: Ehemalige Benediktiner-Abtei*. Bad Homburg vor der Höhe: Verwaltung der Staatlichen Schlösser und Gärten Hessen, 1975.

Oswald, Friedrich, Leo Schaefer, and Hans Rudolf Sennhauser. *Vorromanische Kirchenbauten: Katalog der Denkmäler bis zum Ausgang der Ottonen*. Munich: Prestel: 1971, vol. 3, pp. 309–312.

Rebecca W. Corrie

SEE ALSO

Carolingian Art and Architecture; Charlemagne; Frankfurt am Main; Fulda; Lorsch; Louis the Pious; Romanesque Art and Architecture; Steinbach

Sempach, Battle of (July 9, 1386)

Provoked by the Swiss conquest of Luzern and the sacking of several castles, the Austrian Habsburgs once more decided to teach the Swiss a lesson and reclaim their lordship in the western Alps. With a force of several thousand, Duke Leopold III was marching through the town of Sempach toward Luzern on July 9, 1386, when he and the Swiss came upon each other. Because their cavalry had been defeated by infantry at the battles of Morgarten and Laupen, this time the Habsburgs tried to adapt to their enemy's tactics. Leopold dismounted his cavalry and had them march on foot with their lances toward the Swiss, who were lodged on high ground. But the Austrians lost their initial advantage, perhaps because Swiss reinforcements arrived or the Austrians grew weary in their hot plate armor. The story of the Swiss hero Arnold of Winkelried, who threw himself on the Austrian lances to open a gap for his comrades to rush in, is purely legendary.

The victorious Swiss slew over six hundred knights, including Duke Leopold himself. Thereafter the Habsburgs could do little to prevent Swiss independence.

BIBLIOGRAPHY

Delbrück, Hans. *Medieval Warfare*, trans. Walter J. Renfroe Jr. Lincoln: University of Nebraska Press, 1982.

Oman, Charles. *A History of the Art of War in the Middle Ages*. 2 vols., 2d ed. London: Methuen, 1924.

Wheatcroft, Andrew. *The Habsburgs: Embodying Empire*. New York: Viking, 1995.

Brian A. Pavlac

Sermons

See Preaching and Sermons, Dutch; Preaching and Sermons, German.

Servatius

Composed around 1185 by an unknown author (whose name most likely appeared at the work's end, now lost), the *Oberdeutscher Servatius,* a version of the life of St. Servatius in an Upper German dialect, tells of the life, death, and posthumous acts and miracles of Servatius, the fourth-century bishop of Tongres in modern-day Belgium. The legend focuses on events in the history of Maastricht, the city with which Servatius is the most closely identified, and describes the actions of a number of rulers (Attila, Charlemagne, Otto I and II, Henry I, II, and III). It also deals with topics such as purgatory, absolution, the power to forgive sins, and heresy. While the Upper German *Servatius* conforms to the expectations of its genre—the saint's life—its author digressed significantly in several passages from the source(s) and thus created what has been called by several commentators a "courtly legend."

In 1172 Agnes of Loon, the patroness (or her daughter) of Heinric von Veldeke, who composed a life of Servatius in his native Limburg dialect, married Otto of Wittelsbach. In her new home, she apparently commissioned a local poet to compose a work honoring her patron saint in the Upper German dialect. Though related to the perhaps more famous version of the saint's life composed by Veldeke, the Upper German version is not a translation of that earlier work. There is textual evidence that the writer consulted Veldeke's work, but the primary source used by the Bavarian author had to have been the late-eleventh-century Latin *Gesta Sancti Servatii.*

The *Oberdeutscher Servatius* is found (missing several final pages) in the Austrian Nationalbibliothek in Vienna (manuscript no. 2696); fragments of four other manuscripts also attest to the work.

BIBLIOGRAPHY

Walter, James K. "The Upper German Life of St. Servatius: Text, Notes and Commentary." Ph.d. diss., University of Wisconsin-Madison, 1989.

Wilhelm, Friedrich. *Sanct Servatius oder Wie das erste Reis in deutscher Zunge geimpft wurde.* Munich: Beck, 1910.

Wolff, Ludwig. "Der Servatius Heinrichs von Veldeke und der Oberdeutsche Servatius," in *Sagen mit Sinne. Festschrift für Marie-Luise Dittrich zum 65. Geburtstag.* Göppingen: Kümmerle, 1976, pp. 51–62.

James K. Walter

SEE ALSO

Charlemagne; Heinrich von Veldeke; Henry I; Henry III; Otto I; Otto II

Servitium

See Fodrum, Gistum, Servitium.

Seuse, Heinrich (1295/1297–1366)

This Dominican priest served as a confessor, preacher, and teacher to religious men and women in the German south. His poetic works in the mystical tradition served to inspire those in his care.

Born into a patrician family in or near Constance, Seuse did not seek out ministerial service but followed in the footsteps of his religiously oriented mother, whose name he chose to use. At thirteen he entered the monastery at Constance. Following a general course of study there, he may have studied briefly in Strasbourg before attending the *studium generale* (early form of university education) in Cologne around 1324 or 1325, where he studied with Meister Eckhart. Seuse probably remained in Cologne until the master's death in 1327, when he returned to Constance and was appointed lector at the monastery. At the age of forty, around 1335, Seuse was told by God to abandon the ascetic practices he had followed for twenty-two years. This turning point in his personal life also marked a change in his professional career: Seuse became an itinerant preacher and spiritual adviser, concentrating his activities in Switzerland, the Alsace, and along the Upper Rhine. Because he supported the pope in a power struggle with Ludwig of Bavaria, Seuse was forced to leave Constance in 1338 or 1339; some eight years later he probably returned. Around 1348 he was transferred to the Dominican monastery in Ulm, where he remained until his death more than fifteen years later. He was canonized in 1831.

In his last years, Seuse undertook the editing of his works for publication, his *Ausgabe letzter Hand;* the works he chose make up the *Exemplar.* Included are his life *(Vita),* which chronicles in third-person narrative the life of the *Diener der ewigen Weisheit* (Servant of Eternal Wisdom), Seuse himself. The authorship of the *Vita* is disputed; the Töß sister Elsbeth Stagel, one of Seuse's spiritual charges, probably played a role in the editing, if not the writing of the work. Following are Seuse's earliest works, the *Büchlein der ewigen Weisheit (Little Book of Eternal Wisdom)* and the *Büchlein der Wahrheit (Little Book of Truth),* two of the most popular devotional tracts in the late medieval mystical tradition. Both are written as dialogues between the Servant and the personification of eternal wisdom and truth, respectively. The *Exemplar* concludes with the *Briefbüchlein (Little Book of Letters),* an edited version of Seuse's correspondence with the Dominican sisters in his charge, primarily those at the convent of Töß. The *Little Book of Love (Minnebüchlein)*, whose authenticity is doubtful, and a larger collection of letters, the *Großes Briefbuch* (Great Book of Letters), also survive. Both sets of letters by Seuse are more characteristic of the homiletic rather than the epistolary genre. Indeed, few of his homiletic works are extant, although he was charged with the responsibility of preaching; only two German sermons are accepted as authentic works of the Dominican friar, but neither is included in the *Exemplar*. The *Horologium sapientiae (Clock of Wisdom)* is the only extant work of the Dominican in Latin; it is an expanded version of the *Büchlein der ewigen Weisheit*.

The religious content of Seuse's work, which draws on the Bernhardian tradition, stands in marked contrast to the speculative mystical theology of his teacher Eckhart. Because of his poetic style and the preeminence of love imagery in his writings, Seuse often is characterized as the *Minnesänger* among the medieval German mystics.

BIBLIOGRAPHY

Bihlmeyer, Karl, ed. *Heinrich Seuse. Deutsche Schriften.* 1907; rpt. Frankfurt am Main: Minerva, 1961.

Boesch, Bruno. "Zur Minneauffassung Seuses." *Festschrift Josef Quint anläßlich* seines 65. Geburtstages überreicht, ed. Hugo Moser, Rudolf Schutzeichel, and Karl Stackmann. Bonn: Semmel, 1964, pp. 57–68.

Clark, James M. *The Great German Mystics: Eckhart, Tauler and Suso.* Oxford: Blackwell, 1949.

Colledge, Edmund, and J. C. Marler. "'Mystical' Pictures in the Suso 'Exemplar' *Ms Strasbourg 2929*." *Archivum Fratrum Praedicatorum* 54 (1984): 293–354.

Filthaut, Ephrem M., ed. *Heinrich Seuse. Studien zum 600. Todestag, 1366–1966.* Cologne: Albertus Magnus, 1966.

Haas, Alois M., and Kurt Ruh. "Seuse, Heinrich OP," in *Die deutsche Literatur des Mittelalters: Verfasserlexikon,* 2d ed., ed. Kurt Ruh et al. Berlin: de Gruyter, 1992, vol. 8, cols. 1127–1129.

Hamburger, Jeffrey E. "The Use of Images in the Pastoral Care of Nuns: The Case of Heinrich Suso and the Dominicans." *Art Bulletin* 71 (1989): 20–46.

Künzle, Pius. *Heinrich Seuses Horologium sapientiae.* Spicilegium Friburgense 23. Freiburg im Breisgau: Universitätsverlag, 1977.

Stoudt, Debra L. "The Structure and Style of the Letters of Seuse's *Großes Briefbuch*." *Neuphilologische Mitteilungen* 90 (1989): 359–367.

Tobin, Frank. "Coming to Terms with Meister Eckhart: Suso's Buch der Wahrheit." *Semper idem et novus. Festschrift for Frank Banta,* ed. Francis G. Gentry. Göppingen: Kümmerle, 1988, 321–344.

Tobin, Frank. *Henry Suso: The Exemplar, with Two German Sermons.* Mahwah, N.J.: Paulist, 1989.

Walz, Angelus. "Bibliographiae susonianae conatus." *Angelicum* 46 (1969): 430–491.

Debra L. Stoudt

SEE ALSO

Meister Eckhart; *Minnesang;* Preaching and Sermons, German; Sister-Books; Visionary Literature

Siegburg, Abbey

A Benedictine abbey founded in 1064 by Archbishop Anno II of Cologne (r. 1056–1075) as part of an ambitious building program for abbeys, parish churches, and chapels within his archdiocese. Of the three cloisters he founded outside Cologne, Siegburg Abbey was his favorite (the other two were in Grafschaft and Saalfeld). The richly decorated abbey, whose patrons were St. Michael and St. Maurice, was located on the Michaelsberg in the town of Siegburg, just northeast of Bonn at the confluence of the Sieg and Agger Rivers.

Initially populating the cloister with monks from St. Maximin in Trier, Anno sent them back around 1070 and installed a dozen Italian monks from Fruttuaria in hopes of spreading the Cluniac reform movement throughout his archdiocese. He also forcibly replaced the Benedictine communities of St. Pantaleon and Grafschaft with Fruttuarians. This imposed reform proved so unpopular that the Cluniac monks were said to have barely escaped with their lives from an uprising against the archbishop in 1074. After dealing harshly with the rebels, Anno retired to his favorite monastery, where he died and was buried in 1075. The reformed monks at Siegburg perpetuated the memory of the archbishop with a *vita* (saint's life) and accounts of his miracles at the abbey. Their archiepiscopal patron soon became their patron saint when the abbot of Siegburg obtained Anno's canonization from Rome in 1183, after which a golden shrine was established in the cloister for the archiepiscopal relics. Siegburg Abbey served (along with the monastery of St. Blasien) as a center of Cluniac reform in Germany and produced several reform-minded churchmen, like Bishop Kuno of Regensburg (1126–1132). The cloister continued to enjoy special archiepiscopal benefaction until its suppression by Napoleonic authority in 1802.

BIBLIOGRAPHY

Delvos, Christian Hubert Thaddaus. *Geschichte der Pfarreien des Dekanates Siegburg.* Cologne: J.P. Bachem, 1896.

Mittler, Mauritius. *Beiträge zur Geschichte der Abtei Siegburg.* Siegburg: Respublica, 1977.

———, ed. *Museum der Stadt Siegburg: Katalog.* Siegburg: Respublica Verlag, 1983.

Semmler, Josef. *Die Klosterreform von Siegburg, ihre Ausbreitung und ihr Reformprogram im 11. und 12. Jahrhundert.* Bonn: Rohrscheid, 1959.

Wisplinghoff, Erich. *Die Benediktinerabtei Siegburg.* Berlin: de Gruyter, 1975.

———. *Urkunden und Quellen zur Geschichte von Stadt und Abtei Siegburg.* 2 vols. Siegburg: Respublica, 1964, 1985.

Joseph P. Huffman

SEE ALSO

Anno; Cologne, Archdiocese; Monasteries; Trier

Siegburg, Art

The Siegburg settlement arose near the Sieg River, at the foot of the Michaelsberg (Mount Saint Michael), where Archbishop Anno II of Cologne established a monastery in 1064. The first abbey church (now destroyed) was a late Ottonian/early Saxon flat-roofed, three-aisle, cross-plan basilica with a square choir, four round crossing towers, and wide apse. A western tower, Gothic rib vaulting, and expansion to seven aisles were later modifications. Anno (d. 1075) chose to be buried here, in his favorite foundation, dedicated to the Archangels Michael and Mauritius and companions. Anno's cult soon flourished, with graveside miracles beginning 1076–1078. His memorial, commissioned by Abbot Reginhard (1076–1105), perhaps included the famous Siegburger Madonna, a Cologne work of circa 1150. The thriving Siegburg pilgrimage center amassed a rich treasury, commissioning numerous liturgical objects, although few were locally produced.

Local Siegburg creations existed, however. Evidence of a monastic scriptorium from circa 1100 includes script and painting, similar to Cologne and Echternach work—until a distinctive Siegburg style emerged in the thirteenth century. Original literary production includes the *Vita Annonis (Life of Anno),* the epic poem *Annolied (Song of Anno),* local chronicles, theological treatises, liturgical music, and office and prayer books.

Vita Annonis (Darmstadt, Hessische Landes- und Hochschulbibliothek, Hs. 945), fol 1v: Archbishop Anno and his foundations Siegburg, St. Georg and St. Maria ad gradus in Cologne, Grafschaft, and Saalfeld. *Photograph: Rheinisches Bildarchiv der Stadt Köln*

Perhaps most noteworthy was Siegburg pottery, from the Aulgasse kiln from the mid–twelfth through the early nineteenth century. Early types were derivative of Pingsdorf and Paffrath wares, but by the thirteenth century, local shapes and decoration emerged. Indigenous clay withstood kiln temperatures well, resulting in a thin, grayish ware, decorated with various color slips and paints, notably brown, violet brown, red, sand, and gray. Both handbuilt and wheelthrown Siegburg wares supplied local and export markets.

BIBLIOGRAPHY

Beckmann, Bernard. "The Main Types of the First Four Production Periods of Siegburg Pottery," in *Medieval Pottery from Excavations,* ed. Vera I. Evison et al. New York: St. Martin's Press, 1974, pp. 183–220.

Klinge, Ekkart. "Siegburger Keramik," in *Die Zeit der Staufer: Geschichte, Kunst, Kultur,* ed. Reiner Haussherr, 5 vols. Stuttgart: Württembergisches Landesmuseum, 1977, vol. 1, pp. 223–224.

Legner, Anton. *Deutsche Kunst der Romanik.* Munich: Hirmer Verlag, 1982, pp. 41–43, 81, 92–101.

Monumenta Annonis: Köln und Siegburg—Weltbild und Kunst im Hohen Mittelalter, ed. Anton Legner. Cologne: Schnütgen Museum, 1975.

Wisplinghoff, Erich. *Das Erzbistum Köln 2: Die Benediktinerabtei Siegburg.* Germania sacra N.F. 29. Berlin: de Gruyter, 1975.

Rita Tekippe

SEE ALSO

Anno; Cologne, Art; Echternach; Ottonian Art and Architecture; Romanesque Art and Architecture

Sigenot

Two versions of the tale of the giant Sigenot survive. An *aventiurehafte* (episodic) Dietrich epic composed in the complicated verse form known as Bernerton (melody of Verona), *Der ältere Sigenot (The Earlier Sigenot)* is an abbreviated version functioning as an introduction to the *Eckenlied* in manuscript "L." Variants of *Der jüngere Sigenot (The Later Sigenot)* are preserved in seven manuscripts (including the Dresden Book of Heroes, or *Heldenbuch*) and at least twenty printed versions dating from the fifteenth through the late seventeenth century.

In the earlier *Sigenot,* Dietrich finds Sigenot, a giant, sleeping in the woods. They duel. Sigenot wins, avenging Grine's death. Throwing Dietrich into a dungeon, he goes to find Hildebrand. He defeats him temporarily, but Hildebrand rallies and kills him. Hildebrand and Eggerich, a dwarf, free Dietrich. Hildebrand and Dietrich return home to Bern.

The later *Sigenot* begins in Bern, from which Dietrich, rejecting Hildebrand's efforts to dissuade him, departs to fight Sigenot. On the way he rescues Baldung, a dwarf, who gives him a magic stone. The duel takes place as in the earlier *Sigenot.* Dietrich is thrown into a cave of serpents, but the stone protects him. Hildebrand and Sigenot meet and duel. Sigenot wins and drags Hildebrand to his cave, but Hildebrand rallies and kills him. As in the earlier *Sigenot,* Hildebrand and Eggerich free Dietrich, then Hildebrand and Dietrich return home.

Sigenot helps document a lost Dietrich epic involving a duel with the giants Grine and Hilde on which a similar episode in the Norse version (*Thidrekssaga*) might have been based. It also features a traditional motif in the Dietrich story—the rescue of the hero by a companion—that occurs in the Old English *Waldere* as well as in *Virginal,* another Dietrich epic in Bernerton. Sigenot thus employs the highly literary *Bernerton* strophe to narrate a traditional tale of rescue. The combination had lasting appeal: *Sigenot* was popular longer than any other Dietrich epic.

BIBLIOGRAPHY

Heinzle, Joachim. *Mittelhochdeutsche Dietrichepik.* Zurich: Artemis, 1978.

Schoener, A. Clemens, ed. *Der jüngere Sigenot.* Heidelberg: Winter, 1928 [later version].

Zupitza, Julius, ed. *Sigenot.* Deutsches Heldenbuch 5, 2d ed. 1870; rpt. Dublin: Weidmann, 1968, pp. 207–215 [earlier version].

Ruth H. Firestone

SEE ALSO

Albrecht von Kemenaten; *Eckenlied; Virginal*

Siger of Brabant (ca. 1240–November 10, 1284)

This scholastic philosopher, an important representative of thirteenth-century heterodox Aristotelianism, played a prominent role in the debate on the proper place of philosophy with respect to theology and Christian faith.

The details of Siger's biography are largely unknown. He was born around 1240 or shortly thereafter in Brabant and started his academic career circa 1255–1260 in Paris, where he received an M.A. in 1260–1265. On November 10, 1284, he died in Orvieto, killed by his secretary.

His oeuvre includes commentaries on Aristotle's *Physics, Metaphysics,* and *On the Soul,* and a number of separate questions dealing with logic, philosophy of nature, metaphysics, and ethics. Most of his writings resulted from his teaching as a master of arts at Paris. His published work probably dates from around 1270 and thereafter.

In his early writings, Siger professes the ideal of the pure philosopher searching for truth unaided by Christian revelation and trying to reveal the exact teachings of Aristotle, the philosopher par excellence. This attitude was seen as a serious threat to theology by a number of theologians, whose reaction was reflected in the famous Parisian Articles of 1270 and 1277, issued by Bishop Stephen Tempier. In his later work, however, Siger is less radical and steers a middle course between philosophy and Christian faith.

Of central importance was Siger's theory of the human intellect. In line with the teachings of Averroës, Siger holds that humans receive intellectual knowledge from a single, pure intellectual substance, which is the last of the hierarchy of intellectual substances and which consists of an active and a potential part. Only this pure intellectual substance is immortal; final personal responsibility therefore has no place. The theory evoked a sharp and detailed criticism of Thomas Aquinas. Toward the end of his career, Siger no longer defended it, mainly because of the attack of Thomas Aquinas, which seems to have convinced him that he was wrong.

BIBLIOGRAPHY

Philosophes Médiévaux 3 (1954): 12–14; (1972–1974): 24–25; (1981–1983) [editions of most of Siger's works].

Gauthier, R. A. "Notes sur Siger de Brabant." *Revue des sciences philosophiques et théologiques* 67 (1983): 201–232; 68 (1984): 3–49.

Hissette, Roland. *Enquête sur les 219 articles condamnés à Paris le 7 mars 1277.* Louvain: Publications Universitaires de Louvain, 1977.

Van Steenberghen, Fernand. *Maître Siger de Brabant.* Louvain: Publications Universitaires de Louvain, 1977.

———. "Publications récentes sur Siger de Brabant," in *Historia Philosophia Medii Aevi,* ed. Burkhard Mojsisch and Olaf Plua, vol. 2. Amsterdam: Grumer, 1991, pp. 1003–1011 [bibliography].

Maarten J. F. M. Hoenen

Sion

Located in the Swiss canton of Valais, the city of Sion (German, Sitten) is situated at the base of two small hills in the Rhône valley. The Romans called the settlement Sedunum—*sedo* meaning "seat" and *dunum* meaning "hill" or "stronghold"—and the Celtic tribe that occupied the region the Seduni. Sion's many important medieval monuments and objects testify to the power of the church there and its dedication to the arts throughout the Middle Ages.

Lombard raids in 565 and 585 forced the episcopal see to move from Martigny to Sion further north. It was also for reasons of safety that the earliest cathedral of Sion was built on top of one of the two hills called Valeria. This structure was then dismantled and a new one built on the valley floor in the first half of the twelfth century, the new center of the city, now protected by defensive walls. However, the new cathedral was destroyed in 1418 in battles between the Zenden in the upper Valais and the barons of Raron. With only the tower and the foundations remaining, rebuilding began again under Bishop Walter Supersaxo (1457–1482) and continued under Cardinal Schiners (1499–1522). Although Notre-Dame-du-Glarier qualifies as a late Gothic structure, its adherence to the Romanesque foundation produced an archaic appearance. It was the last cathedral built in Switzerland in the Middle Ages. In the interior, south of the choir in the chapel dedicated to St. Barbara, is a carved and polychromed (multicolored) altar given by Bishop Supersaxo in 1474. In the cathedral treasury are many outstanding objects dating from the late Antique to the late Gothic. Of note are the rich collection of Roman, Byzantine, and Oriental silks used for the wrapping of relics and two early medieval reliquaries: the Adalricus reliquary made out of bone from the eighth century, and the Altheus reliquary, named after a bishop of Sion, made out of silver and gold-plated silver with enamels from the late eighth century.

Next to the cathedral is the late Gothic church dedicated to St. Theodore, a bishop of Sion in the fourth century. Excavations from 1960 to 1964 revealed that the sixteenth-century church rests on foundations from the Carolingian and Roman periods and that the crypt beneath the altar was built to house the relics of the saint.

Atop the hill Valeria, a new and imposing church, Notre-Dame-de-Valère, was rebuilt at the end of the eleventh and beginning of the twelfth century. The rounded apse, the southern choir chapels, the transept, and the first nave bay to the west, as well as all the remaining foundations, were all completed between 1100 and 1130. The acanthus leaf and figural capitals in the choir are loosely executed, signaling a new direction in the third quarter of the twelfth century. Construction then proceeded sporadically; the tower was added at the end of the twelfth century and the nave in the thirteenth. Many medieval objects from the Notre-Dame-de-Valère are now preserved in the Musée Cantonal in Sion.

BIBLIOGRAPHY

DuBuis, François Olivier. "Archéologie, tradition et légende: Saint Théodor, éveque d'Octodure, son souvenir et son culte en Valais jusqu'au XVIᵉ siècle," in *Helvetia Antiqua: Festschrift Emil Vogt.* Zurich: Conzett und Huber, 1966, pp. 317–326.

Jacobsen, Werner, Leo Schaefer, and Hans Rudolf Sennhauser. *Vorromanische Kirchenbauten: Katalog der Denkmäler bis zum Ausgang der Ottonen, Nachtragsband* [Supplement]. Munich: Prestel, 1991, pp. 387–389.

Reinle, Adolf. *Kunstgeschichte der Schweiz 1: Von den helvetisch-römischen Anfängen bis zum Ende des romanischen Stils,* 2d ed. Frauenfeld: Huber, 1968.

Schmedding, Brigitte. *Mittelalterliche Textilien in Kirchen und Klöstern der Schweiz.* Bern: Stämpli, 1978, pp. 234–301.

Speich, Klaus, and Hans Schläpfer. *Kirchen und Klöster in der Schweiz.* Zurich: Ex Libris, 1978.

Elsa Gontrum

SEE ALSO

Gothic Art and Architecture; Relics and Reliquaries; Romanesque Art and Architecture

Sister-Books

Also referred to as Convent Chronicles, this body of literature comprises nine texts from different Dominican women's monasteries in the southwest of the German-speaking area from circa 1318 to 1350. The two oldest books were originally composed in Latin, the others in Middle High German. While the nine texts differ slightly as to their literary significance and as to their cultural and sociohistorical relevance, the texts are more or less identical in structure, contents, and style. The language is deliberately simple; characteristic for the style is the lively contact the authors establish with their intended monastic women audience. Most texts have an initial chronicle dealing with the circa 100-year-old history of the particular monastic community; all Sister-Books contain a series of entries on selected saintly women of the community past and present. Only five authors are known by name.

The Sister-Books are modeled after the Dominican friar Gerard de Frachete's late-thirteenth-century *Vitae fratrum (Lives of the Brothers)* and are presumably intended as a feminine counterpart.

To recognize the fact that the Sister-Books' authors meticulously observed the rules of rhetoric is the point of divergence between condemning and appreciating these texts. For the repetitive description of visions, auditions, and various other charisms make sense only when interpreted as hagiographic topoi (recurring themes).

Most of the Sister-Books have never been critically edited, and only minor excerpts have ever been translated into English. In a roughly chronological order, the nine Sister-Books and their known authors are as follows:

The Adelhausen Sister-Book, circa 1318, author: Anna von Munzingen of Adelhausen in Freiburg, Black Forest; Middle High German translation circa 1345–1350.

The Unterlinden Sister-Book, circa 1320, author: Katharina von Unterlinden (von Gueberschwihr) in Colmar, Alsace; Middle High German translation by Elisabeth Kempfin, Unterlinden, late fifteenth century.

The Gotteszell Sister-Book, circa 1320/1330, community of Gotteszell (Cella Dei) outside of Schwäbisch-Gmünd, Württemberg; author unknown.

The Engeltal Sister-Book, circa 1340, entitled: *von der genaden uberlast;* author: Christine Ebner of Engeltal near Nuremberg. Christine Ebner was also the author of *Revelations,* a work that markedly differs in style from her Sister-Book.

The Kirchberg Sister-Book, before 1340; author: Elisabeth von Kirchberg in Sulz, Neckar (Baden-Württemberg).

The Töss Sister-Book, circa 1340; one of several authors is Elsbet Stagel of the monastery of Töss near Winterthur, Switzerland.

The Oetenbach Sister-Book, after 1340; the Oetenbach monastery was in Zurich; author(s) unknown.

The Diessenhofen Sister-Book (also referred to as the *Katharinental Sister-Book*), before 1343 in the monastery of St. Katharinental near Diessenhofen, Switzerland; author(s) unknown.

The Weiler Sister-Book, 1350 in Weil(er) near Esslingen (Baden-Württemberg); author(s) unknown.

BIBLIOGRAPHY

Blank, Walter. *Die Nonnenviten des 14. Jahrhunderts; eine Studie zur hagiographischen Literatur des Mittelalters.* Freiburg: Müller, 1962.

Gehring, Hester Reed. "Dominican Convent Chronicles of the 14th Century." Ph.d. diss., University of Michigan, 1957.

Hindsley, Leonard P. *The Mystics of Engelthal: Writings from a Medieval Monastery.* New York: St. Martin's Press, 1999.

Lewis, Gertrud Jaron. *By Women, for Women, about Women: The Sister-Books of Fourteenth-Century Germany.* Toronto: Pontifical Institute of Mediaeval Studies,

1996 [complete listing of all manuscripts known prior to 1995; comprehensive bibliography of all texts in print with microfiches of all the Sister-Book texts save the critically edited Diessenhofen Book; all secondary sources until 1995].

Meyer, Ruth. *Das St. Katharinentaler Schwesternbuch. Untersuchung, Edition, Kommentar.* Tübingen: Niemeyer, 1995.

Gertrud Jaron Lewis

SEE ALSO
Ebner, Margaretha; Elisabeth von Schönau; Langmann, Adelheid

Slavery

Slavery was practiced throughout Germany in late Antiquity and the early Middle Ages. In those territories, west of the Rhine and south of the Danube, that were accustomed to the Roman system, there were large numbers of slaves who worked the fields of big plantations. Slavery was also common to the north and east, among the Saxons, Bavarians, and Franks, and among the Lombards after they moved into Noricum and northern Italy. Significant portions of the Lombard law codes of the seventh and eighth centuries concern either unfree Germans or household slaves of Roman descent.

Although it is often presumed that slavery disappeared outside the former territories of the Roman Empire, in fact it continued in German lands throughout the ninth and tenth centuries. Most slaves came from the eastern borders—Slavs captured in raids and sold at markets in Prague and throughout Bohemia. There was an important slave trade in southern Germany as well, especially among Jewish merchants. Trade routes ran through Alpine passes to the Mediterranean, from the Elbe toward the valley of the Rhine, and along the Meuse and Moselle Rivers toward Verdun, where captives were castrated and sold as eunuchs.

But by the late twelfth century slavery had for all intents and purposes come to an end in Germany. As the wars against the Slavs slowed and the number of Christian converts rose, slavery ceased to fulfill the function it did in the ancient world. The word *servus* took on a new meaning and a new legal definition as slaves were gradually transformed into serfs, an arrangement much better suited to the seigniorial system.

BIBLIOGRAPHY

Bloch, Marc. *Slavery and Serfdom in the Middle Ages*, trans. William R. Beer. Berkeley: University of California Press, 1975.

Bosl, Karl. "Freiheit und Unfreiheit. Zur Entwicklung der Unterschichten in Deutschland und Frankreich," in *Frühformen der Gesellschaften im mittelalterlichen Europa. Ausgewählte Beiträge zu einer Strukturanalyse der mittelalterlichen Welt.* Munich: Oldenbourg, 1964, pp. 180–203.

Nehlsen, Hermann. *Sklavenrecht zwischen Antike und Mittelalter: Germanisches und römisches Recht in den germanischen Rechtsaufzeichnungen.* Göttingen: Musterschmidt, 1972.

Verlinden, Charles. *L'Esclavage dans l'Europe médiévale.* 2 vols. Bruges: Rijksuniversiteit te Gent, 1955, 1977.

David R. Blanks

SEE ALSO
Meuse River; Moselle River

Soest

The oldest church in the Westphalian city of Soest was founded in 780 and dedicated to St. Peter. In 954 the archbishop of Cologne founded the church of St. Patroklus, which later became the cathedral. Relics of this saint were brought from Troyes in 964. Located on the trade route across Westphalia known as the Hellweg, Soest achieved great prosperity in the twelfth and thirteenth centuries as a member of the Hanseatic League. In 1179 the town was walled.

The present churches of St. Peter and St. Patroklus both date to the mid–twelfth century. St. Peter is a three-aisle basilica with a single western tower. An imperial gallery inside the tower once connected directly to the neighboring archiepiscopal palace established in the tenth century; remains of the palace are still visible. A sculpted capital gives one of the oldest artist's inscriptions in Germany: *Herenfridus me fecit* (Herenfrid constructed me). The main portal of circa 1150, on the south side, depicts the martyrdom of St. John the Evangelist.

The church of St. Patroklus, dedicated in 1166, was embellished with frescoes and stained glass windows. Paintings in the main apse, which was destroyed in World War II, depicted Christ in Majesty; the north side apse of circa 1230 shows the Adoration of the Magi with the Virgin and Child enthroned in a mandorla (body halo).

Fragments of a Tree of Jesse window are preserved in the north transept; and scenes of the Resurrection, Ascension, Crucifixion, and Israelite spies carrying grapes are set into modern windows in the apse. The glass dates to the time of the church's dedication. The theme of the main apse is echoed in the north portal tympanum, which shows a half-length blessing Christ surrounded by the symbols of the four evangelists.

During the thirteenth century, a number of new churches were built, and the east end of St. Peter was completed. Two of more than twenty small chapels once located in the town are still extant. One of them, St. Nicholas, is a two-aisle church built in 1202 by the Hansa merchants next to St. Patroklus. Its mid-thirteenth-century apse fresco in the Zackenstil (zigzag style) depicts Christ in a mandorla surrounded by the symbols of the evangelists, with the Virgin and saints to the sides, echoing the composition of the main apse of St. Patroklus.

The church of St. Maria zur Höhe (or Hohnekirche) was built circa 1220. Its western tower is slightly earlier. It is entered through a portal on the south side; the tympanum (triangle above door) depicts the Crucifixion in a quadrilobe (with rounded corners) frame, flanked by the Nativity and the Three Maries at the empty tomb. Inside a wooden *Scheibenkreuz* (wheel cross) dating to circa 1220, the earliest example known, was originally placed on a triumphal arch. The cross has lost its central Crucifixion group. It was surrounded by four circles and four outer squares containing scenes of the Passion and Resurrection: Entry into Jerusalem, Christ teaching, Gethsemane, Betrayal, Entombment, Christ in Limbo, Three Maries at the Tomb, and Ascension. The wheel cross is now supported by two fifteenth-century wings. It had great influence on later wheel crosses in Scandinavia. The frescoes decorating the east end of St. Maria zur Höhe are the most elaborate in the city. The domical vault before the main apse (ca. 1240) depicts the Virgin and a circle of angels. The paintings from the 1250s in the north side apse represent the Coronation of the Virgin in the conch and the legend of St. Katherine on the side walls. In the north side aisle there is a Holy Sepulchre niche also decorated with frescoes.

Other churches built in the thirteenth and fourteenth centuries include Alt St. Thomas (Old St. Thomas), begun in 1181 and enlarged 1250–1270, which was the first church in Soest built in the Gothic style. Neu St. Thomas (New St. Thomas) was built for the Franciscans after their arrival in 1237. The church itself is fourteenth century in date. The church of St. Paul is a mid-fourteenth-century hall church with somewhat later statues of the Virgin and apostles on the piers of the choir, in the tradition of Cologne Cathedral. The most famous of the Gothic churches is the hall church St. Maria zur Wiese, begun in 1313 and finished only in 1530. Stained glass windows in the east end include some of mid-fourteenth-century date depicting the Virgin and saints under baldachins. The main portal on the south side dates to circa 1400 and has the Virgin on the trumeau (inner door frame on double door) and two saints on either jamb (outside door frame). Statues are also arranged on piers around the choir.

Panel painters and manuscript illuminators were also active in Soest. The oldest panel painting is an antependium (front altar panel) of the 1170s from the cloister of St. Walburgis depicting Christ in Majesty, the Virgin with the gifts of the Holy Spirit, John the Baptist, and Saints Walburgis and Augustine (now in the Landesmuseum in Münster). Two later thirteenth-century altarpieces—the first depicting the Crucifixion, Christ before Caiaphas, and the three Maries at the Tomb; the second depicting the Throne of Grace—are both in Berlin, as is a mid-fourteenth-century antependium from the Wieskirche depicting Christ in a quadrilobe frame flanked by eight saints. Illuminated manuscripts from the nearby Cistercian convent of Welver and the Dominican nunnery of Paradies, and the well-known *Nequambuch (Book of Misdeeds)* of 1315 are further evidence of flourishing artistic activity. Fragments of thirteenth-century stained glass have migrated to museums in Burg Altena and Cologne. A splendid series of seven windows of the 1240s from Lohne near Soest is now preserved in the Landesmuseum in Münster. Goldsmiths were also active. A shrine of St. Patroklus by the artist Siegfried was commissioned in 1313. Once in the Deutsches Museum in Berlin, it was destroyed, with the exception of some of its figures, in World War II. An embroidered altar hanging of circa 1375 in whitework depicting the Coronation of the Virgin, the Noli me tangere, and the Annunciation in quadrilobes is still preserved in the Wieskirche. In the early fifteenth century, the city's most famous artist, Conrad von Soest, and his atelier painted altarpieces for many churches in the city.

BIBLIOGRAPHY

Deus, Wolf-Hubert. *Scheibenkreuze in Soest, auf Gotland und anderswo.* Soester Wissenschaftliche Beiträge 30. Soest: Mocker und Jahn, 1967.

Engemann, Josef. *Das Hauptportal der Hohnekirche in Soest: Die Reliefdarstellungen und ihre Bedeutung.* Münster: Aschendorff, 1991.

Haussherr, Reiner. "*Si tu es Christus, dic nobis palam!* Ein Notiz zum Soester Retabel der Berliner Gemäldegalerie," in *Florilegium in honorem Carl Nordenfalk.* Stockholm: Nationalmuseum, 1987, pp. 81–90.

Der heilige Patroklus: Festschrift zur Tausend-Jahrfeier der Reliquienübertragung nach Soest am 5. Juli 1964. Soester Wissenschaftliche Beiträge 26. Soest: Propstei-Kirchengemeinde St. Patrokli, 1964.

Kohl, W., ed. *Das Soester Nequambuch: Neuausgabe des Acht- und Schwurbuchs der Stadt Soest.* Veröffentlichungen der Historisches Kommission für Westfalen 14. Wiesbaden: L. Reichert, 1980.

Korn, Ulf-Dietrich. *Die romanischen Farbverglasung von St. Patrokli in Soest.* Westfalen Sonderheft 17. Münster: Aschendorff, 1967.

Landolt-Wegener, Elisabeth. *Die Glasmalerei im Hauptchor der Soester Wiesenkiche.* Westfalen Sonderheft 13. Münster: Aschendorff, 1959.

Oliver, Judith. "The Walters Homilary and Westphalian Manuscripts." *Journal of the Walters Art Gallery* 54 (1996): 69–85.

Schwartz, Hubertus. *Soest in seinen Denkmälern,* 6 vols. Soester Wissenschaftliche Beiträge 14–17. Soest: Mocker und Jahn, 1955–1958.

———. *Die Kirchen der Soester Börde.* Soester Wissenschaftliche Beiträge 18. Soest: Mocker und Jahn, 1961.

———. *Gesammelte Aufsätze.* Soester Wissenschaftliche Beiträge 24. Soest: Mocker und Jahn, 1963.

Soest: Geschichte der Stadt, vol. 2, *Die Welt der Bürger, Politik, Gesellschaft und Kultur im spätmittelalterlichen Soest,* ed. Hans-Dieter Heimann et al. Soest: Mocker und Jahn, 1996.

Thümmler, H. "Die Patroklussäule in Soest." *Westfalen* 45 (1967): 78–96.

Judith H. Oliver

Song of Songs

There are two early Middle High German versions of *Das Hohelied (The Song of Songs)*: a paraphrase by Williram, abbot of Ebersberg (Bavaria), written about 1060, and the *St. Trudperter Hohes Lied* (so named after the source of the oldest complete manuscript) about one hundred years after Williram by an unknown author. Both are written in prose but have different accents, even though the younger version uses Williram's translation of the biblical text. Williram begins his work with a Latin preface, after which the main text follows in three columns: the Vulgate Latin text in the middle, a Latin interpretation in leonine hexameters on the left, and a German translation with a prose version of the Latin interpretation on the right. The German text is liberally larded with Latin words, phrases, even sentences, reminiscent of Notker Labeo's translations. Williram follows the interpretation of the Song of Songs as a dialogue between Christ (the bridegroom) and the Church (the bride), whereas in the St. Trudpert version the dialogue is between the Holy Spirit and the Virgin Mary, who prefigures the individual soul. Williram's institutional emphasis can be seen against the background of his day, the period of church and monastic reform, and the developing Investiture Controversy. The St. Trudpert version represents the more personal, mystical approach of a later period. Both works must have attained considerable popularity. There are over twenty two extant manuscripts of Williram's text and about six of the St. Trudperter.

BIBLIOGRAPHY
Bartelmez, Erminnie, ed. *The 'Expositio in Cantica Canticorum' of Williram, Abbot of Ebersberg (1048–1085): A Critical Edition.* Philadelphia: American Philosophical Society, 1967.

Dittrich, Marie-Louise. "Die literarische Form von Willirams Expositio in Cantica Canticorum." *Zeitschrift für deutsches Altertum* 84 (1953): 179–197.

Küsters, Urban. *Der verschlossene Garten. Hohelied-Auslegung und monastische Lebensform im 12. Jahrhundert.* Düsseldorf: Droste Verlag, 1985.

Menhardt, Hermann. *Das St. Trudperter Hohe Lied. Kritische Ausgabe.* Halle (Saale): Niemeyer, 1934.

Ohly, Friedrich, ed. *Das St. Trudperter Hohelied: eine Lehre der liebenden Gotteserkenntnis.* Frankfurt am Main: Deutscher Klassiker Verlag, 1998.

Sidney M. Johnson

Speyer

A fortified town under the Roman Empire, Speyer (Rheinland-Pfalz) was destroyed around 450. Rebuilt and later made a bishopric in the seventh century, the town became important in the early eleventh century when the Emperor Conrad II (r. 1024–1039) designated it as the burial place for the Salian emperors and began the construction of a new cathedral for that purpose. Work on the cathedral began by 1029 and was completed circa 1061. A second phase of building saw the construction of vaults and their supports between circa 1080 and 1125. The town was strongly fortified in the twelfth and thirteenth centuries.

The cathedral has a semicircular east apse behind a trapezoidal choir with barrel vaults, a three-bay transept, a crossing with octagonal lantern tower, a long nave with side aisles, and a massive western entry structure, or westfront. The hall crypt is among the largest of the Middle Ages and extends under the crossing, transepts, choir, and apse. There is no evidence of earlier buildings beneath the Romanesque cathedral, and a study of the early liturgy at Speyer indicates that there was not a strong cult of a local saint or an elaborate processional liturgy at the time of the initial construction. In the following years the emperors donated a number of relics to the cathedral that added to the liturgical and religious life of the building, including the head of St. Anastasius and the body of St. Guido, given by Henry III in 1047, and relics of Saints Martin and Emmeram and a number of other saints, gifts of Henry IV in the 1050s. *The Golden Evangeliary* (book of gospel readings) of Henry III is the most important liturgical manuscript from Speyer.

The cathedral, erected in two distinct building campaigns, is one of the most significant examples of Romanesque architecture. The first phase of the building was a simpler version of the extant plan. The earliest work saw construction of the crypt under the apse and choir, followed by the construction of the present eastern towers. The crypt was then extended laterally to fill the bays of the transept. Work then proceeded on the transept and the nave, which was extended from an original eight bays to twelve. The cathedral was consecrated in 1061. The original building had vaults only in the apse and the choir, with wooden ceilings in the nave.

The reasons for vaulting the church are not certain; the decision may be due to a combination of damage from flooding as well as to a desire to create a more magnificent and up-to-date cathedral under Henry IV. This monarch was concerned to show his power during the Investiture Controversy, and the imperial burial church provided an opportunity to demonstrate his patronage.

Speyer, cathedral, view of choir from south. *Photograph: Joan A. Holladay*

During the second phase of building, the apse was reconstructed, with niches set into the interior walls and elaborate blind arcades and a dwarf gallery placed on the exterior. The walls of the choir were thickened and additional chapels were inserted into the building, as well as a two-story chapel in the exterior corner between the south aisle and the transept. The walls of the transepts and nave were rebuilt and alternate piers were considerably strengthened in preparation for the construction of groin vaults. These are among the largest Romanesque vaults, with a height of about thirty three meters and width of about fourteen meters. During the final phase of construction the chapel of St. Afra was also built on the south side of the nave. Dwarf galleries and elaborate architectural ornament were added throughout the building. The wealth of ornamental detail owes much to Roman models.

BIBLIOGRAPHY

Klimm, Franz. *Der Kaiserdom zu Speyer,* 2d ed. Speyer: Jaeger, 1953.

Kubach, Hans Erich, and Walter Haas. *Der Dom zu Speyer.* 3 vols. Munich: Deutscher Kunstverlag, 1972.

Lamott, A. "Codex Vindobonensis 1882: Ein *Liber ordinarius* des Speyerer Domes aus dem 13. Jht." *Archiv für mittelrheinische Kirchengeschichte* 13 (1961): 27–48.

Lehmann, Paul. *Die mittelalterliche Dombibliothek zu Speyer.* Sitzungsberichte der Bayerischen Akademie der Wissenschaften, Phil.-hist. Abt., 1934, no. 4. Munich: Bayerische Akademie der Wissenschaften, 1934.

Mark Stansbury-O'Donnell

SEE ALSO
Henry III; Henry IV; Relics and Reliquaries; Romanesque Art and Architecture; Salians

Spielmannsepen

Grouped together in the early nineteenth century, the *Spielmannsepen* (minstrel epics)—*König Rothar, Herzog Ernst, Münchener Oswald, Orendel,* and *Salman und Morolf*—have been known by this designation ever since. Originally this grouping situated the texts between the heroic poetry of the early medieval period and the sophisticated and stylistically harmonious courtly romances. The earliest scholarship was shaped by the romantic concept of minstrels *(Spielleute),* as itinerant, uneducated performers. Scholars thought that in their striving to astonish audiences by embellishing their narratives with magic, fantastic plots, and mythic characters, they diminished the aesthetic quality of their texts. The style of these poems was condemned as inept and repetitive, the language as coarse, the scenes as burlesque, and the narrative as superficial. Whether the minstrel was considered a transmitter of poetry or a genuine poet, he was blamed for narratives that merely offered entertainment.

Defining this group according to the heterogeneous category of minstrels fails to characterize the texts and justify the genre. The customary quotation marks signify the inadequacy of our definitions. Since the early 1970s, scholars have realized that these texts are more complex than previously thought. The scholar Rolf Bräuer suggested that they were produced for townspeople, not a court, whereas Hans Simon-Pelanda emphasized their political dimension, calling them state epics. Unfortunately, these suggestions lose sight of the vitality of the individual texts and their interest in foreign adventure. Alternatively one might recategorize the poems, but this, too, fails because they do not share enough essential characteristics with other narratives to be placed into any single, related category such as heroic epic, romance, or hagiography. Attempts at recategorizing have led to the recognition, however, that they are hybrid forms, exhibiting similarities with all three narrative types. These poems can be understood as attempts to adapt the heroic epic to a Christian ethic. The medieval reception of these texts certainly supports this thesis because the texts were included in heroic as well as religious collections. The *Orendel* with a strong hagiographic thread appears in the *Straßburg* Heldenbuch in the company of the heroes Alexander, Siegfried, and Dietrich. At the same time, the similarly hagiographic *Oswald* is found together with annals of popes, martyr legends, and conversion stories.

These hybrid forms may, nevertheless, be examined together as well as separately because they share plot structure and many significant elements. First of all, these poems draw heavily on oral tradition. Second, each poem has a historical event or person at the center. Third, the bridal quest combined with the crusade ideology dictates both plot structure and motivation (except in *Herzog Ernst).* Fourth, the texts explore popular themes: the political and religious ramifications of the crusade mission, the lives of hero-saints, and the centralization of power in the hands of a king. Finally, in contrast to earlier vernacular poetry, they are secular in that they all convey an ardent curiosity about the physical world, and the political ambition to control foreign lands. Even the most hagiographically drawn heroes—Orendel and Oswald—are theocratic kings who progress to sainthood by serving God in battle.

We know nothing of oral precursors to these poems, but they certainly draw heavily on oral tradition both in their inclusion of heroic characters and in their formulaic style. From Germanic tradition they inherited characters (Orendel, Asprian, Witold, Dietrich), mythic figures (giants, mermaids, dwarfs), and magic. Formulaic phrases in the manuscripts replicate for the reader a performer's typical interjections. These formulas indicate a desire even in written literature to imitate an oral performance. Therefore, minstrels' performances and, consequently, their interpretations had a formative influence on the audience and its reception of literature. What this implies, then, is that however clumsy scholars find these epics, the vitality of transmission and performance must also be considered.

Second, one might call these texts historical legend because they contain a historical kernel and a claim to historical truth. *Orendel* is connected with the seamless cloak of Christ deposited in Trier Cathedral in 1196. *Oswald* is associated with Regensburg, the seat of the Welfs, because St. Oswald was their patron saint. *König Rothar* is connected with the Langobard king Rothari (636–652) and the Norman ruler Roger II (1105–1154), who was unsuccessful in establishing a marriage between his son and a Byzantine princess. The *Salman und Morolf* documents the existence of the Christian Kingdom of Jerusalem (1100–1187). Finally, *Herzog Ernst* may have been inspired by the actual revolt of Ernst II, duke of Swabia, against his stepfather, Conrad II, in 1026. All five "minstrel epics" are likely to have originated in the twelfth-century because of these historical elements. However, we have twelfth-century manuscripts of *Herzog Ernst* and *König Rothar*. But the fact that these two texts are contemporary with courtly romances means they are not necessarily precursors. The other three "minstrel epics" are extant only in fifteenth-century manuscripts and printed books, so we have no knowledge of their earlier form. Since the stories tell of faraway places, they give the appearance of satisfying people's curiosity about the foreign lands, but basically these poems use the foreign and the exotic as a negative contrast by which to define and extend the borders of the familiar.

Most likely, *Herzog Ernst* and *König Rothar* were composed in a form similar to what we find in the earliest manuscripts from the second half of the twelfth century. This was a period of especially rapid social and economic growth and an explosion in literary activity. And within this explosion, the "minstrel epics" are obvious examples of literary experiments that cross boundaries. These narratives were popular but, lacking the concepts of *Minne* (courtly love) and *aventiure* (knight errantry), never became a generic model.

Third, the bridal quest narrative found in the "minstrel epics," but not limited to them, follows a simple pattern: The royal councillors advise the king to marry and produce a successor. Only one princess, usually pagan, has the qualifications of rank, wealth, beauty, and virtue, but her father takes the life of all suitors. In each poem the protagonist accomplishes the courtship and abduction of the chosen princess in a different manner. Although he asks her approval, she is nevertheless vulnera-

ble because the threat of force can compel her to consent. The courtship and abduction process causes a battle that often becomes an invasion of foreign (heathen) territory. The suitor fights in genuinely deadly battles and abducts the bride in an act of violence that isolates her and leaves her completely powerless—so much so that the narrative frequently leaves her nameless.

This plot is often doubled. On the couple's return home, the husband loses his new wife. In *König Rothar* the princess's father sends someone to abduct her, and Rother must then return at great risk to retrieve her. The pattern can vary, and the wife may be lost to him in other ways, but in all cases, the husband must retrieve her. In *Orendel,* the heathens imprison queen Bride during the crusade. The *Salman und Morolf* inverts the bridal theft but also contains two cycles.

Fourth, composed against the background of a crusade ideology that encourages conversion efforts, courtship naturally looks to the heathen lands. The crusade thus provides the religious grounds for political expansion. To save the young woman from paganism, it is justifiable to wrench her from the protection of her kin. As a reward for this violence, the suitor achieves not only purification and salvation by means of his crusading vow but also stands to acquire her property because she is the single heir. Thus the crusade ideology fosters two themes: It supports the hero's attainment of grace, thus bringing these narratives in proximity to the saint's legend, and at the same time it advances the cause of territorial expansion and consolidation. In *Oswald* the typical abduction is transformed into a miracle story in which Christ arrives at the wedding disguised as a beggar to test Oswald by asking him for his possessions, including his new wife in the name of Christ. Oswald passes the test by turning everything, including the wife, over to the beggar. And the *König Rothar* attempts to validate the foundation of the universal empire when the eventual fruit of the union between Rother of Italy and the princess of Constantinople is Charlemagne.

Finally, as the bridal quest plot forces the king to confront strange and foreign lands in pursuit of his bride, his search becomes the vehicle for exploring the compatibility of the crusade with the political questions these works are concerned with. As a group, these epics explore the increasing institutionalization of the monarchy and the way the king strives to augment political advantage by ensuring succession and expanding territorial sovereignty. The progressive institutionalization of kingship unfolds in the later texts only *(Oswald, Orendel, Salman und Morolf)*. As they portray the king's decreasing capacity to make decisions and increasing reliance on advisers, they demonstrate that the office of king loses no credibility or power as a result. The narratives thus experiment with ways to incorporate a new kingship into the inherited literary forms of heroic epic and saint's life. In addition, they describe crusade expeditions in which an entire society may take part. Although nonbelievers are occasionally converted, the purpose of the crusade battles is primarily to extend and consolidate the Christian (and German!) territories. Thus we find here a sense of state planning that extends far beyond courtship and royal succession and emphasizes the consolidation of the monarchy as an institution. It is significant that in most of these epics *(Orendel, Oswald, Herzog Ernst, König Rothar),* the leader (king or exiled warrior) loses his entourage and must collect a new set of supporters. If he proves his ability to gather loyal warriors and to sustain cooperation within the body politic, he wins the bride. This implies that if the king and realm are to achieve stability, they must forge a structured social organization of a magnitude in which the energies of individuals join to support the king's established common goals.

Happily, scholarship has been moving these texts out of the rubric of "minstrel epics" and opening them up to broader comparison. Fruitful research would focus on storytelling strategies, ways of establishing the credibility of the narrator, and the strategies of violence and subjugation that pervade these texts. Also, a more subtle political agenda still needs attention, namely, the way in which courtship texts define an implied German identity by means of the protagonist's encounter with the foreign.

BIBLIOGRAPHY

Bräuer, Rolf. *Literatursoziologie und epische Struktur der deutschen "Spielmanns-" und Heldendichtung. Zur Frage der Verfasser, des Publikum und der typologischen Struktur des "Nibelungenliedes," der "Kudrun," des "Ortnit-Wolfdietrich," des "Buches von Bern," des "Herzog Ernst," des "König Rothar," des "Orendel," des "Salman und Morolf," des "St.- Oswald- Epos," und der "Tristan-Dichtungen."* Berlin: Akademie Verlag, 1970.

Curschmann, Michael. *"Spielmannsepik:" Wege und Ergebnisse der Forschung von 1907–1965. Mit Ergänzungen und Nachträgen bis 1967.* Stuttgart: Metzler, 1968.

Dobozy, Maria. *Full Circle: Kingship in the German Epic. "Alexanderlied, Rolandslied, 'Spielmannsepen.'"* Göppingen: Kümmerle 1985.

———. "The Theme of the Holy War in German Literature, 1152–1190: Symptom of the Controversy between Empire and Papacy?" *Euphorion* 80 (1986): 341–362.

———. "Das Bild der Heidin in der deutschen Kreuzzugsdichtung," in *La Croisade: réalités et fictions. Actes du colloque d'Amiens, 1987,"* ed. Danielle Buschinger. Göppingen: Kümmerle, 1989, pp. 111–118.

———. "Eine Braut aus dem Orient. Traditionelles und Fremdes in der Kreuzzugsdichtung," in *Alles was Recht war: Rechtsliteratur und literarisches Recht: Festschrift für Ruth Schmidt-Wiegand,* ed. Hans Höffinghof et al. Essen: Item, 1996, pp. 45–54.

Haug, Walter. *Literaturtheorie im deutschen Mittelalter. Von den Anfängen bis zum Ende des 13. Jahrhunderts,* 2d ed. Darmstadt: Wissenschaftliche Buchgesellschaft, 1992, ch. 4.

———. "Struktur, Gewalt und Begierde. Zum Verhältnis von Erzählmuster und Sinnkonstitution in mündlicher und schriftlicher Überlieferung," in *Idee. Gestalt. Geschichte. Festschrift Klaus von See. Studien zur europäischen Kulturtradition,* ed. Gerd Wolfgang Weber. Odense: Odense University Press, 1988, pp. 143–157.

Knappe, Karl-Bernhard. *Repräsentation und Herrschaftszeichen. Zur Herrscherdarstellung in der vorhöfischen Epik.* Munich: Arbeo-Gesellschaft, 1974.

Kühnel, Jürgen. "Zur Struktur des *Herzog Ernst.*" *Euphorion* 73 (1979): 248–71.

Kühnert, Karl Helmut. *Die Geschichte von dem Rock Christi: die symbolische Bedeutung des mittelhochdeutschen Epos vom König Orendel (in Trier).* Frankfurt: R.G. Fischer, 1979.

Meves, Uwe. *Studien zu König Rothar, Herzog Ernst und Grauer Rock (Orendel).* Frankfurt: Lang, 1976.

Neudeck, Otto. "Ehre und Demut. Konkurrierende Verhaltenskonzepte im 'Herzog Ernst B.'" *Zeitschrift für deutsches Altertum* 121 (1992): 177–208.

Schroeder, Walter Johannes. *Spielmannsepik.* Stuttgart: Metzler, 1962.

Simon-Pelanda, Hans. *Schein, Realität und Utopie: Untersuchungen zur Einheit eines Staatsromans (Herzog Ernst B).* Frankfurt: Lang, 1984.

Störmer, Wilhelm. "'Spielmannsdichtung' und Geschichte. Die Beispiele Herzog Ernst und König Rother." *Zeitschrift für bayerische Landesgeschichte* 43 (1980): 551–574.

Urbanek, Ferdinand. *Kaiser, Grafen und Mäzene im König Rother.* Berlin: Schmidt, 1976.

Wishard, Armin. *Oral Formulaic Composition in the Spielmannsepik: An Analysis of "Salman und Morolf."* Göppingen: Kümmerle, 1984.

Maria Dobozy

SEE ALSO

Buch von Bern and *Rabenschlacht; Dietrich und Wenzelan; Dietrichepik; Kudrun; Nibelungenlied; Wolfdietrich* and *Ortnit*

Stained Glass

See Gothic Art and Architecture; Romanesque Art and Architecture.

Stainreuter, Leopold (ca. 1340–ca. 1400)

An Austrian by birth, the cleric Leopold Stainreuter studied at the Universities of Paris and Vienna, becoming court chaplain to Duke Albrecht III of Austria (d. 1395). Stainreuter was a prominent translator of Latin theological tracts, having rendered the *Rationale divinorum officiorum* of Guilelmus Durandus (d. 1296) for the ducal court. Apparently at the behest of the duke's steward, Hans von Liechtenstein, Stainreuter translated Latin books on pilgrimage (called *Pilgerbüchlein*). Stainreuter, as translator and popular theologian, joins the so-called *Wiener Schule* (Viennese School), formed from authors with close ties both to the Habsburg court and the University of Vienna: Heinrich von Langenstein, Nikolaus von Dinkelsbühl, Thomas Peuntner, Nikolaus Kempf, and Nikolaus von Astau. (Johannes von Gelnhausen, Rudolf Wintuawer, Friedrich der Karmeliter, and Ulrich von Pottenstein are also associated, however tangentially, with the Viennese School.)

Central concerns of the authors named were religious instruction and edification, to which ends they translated Latin writings into the vernacular. Believing that literature should offer practical instruction for daily living and should promote the conversion of souls, they aimed their catechetical literature at a broad audience, embracing clerics, the laity, common people, and the nobility. Augustinianism was the theological direction of the school, Stainreuter having been active in the monastery of the Augustinian Hermits in Vienna.

Stainreuter also found his voice as historian, translating and composing dynastic history. For his 1385 translation of the *Historia tripartita,* the three-part church history by Cassiodorus, he wrote, as a type of introduction, a panegyric poem to Duke Albrecht III, labeled an "Epistel in daz lob des furstleihen herren herczog Albrechten czw Österreich" (Epistle of praise of his princely duke Albrecht of Austria). In the work Stainreuter identifies himself both as *chapplan, prueder Lewpoltz* (Brother Leopold, chaplain) and *lesmaister* (lector). Noteworthy is his employment of genealogy, a topic carried to fullness in his *Österreichische Chronik von den 95 Herrschaften* (begun in the late 1380s), an influential compendium of Austrian history borrowing the frame of world history, and commissioned by Duke Albrecht III. The *Chronik,* sometimes called the *Chronica patrie,* is a detailed, annalist prose history—based in part on the religious chronicle *Flores temporum* focusing on Austria from its earliest times through the rule of Duke Albrecht. (The concluding events are the death of the duke in 1395 and the pilgrimage of Duke Albrecht IV in 1398.) Stainreuter's *Chronik* is nourished by its vivid historical awareness, as indicated by its opening references to Seneca as helmsman, of the value of memory *(gedechtnüs),* and of history writing itself. There follows a fabulous pseudo-history, insistent in its efforts to legitimate Habsburg rule, placing Austria in a historical context that is both inventive and tendentious. As valuable as any of the Austrian historical events reported by Stainreuter is his allusion to a very early German Bible. He reports (in paragraph 388) that Queen Agnes of Hungary (d. 1364), *het ain bibel, die waz ze deütsche gemachet* (possessed a Bible written in the German tongue).

By the 1980s scholarship on Leopold Stainreuter seemed stable and serene. For all the vague remarks in the critical literature of the type that works were "ascribed" to him, a consensus had emerged that he was a translator and historian of note. Now that consensus has been shattered. Paul Uiblein recently shook Stainreuter research to its foundations, claiming Stainreuter was in fact the beneficiary of a kind of mistaken identity. Uiblein identifies our author, instead, as a certain Leopold of Vienna (Leupoldus de Wienna), a cleric of similar background who studied theology in Paris and taught the same in the theological faculty of the University of Vienna, established in 1384. At some point before this, Leopold had become court chaplain of Duke Albrecht III of Austria. Among his ducal duties was the preparation of translations; for these, as well as for his teaching at the university, he was recognized in 1385. In that year Duke Albrecht interceded on Leopold's behalf with Pope Urban VI, so that the chaplain might receive a benefice. That Leopold of Vienna already enjoyed the favor of the pope is shown by the bestowal of the title "papal honorary chaplain" in 1385.

Suffice it here to say that scholarship on Leopold Stainreuter is in flux; it is not yet certain when, or how, researchers might sort through the claims and counterclaims, and make a cogent case for the achievements of either "Leopold." Until that time, the literary patronage of the Habsburg dukes, primarily Albrecht III, will be more opaque than once believed. What is clear is that in late-fourteenth-century Austria a court historiography arose animated by nobles and confected of genealogy, historical fact, and fable.

BIBLIOGRAPHY

Boot, Christine, ed. *Cassiodorus' Historia Ecclesiastica Tripartita in Leopold Stainreuter's German Translation MS ger.fol.1109.* 2 vols. Amsterdam: Rodopi, 1977.

Uiblein, Paul. "Leopold von Wien (Leupoldus de Wienna)," in *Die deutsche Literatur des Mittelalters. Verfasserlexikon,* 2d ed., ed. Kurt Ruh et al. Berlin: de Gruyter, 1985, vol. 5, cols. 716–723.

William C. McDonald

SEE ALSO
Vienna

Statutum in Favorem Principum

During the latter years of the 1220s, King Henry VII of Staufen followed a policy that favored the towns over the princes. A case in point was a privilege (Statute in the Favor of Princes) that he granted to the burghers of Verdun in March 1227, giving them the rights to elect their own town council and to fortify their town by means of a self-imposed tax; these rights were to be valid even without the consent of their prelate. Opposition from the princes, headed by Archbishop Dietrich II of Trier, forced the king to revoke the privilege the following month.

By early 1231, however, tension between Henry and the princes, particularly the bishops of Würzburg and Strasbourg, reached the point where, on January 23 at Worms, they compelled him to give legal recognition to their lordly rights over the towns in their territories. This was confirmed in April 1231 in the *Statutum in favorem principum.* Frederick II, whose policy regarding Germany at this time was one of identifying the interests of crown and princes by implicitly accepting their point of view vis-à-vis the towns, confirmed the *Statutum in favorem principum* in May 1232 at Cividale. Frederick thereby extended to all princes, lay and spiritual, concessions made in 1213 (the Golden Bull of Eger) and in 1220 *(Confoederatio cum principibus ecclesiasticis)* to the ecclesiastical princes alone.

Whereas in England and in France, the monarchy allied itself with the rising interests of the towns against the princes, the *Statutum* and its predecessors effectively eliminated the possibilities of a strong monarchy in Germany by rejecting the economic and political potential of the towns in favor of continued harmony with the princes. Thirteen of the twenty-three clauses in the *Statutum* make direct reference to towns and markets, control of which was demanded by the princes. They furthermore received guarantees of full control of all courts and jurisdictions within their territories. It was thus the princely territories that emerged from the Middle Ages with strong and effective administrative machinery, rather than the monarchy, as in England and France.

BIBLIOGRAPHY

Boshof, Egon. "Reichsfürstenstand und Reichsreform in der Politik Friedrichs II." *Blätter für deutsche Landesgeschichte* 122 (1986): 41–66.

Klingelhöfer, E. *Die Reichsgesetze von 1220, 1231–2 und 1235 und ihre Wirkung im deutschen Staat Friedrichs II.* Weimar: Böhlhaus Nachfolger, 1955.

Knöpp, Friedrich. *Die Stellung Friedrichs II. und seiner beiden Söhne zu den deutschen Städten.* Berlin: E. Ebering, 1928.

Schrader, E. "Zur Deutung der Fürstenprivilegien von 1220 und 1231/2," in *Stupor mundi. Zur Geschichte Friedrichs II. von Hohenstaufen,* ed. Gunther G. Wolf. Darmstadt: Wissenschaftliche Buchgesellschaft, 1966, pp. 420–454.

Zinsmaier, P. "Zur Diplomatik der Reichsgesetze Friedrichs II. (1216, 1220, 1231/2, 1235)." *Zeitschrift der Savigny-Stiftung für Rechtsgeschichte. Germanistische Abteilung* 80 (1963): 82–117.

Paul B. Pixton

SEE ALSO
Frederick II; Staufen; Verdun

Staufen

The Staufen (also Hohenstaufen, literally "high Staufen") were a great imperial ruling family of the twelfth and thirteenth centuries whose struggles with and eventual defeat by the papacy signaled the decline of the medieval empire. The greatest members of the line were the two Fredericks: Frederick I Barbarossa and his grandson Frederick II Hohenstaufen. Both these rulers embodied the values and desires of their age and also represented the greatness of imperial authority. After the death of Frederick II and that of his heirs, the empire fell into a period of interregnum and then a prolonged period of decentralization and fragmentation.

The Staufen rise to royal and imperial power occurred in the early twelfth century. Possessors of extensive estates in Swabia, the line felt ready to assume the throne on the death of Henry V in 1125, in the person of Duke Frederick of Swabia, but the last of the Salians chose the Welf (Guelf) Lothar III (r. 1125–1137). Opposition among the Staufen to Lothar's succession was strong, and in 1127 the line engineered the election of Conrad as antiking. But the time was not ripe for the Staufen claim to the throne, and only papal schism kept Lothar from a total victory over his rivals. The victory, however, would be short-lived because Conrad (III) would succeed to the throne in 1138. His reign witnessed triumph over his Welf opponents in Germany— although the Welfs would remain among the most important adversaries of the Staufen. Conrad, like many contemporaries and descendants, was attracted to the idea of crusade and joined the ill-fated Second Crusade. His return from the Holy Lands saw him accept another religious obligation—defense of the pope against his Norman enemies. Indeed, Conrad would receive imperial coronation for his efforts, but he died before he could mount a campaign in Italy. His death left the line in a precarious position, particularly with Conrad's heir still a minor. Although the Staufen hold on power was tenuous, Conrad's eventual successor would secure the dynasty's hold on power and raise the line to great heights.

Arguably the greatest of the line, and one of the greatest rulers in all the Middle Ages, Frederick Barbarossa assumed the throne in 1152—favored by Conrad over his own son, who was still a minor. Frederick was also favored because of important family connections with both his own Staufen line and the rival Welfs. It was his great talents that enabled him to exploit his advantages. His reign was marked by three major concerns: Germany, Italy, and crusade. In the homeland of the realm, Frederick skillfully managed the territorial nobles and family relations to strengthen his authority. He maintained the support of his family by making his displaced cousin duke of Swabia. He also manipulated relations with the rival Welfs effectively, granting them important titles and positions but exploiting the violation of feudal relations of their most powerful figure, Henry the Lion. Frederick also married well, acquiring Burgundy in the process, and intervened in disputed episcopal elections and made greater use of *ministeriales* (ministerials, or officials) during his reign to make his authority more effective. More-

over, it was Frederick and his advisers who recognized the value of Roman law in imperial governance and who first used the term *sacrum imperium* to describe the empire and thereby made it a rival with the holy power of Rome.

Frederick's second great concern was with Rome and Italy. His relations with the papacy were stormy and marked by schism. Although crowned emperor by the pope in 1155 and supportive of the pope at the outset of his reign when he helped suppress the Roman republic associated with Arnold of Brescia, he would find himself in conflict with popes in the 1150s and 1160s. There was the unfortunate incident at Besançon concerning the nature of his relationship with Rome and the exact nature of the "gifts" bestowed by the pope on the emperor. He also found himself on the side of the antipopes during the Alexandrine schism of the 1160s and 1170s. Frederick would see success in this struggle and would have Charlemagne declared a saint, but he would also suffer a major defeat by the Lombard League, which weakened his hand in Italy and ultimately recognize the authority of Alexander III.

Barbarossa's last act was his participation in the Third Crusade. A participant in the Second Crusade, Barbarossa led a large force toward the Holy Lands and enjoyed early success along the way. Unfortunately, while crossing the river Saleph on June 10, 1190, Barbarossa drowned. Demoralized, much of his army returned home; with a much weaker crusader army in the field, chances for success were greatly diminished. Despite his unfortunate end, Barbarossa made a lasting impact on the empire and left it at peace and in the relatively capable hands of his son, Henry VI.

Although not the warrior his father was, Henry was nonetheless a skilled and ruthless ruler whose abilities and ambitions offered great promise to the empire. In his short reign, he managed to strengthen the central authority and reinforce the prestige of the imperial title. He struggled successfully in both Italy and Germany to assert his territorial and political rights and sought to create a hereditary monarchy encompassing Germany and Sicily. His untimely death, however, was disastrous for the empire and led to a period of instability and civil strife in the competition for power among Otto IV, Philip of Swabia, and Henry's own heir, the three-year old Frederick.

Frederick II, one of the most interesting and controversial figures of the Middle Ages—the *stupor mundi* (stuporous to the world)—was the least likely to succeed at the death of Henry. He would triumph over the Welf, Otto IV, whose support from Rome dissipated once he sought to expand his authority into Italy. Frederick resurrected the fortunes of the dynasty after the death of his uncle Philip of Swabia, whose death prevented his triumph over Otto, only to fall ultimately in his prolonged struggle with an increasingly power hungry papacy. Like his illustrious grandfather, Frederick II was concerned with matters in Italy—king of his native Sicily, his attentions naturally focused on the peninsula—Germany, and the Holy Lands. His relations with a series of popes, however, beginning with Innocent III and ending with Innocent IV, shaped his reign. It was support from Innocent III that ensured Frederick's rise and successful claim to succession to the throne in Germany. It was the excommunication passed by Gregory IX that strengthened the opposition to Frederick. Indeed, the popes themselves were often in the forefront of opposition to Frederick, in part because of his failure to honor pledges to keep the crowns of Germany and Sicily separate. His failure to launch a crusade in timely fashion—despite his successful negotiation with the sultan of Egypt and his coronation as king of Jerusalem—brought about the first papal excommunication.

Despite his great ability as a ruler and his ruthlessness, Frederick's sudden death while under the ban of excommunication seriously damaged the line's fortunes. Frederick's descendants, especially Manfred of Sicily and Conradin, were unable to secure the power and position of their father and grandfather, and suffered the continued implacable hatred of the papacy. Frederick's sons were killed in battle or died in prison, and the glorious line that had dominated imperial affairs and raised Germany to great heights was finally defeated by its papal rival. But the legend of the return of Frederick persisted, testifying to both the awe in which he was held and the importance of his family to the medieval empire.

BIBLIOGRAPHY

Abulafia, David. *Frederick II: A Medieval Emperor.* Oxford: Oxford University Press, 1988.

Fuhrmann, Horst. *Germany in the High Middle Ages,* trans. Timothy Reuter. Cambridge: Cambridge University Press, 1986.

Haverkamp, Alfred. *Medieval Germany, 1056–1273,* trans. Helga Braun and Richard Mortimer. Oxford: Oxford University Press, 1992, pp. 137–298.

Gillingham, J. B. *The Kingdom of Germany in the High Middle Ages* (900–1200). London: Historical Association, 1971.

Housely, Norman. *The Italian Crusades: The Papal-Angevin Alliance and the Crusades against Christian Lay Powers, 1254–1343.* Oxford: Clarendon, 1982.

Leyser, Karl. "Frederick Barbarossa and the Hohenstaufen Polity," in *Communications and Power in Medieval Europe: The Gregorian Revolution and Beyond,* ed. Timothy Reuter. London: Hambledon Press, 1994, pp. 115–142.

Kantorowicz, Ernst. *Frederick the Second, 1194–1250,* trans. E.O. Lorimer. New York: Ungar, 1957.

Munz, Peter. *Frederick Barbarossa: A Study in Medieval Politics.* Ithaca, N.Y.: Cornell University Press, 1969.

Otto of Freising and his Continuator, Rahewin. *The Deeds of Frederick Barbarossa,* trans. Charles Chrisopher Mierow. Toronto: University of Toronto Press, 1994.

Van Cleve, Thomas Curtis. *The Emperor Frederick II of Hohenstaufen: "Immutator Mundi."* Oxford: Clarendon Press, 1972.

Michael Frassetto

SEE ALSO

Conradin of Kohenstaufen; Crusades; Frederick I Barbarossa; Frederick II; Gerhoh of Reichersberg; Henry VI; Henry the Lion; Lothar III; Manfred of Sicily; Ministerials; Otto of Freising; Rahewin; Rainald of Dassel; Salians; Succession; Welfs

Steinbach

The so-called basilica of Einhard, the only remains of the former Benedictine cloister at Steinbach near Michelstadt in the Odenwald (Bavaria), is one of the most important examples of Carolingian architecture to survive in Germany. It was founded by Einhard, the biographer of Charlemagne, to whom Charlemagne's son Louis the Pious had given the border settlement Michlinstadt in 815. By 827, when the relics of the martyrs Marcellinus and Petrus were transferred from Rome *in basilicam noviter a me costructam sed nondum dedicatam* (to the church recently built in my honor but not yet dedicated, *Translatio* 1887:243), the church was apparently finished but not yet consecrated. A three-part westwork (entrance structure) preceded the three-aisle nave supported on piers; together with the low chapel-like transept wings and the cruciform shafts of the crypt, these features characterize a building of the "compressed, compartmentalized basilica" type *(gestauchte Zellenbasilika)* in the circle of Abbot Gozbert's abbey church at St. Gall and associated with the reform movements of Benedict of Aniane. The rough stone work of the nave was plastered outside; in the eastern parts of the building, by contrast, the ashlar

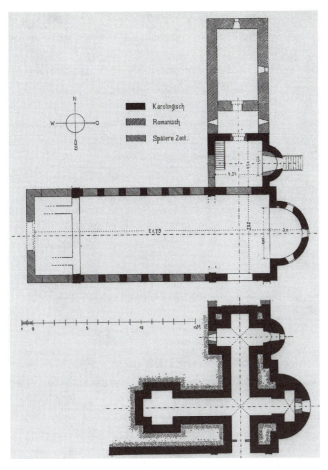

Steinbach, Einhard-Basilica, plan of church (above) and crypt (below) in present state. *Photograph: after Georg Schaefer, Kunstdenkmäler im Grossherzogthum Hessen, A. Provinz Starkenburg, Kreis Erbach,* p. 250 (Darmstadt: Arnold Bergsträsser, 1891)

Mainz, Benedictine nuns were settled at the site. In 1539, the convent was dissolved and the church secularized.

Of the original building only the nave, its arcades walled in since the fourteenth century, the main apse, and the north side choir with its attached two-story "winter choir," added about 1168, still stand. The complex was fully restored between 1968 and 1974.

BIBLIOGRAPHY

Claussen, Hilde, and Matthias Exner. "Abschlußbericht der Arbeitsgemeinschaft für frühmittelalterliche Wandmalerei." *Zeitschrift für Kunsttechnologie und Konservierung* 4 (1990): 283–285.

Jacobsen, Werner. *Der Klosterplan von St. Gallen und die karolingische Architektur: Entwicklung und Wandel von Form und Bedeutung im fränkischen Kirchenbau zwischen 751 und 840.* Berlin: Deutscher Verlag für Kunstwissenschaft, 1992, pp. 265–267.

Ludwig, Thomas, Otto Müller, and Irmgard Widdra-Spiess. *Die Einhards-Basilika in Steinbach bei Michelstadt im Odenwald.* 2 vols. Mainz: Philip von Zabern, 1996.

Schopf, Stefan. "Die Wandmalerei der Einhardsbasilika in Steinbach: Untersuchungen zum Bestand an historischen Putzen, Fassungen und Malschichten," in *Wandmalerei des frühen Mittelalters: Bestand, Maltechnik, Konservierung,* ed. Matthias Exner. ICOMOS—Hefte des Deutschen Nationalkomitees, 23. Munich: Lipp-Verlag, 1998, pp. 75–85.

Translatio et miracula SS. Marcellini et Petri, ed. G. Waitz. Monumenta Germaniae Historica, Scriptores 15/1, 1887; rpt. Hannover: Hirsemann, 1992, pp. 238–264.

Vorromanische Kirchenbauten: Katalog der Denkmäler bis zum Ausgang der Ottonen. Veröffentlichungen des Zentralinstituts für Kunstgeschichte, 3. 2 vols, 1966–1971, vol. 1, rpt. Munich: Prestel, 1990, pp. 320–322; vol. 2, *Nachtragsband.* Munich: Prestel, 1991, pp. 399 [suppl.].

Matthias Exner

SEE ALSO
Sankt Gall; Seligenstadt

masonry of sandstone with light-colored joints was left visible (*pietra rasa* surface). A painted console frieze on the interior below the ceiling remains from the wall painting contemporary with the building's construction; the rest of the walls were whitewashed. Remains of the Carolingian plaster paving are preserved in the apse, but fragments of figural wall painting in the middle apse probably date only from the eleventh century.

Einhard left the site already in 828, taking the bones of the two Roman martyrs with him to the newly erected abbey church at Seligenstadt. Repair work and new building is documented for the years about 1073, when a Benedictine priory was established by Abbot Udalrich of Lorsch, and again about 1160, when two western towers were erected. The towers were pulled down in 1588. In 1232, after the Abbey Lorsch was transferred to the diocese of

Stendal

The original rural settlement grouped around the Petrikirche (church of St. Peter) in the north, still recognizable in today's town plan, received market privileges in 1160 from Margrave Albrecht "the Bear" of Brandenburg. To enhance the importance of the place, the Augustinian chapter at nearby Tangermünde was transferred to Stendal in 1188, and its church, St. Nikolai (the Dom), was established to the south. Between these two poles developed the market town with the Marienkirche (church of the Virgin) and the town hall; finally, the three units became enclosed by a defensive system that gave the town, like Lübeck, an oval shape with its main axis stretching north-south.

The main parish church of St. Marien—begun before 1400 and vaulted in 1447—belongs to a group of similar churches, characteristic of the margraviate of Brandenburg and modeled on St. Sebald's in Nuremberg. Like the churches of St. Nikolai in Berlin and Spandau and those dedicated to St. Katharinen and St. Gotthardt in Brandenburg, St. Marien displays a hall ambulatory choir and shallow chapels filling the space between the inverted buttresses. What distinguishes Stendal from this group, however, is that only here do the seven sides of the exterior correspond to an equal number of the inner apse with six narrowly spaced pillars instead of a single pair that created a portal-like vista.

In contrast, the Dom is a conservative, rather archaic looking monument of the fifteenth century, which in all its aspects re-creates the image of a thirteenth-century building; it is covered throughout by cross-rib vaults and consists of an elongated choir ending in a half bay and five sides of a decagon, with expanding transepts and a hall nave with heavy round pillars and five-partite vaults in the aisles (just as in Magdeburg Cathedral); the latter correspond to the duplication of windows in the outer walls. The result is a spatial clarity and a brightness enhanced by the largely surviving late Gothic stained glass windows.

Both Dom and Marienkirche, like the two smaller parish churches of St. Peter and St. Jakob, have, although Protestant, preserved most of their medieval fittings. Carved in wood, their choir stalls, rood screens, and altar retables contrast in their late Gothic detailing with the sober architecture executed in brick.

The town hall, which creates a screen between the market square and the two-towered facade of St. Marien, represents an ensemble of different parts. In the earlier fifteenth century, the open loggia that served for public court sessions was erected. The long brick building behind, consisting of the northern cloth hall and the southern council hall, was built around 1450, and a wing projecting into the market square was added in the later fifteenth century; this was changed in the subsequent century to a stuccoed Renaissance building with scrolled gable. Of the originally three town gates, two (i.e., the Tangermünder Tor to the northwest and the Uenglinger Tor to the south) have survived. In both, the simple square tower gate built in fieldstone was heightened in the mid–fifteenth century by an impressive superstructure in brick with round corner towers and richly decorated wall surfaces, as well as an ornamental battlement surmounted by a round central tower.

BIBLIOGRAPHY

Schürenberg, Lisa. *Das mittelalterliche Stendal.* Deutsche Bauten 14. Burg: August Hopfer, 1929.

Hans J. Böker

SEE ALSO

Gothic Art and Architecture; Liturgy, Furniture; Lübeck; Magdeburg; Nuremberg

Stoke, Melis (fl. early 13th c.)

The author of an important Dutch chronicle, Melis Stoke is known to have been employed as a town clerk in Dordrecht starting in July 1296. In December 1299 he entered the service of Count Jan II (d. September 11?, 1304) and worked as a chancellery clerk at the court of Holland until November 1305. His *Rijmkroniek van Holland (Rhymed Chronicle of Holland)* is a regional chronicle in the vernacular (more than 13,000 lines long) and is an invaluable source of information about the history of Holland and Zeeland around 1300. Three manuscripts and three fragments of the chronicle have survived. The earliest version (of which no manuscripts have been preserved but which can still be recognized in the part preceding Book 4, l. 242 in later versions) dates from 1278–1282 and was dedicated in the prologue to Count Floris V of Holland. The most important source of this version of the chronicle was the *Chronicon Egmundanum*, written in the monastery of Egmond in Holland. The author aimed to emphasize Floris V's noble ancestry and to show why the subjection of the rebellious Frisians was legitimate. In or around 1305, the early version was rewritten and a continuation was added that devotes a great deal of attention to the murder of Floris V (d. June 27, 1296) and to Holland's conflict with the count of Flanders and the Zeeland nobility. The last remark in the continuation concerns the marriage of Count Willem III of Holland, of the House of Avesnes, to Jeanne of Valois (May 23, 1305). Two versions of the continuation have survived, the later of which was dedicated to Count Willem III.

BIBLIOGRAPHY

Brill, W. G. *Rijmkroniek van Melis Stoke.* 1885, rpt. Utrecht: HES, 1983.

Burgers, J. W. J. "De loopbaan van de klerk Melis Stoke." *Bijdragen en mededelingen betreffende de geschiedenis der Nederlanden* 108 (1993): 20–27.

Peeters, Hugo C. *De Rijmkroniek van Holland, haar auteur en Melis Stoke.* The Hague: Nijhoff, 1966.

Wim van Anrooij

SEE ALSO

Beyeren, Herald; Chronicles, Regional/National, Dutch; Holland

Stoss, Veit (ca. 1445/1450–1533)

The famed sculptor was born in Horb am Neckar and died in Nuremberg on September 20, 1533. Virtually no documentation exists about Stoss's training and earlier years. His earliest secure sculptures show his familiarity with the heightened realism of the art of Nikolaus Gerhaert and Martin Schongauer, suggesting a stay on the Upper Rhine, perhaps in Strasbourg. Rogier van der Weyden's paintings, likely through other artistic intermediaries, also influenced the young sculptor. Although scholars have suggested the Stoss collaborated on altarpieces in Rothenburg (1466) and Nördlingen, nothing is known about his very earliest production. He certainly was an established sculptor when, in 1477, he moved to Kraków from Nuremberg, where he had married before 1476. Between 1477 and 1489 he created the Mary Altarpiece for St. Mary's in Kraków. Measuring 13.95 × 10.68 meters, this is probably the period's largest winged retable. Several of the apostles in the Death and Coronation of the Virgin in the corpus are about 2.8 meters tall. Here and in the relief scenes of the inner and outer wings, Stoss provides his figures with little space. Most are located within a shallow stage with a sharply tilted ground plane. Stoss's virtuosity in cutting highly animated draperies with deep, crisp folds is best observed in the richly polychromed (multicolored) and gilt corpus statues. For a project of this magnitude, the artist employed several assistants likely including a few of his seven sons. The Mary Altarpiece, the red marble Tomb of King Casimir IV Jagiello (1492) in Wawel Cathedral in Kraków, and his cast bronze Tomb Plate of Callimachus (Filippo Buonaccorsi, d. 1496) in the city's Dominican Church, among other works, exerted a tremendous influence on other artists active in Poland and eastern Prussia.

In 1496 Stoss moved back to Nuremberg. Three years later he completed stone statues of the Man of Sorrows and Mater Dolorosa plus three reliefs of the Last Supper, Christ on the Mount of Olives, and the Arrest of Christ that patrician Paulus Volckamer set in the eastern choir wall of St. Sebaldus church. The emotional appeal of the figures, notably Christ and Mary, who look beseechingly at the viewers passing in the ambulatory, coupled with a growing clarity of form define Stoss's more developed style. His career, however, was temporarily sidetracked. Having lost 1,265 guilders speculating on copper, Stoss forged a promissory note in 1503. After being convicted, he was branded on both cheeks and banned from leaving the city. In 1504 Stoss fled and worked briefly in Münnerstadt, where he polychromed Tillmann Riemenschneider's Mary Magdalene Altarpiece (1490–1492) and painted four scenes of the Martyrdom of St. Kilian on the wings. These are Stoss's only documented paintings; he also created ten engravings during this decade. Stoss returned to Nuremberg and through the intercession of Emperor Maximilian resumed his career. For the choir of St. Sebaldus, he made the limewood St. Andrew (1505–1507), in which the clear and stable pose of the apostle contrasts with the marvelous billowing drapery.

Stoss carved both small-scale and large statues throughout the 1510s and 1520s for local patrons and churches. His greatest feat was the Angelic Salutation (1517–1518), an over-life-size Annunciation suspended from the choir vault in St. Lorenz church. Supported by an angel holding *sanctus* bells, Gabriel and Mary float before the high altar. They are enframed by a giant rosary complete with roses, beads, small figured roundels, a group of joyous angels, and, at the apex, God. The ensemble included a great crown above, now lost, and Jakob Pülmann's candelabrum. Commissioned by Anton II Tucher, Nuremberg's highest official, the Angelic Salutation was covered for much of the liturgical year. With the advent of the Reformation in Nuremberg, the whole group was sheathed permanently from 1529 until circa 1806. The Reformation also affected Stoss's final great commission, the Mary Altar (1520–1523) ordered by the artist's son, Andreas Stoss, who was the prior of the local Carmelite convent. Stoss's preparatory drawing is today in the University Museum in Kraków. The sculptor had yet to be paid when the convent was dissolved in 1525.

After a long legal battle, the altarpiece was transferred by Stoss's heirs to Bamberg in 1543 and is now in the cathedral. Like several of Stoss's later carvings, the Mary Altar was stained but never polychromed. Stoss continued working at least until 1532. His impact on regional sculpture, at least before 1525, was considerable.

BIBLIOGRAPHY

Baxandall, Michael. *The Limewood Sculptors of Renaissance Germany*. New Haven, Conn.: Yale University Press, 1980.

Kahsnitz, Rainer. "Veit Stoss in Nürnberg. Eine Nachlese zum Katalog und zur Ausstellung." *Anzeiger des Germanischen Nationalmuseum* (1984): 39–70.

———, ed. *Veit Stoss in Nürnberg: Werke des Meisters und seiner Schule in Nürnberg und Umgebung*. Munich: Deutscher Kunstverlag, 1983.

———, ed. *Veit Stoss: Die Vorträge des Nürnberger Symposions*. Munich: Deutscher Kunstverlag, 1985.

Lutze, Eberhard. *Veit Stoss*, 4th ed. Munich: Deutscher Kunstverlag, 1968.

Oellermann, Eike. "Die monochromen Holzbildwerke des Veit Stoss." *Maltechnik* 82 (1976): 173–182.

Sello, Gottfried. *Veit Stoss*. Munich: Hirmer, 1988.

Skubiszewski, Piotr. *Veit Stoss und Polen*. Nuremberg: Germanisches Nationalmuseum, 1983.

Söding, Ulrich. "Veit Stoss am Oberrhein: Zur Kunstgeschichtlichen Stellung der 'Isenheimer Muttergottes' im Louvre." *Jahrbuch der Staatlichen Kunstsammlungen in Baden-Württemberg* 29 (1992): 50–76.

Jeffrey Chipps Smith

SEE ALSO

Iconographies, Innovative; Maximilian; Nuremberg; Riemenschneider, Tillmann; Rothenburg ob der Tauber; Schongauer, Martin; Strasbourg

Stralsund

The city of Stralsund is located in a strategically prominent position on an elevation dominating the Strelasund, which separates the island of Rügen from the Pomeranian coast, and secured on the landward side by a series of lakes created from swamps. The economically important medieval city grew out of a preexisting Slavic settlement and received trading privileges from Prince Wizlaw of Rügen in 1234. As a result of its speedy economic development, which provoked the envy of Lübeck, Stralsund was conquered and sacked in 1249 by the latter; it soon regained and surpassed its former prosperity, however, and by 1256 there is mention of the Heilig-Geist-Spital (Hospital of the Holy Spirit) in the new town, indicating that the first major urban expansion was well on its way. A fire in 1271 did not halt the urban development either but led to a rebuilding of the city, now surrounded by defensive works in brick. In 1316, Stralsund sided openly with the Baltic cities and was consequently besieged by its territorial lord, the prince of Rügen. In 1325, after the prince's death, Stralsund fell to Pomerania. The treaty of Stralsund, signed in 1370 to end the war between the Hanseatic League and Denmark, marked the first peak of the town's economic and political importance, and in 1429, a Danish fleet was destroyed near Stralsund. The second half of the fifteenth century witnessed the lasting conflict between the city's growing struggle for independence and the territorial interests of the Pomeranian princes, which, in 1512, reached a compromise. Through the subsequent centuries, which saw the Swedish occupation of Stralsund, the city underwent a continuous decline. As a result, the city was able to preserve its late medieval architectural appearance.

The town plan of Stralsund reflects the fusion of two halves, i.e., the old town with town hall and Nikolaikirche (church of St. Nicholas) to the north, and the new town with the Marienkirche (church of the Virgin) to the south. The present Nikolaikirche, which replaced an earlier hall church, was begun after 1276 when the council asked for donations, and—to be more precise—most probably in 1288, when Dietrich von Barth was appointed architect for the building. An inscription near the western portal gives the year 1311, and by the mid–fourteenth century the church itself must have been completed, while its monumental two-towered facade was still under construction. As a basilica with flying buttresses, St. Nikolai can be considered a faithful copy of the exactly contemporaneous Marienkirche in Lübeck, which had applied the scheme of a Gothic cathedral to a parish church erected in brick. Like its prototype, St. Nikolai has no transepts but an ambulatory choir with integrated hexagonal chapels and a two-storied wall elevation with high niches in the clerestory.

The first Marienkirche of the new town—likewise a hall church—was destroyed by the collapse of the tower in 1382 or 1384 and was subsequently rebuilt as a late Gothic variation on the theme of St. Nikolai. Already in

1394, the northern transept received its stained glass window, while the massive western tower was begun in 1416 and completed in 1478. In contrast to its model, St. Marien has a set of transepts with aisles, and the radiating chapels become unified externally to form a large polygon. Despite its late date, the Marienkirche shows a rather austere treatment of all architectural forms in accordance with the brick technique. It still exhibits simple cross-rib vaults, and only the crossing possesses a star vault not unlike that of Amiens Cathedral, but also found in contemporaneous north German brick architecture. The western tower, however, its accompanying transeptlike wings, and even its arcades that pierce the massive walls, show an abundance of late Gothic star vaults. Like a donjon, the square tower, flanked by turrets at all its four corners, rises above the ridgeline of the church in an octagonal superstructure. In the third parish church, the Jakobikirche (church of St. James), the original hall church with straight eastern termination was not, as in the two others, completely rebuilt, but only heightened during the fifteenth century to correspond to the system of the two existing basilicas. Its tower repeats the scheme of St. Marien, but with corner towers flanking the octagon.

The completely preserved Dominican monastery of St. Katharinen (St. Catherine's) with its church—a hall church of eight bays plus choir, consecrated in 1287—serves today as the city's museum, while the Franciscan monastery, founded 1254 and destroyed 1944, survives as a ruin. The Heilig-Geist-Spital, rebuilt in the fifteenth century, consists of a chapel—a hall of four bays, cross-rib vaulted with the exception of a central bay that shows a complicated star pattern—and the hospital as its eastern continuation. The latter consists basically of two wings that prolong the chapel's aisles, while an open courtyard acts as the continuation of the central nave.

Stralsund's town hall is one of the most impressive monuments of this building type. Placed as a barrier between the western facade of the Nikolaikirche and the market square, it consists, like its prototype in Lübeck, of two parallel wings separated by an elongated courtyard, and a northern wing that unites the two buildings; with its six high gables between turrets and opened in tracery, the northern wing presents to anyone who approaches the city from the north a majestic silhouette.

BIBLIOGRAPHY

Zaske, Nikolaus. *Die gotischen Kirchen Stralsunds und ihre Kunstwerke: Kirchliche Kunstgeschichte von 1250 bis zur Gegenwart.* Berlin: Evangelische Verlagsanstalt, 1964.

Hans J. Böker

SEE ALSO

Gothic Art and Architecture; Hanseatic League; Lübeck

Strasbourg

This important medieval city began as a fortified Roman settlement named Argentoratum or Argentina. Because of its location on the Rhine River at the border between German and French lands, Strasbourg has always been a crossroad as its Merovingian name, Strateburg—"the city on the roads"—indicates. It was a prosperous city throughout the Middle Ages. The bishops of Strasbourg controlled the city until the thirteenth century, when, with support of the Staufen rulers, the citizens of Strasbourg assumed control. While its geographic location and economic prosperity made Strasbourg a vital medieval intellectual and artistic center, the ravages of numerous wars, most notably the bombardment by the Germans in 1870 (Franco-Prussian War) and the bombing in 1944 by the Allies, destroyed or damaged many of Strasbourg's medieval monuments.

The best-preserved and restored medieval edifice is the cathedral of Notre-Dame, which represents a mixture of German and French artistic influences. The plan and proportions follow the eleventh-century Ottonian Romanesque church, including the elongated crypt and an octagonal crossing tower. Some of the Romanesque stained glass windows are preserved in the transept. During the thirteenth century, French Gothic styles predominated, first in the sculpture of the south transept, which reflects influences from Chartres, and most important in the nave, which was rebuilt around 1240–1275 in the rayonnant style of Parisian Gothic architecture. The most famous aspect of the cathedral is its "harp string" facade, which was begun around 1277 and completed in the fifteenth century. It is a prime example of Rhenish Gothic architecture.

As a flourishing city, numerous religious foundations were established in medieval Strasbourg. Many of these have been destroyed completely, or the medieval remains have been considerably modified or restored. The Dominican convent, one of the earliest Dominican establishments in southern Germany, was begun in 1254 but was destroyed in 1870. The churches of St. Aurelia, St. Thomas, and St. Stephen were founded during the Car-

Strasbourg, cathedral, south transept façade portals. *Photograph: Joan A. Holladay*

olingian period. Parts of these structures dating from the Romanesque and Gothic periods survive. Two churches were dedicated to St. Peter. The most fully preserved, known as St. Pierre-le-Jeune, is a Gothic structure primarily of the fourteenth century. Little of the medieval walls, gates, streets of commerce, and houses of wealthy burghers remain in their original state.

BIBLIOGRAPHY

Haug, Hans. *Strasbourg.* Paris: Éditions "Tel," 1946.

Pfleger, Luzian. *Kirchengeschichte der Stadt Strassburg im Mittelalter.* Forschungen zur Kirchengeschichte des Elsaß 6. Colmar: Alsatia, 1941.

Reinhardt, Hans. *La Cathédrale de Strasbourg.* Paris: Arthaud, 1972.

Reuss, H. Rodolphe. *Histoire de Strasbourg depuis ses origines jusqu'à nos jours,* 1922. Marseille: Laffitte Reprints, 1981.

Karen Gould

SEE ALSO

Gothic Art and Architecture; Gottfried von Straßburg; Romanesque Art and Architecture; Strasbourg Oaths

Strasbourg Oaths

Recorded in Nithard's Latin history of the Carolingian civil war (Book 3, Chapter 5), the Strasbourg Oaths were the oaths sworn at the city of Strasbourg in Alsace on

February 14, 842, among Louis the German of east Francia (r. 840–876), his (half-)brother Charles the Bald of west Francia (r. 840–877), and their followers. Louis and Charles swore these oaths to reaffirm their fraternal alliance against their elder brother Lothar I (r. 840–855), who had claimed the entire Carolingian Empire for himself on the death of their father, Louis the Pious (r. 814–840). Recorded by Nithard in proto-Romance *(lingua Romana)* and the Rhine-Franconian Germanic dialect *(lingua Teudisca),* the Strasbourg Oaths provide the earliest surviving example of Old French and one of the earliest examples of Old High German. This alliance enabled Louis and Charles to force an equal division of the empire at the Treaty of Verdun in the following year. Because that division gave Louis an east Frankish kingdom and Charles a west Frankish kingdom, scholars in retrospect have interpreted the Strasbourg Oaths as a linguistic and political milestone in the origins of France and Germany.

The Strasbourg Oaths reveal the complexities of aristocratic loyalties and spoken and written communication in Frankish politics. By February 842 the nobility had become weary of civil war. Louis and Charles therefore swore oaths at Strasbourg to reassure their supporters of their fraternal alliance through which they hoped to force permanent concessions out of Lothar. Because Louis and Charles wanted the rank and file of their eastern and western armies to understand their negotiations, they swore not in educated Latin but rather in the vernacular. Before the oaths, Louis and Charles briefly recounted their just grievances against Lothar, with Louis addressing his forces in the German tongue *(lingua Teudisca)* and Charles his forces in a Romance language *(lingua Romana,* i.e., French). Thereupon Louis and Charles swore oaths of mutual help to each other and promised never to enter an alliance with Lothar. This time each swore in the language of his brother's followers—Louis in Romance and Charles in Old High German—thus revealing the kings' facility in both vernacular tongues. Finally Louis's and Charles's supporters swore in their respective vernaculars that they would support their king only as long as he kept his promise to his brother. In this way the eastern and western nobles sought to hold Louis and Charles to their alliance by threatening to withdraw their loyalty if they did not.

Nithard's record of the Strasbourg Oaths functioned as a rhetorical and literary device that reflected his political agenda. Nithard was an illegitimate grandson of Charlemagne who played an active role in the civil war as a politician, counselor, envoy, and warrior. He supported Charles the Bald in the conflict with Lothar, and indeed Charles commissioned him to write his history. By inserting the Germanic and Romance oaths into his Latin history, Nithard sought to convey the political solidarity among the eastern and western nobles that Louis and Charles so desperately hoped to forge at Strasbourg. In reality the linguistic situation was much more complex: as Nithard himself reports, Louis's followers included east Franks, Bavarians, Alemans, and Saxons, and Charles led Bretons and Gascons as well as west Franks. Thus their supporters spoke different dialects and languages, and one therefore cannot take Nithard's record of the oaths as an accurate rendering of the actual words and dialects spoken. Janet Nelson argues that Nithard intended his history to be read aloud at Charles the Bald's court, in which case his vernacular record of the Strasbourg Oaths would have served as a linguistic metaphor for the eastern and western kingdoms that Louis and Charles were striving to create.

BIBLIOGRAPHY

Becker, Siegfried. *Untersuchungen zur Redaktion der Straßburger Eide.* Bern: Lang, 1972.

Bostock, J. Knight. *A Handbook on Old High German Literature,* 2d ed. Oxford: Clarendon, 1976, pp. 187–189.

Murdoch, Brian. "The Strasbourg Oaths," in Will Hasty and James Hardin, eds. *German Writers and Works of the Early Middle Ages: 800-1170.* In *Dictionary of Literary Biography,* vol. 148. Detroit: Gale, 1995, pp. 279–282.

Nelson, Janet. "Public *Histories* and Private History in the Works of Nithard." *Speculum* 60 (1985): 251–293.

Nithardi historiarum libri IIII, ed. Ernst Müller. Monumenta Germaniae Historica. Hanover: Hahn, 3d ed. 1907, new ed. 1956, vol. 3, pt. 5.

Scholz, Bernard Walter, and Barbara Rogers, trans. *Carolingian Chronicles: Royal Frankish Annals and Nithard's Histories.* Ann Arbor: University of Michigan Press, 1970, pp. 161–163.

Eric J. Goldberg

SEE ALSO

Carolingians; Charlemagne; Lothar I; Louis the Pious

Stricker, Der (ca. 1190–ca. 1250)

This itinerant poet, known only by his pseudonym, was probably born toward the end of the twelfth century in the Middle German region. A major portion of his life was spent in Austria, where he died about 1250, if the last poems for which reliable dates exist are taken as *terminus post quem*. Clearly not a member of the nobility, he seems to have worked for various audiences and patrons, although none is known to us by name. His oeuvre, consisting of nearly 170 works and spanning a wide variety of genres, attests not only to his versatility and originality but also to his considerable knowledge of theological and legal issues. He is familiar with the works of Hartmann von Aue and Wolfram von Eschenbach. The paucity of information regarding the poet extends to the chronology of his works. While it is generally assumed that his two longer works, *Daniel von dem Blühenden Tal* and *Karl der Große*, are products of his youth, it remains impossible to establish a sequence for *Pfaffe Amis,* various stories of medium length, and his vast output of short narratives consisting of fables, prayers, didactic poems, and a corpus of *Mären* (stories or tales) that constitute his actual claim to fame. *Daniel von dem Blühenden Tal,* consisting of 8,478 verses and transmitted in four extant manuscripts, is a highly original treatment of the Arthurian romance genre. Denounced by earlier scholarship, which viewed Stricker's *novum* of an unproblematic hero and an active, functioning society as a serious misunderstanding of the genre, it is recognized today as the coherent and skillful text that introduced the notion of *ratio* as a means to avoid the pitfalls of human life. The popularity of Stricker's *Karl* is attested to by twenty-four manuscripts and twenty-three fragments. Whether it was written in the wake of the Charlemagne revival or occasioned by the moving of his remains to Aachen in 1215 or by the transport of Charlemagne reliquaries to Zurich in 1233 still must be determined. Although Stricker's primary source was the *Chanson de Roland,* modern scholarship has been reluctant to label the 12,206 verse narrative simply a reworking of his source. Yet, attempts to explain it in its historical context as a political piece aimed at renewing interest in crusading efforts or as confirmation of the Hohenstaufen emperors as legitimate heirs to Charlemagne are inconclusive as well. A comprehensive interpretation remains a desideratum.

Stricker's shorter narratives are transmitted in fifty-three manuscripts and range from 10 to circa 2,500 verses. Counted among the latter are *Die Frauenehre,* Stricker's praise of women, and *Pfaffe Amis,* a cyclical narrative arranged in twelve episodes that castigates the folly of man. The thematic emphasis on *prudentia* and self-knowledge, either as underlying message or overtly stated, extends to many of the shorter works, which range from purely religious to profane, from entertaining to moralizing. Viewed as a whole, the shorter narratives present a canon of values appropriate to men and women and to all social classes.

BIBLIOGRAPHY

Bartsch, Karl. *Karl der Große von dem Stricker.* Quedlinburg: Basse, 1857; rpt. Berlin: de Gruyter, 1965.

Ehrismann, Otfrid. *Der Stricker: Erzählungen, Fabeln, Reden. Mittelhochdeutsch/Neuhochdeutsch* Stuttgart: Reclam, 1992.

Fischer, Hanns. "Strickerstudien: Ein Beitrag zur Literaturgeschichte des 13. Jahrhunderts." Ph.d. diss., Ludwig Maximilian-Universität, Munich, 1953.

———. *Studien zur deutschen Märendichtung.* Tübingen: Niemeyer, 1968, 2d ed. 1983.

———. *Der Stricker: Verserzählungen I.* Tübingen: Niemeyer, 1960, 4th ed. Johannes Janota, ed. 1979.

———. *Der Stricker. Verserzählungen II.* Tübingen: Niemeyer, 1967, 4th. ed. Johannes Janota, 1983.

Geith, Karl-Ernst. *Carolus Magnus: Studien zur Darstellung Karls des Großen in der deutschen Literatur des 12. und 13. Jahrhunderts,* Bibliotheca Germanica 19. Bern: Francke, 1977.

Henderson, Ingeborg. *Strickers Daniel von dem Blühenden Tal: Werkstruktur und Interpretation.* Amsterdam: Benjamins, 1976.

Henne, Hermann. *Der Pfaffe Amis.* Göppingen: Kümmerle, 1991.

Hofmann, Klaus. *Strickers Frauenehre: Überlieferung, Textkritik, Edition, literaturgeschichtliche Einordnung.* Marburg: Elwert, 1976.

Mettke, Heinz. *Fabeln und Mären von dem Stricker.* Halle: Niemeyer, 1959.

Moelleken, Wolfgang W. *Die Kleindichtung des Strickers,* 5 vols. Göppingen: Kümmerle, 1973–1978.

Räkel, Hans-Herbert. "Die Frauenehre von dem Stricker," in *Österreichische Literatur zur Zeit der Babenberger,* ed. Alfred Ebenbauer. Vienna: Halosar, 1977.

Resler, Michael. *Der Stricker: Daniel von dem Blühenden Tal.* Tübingen: Niemeyer, 1983.

———. *Der Stricker: 'Daniel of the Blossoming Valley' (Daniel von dem Blühenden Tal).* New York: Garland, 1990.

Schwab, Ute. *Die bisher unveröffentlichten geistlichen Bispelreden des Strickers.* Göttingen: Vandenhoeck and Ruprecht, 1959.

———. *Der Stricker, Tierbispel.* Tübingen: Niemeyer, 1960, 3d ed. 1983.

Thamert. Mark Lee. "The Medieval Novelistic 'Märe': Telling and Teaching in Works of the Stricker." Ph.d. diss., Princeton University, 1986.

Wailes, Stephen L. *Studien zur Kleindichtung des Stricker.* Berlin: Schmidt, 1981.

Ziegeler, Hans-Joachim. *Erzählen im Spätmittelalter.* Munich: Artemis, 1985.

Ingeborg Henderson

SEE ALSO

Charlemagne; Hartmann von Aue; Wolfram von Eschenbach

Stuttgart

The Stuttgart valley had been settled by Celts and Romans, long before the Duke Liudolf first established his mares' meadow *(Stutengarten)* on this site in approximately 950. First mentioned in official documents in 1229, the city became the seat of the counts and dukes of Württemberg in the fourteenth century.

Among the earliest monuments built here is the thirteenth-century Altes Schloss (Old Castle), first designed as a fortress surrounded by water and later renovated in the German Renaissance style. The nearby medieval grain storage house (Fruchtkasten) has fourteenth-century origins.

At the center of the old town is the abbey church of the Holy Cross. The oldest sections of this monument are the lower stories of the south tower, which date to about 1175. In the thirteenth century, the church became the burial place of the counts of Württemberg. By 1347, the High Gothic choir was completed. Hänslin and Aberlin Jörg finally finished the nave of the hall church by 1495.

The exterior of the monument retains fragments of its original fourteenth-century sculpture. Of highest importance in the interior is the tomb of the patron couple Count Ulrich (called *Ulrich mit dem Daumen,* "Ulrich with the thumb") and Agnes von Liegnitz. Their elegant and finely worked effigies date to 1300. The north wall of the nave is ornamented with a number of interesting late medieval reliefs, among them the Annunciation, the Adoration of the Magi, and a very unusual Christ of Mercy *(Schutzmantelchristus)* protecting the pious beneath his cloak.

Aberlin Jörg was also responsible for the construction of the church of St. Leonhard, after 1463. The older choir of the hall church suggests the existence of an earlier church, probably a chapel dedicated to Leonhard. The

city's Hospitalkirche (Hospital Church), also built under Jörg, was completed between 1471 and 1493. This three-aisle hall-form structure served as a monastery church from 1473; it was given over to the Dominicans in 1475.

North of the city center, in Stuttgart-Mühlhausen, is the small but important Chapel of St. Vitus, built between 1380 and 1385 under the patronage of the Prague citizen Reinhard von Mühlhausen. Most noteworthy is the chapel's cycle of wall paintings dating to 1428. The legend of St. Vitus is shown in twelve episodes between small interior chapels; the life of the Virgin is depicted over the windows, and a Madonna of Mercy appears on the north wall. Over the choir arch is the Last Judgment.

Leslie Anne Hamel

SEE ALSO

Gothic Art and Architecture; Iconographies, Innovative; Prague

Succession

The tradition of political succession in medieval Germany was characterized by two seemingly contradictory practices: election and inheritance. The tradition of election was a legacy of ancient Germanic custom from before the period of migrations in the late Roman period. This practice found expression among early Germanic peoples and, especially, among the Franks. The usurpation by Pippin III, the Short, was confirmed by the church but also by election of the Frankish people in 751. The practice of election would emerge throughout the Carolingian period, particularly in the later ninth century and would involve the succession of Arnulf of Carinthia. The act of election was important in the end of the Carolingian line and the rise of the Saxon dynasty. Elections would play a role in the succession of the first of the Saxon kings, Conrad I (911), Henry I (918), and Otto I (936), and would confirm the efforts of Henry to ensure the hereditary succession of his son Otto. The electoral process would, perhaps, be most important when the reigning king died childless, as was the case with Otto III (983–1002), Henry II (1002–1024), Henry V (1056–1106), and Lothar of Supplingburg (1125–1137), or when the reigning family faced great opposition and disgrace, as was the case with the election of Rudolf of Habsburg in 1273. Indeed, election was a powerful tool in the hands of the ruler's opponents, as Henry IV discovered when he faced the election of the duke of Swabia, Rudolf of Rheinfelden, as king of Germany in 1077. But just as election could undermine royal and imperial authority, it was used to buttress this authority and secure the nomination of the king's appointed successor, often his son or close family member. Otto the Great, Henry IV, Conrad III, and Frederick I Barbarossa all designated successors whose succession was confirmed by election. The practice of hereditary succession was attempted by many of the same rulers who had been elected and witnessed the election of their sons as successors. Although somewhat of a paradox, the use of elections was a means by which proponents of hereditary succession could confirm the legacy for their sons as successor to the throne. And in the Golden Bull of 1356, the principle and practice of election were confirmed by the emperor, Charles IV, and the great powers, the electors, of the realm. But the terms of this document too would be used to secure the hereditary succession of the Habsburgs. Finally, the succession to the throne was confirmed by the act of coronation and unction by the pope. A practice begun by Pippin at the creation of the Carolingian monarchy and confirmed as the essential act of the ascension to the imperial dignity, coronation would provide divine sanction to the succession to the imperial throne and would be sought after by most rulers of medieval Germany.

BIBLIOGRAPHY

Arnold, Benjamin. *Medieval Germany, 500–1300: A Political Interpretation.* Toronto: University of Toronto Press, 1997.

Gillingham, J. B. *The Kingdom of Germany in the High Middle Ages (900–1200).* London: Cox and Wyman, 1979.

Schmid, Karl. "Die Thronfolge Ottos des Großen." *Zeitschrift der Savigny-Stiftung für Rechtsgeschichte, Germanistische Abteilung* 81 (1964).

Michael Frassetto

SEE ALSO

Carolingians; Charles IV; Conrad I; Coronation; Frederick I Barbarossa; Golden Bull; Henry I; Henry IV; Otto I; Pippin

Suchenwirt, Peter (fl. 14th c.)

Neither the birth date nor death date is known for this most famous German herald of the fourteenth century. The name Suchenwirt is apparently a professional one derived from *such den wirt* (get the innkeeper); he calls himself *chnappe von den wappen* (page of the weapons, poem

30, ll. 169–189). His name appears in twelve documents from 1377 to 1407, all dealing with his house in Vienna. His name also appears in a eulogy by Hugo von Montfort (1357–1423), who was with him on Duke Albrecht III's Prussian crusade of 1377. Suchenwirt's language, perspective, and sympathies suggest that he was an Austrian. The best source of information about his life is found in his poetry.

There are fifty two poems by Peter Suchenwirt extant in at least thirty three manuscripts. The main manuscript containing Suchenwirt's works, called "A," is in the National Library in Vienna (no. a3045, 503 pages from beginning of fifteenth century). The poems range in length from 57 lines to 1,540 lines. They include a number of different genres: four death laments; eighteen elegies *(Ehrenreden);* eleven historical and political occasional poems; fifteen moral allegories and spiritual didactic poems; four comic poems. The general term *Ehrenrede* was coined by Alois Primisser, Suchenwirt's first editor, and was applied to Suchenwirt's poems honoring famous Austrian nobles. These were poems that followed a strict formula: a formal expression of humility; general praise of the hero; description of hero's specific deeds; repetition of general praise; prayer for intercession of his soul (if the hero was already deceased); description of his coat of arms, both shield and helmet; name of the hero; a short closing prayer.

The subject matter of his political comments is especially enlightening. He discusses the ramifications of a division of property, the political consequences of a tax on wine, and the interrelationships among the classes; these are not generally the subject matter for chronicles or historical songs.

Suchenwirt (and a certain Gelre in the Low Lands) are unique in writing *Ehrenreden.* Their poetry places them within a long and illustrious tradition whose origins are in the death lament, the political-historical song, and in the so-called "tournament and siege poetry."

The heroes of the *Ehrenreden* follow similar life patterns with crusades against the heathens in Prussia, pilgrimages to the Holy Land, expeditions into Italy, and in the so-called numerous local campaigns in their homelands.

BIBLIOGRAPHY

Achnitz, Wolfgang. "Peter Suchenwirts Reimtraktat 'Die zehn Gebote' im Kontext deutschspracher Dekaloggedichte des Mittelalters. Mit Textedition und einem Abdruck der Dekalog-Auslegung des Johannes Künlin." *Beiträge zur Geschichte der deutschen Sprache und Literatur* 120 (1998): 53–102.

Blosen, Hans. "Überlegungen zur Textüberlieferung und Textgestaltung bei einem Gedicht von Peter Suchenwirt," in *Probleme altgermanistischer Editionen,* ed. Hugo Kuhn, Karl Stackmann, and Dieter Wuttke. Wiesbaden: Steiner, 1968.

Brinker-von der Heyde, Claudia. "Suchenwirt, Peter," in *Die deutsche Literatur des Mittelalters. Verfasserlexikon,* 2d ed., ed. Kurt Ruh et al. vol. 9. Berlin: de Gruyter, 1995, cols. 481–488.

Busse, Kaarl Heinrich von. "Peter Suchenwirt's Sagen über Livlane." *Mittheilungen aus dem gebiete der Geschichte Liv-, Esthh- und Kurland's,* ed. Gesellschaft für Geschichte und Altertumskund der russischen Ostsee-Provinzen. 3. Riga: Nicolai Kymmel, 1845, pp. 5–21.

Docen, Bernard Joseph. "Die Schlacht bei Sempach. 1386. Von Peter Suchenwirt." *Sammlung für altdeutsche Literatur und Kunst* 1, no. 1 (1812): 152–160.

Friess, Godfried Edmund. "Fünf unedierte Ehrenreden Peter Suchenwirts." *Wiener Sitzungsberichte der Akademie der Wissenschaften, Phil.-hist. Klasse* 88 (1877): 99–126.

Primisser, Alois, ed. *Peter Suchenwirts Werke aus dem vierzehnten Jahrhunderte. Ein Beytrag zur Zeit- und Sittengeschichte.* Vienna: J.B. Wallishausser, 1827; rpt. Vienna: H. Geyer, 1961.

Van D'Elden, Stephanie Cain. *Peter Suchenwirt and Heraldic Poetry.* Vienna: Halosar, 1976.

Stephanie Cain Van D'Elden

SEE ALSO
Hugo von Montfort

Sylvester II (ca. 945–1003)

Pope, archibishop of Ravenna, educator. Born circa 945 into a peasant family in the Auvergne, the young Gerbert was befriended by the monks of the monastery St. Gerald of Aurillac and there received his early education. In 967 he journeyed to Catalonia, where he continued his studies, with special attention to the *quadrivium* (four of the seven liberal arts: geometry, astronomy, arithmetic, music). In the early 970s he began teaching at the cathedral school at Reims and became a close associate of Archbishop Adalbero. Emperor Otto II named him abbot of Bobbio in 982, but he returned to Reims in 984 after Otto's death. As a teacher he was a master of the seven liberal arts: both the lower level, or *trivium* (grammar, logic, rhetoric), and the higher level, or *quadrivium,* although he was probably best

known for his ability in mathematics, particularly for his great skill with the abacus. His students included Fulbert of Chartres, Richer of Saint-Remi and King Robert II. In 991 Gerbert was selected by Hugh Capet (ca. 940–October 24, 966, Duke of Francia) to be archbishop of Reims but failed to gain papal support because the pope would not accept the deposition of Gerbert's predecessor, Arnulf. In 997 having traveled to the court of Otto III, he became the young emperor's teacher. In 998 Otto named him archbishop of Ravenna, and in 999 he was appointed pope as Sylvester II. He worked closely with the emperor until the latter's death in 1002 in seeking the conversion of eastern Europe. In several ways his papacy prepared the way for ecclesiastical developments later in the century. He was a strong supporter of reform in the church, especially in curbing simony (selling of indulgences) and nicolaitism (opposition to celibacy). He also took much interest in the protection of Jerusalem. After his death in 1003 later historians would recall him as one of the most gifted thinkers of the tenth century, even as a magician who received his inspiration from the diabolical forces he found in Islamic Spain. Thus was remembered the pope of the year 1000.

BIBLIOGRAPHY

Lettres de Gerbert, 983–997, ed. J. Havet. Paris: Collection des textes pour servir à l'étude et à l'enseignement de l'histoire, 1889.

The Letters of Gerbert, with His Papal Privileges as Sylvester II, trans. H.P. Lattin. New York: Columbia University Press, 1961.

Correspondance de Gerbert d'Aurillac. 2 vols., ed. and trans. P. Riché and J. P. Callu. Paris: Société d'Édition les Belles Lettres, 1993 [correspondence with French trans.].

Darlington, O. G. "Gerbert the Teacher." *American Historical Review* 52 (1947): 456–476.

Gerberto, scienza, storia e mito: atti del Gerberti Symposium. Bobbio: Archivium Bobiense, 1985.

Riché, P. *Gerbert d' Aurillac, le pape de l'an mil.* Paris: Fayard, 1987.

Daniel F. Callahan

SEE ALSO
Education; Otto III

Sylvester, Trierer

The so-called *Trier Sylvester,* a tale of events from the life of the fourth-century Pope Sylvester, was composed some time after 1150 by an unknown author from the Middle German dialect region. The date of composition is based on the fact that the *Trierer Sylvester* is a reworking of lines 7,806–10,400 from the *Kaiserchronik,* which was completed after 1147. At the center of the legend is the relationship between Pope Sylvester and the Emperor Constantine, which results after Sylvester brings Constantine to the Christian faith, baptizes him, and heals him of a disease that has plagued him. Constantine's own worth, too, is clear; he is favored by God because he has abandoned a plan to gain healing by bathing in the blood of sacrificed infants. Through the depiction of a strong partnership between pope and emperor, a number of key institutions of the Middle Ages are given "historical" justification: a Christian Roman Empire, a Rome-based papacy, and the ideal of the Christian warrior and ruler. Also stressed is the superiority of Sylvester's arguments in disproving the validity of other religious systems; the legend has a strong apologetic tone.

The Trier version exists only in fragmentary form (manuscript no. 364 in the Trierer Stadtbibliothek) and breaks off before Sylvester is able to confound the arguments of learned unbelievers and thus bring the Empress Helena to the Christian faith.

BIBLIOGRAPHY

Roediger. Max. "Trierer Bruchstücke III. Silvester." *Zeitschrift für deutsches Altertum und deutsche Literatur* 22 (1878): 145–209.

Kraus, Carl. *Der Trierer Silvester.* Hannover: Hahn, 1895.

James K. Walter

SEE ALSO
Kaiserchronik

Synod of Frankfurt (794)

In June 794 Charlemagne presided over an assembly of the great men of the realm and a concurrent synod that included bishops from Francia, Italy, Aquitaine, and Provence, along with Alcuin and two papal legates. Although the assembly's *acta,* or official records, have not survived, a summarizing protocol of fifty-six chapters from the synod shows that the impulse to reform church and society articulated in the *Admonitio generalis* (edict of 789) remained strong. Those general reform measures frame three unusual items.

The synod rejected the adoptionist christology of Felix of Urgel and Elipand of Toledo, according to which Jesus, in his divinity the truly begotten Son of God, was the adoptive Son of God in his humanity. A Frankish council had condemned the teaching in 792 and sent Felix to Rome to recant before the pope. When the error continued to spread in the Spanish March, the prelates gathered at Frankfurt renewed the condemnation and wrote three antiadoptionist tracts. Alcuin probably drafted two of these, a letter of the bishops of Francia, and Charlemagne's letter to Elipand and the Spanish clergy. The third is a treatise written on behalf of the bishops of Italy by Paulinus, patriarch of Aquileia.

Image worship was the other major doctrinal issue the synod considered. The arrival at the Frankish court of the iconodule (supporting icon) *acta* of the Second Council of Nicaea (787) had elicited an exhaustive polemic against image worship known as the *Libri Carolini* (793). By contrast, the bishops at Frankfurt denounced only one statement from the Second Nicaean Council, namely, that images are entitled to the same adoration and service that are given the Trinity. While the condemned statement was a translator's corruption of an unobjectionable original, the synod's aversion to image worship remains. The comparatively subdued response in 794 likely reflects a desire to avoid open disagreement with Pope Hadrian I, who had lately informed Charlemagne of his approval of the doctrine of the Second Nicaean Council, and whose legates at Frankfurt may have been instructed to monitor the discussion of images.

The synod also witnessed the final public act of Duke Tassilo of Bavaria. Despite his oaths of loyalty to the Carolingians, Tassilo's taste for autonomy made him a troublesome vassal. In 787 his flagrant recalcitrance gave Charlemagne cause to depose Tassilo and confine him to a monastery. Tassilo appeared before the synod to renounce his duchy in a definitive way, thereby conferring a certain legitimacy on the Frankish annexation of Bavaria.

BIBLIOGRAPHY

Barion, Hans. "Die kirchenrechtliche Charakter des Konzils von Frankfurt 794." *Zeitschrift der Savigny-Stiftung für Rechtsgeschichte,* Kanonistische Abteilung 19 (1930): 139–170.

Concilium Francofurtense, ed. Albert Werminghoff. Monumenta Germaniae historica, Concilia aevi Karolini 1/1. Hannover: Hahn, 1906, pp. 110–171.

Freeman, Ann. "Carolingian Orthodoxy and the Fate of the Libri Carolini." *Viator* 16 (1985): 65–108.

Ganshof, F. L. "Observations sur la Synode de Francfort de 794," in *Miscellanea Historica in honorem Alberti*

De Meyer. 2 vols. Louvain: Bibliothèque de l'Université, 1946, vol. 1, pp. 306–318.

Wallach, Luitpold. *Alcuin and Charlemagne: Studies in Carolingian History and Literature,* rev. ed. Ithaca, N.Y.: Cornell University Press, 1968.

David Appleby

SEE ALSO

Admonitio Generalis; Carolingians; Charlemagne

Syrlin, Jörg the Elder (1420/1430–1491) and Jörg the Younger (1455–1523)

Father and son were highly successful joiners and masons. Based in Ulm (Baden-Württemberg), they supplied furniture, altars, fountains, and other carvings for towns throughout Swabia and southern Germany. Yet were they also sculptors? The answer to this question ultimately determines the level of their fame. Recent scholarship suggests that most carvings attributed to the pair are by other Ulm sculptors with whom they collaborated. The careers of the Syrlins are relatively well documented. Jörg the Elder signed and dated (1458) an oak lectern with sculpted evangelist symbols now in the Ulmer Museum. More important, his signatures appear on the sedilia (chancel seats, 1468) and elaborate choir stalls (1469–1474) in the Münster cathedral in Ulm. This is the finest extant late Gothic cycle in Germany. It includes ninety nine exquisite oak busts and reliefs of philosophers and sibyls, each distinguished by fine facial characterizations and varied natural poses. Traditionally, scholars ascribed the sculpture and the carpentry to Jörg the Elder, though already in 1910 Georg Dehio challenged this view by arguing that Jörg's signatures and monograms pertain only to his production as a joiner. The sculpture of these and other carvings ascribed to Jörg are quite varied in their styles rather than the work of a single hand. In later-fifteenth-century Ulm, it was common for a single master to receive a commission for a complex altarpiece. This artist then engaged a collaborative team of sculptors, joiners, and painters. Between 1474 and 1481, Jörg and his colleagues created the Münster's monumental high altar. Although the altar was destroyed on July 20, 1531, during the Protestants' iconoclastic cleansing of the church, Jörg the Elder's intricate presentation drawing (81 × 231 cm; Stuttgart, Württembergisches Landesmuseum) displays his talents as a designer, notably his adept mastery of architectural ornament. The sculptor of the altar is unknown, though Michel Erhart of Ulm has been suggested.

Jörg the Younger trained with and assisted his father before assuming control of the workshop in early 1482. Under his direction the atelier's production seems to have expanded, though again his role as sculptor is doubtful. Inscriptions and other documentation link him with projects at the Benedictine abbeys of Ochsenhausen, Zweifalten, and Blaubeuren. For Zweifalten Jörg prepared choir stalls, a sacrament house, and seven altars between 1509 and the dedication of the choir in 1517. He was aided by Christoph Langeisen, an Ulm sculptor. Langeisen was likely just one of several participating sculptors. Little survived the rebuilding of the church in the mid–eighteenth century. Passion reliefs from one of these altars, today in the Württembergisches Landesmuseum in Stuttgart, are attributed to Nikolaus Weckmann (active 1481–1526), another Ulm sculptor to whom the majority of carvings once ascribed to Jörg the Younger are now credited. It appears that the son too was primarily a joiner and contractor. In 1493 his workshop created the elaborate choir stalls at Blaubeuren, which while loosely patterned on those in the Ulm Münster include far fewer sculpted busts.

Jörg the Younger, like his father, excelled as a designer. In 1482 one of the Syrlins completed and signed the Fish Trough fountain opposite the city hall in Ulm. The pair probably collaborated on the project; some scholars believe the showy twisting of the spire relates to other architectural drawings, such as the plan for a new western tower for the Münster, ascribed to the son. The three sandstone sculptures of knights, now in the Ulmer Museum, are by yet another hand.

BIBLIOGRAPHY

Baum, Julius. *Die Ulmer Plastik der Spätgotik.* Stuttgart: J. Hoffmann, 1911.

Dehio, Georg. "Über einige Künstlerinschriften des deutschen 15. Jahrhunderts." *Repertorium für Kunstwissenschaft* 33 (1910): 18–24.

Deutsch, Wolfgang. "Der ehemalige Hochaltar und das Chorgestühl, zur Syrlin- und zur Bildhauerfrage," in *600 Jahre Ulmer Münster: Festschrift,* ed. Hans Eugen Specker and Reinhard Wortmann. Forschungen zur Geschichte der Stadt Ulm 19. Ulm: Stadtarchiv, 1977, pp. 242–322

———. "Syrlin der Jüngere oder Niklaus Weckmann?" In *Meisterwerke Massenhaft: Die Bildhauerwerkstatt des Niklaus Weckmann und die Malerei in Ulm um 1500.* Stuttgart: Württembergisches Landesmuseum, 1993, pp. 7–17.

Koepf, Hans. *Die gotischen Planrisse der Ulmer Sammlungen.* Forschungen zur Geschichte der Stadt Ulm, 18. Ulm: Stadtarchiv, 1977, nos. 8, 30, 31, 49.

Schneckenburger-Broschek, Anja. "Ein Niederländer als schwäbisches Genie: Neues zum Ulmer Chorgestühl." *Zeitschrift des deutschen Vereins für Kunstwissenschaft* 40 (1986): 40–68.

Seifert, Hans. *Das Chorgestühl im Ulmer Münster.* Königstein im Taunus: K.R. Langewiesche Nachfolger, 1958.

Vöge, Wilhelm. *Jörg Syrlin der Ältere und seine Bildwerke,* 2 vols. Berlin: Deutsche Verein für Kunstwissenschaft, 1950.

Jeffrey Chipps Smith

SEE ALSO
Erhart, Michel; Gothic Art and Architecture; Ulm; Weckmann, Nicolaus, the Elder

T

Tannhäuser, Der (fl. mid–13th c.)

The lyrical works of Tannhäuser, a thirteenth-century traveling singer and composer, are preserved in the famous Zurich Manesse family and Jena manuscripts of courtly love poetry known as *Minnesang*. The name is toponymic, but as several villages are called Tannhausen, the poet's place of origin cannot be determined. We know only that he was for a time at court in Vienna under the patronage of Duke Frederick II. The first song *(Leich)* can be dated to 1245, the sixth to 1264–1266. The language is South German.

The range and quality of the surviving poetry reveal Tannhäuser as a fine poet of great versatility. All three major categories of Middle High German verse are represented: *Minnesang, Leich,* and *Sangspruch*. The six *Minnelieder,* preserved in the Manesse manuscript, can be grouped as two summer songs, two winter songs—all relatively conventional—and two *Minne* (courtly love) parodies in which the poet's optimism is obviously misplaced in the face of the impossibility of his lady's absurdly exaggerated demands.

The *Leiche,* likewise in the Manesse manuscript, are probably Tannhäuser's best-known pieces. There are seven, five of them *Tanzleiche,* the earliest such dance songs in German literature. The first is a panegyric on Duke Frederick, and princes and patronage return later in *Leich* 6. *Minne* is a theme in several, and 2 and 3 both contain love stories. The shortest, 7, is a riddle. Recurring motifs are nature, May, and dancing, lending the *Leiche* a consistently jovial tone. The poet delights in references to contemporary narrative literature. A passion for geographical locations is no doubt intended to underscore the vast experience of the traveling singer, though some feel that in *Leich* no. 5 this reaches the level of parody.

There are sixteen *Sangsprüche* in three cycles in the Manesse manuscript and—though authenticity is open to question—a further cycle of four in the Jena manuscript. The principle theme of the Manesse *Sangsprüche* is the experience (and the poverty) of the traveling singer, patronage, and the death of the patron. The Jena cycle is more pious, including prayers of atonement. Other lyrical works attributed to Tannhäuser in Jena, Kolmar, and Wiltener manuscripts are at best of dubious authorship.

Tannhäuser was held in particular esteem in ensuing centuries, his love poetry being celebrated by the *Meistersänger,* who named a melody *(Tannhäuserton)* after him and cast him as the thirteenth member at the gathering of the "12 old masters." By contrast, a pious rejection of sexuality underlies the late medieval Tannhäuser legend, in which the poet endangers his soul by his service to Venus but turns to Mary in the end. In the poems *Tannhäuser und Venus* and *Tannhäuser und Frau Welt,* the Minnesinger takes his leave of the goddess despite her allure. The fifteenth-century *Tannhäuser-Ballads* develops this, with Tannhäuser then traveling to Rome to seek absolution. The pope (Urban IV) tells him he can no more be saved than the papal staff can produce life. When the dry stick begins to bud, the pope sends for Tannhäuser, but too late; the poet has returned to Venus and the pope is damned. The most familiar modern version of the legend is Wagner's opera, in which it is merged with the story of the *Wartburgkrieg*.

BIBLIOGRAPHY

Thomas, J.W., trans. *Tannhäuser: Poet and Legend.* Chapel Hill: University of North Carolina Press, 1974.

Graeme Dunphy

SEE ALSO
Meistersinger; *Minnesang;* Versification

Tatian

Latin and Old High German "harmony" (or compilation) of the first four books (gospels) of the New Testament, preserved in the monastery library at St. Gall. This text, called "G," is probably a copy made around 840, embracing a translation made about 830, almost surely at Fulda. The Old High German text, arranged side by side with the Latin, is generally a conservative East Franconian of a Fuldan cast. There is some variation among the six scribes, or translators, one of whom also functions as corrector.

Eduard Sievers thought the Old High German text was a translation of the Latin with which it appears, a theory generally subscribed to into the 1960s. But the German text, although closely tied to the Latin, still deviates significantly. Recent research has made Sievers's theory untenable and elevated the importance of the medieval German version.

Tatian himself was a Syriac monk who fashioned a gospel harmony (synopsis) in Greek or Syriac around 170 C.E., which soon found Latin form as well. In the sixth century Bishop Victor of Capua found a Tatian gospel harmony, in either Greek or Latin, that he caused to be translated or copied into Latin. Sievers believed this manuscript ("F"), brought to Fulda, to be the basis of all later Latin gospel harmonies, including "G." But it now seems clear that Latin "G" is independent of "F" and that the German of "G" derives from neither.

BIBLIOGRAPHY

Baesecke, Georg. *Die Überlieferung des althochdeutschen Tatian.* Hallische Monographien 4. Halle (Saale): Niemeyer, 1948.

Baumstark, Anton. *Die Vorlage des althochdeutschen Tatian,* ed. Johannes Rathofer. Cologne: Böhlau, 1964.

Bostock, J. Knight. *A Handbook on Old High German Literature,* 2d ed., rev. K. C. King and D. R. McLintock. Oxford: Clarendon, 1976, pp. 157–168.

Ehrismann, Gustav. *Geschichte der deutschen Dichtung bis zum Ausgang des Mittelalters,* vol. 1. Munich: Beck, 1932, rpt. 1954, pp. 286–290.

Tatian. Lateinisch und altdeutsch mit ausführlichem Glossar, ed. Eduard Sievers, 1872, 2d ed. Paderborn: Schöningh, 1892; rpt. 1960.

Richard H. Lawson

SEE ALSO
Bible; Notker Labeo; Otfrid

Technology

See Sachliteratur; Tournaments; Warfare; Weapons.

Tegernsee

The Benedictine abbey of Tegernsee, strategically situated on Lake Tegern on the road to the Tyrol, is particularly important in the early history of the Middle Ages. By tradition, the first church was founded by Adalbert and Otker in the mid–eighth century. In 805, the church received the relics of St. Quirinus and took the fifth-century Roman martyr as its major patron. The wealthy monastery was prominent in Carolingian affairs but declined after the disastrous Bavarian defeat by the Magyars in 907, and burned in 975. Tegernsee celebrated its second founding in 979 through Abbot Hartwig (978–982) from St. Maximin in Trier. The Gorze Reform continued with Abbot Gozbert (982–1001), student of Ramwold of St. Emmeram in Regensburg. Tegernsee itself sent monks to found the abbey of Sts. Ulrich and Afra in Augsburg in 1015. The reign of Abbot Ellinger (1017–1026, 1032–1041, d. 1056) was marked both by struggle with local vassals and the flourishing of the convent. In 1041 the exterior crypt was consecrated, an architectural form significant in the reformed spiritual practice of Trier. In Tegernsee, the poet Froumond (d. 1012) was active, and *Ruodlieb,* the earliest poetic romance, was written circa 1050. The monk Edemeram is credited as builder of the new church building, consecrated in 1087.

Under Abbot Rupert I, Count of Neuburg (1155–1186), Tegernsee was involved in conflicts between pope and emperor. It was probably Rupert's brother Otto of Rottenbuch who brought to the library a copy of the pro-imperial *Play of Antichrist (Tegernseer Antichristsspiel).* To the late twelfth century belong the poetic *Quirinalia* of Metellus and the scholastic works of Werenher. While Tegernsee's privileges were repeatedly confirmed, battles between local vassals laid waste to the monastery in 1208 and 1214, and Tegernsee suffered thirteenth-century declines typical of the Benedictines. The monastery burned in 1410, and the church choir collapsed in 1424.

Under the leadership of Kaspar Aindorffer (1426–1461), protégé of Nicholas of Cusa, Tegernsee emerged as a center of the Melk reform in Bavaria. Ulrich

Stöckl, also known as Trunculus, was legate to the Council of Basel from 1432 to 1437 and wrote a valuable account of it, among other poetic works. In 1426 a generous new Gothic choir and sacristy was built, in 1445 a substantial portion of the church was vaulted, and in 1476 the nave was consecrated. Wood-carvers Johannes of Reichenbach and Hans Haldner, and the Master of the Tegernsee *Tabula Magna* created works for the church interior. The church received its baroque appearance in a seventeenth-century remodeling; it was secularized in 1803. Today, Tegernsee's two thousand medieval manuscripts are housed in the State Library in Munich.

BIBLIOGRAPHY

Acht, Peter. *Die Traditionen des Klosters Tegernsee 1003–1242.* Munich: Beck, 1952.

Bange, Ernst Friedrich. *Eine bayerische Malerschule des XI. und XII. Jahrhunderts.* Munich: H. Schmidt, 1923.

Bauereiss, Romuald. *Kirchengeschichte Bayerns.* 5 vols. St. Ottilien: EOS, 1947–1955.

Bezold, Gustav von, et al., eds. *Kunstdenkmale des Regierungsbezirkes Oberbayern,* 2. Theil. Kunstdenkmale des Königreichs Bayerns 1. Munich: Verlag der Vereinigten Kunstanstalten, 1902, pp. 1496–1517.

Eder, Christine. "Die Schule des Klosters Tegernsee im frühen Mittelalter im Spiegel der Tegernseer Handschriften." *Studien und Mitteilungen zur Geschichte des Benediktinerordens und seiner Zweige* 83 (1972): 5–155.

Engel, Johannes. *Das Schisma Barbarossas im Bistum und Hochstift Freising (1159–77).* Ph.d. diss., University of Freiburg in Breigau. Munich: Hueber, 1950.

Günther, Gerhard. *Der Antichrist: Ein mittelalterliches Drama.* Hamburg: Wittig, 1970.

Hartig, Michael. *Die Benediktinerabtei Tegernsee 746–803.* Munich: Schnell und Steiner, 1946.

Jacobsen, Peter Christian. *Die Quirinalien des Metellus von Tegernsee: Untersuchungen zur Dichtkunst und kritische Textausgabe.* Mittellateinische Studien und Texte 1. Leyden: Brill, 1965.

Klemm, Elisabeth. *Die romanischen Handschriften der Bayerischen Staatsbibliothek 2: Die Bistumer Freising und Augsburg, Verschiedene deutsche Provenienzen.* Katalog der illuminierten Handschriften der Bayerischen Staatsbibliothek in München 3. 2 vols. Wiesbaden: Reichert, 1980, pp. 32–53.

Lampl, Sixtus. *Die Klosterkirche Tegernsee: Massanalytische Untersuchungen zum Bestand, zur Baugeschichte und zur Funktion.* Oberbayerisches Archiv 100. Munich: Historisches Verein von Oberbayern, 1975.

Oswald, Friedrich, Leo Schaefer, and Hans Rudolf Sennhauser. *Vorromanische Kirchenbauten: Katalog der Denkmäler bis zum Ausgang der Ottonen.* 3 vols. Munich: Prestel, 1966–1971, vol. 3, pp. 330–331.

Plechl, Helmut. "Studien zur Tegernseer Briefensammlung des 12. Jahrhunderts IV, 1: Tegernsee unter den Äbten Konrad I und Rupert (1126–1186)." *Deutsches Archiv für Erforschung des Mittelalters* 13 (1957): 35–114.

Sanderson, Warren. *Monastic Reform in Lorraine and Architecture of the Outer Crypt, 950–1100.* Philadelphia: University of Pennsylvania Press, 1971.

Schmeidler, Bernhard. *Studien zur Geschichtsschreibung des Klosters Tegernsee vom 11. bis zum 16. Jahrhunderts.* Schriftenreihe der Bayerischen Landesgeschichte 20. Munich: Verlag der Kommission, 1935.

Stange, Alfred. *Deutsche Malerei der Gotik 10: Salzburg, Bayern und Tirol in der Zeit von 1400 bis 1500.* Munich: Deutscher Kunstverlag, 1960, pp. 63–67.

Wright, John. *The Play of Antichrist.* Toronto: Pontifical Institute of Mediaeval Studies, 1967.

Zeydel, Edwin H., ed. and trans. *Ruodlieb.* University of North Carolina Studies in the Germanic Languages and Literatures 23. New York: AMS Press, 1969.

Amelia Carr

SEE ALSO

Augsburg; Gothic Art and Architecture; Melk; Ottonian Art and Architecture; Regensburg; *Ruodlieb;* Trier

Textiles

See Gothic Art and Architecture; Ottonian Art and Architecture; Romanesque Art and Architecture.

Theodoric, Master (fl. ca. 1359–ca. 1381)

During the reign of Holy Roman Emperor Charles IV of Bohemia, this master (also known as Theodoricus of Prague and Zelo) was a principal member of the so-called Bohemian school of painting. Tax records naming Theodoric as the emperor's "master painter" show that he lived in the Hradčany quarter of Prague by 1359 and was deceased by 1381. In a letter dated April 28, 1367, Charles IV thanked Theodoric personally for his "great ingenuity and artistic sense" in the design of the Chapel of the Holy Cross in Karlstein. It is in that chapel that the best example of Theodoric's organization and style of painting is preserved. His panel paintings of bust-length saints cover the walls of the chapel, framed by frescoes in the window recesses of the Annunciation, the Visitation, the Adoration of the Magi, scenes from the life of Mary Magdalene, the Crucifixion, the Entombment, and the Last Judgment; golden vaults embedded with stars span the room. Certainly affected by his predecessor at the Bohemian court, Tommaso da Modena, and his visits to Italy, Theodoric fills out his subjects with solid modeling and naturalistic forms. But his grounding in the art of Bohemia balances these traits with a dark, psychological intensity that gives his holy subjects a massive feel, mirroring their function as protectors of the imperial insignia and crown jewelry housed in the chapel.

BIBLIOGRAPHY

Fajt, Jiri, and Jan Royt. *Magister Theodoricus, Court Painter of Emperor Charles IV: Decoration of the Sacred Spaces at Castle Karlstejn.* Prague: National Gallery of Prague, 1997.

Möseneder, Karl. "*Lapides vivi:* Über die Kreuzkapelle der Burg Karlstein." *Wiener Jahrbuch für Kunstgeschichte* 34 (1981): 39–69.

Stejskal, Karel. *European Art in the 14th Century,* trans. Till Gottheinerová. London: Octopus Books, 1978.

Tracy Chapman Hamilton

SEE ALSO
Charles IV; Prague

Theodulf of Orléans (d. 820/821)

Theodulf, a Visigoth from Spain, came to the court of Charlemagne (r. 768–814) sometime in the 780s, where he became a familiar and central figure in the moral and intellectual reform of Frankish society. He also served Charles's government as a *missus dominicus* (emissary). Appointed bishop of Orléans before 798, he also governed several monasteries. Implicated in the plot against Louis the Pious (814–840), Theodulf was stripped of his offices in 817 and sent into exile in Angers, where he died in 820 or 821. Theodulf was a dedicated pastor and keen-witted intellectual. His poetry provides a lively and detailed window into court life. Principal writer of the *Libri Carolini (Book of the Carolingians),* the Carolingian response to Byzantine iconoclasm, Theodulf also revised the text of the Vulgate Bible and composed several theological tracts. His

works are important sources for Carolingian religion, art, and intellectual and political life.

BIBLIOGRAPHY

Chazelle, Celia. "Matter, Spirit, and Image in the *Libri Carolini.*" *Recherches augustiniennes* 21 (1986): 163–184.

Dahlhaus-Berg, Elisabeth. *Nova antiquitas et antiqua novitas: Typologische Exegese und Isidorianische Geschichtsbild bei Theodulf von Orléans.* Kölner Historischer Abhandlungen 23. Cologne: Böhlau, 1975.

Noble, Thomas F. X. "Some Observations on the Deposition of Archbishop Theodulf of Orléans in 817." *Journal of the Rocky Mountain Medieval and Renaissance Association* 2 (1981): 29–40.

Theodulf of Orléans. *The Poetry of Theodulf of Orleans: A Translation and Critical Study,* ed. and trans. Nikolai A. Alexandrenko. Ann Arbor: University Microfilms, 1970.

John J. Contreni

SEE ALSO
Carolingians; Charlemagne; Louis the Pious

Theophanu (ca. 959–991)

Married to Otto II on Easter 972, Theophanu (also Theophano) was crowned empress on the same occasion. The marriage was the result of an alliance between Otto I and the Byzantine Empire. Otto desired a princess of imperial descent *(porphyrogenita)* for his son to help legitimize Ottonian rule. Instead of a *porphyrogenita,* though, he received Theophanu, a noble kinswoman of the Byzantine usurper John Tzimiskes. Contemporary sources agree that she was not the "longed-for princess," but her Greek sophistication and enormous treasure overcame most dissent to the marriage.

Theophanu, almost certainly born in 959, soon exerted a strong influence over Otto II, as can be seen in her sixty-six interventions among Otto II's 317 extant documents. She traveled with him almost continually, even giving birth to her children at monasteries along the royal itinerary, so she could rejoin her husband quickly. She was blamed for Otto II's ill-fated campaign to southern Italy, although it is unlikely she would have favored the Byzantine government after the Macedonian dynasty was restored in 976.

After Otto II's death on December 7, 983, Theophanu at first made no effort to claim the regency for her infant son Otto III. After Duke Henry the Quarrelsome proved his unsuitability for the post by trying to make himself king, though, the twenty-three-year-old Theophanu stepped into the vacuum that had been created. She gained power especially thanks to the efforts of Archbishop Willigis of Mainz, who summoned her from Italy to help protect her son's rights. She then acted as effective sole regent until her death. Although she did not lead troops herself, Theophanu supported the Saxon margraves's campaigns against the Slavs. Even the frequently hostile Quedlinburg annalist gives her credit for restoring political stability after Otto II's defeat at Cotrone, the Slav revolt of 983, and Otto's untimely death. She reestablished alliances with the Danes, Boleslav II of Bohemia, and Mieszko I of Poland through diplomacy, and was also able to maintain loose German control over Italy. In the fall of 989 she was able to visit Rome for business with only a few followers, acting there as "emperor Theophanius," using the masculine form to give her authority since she could not issue documents in the name of the absent Otto III. Much of her authority as regent came from her close alliance with churchmen who often acted as her agents, especially Gerbert of Aurillac and Bishop Notker of Liège.

Contemporaries accused Theophanu of excessive love of luxury and of talkativeness, perhaps a comment on the unusual role she played as a female ruler. Kinder commentators have called her "eloquent." She appears to have been pious, acting as a typical royal widow of the time in her alms and prayers for her husband's soul. She was about thirty years old when she died on June 15, 991, in Nijmegen, leaving a stable realm for her son. She is buried in the monastery of St. Pantaleon, Cologne.

BIBLIOGRAPHY

Davids, Adelbert, ed. *The Empress Theophano: Byzantium and the West at the Time of the First Millennium.* Cambridge: Cambridge University Press, 1995.

Parisse, Michel, ed. *Veuves et veuvage dans le haut moyen âge.* Paris: Picard, 1993.

von Euw, Anton, and Peter Schreiner, ed. *Kaiserin Theophanu. Begegnung des Ostens und Westens um die Wende des ersten Jahrtausends.* 2 vols. Cologne: Schnütgen-Museum, 1991.

Wolf, Gunther, ed. *Kaiserin Theophanu. Prinzessin aus der Fremde—des Westreichs große Kaiserin.* Cologne: Böhlau, 1991.

Phyllis G. Jestice

SEE ALSO
Adelheid of Burgundy; Otto I; Otto II, Otto III

Theophanu, Art

The empress's political power is reflected in two images that depict her as the equal of her husband, Otto II (d. 983): the byzantinizing ivory coronation image in the Musée de Cluny, Paris, and on an ivory plaque preserved in the treasury of the cathedral of Milan.

It is harder to define her cultural impact than her political power. With the exception of her patronage of St. Pantaleon, Cologne, where she was buried, there is little evidence for artistic commissions. However, Theophanu's arrival in the west coincided with the flowering Ottonian art and with an increase in Byzantine stylistic and iconographic influence. Furthermore, the number of tenth-century objects from Byzantium preserved in German collections is markedly greater than those from earlier and later periods. Scholars have thus assumed that Theophanu brought with her to the west a substantial dowry of Constantinopolitan sacred and secular objects, books, and textiles, and that these provided models for and gave impetus to the fledgling Ottonian scriptoria and workshops. Although not a single object has been linked securely to the empress, a series of liturgical furnishings known to have been in the possession of her children may be assumed to have belonged to Theophanu, such as the ivory plaque depicting the Dormition of the Virgin set into the cover of the Munich Gospels of her son, Otto III, for whom she served as regent, (Bayerische Staatsbibliothek, no. Clm. 4453) assembled at Reichenau circa 1000. In addition, Henry II is said to have taken into his possession the personal treasure of Otto III in addition to the imperial insignia, which may account for the Byzantine objects he presented to a variety of churches and monasteries during his reign. Thus, while careful analysis indicates that Ottonian visual culture resulted from the synthesis of various traditions and cannot be accurately attributed solely to an influx of Byzantine models in the possession of Theophanu, her indirect influence in the evolution of Ottonian art cannot be doubted.

BIBLIOGRAPHY

Kaiserin Theophanu: Begegnung des Ostens und Westens um die Wende des ersten Jahrtausends, ed. Anton von Euw and Peter Schreiner. Cologne: Schnütgen Museum, 1991.

Kunst im Zeitalter der Kaiserin Theophanu, ed. Anton von Euw and Peter Schreiner. Cologne: Locher, 1993.

Wentzel, Hans. "Das byzantinische Erbe der ottonischen Kaiser: Hypothesen über den Brautschatz der Theophano." *Aachener Kunstblätter* 40 (1971): 15–39.

Karen E. Loaiza

SEE ALSO

Cologne, Art; Henry II, Art; Otto II; Otto III; Reichenau; Theophanu

Theophilus Presbyter (fl. ca. 1100)

The best-studied medieval book of instructions on how to do various crafts is the *De diversis artibus,* whose authorship is given on the title pages of the earliest texts to Theophilus Presbyter, possibly a pseudonymn for the renowned metalworker Roger of Helmarshausen. Both the earliest manuscripts of the text and the artist have been associated with the early twelfth century. The use of certain terms has identified the text with northern Europe and specifically with the Rhineland.

The text, divided into three books devoted to painting, stained glass, and metalwork, contains recipes for preparing materials and using them to make certain things. Instructions stemming more from myth and folklore than from actual practice of any period and instructions with only the most tenuous relation to medieval practice are combined with very precise instructions that relate to contemporary practice of the twelfth century. So it is likely that the compiler brought together different sources, including the knowledge of twelfth-century artists.

The "prologues" attached to each book in some manuscript versions of the text have been studied to try to determine the purpose of the book. They reveal an understanding of theology related to Benedictine thinking and have suggested a relation to the Benedictine dispute with the Cistercians about the use of art in the liturgy. The importance to the Benedictines of creating and using precious objects in the liturgy may have been defended and enhanced by the setting down of the text. The prologues also contain a passionate defense of the value of the *artes mechanicae* (mechanical arts), reflecting a trend in thinking of the early twelfth century.

The association of the text with Roger of Helmarshausen and with the Benedictine monasteries of Stavelot, St. Pantaleon in Cologne, and Helmarshausen, and the importance of the arts in all three of these monasteries, has suggested these three sites as possible places where the text may have been assembled.

BIBLIOGRAPHY

Kaufmann, Virginia Roehrig. "Malanleitungen im Buch I *De diversis Artibus* des Theophilus Presbyter und ihre Anwendung im Evangeliar Heinrichs des Löwen," in *Heinrich der Löwe und seine Zeit: Herrschaft und Repräsentation der Welfen 1125–1235,* ed. Jochen Luckhardt and Franz Niehoff. 3 vols. Munich: Hirmer, 1995, vol. 2, pp. 301–311.

Roosen-Runge, Heinz. "Die Buchmalereirezepte des Theophilus." *Münchner Jahrbuch der bildenden Kunst* 3, 4 (1952–1953): 15–27.

Theophilus. *De diversis artibus,* trans. and ed. C. R. Dodwell. London: Nelson, 1961.

Van Engen, John. "Theophilus Presbyter and Rupert of Deutz: The Manual Arts and Benedictine Theology in the Early Twelfth Century." *Viator* 11 (1980): 147–163.

White, Lynn, Jr. "Theophilus Redivivus." *Technology and Culture* 5 (1964): 224–233.

Virginia Roehrig Kaufmann

SEE ALSO

Cologne, Art; Helmarshausen; Roger of Helmarshausen; Romanesque Art and Architecture

Thietmar of Merseburg (975–1008/1018)

Born into the comital house of Walbeck in eastern Saxony, Thietmar received his primary education at the royal convent of Quedlinburg. In 987, his father transferred him from Quedlinburg to the monastery of Berge, outside of Magdeburg. Thietmar remained at Berge for three years, continuing his education, apparently with the expectation that he would eventually join the community. When a place could not be obtained for him there, he was moved to the cathedral at Magdeburg (November 1, 990). Thietmar studied at the cathedral's school, then among the empire's preeminent centers of learning, and was formally admitted to the chapter circa 1000, during the reign of Archbishop Giselher. Professional advancement came to him during the reign of Giselher's successor, Archbishop Tagino. The archbishop elevated him to the priesthood in 1004 at a ceremony attended by Emperor Henry II, and thereafter he seems to have joined the archbishop's entourage. It was due to Tagino's favor, moreover, that Thietmar was chosen by Henry II to succeed the recently deceased bishop of the see of Merseburg (1008). As Bishop of Merseburg, Thietmar inherited a host of problems deriving from that diocese's troubled history. Emperor Otto I had founded the bishopric in 968, in conjunction with his elevation of Magedeburg to the status of archbishopric. For a variety of reasons, it was suppressed in 981, its property being divided among neighboring dioceses and its cathedral transformed into a proprietary monastery of the archbishops of Magdeburg. Although the diocese was restored by Henry II in 1004, its boundaries and property rights remained a matter of dispute. Thietmar seems to have occupied most of his career in attempts to regain diocesan lands ceded to neighboring dioceses during the period of Merseburg's suppression (i.e., 981–1004). Similar issues led to a long running property dispute with the Saxon ducal house of the Billunger.

Thietmar's chief gift to posterity is his history, the *Chronicon,* which he composed between 1012 and his death in 1018. The work is divided into eight books and survives in two manuscripts at Brussels and Dresden, the latter now available only in the form of a facsimile. The Dresden manuscript is particularly valuable as it was produced under Thietmar's direction and includes corrections and additions made in his own hand. In compiling the *Chronicon,* Thietmar drew heavily at times on the work of other historians, but much of his material is based on his own observations and experiences, especially in the later books. Indeed, for events in the reign of Emperor Henry II, he is often our unique informant. It is generally assumed that Thietmar's original intention was to focus on the history of his diocese. If so, his theme must have rapidly expanded to include the history and deeds of the Ottonian kings, their lineage, and other topics as well. Thietmar was nothing if not opinionated and expressed views on subjects ranging from politics to the (in his opinion) shocking character of contemporary women's fashions. He subjected monastic reform and its advocates to a withering critique and offered negative characterizations of Lotharingians, Bavarians, Italians, and others lacking the good fortune to have been born Saxon. With his detailed commentary on the career of Duke Boleslav Chrobry, Thietmar is one of the most important witnesses for the emergence of the medieval Polish state, and his detailed descriptions of Slavic social customs and religion are some of the earliest on record. Thietmar's testimony is especially valuable for the history of Ottonian policy in the east, German relations with the western Slavs, and the family histories of the east Saxon aristocracy.

BIBLIOGRAPHY

Chronicon (Die Chronik des Bischofs Thietmar von Merseburg und ihre Korveier Überarbeitung). ed. Robert Holtzmann. Monumenta Germaniae Historica, Scriptores rerum Germanicarum, nova series 9. Berlin: Weidmann, 1935.

Leyser, Karl. *The Ascent of Latin Europe.* Oxford: Clarendon Press, 1986.

Lippelt, Heinrich. *Thietmar von Merseburg. Riechsbischof und Chronist.* Mitteldeutsche Forschungen 72. Cologne: Böhlau, 1973.

Warner, David A. "Thietmar of Merseburg on Rituals of Kingship." *Viator* 26 (1995): 53–76.

———. *Ottonian Germany.* Manchester: Manchester University Press, 1999.

David A. Warner

SEE ALSO
Otto I

Thomas à Kempis (1379/1380–1471)

An author of spiritual writings, Thomas (Hemerken) à Kempis (also Hamerkein, Malleolus) was born some time between September 29, 1379, and July 24, 1380, at Kempen near Cologne. At the age of thirteen he left for Deventer to attend classes at the chapter's school of the Lebuinus Church. In 1399 he applied for admission to a monastery of the Canons Regular at Zwolle called St. Agnietenberg. This monastery, a daughter-house of Windesheim, was pervaded by the spirit of the *Devotio moderna* (Modern Devotion) movement. After taking the habit in 1406 and after his solemn profession in 1407, Thomas was ordained a priest in 1413 or 1414. He evolved into a prolific transcriber and author of several spiritual writings. From 1425 till 1430 (and in a second term starting in 1433), he performed the task of subprior and combined it with the assignment of a novice master. In this last quality he developed as a musician, preacher, and history teacher. For the job of procurator Thomas turned out to be less suited; he held that office for only one year in 1443. He died on either May 1 or July 24, 1471.

Thomas à Kempis is credited with thirty-one treatises, as well as three cycles of *sermones* (sermons), some *cantica* (catechetic songs), and *epistolae* (letters). Depending on the goal he had in mind or the audience he wanted to reach, he used different genres. He proved to be a pious historian in, e.g., his *Chronicon Montis sanctae Agnetis.* One can discover his qualities as a musician and writer of letters in his *Cantica* and *Epistolae.* His output consists in large part of practical-ascetic works, such as his *Libellus de disciplina claustralium, Vita boni monachi, Manuale parvulorum,* and *Doctrina iuvenum.*

His famous *De Imitatione Christi* is included in this category as well. This work deserves a wider treatment here, as it is one of the most influential spiritual texts of the late Middle Ages and can be considered the most widely read book in Christianity, with the exception of the Bible. In the centuries-old fight about the authorship of this fifteenth-century treatise, forty serious candidates have been taken into account. Among them Augustin, Bernard, Jan van Ruusbroec, Geert Grote, Joannes Gersen, abbot of Vercelli, Jean Gerson, and, finally, Thomas à Kempis, were the most prominent. On the basis of the excellent linguistic and codicological (manuscript) investigations of L.J.M. Delaissé, it is now generally accepted among scholars that Thomas à Kempis has to be regarded as the author of the four *libelli* (books) that form *De Imitatione Christi*. The first four treatises of Thomas à Kempis's autograph of 1441 (Brussels, Koninklijke Bibliotheek, manuscript no. 5855–5861) form, in this order, books I, II, IV, and III of *De Imitatione Christi*. They have the following incipits (first lines):

1. *Qui sequitur me, non ambulat in tenebris*
2. *Regnum Dei intra vos est dicit Dominus*
3. *De sacramento. Venite ad me omnes qui laboratis*
4. *Audiam quid loquator in me Dominus Deus*

In other manuscripts and incunabula, treatises I, II, and IV often appear as a unity. If one considers the contents of these works and the titles given by Thomas in his autograph of 1441, this unity is not purely a coincidence. A codex belonging to a monastery of Canons Regular at Nijmegen, now in the Royal Library in Brussels (manuscript no. 22084), makes clear that the four *libelli* of *De Imitatione Christi* already circulated in 1427, fifteen years before Thomas completed his final redaction in the autograph mentioned above.

In treatise I, *Admonitiones ad spiritualem vitam utiles*, Thomas formulates, for beginners in spiritual life, some points of advice concerning a life in silence, prayer, and study. In treatise II, *Admonitiones ad interna trahentes*, Thomas merely describes the mental state that the young religious has to develop to consider prayer as a privileged place where one is able to meet Christ personally instead of a mechanical duty. Treatise III, *De interna consolatione*, is Thomas's personal testimony of his intimate relationship with Christ in daily life of the monastic community. Thomas points out that the life of a person who is looking for God is not without obstacles. He wrote this book,

furthermore, to provide consolation. Finally, treatise IV of the *De Imitatio Christi* contains reflections on the Holy Eucharist that are characteristic of the time in which the *Imitatio* was composed but not strictly coordinated with the contents of the first three books. It is especially in these books that Thomas develops the concept of a "journey" for the faithful. Here he first describes the inner disposition from which one can be open to Christ and follow Him in the most appropriate and fruitful way. From studies made after those of Delaissé mentioned above, the conclusion can be drawn that Thomas made the stylistic improvements in the *Imitatio* not because of his love for the beauty of the (Latin) language, the *latinitas,* but for catechetical reasons.

Other treatises, like the *Orationes et meditationes de vita Christi,* have a more theological character. In his *Hortulus rosarum* and *Soliloquium animae,* Thomas shows his gifts as a spiritual writer. All but one of his works were composed in Latin; he wrote a small treatise in Middle Dutch: *Van goeden woerden to horen ende die to spreken.* Finally, he compiled his *sermones* in three coherent cycles.

One can easily conclude that the quantity of scholarly contributions on the sources, style, and theology in Thomas à Kempis's *opera omnia* (complete works) stands in no proportion to the enormous amount of literature devoted to his authorship of the *Imitatio.* The study of his theology is in an early stage; up until now, no attempt has been made at a synthesis. Recent investigation has shown that Thomas's originality lies in his view that the ascetic structuring of life is explained by the mystical longing that Thomas wants to develop in each person. In his theological anthropology, mystical aspirations are exclusively nourished and purified by a realization of the self in an ascetic way of life. Furthermore, his spirituality is strongly Christ-centered.

BIBLIOGRAPHY

Ampe, Albert, and Bernhard Spaapen. "Imitatio Christi. I. Le livre et l'auteur.—II. Doctrine," in *Dictionnaire de spiritualité,* ed. Marcel Viller. Paris: Beauchense, 1932ff, vol. 7, cols. 2338–2355.

Delaissé, L. J. M. *Le Manuscrit autographe de Thomas à Kempis et "L'Imitation." Examen archéologique et édition diplomatique du Bruxellensis 5855–5861.* 2 vols. Paris: Erasme, 1956.

Ingram, John K., ed. *The Earliest English Translation of the First Three Books of* De imitatione Christi . . . London: K. Paul, Trench, Trubner, 1893.

Pohl, Michael Joseph, ed. *Thomae a Kempis canonici regularis ordinis S. Augustini Opera Omnia,* 7 vols. Freibourg im Breisgau: Herder, 1902–1922.

Puyol, Pierre-Édouard. *L'auteur du livre De Imitatione Christi. Première section: la contestation.* Paris: Retaux, 1899.

van Dijk, Rudolf, Th.M. "Thomas Hemerken à Kempis," in *Dictionnaire de spiritualité,* ed. Marcel Viller. Paris: Beauchense, 1932ff., vol. 15, cols. 817–826.

van Geest, Paul. "Thomas Hemerken a Kempis," in *Die deutsche Literatur des Mittelalters: Verfasserlexikon,* ed. Kurt Ruh et al., vol. 9. Berlin: de Gruyter, 1978, cols. 862–882.

———. "Introduction," in *Thomas a Kempis: La vallée des Lis.* Bégrolles-en-Mauges: Abbaye de Bellefontaine, 1992, pp. 11–48.

———. "De sermones van Thomas a Kempis; een terreinverkenning." *Trajecta* 2 (1993): 305–326.

———. *Thomas a Kempis (1379/80–1471): een studie van zijn mens- en godsbeeld: analyse en tekstuitgave van de Hortulus Rosarum en de Vallis Liliorum.* Kampen: Kok, 1996.

Weiler, Anton G. "Recent Historiography on the Modern Devotion: Some Debated Questions." *Archief voor de geschiedenis van de katholieke kerk in Nederland* 26 (1984): 161–184.

"The works of Thomas à Kempis," trans. Michael Joseph Pohl. 6 vols. Ph.d. diss., University of London, 1905–1908.

Paul J. J. van Geest

SEE ALSO
Devotio Moderna

Thomasîn von Zerclaere (fl. early 12th c.)

Born into an ancient noble family in Cividale in Friulia, northern Italy, around 1185, Thomasîn was a member of the monastic cathedral of Aquileia and so later came into close contact with Wolfger von Erla, the German patriarch of Aquileia known for his patronage of such famous German poets as Walther von der Vogelweide. We might assume that Wolfger commissioned Thomasîn to compose his famous book of courtly etiquette, *Der Welsche Gast (The Italian Visitor),* consisting of about 14,800 verses. Thomasîn dated his Middle High German poem by telling us that he wrote it twenty-eight years after the loss of Jerusalem to the Arabs in 1187, that is, in 1215. The intention with his treatise was to improve the desolate state of the German nobility. It is the first German *Hofzucht* (courtly primer) ever written, and this by a nonnative speaker; it addresses young noblemen and -women, teaching them the norms of courtly behavior. Thomasîn also added a general lesson about courtly love that he based on his *Buch von der Höfischeit (Book of Courtliness),* which he had previously composed in the Provençal language. In his book the poet emphasizes the value of constancy *(staete),* moderation *(mâze),* law *(reht),* and generosity *(milte).* Thomasîn drew from many different sources but mentions only the *Moralia* by Pope Gregory the Great (d. 604), a highly popular Latin moral treatise. Nevertheless, the text demonstrates Thomasîn's extensive knowledge of theological and secular literature of his time. The poet was clearly opposed to Walther von der Vogelweide's polemics against the pope, warned of the threatening spread of hereticism, and appealed to the German knighthood to embark on a new crusade. For him, knighthood must be subservient to the church and must pursue primarily religious and moral ideals. However, Thomasîn did not hesitate to recommend courtly literature as reading material for young noble people because some of the best-known protagonists in Middle High German literature would provide them with models of ideal behavior. The *Welsche Gast* proved to be an enormously popular didactic treatise and has come down to us in some two dozen manuscripts (thirteen complete, eleven as fragments), of which almost all are illustrated.

BIBLIOGRAPHY

Huber, Christoph. "Höfischer Roman als Integumentum? Das Votum Thomasîns von Zerclaere." *Zeitschrift für deutsches Altertum* 115 (1986): 79–100.

Neumann, Friedrich. "Einführung," in *Der Welsche Gast des Thomasîn von Zerclaere. Cod. Pal. Germ. 389 der Universitätsbibliothek Heidelberg.* Wiesbaden: Reichert, 1974, Kommentarband, pp. 1–65.

Röcke, Werner. *Feudale Anarchie und Landesherrschaft: Wirkungsmöglichkeiten didaktischer Literatur. Thomasîns von Zerclaere "Der Welsche Gast."* Bern: Lang, 1978.

Ruff, E. J. F. *"Der Welsche Gast" des Thomasîn von Zerclaere: Untersuchung zu Gehalt und Bedeutung einer mhd. Morallehre.* Erlangen: Palm und Enke, 1982.

Thomasîn von Zerclaria. *Der Welsche Gast,* ed., Heinrich Rückert. Quedlinburg: Basse, 1852; rpt. ed. Friedrich Neumann. Berlin: de Gruyter, 1965.

Albrecht Classen

SEE ALSO
Gregory VII; Walther von der Vogelweide

Tnugdalus

Around the year 1190, at the urging of three women (Otegebe, Heilke, and Gisel), a priest named Alber composed a Middle High German version of the Latin *Visio Tnugdali* (*Vision of Tnugdalus,* or *Tundalus*), written by a monk Marcus circa 1150. The story is of a certain Tnugdal/Tundalus, an Irish knight who, in the year 1149, lay dead for three days, during which time he traveled to Hell, learned of the various torments to which the damned are subjected, and experienced these in part. In the end he was released from his travails through intercession from Heaven, and returned to his earthly existence. After his experiences he took up the spiritual life and went about calling others to repentance from their sins lest they, too, meet a similar fate. The *Visio* and its vernacular reworkings are important examples of the literary journey to Hell or beyond, a genre that originated in Antiquity and culminated in Dante.

Alber himself cannot be identified with any certainty. He has frequently been placed in the monastery at Windberg (on the Danube east of Regensburg), because two deacons with his name are attested to have died there around 1200. There is also a Windberg (Bavaria) manuscript of the *Visio Tnugdali,* which could well have served as Alber's exemplar. The author says that he rhymed his tale at the behest of a "brother Kuonrat" of Windberg; evidence has been found for the existence of several Conrads in that monastery between 1190 and 1200.

Alber's rendering of the Latin text is reasonably close, though he has added a prologue, an epilogue, and, most interestingly, the story of how St. Patrick converted an Irish king. This tale is also found, in the form used by Alber, in the *Legenda aurea* (Golden Legend) of Jacob of Voragine; a common source for the two has never been identified. Having made these additions, Alber abridged the Latin *Tnugdalus* in a number of places, for the most part by simplifying or omitting passages of theological import. He also omitted an explanation of how pre-Christian Irish heroes received eternal reward by being true to their own pagan religion. Whether this omission was due to Alber's (and his audience's) lack of interest in things Irish or because he chose to sidestep a matter of religious controversy cannot be said.

Alber's style is best described as "didactic"; he frequently addresses his readers in the second person and has added some short passages of a homiletic nature. Though Alber obviously wished to warn his audience of the perils of entering the afterlife unprepared, he did not refrain from a sort of "sensationalism" in his description of Hell's torments and of how the damned suffer, and surely managed in the best medieval sense both to edify and to entertain his readers.

The question of the development of the idea of Purgatory has often occupied scholars of the *Tnugdalus* stories; of the *Visio* (and of Alber), it can probably best be said that the concept of a separate Purgatory is not actually developed, appearing instead as a sort of "higher Hell," though with similar functions.

Alber's *Tnugdalus* is preserved in the Austrian National Library in Vienna (manuscript no. 2696, the *Wiener,* or Viennese, manuscript). An edited text of fragments in the German Middle Franconian dialect is included in Wagner's edition.

BIBLIOGRAPHY

Le Goff, Jacques. *The Birth of Purgatory,* trans. Arthur Goldhammer. Chicago: University of Chicago Press, 1984, pp. 190–193.

Sprenger, Robert. "Albers Tundalus." Ph.d. diss., University of Halle-Wittenberg, 1875.

———. "Nachträgliches zu Albers Tundalus." *Germania* 22 (1877): 264–272.

Wagner, Albrecht. *Visio Tnugdali. Lateinisch und Altdeutsch.* Erlangen: Deichert, 1882.

James K. Walter

SEE ALSO
Legenda Aurea, Alsatian; Saints' Lives, Dutch; Visionary Literature

Toul

Located at the intersection of important Roman roads, ancient Tullum (Tullum Leucorum) was the main center of the Gallic tribe of Leuci. By the mid–fourth century it had become the seat of a bishopric that eventually became a suffragan (subordinate administrative unit) of Trier. During Merovingian times, Toul was the first major port along the Mosel River from which goods were transported as far as Koblenz and Andernach.

In 925 Toul, together with the rest of Lorraine, became part of the east Frankish realm, and during the early eleventh century its bishops played an important role in the empire. Bishop Bruno of Toul was one of Henry III's favorite churchmen, eventually rising to the office of pope in 1049 as Leo IX.

From late Antiquity a wall surrounded the city within which lay the cathedral St. Stephan (St.-Étienne) and, over time, the monasteries, cloisters, and foundations of St. Vaast, Ste. Geneviève, St. John, and St. Gangolf (St.-Gengoult). To the north of the city lay the great abbey of St. Mansuy, while the monastery of St. Evre lay along the main road to the south. About 1240, the bishop and burghers collaborated in building a new wall that extended protection to the area (particularly west of the old wall) that had grown up during the previous centuries of economic expansion.

Until modern times, viticulture was the most important economic activity for the religious houses and foundations of Toul, the patrician families, and the general population as well. The wealth derived from the wine trade is reflected in the cathedral of St. Stephan, the present interior of which was begun in 1204: 321 feet long and 105 feet high, it was a monument to both the piety and the prosperity of the townspeople. The church of St. Gangolf was also expanded; its choir boasts some of the finest thirteenth-century stained glass in eastern France. The west facade of the cathedral was done in the fifteenth century, in the then current flamboyant style.

The same roads that carried trade to and from Toul also facilitated the spread of heretical notions, however, and in 1192 a synod held in Toul condemned the Waldensians. Toul was also infected by the spirit of civic independence that spread across Germany in the thirteenth century. Having been an episcopal city for centuries, it sought liberation from that relationship and, shortly after 1250, we begin to read of conflicts between the bishop and the city, more particularly the leading families.

Toul's proximity to the boundary between the empire and France made it a convenient venue for meetings between monarchs. In 1224, Louis VII of France met with Henry VII for deliberations; and in 1299, Adolf met Philip the Fair near Toul (at Quatrevaux). By the latter year, however, Toul was under French domination. It had ceased to be of much significance as an imperial city since the mid–thirteenth century, and in 1281 the French king took it under his protection; ten years later, the lands of the bishopric of Toul west of the Meuse became French. In 1297, the neighboring bishopric of Metz also came under French control.

BIBLIOGRAPHY

Bönnen, Gerold. *Die Bischofsstadt Toul und ihr Umland während des hohen und späten Mittelalters.* Trier: Verlag Trierer Historische Forschungen, 1995.

Morret, Benno. *Stand und Herkunft der Bischöfe von Metz, Toul und Verdun im Mittelalter.* Ph.d diss., University of Bonn, 1911; Düsseldorf, 1911.

Paul B. Pixton

SEE ALSO
Henry III; Leo IX

Tournaments

Although equestrian military games stretch much further back in time, the three main types of mounted military exercise or sport in medieval Germany are all first recorded in the twelfth century: *buhurt,* joust *(tjost, stechen),* and tourney *(turnei).*

The *buhurt* was a group exercise involving the clashing of shields or lance charges. Full armor was not necessary and there was no pursuit of material gain; rather the *buhurt* was a matter of military training, sport, or display. It was often connected with dancing and other pastimes as an expression of aristocratic joy and was a standard accompaniment of marriages, knightings, and other festivities. The *buhurt* faded out after the end of the thirteenth century as more peaceful forms of the *turnei* emerged.

Jousts were mounted combats of two knights attacking with couched lances, a technique that arose in the eleventh century. They are documented in German literature in the twelfth century and in historical sources from the thirteenth century onward. Jousts enjoyed great popularity throughout the Middle Ages as events that were simpler to organize than the mass tournaments. Jousts figure in two basic types—with blunt lances and with sharp lances—these described, respectively, as *stechen* and *rennen* from the fourteenth century onward. Many variations on these types emerged in the late fifteenth century, when the German areas were foremost in Europe in this field. The books commissioned by Emperor Maximilian I, and other sources, document this variety pictorially. Jousting had strong fictional connections, and knights jousted at times in imitation of characters from Arthurian literature.

The tourney arose in the late eleventh century in France, whence it spread through the rest of Europe, the term first appearing in Germany in the mid–twelfth century. The early tourneys were still close to feud warfare in style. They were prearranged mass encounters in which the participants fought in groups, wearing full battle armor and using lance and sword to take captives who had to buy themselves free. The combatants were usually accompanied by auxiliary squires, who helped particularly in seizing the horses of unseated knights as booty. The events were held on large tracts of open ground, often between two places, or outside a town. Injuries, even fatalities were frequent, and material gain was an important motive. This early tourney was far more bellicose than the *buhurt* and was condemned by the church throughout Christendom. Stronger regulatory tendencies then appeared during the thirteenth century (equal numbers on both sides, the exclusion of or tighter control over auxiliaries, the use of blunt weapons), and new, less bellicose forms of the tournament emerged, notably the "Round Table," which involved jousts with blunt lances. These developments led to the revocation of the papal ban on tourneying in 1316, and they allowed tournaments to become an adornment of aristocratic festivities. They were now commonly held in enclosed spaces in towns, with specially constructed seating for spectators.

After a transitional period in the fourteenth century, the fifteenth century brought a resurgence of interest in the tournament, which had by that time undergone important changes of form and function. The tournaments of the fifteenth century were demonstrations of aristocratic solidarity in a time of social change, and they employed equipment quite different from that of real warfare: maces *(Kolben)* as weapons, and special light armor. Entry to the tournament was now dependent on proof of noble ancestry, and participants who had offended against the honor of the nobility were to be punished by receiving a thrashing. These new measures were codified in detailed ordinances that were agreed by committees representing the nobility of the "Four Lands"—Bavaria, Swabia, Franconia and the Rhinelands (texts of the ordinances in the *Turnierbuch*, "Tournament Book," of Ludwig von Eyb). The tournaments of the Four Lands were large operations involving hundreds of participants and their families. They mark a late and critical phase in the independence of the German nobility. The last such event was held at Worms in 1487. Tournaments continued to be held, and to change in form, during the sixteenth century and beyond, but they were now tied to the courts of rulers, and they were carefully stage-managed affairs, as demonstrations of the power of the ruler in the early modern state.

BIBLIOGRAPHY

Barber, Richard W., and Juliet Barker. *Tournaments: Jousts, Chivalry and Pageantry in the Middle Ages.* Woodbridge, England: Boydell, 1989.

Bumke, Joachim. *Höfische Kultur: Literatur und Gesellschaft im hohen Mittelalter.* 2 vols. Munich: Deutscher Taschenbuch Verlag, 1986, pp. 342–379.

Czerwinski, Peter. "Die Schlacht- und Turnierdarstellungen in den deutschen höfischen Romanen des 12. und 13. Jahrhunderts." Ph.d. diss., Berlin, 1975.

Fleckenstein, Josef, ed. *Das ritterliche Turnier im Mittelalter: Beiträge zu einer vergleichenden Formen- und Verhaltensgeschichte des Rittertums.* Göttingen: Vandenhoeck and Ruprecht, 1985 [major collaborative volume].

Harvey, Ruth. *Moriz von Craûn and the Chivalric World.* Oxford: Clarendon, 1961, pp. 112–258.

Jackson, W. H. "Lance and Shield in the *Buhurt*," in *German Narrative Literature of the Twelfth and Thirteenth Centuries: Studies Presented to Roy Wisbey,* ed. Volker Honemann, et al. Tübingen: Niemeyer, 1994, pp. 39–54.

Peters, Ursula. *Frauendienst. Untersuchungen zu Ulrich von Lichtenstein und zum Wirklichkeitsgehalt der Minnedichtung.* Göppingen: Kümmerle, 1971, pp. 173–205.

Stamm, Heide, ed. *Das Turnierbuch des Ludwig von Eyb (cgm 961).* Stuttgart: Heinz, 1986.

William H. Jackson

SEE ALSO

Armor; Crusade Literature, Dutch; Crusades

Town Planning and Urbanism

The early Middle Ages in Germany (ca. 500–1050) are marked by both the disintegration of the urban fabric inherited from Roman antiquity and the emergence of new forms of settlement that would develop into the cities of the High Middle Ages. While fortified settlements are known to have existed in Germanic territories during the Roman period, the major urban centers on German soil were those founded by the Romans west of the Rhine and south of the Danube (Xanten, Cologne, Bonn, Mainz, Worms, Trier, Augsburg, Regensburg, Salzburg, etc.). With the collapse of the administrative infrastructure of the Roman Empire and the depopulation of these provincial Roman centers, de facto municipal leadership was assumed in large measure by the church, both politically and architecturally. In the Merovingian period, settlements grew up around cathedrals or saints' burial churches, sometimes within the area of the old Roman *civitates* (cities) and *castella* (forts), as at Cologne, Mainz,

Rolthenburg ob der Tauber, *Markusturm. Photograph: Joan A. Holladay*

The twelfth and thirteenth centuries represent the great age of urban expansion in medieval Germany. From the late eleventh century on, inhabitants of existing settlements, above all merchants and craftsmen, won increasing political and economic independence from bishops and feudal overlords. At the same time, kings and other nobles founded and built numerous new towns with charters granting rights and freedoms to the inhabitants; examples of the latter include towns founded by the dukes of Zähringen in southwestern Germany and Switzerland (Freiburg im Breisgau, Bern, Villingen, and others) and by Henry the Lion in the north (Braunschweig, Lübeck, Schwerin), as well as the Hanseatic merchant cities and foundations of the Teutonic Order in the east (Rostock, Stralsund, Prenzlau, Stettin, Danzig, etc.). In this way the city acquired a status as a separate legal entity with political and economic privileges for its citizens, including freedom from servitude; at the same time, such privileges were bound to the clearly demarcated space within the city walls (hence the proverb *Stadtluft macht frei*, "city air sets free"). Thus the significance of the walls built everywhere in the eleventh and twelfth centuries lies not only in their practical function as a means of defense but also in their role as symbol and marker of a political and economic sphere qualitatively distinct from that of the surrounding countryside.

The city wall often served to unite two or more settlements into a single urban area (Braunschweig, Hildesheim) or, reflecting an increase in population and prosperity, to enlarge the total area of the city and incorporate new districts (Nördlingen). In new or extended towns, the urban area was articulated by street systems ranging from a single central artery with alleys branching off (Neuenburg am Rhein, Friedberg), to two or more parallel avenues crossed by a ladderlike series of shorter streets (Bern, Lübeck), to a more or less regular grid plan (Hann, Münden, Neubrandenburg, Breslau). The transition from barter to money economy, central to the growth and proliferation of towns, is reflected in the emergence of the market street or square—an open space furnished with temporary booths or a permanent hall for the sale of produce and wares from town and countryside as well as commodities brought in from greater distances. Such markets, subject to special municipal tolls, were usually located along the main artery or at the intersection of principal streets.

The fully developed city of the High and late Middle Ages was characterized by a high degree of topographic differentiation, with districts and architectural forms

and Trier, and sometimes outside them, as at Xanten and Bonn; in some cases parts of the original Roman walls and street system were preserved (e.g., Cologne). In addition to the old Roman cities, the bishoprics, abbeys, and palaces established under the Carolingian and Ottonian emperors (Aachen, Ingelheim, Paderborn, Münster, Hamburg, Hildesheim, Bamberg, Magdeburg, Quedlinburg, Goslar, and others), often endowed with special market privileges, served as the germ for new settlements. Structurally, these protocities consisted of one or more smaller fortified complexes (cathedral, palace, monasteries, and convents) with craft and trade settlements *(suburbia)* developing outside and along the roads leading to the main centers; the *suburbia* themselves might or might not be fortified. In the eighth and ninth centuries a number of semi-independent trade settlements *(wiks)* also flourished along the North and Baltic seacoasts (Dorestad, Haithabu).

manifesting the variety of social networks in which the lives of individual citizens were embedded. Ecclesiastical and secular overlords maintained an architectural presence in cathedrals and fortresses, although the growing economic and political power of the townspeople sometimes resulted in greater citizen participation in the building and decoration of cathedrals or in the acquisition and demolition of the local castle. Family life and occupation centered around the private house, typically a wooden structure on a narrow rectangular parcel; in the later Middle Ages, houses of the patrician class were increasingly built of stone or brick. Houses and workshops of certain professions were often grouped together in the same district according to the topographical requirements of the trade; tanneries, mills, and dyeworks, for example, were often found on the urban periphery, as were hospitals and the cloisters of the mendicant orders. Ethnic groups of varying origins likewise concentrated in distinct quarters (Jews, but also Frisians and other foreign tradesmen). The civic consciousness of the citizenry found architectural expression in the town hall *(Rathaus),* most often located on the market square and equipped with spaces for council meetings, law courts, archives, state receptions, and dancing, as well as in the often elaborate parish churches and houses of the guilds and religious confraternities.

BIBLIOGRAPHY

Engel, Evamaria. *Die deutsche Stadt des Mittelalters.* Munich: Beck, 1993.

Ennen, Edith. *Die europäische Stadt des Mittelalters,* 4th ed. Göttingen: Vandenhoek and Ruprecht, 1987.

Herzog, Erich. *Die ottonische Stadt.* Berlin: Gebr. Mann, 1964.

Isenmann, Eberhard. *Die deutsche Stadt im Spätmittelalter.* Stuttgart: Ulmer, 1988.

Leudemann, Norbert. *Deutsche Bischofsstädte im Mittelalter.* Munich: Holler, 1980.

Meckseper, Cord. *Kleine Kunstgeschichte der deutschen Stadt im Mittelalter.* Darmstadt: Wissenschaftliche Buchgesellschaft, 1982.

Planitz, Hans. *Die deutsche Stadt im Mittelalter,* 3d ed. Vienna: Hermann Böhlaus Nachfolger, 1973.

Melissa Thorson Hause

SEE ALSO

Aachen; Augsburg; Bamberg; Bern; Bonn; Braunschweig; Cologne, History; Freiburg; Goslar; Hamburg; Henry the Lion; Hildesheim; Ingelheim; Lübeck; Magdeburg; Mainz; Münster; Paderborn; Prenzlau; Quedlinburg; Regensburg; Rostock; Salzburg; Schwerin; Stralsund; Trier; Worms; Xanten

Trier

The Romans founded the city of Trier during Caesar Augustus's reign. They gave it the unusual name of Augusta Treverorum, after a local Celtic tribe, the Treveri. The Romans at first took advantage of its useful location on the Mosel River, across which they soon built a stone bridge to provision the Roman military outposts along the Rhine. The city soon grew into a major center of trade and imperial administration, becoming a provincial capital. At its height, its population probably exceeded sixty thousand, surpassing most of the cities of northern Gaul. A brief decline followed the Roman Empire's troubles of the third century, probably including a sacking by the Alamans in 276. Some of the city walls and the famous Porta Nigra (Black Gate) commemorate this period. Shortly thereafter the city experienced a new revival under Constantius Chlorus and his son, Constantine. Emperor Constantine especially promoted the city as one of his residences, for which he had built his famous basilica and baths.

By the end of the fourth century, with the destabilization of the Roman Empire, Trier had lost its important status. At the beginning of the fifth century invading Germans began to sack the city repeatedly. The Ripuarian Franks finally absorbed the city into their realm by the end of the century. While much of Trier lay in ruins and its population had been reduced to a few thousand, some importance was preserved because the city was the seat of a bishop. Indeed, the bishops of Trier would lead the slow revival of the city's fortunes, and not just as religious prelates. They soon became political rulers, namely, prince-bishops. They would turn the desolate city into the capital of a middle-sized political territory spreading from the lower Moselle across the Rhine and along the lower Lahn Rivers.

The bishops necessarily took on civic leadership because of the chaos created by the Germanic invasions. Soon they began to cooperate with the Frankish kings, who often used the episcopacy as part of their methods of government. By the eighth century, the bishops exercised broad authority in the city and its surroundings. Yet the election of Frankish nobles as bishops also meant the prelates became more secularized, sometimes scandalously leading a noble lifestyle of hunting and warfare. In reaction, the Carolingians trimmed back some of the

Trier, Church of Our Lady, west portal: Adoration of the Magi and Presentation in the Temple. *Photograph: Joan A. Holladay*

bishops' political power to reemphasize the spiritual office. Charlemagne transferred the royal ban and rights to mint money to a local count. At the same time, Charlemagne likewise preserved the bishops' preeminent position in the region, especially in a reorganization of the church hierarchy. Shortly before 800 the prelates were elevated to be metropolitan archbishops with suffragans (representatives) in Metz, Toul, and Verdun.

In the wake of late Carolingian civil wars and invasions by Vikings (who sacked Trier in 882), effective royal authority waned. Again the archbishops slowly rebuilt the city and reasserted their governance over the surrounding area. By the tenth century the patronage of the kings of the Ottonian and Salian dynasties became especially helpful. Emperor Otto I, for example, confirmed or added to their immunity protection, their freedom from tolls, and their possession of a large forest and monasteries. Other kings gave them more forests, minting rights, market privileges for the city of Trier, and even the surrounding counties. The grant of Coblenz in 1018 was

very important for the future. Forming a bridgehead on the Rhine, it provided a motive for the archbishops to connect that city with Trier along the Moselle and through the Eifel and Hunsrück hills to the north and south. By the mid–eleventh century, the archbishops of Trier had become a major political force in the Rhineland.

The Investiture Controversy opened up a period of disturbances as pope and emperor tried to assert control over the bishops throughout the empire. Gradually the archbishops of Trier increased their independence from the king as they tried to preserve and defend order in their diocese. At the same time they faced increasing competition from local dynasts, like the counts Palatine by the Rhine or the counts of Luxembourg, to name the most powerful, who were trying to consolidate their own territorial rule. Meanwhile, the bishops had been increasingly using ministerials, or servile knights for their local administration. Many of these, however, soon began to act like free nobles and sought their own interests before those of their master, the archbishop. At the beginning of Archbishop Albero of Montreuil's reign (1131–1152), the burggrave of Trier had taken political and economic leadership from the previous weak prelates: he commanded the soldiery and controlled the revenues. Albero reclaimed the archbishop's paramount position, reducing Ludwig to the status of servant. Additionally, in a seven-year war over the substantial properties of the abbey of St. Maximin by Trier, Albero also excluded the abbey's advocates, the counts of Luxembourg, from the area around the city.

Tension also began to increase between the archbishop and the citizens of Trier, who increasingly sought to form their own government. In 1157, residents of Trier formed a sworn conspiracy to organize communal government, independent of the prelate. Archbishop Hillin briefly suppressed the movement with the aid of a judgment by Emperor Frederick Barbarossa. Then, while Hillin was on a military campaign in Italy during 1161, the movement revived, this time with the cooperation of Conrad von Staufen, the count Palatine by the Rhine and half brother of Emperor Frederick. Fortunately for the archbishop, once again the emperor reinforced the archbishop's regime.

By the mid–thirteenth century not only the citizens of the towns but also the cathedral chapter began to demand a greater share in political rule. The cathedral chapter's membership was largely drawn from the nobility of the countryside. By the end of the century the chapter was demanding capitulations from candidates before election to archiepiscopal office. These capitulations tended to guarantee more and more power to the canons, limiting the political choices of the archbishops. By the late Middle Ages regional nobles would often join forces with their relatives in the chapter and the city leaders of Trier. Eventually they were able to establish a corporate system where the archbishop shared some power with the estates.

In the late Middle Ages, the most effective of Trier's rulers was Baldwin von Luxembourg (1307–1354), ironically, a member of an old rival noble family. He opposed his own relatives, the counts of Luxembourg, while constructing a more effective archiepiscopal government. First, he checked the local nobility through force (sieges and battles) and the enforcement of laws. He reformed the chancery, both reviewing old and producing new documents. Second, he expanded the territory through purchase, trade, and feudal contracts. Third, Baldwin augmented archiepiscopal power through royal privileges. The most famous, the Golden Bull of 1356, granted by his nephew Charles IV, assured the archbishop's preeminence in the empire as one of the electoral princes and

tightened his control over cities like Trier and Coblenz. From this foundation regional dynasts would never again be able to threaten the core of archiepiscopal rule.

Schisms inflicted by divided cathedral canons did, however, damage the territory's political development. One of the worst occurred in 1430 as one faction elected Jacob von Sierck and another voted for Ulrich von Manderscheid; subsequently the pope rejected both and provided Hraban von Helmstätt, who was already prince-bishop of Speyer. Ulrich and his supporters not only took up arms, they appealed to the Council of Basel. The soon-to-be-famous humanist Nicholas of Cusa went to argue Ulrich's case, even though the prelate was less than the best role model (by the time of his death, he had four natural children). Although the council supported the papal candidate, Hraban of Speyer, Ulrich fought on, financing his efforts by mortgaging the precious rights, privileges, and key places of the territory and diocese. The schism ended with Ulrich's death in Italy in 1437. The territory took decades to recover from this civil war.

And at the end of the Middle Ages, the city of Trier made one last attempt at achieving the status of a free imperial city independent of the archbishop's authority. But the Imperial Chamber Court decided once and for all in favor of the archbishop in 1580. Surviving the famous rebellion of Franz von Sickingen (1522–1523) and the Reformation intact, the Electoral Principality of Trier remained a not insignificant player in German politics. Only the wars of the French Revolution, as they demolished the Holy Roman Empire, likewise destroyed the temporal rule of the archbishops of Trier.

BIBLIOGRAPHY

Anton, Hans Hubert. *Trier im frühen Mittelalter.* Paderborn: Schöningh, 1987.

Erkens, Franz-Reiner. *Die Trierer Kirchenprovinz im Investiturstreit.* Cologne: Böhlau Verlag, 1987.

Mötsch, Johannes, and Heyen, Franz-Josef, ed. *Balduin von Luxemburg: Erzbischof von Trier—Kurfürst des Reiches, 1285–1354: Festschrift aus Anlass des 700. Geburtsjahres.* Mainz: Verlag der Gesellschaft für Mittelrheinische Kirchengeschichte, 1985.

Pauly, Ferdinand. *Aus der Geschichte des Bistums Trier.* Pt. 1, *Von der spätrömischen Zeit bis zum 12. Jahrhundert.* Trier: Selbstverlag des Bistumsarchiv Trier, 1968.

———. *Aus der Geschichte des Bistums Trier.* Pt. 2, *Die Bischöfe bis zum Ende des Mittelalters.* Trier: Paulinus Verlag, 1969.

Pavlac, Brian A. "Excommunication and Territorial Politics in High Medieval Trier." *Church History* 60 (1991): 20–36.

Brian A. Pavlac

Trier, Art

The city of Trier lies nestled between the hills of the Moselle River valley. After the Romans under Augustus conquered the Treveri, the Gallic tribe that inhabited the region, the town was founded as an administrative center and became prosperous through active viticulture and craft industries. With its position on the Moselle and the construction of a bridge over the river, Trier also became an important trading center. The city was laid out in a grid pattern, with the streets *cardo* and *decumanus,* named after thoroughfares in Rome, set along the north-south and east-west axes and a large complex of public buildings in the center of the city. Numerous Roman monuments, many reused throughout the Middle Ages, testify to Trier's prosperity and importance. Following the reorganization of the Roman Empire under Diocletian in the late third century, Trier became the capital of Constantius Chlorus. An important mint was established and numerous new buildings were constructed, including the basilica of Constantine, the imperial baths, and the Porta Nigra (Black Gate).

With the Christianization of the empire, Trier became one of the early centers of the church. Ambrose was educated in Trier, and Augustine and Martin visited the city. Trier's topography was transformed by the construction of churches, mainly outside the city walls in the cemeteries that the Christians had used in the third and fourth centuries. These include the churches of St. Eucharius (later St. Matthias), St. John the Evangelist (later St. Maximin), and St. Paul. A huge double cathedral was founded in the northern quarter of the city.

Trier continued to be an important center throughout the Middle Ages. Its archbishop, along with those of Cologne and Mainz, was influential in the affairs of the church and the Holy Roman Empire and served as elector. Trier was a major center of artistic production, especially during the Ottonian dynasty under Archbishop Egbert (r. 977–993). During this time the archbishops of

Trier were particularly active in establishing their position that Trier was the primary church of Germany as a result of its foundation by St. Eucharius, a disciple of St. Peter who had personally sent the bishop north along with his staff. A number of important relics are attested in Trier during the Middle Ages, including the robe of Christ and a nail from the crucifixion, the body of St. Matthew, and the staff that St. Peter gave Eucharius.

Later medieval sources state that the first cathedral of Trier was built on the grounds of the imperial palace at the instigation of Helena, mother of Constantine. Excavations following World War II revealed the remains of a luxurious residence under the cathedral and suggested that the first building was indeed constructed during the reign of Constantine. This cathedral, whose plan is imperfectly understood, had a long nave preceded by a second basilica hall and possibly atrium, with a total length of about 210 meters. A second, narrower building lay parallel to the south under the present-day Liebfrauenkirche (Church of the Virgin), and a baptistery lay between the two buildings. The dedications of the churches are unknown. The east end of the cathedral was reworked during the middle of the fourth century with a twelve-sided structure. During the last third of the fourth century the entire east end of the cathedral was rebuilt as a large, square building with corner towers and a lantern; the walls of this building still serve as the lower stories of the side walls of the present building.

The cathedral was destroyed in 451 in the attack of the Huns and reconstructed under Bishop Nicetius (r. 525–ca. 566). During the Carolingian period the sanctuary of the cathedral was remodeled, but the building was again destroyed in 882, this time by the Normans. Reconstruction of the east end, still seen in the cruciform piers flanking the lower choir, did not begin until the tenth century under Archbishop Egbert (r. 977–993), but the complete restoration of the cathedral did not take place until the eleventh century. Under Archbishop Poppo (r. 1016–1047) the present western end of the church was constructed, giving the cathedral a double-apse plan and creating an early example of Rhenish Romanesque architecture. A new eastern choir similar in form to the earlier choirs of St. Simeon in Trier and the cathedral of Verdun was added to the cathedral under Hillin (r. 1152–1169) and dedicated in 1196. By the early thirteenth century the entire church was vaulted.

The Liebfrauenkirche stands over the foundations of a fourth-century basilica church that lay parallel to the cathedral and was attached to it by a baptistery and connecting structure. It is possible that this was a church for catechumens, who would then be initiated and taken to the cathedral. The close liturgical and functional relationship of this church to the main cathedral can be seen in its reconstruction under Nicetius following destruction in 451. Its sanctuary was also reorganized during the Carolingian period in a plan similar to the cathedral. Following the destruction in 882, the church was rebuilt before the cathedral in the early tenth century, and had a cloister built at its east end. This Ottonian building remained relatively unchanged during the many phases of the cathedral's reconstruction, but the building was razed and a new Gothic structure was begun in the 1230s. This building is related in style and form to the church of St. Elizabeth in Marburg, but is unusual among Gothic buildings in having a centralized plan. The location of doors on the four axes of the church show that it continued to function with the cathedral in processional liturgy, but the building takes on a more independent character from this point.

The Benedictine abbey of St. Maximin was important in the Gorze reform movement of the tenth century. Excavations have produced the remains of a painted crypt that is a valuable example of late Carolingian and Ottonian mural painting. The crypt was dedicated in 952 and is an example of an outer crypt, a structure projecting beyond the walls of the apse of the church. This was not an uncommon type in Lotharingia.

Between 1147 and 1160 Provost Albero added a choir to the east end of one of the Roman city gates, the Porta Nigra. The church commemorated St. Simeon, the Greek monk from Sicily who came to Trier following the pilgrimage of Archbishop Poppo to the Holy Land and took up residence in the ruins of the Porta Nigra until his death in 1035. In 1042 Poppo had established a chapter of canons and dedicated the building to Christ, Mary, and Simeon. The new Romanesque choir had two floors, one for the laity and one for the canons above. A crypt below held the bodies of Poppo and Simeon. In form it develops the type found in the choir of Verdun that was consecrated in 1147 and precedes the building of the east choir of the cathedral.

Trier was an important center for art production during the Middle Ages, particularly in the tenth and eleventh centuries. The Codex Egberti was probably produced in Trier utilizing monks from Reichenau as scribes, although this is disputed. This work and others have been attributed to the Master of the Registrum Gregorii, who was active in Trier during the last quarter of the tenth century. A variety of reliquaries produced by Trier workshops included those for the nail of the cross, the sandal of St. Andrew, and the staff of St. Peter.

BIBLIOGRAPHY

Borger-Keweloh, Nicola. *Die Liebfrauenkirche in Trier: Studien zur Baugeschichte.* Trier: Rheinisches Landesmuseum, 1986.

Bunjes, Hermann, N. Irsch, G. Kentenich, F. Kutzbach, and H. Lückger. *Die kirchlichen Denkmäler der Stadt Trier mit Ausnahme des Domes.* 1938. Rpt. Trier: Akademische Buchhandlung Interbook, 1981.

Head, Thomas. "Art and Artifice in Ottonian Trier." *Gesta* 36 (1997): 65–82.

Irsch, Nikolaus. *Der Dom zu Trier.* 1931; rpt. Trier: Akademische Buchhandlung Interbook, 1984.

Kurzeja, Adalbert. *Der älteste "Liber ordinarius" der Trier Domkirche.* Münster: Aschendorff, 1970.

Ronig, Franz J., ed. *Der Trierer Dom.* Neuss: Gesellschaft für Buchdruckerei, 1980.

Sanderson, W. "Die frühmittelalterlichen Krypten von St. Maximin in Trier." *Trierer Zeitschrift* 31 (1968): 7–172.

Trier: Ein Zentrum abendländischer Kultur. Neuss: Rheinsicher Verein für Denkmalpflege und Heimatschutz, 1952.

Trier, Kaiserresidenz und Bischofssitz: Die Stadt in spätantiker und frühchristlicher Zeit. Mainz: P. von Zabern, 1984.

Mark Stansbury-O'Donnell

SEE ALSO

Cologne, Art; Mainz; Marburg; *Registrum Gregorii,* Master of the; Reichenau; Relics and Reliquaries; Romanesque Art and Architecture; Trier

Tristan

See Gottfried von Straßburg.

U

Ulenspegel

The hero of a large number of facetious, scatological, and social-critical narratives collected in a jest book perhaps composed by the Brunswick toll collector Hermen Bote (ca. 1463–ca. 1520), *Ulenspegel* (literally, owl's mirror) was one of the most popular and entertaining texts all over Europe from the late Middle Ages until today and has been one of the most influential German contributions to world literature. The earliest printed version dates from 1510/1511 (Strasbourg); later versions were printed in 1515, 1519, and 1531. In the sixteenth century alone at least twenty-eight printed versions appeared in Germany, not counting the considerable number of translations in all major European languages. According to the 1510/1511 edition, the original text was written in 1500; later versions date the text as early as 1483. Apparently a Low German copy was used by the Strasbourg printer that seems to be lost today. The general appeal of these narratives did not decline until the late seventeenth century, but they regained in literary status again since the middle of the nineteenth century (reprint of the 1519 version in 1854 by J. M. Lappenberg).

The collection comprises a prologue and ninty-six *histori* (tales); later versions added up to nine more *histori*. The text is written in early New High German, reflecting some influences of Low German dialects.

Ulenspegel is known as a historical personality from the first half of the fourteenth century who became famous for his jests and skill in fooling others in a rather outrageous manner. Since 1350, when he was supposed to have died, a rich oral tradition kept his memory alive, until Hermen Bote (or somebody else) copied them down in 1500. The tales, each of them a relatively independent narrative, all taken together describe the life of the protagonist who plays tricks with members of all social classes and with men and women alike. Many of his jokes are based on scatology; many rely on linguistic puns and reveal the ambivalence of everyday-life metaphorical speech. In some tales Ulenspegel ridicules the urban intelligentsia, in others the clergy, innkeepers, merchants, and craftsmen. Nobody is spared, not even the protagonist himself. Whereas his most drastic form of criticism relies on the body's anal functions, no references to sexuality or erotic elements can be found throughout the book. The allegedly "bawdy" character of these tales did not diminish their popularity, which explains in part the generic label *Volksbuch* (chapbook), coined in 1807 by Joseph Görres.

Throughout the sixteenth and seventeenth centuries *Ulenspegel* was heavily criticized by theologians, philosophers, and public administrators of all colors, but the general demand for these entertaining tales could not be suppressed. We know of more than 250 poems and other texts written between the sixteenth and the late twentieth century in which Ulenspegel comes to life again, not counting the vast number of *Eulenspiegel* children's books enjoying a vast popularity even in the late 1990s. Richard Strauss composed a symphony with the title *Till Eulenspiegel* in 1895.

BIBLIOGRAPHY

Bollenbeck, Georg. *Till Eulenspiegel, der dauerhafte Schwankheld*. Stuttgart: Metzler, 1985.

Classen, Albrecht. *The German Volksbuch*. New York: Edwin Mellen Press, 1995.

Ein kurtzweilig lesen von Dil Ulenspiegel, ed. Wolfgang Lindow. Stuttgart: Reclam, 1966.

Oppenheimer, Paul. *Till Eulenspiegel: His Adventures*. New York: Garland, 1991.

Ulm

Röcke, Werner. *Die Freude am Bösen.* Munich: Fink, 1987.

Wunderlich, Werner, ed. *Eulenspiegel-Interpretationen.* Munich: Fink, 1979.

Albrecht Classen

Ulm

Situated in Swabia along the Danube River, Ulm slowly developed into one of Germany's foremost mercantile centers. Its name is first recorded in 854 when a Carolingian palace was located on the Weinhofberg. Few vestiges remain from either this period or from the late eleventh century, when Ulm served as a Hohenstaufen residence. The town obtained its civic rights in 1164 and in 1274 was elevated to an imperial free city. Buoyed by its prosperous economy, notably its textile industry, and its growing regional importance, Ulm quadrupled its circumference when it expanded its city walls between 1316 and 1335. Supplemental fortifications were added around 1527 and again in 1616. At its apex during the later fourteenth and fifteenth centuries, Ulm boasted a splendid city hall, the largest parish church in southern Germany, ten other churches, thirty-one chapels, eleven independent cloisters, and ten town residences for other regional monasteries. Ulm controlled more territory than any other imperial free city except Nuremberg. Between 1397 and 1548 representatives of the seventeen guilds shared political power with a slightly smaller group of patricians, thus guaranteeing guilds a leading role in running the city. Ulm supported a sizable community of artists who in many cases exerted considerable regional influence. The painters and sculptors belonged to the Large Shopkeepers' Guild yet since 1402 had their own brotherhood of St. Luke with a chapel in the former Wengen cloister church.

The Münster, dedicated to the Virgin Mary, dominates Ulm's skyline. In the aftermath of an imperial siege

Ulm, cathedral, interior, nave, view to east. *Photograph: Virginia Jansen*

in 1376, when access to their parish church proved difficult, the council decided to erect a new church on a more secure site. The new building, constructed between 1377 and 1531, matched Ulm's own ambitiousness. In his civic encomium, written in 1488, the Dominican Felix Faber stressed that this remarkable church was funded solely by the citizens, and that its remarkable scale surpassed any other German parish church. Indeed the Münster, with exterior dimensions of 139 × 59 meters, rivals in size the cathedrals of Cologne and Vienna. In a stone relief commemorating the laying of the foundation stone in 1377, Bürgermeister (mayor) Lutz Krafft and his wife set a model of the church on the architect's back. The original plans were formulated by Heinrich (fl. 1377–1387), Michael (fl. 1387), and Heinrich the Younger (1387–1392) Parler, a branch of the famed family of architects and sculptors who hailed from Schwäbisch Gmünd. Either Heinrich the Younger or, more likely, his successor, Ulrich von Ensingen (fl. 1392–1419), transformed the initial hall church design into a basilica plan with the addition of a second pair of aisles, a different configuration for the choir, and the introduction of a single massive western tower. Although the church was dedicated in 1405, work continued until 1531. Then measuring 70 meters, the tower would attain its full height of 161 meters and appearance, carefully following von Ensingen's original plan (Ulm, Stadtarchiv), only when construction resumed in 1856–1890. The two smaller towers by the choir were built in 1875–1880.

From the late fourteenth to the early sixteenth centuries, local families and civic groups lavishly decorated the Münster. The church had fifty-two altars, each ornamented with a statue or an altarpiece. Unfortunately, virtually nothing survives of this patrimony since on June 19, 1531, the church was "purified" by order of the Protestant-dominated city council. As followers of Huldrych Zwingli, who held most religious art to be idolatrous, they purged all the altars, the large statues lining the nave, and selected other objects. Only the Hutz Altar from 1521 with its painted wings by Martin Schaffner and its corpus statues attributed to Niklaus Weckmann survived. It had been removed just before the iconoclasm and now serves as the high altar. Because the council so tightly controlled the occasion and specified precisely which works were not to be touched, the Münster still retains much of its original embellishments. Each of the five western portals are ornamented with sculpture, much of it produced in the 1350s for the old parish church and transferred by the end of the century. Most of the Genesis

cycle in the tympanum above the main doorway dates before 1391 and reflects the Prague Parler school style. None of the surrounding statues of Mary and saints matches the evocative power and heightened realism of Hans Multscher's life-size Man of Sorrows (1429), who displays his wounds to all who enter through the central portal.

Faber praised the Münster's interior light that provided both illumination and spiritual mood. He doubtlessly responded to the beauty of the church's cycle of stained glass windows. Best preserved are the windows of the choir, which include four (1385–1404) by the noted Ulm glazer Jakob Acker plus another pair (ca. 1480) by Peter Hemmel von Andlau of Strasbourg. The adjacent Besserer chapel contains the five exquisite windows (ca. 1430) by Hans Acker. The iconoclasts spared Jörg Syrlin the Elder's set of choir stalls (1468–1474), Germany's most famous and most extensive cycle from this period. Complementing Syrlin's skilled carpentry are ninety-nine freestanding and relief busts of philosophers (north side) and sibyls (south side) by several local sculptors. Particularly impressive are the lifelike busts and varied poses of figures such as Ptolemy, Seneca, and Virgil. The eastern wall of the crossing is covered by the monumental Last Judgment fresco from 1471 (145 m^2). Below, at the northern entrance to the choir, stands the 26-meter-tall sacrament house (1467–1471) with its sculpted statues of prophets. These have been unconvincingly attributed to Jörg Syrlin the Elder and Michel Erhart but are likely by a different Ulm workshop. When the iconoclasts removed the statues lining the nave and inner aisles, they left twenty-nine of the original figural consoles fashioned by artists in the Parler workshop between 1383 and 1391; these included several naturalistically painted female busts whose hair metamorphosizes into foliate supports.

None of Ulm's medieval churches, other than the Münster, survives intact. The city's embrace of Protestantism obviated the need for monasteries; the Trinity church and former Wengen cloister were altered later, in keeping with changes in tastes; and the 1944 bombings of Ulm obliterated most of the medieval city. The marketplace before the Münster originally contained a large *Ölberg* (Mount of Olives group) designed by Matthäus Böblinger in 1474 and erected in 1514. The architectural canopy covered life-size statues of Christ in prayer on the Mount of Olives with twelve apostles; the figures were removed in 1534 to discourage their use by Catholics. South of the Münster stands Ulm's city hall. Much of the structure dates to the 1360s, with major alterations of the east wing around 1420. Hans Multscher and others carved the figures of Charlemagne, the imperial electors, and their standard bearers that adorned the eastern show window. Facing the south side of the city hall stands the Fish Trough Fountain from 1482, designed by the Syrlin workshop, perhaps by Jörg the Younger. The fountain's three sandstone knights together with the city hall statues and remnants of the *Ölberg* are today in the Ulmer Museum.

For over a century Ulm was Swabia's major economic and artistic center. By the end of the fifteenth century it was surpassed by Augsburg and never regained its prominence.

BIBLIOGRAPHY

Baumhauer, Hermann. *Das Ulmer Münster und seine Kunstwerke.* Stuttgart: K. Theiss, 1977.

Baxandall, Michael. *The Limewood Sculptors of Renaissance Germany.* New Haven, Conn.: Yale University Press, 1980.

Braunfels, Wolfgang. *Die Kunst im Heiligen Römischen Reich Deutscher Nation.* Munich: Beck, 1979–1989, vol. 3, pp. 138–156.

Geiger, Gottfried. *Die Reichsstadt Ulm vor der Reformation: Städtisches und kirchliches Leben am Ausgang des Mittelalters.* Ulm: Stadtarchiv, 1971.

Jasbar, Gerald, and Erwin Treu. *Ulmer Museum: Bildhauerei und Malerei von 13. Jahrhunderts bis 1600.* Kataloge des Ulmer Museums, 1. Ulm: Ulmer Museum, 1981.

Koepf, Hans. *Die gotischen Planrisse der Ulmer Sammlungen.* Ulm: Stadtarchiv, 1977.

Otto, Gertrud. *Die Ulmer Plastik der Spätgotik.* Tübinger Fotschungen zur Archäologie Kunstgeschichte 7. Reutlingen: Gryphius, 1927.

Reisinger, Claus. *Flandern in Ulm: Glasmalerei und Buchmalerei: Die Verglasung der Bessererkapelle am Ulmer Münster.* Worms: Wernersche Verlagshaus, 1985.

Scholz, Hartmut. *Die mittelalterlichen Glasmalereien in Ulm.* Corpus vitrearum medii aevi, Deutschland, vol. 1, pt. 3. Berlin: Deutscher Verlag für Kunstwissenschaft, 1994.

Specker, Hans Eugen, and Reinhard Wortmann, eds. *600 Jahre Ulmer Münster: Festschrift.* Ulm: Stadtarchiv, 1977.

Specker, Hans Eugen, and Hermann Tüchle, eds. *Kirchen und Klöster in Ulm.* Ulm: Süddeutsche Verlagsgesellschaft, 1979.

Jeffrey Chipps Smith

SEE ALSO

Augsburg; Charlemagne; Erhart, Michel; Gothic Art and Architecture; Iconographics, Innovative; Multscher, Hans; Parler Family; Prague; Schwäbisch Gmünd; Syrlin, Jörg (Elder and Younger); Weckmann, Nicolaus, the Elder

Ulrich von Etzenbach (fl. 2d half of the 13th c.)

A German author who contributed to the emerging German culture at the Bohemian court in Prague of the House of the Přemysl. He began writing his *Alexander* romance around 1270 under the patronage of King Ottokar, and completed it in 1286 under King Wenzel II, Ottokar's son. The legendary romance *Wilhelm von Wenden* was written around 1290, whereas the date of Ulrich's *Herzog Ernst* version D (attribution uncertain) cannot be confirmed.

We do not know much about Ulrich apart from what he mentions about himself in his works. He was born in Northern Bohemia (*Alexander,* vv. 27627f.) and acquired a solid education, though he probably did not become a cleric. His knowledge of Latin was very good, and so his familiarity with "classical" Middle High German literature, to which he refers often.

The *Alexander,* which has been preserved in six manuscripts and several fragments, deals with the famous history of the Macedonian ruler Alexander the Great and follows his conquest of the Persian Empire and all the lands extending to the river Indus. The text is based primarily on the Latin epic poem *Alexandreis* (thirteenth century), composed in hexametric verse by Walther of Châtillon, but then also on the *Nativitas et victoriae Alexandri Magni regis* (*Birth and Victories of Alexander the Great King,* ca. 950–970) by the Archpriest Leo (which again was based on the tenth-century *Historia preliis*).

For both Walther and Ulrich, Alexander's victories laid the foundation for the third of four secular empires that would, according to biblical traditions, come and go before Christ's return and the Day of Judgment. For religious reasons Alexander's activities are cleansed from any negative elements as in the older tradition; even murderous slaughter and killing of enemy troops are exculpated. Moreover, the important aspects of Alexander's curiosity leading to his exploration of the world (dive into the sea in a glass bubble; flight in the air with the help of griffins) are eliminated as well, because he is seen as God's instrument and made to an ideal ruler in the tradition of the

Fürstenspiegel (didactic texts for princes). In many respects, Alexander is modeled after Ottokar II, whom Ulrich wanted to idealize through his work.

In *Wilhelm von Wenden,* preserved only in one manuscript, now in Dessau, King Wenzel II and his wife, Guta of Habsburg, are immortalized in the figure of Prince Wilhelm of Parrit and his wife, Bene (the Good One). Wilhelm secretly departs from his dukedom to make a pilgrimage to Jerusalem and to convert to a Christian. Bene accompanies him but is left behind in a foreign country after she delivers twins, whom Wilhelm sells to Christian merchants to be free of this burden on his pilgrimage. Because of Bene's virtuous lifestyle she is later elected (!) the ruler of that country, and when by chance the family eventually reunites again after many years, they all convert to Christianity and thus missionize the entire country. Both the role of the strong woman and the tolerant attitude toward non-Christian religions are remarkable. Ulrich used as his model either *Guillaume d'Angleterre* by Chrétien de Troyes, or the *Eustachius* legend in the *Legenda aurea (Golden Legendary).*

Herzog Ernst D finally, extant in one manuscript (Gotha, called "d"), follows the tradition of goliardic narratives *(Spielmannsepen)* in which the young Bavarian duke has to leave Germany because of political and military conflicts with his father-in-law, the irrational and impetuous emperor, and explores the world of the Orient. Both this text and the *Alexander* were later translated into Czech.

BIBLIOGRAPHY

Behr, Hans-Joachim. *Literatur als Machtlegitimation.* Munich: Fink, 1989.

Classen, Albrecht: "Ulrichs von Etzenbach *Wilhelm von Wenden*—ein Frauenroman?" *Literaturwissenschaftliches Jahrbuch* 30 (1989): 27–43.

Kohlmayer, Rainer: *Ulrichs von Etzenbach "Wilhelm von Wenden."* Meisenheim: Hain, 1974.

Rosenfeld, Hans-Friedrich, ed. *Ulrich von Etzenbach. "Wilhelm von Wenden."* Berlin: Akademie-Verlag, 1957.

———, ed. *Herzog Ernst D.* Tübingen: Niemeyer, 1991.

Toischer, Wendelin, ed. *Ulrich von Etzenbach: "Alexander."* Prague: Verein für Geschichte der Deutschen in Böhmen, 1888.

Albrecht Classen

SEE ALSO

Legenda Aurea, Alsatian; *Spielmannsepen*

Ulrich von Liechtenstein (ca. 1200–1275)

Ulrich von Liechtenstein's action-filled life as a political *ministeriale* in Austria in the middle two fourths of the twelfth century is well documented in contemporary records. As a literary parallel to his life, Ulrich created with his *Frauendienst (Service of Ladies),* compiled around 1255, though doubtless utilizing songs composed earlier, a fictional verse romance in which his persona, the minnesinger Ulrich, woos a recalcitrant lady with songs, adventures, including a cross-country tournament for which he dresses himself as Venus, and misadventures. In one of these he disables a finger while fighting to gain his lady's approval. When he learns that she doubts he was really injured, he chops the finger off and sends it to her in a jeweled casket, accompanied by a verse booklet proclaiming his love. His misadventures, which often echo literary motifs, are recounted with rollicking humor. His attempted tryst with the lady in her chambers, in the course of which he is hoisted up to and let down (literally: let fall) from her window in a basket and is so distraught at being rejected that he tries to drown himself, forms a high point of his hapless service. Angered by her consistent rejection of him, he turns to the service of a new lady, undertaking yet another marathon tournament, this time as King Arthur. In the midst of all his feverish service of a lady, he explicitly takes some time off to enjoy the company of his wife. Whereas songs more or less punctuate the narrative in the first half of the work (though their motifs often seem to have inspired its plot), they dominate the second half. Here, the framework often becomes little more than a poetological commentary on the songs, though as in many *razos,* or reasons (i.e., prose commentaries), of the troubadours—a possible inspiration for this part of the work—the commentary consists largely of paraphrase, and praise of the songs' excellence. Ulrich's fifty-seven songs and one *Leich* (poem), though accomplished, pale somewhat against the originality of their frame. His models were Walther von der Vogelweide (whom he quotes without attribution), Wolfram von Eschenbach (whose dawn songs he parodies), and Gottfried von Straßburg. He also doubtless learned from singers such as Gottfried von Neifen (whose use of the motif of the lady's rose-red mouth he exaggerates to comic effect) and probably influenced others in turn, such as Steinmar. A set of strophes he shares with Heinrich von Veldeke and Niune (Kraus, no. 58 XII) probably bears the former's name through scribal misascription and was adapted into two shorter songs by the latter.

In addition to the *Frauendienst,* he wrote the *Frauenbuch,* a didactic treatise in debate form in which a lady and a knight discuss who is responsible for the sad state of the world. In the end the lady is declared free of blame. Though it lacks the innovative sparkle (and the occasional narrative tedium) of the former work, its earnestness and apparent sincerity remind us that despite the ubiquity of humor and playfulness in Ulrich's larger work, he seems to have taken the exhortations to be constant, loyal, pure, and kind (good)that permeate both works to heart. Despite all the weaknesses and absurdities that he clearly recognizes in contemporary life and (especially) letters, he valorizes courtly ideals and seeks to promote *hôher muot* (courtly good cheer).

BIBLIOGRAPHY

Bechstein, Reinhold, ed. *Ulrich's von Lichtenstein Frauendienst.* 2 vols. Leipzig: Brockhaus, 1888.

Kraus, Carl von, ed. *Deutsche Liederdichter des 13. Jahrhunderts.* 2 vols.; 2d ed. Gisela Kornrumpf. Tübingen: Niemeyer, 1978.

Lachmann, Karl, ed. *Ulrich von Lichtenstein.* Berlin: Sander, 1841; rpt. Hildesheim: Olms, 1974.

Thomas, J. W., trans. *Ulrich von Liechtenstein's Service of Ladies.* Chapel Hill: University of North Carolina Press, 1969.

Hubert Heinen

SEE ALSO

Arthurian Literature, German; Heinrich von Veldeke; Minesterials; *Minnesang;* Versification; Walter von der Vogelweide; Wolfram von Eschenbach

Ulrich von Türheim (fl. ca. 1230–1245)

After Gottfried von Straßburg had left his *Tristan* as a torso around 1210, two authors picked up the fragment and provided their own conclusions—Heinrich von Freiberg (ca. 1280–1290) and Ulrich von Türheim. The latter composed his *continuatio* (continuation) roughly between 1230 and 1235, adding a total of 3,730 verses. Ulrich's conclusion of the *Tristan* was commissioned by the imperial cup-bearer *(Reichsschenk),* the Augsburg nobleman Konrad von Winterstetten (d. 1243). Sometime after that Ulrich wrote the continuation of Wolfram von Eschenbach's *Willehalm,* the so-called *Rennewart,* comprising more than 36,000 verses, completed before 1250. Among his earliest literary enterprises, however, we find Ulrich's short narrative *Clîges,* which is extant only in a fragment from circa 1230 and based on Chrétien de Troyes's *Cligès.*

An Ulrich von Türheim appears in the documents of the bishop and the cathedral chapter of Augsburg between 1236 and 1244. We assume that he was identical with our poet.

For his *Tristan* continuation, Ulrich relied heavily on the *Tristan* version by Eilhart von Oberg, *Tristrant.* Here, Tristan marries Isolde Whitehand, without sleeping with his newlywed. Her brother Kaedin learns about this scandalous situation and challenges Tristan, who then tells him of Isolde the Fair. Together they travel to England and meet Isolde secretly. Tristan spends one night with her alone, whereas Kaedin is duped by a chambermaid. Later Tristan is falsely accused of having failed in his service for the queen, and the latter orders him to be beaten and chased away when he shows up at court in the guise of a leper. The lovers overcome the conflict and misunderstanding, however, and Tristan can spend some time at court hidden behind his mask, until he is discovered and then returns to Arundel with Kaedin. Now Tristan fully accepts his wife and sleeps with her. When he later helps Kaedin in a secret love affair, Kaedin is killed and Tristan badly wounded. He requests help from Isolde the Fair, and asks that in case of her arrival the ship should set a white sail. When Isolde the Fair approaches the coast, jealous Isolde Whitehand deceives her husband and tells him that the sail is black. Despairing, Tristan dies, and when his true love has finally arrived at the bed, she drops dead next to him. King Marke has both buried together; a rosebush and a grapevine planted on their grave later intertwine, symbolizing the everlasting love of Tristan and Isolde the Fair.

Ulrich's *Rennewart* focuses on the history of the eponymous hero, who is, after the victory over the Saracens (described by Wolfram von Eschenbach in his *Willehalm*), baptized and married to King Loys' daughter Alise. Rennewart assumes the kingdom of Portebaliart and continues with his battles against the heathens. Alise dies at the birth of her child Malefer, who is soon after kidnapped by merchants and brought to Terramer, who wants to raise him as an opponent to Christianity, though to no avail. Rennewart, deeply grieved, joins a monastery where he lives for twenty more years. Two times he enters the battlefield again, however, and there he meets his son and entrusts him with the rulership of Portebaliart. Malefer later conquers the Oriental empire of his grandfather Terramer and marries the queen of the Amazons, Penteselie, who delivers a child with the name Johann who will continue with the religious struggle against the heathens. When Terramer's son Matribuleiz attacks France anew, Willehalm returns from his hermitage, a move that immediately convinces the Saracens, reminded of their previous defeat, to return home. Willehalm erects a monastery near Muntbasiliere where he will eventually meet his death.

This *continuatio* was, along with Wolfram's epic, highly popular and is extant in thirteen manuscripts and twenty-nine fragments. Ulrich relied in part on the French tradition of the *chansons de gestes* (heroic songs), which are focused on Guillaume d'Orange. The Augsburg citizen Otto der Bogner supplied Ulrich, as he indicates in his *Rennewart,* with the manuscripts of the French texts (vv. 10270–10282). Ulrich probably composed his works for the royal court of the Hohenstaufen family.

BIBLIOGRAPHY

Grubmüller, Klaus. "Probleme einer Fortsetzung." *Zeitschrift für deutsches Altertum* 114 (1985): 338–348.

McDonald, William C. *The Tristan Story in German Literature of the Late Middle Ages and Early Renaissance.* Lewiston, Maine: Edwin Mellen Press, 1990.

Spiewok, Wolfgang, ed. *Das Tristan-Epos Gottfrieds von Straßburg. Mit der Fortsetzung des Ulrich von Türheim.* Berlin: Akademie-Verlag, 1989.

Ulrich von Türheim. *Rennewart,* ed. A. Hübner. Berlin: Weidmann, 1938; 2d ed., 1964.

———. *Tristan,* ed. Th. Kerth. Tübingen: Niemeyer, 1979.

Westphal-Schmidt, Christa. *Studien zum Rennewart Ulrichs von Türheim.* Frankfurt am Main: Haage und Herchen, 1979.

Albrecht Classen

SEE ALSO

Eilhart von Oberge; Gottfried von Straßburg; Wolfram von Eschenbach

Ulrich von Zatzikhoven (fl. ca. 1200)

Flourishing in the late twelfth/early thirteenth century, Ulrich von Zatzikhoven was author of the earliest German version of the Lancelot story, *Lanzelet,* a poem of over 9,444 lines in rhymed couplets. This version differs significantly from that of Chrétien and subsequent versions in that it does not contain the affair between Lancelot and Guinevere. Ulrich translated an Anglo-Norman manuscript received from "Hûc von Morville," who was a hostage in 1194 to Duke Leopold of Austria in exchange for King Richard the Lion-Hearted of England. The only historical record of Ulrich's existence is found in a document of 1214, where Ulrich is mentioned as a parish priest of Lommis in the Swiss canton of Thurgau.

Lanzelet's story is one of lost and regained identity and patrimony. Lanzelet, kidnapped as an infant and raised by a sea fairy, leaves at age fifteen to become a knight, without knowing his identity or lineage. The sea fairy promises to reveal it to him if he avenges her by killing a certain Iweret. This search carries Lanzelet through the first half of the romance, where he encounters and wins three ladies and defeats all comers at a tournament. The central episode is the winning of Iblis, which he does by killing Iweret and thereby learning his identity and his place in the Arthurian family (Arthur is his uncle).

The second part of the romance deals with the Arthurian community and the rehabilitation of Lanzelet's patrimony. Lanzelet's activities generally are in collaboration with other Arthurian knights, including the rescue of Ginover from Valerîn and Lanzelet's own rescue from the Queen of Plûrîs. In the end, Lanzelet recovers his lands, and with his wife, Iblis, becomes the ruler of their combined holdings.

BIBLIOGRAPHY

Pérennec, René. "Artusroman und Familie: 'Daz welsche buoch von Lanzelet.'" *Acta Germanica* 11 (1979): 1–51.

Richter, Werner. *Der 'Lanzelet' Ulrichs von Zazikhoven.* Frankfurt: Diesterweg, 1934.

Ulrich von Zatzikoven. *Lanzelet: A Romance of Lancelot,* ed. Roger Sherman Loomis; trans. Kenneth G. T. Webster. New York: Columbia University Press, 1951.

———. *Lanzelet: Eine Erzählung,* ed. K. A. Hahn. Frankfurt am Main: Brönner, 1845; rpt. ed. Frederick Norman. Berlin: de Gruyter, 1965.

Kathleen J. Meyer

SEE ALSO

Arthurian Literature, German

Universities

The university in German-speaking areas of the Middle Ages was a phenomenon that appeared relatively late. The first universities, that is, those centers of learning distinct from the cathedral and monastic schools and developed into viable, independent secular institutions, were exclusively established in the Gallo-Mediterranean area, with the notable exceptions of Oxford and Cambridge, in the early thirteenth century. This development continued throughout the first half of the fourteenth century, and it was not until 1347 that Charles IV established a university in Prague.

The late fourteenth century saw a rapid succession of such university foundings, with Kraków (1364), Vienna (1365), Fünfkirchen (1367), Erfurt (1379), Heidelberg (1385), and Cologne (1388). By the end of the Middle Ages, some fifteen universities existed within the Holy Roman Empire, plus those in Basle and Kraków. This late but determined expansion was based largely on imperial politics and the desire to increase the intellectual and cultural significance of central Europe. It was also driven by the Great Schism of 1378 and the resulting split in church authority, with faculty having to choose sides and often electing to found new centers of study elsewhere.

All medieval universities were small by modern standards, with perhaps a few hundred students enrolled. By the end of the fifteenth century only some three thousand students were matriculated annually in all of Germany. The university was built on the concept of the *studium generale,* that is, a place where a number of disciplines could be studied, and the desire to promulgate the study of the seven liberal arts along with theology and the secular subjects of civil (Roman) law and medicine. German universities developed faculties that sought to develop local reputations and student bodies, in competition with the older international universities such as Paris and Bologna. These faculties soon became independently endowed entities, or colleges, with their own libraries, housing, staff, and curriculum. The German college system tended to be organized around the masters, or professors, and formed the locus for almost all lectures and readings. Students were usually organized along the Paris model of nations based on their place of origin. The university at Prague established four nations: Czech, Bohemian, Bavarian, and Saxon. These student organizations had varying degrees of influence on the administration.

The history and organization of universities must also be seen in conjunction with the rise of the medieval city. Universities were city institutions and served the needs of the ever-increasingly secular and mercantile population. Those who studied there went on to serve the community in any number of capacities, especially administrative, clerical, and pedagogic. The universality of Latin as the language of instruction allowed the exchange of new ideas to spread rapidly, and Germans who had studied in Italy in the fifteenth century succeeded in bringing humanism north of the Alps.

BIBLIOGRAPHY

Cobban, Alan B. *The Medieval Universities: Their Development and Organization.* London: Methuen, 1975.

Pedersen, Olaf. *The First Universities: Studium generale and the Origins of University Education in Europe.* Cambridge, England: Cambridge University Press, 1997.

Rashdall, Hastings. *The Universities of Europe in the Middle Ages,* vol. 2. Oxford, England: Clarendon Press, 1936.

de Ridder-Symoens, Hilde, ed. *Universities in the Middle Ages.* Cambridge, England: Cambridge University Press, 1992.

Rüegg, Walter, ed. *Geschichte der Universität in Europa,* vol. 1. Munich: Beck, 1993.

William Whobrey

SEE ALSO

Charles IV; Cologne, History; Education; Erfurt; Heidelberg; Latin Language; Vienna

Utrecht

A convenient start for the history of this ecclesiastical principality (also known as Het Sticht) is the arrival of the Anglo-Saxon missionary Willibrord in 690. Shortly before, the Frankish Mayor of the Palace Pippin II had captured the part of Friesland (Frisia) in which lay the small Roman *castellum* of Utrecht. The most important settlement in these lands was the *emporium* of Dorestat. Nevertheless, Willibrord chose Utrecht as the place for his *cathedra.* He refounded there a church that had temporarily existed in the reign of Dagobert (d. 638) and maybe also founded a second church, although this is debated. Willibrord, whose interests included the region around Antwerp and the monastery of Echternach, closely cooperated with the Franks, who tried to get a hold in Friesland. After Frisian defeats in 719 and 733–734 the political situation stabilized. The gift of the *castella* in Utrecht and nearby Vechten with their dependent properties to the Utrecht clergy by Charles Martel in

723 marked the beginning of the growth of the temporal domain of the Utrecht church, further stimulated by the grant of immunity circa 753.

Missionary activities to the north and the east dominated the rest of the eighth century. But problems arose over the status of the Utrecht church. Willibrord's rank of archbishop was personal to him; after his death in 739 the bishop of Cologne claimed control on the grounds that the church of Dagobert had been given to Cologne. Boniface, who had been assistant to Willibrord in 719–722, defended the Utrecht case. In old age he had retired to Utrecht to help the mission again. By his violent death by sword at the hands of the Frisians in 754 he became Utrecht's most famous martyr. Between circa 775–811 the relations with Cologne were sorted out: the authority of the bishop of Cologne was recognized; before 811 he became the metropolitan for Utrecht. From circa 775 onward, Utrecht was definitively the see of a bishop. After some bishops, who were related to the Carolingian family, the majority of the bishops between 806 and 975 probably belonged to the same noble family, which had its roots in the *rivierengebied,* roughly the area in the delta of rivers between Amsterdam, Nijmegen and 's-Hertogenbosch. We have here another example of the well-known practice of episcopal dynasties.

Serious trouble arose in the ninth century with the attacks of the Vikings, who plundered Utrecht and Dorestat several times. As a result the Utrecht bishops were exiled (857–ca. 920/929). They took refuge on royal or episcopal domains, first in Odiliënberg, later in Deventer, which together with Tiel had taken over the commercial role of Dorestat. It was bishop Balderik (917–975) who was finally able to return to Utrecht (between 920–929). During his long episcopate he reorganized the Utrecht bishopric. He did compile a list of goods of the Utrecht church in that region, which was formerly occupied by the Vikings, and he probably rebuilt or founded churches in places that were associated with other missionaries such as Elst, Oldenzaal, and Deventer. These places became the focal point of episcopal power, although some of them were later lost or traded off.

In 925 Balderik with the nobility of Lotharingia transferred his allegiance to the kingdom of the East Franks. Although the scholar Rolf Grosse (1987) has suggested that the bishops up until 1010 probably did not approve of the Ottonian system because they disagreed with the idea of a cleric using military force, nevertheless Utrecht was a key point for the German emperors in their attempt to control the unruly nobility of Lotharingia. Brune of Cologne, the brother of Otto the Great, and Henry V were educated at Utrecht; the duke of Bavaria was kept in custody there for the German ruler (978–983); a *vita* (life) of Henry II was written by Bishop Adelbold (r. 1010–1026). The Bishops Willem, Koenraad, and Burchard (1054–1112) were staunch supporters of Henry IV and Henry V in the Investiture Controversy; the hearts of the Emperors Conrad II and Henry V were buried in Utrecht Cathedral. Gifts from German kings and emperors, who had their own palace in Utrecht, started early and greatly enriched the bishops; they laid the foundations for their temporal lordship. In the tenth century the bishops received mainly gifts of lands (sometimes confiscated) and regalia like the mint in Utrecht (936), the toll in Muiden (975), toll and mint in Zaltbommel (999), forestry rights in Drenthe (944), and domains in the *rivierengebied* (944, 949) and Salland (960). In the eleventh century gift continued like toll, mint, and other rights in Deventer and Hamaland (1046) and comital rights in Drenthe (1024) or in (parts of) Teisterbant (1026), Groningen (1040), Holland (1064), and Frisia and Salland (1077, 1086, 1089). Some of these gifts had to be confirmed or were in the end ineffective because the former owners who had forfeited their rights could not be expelled. A natural opponent of the Utrecht bishops was a Westfrisian comital family (later counts of Holland), which had lost (944 and 1064) part of their rights to the bishop owing to rebelling against imperial authority. Westfrisian victories in 1018 and 1076 marked nevertheless the growing power of these counts. Yet the bishop of Utrecht was at that time still the strongest and richest ruler in these northern regions.

Bishop Bernold (1026–1054) enhanced this status by a grandiose building scheme. He rebuilt the churches in Deventer and Emmerich. Stimulated and funded by Emperor Henry III, he transferred an abbey to Utrecht and founded there two more collegiate churches that were symbolically laid out as a cross centered on the cathedral, although some authors are skeptical about this. This scheme was crowned by the foundation of a fifth church circa 1085. Bernold also restructured his bishopric, e.g., by separating the properties of the Utrecht church and giving old and new chapters more control over it. Archdeacons received a part of the episcopal jurisdiction in their districts. Bernold and his successors in the eleventh century ruled lands that would form the nucleus for the later principality, based on their right of immunity and the comital rights they had derived from the emperors and also based on their position of being the sole bishop in these regions. The core was of course Utrecht, which had developed into a busy commercial center. To the far north lay the *vill* of Groningen and rural Drenthe; in between lay Salland, Twente, and Vollenhove (nowadays the province of Overijssel), with Deventer as preeminent center. Important for the future was the fact that the region around Utrecht (the later Nedersticht) was being separated by lands held by the count of Gelre from the other episcopal regions (the Oversticht). Other properties and rights in the west (Holland), south (Odiliënberg), and east (e.g., Emmerich) were lost or traded off in this or the following centuries.

Momentous for the future was the *Grote Ontginning* (great drainage) operation that continued for centuries. Till then Holland and Utrecht were very sparsely populated, because most of the country consisted of vast boggy marshes. From the end of the tenth century, Holland out of the west and the bishop from the east started to clear these wastelands by draining them. Planning and articulation seems to have been greatest on the part of the bishop. The curiously indented frontier with Holland was partly defined by this development. Part of the planning existed in granting the right to organize these clearances to *ministeriales* and clerics. At first this system enlarged the resources of the bishops, but in the twelfth and later centuries successful *ministeriales* would sharply remind them of their growing power. This situation was aggravated by the fact that the Utrecht bishops in the eleventh and twelfth centuries liberally distributed wealth, lands, and rights to their chapters, which became rich institutions. An important reason for the later weakness of the bishops lies in the fact that they were relatively poor, mainly because they had given away too much.

The Concordat of Worms (1122) brought important changes. From that date the bishop lost his backing by the emperor, especially since the attention of the emperor was directed more and more to the south; so the bishop had to stand on his own. After 1122 the counts of Holland and Gelre were driving forces behind the election of every new bishop. Protégés or (financially) weak bishops would the more easily succumb to the pressure of the counts who tried to extend their hold over fiefs, rights of jurisdiction, and *ministeriales* of the bishop. These last ones tried to get more independent by claiming that their lands and offices were allods (lands without obligations), or by becoming the vassals of the neighboring counts. In 1159–1160 they openly rebelled against the bishop. In the thirteenth century this led to the existence of very powerful lords at the borders of the Nedersticht like the

Amstels, Woerdens, Abcoudes, and the *burggraven* of Montfoort. The bishops, in their struggle with the *ministeriales,* had to ask assistance and borrow money from the neighboring counts. At the end of the thirteenth century this resulted in the loss of the lands of Amstel and Woerden to Holland.

Similar problems existed in the Oversticht and Drenthe. Bishop Harthert (r. 1139–1150) made his brothers hereditary prefect in Groningen, and castellan and sheriff in Coevorden and Drenthe. In the beginning of the thirteenth century the prefect of Groningen quarreled with its inhabitants, who were being backed by the castellan of Coevorden in his attempt to get a dominant position in the north. Bishop Otto came with an army to the assistance of his prefect but was slain in 1227. From then on the bishop had to use considerable effort to be recognized in Drenthe. Not until 1395 did he succeed in getting control over Coevorden. From the thirteenth century Groningen was more or less an independent city that succeeded in controlling large tracts of the surrounding countryside. Groningen recognized the bishop merely nominally as overlord of the city and region, and then mostly only in times of crisis, such as in 1469, when the Burgundians tried to annex Groningen.

Utrecht's municipal rights were confirmed as early as 1122. In the eleventh and twelfth centuries it was an important commercial center. Because of the increased silt deposits in its riverways and the growing role of the towns of Holland, Utrecht lost its position in international trade. Nevertheless, it retained a crucial function in regional trade and commerce, its wealth being augmented by the many churches and monasteries within its walls. Till the sixteenth century Utrecht remained the biggest city in the northern Netherlands, with a corresponding influence in politics. In the Oversticht the three towns of Deventer, Kampen, and Zwolle knew rapid growth during the fourteenth and fifteenth centuries. River trade and the transferring of goods from Holland and the Rhineland to northern Germany made them prosperous. What was missing in all these towns was an important industry. Because of their richness, these three towns in the Oversticht became the most influential factors in the politics of this region.

At the end of the thirteenth century and between circa 1320 and 1345, the authority of the Utrecht bishop was at its lowest ebb. He was more or less broke; his lands had become a protectorate of the counts of Holland and Gelre, who in fact twice concluded a secret treaty (1331 and 1420) to divide the temporal goods of the bishopric.

But after circa 1345 the bishop recovered his position. The neighboring counties of Holland and Gelre were weakened by internal strife. Furthermore the bishop got more and more support from the important five Utrecht chapters and from his towns. They had become sufficiently independent to realize the disadvantages of a weak bishop. Central concern for towns and clergy was the damage done by unruly (robber) knights. Nedersticht and Overstricht were lands apart, but in each the towns donated money to the bishop or supported him with troops. In return they got control over castles or functionaries (e.g., 1352 and 1375). In the fourteenth century cooperation among the chapters, Utrecht, and the gentry institutionalized into the Estates of the Nedersticht. In 1375 the bishop was compelled to give them the *Landbrief* in which the rights of the Nedersticht were written down. From circa 1350 bishop and Estates ruled the Nedersticht together. The Overstricht knew a growing tendency to combine the different regions. More and more the three towns consulted with the gentry of those regions, thus forming the Estates of the Overstricht. The rural-oriented and isolated Drenthe, however, kept aloof.

Internal strife and factions in Utrecht caused many problems, the more so because the bishop was obliged to take sides to control his most powerful city, and because both sides combined with factions in Holland and Gelre. Foreign troubles therefore also undermined the stability of the Nedersticht. Wars with Holland (e.g., 1345–1346, 1355–1356, 1373–1375, 1419–1421) and Gelre (1419–1421) were closely connected with these factions and the attempts of the bishops to control their lands. The same can be said of the episcopal elections of 1423 and 1455; these resulted in the "Utrecht schism" (1423–1449) and in a campaign by the count of Holland, Philip of Burgundy, to establish his son as a bishop (1456). From 1455 till 1524 all Utrecht bishops were virtually nominees of the Burgundians/Habsburgs. Consequently rivalry between factions coincided more and more with a general attempt in the Netherlands to ward off the growing Burgundian/Habsburg power. This was especially the case from 1492, when Burgundy and Gelre often warred openly, with the Sticht in between. The results were several campaigns and continuous pressure from Gelre in the Overstricht and Groningen, and civil wars in the Nedersticht (1481–1483 and 1525–1527). In 1527 the bishop asked the assistance of Emperor Charles V to help him win back the Overstricht and Utrecht, which were more or less occupied by Gelre. For his help the bishop translated his authority over the Sticht to the emperor in 1528.

BIBLIOGRAPHY

Alberts, W. J., and Stefan Weinfurter. "Traiectum (Utrecht)," in *Series episcoporum ecclesiae catholicae occidentalis . . .*, pt. 5, l. Stuttgart: Hiersemann, 1982, pp. 167–205.

Algemene Geschiedenis der Nederlanden, vols. 1–4. Haarlem: Fibula-Van Dishoeck, 1979–1982.

Angenendt, Arnold. "Willibrord im Dienste der Karolinger." *Annalen des historischen Vereins für den Niederrhein* 175 (1973): 63–111.

Buitelaar, A. L. P. *De Stichtse ministerialiteit en de ontginningen in de Utrechtse Vechtstreek.* Hilversum: Verloren, 1993.

Dekker, Cornelis, et al. *Geschiedenis van de provincie Utrecht* [in preparation].

Dekker, C. *Het Kromme Rijngebied in de middeleeuwen. Een institutioneel-geografische studie.* Zutphen: Walburg Pers, 1983.

Fritze, W. H. "Zur Entstehungsgeschichte des Bistums Utrecht. Franken und Friesen 690—734." *Rheinische Vierteljahrsblätter* 35 (1973): 107–151.

Grosse, Rolf. *Das Bistum Utrecht und seine Bischöfe im 10. und frühen 11. Jahrhundert.* Cologne: Böhlau, 1987.

Heringa, J. *Geschiedenis van Drenthe.* Meppel: Boom, 1985.

Hoekstra, T. J. "The Early Topography of the City of Utrecht and Its Cross of Churches." *Journal of the British Archaeological Association* 141 (1988): 1–34.

Immink, P. W. A. *De wording van staat en souvereiniteit in de middeleeuwen.* Groningen: Rijksuniversiteit Groningen, 1942.

Janssen, Hans L. "The Castles of the Bishop of Utrecht and Their Function in the Political and administrative development of the bishopric." *Château Gaillard. Études de castellogie médiévale* 8 (1977): 135–157.

Koch, A. C. F. "Die Anfänge der Stadt Deventer." *Westfälische Zeitschrift* 10 (1957): 163–173.

Leupen, Piet H. D. "Sint Salvator en Sint Maarten, Willibrord en Bonifatius," in Petty Bange and Anton G. Weiler, eds. *Willibrord, zijn wereld en zijn werk.* Nijmegen: Centrum voor Middeleeuwse Studies, 1990, pp. 317–327.

Levison, Wilhelm. "St. Willibrord and His Place in History." *Aus rheinischer und frankischer Frühzeit.* Düsseldorf: Schwann, 1948, pp. 314–329.

Marshall, Sherrin. *The Dutch Gentry: 1500–1650. Family, Faith, and Fortune.* New York: Greenwood, 1987 [on Utrecht families].

Moore, S. F. C. "The Cathedral Chapter of St. Maarten at Utrecht before the revolt." Ph.d. diss., University of Southampton, 1988.

Petri, F. "Die Stellung der Südersee- und Ijsselstädte im Flandrisch-Hansischen Raum." *Hansische Geschichtsblätter* 79 (1961): 34–57.

Post, Regnerus R. *Geschiedenis der Urrechtsche bisschopsverkiezingen tot 1535.* Utrecht: Instituut voor middeleeuwse geschiedenis, 1933.

Slicher van Bath, B. H., ed. *Geschiedenis van Overijssel.* Deventer: Kluwer, 1970.

Sneller, Zeger Willem. *Deventer, die Stadt der Jahmärkte.* Weimar: Böhlau, 1936.

Struick, J. E. A. L. *Utrecht door de eeuwen heen.* Utrecht: Spectrum, 1968.

Weiler, Anton G. *Willibrords missie. Christendom en culluur in de zevende en achtste eeuw.* Hilversum: Gooi en Sticht, 1989.

van den Hoven van Genderen, Bram. *Het kapittelgeneraal en de Staten van het Nedersticht in de 15e eeuw.* Zutphen: De Walburg Pers, 1987.

van Winter, Johanna Maria. "Verfassung und Verwaltung im Spätmittelalterlichen Utrecht," in *Verwaltung und Politik in Städten Mitteleuropas,* ed. Walter Ehbrecht. Cologne: Böhlau, 1994, pp. 47–54.

Bram van den Hoven van Genderen

SEE ALSO
Friesland; Holland

V

Van Meckenem, Israhel (ca. 1445–1503)

A highly productive engraver and a goldsmith, van Meckenem worked primarily in Bocholt near the Dutch border. He was taught by his father, who shared the same name but is known also as the Master of the Berlin Passion. Both father and son used the same housemark for their engravings, and the son's early style is similar to that of his father.

Although van Meckenem was a highly creative artist in his own right, he has been maligned for being a prolific copyist of other printmaker's works. Among the artists whose works he copied are Schongauer, the Housebook Master, and Albrecht Dürer. Van Meckenem produced a large body of works, but relatively few—less than one-fourth—are his own design. It is clear from his choice of subject matter as well as his artistic manipulation of certain designs that van Meckenem was a savvy businessman as well as an artist.

Around 1466, van Meckenem visited Constance to study under the Master E. S. When his master died sometime in 1468, van Meckenem assumed many of his plates and reprinted them. By the 1470s, van Meckenem had moved back to Bocholt, where he continued as a printmaker and received several commissions to create silver objects for the city council. Later in his career, van Meckenem's engravings seem to have been influenced by paintings because of their sense of volume, texture, and richness of detail. His style appears to have been affected by Netherlandish art as well as his professional relationship with Hans Holbein the Elder.

BIBLIOGRAPHY

Geisberg, Max. *Verzeichnis der Kupferstiche Israhels van Meckenem †1503.* Strasbourg: J. H. E. Heitz, 1905.

———. "Israhel van Meckenem." *Print Collector's Quarterly* 17 (1930): 212–237.

Shestack, Alan. *Fifteenth-Century Engravings of Northern Europe from the National Gallery of Art.* Washington, D.C.: National Gallery of Art, 1967–1968, pp. 152–154.

Warburg, Anni. *Israhel van Meckenem: Sein Leben, sein Werk und seine Bedeutung für die Kunst des ausgehenden 15. Jahrhundert.* Ph.d. diss., University of Bonn, 1929. Bonn: Schröder, 1930.

Melanie Gesink Cornelisse

SEE ALSO

Constance; E. S., Master; Holbein, Hans the Elder; Housebook, Master of the; Gothic Art and Architecture; Metalwork; Printmaking; Schongauer, Martin

Väterbuch

This rhymed legendary *Väterbuch* (*Book of the Fathers,* ca. 1285–1300) was the first German translation and adaptation of the Latin *Vitas patrum* (*Book of the Fathers*). However, at the end of this collection, five legends from the *Legenda aurea* (*Golden Legendary*) were added by the same poet who wrote the *Passional* (*Passion Stories*) within the Teutonic Order *(Deutschorden).* None of the legends in the *Väterbuch,* comprising 41,542 verses, are repeated in the Passional.

In the *Väterbuch,* the anonymous poet and priest addresses the community of lay brothers to live with humility and devote their lives to conquering heathens and converting them. Against the worldly courtly life, the model of the paters of late Antiquity was widely accepted within German mysticism. Numerous prose renditions followed in the fourteenth and fifteenth centuries in all German, Swiss, Austrian, and Dutch regions, which are based on the *Vitas patrum*. The role that the *Väterbuch* might have played for the prose translations has not quite been established yet.

To date, thirty manuscripts of the *Väterbuch* are reported that were quickly distributed through the Teutonic Order from the fourteenth century, and only two from the fifteenth, including complete texts, selections, and fragments. For *Maria Aegyptiaca (Mary of Egypt)*, the poet used the poetic Latin version of Hildebert von Lavardin as a source. For *Alexius*, it has been possible to discern the influence of Konrad von Würzburg's *Alexius* in addition to the *Legenda aurea* and so-called Latin Version B, and to establish that *Alexius* of the *Väterbuch* was a partial source for the version in other collections of legends, specifically the *Heiligenleben (Saints' Lives)* of Herbort von Fritzlar, and in versions known as *Alexius* "B," and *Alexius* "F."

BIBLIOGRAPHY

Borchardt, Dorothea, and Konrad Kunze. "Väterbuch," in *Die deutsche Literatur des Mittelalters. Verfasserlexikon*, ed. Kurt Ruh et al. Berlin: de Gruyter, 1998f., vol. 10, cols. 164–170.

Jefferis, Sibylle. "Zur Rezeption des *Alexius* Konrads von Würzburg," in *Konrad von Würzburg. Seine Zeit, sein Werk, seine Wirkung (Tagung Würzburg 1987)*, ed. Horst Brunner. *Jahrbuch der Oswald-von-Wolkenstein Gesellschaft* (1988/1989), pp. 195–213.

Kunze, Konrad. *Studien zur Legende der heiligen Maria Aegyptiaca im deutschen Sprachgebiet*. Berlin: Schmidt, 1969, pp. 68–75.

Sibylle Jefferis

SEE ALSO

Deutschorden; Heiligenleben; Herbort von Fritzlar; *Legenda Aurea*, Alsatian; *Passional;* Saints' Lives, Dutch

Verdun

The site of an earlier Gallic fortress on the left bank of the Meuse River, Verodumum (strongly fortified place) grew into a Roman *oppidum* (rural town) and by the fourth century C.E. was a Christian bishop's seat. Located on the Metz-Reims corridor, it enjoyed a favorable location for trade. During the reign of Theodebert I (534–548), Verdun played an important role in the Frankish trade in Slav and Avar slaves captured on the eastern frontier. Gre-gory of Tours tells of the *domus negociatorum* (great bazaar) found in the city in his day and of the rich businessmen who profited from the slave trade. In the days of Charlemagne and as late as the tenth century, merchants of Verdun organized slave caravans bound for both Spain and Italy.

In 843 the three sons of Louis the Pious (d. 840)—Lothar, Louis the German, and Charles the Bald—divided Charlemagne's empire at Verdun. The central portion, including Verdun, fell to Lothar, who also styled himself emperor. In 880, however, the region (now known as Lotharingia, or Lorraine) went to the east Frankish realm; thus, it later belonged to the empire. During the ninth and tenth centuries, the location of Verdun far from the coastal regions provided some security against the depredations of the Vikings.

The economic recovery of western Europe that began in the mid–tenth century affected the region around Verdun as well, and the growing wealth of the city can be seen in the Romanesque cathedral built between 1048 and 1083. The German civil war after 1198 caused the burghers of Verdun to build city walls.

The burghers tried early in the thirteenth century to gain some independence from their bishop, but an imperial diet at Aachen in July 1215 had forbidden them to form a *coniuratio*, to fortify their town, or to tax themselves. A new opportunity arose with the contested election of Rudolf of Thourotte as bishop in 1224. At an audience with King Henry VII early in 1225, representatives of the newly formed commune secured privileges that usurped the rights of their prelate; Archbishop Dietrich II of Trier represented the bishop before the king, demanding that the charter of privileges be retracted. Meanwhile the burghers successfully withstood a siege by their bishop.

The German princes supported the bishop, however, and in April 1227 King Henry was forced to write the burghers, revoking the privileges. At great risk to himself, Archbishop Dietrich went to Verdun to retrieve the document, an act that required two attempts. The tension between the king and the German princes regarding the towns and cities of Germany ultimately resulted in the *Statutum in favorem principum*, which both Henry and his father, Frederick II, recognized.

Being a French-speaking diocese, Verdun became the target of Phillip II Augustus, who sought to secure the election of French bishops to the see. Phillip III continued this aggressive policy, directing French expansion toward the rivers Meuse and Rhone. After 1273, the French were near Verdun, encroaching on German land. By

1297 the French controlled Metz. The bishoprics of Liège, Verdun, and Lyon were the key to the frontier. Owing to his conflict with Phillip IV, Pope Boniface VIII placed anti-French bishops at Verdun, but eventually the French policy prevailed: Louis X was the first French monarch to accord royal protection to the city of Verdun.

BIBLIOGRAPHY

Clouet, L'Abbé. *Histoire de Verdun et du pays verdunois.* Verdun: Impr. de Ch. Laurent, 1867; rpt. Marseille: Laffitte Reprints, 1977.

Hirschmann, Frank G. *Verdun im hohen Mittelalter.* Trierer Historische Forschungen 27. Trier: Verlag Trierer Historische Forschungen, 1996.

Girardot, Alain, ed. *Histoire de Verdun.* Toulouse: Privat, 1982.

Paul B. Pixton

SEE ALSO

Carolingians; Charlemagne; Frederick II; Lothar I; Louis the Pious; Meuse River; Slavery

Versification

Old High German (OHG) verse is structured basically according to one of two principles: *Stabreimvers* (strong-stress alliterative verse) and *Endreimvers* (verse in which the concluding syllable or syllables rhyme, or at least assonate). The oldest form, which is shared in general with Old Saxon (OS), Anglo-Saxon (AS), and Old Norse (ON), is strong-stress alliterative verse, all of which has a long line with a pronounced break in the middle (a caesura). Various systems have been posited to describe this verse, none of which are totally adequate. The commonly accepted definition of OHG and OS alliterative verse, for instance, is so general that it fails to predict which configurations do not occur. More stringent descriptions appropriate for selected texts of AS and ON verse, however, cannot be applied meaningfully to other AS and ON and especially to OHG and OS texts.

Stabreimvers has two strong stresses in each half line. A strong stress can be on either a linguistically long syllable (one containing a long vowel (f*ō*hem) or a diphthong (m*uo*tin) or a short vowel followed by two or more consonants (ri*h*tun) or on a short one plus a single consonant followed by an unstressed one (gar*u*tun). Strong stresses may fall on (most commonly) nouns, full verbs (on the stem syllable), adverbs, or adjectives. One or two of the strong-stressed syllables in the first half line or a-verse

(Anvers) alliterates with the first of the two strong-stressed syllables in the second half line or b-verse *(Abvers).* The rhyme patterns a x / a x and a a / a x are the most common, but x a / a x also is possible (a = strong-stressed syllable with alliteration; x = strong-stressed syllable without—unstressed syllables are not considered here). Since all strong-stressed vowels in the Germanic languages begin with a glottal stop, that is apparently what actually alliterates. At any rate, all vowels count as one alliterative sound, and it is rare for the same vowel to be repeated. However st-, sp-, sc-, and su- (sw-) do not alliterate interchangeably or with s-.

Here is an example from the *Hildebrandslied,* verses 53–57 (alliteration underlined; strong stresses accented):

nu scal mih suásat chínd   suértu háuwen,
bréton mit sinu bílliu,   eddo ih imo ti bánin wérdan.
doh maht du nu áodlíhho,   ibu dir din éllen táoc,
in sus héremo mán   hrústi giwínnan,
ráuba biráhanen,   ibu du dar enic réht hábes.

In the *Hildebrandslied,* most long lines correspond to syntactic units, creating what one terms *Zeilenstil.* Occasionally the syntactic unit begins with the b-verse (and ends with a later a-verse), *Hakenstil* (hook style), which is more common in the Heliand.

her was héroro mán,
férahes frótoro;   her frágen gistúont
fóhem uuórtum,   hwer sin fáter wári
fíreo in fólche —

Otfrid's OHG *Evangelienbuch* is the first extant longer work of European literature to use end rhyme as a consistent structural principle. Otfrid apparently used the Latin Ambrosian (fourth-century) hymn as his model, which has a long line with eight plus eight syllables often, though not always, ornamented with end rhyme. Many of these lines can be read as alternating unstressed and stressed syllables, one of three possibilities for Medieval Latin verse (some ML verse replicates, more or less precisely, the meters of Antiquity; some is accentual; much controls primarily the number of syllables in a line, as does Romance verse). Otfrid may have borrowed this feature as he made the use of rhyme structural. But it is also possible that accentual ML verse reflects a tendency of indigenous vernacular poetry. Otfrid may have thought he was replicating classical meter—he speaks of "feet"—but another feature of his verse is arguably more significant. He praises its "times." Perhaps he realized he had created isochronic verse, verse in which the "feet" might not be perfectly equal but in which the stresses follow at regular intervals. (Book I, Chapter 1, lines 19–26. The accents are in the original and apparently indicate primary stresses.)

> Ist iz prósun slihti   thaz drénkit thih in ríhti
>   odo métres klíni: theist góuma filu réini.
> Sie dúent iz filu súazi,   joh mézent sie thie fúazi,
>   thie léngi joh thie kúrti,   theiz gilústlichaz wúrti.
> Éigun sie iz, bithénkit,   thaz síllaba in ni wénkit,
>   sies álleswio ni rúachent,   ni so thie fúazi suachent;
> Joch állo thio zîti   so záltun sie bi nóti;
>   iz mízit ana bága   al io súlih waga.

If it is simple prose, that quenches your thirst immediately; if, however, there are exquisite meters, that lies cleanly on the palate. They do this with much sweetness; they measure the feet, the longs and the shorts, so that it provides pleasure. They have paid attention that no syllable is missing; they are intent on how they seek the feet. In addition they counted the times carefully; such a scale weighs without deviation.

Some scholars read *Stabreimvers* isochronically, often including weaker stresses as well to reach four beats per half line. That reading is problematic, but if it were accepted it might explain why not just German versifiers but also English and Scandinavian ones, after they had abandoned strong-stress alliterative verse, tended to adopt similar substitutes, for the most part independently. Clearly, in any case, the presence of a regular beat is the primary organizing principle of German verse from Otfrid to the Renaissance literary scholar Opitz. When Opitz in 1624 recommended structuring German verse by iambs (x x́) and trochees (x́ x), substituting (under the influence of Dutch models) stress and its lack for the long and short syllables of classical verse—soon afterward, dactyls (x́ x x) were declared acceptable as well—he shaped the way German poets conceived of their verse and readers understood it from then on. Enough remained of the isochronic tradition, however, sustained perhaps by folk songs, that it shaped much of the irregular verse that became fashionable from the late eighteenth century on.

The sample above of Otfrid's verse may be read as twice three beats, with each rhyme having one stress. But when we look at other passages, twice four beats seems more likely, with two stresses on each disyllabic rhyme word. A fair number of verses (both a and b ones) end with a single stressed syllable; these appear to have four beats, though some are ambiguous (I, 1, 65–66 and 69–70).

> Sie búent mit gizíugon — ioh uuarun ío thes giuuón —
>   in gúatemo lánte: bi thíu sint sie únscante. . . .
> Zi núzze grébit man ouh thár   ér inti kúphar,
>   ioh bi thía meina   ísina steina,

The first and the third line rhyme only the final syllable. The second, third, and fourth are irregular—the "feet" are defective—but the lines work perfectly well as isochronic verse. (In the following schema, x denotes a syllable of indeterminate length, long or short, and a linguistically long one. The vertical lines divide the beats [lifts, *Hebungen*] and unaccented syllables [dips, *Senkungen*] into measures, which need not have metronomic precision.)

```
x | x́   x | x́   x | ⸓   | x̀       x | x́   x | x́   x | x́   x | x́
x | ⸓   | x̀   x | ⸓   | x̀       x | x́  x x | ⸓   | ⸓   | x̀
x | x́   x | x́   x | x́   x | x́       | ⸓   | x̀   x | ⸓   | x̀
| x́   x | x́   x | ⸓   | x̀       | ⸓   | x̀   x | ⸓   | x̀
```

This general pattern of verse prevails in the Middle High German (MHG) and Early New High German periods, though with time internally rhymed *(binnengereimte)* half lines became regarded as couplets.

A passage from the *Rolandslied (Song of Roland)* can provide an example of MHG couplets as they existed in the period between Otfrid and the *Blütezeit* (or high period, 1185–1230). (ll. 6681–88. In the schema, u stands for a linguistically short syllable where length may be metrically significant.)

> Rolant was do aine. | x́   x | x́   x | ⸓ | x̀
> do wanten di haiden   x | x́   x | x́   x | ⸓ | x̀
> si scolten in erslahen: x | x́   x | x́   x | ú u
> an dem lîbe nemacht im do niemen geschaden.
>   x x | x́   u u | x́   x x | x́   x x | ú
> Rolant sach in allenthalben sin, | x́   x | x́   x | x́   x | x́ | x́
> wi Olivir unt Turpin   x | x́   x | x́   x | ⸓ | x̀
> unt ander sine gesellen   x | x́   x | x́   u u | ⸓
> in plûte lagen bewollen.   x | x́   x | x́   x x | ⸓

The basic verse line has four beats, but three-beat and five-beat (called, respectively, hypometric and hypermetric) lines do occur, and the reading given above of the fifth line as having six beats is not absurd. Given the freedom with which a measure can be filled *(Füllungsfreiheit)*, it may make no sense to distinguish between three-syllable measures in which the first two or last two are short (| x́   u u | or | ú   u x |) and others where at least the second of the syllables is long (| x́   x x |). However, in the verse (both of narrative couplets and of song) of the *Blütezeit,* the former patterns are common and the latter is fairly rare. (Modern editors have often rewritten the verse to make it even rarer.) The line may begin with the first beat or there may be one or two (rarely more) syllables before the beat (the *Auftakt,* or anacrusis). Note that many of the "rhymes" are really assonances, i.e., the vowels correspond but the consonants do not. This is a typical feature of archaic MHG verse. Inexact correspondences in vowel quality, which sporadically occur even in works of the *Blütezeit,* probably reflect dialect variation. In the example "gesellen : bewollen," however, it may be that only the last syllable was intended to rhyme (an identical rhyme of "-len").

In general, the verse of the *Blütezeit* is more regular; the model of Romance octosyllabic couplets and songs with syllabic verses with pure rhymes seems to have led to a modification of German verse. Three-beat lines are rare in narrative verse, and five-beat ones are virtually nonexistent. Three-syllable measures are fairly rare except for the special cases where the first or last two of the syllables are short. Narrative verse has three cadences (cadence is the rhythmic treatment of the end of a line or half line): masculine (| x́), split masculine (| ú u), and double-stressed (| ´ | x̀). Some modern readers find the last cadence implausible, and they read it as a feminine one (| x́   x). If one chooses to do so, one must then explain why (with few exceptions) all verses in narrative couplets with "feminine" cadence have three beats, while those with the two varieties of masculine cadence have four. (Some Germanists eschew the terms *masculine* and *feminine,* but the substitutes they use create more problems than they solve; the traditional terms derive from French, where the masculine adjective, e.g., *grand,* typically has one syllable, while the feminine adjective, e.g., *grande,* has two.) It is best to speak of cadence rather than rhyme, since not all verse endings are rhymed. Regularity does not necessarily mean rigidity. MHG narrative verse often has a richness of rhythmic variation absent from modern verse in rhyme couplets. (That is one reason why modern verse translations of MHG works can seem so stiff.) In the ten lines of the following passage from *Der arme Heinrich* by Hartmann von Aue (ll. 16–25), we find eight different expressions of the basic pattern.

nu beginnet er iu diuten	x x | x́ x | x́ x | ´ | x̀
ein rede, die er geschriben vant.	x | ú u x | x́ x | x́ x | x́
dar umbe hât er sich genant,	x | x́ x | x́ x | x́ x | x́
daz er sîner arbeit,	| x́ x | x́ x | ´ | x̀
die er dar an hât geleit,	| x́ x | x́ x | x́ x | x́
iht âne lôn belîbe,	x | x́ x | x́ x | ´ | x̀
und swer nâch sînem lîbe	x | x́ x | x́ x | ´ | x̀
sî hœre sagen oder lese,	x | x́ x | x́ x | x́ x | ú
daz er im bittende wese,	x | x́ x | ´ | x̀ x | ú u
der sêle heiles hin ze gote.	x | x́ x | x́ x | x́ x | ú u

The verse of the *Nibelungenlied* (as of most other heroic epics and many archaic songs) utilizes a long line. In general, the caesura does not rhyme; the long lines typically rhyme in pairs and are collected in strophes. One major difference between Otfrid's verse and the long-line strophes is that the a-verse and b-verse in MHG usually differ in form. In the following pattern for the Nibelungen strophe, m = masculine cadence; k = double-stressed cadence *([schwer]klingend);* a and b indicate the rhymes; x designates the unrhymed caesura (also indicated with a colon); and the numbers give the number of realized beats. (Since the split masculine and the regular masculine cadence may be used interchangeably, a generalized schema need not differentiate; a description of a given set of verses should, in which case gm *[gespalten männlich]* may be used for the former.)

4kx : 3ma 4kx : 3ma 4kx : 3mb 4kx : 4mb

Some read the double-stressed cadence as feminine = w *(weiblich),* but if we accept that such cadences in rhyme couplets are double-stressed, it would make sense to read them the same way here, especially since we can assume that the performance of heroic strophes more closely resembled chant than that of courtly couplets (in chant and song, double-stressed cadences still occur today, as in the children's verse "Backe, backe, Kuchen" | x́   x | x́   x | ´ | x̀). In addition, the same linguistic patter (long, normally stressed syllable followed by two of indeterminate length), when it occurs within a verse line, generally leads to an augmented lift (*beschwerte Hebung*), e.g., 13,4b "nimmer ge-" | ´ | x̀   x. Roughly half of the 4b verses of the *Nibelungenlied* achieve their fourth beat in this way. Others consider the first three b-verses to have an additional beat in the pause (as one sometimes finds today in marching songs), but the prevalence of enjambment (a syntactic period extending over a verse boundary) and *Hakenstil* would seem to speak against this, as do the fairly rare examples of cadence switching *(Kadenztausch),* where a masculine cadence creates the fourth beat in the a-verse or a double-stressed one fills the second and third beats of one of the first three b-verses. In the following example 13,1b is most easily read as 4ka; only the pattern of the other strophes would lead us to posit a disyllabic anacrusis. The demotion (from a stress or lift to an un-stressed syllable or dip) of the 13,2b anacrusis "starc" is a normal treatment of the initial element of an extended se-ries (one that occurs even in modern verse).

> 13 In disen hôhen êren   troumte Kriemhilde,
>   wie si züge einen valken,   starc schœn' und wilde,
>   den ir zwêne arn erkrummen.   daz si daz muoste sehen:
>   ir enkunde in dirre werlde   leider nimmer geschehen.
> 14 Den troum si dô sagete   ir muoter Uoten.
>   sine kundes niht bescheiden   baz der guoten:
>   "der valke den du ziuhest,   daz ist ein edel man.
>   in welle got behüeten,   du muost in schiere vloren hân."

```
x | x́   x | x́   x | -́   | x̀        x x | -́   | -́   | x̀
x x | x́   x | x́   x | -́   | x̀          x | x́   x | -́   | x̀
x x | x́   x | x́   x | -́   | x̀          x | x́   x | x́   x | ú  u
x x | x́   x | x́   x | -́   | x̀          | x́   x | -́   | x̀   x | ú  u
x | -́   | x̀   x | ú  u | x̀          x | x́   x | -́   | x̀
x x | x́   x | x́   x | -́   | x̀          | x́   x | -́   | x̀
x | x́   x | x́   x | -́   | x̀          x | x́   x | x́   x | x́
x | x́   x | x́   x | -́   | x̀          x | x́   x | x́   x | x́   x | x́
```

There are a fair number of trisyllabic double-stressed ca-dences like 14a "sagete" in the *Nibelungenlied,* most of them with the first two or (as here) all three of the sylla-bles short. Many would consider a measure anomalous if it contained only u u, since the symbols -, x, and u for isochronic verse are often explained as equivalent to half, quarter, and eighth notes, and the verse is thought of as performed in two four time. But since it is highly un-likely, even if we assume that the verse had a fairly regular beat, that the "metrical" length of each syllable was pre-cisely measured in performance, it makes better sense to retain - and u to indicate a necessity for linguistically long and short syllables and use x where the syllable may be ei-ther short or long. A word is in order here about the pres-ence or absence of hiatus in MHG verse. The manu-scripts often omit (elide) a final unstressed vowel before a following vowel; modern editors have regularized this practice, sometimes indicating the elision with an apos-trophe (as in "schœn'") or a dot under the vowel to be elided (medieval correctors often used subscribed dots to indicate desired deletions). One point, however, not all

editors (and other scholars) have considered is that hiatus is permissible, even likely, if the following vowel is stressed, since the glottal stop that introduces stressed vowels would have inhibited elision.

Variations of the Nibelungen strophe are used in most heroic epics and for much archaic song. The Kürenberg strophe is virtually identical, though the first two strophes ascribed to Kürenberg have an additional a-verse between the first and second long-line couplets, and there are more irregularities throughout than can be easily explained by a faulty transmission. For the most part, the strophes used by other early singers are somewhat more complicated, often with more lines. Other early song forms are simple strings of rhyme couplets, often concluded by a tercet in which a couplet encloses an orphan *(Waisenterzet).* The Burggraf von Rietenburg may be an early adapter of Occ-itan strophic forms, or his cross rhyme quatrains may be a further development of couplet strings. His "Ich hôrte wî-lent sagen ein maere" (MF 16,25), for example, probably has the following form (A = anacrusis):

> A5ka A4mb A5ka A4mb A4mb A5ka A5ka 3mc
> A4mc A4mc

The masculine rhymes are, in part, assonances (and thus archaic) and the prosody (the way the words fit the meter) is rough; otherwise, the strophic form shows con-siderable sophistication and an economy of rhyme sounds reminiscent of Romance songs. The choice of double-stressed cadences over feminine ones is based on deference to the archaic traits (feminine rhymes seem to be one of the innovations borrowed from Romance and Latin verse). In addition, the anacrusis in lines 2, 4, and 6 (it is lacking in 7) provides an ideal precondition for them. If the following line begins with a beat, the clash of a secondary accent followed by a primary one would be awkward (though not impossible). Sometimes such clashes, which also can occur if a masculine cadence is fol-lowed by a line without anacrusis, mark a structural break in the strophe, a pause, as they may here (against the syn-tax) between lines 7 and 8. In a large number of songs the anacrusis is facultative (sometimes present, sometimes ab-sent, with no discernible pattern). Many scholars would read this strophe (ignoring the presence or absence of anacrusis) as follows:

> 4wa 4mb 4wa 4mb 4mb 4wa 4wa 3mc 4mc 4mc

If one posits that the arguably consistent use of anacrusis deceives and that anacrusis is actually facultative (i.e., has no relevance for the underlying structure), this simpler schema is preferable to the previous, cumbersome one. (Since only one strophe in precisely this form is transmitted, we cannot tell whether, for example, the seventh line lacks anacrusis in some significant way or purely by accident. The differences between the MF text of the strophe, following codex C, and the parallel transmission—from a common exemplar—in the Budapest fragment do not go beyond word choice; the strophic form is identical.) Scarcely anything with respect to medieval German meter is uncontested. Most of the conclusions are based on matching the evidence (which all too often consists of texts reworked by editors to match some posited ideal) to one's preconceptions. Even the conventions about what to call what one is describing and the symbols used to denote them vary from scholar to scholar. Fortunately, if one spends some time examining examples, it is fairly simple to translate from one ad hoc system to another. To uncover preconceptions, one must sometimes read between the lines; not all scholars admit (or realize) that they have them.

Combinations of long lines and couplets also occur, for example, in some of the songs of Dietmar von Eist (for whom we have such a wide range of forms and styles that some scholars suggest several generations of singers created the songs ascribed to him). Dietmar also mixes lengthy lines and short ones. A lengthy line *(lange Zeile)* is one with five or more beats that does not resemble the archaic long line *(Langzeile)* of the heroic epic, with its relatively rigid pattern of a-verses and b-verses. Spervogel utilizes all three—short lines, long lines, and lengthy lines—in one strophic pattern, which he uses for a number of didactic songs *(Sangsprüche),* e.g., "Swer in vremden landen vil der tugenden hât" (MF 20,1). (Note that anacrusis, which is facultative for Spervogel, is not indicated.)

6ma 6ma 4mb 4mb 4mx : 4kc 4mx : 4kc

When minnesingers began to emulate Occitan models, they made a common form almost a universal one. The tripartite *Kanzone* (from an Italianate variant of Occitan *canso,* "song") consists of a unit (two or more lines) followed by a metrically and (presumably) musically identical one, followed by a different unit. The two initial units, termed *Stollen* by the later Meistersinger, form the *Aufgesang.* The third unit concluding the strophe, the *Abgesang,* usually differs in meter and rhyme scheme from and is typically longer than a *Stollen.* Lines may vary

in length from two to eight beats, though four beats are the most common. A strophe might have the form 3 3 4 / 3 3 4 // 3 3 3 4, for example. Rhymes, which tend to be pure, usually link the two *Stollen* (e.g., a b c / a b c). Though the rhymes are occasionally echoed in the *Abgesang,* it more often has new ones (e.g., d d x d—with x signaling a line that does not rhyme, a *Waise,* "orphan"). An orphan that rhymes with the corresponding line in a subsequent strophe is termed a *Korn* (K). In general, German songs, even those directly imitating Romance ones, have more different rhymes. Many strophes have a bridge *(Steg)* between the *Aufgesang* and the *Abgesang* proper, though this bridge is generally regarded by scholars to be part of the *Abgesang* that does not constitute a separate unit. Refrains, which are common in Romance songs, occur exceedingly rarely; when they do, they are signaled in a schema by a capital R or by capitalizing the letter used to designate the rhyme.

Interestingly enough, though the elements that make up a strophe are fairly restricted, few of the thousands of extant love songs share precisely the same form, and many of those that do seem to replicate the form of a given song as a parody or response to it. Scholars who eschew noting the presence or absence of anacrusis or do not attempt to differentiate between double-stressed and feminine cadences find more shared patterns. Since variation in the use of anacrusis and possibly even the type of cadence can occur from one version of the same song to another, marking them may indeed create false distinctions.

Two types of meter occur in the *Kanzone.* One, which is similar to the meter of narrative couplets, is basically alternating (lift plus dip), perhaps with less freedom to add or drop a dip than in narrative verse (in most editions, many irregularities that show up in the manuscripts have been excised). The other, so-called dactylic, is less common and seems to have fallen into disfavor by 1250. Heinrich von Morungen delighted in combining dactyls with alternating lines, so one of his strophes can demonstrate both forms. Its overall schema would need to be accompanied by a note that the fifth (long) line is alternating, while the others are dactylic. (The anacrusis of the sixth line is anomalous; none is present in the other two strophes.)

8ka 7mb / 8ka 7mb // 3mx : 4mb A8ka 7mb

Leitlîche blicke und grôzlîche riuwe
hât mir daz herze und den lîp nâch verlorn.

mîn alte nôt,   die klage ich vür niuwe,
wan daz ich vürhte der schimpfære zorn.
singe aber ich dur die,   diu mich vröuwet hie bevorn,
so velsche dur got nieman mîne triuwe,
wan ich dur sanc bin ze der welte geborn.

| ´ x̀   x | ´ x̀   x | ´ x̀   x | ´ x̀
| ´x̀   x | ´ x x̀   x | ´ x̀   x | ´
| ´ x̀   x | ´ ´ | x́   x x̀   x | ´ x̀
| ´ x̀   x | ´ x̀   x | ´ x̀   x | ´
| x́ u   u u | x́   x | x́ | x́   x | x́   x | x́   x | x́
x | ´ x̀   x | ´ ´ | ´ x̀   x | ´ x̀
| ´ x̀   x | x́   x x̀   x | ´ x̀   x | ´

Many scholars ignore the secondary stresses in MHG dactyls. However, only through them can one explain the common substitution of | x́   x x̀   x | for | ´ x̀   x |. If one reads the verse as strings of | x́   x x |, one cannot explain why the first syllable must be long; if as | ´   x x |, why there is no secondary stress on the second syllable. In addition, one must, when reading the texts as they occur in the manuscripts, either assume very imperfect verses or attempt to rewrite the lines. Even positing the patterns | ´ x̀   x |, | x́   x x̀   x |, and | ´ ´ | does not enable us to scan every apparently dactylic verse transmitted; scribes copying songs long after dactyls had fallen out of fashion may well have corrupted them. But, anomalies are rare. Dactyls represent a musical rhythm, probably one used in dance, that caused the singers to shape their verse in an unusual and artificial manner. All metrical accentuation bends and stylizes the normal patterns of speech, but the dactyls do so most strikingly.

Though scholars of MHG meter commonly treat the lifts and dips of alternating verses as having equal length, the music may have made distinctions not reflected in the language. Most of the music sparsely transmitted with medieval German songs is not mensural, i.e., we cannot discern what values were intended. An exceptional mensural notation, for a song by Neidhart, does suggest triple meters rather than duple ones (of the sort one would assume following the metrical conventions proposed in this sketch). Triple meters are often suggested for Romance songs. They are also described in Medieval Latin treatises, where dactyls appear as the third rhythmic mode: 3 1 2.

Not all songs of the *Blütezeit* and beyond have the form of the *Kanzone*, but it is by far the most common (its hegemony continues through the fifteenth and into the sixteenth century). Another type of song, the *Leich* (lay), differs radically. This through-composed, non-strophic form parallels the Latin sequence. It also has affinities to Romance dance songs such as the *estampie*. As a rule, a *Leich* is longer and more complex than minnesongs or didactic songs. The *Leich* does have units, versicles, comparable to the *Stollen,* which are often doubled, and some *Leichs* seem to double the overall assemblage of versicles.

Neidhart uses the *Kanzone* for his winter songs; for his summer ones, however, he utilizes through-composed strophes that may echo dance songs. Other singers occasionally seem to use a series (three or, more commonly, four) versicles from a *Leich*. For the most part, the strophes of didactic songs tend to be longer and more complex than those of minnesongs, though the brooding contemplations of Reinmar der Alte, for example, often exhibit both the form and the tone of the former. Lengthy lines, which lack, almost by definition, a consistent caesura can be broken by internal rhymes either sporadically or at fixed spots within the line. These internal rhymes, which may (initially, in what is termed a *Pausenreim*) fall on the offbeat, do not seem to signal that the line is to be broken into small units. In those cases where we have music (such as for songs by the fourteenth-century Mönch von Salzburg or the fifteenth-century Oswald von Wolkenstein), the melodic line disregards internal rhymes. The complexity of metrical forms for strophic songs may not correlate well to the simplicity or complexity of the music, though so little music is preserved for most twelfth-century and even thirteenth-century songs that there can be no certainty in the matter. The archaic long-line strophe seems to have been sung more simply than the *Kanzone,* and the *Leichs,* especially those with religious themes, were the most complex.

BIBLIOGRAPHY

Beyschlag, Siegfried. *Altdeutsche Metrik in Grundzügen,* 6th ed. Nuremberg: Carl, 1969.

Hoffmann, Werner. *Altdeutsche Metrik.* Stuttgart: Metzler, 1967.

Paul, Otto, and Ingeborg Glier. *Deutsche Metrik,* 9th ed. Munich: Hueber, 1974.

Tervooren, Helmut. *Minimalmetrik zur Arbeit mit mittelhochdeutschen Texten.* Göppingen: Kümmerle, 1979.

Touber, A. H. *Deutsche Strophenformen des Mittelalters.* Stuttgart: Metzler, 1975.

von See, Klaus. *Germanische Verskunst.* Stuttgart: Metzler, 1967.

Hubert Heinen

SEE ALSO
Heinrich von Morungen; *Hildebrandslied;* Meistersinger; *Minnesang;* Neidhart; *Nibelungenlied;* Otfrid; Oswald von Wolkenstein; Reinmar der Alte

Vienna

The medieval (and modern) capital of Austria is situated south of the Danube in the naturally well-protected area of the "Bay of Vienna" formed by the foothills of the Viennese forest and opening eastward to the Pannonian plains. A Roman military camp, Vindobona, intended as part of the protection of the important city of Carnuntum on the Danube, represents the urban nucleus of medieval Vienna; it dated from the first century C.E. and was subsequently enlarged in the third century. With its square form it is sill recognizable in the modern plan of the city, while a civic settlement grew up to the east. Not much is known about the intermediate time period after the withdrawal of the Roman forces in 433, although a continuity of settlement can be assumed. The early parish churches St. Peter and St. Ruprecht, which were constructed at the south and north boundaries, respectively, point through their patron saints to the archbishopric of Salzburg as the missionary center for early medieval Vienna. In 881 the place, known under the name Wenia, is mentioned in connection with the Hungarian expansion, which dominated Vienna through the tenth century, until, in 976, Emperor Otto I granted Austria as a margravia to the new dynasty of the Babenberger. After having suffered a major defeat against the Hungarians in 1030 at Vienna, Emperor Henry III held an imperial diet here in 1042. In 1137 Vienna is already called a *civitas,* and its parish system became firmly established with a new parish church built outside the southeast corner within a developing suburb. The first Austrian duke, Henry II Jasomirgott, erected his residence in the southwest corner of the former Roman camp (Am Hofe), which, with its wall system, still enclosed the city, and in 1155 he founded a monastery of Irish monks, the Schottenkloster, in its vicinity; its Romanesque basilica still survives under baroque disguise. During the next half century, Vienna experienced major economic growth and urban extension, especially to the east around the new church of St. Stephan. By 1200, when a new city wall enclosed all the settlements outside the Roman walls, Vienna had already reached its medieval extension within the Ring.

In 1208 and again in 1221, Duke Frederick I (1196–1230) gave civic rights to the city, to which he moved the ducal residence. At the same time, a rebuilding of the parish church of St. Stephan, situated just outside the Roman town walls, was undertaken in the form of a major basilica whose Romanesque exterior enclosed a space that, with its cross rib vaults over compound pillars, made full use of the new Gothic system. Furthermore, a number of monastic churches were founded under ducal patronage, such as the nearby monasteries of the Augustinian Hermits and the Minorites, or the Teutonic Knights and the Knights of Malta. The new parish church of the ducal residence became St. Michael's, which like St. Stephan's was built in an early Gothic style. The pretensions of Duke Frederick II and his struggle with his namesake, Emperor Frederick II, caused the seizure of the city in 1237 by the emperor, who granted it—although only for one year—an imperial status. Duke Frederick's death, and with it the end of the dynasty, in 1246 brought Vienna finally under the rule of King Ottokar Přemysl of Bohemia, which was ended only by Rudolph of Habsburg's victory in 1278; Rudolph assigned Austria to his son, Albrecht I. Under Albrecht, in 1287–1288, and following his death in 1308, the city revolted against Habsburg rule but was subjected again. Under Albrecht II and his brother Frederick the Fair, who unsuccessfully claimed the crown of the Holy Roman Empire against Louis of Bavaria, the city experienced a new period of urban growth. The ducal castle (Hofburg) was built at a strategically important position controlling the Weidmer Tor, one of the city's gates. The medieval courtyard with its fifteenth-century chapel has survived within the extended complex of buildings from the seventeenth through nineteenth centuries.

By 1300 the civic constitution was firmly established, and the new town hall was erected at its present location; it was expanded again in 1316 by the adjacent building, which, after the insurrection of 1308, had been confiscated by the duke and given to the city. A projected rebuilding as a highly ornate monument of three stories with tower and chapel for which Laurenz Spenyng had prepared the drawings in 1456, however, remained on paper.

After the Black Death in 1348, the brief but important rule of Rudolph IV (1358–1365) is marked by the foundation of a collegiate chapter at St. Stephan's, to which the new university, the Rudolphinum, was linked. To house this chapter, Rudolph apparently expanded—in

1359—the choir of St. Stephan's to the existing hall choir and laid the foundation stone to the south tower. Completed only in 1433, this tower is closely linked to the building project of Rudolph's father-in-law, Emperor Charles IV, at Prague Cathedral. The western chapels added by Rudolph IV were, in 1396, topped by the ducal chapel, which originally housed the cycle of stained glass windows with the genealogy of the Habsburg dukes (Herzogenfenster), now mainly in the municipal museum. The church's nave, integrating the two princely portals (Fürstenportale) of Rudolph's time, however, is basically the work of the first half of the fifteenth century, erected under Duke Albrecht V, who, in 1438, secured the crown of the Holy Roman Empire for the Habsburg dynasty.

In the fifteenth century, however, the city experienced political disturbances and an economic decline, even though a bridge over the Danube was constructed in 1439. In 1407–1408, a revolt against the ruling circle caused an interruption of work at St. Stephan's, and in 1420 the Jewish community was expelled from the city in response to religious pressure. In 1461, Emperor Frederick III granted the city a new (imperial) coat of arms, but the subsequent year the city revolted openly against him and besieged him in the Hofburg, although it finally surrendered to imperial rule. After this event the emperor made Vienna his main residence for the next two decades and, in 1469, achieved the promotion of the collegiate church of St. Stephan's to the rank of a cathedral. By this time the church was basically completed with the exception of its northern tower, mainly the work of Laurenz Spenyng from Dresden; the construction of the tower had begun in 1467, but it was finally abandoned in its present unfinished state in 1513. The tomb monument of Frederick III with the highly realistic figure of the deceased, begun in 1469 by Nicolaus Gerhaert van Leyden and completed only in 1517, is the largest of its type.

Another important ecclesiastical monument is the church St. Maria am Gstade. Originally one of the early parish churches of the city, it became, next to St. Stephan's, the most important late Gothic monument. The choir, with its important cycle of stained glass windows, dates back to the early fourteenth century, while its nave was begun in 1398 under the influential Hans of Liechtenstein, but completed in 1414 after his downfall under Duke Albrecht IV. Its design is by the duke's architect, erroneously named "Chnab," who is supposed to have been involved briefly in the construction of St. Stephan's.

In 1485 the city was besieged and finally conquered by Matthias Corvinus, King of Hungary, and held until his death in 1490. Civic self-administration came to its end in the unsuccessful uprising of 1522, after which Ferdinand I terminated the constitution and integrated the city into the early absolutistic system in which it was to become, until 1918, the political center of the large complex of territories under Habsburg rule.

BIBLIOGRAPHY

Achthundertfünfzig Jahre St. Stephan Symbol und Mitte in Wien 1147–1997. 22. Sonderausstellung Historisches Museum der Stadt Wien. Vienna: Museen der Stadt Wien, 1997.

Csendes, Peter. "Stadtherr und bürgerliche Führungsschicht im Wien des 14. Jahrhunderts." *Stadt und Stadtherr im 14. Jahrhundert: Entwicklungen und Funktionen,* ed. Wilhelm Rausch. Beiträge zur Geschichte der Städte Mitteleuropas 2. Linz: Österreichischer Arbeitskreis für Stadtgeschichtsforschung, 1972, pp. 251–256.

Feuchtmüller, Rupert. *Der Wiener Stephansdom.* Vienna: Domverlag, 1978.

Flieder, Viktor. *Stephansdom und Wiener Bistumsgründung: Eine diözesan- und rechtsgeschichtliche Untersuchung.* Veröffentlichungen des kirchenhistorischen Instituts der katholisch-theologischen Fakultät der Universität Wien 6. Vienna: Domverlag, 1968.

Frodl-Kraft, Eva. *Die mittelalterlichen Glasgemälde in Wien.* Corpus vitrearum medii aevi, Österreich 1. Graz: Böhlau, 1962.

Grass, Nikolaus. *Der Wiener Dom, die Herrschaft zu Österreich und das Land Tirol.* Innsbruck: Rauch, 1968.

Perger, Richard, and Walther Brauneis. *Die mittelalterlichen Kirchen und Klöster Wiens.* Wiener Geschichtsbücher 19–20. Vienna: Zsolnay, 1977.

Phanka, Reinhard. *Hinter den Mauern der Stadt: Eine Reise ins mittelalterliche Wien.* Vienna: Herold, 1987.

Tietze, Hans. *Geschichte und Beschreibung des St. Stephansdomes in Wien.* Österreichische Kunsttopographie 22. Vienna: Filser, 1931.

Zykan, Marlene. *Der Stephansdom.* Wiener Geschichtsbücher 26–27. Vienna: Zsolnay, 1981.

Hans J. Böker

SEE ALSO

Charles IV; Frederick III; Gothic Art and Architecture; Nicolaus Gerhaert von Leyden; Otto I; Prague; Romanesque Art and Architecture; Salzburg

Viktring

Founded in 1142 by Duke Bernhard of Spanheim, Viktring Abbey became one of the most important Cistercian cloisters in Carinthia (southern Austria). The abbey, just south of Klagenfurt, had extensive land holdings that were a frequent source of strife with secular rulers until the jurisdiction of the abbey *(Burgfried)* was officially recognized, although in a significantly reduced state, in 1418.

The abbey became famous under the direction of Abbot Johann of Viktring (1312–1345), whose work, *Liber certarum historiarum,* established his reputation as one of the most important historians of the late middle ages. The comprehensive nature of Johann's writing attests to the presence of a large library at Viktring during the fourteenth century.

In 1202, the abbey church, a late Romanesque three-aisle pillared basilica with barrel vaults, was consecrated. In its interior space, the church is reminiscent of that at Fontenay abbey in Burgundy; it is perhaps the most important extant example of Burgundian Cistercian architecture in the German-speaking realm. The rib-vaulted apse, added during the early fourteenth century, houses three of the most famous Gothic stained glass windows (1380–1390) in Austria. An altar from the abbey church (1447) is now in St. Stephan's Cathedral in Vienna.

During the late Middle Ages, a moat was constructed on three sides of Viktring, and although the abbey itself never fell, it suffered during various military encounters with Hungarian and Turkish forces. Inner turmoil under Abbot Matthäus (1467–1481) hastened the decline of Viktring Abbey.

BIBLIOGRAPHY

Fräss-Ehrfeld, Claudia. *Geschichte Kärntens* 1: *Das Mittelalter.* Klagenfurt: Heyn, 1984, pp. 196–208.

Ginhart, Karl. *Kunstdenkmäler Kärntens* 5: *Viktring.* Klagenfurt: Kollitsch, 1962.

Ruth M. W. Moskop

SEE ALSO

Cistercian Art and Architecture; Gothic Art and Architecture; Romanesque Art and Architecture; Vienna

Virginal

This *aventiurehafte* (episodic) Dietrich epic composed in the complicated verse form known as Bernerton (Melody of Verona), also known as *Dietrichs erste Ausfahrt (Dietrich's First Sojourn)* or *Dietrich und seine Gesellen (Dietrich and his Companions),* is preserved in twelve fifteenth-century manuscripts, three of which are complete. There are two main versions, that of a manuscript from Hagenau ("h") and that of the *Dresdener Heldenbuch (Dresden Book of Heroic Tales,* "d"). A third version, that of *Lienhard Scheubels Heldenbuch* (the Viennese *Piaristenhandschrift,* "w"), is a combination of the other two. The narrative probably originated in Alemannic territory in the second half of the thirteenth century.

In version "h," Hildebrand takes a reluctant Dietrich to the Alps to instruct him in adventure: Dietrich is supposed to help Queen Virginal, whose country has been invaded by the heathen Orkise. Leaving Dietrich, Hildebrand rescues a maiden sent by Virginal as annual tribute to Orkise, killing Orkise in the process. He then helps Dietrich defeat a band of heathens. The maiden invites them to Jeraspunt, Virginal's residence. On learning from her of the visit, Virginal sends Bibung, a dwarf, to bring the heroes to court. Hildebrand rescues Rentwin, his grandnephew, from the maw of a dragon. They find Dietrich fighting a dragon, which he kills with Rentwin's sword. They visit Arona, where Rentwin lives with his parents. Bibung brings Virginal's invitation and is sent back and forth to transmit plans for the visit. On the way Dietrich gets lost and is captured by Wicram, one of a dozen giants who serve Nitger, master of Muter. At Muter Ibelin, Nitger's daughter helps Dietrich contact the group at Jeraspunt. They decide to send for Dietrich's men. Messengers crisscross the territory arranging for Dietrich's rescue. In a series of duels Dietrich and his men defeat the giants. Fighting giants and dragons along the way, the heroes finally reach Jeraspunt, where a feast awaits them. A messenger announces that Bern is in danger. Dietrich and his men arrive there and are welcomed. His men depart for their home territories.

In the *Dresdener Heldenbuch* there is no Muter episode. In Arona Dietrich fights a duel with Prince Libertin of Palermo and they become friends. They depart for Jeraspunt. Orkise's son Janapas invites them to Castle Orteneck, where they are attacked by his men and also by lions. Victorious, they rescue three more maidens sent to Orkise as tribute. Dietrich then defeats a boar and a giant, then all go to Jeraspunt. Dietrich and Virginal marry at the feast, then go to live in Bern. The *Piaristenhandschrift* includes not only the Libertin and Janapas episodes but also an abbreviated version of the Muter episode, which takes place just before the arrival and wedding feast at Jeraspunt.

Virginal consists of stock situations of the Dietrich story coupled with clichés of courtly literature. Because of its uncritical absorption of heterogeneous narrative material, its plot is very confused. Literary scholars try to excavate and date an original narrative underneath the layers of accretion or attempt to find consistency in the narrative goals of each version.

BIBLIOGRAPHY

Heinzle, Joachim. *Mittelhochdeusche Dietrichepik.* Zurich: Artemis, 1978.

Zupitza, Julius, ed. *Virginal.* Deutsches Heldenbuch 5, 2d ed. 1870; rpt. Dublin: Weidmann, 1968, pp. 1–200.

Ruth H. Firestone

SEE ALSO
Dietrichepik

Visionary Literature

Otherworldly journeys, apocalyptic eschatologies (interpretations), miraculous visits, and mystical unions abounded in medieval German vernacular and Latin literature. This literature recounted contact with the supernatural realm, either through human transport out of the world or miraculous visits into the world by figures such as angels, saints, Mary, Christ, or the devil. Some vision narratives comprised segments within larger works, but many constituted entire works themselves. Their authors chronicled a variety of dreams, journeys, apparitions, ecstasies, passion accounts, apocalyptic furies, and mystical unions.

Medieval visionary authors drew on several models. Classical examples included Virgil's *Aeneid* and Cicero's *Dream of Scipio.* Scriptural models came from the Old Testament (Isaiah, Ezekial, and Daniel), the New Testament (Revelation of John), and the apocrypha *(Vision of Paul).* Early church figures such as Augustine, who distinguished three types of visions (corporeal, spiritual, intellectual), Gregory the Great, and Boniface continued the visionary tradition. The twelfth century witnessed the greatest development of visionary literature and a major shift in types of visions. Prior to the mid–twelfth century, vision literature outlined unique, lengthy tours through the otherworld for the purpose of conversion. Thereafter it described short, repeatable encounters with heavenly figures for specific theological instruction or the vision-ary's own sanctity. By the later Middle Ages visions formed the basis for popular literature, most famously the *Roman de la Rose* and *The Divine Comedy.*

One of the best-known accounts from Germany was the *Vision of Tundal* (ca. 1149). This clearly structured, popular tale told of an Irish monk in Regensburg traveling through a fantastic otherworld. Hundreds of manuscripts in Latin and many vernaculars attest to its popularity. In the *Vision of Gottschalk* (ca. 1189–1190) a peasant farmer from Holstein returned from a near-death experience to retell highlights from his angel-guided tour of the otherworld.

Much of the most popular German visionary literature hails from the context of monasticism and developing religious movements in the form of saints' lives, spiritual guidebooks, and mystical texts. The Benedictine Rupert of Deutz (d. 1129), for example, tied his visionary experiences to his exegetical teaching. Women were highly represented in this literature. Hildegard of Bingen (d. 1179), the "Sibyl of the Rhein," gained notoriety as prophet and apocalyptic reformer through her visionary activity. She considered her visions a capacity of her soul and was adamant that they occurred neither in dream states nor rapture. Elizabeth of Schönau (d. 1165), even more widely read in the Middle Ages, mediated messages from angels and sought reform in church teaching and politics. The Beguine Mechthild of Magdeburg (d. ca. 1282) wrote otherworldly journeys and mystical unions to teach people the path to God. The visions of the Helfta nuns helped fortify the monastery's reputation as a thriving center of devotion. Visionary literature predominated among fourteenth-century German Dominicans as Margaret Ebner (d. 1351), Christina Ebner (d. 1356), Adelheid Langmann (d. 1375), and the Engelthal Sister-Books illustrate. German authors thus used visionary literature throughout the Middle Ages in a variety of contexts both to warn and to inspire their readers.

BIBLIOGRAPHY

Benz, Ernst. *Die Vision: Erfahrungsformen und Bilderwelt.* Stuttgart: Klett, 1969.

Dinzelbacher, Peter. *Vision und Visionsliteratur im Mittelalter.* Stuttgart: Hiersmann, 1981.

McGinn, Bernard. *The Presence of God: A History of Western Christian Mysticism.* 3 vols. New York: Crossroad, 1991–1998.

Medieval Women's Visionary Literature, ed. Elizabeth Alvilda Petroff. New York: Oxford University Press, 1986.

Mittelalterliche Visionsliteratur: Eine Anthologie, transl. and ed. Peter Dinzelbacher. Darmstadt: Wissenschaftliche Buchgesellschaft, 1989.

Patricia Zimmerman Beckman

SEE ALSO

Ebner, Margaretha; Gertrud von Helfta; Hildegard von Bingen; Langmann, Adelheid; Saints' Lives, Dutch; Sister-Books

Vita, Vitae

See Saints' Lives.

Vom Rechte

An early Middle High German poem, *Vom Rechte (On the Right Way)* deals specifically with social matters in relation to salvation. It is difficult to find a good, short expression in English for *Recht.* It certainly means "justice," the "right," or the "law," but here it seems to stand for the broader concept of the divinely ordained, established order of things in the world. Naturally, that order would be "just" or "right," but the poet spares no words in explaining that such order is not always observed by man and that no one is indeed so noble, high, or mighty as *Das Recht.* Putting oneself above the "law" will surely have dire consequences for the salvation of one's soul. The proper Christian life is characterized by loyalty, truthfulness, and reliability. Wealth and power lead to pride and exploitation of the poor. Masters and mistresses should be fair in their treatment of their servants and share the profits of their common work. Lies and slander are to be avoided. Greed is a shameful trait. The relation between man and woman should also be subject to God's laws, and by all means one should consult one's priest on how to lead a proper life. The descriptions of human behavior are taken very vividly from everyday country life and show a keen appreciation of human foibles. All in all, it is a fascinating, lively sermon-in-verse *(Reimpredigt),* and impresses with its style and seriousness of purpose.

Vom Rechte is found in the Millstadt *Sammelhandschrift* (manuscript containing a number of texts). The text is in poor condition and presents editorial problems. There are 549 lines in rhymed couplets in thirty stanzas of varying length, or half that many long lines. The dating of the text is also difficult (1150–1160); its language is Austrian (Carinthian).

BIBLIOGRAPHY

Haug, Walter, and Benedikt Vollmann. *Frühe deutsche Literatur und lateinische Literatur in Deutschland, 800–1150.* Frankfurt am Main: Deutscher Klassiker Verlag, 1991, pp. 752–83 [with German trans.].

Maurer, Friedrich, ed. *Die religiösen Dichtungen des 11. und 12. Jahrhunderts. Nach ihren Formen besprochen,* 3 vols. Tübingen: Niemeyer, 1964–1970, vol. 2, no. 29.

Schröbler, Ingeborg. "Das mhd. Gedicht vom 'Recht'." *Beiträge zur Geschichte der deutschen Sprache und Literatur* 80 (1958): 219–252.

Speicher, Stephan. *'Vom Rechte.' Ein Kommentar im Rahmen der zeitgenössichen Literaturtradition.* Göppingen: Kümmerle, 1986.

Sidney M. Johnson

SEE ALSO

Preaching and Sermons, Dutch

Walahfrid Strabo (ca. 809–August 18, 849)

Despite a tragically brief life (ca. 809–849), Walahfrid Strabo (alternatively, Strabus—the nickname refers to the cast in his eye) played a major role in ninth-century intellectual activity. Of Swabian origin, he studied first at Reichenau and then, under Hrabanus Maurus, at Fulda. In forty years Walahfrid left a lasting mark in Reichenau as monk, teacher, and abbot (838–849) and elsewhere, thanks to his achievements as poet, theologian, liturgist, naturalist, and royal tutor (829–838) of the future Charles the Bald.

His most substantial poem is also very precocious: he composed "Wetti's Vision" when he was eighteen years old. It relates the deathbed visions of heaven and hell that the monk Wetti (one of his teachers, d. 824) experienced when Walahfrid was fifteen years old. A highly literary recasting of an earlier prose account, it is seen as anticipating Dante's *Divine Comedy* in its emphasis on purgation and purgatory. Among Walahfrid's other poems (which employ a considerable number of different meters), particular importance has been attached by modern scholars to a polemic against the erection of a statue to the Ostrogothic king Theodoric in Aachen and to a didactic work on horticulture that describes the medicinal plants found in the monastic garden of Reichenau and their properties.

Among his other works are found commentaries on various books of the Bible (both Old and New Testaments), a history of various ecclesiastic institutions and practices, redactions of saints' lives and Einhard's *Life of Charlemagne,* and homilies.

BIBLIOGRAPHY

Dümmler, Ernst, ed. *Walahfridi Strabi carmina,* in *Monumenta Germaniae Historica Poetae Latini Aevi Carolini,* vol. 2. Berlin: Weidmann, 1884, pp. 259–428.

Godman, Peter. *Poetry of the Carolingian Renaissance.* London: Duckworth, 1985.

Payne, Raef, trans., and Wilfrid Blunt, commentary. *Hortulus: Walahfrid Strabo.* Pittsburgh: Hunt Botanical Library, 1966.

Traill, David A., ed. and trans. *Walahfrid Strabo's Visio Wettini.* Bern: Lang, 1974.

Jan M. Ziolkowski

SEE ALSO

Charlemagne; Fulda; Hrabanus Maurus; Latin Language; Reichenau

Waltharius

The *Waltharius,* which could be translated into English as *The Poem of Walter,* is a Latin epic of 1,456 dactylic hexameters written by a speaker of a Germanic language dealing with peoples and individual characters of interest to a Germanic audience. Its narrative action divides into three main sections. After a brief preface (1–10), the first (11–418) describes the subjugation of assorted Germanic peoples by the Huns; the exploits of Walter of Aquitaine in Hunland with his fellow hostage, the Frank Hagen; and Walter's escape from there with another captive, his betrothed Hildegund of Burgundy. The second (419–1061) enumerates a sequence of nine combats, most of them duels between Walter and individual Franks who seek to vanquish him to gain from him possession of the treasure he has taken from the Huns. The third (1062–1452) is devoted to the final combat that Gunther and his retainer Hagen wage against Walter. Gunther loses a leg, Hagen an eye and some teeth, and Walter his right hand. After the battle ends the warriors drink wine and taunt each other. The poem concludes with a short epilogue (1453–1456).

The dating and authorship of the *Waltharius* are as notoriously controverted as are those of another famous early Germanic heroic epic, *Beowulf*. The three main possibilities for the author are an otherwise unidentified Gerald, Ekkehard I of St. Gall (900–973), and an anonymous. Gerald, who wrote a prologue of twenty-two hexameters that is included in four manuscripts, need not have been the author of the entire poem. Alternatively, he could have been a copyist who composed a poem to his patron, Erckambald (perhaps the man by this name who served as Bishop of Strasbourg from 965 to 991), to accompany a manuscript of the poem that he had produced. As for dating, the earliest manuscript evidence is a fragment of 975; scholars place the composition of the poem variously in the early ninth century (Charlemagne), late ninth century (Charlemagne's successors), and mid–tenth century (Ottonian emperors).

The story or stories that the poet had at his disposal cannot be easily reconstructed, although evidence in other medieval languages supplements what is found in the Latin. In Old Norse we have a lay about Attila and the *þ∂rekssaga*, in Old English the short and fragmentary *Waldere*, in Middle High German a mention of the tale in the *Nibelungenlied*, and even several accounts in Polish; but none of these is nearly as elaborate as the *Waltharius* itself, and nothing appears to be even closely related to a possible source of it. Furthermore, in none of these is evident the same fusion of Germanic, classical, and Christian features that characterizes the *Waltharius*. Alongside a close knowledge of such poets as Vergil and Prudentius, the poet shows an insider's appreciation for the basic workings of oral German epic and considerably more than a passing interest in the Germanic past.

BIBLIOGRAPHY

D'Angelo, Edoardo, ed. and transl. *Waltharius. Epica e saga tra Virgilio e i Nibelunghi*. Milan: Luni Editrice, 1998.

Kratz, Dennis, ed. and trans. *"Waltharius" and "Ruodlieb."* New York: Garland, 1984.

Langosch, Karl. *"Waltharius." Die Dichtung und die Forschung*. Darmstadt: Wissenschaftliche Buchgesellschaft, 1973.

Magoun, F. P., Jr., and H. M. Smyser, trans. *Walter of Aquitaine: Materials for the Study of His Legend*. New London, Conn.: Connecticut College, 1950.

Strecker, Karl, ed., and Peter Vossen, trans. *Waltharius*. Berlin: Weidmannsche Verlagsbuchhandlung, 1947.

———, ed. *Waltharius*, in *Poetae Latini Medii Aevi* 6, fasc. 1. Monumenta Germaniae Historica. Weimar: Hermann Böhlaus Nachfolger, 1951.

Jan M. Ziolkowski

SEE ALSO

Latin Language; *Nibelungenlied;* Sankt Gall; Versification; *Walter und Hildegund*

Walter und Hildegund

The legend of Walther of Aquitaine (or of Spain, in most medieval German sources) found its way into writing quite early. We find a Latin epic, *Waltharius,* probably from St. Gall, and an Old English epic, *Waldere,* which unfortunately exists only in fragments, both of which are probably products of the tenth century. The Middle High German version was almost certainly of epic breadth as well, if the surviving fragments are any indication. It was composed in a strophic form much like that of the *Nibelungenlied*. Parchment fragments of two different manuscripts of the epic were later used in the bindings of books and thus survive, albeit as tiny scraps of a large poem. There is also a version of the story in the Norwegian *Thidrekssaga af Bern*.

The story of Walther remains essentially the same in all versions. Walther is a noble hostage at the court of Attila/Etzel. He is in love with his fellow hostage Hildigund. He steals a considerable amount of treasure and his beloved and, taking advantage of the Huns' drunkenness, escapes from Attila's court. Underway he is attacked by Gunther and Hagen as he crosses the Rhine. He holds off an attack in the Vosges Mountains by placing himself in such a position that only one of his attackers can reach him at a time. After defeating all his attackers but Gunther and Hagen, he finally fights to a draw with his old friend Hagen, and Hildigund binds the wounded men. The Middle High German versions included a festival in Walther's homeland after his return.

BIBLIOGRAPHY

Hoffmann, Werner. *Mittelhochdeutsche Heldendichtung*. Grundlagen der Germanistik 14. Berlin: Schmidt, 1974, pp. 112–116.

Smyser, H.M., and F. P. Magoun Jr. *Walter of Aquitaine: Materials for the Study of His Legend*. New London: Connecticut College, 1950.

Edward R. Haymes

SEE ALSO
Nibelungenlied; Waltharius

Walther von der Vogelweide (ca. 1170–ca. 1230)

In service largely at the Hohenstaufen courts, Walther is considered the greatest of the German courtly singers of the High Middle Ages. Some would argue for his poetic primacy among European singers in any language. Internal evidence in his songs suggests he was active between the early 1190s and the late 1220s. His *Minnesang* (love singing), in which he sang the painful joy of unrequited love for a woman of high station *(hôhe minne),* shows influences of fashionable German courtly singers such as Heinrich von Morungen and Reinmar der Alte. Walther also sang of the so-called *nidere minne* (down-to-earth love), an amorous relationship both physical and mutual that has close parallels in Latin secular love songs. His political, personal, didactic, and religious songs *(Sangspruch)* reflect the vicissitudes of his career as well as the turbulent political events of the *sacrum imperium,* known later as the Holy Roman Empire.

Extant today are over six hundred stanzas in some three dozen manuscripts. Walther's music has been entirely lost save for five melodies, two of them fragmentary and another two from manuscripts written three centuries later. Accordingly, readers must use their imaginations to re-create the conditions of performance and the effect of the melodies and their accompaniments.

Walther's name appears only once in nonliterary documents of his lifetime, a 1203 entry in the travel accounts of Bishop of Passau directing that five shillings be given the singer *(cantor)* for a fur coat. But other thirteenth-century singers and romanciers provide ample encomia, or formal praise, for this towering figure of German lyric singing. Gottfried of Straßburg in his *Tristan* (ll. 4751–4820) calls him the nightingale carrying the banner of *Minnesang,* praising Walther's high (tenor?) voice and his dexterity in the polyphonic style of the day (organum). His artistry is also celebrated by, among others, Reinmar von Zweter, Bruder Werner, and Rudolf von Ems. In the waning Middle Ages he is enthroned by the Meistersinger as one of the Twelve Old Masters. Only one contemporary provides negative criticism: Thomasin von Zerklaere castigates him as a slanderer of Pope Innocent III and a deceiver of men *(Der welsche Gast,* 11. 11091–11268).

The songs classified as *Minnesang*—the sequence can only be surmised—are normally categorized in the following major groups: early songs of elevated love *(hôhe minne)* linked to Reinmar at the Viennese court; later *Minnesang;* songs of down-to-earth love *(nidere minne);* and late songs. Augmenting the difficulties of dating these songs is the strong possibility of revision in the course of the singer's career or changes developing from the orality of the pieces.

Walther's assumed apprenticeship at the Viennese court, in the 1190s under the tutelage of Reinmar der Alte (Reinmar von Hagenau), produced a number of early songs. Some of these have been linked to a "Reinmar feud" *(Reinmar-Fehde),* a quasi debate revealing the outlines of a serious polemic with his former mentor on the nature of *minne.* Reinmar is the representative of the traditional (since the 1160s) ideas inherent in the troubadour lyric: his love, unrequited and unconsummated, is for an unapproachable lady of a higher station. Walther, on the other hand, hints at a more mutual love; his lady is valued not for her cold, Turandot-like majesty but for a more immediate and shared joy. The Reinmar debate began in the 1190s and seemed to continue until after Walther's departure from Vienna in 1198. Emblematic of this exchange is Walther's *Ein man verbiutet âne pfliht* (no. L. 111,22ff), a response to Reinmar's *Ich wirbe umb allez daz ein man* (*Minnesangs Frühling,* no. 159,1ff), in which, using the same melody and stanzaic form, he weaves Reinmar's key motifs into his song to produce an ironically critical response to his mentor.

It is difficult to separate what seem to be the more mature songs of the Reinmar debate from Walther's non-Reinmar–related songs of the period circa 1205–1215, a time in which he achieved mastery of language. Here the singer composed his most effective and inventive songs, sharply breaking with the traditional German *Minnesang* (as performed by Heinrich von Morungen, Reinmar, and others), with its prickling tensions and the incessant conjectures about an impossible love. Walther's style now becomes pointed, ironic, playful, and original. Though still dancing around the theme of *hôhe minne,* many of his songs now suggest an equal relationship with a young woman whose station is not of importance and whose designation increasingly becomes the generically female *wîp* (woman) rather than the socially hierarchical *frouwe* (lady). In *Si wunderwol gemachet wîp,* (L. 53,25ff), he sings of the physical attributes of a woman not of the nobility, completing his catalog of adulation with an unprecedented image of the woman, unclothed, stepping cleanly from her bath.

Among the songs of this period are some that appear outside the scope of the *Minne* theme. The so-called

Preislied (panegyric) *Ir sult sprechen willekomen* (L. 56, 14ff) is possibly a response to the troubadour Peire Vidal (fl. ca. 1187–1205), whose unkind characterizations of German deportment probably rankled at German-speaking courts. Walther's praise of German *(tiutschiu)* woman and, by extension, German culture is unique in medieval song.

During these years Walther also composed songs with bucolic settings about the real and physical love of a young woman who seems tangential to courtly circles (songs of *nidere Minne,* sometimes called *Mädchenlieder).* In "Herzeliebez frouwelîn" (L. 49, 25ff) he is charmed by a woman or girl whose glass ring he values more than the gold ring of a queen. "Nement, frowe, disen cranz" (L. 74, 20ff) projects a dream vision of his beloved, a pretty girl *(wol getânen maget)* portrayed in the scenery of the *Carmina Burana,* that is, under a blossoming tree on a meadow graced by flowers and the singing of the birds.

"Under der linden" (Beneath the Linden Tree, no. L. 39,11ff) is Walther's most celebrated love song. In the tradition of the Latin *pastourelle,* it contains the same predictable imagery as in "Nement, frowe, disen cranz." But Walther brings to this tradition a deceptively simple language expressing the essence of the lovers' joy, deftly combined with a playful and delicate web of motifs to form a song with complex levels of meaning.

Walther's position at court required him also to excel at the art of *Sangspruch.* The term pertains to songs in which love is not the primary matter: political pieces, songs of personal invective, requests for favors from a patron, crusade songs, and songs with a didactic or religious content. Each piece is normally restricted to one stanza, though in some cases several stanzas composed in the same tune (*Ton,* plural *Töne*) can be bound together to form a performance piece. Walther's *Sangspruch* provides a glimpse of the events of his life as well as the fortunes of the empire under the Hohenstaufen rulers and its ongoing struggle with the papacy. These songs were composed largely for patrons at the electoral courts—kings, dukes, counts, and bishops—who expected from the singer both workmanlike compositions and persuasive performances. Occasional songs in the best sense, they were composed about specific events or personalities. In editions of Walther they are usually grouped into cycles of stanzas of identical metrical and musical form *(Ton).* Some, though not all, of the stanzas of a *Ton* have the same general thematic content. Modern scholarship has given them associative names that apply to some though not all of the stanzas in the *Ton.* In the "König-Friedrichston" (King

Friedrich Tune, no. 26,3ff), for example, King Friedrich (later the emperor Friedrich II) plays a major role only in a few of the stanzas. Each of these *Töne* contains between three and eighteen stanzas.

Walther's best-known *Ton,* the "Reichston" (Imperial Tune, L. 8,4ff), may well be the earliest. A triad of long stanzas (twenty-four lines each), it begins pensively with the trademark image of Walther sitting on a stone in the pose of the philosopher (*Ich saz ûf eime steine,* I sat upon a stone). In the second song (L. 8,28), Walther moves out of the meditative mode and into the political, calling for the crowning of the true emperor, the Hohenstaufen candidate Philipp of Swabia rather than the papally sanctioned Otto of Brunswick, dynastic leader of the Welf party. With pointed imagery he declares the clergy of Rome corrupt and the times out of joint. In the third song (L. 9,16), assuming the persona of a pious hermit, he indicts the pope as being too young (Innocent III was only thirty-nine), an anomaly symptomatic of the ills besetting the curia at Rome and its imperial policy.

In 1198 Walther left Vienna and attached himself to various Hohenstaufen courts in the middle German regions, continuing both positive and negative associations with Philipp of Swabia (in the five stanzas of the first "Philippston," Philipp Tune, L. 18,29ff). Despite Walther's ardent propaganda for the imperial candidate, he complains of Philipp's parsimony. This theme of a patron's miserly qualities would become a favorite of the later generation of *Sangspruch* singers in the thirteenth century.

The "Wiener Hofton" (Viennese Court Tune, L. 20,16ff), largely composed after Walther's departure from Vienna in 1198, reveals an ambivalence about the Viennese court, combining a longing to return to this desirable venue with an uneasiness about his relations with the reigning Duke Leopold VI. Walther continues to sing in the causes of Philipp until the would-be emperor's death in 1208, but gradually in the course of the first decade of the thirteenth century, he forms new courtly associations, most prominently with Hermann, Landgrave of Thuringia, and his son-in-law, Dietrich, Margrave of Meißen. These princes are forced to change allegiance after Philipp's death, leaving the imperial candidacy open to his archrival, Otto of Brunswick. Walther reflects the new loyalties in the "Ottenton" (Otto Tune, L. 11,6ff), in which he welcomes the new kaiser to the Reichstag (imperial diet) in Frankfurt, declaring that his patron, the Margrave of Meißen, is as loyal to the emperor as an angel is to God. Less than a year later the margrave and other princes (like the fallen angels) are in open rebellion, preparing the way for a new Hohenstaufen pretender, the young Friedrich II, grandson of Barbarossa.

As was the lot of singers employed by the courts, Walther continued the propaganda commissioned by his various patrons. In one of his sharpest and most amusing pieces, "Unmutston" (Disgruntled Tune, L. 34,4), Walther rants against that most ardent enemy of the Hohenstaufen interests, Pope Innocent III, for his collecting of German monies to finance the Albigensian Crusade in 1213, accusing the Roman clergy of feasting on capons and wine while the German laity grows lean from fasting.

There is evidence that Walther was able to gain a modicum of independence as overseer of a fief. In 1220 he composed a song of request to King Friedrich for his own house, playing on his lord's sympathy for a homeless singer whose wearisome life was a procession of one-night stands. ("König-Friedrichston," L. 28,1). Apparently Walther was successful, for in the same *Ton* (L. 28,31) he proclaims triumphantly his thanks to the king, grateful that he need no longer go begging at the courts of base lords for shelter.

Since these songs of praise and political propaganda were produced on demand to suit the shifting political alliances of a turbulent period of imperial history, one might properly ask to what extent Walther's songs reflect his own values. Many are outright propaganda, although of a kind wrought with the highest poetic skills and a deft sense of language. And yet many pieces reveal a personality sharply troubled by the woeful state of the mutable world and impelled by a desire to return to the established, predictable, and more ethical patterns of time past. The "Wiener Hofton" bewails the uncouth behavior of courtly youth (L. 24,3), marking its disparity with the days when one did not spare the rod with ill-mannered children. More personal and sadder echoes of this nostalgia permeate the "Elegie" (Elegy, L. 124,1 ff), generally held to have been composed in Walther's old age. It too complains of the uncourtly behavior of young people, but combines it with what must have been an old man's deeply personal sense of an irretrievable past. And yet, in the last stanza, it is clear that it is a song of outright propaganda, urging knights to undertake a crusade, possibly that of Frederick II in 1227. Walther was still the paid entertainer whose patron called the tune.

The manuscripts also contain a scattering of personal and religious songs of one or more stanzas that cannot properly be called *Sangspruch*. One is the "Palästina-Lied" (Palestine Song, L. 14,38ff), also a recruiting song for a crusade, containing the only complete and proven melody among Walther's songs. Another is the *Leich* (L. 3,1ff). This most virtuosic of all medieval lyric forms—derived from the liturgical sequence—is a large-format song built on a series of versicles and responses that undergo repetition and variation. It may have been specifically composed for groups of singers and instrumentalists, who would have sung and played it antiphonally in unison or possibly with rudimentary polyphony (*organum*). With its many repetitions and variations, it often approached the complexity of a fugue. This is Walther's longest single performance piece, a prayer to the Mother of God (hence called a *Marienleich*), marked by lush praise of the Virgin commingled with references to the Trinity, biblical prefigurations, and elements of Christian theology. Yet even in this, Walther's most pious work, the singer cannot refrain from references to the Roman curia and its "unchristian things" (*unchristliche dinge*).

The legacy of Walther's *Sangspruch* was a set of models and patterns for a century of professional singers who followed. His love songs, on the other hand, marked in a sense the end of *Minnesang*. The art had soared in the songs of Morungen and Reinmar. Walther moved through the exhausted concept of *hôhe minne* and brought the love song back to earth. But after him no other Minnesinger approached his or his predecessors' mastery of the art.

BIBIOGRAPHY

Bäuml, Franz, ed. *From Symbol to Mimesis: The Generation of Walther von der Vogelweide.* Göppingen: Kümmerle, 1984.

Bein, Thomas. *Walther von der Vogelweide.* Stuttgart: Reclam, 1997.

Brunner, Horst, et al. *Walther von der Vogelweide: Die gesamte Überlieferung der Texte und Melodien—Abbildungen, Materialien, Melodiestranskription.* Göppingen: Kümmerle, 1977.

———, et al. *Walther von der Vogelweide: Epoche—Werk—Wirkung.* Munich: Beck, 1996.

Cormeau, Christoph, ed. *Walther von der Vogelweide: Leich, Lieder, Sangsprüche.* Berlin: de Gruyter, 1996.

Goldin, Friedrich. "Walther versus Reinmar," in *The Regeneration of Poetic Language in Medieval German Literature: Vernacular Poetics in the Middle Ages,* ed. Lois Ebin. Kalamazoo: Western Michigan University, 1984, pp. 57–92.

Hahn, Gerhard. *Walther von der Vogelweide: Eine Einführung.* Munich: Artemis, 1986.

Halbach, Kurt Herbert. *Walther von der Vogelweide,* 4th ed. Stuttgart: Metzler, 1983.

Jones, George Fenwick. *Walther von der Vogelweide.* New York: Twayne, 1968.

McFarland, Timothy, and Silvia Ranawake, eds. *Walther von der Vogelweide: Twelve Studies.* Oxford: Oxford University Press, 1982.

Mück, Hans-Dieter. *Walther von der Vogelweide: Beiträge zu Leben und Werk.* Stuttgart: Stöffler and Schütz, 1989.

Müller, Jan-Dirk, and Franz Josef Worstbrock, eds. *Walther von der Vogelweide: Hamburger Kolloquium 1988 zum 65. Geburtstag von Karl-Heinz Borck.* Stuttgart: Hirzel, 1989.

Nix, Matthias. *Untersuchungen zur Funktion der politischen Spruchdichtung Walthers von der Vogelweide.* Göppingen: Kümmerle, 1993.

Scheibe, Fred Karl. *Walther von der Vogelweide, Troubadour of the Middle Ages: His Life and His Reputation in the English-Speaking Countries.* New York: Vantage, 1969.

Peter Frenzel

SEE ALSO

Carmina Burana; Crusades; Frederick II; Heinrich von Morungen; *Mariendichtungen;* Meistersinger; *Minnesang;* Reinmar der Alte; Rudolf von Ems; *Sangspruch;* Staufen; Thomasîn von Zerclaere; Versification

Warbeck, Veit (ca. 1490–1534)

The fifteenth century saw the rise of a new literary genre, the chapbook. Although precise definitions are still missing, the large number of prose novels, often based on medieval themes and motifs, if they are not direct translations, which were soon printed and made available for an increasingly expanding readership, are generally called *Volksbücher* (literally, books of the folk). Veit Warbeck was born shortly before 1490 as the second son of a wealthy patrician in Schwäbisch Gmünd. In 1527, he translated, on the occasion of the wedding of his student, Prince Johann Friedrich of Saxony, the chapbook *Magelone* into German on the basis of a French version, composed between 1453 and 1457, which again can be traced back to many Oriental sources. This text was to become one of the very successful early modern chap-

books when it was posthumously printed in 1535 by Georg Spalatin.

In 1505 Veit began with his university studies at the Sorbonne in Paris and passed his master exam in 1508. In 1514 he continued with the study of law at Wittenberg but soon switched to theology under Martin Luther and became a minister. In 1519 he celebrated his first church service. Subsequently, the Saxon court librarian Georg Spalatin befriended him and arranged his employment at court in many different functions since 1523, especially as tutor and teacher for the young princes. When Johann Friedrich assumed the throne in 1532, Veit was appointed councillor and vice chancellor. He died on June 4, 1534. His daughter Anna married one of Luther's sons.

In *Magelone,* young Peter, son of the count of Provence (France), wins the love of the princess Magelone, but the parents oppose their marriage. The couple escapes from home, but they lose each other in the woods because Peter, erotically aroused, had opened Magelone's dress while she was asleep, which in turn had made it possible for a bird to steal a cloth of hers, suggesting romance. While Peter tries to catch the bird and recover the cloth, he is captured by pirates and sold to the Egyptian sultan. Whereas Peter develops into a loyal servant of the sultan, Magelone builds a hospital in Peter's home country. Here the two lovers eventually meet again and can finally join hands in marriage. The novel specifically emphasizes morality, virtues, and highly affectionate relationships. The narrator strongly admonishes parents to keep better watch over their children, but still idealizes the young people's love and loyalty.

BIBLIOGRAPHY
Bolte, Johannes, ed. *Die schöne Magelone, aus dem Französischen übersetzt von Veit Warbeck 1527.* Weimar: Felber, 1894.

Classen, Albrecht. *The German "Volksbuch": A Critical History of a Late-Medieval Genre.* Lewiston, N.Y.: Mellen, 1995.

Müller, Jan-Dirk, ed. *Romane des 15. und 16. Jahrhunderts.* Frankfurt: Deutscher Klassiker Verlag, 1990.

Theiß, Winfried. "Die *Schöne Magelona,* und ihre Leser. Erzählstategie und Publikumswechsel im 16. Jahrhundert." *Euphorion* 73 (1979): 132–148.

von Ertzdorff, Xenja. *Romane und Novellen des 15. und 16. Jahrhunderts in Deutschland.* Darmstadt: Wissenschaftliche Buchgesellschaft, 1989.

Albrecht Classen

Warfare

Warfare was a dominant feature of medieval German history. After the late fourth century, Germanic tribes penetrated the western Roman Empire in force, bringing important changes to the military system. Roman discipline and organization gave way to badly organized forces with poor training, few arms, and almost no discipline. Military recruitment and payment for services were based on the amount of booty a leader could provide his soldiers, and loyalty to this leader was dependent on the continued success of his conquest. Soldiers generally were equipped with only a rudimentary shield and helmet, and their arms consisted of a sword, ax, or spear. These militaristic barbarians had an almost Homeric sense of heroism and revered martial skills. Their names, both male and female, reflected the constant presence of war, and warriors were the elite of the wergeld (literally, man money) system of compensation and given elaborate burials with their equipment and booty.

By the sixth and seventh centuries, the Merovingian Franks, who required military service of all free men, had an effective army based on infantry. Their special weapon was the francisca, a throwing ax. They adopted body armor only gradually. With this army, they conquered most of the land of what would become Germany. They protected their lands with fortifications, which, other than those inherited from the Roman Empire, were simple earth and wood ramparts.

When the Carolingians came to power in the eighth century, the requirements of a large empire led to new military institutions that presaged the military obligation patterns of a later time. Rulers granted income-producing estates to followers who promised to render full-time military service at their own expense. The expanding role of the stirrup gradually encouraged the development of heavy cavalry and eventually the archetypical medieval knight.

The system of land grants and oaths of loyalty enabled Charlemagne to muster an effective cavalry force almost annually. His armies were not large, but they were powerful and dominated their opponents. He generally led them himself, and although there were few "formal" military tactics, they were successful in most engagements and in adding much new land to his empire. Among these lands were Saxony and Lombard Italy.

As the ruins of the Carolingian Empire gave way to Ottonian, Salian, and eventually Hohenstaufen Germany, rulers stayed in power largely by dint of their military capabilities, and some suffered serious political rever-sals when defeated in war. Recruitment of soldiers increasingly depended on administrative institutions of obligation in the eleventh and twelfth centuries, and emperors and other nobles sometimes could not muster sufficient troops to fight their wars. As they began to acquire more resources, they began to supplement traditionally recruited troops with paid professionals.

Mounted soldiers were still the core of the army. With improved weapons and armor and mounted on expensive warhorses, they usually decided the course of each battle, fighting with couched lance in a tournament-like fashion. Most cavalry soldiers of the twelfth and thirteenth centuries were knights supported by fiefs. Large battles were infrequent, and those that were fought often included only rudimentary tactical combinations.

While the cavalry was the core of the army, the most numerous forces were still the infantry. Levied from among the freemen of the kingdom, these troops were armed much less well than their mounted counterparts. While some were protected by a helmet, a small shield, and a leather hauberk, infantry soldiers frequently served without armor. Offensive infantry weapons included the spear, sword, lance, and pike, with little standardization among these weapons. Archers also served in infantry contingents, initially being equipped with traditional wood bows. In the course of the twelfth century, these began to be replaced with the more powerful crossbow.

Following the Carolingian period, the siege replaced the battle as the primary form of military engagement. Though Charlemagne had effectively altered the standard of battlefield fighting, he and his successors tended to neglect fortifications, leaving the empire vulnerable to the raids of Vikings and, especially in Germany, Hungarians. In the eleventh century, local rulers led in the construction of fortifications, at first small earth and wood castles, but soon larger and stronger structures of masonry. These more intricate and costly fortifications provided valuable defenses. Although mining, sapping, and stone-throwing engines were used against them, a castle or town with strong stone walls could generally be reduced only by starvation.

In the late Middle Ages, five significant developments altered warfare. First, armies fighting on foot began again to predominate. The stunning defeats of German cavalry armies at Mortgarten in 1316 and Vottem in 1346 were followed by several others in the Holy Roman Empire over the next two centuries. The second development was the continual fighting that beset Germany between the early thirteenth and sixteenth centuries. This long military struggle exhausted the German military and eventually required a stricter and often less noble military bureaucracy, which would not be fully achieved until the reign of Emperor Charles V. As well, the emergence of condottieri, paid mercenaries without traditional military obligation, weakened medieval military institutions. The third factor was the Black Death of 1348–1349, which significantly reduced the numbers available to fight on the battlefield and defend German towns and castles. The fourth was the advent of frequent and often violent popular rebellions by German peasants, townspeople, and nobles, the suppression of which required changes in military tactics.

Finally, warfare was changed by the advent and proliferation of missile weapons employing gunpowder. Appearing initially in the early fourteenth century, they began influencing warfare by the 1380s, when they were used effectively against fortifications and on the battlefield. By 1400, no siege was free of their use, as they reduced substantially the time needed to destroy walls. No longer was it necessary to rely on starvation to force the capitulation of castles or towns. By the 1430s, hand-held gunpowder weapons began to take their place among infantry contingents, changing the face of battlefield engagements. By the Swiss and Burgundian Wars of 1475–1477, one third of the infantry on each side was outfitted with handguns. These late medieval changes brought an end to medieval forms of warfare and encouraged the development of states capable of financing modern armies.

BIBLIOGRAPHY

Contamine, Philippe. *War in the Middle Ages,* trans. M. Jones. London: Blackwell, 1984.

DeVries, Kelly. *Medieval Military Technology.* Peterborough, Ont.: Broadview, 1992.

Lot, Ferdinand. *L'Art militaire et les armées au moyen âge,* 2 vols. Paris: Payot, 1946.

Oman, Sir Charles. *A History of the Art of War in the Middle Ages,* 2d ed. 2 vols. London: Methuen, 1924.

Verbruggen, J. F. *The Art of Warfare in Western Europe During the Middle Ages: From the Eighth Century to 1340,* trans. S. Willard and S. C. M. Southern, 2d ed. Woodbridge: Boydell Press, 1997.

Kelly DeVries

SEE ALSO

Archer/Bowman; Armor; Carolingians; Charlemagne; Clovis; Salian; Staufen; Weapons

Wartburg

The palace of the langraves, or counts, of Thuringia on the Wartburg occupies a dramatic and easily defensible site in the hills outside Eisenach at the edge of the Thuringian forest. As part of his successful attempt to consolidate Thuringia as a separate territory, Count Ludwig der Springer built a castlelike fortress on this site about 1067. Sometime after King Lothar conferred the title of landgrave on Ludwig's son in 1130, the decision was made to erect a building more representative of the family's power and aspirations to the south of the modest living structure. The once controversial dating of the present palace building now seems to have been settled by dendrochronological investigation. The oak trees that provided ceiling beams for the ground floor were felled about 1162 and those for the second story within five years of 1168. The lack of original wood beams in the third story makes it impossible to date this area accurately. While it is generally accepted that the third story was not part of the original plan for the building, the previously accepted delay between the erection of the two lower stories and the third, upper story is now discounted, as is the legendary association of the building with Landgrave Hermann (r. 1190–1217). The building was erected at the latest under his predecessor, his brother Ludwig III (1172–1190), and if Hermann was involved

Wartburg, palace, courtyard façade. *Photograph: after G. Voss, Die Wartburg (Jena: Verlag Gustav Fischer, 1917)*

at all, his role must have been limited to completing a nearly finished structure.

A number of devices make clear the importance of this structure in the landgraves' self-definition. The Singers' Hall on the second floor, the supposed site of the famous *Sängerkrieg* (poets' competition) sponsored by Landgrave Hermann in 1207, competes in scale with the ceremonial halls of the imperial palaces erected about this time. Likewise the arcaded open gallery facing onto the courtyard was a standard feature of these imperial palaces. Stylistic relationships between capitals in the palace and those at the church of Schwarzrheindorf near Bonn indicate the importation of sculptors from important Rhenish sites in an effort to insure the quality of the building. The use of a number of columns of *Kalksinter* (literally *limestone*) serves a similar purpose. These columns, made from the mineral deposits found in the Roman aqueducts that had supplied Cologne with water from the Eifel, were as highly prized in the Rhineland as marble, which was not available locally. Their discovery this far to the east is unusual and, together with the references to imperial palaces, makes it clear that the landgraves spared no expense in the building of the Wartburg, which they intended as an expression of their political position in the empire. The incorporation of the Wartburg into the early legends of the *Sängerkrieg* and the story of St. Elizabeth and Luther's translation of the New Testament here in 1521–1522 helped to secure the status of the complex as a national monument.

BIBLIOGRAPHY

Asche, Sigfried. *Die Wartburg.* Dresden: Sachsenverlag, 1960.

Eckstein, Dieter, Thomas Eißing, and Peter Klein. *Dendrochronologische Datierung der Wartburg und Aufbau einer Lokalchronologie für Eisenach/Thüringen.* Cologne: Abteilung Architekturgeschichte des Kunsthistorischen Instituts der Universität zu Köln, 1992.

Holladay, Joan A. "Hermann of Thuringia as Patron of the Arts: A Case Study." *Journal of Medieval History* 16 (1990): 191–216.

Noth, Werner. *Die Wartburg: Denkmal und Museum.* Leipzig: Koehler and Amelang, 1983.

Joan A. Holladay

Wartburgkrieg

The *Wartburgkrieg* (Wartburg Contest) is a collection of anonymous poems from the thirteenth to the fifteenth centuries written in two different melodies—the *Türinger Fürstenton* (Thuringian Emperor's Melody) and *Klingsors schwarzer Ton* (Klingsor's Black Melody). The best manuscript versions are in the Heidelberg, Jena, and Colmar manuscripts ("C," "J," and "k," respectively). There is as yet no complete edition. The complex tells the story of a singers' contest at the Wartburg, material that Richard Wagner later incorporated in his opera *Tannhäuser* (1845). Manuscript "C" has a famous miniature depicting the contest. The dramatis personae consists of the landgraf of Thuringia and his wife, who speak little but host the contest, six singer-poets (Walther von der Vogelweide, Wolfram von Eschenbach, Reinmar von Zweter, Biterolf, Der Tugendhafte Schreiber—"the virtuous scribe"—and Heinrich von Ofterdingen), Wolfram's mysterious adversary, Klingsor of Hungary, and various spirits. All the singers apart from Heinrich von Ofterdingen are known from other sources as composers of *Minnesang* (courtly love poetry) and *Sangspruch* (political poetry), and it is assumed that Heinrich was likewise a contemporary poet of note. The character of Klingsor, on the other hand, the "master-priest" and authority on astronomy and necromancy, is derived from Wolfram's grail epic *Parzival,* where Clinschor is the magician and foe of the Grail Knights.

The most important pieces in the complex are the long poems *Fürstenlob (Praise of Lords)* and *Rätselspiel (Guessing Game).* The latter appears to be the oldest part of the *Wartburgkrieg,* with the former designed as a prequel. The *Fürstenlob* tells how six singers compete to see who can best sing the praises of a generous patron, one of the set-piece motifs of *Sangspruchdichtung.* The poets compete in turn; Walther finally defeats Heinrich by a ruse, whereupon Heinrich insists that Klingsor be called to arbitrate. The *Rätselspiel* then takes up the story with Klingsor and Wolfram facing each other in a riddle competition, Klingsor setting abstruse puzzles with spiritual meanings and Wolfram as the pious layman proving his equal by solving each riddle. In one riddle a father tries to waken a child sleeping by a dam, but the child sleeps on until the dam breaks. The solution: the sinner who ignores God's warnings until surprised by death. A version of the *Rätselspiel,* incidentally, forms the prologue to the courtly novel *Lohengrin.*

Other poems in the *Wartburgkrieg* cycle are less well integrated into the narrative setting. The *Totenfeier* begins with a contest between the "Tugendhafte Schreiber" and another voice (possibly Biterolf) in the art of lamenting the dead. The Tugendhafte Schreiber describes a vision of the personified Justice and Compassion, who stand by the grave of a Thuringian lord and dispute whether the occupant has deserved a song of praise. *Zabulons Buch* tells how after the contest recounted in the *Rätselspiel*, Wolfram calls on St. Brandan for support, and Klingsor on the magic Book of Zabulon; the bulk of the poem describes the history of the book. *Aurons Pfennig (Auron's Penny)* is an account of a conflict between monks and secular priests in which the latter are accused of corruption. A letter written in Aramaic, passed to Klingsor by a neutral angel, contains the charges against them.

BIBLIOGRAPHY

Parodie und Polemik in mittelhochdeutscher Dichtung: 123 Texte von Kürenberg bis Frauenlob, samt dem Wartburgkrieg nach der Grossen Heidelberger Liederhandschrift C, ed. Gunther Schweikle. Stuttgart: Helfant, 1986.

Wachinger, Burghart. *Sängerkrieg; Untersuchungen zur Spruchdichtung des 13. Jahrhunderts.* Munich: Beck, 1973.

Graeme Dunphy

SEE ALSO

Minnesang; Sangspruch; Versification; Walther von der Vogelweide; Wartburg; Wolfram von Eschenbach

Weapons

The Roman soldiers who faced the barbarian invasions of the fourth and fifth centuries were outfitted with offensive armaments that varied little from those carried by the first-century legionnaires. The barbarian soldiers whom they faced in the fourth and fifth centuries had different weapons and different attitudes to them than did the Romans. Although there was little standardization among, or even within, the various tribal armies that invaded the Roman Empire, their infantries tended to use spears as their chief weapon. They also were outfitted with axes, bows with iron-tipped arrows, and swords. The chief weapon of the cavalry was a long, two-edged sword. Although the weapons of the barbarians were in most instances not as effective as those of the Romans, the invaders seemed to recognize these limitations and modified their tactics until they could more effectively use their "inferior" weapons.

By the time of the Carolingians, the standardization and effectiveness of offensive weapons had greatly improved. The principal weapon remained the spear, and it was to be carried by both infantry and cavalry troops. As early as 792–793 Carolingian laws required the lance as a weapon for all horsemen, with the infantry outfitted likewise with a lance, as decreed in 802–803. From this time throughout the end of the Middle Ages, the spear, both as an infantry weapon and as a cavalry weapon, took on a new importance in warfare. It continued to be used sometimes as a javelin but mostly as a thrusting weapon, the soldier either thrusting downward with his spear, in a stabbing motion, or thrusting upward, in an attempt to strike an opponent under his armor or to lift him from his horse. Yet using the lance only as a thrusting weapon when mounted made the warhorse merely a fighting platform and did not incorporate either its power or speed into the attack. This was accomplished only when the lance was held fixed under the horseman's arm in a couched position. Then, in what is now called mounted shock combat, as the horse charged an opponent, the lance blow was delivered by a combination of the lance, the rider, and the horse, producing a far greater impact to the attack than a manual thrust ever could. In the fourteenth and fifteenth centuries the infantry spear lengthened to become a pike. In this form it continued to dominate infantry warfare until well into the eighteenth century.

The sword was also prominent in Charlemagne's army. When a warhorse was owned, so too should a sword be owned. Carolingian swords also set the technological standard for sword making for several centuries. The swords on both sides of the Norman conquest of England were Carolingian-influenced. They were also the swords of the Spanish Reconquista and the First Crusade. This was mostly because of the chain mail armor they faced, armor that was most easily destroyed by using the sword as a slashing weapon. Thus, sword blades remained flat and light, with sharp edges emphasized rather than a point. With the fourteenth-century change in armor, from chain to plate, a change in sword fabrication was also needed. Plate armor easily resisted the slashing attacks of the Carolingian-style sword but was more easily penetrated than chain mail had been. Thus the sword needed to be modified to take advantage of that handicap. It became a thrusting weapon, its point used more than its edge to attack an opponent. Swords of the late Middle Ages became shorter and stiffer, often with reinforced, sharp points. Daggers, too, were used throughout the Middle Ages, both for military and for nonmilitary functions.

The ax as a weapon continued to be used until the end of the eleventh century. By that time it began to be replaced by the mace. Derived from the cudgel or club, the mace consisted of a flanged or knobbed iron head mounted on a wooden haft, although by the fourteenth century, some maces were being constructed completely in metal. The mace proved to be a popular weapon, with soldiers using it in a tournament or battle causing great damage to their opponents' shields and armor. But with its variation, the war hammer, the mace tended to be used most frequently by cavalry soldiers.

A late medieval infantry variation of the mace was the staff weapon. The staff weapon describes an entire category of offensive weapons. In their simplest form, staff weapons united the spear or lance with an ax, hammer, or mace to produce a long-hafted infantry weapon that combined the capabilities of a lance against the charge with those of the axe or mace in close-combat melee. In the early years of the fourteenth century, infantry-based armies began to witness their first substantial and constant victories over cavalry-based armies. Although these victories were not determined by weapons alone, the long-hafted weapons that the infantry used at these battles was recognized, as well as that more and more improved, long-hafted weapons would continue to be needed. This led ultimately to the development of many different staff weapons in the next few centuries. These included instruments with names such as halberd, pole axes, goededages, military forks, glaives, guisarmes, ahlspiesses, bardiches, vouges, bills (or billhooks), chauvesourises, couseques, partisans, and rawcons.

Finally, missile weapons, bows, and crossbows were also frequently used on the battlefield, with slings used less frequently.

BIBLIOGRAPHY

Contamine, Philippe. *War in the Middle Ages,* trans. M. Jones. London: Blackwell, 1984.

DeVries, Kelly. *Medieval Military Technology.* Peterborough, Ont.: Broadview, 1992.

Nicolle, David C. *Arms and Armour of the Crusading Period, 1050–1350.* 2 vols. White Plains, N.Y.: Kraus, 1988.

———. *Medieval Warfare Source Book.* 2 vols. London: Arms and Armour, 1995–1996.

Kelly DeVries

SEE ALSO

Archer/Bowman; Armor; Carolingians; Charlemagne; Crossbow; Warfare

Weckmann, Nicolaus, the Elder (d. ca. 1526)

Nicolaus Weckmann became a citizen of Ulm in 1481, and documents reveal that he subsequently became a highly successful wood sculptor. His large oeuvre was not recognized, however, until Wolfgang Deutsch's research was published in 1968 following the discovery four years earlier of a signature on the base of an over-life-size linden wood statue of the *Ritter* (Knight) Stefan von Gundelfingen at the parish church in Neufra. The inscription "niclaus weckman bildhauer . . . 1528" (Nicolaus Weckman Sculptor . . . 1528) revealed during a cleaning of the Neufra sculpture is likely that of the younger Weckmann, but its discovery has resulted in a reevaluation of sculpture in Ulm during the years around 1500 and of the recognition of Weckmann the Elder as a major artistic personality.

Prior to 1964 Michel Erhart and Jörg Syrlin the Younger were considered the major wood sculptors in Ulm active around 1500. Deutsch has recognized, however, that the younger Syrlin was primarily a contractor who acted as an agent in securing wood carvers and decorators for the production of altarpieces. Much of the work previously attributed to the younger Syrlin has now been given to Weckmann. Some of the key monuments are a figure of Saint Sebastian in the Neidhart chapel of Ulm Münster, the Virgin with Saints Peter and Paul from Ochsenhausen now at Ballamont, a Holy Kindred in the parish church of Haldenwang, the center of the altarpiece from Talheim now in the Württembergisches Landesmuseum in Stuttgart, and the Virgin Enthroned on the Crescent Moon in the Kunsthistorisches Museum in Vienna.

Weckmann maintained a large workshop, and there is consequently some inconsistency in the generally high quality of its output, as well as a formulaic approach to such features as drapery carving and hair. Nicolaus Weckmann the Elder is last mentioned in documents in 1526 when he was characterized as "old."

BIBLIOGRAPHY

Deutsch, Wolfgang. "Jörg Syrlin der Jüngere und der Bildhauer Niklaus Weckmann." *Zeitschrift für Württembergische Landesgeschichte* 27 (1968): 39–82.

———. "Der Altar in der Adelberger Ulrichskapelle." In *Heilige Kunst: Mitgliedsgabe des Kunstvereins der Diözese Rottenburg-Stuttgart* (1979–1980), pp. 13–51.

Meisterwerke Massenhaft: Die Bildhauerwerkstatt des Niklaus Weckmann und die Malerei in Ulm um 1500. Stuttgart: Württembergisches Landesmuseum, 1993.

Schädler, Alfred. "An Unknown Late Gothic Masterpiece: The 'Adoration of the Magi' by Niclaus Weckmann the Elder." *Apollo* 129 (1989): 173–178.

Peter Barnet

SEE ALSO

Erhart, Michel; Gothic Art and Architecture; Iconographies, Innovative; Syrlin, Jörg (Elder and Younger); Ulm

Weddings and Funerals

See Birth, Marriage, Burial; Marriage and Divorce.

Welfs

The Welfs (also Guelfs) came originally from Alsace. A Frankish noble called Ruthard, count of Argengau in the reign of Pippin III, the Short, is now recognized as one of the founders of the family.

When Louis the Pious married Judith, the eldest daughter of Count Welf, possibly Ruthard's son or grandson, in 819, her brothers Conrad the Elder and Rudolph advanced rapidly at court, and her younger sister Hemma married Louis the German, Judith's stepson. Conrad the Elder in particular acquired much land in Swabia. Conrad's sons Conrad the Younger and Hugo, and Rudolph and Welf were deeply involved in the problems of the Carolingian Empire after 841. Their Swabian power base committed them initially to Louis the German of east Francia, but in 859 Conrad the Younger chose to ally himself with the west Frankish Charles the Bald, and he married the Carolingian Waltrada. In 865, Conrad acquired the former Burgundian "kingdom." Burgundy was a Germanic settlement in the northern Rhône valley, the eastern Alps and the Upper Rhine. In the fifth century their leader Sigismund had become a Christian, but Attila's Huns seriously damaged the fragile kingdom, and the expanding Merovingian Franks destroyed it soon after. Little remained but legends later turned into the *Waltharilied* (ninth century) and the *Nibelungenlied* (thirteenth century).

Conrad's son Rudolph, cognizant of his Carolingian heritage, called himself "King of Burgundy" in 888. His ambitions suffered a serious setback, however, at the hands of Arnulf of Carinthia, the new ruler of East fran-

cia, who blocked Rudolph's expansion into Lotharingia. Rudolph bequeathed his dreams and his kingdom to his son in 912. Rudolph II also tried to move westward into Vienne, south into Provence and Italy, and eastward into the areas around Basel. Italy was beyond his grasp, but he managed to move into Provence. In 922 he married Bertha of Swabia and in 926 he became an ally of the German king Henry I. Rudolph II died in 937; his son Conrad "the Peaceable" eventually succeeded him in circa 941; his daughter Adelheid first married Lothar of Italy in 947 (d. 950) and then the German king Otto I. Conrad died in 993; his son Rudolph III ruled Burgundy until 1032, when he died without heirs. The senior branch of the Welfs ended and Burgundy became part of Conrad II's empire.

The younger branch of the Welf family descended from Welf I (d. 876), left behind as Count of Argengau when his elder brothers defected to Charles the Bald. His grandson Henry *(Heinrich mit dem goldenen Pflug)* recovered some of their lost lands in Swabia, and in 935 he founded the convent of Altdorf. His marriage to Atha von Hohenwarth brought him lands in Bavaria; one of his sons, Conrad, became bishop of Constance (934–975). His great grandson Welf II (ca. 970–1030) married Imiza (Irmentrud) (ca. 985–after ca. 1057), daughter of Frederick of Luxemburg. Welf II and Imiza had two children: a daughter, Kunigunde (Cuniza) (ca. 1010–ca. 1040), married to Azzo II marquis of Este about 1030, and a son, Welf III (born ca. 1005), duke of Carinthia. He relocated the family monastery of Altdorf on the Martinsberg, now called Weingarten. Unmarried, Welf III willed the Welf lands to Weingarten. On his death in 1055, however, his mother, Imiza, challenged his will on the grounds that she had not consented to his bequests; her Italian grandson Welf IV (d'Este) inherited instead. Welf, then about twenty, began his long career in Swabia and Bavaria under the Salian emperors Henry III and Henry IV, becoming duke of Bavaria in 1070. He died in 1101. He married three times but had children only by his third wife, Judith of Flanders (d. 1094), the widow of Tostig Godwinson (d. 1066). His eldest son, Welf V, born circa 1073, married the middle-aged Mathilda of Tuscany in 1089, but the marriage was dissolved in 1095. In 1101 Welf V became duke of Bavaria, dying on September 24, 1120; his successor was his younger brother Henry the Black (Heinrich der Schwarze), born 1074 and died December 13, 1126. In 1095/1100 Henry married Wulhild of Saxony, heiress of Magnus Billung duke of Saxony (she died on December

29, 1126). Henry the Black thus established a foothold in Saxony for the Welf family; he and his wife had seven children, among them Judith (1100–1130), the wife of Frederick of Staufen, duke of Swabia, and the mother of Frederick Barbarossa; Welf VI, who inherited all the Italian lands (Spoleto and Tuscany) and died in 1191, his only son, Welf VII, having predeceased him in 1167. The eldest son, Henry the Proud (Heinrich der Stolze), born circa 1100, became duke of Bavaria in 1126, married Gertrude, daughter of Lothar III, in 1127, and became duke of Saxony in 1137. Henry the Proud had fully expected to follow his father-in-law as ruler of the Holy Roman Empire in 1137, but he was passed over for Conrad of Staufen. A civil war ensued, but Henry died suddenly on September 24, 1139, and the Welfs' power seemed at an end. Henry and Gertrude had one son, Henry the Lion (Heinrich der Löwe), (ca. 1129/1131–August 6, 1195), whose guardians managed to save his Saxon lands. Henry the Lion rose to great heights as duke of Saxony and Bavaria in the reign of his cousin, Frederick I, only to lose everything through arrogance and political miscalculation. Henry the Lion's marriage to Mathilda of England (1156 to June 28, 1189) produced at least eight children, among them Henry of Braunschweig (1173–1227), Otto IV (1177–1218), and William of Winchester (1184–1213). William and his wife, Helena of Denmark, had one son, Otto the Child (Otto das Kind, 1204–1252), who became duke of Braunschweig-Luneburg. His descendants were the electors of Hanover (1699) and kings of England (1714).

The Welfs are one of the oldest noble families of Europe, beginning in the eighth century. In the twelfth century a Swabian cleric in the employ of Welf VI wrote a family history, *Historia Welforum.* Embellished with legendary details, this chronicle bears witness to the Welfs' pride as a noble clan. Though dimly aware of their Frankish past, the Welfs saw themselves as proud Swabians connected to the most powerful families of Germany and Italy; their name "Welf," so they believed, derived from *welp* (cub), particularly the lion's cub. A lion was their heraldic symbol.

BIBLIOGRAPHY

Hlawitschka, Eduard. *Stirps regia: Forschungen zum Königtum und Führungsschichten im frühen Mittelalter,* ed. Gertrud Thoma and Wolfgang Giese. Frankfurt: Lang, 1989.

Jordan, Karl. *Henry the Lion,* trans. P. S. Falla. Oxford: Clarendon, 1986.

König, Erich. *Historia Welforum.* Sigmaringen: Thorbecke, 1978.

Schmid, Karl. *Gebetsgedanken und adliges Selbstverständnis im Mittelalter.* Sigmaringen: Thorbecke, 1983.

Tellenbach, Gerd. *Studien und Vorarbeitungen zur Geschichte des Großfränkischen Adels.* Freiburg: E. Albert, 1957.

Madelyn Bergen Dick

SEE ALSO

Adelheid of Burgundy; Billunger; Carolingians; Conrad II; Frederick I Barbarossa; Henry III; Henry IV; Henry the Lion; Louis the Pious; Matilda, Empress; *Nibelungenlied;* Otto I; Otto IV; Pippin; Salians; Staufen

Wenceslas (November 26, 1361–August 6, 1419)

Wenceslas IV (Václav, Wenzel, king of the Romans 1378–1400, king of Bohemia until 1419) was the eldest son of Charles IV by his third wife, Anna of Schweidnitz. Wenceslas was born on November 26, 1361, in Nuremberg. He was elected king of the Romans on June 10, 1376, and assumed control of imperial affairs as Staathalter in February of the following year. After Charles's death, he inherited the Bohemian crown. Wenceslas has not enjoyed the good reputation of his father. In particular, he has been generally condemned for his sloth, vacillation, and drunkenness.

Wenceslas was faced immediately with several serious problems. First was the Swabian City League, established July 4, 1376. The growth of the league, aimed directly against the mortgage policies of his father, led to a major war, lasting until 1389. The second problem was the Great Schism, which broke out in the fall of 1378. Wenceslas supported the pope in Rome, Urban VI. In 1380 he traveled to Paris in an attempt to convince French King Charles V to withdraw support from the Avignon pope, Clement II. When this effort failed, on the advice of Urban VI, Wenceslas allied himself with Richard II of England. The alliance and resulting marriage between the English king and Wenceslas's sister Anna marked a total break with the traditional pro-French Luxembourg policy. Within the empire, a group of southern principalities, led by Leopold III of Austria and Archbishop Pilgrim II of Salzburg, supported Clement VII.

During the first years of his reign, Wenceslas sought to resolve the problems of the cities. The *Landfriede* (peace)

of Nuremberg (1383) marks the first attempt to divide the empire into districts or counties *(Kreise),* anticipating the later reforms of Albrecht II and Maximilian I. After the league's defeat at Döffingen (1388), the *Landfriede* of Eger (1389) provided a modicum of stability for the next several decades. The political autonomy of the cities was recognized, while they were banned from making further leagues.

After 1390, problems in Bohemia consumed most of Wenceslas's energy. He tended to support the towns and lower nobility; this provoked resistance from the great nobles and higher clergy. The archbishop of Prague, Jan z Jenštejna (1379–1396) in particular proved a serious opponent of the crown. The torture and murder of the vicar general of Prague, John of Pomuk (March 20, 1393) by royal officials provoked a noble Fronde in 1394. Wenceslas's cousin, Margrave Jost of Moravia, joined with the nobles and took the king prisoner (May 8, 1394) with the collusion of Duke Albrecht III of Austria. Jost was named regent, but the intervention of Wenceslas's half-brother John of Görlitz and Ruprecht II of the Palatinate led to the king's release. As Wenceslas now turned on his opponents, a civil war broke out. The deaths of Albrecht III (August 29, 1395) and John of Görlitz (March 1, 1396) brought an end to the fighting. Wenceslas's other half-brother, king Sigismund of Hungary, was able to negotiate a peace settlement among Jost, Wenceslas, and the nobles. In return, Sigismund was recognized as Wenceslas's heir and named imperial vicar.

After the battle of Nikopolis (September 28, 1396), Sigismund turned to securing his Hungarian lands. This left Wenceslas, after a ten-year absence from Germany, faced with an angry crowd of princes at the imperial diets of Nuremberg (1397) and Frankfurt (1398). The four Rhenish electors issued a series of demands. The *Landfriede* and Schism were perennial sticking points. Wenceslas's elevation of Giangalleazzo Visconti to the duchy of Milan (April 11, 1395) also provoked the electors' ire. In June 1400 the Rhenish electors demanded that Wenceslas appear before them to answer to their complaints. Their request coincided with a renewal of hostilities among Wenceslas, Jost, and the nobles. Wenceslas's Bohemian problems did not, in the eyes of the electors, excuse his refusal to appear. On August 20, 1400, the four Rhenish electors declared Wenceslas deposed and elected the count palatine, Ruprecht III, king of the Romans.

Wenceslas refused to recognize his deposition, but he was too occupied with Bohemian affairs to do much about it. The death of Ruprecht of the Palatine in 1401

presented Wenceslas with an opportunity to regain the German throne. Unfortunately he could not count on support from his family. Indeed, both Sigismund and Jost were able to secure election to the imperial throne. Jost's death—perhaps from poison—in January 1411 cleared the way for an agreement between Sigismund and Wenceslas. The latter agreed to relinquish his German crown in return for half the imperial revenues and recognition of his position in Bohemia.

The last years of Wenceslas's reign in Bohemia saw the beginnings of a religious and political crisis that would later erupt in the Hussite revolution. Since the time of Charles IV, a series of radical preachers, among them Conrad Waldhause, Jan Milíc, and Matthew of Janov, had been attacking the higher clergy. The marriage between Anne of Bohemia and Richard II of England led to the growth of a Wycliffite faction among Czech scholars at the University of Prague. Jerome of Prague, along with his student Jan Hus, appeared as leaders of the Wycliffite Czechs. The ideological struggles were connected with political struggles in the university between the Czech minority and the three German-dominated "nations."

After the Roman pope Boniface IX (1389–1404) supported the Rhenish electors in 1400, Wenceslas turned to support the Czech reformers. He agreed to recognize the Council of Pisa (1408) and at the council of Kutná Hora ordered the German masters of the university to do so as well. The Kutná Hora decrees (January 18, 1409) broke the Germans' control over the university, giving the Czech nation three votes to one for all three of the German nations. A number of German masters left, later forming the core of the University of Leipzig.

The principal architects of the Czech victory were Jerome of Prague, Jan Hus, and Jakoubeck of Stríbro. In the wake of the Kutná Hora decrees, Archbishop Zdynek of Prague (1399–1411) excommunicated a number of royal officials and placed Prague under the interdict. Wenceslas ordered the city's clergy to ignore the decree. Zydnek agreed to submit to the king, but then fled the kingdom, seeking the aid of Emperor Sigismund. The archbishop died in Bratislava in September 1411, and after his departure, the Hussite movement became more radical. A group of reformers began calling for the administration of the cup to the laity *(utraquism).* In 1412 Hus and Jakoubek publicly declared the Roman pontiff to be antichrist, leading to their excommunication. Along with the new archbishop, Conrad of Vechta, Wenceslas made a furtive attempt to restore Catholicism. Hus turned to the nobility for support, and at a synod in February 1413,

Wenceslas again changed his mind, ordering the archbishop's commission to declare that there was no heresy in Bohemia.

In 1414 Emperor Sigismund requested that Hus appear before the Council of Constance to explain his program. Under a guarantee of safe-conduct, Hus went to Constance but soon found himself imprisoned. Over 250 Czech nobles protested this action, but to no avail. On July 6, 1415, Hus was burnt as a heretic in Constance. Reprisals against other Hussites had already begun. The German burghers of Olomouc had burned two lay preachers a week earlier; Jerome of Prague was burnt in May of the following year. Hus's death led fifty-eight Hussite nobles to form a Hussite league in September 1415. A Catholic alliance followed a month later. In 1416 Wenceslas again tried to restore Catholicism in Prague, but resistance from the university faculty and nobility forced a compromise on the question of *utraquism.*

The election of Pope Martin V in 1417 increased pressure on Wenceslas to take a hard line against the heretics. In the spring of 1419, Wenceslas arrested priests in Prague who granted the cup to the laity, and appointed Czech and German Catholics as *Bürgermeister* (mayors) in the Nové Mesto. On July 30, 1419, the radical preacher Jan Zelivsky led a procession through the city to the New Town Hall demanding the release of imprisoned Utraquist priests. A scuffle broke out, and thirteen of the council members were thrown out the window. The first defenestration of Prague led to the outbreak of a great revolt. Not long after, on August 6, 1419, Wenceslas died. While most works ascribe his death to a stroke, research by a Czech neurologist suggests that the actual cause of death was acute alcohol poisoning.

Wenceslas was married twice, to Johanna of Bavaria (d. 1386) and Sophia of Bavaria (d. 1425). He had no children and all his lands fell to Emperor Sigismund.

BIBLIOGRAPHY

Baethgen, Friedrich. *Schisma und Konzilzeit, Reichsreform und Habsburg Aufstieg.* Munich: Deutscher Taschenbuch Verlag, 1973.

Gerlich, Alois. *Habsburg-Luxembourg-Wittelsbach im Kampf um die deutschen Königsthrone: Studien zur Vorgeschichte Königtums Ruprechts von der Pfalz.* Wiesbaden: Steiner, 1960.

Hlaváček, Ivan. *Das Urkunden- und Kanzleiwesen des böhmischen und römischen Königs Wenzel (IV.) 1376–1419: Ein Beitrag zur spätmittelalterlichen Diplomatik.* Stuttgart: Hiersemann, 1970.

Kaminsky, Howard. *A History of the Hussite Revolution.* Berkeley: University of California Press, 1967.

Lindner, Theodor. *Geschichte des deutschen Reiches unter König Wenzel.* Braunschweig: C. A. Schwetschkte und Sohn, 1875/1880.

Speváček, Jiří. *Václav IV. 1361–1419. K predpokladûm hustiské revoluce.* Prague: Svoboda, 1986.

William Bradford Smith

SEE ALSO
Charles IV; Constance; Luxemburger

Wenezlan

See Dietrich and Wenezlan.

Werden

Located near Essen on the Ruhr River, Werden was founded as a private monastery about 800 by Liudger (or Ludger), the missionary to Friesland (Frisia) and the first bishop of Münster in Westphalia; after his death in 809 he was buried here. Richly endowed and stamped by Anglo-Saxon influence, the abbey possessed an important scriptorium, a large library, and several early medieval church buildings. Of Liudger's original three-aisle church, only the foundations of the nave and the west wall have been excavated. Building II, a basilica structure with a triapsidal sanctuary and a hall crypt where Liudger's grave was located, was consecrated in 875. Its basic forms are visible in the Romanesque ring crypt from the eleventh and thirteenth centuries and in the outer walls of the choir integrated into the new, late Romanesque church. A "westwork," or side of the structure facing west, known as the tower of the Virgin *(turris Sanctae Mariae)* and later as the church of St. Peter, was added onto the late Carolingian building in the second quarter of the tenth century and consecrated in 943; its middle tower with flanking two-story side spaces is also largely preserved, although changed as a result of its incorporation into the thirteenth-century building. In 1892 and 1953–1954, wall paintings were uncovered in the westwork. Architectural features, such as the undersides of the arches of the gallery, were decorated with color and, in places, ornamental detail, and remains of unidentified scenes occupied two niches in the side walls of the aisles. These may well be the oldest known Ottonian wall paintings. After a fire in 1256, Abbot Albero rebuilt the church (now the parish church of St. Ludger) almost completely in the mature forms of the Rhenish late Romanesque; it was consecrated in 1275.

The treasury of the secularized cloister was partially auctioned off; a Frankish reliquary casket made of bone in the eight century, the so-called chalice of St. Liudger of the ninth-tenth century, and a Romanesque bronze crucifix from the daughter cloister of Helmstedt (about 1060) attest to its former richness. Still preserved in the church are seven limestone reliefs representing two standing deacons and fourteen seated figures, mostly women, under individual arcades; these panels, which probably came from a rearrangement of Liudger's tomb about 1058, represent an important early step in the development of stone sculpture in the Rhineland.

The eastern parts of the three-apse choir of the affiliated church St. Clemens, which stood on the hill above the abbey church, have been excavated; this church was consecrated in 957 and razed in 1817. The remains of the eleventh-century parish church St. Lucius, a three-aisle basilica with alternating supports dedicated in 1063, have been severely altered as a result of partial demolition in the eighteenth and nineteenth centuries, secularization in 1803, and rebuilding in 1958. Some figural painting remains in the niches of the square choir bay.

BIBLIOGRAPHY

Clemen, Paul. *Die Kunstdenkmäler der Stadt und des Kreises Essen.* Die Kunstdenkmäler der Rheinprovinz 2, 3. Düsseldorf: L. Schwann, 1893, pp. 76–104.

———. *Die romanische Monumentalmalerei in den Rheinlanden.* Düsseldorf: L. Schwann, 1916, pp. 77–87.

Effmann, Wilhelm. *Die karolingisch-ottonischen Bauten zu Werden.* 2 vols. Strasbourg: Heitz, 1899; rpt. Berlin: Deutscher Kunstverlag, 1922.

Haacke, Rhaban. *Die Benediktinerklöster in Nordrhein-Westfalen.* Germania Benedictina 8. St. Ottilien: Eos, 1980, pp. 575–607.

Kubach, Hans E., and Albert Verbeek. *Romanische Baukunst an Rhein und Maas: Katalog der vorromanischen und romanischen Denkmäler.* 4 vols. Berlin: Deutscher Verlag für Kunstwissenschaft, 1976–1989, vol. 2, pp. 1219–1237; vol. 4, pp. 23f., 647 passim.

Schaefer, Leo, and Hilde Claussen. "Neue Funde zur frühen Baugeschichte der Abtei Werden," in *Beiträge zur Rheinischen Kunstgeschichte und Denkmalpflege 2.* Die Kunstdenkmäler des Rheinlandes, Beiheft 20. Düsseldorf: L. Schwann, 1974, pp. 293–334.

Vorromanische Kirchenbauten: Katalog der Denkmäler bis zum Ausgang der Ottonen. Veröffentlichungen des Zentralinstituts für Kunstgeschichte in München 3. 1966–1971. Munich: Prestel, 1990, pp. 368–372. *Nachtragsband* [suppl.], Munich: Prestel, 1991, pp. 453–455.

Zimmermann, Walther. *Die Kirchen zu Essen-Werden.* Die Kunstdenkmäler des Rheinlandes, Beiheft 7. Essen: Fredebeul und Koenen, 1959.

Matthias Exner

Werner der Gärtner (fl. circa 1250–1280)

The creator of one of the most realistic narratives of the Middle Ages, Werner der Gärtner (the gardener) composed *Helmbrecht*, a short epic of 1,934 lines written in rhyming couplets, between 1250 and 1280, although some dispute this dating. Detailing a drastic picture of contemporary life, Werner depicts the decline of chivalry as well as the moral decay of the peasantry. The work has been variously described as a *Dorfgeschichte* (village tale), *Verspredigt* (rhymed sermon), and exemplum (moral tale). *Helmbrecht* survives in two manuscripts: "A" refers to the famous *Ambras Book of Heroes* (Heldenbuch) from 1504 to 1515, a costly parchment manuscript in Vienna (Nationalbibliothek) copied by Hans Ried; and "B," the "Leombach Manuscript" (1413), a paper manuscript. A third, illustrated manuscript, now lost, was still extant at the start of the nineteenth century. Manuscript "A," regarded as the original version, points to the Austrian-Bavarian region as its place of composition. Little is known of Werner, who is generally thought to have been a cleric, a wandering minstrel, or an occasional poet. He was an educated man whose work was intended for a sophisticated, noble audience.

This moral-didactic tale centers on the generation gap between father and son, between older conservative values and newer progressive aspirations. Werner begins with a description of the elaborate and highly inappropriate cap with which Helmbrecht, the farmer's son, hopes to find acceptance among the knights. The younger Helmbrecht rejects the farmer's life and instead aspires to become a knight, a calling for which he is clearly unsuited. His mother and sister provide him with expensive clothing (a contravention of the sumptuary laws); father Helmbrecht provides him with a costly steed, but only after trying to dissuade his son from leaving the farm (vv. 233–258; 279–298; 329–360). Helmbrecht easily finds acceptance with a band of robber knights and soon becomes the worst in his gang. After a year of plundering, he returns home and tells his father about the depravity and immorality of the knights. The elder Helmbrecht again tries to convince his son to remain on the farm and offers to share all that he has with him (vv. 1098–1114). Helmbrecht scoffs at this offer and returns to his band of robber knights, taking with him his sister Gotelint, who secretly has agreed to marry his friend Lemberslint. The marriage proves ill-fated, for after the wedding breakfast the judge and his hangmen appear and try them on the spot. Helmbrecht's nine companions are summarily hanged. Helmbrecht's life is spared but only after he has been maimed and blinded as punishment for his behavior toward his parents. It is in this pitiful condition that Helmbrecht returns home for the last time. Unlike before, he does not find a compassionate father ready to help him, but rather a disdainful father who turns him out (vv. 1713–1760; 1775–1813). Helmbrecht suffers a miserable existence in the forest until he is finally captured by peasants whom he had wronged and is hung.

The three conversations between father and son mark the tale's progress. The lesson is clear: parents should be strict in educating their children; children should obey their parents (the Fourth Commandment); one should be content with one's station in life *(ordo mundi)*. Whether or not Werner actually witnessed the events he describes, these events accurately reflect the social unrest occasioned by the end of the Hohenstaufen reign in the late thirteenth century. Werner addresses the major social issues of his time by depicting the collapse of the feudal system, the decline of chivalry, and the new self-assertiveness of the peasants; his social criticism is directed at peasants and knights alike.

BIBLIOGRAPHY

Banta, Frank G. "The Arch of Action in Meier Helmbrecht." *Journal of English and German Philology* 63 (1964): 696–711.

Helmbrecht, ed. and trans. Helmut Brackert, Winfried Frey, and Dieter Seitz. Frankfurt am Main: Fischer-Taschenbuch Verlag, 1972; rpt. 1990.

Jackson, W. T .H. "The Composition of Meier Helmbrecht." *Modern Language Quarterly* 18 (1957): 44–58.

Kolb, Herbert. "Der 'Meier Helmbrecht' zwischen Epos und Drama." *Zeitschrift für deutsche Philologie* 81 (1962): 1–23.

Meier Helmbrecht von Wernher der Gartenaere, ed. Friedrich Panzer. Halle: Niemeyer, 1902; 10th ed., Hans-Joachim Ziegeler. Tübingen: Niemeyer, 1993.

Seelbach, Ulrich. *Bibliographie zu Wernher der Gartenaere.* Berlin: Schmidt, 1981.

———. *Kommentar zum Helmbrecht von Wernher dem Gartenaere.* Göppingen: Kümmerle, 1987.

Sowinski, Bernhard. *Wernher der Gartenaere: Helmbrecht. Interpretation.* Munich: Oldenbourg, 1971.

Wernher der Gartenaere: Helmbrecht, trans. Linda Parshall, ed. Ulrich Seelbach. New York: Garland, 1987.

Lynn D. Thelen

SEE ALSO

Exemplum; *Heldenbücher;* Staufen

Westphalia

This region of northwest Germany (German, Westfalen) was originally the territorial home of one of the three ancient Saxon groups: Westphalians, Eastphalians, and Angarians (or Engern). The Westphalian Saxons had settled in the plains around the Hunte and Ems Rivers around the late seventh century and migrated southward thereafter almost as far as Cologne. They became the target of missionary activity but resisted Charlemagne's attempts to extend Frankish power in the region. Westphalia retained a separate identity for the next three centuries, during which the traditional distinction between the Westphalians and Angrians fell into disuse. In spite of the formation of a Saxon tribal stem duchy under the Liudolfinger (Ottonian) dynasty, the Weser River remained the dividing line between Westphalia and the duchy of Saxony as it emerged east of the Weser in the tenth century.

After rising to royal status, the Saxon princes of the Liudolfinger line retained Westphalia as crown land after establishing a new Saxon duchy under the Billung dynasty by the mid–tenth century. After the extinction of the Saxon royal dynasty, however, the many local secular and ecclesiastical lords increased their power and independence in Westphalia as a result of the Investiture Controversy wars and other rebellions against the Salian royal dynasty. When the Billung ducal house also died out (in 1124), the Saxon duchy (east of the Weser) and the territory of Westphalia were reunited in 1142 and placed in the hands of the Welf, Henry the Lion (thus the duke of Saxony and Bavaria). This reunification of Saxony under ducal leadership was short-lived, however. An anti-Welf alliance of Bishop Ulrich of Halberstadt (recently deposed by Henry the Lion) and the Cologne archbishop, Philip of Heinsberg (who was seeking to recover his nephew's confiscated Saxon inheritance as well as to extend his lordship into western Westphalia) led to increasing feuds with the Welf in Westphalia. The result was Henry the Lion's famous deposition in 1180 at the hands of the emperor (Frederick I Barbarossa), at which Barbarossa gave Westphalia to the archbishop of Cologne as the new duchy of Westphalia. This duchy would be ruled by the archbishops of Cologne until 1803, with its own political and administrative institutions and capital (first at Arnsberg, then from 1434 at Werl). In actuality, effective archiepiscopal lordship was confined mainly to the Sauerland, an area just north and east of Cologne. The other regions of Westphalia were ruled by the bishops of Münster, Paderborn, Osnabrück, and Minden, with the counts of Waldeck, Schaumburg, Lippe, Ravensberg, and Mark (with the Limburg), the imperial city of Dortmund, and the abbey of Essen.

With regard to trade and commerce, the cities of Westphalia tended to follow the city of Cologne throughout the eleventh and twelfth centuries. This is best seen in their coinage, which they minted as replicas of the Cologne penny *(pfennig)*. But by the mid–thirteenth century they had become vital centers of trans-European trade in their own right, and were among the first in Germany to form an urban league for the advancement of their economic interests. The Westphalian city league was created in 1246, lead by such cities as Münster, Osnabrück, and Minden.

BIBLIOGRAPHY

Berghaus, Peter. "Der Kölner Pfennig in Westfalen," in *Dona Numismatica. Walter Havernick zum 23. Januar 1965 dargebracht,* ed. Peter Berghaus and Gert Hatz. Hamburg, 1965, pp. 193–204.

Berns, Jürgen Karl W. *Propter communem utilitatem: Studien zur Bundnispolitik der westfälischen Städte im Spätmittelalter.* Düsseldorf: Droste, 1991.

Droege, G. "Das kölnische Herzogtum Westfalen," in *Heinrich der Löwe,* ed. Wolf-Dieter Mohrmann. Göttingen: Vandenhoeck and Ruprecht, 1980, pp. 275–304.

Fricke, Wilhelm. *Das mittelalterliche Westfalen, oder, Die alten Sitten, Gesetze, Gerichte, Zustände und Gewohnheiten der roten Erde.* Minden: Bruns, 1890; rpt. Walluf: Sandig-Reprint, 1976.

Heimann, Heinz-Deiter. *Von Soest—aus Westfalen: Wege und Wirkung abgewanderter Westfalen im späten Mittelalter und in der frühen Neuzeit.* Paderborn: Schöningh, 1986.

Ilisch, Peter. *Münzfunde und Geldumlauf in Westfalen in Mittelater und Neuzeit: numismatische Untersuchungen und Verzeichnis der Funde in den Regierungsbezirken Arnsberg und Münster.* Ph.d. diss., University of Münster, 1975. Münster: Aschendorff, 1980.

Janssen, Wilhelm. "Die Erzbischöfe von Köln und ihr Land." Westfalen im Spätmittelalter." *Westfalen* 58 (1980): 82–95.

Kallen, Gerhard. "Das Kölner Erzstift und der ducatus Westfalie et Angarie (1180)." *Jahrbuch des Kölnischen Geschichtsvereins* 31/32 (1956–1957): 78–107.

Rothert, Hermann. *Westfälische Geschichte, I: Das Mittelalter,* 2d ed. Gütersloh: Bertelsmann, 1962.

Stievermann, Dieter. *Städtewesen in Südwestfalen: die Städte der Mark Sauerlandes im späten Mittelalter und in der frühen Neuzeit.* Stuttgart: Klett-Cotta, 1978.

Joseph P. Huffman

SEE ALSO

Billunger; Charlemagne; Cologne, History; Essen; Henry the Lion; Investiture Controversy; Liudolfinger; Minden; Münster; Osnabrück; Salians; Welfs

Widukind of Corvey (fl. 760s–770s)

Little is known of Widukind's personal life. It has been suggested that the future historian may have entered Corvey at the age of fifteen, during the reign of Abbot Folkmar (d. 942), and that, given the community's social profile, he would have stemmed from the high Saxon aristocracy. Indeed, he may well have been related in some way to "Duke" Widukind, the ninth-century leader of Saxon resistance to Charlemagne's conquest. If so, he would also have been distantly related to the wife of King Henry I, Mathilda, and to her nephew, Count Wichmann. Widukind is known to have composed two works of hagiography: a passion of Thecla the Virgin, and a life of Paul the Hermit. Neither of these has survived. His only extant work, then, is his Saxon history. The work survives in three versions. The first and earliest ("A") is dedicated to Abbess Mathilda of Quedlinburg (d. 999) and includes appropriate prefaces for each book and additional material, most of it intended to edify or flatter her. Widukind apparently hoped that Mathilda, a royal princess, would use her influence at court to help the monks of Corvey.

This version of the text extends as far as Book 3, Chapter 69, and is thought to have been completed by 968. Version "B," the so-called *Hand-* or *Klosterexemplar* (monastery copy), remained at Corvey. It preserves most though not all the additions included in "A." Widukind subsequently added material to this text that now extended through the death of Emperor Otto I in 973. Version "C" also continues Widukind's text up to the death of Otto I but shows evidence of revisions that differ from both version "A" and "B." It is generally thought to have arisen after 973 and to have been based on "B." The text itself is organized into three books. The first book considers the origins of the Saxon folk, especially their early relations with the Franks, the early history of the Liudolfing lineage (i.e., the future royal dynasty), and the rise to power of King Henry I. Here, too, one encounters Widukind's observation that Henry had refused the right of royal anointing, a passage whose significance has intrigued historians for generations, and his equally problematic reference to the *agrarii milites* (armed farmers) who manned the king's fortresses. The second book covers the history of Otto the Great through the death of Queen Edith (946). It includes a unique and particularly detailed description of the king's coronation at Aachen and deals extensively with the uprisings and feuds that plagued much of his reign. The third book continues the story of Otto's reign up to the death of Count Wichmann the Younger (967), who ended his life as a rebel against King Otto I. As already noted, versions "B" and "C" continue the story to Otto's own death and the election of his successor, Otto II. Widukind appears to have known the more familiar historical works of the era, especially Bede and Einhard, and had access to works, such as the anonymous *Translation of St. Vitus,* produced by members of his own community. Among classical authors, he is thought to have been influenced in particular by the Latin poet Sallust, although recent study has raised strong arguments to the contrary.

BIBLIOGRAPHY

Beuman, Helmut. *Widukind von Korvei. Untersuchungen zur Geschichtesschreibung und Ideengeschichte des 10. Jahrhunderts.* Weimar: Böhlaus Nachfolger, 1950.

Keller, Hagen. "Machabaeorum pugnae. Zum Stellenwert eines biblischen Vorbilds in Widukinds Deutung der ottonischen Königsherrschaft," in *Iconologia Sacra. Mythos, Bildkunst und Dichtung in der Religions- und Sozialgeschichte Alteuropas. Festschrift Karl Hauck zum 75. Geburtstag,* ed. Hagen Keller and Nikolaus Staubach. Berlin: de Gruyter, 1994, pp. 417–437.

Quellen zur Geschichte der sächsischen Kaiserzeit ed. Albert Bauer and Reinhold Rau. Darmstadt: Wissenschaftliche Buchgesellschaft, 1977.

Rerum gestarum Saxonicarum libri tres (die Sachsengeschichte des Widukind von Korvei), 5th ed. ed. Hans-Eberhard Lohmann and Paul Hirsch. Monumenta Germaniae Historica, Scriptores rerum Germanicarum, 60. Hannover: Hahn, 1935.

David A. Warner

SEE ALSO
Aachen; Charlemagne; Coronation; Henry I; Liudolfinger; Otto I; Otto II

Wiener Neustadt

Not commonly referred to as Wiener Neustadt (literally, Vienna New City) until the seventeenth century, Neustadt was founded by Leopold V, duke of Austria and Styria, in 1194. He intended that Neustadt fortify the eastern boundary of his realm against Hungarian invasion and protect the roads through that frontier area. According to tradition, Leopold's share of the ransom paid by Richard the Lionhearted (50,000 pounds sterling) financed the city walls. The task of building the town, however, fell to Leopold VI, as his father died within a few months of its founding.

The military colony was laid out as a parallelogram with four main streets leading from a rectangular plaza in the center of the city out through four city gates, each dominated by a massive, four-cornered tower. A canal was constructed to divert water from the Schwarza River to the city, then into a moat between a high inner wall and a lower outer wall around the town; the moat provided additional protection for Neustadt as well as its water supply.

To draw inhabitants to the new military colony, the duke transferred market rights from Neunkirchen to Neustadt. Throughout the Middle Ages, moreover, the ruling lords encouraged the Neustadt economy by granting its citizens special trading privileges as well as exemption from tolls and taxes. The special privileges and protection afforded the town sparked jealousy in the surrounding area. Indeed, Neustadt's history during the second half of the fourteenth century is marked by repeated, sometimes violent quarrels with Vienna over the smaller town's preferential treatment. Impressive works of art like the intricate Gothic cross base, the so-called *Spinnerin Kreuz* (weaver's cross), commissioned about 1380 by wealthy citizens and trade guilds, are a testament to Neustadt's prosperity during this period.

The presence of cloisters and churches contributed significantly to the character of Neustadt. Construction of the parish church dedicated to the Virgin (Liebfrauenpfarrkirche), a spacious three-aisle basilica, was completed in 1279. The two imposing towers on either side of the west portal are a prominent feature of the city skyline. Although the church has a Romanesque exterior, the interior displays predominately Gothic elements. A Gothic choir and transept were added to the church in the early fourteenth century. In 1469, Pope Paul II established the bishopric of Neustadt and elevated this parish church to a cathedral. The church's new status required that appropriate embellishments be undertaken. During the later fifteenth century, late Gothic auxiliary chapels were added, four new altars were consecrated, and splendid sculptures and paintings were produced to adorn the interior of the cathedral. Among these were grand, two-meter-high figures of the apostles with companion paintings of twelve prophets.

Before 1250, Cistercians, Dominican friars, Dominican nuns, and Franciscans had established houses within the city walls. The exterior walls of the Dominican cloisters were incorporated into the city walls so that these buildings, too, contributed to Neustadt's fortification. The choir of the Franciscan church (Minoritenkirche), built around 1300, provides the most impressive example of Gothic architecture in Neustadt. Later, Augustinians as well as Teutonic Knights and Knights of St. George all had houses within the town's walls.

Additional fortification was added to the frontier town in the early fourteenth century when Duke Frederick II (Babenburg) built a new castle against the southeast corner of the city walls. This castle was then the largest four-towered Gothic castle in Babenberg territory. During the fifteenth century, under Habsburg rule, the castle was improved and transformed into a Renaissance palace. An already famous walled garden, the Tiergarten, on the east side of the castle was enhanced. A new church, St. George's, was constructed on top of the western gate of the palace and furnished with rich carvings and stained glass windows. The famous Wappenwand, on the exterior of the church, which boasts 107 coats of arms around three Gothic windows, was completed in 1453.

By around 1250, one of the most important Jewish congregations in the empire had developed in Neustadt, where its members experienced greater tolerance than did their counterparts in other cities. Neustadt's Talmud school attracted students from all over the empire, as well as from Hungary and Bulgaria. The school reached the height of its fame under Rabbi Israel Isserlein. After his death in 1460, its importance waned. In 1496, Maximilian I ordered the Jewish community to leave Neustadt. By 1500 this exodus was complete.

Neustadt became the primary residence of the Habsburgs in 1412. Their continued presence increased the city's stability and fostered a period of tremendous economic and cultural growth, particularly during the period of Frederick III (1433–1493). When Duke Frederick was elected king in 1440 and crowned emperor in 1452, the political importance, prosperity, and outward splendor of Neustadt increased accordingly. A richly gilded altar that Frederick commissioned for the Neuklosterkirche was completed in 1447. It is one of Austria's most important late Gothic works of art. During this period of Habsburg residency, Neustadt was second only to Vienna as an important center of Gothic architecture in the eastern realm.

When Frederick III left Neustadt to reside primarily in Graz and Linz, the city's population and glory began to decline. In 1483, Neustadt was captured by the Hungarian king Matthias Corvinus after a siege of seventeen months. Maximilian I recaptured the city and, although he moved his court to the more centrally located Innsbruck, he returned frequently to a hermitage built onto the Neustadt castle for him. His tomb is there in St. George's. A fire in 1497 destroyed much of the city and accelerated a decline in population.

BIBLIOGRAPHY

Gerhartl, Gertrud. *Wiener Neustadt: Geschichte, Kunst, Kultur, Wirtschaft.* Vienna: Braumüller, 1978.

Ruth M. W. Moskop

SEE ALSO

Cistercian Art and Architecture; *Deutschorden;* Frederick III; Gothic Art and Architecture; Jews; Linz; Maximilian; Romanesque Art and Architecture; Vienna

Wienhausen

A nuns' cloister of Cistercian observance dedicated to the Virgin and St. Alexander was first documented on the Aller River northwest of the village of Wienhausen (Lower Saxony) in 1229. Founded by Agnes of Meißen, a daughter-in-law of Henry the Lion, it received rich donations from the dukes of Brunswick-Lüneberg as well as from the early nuns who were from noble families. Its building and decoration reached a high point in the fourteenth and early fifteenth centuries, and it is remarkable today for the number and quality of original artworks, interiors, and furniture still existing in the original setting. An economic decline that began with a Windesheim reform in 1469 and continued in the sixteenth century with the successful efforts to force a Lutheran reform ensured that no extensive baroque changes replaced the early arrangement.

Today, the interior of the All Saints' Chapel (ca. 1300), the west wing of the cloister (ca. 1310), and the nuns' church (ca. 1330) remain from the original buildings. The latter two, both with stepped gables, ogival (diagonal) blind niches, and high ridge roofs, as well as stairway towers at the corners, are early examples of brick Gothic building in the Lüneberg Heath. In the west wing at the former entrance to the winter refectory, fragments of wall painting (ca. 1320) show the donor Agnes with the church, its patron saints, and the abbess and provost with the west wing, which was built in their time. The oldest stained glass windows of the cloister (1290–1300) are found in the All Saints' Chapel and on the upper level of the south cloister (ca. 1330), where six Passion scenes and a Crucifixion by the Virtues are found. In an adjoining new chapel are the half-life-size figures of the Throned Madonna and Child and the Resurrected Christ from the late thirteenth century.

The nuns' choir is a rare example of completely preserved, although often restored, wall and ceiling painting showing the lives of saints, Old and New Testament scenes, and the Heavenly Jerusalem (ca. 1335). In the middle is a house-shaped Holy Tomb consecrated in 1448; it is painted inside with the Life and Passion of Christ and contains a wooden Christ figure of the late thirteenth century. High wooden candlesticks with scenes of the Life of the Virgin and Passion of Christ from about 1400 now stand at its four corners. The late Gothic altar retable from 1519 has in the center an almost life-size Virgin on a Half-Moon and, flanking her, wings containing relief scenes from her life.

The cloister museum displays a large number of small medieval devotional objects and items for daily use found in 1953 under the floorboards of the choir. Each year, in the second week after Pentecost, the nine famous wool-embroidered tapestries on linen dating from the fourteenth and fifteenth centuries are shown to the public. Their subjects vary from the important and early Tristan tapestry and one with Hunting Scenes, to Old Testament Prophets, a typological *Speculum* (mirror, or primer) tapestry, and Legends of St. Thomas, St. Anne, and St. Elisabeth. Most of the available literature on the cloister is descriptive and historical; only since 1990 have studies relating its furnishing to the practices of north German women's cloisters been published.

BIBLIOGRAPHY

Appuhn, Horst. *Kloster Wienhausen.* Wienhausen: Das Kloster, 1986.

Becksmann, Rüdiger, and Ulf-Dietrich Korn. *Die mittelalterlichen Glasmalereien in Lüneburg und den Heideklöstern.* Corpus vitrearum medii aevi, Deutschland 7/2. Berlin: Deutscher Verlag für Kunstwissenschaft, 1992, pp. 203–249.

Hengevoss-Dürkop, Kerstin. "Der Wienhauser Auferstehungs-Christus: Überlegungen zum Frauenkloster als Formgelegenheit," in *Studien zur Geschichte der Europäischen Skulptur im 12./13. Jahrhundert,* ed. Herbert Beck und Kerstin Hengevoss-Dürkop. Schriften des Liebieghauses. Frankfurt: Heinrich, 1994, vol. 1, pp. 483–493.

Maier, Konrad. *Die Kunstdenkmale des Landkreises Celle im Regierungsbezirk Lüneburg 2: Wienhausen. Kloster und Gemeinde.* Die Kunstdenkmale des Landes Niedersachsen 4/2. Hanover: Niedersächsisches Landesverwaltungsamt, 1970.

Zimmer, Petra. "Die Funktion und Ausstattung des Altares auf der Nonnenempore: Beispiele zum Bildgebrauch in Frauenklöstern aus dem 13. bis 16. Jahrhundert." Ph.d. diss., University of Cologne, 1990, pp. 36–74, 233–251.

Marta O. Renger

SEE ALSO

Cistercian Art and Architecture; Gothic Art and Architecture; Gottfried von Straßburg, *Tristan,* Illustrations; Henry the Lion, Art; Iconographies, Innovative; Ludolf of Saxony; Lüneburg

Wigamur

This Arthurian romance was written by an anonymous poet of unknown social status, presumably around 1250. Subsequent references to this 6,106-verse work by Der Tannhäuser and Ulrich Füeterer and in *Jüngerer Titurel* and *Friedrich von Schwaben* provide no help in more precise dating. East Franconia has been named as a possible place of origin. The text is transmitted in one paper manuscript (Wolfenbüttel) from the end of the fifteenth century and two fragments written on parchment (now in Salzburg and Munich) dating from the mid–fourteenth century and from around 1300, respectively. The fragments have played a crucial role in emendating the text of the head manuscript, which is, in part, seriously flawed by lacunae and interpolations.

While earlier scholarship viewed the romance as a primitive compilation of traditional episodes and motifs derived from the vast body of Arthurian literature, most notably *Lanzelet* and *Wigalois,* contemporary critics have pointed to a sequence of narrative elements that is structured as follows: Prelude: Wigamur's abduction and childhood; Probationary Period: From precourtly state to knight errant; Affirmation: Wigamur in the Arthurian world; Reintegration: Wigamur's homecoming and wedding; Postlude: Abduction and rescue of Wigamur's bride. The achievement of the *Wigamur*-poet is seen in his unique emphasis on the hero's reintegration into family and society, which begins with Wigamur's personal quest of identity and ends with the assumption of royal duties and the administration of justice. These themes are supported and elaborated in the Wolfenbüttel manuscript by an impressive picture cycle consisting of sixty-seven framed drawings. Not only do they exhibit a distinct narrative structure of their own, but they also bear testimony to the positive reception of the work in fifteenth-century Germany.

BIBLIOGRAPHY

Buschinger, Danielle. *Wigamur.* Göppingen: Kümmerle, 1987.

Ebenbauer, Alfred. "Wigamur und die Familie," *Artusrittertum im säpten Mittelalter: Ethos und Ideologie,* ed. Friedrich Wolfzettel. Giessen: Schmitz, 1984.

Henderson, Ingeborg. "Illustrationsprogramm und Text der Wolfenbütteler *Wigamur*-Handschrift," in *In hohem prise: A Festschrift in Honor of Ernst S. Dick.* ed. Winder McConnell. Göppingen: Kümmerle, 1989.

Linden, Walter. "Studien zum Wigamur: Überlieferung und Sprache." Ph.d. diss., University of Halle, 1920.

Sarrazin, Gregor. *Wigamur: Eine litterarhistorische Untersuchung.* Strasburg: Trübner, 1879.

von der Hagen, Friedrich Heinrich, and Johann Gustav Büsching. *Deutsche Gedichte des Mittelalters.* Berlin: Realschulbuchhandlung, 1808.

Ingeborg Henderson

SEE ALSO

Arthurian Literature, German; Fuetrer, Ulrich; Tannhäuser, Der; Wirnt von Grafenberg

Willehalm
See Wolfram von Eschenbach.

Willem of Hildegaersberch (ca. 1350–1408/1409)

The most important author and performer of *sproken* (short verse narratives) in Middle Dutch literature, Willem was born around 1350 in Hillegersberg, near Rotterdam (county of Holland). He died between June 1408 and April 1409. He was not of noble heritage and seems to have received a rather restricted education. We can probably take seriously the verses in which he states that he is ashamed of his lack of knowledge of Latin. Willem was an itinerant poet, performing at aristocratic courts, in abbeys, and in towns. He maintained a close relationship with the court in The Hague, judging by his frequent appearances in the writings about the counts of Holland. Between 1383 and 1403, Willem is mentioned no fewer than thirty-two times.

Much of Willem's oeuvre survives; 120 *sproken* can be attributed to him. His name is mentioned in forty of them. Two manuscripts contain almost all known *sproken* written by him: The Hague, Koninklijke Bibliotheek (manuscript no. 128 E 6) and Brussels, Koninklijke Bibliotheek (manuscript no. 15.659–661), preserving 117 and 119 *sproken,* respectively. Fragments and *sproken* in other miscellanies prove that Willem of Hildegaersberch was very esteemed in his days.

The *sproke,* a short poetic genre, was performed from the fourteenth century onward by itinerant artists in the Middle Dutch area. It has an average length of 180 to 200 verses, but shorter as well as longer *sproken* are found. The *sproke* can be mainly narrative as well as demonstrative, mostly with no lyrical tenor. It generally implicitly or explicitly moralizes or serves a didactic purpose. Moral truth and Christian or worldly ethics are often stressed. The genre of the *sproke* is very close to the exemplum, the parable, and the sermon. Willem mostly writes rhyming couplets, but he sometimes switches to a strophic form.

Willem's poems treat a large diversity of themes. He speaks about religious subjects, such as Christian virtues or the Easter gospel. On the other hand, he does not hesitate to criticize the clergy. An important part of Willem's oeuvre was meant to be recited at court, and these texts are consequently directly addressed to the lords. Here he is concerned with worldly virtues like honor and justice, especially complaining about their decline. He considers it to be his duty to advise the lords in matters of government and to confront them with the truth. His criticism concerns especially the rogues who surround the lords and deceive them. Willem of Hildegaersberch was conscious that he depended to a very large extent on the favor of the lords. This is why he sometimes felt obliged to soften the truth. In those cases he formulated his criticism in an indirect way. Thus, no one had to feel offended, and the person in question always had the possibility to say the criticism did not apply to him or her. The way to make his criticism indirect is fiction. Willem uses dissociating elements: he wraps his criticism in exempla, allegories, or (animal) fables, for example.

BIBLIOGRAPHY

Bisschop, Willem, and Eelco Verwijs, eds. *Gedichten van Willem van Hildegaersberch.* The Hague: Nijhoff, 1870.

Hogenelst, Dini. *Sproken en sprekers. Inleiding op en repertorium van de Middelnederlandse sproke.* 2 vols. Amsterdam: Prometheus, 1997.

Meder, Theo. *Sprookspreker in Holland. Leven en werk van Willem van Hildegaersberch (circa 1400).* Amsterdam: Prometheus, 1991 [German summary].

van Oostrom, Frits P. *Court and Culture: Dutch Literature, 1350–1450.* Berkeley: University of California Press, 1992.

An Faems

SEE ALSO
Exemplum; Literature, Dutch

Wimpfen

The lower town of medieval Wimpfen—known as Wimpfen im Tal (Wimpfen in the Valley)—was constructed on the ruins of a Roman garrison built to protect the imperial frontier. From the ninth century, Wimpfen belonged to the bishopric of Worms. Little is known about the first church built here, the foundations of which were uncovered in 1901, during the restoration of the abbey church of Saints Peter and Paul. The floor plan shows a central-plan structure, which according to a report of Burkhard von Hall was destroyed in 905 by the Huns. The church was subsequently rebuilt and enlarged; its Romanesque western end still survives. This two-story

Wimpfen am Berg, remains of the imperial palace, from left: gallery, stone house, Blue Tower. *Photograph: Joan A. Holladay*

narthex (entrance hall), with its eight-sided towers, dates to before 1000. It probably stands today only because the building campaign for a new three-aisle Gothic church, after 1269, ran out of money before the demolition and rebuilding of the western end.

Burkhard von Hall, in his chronicle of the Gothic campaign, reported that a builder was called on to construct a new church in the French manner *(opus francigenum).* The south side of the Gothic nave and choir has a more fully developed ornamental program than the north side, which is attached to the monastery's Gothic cloister. Within a gabled porch is a Crucifixion relief in the tympanum, a Virgin and Child sculpture on the trumeau, jamb figures of martyrs bearing palms, and figures of Peter and Paul within niches on either side of the portal. The gable is crowned with a figure of the resurrected Christ. The slender, elegantly proportioned choir, lined with figures of saints on consoles between its windows, is one of a number of German monuments inspired by Ste.-Chapelle in Paris. The oak choir stalls here, commissioned in 1298, are among the earliest examples of wood carving of this kind in Germany. Fresco fragments in the west transept depict Christ Carrying the Cross.

The upper town, Wimpfen am Berg (Wimpfen on the Mountain), was the site of the Hohenstaufen's largest and favorite palace on German soil. Between the so-called Red Tower in the east and the Blue Tower in the west, stretches a 25 meter wide and 89 meter long fortified settlement that was probably established by Emperor Frederick I Barbarossa at the end of the twelfth century. He was here in 1182, at which time he may have commissioned the construction of the imperial palace. The most frequent resident here was King Heinrich (Henry) VII, who held court nine times at Wimpfen in the period between 1224 and 1235. In addition to the two towers, which are accessible to the public, a long section of the north wall of the palace survives. Here, overlooking the Neckar River, one finds remnants of a delicately sculpted arcade dating to about 1200. Twin columns, each with its own abstract capital design, and in some cases shaft ornaments, support a series of round window arches. The Romanesque palace chapel, greatly altered in the nineteenth century, has since been restored.

The well-preserved Steinhaus (stone house) largely dates to the twelfth century. Long thought to be the storehouse for the fortification's provisions, it is now believed to have been the original residence of the queen. The second story is occupied by a large hall with a semi-circular Romanesque hearth and decorative wall paintings believed to have been done in the thirteenth century. The ground floor probably originally served as a kitchen; it was converted in the later Middle Ages for use as a prison. At the same time, the upper hall served as the town's courtroom. Although most of the town's half-timbered *(Fachwerk)* houses were destroyed in the Thirty Years' War, several fine examples survive. Among the oldest is the Bürgerspital (Citizens' Hospital) from circa 1233, with each of its upper stories overhanging the one beneath it.

The Stadtkirche (Munincipal Church) in the upper town is a Gothic hall church, the construction of which began in 1234. A Romanesque church on this site, predating the imperial palace, was demolished to make way for the larger Gothic building. The lower sections of the square-based eastern towers are all that remain of the Romanesque monument. The decorative programs on and within the church, including its sculptural works and decorative vaults, largely date to the later part of the Middle Ages. Fine examples of stained glass from this monument (ca. 1300) are preserved in the Württembergisches Landesmuseum in Stuttgart.

BIBLIOGRAPHY

Arens, Fritz. *Die Kunstdenkmäler in Wimpfen am Neckar,* 2d ed. Mainz: Schmidt, 1958.

———. *Die Königspfalz Wimpfen.* Denkmäler deutscher Kunst. Berlin: Deutscher Verlag für Kunstwissenschaft, 1967.

Frisch, Teresa G. *Gothic Art, 1140–c. 1450: Sources and Documents.* Sources and Documents in the History of Art Series. Englewood Cliffs, N.J.: Prentice-Hall, 1971, p. 56.

Klotz, Heinrich. *Die Ostbau der Stiftskirche zu Wimpfen im Tal.* Ph.d. diss., University of Göttingen, 1963. Kunstwissenschaftliche Studien 39. Munich: Deutscher Kunstverlag, 1967.

Leslie Anne Hamel

SEE ALSO

Frederick I Barbarossa; Gothic Art and Architecture; Romanesque Art and Architecture; Worms

Winterthur

The city of Winterthur/Oberwinterthur in Switzerland was founded around 1170 by Count Hartmann III of Kyburg to serve as a marketplace and stockyard. Hartmann was a member of the powerful Kyburg family, which owned lands in the present-day cantons of Zurich and Aargau in the twelfth and thirteenth centuries. After the extinction of the Kyburgs in the mid–thirteenth century, the Habsburgs under the leadership of Count Rudolph acquired Winterthur and used it as a point of defense against the Swiss confederation in 1264.

After its founding in 1170, a small church dedicated to St. Lawrence was erected in Winterthur but was destroyed by fire in 1313. In the section of the city known as Oberwinterthur, a Romanesque parish church is still preserved. There, unique early Gothic frescoes can be found. Oberwinterthur was the site of excavations in the nineteenth century and then again in 1949–1951 and 1958–1959. These revealed first a Roman fort, known as *vitudurum*. Also found were the foundations of an early medieval church erected under the patronage of the Frankish Bishop Arbogast. This church, first mentioned in the sources as Winteraduro in 856, included a rounded apse. Arbogast's church was enlarged in the twelfth century to a basilica with a nave and flanking aisles, and later a choir and tower. The churchyard walls of this church still follow the defensive walls of the Roman fort. The frescoes in the twelfth-century nave were executed around 1340, probably by a workshop from Zurich or Constance. The style of the images can be compared to the Manesse Codex (Heidelberg, Ms. Pal. germ. 848) and the gradual from St. Katharinenthal (Zurich, Schweizerisches Landesmuseum), as well as to the stained glass produced in eastern Switzerland. On the south wall of the nave is a Passion cycle, and on the north, the life of St. Arbogast; both are framed by decorative bands. Portraits of apostles and saints appear between the windows above, in the tradition of basilican wall painting in Rome. During the Reformation in the sixteenth century, the frescoes were whitewashed; they were rediscovered only in 1835.

BIBLIOGRAPHY

Dejung, Emanuel, and Richard Zürcher. *Die Kunstdenkmäler des Kantons Zürich* 6: *Die Stadt Winterthur.* Basel: Birkhäuser, 1952.

Eggenberger, Christoph, and Dorothee Eggenberger. *Malerei des Mittelalters.* Disentis: Desertina, 1989, pp. 200–205.

Häberle, Alfred. "Die Grafen von Kyburg und ihre kirchliche Stiftungen," in *Die Grafen von Kyburg: Kyburger-Tagung 1980 in Winterthur.* Schweizer Beiträge zur Kulturgeschichte und Archäologie des Mittelalters 8. Olten/Freiburg im Breisgau: Walter, 1981, pp. 53–68.

Speich, Klaus, and Hans R. Schläpfer. *Kirchen und Klöster in der Schweiz,* 3d ed. Zurich: Ex Libris, 1982, pp. 108–109.

Elsa Gontrum

SEE ALSO

Constance; Gothic Art and Architecture; *Liederhandschriften;* Zurich

Wirnt von Grafenberg (fl. 1204–1210)

Author of the Middle High German Arthurian romance *Wigalois,* written between 1204 and 1210, Wirnt is thought to be a *ministerial* (clerical administrator) from the town of Gräfenberg north of Erlangen.

No documents associate him with any particular court at which *Wigalois* might have been written, but Berthold IV, count of Andechs and duke of Meran, is his most likely patron. References to characters from *Erec* and *Iwein* as well as the first part of *Parzival* attest to the author's familiarity with the works of his famous contemporaries Hartmann von Aue and Wolfram von Eschenbach. Although earlier treatments of the *Wigalois* story, such as Renaud de Beaujeu's *Le Bel Inconnu,* existed outside of Germany, Wirnt insists that his source was a story told by a squire. It has been suggested that the citing of an oral source served as a pretext to set his own emphasis rather than following slavishly the demands of the genre.

The *Wigalois* romance consists of 11,708 verses and is written in rhymed couplets. The story of Gawein's son, it is divided into five distinct parts: the hero's upbringing in his mother's fairy kingdom; his arrival at Arthur's court and his adventures in the Arthurian realm; his adventures in the otherworldly realm of Korntin and ultimate triumph over the prince of darkness, the heathen King Roaz of Glois; the hero's wedding and coronation; and the avenging of the murder of a wedding guest. While earlier scholarship insisted on viewing Wirnt's hero as the unproblematic knight of fortune's wheel, more recent work detects a flawed character in need of God's mercy who submits to the will of God. It is God who provides the supreme guidance through the supernatural obstacles of Korntin and grants victory. Wirnt's novelty is the Arthurian knight as God's champion in the eschatological conflict between heaven and hell. He uses the genre to send a message of apocalyptic urgency to his contemporary society, drawing obvious parallels between that society and Wigalois's antagonist. Both have lost sight of the ultimate good, and thus the story of Wigalois serves as a vehicle to reaffirm God's grace as our only hope for salvation. Wirnt's romance has enjoyed surprising popularity, judging not only by the relatively large number of extant manuscripts but also by its influence on contemporary as well as subsequent German authors writing in the latter thirteenth and fourteenth centuries. Noteworthy later adaptations of the story include a fifteenth-century chapbook, a Yiddish rendition transmitted in manuscripts from the sixteenth century, and a nursery tale dated 1786. Wirnt himself became the hero of Konrad von Würzburg's verse narrative *Der Welt Lohn,* in which he is depicted as a knight who learns to forsake the things of the world and to serve God. The story of Wigalois has also contributed valuable material to the body of Arthurian iconography, ranging from the Wigalois frescoes in Runkelstein castle near Bolzano in South Tyrol and woodcuts illustrating the chapbook version to picture cycles in two of the manuscripts. One of these, the parchment codex no. *Ltk 537* of Leyden, is considered the only significant illuminated Arthurian manuscript of the fourteenth century.

BIBLIOGRAPHY

Cormeau, Christoph. *'Wigalois' und 'Diu Crone': Zwei Kapitel zur Gattungsgeschichte des nachklassischen Aventiureromans.* Zurich: Artemis, 1977.

Freeland, Beverly M. "*Wigalois A*: A Prototype Edition of Wirnt von Gravenberg's *Wigalois.*" Ph.d. diss., University of California, Los Angeles, 1993.

Henderson, Ingeborg. "Manuscript Illustrations as Generic Determinants in Wirnt von Gravenberg's *Wigalois,*" in *Genres in Medieval German Literature,* ed. Hubert Heinen and Ingeborg Henderson. Göppingen: Kümmerle, 1986.

Kapteyn, J. M. N. *Wigalois, der Ritter mit dem Rade.* Bonn: Klopp, 1926.

Thomas, J. W. *Wigalois, The Knight of Fortune's Wheel.* Lincoln: University of Nebraska Press, 1977.

Ingeborg Henderson

SEE ALSO

Hartmann von Aue; Konrad von Würzburg; Manuscripts, Painting and Production; Runkelstein; Wolfram von Eschenbach

Wismar

The historic importance of Wismar results from its fortunate geographical position at the southern end of a bay naturally suited to the placement of a harbor, which was mentioned for the first time in 1211; its importance was enhanced by the land connection to Lübeck along the coastline. The nucleus of urban development is the northern quarter around the Nikolaikirche (church of St. Nicholas) in the immediate vicinity of the old harbor. The town itself developed during the first half of the thirteenth century along the axis of the road to Lübeck. In 1256, the dukes of Mecklenburg moved their residence from the nearby castle of Mecklenburg—destroyed in 1358 and today a mere village—to a castle just outside Wismar and in 1300, after conflicts between prince and citizens, to an unfortified court palace within the town itself. Even though Schwerin became the new capital of the duchy after its acquisition in 1358, the dual function of Wismar both as a prosperous trading center, centered around the market square, town hall, and Marienkirche (church of the Virgin), and as a princely residence with Fürstenhof (the Princes' Court) and Georgenkirche (church of St. George), determined its development and architectural appearance. The first half of the fifteenth century was characterized by civic unrest between patriciate and artisans, between the city and the duke, who demonstrated his continued interest in the civic administration, and by tensions between Wismar and Lübeck.

Despite the severe damage it suffered in 1945 during World War II, Wismar largely still preserves the character of a medieval Hanseatic town. Among the three Gothic parish churches, only the Nikolaikirche is well preserved. Begun in 1381 by Heinrich von Bremen and largely completed in 1459, its tower was finished only in 1508; it is, although a century later, a faithful copy of Lübeck's Marienkirche as a transeptless basilica with ambulatory choir and hexagonal chapels. Of the fourteenth-century Marienkirche, which followed the same model, only the western tower escaped destruction in 1945 and subsequent demolition in 1960. The present Georgenkirche, while integrating a straight-ended choir of circa 1300, was erected in 1404–1497 as a cruciform basilica with expanded transepts and a short nave of three bays covered by star vaults. Partly destroyed in 1945, its ruined state was only recently restored to its original appearance.

Of the town's fortifications as built in the mid–thirteenth century, only the late Gothic Wassertor (Water Gate) from the later fifteenth century has survived intact, and among the many medieval houses with their brick facades, although mostly remodeled, the house Zum Alten Schweden (The Old Swede) on the market square with its splendid Gothic gable represents the best example of its type. The Gothic town hall, a brick building of the mid–fourteenth century stretching along the entire north side of the market square, was rebuilt 1817–1819 in classical forms, but incorporating the original vaulted basement. Of the two mendicant monasteries in the town, only the choir of the Dominican church, consecrated in 1397, exists today; its nave was demolished in 1876 for a rebuilding of the school into which the Reformation had turned the monastic institution. The chapel of the Heilig-Geist-Spital (Hospital of the Holy Spirit), founded around 1250, an unvaulted single-aisled structure, dates from the same period. The Fürstenhof was rebuilt in 1512–1513 and 1553–1554 in Renaissance forms with terra-cotta decoration.

BIBLIOGRAPHY

Albrecht, Anna Elisabeth, and Stephan Albrecht. *Die mittelalterlichen Flügelaltäre der Hansestadt Wismar.* Kiel: Ludwig, 1998.

Hans J. Böker

SEE ALSO
Hanseatic League; Lübeck

Wittenwiler, Heinrich (ca. 1350–ca. 1450)

Author of the *Ring,* a comic-didactic verse satire of the early fifteenth century, Heinrich Wittenwiler employs chiefly High Alemannic language in the poem, with occasional Bavarianisms. As shown by his knowledge of the local dialect, which he places in the mouths of the peasants in the *Ring,* Wittenwiler probably stemmed from the Toggenburg area of Switzerland. The poem exists in only one manuscript, located in the Meiningen (Thuringia) archives.

Wittenwiler served as *advocatus curiae* at the episcopal court in Constance, where, as a high official of the bishop, he would have moved in circles favorable to the Austrian nobility and inimical to disruptive forces such as the city guilds and the Bund ob dem See (Dutch marine commerce alliance). His use of *Sachliteratur* (technical writing) shows him to have been a man of great learning and wide-ranging interests. He is mentioned in documents from the last two decades of the fourteenth century, although the composition of the *Ring* falls in the first decade of the fifteenth, probably during the episcopate of Albrecht Blarer.

Wittenwiler derived the basic structure of the *Ring* from the short farce *Metzen hochzît (Metz's Wedding),* but expanded it to almost ten thousand lines with extensive allegorical, didactic, and satirical passages. Set in the village of Lappenhausen, the first of three sections deals with Bertschi Triefnas's devotion to Mätzli Rüerenzumph, the antipode of all ideals of courtly beauty. During his wooing, Bertschi accidentally inflicts a head wound on Mätzli, who, while receiving treatment, is impregnated by the doctor Chrippenchra. To cover up his misdeed, the doctor persuades Mätzli to marry Bertschi.

In the second section, a lengthy debate on the pros and cons of marriage, as well as instruction for Bertschi in religion, manners, virtue, hygiene, and home economics, precede the wedding. At the wedding feast, the villagers display every possible form of bad manners and finally abandon themselves to wild dancing. A minor incident at the dance leads, in the third section, to an all-out war between Lappenhausen and neighboring Nissingen. The conflict escalates until it involves most of southwestern Germany and figures from the Germanic epics. Fro Laichdenman, the local astrologer, betrays Lappenhausen to its enemies, and the village burns to the ground. Bertschi, the only survivor, laments his failure to follow the wise teachings of his mentors and moves to the Black Forest to lead the life of a hermit.

To underscore Wittenwiler's method of alternating didacticism with bucolic bawling (*gpauren gschrai),* the manuscript differentiates by means of red or green marginal stripes those passages that can serve as stylistic models (red) from those that satirize peasant mores (green). Read as an allegorical work, the *Ring* strongly associates peasants with images of a carnal and sinful humanity; read politically, it expresses the disgust of an urban nobility faced with a series of peasant revolts.

BIBLIOGRAPHY

Jones, George Fenwick, trans. *Wittenwiler's Ring and the Anonymous Scots Poem Colkelbie Sow.* Chapel Hill: University of North Carolina Press, 1956; rpt. New York: AMS, 1969.

Lutz, Eckhart Conrad. *Spiritualis Fornicatio.* Sigmaringen: Thorbecke, 1990.

Plate, Bernward. *Heinrich Wittenwiler.* Darmstadt: Wissenschaftliche Buchgesellschaft, 1977.

Riha, Ortrun. *Die Forschung zu Heinrich Wittenwilers "Ring" 1851–1988.* Würzburg: Königshausen and Neumann, 1990.

Wießner, Edmund. *Heinrich Wittenwilers "Ring."* Leipzig: Reclam, 1931; rpt. Darmstadt: Wissenschaftliche Buchgesellschaft, 1964.

Wittenwiler, Heinrich. *Der Ring,* ed. Rolf Bräuer, George F. Jones, and Ulrich Müller. Göppingen: Kümmerle, 1990 [facsimile ed.].

Jim Ogier

SEE ALSO
Fastnachtspiele; *Sachliteratur*

Witz, Konrad (ca. 1400/1410–1445/1446)

In 1896, Daniel Burckhardt of the Öffentlichen Kunstsammlung in Basle published his observations on the stylistic similarity between the panels of an incomplete Heilsspiegel Altar (Altar of Human Salvation) in Basle and the panels from the St. Peter Altar in Geneva, which are signed by Konrad Witz and dated 1444. This artist, whose distinctive style had little influence on later German art, had been forgotten since his death.

Konrad Witz was probably born in Rottweil in Württemberg circa 1400–1410; he is first documented by his entrance into the Basel painters' guild on June 21, 1434.

Konrad Witz, Saints Mary Magdalene and Katharine (Strasbourg, Musée de l'Oeuvre Notre-Dame). *Photograph: Joan A. Holladay*

The Council of Basle (1431–1437), which brought high church officials to the city, thus increasing the possibilities for important artistic commissions, was probably the motivation for his move. On January 10, 1435, he became a citizen of Basle, and he married shortly thereafter. In 1441 and 1442 he was paid for unknown paintings in the Kornhaus (granary). One of the wings of his altarpiece for the high altar of St. Peter in Geneva is signed and dated 1444. In 1446 he is recorded as dead, leaving his widow and five young children.

The Heilsspiegel Altar, dated circa 1435 and partially destroyed and dismembered in the iconoclasm of 1529, was painted for the choir of the church of St. Leonhard in Basle. Based on the *Speculum humanae salvationis (Mirror of Human Salvation),* which places Old Testament and other prefigurations next to their fulfillment in the New Testament and Last Judgment, it is the earliest and largest altar in this tradition in the fifteenth century. The center and predella (lower alter panel) are lost, but seven of the eight scenes from the inner wings survive. Five are in the Kunstmuseum in Basle and the other two in the Gemäldegalerie in Berlin and the Musée des Beaux Arts in Dijon. Since they show Old Testament or historical scenes with two figures standing before a gold background, the missing center must have shown their fulfillment: an Adoration of the Magi or a *Christus Salvator* (Christ as Savior) are most often suggested. The outside panels seen on the closed altar showed single figures standing in narrow rooms. Five of the original eight survive: four in Basle and one in Dijon.

The St. Peter Altarpiece (Geneva, Musée d'Art et d'Histoire) also lacks its center and predella, probably destroyed by iconoclasts in 1535, when the remaining panels were separated. Today the inner wings show the Adoration of the Magi on the left and the donor presented to the Virgin by St. Peter on the right. The left outside wing represents the Miracle of Fishes and Calling of St. Peter, and the right outside wing the Freeing of St. Peter from Prison. The landscape of the Miracle of Fishes gives an accurate view of the shores of Lake Geneva with the Savoy Alps and Mont Blanc and is considered to be the first topographical landscape portrayed in northern European art. New research considers the connection of this panel to the politics of Savoy. Other undated paintings attributed to Witz are the Annunciation (Nuremberg, Germanisches Nationalmuseum), the Meeting at the Golden Gate (Basel, Kunstmuseum), and Saints Catherine and Mary Magdalene in a Church (Strasbourg, Musée de l'Oeuvre Notre-Dame).

The physical presence of figures and materials is more important in Witz's paintings than depiction of rich costumes or detailed settings. His tempera technique and strong, simple colors increase the immobility that characterizes his figures, and strong shadows help to define his space. The forms on the outside wings in their narrow rooms resemble those in some miniatures of the Utrecht school circa 1430.

BIBLIOGRAPHY

Deuchler, Florens. "Konrad Witz, la Savoie et l'Italie: Nouvelles hypothèses à propos du retable de Genève." *Revue de l'art* 71 (1986): 7–16.

Gantner, Joseph. *Konrad Witz.* Vienna: A. Schroll, 1942.

Rott, Hans. *Quellen und Forschungen zur südwestdeutschen und schweizerischen Kunstgeschichte im XV. und XVI. Jahrhundert 3: Der Oberrhein* 2. Stuttgart: Strecker und Schröder, 1936, pp. 20–25.

Schauder, M. "Konrad Witz und die Utrechter Buchmalerei," in *Masters and Miniatures: Proceedings of the Congress on Medieval Manuscript Illumination in the Northern Netherlands (Utrecht, 10–13 December 1989),* ed. K. van der Horst and Johann-Christian Klamt. Doornspijk: Davaco, 1991, pp. 137–147.

Marta O. Renger

SEE ALSO

Basel; Gothic Art and Architecture; Ludolf of Saxony; Rottweil

Wolfdietrich and *Ortnit*

Two of the most important strophic heroic narratives written down in numerous versions throughout the later Middle Ages. The differing versions of the *Wolfdietrich* poem vary so widely that they can properly be called different works. There are two major branches of the story, identifiable by the incompatible stories of the hero's birth. The version that appears in the most manuscripts and in the printed *Heldenbuch* (Book of Heroes) is the longest version, referred to in the literature as *Wolfdietrich D* (editions Holtzman, 1865; Amelung-Jänicke, 1870). The "B" version is apparently a condensation of "D" and appears only in three late manuscripts. Most scholars consider all versions to be products of the thirteenth century, probably from around the middle, but the dating will probably remain uncertain because almost all surviving manuscripts derive from the fifteenth and sixteenth centuries.

Version "D" begins with the bride-winning romance of the hero's father, Hugdietrich, who wins his bride by posing as an exiled princess. The son of this union is Wolfdietrich, who is exiled by his younger brothers upon Hugdietrich's death. The hero passes through many adventures involving giants, heathen rulers, dragons, and morally ambiguous females before returning to regain his rightful throne and free his imprisoned faithful vassals. After reigning for many years he retires to a monastery, where he helps defend the monks against Saracen raiders. In an unusual episode, Wolfdietrich does penance for his heroic life by once again battling all the men he had killed in a single night's dream.

Version "A" (edition Schneider, 1919) is transmitted only in the *Ambras Heldenbuch,* where it is a fragment. Here Wolfdietrich is the youngest son, born during his father's absence, and he is forced out of his rightful position when his brothers claim he is illegitimate. The conclusion of the fragment is derived from the "D" version. There is a much shortened version of "A" in the *Dresden Heldenbuch.* Version "C" survives only in fragments rescued from the binding of later books. The fragments are insufficient to provide a coherent view of a version that is apparently as different from the other two as they are from each other. Wolfdietrich appears in all versions except "B" together with Ortnit, which forms something of a prelude to Wolfdietrich's encounter with Ortnit and his later marriage to Ortnit's widow.

Ortnit is presented as emperor in Lombardy. His story is a bride-winning romance in which the young emperor receives help from his father, a dwarf with supernatural powers named Alberich. He goes to the Near East to win his bride. After his abduction of the bride, his father-in-law seeks revenge by sending dragon eggs to Ortnit's land. When the dragon hatches and begins to ravage the countryside, Ortnit sets out to slay the beast. Along the way he rests under a tree and magically falls into a deep sleep. The dragon takes him to her cave to feed him to her young.

The story is repeated in *Wolfdietrich D* (although the full text of Ortnit appears in all manuscripts of *Wolfdietrich D*), after which Wolfdietrich sets out to avenge his friend. He kills the dragon and returns to Ortnit's court, where he marries the emperor's widow.

Wolfdietrich is identified in various versions as being from Constantinople, Saloniki, or simply from Greece. In "D" he is identified as the grandfather of Dietrich von Bern. The attempts to find historical sources for the story are unconvincing, and the poems are best understood as heroic romances based on traditional narrative materials that may or may not have historical roots.

All versions are composed in the four-line stanza known as the *Hildebrandston,* a version of the *Nibelungen* stanza in which all four lines are metrically identical. The rhyme scheme is *aabb,* with frequent rhyme at the caesura (gap between first and second half of each line. The formulaic language and strophic form suggest roots in the same, presumably oral tradition of heroic poetry that lay behind the *Nibelungenlied, Kudrun, Alpharts Tod, Ortnit,* and *Der Rosengarten zu Worms.*

BIBLIOGRAPHY

Amelung, Arthur, and Oskar Jänicke, eds. *Deutsches Heldenbuch* [all versions], vols. 3–4. Berlin, 1872–1873; rpt. Zurich: Weidmann, 1968.

Haymes, Edward R. "Die *Wolfdietrich-B*-Überlieferung zwischen Franken und Tirol." *Jahrbuch der Oswald von Wolkenstein Gesellschaft* 2 (1982–1983): 89–98.

Hoffmann, Werner. *Mittelhochdeutsche Heldendichtung.* Berlin: Schmidt, 1974, pp. 133–158.

Holtzmann, Adolf, ed. *Der große Wolfdietrich.* Heidelberg: Mohr, 1865 [version "D"].

Schmid-Cadalbert, Christian. *Der 'Ortnit AW' als Brautwerbungsdichtung. Ein Beitrag zum Verständnis mittelhochdeutscher Schemaliteratur.* Bern: Francke, 1985.

Schneider, Hermann. *Die Gedichte und die Sage von Wolfdietrich.* Munich: Beck, 1913.

Thomas, J.W., trans. *Ortnit and Wolfdietrich: Two Medieval Romances.* Columbia, S.C.: Camden House, 1986.

Edward R. Haymes

SEE ALSO

Alpharts Tod; Dietrichepik; Heldenbücher; Hildebrandslied; Kudrun; Nibelungenlied

Wolfram von Eschenbach (fl. first half of the 13th c.)

The greatest German epic poet of the High Middle Ages, Wolfram wrote *Parzival, Willehalm, Titurel,* and nine lyric poems. Internal evidence in his works makes it likely that he composed *Parzival* between 1200 and 1210, worked on *Willehalm* after 1212, and left it unfinished sometime after 1217, possibly as late as the 1220s. Wolfram's few lyric poems, most of them amorous exchanges between two lovers ("dawn songs"), were probably completed early in his career, and the two fragments that make up *Titurel* were composed either during or after his work on *Willehalm.* Wolfram must have lived from about 1170 to the 1220s. He names himself in both *Parzival* and *Willehalm* and characteristically interjects remarks about his personal life and circumstances, so that we seem to have ample biographical information about Wolfram. Yet it is difficult to know how much of it is true or how much is only a pose.

If we take Wolfram at his word, he was a poor man, probably not a ranked administrator (*ministeralis,* ministerial), dependent on wealthy patrons for support. He must have been at the court of Landgrave Hermann of Thuringia, who, he says, provided the French source for *Willehalm,* and he claims to have been a military man with a wife and young daughter. Wolfram was probably born in the Middle Franconian town of Ober-Eschenbach, today renamed Wolframs-Eschenbach. His grave was seen there in the fifteenth century and again in the early seventeenth century, but there is no sign of it today. He was well acquainted with the works of the leading poets of his day: Heinrich von Veldeke, Hartmann von Aue, Gottfried von Straßburg, Walther von der Vogelweide, and Neidhart von Reuental. He surely knew Eilhart von Oberge's *Tristant,* the German *Alexanderlied, Rolandslied, Kaiserchronik, Nibelungenlied,* and other heroic sagas. Yet Wolfram claims not to be able to read or write (see *Parzival* strophe 115, ll. 27–30; *Willehalm* 2,16–22). Such remarks may well have been made in reaction to poets like Hartmann and Gottfried, who boasted of their learning and their literary abilities.

Wolfram's *Parzival,* an Arthurian romance of over 25,000 lines in rhymed couplets, is based on Chrétien de Troyes's *Perceval* (also called *Le Conte del Graal*). It is not a translation in the modern sense, rather an adaptation, expansion, and completion of Chrétien's work. There are several important differences. Chrétien's romance is unfinished. Although there are several continuations, his work stops after 9,234 lines. Wolfram provides his *Parzival* with a detailed prehistory and brings his story to a logical conclusion, while maintaining the general sequence of events found in his source. The prehistory (the first two books) deals with Parzival's father, Gahmuret, and how he eventually marries Herzeloyde, but is killed in battle. Striken by the news of Gahmuret's tragic death, Herzeloyde gives birth to Parzival and resolves to raise him in the wilderness, far from the knightly world of the court.

Wolfram takes Chrétien to task in an epilogue for not having told the story properly then goes on to say that a certain "Kyot," who told the true tale, might well be angry about that (*Parzival* 827,1–4). Earlier Wolfram had claimed Kyot as his source on several occasions and had gone into great detail about how Kyot had found the true story of the Grail in a discarded Arabic manuscript in Toledo. In the manuscript there was a report about the Grail and the Grail family by a part-Jewish astronomer named Flegetanis, who had read about the Grail in the stars. Kyot, a Provençal Christian, had to learn Arabic to read the manuscript. Then he read in Latin chronicles and finally found the story of the Grail Family, which he eventually located in Anjou. All in all, an elaborate invention, especially since we have no real evidence of such a Kyot.

Another striking difference between Wolfram and his source is the nature of the Grail. In Chrétien it is a dish or bowl, in Wolfram a fantastic stone with the pseudo-Latin name of *lapsit exillis*. The angels, who had remained neutral during Lucifer's rebellion, were banished to the stone. Later, a human family became the guardians of the Grail and lived from the food and drink that the Grail miraculously provided. Anyone who has been in the presence of the Grail will not die for a week thereafter, only a virgin can carry the Grail, and inscriptions appear on the stone to name children who are called to the Grail. They grow up to become knights and ladies and are sent out to occupy thrones that lack rulers. The knights defend the Grail Castle and are forbidden to marry or to have a love relationship with a woman (Wolfram calls them "templars"). Only the Grail King may have a wife, but King Anfortas had been wounded by a poisoned spear while performing chivalric deeds in the service of a lady, and been kept alive by the power of the Grail, yet suffering excruciating pain. Nevertheless, although the Grail cannot be found by any seeker, an inscription on the Grail announced that a stranger would come and Anfortas would be healed if he asked the question without prompting during the first night. The stranger would then become Grail King.

Of course, Parzival is destined to be that stranger. He grows up ignorant of knighthood until he encounters some knights, riding through the forest. Impressed by their armor, Parzival is intent on becoming a knight himself. His desire for knighthood stems from the paternal side of his genetic makeup, and his mother reluctantly allows him to leave. Still, she dresses him in fool's clothing in the hope that the ridicule he will surely receive will force his return. However, Parzival's handsome appearance impresses people, and he eventually reaches King Artus's court, only to be told that he should get his own armor by attacking Ither, a knight outside the court who is feuding with Artus, if he wants to become a knight.

Parzival kills Ither with his crude javelin, unaware that Ither is a blood relative, strips him of his armor, puts it on, and rides off on Ither's horse. He arrives at the castle of Gurnemanz, who gives him a short course in knightsmanship and admonitions about how to behave as a knight. Traveling on to Pelrapeire, Parzival wins the beautiful Condwiramurs by defeating her besiegers. After some time, Parzival leaves Condwiramurs to visit his mother, but he arrives instead unwittingly at Munsalvæsche, the Grail Castle. There he is received with great honor, sees the Grail procession and the bloody lance, hears the lamenting of the people, and receives a sword from King Anfortas, who is obviously in great pain. But Parzival, mindful of Gurnemanz's advice not to ask too many questions, remains silent. The next morning the Grail company has disappeared, and Parzival leaves to try to find them. Two days later, he comes to King Artus's court, which has been eager to meet the Red Knight, as he was called by the knights he had defeated, and sent to Artus. His arrival occasions a feast at the Round Table, and Parzival is duly admitted to that select company. At this crowning moment of Parzival's knightly career, the ugly Grail messenger, Cundrie, appears and castigates him verbally for having failed to ask about Anfortas's suffering. Publically humiliated, Parzival leaves, angrily blaming God for his shame and determined to find the Grail and rectify things.

After Parzival's humiliation by Cundrie in front of Artus and his knights, that other paragon of chivalry, Gawan, is challenged to defend his honor. He then takes over center stage of the narrative with his quest for four queens and four hundred maidens held captive at Schastel Marveille. His adventures predominate from Book VII through XIV, except for Book IX, where the story returns to Parzival. Book IX is crucial for Parzival, angry as he is at God but with his thoughts on the Grail and his wife, Condwiramurs. Four and one-half years have passed since Parzival was at the Munsalvæsche and had failed to ask the question. Now, on Good Friday, he is directed to his uncle, the hermit Trevrizent, who tells him about his family and his relationship to the Grail King Anfortas. In addition, Parzival learns all about the Grail, about his mother's death, and the fact that he had killed a relative, Ither, in his effort to become a knight. Hesitatingly, Parzival admits that he was the one who had visited the Grail Castle but had not asked the question. After this confession, Trevrizent gives Parzival a new understanding of the relationship of God and humans, so that he makes his peace with God through penance. Nevertheless, he will still wander in search of the Grail Castle.

Gawan, in the meanwhile, has cleared his family name, rescued the queens from Schastel Marveille, and won the hand of Orgeluse. He has one last task to complete: single combat with Gramoflanz in the presence of his uncle, King Artus, who arrives with all his court. Before that can happen, Gawan fights with Parzival but is spared when they recognize each other. Parzival fights in place of the wounded Gawan against Gramoflanz and defeats him. King Artus then arranges a reconciliation among all the parties involved, and a joyous nuptial celebration ensues. Parzival leaves the festivities alone and encounters his heathen half-brother, Feirefiz, in combat. Just when it appears that Parzival will be defeated, Feirefiz throws aside his sword and magnanimously discloses his identity first. Now Parzival, with his new awareness of God and having been tested to the point of death, is ready to be summoned to the Grail. Cundrie appears, announces that Parzival has been called, and they leave for Munsalvæsche accompanied by Feirefiz. There Parzival asks the question, Anfortas is healed, and a short time thereafter Parzival is reunited with Condwiramurs, who arrives at the castle with their twin sons.

In Wolfram's *Parzival* we see two ideal realms, that of King Artus and that of the Grail. The knights of Artus's Round Table represent the highest secular ideal of chivalry, epitomized in the person of Gawan. The Grail knights on the other hand have a special relationship to God. They are chosen for divine purposes. Parzival belongs to both realms by virtue of his inheritance: from his father, the skill and desire to excel in knightly combat; from his mother, his genealogical relationship to the Grail family and his destiny to succeed Anfortas as King of the Grail Castle. We see in his story first his misguided striving to become an exemplary knight, then his angry confusion when he is humiliated at what should have been his moment of highest honor. Finally, he learns to adjust his sights from the goals of his own ambition and accept the purposes that God has for him. The twofold structure of the work embodied in the figures of Gawan and Parzival shows both knights succeeding in their particular tasks of freeing two groups of people. For one it is a worldly success, for the other, a transcendent, spiritual achievement.

Wolfram's other major work, *Willehalm,* is quite different from *Parzival.* Not only is it unfinished, but it is also not an Arthurian romance. Its source is the Old French *chanson de geste, La Bataille d'Aliscans,* one of the twenty-four poems in the cycle about Guillaume d'Orange and his family. This is heroic poetry that revels in combat and death, Christians against heathens, good against evil. Wolfram himself takes notice of the difference when he states: "Whatever I recounted earlier about fighting [. . .] ended in some way other than in death. *This* fighting will settle for nothing less than death and loss of joy" (*Willehlm* 10, 22–26). Yet for Wolfram, love and courtly attitudes are not lacking. *Willehalm* deals with the conflict between religions and the love that makes the religious conflict tragic. It involves immense slaughter and suffering on both the Christian *and* the heathen sides, and the religious differences and the human experience of the struggle give the work a much greater depth. Although he has transformed the material of his source perhaps to an even greater extent than in *Parzival,* Wolfram still preserves the essential sequence of events of his source as far as his story goes. One final difference: the *chanson* is written in tirades—stanzas of a varying number of ten-syllable lines, with each tirade, or *laisse,* having the same assonance. Wolfram uses the rhymed couplets of the courtly romance.

Willehalm begins in the midst of the first great battle of Aliscans. The heathen emperor Terramer had summoned huge armies and landed not far from Willehalm's fortified city of Oransche. Terramer's purpose is to force the return of his daughter Arabel to her husband, Tybalt, and to the religion of her people. Arabel, now called Gyburg after her baptism, had fallen in love with Willehalm when he was a prisoner in heathendom. She had helped him escape, left Tybalt to flee with Willehalm, and converted to Christianity. Her former husband and her son have come with the Saracen forces.

In the course of the first battle, Willehalm loses all his knights, including young Vivianz, who is the outstanding fighter for the Christians. Willehalm himself is barely able to escape the slaughter by donning the armor of King Arofel, whom he had slain, and riding away through the heathen ranks, almost unnoticed. He spends the night at Oransche with Gyburg, then leaves early the next morning to seek help from King Louis. Gyburg is left to defend the fortress with her ladies and a handful of survivors.

Having arrived in Laon, Willehalm receives an extremely cold welcome. King Louis and the queen, Willehalm's sister, are most reluctant to do anything for him. Willehalm, in great rage at the insulting treatment and deeply concerned about Gyburg's fate, grabs the queen by her braids and threatens to cut her head off. When Willehalm's father, mother, and brothers, who are present at court, hear what has happened at Aliscans and Oransche, they immediately pledge help. Eventually, Willehalm's anger is appeased by the intervention of his niece, Alyze; Louis, whose life had also been threatened by Willehalm, is mollified so that he, too, offers to send imperial forces under Willehalm's command to raise the siege at Oransche.

Before setting out for Oransche with the French troops, Willehalm obtains from Louis the services of Rennewart, a huge young heathen who had been working as a kitchen boy, having rejected baptism. Rennewart is eager to fight, believing that his relatives had refused to ransom him after he was abducted by merchants. He asks for a gigantic club, bound with iron bands, as his weapon, but he forgets it repeatedly on the way to Oransche. (In *Aliscans,* Rainouras is a burlesque figure who eventually dominates the fighting in the second battle. Wolfram's Rennewart, however, despite some boorish acts, is portrayed as a young nobleman in undeserved circumstances. He is actually Gyburg's long-lost brother!)

Willehalm hastens back to Oransche with the French troops, only to discover that Terramer's forces had withdrawn to the coast where the air was better without having stormed the fortress successfully. Gyburg and her meager forces had been able to hold them off. One by one, Willehalm's father and his brothers arrive with their armies, and the stage is set for the second battle. However, before it begins, a meeting of all the leaders takes place, at which all voice their resolve and support for the battle. Gyburg alone adds a temporizing voice. Tearfully she expresses her sorrow that she is the cause for the huge loss of life on both sides and makes a moving plea for the Christians to spare the heathens, if possible.

In the ensuing battle the Christians are victorious, but the loss of life on both sides is immense. Rennewart, who had forcibly "persuaded" the wavering French not to desert, plays a leading role in the victory. Terramer manages to escape to his ships, and the expected confrontation between Rennewart and his father does not take place. Indeed, when the battle is over Rennewart is missing. Willehalm grieves at the apparent loss of Rennewart and about the terrible slaughter that has occurred. In a gesture of respect for the noble heathens, he gives orders to have their fallen kings embalmed and buried according to their own rites. At this point the narrative breaks off.

Most scholars believe that *Willehalm* is a fragment, basing their argument on the fact that too many narrative strands are left untied. Others feel that, for whatever reasons, Wolfram may have been unable to finish it and devised an emergency conclusion (the *Notdach* theory). Still others maintain that *Willehalm* is complete as it stands, that with the tragic quality of the poem Wolfram has put an entirely new meaning into the substance of his source and that for him any continuation of the Rennewart story had become irrelevant. One further, more recent position is that Wolfram intended it to be a fragment. No matter how one looks at the ending, or lack thereof, *Willehalm* is still a powerfully moving work, dealing with problems that have been with us, as Wolfram says: "since Jesus was plunged into the Jordan to be baptized" (*Willehalm* 4, 28f). Wolfram seems to have been deeply affected himself by the tragedy of it all, if one can judge by his numerous self-reflective remarks throughout the poem.

The two fragments usually called *Titurel* from the name of the old Grail King in the first line of the first fragment deal with the two young lovers, Schionatulander and Sigune, from Wolfram's *Parzival*. It is as if Wolfram attempted to flesh out the briefly mentioned story of their tragic love. Written in four long-line strophes that resemble the *Nibelungenlied* strophes to a limited degree, the first fragment deals with the discovery of the mutual love of the two young people, and the second fragment describes an idyll in the woods that is interrupted by the catching of a hunting dog who had been running through the woods trailing a fantastically elaborate leash with a story depicted on it. Sigune wishes to read the story to its end, but the dog escapes as she loosens the leash to read more and carries the leash away. She promises Schionatulander her love as a reward for retrieving the leash. We know from *Parzival* that Schionatulander gets killed in the attempt, and Sigune is left mourning over his dead body when Parzival meets her. A later poet named Albrecht (von Scharfenberg?) took on the task of completing *Titurel,* and he did so with a vengeance. There are over 6,000 strophes in his so-called *Jüngerer Titurel,* compared with Wolfram's 170! Although it is poetically inferior, Albrecht's work was thought for a long time to be Wolfram's because he identifies himself as Wolfram early on in the work, disclosing his own name only at almost the very end.

There are many problems in *Titurel.* These include the manuscript tradition, the precise text of the poem, and the relationship of the two fragments to each other. Even the theme of love is treated strangely, portraying the exuberance and joy of the naive young lovers trying to act so properly as courtly lovers, yet with a background of impending tragedy on the basis of family history. It is a work of changing moods with somberness predominating.

Wolfram's lyric poems generally describe the parting of lovers at dawn and follow a tradition found in Provençal and Old French poetry. For the most part the lady is the dominant figure. She is the one who is awake as dawn is breaking and must wake her lover so that he can leave without being seen. But Wolfram also includes a sympathetic watchman in several instances, and in one poem he is the dominant speaker. The poems generally end with one last embrace and then the tearful parting as the sun rises higher. Wolfram's dawn songs, among the first in German of that genre, are marked by their striking imagery and their sensitive portrayal of the lovers. His few other poems are similar to more traditional *Minnelieder* (courtly love songs) but show his complete mastery of that type.

BIBLIOGRAPHY

Bumke, Joachim. *Die Wolfram von Eschenbach Forschung seit 1945. Bericht und Bibliographie.* Munich: Wilhelm Fink, 1970.

———. *Wolfram von Eschenbach,* 6th ed. Stuttgart: Metzler, 1991; 7th ed., 1997.

Gibbs, Marion E., and Sidney M. Johnson, trans. *Wolfram von Eschenbach: Willehlam.* Harmondsworth: Penguin, 1984.

Gibbs, Marion E., and Sidney M. Johnson. *Wolfram von Eschenbach: "Titurel" and the "Songs."* New York: Garland, 1988 [with English trans.].

———. *Medieval German Literature: A Companion.* New York: Garland, 1997, pp. 174–205.

Green, D. H. *The Art of Recognition in Wolfram's "Parzival."* Cambridge: Cambridge University Press, 1982.

Groos Arthur. *Romancing the Grail.* Ithaca, N.Y.: Cornell University Press, 1995 [on *Parzival*].

Hatto, Arthur T., trans. *Wolfram von Eschenbach: Parzival.* Harmondsworth: Penguin, 1980.

Heinzle, Joachim. *Stellenkommentar zu Wolframs "Titurel."* Tübingen: Niemeyer, 1972.

Heinzle, Joachim, ed. *Wolfram von Eschenbach: Willehlam.* Frankfurt am Main: Verlag Deutscher Klassiker, 1991 [with German trans.].

———, ed. *Willehalm: nach der Handschrift 857 der Stiftsbibliothek St. Gallen.* Tübingen: Niemeyer, 1994.

Kiening, Christian. "Wolfram von Eschenbach: *Willehalm,*" in *Mittelhochdeutsche Romane und Heldenepen,* ed. Horst Brunner. Stuttgart: Reclam, 1993, pp. 212–232.

Kühn, Dieter, trans. *Wolfram von Eschenbach: Parzival.* Frankfurt am Main: Insel, 1986.

Lachmann, Karl, ed. *Wolfram von Eschenbach,* 6th ed. Berlin: de Gruyter, 1926 [reprinted often].

Leitzmann, Albert, ed. *Wolfram von Eschenbach,* 5 vols. Halle (Saale): Niemeyer, 1902–1906 [reprinted often].

Lofmark, Carl. *Rennewart in Wolfram's "Willehlm": A Study of Wolfram von Eschenbach and His Sources.* Cambridge, England: Cambridge University Press, 1972.

Mertens, Volker. "Wolfram von Eschenbach: *Titurel,*" in *Mittelhochdeutsche Romane und Heldenepen,* ed. Horst Brunner. Stuttgart: Reclam, 1993, pp. 196–211.

Mohr, Wolfgang. *Wolfram von Eschenbach. Titurel. Lieder.* Göppingen: Kümmerle, 1978, pp. 101–161.

Mustard, Helen M., and Charles E. Passage, trans. *Wolfram von Eschenbach: Parzival.* New York: Vintage Books, 1961.

Nellmann, Eberhard, ed. *Wolfram von Eschenbach: Parzival.* Frankfurt am Main: Verlag Deutscher Klassiker, 1994 [German trans. Dieter Kühn].

Passage, Charles E., trans. *Wolfram von Eschenbach: Willehlam.* New York: Ungar, 1977.

———. trans. *Wolfram von Eschenbach: Titurel.* New York: Ungar, 1984.

Poag, James F. *Wolfram von Eschenbach.* New York: Twayne, 1972 [good general introduction in English].

Pretzel, Ulrich, and Wolfgang Bachofer. *Bibliographie zu Wolfram von Eschenbach,* 2d ed. Berlin: Schmidt, 1968.

Schmidt, Elisabeth. "Wolfram von Eschenbach: *Parzival,*" in *Mittelhochdeutsche Romane und Heldenepen,* ed. Horst Brunner. Stuttgart: Reclam, 1993, pp. 173–195.

Schröder, Werner, ed. *Wolfram von Eschenbach: Willehalm.* Berlin: de Gruyter, 1978 [with German trans. Dieter Kartschoke; rev. 1989].

Walshe, Maurice O'C. *Medieval German Literature.* Cambridge, Mass.: Harvard University Press, 1962, pp. 156–175 [concise treatment].

Wapnewski, Peter. *Die Lyrik Wolframs von Eschenbach: Edition. Kommentar. Interpretation.* Munich: Beck, 1972 [songs, with German trans.].

Sidney M. Johnson

SEE ALSO

Alexanderlied; Eilhart von Oberge; Gottfried von Straßburg; Hartmann von Aue; Heinrich von Veldeke;

Kaiserchronik; Neidhart; *Nibelungenlied;* Walther von der Vogelweide; Wolfram von Eschenbach, *Parzival,* Illustrations; Wolfram von Eschenbach, *Willehalm,* Illustrations

Wolfram von Eschenbach, *Parzival,* Illustrations

The thirteen visual manifestations of the Parzival material that can be cataloged for the German language area—eight books, one embroidery, two mural cycles, and two other wall paintings—reflect a broad range of responses to the story of Parzival.

At one extreme we may locate the well-known illuminations in the mid-thirteenth-century Munich manuscript (Bayerische Staatsbibliothek, no. cgm 19). In twelve scenes on the two sides of a single bifolio, presumably part of a larger lost or incomplete program of illumination, the layout of the illuminations in three registers, the choice of scenes culminating in Feirefiz's baptism and his destruction of heathen idols, and the iconography, with its resonances of the Last Supper and the baptism of Constantine, suggest an equation of knighthood with salvation and a profound religious meaning for the work as a whole.

At the other extreme are perhaps the illumination programs of the Parzival manuscripts produced in the Alsatian workshop of Diebolt Lauber in the middle of the fifteenth century, in which the story is radically deproblematized and largely stripped of any transcendence, becoming a story of a knightly career with almost exclusively social significance. The mid-fourteenth-century Braunschweig embroidery, with twenty scenes from the story of Gawain and Orgeluse, probably fits into this category as well.

The two mural cycles are difficult to analyze, given their fragmentary state of preservation. The early- to mid-fourteenth-century Lübeck cycle appears to have taken Parzival from youth to the Grail kingship. Its ten scenes—of originally twenty or more—were discovered

Parzival in the Red Knight's armor before Arthur, Ginover, and their guests, Haus zur Kunkel, Constance. *Photograph: Joan A. Holladay*

in 1929 and destroyed soon after. Also from the early fourteenth century, the approximately twenty-two scenes of poorly preserved wall painting in the Haus zur Kunkel in Constance appear to concentrate on Parzival's youth as well, although the extent of the narrative is difficult to determine.

Two wall paintings remove Parzival entirely from his narrative context, presenting him as an exemplary figure. He appears among the Slaves of Love in the Haus zur Kunkel (mid-fourteenth century) and as one of the three best Arthurian knights—with Iwein and Gawein—in the "Triads" at Runkelstein circa 1400–1405.

BIBLIOGRAPHY

Ott, Norbert H. "Zur Ikonographie des Parzival-Stoffs in Frankreich und Deutschland: Struktur und Gebrauchssituation von Handschriftenillustration und Bildzeugnis." *Wolfram-Studien* 12 (1992): 108–123.

Saurma-Jeltsch, Lieselotte E. "Zum Wandel der Erzählweise am Beispiel der illustrierten deutschen 'Parzival'-Handschriften." *Wolfram-Studien* 12 (1992): 124–152.

Schirok, Bernd. *Wolfram von Eschenbach: Parzival: Die Bilder der illustrierten Handschriften.* Göppingen: Kümmerle, 1985 [illustrations].

James A. Rushing Jr.

SEE ALSO

Braunschweig; Constance; Gothic Art and Architecture; Lauber, Diebolt; Lübeck; Wolfram von Eschenbach; Wolfram von Eschenbach, *Willehalm*, Illustrations

Wolfram von Eschenbach, *Willehalm,* Illustrations

The illustration of the Willehalm trilogy—Wolfram's *Willehalm*, Ulrich von dem Türlin's *Arabel*, and Ulrich von Türheim's *Rennewart*—is characterized by an opulence rare in the illustration of German vernacular literature, reflecting the status of the Willehalm material as something closer to historical and salvific truth than "mere" romance.

Among the most lavishly decorated Willehalm manuscripts are royal and princely codices such as Vienna, Österreichishe Nationalbibliothek (no. Cod. ser. nov. 2643), made in 1387 for King Wenzel I of Bohemia, with 247 miniatures; and Kassel, Murhardsche Bibliothek und Landesbibliothek (no. 2° Ms. poet. et roman. 1), made for Landgrave Heinrich II of Hesse in 1334, with spaces

Willehalm (Kassel, Hessische Landesbibliothek, 2° Ms. poet. et roman. 1), fol. 1v: Frontispiece with Christ in Majesty and Heinrich II, Landgrave of Hesse. *Photograph: Hessische Landesbibliothek*

for 479 miniatures, of which 62 were brought to varying stages of completion. That the Willehalm material was regarded as history in the later Middle Ages is also indicated by the adoption of excerpts from all three parts of the trilogy, sometimes with illustrations, into the *Weltchronik* of Heinrich von München.

Unique among illuminated vernacular literary manuscripts, the fragmentarily preserved *Große Bilderhandschrift* (Munich, Bayerische Staatsbibliothek, no. Cgm 193/III; no. Cgm 197/III, A; no. Cgm 197/III, 3b; and Nuremberg, Germanisches Nationalmuseum, Graphische Sammlung, no. Hz 1104–1105 Kapsel 1607), which might have contained up to 1,380 miniatures, attempts to illustrate practically every moment in the narrative in a format derived from *Sachsenspiegel* illustration, with the inner column of each page devoted to text and the outer one to pictures.

A provisional catalog of German Willehalm illustrations would include approximately sixteen manuscripts and fragments of all or part of the trilogy, with miniatures, space left for miniatures, or rubrics suggesting a lost illustrated source, as well as at least three manuscripts of the *Weltchronik* that include Willehalm illustrations.

BIBLIOGRAPHY

Diemer, Peter, and Dorothea Diemer. "Miniaturen zum Willehalm," in *Wolfram von Eschenbach. Willehalm: Nach der Handschrift 857 der Stiftsbibliothek St. Gallen,* ed. Joachim Heinzle. Bibliothek des Mittelalters 9. Frankfurt: Deutscher Klassiker Verlag, 1991, pp. 1093–1115.

Holladay, Joan A. *Illuminating the Epic: The Kassel Willehalm Codex and the Landgraves of Hesse in the Early Fourteenth Century.* College Art Association Monographs 54. Seattle: University of Washington Press, 1996.

Schmidt, Ronald Michael. *Die Handschriftenillustrationen des "Willehalm" Wolframs von Eschenbach: Dokumentation einer illustrierten Handschriftengruppe.* 2 vols. Wiesbaden: Reichert, 1985.

James A. Rushing Jr.

SEE ALSO

Gothic Art and Architecture; Ulrich von Türheim; Wolfram von Eschenbach; Wolfram von Eschenbach, *Parzival,* Illustrations

Wolgemut, Michael (1434/1437–1519)

Born in Nuremberg between 1434 and 1437, Michael Wolgemut was the city's foremost painter and printmaker in the late fifteenth century. Wolgemut trained with his father, Valentin, a painter, and worked as a journeyman with Gabriel Mälesskircher in Munich before returning to Nuremberg in 1471. A year later he married Barbara, the widow of the noted painter Hans Pleydenwurff. Whether he had collaborated earlier with Hans is uncertain. Wolgemut developed a large workshop that specialized in the production of large retables, woodcuts, and designs for stained glass windows. The artist's pupils included his stepson, Wilhelm Pleydenwurff, and Albrecht Dürer, who was in the shop from 1486 until 1489.

Wolgemut's first documented painting is the high altar completed in 1479 for the St. Marienkirche in Zwickau. This complex polyptych includes painted wings depicting the Passion of Christ (exterior) and Infancy (middle)

that cover the nine life-size standing statues of saints on the inner wings and in the corpus, a painted and carved winged predella (lower altar panel), and a Last Judgment covering the back of the altar. Wolgemut employed a team of now anonymous joiners, painters, and sculptors on this and similar elaborate projects, notably the Peringsdorfer Altar made circa 1486 for the Augustinian Cloister in Nuremberg (today in the Friedenskirche) and the high altar (1506–1508) in the church of St. Johannes and St. Martinus in Schwabach. In his paintings, including his independent portraits, such as that of Levinus Memminger circa 1485 (Madrid, Museo Thyssen-Bornemisza), Wolgemut displayed his familiarity with Netherlandish art, notably the works of Rogier van der Weyden and Dirk Bouts. His clearly defined figures are located in the extreme foreground before deep landscapes.

Today the artist is best known for his prints. In addition to independent woodcuts, Wolgemut recognized the potential of illustrating books. The artist, his stepson, and his shop supplied 96 woodcuts for Stephan Fridolin's *Schatzbehalter* (1491) and 1,809 woodcuts using 645 different blocks for Hartmann Schedel's *Liber Chronicarum (Nuremberg Chronicle,* 1493), both published by Anton Koberger in Nuremberg. The latter with its maps, city views, portraits, and elaborate illustrations was the century's most ambitious publishing project and was marketed across Europe.

Wolgemut's career spanned four decades. His last major picture, the *Epitaph of Anna Gross* (Nuremberg, Germanisches Nationalmuseum), dates around 1509. In 1516 Albrecht Dürer affectionately recorded his mentor's likeness in a portrait (Nuremberg, Germanisches Nationalmuseum). Wolgemut died on November 30, 1519, in Nuremberg.

BIBLIOGRAPHY

Bellm, Richard. *Wolgemuts Skizzenbuch im Berliner Kupferstichkabinett.* Studien zur deutschen Kunstgeschichte 322. Baden-Baden: P. H. Heitz, 1959.

Fridolin, Stefan. *Der Schatzbehalter: Ein Andachts- und Erbauungsbuch aus dem Jahre 1491,* ed. Richard Bellm. 2 vols. Wiesbaden: G. Pressler, 1962.

Füssel, Stephan, ed. *500 Jahre Schedelsche Weltchronik.* Pirckheimer Jahrbuch 9. Nuremberg: Carl, 1994.

Rücker, Elizabeth. *Die Schedelsche Weltchronik: Das größte Buchunternehmen der Dürer-Zeit,* 33d rev. ed. Munich: Prestel, 1988.

Scholz, Hartmut. *Entwurf und Ausführung: Werkstattpraxis in der Nürnberger Glasmalerei der Dürerzeit.*

Ph.d. diss., University of Stuttgart, 1988. Berlin: Deutscher Verlag für Kunstwissenschaft, 1989.

Stadler, Franz Izra. *Michael Wolgemut und der Nürnberger Holzschnitt im letzten Drittel des XV. Jahrhunderts.* 2 vols. Studien zur deutschen Kunstgeschichte 161. Strasbourg: J. H. E. Heitz, 1913.

Strieder, Peter. *Tafelmalerei in Nürnberg, 1350 bis 1550.* Königstein im Taunus: K. Robert, 1993, pp. 65–85, 200–219.

Wilson, Adrian. *The Making of the Nuremberg Chronicle.* Amsterdam: Nico Israel, 1976.

Jeffrey Chipps Smith

SEE ALSO

Gothic Art and Architecture; Munich; Nuremberg; Printmaking

Women

Most medieval source documents about German women reveal more about reigning cultural ideologies of gender and concepts of the feminine than they do about actual females who lived. Indeed, the terms "woman" and "women," vigorously debated by feminist theorists, remain as slippery when viewed in the past. For theologians, the figure or concept of woman embodied both original sin (being descended from Eve) and the path to redemption (through the mercy of the Virgin Mary); for hagiographers, woman's greater susceptibility to sin made her sanctity that much closer to the divine; for natural philosophers, women's bodies represented imperfection in juxtaposition to the perfection of men; for the courtly poet, the lofty lady's ideal beauty and behavior lifted him to new heights of virtue; and for the male heroes of romance, women made men complete. Nevertheless, women were neither silent in nor absent from medieval German history and literature. Chronicles report of influential and charismatic queens. Female-authored texts offer readers both alternative views of women and responses to prevalent ideas about gender. Finally, recent and ongoing research into primary source documents such as wills and tax and church records reveals women active on every level of society.

The negative images of women circulating in medieval German culture had their roots in the complex tradition of Judeo-Christian misogyny. Condemned in the Bible as the origin of sin and more bitter than death (Ecclesiastes 25:33; 7:27), women were declared inferior and subservient to men. In the letters of Paul recorded in the New Testament, women's subordination to men justified a ban on both public speaking and teaching (Timothy 2:11–12). With the Bible as their authority, later commentators could claim that women were the gateway of the devil (Tertullian, ca. 160–225), the source of all evil (Jerome, d. 420), or the servants of men, according to natural order (Augustine, 354–430). Made at different times, for differing purposes and often met with debate, such statements became fodder for medieval theologians like Gratian (d. ca. 1160), who codified women's subservience into canon law *(Decretum)* or scholastic theologians like Thomas Aquinas (1225–1274), who reinforced these laws with the rediscovered natural philosophy of Aristotle, thereby linking the perceived inferiority of women to matters of "science."

In stark contrast to these negative conceptualizations of women and female nature stands the poetry of courtly love (a term, it should be noted, invented by modern scholars) known in German scholarship as *Minnesang.* Poems singing the praises of an inaccessible lofty lady, or *domna,* became popular in the courts of northern France and the southeastern region of Provence in the mid-twelfth century.

Poets decried the strength of their love inspired by the unsurpassable beauty and virtue of the lofty lady (often the wife of the poet's patron). The lady's inaccessibility on the other hand meant that the ideal remained forever beyond the poet's grasp. In its German incarnation, courtly poetry grew out of and coexisted with a "native" tradition of "woman's song" in which female voices offer laments about love as in the poetry of Der von Kürenberg. Later poets portrayed a lofty lady (Middle High German *vrouwe*) who came to represent not only ideal female beauty but also ideal virtue and perfection. The poets' desire for the lady's love inspired them to serve her, a service through which they became better men. Among the classic composers of *Minnesang* are Reinmar der Alte, Heinrich von Morungen, and Friedrich von Hausen. Not all poets adhered to these conventions, however. Walther von der Vogelweide wrote in his later poetry of consummating his passion with a less than ideal but real woman, and Neidhart von Reuental's poetry turns the conventions of courtly love into burlesque comedy.

The women figures in the courtly epic and romance tend to be more realistic, which is to say, they reflect not only the ideal but also the dangerous characteristics of womanhood. Particularly in the romances of Hartmann von Aue *(Erec* and *Iwein),* women inspire a love that is consummated in marriage, indirectly cause dishonor, and become the means through which honor is regained. Hartmann depicts his women characters as beautiful, virtuous, and sensible (though to varying degrees: one thinks here of Lunete, who is far more politically savvy than Queen Laudine, whom she serves), but also as struggling to negotiate the rules for gendered behavior by which they live (Enite). In Gottfried's *Tristan,* the elder Queen Isolde not only practices medicine but also deftly maneuvers for the authority to speak for the King, primarily to secure a position like her own for her daughter through marriage. Portrayals of powerful women are consistently ambiguous, however, as evident in the *Nibelungenlied,* where Brünhild's physical strength vanishes once she is vanquished in the marriage bed, and Kriemhild's excessive desire for revenge leads to the fall of a dynasty. In late medieval short narratives, strong women are most often caricatured as shrewish wives or mothers (see Der Stricker), though with some interesting exceptions like the anonymous tale of the ladies tournament *(der vrouwenturnei).*

While in France a small group of women contributed to the tradition of courtly love lyric (*Trobairitz,* or women troubadours) and one to the tradition of romance (Marie de France), in Germany women wrote within the context of the church. In the tenth century, Hrosvit of Gandersheim wrote a series of plays on the virtues and saints for the edification of her community. In the twelfth century, Herrad of Landsberg wrote an encyclopedia of natural history interlaced with biblical passages. The twelfth through fourteenth centuries produced religious women both in and outside of the cloister who wrote compelling and original treatises on their visionary experiences (Hildegard of Bingen, Elisabeth of Schönau, Mechthild von Magdeburg, Gertrude the Great, Mechthild of Hackeborn, Adelheid Langmann, and Margaretha Ebner, among others). These texts offer insights into how women negotiated the images of women and femininity circulating in their differing cultural milieus, as well as the hierarchical power structures in which they lived. Of those listed, Hildegard, an abbess of a Benedictine convent, received sanction both to write and to teach from the pope, and Mechthild of Magdeburg, a Beguine, was the first woman to write in German. Mechthild's text evokes special literary interest (as does a contemporary Middle Dutch text attributed to Hadewijch of Antwerp), for it engages not only with ecclesiastical discourse but also with the courtly poetry of her day.

These women writers and the women portrayed in literature come from the upper tiers of the medieval social hierarchy—namely, the nobility. The women writers are exceptional, the noble women of literature, ideals. The majority of the female population, however, was busy doing other things such as cooking, washing, and mending. Recent research, focusing for example on women peasants in the countryside (Bennett), women in cities (Wunder), and widows (Mirrer) proves that women's contributions to society extended beyond servicing men and having children to entering professions like medicine, textiles, and trade.

BIBLIOGRAPHY

Affeldt, Werner, et al., eds. *Frauen im Frühmittelalter. Eine ausgewählte, kommentierte Bibliographie.* New York: Lang, 1990.

Bennett, Judith. *Ale, Beer and Brewsters in England: Women's Work in a Changing World, 1300–1600.* New York: Oxford University Press, 1996.

Blamires, Alcuin. *The Case for Women in Medieval Culture.* New York: Oxford University Press, 1997.

Blamires, Alcuin, Karen Pratt, and C. W. Marx, eds. *Woman Defamed and Woman Defended: An Anthology of Medieval Texts.* New York: Oxford University Press, 1992.

Bynum, Caroline Walker. *Holy Feast and Holy Fast: The Religious Significance of Food to Medieval Women.* Berkeley: University of California Press, 1987.

Cadden, Joan. *Meanings of Sex Difference in the Middle Ages,* ed. Charles Webster. Cambridge: Cambridge University Press, 1993.

Echols, Anne, and Marty Williams, eds. *An Annotated Index of Medieval Women.* New York: Wiener, 1992.

Lewis, Gertrud Jaron. *By Women, For Women, About Women: The Sister-Books of Fourteenth Century Germany.* Toronto: Pontifical Institute of Mediaeval Studies, 1996.

Mirrer, Louise. *Upon My Husband's Death: Widows in the Literatures and Histories of Medieval Europe.* Ann Arbor: University of Michigan Press, 1992.

Rasmussen, Ann Marie. *Mothers and Daughters in Medieval German Literature.* Syracuse: Syracuse University Press, 1997.

Westphal-Wihl, Sarah. *"The Ladies' Tournament:* Marriage, Sex and Honor in Thirteenth Century Germany." *Signs* 14 (1989): 371–398.

Wilson, Katharina M., ed. *Medieval Women Writers.* Athens: University of Georgia Press, 1984.

Wunder, Heide, et al., eds. *Eine Stadt der Frauen: Studien und Quellen zur Geschichte der Baslerinnen im späten Mittelalter und zu Beginn der Neuzeit.* Basel: Helbing and Lichtenhahn, 1995.

Sara S. Poor

Women and Art

In medieval Germany, women were included as the subjects of visual representation certainly just as often as men. Depictions of women abounded: images of the Virgin, other biblical women and female saints, female personifications of virtues and vices, female figures depicting the labors of the months, images of women donors, and self-portraits by women artists. Recent scholarship has explored the ways in which these images helped to shape gender roles within specific historical and social contexts. Women likewise played important roles in the making and using of what later generations have called "art." They initiated, commissioned, financed, and donated art and architecture. Among the best-known female sponsors of art in German-speaking lands during the early and High Middle Ages were empresses Theophanu, Kunigunde, and Agnes, Queen Gisela, Duchess Hedwig, and Abbess Hildegard von Bingen. With the expanding base of patronage during the late Middle Ages, many bourgeois women commissioned epitaphs and altarpieces in urban centers. Women also participated directly in the production of art, especially as embroiderers and manuscript illuminators (e.g., Guda, Clarissa, Barbara Gwichtmacherin). During the late Middle Ages they served important roles as workshop wives who managed business affairs and sometimes took part in hands-on activities in what were family enterprises (e.g., wife of Adam Kraft). When widowed, these women occasionally led workshops themselves (e.g., Barbara Wolgemut, widow of Valentin), and through remarriage they frequently determined the new master of the shop (e.g., Barbara Pleydenwurff, the widow of Hans, who married Michael Wolge-

Madonna, Magdeburg cathedral. *Photograph: Joan A. Holladay*

mut). Women were also significant as users, owners, consumers, and audiences—not only of works made exclusively for them but also as individuals and members of groups that viewed works differently than their male counterparts.

Art history has traditionally excluded women from the discourses on art in the Middle Ages in several ways. For one, scholarship has focused on the maker—an area in which women were underrepresented. Moreover, even though much medieval production resulted from the collaborative efforts of anonymous craftspersons, some of whom were women, male artists shaped in the mold of the nineteenth-century solitary romantic genius have been invented for the Middle Ages. Moreover, valorizing architecture and sculpture as the premier art forms of the Middle Ages has effectively marginalized not only the so-called minor arts but also their makers, many of whom were women. Second, when attention is focused on the sponsors—an area in which women were well represented—men are given credit for the projects. Indeed, numerous sources show that decisions were made jointly by a couple or that surviving women utilized their own or inherited capital to initiate memorials for themselves and their families. Third, when audiences are considered, the position of the dominant is usually taken for the whole, and women's alternative readings of works are thus not taken into account. Feminist medievalists are now beginning to use the art and history of the Middle Ages to challenge art history's paradigms and change its time-honored habits.

BIBLIOGRAPHY

Ashley, Kathleen, and Pamela Sheingorn, eds. *Interpreting Cultural Symbols: Saint Anne in Late Medieval Society.* Athens: University of Georgia Press, 1990.

Bell, Susan Groag. "Medieval Women Book Owners: Arbiters of Lay Piety and Ambassadors of Culture." *Signs* 7 (1982): 742–768.

Callahan, Leslie. "The Torture of Saint Apollonia: Deconstructing Fouquet's Martyrdom Stage." *Studies in Iconography* 61 (1994): 119–138.

Carr, Annemarie Weyl. "Women Artists in the Middle Ages." *Feminist Art Journal* (Spring 1976): 5–9, 26.

Caviness, Madeline H. "Anchoress, Abbess, and Queen: Donors and Patrons or Intercessors and Matrons?," in *The Cultural Patronage of Medieval Women,* ed. June Hall McCash. Athens: University of Georgia Press, 1996, pp. 105–154.

Easton, Martha. "Saint Agatha and the Sanctification of Sexual Violence." *Studies in Iconography* 61 (1994): 83–118.

Hamburger, Jeffrey F. "Art, Enclosure, and the *Cura Monialium*: Prolegomena in the Guise of a Postscript." *Gesta* 31 (1992): 108–134.

———. *The Rothschild Canticles: Art and Mysticism in Flanders and the Rhineland ca. 1300.* New Haven, Conn.: Yale University Press, 1990.

———. *Nuns as Artists: The Visual Culture of a Medieval Convent.* Berkeley: University of California Press, 1997.

Medieval Feminist Newsletter, especially 1991 and 1993.

Miner, Dorothy. *Anastaise and Her Sisters: Women Artists of the Middle Ages.* Baltimore: Walters Art Gallery, 1974.

Möbius, Helga. "Geschlechterdifferenz: Ihre Darstellung und Wahrnehmung im Mittelalter," in *Kunst und Sozialgeschichte: Festschrift für Jutta Held.* Pfaffenweiler: Centaurus-Verlagsgesellschaft, 1995, pp. 295–305.

Parker, Rozsika. *The Subversive Stitch: Embroidery and the Making of the Feminine.* London: Women's Press, 1984.

Schleif, Corine. "The Many Wives of Adam Kraft: Early Modern Artists' Wives in Legal Documents, Art-historical Scholarship, and Historical Fiction." *Georges-Bloch-Jahrbuch* 5 (1998): 61–74.

Schraut, Elisabeth. *Stifterinnen und Künstlerinnen im mittelalterlichen Nürnberg.* Nuremberg: Selbstverlag der Stadt Nürnberg, 1987.

———, and Claudia Opitz. *Frauen und Kunst im Mittelalter.* Braunschweig: Braunschweigisches Landesmuseum, 1983.

Sheingorn, Pamela. "'The Wise Mother': The Image of St. Anne Teaching the Virgin Mary." *Gesta* 32/1 (1993): 69–80.

Vavra, Elisabeth. "Überlegungen zum 'ild der Frau' in der mittelalterlichen Ikonographie," in *Frau und Spätmittelalterlicher Alltag. Internationale Kongress Krems and der Donau 2. bis 5. Oktober 1984.* Sitzungsberichte der Österreichischen Akademie der Wissenschaften, Philosophisch-historische Klasse 473. Vienna: Verlag der Österreichischen Akademie der Wissenschaften, 1986, pp. 283–299.

Wolfthal, Diane. "'A Hue and a Cry': Medieval Rape Imagery and Its Transformations." *Art Bulletin* 75 (1993): 39–64.

Corine Schleif

SEE ALSO
Gothic Art and Architecture; Hildegard von Bingen; Kraft, Adam; Manuscripts, Painting and Production; Pleydenwurff, Hans; Romanesque Art and Architecture; Theophanu; Wolgemut, Michael; Women

World Chronicles
See Chronicles, World.

World Maps
By far the dominant genre of medieval cartography, world maps (German, *Weltkarten;* Latin, *mappaemundi*) range from the mere schematic diagrams to elaborately descriptive images in which pictorial and textual elements are densely interwoven. Regardless of their simplicity or complexity, they fall into two broad categories in terms of

content: either they are focused exclusively on the inhabited portion of the world (the *oikumene*) surrounded by ocean; or they portrayed in plan a longitudinal section of the entire globe showing half the Northern Hemisphere (which contained the *oikumene*) separated by an equatorial ocean from half the Southern Hemisphere, the two quadrants encircled by an ocean running through the poles. Typologies based on purely formal criteria have been proposed, but such arbitrary systems of classification obscure the essential fluidity of cartographic representation throughout the Middle Ages. Modes of figuration remained highly contingent on the specific contexts in which maps were embedded and on the particular purposes they served. Seemingly (i.e., to us) contradictory models of geographical space coexisted, even commingled, because they facilitated visualization, hence understanding, of different aspects of reality.

World maps circulated within manuscripts as illustrations, glosses, résumés of or programmatic introductions to texts, scientific and spiritual. Display outside the codex entailed the use of a variety of supports: *mappaemundi* could be made of precious metals as treasury objects or incorporated into the monumental decoration of diverse architectural spaces as mosaic pavements, mural paintings, and large wall hangings on vellum or cloth. In schools, palaces, and churches, world maps performed multiple cognitive and symbolic functions.

A key monument from the high medieval period is the giant Ebstorf map (destroyed in World War II), named after the Benedictine nunnery in lower Saxony where it was discovered. Art historians have now convincingly linked the map, painted on thirty goatskin panels stitched together, to works produced circa 1280–1300 by and for women in convents of the region. As places featured on the map reveal a Guelph political agenda current during the reigns of Otto IV or Otto the Child, an earlier work displayed at the palace at Braunschweig or Lüneberg may have served as a model. Gervasius of Tilbury is known to have made a world map to accompany his *Otia imperialia* (ca. 1214), dedicated to Otto IV. Whether the exemplar from Ebstorf ultimately reflects Gervasius's ideas is open to debate.

BIBLIOGRAPHY

Arentzen, Jörg-Geerd. *Imago Mundi Cartographica: Studien zur Bildlichkeit mittelalterlicher Welt- und Ökumenekarten unter besonderer Berücksichtigung des Zusammenwirkens von Text und Bild.* Ph.d. diss., University of Münster. Munich. Fink, 1984.

Edson, Evelyn. *Mapping Time and Space: How Medieval Mapmakers Viewed Their World.* London: British Library, 1997.

Gautier Dalché, Patrick. *La "Descriptio mappae mundi" de Hugues de Saint-Victor: Texte inédit avec introduction et commentaire.* Paris: Études augustiniennes, 1988.

———. "De la glose à la contemplation. Place et fonction de la carte dans les manuscrits du haut moyen age," in *Testo e immagine nell'alto medioevo.* Settimane di studio del Centro italiano di studi sull'alto medioevo 41. Spoleto: Centro Italiano di Studi sull'Alto Medioevo, 1994, 2 vols, vol. 2, pp. 693–771.

Harley, J. B., and David Woodward, eds. *Cartography in Prehistoric, Ancient, and Medieval Europe and the Mediterranean.* Chicago: University of Chicago Press, 1988, pp. 286–370.

Kugler, Hartmut, ed. *Ein Weltbild vor Columbus: Die Ebstorfer Weltkarte.* Weinheim: VCH, 1991.

Kupfer, Marcia. "Medieval World Maps: Embedded Images, Interpretive Frames." *Word & Image* 10 (1994): 262–288.

von den Brincken, Anna-Dorothee. *Kartographische Quellen: Welt-, See- und Regionalkarten.* Typologie des sources du moyen-age occidental 51. Turnhout: Brepols, 1988.

———. *Finis Terrae: Die Enden der Erde und die vierte Kontinent auf mittelalterlichen Weltkarten.* Schriften der Monumenta Germaniae Historica 36. Hanover: Hahnsche Buchhandlung, 1992.

Marcia Kupfer

SEE ALSO
Braunschweig; Lüneburg; Otto IV; Welfs; Zillis

Worms

Located in the Rhineland-Palatinate, the city of Worms was first settled by the Celts in the fifth century C.E. as Borbetomagus and later served as a Roman garrison town (Civitas Vangionum) and capital of the Vangiones region through the fourth century C.E. Parts of the original Roman city wall still stand. In 413 C.E. the city became the capital of the Burgundian Empire, and later was completely destroyed by the Huns in 436. It was rebuilt by the Merovingians, especially Brunhilda and Dagobert, in the first half of the seventh century. Worms may have been a bishopric as early as the fourth century, although the earliest recorded date is 614.

Beginning in the eleventh century, Worms became one

Worms, cathedral, west choir. *Photograph: Joan A. Holladay*

of the most important medieval cities and played an integral role in the antagonism among the Holy Roman Empire, the pope, and local dukes and bishops. The ascension of Worms can be traced to Bishop Burchard I (1000–1025), who was instrumental in creating the religious landscape of the area, and the local dynasty, the Salian family, from which Emperor Konrad II (1024–1035) stemmed. The city's political and religious freedom was defined by the Investiture Controversy, a struggle between Emperor Heinrich IV (1056–1106) and Pope Gregory VII (1073–1085) concerning the nomination of bishops. The dispute arose when the citizenry of Worms supported Heinrich in a conflict with other princes and clergy, including Bishop Adelbert of Worms. For the next half century, tension between citizenry and clergy was high; the dispute finally ended in 1122 with the Concordat of Worms. Edicts in 1156 and 1184 by Emperor Frederick I guaranteed the freedoms of the city, which in 1184 became an imperial free city. Throughout

the thirteenth century the bishops of Worms attempted unsuccessfully to reassert their control over the city. In 1254 Worms founded the Rhine League with Speyer and Mainz. As an imperial city, Worms was the site of more than one hundred imperial diets from the eighth to the sixteenth centuries, most notably that of 1521, at which Martin Luther and his associates were condemned. A Jewish community existed in Worms from around the tenth century; its synagogue, dating from the tenth century, was completed in 1174, destroyed during the Nazi Kristallnacht (Night of the Broken Crystal) pogrom in 1938, and completely rebuilt after World War II. Adjacent to the synagogue is one of the largest Jewish cemeteries in Europe, with more than two thousand graves dating from as early as the eleventh century.

The architecture of Worms is dominated by the imposing cathedral dedicated to St. Peter, built over remains dating from late Antiquity. The current cathedral stands on the foundations of a church constructed under Bishop Burchard I and consecrated in 1018. It was a cross-shaped basilica; little survives from this structure other than the bases of the west towers and the tenth-century tombs of members of the Salian dynasty. Along with the cathedrals at Mainz and Speyer, the current cathedral in Worms is one of the greatest examples of High Romanesque architectural style in Germany. The fully vaulted basilica, built primarily from red sandstone, has a double choir, two slightly different, octagonal towers over the east and west choirs, and two round towers flanking each choir. Construction of the cathedral began in the first half of the twelfth century under Bishops Burchard II and his successor Konrad II; it was consecrated in 1181. External architectural ornamentation is limited; notable are the sculptures of animals on the eastern façade. A few examples of twelfth-century wall painting survive in the north transept.

Although the city was completely destroyed in 1689 by the French and again during World War II, several other examples of medieval, specifically Romanesque, architecture still stand. Most notable is perhaps the church of St. Paul, which stands on the site of a former Salian castle. After Bishop Burchard I procured the castle, it was modified in the first quarter of the eleventh century to accommodate the church. The originally three-story basilica incorporated two former castle towers. Of specific interest are the stone cupolas on the west towers, which give the impression of a small, squat Byzantine church. These changes, along with those of the east choir and west façade, may have been inspired by the Crusades of the early thirteenth century. Two other churches can be directed to Bishop Burchard's involvement: the church of St. Andreas, a three-story basilica, was built in the eleventh century and renovated in the early thirteenth century, and the church of St. Martin, a vaulted basilica with two towers, begun in the eleventh century, renovated in the thirteenth century, and consecrated in 1265.

Worms and its history are closely linked to the anonymous German heroic epic, *Das Nibelungenlied,* from around 1200. The Burgundian empire and Queen Brunhild form the historical basis of the work, which conveys the historical, political, and cultural importance of the city. The north portal of the cathedral, the portal of the emperors, is the site of the legendary fight between rival queens Brunhild and Kriemhild. With the recovery of and new-found emphasis placed on *Das Nibelungelied* in the nineteenth century, Worms began to commemorate its role in the epic.

BIBLIOGRAPHY

Hotz, Walter. *Der Dom zu Worms.* Darmstadt: Wissenschaftliche Buchgesellschaft, 1981.

———. *Die Wormser Bauschule 1000–1250.* Darmstadt: Wissenschaftliche Buchgesellschaft, 1985.

Illert, Georg. *Worms.* Munich: Deutscher Kunstverlag, 1970.

Kautzsch, Rudolf. *Der Dom zu Worms.* 3 vols. Berlin: Deutscher Verlag für Kunstwissenschaft, 1938.

Keilmann, Burkard. *Der Kampf um die Stadtherrschaft in Worms während des 13. Jahrhunderts.* Darmstadt: Hessische Historische Kommission, 1985.

Winterfeld, Dethard von. *Der Dom zu Worms.* Königstein/Taunus: H. Köster, 1985.

———. *Die Kaiserdome Speyer, Mainz, Worms.* Würzburg: Zodiaque-Echter, 1993, pp. 165–206.

Zorn, Friedrich. *Wormser Chronik,* ed. Wilhelm Arnold, 1857. Amsterdam: Rodopi, 1969.

Gregory H. Wolf

SEE ALSO
Conrad II; Henry IV; Investiture Controversy; Jewish Art and Architecture; Jews; Mainz; *Nibelungenlied;* Romanesque Art and Architecture; Speyer

Worringen, Battle of (June 5, 1288)

During a long fight between the Archbishop Siegfried von Westerburg of Cologne (1275–1297) and the city of Cologne, which was trying to become independent of the archiepiscopal government, a dispute over the inheritance of Limburg sparked a broader regional war. Allied with powerful lords like the counts of Luxemburg and Nassau, the archbishop faced an alliance of Cologne and the counts of Berg, Jülich, and Cleves, as well as the duke of Brabant. The Brabantine and Cologne forces met the archbishop's army near his castle of Worringen. In the course of the massive battle on June 5, 1288, over two thousand were killed, including the commander of the Cologne city troops. But Brabant and the city prevailed, managing to surround and capture the archbishop.

This defeat left Cologne as an independent, self-governing city, forcing the archbishops to move their main residence to Bonn. The territorial rule of the archbishops on the lower Rhine also continued to decline in competition against the secular dynasts.

BIBLIOGRAPHY

Delbrück, Hans. *Medieval Warfare,* trans. Walter J. Renfroe Jr. Lincoln: University of Nebraska Press, 1982.

Der Tag bei Worringen, 5. Juni 1288, ed. Wilhelm Janssen and H. Stehkämper. Cologne: Böhlau, 1988; special issue of *Blätter für deutsche Landesgeschichte* 124 (1988).

Torunsky, Vera. *Worringen 1288: Ursachen und Folgen einer Schlacht.* Cologne: Rheinland-Verlag, 1988.

Ulrich, Lehnart. *Die Schlacht von Worringen 1288: Kriegführung im Mittelalter: der Limburger Erbfolgekrieg unter besonderer Brücksichtigung der Schlacht von Worringen, 5. 6. 1288.* Frankfurt am Main: AFRA-Verlag, 1994.

Brian A. Pavlac

SEE ALSO
Cologne

Würzburg

The city developed on the Main River near where the Irish missionary Saint Kilian was martyred in about 688. A *castellum Virteburh* on a hill west of the Main, first mentioned as the center of an expansive agrarian settlement in 704, seems to have been an important residence of the Frankish dukes. The castle walls enclosed the Marienkapelle (Chapel of the Virgin), the oldest round church east of the Rhine. St. Boniface established a bishop's see at Würzburg in 741, and the Andreas Cloister (*Andreaskloster*), housing a school, a library, and a scriptorium, was founded soon after by the first bishop, Burchard. The original cathedral, dedicated to the Savior, was built during the second half of the eighth century but burned to the ground after being struck by lightning in 855. Bishop Arno began a new cathedral dedicated to Saint Kilian, the Kiliandom, and a bishop's residence, thereby drawing craftsmen to Würzburg. The Kiliandom was rebuilt in 1045.

Through the eighth and ninth centuries, Würzburg developed under Carolingian patronage. Indeed, since the time of Charles Martel, members of the royal court, including Charlemagne, had resided there in the Wirtschaftshof, a center of local commerce. Located at a ford across the Main, Würzburg lay at the crossing of an important east-west travel route and a north-south pilgrimage route from Denmark to Rome. The bishop's see and the Carolingian palace encouraged development of urban settlement so that by the end of ninth century, Würzburg was an important trade center. A market thrived near the cathedral, and a community of fishermen and shippers flourished along the riverbank. The presence of a mint in Würzburg further attests to the city's commercial importance during this period.

Centrally located and the see of one of the empire's most powerful bishoprics, Würzburg continued to be a popular place for emperors to reside and hold court. In 1127, the first known German tournament took place in Würzburg. The Staufer rulers, Konrad III and Frederick Barbarossa, the latter in particular, visited the city numerous times. Frederick celebrated his marriage to Beatrix of Burgundy here in 1156.

Over the course of the eleventh and twelfth centuries, the bishop became the absolute authority in Würzburg; the *Goldene Freiheit* (Golden Freedom) of 1168 extended the bishop's power over the whole city. The five-cornered city wall, known as the Bischofshut (bishop's hat), dates from the eleventh century, and a number of important churches and cloisters were established in and around Würzburg during this period. In 1042, St. Burkard, a three-aisle Romanesque basilica of which the original western portion is still standing, was dedicated. A late Gothic transept and choir was added to this church in 1490. The Neumünster (new cathedral) was built between 1045 and 1090. In the thirteenth century Albertus Magnus laid the cornerstone for the church of the Dominican cloister. The Würzburg cathedral school and library, with its rare manuscripts dating from the fifth to the tenth centuries, were particularly well respected.

Many of these manuscripts are still preserved in the University Library.

In 1230, the minnesinger Walther von der Vogelweide died in Würzburg, where Friedrich II had granted him permanent residence. His gravestone is in the Neumünster.

As long as bishops controlled the city, the citizens had little opportunity to regulate and govern their own business, and in the late thirteenth century, the townspeople began to assert themselves against bishops and clerics by plundering and burning their residences. The bishops retaliated with high taxes and punishments so that citizens who could manage it moved elsewhere. Nuremberg began to replace Würzburg as an important center of commerce, at least in part because of the social unrest that marked the history of the older center during the fourteenth and fifteenth centuries. Beginning in 1372, bitter battle raged for over twenty years between the bishop in the Marienburg castle on the hill and the citizens of Würzburg below. Between 1376 and 1475, the townspeople built their own church, the Marienkapelle—a three-aisle, late Gothic hall church with portal decorations that rank among the masterpieces of the period.

The bishops of Würzburg amassed tremendous debt, and the secular rulers repeatedly allowed them to raise taxes to repay their debts. Würzburg became a depopulated, impoverished city and remained so well into the second half of the fifteenth century. The city was also involved in the turmoil of religious reform; Hans Bohm, who preached reform in the church, was burned at the stake in Würzburg in 1476.

BIBLIOGRAPHY

Otremba, Heinz. *15 Jahrhunderte Würzburg: Eine Stadt und ihre Geschichte.* Würzburg: Echter Verlag, 1979.

Ruth M. W. Moskop

SEE ALSO

Albertus Magnus; Bookmaking and Production; Carolingian Art and Architecture; Charlemagne; Frederick I Barbarossa; Frederick II; Gothic Art and Architecture; *Minnesang;* Nuremberg; Ottonian Art and Architecture; Riemenschneider, Tillmann; Romanesque Art and Architecture; Walther von der Vogelweide

Xanten

About 105 C.E. the Roman emperor Trajan established the city Colonia Ulpia Traiana on the left bank of the Rhine near the sites of a smaller settlement and two earlier Roman forts. It would become, after Cologne some eighty kilometers (fifty miles) to the southeast, the most important trading center and harbor in the Roman province of Lower Germany. About the middle of the fourth century, the Romans were forced to abandon the recently fortified city to the local Germanic tribes, who built up a new settlement outside the city wall along the main road leading to the south. Here in the Roman cemeteries, which typically lined the main traffic axes leading out of town, were buried the remains of the third-century martyr St. Victor and his companions of the Theban legion. The name "Xanten" comes from the Latin *ad sanctos,* meaning "near the saints." The development of the site is typical: an early oratory over the burial site, supposed to have been erected by Saint Helen, the mother of the emperor Constantine, was replaced by a succession of later churches dedicated to the saint. In this case, a Carolingian building from the mid–eighth century, which burned in 1109, was supplanted by a Romanesque church. During the High Middle Ages, the foundation developed into one of the wealthiest landholders on the Lower Rhine; its well-placed canons built houses inside a walled area that included the cathedral and the palace of the archbishop of Cologne.

In 1263, Prior Friedrich von Hohenstaufen, brother of the archbishop, laid the cornerstone to the new cathedral of St. Victor, which incorporated the towers and Westwerk (entry structure on the side facing west) of its predecessor. Destroyed with much of the rest of the city in 1945, it has been completely rebuilt in its medieval form,

which reflects the long building period extending into the sixteenth century. The Gothic cathedral has the same dimensions as its predecessor, suggesting that the decision to rebuild in the new style had more to do with the canons' self-perception, and with fashion and prestige, than with the need for more space. In the two-story elevation, the building reveals the influence of the recently built church of the Virgin (Liebfrauenkirche) at Trier; likewise the chapels set diagonally between the choir and the east ends of the aisles are taken over from the Trier plan. The influence of the Gothic cathedral underway at Cologne since 1248 is visible in the stone statues adorsed (attached back to back) to the columns of the choir and nave. Among the oldest figures, sculpted in a style related to Cologne works, number those of Saints Helena and Victor in the choir. The short nave without transepts is flanked by a double aisle on each side, which gives the impression of great width. Much of the interior decoration of the cathedral has been preserved; in addition to the Romanesque shrine for the relics of St. Victor, now incorporated into the later high altar, the oldest carved choir stalls in the Rhineland, from the middle of the thirteenth century, and some of the stained glass windows from the earliest building period are still to be seen in the choir. Some twenty elaborate, carved altarpieces, many of them from the first half of the sixteenth century, are also preserved at St. Victor's.

In 1228 Archbishop Heinrich von Molenark granted city rights to the market settlement just to the south of the walled cathedral area. Trade with Flanders and the Hansa cities made the strategically located city wealthy; it also made its control important to the surrounding political powers, the archbishop and the counts of nearby Kleve. At the end of the fourteenth century, the archbishop decided to protect the city with a wall, some of whose towers still stand. But in 1392, before the fortification was completed, the counts' men occupied the northern half of the city. After a half-century in which the city was divided between the two powers, the pope granted it to Kleve in 1444.

Siegfried, the hero of the *Nibelungenlied,* is supposed to have been born in Xanten.

BIBLIOGRAPHY

Bader, Walter. *Der Dom zu Xanten.* Kevelaer: Butzon und Bercker, 1961.

Beissel, Stefan. *Die Bauführung des Mittelalters: Studie über die Kirche des hl. Viktor zu Xanten.* 1889; rpt. Osnabrück: Zeller, 1966.

Hilger, Hans Peter, Udo Grote, and Heinrich Heidbüchel. *Der Dom zu Xanten und seine Kunstschätze,* 2d ed. Königstein im Taunus: Langewiesche, 1997.

Knoll, Gabriele M. *Xanten. Stadtführer am Niederrhein.* Kleve: Boss, 1991.

Studien zur Geschichte der Stadt Xanten 1228–1978: Festschrift zum 750jährigen Stadtjubiläum. Cologne: Rheinland, 1978.

Joan A. Holladay

SEE ALSO

Cologne, Art; Gothic Art and Architecture; *Nibelungenlied;* Town Planning and Urbanism; Trier

Z

Zeitblom, Bartholomäus
(ca. 1460–1518/1522)

Also known as Hausner, this painter and polychromer, who was probably born about 1460 in Nördlingen, appears for the first time in Ulm documents in 1482, where he is listed as an unmarried citizen. The first two of his three later wives were the daughters of the painters Hans Schüchlin of Ulm and Friedrich Herlin of Nördlingen. His use of Herlin's technique and the appearance of ornamental patterns from Schüchlin's workshop in the backgrounds of his paintings make it probable that he was trained by these two painters. From 1499, Zeitblom paid taxes on a house in Ulm and a pew in the city's cathedral. His death date lies between 1518 and 1522.

Zeitblom's reputation reached far beyond the city walls of Ulm. His shop exported numerous winged altarpieces, many of them made in collaboration with the wood sculptor Nicolas Weckmann and the painters Schüchlin, Bernhard Strigel, and the anonymous Master of the Pfullendorf Altar. Characteristic of his thinly painted panels are introverted saint figures whose monumentality radiates a great calm.

Two altars signed by Zeitblom are preserved. The winged altarpiece from Heerberg near Schwäbisch Hall—a collaborative project with Weckmann dated 1497–1498—is now in the Württembergisches Landesmuseum in Stuttgart, as is the slightly earlier one from Kilchberg near Tübingen. Written sources document an altar at Süßen from 1507, now destroyed, and polychromy on a Mount of Olives group by Michel Erhart at the south side of Ulm Cathedral.

Fragmentarily preserved altarpieces from Donzdorf (about 1490, now in the Fürstenbergische Gemäldegalerie in Donaueschingen), Eschach (1496; Stuttgart, Staatsgalerie), Söflingen near Ulm (ca. 1500; Kempten, Alpenländische Galerie), and the Wengenkirche in Ulm (ca. 1510; Ulm, Ulmer Museum) can be attributed to Zeitblom's workshop on the basis of technical and stylistic similarities to his documented works. Conversely, Zeitblom's participation as a member of Schüchlin's workshop on the panels of the Hausen altarpiece from 1488 (Stuttgart, Württembergisches Landesmuseum) and those for the Blaubeuren altar from 1493–1494 has been demonstrated conclusively, as has his work with Weckmann on the retable dated 1511 at Adelberg, near Schwäbish Hall.

BIBLIOGRAPHY

Bach, Max. "Zur Kenntnis der Werke Bartholomäus Zeitbloms." *Diözesan-Archiv von Schwaben* (1894): 81–88.

Bushart, Bruno. "Studien zur altschwäbischen Malerei." *Zeitschrift für Kunstgeschichte* 22/1 (1959): 143–149.

Roth, Michael, and Hanns Westhoff. "Beobachtungen zu Malerei und Fassung des Blaubeurer Hochaltars," in *Flügelaltäre des späten Mittelalters,* ed. Hartmut Krohm and Eike Oellermann. Berlin: Dietrich Reimer, 1992, pp. 167–188.

von Pfeil, Daniela. "Notizen zu Leben und Werk des Bartholomäus Zeitblom," in *Meisterwerke massenhaft: Die Bildhauerwerkstatt des Niklaus Weckmann und die Malerei in Ulm um 1500.* Ulm: Süddeutsche Verlagsgesellschaft, 1993, pp. 168–183.

Brigitte Schliewen

SEE ALSO
Erhart, Michel; Herlin, Friedrich; Schwäbisch-Hall; Ulm; Weckmann, Nicolas, the Elder

Bartholomäus Zeitblom, John the Baptist, wing of the Kilchberg Altar (Stuttgart, Württembergisches Landesmuseum).
Photograph: Württembergisches Landesmuseum Stuttgart

Zillis

The village of Zillis, Switzerland, lies above the Schams valley to the south of the ravine of the Via Mala. Already settled in the Roman era, Zillis lies on the important Alpine route leading through the Splügen Pass. The settlement of Ciranes (Zillis), mentioned circa 831, already contained the principal church of the Schams valley—the parish church *(ecclesia plebia)* of St. Martin. The seat of

the criminal justice system of the entire Schams region, the village of Zillis was thus both the spiritual and the legal center of the area, owing principally to its location on the trade route. Initially under control of Pfäffers Monastery, Zillis was given over to the bishop of Chur by Otto I in 940. In the early twelfth century the Schams valley, including Zillis, became the property of the lords of Vaz. In the fourteenth century it is again named as property of the chapter of the cathedral of Chur.

The most significant monument in Zillis is the parish church of St. Martin. Four building phases can be discerned. An early Christian church (ca. 500) in rectangular form with a large parabolic apse appears to be the earliest structure on the site. Immediately to the north, a tripartite structure may have been a baptistery/sacristy. This was replaced circa 800 by a three-apse hall church, typical of Carolingian Raetia, as seen at Müstair. The present Romanesque church was constructed circa 1130 with a single rectangular nave, narrow square chancel, and flat wooden roof. At this time too was constructed the tower on the south flank. The Romanesque chancel was replaced with the present star-vaulted, Gothic polygonal chancel and sacristy, signed "1509 meister andres büchler" (1509 Master Andres Büchler).

Zillis, St. Martin's, detail of painted ceiling: central panel of Last Supper with Judas, John the Evangelist, Christ, and Peter.
Photograph: Eidgenössiches Archiv für Denkmalpflege/Boissonas, Geneva

Of particular importance is the painted wooden ceiling, the earliest extant painted Romanesque wooden ceiling, and the only surviving example of its kind from the twelfth century. While dated variously from 1140 to 1200, a date of circa 1160 seems the most probable and is popularly accepted in recent scholarship. Comprising 153 panels, painted in a limited palette of green, red, gray, white, and black, the ceiling appears to have been polychromed prior to installation. Strong stylistic and iconographic affinities have been noted between the ceiling and manuscript illumination of the twelfth century, suggesting that the artists came from the scriptorium at Chur.

The ceiling, arranged in seventeen rows of nine panels running east to west, depicts scenes from the lives of Christ and St. Martin, surrounded by a border. At the four corners angels, labeled as the four winds, blow trumpets. The remaining forty-four border scenes portray lively, fantastic aquatic animal hybrids and two episodes of fishermen in boats (Peter and Andrew, Jonah). The inner scenes run from east to west, beginning with three Old Testament kings and allegorical figures of Synagogue and Church. The narrative cycle of scenes from Christ's life, including both scriptural and apocryphal episodes, begins with the Annunciation and concludes with the Crowning with Thorns. The final seven panels contain scenes from the life of St. Martin, the church's patron.

While the conclusion of the Christ cycle with the Crowning with Thorns is unusual, it appears to follow a strong regal theme in the cycle, beginning with the three Old Testament kings and continuing through a strong emphasis on the Three Magi. This emphasis may reflect the passage of the relics of the Three Magi through Zillis during their translation from Milan to Cologne in 1161. Peculiar too is the absence of the Crucifixion, although it is alluded to in the cross pattern, formed by parallel rows of bold wavy lines, extending along the central east-west and north-south axes of the entire ceiling. The lost Romanesque chancel may also have contained additional imagery.

The entire ceiling seems to present a spiritual *mappa mundi*—an image of the world as the triumphal route of Christ. The role of the church in administering this path is adumbrated in the appended scenes of the titular saint, Martin, and also in the complex number symbolism employed. The number of panels reflects the 153 fish drawn by Peter in the miraculous draught described in John 21:11. The ceiling thus functions as a vision in which Christian time and space are "mapped" out.

BIBLIOGRAPHY

Brugger-Koch, Susanne. "Die romanische Bilderdecke von Sankt Martin, Zillis (Graubünden): Stil und Ikonographie." Ph.d. diss., University of Basel, 1981.

Eggenberger, Christoph. "Die Bilderdecke von St. Martin Zillis," in *Geschichte und Kultur Churrätiens. Festschrift für Pater Iso Müller OSB zu seinem 85.* Geburtstag. Disentis: Desertina, 1986, pp. 233–270.

Murbach, Ernst. *The Painted Romanesque Ceiling of St. Martin in Zillis,* trans. Janet Seligman. New York: Praeger, 1967.

Myss, Walter. *Bildwelt als Weltbild: Die romanische Bilderdecke von St. Martin zu Zillis.* Beuron: Beuroner Kunstverlag, 1965.

Poeschel, Erwin. *Die romanischen Deckengemälde von Zillis.* Erlenbach-Zürich: E. Rentsch, 1941.

Rudloff, Diether. *Zillis, die romanische Bilderdecke der Kirche St. Martin.* Basel: Verlag Peter Heman, 1989.

Wiesmann, Peter. "Zur Formensprache der Deckenbilder von Zillis." *Zeitschrift für schweizerische Archäologie und Kunstgeschichte* 11 (1950): 17–21.

Scott Bradford Montgomery

SEE ALSO

Chur; Cologne, Art; Müstair; Otto I; Romanesque Art and Architecture; World Maps

Zug

First mentioned as a city in 1246, Zug, Switzerland, owes its founding to the counts of Kyburg. Rudolph von Habsburg acquired the town in 1273 and used it as a strategic point of defense against the original Swiss cantons in the battle of Morgarten in 1315. A fifteen-day siege by the confederates led to Zug's entry into the union in 1352.

Zug is home to one of the most richly decorated late Gothic churches in Switzerland. St. Oswald's was built on the site of a fourteenth-century church dedicated to the other patron saint of Zug, St. Michael. St. Oswald's was begun in 1478 by Hans Felder from Oettingen in Swabia. Felder was also responsible at this time for the second city wall. Later additions to St. Oswald's included the elongation of the polygonal choir (1494–1496) and, in the sixteenth century, the aisles to flank the nave as well as the steeple. Of particular interest are the figural sculptures on the west facade executed by an unknown sculptor. These include figures of saints Oswald and Michael, a Madonna and Child, German emperors, and saints—all standing in niches and partially enclosed by baldachins.

BIBLIOGRAPHY

Birchler, Linus. *Die Kunstdenkmäler des Kantons Zug 2: Die Kunstdenkmäler von Zug-Stadt.* Basel: Birkhäuser, 1935.

Gerber, Roland. "Finanzierung und Bauaufwand der ersten St. Oswaldskirche in Zug (1478–1486): Der Einfluss der Baufinanzen auf die gebaute Architektur." *Unsere Kunstdenkmäler* 43/1 (1992): 51–66.

Rothkegel, Rüdiger. "Die Befestigung der Stadt Zug im ausgehenden Mittelalter." *Tugium* 8 (1992): 111–135.

Speich, Klaus, and Hans R. Schläpfer. *Kirchen und Klöster in der Schweiz.* Zurich: Ex Libris, 1978.

Elsa Gontrum

SEE ALSO
Gothic Art and Architecture

Zurich

The strategic site where the Limmat exits the northern end of Lake Zurich (Switzerland) was inhabited as early as the Neolithic age, but the Romans were responsible for the permanent settlement of this area. A toll station was established here in Augustan times, and under Emperor Valentinian I (364–375) a fort was erected on the Lindenhof, a hill on the left bank, and a bridge nearby spanned the river. A Christian church may also have stood near here at this time, on the site of the later church of St. Peter. Burials near here attest to the continuous use of the site in the fifth through seventh centuries, even after withdrawal of the Romans in 401. More modest graves on the right bank signal an early settlement in this area as well.

Medieval Zurich enjoyed two periods of extended prosperity. In the middle of the ninth century, Charlemagne's grandson, Louis the German, and Louis's daughter Hildegard founded the women's abbey known as the Fraumünster on the left bank. Hildegard served as the convent's first abbess, establishing what would be a long tradition of the personal power of the abbess and the foundation's proximity to the highest political instances. At the same time as the building of the Fraumünster, which was consecrated in 874, a new palace was built on the Lindenhof, with material quarried from the remains of the Roman fort. The Grossmünster (big church) stood on a hill on the right bank of the Limmat directly opposite the Fraumünster, on the site of the cemetery where the town's patron saints Felix and Regula were buried; it served the religious needs of the men's abbey.

After the death of the last male heir of the house of Zähringen in 1217, the Emperor Frederick II granted Zurich its freedom from a territorial overlord (Reichsfreiheit), and the city experienced a political and economic boom. The palace on the Lindenhof, which had been rebuilt in the tenth century under the Ottonian emperors and later under the Zähringer dukes, was razed to symbolize the city's independence; a new town hall (Rathaus) was built along the river; and the city was ringed with a protective wall. The church of St. Peter and the Wasserkirche (Water Church), on the island below the Grossmünster where Felix and Regula had been martyred, were rebuilt, and building on both the Grossmünster and Fraumünster, which had been started in the previous century, was completed. The newly arrived Franciscans, Dominicans, and Augustinians constructed churches and convents near the city wall. Well-placed citizens built and enlarged stone houses in both the *mindere Stadt* (lesser town) on the left bank and the *merere Stadt* (larger town) on the right; a number of these still preserve interior wall painting—both decorative and figural—from the period about 1300 and the fourteenth century. These same patrons, like the well-known patron of *Minnesang* Rüdiger Manesse, also commissioned lavish manuscripts, like the *Große Manessische Liederhandschrift* (*Great Mannessian Song Manuscript,* Heidelberg, Universitätsbibliothek, no. cpg 848) and the world chronicles in St. Gall (Vadiana, no. 302) and Berlin (no. mgf 623). Whether these and other commissions were executed in lay shops or in scriptoria at the Grossmünster, the Dominican men's cloister, or the Dominican women's convent Oetenbach at the northern tip of the *mindere Stadt,* has not been definitively settled.

The craftspeople, who had significantly contributed to the city's financial success, finally managed to better their political and legal situation in 1336. In an uprising led by the knight Rudolf Brun, they stormed the Rathaus and exiled some members of the city council. Brun was named mayor, and the new constitution, based on that of Strasbourg, gave the thirteen newly formed guilds political representation equal to that of the nobles and the wealthy who had traditionally ruled.

Huldrych Zwingli began preaching the Reformation in Zurich in 1519, and five years later the iconoclasts under his influence emptied the city's churches of crucifixes, altars, metalwork objects, and manuscripts used in the Catholic rite and dissolved the foundations. Despite the "cleansing" of Zurich's churches and the rededication of some of them to other purposes, the street plan and

Zurich, *mindere Stadt,* with (from left) towers of the *Fraumünster* and of St. Peter and trees on the *Lindenhof. Photograph: Joan A. Holladay*

many of the buildings of the medieval city are still more or less intact.

BIBLIOGRAPHY

Brinker, Claudia, and Dione Flühler-Kreis. *edele frouwen—schoene man: Die Manessische Liederhandschrift in Zürich.* Zurich: Schweizerisches Landesmuseum, 1991.

Die Liber ordinarius des Konrad von Mure: Die Gottesdienstordnung am Grossmünster in Zürich, ed. Heidi Leuppi. Spicilegium Friburgense 37. Fribourg: Universitätsverlag, 1995.

Escher, Konrad. *Die Stadt Zürich.* Die Kunstdenkmäler des Kantons Zürich 4. 2 vols. Basel: E. Birkhäuser, 1939–1949.

Gutscher, Daniel. *Das Grossmünster in Zürich: Eine baugeschichtliche Monographie.* Beiträge zur Kunstgeschichte der Schweiz 5. Bern: Gesellschaft für Schweizerische Kunstgeschichte, 1983.

Schneider, Jürg E. "Zürich," in *Stadtluft, Hirsebrei und Bettelmönch: Die Stadt um 1300,* ed. Marianne Flüeler and Niklaus Flüeler. Stuttgart: Theiss, 1992, pp. 69–91.

Schneider, N. Jürg E., and Jürg Hanser. *Wandmalerei im alten Zürich.* Zurich: Hochbauamt der Stadt Zürich, 1986.

Joan A. Holladay

SEE ALSO

Carolingian Art and Architecture; Gothic Art and Architecture; Iconographies, Innovative; *Minnesang;* Ottonian Art and Architecture

Zwettl

The Cistercian monastery of Zwettl was founded in 1137 by Hadmar of Kuenring, a member of the dynasty of dominant influence in Lower Austria. The events of the foundation and its ongoing support by subsequent generations of the family and others are described in the lavish *Founders' Book (Liber fundatorum)* compiled between 1310 and about 1320 from earlier sources. Its figural decoration consists of fifteen mostly full-page family trees and sixteen images of other donors.

The first, Romanesque, abbey church, the western part of which survived until 1722, was a basilica with transepts and a "Benedictine" choir. The present Gothic abbey church is, despite its stylistic uniformity, the result of different building campaigns of the fourteenth, fifteenth, and eighteenth centuries. On the initiative of Albrecht II, a new ambulatory choir was begun in 1343; its radiating chapels were consecrated in 1348. Under the patronage of Charles IV, work was resumed in 1360, and after a change of plans, the first hall-ambulatory choir in Austria was completed in 1383. A reconsecration of the church and main altar is recorded for 1437, and by this time the two easternmost bays of the nave, which contained the choir stalls of the monks, were built as a hall church in continuation of the existing choir. The westernmost bays of the church, finally, were constructed, still in Gothic forms, when the Baroque facade was added in 1722. In 1471, the monastery was thoroughly fortified, and the church, after a fire in 1511, was reroofed and equipped with defendable towers and a central spire. At the same time, a refurbishing of the church took place. The eight stained glass windows that Abbot Koloman Bauernfeind ordered for the north side of the church from master Michael at Steir in 1490 got lost in transit; of their replacements, only one panel, with the Trinitarian Coronation of the Virgin, a subject popular at the court of Frederick III, has survived. A late Gothic altarpiece, carved by Andreas Morgenstern from Budovice and stylistically related to the one at Kefermarkt, was installed in the choir in 1525.

The town of Zwettl, first documented in 1139 and founded as a town at the present site in 1200, is located about two miles west of the abbey. The first parish church of Zwettl, however, was the Romanesque church of St. John, situated on a hillside overlooking the Kamp valley within the original castle of the Kuenrings. In 1483, Emperor Frederick III founded a collegiate chapter at the church and advised its subsequent fortification.

BIBLIOGRAPHY

Buberl, Paul. *Die Kunstdenkmäler des Zisterzienserklosters Zwettl.* Ostmärkische Kunsttopographie 29. Baden bei Wien: Rudolf M. Rohrer, 1940.

Liber fundatorum zwetlensis monasterii: "Bärenhaut," ed. Joachim Rössl. Codices selecti 73. Graz: Akademische Druck- and Verlagsanstalt, 1981 [facsimile].

Hans J. Böker

SEE ALSO

Charles IV; Cistercian Art and Architecture; Frederick III; Gothic Art and Architecture; Romanesque Art and Architecture

Index

Entries with page numbers in **bold** indicate main entries.

Index

Index

Index

Index

Index

Index

Index

Index

Index

Index

Index

Index

Index

Index